CHRISTIANITY IN CHINA

A Scholars' Guide to Resources
in the Libraries and Archives
of the United States

CHRISTIANITY IN CHINA

A Scholars' Guide to Resources in the Libraries and Archives of the United States

ARCHIE R. CROUCH
STEVEN AGORATUS
ARTHUR EMERSON
DEBRA E. SOLED

Foreword
by
John King Fairbank

M. E. Sharpe, Inc.
Armonk, New York
London, England

Library of Congress Cataloging in Publication Data

Christianity in China: a scholars' guide to resources in the libraries and
    archives of the United States / edited by Archie R. Crouch . . .
    [et al.].
        p. cm.
    Includes index.
    ISBN 0-87332-419-6
    1. Christianity—China—Library resources—United States—Directo-
ries. 2. China—Church history—Library resources—United States—
Directories. 3. Christianity—China—Archival resources—United
States—Directories. 4. China—Church history—Archival resources—
United States—Directories. I. Crouch, Archie R.
Z7757.C6C46   1989
[BR1285]
016.2751—dc19   88-18524
                                                                  CIP

Printed in the United States of America

The paper used in this publication meets the minimum
requirements of American National Standard for
Information Sciences—Permanence of Papers for
Printed Library Materials, ANSI Z39.48–1984.
The book is Smyth sewn and casebound in F-grade Library
Buckram, which contains no synthetic fibers.

BB 10 9 8 7 6 5 4 3 2 1

DEDICATED TO

Edward H. Johnson

*Friend and Colleague
in the Service of
Christian Missions in China
Student Christian Movement in the U.S.A.
Church Administration in North America*

"To find out how Protestant and Catholic missionaries really contributed to American policy in East Asia, as well as to the rise of modern China, will require historical research of the multi-archival kind. . . . One fact is plain: mission history in China cannot be separated from the history of the Christian church there, and together they touch on all aspects of Chinese life over many decades."

John K. Fairbank
in *The Missionary Enterprise
in China and America*, 1974

Contents

CONTENTS

CONTENTS

CONTENTS

CONTENTS

CONTENTS

CONTENTS

CONTENTS

CONTENTS

CONTENTS

CONTENTS

CONTENTS

CONTENTS

CONTENTS

CONTENTS

CONTENTS

CONTENTS

Foreword

CHINA WAS ONCE A UNIVERSE IN ITSELF, but it has gradually entered the modern international world and is indeed becoming a major part of it. In this long and still unfinished process of cultural transfer and assimilation, the shocks and benefits have flowed in both directions and Christian missionaries have been the principal agents. From the beginning, the missionaries found themselves trying both to change China and to change foreigners' views of China. Their roles in their homelands were sometimes as important as their roles in the field, for they were the only persons who maintained direct contact with the common people both in China and in the West.

Foreign missions are deeply embedded in American history, which, of course, began in New England under predominantly religious auspices. The migration of American Protestant missionaries overseas got underway early in the nineteenth century, in the same period as the rise of free trade in England. American trade, the flag, and the Bible went abroad in quick succession. The merchant, the consular official, and the preacher appeared as an expansive triumvirate first in the Near East, then in India, and soon after in Southeast Asia and China. This American expansion went by way of the Mediterranean, where the United States Navy first operated abroad, into the Levant, and thence eastward, reaching the Far East by way of the Indian Ocean.

From the beginning, American missionaries found helpful colleagues as well as competitors among their British cousins. The London Missionary Society of 1795 antedated the American Board of Commissioners for Foreign Missions by fifteen years, just as the British Navy fought for wider access to China in the Opium War fifteen years before Commodore Perry's black ships secured the opening of Japan in 1854. Despite the very different concerns of the missionaries, as opposed to merchants and diplomats, they all functioned within the predominantly Anglo-American community in Asia.

Within the young American nation, Protestant missionaries going overseas were the maritime counterpart of the American migration by barge and wagon across the Alleghenies into the Middle West and on across the Mississippi. The Old China Trade during the era from 1784 to the Civil War was part and parcel of the movement from New England and the Atlantic states across the continent. In the sailing ships of traders, American missionaries reached China long before they arrived in California.

Where American merchants risked their venture capital, missionaries more directly risked their health. Both were on a cultural frontier vis-à-vis the crowded societies of Asia, in situations that demanded initiative, fortitude, and ingenuity quite as much as the taming of the wilderness required such qualities in North America. As trade expanded into an era of large corporations and trusts, overseas missions grew to require centralized business management. The mission boards indeed pioneered in the administration of transnational and multinational enterprises: recruiting, supporting, and replenishing personnel in far distant places.

The missionary experience and the record it left are thus a great key to the historical understanding of modern world history, but until now, this record has been scattered in fragments all over the globe. Consequently, this bibliographical guide is not simply a tool with which to finish the job. It is a map of a job still to be done, one of the greatest tasks of the twenty-first century. The care and thoroughness with which the compilers have done their work of survey and appraisal are already having effect. Librarians and archivists are being given a new awareness, researchers a new vision of opportunity.

John K. Fairbank

Acknowledgments

THE COMPLETION OF *Christianity in China: A Scholars' Guide to Resources in the Libraries and Archives of the United States* is due to more contributors than we can possibly list. In naming a few of those most closely involved, we express appreciation to the many others who helped bring it to fruition.

*The librarians and archivists who collaborated in providing information and in verifying the entries.

*The members of the Advisory Committee who assisted with their expertise as archivists, librarians, and China scholars: James Armstrong, Princeton Theological Seminary, Speer Library; William Brackney, Eastern Baptist Theological Seminary; Gerald Gillette, Presbyterian Historical Society; Donald MacInnis, Maryknoll Fathers and Brothers; Robert Maloy, Southern Methodist University; Leslie R. Marchant, University of Western Australia, East Asian Studies; Peter Mitchell, University of Toronto/York University, Centre for Asia Pacific Studies; Stephen Peterson, Yale Divinity School Library; Nancy Sahli, National Historical Publications and Records Commission; Richard D. Spoor, Union Theological Seminary, Burke Library; Faith Johnson Vance, National Association for Foreign Student Affairs; Charles West, Princeton Theological Seminary, Christian Ethics; Edwin Winckler, Columbia University, East Asian Institute; and Franklin Woo, National Council of Churches, China Program.

*Louis Charles Willard, now at Harvard Divinity School, Andover-Harvard Theological Library, who chaired the Advisory Committee, helped organize the committee in 1976, and arranged for Princeton Theological Seminary to act as the sponsoring institution.

*Princeton Theological Seminary, the sponsoring institution, which served as administrative center and provided complete accounting services.

*The late Edward H. Johnson, who dreamed with the author of the need for the *Guide* long before it took shape, who encouraged the production of a companion guide for Canada, and who contributed a loan toward the printing costs of the sample fascicle. "Ted" Johnson died suddenly of heart failure on December 9, 1981. The work is dedicated to his memory.

ACKNOWLEDGMENTS

*Nancy Sahli, consultant, editor of the *Directory of Archives and Manuscript Repositories in the United States*, 1978, and currently, director of the Records Program of the National Historical Publications and Records Commission, who advised on technical standards.

*John K. Fairbank, Francis Lee Higginson Professor of History, Emeritus, at Harvard University and pioneer in the study of Christian missions in China, for his encouragement and assistance.

*Paul T. Lauby, past-president of the United Board for Christian Higher Education in Asia, whose assistance led to major financial support for the project.

*Arthur Emerson, Peter Hauth, David Kamen, Edward Malatesta, Debra Soled, and Philip Slutz, who did the translations.

*Kathleen Lodwick, whose *Chinese Recorder Index* was a valuable resource for checking the Personal Names Index.

*Ellen Crouch, who assisted in every part of the work.

*Staff colleagues whose skill and labor brought the project to fruition: Steven Agoratus, Research Assistant; Arthur Emerson, Bibliographer; Michael Gorman, Bibliographer; David Kamen, Computer Consultant and Translator; and Debra E. Soled, Editor and Indexer.

*Douglas Merwin, Editorial Director for M. E. Sharpe, Inc., whose technical expertise and patience guided the staff through the complications of producing the manuscript.

*The Henry Luce Foundation, whose major grant made it possible to employ a full research staff, the Starr Foundation together with Mr. Mansfield Freeman whose grant underwrote the final section of the work, and other institutions whose grants supplemented the underwriting of the Luce Foundation and the Starr-Freeman group: the American Baptist Foreign Mission Society, the California Jesuit Missionaries, The Institute for Chinese-Western Cultural History at The University of San Francisco, Charles Johnson Charitable Trust, Maryknoll Fathers and Brothers, Maryknoll Sisters of St. Dominic, National Council of Churches of Christ China Program, Presbyterian Church (U.S.A.) Division of International Mission, Presbyterian Church (U.S.A.) Program Agency, The Society of Jesus-Oregon Province, Trustees of Lingnan University, United Board for Christian Higher Education in Asia, United Methodist Church, General Board of Global Ministries—China Program.

*The friends whose gifts symbolized the wide range of support for the project: Richard Baird, Phillip Ball, Entré Computer Company of Princeton-New Jersey, William and Cynthia Gott, E. H. Johnson, Paige Kempner, Koinonia of Englewood-New Jersey, Raymond Lindquist, Armand Nigro, Robert Maloy, Harold and Evelyn Meltzer, Douglas Merwin, George and Hannah Sgalitzer, Sidney and Esther Silverman, Harry Stearns, Rev. and Mrs. David Wong, and Mei-mei Woo.

Introduction

THE OLDEST RECORD OF CHRISTIAN COMMUNITIES IN CHINA is the Nestorian Monument, erected in Xi'an in 781 A.D., 711 years before Christopher Columbus landed in America. From that beginning, the missionary presence fluctuated, growing from none at all for centuries to over 10,000 in the 1920s, the high water mark of the missionary enterprise in China. Living close to the Chinese people for extended periods of time, often for a professional lifetime of thirty to forty years, the missionaries learned the language and customs of the people and thus became the agents of cross-cultural communication between China and the West. Most of them were required to prepare detailed and regular reports and to keep in constant touch with relatives and friends in their home communities. Since the content of this vast accumulation of records extended beyond the ecclesiastical concerns of the Church—touching on activities in the fields of agriculture, education, medicine, famine relief, science, and others—the records created by this encounter are indispensable resources for the study of China as a whole.

John King Fairbank, in his introduction to *The Missionary Enterprise in China and America*, points out that the missionaries pioneered

> the spread of literacy to ordinary people, the publication of journals and pamphlets in the vernacular, education and equality of women, the abolition of arranged child marriages, the supremacy of public duty over filial obedience and family obligations, increased agricultural productivity through the sinking of wells and improved tools, crops, and breeds, dike and road building for protection against flood and famine, public health clinics to treat common ailments and prevent disease, discussion groups to foster better conduct, student organizations to promote healthy recreation and moral guidance, and the acquisition and Sinification of western knowledge for use in remaking Chinese life.

The first guide to resources relating to Christianity in China was *A Guide to the Archives and Records of Protestant Christian Missions from the British Isles to China, 1796–1914*, by Leslie R. Marchant, published by the University of Western Australia Press in 1960. As the title indicates, it only covers a limited historical period, is limited to the British Isles, and does not include either China-based institutions or the personal papers of missionaries.

A few more general guides include some, but by no means all, of the records related to missions in China. The History Department at Harvard University pioneered bibliographical research for China studies in the United States under the guidance of the Committee on American Far Eastern Policy Studies, beginning in about 1957. *Americans and Chinese: A Historical Essay and a Bibliography*, by Kwang-ching Liu, was published in 1962 under the sponsorship of that committee. The bibliographic data relates to three groups: traders and entrepreneurs, missionaries, and Chinese who studied or worked in the United States. The material is organized into four classifications: manuscripts and archives, biographies, memoirs and published letters, and reference works. The author states that the work was not meant to be a comprehensive research guide. For example, there are letters and documents reported for 55 missionaries, yet over 5,000 Americans served as missionaries in China at the peak of the enterprise. Canadian resources are not included. *Modern China, 1840–1972: An Introduction to Sources and Research Aids*, by Andrew J. Nathan, was published as *Michigan Papers in Chinese Studies*, No. 14, in 1973. It contains less than a page of references to missionary archives.

G. Raymond Nunn, of the Center for Asian and Pacific Studies at the University of Hawaii, published *Asia and Oceania: A Guide to Archival and Manuscript Sources in the United States* in 1985. This guide includes manuscripts of every category: diplomatic, military, commercial, financial, missionary, educational, scientific, etc. However, its extensive geographic scope and wide variety of manuscript sources omit some of the small but important collections, and it does not include union lists of serials, dissertations/theses, and oral histories. *A Guide to Archival Resources on Canadian Missionaries in East Asia: 1890–1960*, by Peter M. Mitchell, was published by the Joint Centre on Modern East Asia at the University of Toronto-York University in 1988. The Canadian guide covers China, Japan, and Korea as represented in nineteen repositories. A guide for Protestant Europe is being compiled by Leslie R. Marchant at the University of Western Australia Centre for East Asian Studies. Fr. Jerome Heyndrickx at the University of Leuven in Belgium has initiated a project which will include all of Catholic Europe. A project under the direction of John T. Wilson and Arthur Waldron at Princeton University is encouraging scholars in the People's Republic of China to produce a guide to documents in the libraries and archives of universities which were formerly part of a group known as the "Christian Colleges of China." Fr. Edward Malatesta at the University of San Francisco is stimulating similar work among institutions which were at one time a part of Catholic higher education in China.

The goal of Christian missions in China was to spread the Christian faith and to develop a self-propagating, self-supporting, and self-governing Christian church. As the church grew, Chinese Christians produced an increasingly important part of the records documenting its history, but these records are in China, and so are outside the purview of this project. Also, since some Chinese-language materials exist in American libraries, this guide provides brief descriptions of them under the category CHINESE LANGUAGE MATERIALS. An exhaustive description of Chinese-language materials deserves fuller attention than this project has been able to provide.

The *Christianity in China* guide is offered not only as an aid to scholars outside China, but also as indirect help to the growing number of Chinese historians within China who are beginning to research and appraise the history of the Christian church in China in all its aspects, both for itself and as a factor in the great drama of China's modernization.

This guide has several unique characteristics: (1) It is comprehensive, ranging from the massive group of collections at Yale Divinity School and Yale University, to the handful of papers at Grove Farm Homestead in Lihue, Hawaii. (2) It contains union lists which are the first of their kind. The list of serials identifies and locates over 700 serial titles produced by the Christian enterprise in and related to China, from the omnipresent *Chinese Recorder* to the one and only collection of the *Yunnan Christian*. The list of dissertations/theses contains over 550 titles, including some in European languages. The list of oral histories locates about 650 interviews with both well-known figures such as Walter Judd and the relatively unknown such as Wu Pak-seng. (3) It includes all Roman Catholic orders in the United States with missions in China, together with missions of all Protestant churches and organizations. (4) It identifies and includes documents relating to institutions and organizations with close ties to the Christian mission in China, i.e., Oberlin-in-China, Carleton-in-China, Dickinson College-in-China, Rockefeller Foundation, China Medical Board, China International Famine Relief Commission, United China Relief, and others. (5) It locates and describes Chinese-language materials, in addition to English and European-language materials. (6) It includes data from the earliest beginnings of Christianity in China in the early 700s through 1952 to the present.

This publication concentrates on mainland China, even though there is a significant extension of data from the mainland to Taiwan and Hong Kong, particularly during and after the late 1940s. The magnitude of the data emanating from the mainland does not diminish the importance of Christianity in Taiwan and Hong Kong, but the logistics of creating a guide to materials there require that it be done as a separate project.

These beginnings are the tip of a huge iceberg of primary and secondary resources produced by the Christian enterprise in China. Therefore, this guide should be considered merely an introduction to resources documenting the history of Christianity in China. Already, material is accumulating for a second edition, which will contain a large amount of new information, in addition to corrections and updates.

When the guides for the United States, Canada, all of Europe, and China are completed, microform reproduction of all the documents located by the guides would enable access to materials related to Christianity in China in a few strategic centers, facilitating and enhancing all scholarship related to China. Microfilming such a vast collection of documents in so many parts of the world may seem like an undertaking too large and too expensive to be realized. However, the technology of electronic record preservation is progressing so rapidly that what seems impossible today may be routine within a few years. The current guides constitute a first step which makes further progress possible. Improved access to such a vast library of human experience between the people of China and the people of North America and Europe may bring us all closer to the ancient Chinese concept that ''all men are brothers.''

The archival collections are as dynamic as a growing fetus, changing shape, size, and location daily. As the resources become known, momentum is created which leads to the discovery of more data. Even now, before publication of this guide, librarians and archivists are reminded of material which has been overlooked, or they are finding material they did not realize was in their repositories. Some large and significant collections, still boxed and stored in library basements, are awaiting the time when there will be enough money and staff to open the boxes and process the papers. Moreover, individuals with private collections of correspondence with relatives who were missionaries in China—some of the letters dating back to the 1880s—are making their collections known and are being encouraged to contribute them to a repository for permanent professional management.

Over 1,200 libraries, archives, historical societies, religious orders, and denominational headquarters were surveyed to ascertain the location of the collections described in the 554 repositories in this guide. The information was solicited by letters explaining the nature of the project, then further contacts were made by telephone, and personal visits were arranged where required. To ensure accuracy, draft entries were sent to each repository for review.

The table of contents reflects all the states which had collections containing relevant material at the time of publication (no collections were found in Montana and Nevada).

In spite of all efforts to be thorough and accurate, important sources may have been overlooked, or the data may need to be corrected. Users who discover such problems are encouraged to contact the Christianity in China Resources Project, c/o M. E. Sharpe, Inc., 80 Business Park Drive, Armonk, NY, 10504.

A. R. C., March 1989

Abbreviations and Acronyms

Miscellaneous

A.B.	Bachelor of Arts
A.B.C.C.C.	Associated Boards for Christian Colleges in China
A.B.C.F.M.	American Board of Commissioners for Foreign Missions
A.B.F.M.S.	American Baptist Foreign Mission Society
A.M.	Master of Arts
American Board	American Board of Commissioners for Foreign Missions
A.P.B.	Adorers of the Precious Blood
A.S.C.	Adorers of the Blood of Christ
b.	born
B.A.	Bachelor of Arts
B.D.	Bachelor of Divinity
B.Div.	Bachelor of Divinity
B.L.	Bachelor of Letters
Br.	Brother
B.R.E.	Bachelor of Religious Education
B.S.L.	Bachelor of Sacred Literature
B.Th.	Bachelor of Theology
ca.	circa
Cap.	Capuchin
c.f.	cubic feet
C.F.X.	Congregation of the Brothers of St. Francis Xavier
C.I.C.	China Industrial Cooperatives
C.I.F.R.C.	China International Famine Relief Commission
C.I.M.	China Inland Mission
C.L.S.	Christian Literature Society of China
C.M.	Congregation of the Mission
C.M.A.	Christian and Missionary Alliance
C.M.B.	China Medical Board
comp.	compiled
C.P.	Congregation of the Passion
C.S.J.	Convent of St. Joseph
C.S.M.	Community of St. Mary

C.T.	Community of the Transfiguration
d.	died
D.B.	Bachelor of Divinity
D.C.	Daughters of Charity
D.Min.	Doctor of Ministry
D.Miss.	Doctor of Missiology
D.R.E.	Doctor of Religious Education
ed.	edited
Ed.D.	Doctor of Education
etc.	*et cetera*
F.M.C.	Committee on Relief in China
Fr.	Father
F.S.P.A.	Congregation of the Sisters of the Third Order of St. Francis of Perpetual Adoration
ft.	foot/feet
in.	inch(es)
inc.	incomplete
Inc.	Incorporated
K.S.G.	Knights of St. Gregory
l.f.	linear feet
L.W.F.	Lutheran World Federation
M.A.	Master of Arts
M.C.T.	Master of Christian Theology
M.Div.	Master of Divinity
M.E.C.	Methodist Episcopal Church
M.E.P.	Société des Missions Etrangères de Paris
M.Litt.	Master of Letters
mm.	millimeter(s)
M.M.	Maryknoll Missioner (Maryknoll Fathers and Brothers/Maryknoll Sisters of St. Dominic)
M.R.E.	Master of Religious Education
M.S.	Master of Science
Msgr.	Monsignor
M.S.I.C.	Missionary Sisters of the Immaculate Conception
M.S.T.	Master of Sacred Theology
M.Th.	Master of Theology
N	number
n.a.	no author
N.C.C.(C.)	National Christian Council (of China)
N.C.C.R.E.	National Committee for Christian Religious Education
n.d.	no date
n.p.	no pages/no place/no publisher
n.s.	new series
n.v.	no volume number
O.F.M.	Order of Friars Minor
O.F.M., Cap.	Order of Friars Minor, Capuchin
O.M.S.	Oriental Missionary Society
O.P.	Order of Preachers
O.S.B.	Order of St. Benedict
O.S.F.	Order of St. Francis
P.C.U.S.	Presbyterian Church of the United States (South)
P.C.U.S.A.	Presbyterian Church of the United States of America (North)

p(p).	page(s)
Ph.D.	Doctor of Philosophy
pt.	part
P.U.M.C.	Peking Union Medical College
RG	Record Group
R.C.S.J.	Society of the Sacred Heart
repr.	reprinted
rev.	revised
Rev.	Reverend
Rt. Rev.	Right Reverend
S.C.	Sisters of Charity
S.D.A.	Seventh-Day Adventist
ser.	series
S.J.	Society of Jesus
s.l.	*sine loco* (no place)
S.L.	Sisters of Loretto
S.M.	Society of Mary (Marianist)
S.N.D.N.	Sisters of Notre Dame de Namur
S.P.	Sisters of Providence
Sr.	Sister
srs.	sisters
S.S.F.	Sisters of St. Francis
S.S.J.	Sisters of St. Joseph
S.S.M.	Sisters of St. Mary
S.S.S.F.	School Sisters of St. Francis
St.	Saint
S.T.B.	Bachelor of Sacred Theology
S.T.D.	Doctor of Sacred Theology
S.T.M.	Master of Sacred Theology
S.V.D.	Society of the Divine Word
Th.B.	Bachelor of Theology
Th.D.	Doctor of Theology
Th.M.	Master of Theology
trans.	translated
U.B.C.C.C.	United Board for Christian Colleges in China
U.B.C.H.E.A.	United Board for Christian Higher Education in Asia
U.C.R.	United China Relief
U.S.	United States
U.S.M.A.	United States Military Academy
V	volume
vols.	volumes
W.A.B.F.M.S.	Women's American Baptist Foreign Mission Society
Y.M.C.A.	Young Men's Christian Association
Y.W.C.A.	Young Women's Christian Association

ABBREVIATIONS AND ACRONYMS

States of the United States of America as authorized by the U.S. Postal Service

Alabama	AL	Montana	MT
Alaska	AK	Nebraska	NB
Arizona	AZ	Nevada	NV
Arkansas	AR	New Hampshire	NH
California	CA	New Jersey	NJ
Colorado	CO	New Mexico	NM
Connecticut	CT	New York	NY
Delaware	DE	North Carolina	NC
District of Columbia	DC	North Dakota	ND
Florida	FL	Ohio	OH
Georgia	GA	Oklahoma	OK
Hawaii	HI	Oregon	OR
Idaho	ID	Pennsylvania	PA
Illinois	IL	Rhode Island	RI
Indiana	IN	South Carolina	SC
Iowa	IA	South Dakota	SD
Kansas	KS	Tennessee	TN
Kentucky	KY	Texas	TX
Louisiana	LA	Utah	UT
Maine	ME	Vermont	VT
Maryland	MD	Virginia	VA
Massachusetts	MA	Washington	WA
Michigan	MI	West Virginia	WV
Minnesota	MN	Wisconsin	WI
Mississippi	MS	Wyoming	WY
Missouri	MO		

How to Use the Guide

The *Guide* is organized according to a system of hierarchic code numbers based on a program developed by the National Historical Publications and Records Commission for the purpose of indexing guides relating to historical research.

States are identified by the two-letter abbreviations used by the U.S. Postal Service. Cities within states are listed alphabetically. Within each city, institutions are listed alphabetically. Example:

CALIFORNIA

BERKELEY

AMERICAN BAPTIST SEMINARY OF THE WEST
CA-10 Library
    2515 Hillegass Avenue
    Berkeley CA 94704
    (415) 841-1905

GRADUATE THEOLOGICAL UNION
CA-15 Library
    2400 Ridge Road
    Berkeley CA 94709
    (415) 649-2400

PACIFIC SCHOOL OF RELIGION
CA-20 Charles Holbrook Library
    1798 Scenic Avenue
    Berkeley CA 94709
    (415) 843-0528

Within each institution, libraries are listed alphabetically. Example:

BERKELEY

UNIVERSITY OF CALIFORNIA, BERKELEY

CA-25 Anthropology Library
    230 Kroeber Hall
    Berkeley CA 94720
    (415) 642-2400

CA–30 Astronomy Library
University of California, Berkeley
100 Evans Hall
Berkeley CA 94720
(415) 642–3381

CA–35 The Bancroft Library
University of California, Berkeley
Berkeley CA 94720
(415) 642–3781

CA–40 Biology Library
3503 Life Science Building
University of California, Berkeley
Berkeley CA 94720
(415) 642–2531

Where several distinct repositories are housed in the same building and the general library holdings contain resources on Christianity in China, the repositories are listed alphabetically, with the general library listed last under the full library name. Example:

WINSTON-SALEM

WAKE FOREST UNIVERSITY

NC–100 North Carolina Baptist Historical Collection
Room 207, Z. Smith Reynolds Library
P. O. Box 7777, Reynolda Station
Winston-Salem NC 27109
(919) 761–5472

NC–105 University Archives
Z. Smith Reynolds Library
P. O. Box 7777, Reynolda Station
Winston-Salem NC 27109
(919) 761–5472

NC–110 Z. Smith Reynolds Library
Wake Forest University
P. O. Box 7777, Reynolda Station
Winston-Salem NC 27109
(919) 761–5480

Where there is no distinct repository name within an institution the index code precedes the name of the institution. Example:

MO–30 KANSAS CITY PUBLIC LIBRARY
311 East 12th Street
Kansas City MO 64106
(816) 221–2685

Within a repository, collection titles are listed alphabetically. Resources which are not in titled collections are listed last under GENERAL HOLDINGS. Example:

DAYTON

UNITED THEOLOGICAL SEMINARY
OH–120 Library
> 1810 Harvard Boulevard
> Dayton OH 45406
> (513) 278–5817 Ext. 120

1-EUNICE MITCHELL BENNETT PAPERS
2-CHURCH OF THE UNITED BRETHREN IN CHRIST
3-SCHUYLER COLFAX ENCK
4-EVANGELICAL ASSOCIATION OF NORTH AMERICA
5-EVANGELICAL CHURCH
6-EVANGELICAL UNITED BRETHREN CHURCH
7-MISSIONARY LETTERS
8-CHARLES AND KATHRYN SHOOP PAPERS
9-UNITED EVANGELICAL CHURCH
10-SAMUEL G. ZIEGLER PAPERS
11-GENERAL HOLDINGS

Standard Entry Form: The description of the materials in each repository is organized according to a standard entry form so that categories of information follow each other in identical sequence for every repository. Captions for each category of information are repeated in the descriptions. A caption omitted in the description of a repository's holdings indicates that there are no materials in that category. The Standard Entry form is reproduced on the following page.

Access Information: This section of the entry form includes the name, address, and telephone number of the repository; the name and title of the staff contact; restrictions on access and use of materials; a background note where applicable; and finding aids which apply to all the collections listed (finding aids to individual collections are indicated under that collection title).

Background note: Comments on the origin of the collection, biographical information on the subject of the collection, or other miscellaneous details concerning the collection are noted. Biographical notes on an individual are attached to one collection only; other collections of the same person contain reference to the location of these notes. The main personal data noted relates to the location, dates, and nature of the subject's mission service in China. The Personal Names Index indicates which entry contains biographical notes.

Collection Titles: Collection titles in the *Guide* are *identical to those used by the repository in which the collection is held*. Each collection title is followed by inclusive dates and volume of relevant material in that collection. A background note may also be included, to provide some additional information on the collection. Collection titles are listed alphabetically, with the exception of GENERAL HOLDINGS. "General Holdings" covers items which are not part of a titled collection.

Inclusive dates: Inclusive dates refer to the dates covered by the materials described, wherever that is known. Where it was not possible to determine the inclusive dates, "n.d." is used.

Total volume: Repository records are uneven. Some are measured in cubic feet, some in linear feet, some in numbers of boxes or folders. The *Guide* uses the measurements provided by the repositories. Where the volume was not available or it was not possible to estimate, "quantity undetermined" is used.

Category Headings: Description of the items in each collection is organized by the broad type of material as indicated by the category headings (see STANDARD ENTRY FORM), generally in the following sequence: subject, volume and dates, and any distinguishing features. Where long lists of items are related to the same subject or institution, as with mission station reports, the subject or institution is at the beginning of the list, covering all the subsequent items until the introduction of a new subject or institution. Occasionally, items listed appear unrelated to the subject, due to the vagaries of arrangement in the collections.

Note on Romanization: The *Guide* uses the spelling of names, places, and titles exactly as they appear in the repository records. This is done because any attempt on the part of the *Guide* to shift from their original spellings to a standard system, however official, would present difficulties to the researcher in trying to retrieve the material.

In most library cataloging, the Wade-Giles system of romanization is used. Variations are due to authors who used different romanization systems or who used ad hoc spellings of their own invention, often representing non-Mandarin dialects. The romanization system now used in the People's Republic of China, *pinyin*, is beginning to be used in publications originating outside of China.

For place names, the *Guide* includes a conversion table, showing the original repository spelling, the Wade-Giles equivalent, and the *pinyin* equivalent.

STANDARD ENTRY FORM

STATE

CITY

CUSTODIAL INSTITUTION
Index code   Repository
              Address
              Telephone
              Name and title of director or section head

Restrictions:
Background note:
Finding aids:

1-COLLECTION TITLE, inclusive dates, total volume
MINUTES/RECORDS/REPORTS:
CORRESPONDENCE:
DIARIES:
MANUSCRIPTS:
PAMPHLETS:
MEMORABILIA:
ORAL HISTORIES:
MAPS/DESIGNS/DRAWINGS:
AUDIO-VISUAL MATERIALS:
SERIALS:
DISSERTATIONS/THESES:
CHINESE LANGUAGE MATERIALS:
FINDING AIDS:

Conversion Table of Place Names
in China

Spelling as it appears in text	Wade-Giles romanization	Pinyin romanization (Mandarin)
Ai-wa*	—	—
Amoy	Hsia-mên	Xiamen
Anfu	An-fu	Anfu
Anhui, Anhwei	An-hui	Anhui
Anki	An-chi	Anji
Anking	An-ch'ing	Anqing
Anlu	An-lu	Anlu
Anlung	An-lung	Anlong
Anning	An-ning	Anning
Antung	An-tung	Andong
Anyang	An-yang	Anyang
Ashiho	A-shen-he	Ashenhe
Barim (Barin)	Pa-lin	Balin
Batang	Pa-t'ang	Batang
Bin Hsien	Pin-hsien	Binxian
Canton	Kuang-chou	Guangzhou
Chahar	Ch'a-ha-êrh	Chahaer
Chai Wan	Chai-wan	Chaiwan
Chakow	Ch'a-kou	Chagou
Chang Chow, Changchow	Chang-chou	Zhangzhou
	Ch'ang-chou	Chang-zhou
Changli	Chang-li	Zhangli
	Ch'ang-li	Chan-gli
Changpu	Chang-p'u	Zhangpu
Changsa	Ch'ang-sa	Changsa
Changsha	Ch'ang-sha	Changsha
Changshu	Ch'ang-shu	Changshu
Changte, Changteh (Changteho, Changtecho)	Ch'ang-teh	Changde

PLACE NAME CONVERSION TABLE

Spelling as it appears in text	Wade-Giles romanization	Pinyin romanization (Mandarin)
Changtek*	—	—
Chang Tien	Chang-tien	Zhangdian
	Ch'ang-tien	Changdian
Ch'ang-yuan	Ch'ang-yüan	Changyuan
Chao Cheng	Chao-ch'eng	Zhaocheng
	Ch'ao-ch'eng	Chaocheng
Chaochow, Chaochowfu	Ch'ao-chou	Chaozhou
Chao hsien	Chao-hsien	Zhaoxian
	Ch'ao-hsien	Chaoxian
Chaotung	Chao-t'ung	Zhaotong
Chaoyang	Ch'ao-yang	Chaoyang
Chaoyangchen	Ch'ao-yang-chen	Chaoyangzhen
Chaoyangchun	Ch'ao-yang-ch'un	Chaoyangchun
Chapei	Cha-pei	Zhabei
Cheefoo, Chefoo	Yen-t'ai (Chih-fou/ Chi-fau/Chih-fu)	Yantai (Zhifu)
Chekiang	Chê-chiang	Zhejiang
Chenchow	Ch'en-chou	Chenzhou
Cheng An	Ch'eng-an	Cheng'an
Chengchow	Cheng-chou	Zhengzhou
Chengku	Ch'eng-ku	Chenggu
Chengteh	Ch'eng-tê	Chengde
Chengtong	Cheng-tung	Zhengdong
	Ch'eng-tung	Chengdong
Chengtu	Ch'eng-tu	Chengdu
Chengyang	Chengyang	Zhengyang
Chenhsi	Ch'en-hsi	Chenxi
Chenhsien	Ch'en-hsien	Chenxian
Chen-Kon-Tien	Chou-k'ou-tien	Zhoukoudian
Chenlingchi	Ch'en-ling-chih	Chenlingzhi
Cheungchow*	—	—
Chiashanchai	Chia-shan-chai	Jiashanzhai
Chichow	Ch'i-chou	Qizhou
Chihli	Chih-li	Zhili
Ch'i-hsien	Ch'i-hsien	Qixian
Chikiang	Chih-chiang	Zhijiang
Chikkai	Ch'ih-ch'i	Chiqi
Chikkung (Chiklung)	Chih-kung	Zhigong
Chin Fu	Chin-fu	Jinfu
	Ch'in-fu	Qinfu
Chinchew	Ch'üan-chou	Quanzhou
Chinchow, Chinchowfu	Chin-chou	Jinzhou
Ching-chao	Ching-chao	Jingzhao
	Ch'ing-chao	Qingzhao
Ching-ho	Ch'ing-ho	Qinghe
Ching-I	Ch'ing-yi	Qingyi
Chinkiang	Chen-chiang	Zhenjiang
Ching lien li	Ch'ing-lien-li	Qinglianli

PLACE NAME CONVERSION TABLE

Spelling as it appears in text	Wade-Giles romanization	Pinyin romanization (Mandarin)
Chiuling	Chiu-ling	Jiaoling
Cho k'e chi	Chou-k'e-chi	Zhoukeji
Chongpu	Ch'ang-p'u	Changpu
Chou-k'ou-tien	Chou-k'ou-tien	Zhoukoudian
Chowkiakow	Chou-k'ou-chen	Zhoukouzhen
Chowkow	Chou-k'ou	Zhoukou
Chowtsun	Chou-ts'un	Zhoucun
Chu Chia (Tsai Tzu)	Chu-chia	Zhujia
Chu chou, Chu chow	Chu-chou	Zhuzhou
Chuanchow, Chuanchowfu	Ch'uan-chou	Quanzhou
Ch'u-hsien-chen	Ch'ü-hsien-chen	Quxianzhen
Chulan*	—	—
Chumatien	Chu-ma-tien	Zhumadian
Chungchen	Chung-chen	Zhongzhen
Chungchow	Chung-chou	Zhongzhou
Chungking	Ch'ung-ching	Chongqing
Chungsun	Chung-hsin	Zhongxin
Chusan	Chou-shan	Zhoushan
Ciuyuankow	Chiu-yuan-k'ou	Jiuyuankou
Cong-chow	Chung-chou	Zhongzhou
Dairen	Ta-lien	Dalian
Di Ho*	—	—
Diongloh	Ch'ang-le (Diong-lo)	Changle
Enshih	En-shih	Enshi
Erhpatan	Erh-pa-tan	Erbadan
Fachow	Hua-chou	Huazhou
Fakumen	Fa-k'u-mên	Fakumen
Fan	Fan	Fan
Fancheng	Fan-ch'eng	Fancheng
Fanhsien	Fan-hsien	Fanxian
Fati	Fa-ti	Fadi
Fatshan, Foh-shan, Fo-shan	Fo-shan	Foshan
Fenchow	Fen-chou	Fenzhou
Feng chan*	—	—
Feng Tien, Fengtien	Feng-t'ien	Fengtian
Fenyang	Fen-yang	Fenyang
Foochow, Fuhchau	Fu-chou	Fuzhou
Fuh-ning	Fu-ning	Funing
Fukien, Fuhkien	Fu-chien	Fujian
Fukou	Fu-kou	Fugou
Funing	Fu-ning	Funing
Funing	Fu-ning	Funing
Fushan	Fu-shan	Fushan
Fushun	Fu-shun	Fushun
Fusing	Fu-hsing	Fuxing
Futsing	Fu-ch'ing	Fuqing
Haian	Hai-an	Hai'an
Haichow	Hai-chou	Haizhou
Hainan	Hai-nan	Hainan
Haitang	Hai-t'ang	Haitang

PLACE NAME CONVERSION TABLE

Spelling as it appears in text	Wade-Giles romanization	Pinyin romanization (Mandarin)
Hanchung	Han-chung	Hanzhong
Hangchow	Hang-chou	Hangzhou
Hankong	Han-kung	Hankong
Hankow	Han-k'ou	Hankou
Hanyang	Han-yang	Hanyang
Harbin	Ha-êrh-pin	Haerbin
Heilungkiang	Hei-lung-chiang	Heilongjiang
Hengchow	Heng-chou	Hengzhou
Hengyang	Heng-yang	Hengyang
Hiao-Kan	Hsiao-kan	Xiaogan
Hingan	Hsing-an	Xing'an
Hinghwa, Hing-Hua	Hsing-hua	Xinghua
Hingking	Hsing-ching	Xingjing
Hingning	Hsing-ning	Xingning
Hoch'ienfu	Ho-ch'ien	Heqian
Hofei	Ho-fei	Hefei
Hoighan	Hai-yen	Haiyan
Hoihow	Hai-k'ou	Haikou
Hoikow	Hai-k'ou	Haikou
Hoimoon	Hai-mên	Haimen
Hokchia	Ho-chia	Hejia
Hokshiha	Ho-shih-hsia	Heshixia
Homantin	Ho-wen-tien	Hewentian
Honan	Ho-nan	Henan
Hong Kew	Hong-k'ou	Hongkou
Hong Kong	Hsiang-kang	Xianggang
Horchow	Hai-k'ou	Haikou
Hopeh, Hopei	Ho-pei	Hebei
Hsianfu	Hsi-an	Xi'an
Hsiang-Si	Hsiang-hsi	Xiangxi
Hsichang	Hsi-ch'ang	Xichang
Hsichow	Hsi-chou	Xizhou
Hsiengtang	Hsiang-t'ang	Xiangtang
Hsienhsien	Hsien-hsien	Xianxian
Hsi-hua	Hsi-hua	Xihua
Hsinpin	Hsin-pin	Xinbin
Hsuchang	Hsü-ch'ang	Xuchang
Hsü-chia-hui	Hsü-chia-hui	Xujiahui
Huachung	Hua-chung	Huazhong
Huaiyuan, Hwaiyuan	Huai-yuan	Huaiyuan
Huangho	Huang-ho	Huanghe
Huchow	Hu-chou	Huzhou (Wuxing)
Hulan	Hu-lan	Hulan
Hunan	Hu-nan	Hunan
Hungkialou	Hung-chia-lou	Hongjialou (Licheng)
Hupeh, Hupei	Hu-pei	Hubei

PLACE NAME CONVERSION TABLE

Spelling as it appears in text	Wade-Giles romanization	Pinyin romanization (Mandarin)
Huping	Hu-p'ing	Huping
Hwaianfu	Huai-an	Huai'an
Hwai King, Hwaikingfu	Huai-ch'ing	Huaiqing
Hwaining	Huai-ning	Huaining
Hwai-Yuen, Huaiyuan	Huai-yuan	Huaiyuan
Hwangchuan	Huang-ch'uan	Huangchuan
Hwanghien, Hwanghsien, Hwangsien	Huang-hsien	Huangxian
Hwang Shih	Huang-shih	Huangshi
Hwang-shih-kang	Huang-shih-kang	Huangshigang
Hwasipa	Hua-hsi-pa	Huaxiba
Hwayang	Hua-yang	Huayang
Hwa Yung	Hua-yung	Huayong
Hweian	Hui-an	Hui'an
Ichang	I-chang	Yizhang
	I-ch'ang	Yichang
Icheng	I-cheng	Yizheng
	I-ch'eng	Yicheng
Ichow(fu) (Ichau)	I-chou	Yizhou
Ilangchow	I-lang-chou	Yilangzhou
Imen	I-mên	Yimen
Ing Hok	Yung-fu	Yongfu
Ingtai, Ing-tai	Ying-t'ao	Yingtao
Ipoh*	—	—
Jaochow	Jao-chou	Raozhou
Jehol	Ch'eng-teh	Chengde
Jenshow	Jen-shou	Renshou
Jiherchueh	Jih-êrh-chüeh	Rierjue
Jinghsien	Ching-hsien	Jingxian
Juancheng	Chüan-ch'eng	Juancheng
Jugu*	—	—
Jukao (Jukau)	Ju-kao	Rugao
Junan	Ju-nan	Runan
Kachek	Chia-chi	Jiaji
Kahsing	Chia-hsing	Jiaxing
Kaichow	K'ai-chou	Kaizhou
Kaifeng	K'ai-feng	Kaifeng
Kai Kwong*	—	—
Kai-tseou	K'ai-chou	Kaizhou
Kaiyuan	K'ai-yüan	Kaiyuan
Kakchie	Chüeh-shih	Jueshi
Kalgam, Kalgan, Kalgon	Chang-chia-k'ou	Zhangjiakou
Kanchow	Kan-chou	Ganzhou
Kanhsien	Kan-hsien	Ganxian
Kansu	Kan-su	Gansu
Kaohsiung	Kao-hsiung	Gaoxiong
Kao-t'un	Kao-ts'un	Gaocun
Kashing, Chiahsing	Chia-hsing	Jiaxing
Kaying	Chia-ying	Jiaying
Kho-Khoi, Kowkoi	Ku-ch'i	Guqi

PLACE NAME CONVERSION TABLE

Spelling as it appears in text	Wade-Giles romanization	Pinyin romanization (Mandarin)
Kiahsien	Chia-hsien	Jiaxian
Kian	Chi-an	Ji'an
Kiangan, Kiang-an	Chiang-an	Jiang'an
Kiang kia	Chiang-chia	Jiangjia
Kiangnan	Chiang-nan	Jiangnan
Kiangsi	Chiang-hsi	Jiangxi
Kiangsu	Chiang-su	Jiangsu
Kiangyin	Chiang-yin	Jiangyin
Kiaotow	Chiao-t'ou	Jiaotou
	Ch'iao-t'ou	Qiaotou
Kiating	Chia-ting	Jiading
Kichow	Ch'i-chou	Qizhou
Kich-yang	Ch'ieh-yang	Qieyang
Kienchow	Ch'ien-chou	Qianzhou
Kienning-Fu	Chien-ning	Jianning
Kienow	Chien-ou	Jian'ou
Kien yang	Chien-yang	Jian-yang
Kikungshan	Chi-kung-shan	Jigongshan
Kingchow	Ching-chou	Jingzhou (Jiangling)
Kingmen	Ching-mên	Jingmen
Kingtehchen	Ching-têh-chen	Jingdezhen
Kinhwa	Chin-hua	Jinhua
Kinkiang	Chin-chiang	Jinjiang
Kinmen	Chin-mên	Jinmen
Kinwa	Chin-hua	Jinhua
Kioshan	Ch'üeh-shan	Queshan
Kirin	Chi-lin	Jilin
Kityang	Chieh-yang	Jieyang
Kiukiang	Chiu-chiang	Jiujiang
Kiulikiang	Chiu-li-chiang	Jiulijiang
Kiulungkiang	Chiu-lung-chiang	Jiulongjiang
Kiungchow, Kiung Chow	Ch'iung-chou	Qiongzhou
Kochow, Kochau	Kao-chou	Gaozhou
Kongmoon	Chiang-mên	Jiangmen
Kowloon	Chiu-lung	Jiulong
Kuanhsien	Kuan-hsien	Guanxian
Kucheng (Kutien)	Ku-ch'eng (Ku-t'ien)	Gucheng (Gutian)
Kulang(su), Kulansu	Ku-lang	Gulang
Kuliang, Kuling	Ku-ling	Guling
Kunming	K'un-ming	Kunming
Kunyang	K'un-yang	Kunyang
Kutien	Ku-t'ien	Gutian
Kutsing	Ch'ü-ching	Qujing
Kwaiping	K'uai-p'ing	Kuaiping
Kwancheng(tze)	K'uan-ch'eng	Kuancheng
Kwangchow, Canton	Kuang-chou	Guangzhou
Kwanghsien	Kuang-hsien	Guangxian
Kwangpingfu	Kuang-p'ing	Guangping
Kwangshan	Kuang-shan	Guangshan
Kwangsi	Kuang-hsi	Guangxi

PLACE NAME CONVERSION TABLE

Spelling as it appears in text	Wade-Giles romanization	Pinyin romanization (Mandarin)
Kwangtung	Kuang-tung	Guangdong
Kweichow	Kuei-chou	Guizhou
Kweifu	Kuei-fu	Guifu
Kweilin	Kuei-lin	Guilin
Kweiyang	Kuei-yang	Guiyang
Laichow	Lai-chou	Laizhou
Laipo	Li-p'u	Lipu
Laitsui	Li-tsui	Lizui
Laiyang	Lai-yang	Laiyang
Lanchow	Lan-chou	Lanzhou
Lankai-siong*	—	—
Lantien	Lan-t'ien	Lantian
Laohokow	Lao-ho-k'ou	Laohekou
Laohukow	Lao-hu-k'ou	Laohukou
Laoling	Lao-ling	Laoling
Laopehchai	Lao-pei-chai	Laobeizhai
Lekwangchiao	Le-kuang-chiao	Leguangjiao
Leling	Le-ling	Leling
Lewchew	Liu-ch'iu	Liuqiu
Lhasa	La-sa	Lhasa
Liangshan	Liang-shan	Liangshan
Liao Chou	Liao-chou	Liaozhou
Liaoyang	Liao-yang	Liaoyang
Lichwan	Li-ch'uan	Lichuan
Lien-chou, Lienchow	Lien-chou	Lianzhou (Hepu)
Liling	Li-ling	Liling
Linchow	Lin-chou	Lhünzhub/Poindo
Ling Ching	Ling-ching	Lingjing
Ling-ling	Ling-ling	Lingling
Lingshan	Ling-shan	Lingshan
Linhsiang	Lin-hsiang	Linxiang
Linhsien	Lin-hsien	Linxian
Linju	Lin-ju	Linru
Linkiang	Lin-chiang	Linjiang
Lin Mei	Lin-mei	Linmei
Lintaan	Lin-t'an	Lintan
Lintin	Lin-ting	Linding
Lintsing	Lin-ch'ing	Linqing
Liuho	Liu-ho	Liuhe
Lobochai	Lao-pei-chai	Laobeizhai
Loking	Lo-ching	Luojing
Loting, Lo Ting	Lo-ting	Luoding
Loyang	Lo-yang	Luoyang
Loyuan	Lo-yüan	Luoyuan
Loyung	Lo-yung	Luoyong
Lu Ho	Lu-ho	Luhe
Luchow(fu)	Lu-chou	Luzhou
Luichow	Lei-chou	Leizhou

PLACE NAME CONVERSION TABLE

Spelling as it appears in text	Wade-Giles romanization	Pinyin romanization (Mandarin)
Lumchai	Lin-chai	Linzhai
Lungchingtsun	Lung-ching-ts'un	Longjingcun
Lungch'iu	Lung-ch'iu	Longqiu
Lungchow	Lung-chou	Longzhou
Lungling	Lung-ling	Longling
Lungnan	Lung-nan	Longnan
Lungshan	Lung-shan	Longshan
Lungwanshan	Lung-wan-shan	Longwanshan
Lungwoh	Lung-wô	Longwo
Lungyen	Lung-yen	Longyan
Luyi	Lu-i	Luyi
Macao	Ao-mên	Aomen
Manchukuo, Manchuria	Man-chou-kuo	Manzhouguo
Matsu	Ma-tzu	Mazu
Meihsien	Mei-hsien	Meixian
Mi-ow	I-yu shan	Yiyu shan
Miao-chen-t'o	Miao-chen	Miaozhen
Miaochien	Miao-ch'ien	Miaoqian
Mienchuhsien	Mien-chu-hsien	Mianzhuxian
Ming-chiang	Ming-chiang	Mingjiang
Mintsing, Mintsinghsien	Min-ch'ing	Minqing
Miyang	Mi-yang	Mi-yang
Mosha*	—	—
Mosimien	Mo-hsi-mien	Moximian
Moukden, Mukden	Shen-yang	Shenyang
Mutao	Mu-t'ou	Mutou
Nachang	Na-chang	Nachang
Nachang	Na-chang	Nachang
Nanch'ang	Nan-ch'ang	Nanchang
Nancheng	Nan-cheng	Nanzheng
	Nan-ch'eng	Nancheng
Nanchung	Nan-chung	Nanzhong
Nanking	Nan-ching	Nanjing
Nankuan	Nan-kuan	Nanguan
Nanning	Nan-ning	Nanning
Nanping	Nan-p'ing	Nanping
Nansuchow	Nan-sü-chou	Nanxuzhou
Nantai	Nan-tai	Nantai
Nantung(chow)	Nan-t'ung	Nantong
Nanwenchuan	Nan-wen-ch'uan	Nan-wen-chuan
Nanyang, Nan Yang Fu	Nan-yang	Nanyang
Ngai Moon, Ngaimoon	Hai-mên	Haimen
Ngucheng	Lung-t'ien	Longtian
Ngwa	Wu-hua	Wuhua
Nien-tcheou	Nien-chou	Nianzhou
Ningpo	Ning-po	Ningbo
Ningteh	Ning-têh	Ningde
Ningtu	Ning-tu	Ningdu
Ningyuan	Ning-yüan	Ningyuan
Nodoa	Na-ta	Nada
On Fun	An-feng(?)	Anfeng(?)

PLACE NAME CONVERSION TABLE

Spelling as it appears in text	Wade-Giles romanization	Pinyin romanization (Mandarin)
Oshan	Oshan	Eshan
Paak Hok Tung	Pai-he-tung	Baihedong
Pa-an	Pa-an	Ba'an
Pakhoi	Pei-hai	Beihai
Pakkai	Pei-chie	Beijie
Pangchia	P'ang-chia	Pangjia
Pang-chuang*	—	—
Pangkhau, Pinghong	P'ing-kang	Pinggang
Pangkiachuang, Pangkiachwang	P'ang-chia-ch'uang	Pangjiachuang
Pan-ku	P'an-ku	Pangu
Paoki	Pao-ch'i	Baoqi
Paoking, Pao King	Pao-ch'ing	Baoqing
Paoning	Pao-ning	Baoning
Paotingfu	Pao-ting-fu	Baodingfu
Pato, Patow	Pa-t'ou	Batou
P'e cheng	P'ei-ch'eng	Peicheng
Pehcheng	Pei-ch'eng	Beicheng
Peichen	Pei-chen	Beizhen
Pei chow	Pei-chou	Beichou
Peiping	Pei-p'ing	Beijing
Peitaiho	Pei-tai-ho	Beidaihe
Peking	Pei-ching	Beijing
P'englai	P'eng-lai	Penglai
Pétang	—	—
Pettochai	Pei-t'ou-chai	Beitouzhai
Pichieh	Pi-chieh	Bijie
P'ing Chang Hien	P'ing-ch'ang-hsien	Pingchang
Pingkiang	P'ing-chiang	Pingjiang
Pinglo	P'ing-lo	Pingluo
Pingnam	P'ing-nan	Pingnan
Ping-tan	P'ing-t'an	Pingtan
Pingtichuan	P'ing-ti-ch'uan	Pingdiquan
Ping Ting Chou, Pingtingchow	P'ing-ting-chou	Pingdingzhou
Pingtu	P'ing-tu	Pingdu
Pingyang, Pingyangfu	P'ing-yang	Pingyang
P'ing Yin	P'ing-yin	Pingyin
Pochow	Po-chou	Bozhou
Ponasang	Pao-fu-shan	Baofushan
Potowchen	Pao-t'ou-chên	Baotouzhen
Puchow	P'u-chou	Puzhou
Pusih	P'u-hsi	Puxi
Putien	P'u-tien	Putian
Putsi	P'u-ch'i	Pugi
Puyang	P'u-yang	Puyang
Safang*	—	—
Salachi	Sa-la-ch'i	Salaqi
Samhopa	San-ho-pa	Sanheba
Sancian	Shang-ch'uan	Shangchuan
Sanhsien	San-hsien	Sanxian
San kiang kow, San Kiong Ko	San-chiang-k'ou	Sanjiangkou
Sanning	San-ning	Sanning

Spelling as it appears in text	Wade-Giles romanization	Pinyin romanization (Mandarin)
Sa Pu Shan*	—	—
Seung Kei	Shuang-chi	Shuangqi
Shahokou	Sha-ho-k'ou	Shahekou
Shakchin	Shih-cheng	Shizheng
Shanchengtze	Shan-ch'eng-tze	Shanchengzi
Shanghai	Shang-hai	Shanghai
Shansi	Shan-hsi	Shanxi
Shantung	Shan-tung	Shandong
Shaohing, Shaohsing	Shao-hsing	Shanxing
Shaowu, Shao Wu	Shao-wu	Shaowu
Shao Yang	Shao-yang	Shaoyang
Shasi	Sha-shih	Shashi
Shatin	Sha-t'ien	Shatian
Shekhang	She-kang	Shegang
Shekichen	She-ch'i	Sheqi
Sheklung	Shih-lung	Shilong
Shekow	She-k'ou	Shekou
Shenchow, Shenchowfu	Shen-chou	Shenzhou
Shenkiu	Shen-ch'iu	Shenqiu
Shensi	Shen-hsi	Shaanxi
Shentang*	—	—
Shih Yu	Shih-yü	Shiyu
Shihchiachwang	Shih-chia-chuang	Shijiazhuang
Shih-erh-li-chwang	Shih-êrh-li-chuang	Shi'erlizhuang
Shihnan	Shih-nan	Shinan
Shima	Shih-ma	Shima
Shimenk'an	Shih-mên-k'an	Shimenkan
Shintting	Hsin-hsing	Xinxing
Shiuchow	Shao-chou	Shaozhou
Shou Yang	Shou-yang	Shouyang
Showchow	Shou-chou	Shouzhou
Showhsien	Shou-hsien	Shouxian
Shuichai	Shui-chai	Shuizhai
Shui Hing	Chao-ch'ing	Zhaoqing
Shui-p'o	Shui-p'o	Shiupo
Shunhwachen	Shun-hua-chen	Shunhuazhen
Shunteh, Shuntefu	Shun-têh	Shunde
Sian, Si-ngan	Hsi-an	Xi'an
Siangtan	Hsiang-t'an	Xiangtan
Siangyang	Hsiang-yang	Xiangyang
Siaochang	Hsiao-chang	Xiaozhang
Siaokan	Hsiao-kan	Xiaogan
Siaoloc	Sou-lo	Souluo
Siaolu	Hsiao-lü	Xiaolu
Siaoyi	Hsiao-i	Xiaoyi
Siau liu dja	Hsiao-liu-chia	Xiaoliujia
Sienhsien	Hsien-hsien	Xianxian
Sienyu	Hsien-yü	Xianyou
Sihsien	Hsi-hsien	Xixian
Sikang	Hsi-kang	Xigang
Si-ka-wei	Hsü-chia-hui	Xujiahui
Sinchai	Hsin-chai	Xinzhai

PLACE NAME CONVERSION TABLE

Spelling as it appears in text	Wade-Giles romanization	Pinyin romanization (Mandarin)
Sinchang	Hsin-chang	Xinzhang
Sinfeng	Hsin-feng	Xinfeng
Singju*	—	—
Sin-hii*	—	—
Sinhwa	Hsin-hua	Xinhua
Sining	Hsi-ning	Xining
Sinkiang	Hsin-chiang	Xinjiang
Sinminfu	Hsin-min-fu	Xinminfu
Sinping	Hsin-p'ing	Xinping
Sinsiang	Hsin-hsiang	Xinxiang
Sinyang, Sinyangchow	Hsin-yang	Xinyang
Siokhe	Hsiao-ch'i	Xiaoqi
Siufu*	—	—
Siulan, Siu Laam	Hsiao-lan	Xiaolan
Siu San Hsien	Hsiu-shan hsien	Xiu-shan xian
Siu Tung	Hsiu-tung	Xiudong
Siwantzu	Hsi-wan-tzu	Xiwanzi
Soeilok*	—	—
Songpan	Sung-p'an	Songpan
Soochow, Suchowfu	Su-chou	Suzhou
Soonchun*	—	—
Suchien	Su-ch'ien	Sugian
Süchow	Sü-chou	Xuzhou
Suichow	Sui-chou	Suizhou
Suifu	Sü-fu	Xufu
Suiling	Sui-ling	Suiling
Suining	Sui-ning	Suining
Suiyuan	Sui-yuan	Suiyuan
Sunchong	Hsin-ch'ang	Xinchang
Sung-Ka-Hong*	—	—
Sungkiang	Sung-chiang	Songjiang
Sungkow	Sung-k'ou	Songkou
Sunwui	Hsin-hui	Xinhui
Sutsien	Su-ch'ien	Suqian
Swabue	Shan-wei	Shanwei
Swatow	Shan-t'ou	Shantou
Szechuan, Szechwan	Ssu-ch'uan	Sichuan
Szwong	Ssu-wang	Siwang
Ta Chia Chi	Ta-chia-chi	Dajiaji
Tah Chien Kia*	—	—
Taianfu	T'ai-an-fu	Tai'an
Taichow, T'aichow	T'ai-chou	Taizhou
Tai chung	T'ai-chung	Taizhong
Taihu	T'ai-hu	Taihu
Taihuan	T'ai-huan	Taihuan
Taikam	Ta-chin	Dajin
Taiku, T'ai ku, Taikuhsien	T'ai-ku	Taigu
Tainan	T'ai-nan	Tainan
Taipathu	Ti-pa-hsü	Dibaxu
Taipei	T'ai-pei	Taibei

PLACE NAME CONVERSION TABLE

Spelling as it appears in text	Wade-Giles romanization	Pinyin romanization (Mandarin)
Taipingtien	T'ai-p'ing-tien	Taipingdian
Taiwan	T'ai-wan	Taiwan
Taiyuan, T'ai-yuen-fu	T'ai-yüen Fu	Taiyuan
Taku	Ta-ku	Dagu
Tali	Ta-li	Dali
Talien	Ta-lien	Dalian
Taming, Tamingfu	Ta-ming	Daming
Tangshan	T'ang-shan	Tangshan
Taohwalun	T'ao-hua-lun	Taohualun
Tatsienlu	Ta-chien-lu	Dajianlu
Tatung, Tatungfu	Ta-t'ung	Datong
Tayeh	T'a-yeh	Taye
Tehchow, Te Chow	Teh-chou	Dezhou
Tehsien	Teh-hsien	Dexian
Teian	Teh-an	De'an
Tengchen	Teng-chen	Dengzhen
Tengchow	Teng-chou	Dengzhou
Tenghsien	T'eng-hsien	Tengxian
	Teng-hsien	Deng-xian
Tengshek	Teng-shih	Deng-shi
Tibet	Tibet	Xizang
Tiehling	T'ieh-ling	Tieling
Tienfu	T'ien-fu	Tianfu
Tienshui	T'ien-shui	Tianshui
Tientsin	T'ien-chin	Tianjin
Tingchow	T'ing-chou	Tingzhou (Changting)
Tinghsien	Ting-hsien	Dingxian
Toisan, Toishan	T'ai-shan	Taishan
Tongan, Tungan	T'ung-an	Tong'an
Tong King*	—	—
Topong	Tu-pang	Dubang
T'ou-se-wei*	—	—
Toyshan, Toishan	T'ai-shan	Taishan
Tsakulao	Tsa-ku-nao	Zagunao (Lixian)
Tsam Kong	Chan-chiang	Zhanjiang
Tsangchow	Ts'ang-chou	Cangzhou
Tsan yuk	Tsan-yai	Can-yai
Tsaohsien	Ts'ao-hsien	Caoxian
Tsaoshih	Tsao-shih	Zaoshi
Tsechow	Tse-chou	Zezhou
Tseliutsing	Tse-liu-ch'ing	Zeliuqing
Tsiahang	Yü-k'eng	Yukeng
Tsienkiang	Ch'ien-chiang	Qianjiang
Tsimo	Chi-mo	Jimo
Tsinan, Tsinanfu	Chi-nan	Jinan
Tsinchow, Tsinchou	Ch'in-chou	Qinzhou
Tsingchow, Tsingchowfu	Ch'ing-chou	Qingzhou
Tsinghai	Ching-hai	Qinghai
Tsing Kiang Pu, Tsingkiangpu	Ch'ing-chiang-p'u	Qingjiangpu
Tsingpoo	Ch'ing-p'u	Qingpu
Tsingtao	Ch'ing-tao	Qingdao

Spelling as it appears in text	Wade-Giles romanization	Pinyin romanization (Mandarin)
Tsingyuen	Ch'ing-yuan	Qingyuan
Tsining	Chi-ning	Jining
Tsowping	Tsou-p'ing	Zouping
Tsuenchaufu	Ch'üan-chou	Quanzhou
Tsun Hua, Tsunhua	Tsun-hua	Zunhua
Tszho	Tz'e-ho	Ci ho
	Tze-ho	Zi ho, Zihag
Tu tu fu*	—	—
Tung-an	Tung-an	Dong-an
Tungchou, Tungchow	T'ung-chou	Tongzhou
Tungchwan	Tung-ch'uan	Dongchuan
Tunghsien, T'unghsien	T'ung-hsien	Tongxian
Tunghwa	T'ung-hua	Tonghua
Tungkun	Tung-kuan	Dongguan
Tungming	Tung-ming	Dongming
Tungshanfu	Tung-shan	Dong-shan
Tungshek	Tung-shih	Dongshi
Tungshien	T'ung-hsien	Tongxian
Tung-sho	Tung-shou	Dongshou
Tungtsiu Wan	Tung-ch'iu	Dongqiu
Tze Kung	Tze-kung	Zegong
Ungchun	Yung-chun	Yongchun
Ungkung	Huang-kang	Huanggang
Vihsien	Wei-hsien	Weixian
Wai Chow*	—	—
Wai Hui	Wai-hui	Waihui
Wanhsien	Wan-hsien	Wanxian
Watlam	Yü-lin	Yulin
Watnam	Yü-nan	Yunan
Wei Hien, Wei Hsien	Wei-hsien	Weixian
Weihu*	—	—
Weihwei	Wei-hui	Weihui
Weishih	Wei-shih	Weishi
Wenchow	Wen-chou	Wenzhou
Wenshang	Wen-shang	Wenshang
Whampoa	Huang-p'u	Huangpu
Woosung	Wu-sung	Wusong
Wuchang	Wu-ch'ang	Wuchang
Wuchow	Wu-chou	Wuzhou
Wuhan	Wu-han	Wuhan
Wuhu	Wu-hu	Wuhu
Wuki	Wu-chi	Wuji
Wukiaho	Wu-chia-ho	Wujiahe
Wukingfu	Wu-ching-fu	Wujingfu
Wusih	Wu-hsi	Wuxi
Wuwei	Wu-wei	Wuwei
Yaan	Ya-an	Ya'an
Yachow	Ya-chou	Yazhou
Yanchow	Yen-chou	Yanzhou
Yang chau, Yangchow	Yang-chou	Yangzhou
Yangchun	Yang-chun	Yangchun

PLACE NAME CONVERSION TABLE

Spelling as it appears in text	Wade-Giles romanization	Pinyin romanization (Mandarin)
Yangkow	Yang-k'ou	Yangkou
Yang Lou Szi	Yang-lou-ssu	Yanglousi
Yangsin	Yang-hsin	Yangxin
Yangtzepoo	Yang-shu-p'u	Yangshupu
Yaochow	Yao-chou	Yaozhou
Yaowan	Yao-wan	Yaowan
Yen Cheng	Yen-ch'eng	Yancheng
Yenan	Yen-an	Yan'an
Yenchiao	Yen-chiao	Yanjiao
Yenchiaping*	—	—
Yenchowfu	Yen-chou	Yanzhou
Yenping	Yen-p'ing	Yanping
Yenshan	Yen-shan	Yanshan
Yentou	Yen-t'ou	Yantou
Yeung Kong, Yeungkong	Yang-chiang	Yangjiang
Yihsien	I-hsien	Yixian
Yinchuan	Yin-ch'uan	Yinchuan
Yinglak*	—	—
Yingtak	Ying-têh	Yingde
Yingtau	Ying-t'ao	Yingtao
Yi Yang, Yiyang	I-yang	Yiyang
Yochow	Yochou	Youzhou
Yong-tak-hia	Yung-t'ai-hsien (?)	Yongtaixian (?)
Yoyang	Yo-yang	Yoyang
Yuanchow	Yuan-chou	Yuanzhou
Yuankiang	Yuan-chiang	Yuanjiang
Yuanling	Yüan-ling	Yuanling
Yuhsien	Yü-hsien	Yuxian
Yuki	Yu-ch'i	Yuqi
Yukiang	Yü-chiang	Yujiang
Yulin(fu)	Yü-lin	Yulin
Yungan	Yung-an	Yong'an
Yungchen	Yung-chen	Yongzhen
Yungchow	Yung-chou	Yongzhou
Yung Chun	Yung-ch'un	Yongchun
Yungfeng	Yung-feng	Yongfeng
Yunghui	Jung-hsü	Rongxu
Yungling	Yung-ling	Yongling
Yunnan	Yun-nan	Yunnan
Yunyang	Yün-yang	Yunyang
Yutu	Yü-tu	Yudu
Yuyao	Yü-yao	Yuyao
Yuyiao*	—	—
Zakelao	Tsa-ku-nao	Zagunao (Lixian)
Zangzok*	—	—
Zikawei	Hsü-chia-hui	Xujiahui
Zo-se*	—	—

*Standard romanization undetermined

CHRISTIANITY IN CHINA

A Scholars' Guide to Resources
in the Libraries and Archives
of the United States

ALABAMA

AUBURN

AUBURN UNIVERSITY
AL–5   Auburn University Archives
Ralph Brown Draughon Library
Auburn AL 36849–3501
(205) 826–4465
Dwayne Cox, University Archivist

1-DENSON FAMILY PAPERS, 1900–1933, 3 folders
Background note: Carrie Vernon Denson was the wife of Nimrod Davis Denson, Sr., a prominent lawyer and judge in Alabama.
CORRESPONDENCE/MANUSCRIPTS/MEMORABILIA: Folder of correspondence between Carrie Vernon Denson and missionary Virginia M. Atkinson, including clippings and a travelogue of Atkinson's trip to China; folder of postcards of China.
AUDIO-VISUAL MATERIALS: Folder of photos of Atkinson, n.d.
FINDING AIDS: In-house guide.

BIRMINGHAM

WOMEN'S MISSIONARY UNION
AL–10   Archives
P.O. Box C–10
Birmingham AL 35283–0010
(205) 991–8100
Eljee Bentley, Archivist

Background note: The Women's Missionary Union (WMU) was founded in 1888 as an independent auxiliary of the Southern Baptist Convention. In addition to the materials listed below, the Special Collections Library holds books published by state WMU organizations and other missionary publishers, with an emphasis on Southern Baptist missions in China. See also Southern Baptist Convention Historical Commission, Library and Archives, 901 Commerce Street, Suite 400, Nashville, TN, 37203-3260; and Southern Baptist Convention, Foreign Mission Board, Box 6767, 3806 Monument Avenue, Richmond, VA, 23230.

1-COLLECTIONS, PAPERS, n.d., quantity undetermined
CORRESPONDENCE: Letters from Lottie Moon to Emma Hampton, and to friends in Cartersville, Georgia, ca. 1880; letter on rice paper from Earnest Provence, a printer in Shanghai, at the request of Southern Baptist Foreign Mission Board, 1909.
MEMORABILIA: Miscellaneous memorabilia belonging to Lottie Moon; clippings and articles about Lottie Moon, n.d.

2-WOMEN'S MISSIONARY UNION ARCHIVES, 1887-, quantity undetermined
MINUTES/RECORDS/REPORTS: Executive Committee/Board, minutes, records, and reports, 1888-; Women's Missionary Union,

Annual Meeting, minutes, records, and reports, including reports from women's organizations in China, 1913–53; reports and printed letters from China missionaries in WMU-published magazines, *Our Mission Fields*, 1906–14; *Royal Service*, 1914-; *World Comrades*, 1922–53; and *The Window of YWA*, 1929–70.
CORRESPONDENCE: Letters from China missionaries to staff, n.d.
MANUSCRIPTS: Research materials used to write and publish *The New Lottie Moon Story*, by Catherine B. Allen (published in 1980), and *Blanche Groves of China: Indomitable Lady*, by Jean F. Bond (published in 1982).
PAMPHLETS: Pamphlets published by WMU and others about China missions, 1887-.
MEMORABILIA: Publications by and other miscellaneous memorabilia from women's organizations in China, ca. 1936; gifts from Chinese Baptists; gifts from missionaries.
ORAL HISTORIES: Recorded oral histories of Lottie Moon and Blanche Groves, n.d.
AUDIO-VISUAL MATERIALS: Photo album and loose photos which belonged to missionaries in Shantung, 1900–1920; photos from Blanche Groves, who was in Soochow from 1920 to 1950.
FINDING AIDS: In-house indicies of minutes and magazines, and lists of pamphlets.

MOBILE

MOBILE COLLEGE
AL–15   J. L. Bedsole Library
P.O. Box 13220
Mobile AL 36571
(205) 675–5990
Brantley H. Parsley, Director

1-GENERAL HOLDINGS
AUDIO-VISUAL MATERIALS: *Journey Home: Lottie Moon of China*, video-cassette by the Southern Baptist Convention, Foreign Mission Board, 1983.

ARIZONA

TUCSON

UNIVERSITY OF ARIZONA
AZ–5   Library
Tucson AZ 85721
(602) 621–2010
W. David Laird, Director
Lois Olsrud, Central Reference Librarian

1-ORIENTAL STUDIES COLLECTION, 1946–81, 12 items
SERIALS: Catholic University of Peking, *Bulletin*, 1926–34.
CHINESE LANGUAGE MATERIALS: 11 volumes, 1946–81, on Young J. Allen, Baptist missions, Ch'ing emperors K'ang-hsi and Ch'ien-lung and the Catholic missionaries, Christianity, diplomatic relations between the K'ang-hsi emperor and Rome, education, embassies from the Vatican to China, J. Hudson Taylor, and missionaries and modern China.

2-SPECIAL COLLECTIONS, 1947, 1 item
MANUSCRIPTS: "A próposito dum livrinho xilográfico dos Jesuítas de Pequim (século XVIII)," by Charles Ralph Boxer, 1947.

3-GENERAL HOLDINGS
MINUTES/RECORDS/REPORTS: Federation of Woman's Boards of Foreign Missions of North America, report of deputation to the Shanghai conference, 1920.
SERIALS: China International Famine Relief Commission, *News Bulletin*, 1939; Publications, series A, 1924–26, 1929–30, 1933–36, 1938. *China Mission Year Book*, 1910–14. *China Monthly*, 1939–47. *Chinese Recorder*, 1868–1941. *Lingnan Science Journal*, 1922–23, 1936–38, 1941–48. *Monumenta Serica*, 1935–. *Yenching Journal of Social Studies*, 1938–41.
DISSERTATIONS/THESES: *China und die katholische Mission in Süd-Shantung, 1882–1900: die Geschichte einer Konfrontation*, by Jacobus Joannes Antonius Mathias Kuepers, 1974. *Chinese, Missionary, and International Efforts to End the Use of Opium in China, 1890–1916*, by Kathleen Lorraine Lodwick, 1976. *Missionary Activities as a Cause of the Boxer Rebellion*, by James Charles Sherman, 1966. *The Negotiations between Ch'i-ying and Lagrené, 1844–1846*, by Angelus Francis J. Grosse-Aschhoff, 1950.

ARKANSAS

BENTON

SALINE COUNTY ART LEAGUE HISTORICAL MUSEUM
AR–5   Schupper House
512 North Main Street
Benton AR 72105
No phone
Pat Dunnahoo, contact person

Restrictions: Access by appointment only. The Schupper House is not open to the public on a regular basis. Contact Pat Dunnahoo at (501) 778-7834 for access.

1-JOHN CLINE PAPERS, ca. 1897–1955, quantity undetermined
Background note: John Wesley Cline (1868–1955) served in China from 1897 to 1955 as a Methodist missionary, president of Soochow University, pastor of the Soong family, and confidant of Generalissimo and Madame Chiang K'ai-shek (Soong Mei-ling).

CORRESPONDENCE/MANUSCRIPTS: Uncatalogued letters and papers of John Cline, ca. 1897–1955.
DIARIES: Four diaries of Cline, ca. 1897–1955.

CALIFORNIA

ANGWIN

PACIFIC UNION COLLEGE
CA–5   Nelson Memorial Library
Angwin CA 94508-9705
(707) 965-6241
Gary Shearer, Special Collections Librarian

1-GENERAL HOLDINGS
MANUSCRIPTS: "The Rains Descended and the Floods Came: A Survey of the Seventh-Day Adventist Church in Communist China," by Ralph and Beatrice Neall, 1971.
PAMPHLETS: *What About Hobbies? The Story of How the Lord Once Used a Hobby to Advance the Third Angel's Message in a Foreign Field*, by Herbert C. White, 1930(?).
MEMORABILIA: Vertical file of clippings from journals and magazines on Seventh-Day Adventists in China, n.d.
ORAL HISTORIES: Tape of a 1985 interview with Paul E. Quimby, an SDA missionary in China; tape of a 1985 interview with Hsu Hua, who headed the SDA church in the 1940s and 1950s.
DISSERTATIONS/THESES: *A History of Seventh-Day Adventist Higher Education in the China Mission, 1888–1980*, by Handel Hing-tat Luke, 1983.

BERKELEY

AMERICAN BAPTIST SEMINARY OF THE WEST
CA–10   Library
2515 Hillegass Avenue
Berkeley CA 94704
(415) 841-1905
Rose Johnson, Librarian

Background note: For other holdings of the American Baptist Seminary of the West, see also Graduate Theological Union Library, 2400 Ridge Road, Berkeley, CA, 94709.

1-GENERAL HOLDINGS
MINUTES/RECORDS/REPORTS: American Baptist Foreign Mission Society, Chekiang-Shanghai Baptist Convention, and Woman's American Baptist Foreign Mission Society, East China projects, n.d.; China Baptist Council, minutes and constitution, 1930; South China Baptist, annual, 1916–17.
CORRESPONDENCE: Letter from Thomas Wang, describing the goals of the Chinese Christian Mission, n.d.

PAMPHLETS: China Baptist Publication Society pamphlet, 1904; Chinese Christian Mission brochure and pamphlet, n.d.; China Inland Mission pamphlets, 1891, 1955.

MAPS/DESIGNS/DRAWINGS: China Inland Mission map of China, 1898.

SERIALS: *Challenger*, 1973. *China and the Gospel*, 1909. China Graduate School of Theology, *Bulletin*, 1972. *China Mission Year Book*, 1915, 1924. *Land of Sinim*, 1905. *Star of Cathay*, 1946.

DISSERTATIONS/THESES: *A Comparative History of the East and South China Missions of the American Baptist Foreign Mission Society, 1833–1935*, by Kenneth Gray Hobart, 1937.

CHINESE LANGUAGE MATERIALS: *Christ's Sermon on the Mount*, by J. Goddard and E. C. Lord, 1851; bilingual Ginling College calendar, n.d.; *An Epitome of the Religion of Jesus*, by E. C. Lord, 1850; unidentified calling card, calligraphy, and book.

GRADUATE THEOLOGICAL UNION
CA–15   Library
2400 Ridge Road
Berkeley CA 94709
(415) 649-2400
Diane Choquette, Head of Public Services

Background note: The Graduate Theological Union Library serves American Baptist Seminary of the West (formerly Berkeley Baptist Divinity School), Church Divinity School of the Pacific, Dominican School of Philosophy and Theology, Franciscan School of Theology, Institute of Buddhist Studies, Jesuit School of Theology (formerly Alma College, Los Gatos), Pacific Lutheran Theological Seminary, Pacific School of Religion, and Starr King School for the Ministry, all in Berkeley; Saint Albert's College, Oakland; and San Francisco Theological Seminary, San Anselmo.

1-RARE BOOK COLLECTION, 1911, 1 item
SERIALS: *American Church Mission Newsletter*, 1911.

2-GENERAL HOLDINGS
MINUTES/RECORDS/REPORTS: American Board of Commissioners for Foreign Missions, Fenchow Station, report, 1920–35; China Continuation Committee, National Missionary Conference, proceedings of the annual meeting, 1920; Chinese Religious Tract Society, annual report, 1879–88; Christian Conference of Asia, report on a visit to China, 1980; Christian Literature Society for China, annual reports, 1888–1947; National Christian Council of China, annual report, 1922–28.

MANUSCRIPTS: "The American Board in China: 1830–1950, Review and Appraisal," by Fred Field Goodsell, 1969–72 (microfilm copy of original in American Congregational Association Library, 14 Beacon Street, Boston, MA, 02108); "A Bibliography of the History of Christianity in China: A Preliminary Draft," by Jonathan T'ien-en Chao, 1970; "The Christian Church in Communist China," by Helen Ferris, 1952; "The Foochow Area Parish Abroad and Our Boys and Girls: A Manual for Leaders of Children," by Alice Louise Brown, 194?; microfiche reproduction of the inventory to papers of William Blount Burke, 1978 (papers and original inventory are held by Emory University, Robert Woodruff Library, Special Collections Department, Atlanta, GA, 30322).

PAMPHLETS: 13 titles, 1841–1980, on Benedictine missions, British Protestant evangelists, Congregational missions, Karl Gützlaff, Luella Miner, Mary Porter, Presbyterian missions, and Russian missions in China.

AUDIO-VISUAL MATERIALS: "China Mission Institute," audio recording, 1980.

SERIALS: *Bridge*, 1983-. *China and the Church Today*, 1987-. *China Bulletin*, 1947–62. *China Christian Advocate*, 1914–41. China Christian Educational Association, *Bulletin*, 1928. *China Christian Year Book*, 1926–39. *China Letter*, 1955–66. *China Medical Journal*, 1907–22. *China Medical Missionary Journal*, 1887–1907. *China Mission Advocate*, 1839. *China Mission Year Book*, 1910–25. *China Notes*, 1962-. *Chinese Recorder*, 1903–40. *Chinese Repository*, 1833–51. *Chinese Theological Review*, 1985-. *Directory of Protestant Missions in China*, 1916. *District of Anking Newsletter*, 1937–41, 1945–48. Educational Association of China, *Monthly Bulletin*, 1907–8. *Educational Review*, 1909–38. *Foochow Messenger*, 1903–40. *Hainan Newsletter*, 1912–49. *Mission Bulletin*, 1951–59. *Missionary Recorder*, 1867. National Christian Council of China, *Bulletin*, 1922–37. *West China Missionary News*, 1899–1943. *Yi (China Message)*, 1987-. *Your China Letter*, 1953–54.

DISSERTATIONS/THESES: *The Anti-Christian Movement in China, 1922–27: With Special Reference to the Experience of Protestant Missions*, by Ka-che Yip, 1970. *China Missions in Crisis: Bishop Laimbeckhoven and His Times, 1738–1787*, by Joseph Krahl, 1964. *Christianity and Social Change: The Case in China, 1920–1950*, by Lee-ming Ng, 1971. *Chosen for China: The California Jesuits in China, 1928–1957, A Case Study in Mission and Culture*, by Peter Fleming, S.J., 1986. *A Collection of Hymns for Use in Chinese Churches, Centers, and Schools in China*, by Mavis Shoa-ling Lee, 1951. *The Cultural and Religious Heritage of China as Related to the Communication of the Christian Faith*, by Charles Shwee Lin Chou, 1967. *The Development of the Motive of Protestant Missions to China, 1807–1928*, by George Bell Workman, 1928. *The Employment of Chinese Classical Thought in Matteo Ricci's Theological Contextualization in Sixteenth-Century China*, by David Chusing Wu, 1983. *An Experiment in Teaching the Christian Religion by Life Experiences in Fan Village, China*, by Mabel Ellis Hubbard, 1938. *The First Nestorian Mission to China: A Discussion of the History and Strategy of China's Earliest Christian Missionaries*, by Raymond L. Oppenheim, 1969. *A History of the Evangelical Lutheran Church of America's Mission Policy in China, 1890–1949*, by Roger Keith Ose, 1970. *Die katholische Missionsmethode in China in neuester Zeit (1842–1912)*, by Johannes Beckmann, 1931. *Lutheran Missions in a Time of Revolution: The China Experience, 1944–1951*, by Jonas Jonson, 1972. *The Mission Compound in Modern China: The Role of the United States Protestant Mission as an Asylum in the Civil and International Strife of China, 1900–1941*, by Gladys Robina Quale, 1957. *The Mission Enterprise of the Lutheran Church-Missouri Synod in Mainland China, 1913–1952*, by Roy Arthur Suelflow, 1971. *The New Life Movement and Its Significance to the Christian Church of China*, by Albert S. L. Lau, 1940. *Present Day Problems in Chinese Christianity*, by Po-chin Chou, 1926. *Die protestantische Christenheit in der Volksrepublik China*, by Ilse Hass, 1974. *Protestant Missions in Communist China*, by Creighton Lacy, 1953. *The Role in National Leadership of the East China Baptist Convention: Otherwise Known as the Chekiang-Shanghai Baptist Convention*, by Charles Ho, 1960. *Seeking the*

Common Ground: Protestant Christianity, the Three Self Movement, and China's United Front, by Philip Lauri Wickeri, 1985. *A Survey of Religious Education in Chinese Christian Middle Schools*, by Estelle Miao, 1950. *Timothy Richard's Contribution to the Christian Church in China*, by David C. P. Kwok, 1957. *Timothy Richard's Theory of Christian Missions to the Non-Christian World*, by Rita Thérèse Johnson, 1966.

PACIFIC SCHOOL OF RELIGION
CA-20   Charles Holbrook Library
1798 Scenic Avenue
Berkeley CA 94709
(415) 848-0528
Jeff Zorn, Librarian

Background note: For other holdings of the Pacific School of Religion, see also Graduate Theological Union Library, 2400 Ridge Road, Berkeley, CA, 94709.

1-WOMAN'S BOARD OF MISSIONS FOR THE PACIFIC, 1874-27, quantity undetermined
MINUTES/RECORDS/REPORTS: Annual reports, 1874(?)–1927, containing sections on China mission work.
CORRESPONDENCE: Ca. 1 in. of letters from missionaries in China to the mission board, 1921-24, including Bertha H. Allen, Elmer L. Cook, Emily S. Hartwell, Maude M. McGwingan, and Laura D. Ward.
MEMORABILIA/AUDIO-VISUAL MATERIALS: Clippings and photos relating to China.

UNIVERSITY OF CALIFORNIA, BERKELEY

CA-25   Anthropology Library
230 Kroeber Hall
Berkeley CA 94720
(415) 642-2400
Dorothy Koenig, Reference Librarian

1-GENERAL HOLDINGS
SERIALS: *Asian Folklore Studies*, 1942-; supplement, 1952. Yenching University, Department of Sociology and Social Work, *Social Research Series*, 1930.

CA-30   Astronomy Library
University of California, Berkeley
100 Evans Hall
Berkeley CA 94720
(415) 642-3381
Kimiyo Hom, Reference Librarian

1-GENERAL HOLDINGS
SERIALS: Zi-ka-wei, China, Observatoire, *Annales de l'observatoire astronomique de Zo-se*, 1929, 1936-40, 1942.

CA-35   The Bancroft Library
University of California, Berkeley
Berkeley CA 94720
(415) 642-3781
Irene Moran, Head of Public Services
Bonnie Hardwick, Head of Manuscripts Division

Background note: In addition to the materials listed below, items by or about individuals affiliated with the University of California, Berkeley, may be found in other collections. Consult with reference staff for assistance.

1-CHARLES WILLIAM BATDORF CORRESPONDENCE, 1912-28, 1 portfolio
CORRESPONDENCE: Letters by Charles William Batdorf, Elmer Edgar Hall, and Nels Christian Nelson concerning the work of Canadian Methodist missionaries in China, and arrangements for Batdorf's journey to China.

2-CHINA MISSIONARIES ORAL HISTORY PROJECT, 1973, 45 items
MANUSCRIPTS: "China Missionaries Oral History Project: An Overview," a report prepared by staff members of the China Missionaries Oral History Project, including a statement of project goals, staff, and procedures by Enid H. Douglass, a report by Cyrus H. Peake, and a summary statement and evaluation of findings by Arthur L. Rosenbaum.
ORAL HISTORIES: *China Missionaries Oral History Collection*, ed. by Cyrus H. Peake and Arthur L. Rosenbaum (Claremont Graduate School, Oral History Program), 1973. See Oral Histories Union List for the names of participants.

3-MATTHEW SIMPSON CULBERTSON PAPERS, 1843-60, 1 box
Background note: Matthew Simpson Culbertson (1819-62) was a missionary in Macao and Ningpo.
CORRESPONDENCE: Letter from Culbertson to his brother, 1844.
DIARIES: Diaries kept by Culbertson as a divinity student at Princeton and as missionary in China, 1844-60(?).
MANUSCRIPTS: Manuscripts of Culbertson's sermons and writings, including *Darkness in the Flower Land* and comments on the siege of Shanghai in 1853.
MEMORABILIA: Culbertson's obituary, n.d.

4-McINTYRE FARIES, 1973, 1 item
ORAL HISTORIES: Photocopy of typed transcript of tape-recorded interviews with McIntyre Faries conducted in 1970 and 1971, including an account of his boyhood in China as son of a medical missionary.

5-ELI LUNDY HUGGINS CORRESPONDENCE AND PAPERS, 1900, ca. 1 box
Background note: Eli Lundy Huggins' career as a U.S. Army officer included service in China during the Boxer Rebellion.
CORRESPONDENCE: Letters written in China by Huggins to family members describing the political chaos and activities of missionaries in the aftermath of the Boxer Rebellion, 1900.

6-HARRY LEES KINGMAN CORRESPONDENCE AND PAPERS, 1921-73, 2 volumes, ca. 2 boxes
Background note: Harry Lees Kingman (b. 1892) was born in

Tientsin, the son of a Congregational missionary. He worked in China for the International Committee of the American YMCA from 1921 until 1928. This collection, totalling 8 boxes and 5 cartons, concentrates on his later career as executive director of the University of California YMCA (Stiles Hall) and other activities in the United States.

MINUTES/RECORDS/REPORTS: Typescript of annual report by Kingman on his YMCA work, 1925.

CORRESPONDENCE: Ca. 1 box of letters mainly by Kingman, relating to his career with the YMCA in China, 1921–27; printed New Year's letters, 1925–26; letter from Eugene Epperson Barnett to R. H. Edwards, containing comments on Kingman's YMCA work, 1928; letter from David Prescott Barrows, congratulating Kingman on his publication on Chinese nationalism in Manchuria, 1932; letters in scrapbook (see MEMORABILIA below), 1926–27, including such correspondents as Jerome Davis, William Horace Day, Harry Emerson Fosdick, Charles James Fox, Mohandas Gandhi, O. M. Green, John Haynes Holmes, Henrietta Lindsay, Robert Morse Lovett, Garfield Bromley Oxnam, Kirby Page, and Bertrand Russell; letter from Harry T. Hodgkin regarding the use of troops in Shanghai, 1927; letter from Stanley Kuhl Hornbeck regarding Kingman's publication on Manchuria, 1932.

MANUSCRIPTS: Writings by Kingman on Chinese people, communism, labor policy in China, physical education, social service in mission work, sports, and Sun Yat-sen, 1921–42.

MEMORABILIA: Notes and clippings, many by Kingman; scrapbook containing clippings of articles by Kingman and letters to Kingman, relating mainly to the "Shanghai Incident" of 1925; tearsheets and reprints of writings by Kingman.

ORAL HISTORIES: "Citizenship in a Democracy," photocopy of a 292-page typed transcript of tape-recorded interviews conducted in 1971–72, including comments on his service in China with the International YMCA from 1921 to 1928.

FINDING AIDS: In-house register.

7-HENRY KINGMAN LETTERS AND DIARIES, 1881–93, 1 box
Background note: Henry Kingman (b. 1863) was a missionary in Tientsin.

CORRESPONDENCE: Letters written from China, mainly mimeographed, some incomplete, describing travel, missionary duties, study of the Chinese language, and social life, mainly in and around Tientsin.

DIARIES: Diaries covering life and schooling in the east, ordination as a minister, and life in China as a missionary.

8-PRUDENCE (WINTERS) KOFOID, 1915–16, 40 items
CORRESPONDENCE: "Carrie's Observations during the Kofoid Trip to the Orient: A Series of Letters to Her Mother," typed transcripts of letters from Prudence (Winters) Kofoid to her mother, Flora D. Winters, while travelling with her husband, Charles Atwood Kofoid, including comments on missionary work with the YMCA, 1915–16.

9-GRACE JOSEPHINE SERVICE, 1904–54, 4.6 l.f. (11 boxes)
Background note: Grace Josephine (Boggs) Service (1879–1954) and her husband, Robert Roy Service, were YMCA missionaries in Chengtu, Chungking, and Shanghai. She remained in China after Roy Service's death in 1935 until the late 1940s when she returned to the United States. See also Young Men's Christian Association of the U.S.A. Archives, University of Minnesota,

Social History Welfare Archives, 2642 University Avenue, St. Paul, MN, 55114.

CORRESPONDENCE: 5 boxes of correspondence with family and friends to and from Grace Service, 1904–31.

DIARIES: 57 diaries of Grace Service, discussing daily actions and feelings, 1908–54.

MANUSCRIPTS: "Golden Inches," a 475-page typescript of memoirs by Grace Service, ca. 1937, recording her experiences in China while her husband served as secretary of the International Committee of the YMCA and after his death, including comments on Chinese culture, domestic life in Chengtu, Chungking, and Shanghai, foreign settlements, work of Protestant missionaries, Chinese servants, travel, Grace Service's work for the National Committee of the YMCA and American Women's Club, the 1911 revolution, the Nanking Incident, the 1937 bombing of Shanghai, and Grace Service's departure from China in 1937; 19 notebooks, 1911–37, containing stories, quotations, notes for a planned novel, and other writings; 8 folders of stories, poems and untitled stories, 1927–48.

MEMORABILIA: Clipping from *The North China Herald* on missionaries and politics, 1917.

FINDING AIDS: In-house inventory.

10-JOHN STEWART SERVICE PAPERS, 1933–77, 1 volume
Background note: John Stewart Service (b. 1909) was a Foreign Service Officer who grew up in China as the child of Roy and Grace Service, YMCA missionaries to China. A separate collection in the Bancroft Library contains papers of John Service relating to his work as a Foreign Service Officer and the *Amerasia* affair.

MINUTES/RECORDS/REPORTS/CORRESPONDENCE/MEMORABILIA/AUDIO-VISUAL MATERIALS: Documentation and photos supporting an oral history interview of John Stewart Service.

ORAL HISTORIES: Photocopy of a 565-page typed transcript of a 1977–78 interview of John Stewart Service, including comments on Service's parents, Roy and Grace Service, their YMCA missionary work in China, and growing up in China.

11-EDWARD THOMAS WILLIAMS, 1882–96, 1 box, 10 cartons, and 1 portfolio
Background note: Edward Thomas Williams (1854–1944) was a Disciples of Christ missionary to China from 1887 to 1896, and later was professor of oriental languages at the University of California, Berkeley, and diplomat in China. The collection mainly concentrates on his diplomatic service and teaching career.

MINUTES/RECORDS/REPORTS: Account book, 1887–90.

CORRESPONDENCE: Carbon copies of letters by Williams, concerning Chinese problems, 1882–1926; letterpress copy book of letters written while stationed in Nanking, 1888–96.

DIARIES: Diary, 1893–95, concerning his missionary activities; journal of voyage from San Francisco to Shanghai, 1887.

MANUSCRIPTS: Williams' writings on Chinese politics, social life, folklore, customs, religion, education, and philosophy; miscellaneous recollections; notebook with English-Chinese vocabulary by Williams.

MEMORABILIA/AUDIO-VISUAL MATERIALS: Clippings of articles and photos of China.

MAPS/DESIGNS/DRAWINGS: Maps of China, Shantung, and Mongolia, n.d.
FINDING AIDS: In-house guide.

12-GENERAL HOLDINGS
PAMPHLETS: *Medical Missions at Home and Abroad*, by J. G. Kerr, 1878; *Reflexions upon the Idolatry of the Jesuits, and Other Affairs Relating to Religion in China*, 1709; *A True Account of the Present State of Christianity in China, with Full Satisfaction as to the Behavior of the Jesuits*, 1709.
SERIALS: *Chinese Recorder*, 1868.
CHINESE LANGUAGE MATERIALS: *A History of the Chinese-American Presbyterian Missionary Society, 1871–1971*, by Kei Tin Wong, 1972.

CA-40   Biology Library
3503 Life Science Building
University of California, Berkeley
Berkeley CA 94720
(415) 642-2531
Ingrid Radkey, Librarian

1-GENERAL HOLDINGS
MINUTES/RECORDS/REPORTS: Peking Union Medical College, annual announcement, 1918–31.
PAMPHLETS: *Technical Methods of the Parasitology Laboratory*, by the Peking Union Medical College, 1934.
SERIALS: *China's Medicine*, 1966, 1968. *Chinese Medical Journal*, 1963–66, 1977–78. *Lingnan Science Journal*, 1922–45, 1950. Lingnan University, *Science Bulletin*, 1930–44. *Peking Natural History Bulletin*, 1926–49. Peking Union Medical College, Department of Anatomy, *Contributions*, 1918–20; *Contributions from the Peking Union Medical College*, 1921–22. St. John's University, *Biological Bulletin*, 1931–35. Université de l'Aurore, *Notes d'ornithologie*, 1943. Yenching University, Department of Biology, *Bulletin*, 1930.

CA-45   Center for Chinese Studies
Barrows Hall, Room 64
2223 Fulton Street
University of California, Berkeley
Berkeley CA 94720
(415) 642-6510
Chi-ping Chen, Librarian

1-GENERAL HOLDINGS
PAMPHLETS: *Christians, White Lotus, and the Boxers in Shantung*, by David D. Buck, 1979.
SERIALS: *China Monthly*, 1946–49.
CHINESE LANGUAGE MATERIALS: 5 volumes, 1951–61, on Christians in China, Communism and Christianity, and the Taiping Rebellion.

CA-50   Earth Sciences Library
230 Earth Sciences Building
University of California, Berkeley
Berkeley CA 94720
(415) 642-2997
Michael Conkin, Reference Librarian

1-GENERAL HOLDINGS
MAPS/DESIGNS/DRAWINGS: *An Index to Every Name on the Map of China, with the Province in Which It Will Be Found and the Latitude and Longitude of the Place*, by the China Inland Mission, 1928.
SERIALS: *Peking Natural History Bulletin*, 1928–30.

CA-55   East Asiatic Library
Durant Hall, Room 208
University of California, Berkeley
Berkeley CA 94720
(415) 642-2556
P. Y. Chang, Librarian

Background note: In addition to the materials listed below, the East Asiatic Library also has several books in Japanese on Christianity, Christians, Christian missions, Jesuits, and Nestorians in China.

1-GENERAL HOLDINGS
MINUTES/RECORDS/REPORTS: Lingnan University, information and curriculum, 1946–48.
SERIALS: *Monumenta Serica*, 1935–46, 1948-; monograph series, 1937-. *T'oung Pao*, 1890-. *Variétés Sinologiques*, 1894, 1896.
CHINESE LANGUAGE MATERIALS/MINUTES/RECORDS/REPORTS: World Missionary Conference, Edinburgh, report, 1910.
CHINESE LANGUAGE MATERIALS/MANUSCRIPTS: "Pu tê i," by Yang Kuang-hsien, 1934(?).
CHINESE LANGUAGE MATERIALS/SERIALS: *Chung-hua Chi-tu chiao hui nien ling (China Church Yearbook)*, 1914. *Chung hsi chiao hui pao (Missionary Review)*, 1891. *Ginling College Magazine*, 1924. *Yüeh pao (The Child's Paper)*, 1876(?).
CHINESE LANGUAGE MATERIALS/DISSERTATIONS/THESES: *I pa ch'i ling nien T'ien-chin chiao an chih yen chiu (The Tientsin Massacre of 1870)*, by Wang Man-p'ing, 1975.
CHINESE LANGUAGE MATERIALS: Books on Baptist missions, Catholic Church, Christianity, Jesuits, missionaries, Muslims, Nestorians, Protestant churches, relations with foreign countries, rural reconstruction, and sectarian cases, ca. 1870s–1983; *Chung-hua Chi-tu chiao wen tzu so yin (A Classified Index to the Chinese Literature of the Protestant Christian Churches in China)*, 1933; *Chiao an shih liao pien mu (A Bibliography of Chinese Source Materials Dealing with Local or International Cases Involving Christian Missions)*, by Wu Shêng-tê, 1941; *Chung-kuo Chi-tu chiao shi yen chiu shu mu (A Bibliography of Christianity in China)*, 1981.

CA-60   Law Library
Boalt Hall, 2nd floor
University of California, Berkeley
Berkeley CA 94720
(415) 642-4044
Ellen Gilmore, Reference Librarian

1-GENERAL HOLDINGS
SERIALS: *China Law Review*, 1922–37.

CA-65 News Department
444 Main Library
University of California, Berkeley
Berkeley CA 94720
(415) 642-3536
Susan Edelberg, Reference Librarian

1-GENERAL HOLDINGS
SERIALS: *Monumenta Serica*, 1947.

CA-70 General Library
350 Main Library
University of California, Berkeley
Berkeley CA 94720
(415) 642-2568

1-GENERAL HOLDINGS
MINUTES/RECORDS/REPORTS: China International Famine Relief Commission, annual reports, 1922-36; Institution for the Chinese Blind (Shanghai), report, 1912-25; International Institute of China, report, 1908-27; report of the mission among the higher classes in China, 1903; Lingnan University, report of the president, 1919-24; Peking Blind Mission, 1896(?); St. John's University, catalogue, 1906-40; University of Nanking, report of the president, 1918-26; University of Shanghai, catalogue, 1911-34.
MANUSCRIPTS: "An Agricultural Survey of Szechwan Province, China," by John Lossing Buck, 1943; "Souvenir of the Missionary Home, Shanghai, China, 1890-1910," 1910.
PAMPHLETS: *La bonne foy des anciens Jésuites missionnaires de la Chine sur l'idolatrie des chinois dans le culte qu'ils rendent à Confucius et aux morts, démontrée par des extraits fidèles des livres des RR. pères Athanase Kirchère, Nicolas Trigault, Alexandre de Rhodes, et autres*, 1700; *The Catholic Missions in China during the Middle Ages, 1294-1368*, by Paul Stanislaus Hsiang, 1949; *The Cause of the Riots in the Yangtse Valley: A 'Complete Picture Gallery,'* n.a., 1891; *The Missionary Question in China: How to Lessen the Recurrence of Anti-Christian and Anti-foreign Riots*, by Christopher Thomas Gardner, 1894; *Our University in Peking [Yenching University]*, 1930(?).
MAPS/DESIGNS/DRAWINGS: *Distribution des pluies en Chine par mois, saison, année*, 1928.
SERIALS: American Friends Service Committee, *Bulletin on Work in China*, 1942-44. *China Christian Year Book*, 1910-12, 1916, 1923, 1926-28, 1931, 1936-39. China International Famine Relief Commission, Publications, series A, 1922-36; series B, 1922-35; series E, 1932. *China Mission Studies Bulletin*, 1979-. *China Monthly: The Truth about China*, 1939-50. *China's Millions* (London), 1881. *Chinese Recorder*, 1868-1941. *Chinese Repository*, 1833-43, 1845-51. College of Chinese Studies (Peking), *Miscellaneous Publications*, 1934-41. *El Correo sino-annamita*, 1889, 1905. *Folklore Studies*, 1942-1960; supplement, 1952. Ginling College, *Bulletin*, 1920-35. *Kitaiskii Blagoviestnik: Ezhemiesiachoe Izdanie Rossiskoi Dukhovnoi Missii v Kitae*, 1936, 1941. Lingnan University, *Bulletin*, 1909-35. *Missionary Recorder*, 1867. *Missions en Chine et au Congo*, 1889-99. Nanking Theological Seminary, *English Publications*, 1940. *New Horizons*, 1982-. *New Mandarin*, 1926. *News of China*, 1942-49. St. John's *University Studies*, 1922. University of Nanking, *Bulletin*, 1915-34; College of Agriculture and Forestry: *Agriculture and Forestry*

Notes, 1924-36, 1939-41; *Agriculture and Forestry Series*, 1920-25; *Bulletin*, 1926, 1932-38; *Economic Facts*, 1936-46; *Miscellaneous Bulletin Series*, 1924-25; *Special Report*, 1935. *Variétés Sinologiques*, 1892-1938, n.d. West China Border Research Society, *Journal*, 1922-46. *Yenching Journal of Social Studies*, 1938-50. Yenching University: *Bulletin*, 1925-48; Department of Sociology and Social Work, *Social Research Series*, 1930. Zi-ka-wei Observatoire: *Bulletin aérologique*, 1931-37; *Bulletin des observations*, 1874-88, 1892-93, 1895-1900, 1910-38; *Notes de météorologie physique*, 1934-39; *Revue mensuelle*, 1913-40.
DISSERTATIONS/THESES: *Die Akkommodationsmethode des P. Matteo Ricci S.I. in China*, by Johannes Bettray, 1955. *American Influence in Chinese Higher Education since 1900*, by Lola Chun, 1948. *Apostolic Legations to China of the Eighteenth Century*, by Antonio Sisto Rosso, 1948. *Christian Missions in China*, by Charles Sumner Estes, 1895. *Double-edged Sword: Christianity and Twentieth Century Chinese Fiction*, by Lewis Stewart Robinson, 1982. *L'Euchologe de la mission de Chine; editio princeps 1628 et développements jusqu' à nos jours*, by Paul Brunner, 1964. *Imperial Government and Catholic Missions in China during the Years 1784-1785*, by Bernward Henry Willeke, 1948. *Die katholische Chinamission im Spiegel der rotchinesischen Presse; Versuch einer missionarischen Deutung*, by Johannes Schütte, 1957. *Louis the Fourteenth's Jesuit Missionary Company to China in 1685*, by Edwin Theodore Turnbladh, 1930. *Lutheran Missions in a Time of Revolution: The China Experience, 1944-1951*, by Jonas Jonson, 1972. *The Missionary and Western Education in Nineteenth-century China*, by George F. Drake, 1959. *The Negotiations between Ch'i-ying and Lagrené, 1844-1846*, by Angelus Francis J. Grosse-Aschhoff, 1950. *La politique missionnaire de la France en Chine, 1842-1856: L'Ouverture des cinq ports chinois au commerce étranger et la liberté religieuse*, by Louis Tsing-sing Wei, 1960. *Protestant Christianity in China and Korea: The Problem of Identification with Tradition*, by Spencer John Palmer, 1964. *Protestant Mission Schools for Girls in South China (1827 to the Japanese Invasion)*, by Mary Raleigh Anderson, 1943. *A Record of the Activities of the Finnish Missionary Society in Northwest Hunan, China, 1902-1952*, by Ilma Ruth Aho, 1953. *Ritual as Ideology in an Indigenous Chinese Christian Church*, by Morris Aaron Fred, 1975.
CHINESE LANGUAGE MATERIALS/SERIALS: *Kuo chi kung pao (International Journal)*, 1926-29, 1940.

CLAREMONT

CLAREMONT COLLEGES

Background note: The Claremont Colleges consist of Pomona College, Scripps College, Claremont McKenna College, Harvey Mudd College, and Pitzer College. Claremont Graduate School is the academic arm of Claremont University Center, the central coordinating institution of the Claremont Colleges. Honnold Library is the joint library serving the Claremont Colleges.

CA-75 Asian Studies Collection

Honnold Library
Claremont Colleges
Eighth and Dartmouth Streets
Claremont CA 91711
(714) 621-8000 Ext. 3970
Frances Wang, Curator

1-CALIFORNIA COLLEGE IN CHINA JOURNALS, 1923-38, 3 items

Background note: This collection contains the journals held by the California College in China Library, totalling 41 titles, dating from 1911 to 1938. The book collection from the California College in China Library was added to the general collection of Honnold Library and to the Asian Studies Collection.

CHINESE LANGUAGE MATERIALS/SERIALS: *Kuo chi kung pao* (*International Journal*), 1923-28. *Shih hsüeh nien pao* (*Historical Annual*), 1929-33, 1935-38. *Yen-ching hsüeh pao* (*Yenching Journal of Chinese Studies*), 1927-36.

FINDING AIDS: In-house inventory.

2-CHINA MISSIONARIES COLLECTION, 1861-1971, 23 boxes

Restrictions: Access restricted.

Background note: The items described below were given to Claremont Colleges by the missionaries who participated in the China Missionaries Oral History Project, the transcripts of which are held by the Special Collections Department. The contents are not inventoried, but are roughly organized in files and boxes according to donor.

MINUTES/RECORDS/REPORTS: Christian Herald Orphanage and Industrial Works, Foochow, report, 1932, 1935, 1937; Fenchow Girls' School, report, 1918; Foochow Medical Missionary Hospital, annual report, 1881, 1901-4, 1913; Foochow Mission, report, 1895-96, 1898, 1900, 1904; Fukien Christian University, Department of Philosophy syllabus, 1926; rules and ideals, 1929; Hong Kong Mission, report, 1883-92; Hope Hospital, Kulangsu, report, 1947-49; Horticultural Experiment Station in Peitaiho, report by Alice and Willard Simpson, 1937; Ichowfu Station, report, 1933-34; International Institute of China, report, 1914; International Relief Committee of Kulangsu, report and financial statement, 1939; Kuliang handbook, 1919; National Christian Council of China, constitution, 1929; Shantung annual conference, 1903-28; Shantung Mission, report, 1861-1913; South China Missionary Directory, 1936; University of Nanking, College of Agriculture and Forestry, Department of Sericulture, annual reports, 1925-26; Weihsien Station, report, 1919, 1921-26, 1939-40; report on conditions in girls' country schools, Weihsien, 1922; West China Union University, bound volume of Senate minutes, belonging to R. L. Simkin, 1916-30; Yihsien Station, annual report, 1936-38; station report, 1937-42; notes for station report, n.d.

CORRESPONDENCE: Photocopy of letter from Rowland Cross to Fred Goodsell, 1965; 3 folders of miscellaneous correspondence and memos of Lois Ely, 1941, 1960s, and n.d.; bound volume of letters to Lois Ely, Nantung Middle School, from her students and others, 1928-65; large folder of correspondence and circular letters of Lyda Houston, 1932-50; circular letters of Ernest Ikenberry, 1930-31, 1934-36, 1939-40, 1948, 1953; ca. 50 letters of family correspondence, mainly from Jean Lingle, 1889-1907; correspondence of Lingle, 1930s-1940s; correspondence to Lingle, after she left China, mostly 1933; correspondence

from Lingle to her sister, Stella Sears, 1915-33; envelope of undated letters, with clippings and programs, of Hortense Potts; large envelope of letters from Potts to her family, 1922-28; correspondence of Mary Rowley, 1938-45; correspondence of Grace M. Rowley, 1902-49 (?); circular letters of Robert and Margaret Simkin, n.d.; correspondence of Marjorie Rankin Steurt, mostly with her family, 1913-ca. 1929, and n.d.; printed letters of Steurt, 1915, 1931; 3 folders of photocopies of correspondence of William Topping, 1911-50; bound collection of printed missionary letters, n.d.

DIARIES: Bound volume of clippings and diary of Lois Ely, 1941-42; photocopy of diary of Lyda Houston, 1944-45; 13 diaries of Hortense Potts, 1913-20, 1922-26; diaries of Grace M. Rowley, 1910-32, 1938-62; diaries of Marjorie Rankin Steurt, 1911-15, 1917-32, 1935, 1937-40, 1942-43, 1945-46, and n.d.; diary fragments, by Steurt, 1921, 1927, 1931.

MANUSCRIPTS: Manuscript on Christian work in liberated areas, by M. S. Ady, n.d.; "Motor Highways in China," and supplement, by R. L. Armacost, 1929; "China's National Highway Budget," by R. L. Armacost, 1930; "The Christian Response to Revolutionary Change in China," photocopy of typescript by Rowland Cross, ca. 1949; "China's Christian Youth," by Cross, 1945; "Is It Nothing to You?," by Cross, n.d.; 2 manuscripts by Lois Ely, n.d.; manuscript on Tibetan religion and on relief in Tibet, by Ikenberry and J. Andrews, 1922; autobiography by Frances P. Jones, n.d.; list of property belonging to Jean Lingle and its value, n.d.; "Christianity and Marxism-Leninism," by Kiang Wen-han, 1952; "Songs of My Life," by C. F. Lung, presented to Robert Armacost, 1933; "My Personal Experiences at the Fall of Nanking," by Edwin Marx, n.d.; "Sunshine Book," notebook of Hortense Potts, n.d.; 3 manuscripts by Potts on social and religious education of Chinese students, n.d.; "The Church in China Today," by Frank W. Price, n.d.; mimeo of *Chinese Music*, by Mrs. Timothy Richard, 1890; "Events in Yihsien—May 4th to June 15th," signed by Grace M. Rowley, Maria M. Wagner, Nettie D. Junkin, and W. C. D'Olive, n.d. (ca. 1938), in papers of Margaret Simkin; notes on students by Mary Rowley, n.d.; manuscript on Presbyterian missions in wartime, 1940, by Mary Rowley; folder of mimeos and manuscripts by Roderick Scott, including outlines, speeches, lectures, and articles, on Christian colleges, Christianity, and missions, 1940s; "Yours in the Bonds of Love," by Clara and George Shepherd, n.d.; looseleaf notebook of typescripts, by the Shepherds, n.d.; "Some Agriculture and Economy Notes on a Trip to Szechwan Province," n.d.; articles of Robert and Margaret Simkin; "The Theological Basis for Cultural Change," by Lewis Smythe, n.d.; several notebooks of Marjorie Rankin Steurt containing recipes, poetry, and writings on China, 1920s-1930s; 8 manuscripts by Steurt, 1927-30 and n.d.; autobiography of Steurt, 1937; manuscript of Steurt's book containing sketches of Chinese cities, 1912-26; fragment by George Tootell, n.d.; 2 manuscripts by Pearl Winans, n.d.; typescript of Winans' dissertation on John Dewey, 1940; "Passport to Hades," n.a., n.d.; list of missionaries' Chinese names, 1948; manuscript on occupation of Nanking, n.a., n.d.; autobiography of Chen Weiping, n.d.; articles on Christian education, n.d.

PAMPHLETS: Reprints from *Chinese Recorder*, n.d.; article on the Kilborn family, 1967; pamphlets, 1896-1948, on agricultural reciprocity between America and China, Changsha, China Cities Evangelization Project, Chinese church, Christian colleges, Christianity in revolutionary China, Disciples of Christ in China, Foochow College, Fukien Christian University, Fukien Mission, William Hill Lingle, Manchuria, missionary work, North China Mission, rural church, Southwest China, United Christian Missionary Society, and Weihsien Station

ORAL HISTORIES: Typed transcript of interview with Grace M. Rowley, 1942.

MEMORABILIA: 2 Canton license plates, n.d.; Chinese wood-block print calendar for 1925; Chinese chess set; brass mirror; miscellaneous personal items and clothing, including women's shoes for bound feet and ear pillow; Chinese currency; Nationalist flag; handpainted lightshade; banners; hand-sewn wall hanging of the Immortals; wooden doll-house furniture and other children's toys; men's clothing belonging to Margaret Simkin; several American journals and U.S. government publications of the 1930s belonging to Robert Armacost; miscellaneous clippings of Mary Rowley, n.d.; address book of Marjorie Rankin Steurt, n.d.; handwriting analysis of Steurt, 1924; passport of Steurt; obituary of William Lingle, n.d.; folder of miscellaneous memorabilia of Roderick Scott; calendars, 1924, 1933, 1941; photocopy of Rowland Cross' passport, n.d.; clippings on Cross, n.d.; scrapbook of Grace Rowley, 1901–52; clippings on Weihsien Station, n.d.; several small envelopes of clippings on New Life Movement, mass education, and Manchukuo; box of postcards of Mukden, Peking, and Lingnan University; card file of Miln Gillespie, n.d.; music books and scrapbooks of Lois Ely, n.d.; 14 unidentified scrapbooks.

MAPS/DESIGNS/DRAWINGS: 3 handpainted Chinese watercolors of flowers and birds, n.d.; 2 handpainted children's "newspapers," n.d.; 2 Tibetan Buddhist scrolls; 3 maps; 16 Chinese scrolls belonging to Lois Ely; map of Tsinan; 2 boxes containing papercuts, embroidery, and woodblock prints; Tibetan prints; stone lithograph in papers of Ikenberry; map of West China Union University, in papers of Pearl Winans, 1938.

AUDIO-VISUAL MATERIALS: Folder of photos of Chinese shop signs, n.d.; 7 painted photoportraits of Chinese women, pre–1911; envelope of photos of China, mostly undated, including YMCA of Shantung Christian University, 1927, in papers of Steurt; photo of one of Steurt's students, 1932; large folder of photos by Roderick and Agnes Scott of the Min River near Fukien Christian University, n.d.; small folder of photos and clippings of the Ming Tombs and Nanking, belonging to Lyda Houston, 1893–96; box of unidentified glass slides and negatives; unidentified photos in papers of Grace Rowley, n.d.; 26 unidentified mounted photos of George and Clara Shepherd; photo of Nanking Theological Seminary, 1950, in folder of Ady and McCallum; miscellaneous photos; large box of photos of Rowley; 2 photo albums and folder of loose photos of Rankin; photo album of Lois Ely; 2 framed photos and miscellaneous loose photos of Simkin; small box of loose photos of Rowley; 20 glass slides and loose photos of Rankin.

SERIALS: China Christian Educational Association, *Bulletin*, 1925, 1928–29. *China Newsletter*, 1947–49. *Ching Feng*, 1964. *The Church*, 1950. *East Asia Millions* (Philadelphia), 1971. *Foochow Messenger*, 1912–13, 1916, 1925–26, 1928–29, 1936–40. *Loose Leaves from Missionaries' Diaries*, 1919. *St. John's Echo*, 1929. University of Nanking, College of Agriculture and Forestry, *Agriculture and Forestry Notes*, 1924–27; *Agriculture and Forestry Series*, 1920; *Bulletin*, 1926; *Daily Meteorological Records*, 1925; *Miscellaneous Bulletin Series*, 1924–25. University of Nanking, *Bulletin*, 1926–27.

DISSERTATIONS/THESES: *Songs of Chinese Children: The Re-*

ligious Education of Youth in the New China, by Anna Hortense Potts, 1927.

CHINESE LANGUAGE MATERIALS: Ca. 20 printed handbills and posters, some on Buddhist subjects, belonging to Simkin; miscellaneous handbills; St. Luke in Bunan and Ladakhi dialects, and Tibetan; poster on Bible study; Bible readers; unidentified letter in papers of Steurt, 1924; songbooks and sheet music in papers of Scott; Chinese Sunday School Union, evangelistic booklet, n.d.; miscellaneous handbills and posters; bible study course; illustrated bible passages; bilingual passport application of Rowland Cross; wall hanging with Christian interpretation in papers of Grace Rowley; letter, 2 exercise books, and 2 folders of miscellaneous items of Clara and George Shepherd; unidentified manuscript; tracts, n.d.; posters; bible study pamphlets; handwritten and illustrated booklet on the situation of Chinese workers, n.d.

3-GENERAL HOLDINGS

MINUTES/RECORDS/REPORTS: American Bible Society, catalogue of Peiping sub-agency exhibition of Bibles, 1937; American Presbyterian Mission Press, catalogues, 1899, 1901; National Committee for Christian Religious Education in China, catalogue of religious education books, 1934; S.D.K., publications catalogue, 1897, 1902–4; Society for the Diffusion of General Knowledge among the Chinese, annual report, 1898; True Light Middle Schools, alumni directory, 1872–1972.

PAMPHLETS: *Calendar of the Gods in China*, by Timothy Richard, 1906; *China Mission Studies (1550–1800): Directory*, by David E. Mungello, 1978; *The Church of Christ in China, 1939–40*; *Directory of Protestant Missionaries in China, Corrected to April, 1896*, 1896; *Stranger Than Fiction: A Thrilling Story of Modern Christian Missions among the Aborigines of Formosa*, by James Dickson, n.d.; *Suggested Plan for the Formation of the Christian Church in China Szechwan Branch and Tentative Constitution*, 1913; *Two Lists of Selected Characters Containing All in the Bible and Twenty-seven Other Books, with Introductory Remarks by William Gamble*, 1861.

SERIALS: *China Christian Year Book*, 1910–39. *Directory of Protestant Missions in China, Japan, and Corea*, 1912, 1917. *Directory of Protestant Missions in China*, 1916–19, 1923, 1928, 1930, 1939. Educational Association of China, *Mission Education Directory*, 1910. *West China Missionary News*, 1907–43.

CHINESE LANGUAGE MATERIALS/SERIALS: *Chiao yü chi k'an (China Christian Educational Quarterly)*, 1925, 1939. *Chiao yü hsüeh pao*, 1936–41. *Chung-hua Chi-tu chiao hui nien chien (China Church Year Book)*, 1911–37 (repr. 1983). *Chung-hua Chi-tu chiao ch'ing nien hui nien ling (YMCA Yearbook)*, 1938. *Fu jen hsüeh chih (Fu jen Sinological Journal/Series Sinologica)*, 1928–47. *Hsiao hai yüeh pao*, 1870(?). *Hsieh he chung hsüeh san shih chou nien chi nien k'an* (Union Middle School, Amoy, 30th anniversary yearbook), 1941. University of Nanking, Library publications, 1924. *Wan kuo kung pao (The Globe Magazine: A Review of the Times)*, 1868–1908. *Yen-ching hsüeh pao (Yenching Journal of Chinese Studies)*, 1948–51. *Yen-ching ta hsüeh tsung chiao hsüeh yüan ts'ung shu ti wu chung* (Yenching School of Religion Series), 1941. *Yen-ta nien k'an (The Yenchinian)*, 1929–50. *Yi chi hsin lu (The Monthly Educator)*, 1877. *Yüeh pao (The Child's Paper)*, 1891.

CHINESE LANGUAGE MATERIALS: Ca. 250 titles by Western missionaries and Chinese Christians, 1859–1982 (many uncatalogued and undated), including Bible stories, dictionaries, reference works, religious tracts, and translations on the history of Western religion in China, missionaries and missionary activities, Nestorians, religious philosophy, social reform, social sciences and education, theology, Western history and sciences, women's issues and concerns, and miscellaneous subjects.

CA–80   Special Collections Department
Claremont Colleges
Honnold Library
Eighth and Dartmouth Streets
Claremont CA 91711
(714) 621–8000 Ext. 3977
Tania Rizzo, Head

Background note: The interviews described below form the China Missionaries Oral History Project, conducted by the Claremont Graduate School Oral History Program in 1970 and 1971 to record and transcribe the experiences of former missionaries to China. The Christian workers interviewed were chosen to represent several denominations, career lines, and geographic locations of missionary work in China. The interviews were intended to produce research material on the interaction of Western Christianity with the emergence of modern China. The Special Collections Department is the depository for the transcripts; tape recordings of the interviews are held by the Oral History Program Office, History Department, Claremont Graduate School, under the direction of Enid H. Douglass.

The Boynton, Edmunds, and Pettus collections are part of the Archives of the Claremont Colleges, also in Special Collections.

Finding aids: *Claremont Graduate School Oral History Program: A Bibliography*, by the Claremont University Center, 1978.

1-MERRILL STEELE ADY INTERVIEWS, 1970–71, 3 items
ORAL HISTORIES: 97-page transcript of an interview with Merrill Steele Ady on his work in Yeung Kong under the Presbyterian Board of Foreign Missions, 1924–41; as executive secretary of the South China Mission of the Presbyterian Church in Canton, 1941–49; and in Hong Kong, 1950–65.
AUDIO-VISUAL MATERIALS: 2 photos of Ady.

2-NETTA POWELL ALLEN INTERVIEW, 1970–71, 1 item
Background note: For biographical notes, see Columbia University, Rare Book and Manuscript Library, Butler Library, 535 West 114th Street, New York, NY, 10027.
ORAL HISTORIES: 86-page transcript of an interview with Netta Powell Allen on her experiences in China with her husband, Arthur J. Allen, who served as YMCA secretary in Nanchung, 1918–31, as a teacher in Boone School in Hankow under the sponsorship of the Episcopal Church, and as mission treasurer in Shanghai and West China, 1932–51.

3-JOHN NEVINS ANDREWS INTERVIEW, 1970, 2 items
ORAL HISTORIES: 34-page transcript of an interview with John Nevins Andrews on his experiences as a medical missionary under the Seventh-Day Adventist Church in Chungking and Tatsienlu on the Tibetan border, 1916–32.
AUDIO-VISUAL MATERIALS: Photo of Andrews.

4-JAMES CHAMBERLAIN BAKER INTERVIEW, 1969, 1 item
ORAL HISTORIES: 26-page transcript of an interview with Methodist Bishop James Chamberlain Baker on the missionary movement in China and American policy in China.

5-CHARLES LUTHER BOYNTON PAPERS, 1906–60, ca. 4 boxes
Background note: A graduate of Pomona College, Charles Luther Boynton (1881–1967) first travelled to China in 1906 and returned to the United States in 1948. An American Baptist minister, he worked with the YMCA in the early years. This collection traces his life from his college days until 1961, totalling 14 boxes of material. For other papers of Charles Luther Boynton, see also Union Theological Seminary, Archives, 3041 Broadway at Reinhold Niebuhr Place, New York, NY, 10028, and Hoover Institute, Archives, Stanford University, Stanford, CA, 94305.
MINUTES/RECORDS/REPORTS: Proposed itinerary of Boynton, 1913; Chapei Civilian Assembly Center (CCAC), census, 1943; transcription of minute book of the Protestant Church of the CCAC, 1943–45; notebook record of CCAC, ca. 1943–1945; expense account for travel to the United States, 1946; resolution of the National Christian Council of China on the Boyntons' services on the occasion of his approaching retirement, 1946.
CORRESPONDENCE: Duplicates of letters home, 1906–9, covering preparation for China, beginnings in China, and his marriage; folder of correspondence, 1906, including Leslie E. Fuller, Harold Hartshorn, William G. Renwick, Augusta Sassen, Hope Braithwaite Smith, Milton F. Wittler, and Frank Y. Young; correspondence with Alice Maria Parker, 1906–49, and Gertrude and Arthur Stewart, 1906–64; transcripts of letters from Charles Boynton from the date of his first departure from San Francisco for Shanghai, 1906; 14 folders of correspondence, 1909–49; circular letters, 1913, 1926, 1929–49; correspondence with Arthur H. Smith, 1916; transcripts of postals and postcards of Leila Dozier Boynton (Mrs. Charles Boynton), 1938; "Shanghai in Wartime, But after Pearl Harbor," from letters of Leila Boynton to members of Boynton and Dozier families, n.d.; correspondence with Edmund Boynton, Rowland Cross, J. W. Decker, and Wynn C. Fairfield, 1945.
DIARIES: Transcript from five-year diary of Leila Boynton, 1928–32; diary transcript, 1945–46.
MANUSCRIPTS: "Christian Leaders in China and the United States: Members of Organizations of Fellow-secretaries with Charles L. Boynton," n.d.; "How to Learn English: A Brief Catechism in Chinese with Examples of the Method," 1910; "Fellowship Notes," by S. E. Hening, 1913; "Special: Regarding Outbreak near Kulin," by S. E. Hening, 1913; folder of writings by Boynton, including "The Community Church of Shanghai, China, 1920–1950, with Introduction Notes"; "Pomona College Students in China," n.d.; "What is Happening at Shanghai," 1932; list of churches, clubs, and associations in Shanghai and Hong Kong, 1937; "How War Came to Shanghai," 1937; "The Boynton Family," n.d.; "Five Faithful Witnesses," address by Charles Boynton in Community Church, Shanghai, 1941; "Since Pearl Harbor," n.d.; Chapei Civilian Assembly Internment Camp addresses, 1943–45; preliminary checklist of manuscripts Boynton produced while interned, and manuscripts, 1943–45; "Missionaries, 1835–1906, Known by C. L. Boynton," n.d.; "Old China Hands in Claremont Area," 1947; inventory of China material sent to the Missionary Research Library, 1956; "Sketches of Chinese Who Have Influenced My Life and Work," ca. 1960; autobiographical sketch, ca. 1960.
PAMPHLETS: "A Dream or a Nightmare?," reprinted from *The Chinese Recorder*, 1939.

MEMORABILIA: Biographical materials, 1918–19; unidentified material relating to Ginling College, St. John's University, and Yenching University, ca. 1957.
FINDING AIDS: In-house register.

6-HOMER VERNON BRADSHAW INTERVIEWS, 1971, 2 items
Background note: For biographical notes, see Presbyterian Historical Society, Archives and Library, 425 Lombard Street, Philadelphia, PA, 19147.
ORAL HISTORIES: 56-page transcript of interviews with Homer Vernon Bradshaw on his service as a medical missionary in Van Norden Hospital in Kwangtung Province, 1928–41, 1947–55, and experiences under Communist rule.
AUDIO-VISUAL MATERIALS: Photo of Bradshaw.

7-EARL CRANSTON INTERVIEW, 1969–70, 1 item
ORAL HISTORIES: 130-page transcript of an interview with Earl Cranston on his career as a missionary teacher and administrator in China, 1920–28, including comments on Christian missions in China.

8-MILDRED (WELCH) CRANSTON INTERVIEW, 1971, 2 items
ORAL HISTORIES: 78-page transcript of an interview with Mildred Cranston, a missionary under the Women's Board of the Methodist Church, on her career teaching in Chengtu and views on missionary activities, 1922–27.
AUDIO-VISUAL MATERIALS: Photo of Cranston.

9-ROWLAND McLEAN CROSS INTERVIEW, 1969, 1 item
Background note: For biographical notes, see Hoover Institute, Archives, Stanford University, Stanford, CA, 94305–2323.
ORAL HISTORIES: 200-page transcript of an interview with Rowland McLean Cross on his experiences as a missionary in evangelical and rural reconstruction work, and service with the National Christian Council in China, 1917–44.

10-HELEN DIZNEY INTERVIEW, 1970, 1 item
ORAL HISTORIES: 25-page transcript of an interview with Congregational Church missionary Helen Dizney on her work supervising nursing school and public health training in China, 1920–38 and 1946–50.

11-CHARLES K. EDMUNDS PAPERS, n.d., 3 files
Background note: Charles K. Edmunds was president of Canton Christian College in the 1920s and president of Pomona College from 1928 to 1941.
MANUSCRIPTS: "Chinese Water Wheels," n.d.; "Irrigation of Chengtu Plain or Beyond," n.d.; "Variations on the Value of the Chinese Foot (*chih*)," n.d.; "Weights and Measures among the Chinese," including bibliography, n.d.; untitled manuscript on Kuanhsien.
MEMORABILIA/MAPS/DESIGNS/DRAWINGS/AUDIO-VISUAL MATERIALS: Clippings of articles and photos relating to flood relief, drainage plan, 1918, and maps of Canton River; folder of photos on saltmines; folder of miscellaneous photos.

12-CYRIL FAULKNER INTERVIEW, 1971, 1 item
ORAL HISTORIES: 54-page transcript of an interview with China Inland Mission missionary Cyril Faulkner, on his experiences from 1935 to 1951.

13-GLENN V. FULLER INTERVIEW, 1970, 2 items
ORAL HISTORIES: 28-page transcript of an interview with Glenn V. Fuller on his experiences in starting a school of business administration in Tientsin and working as an administrator for the Methodist Board of Foreign Missions in Shanghai, 1921–?
AUDIO-VISUAL MATERIALS: Photo of Fuller.

14-OSWALD JOHN GOULTER INTERVIEW, 1971, ca. 3 items
ORAL HISTORIES: 54-page transcript of an interview with Oswald John Goulter on agricultural improvement activities in Hofei and Anhwei provinces and Chu-chou, near Nanking, 1922–51, including comments on bandits, warlords, politics, and Communists.
AUDIO-VISUAL MATERIALS: 3 photos of Oswald.

15-EDWARD PEARCE HAYES INTERVIEW, 1970, 1 item
ORAL HISTORIES: 24-page transcript of an interview with Edward Peace Hayes on his experiences in Fukien as a Methodist missionary and with the Communists, ca. 1920–1949.

16-EGBERT M. HAYES INTERVIEWS, 1969, 2 items
ORAL HISTORIES: 42-page transcript of an interview with Egbert M. Hayes on his experiences as YMCA secretary and director of religious and social work at Peking Union Medical College, 1913–35.
AUDIO-VISUAL MATERIALS: Photo of Hayes.

17-ALFRED DIXON HEININGER INTERVIEWS, 1970–71, 2 items
ORAL HISTORIES: 65-page transcript of interviews on Alfred Dixon Heininger's experiences in evangelical work and teaching in Shantung under the sponsorship of the Congregational Church, 1917–27, and Heininger's return to China for postwar rehabilitation work, 1945–48.
AUDIO-VISUAL MATERIALS: Photo of Alfred Dixon Heininger.

18-CLARENCE H. HOLLEMAN INTERVIEW, 1969, 2 items
Background note: For biographical notes, see Western Theological Seminary, Beardslee Library, 85 East 13th Street, Holland, MI, 49423.
CORRESPONDENCE: Letter by Clarence H. Holleman describing his capture by the Communists in 1969, appended to the transcript.
ORAL HISTORIES: 95-page transcript of an interview with Holleman on his experiences as a medical missionary in Lungyen and Amoy from 1919 to 1950.

19-LYDA SUYDAM HOUSTON INTERVIEW, 1970–71, 1 item
ORAL HISTORIES: 83-page transcript of an interview with Lyda Suydam Houston on her missionary and teaching activities in Fukien from 1924 to 1950, and on life under Japanese occupation and the Communists.

20-ETHEL LACEY HYLBERT INTERVIEW, 1970, 2 items
ORAL HISTORIES: 32-page transcript of an interview with Ethel Hylbert on her experiences, 1920–43 and 1946–48, as treasurer for Baptist missions in China and assisting her husband, Lewis C. Hylbert, secretary of the East China Mission.
AUDIO-VISUAL MATERIALS: Photo of Ethel Hylbert.

21-ERNEST LEROY IKENBERRY INTERVIEW, 1971, 2 items
ORAL HISTORIES: 35-page transcript of an interview with Ernest Leroy Ikenberry on his experiences as a missionary under the Church of the Brethren from 1922 to 1941, working with the YMCA, evangelizing in rural areas, and serving with the National Christian Council of China in Shanghai from 1945 to 1951.
AUDIO-VISUAL MATERIALS: Photo of Ikenberry.

22-LYDIA JOHNSON INTERVIEW, 1970–71, 1 item
ORAL HISTORIES: 38-page transcript of an interview with Lydia Johnson on her experiences in personnel training and educational projects with the YWCA in China, 1926–43, including comments on evangelizing by church missions.

23-FRANCIS PRICE JONES INTERVIEW, 1969–70, 1 item
ORAL HISTORIES: 69-page transcript of an interview with Francis Price Jones on his experiences as an educational missionary at the University of Nanking and Nanking Theological Seminary, 1915–50, including discussion of his translations of theological textbooks and Christian classics into Chinese.

24-LUCILE (WILLIAMS) JONES INTERVIEW, 1970, 1 item
ORAL HISTORIES: 47-page transcript of an interview with Lucile Jones on her life as a missionary's wife in China, 1915–50, with discussion of teaching in mission schools, and World War II.

25-CLAUDE RUPERT KELLOGG INTERVIEW, 1970, 4 items
ORAL HISTORIES: 30-page transcript of an interview with Claude Rupert Kellogg.
AUDIO-VISUAL MATERIALS: 3 photos of Kellogg.

26-MARY LEE (NELSON) LATIMER INTERVIEW, 1971, 2 items
ORAL HISTORIES: 45-page transcript of an interview with Mary Lee Latimer on her experiences as the daughter of missionary parents, and teaching in both mission and non-mission schools, from 1923 to 1927 and 1929 to 1943.
AUDIO-VISUAL MATERIALS: Photo of Latimer.

27-JOHN JOSEPH LOFTUS INTERVIEW, 1971, 4 items
ORAL HISTORIES: 52-page transcript of an interview with John Joseph Loftus on his experiences as a Catholic priest in China from 1926 to 1935.
AUDIO-VISUAL MATERIALS: 3 photos of Loftus.

28-JAMES HENRY McCALLUM INTERVIEW, 1970, 2 items
ORAL HISTORIES: 29-page transcript of an interview with James Henry McCallum on his experiences as a missionary in Nanking with the United Christian Missionary Society from 1921 to 1951.
AUDIO-VISUAL MATERIALS: Photo of McCallum.

29-SISTER MARY COLMCILLE McCORMICK INTERVIEW, 1971, 2 items
ORAL HISTORIES: 29-page transcript of an interview with Sister Mary Colmcille McCormick on her experiences teaching Catholic doctrine from 1929 to 1939.
AUDIO-VISUAL MATERIALS: Photo of Sister Mary.

30-JAY CHARLES OLIVER INTERVIEW, 1970, 1 item
Background note: For biographical notes, see University of Oregon, Special Collections, Eugene, OR, 97403–1299. See also Young Men's Christian Association of the U.S.A. Archives, University of Minnesota, Social History Welfare Archives, 2642 University Avenue, St. Paul, MN, 55114.
ORAL HISTORIES: 122-page transcript of an interview with Jay Charles Oliver.

31-WILLIAM B. PETTUS PAPERS, 1930–46, ca. 30 boxes
Background note: The papers described below pertain to the California College in China (College of Chinese Studies) Foundation and are in storage, uncatalogued. Some of the printed materials originally part of this collection were removed and placed in the general holdings of the library. For biographical notes, see Hoover

Institution, Archives, Stanford University, Stanford, CA, 94305.
MINUTES/RECORDS/REPORTS: Minutes of meetings, reports, lists of trustees, articles of incorporation (1930), by-laws, and other typescript records, 1930–46.

32-ALICE CLARA REED INTERVIEW, 1969, 1 item
ORAL HISTORIES: 122-page transcript of interview with Alice Clara Reed on her experiences as an educational missionary to China in various Congregational mission stations between 1916 and 1948.

33-GRACE MAY ROWLEY INTERVIEWS, 1970–71, 4 items
ORAL HISTORIES: 52-page transcript of interviews with Grace May Rowley.
AUDIO-VISUAL MATERIALS: 3 photos of Rowley.

34-AGNES (KELLY) SCOTT INTERVIEWS, 1969–72, 2 items
ORAL HISTORIES: 57-page transcript of interviews on educational missionary Agnes Scott's career teaching music and directing choral groups at high school in Foochow and at Fukien Christian University.
AUDIO-VISUAL MATERIALS: Photo of Agnes Scott.

35-RODERICK SCOTT INTERVIEW, 1969–70, quantity undetermined
Background note: For biographical notes, see Hoover Institution, Archives, Stanford University, Stanford, CA, 94305–2323.
CORRESPONDENCE/MANUSCRIPTS: Correspondence and written materials of Scott.
ORAL HISTORIES: 117-page transcript of interviews with Roderick Scott, a professor at Fukien Christian University, on his missionary career, 1916–51, including discussion of the influence of the Christian missionary movement in China.

36-MARGARET (TIMBERLAKE) SIMKIN INTERVIEWS, 1970–71, 2 items
ORAL HISTORIES: 62-page transcript of interviews with Margaret Simkin on her life as the wife of a Quaker missionary, 1923–44, stationed primarily in Chengtu at West China Union University.
AUDIO-VISUAL MATERIALS: Photo of Simkin.

37-LEWIS STRONG CASEY SMYTHE INTERVIEWS, 1970–71, 2 items
Background note: See also American Lutheran Church, Archives, 2481 Como Avenue, St. Paul, MN, 55108.
ORAL HISTORIES: 118-page transcript of interviews with Lewis Strong Casey Smythe on his work as a missionary with the United Christian Missionary Society in Nanking and West China, 1928–51, including comments on Chinese culture, society, politics, work on sociological surveys, and the development of industrial cooperatives.
AUDIO-VISUAL MATERIALS: Photo of Smythe.

38-MARGARET (GARRETT) SMYTHE INTERVIEWS, 1971–72, 1 item
ORAL HISTORIES: 84-page transcript of interviews with Margaret Smythe on her childhood in China as the daughter of missionary parents, her medical missionary work, the Sino-Japanese War, and life under the Communists until 1951.

39-LOUISE CLAIRE (HATHAWAY) STANLEY INTERVIEW, 1971, 2 items
ORAL HISTORIES: 83-page transcript of an interview with Louise Stanley on her experiences as a missionary in Tientsin and

Shantung, 1904–41, as the wife of a Congregational Board missionary, Charles A. Stanley, including comments on her husband's family and early missionaries in China.
AUDIO-VISUAL MATERIALS: Photo of Louise Stanley.

40-MARJORIE (RANKIN) STEURT INTERVIEW, 1970, 2 items
Background note: For biographical notes, see Mount Holyoke College, College History and Archives, Williston Memorial Library, South Hadley, MA, 01075–1493.
ORAL HISTORIES: 133-page transcript of interviews with Marjorie Steurt on her teaching career under sponsorship of the Presbyterian Mission Board, 1912–27; her return to China as director of experimental education, Nankai University, 1929–32; her views on education; and comments on missionaries.
AUDIO-VISUAL MATERIALS: Photo of Steurt.

41-F. OLIN STOCKWELL INTERVIEW, 1971, 2 items
ORAL HISTORIES: 48-page transcript of an interview with Francis Olin Stockwell on his missionary experiences in rural evangelistic work in Foochow, 1929–34, and in Chengtu, 1935–41; teaching at West China Union Theological Seminary, 1942–49; and imprisonment by the Communists, 1950–51.
AUDIO-VISUAL MATERIALS: Photo of Stockwell.

42-GEORGE THOMAS TOOTELL INTERVIEW, 1969, 1 item
Background note: For biographical notes, see University of Oregon, Special Collections, Eugene, OR, 97403–1299.
ORAL HISTORIES: 35-page transcript of an interview with George Thomas Tootell on his experiences as a Presbyterian medical missionary to China from 1913 to 1949.

43-WILLIAM HILL TOPPING INTERVIEW, 1970, 1 item
ORAL HISTORIES: 25-page transcript of an interview with William Hill Topping on his experiences as a missionary in Foochow under the Synod of the Church of Christ in China from 1911 to 1951.

44-KATHERINE BERTHA (BOEYE) WARD INTERVIEW, 1971, 2 items
Background note: See also American Lutheran Church, Archives, 2481 Como Avenue, St. Paul, MN, 55108.
ORAL HISTORIES: 92-page transcript of an interview with Katherine Bertha Boeye Ward on her experiences as a missionary in China, 1925–39, teaching in Nanking and Chungking, and as a bishop's wife, 1948–58, in Shanghai and Taiwan.
AUDIO-VISUAL MATERIALS: Photo of Ward.

45-MARTHA WILEY INTERVIEW, 1969, 1 item
Background note: For biographical notes, see Yakima Valley Museum and Historical Association, 2105 Tieton Drive, Yakima, WA, 98902.
ORAL HISTORIES: 106-page transcript of an interview with Martha Wiley on her experiences as a Congregational missionary in China, primarily in the Foochow area, 1900–1947, including recollections of Wiley by Dr. and Mrs. Roderick Scott.

46-ELEUTHERIUS WINANCE INTERVIEW, 1969, 2 items
ORAL HISTORIES: 131-page transcript of an interview with Eleutherius Winance on his experiences as a Benedictine missionary in Szechuan Province, 1936–52, including his trial and expulsion by the Communists in 1952.
AUDIO-VISUAL MATERIALS: Photo of Winance.

47-PEARL BEATRICE (FOSNOT) WINANS INTERVIEWS, 1970, 1 item
ORAL HISTORIES: 47-page transcript of interviews with Pearl Beatrice Winans.

48-GENERAL HOLDINGS
MANUSCRIPTS: *China Missionaries Oral History Project: An Overview*, a report prepared by staff members of the China Missionaries Oral History Project, including a statement of project goals, staff and procedures by Enid H. Douglass, a report by Cyrus H. Peake, and a summary statement and evaluation of findings by Arthur L. Rosenbaum.
PAMPHLETS: *California College in China...to the Heart of China Through the Doorway of the North China Union Language School*, n.d.; *The Spirit and Purpose of Lingnan*, 1928(?).
CHINESE LANGUAGE MATERIALS: *Research Guide to the 'Chiao hui hsin pao,' 1868–1874*, by Adrian Arthur Bennett, 1975; *Research Guide to the 'Wan kuo kung pao,' 1874–1883*, by Adrian Arthur Bennett, 1976.

CA–85   Honnold Library
Claremont Colleges
Ninth and Dartmouth Streets
Claremont CA 91711
(714) 621–8150
Patrick Barkey, Director of Libraries
  for the Claremont Colleges

1-GENERAL HOLDINGS
MINUTES/RECORDS/REPORTS: American Board of Commissioners for Foreign Missions, North China Mission, report, 1898; Board of Missionary Preparation, report, 1914; Canton Missionary Conference, South China Missionary Diary and Calendar, 1924; Christian Literature Society for China, report, 1899–1900; Church Committee for China Relief, records, 1940(?); Foreign Missions Conference of North America, addresses on China, 1927; International Institute of China, prospectus, 1910(?); reports, 1913.
MANUSCRIPTS: Circulars sent out in behalf of the Diffusion Society and the Christian Literature Society between 1891 and 1901, collected by Timothy Richard, n.d.
PAMPHLETS: 18 titles, 1901–38, on subjects such as anti-Christian movements, Canton Hospital, Christian education, health of missionary families, David Nelson Lyon, Mandana E. Lyon, political obstacles to missionary success, self-supporting church, and the Siege of Peking.
SERIALS: *China and the Gospel*, 1908. *China Christian Year Book*, 1910–39. China International Famine Relief Commission, *Bulletin*, 1923–26; *News Bulletin*, 1935–39; Publications, series A, 1923–37; series B, 1924–26, 1928–31, 1933. *China Law Review*, 1922–24. *China's Millions* (Philadelphia), 1893–94, 1913–36, 1938, 1949. *Chinese Recorder*, 1868–1941. *Chinese Repository*, 1832–51. *Educational Review*, 1916–38. *Folklore Studies*, 1942–46. *Land of Sinim*, 1904. *Lingnan Science Journal*, 1922–45. *Missionary Recorder*, 1867. *Monumenta Serica*, 1935-. *Peking Natural History Bulletin*, 1926–40. *Yenching Gazette*, 1932–33. *Yenching Journal of Social Studies*, 1938–41.
CHINESE LANGUAGE MATERIALS/SERIALS: *Ling-nan hsüeh pao*, 1929–33. *Yen-ching hsüeh pao*, 1927–51.

SCHOOL OF THEOLOGY AT CLAREMONT
CA-90   Library
Foothill Boulevard at College Avenue
Claremont CA 91711
(714) 626-3521 Ext. 270
Caroline Whipple, Director

1-GENERAL HOLDINGS
MINUTES/RECORDS/REPORTS: National Christian Council, report on rural church, 1924–25; National Council of the Churches of Christ in the U.S.A., report on China, 1958; North China Institute for Supervisors of Rural Work, Tunghsien, report, 1935.
PAMPHLETS: 12 pamphlets, 1906–57, on Miner Searle Bates, Christian education, Chung-hua Sheng Kung Hui, College of Chinese Studies, Disciples of Christ missions, indigenous church, Emma A. Lyon, Methodist Episcopal Church, Robert Morrison, rural China, and Clara Swain.
SERIALS: *China Christian Year Book*, 1911–12, 1916–23, 1931. *Chinese Repository*, 1832–46.

DAVIS

UNIVERSITY OF CALIFORNIA

CA-95   Carlson Health Sciences Library
Davis CA 95616
(916) 752-1214
Jo Anne Boorkman, Health Sciences Librarian

1-GENERAL HOLDINGS
SERIALS: *China's Medicine*, 1966–68. *Chinese Medical Journal*, 1956–65, 1975-.

CA-100   Department of Special Collections
University of California
Davis CA 95616
(916) 752-1621
Donald Kunitz, Head of Special Collections

1-GENERAL HOLDINGS
DISSERTATIONS/THESES: *Christianity and Confucianism: The Writings of Matteo Ricci (1552-1610) and Yang Kuang-hsien (1597-1669)*, by John Dragon Young, 1972. *Community and Bureaucracy in Rural China: Evidence from "Sectarian Cases (chiao an)" in Kiangsi, 1860-1895*, by Alan Richard Sweeten, 1980. *Confucianism and Christianity: The Jesuits, Their Converts, and Their Critics, 1552-1669*, by John Dragon Young, 1976. *The Jesuit Mission of Matteo Ricci: Christianity and the Chinese World View*, by Richard Edward Negron, 1984. *John Fryer and the Introduction of Western Science and Technology into Nineteenth-century China*, by Adrian Arthur Bennett, III, 1966. *Mary Ann Aldersey and the Beginning of Christian Schools for Women in China*, by George Chester Burnett, 1975. *The Middle Kingdom Revisited: The Validity of S. Wells Williams' Book and Its Sources*, by Mark Sherman Farber, 1972. *Missionary Journalism in Nineteenth-century China: Young J. Allen and the Early 'Wan kuo kung pao,'* by Adrian Arthur Bennett, III, 1970. *The Politics of Escha-*

tology: Hung Hsiu-ch'uan and the Rise of the Taipings, 1837-1853, by Paul Richard Bohr, 1978. *Temple Community and Village Cultural Integration in North China: Evidence from "Sectarian Cases (chiao an)" in Chihli, 1860-1895*, by Charles Albert Litzinger, 1983.

CA-105   Law Library
University of California
Davis CA 95616
(916) 752-3326
Mortimer Schwartz, Librarian

1-GENERAL HOLDINGS
SERIALS: *China Law Review*, 1922–24, 1937–40.

CA-110   University Library
University of California
Davis CA 95616
(916) 752-1136
Gregor A. Preston, Head of Cataloging

1-ASIAN COLLECTION, 1927–81, 18 volumes
SERIALS: *Folklore Studies*, 1942–52.
CHINESE LANGUAGE MATERIALS/SERIALS: *Yen-ching hsüeh pao (Yenching Journal of Chinese Studies)*, 1927–50. *Yen-ching hsüeh pao chuan hao (Yenching Journal of Chinese Studies, Monograph)*, 1933–48 (repr. 1973). Yen-ching ta hsüeh: *K'ao ku hsüeh she she k'an*, 1934–37; *Shih hsüeh nien pao (Historical Annual)*, 1929–40 (repr. 1969).
CHINESE LANGUAGE MATERIALS: 13 volumes, 1960–81, on Young J. Allen, anti-missionary activity, Christianity, controversial literature, land utilization, Nanking, Nestorians in China, Peking University, and sectarian cases.

2-GENERAL HOLDINGS
MINUTES/RECORDS/REPORTS: University of Nanking, College of Agriculture and Forestry and Experiment Station, annual report, 1917–19, 1920–21, 1923–27.
MANUSCRIPTS: "An Experiment in the Registration of Vital Statistics in China," by Ch'iao Ch'i-ming, 1938.
PAMPHLETS: *The Catholic Missions in China during the Middle Ages, 1294-1368*, by Paul Stanislaus Hsiang, 1949; *Nanking: The Capital, Symbol of the New Life of China*, by Ralph Ansel Ward, 1935; *A Retrospect of Sixty Years: A Paper Read at a Meeting of the Hangchow Missionary Association*, by George Evans Moule, 1907.
SERIALS: *China Christian Year Book*, 1911–12, 1914–17, 1919, 1923–26, 1929, 1931. China International Famine Relief Commission, Publications, series B, 1930. *Chinese Christians Today*, 1986-. *Chinese Recorder*, 1887, 1893–95. *Chinese Repository*, 1832–51. *Monumenta Serica*, 1935-. University of Nanking, College of Agriculture and Forestry: *Agriculture and Forestry Notes*, 1924–41; *Agriculture and Forestry Series*, 1920–26; *Miscellaneous Bulletin Series*, 1924–25. *Yenching Journal of Social Studies*, 1938–50.

FRESNO

CENTER FOR MENNONITE BRETHREN STUDIES
CA-115 Archives and Historical Library

Mennonite Brethren Biblical Seminary
4824 East Butler
Fresno CA 93727
(209) 453-2225
Kevin Enns-Rempel, Archivist

Restrictions: Personnel files are restricted. Permission required for use.
Background note: This repository is the archive for the General Conference of Mennonite Brethren Churches of North America. See also Bethel College, Mennonite Library and Archives, North Newton, KS, 67117-9998; Eastern Mennonite College and Seminary, Menno Simons Historical Library and Archives, Harrisonburg, VA, 22801-2462; and Goshen College, Archives of the Mennonite Church, 1700 South Main Street, Goshen, IN, 46526.

1-MENNONITE BRETHREN MISSIONS/SERVICES, 1900-1950,
 ca. 2 l.f., 4 cassette tapes, 2 volumes
MINUTES/RECORDS/REPORTS/CORRESPONDENCE/
PAMPHLETS/MAPS/DESIGNS/DRAWINGS: Correspondence, photos, pamphlets, and maps relating to China, 1900-1950; General Conference China Mennonite Mission, report, 1940.
CORRESPONDENCE: Personal correspondence in personnel files: Harold and Elaine Baltzer, 1946-57; Peter and Lydia Baltzer, 1919-64; Bena Bartel and Emma Bartel, 1931-59; Henry C. and Nellie Bartel, 1919-65; John S. and Tina Dick, 1919-53; Henry and Aganetha Epp, 1943-64; Paulina Foote, 1922-62; Sara Heinrichs, 1933-40; Helen (Quiring) Heppner, 1919-30; Elizabeth Hofer, n.d.; Peter D. Kiehn, Mary Kiehn (his first wife), and Susie Kiehn (his second wife), 1942-57; Anna Klassen, 1947-58; Tina Kornelson, 1920-32; Adelgunda Priebe, 1926-58; Marie Richert, 1921; Sophie Richert, 1920-44; Mary Schmidt, 1922; Abraham K. and Gertrude Buhler Wiens, 1945-51; Bernard and Sarah Wiens, 1920-59; Frank J. Wiens, Agnes Harder Wiens (his first wife), and Agnes Koop Wiens (his second wife), 1936-59; Roland and Anna Wiens, 1945-51; George K. and Mary Willems, 1922.
MANUSCRIPTS: "China: Communism But God," by Roland and Anna Wiens, n.d.; "China Retrospect," by Roland and Anna Wiens (?), 1955; "Krimmer Mennonite Brethren Mission Work in China," by Abraham K. Wiens, n.d. (draft of dissertation listed below under DISSERTATIONS/THESES); "My Heart Looks Back," by Tina Harder Dick, n.d.; "Our Brethren Behind the Bamboo Curtain," by Roland Wiens, 1952 (?); "A Sketch of Your Life," article about Harold and Elaine Baltzer, n.d.; "The Wiens Bicycle," biography of Frank J. Wiens, n.d.
PAMPHLETS: *China Revisited*, by Roland and Anna Wiens, 1955; *Foreign Missions*, containing a section on China, 1945; *Have Cart Will Travel* (the life of Paulina Foote), by Katie Funk Wiebe, 1974; *The Lord's Way for Me to Escape War Imprisonment*, by Paulina Foote, 1948; *1909-1934: The Celebration of the Twenty-fifth Anniversary of Rev. H. J. and Maria Brown's Missionary Service in China*, by Henry J. Brown, 1934.
ORAL HISTORIES: 4 taped interviews with Susan Schultz Bartel in 1978 and 1979, including discussion of her experiences in China to the time of the Japanese occupation, evacuation of missionaries,

internment and release, Chinese Communists, departure from China, her adjustments after return to the United States, and the life of her father-in-law, Henry Bartel (see also Wheaton College, Billy Graham Center, Archives, Wheaton, IL, 60187).
DISSERTATIONS/THESES: *Evangelism in the Chinese Church*, by David H. Purnomo, 1981. *The Work of the Mennonite Missions in China*, by Abraham K. Wiens, 1951.
FINDING AIDS: Index to articles in denominational periodicals, *Christian Leader* and *Zionsbote*, in individual personnel files.

2-GENERAL HOLDINGS
MANUSCRIPTS: "A Review of Mennonite Mission and Church History in China," by S. F. Pannabecker, n.d.
PAMPHLETS: *Foreign Missions: M. B. Mission in West China*, 1949.
DISSERTATIONS/THESES: *The Work of the Mennonite Missions in China*, by Abraham K. Wiens, 1951.

FULLERTON

CALIFORNIA STATE UNIVERSITY
CA-120 Library

800 North State College Boulevard
P.O. Box 4150
Fullerton CA 92634
(714) 773-2633
Joyce Wilder-Jones, Chair of Public Services

1-GENERAL HOLDINGS
PAMPHLETS: *Religious Suppression in Mainland China*, by Peter Humphrey, 1983.
DISSERTATIONS/THESES: *The Bible Institute of Los Angeles in China: An American Missionary Experience as Viewed from the Stewart Papers*, by Charles Everleigh Clements, 1975.

LA JOLLA

UNIVERSITY OF CALIFORNIA, SAN DIEGO
CA-125 University Library

La Jolla CA 92093
(619) 534-3336
Irene Hurlbut, Reference Librarian
Geoffrey Wexler, Manuscripts Librarian

1-J. STUART INNERST PAPERS, 1920s-1970s, ca. 10 boxes
Background note: J. Stuart Innerst (1894-1975) was a Quaker missionary to China, the first Western missionary to leave China at the onset of the revolution and the first to be invited back by the Communists in 1972. He was editor of *Understanding China Newsletter*, published by the American Friends Service Committee. This collection is unprocessed. Some of the printed materials have been removed from the collection and distributed among the library's general holdings.
MINUTES/RECORDS/REPORTS/MANUSCRIPTS/DIARIES: Ca. 10 folders of manuscripts, notes, and journals; 20 folders of manuscript notes; notes, typescripts, and articles on U.S.-China relations, post-1960s; folder of notes and manuscripts of "Modern Industrialization in China," by Innerst (published in the 1920s); 2

stenographer's notebooks of Innerst's comments on a trip to Asia in 1968 to investigate China and surrounding countries; notes on Innerst's 1972 trip to China, including memobooks and loose notes.

CORRESPONDENCE: Ca. 25 folders of correspondence to Innerst regarding China and U.S.-China relations, and ca. 12 folders of mimeographed letters for distribution to friends and associates; folder of ca. 60 pages of letters to Rev. and Mrs. R. H. Lefever, regarding Innerst's trip to China; 30 pages of correspondence between Innerst and Anna Louise Strong regarding China, 1920s–1930s.

MANUSCRIPTS: "China and the Quakers: A Century of Sino-British Team Work," by H. T. Silcock, n.d. (ca. 1960?).

PAMPHLETS: *The Force of Missions in a New China*, by Ira M. Condit, D.D., n.d.; *Quaker Mission to China: W. Grigor McClelland's Diary, 26th September–29th October 1955*; miscellaneous publications by Innerst.

MEMORABILIA: 20 folders of clippings and articles by and about Innerst, in particular, regarding his trip to China after Nixon's trip in 1972; folder of clippings, articles, and other materials relating to the life and work of Anna Louise Strong, including issues of her publications, *Letter from China* and *Today*; obituary of Innerst, 1975.

AUDIO-VISUAL MATERIALS: 6 audio cassettes of notes during and after his 1972 trip to China; 65 photos from 1972 trip to China; 34 slides, with 12-page narrative for presentation; ca. 300 slides from 1972 trip.

2-GENERAL HOLDINGS

PAMPHLETS: *Nestorians in China: Some Corrections and Additions*, by Arthur Christopher Moule, 1940.

SERIALS: *Educational Review*, 1920–37. *Monumenta Serica*, 1935–83.

LA MIRADA

BIOLA UNIVERSITY
CA–130 Rose Memorial Library
    13800 Biola Avenue
    La Mirada CA 90639
    (213) 944–0351
    Gerald Gooden, Associate Librarian

Background note: Biola University, formerly the Bible Institute of Los Angeles, founded the Hunan Bible Institute (HBI) in 1916 on the outskirts of Changsha, financially supported by Lyman Stewart, founder of the Union Oil Company and the first president of Biola, and his brother, Milton Stewart. The first superintendent and pioneer of HBI was Frank A. Keller, who went to China as a medical missionary under the China Inland Mission in 1897. His innovation was the creation of river evangelism—riverboat bands or floating Bible schools—between 1906 and 1909. Charles Roberts succeeded him as superintendent, followed by William Ebeling. "Biola in China: The Hunan Bible Institute and Its Ongoing Legacy," by Robert Harrison, 1985, contains a history of the Hunan Bible Institute and its relationship with Biola (see MANUSCRIPTS under GENERAL HOLDINGS below).

1-HUNAN BIBLE INSTITUTE PAPERS, 1904–50, 19 folders, 10 volumes

MINUTES/RECORDS/REPORTS: Memorandum on China, 1935; agreement between the British Red Cross and HBI to establish a hospital base in Changsha, 1942; balance sheet for HBI, 1946; freight lists and shipping documents, 1947; Hudson Taylor Memorial Hospital, Changsha (China Inland Mission), list of equipment, 1947; statements of accounts, 1947; list of donations and donors, 1947, 1949; minutes and report of business meeting, 1947; lease agreement for Taylor Hospital between HBI and China Inland Mission (CIM), 1947; HBI, minutes, 1948; invoices and bills of lading for miscellaneous office and medical supplies, and used Bibles to be sent to HBI, 1948; monthly budget, 1948; receipts for funds from Biola to the China Inland Mission for transmission to HBI, 1949; excerpt from minutes, Biola Board of Directors, China Department, 1948; report to Board of Directors of Biola on HBI, 1949.

CORRESPONDENCE: HBI correspondence, 1904–50, including correspondents James R. Allder (business manager of Biola), A. B. Brown, A. G. Carpenter, China Inland Mission, Chinese Consulate in Los Angeles, Eleanor and Edwin Cory, Rowland Cross, Russell Davis, Henry Frost, Minnie Moore Gray, William Haven (American Bible Society), Frank Keller, Mary E. Knox, Howard Lucy, Ray Myers (chairman of the Board of Directors of Biola), William Orr, Francis Price, Helen Pufield, Charles Roberts, Paul Rood (president of Biola), Ralph D. Smith, Lyman Stewart, Milton Stewart and Mary W. Stewart, Louis Talbot (president of Biola), the U.S. State Department (regarding claims for war damages), G. G. Warren, Mrs. J. Woodberry, and R. K. Yeryard (?); typed extracts of a letter from Keller to William G. Nyman, 1933; circular letters from Eleanor and Edwin Cory, 1947; telegrams of Russell Davis and Charles Roberts, 1948; correspondence concerning requests for medical supplies for a hospital in Changsha, 1948; letter from Davis to Frances Neilson, Church of the Open Door, regarding requests for children's clothing, with a list of measurements of children at HBI orphanage, 1948.

MANUSCRIPTS: List of points for discussion, 1937; names and addresses of HBI staff, n.d.; Hudson Taylor Memorial Hospital, list of medicines, n.d.; untitled manuscript from the China Department of the Bible Institute of Los Angeles, 1938; list of merchandise for shipment to HBI, 1948; Robert Harrison's research and interview notes for his paper, "Biola in China: The Hunan Bible Institute and Its Ongoing Legacy," 1985.

PAMPHLETS: Printed list of Biola missionaries, including those in China, 1939; *Manual of the Hunan Bible Institute, China Department of the Bible Institute of Los Angeles*, n.d.

MEMORABILIA: Clipping from *Evening Outlook*, Santa Monica, California, on the return to China of Mr. and Mrs. J. R. Saunders.

MAPS/DESIGNS/DRAWINGS: Folder of maps and graphics, n.d.; hand-drawn maps of HBI compound, n.d.; map of Changsha, n.d.

AUDIO-VISUAL MATERIALS: 11 folders of loose photos of HBI campus, Chinese scenes, Communist takeover of Hunan, orphanage, staff and students, Evangelistic Bands, Keller, Roberts, ministry and Christian service, and the Nanyoh Bible Conference site; printed photo of Door of Hope missionary E. Gladys Dieterly with Chinese children in Shanghai, n.d.; film footage of HBI taken by Charles Roberts, 1930–37; photographic diary of

Thirteen Floating Biola Bands in Hunan, 1926.
SERIALS: *Hunan Bible Institute Bulletin*, 1949–50. *The Word for God in Chinese*, 1914–15.
CHINESE LANGUAGE MATERIALS: 10 handwritten Evangelistic Band diaries, 1939–41; HBI yearbook, 1936; HBI workplans, n.d.; letter from Yan Hsi Shao to Lyman Stewart, with translation, n.d.

2-PRESIDENT'S FILES, 1912–68, quantity undetermined
MINUTES/RECORDS/REPORTS: Hunan property deeds, 1912–24; report on Biola Schools and Colleges by the Foreign Claims Settlement Commission of the United States, 1968.
CORRESPONDENCE: Letters from Al Sanders, vice president of Biola Public Relations, to Paul Schwepker, Biola Controller, 1961, regarding property in Hong Kong; correspondence relating to foreign claims settlement, 1970–71.

3-LYMAN STEWART PAPERS, 1904–73, 9 volumes
Background note: The section on China in Lyman Stewart's papers represents only a part of a larger uncatalogued collection. There may be more material on China in addition to the items listed below, but it has not yet been identified. The materials described are in several binders, photocopied by Charles Everleigh Clements in 1972 in preparation of his dissertation (see DISSERTATIONS/THESES under GENERAL HOLDINGS below). Of the 9 volumes, 6 largely overlap with the Hunan Bible Institute papers, and all are heavily marked and annotated by Clements.
MINUTES/RECORDS/REPORTS: Hunan Bible Institute: bound volume of financial reports, 1936–49; tentative constitution, n.d.
CORRESPONDENCE: Bound volume of correspondence between Biola University and HBI, n.d.; bound volume of typed copies of letters from Frank Keller, 1918–50; bound volume of copies of HBI correspondence and typed transcripts, including correspondents Ralph Smith, Charles Roberts, Frank Keller, Lyman Stewart, Milton Stewart, 1904–23; 4 bound volumes of correspondence of Lyman Stewart, 1932–51.
MANUSCRIPTS: List of missionary and Chinese staff of HBI, ca. 1949; history and background of HBI, n.d.; manual of HBI, n.d.; list of cable phrases for Biola in case of Changsha bombing, n.d.; "Facts about the Hunan Bible Institute for Board Consideration," n.d.; "A Message from Chinese Christians to Mission Board Abroad," n.d.
MEMORABILIA: Typed extracts from the *King's Business*, 1917–50, with copies of articles by Frank Keller, Everett Harrison, and Charles Roberts.
MAPS/DESIGNS/DRAWINGS: Map of HBI compound with explanatory notes.
ORAL HISTORIES: Typed transcript of an interview with William Ebeling in 1969 and 1973 on his experiences as a missionary under the China Inland Mission in Changsha.

4-GENERAL HOLDINGS
MINUTES/RECORDS/REPORTS: Reports on work in China in *King's Business*, ca. 1912-ca. 1952; China Inland Mission, report, 1934.
MANUSCRIPTS: "Bethel Heartthrobs of Revival," 1931; "Biola in China: The Hunan Bible Institute and Its Ongoing Legacy," by Robert T. Harrison, 1985; "A Collection of Missionary Biographies," by students of Talbot Theological Seminary, 1965, including James Gilmour, Jonathan Goforth, George Leslie MacKay,

Robert Morrison, John and Betty Stam, and J. Hudson Taylor; "God in Ka Do Land," by H. A. Baker, n.d.; "The Missions Situation in China since 1949," by Lanny R. Johnson, 1966.
PAMPHLETS: *Afloat in Hunan, China*, by Frank Keller, n.d.; *Kept and Led during China's War Years: A Continuation of the Hebron Mission*, by Ruth Hitchcock, 1947; *Through the Gates into the City*, by Isabella C. Campbell, n.d.
ORAL HISTORIES: *China Missionaries Oral History Collection*, ed. by Cyrus H. Peake and Arthur L. Rosenbaum (Claremont Graduate School, Oral History Program), 1973. See ORAL HISTORIES Union List for the names of participants.
SERIALS: *China and the Gospel*, 1910. *China Christian Year Book*, 1910–35. *China's Millions* (London), 1886–88. *China's Millions* (Toronto), 1895–1901, 1932–34, 1937–52. *Chinese Around the World*, 1984–85. *Chinese Christians Today*, 1980. *Chinese World Pulse*, 1981. *Directory of Protestant Missions in China*, 1920, 1930. *East Asia Millions* (Philadelphia), 1961–70, 1985–86. *Millions* (Philadelphia), 1953–60. *Monumenta Serica*, 1935–65, 1974-. *The Story of the China Inland Mission*, 1935, 1937, 1940, 1942, 1945–46, 1949–55, 1957.
DISSERTATIONS/THESES: *The Bible Institute of Los Angeles in China: An American Missionary Experience as Viewed from the Stewart Papers*, by Charles Everleigh Clements, 1975. *The Work of the Mennonite Missions in China*, by Abraham K. Wiens, 1951.

LOMA LINDA

LOMA LINDA UNIVERSITY
CA–135 Vernier Radcliffe Memorial Library
Loma Linda CA 92354
(714) 824-4942
Dorothy Womack, Library Associate

Background note: In addition to the materials listed below, information on activities of Seventh-Day Adventists (SDA) in China can be found in the denominational periodicals, *Health Alert*, *Medical Bulletin*, *Medical Evangelist*, *Review and Herald*, *Signs of the Times*, and *The Youth's Instructor*, all of which are indexed in the *Seventh-Day Adventist Periodical Index*.

1-GENERAL HOLDINGS
CORRESPONDENCE: Correspondence between Dr. H. W. Miller and P. T. Magan, C. C. Crisler, W. A. Spicer, and J. L. Shaw regarding the establishment of a medical school in China, 1929; letter to F. L. Hawks Pott, president of St. John's University, n.d.; unidentified telegram, 1929; letter from W. C. White to Abram La Rue, 1889; copy of a 1902 letter from E. H. and Susan Wilbur, who are reported to have been the first SDA missionaries in China; uncatalogued file of ca. 100 letters between Loma Linda University and medical workers in China, 1911–49.
DIARIES: Unidentified diary fragments, n.d.
MANUSCRIPTS: "An Appraisal of Administrative Policy and Practice in S. D. A. Missions," by David Lin, n.d.; talk by C. Conard on educational work in China, 1934; talk by J. Harold Schultz on Chinese history, 1935; list of presidents of the SDA China division, 1931–50; historical data on the China division from 1888 to 1951; "Medical Missions Miscellany," by William Clarence White, n.d., a compilation of copies of published articles, which may include China.

PAMPHLETS: Promotional brochures for establishing a medical school, n.d.
ORAL HISTORIES: Oral history tapes containing interviews with Hsu Hua, Dr. Harry Miller, and Paul Quimby, n.d.
SERIALS: *Asiatic Division Mission News*, 1914–16. *Asiatic Division Outlook*, 1917–24. *China Division Reporter*, 1931–41, 1947–51. *China Evangelism*, 1977–80. *China Medical School News*, 1950–52. *Far Eastern Division Newsletter*, 1980–85. *Far Eastern Division Outlook*, 1924–41, 1944–85. *Far Eastern Division Voice*, 1981–85. *Far Eastern Promoter*, 1925. Nanking Theological Seminary, English publications, 1940. *Newsletter for the Asiatic Division*, 1913–14.
DISSERTATIONS/THESES: *The Development and History of the Seventh-Day Adventist Church in China since the Communist Take-over*, by Lien-chieh Tsao, 1975. *A History of Seventh-Day Adventist Higher Education in the China Mission, 1888–1980*, by Handel Hing-tat Luke, 1983. *A Study of the Christian Church [ching chiao] in T'ang China: A.D. 618 to 906*, by James Harold Shultz, 1970.
CHINESE LANGUAGE MATERIALS: Medical pamphlet, n.d.; *Knowledge and Progress*, by the Editorial Department of the Signs Publishing House with Denton Edward Rebok and A. L. Tai, 1931.

LOS ANGELES

CA-140 LOS ANGELES COUNTY LAW LIBRARY
301 West First Street
Los Angeles CA 90012
(213) 629–3531
Earl Weisbaum, Foreign and International
  Law Librarian

1-GENERAL HOLDINGS
SERIALS: *China Law Review*, 1922–37.

LOS ANGELES COUNTY MEDICAL ASSOCIATION
CA-145 Library
634 South Westlake Avenue
Los Angeles CA 90057
(213) 483–4555
Elizabeth Crahan, Librarian

1-GENERAL HOLDINGS
MINUTES/RECORDS/REPORTS: China Medical Board, annual report, 1916; Peiping, First Health Station, annual report, 1935; Peiping Union Medical College, addresses and papers, 1922; annual announcements, 1933–34; Peiping Union Medical College Hospital, report of the superintendent, 1933–40; Shantung Christian University, Cheeloo School of Medicine, report, 1932.
SERIALS: *China Medical Journal*, 1928, 1931. *China's Medicine*, 1966–68. *Chinese Medical Directory*, 1932. *Chinese Medical Journal*, 1932, 1934–41, 1943–45, 1947–66, 1973–; supplement, 1936, 1952.

CA-150 LOS ANGELES PUBLIC LIBRARY
Philosophy, Religion, and Social Science Department
630 West Fifth Street
Los Angeles CA 90071
(213) 626–7555
Marilyn C. Wherley, Subject Department Manager
Richard P. Giannini, Senior Librarian

Background note: In addition to the materials listed below, the LAPL may have monographs and serials related to Christian missionary work in China. However, finding aids and materials will not be available until reparations from the recent fire have been completed.

1-GENERAL HOLDINGS
PAMPHLETS: *Catholic Church Activities in War Afflicted China*, n.d.; *China's Spiritual Mobilization: Outline of the Plan*, 1939; *Outline Story of the China Inland Mission*, 1934.
SERIALS: *China Bulletin*, 1959–67. *China Mission Year Book*, 1918–39. *ECF News*, 1970.

MOUNT ST. MARY'S COLLEGE
CA-155 Charles Willard Coe Library
12001 Chalon Road
Los Angeles CA 90049
(213) 476–2237
Erika Condon, Director

1-GENERAL HOLDINGS
DISSERTATIONS/THESES: *Maryknoll in Manchuria, 1927–1947: A Study of Accommodation and Adaptation*, by Kathleen Kelly, 1982.

UNIVERSITY OF CALIFORNIA AT LOS ANGELES

CA-160 Biomedical Library
Los Angeles CA 90024
(213) 825–6098
Julie Kwan, Head of Reference

1-GENERAL HOLDINGS
SERIALS: *China's Medicine*, 1966–68. *Chinese Medical Journal*, 1932–34, 1937–52, 1954–66, 1975–; supplement, 1936. *Lingnaam Agricultural Review*, 1925–27. *Lingnan Science Journal*, 1927–48. *Peking Natural History Bulletin*, 1926–41.

CA-165 Department of Special Collections
University Research Library
University of California at Los Angeles
405 Hilgard Avenue
Los Angeles CA 90024
(213) 825–4879
Anne Caiger, Manuscripts Librarian

1-GENERAL HOLDINGS
MANUSCRIPTS: Chinese-Latin dictionary, "Chinarum librum litteracaracter," n.a., n.p., ca. 1725; "Collection of Four Works on the Chinese Language," ca. 1721–1723, containing: "Table of Chinese Characters," comp. by Basilio da Gemona, O.F.M.;

"Spanish-Chinese Dictionary," comp. by Francisco Varo, O.P., trans. into Italian by Barthelemy Ferrari; "A Compendium Compiled from the Dictionary of Basilio da Gemona," by Barthelemy Ferrari; and "Chinese-Latin Dictionary," comp. by Barthelemy Ferrari.
PAMPHLETS: *Annua della Cina del MDCVI e MDCVII*, by Matteo Ricci, 1610; *Catholic Missions and the Chinese Republic*, by Andrew Hilliard Atteridge, 1915 (?); *A Chinese Hero* (Fong Ping), by Frederic J. Masters, n.d.
DISSERTATIONS/THESES: *G. W. von Leibniz und die China-Mission*, by Franz Rudolf Merkel, 1920.

CA–170 Law Library
University of California at Los Angeles
Law Building
Los Angeles CA 90024
(213) 825–4743
Myra Saunders, Head of Public Services

1-GENERAL HOLDINGS
SERIALS: *China Law Review*, 1922–37.

CA–175 Map Library
University of California at Los Angeles
Los Angeles CA 90024
(213) 825–3493
Carlos Hagen, Head of Library

1-GENERAL HOLDINGS
MAPS/DESIGNS/DRAWINGS: *Atlas of the Chinese Empire Containing Separate Maps of the Eighteen Provinces of China Proper on the Scale of 1:3,000,000 and of the Four Great Dependencies on the Scale of 1:7,500,000, Together with an Index to All the Names on the Maps and a List of All Protestant Mission Stations, etc.*, by Edward Stanford, 1908, 1917.

CA–180 Richard C. Rudolph Oriental Library
University of California at Los Angeles
405 Hilgard Avenue
Los Angeles CA 90024
(213) 825–4836
James Cheng, Head of Library

1-GENERAL HOLDINGS
CHINESE LANGUAGE MATERIALS/DISSERTATIONS/THESES: *Ma-li-no hui tsai Hua ch'uan chiao chien shih (A Short History of Maryknoll Missions in China)*, by Wen Shun-t'ien, 1977.
CHINESE LANGUAGE MATERIALS: 21 volumes, 1937–78, on Young J. Allen, anti-Christian activities, Buddhism and Christianity, church history in the Middle Ages, history of Christianity, Lingnan University, Gregorio Lopez, missions, sectarian cases, and Sun Yat-sen, and translations by Jesuits.

CA–185 University Research Library
University of California at Los Angeles
Los Angeles CA 90024
(213) 825–1323
Janet Zeigler, Reference Librarian

1-GENERAL HOLDINGS
MINUTES/RECORDS/REPORTS: Missionary Conference, Shanghai, report, 1890.
MANUSCRIPTS: "An Agricultural Survey of Szechwan Province, China," by John Lossing Buck, 1943; "The Catholic Church in China: Backgrounder," 1959(?); Methodist Missionary Society, "Inventories," 1978, microfiche reproduction of indexes to documents of the Methodist Missionary Society, including sections on China missions.
PAMPHLETS: *An Autobiographical Sketch, Read before the Afternoon Club of Claremont, California*, by Henry Poor Perkins, 1921; *The Catholic Missions in China during the Middle Ages, 1294–1368*, by Paul Stanislaus Hsiang, 1949; *China's Attempt to Absorbe [sic] Christianity: The Decree of March 15, 1899*, by George Nye Steiger, 1926; *The Growth of Knowledge of China in the West: A Lecture Delivered at the College of Chinese Studies in Peking*, by Frederick Dwight Schultheis, 1936; *Guds ledning i mitt liv.: Till svenska av D. R. Wahlquist*, by Petrus Hsi, 1940; *Peking Pigeons and Pigeon-flutes: A Lecture Delivered at the College of Chinese Studies, Peking*, by Harned Pettus Hoose, 1938; *Relation de ce qui s'est passé à la Chine en 1697–1698 et 1699 à l'occasion d'un établissement que m. l'Abbé de Lyonne a fait à Nien-Tcheou, ville de la province de Tche-Kiang*, by Jean de Fonteney, 1700; *Windows into China: The Jesuits and Their Books, 1580–1730*, by John Parker, 1978; *Yuen ming yuen: L'Oeuvre architecturale des anciens jésuites au XVIIIe siècle*, by Maurice Adam, 1936.
SERIALS: Catholic University of Peking, College of Education, publications, 1939–40. *China Christian Year Book*, 1931. China International Famine Relief Commission: *News Bulletin*, 1935, 1938–39; Publications, series A, 1934; series B, 1935. *China Notes*, 1967-. *Chinese Repository*, 1832–51. *Folklore Studies*, 1942–62. *Monumenta Serica*, 1935–78. Nanking Theological Seminary, English publications, 1940. *South China Collegian*, 1904. Université de l'Aurore, *Monthly Bulletin*, 1946–48. University of Nanking, College of Agriculture and Forestry, *Bulletin*, 1932–36.
DISSERTATIONS/THESES: *Die Akkommodationsmethode des P. Matteo Ricci S. I. in China*, by Johannes Bettray, 1955. *China Missions in Crisis: Bishop Laimbeckhoven and His Times, 1738–1787*, by Joseph Krahl, 1964. *Chinese Hostility to Christianity: A Study in Intercultural Conflict, 1860–1870*, by Paul A. Cohen, 1960. *Christianity and Social Change: The Case in China, 1920–1950*, by Lee-ming Ng, 1971.

UNIVERSITY OF SOUTHERN CALIFORNIA
CA–190 Von Kleinsmid Center Library
University Park
Los Angeles CA 90089–0182
(213) 743–6050
Kenneth Klein, East Asian Librarian

1-CHEN COLLECTION, 1923–78, 5 items
PAMPHLETS: *From Foochow to the Nation: A Souvenir of the Eastern Asia Jubilee Celebrating the Seventy-fifth Anniversary of Methodism's Beginnings in Eastern Asia*, by Frank Thomas Cartwright, 1923.

CHINESE LANGUAGE MATERIALS/DISSERTATIONS/ THESES: *Ma-li-no hui tsai Hua ch'uan chiao chien shih (A Brief History of Maryknoll Missions in China)*, by Wen Shun-t'ien, 1977.

CHINESE LANGUAGE MATERIALS: Biographies of Young J. Allen and Stephen Douglas Sturton, and a study of religious persecution in modern China, 1947–78.

2-GENERAL HOLDINGS

SERIALS: *Asia*, 1964. *China Christian Year Book*, 1932–33. China International Famine Relief Commission, Publications, series A, 1922–36. *China Notes*, 1962–84. *Directory of Protestant Missions in China*, 1929. *Yenching Journal of Social Studies*, Monograph series, ca. 1936(?).

DISSERTATIONS/THESES: *An Educational Program for Young Adults Adaptable to the Christian Churches in China*, by Liu I-hsin, 1952. *Maryknoll in Manchuria, 1927–1947: A Study of Accommodation and Adaptation*, by Kathleen Kelly, 1982. *A Study of the Christian Church [ching chiao] in T'ang China: A.D. 618 to 906*, by James Harold Shultz, 1970. *A Study of the Indigenous Elements in Chinese Christian Hymnody*, by David Sheng, 1964. *The Work of the Mennonite Missions in China*, by Abraham K. Wiens, 1951.

LOS GATOS

CALIFORNIA PROVINCE OF THE SOCIETY OF JESUS
CA–195 Archives
Jesuit Provincial Office
300 College Avenue
P.O. Box 519
Los Gatos CA 95031
(408) 354-6143
Thomas A. Marshall, S.J., Archivist

Background note: In addition to the materials listed below, the Archives hold complete sets of *Jesuit Missions*, *The Western Jesuit*, and *Woodstock Letters*, which contain information on the China mission work of the California Province. The California Province *Catalogue* contains the names of the missionaries, with their Chinese names and their year-by-year assignments. The Archives also have extensive holdings on their work in Macao, Taiwan, and Hong Kong, including the papers of José Peña (Xavier House, Kowloon).

1-CALIFORNIA PROVINCE CHINA MISSION ARCHIVE, 1926– 57, ca. 8,000 items
MINUTES/RECORDS/REPORTS: California Province of the Society of Jesus: personnel records, including academic records, correspondence, and other materials; Yangchow Mission, catalogues, 1948–51; Gonzaga College, Shanghai, catalogue, 1931– 33; Spanish Jesuit Mission, Wuhu Mission and Diocese, 5 folders of records, 1930s.

CORRESPONDENCE: Folder of correspondence on the China Mission History project, 1968–70; correspondence between California Province and personnel in China, 1925–45, with register leaves synopsizing contents; curial correspondence with American Jesuits in China, 1949–67; 3 folders of correspondence relating to the formation of the California Jesuit Mission in China and property deeds of Yangchow Missions lands; California Jesuit Missionaries, San Francisco office, curia correspondence, 1970–78; Far East Province of the Society of Jesus, curia correspondence, 1958– 70; Province of China, Society of Jesus, brochures and correspondence, 1972.

DIARIES: Diaries of Charles D. Simons, S.J., 1933–35; diary of Eugene Fahy, S.J., 1941–45; photocopy of diary of William J. Klement, S.J., 1937(?).

MANUSCRIPTS: Typescripts of promotion brochure with curial correspondence, including "Zikawei: Mother of the Mission," "Death by Bandits" (on the assassination of Charles D. Simons in 1940), and "Yangchow Mission History," ca. 1949; "Historia collegii Hung Kuang apud Nanking in Sinis," 1949; 6 notebooks of religious thoughts of Charles D. Simons, S.J., 1920–24; "In the Footsteps of the Great Shepherd," by Wilfred J. LeSage, S.J., n.d.

MEMORABILIA: 2 file drawers of memorabilia, including miscellaneous newletters, promotional materials, relics, and commercially-produced slides, belonging to Pius Moore, S.J., the first Mission Procurator.

ORAL HISTORIES: Tape of interview with Mark A. Flavey, S.J., recounting the death of Charles D. Simons, S.J., 1969; interview of John Houle, S.J., after his release from Chinese prison, 1958; oral histories of John Brennan, S.J., 1969; John W. Clifford, S.J., n.d.; Ralph Deward, S.J., on his China experiences 1934–48, recorded 1968–69; Eugene Fahy, S.J., n.d.; Albert Klaeser, S.J., n.d.; Charles McCarthy, S.J., n.d.; Edward Murphy, S.J., n.d.; Albert O'Hara, S.J., 1969; Thomas Phillips, S.J., n.d.; Gerald Pope, S.J., 1969; Francis Rouleau, S.J., n.d.; James Rude, S.J., 1967; Arthur Rutledge, S.J., 1970; Dominic Tang, S.J., Archbishop of Canton, n.d.; Stephen Vaskco, S.J., n.d.; and Norman Walling, S.J., 1969.

MAPS/DESIGNS/DRAWINGS: Canonical division of the Diocese of Schiamhaeven into the Apostolic Prefectures of Yangchow and Haichow, n.d.

AUDIO-VISUAL MATERIALS: 5 volumes of 2,000 black and white photos and 2 boxes of negatives (some of which have been made into slides), 1949-early 1960s, including some on the work of Jean Barry, S.J.; 20 cm. photo archives of American Jesuits on Mainland China, n.d.; *California Province News*, 1926–35, read aloud on reel-to-reel tape by John J. Dalheimer, S.J., including an account of the Ricci Mutiny; reel-to-reel tape of Dalheimer reading letters from 1920s and 1930s initiating the mission; "The Exchange at Goa," by Pius Moore, S.J., and "Between the Lines," by Charles D. Simons, read on tape by Dalheimer, n.d.; addresses of Women for America rally by John Houle, S.J., recorded 1961; motion picture films: "Ageless China," by Bernard Hubbard, S.J., 1948; "The California Jesuits in China," 1937; "New China," by William J. Klement, S.J., 1948; 2 untitled by William J. Klement, S.J., 1948; "New Bamboo," by Frederick Foley, 1961.

SERIALS: *American Jesuits in China*, 1949. *Bamboo Wireless*, 1952–58. *Catholic Review*, 1941–49. *China Letter of the American Jesuits to Their Friends in the States*, 1929–41. *Epistola Familiae Missionis*, 1949–50. *Hua Ming News Service*, 1949. *Mission Chronicle*, 1949. *Mission News Jottings*, 1949–52. *Your China Letter*, 1952–54.

DISSERTATIONS/THESES: *Chosen for China: The California Jesuits in China, 1928–1957, A Case Study in Mission and Culture*, by Peter Fleming, S.J., 1986.

CHINESE LANGUAGE MATERIALS: Gonzaga College, Shanghai, catalogue, 1931–33.

MONROVIA

WORLD VISION INTERNATIONAL
CA–200 Research and Information Division
  919 West Huntington Drive
  Monrovia CA 91016
  (818) 357–7979
  John E. Cooper, Director

Background note: In addition to the materials listed below, WVI also holds issues of the following serials for the current year only: *China Notes, China Prayer Letter, China Spectrum, Chinese Churches Today, Pray for China Fellowship*, and *Religion in the People's Republic of China*.

1-GENERAL HOLDINGS
MINUTES/RECORDS/REPORTS/MANUSCRIPTS: Internal confidential reports and papers on China.
PAMPHLETS/MEMORABILIA: Miscellaneous pamphlets and brochures, and clippings of newspaper and magazine articles since 1970, emphasizing Christianity, missions, and mission agencies.
SERIALS: *China and the Church Today*, 1979–81, 1985–86. *Chinese Around the World*, 1979-. *Chinese World Pulse*, 1971.
DISSERTATIONS/THESES: *The Responsibility and Prospects of Overseas Chinese Christians to Evangelize Mainland China When It Reopens*, by Lukas Tjandra, 1973.

PASADENA

FULLER THEOLOGICAL SEMINARY
CA–205 McAlister Library
  135 North Oakland Avenue
  Pasadena CA 91182
  (818) 584–5200
  Shieu-yu Hwang, Reference Librarian

1-GENERAL HOLDINGS
MINUTES/RECORDS/REPORTS: China Inland Mission, annual report, 1947; Christian Conference of Asia, 1981.
MINUTES/RECORDS/REPORTS/CORRESPONDENCE: Presbyterian Church in the U.S.A., Board of Foreign Missions, missions correspondence and reports on China on 54 reels of microfilm, 1837–1911, and index to correspondence with abstracts (see also Presbyterian Historical Society, Archives and Library, 425 Lombard Street, Philadelphia, PA, 19147).
CORRESPONDENCE: "China Log," 150 pages of letters from Annie Eloise Bradshaw to Flora Bonsack Stanley, 1965(?).
MANUSCRIPTS: "The Mission Work of the Presbyterian Church in the United States in China, 1867–1952," by James Edwin Bear, 1963–73; "Notes on the Chronological List of Missionaries to China and the Chinese, 1807–1942," by Charles Luther Boynton, n.d.
PAMPHLETS: *The Chinese Church Rides the Storm*, by Richard Orlando Jolliffe, 1946; *The Chinese Indigenous Church Movement: Some of Its Problems*, by Violet M. Grubb, n.d.; *Indigenous*

Ideals in Practice: Evangelistic Policy and Work in Siaochang Field in North China, by William Francis Rowlands, 1932; *Kept and Led during China's War Years: A Continuation of the Story of the Hebron Mission*, by Ruth Hitchcock, n.d.; *The Needed Gesture to the Church in China*, by Alice Mildred Cable, 1927; *Tales from Free China*, by Robert Baird McClure, 1941.
ORAL HISTORIES: *China Missionaries Oral History Collection*, ed. by Cyrus H. Peake and Arthur L. Rosenbaum (Claremont Graduate School, Oral History Program), 1973. See ORAL HISTORIES Union List for the names of participants.
AUDIO-VISUAL MATERIALS: Audio tapes containing lectures by Ralph R. Covell for his course, "The Gospel in Chinese," School of World Mission, Fuller Seminary, 1982; *The Chinese Religious Experience*, audio cassette by Ninian Smart, 1980.
SERIALS: *Bridge*, 1983–86. *China and the Church Today*, 1979–86. *China Christian Year Book*, 1910–39. *China Mission Studies Bulletin*, 1979–86. *China Notes*, 1964–86. *China Update*, 1983–86. *China's Millions* (Toronto), 1937–52. *Chinese around the World*, 1983, 1986. Chinese Church Research Center, *Occasional Papers*, 1979. *Chinese Churches Today*, 1982–86. *Chinese Recorder*, 1884–1912. *Chinese Recorder and Missionary Journal*, 1912–30. *Ching Feng*, 1966–86. *East Asia Millions* (Philadelphia), 1961- . *Millions* (Philadelphia), 1952–61.
DISSERTATIONS/THESES: *American Catholic Missions and Communist China, 1945-1953*, by Virginia F. Unsworth, 1977. *American Missionaries and the Chinese Communists: A Study of Views Expressed by Methodist Episcopal Church Missionaries, 1921-1941*, by Milo Lancaster Thornberry, 1974. *China's Opposition to Western Religion and Science during Late Ming and Early Ch'ing*, by George Ho Ching Wong, 1958. *Chinese Family Mission-church: A Contextualized Model for Holistic Christian Mission in Mainland China*, by Thomas M. C. Au-Yeung, 1985. *Christianity and Animism: China and Taiwan*, by Alan Frederick Gates, 1971. *Christianity and Social Change: The Case in China, 1920-1950*, by Lee-ming Ng, 1971. *Christliche Theologie in China: T. C. Chao, 1918-1956*, by Winfried Glüer, 1978. *Cognitive Processes and Linguistic Forms in Old Testament Hebrew and Chinese Cultures: Implications for Translation*, by Guek-eng Violet Lee Lim, 1986. *A Comparative Selection Process among Four Chinese Leaders*, by Samuel Mau-cheng Lee, 1985. *The Covenant Missionary Society in China*, by Earl C. Dahlstrom, 1950. *The Development of the Motive of Protestant Missions to China, 1807-1928*, by George Bell Workman, 1928. *The Emergence of a Protestant Christian Apologetics in the Chinese Church during the Anti-Christian Movement in the 1920s*, by Wing-hung Lam, 1978. *Faith and Facts in the History of the China Inland Mission, 1832-1905*, by Moira Jane McKay, 1981. *God's Communication Media on Church Growth in Korea and Mission Broadcasting toward Iron Walls*, by Ho Won Cha, 1983 (in Korean, with summary in English). *The Gospel Mission Movement within the Southern Baptist Convention*, by Adrian Lamkin, 1980. *John Leighton Stuart: The Mind and Life of an American Missionary in China, 1876-1941*, by Shaw Yu-ming, 1975. *Lutheran Missions in a Time of Revolution: The China Experience, 1944-1951*, by Jonas Jonson, 1972. *The Other May Fourth Movement: The Chinese "Christian Renaissance," 1919-1937*, by Samuel D. Ling, 1980. *Sin in the Chinese Religions*, by Charles L. Culpepper, 1945. *Suffering in the Experience of the Protestant Church in China (1911-1980): A Chinese Perspective*, by Paul Cheuk-ching Szeto, 1980. *A Theological Dialogue between Christian Faith and Chinese Belief in the Light of*

"Sin": An Inquiry into the Apparent Failure of the Protestant Mission in Late Nineteenth-century China, Especially among Chinese Intellectuals, by Christopher Chou, 1981.
CHINESE LANGUAGE MATERIALS/SERIALS: *Ching Feng*, 1966-. *Tian Feng*, 1985-. *Zhongguo yu jiaohui*, 1978-.
CHINESE LANGUAGE MATERIALS/DISSERTATIONS/THESES: *A Chinese Adaptation of "Church Growth and the Word of God"*, by Bill Tung Chuan Yang, 1974. *A Chinese Adaptation of "Discipling the Nations," by Richard T. De Ridder*, by David Tsang, 1976. *The Chinese Church: A Bridge to World Evangelization*, by Cyrus On-kwok Lam, 1983. *Essential Knowledge of Missionary Work* (a Chinese adaptation of *Understanding Christian Missions*, by J. Herbert Kane), by Peter Wongso, 1976. *Gospel and Culture*, by James Shih-chia Tai, 1974 (brief English synopsis). *A New Missiological Approach to Chinese Confucianism*, by David Tsang, 1977. *Reflection on the Expansion of the Christian Movement among the Chinese People*, by Joseph Young, 1974. *A Study of Mission for Chinese Churches*, by Bill Tung Chuan Yang, 1975.
CHINESE LANGUAGE MATERIALS: *Chinese Monograph and Serials Collection*, a collection of monographs and serials on Christianity in China on 71 reels of microfilm (for details, see Union Theological Seminary, Archives, 3041 Broadway at Reinhold Niebuhr Place, New York, NY, 10027); books on Christianity and Communism, church history, missions, and evangelistic work.

REDLANDS

UNIVERSITY OF REDLANDS
CA–210 George and Verda Armacost Library
1200 East Colton Avenue
Redlands CA 92373
(714) 793–2121
Irene Matthews, Librarian

1-MACNAIR COLLECTION, 1908–44, 3 items
MAPS/DESIGNS/DRAWINGS: *Atlas of the Chinese Empire Containing Separate Maps of the Eighteen Provinces of China Proper on the Scale of 1:3,000,000 and of the Four Great Dependencies on the Scale of 1:7,500,000, Together with an Index to All the Names on the Maps and a List of All Protestant Mission Stations*, by Edward Stanford, 1908.
SERIALS: *China Christian Year Book*, 1918, 1923, 1925–26, 1928–29, 1936–37.
DISSERTATIONS/THESES: *The Jesuits in China in the Last Days of the Ming Dynasty*, by George Harold Dunne, 1944.

2-HARLEY FARNSWORTH MACNAIR COLLECTION, 1912–43, quantity undetermined
Background note: Florence Wheelock Ayscough MacNair (1878–1942) and Harley Farnsworth MacNair (1891–1947), her second husband, graduated from the University of Redlands. This collection contains materials from their stay in China as missionaries, as well as from his later career as professor of Far Eastern history at the University of Chicago. Only part of their vast memorabilia is here, the rest having been donated to the Library of Congress and the Claremont Colleges. From 1912 to 1927, Harley MacNair was professor of history and government at St. John's University, Shanghai. He also served as secretary of the Advisory Council of East China Christian Colleges and Universities, and in 1924, as dean of the East China Summer School. Florence Wheelock Ayscough was born in Shanghai, and worked as a librarian in Shanghai from 1907 to 1922. They married in 1935.
CORRESPONDENCE/MEMORABILIA: Indexed scrapbooks of newspaper clippings on China Educational Association and Christian schools in Wuhan, with letters from missionaries, 1927; 6 boxes of uncatalogued correspondence including 3 letters from Pearl Buck to Florence MacNair (1939 and n.d.) and letters to Harley MacNair, 1930–36, from David Gray Poston, J. Leighton Stuart, Wu Lien-têh, John K. Fairbank, and L. Carrington Goodrich; 2 boxes of letters from Harley MacNair in China to his family, 1912–18; bound volume of letters from students to Harley MacNair, including some Chinese students, n.d.; bound volume of professional correspondence, 1931–43; letters to and from Florence Ayscough, 1923–27; miscellaneous correspondence.
MANUSCRIPTS: 4 typescript notebooks, 1912–16, containing passages on the history of Christianity in England and a draft of "The Story of Chang K'ien," 1912; "Present Political Tendencies in China," by Harley MacNair for *China Mission Year Book*, 1922; translations of Chinese poetry.
MEMORABILIA: Tibetan banknote, n.d.; clippings and printed materials on Chinese Industrial Cooperatives, n.d.
AUDIO-VISUAL MATERIALS: Photo album on St. John's University, Shanghai, n.d.; photo album and miscellaneous loose photos of China, n.d.
FINDING AIDS: Vault list, comp. by Irene Matthews.

3-ARCHIVES, 1832–43, 1 item
SERIALS: *Chinese Repository*, 1832–43.

RICHMOND

UNIVERSITY OF CALIFORNIA
CA–215 Northern Regional Library Facility
Richmond Field Station
South 47th and Hoffman Boulevard
Richmond CA 94804–4698
(415) 232–7767
Gloria Stockton, Librarian

1-GENERAL HOLDINGS
SERIALS: *Lingnan Science Journal*, 1922–48.

RIVERSIDE

LOMA LINDA UNIVERSITY
CA–220 Library
La Sierra Campus
4700 Pierce Street
Riverside CA 92515
(714) 785–2397
William H. Hessel, Associate Director

1-GENERAL HOLDINGS
MANUSCRIPTS: "The Rains Descended and the Floods Came: A Survey of the Seventh-Day Adventist Church in Communist China," by Ralph and Beatrice Neall, 1971.

SERIALS: *China Division Reporter*, 1931–51. *Far Eastern Division Outlook*, 1923, 1927–42, 1944-.
DISSERTATIONS/THESES: *The Development and History of the Seventh-day Adventist Church in China since the Communist Takeover*, by Tsao Lien-chieh, 1975. *A History of Seventh-Day Adventist Higher Education in the China Mission, 1888–1980*, by Handel Hing-tat Luke, 1983. *Protestant Mission Schools for Girls in South China (1827 to the Japanese Invasion)*, by Mary Raleigh Anderson, 1943.

RIVERSIDE

UNIVERSITY OF CALIFORNIA
CA–225 University Library
P.O. Box 5900
Riverside CA 92517
(714) 787-4392
Venita Jorgensen, Reference Librarian

1-GENERAL HOLDINGS
SERIALS: *China Notes*, 1962-.

SACRAMENTO

CA–230 CALIFORNIA STATE LIBRARY
Courts Building
P.O. Box 942837
Sacramento CA 94237–0001
(916) 445-2585
Richard Terry, Senior Librarian

1-GENERAL HOLDINGS
SERIALS: American Friends Service Committee, *Bulletin on Work in China*, 1942–44. *China Law Review*, 1922–37. University of Nanking, College of Agriculture and Forestry, *Bulletin*, 1932.

SAN ANSELMO

SAN FRANCISCO THEOLOGICAL SEMINARY
CA–235 Library
2 Kensington Road
San Anselmo CA 94960
(415) 258-6635
John David Baker-Batsel, Director
Michael D. Peterson, Branch Librarian

Background note: This is a branch library of the Graduate Theological Union Library.

1-CHINESE PAMPHLET COLLECTION, 1847–1946, quantity undetermined
MINUTES/RECORDS/REPORTS: Associated Boards for Christian Colleges in China, annual report, 1936, 1944, 1946; Canton Hospital, annual report, 1935–36; Charles Rogers Mills Memorial School for the Deaf, report, 1925–26; Christian Literature Society for China, annual report, 1934–36; Church of Christ in China, important actions of the enlarged General Assembly, 1946; Foreign Missions Conference of North America, addresses on China, 1927; General Missionary Society, abstract of report, 1870; Medical Missionary Society in China, report, 1847; Ming Deh Girls' School, 1935; National Christian Council of China, constitution and by-laws, 1931; findings of the National Conference on Christianizing Economic Relations, 1927; proposals in relation to reorganization, 1928; report on the Church Literacy Movement, 1931.

Presbyterian Church in the U.S.A.: Central China Mission, annual report, 1922–27, 1931–32; Hangchow Station, report, 1926; Soochow Station, report, 1937; Nanking Station, report, 1935–36; North China Presbyterian Mission, Peiping Station, report, 1934–35; Paotingfu Station, annual report, 1934–35; South China Mission, report, 1936; Tengchow Station, annual report, 1925–26; Yihsien-Shantung, report, n.d.; Yunnan Mission, Kiulungkiang and Yuankiang Station, reports, 1930–34.

Presbyterian Union Theological Seminary, catalogue, 1907–8; University of Nanking, College of Agriculture and Forestry and Experiment Station, annual report, 1926–27; folder of biographical profiles of missionaries, 1942–44, including Stanton Lautenschlager, James P. Leynse, Arthur W. March, Edith F. Millican, Frank W. Newman, Elizabeth Newman, Frederick G. Scovel, Myra Scovel, J. Claude Thomson, Margaret C. Thomson, George Tootell, and Kepler and Pauline W. Van Evera; folder of miscellaneous papers relating to mission work in China, 1928; folder on middle schools in China, ca. 1944.
CORRESPONDENCE: Church workers, folder of letters from the field, 1940–44, including Lillian and Richard Jenness, Mabel Jones, Marjorie Judson, Nettie D. Junkin, Jeanette Fitch Kepler, Stanton Lautenschlager, Florence L. Logan, Lois D. Lyon, G. Gordon Mahy, Helen B. McClain, Elizabeth McKee, Wallace C. Merwin, Aimee Millican, Elizabeth Mitchell, Rachel Owens, Florence Pike, Mrs. H. H. Pommerenke, Charles V. Reeder, Lucy Romig, Francis H. Scott, C. Stanley Smith, Reuben A. Torrey, Mrs. Courtland Van Deusen, Kepler Van Evera, Mrs. D. K. West, Vella M. Wilcox, Kenneth W. Wilson, Gardner Winn, Paul and Anne Winn, and Catherine Woods; educators, folder of letters from the field, 1940–44, including William P. Fenn, Arthur W. March, Helen B. McClain, Grace M. Rowley, Matilda C. Thurston, Andrew Torrance, Ralph M. White, and University of Nanking; medical workers, folder of letters from the field, 1939–44, including Edith Adlam, W. L. Berst, William Cochran, Mr. and Mrs. J. Horton Daniels, William H. Dobson, Myrtle Hinkhouse, J. F. Karcher, Ralph C. Lewis, Caroline McCreery, Edith F. Millican, Margaret Murdoch, Mrs. E. E. Murray, Myra Scovel, Mrs. Charles C. Selden, Dorothy Jean Snyder, James A. Stringham, George T. Tootell, Maria M. Wagner, and James L. Young.
PAMPHLETS: Ca. 60 pamphlets, 1849–1940s (many undated), on Baptist missions, Cantonese Church, Central China Mission, Cheefoo Mission, Cheeloo School of Theology, Chinese literature, Christian Colleges, Christian education, Christian missionaries during the war, Church of Christ in China, girls' education, Ichowfu Station, medical missionaries, missionary thought, Nanking Incident, National Christian Council, Ningpo, North China Mission, William Winston Pettus, Princeton-Yenching Foundation, rural China, Shantung Mission, Sino-Japanese conflict, South China Mission, James Hudson Taylor, Weihsien Mission, West China, Eleanor Wright, Yenching University, and YMCA; bound volumes of Chinese pamphlets including *Connection between Foreign Missionaries and the Kwang-Se Insurrection*, n.d., *The T'ai-ping Rebellion: A Lecture*, by Rev. M. T. Yates, n.d., and

Personal Recollections of the T'ai-p'ing Rebellion, 1861–1863, by Ven Archdeacon Moule, 1884.

MEMORABILIA: Tearsheet of "Christianity and Treaties: Individual Missionary Opinion," including interviews of China missionaries, n.d.; "Now, Where Is My Home?," by Grace Boynton, in *The Woman's Press*, 1943.

MAPS/DESIGNS/DRAWINGS: "A Sketch of Missionary Work in the Old Capital of China," a map of the missions in Peking, n.d.

2-GENERAL HOLDINGS
MINUTES/RECORDS/REPORTS: Shanghai Community Church, annual report, 1932.
PAMPHLETS: *Christian Cooperation in China*, by the National Christian Council of China, 1937; *John, Archbishop of Cambaleigh*, by Dwight C. Baker, 1929; *Lecture on the Chinese Empire*, by Rev. William Anderson Scott, 1854; *An Outline for Study of the Chinese Christian Church*, by the Mid-China Southern Presbyterian Church, n.d.; *The Religious Condition of the Chinese, and Their Claims on the Church: A Sermon Preached for the Board of Foreign Missions of the Presbyterian Church*, by Michael Simpson Culbertson, 1857; *"...To Make the Dream a Reality,"* by Henry Winters Luce, n.d.
AUDIO-VISUAL MATERIALS: Ca. 70 monochrome photos of China which may have belonged to William Speer, n.d.; ca. 100 colored glass projection slides made between 1920 and 1940 by the Missions Agency of the Presbyterian Church.
SERIALS: *Bible for China*, 1925–27. Bible Union of China, *Bulletin*, 1921–25. Canton Committee for Justice to China, *Bulletin*, 1938. *China Bookman*, 1948, 1950. China Graduate School of Theology, *Bulletin*, 1973–? *China Sunday School Journal*, 1927. *China's Millions* (London), 1875–93, 1950–52. *Chinese Recorder*, 1870–1941. *Chinese Repository*, 1833–51. *Ching Feng*, 1976, 1979. *The Church*, 1947–50. *Directory of Protestant Missions in China*, 1927. *Educational Review*, 1934. *Hainan Newsletter*, 1922–38, 1947–49. *Information Service of the Church of Christ in China*, 1937. *Missionary Recorder*, 1867. National Christian Council of China, *Bulletin*, 1922–37. *New Horizons*, 1945–55. *News of China*, 1943–45, 1948–49. *Shanghai Young Men*, 1924. *The Story of the China Inland Mission*, 1950. University of Nanking, College of Agriculture and Forestry, *Bulletin*, 1926. *Yenching News*, 1946.
DISSERTATIONS/THESES: *Christianity and the New Life Movement in China*, by Christopher Tang, 1941.
CHINESE LANGUAGE MATERIALS: 13 Chinese evangelistic posters, ca. 1923, with English translations added; Chinese hymnal, 1907.

SAN BERNARDINO

INTERNATIONAL CHRISTIAN GRADUATE UNIVERSITY
CA-240 International School of Theology Library
Arrowhead Springs
P.O. Box 50015
San Bernardino CA 92412
(714) 886-7876
George A. Mindeman, Library Director

1-GENERAL HOLDINGS
SERIALS: *China and the Church Today*, 1985–86. *China Prayer Letter*, 1986–. *Chinese around the World*, 1983, 1985–.
DISSERTATIONS/THESES: *The House-Church Movement in China: A Biblical Model for Church Growth*, by Chan-kei Thong, 1985.

SAN FRANCISCO

CA-245 INSTITUTE FOR CHINESE-WESTERN CULTURAL HISTORY
University of San Francisco
Ignatian Heights
San Francisco CA 94117
(415) 666-6401
Edward J. Malatesta, S.J., Director
Mary Celeste Rouleau, S.M., Archivist

Restrictions: Access by appointment.
Background note: The Institute for Chinese-Western Cultural History is sponsored by the California Province of the Society of Jesus. Among the projects undertaken by staff of the Institute in its on-going research relating to Christianity in China is the completion of Francis Rouleau's study of the legation to China of Cardinal Charles Maillard de Tournon by Edward Malatesta, S.J. (see Francis A. Rouleau Microfilm Archive Collection below).

1-ALBERT CHAN COLLECTION, 16th-early 20th centuries, ca. 70,000 volumes
Background note: Albert Chan (b. 1915) is a Jesuit priest who has been collecting Chinese books and documents since the 1930s on Chinese-Western relations. The history of this collection is described in *Fleet Flashes* (Lykes Steamship Company), 1985.
CHINESE LANGUAGE MATERIALS: Books and documents on the histories of the Ming and Qing dynasties, including the advent of Christianity in China, mostly in Chinese but including several hundred in other Asian and Western languages.

2-FREDERICK FOLEY PHOTOGRAPH COLLECTION, ca. 1940s–1950s, ca. 4,000–6,000 items
AUDIO-VISUAL MATERIALS: Photos of China taken by Frederick Foley while a Jesuit, ca. 1940s–1950s.

3-THEODORE FOSS COLLECTION, 16th–18th centuries, ca. 3,000 volumes
Background note: This collection consists of specialized reference works, monographs, catalogues, and offprints on the history of cultural interaction between China and the West. It is currently uncatalogued.

4-ROMAN CATHOLIC DIOCESE OF CANTON ARCHIVES, 19th–20th centuries, 7 boxes
Background note: This uncatalogued collection consists of copies of original materials from the archives of the Roman Catholic Diocese of Canton.
MINUTES/RECORDS/REPORTS/CORRESPONDENCE/ CHINESE LANGUAGE MATERIALS: Approximately 10,000

documents, consisting of correspondence, reports, and other printed materials in French, Latin, English, Italian, and Chinese.

5-ROULEAU COLLECTION, 16th–20th centuries, ca. 200 volumes
Background note: This collection consists of books, monographs, reference works, and offprints of articles on China in European languages collected by Francis A. Rouleau, S.J., on Jesuits, missions and missionaries, and the rites controversy.
MANUSCRIPTS: "Histoire d'une dame chrétienne, Candide Hiu," by Philippe Couplet, S.J., n.d.; "Incrementa Sinicae ecclesiae a Tartaris oppugnatae," by Jean-Dominiques Gabiani, S.J., 1673; "Il P. Matteo Ricci, apostolo della Cina," by Fernando Bortone, S.J., 1963; "A Virgin and Child in Mediaeval China," by John Foster, 1956.
FINDING AIDS: Partial card catalogue.

6-FRANCIS A. ROULEAU MICROFILM ARCHIVE, 17th–18th centuries, 43 reels microfilm
Background note: The originals of this collection are in the archives of the Society of Jesus in Rome and Paris, the British Museum in London, Vatican Archives, and other archives in Europe and the Philippines. The copies were collected by Rouleau as part of his research on Cardinal Charles Maillard de Tournon's mission to China and the rites controversy.
MINUTES/RECORDS/REPORTS/CORRESPONDENCE/MANUSCRIPTS/PAMPHLETS: Microfilm copies of 50,000 folios of documents and excerpts in European languages pertaining to Jesuit missions to China, particularly on the rites controversy, including reports, treatises, correspondence, and lists of documents.
MANUSCRIPTS: Notes and drafts by Rouleau on various subjects pertaining to Jesuit missions in China, in preparation for his book on the rites controversy which he did not live to complete.
FINDING AIDS: In-house catalogue.

7-GENERAL HOLDINGS
MANUSCRIPTS: 1,000-page manuscript of a catalogue by Albert Chan, S.J., describing over 200 volumes of documentation about China, including many original letters about the missions, in the archives of the Society of Jesus in Rome, dating from the 16th century.
MEMORABILIA: Clippings and journal articles on the church in China in general and Jesuits in China, 1923–68.
MAPS/DESIGNS/DRAWINGS: Rubbing of a Christian tombstone discovered in Yangzhou, with inscription dated 1342, said to be the oldest representation of Mary found in China to date.
AUDIO-VISUAL MATERIALS: 28 panels of photos and other materials mounted on posterboard for an exhibit on California Jesuit works in China and Taiwan, 1928–84.
SERIALS: *Bridge*, 1983-. *China and the Church Today*, 1979-. *China Bulletin* (Rome), 1979-. *China Mission Studies Bulletin*, 1979-. *China Talk*, 1984-. *China Update*, 1982-. *Ding*, 1981-. *Zhonglian*, 1985-.
DISSERTATIONS/THESES: *A Jesuit Encyclopedia for China: A Guide to Jean-Baptiste du Halde's "Description . . .de la Chine" (1735)*, by Theodore N. Foss, 1979.
CHINESE LANGUAGE MATERIALS: Original document printed by the Kangxi emperor in 1716 concerning envoys he sent to Rome regarding the rites controversy.

UNIVERSITY OF CALIFORNIA
CA–250 Medical Library
257 Medical Sciences Building
San Francisco CA 94143
(415) 476-2334
(415) 476-8101 (Oriental Medical Collection)
Atsumi Minami, Librarian, Oriental Medical Collection
Elisabeth Bell, Reference Librarian

1-ORIENTAL MEDICINE COLLECTION, 1838–1921, 6 items
MINUTES/RECORDS/REPORTS: Medical Missionary Society in China, 1841.
PAMPHLETS: *The Medical Missionary Society in China*, 1838; *The North China Union Medical College for Women, Peking, China, 1908–1921*, by the Joint Committee of the Women's Union Christian Colleges, 1921.
CHINESE LANGUAGE MATERIALS: *Ch'uan t'i hsin lung (New Discussion of the Entire Body)*, by Benjamin Hobson, 1851; *Hsi i lüeh lun (Outline of Western Medicine)*, by Benjamin Hobson, 1857; *Nei k'o hsin shuo (New Theory on Internal Medicine)*, by Benjamin Hobson, 1858.

2-GENERAL HOLDINGS
SERIALS: *Chinese Medical Journal*, 1924-.
CHINESE LANGUAGE MATERIALS/SERIALS: *The Leper Quarterly*, 1928–38.

SAN JOSE

SAN JOSE BIBLE COLLEGE
CA–255 Archives
790 South 12th Street
P.O. Box 1090
San Jose CA 95108
(408) 293-9058
(408) 293-7650
Kay Llovio, Librarian

1-GENERAL HOLDINGS
SERIALS: *For Christ in China*, 1947–49. *The Tibetan Missionary*, 1946–47, 1949. *The Yunnan Christian*, 1947–49. Untitled newsletters of the Lisuland Churches of Christ, 1946–51 (published in Aiwa, Yunnan, and Kachin, Burma).

SANTA BARBARA

MISSION SANTA BARBARA
CA–260 Archive Library
Old Mission
Upper Laguna Street
Santa Barbara CA 93105
(805) 682-4713
Virgilio Biasiol, O.F.M., Archivist

Restrictions: Access by appointment.

1-FRANCISCAN MISSIONARIES OF THE PROVINCE OF SANTA BARBARA IN CHINA, 1907–86, 25 folders
MINUTES/RECORDS/REPORTS: Yunyang Mission, annual report of the pharmacy, 1914.
CORRESPONDENCE: 5 letters from Benedict Jensen, O.F.M., to the mission, 1934, 1947; 4 letters about Jensen, 1947; 10 letters from Walter Tracy in Tungshanfu, 1935–39; 4 letters to Fr. Fabian from Fr. Edgar in Sutsien, 1946; letter from Fr. Brice Moran, Suining, to Fr. Fabian, 1946; correspondence of Fr. Edward Lunney, 1915; 5 letters to Fr. Ralph, from Fr. Fabian, Fr. Sebastian, and Fr. Paschal, 1945–48; letter from Br. Benedict to Fr. Angelus, 1934; printed letter from the Kongmoon mission, 1927; folder of correspondence of Donald Gander, O.F.M., 1934–39; ca. 1 file of letters from Br. Benedict Jensen to Br. Bernardine Brophy, 1938–46.
DIARIES: 3 diaries of Adrian Erlenheim, O.F.M., 1938–39; 5 diaries of Maynard Geiger, O.F.M., 1939–43; Rt. Rev. Msgr. Fabiano Landi, O.F.M., Vicar Apostolic of Northwest Hupeh, diary of a visit to the Hupeh mountains, 1915; diary of Fr. Edward Lunney, 1914.
MANUSCRIPTS: "Un bijogno urgente," by P. C. Silvestri, 1915; "Brother Benedict Jensen, O.F.M. (1899–1947)," n.d.; "Catholic Missionary Endeavor in Modern China," n.a., ca. 1960s; "Circumstances Concerning the Death of the Two Franciscans, Fr. Augustine Holzum and Br. Benedict Jensen, O.F.M., at Yentou, January 1–2, 1947," n.a., with a map of the mission; resumé of Jensen to 1945; "Little Rosebud," by R. Gaudissart, S.J., on the orphanage of Kai-tseou, n.d.; "La Missione dei Monti," by Egidio Santoro, 1917; "La Missione di Yunyang," n.a., ca. 1916(?); "Missions in China (The Past)," by Fr. Marius, O.F.M., ca. 1960; "The Purpose of the Missions," n.a., ca. 1960s; "This Was China," by Adrian Erlenheim, O.F.M., including a map of Shantung province, 1986; untitled manuscript in Italian, 1916; statistics on the Regular Mission of Yaowan, n.d.; 1 folder of mission statistics, Laohokow, 1914–16, Vicariate Northwest Hupeh, 1913–18; account of a trip to Shanghai, by Br. Benedict [Jensen], 1934.
PAMPHLETS: *Yentou New Year: A Life of Brother Benedict Jensen, Franciscan Missionary in China*, by Br. Giles, O.F.M., 1959.
MEMORABILIA: Miscellaneous clippings, 1915; clippings in Italian on the China mission, n.d.; clippings and obituary of Lunney, n.d.; personnel brochure, ca. 1945(?); clippings in Italian on the mission in Siangyangfu, 1907; clippings on Fr. Walter in China, ca. 1937; souvenir passenger lists, *S.S. Manchuria*, n.d.; envelope of miscellaneous memorabilia, including a postal rate chart, n.d.; *Smiles from the Mixed Court*, clippings on China, n.d.
AUDIO-VISUAL MATERIALS: 2 reels of 8-mm. film showing missionary activities, n.d.; small photo album of the girls' school at Laohokow, ca. 1911–15, containing photos of Fr. Edward and other Franciscans, Catholic school students, native clergy, Chinese sisters, and orphanage at Ciuyuankow; small envelope of about 15 loose photos of sisters and Franciscans, Shantung, 1936; photo of Fr. Edward Lunney in Chinese clothing, ca. 1914; 6 large loose photos, some of Kinmen, 1958; 11 loose photos of Peking, 1948; photo album of the Laohokow Mission, ca. 1915; mounted photo of Oriolo Romano, 1914; loose photos of Peking, 1948; 2 mounted photos of Apostolic Delegate Msgr. Mario Zanin and the community at Lekwangchiao, 1939.
MAPS/DESIGNS/DRAWINGS: Maps of China, Pearl River, Canton, Lower Yangtze River, and Hupeh Plain, n.d.

SERIALS: *The Herald of the Rice Fields*, 1929–31. *The Sutsien Tower*, 1942–43.
CHINESE LANGUAGE MATERIALS: Chinese Christian poster, n.d.; poster regarding Laohokow school regulations, n.d.

2-GENERAL HOLDINGS
MANUSCRIPTS: "Santa Barbara in China," n.a., n.d.
PAMPHLETS: *Franciscan Missionaries in China*, 1934.

CA-265 Institute for Franciscan Studies Library
Old Mission
Upper Laguna Street
Santa Barbara CA 93105
(805) 682-4713

Background note: The Institute for Franciscan Studies maintains a small library of books in European languages on Franciscan activity, including several on China, some of which may not be found elsewhere. Works on Franciscan work in China include *Liber Missionalis: Vicariatus Apostolici di Kichow* (Wuchang, 1929), *Catalogus Fratrum Minorum in Sinis* (Peking, 1948), and *Missiones ordinis fratrum minorum in Sinis et Iaponia in 1908–1909* (Florence, 1910).

1-GENERAL HOLDINGS
PAMPHLETS: *Around the Franciscan Missions*, by Walter Hammon, 1952; *Catholic Missions in the Middle Ages*, by Paul Stanislaus Hsiang, 1949; *Fra. Giovanni di Pian del Carpine: Ambasciadore di Roma*, by P. M. Alfonso Orlini, O.F.M. Conv., 1943; 4 undated pamphlets by Otto Maas, O.F.M.: *Die Franziskanermission in China um die Wende des 17 jahrhunderts*, *Die Franziskanermission in China des 18 jahrhunderts*, *Die Franziskanermission in China während des 19 jahrhunderts*, and *Franziskanermission in China vom jahre 1900 bis zu Gegenwart*; *Fra. Fellegrino da Città di Castello, O.Min. 110 Vescovo di Zayton in Cina (7 luglio 1322) et l'autenticità della sun "lettera" (30 dic. 1318): dopo l'instituzione della Gerarchia Episcopale in Cina (11 Aprile 1946) e nel VII Centenario della nascita de Fra. Giovanni da Montecorvino, O.Min. (1247–1947)*, by P. Giovanni Bastiannini, O.F.M. Conv., 1947.
SERIALS: *Sinica Franciscana*, 1929–54.

UNIVERSITY OF CALIFORNIA

CA-270 Department of Special Collections
Santa Barbara CA 93106
(805) 961-2741
Christian Brun, Special Collections

1-WYLES COLLECTION, 1874–1935, 3 items
MINUTES/RECORDS/REPORTS: Baptist mission, Chusan Islands, annual report, 1915.
SERIALS: *China Christian Year Book*, 1912–13, 1918, 1928, 1931, 1934–35. *Chinese Recorder*, 1874.

CA-275 University of California Library
Santa Barbara CA 93106
(805) 961-2741
Allan Cohen, Head, Cataloging Department
Henry Tai, Oriental Cataloguer

1-ORIENTAL COLLECTION, 1927–83, 22 items
CHINESE LANGUAGE MATERIALS/SERIALS: *Chung-kuo hsin t'u yüeh k'an (Chinese Christians Today)*, 1973-.
CHINESE LANGUAGE MATERIALS/DISSERTATIONS/THESES: *Tsao ch'i Mei-kuo chiao hui tsai Hua chiao yü shih yeh chih chien li (The Establishment of Early American Educational Missions in China)*, by Hu Kuo-t'ai, 1980.
CHINESE LANGUAGE MATERIALS: 20 volumes, 1927–83, on Young J. Allen, American missions, anti-missionary activity, Catholic missions and missionaries, educational missions, Vincent Lebbe, missions in Szechwan, and sectarian cases.

2-GENERAL HOLDINGS
PAMPHLETS: *The Harrowing of Hell in China: A Synoptic Study of the Role of Christian Evangelists in the Opening of Hunan Province*, by Leslie Ronald Marchant, 1977.
SERIALS: *Chinese Medical Journal*, 1975-. *Ching Feng*, 1964–76. *Folklore Studies*, 1942–47; supplement, 1952. *Monumenta Serica*, 1948-. *Yenching Journal of Social Studies*, 1938–50.
DISSERTATIONS/THESES: *American Catholic China Missionaries, 1918–1941*, by Thomas A. Breslin, 1972. *American Missionaries and the Chinese Communists: A Study of Views Expressed by Methodist Episcopal Church Missionaries, 1921–1941*, by Milo Lancaster Thornberry, 1974. *Christianity and Social Change: The Case in China, 1920–1950*, by Lee-ming Ng, 1971. *John Leighton Stuart: The Mind and Life of an American Missionary in China, 1876–1941*, by Shaw Yu-ming, 1975. *The Mission Enterprise of the Lutheran Church-Missouri Synod in Mainland China, 1913–1952*, by Roy Arthur Suelflow, 1971. *Missionary Intelligence from China: American Protestant Reports, 1930–1950*, by Bruce Stephen Greenawalt, 1974. *The Oriental Educational Commission's Recommendations for Mission Strategy in Higher Education*, by David Lloyd Lindberg, 1972. *The Protestant Missionary Understanding of the Chinese Situation and the Christian Task from 1890 to 1911*, by C. William Mensendiek, 1958. *Reciprocal Change: The Case of American Protestant Missionaries to China*, by Paul Voninski, 1975. *Revolutionary Faithfulness: The Quaker Search for a Peaceable Kingdom in China, 1939–1951*, by Cynthia Letts Adcock, 1974. *A Search for a Dialogue between the Confucian "Sincerity" and the Christian "Reality": A Study of the Neo-Confucian Thought of Lee Yu-lok and the Theology of Heinrich Ott*, by Young Chan Ro, 1982. *Strangers in the House: J. Lewis Shuck and Issachar Roberts, First American Baptist Missionaries to China*, by Margaret Coughlin, 1972.
CHINESE LANGUAGE MATERIALS/SERIALS: *Fu jen hsüeh chih (Fu jen Sinological Journal/Sinologica Sinica)*, 1928–47. *Ling-nan hsüeh pao (Lingnan Journal)*, 1948–50. *Wan kuo kung pao (The Globe Magazine: A Review of the Times)*, 1868–1907. *Yen-ching hsüeh pao (Yenching Journal of Chinese Studies)*, 1927–51.

SANTA CLARA

SANTA CLARA UNIVERSITY
CA–280 Michel Orradre Library
Santa Clara CA 95053
(408) 554–6830
Alice Whistler, Assistant University Librarian

1-GENERAL HOLDINGS
PAMPHLETS: *The Catholic Missions in China during the Middle Ages, 1291–1368*, by Paul Stanislaus Hsiang, 1949.
SERIALS: *Variétés Sinologiques*, 1932–34.
CHINESE LANGUAGE MATERIALS: *T'ien-chu-chiao chüan hsing Chung-kuo kao*, by Joseph Siao, 1923.

SANTA CRUZ

UNIVERSITY OF CALIFORNIA
CA–285 McHenry Library
Santa Cruz CA 95064
(408) 429–2801
Allan Dyson, Librarian

1-METHODIST MISSIONARY SOCIETY ARCHIVES, 1829–1954, 1,760 microfiches
Background note: These materials are microfiche reproductions of the original archives, now housed in the Library of the School of Oriental and African Studies in London. The collection is divided into three components, two of which—the Wesleyan Methodist Missionary Society records and the Women's Work Collection—contain extensive materials concerning Methodist missions in China.
MINUTES/RECORDS/REPORTS: China Synod, minutes, 1853–1946; overseas schedules, China, 1923–46.
CORRESPONDENCE: 820 microfiches of letters in the Wesleyan Methodist Missionary Society records, divided into 11 series: Canton (1851–1905), China General (1936–45), China Miscellaneous (1924–34), Hunan (1907–45), Hupeh (1905–45), Ningpo (1933–46), North China (1933–45), South China (1905–45), South West China (1932–45), Wenchow (1933–45), and Wuchang (1876–1905); 281 microfiches of letters in the Women's Work Collection, divided into 3 series: Hunan, Hupeh, Ningpo, and Wenchow (1921–54); North, South, and South West China (1920–47); and Missionaries on Furlough (China, 1925–30).
MANUSCRIPTS: 330 microfiches of biographical materials and personal papers of Methodist missionaries in China, including David Hill, Samuel Pollard, and G. Stephenson, 1829–69.
FINDING AIDS: Microfiche reproductions of typescript inventories of correspondence.

2-GENERAL HOLDINGS
ORAL HISTORIES: *China Missionaries Oral History Collection*, ed. by Cyrus H. Peake and Arthur L. Rosenbaum (Claremont Graduate School, Oral History Program), 1973. See ORAL HISTORIES Union List for the names of participants.
DISSERTATIONS/THESES: *Imperial Government and Catholic Missions in China during the Years 1784–1785*, by Bernward Henry Willeke, 1948. *The Mission Compound in Modern China: The Role of the United States Protestant Mission as an Asylum in the Civil and International Strife of China*, by Gladys Robina Quale, 1957. *The Role of the Christian Colleges in Modern China before 1928*, by Jessie Gregory Lutz, 1955. *Strangers in the House: J. Lewis Shuck and Issachar Roberts, First American Baptist Missionaries to China*, by Margaret Coughlin, 1972. *Zion's Corner: Origins of the American Protestant Missionary Movement in China, 1827–1839*, by Murray A. Rubinstein, 1976.

STANFORD

HOOVER INSTITUTION ON WAR, REVOLUTION, AND PEACE

CA–290 Archives
Stanford University
Stanford CA 94305–2323
(415) 723–3563
Charles G. Palm, Archivist

Finding aids: "Hoover Institution Archives Holdings on China," 1986.

1-FRANK ARGELANDER, n.d., 1 folder
Background note: Frank Argelander was an American missionary teacher in China from 1919 to 1931.
MANUSCRIPTS: Typescript memorandum based on his diaries relating to the 1927 uprising of the Communist party in China.

2-GEORGE BROWN BARBOUR PAPERS, 1911–34, 2 boxes, 1 envelope, 1 reel film
Background note: George Brown Barbour was professor of geology at Yenching University from 1923 to 1932 and visiting physiographer for the Rockefeller Foundation, Peking, 1934.
CORRESPONDENCE/MEMORABILIA/MAPS/DESIGNS/DRAWINGS/AUDIO-VISUAL MATERIALS: Correspondence, postcards, drawings, photo, and a reel of motion picture film relating to political and social conditions, missionary service, and university education, 1911–34.

3-CHARLES LUTHER BOYNTON PAPERS, 1901–67, 9 boxes, 2 envelopes
Background note: For biographical notes, see Claremont Colleges, Special Collections Department, Honnold Library, Claremont, CA, 91711. See also Union Theological Seminary, Archives, 3401 Broadway at Reinhold Niebuhr Place, New York, NY, 10027.
CORRESPONDENCE/DIARIES/MANUSCRIPTS/PAMPHLETS/MEMORABILIA/AUDIO-VISUAL MATERIALS: Correspondence, diaries, writings, pamphlets, and photos relating to missionary work in China in Shanghai, the Shanghai American School, and conditions in China, 1901–67, including "How War Came to Shanghai," a letter written by Charles L. Boynton to E. C. Lobenstine, 1937, and "The Chapei Civil Assembly Center: Shanghai, 1943–1945: Internment for American, Belgian, British, and Dutch Civilians," by Charles Luther Boynton, n.d.
FINDING AIDS: In-house guide.

4-R. F. BRADY PAPERS, 1933–41, 1 folder
MINUTES/RECORDS/REPORTS/MANUSCRIPTS/PAMPHLETS: Notes and printed matter including "Ginling College, 1915–1940"; "Sketches of Nanking," 1933; and a University of Nanking Hospital report, 1940.
SERIALS: *Notes and Notices of the Nanking Union Church and Community*, 1941.

5-JOHN STEWART AND STELLA FISHER BURGESS PAPERS, 1910–35, 1 folder
Background note: For biographical notes, see Princeton University, Firestone Library, Manuscript Division, Princeton, NJ, 08544. See also Young Men's Christian Association of the U.S.A. Archives, University of Minnesota, Social History Welfare Archives, 2642 University Avenue, St. Paul, MN, 55114.
CORRESPONDENCE/MANUSCRIPTS/PAMPHLETS: Letters, poems, and printed matter relating to the missionary work of the YMCA and to revolutionary movements in China, 1910–35.

6-WILLIAM M. CORNWELL PAPERS, 1909–24, 1 box
Background note: William M. Cornwell was the son of a Presbyterian missionary in China.
CORRESPONDENCE/MEMORABILIA/MAPS/DESIGNS/DRAWINGS: Correspondence, clippings, memorabilia, and a map of Tsingtao, relating to Cornwell's experiences and events in the Far East, chiefly China, 1909–24.

7-ROWLAND McLEAN CROSS PAPERS, 1921–63, 1 box
Background note: Rowland McLean Cross was a missionary to China under the American Board of Commissioners for Foreign Missions. See also Claremont Colleges, Honnold Library, Claremont, CA, 91711; and American Lutheran Church, Archives, 2481 Como Avenue, St. Paul, MN, 55108.
MINUTES/RECORDS/REPORTS/CORRESPONDENCE/PAMPHLETS: Reports, correspondence, and printed material dealing with Cross's activities in revolutionary and Communist China, 1921–63.

8-PAUL C. DOMKE, 1936–45, 8 reels film, 1 envelope
Background note: Paul C. Domke was a teacher with Carleton-in-China from 1937 to 1939, and a member of the U.S. Observer Mission to Yenan, 1944–45. See also American Lutheran Church, Archives, 2481 Como Avenue, St. Paul, MN, 55108.
AUDIO-VISUAL MATERIALS: Films and loose photos depicting missionary schools, the effects of Japanese bombing, U.S. Army headquarters in Chungking, and various other scenes in China, 1936–45.

9-JAMES ARTHUR DUFF, n.d., ca. 6 boxes
Restrictions: This collection is closed until January 1995.
Background note: James Arthur Duff (b. 1899) was a Canadian businessman in China.
CORRESPONDENCE/MANUSCRIPTS/PAMPHLETS/MEMORABILIA/AUDIO-VISUAL MATERIALS: Memoirs and other writings, correspondence, printed materials, memorabilia, and photos, relating to missionaries in China.

10-PAUL FRILLMAN, 1941–69, 3 boxes, 3 envelopes, 1 oversize box, 3 framed certificates
Background note: Paul Frillman (b. 1911) was an American missionary in China from 1936 to 1941, chaplain for the Flying Tigers from 1941 to 1945, and consular official in China and Hong Kong from 1946 to 1950.
CORRESPONDENCE/MANUSCRIPTS/AUDIO-VISUAL MATERIALS: Correspondence, memoranda, orders, notes, and photos, relating to activities of the American Volunteer Group (Flying Tigers) during World War II, U.S. relations with China, and conditions in China during the Civil War.

11-BETTIS ALSTON GARSIDE PAPERS, 1897–1980, 4 boxes
Background note: Bettis Alston Garside was an educator, missionary, and official of various relief agencies in China, 1922–26.
MINUTES/RECORDS/REPORTS/CORRESPONDENCE/MANUSCRIPTS/PAMPHLETS/MEMORABILIA: Minutes, correspondence, speeches, writings, memoranda, and printed matter, relating to Communism in China, Henry W. Luce, mission

schools in China, post-World War II relief, and refugees from China, 1897–1980.

12-SELKSAR M. GUNN, 1934, 1 folder
MINUTES/RECORDS/REPORTS: "China and the Rockefeller Foundation," 1934, a mimeographed report on educational, scientific, technical, and cultural assistance activities of the Rockefeller Foundation, and proposals for future activities.

13-JOHN AND THEODORA INGLIS PAPERS, 1898–1902, 1 box, 1 envelope
Background note: John Inglis was a missionary at An Ting Hospital, Peking, from 1898 to 1900.
CORRESPONDENCE/MANUSCRIPTS/MEMORABILIA: Correspondence, manuscript, memoirs, clippings, 3 medals, and a printing block relating to the Boxer Rebellion, the Siege of Peking, and John and Theodora Inglis' service at An Ting Hospital, 1898–1902.

14-MARTHA JOB, 1920–41, 1 box, 3 envelopes
Background note: Martha Job worked with the YWCA in China from 1919 to 1929.
PAMPHLETS/DIARIES/MAPS/DESIGNS/DRAWINGS/MEMORABILIA/AUDIO-VISUAL MATERIALS: Booklets, diary, maps, posters, photos, and clippings, relating to the YWCA in China, flood relief, the University of Peking, and internal problems in China from 1920 to 1928.

15-WALTER JUDD, 1926–84, quantity undetermined
Background note: This collection consists of ca. 300 boxes, of which the portion relating to missionary work has not been determined.
CORRESPONDENCE/MANUSCRIPTS/PAMPHLETS/AUDIO-VISUAL MATERIALS: Correspondence, speeches and writings, printed matter, and audio-visual material, relating to the Chinese civil war and aid to Chinese refugees.

16-LUCERNE H. KNOWLTON PAPERS, 1922–53, 1 box, 1 envelope
MINUTES/RECORDS/REPORTS: Hwa Nan College, annual report, 1927, 1930, 1940, 1949; Methodist Episcopal Church, Women's Foreign Mission Society, Women's Work Conferences at Foochow, proceedings, 1922, 1924–26, 1928–29.
CORRESPONDENCE/MANUSCRIPTS/PAMPHLETS: Letters, typescript history, and printed matter relating to missionary work in China.
SERIALS: *China Christian Advocate*, 1937. *Foochow News*, 1931–32, 1934–40.

17-VINCENT LEBBE PAPERS, 1893–1982, 2,532 microfiches, 1 box
Background note: The originals for this collection, representing ca. 70,000 pages of documents, are deposited at the Université Catholique de Louvain-la-Neuve, Belgium. Vincent Lebbe (1877–1940) was a Belgian missionary in China from 1901 to 1913, 1917 to 1920, and 1927 to 1940. J. Leclercq based his biography of Lebbe, *La Vie du Père Lebbe*, on these documents.
MINUTES/RECORDS/REPORTS/CORRESPONDENCE/MANUSCRIPTS/PAMPHLETS/CHINESE LANGUAGE MATERIALS: Correspondence, writings, reminiscences, reports, memoranda, and printed matter in French and Chinese, relating to Roman Catholic missions in China, diplomatic relations between China and the Vatican, and activities of Chinese students in Belgium and elsewhere in Europe, including 4 volumes of printed copies of selected documents from the papers (*Recueil des archives Vincent Lebbe*, by C. Soetens).
FINDING AIDS: *Inventaire des archives Vincent Lebbe*, by C. Soetens (*Cahiers de la Revue Théologique de Louvain*, Publications de la Faculté de Théologie, Louvain-la-Neuve, N 4, 1982).

18-FRANÇOIS LEGRAND DIARY, 1945–46, 1 volume
Background note: François Legrand was a Belgian Roman Catholic missionary in Siwantzu and North China from 1929 to 1947.
MINUTES/RECORDS/REPORTS/DIARIES: Diary in French relating to Legrand's experiences in Siwantzu and political events in North China, including typewritten carbon copies of reports in English, French, and Dutch from members of the Catholic mission in North China regarding daily living conditions in the Communist zone and the behavior of the Communists toward the mission, 1945–46.

19-HAROLD SHEPARD MATTHEWS PAPERS, 1936–68, 3 boxes
Background note: Harold Shepard Matthews was an American missionary in North China from 1922 to 1942 and American Board of Commissioners for Foreign Missions secretary from 1944 to 1953.
MINUTES/RECORDS/REPORTS/CORRESPONDENCE/PAMPHLETS: Reports, correspondence, writings, and printed materials relating to Christian missionary work in China and Japan, and to the Communist movement in China, 1936–68.

20-ELMER L. MATTOX PAPERS, 1905–66, 2 boxes
Background note: Elmer L. Mattox was a Presbyterian missionary teacher at Hangchow Christian College.
CORRESPONDENCE/MANUSCRIPTS/PAMPHLETS/AUDIO-VISUAL MATERIALS: Correspondence, writings, pamphlets, and photos relating to Hangchow Christian College, missionary work in Hangchow, and to social conditions in China, 1905–66.

21-PAUL C. MELROSE PAPERS, 1906–49, 1 box
Background note: For biographical notes, see University of Oregon, Special Collections, Eugene, OR, 97403.
MINUTES/RECORDS/REPORTS/MEMORABILIA: American Presbyterian Mission, Hainan, annual reports, 1906, 1910, 1930–31; annual meeting, report, 1928–29, 1931, 1938; reconstituting assembly, minutes, n.d.
SERIALS: *Hainan Newsletter*, 1914, 1917–27, 1930–38, 1947–49.

22-IVA M. MILLER PHOTOGRAPHS, ca. 1910–1930, 1 envelope
Background note: Dr. Iva M. Miller was medical director of the Isabella Fisher Hospital in Tientsin.
AUDIO-VISUAL MATERIALS: 90 photos of scenes at the Isabella Fisher Hospital, Tientsin, ca. 1910–1930.

23-HUGH ANDERSON MORAN, 1916–33, 2 boxes
Background note: Hugh Anderson Moran (b. 1881) was an American Presbyterian clergyman who worked with the YMCA in Siberia and China from 1909 to 1918. See also Cornell University, Department of Manuscripts and University Archives, John M. Olin Library, Room 101, Ithaca, NY, 14853–5301.
CORRESPONDENCE/MANUSCRIPTS/MEMORABILIA/MAPS/DESIGNS/DRAWINGS/AUDIO-VISUAL MATERIALS: Correspondence, writings, clippings, posters, maps, and photos, relating to political and economic conditions, and relief

work in prisoner of war camps, in Manchuria and Siberia during the Russian Civil War.

24-WILLIAM PETTUS, 1939, 1 folder
Background note: William Bacon Pettus (b. 1880) was president of the College of Chinese Studies (California College in China), Peking, from 1916 to 1945, and a trustee of California College in China Foundation. See also Claremont Colleges, Special Collections Department, Honnold Library, Eighth and Dartmouth Streets, Claremont, CA, 91711.
MINUTES/RECORDS/REPORTS/CORRESPONDENCE: Letters to Robert Swain, on the Sino-Japanese War and political conditions in China and Japan, including reports by Pettus and John Leighton Stuart, 1939.

25-IDA PRUITT PAPERS, 1911–48, 1 folder
Background note: For biographical notes and other papers of Ida Pruitt, see Radcliffe College, Schlesinger Library, Cambridge, MA, 02138.
MINUTES/RECORDS/REPORTS/CORRESPONDENCE/PAMPHLETS: Reports, letters, and printed matter relating to missionary and social work in China, the Sino-Japanese conflict, and Chinese Industrial Cooperatives, 1911–48.

26-ALICE C. REED EXCERPTS FROM LETTERS, 1916–48, 1 folder
CORRESPONDENCE: Correspondence excerpts relating to social conditions and Christian missionary work in China, 1916–48.

27-HARRIET RIETVELD PAPERS, 1925–41, 1 box
MANUSCRIPTS/PAMPHLETS/MEMORABILIA: Notes, educational material, and printed matter, relating to missionary work of the YWCA in Chefoo, flood relief, and other missionary activities in China, 1925–41.

28-CLYDE BAILEY SARGENT, 1941, 1 folder
Background note: Clyde Bailey Sargent was a professor at Cheeloo University, Chengtu, in 1941.
CORRESPONDENCE: Typescript extracts from letters, including those on the Sino-Japanese War and social conditions in China, 1941.

29-RODERICK SCOTT PAPERS, 1916–58, 2 boxes
Background note: Roderick Scott, a missionary educator, was professor of Western culture, dean, and president of Fukien Christian University, Foochow, from 1917 to 1949. See also Claremont Colleges, Honnold Library, Claremont, CA, 91711.
MINUTES/RECORDS/REPORTS/CORRESPONDENCE/MANUSCRIPTS/AUDIO-VISUAL MATERIALS: Reports, correspondence, and photos of Scott and his wife, Agnes, chiefly relating to Fukien Christian University, Foochow, including lists of alumni, an historical sketch of the university written by Scott, and textbooks for college reading.
SERIALS: Fukien Christian University: *FCU Family Newsletter in America*, 1951–54, 1956; *FCU News*, 1930; *Fukien News*, 1934, 1937.
DISSERTATIONS/THESES: Untitled thesis by Peter Ping-k'ang Hsieh, on Karl Barth and predestination, Fukien Christian University, 1943(?).

30-GEORGE WILLIAM SHEPHERD PAPERS, 1895–1980, 1 box
Background note: George William Shepherd was an American

missionary to China and adviser to Chiang K'ai-shek from 1918 to 1939.
MANUSCRIPTS/MEMORABILIA/AUDIO-VISUAL MATERIALS: Memoirs, studies certificates, other memorabilia, and photos. relating to social and political conditions, Chiang K'ai-shek, and the New Life Movement, 1895–1980.

31-JOHN LEIGHTON STUART, 1946–49, 1 folder
DIARIES: Photocopy of typewritten diary on Chinese Civil War and Sino-American relations, 1946 and 1949.

32-LAURA M. WHITE ULMER DIARY, 1932–38, 1 box
Background note: Laura M. White Ulmer was an American missionary in China from 1924 to 1930 and from 1932 to 1939. See also Nebraska State Historical Society, Library, 1500 R Street, Box 82554, Lincoln, NB, 68501.
DIARIES: Typewritten diary relating to social conditions and medical missionary activities in China, 1924–30 and 1932–39.

33-JAMES BENJAMIN WEBSTER PAPERS, 1903–31, ca. 22 boxes
CORRESPONDENCE/DIARIES/MANUSCRIPTS/MEMORABILIA/AUDIO-VISUAL MATERIALS: Correspondence, diaries, writings, notebooks, and 3 photos relating to theology, missionary activities, and Christian education in China, 1903–21.
FINDING AIDS: In-house guide.

CA–295 East Asian Collection
Hoover Institution on War, Revolution, and Peace
Stanford University
Stanford CA 94305–6010
(415) 723–1754
Ramon H. Myers, Curator

1-GENERAL HOLDINGS
DISSERTATION/THESES: *Russian (Greek Orthodox) Missionaries in China, 1689–1917: Their Cultural, Political, and Economic Role*, by Albert Parry, 1938.
CHINESE LANGUAGE MATERIALS/MINUTES/RECORDS/REPORTS: Chung-hua Chi-tu chiao ch'ing nien hui (YMCA of China), reports, 1920–21; Chung-kuo chung pu chin hui nü ch'ai hui lien hui (Central China Baptist Women's Conference), records of annual meeting, 1918; Liang Kuang Baptist Conference, report, 1927.
CHINESE LANGUAGE MATERIALS/MANUSCRIPTS: Mimeographed copy of *Revised Directory of the Protestant Christian Movement in China*, 1949.
CHINESE LANGUAGE MATERIALS/SERIALS: *Ai kuo pao (Patriotic Journal)*, 1923. *Chen kuang tsa chih (True Light Magazine)*, 1927–29. *Ch'i-ta chi k'an (Cheeloo University Journal)*, 1932–37. *Chiao yü chi k'an (China Christian Educational Quarterly)*, 1927–29, 1942. *Chung-hua Chi-tu chiao hsüeh sheng li chih ch'uan tao t'uan chi k'an (Volunteer Bulletin)*, 1924. *Chung-hua Chi-tu chiao hui nien chien (China Church Year Book)*, 1934, 1936. *Chung-kuo hsin t'u yüeh k'an (Chinese Christians Today)*, 1962, 1972–77. *Chung wai hsin pao (Chinese and Foreign Bulletin)*, 1859. *Hsieh chin* (National Christian Council of China, *Bulletin*), 1951. *Hsing hua (Chinese Christian Advocate)*, 1927. *P'an shih tsa chih (The Rock)*, 1935–36. *Shang-hai Chung-hua Chi-tu chiao hui yüeh pao (Shanghai Chinese Christian Monthly)*, 1918, 1920, 1922. *Shang-hai Hu-pei chin hui t'ang nien k'an* (Shanghai Baptist Church, Hupei, *Yearbook*), 1925. *T'ung wen pao (Chinese*

Christian Intelligencer), 1946. *Yang-tzu chi pao* (*Yangtse Quarterly*), 1922–23.

CHINESE LANGUAGE MATERIALS: Biographies of China missionaries, and pamphlets and monographs on the history of Christianity in China, including such subjects as anti-Christian movements, Baptist missions, Boxer Rebellion, Chinese Christian Medical Association, Chung-hua Sheng Kung Hui, diplomatic relations between the K'ang-hsi emperor and Rome, educational administration, evangelistic work, medical missions, imperialism, Nestorians, northwest China, Protestant church, rural development, sectarian cases, and *Wan kuo kung pao*.

CA–300 Library

Hoover Institution on War, Revolution, and Peace
Stanford University
Stanford CA 94305
(415) 723-2058
Neil J. McElroy, Head of Readers' Services

1-GENERAL HOLDINGS

MANUSCRIPTS: "The Interesting Life of the Ordinary Missionary—China—1912–1949," by Augustus I. Nasmith, n.d.

PAMPHLETS: *Life in Communist China*, by Edward MacElroy, 1957; *Memorandum on Missions*, by Henry T. Hodgkin, 1927; *The Present Situation in China and Its Significance for Christian Missions*, by the Foreign Missions Conference of North America, Committee of Reference and Counsel, 1925.

SERIALS: *China Bulletin*, 1947–62. *China Christian Advocate*, 1914–41. China Christian Educational Association, *Bulletin*, 1926, 1928. *China Christian Year Book*, 1910–35, 1938–39. *China Colleges*, 1934–35, 1937–48. *The China Fundamentalist*, 1936. China Inland Mission, *Occasional Papers*, 1872–75. China International Famine Relief Commission, Publications, series A, 1922, 1926, 1928, 1930–36. *China Notes*, 1962–74. *Chinese Repository*, 1832–51. *Directory of Protestant Missions in China*, 1916, 1930. Educational Association of China, *Mission Educational Directory*, 1910. *Educational Review*, 1907–11, 1913–38. *Fu Jen Magazine*, 1932–33. *Fu Jen Newsletter*, 1931–32. *Letters from China*, 1948–49. *Lingnan*, 1938. *Szechuan Weekly Bulletin*, 1936–38. *Yenching Journal of Social Studies*, 1938–41, 1948–50. Yenching University, Department of Sociology and Social Work, *Social Research Series*, 1930; Publications, series C, 1929–30, 1933.

DISSERTATIONS/THESES: *Die katholische Chinamission im Spiegel der rotchinesischen Presse; Versuch einer missionarischen Deutung*, by Johannes Schütte, 1957. *Suomen lähetysseuran työ Kiinassa vuosina, 1901–1926* (*The Work of the Finnish Missionary Society in China in the Years 1901–1926*), by Toivo Saarilahti, 1960.

STANFORD UNIVERSITY
CA–305 Green Library

Stanford CA 94305–2393
(415) 723-9108
David C. Weber, Director

1-GENERAL HOLDINGS

MINUTES/RECORDS/REPORTS: Christian Literature Society for China, annual reports, 1900, 1910–11, 1920; International Institute of China, constitution, 1907; reports, 1903–19, 1927; Methodist Episcopal General Hospital, Chungking, annual report, 1897.

PAMPHLETS: *The Catholic Missions in China during the Middle Ages, 1294–1368*, by Paul Stanislaus Hsiang, 1949; *The Present Situation in China and Its Significance for Christian Missions*, by the Foreign Missions Conference of North America, Committee of Reference and Counsel, 1925; *The Sericulture Industry of South China*, by Charles Walter Howard, 1923; *Sketch of the History of Protestant Missions in China*, by David Willard Lyon, 1895.

ORAL HISTORIES: *China Missionaries Oral History Collection*, ed. by Cyrus H. Peake and Arthur L. Rosenbaum (Claremont Graduate School, Oral History Program), 1973. See ORAL HISTORIES Union List for the names of participants.

MAPS/DESIGNS/DRAWINGS: *Atlas of the Chinese Empire, Containing Separate Maps of the Eighteen Provinces of China Proper on the Scale of 1:3,000,000 and the Four Great Dependencies on the Scale of 1:7,500,000, Together with an Index to All Names on the Maps and a List of All Protestant Mission Stations*, by Edward Stanford, 1908.

SERIALS: *Anking Newsletter*, 1937–41, 1945, 1947–48. *Asian Folklore Studies*, 1942–; supplement, 1952-. Catholic University of Peking, *Bulletin*, 1928; College of Education, *Publications*, 1939–40. *China Christian Advocate*, 1914–41. China Christian Educational Association, *Bulletin*, 1928. *China Christian Year Book*, 1910–39. China International Famine Relief Commission, *Bulletin*, 1929; Publications, series A, 1922–36; series B, 1922–30 (?). *China Mission Advocate*, 1839. *Chinese Medical Journal*, 1887–1921. *Chinese Recorder and Missionary Journal*, 1868–1941. *Chinese Repository*, 1832–51. Diocesan Association for Western China, *Bulletin*, ?, 1951–57. *Educational Review*, 1907–11, 1913–38. *Fenchow*, 1919–36. *The Foochow Messenger*, 1903–40. *The Green Year*, supplement, 1925. *Hainan Newsletter*, 1912–49. *Lingnan Science Journal*, 1922–50. *Missionary Recorder*, 1867. *Monumenta Serica*, 1935-; Monograph Series, 1942–43, 1945–46, 1948, 1961, 1966. Nanking Theological Seminary, English Publications, 1940. *Notes and Queries on China and Japan*, 1867–70. University of Nanking, College of Agriculture and Forestry, *Bulletin*, 1926, 1933–35. *Variétés Sinologiques*, 1892–1938, 1982-. *West China Missionary News*, 1899–1943. *Yenching Journal of Chinese Studies*, Supplement, 1932. *Yenching Journal of Social Studies*, 1938–50. Yenching University, Department of Sociology and Social Work, Publications, series C, 1929, 1933; *Social Research Series*, 1930.

DISSERTATIONS/THESES: *The American and British Missionary Concept of Chinese Civilization in the Nineteenth Century*, by James Miller McCutcheon, 1959. *American Catholic China Missionaries, 1918–1941*, by Thomas A. Breslin, 1972. *American Catholic Missions and Communist China, 1945–1953*, by Virginia F. Unsworth, 1977. *Die Anfänge der neuen Dominikanermission in China*, by Benno M. Biermann, 1927. *The Anti-Christian Movement in China, 1922-1927*, by Ka-che Yip, 1970. *A Century of Chinese Christian Education: An Analysis of the True Light Seminary and Its Successors in Canton and Hong Kong*, by Chen Kuanyu, 1972. *The China Inland Mission and Some Aspects of Its Work*, by Hudson Taylor Armerding, 1948. *Chinese, Missionary, and International Efforts to End the Use of Opium in China, 1890–1916*, by Kathleen L. Lodwick, 1976. *The Chinese State and the Catholic Church: The Politics of Religion within the Confucian-Sectarian Dynamic*, by Eric Osborne Hanson, 1976. *Christliche*

Theologie in China, by Winfried Glüer, 1978. *An Enduring Encounter: E. T. Williams, China, and the United States*, by Dimitri D. Lazo, 1977. *The Influence of American Missionaries in China upon the Foreign Policy of the United States, 1931–1941*, by Stephen H. Johnsson, 1956. *Issachar Jacox [i.e., Jacob] Roberts and American Diplomacy in China during the Taiping Rebellion*, by George Blackburn Pruden, Jr., 1977. *The Life and Thought of W. A. P. Martin: Agent and Interpreter of Sino-American Contact in the Nineteenth and Early Twentieth Centuries*, by Ralph M. Covell, 1974. *The London Missionary Society in India and China, 1798–1834*, by Laurence Kitzan, 1965. *The Mission Compound in Modern China: The Role of the United States Protestant Mission as an Asylum in the Civil and International Strife of China, 1900–1941*, by Gladys Robina Quale, 1957. *The Mission Enterprise of the Lutheran Church-Missouri Synod in Mainland China, 1913–1952*, by Roy Arthur Suelflow, 1971. *The Mission of Matteo Ricci, S.J.: A Case Study of an Effort at Guided Culture Change in China in the Sixteenth Century*, by George L. Harris, 1967. *Missionary Conscience and the Comprehension of Imperialism: A Study of the Children of American Missionaries to China, 1900–1949*, by Sarah Mason, 1978. *Missionary Journalism in Nineteenth-century China: Young J. Allen and the Early "Wan kuo kung pao," 1868–1883*, by Adrian A. Bennett, III, 1970. *The Modern Phase and Conclusion of the Chinese Rites Controversy*, by George Hisaharu Minamiki, 1977. *The Negotiations between Ch'i-ying and Lagrené, 1844–1846*, by Angelus Francis J. Grosse-Aschhoff, 1950. *Oberlin-in-China, 1881–1951*, by Mary Tarpley Campfield, 1974. *The Problem of Missionary Education in China, Historical and Critical*, by Yau S. Seto, 1927. *Protestant Mission Schools for Girls in South China (1827 to the Japanese Invasion)*, by Mary Raleigh Anderson, 1943. *The Protestant Missionary Understanding of the Chinese Situation and the Christian Task from 1890 to 1911*, by C. William Mensendiek, 1958. *Protestant Missions in Communist China*, by Creighton B. Lacy, 1953. *Reciprocal Change: The Case of American Protestant Missionaries to China*, by Paul Voninski, 1975. *Revolutionary Faithfulness: The Quaker Search for a Peaceable Kingdom in China, 1939–1951*, by Cynthia Letts Adcock, 1974. *The South Shensi Lutheran Mission*, by Sigurd Olaf Aske, 1951. *Strangers in the House: J. Lewis Shuck and Issachar Roberts, First American Baptist Missionaries to China*, by Margaret M. Coughlin, 1972. *The Yangtze Valley Antimissionary Riots of 1891*, by Roberto M. Paterno, 1967. *Zion's Corner: Origins of the American Protestant Missionary Movement in China, 1827–1839*, by Murray A. Rubinstein, 1976. CHINESE LANGUAGE MATERIALS: *Hankow Syllabary*, by James Addison Ingle, 1899. CHINESE LANGUAGE MATERIALS/SERIALS: *Yen-ching hsüeh pao*, 1927–32.

CA–310 Lane Medical Library

Stanford University Medical Center
Stanford CA 94305
(415) 723-6831
Betty Vadeboncoeur, Librarian, Historical Collection

1-GENERAL HOLDINGS
MINUTES/RECORDS/REPORTS: China Medical Missionary Association, constitution and by-laws, n.d., with proposed membership list.
PAMPHLETS: American Bureau for Medical Aid to China pamphlets; *A Comparative Study of the Health of Missionary Families in Japan and China and a Selected Group in America*, by William G. Lennox, 1921; *China Medical Journal*, reprinted articles, n.d.; West China Union University, College of Medicine and Dentistry, *Collected Reprints*, 1938–45.
SERIALS: *China Medical Journal*, 1913, 1916–31. *China Medical Missionary Journal*, 1887–88, 1891–97. *China's Medicine*, 1966–68. *Chinese Medical Journal*, 1932–52, 1955–66, 1973–; supplement, 1936–40. *Chinese Medical Journal* (Chengtu), 1942–45. West China Border Research Society, *Journal*, 1932.
CHINESE LANGUAGE MATERIALS/SERIALS: *Chung-hua i hsüeh tsa chih* (*Chinese Medical Journal*), 1973–74.

CA–315 Special Collections Department

Stanford University Libraries
Stanford CA 94305-2393
(415) 723-4054
Carol A. Rudisell, Manuscripts Librarian

1-MIRIAM BOYD LETTERS, 1923–24, 1 volume
Background note: Miriam Boyd was a professor of chemistry at the University of Peking from 1923 to 1924.
CORRESPONDENCE: Bound volume of 18 transcribed letters from Miriam Boyd to her mother, including descriptions of Christian missionaries Boyd met during her stay in Peking.

2-CLARKE FAMILY PAPERS, ca. 1904–1937, 15 l.f.
Background note: J. Eric G. and Ruth Elliott (Johnson) Clarke were in Shanghai from 1904 to 1943. They were interned by the Japanese from 1943 to 1945.
MINUTES/RECORDS/REPORTS/CORRESPONDENCE/MANUSCRIPTS/AUDIO-VISUAL MATERIALS: Uncatalogued letters, business records, and notebooks pertaining to the Clarkes' stay in Shanghai, 1904–37; photos of the China Medical Missionary Association Conference, 1910, and of missionaries in China.

3-GENERAL HOLDINGS
SERIALS: *Chinese Repository*, 1832–51.

STOCKTON

UNIVERSITY OF THE PACIFIC

CA–320 J. A. B. Fry Research Library

Commission on Archives and History
The United Methodist Church
The California-Nevada Conference
Stockton CA 95211
(209) 946-2269
William B. Jefferies, Archivist
Nadine Johnson, Librarian

Restrictions: Access by appointment. Contact William B. Jefferies, c/o Biggs Community United Methodist Church, P.O. Box 425, 441 C Street, Biggs, CA, 95917.

1-GENERAL HOLDINGS
MINUTES/RECORDS/REPORTS: Methodist Episcopal Church: Central China Conference, report, containing sections on conferences of Foochow, Hinghwa, Kalgan, Kiangsi, North China, Shantung, West China, and Yenping, 1946(?); North China Woman's

Conference, minutes, 1893–99, 1901–25, 1927–28; Pacific Chinese Mission, minutes and reports, 1918–20, 1922, 1926, 1935–37; Methodist Episcopal Church, South, China Conference, Golden Jubilee report, 1935; Moore Memorial Church, Shanghai, reports, 1935, n.d.; Soochow University, President's report, 1933–34.

CORRESPONDENCE: Circular letters from Sid and Olive Anderson, 1933, 1947–48, 1951; 2 circular letters from Katherine and Ralph A. Ward, Shanghai, 1949; circular letters from Bliss and Mildred Wiant, 1965, 1968 (on Nestorian crosses), and n.d. (on Wiant Memorial Residence at Yenching University).

MANUSCRIPTS: "Index to Missions," containing a section on China with statistics on missions, ca. 1943; miscellaneous handwritten notes, n.a., n.d.

PAMPHLETS: *The China Mission of the Methodist Episcopal Church*, by Rev. Arthur Bowen, ca. 1915; *China's Industrial Wall*, by Ida Pruitt, 1940; *I Bear My Witness*, by Chiang K'ai-shek, n.d.; *I Confess My Faith*, by Mei-ling Soong Chiang, n.d.; *Bible Stories of 1935–36* and *Frontiers of Faith*, by Carleton Lacy, n.d.; *Christ for the Children of China*, n.a., n.d.; *Christianity in China*, by Mei-ling Soong Chiang, n.d.; Soochow Hospital, 50th anniversary pamphlet, 1933; China Sunday School Union, 10th anniversary pamphlet, n.d.

MEMORABILIA: Clippings on China in *The Christian Advocate*, 1937; *The Bible Society Record*, 1923; *Christian Education*, 1927; *Sunday School Times*, 1934; *Together*, 1961; *World Outlook*, 1934, 1937 (special issue on China), 1939, 1942, 1950; brochures by Ralph Ward and F. Olin Stockwell, n.d.

SERIALS: *Foochow News*, 1940.

CHINESE LANGUAGE MATERIALS: Programs and songs commemorating the 50th anniversary of Changli Conference, n.d.

CA–325 Holt-Atherton Center for Western Studies
William Holt Knox Memorial Library
University of the Pacific
Stockton CA 95211
(209) 946–2945
Ron Limbaugh, Director
Daryl Morrison, Special Collections Librarian

1-ELLEN DEERING COLLECTIONS, 1912, 1 item
CORRESPONDENCE: Typescript copy of a letter from Tong Sing Kow, a University of the Pacific graduate, discussing American missionary activities in China and rising European influence, Tu Tu Fu, Chang Sa, 1912.

WHITTIER

WHITTIER COLLEGE
CA–330 Bonnie Bell Wardman Library
7031 Founders Hill Road
Whittier CA 90608
(213) 693–0771
Joseph Dmohowski, Special Collections Librarian

Background note: Wardman Library has particularly strong holdings on Quakers (Society of Friends) and may have other materials in addition to those listed below.

1-QUAKER COLLECTION, 1925–75, 2 items
MINUTES/RECORDS/REPORTS: Ohio Yearly Meeting of Friends, record of missionary work in China, 1925.

DISSERTATIONS/THESES: *Revolutionary Faithfulness: The Quaker Search for a Peaceable Kingdom in China, 1939–1951*, by Cynthia Letts Adcock, 1974.

COLORADO

COLORADO SPRINGS

NAZARENE BIBLE COLLEGE
CO-5 Trimble Library
1111 Chapman Drive
P.O. Box 15749
Colorado Springs CO 80930
(303) 596-5110 Ext. 110
Roger M. Williams, Librarian

Background note: See also Church of the Nazarene International Headquarters, Nazarene Archives, 6401 The Paseo, Kansas City, MO, 64131.

1-GENERAL HOLDINGS
PAMPHLETS: *Hitherto! 1914-1939: Silver Anniversary of the Church of the Nazarene in China*, by the missionary staff of the Church of the Nazarene in China, n.d.

DENVER

DENVER CONSERVATIVE BAPTIST SEMINARY
CO-10 Carey S. Thomas Library
3401 South University Boulevard
P.O. Box 10,000
University Park Station
Denver CO 80210
(303) 761-2482
Sarah Lyons, Librarian

1-RALPH COVELL COLLECTION, 1947-51, quantity undetermined
Background note: Ralph Covell is the academic dean at Denver Seminary.
CORRESPONDENCE: Personal letters from Ralph Covell to his parents and to the Conservative Baptist Foreign Mission Society, from Shanghai, Chengtu, Hsichang, Jugu, and Ya'an, 1947-51.

2-RUTH MAYO PAPERS, 1927-50, quantity undetermined
Background note: Ruth Mayo was a missionary of the Conservative Baptist Foreign Mission Society (CBFMS) in mainland China and then in Taiwan. The major portion of her correspondence is from Taiwan.
CORRESPONDENCE: Letters from Ruth Mayo, Shanghai, to the Brill family of Elk Mound, Wisconsin, 1927-30, and circular let-

ters submitted by Mayo, at the Ch'uen Yu Orphanage in Kanhsien, Kiangsi, to the files of the CBFMS, 1947-50.
MEMORABILIA/AUDIO-VISUAL MATERIALS: 3 autograph books, two of which contain pictures with the autographs, n.d.

3-GENERAL HOLDINGS
MINUTES/RECORDS/REPORTS: China Inland Mission, annual report, 1953, 1958; Consultation on World Evangelization, report, 1980.
PAMPHLETS: *The Indigenous Church*, by Sidney James Wells Clark, n.d.; *Indigenous Ideals in Practice: Evangelistic Policy and Work in the Siaochang Field in North China*, by W. F. Rowlands, 1931.
SERIALS: *China and Ourselves*, 1981-86. *China and the Church Today*, 1979-86. *China Mission Advocate*, 1839. *China Notes*, 1962-76, 1978-. *Chinese Recorder*, 1868-1941. *Chinese World Pulse*, 1977-83. *Ching Feng*, 1964-86. *Missionary Recorder*, 1867. *Variétés Sinologiques*, 1985.
DISSERTATIONS/THESES: *The American Board in China: The Missionaries' Experiences and Attitudes, 1911-1952*, by Janet E. Heininger, 1981. *A History of the Evangelical Lutheran Church of America's Mission Policy in China, 1890-1949*, by Roger Keith Ose, 1970. *A History of Seventh-Day Adventist Higher Education in the China Mission, 1888-1980*, by Handel Hing-tat Luke, 1983. *Lutheran Missions in a Time of Revolution: The China Experience, 1944-1951*, by Jonas Jonson, 1972. *The Modern Phase and Conclusion of the Chinese Rites Controversy*, by George Hisaharu Minamiki, 1977. *The Protestant Missionary Understanding of the Chinese Situation and the Christian Task from 1890 to 1911*, by C. William Mensendiek, 1958. *A Symbolic Interactionist Approach to the Religious Stranger Concept: Protestant Missionaries to China, 1845-1900*, by Nishan J. Najarian, 1982. *A Theological Dialogue between Christian Faith and Chinese Belief in the Light of "Sin": An Inquiry into the Apparent Failure of the Protestant Mission in Late Nineteenth-century China, Especially among Chinese Intellectuals*, by Christopher Chou, 1976. *Timothy Richard's Theory of Christian Missions to the Non-Christian World*, by Rita T. Johnson, 1966.
CHINESE LANGUAGE MATERIALS: *Research Guide to the "Wan kuo kung pao," 1874-1883*, by Adrian Arthur Bennett, 1976.

THE ILIFF SCHOOL OF THEOLOGY
CO-15   Ira J. Taylor Library
2201 South University Boulevard
Denver CO 80210
(303) 744-1287
Sara J. Myers, Director

Restrictions: Interview with the archivist, librarian, or their representatives required for access.
Background note: This library contains the joint archives of the Iliff School of Theology and the Rocky Mountain United Methodist Conference and persons connected with it. Most of the material is at present unprocessed, so the extent of the collection has not yet been determined. It does, however, include records of some of the Methodist, Evangelical United Brethren, and United Methodist churches in Colorado, and correspondence and other personal papers of several prominent figures in Colorado Methodism.

1-GENERAL HOLDINGS
MINUTES/RECORDS/REPORTS: Methodist Episcopal Church, minutes of the seventh annual session of the South Fukien annual conference, 1933; National Council of Churches of China, China consultation, 1958.
PAMPHLETS: *The Awakening of China*, by James Whitford Bashford, 1906; *The Bible and China*, by Will H. Hudspeth, 1952; *Die chinesische Mission im Gerichte der deutschen Zeitungspresse*, by Gustav Warneck, 1900; *From China and Tibet: A Commentary on Letters Written by Missionaries Working in the Interior, 1844-1865*, by Robson Lowe, 1981.
SERIALS: *China Mission Year Book*, 1911, 1917-19, 1925-26, 1928-29, 1931-37. Nanking Theological Seminary, English Publications, 1940.

UNIVERSITY OF DENVER
CO-20   Penrose Library
University Park
Denver CO 80208
(303) 871-2422
Patricia A. Fisher, Assistant Director
for Public Services

1-GENERAL HOLDINGS
PAMPHLETS: *Windows into China: The Jesuits and Their Books, 1580-1730*, by John Parker, 1978.
DISSERTATIONS/THESES: *A Comparative Study of Missionary Families in Japan, China, and a Selected Group in America*, by William Gordon Lennox, 1921. *The Life and Thought of W. A. P. Martin: Agent and Interpreter of Sino-American Contact in the Nineteenth and Early Twentieth Centuries*, by Ralph M. Covell, 1974. *Political Activities of the Christian Missionaries in the T'ang Dynasty*, by Lam Ch'i-hung, 1975.

CONNECTICUT

BRIDGEPORT

CT-5   BRIDGEPORT PUBLIC LIBRARY
Burroughs Building
925 Broad Street
Bridgeport CT 06604
(203) 576-7777
David W. Palmquist, Head, Historical Collections

1-HAZEL M. KIRK PAPERS, 1927-41, 1 folder
CORRESPONDENCE: Correspondence received from Elizabeth C. Wright of the Presbyterian Mission in Peking, 1927-41.

HARTFORD

HARTFORD SEMINARY FOUNDATION

CT-10 Archives
Case Memorial Library
77 Sherman Street
Hartford CT 06105
(203) 232-4451 Ext. 260
William Peters, Librarian

Background note: The following collections are uncatalogued.

1-CHARLES PAUL, 1902–40, 1 pamphlet box

Background note: Charles Paul, the president of the College of Missions, Irvington, Indiana, was a missionary educator at the University of Nanking. He went to China in 1905.
MANUSCRIPTS: "Notes of Confucian Literature," n.d.; galleys for a book on Christian work among Buddhists, n.d.; typescript extracts of articles on Buddhism, n.d.
PAMPHLETS: *The Story of Christian Colleges in China*, ca. 1940; pamphlet on the University of Nanking in Chengtu, n.d.; *Manchuria before November 16* (supplement to *The Chinese Christian Student*, 1931); *Un pélerinage bouddhique en China: Le Mont Omi*, by P. le Roux, 1925.
MEMORABILIA: "Mencius and Some Other Reformers of China," by W. E. Macklin, *Journal of the China Branch of the Royal Asiatic Society*, V 33, n.d.; clipping on Paul's experiences at University of Nanking and on Patros Rijnhart's experiences in Tibet, *Detroit News*, 1910.
SERIALS: *T'oung pao*, 1928. *Variétés Sinologiques*, 1902.

2-GENERAL HOLDINGS

Background note: The materials listed below are contained in 3 pamphlet boxes marked "Missions."
MINUTES/RECORDS/REPORTS: Foochow Mission, report on medical work, 1891; memos of F. N. Chapin regarding Foochow Mission and federation, 1905; YMCA, annual reports by W. B. Pettus, 1918; personal report by Charles Ernest Scott, 1918; general report of evangelistic work, Fenchow, 1923; bulletin from A. L. Warnshuis regarding compensation for property losses in Nanking, 1923; newsletter from Kuling Mission, 1937; North China Union Language School, *The Peking Mandarin* (yearbook), 1922–23; Synod of Church of Christ in China, mid-Fukien, announcement of scholarships, 1938; bulletin from the Kiangsi Christian Rural Service Union, Lichwan, 1940–41; United Board for Christian Colleges in China (UBCCC), general progress report of the literature program, 1952–53.
CORRESPONDENCE: Letters to J. M. Hobbes from Charles Hartwell, Foochow, 1885; Henry Perkins, Pangchia, 1885; and F. N. Chapin, Tientsin, 1885; letter from "Will" to "Ed" in Paotingfu, 1903; 33 circular letters from Alice Seymour Browne to Women's Board of Missions, Boston, 1906–26; letter from Matilda Thurston, Kuling, to Lydia (Capen?), 1908; letter from George Sherwood Eddy to the International Committee of YMCAs in New York, 1914; letter from Reuben, Tsinanfu, to "old Frank," 1917; 2 letters from Charles Ernest Scott, Tsingtao, to Edward Warren Capen, with a brochure on work in China by Scott, 1917–18; letter from Dwight Edwards en route to China, 1918; 2 letters from Ch'uan Ch'in Liang, Nantao Christian Insti-

tute, to Robbins W. Barstow, 1933, 1938, and his reply, 1934; letter from Barstow to Liang, 1940; letter from Nettie Senger, PUMC Hospital, Peking, to Barstow, 1938, and his reply; letter from Jean Pommerenke, Yeungkong, to Barstow, 1939, and his reply; letter from Harry Worley, Foochow, to Malcolm Pitt, 1941; letter from Ernest J. Swift to Mr. [William Rockwell] Leete, 1939; letter from Ralph Sell, American Lutheran Mission, Tsimo, 1939; letter from Marguerite Twinem, Changli, 1939; letter from Alice Weed, 1940; letters to the Associated Boards for Christian Colleges in China (ABCCC) from Charles Corbett, Y. C. Yang, and H. Y. Loh, 1945; letter from Russell Henry Stafford to Dung-hwe Zi, 1947; 2 letters from Harriet, Hainan, to Lydia Capen, 1947–48; letter from Russell Henry Stafford to Kimber Den, 1948; 2 letters from Jean Stewart, Chungking, to Lydia Capen, 1950; letter from Lyda Houston to Lydia Capen, 1950, with printed letter; letter from Jean Stewart, Chungking, 1950.

Letters to Lewis Hodous from the following correspondents: Lois Armentrout, Canton, 1941; Earle Ballou, 1943, 1947; Willard Beard, Foochow, 1940; Margaret H. Brown, 1941–42; Mr. and Mrs. Leonard J. Christian, Foochow, 1923, 1928; Harriet Chue, 1942; Clarence B. Day, 1943; Kimber H. K. Den, Kiangsi Rural Service Union, Lichwan, 1939, 1941; Mary L. Donaldson, 1938, 1940, 1942; Woodrow Ging, Shanghai, 1941; Enid P. Johnson, American Baptist mission, Swatow, 1939, 1941; Wayne Jordan, 1923; William Rockwell Leete, 1943; Ching Lien Li, 1940; Alice Murphy, 1940–41; Herbert and Jean Pommerenke, 1940, 1942, 1944; Clyde B. Sargent, Chengtu, with resume, 1940; Evelyn (Sites), 1948; "Ned" (Edward H. Smith), Ingtai, 1923–24, 1927–28, 1940, 1948, n.d. ; Florence Smith, 1940–41; T. Janet Surdam, 1948; Mary Fine Twinem, 1948; Emma B. Tucker, 1941; Francis Tucker, 1941; Ralph A. Ward, Chungking, 1940; Gertrude Waterman, College of Chinese Studies, Peking, 1939, 1941; E. J. Winans, 1941; Benny and Lucy Zi, Garbour-Ley Theological College, Shanghai, 1939; D. H. Zi, Swatow, 1938; unsigned from Taiyuan, 1923; unsigned from Foochow, 1948; Marion C., American Board Mission in Peking, 1924; and Mary, Chungking, 1938.

Circular letters from Lois Armentrout, Canton, 1940; Percival R. Bakeman, American Baptist Foreign Mission Society, Shanghai, 1927; Searle Bates, Nanking, 1946; John Bickford, Paoting, 1947; H. Brewster, Wiley General Hospital, Kutien, 1943; Harold Brewster Brockton, 1950; Margaret H. Brown, Chengtu, 1944, 1947; Henry H. Bucher, Kiungchow, 1947; Canadian Missionary Hospital, Chungking, 1942; Robert and Helen Chandler, 1938, 1941, 1947; Leonard and Agnes Christian, 1939, 1941, 1944, 1947; Ralph Coonradt, Kunming, 1947; D. S. Corpron, Luchowfu Christian Hospital, 1940; Kimber H. K. Den, 1947; Jean Dickinson, 1923–24; Mary L. Donaldson, 1938; Aganetha Fast, Taming, 1938–39, 1941; A. J. Fisher, Church of Christ in China, Kwangtung Synod, 1939; Elmer Galt, 1944; Gilberts, Tungchow, 1939; Charles L. Gillette, Pagoda Hospital, Fukien, 1938; Oswald Goulter, Hofei, 1939, 1943; Anne Guthrie, 1940; H. G. C. Hallock, Shanghai, 1929; George K. and Winifred Harris, Sining, 1947–48; Earl Hibbard, Tientsin, 1940, 1942; Donald and Catherine Hsueh (with notes to Hodous), Foochow College, 1946; J. W. Hawley, Methodist Episcopal Church, Hinghwa Conference, 1916; Lyda S. Houston, Foochow, 1939, 1949; Donald A. Irwin, Hangchow, 1947; Anna E. M. Jarvis, Union Hospital, Foochow, 1946; Wayne Jordan, YMCA, Sian, 1922, with memo to Hodous; Wilhelmina Kuyf, Taming, 1938; Walter N. Lacy, 1940–41; William R. Leete, 1944, 1949–50; Samuel H. Leger, 1942, 1945; Mabel Leger, Fukien Christian University, Shaowu, 1940; Jenny Lind, Kiukiang, 1939; Bruno and Katherine Luebeck, Ungkung, 1939, 1941; Harold Martinson, 1950; Paul C. Melrose, Kiungchow, 1947; William Meyer, Chenhsien, 1947; Robert Miller, Peking, 1947; Aimee Millican, Shanghai, 1947; Wallace H. Miner, Methodist Episcopal Church, Foochow Conference, 1916; Anna Moffet, 1942–43; Alice Murphy, 1928, 1939; Russell Nelson, 1950; Richard B. Norton, Hangchow, 1947; Herbert and Jean Pommerenke, 1939, 1944, 1946–48; Presbyterian Board of Foreign Missions, Hwaiyuan Station, 1947; P. Frank Price, 1923, 1925, 1940–41, 1943–44, 1948; Watts O. Pye, Fenchow, 1914; H. W. Robinson, Tunghsien, 1947–48; Mary Robinson, 1943; Lloyd S. Ruland, 1944; Roderick Scott, 1940, 1946–48; Margaret Seeck, Yutu, 1942; George W. Shepherd, Hankow, 1938; Peter Y. F. Shih, West China Theological College, Chengtu, 1942–43; Clement and Evelyn Sites, 1948; Edward H. Smith, Foochow, 1947; Elleroy M. Smith, Ningpo, 1947; Florence W. Smith, Methodist Mission, Putien, 1939–41; Lewis and Margaret Smythe, Chengtu, 1939; William B. Steele, Tunghsien, 1928; William and Anna White Stewart, North China Union Language School, Peking, 1928, YMCA residence, Kaifeng, 1939; Charles L. and Mary Storrs, Shaowu Mission, 1923, 1928 (with personal notes to Hodous), 1934, 1939–40, 1943; T. Janet Surdam, Su Deh Girls' School, 1940–44, 1947–48; Luella Tappan, Kiungchow, 1947; Anna K. Tootell, Changteh, 1947; Francis and Emma Tucker, 1940, 1947; Marguerite Twinem, Changli, 1941; David B. Van Dyke, Showhsien, 1947; Laura Ward, Diong-loh, 1938, 1940; Ralph Ward, Shanghai, 1941; Gertrude Waterman, 1943; Alice Weed, 1940–45, 1947–51; Katherine King and Louis E. Wolferz, 1938, 1940–41, 1943–44; Zela and Harry Wiltsie Worley, 1939–40, 1942–45, 1947 (with handwritten notes to Chandler and Worley on reverse from Hodous), 1948; Elizabeth C. Wright, Peking, 1947; and Herrick B. Young, 1947.

Printed letters from Earle Ballou, Peking, 1941, 1946–47; Margaret Brown, Christian Literature Society, Shanghai, 1939; Helen and Robert Chandler, 1941; Leonard and Agnes Christian, 1940; William B. and Sarah F. Pettus, 1945; Aganetha Fast, Taming, with photo of YW Home and Bible Training School, 1939–40; Lewis and Lois Gilbert, North China Mission, Techow, 1939; Myrtle M. Lefever, Miller Seminary, Siu Laam, 1948; Alice E. Murphy, Tehchow, 1940; Clara A. Nutting, 1939, 1940; John De F. Pettus, Kunming, 1947; H. W. Robinson, 1942, 1944; Roderick Scott, Shaowu, 1940; Margaret Seeck, Baldwin School for Girls, Yutu, 1940–41; Nettie M. Senger, Tsinchou, 1936; Edward H. Smith, Foochow, 1948 (one with handwritten notes to Hodous); Matilda Thurston, Nanking, 1939; W. Reginald Wheeler, Nanking, 1933–35; and Mr. and Mrs. Harrison K. Wright, Shanghai, Christian Literature Society, 1922–23.

MANUSCRIPTS: Bibliography on Nestorians in China, with "The Nestorians in China," 1916; "The Place of Christianity in China" with outline, 1925; poem by Anna White Stewart on life in China, 1939; outfit lists for Kiangan Mission, 1941, South China, 1941, Hunan, 1945, West China, 1947, and general, 1946; 16 typescripts, 1922–47, on the church and war conditions, church-mission relationships, evangelism, medical mission work, mission work, and Christian education in post-war China, Islam in China, Kiangsi Rural Service Union, Kochow nut, rehabilitative campaign, travel in China, Yenching University, and YMCA, by Merrill S. Ady, Nathaniel Bercowitz, O. C. Crawford, Archie R.

Crouch, Kimber H. K. Den, L. Carrington Goodrich, A. R. Kepler, Howard Lair, G. Gordon Mahy Jr., W. C. Merwin, Anna E. Moffet, Joseph C. D. Sing, Tracy Strong, and John Leighton Stuart.

DIARIES: Printed diary extracts by Zela and Harry Worley, 1941.

PAMPHLETS: *Mrs. Cheng and Cinnamon Flower*, by Mary Williams Hemingway, extracted from *Missionary Herald*, 1913; *Where Dragons Sleep*, by Robert Case Beebe, 1924; pamphlet on the Presbyterian mission in Peking; *A Message to the West from a Former Westerner*, by Mary Fine Twinem, 1937.

MEMORABILIA: Brochure on South China Mission, 1900; memorial for Harrison King Wright, 1923; 3 articles by Paul G. Hayes, *Chinese Recorder*, 1928, 1934; program for biennial meeting of the National Committee of YMCAs of China, 1947; clipping on Earl C. Dahlstrom, *Hartford Courant*, 1948; "What About China Now?," American Board flyer, 1949; clipping on changes at Yenching University, 1950; clipping on Earl Cressy, *Hartford Courant*, 1950; brochure on "Kingdom Investments under the American Board" in China, n.d.; clipping on station XLAK-3, Shanghai Christian Broadcasting Station, by Aimee Millican, ca. 1950s.

SERIALS: *China Mission Newsletter*, 1947–48.

CT–15   Case Memorial Library

Hartford Seminary Foundation
77 Sherman Street
Hartford CT 06105
(203) 232–4451 Ext. 260
William Peters, Librarian

Background note: The Kennedy School of Missions was established in 1911, but became a part of the Hartford Seminary Foundation in 1913 and merged completely in 1961.

Finding aids: "The Archives of the Case Memorial Library," by Nafi Donat, 1972.

1-PEARL BUCK, 1942–43, 13 items
CORRESPONDENCE: 8 letters to and from E. E. Calverly, 1942–43; letter to Malcolm Slack Pitt and his reply, 1943; copies of 3 letters to Lewis Hodous, 1942.
FINDING AID: In-house index.

2-EDWARD WARREN CAPEN, 1902–15, quantity undetermined
Background note: Materials in this collection on China relate primarily to Capen's trip to China as part of a world tour under the auspices of the American Board of Commissioners for Foreign Missions (ABCFM) from 1907 to 1909.
MINUTES/RECORDS/REPORTS: Reports on South China, Foochow Mission, Shansi Mission, and North China Mission.
CORRESPONDENCE: Letter about Capen from Yeungkong, 1939; ca. 13 folders of correspondence relating to his world tour, 1907–8; letter listing locations of mission stations and ministers in China, ca. 1907–1908.
MANUSCRIPTS: "Foochow Mission, Progress at Foochow," "South China Mission," and "North China Mission," 1906; "Shansi Mission," n.d.; "Western Influence in China," n.d.; description of the China Continuation Committee, n.d.; notes for "Social Aspects of Village Life in China and India," 1903–15; miscellaneous notes on China, 1915, n.d.
MEMORABILIA: Clippings on Horace Bushnell, 1902; obituary

of his father, Samuel Capen, 1914; leaflet, "Home Again from Nanking," by William A. Mather, ca. 1950.
FINDING AIDS: In-house index.

3-EARL CRESSY, 1943–60, 2 folders
CORRESPONDENCE: 4 letters from Cressy to Lewis Hodous, 1943–44, 1947–48; letter from Clarence Hamilton to Hodous, with his reply on reverse, 1944; circular letter from Earle Ballou, 1948.
MANUSCRIPTS: A general statement on the Institute for Research on Religion in China, 1943; resumé, 1954–55; outline report on China trip, 1948; biography of Mrs. Cressy, 1960; proposal for a research center in Nanking, n.d.
AUDIO-VISUAL MATERIALS: Photo of Cressy, n.d.

4-GEORGE SHERWOOD EDDY, 1911–12, 8 items
CORRESPONDENCE: 8 letters to and from Edward Capen, 1911–12.
FINDING AIDS: In-house index.

5-LEWIS HODOUS PAPERS, 1907–50, 22 folders
Background note: Lewis Hodous (1872–1949), a professor in the Chinese department at the Kennedy School of Missions until 1945, was a Congregational missionary in Foochow from 1901 to 1917. He was president of the Foochow Theological Seminary from 1902 to 1912 and of Union Theological Seminary in Foochow (which he founded) from 1914 to 1917.
MINUTES/RECORDS/REPORTS: Ingtai Medical Work, report by Fred Donaldson, 1924.
CORRESPONDENCE: Letters from Hodous to Edward Capen, 1907; to his wife, Anna, 1917; and to his professors at Hartford Theological Seminary, 1907–12; letters to Hodous from: Willard Beard, 1924; S. M. Bosworth, 1927; Frank T. Cartwright, 1930; Marion H. Chatfield, 1924; Charles H. Corbett, 1943; E. H. Cressy, 1922, 1946; Clarence B. Day, 1946; Fred F. G. Donaldson, 1924; Lora Dyer, 1926; B. A. Garside, 1930; Ralph G. Gold, 1926; Edwin Jones, 1920; H. N. Kinnear, 1926; Kenneth Scott Latourette, 1930; C. J. Lin, 1930; Mrs. [Jean?] Lingle, 1919; E. C. Lobenstine, 1919–20, 1929; Donald MacGillivray, 1919; W. B. Pettus, 1927; P. Frank Price, 1924; Frank Rawlinson, 1929; Richard Ritter, 1928; Sisto Rosso, 1942; Rilla Scherick, 1924; A. Schmüser, 1924; Clement and Evelyn Sites, 1943; John Leighton Stuart, 1920; and A. L. Warnshuis, 1920; copy of a letter from P. L. Gillett in Nanking to Mrs. M. G. Warren, 1923; letter from Hodous in Peking, 1934; letter from Catherine Hsueh, Foochow College, to R. H. Potter, 1946; letter from Nettie Senger to Mr. and Mrs. Ritter, n.d.; circular letters from Mary Shearer, 1947; Frank Price, 1928, n.d.; and A. R. Kepler, 1928.
DIARIES: Hodous' diaries, 1903–7, 1928–50.
MANUSCRIPTS: Bibliographies, 1917–18, 1937, 1949; "The President of China Dons Christianity," n.d.; autobiography, including years in China, ca. late 1940s; miscellaneous biographical writings; "Foism and the Buddhists of China," 1923; "The Educational Situation in Hunan," 1927; "The Mysticism of Lao-tzu and Chuang-tzu,", n.d.; "The Development of Logical Methods in Ancient China," n.d.; "The Ministry of Chinese Religions," n.d.; manuscript of his book, *Folkways in China*, chapters 1–18, n.d.; list of periodical articles on Chinese subjects, 1933, n.d.
MEMORABILIA: Article on Chinese language by Hodous from the *Missionary Herald*, 1913; "The Literature of China," by Hodous, *China*, 1937; "A Precursor of the Modern Renaissance in

China," by Hodous, *Chinese Recorder*, n.d.; "China's New Religion," by Edwin R. Thiele, *Signs of the Times*, n.d.; notices of memorial service for Hodous, 1950.
AUDIO-VISUAL MATERIALS: Photos of Hodous, n.d.; photo of Hodous with President C. J. Lin of Fukien Christian University at commencement, 1935.
CHINESE LANGUAGE MATERIALS: 3 unidentified letters.
FINDING AIDS: Partial in-house index.

6-JAMES HUDSON ROBERTS PAPERS, 1872–1941, 6 volumes
Background note: James Hudson Roberts (1851–1945), a 1907 graduate of Hartford Theological Seminary, was a Congregational missionary in Kalgan.
CORRESPONDENCE/MANUSCRIPTS: Correspondence, appreciations of missionaries in Kalgan, and poems, by Roberts.

7-GENERAL HOLDINGS
MINUTES/RECORDS/REPORTS: Chinese Students' Christian Association in North America, 1914, annual reports, 1911, 1922–28.
PAMPHLETS: *Christianity and Confucianism*, by John Leighton Stuart, 1928.
DISSERTATIONS/THESES: *An Analysis of Religion as Found in the Works of Hsün-tzu*, by Sigurd Aske, 1949. *Ancestor Worship and the Progress of Christianity in China*, by Earle Hoit Ballou, 1916. *The Anti-missionary Movement in China, 1922–1927: A Case Study of the Effect of Modernization on the Attitude toward Christian Missions*, by John Kenneth Reynold Luoma, 1970. *Certain Fundamental Religious Characteristics of the Chinese with a Brief Reference to the Proper Application of Christianity to Them*, by Warren Bartlett Seabury, 1903. *The Christian Church in Rural China*, by Hsieh Ching-shen, 1942. *A Compendium of Basic Characters in Chinese Christian Thought*, by Daniel Nelson, 1943. *The Covenant Missionary Society in China*, by Earl C. Dahlstrom, 1950. *Facing Family Problems with Chinese Youth*, by Mary Lois Donaldson, 1938. *The Fellowship of Goodness (Tung Shan She): A Study in Contemporary Chinese Religion*, by John Cornelius De Korne, 1941. "*Folkways and Religion,*" Translations of Chapters Nine and Ten from "*Ting-Hsien, A Social Survey,*" by Aganetha Helen Fast, 1936. *Franciscans at the Court of the Khan: An Essay in World Unity*, by Richard H. Ritter, 1937. *The Idea of the Church in the Minds of Protestant Missionaries to China*, by Herbert Henry Pommerenke, 1937. *The Idea of God in the Chinese Classics*, by Dung-hwe Zi, 1930. *Imperial Government and Catholic Missions in China during the Years 1784–1785*, by Bernward Henry Willeke, 1948. *The Influence of the Chinese Renaissance upon Protestant Christianity in China*, by Samuel James Russell Ensign, 1930. *Nestorianism in the T'ang Dynasty (618–906 A.D.)*, by Woodrow Ging, 1930. *The New Life Movement in China*, by Mabel Heebner Reiff, 1945. *Peasant Religion in Northern Chekiang*, by Clarence Burton Day, 1930. *Present-day Mission Work in Rural China*, by Ora Margaret Anderson, 1934. *A Program of Religious Education for Christian Churches in China*, by Chen Chang-yu, 1926. *The Renaissance in China in the Twentieth Century (Especially with Reference to Education and Religion)*, by Ching-lien Li, 1930. *Some Aspects of the Religion of the Former Han Dynasty as Found in the Annals Section of the Dynastic History*, by Earl Carl Dahlstrom, 1949. *Some Chinese Roads to Christianity*, by Thomas Lowry Sinclair, 1926. *The South Shensi Lutheran Mission*, by Sigurd Aske, 1951. *The Spiritual Awakening in the Lutheran Churches of China*, by Talbert Rorem Ronning, 1947. *A*

Study of Some Phases of the Christian Religious Education of Adults in China, by Maud Risher Jones, 1929. *A Study of the Experiences of Chinese Children and Their Implications for Religious Education*, by Ella Gryting Ronning, 1947. *Toward a Religious Program for Youth in North China*, by Jessie Marguerite Twinem, 1938. *The Training of Laymen for Christian Service in North China*, by Alice Eugenia Murphy, 1938. *Working Out of a New Approach to Chinese Social Units: Particularly Village and Klan*, by Jeno Kunos, 1948.

HARTFORD

TRINITY COLLEGE

CT–20   Watkinson Library
300 Summit Street
Hartford CT 06106
(203) 527–3151 Ext. 307
Jeffrey H. Kaimowitz, Curator

1-GENERAL HOLDINGS
MANUSCRIPTS: "The Real Chinaman," by Chester Holcombe, 1898.
SERIALS: *Chinese Repository*, 1833–44, 1851.
CHINESE LANGUAGE MATERIALS: New Testament, 1894; 3 tracts by William Milne, 1816–34; tract by Walter Henry Medhurst, ca. 1830s.

CT–25   Trinity College Library
300 Summit Street
Hartford CT 06106
(203) 527–3151
Ralph Emerich, Librarian

1-GENERAL HOLDINGS
SERIALS: *Lingnaam Agricultural Review*, 1922–27. *Lingnan Science Journal*, 1927–48.
DISSERTATIONS/THESES: *Imperial Government and Catholic Missions in China during the Years 1784–1785*, by Bernward Henry Willeke, 1948.
CHINESE LANGUAGE MATERIALS/SERIALS: *Yen-ching hsüeh pao (Yenching Journal of Chinese Studies)*, 1927–40, 1946–50. *Yen-ching hsüeh pao chuan hao (Yenching Journal of Chinese Studies*, Monograph series), 1933–50.

MIDDLETOWN

WESLEYAN UNIVERSITY
CT–30   Special Collections and Archives
Wesleyan University Library
Middletown CT 06457
(203) 347–9411 Ext. 2456
Elizabeth A. Swaim, Special Collections
Librarian and University Archivist

Background note: Wesleyan students and alumni contributed to missionary work in China for about 110 years. In 1835, four years after the founding of the university, the Missionary Lyceum, an early student organization devoted to furthering interest in foreign missions, passed a resolution regarding the particular desirability of establishing Methodist missions in China. Erastus Wentworth, Class of 1837, later co-founded the Methodist Episcopal Mission in Foochow. Some 30 Wesleyan graduates were missionaries in China, mostly during the period from 1895 until shortly after World War II. Joseph Beech, an 1899 graduate, founded the Wesleyan Chungking Institute, which came under the financial patronage of Wesleyan Unversity students and alumni in 1902; in 1909 he helped to found West China Union University in Chengtu, where many of Wesleyan's missionaries later taught. Other Wesleyan missionaries were associated with Tsinghua College and the Wiley School of Theology in Peking, the University of Nanking, and Foochow College. Wesleyan graduates became presidents of the Anglo-Chinese College and Fukien Union College, both in Foochow. For Wesleyan alumni listed, class year is indicated in parentheses.

1-JOSEPH BEECH (1899), 1919–54, 1 folder
CORRESPONDENCE: Letter from Joseph Beech's daughter, Katharine, about a portrait of Beech donated to Wesleyan; 2 letters from Beech's daughter, Miriam, about his obituary in *Wesleyan Alumnus*.
MANUSCRIPTS: "Tribute to Dr. Joseph Beech," a copy of an address by F. Olin Stockwell.
MEMORABILIA: Articles by and about Beech in *Wesleyan Alumnus*, 1919, and obituary, 1954.

2-CIU DO GIENG (1916), 1921, 1 folder
MEMORABILIA: Articles in *Middletown Press* and *Christian Advocate* on Ciu Do Gieng's missionary work and return from the United States, 1921.

3-WILLIAM HARRY CLEMONS (1902), 1927–68, 2 items
MEMORABILIA: Article about William Harry Clemons in *Wesleyan Alumnus*, 1927, and his obituary, 1968.

4-EDWARD EVERETT DIXON (1920), 1922–73, 1 folder
CORRESPONDENCE: Letter from Edward Everett Dixon to Herman D. Berlew, in *Wesleyan Alumnus*, 1922, recounting experiences with the Shantung International Relief Committee.
MEMORABILIA: Obituary in *Wesleyan Alumnus*, 1973.
SERIALS: *The Clasped Hands*, 1931, 1934.

5-JOHN (1897) AND ELIZABETH THOMPSON GOWDY (1898), 1866–1940, 1 folder
CORRESPONDENCE: 2 letters from John Gowdy to George Dutcher, 1939–40.
PAMPHLETS: *Szechwan Revisited*, 1935, an account of their trip to Szechwan and conditions at missions.
SERIALS: *Foochow News*, 1940.
CHINESE LANGUAGE MATERIALS: *The Diamond Sutra*, printed in Foochow, 1866.

6-EDWIN CHESTER JONES (1904), 1917–24, 1 folder
MEMORABILIA: "A New College President in China," in *Wesleyan Alumnus*, 1917.
SERIALS: *Fukien Star*, 1924.

7-JAMES LUKENS McCONAUGHY, 1942–43, 1 folder
Background note: James Lukens McConaughy was president of Wesleyan University from 1925 to 1943. He resigned to become full-time director of United China Relief.

MEMORABILIA: Articles in *Wesleyan Alumnus*, regarding McConaughy's relief work, 1942, and his resignation, 1943.

8-MISSIONARY LYCEUM RECORDS, 1835, 3 folders
MINUTES/RECORDS/REPORTS: Minutes, 1835; report on missions; resolution concerning dispatching missionaries and a printing press to China; election of Peter Parker to honorary membership.
CORRESPONDENCE: 7 letters from James Fulton to D. P. Kidder of the Missionary Lyceum regarding methods of setting Chinese characters in type; establishment of print shops in China to publish religious tracts, 1835.

9-RUTHVAN BEEBE NICHOLS (1913), 1938, 1 item
CORRESPONDENCE: Typed transcript, unsigned, of a letter from Shanghai, describing ill treatment of Chinese and foreigners, including some missionaries, by the Japanese, 1938.

10-FREDERIKA VAN BENSCHOTEN (1901), 1975, 1 item
MEMORABILIA: Obituary in *Wesleyan Alumnus*, 1975.

11-ERASTUS WENTWORTH (1837), 1859, 1 item
CHINESE LANGUAGE MATERIALS: *Amoy Hymns*, by Erastus Wentworth, 1859.

12-WEST CHINA UNION UNIVERSITY COLLECTION, 1905–43, 10 items
Background note: See also Yale Divinity School, Special Collections, 409 Prospect Street, New Haven, CT, 06510.
PAMPHLETS: *West China Union University, Chengtu, Szechwan*, 1919; *Wesleyan and the West China University*, a financial appeal with a summary of activities in China sponsored by American colleges and universities, 1910(?).
MEMORABILIA: Articles on West China Union University, and Wesleyan-in-China in *Wesleyan Alumnus*, 1936, 1939, 1943; and on Chungking Institute in *Olla Podrida*, 1905.
AUDIO-VISUAL MATERIALS: Photo of 2 newly-constructed administrative buildings; photo of a ceremony, which may be a commencement.

13-MOSES CLARK WHITE (1845), 1847–1901, 1 volume, 1 folder
MANUSCRIPTS: Bound volume of late 19th-century transcripts by Moses Clark White, a missionary doctor, relating to the founding of Methodist missions in Foochow, 1847–53.
MEMORABILIA: Several obituary notices of White, 1901; common-place book, including a description of the Fukien Examination Hall in Fuhchau, with White's notes on learning Chinese.
CHINESE LANGUAGE MATERIALS: *Yesu yu shan lundao*, a tract, ca. 1852.

14-STANLEY WILSON (1909), 1930s, 1 folder
PAMPHLETS: 6 pamphlets on scholarly work at Yenching University, Department of Chemistry.

15-GENERAL HOLDINGS
MINUTES/RECORDS/REPORTS: Methodist Episcopal Church, mission conferences, minutes: Foochow, 1902, 1905; Hinghwa, 1924–25, 1923; North China, 1887, 1891; South Fukien, 1924–25, 1927–33; West China, 1905–6; Williams Hospital, Pangkiachwang, report, 1908.
PAMPHLETS: *Wesleyan's Outposts*, by William North Rice, 1917 (includes a list of Wesleyan missionaries in China through 1916).

MEMORABILIA: "Useful Work of 30 Alumni in China," in *Wesleyan Alumnus*, 1922.
SERIALS: *China Mission Year Book*, 1924.
CHINESE LANGUAGE MATERIALS: Bible, Books of Ezra and Job, n.d.; *A Part of the New Testament of Our Lord and Savior Jesus Christ*, n.d.; *John's Gospel*, Shanghai version, n.d.
FINDING AIDS: In-house list.

MYSTIC

MYSTIC SEAPORT MUSEUM
CT–35   G. W. Blunt White Library
Greenmanville Avenue
Mystic CT 06355
(203) 572-0711
Douglas Stein, Curator of Manuscripts

1-ALBERT L. FREEMAN LETTERS, ca. 1850s, 125 items
CORRESPONDENCE: 125 letters from Albert L. Freeman, a shipping agent in Shanghai, to his friend, Charles Cullis, in Boston, detailing his passages to China, descriptions of Shanghai, conditions in China, and missionary work.
FINDING AIDS: In-house box and folder description.

2-SAMUEL M. WHITING LETTERS, 1850–51, 4 items
CORRESPONDENCE: 4 letters from Samuel M. Whiting to J. S. Eaton, of Portland, Maine, describing his trip to China to serve as a missionary, 1850–51.

NEW BRITAIN

CENTRAL CONNECTICUT STATE UNIVERSITY
CT–40   Elihu Burritt Library
1615 Stanley Street
New Britain CT 06050
(203) 827-7531
Frank Gagliardi, Associate Director
   of Library Services

Background note: The serial title listed below is uncatalogued.
1-GENERAL HOLDINGS
CHINESE LANGUAGE MATERIALS/SERIALS: *Yen-ching hsüeh pao (Yenching Journal of Chinese Studies)*, 1927–30, 1949.

NEW HAVEN

CT–45   NEW HAVEN COLONY HISTORICAL SOCIETY
114 Whitney Avenue
New Haven CT 06510
(203) 562-4183
Ottilia Koel, Librarian and Curator of Manuscripts

1-FOOTE COLLECTION, 1857, quantity undetermined
CORRESPONDENCE: Letters to Andrew Hull Foote, a U.S. naval commander stationed in Canton, from Eliza Gillette and Elijah Coleman Bridgman, 1857.

NEW HAVEN

YALE DIVINITY SCHOOL

CT-50   Special Collections
409 Prospect Street
New Haven CT 06510
(203) 432-5301
Martha L. Smalley, Archivist

Background note: The Yale Divinity School Library archival collections include the China Records Project (Record Groups 1–17 below), which was begun in 1968 by the National Council of Churches and became part of the Divinity Library in 1971. It currently includes nearly 700 linear feet of manuscript material from missionaries and organizations active in China beginning in the early 1800s.

Finding aids: "Archives and Manuscripts at the Yale Divinity School Library," an in-house listing of the collections.

1-AMERICAN BOARD OF COMMISSIONERS FOR FOREIGN MISSIONS PAPERS (film MS 32), 1827–1919, 94 reels microfilm

Background note: The originals for this collection are at Harvard University, Houghton Library, Cambridge, MA, 02138. See the entry on Harvard University for a more detailed description. China-related material may also be found in Unit I of this collection, letters from foreign correspondents.

MINUTES/RECORDS/REPORTS/CORRESPONDENCE: American Board of Commissioners for Foreign Missions, reports, minutes, documents, and correspondence of the following missions: Amoy, 1827–59; Foochow, 1860–1929; South China, 1829–1922; North China, 1860–1930, including Fukien Christian University, North China Union College, Peking Union Medical College, Shantung Christian University, Yenching College for Women, and Yenching University; Shansi, 1880–1914.

FINDING AIDS: *Papers of the American Board of Commissioners for Foreign Missions: Guide to the Microfilm Collection, Units 1–6*, of which units 1 and 2 are on China (Research Publications, Inc.: Woodbridge, CT).

2-MINER SEARLE BATES PAPERS (RG 10), 1920–78, 55 l.f.

Background note: Miner Searle Bates (1897–1978) was a professor of history at the University of Nanking from 1920 to 1950. He remained in Nanking during the evacuation of the university to Chengtu from 1937 to 1941, and was chairman of the Nanking International Relief Committee. Much of the collection consists of the raw materials and drafts for the survey of the Christian effort in China from 1900 to 1950 which he did not live to complete. "Gleanings from the Manuscripts of M. Searle Bates" contains an outline and summaries of the material in this collection (see FINDING AIDS below).

MINUTES/RECORDS/REPORTS: Bible Union of China, 1921–29; China Christian Educational Association, Council of Higher Education, 1924–25, 1943–46; China Inland Mission, 1925–51; Chinese Theologians' Colloquium, 1978–79; Church of Christ in China: General Assembly, 1942–51; Hunan Synod, 1950; Kwangtung Synod, 1949–50; Yunnan Mission committee, 1941–51; Joint Conferences of Representatives of Mission Boards cooperating with the CCC, 1947–50; North American Advisory Committee, 1950–51; miscellaneous reports, 1969–70; Foreign Missions Conference of North America, China Committee bulletins, 1947–50;

International Institute of China, 1897–1927; International Missionary Council, China Study Group, 1953–57; Nanking Church Council, 1939–41; University of Nanking, 1925–50; National Christian Council of China, reports, ca. 1922–48; Rural church department, 1950; National Council of Churches of Christ in the U.S.A.: Far Eastern Joint Office, China Committee, minutes and bulletins, 1951–64; Asia department, China Committee, minutes and bulletins, 1965–67; Asia department, China study group, 1965–66; Asia department, China program, 1968; East Asia department, China program, 1969–76; North China Christian Rural Service Union, 1949–50; United Christian Missionary Society, report on mission stations in China to 1922; conference reports: General Conference of Missionaries to China, 1890; Second Shantung Missionary Conference at Wei-h[s]ien, 1898; West China conference, 1899; Women's Conference in China on Homelife of Christian Women, 1900; China Centenary Missionary Conference, 1907; World Missionary Conference, Edinburgh, 1910; China Continuation Committee Conference, 1913; National Christian Conference, 1922; Conference on Christianizing Economic Relations, Shanghai, 1927; Central China Church Conference, Wuchang, 1929; miscellaneous, 1951–77; unidentified reports and memoranda from China, 1927–28, 1935–41.

CORRESPONDENCE: Correspondence with family members, 1937–38, describing relief work under Japanese occupation; letter from Bates to his sister regarding the mental health of a Ginling College professor, n.d.; circular letters by Bates, 1927–42, 1945–74; correspondence relating to Bates' work in China, 1927–50, including such correspondents as the China International Famine Relief Commission, William Fenn, Kenneth Scott Latourette, Henry Luce, Nanking International Famine Relief Committee, University of Nanking Board of Founders, National Christian Council-Shanghai, United Board for Christian Colleges in China, United China Relief, United States Embassy in Nanking, and Henry Van Dusen.

General correspondence, 1950–78, including such correspondents as Charles L. Boynton, China Records Project, John King Fairbank, William P. Fenn, China Study Project, Creighton Lacy, Kenneth Latourette, Wallace C. Merwin, Valentin Rabe, United Board for Christian Colleges in China, United Board for Christian Higher Education in Asia, Henry Van Dusen, World Council of Churches, and N. Z. Zia; circular letters from China missionaries; correspondence relating to *China in Change: An Approach to Understanding*, 1967–68.

DIARIES: Diaries and memo books, 1917–18, 1944–78.

MANUSCRIPTS: 7 boxes of notes and sources for Bates' survey of Christian work in China, arranged in an outline, 1836–1978; folder of mixed notes on periodicals, 1923–31; 23 boxes of unsorted notecards; folder of notes on the National Christian Council of China, covering 1930s–1940s; 3 boxes of miscellaneous notes on topics such as anti-Christian movement, Chinese religions, missionaries and Chinese law, political and religious situation, Nanking during Japanese occupation, n.d.; 12 boxes containing several stages of drafts, arranged according to outline, including statements on progress up to 1971, outline and proposed introductory materials.

17 boxes of source materials arranged by author or editor, 1903–78, including dissertations (see DISSERTATIONS/THESES below), a typescript (auto-)biography of Edward Bliss, lists of Protestant missionaries to China by Charles L. Boynton, "China Log," a memoir by N. E. Eloise Bradshaw, and papers on

such subjects as agricultural problems, Young J. Allen, American Catholic missionaries, Boxers, Canadian missions in Manchuria and Honan, Chang Heng-ch'iu, Christian universities, Communism, Confucianism, extraterritoriality, Fukien Christian University, Japanese Christians, Liang Ch'i-ch'ao, Liao Chung-k'ai, Donald MacGillivray, May Fourth movement, medical schools, Lottie Moon, Nanking Incident, Nanking Theological Seminary, NCCC, peasant violence, Protestant missions, Bernard Emms Read, South China mission, Southwest Associated University, student movements, Western medicine, and the YMCA.

Authors of the above include M. S. Ady, R. K. Anderson, Eugene E. Barnett, Bau Ming-chien, Kenneth J. Beaton, Karl H. Beck, Derk Bodde, Howard L. Boorman, H. A. Boyd, Thomas A. Breslin, Rachel Brooks, Margaret H. Brown, John L. Buck, Lawrence J. Burkholder, Arthur V. Casselman, Wilbur J. Chamberlin, F. Gilbert Chan, Robert E. Chandler, Jonathan Chao, H. Owen Chapman, Chen Chi-yun, Ellen Marie Chen, Theodore H. E. Chen, C. Y. Cheng, Julia Ching, J. G. Cormack, Archie R. Crouch, William T. DeBary, Knud Faber, John K. Fairbank, Wilma Fairbank, Morton H. Fried, Robert B. Fulton, E. H. Giedt, Merle Goldman, Han Yü-shan, Edward H. Hume, Irwin Hyatt, Yoshiaki Iisaka, John Israel, Rita Johnson, F. C. Jones, Kiang Wen-han, Leslie G. Kilborn, Ku Tun-jou, Creighton Lacy, S. C. Leung, Lin Ching-jin, Jessie G. Lutz, D. MacGillivray, Donald MacInnis, H. F. MacNair, John W. Masland, Harold S. Matthews, Wallace C. Merwin, Chester Miao, Anna Moffet, Elizabeth Perry, Joachim Pillai, Frank W. Price, Katherine L. Read, Murray A. Rubinstein, Randolph C. Sailer, Irwin J. Schulman, Vera Schwarcz, Lewis S. C. Smythe, Absalom Sydenstricker, Joseph Taylor, S. Y. Teng, J. O. Thomson, Paul A. Varg, Ezra F. Vogel, Francis Cho-min Wei, Raymond L. Whitehead, M. O. Williams, H. G. W. Woodhead, Y. T. Wu, Philip Yang, and David Z. T. Yui.

5 boxes of drafts, lists, biographical sketches, notes, and cover letters relating to documentation of prominent Chinese Christians; mixed format notes and collected materials, 1928–78, some on notecards, on organizations including Nanking Theological Seminary Board of Founders and UBCHEA, and on miscellaneous topics; 12 folders of sermons, addresses, and interviews, 1925–74; box of drafts and notes for *China in Change: An Approach to Understanding* (1969); "The Theology of American Missionaries in China," handwritten and typescript drafts, 1972–73; source materials, notes, exams relating to courses, 1952–64.

MANUSCRIPTS/PAMPHLETS/MEMORABILIA: 5 boxes of articles, pamphlets and papers, 1924–75, relating to China in general, Chinese church, Tibet, Christianity, missions, Chinese political situation, and Yale-in-China; 6 folders of book reviews, 1928–74.

MEMORABILIA: Box of clippings and articles, 1928–76, on missions and other subjects as material for his study; address books and cards, n.c.; miscellaneous memorabilia, 1921–78; medical records, 1941–78; travel documents, 1916–68.

AUDIO-VISUAL MATERIALS: Folder of unidentified, undated photos of China scenes and groups.

SERIALS: *China Bookman*, 1922–37. *China Christian Year Book*, 1928–29, 1932–37. *China Mission Year Book*, 1910–19, 1923–26. *China Missionary Bulletin*, 1948–63. *China's Millions* (Philadelphia), 1899–1937. *Chine-Madagascar*, 1949. *Chinese Recorder*, 1871–1911, 1922–29, 1932–40. *Ching Feng*, 1965–72. *Educational Review*, 1907–10, 1920–38.

DISSERTATIONS/THESES: *The Rural Work of American Protestant Missionaries in China, 1911–1937*, by William J. Megginson, 1968. *Winning Chinese Youth to Christ*, by Ellen M. Studley, 1956.

The collection also contains portions of the following, with Bates' notes: *American Lutheran Mission in China*, by Rolf A. Syrdal, 1942; *The China Inland Mission and Some Aspects of Its Work: Pre-1948*, by Hudson T. Armerding, 1948; *China's Old Culture and New Order*, by Finley M. Chu, 1955; *The Chinese Mind and the Missionary Approach*, by George B. Workman, 1939; *Confucianism in Modern China*, by Luther G. Cooper, 1937; *The History of Early Relations between the United States and China, 1784–1844*, by Kenneth Scott Latourette, n.d.; *History of Nursing in China*, by Willie P. Harris, 1953; *The Opening of Hunan*, by Charlton Lewis, 1965; *Rural Reconstruction in Underdeveloped Areas and the Contributions of the Christian Movement*, by Fu Siang Chang, n.d.; and *Southern Baptist Missions in China, 1945–1951*, by Garnett L. White, 1967.

CHINESE LANGUAGE MATERIALS/SERIALS: *Ch'ing-ch'ao hsü wen hsien t'ung k'ao*, 1885–1908. *Chung-hua Chi-tu chiao hui nien ling (China Church Year Book)*, 1914–36. *Chiao yü chi k'an (China Christian Educational Quarterly)*, 1930–33. *Ching Feng*, 1922–72. *Hsin ts'uan yo chang*, ca. 1900–1909. *Shih lu*, 1902–10, 1970. *Truth and Life*, 1926–31. *Yang sen fu*, ca. 1897–1921.

CHINESE LANGUAGE MATERIALS: Bibliographies, ca. 1912–71; folder of materials on Christian histories, folder on Communist histories, and folder of general histories; 4 folders of notes and bibliographic references on notecards; 8 folders of unidentified printed materials; folder of unidentified handwritten notes; folder of unidentified printed material and notes; unidentified memorabilia.

FINDING AIDS: "Gleanings from the Manuscripts of M. Searle Bates: The Protestant Endeavor in Chinese Society, 1890–1950," by Cynthia McLean (New York: National Council of Churches of Christ in the U.S.A.), 1984; in-house register.

3-BEACH FAMILY PAPERS (RG 60), 1871–1933, 12 folders
Background note: Harlan Page (1854–1933) and Lucy Ward Beach went to China from 1883 to 1890 under the American Board of Commissioners of Foreign Missions. The materials listed below are only part of a large collection.
CORRESPONDENCE: Correspondence of Harlan Beach to family, 1871–1933, and general, 1892, including discussion of missionary experiences.
AUDIO-VISUAL MATERIALS: Folder of unidentified photos, n.d.
FINDING AIDS: In-house register.

**4-BORDER SERVICE DEPARTMENT OF THE CHURCH OF
  CHRIST IN CHINA, (RG 17), 1932–50, ca. 260 items**
Background note: The Border Service Department of the Church of Christ in China was organized by Chinese church leaders in 1939 during the period that the church had its temporary war-time headquarters in Chungking. Also known as the Border Mission, the Border Service Department concentrated its work among the Nosu (Lolo, now Yi), Ch'iang, and Chia-rung national minorities. W. B. Djang was the director of the Border Mission and Archie R. Crouch was the English-language secretary.
MINUTES/RECORDS/REPORTS: Border Service Department, administrative memos and reports, board of directors, budgets, constitutions, financial statements, and minutes, 1939–47.

CORRESPONDENCE: Ca. 175 items of administrative correspondence, 1944–50, between W. B. Djang and Archie Crouch, and organizations such as the American Embassy in Chungking, Baptist Missionary Society (London), British Embassy in Chengtu, British Information Service, Canadian Mission Press, China Inland Mission, Cornell University, China Dental Dispensary, Friends Ambulance Unit—China Convoy, Lifan County Magistrate, Presbyterian Board of Foreign Missions, Society of Friends of Moslems in China, United China Relief, U.S. Department of Agriculture, and Yunnan Mission of the Church of Christ in China; ca. 57 letters between W. B. Djang and Archie R. Crouch, 1944–50; ca. 75 letters thanking contributors, 1944–50; 4 letters from Henry Tsui to Archie Crouch, 1980–83, concerning Tsui's confinement during the Cultural Revolution and the death of W. B. Djang; 4 letters between Kiang Wen-han and Archie R. Crouch, 1982–84, and 1 from Yao Hsien-hwei (Mrs. Kiang Wen-han), regarding Kiang's death, 1984; "Letters to Supporting Groups and Friends," a volume containing circular letters, correspondence, and clippings from Archie Crouch and the Border Service Department, 1943–47.

MANUSCRIPTS: "China's Wild West," n.a., n.d.; "The Churches in the West and the Rehabilitation of the Church in China," n.a., n.d.; "The Decline and Possible Future of a Great Race—The Ch'iang People," by W. B. Djang, ca. 1948; "Ethnobotany of the Gia-rung Tribe," by S. Y. Hu, n.d.; "Facts about the Lolos," ed. by Archie Crouch, n.d.; "Mission to West China," a volume of clippings of "The Christian Front in China," a column by Archie Crouch published in *The Church Times*, 1944–46, and *The Presbyterian*, 1946–47; "A New Age for Christian Missions in China," by Archie R. Crouch, 1945; "An Oasis in a Vast Human Desert: The Story of the Border Mission of the Church of Christ in China," by W. B. Djang, n.d.; "An Outline of the Ethnography of China," by Archie Crouch, 1948, including a map showing the distribution and classification of Southwestern minority peoples, n.d. (ca. late 1930s-early 1940s); "Why a Daughter-in-law Avoids Her Father-in-law and Her Brother-in-law," by Archie Crouch, n.d.

PAMPHLETS: *China's Wild West*, 1949.

CHINESE LANGUAGE MATERIALS/SERIALS: *Pien chiang fu wu (Border Mission Bulletin)*, 1932–33, 1936.

CHINESE LANGUAGE MATERIALS: Letter from W. B. Djang to Y. S. Djang, International Relief Committee, requesting funds for rehabilitation from the Committee on Aid to Social Workers, 1946; copy of a letter from W. B. Djang to Mr. Chung at the Border School in Nan Wen Chuan, 1935; letter to Archie Crouch from students, thanking him for Christmas gifts, 1937; letter to Crouch family in Lolo script, thanking them for Christmas gifts, n.d.; photostatic copies of 3 letters in Chinese and Tibetan, with translations, requesting the Border Service Department to open a hospital in Cho k'e-chi, 1947; report on budget, new personnel, and support of personnel, n.d.; unidentified letter, n.d.

FINDING AIDS: In-house register.

5-ARTHUR JUDSON BROWN PAPERS (RG 2), 1900–1958, quantity undetermined

Background note: Arthur Judson Brown (1856–1963), a Protestant clergyman and missionary, made a world trip to missions in Asia, including China, in 1901 and 1902, and again in 1909, as administrative secretary of the Presbyterian Board of Foreign Missions.

CORRESPONDENCE: General correspondence, 1900–1963, including Chinese Legation, 1900, 1903, 1917, 1922, and Yuan Shih-k'ai, 1901, 1912; correspondence relating to his publications, 1902–58; correspondence relating to missions in China, 1901–46.

DIARIES: 17 volumes entitled "Diary of Arthur J. Brown on Tour of Asia," 1901–2, describing professional conferences and meetings, visits to hospitals, schools, churches, personal impressions, travel adventures, conflicts between Protestant and Roman Catholic missionary interests, the Paotingfu mission, Yuan Shih-k'ai, Boxers and the reconstruction of the missionary compound; 5 volumes entitled "Journal of Arthur J. Brown World Tour 1909," describing professional conferences and meetings, visits to missions and institutions, personal reflections and travel descriptions, discussion of Christian church cooperation, and interview with Yuan Shih-k'ai's son.

MANUSCRIPTS/PAMPHLETS/MEMORABILIA: Clippings, receipts, notes, pamphlets, travel schedules, calling cards, and other papers enclosed in the diaries above, 1901–2, 1909; addresses welcoming Brown to China, 1901–2; letters of introduction; reviews and articles regarding Brown's book, *New Forces in Old China*, 1904–6, and *The Chinese Revolution*, 1912; travel documents, Chefoo, 1901; Boxer poster distributed in Shantung, 1900–1901.

MAPS/DESIGNS/DRAWINGS: 4 maps of Shantung: a route suggested by F. H. Chalfant, the locations of Protestant missions, "Mail Routes of Am. Pres. Miss. Service," and "Part of Shantung Showing F. H. Chalfant's Itineraries 1897."

AUDIO-VISUAL MATERIALS: 5 folders of photos of Paotingfu and Yuan Shih-k'ai's troopers, 1901–2, 1909.

CHINESE LANGUAGE MATERIALS: Unidentified correspondence, n.d.

FINDING AIDS: In-house register.

6-CAMPBELL FAMILY PAPERS (RG 7), 1855–1972, 31 boxes (13 l.f.)

Background note: George (1858–1927) and Jennie Wortman (1863–1939) Campbell were Baptist missionaries in South China from 1887 to 1900, 1908 to 1912, and from 1914 to 1916. Jennie Campbell returned to China from 1927 to 1933, while several of her children were there. Louise Campbell (1883–1968) worked as a missionary for 40 years as principal of the Kwong Yit Girls' School in Meihsien and among the Hakkas. Margaret Larue Campbell Burket (1891–1952) worked in China among the Hakkas with her husband, Everett Burket, from 1916 to 1946. Dorothy McBride Campbell (1892–1972) served in China from 1926 to 1944. David Miles Campbell (1901-ca. 1972) was a missionary in China from 1926 to 1942.

MINUTES/RECORDS/REPORTS: Account books of George Campbell, 1912; record of Louise Campbell's first year as a missionary, 1911.

CORRESPONDENCE: 11 boxes of family correspondence, ca. 1880s–1972, including letters from Kenneth Campbell to his parents while he attended the China Inland Mission Boy's School in Chefoo from 1909 to 1912, and letters of Louise and Dorothy on war-time conditions; other correspondents include Edith Traver, ca. 1940s, Chi Ki-kwong (regarding piracy incident), Marion Reith, 1936, and Marguerite Everham, ca. 1938–1944; letters from Woman's American Baptist Foreign Mission Society to Dorothy Campbell, 1946; copies of letters to Dorothy Campbell regarding an article from Pearl Buck, 1955.

DIARIES: Diaries of George Campbell, 1874–1927; Jennie Campbell, 1879–1939; Louise Campbell, 1895–1968; Dorothy Campbell, 1908–66; Margaret Campbell Burket, 20-page copy, 1904–7.

MANUSCRIPTS: Autobiographical writings of Jennie Campbell, 1933, and Dorothy Campbell, 1946, ca. 1960; notebooks of George Campbell, 1913–14, 1924–27; "Chinese Medical Remedies, Notes by Anna Foster," cures practiced by the Hakka, n.d.; notebooks of Dorothy Campbell, 1920–66; writings of Jennie Campbell on Baptist missionary work among the Hakka, 1932; term papers of Louise Campbell on China, 1926–27; "Japanese Prisoner: A Play," by Dorothy Campbell, 1945; folder of autobiographical material regarding China, n.d.; "Account of His Adventures," by David Campbell, 1927; essays and case studies of Dorothy Campbell, ca. 1930–1946; "Origin and Migration of the Hakkas," by George Campbell, 1912.

PAMPHLETS: 3 unidentified pamphlets among papers of George Campbell; *Missionary Cameralogs*; *Who's Who in the South China Mission?*; *Then and Now*; *Second Annual Report of the Hakka Work, 1906*.

MEMORABILIA: Autograph book of George Campbell, 1879–94; autograph book of Jennie Campbell, 1879, 1881; family genealogy; 3 clippings on 1929 piracy incident which directly involved Jennie, Louise, and Dorothy Campbell; biographical materials on George and Jennie Campbell and Louise Campbell; newspaper and magazine clippings by Louise Campbell from Baptist and Chinese publications, n.d.; folder of obituaries of former missionaries, n.d.; "Echoes from Our Missionaries in Troubled China," an article by Louise Campbell, 1932.

ORAL HISTORIES: 14-page transcript of a tape by Louise Campbell about Kaying Girls' School and other experiences in China, 1967.

MAPS/DRAWINGS/DESIGNS: 2 maps of China, n.d.

AUDIO-VISUAL MATERIALS: Box of photos and identification lists, with views of life at China Inland Mission School in Chefoo, 1909–12, including Thornton Wilder, a classmate of Kenneth Campbell; scrapbook of postcards of China, n.d.

CHINESE LANGUAGE MATERIALS: Notebook of Louise Campbell, n.d.; unidentified pamphlet.

FINDING AIDS: In-house register.

7-CHINA RECORDS PROJECT: PERSONAL PAPERS COLLECTION (RG 8), 1834–1978, ca. 128 l.f.

Background note: This collection represents an on-going project which currently contains material from over 300 individuals, with no individual's papers accounting for more than 3 linear feet. The papers are arranged alphabetically by name, noting each missionary's sending agency, geographic location, and period of service where available. The records in this collection include biographical information, correspondence, diaries and journals, writings, printed material, tape recordings, artifacts, and maps, reflecting the medical, educational, and evangelical work of the missionaries. The items described represent only a sampling of the materials in the collection.

Individuals in this collection, not named below, include: Archibald Adams, Arthur Adams, Marie Adams, Merrill Steele and Lucile Meloy Ady, Martin Albert, Alice Alsup, Mrs. Carl L. Anderson, Irrenius J. Atwood, Benjamin Parke Avery, John Gilbert Hindley Baker, Earle H. Ballou, George B. and Dorothy (Dickinson) Barbour, Margaret Hart (Bailey) Barbour, Eugene E. Barnett, Myrth Bartlett, Robert Lord and Euva Evelyn (Majors) Bausum, Frederick P. Beach, James E. and Margaret W. Bear, Karl H. Beck, Harold and Marian Belcher, L. Nelson Bell, Alice (Ware) Berry-Hart, Brewster Bingham, Susan Rowena Bird, Wesley S. Bissonnette, Henry Blodget, Ruth A. Brack, Grace Breck, Dorothy Brewster, Jennie B. Bridenbaugh, Eliza Jane (Gillette) Bridgman, Richard Briggs, J. Calvin Bright, L. Emma Brodbeck, Fanny Pomeroy Brown, Velva V. Brown, Elizabeth Gordon Bruce, Harry A. Brunger, Mina Van Cleave Buck, Robert E. Bundy, Rosa May Butler, Mary W. Caldwell, Mary Elaine Carleton, Ruth M. (White) Carr, F. Stanley Carson, Chang Fu-liang, Cheng Ching-yi, Ruth M. Chester, Irving B. Clark, Arthur Bradden Coole, Douglas S. Corpron, Marian Craighill, O. C. Crawford, Edith Loree Crook, Helen C. Silsby Cross, Edith Curtis, Sydney Arthur Davidson, Jr., Mary E. S. Dawson, John W. Decker, Nettie R. De Jong, Philippe de Vargas, Mary Reed Dewar, Carol M. Dewey, Frederick and Mary Grace (French) Dilley, Dodd family, Florence Drew, Leighton W. Eckard, Emery Ward Ellis, Lois Anna Ely, Philip S. Evans, Jr., Elizabeth H. Falck, S. C. Farrior, Aganetha Fast, John C. Ferguson, Alzo John Fisher, Alice Seymour (Browne) Frame, Grace A. Funk, Curtis M. and Mabel (Moore) Galt, Howard S. Galt, Sidney D. Gamble, Frank and Verna Waugh Garrett, Raymond H. and Jean Giffin, Dean Goddard, Ralph G. Gold, Chauncey and Sarah Boardman (Clapp) Goodrich, Luther Carrington Goodrich, Fred Field Goodsell, Lucy J. Graves, Dorothy D. Brewster Grayson, Pansy P. Griffin, Anne M. Groff, James W. Hall, Henry Galloway Comingo Hallock, Katharine W. Hand, Emily Susan Hartwell, Albert Carl Hausske, John David Hayes, Watson McMillan Hayes, Mrs. Walter J. Heisey, Elizabeth (Rue) Hembold, Earl R. Hibbard, Harris G. Hilscher, Kate (Bailey) Hinman, George H. Hubbard, James A. and Maude Hunter, Huntington family, Bruce W. Jarvis, Wenona (Wilson) Jett, Charles F. Johannaber, Tracey K. Jones, Walter H. Judd, J. H. and Jennie (Filley) Judson, Victoria Kavooghian, Raymond F. Kepler, Esther E. Kreps, John F. Krueger, Thyra Lawson, Lucy (Chaplin) Lee, Samuel Howard Leger, Marie and Sarah LeTourneau, Wilson Seeley Lewis, James P. Leynse, Jenny Lind, Edwin C. Lobenstine, Josiah Calvin McCracken, Gertrude F. McCulloch, William A. McCurdy, James McCutcheon, Winfield A. McLean, Manly family, A. W. March, Charlotte E. Merrell, Wallace C. Merwin, Samuel John and Emily Ingersoll (Case) Mills, John P. Minter, Maude Moler, Martha R. Moore, Julia Morgan, Robert Morrison, Augustus I. Nasmith, Charles and Jennie Nelson, E. A. Nelson, Y. T. Zee New, Mabel Ruth Nowlin, Dorothy Nyland, Frank and Bertha (Schweinfurth) Ohlinger, Henry James and Lona (Van Valkenburgh) Openshaw, Daryl M. Parker, Elizabeth S. Perkins, Eleanor Elizabeth (Whipple) Peter, Dryden Linsley Phelps, Grace (Darling) Phillips, Christine Hubbard Pickett, Florence M. Pierce, Margaret May Prentice, Elsie May Priest, Ruth Rawlinson, Alice C. Reed, Elsie Reik, August H. Reinhard, Otto G. and Martha Reuman, Paul Russell and Charlotte (Belknap) Reynolds, Robert Price and Agnes Richardson, Harriet A. Rietveld, Richard H. Ritter, William P. Roberts family, Jay Robinson, Olga (Olsen) Robinson, Mae Rohlfs, Jean B. Rothe, Henry Hosie and Mildred May (Ament) Rowland, Marion Jean Rowland, Margaret Mary Rue, Bertha Harding (Allen) St. Clair, Robert J. and Frances (King) Salmon, Abbie G. Sanderson, Katherine Scott, Stuart P. Seaton, Charles C. and Gertrude Selden, Esther I. Sellemeyer, Elizabeth Selsbee, Nettie Mabelle Senger, Ella C. Shaw, Ernest T.

Shaw, Dwight Lamar and Margarita (Park) Sheretz, Arthur M. and Margaret (Marston) Sherman, Randolph T. Shields, Elizabeth T. Shrader, Horace and Gertrude (Haugh) Sibley, John Alfred Silsby, Edith Simester, Winifred Simester, Willard J. Simpson, Evelyn Sites, Philip and Phyllis Slater, B. Ward and Trissa (Darnall) Smith, Grace Goodrich Smith, Hart Maxcy and Margaret (Jones) Smith, Iona Smith, Margaret E. Smith, J. W. Spreckley, Mrs. Raymond E. Stannard, Adelia (Dodge) Starrett, Albert Newton and Celia Belle (Speak) Steward, Catherine Stirewalt, Eugene Stockwell, Everett M. Stowe, Minnie Stryker, John Leighton Stuart, Warren Horton Stuart, Clifford Morgan Stubbs, John Calvin and Marie Stucki, Lennig Sweet, David Stanton Tappan, Lyrel G. Teagarden, Mrs. Steve Terani, Myron E. Terry, M. Gardner Tewksbury, Joseph Oscar Thomson, Edward Payson Thwing, Ting Me Iung, Olive B. Tomlin, Mary Bosworth Treudley, Francis Fisher and Emma Jane (Boose) Tucker, Andrew Yu-yue Tsu, Nellie M. Walker, Alta Harper Wallace, Lewis Walmsley, Laura D. Ward, Percy Theodore Watson, Katherine H. Wead, Georgia Weist, Amy Welcher, Felix B. and Frances Welton, Charles Hart and Louise Westbrook, Mary Culler White, Minerva S. (Weil) White, Sterling Wilfong Whitener, Emily C. Wilcox, Gertrude Wilder, Martha Wiley, Maynard Owen Williams, Stanley Davis and Anna (Lane) Wilson, Jesse B. Wolfe, Clara Husted Whiting, Harry Westcott and Zela W. Worley, Eleanor Wright, Elizabeth Curtis Wright, Ellen Gertrude Wyckoff, Helen Grace Wyckoff, Carroll Harvey and Helen Nevius (Eckard) Yerkes, Lois Young, and Elinor J. Zipf.

MINUTES/RECORDS/REPORTS: Reports and other printed materials on Yenching University, in papers of Randolph Sailer, 1932–50; other reports in papers of individuals listed above.

CORRESPONDENCE: 46 letters from Willard Livingston Beard in Foochow or Kuliang, to his family, 1900, 1915–33; 110 letters of Gladys (Wilson) Bundy discussing political conditions around Boone University in Wuchang, ca. 1924–1926; 34 folders of correspondence from Elsie Clark Krug, in Foochow, Kuliang, or Haitang, to her family in Baltimore, 1912–18; 7 folders of letters to or from Chinese friends and students of Elsie Clark Krug; over 200 letters between Chester Garfield and Phebe (Meeker) Fuson and their family, 1918, 1934–50; over 100 items of general correspondence, including printed and typescript report letters, to and from Chester Fuson, 1906–48; 17 folders of correspondence from Lewis Loder and Lois (Chandler) Gilbert to their families in the United States, 1925–41; 24 bound volumes of correspondence from Lewis and Lois Gilbert, edited and compiled by Josephine Cowin Gilbert, 1925–80; more than 85 photocopies of mimeographed circular letters of Thomas Lee, 1947–58, describing the Communist takeover and missionaries who remained; correspondence of Jeanie Graham McClure, in Fukien, to her family, 1916–37; 45 folders of correspondence of the Mead family, 1894; ca. 100 folders of correspondence of the Poteat family, n.d.; over 50 folders and 1 roll of microfilm of correspondence of Frank and Florence Rawlinson, 1902–52; ca. 49 folders of correspondence of Bliss Wiant, 1922–72; other correspondence in papers of individuals listed above.

DIARIES: 3 diaries of Willard Beard, 1895–97; journals of Willard Beard, with daily accounts of voyages from Foochow to Connecticut and from Foochow to Shaowu, with details on typical missionary work, 1903, 1906–7; journal of Elijah Coleman Bridgman with notes, 1834–38; 3 diaries of Elsie Clark Krug, 1912–14; 254-page diary of Courtney Hughes Fenn, 1866–1927; "How We Got to China," journal of Lewis and Lois Gilbert, 1925–26; "Let-

ters from China, 1920–1949," journal of Anna (Moffet) Jarvis; diaries of Jeanie McClure, 1917–37; 109-page diary of Elizabeth Ellen and Emma Estelle Martin, 1900–1923, describing the siege of Peking; 41 diaries of Elleroy and Mabelle Smith, 1916–52; microfilm diary of Wilhelmina Vautrin, 1937–40, describing life and work at Ginling College, used by Mary Bosworth Treudley in her biography of Vautrin, *This Stinging Exultation*.

MANUSCRIPTS: 13 folders of typescript autobiography by Elizabeth Fisher Brewster, 1917; autobiographical writings of Elijah Bridgman, 1856, 1865; "History of the Peking Station of the North China Mission of the Women's Foreign Missionary Society of the Methodist Episcopal Church," by Mary Porter Gamewell, a 218-page handwritten history in a scrapbook, ca. 1938; typescript and handwritten copies of a report and history of Lingnan University, with summaries of letters, annual reports, and transcribed minutes of early Presbyterian mission meetings, by J. Stewart and Julia Mitchell Kunkle; "Seventy-five Years of the American Board in North China, 1860–1935," "The Foochow Mission of the American Board," 1942, and "Some Historical Notes Concerning the North China Mission of the American Board, 1935–1960," 1970, by Harold Matthews; "The Story of the Church of the Brethren in China, 1932 to 1950," compiled from letters, diaries, articles, interviews with missionaries, and other historical materials, by Martha (Neiderhiser) Parker, 1973; "Frank Joseph Rawlinson: A Bio-bibliography," by Helen Ann Rawlinson, n.d.

ORAL HISTORIES: *China Missionary Oral History Collection*, transcripts, ed. by Cyrus H. Peake and Arthur L. Rosenbaum (Claremont Graduate School, Oral History Program), 1973 (see ORAL HISTORIES Union List for the names of participants); transcript of Midwest China Oral History and Archives project interview of Anne (Edwards) and Robert Brank Fulton; transcript of interview with Randolph Sailer, 1979; 13 tapes of interviews with William E. Schubert, n.d.

DISSERTATIONS/THESES: *Women in a Changing China: The YWCA*, by Jean McCown Hawkes, 1971. *Francis Lister Hawks Pott—1864–1947: China Missionary and Educator*, by John N. Hawkins, 1971. *The Cross in Conquest over China*, by Clara Jones, 1971.

FINDING AIDS: In-house register.

8-ARCHIVES OF THE CHINESE STUDENTS' CHRISTIAN ASSOCIATION IN NORTH AMERICA (RG 13), 1909–52, 1.5 l.f.

Background note: The Chinese Students' Christian Association (CSCA) in North America was founded in 1909 and was affiliated with the Committee on Friendly Relations Among Foreign Students of the International Committee of the YMCAs of North America, the National Committee of the YMCA in China, the Chinese Students' Christian Union of Great Britain and the Chinese YMCA in France. The Association provided Christian training and practical services to Chinese students arriving from or going to China.

MINUTES/RECORDS/REPORTS: Constitution and by-laws, 1909–22; financial records, 1927–51; minutes, 1914–50; officers and staff, 1916–34; reports, 1911–50.

CORRESPONDENCE: 12 folders of correspondence, 1918–50, including the following correspondents: Welthy H. Fisher, Lyman Hoover, Stanton Lautenschlager, J. Leighton Stuart, the United Board for Christian Colleges in China, and West China Union University in Chengtu.

MANUSCRIPTS: Notes on CSCA history and documents, n.d.

FINDING AIDS: In-house register.

9-ARCHIVES OF THE COUNCIL FOR WORLD MISSION (RG 59), 1821–1951, 372 microfiches

Background note: The originals of these materials are at the library of the School of Oriental and African Studies, London.

MINUTES/RECORDS/REPORTS: London Missionary Society, minutes, 1856–1939; papers of Robert Morrison, n.d.: Anglo-Chinese College, report on missions; Tyerman and Bennet deputation, report, 1821–29; Fukien, 1866–1939; South China, 1866–1939; North China, 1866–1939; Central China, 1866–1940; Peking Union Medical College, minutes, n.d.; Siaokan Hospital, n.d.; Amoy district, committee minutes, 1903–24, 1878–1912; North China district, committee minutes, 1874–1920; Hong Kong and New Territories Evangelical Society, minutes, 1904–32; F. H. Hawkins, deputation, 1917; Central China district, committee minutes, 1932–37; Lockhart, records and accounts(?), n.d.

CORRESPONDENCE: London Missionary Society, outgoing letters to China, 1822–1914; Fukien, incoming letters, 1845–1939; outgoing letters, 1928–39; South China, incoming letters, 1803–1939; outgoing letters, 1928–39; North China, incoming letters, 1860–1939; outgoing letters, 1928–39; Central China, incoming letters, 1843–1939; outgoing letters, 1928–39; letters of Robert Morrison, n.d.; miscellaneous letters from missionaries to friends, n.d.; letters from Marjorie Clements in North China, 1930–33; George and Dorothy Barbour, letters from North China, 1920–36; correspondence of J. Legge, n.d.; letters, letterbook of Mrs. L[egge], n.d.; correspondence of Peking Union Medical College, n.d.; letters regarding a book by M. Aldersey, n.d.; correspondence of W. H. Somervell regarding British Foreign Bible Society Chinese Bible, n.d.

DIARIES: South China, journals, 1807–42; North China, journals, 1863–64; Central China, journals, 1888–96; George and Dorothy Barbour, diary, 1920–36; Terrell diaries, n.d.

MANUSCRIPTS: Sermons by J. Legge, n.d.; articles and notes on literary and language work, by J. Legge; address by J. Legge on Amoy Induction, 1874; papers of E. Hope Bell, n.d.; "Discipleship," by Eric Liddell, n.d.; autobiographical sketch by F. A. Brown, 1935–51; notes on Peking Hospital by Dudgeon, n.d.; Hankow Medical Planning papers, n.d.; notes by Medhurst, 1848–52; Boxer Indemnity papers, n.d.; miscellaneous notes on Chinese Church leaders, n.d.

MEMORABILIA: Biographical materials on Legge, including clippings, obituaries, and reviews; obituary of Griffith John, n.d.; Chinese medal.

MAPS/DESIGNS/DRAWINGS: Rubbings of Nestorian Tablet, n.d.

FINDING AIDS: "Guide to the Archives of the Council for World Mission," by the Interdocumentation Company, Switzerland.

10-GEORGE SHERWOOD EDDY PAPERS (RG 32), 1911–61, ca. 15 folders

Background note: George Sherwood Eddy (1871–1963) travelled to China in the early part of the century holding evangelistic meetings with John Mott, as part of their tours of Asia. The items listed below are only part of a much larger collection.

MINUTES/RECORDS/REPORTS/CORRESPONDENCE: 7 folders of "report letters" from China, 1914–16, 1918, 1922, 1931–32, 1934.

CORRESPONDENCE: Correspondence with Eugene Barnett, 1952, 1960–61, and Kenneth S. Latourette, 1953, 1955.

MANUSCRIPTS: 13 essays, 1922–49, on subjects including Feng Yü-hsiang, South China, Manchuria, U.S. China policy, Civil War in China, and the use of Chiang K'ai-shek's troops; folder of notes on China, 1935, n.d.

MEMORABILIA: File of clippings on China, 1955, n.d.; file of clippings on Y. T. Wu, ca. 1949.

PAMPHLETS: *How China's Leaders Received the Gospel*, n.d.

AUDIO-VISUAL MATERIALS: Folder of photos documenting meetings led by Eddy in Foochow and Hong Kong, 1913–14; folder of miscellaneous photos of China, ca. 1915–1936, n.d.; folder of photos from souvenir album, 1914–15.

FINDING AIDS: In-house register.

11-DWIGHT EDWARDS PAPERS (RG 12), 1906–49, 19 boxes (8 l.f.)

Background note: Dwight Woodbridge Edwards (1883–1967) first went to China under the YMCA, serving in several administrative positions until 1946. His wife, Mary E. Vanderslice Edwards, was a missionary under the American Board of Commissioners for Foreign Missions serving as director of kindergarten training at the North China College for Women. Edwards was also executive secretary of the Peking United International Famine Relief Committee from 1920 to 1922, which led to the formation of the China International Famine Relief Commission, and field director of United China Relief (later known as United Service to China). After retiring from the YMCA in 1946, he was executive secretary of the Administrative Committee of Yenching University. He and his family returned to the United States in 1949.

MINUTES/RECORDS/REPORTS: Annual reports and conference reports relating to YMCA, Princeton-in-Peking and Princeton-Yenching Foundation, 1907-ca. 1942, including reports on North China, Tatungfu, Suiyuan, Lanchow, Princeton-Yenching Rural Demonstration Center at Ching-ho, Northwest China, and Mukden; reports and printed material of the following organizations: California College in China, 1951; China International Famine Relief Commission, 1923–49; Church World Service—China office, 1948–50; Peking Union Church, 1954–55; Princeton-in-Peking/Princeton-Yenching Foundation, ca. 1905–1958; United China Relief, ca. 1945; United Service to China, 1948–51; Yenching Alumni Association, 1951–59; Yenching University, 1949; YMCAs of China and Korea, 1912, 1917; YMCA-World Service Fellowship; miscellaneous reports on China Christian colleges, the political and religious situation in China, famine relief and social welfare, 1912–49.

CORRESPONDENCE: Correspondence, 1924–65, including the following correspondents: Eugene E. Barnett, 1927–50; China International Famine Relief Commission, 1951–64; William P. Fenn, 1948–58; Robert Gailey, 1924, and W. B. Pettus, 1927, documenting disputes within the missionary ranks; B. A. Garside, 1947–49; Wallace C. Merwin, 1956; Princeton-Yenching Foundation, 1949–52; J. Leighton Stuart, 1954, 1956; United Board for Christian Colleges in China, 1948–54; United Board for Christian Higher Education in China, 1958; United Service to China, 1948–50; and George D. Wilder, 1927.

MANUSCRIPTS: "The Mission to China of Dwight Woodbridge and Mary Vanderslice Edwards," by Robert Brank Fulton (their son-in-law), 1982; addresses, articles and reports written by Edwards, including 5 folders on analysis of the China situation, 1911–1940s; folder on anti-Christian movement in China, 1922–ca.1925; 7 folders of biographical sketches on Djang Bo-ling and Ding Li-mei, Courtney H. Fenn, William P. Fenn, Robert Gailey, Walter Lowrie, and Hollis Wilbur; 5 folders on famine relief, ca.

1920-ca. 1943; 2 folders of miscellaneous manuscripts, 1916–51; 2 boxes of handwritten and typescript drafts, notes, source material, and card file for Edwards' history of Yenching University, ca. 1956, later published by UBCHEA; box of notes, including a folder apiece on Peking University from 1890 to 1922, the Peking YMCA and Princeton-in-Peking, 1912, 1918, and United Service to China, 1949.

MEMORABILIA: Edwards' address book, n.d.; biographical documentation, 1918–38, 1943–49, 1951–67; travel documents, 1918, 1939–45, n.d.

MAPS/DESIGNS/DRAWINGS: Map of famine area, n.d.

FINDING AIDS: In-house register.

12-FOSTER FAMILY PAPERS, (RG 1), 1888–1916, 7 l.f.

Background note: John Barton Foster (1822–97), his son, John Marshall Foster (1857–1924), and Clara (Hess) Foster (1859–1948), were Baptist missionaries. John Marshall Foster, who graduated from Colby College (Class of 1877), served as a missionary in Swatow under the American Baptist Missionary Union beginning in 1887. Clara Hess joined the South China mission in 1886 or 1887 to assist Adele M. Fielde, before her marriage to John Marshall Foster. In 1894 John Marshall and Clara Foster left China, returning in 1897 and 1898 until the Boxer Rebellion forced their departure in 1900. Foster returned again in 1914 and Clara joined him the following year; he left China in 1921, but she stayed with her children until she died in 1948.

Anna E. Foster (d. 1968), their daughter, went to China in 1917 under the American Baptist Mission Society; she taught in Meihsien until 1940. Frank Clifton Foster (1894–1973), also a graduate of Colby College (Class of 1916), was a Presbyterian minister who taught at the Swatow Academy in Swatow from 1916 to 1919, and served with the YMCA in Siberia and Manchuria for six months during World War I. Their other son, John Hess Foster (b. 1891), and his wife, Helen Thomas Foster, graduates of Colby College, Classes of 1913 and 1914, respectively, both served as medical missionaries. Born in Swatow, John Hess Foster returned to China in 1919 as Yale Medical School's appointee to its Medical School in Changsha and served on the staff of the Hunan-Yale (Hsiang-Ya) Hospital until 1927. See also Colby College, Miller Library, Waterville, ME, 04901; and Yale-in-China collection at Yale University, Department of Manuscripts and Archives, Sterling Library, 120 High Street, New Haven, CT, 06520.

CORRESPONDENCE: 6 boxes of correspondence containing: letter from Adele M. Fielde to Elizabeth B. Foster, 1888; letters to John Marshall Foster, 1884–1921, including such correspondents as William Ashmore, Mr. and Mrs. John Barton Foster, and other family members; correspondence of Clara Hess Foster, 1889–1916, mostly to her husband's parents, Mr. and Mrs. John Barton Foster, and other family members; letters from William Ashmore to John Barton Foster, 1891, n.d., and to Elizabeth B. Foster, 1888, 1894, 1900; correspondence of John Hess Foster, including Edward H. Hume, 1922, 1927; Roger S. Greene, 1923; W. H. Lingle, 1927; Dickson H. Leavens, 1927, 1936–40; and Z. M. Tien, 1928–29.

DIARIES: Ca. 3,400 typed and hand-written pages of journals of John Marshall Foster, 1888–1903, 1908–16, recording daily life in South China, with notes on political and religious matters, the Boxer Rebellion, and Foster's travels; journal of Clara Hess Foster, 1915–16, containing family and travel news; diaries of John Hess Foster, 1918–19, 1925, 1944–49.

MANUSCRIPTS: "The Situation at Swatow—Missionaries" and "The Sunday School at Swatow," both by John Marshall Foster, ca. 1890; 3 sermons by John Marshall Foster, 1892; medical writings by John Hess Foster, including 2 notebooks of "Medical Service" at Hsiang-Ya Hospital, 1922–74.

PAMPHLETS: Miscellaneous printed materials on Adele M. Fielde, n.d.

MEMORABILIA: Genealogical and biographical study of the Foster family, written in 1974 by John Hess Foster; biographical information on John Marshall and Clara Hess Foster, including notes on Adele M. Fielde; directory of the American and European Community, Changsha, 1925–26.

MAPS/DESIGNS/DRAWINGS: Map of China, Changsha, mission fields of Northern Baptists in China, 1940, showing mission stations except the Roman Catholics.

AUDIO-VISUAL MATERIALS: 12 folders of photos, mostly undated, including Adele M. Fielde, Foster family, unidentified individuals in China, China scenes and Swatow, and students at Lingnan University in 1927.

CHINESE LANGUAGE MATERIALS: Hymnal of John Marshall Foster, n.d.; workbook of Chinese language, possibly written by Adele M. Fielde, 1869; miscellaneous unidentified written and printed materials.

FINDING AIDS: In-house register.

13-HARTWELL FAMILY PAPERS (RG 4), 1849–1975, 7 l.f.

Background note: Jesse Boardman Hartwell, Jr. (1835–1912), organized the first Protestant church in China north of Shanghai and aided refugees during the Taiping Rebellion. Hartwell first went to China in 1858, moving from Shanghai to Chefoo in 1860 and then to Tungchow, where he remained until 1875. After a brief return to the United States, he went back to China from 1893 until his death. His children, Anna Burton Hartwell (1870–1961), Charles Norris Hartwell (1884–1927), Lottie (Hartwell) Ufford (b. 1882), and Nellie (Hartwell) Beattie also worked in China.

MINUTES/RECORDS/REPORTS: East China Baptist mission, 1934, 1948; minutes and reports on Hangchow, 1946, 1948; Shanghai, 1937; Chekiang Shanghai Baptist Convention, 1949; Shaohing, 1933, 1936–37; Principal's report, 1947–48.

CORRESPONDENCE: Family correspondence, 1849–1941, including letters of Hartwell and his first wife, Eliza Jewett, during their married life in China, letters of Matthew Yates (1871, 1875) and discussions of anti-foreign sentiment, mission history, and living conditions.

DIARIES: 24 private notebooks of Anna B. Hartwell, 1889–1944.

MANUSCRIPTS: 2 notebooks of A. Frank Ufford, Shaohing, ca. 1934–48; typescripts on Christianity, Communism, relief work, T. C. Bau, William H. Warren, travel, work in East China, by Ufford, 1938–53, and n.d.; manuscript and draft of "The Burning Bridge," an autobiography and interpretative history by Ufford; "China in Retrospect," by K. K. Thompson, n.d.; notes for essays on missions, Christianity, Communism, Japan, and Chekiang, 1929–51; sermons by Ufford, n.d.; "Christian Experience," by Mrs. Wilson Chen, n.d.; play script, n.d.; "Experience of Anna B. Hartwell in Hwanghien, China," n.d.; travel sketches, by Ufford, n.d.; "Shaohing Pioneer Missionaries," by Ufford, n.d.; "Clarissa Hewey's Story of Her Early Days in Kinhwa," 1960.

MEMORABILIA: Autograph collection of Ufford, 1910–51; articles by Ufford, 1932–38; miscellaneous printed materials on missions; travel pass of Ufford and his wife, Lottie, from American

Consular Service, Shanghai, 1925; biographical information on the Uffords.
ORAL HISTORIES: "Refugee Recordings," by Martha Wilson, 1939.
AUDIO-VISUAL MATERIALS: 32 folders of undated photos including views of Chinese buildings, people, and scenes, missionaries and friends, schools in China, Northern Presbyterian mission, Hartwells, Harry Luce, his son Henry Luce, the burning of the Chapei section of Shanghai in 1937, and mission work in Shaohing; 2 photo albums, one of Shaohing, n.d.; "The Future of Christian Missions in China," a memorandum of informal discussions by China missionaries returning on the USS *Breckinridge*, 1938.
CHINESE LANGUAGE MATERIALS: 4 letters to Jesse Boardman and Eliza Jewett Hartwell, 1870; memorial pamphlet with photos of Hartwell family; Bible reference and unidentified pamphlet of Anna Burton Hartwell; folder of miscellaneous unidentified materials.
FINDING AIDS: In-house register.

14-ELLISON AND LOTTIE HILDRETH PAPERS (RG 15), 1901–1940s, ca. 6 l.f.
Background note: Ellison Story (1884–1962) and Lottie Rowe Lane Hildreth (1882–1977) were American Baptist missionaries in South China from 1913 to 1937. After two years of language study in Kakchieh, they were assigned to Chaochowfu and Swatow as teachers. See also Mount Holyoke College, Williston Memorial Library, College History and Archives, South Hadley, MA, 01075–1493.
CORRESPONDENCE: Ca. 5 boxes of correspondence between the Hildreths and family members, friends, mission associates, and others, ca. 1913–1940, including Mabel Adams, Benjamin F. Allen, American Baptist Foreign Mission Society, William Ashmore, Alice and Ben Baker, Bob Bartholomew, Charlton Bolles, C. W. Brinstad, E. S. Butler, [Edward ?] Capen, Brooks Clark, [?] Haggard, [H. G. C.?] Hallock, W. B. Herrick, Kenneth and Waneta Hobart, Enid Johnson, Hellen Barrett Montgomery, John R. Mott, Helen Smith, William K. Towner, Edith Traver, Ruth Van Kirk, and Fanny Wickes; abstract of letter regarding Baptist Central China Mission, 1914.
MANUSCRIPTS: "The Anti-Christian Movement in Swatow," 1926; "Early Mission History of the Swatow Region Brought Down to the Present for the American Baptist Mission," by Emanuel H. Giedt, 1946–53, n.d.; "The Present Apparent Conflict between Foreign and Nationalist Interests in China, with a Suggested Plan of Reconciliation," by Ellison Story Hildreth, 1927 (thesis submitted to Rochester Theological Seminary); miscellaneous writings by Ellison Hildreth, 1925, n.d.; 4 folders of writings by Lottie Lane Hildreth on China, 1914–40, n.d.; untitled skit, n.d.; other miscellaneous writings about China.
DIARIES: "South China Diary," by A. S. Adams, 1928–33; diary fragments by Lottie Hildreth, 1901–28.
MEMORABILIA: Miscellaneous memorabilia of Lottie Hildreth, 1901–28; travel documents, 1917–27; Chinese calling cards, n.d.; postcards of China; straw slippers, models of bound feet, and other artifacts.
MAPS/DESIGNS/DRAWINGS: Bamboo artwork, scrolls, and rubbing of a granite memorial to Ellison Story and others, n.d.
AUDIO-VISUAL MATERIALS: Photos of Hildreth family, 1901–42; individual and group portraits of China missionaries and their children, 1913–42, n.d., and of Chinese people, 1914–40; photos of China, 1914–35.
SERIALS: *Kakchieh Weakly News*, 1914.
CHINESE LANGUAGE MATERIALS: New Testaments and hymnal, 1908, 1931, n.d.; unidentified materials, n.d.
FINDING AIDS: In-house register.

15-LYMAN HOOVER PAPERS (RG 9), 1900–1977, 22 l.f.
Background note: Lyman Hoover (1901–86) worked as a missionary under the auspices of the YMCA from 1930 to 1949, based in Shanghai, Peking, and Chungking. See also Young Men's Christian Association of the U.S.A. Archives, University of Minnesota, Social History Welfare Archives, 2642 University Avenue, St. Paul, MN, 55114.
MINUTES/RECORDS/REPORTS: YMCA in China: financial material, 1939–48; meeting minutes, 1928–49; reports and statements, 1927–55.
CORRESPONDENCE: Correspondence between Hoover and his family, 1924–67; correspondence with individuals, organizations, and YMCA staff, 1923–75, including such correspondents as Bertha and Eugene Barnett, Fletcher Brockman, Chinese Students' Christian Association, Chungking Missionary Association, Harold and Reba Colvin, Community Church of Shanghai, Rowland Cross, Dwight and Mary Edwards, John King Fairbank, George and Geraldine Fitch, Friends Ambulance Unit, Chungking, William Hines, C. S. Richard Hu, Charles and Dorothy Jorgensen, Walter and Miriam Judd, Kiang Wen-han, Carleton and Harriet Lacy, Kenneth S. Latourette, S. C. Leung, Orrin and Ellen Magill, Herbert Minard, Paul and Margaret Moritz, John R. Mott, National Christian Council of China, Jay C. and Lucile Oliver, George and Betty Osborn, David M. Paton, Peking Union Church, Claude L. and Elizabeth Pickens, Frank W. Price, Andrew and Margaret Roy, Dwight and Gertrude Rugh, Society of Friends of Moslems in China, Lennig and Helen Sweet, Winburn Thomas, Y. C. Tu, Luther and Jo Tucker, United Board for Christian Colleges in China, United Board for Christian Higher Education in China, United China Relief, United Service to China, Henry P. Van Dusen, Hollis Wilbur, Robert Parmelee Wilder, Y. T. Wu, YMCA, YWCA, Walter Zimmerman, and Samuel Marinus Zwemer.
DIARIES: Diaries and appointment books, 1926–74.
MANUSCRIPTS: Essays and articles by Hoover, 1918–48, primarily on his personal beliefs and relationship to the missions movement, YMCA student work and Muslims in China; manuscripts and notes, 1900–1976, on subjects such as Chinese Protestant leaders, Chinese organizations, Muslims in China, missionary preparation, Peiping Union Church, student situation in China, United Board for Christian Higher Education in China, United Service to China, YMCA in China (student work, study groups, training programs, relief, personnel), and the Chinese Students' Christian Association.
MEMORABILIA: 3 folders of biographical material, 1907–76; 2 folders of miscellaneous unidentified memorabilia, 1922–62 and n.d.; travel documents, legal documents, 1930–66.
AUDIO-VISUAL MATERIALS: Folder of photos relating to Muslims in China, 1931–41, n.d.; 8 folders of photos, mostly unidentified, 1919–70.
SERIALS: *Chinese Recorder*, 1931–40. YMCA of China: *Chinese Y's Men's Bulletin*, 1946; *Fellowship Notes*, 1930–31, 1933, 1935.

CHINESE LANGUAGE MATERIALS/SERIALS: *Hsiao-hsi (News)*, 1947–48. *The Student China*, V 1, N 1–2, n.d.
CHINESE LANGUAGE MATERIALS: 8 folders of language-study materials, ca. 1931–1932; 5 folders of miscellaneous advertisements and printed materials, n.d.; worship manual; 4 folders of miscellaneous YMCA publications, 1934–49; miscellaneous YMCA periodicals, n.d.; passports and travel documents, n.d.
FINDING AIDS: In-house register.

16-WILLIAM RICHARD JOHNSON PAPERS (RG 6), 1836–1966, 17.5 l.f.

Background note: William Richard Johnson (1878–1967) was a Methodist missionary. He and his wife, Ina Buswell Johnson, sailed for China in 1906. They went to Shanghai, then to Nanch'ang until 1927, returning from 1929 until repatriated in 1942.
MINUTES/RECORDS/REPORTS: University of Nanking, minutes, 1909–10; Educational Union, constitution, 1911; Kiangsi mission, minutes, 1913; Nanchang Academy, catalogue, 1923; Nanchang, individual accounts, 1927; China Famine Relief Fund, 1928; Kiangsi International Famine Relief Committee, 1931–33; Kuling Estate Council, minutes, 1935; Nanking Theological Seminary, program, 1935; Yungfeng Refugee Camp, 1939; American Red Cross China Relief Unit, 1940; Kiangsi Christian Rural Service Union, 1943–44, 1949–50; Peking Christian Conference, 1951; personal financial records of William Johnson, 1901–66; budgets and reports regarding mission affairs, 1911, 1914–20, 1926, 1930, 1933–39, 1941; Nanchang Building Academy Building Committee, agreement, 1925; Kuling Estate, agreement, 1935; mission finances, n.d.; family medical records, 1929–66.
CORRESPONDENCE: 10 boxes of family correspondence, 1836–1966; 15 boxes of general correspondence, 1852–1966, including such correpondents as James Whitford Bashford, Lauress J. Birney, Soong Mei-ling, F. C. Gale, J. G. Vaughan, Fred R. Brown, Ralph A. Ward, R. E. Dieffendorfer, L. R. Craighill, Walter Judd, Hwa Hsing Tung, Hsu Hsi Chi, Wilbur Emory Hammaker, C. K. Shaw, and Herbert Welch; printed newsletters from missionaries.
DIARIES: "Mrs. Brown's Diary of Nanchang Events," 1926–27; diaries of William Johnson, 1887–88, 1890–94, 1896, 1898, 1905–8, 1938; diaries of Ina Johnson, 1906, 1910, 1922, n.d.
MANUSCRIPTS: 5 boxes of writings by William Johnson, 1909–61, on subjects such as Nanchang Academy, famine relief, Communism, Methodist work in Nanchang, Chiang K'ai-shek, Protestantism, U.S. foreign policy and China, persecution of Chinese Christians, and rural reconstruction; 5 boxes of writings by others, 1897–1961, including subjects such as Christian colleges, Japan, famine and famine relief, rural reconstruction, Kuling, Soong Mei-ling, Nanchang Academy, Sun Yat-sen, and Communism; box of miscellaneous notes of William Johnson, 1908–66, n.d.; 2 folders of miscellaneous notes of Ina Johnson, 1936–37, 1961, n.d.
MEMORABILIA: Address books and lists, 1943–62, n.d.; card file, 1950–53; date books, 1919–63; address books of Ina Johnson, n.d.; biographical information on Johnson family, 1897–1956; announcements, 1939–65; autograph albums, 1885, 1890; bon-voyage book for Laura S. Buswell on her trip to China, n.d.; Chinese postcards, n.d.; Chinese greeting cards, n.d.; currency, 1915, 1918, n.d.; deacon's credentials, 1908; elder's credentials, 1908; Shanghai Tiffin Club, list of members, 1928.

MAPS/DESIGNS/DRAWINGS: 3 folders of miscellaneous maps and drawings, 1925–32, n.d.
AUDIO-VISUAL MATERIALS: Folder of photos of buildings in China, 1897–1938; folder of photos of Chinese individuals, 1922–64; 2 folders of photos, including Japanese atrocities in China, and family, 1937–64.
CHINESE LANGUAGE MATERIALS: 4 folders of unidentified materials, 1927, 1936–37, n.d.
FINDING AIDS: In-house register.

17-KENNETH SCOTT LATOURETTE PAPERS (RG 3), 1861–1968, quantity undetermined

Background note: Kenneth Scott Latourette (1884–1968) was a professor of missions and Oriental history at Yale University. He taught at the College of Yale-in-China, in Changsha, from 1910 to 1912 and later served on the United Board for Christian Colleges in China and the Yale-in-China Association. The materials listed below represent only a portion of a large collection.
CORRESPONDENCE: Correspondence of Latourette with his family and organizations including American Baptist Foreign Mission Society, American Bible Society, China Medical Board, Federal Council of Churches of Christ in America, International Board of the YMCA, Oberlin-in-China Association, United Board for Christian Colleges in China, United China Relief, World Council of Churches, World's Student Christian Federation, and Yale-in-China Association; correspondents include Miner Searle Bates, Harlan Page Beach, Robert Brank Fulton, Kenneth Gray Hobart, Lyman Hoover, Dickson Leavens, John R. Mott, David R. Porter, Frank Price, Dwight Rugh, Henry Pitney Van Dusen, Luther Allan Weigle, and Frederick Wells Williams.
DIARIES: 5 volumes of diaries, 1905–16, documenting Latourette's experiences as a faculty member of Yale-in-China.
MANUSCRIPTS/PAMPHLETS/MEMORABILIA: Manuscript drafts, 1933–68, of book reviews, articles, papers, lecture notes, clippings, pamphlets, memorabilia, printed material and other papers; 2 drafts of "The Chinese: Their History and Culture"; "The China That Is to Be," 1949; "Protestant Higher Education in China: An Historical Sketch and Appraisal," n.d.; clippings of published articles on Christian missions in China from serials such as *Chinese Recorder* and *International Review of Missions*, 1916–67.
FINDING AIDS: In-house register.

18-ARCHIVES OF THE TRUSTEES OF LINGNAN UNIVERSITY (RG 14), 1898–1982, 29 l.f.

Background note: This collection represents the official archives of the Trustees of Lingnan University from 1952 to the present, complementing the earlier archives which were sent to Harvard University in the late 1950s. The majority of material relates to Lingnan after the trustees diverted funds to institutions outside the mainland. Materials on these institutions, the Chinese University of Hong Kong, Chung Chi College, Hong Kong Baptist College, Lingnan College, Lingnan Institute of Business Administration, and Lingnan Middle School, are also included in the collection. See also Harvard University, Harvard-Yenching Library, 2 Divinity Avenue, Cambridge, MA, 02138.
MINUTES/RECORDS/REPORTS/CORRESPONDENCE: Documents and correspondence, 1927–80, including: agreements of Trustees of Lingnan, alumni associations, Lingnan University Medical College, and United Board for Christian Colleges in

China; agendas, minutes, records, and documents, 1945–82, including constitution and by-laws, 1949–62; annual and semi-annual meetings of the Board of Trustees, 1946–82; financial records, 1919–81.

AUDIO-VISUAL MATERIALS: 15 boxes of photos including scenes of Lingnan University buildings and grounds, 1906–73, campus life, 1903–49, portraits of students and staff, 1900–1977, portraits of trustees and directors, 1905–66, South China, 1908–33, and miscellaneous subjects, 1900–1939.

FINDING AID: In-house register.

19-METHODIST MISSIONARY SOCIETY ARCHIVES (RG 69), 1829–1947, 1,760 microfiches

Background note: The originals of these materials are housed in the library of the School of Oriental and African Studies, London.

MINUTES/RECORDS/REPORTS: Wesleyan Methodist Missionary Society, China Synod minutes, 1853–1946; Women's Work Collection, China reports, 1939–41; overseas schedules, 1923–46.

CORRESPONDENCE: Wesleyan Methodist Missionary Society correspondence with Canton, 1851–1905; Hunan, 1907–45; Hupeh, 1905–45; Ningpo, 1933–46; North China, 1933–45; South China, 1905–45; South West China, 1932–45; Wenchow, 1933–45; Wuchang, 1876–1905; China (general) 1924–34, 1936–37; Women's Work Collection correspondence with South China, 1920–47; South West China, 1943–45; North China, 1933–45; Hunan, 1921–45; Hupeh, 1921–45; Ningpo, 1933–45; Wenchow, 1933–45.

MEMORABILIA: 9 folders of biographical data on China personnel, including David Hill, Samuel Pollard, and G. Stephenson, 1829–69.

FINDING AIDS: "Guide to the Methodist Missionary Society Archives," by the Interdocumentation Company, Switzerland.

20-MISSIONS PAMPHLET COLLECTION (RG 31), 1706–1976, ca. 20 l.f.

Background note: The Missions Pamphlet Collection, totalling 225 l.f., consists primarily of printed materials, such as reports, brochures, short monographs, maps, and hymn books.

MINUTES/RECORDS/REPORTS/PAMPHLETS: Reports, pamphlets, and other printed materials of the following organizations: Series I: Agricultural Missions, 1931–50; Allegemeiner Evangelische Protestantischer Missionsverein, 1884–1905; American and Foreign Bible Society, 1836–40; American Baptist Foreign Mission Society: China (general), 1894–1953; East China Mission, 1909–50; South China Mission, 1911–51; West China Mission, 1923–50; American Board of Commissioners for Foreign Missions: China (general), 1892–1951; Foochow Mission, 1896–1950; North China Mission, 1886–1952; Shaowu Mission, 1900–1923; South China Mission and Hong Kong Mission, 1892–1933; American Bureau for Medical Aid to China, 1942–46; American Chinese Educational Committee, n.d.; American Friends Board of Missions, 1892–1957; American Friends Service Committee, 1941–71; American Leprosy Missions, 1924–68; Associated Boards for Christian Colleges in China, 1932–47; Association for the Chinese Blind, 1915–51; Augustana Evangelical Lutheran Church, Board of Foreign Missions, 1927–58; Baptist Missionary Society, 1794–1942; Berliner Frauen-Missionsvereins für China, 1910–11, 1921; British and Foreign Bible Society, 1842; Catholic Mission stations, 1899–1952; China's Children Fund, 1943–51;

China Famine Relief Fund, 1878; China Christian Universities Association, 1948; China Inland Mission, 1872–1950; China International Famine Relief Commission, 1929–36; China Medical Board: by-laws, 1934–48; minutes, 1934–61; financial reports, 1935–49; China Mennonite Missions Society, 1919; Christian Literature Society for China, 1835, 1894–1931; Christliche Blindenmission im Orient, 1948, 1950; Church Committee for China Relief, 1938–44; Church Missionary Society, 1886–1917; Church of England, 1879–1952; Church of Scotland, 1796–1936; Church of the Brethren, General Brotherhood Board, 1939–56; Church World Service, 1946–56; Council on Higher Education in Asia, 1957; Det Danske Missionsselskab, 1880–1928; Deutsche China-Allianz-Mission, n.d.; Deutsche Evangelische Missions-Hilfe, 1927; The Evangel Mission, Shanghai, 1918, 1920; Evangelische Missionsgesellschaft in Basel, 1818–52; "Evangelize China" Fellowship, 1963; Foreign Missions Conference of North America: Commission on mission policies and methods in China, 1927–29; Committee on relief in China, 1938; Far Eastern Joint Office Committee, China Committee, 1946–50; Hakka Mission, n.d.; Hildesheimer China-Blinden-Mission, 1914; International Institute of China, 1895–1931; International Missionary Council, 1925–57; Kieler-China-Mission, 1909, 1921; Liebenzeller Mission, 1931–49; London Missionary Society, 1846–1922; Lutheran Church-Missouri Synod, Board of Foreign Missions, 1951.

Methodist Church, Board of Missions: newsletters, 1940–64; miscellaneous, 1939–48; China conference, 1940–41; Foochow conference, 1939–40, 1945–49; Hinghwa conference, 1939–40; Kalgan conference, 1939; Kiangsi conference, 1940; North China conference, 1939–40; Shantung conference, 1939–40; Yenping conference, 1939–40; Methodist Episcopal Church, Board of Foreign Missions: news releases, 1938; schools and hospitals, 1902–37; periodicals, 1924–35; miscellaneous, 1864–1939; Central conference, 1897; Chengtu West China conference, 1928, 1934; Chengtu Women's conference, 1926–30; Chungking West China conference, 1925–34; Chungking West China Women's conference, 1925; Eastern Asia Central conference, 1915, 1920, 1923, 1928, 1930, 1934, 1937; Hinghwa Women's conference, 1899, 1903, 1916, 1923, 1930; Shanghai district, 1904–18; Shantung conference, 1928, 1930–32, 1934, 1937; Shantung Women's conference, 1926; South Fukien conference, 1923–25, 1929–33; West China Women's conference, 1913–17, 1922–23, 1931, 1933, 1936–37, 1939; Yenping conference, 1917–18, 1920–22, 1926–28, 1931–32, 1934–38; Yenping Woman's conference, 1926–28, 1931; Methodist Episcopal Church, South, Board of Missions: miscellaneous, 1891–1940; schools and hospitals, 1917–39; conference reports, 1920–38.

Missionary Society of the Church of England in Canada, 1934–59; Nanking Theological Seminary, Board of Founders, 1951–63; National Council of the Churches of Christ in the U.S.A., Division of Overseas Ministries, Far Eastern Office, China Committee, 1950–64; Norwegian Lutheran Church of America, Women's Missionary Federation, 1921–26; Oberlin Shansi Memorial Association, 1908–56; Presbyterian Church in the United States, Board of World Missions, 1919–58; Presbyterian Church in the U.S.A., Board of Foreign Missions: China (general), 1888–1946; Canton Mission, 1887–1941; Hunan Mission, 1929–45; other stations, 1896–1950; Presbyterian Mission Press, 1875–1924; Chefoo School for the Deaf, 1918–41; Presbyterian Church of England,

Overseas Missions Committee and Women's Missionary Association, 1911–38; Presbyterian Church of New Zealand, Overseas Missions Committee, 1897–1927; Princeton University Center in China, 1906–20; Protestant Episcopal Church of the United States of America, Domestic and Foreign Missionary Society, China, 1837–1954; Reformed Church of America, 1863–1946; Reformed Presbyterian Church in North America, General Synod, Board of Foreign Missions, 1910; Rheinische Missionsgesellschaft, 1865–1904, 1941; South Chihli Mission, 1906–7; South China Baptist Mission, 1940; South China Boat Mission, 1951–52; Suomen Lähetysseura (Finska Missionssällskapet), 1947, 1960; United Board for Christian Colleges in China, 1945–56; United Board for Christian Higher Education in Asia, 1956–74; United China Relief, 1941–44; United Christian Missionary Society, 1921–50; United Church of Canada, Board of Foreign Missions, 1928–48; United Church of Christ, Western Reserve Association, China Task Force, 1970–71; United Committee for Christian Universities of China, n.d.; United Free Church of Scotland, 1901–21; United Lutheran Church in America, Board of World Missions, 1928, 1935; United Methodist Church (United States), Board of Global Ministries, n.d.; United Service to China, 1947–49; University of Pennsylvania Christian Association, 1912–16; Wesleyan Methodist Missionary Society, 1808–1927; Woman's Christian Medical College, Shanghai, American Board of Founders: lists of members and historical sketch, 1943–73; minutes, 1938–74; legal materials, 1924–74; financial material, 1932–74; scholarships and grants, 1961–75; operations, 1920–68; Woman's Union Missionary Society of America, 1875–1961; World Missionary Conference, Edinburgh: Commission I, 1910; Commission IV, 1910; Continuation Committee, 1913–24; World Student Christian Federation, 1909, 1936, 1967.

Series II, 1838–1952: American-Chinese Educational Commission, Canton Baptist Missionary Society, China Baptist Council, China Baptist Publication Society, China Bible House, China Bible School Movement, China Christian Education Association, China Christian Endeavor Union, China Fellowship of Reconciliation, China-for-Christ Movement, China Medical Association, China Medical Missionary Association, Chung-hua Sheng Kung Hui, Church of Christ in China, Committee on Christian Education in China, Committee on Church Union in West China, Conference of Hunan Missionaries, East China Educational Association, Educational Association of China, Evangelistic Association of China, Fookien Provincial Union, Hangchow Missionary Association, Kwangtung Christian Council, Kwongtung Christian Educational Association, The Life Fellowship, Medical Missionary Society in China, Mission Photo Bureau, Mount Zion in China, Nanking Church Council, Nanking International Relief Committee, Nanking Union Church, National Christian Conference of China, National Christian Council of China, National Committee for Christian Religious Education in China, North China Christian Rural Service Union, North Fukien Religious Tract Society, International Christian Workers' Fellowship Union, Peking Missionary Association, Peking Union Church, Ricksha Mission, Shanghai Christian Broadcasting Association, Shanghai Christian Evangelistic Association, Shanghai Community Church, Fitch Memorial Church, Shanghai-for-Christ Crusade, St. Peter's Church, South Fukien Religious Tract Society, Student Christian Movement of China, Tientsin Missionary Association, Union Lutheran Conference, West China Christian Educational Union, West China General Conference, West China Missions Advisory Board, West China Religious Tract Society, Woman's Missionary Association in China, Woman's Missionary Society—China conference, Young Men's Christian Association of China, Young Women's Christian Association of China, Youth and Religion Movement Mission to Southwest and West China.

Educational and Medical Institutions: The American Hospital for Refugees, Anglo-Chinese College, Blind Girls' School, Canton Christian College, Canton Hospital, Canton School for the Blind (Ming Sam School), Canton Union Theological College, Central China Teachers' College, Central China Union Lutheran Theological Seminary, Central China University, Cheeloo University, Chefoo Industrial Mission Schools, Christian Herald Fukien Orphanage and Industrial work, The Christian Hospital, College of Chinese Studies, David Hill School for the Blind (Hankow), Elizabeth Blake Hospital (Soochow), Foochow College, Foochow Missionary Hospital, Fukien Christian University, Ginling College, Goodrich Girls' School (Tunghsien), Hangchow Christian College, Hangchow Union Girls' High School, Hankow Union Hospital, Hill-Murray Institute for the Blind, Hope Hospital, Hopkins Memorial Hospital, Hospital for Women and Children, Hsiang-Ya Medical College, Huachung University, Hwa Mei Hospital, Hwa Nan College, I Fang Girls' Collegiate School, Jefferson Academy, Jenshow Industrial School (Szechwan), John G. Kerr Hospital for the Insane, Kuling School for Missionary Children, Ling Naam Hospital, Lingnan University, Lockhart Union Medical College, Lowrie High School, Lutheran Hospital, Margaret Williamson Hospital, Martyrs' Memorial Hospital, Mei Wa School, Mukden Medical College, Nantao Christian Institute, Nanking Theological Seminary, University of Nanking, North China American School, North China Theological Seminary, North China Union College, North China Union Language School, Orthopedic Hospital of Shanghai, Peiping Union Medical College, Peking Theological Seminary, Peking University, Ping Ting Hospital, Presbyterian Union Theological Seminary of Central China, Refuge for the Insane, Roberts Memorial Hospital, Shanghai American School, Shanghai Baptist College and Theological Seminary, Shanghai College, Shantung Christian University, Shantung Protestant University, Soochow University, Swatow Christian Institute, True Light Seminary, Tsinanfu Institute, Tsing Hua College, Tung Chow Rural Institute, Tungwen College, Université l'Aurore, West China Union University, Westminster College, Wiley Institute, and Yenching University; ca. 400 items (Appendix B), 1833–1971, not identified with organizations listed above.

MAPS/DESIGNS/DRAWINGS: 3 folders of maps and directories, 1910–53 and n.d.

DISSERTATIONS/THESES: *Missionary Participation in the Diplomacy of the United States in China: A Study of the Work of the Missionaries Bridgman, Parker, and Martin*, by C. G. G. Moss, 1926.

CHINESE LANGUAGE MATERIALS: Miscellaneous posters, n.d.; "Collection of Missionary Works in Chinese," 1835–72, n.d.; miscellaneous pamphlets, 1863–1966, n.d.

FINDING AIDS: In-house register.

21–JOHN R. MOTT PAPERS (RG 45), ca. 1896–1949, quantity undetermined

Background note: The materials listed below represent a small portion of an extensive collection.

MINUTES/RECORDS/REPORTS: Trip reports to Asia, 1907, 1913, 1935.

CORRESPONDENCE: General correspondence, 1886–1955, including such correspondents as Eugene E. Barnett, Fletcher S. Brockman, Arthur Judson Brown, Cheng Ching-yi, Chiang K'ai-shek, George Sherwood Eddy, Feng Yu-hsiang, S. P. Fenn, Fred Field Goodsell, Griffith John, T. Z. Koo, H. H. K'ung, Kenneth Scott Latourette, S. C. Leung, Walter Lowrie, Calvin and Julia Mateer, Frank W. Price, Ernest Pye, Ronald Rees, Arthur H. Smith, Anson Phelps Stokes, J. Hudson Taylor, Chengting Wang, A. L. Warnshuis, Luther A. Weigle, Robert P. Wilder, Wu Yi-fang, David Z. T. Yui, and Yun Chi Ho.

MANUSCRIPTS: Notes and notebooks on China, 1896–1949, and Chinese YMCA, 1896–98; addresses and articles on Fletcher Brockman (n.d.), Sherwood Eddy (1931), missions in Asia (1902), conferences of students and Christian workers in China (n.d.) and lessons for the student movement from evangelistic work among students in the Orient (n.d.).; drafts of C. Howard Hopkins' biography of Mott, including a chapter on the YMCA Foreign Department China work, n.d.

MEMORABILIA: Biographical data. including clippings, programs, posters, bulletins and publicity from Mott's trips to China in 1901, 1913, 1929, conferences and visits in China in 1906–7 and 1922, Pacific Basin tour in 1926, conferences and visits to Shanghai, Nanking, Peiping, and Hankow in 1935; biography files, including clippings, articles, brochures, reports and other printed materials on such individuals as Fletcher S. Brockman, Sherwood Eddy, Sun Yat-sen, and Dowager Empress Tze-hsi; subject files on education, evangelism, and missions in China, and YMCA International Committee work in China (ca. 1901–1912).

AUDIO-VISUAL MATERIALS: Folder of photos of WSCF conference in China, 1922; folder of unidentified photos in China, 1920s.

FINDING AIDS: In-house register.

22-SMITH FAMILY PAPERS (RG 5), 1894–1971, 6 l.f.

Background note: Edward Huntington Smith (1873–1968) and his daughter, Helen Huntington Smith (1902–71), were missionaries in Ing Tai and Foochow under the American Board of Commissioners for Foreign Missions. Edward Smith and his wife, Grace W. (Thomas) Smith (1874–1939), sailed for China in 1901 and they remained until he was expelled in 1950. Helen Smith taught at the Wen Shan Girls' School (also known as the Orlinda Childs Pierce Girls' School) in Foochow beginning in 1929, and participated in relief work in the 1940s. After leaving China, she was research consultant for the China Records Project at Yale University.

MINUTES/RECORDS/REPORTS: Minutes and reports of the International Anti-Opium Association, Fukien branch, 1922, and Chinese Industrial Cooperatives, 1939–40; 4 account books of Edward Smith, 1904–49; unidentified academic catalogues, 1916, 1924, n.d.; unidentified minutes and reports, 1900–1965.

CORRESPONDENCE: Letters from Edward Smith to his family in Norwich, Connecticut, including discussion of social change, missionary finances, education, bandits, travel, and the political situation in China; correspondence of Edward Smith, 1899–1945, including such correspondents as Harlan P. Beach, E. H. Cressy, Donald and Catherine Lin Hsueh, and Samuel Leger; box of correspondence of Helen Smith, 1910–70, including 4 letters to and from the YWCA of China in 1933; folder of excerpts of letters from Lewis Hodous to James Barton regarding the establishment

of Fukien University, 1912–14; 2 folders of memorial letters to Mary Lou Dixon regarding the death of Helen Smith, 1972.

MANUSCRIPTS: 2 boxes of notes and notebooks of Edward Smith, on Foochow Mission history and missions in general, including undated biographical essays, "My Friend, E. H. Smith," by Arthur O. Rinden and "The Man They All Love (Rev. Edward H. Smith)"; papers and short stories by Helen Smith, 1950–66; writings by others: "Experiences and Awakening of Uong Cu Buoi and Ing Hok Foochow Prefecture, Fukien Province, China," 1904; "Chinese Education," ca. 1910; "My Dung Jen School," 1947; "Memories of HHS Collected at the Time of Her Death," by Mary Lou Dixon and Gertrude Rinden, 1971; lists of students by Edward Smith, 1904–28.

PAMPHLETS: Printed materials including publications by the ABCFM on Foochow, papers by Sherwood Eddy, Frank Price, and others, news bulletins, flyers on missions, and other China-related pamphlets and reprints.

MEMORABILIA: Biographical material on the Smith family; clippings; music; poster, "60th Anniversary of Our Mother School," 1961; elementary school poster; "First Draft of Ingtai City Church, 1914"; document of rights of ownership and property from the U.S. Consulate, Foochow, 1938.

ORAL HISTORIES: Tape recordings by Helen Smith, n.d.

AUDIO-VISUAL MATERIALS: Box of loose photos of the Smith family, groups, and Chinese Christian religious art; 4 albums of unidentified photos; album/scrapbook entitled "Ing Hok District of Foochow Mission, China."

SERIALS: *China Bulletin*, 1950–52.

CHINESE LANGUAGE MATERIALS: Folder of unidentified pamphlets, n.d.; Ing-Tai High School and Elementary School, student directory and by-laws, 1913–37; Foochow Union Seminary, commencement program and classbook; calling cards, invitations, envelopes, church material, compositions, correspondence; ABCFM annual report, maps, block print, n.d.

FINDING AIDS: In-house register.

23-STM RESEARCH PAPERS (RG 41), 1948–51, 3 items

DISSERTATIONS/THESES: *The Development of Protestant Higher Education in China*, by Iver A. Sonnack, 1951. *The Evangelistic Campaigns of Sherwood Eddy in India and China, 1896–1931*, by William A. Imler, 1953. *Pioneer Protestant Educational Missionaries to China, 1807–1857*, by John William Arnold, 1948.

24-THOMAS TORRANCE PAPERS (RG 16), 1883–86, 4 l.f.

Restrictions: The Vale-Torrance Case correspondence is restricted until 1999.

Background note: Thomas Torrance (1871–1959) was a missionary under the China Inland Mission (CIM) in West Szechuan, beginning in 1895. After leaving the CIM in 1909, he returned to China in 1910 to head the West China Agency of the American Bible Society in 1910, and later was also in charge of the British and Foreign Bible Society in Chengtu until the early 1930s. Together with David Graham, he was instrumental in founding the West China Union University Archaeological Museum. His wife, Annie Elizabeth (Sharpe) Torrance, was a CIM missionary in Kuanhsien, near Chengtu. The collection is not yet fully processed.

MINUTES/RECORDS/REPORTS: Reports on work in Chengtu, 1915–33, n.d.; Songpan, Szechuan, 1932; Szechuan, 1933–34; hospital work, n.d.; and unidentified, 1934.

CORRESPONDENCE: 14 folders of correspondence between Torrance and his wife, 1928–35; 12 folders of correspondence between Torrance and his children, 1928–35; 10 folders of general correspondence, including such correspondents as the American Bible Society, 1911–12; John R. Hykes, 1917–20; Carleton Lacy, 1923–31; D. Z. Koo, 1937; Clarence H. C. Ramsey, 1935; and Johanna Madson Reynolds, 1955; letterbox of correspondence with the China Inland Mission and American Bible Society, regarding the Vale-Torrance Case, 1909–23; box of correspondence and papers of Archie R. Crouch, relating to the Church of Christ in China, 1945–49; National Christian Council of China, 1944–46; Stephen L. Peterson, 1985–86; and Thomas F. Torrance, 1985–86; correspondence between Crouch and Dennis A. Leventhal (Jewish Historical Society, Hong Kong) regarding an article on the Ch'iang 1987 (see PAMPHLETS below).

MANUSCRIPTS: Bibliography of Torrance's published works, n.d.; drafts and manuscript of unpublished book, *Conversion Stories of Chinese Christians*, 1896–1935; "The Decline and Possible Future of a Great Race: The Ch'iang People," by W. B. Djang, ca. 1948; miscellaneous stories and story fragments on Chinese Christians, n.d; memoirs of Annie Elizabeth Sharp Torrance, 1883–1927; "The Late Dr. J. H. McCartney of Chungking," n.d.; list of directors, members of councils, missionaries, and stations of the China Inland Mission, 1937.

PAMPHLETS/MEMORABILIA: Articles and leaflets by Torrance, 1910–52, including articles on the Ch'iang of West China; reviews of Torrance's writings, 1937; miscellaneous articles and publications collected by Torrance, 1902–84, n.d.; "The Jews in China: A Bibliography," by Rudolf Lowenthal, in *Yenching Journal of Social Studies*, 1939; "A Century of Bible Work in China," in *Chinese Recorder*, 1934; "A Resume of Border Research and Researchers," in *Journal of the West China Border Research Society*, 1934; statement of investment certificate, 1934; "Some Comments on the Origin and Beliefs of the Ch'iang People," by Schuyler V. R. Cammann, in *Hong Kong Jewish Chronicle*, 1986.

AUDIO-VISUAL MATERIALS: 60 slides, taken by Archie Crouch, of Ch'iang people in the villages of the Min River Valley in northern Szechwan (Lobochai, Chiashanchai, Jiherchueh, and Tsakulao), including views of an ancient swastika built into a wall and a Nestorian cross, 1945.

SERIALS: *West China Missionary News*, 1926.

CHINESE LANGUAGE MATERIALS: Tracts, including, "World's Foremost Question" and tract by a Ch'iang convert, ca. 1935; *Ch'iang Sacrificial Rites*, 1925; "The Sacrifice of the Lamb in the Old Testament is Just the Same as the Practice of Our Tribe," including translation, n.d.; unidentified letter, n.d.; 4 travel passes, 1916–35; Chinese scroll containing a tribute to Torrance, n.d.

CHINESE LANGUAGE MATERIALS/SERIALS: *Pien chiang fu wu (Border Mission Bulletin)*, 1945–47.

25-ARCHIVES OF THE UNITED BOARD FOR CHRISTIAN HIGHER EDUCATION IN ASIA (RG 11), 1882–1974, 206 l.f.

Background note: With the goal of coordinating educational policies and programs in China and coordinating financial assistance in the West, representatives of the boards of several colleges in China established the Permanent Committee for the Coordination and Promotion of Christian Higher Education in China in 1925. This predecessor of the United Board for Christian Higher Education in

Asia (UBCHEA) went through several name changes: Committee for Christian Colleges in China, 1928; Associated Boards for Christian Colleges in China (ABCCC), 1932; United Board for Christian Colleges in China (UBCCC), 1945; UBCHEA, 1955, which continues to the present. The original member colleges of the Associated Boards for Christian Colleges in China were: Central China College, Fukien Christian University, Ginling College, Hangchow Christian College, Lingnan University, University of Nanking, Shantung Christian College, Soochow University, West China Union University, and Yenching University, later joined by Hwa Nan College and the University of Shanghai. St. John's University, Huachung University, and Hangchow University were later members of the United Board for Christian Colleges in China. This collection represents the official archives, concentrating on materials from 1922 to 1957. The materials listed below represent only a sampling of this vast collection. See also Center for Research Libraries, 5721 Cottage Grove Avenue, Chicago, IL, 60637.

MINUTES/RECORDS/REPORTS/CORRESPONDENCE: General files from the ABCCC headquarters in New York, containing printed materials and correspondence, 1918–57, including the following: American Board of Commissioners for Foreign Missions, American Bureau for Medical Aid to China, China Christian Educational Association, China Medical Board, Christian Character, Church Committee for China Relief, William P. Fenn, L. Carrington Goodrich, Dr. and Mrs. Phillips Greene, Edward H. Hume, Oberlin-Shansi Memorial Association, Frank W. Price, Anson Phelps Stokes, United China Relief, and United Committee for Christian Universities of China (London).

General files of UBCCC headquarters in New York, containing printed materials and correspondence, 1924–65, including the following: audits from member colleges, Eugene E. Barnett, M. Searle Bates, Grace M. Boynton, Cheeloo University, China Christian Educational Association, China Christian Universities Association, China Medical Board, consent to use of names by Wellesley-Yenching Committee, East China Union University, enrollments and faculty of member colleges, reports from member colleges, insurance data on member colleges, Kenneth Scott Latourette, Roy S. Lautenschlager, minutes from meetings of member colleges, University of Nanking student records, mission boards, Oberlin-in-China Memorial Association, Dwight Rugh, St. John's Alumni Association in the U.S., Smith College, John Leighton Stuart, tax exemption papers for member colleges, Wellesley-Yenching committee, Yale-in-China Association, and Yenching College for Women.

Supplemental general files, containing printed reports, minutes, documents, records, and correspondence, 1912–74, of the following: Central Office of the China Union Universities, Permanent Committee for the Coordination and Promotion of Christian Higher Education in China, Committee for Christian Colleges in China, Associated Boards for Christian Colleges in China, United Board for Christian Colleges in China, United Board for Christian Higher Education in Asia; China College files, containing administrative, academic, and financial records, reports, and correspondence of the member colleges, 1882–1965.

General files on related organizations, 1906–61, including the China Christian Universities Association, East China Christian Educational Association, National Committee for Christian Religious Education in China, North China Union Language School,

Princeton-in-Asia, Princeton-in-Peking/Princeton-Yenching Foundation, Union Medical College, United Committee for Christian Universities of China, United Service to China, Wellesley-Yenching Committee, and Yale-in-China; financial record book of Huachung University, 1948–57; cash disbursements record book of UBCHEA, 1956–57; student records of University of Nanking, n.d.; financial record book of Yenching University, 1929–49.

PAMPHLETS: *Chinese Universities and the War*, by Oliver J. Caldwell, 1942; *Christianity in China*, by Hollington K. Tong, 1957; *Educational Problems in China*, by George B. Cressey, 1945; *An Evaluation of the Christian Universities in China*, by S. C. Leung, 1958; *The Foundations and Growth of Shantung Christian University*, by William M. Decker, 1948; *The Gripsholm*, by George Sokolsky, 1943; *Huachung University*, by John L. Coe, 1962; *Medical Education in China*, by Randolph Shields, 1936; *The Outlook for Christian Education in China*, by E. W. Wallace, 1936; *The Present Status of Christian Schools*, by Earl Herbert Cressy, 1936; list of educational institutions and organizations in China, n.d.; miscellaneous typescript and mimeographed material on medical work and medical education; publications of related organizations, 1920–61, on education, medical work and medical education, missionary activity and religion in China, teaching of English and miscellaneous subjects.

MEMORABILIA: Miscellaneous newspaper and magazine articles related to the China colleges; charters, diplomas, and certificates of member colleges; certificate of name change, Princeton-Yenching Foundation, 1956.

MAPS/DESIGNS/DRAWINGS: Pen and ink/pencil sketches of Ginling College, by Mary V. Thayer, ca. 1925–1926; maps of China and cities; blueprints and architectural drawings of member colleges.

AUDIO-VISUAL MATERIALS: 5 general films on China; film on Fukien Christian University; 9 films on Ginling College; film on Lingnan University; 2 films on University of Nanking; film on Shantung Christian University; film on UBCCC; film on West China Union University; 5 films on Yenching University; box of miscellaneous filmstrips.

Photos: 2 boxes of ABCCC conferences and dinners, 1935–40, and UBCCC students and other individuals, 1952–55; 4 albums and 2 boxes of Fukien Christian University, 1919–68, including buildings, scenes, students and faculty; 4 boxes and 4 albums of Ginling College, 1916–58, including alumnae, faculty, buildings and scenes; box of Hangchow Christian College, 1917–51, including student life, students, faculty and alumnae; box of Huachung University, 1931–48, including buildings and scenes, faculty, and students; box of Hwa Nan College, 1938–46, including buildings and scenes, faculty, students and alumnae; box of Lingnan University, 1899–1950, including buildings and scenes; 6 boxes and an album of the University of Nanking, 1912–47, including buildings and scenes, commencements and ceremonies, alumni, faculty and campus life; 4 folders of St. John's University, n.d., including buildings and scenes, faculty, and campus life; 2 folders of Shanghai University, n.d., including general scenes, individuals, and scenes of war damage; 3 boxes of Shantung Christian University, 1919–46, including buildings and scenes, faculty, graduates, and campus life; box of Soochow University, 1935–49, including buildings and scenes, faculty, students, and campus life; 3 boxes of West China Union University, 1934–47, including buildings and scenes, faculty, and campus life; 10 boxes and 4 albums of Yen-

ching University, 1920–50, including buildings, activities, faculty, and students; 5 boxes of miscellaneous and unidentified photos of China, 1890–1948; miscellaneous oversize photos of member colleges.

Slides: box of Ginling College, 3 boxes of the University of Nanking, box of West China Union University, 8 boxes of Yenching University, and 4 boxes of miscellaneous and unidentified slides, n.d.; 2 phonograph records, "Chinese College Women in War Time," produced by Ginling College, 1940; 17 soundscript discs of an ABCCC annual meeting, 1945; 2 cases of lantern slides of Shantung Christian University, n.d.

SERIALS: *Bulletin on China's Foreign Relations* (University of Nanking), 1931–35. *Campus Life* (Hangchow Christian College), 1930–34. Cheeloo University: *Cheeloo Magazine*, 1924–26; *Cheeloo News*, 1944–45; *Cheeloo Notes*, 1926; *Cheeloo Sketches*, 1927, 1929; *Cheeloo Weekly Bulletin*, 1923–30, 1932–33, 1937, 1948–49; *Monthly Bulletin*, 1933–41, 1946; *News Bulletin*, 1948–49; *Occasional Notes*, 1921–24; *Shantung Christian University Bulletin*, 1917–36, 1940–42. China Christian Educational Association, *Bulletin*, 1924–26, 1928–34, 1937–40. *China Colleges*, 1934–35, 1937–48. *Christian Colleges in China Progress Bulletin*, 1942–43. *Christian Colleges Newsletter*, 1943. *Dragon Flag* (St. John's University), 1904, 1907. *Fukien Agricultural Journal*, 1947–50. Fukien Christian University: *FCU Family Newsletter in America*, 1956; *FCU News*, 1930, 1932; *Fukien Leaflet*, 1935; *Fukien News*, 1934, 1937; *Fukien Star*, 1923–25; *Fukien Voice*, 1935; *Weekly Bulletin*, 1933–38. Ginling College: *College Letter*, 1924–26; *Ginling Association in America Newsletter*, 1951–64; *Ginling News*, 1942, 1945; *Magazine*, 1924–30; *News Letter*, 1934. Hua Chung University: *Hua Chung College Bulletin*, 1937, 1939–41; *Hua Chung College News*, 1940–41; *Hua Chung News*, 1938; *Hua Chung Newsletter*, 1947–50. *Hua Nan News*, 1939. *Latest News from China Colleges*, 1945–46, 1948–49. *Lingnaam*, 1924. *Lingnaam Agricultural Review*, 1922–27. *Lingnan: A Monthly Magazine*, 1944, 1946–49. *Lingnan News*, 1949–50. *Lingnan Science Journal*, 1927, 1929–50. *The Linguist* (University of Nanking), 1922–24. *Nanking Bulletin of Church and Community*, 1925. *Nanking Notes and Notices*, 1939. *New Horizons*, 1952–58. *New Mandarin* (Yenching University), 1926. *Notes and Notices of the Nanking Union Church and Community*, 1940–41. *Peking News* (Yenching University), 1921–30. *Princeton Peking Gazette*, 1925–29. *Princeton-Yenching Gazette*, 1930–39. *Princeton-Yenching News*, 1942–54. *St. John's Echo*, 1900–1901, 1904–5. *Shanghai Spectator*, 1947. *Tsinan Medical Review* (Shantung Christian University), 1921. *Tung Wu Magazine* (Soochow University), 1937. University of Nanking, School of Agriculture and Forestry: *Agriculture and Forestry Notes*, 1923–27, 1931–41; *Bulletin*, 1933–35; *Daily Meteorological Records*, 1925; *Economic Facts*, 1939, 1943, 1945–46; *Economic Weekly*, 1947–49; *Special Reports*, 1934–35; *University of Nanking Magazine*, 1909–14, 1916, 1918, 1922–24, 1930. West China Border Research Society, *Journal* (West China Union University), 1922–23, 1939–40. West China Union University, *College of Science Newsletter* 1940–42; *News Bulletin*, 1946–48; *Studia Serica*, 1940. Yenching University: *Arts and Letters News*, 1941; College of Public Affairs, *News Bulletin*, 1938–40; *Peking University Magazine*, 1919–20; College of Public Affairs, *Public Affairs*, 1934–35; *Quarterly News*, 1935–37; College of Natural Science, *Science Notes*, 1934–41, 1947; Department of Sociology and Social Work, *Sociology Fel-*

lowship News, 1930; *Yenching Catalyst*, 1945–46; *Yenching Faculty Bulletin*, 1928–34, 1936–41, 1945–46; *Yenching Fortnightly*, 1945–46; *Yenching Gazette*, 1932, supplement, 1931; *Yenching Index Numbers*, 1940–41, 1947–48; *Yenching News* (China ed.), 1935–41, 1943–45; (U.S. ed.) 1931–41, 1943–50; *Yen-ta Journalism News*, 1934.
DISSERTATIONS/THESES: *Winning Chinese Youth to Christ*, by Ellen M. Studley, 1956.
CHINESE LANGUAGE MATERIALS/SERIALS: Fukien Christian University: *Biological Bulletin*, 1947; *The FCU Student*, 1931; *FCU Students Quarterly*, 1931; *The FCU "Y"*, 1931; *Fukien Bi-weekly*, 1930, 1932; *Fukien Culture*, 1932; *Hsieh Ta Hsio Shu*, 1930, 1932; *Hsieh Ta Journal of Chinese Studies*, 1949. Soochow University, *Tung Wu Magazine*, 1935. University of Nanking, *Film and Radio News*, 1942, 1945. Yenching University: *Truth and Life*, 1930; *Yen-ching hsüeh pao (Yenching Journal of Chinese Studies)*, 1927–29; *Yen-ta nien k'an (The Yenchinian)*, 1928–41.
CHINESE LANGUAGE MATERIALS: Fukien Christian University, catalogue, 1928–29.
FINDING AID: In-house register.

26-ARCHIVES OF THE UNITED BOARD FOR CHRISTIAN HIGHER EDUCATION IN ASIA ADDENDUM (RG 11A), 1917–76, ca. 11 l.f.

Background note: This collection represents a continuation of the official archives of the United Board for Christian Higher Education in Asia (see Archives of the United Board for Christian Higher Education in Asia, RG 11, above). Transferred to Yale Divinity Library in 1984, it supplements and overlaps with the records in RG 11, documenting the work of the United Board as it redefined its goals and policies following the closing of mainland China in 1951. The records comprise 115 l.f. in total, dating from 1904 to 1981.
MINUTES/RECORDS/REPORTS/CORRESPONDENCE: Ca. 1 l.f. of materials in the United Board Consolidated General File, 1925–71, including China colleges, China Medical Board of New York, Ginling Association in America, Ginling College, Reginald Helfferich, mission boards, Nanking Theological Seminary, Oberlin-Shansi Memorial Association, United Service to China, University of Nanking, Wellesley-Yenching Committee, and Yale in China Association; 4 boxes of administrative records of the United Board for Christian Colleges in China, 1945–55, including annual reports, 1948–55; Program Files, containing correspondence, memoranda, questionnaires, grant applications, and notes for a proposed book on Christian colleges in China, 1953–62; financial records, affidavits, correspondence, and other papers relating to Japanese war claims of the China colleges, 1930–67; UBCHEA, annual reports, news releases, policy statements, brochures, 1956–76; China Medical Board, annual reports, 1958–67; papers of Princeton-in-Asia (formerly Princeton-in-Peking and Princeton-Yenching Foundation), consisting of 4 boxes of administrative records, 1923–48; 11 boxes of consolidated general files, 1917–49, including J. Stewart Burgess, Henry J. Cochran, Edward S. Corwin, Dwight W. Edwards, fund-raising reports, Robert R. Gailey, Sidney Gamble, history and development, incorporation, certificate and by-laws, Cyrus H. McCormick, Peking University, reorganization of Princeton-in-Peking, Rockefeller Foundation, T. H. P. Sailer, H. Alexander Smith, J. Leighton Stuart, Yenching University, and Young Men's Christian Association; box of papers

relating to Smith-Ginling, including correspondence and miscellaneous records, 1924–49; box of papers relating to Wellesley-Yenching, including correspondence and reports, 1939–54.
MANUSCRIPTS: Outlines, chapters, and reports for proposed book on Christian colleges, in Program Files, including "An Appraisal of Christian Women's Education in China," by Grace Shu, ca. 1954; "Beginnings of English Baptist Educational Work" (on Cheeloo University), ca. 1926; "Cheeloo and Yenching Universities Agricultural Sanitation Investigation," by G. F. Winfield, S. D. Wilson, and J. S. Scott, 1939; "The China Colleges and Instruction in the Natural Sciences," by William Band, 1956; "The Christian Colleges and the Chinese Church," 1958; excerpts from *History of Hwa Nan College*, by Ethel Wallace, n.d.; "The Humanities and the Fine Arts: Oriental," by William Hung, n.d.; "Instruction, Research, and Extension in Agriculture," by C. W. Chang, 1954; "Journalism," by M. E. Votaw, n.d.; "The Magnetic Survey of China," by F. C. Brown, 1933; "Nanking College of Agriculture," by J. B. Griffin, 1954; "Science in the Christian Universities at Chengtu, China," by William Band, 1944; science reports by C. T. Kwei and C. F. Wu, 1931–44; "Soochow University Science College," by J. W. Dyson, 1956; and "The Tengchow College," n.d.; statements and articles relating to history of UBCHEA, including authors such as B. A. Garside, William P. Fenn, and Eric North, 1922–73; "Fifty Years of Work by Princeton-in-Peking and Princeton-Yenching Foundation," by C. A. Evans, 1949, including notes, source materials, and correspondence, 1927–49; "The Significance for Religious Education of Modern Educational Trends in China," by Chen Ching-szu, 1940.
AUDIO-VISUAL MATERIALS: Photo album of Princeton-in-Asia, n.d.
SERIALS: *China Colleges*, 1948–55. *New Horizons*, 1955–61, 1972–76. *Yenching Journal of Social Studies*, 1938–40.
FINDING AIDS: In-house register.

27-ARCHIVES OF THE WORLD STUDENT CHRISTIAN FEDERATION (RG 46) 1891–1945, ca. 10 boxes (5 l.f.)

Background note: The records of the World Student Christian Federation at Yale Divinity School Library, collected under the direction of John Mott, a founder of the organization, represent the official archives of the WSCF from 1895 to 1925. The official archives from 1925 on are located at the organization's headquarters in Geneva, Switzerland. RG 46 also contains the books and periodicals which constituted the library of the WSCF.
MINUTES/RECORDS/REPORTS: Association Press of China (YMCA), publishers' prospectuses, trade lists and announcements, 1914–15, 1919; YMCA of Tientsin, constitution, n.d.; reports, 1901, 1909, 1913, 1917; YMCA-Canton, report, 1919; YMCA-Hong Kong, reports, 1909–10; European YMCA, Hong Kong, reports, 1910; YMCA-Shanghai, reports, 1908–9, 1914, 1921; West China Union University, catalogue, 1919; Canton College Hall charts, n.d.; Academy College at Tung-sho, course of study, n.d.; Canton Christian College, catalogue, 1917–18; Methodist Missionary Peking University, catalogue, n.d.; Hangchow Christian College, catalogue, 1917–18; Shanghai American School, prospectus, 1916–17; University of Nanking, constitution, n.d.; Moukden Medical College, annual statement, 1916; report, 1917; Tsechowfu Mission, prospectus, n.d.; Christian Literature Society for China, report, 1925–26; reports from Chinese YMCA workers, 1911, 1919–26; reports from G. S. Eddy and T. Tatlow, 1920–22; miscellaneous reports on China, 1920–23; re-

ports on conferences, 1920–24; YMCA, annual reports, 1903–21; YWCA, annual reports, 1915; reports by Brockman, Koo, Seescholtz, and Lyon on YMCA work, 1906, 1920, 1925; YWCA, reports, 1915–29; Peking Christian Student Union, report, 1920–21; YMCA directory card; World's Chinese Students' Federation, rules, regulations, and by-laws, 1905; Student Relief in China, reports, 1937–40.

CORRESPONDENCE: Correspondence of John Mott with F. S. Brockman, 1907; T. Z. Koo, 1921–25; Walter Lowrie, ca. 1918, 1920–21; Robert P. Wilder, 1897–1916, 1919–20; and YMCA associations, n.d.; correspondence of Ruth Rouse with Grace Coppock, 1911–21; Henry Hodgkin, 1920–24; Estelle Paddock, 1908–14; Anne Seescholtz, 1920; Philippe de Vargas, 1916; and Ingeborg Wikander, 1915–27.

PAMPHLETS: Ca. 7 boxes of pamphlets, 1891–1940, on athletics and hygiene, Bible study, biographies, Christian colleges, Christianity, employment, entertainment, evangelistic and philanthropic work among students, finances, missions study and service, prayer, social work, student life, and YMCA/YWCA.

MEMORABILIA: Postcards of St. John's University, n.d.

SERIALS: Nanking Theological Seminary, *Bulletin*, 1916–17. National Christian Council, *Bulletin*, 1925. Miscellaneous publications of St. John's University, YMCA school, n.d. *Shanghai Young Men*, 1917–18. *South China Alliance Tidings*, 1914. *University of Nanking Magazine*, 1919.

CHINESE LANGUAGE MATERIALS: Unclassified materials (posters, etc.), n.d.; books, pamphlets and essays on Bible study, evangelistic and philanthropic work among students, prayer, Protestant missions, social work, WSCF and YMCA, and biographies; YMCA, constitutions, 1902–12; manual, 1918, handbook, 1911; St. John's University YMCA school, report, n.d.; reports of L. Hwang, WSCF delegate to Versailles conference, 1900; YMCA secretaries conference, report, 1912, 1919; WSCF conference in Tokyo, report, 1907; Chinese student conferences, report, 1921; summer conference handbooks, 1921, 1923.

FINDING AIDS: "Hints to Research Workers in the John R. Mott Library," by Ruth Rouse, 1945; in-house register; Appendix A to John R. Mott papers described above (for Mott correspondence).

CT–55   Yale Divinity School Library

409 Prospect Street
New Haven CT 06510
(203) 432-5274
Stephen Peterson, Director of the Library

Background note: Evolving methods of description in the long history of the Yale Divinity School Library have resulted in the scattering of missions-related reports and pamphlets throughout different classification systems. Researchers interested in the library's extensive China-related resources are advised to consult with the Archivist.

In addition to the serials listed below, the library also holds uncatalogued issues of *The Chinese Illustrated News*, *Nanking Journal*, *Nanking Theological Seminary Bulletin*, *University of Nanking Magazine*, and *The New East* (China Baptist Publication Society of Shanghai).

1-DAY MISSIONS COLLECTION, 1700–1952, quantity undetermined

Background note: The Day Missions Library was established in 1891 by Professor George Edward Day. By 1921 it contained more than 20,000 items, divided almost evenly between books and pamphlets. The holdings more than doubled during the subsequent thirty years. Since approximately 1950, no items have been catalogued using the Day Missions Library classification system. Since that time, monographs and pamphlets have been added to the library's general collection or to the library's Missions Pamphlet Collection. In 1976 nearly all pamphlets catalogued by the Day Missions classification system were withdrawn from the Day Collection and added to the Missions Pamphlet Collection. Due to ambiguities of definition and description, a small amount of pamphlet material remains in the Day Collection. It is expected that these items will eventually be located in the Missions Pamphlet Collection, Record Group 31.

MINUTES/RECORDS/REPORTS: American Baptist Foreign Mission Society: East China Mission, 1906–7, 1909–13, 1921–24; South China Mission, 1908, 1911; South China Mission, annual report, 1917–20; West China Mission, 1910–14, 1920–23; American Board of Commissioners for Foreign Missions: Foochow Mission, report, 1895–99, 1901, 1912, 1915–16; Inghok Station, report, 1897, 1906, 1911; North China Mission, minutes, 1928; report, 1888–99, 1902–14; Chihli district, report, 1914; Tungchow, 1916; Shansi district, report, 1897, 1910–13; Fenchow, annual report, 1914, 1918.

Bible, Book and Tract Depot, report, 1912; British and Foreign Bible Society, China agency, report, 1896; Shanghai agency, report, 1892; California Chinese mission, annual report, 1900–1901; Central China Religious Tract Society, annual report, 1884–89, 1892, 1897–1915; Cheeloo University, School of Medicine, reports, 1917–38; Tsinanfu Institute, report, 1912, 1917; Charles Rogers Mill School for Deaf Children, reports, 1916–41; Chefoo Industrial Mission, report, 1908, 1913–14; China Baptist Council, report, 1930; China Baptist Publication Society, annual report, 1902, 1904–6, 1917–18, 1926–27; China Bible House, report, 1939, 1948; China Continuation Committee, minutes, 1915–21; China International Famine Relief Commission, annual report, 1931, 1935–36; China Mennonite Mission Society, field report, 1922, 1924; China Sunday School Union, report, 1925; Chinese Evangelization Society, annual report, 1851–55; Chinese Religious Tract Society, annual report, 1888–89; Chinese Students' Alliance, annual bulletin, 1908; Chinese Tract Society, report, 1910–11, 1915–19; Christian and Missionary Alliance, South China Mission, report, 1916; Christian Literature Society for China, report, 1927–28, 1935–39; Women's branch, report, 1938; Chung-hua Sheng Kung Hui, General Synod, report, 1912–37; Board of Missions, triennial report, 1915–17, 1921–37; Kiangsu Synod, journal, 1918; Church of England, Diocesan Association for Western China, financial report, 1930–36; Deutsche China-Allianz-Mission in Barmen, yearbook, 1909–13; Evangelical Church in China, East Hunan Mission, annual report, 1927–28; Foochow Missionary Hospital, annual report, 1872, 1880, 1883–87, 1896, 1901–4, 1907–20; Fukien Christian University, annual report, 1929–32; catalogue, 1921–24, 1934–36; Hauptverein für die evangelische Mission in China zu Berlin, yearbook, 1860, 1865–69; Hildesheimer Verein für die deutsche Blindenmission in China, yearbook, 1898–1917, 1921–28; report, 1912; Hill-Murray Institute for the Blind, annual report, 1924–30, 1932–34; report, 1909–18, 1921, 1923–24, 1932–39; Huapei Kung Li Hui, minutes, 1926–27; Institute of Social Research, annual report,

1926–27; Ling-nan ta-hsüeh, treasurer's report, 1911–16; London Missionary Society, China Advisory Council, report, 1928; Lutheran Church of China, General Assembly, proceedings, 1933–34.

Methodist Episcopal Church: Central China annual conference, minutes, 1887–88, 1890–92, 1897–1922, 1928–39; yearbook, 1911; Central China Women's Conference, report, 1921, 1925, 1936, 1940; Central Conference in China, minutes, 1897–99, 1907, 1911; Foochow annual conference, minutes, 1884–85, 1890–95, 1897–1938, 1946–49; Foochow Women's Conference, minutes, 1887, 1894, 1900, 1902–4, 1906–9, 1911–16, 1918, 1920, 1926, 1928, 1931; Hinghwa annual conference, 1896–1901, 1905, 1907, 1909, 1915, 1918–23, 1925, 1928–29, 1932–35, 1938; Kiangsi annual conference, minutes, 1913, 1915–18, 1920–23, 1925, 1927–36; Women's Conference, minutes, 1913–14, 1918–35; North China annual conference, minutes, 1882–88, 1890–1924, 1937–38; North China Women's Conference, minutes, 1895–1904, 1907–16, 1923–24, 1931–35, 1937–39; Pacific Coast Chinese Mission, annual meeting, 1904–12; West China annual conference, minutes, 1894–95, 1902–17, 1920–22, 1938–39.

Nanking Theological Seminary, minutes, 1917, 1926, 1931–37, 1939, 1941; Nanking University, catalogue, 1910–21, 1924–25, 1931–32; report of the president, 1910–26; Department of Missionary Training, announcements, 1918–19, 1921–26; East China Union Medical College, report, 1912–13; National Committee for Christian Religious Education in China, annual meeting, 1935–36; New York, Central Presbyterian Church, General Missionary Committee, annual report, 1914, 1917, 1924–38; Norske Lutherske Kinamisjonsforbund, yearbook, 1898–1900, 1907, 1910, 1913–25, 1933; North China Tract Society, annual report, 1894, 1911–12; North Fukien Religious Tract Society, annual report, 1918–19, 1921; Oberlin-Shansi Memorial Academy, annual report, 1909; Peiping Union Medical College, report, 1910–12, 1920–23, 1925–42; hospital, annual report of the superintendent, 1908–9, 1914–40; Peking Chinese hospital, report, 1863–65, 1867, 1869, 1872, 1875–83; Presbyterian Church in Canada, North Formosa mission, 1912; North Honan Mission, annual report, 1910; Presbyterian Church in Ireland, Manchuria mission, 1912–14, 1916–21, 1927–32, 1934–39.

Presbyterian Church in the U.S.A.: Central China Mission, minutes, 1894, 1905, 1908, 1916–28, 1930, 1932–34, 1936–37; station reports, 1891–92, 1909–13, 1919–20, 1922–23; Ningpo Station, report, 1925–26; Soochow Station, report, 1925–26; China Council, annual meeting, 1911–22, 1924–25, 1928–30, 1935–36, 1939–40; East China Mission, minutes, 1939–41; Hainan Mission, annual report, 1906; minutes, 1913, 1916–26, 1935–39; Hunan Station, minutes, 1914, 1919–26, 1929–30, 1935–41; Kiangan Mission, 1909–11, 1914–17; minutes, 1907–8, 1912, 1914, 1919, 1921–26, 1929–30, 1932, 1934–41; station reports, 1905–6; Nanking Station, report, 1926–29; North China Mission, minutes, 1918–41; Shantung Mission, minutes, 1918–34, 1936–41; Shantung Mission (East), reports, 1906–7; Shantung Mission (West), reports, 1904–5; Chefoo Station, annual report, 1916–18; Tengchowfu Station, annual report, 1917–18; Weihsien Station, report, 1922–23, 1928–35; South China Mission, report, 1923–24; Canton Station, report, 1889–91, 1896–97, 1900–1901; Synod of China, minutes, 1870, 1874, 1883; Yunnan Mission, minutes, 1924–25; station reports: Kiulungkiang Station and Yuankiang

Station, 1923–25.

Presbyterian Church of England, Scottish auxiliary of the China mission, annual report, 1933–52; Presbyterian Mission Press, annual report, 1875, 1917–24; Protestant Episcopal Church in the U.S.A., Shanghai, journal of the synod, 1917–18; Reformed Church in America (Dutch), Amoy Mission, report, 1910; report of women's work, 1901; Reformed Church in the U.S. (German), Board of Foreign Missions, annual survey, 1918; Reformed Church in the United States, China Mission, minutes, 1925–26; Religious Tract Society, East China branch, annual report, 1891; Religious Tract Society in China, annual report, 1921–40; Religious Tract Society for North and Central China, annual report, 1915–19; St. John's University, catalogue, 1913–26, 1928–40; Shanghai Baptist College and Theological Seminary, annual catalogue, 1912–25; Skandinaviska alliansmissionen, Jönköping, Arsmeddelande, jönköping, 1911–12; South Fukien Religious Tract Society, report, 1908–41; Southern Baptist Convention, South China Mission, annual report, 1918; Svenska missionen i Kina, report, 1894–95, 1907; University of Peking, Student Volunteer Band, yearbook, 1915–17; West China Christian Educational Union, report, 1905–6, 1907–8, 1912–15; West China Council on Health Education, report, 1931; West China General Conference, Committee on Literature, report, 1921; Committee on "The Worker," report, 1921; West China Religious Tract Society, annual report, 1903–4, 1916–22; Woman's American Baptist Foreign Mission Society, annual reports in *Our Work in the Orient*, 1909–27.

MANUSCRIPTS/PAMPHLETS: Manuscripts, typescripts, and other printed materials, ca. 1700–1944, on such subjects as American church mission in Shanghai, Baptist missions, Canton Christian College, Catholicism in China in the eighth century, China Inland Mission, Chinese Christians, Christian education, Hangchow, Jesuits, Kiangnan mission, Liebenzeller mission in Changsha, Methodist Church in China, medical missions, mission organization and policy, missionary education, missionary problems, Nanking Theological Seminary, Nanking University—College of Agriculture and Forestry, North China Union College, Peter Parker, rural China, Shensi Mission, South China, and West China.

MAPS/DESIGNS/DRAWINGS: *Carte des préfectures de Chine et de leur population chrétienne en 1911*, by J. de Moidrey, 1913; *Atlas of China in Provinces*, 1913; *Wesleyan Methodist Church Missionary Atlas: China Section*, 1892(?).

SERIALS: Canton Christian College (Lingnan University), *Bulletin*, 1909–30; *Newsletter*, 1915–19. Catholic University of Peking, *Bulletin*, 1926–31. China Christian Educational Association, *Bulletin*, 1924–33. China International Famine Relief Commission, Publications, series A, 1932, 1936–37. *Ginling College Bulletin*, 1915, 1919–20, 1922, 1925, 1928, 1931, 1933–35. Nanking Theological Seminary, English publications, 1940. *North China American School Bulletin*, 1919–23. University of Nanking, College of Agriculture and Forestry, *Bulletin*, 1920–21, 1923–27, 1931, 1934. University of Peking, College of the Arts, *Bulletin*, 1895–1925. *Variétés Sinologiques*, 1895–1902, 1914.

DISSERTATIONS/THESES: *The History of the Educational Work of the Methodist Episcopal Church in China*, by Eddy Lucius Ford, 1936.

CHINESE LANGUAGE MATERIALS: Fukien Christian University, catalogue, 1928–29.

2-GENERAL HOLDINGS

MINUTES/RECORDS/REPORTS: American Board of Commissioners for Foreign Missions, reports, 1907; Berliner Missionsgesellschaft, yearbook, 1825–26, 1830–32, 1833–1905, 1908–35; Canton Hospital, report, 1908–10, 1913–41; China Christian Educational Association, records of the triennial meeting, 1902, 1905, 1909; China Inland Mission, Hospital, report, 1918; China Medical Board, annual report, 1950–54; China Medical Board of New York, annual report, 1954–71, 1975–78, 1980–84; Christian Literature Society for China, report, 1887–1940, 1946; Deutsche Ostasien-Mission, yearbook, 1892–1908, 1910–12, 1921–35, 1937–39; Junk Bay Medical Relief Council, report, 1957–61; London Missionary Society, report, 1795–1966; report of deputation, 1928; review of the work, 1910–57; Medical Missionary Society in China, report, 1838, 1843, 1845–46, 1850, 1852, 1861–67, 1869–86, 1888–91, 1893; Ming Sam School for the Blind, report, 1906–10; National Christian Council of China, report, 1922–37; National Committee for Christian Religious Education in China, Survey Commission, 1935, 1945; Presbyterian Church in the U.S.A., South China Mission, minutes, 1917–41; Shanghai Mission to Ricksha Men, report, 1919–20, 1927–28; Young Men's Christian Associations, report, 1908–9, 1911–13, 1916, 1918–21; yearbook, 1934–38.

MANUSCRIPTS/PAMPHLETS: Typescripts, mimeographs, pamphlets, and other printed materials, 1711–1978, on such subjects as Young J. Allen, American Baptist missions in Swatow, American Board mission in Foochow, American Board missions, American Church mission in Shanghai, Anking missions, Baptist missions, Bible, British Protestant Christian Evangelists, Catholic missions, Catholicism in China in the eighth century, China Inland Mission, Communist persecution of churches, Dublin University Fukien mission, Fan village, Feng Yü-hsiang, Finnish Missionary Society, Franciscans, Karl Friedrich Gützlaff, health of missionaries, Hsi Sheng-mo, Jesuit missions, Lee Ying-liu, Lu Po-hung, Lutheran Church missions, Walter Henry Medhurst, medical missions, Mennonite missions, Methodist Episcopal missions, native Christians, Nestorian monument, Johannes Abraham Otte, Horace Tracy Pitkin, Presbyterian missions, Protestant missionaries, rural life, rural reconstruction, Tsingtao Lutheran Hospital, vernacular Chinese, Vincentian missions, and YMCA of China.

MAPS/DESIGNS/DRAWINGS: *Map of China Showing the Distribution of the Missionary Body*, by the China Continuation Committee, 1917(?).

SERIALS: *Advent Christian Missions*, 1920–79. *Anking Newsletter*, 1920–41, 1945, 1947–48. *Annuaire des missions catholiques de Chine*, 1924–41. *Asia*, 1948–60. *Boletim eclesiastico da diocese de Macau*, 1957–79. *Bulletin of the Diocese of Western China*, 1934–37. *Bulletin of the Diocesan Association for Western China*, 1937–51. *Catholic Church in China*, 1928–41, 1945–46. *China and the Church Today*, 1982–83. *China Bookman*, 1919, 1925–28, 1931–39, 1947–50. *China Bulletin*, 1947–62. *China Christian Advocate*, 1914–29, 1931–41. China Christian Educational Association, *Bulletin*, 1928. *China Christian Newsletter*, 1928. *China Christian Year Book*, 1910–39. *The China Fundamentalist*, 1929–40. China Inland Mission, *Review*, 1903–45, 1947–65. *China Medical Journal*, 1907–21. *China Medical Missionary Journal*, 1887–1907. *China Mission Advocate*, 1839. *China Mission Newsletter*, 1927–29, 1940–42, 1948–49. *China Mission Studies Bulletin*, 1979–83. *China Mission Year Book*, 1910–25. *China News*, 1927. *China Notes*, 1962–83. *The China Sunday School Journal*,

1913–28, 1930, 1933–34. *China: The Quarterly Record of the Christian Literature Society for China*, 1905, 1911–15. *China Update*, 1983–84. *De Chinabode*, 1908–21. *China-Bote*, 1908–12. *Der Chinabote für den Amerikanischen Freundeskreis der Rheinischen Mission in China*, 1937–38. *Chinas millionen vereinigt met dem missionsboten aus der Deutschen Sudsee*, 1900–1906, 1910–17, 1920–40. *China's Young Men*, 1906–16. *Chine, Madagascar*, 1899–1939, 1944–82. *Chinese Evangelist*, 1889–90. *Chinese Medical Journal*, 1887, 1893–97, 1901, 1908–51. *Chinese Missionary Gleaner*, 1851–55. *Chinese Recorder*, 1868–1941. *Chinese Repository*, 1832–50. *Ching Feng*, 1957–60, 1963–84. *El Correo Sino-Annamita*, 1886–91, 1893–95. *Danziger Evangelischer Missions-Verein für China*, 1852–78. *Directory of Protestant Missions in China*, 1916, 1921, 1923–24, 1926–30, 1932–36, 1940, 1950. *East Asia Millions* (London), 1875–1979. *East Asia Millions* (Philadelphia), 1892–1985. *East China Christian Educational Association Bulletin*, 1923–28. Educational Association of China, *Monthly Bulletin*, 1907–8. *Educational Directory of China*, 1917, 1921. *Educational Review*, 1907–9, 1913–38. *En Chine avec les soeurs missionnaires Notre-Dame des Anges*, 1939–45. *Evangelischer reichsbote*, 1851–65, 1867–73. *Far East*, 1876–78. *Fenchow*, 1919–26, 1928–36. *The Foochow Messenger*, 1903–7, 1909–17, 1922–30, 1935–40. *Foochow News*, 1927–32, 1935, 1938–41. *Four Streams*, 1934–59. *Franciscans in China*, 1923–41. *Free Wan-kan*, 1942–44. *Friends of Moslems*, 1927–51. *Hainan News Letter*, 1912–49. *Land of Sinim*, 1893–1951. *The Light*, 1932–67. *Ling Naam*, 1924–25, 1927–31, 1936. *Looking East at India's Women and China's Daughters*, 1882–83, 1899–1900, 1902–4, 1911–57. *Missionary Recorder*, 1867. *Les Missions de Chine*, 1916–17, 1919, 1923, 1925, 1927, 1929, 1931, 1933–35, 1938–39. *Missionstidningen Sinims land*, 1925–81. *Monde et mission*, 1889–1902, 1927–75. Nanking Theological Seminary, English publications, 1940–41. National Christian Council of China, *Bulletin*, 1922–41. *New Mandarin*, 1926. *Newsletter of the Diocesan Association for Western China*, 1951–59. *Norsk misjonstidende*, 1848–54, 1858–59, 1861, 1863–69, 1871–77, 1879–81, 1884–1911, 1919–41, 1948–57, 1959–83. *Quartelberichte der chinesischen Stiftung*, 1850–51. *Relations de Chine*, 1921–40. *Religion in the People's Republic of China*, 1980–83. *Religious Education*, 1937–40. *St. John's Echo*, 1890–1925. *Shanghai Newsletter*, 1928, 1940, 1944. *Sinica Franciscana*, 1929. *South China Collegian*, 1904. *Star of Cathay*, 1940–48. *West China Missionary News*, 1899–1943.

DISSERTATIONS/THESES: *Accommodatie in de Chinese zendingagescheidenis*, by Johannes Maarten van Minnen, 1951. *Die akkommodationsmethode des P. Matteo Ricci S.I. in China*, by Johannes Bettray, 1955. *American Missionaries and the Policies of the United States in China, 1898–1901*, by John Lindbeck, 1948. *The Central Conference of the Methodist Episcopal Church*, by Harry Wescott Worley, 1938. *Changes in the Christian Message for China by Protestant Missionaries*, by Lewis Strong Casey Smythe, 1928. *China und die katholische Mission in Süd-Shantung, 1882–1900: die Geschichte einer Konfrontation*, by Jacobus Joannes Antonius Mathias Kuepers, 1974. *Christian Missions in China*, by Charles Sumner Estes, 1895. *The Development of the Motive of Protestant Missions to China, 1807–1928*, by George Bell Workman, 1928. *A Comparative History of the East and South China Missions of the American Baptist Foreign Mission Society, 1833–1935*, by Kenneth Gray Hobart, 1937. *Education of Christian Ministers in China*, by Samuel H. Leger, 1925. *The Emer-*

gence of a Protestant Christian Apologetics in the Chinese Church during the Anti-Christian Movement in the 1920s, by Lam Wing-hung, 1978. *Etude sur les missions nestoriennes en Chine au VIIe et au VIIIe siècles d'après l'inscription Syro-Chinoise de Si-Ngan-Fou*, by Augustin Cleisz, 1880. *L'Euchologe de la mission de Chine*, by Paul Brunner, 1964. *The Evangelistic Campaigns of Sherwood Eddy in India and China, 1896–1931*, by William Alfred Imler, 1953. *An Experiment in Teaching the Christian Religion by Life Situations in Fan Village, China*, by Mabel Hubbard, 1938. *Imperial Government and Catholic Missions in China during the Years 1784–1785*, by Bernward Henry Willeke, 1948. *The Interpretation of History in Chinese Christianity*, by Sterling Hegnauer Whitener, 1952. *The Jesuits in China in the Last Days of the Ming Dynasty*, by George Harold Dunne, 1944. *Kilian Stumpf, 1655–1720: ein Würzburger Jesuit am Kaiserhof zu Peking*, by Sebald Reil, 1978. *John Leighton Stuart: The Mind and Life of an American Missionary in China, 1876–1941*, by Yu-ming Shaw, 1975. *The Mission Compound in Modern China: The Role of the United States Protestant Mission as an Asylum in the Civil and International Strife of China, 1900–1941*, by Gladys Robina Quale, 1957. *The Missouri Evangelical Lutheran Mission in China, 1913–1948*, by Richard Henry Meyer, 1948. *The Negotiations between Ch'i-ying and Lagrené, 1844–1846*, by Angelus Francis J. Grosse-Aschhoff, 1950. *The Planting of Protestant Christianity in the Province of Kwangtung, China*, by Emanuel Herman Giedt, 1936. *La Politique missionnaire de la France en Chine, 1842–1856; l'ouverture des cinq ports chinois au commerce étranger et la liberté religieuse*, by Louis Tsing-sing Wei, 1960. *Protestant Christianity and Marriage in China*, by Calvin H. Reber, 1958. *The Protestant Missionary Understanding of the Chinese Situation and the Christian Task from 1890 to 1911*, by C. William Mensendiek, 1958. *Protestant Missions in Communist China*, by Creighton Boutelle Lacy, 1953. *The Development of Protestant Theological Education in China*, by Charles Stanley Smith, 1938. *Die protestantische Christenheit in der Volksrepublik China und die Chinaberichterstattung in der deutschen evangelischen Missionsliteratur*, by Ilse Hass, 1974. *The Relation of the Board of Foreign Missions of the Presbyterian Church in the United States of America to the Missions and Church Connected with It in China*, by Samuel Hugh Moffett, 1945. *La rencontre et le conflit entre les idées des missionnaires chrétiens et les idées des chinois en Chine depuis la fin de la dynastie des Ming*, by Liang Si-ing, 1940. *Roland Allen, sein Leben und Werk; kritischer Beitrag zum Verständnis von Mission und Kirche*, by Hans Wolfgang Metzner, 1970. *The Rural Work of American Protestant Missionaries in China, 1911–1937*, by William James Megginson, 1968. *Some Adjustment Problems of Chinese High School Students*, by Ralph Raymond Shrader, 1933. *Some Guiding Principles for Christian Education in China Today*, by Roxy Lefforge, 1933. *Die Sonn- und Festtagsfeier in der katholischen Chinamission; eine geschichtlich-pastorale Untersuchung*, by Franz Xaver Bürkler, 1942. *South Shensi Lutheran Mission*, by Sigurd Aske, 1951. *Suomen lähetysseuran työ Kiinassa vuosina, 1901–1926 (The Work of the Finnish Missionary Society in China in the Years 1901–1926)*, by Toivo Saarilahti, 1960.
CHINESE LANGUAGE MATERIALS/SERIALS: *Chung-hua Chi-tu chiao hui nien chien (China Church Year Book)*, 1914–36. *China's Young Men*, 1896–1917. *Chinese Christian Advocate*, 1921–22. *Chinese Methodist Message*, 1967–72. *Ching Feng*, 1970–80. *Kuo chi kung pao (International Journal)*, 1929–37(?).

Nanking Seminary Review, 1932–34, 1936–41, 1947–49. *Tien Feng*, 1949–52. *Truth and Life: A Journal of Christian Thought and Practice*, 1930–38.
CHINESE LANGUAGE MATERIALS: 13 volumes, 1916–81, on such subjects as Baptist missions, theological studies, missionaries and modern China, church in rural China, religious education and the history of Christianity in China.

YALE UNIVERSITY

CT–60   Department of Manuscripts and Archives
Sterling Library
120 High Street
New Haven CT 06520
(203) 432-1775
Judith Ann Schiff, Chief Research Archivist
Katharine D. Morton, Head, Manuscripts and
    Archives

Finding aids: "Primary Sources for the Study of China in the Department of Manuscripts and Archives, Yale University Library," comp. by Judith Ann Schiff, 1984; "Bibliography on English-language Source Material at Yale University for the Study of Chinese History," by Joanna Waley-Cohen, 1985.

1-BIDWELL FAMILY PAPERS (MS 79), 1853–77, 28 items
CORRESPONDENCE: 4 letters from Samuel Wells Williams, 1853–54, with observations on the Taiping Rebellion and other disturbances; 24 letters from Leonard W. Kip, Jr., 1857–77, on the Taiping Rebellion, a visit to Taiwan, and missionary experiences.
FINDING AIDS: In-house register.

2-OLIVE BIRD PAPERS, 1917–50, 31 items
CORRESPONDENCE: 31 letters from Olive Bird, a missionary teacher at St. Hilda's School in Hankow and the Boone School in Wuchang, to her friend, Alice Chamberlain Darrow Rounds, 1917, and describing educational and social life at the school and mission, and the difficulty in staying at her post, 1940–42, 1945–50.

3-H. HUGH AND NORA BOUSMAN PAPERS, 1924–42, 1 folder
Background note: This collection is in the Miscellaneous Manuscripts Collection.
CORRESPONDENCE/MANUSCRIPTS: Correspondence and other documents concerning missionary work of the Bousmans in China, 1924–42.

4-SAMUEL CLARKE BUSHNELL PAPERS (MS 1292), 1877–78, 5 ft.
Background note: Samuel Clarke Bushnell was a Congregational minister of New Haven and Massachusetts. The collection relates to his tour of the Far East beginning in 1877.
DIARIES: 2 diaries of a world tour, including Hong Kong, Canton, and Shanghai, 1877–78.

5-CATHOLIC MISSION TO CHINA PAPERS, 1705–13, 29 items
Background note: This collection is in the Miscellaneous Manuscripts Collection.

CORRESPONDENCE/MANUSCRIPTS: 28 letters, in Italian, French, Latin, Spanish and Portuguese, and a manuscript, concerning Catholic missionary work in China and Macao, including such correspondents as Clement XI, Cardinal Charles Maillard de Tournon, and the Patriarch of Antioch, 1705–13.

6-EDWIN ROGERS EMBREE PAPERS (MS 198), 1921, 2 folders
Background note: Edwin Rogers Embree (1883–1950) held several executive positions at the Rockefeller Foundation between 1917 and 1927. See also Rockefeller University, Rockefeller Archive Center, Pocantico Hills, North Tarrytown, NY, 10591.
DIARIES: Ca. 38 pages of typescript journals from trips to China in 1921 and 1922, in connection with Peking Union Medical College administration, including comments on missionaries.
FINDING AIDS: In-house register.

7-FARNAM FAMILY PAPERS (MS 203), 1924–33, 5 folders
Background note: Henry W. Farnam (1853–1933) was an economist and professor at Yale University. In addition to the materials described below, there may also be some material relating to the Yale-China Association among the correspondence.
CORRESPONDENCE/MANUSCRIPTS/PAMPHLETS/MEMORABILIA: Folder of correspondence, notes, printed materials, and miscellanea relating to China, 1924–25; 4 folders relating to Yale-in-China, 1924–33.
FINDING AIDS: In-house register.

8-GOODRICH FAMILY PAPERS (MS 242), 1848–58, 13 items
CORRESPONDENCE: 13 letters from missionary William Allen Macy to his friend, William Henry Goodrich, 1848–58, describing his work as director of the Morrison Education Society's School for Chinese Youth in Hong Kong (1848–49), his preparation for assignment to an inland mission in northern China (1856), and life in Canton and Shanghai.
FINDING AIDS: In-house register.

9-PHILLIPS AND RUTH GREENE PAPERS (MS 797), 1921–68, ca. 3 l.f.
Background note: Phillips Foster Greene (1892–1967) was a faculty member and surgeon at Hsiang-Ya (Hunan-Yale) Medical School and Hospital in Changsha from 1923 to 1927 and 1931 to 1941, and director of the American Red Cross in China from 1942 to 1943. His wife, Ruth Peabody Altman Greene (b. 1896), taught English to Hsiang-Ya students and later served on the Wellesley-Yenching College Board in 1948 and 1949. Her letters from China from 1923 to 1943 were later published as *Hsiang-Ya Journal* (1977).
MINUTES/RECORDS/REPORTS: Financial records, 1923–46; health reports, 1931; Hsiang-Ya Hospital and College, reports, 1939–46; Changsha International Relief Committee, report, 1939–40.
CORRESPONDENCE: 4.5 boxes of correspondence from Changsha to family, friends and Yale-in-China colleagues, 1923–68, including discussion of social and political conditions in Changsha and Hunan, Greene's medical work and Yale-in-China administrative matters.
DIARIES: Diary of a trip to inland China, by Ruth Greene, 1940.
MANUSCRIPTS: Mailing lists, n.d.; meeting notes and agenda, 1933–44; miscellaneous notes, n.d.; letter of Phillips Greene to *The New York Times*, 1944; 4 essays on medical work in China, by Phillips Greene, 1944–46; 5 essays by Ruth Greene: "Fragments

from a Chinese Journal," 1941; "Chinese Women and War," 1944; "From a Chinese Dug-out," n.d.; "War-time Hsiang-Ya," n.d.; "Broken Jade," n.d.; research notes for *Hsiang-Ya Journal*, n.d.
MEMORABILIA: Newspaper clippings containing biographical material on the Greenes, n.d.
AUDIO-VISUAL MATERIALS: Photo of Phillips and Ruth Greene, n.d.; 48 photos collected by Phillips Greene during the Sino-Japanese War, 1937–45.
CHINESE LANGUAGE MATERIALS: Chinese newspapers, 1932, 1949.
FINDING AIDS: In-house register.

10-WILFRED T. GRENFELL PAPERS, 1924–25, 315 items
AUDIO-VISUAL MATERIALS: 315 photos of China, 1924–25, taken by Wilfred T. Grenfell, a medical missionary.
FINDING AIDS: In-house register.

11-HOWARD LEE HAAG PAPERS (MS 621), 1921–61, 4 ft.
Background note: Howard Lee Haag (b. 1893) held several executive positions in the YMCA, serving as the secretary in Harbin from 1921 to 1935. He worked with Russian refugees there and established several schools, including an English-speaking junior college. While in Manchuria, he also worked with relief organizations and reconstructed the Harbin YMCA building.
MINUTES/RECORDS/REPORTS: Reports and conference material on YMCA in China, 1926–43 and undated; YMCA in Harbin, annual reports, 1928, 1935; other reports, 1923–36 and n.d.
CORRESPONDENCE: Correspondence relating to Haag's work for the YMCA in Harbin, its financial difficulties and general local conditions, including correspondence with YMCA secretaries in China, Japan, and the Soviet Union, 1921–61; excerpts from Haag's correspondence to his parents from Harbin, published as newspaper articles, 1921–42.
DIARIES/MANUSCRIPTS: 4 notebooks, 1921–35, containing addresses, notes on Christianity and YMCA work, outlines for religious services, and sporadic diary entries, describing trips to Barim [Barin] and Mukden in Manchuria; miscellaneous essays and notes describing Harbin, YMCA work and Christianity; outlines for speeches, 1942–60; "On the Manchurian-Soviet Border," 1931; "Manchuria, A Backward Glance," n.d.
MEMORABILIA: Newspaper clippings about Haag, 1921–61; programs and souvenirs, 1924–56; biographical material on Haag, 1946, 1962; clippings and memoranda on YMCA work in Harbin, 1921–67; 2 folders of unidentified printed materials on Manchuria, 1925–35.
MAPS/DESIGNS/DRAWINGS: 2 maps of Manchuria, 1939, 1952.
AUDIO-VISUAL MATERIALS: 67 postcards and photos, almost all of Manchuria in the 1920s and 1930s.
FINDING AIDS: In-house register.

12-GEORGE HENRY HUBBARD PAPERS (MS 965), 1897–1918, ca. 1 box
Background note: George Henry Hubbard (1855–1928) was a missionary under the American Board of Commissioners for Foreign Missions from 1885 to 1925, stationed in Foochow until 1891 and then posted to Fukien until his retirement in 1925. He taught at the Union Theological Seminary in Foochow and served as superintendent of Ponasang Hospital, secretary of the Foochow Missionary Union, 1888–90, and as president of United Society of Christian

Endeavor for China, 1900–1905, in addition to translating Sunday school lessons into Foochow dialect. His wife was Ellen L. Peet, whose papers (and those of her mother, Hannah Louise Plimpton Peet) are at Mount Holyoke College, Williston Memorial Library, College History and Archives, South Hadley, MA, 01075–1493.
MINUTES/RECORDS/REPORTS: Hubbard's account books, with receipts and notes, 1897–98, 1915–18.
CORRESPONDENCE: 4 letters to Hubbard concerning mission business, 1897, 1918.
DIARIES: 3 folders of Hubbard's diaries, 1896–97 and 1908, describing Hubbard's travels and activities in Fukien as administrator of various schools, hospitals, and missions; diary, 1894, containing school lessons by Hubbard's mother-in-law, Hannah Peet, later Mrs. Charles Hartwell, in Foochow.
FINDING AIDS: In-house register.

13-EDWARD HICKS AND LOTTA C. HUME PAPERS (MS 787), 1907–72, ca. 6 l.f.
Background note: Edward Hicks Hume (1876–1957) went to China with the Yale Mission in Changsha in 1905. He organized the Yale Mission Hospital there and served as its senior physician until 1923. In 1914 he founded Hsiang-Ya (Hunan-Yale) Medical College, serving as dean and professor of medicine until 1927. From 1923 to 1927 he was president of the colleges of Yale-in-China and held a succession of executive positions in the Yale-in-China Association between 1934 and 1957. He resigned his offices at Hsiang-Ya in 1927. Among the organizations and institutions which Hume served as trustee were the Associated Boards for Christian Colleges in China, the Harvard-Yenching Institute, and Lingnan University.
Helen Charlotta (Lotta) Carswell Hume (1876–1976) assisted her husband in Changsha as a nurse and research assistant and later started the first Social Service League in Changsha.
See also Columbia University, Rare Book and Manuscript Library, Butler Library, 535 West 114th Street, New York, NY, 10027; and Union Theological Seminary, Archives, 3041 Broadway at Reinhold Niebuhr Place, New York, NY, 10027.
MINUTES/RECORDS/REPORTS: Hua Chung College, draft of constitution, n.d.; medical reports, 1913–25; Yale Mission, memoranda on plans and policy, 1906–24; miscellaneous memoranda, 1925–27; reports to the trustees, 1924–25; financial records, 1907–26.
CORRESPONDENCE: Correspondence of Edward Hume with Yale-in-China staff and other individuals, including such correspondents as Harlan Page Beach (1905–19), Palmer Bevis (1924–30), Boone University (1924), Henry W. Farnam (1925–26), Kenneth Scott Latourette (1925–30), Dickson H. Leavens (1919–27), Sidney Lovett (1935–36), North China Union Language School (1923), Rockefeller Foundation (1923–24), Warren Seabury (1906–7), Anson Phelps Stokes (1903–32), Wesleyan Methodist Missionary Society (1924), Amos Wilder (1914–19), F. Wells Williams (1911–24), and F. C. Yen (1924–37), with discussion of organizational and building plans for the Yale Mission in Changsha, Hume's efforts to build a quality medical school and hospital, political conditions in Changsha and Hunan, the attitude of Chinese students towards western education and culture and routine administrative matters; correspondence of Lotta Hume with friends and Yale-in-China Association staff, with an account of the

1910 Changsha riots, 1910–72; correspondence of Lotta Hume with Norman Freeman and other family members, including discussion of her writings and Edward Hume's activities, 1930–72; 14 folders of correspondence between Edward and Lotta Hume, 1919 and 1931–51 (restricted); correspondence and memoranda regarding student strike at Yali, 1925.
MANUSCRIPTS: Folder of miscellaneous research notes, 1920–24; folder of historical notes on Yale-in-China, 1909–20; inventory of Hume materials in the Missionary Research Library, 1928–57; 2 boxes of mostly undated manscripts by Edward Hume (ca. 1907–1956), including 2 bibliographies of addresses and articles by Hume; 125 articles and professional papers on medical work in China, Christian medicine, missions, education, communism, American colleges in China, medical education in China, Peter Parker, Sino-Western relations, Sino-Japanese relations, Yale and China, and Yung Wing; 3 folders of sonnets; folder of book reviews, 1925, 1943, 1946; folder of memorials to friends and colleagues, including William Henry Welch and Warren Seabury; 3 folders of research notes, n.d.; "The Human Touch at Yali," by Lotta Hume, n.d.; "Marriage Customs in Changsha," by Lotta Hume, n.d.; 5 folders of Chinese and Tibetan folktales, by Lotta Hume, n.d.; 6 folders of research notes by Lotta Hume, n.d.
MEMORABILIA: Folder of clippings on anti-foreign disturbances, 1920s; Hsiang-Ya school song, 1945; folder of clippings relating to the inauguration of Edward Hume as president of the Colleges of Yale-in-China, 1924; address book and addresses, n.d.; biographical information on Edward Hume and curriculum vitae, n.d.; 4 folders of clippings on Hume and his publications, 1907–52; 2 folders of miscellaneous clippings, n.d.; clippings and programs on honorary degrees, 1912–25; Hume family genealogical data, 1931; 4 folders of travel memorabilia, 1918–46; biographical data and obituaries of Lotta Hume, 1976.
MAPS/DESIGNS/DRAWINGS: Architect's rendering of a scheme for a hospital in Changsha by Hume, n.d.
AUDIO-VISUAL MATERIALS: 8 folders of photos, including Yale-in-China staff, E. H. Hume and family members, and scenes in Changsha, n.d.
FINDING AIDS: In-house register.

14-NELSON TRUSLER JOHNSON REMINISCENCES, 1954, 1 item
Background note: The originals for this collection are at Columbia University, Rare Book and Manuscript Room, New York, NY, 10027, as part of the Columbia University Oral History Collection.
ORAL HISTORIES: Transcript of an interview with Nelson Trusler Johnson, including discussion of his Yale-in-China activities, 1954.
FINDING AIDS: Published guide.

15-DICKSON HAMMOND AND MARJORIE LEAVENS PAPERS (MS 715), 1908–72, 5 ft.
Background note: Dickson Hammond Leavens (1887–1955) was a missionary, teacher, and economist. He taught at the Yale Mission College in Changsha from 1909 to 1912 and returned from 1915 to 1921. At this point he went to Paotingfu to assist in famine relief for four months. After a brief leave in the United States, he again returned to the college in Changsha, where he stayed until the Yale-in-China facilities were closed in 1927. Unlike most of the staff, he remained in China, as the representative of the Yale-in-

China Association's trustees, in Shanghai. In 1928, he was able to return to Changsha and make arrangements for the resumption of work with a Chinese staff. He left China later that year. His wife, Marjorie Browning Leavens (1888–1977), taught mathematics and astronomy at Yale Mission College. For biographical notes and papers relating to his sister, Delia, see Smith College, College Archives, Alumnae Gymnasium, Northampton, MA, 01063.

MINUTES/RECORDS/REPORTS: Changsha University Club, abstract of constitution, n.d.; Conference on the Support of the Hunan-Yale Medical College, report, 1926; Continuation committee, memoranda and minutes, 1928; Finance Committee, agenda and minutes, 1919–25; Hunan Christian Educational Association, bulletins, 1923–24; Leavens' trip to Changsha, memoranda, 1934; retirement plan for Yali Union Middle School faculty, memoranda, 1940; Yale Foreign Missionary Society, memoranda on qualifications, 1910–12.

CORRESPONDENCE: Letters from Leavens to his parents and sisters, Delia and Faith, 1909–22, including detailed accounts of day-to-day activities as a faculty member and treasurer of Yale Mission College and his observations on political conditions in Changsha and Hunan; correspondence between Leavens and Yale-in-China Association staff, 1909–58, including such correspondents as Palmer Bevis, Rachel Dowd, John Hess Foster, Edward H. Hume, Kenneth Scott Latourette, J. Leighton Stuart, Matilda C. Thurston, H. H. Vreeland, Frederick Wells Williams, and Amos Wilder, with discussion of financial matters, mission activities, and political conditions in Changsha; letters from Marjorie Leavens to her family and Yale-in-China staff, 1908–72, primarily 1915–27 from Changsha, including discussion of day-to-day activities as a mission housewife, family matters, and her reactions to Chinese people and culture; correspondence relating to the Conference of Christian Colleges and Universities, 1923–24; Yale-in-China staff circular letters, 1910–46.

MANUSCRIPTS: "The History of Yale-in-China," 1921–22; "Memoirs of Yale-in-China," 1921–22; "Student Activities at Yali," 1913–14; staff address list, 1930; student lists, 1910; notebook showing distances from New Haven in great circles, with essay, "Names of Yale Men," n.d. [1949?].

PAMPHLETS: China Christian Educational Association pamphlets, 1926–30; Kuling information pamphlet for visitors, 1909.

MEMORABILIA: Obituaries and biographical clippings; clippings relating to his Yale-in-China activities, Changsha riots, Nanking Incident, and Wanhsien Incident; 2 files of notices to Yale Mission staff, n.d.; staff party at Changsha, program, 1932; unpublished speeches and sermons by Leavens, 1912–28; miscellaneous Yale-in-China memorabilia, n.d.

AUDIO-VISUAL MATERIALS: 50 photos, including Dickson and Marjorie Leavens, Yale Mission staff, landscapes and urban scenes in Hong Kong, and damage from the Changsha riot of 1910, 1910–1920s.

CHINESE LANGUAGE MATERIALS: Yenching University, bulletin, n.d.

FINDING AIDS: In-house register.

16-CHARLES TEMPLEMAN LORAM PAPERS (MS 10), 1936–39, 3 folders

MINUTES/RECORDS/REPORTS/CORRESPONDENCE: Folder of correspondence regarding Lingnan University, 1936; folder of correspondence regarding Yale-in-China, with minutes of meetings, reports and notes on missions, 1936–39.

MANUSCRIPTS: "Yale and China," n.d.; "Hua Chung College," 1937; bibliography on education in China, 1937.

FINDING AIDS: In-house register.

17-A. SIDNEY LOVETT, JR. PAPERS (MS 1089), 1933–79, 1.25 l.f.
Background note: Augustus Sidney Lovett, Jr. (1890–1979), was chaplain of Yale University until 1958 and executive vice-president of Yale-in-China from 1959 on.

MINUTES/RECORDS/REPORTS/CORRESPONDENCE/PAMPHLETS: 2 boxes of general correspondence relating to Yale-in-China, 1933–79; box of correspondence, printed materials and reports relating to the Far Eastern Conference, 1941–75, including correspondents such as Mimi Kuo, Ng Kam Yan, and Alphonse Park.

CHINESE LANGUAGE MATERIALS: Folder of correspondence, 1962–67.

FINDING AIDS: In-house register.

18-MORSE FAMILY PAPERS (MS 358), 1854–57, ca. 3 folders
Background note: Richard Cary Morse, founder and editor of the religious newspaper, *The New York Observer*, and his son, Sidney Edwards Morse, travelled in China in the 1850s.

CORRESPONDENCE: Folder of correspondence from Richard Morse, Hong Kong, Canton, and Macao, 1854, and from Sidney Morse, Hong Kong, 1856–57.

DIARIES: Fragment of a journal extract of Richard Morse, 1854; Sidney Morse's 131-page journal of a trip to China in the *N. B. Palmer*, 1856–57.

19-WILLIAM WINSTON PETTUS PAPERS (MS 786), 1928–45, 1 ft.
Background note: William Winston Pettus (1912–45) was a surgeon at Hsiang-Ya Hospital from 1928 to 1945.

CORRESPONDENCE/DIARIES/MANUSCRIPTS: 3 boxes of correspondence, diaries and notes on his day-to-day activities as a doctor before and during the second Sino-Japanese war, 1928–45.

FINDING AIDS: In-house register.

20-FRANK LYON POLK PAPERS (MS 656), 1919, 1 folder
CORRESPONDENCE: Letters regarding the repatriation of Catholic missionaries, 1919.

FINDING AIDS: In-house register.

21-HOWARD RICHARDS PAPERS (MS 1057), 1907–12, 8 folders
Background note: Howard Richards (1877–1940) was an engineer who served as a missionary at Boone College in Wuchang from 1905 to 1916 and secretary to Yale-in-China.

MINUTES/RECORDS/REPORTS/PAMPHLETS/MEMORABILIA/CHINESE LANGUAGE MATERIALS: Printed material and memorabilia including annual reports of the Yale Mission College in Changsha, pamphlets, and religious tracts in Chinese.

CORRESPONDENCE: 7 folders of correspondence relating to Yale-in-China, 1907–12.

FINDING AIDS: In-house register.

22-CHARLES P. ROCKWOOD PAPERS (MS 1159), 1939–40, ca. 10 folders
Background note: Charles Parkman Rockwood was an instructor at Yale-in-China in Yuanling from 1939 to 1940.

CORRESPONDENCE: Typescript copies of letters, mostly to his parents and sister, describing activities of Yali Middle School and

life in wartime China, 1939–40.
FINDING AIDS: In-house register.

23-CHARLES ERNEST SCOTT PAPERS, 1920, 1 item
Background note: This collection is in the Miscellaneous Manuscripts Collection.
MANUSCRIPTS: "Sinister Methods in Shantung," a description of Japanese behavior in Shantung, 1920.

24-WARREN BARTLETT SEABURY PAPERS (MS 790), 1901–36, 8 ft.
Background note: Warren Bartlett Seabury (1877–1907) was an organizer of the Yale Foreign Missionary Society (YFMS). After his ordination as a minister in 1904, he went to China to help organize the Yale Mission's educational work. He spent the first two years studying Chinese in Hankow and negotiating the purchase of a mission site in Changsha. By 1906, he had established a middle school in temporary quarters, which was later known as Yale Union (Yali) Middle School.
CORRESPONDENCE: Correspondence from Seabury to his family, 1901, 1904–7, summarizing his work for the Yale Foreign Missionary Society and his comments on Chinese culture, including discussion of his efforts to buy land for the Yale Mission, and the founding of Yali Middle School; correspondence with members of the Yale Foreign Missionary Society staff, including correspondents such as Harlan Page Beach, 1903–7, and John Lawrence Thurston, 1902–3; correspondence between Seabury's father and the YFMS staff, regarding Seabury's death and the establishment of a memorial fund, 1909–14.
MANUSCRIPTS: 25 short essays and sketches written between 1904 and 1907 on various aspects of his life in China, including subjects such as Griffith John, missionaries, and the Yale University mission in China; draft of "Rules and Regulations of Yale Mission College," n.d.
MEMORABILIA: Several obituaries and memorials of Seabury.
AUDIO-VISUAL MATERIALS: Photo of Seabury, n.d.
FINDING AIDS: In-house register.

25-EDWARD COMFORT STARR PAPERS (MS 1166), 1854–1916, .5 l.f.
CORRESPONDENCE: Correspondence of family members and associates sent to Edward Comfort Starr, from China, including letters from his sister-in-law, Lizzie DeForest, describing famine in Nanking (1907), from missionaries in Asia, and to family members involved in mission work, 1854–1916.
FINDING AIDS: In-house register.

26-ANSON PHELPS STOKES FAMILY PAPERS (MS 299), 1901–56, 28 folders
Background note: Anson Phelps Stokes (1874–1958) was secretary of Yale University for 22 years beginning in 1899. Yale-in-China, an organization to which he was to give many years of service as a member of the executive committee, was organized in 1902 in his home.
MINUTES/RECORDS/REPORTS/CORRESPONDENCE: 17 folders of memoranda, minutes, offical correspondence, and reports relating to Yale-in-China, including correspondents such as Edward H. Hume, F. D. Yen, Frederick Wells Williams, and Palmer Bevis, 1901–51, 1956.
MEMORABILIA: Folder of miscellaneous memorabilia, 1912–43 and undated.

AUDIO-VISUAL MATERIALS: 10 folders of photos of Yale-in-China faculty, students and Yali facilities, 1909–50.
FINDING AIDS: In-house register.

27-JOHN LAWRENCE THURSTON (MS 493), 1903, 3 folders
Background note: John Lawrence Thurston (1874–1904) was the first missionary sent out by the Yale Foreign Missionary Society. His wife, Matilda Calder Thurston, founded Ginling College. For other papers regarding John Thurston, see Dartmouth College Archive, Hanover, NH, 03755; for papers and biographical notes relating to Matilda Thurston, see Union Theological Seminary, Archives, 3041 Broadway at Reinhold Niebuhr Place, New York, NY, 10027.
CORRESPONDENCE: 2 folders of correspondence, some to his family, 1903.
MANUSCRIPTS: Fragment of a long article or memorandum discussing Yale Missionary activity in China, n.d.
FINDING AIDS: In-house register.

28-U.S. DEPARTMENT OF STATE: CONSULAR DESPATCHES, 1790–1906, quantity undetermined
Background note: Originals of this collection are in the National Archives and Records Service, Eighth Street and Pennsylvania Avenue NW, Washington, DC, 20408 (RG84).
MINUTES/RECORDS/REPORTS: Consular dispatches including reports on missionary activities from U.S. consulates in Amoy, 1844–1906; Canton, 1790–1906; Cheefoo, 1863–1906; Chungking, 1896–1906; and Hangchow, 1904–1906.
FINDING AIDS: Published guide.

29-ABBE LIVINGSTON WARNSHUIS REMINISCENCES, 1951–52, 1 item
Background note: The originals for this collection are at Columbia University, Rare Book and Manuscript Room, New York, NY, 10027, as part of the Columbia University Oral History Collection. For biographical notes, see Union Theological Seminary, Archives, 3041 Broadway at Reinhold Niebuhr Place, New York, NY, 10027.
ORAL HISTORIES: Transcript of an interview with Abbe Livingston Warnshuis, including discussion of his experiences in Amoy, 1951–52.
FINDING AIDS: Published guide.

30-SAMUEL WELLS WILLIAMS FAMILY PAPERS (MS 547), 1824–1939, ca. 10 l.f.
Background note: This collection contains the papers of Samuel Wells Williams (1812–1884) and his son, Frederick Wells Williams (1857–1928). Samuel W. Williams (SWW) went to China in 1833, first going to Canton for several months to study Chinese and Portuguese and at the same time managing a printing press and contributing to the *Chinese Repository*, edited by Elijah Coleman Bridgman. In 1835 he and the press moved to Macao. During the next decade he aided Bridgman in preparing several reference works on Chinese language, geography, and commerce. He left for the United States in 1845, but later returned to China to become secretary and interpreter of the American legation to China from 1856 until 1876, not returning to the United States until 1877. At this time, he began his revision of *The Middle Kingdom*, assisted by his son, Frederick.

Frederick W. Williams (FWW) taught Oriental history at Yale and was chairman of the executive committee of Yale-in-China and its board of trustees.

Items listed below are those of SWW unless otherwise identified.

MINUTES/RECORDS/REPORTS: Account books, 1844–48, 1858–65, 1875–76; account statements for books, 1852, 1871–84; accounts, correspondence, and circulars regarding SWW's work for the Japan Expedition and for the Legation in Peking, 1854–63; register of receipts from an auction of SWW belongings, 1876.

CORRESPONDENCE: 10 boxes of correspondence, 1824–1939, relating mostly to SWW and his life in China and the United States, including the following correspondents: Henry Blodget, William Jones Boone, Elijah Coleman Bridgman, Pearl Buck, Anson Burlingame, James Dwight Dana, William Dean, Andrew Patton Happer, William Alexander Parsons Martin, Calvin Wilson Mateer, Peter Parker, Matthew Perry, William Bradford Reed, William Henry Seward (with discussion of revolution in China and the struggle of foreign powers seeking greater freedom and toleration of missionaries), Arthur Henderson Smith, Matthew Tyson Yates, missionaries in China, the American Bible Society, and Scribners (regarding publication of *The Middle Kingdom*); bound volume of letters, 1831–51; annotated reprint of a letter to President Rutherford Hayes by the Faculty of Yale College, on Chinese immigration, 1879; draft of a letter to the editor of the New York *Tribune* on Chinese immigration, 1880; notes and extracts from letters on treaty provisions for Americans, 1880(?); correspondence of FWW with Hunan-Yale College of Medicine, 1910–16.

MANUSCRIPTS: Manuscript of *A Syllabic Dictionary of the Chinese Language*, 1874; list of missionaries who received copies, 1874–75; portion of a printed copy of *The Middle Kingdom*, with manuscript corrections, lithographs and proofs of illustrations, and publicity, 1883; "List of Articles by S. Wells Williams in the *Chinese Repository*," n.d.; autobiographical sketch, 1878, 1889; "Notes of Remarks to Linonians," on Chinese immigration, 1879; "Our Treaties with China," n.d.; manuscripts of articles on Lewchew Islands, extraterritoriality, women in Chinese society, tea culture, Chinese religious and political institutions, the proper translation of the words "God" and "spirit" into Chinese, and Mormonism; drafts of articles on Chinese language, early Chinese records, and missions in Japan; translation of *Lieh Kwoh Chi*, 1880; review of 2 books on Christian merchants' missionary work in China; lecture on Chinese religion and philosophy, 1882; circulars, 1869, 1875; notes and lists of Chinese orthography; "System of Orthography Commonly Used in Writing the Amoy Dialect," n.d.; gazetteer of Chinese districts and cities, n.d.; survey of Chinese history; legal claim against Chinese government for losses, ca. 1856, 1859; agreement between British and Foreign Bible Society and the American Bible Society, regarding editions of translations of the Bible, 1861; agreements with printers and publishers, 1874, 1882; power of attorney and memorandum concerning lease of legation in Peking, 1875–76; outline of will; writings about SWW, some by family members, and a resolution adopted by the Peking Missionary Association at his death, 1877–88, n.d.; Williams family genealogies, 1880, 1882; writings by Elijah Coleman Bridgman, 1828–46, 1859, 1861; "Yun-nan Inquiry," by Thomas George Grosvenor, 1875–78; poetry dedicated to SWW by Ko Kun-hua, 1881–82; "A Few Lines on the Occasion of Dr. Williams' Leaving China"; "Translations of the Bible into Chinese," by Sarah (Walworth) Williams (Mrs. Samuel Wells Williams), n.d.

DIARIES: SWW's journal of a trip to Peking, 1858–59.

MEMORABILIA: Clippings of letters to editors, 1858–84; clippings, 1877, 1879; miscellaneous receipts, accounts and bills of sale, 1863, 1865, 1876–83 and n.d.; biographical notices and obituaries of SWW and review of *Life and Lectures of SWW*, 1875–1905; scrapbook of obituary clippings on SWW, 1884; reviews of *A Syllabic Dictionary of the Chinese Language*, 1874–76; reviews of *The Middle Kingdom*, 1848, 1883–84; miscellaneous printed material, 1835–83, n.d.; lock of SWW's hair, 1884; scrapbook of calling cards, correspondence and printed memorabilia, ca. 1854–74.

MAPS/DESIGNS/DRAWINGS: Manuscript maps of China, in Chinese, n.d.; printed map of China, in English, n.d.; 8 manuscript maps of Manchuria, Tibet and Mongolia, mounted on Chinese scrolls, n.d., captioned by SWW or FWW, n.d.

AUDIO-VISUAL MATERIALS: Photos of SWW, with illustration, 1876, n.d.; photos of members of the North China mission, 1874; photo of Macao Protestant Cemetery, 1888.

CHINESE LANGUAGE MATERIALS: "Lists of Plants in the Treatise on Grains and Planting," n.d.; documents, some with SWW translations or annotations, and one with silk envelope, 1843, 1866, 1871, 1874–76, n.d.; books, including translations of English works, n.d.

FINDING AIDS: In-house register.

31-STANLEY WILSON PAPERS (MS 1362), 1914–18, 127 items
AUDIO-VISUAL MATERIALS: 127 lantern slides taken by Stanley Wilson, the supervising architect for Yale-in-China, showing the construction of the campus and scenes of everyday life, 1914–18.

32-RECORDS OF THE YALE-CHINA ASSOCIATION (YRG 37-A), 1869–1976, 105 l.f.
Restrictions: Permission required; Series IX-Motion Picture Film, is restricted.
Background note: This collection represents the official archives of the Yale-China Association and its predecessors. The Yale-China Association originated from plans by a small group of Yale students and faculty for a Yale mission in China in 1901. The following year, the Yale Foreign Missionary Society was organized and its first representative, Lawrence Thurston, was sent to China to seek a site on which to locate the mission. In 1903, as a result of Thurston's efforts, the First Conference of Protestant Missions of Hunan invited the Yale group to settle in Changsha. During 1905, Brownell Gage, Warren Seabury, and Edward Hume went to Changsha. They founded the Yali Middle School in 1906 (which temporarily took refuge in Yuanling during World War II) and the College of Arts and Sciences in 1914. In 1927 all Americans withdrew from Hunan due to political circumstances. The leadership of Yale-in-China came to the conclusion that their efforts could only continue in cooperation with other missionary groups. Their School of Science of Yale-in-China College then became part of Central China (Hua Chung) College.

Yale-in-China was also instrumental in the founding of Hsiang-Ya Medical School in 1916, which grew out of the Yale-in-China College of Nursing, begun in 1910. Hsiang-Ya (Hunan-Yale) Hospital was the first institution in China to employ western-educated Chinese as full members of their permanent faculty on equal terms with Americans. During the war, the Medical College moved to Kweiyang, then to Chungking in 1945. Although plans were begun to reconstruct Yali and Hsiang-Ya immediately after the war, the political situation prevented its completion. In 1948, most of the

Yale-in-China staff remaining in Changsha was evacuated. Yali, renamed Hunan Private Liberation Middle School, and Hsiang-Ya both continued to function, but Yale-in-China removed its headquarters to Hong Kong in 1951.

First incorporated as the Yale Foreign Missionary Society in 1903, the organization name was the Yale-in-China Association from 1934 to 1975, and the Yale-China Association after 1975.

MINUTES/RECORDS/REPORTS: Minutes of the following: Executive Committee, 1901–70; Board of Trustees, 1921–73; Yali Governing Board, 1909–37; Monthly College Faculty Meetings, 1917–29; Executive Committee of the Yale-in-China Mission, 1932–35; Executive Committee of Hua Chung College, 1938–41; Executive Committee of Hsiang-Ya, 1944; Executive Committee of Yali Middle School, 1933–35; Yale-China Association annual meetings, 1902–71; reports of the following: Yale-China Association, 1909–76; Executive Committee and Board of Trustees, 1903–73; Trustee's Representatives, 1929–72.

Chairman of the Governing Board, 1913–14, 1916, 1921, 1923–24, 1926–27; Executive Secretary to the Trustees, 1926–58; Executive Director to the Trustees, 1966–73; account books, 1902–71; budgets, 1909–68; treasurer's reports, 1902–39; financial statements and audit reports, 1905–72; reports on fund-raising campaigns, 1911–12, 1923–24, 1947–48; miscellaneous financial files, 1934–73; real estate and architectural records, including Changsha building plans, Hsiang-Ya financing and construction bills, war damage claims, 1902–72; Hua Chung College, catalogues, 1931–36; yearbook, 1932; Hunan-Yale College of Medicine, catalogues and announcements, 1918–19, 1926–27; Hunan-Yale School of Nursing, catalogues, 1924–26; Yale-in-China School of Science, Hua Chung College, newsletter, 1940; Yale College in China, catalogue of the Preparatory Department, 1913; Yale in China College, catalogues, 1919–23; Yale Mission in China, catalogue, 1906–8; Yali Middle School, catalogue, 1931.

MINUTES/RECORDS/REPORTS/CORRESPONDENCE: 16 l.f. of reports, memoranda and correspondence, titled "New Haven Office Subject Files," 1901–75, including materials of the following: American Board of Foreign Missions, 1901, 1948–51; Hsiang-ya Medical Education Association, n.d.; American Bureau for Medical Aid to China, 1939–42, 1946–47, 1950s; American Presbyterian Mission, 1950–51; David Anderson, 1936–46; Associated Boards for Christian College in China, 1943–47; bachelor applications, 1939–72; M. Searle Bates, 1942–48; J. V. W. Bergamini, 1937–46; Bible Union of China, 1921–22; John Crosby Brown, 1924; Brown University-in-China, 1920; by-laws, 1934–48; candidates for representative, 1938; candidate information, 1923–24; medical candidates, 1915–48; rejected candidates, 1920–22; Arthur V. Casselman, 1937–43; Changsha, 1923–50; Changsha International Relief Committee, 1940–41; Changsha Missionary Association; Generalissimo and Madame Chiang K'ai-shek, 1937–49; children at Yali, 1904–29; Rockwood Q. P. and Wesley Chin, 1934–46; China Association for Christian Higher Education, 1926; China Educational Commission, 1921–22; China Medical Board, 1914–71; China Union University, 1923–27; Committee on Christian Colleges in China, 1928–32, 1942–43; Christian Medical Council for Overseas Work, 1938–52; Communism in China, 1940–54; continuation committee, 1927–29; Council on Christian Higher Education in Asia, 1953–58; Arnold G. Dana, 1944; Dartmouth-Williams-Yale-in-China, 1965–68; Dayton-Bevis Changsha trip, 1925; Educational Policy Committee, 1922–26, 1938; Episcopal Board, Department of Missions, 1929–31; Evangelical and Reformed Mission, 1946; Fellowship fund, 1931–50; Foreign Missions Conference of North America, 1936–56; forestry in China, 1916–19; future of Yale-in-China, 1943–46; future of Yali, 1926–28; Gage Fellowship, 1924–33; Ginling College, 1937–49; Roger S. Greene, 1925–29; Thomas Griffen, 1909–10; Hamilton College, 1919–21; Hsiang-Ya, 1919–60; J. C. Hsiung, 1934–35; Hua Chung, 1928–51; Huachung College, president's reports, n.d.; Hunan University, 1938; International Missionary Council, 1930–57; Jeme Tien-yoh Memorial, 1924–25; Nelson T. Johnson, n.d.; Walter H. Judd, 1945–48; Laymen's Foreign Missions Inquiry, 1932–33; Li Chen-nan, 1929–47; Stephen C. Liu, 1928; Henry W. Luce, 1904–42; Martinsburg Missouri Church, 1935–41; Medical Advisory Board, 1915–20; Medical cooperation, 1913–21; medical education, 1919–32; medical mission boards, 1920; medical work at Changsha, 1950; Methodist Episcopal Church, Board of Missions, 1922–24; Mission boards, 1901–9; mission policy, 1911; mission rules, 1914–23; missionary conditions, 1917–19; Modern Missions Movement, 1934–35; National Christian Council, 1948–50; National Christian Council of China, 1925–27; National Council of Churches, 1950–71; National Council Protestant Episcopal Church, 1929–43; Nursing Board of Residence, 1920–22; Nursing School, 1921–48; Oberlin-in-China, 1925–56; J. Hall Paxton, 1948–51; Erwin S. Penn, 1949–57; Personnel committee, 1933–55; Ru-Chen Educational Association, 1914; physical training, 1920–23; proposed Yale Mission, 1907; policy and budget formation committee, 1940–43; Presbyterian Board of Foreign Missions, 1946–52; Princeton University, 1920; promotion, 1923–50; reconstruction fund, 1942–46; Red Cross Headquarters, 1938–43; reunions of staff, 1927–45; rules and regulations, 1919–36; scholarships, 1922–68; Seabury memorial library, 1913–36; Yale-in-China seal, 1939; Shanghai National Conference, 1913; Shanghai Yale Club, 1924–46; Sino-American Yale Alumni Association in China, 1944; Sino-Japanese situation, 1937–38; speeches, 1916–46; staff families, 1931–32; staff information, 1918–26; John Leighton Stuart, 1948–49; Syracuse-in-China, 1925–48; Tech-Harvard Cooperation, 1921; Hillstone High School and Yali track meet, 1935–36; Tsinghu Cooperation, 1936; United Board for Christian Colleges in China, 1948–51; United Board for Christian Higher Education in Asia, 1967–71; United China Relief, 1942–50; Wesleyan Methodist Missionary Society, 1930–31; Williams scholarship, 1938; Williams-Yali library, 1928–59; Wuhan proposed transfer, 1921–24; Yale College in China, 1910–27; Yale Mission College, n.d.; Yale-in-China Association, 1947–54; Yale-in-China future plans, 1935–46; Yale-in-China Women's League, 1912–49; Yale Foreign Missionary Society, 1901 (?); Yali Alumni Association, 1920–46; Yali students and faculty, 1908–24; *Yali Pao*, 1936; Yali Student Association in Peking, 1920; Yali Union Middle School, 1919–51; Y. C. Yen, 1943; Yenching University, 1925–42.

CORRESPONDENCE: 53 boxes of staff correspondence, including: Harlan P. Beach, 1901–33; Palmer Bevis, 1926–30; Samuel Bushnell, 1923–25; John Hess Foster, 1919–27; Brownell Gage, 1903–45; Francis S. Hutchins, 1913, 1923–70; Paul C. T. Kwei, 1917–53; C. C. Lao, 1927–50; Kenneth Scott Latourette, 1909–68; Edwin Lobenstine, 1907–59; Sidney Lovett, 1942–61; Edward Reed, 1900–1947; Dwight Rugh, 1930–57; William H. Sallmon, 1902–13; B. Preston Schoyer, 1933–70; Anson Phelps Stokes, 1902–59; Francis C. M. Wei, 1930–51; Luther A. Weigle,

1933–57; Richard D. Weigle, 1931–58; Frederick Wells Williams, 1900–1929; Yen Fu-chun, 1909–47; radiograms and cables, 1904–51; box of donor correspondence, 1916–67; correspondence and statistics on donors and contributions, organized by city, 1930s and 1940s; New Haven office administrative files, including *Hsiang-Ya Journal* correspondence and reviews, 1970s; 4 letters from John D. Shove, in Changsha, to his family, 1917; Maude Powell correspondence relating to famine relief, n.d.

DIARIES: "China Journal, 1921–1923," by Morris Sanders, a 400-page typescript, describing his trip to China, activities as a surgeon at Hsiang-Ya and walking tours of the countryside; diary by Robert Platt, n.d.

MANUSCRIPTS: "Abstracts of the Minutes of the Yale-in-China Trustees, 1949–1965," by Geoffrey K. Walker, n.d.; "China as I Knew It," by Ruth Hoadley Wilson, n.d.; "History of the Association until Approximately 1945," collected memoranda; "A History of Yale-in-China," by Arthur Birsh and Roland Vance, 1952; "The History of Yale-in-China Pertaining Only to Yali Middle School and the College," by Catherine Ready, 1956; "Sino-American Cooperation in Medicine: The Origins of Hsiang-Ya, 1902–1914," by William Reeves, n.d.; "The Yale Foreign Mission Founding and Early Years," by Gerald Jones, 1955; "Yali Union Middle School and the War Years, 1937–1945," by S. Y. Teng, 1964; "Flight to Cathay, An Aerial Journey to Yale-in-China," by W. Reginald Wheeler, 1949; "A Visit to Yale-in-China," by Anson Phelps Stokes, 1920; Hsiang Len Tsing memoir of Changsha, ca. 1932; Vernon Farnham autobiography, 1977.

PAMPHLETS: *The Story of Yale-in-China*, 1945.

MEMORABILIA: Real estate deed photostats of Changsha property, n.d.; 17 scrapbooks of clippings on Yale-in-China activities, publicity materials, Sino-Japanese war, Chinese political events, and the communist looting of Changsha, 1902–64; 19 folders of articles on Yale-in-China, 1900–1959; 25 folders of clippings on Yale-in-China activities, 1900–1959; publicity form letters and brochures, 1906–77; Yale Foreign Missionary Society seal; College of Yale-in-China diplomas; copies of "thank you" inscriptions sent to Governor Chao Heng-li for protecting Yali buildings from mob attack, 1925; annual meeting announcement posters; proclamation by Changsha military authorities on using Yale Missions property as barracks, 1920s; notice posted on Yale mission property during 1910 riot; miscellaneous items from Maude Powell collected by her husband, Ralph Powell, in the 1920s–1930s.

ORAL HISTORIES: Transcript of Harry Rudin oral history, 1981.

MAPS/DESIGNS/DRAWINGS: Map of the College of Yale-in-China, 1925; folio of 13 blueprints and drawings of Yali, Yale-in-China chapel, Hua Chung College, Yale-in-China library, hospital in Changsha, and Changsha, 1911–46; drawings, paintings and cartoons with primarily anti-Japanese themes, 1930s–1940s; map of Changsha, showing locations of various missions sites, n.d.

AUDIO-VISUAL MATERIALS: 10 boxes of photos, n.d., of Yale-in-China, Changsha, including views of buildings, campus, interiors, students, missionary groups, cities other than Changsha, faculty, festivities, graduations, Hua Chung College, Kuling, landmarks, Leiyang Branch Hospital, medical and hospital staff, nursing school staff and students, Chinese scenes, Warren Seabury, war, Yuanling, and Yung Wing; 23 photo albums of Changsha, 1901–50, including those of Arthur C. Williams, Dickson Leavens, Changsha riot, Morris B. Sanders, Francis S. Hutchins,

Robert Ashton Smith, and R. Brank Fulton; box of negatives, n.d.; box of lantern slides of Yale-in-China, Changsha, including general Chinese scenes, technical slides, Yali and Hsiang-Ya; 229 glass negatives of Yale-in-China, Changsha; 35 mm. slides of Changsha, Yali, Hsiang-ya, and Yuanling; folder of negatives of prints made from broken lantern slides and from frames of motion picture film; 72 reels of original 16 mm. motion picture film taken by members of the Yale-China Association staff, 1932–51, some with negatives and prints, including views of Hsiang-Ya, Yali Middle School, Hua Chung College, Hsi Pai Lao Clinic, Changsha, Phillips Greene family, Yale-China friends, Yuanling, Yale-in-China 70th Anniversary activities, Yale-in-China trustees, rural China, student life, faculty and staff; phonograph record of a fund-raising campaign speech by Henry R. Luce, 1947; ca. 12 photos of personnel of Hsiang-Ya Hospital, 1925–37, belonging to Jessie P. Norelius; 5 photos of Middle School students and staff, 1921, belonging to Harry Rudin; ca. 35 photos of Changsha street scenes, Yali campus, and College staff, 1924, belonging to Paul Penfield.

SERIALS: *Hua Chung College News*, 1940–41. *The Hunan-Yale Bulletin*, 1932. *News Bulletin of the Yale Collegiate School and Hospital*, 1912. *Nurse-in-China*, 1946–47. *Yale-in-China Newsletter*, 1924, 1963–73. *Yale-in-China Newsletter to Contributors*, 1937–38. *Yale-in-China Occasional Bulletin*, 1918–20, 1937–38. *Yale-in-China Occasional Notes*, 1904–5. *The Yale-in-China Student*, 1917–21. *Yale Mission in China Newsletter*, 1908–9. *Yali News*, 1934. *Yali News Bulletin*, 1938–49, 1951–57. *Yali Quarterly*, 1916–38.

CHINESE LANGUAGE MATERIALS/SERIALS: *Hunan Student Union Save the Nation Weekly*, 1917, 1919. *Hunan-Yale Monthly*, 1923. *Yali Biweekly*, 1926. *Yali High School Monthly*, 1932. *Yali Magazine*, 1922–24. *Yali Report*, 1934. *Yali Weekly*, 1925, 1936, 1946–47.

CHINESE LANGUAGE MATERIALS: Yale College in China, bulletin, 1907–8; Hsiang-Ya Middle School, bulletin; Hunan-Yale College of Medicine, yearbook, 1924; Hunan-Yale School of Nursing, rules of admission; Nationalist pamphlets and broadsides; pamphlets and posters on health care; pamphlets and broadsides on radical, labor and nationalist movements; Yali Medical School, regulations and rules book, 1935; *History of the Class of 1934*; 16 volumes on religion, science, Hu-hsi, and medicine, 1890–1943; bill of mason and contractors for work on Yale Hospital, 1906–7; Chinese New Year decorations.

FINDING AIDS: In-house register.

33-GENERAL HOLDINGS
SERIALS: *Chinese Miscellany*, 1849.

CT–65   Kline Science Library

Yale University
C–8, Kline Biology Tower
219 Prospect Street
New Haven CT 06510
(203) 432–3439
Elizabeth E. Ferguson, Reference Librarian

1-GENERAL HOLDINGS
SERIALS: *Lingnan Science Journal*, 1922–42, 1945, 1948. *Peking Natural History Bulletin*, 1926–41, 1948–51.

CT-70 Law Library
Yale University
127 Wall Street
P.O. Box 401A
New Haven CT 06510
(203) 432-1601
Morris L. Cohen, Librarian

1-GENERAL HOLDINGS
SERIALS: *China Law Review*, 1922-40.

CT-75 Medical Library
Yale University
333 Cedar Street
New Haven CT 06510
(203) 785-4356
R. Kenny Fryer, Reference Librarian
Ferenc A. Gyorgyey, Special Collections

1-GENERAL HOLDINGS
SERIALS: *China Medical Journal*, 1907-31. *China Medical Missionary Journal*, 1887-90, 1894, 1898, 1900-1907. *China's Medicine*, 1966-68. *Chinese Medical Journal*, 1975-. *Chinese Medical Journal* (foreign ed.), 1932-66.

CT-80 Sterling Memorial Library
Yale University
120 High Street
P.O. Box 1603A, Yale Station
New Haven CT 06520
(203) 432-1776 (Main Reference)
Alan C. Solomon, Head Librarian, Reference
  Department
Hideo Kaneko, Curator, East Asian Collection

1-GENERAL HOLDINGS
MINUTES/RECORDS/REPORTS: Reports on the China mission in *Annals of the Propagation of the Faith*, 1907-; Medical Missionary Society in China, address and minutes, 1838; China International Famine Relief Commission, annual reports, 1922-38 (see SERIALS below).
MANUSCRIPTS: "Christian Missions in China," by Edward Wilson Wallace, 1929; China International Famine Relief Commission, lists of publications, n.d.
PAMPHLETS: *British Protestant Christian Evangelists and the 1898 Reform Movement in China*, by Leslie Ronald Marchant, 1975; *Robert John Davidson: A Memoir of the Pioneer Quaker Missionary in West China*, by C. G. Naish, 1943; miscellaneous pamphlets on the church history of China.
SERIALS: *Bulletin on China's Foreign Relations*, 1931-35. Catholic University of Peking, *Bulletin*, 1926-34; Agricultural Extension Service, *Bulletin*, 1948. *China Christian Year Book*, 1910-14, 1916-19, 1923-39. China International Famine Relief Commission: *News Bulletin*, 1937-39; Publications, series A (annual reports), 1922-37; series B, 1923-24, 1926, 1929-30, 1977. *China Monthly*, 1939-50. *Chinese Recorder*, 1868-1928, 1933, 1939. *Chinese Repository*, 1832-51 (also Japanese edition). *Educational Review*, 1909, 1914-17, 1921-22, 1924-38. *Folklore Studies*, 1942-62. *Fu jen Newsletter*, 1931-32. *Lingnan*, 1941. *Missionary Recorder*, 1867. *Monumenta Serica*, 1935-83; Monograph Series, 1937, 1939, 1941-48, 1961. Nanking Theological

Seminary, English publications, 1940-41. *New Horizons*, 1934-35, 1938-44, 1945-47, 1952-59, 1972. University of Nanking, College of Agriculture and Forestry, *Bulletin*, 1926, 1932-34. West China Border Research Society, *Journal*, 1922-36, 1939-44; supplement, 1932. *Yenching Journal of Social Studies*, 1938-50. *Yenching News Letter*, 1936.
DISSERTATIONS/THESES: *The American College in the Orient: A Study of the Transplanting of a National Institution with Special Reference to the College of Yale in China*, by Brownell Gage, 1924. *American Missionaries and Policies of the United States in China, 1898-1901*, by John M. H. Lindbeck, 1948. *Apostolic Legations to China of the Eighteenth Century*, by Antonio Sisto Rosso, 1948. *The Central Conference of the Methodist Episcopal Church*, by Harry Wescott Worley, 1938. *Christian Education of Adults in China*, by Arthur Owen Rinden, 1941. *Church and State in Republican China: A Survey History of the Relations between the Christian Churches and the Chinese Government, 1911-1945*, by Arne Sovik, 1952. *A Comparative History of the East and South China Missions of the American Baptist Foreign Mission Society, 1833-1935*, by Kenneth G. Hobart, 1937. *An Educational Experiment in China: The Story of the Development of Yale-in-China*, by Reuben Andrus Holden, 1951. *A History of the Development of the Chinese Indigenous Christian Church under the American Board in Fukien Province*, by Peter Siebert Goertz, 1933. *Imperial Evangelism: American Women Missionaries in Turn-of-the-century China*, by Jane Harlow Hunter, 1981. *Imperial Government and Catholic Missions in China during the Years 1784-1785*, by Bernward Henry Willeke, 1948. *Missionary Journalism in Nineteenth-century China: Young J. Allen and the Early "Wan kuo kung pao," 1868-1883*, by Adrian Arthur Bennett III, 1970. *The Negotiations between Ch'i-ying and Lagrené, 1844-1846*, by Angelus Francis J. Grosse-Aschhoff, 1950. *The Planting of Protestant Christianity in Kwangtung, China*, by Emanuel Herman Giedt, 1936. *La Politique missionnaire de la France en Chine, 1842-1856: l'ouverture des cinq ports chinois au commerce étranger et la liberté religieuse*, by Louis Tsing-sing Wei, 1960. *Protestant Missions in Communist China*, by Creighton Boutelle Lacy, 1953. *The Development of Protestant Theological Education in China*, by Charles Stanley Smith, 1938. *The Relation of the Board of Foreign Missions of the Presbyterian Church in the U.S.A. to the Missions and Church Connected with It in China*, by Samuel H. Moffett, 1945. *Religious Liberty and Christian Education in China*, by Luther Ching-san Shao, 1934. *The Rural Church in China*, by Frank W. Price, 1938. *Sherwood Eddy: Evangelist and YMCA Secretary*, by Deane William Ferm, 1954. *The Use of Material from China's Spiritual Inheritance in the Christian Education of Chinese Youth*, by Warren Horton Stuart, 1932.
CHINESE LANGUAGE MATERIALS/SERIALS: *Chiao hui hsin pao (Church News)*, 1868-74. *Chin-ling hsüeh pao (Nanking Journal)*, 1931-41. Chin-ling ta-hsüeh chung kuo wen hua yen chiu so ts'ung k'an, chia chung, Publications, series A, 1932, series B, 1944. *Chung-hua i hsüeh tsa chih (Chinese Medical Journal)*, 1973-74, 1979. *Economic Facts*, 1936-39. *Fu jen hsüeh chih (Fu jen Sinological Journal)*, 1929-47. *Fu Sheng*, 1931-? *Ling-nan hsüeh pao (Lingnan Journal)*, 1929-52. Ling-nan ta hsüeh, wen hsüeh yuan wen shih ts'ung k'an ti i chung, Publications, series A, 1936. *Pien chiang yen chiu lun ts'ung (Frontier Studies)*, 1941-44. *Wan kuo kung pao (The Globe Magazine: A Review of the Times)*, 1874-1907. *Wen hsüeh nien pao (Chinese Literature Annual)*, 1932-41. *Yen-ching hsüeh pao (Yenching Journal of Chinese Stud-*

ies), 1927–51; *Chuan hao* (Monograph series), 1933–50.
CHINESE LANGUAGE MATERIALS/DISSERTATIONS/
THESES: *Ch'ing mo yü Hua hsi chiao shih chih cheng lun chi ch'i ying hsiang (The Political Commentaries of Western Missions in China and Their Influence on Late Ch'ing Government)*, by Huang Chao-hung, 1970. *Hsi fang ch'uan chiao shih tsai Hua tsao ch'i ti pao yeh t'an t'ao (Newspaper Publishing among Early Western Missionaries in China)*, by Chu Li-chih, 1977. *I pa ch'i ling nien T'ien-chin chiao an chih yen chiu (The Tientsin Massacre of 1870)*, by Wang Man-p'ing, 1975.
CHINESE LANGUAGE MATERIALS: *Research Guide to the "Wan kuo kung pao (The Globe Magazine)," 1874–1883*, comp. by Adrian A. Bennett, 1976; 35 volumes, 1928–82, on such subjects as Christianity and the rural reconstruction movement, missionaries and modern China, Vincent Lebbe, anti-foreign religion movement among Chinese gentry, Catholic missions, relations with Europe, religious education, Communism and missions, Antoine Cotta, Matteo Ricci, Young J. Allen, Meng Hsiao-ch'ih, imperialism, Jesuits in China in the sixteenth century, Sister Dominique, agricultural periodicals, University of Nanking, agricultural trade, Chung Jung-kuang, and the Agricultural Bank of China.

NEW LONDON

CONNECTICUT COLLEGE
CT–85 C. E. Shain Library
New London CT 06320
(203) 447–7622
W. James MacDonald, Reference Librarian

1-GENERAL HOLDINGS
SERIALS: China Christian Educational Association, *Bulletin*, 1926.
CHINESE LANGUAGE MATERIALS: Book on anti-missionary activities, 1958.

STORRS

UNIVERSITY OF CONNECTICUT
CT–90 Homer Babbidge Library
Box U–5, Room 132
369 Fairfield Road
Storrs CT 06268
(203) 486–2524
Richard Schimmelpfeng, Special Collections

1-GENERAL HOLDINGS
DISSERTATIONS/THESES: *A Century of Chinese Christian Education: An Analysis of the True Light Seminary and Its Successors in Canton and Hong Kong*, by Chen Kuan-yu, 1972. *The Educational Philosophy and Work of Welthy Honsinger Fisher in China and India: 1906–1980*, by Colleen Adele Kelly, 1983. *Matteo Ricci, S.J. in China, 1583–1610: A Case Study of a Precursor in Educational Anthropology*, by Rosalie Judith Ford, 1985.

DELAWARE

NEWARK

UNIVERSITY OF DELAWARE
DE–5 Morris Library
Newark DE 19717–5267
(302) 451–2965
Susan Brynteson, Director of Libraries

1-AMERICAN BOARD OF COMMISSIONERS FOR FOREIGN MISSIONS PAPERS, 1827–1930, 94 reels microfilm
Background note: The originals of this collection are at Harvard University, Houghton Library, Cambridge, MA, 02138. See the entry on Harvard University for a more detailed description. China-related material may also be found in Unit I of this collection, letters from foreign correspondents.
MINUTES/RECORDS/REPORTS/CORRESPONDENCE: American Board of Commissioners for Foreign Missions, reports, minutes, documents, and correspondence of the following missions: Amoy, 1827–59; Foochow, 1860–1929; South China, 1829–1922; North China, 1860–1930, including Fukien Christian University, North China Union College, Peking Union Medical College, Shantung Christian University, Yenching College for Women, and Yenching University; Shansi, 1880–1914.
FINDING AIDS: *Papers of the American Board of Commissioners for Foreign Missions: Guide to the Microfilm Collection, Units 1–6*, of which units 1 and 2 are on China (Research Publications, Inc.: Woodbridge, CT).

2-GENERAL HOLDINGS
MINUTES/RECORDS/REPORTS: Medical Missionary Society in China, hospital in Macao, reports, 1841–42.
PAMPHLETS: *Quaker Mission to China: W. Grigor McClelland's Diary, 26 September–29 October, 1955*, by W. Grigor McClelland, 1955.
SERIALS: *Asia*, 1970. *Chinese Recorder*, 1867–1941. *Les Missions de Chine et du Japon*, 1916–17, 1919.

WILMINGTON

HAGLEY MUSEUM AND LIBRARY
DE–10 Manuscripts and Archives Department
Wilmington DE 19807
(302) 658–2400
Michael Nash, Curator

1-CHARLES L. HUSTON PAPERS, 1916–51, 700 items
Background note: Charles Lukens Huston (1856–1951) was vice president of the Lukens Steel Company, and a life-long Ruling Elder of the Presbyterian Church of Coatesville, Pennsylvania.
CORRESPONDENCE/PAMPHLETS/AUDIO-VISUAL MATERIALS: Ca. 700 letters to and from correspondents including Pearl Buck, the China Inland Mission, China Relief Legion, China's Children Fund, Christian and Missionary Alliance, Christian Fundamentals Association, Rev. W. Carlew Chapman, Institute for the

Chinese Blind, W. Percy Knight, E. C. Munson, Charles E. Scott, J. Ross Stevenson, Leland Wang, Roger B. Whittlesey, and the YMCA of China, on subjects including the rise of communism, increase/decrease in converts, mission needs, religious theory, and daily life, 1916–51; miscellaneous pamphlets, some in Chinese language, and photos with the letters.

DISTRICT OF COLUMBIA

WASHINGTON DC

AMERICAN UNIVERSITY
DC–5   Library
4400 Massachusetts Avenue, NW
Washington DC 20016
(202) 686-2325
H. K. Schmidt, Reference Librarian

1-GENERAL HOLDINGS
DISSERTATIONS/THESES: *Issachar Jacox [i.e., Jacob] Roberts and American Diplomacy in China during the Taiping Rebellion*, by George Blackburn Pruden, Jr., 1977.

CATHOLIC UNIVERSITY OF AMERICA

DC–10   Institute of Christian Oriental Research (ICOR) Library
John K. Mullen of Denver Memorial Library, Room 18
620 Michigan Avenue, NE
Washington DC 20064
(202) 635-5084
Monica Blanchard, Librarian

Restrictions: Access by appointment.
Background note: The Institute holds approximately 100 uncatalogued rare books on China, mostly written by Western travelers and missionaries from the sixteenth to the nineteenth centuries. Consult staff to locate a particular work. Titles include: *Divers voiages du P. Alexandre de Rhodes en la Chine, & autres roiaumes de l'Orient, avec son retour en Europe par la Perse & l'Armenie*, by Alexandre de Rhodes, 1666, and *Nouvelle relation de la Chine*, by Gabriel de Magalhães, 1688.
Finding aids: *A Guide to the Far Eastern Holdings of the Institute of Christian Oriental Research (ICOR) Library*, by Monica J. Blanchard, 1986.

1-GENERAL HOLDINGS
PAMPHLETS: *Origin and Causes of the Chinese Crisis*, by J. Freri, 1902.
MAPS/DESIGNS/DRAWINGS: Map of western China, by R. Hausermann (Paris: Edgar Quinet), 1913; supplement to the journal *Les Missions Catholiques*, 1913.

DC–15   Oliveira Lima Library
Catholic University of America
John K. Mullen of Denver Memorial Library
620 Michigan Avenue, NE
Washington DC 20064
(202) 635-5059
Ralph J. Annicharico, Assistant Curator

Restrictions: Access by appointment.
Background note: Donated to Catholic University by Brazilian scholar and diplomat Manoel de Oliveira Lima (1867–1928) in 1916, the Oliveira Lima Library's collections center on the history and culture of Portuguese-speaking peoples. Its materials on Portugal include strong holdings on the Society of Jesus and the missionary enterprise. Among the approximately 20 books pertaining to Christianity in China is *Imperio de la China, y cultura evangelica en el, por los Religiosos de la Compañia de Jesus. Sacado de las noticias del Padre Alvaro Semmedo de la propia Compañia*, by Manuel del Faria y Sousa, 1731. The library also holds Chinese-language grammars, lexicons, and dictionaries, such as *Arte China constante de Alphabeto e Grammatica comprehendendo Modelos das Differentes Composiçoens*, 1829, by Joaquim Affonso Gonçalves, a Lazarist missionary in Macao.
Finding aids: *Bibliographical and Historical Description of the Rarest Books in the Oliveira Lima Collection at the Catholic University of America*, comp. by Ruth E. V. Holmes (Washington DC: Catholic University of America), 1926. *Catalog of the Oliveira Lima Library* (Boston: G. K. Hall), 1970.

DC–20   John K. Mullen of Denver Memorial Library
Catholic University of America
620 Michigan Avenue, NE
Washington DC 20064
(202) 635-5077 (Reference)
(202) 635-5088 (Philosophy and Theology)
Adele R. Chwalek, Interim Director
R. Bruce Miller, Philosophy and Theology

1-GENERAL HOLDINGS
SERIALS: *Annuaire des missions Catholiques de Chine*, 1901–47. *Asia*, 1960. Catholic University of Peking, *Bulletin*, 1926–31, 1934. Catholic University of Peking, College of Education, *Publications*, 1939. *China Missionary*, 1948–49. *China Missionary Bulletin*, 1950–53. *China Monthly*, 1947–49. *Collectanea Commissionis Synodalis*, 1928–47. *Far East*, 1920–24, 1926–41, 1943–53, 1956–57. *Franciscans in China*, 1923–27. *Maryknoll Mission Letters*, 1927, 1942–43, 1946. *Mission Bulletin*, 1953–54, 1956–57. *Les Missions de Chine*, 1916, 1925–33, 1938–41. *Monumenta Serica*, 1935–38, 1940–41, 1949–55, 1957–62, 1964–76. *The Torch*, 1927–37, 1941–43, 1945–53, 1955–56. University of Nanking, College of Agriculture and Forestry, *Bulletin*, 1932. *Yenching Journal of Social Studies*, 1938–41, 1948–49.
DISSERTATIONS/THESES: *Die Akkommodationsmethode des P. Matteo Ricci S.I. in China*, by Johannes Bettray, 1955. *Apostolic Legations to China of the Eighteenth Century*, by Antonio Rosso, 1948. *The Catholic Missions in China during the Middle Ages (1294–1368)*, by Paul S. Hsiang, 1950. *The Constitution and Supreme Administration of Regional Seminaries Subject to the Sacred*

Congregation for the Propagation of the Faith in China, by Marcian J. Mathis, 1953. *Diplomatic Correspondence Concerning the Chinese Missions of the American Vincentians, 1929–1934*, by Julius M. Schick, 1951. *The History of Privately Controlled Higher Education in the Republic of China*, by Anthony C. Li, 1954. *An Image of the French Religious Protectorate in China, as Reflected in the Catholic and Moderate Press at the Time of the Third Republic*, by Lawrence Nemer, 1967. *Imperial Government and Catholic Missions in China during the Years 1784–1785*, by Bernward Henry Willeke, 1948. *Die katholische Chinamission im Spiegel der rotchinesischen Presse; Versuch einer missionarischen Deutung*, by Johannes Schütte, 1957. *The Maryknoll Movement*, by George Cornelius Powers, 1926. *The Mission of Matteo Ricci, S.J.: A Case Study of an Effort at Guided Culture Change in China in the Sixteenth Century*, by George L. Harris, 1967. *The Negotiations between Ch'i-ying and Lagrené, 1844-1846*, by Angelus Francis J. Grosse-Aschhoff, 1950. *Protestant Mission Schools for Girls in South China (1827 to the Japanese Invasion)*, by Mary Raleigh Anderson, 1943. *Die Sonn- und Festtagsfeier in der katholischen Chinamission; eine geschichtlich-pastorale Untersuchung*, by Franz X. Bürkler, 1942.

CHINESE LANGUAGE MATERIALS/SERIALS: *Fu jen hsüeh chih (Fu jen Sinological Journal/Series Sinologica)*, 1929–47.

CHINESE LANGUAGE MATERIALS: Microfilm of work on laws and memorials concerning Christianity during the Qing dynasty, n.d.

DC–25 Special Collections Section
Catholic University of America
John K. Mullen of Denver Memorial Library
620 Michigan Avenue, NE
Washington DC 20064
(202) 635–5091
Carolyn Lee, Curator

Restrictions: Access by appointment.

1-CLEMENTINE LIBRARY, ca. 1600–1900, ca. 30 volumes
Background note: This collection is part of the collection of the family of Pope Clement XI (Gian Francesco Albani), during whose reign (1700–1721) the Chinese rites controversy was resolved. The nearly 10,000-volume Clementine Library contains books relating to the rites controversy and the history of Christianity in China, such as: *Apologia de' Padri Domenicani Missionarii della China, overo risposta al libro del P. de Tellier, Giesuita*, by Charles Le Gobien, 1699; *De Christiana expeditione apud Sinas suscepta ab societate Iesu. ex p. Matthaei Ricci eiusdem societatis commentarius*, by Nicholas Trigault, 1615; *Difesa de missionarii Cinesi della de Giesu, in risposta all'Apologia de PP. Domenicani missionarii della Cina, intorno à gli onori di Confusio, e de' Morti: Opera di un religioso*, 1700.
PAMPHLETS: 5 pamphlets on the rites controversy from the 17th and early 18th centuries.

2-GENERAL HOLDINGS
Background note: The Special Collections Section holds ca. 30 books, 1667–1833, mostly uncatalogued, about mission history, missionary travel, Chinese civilization and culture, the rites controversy, Chinese and Tibetan language instruction, grammars, and chrestomathies. Examples include: *China monumentis, qua sacris qua profanis, nec non variis naturae et autis spectaculis, aliarumque rerum memorabilium argumentis illustratae*, by Athanasius Kircher, 1667; *Description géographique, historique, chronologique, politique, et physique de l'empire de la Chine et de la Tartarie chinoise, enrichie des cartes générales et particulières de ces pays, de la carte générale & des cartes particulières du Thibet, & de la Corée; & ornée d'un grand nombre de figures & de vignettes gravées en tailledouce*, by Jean Baptiste du Halde, 1735; *Eléments de la grammaire Chinois, ou principes généraux du 'kou-wen' ou style antique et du 'kouan-hua,' c'est-à-dire, de la langue commune généralement utilisée dans l'empire Chinoise*, by Jean Pierre Abel-Remusat, 1822.

MINUTES/RECORDS/REPORTS: Reports on China mission work in *Annales de l'Association de la Propagation de la Foi*, 1827–1931.

SERIALS: *Chinese Repository*, 1833–51.

CHINESE LANGUAGE MATERIALS: Picture book in Chinese and Latin for Chinese Christians, n.a., 1900.

DOMINICAN HOUSE OF STUDIES

DC–30 Library
487 Michigan Avenue, NE
Washington DC 20017–1584
(202) 529–5300
J. Raymond Vandegrift, O.P., Librarian

Background note: In addition to the materials listed below, the Dominican College library also located here holds several books on the work of Dominican missionaries in China, including titles written in Spanish about Spanish missionaries and a small collection dating between 1699 and 1752.

1-GENERAL HOLDINGS
PAMPHLETS: *Kienning-Fu Chronicle: Twenty-five Years in China with the Dominican Fathers and Brothers, Province of St. Joseph, U.S.A.*, by William F. Cassidy, 1948.
DISSERTATIONS/THESES: *The Constitution and Supreme Administration of Regional Seminaries Subject to the Sacred Congregation for the Propagation of the Faith in China*, by Marcian J. Mathis, 1953.

DC–35 Province of St. Joseph Archives
Dominican House of Studies
487 Michigan Avenue, NE
Washington DC 20017
(202) 529–5300
Adrian Wade, O.P., Archivist

1-MISCELLANEOUS MISSION MATERIALS, 1926–51, quantity undetermined
MINUTES/RECORDS/REPORTS: Financial reports of Kienning-fu Mission, 1926–36.
MANUSCRIPTS: Manuscript of a play relating to the murder of Fr. Devine at Kienning-fu by Communist guerillas, 1947.
MEMORABILIA: Clippings from the *Hong Kong Standard* relating to persecution of Chinese Christians, 1951.
MAPS/DESIGNS/DRAWINGS: Miscellaneous maps of China.
AUDIO-VISUAL MATERIALS: Miscellaneous loose photos of China mission activities.

2-PAPERS OF MISSIONARIES OF KIENNING-FU MISSION, 1922-ca. 1950, quantity undetermined
MINUTES/RECORDS/REPORTS/CORRESPONDENCE/MEMORABILIA: Personal correspondence (some of which contains details of mission activities), copies of official reports, and miscellaneous memorabilia, filed by name of missionary.

3-RECORDS OF THE KIENNING-FU MISSION: INSTITUTIONAL RECORDS, 1922-ca. 1950, 1.5 l.f.
MINUTES/RECORDS/REPORTS/CORRESPONDENCE: Administrative correspondence, financial reports, statistical reports.
MANUSCRIPTS: Papers relating to land transactions; other papers, 1950-55.
MAPS/DESIGNS/DRAWINGS: Map of Kienning-fu Mission area in Chinese and English.
AUDIO-VISUAL MATERIALS: Photo album of Kienning-fu Mission and ca. 250 loose photos.

GENERAL CONFERENCE OF SEVENTH-DAY ADVENTISTS

DC-40 Archives
6840 Eastern Avenue, NW
Washington DC 20012
(202) 722-6375
Bert Haloviak, Assistant Archivist

Background note: Seventh-Day Adventist mission work began in China in 1901. The China mission came under the auspices of the Asiatic Division from 1909 to 1919, when all Asian work was reorganized as the Far Eastern Division. Responsibility for the China work was spun off into a separate China division in 1931. Organizations in mainland China severed all connections with the world-wide church organization in 1951 and became an autonomous Chinese church with 278 churches and 21,168 members. Remaining Adventist missions in Hong Kong and other regions, as well as those on Macao and Taiwan, continued with the Far Eastern Division.

The Seventh-Day Adventist Library is currently being consolidated from twenty or more departmental libraries. Finding aids to collections are incomplete but in preparation. See also Andrews University, James White Library, Berrien Springs, MI, 49104.

1-GENERAL HOLDINGS
Restrictions: Fifty-year hold on correspondence.
Background note: The archives of the General Conference contain records of the Seventh-Day Adventist Church. Many China records are scattered throughout the archives and may be traced through names of the missionaries or organizations.
MINUTES/RECORDS/REPORTS: Box of minutes on the China mission, with those of other Asian countries in the records of the Asiatic and Far Eastern Divisions, 1909-31; box of minutes of the China division, 1931-51; ca. 10 pages per year of references to decisions and actions on China activities in the records of the General Conference Committee, consisting of minutes, sessions, financial statements, statistics, and sustentation (retirement) records, 1901-51.
CORRESPONDENCE: 10 boxes of correspondence between the office of the secretary of the General Conference and missionaries:

1901-30 filed by missionary's name in the corresponding secretaries' files; 1931-51 in separate China files.
AUDIO-VISUAL MATERIALS: Ca. 50 glass slides and 50 photos of missionaries, Bible students, Bible class, general meetings, and workers, 1920-30.
SERIALS: *Asiatic Division Mission News*, 1914-17. *Asiatic Division Outlook*, 1917-24. *China Division Reporter*, 1931-51. *Far Eastern Division Outlook*, 1924-. *Newsletter for the Asiatic Division*, 1912-14.
FINDING AIDS: *The General Conference Yearbook* and the *Obituary Index* contain listings of mainland missionaries from 1900 to 1951.

GEORGE WASHINGTON UNIVERSITY

DC-45 Gelman Library
2130 H Street, NW
Washington DC 20052
(202) 676-7497
Sharon D. Galperin, University Archivist

1-JONATHAN TILSON DIARY, 1842-59, 1 volume
Background note: Jonathan Tilson (1818-1908), a Baptist minister in Massachusetts, graduated from Columbian College, a precursor of George Washington University.
DIARIES: Diary including references to China missionaries home on furlough and to Chinese converts accompanying them.

2-GENERAL HOLDINGS
DISSERTATIONS/THESES: *The Rural Work of American Protestant Missionaries in China, 1911-1937*, by William James Megginson, 1968.

GEORGETOWN UNIVERSITY

DC-50 John Vinton Dahlgren Medical Library
Georgetown University Medical Center
3900 Reservoir Road, NW
Washington DC 20007
(202) 624-8348
Naomi Broering, Librarian

1-GENERAL HOLDINGS
SERIALS: *Chinese Medical Journal*, 1943-44, 1962-66.

DC-55 Fred O. Dennis Law Library
Georgetown University Law School
600 New Jersey Avenue, NW
Washington DC 20001
(202) 662-9140
Robert L. Oakley, Director

1-GENERAL HOLDINGS
SERIALS: *China Law Review*, 1928.

DC-60 Joseph Mark Lauinger Library
Georgetown University
37th and O Streets, NW
Washington DC 20057
(202) 625-4173
Joseph E. Jeffs, Director

1-GENERAL HOLDINGS
PAMPHLETS: *The Missions in China*, by Bernard H. Wilke, 1943; *Schism in China: The Encyclical Ad Apostolarum Principis of Pope Pius XII*, 1958.
SERIALS: *China Christian Year Book*, 1925. *Folklore Studies*, 1948, 1951–53, 1955–61. *Monumenta Serica*, 1935–.
DISSERTATIONS/THESES: *The American Community in Canton, 1784–1844*, by Jacques Downs, 1961. *Americans and the Taiping Tien Kuo: A Case of Cultural Confrontation*, by Teng Yuan-chung, 1961. *The Bases and Tactics of the Anti-Vatican Movement in Communist China*, by Philip Shung-tse Sha, 1960. *A Critical Survey of French Sinology, 1870–1900*, by John P. Martin, 1966. *An Eighteenth-century Frenchman at the Court of the K'ang-hsi Emperor: A Study of the Early Life of Jean François Foucquet*, by John W. Witek, 1973. *The Influence of American Missionaries in China upon the Foreign Policy of the United States, 1931–1941*, by Stephen Henning Johnsson, 1956. *Sino-American Relations, 1882–1885: The Mission of John Russell Young*, by Victoria M. Cha-tsu Siu, 1975.
CHINESE LANGUAGE MATERIALS: *Anti-Christian Movement by Chinese Officials and Gentry, 1860–1874*, by Lü Shih-ch'iang, n.d.

DC-65   Special Collections Division
Georgetown University
Joseph Mark Lauinger Library
37th and O Streets, NW
Washington DC 20057
(202) 625-3230
Nicholas B. Scheetz, Manuscripts Librarian

1-GEORGE SCHWARZ COLLECTION, 1674–82, 1 volume
CORRESPONDENCE: Letters from Gabriel de Magalhães to Juan Cardoso on the visit of the Chinese emperor to the Jesuit church; from Thomas Pereira to Simon Rodriguez on the death of Gabriel de Magalhães; and from Simon Rodriguez, in China, to the Provincial of the Philippines, in "Relationes P. P. Missionariorum Societatis Jesu in America Septemtrionali et in China 1672–1682" (Prague, 1685), a bound collection of over 30 letters concerning Jesuit missionaries in the Americas, the Pacific, and Asia, mostly addressed to Rev. Matthias Tanner.

2-GRANGER-TEILHARD DE CHARDIN COLLECTION, 1924–35, 18 items
CORRESPONDENCE: 18 letters by French Jesuit theologian Pierre Teilhard de Chardin to Walter Granger, chief paleontologist of the Central Asiatic expedition, on paleontological discoveries, 1924–35.

3-LUKAS-TEILHARD DE CHARDIN COLLECTION, ca. 1919–1958, 2 l.f.
Restrictions: Access by appointment.
Background note: Mary and Ellen Lukas amassed this collection of research files in the writing of their book, *Teilhard, A Biography* (1977).
CORRESPONDENCE/AUDIO-VISUAL MATERIALS: Letters, photo reproductions of unpublished letters, and photos of Pierre Teilhard de Chardin, his family, friends, and associates.

DC-70   Woodstock Theological Center Library
Georgetown University
Joseph Mark Lauinger Library
37th and O Streets, NW
Washington DC 20057
(202) 625-3120
Eugene M. Rooney, S.J., Librarian

Background note: The library of the former Woodstock College, the Woodstock Theological Center Library is part of the Woodstock Theological Center, an independent research institute. Housed in Lauinger Library, the Woodstock collection concentrates on sixteenth- and seventeenth-century encounters between Europe and Asia, and the history of Christian missions.
    Dated 1581 through 1950, the collection includes 55 volumes by and about Pierre Teilhard de Chardin, and early writings by missionaries of other Catholic orders, in addition to those by Protestant pioneers.

1-GEORGE B. BARBOUR COLLECTION OF PIERRE TEILHARD DE CHARDIN MATERIALS, 1928–72, ca. 1,500 items
Background note: For biographical notes on George B. Barbour, see Hoover Institution on War, Revolution, and Peace, Archives, Stanford University, Stanford, CA, 94305-2323.
CORRESPONDENCE: 200 photocopies of letters from Pierre Teilhard de Chardin, including correspondents such as American sculptor Melvina Hoffman, n.d.; ca. 185 pages of correspondence from George Barbour in China during the Yangtze Expedition of 1934, mainly to his wife, 1928–54; ca. 900 letters to George Barbour regarding Teilhard, n.d.
MANUSCRIPTS: Typescripts of 2 lectures on Teilhard by George Barbour, n.d.
PAMPHLETS/MEMORABILIA: Ca. 900 clippings, pamphlets, and articles regarding Teilhard, n.d.; bust of Teilhard by Melvina Hoffman, n.d.
AUDIO-VISUAL MATERIALS: Film biography of Teilhard, 1965; ca. 150 photos and negatives of work in China, including work at Chen-Kon-Tien and the Yangtze expedition of 1934.
FINDING AIDS: In-house directory.

2-SHRUB OAK COLLECTION, 17th and 18th centuries, ca. 50 items
Background note: This collection contains ca. 50 published reports, letters, and biographies by and about seventeenth- and eighteenth-century Jesuit missionaries in China.

3-SPECIAL COLLECTION, 17th–19th centuries, ca. 500 volumes
Restrictions: Access by appointment.
Background note: Among the many books in its Special Collection which detail the life and work of Jesuits in China from the early seventeenth through the mid-nineteenth centuries, the Woodstock Library contains one of the rare surviving examples of blockbooks printed under the direction of the Jesuits in Peking, *Innocenta Victrix, sive Sententia Comitiorum Impeii Sinici pro Innocenta*, by Giovanni Lobelli, S.J., 1669.
MANUSCRIPTS: Anonymous, bound, handwritten manuscript of a Chinese-Latin dictionary, attributed to Basile de Gemona, pre-19th century.
FINDING AIDS: "Resources on China and Japan among the Jesuit Publications in the Woodstock Theological Center Library, Georgetown University," by Ann Nottingham Kelsall, 1977.

4-GENERAL HOLDINGS

Background note: Woodstock Library's holdings include many reference works which aid in locating and researching the life and career of any member of the Society of Jesus from its beginnings to the present. Ca. 1,200 volumes known collectively as "Jesuit Personnel Catalogues" list the names, mission stations, and activities of Jesuits from the seventeenth century to the present. Examples are *Notices biographiques et bibliographiques sur les Jésuites de l'ancienne mission de Chine, 1552–1773*, by Louis Pfister, S.J., 1932, and *Catalogus Patrum ac Fratrum S.J. qui Evangelio Christi Propagando in Sinis Adlaboraverunt. Pars secunda: 1842–1908; addito catalogo sacerdotum saecularium missionis Nankinensis*, ed. by Ignatius Henri Dugout, S.J., 1908. Short "pocket" biographies of Jesuits running from the seventeenth century to the present are found in the *Ménologe de la Compagnie de Jésus*, ed. by Elesban de Guilhermy, S.J. (Poitiers: H. Oudin, 1867–1902, and others), and from 1814 to 1970 in the *Catalogus Defunctorum in renata Societate Iesu, ab a.1814 ad 1970*, ed. by Rufo Mendizábal, S.J., 1972.

Various collections of correspondence such as *Lettres édifiantes et curieuses* date back to the sixteenth century and number in the hundreds. Some volumes are on China alone, while others contain China correspondence among that of other areas. Listings for Taiwan, Macao, and Hong Kong continue to the present.
MINUTES/RECORDS/REPORTS: Records and reports on the China mission in the serials *Annales de la Congregation de la Mission ou Receuil de Lettres Edifiantes*, 1852–88; *Annales de la Propagation de la Foi* (Lyon ed.), 1822–54, 1860–96; *Annales de la Propagation de la Foi pour la Province de Québec*, 1880–87; *Annales de la Société des Missions*, 1910–23; *Annales domus Zi-Ka-Wei S.J. Pars prima ab ejus primordio ad finem anni, 1847–1860*; *Annals of the Propagation of the Faith* (London ed.), 1839–66; (Paris ed.), 1838–40; and *Archivum Historicum Societatis Iesu*, 1932-.
PAMPHLETS: *The Basic Strategy of Matthew Ricci, S.J., in the Introduction of Christianity to China*, by Richard V. Lawlor, 1951; *Biographie du Père Etienne Le Fèvre de la Compagnie de Jésus; décédé en Chine le 22 mai 1659*, by Leopold Gain, 1922.
SERIALS: *American Jesuits in China*, 1952. *Asia*, 1948–60. *China Letter*, 1955–63. *Chine, Ceylan, Madagascar*, 1898, 1901–2, 1906, 1920, 1925–26. *Lettres des nouvelles missions de Chine*, 1843–44. *Missionariorum Ministeria et Opera in Provincia Kiangnan ab Anno MDCCCXLVII ad MDCCCLXXXI*, 1881. *Missions de Chine et du Japon*, 1929. *Oeuvres de la mission de Kiang-nan*, 1891–1912. *Relations de Chine*, 1925–38. *Variétés Sinologiques*, 1932 (repr. 1971). *Your China Letter*, 1952–54.

HOWARD UNIVERSITY
DC–75   Moorland-Spingarn Research Center
2400 Sixth Street, NW
Washington DC 20059
(202) 636–7480
Esme E. Bhan, Research Associate

Restrictions: Access by appointment.

1-JESSE MOORLAND PAPERS, 1898–1923, 2 in.
MINUTES/RECORDS/REPORTS: "China and India," reports, n.d.

PAMPHLETS: *The Y.M.C.A. in China*, n.a., 1922.
CHINESE LANGUAGE MATERIALS: *The Red Triangle: Helping China's River Conservancy*, n.a. (Shanghai: National Committee of the YMCA), ca.1923.
FINDING AIDS: In-house directory (Coll. 126, Box 64, Folder #1224).

LIBRARY OF CONGRESS

Background note: Because more than 75 million items are held by the Library of Congress (LC), it is not possible to detail holdings on Christianity in China. Rather, relative strengths of the divisions are described, with a few exemplary collections indicated. Bibliographic aids, the most current of which are at the LC itself, and on-site consultation with staff are necessary to locate specific items. The nature of certain types of material creates subject titling and cross-referencing difficulties, limiting the usefulness of card catalogues in some divisions.

Researchers working on Christianity in China should begin with consultations at the Asian division, where staff and specialized bibliographies will identify appropriate materials.
Finding aids: *Scholars' Guide to Washington DC for East Asian Studies (China, Japan, Korea, and Mongolia)*, by Hong N. Kim (Washington DC: Smithsonian Institution Press for the Woodrow Wilson International Center for Scholars), 1979.

DC–80   Asian Division
Library of Congress
Thomas Jefferson Building
10 First Street, SE
Washington DC 20540
(202) 287–5423
Warren M.Tsuneishi, Chief
Chi Wang, Head, Chinese and Korean Section

Background note: The Asian Division's specialized staff and bibliographic resources can assist in securing current references and locating uncatalogued or unclassified materials on LC holdings about Christianity in China. The following are examples of the division's special collections.

The division's general holdings include printed works in Asian languages, which are included in the main shelflist and catalogues of the LC for post-1958 catalogued items. Titles catalogued before 1958 are in separate card catalogues maintained by the Asian Division. The number and kind of items relating to Christianity in China has not been determined. Serial titles in Chinese language relating to Christianity in China are listed in the general collections (see CHINESE LANGUAGE MATERIALS/SERIALS under Library of Congress, GENERAL HOLDINGS below).
Finding aids: *Chinese Collections in the Library of Congress: Excerpts from the Annual Reports of the Librarian of Congress, 1898–1971*, comp. by Ping-kuen Yu (Washington DC: Center for Chinese Research Materials, Association of Research Libraries), 1974, 3 V; *Chinese Cooperative Catalog*, 1975-; *Chinese-English and English-Chinese Dictionaries in the Library of Congress*, by Robert Dunn, 1977; *Chinese Periodicals in the Library of Congress*, by Han-chu Huang, 1979; *A Descriptive Catalog of Rare*

Chinese Books in the Library of Congress, comp. by Chung-min Wang, ed. by T. L. Yuan, 1957, 2 V; *Far Eastern Languages Catalog* (Boston: G. K. Hall and Co.), 1972, 22 V (includes publications catalogued between 1958 and 1971).

1-ARCHIVES IN THE JAPANESE MINISTRY OF FOREIGN AFFAIRS, 1912–43, 2 reels microfilm
MINUTES/RECORDS/REPORTS: 1 reel of microfilm of general records, 1931–43, and records referring to the United States, 1928–41, relating to missionary work and education in China (SO.2.3.0-(1–2); 1 reel of microfilm of documents relating to the right to proselytize in the hinterland of China, 1912–20 (MT 3.10.1.15).
FINDING AIDS: *Checklist of Archives: In the Japanese Ministry of Foreign Affairs, Tokyo, Japan, 1868–1945; Microfilmed for the Library of Congress, 1949-1951*, comp. by Cecil H. Uyehara (Washington DC: Library of Congress Photoduplication Service), 1954.

2-WILLIAM GAMBLE COLLECTION, ca. 1800–1870, 427 items
Background note: A printer for the Presbyterian Board of Foreign Missions, William Gamble (1830–86) worked in Ningpo from 1858 to 1860 and in Shanghai from 1860 to 1870, when he left China.
MINUTES/RECORDS/REPORTS: 120 reports and other items from mission hospitals, presses, and other institutions at Ningpo and Shanghai, ca. 1800–1858.
AUDIO-VISUAL MATERIALS: Ca. 30 photos of William Gamble's acquaintances, including missionaries, 1858–70.
CHINESE LANGUAGE MATERIALS/MAPS/DESIGNS/DRAWINGS: *Yu ti ch'uan t'u (Map of the World)*, by Ma Chün-liang, ca. 1755.
CHINESE LANGUAGE MATERIALS: Ca. 277 scriptures and tracts in 493 volumes, ca. 1800–1850, printed in Malacca, Hong Kong, Amoy, Foochow, Ningpo, and Shanghai, including translations of geographies, astronomy, mathematics, botany, medical texts, hymnals, cookbooks, and others; tracts by Elijah Coleman Bridgman, William C. Burns, Joseph Edkins, William Gamble, Samuel Wells Williams, and Alexander Wylie, and others; tracts by Henry Blodget, David Collie, Karl F. A. Gützlaff, Walter Macon Lowrie, Divie Bethune McCartee, William Alexander Parsons Martin, Walter Henry Medhurst, William Milne, William Muirhead, John Livingston Nevius, James Summers, and Alexander Williamson, and others.
FINDING AIDS: In-house guide.

3-PEKING UNION MEDICAL COLLEGE COLLECTION, ca. 13th–19th centuries, 305 reels microfilm
Background note: This is a collection of Chinese medical books from the library of Peking Union Medical College, focusing on the fifteenth, sixteenth, and seventeenth centuries.
CHINESE LANGUAGE MATERIALS: Microfilms of 3,600 printed or manuscript volumes representing 654 Chinese medical works, mostly on fevers and infectious diseases.

4-SELECTED ARCHIVES OF THE JAPANESE ARMY, NAVY, AND OTHER GOVERNMENT AGENCIES, ca. 1930, 1 reel microfilm
MINUTES/RECORDS/REPORTS: Microfilmed documents on the anti-Christian movement in China, ca. 1930 (T100. SHINA KYOSANTO UNDO, SONO TA).
FINDING AIDS: *Checklist of Microfilm Reproductions of Selected Archives of the Japanese Army, Navy, and Other Government Agencies*, by John Young (Washington DC: Georgetown University Press), 1959.

DC–85   Geography and Map Division
Library of Congress
James Madison Memorial Building
10 First Street, SE
Washington DC 20540
(202) 287–5000
John A. Wolter, Chief

Background note: East Asian materials held by the Geography and Map Division number 21,000 items, including maps and charts, atlases, globes, and three-dimensional relief models. The proportion of the collection which relates to Christianity in China has not been determined. A few of the division's special collections are described below.

Approximately 55 percent of the 3.9 million maps are individual sheets of large and medium-scale series maps and charts published during the nineteenth and twentieth centuries, of which approximately 5,283 single and multi-sheet thematic maps are of China. Shelflist measurements also reveal approximately 447 atlases on China.
Finding aids: *List of Geographical Atlases in the Library of Congress, with Bibliographical Notes* (Library of Congress), n.d., 8 V. *Bibliography of Cartography* (Boston: G. K. Hall), 1973, 5 V. *Bibliography of Cartography, First Supplement* (Boston: G. K. Hall), 1980, 2 V. *Geography and Map Division: A Guide to Its Collections and Services* (Library of Congress), 1975.

1-HUMMEL COLLECTION, 1674, 1 item
Background note: This map was obtained by Orientalist Arthur W. Hummel while a resident of China.
MAPS/DESIGNS/DRAWINGS/CHINESE LANGUAGE MATERIALS: *Map of the World*, by Ferdinand Verbiest, 1674, in Chinese, wood-block prints on 8 scrolls.

2-GENERAL HOLDINGS
MAPS/DESIGNS/DRAWINGS: Japanese version of Matteo Ricci's world map, by Sekisui Nagakubo, ca.1600.

DC–90   Manuscript Division
Library of Congress
James Madison Memorial Building
10 First Street, SE
Washington DC 20540
(202) 287–5387
James H. Huston, Chief

Background note: The Manuscript Division's total holdings relating to Christianity in China have not been determined. Staff help is indispensable for locating specific items. Collections described below are only a sample of what is held by the division.
Finding aids: The most current finding aid is *The National Union Catalog of Manuscript Collections* (Library of Congress), 1959-. Earlier publications include: *Guide to Archives and Manuscripts in the United States*, by Philip Hamer (New Haven, CT: Yale Univer-

sity Press), 1961; *Handbook of Manuscripts in the Library of Congress* (Library of Congress), 1918; *List of Manuscript Collections in the Library of Congress to July 1931*, by Curtis W. Garrison, 1932; and *List of Manuscript Collections Received in the Library of Congress, July 1931 to July 1938*, by C. Percy Powell, 1939.

The Annual Report of the Library of Congress, 1898-, and the *Quarterly Journal of the Library of Congress*, 1943-, describe current manuscript acquisitions.

An unpublished computerized listing, updated every six months, provides the most complete holdings list. Other unpublished guides include: "Manuscript Division: Library of Congress," and "Catalogs, Indexes, Finding Aids."

1-JAMES COLDER PAPERS, 1851-53, 2 volumes
Background note: James Colder was an American missionary and U.S. Vice Consul in Foochow.
DIARIES: "Voyage to China," a journal on Colder's trip to China on the ship *Russell*, 1851; private journal covering Colder's time in China, mostly in "Fuchan," 1851-53.

2-CALVIN COOLIDGE PAPERS, 1925, 12 pages
MINUTES/RECORDS/REPORTS: Canton Christian College, 1925 (Case File 2904).
FINDING AIDS: *Index to the Calvin Coolidge Papers* (Washington DC: Library of Congress), 1965.

3-FRANCIS DUNLAP GAMEWELL PAPERS, 1900-1937, 1 volume
Background note: Francis Dunlap Gamewell was an American missionary to China from 1900 to 1906 and 1937.
MEMORABILIA: Scrapbook containing letters, photos, clippings, and other memorabilia, mainly concerning Gamewell's work as a missionary in China and his service in Peking during the Boxer Rebellion, 1900-1906, 1937.

4-HENRY ROBINSON LUCE PAPERS, 1935-65, 7 boxes
Background note: The son of missionary Henry Winters Luce, publisher Henry Robinson Luce (1898-1967) was born on the campus of Shantung Christian University. A supporter of Christian education in China, Luce became particularly involved with war and famine relief in China during and after World War II.
MINUTES/RECORDS/REPORTS/CORRESPONDENCE/PAMPHLETS: Mostly correspondence, with some records, reports, and pamphlets, as enclosures with the letters, including 2.5 boxes on the United Board for Christian Higher Education in China, 1935-65; 2 boxes on United China Relief, 1941-45; box on United Service to China, 1946-58 (mostly 1948-49); and 1.5 boxes on the Yale-in-China Association, 1941-46.
CORRESPONDENCE: Folder of Luce's correspondence with Pearl S. Buck and Walter H. Judd, 1941-48.
FINDING AID: In-house directory.

5-MISCELLANEOUS MANUSCRIPTS, 1699, 1 volume
DIARIES: Journal describing trip to China and Jesuits, by Giovanni Gherardini, 1699 (in French prose and Italian verse).

6-MORAL RE-ARMAMENT, INC. RECORDS—FRANK N. D. BUCHMAN, 1916-19, 1 folder
MINUTES/RECORDS/REPORTS: Ca. 1/2 folder of records on Chinese missions, 1916-19.

CORRESPONDENCE: Ca. 1/2 folder of correspondence with Christiana Tsai, 1918, n.d.

7-JOHN SHERMAN PAPERS, 1897-98, ca. 1 volume
MINUTES/RECORDS/REPORTS: Correspondence concerning Secretary of State John Sherman's discussions with President William McKinley on Chinese internal attitudes to missionaries and converts, 1897-98.

8-SOCIETY FOR PROPAGATION OF THE GOSPEL RECORDS IN LAMBETH PALACE LIBRARY, 1701-1901, ca. 1 reel microfilm
CORRESPONDENCE: Correspondence on China, 1701-1901.

DC-95 Motion Picture, Broadcasting, and Recorded Sound Division
Library of Congress
Motion Picture Section
Thomas Jefferson Building, Room 1046
10 First Street, SE
Washington DC 20540
(202) 287-5840
Erik Barnouw, Chief

Background note: The Motion Picture Section holds approximately 100 items on China, including the People's Republic of China. Computer disk technology is available for viewing purposes.
Finding aids: *Motion Pictures from the Library of Congress Paper Print Collection*, by Kemp R. Niver (Berkeley, CA: University of California Press), 1967; *Library of Congress Catalog—Films and Other Materials for Projection*, issued quarterly and as part of the library's *National Union Catalog*; and *Motion Pictures and Filmstrips*, also part of the *National Union Catalog*.

1-PAPER-PRINT COLLECTION, 1894-1912, 7 items
AUDIO-VISUAL MATERIALS: 7 paper print reproductions, varying from 20 to 100 feet in length, of motion pictures made in the early twentieth century: "The Forbidden City," "Peking," "Ch'ien-men Gate, Peking," "Landing Wharf at Canton," "Canton River Scene," "Canton Steamboat Landing Chinese Passengers," and "Chinese Procession."

2-GENERAL HOLDINGS
AUDIO-VISUAL MATERIALS: 3 motion pictures: *A Christian in Communist China*, by Jan Sadlo (Film Services), 1960; *My Name is Han*, by Paul F. Heard (Protestant Film Commission, 1948); *Thy Will Be Done*, by Cathedral Films, 1949.

DC-100 Music Division
American Folklife Center—Archive of Folk Song
Library of Congress
Library of Congress Building
Ground Floor, G152
10 First Street, SE
Washington DC 20540
(202) 287-5510
Joseph C. Hickerson, Head

Restrictions: Access by appointment.
Background note: The Archive of Folk Song houses recordings containing folksongs, folk music, folk tales, oral history, and other

types of folklore, some of which were prepared by missionaries in China. In addition to materials from the United States, the Archive maintains representative collections of traditional music and lore from foreign countries, some of which were prepared by missionaries in China. The number and kind of items relating to Christianity in China has not been determined.

Finding aids: *Music, Books on Music and Sound Recordings*, a part of the *National Union Catalog*; *The Music Division: A Guide to its Collections and Services*, 1972.

1-GENERAL HOLDINGS, n.d., 5 12-inch records
AUDIO-VISUAL MATERIALS: Chinese songs recorded by Chao Rulan, Margaret Speaks, and students and faculty of the former California College in China, n.d.

DC-105 Prints and Photographs Division
> Library of Congress
> Thomas Jefferson Building
> 10 First Street, SE
> Washington DC 20540
> (202) 287-9156
> Steven Ostrow, Chief

Background note: The number and type of materials on Christianity in China in the Prints and Photographs Division has not been determined. Estimates reveal at least 174 collections on China, ranging from 25 to 2,500 items in each collection, 1,730 stereographs from the early 1900s, and a large number of unprocessed prints. Staff assistance is recommended. Computer disk technology is available for viewing purposes.

Finding aids: *Guide to the Special Collections of Prints and Photographs in the Library of Congress*, by Paul Vanderbilt (Library of Congress), 1955, locates major collections catalogued before 1955.

1-GAMBLE COLLECTION, 1860-80, 50 items
Background note: This collection of photos, from William Gamble of the Presbyterian Board of Foreign Missions, is specifically related to Christianity in China. The larger part of William Gamble's materials is described above in the Asian Division.
AUDIO-VISUAL MATERIALS: Photos and photocopies of pictures of missionaries and Chinese daily life made in the 1860s and 1870s and collected by William Gamble, a printer for the Presbyterian Board of Foreign Missions in Ningpo and Shanghai.

DC-110 Rare Book Division
> Library of Congress
> Library of Congress Building
> Second Floor, Room 256
> 10 First Street, SE
> Washington DC 20540
> (202) 287-5434
> William Mathison, Chief

Background note: The Rare Book Division's complete holdings relating to Christianity in China have not been determined. The Asian Division holds most rare Chinese language materials. Western language materials are held by this division. Examples are *Dell' historia della China Genova*, by Juan Gonzalez de Mendoza,

1586, and travel books by early Western visitors and missionaries.
Finding aids: *Rare Book Division: A Guide to Its Collections and Services*, 1965. *Some Guides to Special Collections in the Rare Book Division*, 1947.

1-GENERAL HOLDINGS
SERIALS: *Chinese Repository*, 1832-51.

DC-115 Recorded Sound Section
> Library of Congress
> Library of Congress Building
> Ground Floor, G152
> 10 First Street, SE
> Washington DC 20540
> (202) 287-5508/9
> Robert Carneal, Head of Recorded Sound

Background note: The number and kind of items held by the Recorded Sound Section which are related to Christianity in China have not been determined.
Finding aids: Catalogued materials in *Music, Books on Music, and Sound Recordings*, issued as part of the *National Union Catalog*. *National Union Catalog 1963-1967: Music and Phonorecords V 1-2* (Ann Arbor, MI: J. W. Edwards), 1969.

1-GENERAL HOLDINGS
AUDIO-VISUAL MATERIALS: 2 12-inch records of *A Chinese Christmas*, carols performed in Cantonese and English by the St. Paul's Children's Choir of Hong Kong (Sisters of St. Paul of Chartres, Hong Kong), with orchestra, 1965.

DC-120 General Reading Rooms Division
> Library of Congress Building
> 1st Floor, Room 144
> 10 First Street, SE
> Washington DC 20540
> (202) 287-5000
> (202) 287-5530 (Reading Room Division)
> James Billington, Librarian of Congress
> Ellen Zabel Hahn, Chief, General Reading
>   Rooms Division

Restrictions: Appointments recommended.
Background note: Various LC divisions hold serials. Although most bound periodicals are shelved in the general collections, cataloging aids should be checked to determine the exact location of a particular title. The titles listed below are those catalogued in the *National Union List of Serials*.
Finding aids: *The National Union Catalog* (London: Mansell), 610 V, which includes pre-1956 imprints; *The Catalog of Books Represented by Library of Congress Printed Cards Issued (August 1898-July 1942)*, 167 V, and its *Supplement: August 1, 1942-December 31, 1947*, 42 V (Washington DC: Library of Congress). *The Library of Congress Author Catalog: A Cumulative List of Works Represented by Library of Congress Cards, 1948-1952*, 24 V (Washington DC: Library of Congress); *Library of Congress Catalog-Books: Subjects, A Cumulative List of Works Represented by Library of Congress Printed Cards*, multiple volumes, 1945-74 (reprint cumulations for 1950-59 from Rowman and Littlefield;

1960–77 from J. W. Edwards; 1978–present, LC Cataloging Distribution Service Division); *Library of Congress Subject Catalog*, (Washington DC: Library of Congress), 1975–, quarterly issues with an annual cumulation.

National Union Catalog: Reference and Related Services (Washington DC: Library of Congress) 1973; *Combined Indexes to the Library of Congress Classification Schedules*, comp. by Nancy Olson (Washington DC: U.S. Historical Documents Institute), 1974–, 15 V. *Union List of Serials in Libraries of the United States and Canada*, by Edna B. Titus, 5 V, 1965. *New Serial Titles: A Union List of Serials Commencing Publication after December 31, 1949*, 1950–70, 4 V (R. R. Bowker, 1971–74, plus current cumulations, LC Cataloging Distribution Service Division). *Dissertation Abstracts International* (University Microfilms, Inc., Ann Arbor, MI). *Doctoral Dissertations on China: A Bibliography of Studies in Western Languages, 1945–1970*, by Frank Joseph Shulman (Seattle: University of Washington Press), 1972. *Doctoral Dissertations on China, 1971–1975: A Bibliography of Studies in Western Languages*, by Frank Joseph Shulman (Seattle: University of Washington Press), 1978. *Doctoral Dissertations on Asia: An Annotated Bibliographical Journal of Current International Research*, by Frank Joseph Shulman (Ann Arbor, MI: Association of Asian Studies), 1975–81, 4 V.

Other published and unpublished (on-site) auxiliary union catalogues available in the Union Catalog Reference Section.

For assistance on Library of Congress General Holdings, also consult:

Main Reading Room Section
(202) 287–2116
Josephus Nelson, Head

Thomas Jefferson Reading Rooms Section
(202) 287–4438
Gary Jensen, Head

Union Catalog Reference Section
(202) 287–6300
Dorothy G. Kearney, Head

1-GENERAL HOLDINGS
MINUTES/RECORDS/REPORTS: Cheeloo University, School of Medicine, report, 1919–38; Lingnan University, College of Medicine, report, 1928–30.
SERIALS: *Bulletin Catholique de Pékin*, 1936–37. Catholic University of Peking, *Bulletin*, 1926–31, 1934. Cheeloo University, School of Medicine, *Bulletin*, 1920–21, 1932. China Christian Educational Association, *Bulletin*, 1924–26, 1932–36. *China Christian Year Book*, 1911–19, 1923–39. China International Famine Relief Commission, *Publications*, series A, 1922–?; series B, 1922–?; series E, 1932?. *China Law Review*, 1922, 1937–40. *China Monthly*, 1939–41, 1944–46, 1949–50. *China Notes*, 1962–68. *China's Millions* (Philadelphia), 1903–4, 1919, 1924–61. *Chinese Medical Journal*, 1908–14, 1916, 1937–39, 1941, 1945, 1950–57. *Ching Feng*, 1968–86. *Educational Review*, 1915–38. *Far East*, 1896–98. *Foochow Messenger*, 1909–16. *Fu-Jen Magazine*, 1932–35. *Fu Jen News Letter*, 1931–32. *Johannean*, 1924. *Lingnan Science Journal*, 1922–23, 1926, 1929–42. Lingnan University, *Daily Meteorological Record*, 1921–26; *Science Bulletin*, 1930, 1936–37. Lingnan Natural History Survey and Museum,

Special Publications, 1947(?)–1950. *Maryknoll Mission Letters*, 1929–49. *Missions de Chine*, 1940–41. Nanking Theological Seminary, English Publications, 1940. *News of China*, 1945, 1948–49. *New Horizons*, 1934–44. *Peking Natural History Bulletin*, 1926–41, 1948–50. University of Nanking, College of Agriculture and Forestry, *Agriculture and Forestry Notes*, 1935–36; *Agriculture and Forestry Series*, 1920; *Bulletin*, 1932, 1934–36, 1938–41; *Special Report*, 1935. West China Border Research Society, *Journal*, 1922–32. *West China Missionary News*, 1915–17, 1920, 1924–26. Yenching University: Department of Biology, *Bulletin*, 1930; Department of Sociology and Social Work, *Sociology Fellowship News*, 1930.
DISSERTATIONS/THESES: Microfilm copies of nearly all the doctoral dissertations listed in *Dissertation Abstracts International*.
CHINESE LANGUAGE MATERIALS/SERIALS: *Ch'i-ta chi k'an (Cheeloo University Journal)*, 1932. *Fu jen hsüeh chih (Fu jen Sinological Journal/Series Sinologica)*, 1929–47. *Fukien wên hua (Fukien Culture)*, 1931–32, 1935–36, 1939, 1941–48. *Ling-nan hsüeh pao (Lingnan Journal)*, 1929–52. *Shang hsien t'ang chi shih (Institute Record)*, 1910–17. *Tung wu hsüeh pao (Soochow Journal)*, 1919–22, 1933–37. Yen-ching ta hsüeh, *She hui wen t'i* (Sociological Society, *Organ*), 1930–31; *Shih hsüeh nien pao (Historical Annual)*, 1929–40; *Wen hsüeh nien pao (Chinese Literature)*, 1932–41; *Yen-ching hsüeh pao (Yenching Journal of Chinese Studies)*, 1927–51.

DC–125 NATIONAL ARCHIVES AND RECORDS SERVICE

Eighth Street and Pennsylvania Avenue, NW
Washington DC 20408
(202) 523–3099
(202) 523–3238 (Diplomatic branch)
Donald W. Wilson, Archivist of the United States

Restrictions: Researcher identification card issued by the National Archives required. Contact staff regarding access to materials, as certain records are under time and security restrictions.
Background note: The National Archives and Records Service (NARS) houses and administers records produced by the United States government's executive, legislative, and judicial branches, as well as most of the independent regulatory commissions and agencies from 1774 to the present.

Records in the NARS are generally arranged by agency of origin, not by subject. The combined records of a particular government agency, such as the Department of State, are referred to as a record group. Record groups are maintained in chronological order of acquisition.

Materials on Christianity in China are found in areas of interaction of U.S. government agencies and Christians in China. The greatest concentration of holdings can be found in the Records of the Department of State (RG 59), the Records of the Foreign Service Posts of the Department of State (RG 84), groups related to military activities abroad, Department of Commerce, and a number of other U.S. government agencies. The collections listed below are only an indication of the kind of materials maintained by the National Archives and Records Service.

Finding aids: *Guide to the National Archives of the United States*, 1974. Folders for each record group, which contain inventories, special lists, and other reference materials, are held in Room 200-B of the National Archives Building. Individual branches also maintain reference materials specific to the record groups under their care. *Catalogue of National Archives Film Publications*, 1974, lists records available on microfilm. Consult staff for regulations concerning holdings, finding aids, and reference materials.

1-NATIONAL ARCHIVES COLLECTION OF FOREIGN RECORDS SEIZED (RG 242), 1937–45, ca. 15 folders, 6 reels microfilm
Background note: Among materials of the *National Archives Collection of Foreign Records Seized* are those of the German consulates at Hankow and Tsingtao.
MINUTES/RECORDS/REPORTS/CORRESPONDENCE/MEMORABILIA: Ca. 1 folder of reports, correspondence, and clippings in the records of the Hankow Consulate on German mission finance, conditions, damage claims, and relations with Chinese and Japanese during World War II, 1937–44; and on wartime conditions of the Katholische Mission at Sinyang, 1941–45.

Reports, correspondence, and clippings in the records of the Tsingtao Consulate on Deutsche Kirchengemeinde in Harbin, 1929; Katholische Mission, 1942–45; educational and cultural mission activities, 1945; "Deutsches Heim (ehem. Christl. Soldatheim)," school and hospital, 1911–37; radio broadcasts of missions, 1942–45; mission-owned property, 1927–45; and finances and property of German Protestant and Catholic missions, 1927–38; 6 reels of microfilm of "Regierung zur Christlichen Kirche."

2-NATIONAL ARCHIVES GIFT COLLECTION (RG 200), 1898–1901, quantity undetermined
CORRESPONDENCE: Letters written by Leslie R. Groves as a U.S. Army chaplain in China, 1898–1901.

3-RECORDS OF BOUNDARY AND CLAIMS COMMISSIONS AND ARBITRATIONS (RG 76), n.d., quantity undetermined
MINUTES/RECORDS/REPORTS: Documents concerning international disputes and their accompanying diplomatic maneuvers, including the "Protocol of 1901-Boxer Rebellion Claims and Indemnity Fund."

4-RECORDS OF THE DEPARTMENT OF STATE (RG 59), 1910–44, ca. 30 folders
MINUTES/RECORDS/REPORTS: Ca. 1 folder of material for each of the following subject headings: American Baptist Mission, 1930–42; American Board of Commissioners for Foreign Missions, 1931–42; American Church Mission, 1932–41; American missions, 1930–44; American missions in Manchuria, 1932–41; American Presbyterian mission, 1932–42; American Reformed Church mission, 1930–43; American schools, 1930–39, 1941–43; American Southern Baptist mission, 1932–39; anti-Christian propaganda and riots, ca. 1910–29; Augustana Synod mission, 1930–39; British missions, 1930–39; Catholic Foreign Missionary Society of America, 1930–32; Catholic foreign missions, 1930–44; Christian and Missionary Alliance, 1940–41; Christian and Missionary Alliance missions, 1937–39; Christian Herald mission, 1938–39; Christian Herald Missionary Organization, 1940–41; Covenant Missionary Society, 1938, 1940–41; Evangelical Church mission, 1931–40; famine relief, 1910–11; Free Methodist mission, 1938–41; Fukien Christian University, 1935–38; Lutheran

United mission at Sinyangchow, 1930–39; Lutheran United mission, 1939–42; Lutheran Brethren mission, 1930–42; Mennonite Brethren mission, 1940–42; Methodist missions, 1931–42; mission schools, ca. 1910–1929; property of American missionaries, 1930–39; Protestant Episcopal Church of the U.S., 1937–38, 1940–41; Seventh-Day Adventist mission, 1932–42; University of Shanghai, 1938–40; Yenching University, 1930–39.
CORRESPONDENCE: Ca. 15 folders of correspondence by diplomats concerning missionaries.
FINDING AIDS: For correspondence above, National Archives Decimal files 393.116/163–189 and 393.11/1415, 1420.

DC–130 Audio-visual Archives Division
Motion Picture, Sound, and Video Branch
National Archives and Records Service
Eighth Street and Pennsylvania Avenue, NW
Washington DC 20408
(202) 786–0042
Leslie C. Waffen, Chief, Motion Picture, Sound, and Video Branch

Restrictions: Access by appointment.
Finding aids: *Motion Pictures in the Audio-visual Archives Division of the National Archives*, by Mayfield S. Bray and William T. Murphy, 1972.

1-MISSIONS-CHINA (RG 11), 1930s and 1940s, 5 motion picture reels
AUDIO-VISUAL MATERIALS: Films of missionaries and converts, Church General Hospital, Bible students, health and child care, education and church services; University of Nanking Theological Seminary, colleges, departments, faculty and students, hospital, and academic and social occasions; "Here Is China," by United China Relief, 1943–44.
FINDING AIDS: Accession NN 368–14; RG 111, Accession 2355.

DC–135 Audio-visual Archives Division
Still-Picture Branch
National Archives and Records Service
Eighth Street and Pennsylvania Avenue, NW
Washington DC 20408
(202) 523–3236
Joseph Thomas, Chief, Still-Picture Branch

Restrictions: Access by appointment.
Finding aids: *Still Pictures in the Audio-visual Archives Division of the National Archives*, by Mayfield S. Bray, 1972.

1-RECORDS OF THE OFFICE OF THE CHIEF OF ENGINEERS (RG 77), 1900–1901, quantity undetermined
AUDIO-VISUAL MATERIALS: Photos of the China Relief Expedition, troops, and scenes, 1900–1901.

THE NATIONAL PRESBYTERIAN CHURCH
DC–140 William S. Culbertson Library
4101 Nebraska Avenue, NW
Washington DC 20016
(202) 537–0800
Mrs. Parkash Samuel, Librarian

Background note: The National Presbyterian Church vault contains unorganized and uncataloged materials on missions in China. Efforts are currently underway to prepare them for microfilming. John D. Hayes served in Peking. James McClure Henry, M.D., worked at Lingnan University. See also Presbyterian Historical Society, 425 Lombard Street, Philadelphia, PA, 19147.

1-GENERAL HOLDINGS

MINUTES/RECORDS/REPORTS: Reports of National Presbyterian Church missionaries in China, Rev. and Mrs. John D. Hayes, and James McClure Henry in their periodical, *The Church Bulletin*, 1939–59.

MEMORABILIA: "Memorial Service Bulletin" for John D. Hayes, 1957.

SMITHSONIAN INSTITUTION

DC–145 Anthropology Library

Smithsonian Institution Libraries
National Museum of Natural History
Tenth and Constitution Avenue
Room 330
Washington DC 20560
(202) 357–1819
Mary Kay Davies, Librarian

1-GENERAL HOLDINGS

PAMPHLETS: *The Legends of the Ch'uan Miao*, by David Crockett Graham (reprinted from the West China Border Research Society, *Journal*, 1938); *Vocabulary of the Ch'uan Miao*, by David Crockett Graham (reprinted from the West China Border Research Society, *Journal*, 1938).

DC–150 Archives

Smithsonian Institution
900 Jefferson Drive, SW
Washington DC 20560
(202) 357–1420
James A. Steed, Assistant Archivist

Background note: The Smithsonian Institution Archives contain papers about the Smithsonian and the fields of science, art, history, and the humanities. Materials are arranged by Record Unit (RU), and indexed in the Smithsonian Institute Archives Subject Index. The materials cited below concerning Christianity in China are connected with people who made expeditions to China on behalf of the Smithsonian. Because nearly 80 percent of the Archives is not indexed, the materials listed are only an indication of total holdings. The Smithsonian's cataloguing numbers appear in order to aid the staff in locating materials described.
Finding aids: *Guide to the Smithsonian Archives* (Washington DC: Smithsonian Institution), 1978. Consult staff for assistance.

1-DIVISION OF MAMMALS FIELD NOTEBOOKS (RU 7217), 1921–38, 1 volume

MEMORABILIA: Notebook by David Crockett Graham, 1921–38.
FINDING AIDS: In-house finding aid.

2-DAVID CROCKETT GRAHAM PAPERS (RU 7148), 1923–36, quantity undetermined

Background note: David Crockett Graham (1884–1961) was an American Baptist missionary and educator, and a field collector for the United States National Museum of the Smithsonian. He served in Shanghai in 1911, and then in Suifu (now Yibin), in Szechuan, for the next 20 years. After that he taught at West China Union University in Chengtu until his retirement in 1948. While on leave at various times, Graham returned to the United States for graduate study in religion, anthropology, and archaeology. From 1919 to 1939, Graham made 14 long summer expeditions and several short trips for the Smithsonian, collecting natural history artifacts and doing anthropological studies in Szechuan, Tibet, and Yunnan.

See also the Human Studies Film Archives and the National Anthropological Archives below; and Whitman College Archives, Penrose Memorial Library, 345 Boyer Avenue, Walla Walla, WA, 99362.

CORRESPONDENCE: Folder of correspondence between William de C. Ravenel and Alexander Westmore of the Smithsonian Institution, concerning the shipment of materials, 1925–36.
DIARIES: 16 diaries of Graham's trips, 1924–35.
MAPS/DESIGNS/DRAWINGS: 3 maps of western China by Graham, 1925–33; map of western China by J. Huston Edgar, Graham's fellow missionary and companion, 1930.
AUDIO-VISUAL MATERIALS: 609 negatives (10 with prints) and 10 lantern slides of Chinese people, countryside, and culture, especially religious items and practices, 1923–30, including negatives of Lolo Christians in ancestral armor, other Chinese Christians and their children, Dr. Tsuang (a Chinese Christian doctor at Suifu Baptist Hospital), patients at Suifu Baptist Hospital, a building at West China Union University, Graham, his house in Suifu, his wife, Alicia May Morey Graham, and their children, n.d.; 2 rolls of microfilm (one positive, one negative) of the 609 negatives.
FINDING AIDS: In-house finding aid.

3-JOSEPH HARVEY RILEY PAPERS (RU 7076), n.d., 1 item

MANUSCRIPTS: Untitled manuscript on birds collected in western China and Tibet, by David Crockett Graham, n.d.

4-ARTHUR DE C. SOWERBY PAPERS (RU 7263), 1911–54, 9.3 c.f.

Background note: Arthur de Carle Sowerby (1885–1954) was the son of Arthur Sowerby, a British Baptist missionary (d.1934). Born in Tai-yuan Fu, Shansi, the younger Sowerby became an explorer and collector in China for the Smithsonian Institution's United States National Museum. These papers largely contain records of his work as a naturalist. In 1911, Sowerby led a relief mission to evacuate missionaries in Shensi and Sianfu.

CORRESPONDENCE/MEMORABILIA: Letter to Robert Lansing concerning Sowerby's 1911 rescue work, 1916; folder of letters to and from Sowerby's father, Arthur Sowerby, 1931, 1934; folder of letters of condolence to Sowerby on the death of his father, 1934; correspondence, genealogical data, and research notes related to Sowerby's work on a family history, "The Sowerby Saga," 1950–54.

MANUSCRIPTS: "The Sowerby Saga," annotated typescript by Arthur de C. Sowerby, ca. 1954; autobiographical memoir, by Arthur de C. Sowerby, 1912–15.

AUDIO-VISUAL MATERIALS: Several photos of Sowerby as leader of the Shensi Relief Expedition, 1911–12.
FINDING AIDS: In-house finding aid.

5-UNITED STATES NATIONAL MUSEUM, 1877–1975, PERMANENT ADMINISTRATIVE FILES (RU 192), 1920–49, ca.165 items
CORRESPONDENCE: Ca.165 letters to and from David Crockett Graham concerning his work for the Smithsonian, 1920–49.

DC–155 Botany Library
Smithsonian Institution
National Museum of Natural History
Tenth and Constitution Avenue
Room W422
Washington DC 20560
(202) 357–2715
Ruth Schallert, Librarian

1-GENERAL HOLDINGS
SERIALS: Lingnan University, *Science Bulletin*, 1930.

DC–160 Freer Gallery of Art Library
Smithsonian Institution
1050 Independence Avenue, SW
Washington DC 20560
(202) 357–2091
Elizabeth Kelly, Archivist
Ellen Nollman, Head Librarian

1-KARL WHITING BISHOP COLLECTION, 1924, 3 items
Background note: Karl Whiting Bishop, an archaeologist whose specialty was ancient China, made archaeological expeditions into China for the Freer Gallery of Art from 1923 to 1927 and again from 1929 to 1934.
AUDIO-VISUAL MATERIALS: Photos with negatives of Nestorian monuments, in Shensi, Sian, and at Pei-lin (Forest of Tablets), Sian, 1924.
FINDING AIDS: In-house finding aid.

2-GENERAL HOLDINGS
Background note: In addition to the following materials, Freer has a large number of articles and books by Henri Cordier, Henri Doré, Arthur Christopher Moule, and others, on the history of missions in China, and Chinese history, international relations, civilization, and natural history.
MINUTES/RECORDS/REPORTS: Deed of gift and of bailment between John C. Ferguson (Chên Yü-kuang), president of the University of Nanking, and Ch'ien T'ung, official in charge of the Museum of the Board of Interior, 1934.
CORRESPONDENCE: 5 letters of Jean-François Gerbillon, S.J., missionary in Peking, ca.1700, published in *T'oung pao*, 1906; letters from missionaries at Peking, relating to the Macartney embassy (1793–1803), ed. by E. H. Pritchard, published in *T'oung pao*, 1934.
PAMPHLETS: Reprints of 14 articles by David Crockett Graham from the West China Border Research Society, *Journal*, 1934–39; *Christian Art in China*, by Berthold Laufer, 1910; *Nestorians in China: Some Corrections and Additions*, by Arthur Christopher Moule, 1940; *On Some Neolithic (and Possibly Paleolithic) Finds in Mongolia, Sinkiang, and West China*, by Pierre Teilhard de

Chardin, 1932; *Wang An-shih: Lecture Delivered at the College of Chinese Studies, Peiping*, by H. R. Williamson, 1935.
MAPS/DESIGNS/DRAWINGS: *Atlas of the Chinese Empire: Containing Separate Maps of the Eighteen Provinces of China Proper on the Scale of 1:3,000,000 and of the Four Great Dependencies on the Scale of 1:7,500,000, Together with an Index to All the Names on the Maps and a List of All Protestant Mission Stations, &c.*, 2nd ed., by Edward Stanford (Philadelphia: Morgan and Scott, Ltd.), 1908; *Complete Atlas of China: Containing Separate Maps of the Eighteen Provinces of China Proper on the Scale of 1:3,000,000 and of the Four Great Dependencies on the Scale of 1:7,500,000, Together with an Index to All the Names on the Maps with the Latitude and Longitude of Each Place, Railways, Telegraph Stations, Ports, & Protestant Mission Stations Marked*, 2nd ed., by Edward Stanford (Philadelphia: Morgan and Scott, Ltd.), 1917.
SERIALS: Catholic University of Peking, *Bulletin*, 1928, 1930–31. *Monumenta Serica*, 1935-. *T'oung pao*, 1890-. *Variétés Sinologiques*, 1895–98, 1909–29. West China Union University, *Museum Guidebook Series*, 1945.
CHINESE LANGUAGE MATERIALS/SERIALS: University of Nanking, *Library Publications*, 1935. *Yenching Journal of Chinese Studies*, 1928–29, 1931, 1946–47.
FINDING AIDS: *Dictionary Catalog of the Freer Gallery of Art* (Washington DC: Smithsonian Institution), 1967.

DC–165 Human Studies Film Archives
National Museum of Natural History
Smithsonian Institution
Tenth and Constitution Avenue
Washington DC 20560
(202) 357–3356
W. Shay, Film Archivist

1-GENERAL HOLDINGS
MANUSCRIPTS: "Explanation of the Moving Picture Film Showing the Ch'uan Miao and Some of Their Customs," by David Crockett Graham, ca. 1936.
AUDIO-VISUAL MATERIALS: 650-foot black and white movie of the Ch'uan Miao hill people of southwest China, showing people posing for the camera, a reception for Graham and party, religious leaders performing exorcism, divining, and conducting funeral ceremonies, filmed by David Crockett Graham, ca. 1936.

DC–170 National Anthropological Archives
National Museum of Natural History
Smithsonian Institution
Tenth and Constitution Avenue
Washington DC 20560
(202) 357–1976
Kathleen T. Baxter, Reference Specialist

Restrictions: Access by appointment; some records are restricted.
Finding aids: *Catalog to Manuscripts at the National Anthropological Archives* (Washington DC: Smithsonian Institution), 1975.

1-DIVISION OF ETHNOLOGY (UNITED STATES NATIONAL MUSEUM) PHOTOGRAPH COLLECTION, 1844–1948, 107 items

Background note: Among the Division of Ethnology's photographs are 107 photos taken by missionaries Divie Bethune McCartee and David Crockett Graham. Divie Bethune McCartee served as a medical missionary in Ningpo from 1844 to 1872. His travels also took him to Hong Kong, Shanghai, and Chefoo. David Crockett Graham was an American Baptist missionary and educator, and a field collector for the United States National Museum of the Smithsonian. See also the David Crockett Graham Papers (RU 7148) in the Smithsonian Institute Archives (above). The Graham and McCartee photos are interfiled with other photos on China.
AUDIO-VISUAL MATERIALS: Ca. 100 photos taken by Graham of the culture and civilization of Szechuan, including native scenes, Lolo and Miao tribesmen, and especially religious practices, shrines, and priests, 1911–48; 7 photos of a Chinese bride and bridegroom, Buddhist priest, and other aspects of Chinese culture, taken by McCartee, 1844–72.

2-GENERAL HOLDINGS
CORRESPONDENCE: 9 pages of correspondence between William Harrison Hudspeth, a missionary to China, and the Smithsonian Institution, concerning the accession of his manuscript on the Hua Miao of southwest China (see MANUSCRIPTS below), 1968.
MANUSCRIPTS: "The Hua Miao of South West China," by William Harrison Hudspeth, 1967 (Collection #4809).
CHINESE LANGUAGE MATERIALS: A 1-page chrestomathy by Elijah Coleman Bridgman, ca.1880 (Collection #2372).

DC–175 National Museum of Natural History Branch Library
Smithsonian Institution Libraries
Tenth and Constitution Avenue
Washington DC 20560
(202) 357-1496
Ann Juneau, Branch Chief

1-GENERAL HOLDINGS
SERIALS: Fukien Christian University, *Biological Bulletin*, 1947; *Science Journal*, 1938. *Lingnan Science Journal*, 1922–50. Lingnan University, *Science Bulletin*, 1944. Natural History Society, *Proceedings*, 1928–30. *Peking Natural History Bulletin*, 1926–41. Yenching University, Department of Biology, *Bulletin*, 1930.

U.S. DEPARTMENT OF EDUCATION
DC–180 Educational Research Library
Office of Educational Research and Improvement
555 New Jersey Avenue, NW
Washington DC 20208
(202) 357-6273
John N. Blake, Jr., Reference Librarian

Finding aids: United States Department of Health, Education, and Welfare, Washington DC, *Author/Title Catalog of the Department Library*, 1965 (supp. 1972).

1-GENERAL HOLDINGS
PAMPHLETS: *Christian Education in China: A Statement of Educational Principles*, by the General Board of the China Christian Educational Association, 1925.
SERIALS: China Christian Educational Association, *Bulletin*, 1924–26, 1929, 1931, 1933.

FLORIDA

CLEARWATER

CLEARWATER CHRISTIAN COLLEGE
FL–5   Library
3400 Gulf-to-Bay Boulevard
Clearwater FL 33519
(813) 726-1153 Ext. 218
Elizabeth Werner, Director

Background note: This library has a collection of books by and about Watchman Nee (Nee To-Sheng), written in exile after 1958.

1-GENERAL HOLDINGS
PAMPHLETS: *Attacking on All Fronts: Part of the Story of the China Inland Mission in 1941*, by Frank Houghton, 1942; *The Far East Broadcasting Company Story as of March 1964*, n.a., 1964; *Gladys Aylward*, by R. O. Latham, 1950; *His Witness*, by Loretta Baltau, 1968; *An Hour with Jonathan and Rosalind Goforth, Missionaries to China*, n.a., n.d.; *My Christian Experience*, by Gilbert Chibee Nee, n.d.

DE LAND

STETSON UNIVERSITY
FL–10   DuPont-Ball Library
421 North Boulevard
De Land FL 32720-3769
(904) 734-4121
Earl Joiner, Curator, Baptist Collection

Restrictions: Permission of the curator required for access.

1-BAPTIST COLLECTION, 1916–43, 2 items
MINUTES/RECORDS/REPORTS: Southern Baptist Convention, North China Mission, Chefoo, 1916, 1927–29, 1932–35, 1939.
DISSERTATIONS/THESES: *Protestant Mission Schools for Girls in South China (1827 to the Japanese Invasion)*, by Mary Raleigh Anderson, 1943.

GAINESVILLE

UNIVERSITY OF FLORIDA
FL–15   University of Florida Libraries
Gainesville FL 32611
(904) 392-0361
Fleming Montgomery, Associate Librarian, Reference and Bibliography

1-GENERAL HOLDINGS
MINUTES/RECORDS/REPORTS: National Christian Council of China, biennial report, 1933–35.

PAMPHLETS: *Our Mission in the East: Being the Substance of an Address before the General Assembly of the Presbyterian Church in Ireland, on the 7th of June, 1878*, by William Fleming Stevenson, 1878.
SERIALS: National Christian Council of China, *Bulletin*, 1922–37.

LAKELAND

FLORIDA SOUTHERN COLLEGE
FL–20   Roux Library
111 Lake Hollingsworth Drive
Lakeland FL 33801–5698
(813) 680–4164
T. M. Haggard, Director

1-GENERAL HOLDINGS
SERIALS: *China Christian Year Book*, 1931. *Directory of Protestant Missions in China*, 1930.

TALLAHASSEE

FLORIDA STATE UNIVERSITY
FL–25   Robert Manning Strozier Library
Tallahassee FL 32306
(904) 644–2706
Charles Miller, Director

1-GENERAL HOLDINGS
SERIALS: *Chinese Recorder*, 1870–71, 1874–77, 1879, 1881–86, 1888–1941. *Relations de Chine*, 1903–7. *Variétés Sinologiques*, 1892–1938(?).
DISSERTATIONS/THESES: *An Eighteenth-century Frenchman at the Court of the K'ang-hsi Emperor: A Study of the Early Life of Jean François Foucquet*, by John W. Witek, 1973.

GEORGIA

ATHENS

UNIVERSITY OF GEORGIA
GA–5   University of Georgia Libraries
Athens GA 30602
(404) 542–2716
Beth Williams, Reference Librarian

1-GENERAL HOLDINGS
ORAL HISTORIES: *China Missionaries Oral History Collection*, ed. by Cyrus H. Peake and Arthur L. Rosenbaum (Claremont Graduate School, Oral History Program), 1973. See ORAL HIS-TORIES Union List for the names of participants.
SERIALS: *China Christian Year Book*, 1926, 1934–35. *China Mission Year Book*, 1911. *Chinese Medical Journal*, 1937–51, 1978-. *Chinese Recorder*, 1868–1940. *Lingnan Science Journal*, 1922–50. University of Nanking, College of Agriculture and Forestry, *Bulletin*, 1926, 1934–36.
DISSERTATIONS/THESES: *The Confrontation: American Catholicism and Chinese Communism, 1945–1952*, by William C. Hearon, 1975. *Protestant Mission Schools for Girls in South China (1827 to the Japanese Invasion)*, by Mary Raleigh Anderson, 1943.

ATLANTA

EMORY UNIVERSITY
GA–10   Manuscripts and Archives Department
Emory University
Pitts Theology Library
Candler School of Theology
Atlanta GA 30322
(404) 727–4166
Cynthia Crouch, Curator of Archives and Manuscripts

1-WALTER ANDERSON HEARN PAPERS, 1918–35, ca. 900 items
Background note: Walter Anderson Hearn, the son of Thomas A. Hearn, a Southern Methodist missionary, was born in China and later became a Methodist missionary and teacher to China. He taught in Shanghai from 1916 to 1919 and was professor of religion and religious education at Soochow University from 1923 to 1927. Between 1924 and 1925 he also served as acting superintendent of the Hong Kong Institutional Church in Soochow. In 1927, the China Annual Conference dismissed Hearn from missionary service because of his public statement of disbelief in the resurrection of Christ and he returned to the United States.
MINUTES/RECORDS/REPORTS: China Mission, minutes and reports, 1926–28; Special Committee of the Board of Missions, proceedings concerning Hearn's case, 1927.
CORRESPONDENCE: Ca. 400 letters, 1918–35, consisting of a folder to and from family members concerning his work in China and his stance before the Board of Missions, 1927–28, and the remainder to and from members of the China Annual Conference, the China Mission, and the Board of Missions, including such correspondents as Bishop William Newman Ainsworth, Sidney R. Anderson, W. O. Cram, O. E. Goddard, W. B. Nance, Charles W. Rankin, Frank Rawlinson, and Mary Culler White.
MANUSCRIPTS: Notes and statements to the Board of Missions, 1927–28.
MEMORABILIA: Newspaper clippings, 1921–28.
FINDING AIDS: In-house inventory.

GA–15   Pitts Theology Library
Emory University
Candler School of Theology
Atlanta GA 30322
(404) 727–4166
Gary Hauk, Reference Librarian

1-CHINESE COLLECTION, 1823–1982, ca. 200 volumes
CHINESE LANGUAGE MATERIALS/MINUTES/RECORDS/
REPORTS: Church of Christ in China, General Assembly, consti-
tution, 1932; minutes and reports, 1933; records and minutes,
1931; reports, 1930; National Christian Conference, Shanghai,
1922; Siangtan Community Guild, yearbook, 1918–19.
CHINESE LANGUAGE MATERIALS/SERIALS: *Chê pao
(Spiritual Record)*, 1922–23. *Chiao yü chi k'an (China Christian
Educational Quarterly)*, 1936. *Chung-hua Chi-tu chiao hui nien
chien (China Church Year Book)*, 1915–18, 1921, 1934. *Ch'ing
nien chin pu (Association Progress: The Official Organ of the
YMCA of China)*, n.d. *Ch'ing nien wên t'i (Christian Youth)*, 1946–
51. *Gin-ling hsieh ho shen hsüeh chih (Nanking Seminary Quarterly)*, 1919–28. *Hsia êrh kuan chên (Chinese Serial)*, 1853–56. *Hua
mei chiao pao (Chinese Christian Advocate)*, 1923–29 (?). *Sheng
ming yüeh k'an (Truth and Life)*, 1924–26. *Tao Feng*, 1934. *Yenching hsüeh pao (Yenching Journal of Chinese Studies)*, 1927,
1930–32, 1935–37, 1939–40, 1947.
CHINESE LANGUAGE MATERIALS: Ca. 125 Bibles, New Testament and Old Testament, 1823–94, including romanized versions
in Amoy, Ch'aochow, Foochow, Hainan, Hangchow, Ningpo,
Swatow, Taichow, and Wenchow dialects; ca. 140 books, catechisms, hymnals, pamphlets, prayer books, and translations,
1825–1982, on subjects including Young J. Allen, anti-Christian
activities, atheism, Augsburg Confession, the Bible, Boxers,
Christian education, church history, Hung Hsiu-ch'uan, Martin
Luther, Lutheran Church, medicine and religion, Nestorians, persecution, Protestant missionaries, religious thought, Religious
Tract Society, Seventh-Day Adventist Church, theology, and John
Wesley.

2-MAP COLLECTION, 1899–1922, 3 items
MAPS/DESIGNS/DRAWINGS: *Carte de Se-tch'ouan occidental,
levée en 1908–1910*, by François Roux, 1915.
SERIALS: *Variétés Sinologiques*, 1899, 1922 (which contain maps
of Kiangsu and Nanking, respectively).

3-SPECIAL COLLECTION, 1773–1948, 25 items
MINUTES/RECORDS/REPORTS: Nanking Station, report,
1934–35; National Christian Council, report on rural and literacy
work, 1933; North China Kung Li Hui, minutes, 1937.
MANUSCRIPTS: "The Situation of Missionaries in China," by
Abbe Livingston Warnshuis, 1925.
PAMPHLETS: *Address in Behalf of the China Mission*, by Wil-
liam Jones Boone, 1837; *Advance Program for Children's Work in
China*, by the National Conference of Children's Workers, 1948;
China Story: Chapter on the Church, by Reuben A. Torrey, 1946;
*Lettre de Pekin, sur le génie de la langue chinoise, et la nature de
leur écriture symbolique...*, by Pierre Martial Cibot, 1773; *Why
Lay Training?*, by Paul R. Lindholm, 1948; *A Letter in Reply to an
Article of "The State Religion of China,"* by William Muirhead,
1881; *New Days in Nanking*, by William Reginald Wheeler, 1934;
*The Responsibility of the Church as Regards the Opium Traffic with
China*, by Arthur Evans Moule, 1881.
SERIALS: University of Nanking, *Bulletin*, 1921.
CHINESE LANGUAGE MATERIALS/SERIALS: *Chiao hui hsin
pao (Church News)*, 1868–73. *Liu ho ts'ung t'an (Shanghae Ser-
ial)*, 1857. *Wan kuo kung pao (The Globe Magazine: A Review of
the Times)*, 1868–1907.

CHINESE LANGUAGE MATERIALS: *China and Her Neigh-
bors: A Tract for the Times*, by Young John Allen, 1876, 1892;
Chung tung chan chi pen mo, by Young John Allen, 1896; *The
Eastern Question*, trans. by Young J. Allen and Ch'ü Ang-lai,
1880; *Hsi to*, by Timothy Richard, 1895; *Lin Lo-chih hsien shen
chuan*, by P'i Huei, 1924; *The Queen's Regulations*, 1880; *Russia
and Her Peoples*, trans. by Young J. Allen and T. H. Yun, 1900;
The Statesman's Yearbook, ed. by F. Martin, trans. by Young J.
Allen, 1898; *Wei-ssu-li chiang tao chen chüan*, five sermons of
John Wesley, trans. by Young J. Allen, 1896.

**4-UNITED METHODIST CHURCH (U.S.) BOARD OF GLOBAL
  MINISTRIES RECORDS, 1847–1955, ca. 218 reels microfilm**
Background note: The originals of this collection are held by the
General Board of Global Ministries, 475 Riverside Drive, New
York, NY, 10115; see entry for details on the collection. The
Records consist of 302 rolls of microfilm, covering mission work
in Asia, South America, and Africa, in addition to China.
MINUTES/RECORDS/REPORTS/CORRESPONDENCE: Re-
ports and correspondence of bishops, 1847–1912; general files and
reports on China mission work, 1917–55; missionary correspon-
dence, 1911–49.
FINDING AIDS: "Index to Methodist Missionary Documents."

5-GENERAL HOLDINGS
Background note: In addition to the reports listed below, Pitts
Theology Library also has extensive holdings of reports of the
Methodist Episcopal Church, South, including reports of its Missionary Society and Woman's Missionary Council, 1846–1940.
MINUTES/RECORDS/REPORTS: American Board of Commissioners for Foreign Missions, report of a deputation to China,
1904; American Presbyterian Mission Press, catalogue of books,
1871; Baptist Missionary Society, report of a deputation to China,
1920; China Continuation Committee, Executive Committee,
minutes, 1915, 1918, annual meeting, 1915–18; China Inland Mission, list of missionaries and stations, 1907; Christian Colleges in
China, statistics, 1932–33; Christian Conference of Asia, consultation with church leaders from China, 1981, 1983; Christian
Literature Society for China, annual report, 1889–99, 1900, 1905–
7, 1909–10, 1919–20, 1924–27, 1933–40; Door of Hope, annual
report, 1921, 1924–25, 1927–31, 1933–34; Evangelical Alliance,
Shanghai and Hankow Committee, memorandum, 1885; Inter-
board Committee for Christian Work in Japan, report of the Japanese delegation to China, 1957; International Institute of China,
reports, 1907–8; International Missionary Council, meeting in
Hangchow, 1938; Irish Presbyterian Mission in Manchuria, report, 1914, 1916, 1918, 1920; Japanese Christian Delegation to
China, report, 1958.

Methodist Church (China) Conference: Central China, minutes, 1941; China Conference, minutes, 1940; East China, minutes, 1941; Foochow, yearbook and minutes, 1947–49; Kiangsi,
minutes, 1940; Shanghai, minutes, 1940; North China, minutes,
1940; Yenping, minutes, 1939.

Methodist Episcopal Church, Board of Foreign Missions, report on China, 1927; Missions and Mission Conferences, minutes:
Central China, 1897, 1899, 1907, 1911, 1915–18, 1920–22; Foochow, 1882, 1902, 1915–22; Hinghwa, 1922; Kiangsi, 1916–17;
Kiangsi Woman's Conference, 1929–30, 1933; North China,

1883, 1892, 1905, 1907–10, 1913, 1919, 1939; South Fukien Conference, 1928; West China, 1905–7; Yenping, 1918–20.

Methodist Episcopal Church, South, China Annual Conference, minutes, 1886–88, 1890–94, 1897–1901, 1903–18, 1920, 1923–24, 1926–28, 1930–31, 1935; China Mission Meeting, minutes, 1917; golden jubilee, 1935; Mission Among the Higher Classes in China, prospectus, 1910; regulations, 1897; Nanking Theological Seminary, report on rural church, 1926; National Christion Council of China, Conference of Christian Workers, report, 1926; Conference on Christianizing Economic Relations, report, 1927; National Council of Churches World Order Study Conference, 1958; National Committee for Christian Religious Education in China, report, 1935; National Council of Churches of Christ, report on deputation of Australian churchmen to China, 1957; Preliminary Committee on Higher Christian Education in Fukien Province, minutes, 1916; Presbyterian Church in the U.S.A., reports on China, 1910, 1946; St. John's University, report, 1907–10, 1912–18; Shantung Christian University, annual report, 1916–18; Soochow Hospital, annual report, 1884–85, 1918; United Board for Christian Colleges in China, annual report, 1939–56; West China missions advisory board, mission directory, 1924, 1926, 1933, 1935, 1939; World Conference of Christian Youth, reports of Chinese delegates, 1939; World Student Christian Federation, reports on China, 1967–68; Yangtzepoo Social Center, Shanghai, annual report, 1919–20.

DIARIES: "The Diary of Lois Anna Thorne, 1858–1904," 1985.
MANUSCRIPTS: "A Century of Baptist Missions to the Chinese," by Francis Wayland Goddard, 1935; "China Log," by Sterling Gardner Brinkley, 1973; "From Six to Sixty to Six: A Narrative of the China Mission of the Reformed Church in the U.S. and the Later Evangelical and Reformed Church," by Arthur Vale Casselman, 1951; "History of Nanking Theological Seminary, 1911 to 1961: A Tentative Draft," by Frank W. Price, 1961; "Lessons to be Learned from the Experiences of Christian Missions in China," by Harold S. Matthews, 1951; "Letters from China and the Far East," a miscellaneous collection of letters, reports, bulletins, etc., collected by Homer Dubs, 1945–47; "My Moving Tent: A Biographical Sketch of Lois Anna Thorne, 1858–1904," by R. Keith Parsons, 1985; "Sketches of a Country Parish," by Arthur Henderson Smith, n.d.; "West of the Yangtze Gorges," by Joseph Taylor, 1936.
PAMPHLETS: 61 titles, 1819–1979, on American Methodist missions, B. J. Bettelheim, the Bible, Catholic missions, Marcus Cheng, Chinese Educational Commission, Danish missions, evangelistic work in Siaochang, Walter Russell Lambuth, Duncan Main, missions of the ABCFM, Nestorians, Nanking International Relief Committee, Nanking monument of the Beatitudes, Karl Ludvig Reichelt, and Charles Taylor; "Chinese Missions," a bound volume of 10 pamphlets, 1896–1938, including a report of Soochow University to the annual conference, China Mission, Methodist Episcopal Church, South (1929).
MEMORABILIA: Shanghai Union Language School, souvenir, 1912.
MAPS/DESIGNS/DRAWINGS: *Atlas of China in Provinces: A Companion Work to "A Survey of the Missionary Occupation of China"*, 1913; *Atlas of the Chinese Empire, Containing Separate Maps of the Eighteen Provinces of China Proper...Together with an Index to All the Names on the Maps and a List of All Protestant Mission Stations*, by Edward Stanford, 1908; *Carte des préfec-*

tures de Chine et de leur population Chrétienne en 1911, by Joseph de Moidrey, 1913; *Carte de Se-tch'ouan occidental, levée en 1908-1910*, by François Roux, 1915; map of China, showing stations of the China Inland Mission, 1911; University of Peking, plans for new buildings, 1920s.

SERIALS: *Bible for China*, 1926. Bible Union of China, *Bulletin*, 1921. *Bridge*, 1983-. *Challenger*, 1977. *China and the Church Today*, 1979–86. *China and the Gospel*, 1906, 1908, 1912–55. *China Bookman*, 1918–28, 1935–38, 1948–49. *China Bulletin*, 1947–62. *China Christian Advocate*, 1914–18, 1925–36, 1938–41. China Christian Educational Association, *Bulletin*, 1926–28, 1932–33. *China Christian Year Book*, 1910–39. China Continuation Committee, *Bulletin*, n.d. *The China Fundamentalist*, 1933–35, 1937. *China Medical Missionary Journal*, 1892–95, 1900–1901. *China Mission Studies Bulletin*, 1979–85. *China Notes*, 1962–84. *China Study Project Bulletin*, 1986-. *The China Sunday School Journal*, 1913–28. *China Talk*, 1975–82. *China's Millions* (London), 1892, 1929–42. *Chinese Recorder*, 1868–74, 1876–77, 1885–86, 1898–1941. *Chinese Repository*, 1832–51. *Ching Feng*, 1964–83. Christian Literature Society for China, *Link*, 1937. *Directory of Protestant Missions in China*, 1916–17, 1921, 1924, 1930, 1932. *East Asia Millions* (Philadelphia), 1949–78, 1980–82. *Educational Review*, 1909–38. *The Foochow Messenger*, 1903–8, 1910–17, 1926, 1928–29. *Ginling College Magazine*, 1924–26, 1929. *India's Women and China's Daughters*, 1881, 1888–89, 1912–16, 1920–38. *Johannean*, 1917–18. *Land of Sinim*, 1904. *Looking East at India's Women and China's Daughters*, 1940–57. *Lutheran Orient Mission*, 1941–44, 1946–57. Lutheran World Federation, *Information Letter*, 1977–80. *Millions* (Philadelphia), 1952–61. *New Horizons*, 1952, 1954, 1958–77. *New Mandarin*, 1926. *News Of China*, 1943–44. *Quarterly Notes on Christianity and Chinese Religion*, 1957–63. *Religion in the People's Republic of China*, 1984–85. *St. John's Echo*, 1893–1908, 1912, 1915. St. John's University, *Bulletin*, 1911–15. *Sign*, 1930–82. *T'oung pao*, 1890–1944. *Tripod*, 1984–85. University of Nanking, College of Agriculture and Forestry: *Agriculture and Forestry Notes*, 1925, 1934; *Agriculture and Forestry Series*, 1923. *Variétés Sinologiques*, 1905, 1917. West China Border Research Society, *Journal*, 1926–31. *West China Missionary News*, 1918–42. *Yenching Journal of Social Studies*, 1938–39. *Zhonglian*, 1981–85.

DISSERTATIONS/THESES: *American Missionaries and the Chinese Communists: A Study of Views Expressed by Methodist Episcopal Church Missionaries*, by Milo Lancaster Thornberry, 1974. *A Century of Chinese Christian Education: An Analysis of the True Light Seminary and Its Successors in Canton and Hong Kong*, by Chen Kuan-yu, 1981. *The Chinese Church: A Bridge to World Evangelization*, by Cyrus On-kwok Lam, 1983. *Christian Colleges and the Chinese Revolution, 1840-1940: A Case Study in the Impact of the West*, by Loren William Crabtree, 1972. *Christianity and Social Change: The Case in China, 1920-1950*, by Lee-ming Ng, 1971. *A Comparative Study of the Religious Thought of Chitsang and H. Richard Niebuhr: A Comparison and Contrast of the Buddhist and Christian*, by Yee-heum Yoon, 1979. *The Covenant Missionary Society in China*, by Earl Carl Dahlstrom, 1950. *Education of Christian Ministers in China: An Historical and Critical Study*, by Samuel H. Leger, 1925. *A History of the Evangelical Lutheran Church of America's Mission Policy in China, 1890-1949*, by Roger Keith Ose, 1970. *A History of the Educational Development of China*, by C. R. McKibben, 1922. *A History of the*

Southern Methodist Church in China, by Joseph Stephen Shen, 1925. *The Missionary Life and Work of W. R. Lambuth*, by H. D. Hart, 1924. *The Missionary Policy of the Methodist Episcopal Church, South, in China, 1848–1911*, by Robert Fielden Lundy, 1944. *The Modern Phase and Conclusion of the Chinese Rites Controversy*, by George Hisaharu Minamiki, 1977. *The Negotiations between Ch'i-ying and Lagrené, 1844–1846*, by Angelus J. Grosse-Aschhoff, 1950. *The New China: An Eastern Version of Messianic Hope*, by Seung-ik Lee, 1982. *La Politique missionnaire de la France en Chine, 1842–1856: l'ouverture des cinq ports chinois au commerce étranger et la liberté religieuse*, by Louis Tsing-sing Wei, 1960. *The Present Religious Situation in China*, by G. S. Reamey, 1922. *Prophet Sage and Wise Man: A Comparative Study of Intellectual Tradition in Ancient China and Israel*, by Nathaniel Yung-tse Yen, 1977. *Seeking the Common Ground: Protestant Christianity, the Three Self Movement, and China's United Front*, by Philip Lauri Wickeri, 1985. *The South Shensi Lutheran Mission*, by Sigurd Olaf Aske, 1979. *A Study of Southern Methodist Schools in China*, by Marion Olin Burkholder, 1937. *Suffering in the Experience of the Protestant Church in China (1911–1980): A Chinese Perspective*, by Paul Cheuk-ching Szeto, 1980. *A Symbolic Interactionist Approach to the Religious Stranger Concept: Protestant Missionaries in China, 1845–1900*, by Nishan J. Najarian, 1982. *A Theological Dialogue between Christian Faith and Chinese Belief in the Light of "Sin"—An Inquiry into the Apparent Failure of the Protestant Mission in Late Nineteenth-century China, Especially among Chinese Intellectuals*, by Christopher Chou, 1976. *The Use of Material from China's Spiritual Inheritance in the Christian Education of Chinese Youth*, by Warren H. Stuart, 1932.

CHINESE LANGUAGE MATERIALS/DISSERTATIONS/THESES: *A Comparative Study of Leadership Selection Processes among Four Chinese Leaders*, by Samuel Mau-cheng Lee, 1985.

CHINESE LANGUAGE MATERIALS: *Chung-kuo T'ien chu chiao chih nan (Guide to the Catholic Church in China)*, 1986; *List of Chinese-Moslem Terms*, by Isaac Mason, 1919.

GA-20   Special Collections Department

Emory University
Robert W. Woodruff Library
Atlanta GA 30322
(404) 727-6887
Linda Matthews, Director of Special Collections
Beverly D. Bishop, Reference Archivist

Background note: In addition to the materials listed below, scattered references to Christianity in China can be found in the papers of Joseph Reid Bingham, Mississippi businessman and prominent layman in the Methodist Episcopal Church, South; Bishop Warren Akin Candler, Methodist clergyman and chancellor of Emory University; Thomas Henry Haden, Methodist missionary and educator in Japan; and Alpheus Waters Wilson, Methodist bishop.
Finding aids: "A Guide to Manuscript Sources for China, Japan, and Korea," by Richard H. F. Lindemann, 1983; "Resources on China, Japan, and Korea in Special Collections, Woodruff Library, Emory University," by Richard H. F. Lindemann, in *Asian Resources in the Southeastern United States: Archival and Manuscript Resources on East Asia in Georgia*, ed. by Kenneth W. Berger, 1985.

1-YOUNG JOHN ALLEN PAPERS, 1854–1924, ca. 7,230 items
Background note: Young John Allen (1836–1907) was a Methodist missionary and journalist in China from 1860 to 1907. He served as a translator at the Kiangnan Arsenal, editor of the *North China Herald* (1858–61), editor of the *Shang-hai hsin pao* (*Shanghai News*), 1864–68, president of the Anglo-Chinese College (1885–95), and editor of the *Chiao hui hsin pao* (*Church News*), later called the *Wan kuo kung pao* (*The Globe Magazine: A Review of the World*), 1868–1907.

The collection is divided into two parts: Part I, an early accession of about 700 items, consisting largely of letters from 1857 to 1901, diaries (1855, 1878), and miscellanea; and Part II, a later accession of over 6,000 items, consisting of letters, diaries, records, manuscripts, and secondary sources about Allen's life and work.

MINUTES/RECORDS/REPORTS: 2 account books, 1859–65, 1882; Educational Association of China, minutes, 1893, 1899, 1902, 1905; inventory of Allen's personal library by George R. Loehr, Jr.; letter registers, 1878–1903; lists of missionaries in south, east, and north China; 24 memoranda; 8 notebooks of accounts, memos, addresses, and appointments; Shanghai Mission, report, 1862–63.

CORRESPONDENCE: Letter press copies of ca. 700 letters, mostly 1877–91, a few items from 1857 to 1907; 4,576 letters and 3 letter books, 1885–88, including such correspondents as Mary Allen (Mrs. Young J. Allen), Asa Griggs Candler, Warren A. Candler, Alice Cobb, W. G. E. Cunnyngham, Charles B. Galloway, Atticus G. Haygood, Laura Haygood, Edward Jenkins, J. W. Lambuth, Walter Lambuth, George R. Loehr, Sr. (Allen's son-in-law), William C. Lovett, John B. McFerrin, Mrs. D. H. McGavock, Enoch Mather McTyeire, Charles K. Marshall, Alexander Means, W. P. Pattillo, George Foster Pierce, Lochie Rankin, Timothy Richard, Nathan Scarritt, John W. Simmons, George Gilman Smith, Osborne L. Smith, Seth Ward, H. E. Yang, George W. Yarborough, T. H. Yun, and Allen's children, Arthur, Edgar, and Malvina.

DIARIES: 5 diaries, 1855, 1867–68, 1878.

MANUSCRIPTS: 4 notebooks containing poems, writing exercises, draft sermons and speeches, and reading notes from Allen's days at Emory College; 7 folders of draft speeches, sermons, articles, and essays; one folder of notes with the heading "History of China-Japan War—Pirating of"; "Comments and References," concerning Allen's literary writings; 5 folders of draft writings, including "Methodist Mission History," "Sunday School and College Reports," "A Survey of Chinese History," "Woman in All Lands," and poems by Allen; "Young J. Allen, A Selection of Chinese Proverbs and Elegant Sentences Gleaned from Books and Conversation, Nov. 1st, 1865," n.a.; 3 volumes of notes by George R. Loehr, Jr. (Allen's grandson), lists of Allen's letters to the *Wesleyan Christian Advocate*, and extracts from books about Allen; 13 folders and 2 bound volumes of Alleniana, including draft articles, notes, and biographical sketches by George R. Loehr, Jr.

PAMPHLETS: *China for Christ: A Call to the Epworth Leagues*, by Young J. Allen, 1898; miscellaneous leaflets.

MEMORABILIA: 8 folders of newspaper clippings and article

reprints on Allen, Mme. Chiang K'ai-shek, Chinese education, general Chinese and ecumenical conferences, Sir Robert Hart, George R. Loehr, Sr., William Hector Park, and W. W. Royall; 11 folders containing materials on the Anglo-Chinese College (Chung hsi shu yüan), the Exclusion Act of 1889, foot binding, McTyeire School, Shanghai School for Girls, Society for the Diffusion of Christian and General Knowledge among the Chinese, Soochow University, Trinity Church (Shanghai), and *Wan kuo kung pao*.
MAPS/DESIGNS/DRAWINGS: Rubbing from a commemorative tablet honoring Allen as the founder of the Anglo-Chinese College, 1907.
AUDIO-VISUAL MATERIALS: Photo of George R. Loehr, Sr., and his class at Huchow Middle School, 1917.
CHINESE LANGUAGE MATERIALS: A set of Chinese vocabulary flash cards.
FINDING AIDS: In-house inventory of Part II of the collection.

2-WILLIAM BLOUNT BURKE PAPERS, 1887–1964, 390 items
Background note: William Blount Burke (1864–1947) was a Methodist missionary in China from 1887 to 1943. He served as principal of Soochow University Bible School, secretary of the Board of Trustees of Soochow University, chairman of the Sungkiang Public Health Association, and head of the Sungkiang Orphanage. He was imprisoned by the Japanese in 1942 and 1943. See also University of North Carolina at Chapel Hill, Southern Historical Collection, Wilson Library, Chapel Hill, NC, 27514–6080.
CORRESPONDENCE: 4 letters to Burke from his younger brother, John, 1887–93; 168 letters from Burke to his son, James Cobb Burke, 1933–41, including discussion of Bishop Arthur J.Moore, the Sino-Japanese political situation in the 1930s and 1940s, the New Life Movement, and student protests over Japanese activities in China; 19 letters from Burke to his wife, Leila, 1936–41.
MANUSCRIPTS: Draft of two chapters of *My Father in China* (1941), a biography of Burke by his son, James; articles written by Burke for the *North China Daily News*, a translation of the petition to save the memorial arch erected in honor of Burke.
PAMPHLETS: *In Remembrance of Rev. W. B. Burke and His Work in Sungkiang*, n.d.
MEMORABILIA: Clippings from Chinese newspapers on Burke's retirement.
AUDIO-VISUAL MATERIALS: 2 photos of Burke in China, n.d.
FINDING AIDS: In-house inventory.

3-CHARLES BETTS GALLOWAY PAPERS, 1883, 1 item
Background note: Charles Betts Galloway (1849–1909) was a bishop in the Methodist Episcopal Church, South, who travelled extensively in Asia.
CORRESPONDENCE: Letter from Galloway in Shanghai discussing Chinese xenophobia and disinclination to distinguish among different types of foreigners, 1883.

4-ATTICUS GREENE HAYGOOD PAPERS, 1864–68, 1 item
Background note: Atticus Greene Haygood was a Methodist clergyman and president of Emory College from 1875 to 1884. His sister, Laura Askew Haygood (1845–1900), was a Methodist missionary in China and founder of Christian girls' schools in Shanghai and Soochow. The collection, which spans 1861–1952, totals 2 boxes and 435 items.

DIARIES: Diary and letterbook of Laura Askew Haygood, 1864–68.
FINDING AIDS: In-house inventory.

5-HAROLD HARBER MARTIN PAPERS, 1925–27, ca. 1 box
Background note: Nancy Hamilton Ogden, whose papers are a part of this collection, served with the American Red Cross at Canton Christian College from 1925 to 1927. The collection, which spans 1837–1983, totals 47 boxes.
CORRESPONDENCE/DIARIES: Ca. 200 pages of typed copies of Nancy Hamilton Ogden's letters and diary from China, 1925–27, including discussion of anti-foreignism, Chinese customs, political strife, and the suppression of Communists.
FINDING AIDS: In-house inventory.

6-METHODIST MISCELLANY, 1883–1940, 2 items
Background note: The collection totals 3 boxes.
CORRESPONDENCE: Letter by Ralph A. Ward, bishop of Chengtu, Szechuan, discussing the Christian church in Japan, 1940.
MANUSCRIPTS: A draft address given by Mrs. V. E. Manget, vice president of the Women's Foreign Missionary Society, describing the society's work in China, 1883.

7-ARTHUR JAMES MOORE PAPERS, 1934–54, 4 folders
Background note: Arthur James Moore (1888–1974) was president of the Methodist Church's Board of Missions and Church Extensions from 1940 to 1954. This collection of his papers is partially catalogued; it spans 1888–1974 and totals 25 boxes.
MINUTES/RECORDS/REPORTS/CORRESPONDENCE: Correspondence on general administrative matters of the church in China, daily activity of specific missions, the cost of living and local living conditions, the effects of the Japanese invasion on Chinese mission work, and concerns about strikes, civil unrest, and Communist advances in the post-World War II period, consisting of one folder of letters and records concerning China, 1940–54; folder of letters and records concerning Christian colleges in China, 1945–51; folder of letters and records concerning the China Rehabilitation Fund, 1940–50; folder of letters and records concerning Soochow University, 1934–49.
FINDING AIDS: In-house inventory.

8-SAVANNAH INDEPENDENT PRESBYTERIAN CHURCH RE-CORDS, 1918–24, 15 reels microfilm
Background note: The Women's Foreign Mission Society in Savannah provided financial support for the work of Waddy H. Hudson, a Presbyterian missionary with the Kashing [Chiahsing] Mission. This collection consists of microfilmed copies of originals and is partially catalogued.
MINUTES/RECORDS/REPORTS: Uncatalogued reports of the Kashing Mission, 1918–22.
CORRESPONDENCE: Uncatalogued correspondence from Waddy Hudson, 1917–24; correspondence relating to Kashing Mission, 1918–22.
MANUSCRIPTS: "The Kashing Story," by Waddy Hudson, 1957, including biography of Hudson.
MAPS/DESIGNS/DRAWINGS: A map of Kashing, n.d.
AUDIO-VISUAL MATERIALS: 8 photos of Kashing Mission,

n.d.; folder containing photos of mission work in Kashing, 1918–24.
CHINESE LANGUAGE MATERIALS: A deed for church property in Shentang, n.d.; Kashing Presbytery, minutes, 1920.

9-MILDRED SEYDELL PAPERS, 1935–38, 7 items
Background note: The collection, which spans 1842–1978, totals 68 boxes.
CORRESPONDENCE: 7 letters from Gene Turner, a YMCA official in Hangchow, discussing the New Life Movement and conditions in Hangchow during the Sino-Japanese War.

10-GENERAL HOLDINGS
MANUSCRIPTS: "China Log," by Sterling Gardner Brinkley, 1973.

GA–25   Robert W. Woodruff Library
Emory University
Atlanta GA 30322
(404) 727–0149
Bettsey Patterson, Head of General Reference

1-GENERAL HOLDINGS
MINUTES/RECORDS/REPORTS/CORRESPONDENCE: Presbyterian Church in the U.S.A., Board of Foreign Missions, missions correspondence and reports on China on 3 reels of microfilm, 1837–1911, and index to microfilm (see also Presbyterian Historical Society, Archives and Library, 425 Lombard Street, Philadelphia, PA, 19147).
PAMPHLETS: *The Chinese Educational Mission and Its Influence: Also an Address on the Influence of Dr. Yung Wing on Chinese Development Given at the Shanghai American School, Together with the Autobiography of the Author*, by Shang Him Yung, n.d.; *Tales from Free China*, by Robert Baird McClure, 1941; *Walter Russell Lambuth*, by E. H. Rawlings, 1921.
ORAL HISTORIES: *China Missionaries Oral History Collection*, ed. by Cyrus H. Peake and Arthur L. Rosenbaum (Claremont Graduate School, Oral History Program), 1973. See ORAL HISTORIES Union List for the names of participants.
SERIALS: *Chinese Repository*, 1834–36, 1840–41, 1851. *Monumenta Serica*, 1954; monograph series, 1939. Nanking Theological Seminary, English publications, 1940. *Variétés Sinologiques*, 1917.
DISSERTATIONS/THESES: *The American and British Missionary Concept of Chinese Civilization in the Nineteenth Century*, by James M. McCutcheon, 1959. *American Catholic China Missionaries, 1918–1941*, by Thomas A. Breslin, 1972. *Aspects of Religious Education in China with Particular Reference to Developments in the Hinghwa Annual Conference*, by Carol Shu Ngo Huang, 1948. *The Bible Institute of Los Angeles in China: An American Missionary Experience as Viewed from the Stewart Papers*, by Charles Everleigh Clements, 1975. *Missionary Conscience and the Comprehension of Imperialism: A Study of the Children of American Missionaries to China, 1900–1949*, by Sarah R. Mason, 1978. *Missionary Intelligence from China: American Protestant Reports, 1930–1950*, by Bruce Stephen Greenawalt, 1974. *Missionary Journalism in Nineteenth-century China: Young J. Allen and the Early "Wan kuo kung pao," 1868–1883*, by

Adrian Arthur Bennett, 1970. *The Mission Compound in Modern China: The Role of the United States Protestant Mission as an Asylum in the Civil and International Strife of China, 1900–1941*, by Gladys Robina Quale, 1957. *Protestant Christianity and Marriage in China*, by Calvin H. Reber, 1958. *Protestant Christianity in China and Korea*, by Spencer J. Palmer, 1964. *The Protestant Missionary Understanding of the Chinese Situation and the Christian Task from 1890 to 1911*, by C. William Mensendiek, 1958. *Reciprocal Change: The Case of American Protestant Missionaries to China*, by Paul Voninski, 1975. *Strangers in the House: J. Lewis Shuck and Issachar Roberts, First American Baptist Missionaries to China*, by Margaret M. Coughlin, 1972. *T. C. Chao's Struggle for a Chinese Christianity*, by Clyde H. Dunn, 1974. *Zion's Corner: Origins of the American Protestant Missionary Movement in China, 1827–1839*, by Murray A. Rubinstein, 1976.

CARTERSVILLE

FIRST BAPTIST CHURCH
GA–30   Lottie Moon Room
114 West Cherokee Avenue
Cartersville GA 30120
No phone
Margie A. Black, contact person

Restrictions: Access by appointment only. For access, contact Margie Black at the Georgia Women's Missionary Union, 2350 South Flowers Road, South Atlanta, GA, 30341, or at (404) 455–0404.

1-LOTTIE MOON LETTERS, 1873–99, 20 items
Background note: Charlotte (Lottie) Moon (1840–1912) was a Southern Baptist missionary in China from 1873 to 1912. Some of her letters are contained in Volumes I and II (1873–1903) of the minutes of the Woman's Missionary Society, First Baptist Church, Cartersville, Georgia. See also Hollins College, Fishburn Library, Hollins College, VA, 24020; and Virginia Baptist Historical Society, University of Richmond, Boatwright Memorial Library, Box 95, Richmond, VA, 23173.
CORRESPONDENCE: 20 letters from Lottie Moon to the Woman's Missionary Society in Cartersville, 1873–99, including letters on such topics as Chinese government pronouncements concerning missionaries, persecution of Chinese Christians, Southern Baptist cooperation with other Baptist missions in China, and missions in Shanghai, Tungchow, and rural Shantung.
FINDING AIDS: Unpublished index created by Margie A. Black.

DECATUR

COLUMBIA THEOLOGICAL SEMINARY
GA–35   John Bulow Campbell Library
701 Columbia Drive
Decatur GA 30031
(404) 378–8821 Ext. 47
James A. Overbeck, Librarian
Christine Wenderoth, Reader Services Librarian

1-GENERAL HOLDINGS
PAMPHLETS: *Essential Facts about Our Mission Work in China*, by Egbert W. Smith, n.d.; *"I Am Not Afraid" The Story of John W. Vinson, Christian Martyr in China*, by E. H. Hamilton, n.d.; *The Last Hundred Days: A Diary of Frank A. Brown, Shanghai, 1949*, by Frank A. Brown, n.d.; *"Not Worthy to Be Compared," The Story of John and Betty Stam* and *The Miracle Baby, Helen Priscilla Stam*, by E. H. Hamilton, 1935; *We Went to West China*, by Frank W. Price, 1943.
AUDIO-VISUAL MATERIALS: "The Christian Church in China and Taiwan," by Chen Wei-ping, 1959 (one side of an audio cassette).
SERIALS: *Bible for China*, 1922, 1932. *The China Fundamentalist*, 1928–36.
DISSERTATIONS/THESES: *The History of Christian Missions in China and Preparation for New Beginnings*, by Chen Hsien-ping, 1973–74.

SAVANNAH

GA–40   GEORGIA HISTORICAL SOCIETY
501 Whitaker Street
Savannah GA 31499
(912) 944–2128
Tracy D. Bearden, Archivist

1-NORTHEN FAMILY PAPERS, 1936–40, 3 items
Background note: This collection consists of 2.5 l.f. of papers (1832–1944) belonging to the Northen and Traylor families, who were prominent in the fields of politics, business, education, and church affairs in Georgia.
CORRESPONDENCE: 3 letters from medical missionary Fred P. Manget of Huchow General Hospital, 1936, 1939–40.

HAWAII

HONOLULU

HAWAII CHINESE HISTORY CENTER
HI–5   Library
111 North King Street
Room 410
Honolulu HI 96817
(808) 521–5948
Violet L. Lai, Librarian

1-GENERAL HOLDINGS
MANUSCRIPTS: "Johanneans of Hawaii: Highlights of Activities and Events of Former Hawaii Students at St. John's University, Shanghai, China," by Francis H. Woo, 1981; "Nineteenth-century Christian Missions in China," by Dennis A. Kastens, 1977.

MISSION HOUSES MUSEUM
HI–10   Hawaiian Mission Children's Society Library
553 South King Street
Honolulu HI 96813
(808) 531–0481
Lela Goodell, Assistant Librarian

Background note: The Hawaiian Mission Children's Society was founded in 1852 by the children of American Protestant missionaries, who were sent to Hawaii between 1820 and 1848. In the nineteenth century, the Society sponsored and financed missionary work in the Pacific Islands.
    In addition to the collections listed below, there is some scattered information on Chinese missions in the Hawaiian Evangelical Association (later, the United Church of Christ, Hawaii Conference) Archives Collection, containing correspondence between Hawaii and China.
Finding aids: *A Guide to the Manuscript Collections in the Hawaiian Mission Children's Society Library* (Honolulu, 1980).

1-CASTLE FOUNDATION PAPERS, 1900–1935, quantity undetermined
MINUTES/RECORDS/REPORTS/CORRESPONDENCE: Large folder containing letters and reports on funding and other subjects relating to China missions, ca. 1900–1935.

2-CHILDREN OF THE MISSION, 1876–89, quantity undetermined
CORRESPONDENCE: 12 letters from China, 1876–89, to Luther Halsey Gulick, the agent for the American Bible Society; letters from China to friends and family in Hawaii and China scattered through his general correspondence, ca. 1870s–1880s.

3-SANDWICH ISLAND MISSION, 1830s–1840s, ca. 50–75p.
CORRESPONDENCE/MANUSCRIPTS: Ca. 50–75 pages of manuscripts and printed general letters between missionaries of the American Board of Commissioners for Foreign Missions in China and Hawaii, including letters from a mission in Canton, 1838–43; letters to Canton by Titus Coan and D. B. Lyman, 1843–40; material regarding a trip to China by Levi Chamberlain, one of the missionaries stationed in Hawaii, 1845; and form letters sent from Macao in the 1830s and 1840s.

UNIVERSITY OF HAWAII
HI–15   Thomas Hale Hamilton Library
2550 The Mall
Honolulu HI 96822
(808) 948–7214
(808) 948–8042 (Asia)
Nancy Morris, Head, Humanities and Social Science Reference
Mrs. Chau Mun Lau, China Specialist

1-ASIA COLLECTION, 1906–78, quantity undetermined
MINUTES/RECORDS/REPORTS: Reports on the China mission in Rheinischen Missionsgesellschaft, yearbook, 1906–20.
MANUSCRIPTS: "Anglo-Saxon Missionary Reactions to the Chinese Reform Movement: 1860–1912," by Paul F. Hooper, 1964.
PAMPHLETS: *Catholic Missions in China during the Middle Ages, 1294–1368*, by Paul Stanislaus Hsiang, 1949; *China Mission Studies (1550–1800) Directory*, ed. by David E. Mungello, 1978; *The L.M.S. and the Regeneration of New China*, by Nelson Bitton, ca. 1914; *Robert Morrison: The Scholar and the Man, An Illustrated Catalogue of the Exhibition Held at the University of Hong Kong, September Fourth to Eighteenth, 1957, to Commemorate the 150th Anniversary of Robert Morrison's Arrival in China*, by Lindsay Ride, 1957.
ORAL HISTORIES: *China Missionaries Oral History Collection*, ed. by Cyrus H. Peake and Arthur L. Rosenbaum (Claremont Graduate School, Oral History Program), 1973. See ORAL HISTORIES Union List for the names of participants.
SERIALS: *China Christian Year Book*, 1915, 1936–37. *China Mission Studies Bulletin*, 1979-. *China Notes*, 1968-.
DISSERTATIONS/THESES: *The American and British Missionary Concept of Chinese Civilization in the Nineteenth Century*, by James Miller McCutcheon, 1959. *An Eighteenth-century Frenchman at the Court of the K'ang-hsi Emperor: A Study of the Early Life of Jean François Foucquet*, by John W. Witek, 1973. *Protestant Christianity and Marriage in China*, by Calvin H. Reber, Jr., 1958.
CHINESE LANGUAGE MATERIALS/SERIALS: *Chen kuang tsa chih (True Light Review)*, 1929–31. *Chiao hui hsin pao (Church News)*, 1868–74. *Ch'ing nien chin pu (Association Progress)*, 1922, 1924–32. *Sheng ming (Life)*, 1925–26. *Wan kuo kung pao (The Globe Magazine: A Review of the Times)*, 1889–1907. *Wen she yüeh k'an*, 1927–28.
CHINESE LANGUAGE MATERIALS/DISSERTATIONS/THESES: *Hsi fang ch'uan chiao shih tsai Hua tsao ch'i ti pao yeh t'an t'ao (Newspaper Publishing among Early Western Missionaries in China)*, by Chu Li-chih, 1977.
CHINESE LANGUAGE MATERIALS: Ca. 50 volumes, 1896–1981, on Young J. Allen, Catholic church, Christianity and Buddhism, Christians in China, church history, education, ethics, Jesuit missions, K'ang-hsi and Ch'ien-lung emperors, Macao, missions in Fukien, missions in Szechwan, Nestorians, T'aiping Rebellion, and Francis C. M. Wei.

2-GENERAL HOLDINGS
MINUTES/RECORDS/REPORTS: National Christian Council, conference on the church in China, 1926.
MANUSCRIPTS: "China Papers," by the Church Missionary Society, 1869 (microfilm copies of originals at the Church Missionary Society in London); "Christian Missions to China," by Edward Wilson Wallace, 1929(?); "Missions in Far Eastern Cultural Relations," by Miner Searle Bates, 1942.
PAMPHLETS: *China Consultation*, by A. Doak Barnett, et al., 1958(?); *China's Call*, by J. S. Burdon, 1882; *Facing the Future of the Missionary Movement*, by Edward Hicks Hume, 1927; *Historical Sketch of the Missions of the American Board in China*, by Samuel Colcord Bartlett, 1876; *Memorandum on Missions*, by

Henry Theodore Hodgkin, 1927; *Nestorians in China: Some Corrections and Additions*, by A. C. Moule, 1940
SERIALS: *China Christian Year Book*, 1926–39. *China's Millions* (London), 1875–1981. *Chinese Recorder*, 1874–1941. *Directory of Protestant Missions in China*, 1923.
DISSERTATIONS/THESES: *American Catholic China Missionaries, 1918–1941*, by Thomas A. Breslin, 1972. *The Anti-Christian Movement in China, 1922–1927: With Special Reference to the Experience of Protestant Missions*, by Ka-che Yip, 1971. *The Educational Association of China, 1890–1912: Its History and Meaning in the Missionary Education in China*, by Shu-hwai Wang, 1963. *The Impact of Christianity on China with Concentration on the Time of the Jesuits*, by Marya Roy, 1973. *Die katholische Chinamission im Spiegel der rotchinesischen Presse; Versuch einer missionarischen Deutung*, by Johannes Schütte, 1957. *The Missionary Factor in Anglo-Chinese Relations, 1891–1900*, by Edmund S. Wehrle, 1962. *The Mission Compound in Modern China: The Role of the United States Protestant Mission as an Asylum in the Civil and International Strife of China, 1900–1941*, by Gladys Robina Quale, 1957. *The Negotiations between Ch'i-ying and Lagrené, 1844–1846*, by Angelus Francis J. Grosse-Aschhoff, 1950. *The Protestant Missionary Understanding of the Chinese Situation and the Christian Task from 1890 to 1911*, by C. William Mensendiek, 1958. *Russian (Greek Orthodox) Missionaries in China, 1689–1917: Their Cultural, Political, and Economic Role*, by Albert Parry, 1938. *Strangers in the House: J. Lewis Shuck and Issachar Roberts, First American Baptist Missionaries to China*, by Margaret M. Coughlin, 1972.

LIHUE

HI-20   GROVE FARM HOMESTEAD
Waioli Mission House
P.O. Box 1631
Lihue HI 96766
(808) 245-3202
Robert J. Schleck, Curator

1-ELSIE HART WILCOX PAPERS, 1940–48, ca. 50 items
Background note: A prominent social worker in Hawaii, Elsie Hart Wilcox (1879–1954), with Frank Atherton, organized the YMCA Pan-Pacific Conference in 1923 and the Institute of Pacific Relations. She visited China in 1926 and subsequently supported Lingnan University, the Peking Christian Student Work Union, Yenching University, and such missionary leaders as Frank Rawlinson and Hugh Hubbard. The collection, which totals 27 l.f., spans from 1897 to 1954.
MINUTES/RECORDS/REPORTS: National Committee of the YMCA of China, report/letter, 1940.
CORRESPONDENCE: Correspondence, including requests and letters of thanks, between Wilcox and such organizations as the American Committee in Aid of Chinese Industrial Cooperatives, the Association for the Chinese Blind, China Relief Legion, Trustees of Lingnan University, United Board for Christian Colleges in China, United Service to China, and Wellesley-Yenching.
FINDING AIDS: In-house register.

IDAHO

MOSCOW

UNIVERSITY OF IDAHO
ID–5 Special Collections
University of Idaho Library
Moscow ID 83843
(208) 885–7951
Terry Abraham, Head, Special Collections

1-RECORDS OF PHI BETA KAPPA, ALPHA OF IDAHO, 1939–55,
6 items
CORRESPONDENCE: 6 letters from Baptist missionary, Joshua
C. Jensen, in Suifu, Szechwan, 1939–40, 1955 (from New York).

2-GENERAL HOLDINGS
SERIALS: *Lingnan Science Journal,* 1922–45.

ILLINOIS

ARLINGTON HEIGHTS

IL–5 BAPTIST GENERAL CONFERENCE
Board of World Missions
2002 South Arlington Heights Road
Arlington Heights IL 60005
(312) 228–0200
(800) 323–4215
June E. Bruce, Administrative Assistant

Background note: The Baptist General Conference had missionaries in China from 1945 to 1951. For further information on Swedish Baptist missions in China see Bethel Theological Seminary,
Archival Center of the Baptist General Conference, 3949 Bethel
Drive, New Brighton, MN, 55112. The materials listed below are
uncatalogued.

1-GENERAL HOLDINGS
CORRESPONDENCE: Letters from Dale Bjork to the Board of
World Missions, 1948–50; letters from Sten Lindberg to the Board
of World Missions, 1945–50.

AURORA

AURORA UNIVERSITY
IL–10 Charles B. Phillips Library
Jenks Memorial Collection of Advental Materials
347 South Gladstone Avenue
Aurora IL 60507
(312) 892–6431
David T. Arthur, Curator

Background note: The China mission of the Advent Christian
Church was first established in Nanking in 1898 as the American
Advent Mission Society (Lai Fu Hui). Other mission stations were
later established in Anhui. The China materials in the Jenks Collection are partially catalogued.

In addition to the materials listed below, references to China
missions can also be found in the following periodicals in the Jenks
Collection: *Advent Christian Missions*, 1920–52; *The Herald of
Life and of the Coming Kingdom*, 1909–52; *Prophetic and Missionary Quarterly*, 1896–1902; *Prophetic and Missionary Record*,
1909–20; and *The World's Crisis and Advent Christian Messenger*,
1897–1952. *Advent Christian Missions* and *Prophetic and Missionary Record* have been partially indexed.

See also Advent Christian General Conference, Headquarters
Archives, P.O. Box 23152, 14601 Albemarle Road, Charlotte,
NC, 28212; and Berkshire Christian College, Carter Library, 200
Stockbridge Road, Lenox, MA, 01240.

1-Z. CHARLES BEALS COLLECTION, 1901–46, 1 box
Background note: Zephaniah Charles Beals and his wife estab-
lished the Advent mission in Wuhu in 1901.
CORRESPONDENCE: 522 letters of Z. Charles Beals, 1917–46;
letter from Beals' third wife, Effie Pinkham Beals, to R. S.
Bezanson, Jr., n.d., concerning Beals' later life.
MANUSCRIPTS: "Tribute to Dr. Z. Charles Beals," by Edward
Jones, n.d.
MEMORABILIA: Scrapbooks of Z. Charles Beals, 1891–1903,
1916–46; 10 articles by and about Beals, n.d.
ORAL HISTORIES: Audio tape of Bertha Cassidy's reminis-
cences of Z. Charles Beals, n.d.
FINDING AIDS: Index of articles by and about Z. Charles Beals in
Prophetic and Missionary Record and *Advent Christian Missions*.

2-BERTHA CASSIDY COLLECTION, ca. 1905–1980, 1 box
Background note: Bertha Cassidy was the stepdaughter of Z.
Charles Beals. She arrived at the Advent mission in Wuhu in 1905.
CORRESPONDENCE: 22 letters of Bertha Cassidy, n.d.
DIARIES: Prayer-diary of Bertha Cassidy, 1935–37.
MANUSCRIPTS: "China Adventure," by Bertha Cassidy, n.d.
AUDIO-VISUAL MATERIALS: 143 photos belonging to Bertha
Cassidy, n.d.

3-VERTICAL FILE, ca. 1898–1975, 2 in.
CORRESPONDENCE: 2 letters of Hannah Stocks Baird, n.d.; 2
letters of Z. Charles Beals, n.d.; 4 letters of Bertha Cassidy, n.d.; 7
letters of Robin Cheo (Mrs. Paul T. Chan), n.d.; 107 letters to and
from David Yang in Nanking during the 1970s, including correspondence with Bertha Cassidy, James Asa Johnson, and Moses C.
Crouse; letter of Grace Hsuen Young, n.d.

MANUSCRIPTS: "A Bachelor's Lonely Mission" (biography of Joseph Wharton), by Carole Douglas, 1970; "History and Difficulties of Advent Christian Mission Work in China," by Douglas Clack, 1985; "Leonidas Motley Spaulding," by Merry Stone, 1967; "The Life of Bertha Cassidy," by Randall S. Wright, 1966; "The Nanking Outrage of 1927," by Margaret Singleterry, 1952; "Pioneering for Christ: A Missionary Biography of Z. Charles Beals, D.D.," by Ronald S. Bezanson, Jr., 1959; "A Survey of the Advent Christian Mission in Wuhu and Chao Hsien, China," by Barbara Fourmont, 1953; "What Next in China? A Study of the Road Ahead for Missions in China," by George Singleterry, 1949; a description of the 1927 Nanking Incident by Orrin O. Singleterry, n.d.
MEMORABILIA: 3 articles on Bertha Cassidy, n.d.; 2 newspaper articles on Robin Cheo, n.d.; biographical article on Orrin O. Singleterry, n.d.; 2 articles on Grace Hsuen Young, n.d.; articles and clippings on Advent mission work in China, n.d.
ORAL HISTORIES: Interview of Bertha Cassidy, 1958.
AUDIO-VISUAL MATERIALS: 2 photos of Hannah Stocks Baird, n.d.; 8 photos of Z. Charles Beals, n.d.; 8 photos of Bertha Cassidy; photos of the Advent Church mission field, property, and missionaries, n.d.; 2 audio recordings of Grace Hsuen Young, n.d.

4-JOSEPH WHARTON COLLECTION, ca. 1909–1950, 1 box
Background note: Joseph Wharton arrived at the Advent mission in Wuhu in 1909, serving for a time as treasurer of the mission. He remained on the mainland long after 1949.
CORRESPONDENCE: 41 letters to and from Wharton, n.d.
MANUSCRIPTS: Notes of interviews of Wharton by Doris Colby and Elsie Kirby, n.d.; sermon manuscripts by Wharton, n.d.
MEMORABILIA: Articles about Wharton, n.d.; 2 medals, including 1 from the Chinese government, awarded to Wharton, n.d.
AUDIO-VISUAL MATERIALS: Photos of Wharton, n.d.
CHINESE LANGUAGE MATERIALS: English-Mandarin New Testament belonging to Wharton, n.d.
FINDING AIDS: Index of articles by and about Joseph Wharton in *Prophetic and Missionary Record* and *Advent Christian Missions*.

5-GENERAL HOLDINGS
PAMPHLETS: *From Buddhism to Christianity*, by Hannah Stocks Baird, n.d.; *Little Deaf One*, by Bertha Cassidy, n.d.; *A Trip to the China Field*, by Gussie M. Pierce, n.d.
DISSERTATIONS/THESES: *Floods, Famine, and Wars: A History of the Advent Christian Mission Work in China*, by David E. Dean, 1976. *Politics and Prayer: A Study of the Advent Christian Denomination's Mission Efforts in China*, by Donna A. Behnke, 1971.

BLOOMINGTON

ILLINOIS WESLEYAN UNIVERSITY
IL–15   Archives
Bloomington IL 61702
(309) 556–3172
Robert W. Frizzell, Archivist and Social Sciences Librarian

1-GENERAL HOLDINGS
CORRESPONDENCE: Letter written in Foochow by M. C. Wilcox, travelling inspector of Methodist missions, regarding his par-

ticipation in a "non-resident and graduate degree program" at Illinois Wesleyan University for overseas missionaries, 1891.
MANUSCRIPTS: "Materialism and Its Relation to Christian Morals," written in China by M. C. Wilcox, 1895.

CHICAGO

CATHOLIC THEOLOGICAL UNION
IL–20   Library
5401 South Cornell Avenue
Chicago IL 60615
(312) 324–8000
Kenneth O'Malley, Director

1-GENERAL HOLDINGS
PAMPHLETS: *Franciscans in the Middle Kingdom: A Survey of Franciscan Missions in China from the Middle Ages to the Present Time*, by Otto Maas, 1938; *Die Franziskanermission in China vom Jahre 1900 bis zur Gegenwart*, by Otto Maas, O.F.M., 1934; *Die Franziskanermission in China während des 18. Jahrhunderts*, by Otto Maas, O.F.M., 1934; *Der Franziskanischen Ordensnachwuchs in China*, by Otto Maas, O.F.M., 1938; *The Problem of Culture in Missionary Fields*, by Celso Constantini, 1931; *The Systematic Destruction of the Catholic Church in China*, by Thomas J. Bauer, 1954.
SERIALS: *Asia*, 1960. *Asian Folklore Studies*, 1978-. *China and the Church Today*, 1981–86. *China Bulletin* (Rome), 1983-. *China Heute*, 1985-. *China Missionary*, 1948–53. *China Update*, 1983-. *Collectanea Commissionis Synodalis*, 1928–47. *Franciscans in China*, 1922–42. *Mission Bulletin*, 1953–59. *Sign*, 1921–82.
DISSERTATIONS/THESES: *Die Akkommodationsmethode des P. Matteo Ricci S. I. in China*, by Johannes Bettray, 1955. *American Missionaries and the Policies of the United States in China, 1898–1901*, by John M. H. Lindbeck, 1948. *China Missions in Crisis: Bishop Laimbeckhoven and His Times, 1738–1787*, by Joseph Krahl, 1964. *Imperial Government and Catholic Missions in China during the Years 1784–1785*, by Bernward Henry Willeke, 1948. *Missionary Intelligence from China: American Protestant Reports, 1930–1950*, by Bruce Stephen Greenawalt, 1974. *The Negotiations between Ch'i-ying and Lagrené, 1844–1846*, by Angelus Francis J. Grosse-Aschhoff, 1950.

IL–25   CENTER FOR RESEARCH LIBRARIES
5721 Cottage Grove Avenue
Chicago IL 60637
(312) 955–4545
Esther Smith, Collection Development Librarian

Background note: The Center for Research Libraries is a cooperative research facility providing scholarly materials to over 100 member institutions throughout North America via interlibrary loan. It has large and growing holdings of foreign dissertations; specific titles can be requested through interlibrary loan at a member institution, however, U.S. dissertations and U.S. or foreign masters' theses are not available.

1-ARCHIVES OF THE COUNCIL FOR WORLD MISSION, 1821–1951, ca. 372 microfiches
Background note: The originals of these materials are at the library

of the School of Oriental and African Studies, London.

MINUTES/RECORDS/REPORTS: London Missionary Society, minutes, 1856–1939; papers of Robert Morrison, n.d.: Anglo-Chinese College, report on missions; Tyerman and Bennet deputation, report, 1821–29; Fukien, 1866–1939; South China, 1866–1939; North China, 1866–1939; Central China, 1866–1940; Peking Union Medical College, minutes, n.d.; Siaokan Hospital, n.d.; Amoy district, committee minutes, 1903–24, 1878–1912; North China district, committee minutes, 1874–1920; Hong Kong and New Territories Evangelical Society, minutes, 1904–32; F. H. Hawkins, deputation, 1917; Central China district, committee minutes, 1932–37; Lockhart, records and accounts(?), n.d.

CORRESPONDENCE: London Missionary Society, outgoing letters to China, 1822–1914; Fukien, incoming letters, 1845–1939; outgoing letters, 1928–39; South China, incoming letters, 1803–1939; outgoing letters, 1928–39; North China, incoming letters, 1860–1939; outgoing letters, 1928–39; Central China, incoming letters, 1843–1939; outgoing letters, 1928–39; letters of Robert Morrison, n.d.; miscellaneous letters from missionaries to friends, n.d.; letters from Marjorie Clements in North China, 1930–33; George and Dorothy Barbour, letters from North China, 1920–36; correspondence of J. Legge; letters, letterbook of Mrs. L[egge]; correspondence of Peking Union Medical College; letters regarding a book by M. Aldersey, n.d.; correspondence of W. H. Somervell regarding British Foreign Bible Society Chinese Bible, n.d.

MANUSCRIPTS: Sermons by J. Legge, n.d.; articles and notes on literary and language work, by J. Legge; address by J. Legge on Amoy Induction, 1874; papers of E. Hope Bell, n.d.; "Discipleship," by Eric Liddell, n.d.; autobiographical sketch by F. A. Brown, 1935–51; notes on Peking Hospital by Dudgeon, n.d.; Hankow Medical Planning papers; notes by Medhurst, 1848–52; Boxer Indemnity papers; miscellaneous notes on Chinese Church leaders, n.d.

MEMORABILIA: Biographical materials on Legge, including clippings, obituaries, and reviews; obituary of Griffith John, n.d.; Chinese medal.

DIARIES: South China, journals, 1807–42; North China, journals, 1863–64; Central China, journals, 1888–96; George and Dorothy Barbour, diary, 1920–36; Terrell diaries, n.d.

MAPS/DESIGNS/DRAWINGS: Rubbings of Nestorian Tablet, n.d.

FINDING AIDS: "Guide to the Archives of the Council for World Mission," by the Interdocumentation Company, Switzerland.

2-METHODIST MISSIONARY SOCIETY ARCHIVES, 1829–1954, 1,760 microfiches

Background note: This collection consists of microfiche reproductions of the original archives, now housed in the Library of the School of Oriental and African Studies in London. The collection is divided into three components, two of which—the Wesleyan Methodist Missionary Society records and the Women's Work Collection—contain extensive materials concerning Methodist missions in China.

MINUTES/RECORDS/REPORTS: China Synod, minutes, 1853–1946; overseas schedules, China, 1923–46; Women's Work Collection, China reports, 1939–41.

CORRESPONDENCE: 820 microfiches of letters in the Wesleyan Methodist Missionary Society records, divided into 11 series: Canton (1851–1905), China General (1936–45), China Miscellaneous (1924–34), Hunan (1907–45), Hupeh (1905–45), Ningpo

(1933–46), North China (1933–45), South China (1905–45), South West China (1932–45), Wenchow (1933–45), and Wuchang (1876–1905); 281 microfiches of letters in the Women's Work Collection, divided into 3 series: Hunan, Hupeh, Ningpo, and Wenchow (1921–54), North, South, and South West China (1920–47), and Missionaries on Furlough (China, 1925–30).

MANUSCRIPTS: 330 microfiches of biographical materials and personal papers of Methodist missionaries in China, including David Hill, Samuel Pollard, and G. Stephenson, 1829–69.

FINDING AIDS: Microfiche reproductions of typescript inventories for correspondence.

3-UNITED BOARD FOR CHRISTIAN HIGHER EDUCATION IN ASIA ARCHIVES, 1899–1953, 27 reels microfilm

Background note: See also Yale Divinity School, Special Collections, 409 Prospect Street, New Haven, CT, 06510.

MINUTES/RECORDS/REPORTS/CORRESPONDENCE/MANUSCRIPTS/PAMPHLETS: Reports, minutes of the trustees and other bodies, correspondence, publications, and other documents of the United Board for Christian Higher Education in Asia relating to Yenching University, 1899–1953.

4-GENERAL HOLDINGS

MINUTES/RECORDS/REPORTS: American Baptist Foreign Mission Society, East China Mission, annual reports and missions, 1907, 1909–10; American Board of Commissioners for Foreign Missions, Foochow Missionary Hospital, annual reports, 1910, 1922–24; Peking Hospital, annual reports, 1865–67, 1869–74; Peking Union Medical College: addresses, papers, dedication ceremonies, and medical conference, 1921; Hospital, annual reports of the superintendent, 1928–40; St. John's University, annual reports, 1906–9; United Board for Christian Colleges in China, annual reports, 1947–55; Yale Mission, College of Yale in China, annual report of the Collegiate and Medical Departments, 1914.

PAMPHLETS: *China*, comp. by the American Board of Commissioners for Foreign Missions, 1867.

SERIALS: *Anking Newsletter*, 1945, 1947–48. *Bulletin of the Diocesan Association for Western China*, 1937–46. *Bulletin of the Diocese of Western China*, 1934–37. *China Christian Advocate*, 1914–41. *China Christian Year Book*, 1926–39. China International Famine Relief Commission, Publications, series A, 1936. *China Medical Journal*, 1907–31. *China Medical Missionary Journal*, 1887–1907. *China Mission Advocate*, 1839. *China Mission Year Book*, 1910–25. *China Relief Notes*, 1946–48. *Chinese Medical Directory*, 1932, 1936. *Chinese Medical Journal*, 1965–66. *District of Anking Newsletter*, 1937–41. *Educational Review*, 1909–38. *Fenchow*, 1919–36. *Folklore Studies*, 1942, 1947, 1957–62. *The Foochow Messenger*, 1903–40. *Four Streams*, 1947–51. *Hainan Newsletter*, 1912–49. Hsü-chia-hui kuan hsiang t'ai (Zi-ka-wei Observatoire): *Bulletin des observations. Fasc. A: Magnétisme terrestre*, 1905–7; *Bulletin des observations. Fasc. B: Météorologie*, 1906–7; *Bulletin des observations. Fasc. C: Sismologie*, 1905; *Bulletin mensuel de l'Observatoire magnétique et météorologique de Zi-ka-wei*, 1882–85, 1887–88, 1893. *Lingnan Science Journal*, 1930–31, 1935–40, 1948. National Christian Council of China, *Bulletin*, 1928–37. Peking Union Medical College: *Bibliography of Publications from the Laboratories and Clinics of the College and Hospital*, 1925–29, 1932–38; *Contributions*, 1921–26. *USC Envoy*, 1946–47. *University of Nanking Magazine* (*Chin-ling kuang*), 1910–16, 1918–19. *West China Missionary News*, 1901–43.

FINDING AIDS: *The Center for Research Libraries Catalogue: Monographs* (Chicago: The Center for Research Libraries), 1969, 5 V; *The Center for Research Libraries Catalogue: Serials* (Chicago: The Center for Research Libraries), 1972, 2 V; *The Center for Research Libraries Catalogue: Serials, First Supplement* (Chicago: The Center for Research Libraries), 1978.

CHICAGO HISTORICAL SOCIETY
IL–30   Archives and Manuscripts Department
Clark Street at North Avenue
Chicago IL 60614
(312) 642-4600
Archie Motley, Curator of Manuscripts

1-WILLIAM DEAN LETTER, 1852, 1 item
CORRESPONDENCE: Letter from William Dean in Hong Kong to the president of Madison University, stressing the value of the *Chinese Repository* for colleges and seminaries, 1852.
FINDING AIDS: Card catalogue.

EVANGELICAL COVENANT CHURCH
IL–35   Covenant Archives and Historical Library
5125 North Spaulding Avenue
Chicago IL 60625-4987
(312) 478-2696 Ext. 5267
Sigurd F. Westberg, Archivist

Background note: The Evangelical Covenant Church (formerly, the Evangelical Mission Covenant Church of America) supported mission work in Hupei from 1890 to 1951 in cooperation with other Swedish Lutheran groups under the name "Covenant Missionary Society." The materials described below are largely uncatalogued.

1-CHINA MISSIONS AND PETER MATSON COLLECTION, 1890–1950, 2 file drawers
MINUTES/RECORDS/REPORTS: Bethesda Hospital, Siangyang, records, 1935-36, 1942-43; Carl Branstrom, personal records and accounts, 1947-51; China Mission Education Committee, records, 1950; China Mission Jubilee Fund, records, 1915; Chungking Theological Seminary, records, 1949-50; Covenant Missionary Society, miscellaneous records and correspondence, 1890-1901, 1932-43, 1948-50; Kingchow Theological Seminary, records, 1908-10, 1923; Lutheran Missions Home and Foreign Agency, Hankow, minutes and reports, 1948-51; Peter Matson, financial and personal records, 1890, 1925-42.
CORRESPONDENCE: Folder of letters by Carl Branstrom, 1947-51; folder of correspondence between Carl Branstrom and Edward Nelson, 1949-50; uncatalogued letters of Marcus Ch'eng, 1949-50; folder of letters by Albert Dwight, 1948-51; 6 folders of letters by E. G. Hjerpe on China, 1890-1901, 1908-21, 1923-27; uncatalogued letters by Peter Matson, n.d.; folder of letters concerning the occupation of mission stations by government troops, 1929-33; partially catalogued letters by various Covenant missionaries, 1892-1950, including letters to S. J. Hjerpe (1916-17), J. Hudson Taylor (1892), N. P. Waldenstrom (1907), and various Chinese Christians.
MANUSCRIPTS: Uncatalogued sermons, addresses, and Bible study notes by Peter Matson, n.d.; "All Aboard on the Han River," by Esther Matson, n.d.

MEMORABILIA: Silk poster of a church with an inscription in Chinese, n.d.
AUDIO-VISUAL MATERIALS: Photo of Covenant missionaries in China, 1912; uncatalogued photos, n.d.
CHINESE LANGUAGE MATERIALS: Mandarin hymnal, n.d.; *Chiu yüeh shih chi ts'uo yao (Synopsis of Old Testament History)*, by Peter Matson, n.d.; Covenant Missionary Society, minutes of meetings, 1926-32, 1935, 1936; *Hsin yüeh shih chi ts'uo yao (Synopsis of New Testament History)*, by Peter Matson, n.d.; New Testament in Mandarin, n.d.; uncatalogued letters by Peter Matson, n.d.

2-WORLD MISSIONS COLLECTION, 1890–1970, 99 Hollinger boxes
MINUTES/RECORDS/REPORTS/CORRESPONDENCE: China Covenant Council, minutes, records concerning Hong Kong and Formosa, and financial reports, 1939-70; China Field Conference and Covenant Missionary Society, minutes, 1960-70; Covenant Missionary Society, financial records, minutes, and correspondence, 1930-49; Covenant Missionary Society, general conference records, 1961-70; Covenant Missionary Society, missionary biographical records and general correspondence, 1943-47; National Christian Council of China, financial records and correspondence, 1930s and 1940s; Shanghai Lutheran Center, financial records and correspondence, 1930s and 1940s; 28 boxes of letters from Covenant missionaries in China, 1930-70; 2 boxes of uncatalogued minutes and reports concerning China, n.d., discussing the American School at Kilungshan, the Augustana Synod Mission, Kingchow Theological Seminary, mission properties in Kingchow and Shasi, missions in Kweichow, salary rules for missionaries, and the Swedish Missionary Society in Hupei.
CHINESE LANGUAGE MATERIALS: Deeds to mission properties in Icheng, Kingmen, Ta Chia Chi, Tungtsiu Wan, Tsienkiang, and Wukiaho; lists of Chinese mission workers, n.d.; uncatalogued letters and documents, n.d.

3-GENERAL HOLDINGS
MINUTES/RECORDS/REPORTS: Covenant Missionary Society, annual conference minutes, 1927-38; National Christian Council of China, annual report, 1924-25.
PAMPHLETS: *Covenant Missions in China/Taiwan*, by Russell A. Cervin, 1920; *Lee Ming and His Sisters*, by Edla Matson, 1929.
DISSERTATIONS/THESES: *The Covenant Missionary Society in China*, by Earl C. Dahlstrom, 1950. *Marcus Ch'eng, Apostle or Apostate? Relations with the Covenant Mission in China*, by O. Theodore Roberg, 1982.
CHINESE LANGUAGE MATERIALS: *Fortieth Anniversary Publication: A Brief Sketch of the Work of the Covenant Missionary Society in Central Hupeh*, ed. by K. S. Cheng, Abel Yin, and A. L. Dwight, 1932; *Gospel Hymns*, comp. by Covenant Missionary Society, n.d.; *New Testament History*, by Peter Matson, n.d.; *A People's Life of Christ: Credentials of Jesus*, by Hjalmar Sundquist, trans. by Peter Matson, n.d.

FIELD MUSEUM OF NATURAL HISTORY
IL–40   Library
Roosevelt Road and Lake Shore Drive
Chicago IL 60605-2498
(312) 922-9410
Michele Calhoun, Reference Librarian

1-GENERAL HOLDINGS

MINUTES/RECORDS/REPORTS: University of Nanking, reports of the president and the treasurer, 1920–26.

PAMPHLETS: *Fukien Christian University in the Second Year of the War*, n.a., 1939; *Publications du Musée Heude*, n.a., 1946.

SERIALS: *Chinese Repository*, 1832–51. *Folklore Studies*, 1942–47. Fukien Christian University, *Biological Bulletin*, 1939. *Lingnan Science Journal*, 1922–42, 1945, 1948. Lingnan University, *Science Bulletin*, 1944. *Monumenta Serica*, 1935–41, 1946, 1948–83. Natural History Society, *Proceedings*, 1928–30. *Peking Natural History Bulletin*, 1926–41, 1948–49. Université l'Aurore, *Notes de botanique chinoise*, 1931–46; *Notes d'entomologie chinoise*, 1929–47; *Notes d'ornithologie*, 1943, 1946. University of Nanking, College of Agriculture and Forestry, *Bulletin*, 1933–36. West China Border Research Society, *Journal*, 1922–42, 1944–46. West China Union University, *Museum Guidebook Series*, 1945, 1947; *Studia Serica*, 1940–41. *Yenching Journal of Social Studies*, 1938–41.

DISSERTATIONS/THESES: *L'Oeuvre de T'ang T'ai-tsong*, by Hsü Hsiang-ch'u, 1924.

CHINESE LANGUAGE MATERIALS/SERIALS: *Chin-ling hsüeh pao* (*Nanking Journal*), 1931–33. *Yen-ching hsüeh pao* (*Yenching Journal of Chinese Studies*), 1927–41.

LOYOLA UNIVERSITY OF CHICAGO
IL–45   Elizabeth M. Cudahy Memorial Library
6525 North Sheridan Road
Chicago IL 60626
(312) 274-3000

1-RARE BOOK COLLECTION, 1537–1772, 37 volumes

Background note: This collection contains books on Christianity in China written in the sixteenth, seventeenth, and eighteenth centuries, the majority of which are by Jesuit missionaries, with a particular focus on the rites controversy of the seventeenth and eighteenth centuries. Representative titles include: *Apologie des Dominicains missionaires de la Chine*, by Noel Alexandre, O.P., 1700; *De Christiana expeditione apud Sinas…*, by Nicholas Trigault, S.J., 1617; and *Historica narratio de initio et progressu missionis Societatis Jesu apud Chinenses…*, by Adam Schall, S.J., 1665.

2-GENERAL HOLDINGS

SERIALS: *China Mission Studies Bulletin*, 1979-.

LUTHERAN CHURCH IN AMERICA
IL–50   Archives
1100 East State Street
Chicago IL 60615-5199
(312) 753-0766
Reuben T. Swanson, Archivist
Elisabeth Wittman, Associate Archivist

Finding aids: *Preserving Yesterday for Tomorrow: A Guide to the Archives of the Lutheran Church in America*, by Joel W. Lundeen (Chicago: Archives of the Lutheran Church in America), 1977.

1-RECORD GROUP 8 (WORLD MISSIONS), 1913–56, ca. 500 items

MINUTES/RECORDS/REPORTS: Paul P. Anspach, report on United Lutheran Church Mission, Shantung, 1946; Augustana Mission in China, field minutes, 1913–56; Joint Lutheran work in China, minutes, 1948–62; Kiahsien Mission Hospital, report, 1939; Lu Shao Dwan (Chinese pastor), report on trip to Augustana Synod mission stations in Honan after the Communist takeover, n.d.; Lutheran Church in China, draft constitution, n.d.; Lutheran Church of America, reports on mission work in Shanghai, the political situation in China, and miscellaneous reports, 1946–51; Lutheran College in China, reports, 1947–48, 1955–56; Lutheran Mission Hospital, Hsuchang, Honan, reports, 1937, 1940, 1948; Lutheran Missions Home and Foreign Agency, Hankow, records, 1948–53; Lutheran Missions Literature Society, minutes, 1948, 1950–53; Lutheran Theological Seminary, Shekow, Hupeh, minutes and reports, 1913, 1917–35, 1938–39, 1945, 1948–53; Lutheran World Federation, China Advisory Committee, minutes, 1965–73; National Lutheran Council, Division of World Missions Cooperation, report by Burton St. John on "orphaned" missions with statistics on all German missions in Asia, 1915; United Lutheran Church Mission, Shantung, minutes, personal property inventories, property deeds, and reports, 1900–1951; United Lutheran Church Mission, Shantung, report from Chinese Lutheran pastors Cheo, Wei, and Tu on the Chinese church in the early 1950s; United Lutheran Church Mission, Rural Service Institute, Luichow, Kwangsi, report on mission activities in Luichow and the transfer of Lutheran mission work to Japan, 1949; Harold Whatstone, report on "The Future of Christianity in China," 1950.

CORRESPONDENCE: Letters of Augustana Synod missionaries in China, 1922–30, 1937–54; copybook of letters of A. W. Edwins, Augustana Synod missionary in China, 1909–13; correspondence concerning Lutheran Theological Seminary, Shekow, Hupeh, 1948–53; correspondence of Lutheran World Federation, Joint Committee on Lutheran Work in China, 1948–53; correspondence of Helen M. Shirk, United Lutheran Church of America Secretary for China, with field stations, 1947–51.

MANUSCRIPTS: Biographical sketch of Martin Yang of the Rural Service Institute in Luichow, n.d.; "The Changing China Scene; Account of the Lutheran Theological Seminary, Shekow, Hupeh," by Gustav Carlberg, 1958; "The General Situation in Shantung, China, the Field of the American Lutheran Mission," by Grady L. Cooper, ca. 1946–47; "The New China," by Daniel Chu (excerpt from letter to Helen Shirk), 1951; "Newsletter from China," by Helen M. Shirk, 1950; "Open and Closing Doors in the Orient," by Helen M. Shirk and Luther A. Gotwald, 1949; "Our Rural Medical Service," n.a. (possibly Martin Yang), n.d.; "A Trip to Loyung Farm," by Martin Yang, n.d.

PAMPHLETS: *China: Chung Hwa*, ed. by Augusta Highland, 1945.

SERIALS: *China Newsletter*, 1949–56. *Honan Glimpses*, 1922–27. *Lutheran Literature Society for China Bulletin*, 1958–63.

CHINESE LANGUAGE MATERIALS/SERIALS: *Sin I Bao* (journal of the Lutheran Church in China), 1913–47.

MOODY BIBLE INSTITUTE
IL–55   Library
820 North LaSalle Drive
Chicago IL 60610
(312) 329-4140
Walter Osborn, Special Collections

1-GENERAL HOLDINGS

SERIALS: *China Bulletin*, 1977–87 (current 10 years). *China*

Fundamentalist and Anti-Bolshevick Bulletin, 1928. *China's Millions* (London), 1886–87, 1891–92, 1895, 1902–3, 1906, 1932, 1934–52. *China's Millions* (Philadelphia), 1893–1910, 1933–52. *East Asia Millions* (Philadelphia), 1977–87 (current 10 years). *Millions* (London), 1952. *Millions* (Philadelphia), 1952–61.

IL–60 NEWBERRY LIBRARY
60 West Walton Street
Chicago IL 60610
(312) 943-9090
Charles T. Cullen, President and Librarian
Carolyn Sheehy, Administrative Curator,
  Special Collections

1-AYER COLLECTION, 1575–1736, 9 items
MINUTES/RECORDS/REPORTS: Royal decrees from Spain to Manila mentioning missions in China, 1682–1736.
CORRESPONDENCE: Letter from Francisco Capillas, O.P., in China, to Juan de los Angeles, O.P., 1647; 4 letters from Miguel de Elorriaga, Manila, to Marcelo Angelita, chancellor of Cardinal Charles Maillard de Tournon, 1712–14, including discussion of Jesuit missions in China, the rites controversy, and the imprisonment of missionaries in Macao by the Portuguese; letter from Cristóbal Pedroche, O.P., Manila, to Tomás Reluz, bishop of Oviedo, 1708, including discussion of the rites controversy and the persecution of Spanish Dominicans in Macao by the Portuguese.
MANUSCRIPTS: "Relacion de las cosas la china que propriamte. se llama taybin" and "Relacion del viage que se hizo a la tierra de la China de 1575," by Martín de Rada, O.S.A., 1575 (photostats of leaves 15–30 from MS 325, contemporary copies of the originals in the Bibliothèque Nationale de Paris); "Revolución contra el Emperador de China," n.a., 1648?
FINDING AIDS: *Calendar of Philippine Documents in the Ayer Collection of the Newberry Library*, ed. by Paul S. Lietz (Chicago: The Newberry Library), 1956.

2-GREENLEE COLLECTION, 1611–1963, 45 volumes
Background note: The Greenlee Collection contains books in English, Portuguese, and Spanish emanating from and relating to Catholic missions in China from the seventeenth and eighteenth centuries, including travelogues, discussions of the rites controversy, and anthologies of reprinted correspondence from Catholic missionaries in China. Representative titles include: *Due lettere annue della Cina del 1610, e del 1611...*, by Claudio Acquaviva, 1615; *Histoire de l'expedition Chrestienne en la Chine...*, by Nicholas Trigault, 1618; *Relaçam annal das cousas que fizeram os padres da Companhia de Iesus...*, by Fernao Guerreiro, 1611.
CORRESPONDENCE: Circular mission letter of Antoine Thomas, describing Ferdinand Verbiest's work at the College of Peking, 1691.
MANUSCRIPTS: "A Brief Reply to the Ambassador of Portugal about the Pretensions of Portugal to the Patronage of the Church in the Orient" (in Italian), n.a., 1674; "Problems and Regulations Relating to Missionary Activity in China" (in Latin), by Domingo Fernández Navarrete, 1674.
PAMPHLETS: *A Igreja de S. Domingos e os Dominicanos em Macau*, by José Maria Braga, 1939; *The Portuguese Padroado in East Asia and the Problem of the Chinese Rites, 1576–1773*, by Charles Ralph Boxer, 1948; *A Propósito dum Livrinho Xilográfico dos Jesuítas de Pequim (século XVIII)*, by Charles Ralph Boxer,

1947; *Relaçao da Gloriosa Morte de Qvatro Embaizadores Portuguezes, da Cidade de Macao, com Sincoenta, & Sete Christaos de Sua Companhia, Degolados Todos Fella Fee de Christo em Nangassaqui, Cidade de Iappao, a Tres de Agoso de 1640...*, by Antonio Francisco Cardim, 1643; *Sermam qve Pregov o R. Padre Simam de Graças de Felice Acclamaçao del Rey...Dom Ioao o Quarto na Cidade da Madre de Deos de Macao...*, by Simao da Cunha, 1644.
DISSERTATIONS/THESES: *Die Akkommodationsmethode des P. Matteo Ricci S.I. in China*, by Johannes Bettray, 1955.
FINDING AIDS: *Catalogue of the Greenlee Collection, The Newberry Library, Chicago* (Boston: G. K. Hall and Co.), 1970.

NORTH PARK COLLEGE AND THEOLOGICAL SEMINARY
IL–65 Wallgren Library
5125 North Spaulding Avenue
Chicago IL 60625
(312) 583-2700
Sonia Bodi, Reference Librarian

1-GENERAL HOLDINGS
MINUTES/RECORDS/REPORTS: National Christian Council of China, annual report, 1925–26.
MAPS/DESIGNS/DRAWINGS: *Atlas of the Chinese Empire*, by Edward Stanford, 1908.
SERIALS: *China and the Gospel*, 1906–8. *Chinese Recorder*, 1903, 1905–41. *Ching Feng*, 1964–79.
DISSERTATIONS/THESES: *Marcus Ch'eng, Apostle or Apostate? Relations with the Covenant Mission in China*, by O. Theodore Roberg, 1982. *The South Shensi Lutheran Mission*, by Sigurd Aske, 1951.
CHINESE LANGUAGE MATERIALS: *The Chinese Hymnary*, n.a., 1934.

UNIVERSITY OF CHICAGO

IL–70 John Crerar Library
5730 South Ellis Avenue
Chicago IL 60637
(312) 702-7715
Pat Swanson, Assistant Director

1-GENERAL HOLDINGS
MINUTES/RECORDS/REPORTS: China Medical Board of New York, reports, 1954–60.
SERIALS: *Chinese Medical Directory*, 1928, 1930. *Chinese Medical Journal*, 1931–66, 1973–; supplement, 1936–40.

IL–75 Department of Special Collections
University of Chicago
Joseph Regenstein Library
1100 East 57th Street
Chicago IL 60637-1502
(312) 702-8705
Daniel Meyer, Assistant Curator for Manuscripts
  and Archives
Richard L. Popp, Archives Assistant

Background note: The Oriental Educational Commission, mentioned in several of the collections listed below, was sponsored by the University of Chicago in 1908 and 1909 to report on educational, social, and religious conditions in East Asia.

1-ARCHIVAL PHOTOGRAPHIC FILES, ca. 1925, 26 items
AUDIO-VISUAL MATERIALS: 5 photos of Ernest D. Burton, including a picture of his funeral in 1925; 4 photos of Thomas C. Chamberlin, n.d.; 11 photos of Franklin C. McLean, including a scene at Peking Union Medical College, n.d.; 2 photos of Helen Vincent McLean, n.d.; 4 photos of Robert Redfield, n.d.

2-ERNEST DeWITT BURTON PAPERS, 1909–23, 2 boxes, ca. 50 folders
Background note: Ernest DeWitt Burton (1856–1925) served as head of the University's Department of New Testament Literature and Interpretation. He travelled to China in 1908 and 1909 as a member of the Oriental Educational Commission, and again in 1921 and 1922 on behalf of the China Educational Commission, under the sponsorship of the Foreign Missions Conference of North America.

In addition to the materials listed below, this collection contains 8 boxes of Burton's correspondence on foreign education and missions, some of which deals with China, and 3 folders of correspondence on the YMCA, which includes some China-related material.
MINUTES/RECORDS/REPORTS: China Educational Commission, minutes and conference transcripts, 1920–22; "Conference of Representatives of Educational Institutions in China with Dr. Ernest D. Burton, May 29–30, 1920" (transcript of proceedings); Oriental Educational Commission, draft report to the president and trustees of the University of Chicago, 1909; reports by Burton after his return from Asia, 1909; University of Nanking, memos and reports, n.d.; West China Union University, constitution with revisions, n.d.
CORRESPONDENCE: 18 letters from Burton in China to Edgar J. Goodspeed, 1909; letter from Burton to H.P. Judson regarding the disposition of records from the Oriental Educational Commission, 1918; folder of letters relating to Canton Christian College, 1909–22; folder of letters relating to Central China University, n.d.; folder of letters relating to Chengtu College, 1909; 3 folders of letters relating to the China Medical Board of the Rockefeller Foundation, 1915–23; folder of letters relating to East China Union Medical College, n.d.; folder of letters relating to the Oriental Educational Commission, 1908–10; folder of letters relating to Peking Federated University, n.d.; folder of letters relating to Shanghai Baptist College, 1911–21; 9 folders of letters relating to the University of Nanking, 1910–22; 2 folders of letters relating to West China Union University, 1909–22.
DIARIES: 2 copies of a journal and record of interviews and observations by Burton for the Oriental Educational Commission, 1908–9; personal journals of his China trip, 1908–9; China Educational Commission, diary, 1921.
MANUSCRIPTS: "Education in China," n.d.; "Educational Conditions in Eastern Lands," 1910; "The Situation in China," n.d.; "Some Recent Developments of Christian Education in China," n.d.; speech by Burton before the students of Soochow University, n.d.; "The Oriental Education Commission," n.a., 1909–10; "Record of Observations of Schools for Girls in China," by Margaret E. Burton, 1909; "An Unofficial Record of

an Unscientific Journey on the Yangtze Kiang," by Burton, n.d.; "The Urgency of a Special Missionary Work to be Started among the Buddhists in China," a draft address by Karl Reichelt, n.d.
PAMPHLETS: Miscellaneous pamphlets relating to Asian mission work and the Oriental Educational Commission, n.d.; "Suggestions by Mr. J. R. Mott on the Oxford and Cambridge Scheme for a University in China," article reprint, n.d.; "Education, Old and New, in China," n.d., and "Educational Work in China," reprints of articles by Burton, 1910.
MEMORABILIA: 3 folders of newspaper clippings concerning the Oriental Educational Commission, 1908–9; postcards sent by Burton to Edgar J. Goodspeed, 1908–9; "Oriental Educational Investigation," a scrapbook, 1908–9.
MAPS/DESIGNS/DRAWINGS: Maps of the University of Nanking, n.d.
AUDIO-VISUAL MATERIALS: Photos of the University of Nanking, n.d.; photos sent by Burton in Asia to Edgar J. Goodspeed, 1908–9.
CHINESE LANGUAGE MATERIALS: Documents relating to the Oriental Educational Commission, n.d.
FINDING AIDS: In-house guide.

3-THOMAS CHROWDER CHAMBERLIN PAPERS, 1908–29, ca. 14 folders
Background note: Thomas Chrowder Chamberlin (b. 1848), head of the Department of Geology at the University of Chicago, went to China as a member of the Oriental Educational Commission in 1908 and 1909. In addition to the materials listed below, some of Chamberlin's correspondence pertaining to the Commission is interfiled with other items in 3 boxes of miscellaneous letters, n.d., and a letterbook, 1907–8.
MINUTES/RECORDS/REPORTS/CORRESPONDENCE: 12 folders of letters, notes, and reports concerning the Oriental Educational Commission, 1909 and n.d.
MANUSCRIPTS: 2 folders containing a draft address by Chamberlin on his trip to China, n.d., and recollections of the trip by Rollin T. Chamberlin, 1929.
MEMORABILIA: Uncatalogued clippings related to the Commission, 1909.
FINDING AIDS: In-house guide.

4-CHINESE RITES, CONTROVERSIAL PAMPHLETS, ca. 1710, 1 item
MANUSCRIPTS/PAMPHLETS: Codex of copies of printed pamphlets in Italian and Latin with supporting memorials, letters, and edicts, relating to Charles Thomas Maillard de Tournon's mission to China and Chinese religion in the context of the rites controversy.
FINDING AIDS: In-house guide.

5-JOHN M. COULTER PAPERS, 1845-ca. 1870, 1 box
Background note: This collection contains papers of Moses S. Coulter, Presbyterian missionary in China from 1849 to 1853, and Caroline E. Coulter, Presbyterian missionary in China from 1849 to 1906.
CORRESPONDENCE: Letters of Moses and Caroline Coulter, ca. 1850–1870, mostly letters to Caroline Coulter from friends in China.
DIARIES: Diaries of Moses Coulter, 1848–49, and Caroline Coulter, 1849.

MANUSCRIPTS: Commonplace book with essays by Moses Coulter, 1845.
MEMORABILIA: Moses Coulter's will, 1851.
FINDING AIDS: In-house guide.

6-KERMIT EBY PAPERS, 1933, 1 volume
Background note: Kermit Eby (1903–62) was a sociologist and minister of the United Brethren Church.
MEMORABILIA: Scrapbook of the Friends' Goodwill Mission to the Orient, 1933, containing itineraries, letters of introduction, postcards, photos, and souvenirs.
FINDING AIDS: In-house guide.

7-FRANKLIN C. McLEAN PAPERS, 1922–23, ca. 5 folders
Background note: Franklin C. McLean (1888–1968) was a physician and staff member of the Rockefeller Institute from 1914 to 1923. He made two trips to China between 1916 and 1919 to supervise the development of Peking Union Medical College (PUMC), and served as chairman and professor of medicine at PUMC until 1923. See also Rockefeller University, Rockefeller Archive Center, Pocantico Hills, North Tarrytown, NY, 10591.
MINUTES/RECORDS/REPORTS: Peking Union Medical College and China Medical Board, reports and records, 1915–65.
CORRESPONDENCE: 2 folders of letters to and from McLean while head of the Department of Medicine at PUMC, 1922–23, including correspondence with Alfred E. Cohn, Rufus Cole, Simon Flexner, and Donald D. Van Slyke, on topics such as the administration of PUMC, the research conducted there, and its relations with the Rockefeller Institute; correspondence with Harold H. Loucks and Mary E. Ferguson concerning the China Medical Board, PUMC, and current medical education in China, 1950–68.
DIARIES: 2 diaries of McLean's trip to China, ca. 1915.
MANUSCRIPTS: "History of Peking Union Medical College and the China Medical Board," typescript by Mary Ferguson, 1965.
MEMORABILIA: Program of a medical conference at Peking Union Medical College, 1921.
AUDIO-VISUAL MATERIALS: Audio cassettes of readings of McLean's letters and journals, including China-related correspondence, 1911–16, 1919–31, and a diary of McLean's first trip to China, 1916; photos of trips to China, 1916–25.
FINDING AIDS: In-house guide.

8-ROBERT S. PLATT PAPERS, 1910–22, ca. 9 folders
Background note: Robert S. Platt (1891–1964) was professor of geography at the University of Chicago, and an instructor at the College of Yale-in-China from 1914 to 1915. See also Yale University, Department of Manuscripts and Archives, Sterling Memorial Library, 120 High Street, New Haven, CT, 06520.
CORRESPONDENCE: Folder of letters concerning the College of Yale-in-China at Changsha, 1917–22.
MANUSCRIPTS: "Life in a Chinese City," by Platt, 1921; "How It Strikes the Newcomer," by Platt, n.d.; 2 folders of teaching notes on Chinese geography and related topics, 1914–15.
PAMPHLETS: Brochure on Yale-in-China, ca. 1910.
MAPS/DESIGNS/DRAWINGS: Map of Changsha, n.d.
AUDIO-VISUAL MATERIALS: Ca. 3 folders of negatives, hand-painted glass slides, and film slides concerning tours of China and the activities of Yale-in-China, 1913–15.
FINDING AIDS: In-house guide.

9-PRESIDENTS' PAPERS, SERIES I, 1889–1925, ca. 12 folders
CORRESPONDENCE: Correspondence concerning the China Medical Board of the Rockefeller Foundation, Chinese students and universities, Christian missionaries and missions in China, and the Oriental Educational Commission, 1889–1925.
FINDING AIDS: In-house guide.

10-ROBERT REDFIELD PAPERS, 1948–49, 2 folders
Background note: Robert Redfield (1897–1958) was a professor of anthropology and dean of the Social Sciences Division at the University of Chicago. He taught at a number of universities in China from 1948 to 1949.
CORRESPONDENCE: 5 folders of letters, 1943–49, concerning Redfield's visit to China; teaching at Lingnan University, National Tsinghua University, and Yenching University; and conditions in China immediately prior to the Communist takeover.
FINDING AIDS: In-house guide.

IL–80   Law Library
University of Chicago
1121 East 60th Street
Chicago IL 60637
(312) 962-9615
Judith M. Wright, Director

1-GENERAL HOLDINGS
SERIALS: *China Law Review*, 1922–40.

IL–85   Joseph Regenstein Library
University of Chicago
1100 East 57th Street
Chicago IL 60637–1502
(312) 702-8442
Curtis Bochanyin, Divinity and Philosophy
 Bibliographer
Wen-pai Tai, Chinese Bibliographer

Finding aids: *Author-Title Catalog of the Chinese Collection* (Boston: G. K. Hall), 1973, 8 V; *Author-Title Catalog of the Chinese Collection: First Supplement* (Boston: G. K. Hall), 1981, 4 V; *Classified Catalog and Subject Index of the Chinese and Japanese Collections* (Boston: G. K. Hall), 1973, 6 V; *Classified Catalog and Subject Index of the Chinese and Japanese Collections: First Supplement* (Boston: G. K. Hall), 1981, 4 V; *Far Eastern Serials* (Chicago: University of Chicago Library), 1977.

1-GENERAL HOLDINGS
MINUTES/RECORDS/REPORTS: China Baptist Publication Society, reports, 1906, 1910; China Inland Mission, annual reports, 1945–47; China International Famine Relief Commission, annual reports, 1922–36, 1938; China Medical Board of New York, reports, 1954–60; General Conference Mennonite Church, China mission, 1940; National Council of the Churches of Christ in the United States of America, reports on deputation of Australian churchmen to China, 1957; Shanghai Mission to Ricksha Men, annual report, 1923–30; World Missionary Conference, Edinburgh, Continuation Committee, China, proceedings, 1910.
MINUTES/RECORDS/REPORTS/CORRESPONDENCE: Presbyterian Church in the U.S.A., Board of Foreign Missions, missions correspondence and reports on China on 55 reels of microfilm, including some early files from the American Board of

Commissioners for Foreign Missions, 1837–1911, and index to correspondence with abstracts (see also Presbyterian Historical Society, Archives and Library, 425 Lombard Street, Philadelphia, PA, 19147).

MANUSCRIPTS: "As I Look Back: Recollections of Growing Down in America's Southland and of Twenty-six Years in Pre-Communist China, 1888–1936," by Eugene Epperson Barnett, 1964.

PAMPHLETS: *Benedictine Mission to China*, by M. Wibora Muehlenbein, 1980; *The Bible and China*, by William Harrison Hudspeth, 1952; *British Protestant Christian Evangelists and the 1898 Reform Movement in China*, by Leslie R. Marchant, 1975; *Children of Bubbling Well*, by Marguerite Harmon Bro and Harriet Harmon Dexter, 1913(?); *The Harrowing of Hell in China: A Synoptic Study of the Role of Christian Evangelists in the Opening of Hunan Province*, by Leslie R. Marchant, 1977; *Nestorians in China: Some Corrections and Additions*, by Arthur Christopher Moule, 1940; *Russian (Greek Orthodox) Missionaries in China, 1689–1917: Their Cultural, Political, and Economic Role*, by Albert Parry, 1940; *Theorie und praxis eines protestantischen missionars in China*, by Ernst Faber, 1902; *Windows into China: The Jesuits and Their Books, 1580–1730*, by John Parker, 1978; other uncatalogued pamphlets.

ORAL HISTORIES: *China Missionaries Oral History Collection*, ed. by Cyrus H. Peake and Arthur L. Rosenbaum (Claremont Graduate School, Oral History Program), 1973. See ORAL HISTORIES Union List for the names of participants.

MAPS/DESIGNS/DRAWINGS: *Atlas of the Chinese Empire Containing Separate Maps of the Eighteen Provinces of China Proper on the Scale of 1:3,000,000 and of the Four Great Dependencies on the Scale of 1:7,500,000, Together with an Index to All the Names on the Maps and a List of All Protestant Mission Stations*, by Edward Stanford, 1908.

SERIALS: American Friends Service Committee, *Bulletin on Work in China*, 1942–44. *Asia*, 1957–60. *Asian Folklore Studies*, 1942-. *China and the Gospel*, 1905–30. *China Bulletin*, 1947–62. China Christian Educational Association, *Bulletin*, 1926, 1928. *China Christian Year Book*, 1910–37. China International Famine Relief Commission: Publications, series A, 1922–36; series B, 1924–34. *China Monthly*, 1939–50. *China Notes*, 1962–72. *Chinese Recorder*, 1870–1940. *Chinese Repository*, 1832–51. *Ching Feng*, 1964-. *Directory of Protestant Missions in China*, 1916–17, 1928, 1930. *Lingnan Science Journal*, 1927–50. *Les Missions de Chine et du Japon*, 1927. *Monumenta Serica*, 1935-. National Christian Council of China, *Bulletin*, 1922–37. Peking Society of Natural History, *Bulletin*, 1926–27. Peking Union Medical College: *Bibliography of the Publications from the Laboratories and Clinics*, 1915–32; Department of Pharmacology, *Contributions*, 1921–26. University of Nanking, College of Agriculture and Forestry: *Agriculture and Forestry Series*, 1932–36; *Bulletin*, 1932–36; *Special Report*, 1935–36. West China Border Research Society, *Journal*, 1922–45. Yenching University: Department of Sociology, Publications, series C, 1929–30; *Yenching Journal of Social Studies*, 1938–50; *Yenching Series on Chinese Industry and Trade*, 1930, 1934.

DISSERTATIONS/THESES: *Die Akkommodationsmethode des P. Matteo Ricci S.I. in China*, by Johannes Bettray, 1955. *American Catholic China Missionaries, 1918–1941*, by Thomas A. Breslin, 1972. *Changes in the Christian Message for China by Protestant Missionaries*, by Lewis Strong Casey Smythe, 1928. *The China Inland Mission and Some Aspects of Its Work*, by Hudson T. Armerding, 1948. *China Missions in Crisis: Bishop Laimbeckhoven and His Times, 1738–1787*, by Joseph Krahl, 1964. *The Chinese Bible: Being a Historical Survey of Its Translation*, by Paul Henry Bartel, 1946. *Christian Higher Education in China: Contributions of the Colleges of Arts and Sciences to Chinese Life*, by J. Dyke Van Putten, 1934. *Christian Missions in China*, by Charles Sumner Estes, 1895. *Cultural Interpretation in a Local Community in China*, by Marie Johanna Regier, 1936. *A History of the Evangelical Lutheran Church of America's Mission Policy in China, 1890–1949*, by Roger Keith Ose, 1970. *Indications of Primitive Chinese Religion in the Confucian Classics*, by David Crockett Graham, 1919. *The Influence of the Modern Christian Missionaries on Social Conditions of China*, by Harold Shepard Matthews, 1920. *A Jesuit Encyclopedia for China: A Guide to Jean-Baptiste du Halde's "Description...de la Chine" (1735)*, by Theodore Nicholas Foss, 1979. *The Jesuits in China in the Last Days of the Ming Dynasty*, by George Harold Dunne, 1944. *John Leighton Stuart: The Mind and Life of an American Missionary in China, 1876–1941*, by Shaw Yu-ming, 1975. *Karl Gützlaff als Missionar in China*, by Herman Schlyter, 1946. *Die katholische Chinamission im Spiegel der rotchinesischen Presse; Versuch einer Missionarischen Deutung*, by Johannes Schütte, 1957. *Die katholische Missionsmethode in China in neuester Zeit (1842–1912)*, by Johannes Beckmann, 1931. *The Lost Churches of China: A Study of Contributing Factors in the Recurring Losses Sustained by Christianity in China during the Last Thirteen Hundred Years*, by Leonard M. Outerbridge, 1952. *Lutheran Missions in a Time of Revolution: The China Experience, 1944–1951*, by Jonas Jonson, 1972. *Methods of Mission Work in China*, by John Thomas Proctor, 1896. *The Mission Enterprise of the Lutheran Church-Missouri Synod in Mainland China, 1913–1952*, by Roy Arthur Suelflow, 1971. *The Missionary Factor in Anglo-Chinese Relations, 1891–1900*, by Edmund S. Wehrle, 1962. *Missionary Status and Influence in Early Nineteenth-century China*, by Richard Bryant Drake, 1950. *The Missouri Evangelical Lutheran Mission in China, 1913–1948*, by Richard Henry Meyer, 1948. *The Negotiations between Ch'i-ying and Lagrené, 1844–1846*, by Angelus Francis Grosse-Aschhoff, 1950. *The Oriental Education Commission's Recommendation for Mission Strategy in Higher Education*, by David Lloyd Lindberg, 1972. *La Politique missionaire de la France en China, 1842–1856: l'ouverture des cinq ports chinois au commerce étranger et la liberté religieuse*, by Louis Tsing-sing Wei, 1960. *Protestant Mission Schools for Girls in South China (1827 to the Japanese Invasion)*, by Mary Raleigh Anderson, 1943. *Protestant Missionary Publications in Modern China, 1912–1949: A Study of Their Programs, Operations, and Trends*, by Ho Hoi-lap, 1979. *The Protestant Missionary Understanding of the Chinese Situation and the Christian Task from 1890 to 1911*, by C. William Mensendiek, 1958. *Religion in Szechuan Province*, by David Crockett Graham, 1927. *Russian (Greek Orthodox) Missionaries in China, 1689–1917: Their Cultural, Political, and Economic Role*, by Albert Parry, 1938. *Social Implications of the Teaching of Agriculture in the Mission Schools of China*, by Ely Martin Stannard, 1925. *Some Adjustment Problems of Chinese High School Students*, by Ralph Raymond Shrader, 1933. *Songs of Chinese Children: The Religious Education of Youth in the New China*, by Anna Hortense Potts, 1927. *The Transfer of the Functions of Christian Missions and the Assumption Thereof by the Chinese Church*, by Lewis Frederick Havermale, 1932. *The Transformation of Religious Concepts in North China*, by Leonard Mallory Outerbridge, 1933. *The Young Men's Christian Associations of China*, by Kirby Page, 1916.

CHINESE LANGUAGE MATERIALS/SERIALS: *Chen li chou k'an* (*The Truth Weekly*), 1923–26. *Chen li yü sheng ming* (*Truth and Life*), 1926–41. *Ch'i lu hsüeh pao*, 1941. *Ch'i-ta chi k'an* (*Cheeloo University Journal*), 1932–37. *Ch'i-ta kuo hsüeh chi k'an*, 1941. *Chi-tu chiao ts'ung k'an* (*Series on Christianity*), 1943–46?. *Chi-tu hao* (*The Call of Jesus*), 1935–37. *Chiao hui hsin pao* (*Church News*), 1868–74. *Chin-ling hsüeh pao* (*Nanking Journal*), 1931–41. *Ching feng*, 1972–75. Chung-hua Chi-tu chiao chiao yü hsüeh hui, *Chiao yü chi k'an* (China Christian Educational Association, *Education Quarterly*), 1925–41. *Chung-hua Chi-tu chiao ch'üan kuo tsung hui kung pao* (*Bulletin of the National Assembly of Chinese Christians*), 1929–54. *Chung-hua Chi-tu chiao hui nien chien* (*China Church Yearbook*), 1914–33. *Chung-hua Chi-tu chiao nü ch'ing nien hui ch'üan kuo hsieh hui hui wu niao k'an* (*Summaries of the National Meetings of the YWCA of China*), 1930–37. *Chung-hua kung chiao ch'ing nien hui chi k'an* (*Periodicum Trimestre Consociationis Juventutis Catholicae*), 1929–30. *Chung-kuo hsin t'u yüeh k'an* (*Chinese Christians Today*), 1962–. *Fu jen hsüeh chih* (*Fu jen Sinological Journal/Series Sinologica*), 1928–47. *Hsieh chin* (National Christian Council of China, *Bulletin*), 1953–53. *Hsieh ho hsüeh pao* (*Journal of Canton Union Theological Seminary*), 1937. *Hua-hsi hsieh ho ta hsüeh Chung-kuo wen hua yen chiu so chi k'an* (West China Union University, *Studia Serica*), 1940–44, 1948, 1950. *I shih pao* (*Social Welfare*), 1936–37. *Ling-nan hsüeh pao* (*Lingnan Journal*), 1929–52. *Ming teng* (*Beacon*), 1921–41. *Nü to* (*Woman's Messenger*), 1912–49. *Pien chiang yen chiu lun ts'ung* (*Frontier Studies*), 1941–44. *Sheng kung hui pao* (*Chinese Churchman*), 1925–35. *Sheng ming* (*Life*), 1919–. *T'ien feng*, 1962. *Tung wu hsüeh pao* (*Soochow Journal*), 1934. *Wan kuo kung pao* (*The Globe Magazine: A Review of the Times*), 1874–1907. *Wen she* (*Literature and Society*), 1925–28. *Yen-ching hsin wen* (*Yenching News*), 1934–36. *Yen-ching hsüeh pao* (*Yenching Journal of Chinese Studies*), 1927–51. *Yen-ching she hui k'o hsüeh* (*Yenching Social Sciences*), 1948–49. Yen-ching ta hsüeh, *T'u shu kuan pao* (Yenching University, *Library Bulletin*), 1933–35.

CHINESE LANGUAGE MATERIALS/DISSERTATIONS/THESES: *Chi-tu chiao Chung-wen ch'i k'an chih tiao ch'a, 1950–1975* (*An Examination of Chinese Christian Periodicals*), by Pai Chia-ling, 1976.

CHINESE LANGUAGE MATERIALS: Ca. 250 titles, including translations of the Bible and the writings of ante-Nicene fathers, Augustine, St. Bernard, John Bunyan, John Calvin, Jonathan Edwards, Martin Luther, Reinhold Niebuhr, Walter Rauschenbusch, John Wesley, and other Western religious thinkers; translations and scholarly treatises by Young J. Allen, Louis Buglio, Li Chih-tsao, W.A.P. Martin, Walter Medhurst, Robert Morrison, and Matteo Ricci; and works on such subjects as Anglicanism, anti-Christian sentiment in China, Baptist churches in China, the Bible, the Boxer Uprising, Catholicism in China, the Chinese Christian Student's Movement, the Chinese Rhenish Mission Church, the Christian Literature Society for China, Christian views on ancestor worship and other facets of Chinese culture, Christian youth work, Christianity in the People's Republic of China, church history, the

church and the Chinese economy, Feng Yü-hsiang, Fu-jen University, missions in Hong Kong and Taiwan, Jesuit missions, Vincent Lebbe, Jesus, Lingnan University, missions to Buddhists and to Chinese Moslems, Nanking Theological Seminary, the National Christian Council of China, Nestorianism, Protestantism in China, Timothy Richard, rural missions, theology, the University of Nanking, Vatican II, West China Union University, the writings of Chinese Christians, and Yenching University; translation of the Gospel of Luke in Manchu.

DEERFIELD

TRINITY EVANGELICAL DIVINITY SCHOOL
IL–90   Library
2077 Half Day Road
Deerfield IL 60015
(312) 945–8800
Keith P. Wells, Reference Librarian

Background note: Trinity Evangelical Divinity School houses the Archives of the Evangelical Free Church of America, which first sent missionaries to China under the auspices of the Scandinavian Alliance Mission. The archives contain published books on Free Church missions in China and serials which include information on China mission work in Swedish and English, 1877–1952.

1-GENERAL HOLDINGS
MINUTES/RECORDS/REPORTS: China Inland Mission, annual reports, 1945–46, 1949, 1952; Reformed Church in the United States, China Mission, minutes of annual meetings, 1920, 1922, 1924, 1926.

PAMPHLETS: *Chinese Communist Religious Policy and the Prospects for Future Mission Work in China*, by Jonathan T'ien-en Chao, 1975; *Forty Blessed Years: The Ministry of Rev. Andrew Gih*, by Richard Chen, 1965; *Frederik Franson: World Evangelist and Missionary Leader*, by J. F. Swanson, 1952.

SERIALS: *Bridge*, 1984–. *China and the Church Today*, 1979–86. *China Christian Year Book*, 1936–37. *China Evangelical Seminary News Bulletin*, 1975, 1977–. *The China Fundamentalist*, 1932–33. *China Missionary*, 1948–49. *China Missionary Bulletin*, 1950–53. *China Notes*, 1962–. *China Prayer Letter*, 1986–. *China Update*, 1985. *Chinese Christians Today*, 1972–. *Chinese World Pulse*, 1977–83. *Ching Feng*, 1964–. *East Asia Millions* (Philadelphia), 1961–. *Mission Bulletin*, 1954–56.

DISSERTATIONS/THESES: *An Analysis of Watchman Nee's Doctrine of Dying and Rising with Christ as It Relates to Sanctification*, by Robert Kingston Wetmore, 1983. *The China Inland Mission and Some Aspects of Its Work*, by Hudson T. Armerding, 1948. *A Comparative Study of the Concept of God in Chinese Thought and Christian Theology as Represented by Selected Evangelical Theologians*, by Joseph Chi-choi Wong, 1979. *The Ecclesiology of the "Little Flock" of China Founded by Watchman Nee*, by James Mo-oi Cheung, 1970. *The Influence of Hudson Taylor on the Faith Missions Movement*, by Daniel W. Bacon, 1983. *The Missions' Responsibilities Toward the Reopening of China*, by Lo Ka-man, 1971. *The Responsibility and Prospects of Overseas Chinese Christians to Evangelize Mainland China When It Reopens*,

by Lukas Tjandra, 1973. *A Study of Frederik Franson: The Development and Impact of His Ecclesiology, Missiology, and Worldwide Evangelism*, by Edvard P. Torjeson, 1984.
CHINESE LANGUAGE MATERIALS/SERIALS: *Chung-kuo hsin t'u yüeh k'an (Chinese Christians Today)*, 1973–84.

DeKALB

NORTHERN ILLINOIS UNIVERSITY
IL–95 University Libraries
DeKalb IL 60115–2868
(815) 753–1094
Doris Miller, Reference Librarian

1-GENERAL HOLDINGS
DISSERTATIONS/THESES: *Imperial Government and Catholic Missions in China during the Years 1784–1785*, by Bernward Henry Willeke, 1948. *Missionary Conscience and the Comprehension of Imperialism: A Study of the Children of American Missionaries to China, 1900–1949*, by Sarah Margaret Refo Mason, 1978. *Protestant Mission Schools for Girls in South China (1827 to the Japanese Invasion)*, by Mary Raleigh Anderson, 1943.

DOWNERS GROVE

GEORGE WILLIAMS COLLEGE
IL–100 Library
555 31st Street
Downers Grove IL 60515
(312) 964–3100
Marilyn T. Thompson, Director

Background note: This institution was founded in 1884 as the Young Men's Christian Association Training School. From 1903 to 1910, it was called the Institute and Training School of the Young Men's Christian Associations. In 1913 the name was changed to Young Men's Christian Association College; it adopted the present name in 1933. See also Young Men's Christian Association of the U.S.A. Archives, University of Minnesota, Social History Welfare Archives, 2642 University Avenue, St. Paul, MN, 55114.

1-GENERAL HOLDINGS
MINUTES/RECORDS/REPORTS: YMCA of China, reports, 1930–31; YMCA of China, yearbooks and rosters, 1931–38.
DISSERTATIONS/THESES: *A Brief History of the Young Men's Christian Association of China, with Particular Emphasis on Its Department of Physical Education*, by H. Ross Bunce, 1914. *The Opportunity of the Young Men's Christian Association Service of Physical Education in the Reconstruction of Chinese Society*, by Chang Tien-be, 1920. *A Policy and Program for Physical Development of the Young Men's Christian Association in China*, by Fred Meichong Chu, 1918. *A Study of the Young Men's Christian Association in China*, by Charles P. Tshia, 1924. *The Young Men's Christian Association in China, Hong Kong, and Korea*, by Thomas Bodin, 1906. *The Young Men's Christian Associations of China*, by Kirby Page, 1916.

ELGIN

CHURCH OF THE BRETHREN GENERAL BOARD
IL–105 Brethren Historical Library and Archives
1451 Dundee Avenue
Elgin IL 60120
(312) 742–5100
James R. Lynch, Archivist

Restrictions: Access by appointment.
Background note: The Church of the Brethren opened its mission in China in 1908, sending five missionaries, who by 1910 had established a mission at Ping Ting Chou in Shansi. A second station was opened at Liao Chou in 1912 and congregations were organized at both stations later that year. A station at Shou Yang was opened in 1919. A primary school was established at Ping Ting in 1911; by 1924 the mission operated 27 schools, including four Bible schools and two secondary schools, serving 1,030 students. Medical work began in 1914 and reached its height in 1924, with three hospitals—Hiel Hamilton Memorial Hospital in Liao Chou, Brethren Hospital in Ping Ting Chou, and Women's Hospital in Shou Yang—staffed by 16 missionary and Chinese workers, and extensive outpatient and public health work. A School for Nurses was maintained at Ping Ting Chou with twelve male and seven female students in 1924. By 1939 there were 2,670 members in five congregations with three Chinese pastors and 48 paid evangelists, of whom 29 were women.

A South China Mission supported by Brethren was begun in 1916 at On Fun village in Kwangtung. In 1948 that congregation had 340 members scattered in 55 villages and an elementary school of 270 students. In 1949 it joined the Kwangtung Synod of the Church of Christ in China. Brethren missionaries left China in 1949 and 1950, and by 1953 missionary activity of the Church of the Brethren in China had ended. Approximately 100 Brethren missionaries had served in China from 1908 to 1953.

In 1941 Brethren Civilian Public Service (CPS) initiated the China Unit, intended to perform ambulance and emergency relief work in China. The unit was disbanded in 1942 when the State Department refused to issue passports to conscientious objectors. The Brethren Service-United Nations Relief and Rehabilitation Administration Unit, which operated in both Nationalist and Communist-held areas from 1946 to 1948, reported reclamation of 50,000 acres of farmland and the training of 600 Chinese tractor operators. The Heifers for Relief Committee of the Brethren Service Committee in 1946 sent a shipment of heifers to China with "seagoing cowboys" as attendants. In addition, substantial shipments of used clothing, bedding, and other material aid were sent.

Yin Jizeng, son of the first Brethren elder in China, emerged as pastor at the Rice Market Street Church in Beijing in 1971. He continued active pastoral leadership there until the early 1980s and is now serving the Chongwenmen Church and Yanjing Theological Seminary in Beijing.

See also General Commission on Archives and History—The United Methodist Church, United Methodist Archives and History Center, Archives, 36 Madison Avenue, P.O. Box 127, Madison, NJ, 07940; and United Theological Seminary, Library, 1810 Harvard Boulevard, Dayton, OH, 45406.

1-AUDIO-VISUAL COLLECTION, ca. 1935–1964, 294 items
ORAL HISTORIES: Audio tape and 29-page transcript of an interview with Anna Crumpsacker, 1964, discussing the history of the Brethren China mission from 1908 to 1941; audio tape of an interview with Clara Li K'an, 1950, discussing the Church of the Brethren in China and deputation work in the United States; audio tape of an interview with Kenneth K'an, 1950, describing a religious experience while imprisoned by the Japanese in 1937.
AUDIO-VISUAL MATERIALS: ''BSC in China,'' original film footage, 1947; audio tape of an address by Calvin Bright, 1951, describing the imprisonment of Bright and other faculty members of West China Union University by Communist forces in 1951; *China Still Survives* (51 color slides with script), 1949; *China's Ancient Glories* (46 color slides with script), 1950; *The Church of the Brethren at Work in China* (black-and-white film), 1935; *The Church in Changing China* (40 color slides with script), 1951; *Free China's Struggle* (black-and-white film), 1944; *In North and West China* (41 color slides with script), 1949; *In the Land of Szechwan (Four Rivers)* (61 color slides with script), 1949; *Rural China and Her People* (45 color slides with script); audio tape of a chapel address by C.C. Wang to the Brethren Publishing House Morning Worship Group, 1950.

2-CHURCH OF THE BRETHREN, BRETHREN SERVICE COMMITTEE, GENERAL SUBJECT FILE, 1941–47, ca. 7 reels microfilm
CORRESPONDENCE: Ca. 2 reels of correspondence relating to the China CPS Unit, 1941–42; ca. 2 reels of correspondence relating to the China Tractor Unit, 1946–47; ca. 1 reel of correspondence relating to Heifers for Relief, 1945–46; ca. 2 reels of correspondence relating to relief and rehabilitation work, 1946.

3-CHURCH OF THE BRETHREN, GENERAL BROTHERHOOD BOARD, FOREIGN MISSION COMMISSION RECORDS, 1910–54, 8.4 c.f.
Restrictions: Access to personnel records is restricted until 25 years after the employee's death.
MINUTES/RECORDS/REPORTS: Records of the Foreign Mission Commission interfiled with correspondence, 1910–54.
CORRESPONDENCE: Missionary personnel/correspondence files—China, 1910–53; correspondence subject files, China, 1925–53; and correspondence subject files, South China, 1914–16, 1947–53, including correspondence between headquarters staff, and missionaries and mission stations; correspondence of General Mission Board interfiled with that of Foreign Mission Commission; correspondence of international nationals in China, 1931–54; correspondence relating to Chinese nationals assisted in education in the United States by the church, and deputation work in the United States by Chinese nationals.
PAMPHLETS: Uncatalogued pamphlets interfiled with correspondence, 1910–54.
MAPS/DESIGNS/DRAWINGS: Uncatalogued maps interfiled with correspondence, 1910–54.
AUDIO-VISUAL MATERIALS: Photos of missionaries in the personnel files, 1910–54.
SERIALS: Uncatalogued periodicals interfiled with correspondence, 1910–54.

4-CHURCH OF THE BRETHREN GENERAL BOARD, WORLD MINISTRIES COMMISSION, PEACE AND INTERNATIONAL AFFAIRS CONSULTANT, EXCHANGE PROGRAM PERSONNEL FILES, 1981–85, .2 c.f.
Restrictions: 25-year restriction on personnel files.
MINUTES/RECORDS/REPORTS: Brethren-Chinese Agricultural Exchange Program, personnel files, 1981–85.

5-CHURCH OF THE BRETHREN MISSION, SHANSI, CHINA, RECORDS, 1912–40, 2.3 c.f.
MINUTES/RECORDS/REPORTS: Church of the Brethren Mission: agendas, 1920, 1922–25, 1928–35, 1937, 1939–40; Building Committee reports, 1915–29; Educational Committee, records, 1916–31; Evangelistic Department, records, 1920–28; Executive Committee, 1926–29; Famine Relief Committee, records, 1917–22, 1938–39, 1947; Field Committee, records, 1912–20; Field Treasurer's reports, 1913–39; Financial Committee, records, 1930–33; financial records, ca. 1924–1935; minutes, 1908–16, 1918–26; Ping Ting Chou Station Meeting, records, 1912–22; minutes and reports from 30 ad hoc committees, n.d.; miscellaneous records and papers, n.d.; reports from stations, schools, and hospitals on evangelistic work, 1916–36; records on language, 1917–23; records on medical work, 1915–36; record of missionaries, 1908–50; records on schools, 1915–32; records on women's work, 1917–33; register of deeds, 1912–23; Yearly Meeting of the Church of the Brethren in China, records, 1923–35.
CORRESPONDENCE: Correspondence between the mission's Field Committee and F.J. Wampler, 1915–18; correspondence of the mission treasurer, 1928, 1936, 1951.
MEMORABILIA: 9 banners, n.d.
MAPS/DESIGNS/DRAWINGS: Plans and architectural drawings, 1915–29 (some interfiled with the Building Committee reports, oversize filed separately).

6-ELGIN SYLVESTER MOYER PAPERS, n.d., .35 c.f.
MINUTES/RECORDS/REPORTS: Materials relating to the South China Missionary Society, the South China Mission, and the Chinese Sunday School of the First Church of the Brethren in Chicago, n.d.
CORRESPONDENCE: Letters from Moy Gwong, in On Fun, Kwangtung, n.d.; letters related to the South China Missionary Society and the Chinese Sunday School, n.d.

7-PHOTOGRAPHIC COLLECTION, ca. 1912–1951, ca. 3,700 items
AUDIO-VISUAL MATERIALS: ''Brethren Service Photo Album II, Section A: China Relief—General,'' containing 24 photos from Brethren Service, CWS, French Press and Information Service, Isaiah Ebersole Oberholtzer, United China Relief, United Nations Relief and Rehabilitation Administration (UNRRA), and unidentified photographers, n.d.; ''Brethren Service Photo Album II, Section B: China Relief—Tractor Unit,'' containing 259 photos from International Harvester Co., UNRRA, and unidentified photographers, n.d.; 4 photo albums of the Foreign Mission Commission containing 2,494 photos, ca. 1912–1950, including pictures of bombed villages, the Brethren mission in Shansi, the Brethren service project at Hsiengtang in Kiangsi, Chinese church groups, daily life, educational work, evangelistic work, medical work, missionaries, relief and refugee assistance, scenes from the South China Mission in Kwangtung, and war scenes; ca. 400 negatives from the Foreign Mission Commission, ca. 1947–1951, taken by

Wendell Flory, Howard Sollenberger, and J.K. Miller; 200 negatives taken by Leland S. Brubaker on a deputation trip, 1948–49; ca. 150 photos of the China mission by Winifred E. Cripe, 1908–17; 56 prints of the China mission in Shansi and 10 prints of the Brethren Service Tractor Unit from the Central Photo File, n.d.; ca. 100 slides, ca. late 1940s.

8-PING TING CHOU CHURCH OF THE BRETHREN, SHANSI, CHINA, RECORDS, 1912–40, .35 c.f.
MINUTES/RECORDS/REPORTS: Council meeting minutes, 1912–40; membership records, ca. 1939.

9-NETTIE MABELLE SENGER COLLECTION, ca. 1932–1939, 1 c.f.
MANUSCRIPTS: Uncatalogued papers relating to Nettie Mabelle Senger's work with women in Chinese villages, n.d.; draft of a dissertation for Hartford Theological Seminary, ca. 1935, concerning women in Chinese history and culture.
CHINESE LANGUAGE MATERIALS: *Gospel Truth for Village Women*, by Nettie M. Senger, 1933; *Gospel Truth for Village Women*, V 2, by Nettie M. Senger, 1938; hymnbook for villagers by Nettie Senger, n.d.; *People's Home Education*, by Dorothy Dickinson Barbour, Ts'ai Yung-ch'un, Nettie Senger, Sun Tsun-ying, and M. R. Rowlin, 1938; *Principles in Child Training*, by Dorothy Dickinson Barbour and Nettie Senger, 1932; *Principles in Child Training, Book II*, by Dorothy Dickinson Barbour, Nettie Senger, and C. C. Shih, 1932; *Special Bulletin of Christianizing the Home Movement of the Churches in China*, comp. by T. C. Kuan and N. M. Stallings, 1932; other uncatalogued material.

10-WANG T'UNG PAPERS, ca. 1940–1981, .6 c.f.
Restrictions: For access, contact the archivist or the Peace and International Affairs Consultant, Church of the Brethren General Board.
Background note: Wang T'ung (1906–85) was educated at Brethren mission schools and Yenching University, and was engaged in YMCA work in China and the United States from 1935 through 1957. He was the first member of the Church of the Brethren in China to visit the United States.
CORRESPONDENCE: Correspondence, ca. 1940–1943, with YMCA International Committee, YMCA of China National Committee, Churches of the Brethren in the United States, Seattle YMCA, Church of the Brethren General Board, China missionaries, and others.
MANUSCRIPTS: "What Has Happened to Me on the Journey of My Life," by Wang T'ung, 1981 (autobiographical description of his youth, education, and experiences under the Communist government); speeches on Christianity in China, post-war reconstruction, and Chinese students, given to YMCA and Church of the Brethren audiences, ca. 1940–1943.

11-GENERAL HOLDINGS
MINUTES/RECORDS/REPORTS: References to China in Brethren General Mission Board, minutes, 1908–47; Church of the Brethren General Brotherhood Board, Foreign Mission Commission and Brethren Service Commission, minutes, 1947–68; Church of the Brethren General Board, World Ministries Commission, minutes, 1969-; and the serials, *Brethren Service News*, 1945–66; *Gospel Messenger*, 1883–1964; *Messenger*, 1965-; *Missionary Visitor*, 1902–30; and *Missiongrams*, 1929–58.

MANUSCRIPTS: "Called to His Purpose: The Story of Nettie Senger in China," by Shirli Strehlow, n.d.; "How a Mission Started in China," by Anna Crumpsacker, n.d.; "Memoirs," by Minnie Flory Bright, n.d.; "Some Reminiscences of a China Missionary in Her Eighty-fourth Year," by Mrs. Walter J. Heisey, n.d.; "The Story of the Church of the Brethren in China, 1932–1950," comp. by Martha Neiderhiser Parker, n.d.; "Thank God for Nettie! Or Nettie Senger as We Remember Her," comp. by Anne M. Albright, 1980;
PAMPHLETS: Ca. 20 mission interpretation pamphlets and tracts, n.d.
ORAL HISTORIES: 35-page transcript of a taped interview with Ernest Ikenberry, for the *China Missionaries Oral History Project*, Claremont Graduate School, Oral History Program, 1971.
SERIALS: *Chinesegrams*, 1931–66. *Star of Cathay*, 1933–35, 1939–48.
DISSERTATIONS/THESES: *Brethren Rural Reconstruction in China, 1920–1950*, by Bradley Kent Geisert, 1975. *The China Tractor Boys*, by Francis P. McMurry, 1969. *Devolution of Missionary Administration in China*, by Herbert Spenser Minnich, 1926.

EVANSTON

GARRETT-EVANGELICAL AND SEABURY-WESTERN THEOLOGICAL SEMINARIES
IL–110 United Library
2121/22 Sheridan Road
Evanston IL 60201
(312) 866–3909
Alva R. Caldwell, Librarian
David K. Himrod, Assistant Librarian
for Reader Services

1-GENERAL HOLDINGS
MINUTES/RECORDS/REPORTS: American Board of Commissioners for Foreign Missions: Foochow Mission, annual reports, 1895, 1898–1901; China Inland Mission, annual report, 1938; Foochow Missionary Hospital, annual report, 1913; North China Mission, reports, 1890–95, 1897–99; Shansi Mission, annual reports, 1897, 1911–13.

China Continuation Committee, proceedings of annual meetings, 1916–21; China Inland Mission, reports, 1904–9, 1911–19, 1921–22; China Medical Board of New York, annual report, 1918, 1920, 1923; Conference on Christian Education in China, report, 1925; Hangchow Medical Mission, annual report, 1905.

Methodist Church (U.S.), conferences: Central China, English journal, 1947; Foochow, minutes, 1939–40, 1945–49; Hinghwa, English journal, 1939–40, 1943, 1945–48; Kiangsi, journal, 1940; North China, official journals, 1940, 1947; Yenping, English journal, 1939–40.

Methodist Episcopal Church: Central Conference, China, minutes, 1897, 1899, 1903, 1907, 1911; Central Conference, Eastern Asia, minutes, 1915, 1920, 1923, 1930, 1934, 1937; Central Conference of Eastern Asia, episcopal address, 1915; conferences: Central China, minutes, 1894–96, 1899, 1901, 1903–12, 1914–22, 1924, 1931–36, 1938–39; Central China Woman's Conference, minutes, 1905; Chengtu West China, minutes, 1928–34; Chungking-West China, minutes, 1926–35; Foochow, minutes, 1885, 1887–88, 1892, 1894–1905, 1907–23, 1925, 1929–31, 1933–38; Hinghwa, minutes, 1896–1902, 1904–10, 1912, 1914–29, 1933–38; Kiangsi, minutes, 1913–31, 1934–36; North China, minutes, 1888–91, 1894–98, 1901–24; South Fukien, minutes, 1923–33; West China, minutes, 1895, 1903–15, 1917–19, 1921–22; West China, journal and year book, 1938; Yenping, minutes, 1917–23, 1925, 1936–38; Woman's Foreign Missionary Society, Shantung, minutes, 1927; Woman's Missionary Conference: Central China, annual reports, 1912–13, 1916, 1921–26, 1929, 1932, 1935; Foochow, annual reports, 1886, 1890, 1892, 1894, 1896, 1899–1900, 1903, 1905–12, 1915, 1918, 1920, 1923–24, 1926–31, 1933; Hinghwa, annual reports, 1917, 1919, 1923–25, 1927, 1929–30; Kiangsi, annual reports, 1913, 1916, 1919, 1921–34; North China, annual reports, 1905–16, 1922–26, 1930, 1933, 1938–40; West China, minutes, 1913, 1917, 1921, 1923, 1931, 1935, 1939; West China (Chengtu), minutes, 1925–26, 1929–30; West China (Chungking), minutes, 1924, 1926, 1929; Yenping, annual reports, 1923–31, 1934–39.

Methodist Episcopal Church, South, China Conference, minutes, 1894, 1916–17, 1926–29; Nanking Theological Seminary, catalogue, 1914, 1931; United Board for Christian Colleges in China, annual report, 1949–50, 1952; West China Missionary Conference, report, 1908.
MANUSCRIPTS: "Christianity and Chinese Life," by Samuel Floyd Pannabecker, 1933; "History of the Evangelical Church in China," by Raymond Hanson, et al., 1936; "West of the Yangtze Gorges," by Joseph Taylor, 1936.
PAMPHLETS: *Address to the First and Organizing Session of the China Central Conference of the Methodist Church*, by John Gowdy and Ralph Ward, 1941; *China and What the Methodists Are Doing There*, n.a., 1941; *David Hill, the Apostolic Chinese Missionary*, by William Arthur Cornaby, ca. 1890; *Methodism in China: The War Years*, by Richard Baker Terrill, 1946; *Three Friends*, by Mary E. Darley, 1912.
SERIALS: *Animus*, 1899–1901. *Central China Record*, 1901–5. *Central China Year Book*, 1911. *China Bulletin*, 1951–62. *China Christian Advocate*, 1914–41. *The China Fundamentalist*, 1930–34. *China Mission Year Book*, 1912. *China Notes*, 1962–69. *China's Millions* (London), 1883–89, 1904, 1908, 1927, 1934–35. *China's Millions* (Philadelphia), 1893–1952. *China's Young Men*, 1908–16. *Chinese Medical Journal*, 1905–11. *Chinese Recorder*, 1912–39. *Chinese Recorder and Educational Review*, 1939–41. *Chinese Recorder and Missionary Journal*, 1870–81, 1886, 1888–1912. *Chinese Repository*, 1832–51. *Ching Feng*, 1964-. *East Asia Millions* (Philadelphia), 1961–84. *Educational Review*, 1914–38. *Foochow News*, 1938. *Fuhkien Witness*, 1905. *India's Women and China's Daughters*, 1897–1902, 1928–39. *Looking East*, 1940–57. *Millions* (Philadelphia), 1952–61. *Mission Bulletin*, 1953–59. *Phoenix*, 1926. *Yungchun Herald*, 1924–33.
DISSERTATIONS/THESES: *Die Akkommodationsmethode des P. Matteo Ricci S.I. in China*, by Johannes Bettray, 1955. *China Missions in Crisis: Bishop Laimbeckhoven and His Times, 1738–1787*, by Joseph Krahl, 1964. *Protestant Mission Schools for Girls in South China (1827 to the Japanese Invasion)*, by Mary Raleigh Anderson, 1943. *Devolution of Missionary Administration in China*, by Herbert Spenser Minnich, 1926. *The History of the Educational Work of the Methodist Episcopal Church in China: A Study of Its Development and Present Trends*, by Eddy Lucius Ford, 1936.

Missionary Journalism in Nineteenth-century China: Young Allen and the Early "Wan kuo kung pao," 1868–1883, by Adrian A. Bennett, 1970. *Politics and Prayers: A Study of the Advent Christian Denomination's Mission Effort in China*, by Donna Alberta Behnke, 1971.
CHINESE LANGUAGE MATERIALS/SERIALS: *Hwa Mei Kiao Pao (Chinese Christian Advocate)*, 1904–33.

EVANSTON

NORTHWESTERN UNIVERSITY
IL–115 Library
1935 Sheridan Road
Evanston IL 60201
(312) 491–2170
Brian Nielsen, Head, Reference Department

1-GENERAL HOLDINGS
MINUTES/RECORDS/REPORTS: International Institute of China, reports, ca. 1906.
MANUSCRIPTS: "Christian Higher Education in China: Contribution of the Colleges of Arts and Sciences to Chinese Life," by J. Dyke Van Putten, 1937.
ORAL HISTORIES: *China Missionaries Oral History Collection*, ed. by Cyrus H. Peake and Arthur L. Rosenbaum (Claremont Graduate School, Oral History Program), 1973. See ORAL HISTORIES Union List for the names of participants.
SERIALS: *Asia*, 1952–60. *China Christian Year Book*, 1924–28, 1930–35, 1940. *China Monthly: The Truth About China*, 1939–47. *Monde et Mission*, 1899–1971. West China Border Research Society, *Journal*, 1922–37, 1944. *Yenching Index Numbers*, 1940–41. *Yenching Journal of Social Studies*, 1938–39.
DISSERTATIONS/THESES: *Apostolic Legations to China of the Eighteenth Century*, by Antonio Sisto Rosso, 1948. *Christian Missions in China*, by Charles Sumner Estes, 1895. *A Comparative Study of the Religious Thought of Chi-tsang and H. Richard Niebuhr: A Comparison and Contrast of the Buddhist and Christian*, by Yee-heum Yoon, 1979. *Devolution of Missionary Administration in China*, by Herbert Spenser Minnich, 1926. *The History of the Educational Work of the Methodist Episcopal Church in China: A Study of Its Development and Present Trends*, by Eddy Lucius Ford, 1936. *Politics and Prayer: A Study of the Advent Christian Denomination's Mission Efforts in China*, by Donna A. Behnke, 1971.
CHINESE LANGUAGE MATERIALS: *Chung-kuo kuan shen fan chiao ti yüan yin (The Origin and Cause of the Anti-Christian Movement by Chinese Officials and Gentry)*, by Lü Shih-ch'iang, 1966.

GREENVILLE

GREENVILLE COLLEGE
IL–120 Dare Library
315 East College Avenue
Greenville IL 62246
(618) 664–1840
Ruth Scandrett, Periodicals Librarian

1-GENERAL HOLDINGS
SERIALS: *China Christian Year Book*, 1911.

LISLE

IL-125 AMERICAN CASSINESE CONGREGATION (BENEDICTINES)

St. Procopius Abbey
Lisle IL 60532
(312) 969-6410
Vitus Buresh, O.S.B., Abbey Archivist

1-GENERAL HOLDINGS
CORRESPONDENCE: Ca. 3 folders of correspondence between St. Procopius Abbey members as missionaries in China, the Holy See, and the superior (abbot) of the abbey in the files of past abbots, 1936-61.

MUNDELEIN

ST. MARY OF THE LAKE SEMINARY
IL-130 Feehan Memorial Library

Mundelein IL 60060
(312) 566-6401
Gloria Sieben, Librarian

1-GENERAL HOLDINGS
PAMPHLETS: *The Systematic Destruction of the Catholic Church in China*, by Thomas J. Bauer, 1954.
SERIALS: *Asia*, 1960. *China Missionary*, 1948-49. *China Missionary Bulletin*, 1950-53. *Far East*, 1946-54. *Mission Bulletin*, 1953-59.
DISSERTATIONS/THESES: *Die Akkommodationsmethode des P. Matteo Ricci S.I. in China*, by Johannes Bettray, 1955. *China Missions in Crisis: Bishop Laimbeckhoven and His Times, 1738-1787*, by Joseph Krahl, 1964. *Imperial Government and Catholic Missions in China during the Years 1784-1785*, by Bernward Henry Willeke, 1948. *The Negotiations between Ch'i-ying and Lagrené, 1844-1846*, by Angelus Francis J. Grosse-Aschhoff, 1950.

OAK BROOK

BETHANY AND NORTHERN BAPTIST THEOLOGICAL SEMINARIES
IL-135 The Seminary Library

Butterfield and Meyers Roads
Oak Brook IL 60521
(312) 620-2214
Kenneth M. Shaffer, Jr., Director

1-GENERAL HOLDINGS
MINUTES/RECORDS/REPORTS: Church of the Brethren, rules of the China mission, 1915; National Christian Council of China, annual report, 1925-26.
MANUSCRIPTS: "Devolution of Missionary Administration in China," by H. S. Minnich, n.d.; "The Memoirs of Minnie F. Bright," by Minnie (Flory) Bright, n.d.
PAMPHLETS: 10 pamphlets, most undated, on Brethren martyrs,

Emma Brodbeck, Chinese church, internment, medical missions, missionary women, native Christian women, and the Presbyterian mission in Peking.
SERIALS: *China Christian Year Book*, 1928, 1931. *China's Millions* (Philadelphia), 1925, 1930-52. *Chinese Recorder*, 1915-24, 1927-40. *East Asia Millions* (Philadelphia), 1961-78. *Millions* (Philadelphia), 1952-61.
DISSERTATIONS/THESES: *American (Northern) Baptist Work in East China*, by George Estel Hines, 1951. *China and Her People*, by Anna M. Hutchison, 1919. *Devolution of Missionary Administration in China*, by Herbert Spenser Minnich, 1926. *Interpretation of Christianity to China*, by N. M. Senger, 1923. *The Religious Background of the Chinese Villager and Its Implication to Mission Work*, by Mary Schaeffer, 1942.

RED BUD

IL-140 ADORERS OF THE BLOOD OF CHRIST

Provincial House—Ruma
Rural Route 1
Box 115
Red Bud IL 62278-9749
(618) 282-3848
Sister Mary Joan Weissler, A.S.C., Archivist

Background note: In 1933, five sisters of the Congregation of Sisters Adorers of the Most Precious Blood, Province of Ruma, sailed to China with three Franciscan fathers headed for the Prefecture of Changtien in Shantung. The sisters began their mission work in Siau Liu Dja, Yangsin, starting in 1934. They established primary schools and, later, the first cathechists' training school in the prefecture. Subsequently, they opened schools and a dispensary in Kiang Kia in 1935. In 1937, due to war conditions, the sisters left Kiang Kia and Siau Liu Dja, but returned in mid-1938. A third mission was opened in Bin Hsien in 1940. Their work continued, though interrupted by internment by the Japanese, until about 1953. The history of Ruma Province and their work in China is recounted in *Ruma: Home and Heritage*, by Sister M. Pauline Grady, A.S.C. (1984).

1-CHINA MISSION COLLECTION, ca. 1933-1946, ca. 2 c.f.
CORRESPONDENCE/AUDIO-VISUAL MATERIALS: Letters, photos, and lantern slides relating to work in China.

ROCK ISLAND

AUGUSTANA COLLEGE

IL-145 Denkman Memorial Library

35th Street and Seventh Avenue
Rock Island IL 61201
(309) 794-7266
John Caldwell, Director

1-GENERAL HOLDINGS
MINUTES/RECORDS/REPORTS: Augustana Synod Mission in China, minutes, 1918-25, 1935-41.

IL-150 Swenson Swedish Immigration Research Center
Box 175, College Center
Rock Island IL 61201
(309) 794-7221
Kermit B. Westerberg, Archivist

Background note: The Center was established in 1981 to serve as national research center for the study of the impact of Swedish immigrants on American life. In addition to the materials listed below, the Center has a number of published works in Swedish that contain scattered references to the Augustana Synod Mission in China. Some representative serial titles are: *Missionären*, 1894–1914; *Missions Wännen*, 1874–80; *Missionsförbundet*, 1908–20, 1928–31; *Missionstidningen*, 1911–16, 1918–19, 1924; and *Missionstidning Budbäraren*, 1855–56, 1884, 1891–92, 1915, 1928–41, 1945–48, 1956. An example of the Center's book holdings is *Korsets Seger; Illustrerad skildring av Svenska Evangeliska Missionsförbundets i Amerika. Kinamission, 1890–1915*, by E. G. Hjerpe and P. Matson, 1915.

1-ALMA STRAND PAPERS, 1897–1930, 1 reel microfilm
Background note: Alma Strand served as a Scandinavian Alliance missionary in China from 1892 to 1910.
MINUTES/RECORDS/REPORTS: Scandinavian Alliance Mission of North America, constitution, principles, and rules, 1930.
CORRESPONDENCE: A 79-page copybook of Alma Strand's letters to friends and supporters of the Scandinavian Alliance Mission, 1897–1905.
MANUSCRIPTS: "Missionär F. Franson," n.a., 1897.
AUDIO-VISUAL MATERIALS: 3 photos from the mission field in China, 1896–97, 1905.
FINDING AIDS: In-house inventory.

2-GENERAL HOLDINGS
SERIALS: *Kina Missionären*, 1923–24.

SPRINGFIELD

HOSPITAL SISTERS OF THE THIRD ORDER OF ST. FRANCIS
IL-155 St. Francis Convent Archives
Sangamon Road
Springfield IL 62794-9431
(217) 522-3386
Sister Dominica McGuire, O.S.F., Archivist

Background note: The Hospital Sisters of the Third Order of St. Francis were engaged in mission work in China from 1925 to 1947. The China materials in the archives at St. Francis Convent are only partially processed.
The Community Bulletin of the Hospital Sisters of the Third Order of St. Francis, 1931–54, contains scattered references to the Order's work in China, reports on hospitals and dispensaries in China, articles on fund-raising efforts for China missions, and copies of correspondence written by China missionaries. Individual articles on China can be found using the archives' subject card catalogue.

1-GENERAL HOLDINGS
MINUTES/RECORDS/REPORTS: Mother Magdalene Wiedlocher, records concerning passports, immigration, and naturalization of Chinese sisters, 1948–57.
CORRESPONDENCE: Correspondence regarding the training of Chinese sisters, 1933–40; correspondence with the Vatican concerning the evacuation of sisters from China, 1948; letters of sisters serving in China, 1925–53; letters of sisters volunteering for missionary work in China, 1925–35.
MANUSCRIPTS: "China for Christ," by Sr. Angelus Gardiner, 1943; "The Hospital Sisters of St. Francis in China," by Sr. DeMontfort Schmitz, 1949; "Mission Life," by China missionary Sr. Euphrosine, 1953; travel notes of sisters in China, 1925–48.
ORAL HISTORIES: "History of Our Mission in China," by Sr. Clementia, head of the China mission from 1925 to 1949 (on 4 audio tapes).
AUDIO-VISUAL MATERIALS: 4 films, regarding sisters' departure for and work in China, 1925–32; ca. 500 photos of American missionaries in China, Chinese religious, the Order's hospitals, dispensaries, and orphanages in China, and Chinese churches and chapels; 34 slides on China, n.d.

SPRINGFIELD

IL-160 ILLINOIS STATE HISTORICAL LIBRARY
Old State Capitol
Springfield IL 62706
(217) 782-4836
Laurel G. Bowen, Curator of Manuscripts

1-FIRST METHODIST CHURCH OF SPRINGFIELD RECORDS, 1895, quantity undetermined
MINUTES/RECORDS/REPORTS/MANUSCRIPTS: Descriptions of work in China in the "History of the Woman's Foreign Missionary Society," 1895.

URBANA

UNIVERSITY OF ILLINOIS AT URBANA-CHAMPAIGN

IL-165 American Library Association Archives
19 Main Library
1408 West Gregory Drive
Urbana IL 61801
(217) 333-0798
Maynard Brichford, University Archivist

Background note: These records, while distinct from the University Archives, are housed by the University, and archival service is provided by the University Archives staff.

1-CHINA PROJECTS FILE, 1938–48, ca. 2 c.f.
MINUTES/RECORDS/REPORTS: Records relating to the library school at Boone College, 1944–48, and other mission-related institutions, such as Cheeloo University and Nanking Theological Seminary.

IL-170 Asian Library

University of Illinois at Urbana-Champaign
325 Main Library
1408 West Gregory Drive
Urbana IL 61801
(217) 333-1501
William Wong, Librarian

1-GENERAL HOLDINGS

Background note: The collection also contains works on church history in Japanese.

CHINESE LANGUAGE MATERIALS: 21 books, 1876–1981, on Young J. Allen, anti-Christian sentiment, Catholic missions in China, church and mission history, modern Chinese religious thought, Protestantism in China, sources in the history of Christianity in China, and Wang Ming-tao.

IL-175 Law Library

University of Illinois at Urbana-Champaign
504 East Pennsylvania Avenue
Champaign IL 61820
(217) 333-2914
Richard Surles, Director

1-GENERAL HOLDINGS

SERIALS: *China Law Review*, 1922–40.

IL-180 University Archives

University of Illinois at Urbana-Champaign
19 Main Library
1408 West Gregory Drive
Urbana IL 61801
(217) 333-0798
Maynard Brichford, University Archivist

1-PAUL B. ANDERSON PAPERS, 1913–80, ca. 20 folders

MINUTES/RECORDS/REPORTS: Paul B. Anderson, field reports from China, 1913–17; Foreign Missions Conference of North America, China Committee, memoranda, notes, and reports, 1948–49; Guenther Feuser, Tore Littmarck, and David Robinson, report on visit to China, 1956; United China Relief, Inc., annual report, 1943; YMCA in China, records, 1948–51; YMCA International Committee, field reports from China, 1948–50; YMCA World Alliance, reports and newsletters on Christianity in China, 1948–58.

CORRESPONDENCE: Correspondence of A. Doak Barnett concerning his father, Eugene Epperson Barnett, 1963; correspondence concerning the memorial service for Eugene Epperson Barnett, 1970; correspondence of the Foreign Missions Conference of North America, China Committee, concerning the prospects for religious work in China under the Communists, 1948–49; correspondence concerning Howard L. Haag's work for the YMCA in Harbin, 1925–28, 1931–36, including discussion of the school for the Russian community in Harbin; letters regarding the YMCA in Harbin, Manchuria, 1925, 1927; correspondence of the YMCA World Alliance concerning Christianity in China, 1948–58; miscellaneous correspondence on China, 1913–19, 1946, 1949–50, 1952.

MANUSCRIPTS: "The Chinese YMCA as an Institution," by Anderson, 1951; Eugene Epperson Barnett's memoirs of his work with the YMCA in China, 1963; field notes from China, 1913–19; miscellaneous notes on China, 1973–77; "The Nature and Objective of the Communist Party as It Affects the YMCA," by Anderson, n.d.; "Revolution in Hankow, 1913–1928," by Arthur Guttery, 1975; 105 pages of talks on China by Mr. and Mrs. B. W. Smith, ca. 1936.

PAMPHLETS: *Conversations of Jesus*, by W. W. Lockwood, 1935; *Foundation Truths of the Christian Religion*, n.a., 1914; "*Religion in Communist China*, by Richard C. Bush, Jr.," reprint of a review by Anderson, 1971.

MEMORABILIA: Christmas card from the Mead family at Yenching University, n.d.; ca. 2 folders of newspaper clippings pertaining to the prospects for religious work in China under the Communists, 1948–58; newspaper extracts and clippings on China, 1946, 1949–50, 1952; program for a memorial service for Eugene Epperson Barnett and his obituary, 1970.

AUDIO-VISUAL MATERIALS: Miscellaneous photos from China, 1913–19; photos of the YMCA Student Conference in Soochow and the YMCA in China National Committee Shanghai office staff, 1915–16.

SERIALS: *China Bulletin*, 1952. *Ching Feng*, 1971.

CHINESE LANGUAGE MATERIALS/SERIALS: *T'ien Feng*, 1949–61.

FINDING AIDS: In-house guide.

2-ERNEST FAUST PAPERS, ca. 1919–1928, ca. 100 items

Background note: Ernest Faust was a parasitologist at Peking Union Medical College from 1919 to 1928.

CORRESPONDENCE: Ca. 100 letters between Faust and Henry B. Ward, ca. 1919–1928.

3-GEORGE W. MYERS PAPERS, ca. 1900, 2 items

AUDIO-VISUAL MATERIALS: 2 photos of a mission school in Chungking, ca. 1900.

4-PRESIDENTS' SUBJECT FILE, 1930–1933, 1933, 1 item

MINUTES/RECORDS/REPORTS: Report by David Kinley on educational institutions containing information on mission education in China, 1933.

5-MAURICE T. PRICE PAPERS, 1916–32, ca. 10 folders

Background note: Maurice T. Price (1888–1964) was a sociologist who studied, among other topics, the impact of Christian missions in east Asia. He was in China from 1917 to 1927.

CORRESPONDENCE: 2 letters from Winifred Rauschenbusch regarding Chinese students and publishing in China, 1916–17; correspondence with Robert E. Park of the University of Chicago and Herbert Rudd of West China Union University, 1921–22, regarding Price's book, *Christian Missions and Oriental Civilizations* (1924).

MANUSCRIPTS: Draft of *Christian Missions and Oriental Civilizations*, 1923; 2 boxes of notes on China missionaries and converts, and missions and social change, n.d.

PAMPHLETS: Copies of reviews of *Christian Missions and Oriental Civilizations* by H. L. Mencken and others, 1924–27.

MEMORABILIA: Ca. 2 folders of magazine and newspaper clippings on China missions, 1924–27; 2 books of newspaper clippings, 1925–26, containing articles on anti-Christian sentiment, missionaries, and St. John's University, among other items.

SERIALS: National Christian Council of China, *Bulletin*, 1931–32.

CHINESE LANGUAGE MATERIALS: Handbills on missionaries and anti-Christian sentiment, 1924–25.
FINDING AIDS: In-house guide.

IL–185 University Library

University of Illinois at Urbana-Champaign
300 Main Library
1408 Gregory Drive
Urbana IL 61801
(217) 333–1900
Richard Goff Smith, Associate Reference Librarian

1-GENERAL HOLDINGS
MINUTES/RECORDS/REPORTS: American Board of Commissioners for Foreign Missions: North China Mission, Fenchow, annual report, 1915; Fenchow Station, annual report, 1914; Foochow Mission, annual report, 1897; North China Mission, reports, 1889–98, 1903–4, 1914; Christian Literature Society for China, annual reports, 1914–15, 1924–40, 1946–47; International Institute of China, semi-annual reports, 1906, 1908, 1912–16, 1919, 1922–23, 1927.
PAMPHLETS: *China Mission Studies (1550–1800) Directory*, ed. by David E. Mungello, 1978; *The Harrowing of Hell in China: A Synoptic Study of the Role of Christian Evangelists in the Opening of Hunan Province*, by Leslie R. Marchant, 1977.
SERIALS: Catholic University of Peking, *Bulletin*, 1926–34. China Christian Educational Association, *Bulletin*, 1924, 1926, 1928. *China Christian Year Book*, 1911, 1913–15, 1924, 1929, 1932–39. *China Colleges*, 1934–35, 1938–51. China International Famine Relief Commission, Publications, series A, 1923, 1931–37; series B, 1923–24, 1926, 1928–31. *China Monthly: The Truth About China*, 1940–50. *China's Medicine*, 1966–68. *China's Millions* (London), 1933. *Chinese Medical Journal*, 1908–41, 1943, 1947–60, 1965–66; supplement, 1936, 1940. *Chinese Recorder*, 1925–26, 1939–41. *Chinese Repository*, 1833–51. *East Asia Millions* (London), 1973–84. *Educational Review*, 1924–38. *Fu-Jen Magazine*, 1934–49. *Fu Jen News Letter*, 1931–32. *Fukien Agricultural Journal*, 1948–51. *Lingnan Science Journal*, 1922–50. *New Horizons*, 1965–82, 1984. *Peking Natural History Bulletin*, 1926–41. *St. John's University Studies*, 1922. *The Story of the China Inland Mission*, 1914–40, 1942–47, 1949–51. University of Nanking, Botany Department, Plant Pathology Laboratory, *Contribution*, 1933 (?), 1934. University of Nanking, College of Agriculture and Forestry, *Agriculture and Forestry Series*, 1920–21, 1924; *Bulletin*, 1926, 1932–36; *Special Report*, 1935. West China Border Research Society, *Journal*, 1924–46. *Yenching Journal of Social Studies*, 1938–50.
DISSERTATIONS/THESES: *An Enduring Encounter: E. T. Williams, China, and the United States*, by Dimitri Daniel Lazo, 1977. *Lutheran Missions in a Time of Revolution: The China Experience, 1944–1951*, by Jonas Jonson, 1972. *Die Protestantische Christenheit in der Volksrepublik China und die Chinaberichterstattung in der deutschen evangelischen Missionsliteratur*, by Ilse Hass, 1974.
CHINESE LANGUAGE MATERIALS/SERIALS: China International Famine Relief Commission, Publications, series B, N 1, 6, 17, 23, 25, 31, 33, 35, 39–40, 43–44, 46, 48, 1923–31. *Chinling hsüeh pao (Nanking Journal)*, 1931–34. University of Nanking, Library Publications, 1924–36.

WHEATON

WHEATON COLLEGE

IL–190 Department of Special Collections and Archives

Buswell Memorial Library
Wheaton IL 60187–5593
(312) 260–5101
Mary Dorsett, Head of Special Collections

1-GENERAL HOLDINGS
DISSERTATIONS/THESES: *The China Inland Mission and Some Aspects of Its Work*, by Hudson Taylor Armerding, 1948. *The Missionary Approach to the Religions of China*, by Rachel Mostrom Chappell, 1946. *A Survey of Sunday School Work in China from 1930 to 1945*, by Edwin William Fisch, 1947. *Why Christianity Failed to Take Root in the Soil of China*, by Violet B. James, 1978.

IL–195 Buswell Memorial Library

Wheaton College
Wheaton IL 60187–5593
(312) 260–5169
Jolene Carlson, Head of Public Services

1-GENERAL HOLDINGS
MINUTES/RECORDS/REPORTS: China Inland Mission, annual report, 1930–31.
SERIALS: *China Christian Year Book*, 1929.

IL–200 Billy Graham Center Archives

Wheaton College
Wheaton IL 60187
(312) 260–5910
Robert Shuster, Director of Archives

Background note: The Billy Graham Center, founded in 1974, is a division of Wheaton College. The overall purpose of the Center is to serve as a resource center for evangelistic and missionary activities. The Archives collect unpublished documents that relate to North American, Protestant, nondenominational mission work.

1-HAROLD ADOLPH (CN 169), 1981, 2 reels audio tape
ORAL HISTORIES: Interview with Harold Adolph describing his boyhood in China as the son of China Inland Mission workers, 1981.
FINDING AIDS: In-house guide.

2-AMERICAN BOARD OF COMMISSIONERS FOR FOREIGN MISSIONS (SC 70), 1852–89, quantity undetermined
MEMORABILIA: Donation certificates in receipt of funds for China missions, ca. 1852–59.

3-IAN RANKIN AND HELEN MOUNT ANDERSON PAPERS (CN 231), 1928–81, ca. 1 box
Background note: Ian Rankin Anderson (1912–82) joined the China Inland Mission (CIM) in 1934 and was initially assigned to Shenkiu. Helen Mount (b. 1909) was accepted by the CIM in 1934 and attended language school in Yangchow until early 1935, when she was assigned to work in Chowkiakow. After their marriage in 1941 they worked in Shenkiu and were later stationed in Shekichen, Chengku, and Paoki, before being expelled in 1951.

CORRESPONDENCE: 9 folders of correspondence from Helen Anderson to her mother and other members of her family, from Ian Anderson to Helen Anderson and his mother, and their periodic prayer letters, 1934–51.

DIARIES: Diaries of Ian Anderson, 1944–49; diaries of Helen Anderson, 1934–39.

MANUSCRIPTS: "As I've Seen It...," 1946; Ian Anderson's notes on an ongoing evangelistic discussion; Ian Anderson's lecture notes on topics including foreign missions and J. Hudson Taylor, post–1974.

MEMORABILIA: Personal effects, ca. 1940, including Chinese clothing, ink block and carbon rubbing plate, and 2 wooden address chops and endorsement chop for letters and legal documents.

MAPS/DESIGNS/DRAWINGS: CIM map of China, 1948.

AUDIO-VISUAL MATERIALS: 3 group photos of Anderson and other CIM workers, 1938, n.d.; 2 photos of Chinese laborers in Choukiakow, ca. 1936; 8 photos of Chowkiakow, ca. late 1930s; photo of Chinese New Year in Shekichen, 1938; 9 photos of Yangchow, n.d.; photo of CIM home in Shekichen, n.d.

CHINESE LANGUAGE MATERIALS: Correspondence of a Chinese co-worker of Helen Anderson during her term of service in Chowkiakow; Chinese songbooks; romanized songsheets for work with Chinese children, including part of an evangelistic talk for children, n.d.; 14 evangelistic and instructional posters, 1938, n.d.

FINDING AIDS: In-house guide.

4-BAPTIST MISSIONARY SOCIETY ARCHIVES (CN 223), 1860–1914, 8 reels microfilm

Restrictions: Literary rights for these materials are retained by the Baptist Missionary Society. To obtain permission to cite these materials, researchers should contact the Society at 93/97 Gloucester Place, London, W1H 4AA, England.

Background note: This collection is a microfilm reproduction of the Archives of the Baptist Missionary Society of England (1792–1914), currently housed in London.

MINUTES/RECORDS/REPORTS: Baptist Missionary Society, application forms and references for all missionary candidates, 1881–1914; Baptist Missionary Society, China Committee, records, 1884–1914; Baptist Missionary Society, China, Ceylon and France Sub-Committee, minute books, 1861–67; Baptist Missionary Society, China Sub-Committee, 1884–1914.

CORRESPONDENCE/DIARIES: Correspondence and journals of Jennie Beckinsale, 1898–1913; journals and 5 letters from Herbert Dixon, 1887–88, including information about Timothy Richard; journal and letter from George Edwards, 1916; journals and 86 letters of George Farthing, 1887–1900, including discussions of mission finances, missions in Shansi, and Timothy Richard; 3 letters from Richard Glover (Baptist minister in Bristol) to Alfred Henry Baynes (Secretary of the Baptist Missionary Society), discussing the health of Herbert S. Jenkins; 9 letters from Francis H. James, including discussions of famine relief work and Timothy Richard; 5 letters from Herbert S. Jenkins, 1903–13; 316 letters, 4 telegrams, and journals of Alfred G. Jones, 1868, 1877–1905, with such correspondents as Clement Bailhache (Secretary of the Baptist Missionary Society), Alfred Henry Baynes, Richard Glover, Timothy Richard, and Arthur DeC. Sowerby, discussing famine relief work, mission finances, missions in Shantung, and the political situation in China; journal and letter of R. F. Laughton to Alfred Henry Baynes concerning finances at the Chefoo mission,

1868; uncatalogued correspondence and journal of M. Lewis, Baptist missionary to China, 1912–14; journal and correspondence of E. F. Kingdon, 1864–67; 4 letters from Mary Richard (Mrs. Timothy Richard) to Albert Henry Baynes, 1895, including discussion of Chinese officials' hostility to missionaries; 227 letters to and from Timothy Richard, 1877–78, 1883–99, 1901–5, with such correspondents as Albert Henry Baynes, Richard Glover, Alfred G. Jones, William Muirhead, and Sir Harry Parkes (British consul in China), discussing the Boxer Uprising, famine relief work, missions in Shansi, missions in Shantung, the persecution of Chinese Christians, and translations of the Bible.

DIARIES: Diaries of Timothy Richard, 1888–92, 1895, 1897–1903.

MANUSCRIPTS: 18 papers prepared by, or commenting on, Timothy Richard, 1894; unpublished description of Timothy Richard's work in Shansi by Mary Richards, 1887.

MEMORABILIA: Insurance policy issued in Shanghai for E. F. Kingdon, 1867; press cuttings on Herbert S. Jenkins, 1904.

FINDING AIDS: "Baptist Missionary Society: Papers Relating to China, 1860–1914," by Mary M. Evans, 1965.

5-SUSAN SCHULTZ BARTEL (CN 57), 1927–78, 30 items

Background note: Susan Schultz and Loyal Bartel were missionaries of the China Mennonite Society in Shantung from 1927 to 1948.

ORAL HISTORIES: Interview with Susan Schultz Bartel on 4 reels of audio tape, 1978–79, describing the Bartels' work in China, her return to the United States in 1948, and his captivity until 1971.

AUDIO-VISUAL MATERIALS: 26 photos of Loyal and Susan Bartel, 1927–48.

FINDING AIDS: In-house guide.

6-CHARLES ISAAC BLANCHETT EPHEMERA (SC 61), 1908, 1 item

Background note: Charles Isaac Blanchett was a Church Missionary Society missionary stationed near Hong Kong in the early 1900s.

MANUSCRIPTS: "The Cannibal Queen of Pakhoi," a handmade booklet of watercolors and a limerick about missions in China by Margery Stuart for Blanchett, 1908.

FINDING AIDS: In-house guide.

7-BOSTON RECORDER, 1819, 1 item

MEMORABILIA: Single issue of *Boston Recorder*, containing articles on China missions, 1819.

8-J. WESLEY AND ANNA ELLMERS BOVYER COLLECTION (CN 131), 1937–40, 1 folder, 8 items

Background note: J. Wesley and Anna Ellmers Bovyer ran the Nazarene Mission, an orphanage in Chinkiang, from 1908 to 1940.

CORRESPONDENCE: Folder of letters, 1937–40.

AUDIO-VISUAL MATERIALS: 8 photos, 1937–40.

FINDING AIDS: In-house guide.

9-CAROL CARLSON COLLECTION (CN 58), 1978, 1 reel audio tape

Background note: Carol and Edwin Carlson were missionaries of the Christian and Missionary Alliance on the Chinese-Tibetan border for 27 years.

ORAL HISTORIES: Interview with Carol Carlson, describing her experiences as a missionary, ca. 1920s–1940s.

FINDING AIDS: In-house guide.

10-ROBERT DEAN CARLSON COLLECTION (CN 205), 1982, 2 reels audio tape
Background note: Robert Dean Carlson is the son of Carol and Edwin Carlson (see Carol Carlson Collection above).
ORAL HISTORIES: Interview with Carlson in which he describes his childhood in west China, 1920s–1940s, and his experiences teaching at the Christian and Missionary Alliance Seminary in Hong Kong, 1960–68.
FINDING AIDS: In-house guide.

11-JOHN C. CHIN (CN 206), 1982, 1 reel audio tape
ORAL HISTORIES: Interview with John C. Chin (Chin Chung-an) in which he discusses his childhood in China, medical training, Chinese Christian church, Mary Stone, Japanese occupation, the political situation in China, and the work of the China Inland Mission in Honan, Szechwan, and Yunnan.
FINDING AIDS: In-house guide.

12-CHINA MISSIONARIES ORAL HISTORY PROJECT, CLARE-MONT COLLEGES (CN 145), 1969–73, 3,320p.
ORAL HISTORIES: *China Missionaries Oral History Collection*, ed. by Cyrus H. Peake and Arthur L. Rosenbaum (Claremont Graduate School, Oral History Program), 1973. See ORAL HISTORIES Union List for the names of participants.
FINDING AIDS: Index for each transcript.

13-CHINA MISSIONS ARTICLE, 1900, 1 item
MEMORABILIA: Single issue of *The Literary Digest*, containing an article with photos of missionaries in China, 1900.

14-ARCHIVES OF THE COUNCIL FOR WORLD MISSION (CN 161), 1821–1951, ca. 2,200 microfiches
Background note: The originals of these materials are at the library of the School of Oriental and African Studies, London.
MINUTES/RECORDS/REPORTS: London Missionary Society, minutes, 1856–1939; papers of Robert Morrison, n.d.: Anglo-Chinese College, report on missions; Tyerman and Bennet deputation, report, 1821–29; Fukien, 1866–1939; South China, 1866–1939; North China, 1866–1939; Central China, 1866–1940; Peking Union Medical College, minutes, n.d.; Siaokan Hospital, n.d.; Amoy district, committee minutes, 1903–24, 1878–1912; North China district, committee minutes, 1874–1920; Hong Kong and New Territories Evangelical Society, minutes, 1904–32; F. H. Hawkins, deputation, 1917; Central China district, committee minutes, 1932–37; Lockhart, records and accounts(?), n.d.
CORRESPONDENCE: London Missionary Society, outgoing letters to China, 1822–1914; Fukien, incoming letters, 1845–1939; outgoing letters, 1928–39; South China, incoming letters, 1803–1939; outgoing letters, 1928–39; North China, incoming letters, 1860–1939; outgoing letters, 1928–39; Central China, incoming letters, 1843–1939; outgoing letters, 1928–39; letters of Robert Morrison, n.d.; miscellaneous letters from missionaries to friends, n.d.; letters from Marjorie Clements in North China, 1930–33; George and Dorothy Barbour, letters from North China, 1920–36; correspondence of J. Legge; letters, letterbook of Mrs. L[egge]; correspondence of Peking Union Medical College; letters regarding a book by M. Aldersey, n.d.; correspondence of W. H. Somervell regarding British Foreign Bible Society Chinese Bible, n.d.
MANUSCRIPTS: Sermons by J. Legge, n.d.; articles and notes on literary and language work, by J. Legge; address by J. Legge on Amoy Induction, 1874; papers of E. Hope Bell, n.d.; "Discipleship," by Eric Liddell, n.d.; autobiographical sketch by F. A.

Brown, 1935–51; notes on Peking Hospital by Dudgeon, n.d.; Hankow Medical Planning papers; notes by Medhurst, 1848–52; Boxer Indemnity papers; miscellaneous notes on Chinese Church leaders, n.d.
MEMORABILIA: Biographical materials on Legge, including clippings, obituaries, and reviews; obituary of Griffith John, n.d.; Chinese medal.
DIARIES: South China, journals, 1807–42; North China, journals, 1863–64; Central China, journals, 1888–96; George and Dorothy Barbour, diary, 1920–36; Terrell diaries, n.d.
MAPS/DESIGNS/DRAWINGS: Rubbings of Nestorian Tablet, n.d.
FINDING AIDS: "Guide to the Archives of the Council for World Mission," by the Interdocumentation Company, Switzerland.

15-MARGARET RICE ELLIOTT AND VINCENT LEROY CROSSETT INTERVIEWS, 1984–85, 4 reels audio tape
Background note: Margaret Rice Elliott Crossett, the sister of Ruth Elliott, grew up in China. She and her husband, Vincent Leroy Crossett, were missionaries under the China Inland Mission, and later, the Overseas Missionary Fellowship in Taiwan. The collection is unprocessed at present. See also Eleanor Ruth Elliott papers below.
CORRESPONDENCE: Folder of correspondence of Margaret Elliott Crossett, 1935.
ORAL HISTORIES: 2 interviews each with Margaret and Vincent Crossett, 1984–85.
MEMORABILIA: Clippings on China of Margaret Elliott Crossett, 1971 and n.d.
SERIALS: *China's Millions* (Philadelphia), 1934–47.

16-MIRIAM J. TOOP DUNN COLLECTION (CN 80), 1978, .5 c.f.
Background note: Miriam J. Toop Dunn was the daughter of China missionaries. After training as a nurse, she joined the China Inland Mission in the 1930s and served in various parts of China until 1951. From 1951 to 1974 she and her husband, Marvin Dunn, worked as missionaries in Hong Kong, Singapore, and Malaysia.
MANUSCRIPTS: "I Get Your Message, Father," by Miriam J. Toop Dunn, relating her experiences with the China Inland Mission, 1978.
FINDING AIDS: In-house guide.

17-EMMA EKVALL, 1960, 5 items
Background note: This collection is unprocessed at present.
MANUSCRIPTS: Biography of Emma Ekvall, n.d.
MEMORABILIA: Journal article on Ekvall, n.d.
ORAL HISTORIES: Radio interviews with Ekvall, and Howard and Gertrude Smith, 1960, on 3 audio cassettes, including discussion of Howard Smith's capture and escape in 1934.

18-ROBERT BRAINERD EKVALL (CN 92), 1979, 2 reels audio tape
ORAL HISTORIES: Interview with Robert Brainerd Ekvall discussing his work with the Christian and Missionary Alliance in Kansu and Tibet from 1922 to 1941 and his activities during World War II.

19-ELEANOR EDWARDS ELLIOT EPHEMERA, n.d., 1 item
MEMORABILIA: Daily Light Birthday Book, containing autographs of missionaries on their birthdays, n.d.

20-ELEANOR RUTH ELLIOTT (CN 187), 1931–81, 1 box, 7 reels audio tape

Background note: See also Margaret Rice Elliott Crossett Interviews above.

CORRESPONDENCE: 12 folders of correspondence of E. Ruth Elliott from China, 1931–51; 3 folders of correspondence of Walter Scott Elliott on conditions in China and his work as an American Bible Society supervisor, 1910–11, 1931, 1934; folder of correspondence of Curtis Elliott, 1940; prayer letter of the Berachen Gospel Work to Boat Men, China, 1931; prayer letters of the China Inland Mission, 1935.

MANUSCRIPTS: "The Emergency Preparatory School," by Eleanor Ruth Elliott, describing the establishment of a Chefoo School for children of missionaries during the war, 1941; "Trio," by E. Ruth and Margaret Elliott, 1928; list of birds seen in China, by Eleanor Ruth Elliott, n.d.

PAMPHLETS: Brochure on Chinese Christian Mission Ministry, 1978.

ORAL HISTORIES: Interviews with Eleanor Ruth Elliott on 7 reels of audio tape, 1981, discussing her youth in Changsha helping her father, Walter Scott Elliott, distribute Bibles for the American Bible Society (ca. 1908), her education at the Kuling American School, and missionary work with the China Inland Mission from 1931 to 1951.

FINDING AIDS: In-house guide.

21-DORIS EMBERY (CN 208), 1980, 1 reel audio tape
ORAL HISTORIES: Interview with Doris Embery, the daughter of China Inland Mission missionaries Mr. and Mrs. William James Embery, discussing such topics as the children of missionaries, the Door of Hope Mission, and missions in Shanghai.

22-EVANGELICAL FOREIGN MISSIONS ASSOCIATION, RECORDS OF THE EXECUTIVE SECRETARY (CN 165), 1944–78, 18.5 c.f.
Background note: Originally an arm of the National Association of Evangelicals, the Evangelical Foreign Missions Association became an independent body in 1945. Its membership includes representation from denominational and independent mission boards, and it was designed to serve the common interests of members in relations with governments, cooperative purchasing, travel, intermission relations, and spiritual fellowship.

MINUTES/RECORDS/REPORTS: Evangelical Foreign Missions Association, convention records, 1945 (mission opportunities in post-war China), 1972 (effect of Richard Nixon's China policy on missions).

CORRESPONDENCE: 20 files of correspondence of the Executive Secretary concerning China, 1944–78, including discussions of the Bethel Mission, the Evangelical Fellowship of Hong Kong, the Far East Broadcasting Company, the Far Eastern Gospel Crusade, the North America Congress of Chinese Evangelicals, the South China Boat Mission, and the Voice of China radio network.

FINDING AIDS: In-house guide.

23-BEREA ST. JOHN FEINER (CN 202), ca. 1860–1950, 3 folders
Background note: Lucy Ann (St. John) Knowlton (1830-ca. 1902) was the wife of Miles J. Knowlton (1825–74). They were missionaries in Ningpo from 1853 to 1874. Berea St. John Feiner is her half-brother's granddaughter.

CORRESPONDENCE: Folder of correpondence of Lucy Ann Knowlton, 1862; letter from Mary Stone, director of the Bethel Mission of China, to Clyde W. Taylor, describing continuation of mission work in China by Chinese Christians, 1950.

PAMPHLETS: *Separation and Service*, by James Hudson Taylor, n.d.

MEMORABILIA: Folder of China mission ephemera belonging to Allen Noah and Jennie Cameron, missionaries in Changsha, including a printed letter, a coal bill in Chinese presented to the mission, and embroidery by girls at the mission orphanage, 1905-ca. 1930.

AUDIO-VISUAL MATERIALS: 11 photos of Changsha, Lucy Ann Knowlton, Allen Noah Cameron, and Knowlton and St. John family members, ca. 1860–1937.

FINDING AIDS: In-house guide.

24-THEODORE FISCHBACHER EPHEMERA (SC 91), 1941–47, 1 folder
MANUSCRIPTS: An article by Phyllis Thompson about the North-West Bible Institute in Shensi, sponsored by the China Inland Mission and the Free Methodist Mission, describing the work of Theodore and Olive Fischbacher at the Institute and the development of the Back to Jerusalem Gospel Band, an organization of Chinese Christians, n.d.

AUDIO-VISUAL MATERIALS: Photocopies from photo album of the North-West Bible Institute, 1941, 1947; photocopies of photo album of the Fischbacher family, 1942–44.

25-JENNIE KINGSTON FITZWILLIAM PAPERS AND INTERVIEWS (CN 272), 1926–85, quantity undetermined
Background note: Jennie Kingston Fitzwilliam (b. 1903) went to China under the China Inland Mission (CIM) in 1926 and began her language training in Yangchow. She married Francis Julius Fitzwilliam in 1927 and they were assigned to work among the Lisu in Yunnan. They principally served as Bible teachers and consultants to the church. After furlough in 1935, they began working among the Atsi Kachin along the Burmese border and lived in Lungch'iu. After her husband's death in 1940, Jennie Fitzwilliam was reassigned to work in the preparatory school at the mission's Chefoo School in Chefoo. She was interned by the Japanese and later transferred to the Weihsien internment camp before being repatriated. Upon her return to the United States, Fitzwilliam joined with other repatriated CIM staff to operate a temporary youth hostel for CIM children who had been repatriated, but whose parents remained in China.

ORAL HISTORIES: Interviews with Jennie Fitzwilliam on 5 audio cassettes, 1984–85, on the Fitzwilliams' work among the Lisu and Kachin, her work in Chefoo, and early influences toward mission work, covering the period 1903 through 1969.

AUDIO-VISUAL MATERIALS: 14 photos including group photos of CIM missionaries, Mrs. J. O. Fraser, Kachin and Lisu people and places, and CIM language school in Anking, 1930s; slide of Lisu in traditional dress, n.d.

SERIALS: *China's Millions* (Philadelphia), containing testimonies by the Fitzwilliams, 1926.

CHINESE LANGUAGE MATERIALS: Atsi Kachin catechism, n.d.; Lisu New Testament, 1939; letters in Lisu, some with translation, 1945–50.

FINDING AIDS: In-house guide.

26-HERBERT W. AND MINNIE E. GREEN FLAGG EPHEMERA (SC 86), 1927, 2 items
CORRESPONDENCE: 2 newsletters for circulation entitled "Missionary Paragraphs" by Herbert W. and Minnie E. Green Flagg of the China Inland Mission, 1927, describing attempts by

missionaries to cope with the turmoil caused by fighting among the Communists, the Nationalists, and robber bands in the Shanghai area.

27-HELEN NOWACK FRAME (CN 255), 1983, 2 reels audio tape
Background note: See also Esther Nowack Hess and William H. Nowack collections below.
ORAL HISTORIES: Interviews with Helen Nowack Frame, discussing her childhood in China as the daughter of China Inland Mission (CIM) missionaries William Henry and Katherine Plantz Nowack, her work as a CIM missionary, her marriage to Raymond Frame, and life in China until their evacuation in 1950.
FINDING AIDS: In-house guide.

28-FREDERIK FRANSON PAPERS (CN 87), 1872-1909, 2 reels microfilm
Background note: Among other evangelical endeavors, Frederik Franson (1852-1908) worked with J. Hudson Taylor to recruit China missionaries in Europe and the United States. Most of the materials in this collection are in Swedish.
MINUTES/RECORDS/REPORTS/CORRESPONDENCE/ MANUSCRIPTS: Reports, letters, and articles, 1872-1909, on such topics as the China Inland Mission, Christian Missionary Alliance, Franson's trip to China in 1904, German-China Alliance mission, missions in Tibet and Mongolia, opium addiction, recruitment of missionaries, Scandinavian missions in China, and A. B. Simpson's trip to China in 1893.
FINDING AIDS: In-house guide.

29-EMERSON AND GRACE FREY PAPERS, 1938-51, 1 folder
Background note: Emerson and Grace Frey served in China under the China Inland Mission. The collection is unprocessed at present.
CORRESPONDENCE/PAMPHLETS/AUDIO-VISUAL MATERIALS: Correspondence, printed matter, and photos relating to the Freys' work in China, 1938-51.

30-PAUL KENNETH GIESER PAPERS (CN 88), 1934-78, .5 c.f.
Background note: Paul Kenneth Gieser (b. 1908) was a medical missionary at Southern Presbyterian Hospital, Tsing Kiang Pu, from 1934 to 1940, and at Chinkiang Hospital from 1940 to 1941.
CORRESPONDENCE/DIARIES: 3 folders containing letters to the Southern Presbyterian Mission Board, 1934-36, and a diary, 1934-40.
MANUSCRIPTS: Partial autobiography.
ORAL HISTORIES: 3 reels of audio tape, 1978, including discussion of the Christian Medical Society, church-state relations in China, leprosy, missions in Anhwei, Kiangsu, and Fukien, the Sino-Japanese War, and John and Elizabeth Stam.
FINDING AIDS: In-house guide.

31-JONATHAN AND ROSALIND BELLSMITH GOFORTH PAPERS (CN 188), 1888-1981, 3 c.f.
Background note: Jonathan (1859-1936) and Rosalind (Bellsmith) Goforth (1864-1942) were Presbyterian missionaries in Honan from 1888 to 1926 and in Manchuria from 1927 to 1934. See also Mary Goforth Moynan Papers below.
MINUTES/RECORDS/REPORTS: Jonathan and Rosalind Goforth, reports, 1931-37; Rosalind Goforth's datebook, 1936.
CORRESPONDENCE: Folder of correspondence, 1893-1942, covering such topics as the Boxer Uprising, Catholic missions in China, the China Inland Mission, Chinese proverbs, Communism, famines, Feng Yü-hsiang, marriage customs in China, missions in Honan, missions in Manchuria, the Mukden Incident, Presbyterian missions in China, relief work in China, the Sino-Japanese War, John and Elizabeth Stam, J. Hudson Taylor, and the World Missionary Conference of the Presbyterian Church in Canada in 1910.
DIARIES: 3 desk diaries, 1897, 1902-8; 17 journals, 1888-89, 1907-22, 1932-33; 2 journals of Rosalind Goforth, 1910, 1914-16.
MANUSCRIPTS: "Escape of the Canadian Presbyterian Missionaries from North Honan during the Boxer Uprising of 1900," by Jonathan Goforth, ca. 1901; untitled manuscript on the Sabbath by Jonathan Goforth, n.d.; manuscript of *Climbing: Memories of a Missionary's Wife*, by Rosalind Goforth, ca. 1940; manuscript of *Goforth of China*, by Rosalind Goforth, 1937; manuscript of *The Land of Sinim*, by Jonathan Goforth, 1894; "The Missionary at Work," by Jonathan Goforth, ca. 1901; "My Casket of Jewels," comp. by Rosalind Goforth, n.d.; "Present Responsibility of the Canadian Presbyterian Church to the Heathen," by Jonathan Goforth, 1901; "Who Caused the Boxer Rebellion (China 1900)," by Jonathan Goforth, 1901; folder of miscellaneous manuscripts, n.d.; notes on "Common Chinese Sayings or Proverbs," n.d.; notebooks, 1894, 1899, 1902-6; notes on the Kuling Conference, 1921; sermons by Jonathan Goforth, 1909-36, n.d.; 9 sermon notebooks, 1910-11, 1924-30, n.d.
MEMORABILIA: 2 folders of articles about China and the Goforths, 1908-81 and n.d.; folder of articles by Jonathan Goforth, 1910-25 and n.d.; 2 folders of articles and article fragments by Rosalind Goforth, 1920-ca. 1933 and n.d.; memorial book, 1942; scrapbook, n.d.; watercolor by Jonathan Goforth, 1936.
MAPS/DESIGNS/DRAWINGS: Hand-drawn map of Manchuria (original and photographic negative), ca. 1890; woodblock print of the Goforth home in Honan, n.d.
AUDIO-VISUAL MATERIALS: 12 photos and 49 slides, 1901-80 and n.d., including pictures of Chinese Christians, Feng Yü-hsiang and his army, the Goforth family and home, the Goforth Mission headquarters in Manchuria, a map of China, William McClure, Robert Morrison, and J. Hudson Taylor; photo of Jonathan Goforth, n.d.; photo of Rosalind Goforth, n.d.
FINDING AIDS: In-house guide.

32-GOSPEL RECORDINGS, INC., COLLECTION (CN 36), 1945-50, 7 folders, 20 audio tapes
Background note: Gospel Recordings, Inc., was founded in 1938 to provide recordings of scripture verses and gospel messages in foreign languages for distribution by overseas missionaries.
MINUTES/RECORDS/REPORTS: Subject files on Cantonese, 1943-50, and Mandarin, 1945-49.
CORRESPONDENCE: 5 folders of correspondence with missionaries in China, Manchuria, Mongolia, and Tibet, 1945-50.
AUDIO-VISUAL MATERIALS: 20 audio cassette recordings of scripture verses and gospel messages in Bana', Cantonese, Foochow dialect, Hainanese, Hakka, Hing Hwa, Hokchia, Lanten, Lisu, Mandarin, Meo, Nung, Shanghainese, Taiwanese, Tibetan, and Yunnanese, n.d.; photo of Gladys Ward and Esther Schell, n.d.

33-HAROLD DEWEY AND HELEN M. HAYWARD EPHEMERA (SC 85), 1926, 1 item
CORRESPONDENCE: Prayer/newsletter from Harold Dewey and Helen M. Hayward of the China Inland Mission, 1926, describing their work in the city of Sining in Kansu.

34-ESTHER NOWACK HESS (CN 232), 1932–59, 1 box
Background note: Esther Marguerite Nowack Hess (b. 1906) was the child of missionaries William Henry and Katherine Plantz Nowack. Accepted by the China Inland Mission (CIM), she began her language training in 1931 and served as a nurse and teacher of nurses in Kansu Province from 1932 to 1934 and in Honan Province from 1935 to 1941. In 1941 she married Lawrence Hess, who died several months later. Soon after, she was interned, first at the Temple Hill Concentration Camp, and then at Weihsien Camp, from 1942 to 1945. Her sisters, Helen Nowack Frame and Ruth Nowack, also served with the CIM in China. See also Helen Nowack Frame and William H. Nowack collections.
CORRESPONDENCE: Prayer letters from China, 1932–41, 1945.
PAMPHLETS: Photocopy of article from *China's Millions*, 1945; 1959 article by Esther Hess, about her confrontation with Communists in 1948.
MEMORABILIA: Packet of teaching materials compiled by Hess for teaching Chinese children, n.d.
AUDIO-VISUAL MATERIALS: 14 photos of Weihsien after the Japanese surrender; 11 photos, including Helen Nowack Frame, Esther Nowack Hess, Ruth Nowack, missionaries in Tsingtao, missionary conference in Kansu, and Women's Language School in Yangchow group photo.

35-RUTH HITCHCOCK PAPERS, 1920–57, .3 c.f.
Background note: This collection is unprocessed at present.
MANUSCRIPTS/PAMPHLETS: Printed matter and manuscript of Ruth Hitchcock's autobiography from 1928 to 1934, *Good Hand of Our God*, 1920–57.

36-ROBERT WILLIAM HOCKMAN AND WINIFRED THOMPSON HOCKMAN COLLECTION (CN 200), 1982, 2 reels audio tape
Background note: Robert William Hockman (1906–35) was the son of missionaries in Szechwan, and lived in China from 1906 to 1924. He and his wife, Winifred Thompson Hockman (b. 1906), were missionaries in Ethiopia in the 1930s.
ORAL HISTORIES: Interview with Robert and Winifred Hockman, discussing the China Inland Mission, Chinese civil wars, the education of missionary children, Katie Elizabeth Rogers Hockman, Robert William Hockman, Sr., and J. Hudson Taylor.
FINDING AIDS: In-house guide.

37-JOHN HSU LECTURE (CN 94) 1979, 2 reels audio tape,
AUDIO-VISUAL MATERIALS: Lecture by Wheaton College alumnus John Hsu after a trip to the People's Republic of China in 1979, including discussion of the Cultural Revolution, home churches, the Religious Affairs Bureau, and the Three-Self Movement.
FINDING AIDS: In-house guide.

38-BRUCE FINLEY HUNT (CN 104), 1980, 4 reels audio tape
Background note: For biographical notes, see Orthodox Presbyterian Church, Committee on Foreign Missions Archives, 7401 Old York Road, Philadelphia, PA, 19126.
ORAL HISTORIES: Interview with Bruce Finley Hunt, discussing his experiences from 1936 to 1941 as an Orthodox Presbyterian missionary in Manchuria.
FINDING AIDS: In-house guide.

39-HWA NAN COLLEGE PAPERS (SC 41) 1920–31, 1 folder
Background note: Hwa Nan College was founded in 1914 as a women's college in Foochow by Lydia A. Trimble of the Women's Foreign Missionary Society, Methodist Protestant Church.
CORRESPONDENCE: Letter from missionary Dorthea Kenney, 1930, describing the inauguration of Lucy C. Wang as the first Chinese president of the college, the college commencement, and the wedding of a staff member.
MEMORABILIA: Articles relating to Hwa Nan College, including one by Lucy Wang describing the background of the college and the careers of its graduates, n.d.
AUDIO-VISUAL MATERIALS: Photo of the family of Foochow missionary Frank Cartwright, Sr., n.d.; 3 photos of Frederick T. Kenney and his family, 1920 and n.d.
FINDING AIDS: In-house guide.

40-JAMES HERBERT AND WINNIFRED MARY KANE COLLECTION (CN 182), 1934–82, 2 c.f.
Background note: James Herbert and Winnifred Mary Kane were China Inland Mission workers in Anhwei from 1936 to 1950.
CORRESPONDENCE: .5 c.f. of letters to and from the Kanes, 1934–76.
ORAL HISTORIES: Interview with James and Winnifred Kane on 2 reels of audio tape, 1982, including discussions of President and Mme. Chiang K'ai-shek, the China Inland Mission, Chinese marriage customs, Chou En-lai, medical care in China, Watchman Nee, Ruth Nowack, Otto F. Schoerner, the Sino-Japanese War, Oswald J. Smith, and John and Elizabeth Stam.
FINDING AIDS: In-house guide.

41-ISOBEL MILLER KUHN EPHEMERA (SC 77), 1928–57, ca. 1 folder
CORRESPONDENCE: 2 letters and a prayer/newsletter of Isobel Miller Kuhn of the China Inland Mission, discussing her journey to China, the city of Yangchow in Kiangsu, and cultural differences between Chinese and Westerners, 1928–29; uncatalogued letters and photos, 1929–57.

42-A. B. LEWIS EPHEMERA (SC 81), 1937, 1 item
CORRESPONDENCE: Prayer/newsletter of A. B. Lewis of the China Inland Mission, describing mission work in Kiangsi and the involvement of Chinese Christians in evangelism, 1937.

43-MARIE HUTTENLOCK LITTLE (CN 315), 1985, 3 reels audio tape
ORAL HISTORIES: Interview with Marie Huttenlock Little, describing her work with the China Inland Mission in Lanchow and Wu Wei in Kansu from 1947 to 1951.
FINDING AIDS: In-house guide.

44-JESSIE McDONALD PAPERS (CN 246), 1907–51, ca. 32 folders
Background note: Jessie McDonald (1888–1980) first went to China as a missionary surgeon with the China Inland Mission (CIM) in 1913. She worked at Kaifeng Hospital from 1913 to 1939, serving as a surgeon, medical teacher, and administrator. With the evacuation of the hospital, she did some itinerant medical work before being stationed from 1940 to 1952 in Tali, Yunnan, near the Burma Road. On several occasions, Dr. McDonald also studied and worked at Peking Union Medical College. She left China in 1952.
MINUTES/RECORDS/REPORTS: China Inland Mission hospital, Kaifeng, annual reports, 1907, 1915–24, 1926, 1930, 1933, 1936–38; CIM hospital, Tali, annual reports, 1947–49.
CORRESPONDENCE: 25 folders of correspondence, from

McDonald to her mother and other family members, and between McDonald and co-workers including Paul and Vivian Adolph, Edith G. Dreyer, G. Whitfield Guinness, and Lawrence and Esther Nowack Hess, describing the medical missions station, how medical work augmented evangelistic outreach, and the nature of health conditions in China, 1914–50.
DIARIES: Undated diary.
MANUSCRIPTS: Medical notebooks, 1950, n.d.; 3 folders of notes on the role of Jews in Chinese religious history, Chinese language, and other subjects, n.d.
PAMPHLETS: Folder of unidentified pamphlets, ca. 1948; *Pearl's Secret* (notes on McDonald), 1951.
MEMORABILIA: Folder of unidentified clippings.
AUDIO-VISUAL MATERIALS: 2 photos of medical facilities, including the Good News Hospital in Kaifeng; photo of medical staff of Kaifeng hospital, 1936.
FINDING AIDS: In-house guide.

45-METHODIST MISSIONARY SOCIETY ARCHIVES (CN 163), 1829–1954, 1,760 microfiches
Background note: These materials are microfiche reproductions of the original archives, now housed in the Library of the School of Oriental and African Studies in London. The collection is divided into three components, two of which—the Wesleyan Methodist Missionary Society records and the Women's Work Collection—contain extensive materials concerning Methodist missions in China.
MINUTES/RECORDS/REPORTS: China Synod, minutes, 1853–1946; overseas schedules, China, 1923–46.
CORRESPONDENCE: 820 microfiches of letters in the Wesleyan Methodist Missionary Society records, divided into 11 series: Canton (1851–1905), China General (1936–45), China Miscellaneous (1924–34), Hunan (1907–45), Hupeh (1905–45), Ningpo (1933–46), North China (1933–45), South China (1905–45), South West China (1932–45), Wenchow (1933–45), and Wuchang (1876–1905); 281 microfiches of letters in the Women's Work Collection, divided into 3 series: Hunan, Hupeh, Ningpo, and Wenchow (1921–54); North, South, and South West China (1920–47); and Missionaries on Furlough (China, 1925–30).
MANUSCRIPTS: 330 microfiches of biographical materials and personal papers of Methodist missionaries in China, including David Hill, Samuel Pollard, and G. Stephenson, 1829–69.
FINDING AIDS: Microfiche reproductions of typescript inventories for correspondence.

46-MISSION AVIATION FELLOWSHIP COLLECTION (CN 136), 1944–69, 5 folders
Background note: The Mission Aviation Fellowship was founded in 1944 as a nonsectarian service agency to Protestant missions, providing transportation of people and supplies to remote areas of the world.
CORRESPONDENCE: Folder of correspondence with Daniel Nelson, China Field Director for the Lutheran World Federation, 1946; folder of correspondence relating to Lutheran World Federation mission work, 1947–69, including its work in China; folder of correspondence relating to the work of the Oriental Mission Society, 1946–69, including its work in China; folder of correspondence with the China Inland Mission, 1944–64.

MEMORABILIA: Clippings of the Lutheran World Federation *China Newsletter*, concerning the *St. Paul*, a mission plane flown into China by Daniel Nelson, 1946–50.
SERIALS: *China Newsletter*, 1947.
FINDING AIDS: In-house guide.

47-MARY GOFORTH MOYNAN PAPERS (CN 189), 1980–81, 16 items
Background note: Mary Goforth Moynan is the daughter of China missionaries Jonathan and Rosalind Goforth. She grew up in China and served as a missionary there briefly in the 1920s. See also Jonathan and Rosalind Bellsmith Goforth Papers above.
ORAL HISTORIES: Interview with Mary Moynan on 3 reels of audio tape, 1980–81, discussing such topics as the Boxer Uprising, Pearl Buck, the China Inland Mission, famine, Feng Yü-hsiang, Jonathan and Rosalind Goforth, house churches, missions in Manchuria, smallpox in China, Oswald Smith, John and Elizabeth Stam, and trips to Taiwan and the People's Republic of China.
AUDIO-VISUAL MATERIALS: 13 color slides, n.d.
FINDING AIDS: In-house guide.

48-PHILIP W. NELSON MEMOIRS, n.d., 1 item
MANUSCRIPTS: Memoirs of Philip W. Nelson on his work in China under the Swedish Alliance Mission, n.d.

49-WILLIAM H. NOWACK PAPERS, 1903–50, .3 c.f.
Background note: This collection is unprocessed at present. See also Helen Nowack Frame and Esther Nowack Hess collections above.
CORRESPONDENCE: Circular prayer letters of William H. Nowack, Helen Frame's father, 1903–23.
MANUSCRIPTS: Sermon notes, study guide, and other notes.
CHINESE LANGUAGE MATERIALS: 2 unspecified serials containing references to the Nowacks, n.d.

50-OVERSEAS MISSIONARY FELLOWSHIP, UNITED STATES HOME COUNCIL RECORDS (CN 215) 1853–1957, 5.5 c.f., 224 items
Restrictions: Some items are subject to 50-year restriction.
Background note: The North America Council of the China Inland Mission was created in 1901 to recruit and channel support to China missionaries from the United States and Canada. The United States and Canadian Home Councils were created as separate divisions of the Overseas Missionary Fellowship in 1969. The China Inland Mission (CIM) officially changed its name to Overseas Missionary Fellowship (OMF) in 1964. See also Overseas Missionary Fellowship, 404 South Church Street, Robesonia, PA, 19551.
Among the missions associated with the China Inland Mission until 1951 were: Alliance China Mission, Danish Missionary Union, Finnish Free Mission Society, Free Church of Finland Mission, Friedenshort Deaconess Mission, German Women's Bible Union, German Women's Missionary Union, Liebenzeller Mission, Norwegian Alliance Mission, Norwegian Mission in China, Evangelical Alliance Mission, Swedish Alliance Mission, Swedish Holiness Union, Swedish Mission in China, and the Yunnan Mission.
MINUTES/RECORDS/REPORTS: Biblical Seminary for Women, reports, 1935–36; Borden Memorial Hospital, reports, 1934–35; legal records concerning the estate of William Borden, 1913–

29, n.d.; China Council, minutes, 1897–1945, 1947; China Council, staff meetings and notes, 1942–52.

China Inland Mission: book catalogues, 1932–36; by-laws, 1894; constitution, 1890; field manuals, 1886–1928, 1938, 1947; marriage register, 1890–1950; medical reports from Paoning, 1943–46; records of the Conference of North American Officers, 1930, 1936, 1941, 1946–48, 1950–52; records of conference at Bournemouth, England, and preliminary meetings, 1951; records of conference at Kelorama, Australia, 1951; surveys, 1951–52.

Legal records concerning the estate of Laura Cunningham, 1905; Henrietta Bird Memorial Hospital, reports, 1938; property records of Charlesanna Huston, 1902–20; Kaifeng Hospital, reports, 1919–38; Kansu Provincial Conference, reports, 1941; senior missionary certificate for L. E. Pflauger, 1923; Shanghai United Conference, reports, 1922; Toronto Council, minutes, 1888–1949, 1951; Toronto Council, speech by Frederick Dreyer on "Training Chinese Workers," 1944.

U.S. Council: announcement of valedictory service for the last missionaries going to China, 1949; cables and telegrams, 1930–33; cash disbursal books, 1889–92; corporate records, 1932; corporation documents signed by the General Director, 1935, 1943; handbooks, ca. late 1940s; minutes, 1902–52; minutes of corporate meetings, 1932–52; minutes of staff meetings, 1929–33, 1943–45; miscellaneous documents, lists, memos, procedural guidelines, and reports, 1927–30; personnel cards giving information on individual missionaries, n.d.; property deeds, 1891–1945; property deeds from China, 1946–49; property deeds from North America, 1891–1929; register of candidate information, 1898–1934; World Missionary Conference, Continuation Committee, report, n.d.; Wilmay Memorial Hospital, reports, 1935.

CORRESPONDENCE: 2 folders of CIM headquarters correspondence, 1947–51; 15 folders of letters from headquarters to Home Councils, 1927–39, 1946–51; folder of correspondence of Paul and Vivian Adolph, discussing medical missions in Shansi and the birth of their son, Harold, 1933; folder of correspondence of Mr. and Mrs. Matthew G. Anderson, 1933; folder of correspondence of Herman and Auguste Becker, describing their work at a Hunan orphanage, 1932; folder of correspondence of William Borden, 1908–28, with such persons as Henry Frost and discussing Borden's education, his missionary training, his Christian beliefs, and his death in Egypt in 1913 en route to China; 2 folders of correspondence regarding the estate of William Borden, 1913–29, n.d.; folder of correspondence of Ernest Carlberg, including a description of his wedding, 1933; folder of correspondence of Howard and May Cliff, including descriptions of a Christian revival in Shunteh, 1933; 10 folders of correspondence of Allyn and Leila Cooke, describing their mission work among the Lisu tribe in Yunnan, 1933–41 and n.d.; folder of correspondence regarding the estate of Laura Cunningham, 1905; folder of correspondence of Mr. and Mrs. George Torr Denham, including an assessment of the growth of the church in Chowkow, Szechwan, during the civil war, 1885–1958; folder of correspondence of Arthur Dieffenbacher, including a description of a day in the life of a missionary in Anking, 1933; folder of correspondence of Gertrude C. Dreyer, including prayer letters, one of which was written during the Boxer Uprising, 1900–1940; folder of correspondence relating to the work of Friedenshort, describing its work among orphans in China, 1933; 2 folders of correspondence of Home Director for North America Henry Frost, 1904–33; 2 folders of correspondence of the

Home Director, Great Britain Council, 1930–33; folder of correspondence of Estella Hayes, 1933; 2 folders of correspondence of the assistant China director, 1929–33; folder of correspondence of the deputy director, 1927–33; 3 folders of correspondence of the Financial Department, 1944–46; 2 folders of correspondence of the general director, 1929–33; 2 folders of correspondence of the secretary, 1930–33; folder of correspondence of O. and L. Hollenweger, 1933; folder of correspondence of Maude Knight, including descriptions of CIM's headquarters in Shanghai and the six new missionaries (including Otto Schoerner) being taken by George Hunter to the mission station in Sinkiang, 1933; 11 folders of correspondence of John and Isobel Kuhn, including prayer letters concerning their work among the Lisu tribe and a description of the Kuhns' courtship, marriage, and family life, 1933–36, 1938–43, ca. 1946; 5 folders of correspondence relating to the Kuling School for the Children of Missionaries in China, 1949–52, 1954; folder of correspondence of A. Bertram Lewis, 1933; folder of correspondence of Henry Lyons, 1933; folder of correspondence of James H. and Frances M. Mellow, discussing prayer life and their experiences in Siaoyi, 1934; folder of prayer letters, 1928–33; folder of correspondence relating to the death of Leighton P. Rand, 1928–29; folder of correspondence relating to the distribution of *Hudson Taylor—The Man Who Believed God*, 1929; folder of correspondence regarding "The Two Hundred," 1931–33; folder of correspondence of A. and J. Robinson, including descriptions of a boat ride up the Yangtze River and disruptions caused by the conflict between the Nationalists and the Communists, 1933; folder of correspondence of Laura Robinson, 1933; folder of sailing and booking notices, 1930–31; folder of correspondence of Alice I. Saltmarsh, 1933; folder of correspondence of Otto Schoerner, including a description of his trip to Sinkiang across the Gobi Desert, 1933; folder of correspondence of F. Howard Taylor, 1928–33; folder of correspondence of Herbert and Jane Taylor, 1933; 3 folders of correspondence of J. Hudson Taylor, including letters to Henry Frost and discussions of Taylor's retirement from the directorship of the China Inland Mission, 1891–93; 2 folders of correspondence of the Toronto Council Editorial Secretary, 1929–33; folder of correspondence of E. Welsh, 1933.

MANUSCRIPTS: 4 folders of notes and manuscripts relating to the composition of a Mongolian-English dictionary, 1932; notebook belonging to J. Hudson Taylor's mother, 1853, describing Taylor's departure for China; miscellaneous papers of J. Hudson Taylor, 1890–1903.

PAMPHLETS: 28 folders of tracts, brochures, and pamphlets, 1890–1951, including outlines of CIM work, preparation for mission work, missionaries' experiences in China, medical work, missions among Tibetans, Moslems, and other non-Han peoples, mission newsletters, story tracts, student work, and prayer tracts.

MEMORABILIA: Folder of CIM currency, 1904, 1921; "Leaving China," article by Nellie DeWard, 1951; eulogy of J. O. Fraser, 1938; eulogy of D. E. Hoste, 1946; scrapbook of brochures, tracts, and newsletters published by the CIM, ca. 1940s.

MAPS/DESIGNS/DRAWINGS: Cloth-backed topographical map of the Burmese-Chinese border, n.d.; cloth-backed topographical map of Assam, Burma, and Yunnan, n.d.; hand-made chart indicating the locations of CIM workers in Yunnan, n.d.

AUDIO-VISUAL MATERIALS: 224 photos, 1853–1962, including group photos of mission officials and participants at mission conferences; pictures of schools, churches, and other mission fa-

cilities; portraits of missionaries, CIM officials, and prominent Chinese; and scenes of Chinese life.
SERIALS: China Inland Mission, *Directory*, 1900–1937, 1939–50, 1952; *Monthly Notes*, 1896–1938. *China's Millions* (Philadelphia), 1938–40. *Young China*, 1931.
CHINESE LANGUAGE MATERIALS: Unidentified letter, 1927.

51-MARTHA POHNERT EPHEMERA (SC 80), 1929, 1 item
CORRESPONDENCE: Prayer/newsletter of Martha Pohnert, missionary in Mukden, describing mission work, a famine in Manchuria, and conditions in an outlying town which had been invaded by Communists, 1929.

52-ROBERT W. PORTEOUS EPHEMERA (SC 74), 1928, 1 item
CORRESPONDENCE: Prayer/newsletter of Robert W. Porteous of the China Inland Mission, describing mission work in Yuanchow in Kiangsi, 1928.

53-PAUL RADER COLLECTION (CN 38), 1923–31, 3 folders
Background note: Daniel Paul Rader (1879–1938) was a Chicago pastor and evangelist who travelled to China in 1931.
MINUTES/RECORDS/REPORTS: Reports relating to Rader's trip to China, 1931.
MANUSCRIPTS: Sermons on China missions delivered at missionary rallies relating to R. B. Ekvall, Moseley, Stewart, Stuart, and Howard Van Dyke, 1923, 1929.
MEMORABILIA: Mementos from 1931 trip.

54-HANNAH L. REID EPHEMERA (SC 82), 1934, 1 item
CORRESPONDENCE: Prayer/newsletter of Hannah L. Reid of the China Inland Mission, discussing the illness, medical treatment, death, and funeral of her sister, Lilias Reid, 1934.

55-HELEN G. RENICH INTERVIEW (CN 124), 1980–82, 2 reels audio tape
Background note: Helen Torrey Renich (b. 1916) is the daughter of missionaries in Tsinan. She spent the first 20 years of her life in China, and served as a missionary in China from 1948 to 1949 with her husband, Frederick Renich. See also Reuben Archer Torrey, Sr., Collection and Reuben Archer Torrey III Interview below.
ORAL HISTORIES: Interview with Helen Renich, discussing such topics as acupuncture, the Boxer Uprising, Pearl Buck, Chiang K'ai-shek, Chinese attitudes toward Westerners, Chinese medicine, famine relief, foot binding, the Sino-Japanese war, Reuben Archer Torrey, Sr., and the war between the Kuomintang and the Communists.
FINDING AIDS: In-house guide.

56-ESTHER I. SALZMAN (CN 52), 1978, 1 reel audio tape
Background note: Esther I. Salzman (b. 1906) went to China in 1939 as a missionary under the American Baptist Foreign Mission Society. She was the only nurse at a hospital in Kinwa.
ORAL HISTORIES: Interview with Esther I. Salzman, describing her experiences as a medical missionary in China from 1939 to 1948.
FINDING AIDS: In-house guide.

57-HELEN IRVIN AND MALCOLM SAWYER INTERVIEW (CN 256), 1983, 4 reels audio tape
Restrictions: Portions of interview are restricted until 1993.
ORAL HISTORIES: 2 interviews each with Helen Irvin and Malcolm Sawyer, discussing their childhoods, schooling, and working in China under the Christian and Missionary Alliance from 1948 to 1949, and later work in Vietnam and Laos.
FINDING AIDS: In-house guide.

58-KATHERINE HASTINGS DODD SCHOERNER (CN 51), ca. 1931–1980, 6 items
Background note: Katherine Hastings Dodd Schoerner (b. 1908) went to China in 1932 under the China Inland Mission (CIM) and worked with women in Anhwei. Otto Frederick Schoerner (b. 1906) left for China in 1932. After attending language school in Anking, he and six others went to Sinkiang to work with George Hunter, and spent the next six years there. In 1938 he traveled to Shanghai to marry Katherine Dodd, and they subsequently went to Hwangchuan, Honan. They later moved to Lanchow in Kansu, where he became business manager of the Borden Memorial Hospital. The Schoerners returned to the United States in 1951. See also Otto Frederick Schoerner collection below.
CORRESPONDENCE: 5 letters by Katherine Schoerner, describing her life in China, n.d.
ORAL HISTORIES: Interview with Katherine Schoerner on 1 reel of audio tape, 1980, describing her childhood in Shantung (ca. 1910s) and work under the CIM in Sinkiang, Honan, and Kansu from 1931 to 1951.
FINDING AIDS: In-house guide.

59-OTTO FREDERICK SCHOERNER (CN 55), 1978–79, 3 items
Background note: See Katherine Hastings Dodd Schoerner collection above.
ORAL HISTORIES: Interview with Otto Schoerner on 2 reels of audio tape, discussing his work with the China Inland Mission in Sinkiang, Honan, and Kansu from 1932 to 1951.
AUDIO-VISUAL MATERIALS: Photo of the staff of Borden Memorial Hospital in Lanchow, Kansu, n.d.
FINDING AIDS: In-house guide.

60-RALPH C. AND HELEN E. SCOVILLE EPHEMERA (SC 78), 1928–29, 3 items
Background note: Ralph C. and Helen E. Scoville were missionaries with the China Inland Mission in Kansu during the 1920s.
CORRESPONDENCE: 3 prayer/newsletters written by the Scovilles, discussing their journey from Shanghai to Yinchuan (now Ningxia), the temporary occupation of Yinchuan by Moslem soldiers, and mission work in Kansu, 1928–29.

61-ELIZABETH STAIR SMALL (CN 164), 1980, 1 reel audio tape
ORAL HISTORIES: Interview with Elizabeth Stair Small, describing her work with the China Inland Mission from 1931 to 1948.

62-JUDSON SMITH COLLECTION (CN 173), 1898, 8 folders
Background note: Judson Smith (1837–1906) was secretary of the American Board of Commissioners of Foreign Missions from 1884 to 1906. From January to June 1898 he travelled in China and Japan.
MINUTES/RECORDS/REPORTS: Typed reports from Smith and his companions to American Board members concerning their tour of China, 1898.
CORRESPONDENCE: 8 folders of letters concerning Judson Smith's trip to China in 1898 discussing various Protestant missions in Hong Kong, Peking, Shanghai, and Tientsin, and giving an

overall assessment of the problems and successes of American mission work in China.

63-CHARLES OLIVER AND MARION ELIZABETH SPRINGER EPHEMERA, (SC 83), 1937, 1 item
CORRESPONDENCE: Prayer/newsletter written by Charles Oliver "Dick" and Marion Elizabeth Springer of the China Inland Mission, describing their arrival in Shanghai, their journey from Shanghai to Hwaining in Anhui, and their feelings about their work as missionaries, 1937.

64-RUTH SUNDQUIST (CN 266), 1984, 2 reels audio tape
ORAL HISTORIES: Interviews with Ruth Sundquist, discussing her work with war orphans in China between 1947 and 1949 under the Free Church, and later work in Hong Kong as administrator of a Sunday school and orphanage.
FINDING AIDS: In-house guide.

65-MELVIN SUTTIE INTERVIEWS, 1985, 2 reels audio tape
ORAL HISTORIES: Interviews with Melvin Suttie, 1985, discussing his work under the China Inland Mission.

66-HERBERT JOHN TAYLOR PAPERS, 1941–50, 3 folders
CORRESPONDENCE: Correspondence relating to missionary organizations active in China, between Christian Workers' Federation (CWF) and Salvation Army Chinese Campaign, 1941; between CWF and China Intervarsity Christian Fellowship, 1948–49; and correspondence of Inter-Varsity, China, 1947–50.
FINDING AIDS: In-house guide.

67-JAMES HUDSON TAYLOR EPHEMERA (SC 92), 1896–98, 2 items
CORRESPONDENCE: 2 letters from J. Hudson Taylor to a Mr. Sloan, describing various aspects of the work of the China Inland Mission, 1896, 1898.

68-HELEN MARGARET JADERQUIST TENNEY COLLECTION (CN 44), 1910–69, 1.5 c.f.
Background note: Helen Margaret Jaderquist Tenney (1904–78) was a teacher and writer who authored *No Higher Honor*, a history of the Women's Union Missionary Society. Chapters 10 and 11 of this work describe the Society's work in China.
MINUTES/RECORDS/REPORTS/MANUSCRIPTS/MEMORABILIA: Minutes, reports, manuscripts, and memorabilia, on such topics as the Margaret Williamson Hospital in Shanghai, medicine in China, mission work among women in China, and the Shanghai Union School of Nursing, 1910–69; drafts of Chapters 10 and 11 and complete manuscript of *No Higher Honor*.
FINDING AIDS: In-house guide.

69-CHARLES THOMSON EPHEMERA (SC 79), 1929, 1 item
CORRESPONDENCE: Prayer/newsletter of Charles Thomson, Pacific Northwest District Secretary for the China Inland Mission, discussing the mission's evangelistic work in China, 1929.

70-REUBEN ARCHER TORREY, SR., COLLECTION (CN 107), 1919–21, .5 c.f.
Background note: Reuben Archer Torrey, Sr. (1856–1928), was a Presbyterian evangelist and writer, and dean of the Bible Institute of Los Angeles. In 1919 and 1921 he travelled to China to inspect China Inland Mission stations and the Hunan Bible Institute. See also Helen G. Renich Interview above.
CORRESPONDENCE: Letters from Torrey to his wife, Claire, during his China visits, concerning such topics as the China Inland

Mission, Hunan Bible Institute, and Kuling General Hospital in Shanghai, 1919, 1921.
FINDING AIDS: In-house guide.

71-REUBEN ARCHER TORREY III INTERVIEW (CN 331), 1986, .2 c.f.
Background note: This collection is unprocessed at present. See also Helen G. Renich Interview and Reuben Archer Torrey, Sr., Collection above.
ORAL HISTORIES: Interview with Reuben Archer Torrey III on 2 reels audio tape and 1 video cassette, 1986, describing his childhood in China, his parents and grandparents, and his work as a missionary in Korea.

72-DORIS TREFREN PAPERS, 1931–48, .1 c.f.
Background note: This collection is unprocessed at present.
CORRESPONDENCE/MANUSCRIPTS/DIARIES: Correspondence, writings, and diary, relating to Doris Trefren's work under the China Inland Mission, 1931–48.

73-NATHAN AND LOIS WALTON EPHEMERA (SC 84), 1927–40, 1 folder
Background note: Nathan and Lois Walton were missionaries with the China Inland Mission in Hopei.
MINUTES/RECORDS/REPORTS: R. W. Middleton, report of a raft trip down the Yellow River in Kansu by 38 missionaries and their families, 1927.
PAMPHLETS: Prayer letters of the Waltons containing an account of their work in the city of Shunteh in Hopei, a description of a Bible conference attended by 500 Chinese Christians, news items from other missionaries, an open letter from Dixon E. Hoste, and financial and statistical data from the China Inland Mission, 1939–40.
SERIALS: China Inland Mission, *Monthly Notes*, n.d.

74-ELIZABETH HOWARD WARNER (CN 75), 1979, 1 reel audio tape
Background note: Elizabeth Howard Warner (b. 1912) grew up in Canton, where her father taught in a Christian college until 1928. In 1936 she went to China as a staff member of the Door of Hope Mission in Canton, where she worked with girls.
ORAL HISTORIES: Interview with Elizabeth Warner, describing her experiences growing up in Canton and her work with the Door of Hope Mission until 1941.
FINDING AIDS: In-house guide.

75-JOSEPH K. WRIGHT EPHEMERA (SC 65) 1856, 1 item
CORRESPONDENCE: Letter from China missionary Joseph K. Wright to his brother, William, describing his sea voyage to China, conditions in Shanghai, his mission work, and the Taiping Rebellion, 1856.

IL–205 Billy Graham Center Library
Wheaton College
Wheaton IL 60187–5593
(312) 260–5194
Ferne Weimer, Director

Finding aids: *Guide to Resources for the Institute of Chinese Stud-*

ies, by Eric Norregaard (Wheaton, IL: Institute of Chinese Studies, Billy Graham Center), 1986.

1-GENERAL HOLDINGS

MINUTES/RECORDS/REPORTS: China Inland Mission, annual reports, 1904, 1908, 1910–11, 1919, 1927, 1931, 1935–37, 1939–47, 1949–52; Peking Union Medical College, annual reports, 1924–28.

MANUSCRIPTS: "Christianity and China/Chinese: A Periodical Bibliography," by Sharon Mumper, 1982; "The Ecumenical Movement and Church-Mission Relationships in China, 1877–1927: The History of a Missiological Problem," by Samuel D. Ling, 1976; "The History of Christianity in China: Success or Failure?," by Samuel D. Ling, 1975; "I Am a Violin: The Story of One Missionary Who Worked as a Nurse for Ten Years (1940–1950) in China and the Philippine Islands," by Bessie M. Crim, 1984; "An Inspiring Story of a 'Beautiful Person'—Catharine E. Sutherland, Oct. 30, 1893–August 1, 1977," by Ruby Chen, n.d.; "Matthew Brown Birrell—Missionary to the Chinese: Jottings—An Autobiography," 1981; "A Selected Bibliography on Chinese Theological Education (Arranged in Chronological Order)," by Jonathan Chao, 1972; "The Student Christian Movement and Chinese Nationalism: 1927–1937," by Richard P. Madsen, 1973; "Theology in Chinese Historical Perspective: Bibliographical Suggestions," by Samuel D. Ling, 1982; "Treasure of Darkness—The True Story of a Missionary Mother: Katie E. Hockman," by Kathleen Hockman Friedericksen, 1981.

PAMPHLETS: 51 pamphlets, 1893–1978 and n.d., on such topics as the Baptist Missionary Society, bibliography of Jesuit missions, the Boxer Uprising, Harry Brown, the China Inland Mission, the China Missionary Survey, Christians and the 1898 reform movement, Chungking Theological School, James Gilmour, medical missions, missions in Amoy, Tibet, Tientsin, and Yunnan, missions to Hakkas, Horace Tracy Pitkin, Mrs. Robert W. Porteous, Mary H. Porter, Presbyterian missions in China, religious policy in the People's Republic of China, John and Betty Stam, and Beryl Audrey Weston.

SERIALS: *Anking Newsletter*, 1937–48. *Bridge*, 1983–. *Bulletin of the Diocesan Association for Western China*, 1934–51. *China and Ourselves*, 1981–. *China and the Church Today*, 1979–86. *China Bulletin* (Rome), 1980–. *China Christian Advocate*, 1914–41. *China Christian Year Book*, 1910–39. *China Colleges*, 1934–42. China Inland Mission, *List of Missionaries*, 1912–21. *China Medical Journal*, 1887–1921. *China Mission Advocate*, 1839. *China Missionary*, 1949. *China Missionary Bulletin*, 1949–53. *China Notes*, 1962–. *China Prayer Letter*, 1979–. *China's Millions* (London), 1875–99, 1914–52. *Chinese around the World*, 1980–. *Chinese Churches Today*, 1979–. *Chinese Recorder*, 1868–1941. *Chinese Repository*, 1832–51. *Chinese World Pulse*, 1977–83. *Ching Feng*, 1964–. *Fenchow*, 1919–36. *The Foochow Messenger*, 1903–40. *Franciscans in China*, 1922–40. *Hainan Newsletter*, 1919–49. National Christian Council of China, *Bulletin*, 1922–37. *Oriental and Inter-American Missionary Standard*, 1946–49. *Quarterly Notes on Christianity and Chinese Religion*, 1957–63. *West China Missionary News*, 1901–43.

DISSERTATIONS/THESES: *The American and British Missionary Concept of Chinese Civilization in the Nineteenth Century*, by James Miller McCutcheon, 1959. *The American Board in China: The Missionaries' Experiences and Attitudes, 1911–1952*, by Janet Elaine Heininger, 1981. *American Catholic Missions and Commu-nist China, 1945–1953*, by Virginia F. Unsworth, 1977. *American Missionaries and the Chinese Communists: A Study of Views Expressed by Methodist Episcopal Church Missionaries, 1921–1941*, by Milo Lancaster Thornberry, 1974. *American Missionaries and the Policies of the United States in China, 1898–1901*, by John M. H. Lindbeck, 1948. *The Anti-Christian Movement in China, 1922–1927: With Special Reference to the Experience of Protestant Missions*, by Ka-che Yip, 1970. *The Baptist Problem of the Indigenous Church in China*, by Frank T. Woodward, 1934. *The Bible Growing a Christian Culture in China*, by Ira Dennis Eavenson, 1928. *Catholic Activities in Kwangtung Province and Chinese Responses, 1848–1885*, by Jean-Paul Wiest, 1977. *The Catholic Missions in China During the Middle Ages, 1294–1368*, by Paul Stanislaus Hsiang, 1949. *A Century of Chinese Christian Education: An Analysis of the True Light Seminary and Its Successors in Canton and Hong Kong*, by Chen Kuan-yu, 1972. *The Challenge of China to America*, by Augustus Young Napier, 1922. *Changes in the Christian Message for China by Protestant Missionaries*, by Lewis Strong Casey Smythe, 1928. *The China Inland Mission and Some Aspects of Its Work*, by Hudson T. Armerding, 1948. *China's Opposition to Western Religion and Science during Late Ming and Early Ch'ing*, by George Ho Ching Wong, 1958. *The Chinese Church: A Bridge to World Evangelization*, by Cyrus On-kwok Lam, 1983. *Christian Missions and Foreign Relations in China: An Historical Study*, by Clifford Merrill Drury, 1932. *Christianity and Animism: China and Taiwan*, by Alan Frederick Gates, 1971. *Christianity and Social Change in China, 1912–1942*, by John Glenn Morris, 1946. *Christianity and Social Change: The Case in China, 1920–1950*, by Lee-ming Ng, 1971. *Church and State in Republican China: A Survey History of the Relations Between the Christian Churches and the Chinese Government, 1911–1945*, by Arne Sovik, 1952. *A Critical Examination of the National Christian Council of China*, by Milledge Theron Rankin, 1928. *The Development of the Motive of Protestant Missions to China, 1807–1928*, by George Bell Workman, 1928. *Education of Women by Baptists in South China*, by Pauline Frances Brammer, 1947. *Faith and Facts in the History of the China Inland Mission, 1832–1905*, by Moira Jane McKay, 1981. *The Gospel Mission Movement within the Southern Baptist Convention*, by Adrian Lamkin, 1980. *The History of Baptist Missions in Hong Kong*, by Paul Yat-keung Wong, 1974. *A History of Seventh-Day Adventist Higher Education in the China Mission, 1888–1980*, by Handel Hing-tat Luke, 1983. *A History of the Evangelical Lutheran Church of America's Mission Policy in China, 1890–1949*, by Roger Keith Ose, 1970. *The House-Church Movement in China: A Biblical Model for Church Growth*, by Thong Chan-kei, 1985. *Hsu Kuang-chi: Chinese Scientist and Christian (1562–1633)*, by Joseph King-hap Ku, 1973. *Indigenous Churches in China*, by Hendon Mason Harris, 1927. *The Jesuits in China in the Last Days of the Ming Dynasty*, by George Harold Dunne, 1944. *John Leighton Stuart: The Mind and Life of an American Missionary in China, 1876–1941*, by Shaw Yu-ming, 1975. *Lessons for China Missionaries from Paul, the Herald of the Gospel*, by Robert Johnston McMullen, 1930. *The Mission Compound in Modern China: The Role of the United States Protestant Mission as an Asylum in the Civil and International Strife of China, 1900–1941*, by Gladys Robina Quale, 1957. *The Mission Enterprise of the Lutheran Church-Missouri Synod in Mainland China, 1913–1952*, by Roy Arthur Suelflow, 1971. *The Mission of Matteo Ricci, S.J.: A Case Study of an Effort at Guided Cultural*

Change in China in the Sixteenth Century, by George L. Harris, 1967. *The Missionary Approach to the Religions of China*, by Rachel Mostrom Chappell, 1946. *Missionary Conscience and the Comprehension of Imperialism: A Study of the Children of American Missionaries to China, 1900–1949*, by Sarah Margaret Refo Mason, 1978. *Missionary Intelligence from China: American Protestant Reports, 1930–1950*, by Bruce Stephen Greenawalt, 1974. *Missionary Mother and Radical Daughter: Anna and Ida Pruitt in China, 1887–1939*, by Marjorie King, 1985. *Oberlin-in-China, 1881–1951*, by Mary Tarpley Campfield, 1974. *The Oriental Educational Commission's Recommendation for Mission Strategy in Higher Education*, by David Lloyd Lindberg, 1972. *The Other May Fourth Movement: The Chinese "Christian Renaissance," 1919–1937*, by Samuel D. Ling, 1980. *Outline of a History of Missions in China*, by E. B. Atwood, 1911. *The Place of Education in the Religious Redemption of China*, by James Toy Williams, 1921. *Political Activities of the Christian Missionaries in the T'ang Dynasty*, by Lam Ch'i-hung, 1975. *Protestant Christianity and Marriage in China*, by Calvin H. Reber, 1958. *Protestant Christianity in China and Korea: The Problem of Identification with Tradition*, Spencer John Palmer, 1964. *The Protestant Church in Communist China, 1949–1958*, by James Herbert Kane, 1958. *Protestant Missionary Publications in Modern China, 1912–1949: A Study of Their Programs, Operations, and Trends*, by Ho Hoilap, 1979. *The Protestant Missionary Understanding of the Chinese Situation and the Christian Task from 1890 to 1911*, by C. William Mensendiek, 1958. *Protestant Missions in Communist China*, by Creighton Lacy, 1953. *Reciprocal Change: The Case of American Protestant Missionaries to China*, by Paul Voninski, 1975. *The Role of the Chinese Church in World Missions*, by Henry T. Ang, 1985. *The Situation in China from a Sociological Point of View*, by Charles R. Shepherd, 1913. *Southern Baptist Contributions to Missions in China: A Survey of Investments and Achievements*, by Park Harris Anderson, 1947. *Southern Baptist Missions in China, 1945–1951*, by Garnett Lee White, 1967. *Strangers in the House: J. Lewis Shuck and Issachar Roberts, First American Baptist Missionaries to China*, by Margaret M. Coughlin, 1972. *Suffering in the Experience of the Protestant Church in China (1911–1980): A Chinese Perspective*, by Paul Cheuk-ching Szeto, 1980. *A Survey of Sunday School Work in China from 1930 to 1945*, by Edwin William Fisch, 1947. *A Symbolic Interactionist Approach to the Religious Stranger Concept: Protestant Missionaries in China, 1845–1900*, by Nishan J. Najarian, 1982. *Teaching the Christian Faith in the Chinese Educational Context*, by Jack L. Gentry, 1971. *A Theological Dialogue between Christian Faith and Chinese Belief in the Light of "Sin": An Inquiry into the Apparent Failure of the Protestant Mission in Late Nineteenth-century China, Especially among Chinese Intellectuals*, by Christopher Chou, 1976. *Timothy Richard's Theory of Christian Missions to the Non-Christian World* by Rita T. Johnson, 1966. *The Use of Literature in the Protestant Missionary Enterprise Among the Chinese People*, by Paul Henry Bartel, 1962. *Zion's Corner: Origins of the American Protestant Missionary Movement in China, 1827–1839*, by Murray Aaron Rubinstein, 1976.
CHINESE LANGUAGE MATERIALS/SERIALS: *Chung-kuo hsin t'u yüeh k'an (Chinese Christians Today)*, 1972, 1978-.
CHINESE LANGUAGE MATERIALS: Bible in Fukienese and romanization, signed by J. Hudson Taylor, 1869; translation of *How I Know God Answers Prayers*, by Rosalind Goforth, n.d.

IL–210 Billy Graham Center Museum
Wheaton College
Wheaton IL 60187
(312) 260–5909
James Stambaugh, Director

1-GENERAL HOLDINGS
MEMORABILIA: 2 banners prepared for the Jonathan Goforth family's departure from China, n.d.; 2 of the Goforths' business cards, n.d.; painting of a Bible quotation by Rosalind Goforth, 1940; Pioneer Service Pin presented to Rosalind Goforth after 41 years in China, 1929; silver engraved plaque, n.d.
CHINESE LANGUAGE MATERIALS: Bible, n.d.

INDIANA

ANDERSON

IN–5   CHURCH OF GOD
Foreign Missionary Board
Box 2498
Anderson IN 46018
(317) 642–0256
Lester Crose, Archivist

Background note: William A. Hunnex and Charles E. Hunnex, born of English missionaries in China, established the first Church of God mission in Chinkiang in 1909–10.

1-HISTORICAL FILES, ca. 1910-ca. 1949, quantity undetermined
MINUTES/RECORDS/REPORTS/CORRESPONDENCE: Records, reports, and correspondence of Church of God missionaries Lovena Billings (Mrs. Peter Jenkins), Milton Buettner, David Gaulke, Charles E. Hunnex, William A. Hunnex, Karl M. Kreutz, Daisy V. Maiden (Mrs. Boone), Belle M. Watson, and Edgar Williams.

BLOOMINGTON

INDIANA UNIVERSITY

IN–10   Manuscripts Department
Lilly Library
Seventh Street
Bloomington IN 47405–3301
(812) 335–2452
Rebecca Campbell Gibson, Manuscripts Cataloguer

1-FAIRBANKS MANUSCRIPTS, 1906, 1 item
CORRESPONDENCE: Letter from James Whitford Bashford, Methodist missionary bishop of Shanghai, to Charles Warren Fairbanks, Vice President of the United States, 1906.

2-MISCELLANEOUS MANUSCRIPTS, 1796, 1 item
MANUSCRIPTS: "Memorias sobre la fundación de la Congregacion de las Missiones Extranjeras en Paris," 1796.

3-PHILIPPINE MANUSCRIPTS, 1645–1721, 3 items
MANUSCRIPTS: "Papeles de Importancia Pertenecientes a la Mission de China, 1645–1721," comp. by Pedro Orense, 1721, 2 volumes containing letters and other documents by Augustinian missionaries in China, letters from Jesuit and Franciscan missionaries, and from various vicars-Apostolic; "Minuta Provincia S. Gregorii," by Antonio Tadeo Morales, et al., on the mission of the Franciscan Province of St. Gregory in China; "Relacion de Algunas Cosas Pertenecientes a la Mission de China," a collection of contemporary transcripts written in Macao about Charles Thomas Maillard de Tournon's embassy to China as a papal legate from 1705 to 1710, Chinese rites, and ecclesiastical jurisdiction.
FINDING AIDS: *Catalogue of Philippine Manuscripts in the Lilly Library*, by C. R. Boxer (Bloomington, IN: Asian Studies Research Institute), 1968.

4-PHILIPPINE MANUSCRIPTS II, ca. 1500–1696, 4 items
CORRESPONDENCE: Letter from Juan de Zarzuela to Jerónimo Guerrero on missionary activity, 1685.
MANUSCRIPTS: "De la Historia de las Philipinas, que Trata de la Conquista...," including accounts of China, n.a., 15??; "Dificultades," n.a., on the difficulties of mission work in the Orient, 1696; "Informe Sobre Ciertos Puntos que los Jesuitas Observan, Practican, Permiten y Enseñan en la China," by Antonio de Santa Maria, 16??.

5-PORTUGAL HISTORY MANUSCRIPTS, 1700–1719, 9 items
MINUTES/RECORDS/REPORTS: "Relazione delle Operazioni di Monsr. Patriarca di Antiochia Hoggi Cardinale di Tournon si nell' Arrivo alla Citta di Macao, Come ande Prima nel Territorio Chinese...," six reports by Charles Thomas Maillard de Tournon (Carlo Tommaso Maillard de Tournon) on his missionary activities in Macao, 1706–8.
CORRESPONDENCE: Letter from Basilio da G[l]emona to Congregatio de Propaganda Fide referring to treatment of the bishop of Peking, 1700; letter from Bernardino della Chiesa to Pope Innocentius XII reporting that he has taken possession of his cathedral despite Jesuit protests, and other news, 1700; letter from Manuel de Sá to Francisco Xavier de Menezes, conde da Ericeira, on the difficulties of Jesuit missions caused by the Papal denunciation of Chinese rites, 1719.

IN-15   Lilly Library
Indiana University
Seventh Street
Bloomington IN 47405-3301
(812) 335-2452
Joel Silver, Head of Reader Services

Background note: The Lilly Library holds the Mendel Collection, focussing on Spanish overseas expansion, as well as the collection of the eminent historian, Charles R. Boxer, devoted primarily to Dutch and Portuguese overseas activity, particularly in the Far East. In addition to the materials listed below, the collection includes a number of books of the seventeenth and eighteenth centuries, such as *Informatio pro Veritate*, authored by the Jesuits in their own defense during the rites controversy, and printed by the Jesuit Xylographic Press in China.

1-GENERAL HOLDINGS
CORRESPONDENCE: Letters from early Christian missionaries in China, each about 12 pages long, among 122 volumes of letters, ca. 1544-ca. 1649.
PAMPHLETS: *Brevis relatio de numero et qualitate Christianorum apud Sinas*, by Martino Martini, 1655; *Carta Circular Acerca de la Muerte del P. Fernando Verbiest; Rector del Colegio de Pekin, Corte de la China, que Murió á 28 del Mes de Enero del Año 1688*, by Antoine Thomas, 1692; *Carta escrita por el R. P. Fr. Victorio Riccio de la sagrada orden de Predicadores, vicario provincial en los reynos de la China; al muy R. P. Fr. Juan de los Angeles, provincial de la misma orden en las Islas Filipinas...*, by Victorio Ricci, 1667; *Exemplar Epistolae*, by Antonio de Gouveia, 1704; *Innocentia Victrix sive Sententia Comitio-Imperij Sinici pro Innocentia Christianae Religionis lata Juridice per Annum 1669*, by Antonio de Gouveia, 1671; *Memorial, que por Parte de la Provincia de San Gregorio de Philipinas, y sus Religiosos, que Assisten en las Missiones de...Cochinchina*, by Pedro Juan de Molina, 1740; *O padroado Portuguez na China*, by Feliciano Antonio Marques Pereira, 1873; *Relaçao da conversao anosta sancta feda rainha & principe da China, & de outras pessoas da casa real, que se baptizarao o anno de 1648*, by Mathias da Maya, 1650; *Relaçao summaria da prizam, tormentos, e glorioso martyro dos veneraveis padres Antonio Joseph portuguez, e Tristam de Attimis italiano, ambos da Companhia de Jesus, da V. Provincia da China*, by Luis de Sequeira, 1751.
MAPS/DESIGNS/DRAWINGS: *Evangelicae Historiae Imagines (Pictures of the Gospel Story)*, by Geronimo Nadal, S.J., 1596, a series of 153 engravings prepared by Nadal to illustrate his own *Annotationes et Meditationes in Evangelia (Notes and Meditations on the Gospels)*, 1596.
CHINESE LANGUAGE MATERIALS/MAPS/DESIGNS/DRAWINGS: *Holy Pictures of Jesus Christ Who Came to Earth*, ed. Julio Aleni, S.J., 1635, 54 images from Nadal's *Evangelicae Historiae Imagines* recut on wood by Chinese artists.
CHINESE LANGUAGE MATERIALS: "The Red Manifesto," a 1716 broadside in Manchu by the Kangxi emperor, in search of the Jesuit envoys Antonio de Barros and Antoine Beauvolier, with Chinese and Latin translations; *Ephemerides of the Planets for the Year 1684*, by Ferdinand Verbiest, S.J., 1683.

IN-20   University Libraries
Indiana University
Main Library, E860
Bloomington IN 47405
(812) 335-8028
Thomas H. Lee, East Asian Librarian

1-EAST ASIAN COLLECTION, 1930–83, 26 items
CHINESE LANGUAGE MATERIALS/SERIALS: *Chiao hui hsin pao (Church News)*, 1868–74 (repr. 1970). *Hua t'u hsin pao (Chinese Illustrated News)*, 1880–81 (repr. 1966). *Yen-ching hsüeh pao (Yenching Journal of Chinese Studies)*, 1927–33.
CHINESE LANGUAGE MATERIALS: 24 books, 1930–83, on Young J. Allen, Bible, Catholics in China, church history, Leung Faat, the K'ang-hsi and Ch'ien-lung emperors and Catholic mis-

sionaries, Martin Luther, missions in Shanghai, Protestant church, Matteo Ricci, Timothy Richard, and John Wesley.

2-GENERAL HOLDINGS

MINUTES/RECORDS/REPORTS: China Foundation for the Promotion of Education and Culture, report, 1939.

MANUSCRIPTS: "Die katholische Missionen in Indien, China, und Japan; ihre Organisation und das portugiesische Patronat vom 15. bis ins 18. Jahrhundert," by Adelhelm Jann, 1915.

PAMPHLETS: *Communist China: What of the Church?*, by Henry August Wittenbach, 1950; *Nestorians in China: Some Corrections and Additions*, by Arthur Christopher Moule, 1940.

MAPS/DESIGNS/DRAWINGS: *Atlas of China in Provinces: A Companion Work to "A Survey of the Missionary Occupation of China,"* by Thomas Cochrane, 1913.

SERIALS: *Boletim Eclesiástico*, 1941, 1960–61, 1963. *China Law Review*, 1922–40. *China Mission Year Book*, 1917. *China Monthly*, 1939–50. *China's Medicine*, 1966. *Chinese Recorder*, 1912–38. *Chinese Recorder and Educational Review*, 1939–40. *Chinese Recorder and Missionary Journal*, 1868–1912. *Chinese Repository*, 1832–51. *Folklore Studies*, 1942–. *Lingnan Science Journal*, 1939–41, 1945, 1948. *Missions en Chine et au Congo*, 1902–3.

DISSERTATIONS/THESES: *Die Akkomodationsmethode des P. Matteo Ricci S.I. in China*, by Johannes Bettray, 1955. *The Canton Hospital and Medicine in Nineteenth-century China*, by Sara Tucker, 1982. *China Missions in Crisis: Bishop Laimbeckhoven and His Times, 1738–1787*, by Joseph Krahl, 1964. *Henry Andrea Burgevine in China: A Biography*, by Robert H. Detrick, 1968. *Protestant Mission Schools for Girls in South China (1827 to the Japanese Invasion)*, by Mary Raleigh Anderson, 1943.

CHINESE LANGUAGE MATERIALS: *Chin tai Chung-kuo fan yang chiao yün tang*, by Li Shih-yüeh, 1958 (repr. 1969); *T'ien hsia ti i shang hsin jen (p'i hsieh chi shih)*, 1871.

ELKHART

ASSOCIATED MENNONITE BIBLICAL SEMINARIES
IN–25 Library
3003 Benham Avenue
Elkhart IN 46517
(219) 295-3726
Eileen Saner, Librarian

Background note: The Associated Mennonite Biblical Seminaries Library serves the Goshen Biblical Seminary and the Mennonite Biblical Seminary.

1-AGATHA FAST LETTERS AND CLIPPINGS, 1924–30, 1 folder

CORRESPONDENCE/PAMPHLETS/MEMORABILIA: Letters and clippings from Agatha Fast's mission work in China, n.d., including "The Celebration of the Twenty-Fifth Anniversary of Rev. H. J. and Maria Brown's Missionary Service in China," "Amoy Today," by Anthony Van Westenburg, "A Missionary Warrior Called Home," by James T. Robertson, "China: A Magnificent Ally," by James T. Robertson, "In China—China General Conference Mennonite Mission Field," 1925; "The Week in China for the Week Ending January 4, 1930," *The Gospel Hall Messenger*, 1928, and *The Mandarin*, 1924.

2-STUDENT PAPERS, n.d., 1 item

MANUSCRIPTS: "The China Mission Field of the General Conference," by Esko Loewen, n.d.

3-GENERAL HOLDINGS

MINUTES/RECORDS/REPORTS: American Board of Commissioners for Foreign Missions, Chihli district, standing rules, 1917; Anderson-Smith report on theological education in southeast Asia, 1952; China Inland Mission, annual report, 1952; China General Conference Mennonite mission field, report, 1924; Mennonite Brethren Church, mission in West China, 1949.

MANUSCRIPTS: "Christianity in China: Papers on the Current Situation, 1949–1951," a collection of materials from the China Committee, Far Eastern Joint Office, Foreign Missions Conference of North America, 1948–51, with essays by E. E. Barnett, Kermit Eby, Victor E. W. Hayward, Harold S. Matthews, W. P. Mills and T. C. Young; "Lessons to be Learned from the Experiences of Christian Missions in China," by Harold S. Matthews, 1951.

PAMPHLETS: *The Country Church and Indigenous Christianity*, by Sidney J. W. Clark, 1920; *"God's Sufficient Grace,"* by Frieda Dirks, ca. 1944; *Hitherto: 1914–1919, Silver Anniversary of the Church of the Nazarene in China*, n.a., 1939; *Internment Echoes*, by Wilhelmina Kuyf, 1949(?); *I Was in Prison*, by Annie James, 1952; *Mission Work in China*, by Pauline Goering, 1940; *Out of the Fire*, by Samuel Floyd Pannabecker, 1938; *Stories of China*, n.a., 1947; *We Enter China: A Statement of Historical Development, Present Progress, Plans, Ideals, Description of Our Mennonite Mission in China*, by Joseph Daniel Graber, 1947; *What Happened in China*, by Matilda Kliew Voth, 1947(?).

SERIALS: *Bulletin of the Hopei Bible School*, 1932–33. *China and the Church Today*, 1979–85. *China Bulletin*, 1952–62. *China Christian Year Book*, 1924. *China News Letter*, 1948–51. *China Notes*, 1962–. *China Relief Notes*, 1945–48. *China-Home Bond*, 1939–41. *China's Millions* (Philadelphia), 1951. *Chinese Christians Today*, 1962–63, 1972, 1977–. *Chinese Recorder*, 1871, 1874–76, 1878–80, 1887–1917. *Ching Feng*, 1964–84. *East Asia Millions* (Philadelphia), 1959–84. *Millions* (Philadelphia), 1952–61.

DISSERTATIONS/THESES: *The Beginning and Growth of the Educational Mission Work in China of the Mennonite General Conference of North America*, by John E. Kaufman, 1924. "Folkways and Religion," Translations of Chapters Nine and Ten from *"Ting-Hsien, a Social Survey,"* by Aganetha Helen Fast, 1936. *Lutheran Missions in a Time of Revolution: The China Experience, 1944–1951*, by Jonas Jonson, 1972.

FORT WAYNE

INTERNATIONAL HEADQUARTERS OF THE MISSIONARY CHURCH
IN–30 Archives
3901 South Wayne Avenue
Fort Wayne IN 46807
(219) 456-4502
Lois Luesing, Librarian

Restrictions: Access by appointment.
Background note: Formed in 1969 through a merger of the United

Missionary Church and the Missionary Church Association, the Missionary Church is evangelical and conservative. The archives are in the basement of the headquarters building, and are unorganized. See also Bethel College Library, 1001 West McKinley Avenue, Mishawaka, IN, 46544.

1-CHINA MISSION COLLECTION, 1891–1951, quantity undetermined
MINUTES/RECORDS/REPORTS: Reports from United Missionary Church and Missionary Church Association missionaries in China, 1891–1951; records of the China mission in the Missionary Church Association periodical, *Missionary Worker*, 1892–1951, and the United Missionary Church periodicals, *Gospel Banner*, 1895–1951, and *Missionary Banner*, 1938–51.
CORRESPONDENCE: Ca. 1 folder each of letters from Missionary Church Association missionaries to China: Fannie (Chapman) Baumgartner, John C. Birkey, Mr. and Mrs. Roy J. Birkey, Nellie Bowen, Kathryn Burkey, Lydia Burkey, Mary DeGarmo, Lena Gerber, Eliza Von Gunten, Elizabeth Hilty, Minnie Hilty, Rhoda (Hinkey) Lugibihl, Mr. and Mrs. Henry Maier, Solomon Miller, Charles and Florence (Suter) Roberts, Mr. and Mrs. Ezra G. Roth, and Henry Zehr, 1892–1947; ca. 1 folder each of letters from United Missionary Church missionaries to China: Daniel Brenneman, Bessie Cordell, William Shantz, and Calvin F. and Phoebe (Brenneman) Snyder, 1895–1951.
AUDIO-VISUAL MATERIALS: Photos of United Missionary Church and Missionary Church Association missionaries to China, and Chinese civilization and culture.

GOSHEN

GOSHEN COLLEGE
IN–35 Archives of the Mennonite Church
1700 South Main Street
Goshen IN 46526
(219) 533-3161 Ext. 477
Rachel Shenk, Associate Archivist

Background note: See also Bethel College, Mennonite Library and Archives, North Newton, KS, 67117-9998; Center for Mennonite Brethren Studies, 4824 East Butler, Fresno, CA, 93727; and Eastern Mennonite College and Seminary, Menno Simons Historical Library and Archives, Harrisonburg, VA, 22801-2462.

1-MENNONITE BOARD OF MISSIONS, EXECUTIVE OFFICE, CORRESPONDENCE, 1906–1945 (IV–7–1), 1921–32, 2 folders
CORRESPONDENCE: Folder of correspondence concerning China famine relief, 1929–32; folder of correspondence concerning the China Mennonite Mission Society, 1921–32.

2-MENNONITE BOARD OF MISSIONS, EXECUTIVE OFFICE, CORRESPONDENCE, 1944–1950 (IV–7–5), 1944–50, 12 folders
MINUTES/RECORDS/REPORTS: Records from the Mennonite China mission, including passports, visas, an equipment list, travel information, a mission study, personal records of Don and Dorothy McCammon, and materials pertaining to relief work, 1944–50.
CORRESPONDENCE: Folder of China-related correspondence, 1944–50.
MANUSCRIPTS: "We Enter China," by Joseph D. Graber, n.d.
MEMORABILIA: Folder of articles relating to the China mission, 1944–50.

3-MENNONITE BOARD OF MISSIONS, OVERSEAS MISSIONS, JOSEPH D. GRABER FILES (IV–18–10), 1951, 1 folder
MINUTES/RECORDS/REPORTS: China records, 1951.

4-MENNONITE BOARD OF MISSIONS, RELIEF AND SERVICE, FOREIGN RELIEF (IV–19–11), n.d., 1 folder
MINUTES/RECORDS/REPORTS: Miscellaneous China records, n.d.

5-MENNONITE BOARD OF MISSIONS, TREASURER, CORRESPONDENCE FOREIGN, 1949–1951 (IV–8–14), 1949–51, 7 folders
MINUTES/RECORDS/REPORTS: Financial reports, 1949–51; miscellaneous China records, 1949–50.
CORRESPONDENCE: Folder each of correspondence with Ruth M. Bean, Clayton Beyler, Eugene Blosser, Don and Dorothy McCammon, and Christine Weaver, 1949–51.

6-MENNONITE CENTRAL COMMITTEE, AKRON DATA FILES (IX–12, #1, 3, 5–6), n.d., 17 folders
MINUTES/RECORDS/REPORTS: 13 folders containing reports and records concerning the Associated Boards for Christian Colleges in China, China Aid Council, China Children's Fund, Inc., China Honan International Relief Committee, a China research project by John Andrew Hostetler, Mennonite relief in China, Protestant missions in China, United Nations Relief Rehabilitation Administration, United Service to China, Inc., and war orphanages; 2 folders of miscellaneous China records, n.d.
SERIALS: *China Aid Council Newsletter*, 1938–49.
CHINESE LANGUAGE MATERIALS: Folder of miscellaneous materials, n.d.

7-MENNONITE CENTRAL COMMITTEE, AKRON GENERAL CORRESPONDENCE (IX–6), 1946–52, 10 folders
CORRESPONDENCE: Correspondence with the China Office, 1946–52.

8-MENNONITE CENTRAL COMMITTEE, FAR EAST OFFICE (IX–48) 1949–52, 3 folders
Restrictions: Permission of the archivist required.
MINUTES/RECORDS/REPORTS: China reports, 1950; records from Shanghai, 1949–52; general China mission records, 1950–51.

9-MENNONITE CENTRAL COMMITTEE, C. L. GRABER FILES, COMMISSIONER TO CHINA AND THE PHILIPPINES 1945–1946 (IX–9), 1945–46, 5 folders
MINUTES/RECORDS/REPORTS: Records relating to relief work, 1945–46; miscellaneous records, 1945–46.
CORRESPONDENCE: Folder of cablegrams, 1945–46; folder of correspondence, 1945–46.
MANUSCRIPTS: Folder of manuscript notes, 1945–46.

10-MENNONITE CENTRAL COMMITTEE, HONG KONG AND CHINA FILES (IX–32), 1941–48, 4 boxes
Background note: In addition to the materials listed below, this collection contains 4 boxes and materials relating to Mennonite mission work in Hong Kong from 1950 to 1973.
MINUTES/RECORDS/REPORTS: American Advisory Committee and Honan International Relief Committee reports, 1946–47; reports and information on China, 1943–45; materials on China unit planning, 1943.
Records on projects sponsored by the Mennonites in China: Agricultural Loans, Shui-p'o, 1946–47; Changte Refugee School,

1947; Ch'ang-yuan Clinic, 1946; Ch'ang-yuan Cotton Loans, 1946–47; Cheng-chow Refugee School Grant, 1946; Ch'i-hsien Hospital, 1946–47; Ch'ü-hsien-chen Clinic, 1946–47; Ch'ü-hsien-chen Cotton Loans, 1946; Ch'ü-hsien-chen Milk Project, 1946–47; Clothing Distribution, 1946–47; CNRRA Cotton Loans, 1947; Cong-chow Industrial School, 1946–47; Fukou Flood Relief, 1946–47; Heifers Project, 1946–48; Hsi-hua Clinic, 1947; Kaifeng, Loans for Displaced Persons, 1946–48; Kao-t'un Clinic, 1946–47; Lithograph Training School, 1946–47; Miao-chen-t'o Wheat Loans, 1946–47; Puyang General Hospital, 1947; Tractor Project, 1946–47; Tung-ming Cotton Loans, 1946–47; Tung-ming Flood Relief, 1946; Weishih Hospital, 1947; Wheat Project, 1947. CORRESPONDENCE: General China correspondence, 1941–44; correspondence of Dale Nebel, 1946–47; correspondence with mission groups, 1946–47. PAMPHLETS: 1 l.f. of reports, letters, and publications on China of the Mennonite Central Committee, 1941–48.

11-PAUL MININGER COLLECTION (1–158), n.d., 1 folder
CORRESPONDENCE: Correspondence relating to fund-raising for China relief, n.d.

12-SARAH ALICE TROYER YOUNG COLLECTION (1–428), ca. late 1800s-early 1900s, 2 folders
CORRESPONDENCE: Letters from Sarah Alice Troyer Young, a missionary in China, 1896–1901. DIARIES: Young's diary, ca. late 1800s-early 1900s. AUDIO-VISUAL MATERIALS: Photos of Young in China, ca. late 1800s-early 1900s.

GREENCASTLE

DEPAUW UNIVERSITY

IN-40 Archives of DePauw University and Indiana United Methodism
Roy O. West Library
P. O. Box 137
Greencastle IN 46135
(317) 658-4500
Wesley W. Wilson, Coordinator of Archives and Special Services

1-MARIE ADAMS PAPERS, 1934–50, 19 items
CORRESPONDENCE: Folder of Marie Adams' correspondence, n.d. MANUSCRIPTS: Autobiographical sketch of Adams, n.d.; "The Charm of Old Peking," with photos, n.d.; "Chinese Cave Temples," with photos, 1934; "The Jumping-off Place," 1979; "Leaves from a War Prisoner's Devotional Diary," 1941–43; "Talks on Chinese Youth," 1929–30. MEMORABILIA: Folder of clippings from DePauw student newspaper, 1936–50. CHINESE LANGUAGE MATERIALS: 6 books written by Adams for a course on the Bible, translated by Hu Lueh Shah: *The Early Church, Early Hebrew Stories, The Hebrew Kingdom, Jesus, the Interpreter of God, The Makers of Judaism,* and *The Building of the Hebrew Nation.*

2-ROXY LEFFORGE PAPERS, 1947–72, 1 folder
CORRESPONDENCE: 18 letters between Roxy Lefforge and President Wildman, 1947–49; circular letters, 1948–72.

3-ELLEN M. STUDLEY PAPERS, 1925–73, 1 folder
Background note: Ellen M. Studley began her missionary work in rural North China in 1924. She was soon appointed principal of the Woman's Union Bible Training School in Peking, where she served until 1951. She was interned by the Japanese during World War II, but was released in 1943 and returned to the United States. After the war, she returned to Peking.
CORRESPONDENCE: Circular letter, 1964; 12 circular letters from Hazel Day Longden, 1930–48. MANUSCRIPTS: Biography of Studley, n.d. MEMORABILIA: "The Ordination of the Reverend Miss Ellen Masia Studley," an article in alumni newsletter, 1956; "Home from China," in *DePauw Alumnus,* n.d.; clippings on Studley, 1961, 1967. AUDIO-VISUAL MATERIALS: Photos of Studley, 1927, 1931, 1952, 1958, 1973, and n.d.; "Changli Views," a photo album, n.d.; 20 photos, in and around the Alderman's School, ca. 1925–1935.

4-WILBUR FISK WALKER PAPERS, 1873–1921, 34 items
Restrictions: Access to "The Siege of Peking," is restricted.
Background note: Wilbur Fisk Walker (1846–1932) was a Methodist missionary to China.
DIARIES: Walker's journal on the Boxer Rebellion, 1900–1901. MANUSCRIPTS: Autobiographical sketch of Walker. MEMORABILIA: Notes by Walker, n.d.; newspaper clippings; scrapbook on Wilbur and Mary Florence (Morrison) Walker. AUDIO-VISUAL MATERIALS: "The Siege of Peking," a photo album; photos of Chinese paintings and China.

5-GENERAL HOLDINGS
MINUTES/RECORDS/REPORTS: Methodist Church, North China Woman's Conference, minutes, 1929. CORRESPONDENCE: Letters from China missionaries L. J. Birney, 1923; Mary Mann, 1923; Ruth L. Myers, 1923; J. Stewart Nagle, 1920; Ruth Pierce, 1923; Francis T. Pyke, 1923; and Frederick M. Pyke, 1923. DIARIES: Journal of Wilbur Fisk Walker, 1873–1880, 1891. MANUSCRIPTS: Autobiographical sketch by Wilbur Fisk Walker, n.d. AUDIO-VISUAL MATERIALS: Photos of Catherine Corey, 1890; Grace A. Crooks, 1890; Lizzie M. Fisher, 1890; Anna M. Gloss, 1880s; Jennie V. Hughes, 1880s; Charlotte Jewell, 1880s; Mary Luella Masters, 1890; Lucy Rider Mayer, 1880s; Florence Nickerson, 1880s; Florence Perine, 1880s; Frederick M. Pyke, 1940; F. M. and Frances Pyke, 1945; Catharine E. Queal, 1880s; Mary Stone, 1880s; Lydia A. Trimble, 1880s; Frances O. Wheeler, 1880s; and Frances O. Wilson, 1893.

HUNTINGTON

HUNTINGTON COLLEGE

IN-45 United Brethren in Christ Archives
Huntington College Library
2303 College Avenue
Huntington IN 46750
(219) 356-6000
Jane E. Mason, Archivist

Background note: In addition to the materials listed below, miscellaneous articles on United Brethren missions can be found in the Huntington College Archives. United Brethren work continued in Hong Kong after 1957.

1-GENERAL HOLDINGS
Background note: Yan Tze Chiu, of Lingnan University, began missionary work in the Canton area in 1924 under the Women's Missionary Association of the Church of the United Brethren in Christ. He was later a professor of chemistry at Huntington College.
MINUTES/RECORDS/REPORTS: Reports on the China mission field in the *Annual Reports and Minutes* of the Department of Missions of the Church of the United Brethren in Christ, 1924–57; miscellaneous annual reports with Yan Tze Chiu's letters (see CORRESPONDENCE below), 1956–69.
CORRESPONDENCE: 8 letters between Cora Loew, Women's Missionary Association secretary, and Moy Ling, concerning the possibility of missionary work in China, 1922–24; 365 letters between Yan Tze Chiu and the missionary secretaries, 1956–69; 5 letters between C. C. Au Yeung and Bishop Duane Reahm, 1969; letters from China missionaries reprinted in *Missionary Monthly*, 1924–54.
MANUSCRIPTS: "Christian Faith in China Today," by Y. T. Chiu, 1966.
PAMPHLETS: *China*, by Laura Shock, 1942; *Ka Fook*, by Mrs. K. Y. Tse, n.d.; *Kit Ling*, by Y. T. Chiu, n.d.; *May Ying*, by Mrs. Y. T. Chiu, n.d.; *Our Mission in China*, by Ellen Bowman, 1959; *Our Mission in China*, by Effie Hodgeboom, 1942; *Our Work in China*, 1922; *Present Work in China*, 1947; *The Way to Happiness*, a play by Mrs. Y. T. Chiu, ca. 1920s or 1930s.
AUDIO-VISUAL MATERIALS: 104 photos and postcards of views of China, staff, and pupils of Lingnan University, 1927–46; 38 photos of the Chiu family, 1930–66; unprocessed slide collection.
CHINESE LANGUAGE MATERIALS: 18 books of hymns and theological study, by Y. T. Chiu; 2 books by Clyde Meadows, 1950–51; unidentified Chinese book.
FINDING AIDS: In-house guide.

INDIANAPOLIS

BUTLER UNIVERSITY
IN–50 Irwin Library
4600 Sunset Avenue
Indianapolis IN 46208
(317) 283–9225
John Kondelik, Director

1-GENERAL HOLDINGS
SERIALS: *China Christian Year Book*, 1910, 1926–27.

CHRISTIAN CHURCH (DISCIPLES OF CHRIST)
IN–55 Library
222 South Downey Avenue
P. O. Box 1986
Indianapolis IN 46206
(317) 353–1491
Doris A. Kennedy, Librarian

1-GENERAL HOLDINGS
MINUTES/RECORDS/REPORTS: Christian Literature Society for China, annual report, 1927–40; Church of Christ in China, minutes, 1927, 1929, 1930, 1932; general council meeting, important actions, 1946; Stephen Jared Corey, report on China visit, 1927–28; Foreign Missions Conference of North America, Committee on East Asia, special mission to China, report, 1946; Luchowfu Christian Hospital, annual report, 1925–26, 1934–35, 1937–40; Nantungchow Christian Hospital, report, 1917–36; National Christian Council, Commission on Cooperation, report, 1933.
  National Christian Council of China: annual report, 1922–23, 1926–28; biennial report, 1929–33, 1937–46; Conference on Christianizing economic relations, report, 1927; constitution, 1929; Executive Committee and ad interim Committee, minutes, 1941–42; rural and literacy work, report, 1933; staff minutes, 1941–42; National Committee for Christian Religious Education in China, report, 1931; National Council of the Churches of Christ in the U.S.A., Division of Foreign Missions, Australian deputation, report, 1957; Peking United International Famine Relief Committee, Personnel Committee, International Cooperation, report, 1921.
  Tsong Ing Girls' School, catalogue, 1935; United Christian Missionary Society: China Mission estimates, 1929–31; constitution, 1925; executive committee statement and report of the China mission, 1922; handbook, 1907, 1917; reports, 1889–1931.
PAMPHLETS: 49 pamphlets, 1924–69, on Chinese civilization and culture, Chinese church, Christian education, cooperative church work, Disciples of Christ, Fan Village, lay service, missionary method and programs, Nanking population, National Christian Council, native Christians, travel, United Christian Missionary Society biographies, war, and west China.
SERIALS: *Central China Christian*, 1900–1909. *China Christian Year Book*, 1910–31, 1938–39. *Directory of Protestant Missions in China*, 1919, 1923. National Christian Council of China: *Broadcast Bulletin*, 1941–42; *China News Letter*, 1941; *Day by Day*, 1941–42; *Special Orient Bulletin*, 1942–43.

CHRISTIAN THEOLOGICAL SEMINARY
IN–60 Library
1000 West 42nd Street
Box 88267
Indianapolis IN 46208
(317) 924–1331
Les R. Galbraith, Director

1-ABRAM EDWARD CORY PAPERS, 1902–3, 2 volumes
Background note: Abram Edward Cory (1873–1952) served as a missionary to China under the Foreign Christian Missionary Society.
DIARIES: 2 diaries by Cory on his mission experiences, 1902–3.
FINDING AIDS: In-house guide (also available at the Disciples of Christ Historical Society, Library and Archives, 1101 Nineteenth Avenue South, Nashville, TN, 37212, and at the Indiana State Library, Indiana Division, 140 North Senate Avenue, Indianapolis, IN, 48204).

2-GENERAL HOLDINGS
MANUSCRIPTS: ''Missions in Far Eastern Cultural Relations,'' by Miner Searle Bates, 1942.
PAMPHLETS: *Far West in China,* by Stanton Lautenschlager, 1941; *The Systematic Destruction of the Catholic Church in China,* by Thomas J. Bauer, 1954.
SERIALS: *Central China Christian,* 1906. *China Bulletin,* 1952–62. *China Christian Year Book,* 1910, 1912–35, 1938–39. *Chinese Recorder,* 1869–1941.

IN–65   INDIANA STATE LIBRARY
   140 North Senate Avenue
   Indianapolis IN 48204
   (317) 232–3675
   Charles Ray Ewick, Director

Background note: In addition to the items listed below, the Indiana State Library also holds a copy of the guide to the Abram Edward Cory Papers, located at the Christian Theological Seminary Library, 1000 West 42nd Street, Indianapolis, IN, 46208.

1-GENERAL HOLDINGS
SERIALS: American Friends Service Committee, *Bulletin on Work in China,* 1942–44.

INDIANA UNIVERSITY
IN–70   School of Medicine Library
   635 Barnhill Drive
   Indianapolis IN 46223
   (317) 274-7182
   Fran Brahmi, Head of Reference

1-GENERAL HOLDINGS
SERIALS: *China Medical Journal,* 1917–19, 1928–31. *Chinese Medical Journal,* 1932–51, 1957–66, 1973–75, 1979, 1983–.

MARION

WORLD GOSPEL MISSION
IN–75   Archives
   Box 948
   Marion IN 46952
   (317) 664-7331 Ext. 353
   Jean Tucker, Publications Director

Background note: Begun as the National Holiness Missionary Society in China in 1910, the World Gospel Mission expanded its work to other countries in 1931. Work on the mainland ended in 1952. The records are organized in looseleaf binders and catalogued.

1-GENERAL HOLDINGS
MINUTES/RECORDS/REPORTS: 2 looseleaf volumes of records of the National Holiness Missionary Society and the World Gospel Mission, 1900–1952.
CORRESPONDENCE: Large looseleaf volume of letters from National Holiness Missionary Society and World Gospel Mission missionaries, including Dr. and Mrs. James Bishop, L. Leona Aggola, Ruth Benton, Amy Brown, Pearl Congdon, Mr. and Mrs. Clifford Cooley, Bessie Cordell, Clara Cortmeyer, Mr. and Mrs.

Dixon, Catherine Flagler, Rebecca Fleming, Edith Glenk, Rev. and Mrs. Harold Good, Miriam Gregory, Esther Gulley, Mary Hill, Gayle Kaiser, Mr. and Mrs. B. J. Kronenburg, Mr. and Mrs. C. C. James, Mr. and Mrs. John Moe, Lillian Morrison, and Earle and Eva Newton, 1926–38.
MANUSCRIPTS: 7 looseleaf volumes of manuscripts on work in China by National Holiness Missionary Society and the World Gospel Mission missionaries, 1900–1952.
AUDIO-VISUAL MATERIALS: 2 large looseleaf photo albums containing photos of National Holiness Missionary Society and World Gospel Mission missionaries to China, 1900–1952.
SERIALS: *Call to Prayer,* 1900- (exclusively on China until 1930—China coverage ends in 1952).
CHINESE LANGUAGE MATERIALS/MEMORABILIA/AUDIO-VISUAL MATERIALS: ''China—Land and Culture,'' 2 looseleaf scrapbooks containing clippings, some in Chinese, from Chinese newspapers, photos, maps, and pamphlets on China, 1900–1952; ''China—Its Peoples,'' a looseleaf scrapbook containing clippings, some in Chinese, from Chinese newspapers, and photos of the Chinese, 1900–1952.

MISHAWAKA

BETHEL COLLEGE
IN–80   Library
   1001 West McKinley Avenue
   Mishawaka IN 46544
   (219) 259-8511 Ext. 333
   Dennis C. Tucker, Director

Background note: Formed in 1969 through a merger of the United Missionary Church and the Missionary Church Association, the Missionary Church is evangelical and conservative. See also International Headquarters of the Missionary Church, Archives, 3901 South Wayne Avenue, Fort Wayne, IN, 46807.

1-MISSIONARY CHURCH HISTORY COLLECTION, 1891–1951,
   quantity undetermined
MINUTES/RECORDS/REPORTS: Reports from United Missionary Church missionaries in China, 1891–1951; records of the China mission in United Missionary Church periodicals, *Gospel Banner,* 1895–1951, and *Missionary Banner,* 1938–51.
CORRESPONDENCE: Ca. 1 folder each of letters from United Missionary Church missionaries to China: Daniel Brenneman, Bessie Cordell, William Shantz, and Calvin F. and Phoebe (Brenneman) Snyder, 1895–1951.
AUDIO-VISUAL MATERIALS: Photos of United Missionary Church missionaries to China, and Chinese civilization and culture.

NORTH MANCHESTER

MANCHESTER COLLEGE
IN–85   Funderberg Library
   College Avenue
   North Manchester IN 46962
   (219) 982-2141
   Robin J. Gratz, Reference Librarian

1-BRETHREN COLLECTION—CHURCH OF THE BRETHREN, MISSIONS, 1908–59, 6 items
Background note: See also Church of the Brethren General Board, Brethren Historical Library and Archives, 1451 Dundee Avenue, Elgin, IL, 60120.
PAMPHLETS: *A Brief History of the Church of the Brethren in China (1908–1959)*, n.a., n.d.; *China—A Challenge to the Church: Appeals from the Church of the Brethren in China*, n.a., 1919; *The Preparation of Missionaries Appointed to China: The Report of a Committee Appointed by the Board of Missionary Preparation*, n.a., 1914; *Twice Born Women: A Sketch of the Evangelistic Work of the Church of the Brethren as Conducted among Women in India and China*, n.a., n.d.
SERIALS: *Star of Cathay*, 1939–40.
DISSERTATIONS/THESES: *Devolution of Missionary Administration in China*, by Herbert Spenser Minnich, 1926.

NOTRE DAME

UNIVERSITY OF NOTRE DAME

IN–90　Archives
　　　607 Memorial Library
　　　Notre Dame IN 46556
　　　(219) 239–6447/6448
　　　Wendy Clauson Schlereth, Director

1-FATHER V. A. SCHOEFFLER, 1846–49, 1 item
Background note: V. A. Schoeffler was a French apostolic missionary to Ton King, Vietnam.
CORRESPONDENCE: Letter from V. A. Schoeffler, in Hong Kong, describing his ocean voyage and Hong Kong, ca. 1846–1849.

IN–95　Memorial Library
　　　University of Notre Dame
　　　Notre Dame IN 46556
　　　(219) 239–5252
　　　C. Ann Lonie, Reference Librarian

1-GENERAL HOLDINGS
MANUSCRIPTS: "The Catholic Church in China: Research Backgrounder," n.a., 1960; "The Catholic Church in Mainland China," a collection of seven articles by Leon Triviere, 1959.
PAMPHLETS: *Catholic Church Activities in War Afflicted China*, by the China Information Committee, 1938?; *The Catholic Missions in China during the Middle Ages, 1294–1368*, by Paul Stanislaus Hsiang, 1949; *Windows into China: The Jesuits and Their Books, 1580–1730*, by John Parker, 1978.
ORAL HISTORIES: *China Missionaries Oral History Collection*, ed. by Cyrus H. Peake and Arthur L. Rosenbaum (Claremont Graduate School, Oral History Program), 1973. See ORAL HISTORIES Union List for the names of participants.
SERIALS: *China Christian Year Book*, 1910–39. *China Notes*, 1962-. *Chinese Recorder*, 1868–1941. *Educational Review*, 1907–38. *Lingnan Science Journal*, 1922–45. Université de l'Aurore, *Bulletin*, 1947–49. *Variétés Sinologiques*, 1914.
DISSERTATIONS/THESES: *Apostolic Legations to China of the Eighteenth Century*, by Antonio Sisto Rosso, 1948. *The Anti-Christian Movement in China, 1922–1927: With Special Reference to the Experience of Protestant Missions*, by Ka-che Yip, 1970. *China and Educational Autonomy: The Changing Role of the Protestant Educational Missionary in China, 1807–1937*, by Alice Henrietta Gregg, 1945. *The Chinese State and the Catholic Church: The Politics of Religion within the Confucian-Sectarian Dynamic*, by Eric Osborne Hanson, 1976. *Imperial Government and Catholic Missions in China during the Years 1784–1785*, by Bernward Henry Willeke, 1948. *John Leighton Stuart: The Mind and Life of an American Missionary in China, 1876–1941*, by Yu-ming Shaw, 1975. *Missionary Intelligence from China: American Protestant Reports, 1930–1950*, by Bruce Stephen Greenawalt, 1974. *The Modern Phase and Conclusion of the Chinese Rites Controversy*, by George Hisaharu Minamiki, 1977. *The Negotiations between Ch'i-ying and Lagrené, 1844–1846*, by Angelus Francis J. Grosse-Aschhoff, 1950. *La Politique missionnaire de la France en Chine, 1842–1856; l'ouverture des cinq ports chinois au commerce étranger et la liberté religieuse*, by Louis Tsing-sing Wei, 1960. *The Protestant Missionary Understanding of the Chinese Situation and the Christian Task from 1890 to 1911*, by C. William Mensendiek, 1958.
CHINESE LANGUAGE MATERIALS/SERIALS: *Chên li yü shêng ming yüeh k'an (Truth and Life Journal)*, 1927–36.

RICHMOND

EARLHAM COLLEGE
IN–100　Lilly Library
　　　Richmond IN 47374
　　　(317) 962–6561 Ext. 360
　　　James R. Kennedy, Jr., Reference Librarian

1-GENERAL HOLDINGS
PAMPHLETS: *The Catholic Missions in China during the Middle Ages, 1294–1368*, by Paul Stanislaus Hsiang, 1949.
SERIALS: American Friends Service Committee, *Bulletin on Work in China*, 1942–44. *Variétés Sinologiques*, 1985.

SAINT MARY-OF-THE-WOODS

SISTERS OF PROVIDENCE
IN–105　Archives
　　　Saint Mary-of-the-Woods IN 47876
　　　(812) 535–3131 Ext. 211
　　　Sister Ann Kathleen Brawley, Archivist

1-SISTER CARMEL BAKER COLLECTION, 1931–48, 3 items
CORRESPONDENCE: Letter from Sr. M. Baptista, S.S.J., to Sr. Carmel referring to Sr. Marie Gratia's trip to Taiwan in order to relocate her mission work, 1948.
DIARIES: Sr. Carmel Baker's journal of her trip to China and her work in Kaifeng, 1931–38, describing the progress of the Ching-I Middle School, student and teacher protests, anti-foreignism, the Japanese invasion and occupation of Kaifeng, and refugees at Ching-I; Sr. Carmel Baker's journal of her work in Peiping, 1945–48, describing the purchase of a house and establishment of the order in Peiping, the spread of Communist activity, and the death of Sr. Elizabeth Cecile in 1947.
FINDING AIDS: In-house inventory.

2-CHINA/TAIWAN COLLECTION, 1920–67, 11 l.f.

Restrictions: Permission of the archivist required to research the correspondence of Sr. Eugene Marie Howard and Sr. Mary Evangela O'Neill.

MINUTES/RECORDS/REPORTS: Code used by the sisters during World War II; contract with the Diocese of Kaifeng and Archbishop Tacconi, 1920; enrollment figures for Ching-I Middle School, 1947; copy of a questionnaire requested by the Propagation of the Faith for a study sponsored by the Vatican, 1920–42; notes on the Archbishop's first visitation, 1931; summary of the sisters' work in China, 1947.

CORRESPONDENCE: Correspondence of Sr. Carmel Baker, 1931–62; correspondence of Sr. Joseph Henry Boyle, 1923–27; correspondence from Sr. Berchmans Collins in Kaifeng, 1931; correspondence of Sr. Theodata Haggerty, 1936–48; correspondence of Bruno Hagspiel, S.V.D., 1923–29; correspondence of Sr. Elizabeth Cecile Harbison, 1934–38, 1947–48; correspondence of Sr. Eugene Marie Howard, 1920–27; correspondence of Sr. Mary Liguori (Mary Loretta) Hartigan, 1929–68; miscellaneous correspondence, 1920–47, including letters of F. H. Clougherty, O.S.B., 1920–29; letters of Sr. Marie Gratia Luking, 1902–8, 1923–63, including correspondence with her family, a 1948 letter discussing the death of Sr. Theodata Haggerty, and letters written in 1953 to Sr. St. Francis; letters from Sr. Marie Gratia and other sisters in Shanghai, 1948; letter from Fr. Ildephonse, O.S.B., 1927, on the opening of a new school in Tientsin; letter from Noble Johnson, M.C., on the closing of a school in Kaifeng by the Japanese, 1939; correspondence of Edward McCarthy, 1920–21; correspondence of Sr. Agatha McFadden, 1931–35; correspondence of Bishop Thomas M. Megan of Sinsiang, including a request for a school in Sinsiang and a copy of a letter from Bishop Megan on the internment of sisters and priests at Wei Hsien, Shanghai, by the Japanese, 1937–43; correspondence of Sr. Clare Mitchell, 1920–30, including an account of her trip to and early years in China; correspondence of Sr. Winifred Patrice O'Donovan, 1920–25; correspondence of Sr. Mary Evangela O'Neill, 1937–48; correspondence of Msgr. Michael J. Read, Secretary of the NCWC, 1937–42; letter from Ralph Reilly, O.F.M., requesting sisters for Shasi, 1937; correspondence of Sr. Mary Elise Reno, 1919–23; letters sent to Mrs. L. Mahoney, sister of Sr. Mary Elise, after her death, 1923; correspondence of Sr. Monica Marie Rigani, 1934–46; correspondence of Sr. Francis de Sales Russell from Kaifeng, Sinsiang, and Taiwan, 1934–59; correspondence from Sr. St. Francis Schultz, in Kaifeng, Shanghai, and Taiwan, 1934–66; correspondence of Sr. Marie Patricia Shortall, from Kaifeng, Dairen, Korea, and Peiping, 1920–45, and a copy of a letter to Sr. Marie Patricia from Sr. Marie Gratia, 1949; copy of letter announcing the sisters' departure to Taiwan, 1948; correspondence of Vicar Apostolic Joseph N. Tacconi in Kaifeng, 1920–36; correspondence of Sr. Agnes Loyola Wolf, 1936–70; correspondence of Sr. Ann Colette Wolf, 1947–67; letters from Teresa Yang to Sr. Eugene Marie Howard, 1920–31.

DIARIES: Unidentified diary, ca. 1931; Sr. Ann Colette Wolf's diary, 1946–67; Kaifeng diary by Sr. Carmel, 1931; excerpts from journal of Sr. Theodata, 1937–38.

MANUSCRIPTS: History of the China mission by Sr. Mary Liguori Hartigan, 1920–56; account of her trip to China by Sr. Eugene Marie Howard, 1920; "History of the Foundation of Providence in China," by Sr. Marie Gratia, 1920.

MEMORABILIA: Newspaper accounts describing the death of Sr. Elizabeth Cecile Harbison in a plane crash in Tsingtao, 1947; newspaper account from Peking and Tientsin describing Sr. Joseph Henry Boyle's travels; newspaper account of the deaths of Sr. Theodata Haggerty and Sr. Theodore, P.C., 1948; newspaper clippings and magazine articles belonging to Sr. Francis Schultz, n.d., describing mission work on the mainland and Taiwan; clippings belonging to Sr. Eugene Marie, 1920–31.

AUDIO-VISUAL MATERIALS: 2 photos of Sr. Francis Schultz, n.d.; photo of Sr. Francis de Sales and Sr. St. Francis, n.d.; snapshots by Sr. Eugene Marie, 1920–31.

SERIALS: *Bugle Call*, 1923. *Ching I Digest*, 1940–42.

CHINESE LANGUAGE MATERIALS: 4 unidentified pamphlets.

FINDING AIDS: In-house inventory.

3-SISTER THEODATA HAGGERTY COLLECTION, 1937–38, 2 folders

MINUTES/RECORD/REPORTS: Data sheet recording treatment of the wounded and baptisms in Kaifeng, 1937.

CORRESPONDENCE: Excerpts from Sr. Theodata Haggerty's letters, 1937.

DIARIES: Sr. Theodata's journal of her trip to China and life in Kaifeng, 1937–38, describing air raids, bombings, evacuation to Sinsiang, and the care of wounded soldiers, refugees, and orphans; excerpts from Sr. Theodata's journal, 1937.

4-SISTER MARY LIGUORI (MARY LORETTA) HARTIGAN COLLECTION, 1920–56, 4 folders

MANUSCRIPTS: Daily account of the sisters' mission in China by Sr. Mary Liguori Hartigan, based on information from the foundress and her companions, correspondence, and the experiences of Sr. Mary Liguori and her companions, 1920–27; account of the establishment of the sisters' China mission covering the years 1920 to 1924, n.a., n.d.; "Historical Account of the China Mission of the Sisters of Providence," by Sr. Mary Liguori, 1926–56.

5-MOTHER MARIE GRATIA (JOSEPHINE) LUKING COLLECTION, 1920–64, 1.5 l.f.

Background note: Mother Marie Gratia Luking established the Ching-I Middle School for Girls in Kaifeng in 1920, and served as directress from 1920 to 1949. After the Communist takeover she continued her mission work in Taiwan.

CORRESPONDENCE: 26 folders of administrative correspondence from Sr. Marie Gratia to the Superior General at Saint Mary-of-the-Woods, 1920–43, 1945–47.

DIARIES: Daily record of her activities from 1920 to 1925 in the manuscript history by Sr. Marie Gratia described below.

MANUSCRIPTS: "History of Providence in China," by Sr. Marie Gratia, 1920–25, containing decriptions of Chinese life and culture, the death of Sr. Mary Elise, Sr. Marie Gratia's work during this period, and educational programs at Ching-I Middle School; a copy of "History of Providence in China" with some revisions, n.a., 1925; "Chronology of Providence in China and Taiwan, 1919–65," n.a., 1925–65.

PAMPHLETS: Uncatalogued brochures and catalogues, n.d.

MEMORABILIA: Scrapbooks and newspaper clippings, 1920–64, containing information about and accounts of the deaths of Srs. Mary Elise, Agatha McFadden, Elizabeth Cecile Harbison, Theodata Haggerty, and Mother Marie Gratia; miscellaneous uncatalogued memorabilia, n.d.

MAPS/DESIGNS/DRAWINGS: Map of Kaifeng, 1939; interior and exterior plans of the Providence in China compound at Kaifeng, n.d.; construction plans, n.d.

AUDIO-VISUAL MATERIALS: Photos, n.d., of students, activities, buildings, the Ching-I Middle School, class and other group pictures, parades, Chinese funerals, athletic events, and the Providence Catechist sisters in Kaifeng.

CHINESE LANGUAGE MATERIALS: Golden Jubilee book, Providence in China, 1920–70.

FINDING AIDS: In-house inventory.

6-SISTER MARY EVANGELA O'NEILL COLLECTION, ca. 1926–1948, 29 folders

MINUTES/RECORDS/REPORTS: Miscellaneous accounts, n.d.

CORRESPONDENCE: Folder of correspondence with Sr. Berchmans Collins, n.d.; letter signed "Don," n.d.; folder of correspondence with Sr. Margaretta Grussinger, n.d.; folder of correspondence with Bruno Hagspiel, S.V.D., and Cardinal Tien, n.d.; folder of correspondence with Sr. Elizabeth Cecile Harbison, n.d.; folder of correspondence (originals and copies) with Sr. Marie Gratia, n.d.; folder of correspondence with and about Sr. Mary Elise Reno, including letters from Bruno Hagspiel, S.V.D., and Sr. Agnes Clare, n.d.; folder of correpondence with Sr. Francis de Sales Russell, n.d.; folder of correspondence with Sr. St. Francis Schultz, n.d.; folder of correspondence with Sr. Marie Patricia Shortall, n.d.; folder of correspondence with Sr. Agnes Loyola Wolf, n.d.; letter to the Sisters of Providence in Ruille, n.d.; folder of letters and telegrams dealing with Sr. Mary Evangela's departure in 1920.

DIARIES: Sr. Mary Evangela's journal, 1936; Sr. Elizabeth Cecile Harbison's diary, n.d.; Sr. Agnes Loyola Wolf, diary, n.d.

MANUSCRIPTS: "From the Wabash to the Huang Ho," by Sr. Eugene Marie Howard, n.d.; a story about Sr. Agnes Joan Li, n.d.; 2 copies of "The History of Providence in China," by Sr. Marie Gratia, 1920–25.

MEMORABILIA: Bishop's sermon from the departure ceremony, n.d.; article on the sisters' work in Kaifeng by Father Cahill, n.d.; article by Sr. Mary Elise Reno, n.d.; materials concerning a mission rally, 1932; newspaper clippings on the first group of sisters going to China, n.d.

MAPS/DESIGNS/DRAWINGS: Map of Kaifeng, 1939; plans and sketches of the Providence in China mission compound by Sr. Mary Evangela, n.d.

AUDIO-VISUAL MATERIALS: Folder of photos, n.d.

SERIALS: Catholic University of Peking, *Bulletin*, 1926, 1928.

FINDING AIDS: In-house inventory.

7-SISTER MARY JOSEPH POMEROY COLLECTION, ca. 1939–1954, 16 folders

Background note: This partially processed collection contains materials relating to the sisters' mission in Taichung and 1 folder of miscellaneous materials in addition to the items listed below.

MINUTES/RECORDS/REPORTS: Accounts for *Bugle Call*, n.d.; annual reports, n.d.; copies of loans made by the Swiss Government to sisters in internment, 1944–45; mission accounts, receipts, and check stubs, n.d.; statements from the U.S. government, 1942–48; records concerning transfer of funds, 1947–53.

CORRESPONDENCE: Letters related to the financial transactions described above, 1942–53; folder of correspondence of the Mission Secretariat, n.d.; folder of miscellaneous correspondence,

n.d.; folder of correspondence with the NCWC, and a copy of a letter from the State Department, n.d.; letters from Kaifeng, 1939–40, 1947.

AUDIO-VISUAL MATERIALS: Ca. 1 folder of photos from Peiping, 1946.

FINDING AIDS: In-house inventory.

8-PROVIDENCE CATECHIST SOCIETY RECORDS, 1929-, .5 l.f.

Background note: This group of religious women was established by Sister Marie Gratia in 1929. It was made up of native Chinese trained by the Sisters of Providence and closely associated with them in their work in Kaifeng and Taiwan. In 1962 they became an independent religious congregation with "Pontifical" status. This collection of their records is unprocessed.

MINUTES/RECORDS/REPORTS: Providence Catechist Society, records, 1929-.

9-SISTER FRANCIS DE SALES RUSSELL COLLECTION, 1934–59, 4 folders

CORRESPONDENCE: Folder of correspondence of Sr. Francis de Sales Russell, 1934–59.

MANUSCRIPTS: "Stories of Chinese Martyrs," by Sr. Francis de Sales Russell, 1946; "The Story of Providence in China," by Sr. Francis de Sales Russell, n.d. (historical account of Providence in China, describing the early days of the mission, exile, schools, the mission's orphanage, the Japanese invasion, and the establishment by Sr. Marie Gratia of the Providence Catechist Society), 1940; account of the work of priest missionaries in China, n.a., ca. 1925.

FINDING AIDS: In-house register.

10-SISTER FRANCIS SCHULTZ COLLECTION, 1919–66, 3 folders, 14 volumes

MINUTES/RECORDS/REPORTS: Official documents in Sr. Francis Schultz's diaries, 1920–66.

CORRESPONDENCE: Correspondence of Sr. Francis with her sister, Valentine, clergy, and other missionaries, 1934–66, including a description of her internment by the Japanese at Camp Weihsien; personal letters to sisters included in Sr. Francis' diaries, 1920–66.

DIARIES: Day-by-day account in 9 volumes (both original and typescript copy) of Sr. Francis' experiences in Kaifeng, 1934–49, including a description of her work at Ching-I Middle School, completed in 1972.

MANUSCRIPTS: Chronology of Sisters of Providence in Kaifeng, China, and other areas, 1920–49, by Sr. Francis Schultz, n.d.; China/Taiwan chronology, 1919–65.

AUDIO-VISUAL MATERIALS: Photos of students included in Sr. Francis' diaries, 1920–66.

11-SISTER ST. FRANCIS SCHULTZ COLLECTION, 1917–70, 73 folders, 1 box

Background note: This collection contains materials relating to the sisters' mission in Taiwan in addition to the items listed below.

MINUTES/RECORDS REPORTS: Account book, n.d.; travel permit for Sr. Carmel Baker, n.d.

CORRESPONDENCE: Folder of letters from Sr. St. Francis to her sister, Valentine, 1920–70; folder of reference letters for former students, n.d.; portion of a letter describing the Japanese occupation, n.d.; letter from Kaifeng Bishop authorizing the conferral of a habit, 1948; folder of letters in French, n.d.; folder of letters and telegrams relating to the death and funeral of Sr. Mary Elizabeth Harbison, 1947; folder of letters to Sr. Marie Gratia from various persons, n.d.; folder of letters of various sisters of Providence in China, 1945–46; folder of letters from Sr. Agnes Loyola Wolf to her family, 1917–42, and a postcard from Sr. Agnes Loyola during her internment; folder of letters relating to death of Mother Marie Gratia, n.d..

DIARIES: Sr. St. Francis' diary and chronology of the China mission, 1948–51; diary notes of Sr. Agnes Joan Li, 1941–42; diary of Sr. Agnes Loyola Wolf, n.d.

MANUSCRIPTS: "Our Trip from Tokyo," by Srs. Joseph Henry and Mary Margaretta, n.d.; folder of notes relating to the internment camp at Weihsien; folder of notes relating to the church in Kaifeng, n.d.; "Missionary in China," n.a., n.d.; folder of miscellaneous notes on the China mission and Taiwan, n.d.; "Providence in North Honan," n.a., n.d.; "The Work of the Sisters of Providence in China," n.a., n.d.; folder of spiritual notes, n.d.

PAMPHLETS: Folder of leaflets and offprints on the Cultural Revolution, ca. 1970; folder of SMWC brochures mentioning Sr. St. Francis, n.d.

MAPS/DESIGNS/DRAWINGS: Diagram of the Providence in China compound, n.d.; drawing given in memory of English lessons in Weihsien, n.d.

AUDIO-VISUAL MATERIALS: 2 folders of photos from the mainland and Taiwan, n.d.; folder of photos of the Ching-I Middle School's Board of Directors, including Sr. Agnes Joan Li's father, n.d.; folder of photos of bishops, priests, seminarians, and parishioners, n.d.; folder of photos from the mainland, including views of Peking, n.d.; 4 folders of photos from Ching-I Middle School in Kaifeng, n.d., including pictures of teachers, students, workers, athletic events, buildings, construction, and refugees; folder of photos relating to the funerals of Srs. Mary Elise and Agatha, n.d.; folder of family pictures from Kaifeng, n.d.; folder of pictures of bound feet, n.d.; 2 folders of photos of sisters' and alumnae's friends and relatives, n.d.; folder of photos of Chinese funerals, n.d.; folder of photos from Kaifeng, n.d., including pictures of beggars, buildings, street scenes, anti-foreign demonstrations, and parades; 2 folders of miscellaneous photos, n.d.; folder of photos of mission exhibits, n.d.; folder of photos related to Holy Childhood Orphanage, n.d.; folder of photos related to the Providence Catechists at Nan Kuan, n.d., including pictures of sisters, novices, postulants, and school children; folder of photos of the Providence in China compound, n.d.; folder of photos of other religious congregations in China, n.d.; folder of photos of various sisters of the China mission, n.d., including pictures of Chinese sisters and Mother M. Raphael; folder of photos of sisters departing for and arriving in China, 1920, ca. 1936; folder of photos of Chinese virgins, n.d.; 5 photos of Sr. Eugene Marie and her family, n.d.; photo of the grave of Sr. Mary Elise, n.d.; photo of an unidentified Benedictine priest, n.d.; photo of the foundresses of the Kaifeng Mission and Chinese virgins, n.d.; photo of Father Clougherty with a baptismal class of men, n.d.; photo of the Ying family, n.d.; class and other group photos from Ching-I Middle School, n.d.; photo of young girls (perhaps orphans) with dolls, n.d.

CHINESE LANGUAGE MATERIALS: Folder of religious and language textbooks, n.d.; folder of letters (one with English translation appended) to Sr. St. Francis from the principal at Ching-I Middle School, 1948; folder of miscellaneous materials, n.d.; 2 volumes of regulations from the Ministry of Education, n.d.; a

New Testament, n.d.; posters against the practice of foot-binding, n.d.

FINDING AIDS: Card catalogue.

12-SISTER AGNES LOYOLA WOLF COLLECTION, 1937–41, 1 folder
MINUTES/RECORDS/REPORTS: Code used by the sisters during World War II, 1941.
CORRESPONDENCE: Correspondence of Sr. Agnes Loyola Wolf in Kaifeng with her family, 1937–38.
DIARIES: Excerpt from Sr. Agnes Loyola's diary, 1937–38.

13-SISTER ANN COLETTE WOLF MANUSCRIPT, 1946–67, 1 folder
MANUSCRIPTS: Account of the sisters' last years in Kaifeng and the establishment of their mission in Taiwan, by Sr. Ann Colette Wolf, 1946–67.

UPLAND

TAYLOR UNIVERSITY
IN–110 Archives

Ayres Alumni Memorial Library
Upland IN 46989
(317) 998–2751 Ext. 241
Roger Phillips, Reference Librarian

1-WORLD GOSPEL MISSION COLLECTION, ca. 1925–45, 1 box
Background note: The World Gospel Mission was known as the National Holiness Association Missionary Society from ca. 1925 to ca. 1945.
MINUTES/RECORDS/REPORTS: Consultation of World Evangelization, report, 1980.
PAMPHLETS: *What Is the Truth about China?*, by Walter H. Judd, 1945; China information tract/booklet, by the National Holiness Association, n.d.; envelope of tracts and pamphlets on Chinese gods; *The Tientsin Bible School: A Center of Spiritual Power and Influence in China*, by the National Holiness Association Missionary Society, n.d.; miscellaneous unidentified "booklets."
MEMORABILIA: Clipping on John Jacob Trachsel, 1943; 3 newspaper clippings on missionary Cecil W. Troxel, 1943–44; poster for the Tientsin Bible School, 1936; American Bible Society Poster, *Rejoicing in Hope*; cloth/cardboard cross; card bearing Matthew 1:23; brightly colored sheets with figures; banner from the Christian Book Room, Shanghai; printed banner.
MAPS/DESIGNS/DRAWINGS: "Sketch of the Thirteen Tombs of the Ming Emperors," a bi-lingual map; unidentifed map sketch; map of National Holiness Association Missionary Society mission goals.
AUDIO-VISUAL MATERIALS: Picture of "'way' from death to life"; photo of John Jacob Trachsel and his daughter, Carol, 1943; posters with illustrated Bible phrases; Religious Tract Society posters, Hankow and Shanghai; other unidentified posters and pictures, some on cloth.
SERIALS: *Bulletin of the Tientsin Bible Seminary*, 1938–39.
CHINESE LANGUAGE MATERIALS: 43 Bibles; kuoyü primer; 3 children's books; study books and exercises; small Bible booklet; box of Chinese (kuoyü) flash cards; Christian literature on the war;

character drill cards of the College of Chinese Studies; book with "cut-out" objects; 3 cloth/cardboard hearts containing Chinese flashcards; card with Chinese letters.

WEST LAFAYETTE

PURDUE UNIVERSITY
IN-115 Humanities, Social Science, and Education Library
Stewart Center
West Lafayette IN 47907
(317) 494-2900
Laszlo Kovacs, Head

1-GENERAL HOLDINGS
SERIALS: *Lingnan Science Journal*, 1924-29, 1945. *Peking Natural History Bulletin*, 1930-41.

WINONA LAKE

FREE METHODIST CHURCH OF NORTH AMERICA
IN-120 Marston Memorial Historical Center of the Free Methodist Church
901 College Avenue
Winona Lake IN 46590
(219) 267-7656
Evelyn Mottweiler, Librarian

Restrictions: Access by appointment.

1-MISSION FIELD MATERIALS IN STOREROOM BOOKCASE—E. P. ASHCRAFT, 1904-52, 22 items
DIARIES: E. P. Ashcraft's diaries, 1931, 1945-48.
MANUSCRIPTS: Deputation notebook, 1949-52; prayer list notebook, 1952; sermon notebook, n.d.; "Book of Memories," n.a., n.d.; "Memory Book," containing pictures and autographs, by Harriet Ashcraft (Mrs. E. P. Ashcraft), 1939-43.
MEMORABILIA: Greek New Testament, 1904; Bible, 1945; Harriet Ashcraft's Bible, dated 1928, 1950, 1958; China clippings, 1921-38; magazine pictures of Chinese life, with notes, 1920; hymnal, n.d.; miscellaneous Chinese artifacts.
MAPS/DESIGNS/DRAWINGS: Map of China by E. P. Ashcraft, n.d.
AUDIO-VISUAL MATERIALS: Picture album, 1925-27.
CHINESE LANGUAGE MATERIALS: Phonetic Chinese Bible, n.d.; "Chinese Characters Copied from Jewish Historical Tablets," n.d.

2-MISSION FIELD MATERIALS IN STOREROOM BOOKCASE—KATE LEINENGER, 1916-69, 6 items
MANUSCRIPTS: 2 memory books by Kate Leinenger, 1956-63.
PAMPHLETS: Memorial booklet on Kate Leinenger, 1969.
MEMORABILIA: Chinese purse and coins, n.d.; Bible, n.d.
AUDIO-VISUAL MATERIALS: China pictures, 1916-51.
CHINESE LANGUAGE MATERIALS: New Testament, n.d.

3-MISSION FIELD MATERIALS IN STOREROOM BOOKCASE—GENEVA SAYRE, 1918-69, 21 items
MINUTES/RECORDS/REPORTS: Official papers, China, 1945-50.
DIARIES: Geneva Sayre's diaries, 1922-24, 1931.
MANUSCRIPTS: "Memory Book—Cavalcade of Missions," by Geneva Sayre, 1969.
MEMORABILIA: Scrapbooks, 1921; passports, n.d.; miscellaneous artifacts.
MAPS/DESIGNS/DRAWINGS: Silk sketch of a church, n.d.
AUDIO-VISUAL MATERIALS: "Taiwan Album," by Geneva Sayre, n.d.; pictures of Taiwanese nationals and missionaries, n.d.; pictures of funeral of "Grandma Wang," a Chinese Christian, n.d.; Chinese pictures, 1918-32; pictures, mostly of Tainan church, Formosa, n.d.

4-MISSION FIELD MATERIALS IN STOREROOM BOOKCASE—VARIOUS, 1854-1942, 15 items
AUDIO-VISUAL MATERIALS: Photo album by Bernie Wood, 1916-41.
MEMORABILIA: Scrapbook of Tidings articles, by Laura (?) Appleton, n.d.; scrapbook on China, by Appleton, n.d.; Mattie Peterson's Bible, 1942; scrapbook on the Peterson family, compiled by Geneva Sayre, n.d.; scrapbook on the early days in China, by Gertrude Keaslilg, n.d.; study books by Tom Bear, n.d.; 2 albums to "Effie," 1929.
CHINESE LANGUAGE MATERIALS: Mattie Peterson's hymn book, 1942; booklets, n.d.; China Annual Conference of the Free Methodist Church, reports, 1933; Pearl Schaffer's hymnbook and Bible, 1954; Bessie Reid Kresge's Bible, 1937; Pearl Reid's Mandarin Bible, n.d.

5-PAMPHLET FILES, 1905-1977, quantity undetermined
MINUTES/RECORDS/REPORTS: China Annual Conference of the Free Methodist Church, constitution, 1937.
CORRESPONDENCE: Ca. 100 letters from China missionaries E. P. and Harriet Ashcraft, 1942-47; Gertrude Groesbeck, 1948; Edith Frances Jones, 1907-45; Kate Leinenger, 1943-48; Florence Murray, 1950; Elmer Parsons, 1948; N. B. Peterson, 1907; Bessie Reid, 1939-1947; Pearl Reid, 1939-43, 1946-48; I. Stanley Ryding, 1943-51; Geneva Sayre, 1938-48; Pearl Schaffer, 1948-49; John Schlosser (son of Mary Schlosser), 19?-49; Mary Schlosser, 1925-49; James Hudson and Alice Taylor II, 1943-44; Irma Wickman, 1948; Bernie Wood, 1940; postcard from Edith Graves to her sister, 1907; 4 letters from Clara Leffingwell, 1903-5; letter from Mattie Peterson, 1935; letter from Pearl Reid, 1934; 4 letters from Mary O. Schlosser, 1946-47; letter from American Legation to Free Methodist Mission, 1911.
MANUSCRIPTS: "History of the Free Methodist Church in Taiwan," by Geneva Sayre, 1973; "Hakka Village," by Geneva Sayre, 1973; miscellaneous writings on China by Laura Appleton, n.d.; manuscript notes for her book, *On the Brink*, by Geneva Sayre, 1974; "Pioneer in Free Methodist Work in China," by Laura Appleton, n.d.; "Pioneering in China," by Laura Appleton, ca. 1938; sketches by Edith Graves of missionary colleagues E. P. and Harriet Ashcraft, Edith Frances Jones, Kate Leinenger, Florence Murray, Mattie Peterson, Paul Reid, I. S. W. Ryding, Geneva Sayre, Pearl Schaeffer, John and Mary Schlosser, and James Hudson and Alice Taylor II, 1906.

PAMPHLETS: *A Challenge from China*, by Frances Schlosser, 1940; *James Hudson Taylor II, God's Man in China*, by Leona Fear, n.d.; *Kaifeng Bible School, Free Methodist Church*, 1949; memorial folder on Grinnell Memorial Hospital, by John Dryer Green, 1937; *Our China Mission*, by Helen I. Root, 1932; *Our Church in China*, by Helen Root, 1932; 2 pamphlets from China missionaries, 1917, 1923; a tribute to Edith Frances Jones, by Mattie Peterson, 1951.

MEMORABILIA: Harriet Ashcraft's obituary, 1967; Edith Graves' metal slate; Edith Graves' notes on missionary colleagues, 1905–7; 4 rubbings from Chinese stone slabs, by E. P. Ashcraft, n.d.; missionaries' and elders' licenses, ordination service program, 1921; prayer letter, 1965; clipping on Lora Jones, 1980; visa for Lily Peterson, 1907; 3 clippings of tributes to Mattie Peterson on her death by Norman Edwards and Lydia Green, 1977.

MAPS/DESIGNS/DRAWINGS: 9 large charts and maps, 1936–51; 5 Bible study charts, 1922–41; map of China, with a "chart on the prophesies fulfilled concerning Jesus Christ," by E. P. Ashcraft, 1932; map of China by E. P. Ashcraft, 1924.

AUDIO-VISUAL MATERIALS: Photo of Edith Graves.

SERIALS: *Chinese Back to Jerusalem Evangelistic Band*, 1949. *Nurse in China*, 1946. *Praise and Prayer*, 1927–35, 1937.

CHINESE LANGUAGE MATERIALS: Metal slate bearing writing, n.d.

6-LILY AND MATTIE PETERSON CORRESPONDENCE FILE, 1906–41, ca. 200 items

Background note: Lily (d. 1908) and Mattie Peterson were Free Methodist missionaries in Cheng Chow.

CORRESPONDENCE: Several hundred letters to their parents from Lily Peterson, 1906–7, and Mattie Peterson, 1909–41; letters to the parents of Lily and Mattie Peterson from Free Methodist missionaries C. F. Appleton, 1906; Laura Appleton, 1908, 1913; Letitia Chandle, 1914; Edith Frances Jones, 1908–18; Aimee Millican, 1913–14; Laura Millican, 1906; Frank Millican, 1909; Bessie Reid, 1939; Pearl Schaffer, 1937; and Mary Schlosser, 1913.

7-WALTER A. SELLEW DIARIES, 1906–11, 2 items

Background note: Walter A. Sellew, a bishop of the Free Methodist Church, traveled to China in 1906 and 1911.

DIARIES: 1906 diary including passages describing his travels in Hong Kong, Shanghai, Hankow, Chang Chow, and Yen Cheng Shen; 1911 diary including passages describing his travels in Shanghai and Chengchow.

8-GENERAL HOLDINGS

MINUTES/RECORDS/REPORTS: Missionary Board records of China missionaries, 1905–51; reports on China mission in denominational periodical, *Missionary Tidings*, 1897–51.

CORRESPONDENCE: 6 file drawers of letters from Free Methodist missionaries in China, 1905–51; 2 file drawers of letters from Free Methodist missionaries in Taiwan.

DIARIES/MEMORABILIA/AUDIO-VISUAL MATERIALS: Ca. 9 l.f. of diaries, journals, notebooks, scrapbooks, and photo albums created by Free Methodist missionaries to China, 1907–51; several hundred loose photos and photo albums of Chinese civilization and culture, and Free Methodist missions and missionaries, n.d.

CHINESE LANGUAGE MATERIALS: *Songs of Victory* (Free

Methodist Church, Kaifeng, Honan), n.d.; prospectus of the Kaifeng Bible School, n.d.; Book of Discipline of the Free Methodist Church, n.d.

GRACE COLLEGE AND THEOLOGICAL SEMINARY
IN–125 Morgan Library
200 Seminary Drive
Winona Lake IN 46590
(219) 267–8191
Floyd M. Votaw, Head of Technical Services

1-GENERAL HOLDINGS

AUDIO-VISUAL MATERIALS: "Asia: Mt. 13: 1–8," an audio cassette by Herbert Kane, 1977.

DISSERTATIONS/THESES: *The Role of the Chinese Church in World Missions*, by Henry T. Ang, 1985.

IOWA

AMES

IOWA STATE UNIVERSITY
IA–5 University Library
Ames IA 50011
(515) 294–1442
Olivia Madison, Head, Monographs Department

1-GENERAL HOLDINGS

MINUTES/RECORDS/REPORTS: Christian Literature Society for China, annual report, 1907–8; University of Nanking, College of Agriculture and Forestry, annual report, 1922–34.

ORAL HISTORIES: *China Missionaries Oral History Collection*, ed. by Cyrus H. Peake and Arthur L. Rosenbaum (Claremont Graduate School, Oral History Program), 1973. See ORAL HISTORIES Union List for the names of participants.

SERIALS: Catholic University of Peking, *Bulletin*, 1926–34. *China Christian Advocate*, 1914–41. *China Christian Year Book*, 1910–39. China Inland Mission, *Occasional Papers*, 1872–75 (repr. 1973). *China Medical Journal*, 1887–1921. *China Mission Advocate*, 1839. *China Monthly*, 1941–50. *Chinese Medical Journal*, 1979-. *Chinese Repository*, 1832–51. *District of Anking Newsletter*, 1937–48. *Educational Review*, 1907–38. *Fenchow*, 1919–36. *The Foochow Messenger*, 1903–40. *Fukien Agricultural Journal*, 1948–51. Fukien Christian University, *Science Journal*, 1938. *Hainan Newsletter*, 1912–38, 1947–49. *Lingnan Science Journal*, 1922–48. Lingnan University, *Science Bulletin*, 1930–36, 1944. *Monumenta Serica*, 1935-. Natural History Society, *Proceedings*, 1928–30. *Newsletter of the Diocesan Association for Western China*, 1934–51. *Peking Natural History Bulletin*, 1926–

49. Peking Union Medical College, *Bibliography of the Publications from the Laboratories and Clinics*, 1915-33, 1939-40; *Contributions*, 1921-26. University of Nanking, College of Agriculture and Forestry, *Agriculture and Forestry Notes*, 1932-33; *Bulletin*, 1926, 1932-35; *Economic Facts*, 1936-46. West China Border Research Society, *Journal*, 1939-46. *West China Missionary News*, 1901-43. *Yenching Journal of Social Studies*, 1938-48, 1950.

CEDAR RAPIDS

COE COLLEGE
IA-10   Stewart Memorial Library
   1220 First Avenue, NE
   Cedar Rapids IA 52402
   (319) 399-8585
   Betty Rogers, Reference Librarian

1-GENERAL HOLDINGS
SERIALS: *China Mission Studies Bulletin*, 1979-.

DECORAH

LUTHER COLLEGE
IA-15   Archives
   Preus Library
   Decorah IA 52101
   (319) 387-1164
   Duane Fenstermann, Associate Librarian and Head of Technical Services

1-NIKOLAI ASTRUP LARSEN PAPERS, 1896-1967, 11 boxes
Background note: A missionary to China from 1913 to 1927, Nikolai Astrup Larsen (1878-1961) served as president of the Lutheran Church of China from 1924 to 1927.
MINUTES/RECORDS/REPORTS: British and American missionaries in Shanghai, statement, 1932; "Resolution to the British Chamber of Commerce," 1923; Board of Foreign Missions, resolutions, 1924; statement to the Board of Foreign Missions, 1924; general statement, building expenses at Tsinan, n.d.; China Continuation Committee, Shanghai, proceedings, 1910; China mission, report, 1917, n.d.; Church of Sweden school, constitution, 1927; report from *Faelles motet i Sinyangchow*, by Edward Sovik, 1916; Foreign Resident's Committee, report, 1922; "Fra Kinamissionen," report, 1917; Foreign Resident's Committee, resolution, 1923; Kwangchow Station, accounting sheet, 1916-17; Kwangchow District Station, report, 1919; Lutheran Board of Publication, report, 1934; Lutheran Church Council, minutes, 1935; report, 1926; Lutheran Church of China, Temporary Council, minutes, 1916; Lutheran College, Taohwalun, Yiyang, Hunan, catalogue, 1926-27; tentative plan, 1928-29; receipt to Lutheran Synod Mission from American Consul, 1917; Lutheran Synodical Representatives, Third Assembly Educational Resolutions, Kuling, minutes, 1928; Lutheran Theological Seminary, report, 1922; Board of Directors of Lutheran Theological Seminary, minutes, 1923; Lutheran United Mission at Kikungshan, Honan, annual conference report, 1923-24; Lutheran United Mission, Executive Committee, meeting minutes, 1925; Lutheran Synod of Honan and

Hupeh, organization meeting, report, 1923; National Christian Council of China, report, 1924-25; inventory list of Larsen's possessions, 1927; statement of receipts and expenditures, Larsen, 1927; *Regulations Governing the Recognition of Educational Institutions Established by Funds Contributed from Foreigners*, 1925; Shanghai Lutheran Church, report and plan, 1929-30; list of synod's property in China and estimate of value, n.d.; K. N. Tvedt, Sihsien Mission, report, 1916; P. E. Thorson, report, 1916-17; treaty between United States and China, n.d.; list of workers in Kwangchow, n.d.
CORRESPONDENCE: Ca. 700 letters, telegrams, and postcards, 1913-59, between Larsen family and friends, including such correspondents as Eliot Aandahl, J. A. Aasgaard, American Consul General-Hankow, Einar C. Andreassen, P. E. Anspach, [Olaf?] Behrents, J. L. Benson, Nels Benson, J. R. Birkeland, John M. Bly, Board of Directors of the Lutheran College, Board of Foreign Mission, L. W. Boe, Louis Henry Braafladt, Ch'i Ch'ang-ch'un, China Mission Committee, H. R. Chu (Chu Hao-ran), Conference of the Lutheran United Mission; "co-workers," Edwin S. Cunningham, L. J. Davies, A. W. Edwins, B. C. Elsom, Mathide Elstad, Nathanael Fedde, L. C. Foss, Clemens Granskou, Roger S. Greene, O. E. Hesla, H. C. Holm, David Hong, Bjarne Houkom, Helge Hoverstad, I. W. Jacobson, Alfred O. Johnson, K. S. Kiang, Martha Kulberg, O. J. Kvale, C. W. Landahl, G. T. Lee, Lutheran United Mission, George O. Lillegard, Olaf Lysnes, [?] Lutie, Raymond C. MacKay, O. G. Malmin, R. Malmin, Herbert J. Masen, missionary conference in China, J. A. E. Ness, J. E. Nilssen, K. R. Palmer, Watts O. Pye, Karl Ludvig Reichelt, Horace Remillard, Herman Roe, O. E. Rolvaag, M. Saterlie, Casper C. Skinsnes, G. Smedal, Sigurd T. Sorenson, Erik Sovik, H. G. Stub, J. A. O. Stub, Victor E. Swenson, Joseph Tetlie, Roy F. Thelander, Peter E. Thorson, Alfred Trued, Tu Chen Chung, Fennell P. Turner, [?] Valdemar, Knut B. Westman, O. R. Wold, Lauritz S. Ylvisaker, and Nils M. Ylvisaker; circular letters and mimeographed letters to Board of Foreign Missions and Conference of the Lutheran United Mission.
DIARIES: Larsen's diary for 1916.
MANUSCRIPTS: 30 articles by Larsen, some in Norwegian, on Lutheran work in China, recognition of the People's Republic of China, and other subjects, 1916-27, 1959, and n.d.; sermons, 1913-28; speeches on China, 1921, 1927, 1929, 1930, 1932, 1936, 1939, 1946, 1953, and n.d.; "Outline of History of China and Japan in Modern Times," by John M. Bly, n.d.; "School Problems in the Lutheran Church (in China)," by Knut B. Westman, 1928; "Some Suggestions for Missionaries in China," by C. N. Li, 1924; autobiography of Louis Henry Braafladt, n.d.; autobiography of Larsen, 1955.
PAMPHLETS: 12 pamphlets, 1918-50, on Buddhists, China, Christian education and schools, Chungking, Lauritz Larsen, Lutheran Church of China, mission work, and missionary preparation.
MEMORABILIA: Clippings on China, 1913-14, 1918, 1923, 1927, 1928, 1959; dedication of Central China Union Lutheran Theological Seminary, 1913; clipping on missionary method, 1919; notes on article by Knut B. Westman, n.d.; interview questions and answers on Karl Ludvig Reichelt and the Christian Mission to Buddhists, 1955; 16 datebooks, 1913-27.
MAPS/DESIGNS/DRAWINGS: Map of Honan and Hupeh, n.d.
AUDIO-VISUAL MATERIALS: Photo of the American School in China and Astrup and Marie Larsen, n.d.

SERIALS: *Christian Industry*, 1926. *Gleanings*, 1922. National Christian Council, *Bulletin*, 1926.
CHINESE LANGUAGE MATERIALS: Map of Honan and Hupeh; 2 datebooks, 1925 and n.d.; 22 letters, 1923 and n.d.; unspecified map; *Lesson XXIII*, a study booklet for language instruction, n.d.; 16 other miscellaneous items.
FINDING AIDS: In-house guide.

2-GENERAL HOLDINGS
MINUTES/RECORDS/REPORTS: Council of the Lutheran Church of China, report, 1928; Hauge's Norwegian Evangelical Lutheran synod, report, 1896–98; Religious Tract Society for China, annual report, 1927–28.
PAMPHLETS: *China Consultation*, by A. Doak Barnett, 1958; *Hedningemissionens frugter*, by O. S Nestegaard, 1891; *Louis Henry Braafladt, Medical Missionary*, by F. Hope Braafladt, 1935.
SERIALS: *China Christian Year Book*, 1913–19, 1923–26, 1928–29. *Kinamissionären*, 1891–95.

DUBUQUE

IA–20   MOUNT ST. FRANCIS
Sisters of St. Francis of the Holy Family (O.S.F.)
3390 Windsor Avenue Extension
Dubuque IA 52001
(319) 583-9786
Sister Helen Larsen, Librarian

Background note: The Sisters of Saint Francis of the Holy Family (O.S.F.) maintained a mission school, conducted a dispensary, and provided health care in China from 1931 to 1949. The materials listed below are held in the office of the Community Secretary.

1-GENERAL HOLDINGS
MINUTES/RECORDS/REPORTS: Enrollment figures of the Sisters of Saint Francis of the Holy Family (O.S.F.) mission school in China, n.d.; folder of bills for the subsistence of sisters in concentration camps in China, 1942–44.
CORRESPONDENCE: Several letters written by the sisters in China to the Community, 1940s.
MANUSCRIPTS: 58-page typescript account of missionary sisters efforts to establish and maintain their mission in China, 1931–47.
MEMORABILIA: 3 clippings about missionary sisters in China, 1938–47.
AUDIO-VISUAL MATERIALS: Ca. 10 photos of missionary sisters with students.

GRINNELL

GRINNELL COLLEGE

IA–25   Archives
Burling Library
Grinnell IA 50112-0811
(515) 269-3364
Anne Kintner, College Archivist

1-GRINNELL-IN-CHINA PAPERS, 1910–86, 2 boxes
MINUTES/RECORDS/REPORTS: American Board of Foreign Missions, North China Mission, annual report, 1912–13; Grin-nell-in-China: annual reports, 1924–25; financial statements, 1922–24; minutes, 1925; report, 1923–24.
CORRESPONDENCE: 200 letters from Grinnell-in-China missionaries M. F. Bradshaw, A. D. Heininger, Paul MacEachron, Harold S. Matthews, and Nelson W. Wehrhan, 1922–27; 2 letters from Paul and Helen Dunham MacEachron, 1919–20; 2 letters from Alice Reed, 1919–20; 2 letters from Alice Reed and Mrs. Harold Matthews to Grant Gale, 1979; 2 letters from Nelson W. Wehrhan, 1927; circular letter from John Scholte Nollen, 1934.
MANUSCRIPTS: "Alice Reed's Letters from China," by David Alperin, 1978; "Excerpts from Letters from China, 1916–1948," by Alice C. Reed, n.d.; "Fifty Years of Change—China Revisited," by Donald R. Fessler, 1986; "Grinnell-in-China: (Reminiscences)," by Helen MacEachron, n.d.; "Grinnell-in-China's Role in the Educational Life of China," by Donald R. Fessler, 1986; "A History of Grinnell-in-China, 1910 to 1930," by Lisa M. Bowers, 1980; "Porter Middle School," by Harold S. Matthews, ca. 1925.
PAMPHLETS: 7 pamphlets on Grinnell-in-China, Tehchow Mission Station, Shantung Christian University, and Tien Tsin Hsin Hsin, 1917–40.
MEMORABILIA: 53 pages of photocopied correspondence, articles, and clippings from China missionary A. B. De Haan, n.d.; clipping on Grinnell missionaries in China, 1917; folder of clippings on fund-raising for Grinnell-in-China, 1916–28; articles on Grinnell-in-China appearing in the Grinnell College publication, *Tanager*, 1926, and the student newspaper, *Scarlet and Black*, 1910–39.
AUDIO-VISUAL MATERIALS: Photo of Alice C. Reed (with "Excerpts from Letters from China, 1916–1948," above), n.d.; 23 photos of the Grinnell-in-China project, ca. 1924; photo of Dr. [Duncan?] Main with Grinnell-in-China staff, n.d.
FINDING AIDS: Card catalogue.

IA–30   Burling Library
Grinnell College
Grinnell IA 50112-0811
(515) 236-2519
Anne Kintner, Assistant Director

1-GENERAL HOLDINGS
MAPS/DESIGNS/DRAWINGS: *Atlas of the Chinese Empire, Containing Separate Maps of the Eighteen Provinces of China Proper...and of the Four Great Dependencies, and a List of All Protestant Mission Stations*, by Edward Stanford (London: China Inland Mission), 1908.

IOWA CITY

IOWA STATE HISTORICAL DEPARTMENT
IA–35   Manuscript Collection
402 Iowa Avenue
Iowa City IA 52240
(319) 338-5471
David Kinnett, Manuscript Librarian

1-GENERAL HOLDINGS
CORRESPONDENCE: Form letter from H. G. C. Hallock, missionary in Shanghai, requesting donations for Christmas gifts for Chinese children, 1938.

MAPS/DESIGNS/DRAWINGS: Colored drawing of Pan-ku, illustrating the Chinese creation story, with letter above.

UNIVERSITY OF IOWA
IA-40   University of Iowa Libraries
Iowa City IA 52242
(319) 335-5884
Robert Felsing, Oriental Cataloguer

1-GENERAL HOLDINGS
MINUTES/RECORDS/REPORTS: American Board of Commissioners for Foreign Missions, 94 reels microfilm of minutes, reports, correspondence, and documents on China missions, 1827–1930 (see Yale Divinity School, Special Collections, 409 Prospect Street, New Haven, CT, 06520, and Harvard University, Houghton Library, Cambridge, MA, 02138, for detailed description); Augustana Synod, China mission, reports, 1937; Canton Christian College (Lingnan University), catalogue, 1942–43; Catholic University of Peking, catalogue, 1939–40; China Medical Board of New York, report, 1952; Christian Literature Society for China, report, 1910–16, 1924–29; Fukien Christian University, catalogue, 1942; Hua Chung College, catalogue, 1943; Hwa Nan College, catalogue, 1943; University of Nanking, catalogue, 1942; West China Union University, prospectus, 1942.
PAMPHLETS: 12 titles, 1878–1978, on such topics as the American Board of Commissioners for Foreign Missions missions to China, anti-missionary riots, Catholic University of Peking, Ginling College, Jesuits, Peiping Union Medical College, Nestorian tablet, Shantung Christian University, Szechuan wilderness, and James Hudson Taylor.
SERIALS: *China Christian Year Book*, 1917, 1919, 1926, 1938–39. *China's Millions* (London), 1875–99. *Chinese Recorder*, 1868–1941. *Monumenta Serica*, 1948–; monograph series, 1939–67. Nanking Theological Seminary, English Publications, 1940. University of Nanking, College of Agriculture and Forestry, *Bulletin*, 1933; *University of Nanking Magazine*, 1910. Yenching University, *Social Research Series*, 1930.
DISSERTATIONS/THESES: *Oberlin-in-China, 1881–1951*, by Mary Tarpley Campfield, 1974.
CHINESE LANGUAGE MATERIALS/PAMPHLETS: *Lingnan ta-hsüeh*, 1894–1905.
CHINESE LANGUAGE MATERIALS/SERIALS: *Chin-ling hsüeh pao (Nanking Journal)*, 1931–41. Chin-ling ta hsüeh, *T'u shu kuan ts'ung k'an (Library Bulletin)*, 1934. *Ling-nan hsüeh pao (Lingnan Journal)*, 1929–52. *Yen-ching hsüeh pao (Yenching Journal of Chinese Studies)*, 1927–41, 1946–51. *Yen-ching hsüeh pao, chuan hao (Yenching Journal of Chinese Studies*, monograph series), 1961–74 (repr.). Yen-ching ta-hsüeh, *Wen hsüeh nien pao* (Yenching University, *Literature Annual*), 1932–44. Yen-ching ta hsüeh, *Shih hsüeh nien pao (Historical Annual)*, 1924–40.

ORANGE CITY

NORTHWESTERN COLLEGE
IA-45   Ramaker Library
Orange City IA 51041
(712) 737-4821 Ext. 146
Nella Kennedy, Archivist

1-CHINESE ARTIFACTS COLLECTION, ca. 1920–1940, ca. 100 items
MEMORABILIA: Miscellaneous objects of daily life and culture in China, including a wall hanging, inscribed, ''Pray to Christ''; calendars from the Christian Book Room in Shanghai; hymnbook; ancestral tablets; samples of papers used in non-Christian rites from Fukien, ca. 1919; paper charms and calling cards; assorted invitations; posters on prayer and Chinese deities.
AUDIO-VISUAL MATERIALS: A series of pictures depicting the story of the Prodigal Son.
CHINESE LANGUAGE MATERIALS: *The Heidelberg Catechism*, trans. by Abbe Livingston Warnshuis, n.d.

2-GENERAL HOLDINGS
Background note: In addition to the report listed below, the library also holds *South Fukien: A Missionary's Miscellany*, by William Angus, containing his correspondence and reminiscences.
MINUTES/RECORDS/REPORTS: Report on a trip to China by Jeane Noordhoff, an American missionary to Japan who traveled in China in 1931, commenting on Peking, the Forbidden City, the Winter and Summer Palaces, and temples.
SERIALS: *China Bulletin*, 1952–62. *China Notes*, 1962–67.

KANSAS

ABILENE

KS-5   DWIGHT D. EISENHOWER LIBRARY
National Archives and Records Administration
SE Fourth Street
Abilene KS 67410
(913) 263-4751
John E. Wickman, Director

Restrictions: Access by research application.

1-HENRY S. AURAND PAPERS, 1945, 1 folder
MINUTES/RECORDS/REPORTS: References to missions and mission hospitals in China near the end of World War II in ''Report on Economic, Geographic, and Political Situation in Southeast Asia,'' 1945.
FINDING AIDS: In-house guide.

2-JACQUELINE COCHRAN PAPERS, 1945, 3 folders
CORRESPONDENCE/MANUSCRIPTS: Ca. 90 pages of typed notes, reports, articles, correspondence, and handwritten drafts describing Jacqueline Cochran's 1945 trip to the Pacific and China, with brief references to her visits to mission facilities in China, including a Chinese Catholic convent in Shanghai.
FINDING AIDS: In-house guide.

3-ELEANOR LANSING DULLES PAPERS, 1894, 4 folders
Background note: Mary Parke Foster was John Foster Dulles' grandmother.
CORRESPONDENCE: Several letters by Mary Parke Foster on a trip in China, referring to meetings with missionaries, 1894.
FINDING AIDS: In-house guide.

4-C. D. JACKSON PAPERS, 1945, 1 folder
DIARIES: Mimeograph of a 5-page diary by Henry R. Luce, Chungking, 1945, with commentary on conditions in China immediately after the Sino-Japanese war and brief references to Christian missionaries in China, including a Catholic bishop, a Catholic paper, and a Methodist mission.
FINDING AIDS: In-house guide.

5-WALTER H. JUDD INTERVIEW, 1968–70, 1 item
Background note: The originals of this collection are held by Columbia University as part of their Columbia University Oral History Project. See also Columbia University, Rare Book and Manuscript Library, Butler Library, 535 West 114th Street, New York, NY, 10027.
ORAL HISTORIES: 150-page transcript of interviews with Walter H. Judd, a medical missionary to China from 1925 to 1938.
FINDING AIDS: In-house guide.

BALDWIN CITY

BAKER UNIVERSITY

KS–10   Kansas East Commission on Archives and History
Baldwin City KS 66006
(913) 594–6451 Ext. 389
Maxine Kreutziger, Archivist

1-ALUMNI FILES, n.d., quantity undetermined
CORRESPONDENCE/MEMORABILIA: Correspondence, clippings, Baker alumni records, and Baker Alumni questionnaires of alumni who served in China: Cora Shepard Boynton (1897); Cora M. Brown (1904); Arthur Coole (1921); Douglas Coole (1923); Ella Endres Coole (1947); Polly Coole (1924); Thomas Henry Coole (1897); Cammie Gray (1915); Lawrence K. Hall (1910); Freeman Havighurst (1916); Irma Highbaugh (1915); Lyda Houston (1915); Harry Carmichael Jett (1917); Wenona Wilson Jett (1915); Ella Francis Jones (1913); Mary G. Kesler (1910); Geneva Miller (1929); Frances B. Molby (1915); Naomi Muenzenmayer (1932); Anna Ruth Roseberry (1915); Karl Steinheimer (1913); Ray Lavelley Torrey (1905); Edith Rosemond Youtsey (1909); and Yung Liang Hwang (1904).

HESSTON

HESSTON COLLEGE

KS–15   Mary Miller Library
Box 3000
Hesston KS 67062–3000
(316) 327–4221 Ext. 245
Margaret Wiebe, Librarian

1-GENERAL HOLDINGS
PAMPHLETS: *We Enter China: A Statement of Historical Development, Present Progress, Plans, Ideals, and Description of Our Mennonite Mission in China*, by Joseph Daniel Graber, 1947.

KANSAS CITY

CENTRAL BAPTIST THEOLOGICAL SEMINARY

KS–20   Library
Seminary Heights
Kansas City KS 66102
(913) 371–5313
Henry R. Moeller, Director

1-GENERAL HOLDINGS
PAMPHLETS: *China Consultation, 1958*, by A. Doak Barnett, 1958; *The Church and China*, by John Foster, 1943; *A Comparative Study of the Health of Missionary Families in Japan and China, and a Selected Group in America*, by William Gordon Lennox, 1922.
SERIALS: *China Christian Year Book*, 1916–17, 1919, 1926, 1929. *China Mission Advocate*, 1839. *Chinese Recorder*, 1892–96, 1923–40.
DISSERTATIONS/THESES: *Protestant Mission Schools for Girls in South China (1827 to the Japanese Invasion)*, by Mary Raleigh Anderson, 1943.

LAWRENCE

UNIVERSITY OF KANSAS

KS–25   East Asian Library
Watson Library
University of Kansas
Lawrence KS 66045–2800
(913) 864–4669
Eugene Carvalho, Director

1-GENERAL HOLDINGS
CHINESE LANGUAGE MATERIALS: 15 books, 1922–82, on such topics as Christian education, Communist views on the church, the history of Christianity in China, rural missions, Wang Ming-tao, and Watchman Nee.
CHINESE LANGUAGE MATERIALS/SERIALS: *Chin-ling hsieh ho shen hsüeh chih (Nanking Theology Review)*, 1984-. *Ching Feng*, 1958-. *Chung-hua Chi-tu chiao hui nien chien (China Church Year Book)*, 1914–36 (repr. 1983).

KS–30   Kenneth Spencer Research Library
University of Kansas
Department of Special Collections
Lawrence KS 66045–2800
(913) 864–4274
Alexandra Mason, Spencer Librarian

1-GENERAL HOLDINGS
MANUSCRIPTS/PAMPHLETS: *Mongolian Solar Ephemeris for*

1680, by Ferdinand Verbiest, 1679 (?), printed from woodblocks, with manuscript notes in Latin and French.
MAPS/DESIGNS/DRAWINGS: "Epistola P. Ferdinandi Verbiest vice provincialis missionis Sinensis anna 1678, die 15 e. Augusti ex curia Pekinensi in Europam ad socias missa," by Ferdinand Verbiest, 1678, printed from woodblocks in facsimile of original manuscript.

KS-35 Watson Library
University of Kansas
Lawrence KS 66045-2800
(913) 864-3366
James Neeley, Head of Reference

1-ARCHIVES OF THE COUNCIL FOR WORLD MISSION, 1821-1951, 372 microfiches
Background note: The originals of these materials are at the library of the School of Oriental and African Studies, London.
MINUTES/RECORDS/REPORTS: London Missionary Society, minutes, 1856-1939; papers of Robert Morrison, n.d.: Anglo-Chinese College, report on missions; Tyerman and Bennet deputation, report, 1821-29; Fukien, 1866-1939; South China, 1866-1939; North China, 1866-1939; Central China, 1866-1940; Peking Union Medical College, minutes, n.d.; Siaokan Hospital, n.d.; Amoy district, committee minutes, 1903-24, 1878-1912; North China district, committee minutes, 1874-1920; Hong Kong and New Territories Evangelical Society, minutes, 1904-32; F. H. Hawkins, deputation, 1917; Central China district, committee minutes, 1932-37; Lockhart, records and accounts(?), n.d.
CORRESPONDENCE: London Missionary Society, outgoing letters to China, 1822-1914; Fukien, incoming letters, 1845-1939; outgoing letters, 1928-39; South China, incoming letters, 1803-1939; outgoing letters, 1928-39; North China, incoming letters, 1860-1939; outgoing letters, 1928-39; Central China, incoming letters, 1843-1939; outgoing letters, 1928-39; letters of Robert Morrison, n.d.; miscellaneous letters from missionaries to friends, n.d.; letters from Marjorie Clements in North China, 1930-33; George and Dorothy Barbour, letters from North China, 1920-36; correspondence of J. Legge, n.d.; letters, letterbook of Mrs. L[egge], n.d.; correspondence of Peking Union Medical College, n.d.; letters regarding a book by M. Aldersey, n.d.; correspondence of W. H. Somervell regarding British Foreign Bible Society Chinese Bible, n.d.
MANUSCRIPTS: Sermons by J. Legge, n.d.; articles and notes on literary and language work, by J. Legge; address by J. Legge on Amoy Induction, 1874; papers of E. Hope Bell, n.d.; "Discipleship," by Eric Liddell, n.d.; autobiographical sketch by F. A. Brown, 1935-51; notes on Peking Hospital by Dudgeon, n.d.; Hankow Medical Planning papers; notes by Medhurst, 1848-52; Boxer Indemnity papers; miscellaneous notes on Chinese Church leaders, n.d.
DIARIES: South China, journals, 1807-42; North China, journals, 1863-64; Central China, journals, 1888-96; George and Dorothy Barbour, diary, 1920-36; Terrell diaries, n.d.
MEMORABILIA: Biographical materials on Legge, including clippings, obituaries, and reviews; obituary of Griffith John, n.d.; Chinese medal.
MAPS/DESIGNS/DRAWINGS: Rubbings of Nestorian Tablet, n.d.

FINDING AIDS: "Guide to the Archives of the Council for World Mission," by the Interdocumentation Company, Switzerland.

2-METHODIST MISSIONARY SOCIETY ARCHIVES, 1829-1954, 1,760 microfiches
Background note: These materials are microfiche reproductions of the original archives, now housed in the Library of the School of Oriental and African Studies in London. The collection is divided into three components, two of which—the Wesleyan Methodist Missionary Society records and the Women's Work Collection—contain extensive materials concerning Methodist missions in China.
MINUTES/RECORDS/REPORTS: China Synod, minutes, 1853-1946; overseas schedules, China, 1923-46.
CORRESPONDENCE: 820 microfiches of letters in the Wesleyan Methodist Missionary Society records, divided into 11 series: Canton (1851-1905), China General (1936-45), China Miscellaneous (1924-34), Hunan (1907-45), Hupeh (1905-45), Ningpo (1933-46), North China (1933-45), South China (1905-45), South West China (1932-45), Wenchow (1933-45), and Wuchang (1876-1905); 281 microfiches of letters in the Women's Work Collection, divided into 3 series: Hunan, Hupeh, Ningpo, and Wenchow (1921-54); North, South, and South West China (1920-47); and Missionaries on Furlough (China, 1925-30).
MANUSCRIPTS: 330 microfiches of biographical materials and personal papers of Methodist missionaries in China, including David Hill, Samuel Pollard, and G. Stephenson, 1829-69.
FINDING AIDS: Microfiche reproductions of typescript inventories for correspondence.

3-GENERAL HOLDINGS
MINUTES/RECORDS/REPORTS: China Inland Mission, annual report, 1947; Christian Literature Society for China, annual report, 1910-16.
PAMPHLETS: *Windows into China: The Jesuits and Their Books, 1580-1730*, by John Parker, 1978.
SERIALS: *Asia*, 1948-49, 1952-60. *China Christian Year Book*, 1910-14, 1923-25. *Chinese Recorder*, 1912-13, 1915-20, 1925-31. Christian Literature Society for China, *Monthly Link*, 1937. *The Millions* (London), 1880. *Peking Natural History Bulletin*, 1930-49.
DISSERTATIONS/THESES: *Lutheran Missions in a Time of Revolution: The China Experience, 1944-1951*, by Jonas Jonson, 1972. *Missionary and Manchu*, by Ernest Delbert Tyler, 1930. *The Negotiations between Ch'i-ying and Lagrené, 1844-1846*, by Angelus Francis J. Grosse-Aschhoff, 1950. *North China Villages: A Comparative Analysis of Models in the Published and Unpublished Writings of Arthur Henderson Smith, American Missionary to China*, by Harry Maurice Lindquist, 1967.

MCPHERSON

McPHERSON COLLEGE
KS-40 Miller Library
1600 East Euclid
P. O. Box 1402
McPherson KS 67460-1402
(316) 241-0731 Ext. 212
Joan Johnson, Assistant Librarian

1-BRETHREN COLLECTION, 1919–41, 4 items
Background note: See also Church of the Brethren General Board, Brethren Historical Library and Archives, 1451 Dundee Avenue, Elgin, IL, 60120.
MANUSCRIPTS: "China: A Challenge to the Church," n.a., 1919; "The Church of the Brethren in China, 1908–1915," n.a., n.d.; "Message from F. H. Crumpacker," by F. H. Crumpacker, 1932.
SERIALS: *Star of Cathay*, 1940–41.

MANHATTAN

KANSAS STATE UNIVERSITY
KS–45   Farrell Library
    Manhattan and Anderson Avenues
    Manhattan KS 66506
    (913) 532–6516
    Ann Birney, Reference Librarian

1-GENERAL HOLDINGS
SERIALS: *Fukien Agricultural Journal*, 1947–50. *Lingnan Science Journal*, 1922–48. University of Nanking, College of Agriculture and Forestry, *Bulletin*, 1926, 1933–36. Yenching University, Department of Biology, *Bulletin*, 1930.

RILEY COUNTY HISTORICAL MUSEUM
KS–50   Seaton Memorial Library
    2309 Claflin Road
    Manhattan KS 66502
    (913) 537–2210
    D. Cheryl Collins, Archivist/Librarian

1-MARGARET MILLER, ca. 1940s, 1 item
Background note: Margaret Miller served as a missionary to China with the Augustana Synod of the Swedish Lutheran Church during the 1940s.
MEMORABILIA: A page of newspaper clippings about Margaret Miller, n.d.

NORTH NEWTON

BETHEL COLLEGE
KS–55   Mennonite Library and Archives
    North Newton KS 67117–9993
    (316) 283–2500 Ext. 310
    David A. Haury, Director

Background note: The Mennonite Library and Archives at Bethel College was formerly known as the Bethel College Historical Library. The first Mennonite missionaries to enter China were sent out from the United States in the 1890s but served under non-Mennonite boards. Mission work under Mennonite boards began after 1900 and may be summarized under six heads: the China Mission of the General Conference Mennonites, the South and West China Missions of the Mennonite Brethren, the Mongolia Mission of the Krimmer Mennonite Brethren, and the postwar attempts of the United Missionary Society and the Mennonites to establish new work.

The China Mennonite Missionary Society operated from 1905 until 1946, when the Society was dissolved and its work taken over by the participating groups, the Mennonite Brethren and Krimmer Mennonite Brethren taking responsibility for the western field in Szechuan-Kansu and the Evangelical Mennonite Brethren in Shantung-Honan.

The China Mission of the General Conference Mennonites was begun as an independent venture by Mr. and Mrs. H. J. Brown in 1909, and in 1911 was located at Kaichow, Hopeh. In 1914 this work was taken over by the Foreign Mission Board of the General Conference and additional workers sent out. See also Center for Mennonite Brethren Studies, 4824 East Butler, Fresno, CA, 93727; Eastern Mennonite College and Seminary, Menno Simons Historical Library and Archives, Harrisonburg, VA, 22801–2462; and Goshen College, Archives of the Mennonite Church, 1700 South Main Street, Goshen, IN, 46526.

1-HEINRICH JACOB BROWN PAPERS, 1945–58, 1 box
Background note: Heinrich Jacob Brown was a Mennonite missionary to China from 1945 to 1951.
MINUTES/RECORDS/REPORTS/CORRESPONDENCE/PAMPHLETS: Reports, articles, correspondence, articles, and passports relating to Heinrich Jacob Brown, 1945–58.
FINDING AIDS: In-house register.

2-HENRY J. BROWN PAPERS, 1927–61, 1 box
Background note: Henry J. Brown (1879–1959) was an independent missionary in China from 1909 to 1914. He founded the Mennonite General Conference Mission in China in 1914 and served in China until he was released from internment by the Japanese in 1943.
MINUTES/RECORDS/REPORTS: Folder of reports and talks on China, 1940s–1950s; folder on Dr. Tucker and the United Mission, 1931.
CORRESPONDENCE: 4 folders of correspondence from Brown, concerning family matters and refugees in Harbin, 1927, 1931, 1936–37, 1947–49, 1950–52; folder of correspondence with the Mennonite Mission Board, n.d.
MANUSCRIPTS: Folder of articles published by or about Henry J. and Maria Brown, 1927–61; folder of sermons and talks; folder of papers on education, women, and art in China.
PAMPHLETS: *25th Anniversary of Mission Work*, n.d.; eulogy of Talitha Neufeld, missionary to China, n.d.; folder of pamphlets and clippings on China.
MEMORABILIA: Folder of notebooks recording expenses and letters; passports; medal; wood cut of the symbol of the China church; folder of news items on China, 1935; folder of Bible studies; folder of Chinese folksongs.
AUDIO-VISUAL MATERIALS: Family photo, n.d.
CHINESE LANGUAGE MATERIALS: Folder of unidentified letters.
FINDING AIDS: In-house register.

3-AGANETHA HELEN FAST PAPERS, 1917–32, 4 boxes, 58 folders
Background note: A Mennonite missionary to China from 1917 to 1932, Aganetha Helen Fast (1888–1981) served as superintendent of the Ling Sheng Girls' and P'e Cheng Boys' Day Schools from 1926 to 1930, and as treasurer of the Kaichow City Evangelistic and Education Work from 1930 to 1932.
MINUTES/RECORDS/REPORTS: Reports on China, 1920–55; reports, n.d.; Evangelization tour, reports, 1922; deeds to Mennonite property in China, n.d.
CORRESPONDENCE: 14 folders of letters from Fast, 1917–32.
DIARIES: Box and folder of Fast's diaries, n.d.
MANUSCRIPTS: 2 folders of Fast's autobiography, n.d.; folder of manuscripts on mission work in China, n.d.; 2 folders of the manuscript for Fast's *Out of My Attic*; Fast's unpublished autobiography, 1968; "Childhood Memories of Pioneer Years," n.d.; manuscript for *The Power of Christ's Love in China*; folder of meditations and autobiographical sketches; folder of writings on Nankai University.
PAMPHLETS: Folder of printed materials on the Women's Mission Society, n.d.
MEMORABILIA: Box of financial receipts, travel materials, family obituaries, souvenirs, wedding invitations, school notes and practice sessions, and Buddhist studies; folder of missionary prayer studies; ca. 1 folder of clippings on China; folder of Chinese material; folder of miscellaneous notes; ca. 1 box of scrapbooks; 2 folders of issues of *Missionary News and Notes*, *Mission Quarterly (Missions-Quartalblatt)*, *The Mennonite*, *Christlicher Bundesbote*, and *Junior Messenger* containing articles on China missions, 1930–50.
MAPS/DESIGNS/DRAWINGS: Folder of Chinese maps.
AUDIO-VISUAL MATERIALS: 2 folders of photos of China; folder of slides of China; folder of photos of Aganetha Helen Fast; 13 folders of Fast family photos; 2 boxes of photo albums and folders of loose photos, n.d.
SERIALS: *China Newsletter*, 1949. *Chinese Christians Today*, 1962–63.
CHINESE LANGUAGE MATERIALS: Folder of unidentified manuscripts in Chinese and English; unidentified book; folder of Chinese script; folder of Chinese catechism, translated by H. J. Brown, n.d.
FINDING AIDS: In-house register.

4-GENERAL CONFERENCE MENNONITE CHURCH ARCHIVES, BOARD OF MISSIONS PAPERS, 1909–50, ca. 5–6 l.f.
MINUTES/RECORDS/REPORTS/CORRESPONDENCE: Quarterly official reports, informal reports, minutes, financial statements, and other documents, and correspondence from China missionaries to the Mission Board, organized chronologically and interfiled with other mission records, 1909–50.

5-SAMUEL JOSEPH GOERING PAPERS, ca. 1944–1945, ca. 1 folder
Background note: Samuel Joseph Goering (1892–1962) was a Mennonite missionary in China from 1919 to 1935, and Mennonite Central Committee Relief Commissioner to China from 1943 to 1944. The bulk of this collection, which occupies 3 boxes, concerns his administrative work with the Mennonite Church from 1940 until his death. Materials on his China mission work can be found in the files of the General Conference Archives, Board of Missions Papers (see above).

MINUTES/RECORDS/REPORTS: Mennonite Central Committee, reports, n.d.
CORRESPONDENCE: Mennonite Central Committee, correspondence, 1944 and n.d.
FINDING AIDS: In-house register.

6-PETER SIEBERT GOERTZ PAPERS, 1918–26, .75 box, 11 folders
Background note: Peter Siebert Goertz (1886–1948) was a missionary to Foochow from 1918 to 1926 under the American Board of Commissioners for Foreign Missions.
CORRESPONDENCE: 10 folders of correspondence from Goertz while on mission in China, 1918–26.
MANUSCRIPTS: Folder of "China Notes" written by Helen Riesen Goertz, n.d.
MEMORABILIA: Notebooks and miscellaneous papers by Goertz, 1918–26.
FINDING AIDS: In-house register.

7-EDMUND GEORGE KAUFMAN PAPERS, 1917–25, 13 folders
Background note: A Mennonite missionary to China from 1917 to 1925, Edmund George Kaufman (b. 1891) served as superintendent of the Mennonite Mission school and was later president of Bethel College.
MINUTES/RECORDS/REPORTS: Report on Kaufman's China trip, n.d.; folder of mission resolutions, 1919–30; folder of mission reports and building plans, 1924–25; list of contributors, n.d.
CORRESPONDENCE: Folder of correspondence on the Foreign Mission Board in China, 1916–31; folder of letters to churches, n.d.; folder of correspondence with missionaries, 1913–14; folder of Kaufman's correspondence with his parents, 1918–24, 1926–31; 3 folders of correspondence relating to the China mission, 1926–35; folder of miscellaneous correspondence on China, 1955–56, 1968; folder of correspondence concerning Chinese boys, 1928–33.
MEMORABILIA: Folder of China souvenirs and miscellaneous, n.d.
FINDING AIDS: In-house register.

8-ERNST KUHLMAN PAPERS, 1913–48, 7 folders
Background note: Ernst Kuhlman (1883–1975) was a missionary in Tangshan and Tsingtao from 1907 to 1948.
CORRESPONDENCE: 7 folders of correspondence from Ernst and Maria Kuhlman in China to Mrs. Kuhlman's sister, Mrs. Lewis Jansen, 1913–41; set of published letters from China missionaries Paul and Ina Bartel, n.d.
SERIALS: *Ausbreitung-Evangeliums in Tangshan*, 1928. *Missions-Nachrichten aus Tangshan*, 1920–28. *Nachrichten aus China*, 193841. *Preach the Gospel: Mission Reports from Tangshan*, 1939–41. *Verkündigt das Evangelium Nachrichten aus China*, 1929–38.
FINDING AIDS: In-house register.

9-WILHELMINA KUYF PAPERS, 1936–51, 12 folders, 1 box
Background note: Wilhelmina Kuyf (1901–67) was a Mennonite missionary to China under the General Conference Board of Missions in China from 1936 to 1942 and 1948 to 1951.
CORRESPONDENCE: 8 folders of correspondence from Kuyf, 1936–42, 1945–48.
PAMPHLETS: Ca. 1 box of pamphlets on China, n.d.

MEMORABILIA: Folder of miscellaneous clippings on China, n.d.; folder of clippings from the *Gospel Messenger*, n.d.; folder of miscellaneous papers, n.d.
AUDIO-VISUAL MATERIALS: Folder of photos of China, n.d.
FINDING AIDS: In-house register.

10-ABRAHAM M. LOHRENTZ PAPERS, 1922–30, 2 folders
Background note: Abraham Lohrentz (1885–1962) was a Mennonite medical missionary to China from 1922 to 1927.
MINUTES/RECORDS/REPORTS/CORRESPONDENCE/ PAMPHLETS/MEMORABILIA: Miscellaneous materials concerning Abraham M. Lohrentz, 1922–30.
FINDING AIDS: In-house guide.

11-MARIE J. REGIER PAPERS, 1926–49, ca. 2 l.f.
Background note: Marie (Janzen) Regier (b. 1897) was a General Conference Mennonite missionary to China from 1926 to 1948.
MINUTES/RECORDS/REPORTS: China Mission Workers Conference, minutes and reports, 1927–34.
CORRESPONDENCE: Folder of Regier's correspondence with China missionaries, 1933–36; folder of Regier's correspondence with Chinese students, 1946–48; 3 folders of Regier family correspondence, 1940–49; folder of Regier's correspondence while interned by the Japanese, 1943–45; folder of Regier's correspondence with the General Conference Mennonite missionary board, 1934–55.
MANUSCRIPTS: "After Internment," by Marie Regier, 1945–48; "In China, 1926–1932," by Marie Regier, n.d.; "The Cloud Over My Second Term in China," by Marie Regier, n.d.; "Cultural Interpretation in a Local Community in China," by Marie Regier, 1936; "Mennonite Teaching and Practice in a Chinese Community," by Marie Regier, n.d.; folder of skits, 1926–32; folder of talks on China, 1933–40.
PAMPHLETS: 2 folders of articles on China, 1926–40.
MEMORABILIA: Folder of mementos from China, n.d.; folder of mementos of Weihsien internment camp, 1943–45; folder of miscellaneous mementos, n.d.; folder of "Chinese Idols," n.d.
MAPS/DESIGNS/DRAWINGS: Folder of sketches of China, 1940–43; folder of sketches of Weihsien internment camp, 1943–45.
AUDIO-VISUAL MATERIALS: Folder of photos of China, n.d.
CHINESE LANGUAGE MATERIALS: 2 boxes of verse, sketches, art work, and photos, n.d.
FINDING AIDS: In-house register.

12-WILLIAM C. VOTH PAPERS, 1911–76, 20 l.f.
Background note: William C. Voth was a Mennonite missionary to China. The collection is unprocessed.
MINUTES/RECORDS/REPORTS/CORRESPONDENCE: Reports to and correspondence with the mission board, 1919–51.
CORRESPONDENCE: Personal correspondence, 1911–76; correspondence with Mennonite and other Protestant missionaries, 1919–76.
MEMORABILIA/AUDIO-VISUAL MATERIALS: Miscellaneous clippings and photos.

13-GENERAL HOLDINGS
MINUTES/RECORDS/REPORTS: China General Conference Mennonite Mission Field, reports, 1924–25; China International Famine Relief Commission, annual reports, 1931; China Menno-nite Mission Society, reports, 1922–24; China Educational Commission, reports, 1922; General Conference China Mennonite Mission, report, 1940; outfit list, 1940; Mennonite Central Committee China Relief, reports, 1945–49; reports on Mennonite missions to China in denominational serials, *Missionary News and Notes*, 1926–65; and *Missions Today*, 1965–73.
CORRESPONDENCE: Letter from Aganetha Helen Fast in Chengtu to friends, 1948.
MANUSCRIPTS: 16 manuscripts, 1913–80, on Hakkas of South China, Mennonite mission work in China, and Jonathan Schrag.
PAMPHLETS: 28 titles, 1921–74, on H. J. and Maria Brown, China Mennonite Mission Society, Chinese Christians, Aganetha Helen Fast, Ginling College, Flora K. Heebner, Mennonite Brethren missions in China, mission accounts, mission methods, missionary education, war, Katie Funk Wiebe, Yang Lien O, and Yenching College.
AUDIO-VISUAL MATERIALS: Personal Photograph Collection, containing photos of most China missionaries; Subject Photo Collection, containing ca. 1,500 photos and several hundred color slides of Mennonite mission work, Chinese Christian workers, missionaries, and Chinese civilization and culture, 1909–51, filed by subject and later by missionary, including collections of J. W. Kliewer, Talitha Neufeld, S. F. Pannabecker, and Marie J. Regier.
SERIALS: *Bulletin of the Hopei Bible School*, 1932–33. *China Mission Year Book*, 1917–19, 1923–24. *China Notes*, 1980–85. *China Relief Notes*, 1946–48. *China Sheet*, 1945–46. *The China-Home Bond*, 1939–41.
DISSERTATIONS/THESES: *The Beginning and Growth of the Educational Mission Work in China of the Mennonite General Conference of North America*, by John E. Kaufman, 1924. *The Chinese Bible: Being a Historical Survey of Its Translation*, by Paul Henry Bartel, 1946. *A History of the Development of the Chinese Indigenous Christian Church under the American Board in Fukien Province*, by Peter Siebert Goertz, 1933.
CHINESE LANGUAGE MATERIALS: 5 Bibles in Mandarin, 1914, 1920–21, 1931–32.
FINDING AIDS: Card catalogue of missionaries for the Personal Photograph Collection; subject catalogue for the Subject Photograph Collection.

WINFIELD

SOUTHWESTERN COLLEGE
KS–60 Memorial Library
100 College Street
Winfield KS 67156-2498
(316) 221-4150 Ext. 225
Joanne Black, Archivist

1-UNITED METHODIST CHURCH ARCHIVES-KANSAS WEST CONFERENCE, 1941–43, ca. 1 folder
MINUTES/RECORDS/REPORTS: Scattered material on China in the records of the Topeka branch of the Woman's Foreign Mission Society, n.d.
MEMORABILIA: Biographical notes from local churches on Methodist missionary Emma Webber Wilson, who was interned in Tientsin from 1941 to 1943.

KENTUCKY

BEREA

BEREA COLLEGE
KY–5   Special Collections
Hutchins Library
Berea KY 40404
(606) 986–9341 Ext. 5259
Shannon H. Wilson, College Archivist

1-YALE-IN-CHINA ASSOCIATION RECORDS, 1925–70, 2.4 l.f.
Background note: This collection consists of photocopies of materials relating to Francis S. Hutchins' participation in the Yale-in-China program. The originals are part of an extensive collection held by Yale University, Department of Manuscripts and Archives, Sterling Memorial Library, 120 High Street, New Haven, CT, 06520. The son of Berea president William Hutchins, Francis S. Hutchins taught at Oberlin-Shansi Memorial School in Shansi while an undergraduate (see Oberlin College, Archives, Mudd Learning Center, Oberlin, OH, 44074). He later returned to China in 1925 as an English instructor in Changsha with Yale-in-China. From 1928 to 1939, Hutchins was a representative of the American Trustees of the Yale-in-China Association, but was forced to leave China in 1939 during the Japanese invasion. He served as vice-president of the Association from 1939 to 1949. Later he served as president of Berea College until 1967.
MINUTES/RECORDS/REPORTS/CORRESPONDENCE: Photocopies of reports, telegrams, and Hutchins' correspondence with Yale-in-China staff and various family members, ca. 1925–1970.

2-GENERAL HOLDINGS
PAMPHLETS: *Tales from Free China*, by Robert B. McClure, 1941.
ORAL HISTORIES: Copy of transcript of an interview with Louise Gilman Hutchins (Mrs. Francis Hutchins), M.D., daughter of Episcopal Bishop [Alfred?] Gilman who served in China, including discussion of family experiences, and medical and missionary work in China, 1975 (original tape and transcript are held by Radcliffe College, Schlesinger Library, 10 Garden Street, Cambridge, MA, 02138).
SERIALS: *China Mission Year Book*, 1910–15, 1918, 1923, 1925, 1938–39. *Chinese Recorder*, 1870–71, 1923–33, 1935–38. *Educational Review*, 1926–33, 1935.

BOWLING GREEN

WESTERN KENTUCKY UNIVERSITY

KY–10   Helm-Cravens Library
College Heights
Bowling Green KY 42101
(502) 745–6125
Bryan E. Coutts, Coordinator of Collection

1-GENERAL HOLDINGS
SERIALS: *China Christian Year Book*, 1923–36.

KY–15   Kentucky Library
Western Kentucky University
College Heights
Bowling Green KY 42101
(502) 745–6086
Pat Hodges, Manuscript Librarian

1-MAMIE SALLEE BRYAN LETTER (SC 618), 1929, 3 items
CORRESPONDENCE: Letter from Mamie Sallee Bryan (Mrs. R. T. Bryan), of the Baptist Compound in Shanghai, to the Women's Missionary Society of Hartford Baptist Church, Hartford, Kentucky, thanking the Women's Missionary Society of Hartford Baptist Church for funds, 1929.
CHINESE LANGUAGE MATERIALS: 2 sheets of *International Sunday School Lessons*, 1929, published by the China Baptist Publication Society, enclosed with Bryan's letter (above).

COLUMBIA

LINDSEY WILSON COLLEGE
KY–20   Katie Murrell Library
210 Lindsey Wilson Street
Columbia KY 42728
(502) 384–2126 Ext. 239
Edward Seufert, Librarian

1-GENERAL HOLDINGS
SERIALS: *China Mission Year Book*, 1911.

FRANKFORT

FIRST CHRISTIAN CHURCH
KY–25   Philip Fall Memorial Library
316 Ann Street
Frankfort KY 40601–2886
(502) 223–2346
Helen Arnold, Librarian

1-WILLIAM MACKLIN COLLECTION, ca. 1930–ca. 1940, 1 folder, 2 volumes
Background note: William Edward Macklin (1860–1947) was a Disciples of Christ medical missionary to China from Frankfort, Kentucky, from 1894 to 1934.
CORRESPONDENCE: Folder of letters from Macklin, ca. 1930–1940.
MEMORABILIA/AUDIO-VISUAL MATERIALS: Photos of Macklin and family; 2 scrapbooks, containing photos, letters, clippings, and articles on China.

2-GENERAL HOLDINGS
SERIALS: *Central China Christian*, 1906.

LEXINGTON

UNIVERSITY OF KENTUCKY

KY-30 Special Collections and Archives
111 King Library North
Lexington KY 40506-0039
(606) 257-8611
Claire McCann, Manuscript Librarian

1-JOSEPHINE DRUMMOND HUNT PAPERS, 1910-14, 3 items
Background note: Josephine Drummond Hunt practiced medicine in Lexington, Kentucky.
CORRESPONDENCE: 3 letters from "Agnes," a medical missionary in China, apparently a colleague of Hunt's when they attended the Johns Hopkins University School of Medicine together.

KY-35 King Library
University of Kentucky
Lexington KY 40506-0039
(606) 257-1631
Claire McCann, Public Services Coordinator

1-GENERAL HOLDINGS
PAMPHLETS: *Modernism and the Nanking Seminary Board: Why the North Kiangsu Mission Withdrew*, n.a., 1912.
MAPS/DESIGNS/DRAWINGS: *Complete Atlas of China*, by Edward Stanford (Philadelphia: Morgan and Scott), 1908.
SERIALS: *China Mission Advocate*, 1839.

LOUISVILLE

KY-40 LOUISVILLE FREE PUBLIC LIBRARY
Fourth and York Streets
Louisville KY 40203
(502) 561-8615
Charles King, Senior Librarian

1-GENERAL HOLDINGS
SERIALS: American Friends Service Committee, *Bulletin on Work in China*, 1942-44.

LOUISVILLE PRESBYTERIAN THEOLOGICAL SEMINARY

KY-45 Library
1044 Alta Vista Road
Louisville KY 40205
(502) 895-3413 Ext. 250
Milton J. Coalter, Jr., Librarian

1-GENERAL HOLDINGS
ORAL HISTORIES: "Pearl Buck's China: A Conversation with the Noted Author and Orientalist," a conversation between Pearl Buck and her daughter-in-law on the differences between Oriental and Occidental approaches to living, on cassette tape, 1969.
SERIALS: *Chinese Repository*, 1832-51. *Ching Feng*, 1976-84.

SOUTHERN BAPTIST THEOLOGICAL SEMINARY

KY-50 James P. Boyce Centennial Library
2825 Lexington Road
Louisville KY 40280
(502) 897-4807
Ronald F. Deering, Librarian

1-CHINESE COLLECTION, 1847-1923, 75 volumes
CHINESE LANGUAGE MATERIALS: 24 Bibles, 1847-97, in classical Chinese and Shanghai dialect; manuscripts, pamphlets, and books, 1847-1923, on the Bible, Chinese religion, hymns, Mencius, and Sunday School lessons.
CHINESE LANGUAGE MATERIALS/SERIALS: *The True Light Monthly*, 1903.

2-GENERAL HOLDINGS
MINUTES/RECORDS/REPORTS: Board of Missionary Preparation, report, 1917; British Quaker Mission to the People's Republic of China, report, 1956; China Baptist Publication Society, report, 1902-9; China Baptist Theological Seminary, annual report, 1949; catalogues, 1940-50; China Continuation Committee, proceedings, 1916; China Inland Mission, annual reports, 1949-50, 1955; China Mission Society, Kentucky Baptist General Association, proceedings, 1840, 1842-45, 1847; Chinese Tract Society, report, 1910 (bound with *Mission Educational Directory*, see SERIALS below); Door of Hope and Affiliated Homes of the Children's Refuge, annual report, 1932; Educational Association of China, catalogue (bound with *Mission Educational Directory*, see SERIALS below); National Christian Council of China, annual report, 1923-27; National Committee for Christian Religious Education, report of a deputation, 1931; Nordic Consultation on China, Aarhus, Denmark, conference reports, 1972; Shanghai Baptist College and Shanghai Baptist Theological Seminary, prospectus, 1907-8; Shanghai Cantonese Baptist Girls' School, annual record, 1929-30; Southern Baptist Convention: Central China Mission, Church Building Loan Fund, report, 1934; minutes, reference book, 1914-29; North China Mission, annual, 1903, 1905; Pakhoi China Mission, annual report, 1924-28; South China Mission, annual report, 1896-1936; Union Conference of American Baptist Missionaries in China, report, 1905; University of Shanghai, annual report of the president, 1940-41; Warren Memorial Hospital (Hwanghien), annual report, 1907.
CORRESPONDENCE: Letter from Mr. and Mrs. Arthur Raymond Gallimore outlining conditions in Canton after ten years on the field, 1928; letter from Clifford Jackson Lowe, Central China Baptist Missions, Southern Baptist Convention, Shanghai, 1933.
MANUSCRIPTS: "Early Mission History of the Swatow Region Brought Down to the Present for the American Baptist Mission," by Emanuel Herman Giedt, 1946; 5 volumes of materials gathered in connection with preparing and publishing *Lottie Moon*, by Una Roberts Lawrence, including letters from Lottie Moon and other missionaries, and manuscript draft, n.d.; "Rose of Three Countries: A Story of the Life and Service of Miss Rose Marlowe, Native of America, Missionary to China and to Japan," by Alice Johnson Tucker, 1966.
PAMPHLETS: Ca. 100 pamphlets, 1855-1968 (many undated), on American Baptist Missionary Union Central China mission, anti-missionary riots, Baptist missions in China, Baptist Publica-

tion Society, Robert Thomas Bryan, Catholic missions, China Baptist Theological Seminary, Chinese Bible, Chinese civilization and culture, Chinese church, Christian education, Christian missions in China, church in China, Communists, Marion D. Eubank, Silver Flower, Rosewell Hobart Graves, Hong Kong Baptist Theological Seminary, Lucy Hamilton Howard, Willie Hays Kelly, Fannie (Knight) King, Miles J. Knowlton, John Lake, mission methods and problems, missionary accounts, Lottie Moon, Robert Morrison, National Christian Council, Nestorians, North China International Society for Famine Relief, Pooi To School (Hong Kong), I. J. Roberts, Shanghai First Baptist Church, Southern Baptists in China, Southern Baptist Convention missions in Canton, Central China, Kwangsi, North China, South China, and Southwest China, John and Betty Stam, Wong Ping San, and women in China.

SERIALS: *China and the Church Today*, 1979–86. *China Bulletin*, 1959–62. China Christian Educational Association, *Bulletin*, 1926. *China Christian Year Book*, 1910–14, 1916–39. *China Mission Advocate*, 1839. *China Notes*, 1962-. *Chinese Recorder*, 1868–1905, 1910–41. *Chinese Repository*, 1832–51. *Chinese Theological Review*, 1985-. *Chinese World Pulse*, 1977–83. *Directory of Protestant Missions in China*, 1943. *East Asia Millions* (Philadelphia), 1947-. Educational Association of China, *Mission Educational Directory*, 1910. *Land of Sinim*, 1904. Nanking Theological Seminary, English Publications, 1940. National Committee for Christian Religious Education, *Lay Training Bulletin*, 1935. *New East*, 1905–10, 1913–14, 1916–33. *True Light Review*, 1937. *West China Missionary News*, 1931–41.

DISSERTATIONS/THESES: *The Baptist Problem of the Indigenous Church in China*, by Frank T. Woodward, 1934. *The Bible Growing a Christian Culture in China*, by Ira Dennis Eavenson, 1928. *The Challenge of China to America*, by Augustus Young Napier, 1922. *Christianity and Social Change in China, 1912–1942*, by John Glenn Morris, 1946. *Christianizing Chinese Sex Relations: The Fight for Monogamy in China*, by James Hundley Wiley, 1929. *A Critical Examination of the National Christian Council of China*, by Milledge Theron Rankin, 1928. *The Development of Interdenominational and International Cooperation in China: A Study in Missionary Congresses*, by Elizabeth Neal Hale, 1932. *The Gospel Mission Movement within the Southern Baptist Convention*, by Adrian Lamkin, Jr., 1980. *The History of Baptist Missions in Hong Kong*, by Paul Yat-keung Wong, 1974. *Indigenous Churches in China*, by Hendon Mason Harris, 1927. *The Kindergarten in the South China Mission*, by Wilma Jesseline Weeks, 1936. *Lessons for China Missionaries from Paul, the Herald of the Gospel*, by Robert Johnston McMullen, 1930. *An Outline History of Medical Missions in China*, by Ruth L. Cochrane, 1939. *Outlines of a History of Missions in China*, by Elmer Bugg Atwood, 1911. *The Place of Education in the Religious Redemption of China*, by James Toy Williams, 1921. *Present Opportunity for the Missionary in China*, by Myrtle Carolyn Salters, 1934. *Protestant Mission Schools for Girls in South China (1827 to the Japanese Invasion)*, by Mary Raleigh Anderson, 1943. *Reaching the Heart of China through the Home*, by Alice Marjorie Giffin, 1939. *The Situation in China from a Sociological Point of View*, by Charles Reginald Shepherd, 1913. *The Socio-economic Conditions of China as a Mission Field*, by Marion Sandow Crocker, 1935. *A Study of Paul's First Epistle to the Corinthians in the Light of Conditions in China*, by Ming-yung Wu, 1933. *A Study of Progressive Christian Education in Light of the Needs of China*, by Peter

Hsing-hsien Lee, 1950. *The Training of an Efficient Native Leadership for the Christian Churches of China*, by Francis Pugh Lide, 1928. *Training Native Christian Leaders in China*, by Mary Lucile Saunders, 1937. *The Use of Material from China's Spiritual Inheritance in the Christian Education of Chinese Youth*, by Warren Horton Stuart, 1932.

CHINESE LANGUAGE MATERIALS: New Testament in Kuoyu and English, 1935; unidentified Chinese school annual, 193?; *Chinese Christian Hymns, by Chinese Writers, with Chinese Tunes*, trans. by Frank W. Price, 1953; manuscript elementary text in geography with a character table, n.d.

UNIVERSITY OF LOUISVILLE

KY–55 Ekstrom Library
Louisville KY 40292
(502) 588-6747
Craig Dean, Reference Librarian

1-GENERAL HOLDINGS
ORAL HISTORIES: *China Missionaries Oral History Collection*, ed. by Cyrus H. Peake and Arthur L. Rosenbaum (Claremont Graduate School, Oral History Program), 1973. See ORAL HISTORIES Appendix for the names of participants.

KY–60 Kornhauser Health Sciences Library
University of Louisville
Louisville KY 40292
(502) 588-5771
Nancy Lee, Technical Services

1-GENERAL HOLDINGS
SERIALS: *China's Medicine*, 1966–72. *Chinese Medical Journal*, 1932-; supplement, 1936–40.

NERINX

SISTERS OF LORETTO AT THE FOOT OF THE CROSS
KY–65 Archives
Loretto Motherhouse
Nerinx KY 40049
(502) 865-5811
Aurelia Ottersbach, S.L., Archivist

1-GENERAL HOLDINGS
Background note: The Sisters of Loretto maintained an Embroidery School in Han Yang from 1923, and an elementary and a high school in Shanghai from 1933 to 1952.
MINUTES/RECORDS/REPORTS: Sisters of Loretto missionaries, 1 box of alumnae lists, and biographical and historical information on the departure of the first group, 1923; Educational Convention, Shanghai, 1948; Maureen O'Connell's tour, Han Yang Embroidery School, fund-raising, 1938–39; Mothers General, 3 boxes of records, 1923–52.
CORRESPONDENCE: .25 box of correspondence from Bishop Edward J. Galvin, n.d.; .25 box of correspondence from Bishop Quinlan, 1955–70; .25 box of correspondence from other China priests, n.d.

MANUSCRIPTS: Ca. 10 folders of memoirs and biographical material by Nicholas Egging, Florentine Greenwell, Antonella Marie Gutterres, Regina Marie Holland, Justa Justyn, Jane McDonald, Maureen O'Connell, Doloretta Marie O'Connor, Clementia Rogner, and Grace Clare Shanley; "Annals," 1922-52.

AUDIO-VISUAL MATERIALS: Ca 500 pictures and 5 photo albums of Loretto in Han Yang and Shanghai, the Embroidery School, life and street scenes, Loretto Sisters in China, bishop and priest, and Sisters of the Blessed Virgin Mary, 1923-52.

MEMORAEILIA: 8 scrapbooks on the Legion of Mary, Loretto School in Shanghai, war in Wuhan, pictures and other items in Shanghai and Wuhan, Mother Mary Linus' visit, and Mother Ann Marita, including Bishop Galvin's letters, 1924-47; box of miscellaneous items on Loretto School, 1920-56, including magazine and newspaper clippings, on the Legion of Mary, Sodality of Mary, St. Mary's novitiate, 1948 Silver Jubilee, and war and refugee camps; clippings about Edward J. Galvin, n.d.; Golden Jubilee celebration, miscellaneous items, 1983; art book and copy books.

SERIALS: *Han Yang Special*, 1924-29.

DISSERTATIONS/THESES: *Lorettine Education in China*, by Antonella Marie Gutterres, 1961.

CHINESE LANGUAGE MATERIALS: 20 books used for Chinese language instruction and as texts in the Loretto school; 5 prayer books; 5 coin dictionaries; flashcards.

RICHMOND

EASTERN KENTUCKY UNIVERSITY
KY-70 John Grant Crabbe Library
Richmond KY 40475
(606) 622-1778
Rebecca M. Turner, Reference Section Chief

1-GENERAL HOLDINGS
ORAL HISTORIES: *China Missionaries Oral History Collection*, ed. by Cyrus H. Peake and Arthur L. Rosenbaum (Claremont Graduate School, Oral History Program), 1973. See ORAL HISTORIES Union List for the names of participants.

VANCLEVE

KENTUCKY MOUNTAIN BIBLE INSTITUTE
KY-75 Gibson Library
Vancleve KY 41385
(606) 666-5000
Ava Smith, Librarian

1-GENERAL HOLDINGS
SERIALS: *China Notes*, 1970-.

VILLA HILLS

KY-80 ST. WALBURG MONASTERY OF BENEDICTINE SISTERS
2500 Amsterdam Road
Villa Hills KY 41016
(606) 331-6324
Teresa Wolking, O.S.B., Archivist

1-KENTUCKY ARCHIVES, ca. 1930s-1980s, quantity undetermined
CORRESPONDENCE: Letters from Conradin Burtschy, O.F.M., and Nicholas Schneiders, C.P., to the St. Walburg Monastery of Benedictine Sisters, ca. 1930s-1940s; 12 letters from Albert Fedders, M.M., to his sisters in the Benedictine order, Marcella, O.S.B., Mark, O.S.B., Viola, O.S.B., and friends Blandina Farrenkopf, O.S.B., and Grace Zimmer, O.S.B., about his work in China, ca. 1930s-1980s.

MANUSCRIPTS: Recollections of Conradin Burtschy, O.F.M., and Nicholas Schneiders, C.P., 1932-35.

AUDIO-VISUAL MATERIALS: 3 photos by Nicholas Schneiders, C.P., in Hunan, 1939; 6 photos in several family albums of Albert Fedders, M.M., of his sisters in the Benedictine order, Marcella, O.S.B., Mark, O.S.B., and Viola, O.S.B.

MEMORABILIA: Ca. 10 gifts given to Albert Fedders, M.M., of Chinese paintings, a lamp, and wall hangings; newsclippings relating to visit of Albert Fedders, M.M., to Covington (Saint Walburg Monastery).

FINDING AIDS: Archives Index.

WILMORE

ASBURY THEOLOGICAL SEMINARY

KY-85 Department of Special Collections
B. L. Fisher Library
North Lexington Avenue
Wilmore KY 40390
(606) 858-3581
Sylvia U. Brown, Special Collections Librarian

1-OMS INTERNATIONAL COLLECTION, 1925-43, quantity undetermined
Background note: Founded in 1901, OMS International was formerly known as the Oriental Missionary Society. The collection contains information relating to OMS missionaries who served in China, including Elizabeth Adams, Roy and Carrie Adams, Sarah Briggs, Fred and Annie Briggs, Edna Kunkle Chandler, Uri and Margaret Chandler, Helen Deutsch, Orville and Eileen French, Lawrence and Margaret Grant, Richard and Jean Hassell, Esther Helsby, Meredith and Christine Helsby, Howard and Esther Hill, Lee and Maethorne Jeffries, Anne Kartozian, Ernest Kilbourne, Edwin L. and Hazel Kilbourne, Ejnar and Ruth Larson, Mary Maness, Eunice Marias, Katherine McCoy, Duncan McRoberts, Arleta Miller, Florence Munroe, Elbridge and Minnie Munroe, Clara Nelson, Garnett and Elma Phillippe, Rolland and Mildred Rice, Rosalind Rinker, Ina Shreve, W. J. Willis, and Harry and Emily Woods.

MINUTES/RECORDS/REPORTS/CORRESPONDENCE/MANUSCRIPTS/PAMPHLETS/AUDIO-VISUAL MATERIALS: Official records of OMS International, including board minutes, annual reports, policy statements, official correspondence, papers of founders Charles and Lettie Cowman, papers of other OMS missionaries, official publications, photos, films, and audio tapes relating to work in China.

ORAL HISTORIES: Oral histories of Lettie Cowman, 1952; Eugene and Esther Erny, 1976, 1980; Anna Hsio, n.d.; Lee Jefferies, 1960; Edwin L. Kilbourne, 1977; and Garnett Phillippe, 1960, 1977.

SERIALS: *Electric Messages*, 1908–14. *Oriental and Inter-American Standard*, 1944–49. *Oriental Missionary Standard*, 1914–44. *Our Children's Own Magazine*, 1929–41, 1944–55. *Our Prayer Circle Bulletin*, 1933–39, 1941.

2-WILLIAM WESBER WHITE COLLECTION, 1910–35, quantity undetermined
Background note: William Wesber White (1863–1944) founded the Biblical Seminary of New York.
MINUTES/RECORDS/REPORTS/CORRESPONDENCE: Foochow Union Theological School, records of the course of study, correspondence and reports, n.d.; Kuling Convention, minutes, 1910; minutes of unspecified conferences in Nanking.

KY-90   B. L. Fisher Library
Asbury Theological Seminary
North Lexington Avenue
Wilmore KY 40390
(606) 858-3581
D. William Faupel, Director of Library Services

1-GENERAL HOLDINGS
MINUTES/RECORDS/REPORTS: China Inland Mission, annual reports, 1931, 1939, 1945–47, 1949, 1951–53, 1955, 1957; Christian Conference of Asia, reports on visits to China, 1981, 1983; Church of the United Brethren, report of a foreign deputation, 1911–12; Consultation of World Evangelization, report on China, 1980; International Institute of China, report, 1894–1910.

Methodist Episcopal Church: unidentified annual report, 1868–1938; Chungking-West China, Woman's Conference, report, n.d.; Foochow Annual Conference, 1940; Kiangsi Annual Conference, minutes, 1931, 1934; North China Mission, minutes, 1869–1938; Shantung Annual Conference, 1931, 1933; West China Annual Conference, 1915, 1917–19, 1921–22; Yenping Annual Conference, minutes, 1925; records, 1939; Methodist Episcopal Church, South, China Annual Conference, minutes, 1900, 1921; West China Missionary Conference, report, 1908.
MANUSCRIPTS: "Confucius and Christ: A Modern Missionary Strategy for China," by Paul B. Denlinger, 197?; "Het leven en het werk van Dr. John A. Otte: in leven geneesheer-directeur van Nederlands Wilhelmina," n.a., n.d.; "Notes on the Chronological List of Missionaries to China and the Chinese, 1807–1942," by Charles L. Boynton, 194?.
PAMPHLETS: *Bethel Mission of China, Inc.*, n.d.; *British Protestant Christian Evangelists and the 1898 Reform Movement in China*, by Leslie R. Marchant, 1975.
SERIALS: Bethel Mission of China, *Newsletter*, 1950, 1959–74. *Bridge*, 1984–. Catholic University of Peking, *Bulletin*, 1926–34. *China and the Church Today*, 1979–86. *China Christian Year Book*, 1910–39. *China Monthly*, 1939–50. *China News and Church Report*, 1984, 1987–. *China Notes*, 1962–. *China's Millions* (Philadelphia), 1952. *Chinese World Pulse*, 1977–83. *Ching Feng*, 1964–. *East Asia Millions* (Philadelphia), 1961–. *ECF News*, 1957–. *Friends Oriental News*, 1948–62. Lutheran World Federation, *Information Letter* (LWF Marxism and China Study), 1972–. *Millions* (Philadelphia), 1952–61.
DISSERTATIONS/THESES: *American Missionaries and the Chinese Communists: A Study of Views Expressed by Methodist Episcopal Church Missionaries, 1921–1941*, by Milo Lancaster Thornberry, 1974. *A Study of the Development of Christian Education in China*, by Samuel Kun-kang Chen, 1955.

LOUISIANA

BATON ROUGE

LOUISIANA STATE UNIVERSITY

LA-5   Law Center Library
Baton Rouge LA 70803-1010
(504) 388-8802
Lance E. Dickson, Director

1-GENERAL HOLDINGS
SERIALS: *China Law Review*, 1922–40.

LA-10   Troy H. Middleton Library
Louisiana State University
Baton Rouge LA 70803
(504) 388-2217
Sharon A. Hogan, Director

1-GENERAL HOLDINGS
SERIALS: *Lingnan Science Journal*, 1926–27, 1929–30, 1932, 1934, 1936–42, 1945, 1948–49.

NEW ORLEANS

NEW ORLEANS BAPTIST THEOLOGICAL SEMINARY
LA-15   John T. Christian Library
4110 Seminary Place
New Orleans LA 70126
(504) 282-4455
Paul Gericke, Director
George Washburn, Reference Librarian

1-GENERAL HOLDINGS
MINUTES/RECORDS/REPORTS: China Baptist Centenary Celebrations, records and addresses, 1936.
PAMPHLETS: *Church Planting*, by Sidney George Peill, 1924; *The New Situation in China*, by C. J. Thompson, n.d.; *Southern Baptist Missions in China*, by S. J. Porter, n.d.; *Yang Ts'uen-ling, Captive, Soldier, Evangelist*, by George T. Howell, n.d.
SERIALS: *China Christian Year Book*, 1926, 1928–29, 1931–37. *China Mission Year Book*, 1911, 1916, 1919, 1923–25.

DISSERTATIONS/THESES: *Education of Women by Baptists in South China*, by Pauline Frances Brammer, 1947. *Edwin McNeill Poteat: A Study of His Life and Work*, by Henry D. Smith, Jr., 1963. *The Effects of the War on the Future of Our Mission Work in China*, by Frances Audrey Berry, 1945. *Protestant Mission Schools for Girls in South China (1827 to the Japanese Invasion)*, by Mary Raleigh Anderson, 1943. *Southern Baptist Contributions to Missions in China: A Survey of Investments and Achievements*, by Park Harris Anderson, 1947. *A Survey of Chinese Baptist Missions of the Northern and Southern Boards in the United States*, by Pauline Fei Ha Cheung, 1940. *A Survey of Southern Baptist Medical Missions in China*, by Park Harris Anderson, 1946.

SHREVEPORT

CENTENARY COLLEGE OF LOUISIANA
LA-20 **Magale Library**
Woodlawn Avenue at Columbia Street
P. O. Box 4188
Shreveport LA 71134
(318) 869-5170
James G. Volny, Director
Carolyn Garrison, Archivist

1-CENTENARY COLLEGE ARCHIVES, 1878-1947, 118 items
MINUTES/RECORDS/REPORTS: Methodist Episcopal Church: Central China Conference, minutes, 1888, 1892, 1897, 1899, 1906-8, 1916-17, 1920, 1947; Eastern Central Asia Conference, minutes, 1915, 1920, 1923; Foochow Conference, minutes, 1878-79, 1882-83, 1885-89, 1891, 1894-1928; Foochow Woman's Conference, minutes, 1887, 1891, 1895, 1898, 1902, 1926-31; North China mission, minutes, 1885, 1889-92, 1894-96, 1899, 1906-10, 1920-24, 1929, 1935; North China Woman's Conference, minutes, 1898, 1913; South Fukien Conference, minutes, 1923-33; West China Conference, minutes, 1906-7, 1910, 1917-19, 1921-22; Yenping Conference, minutes, 1917-22.

MAINE

BANGOR

BANGOR THEOLOGICAL SEMINARY
ME-5 **Moulton Library**
300 Union Street
Bangor ME 04401
(207) 942-6781
Clifton G. Davis, Librarian

1-GENERAL HOLDINGS
CORRESPONDENCE: Correspondence of Bangor Theological Seminary graduates: Edwin Kellogg, from Shaowu, 1914-40; Harry S. Martin, from Tung Shien, Chihli, 1918-37.
PAMPHLETS: *Jesuit Letters from China, 1583-1584*, ed. and trans. by Howard Rienstra, 1986.
AUDIO-VISUAL MATERIALS: Photocopy of memorial tablet at the Old South Church in Farmington, Maine, to Mary Susan Morrill, a Maine native and Mount Holyoke college graduate who was martyred at Paotingfu in 1900.
SERIALS: *China Christian Year Book*, 1924-26. *Chinese Recorder*, 1927-31.
DISSERTATIONS/THESES: *An Experiment in Teaching the Christian Religion by Life Situations in Fan Village, China*, by Mabel Ellis Hubbard, 1938. *Protestant Mission Schools for Girls in South China (1827 to the Japanese Invasion)*, by Mary Raleigh Anderson, 1943.

BRUNSWICK

BOWDOIN COLLEGE
ME-10 **Library**
Brunswick ME 04011
(207) 725-3000
Dianne M. Gutscher, Curator, Special Collections

1-ABBOTT MEMORIAL COLLECTION, 1898-1902, 2 volumes
CHINESE LANGUAGE MATERIALS: Bible and New Testament, trans. by Samuel I. J. Schereschewsky, 1898, 1902.

2-HUNTINGTON GILCHRIST COLLECTION, 1914-70, ca. 1.5 c.f.
Background note: Huntington Gilchrist (1891-1975) taught at Foochow Methodist College between 1914 and 1916. The collection is not fully catalogued.
CORRESPONDENCE: Ca. 100 letters (averaging 10 pages each), from Gilchrist, primarily to his mother, with discussions of the Methodist mission in Foochow, the American Board mission, and visiting missionaries, ca. 1914-1916.
MANUSCRIPTS: "Hon. Huntington Gilchrist," n.a., 1970.
DIARIES: Diary written by Gilchrist en route to China, ending with his arrival, 1914.
MEMORABILIA: Flyer soliciting contributions to the Sherwood Eddy evangelistic campaign for government students in Peking, 1914, with handwritten note on reverse side by Gilchrist.
AUDIO-VISUAL MATERIALS: Ca. 150 uncatalogued photo negatives taken by Gilchrist, mostly of China.

LEWISTON

BATES COLLEGE
ME-15 **George and Helen Ladd Library**
Lewiston ME 04240
(207) 786-6263
Mary Riley, Special Collections Librarian

1-GENERAL HOLDINGS
SERIALS: *China Mission Year Book*, 1910.

PORTLAND

ME-20 MAINE HISTORICAL SOCIETY
485 Congress Street
Portland ME 04101
(207) 774-1822
Thomas L. Gaffney, Curator of Manuscripts

1-SARAH ELIZABETH KENDALL COLLECTION, 1889-1900, 18 items
Background note: Mary S. Morrill and Annie Allender Gould, both of Portland, were missionaries killed in Paotingfu in 1900. For biographical notes on Annie Allender Gould and other material relating to Mary S. Morrill, see United States Military Academy, Library Special Collections, West Point, NY, 10996. See also Mount Holyoke College, Williston Memorial Library, College History and Archives, South Hadley, MA, 01075.
CORRESPONDENCE: 18 letters from Mary S. Morrill to Sarah Kendall, Paotingfu, 1889-1900.

WATERVILLE

COLBY COLLEGE
ME-25 Miller Library
Waterville ME 04901
(207) 873-1131
Patience-Anne W. Lenk, Special Collections

Background note: Colby College has a long history of graduates who became missionaries. The college maintains biographical files in its College Alumni Archives, including the following who went to China but left no collections at Colby: Hazel E. Barney (1918), Hazel M. Gibbs (1917), Henry Kingman (1884), Arthur Hartstein Page (1898), Ellen Josephine Peterson (1907), Hugh Laughlin Robinson (1918), and Abbie Gertrude Sanderson (1914). The collections below are from the biographical files.

1-EDWIN PALMER BURTT, n.d, 1 item
Background note: Edwin Palmer Burtt (1858-1940), Class of 1884, who later became head of the Evangel mission in Shui Hing, spent 30 years in China. When he first arrived, about 1900, he ran a school for blind girls in Shui Hing, South China.
CORRESPONDENCE: Letter to Colby President Johnson, regarding Burtt's stay in China, n.d.

2-JOHN HESS FOSTER, 1981, 1 folder
Background note: For biographical notes see Yale Divinity School, Special Collections, 409 Prospect Street, New Haven, CT, 06510.
MANUSCRIPTS/AUDIO-VISUAL MATERIALS: "Looking Backward: Random Recollections and Reminiscences," n.a., including photos of experiences in China, n.d.
ORAL HISTORIES: "Changsha Memories of John H. Foster, M.D.," 1981.

3-ARTHUR G. ROBINSON, 1932-64, 1 folder
Background note: For biographical notes, see Wellesley College, Archives, Margaret Clapp Library, Wellesley, MA, 02181. See also Harvard University, Houghton Library, Cambridge, MA, 02138.

MANUSCRIPTS/AUDIO-VISUAL MATERIALS: "Robbie: 1884-1964, An Informal Biography of A. G. Robinson," by his wife, Marian Rider Robinson, including photos, n.d.
PAMPHLETS: *The Senior Returned Students: A Brief Account of the Chinese Educational Commission (1872-1881) under Dr. Yung Wing*, by Arthur G. Robinson, 1932.

4-HENRY ALLEN SAWTELLE, n.d., 1 item
Background note: Henry Allen Sawtelle (b. 1832), Class of 1854 graduate, was ordained as a Baptist minister after studies at Newton Theological Institute. He was appointed by the American Baptist Missionary Union to be a missionary in China in 1859. Stationed in Hong Kong until 1861, he then served in Swatow for several months before returning to California.
MANUSCRIPTS: Bibliography of Sawtelle's publications from 1856 to 1875.

5-CHESTER FRANK WOOD, n.d., 1 item
Background note: Chester Frank Wood (b. 1892), Class of 1914, went to China in 1920 as a missionary under the American Baptist Foreign Missionary Society, serving in Yachow until 1925. He returned to China in 1930 to work in Suifu, Szechuan, where he was director of the YMCA and advisor in school management.
MANUSCRIPTS: "Christian Dynamic and Chinese Determination," by Chester Frank Wood, n.d.

6-GENERAL HOLDINGS
MANUSCRIPTS: "Colby College Missionaries to China," by Erin Foster, 1986.

MARYLAND

BALTIMORE

JOHNS HOPKINS UNIVERSITY

MD-5 Alan Mason Chesney Medical Archives
Johns Hopkins Medical Institutions
35 Turner Auditorium
720 Rutland Avenue
Baltimore MD 21205
(301) 955-3043
A. McGehee Harvey, Archivist
Nancy McCall, Assistant Archivist
Gerard Shorb, Archives/Records Coordinator

1-SIMON FLEXNER CORRESPONDENCE, 1935-40, quantity undetermined
Background note: Simon Flexner was a trustee of the China Medical Board. For other papers relating to Simon Flexner and the China Medical Board, see the American Philosophical Society

Library, 105 South Fifth Street, Philadelphia, PA, 19106, and Rockefeller University, Rockefeller Archive Center, Pocantico Hills, North Tarrytown, NY, 10591.

CORRESPONDENCE: Correspondence relating to William Henry Welch, his work, his family, his visits to China and Peking Union Medical College, including such correspondents as Edward H. Hume, Franklin C. McLean, and H. F. Pierce.

2-WILLIAM HENRY WELCH PAPERS, 1915–21, quantity undetermined

Background note: William Henry Welch was instrumental in the founding of the Johns Hopkins Medical Institutions, the *Journal of Experimental Medicine*, and Peking Union Medical College (PUMC).

MINUTES/RECORDS/REPORTS: "Report of the China Medical Commission to the Rockefeller Foundation," 1916; lists of physicians and nurses at medical schools in China; 3 boxes of Chinese medical school catalogues, 1908–24.

DIARIES: 7 diaries describing Welch's trips to China and Japan, with 7 folders of diary notes and expense accounts, 1915, 1921.

MANUSCRIPTS: Addresses by Welch to the students of PUMC and to Yale students, 1915; miscellaneous papers of the Rockefeller Foundation relating to PUMC, 1916–40(?); outline of an address on medicine in China, 1921.

PAMPHLETS: Travel guides.

MEMORABILIA: 3 boxes of notes on Chinese education and medicine from a trip with China Medical Commission in 1915; 3 boxes of clippings and articles about medicine and PUMC in China; China Medical Board invitation, 1920; invitation to 25th anniversary of Yale-in-China at Changsha, 1931.

FINDING AIDS: In-house directory.

MD–10   Milton S. Eisenhower Library
Johns Hopkins University
Baltimore MD 21218
(301) 338–8000
Ed Rosenfeld, Associate Director for
    Collection Services

1-GENERAL HOLDINGS

MINUTES/RECORDS/REPORTS: International Institute of China (Mission among the Higher Classes in China), reports by Gilbert Reid, 1911, 1918, 1926.

PAMPHLETS: *The Catholic Missions in China during the Middle Ages, 1294–1368*, by Paul Stanislaus Hsiang, 1949; *China's Attempt to Absorb Christianity: The Decree of March 15, 1899*, by George Nye Steiger, 1926; *The Present Situation in China and Its Significance for Christian Missions*, 1925.

SERIALS: Catholic University of Peking, *Bulletin*, 1926, 1928, 1930–31. China International Famine Relief Commission, Publications, series A, 1923–37. *China Law Review*, 1925–29. *China Monthly: The Truth about China*, 1939–50. *Chinese Recorder*, 1925–28. *Collectanea Commissionis Synodalis*, 1928–31. *Les Missions de Chine et du Japon*, 1933. *News of China*, 1942–49. University of Nanking, College of Agriculture and Forestry, *Bulletin*, 1932. *USC Envoy*, 1946–47. *Yenching Journal of Social Studies*, 1938–50. Yenching University, *Social Research Series*, 1930.

DISSERTATIONS/THESES: *Apostolic Legations to China of the Eighteenth Century*, by Antonio Sisto Rosso, 1948. *China and Educational Autonomy: The Changing Role of the Protestant Edu-*

cational Missionary in China, 1807–1937, by Alice Henrietta Gregg, 1946. *Christian Missions in China*, by Charles Sumner Estes, 1895. *Karl Gützlaff als Missionar in China*, by Herman Schlyter, 1946. *The Legal and Political Aspects of the Missionary Movement in China*, by Chao-kwang Wu, 1928. *Lutheran Missions in a Time of Revolution: The China Experience, 1944–1951*, by Jonas Jonson, 1972. *The Mission of Matteo Ricci, S.J.: A Case Study of an Effort at Guided Culture Change in China in the Sixteenth Century*, by George Lawrence Harris, 1967. *The Negotiations between Ch'i-ying and Lagrené, 1844–1846*, by Angelus Francis J. Grosse-Aschhoff, 1950. *Protestant Mission Schools for Girls in South China (1827 to the Japanese Invasion)*, by Mary Raleigh Anderson, 1943.

CHINESE LANGUAGE MATERIALS/SERIALS: *Chin-ling hsüeh pao (Nanking Journal)*, 1931-. *Fu jen hsüeh chih (Fu jen Sinological Journal)*, 1929.

MD–15   Ferdinand Hamburger, Jr., Archives
Johns Hopkins University
3400 North Charles Street
Baltimore MD 21218
(301) 338–8323
Julia B. Morgan, Archivist
James K. Stimpert, Assistant Archivist

Restrictions: Administrative records are restricted for fifty years from the date of creation.

Background note: The Ferdinand Hamburger, Jr., Archives is the official archival repository for the non-medical divisions of Johns Hopkins University. The materials described below are contained in the Records of the Office of the President (RG 02.001), series 1, Numerical Subject Files, 1903–63.

Finding aids: In-house archival inventory and index.

1-ASSOCIATION OF AMERICAN UNIVERSITIES (AAU), 1916–17, 1 file

MINUTES/RECORDS/REPORTS/CORRESPONDENCE: Reports and correspondence relating to President Frank J. Goodnow's activities as chairman of an AAU committee on the rating of Oriental institutions of higher education for the purpose of admissions to the graduate schools of the AAU, 1916–17, including correspondence with C. K. Edmunds (president of Canton Christian College), W. W. Willoughby, R. M. M. Elroy, A. O. Lausthner, Yoohi S. Kuno, S. C. Kiang, and Herman Ames.

2-CHINESE MATTERS, ca. 1914-ca. 1935, 8 files

MINUTES/RECORDS/REPORTS: Peking Union Medical College, Executive Committee, minutes, n.d.

CORRESPONDENCE: Letter from Edward H. Hume on medical education in China, n.d.; letter to John Fryer from E. LeRoy Moore, regarding the arrangement of characters in Chinese dictionaries, n.d.; letter from J. S. Burgess regarding Princeton work in China, n.d.; letter from the Chinese YMCA, introducing Lun Hsi, n.d.; correspondence relating to the China International Famine Relief Commission, 1925–32.

MANUSCRIPTS: "Plea for the Development of Hospitals in China," by B. H. Griswold, n.d.

3-CHINA MEDICAL BOARD, 1919–27, 11 files

Background note: See also Rockefeller University, Rockefeller

Archive Center, Pocantico Hills, North Tarrytown, NY, 10591. MINUTES/RECORDS/REPORTS/CORRESPONDENCE: Papers relating to President Frank J. Goodnow's participation in the China Medical Board, consisting of minutes, memos, and correspondence, including topics such as Peking Union Medical College and building hospitals in China, 1919–27.

4-CHINESE RELIEF, 1920–21, 1 file
MINUTES/RECORDS/REPORTS/CORRESPONDENCE: Correspondence and reports of President Frank J. Goodnow relating to his participation in the China International Famine Relief Commission, including the YMCA and the Bible House, 1920–21.

5-INTERNATIONAL INSTITUTE OF CHINA, 1907–10, 1 file
MINUTES/RECORDS/REPORTS/CORRESPONDENCE: Prospectus and correspondence with President Ira Remsen, 1907–10.

6-ISAIAH BOWMAN, 1937–38, 1 file
CORRESPONDENCE: Correspondence between the Chinese Students' Club and President Isaiah Bowman, to secure his support for a benefit lecture by T. Z. Koo, 1937–38.

7-ORIENTAL LANGUAGES, DEPARTMENT OF, 1912, 1 item
CORRESPONDENCE: Letter from missionary C. Spurgeon Medhurst to President Ira Remsen, requesting the University's sponsorship of his research in Chinese mysticism and philosophy, 1912.

MD-20 George Peabody Institute Library
17 East Mount Vernon Place
Baltimore MD 21202
(301) 659-8197
Robert Bartram, Librarian

Background note: The Peabody Institute Library is administered by the Special Collections division of the Eisenhower Library.

1-GENERAL HOLDINGS
SERIALS: *Chinese Repository*, 1832–51.

LOVELY LANE MUSEUM
MD-25 Library
2200 St. Paul Street
Baltimore MD 21218
(301) 889-4458
Edwin Schell, Executive Secretary

Background note: Lovely Lane Museum is the museum of the Baltimore Conference of the United Methodist Church, which resulted from the 1968 merger of the Evangelical United Brethren Church with the Methodist Church. The Methodist Church had been formed in 1939 from the reunion of the Methodist Episcopal Church, the Methodist Episcopal Church, South, and the Methodist Protestant Church, churches which had broken away from one another before the Civil War.

1-CHINA BISHOPS PAPERS, 1879–1961, 33 items
Background note: John Franklin Goucher was a leader and benefactor of Methodist mission work (see his papers below). The material is arranged alphabetically by writer within the library's files of correspondence.
MINUTES/RECORDS/REPORTS: 2 reports by Bishop J. W.

Bashford, Peking, to John Goucher, on the China mission of the Methodist Episcopal Church, 1913.
CORRESPONDENCE: Letters concerning Methodist mission work in China, especially educational endeavors and financial needs: 3 letters from Bishop I. W. Wiley to John Goucher, 1879–81; 2 letters from Bishop David H. Moore in Shanghai to Goucher, 1901–5; 13 letters from Bishop Bashford in Peking to Goucher, 1902–17; 3 letters from Bishop Wilson S. Lewis in Peking to Goucher, 1912–21; 3 miscellaneous letters of Bishop Bashford; 7 letters of Bishop and Mrs. John Gowdy, mostly to Elsie Krug and her daughter, Dorothy Krug, 1930–61.

2-JOHN FRANKLIN GOUCHER PAPERS, ca. 1881–1922, quantity undetermined
Background note: For biographical notes, see Goucher College, Julia Rogers Library, Towson, MD, 21204. Goucher made at least three trips to China to visit institutions and missions with which he was connected, and he frequently attended meetings in the United States and abroad regarding the same organizations. For correspondence from Methodist Episcopal bishops in China seeking his financial assistance, see the China Bishops Papers described above. See also Union Theological Seminary, Archives, 3041 Broadway at Reinhold Niebuhr Place, New York, NY, 10027.
CORRESPONDENCE/MEMORABILIA: Miscellaneous correspondence, clippings, and other memorabilia relating to Goucher.
DIARIES: 1906–7 diary including a list of places visited (or scheduled for visits) in Hong Kong, Canton, Amoy, Foochow, and Shanghai; travel diary with observations of Shanghai and elsewhere, 1906–7; travel diary containing notes on addresses and meetings in Peking and Tsinan, at West China Union University, and elsewhere, early 1920; 3 daily appointment books with notations about meetings held around the world regarding his interests in China, 1913, 1917, 1921.
MANUSCRIPTS: "John Franklin Goucher, Educator-Missionary Statesman," by Carlyle Reede Earp, 1960.

3-ELSIE (CLARK) KRUG PAPERS, ca. 1940s, 1 folder
Background note: Elsie (Clark) Krug (1888–1982) was a missionary to China from 1912 to 1918 under the Woman's Foreign Missionary Society of the Methodist Episcopal Church. She taught various subjects at Hwa Nan (Women's) College in Foochow. After her return to the United States she married Andrew H. Krug. She subsequently returned to China in 1932 and 1933. Her correspondence and diary are held by the Yale Divinity School, Special Collections, 409 Prospect Street, New Haven, CT, 06510 (Record Group 8).
MINUTES/RECORDS/REPORTS: Foochow Conference, n.d. (ca. 1940s).
AUDIO-VISUAL MATERIALS: Photos of the first two Methodist churches in Asia, Chinese leaders, hospitals, and schools, n.d.
SERIALS: *Foochow News* (report of the Methodist mission in Foochow), 1940.

4-GENERAL HOLDINGS
MINUTES/RECORDS/REPORTS: Mary Porter Gamewell School, Peking, catalogue/yearbook, 1939.
SERIALS: *Foochow News*, 1937–38; anniversary pictorial supplement, n.d. *Tung Wu Magazine*, 1935.
CHINESE LANGUAGE MATERIALS: Mary Porter Gamewell School, Peking, catalogue/yearbook, n.d. (1939?).

MARYLAND HISTORICAL SOCIETY

MD-30 Manuscripts Division

201 West Monument Street
Baltimore MD 21201
(301) 685-3750
Susan Weinandy, Assistant Manuscripts Librarian

Restrictions: Access by appointment.

1-BRUNE-RANDALL FAMILY PAPERS (MS 2004), 1922-23, 1 box
Background note: Harry Richmond Slack served as a Protestant Episcopal medical missionary at Peking Union Medical College (PUMC) from 1922 to 1923.
CORRESPONDENCE: Box of correspondence between Harry and Elizabeth Blanchard Randall Slack, and family members, during Slack's tenure at PUMC, 1922-23; 13 letters mentioning PUMC, 1922-23.
FINDING AIDS: In-house directory.

2-GRAVES-STEWART COLLECTION (MS 1991), 1882-1912, 5 items
Background note: Rosewell Hobart Graves (1833-1912) was a medical missionary to China from 1856 to 1895.
CORRESPONDENCE: Letter from Graves, Canton, to "William," 1882.
MANUSCRIPTS: Bound volume of poetry, essays, and a bound notebook containing an operetta, "Cinderella," by Graves, 1882-86.
PAMPHLETS/MEMORABILIA: Memorial pamphlet of Graves, 1912, and obituary of his wife, Jane W. (Morris) Graves, n.d.

3-HYATT COLLECTION (MS 1007), 1886, 1 item
CORRESPONDENCE: Letter from Adele Marion Fielde to Alpheus Hyatt, describing missionary activities in Swatow, 1886.

4-SHOEMAKER PAPERS (MS 1968), 1917-18, 1 box
Background note: Samuel Moor Shoemaker (1893-1963) was a Protestant Episcopal minister and evangelist.
CORRESPONDENCE: Box of letters of Samuel Moor Shoemaker concerning missionary activity in China, 1917-18.

5-WATERS PAPERS (MS 1457), 1905, ca. 8 items
Background note: A missionary to China with the China Inland Mission from 1901 to 1911, Mary Elizabeth Waters was in China from 1908 to 1911.
MINUTES/RECORDS/REPORTS: Certificate certifying Mary Elizabeth Waters as a Junior Missionary of the China Inland Mission, 1905.
MEMORABILIA: Ca. 7 certificates and passports.

BETHESDA

MD-35 NATIONAL LIBRARY OF MEDICINE

Bethesda MD 20894
(301) 496-6097 (Reference, Public Services Division)
(301) 496-5405 (History of Medicine)
Eva Marie Lacroix, Chief, Public Services Division
John Parascandola, Chief, History of Medicine Division

Background note: Formerly the Library of the U.S. Army Surgeon General, the National Library of Medicine (NLM) has its collection in two divisions: the History of Medicine Division, which contains all pre-1871 publications and all manuscripts and photos; and the Public Services Division, which contains most post-1870 publications.
Finding aids: Several types of finding aids are available for the two collections of the National Library of Medicine. First, there are published catalogs, the most important of which is the *Index-Catalogue of the Library of the Surgeon-General's Office*, which was published in five series between 1880 and 1961. The Surgeon General's library is now part of the National Library of Medicine. The *Index-Catalogues* list books, reports, and articles by subject.

Other important catalogs include the *Armed Forces Medical Library Catalog*, covering 1950-54; the *National Library of Medicine (Current) Catalog*, the *Index of NLM Serial Titles*, and *Biomedical Serials, 1950-1960, A Selective List of Serials in the National Library of Medicine*, comp. by Lela M. Spanier, 1962. The library also has an online catalog, CATLINE, which can be searched at the National Library or at institutions which have online access to the MEDLARS database.

1-HISTORY OF MEDICINE DIVISION, 1827-1940s, quantity undetermined
MINUTES/RECORDS/REPORTS: China Medico-Chirurgical Society, transactions, 1845-46; Chinese Hospital at Shanghai, annual reports, 1862, 1864, 1869, 1874; Hankow Medical Missionary Hospital, annual report, 1864-67; London Mission Hospital, Tientsin, 186?-194?; Medical Missionary Hospital at Swatow, in connection with the Presbyterian Church of England, reports, 1863-79; Medical Missionary Society in China: minutes, proceedings, and report of the Ophthalmic Institution at Macao, 1827-32, 1838-39; Ophthalmic Hospital at Canton, reports, 1836-37, 1839, 1842-51; address and minutes, Canton, 1838; objects of the society, 1838; proceedings and reports of officers to the society, 1838-42, 1844-45, 1858-81, 1884 (some including report for Canton Hospital); papers relative to hospitals in China, 1841; statements respecting hospitals in China, 1841, 1842; report, with history and plans, 1841-42, together with report on Macao hospital, 1841-42, and Parker's report, 1843; minutes of annual meetings and Canton Ophthalmic Hospital, 1850-51; Hospital at Ningpo, 1852; reports, 1858-99 (some including reports of South China Medical College and Canton Hospital); mission hospital (Kam-li-fau Hospital) in the western suburbs of Canton, 1849, 1853-54, 1859-60; Peking Hospital, connected with the London Missionary Society, reports, 1864-68, 1870-71, 1873.
PAMPHLETS: *The Advantages of Medical Missions to China*, n.a., 1852; *An Appeal to the Religious and Benevolent Public on Behalf of a Proposal to Establish a Medical School for the Natives of China in Connection with the Chinese Medical Mission at Hong-Kong*, n.a., 1846; *A Brief Account of an Ophthalmic Institution during the Years 1827-1832, at Macao*, n.a., 1834; *The Medical Missionary Society in China*, by T. R. Colledge, 1838; *Suggestions for the Formation of a Medical Missionary Society*, by T. R. Colledge, P. Parker, and E. C. Bridgman, 1836.
SERIALS: *Chinese Repository*, 1848.

2-PUBLIC SERVICES DIVISION, 1858-, quantity undetermined
MINUTES/RECORDS/REPORTS: American Presbyterian Hos-

pital, Hoihow, 1880-?; American Presbyterian Hospital, Weihsien, Shantung, 1918-24; Cheeloo University (Shantung Christian University), School of Medicine, reports, 1920-ca.1938; China Inland Mission Hospital at Kaifeng, reports, 1905-?, 1914, 1916-21, 1924, 1926; China Medical Board of New York, reports, n.d.; China Medical Board, Rockefeller Foundation, reports, n.d.; China Medical Commission, Rockefeller Commission, reports, 1914; China Medical Missionary Association, proposed revision of the constitution and by-laws, ca. 1924; Chinese Hospital at Shanghai, reports, 1862, 1864, 1869, 1874; Church General Hospital, Wuchang, reports, 1919-25, 1927-38, 1940; medical mission at Taiyuen-fu, Shansi, in connection with the China Inland Mission, report, 1883; Fenchow hospitals, Harwood Memorial Hospital for Men, Kate Ford Whitman Hospital for Women, and Scudder Children's Ward, annual report, 1925-?; Foochow Medical Missionary Hospital, annual report, 1871-90, 1909-12, 1914, 1916-22, 1924-25, including Opium Asylum, Foochow, report, 1878-83, Shaowu medical missionary work in connection with the American Board Mission, annual report, 1889-90, and Hospital for Women and Children, Foochow, annual report, 1889; Foochow Hospital of the Woman's Foreign Missionary Society of the Methodist Episcopal Church, annual report of the physician in charge, 1885-86; Foochow Missionary Hospital, annual report, 1909-?; Foochow Missionary Hospital, Eye Department, 1922; Hangchow Medical Mission in connection with the Church Missionary Society, 1884(?); Hospital for Chinese at the American Episcopal Mission, annual report of the officers, 1885-86; Hospitals and Nursing Services Commission, Shanghai, 1930-31; International Famine Relief Commission, annual report, 1934; Lingnan University, medical department, hospital, and infirmary, 1928-30; London Mission Hospital, Siaochang, 19??-194?; London Mission Hospital, Tientsin, 186?-194?; Medical Missionary Hospital at Fatshan, in connection with the Wesleyan Missionary Society, 1883; Medical Missionary Hospital at Swatow, in connection with the Presbyterian Church of England, 1863-79; Medical Missionary Society in China, 1858-99 (some including reports of South China Medical College and Canton Hospital); Canton Hospital, 1879; Medical Missionary Association of China: list of members, 1914; constitution, by-laws, and list of members, n.d.; Peiping Union Medical College, annual report of the superintendent, 1911-39; Peking Hospital, connected with the London Missionary Society, reports, 1864-68, 1870-71, 1873; Ponasang Missionary Hospital, Foochow, annual reports of the physician-in-charge, 1882-1909; Saint Luke's Hospital for Chinese, Shanghai, 1918-36; Sun Yat-sen Memorial Canton Hospital, Canton, 1858-99, 1902-3, 1905, 1907, 1909-11, 1913-23, 1930-35, 1939-40; T'ai Yüan Medical Mission, annual report, 1882(?)-?; Temple Hill Hospital, Chefoo, 1920-34; Tsan Yuk Hospital, clinical report, 1932-35; University of Nanking Hospital, 1917-22; Yale Foreign Missionary Society, Yale Mission, Changsha, n.d.
PAMPHLETS: *An Additional Fragment of Medical Work in China*, by Mary H. Fulton, 1889; *Arzt in China: Bilder aus der ärztlichen Mission*, by Hans Meister, 1957; *The Field and Methods of Public Health Work in the Missionary Enterprises*, by William Wesley Peter (repr. from *China Medical Journal*), 1926; *Review of the Customs Opium Smoking Returns*, by John Dudgeon, 1882; *Talks on Medical Work in India and China*, by Lilian E. Cox, 1922; miscellaneous publications of the Medical Missionary Society in China, n.d., and of the Yale Mission, Changsha, n.d.

SERIALS: *China Medical Journal*, 1907-22. *China Medical Missionary Journal*, 1887-1907. *China's Medicine*, 1966-68. Chinese Medical Association: Council on Christian Medical Work, *Bulletin*, 1947-49; Council on Medical Missions, *Occasional Leaflet*, 1932-41. *Chinese Medical Directory*, 1928-34. *Chinese Medical Journal*, 1932-66. National Christian Council of China, *Newsletter*, 1950-.
CHINESE LANGUAGE MATERIALS/SERIALS: *The Leper Quarterly*, 1927(?)-43(?). *Leprosy in China*, 1949-.
CHINESE LANGUAGE MATERIALS: *The Principles and Practices of Medicine*, by Sir William Osler (with portions of *Tropical Diseases*, by Sir Patrick Manson), 7th ed., trans. by Philip B. Cousland, 1910; *Hu ping ya shu (Manual of Nursing)*, by the Central China Medical Missionary Association, 1905; *Shan choo mih keuï (Commentaries and Maxims on the Pulse)*, by the Medical College at Peking, n.d.; *A Text-book of Practical Therapeutics, with Especial Reference to the Application of Remedial Measures to Disease and Their Employment upon a Rational Basis*, by Hobart Amory Hare, trans. by James H. Ingram, 1907 (?).

COLLEGE PARK

MD-40   ASIAN STUDIES NEWSLETTER ARCHIVES
c/o East Asia Collection
McKeldin Library
University of Maryland
College Park MD 20742-7011
(301) 454-2819
Frank Joseph Shulman, Curator

Restrictions: This is a privately maintained collection for scholars, containing files of over 1,000 academic newsletters and bulletins dealing with Asia. Access by appointment.
Finding aids: ''Bibliography of Newsletter-type Publications Available within the Asian Studies Newsletter Archives,'' by Frank Joseph Shulman, 1984.

1-GENERAL HOLDINGS
SERIALS: *China and Ourselves*, 1976-. *China and the Church Today*, 1979-86. *China Bulletin* (Rome), 1979-. *China Colleges*, 1949-53. China Graduate School of Theology, *Bulletin*, 1982-. *China Heute*, 1982-. *China Mission Studies Bulletin*, 1979-. *China News* (Atlanta), 1981-86. *China News and Church Report*, 1983-. *China News Update*, 1986-. *China Notes*, 1970-. *China Prayer Letter*, 1978-. *China Talk*, 1976-. *China Update: News in Brief*, 1981-86. *China Update: The Yale-China Association Newsletter*, 1979-. *Christianity in China: Historical Studies*, 1985-. *New Horizons*, 1953-. *Oberlin-in-China*, 1949-56. *Oberlin Shansi Memorial Association Newsletter*, 1957-. *Understanding China Newsletter*, 1965-76. *Yale-China Newsletter*, 1965-79.

UNIVERSITY OF MARYLAND
MD-45   McKeldin Library
College Park MD 20742-7011
(301) 454-2819/5459
H. Joanne Harrar, Director, University Libraries
Frank Joseph Shulman, Curator, East Asia Collection

1-EAST ASIA COLLECTION, 1868–1973, 5 volumes
Background note: In addition to the materials listed below, the East Asia Collection holds 325 serials in Chinese, among which the titles relating to Christianity in China have not yet been identified.
CHINESE LANGUAGE MATERIALS/SERIALS: *Wan kuo kung pao (The Globe Magazine. A Review of the Times)*, 1868–1906. *Yen-ching hsüeh pao (Yenching Journal of Chinese Studies)*, 1927–49.
CHINESE LANGUAGE MATERIALS: 3 volumes on the history of Christianity and Christians in China, 1971–73.

2-GENERAL HOLDINGS
ORAL HISTORIES: *China Missionaries Oral History Collection*, ed. by Cyrus H. Peake and Arthur L. Rosenbaum (Claremont Graduate School, Oral History Program), 1973. See ORAL HISTORIES Union List for the names of participants.
SERIALS: *China Mission Advocate*, 1839. *China Monthly: The Truth about China*, 1944–50. *China's Medicine*, 1966–67. *Chinese Medical Journal*, 1952, 1956–57, 1959–66. *Chinese Recorder*, 1868–1940. *Folklore Studies*, 1942–47, 1952. *Lingnan Science Journal*, 1922–48.
DISSERTATIONS/THESES: *American Missions and American Diplomacy in China, 1830–1900: A Study of the Relations of American Missionaries, American Missions, and the American Missionary Movement to the Official Relations between the United States and China to 1900*, by Allen Thomas Price, 1932. *The Anti-Christian Movement in China, 1922–1927*, by Ka-che Yip, 1970. *The China Tractor Boys*, by Francis P. McMurry, 1969. *La Politique missionaire de la France en Chine, 1842–1856: l'ouverture des cinq ports chinois au commerce étranger et la liberté réligieuse*, by Louis Tsing-sing Wei, 1960. *Protestant Mission Schools for Girls in South China (1827 to the Japanese Invasion)*, by Mary Raleigh Anderson, 1943.

EMMITSBURG

DAUGHTERS OF CHARITY OF ST. VINCENT DE PAUL
MD–50   Saint Joseph's Provincial House Archives
333 South Setor Avenue
Emmitsburg MD 21727
(301) 447–3121
Sister Aloysia Dugan, Provincial Archivist

Background note: The Company of Daughters of Charity of St. Vincent de Paul was founded in France in 1633, spread throughout Europe, and sent its first missionaries to China from France in 1848. The first American daughters went to China in the 1890s. The Emmitsburg province established a China mission in the 1920s. The sisters returned to Emmitsburg in 1931 because of imprisonment, but re-established the mission in 1936. Thereafter, they remained in China until forced to leave in 1952. The Daughters of Charity of the Emmitsburg Province and Vincentian (Congregation of the Mission) priests did parish, educational, social, and medical mission work together in places such as Kanchow, Ningtu, Sing Teng (Sinfeng), and Ningyuan. See also Daughters of Charity of St. Vincent de Paul, De Paul Provincial House, 96 Menands Road, Albany, NY, 12204, and St. John's University, Grand Central and Utopia Parkways, Jamaica, NY, 11439.

1-GENERAL HOLDINGS
MINUTES/RECORDS/REPORTS: Reports on the China mission in the *Provincial Annals*, 1896–1953.
CORRESPONDENCE: Correspondence of Sr. Clara Groell and other Daughters of Charity, mostly 1922–29.
PAMPHLETS: *The Reds Take Bishop O'Shea*, by Joseph Gately, C.M. (reprinted from *Miraculous Medal* magazine), 1953.
MEMORABILIA: Publicity concerning Vincentians, including Bishop John O'Shea, C.M.; holy cards belonging to John Gabriel Perboyre, ca.1835–1840; accounts by and notes on Sr. Vincent de Lude, 1928–31 and 1936–52; wood pieces from coffins of 1870 Tientsin martyrdom; medal awarded by Czar Nicholas II to Sr. Joannes O'Connell for nursing soldiers during the Boxer Rebellion.
MAPS/DESIGNS/DRAWINGS: Map of Vincentian mission area, including Kanchow, Ningtu, Sinfeng, and Ningyuan, n.d.; artist's rendition of 1870 Tientsin martyrdom.
AUDIO-VISUAL MATERIALS: Photos and prints of Bishop John O'Shea, C.M.; François Régis Clet, ca. 1820; John Gabriel Perboyre, ca.1835–40; 1870 martyrs of Tientsin; and other Vincentians and Daughters of Charity engaged in working with orphans, lepers, and the aged; working in dispensaries and hospitals; and teaching, especially practical skills such as needlework and woodworking.
FINDING AIDS: In-house list.

MOUNT ST. MARY'S COLLEGE
MD–55   Special Collections
Archives House
Emmitsburg MD 21727–7799
(301) 447–6122
Kelly Fitzpatrick, Archivist

1-GENERAL HOLDINGS
DISSERTATIONS/THESES: *The Maryknoll Movement*, by George C. Powers, 1926.

FROSTBURG

FROSTBURG STATE COLLEGE
MD–60   Library
Frostburg MD 21532
(301) 689–4888
David Gillespie, Director

1-GENERAL HOLDINGS
PAMPHLETS: *Bishop James Walsh*, containing articles from the *Cumberland News* and the *Cumberland Evening Times*, comp. by Hazel Groves Hansrote, 1981.

TAKOMA PARK

COLUMBIA UNION COLLEGE
MD–65   Theofield G. Weis Library
7600 Flower Avenue
Takoma Park MD 20912
(301) 270–9200
Margaret von Hake, Director of the Library

1-GENERAL HOLDINGS
MINUTES/RECORDS/REPORTS: China Inland Mission, report, 1933; reports on the China mission in Seventh-Day Adventist serials: *Canadian Watchman*, 1921–52; *Life and Health*, 1905–06, 1909–60; *Ministry*, 1928–60; *Review and Herald*, 1865–83, 1887–98, 1900–1965; *Signs of the Times*, 1930–60; *Watchman Magazine*, 1905, 1918–19, 1922–23, 1925, 1927–60; *Youth's Instructor*, 1883–84, 1900–1907, 1910–65.
PAMPHLETS: *The Preparation of Missionaries Appointed to China*, by the Board of Missionary Preparation, n.d.
SERIALS: *Far Eastern Division Outlook*, 1948-.

TOWSON

GOUCHER COLLEGE
MD–70 Julia Rogers Library
Towson MD 21204
(301) 337-6364
Betty R. Kondayan, Librarian
Barbara Simons, Reference Librarian

Background note: Goucher College was founded in 1885, as the Woman's College of Baltimore City, by John Franklin Goucher, a Methodist who promoted Christian missions and educational work. The name was changed to the Woman's College of Baltimore in 1890 and to Goucher College in 1910.

1-JOHN FRANKLIN GOUCHER PAPERS, ca. 1920–1938, 1 box
Background note: John Franklin Goucher (1845–1922) was a Methodist missionary statesman and benefactor of Methodist religious, educational, and medical institutions in the United States and in many foreign countries. In 1881 he founded the West China Mission of the Methodist Episcopal Church. Later he became president of the board of governors of West China Union University in Chengtu and a trustee of the University of Peking.

Goucher made at least three trips to China to visit institutions and missions with which he was connected. He persuaded James N. Gamble of Proctor and Gamble to build Gamble Memorial Hospital in Chungking. Goucher, with his wife, provided the funds for the construction of Isabella Fisher Hospital in Tientsin, as a memorial to Mrs. Goucher's sister. For other papers of John Goucher, see Lovely Lane Museum, Library, 2200 St. Paul Street, Baltimore, MD, 21218; and Union Theological Seminary, Archives, 3041 Broadway at Reinhold Niebuhr Place, New York, NY, 10027.
CORRESPONDENCE: Several letters from John B. Van Meter, acting president of the College, concerning 1907 Goucher's trip to China, 1907.
MANUSCRIPTS: ''The Life of Dr. Goucher,'' by Betsy Woollen, n.d.
MAPS/DESIGNS/DRAWINGS: Hand-drawn map of West China Union University and The Goucher [junior high] School, 1938.
AUDIO-VISUAL MATERIALS: Photo of John Goucher, ca. 1920.

2-GENERAL HOLDINGS
SERIALS: *China's Millions* (Philadelphia), 1893–94, 1901–2, 1904.

MASSACHUSETTS

AMHERST

AMHERST COLLEGE

MA–5 Archives
Amherst MA 01002
(413) 542-2299/2068
Daria D'Arienzo, Archivist of the College

Background note: A few early graduates of Amherst College went to China. Among them was Elijah Coleman Bridgman, Class of 1826; Charles Hartwell, Class of 1849; and Peter Parker, a founder of the Medical Missionary Society, who left Amherst at the end of his junior year to study medicine and theology at Yale University, before becoming a medical missionary under the American Board of Commissioners for Foreign Missions. The *Amherst College Biographical Record* contains brief sketches on each of them in addition to the materials detailed below.

1-ELIJAH COLEMAN BRIDGMAN COLLECTION, n.d., 1 folder
Background note: For biographical notes, see Belchertown Historical Association, Stone House Museum, 20 Maple Street, Belchertown, MA, 01007.
MEMORABILIA: Miscellaneous articles about Bridgman.
AUDIO-VISUAL MATERIALS: Photo of Elijah Bridgman, n.d.; print of a group of mourners in China, one of whom appears to be Bridgman, n.d.; 2 photos of his home in Belchertown, n.d.

2-CHARLES HARTWELL COLLECTION, ca. 1850s–1899, 1 folder
Background note: Charles Hartwell (1825–1905) was a missionary in Foochow under the American Board of Commissioners for Foreign Missions. He translated parts of the New Testament and various tracts into Foochow dialect and was president of the North Fukien Religious Tract Society in 1901, as well as corresponding secretary for the Foochow Mission, was in Foochow from 1853 to 1905.
CORRESPONDENCE: Letter from Hartwell to Edward Hitchcock, describing disease and suffering among the Chinese, 1855; letter from Hartwell to his classmates before the 40th reunion in 1889; letter from Hartwell to his classmates before the 50th reunion in 1899, summing up his life and listing some of his publications; 4 miscellaneous letters, pre-1853.
MEMORABILIA: Miscellaneous articles about Hartwell.
AUDIO-VISUAL MATERIALS: Photo of Mr. and Mrs. Hartwell, 1852, and of Hartwell as an elderly man, n.d.

3-GENERAL HOLDINGS
MINUTES/RECORDS/REPORTS: American Board of Commissioners for Foreign Missions, Foochow Mission, reports, 1896 (including articles by and about Charles Hartwell), 1898, 1900, 1901; North Fukien Religious Tract Society, annual report and catalogue, 1901 (including an address by Hartwell).
SERIALS: *The Foochow Messenger*, 1903–5 (inc.).

MA–10 Special Collections
Amherst College
Amherst MA 01002
(413) 542–2299/2068
Daria D'Arienzo, Special Collections Coordinator

1-GENERAL HOLDINGS
SERIALS: *Chinese Repository*, 1832–48, 1850–51.

UNIVERSITY OF MASSACHUSETTS
MA–15 Library
Amherst MA 01003
(413) 545–0150
Melinda McIntosh, Microforms Reference Librarian

1-ELIJAH COLEMAN BRIDGMAN PAPERS, 1820–39, 1 reel microfilm
Background note: For biographical notes, see Belchertown Historical Association, Stone House Museum, 20 Maple Street, Belchertown, MA, 01007 (which holds the originals of the items in this collection).

CORRESPONDENCE/MANUSCRIPTS/PAMPHLETS/MEMORABILIA: Ca. 60 items, including letters from, to, and about Bridgman, 1826–37, and published and unpublished biographical materials.

2-GENERAL HOLDINGS
PAMPHLETS: *Windows into China: The Jesuits and Their Books, 1580–1730*, by John Parker, 1978.
SERIALS: *China Christian Year Book*, 1928–29, 1931. *China Mission Year Book*, 1919. *Directory of Protestant Missions in China*, 1930. *Lingnan Science Journal*, 1922–42.

BELCHERTOWN

STONE HOUSE MUSEUM
MA–20 Belchertown Historical Association
20 Maple Street
Belchertown MA 01007
(413) 323–6573
Helen F. Lister, Curator

1-ELIJAH COLEMAN BRIDGMAN PAPERS, 1820–39, 60 items
Background note: Elijah Coleman Bridgman (1801–61) and his wife, Eliza Jane Gillette Bridgman, spent most of their lives in China as missionaries. After graduating from Amherst College and Andover Theological Seminary, he arrived as a missionary in China in 1829 and lived there as an educator, translator, and publisher until 1861. A native of Belchertown, Bridgman was editor of the *Journal of the North China Branch of the Royal Asiatic Society* and spent the later years of his life revising a Chinese version of the Bible. He was prominent in the Medical Missionary Society and the Morrison Education Society, editor of the *Chinese Repository* for the entire length of its publication (1832–51), and joint editor of a Chinese chrestomathy. Part of this collection is on microfilm at the University of Massachusetts at Amherst Library, Amherst, MA, 01003. See also Amherst College, Archives, Amherst, MA, 01002.

CORRESPONDENCE: Letters of Elijah Bridgman to his family, 1820–39.
MANUSCRIPTS: Handwritten sermon and "charge" given to Elijah Bridgman at his ordination, n.d.
PAMPHLETS: Article on Elijah Bridgman in *Missionary Herald*, 1862; *An Early American Sinologue, Elijah Coleman Bridgman*, by Susan Reed Stefler, 1935; *American Heroes on the Mission Field #9, Elijah Coleman Bridgman*, by the American Tract Society, n.d.
MEMORABILIA: Chinese clothing and jewelry of the Bridgmans, including ivory brooches and earrings, and nail clips in a small painted cloth case.
AUDIO-VISUAL MATERIALS: Photo of Elijah and Eliza Bridgman, n.d.

BOSTON

AMERICAN CONGREGATIONAL ASSOCIATION
MA–25 Congregational Library
14 Beacon Street
Boston MA 02108
(617) 523–0470
Harold Field Worthley, Librarian

1-AMERICAN BOARD OF COMMISSIONERS FOR FOREIGN MISSIONS, 1812–1962, quantity undetermined
Background note: The minutes of the Prudential Committee of the American Board of Commissioners for Foreign Missions (ABCFM), 1810–1962, are held by the United Church Board for World Ministries (the successor to the ABCFM), located at 14 Beacon Street, Boston, MA, 02108, but permission to consult these records must be obtained from the executive vice-president at 475 Riverside Drive, New York, NY, 10115. See also Harvard Divinity School, Andover-Harvard Theological Library, 45 Francis Avenue, Cambridge, MA, 02138; Harvard University, Houghton Library, Manuscript Department, Cambridge, MA, 02138; and Yale Divinity School, Special Collections, 409 Prospect Street, New Haven, CT, 06510.
MINUTES/RECORDS/REPORTS: ABCFM, annual reports, 1812–1960 (complete set); treasurer's reports, 1907–23, 1925–26, 1929, 1931–45, 1947–49, 1952–61; reports of the following: Foochow Medical Missionary Hospital, 1876–77, 1879–80, 1884, 1918; Foochow Mission, 1895–98, 1900; Foochow Missionary Hospital, 1912–14; North China Mission, 1889–96, 1898–99, 1902–3, 1910–11; Ponasang Missionary Hospital, 1895, 1901–4, 1908; Shansi Mission, 1897, 1907, 1909, 1911–12; Shansi Mission, Dispensary and Hospital, T'ai ku Station, 1896; Hospital for Women and Children, 1898; American Home Missionary Society, reports, 1827–1913.

2-FRED FIELD GOODSELL PAPERS, ca. 1930–1972, 3.5 boxes, 4 volumes
Restrictions: Permission required. Personal sections of the collection are closed.
Background note: Fred Field Goodsell (1880–1976) was the executive vice-president of the American Board of Commissioners for Foreign Missions (ABCFM) from 1930 to 1948. His papers include material on ABCFM missions and missionaries around the world. This extensive collection is unprocessed and uncatalogued.

MINUTES/RECORDS/REPORTS: 2 pamphlet boxes of records relating to ABCFM work in China, n.d.
MANUSCRIPTS: "The American Board in China: 1830–1950, Review and Appraisal," by Fred Goodsell, including a list of personnel and financial statistics, 1969 (typescript in 2 loose-leaf notebooks); "Autobiography of Mr. James Ch'üan," 1972 (typescript in 2 loose-leaf notebooks).
MEMORABILIA: Box of notecards on missionary personnel and part of another box on Foochow, n.d.

3-GENERAL HOLDINGS
MINUTES/RECORDS/REPORTS: American Board of Commissioners for Foreign Missions (ABCFM), general report of the deputation, 1907; almanac of missions, 1908–16; yearbook, 1917–60; China Centenary Missionary Conference, report, 1906–7; China Inland Mission, report, 1907; Medical Missionary Society in China, minutes, 1838; reports, 1840, 1846, 1848, 1850; Mission Among the Higher Classes in China, report, 1895; New York Board of Foreign Missions, Amoy Mission, 1906.
MANUSCRIPTS: "Beloit's First Contacts with China," by David D. Buck, 1985; "China Her Own Interpreter: Chapters by a Group of Nationals Interpreting the Christian Movement of the U.S. and Canada," ed. by Milton Stauffer, 1927; "China Mission," n.a., n.d.; "Lessons to be Learned from the Experiences of Christian Missions in China," comp. by Harold S. Matthews, 1951; "West of the Yangtze Gorges," by Joseph Taylor, 1936.
PAMPHLETS: 18 pamphlets, 1867–1932, on subjects such as the ABCFM, China Inland Mission, Chinese Mission of New England, Congregational missions, Foochow Mission, future missionary policy, opium, rural parishes, and South China Mission.
MEMORABILIA/MAPS/DESIGNS/DRAWINGS: *Pictures of Missionary Work in Fukien, Foochow, China*, ABCFM calendar for 1933.
SERIALS: *China Mission Year Book*, 1912–18, 1923–24. *China's Millions* (London), 1875–1915. *China's Millions* (Toronto), 1915(?). *Chinese Repository*, 1832–51. *Directory of Protestant Missions in China*, 1916.
DISSERTATIONS/THESES: *An Experiment in Teaching the Christian Religion by Life Situations in Fan Village, China*, by Mabel Ellis Hubbard, 1938.

MA-30   BOSTON PUBLIC LIBRARY
666 Boylston Street
Box 286
Boston MA 02117
(617) 536-5400
Katherine K. Dibble, Assistant Supervisor of Research
  Library Services
Roberta Zonghi, Curator of Rare Books and Manu-
  scripts

1-RARE BOOKS AND MANUSCRIPT ROOM, 1846, 1 item
PAMPHLETS: *Ningpo, January 1st [!], 1846...*, by Walter Macon Lowrie, 1846.

2-GENERAL HOLDINGS
MINUTES/RECORDS/REPORTS: China International Famine Relief Commission, annual report, 1922–24, 1926, 1928–34; International Institute in Connection with the Mission Among the Higher Classes of China, regulations, 1897; Methodist Episcopal

Church in the United States: Central Conference in China, official minutes, 1897, 1899; Hinghwa Mission conference, official minutes, 1896, 1898; West China Mission, Suiling, minutes, 1905; Ponasang Missionary Hospital, Foochow, annual report, 1889–93, 1895, 1897–1900; Woman's American Baptist Foreign Mission Society, annual report, 1872, 1874–1915, and reports in *Our Work in the Orient*, 1911–15; T'ai-yuen-fu Medical Mission and Hospital, report by Robert Harold Aynsworth Schofield, 1883.
PAMPHLETS: *Address in Behalf of the China Mission*, by William Jones Boone, 1837; *China and Christian Missions*, by Judson Smith, 1861; *China at the Crossroads*, by Ernest Delbert Tyler, 1929(?); *Das Chinesische Heidenthum*, by August William Dieckhoff, 1859; *Historical Sketch of the Missions of the American Board in China*, by Samuel Colcord Bartlett, 1880; *The Political Obstacles to Missionary Success in China*, by Alexander Michie, 1901; American Board of Commissioners for Foreign Missions pamphlet containing articles on China mission by S. B. Treat, S. Wells Williams, and others, 1867; *Windows into China: The Jesuits and Their Books, 1580–1730*, by John Parker, 1978; *Work for the Blind in China*, by Constance Frederica Gordon-Cumming, 1893(?); Junior Auxiliary pamphlet on Episcopal missions in China, 1893.
MEMORABILIA: "Li Hung Chang's Scrap-book," comp. by Hiram Stevens Maxim, 1913.
MAPS/DESIGNS/DRAWINGS: *Atlas of the Chinese Empire Containing Separate Maps of the Eighteen Provinces of China Proper on the Scale of 1:3,000,000 and of the Four Great Dependencies on the Scale of 1:7,500,000 with an Index to All the Names on the Maps and a List of All Protestant Mission Stations*, by Edward Stanford (London: China Inland Mission), 1908.
SERIALS: American Friends Service Committee, *Bulletin on Work in China*, 1942–44. Catholic University of Peking, *Bulletin*, 1926–32, 1934. *China Christian Year Book*, 1916, 1923–26, 1928–29, 1931–33. China International Famine Relief Commission, Publications, series A, 1922–24, 1926, 1929–34; series B, 1923–24; series E, 1932. *China Monthly*, 1939–50. *China's Millions* (London), 1875–79, 1882–84. *Chinese Evangelist*, 1888–89. *Chinese Repository*, 1832–38, 1840, 1842–46. *News of China*, 1942–49. *St. John's University Studies*, 1922. *Yenching Journal of Chinese Studies*, monograph, 1936.
DISSERTATIONS/THESES: *Christian Missions in China*, by Charles Sumner Estes, 1895.

BOSTON UNIVERSITY
MA-35   **School of Theology Library**
745 Commonwealth Avenue
Boston MA 02215
(617) 353-3034
William E. Zimpfer, Librarian

1-GENERAL HOLDINGS
MINUTES/RECORDS/REPORTS: National Christian Council of China, report, 1926.
MANUSCRIPTS: "Christian Higher Education in China: Contributions of the Colleges of Arts and Sciences to Chinese Life," by J. Dyke Van Putten, 1937.
PAMPHLETS: Missionary Research Library, *Occasional Bulletin*, 7 pamphlets on China, 1950–56; *Adventurous Evangelism*, by

H. F. Wickings, 195?; *China Consultation, 1958*, by the National Council of the Churches of Christ, 1958; *The Clock Man's Mother and Other Stories*, by C. F. Tippett, 1930; *The Healing Art in China*, by James Whitford Bashford, 1907; *Lessons to Be Learned from the Experiences of Christian Missions in China*, by the National Council of the Churches of Christ, 1951.
SERIALS: *China* (Foreign Missions Conference of North America), 1947–48, 1950–52. *China Bulletin*, 1952–62. *China Christian Advocate*, 1931–41. *China Christian Year Book*, 1911, 1916, 1919, 1923–25. *China Notes*, 1962–84. *China Talk*, 1976–85 (inc.). *Chinese Recorder*, 1868–1941. *Chinese Repository*, 1832–51. *Ching Feng*, 1964–84. *Directory of Protestant Missions in China*, 1921. *Missionary Recorder*, 1867. *West China Messenger*, 1903. *West China Missionary News*, 1938–43.
DISSERTATIONS/THESES: *American Missionaries and the Chinese Communists: A Study of Views Expressed by Methodist Episcopal Church Missionaries, 1921–1941*, by Milo Lancaster Thornberry, Jr., 1974. *Attitudes within the Protestant Churches of the Occident towards the Propagation of Christianity in the Orient: An Historical Survey to 1914*, by James Stuart Udy, 1952. *China's Crisis*, by Daniel Onstott, 1894. *The Chinese University of the Past and the Future*, by George Lowry Davis, 1902. *A Comparison of Jesus and Confucius as Ethical Teachers*, by Timothy Yu-hsi Chow, 1952. *The Confucian Civilization*, by Z. K. Zia, 1924. *The Contribution of Religious Education to the Democratization of China*, by Li Gwan-fang, 1927. *The Development of Protestant Theological Education in China*, by Charles Stanley Smith, 1941. *Missionary Journalism in Nineteenth-century China: Young J. Allen and the Early "Wan kuo kung pao,"* by Adrian Arthur Bennett, 1970. *The Protestant Missionary Understanding of the Chinese Situation and the Christian Task from 1890 to 1911*, by C. William Mensendiek, 1958. *The Psychodynamics of Change in Religious Conversion and Communist Brainwashing with Particular Reference to the Eighteenth-century Evangelical Revival and the Chinese Thought Control Movement*, by Duane A. Windemiller, 1960. *The Scope, Organization, and Program of the Christian School of China*, by Timothy Chih-tien Cheng, 1925. *The Significance of the Anti-Christian Movement in China Today*, by H. I. Wang, 1925. *Some Guiding Principles for Christian Education in China Today*, by Roxy Lefforge, 1933.

THE EPISCOPAL DIOCESE OF MASSACHUSETTS
MA–40   Diocesan Library and Archives
One Joy Street
Boston MA 02108
(617) 742-4720
Kathryn Hammond Baker, Archivist

1-ELISE G. DEXTER PAPERS, 1936–39, .5 c.f.
Background note: Elise G. Dexter (1880–1950) worked as a missionary nurse in Wuchang and Hankow. In 1917, she went to Wuchang, where she served under Dr. Mary James at the Church General Hospital and established the nurses' training school. Dexter left for the United States in 1925. She returned to China in 1936 and served under Bishop [Logan H.?] Roots and later Bishop [Alfred?] Gilman, at the American Church Mission. One of her primary tasks was to coordinate public health services with the International Red Cross. Material in this collection relates mostly to her second stay in China, 1936 to 1939. See also Archives and Historical Collections of the Episcopal Church, 606 Rathervue Place, P. O. Box 2247, Austin, TX, 78768.
CORRESPONDENCE: Correspondence from Dexter to her sisters, Polly Dexter Hill (Mrs. Lewis W. Hill) and Christine Dexter Bradshaw (Mrs. William Bradshaw), and other family members, containing reflections on the church, the daily life of the mission, living conditions of the Chinese, the Sino-Japanese war, and the difficulties of Westerners living in China and leaving during the Sino-Japanese war, 1936–37.
MEMORABILIA: Article by Dexter in *District of Hankow Newsletter*, 1937; clipping and transcript of an address by Mme. Chiang K'ai-shek to the missionary community in Hankow, 1938; miscellaneous biographical notes on Dexter, n.d.
AUDIO-VISUAL MATERIALS: 24 photos, including scenes of daily life, other missionaries, hospital students and staff, 1936–39 and n.d., including some from her first stay in China.

2-GENERAL HOLDINGS
MINUTES/RECORDS/REPORTS: Reports on the China mission in *The Militant*, the Diocese of Massachusetts newsletter, and other mission serials, 1828–1960.

THE FIRST CHURCH OF CHRIST, SCIENTIST
MA–45   Records Management (Organizational Archives)
175 Huntington Avenue
Boston MA 02115
(617) 450-2000
Yvonne C. Fettweis, Records Administrator

Restrictions: Some of the materials are restricted.
Background note: The Church of Christ, Scientist, was founded by Mary Baker Eddy in 1879. Sarah Pike Conger, the wife of the American Minister to China, arrived in China in 1898. She was probably the first Christian Scientist to live in China. Mrs. Conger corresponded with Mary Baker Eddy about the Chinese political situation and later published letters she had written from China to her family in *Letters from China*. During the first decade of the twentieth century, Christian Scientists in China became numerous enough to organize church activity, and branches of The Mother Church were formed in Shanghai, Tientsin, and Hong Kong. Relatively few native Chinese became interested in Christian Science and joined these churches. Their membership consisted largely of Britons and Americans. Of these churches, First Church of Christ, Scientist, Hong Kong, is the only one still in existence. In addition to the materials listed below, the archives hold records on its activities in Hong Kong and Taiwan.
Finding aids: Record inventory and schedules for each series and copies of box labels, arranged by series.

1-AR 44A BRANCH CHURCH HISTORIES AND RECORDS, 1913–65, ca. 7 items
CORRESPONDENCE: Letter from the executive board of Christian Science Society, Shanghai, to Mabel B. Fowler, 1913; letter from the clerk, Christian Science Society, Shanghai, to the Clerk of The Mother Church in Boston, 1921; memo from the Archivist of The Mother Church, to the executive assistant of the Christian Science Board of Directors, regarding the purchase of a photo

album of the construction of First Church of Christ, Scientist, Shanghai, 1965; letter from the Archivist of The Mother Church to I. Warsaw in New York regarding the purchase of the above photo album, 1965.

MANUSCRIPTS: History of the Christian Science movement in Shanghai from 1907 to 1934, dated 1934.

MEMORABILIA: Clipping from *The Christian Science Monitor*, containing excerpts from an article in the *North China Daily News* regarding the dedication of First Church, Shanghai, 1935.

AUDIO-VISUAL MATERIALS: Photos of the construction of First Church, Shanghai, and the completed edifice, ca. 1935.

2-BD 6 CORRESPONDENCE, 1913–51, ca. 17 items

MINUTES/RECORDS/REPORTS: Christian Science Society, Shanghai, copy of cash statement, 1913; report on conditions in Churches of Christ, Scientist, in China, by William R. Rathvon, 1913; report of Phyllis Ayrton, Committee on Publication for Canton and Hong Kong, 1942–45.

CORRESPONDENCE: Letter from William R. Rathvon, Christian Science lecturer, to John V. Dittemore, secretary of the Board of Directors, regarding his lecture tour of the Far East, 1913; letter from First Church, Shanghai, to the Board of Directors, regarding the refugee problem in Shanghai, 1937; letter from First Church, Shanghai, to the Board of Directors, regarding relief work in Shanghai, 1938; letter from Mary Edna Sammann to the Board of Directors, and their reply, 1942; letter from Marjorie Smith Marr, member of First Church, Shanghai, to the Clerk of The Mother Church, regarding her internment in China and return to the United States, including a list of members interned, 1944; memo from the Clerk of The Mother Church regarding Marr's letter and letter from the clerk to Marr, 1944; correspondence regarding the efforts of First Church, Shanghai, to regain possession of its edifice after the war, 1945–46; letter from First Church, Shanghai, to the Board of Directors, regarding its activities during the war years, including a list of members and officers, and their reply, 1946; letter from Angie W. Cox to the Board of Directors, quoting a letter she received from Anne Koopman Sun of Shanghai, regarding activities of church members there, and their reply, 1946; memo from Christian Science Camp Welfare Activities to Executive Office of the Board of Directors, regarding the activities of F. R. Halling, a volunteer Christian Science worker in Tsingtao, 1949; correspondence regarding the activities of First Church, Shanghai, and its disbanding, 1950–51.

3-BP 8 BRANCH ACTIVITIES FILES, 1921–55, ca. 12 items

MINUTES/RECORDS/REPORTS: Christian Science Society, Shanghai, minutes, 1928; Christian Science Society, Tientsin, by-laws, n.d., before and after recognition by The Mother Church.

CORRESPONDENCE: Correspondence of First Church, Shanghai, with The Mother Church regarding its listing in *The Christian Science Journal*, 1922; correspondence between Christian Science Society, Shanghai, and The Mother Church, regarding the Society's application to change its title to First Church of Christ, Scientist, Shanghai, 1926–28; letter from First Church of Christ, Scientist, Shanghai, to the Board of Directors, regarding its disbanding, 1951; memo from the Board of Directors withdrawing the listing of First Church, Shanghai, from *The Christian Science Journal*, 1951; memo from the Board of Directors to the Department of Branches and Practitioners of The Mother Church, regard-

ing the disbanding of the Shanghai branch, 1951; correspondence between The Mother Church and the Christian Scientists in Tientsin, regarding their application for recognition, 1921–22; correspondence between The Mother Church and individuals named as references by the Christian Scientists in Tientsin, 1922; memo from the Board of Directors to Theodore E. Metzner, manager of the Department of Branches and Practitioners, regarding the withdrawal of recognition from the Tientsin branch, 1955.

4-CP 3A AREA COMMITTEES—COMMITTEE ON PUBLICATION APPOINTMENTS, 1948–76, ca. 28 items

CORRESPONDENCE: Correspondence regarding the appointment by The Mother Church of Committees on Publication in China, Hong Kong, and Taiwan, 1948–76.

5-CP 3B AREA COMMITTEES—COMMITTEE ON PUBLICATION ANNUAL REPORTS, 1924–71, ca. 47 items

MINUTES/RECORDS/REPORTS: Committees on Publication in China and Hong Kong, annual reports, 1924–71.

6-ID 1 INTERNATIONAL ADVISOR FILES, 1981–82, ca. 10 items

CORRESPONDENCE: Inter-office memos between the International Department of The Mother Church and other Church departments regarding the sending of Christian Science literature to Christian Scientists living in China, 1981; correspondence between the International Department of The Mother Church and Christian Scientists in China, 1981–82.

7-ID 3 AREA DESK FILES, 1980–81, ca. 8 items

MINUTES/RECORDS/REPORTS: China Development Committee of The Mother Church, records and minutes, 1980–81, and a memo regarding the proposed translation of *Science and Health with Key to the Scriptures* by Mary Baker Eddy, into Chinese.

8-JS 7B APPLICATIONS FOR LISTING (PUBLISHING CARD ADVERTISING), 1922, 1 item

MINUTES/RECORDS/REPORTS: Application of Christian Science Society, Tientsin, for listing in *The Christian Science Journal*, 1922.

9-PA 70 LESSON-SERMON TRANSLATION ACTIVITY, 1966–77, ca. 8 items

CORRESPONDENCE: Correspondence between The Mother Church and translators regarding the translation of Bible Lessons from the *Christian Science Quarterly* into Chinese, 1966–77.

10-RM 4 FIELD COLLECTION AND ARCHIVES, 1944–51, 4 items

CORRESPONDENCE: Letter from Marjorie Smith Marr to the Board of Directors, regarding the status and location of members of First Church, Shanghai, and the status of its edifice, 1944; letter from First Church, Shanghai, to the Board of Directors, regarding post-war conditions, including a list of members and officers from 1943 to 1946, 1946; letter from First Church, Shanghai, to the Board of Trustees of The Christian Science Publishing Society, regarding its decision to close, 1951.

MANUSCRIPTS: Unpublished manuscript, ''The Mother Church and Its Branches in World War II (1940–1951),'' by Birse Shepard, containing information on branches in China.

11-TW 28 LESSON-SERMON TRANSLATIONS, 1970, ca. 52 items

CHINESE LANGUAGE MATERIALS: Translations of Bible Lessons from the *Christian Science Quarterly*, 1970.

FRANCIS A. COUNTWAY LIBRARY OF MEDICINE

MA-50 Rare Book and Manuscript Department
10 Shattuck Street
Boston MA 02115
(617) 732-2172
Richard Wolfe, Curator of Manuscripts

Background note: The Francis A. Countway Library of Medicine incorporates the Boston Medical Library and the Harvard Medical Library. In addition to the materials listed below, further data may be found within collections of individuals affiliated with Harvard University.

1-WALTER BRADFORD CANNON, 1921-42, 4 boxes
MINUTES/RECORDS/REPORTS: China Medical Board, minutes and related materials, 1939-42; certificate, 1933; Peking Union Medical College, certificate of incorporation, 1928; minutes and related materials, 1939-40; United China Relief, minutes of meetings and related materials, 1942; progress reports and by-laws, 1941.
CORRESPONDENCE: Correspondence relating to Peking Union Medical College, 1921-42, with Robert S. K. Lim, O. H. Robertson, H. C. Chang, S. C. Chen, Roger S. Greene, G. Canby Robinson, H. S. Houghton, and E. W. Cruikshank; mimeograph letters from John Leighton Stuart, Yenching University, 1939-40; correspondence with Y. C. Tsang at Tsing Hua College, 1928-31; correspondence relating to China Medical Board, 1936-42, with E. C. Lobenstine and Agnes M. Pearce; correspondence relating to American Bureau for Medical Aid to China, 1939-42, with Mrs. A. W. Hartt, Edward H. Hume, Frank Co Tui, Helen Stevens, Donald D. Van Slyke, and Marion Exeter; correspondence with officers and directors of United China Relief, 1941-42, including Edward C. Carter, Robert W. Barnett and James Blaine; correspondence with J. H. Liu, 1942; correspondence with New England Committee for Chinese Relief, China Aid Council, and other aid-to-China organizations, 1937-42; miscellaneous correspondence with others in or relating to China, 1932-42.
FINDING AID: In-house inventory.

2-JEAN ALONZO CURRAN, 1921-28, ca. 1 box
Background note: Jean Alonzo Curran (1893-1977), a 1921 graduate of Harvard Medical School, was a medical missionary in China from 1921 to 1928. After his service in China, he became dean and then president of New York State University's Downtown Medical Center. The collection, altogether 20 boxes, is not yet catalogued.
CORRESPONDENCE/DIARIES: Correspondence and diaries related to his work in China, 1921-28.

3-THEODORE CHASE GREENE, 1927-49, 15 items
CORRESPONDENCE: 15 letters from Theodore Chase Greene to Hugh Lyle Stalker, regarding his work at the Cheeloo University School of Medicine, including discussion of the work at mission hospitals, medical conditions in China, a protest regarding proposed removal of Mr. Dean and Dr. Greene from Peking, experiences in Canton teaching in medical school and working in the hospital, relief, and religion, 1927-49; letter from James Harry Ingram to Greene, 1928; letter from Wang Chi-min to Greene, n.d.; mention of Greene in correspondence between Alexander Taylor Bunts and Stalker, 1932-72, and between John Farquhar Fulton and Stalker, 1937-51.
MANUSCRIPTS: "Notes on Chinese Medicine," n.d.; "Chinese Medical Literature," by Wang Chi-min, 1918.

4-GENERAL HOLDINGS
MINUTES/RECORDS/REPORTS: China Medical Commission, Rockefeller Foundation, report, 1914; Harvard Medical School of China, annual reports and hospital reports, 1911-17; reports and announcements, n.d.; Medical Missionary Society in China, annual reports, 1839, 1841-43, 1845-51, 1858-59, 1864, 1874, 1879; Medical School of China, financial records and forms, 1910-26; Ophthalmic Hospital at Canton, minutes and report, 1836, 1838, 1848-51, 1885.
CORRESPONDENCE: Miscellaneous correspondence by Simon Flexner, n.d.
MANUSCRIPTS: "The China Medical Board," by Frederick Taylor, n.d.; essay by W. H. Welch, 1907; "Harvard Medical School of China," by Jean Alonzo Curran, 1963.
PAMPHLETS: *A Brief Account of an Ophthalmic Institution, During the Years 1827, '28, '29, '30, '31, and 1832, at Macao*, by a philanthropist, 1834; *The Chinese Ministry of Health*, by Jui-heng Liu, 1929; *Lingnan University (Lingnan School, the Orphanage, Canton Hospital, etc.): A Letter*, 1941; *The Medical Missionary Society in China*, by Thomas Richardson Colledge, 1838; *Papers Relative to Hospitals in China*, by the Medical Missionary Society in China, 1841; *Statement Respecting Hospitals in China*, by Peter Parker, 1842; *Suggestions for the Formation of a Medical Missionary Society, Offered to the Consideration of All Christian Nations*, by T. R. Colledge, P. Parker, and E. C. Bridgman, 1836; *A Visit to Yale-in-China, June 1920: An Account of Changsha and of the Conditions and Needs of Yali*, by Anson Phelps Stokes, 1920.
SERIALS: *China Medical Journal*, 1907-14. *China Medical Missionary Journal*, 1887-1907.

MA-55 Francis A. Countway Library of Medicine
10 Shattuck Street
Boston MA 02115
(617) 732-2147
Charles C. Colby 3rd, Associate Librarian for Boston Medical Library Services

1-GENERAL HOLDINGS
MINUTES/RECORDS/REPORTS: China Medical Board, annual reports, 1914-17, 1922, 1950-54; China Medical Board of New York, report, 1954-79, financial report, 1950-51; Lingnan University, report of the medical department, 1928-30.
SERIALS: *China Colleges*, 1934-37. *China Medical Journal*, 1907-32. *China Medical Missionary Journal*, 1887-1907. *China's Medicine*, 1966-68. *Chinese Medical Journal*, 1932-66, 1973-79; Chengtu ed., 1942-45; foreign ed., 1932-66; supplement, 1936-40.
CHINESE LANGUAGE MATERIALS/SERIALS: *Chinese Medical Journal*, 1973-74.
CHINESE LANGUAGE MATERIALS: *Chung wen i hsüeh wen hsien fen lei so yin (Classified Index to Chinese Medical Literature in Periodicals)*, by Kuan Kuo-wu and Hung Chi, 1958; *Preventative Medicine and Hygiene*, trans. by S. M. Woo and J. C. Hwang, 1927; *A Textbook of Histology Arranged upon an Embryological Basis*, trans. by R. T. Shields, 1918.

MA-60 GENERAL THEOLOGICAL LIBRARY
14 Beacon Street
Boston MA 02108
(617) 227-4557
Ruth Pragnell, Librarian

1-GENERAL HOLDINGS
SERIALS: *China Christian Year Book*, 1926, 1928-29, 1931.
China Mission Year Book, 1912-14, 1917, 1919-20, 1923-25.

LIBRARY OF THE BOSTON ATHENAEUM
MA-65 Rare Book Room
10-1/2 Beacon Street
Boston MA 02108-3777
(617) 227-0270
Cynthia English, Head Reference Librarian

1-GENERAL HOLDINGS
PAMPHLETS: *Sermon for the Benefit of the Translation of the Scriptures into the Languages of India and China*, by William Johns, 1812.
SERIALS: *Chinese Repository*, 1832-51 (inc.).

MUSEUM OF FINE ARTS
MA-70 William Morris Hunt Library
465 Huntington Avenue
Boston MA 02115
(617) 267-9300
Bonnie Porter, Interlibrary Services

1-GENERAL HOLDINGS
SERIALS: *Monumenta Serica*, 1935-.

ROMAN CATHOLIC ARCHDIOCESE OF BOSTON
MA-75 Archives
2121 Commonwealth Avenue
Boston MA 02135
(617) 254-0100
Timothy J. Meagher, Archivist

Restrictions: Access by written application.
Finding aids: *Guide to the Archives of the Archdiocese of Boston*, by James M. O'Toole (New York: Garland Publishing, Inc.), 1982.

1-WILLIAM HENRY CARDINAL O'CONNELL PAPERS, 1933-43, 10 items
CORRESPONDENCE: 4 letters from F. F. Bruno, Shihchiachwang mission, 1940-41, with photos; letter from Louis Lapierre, Vicar Apostolic of Manchuria, 1938; letter from Valentine J. Koehler, O.S.B., Catholic University of Peking, 1933; 3 letters from Paul Yu-pin, Vicar Apostolic of Nanking, 1943; letter from O'Connell to Yu-pin, 1943.
FINDING AID: In-house index.

2-SOCIETY FOR THE PROPAGATION OF THE FAITH RECORDS, 1901-70, quantity undetermined
MINUTES/RECORDS/REPORTS: Reports on the China mission of the Society for the Propagation of the Faith, 1901-70, including administrative and financial records of the Boston branch.

SIMMONS COLLEGE
MA-80 Colonel Miriam E. Perry Goll Archives
300 The Fenway
Boston MA 02115
(617) 738-3141
Megan Sniffin-Marinoff, College Archivist

1-MARY ELIZABETH WOOD FILE, ca. 1920s, 1 file
Background note: Mary Elizabeth Wood (1861-1931) was an Episcopal missionary and librarian in China. She first went to China in 1900 to visit her brother, Robert, an Episcopal missionary in Wuchang. Beginning her work as a teacher at the Boone School, she founded China's first Western library and library school there. She remained active in library work in China until her death in 1931. See also Richmond Memorial Library, 19 Ross Street, Batavia, NY, 14020.
PAMPHLETS/MEMORABILIA/AUDIO-VISUAL MATERIALS: Newspaper clippings, a photo of Wood and her students at the Boone School, Wuchang, and booklets about her work at the Boone School, ca. 1920s; biographical sketch of Wood in *Notable American Women*, V 3.

BRIGHTON

ST. JOHN'S SEMINARY
MA-85 Library
127 Lake Street
Brighton MA 02135
(617) 254-2610 Ext. 79
L. W. McGrath, Director

1-GENERAL HOLDINGS
SERIALS: *Far East* (Chinese Mission Society), 1937-44. *Far East* (Maynooth Mission to China), 1936-43. *Maryknoll Mission Letters*, 1923.

CAMBRIDGE

MA-90 FIRST CHURCH IN CAMBRIDGE, CONGREGATIONAL
11 Garden Street
Cambridge MA 02138
(617) 547-2724
Susan Moran, Parish Administrator and Archivist

1-ROBERT E. AND HELEN D. CHANDLER PAPERS, 1910-82, ca. 10 items
CORRESPONDENCE: Printed letters, 1930-41; 3 letters, 1947.
MANUSCRIPTS: Autobiographical sketch and doctrinal statement, by Helen A. Davis Chandler, 1910; "Deep Difficulties: The Personal Story of Certain Stations in the North China Mission of the American Board," an account of an incident in Tientsin involving Francis Tucker and others, by Robert Chandler, 1921; occasional references and photos in manuscript "Autobiography," by John H. Leamon, pastor of First Church in Cambridge from 1940 to 1962.
MEMORABILIA: Memorial service for Helen D. Chandler, First

Church in Cambridge, Congregational, 1982; clippings on the Chandlers, including photos, and 1982 obituary of Helen Chandler.

HARVARD DIVINITY SCHOOL
MA-95 Andover-Harvard Theological Library
45 Francis Avenue
Cambridge MA 02138
(617) 495-5788
Louis Charles Willard, Director
Alan Seaburg, Curator

1-AMERICAN BOARD OF COMMISSIONERS FOR FOREIGN MISSIONS PAMPHLET COLLECTION, 1830-1954, 22 boxes
Background note: This collection is currently unprocessed. It is held in the vault and requires permission from the curator. Most of the correspondence is typed carbon copies regarding mission business, either sent to the American Board of Commissioners for Foreign Missions (ABCFM) headquarters or distributed among colleagues. See also ABCFM collections at Harvard University, Houghton Library, Manuscripts Department, Cambridge, MA, 02138; American Congregational Association Library, 14 Beacon Street, Boston, Ma, 02108; and Yale Divinity School, Special Collections, 409 Prospect Street, New Haven, CT, 06510.
MINUTES/RECORDS/REPORTS: American Bible Society, report on the Boxer movement, 1900; Associated Board for Christian Colleges in China, report of a committee on Christian character, staff, and curriculum for 1946-47, 1940; report on the conditions of Christian colleges in China in 1940; Associated Boards for Christian Colleges in China, Committee for Consideration of Greater Unity, report, 1940; memo on church property in China, 1952; Cheeloo University: British section of the Board of Governors, minutes, 1937; catalogue, 1941-42; bulletins, 1948-49; School of Medicine, statement of policy, 1949; China Continuation Committee, national conference report, 1913; report on general conditions, 1942; China Medical Board, financial report, 1950-51; China Sunday School Union, list of publications, n.d., memo, 1927; Chinese Sunday School Union, statement, 1930; Christian Literature Society for China, annual report, 1938, catalogue of publications, 1930; Church Committee for Relief in Asia, report, 1946; Committee for Christian Colleges in China, minutes, 1928; Conference on Christian Education, report, 1930; Preliminary Committee on Higher Christian Education in Fukien province, minutes, 1916; Chinese Christian Education, conference report, 1925; Christianizing economic relations, conference report, 1927; conference report: "The Effects of the Sino-Japanese Conflict on American Educational and Philanthropic Enterprises in China: II-Higher Education; III-Secondary Education; IV-Medicine and Public Health," by Earl Cressy, 1939; "V-Rural Reconstruction," by John Reisner, 1939; Mott conference, report, 1925; Biennial College Conference, Shanghai College, report, 1926; National Christian Council of China, biennial meeting, minutes, 1935; "The Libraries of the Christian Colleges of China: Report of a Survey Made in 1947-1948," by Charles B. Shaw, 1948; conference on medical and health work in China, conference report, 1945; conference on mission cooperation in China and Japan, report, 1935; English Baptist mission in Taihuan (Shansi), minutes, 1946; Foochow College, Board of Trustees, 1908, 1912,

1916, 1924; Foochow College, constitution, 1909; by-laws, 1928-29; Deputation to China, 1898, 1907, 1909; report to Prudential Committee, 1948; report on missions, 1951; Fukien conference on theological education, 1943; Preliminary Committee on Higher Christian Education in Fukien province, minutes, 1915-16; Foochow Congregational Church, minutes, 1927; Foochow Theological Seminary for Women, report, 1898.

Fukien Christian University (FCU): report by C. J. Lin on FCU, 1946; report of the treasurer, 1945; reports on FCU, 1940, 1942-43; report on FCU in wartime, 1942; memo on personnel, 1935; report on work at FCU, 1934-35, with photos of campus; catalogue, 1926-27, 1934-36; rules and regulations, 1927-28, 1934; annual reports of president and dean, 1931-32; budget, 1931; rules and ideals, 1929; charter and by-laws, 1921; Preliminary Committee on Higher Christian Education in Fukien Province, 1915-16; report on rural service at FCU, 1934; amendment to charter of FCU, 1923.

Inghok Station, report, 1903, 1911-12; meeting of delegates of four mission boards on "China Protection," minutes, 1929; report on referendum on military protection in China with voting tally, 1928; National Christian Council of China: Conference of Christian workers, report, 1926, 1929; conference on Christianizing economic relations, report, 1927; biennial meeting, report, 1937, 1946; conference on People's Livelihood, 1931; report on cooperation in West China, 1940; by-laws, 1933; Mott conference, 1926; meeting in Hangchow, 1931; North China, 1938; memo, 1944; Chengtu conference on post-war planning, 1945; Elgin conference, minutes, 1945; report to China committee, 1946; report on seminar at Walker missionary home, 1949; report, Christian emergency council, Shanghai, 1949; report on program of China Committee, 1948; report, deputation of Australian churchmen, 1957; National Committee for Christian Religious Education in China, minutes, 1932, 1934-36, 1947; North China Kung Li Hui: report, 1929; Shansi Plague Prevention Bureau, report, 1918; Commission on the Chinese Church, report, 1925; North Fukien Council, student volunteer movement for the ministry, annual report, 1923; North China Mission, Prudential Committee, report, 1948; Ching-chao, 1921; tentative committee on federation, Shansi province, report, 1908; North Fuhkien Religious Tract Society, annual report, 1901; North China Mission: Tehsien, report, 1937; Tungchou, report, 1916; Tientsin Christianizing the Home Committee, constitution, n.d.; "Industrialization in China: A Study of Conditions in Tientsin," conference report, 1929; Tehchow, report, 1940; Taikuhsien, report, 1913-14; North Shensi, report, 1936; Shantung, annual report, 1914, minutes of annual meeting, 1917; Shansi Mission, report of a visit by J. H. McCann and G. D. Wilder, 1906; Shansi Mission, rules and regulations, n.d.; Paotingfu, report, 1911-12; Pangkiachuang Station report, 1910; Fenchow, reports, 1914-15, 1935-36, 1938; Fenchow commission of assistance, report, 1930-31; conference on Christian workers in North China, report, 1926, 1929; Chihli district, annual report, 1914; minutes of the Fourth Chinese-Foreign Meeting, 1918; minutes, annual meeting, 1914; North China Union Language School, catalogue, 1924; Pagoda Anchorage Girls' Boarding School, report, 1901; Peking conference on Federation, records, 1905; Peking Mission Station, minutes on petition, 1929; report on educational foreign service in the Christian church, 1935; report of a symposium on Tinghsien Rural Institute, 1933; report by John Leighton Stuart for Jerusalem meeting of International Missionary Council, 1928; report on conditions in the Lower Yangtze Valley, 1949; Shaowu Mission: annual report, 1903; fiscal report, 1919; general report, 1949; Shaowu medical missionary work, annual report, 1878; work for women and children, report, 1900; South China Mission, 1906; Canton Mission, 1922; United China Relief, by-laws, 1941; Willis F. Pierce Memorial Hospital: annual report, 1913, 1931–33, 1942–43; by-laws, 1931, 1932; constitutions, n.d.; chronology, 1847–1936; proposed plan of federation, n.d.; designation of funds, n.d.; minutes, 1932, 1950, 1958, 1966; building committee report, 1933; deed, 1934; Prudential Committee, minutes, 1934; reports, 1943, 1948; outpatient department report, 1944; clinical report, 1943; School of Nursing, report, 1942–43; director's report, 1943–44, 1946–50; treasurer's report, 1943; medical report, 1942; hospital report, 1946; report to the board of trustees, 1950; Winnetka Resolution, minutes, 1927; World Missions Conference, report, 1909; Yenching University: catalogue, 1927–29; faculty bulletin, 1934; report to board of trustees, 1939–40; Board of Directors, minutes, Yenching (Chengtu), 1945; report of women's college, 1944; Yenching in Chengtu, report, 1944; women's college administrative meeting, minutes, 1945; Committee of Yenching College for Women, minutes, 1945; Yenching Board of Trustees, minutes, 1945; Yenching committee, United Board for Christian Colleges in China, 1945; report on damages by the Japanese, 1946; School of Religion, list of faculty publications, 1932–35; catalogue, 1932–33; Yenching Interim Committee, minutes, 1946; survey of attitudes toward religion at Yenching, 1936–37; contract between Yenching University and Pierce Hedrick, Inc. for promotional services, 1932; terms of relationship between Princeton-Yenching Foundation and Yenching University, 1931; Harvard-Yenching Institute, certificate of incorporation and by-laws, 1918.

CORRESPONDENCE: Letter from Earle Ballou to Harold Matthews, 1946, regarding missionary qualifications; Earle Ballou, 1948; B. Willis Beede to R. E. Chandler, 1929; "Bell," in Canton, to "Strong," 1918; Edward Bliss in Shaowu, 1922; Harold N. Brewster, Foochow, to "Friends" regarding medical work, 1949; Constance Buell, Tientsin, 1950; Frank T. Cartwright to Wynn Fairfield, 1929, with a copy of a letter from J. W. Hawley to Cartwright, 1929, regarding the petition; J. P. Chamberlain to A. L. Warnshuis, 1927; Chandler to R. E. Dieffendorfer, 1929; Rowland Cross to Myra Sawyer, 1929; J. A. Curran to Pauline Baker, 1929; Wynn Fairfield, 1931, 1935; Wynn Fairfield to Beverly Heigham, 1960, regarding the withdrawal of missionaries; Fairfield to Edna Lowrey, 1929, and her reply; Fairfield, 1942, to missionaries on furlough; Fairfield, 1929, regarding petition (see below); Lyda L. Houston at Diongloh, 1937; A. S. Johnson in Canton to Rev. W. E. Strong in Tientsin, 1926; Walter Judd to Chandler, 1928; Eula B. Lee (Mrs. Lucius Lee) to Fairfield, 1929; Eula Lee and Chandler from Elmer Galt in Yulinfu, Shansi, 1929; Samuel and Mabel Leger to Carl Gates, 1929; Alden Matthews, on transfers of missionaries, 1950; excerpts of a letter from Alden Matthews, Foochow, 1950; letters from Louise Meebold to the Women's Board of Missions of the Interior, with a printed religious message to women in Chinese, 1941; Spenser Minnich to Chandler, 1929; Chih-kun P'ang, Peking, 1950; Lucius C. Porter, in Peking, to Dorothy Cushing, 1948; Myra Sawyer to Fairfield, 1929; George Shepherd to Russell Stafford, 1943; excerpts of a letter from Helen Smith, Foochow, 1950; telegram from A. L. Warnshuis to Fairfield, 1937, regarding evacuation of missionar-

ies; Warnshuis to Chandler, 1929; Warnshuis to R. E. Chandler, 1927, and J. P. Chamberlain, 1927; Warnshuis, regarding wartime situation, 1937; Samuel Wells Williams in Macao, to Charles Robinson, 1843; Quincy Wright to A. L. Warnshuis, 1928.

Letters to Fairfield, 1929, regarding petition, from: Susan Armstrong, Fred Beach, Grace Breck, Constance Buell, Helen and Robert Chandler, Alice B. Cook, Phillip Dutton, Lora Dyer, Charles Gillette, Daniel Gross, Josie Horn, James McCann, R. W. McClure, Luella Miner, Valley Nelson, Emma B. Noreen, Isabella Phelps, Mary Powers, Gertrude C. Pye, Frank Rawlinson, Paul R. Reynolds, Arthur and Gertrude Rinden, Everett Sandburg, Ralph and Elizabeth Schrader, Mr. and Mrs. Roderick Scott, George and Clara Shepherd, Guy Thelin, F. F. Tricker, Nellie Walker, L. D. Ward, R. B. and Louise Whitaker, Dean Wickes, and Stanley D. Wilson.

Correspondence relating to Cheeloo University: Ruth Chen in Chengtu to Mrs. Plumer Mills, 1945; 2 letters from Edward Phillips in Tsinan, 1946; Ernest Struthers to Annie V. Scott in Tsinan, 1946; 2 letters from Gerald Winfield in New York, 1946.

Correspondence relating to Foochow College: to Donald T. M. Hsueh in Foochow, 1933; Hsueh to H. B. Belcher, regarding funds, 1933; 2 letters from Hsueh to Mary Uline, 1933; Caroline Lin Hsueh in Ingtai, Fukien, to Belcher, regarding damage to Foochow College, 1945; C. L. Hsueh in Foochow to Mrs. Medlicox, 1947.

Correspondence relating to Fukien Christian University: Frank Cartwright to Earle Ballou, 1946; 2 letters from Ching Jung-lin at FCU to "Friends," 1935; John Gowdy to Garside, 1938; C. J. Lin to Dean Chase, 1934, with a list of rare books in the library; to C. A. Evans, 1941; to Caroline Frost, 1946; to E. M. Stowe, 1945; extracts of letters from Mrs. Roderick Scott at FCU, 1938; printed letter of Eunice Thomas at FCU, 1940.

Correspondence relating to the North China Mission: Willard Beard, in Ingtai, 1949; Raymond Blakney, 1948; folder of letters and mimeos related to the Boxer Indemnity, n.d.; Constance Buell to "Robbie," n.d.; L. D. Chapin in Tungchou, 1879; Hugh Hubbard to Robert Chandler, 1938; "Journal of Daily Events in a War-stricken Chinese City," letters of James A. Hunter in Tunghsien to his wife in Peitaiho, 1937; Wallace Merwin to Alice Cary regarding American graves in Peking British cemetery, 1957; Isaac Pierson, in Paotingfu, 1879; 4 letters from Judson Smith to Arthur Smith, 1900–1901; P. H. Wang, regarding student work, 1946.

Correspondence relating to the Willis Pierce Hospital: Harold Brewster, 1948, with a report on a proposed Wiley Hospital in Kutien, 1924; extract of letter from Bruce Jarvis, Foochow, 1933; Henry Lacy in Foochow, 1938; W. H. Topping to Mark Ward, 1944(?); Laura Ward in Newton Highlands to Ferdinand Blanchard, 1937; Mark Ward to J. Gurney Barclay, 1943; Mark Ward to Trustee, 1945.

Correspondence relating to Yenching University: Earle Ballou, on release of John Leighton Stuart (JLS) by Japanese, 1945; letters to the Board of Trustees from JLS, 1937; reprint of letter from Grace Boynton, Peking, 1937; Grace Boynton, Shanghai, regarding occupation conditions, 1939; Grace Boynton, 1944; Lucy R. Burtt, Peking, to faculty on furlough, n.d.; T. C. Chao to B. A. Garside, 1933, 1937, to JLS, 1931, and to E. M. McBrier, 1937; Ch'en Fang-chih, 1944; Rowland Cross to Garside, 1931; R. Brank Fulton to Board of Trustees, 1939; Howard S. Galt to Board of Trustees, 1938; B. A. Garside to E. M. McBrier, 1934; Garside to JLS, 1935; E. R. Hughes to JLS, 1931; Ralph Lapwood, 1944; Lu Hui-ching, 1945; Lucius C. Porter, Peking, to churches, 1938, regarding wartime conditions; excerpts of letter from L. C. Porter, Peking, 1938; Emma and Richard Ritter, Peking, to friends abroad, 1934; Randolph Sailer, Peking, 1946; JLS regarding appointment of Japanese faculty at Yenching, n.d.; JLS, Peking, on his return to Yenching and internal conditions in China, 1946; letters of JLS to the Board of Trustees, 1933–40; JLS to Earle Ballou, 1934; to George Barber, 1933, 1934, and his replies, 1934; to Wynn Fairfield, 1935; to Garside, 1933, 1934, 1937; to McBrier, 1937; Ch'i-yu Wu, 1945.

MANUSCRIPTS: Typescripts, mimeographs, and manuscripts, 1878–1952, on such subjects as the American cemetery in Nantai, basic policies, Boxer Indemnity, Cheeloo College of Medicine, China Incident and its effect on Foochow, China Colleges, Chinese cities, Christian literature in post-war China, Christian work in Tientsin schools, Christian middle schools, Christmas at Yenching, church problems, churches of Diong-loh, co-education, communists and Christian colleges, correlation, cost of China field, displaced missionaries, drought-resistant sorghum, Dudley Church, education, effect of the Sino-Japanese conflict on American education, evaluation of mission work, evangelism, famine relief, Fenchow Mission, Foochow Christian Union Hospital, Foochow Mission, Foochow College, Foreign Missions Conference, French attack of 1884, Fukien Christian University, home life, indigenous church, Ingtai, Japanese Christian work in China, Kang Wei Lu church, Kiangsi Christian Rural Service Union, Kiangsu-Anhwei Christian Rural Service Union, Lintsing Mission, Manifesto of 1950, medical work, military situation in Shansi in war-time, mission work under Japanese occupation, mission work in Southern China, mission work in Fukien, missionary personnel, missionary rights and privileges, national leadership, nationalism, North China Hospital, North China Mission, Oberlin-in-Shansi, orphanages, polygamy, post-war conditions, post-war problems, religious education, religious attitudes at Yenching University, rural church, rural reconstruction, scholarships, 75th anniversary of North China Mission, Shaowu Mission, social work, social work and Peking Protestant churches, Taiku, taxes on church property, theological education, Tungchow, Upper Bridge Church, war-time conditions, women's work in rural Fukien, Wuhan, Yenching University, Yenching School of Religion, and youth.

MANUSCRIPTS/PAMPHLETS: 1 file each of mimeographs and pamphlets related to the Alice Williams School (Taiku), Beacon Hill Farm (Foochow), Bridgman Academy (Peking), Canton Hospital, Canton Union Theological College, Catherine S. Harwood Bible Training School (Fenyang), Charles E. Jefferson Academy (Tunghsien), China Christian Education Association, Christian Herald Industrial Mission (Foochow), College of Chinese Studies (Peking), Diongloh Kindergarten, Elizabeth Memorial Hospital (Lintsing), Ellis Laymen's Christian Training School (Lintsing), Fan Village Rural Center (Hopei), Foochow Christian Women's Industrial Institute, Goodrich Girls' School (Tunghsien), Han Mei School (Shaowu), Harwood Memorial and Kate Ford Whitman Hospital (Fenyang), Health Center (Tientsin), Hwa Nan College (Foochow), Institute of Hospital Technology, Joint Council on Extension Service to the Rural Church in North China, Kate C. Woodhull Hospital for Women, Lombard School (Shaowu), Lu Ho Hospital (Tunghsien), Lu Ho Rural Service Center (Tunghsien),

Lydia Lord Davis School (Fenyang), Mary Morrill Woman's School (Paoting), Ming I Middle School (Fenyang), Nanking Theological Seminary, Nanking University, North China American School, North China Christian Rural Service Union, North China Council for Rural Reconstruction, North China Union College (Tunghsien), North China Union Medical College for Women (Peking), Oberlin-Shansi Memorial School (Taiku), Orlinda Childs Pierce Memorial School, Pagoda Anchorage Hospital (Diongloh), Pang-chuang Hospital, Peking Union Bible Training School for Women, Peking Union Medical College, Peking University School of Theology, Porter-Wyckoff Middle School (Tehsien), Shaowu Bible School for Men, Shaowu Christian Hospital, Stanley Memorial School (Tientsin), Taiku Hospital, Tung Jen Middle School (Paoting), Union High School (Foochow), Union Kindergarten Training School (Foochow), Union Medical College (Foochow), Union Normal School (Canton), Union Theological Seminary (Foochow), United Board for Christian Colleges in China, United Board for Christian Higher Education in Asia, West China Union University, Whitney Hospital (Ingtai), Williams-Porter Hospital (Tehsien), Woman's Bible School (Foochow), Yenching College for Women, and Yu Ying Boys' School (Peking).

PAMPHLETS: Mostly undated pamphlets, including the following subjects: ABCFM in China (general), aftermath of the Boxer Rebellion, Amoy Mission, Cheeloo School of Medicine, Cheeloo University, Chinese Christians, Chinese translation controversy, Chinese language study, Christian colleges in China, Christian students, Christian education, Christianizing economic relations, Church of Christ in China, Diong-loh, education, education of women, evaluation of religious education, Fan Village, Fei Ch'i-hao, Foochow Mission, Foochow College, Fukien Christian University, Ginling College, Grinnell-in-China, Flora K. Heebner, Ho Shen, Hopei Union of Christian Student Associations, Inghok, Institute of Pacific Relations, lay training, Leagues of 10, Li Hung-chang, medical work, missions in China, National Christian Council of China, New Life Movement, North China Mission, North China Union Language School, Oberlin-in-China, Oberlin-Shansi Memorial Association, Peking Union Women's College, Quakers in China, registration of Christian schools with the Chinese government, Schwenkfelder mission in Shansi, Shansi, Shaowu Mission, South China Mission, Taiku, Tehchow, theology, Tientsin, women's work in Fukien, women's work, Yale-in-China, and Yenching University.

MEMORABILIA/AUDIO-VISUAL MATERIALS: Scrapbook belonging to Flora Beard, containing clippings, loose and pasted photos of students, faculty, and activities, programs, certificates, emblem, diploma case relating to the North China American School (NCAS), correspondence to Beard, and NCAS periodicals (*Fall Leaves* and *Mei Hua Pai So*, listed below under SERIALS, are complete issues), pasted in, 1917–32.

MEMORABILIA: Miscellaneous clippings on ABCFM; programs for the centennial service for the Foochow Mission, 1948; clippings on Yenching University and a program for the formal opening of Yenching, 1929; program for the service of dedication for Yenching University, 1929; articles and brochures on ABCFM in China; clippings on location and transfers; program for memorial service for Shansi Memorial Association, 1958; clipping on Willis F. Pierce Hospital; clippings from *Chinese Recorder*, 1935, 1937, 1939; *Chinese Student Monthly*, 1926; *Educational Review*, 1927, 1936–37; *China Medical Journal*, 1927; *Christian*

Century, 1925; *The Congregationalist*, 1928; *Peking and Tientsin Times*, 1929; *Peking Leader*, 1928; *Life and Light*, n.d.; *The Week in China*, 1929; *Missionary Herald*, 1935; *North China Star*, 1935; *United Church Herald*, 1965; and *The Christian Sun*, 1948; brochure on Bangor-in-China, 1923; brochures on South China Girls' School in Canton, n.d., Hong Kong missions, 1892, and Training School in Canton, 1898; clipping from the *Japanese Bible Society Record*, on Robert Morrison, 1958; articles from *Far Eastern Quarterly*, 1954; article on Hung Hsiu-ch'uan, 1954; National Committee on Christian Religious Education in China brochure; brochure on Shensi; miscellaneous memorabilia and clippings on Paotingfu; brochure on Pangchuang; Hua Chung College, brochure, 1943; American Bible Society brochures, 1885, 1894, 1916, 1934; obituary of John Leighton Stuart; brochures on Princeton-in-Peiping, 1948; Fukien Christian University, commencement programs, 1935; reprint from *Proceedings of Natural History Society*, 1928.

MAPS/DESIGNS/DRAWINGS: Map showing churches in Foochow with index in Chinese; chart and map of Cheeloo rural program, 1934; maps and chronology of Shaowu Mission, with statistical charts, 1918–42; 2 charts showing evangelism progress with Chinese in Paoting, 1935; summary chart on flood conditions in Paoting, 1939; statistics on economic losses in Paotingfu; map of Fenchow Mission compound, n.d.; map of Fukien province, 1940, with report on Fukien Christian University.

SERIALS: *Agricultural Missions*, ca. 1935–50. Cheeloo University: *Cheeloo*, 1924–25; *Cheeloo Bulletin*, 1930–31; *Cheeloo College of Medicine Bulletin*, 1948; *Cheeloo Monthly Bulletin*, 1946; *Cheeloo Notes*, 1928–29; *Cheeloo School of Theology Bulletin*, 1933; *Cheeloo Sketches*, 1927, 1929; *Occasional Notes from Shantung Christian University*, 1922, 1924. *China Bulletin*, 1952–62 (inc.). China Christian Education Association, *Bulletin*, 1922, 1936. *China Colleges*, 1951. China International Famine Relief Commission, Publications, series B, 1930. *China News*, 1927. *The China Sunday School Journal*, 1928. Chinese Medical Association, *Occasional Leaflet*, 1935–36, 1938. Christian Literature Society for China, *Periodical Link*, 1936. *Christian Universities of China Bulletin*, 1938. *The Church: Bulletin of the Church of Christ in China*, 1950. *Dragon Tracks*, 1941. *Fall Leaves*, 1932. *Fenchow*, 1936. *Foochow College Quarterly*, 1924. *Foochow Messenger*, 1922. Fukien Christian University: Department of English, *Composition Bulletin*, 1923; *FCU News*, 1930, 1932; *Fukien Leaflet*, 1935; *Fukien News*, 1934, 1937; *Fukien Star*, 1922. *Here and Now*, 1923, 1925–26. *Mei Hua Pai So*, 1932. National Christian Council, *Overseas Newsletter*, 1947. National Committee for Christian Religious Education in China, *Bulletin*, 1935–37; *English Bulletin*, 1935–37. Natural History Society, *Proceedings*, 1928, 1930. *Oberlin-in-China*, 1948. *Oberlin Shansi Memorial Association Newsletter*, 1938. *Peking Union Church Bulletin*, 1928. *Quarterly Notes on Christianity and Religion*, 1960–61. *Taiku Reflector*, 1932. Yenching University, Department of Sociology and Social Work, Publications, series B, 1932; *Science Notes*, 1934–39.

CHINESE LANGUAGE MATERIALS/SERIALS: *Directory of the Protestant Christian Movement in China*, 1950. *Foochow College Magazine*, 1923.

CHINESE LANGUAGE MATERIALS: 30 tracts, ca. 1830–1840, mostly undated, printed in Singapore, including pamphlets by William Milne and Karl Gützlaff, a hand-written personal confession of faith, and an untitled pamphlet with a map of the heavens;

Foochow Mission, "Centennial Celebration, 1847–1948: A Century of Christian Work," 1948; bilingual brochure on Foochow College, n.d.; educational regulations of the Nationalist Government, 1927; regulations governing recognition of educational institutions established by funds contributed by foreigners, 1925; Ingtai Academy, catalogue, 1936; American Board Mission schools, Foochow, catalogue, 1899; letter to Ingtai students and preachers, from E. H. Smith, 1927; rules for Christians at Ingtai, 1914; Ingtai Academy Boy's School, catalogue, 1915; memorabilia related to North China mission's 75th anniversary celebration: programs, commemorative pamphlets, hand-written essay, 1935; brochure on Cheeloo University, 1925(?); painted poster on Christian activities, n.d.; 2 pages of handwritten prayers in characters and romanization, n.d.; 14 posters and tracts, including the Lord's Prayer and other religious messages, 1950.

2–GENERAL HOLDINGS

MINUTES/RECORDS/REPORTS: American Board of Commissioners for Foreign Missions (ABCFM): Foochow Mission, annual report, 1895–1901; minutes of the annual meeting, 1915, 1917–18, 1920–22, 1926, 1931; Foochow Mission, report, 1896; Foochow Mission, Pagoda Hospital and Diong-loh Hospital, annual reports, 1917–40; Foochow Mission, Ing-hok district, annual report, 1897–1903, 1905–7, 1910–13, 1915, 1919; Ing Hok (Ingtai), report, 1897–1945; North China Mission, minutes of the annual meeting, 1908–9, 1911–16, 1918–41; reports, 1888–90; annual reports, 1888–96, 1898–99, 1902–11, 1913–14; standing rules, 1906, 1915, 1930; report of the deputation, 1907; Shansi Mission, annual report, 1897, 1905–13; Bridgman Academy, yearbook, 1928; British and Foreign Bible Society, 1909–10; Cheeloo University, School of Medicine, report, 1915–38; China International Famine Relief Commission, annual report, 1929; China Medical Board of New York, annual report, 1963–66; Chinese Young Men's Christian Association, annual report, 1913; Christian Literature Society for China, annual report, 1913; Church of Christ in China, General Council: records and minutes, 1928–33, 1935; Provisional General Assembly, minutes of the executive committee, 1922, 1925; minutes of the secretarial committee, 1925, 1930; general assembly, digest, 1927, 1933, 1937; Fenchow Hospital, annual report, 1925–30; Foochow Medical Missionary Hospital, report, 1872–83, 1886–88, 1890, 1894, 1896, 1898–1904, 1908, 1911–13, 1918–21, 1925; Foochow Hospital for Women and Children, report, 1901–4; Fukien Christian University: annual report of the President and Dean, 1930–32; catalogue, 1926–27; weekly bulletin, 1934–36; president's reports and letters, 1930–39; Lintsing Memorial Hospital, annual report, 1910–40; Lu Ho Hospital, annual report, 1934–48; Mission among the Higher Classes in China, report, 1896; National Christian Council of China, minutes, 1933–37; report, 1935–37; North China, Kung Li Hui, minutes of the annual meeting, 1915–50; Peking Conference on Federation, records, 1905; Peking Union Bible College Training School for Women, report, 1925–49; Peking Union Medical College, yearbook, 1927; Ponasang Missionary Hospital, annual report, 1902; St. John's University, catalogue, 1913–14; Shensi district association, minutes of the annual meeting, 1915, 1917, 1922–24, 1926; Society for the Diffusion of Christianity and General Knowledge among the Chinese, report, 1902, 1904; Taihu Hospital, report, 1896–1940; United Board for Christian Colleges in China, annual report, 1936, 1938–53; United Board for Christian Higher Education in Asia, annual report,

1955–58, 1961–66; Williams Porter Hospital, Shantung, annual report, 1890–1939; Willis F. Pierce Memorial Hospital, report, 1933–38, 1941–42, 1947; Yale-in-China, annual report, 1945–46, 1949–52; Yenching University, president's report, 1913; minutes of the annual meeting of the Board of Managers, 1891.
MANUSCRIPTS: ''Chinese Christian Papers,'' comp. by David MacDonald Paton, 1958; ''West of the Yangtze Gorges,'' by Joseph Taylor, 1936.
PAMPHLETS: 57 pamphlets, 1853–1983, on subjects such as the American Board, Bible, China Inland Mission, China mission studies, Chinese Christians, Chinese church, Christian colleges, Congregational Union, divine salvation, documents of Christian churches, Foochow Mission, Lingnan University, Medical Missionary Society, Methodism in China, Nestorian monument, Protestant missionary works in Chinese, South China Mission, translations, Union Church (Tientsin), and Universalist women at Ginling College.
SERIALS: *Bridge*, 1983-. Cheeloo University: *Bulletin*, 1922–32; *Cheeloo Bulletin*, 1927–39 (inc.). *China and the Gospel*, 1913. *China Bulletin* (Boston), 1937–46. *China Bulletin* (New York), 1947–62. China Christian Educational Association, *Bulletin*, 1933–36. *China Christian Year Book*, 1911–14, 1916–29, 1934–39. *China Circular Bulletin*, 1951–52. *China Colleges*, 1951–66. China International Famine Relief Commission, Publications, series A, 1923-?; series B, 1931. *China News* (Boston), 1927. *China Newsletter*, 1944–51. *China Notes*, 1962–84. *The China-home Bond*, 1939–41. *China's Millions* (London), 1875–1952. *China's Millions* (Toronto), 1893–94, 1897–1903. Chinese Medical Association, Council on Christian Medical Work, *Bulletin*, 1947–49. *Chinese Recorder*, 1868–78, 1883–95, 1908, 1910–12, 1914–17, 1920, 1925–31, 1933–36, 1939–40. *Chinese Repository*, 1832–51. *Ching Feng*, 1964-. *The Christian Farmer*, 1935. Christian Literature Society for China, *Monthly Link*, 1937, 1939. *The Church: Bulletin of the Church of Christ in China*, 1935–36, 1947–50. *Dragon Tracks*, 1944–46. *East Asia Millions* (London), 1965–84. *East Asia Millions* (Philadelphia), 1959–82. *Educational Association of Fukien Province Journal*, 1907, 1911. *Fenchow*, 1919–35 (inc.). *Foochow Goodwill Trenches*, 1923–24. *The Foochow Messenger*, 1903–17, 1922–31, 1935–40. *Fuhkien Witness*, 1908. *Here and Now*, 1922–30. *Information Service*, 1959–60, 1962–63. *Loose Leaves from Missionaries' Diaries*, 1917–21. *Millions* (London), 1952–64. *Millions* (Philadelphia), 1959–61. *Mission Mirror*, 1932–39, 1941–42. *Missionary Recorder*, 1867. Nanking Theological Seminary, English publications, 1940. National Christian Council of China, *Broadcast*, 1938; *Bulletin*, 1930–40; *News*, 1948, 1950. National Committee on Christian Religious Education, *Religious Education Fellowship Bulletin*, 1933, 1936–37, 1939, 1948, 1950. *New Mandarin*, 1926. North China Union College, *Bulletin*, 1914–16. *Quarterly Notes on Christianity and Chinese Religion*, 1958–63. St. John's University, *Bulletin*, 1911–12. *Shansi Bulletin*, 1930, 1936, 1948. *Shaowu Bulletin*, 1921–26. *Truth and Life*, 1927. Yenching University: *Bulletin*, 1927–40; *Yenching News*, 1922–50.
DISSERTATIONS/THESES: *Die Anfänge der neueren Dominikanermission in China*, by Benno M. Biermann, 1927. *Changes in the Christian Message for China by Protestant Missionaries*, by Lewis Strong Casey Smythe, 1928. *Christian Missions in China*, by Charles Sumner Estes, 1895. *Congregational Missionaries in Foochow during the 1911 Revolution*, by Thomas Eliot Korson, 1963. *Education of Christian Ministers in China*, by Samuel H.

Leger, 1925. *Famine in China and the Missionary: Timothy Richard as Relief Administrator and Advocate of National Reform*, by Paul Richard Bohr, 1971. *Imperial Government and Catholic Missions in China during the Years, 1784–1785*, by Bernward H. Willeke, 1948. *Die katholische Missionsmethode in China in neuester Zeit (1842–1912)*, by Johannes Beckmann, 1931. *The Mission Compound in Modern China: The Role of the United States Protestant Mission as an Asylum in the Civil and International Strife of China, 1900–1941*, by Gladys Robina Quale, 1957. *The Negotiations between Ch'i-ying and Lagrené, 1844–1846*, by Angelus Francis Grosse-Aschhoff, 1950. *The Protestant Church in Communist China, 1949–1958*, by James Herbert Kane, 1958. *The Righteous and the Sage: A Comparative Study on the Ideal Images of Man in Biblical Israel and Classical China*, by Sung-hae Kim, 1981.
CHINESE LANGUAGE MATERIALS/SERIALS: *The Chinese Churchman's Yearbook: A Handbook of the Chung Hua Sheng Kung Hui*, 1914. *T'ien chia pan yüeh pao (The Christian Farmer)*, 1939.
CHINESE LANGUAGE MATERIALS: 4 Bibles, 1934–47; *Chinese Hymnal*, prepared by Henry Blodget and C. Goodrich, 1877, 1907; *A Classified Index to the Chinese Literature of the Protestant Churches in China*, 1933; Fenchow Hospital, annual report, 1935; Fukien Christian University, catalogue, 1926–27; Jefferson Academy, catalogue, 1923–26; North China Council, constitution, 1915, 1917, 1921; North China Kung Li Hui, constitution, bylaws and rules, 1933.

HARVARD UNIVERSITY

MA–100 Arnold Arboretum Library

22 Divinity Avenue
Room 202
Cambridge MA 02138
(617) 495–2366
Barbara Callahan, Librarian

1-GENERAL HOLDINGS
SERIALS: *Lingnaam Agricultural Review*, 1922–27. *Lingnan Science Journal*, 1927–50. Lingnan University, *Science Bulletin*, 1930–40. Peking Society of Natural History, *Bulletin*, 1926–41, 1947–48. University of Nanking, College of Agriculture and Forestry: *Agriculture and Forestry Notes*, 1924–26, 1932–36, 1940–41; *Agriculture and Forestry Series*, 1921–24; *Bulletin*, 1923–27, 1931–34, n.s., 1933–37.

MA–105 Baker Library

Harvard University
Graduate School of Business Administration
Soldiers Field
Boston MA 02163
(617) 495–6411
Florence Lathrop, Curator, Manuscripts and Archives

1-JOHN HOWARD NICHOLS COLLECTION, 1856–1905, ca. 20 items
Background note: John Howard Nichols was a China trader in the 1860s who had a personal interest in missionaries.
CORRESPONDENCE: 6 letters from S. L. Baldwin, 1868; 6 letters from Sue and Alvin Ostrom, 1859–62; 4 letters from M. E.

and J. V. N. Talmage, 1868; letters from Eliza Bridgman, 1859–60, regarding missionary activity in China.
FINDING AIDS: In-house inventory.

2-GENERAL HOLDINGS
SERIALS: *Yenching Series on Chinese Industry and Trade*, 1933–34.

MA–110 Farlow Reference Library
Harvard University
20 Divinity Avenue
Cambridge MA 02138
(617) 495–2369
Geraldine C. Kaye, Librarian

1-GENERAL HOLDINGS
SERIALS: University of Nanking, College of Agriculture and Forestry, *Bulletin*, 1933–36.
CHINESE LANGUAGE MATERIALS/SERIALS: *Chin-ling hsüeh pao (Nanking Journal)*, 1933–34.

MA–115 Fine Arts Library
Harvard University
Fogg Art Museum
Rubel Asiatic Research Collection
32 Quincy Street
Cambridge MA 02138
(617) 495–0570
Yen-shew Chao, Librarian

1-GENERAL HOLDINGS
SERIALS: West China Border Research Society, *Journal*, 1939.
West China Union University, *Museum Guidebook* series, 1945.

MA–120 Monroe C. Gutman Library
Harvard University
6 Appian Way
Cambridge MA 02138
(617) 495–3421
Sarah Buckingham, Reference Librarian

1-GENERAL HOLDINGS
MINUTES/RECORDS/REPORTS: Catholic University of Peking, catalogue, 1936–37.
SERIALS: Catholic University of Peking, *Bulletin*, 1926–30.

MA–125 Harvard-Yenching Library
Harvard University
2 Divinity Avenue
Cambridge MA 02138
(617) 495–3327
Eugene Wu, Librarian
John Yung-hsiang Lai, Associate Librarian
Raymond Lum, Assistant Librarian for
Western Languages

Background note: The nucleus of the missionary collections was presented to the Harvard-Yenching Library in 1949 and 1962 by the successor to the American Board of Commissioners for Foreign Missions. It included many versions and editions of the Chi-

nese Bible and its separate books, as well as catechisms, commentaries, hymnbooks, prayer books, textbooks, serials and small tracts, both religious and secular, which were sent back by the missionaries in the field to Boston. The library later added more items and expanded its coverage to other denominations, and added the collections of papers described below.
Finding aids: *Christianity in China: Early Protestant Missionary Writings*, by Suzanne Wilson Barnett and John King Fairbank, 1985. *Catalog of Protestant Missionary Works in Chinese, Harvard-Yenching Library*, comp. by John Yung-hsiang Lai, 1980 (see CHINESE LANGUAGE MATERIALS under GENERAL HOLDINGS below).

1-GEORGE A. AND GERALDINE FITCH PAPERS, 1909-ca. 1950, 43 boxes
Restrictions: Access by appointment.
Background note: George A. Fitch was a Presbyterian missionary to China from 1870 to 1923. See also Rutherford B. Hayes Presidential Center, Library, Spiegel Grove, Fremont, OH, 43420–2796.
MINUTES/RECORDS/REPORTS/CORRESPONDENCE: Documents, reports, correspondence, clippings, and other papers, relating to the George and Geraldine Fitch's work with Chinese industrial cooperatives, United China Relief, YMCA, Institute for Chinese Blind, and other service organizations, including correspondence regarding John and Betty Stam and Roderick [?] Scott, and with Chiang K'ai-shek and Eleanor Roosevelt.
MANUSCRIPTS: "My 80 Years in China," by George Fitch, n.d., including background materials.

2-PHOTOGRAPHIC COLLECTION, 1925, 50 items
Background note: See also Young Men's Christian Association of the U.S.A. Archives, University of Minnesota, Social History Welfare Archives, 2642 University Avenue, St. Paul, MN, 55114.
AUDIO-VISUAL MATERIALS: The YMCA Collection, consisting of 50 hand-tinted lantern slides of China prepared by the Foreign Committee, 1925, with accompanying booklet, illustrated, describing each slide.

3-CLAUDE L. PICKENS COLLECTION, ca. 1900-ca. 1950, ca. 30 volumes
Restrictions: Access by appointment.
Background note: Claude L. Pickens, Jr. (d. 1984), was an American Episcopalian missionary among Muslims in China. *Friends of Moslems* was published by Pickens and edited by his wife, N. Elizabeth Zwemer Pickens.
MANUSCRIPTS: 25 notebooks containing notes on Islam in China, including manuscript of a Chinese-Muslim biographical dictionary.
PAMPHLETS/MEMORABILIA/CHINESE LANGUAGE MATERIALS: Published materials in English, Chinese, and Arabic on Islam in general and on Islam in China.
AUDIO-VISUAL MATERIALS: Several photo albums depicting Muslim people and structures in China.
SERIALS: *Friends of Moslems*, 1927–36.

4-RECORDS OF THE TRUSTEES OF LINGNAN UNIVERSITY, 1820–1952, 176 boxes
Restrictions: Access by appointment.
Background note: See also Yale Divinity School, Special Collections, 409 Prospect Street, New Haven, CT, 06510.

MINUTES/RECORDS/REPORTS: Lingnan University: catalogues, 1899–1948; field reports, 1820–1951; university survey, 1847–48; financial reports, 1887–1952; statistics; charter of the Board of Regents; minutes, 1886–1952; medical work, 1900–1951.

CORRESPONDENCE: Correspondence arranged by key personalities: Charles K. Edmunds, 1920–23; F. F. Ellinwood, 1884–94; Henry S. Frank, 1946–51; W. Henry Grant, 1895–1919; Andrew P. Happer, 1884–89; B. C. Henry, 1893–94; James M. Henry, 1924–51; Harold B. Hoskins, 1940–45; Y. L. Lee, 1939–47; Olin D. Wannamaker, 1939–51.

FINDING AIDS: "General Guide to the Trustees of Lingnan University Archives" (incomplete). *Asia and Oceania: A Guide to Archival and Manuscript Sources in the United States*, ed. by G. Raymond Nunn (New York: Mansell), 1985.

5-ANDREW STRITMATTER LETTERS, 1869–80, 1 volume
Background note: Andrew Stritmatter (1847–88) was a Methodist missionary in China from 1873 to 1880. See also Ohio University, Vernon R. Alden Library, Department of Archives and Special Collections, Park Place, Athens, OH, 45701–2978.

CORRESPONDENCE: Typed copies of letters from Stritmatter, mostly to his sister living in Ohio and to the *Athens Messenger*, an Ohio newspaper, relating to missionary activities, 1869–80.

6-GENERAL HOLDINGS
MINUTES/RECORDS/REPORTS: Librairie des Lazaristes, catalogue, 1941; Lingnan University, catalogue, 1930–31, 1934–35, 1937–38; National Council of Churches World Order Study Conference, report of the Circuit Riders, 1958; West China Union University, report, 1933; Yenching University History Society, historical annual, 1936.

MANUSCRIPTS: "Books on China in the University of Nanking Library," 1937; "The Catholic Church in China," 1960 (?); "History of Nanking Theological Seminary, 1911 to 1961: A Tentative Draft," by Frank Wilson Price, 1961; "A Selected List of Chinese Characters, North China Language School," n.d.; list of serials, Lingnan University Library, 1936.

PAMPHLETS: *Catalogue of the Nestorian Literature and Relics*, by P. Yoshio Saeki, 1950; *Critical Moments in the History of Christianity in China: A Paper Read before the Shanghai Missionary Association, November 3, 1925*, by Harley Farnsworth MacNair, 1925(?); *A Mighty Invalid: The Story of Bishop Schereschewsky*, by James Arthur Muller, 1942; *Twenty-two Years of Agricultural Economics: A Review of the Work of the Department of Agricultural Economics, College of Agriculture and Forestry, University of Nanking (1920–42)*, by Lien-ken Yin, 1942.

SERIALS: *Bridge*, 1983-. Catholic University of Peking, *Agricultural Extension Service Bulletin*, 1948; *Bulletin*, 1926–34. *China Bulletin*, 1952–62. China Christian Educational Association, *Bulletin*, 1928. *China Christian Year Book*, 1926. *China Colleges*, 1947–48. China International Famine Relief Commission, Publications, series A, 1923–32, 1934–37; series B, 1923. *China Mission Studies Bulletin*, 1979-. *China Missionary*, 1948–49. *China Missionary Bulletin*, 1952–53. *China Notes*, 1962–83. *Chinese Medical Journal*, 1953–66. *Chinese Recorder*, 1872, 1882, 1893, 1902–3, 1905–6. *Chinese Recorder and Missionary Journal*, 1922. *Chinese Repository*, 1832–51. *Ching Feng*, 1957-. *Folklore Studies*, 1942–47, 1951; supplement, 1952. *Friends of Moslems*, 1927–36. *Lingnan Science Journal*, 1933–39, 1945. *Quarterly Notes on Christianity and Christian Religion*, 1957–63. Université

de l'Aurore, *Bulletin de l'Université de l'Aurore*, 1933–49. *Variétés Sinologiques*, 1985. West China Border Research Society, *Journal*, 1922–45; supplement, 1937. *West China Missionary News*, 1933–34. West China Union University, monograph series, 1946; *Museum Guidebook* series, 1945; *Offprint series*, 1945. Yenching University: *Bulletin*, 1927–28, 1932–37, 1940–41, 1947–48; *Journal of Sinological Studies*, 1923; *Occasional Papers*, 1939-?; *Social Sciences Quarterly*, 1922–25; *Yenching Journal of Chinese Studies*, supplement, 1932; *Yenching Journal of Social Studies*, 1938–41, 1948–50; *Yenching News*, 1938, 1941, 1944–50.

DISSERTATIONS/THESES: *Catholic Activities in Kwangtung Province and Chinese Responses, 1848–1885*, by Jean-Paul Wiest, 1977. *China und die katholische Mission in Süd-Shantung, 1882–1900: die Geschichte einer Konfrontation*, by Jacobus Joannes Antonius Mathias Kuepers, 1974. *Chinese Hostility to Christianity: A Study in Intercultural Conflict, 1860–1870*, by Paul Anthony Cohen, 1960. *Patterns at Tengchow: Life Experiences of Three American Missionaries in East Shantung Province, China, 1864–1882*, by Irwin Townsend Hyatt, 1969. *Practical Evangelism: Protestant Missions and the Introduction of Western Civilization into China, 1820–1850*, by Suzanne Wilson Barnett, 1973. *The Russian Ecclesiastical Mission in Peking during the Eighteenth Century*, by Eric George Widmer, 1970. *Yenching University and American-Chinese Relations, 1917–1937*, by Philip West, 1971.

CHINESE LANGUAGE MATERIALS/SERIALS: *Chen i chou k'an*, 1923–26. *Chiao hui hsin pao (The Church News)*, 1869–70. *Chung-hua Chi-tu chiao hui nien chien (China Church Year Book)*, 1914–36 (repr. 1983). *Fu jen hsüeh chih (Fu jen Sinological Journal/Series Sinologica)*, 1929. *Hua t'u hsin pao (Chinese Illustrated News)* 1880-?. *Kuo chi kung pao (International Journal and Institute Record)*, 1923. *Wan kuo kung pao (The Globe Magazine: A Review of the Times)*, 1868–1907.

CHINESE LANGUAGE MATERIALS: Over 1,500 titles in Mandarin and other Chinese languages (some in romanized script), in addition to works in other Asian and Western languages, on Apologetics, Baptist missions, the Bible, Boxers, catechism, Catholic church, Christian education, Christian ethics, Christianity, Jesuits, liturgy, martyrs, Methodist missions, missionaries, Nestorians, Presbyterian church, Protestant church, sermons, Taiping Rebellion, theology, tracts, and other mission-related subjects, institutions, and individuals, dating from the mid–16th to early 20th centuries; microfiche copies of 708 of the aforementioned titles on Protestant missionary works on Christianity in general, the Bible, theological works, church histories and biographies, history and geography, humanities, social sciences, science and technology, physiology and medicine, and ritual, liturgy, and missionary works.

MA–130 Houghton Library
Harvard University
Manuscript Department
Cambridge MA 02138
(617) 495-2449
Rodney G. Dennis, Curator

1-AMERICAN BOARD OF COMMISSIONERS FOR FOREIGN MISSIONS RECORDS, 1820–1952, quantity undetermined
Background note: This collection is the manuscript archive of the

American Board of Commissioners for Foreign Missions (ABCFM), consisting of correspondence with domestic and foreign departments, the Woman's Boards, and world missions. The collection also includes material on the Reformed Church in America and other mission-sending agencies who worked under the ABCFM. Prudential Committee minutes are held by the library of the United Christian Board of World Ministries at 14 Beacon Street, Boston, MA, 02115. See also ABCFM collections at the American Congregational Association Library, 14 Beacon Street, Boston, MA, 02108; Harvard Divinity School, Andover-Harvard Theological Library, 45 Francis Avenue, Cambridge, MA, 02138; and Yale Divinity School, Special Collections, 409 Prospect Street, New Haven, CT, 06510.

MINUTES/RECORDS/REPORTS/CORRESPONDENCE: Reports, documents, and correspondence with missions in China including Amoy, 1820–46; Amoy and Fuh-chau, 1846–54; Fuh-chau and Canton, 1860–80; Foochow, 1871–1952; Foochow Woman's Board, 1901–27; Foochow, Shaowu, South China, 1878–1929; Shanghai, Shantung, 1917–29; Foochow Mission, treasurer accounts, 1872–95, miscellaneous accounts, 1909–40; minutes of the following: Foochow Mission, 1848–1923; Ad Interim Committee, 1918–43; Comity Committee, 1907–17; Anti-Cobweb Society, 1915–50; South China Mission, 1831–60, 1882–1919; Treasury department, 1830–46; miscellaneous, 1836–1918; North China Mission, 1860–1952, Woman's Board, 1903–27; letters from missionaries, 1871–1904; North China colleges, Fukien Christian University, 1916–29; Chihli, Shansi, 1907–29; North China American School, Tunghsien, student records, 1914–41; Shansi Mission, 1880–1914; Shaowu Mission, 1920–52.
MANUSCRIPTS: Sermon by Henry Blodget, 1866; papers relating to memoirs of Harriet Newell, n.d.
FINDING AIDS: In-house inventory.

2-ROGER SHERMAN GREENE PAPERS, 1905–47, ca. 47 boxes
Background note: Roger Sherman Greene (1881–1947) worked with the Rockefeller Foundation's China Medical Commission and China Medical Board, and with Peking Union Medical College. See also Rockefeller University, Rockefeller Archive Center, Pocantico Hills, North Tarrytown, NY, 10591; and State Historical Society of Wisconsin, Archives Division, 816 State Street, Madison, WI, 53706.
MINUTES/RECORDS/REPORTS: 2 boxes of reports and papers relating to the Rockefeller Foundation, 1913–36; 3 boxes of reports and papers relating to the Harvard-Yenching Institute, 1928–46.
CORRESPONDENCE: 8.5 boxes of correspondence relating to the China Medical Commission and China Medical Board, 1914–27, 1935–38, 1940–46; 2 boxes of correspondence relating to Peking Union Medical College, 1927–28; 3 boxes of correspondence with the director of the China Medical Board; folder of correspondence between his wife, Kate Greene, and China Medical Board, 1947–63; 19 folders of correspondence with various relief organizations, 1938–39; 3 boxes of correspondence with the Harvard-Yenching Institute, 1928–46, including West China Union University and the Associated Boards for Christian Colleges in China; 4 folders of correspondence with United China Relief, 1942–45; correspondence with Pearl Buck, ca. 1939–1944, and Pierre Teilhard de Chardin, ca. 1931–1934.
FINDING AIDS: In-house register.

3-ARTHUR GREENWOOD ROBINSON PAPERS, 1913–17, 8 boxes
Background note: For biographical notes, see Wellesley College, Archives, Margaret Clapp Library, Wellesley, MA, 02181. See also Colby College, Miller Library, Waterville, ME, 04901; Washington State University, Manuscripts, Archives, and Special Collections, Pullman, WA, 99164–5610; and Young Men's Christian Association of the U.S.A. Archives, University of Minnesota, Social History Welfare Archives, 2642 University Avenue, St. Paul, MN, 55114. The collection is not yet processed.
MINUTES/RECORDS/REPORTS: Papers relating to Yung Wing's mission and YMCA work in North China, 1913–17.

4-GENERAL HOLDINGS
PAMPHLETS: *Response des jésuites à la lettre qui leur a été écrite. A la Chine, aux dépens de la Société Jésuitique*, 1752.

MA–135 Law School Library
Harvard University
Langdell Hall
Cambridge MA 02138
(617) 495-4295
Harry S. Martin, Librarian

1-GENERAL HOLDINGS
MINUTES/RECORDS/REPORTS: International Institute of China, reports, 1913, 1927.
SERIALS: *China Law Review*, 1922–33.
DISSERTATIONS/THESES: *The Legal Status of Alien Religious Property Situated in China*, by Norman Judson Padelford, 1929.

MA–140 Museum of Comparative Zoology Library
Harvard University
26 Oxford Street
Rooms 209–209P
Cambridge MA 02138
(617) 495-2475
Eva Jonas, Librarian

1-GENERAL HOLDINGS
SERIALS: *Lingnaam Agricultural Review*, 1922–27. *Lingnan Science Journal*, 1927–28. Natural History Society, *Proceedings*, 1929. *Peking Natural History Bulletin*, 1926–41, 1948–49. St. John's University, *Biological Bulletin*, 1935. West China Border Research Society, *Journal*, 1922–29, 1932–34, 1940, 1945. Yenching University, Department of Biology, *Bulletin*, 1930.

MA–145 Peabody Museum Library
Harvard University
11 Divinity Avenue
Cambridge MA 02138
(617) 495-2253

1-GENERAL HOLDINGS
SERIALS: *Lingnan Science Journal*, 1939. *Peking Natural History Bulletin*, 1927. West China Border Research Society, *Journal*, 1922–45. West China Union University, *Museum Guidebook* series, 1943–47; Museum of Archeology, Art, and Ethnology, *Translation Series*, 1946; *Offprint Series*, 1945.

MA–150 Pusey Library
Harvard University Archives
Cambridge MA 02138
(617) 495-2461/2462
Harley P. Holden, Curator

Finding aids: A Descriptive Guide to the Harvard University Archives, comp. by Clark A. Elliott (Cambridge, MA: Harvard University Library), 1976.

1-HARVARD-YENCHING INSTITUTE, 1929-56, 4 volumes
MINUTES/RECORDS/REPORTS: Board of Trustees, Corporation, and Executive Committee, minutes, 1929-31, 1943-51, 1956; library forms and notices; equipment inventory, 1941.

2-YENCHING INSTITUTE, 1949-60, 2 items
Background note: See Harvard-Yenching Library above.
MANUSCRIPTS: "General Guide to the Trustees of Lingnan University Archives (1845-1951)," ca. 1960.
PAMPHLETS: *The Harvard Yenching Institute and the Christian Colleges in China: A Statement of Interest and of Policy*, 1949.

3-GENERAL HOLDINGS
DISSERTATIONS/THESES: *American Missionaries' Outlook on China, 1830-1860*, by Earl Cranston, 1931. *American Missionaries and American Diplomacy in China, 1830-1900*, by Allen Thomas Price, 1932. *The American Protestant Foreign Mission Movement, 1880-1920*, by Valentine H. Rabe, 1965. *Americans as Reformers in Kuomintang China, 1928-1937*, by James Claude Thomson, 1961. *Biblical Influence upon the Ideology of the T'ai p'ing Rebellion*, by Eugene P. Boardman, 1946. *Chinese Hostility to Christianity: A Study in Intercultural Conflict, 1860-1870*, by Paul A. Cohen, 1960. *The Legal Status of Alien Religious Property Situated in China*, by Norman Judson Padelford, 1929. *Missionaries and Chinese: A Descriptive Case Study of the Responses of American Board Missionaries to Selected Aspects of the Setting of Their Work, 1895-1905*, by Sidney A. Forsythe, 1963. *The Missionary Mind and American Far Eastern Policy, 1911-1915*, by James Elden Reed, 1977. *Patterns at Tengchow: Life Experience of Three American Missionaries in East Shantung Province, China, 1864-1912*, by Irvin T. Hyatt, Jr., 1969. *Practical Evangelism: Protestant Missions and the Introduction of Western Civilization into China, 1820-1850*, by Suzanne Wilson Barnett, 1973. *Protestant America and the Pagan World: The First Half Century of American Board of Commissioners for Foreign Missions, 1810-1860*, by Clifton Jackson Phillips, 1954. *The Russian Ecclesiastical Mission in Peking during the Eighteenth Century*, by Eric G. Widmer, 1970. *The Salvation of China: Urban Reform and the Chinese YMCA*, by Shirley Stone Garrett, 1966. *The Treaty of Nerchinsk (Nipchu), 1689: A Case Study of the Initial Period of Sino-Russian Diplomatic Relations Based on the Unpublished Diary of Father Thomas Pereyra of the Society of Jesus*, by Joseph Schobert Sebes, 1958. *The Yangtze Valley Anti-missionary Riots of 1891*, by Roberto M. Paterno, 1967. *Yenching University and American-Chinese Relations, 1917-1937*, by Phillip West, 1971.

MA–155 Widener Library
Harvard University
Cambridge MA 02138
(617) 495-2401
Yen-tsai Feng, Librarian of Harvard College

1-GENERAL HOLDINGS
MINUTES/RECORDS/REPORTS: Canton Christian College, president's report, 1910-12, 1919-24; Canton Hospital, report, 1919; Catholic University of Peking, catalogue, 1936-37, 1946-48; China Baptist Publication Society, report, 1910; Christian Literature Society for China, report, 1912; Foochow Missionary Hospital, report, 1910-14, 1922-23; Fukien Christian University, report of the president and dean, 1930-32; report, 1930-32; 2 reels of minutes, reports, publications, n.d.; Ginling College Archives, 4 reels of reports, n.d.; International Institute of China, reports, 1897, 1913-19, 1921-27; Lingnan University, record of testimonial dinner to Charles K. Edmunds, 1922; president's report, 1910-12, 1919-24; report of the medical department, 1928-30; Medical Missionary Society in China, report, 1845-47, 1858-59; University of Nanking: 6 reels of minutes, reports, publications, catalogues, etc., n.d.; College of Agriculture and Forestry, Experiment Station, report, 1923-26, 1931-34; West China Union University Archives, 2 reels of reports, n.d.; Yenching University, 9 reels of catalogues, minutes, publications, reports, etc., n.d.
CORRESPONDENCE: Letter from Ella (Johnson) Kinnear, Foochow Missionary Hospital, concerning the revolution in Foochow, 1912; letter from Catherine Jones and William Warder Cadbury, Lingnan University, 1948; "Lettre aux rr. pp. jésuites sur les idolatries et sur les superstitions de la Chine," ca. 1700; "China Log," letters from Annie Eloise Bradshaw to Flora Bonsack Stanley, 1965(?).
MANUSCRIPTS: "An Agricultural Survey of Szechwan Province, China," by John Lossing Buck, 1943; "La calunnia convinta, cice Risposta ad un libello publicato da difensori de riti condannati della Cina, sotto il titilo di Lettere d'avviso d'un buon amico, al dottore de Sorbona, autore della Difesa del Giudizio formato dalla Sede Apostolica...," n.a., 1710; "Chinese Christian Papers," comp. by David MacDonald Paton, 1958; "Chinese Communists and Mission Properties," by Mr. Harmon of Shantung University, ca. 1920; "Christian Missions in China," by Edward Wilson Wallace, 1929(?); "Education for the Needs of Life in Lingnan University, Canton, China," n.a., n.d.; "Epistola ad summum pontificem Innocentium XII, scripta a directoribus Seminarii Parisiensis Missionum ad Exteros de idolatricis ac superstitiosis cultibus Sinarum," n.a., n.d.; "Missions in Far Eastern Cultural Relations," by Miner Searle Bates, 1942; "La verità e l'innocenza de missionari della Compagnia de Giesu nella Cina...," n.a., ca. 1710; "Yenching University: Its Sources and Its History," by Howard Spilman Galt, 1939.
PAMPHLETS: Ca. 28 pamphlets, 1709-1941, on subjects such as American Board missions, Emma Brodbeck, Canton Christian College, Christian missions, church in war-time, Fukien Christian University, International Institute of China, Lingnan University, Nestorians, political obstacles to missionary success, Russian missionaries, St. John's University, Shansi massacres, and Yenching University.
MEMORABILIA: "Li Hung Chang's Scrapbook," 1913.
MAPS/DESIGNS/DRAWINGS: *Atlas of the Chinese Empire Containing Separate Maps of the Eighteen Provinces of China Proper on the Scale of 1:3,000,000 and of the Four Great Dependencies on the Scale of 1:7,500,000, Together with an Index to All the Names on the Maps and a List of All Protestant Mission Stations*, by Edward Stanford (London: China Inland Mission), 1908.
SERIALS: American Friends Service Committee, *Bulletin on Work in China*, 1942-44. *Bulletin on China's Foreign Relations*,

1931–35. Catholic University of Peking, *Bulletin*, 1926–30. *China Christian Advocate*, 1914–30, 1932, 1934–41. *China Christian Year Book*, 1926–39. *China Colleges*, 1934–35, 1937–38, 1940–55. China Inland Mission, *Occasional Papers*, 1866–75. China International Famine Relief Commission, *Bulletin*, 1925–28; Publications, series B, 1923, 1930–31; series E, 1932. *China Medical Journal*, 1907–21. *China Medical Missionary Journal*, 1887–91, 1893–97, 1901, 1906–7. *China Mission Advocate*, 1839. *China Mission Year Book*, 1910–25. *China Monthly*, 1939–50. *China Notes*, 1962–. *China, The Quarterly Record*, 1912–13, 1915. *Chine, Ceylon, Madagascar*, 1898–1905. *Chinese Recorder*, 1868–1941. *Chinese Repository*, 1832–51. *El Correo Sino-anna-mita*, 1866–1916. *East Asia Millions* (Philadelphia), 1961–. Educational Association of China, *Directory*, 1905. *Educational Review*, 1909–38. *The Foochow Messenger*, 1903–17, 1922–40. *Fu Jen Newsletter*, 1931–32. *Maryknoll Mission Letters*, 1923–27. *The Millions* (Philadelphia), 1959–61. *Missions de Chine et du Japon*, 1916, 1919, 1929. *Monumenta Serica*, Monograph series, 1948. *New East*, 1909–12. *New Mandarin*, 1926. *Peking Natural History Bulletin*, 1928. *St. John's University Studies*, 1922. Université de l'Aurore: *Bulletin*, 1942, 1945–49; *Monthly Bulletin*, 1946–48. University of Nanking, College of Agriculture and Forestry: *Agriculture and Forestry Notes*, 1924–27, 1934–36, 1938–41; *Agriculture and Forestry Series*, 1924; *Bulletin*, 1926, 1932–36; *Economic Facts*, 1936–37; *Miscellaneous Bulletin Series*, 1924; *Special Report*, 1935. University of Peking, College of Education, Publications, 1939–40. West China Border Research Society, *Journal*, 1922–37. *West China Missionary News*, 1901–43. Yenching University: Department of Sociology and Social Work, *Social Research Series*, 1930; *Yenching Index Numbers*, 1940–41; *Yenching Journal of Chinese Studies*, Supplement, 1932; *Yenching Journal of Social Studies*, 1938–50; *Yenching Political Science Series*, 1929–32; *Yenching Series on Chinese Industry and Trade*, 1937.

DISSERTATIONS/THESES: *Accommodatie in de Chinese Zen-dingageschiedenis*, by Johannes Maarten van Minnen, 1951. *The American Missionaries' Outlook in China, 1830–1860*, by Earl Cranston, 1931. *American Missions and American Diplomacy in China, 1830–1900*, by Allen Thomas Price, 1932. *The American Protestant Foreign Mission Movement, 1880–1920*, by Valentine H. Rabe, 1965. *American Protestant Missionary Movement: Its Impact on China*, by Joseph Patrick O'Neill, 1969. *Americans as Reformers in Kuomintang China, 1928–1937*, by James Claude Thomson, 1961. *Die Anfänge der neueren Dominikanermission in China*, by Benno M. Biermann, 1927. *Apostolic Legations to China of the Eighteenth Century*, by Antonio Sisto Rosso, 1948. *Biblical Influence upon the Ideology of the T'ai-p'ing Rebellion*, by Eugene P. Boardman, 1946. *Chinese Hostility to Christianity: A Study in Intercultural Conflict, 1860–1870*, by Paul A. Cohen, 1960. *Christian Missions in China*, by Charles S. Estes, 1895. *François Pallu, principal fondateur de la Société des missions étrangères*, by Louis Baudiment, 1934. *Die katholische Missionsmethode in China in neuester Zeit (1842–1912)*, by Johannes Beckmann, 1931. *The Legal Status of Alien Religious Property Situated in China*, Norman Judson Padelford, 1929. *Lutheran Missions in a Time of Revolution: The China Experience, 1944–1951*, by Jonas Jonson, 1972. *Missionaries and Chinese: A Descriptive Case Study of the Responses of American Board Missionaries to Selected Aspects of the Setting of Their Work, 1895–1905*, by Sidney A. Forsythe, 1963. *The Missionary Mind and American Far Eastern*

Policy, 1911–1915, by James Elden Reed, 1977. *Missionary Power and Civil Authority in China: The Crisis of 1900*, by Robert Laurence Cook, 1970. *Patterns at Tengchow: Life Experience of Three American Missionaries in East Shantung Province, China, 1864–1882*, by Irvin T. Hyatt, Jr., 1969. *La Politique missionnaire de la France en Chine, 1842–1856; l'ouverture des cinq ports chinois au commerce étranger et à la liberté religieuse*, by Louis Tsing-sing Wei, 1960. *Practical Evangelism: Protestant Missions and the Introduction of Western Civilization into China, 1820–1850*, by Suzanne Wilson Barnett, 1973. *Protestant America and the Pagan World: The First Half Century of American Board of Commissioners for Foreign Missions, 1810–1860*, by Clifton Jackson Phillips, 1954. *La rencontre et le conflit entre les idées des missionnaires chrétiens et les idées des Chinois en Chine depuis la fin de la dynastie des Ming*, by Liang Si-ing, 1940. *The Russian Ecclesiastical Mission in Peking during the Eighteenth Century*, by Eric G. Widmer, 1970. *The Salvation of China: Urban Reform and the Chinese YMCA*, by Shirley Stone Garrett, 1966. *The Treaty of Nerchinsk (Nipchu), 1689: A Case Study of the Initial Period of Sino-Russian Diplomatic Relations Based on the Unpublished Diary of Father Thomas Pereyra of the Society of Jesus*, by Joseph Schobert Sebes, 1958. *The Yangtze Valley Anti-missionary Riots of 1891*, by Roberto M. Paterno, 1967. *Yenching University and American-Chinese Relations, 1917–1937*, by Philip West, 1971.
CHINESE LANGUAGE MATERIALS/SERIALS: *Hua t'u hsin pao (Chinese Illustrated News)*, V 1, N 6, n.d.
CHINESE LANGUAGE MATERIALS: *St. John's University, 1879–1929*, 1929; *What Is Japan Doing in China*, by the faculty of Yenching University, 1931; Harvard Divinity School, catalogue, 1926–27.

MA–160 John G. Wolbach Library
Harvard College Observatory
60 Garden Street
Cambridge MA 02138
(617) 495-5488
Estelle Karlin, Librarian

1-GENERAL HOLDINGS
CHINESE LANGUAGE MATERIALS/SERIALS: *Nanjing da-xue xue-bao*, 1979–.

RADCLIFFE COLLEGE
MA–165 Arthur and Elizabeth Schlesinger Library on the History of Women in America
10 Garden Street
Cambridge MA 02138
(617) 495-8647
Eva S. Moseley, Curator of Manuscripts

Finding aids: *The Manuscript Inventories and the Catalogs of Manuscripts, Books, and Periodicals*, second ed. (Boston: G. K. Hall, 1984), 10 V.

1-GRACE MORRISON BOYNTON PAPERS, 1925–51, 1.25 l.f.
Background note: Grace Morrison Boynton (b. 1890) was a missionary educator in China, a teacher and dean at Yenching University.

CORRESPONDENCE: Letters from Yenchiao in diary, 1925–26; correspondence of Boynton, 1939–44.
DIARIES: 28 folders of diaries and transcripts of diaries, 1925–51.
MANUSCRIPTS: Folder of biographical materials on Boynton, n.d.; folder of miscellaneous papers and notes, n.d.
FINDING AIDS: In-house inventory.

2-FAMILY PLANNING ORAL HISTORY PROJECT, 1975, 1 item
ORAL HISTORIES: Audio tape and transcript of 1975 interview with Louise Gilman Hutchins, discussing her childhood in China and medical missionary work in China (see also Berea College, Hutchins Library, Berea, KY, 40404)

3-AMY RICHARDSON HOLWAY, 1917–32, 8 folders
Background note: Amy Richardson Holway (1894–1949) went to China in 1917 as a missionary. She was the school principal at the Mary Bridgman Normal School in Shanghai from 1920 to 1927, remaining there as a teacher until she left China, ca. 1932. See also Mount Holyoke College, Williston Memorial Library, College History and Archives, South Hadley, MA, 01075–1493.
CORRESPONDENCE: Letters from Holway to her family, 1917–29, 1931–32, commenting on Chinese life; 2 letters from missionary Anna West, 1923–25.
DIARIES: Transcribed diary, 1922, with notes by transcriber (on microfilm).
MANUSCRIPTS: Notes by Holway on Chinese customs, incidents, etc., 1917–18.
MEMORABILIA: Printed biographical sketch of Holway from family history; clippings on Chinese life, 1925, n.d.; form letter and leaflet from missions in China, n.d.
FINDING AIDS: In-house inventory.

4-THYRA PEDERSEN, 1923–25, 12 folders
Background note: Thyra Pedersen (b. 1889?) taught at the Union Girls' School in Hangchow between 1923 and 1925.
CORRESPONDENCE: 9 folders of letters from Pedersen, in Shanghai and Hangchow, 1923–25, concerning her travels.
MANUSCRIPTS: Folder of articles by Pedersen on East Asia, 1924–25, and an introduction to Feng Yü-hsiang's camp, n.d.
AUDIO-VISUAL MATERIALS: Folder of photos of China, n.d.
FINDING AIDS: In-house inventory.

5-PRUITT FAMILY PAPERS, 1891–1970s, 15 boxes, 12 file drawers
Background note: Anna Seward Pruitt was a Southern Baptist missionary to the North China Mission in Shantung from 1887 to 1939. Ida Pruitt, her daughter, was a teacher and principal at the Wai Ling School for Girls in Chefoo from 1912 to 1918, chief of the Department of Social Services at Peking Union Medical College from 1921 to 1939, and American Executive Secretary of the Chinese Industrial Cooperatives from 1939 to 1952. The collection is expected to be acquired in 1988. See also Hoover Institution, Archives, Stanford University, Stanford, CA, 94305–2323.
MINUTES/RECORDS/REPORTS: Peking Union Medical College, annual reports and memos to staff and colleagues, 1921–39; Chinese Industrial Cooperatives, newsletters and annual meeting reports, Board minutes, and Finance and Policy Committee minutes, n.d.
CORRESPONDENCE: Letters of Anna Pruitt to her parents, relatives and friends, 1891–1907; 11 bound volumes of correspondence of Anna Pruitt (ca. 100–200 pages each); originals and carbons (with personal notes) of weekly correspondence of Anna Pruitt, 1908–48; miscellaneous correspondence of Seward family; miscellaneous letters of C. W. Pruitt (Anna Pruitt's husband) to family members; correspondence of Ida Pruitt relating to Chinese Industrial Cooperatives, ca. 1939–1952; correspondence of Ida Pruitt with Rewi Alley, 1938–85, and Edgar and Helen Foster Snow, n.d.; correspondence of Ida Pruitt with her parents during tour of Chinese Industrial Cooperatives region, 1946; copies of miscellaneous correspondence of Ida Pruitt, 1930s–1970s; correspondence from Chinese Industrial Cooperatives staff in China, n.d.
MANUSCRIPTS: Carbon copies of published and unpublished essays of Anna Pruitt, mostly for the mission press, early 1900s–1930s; miscellaneous memos, lists and notes of Anna Pruitt; unpublished Seward family stories and genealogies; 2 drafts of autobiography of C. W. Pruitt; drafts of autobiography of Ida Pruitt covering 1887–1939; notes and copies of Ida Pruitt's lectures on hospital social service, 1930s; notes, papers, and dream records of Ida Pruitt, 1930s–1970s; notes and copies of Ida Pruitt's lectures on China-related subjects, 1930s–1960s; copies of stories and incomplete patient records by Peking Union Medical College hospital case workers, 1921–39; notes and essays on Ida Pruitt's travels in China, 1930s; essay on Japanese occupation of Peking, by Ida Pruitt, 1939; short stories about China and Chinese Industrial Cooperatives, by Ida Pruitt, n.d.; drafts of translations, books, social work articles, and short stories, by Ida Pruitt, n.d.; script to slide show on Chinese Industrial Cooperatives, n.d.; works of other writers and translators given to Ida Pruitt, including drafts of Rewi Alley manuscripts, n.d.
DIARIES: Diaries of Anna Pruitt, n.d.
PAMPHLETS: United China Relief pamphlet, n.d.
ORAL HISTORIES: Transcript of an interview with Ida Pruitt, ca. 1970s.
MEMORABILIA/AUDIO-VISUAL MATERIALS: 7 bound scrapbooks of Anna Pruitt, ca. 1880s–1940s, containing miscellaneous articles by and about her, about her mission work, missionaries, and her children's work, and photos of missionaries and Chinese; photos by Anna Pruitt of Chinese Christians and missionaries, late 19th–early 20th centuries; scrapbook of Baillie School photos; miscellaneous booklets and postcards; social work articles by Ida Pruitt in *Chinese Medical Journal*, 1928–36; miscellaneous small notebooks and index files with addresses relating to Chinese Industrial Cooperatives, n.d.; photos collected by Ida Pruitt of Chinese people, countryside and Chinese Industrial Cooperatives, n.d
MAPS/DESIGNS/DRAWINGS: Papercuts, annotated by Anna Pruitt, ca. late 19th–early 20th centuries; Chinese prints, woodcuts, wood carvings, temple rubbings, silk weavings, original sketches and reproductions of wartime scenes, papercuts; map of Chefoo and P'englai, n.d.
FINDING AIDS: ''Description of Pruitt Papers,'' by Marjorie King, 1986.

6-EDITH G. STEDMAN, 1924–37, 3 folders
Background note: Edith G. Stedman (1888–1978) was a medical social worker at an Episcopal mission in Wuchang, Hankow, from 1920 to 1927.
CORRESPONDENCE/DIARIES/MANUSCRIPTS: Folder of diaries, correspondence, and personal papers relating to her stay in China, 1924, 1937; undated writings on religion.

AUDIO-VISUAL MATERIALS: Folder of photos of Stedman and others in China, 1924.
FINDING AIDS: In-house inventory.

7-MARGARET COOK THOMSON, 1917–83, ca. 2 boxes
Background note: Margaret Cook Thomson (1889–1975) was a teacher and missionary for the United Presbyterian Church in China from 1917 to 1949. Her husband, James Claude Thomson, was chairman of the Chemistry Department at the University of Nanking. The collection is not yet fully catalogued. See also Smith College, College Archives, Alumnae Gymnasium, Northampton, MA, 01063.
CORRESPONDENCE: 28 folders of correspondence with family and friends, describing life in China, including the Nanking Incident, 1917–49; folder of correspondence between Thomson and foreign students in China, n.d.
DIARIES: Diaries of Margaret Thomson, 1940, 1944, 1946–50; diary of James Thomson, 1943.
MANUSCRIPTS: "China Notes, 1951"; 7 small notebooks, n.d.
MEMORABILIA: Address books, guest books, Chinese currency; Cook family scrapbook, 1930–31.
AUDIO-VISUAL MATERIALS: 3 reels of 16 mm. home movies of China, 1930–31, 1937–38, and n.d. (on Ginling College).
ORAL HISTORIES: Folder of transcripts of interviews with the Thomson's children, Anne Thomson Waller, Diana Thomson, James C. Thomson, Jr., and with John Hersey, by Jane M. Rabb, concerning missionary life in China, 1977–83.
FINDING AIDS: In-house preliminary inventory.

CHESTNUT HILL

BOSTON COLLEGE
MA–170 John J. Burns Library
140 Commonwealth Avenue
Chestnut Hill MA 02169
(617) 552-4477
John C. Stalker, Chief Reference Librarian

Background note: Boston College holds a collection of works by and about Jesuits printed before the suppression of the Society in the eighteenth century, including a bound collection of Italian translations of letters from missions from the sixteenth through the eighteenth centuries.
Finding aids: *The Jesuit Collection in the John J. Burns Library of Boston College*, comp. by John C. Stalker, 1986.

1-GENERAL HOLDINGS
SERIALS: *Chinese Repository*, 1832–51. *Maryknoll Mission Letters*, 1942–46.

LENOX

BERKSHIRE CHRISTIAN COLLEGE
MA–175 Linden J. Carter Library
200 Stockbridge Road
Lenox MA 01240
(413) 673-0838 Ext. 77
Oral Collins, Acting Director of Library

Background note: See also Advent Christian General Conference, Headquarters Archives, P. O. Box 23152, 14601 Albemarle Road, Charlotte, NC, 28212; and Aurora University, Phillips Library, 347 South Gladstone Avenue, Aurora, IL, 60507.

1-GENERAL HOLDINGS
MINUTES/RECORDS/REPORTS: Reports on China mission work in Advent Christian denominational periodicals, *Advent Christian Missions*, 1921–79, and *Prophetic and Mission Record*, 1896–99, 1907–20.
MEMORABILIA: Scrapbook of clippings and miscellaneous materials on the Advent Christian mission work in China, by Mrs. L. A. Horne, 1892–1980.
ORAL HISTORIES: *Searching for Yellow Gold*, cassette by Lena Sellon, missionary to China, 1972.
DISSERTATIONS/THESES: *Floods, Famine, and Wars: A History of the Advent Christian Mission Work in China*, by David E. Dean, 1976.

NEWTON CENTRE

ANDOVER NEWTON THEOLOGICAL SCHOOL
MA–180 Franklin Trask Library
169 Herrick Road
Newton Centre MA 02159
(617) 964-1100 Ext. 252
Diana Yount, Special Collections Librarian

1-RECORDS OF THE SOCIETY OF INQUIRY RESPECTING MISSIONS, 1815–59, 15 items
Background note: The Society of Inquiry Respecting Missions (originally called the Society of Inquiry on the Subject of Missions) was a student group formed in 1811 to promote interest in missionary work. The Society disbanded about 1920. In addition to the correspondence listed below, the collection may contain references to China in its minutes and reports.
CORRESPONDENCE: Letters to the Society of Inquiry, from Elijah Coleman Bridgman, 1830, 1832–35, 1837; Lyman B. Peet, 1853; and Caleb C. Baldwin, 1858; letters from Elijah Bridgman used by Elias Loomis in the compilation of *Memoirs of American Missionaries Formerly Connected with the Society of Inquiry in the Andover Theological Seminary*, 1832, 1851, 1855, 1858–59.
MANUSCRIPTS: "On an American Mission to China," by Henry Robinson, 1815.

2-GENERAL HOLDINGS
MANUSCRIPTS: "The Evangelisation of China: Addresses Delivered at Five Conferences, Held during Aug., Sept., and Oct., 1896, at Chefoo, Peking, Shanghai, Foochow, and Hankow," ed. by D. W. Lyon; "West of the Yangtze Gorges," by Joseph Taylor, 1936.
PAMPHLETS: *China as a Mission Field*, by Miles Justin Knowlton, n.d.; *China Consultation*, 1958; *Floodtide in China*, by B. B. Chapman, 1922.
SERIALS: *China Bulletin*, 1955–57. *China Christian Year Book*, 1926–39. *China Mission Advocate*, 1839. *China Mission Year Book*, 1910–25. *China Notes*, 1962–68. *Chinese Recorder*, 1906-9, 1922–41. *Chinese Repository*, 1836–37. *Ching Feng*, 1961-. *Fenchow*, 1919–36? *The Foochow Messenger*, 1903–17, 1922–40.

National Christian Council of China, *Bulletin*, 1922–37. *Quarterly Notes on Christianity and Chinese Religion*, 1961–63.
DISSERTATIONS/THESES: *Christian Missions in China*, by Charles Sumner Estes, 1895. *The Early Eastward Spread of Christianity*, by Gordon D. Barss, 1949. *A Practical Program for Character Training in Yuih Dzae Academy (a Baptist Mission School in China)*, by Daniel C. Koo, 1935. *The Prospect of Student Christian Work in Communist China*, by Wilson Wei-sing Chen, 1950.

NORTHAMPTON

SMITH COLLEGE

MA–185 College Archives
Alumnae Gymnasium
Northampton MA 01063
(413) 584-2700 Ext. 2970
Margery Sly, College Archivist

Background note: To assist in locating the collections, the class year is given for Smith graduates' collections.
Finding aids: "Papers on Asia in the Smith College Archives."

1-RUTH MIRIAM CHESTER (1914), n.d., 5 items
CORRESPONDENCE/MEMORABILIA: 3 letters relating to her years as a teacher to Ginling College, citation, and biographical material.

2-JULIA ADELINE CLARK (1910), 1944, 2 items
Background note: Julia Adeline Clark was superintendent of a primary school in Hankow, Wuchang, and Changsha, and later, the acting principal and dean of St. Hilda's School in Wuchang from 1928 to 1932.
CORRESPONDENCE/MEMORABILIA: Letter, 1944, and a newspaper clipping, n.d.

3-LORA GENEVIEVE DYER (1903), n.d., 3 items
CORRESPONDENCE/MANUSCRIPTS/MEMORABILIA: Letter, press releases, and 5 pages of biographical material, relating to Lora Genevieve Dyer's work as a medical missionary in Foochow.

4-MARY LOUISE FOSTER (1891), 1925, 1 item
PAMPHLETS: *Smith Around the World*, 1925, containing accounts of Smith women working in China as missionaries.

5-MARION SPENCER HALSEY (1913), n.d., 1 item
Background note: Marion Spencer Halsey was secretary to the Medical Superintendent of Peking Union Medical College.
MINUTES/RECORDS/REPORTS: Corrected copy of the 16th annual report of the Superintendent, n.d.

6-GINLING COLLEGE, 1912–75, 6 boxes
Background note: See also Mount Holyoke College, College History and Archives, Williston Memorial Library, South Hadley, MA, 01075-1493; Union Theological Seminary, Archives, 3041 Broadway at Reinhold Niebuhr Place, New York, NY, 10027; and Yale Divinity School, Special Collections, 409 Prospect Street, New Haven, CT, 06510.
MINUTES/RECORDS/REPORTS/CORRESPONDENCE: Alumnae Association, Ginling Record Book, 1975; Alumnae in the United States, 1938–57; Ginling Association in America, 1952-; Alumnae Committee for Ginling College, 1938–54; general correspondence, 1920–75; faculty correspondence; Nanking Teachers' College, 1979-; Associated Boards for Christian Colleges in China, 1937–47; Board of Directors, 1932; Board of Founders, 1941–50; United Board for Christian Colleges in China, 1945–54; newsletter, 1922–57; Ruth Chester's newsletter, 1940–50; miscellaneous bulletins, 1915–35; calendars, 1924–26, 1938; president's reports, 1916–21.
MANUSCRIPTS: "Smith-Ginling History," 1937.
PAMPHLETS: Pamphlets of Ginling College, 1912–42; publications of *Ginling College Magazine*, 1924–29; *Ginling Bulletin*, promotional booklet, 1961.
MEMORABILIA: Brochures, 1915–50; 3 Chinese scrolls, diplomas of the Girls' Academy, and 2 embroidered wall hangings given to Smith College by Ginling College in 1925.
MAPS/DESIGNS/DRAWINGS: Watercolor of Ginling Mirror, 1937; map showing 2,500-mile route to West China, n.d.
AUDIO-VISUAL MATERIALS: Box containing undated photos of Ginling College, Alumnae Association 25th anniversary (1940–41), Alumnae Association exhibits (1949), faculty, and miscellaneous unidentified photos, 1920–41; 11 photos of Ginling College, including students, faculty, buildings, Class of 1926, biology class, practice school, music lesson, and Smith Building.
SERIALS: Ginling College: *Bulletin*, 1915, 1919, 1922, 1925, 1928, 1931, 1933–35; *Ginling Association Newsletter*, 1951–52, 1954, 1957; *Ginling College Letter*, 1924–25; *Ginling College Magazine*, 1924–26, 1928–29.
FINDING AID: In-house inventory.

7-FREDERICA (MEAD) HILTNER (1911), 1921–22, 2 items
Background note: Frederica (Mead) Hiltner taught at Ginling College from 1915 to 1922.
MANUSCRIPTS: 2-page autobiography.
AUDIO-VISUAL MATERIALS: Photos of Hiltner with her class at Ginling College, 1921–22.

8-JULIA (MITCHELL) KUNKLE (1901), n.d., 6 items
CORRESPONDENCE/MANUSCRIPTS: 3 letters and 3 articles, regarding Julia (Mitchell) Kunkle's work as a missionary.

9-DELIA DICKSON LEAVENS (1901), n.d., 7(?) items
Background note: Delia Dickson Leavens was a Smith College missionary in Lungchow from 1909 to 1916. Her brother, Dickson Hammond Leavens, taught at Yale-in-China. See also Yale University, Department of Manuscripts and Archives, Sterling Library, 120 High Street, New Haven, CT, 06520.
MEMORABILIA/AUDIO-VISUAL MATERIALS: 3 photos of Lungchow, North China, photos at the Tungchou School for Boys, obituaries, program of Commission Services (Smith College missionary to North China) and biographical material by her sister, Margaret Leavens, n.d.

10-EVA (ADAMS) MACMILLAN (1915), 1914–40, .5 box
DIARIES: Notebook of memoirs of work at Peking Women's Medical College, 1914–40.

11-MISSIONARY SOCIETY, 1876–1902, .5 box
MINUTES/RECORDS/REPORTS: Missionary Society, minutes and records, 1876–1902.
CORRESPONDENCE/AUDIO-VISUAL MATERIALS: Correspondence and photo album of Angie Martin Myers, a medical missionary in Amoy, 1899–1901.

12-ADA (COMSTOCK) NOTESTEIN (1897), 1945–46, 1 folder
MINUTES/RECORDS/REPORTS/CORRESPONDENCE: Commission on Women's Higher Education in China, minutes and correspondence, 1945–46.

13-ISABELLA (MACK) PATTON (1898), 1935, 2 items
CORRESPONDENCE: 2 letters from Isabella Mack, a medical missionary in Shanghai, to Vera (Scott) Cushman (1898), 1935.

14-OLGA LUCILLE SMITH (1908), n.d., 1 item
Background note: Olga Lucille Smith worked with the YWCA in Shanghai.
CORRESPONDENCE: Letter describing her years in China.

15-MARGARET (COOK) THOMSON (1911), n.d., quantity undetermined
Background note: For biographical notes, see Radcliffe College, Schlesinger Library, 10 Garden Street, Cambridge, MA, 02138.
CORRESPONDENCE: Excerpts from 11 letters written while a missionary at the University of Nanking, n.d.

16-OLIVE BIRD TOMLIN (1913), n.d., 8 (?) items
CORRESPONDENCE/AUDIO-VISUAL MATERIALS: 5 letters and photos relating to Olive Bird Tomlin's years at St. Hilda's School in Wuchang.
MEMORABILIA: "St. Hilda's Becomes a Refugee Camp," in *Smith Alumni Quarterly*, 1938, and biographical material.

17-EDITH MAY WELLS (1902), n.d., 11 items
MEMORABILIA/AUDIO-VISUAL MATERIALS/CHINESE LANGUAGE MATERIALS: 9 photos, biographical material, and a newspaper clipping in Chinese on the YWCA in Tientsin, n.d.

18-ELIZABETH CURTIS WRIGHT (1910), n.d., 2 items
AUDIO-VISUAL MATERIALS: 2 photos of China from Elizabeth Curtis Wright's stay in Peking and Anhwei as an English teacher, n.d.

19-GENERAL HOLDINGS
MINUTES/RECORDS/REPORTS: Missionary Society, reports in *Smith College Monthly*, 1899–1910; Smith College Association for Christian Work, annual reports, 1900-; report on the growth and results of the Missionary Investigation Committee of Smith College, in papers of Helen Virginia Frey (1915), 1915.
CORRESPONDENCE: Letter from Marion Leroy Burton to Frances Fessenden (1916), regarding the China mission, 1915; 14 letters from Adelia Cobb Hallock (1921) to Martha Amelia Kirstein (1921), regarding missionary work, 1923–36.
MEMORABILIA: "History at First Hand," by Laura Edna Lenhart (1908), in *Smith Alumnae Quarterly*, 1938, recounting her medical work from 1912 to 1935 in hospitals in Wusih and Shanghai; "Missionary Society Supports Medical Missionary in China," concerning Grace Louise Russell (1900), in *Smith College Monthly*, 1899.
AUDIO-VISUAL MATERIALS: Photos of sketches of Ginling College, in an accordion folder, n.d.

MA–190 William Allan Neilson Library
Smith College
Northampton MA 01063
(413) 584–2700 Ext. 2960
Elaine Miller, Reference Librarian

1-GENERAL HOLDINGS
PAMPHLETS: *Our Missionaries in Peking: Extracts from Some of Their Letters*, by the London Missionary Society, 1900.
SERIALS: China Christian Educational Association, *Bulletin*, 1926. China International Famine Relief Commission, Publications, series A, 1922–35; series B, 1923, 1930. *News of China*, 1943–49.
CHINESE LANGUAGE MATERIALS/SERIALS: *Yen-ching hsüeh pao (Yenching Journal of Chinese Studies)*, 1927–30.

MA–195 Sophia Smith Collection (Women's History Archive)
Smith College
Alumnae Gymnasium
Northampton MA 01063
(413) 584–2700 Ext. 2970
Susan Boone, Curator

1-RUTH V. HEMENWAY PAPERS, 1924–42, 4 boxes
DIARIES: 20 volumes of diaries, describing the medical and surgical career of Ruth V. Hemenway, a medical missionary, including discussion of the economic, social and political situation in China before World War II, 1924–42.
MEMORABILIA: Obituary and biographical articles on Hemenway.

2-BEATRICE FARNSWORTH POWERS PAPERS, 1913–66, 1 box, 1 volume
Background note: Beatrice Farnsworth Powers (1880–1967) was a nurse and teacher at Changsha Hospital from 1913 to 1915.
MINUTES/RECORDS/REPORTS: Yale-in-China Hospital, annual report, 1915, 1966.
CORRESPONDENCE/MANUSCRIPTS: Letters to and from Powers, 1913–16, notes, and essays describing her career at Yale-in-China Hospital in Changsha, 1913–15, including discussion of the status of Chinese women and the impact of missionaries on China.
MEMORABILIA: Biographical material and obituaries.
AUDIO-VISUAL MATERIALS: Ca. 330 photos in album.

3-RELIGION COLLECTION, 1913–49, 6 items
MINUTES/RECORDS/REPORTS: Foochow Women's Conference of the Methodist Episcopal Church, report of the annual session, 1913; Kiangsi Women's Conference, 1919.
CORRESPONDENCE: Copy of a letter from Lora Gene Dyer, in Foochow, 1949.
PAMPHLETS; *Our Educational Missions in China*, by Mrs. Charles H. Daniels, n.d.
MEMORABILIA: "Gertrude Howe, Pioneer China Missionary," in *Christian Advocate*, 1929; "Katherine E. Scott, A Continuing Life," by Aimee Drake, in *The Churchman*, 1923.

4-GRACE THOMPSON (GALLATIN) SETON PAPERS, 1903–40, 4 folders
MANUSCRIPTS: Typescripts of articles on education and medicine in China, n.d., and material on Mary Stone, a medical missionary in China.
MEMORABILIA: 3 folders of clippings and travel notes on China, n.d.

5-RUTH WOODSMALL COLLECTION, 1932, 2 folders
MANUSCRIPTS: 2 folders of Layman's Foreign Missions Inquiry notes by Ruth Woodsmall, from interviews with 85 individuals in China, including Julean Arnold, May Bagwell, Miss Barnes (Union Bible Training School), Prof. [Miner Searle?] Bates (University of Nanking), Miss Bishoff (Hackett Memorial Hospital), Miss [Julia?] Bonafield (WFMS), Pearl Buck, Miss Carleton (Junior Middle School, Foochow), Mrs. C. C. Chen, G. Chen (University of Nanking), Chen Hsu, Mrs. Chik (Lingnan University), Miss Chin (Ginling College), F. A. Cleveland, H. Cowen (True Light School), Miss Culley, Dr. Davies (Cheeloo University), Irene Dean, Mr. and Mrs. De Pree, Mrs. A. F. Fisher, Margaret Frame, Sally Glass, Dr. Godshall, Miss Ha (YWCA), Lillian Haas, John Hayes, J. M. Henry, Irma Highbaugh, Franklin Ho, Miss Holbekar (Amoy Girls' School), Paul F. Hopkins, Emma Horning, Hu Shih, Miss Johnson, Enid Johnson, Miss Jones (WFMS), Dr. Kady (Cheeloo Theological School), Mrs. L. C. King, T. Z. Koo, H. H. Kung, J. S. Kunkle, Miss Lau (YMCA, Toyshan), Miss Law (general secretary of the YWCA and principal of the True Light Primary School), G. E. Lerrigo, Ida Belle Lewis, Herman Liu, Miss Liu (Yuetwah Girls' School, Macao), Miss Liu (Ginling College), Liu Toi-ching, E. C. Lobenstine, Dr. Love (University of Nanking), Dr. MacKenzie (PUMC), Paul Maslin, Miss Myers (YWCA, Tsinan), Mabel Nowlin, Lulu Patton, Alice Powell, Ida Pruitt, Miss Sanderson, Roderick Scott, Dr. Sheld (Central China College), Dr. Shields (Cheeloo University Medical School), Miss Smith, Miss Sollman, Margaret Speer, Mrs. Speicher, Miss Spicer (Ginling College), Mr. Stanley (Cheeloo Theological School), D. D. Stevenson, P. H. Stevenson, Deaconess Stuart (American Church Mission, Hankow), J. B. Taylor, Mrs. Thurston (Ginling College), Miss Ting, Y. Y. Tsu, Miss Veldman, Miss Wallace (Hwa Nan College), Mrs. C. F. Wang, Francis Wei, Mr. Wiant (Methodist Mission, Foochow), Priscilla Wong, Lucy Wong, Myfanwy Wood, Mrs. Wu (YMCA, Canton), Wu I-Fang, Mrs. Wurley, and Grace Yang.
AUDIO-VISUAL MATERIALS: Ca. 75-100 photos of China, by Woodsmall, n.d.

NORTON

WHEATON COLLEGE
MA-200 Marion B. Bebbie, 1901, Archives and Special Collections
> Madeleine Clark Wallace Library
> Norton MA 02766
> (617) 285-7722 Ext. 513
> Zephorene L. Stickney, Archivist and
> Special Collections Curator

1-EMILY HARTWELL PAPERS, 1881-1964, quantity undetermined
Background note: Emily Susan Hartwell (1859-1951), daughter of Lucy Stearns and Charles Hartwell, was born in Foochow. She taught at Wheaton College after graduating from there in 1883, before going to China as a missionary to replace her late mother. For 20 years she taught at Foochow College, organizing relief work, establishing charitable institutions, such as the Union Kindergarten Training School, the Christian Woman's Industrial Institute, and the Dr. Cordelia A. Green Memorial Home, and receiving the "Order of the Golden Grain" from the president of the Fukien Provincial Government. She was evacuated from Foochow in 1937. For other papers of Emily Hartwell, see Mount Holyoke College, Williston Memorial Library, College Archives and History, South Hadley, MA, 01075-1493.
MEMORABILIA: Newspaper and magazine articles relating to Emily Hartwell, 1881-1964; postcards and labels, 1890s.
AUDIO-VISUAL MATERIALS: 62 photos of Yenching University and industrial school students, buildings, and staff, orphans and orphanages, and others, ca. 1900-1940s; tintype of Hartwell and Elizabeth Studley, Wheaton Female Seminary class of 1883, dated 1883.
CHINESE LANGUAGE MATERIALS/SERIALS: *Yüeh pao (Child's Paper)*, 1889.
CHINESE LANGUAGE MATERIALS: Unidentified letter, with translation, n.d.; *A Few Foochow Hymns*, 1895; 6.5 l.f. of Chinese objects, ca. 1890s, including Mongolian print blocks, ancestral tablets, scrolls, clothing, currency, and fisherman's idol.

2-LUCY HARTWELL PAPERS, 1852-ca. 1883, 13 items
Background note: Lucy Estabrook Stearns taught at Wheaton Female Seminary from 1849 to 1851, when she married Rev. Charles Hartwell. They went to Foochow as missionaries in 1852 and Lucy Hartwell died there in 1883. See also Mount Holyoke College, Williston Memorial Library, College Archives and History, South Hadley, MA, 01075-1493; and Minnesota Historical Society, Division of Archives and Manuscripts, 1500 Mississippi Street, St. Paul, MN, 55101.
CORRESPONDENCE/DIARIES: Letter/diary by Lucy Hartwell, written while on board the *Talbot* en route to Hong Kong, 1852-53.
AUDIO-VISUAL MATERIALS: Copy of a photo of Rev. and Mrs. Charles Hartwell, 1852.
CHINESE LANGUAGE MATERIALS: Pamphlets and tracts published by the Foochow Mission (American Board of Commissioners for Foreign Missions), including tracts on opium and the Gospel (by Elijah Coleman Bridgman), pre-1883.

3-GENERAL HOLDINGS
SERIALS: *Chinese Recorder*, 1868-1940.

PITTSFIELD

BERKSHIRE ATHENAEUM
MA-205 Pittsfield Public Library
> One Wendell Avenue
> Pittsfield MA 01201
> (413) 442-1559
> Ruth T. Degenhardt, Department head,
> Local History and Literature Services

1-GENERAL HOLDINGS
PAMPHLETS: Memorial pamphlet on Susie Parker, of the China Inland Mission, 1889.
MEMORABILIA: Letter from Susie Parker, Yang chau, to her family, reprinted in the *Pittsfield Sun*, 1889; clipping regarding memorial service for Susie Parker in the *Pittsfield Sun*, 1889.

SALEM

ESSEX INSTITUTE
MA–210 James Duncan Phillips Library

132 Essex Street
Salem MA 01970
(617) 744–3390
Eugenia Fountain, Librarian

1-LUCY IRENE MEAD PAPERS, 1910–25, 11 items
CORRESPONDENCE: 9 letters to and from Lucy Irene Mead, a missionary in China, 1910–25, including accounts of life in China, Taoist worship, Chinese women, education and military skirmishes in Peking during 1917.
MEMORABILIA: Copy of the temporary constitution of the Chinese Christian Church in Peking, n.d.
AUDIO-VISUAL MATERIALS: Small photo of Marian Yang, n.d.

2-FREDERICK TOWNSEND WARD CHINA COLLECTION, 1600–
1940, ca. 10,000 volumes
Background note: The Frederick Townsend Ward China Collection is one of the outstanding collections in the United States of western-language materials on Imperial China, containing about 10,000 books, pamphlets, periodicals, etc. The collection is particularly strong in first-hand accounts of Western travellers in China and missionary activities from the early seventeenth to the early twentieth century. The books in the collection authored by missionaries cover a broad range of subject areas.
MINUTES/RECORDS/REPORTS: American Board of Commissioners for Foreign Missions (ABCFM): almanac, 1887–90, 1893, 1895, 1898–99, 1901, 1903–4, 1907–14; Prudential Committee, instructions, n.d.; roster, 1887–1914; China Medical Board, reports, 1914–23; China Mission, report, 1871; Educational Association of China, records of triennial meeting, 1896–1902; Foochow Missionary Hospital, report, 1912–14; Harvard Medical School of China, reports, 1911–16; International Institute of China, report, 1903–9; Medical Missionary Hospital, report, 1874; Medical Missionary Society in China, minutes, 1838, 1850–51; Medical Missionary Society in China, report of the hospital in Canton, 1878; Methodist Episcopal Church: Mission conferences, central conference, 1897; North China conference, 1893, 1895; Women's conference, 1904; Morrison Education Society, report, 1837–38; Peking Union Medical College, announcements, 1919–24; Peking University, catalogue, 1892; Presbyterian Church in Ireland, China mission, 1877; Religious Tract Society, report on Christian literature, 1882; School for Chinese Deaf at Chefoo: leaflets, 1908; report and financial statement, 1901–3; Society for the Diffusion of Christian and General Knowledge Among the Chinese, report, 1903; West China Missionary Conference, records, 1899; Yale mission, Changsha, report, 1911; Yale-in-China, report, 1923.
CORRESPONDENCE/AUDIO-VISUAL MATERIALS: 9 letters from Charles G. Lewis, a missionary in China, to George Chase and other friends and associates, with 20 photos of Lewis, his wife, other missionaries, and Chinese, 1896–1900.
MANUSCRIPTS: Ordination certificate of William Jones Boone, n.d.
PAMPHLETS: Ca. 50 pamphlets, 1667–1932, on subjects such as the ABCFM, Baptist missions, Bible, books on China, Canton Christian College library, Chinese Educational Commission, Christian missions, Confucianism, Epworth League, General Conference of Protestant Missionaries of China, International Institute of China, Jesuits, Lien-chou, Lucy E. Hartwell, Medical Missionary Society in China, missionary meetings, Morrison Education Society, Nestorian Christians, Nestorian monument, Odoric of Pordenone, persecution of Christians, Protestant Episcopal Church in the U.S., Religious Tract Society, Spanish missions, and translations.
MEMORABILIA: Clippings on American missionaries in China, 1892–1905; Catholic missionaries in China, 1898–1906; China and the missionaries, 1892–1901; Church Missionary Society at Fuh-ning, 1900–1903; education, 1909–10; Methodist missionaries to the Chinese, n.d.; and missionaries in China, 1899–1900; clipping on religious tolerance in China, 1904.
MAPS/DESIGNS/DRAWINGS: Scroll of rubbings from Hsian-fu Nestorian tablet, n.d.; *Carte des préfectures de Chine et de leurs population chrétienne en 1911*, by Joseph de Moidrey in *Variétés Sinologiques*, 1913; map of China (Boston: ABCFM), 1881, printed on cloth; map of the Chinese empire, by S. W. Williams, 1884.
AUDIO-VISUAL MATERIALS: 2 albums of China Inland Mission portraits, n.d. (ca. 1890), containing ca. 300 photos (about half identified), some in Chinese dress, with a list of CIM missionaries arranged by date of arrival in China, 1854–86.
SERIALS: *The Boone Review*, 1908. China Inland Mission, *Occasional Papers*, 1866–75. *China Medical Missionary Journal*, 1887–90. *China Mission Year Book*, 1910. *China's Millions* (London), 1875–99, 1902–16; (Toronto), 1893–96, 1898, 1901, 1903–40. *Chinese Advocate*, 1890. *Chinese Recorder and Missionary Journal*, 1868–1932. *Chinese Repository*, 1832–50. *Directory of Protestant Missions in China*, 1918. Educational Association of China, *Mission Educational Directory*, 1910. *Educational Directory of China*, 1914. *The Evangelist*, 1833. *Fenchow*, 1923–24. *Hinghwa*, 1922–24. *Missionary Recorder*, 1867. *The Shanghai*, 1921. *Variétés Sinologiques*, 1901–19.
CHINESE LANGUAGE MATERIALS: Several translations of the Gospel and the Scriptures, 1845–1916, and discussions of the translation of *shang-ti*, 1876–77.
FINDING AIDS: *Catalog of the Books on China in the Library of the Essex Institute*, by Louise M. Taylor (Salem, MA: Essex Institute), 1926.

PEABODY MUSEUM
MA–215 Phillips Library

East India Square
Salem MA 01970
(617) 745–1876
Gregor Trinkaus-Randall, Librarian

1-ANDOVER NEWTON THEOLOGICAL SCHOOL MANU-
SCRIPTS, ca. 1822, ca. 1 box
CORRESPONDENCE: 2 letters to Capt. Sherman from R[obert] Morrison, Canton, 1822.
MANUSCRIPTS: "Introduction to a New...Chinese Sect: Jesus' family," n.a., n.d.
MAPS/DESIGNS/DRAWINGS: Map of China on cloth, n.d.; Chinese posters in folders, n.d.

CHINESE LANGUAGE MATERIALS: Miscellaneous texts and primers.

2-GENERAL HOLDINGS

PAMPHLETS: *Across the Desert of Gobi: A Narrative of an Escape during the Boxer Uprising, June to September, 1900*, by Mark Williams, 1901; *The Foochow Missionary Difficulty: Report of the Case of Chow Chang Hung, Lin King Ching, [and Others]...Versus Rev. John R. Wolfe*, 1879 (repr. *Hong Kong Daily Press*); *The Medical Missionary Society in China*, by Thomas Richardson Colledge, 1838; *Windows into China: The Jesuits and Their Books, 1580–1730*, by John Parker, 1978.
SERIALS: *Chinese Repository*, 1832–51 (repr.).

SOUTH HADLEY

MOUNT HOLYOKE COLLEGE

MA–220 College History and Archives

Williston Memorial Library
South Hadley MA 01075–1493
(413) 538–2441
Anne C. Edmonds, College Librarian
Elaine Trehub, College History and Archives Librarian
Patricia J. Albright, College History and Archives Librarian

Background note: Between 1846 and 1936 approximately a hundred graduates of Mount Holyoke College went to China as missionaries or missionary wives. The College History and Archives Collection contains the record of their experiences.
Finding aids: Lists of Mount Holyoke alumnae in China and a guide to their papers in Mount Holyoke College: Missions/ Missionaries-China collection (see below, collection #37).

1-KATHERINE J. ABBEY, 1910–71, 52 items
Background note: Katherine J. Abbey (Mrs. Horace Vanderbeek) was a missionary teacher in Shanghai and Wusih from 1910 to 1925.
CORRESPONDENCE/MANUSCRIPTS/PAMPHLETS: Correspondence and biographical materials, in part relating to Abbey's work in China.

2-JULIA F. ALLEN, 1915–74, 76 items
Background note: Julia F. Allen was a missionary teacher in Nanking from 1922 to 1926.
CORRESPONDENCE/MANUSCRIPTS/PAMPHLETS: Correspondence and biographical materials, in part relating to Allen's work in China.

3-HARRIETT M. ALLYN, 1917, 1 item
Background note: Harriett M. Allyn was a teacher and administrator at Hackett Medical College from 1913 to 1924.
CORRESPONDENCE: Letter from Harriett Allyn, Canton, describing her work, 1917.

4-LUCY F. BAKER, 1896–1964, 52 items
Background note: Lucy F. Baker (Mrs. Everard P. Miller) was a missionary teacher in Wuchang and Hsichow from 1910 to 1942.
CORRESPONDENCE/MANUSCRIPTS/PAMPHLETS: Correspondence, writings, and biographical materials, relating in part to Baker's work in China.

5-MIRIAM L. BARBER, 1924–75, 61 items
Background note: Miriam L. Barber (Mrs. Walter Judd) was a missionary in Fenchow from 1934 to 1936.
CORRESPONDENCE/MANUSCRIPTS/PAMPHLETS: Correspondence, articles, and biographical materials, relating in part to Barber's missionary work in China.

6-MARY L. BEARD, 1901–64, 19 items
Background note: Mary L. Beard was a missionary teacher in Tungchow from 1914 to 1924.
CORRESPONDENCE/MANUSCRIPTS/PAMPHLETS/AUDIO-VISUAL MATERIALS: Correspondence and biographical materials, relating in part to Beard's work in China, and a photo of students at the North China American School, 1919.

7-LUCY H. BOOTH, 1916–58, 33 items
Background note: Lucy H. Booth (Mrs. Everett E. Murray) was a missionary teacher in Peking and Shantung from 1924 to ca. 1949.
CORRESPONDENCE/MANUSCRIPTS/PAMPHLETS: Correspondence and biographical materials, relating in part to Booth's missionary work in China.

8-HELEN E. BOUGHTON, 1917, 1 item
Background note: Helen E. Boughton was a missionary in Hwaiyuen from 1917 to ca. 1941.
CORRESPONDENCE: Letter from Boughton describing her work, 1917.

9-HARRIET L. BOUTELLE, 1908–66, 77 items
Background note: Harriet L. Boutelle (Mrs. Carleton Lacy) was a missionary teacher in Canton, Kiukiang, and Shanghai from 1915 to 1950.
CORRESPONDENCE/MANUSCRIPTS/PAMPHLETS: Correspondence and biographical materials relating to Boutelle's work in China.

10-EDITH C. BOYNTON, 1902–70, 98 items
Background note: Edith C. Boynton was a missionary in Amoy from 1916 to 1932.
CORRESPONDENCE/MANUSCRIPTS/PAMPHLETS: Correspondence, articles, and biographical materials, relating in part to Boynton's work in China.

11-VIETTE I. BROWN, 1900–1923, 60 items
Background note: Viette I. Brown (Mrs. William P. Sprague) was a missionary in Kalgan from 1893 to 1910.
CORRESPONDENCE/MANUSCRIPTS/PAMPHLETS/AUDIO-VISUAL MATERIALS: Correspondence, writings, biographical materials, and 27 photos, mostly relating to Brown's work in China.

12-ALICE S. BROWNE, 1896–1942, 5 in.
Background note: For biographical notes, see Union Theological Seminary, Archives, 3041 Broadway at Reinhold Niebuhr Place, New York, NY, 10027.
CORRESPONDENCE/MANUSCRIPTS/PAMPHLETS/AUDIO-VISUAL MATERIALS: Correspondence, writings, printed materials, and 10 photos, mostly relating to Browne's work in China.
FINDING AIDS: In-house inventory.

13-GRACE BURROUGHS, 1895–1949, 36 items
Background note: Grace Burroughs (Mrs. William A. Mather) was a missionary teacher in Paoting from 1904 to 1939.
CORRESPONDENCE/MANUSCRIPTS/PAMPHLETS: Correspondence, writings, and biographical materials, mostly relating to Burroughs' work in China.

14-MATILDA S. CALDER, 1892–1978, 5 in.
Background note: For biographical notes, see Union Theological Seminary, Archives, 3041 Broadway at Reinhold Niebuhr Place, New York, NY, 10027.
CORRESPONDENCE/MANSUCRIPTS/PAMPHLETS: Correspondence, writings, and biographical materials, relating in part to work of Matilda S. Calder (Mrs. Lawrence Thurston) in China.

15-MARION H. CHATFIELD, 1915–75, 62 items
Background note: Marion H. Chatfield (Mrs. George B. Cressey) was a missionary in Peking, Shanghai, and Tientsin from 1923 to 1929.
CORRESPONDENCE/MANUSCRIPTS/PAMPHLETS: Correspondence, articles, and biographical materials, relating in part to Chatfield's missionary work in China.

16-HARRIET COGSWELL, 1905–83, 4 l.f.
Background note: Harriet N. Cogswell (Mrs. Paul C. Meyer) taught at Ginling College from 1926 to 1927 and 1929 to 1931. She then married an American diplomat stationed in Nanking, Yunnanfu, and Peking from 1931 to 1941 and 1946 to 1947.
CORRESPONDENCE: Ca. 200 letters describing Cogswell's work at Ginling and her subsequent activities in China.
MANUSCRIPTS/PAMPHLETS/MEMORABILIA: Poems and other writings, biographical material, and miscellaneous memorabilia relating to her experiences in China.
DIARIES: Excerpts from journals by Cogswell, describing activities in Yunnanfu, 1937–39.
AUDIO-VISUAL MATERIALS: Ca. 300 photos of people and scenes in China.
FINDING AIDS: In-house inventory.

17-ALICE H. COOK, 1914–73, 45 items
Background note: Alice H. Cook (Mrs. Otto W. Millner) was a medical missionary in Peking from 1919 to ca. 1927.
CORRESPONDENCE/MANUSCRIPTS/PAMPHLETS: Correspondence, writings, and biographical materials, relating in part to Cook's work in China.

18-MARGUERITE DODDS, 1917, 2 items
Background note: Marguerite Dodds was a missionary teacher at the Bridgman School in Shanghai from 1916 to 1918.
CORRESPONDENCE: 2 letters from Dodds describing her work, 1917.

19-ADELIA M. DODGE, 1908–82, 84 items
Background note: Adelia M. Dodge (Mrs. Oscar G. Starrett) was a missionary teacher in Canton and Chengtu from 1917 to 1937.
CORRESPONDENCE/MANUSCRIPTS/PAMPHLETS: Correspondence and biographical materials, relating in part to Dodge's missionary activities in China.

20-SARA B. DOWNER, 1918–64, 27 items
Background note: Sara Boddie Downer (b. 1896) was a missionary teacher in Chengtu from 1920 to 1951. She served as a missionary under the Women's American Baptist Foreign Mission Society in West China from 1946 to 1950. See also American Baptist Historical Society, 1106 South Goodman Street, Rochester, NY, 14620.
CORRESPONDENCE/MANUSCRIPTS/PAMPHLETS/AUDIO-VISUAL MATERIALS: Correspondence, articles, biographical materials, and 7 photos mostly relating to Downer's missionary work in China.

21-GINLING COLLEGE, ca. 1916–1977, 74 items
Background note: See also Smith College, College Archives, Alumnae Gymnasium, Northampton, MA, 01063; Union Theological Seminary, Archives, 3041 Broadway at Reinhold Niebuhr Place, New York, NY, 10027; and Yale Divinity School, Special Collections, 409 Prospect Street, New Haven, CT, 06510.
MINUTES/RECORDS/REPORTS: Ginling Association in America, directory, 1960 (also includes alumnae outside North America and faculty), 1969; Ginling College: annual report, 1927–28; report of the president, 1915–18; yearbook, 1919; Presbyterian Church in the U.S.A., Nanking Station, Kiangan Mission, report, 1931–32.
CORRESPONDENCE/PAMPHLETS/AUDIO-VISUAL MATERIALS: Correspondence, photos, historical notes, brochures, and other publications of and about Ginling College.
SERIALS: Ginling College: *Bulletin*, 1920, 1925, 1928: *Letter*, 1925; *Magazine*, 1924, 1928; *Newsletter*, 1934.

22-ANNIE ALLENDER GOULD, ca. 1892–1920, 18 items
Background note: For biographical notes, see United States Military Academy, Library Special Collections, West Point, NY, 10996–1799. See also Maine Historical Society, 485 Congress Street, Portland, ME, 04101.
CORRESPONDENCE/MANUSCRIPTS/PAMPHLETS: Mostly biographical materials about Gould's work in China, including a published memorial, ca. 1900, containing extracts from letters and an account of her death during the Boxer Rebellion.

23-KATHARINE R. GREEN, 1903–63, 53 items
Background note: Katharine R. Green was a missionary teacher in Amoy and Shanghai from 1907 to 1938.
CORRESPONDENCE/MANUSCRIPTS/PAMPHLETS/AUDIO-VISUAL MATERIALS: Correspondence, writings, biographical materials, and 8 photos relating in part to Green's work in China.

24-ANNE G. HALL, 1914–29, 20 items
Background note: Anne G. Hall (Mrs. Oscar G. Starrett) was a missionary teacher at the Bridgman School in Shanghai from 1911 to 1921.
CORRESPONDENCE/MANUSCRIPTS/PAMPHLETS: Correspondence and biographical materials, relating in part to Hall's work in China.

25-EMILY S. HARTWELL, 1900–1964, 41 items
Background note: For biographical notes, see Wheaton College, Madeleine Clark Wallace Library, Marion B. Bebbie, 1901, Archives and Special Collections, Norton, MA, 02766.
CORRESPONDENCE/MANUSCRIPTS/PAMPHLETS: Correspondence, writings, and biographical materials, mostly relating to Hartwell's work in China.

26-KATHERINE L. HENDERSON, 1916–79, 52 items
Background note: Katherine L. Henderson (Mrs. Bernard E. Read) was a missionary teacher in Peking and Shanghai from 1919 to 1949.
CORRESPONDENCE/MANUSCRIPTS/PAMPHLETS: Correspondence, articles, and biographical materials relating to Henderson's work in China.

27-RUBY E. HIGGINS, 1919, 1 item
Background note: Ruby E. Higgins (Mrs. Leroy C. Brown) was a missionary teacher at the Bridgman School from 1919 to 1922.
CORRESPONDENCE: Letter from Higgins, Shanghai, describing her work, 1919.

28-AMY R. HOLWAY, 1917–49, 40 items
Background note: For biographical notes, see Radcliffe College, Arthur and Elizabeth Schlesinger Library on the History of Women in America, 10 Garden Street, Cambridge, MA, 02138.
CORRESPONDENCE/MANUSCRIPTS/PAMPHLETS: 2 letters, 1917, 1929, and biographical materials, relating in part to Holway's missionary work in China.

29-GERTRUDE JENNESS, 1922–65, 47 items
Background note: Gertrude Jenness (Mrs. Arthur O. Rinden) was a missionary in Foochow from 1926 to 1949.
CORRESPONDENCE/MANUSCRIPTS/PAMPHLETS: Correspondence, articles, and biographical materials, relating in part to Jenness' missionary work in China.

30-ADALINE D. H. KELSEY, 1878–1931, 23 items
Background note: Adaline D. H. Kelsey was a medical missionary in Feng Chan and Tungchow from 1878 to 1882.
CORRESPONDENCE/MANUSCRIPTS/PAMPHLETS/MEMORABILIA: Correspondence, writings, and biographical material, relating in part to Kelsey's work in China, including extracts of letters from Chefoo and Tungchow, 1878, and describing a missionary tour, 1880.

31-ANNIE L. KENTFIELD, 1914–50, 14 items
Background note: Annie L. Kentfield (Mrs. Clarence M. Wood) was a missionary teacher in Diongloh from 1918 to 1923.
CORRESPONDENCE/MANUSCRIPTS/PAMPHLETS: Correspondence, articles, and biographical materials, relating in part to Kentfield's missionary activities in China.

32-CAROLINE KOERNER, 1904, 1 item
Background note: Caroline Koerner (Mrs. Lyman P. Peet) was a missionary teacher in Foochow from 1887 to 1917.
CORRESPONDENCE: Letter from Caroline Koerner, Foochow, to Anna C. Edwards, mentioning her work in China, 1904.

33-LOTTIE R. LANE, 1901–77, 37 items
Background note: For biographical notes, see Yale Divinity School, Special Collections, 409 Prospect Street, New Haven, CT, 06510.
CORRESPONDENCE/MANUSCRIPTS/PAMPHLETS: Correspondence and biographical materials, relating in part to Lottie R. Lane's work in China.

34-KATHERINE E. LUCCHINI, 1935, 1 item
Background note: Katherine E. Lucchini was a missionary in Hangchow from 1930 to 1934.

PAMPHLETS: *China's New Deal Has Its Flapper*, a newspaper report describing Lucchini's experiences as a missionary in China.

35-LUCY T. LYON, 1835–48, 42 items
Background note: Lucy Thomas Lyon (Mrs. Edward C. Lord) served in Canton from 1846 to 1853.
CORRESPONDENCE/MANUSCRIPTS: 32 letters and biographical materials relating to Lyon's work in Canton.

36-MARIAN G. MacGOWN, 1900–1962, 43 items
Background note: Marian G. MacGown (Mrs. Richard T. Evans) was a missionary teacher in Tientsin from 1908 to 1941.
CORRESPONDENCE/MANUSCRIPTS/PAMPHLETS: Correspondence, writings, and biographical materials, mostly relating to MacGown's work in China.

37-MOUNT HOLYOKE COLLEGE: MISSIONS/MISSIONARIES-CHINA, ca. 1892–1985, 3 in.
MANUSCRIPTS: Guide to papers of Mount Holyoke missionaries to China; lists of Mount Holyoke missionaries to China, classes of 1840–1933; other miscellaneous lists.
PAMPHLETS: *Mount Holyoke Alumnae in China*, 1920, 1931; notes, articles, and other printed materials.
DISSERTATIONS/THESES: *Breaking the Bonds of Womanhood: Prospectives on the History, Ideology, and Courage of American Women Missionaries*, by Janna Sibley, 1985.

38-MARY LOUISE PARTRIDGE, ca. 1888–1900, 7 items
Background note: Mary Louise Partridge was a missionary in Shansi from 1893 to 1900.
MANUSCRIPTS/PAMPHLETS: Biographical material, including a published memorial describing Partridge's work in China and her death during the Boxer Rebellion.

39-MARION B. PATERSON, 1914–69, 48 items
Background note: Marion B. Paterson (Mrs. George T. Blydenburgh) was a missionary in Nancheng from 1920 to 1931.
CORRESPONDENCE/MANUSCRIPTS/PAMPHLETS: Correspondence and biographical materials, relating in part to Paterson's missionary work in China.

40-ELLEN L. PEET, 1877–1930, 30 items
Background note: Ellen L. Peet (Mrs. George H. Hubbard) was a missionary in Foochow and Pagoda Anchorage from 1884 to 1925. Her mother was Hannah (Plimpton) Peet. For George Hubbard's papers, see Yale University, Department of Manuscripts and Archives, Sterling Library, 120 High Street, New Haven, CT, 06520.
CORRESPONDENCE/MANUSCRIPTS/PAMPHLETS: Correspondence and biographical materials, relating in part to Peet's work in China.

41-HANNAH L. PLIMPTON, 1847–1904, 2.5 in.
Background note: Hannah Louise Plimpton (Mrs. Lyman B. Peet [lst]; Mrs. Charles Hartwell [2nd]) was a missionary in Foochow from 1859 to 1908.
CORRESPONDENCE: Letter from Plimpton, in Fuh Chau, to Mrs. Banister, discussing the condition of the Duquoine Seminary and accounts of events in Fuh Chau, 1860.
MANUSCRIPTS/PAMPHLETS/MEMORABILIA: Printed and written materials, a botany notebook, biographical materials, and documents relating to her missionary work.

42-MARJORIE RANKIN, 1908–78, 1.5 l.f.
Background note: Marjorie Rankin (Mrs. Roy Steurt) was a missionary teacher in Weihsien and Tientsin from 1912 to 1932. See also Claremont Colleges, Honnold Library, Claremont, CA, 91711.
CORRESPONDENCE/MANUSCRIPTS/PAMPHLETS: Correspondence and biographical materials, relating to Rankin's work in China.
MANUSCRIPTS: "My First Seven Years in China," reminiscences of her work as a missionary teacher in China; "China Verse," ca. 1923–1927.
FINDING AIDS: In-house inventory.

43-RUTH C. SAVAGE, 1913–73, 71 items
Background note: Ruth C. Savage (Mrs. M. Gardner Tewksbury) was a missionary in Shanghai and Tsingtao from 1918 to 1948.
CORRESPONDENCE/MANUSCRIPTS/PAMPHLETS: Correspondence, article, and biographical materials, relating in part to Savage's missionary activities in China.

44-CAROLYN T. SEWALL, 1910–46, 51 items
Background note: Carolyn T. Sewall was a missionary and minister in Tientsin from 1913 to 1941.
CORRESPONDENCE/MANUSCRIPTS/PAMPHLETS: Correspondence, articles, and biographical materials, chiefly relating to Sewall's work in China.

45-MARY W. SHEPARD, 1908–55, 30 items
Background note: Mary W. Shepard (Mrs. Henry J. Voskuil) was a missionary teacher in Amoy from 1910 to 1920.
CORRESPONDENCE/MANUSCRIPTS/PAMPHLETS: Correspondence and biographical materials, relating in part to Shepard's work in China.

46-MARTHA L. SHERMAN, 1931–77, 40 items
Background note: Martha L. Sherman was a missionary in Wuchang from 1937 to 1939.
CORRESPONDENCE/MANUSCRIPTS/PAMPHLETS: Extracts from letters and biographical materials relating to Sherman's missionary experiences in China.

47-HARRIET H. SMITH, 1923, 1 item
Background note: Harriet H. Smith was a medical missionary at the Hunan-Yale Hospital in Changsha from 1921 to 1923.
CORRESPONDENCE: Letter from Smith describing her work, 1923.

48-HELEN H. SMITH, 1924–71, 54 items
Background note: Helen H. Smith was a missionary teacher in Chengtu, Foochow, and Peking from 1929 to 1950.
CORRESPONDENCE/MANUSCRIPTS/PAMPHLETS: Correspondence, articles, and biographical materials, relating in part to Smith's missionary work in China.

49-LUCY E. STEARNS, 1871, 1 item
Background note: For biographical notes, see Wheaton College, Madeleine Clark Wallace Library, Marion B. Bebbie, 1901, Archives and Special Collections, Norton, MA, 02766.
CORRESPONDENCE: Letter from Stearns, in Foochow, to Anna C. Edwards, describing her activities and problems facing missionaries, 1871.

50-MINNIE STRYKER, 1903–51, 22 items
Background note: Minnie Stryker was a medical missionary in Foochow and Peking from 1901 to 1929.
CORRESPONDENCE/MANUSCRIPTS/PAMPHLETS: Correspondence, writings, and biographical materials, relating in part to Stryker's work in China.

51-HELEN E. TYZZER, 1913–67, 27 items
Background note: Helen E. Tyzzer (Mrs. Charles D. Leach) was a missionary teacher in Huchow and Kinhwa from 1914 to 1928.
CORRESPONDENCE/MANUSCRIPTS/PAMHLETS: 2 letters and biographical materials, relating to Tyzzer's activities as a missionary in China.

52-HELEN VAN DOREN, 1877, 1 item
Background note: Helen Van Doren was missionary teacher in Amoy from 1870 to 1876.
CORRESPONDENCE: Letter describing Van Doren's work in China, 1877.

53-SUSAN M. WAITE, 1894, 4 items
Background note: Susan M. Waite (Mrs. Edward P. Thwing) was a missionary in Canton from 1887 to 1893.
MANUSCRIPTS/PAMPHLETS: Biographical materials, including a published account of Waite's life and work in China.

54-LAURA D. WARD, 1905–72, 5 in.
Background note: Laura Dwight Ward was a missionary in Foochow from 1914 to 1950.
CORRESPONDENCE/MANUSCRIPTS/DIARIES: 6 letters, biographical materials, and 4 diaries regarding Ward's work in China.

55-RUTH P. WARD, 1901–40, 35 items
Background note: Ruth P. Ward (Mrs. Frederick P. Beach) was a missionary teacher in Foochow from 1907 to 1933.
CORRESPONDENCE/MANUSCRIPTS/PAMPHLETS: Correspondence, articles, and biographical materials, chiefly relating to Ward's work in China.

56-LAURA P. WELLS, 1913–61, 24 items
Background note: Laura P. Wells was a missionary nurse in Shanghai from 1915 to 1941.
CORRESPONDENCE/MANUSCRIPTS/PAMPHLETS: 1918 letter, biographical materials, and a collection of stories, relating in part to Wells' missionary experiences in China.

57-MURIEL WOOD, 1919–60, 23 items
Background note: Muriel Wood (Mrs. Frank H. Bowrey) was a missionary teacher at the Bridgman School in Shanghai from 1921 to ca. 1936.
CORRESPONDENCE/MANUSCRIPTS/PAMPHLETS: Correspondence and biographical materials, relating in part to Wood's missionary work in China.

58-CATHARINE T. WOODS, 1900–1964, 24 items
Background note: Catharine T. Woods was a missionary teacher in Siangtan from 1910 to 1946.
CORRESPONDENCE: Correspondence, writings, and biographical materials, relating in part to Woods' experiences in China.

59-MARTHA D. WOODS, 1908–77, 20 items
Background note: Martha D. Woods was a missionary teacher in Hangchow from 1911 to 1918.
CORRESPONDENCE/MANUSCRIPTS/PAMPHLETS: Correspondence and biographical material, relating in part to Woods' work in China.

60-EVELYN M. WORTHLEY, 1895–1972, 49 items
Background note: Evelyn M. Worthley (Mrs. C. M. Lacey Sites) was a missionary teacher in Diongloh, Foochow, and Yenping from 1902 to ca. 1944.
CORRESPONDENCE/MANUSCRIPTS/PAMPHLETS: Correspondence, writings, and biographical materials, chiefly relating to Worthley's work in China.

61-GENERAL HOLDINGS
AUDIO-VISUAL MATERIALS: Photo album of staff, students, buildings, and grounds of Bridgman School, Shanghai, ca. 1919.

MA–225 Williston Memorial Library
Mount Holyoke College
South Hadley MA 01075–1493
(413) 538–2225
Anne C. Edmonds, College Librarian

1-GENERAL HOLDINGS
MINUTES/RECORDS/REPORTS: International Institute of China, reports, 1908–16.
PAMPHLETS: *Windows into China: The Jesuits and Their Books, 1580–1730*, by John Parker, 1978.
SERIALS: *China Christian Year Book*, 1913–39. China International Famine Relief Commission, Publications, series B, 1926, 1930. *Chinese Recorder*, 1931, 1937–41. *St. John's University Studies*, 1922.

SOUTH HAMILTON

GORDON-CONWELL THEOLOGICAL SEMINARY
MA–230 Burton L. Goddard Library
130 Essex Street
South Hamilton MA 01982
(517) 468–7111
Norman E. Anderson, Acting Director

Background note: Goddard Library also holds the papers of Frederic Leonard Chappell, who was dean of the Boston Missionary Training School, including his diaries from 1889 to 1900. Although his papers are not indexed, they may contain some references to China.

1-LIT-SEN CHANG COLLECTION, 1960s–1970s, 5 boxes
Background note: Lit-sen Chang (b. 1904) was founder-president of Kiang-Nan University. A convert to Christianity in mid-life, he graduated from, then taught at, Gordon-Conwell Theological Seminary.
MINUTES/RECORDS/REPORTS: China Evangelistic Literature Committee, quarterly reports of Christian literature work, 1963–79.
CORRESPONDENCE: Large envelope of "Letters to National Leaders," n.d.

DIARIES: Bi-lingual journal, 1971–79.
MANUSCRIPTS: "A Christian Approach to Oriental Religions," n.d.; "Strategy of Missions in the Orient: Christian Impact on the Pagan World," 1968.
PAMPHLETS: *The True Gospel vs. Social Activism*, n.d.; *The True Way of Salvation*, n.d.
MEMORABILIA: Articles in *The Bible Magazine*, n.d.
CHINESE LANGUAGE MATERIALS: 13 manuscripts by Chang, mostly undated, on religious subjects and published editions of them; *Faith on Trial: The Testimony of Dr. Chang Lit-sen*, 1964; *The Power of Gospel*; *A Short Biography*; *The Way: An Investigation of Divine Truth*, 1960; *The Way of Life*, n.d.; translations of *New Bible Commentary: Gospels, Acts, Revelation* and *New Bible Commentary: Romans-Jude*.
FINDING AIDS: Faculty bibliography card catalogue listing Chang's works.

2-MISSION ROOM COLLECTION, 1910–39, 1 item
SERIALS: *China Christian Year Book*, 1910–39.

3-RARE BOOK ROOM, 1931–85, 7 items
DISSERTATIONS/THESES: *American Lutheran Mission Work in China*, by Rolf Arthur Syrdal, 1942. *An Estimate of the Applicability of the Christian Message to Modern China*, by Pauline Poy-ling Senn, 1939. *Fallacy of Pantheism in Respect to the Personality of God*, by Lit-sen Chang, 1958. *The Influence of the Mongol Invasion on the Russian Church Indirect and Negative Rather than Direct and Positive*, by Brenton Joffre Kitchener Arthur, 1944. *Jesus and the Oriental Mind*, by Alexander T. K. Choa, 1931.
CHINESE LANGUAGE MATERIALS: *A Study of Women in the Bible*, by Nancy Chow, 1985; Bible, 1955.

4-GENERAL HOLDINGS
MINUTES/RECORDS/REPORTS: Report by William Adams Brown on missions in the Far East prepared for Union Theological Seminary, 1917; China Inland Mission, report, 1938; Christian Literature Society for China, reports, 1887–1947; Lutheran Theological Reflection on China, report, 1975.
PAMPHLETS: *British Protestant Christian Evangelists and the 1898 Reform Movement in China*, by Leslie R. Marchant, 1975; *The Dutch Reformed Church in Formosa, 1627–1662: Mission in a Colonial Context*, by Jacobus Joannes Antonius Mathias Kuepers, 1978; *Elephant Trails: Platform Talks on Missionary Trails through Siam...into the Tai Country of South China*, by Leila Allen Dimock, 1920(?); *The Harrowing of Hell in China: A Synoptic Study of the Role of Christian Evangelists in the Opening of Hunan Province*, by Leslie R. Marchant, 1977; *The Relation of Church and Mission in China*, by Edwin Carlyle Lobenstine, 1923; *The River Cassia as It Flows through the Life of Pastor Chao*, by J. R. Turnbull, 1937.
SERIALS: *China and the Church Today*, 1979. *China Christian Advocate*, 1914–41. *China Christian Year Book*, 1910–39. *China Evangelical Seminary News Bulletin*, 1978-. China Graduate School of Theology, *Bulletin*, 1978. *China's Millions* (Toronto), 1942–52. *Chinese Christian Digest*, 1962. *Chinese for Christ, Inc. Newsletter*, 1960–63. *Chinese Recorder and Missionary Journal*, 1868–1932, 1937, 1940. *Chinese World Pulse*, 1977–81. *Ching Feng*, 1964–74, 1976-. *East Asia Millions* (Philadelphia), 1954-. *The Foochow Messenger*, 1903–40. *The Millions* (Philadelphia), 1952–61.

WALTHAM

BRANDEIS UNIVERSITY
MA-235 Library
South Street
Waltham MA 02254
(617) 736-4621
Virginia Massey-Burzio, Head of Reference

1-GENERAL HOLDINGS
PAMPHLETS: *Windows into China: The Jesuits and Their Books, 1580-1730*, by John Parker, 1978.
SERIALS: *China Christian Year Book*, 1911.
DISSERTATIONS/THESES: *Christian Missions in China*, by Charles Sumner Estes, 1895. *The Legal and Political Aspects of the Missionary Movement in China*, by Chao-kwang Wu, 1928.

WELLESLEY

WELLESLEY COLLEGE

MA-240 Archives
Margaret Clapp Library
Wellesley MA 02181
(617) 235-0320 Ext. 2129
Wilma R. Slaight, Archivist

Background note: In addition to the materials detailed below, the Archives maintain biographical files on alumnae (class year given), faculty, and staff. Among those who were missionaries or missionary wives in China were: Florence Bell (1901), Miriam E. Boyd (1921), Anna Brown (1909), Gertrude Carter (1896), Martha Cecil (1909), Nina Gage (1905), Frances Gray (1912), Jessie Hall (1905), Lottie Hartwell (1906), Helen Howe (1899), Alnah James (1918), Margaret V. Jones (1909), Elizabeth Kendall, Eliza Kendrick (1885), Edith Knowlton (1905), Augusta List (1909), Alice L. Logan (1901), Ruth Lyon (1904), Abbie Mayhew (1885), Mildred D. Miles (1922), Marion Mitchell (1894), Ada Newell (1890), Marion P. Perrin (1922), Isabella Phelps (1900), Caroline Read (Special student), Mary Scott (1890), Theresa Severin (1909), Frances Taft (1909), Annetta Thompson (1887), Seal Thompson, Ann Torrence (1903), and Augusta F. Wagner (1924).

1-CLASS OF 1912 RECORDS, 1942-47, 4 letters
CORRESPONDENCE: 4 letters from Grace Boynton at Yenching University, 1942-43, 1947.

2-CLASS OF 1918 RECORDS, 1939, 4 in.
MAPS/DESIGNS/DRAWINGS: "Greetings from Tungchou," n.d.; "Map Showing Flood, Drought, Storm, and Insect-plague Areas in Hopei and North-west Shantung," Church Committee for China Relief, 1939, in folder on Marguerite Atterbury.
AUDIO-VISUAL MATERIALS: 4 bound photo albums of China and Yenching, in folder on Marguerite Atterbury.

3-OUTSIDE AFFILIATIONS: CHINA COLLEGES, 1917-79, 1 box, 1 volume
MINUTES/RECORDS/REPORTS/CORRESPONDENCE/PAMPHLETS: Associated Boards for Christian Colleges in China, n.d., 1937-51; Women's Union Christian Colleges of the Ori-

ent, n.d., 1922; correspondence relating to Wellesley-Yenching, 1922-49; miscellaneous publications by and about Yenching University, n.d., 1921-49.
MEMORABILIA: "The China Connection: A Brief History of Wellesley-Yenching," in *Wellesley Alumnae Magazine*, 1979; brochures, n.d., 1917-19, 1934-53, relating to Wellesley-Yenching; clippings about Wellesley-Yenching, n.d., 1922-41; article on Yenching University in *Life*, 1941.
AUDIO-VISUAL MATERIALS: Slides of Yenching University campus, n.d.; photo album of Yenching Women's College, n.d.
SERIALS: *China Colleges*, 1938-54 (inc.).
FINDING AID: In-house inventory.

4-PRESIDENT'S OFFICE: YENCHING UNIVERSITY (1921-64), ca. 1922-1964, 1 folder
Background note: Beginning in 1919, Wellesley College was a sister college of Yenching College for Women, formerly the North China Union Women's College.
MINUTES/RECORDS/REPORTS: Associated Boards for Christian Colleges in China, by-laws, 1933; constitution, 1933; Boston Committee, luncheon meeting, minutes, 1937; Yenching College Committee of the Trustees of Peking University, minutes, 1921; Board of Trustees of Yenching University, resolution, 1944.
CORRESPONDENCE: 41 letters relating to Wellesley's sister college relationship with Yenching University and the United Board for Christian Higher Education in Asia, 1934-64, including such correspondents as Earle Ballou, Mme. Chiang K'ai-shek, Wynn Fairfield, B. A. Garside, Alice Lyman, Eva Macmillan, Kendric Nicols Marshall, Beth Moore, Albert Seely, Margaret Speer, J. Leighton Stuart, and Wellesley College presidents Ellen Pendleton, Mildred McAfee, and Margaret Clapp.
MANUSCRIPTS: "An American Enterprise in China," n.a., n.d.; "Turning the Sod for the First Building of the Yenching College for Women," n.a., n.d.
MEMORABILIA: 2 Yenching College brochures, n.d.; clippings on Wellesley in China, n.d. (ca. 1922); Wellesley-Yenching brochure, n.d.
SERIALS: *Peking News*, 1921.
CHINESE LANGUAGE MATERIALS: Yenching University, reception program, 1920.
FINDING AIDS: In-house list.

5-MARIAN RIDER ROBINSON PAPERS, 1915-37, ca. 2 l.f.
Background note: Marian Rider Robinson was in China with her husband, Arthur Greenwood Robinson (1884-1964), from 1915 to 1926, and again from 1929 to 1937. A 1906 Harvard graduate, he studied in Nanking in 1913 and 1914, served in Tientsin with the YMCA from 1915 to 1926, and worked in government schools under the American Board mission in Tientsin from 1929 to 1934. From 1934 to 1937, the Robinsons owned and operated a store in Tientsin called "Robins' Nest Handicraft and Hobby Shop," which sold mission industrial products. The collection is only partially processed. See also Harvard University, Houghton Library, Cambridge, MA, 02138; and Colby College, Miller Library, Waterville, ME, 04901.
CORRESPONDENCE: Letters to family and friends telling of the Robinsons' experiences in China, family news, and occasional descriptions of Chinese events and customs, 1915-37; correspondence relating to owning and operating their store, 1934-37.
MANUSCRIPTS: "Robbie, 1884-1964: An Informal Biography

of Arthur Greenwood Robinson,'' by Marian Rider Robinson, 1964.
PAMPHLETS: *Chinese Chapters from the Book of the Stanley Club*, 1935; other pamphlets relating to the Stanley Club, n.d.
DIARIES/AUDIO-VISUAL MATERIALS: 4 journal/photo albums of their years in China, 1915–37; several small photo albums, n.d.
MEMORABILIA: Several items, including their license, pertaining to their store; publicity for the store; medal from the Chinese government (7th Order of the Golden Harvest) awarded to Marian Robinson, 1917.

6-GENERAL HOLDINGS
MANUSCRIPTS: Papers from a seminar by Suzanne Barnett in 1973: ''The Impact of Anti-missionary Disturbances in China and Missionary Response, 1870–1900,'' by Helen Feng; ''Missionary Educators D. Z. Sheffield and Charles A. Stanley: The Role of Education in the Chinese Ministry,'' by Rowena Fong; ''Native Clergy in the China Inland Mission, 1870–1900,'' by Micheline Lim; ''On Becoming: The Growth of K'ang Yu-wei as a Reformer and the Influence of Timothy Richard,'' by Anne Shen; ''The Taiping Rebellion and Missionary Approaches to China,'' by Duncan Sze-tu; ''Yenching University and the Conflict of Objectives in Mission Education in China: 1920s and 1930s,'' by Wendy Jo Jester.
MEMORABILIA: ''Wellesley Missionaries in Foreign Lands,'' an article in *The Wellesley College News*, 1914.

MA-245 Margaret Clapp Library
Wellesley College
Wellesley MA 02181
(617) 235-0320 Ext. 2095
Eleanor Gustafson, Head Librarian

1-GENERAL HOLDINGS
PAMPHLETS: *Windows into China: The Jesuits and Their Books*, by John Parker, 1978.
SERIALS: China Christian Educational Association, *Bulletin*, 1926, 1928. *China Christian Year Book*, 1928–29. China International Famine Relief Commission, *Publications*, series B, 1924. *China Mission Year Book*, 1917–23. *China Monthly*, 1942–50. *China Notes*, 1966-. *Chinese Recorder*, 1868–1940. *Chinese Repository*, 1832–51. *Millions* (London), 1875–83. *St. John's University Studies*, 1922. Yenching University, Department of Sociology, *Social Research Series*, 1930; *Yenching Journal of Social Studies*, 1948–50.

WENHAM

GORDON COLLEGE
MA-250 Winn Library
255 Grapevine Road
Wenham MA 01984
(617) 927-2300
John Beauregard, Director

1-VINING COLLECTION, 1845–1911, 9 volumes
CHINESE LANGUAGE MATERIALS: Several New Testaments, including translations by Karl Friedrich August Gützlaff and Robert Morrison, 1845–1911.

2-GENERAL HOLDINGS
SERIALS: *China Mission Year Book*, 1911, 1913.

WEST SPRINGFIELD

CONGREGATION OF THE PASSION OF THE EASTERN UNITED STATES (PASSIONISTS)
MA-255 The Chronicle Office
Mother of Sorrows Retreat House
110 Monastery Avenue
West Springfield MA 01089
(413) 736-0312/3
Caspar Caulfield, C.P., Director
Robert Carbonneau, C.P., Associate Director
Elizabeth A. Marshall, Research Coordinator

Restrictions: Access by appointment.
Background note: The Passionists, a Roman Catholic missionary institute, were sent to China by the Propaganda in Rome. They numbered about 80, more than are represented in the historical collection. Passionists went to China to establish and evangelize the Diocese of Yuanling, Hunan; they arrived in 1921 and remained until they were expelled in 1955. Several orders of religious sisters worked in conjunction with the Passionists, namely, Sisters of Charity of Convent Station, Sisters of St. Joseph, Grey Nuns of Ontario, Sisters of Charity (Hungary), and Sisters of Notre Dame (Kalocsa, Hungary). For other collections on these religious orders, see Sisters of Charity of St. Elizabeth, Generalate Archives, Convent Station, Elizabeth, NJ, 07961; Paterson Diocese Archives, 777 Valley Road, Paterson, NJ, 07013; and Sisters of St. Joseph Archives, Baden, PA, 15005. The Passionist China History File currently covers from 1920 onwards, but material is still in the process of being gathered and catalogued.

1-GENERAL FILE, 1921–55, quantity undetermined
MINUTES/RECORDS/REPORTS/CORRESPONDENCE/MANUSCRIPTS: Procurator File, containing materials on financial policy and activities of the mission, 1921–55; Rome File, containing materials on policy questions to and from Rome, n.d.; Apostolic letters, documents, and missionary biographical studies, including a history of Yuanling; 41 boxes of missionary letters, including Annual Status of Mission reports indicating missionary productivity and direct policy orders from Rome, 1921–55.
MANUSCRIPTS: Untitled manuscript by Cormac Shanahan, C.P., who travelled to Yenan as a reporter in 1944, including interviews with Mao Tse-tung and Chou En-lai, n.d.
DIARIES: Diary of Lambert Budde, translated from Dutch, reviewing early mission years from 1922 to 1928; diary of Sr. Clarissa of the Sisters of St. Joseph, 1926–27; diary by Matthias Mayou, C.P., 1924–25.
MANUSCRIPTS/MEMORABILIA/AUDIO-VISUAL MATERIALS: Individual folders of missionaries' personal effects, including newspaper clippings, notebooks, photos, obituaries, and biographical materials; 3 folders of clippings on historical events, 1923–55.
ORAL HISTORIES: Audio cassette of interviews by Anthony Maloney, C.P., with Justin Garvey, C.P., and Marcellus White, C.P., who were arrested and imprisoned from 1951 to 1955.
MAPS/DESIGNS/DRAWINGS: Unspecified maps.
AUDIO-VISUAL MATERIALS: Unspecified photos.

CHINESE LANGUAGE MATERIALS: Chinese-Latin documents: baptismal certificates, 1903–51; confirmation certificates, 1913, 1915, 1920, 1940–41; matrimonial certificates, 1912–49.
SERIALS: *Caritas*, 1933–43, 1966–67. *China Missionary Bulletin*, 1949–60. *Hunan News*, 1949–56. *The Sign*, 1921–82.

2-TIMOTHY McDERMOTT, C.P., COLLECTION, 1918–41, quantity undetermined
CORRESPONDENCE: Personal letters from Timothy McDermott, C.P., at the Yuanchow Mission, Hunan, to his family and friends, 1918–41.

3-MISSIONARY MURDERS OF 1929 COLLECTION, 1929, quantity undetermined
CORRESPONDENCE: Correspondence with the U.S. State Department concerning the circumstances surrounding the murders of Walter Coveyou, C.P., Godfrey Holbein, C.P., and Clement Seybold, C.P., in 1929.
MEMORABILIA: Commemorative materials, news articles, biographical materials.
AUDIO-VISUAL MATERIALS: Unspecified photos.

4-BISHOP CUTHBERT O'GARA, C.P., COLLECTION, n.d., quantity undetermined
CORRESPONDENCE: Personal letters and business correspondence relating to the Vicariate of Yuanling, Hunan, n.d.
MANUSCRIPTS/PAMPHLETS: Commemorative material celebrating appointment of Cuthbert O'Gara as bishop, including 33 sermons and speeches on religious and political topics, n.d.
MEMORABILIA: Awards and biographical materials, including accounts of his arrests, first by the Japanese in 1941 and 10 years later by the Chinese Communists; newspaper and magazine articles.
AUDIO-VISUAL MATERIALS: Unspecified photos; audio cassettes of a U.S. State Department deposition, "Story of Imprisonment in Red China," n.d.

5-WESTERN PROVINCE COLLECTION, 1922–55, quantity undetermined
Background note: The Passionists are divided geographically into two provinces, east and west. During their time in Hunan, missionaries from both sectors joined forces.
CORRESPONDENCE: Box of letters from western missionaries describing the mission in detail to the Holy Cross Province in Chicago, 1922–55.
DIARIES: 18 small notebooks by Cyprian Frank, C.P., containing daily records, 1921–55; diary by Cyprian Frank, C.P., describing conditions in Chenhsi and Pusih Missions, n.d.; journal by William Westhoven, C.P., 1936–38, 1940–41.
MEMORABILIA/AUDIO-VISUAL MATERIALS/CHINESE LANGUAGE MATERIALS: Assorted teaching aids including Chinese catechisms and 4 large scrapbooks containing photos and clippings.

WOODS HOLE

MARINE BIOLOGICAL LABORATORY
MA-260 Library
Woods Hole MA 02543
(617) 548-3705
Jane Fessenden, Head Librarian

1-GENERAL HOLDINGS
SERIALS: *Lingnan Science Journal*, 1922–50. *Peking Natural History Bulletin*, 1926–50. Yenching University, Department of Biology, *Bulletin*, 1930.

WORCESTER

MA-265 AMERICAN ANTIQUARIAN SOCIETY
185 Salisbury Street
Worcester MA 01609-1634
(617) 755-5221
Marcus A. McCorison, Director and Librarian

Restrictions: Access upon application with letter of reference.
Background note: The American Antiquarian Society, founded in 1812, is the third oldest historical society in the United States. Its holdings consist of manuscripts and printed materials about American history through 1876.
Finding aids: *A Dictionary Catalog of American Books Pertaining to the Seventeenth through the Nineteenth Centuries: Library of the American Antiquarian Society* (Westport, CT: Greenwood), 1971, 20 V. *Catalogue of the Manuscript Collections of the American Antiquarian Society* (Boston: G. K. Hall & Co.), 1979, 4 V.

1-GENERAL HOLDINGS
MINUTES/RECORDS/REPORTS/PAMPHLETS: Medical Missionary Society in China: address with minutes, 1838; prospectus, 1838; reports, 1838–39, 1841–42; minutes and report of its ophthalmic hospital, 1848–51; Morrison Education Society, annual report, 1837–38; catalogue of books in its library, 1838; uncatalogued reports and pamphlets of the following: American Baptist Missionary Union, American Board of Commissioners for Foreign Missions, American Christian Missionary Society, American Church Missionary Society, American Missionary Association, Episcopal Missionary Association, Free Will Baptist Foreign Mission Society, Foreign Missionary Society of the Valley of the Mississippi, German Mission Society of the Mississippi Valley, Reformed Church in America Board of Foreign Missions, Women's Board of Missions, and Women's Union Missionary Society.
SERIALS: *Chinese Recorder and Missionary Journal*, 1869–71, 1874–78. *Chinese Repository*, 1832–36, 1842. *Directory of Protestant Missions in China*, 1866.
CHINESE LANGUAGE MATERIALS: Several translations of the New Testament or portions of it with some other materials, printed by mission presses during the late 19th century.

CLARK UNIVERSITY
MA-270 Goddard Library
Worcester MA 01610
(617) 793-7461
Marla M. Wallace, Reference Librarian

1-GENERAL HOLDINGS
DISSERTATIONS/THESES: *Early History of Christian Propaganda*, by C. L. Smith, 1911. *Protestant Missions in China*, by G. H. Merriam, 1927.

COLLEGE OF THE HOLY CROSS

MA–275 Archives
Dinand Library
Worcester MA 01610
(617) 793–3371
James M. Mahoney, Rare Book Librarian

1-GENERAL HOLDINGS
CORRESPONDENCE: 13 letters to and from Robert Cairns, on Maryknoll mission work in South China, 1921–40; 2 letters from Bishop Frederick Donaghy about converts in Wuchow and his imprisonment, 1940, 1951.
MANUSCRIPTS: "Maryknoll Missionary," a lecture by Robert Cairns, 1931; 2 manuscripts by Cairns on suffering and sacrifice in China and on introducing Chinese immigrants, 1923–31.
MEMORABILIA/AUDIO-VISUAL MATERIALS: Articles and photos about Donaghy's arrest and release, Cairn's capture by bandits, and the plight of Catholic girls in China, 1939, 1951, 1955; articles about Donaghy's appointment as vicar-apostolic of Wuchow mission, 1939; clipping about Cairns' work on Sancian Island, n.d.; articles by Cairns, 1928–37; article by Thomas Breslin on Roman Catholic missions in China, 1975.
AUDIO-VISUAL MATERIALS: 2 photos of Cairns, 1928; 7 photos of Donaghy, including his prison experiences and release, 1955–56, 1966.

MA–280 Dinand Library
College of the Holy Cross
Worcester MA 01610
(617) 793–3371
James M. Mahoney, Librarian

1-GENERAL HOLDINGS
PAMPHLETS: *The Systematic Destruction of the Catholic Church in China*, by Thomas J. Bauer, 1954; *Windows into China: The Jesuits and Their Books, 1580–1730*, by John Parker, 1978.
SERIALS: *Monumenta Serica*, 1948–83. *Variétés Sinologiques*, 1985.

MICHIGAN

ALBION

ALBION COLLEGE
MI–5 Stockwell Memorial and Seeley G. Mudd Libraries
Albion MI 49224
(517) 629–5511 Ext. 285
Keith Fennimore, Archivist

1-JUDSON COLLINS COLLECTION, ca. 1850–1947, quantity undetermined
Background note: For biographical notes, see Bentley Historical Library, Michigan Historical Collections, 1150 Beal Avenue, Ann Arbor, MI, 48109–2113.
MANUSCRIPTS: "Judson Collins before the Mast," a biographical play on Collins' life through 1849, 1947.
MEMORABILIA: Several clippings on Judson in China, ca. 1850–1875.

2-GENERAL HOLDINGS
CORRESPONDENCE: Letter from China missionary Lucy Hoag, in Kiu Kiang, reprinted in Albion College newspaper, *The Annalist*, 1873.

ANN ARBOR

UNIVERSITY OF MICHIGAN

MI–10 Asia Library
Hatcher Graduate Library, 4th floor
Ann Arbor MI 48109
(313) 764–0406
Wei-ying Wan, Asia Librarian

Finding aids: *Catalogs of the Asia Library, the University of Michigan, Ann Arbor* (Boston: G. K. Hall), 1978, 25 V.

1-GENERAL HOLDINGS
SERIALS: *China Medical Journal*, 1907, 1920–54, 1957–64, 1966. *China's Medicine*, 1966–68. *Chinese Medical Journal*, 1975–78, 1980–85. *Lingnan Journal*, 1929–37, 1949–52.
CHINESE LANGUAGE MATERIALS/SERIALS: *Chan wang yüeh k'an (Outlook)*, 1962–63. *Ch'i ta chi k'an (Cheeloo University Journal)*, 1932–37. *Chiao hui hsin pao (Church News)*, 1868–74. *Chin-ling hsüeh pao (Nanking Journal)*, 1931–40. *Chin-ling kuang (University of Nanking Magazine)*, 1930. *Fu jen hsüeh chih (Fu jen Sinological Journal)*, 1928–47. *Hsiang ts'un chiao hui (The Rural Church)*, 1948–49. *Hua hsi hsieh ho ta hsüeh Chung-kuo wen hua yen chiu so hsüeh pao* (West China Union University, *Studia Serica*), 1940–50. *Ling-nan hsüeh pao (Lingnan Journal)*, 1929–48. *Min su hsüeh chih* (Catholic University of Peking, *Folklore Studies*), 1942–52. *Wen hua t'u shu k'o chi k'an (Boone Library School Quarterly)*, 1929–37. *Yen-ching hsüeh pao (Yenching Journal of Chinese Studies)*, 1927–51. *Yen-ching hsüeh pao chuan hao (Yenching Journal of Chinese Studies*, Supplement), 1933–48.
CHINESE LANGUAGE MATERIALS/DISSERTATIONS/THESES: *Des Systèmes agraires en Chine (Chung-kuo nung yeh chih t'u k'ao)*, by Yüan Min-pao, 1922.
CHINESE LANGUAGE MATERIALS: Ca. 250 titles, including translations of the Bible into Mandarin, classical Chinese, and Foochow dialect; translations of the writings of John Lossing Buck, Pearl Buck, and John Leighton Stuart; translations and other works by Young J. Allen, James Legge, W. A. P. Martin, Matteo Ricci, Issachar J. Roberts, and Nicolas Trigault; and works on such subjects as Anglican missions, anti-Christian sentiment, Baptist missions, biblical studies, the Boxer Uprising, Catholic missions, Christianity and Chinese culture, Christianity and indigenous Chinese religion, Christianity and literature, Christianity in contemporary China, churches in Hong Kong, Jesuits, Jesus Christ, Feng

Yü-hsiang, Hsü Kuang-chi, Li Chih-tsao, Liang A-fa, Adam Schall, John Leighton Stuart, John (Shang-chieh) Sung, Archbishop Paul Yü-pin, Lingnan University, Nestorians, Protestantism, rural missions, the Soong family, sources in the history of Christianity in China, theology, the University of Nanking, and Yenching University; 12 titles in Japanese on the history of Christianity in China and Manchuria, Jesuit and other Catholic missions in China, and Matteo Ricci.

MI-15   Bentley Historical Library
Michigan Historical Collections
1150 Beal Avenue
Ann Arbor MI 48109-2113
(313) 764-3482
Nancy Bartlett, Reference Archivist

1-ARTHUR EDWARD ARMSTRONG PAPERS, 1911–38, 3 boxes
Background note: Arthur Edward Marriott Armstrong was the Singer Sewing Machine Company representative in central China. His wife, Elsa Felland Armstrong (b. 1890), was a missionary under the Norwegian Lutheran Church of America from 1911 to 1917. See also St. Olaf College, Archives, Rölvaag Memorial Library, Northfield, MN, 55057.
CORRESPONDENCE: Box of letters between Arthur and Elsa Armstrong, their families, and other missionaries, including Ruth Paxson (YWCA and Student Volunteer Movement) and Daniel Nelson, 1911–38.
MANUSCRIPTS/MEMORABILIA/MAPS/DESIGNS/DRAWINGS: Maps, clippings, posters depicting Chinese revolution and other subjects, and the Armstrongs' reminiscences of China.
AUDIO-VISUAL MATERIALS: Ca. 1 box of photos collected by the Armstrongs, of Elsa Armstrong's trip to China, mission scenes, Chinese civil war, scenes in China, friends and associates, the mission building and churches, and the Singer Sewing Machine Company in China, ca. 1900–1917; postcards of China; 6 folders of stereoptic views of China, with printed guide; 5 photo albums of China, including mission life, the Sinyang Girls' School, urban and rural life, Elsa Armstrong's trip to China, Chinese civil war, and Shanghai and miscellaneous Chinese scenes.
FINDING AIDS: In-house inventories.

2-JUDSON DWIGHT COLLINS DIARIES, 1845(?), 1 volume
Background note: Judson Dwight Collins (1821–52) was a United Methodist missionary to China. See also Albion College, Stockwell Memorial and Seeley G. Mudd Libraries, Albion, MI, 49224.
DIARIES: Diary containing an account of Collins' journey to China, with comments on the people and conditions of the country.

3-MABEL STONE FARLEY LETTER, 1915, 1 item
CORRESPONDENCE: Letter to Mabel Stone Farley, an educational missionary, from Feng Sien Hsii of Nanking, describing his studies, 1915.

4-ESSON MCDOWELL GALE PAPERS, 1940, 1 volume
MANUSCRIPTS: Notebook including lectures on China missions, 1940.
FINDING AIDS: In-house inventory.

5-HAROLD STUDLEY GRAY PAPERS, 1922–26, 18 folders
Background note: Harold Studley Gray (1894–1972) was a teacher

of economics at Huachung (Central China) University, Wuchang, from 1922 to 1926.
CORRESPONDENCE: 16 folders of correspondence, 1922–26, including correspondents such as Chang Fu-liang, Maxwell Chaplin, Kirby Page, and David R. Porter.
MANUSCRIPTS: "A Report on the Causes of Overpopulation in China, 1922 (his master's thesis).
AUDIO-VISUAL MATERIALS: Excerpts of photo album, 1925–27, including China.
FINDING AIDS: In-house inventory.

6-GERTRUDE F. McCULLOCH PAPERS, 1920, 3 items
Background note: For biographical notes, see American Baptist Historical Society, 1106 South Goodman Street, Rochester, NY, 14620.
CORRESPONDENCE: 2 copies of letters sent to the First Baptist Church in Jackson, Michigan, concerning Gertrude McCulloch's life and work in China.
MEMORABILIA: Biographical information on McCulloch.

7-MARGARET WILDER MENZI PAPERS, 1911–40, 1 box
Background note: Margaret Wilder Menzi was the daughter of George D. Wilder (see George D. Wilder Papers below).
CORRESPONDENCE: Letter to Menzi from George D. Wilder concerning China prior to World War II, ca. 1939.
MANUSCRIPTS: Reminiscences of Gertrude Stanley Wilder relating to life on the China mission field, and George D. Wilder on China prior to World War II.
DIARIES: Diaries describing life in a missionary compound in China, 1911–14.

8-HAZEL LITTLEFIELD SMITH PAPERS, ca. 1915–1928, quantity undetermined
Background note: Hazel Littlefield Smith's husband, Dennis V. Smith, was a Methodist Episcopal medical missionary to China. He was head of the optical department in the Methodist Sanitarium and Eye Clinic at Methodist (John L. Hopkins Memorial) Hospital, Peking. See also University of Oregon, Special Collections, Eugene, OR, 97403-1299.
MINUTES/RECORDS/REPORTS: Ledger and notebook kept by Dennis Smith in China, n.d.; subscription list of the Peking Hua Shih Chapel Building Fund, n.d.; invoice for goods shipped to the Smiths in Peking, 1918.
CORRESPONDENCE: Folder of letters from Hazel Smith from Peking and Peitaiho, 1915–27; 5 folders of letters of Dennis Smith en route to China, 1915, and from Peking, 1915–28, describing activities of the hospital, Christian missionaries, family and friends, and China politics; folder of letters from Josiah L. Littlefield (Hazel Smith's father), Peking, 1916–17; letter from Dennis V. Smith on Chinese politics and civil war, 1917; letter from Kuan Fu Ti to Dennis Smith, 1921.
MANUSCRIPTS: "Arrival in Peking," by Dennis Smith, 1915; address by Josiah Littlefield to a group of Chinese Christian theological students in Peking, 1917; poem by Hazel Smith concerning boat trip in China, 1924; "The School Awaits," by Paul Wakefield, concerning Christian mission-sponsored education in China, n.d.; "Boxer Rebellion—Peking," by Dennis Smith, n.d.; "Medicine and Christian Literature," by Dennis Smith, n.d.; "Some Chinese I Have Known," by Dennis Smith, n.d.; "Young China Seeking Health," by Dennis Smith, 1931.

PAMPHLETS: *Messages from the China National Christian Conference*, n.d.
DIARIES: Diaries of Dennis V. Smith on Chinese politics and civil war, 1918–20; 2 diaries of Josiah L. Littlefield, n.d.
MEMORAEILIA: Chinese wedding invitation, passports, pasteboard household gods, clippings on China, and miscellaneous printed materials.
MAPS/DESIGNS/DRAWINGS: Map of Peking, early 1900s.
AUDIO-VISUAL MATERIALS: 13 small photo albums of photos and postcard views of North China, with descriptions, including Peking, western compound in Peking, Methodist Sanitarium in the Western Hills, Peitaiho resort and other holiday travels; small scrapbook of photos by Dennis Smith, taken in Jehol (Chengteh), n.d.; photos of China, including University of Michigan alumni in Peking, and Eye Clinic at Methodist Hospital in Peking; box of lantern slides of China, the Eye Clinic and Methodist Sanitarium; prints of Chinese calendars in pen and watercolor, n.d.
FINDING AIDS: In-house inventories.

9-GEORGE D. WILDER PAPERS, 1904–71, 1 box
Background note: George Durand Wilder (1869–1946) was a missionary to China from 1894 to 1939. There he met and married Gertrude Stanley who had been born in China in 1870 to American Board missionaries in Tientsin. See also Cornell University, Department of Manuscripts and University Archives, John M. Olin Library, Room 101, Ithaca, NY, 14853–5301.
CORRESPONDENCE: Letters from Wilder to his family, describing missionary life, politics, and family matters, 1911–32; letters from Theodore Stanley Wilder and Durand Wilder, to family members describing China experiences, 1910–13; excerpts of letters, 1911–15, selected by Cynthia Ritsher.
MANUSCRIPTS: Translation by George Wilder of *Cat City*, by Lao She, n.d.; "The China Years of George Durand and Gertrude Stanley Wilder," impressions of China, ca. 1900–1912, by Theodore Stanley Wilder, n.d.
DIARIES: Diary by Wilder, describing internment by the Japanese in Peking, 1942–43.
ORAL HISTORIES: Transcript of oral history of Louise Hathaway Stanley for the *China Missionaries Oral History Project*, Claremont Graduate School, Oral History Program, 1971.
MEMORABILIA/AUDIO-VISUAL MATERIALS: Scrapbook concerning International Monetary Commission to Honan, including articles by Wilder on "The Peking-Hankow Overland Route," 1904.
FINDING AIDS: In-house inventory.

10-PHILIP NEWELL YOUTZ PAPERS, 1920–24, ca. 1 l.f.
Background note: Philip Newell Youtz was home secretary of Canton Christian College from 1920 to 1924.
CORRESPONDENCE: Correspondence of Philip Youtz from Canton Christian College to family and friends, 1920–22.
MEMORABILIA: Articles, 1920–24, and notebook by Philip and Frances Youtz on Canton Christian College, 1924–25.
FINDING AIDS: In-house inventory.

11-NELLIE ZWEINER PAPERS, 1907–43, 10 items
Background note: Nellie Zweiner was a Reformed Church in America missionary to China.
CORRESPONDENCE: 10 letters from Zweiner to Christine Brock, 1907–43.

MI-20   William L. Clements Library
University of Michigan
909 South University Avenue
Ann Arbor MI 48109
(313) 764-2347
Glen R. Wilson, Manuscripts Curator

1-MISCELLANEOUS BOUND: McGILL COLLECTION, 1843, 1 item
CORRESPONDENCE: Letter from Andrew Patton Happer to Alexander Taggart McGill, asking advice on how to begin a missionary career, 1843.

2-ROCHESTER LADIES ANTI-SLAVERY SOCIETY COLLECTION, ca. 1850, 1 item
CORRESPONDENCE: Letter from Mary Gutzall to Susan Farley Porter, expressing interest in going to China as a missionary, ca. 1850.

MI-25   Hatcher Graduate Library
University of Michigan
Ann Arbor MI 48109
(313) 764-9373
Wendy P. Lougee, Head of the Graduate Library

1-GENERAL HOLDINGS
MINUTES/RECORDS/REPORTS: American Board of Commissioners for Foreign Missions, report of the deputation to China, 1907.
MANUSCRIPTS: "Christian Higher Education in China: Contributions of the Colleges of Arts and Science to Chinese Life," by J. Dyke Van Putten, 1937.
PAMPHLETS: *British Protestant Christian Evangelists and the 1898 Reform Movement in China*, by Leslie Ronald Marchant, 1975; *Stirring Facts: An Address on China*, by Llewellyn James Davies, 1901.
MAPS/DESIGNS/DRAWINGS: *Atlas of the Chinese Empire Containing Separate Maps of the Eighteen Provinces of China Proper on the Scale of 1:3,000,000, Together with an Index to All the Names on the Maps and a List of All Protestant Mission Stations, etc.*, by Edward Stanford, 1908.
SERIALS: *China Christian Year Book*, 1926–39. China International Famine Relief Commission, Publications, series A, 1922–36; series B, 1923–26, 1929–30; series E, 1932. *China Mission Year Book*, 1910–11, 1913, 1915, 1918–19, 1925. *Chinese Recorder*, 1876–1941. *Chinese Repository*, 1832–51. *Directory of Protestant Missions in China*, 1926. *Folklore Studies*, 1942–83. *Lingnan Science Journal*, 1922–48. Lingnan University, *Science Bulletin*, 1930–35. *Looking East at India's Women and China's Daughters*, 1880–81, 1883–88, 1893–94. *The Millions* (London), 1875–77. Nanking Theological Seminary, *English Publications*, 1940. Natural History Society, *Proceedings*, 1928–30. *Relations de Chine*, 1903–10. University of Nanking: College of Agriculture and Forestry, *Agriculture and Forestry Notes*, 1924–36; *Miscellaneous Bulletin Series*, 1924–25. West China Border Research Society, *Journal*, 1922–45. Yenching University, Department of Sociology and Social Work, *Social Research Series*, 1930.
DISSERTATIONS/THESES: *Die Akkommodationsmethode des P. Matteo Ricci S.I. in China*, by Johannes Bettray, 1955. *The Anti-Christian Persecution of 1616–1617 in Nanking*, by Edward

Thomas Kelly, 1971. *Apostolic Legations to China of the Eighteenth Century*, by Antonio Sisto Rosso, 1948. *China and Educational Autonomy: The Changing Role of the Protestant Educational Missionary in China, 1807–1937*, by Alice Henrietta Gregg, 1946. *Christian Missions in China*, by Charles Sumner Estes, 1895. *The Educational Work of the Missionaries in China*, by Wei-cheng Chen, 1910. *An Eighteenth-century Frenchman at the Court of the K'ang-hsi Emperor: A Study of the Early Life of Jean François Foucquet*, by John W. Witek, 1973. *Imperial Government and Catholic Missions in China during the Years 1784–1785*, by Bernward Henry Willeke, 1948. *Die katholische Missionsmethode in China in neuester Zeit (1884–1912); geschichtliche untersuchung über arbeitsweisen, ihre Hindernisse und Erfolge*, by Johannes Beckmann, 1931. *The Mission Compound in Modern China: The Role of the United States Protestant Mission as an Asylum in the Civil and International Strife of China, 1900–1941*, by Gladys Robina Quale, 1957. *La Politique missionnaire de la France en Chine, 1842–1856; l'ouverture des cinq ports chinois au commerce étranger et la liberté religieuse*, by Louis Tsing-sing Wei, 1960. *Die protestantische Christenheit in der Volksrepublik China und die Chinaberichterstattung in der deutschen evangelischen Missionsliteratur*, by Ilse Hass, 1974. *La rencontre et le conflit entre les idées des missionnaires chrétiens et les idées des Chinois en Chine depuis la fin de la dynastie des Ming*, by Liang Si-ing, 1940. *Women in a Changing China: The YWCA*, by Jean McCown Hawkes, 1971.

MI–30 Law Library
University of Michigan
801 Monroe
Ann Arbor MI 48109
(313) 764-9322
Linda Maslow, Reference Librarian

1-GENERAL HOLDINGS
SERIALS: *China Law Review*, 1922–40.

MI–35 Museum Libraries
University of Michigan
2500 Museums Building
Ann Arbor MI 48109
(313) 764-0467
Patricia Yocum, Reference Librarian

1-GENERAL HOLDINGS
SERIALS: *Peking Natural History Bulletin*, 1926–49.

MI–40 Natural Sciences Library
University of Michigan
3140 Natural Science Building
Ann Arbor MI 48109
(313) 764-1494
Patricia Yocum, Reference Librarian

1-GENERAL HOLDINGS
SERIALS: Fukien Christian University, *Biological Bulletin*, 1939. University of Nanking, College of Agriculture and Forestry, *Bulletin*, 1924–36; Botany Department, Plant Pathology Laboratory, *Contribution*, 1932, 1936.

BERRIEN SPRINGS

ANDREWS UNIVERSITY

MI–45 Adventist Heritage Center
James White Library
Berrien Springs MI 49103
(616) 471-3274
Louise Dederen, Curator

1-JOHN PETER ANDERSON DIARIES, 1943-ca. 1977, 2 boxes
CORRESPONDENCE/DIARIES: Diaries, written as letters, of John Peter Anderson, a Seventh-Day Adventist clergyman in China, 1943–45.
ORAL HISTORIES: Tapes of oral history interviews with Anderson, ca. 1977.

2-FREDERICK GRIGGS PAPERS, n.d., quantity undetermined
Background note: Frederick Griggs (1867–1952) was field secretary (1925–30) and president (1931–36) of the Far Eastern Division of Seventh-Day Adventists, and president (1936–38) of the China Division of Seventh-Day Adventists.
MINUTES/RECORDS/REPORTS/CORRESPONDENCE/DIARIES: Reports, correspondence, and diaries, 1892–1926, including material on Seventh-Day Adventist missions in China.

3-GENERAL HOLDINGS
CHINESE LANGUAGE MATERIALS: Uncatalogued books and pamphlets, 1891–1972; catalogued materials interfiled with other foreign language materials, mostly translations of English-language works on Seventh-Day Adventism.
CHINESE LANGUAGE MATERIALS/SERIALS: *China Christian Educator*, 1923–32. *Fuh In Hsuen Pao (The Gospel Herald)*, 1906–7. *Hsing Chwan Lu*, 1918–20. *Hwa Nan Pao*, 1920. *Sabbath School Lessons*, 1925, 1927–31, 1942. *Sabbath School Lessons* (in Wenli), 1923. *Shi Djao Yüeh Pao (Signs of the Times)*, 1912, 1915, 1919–41, 1951. *Tjen Le [Che] Poh (Present Truth)*, 1920.

MI–50 James White Library
Andrews University
Berrien Springs MI 49103
(616) 471-3275
Warren Johns, Seminary Librarian

1-GENERAL HOLDINGS
MINUTES/RECORDS/REPORTS: China Continuation Committee, proceedings, 1919.
MANUSCRIPTS: "A History of the Evangelical Lutheran Church of America Mission Policy in China, 1890–1949," by Roger Keith Ose, 1966; "Observations and Comments on the Work in China, Past and Present," by S. J. Lee, 1957; "Reminiscences of Post-liberation Days in China, 1951–1957," by S. J. Lee, 1957(?); "Sinicization: The Church as a Living Community in Modern China, 1969–1970," ed. by Delos A. Humphrey, 1971.
PAMPHLETS: *China Consultation*, 1958, 1960, 1962; *Der chinesische Ritenstreit*, by Anton Huonder, 1921.
SERIALS: *Asiatic Division Outlook*, 1918. *China Bulletin*, 1947–62. *China Christian Year Book*, 1911, 1917, 1919. *China Division Reporter*, 1931–45. China Graduate School of Theology, *Bulletin*, 1972–82. *China Notes*, 1962-64, 1966-85. *Chinese Christians*

Today, 1972–86. *Chinese Recorder*, 1909–11, 1913–25, 1927–31, 1933–37, 1939–41. *Ching Feng*, 1964–75. *Far Eastern Division Outlook*, 1926–36, 1939–. *Maryknoll Mission Letters*, 1923, 1943. DISSERTATIONS/THESES: *Apostolic Legations to China of the Eighteenth Century*, by Antonio Sisto Rosso, 1948. *A History of Seventh-Day Adventist Higher Education in the China Mission, 1888–1980*, by Handel Hing-tat Luke, 1983. *Lutheran Missions in a Time of Revolution: The China Experience, 1944–1951*, by Jonas Jonson, 1972. *Missionary Conscience and the Comprehension of Imperialism: A Study of the Children of American Missionaries to China, 1900–1949*, by Sarah R. Mason, 1978.
CHINESE LANGUAGE MATERIALS: *China Has a Ten Thousand-Mile Spiritual Wall*, by Shao Yan Lee, 1946; *A Story of Christian Missionaries in China*, by Zhong-shing Guo, 1983.

DETROIT

MI–55 DETROIT PUBLIC LIBRARY
5201 Woodward Avenue
Detroit MI 48202
(313) 833–1000
Joseph Oldenburg, Assistant Director, Main Library

1-GENERAL HOLDINGS
MINUTES/RECORDS/REPORTS: International Institute of China, annual reports, 1926.
MAPS/DESIGNS/DRAWINGS: *Atlas of the Chinese Empire*, by Edward Stanford (Philadelphia: China Inland Mission), 1908.
SERIALS: Catholic University of Peking, College of Education, Publications, 1939–40. *China Christian Year Book*, 1924–28. China International Famine Relief Commission, Publications, series A, 1921–24, 1926–36; series B, 1926, 1930. *Lingnan Agricultural Review*, 1924–26. *Lingnan Science Journal*, 1936–40, 1942, 1945.
DISSERTATIONS/THESES: *China and Educational Autonomy: The Changing Role of the Protestant Educational Missionary in China, 1807–1937*, by Alice Henrietta Gregg, 1945.

MI–60 Burton Historical Collection
5201 Woodward Avenue
Detroit MI 48202
(313) 833–1485
Mary Karshner, Curator of Manuscripts

1-EDWIN DENBY PAPERS, 1923, 1 folder
CORRESPONDENCE: Letters between Frank D. Gamewell, general secretary of the China Christian Educational Association, and Edwin Denby, Secretary of the Navy, about a petition signed by 400 China missionaries for the reappointment of Judge Lobinger of the China court.

2-DUFFIELD PAPERS, ca. 1845, 2 items
Background note: For biographical notes on Divie Bethune McCartee, see Presbyterian Historical Society, Archives and Library, 425 Lombard Street, Philadelphia, PA, 19147.
CORRESPONDENCE: 2 letters from Divie Bethune McCartee on his work in Ningpo, ca. 1845.

3-GOUX FAMILY PAPERS, 1910–44, 1 box
Background note: Detroit resident Mrs. Goux supported missionaries and mission interests through the First Baptist Church in Detroit.
MINUTES/RECORDS/REPORTS: Women's School in Huchow, catalogue, 1918; curriculum, 1919; and prospectus, 1917; Joint Conference of the East China District, American Baptist Foreign Mission Society and the Central China Mission, Southern Baptist Convention, program on education work, 1916; Shanghai Mission College, annual reports, 1931–32; University of Shanghai, annual report, 1934.
CORRESPONDENCE: Box of letters to Goux from Baptist missionaries in Huchow, 1910–44, from Margaret Cuddeback, Bertha A. Fetzer, Viola C. Hill, Mary I. Jones, Anna M. Martin, Ruth Mather, and Helen M. Rawlings, 1910–44; station letter from Steven G. Goddard, Swatow, 1941; letter from James McKay, executive secretary of the Women's American Baptist Foreign Mission Society, congratulating Goux on her activities on behalf of missionaries, 1938; letter from Nashville Board of YWCA to Goux on missionaries supported in China, 1923; 4 circular letters from Mary I. Jones, 1923, 1925, 1941, n.d.; circular letter from Charles D. Leach, 1924; unidentified circular letter, 1938.
PAMPHLETS: *A Catechism on the Hoochow School of Mothercraft*, by the American Women's Baptist Foreign Mission Society, n.d.; *Life and Conversion of Mrs. Go, the Chinese Bible Woman Who Is Miss Jones' Co-worker*, n.d.; ca. 10 biographical pamphlets of the missionaries, ca. 1910–1914.

4-LEANDER WILLIAM PILCHER PAPERS, 1847–85, 2 items
MANUSCRIPTS: "China Mission (Commenced in 1847)," by William Pilcher, 1847; "Founding of a Mission, Being a Sketch of the Life of the Rev. Judson D. Collins and the Founding of the China Mission of the Methodist Episcopal Church," by Leander William Pilcher, 1885.

5-GENERAL HOLDINGS
CORRESPONDENCE: Circular letter (broadside) from S. A. Rulison, containing extracts from correspondence of 3 female missionaries supported by the Northwestern Branch of the Women's Foreign Missionary Society, Flint, Michigan, 1874.
PAMPHLETS: *Visit to the Chinese Coast*, by Charles Gützlaff, 18?.

MARYGROVE COLLEGE
MI–65 Library
8425 West McNichols Road
Detroit MI 48221
(313) 862–8000 Ext. 212
Anna Mary Waickman, I.H.M., Library Director

1-GENERAL HOLDINGS
SERIALS: *Far East: The Magazine of the Chinese Mission Society*, 1928–29.

UNIVERSITY OF DETROIT
MI–70 Library
4001 West McNichols Road
Detroit MI 48221
(313) 927–1000
Jonathan Gilham, Reference Librarian

1-GENERAL HOLDINGS
MANUSCRIPTS: "Duo responsa centum doctorum Sacrae facultatis theologicae Parisiensis ad Sinarum quaesita in Sacra congregatione S. Officii proponenda," 1700 (on microfilm).

EAST LANSING

MICHIGAN STATE UNIVERSITY
MI-75   University Library
East Lansing MI 48824
(517) 355-2344
Eugene DeBenko, Librarian

Background note: The Asian Studies Center is preparing a project to compile oral histories of Americans in Michigan who lived and worked in Asia prior to 1950, supplemented by mementos, photos, and other materials. Contact Jack F. Williams, director of the Asian Studies Center, for further information.

1-GENERAL HOLDINGS
SERIALS: China International Famine Relief Commission, Publications, series A, 1922–36. *China Monthly*, 1940, 1946–50. *Chinese Recorder*, 1912–41. *Fukien Agricultural Journal*, 1942, 1947–50. *Lingnan Science Journal*, 1922–45. *Peking Natural History Bulletin*, 1926–50. University of Nanking, College of Agriculture and Forestry, *Bulletin*, 1926, 1932–36.

GRAND RAPIDS

CALVIN COLLEGE AND SEMINARY

MI-80   Archives
Denominational Historical Collection of the Christian Reformed Church
3207 Burton Street NE
Grand Rapids MI 49506
(616) 957-6297
Z. C. Janssens, Archivist, Historical Collections

Background note: The Synod of the Christian Reformed Church adopted China as a mission field in 1920.

1-HENRY BEETS PAPERS, 1895–1947, 17 l.f.
Background note: Henry Beets, a minister of the Christian Reformed Church, was director of Foreign Missions and edited *The Banner* and *The Missionary Monthly*.
MINUTES/RECORDS/REPORTS/CORRESPONDENCE/MANUSCRIPTS/PAMPHLETS/SERIALS: Personal papers, including reports, articles, correspondence, speeches, and newsletters concerning the Christian Reformed Church's China missions.

2-RICHARD BLAUW, 1964, 1 item
MANUSCRIPTS: "Christian Reformed Missions in China," student paper by Richard Blauw, 1964.

3-BOARD FOR CHRISTIAN REFORMED WORLD MISSIONS, 1918-, 5 reels microfilm, ca. 2 l.f.
Restrictions: Written permission from the Board for Christian Reformed World Missions, 2850 Kalamazoo Avenue SE, Grand Rapids, MI, 49560, required for access to minutes and reports.

MINUTES/RECORDS/REPORTS: Board for Christian Reformed World Missions, China mission, minutes and reports on microfilm, 1918–83; Jukao Leper Clinic, Jukao, Kiangsu, annual report, 1937; National Christian Council of China, annual report, 1923–28.
CORRESPONDENCE: Correspondence of Board of World Missions missionaries: Peter De Jong, 1 in., 1944–55; John C. De Korne, 4 in., 1938–51; Marion De Young, 1 in., 1947–51; Harry A. Dykstra, 5 in., 1936–63; Simon A. Dykstra, 1 in., 1934–51; Elisabeth Heerema, 1 in., 1948–55; Magdalena Koets, 2 in., 1939–56; Albert H. Selles, 5 in., 1937–67; Albert H. Smit, 5 in., 1924–53; Henry Everett Van Reken, 2 in., 1945–55; Bernard J. Voss, 1 in., 1945–47.
MANUSCRIPTS: Manuscripts of the China mission, 1920–73.

4-JOHN CORNELIUS DE KORNE PAPERS, 1910–51, 3 l.f.
Background note: John Cornelius De Korne, a minister of the Christian Reformed Church, was a missionary to China, director of Foreign Missions, and editor of *The Missionary Monthly*.
MINUTES/RECORDS/REPORTS/CORRESPONDENCE/MANUSCRIPTS/PAMPHLETS/MAPS/DESIGNS/DRAWINGS/MEMORABILIA: Personal papers, including files concerning the Christian Reformed Church's China missions: account books (1923–34), records, reports, correspondence, speeches, articles, sermons, programs, China maps, and China liturgical forms.
MANUSCRIPTS: "Chinese Altars to the Unknown God," by John C. De Korne, 1926; "The Christian Approach to the Heart and Mind of China," John C. De Korne, n.d.; "The Fellowship of Goodness," by John C. De Korne, 1941; translation of "Guide to Seekers of the Tao," by Lis Yin Shan Yen, n.d.

5-WILLIAM C. HAVERKAMP, 1967, 1 item
MANUSCRIPTS: "Dr. Lee S. Huizenga and the China Mission, 1930–1939," student paper by William C. Haverkamp, 1964.

6-LEE SJOERDS HUIZENGA PAPERS, 1901–48, 8 l.f.
Background note: Lee Sjoerds Huizenga was a minister of the Christian Reformed Church and a medical missionary to China.
MINUTES/RECORDS/REPORTS/CORRESPONDENCE/MANUSCRIPTS/MEMORABILIA/AUDIO-VISUAL MATERIALS: Reports to supporting churches, correspondence, manuscripts of books and articles, sermon notes, newspaper clippings, and photos on leprosy, 1901–48.

7-MARK KNOPER, 1978, 1 item
MANUSCRIPTS: "The China Mission of the Christian Reformed Church, 1920–1950," student paper by Mark Knoper, 1978.

8-RENA D. WESTRA, 1951, 2 items
MANUSCRIPTS: "Communism in China" and "Under Communism," papers by Rena D. Westra, 1951.

9-GENERAL HOLDINGS
ORAL HISTORIES: 2 undated audio tapes by Edward Van Baak on missions in China.
PAMPHLETS: *Christus' Gang Door China*, by J. A. C. Rullman, n.d. *Griffith John, de Vader van de Hankow-Zending in China*, by M. Schuurman, n.d.; *Het Echtpaar Stam; de Martelaren van Miaosheo (China)*, 1938; *History on Leprosy in China*, by Lee Sjoerds Huizenga, 1934; *Legislation and Leprosy*, by Lee Sjoerds Huizenga, 1937; *In Memoriam. Rev. John A. Otte, M.D. In Leven*

Medisch Zendeling van de Gereformeerde Kerk in Amerika, to Siokhe en Amoy, China, 1910; *Presbyterians at Work in China*, by the Presbyterian Church in the U.S.A., Board of Foreign Missions, 1929; *Sketch of the Amoy Mission, China*, by Abbe Livingston Warnshuis, 1906.
AUDIO-VISUAL MATERIALS: "China Missions," a film by Albert H. Smit on activities in Jukao, Haian, and Shanghai, 1947.

MI–85 Calvin College and Seminary Library
3207 Burton Street NE
Grand Rapids MI 49506
(616) 957–6297
Conrad J. Bult, Reference Librarian

1-GENERAL HOLDINGS
MANUSCRIPTS: "The Mission Work of the Presbyterian Church in the United States in China, 1867–1952," by James Edwin Bear (microfilm copy of original at Union Theological Seminary, Richmond, VA, 23227), 1963–73.
PAMPHLETS: *The Catholic Missions in China during the Middle Ages, 1294–1368*, by Paul Stanislaus Hsiang, 1949; *An Hour with John and Betty Stam: Martyred Missionaries to China*, by Theodore Wilhelm Engstrom, 1942; *Jesuit Letters from China*, trans. by M. Howard Rienstra, 1986.
SERIALS: *China Christian Year Book*, 1911–16, 1918, 1928–38. *Chinese Recorder*, 1921–41. *Variétés Sinologiques*, 1985.
DISSERTATIONS/THESES: *Accomodatie in de Chinese Zendingagescheideris*, by Johannes Maarten van Minnen, 1951. *China Missions in Crisis: Bishop Laimbeckhoven and His Times, 1738–1787*, by Joseph Krahl, 1964. *The Fellowship of Goodness (Tung Shan She): A Study in Contemporary China Religion*, by John Cornelius De Korne, 1941. *Lutheran Missions in a Time of Revolution: The China Experience, 1944–1951*, by Jonas Jonson, 1972.

GRACE BIBLE COLLEGE
MI–90 Library
1011 Aldon, SW
P. O. Box 910
Grand Rapids MI 49509
(616) 538–2330
G. Olson, Director of Library Services

1-GENERAL HOLDINGS
PAMPHLETS: *Christianity and China/Chinese: A Periodical Bibliography*, by Sharon E. Mumper, 1982.
AUDIO-VISUAL MATERIALS: 2 photos of Isobel Kuhn, ca. 1920.

REFORMED BIBLE COLLEGE
MI–95 Library
1869 Robinson Road SE
Grand Rapids MI 49506
(615) 458–0404 Ext. 11
Lavonne Nettleton, Librarian

1-GENERAL HOLDINGS
MINUTES/RECORDS/REPORTS: Ecumenical Seminar, report on China, 1974; International Reformed Bulletin, report on missions to China, 1975.

MANUSCRIPTS: "Christian Concern for China," by Paul Szto, 1973; "A Model for United Evangelical Witness to China," by Paul Szto, 1973.
PAMPHLETS: *China Inland Mission Handbook*, n.a., 1949.
AUDIO-VISUAL MATERIALS: "China Consultation," 2 cassette tapes of a conference at Reformed Bible College, 1975, containing discussions on aspects of Christianity in China by A. F. Glasser, Paul Szto, Edward Van Baak, Donald MacInnis, and Jonathan Chao; *J. Hudson Taylor, Apostle to Inland China*, flashcards and script, 1964.
SERIALS: *China and the Church Today*, 1979–86. *China News and Church Report*, 1984-. *Chinese World Pulse*, 1978, 1980–82.

HANCOCK

SUOMI COLLEGE
MI–100 Finnish-American Historical Archives
Hancock MI 49930
(906) 482–5300 Ext. 273
Marsha Penti, Director

Restrictions: Access by appointment.
Background note: The missionary activities of the Suomi Synod were closely tied to those of the Evangelical Lutheran Church of Finland. The correspondence below documents the relationship between the Suomi Synod and Suomen Lähetysseura, Finland's Mission Society. References to work in China may also be found in the calendars and yearbooks of the Suomi Synod, and in the synod periodical, *Paimen Sanomat*.

Two missionaries from the Suomi Synod, Evangelical Lutheran Church in America, served in China: Niilo Korhonen (1916–22) and Onni Könönen (1937–41). Their correspondence stored at FAHA refers only to their American pastorates following return from China.

1-SUOMI SYNOD COLLECTION, 1916–62, .5 l.f.
CORRESPONDENCE: Ca. 1 in. of Suomi Synod correspondence with the Lutheran Church of China in Shekow and the Finnish Missionary Society in Helsinki, scattered throughout the archive's "Foreign Mission"-correspondence files, 1917–62.
DISSERTATIONS/THESES: *A Record of the Activities of the Finnish Missionary Society in Northwest Hunan, China, 1902–1952*, by Ilma Ruth Aho, 1953.

HOLLAND

HOPE COLLEGE

MI–105 Archives
Van Zoeren Library
Holland MI 49423
(616) 394–6992
Andrew Vander Zee, Archivist

Background note: Affiliated with the Reformed Church of America, the Hope College Archives contain materials reflecting the work of alumni in China missions. For other Reformed Church in America archives, see New Brunswick Theological Seminary, Archives of the Reformed Church in America, Gardner A. Sage

Library, 21 Seminary Place, New Brunswick, NJ, 08901; and Netherlands Museum, Holland, MI, 49423.

1-WILLIAM R. ANGUS PAPERS, 1925–62, 800 items
Background note: For biographical notes, see New Brunswick Theological Seminary, Archives of the Reformed Church in America, Gardner A. Sage Library, 21 Seminary Place, New Brunswick, NJ, 08901.
MANUSCRIPTS: "A Missionary's Miscellany," containing several hundred sketches of life among Chinese Christians in prose and poetry.
MEMORABILIA/AUDIO-VISUAL MATERIALS: Photos of missionaries, Chinese people, and scenic views, and clippings.

2-WALTER DE VELDER PAPERS, ca. 1944, 2 items
Background note: For biographical notes, see Western Theological Seminary, Beardslee Library, 85 East 13th Street, Holland, MI, 49423.
MANUSCRIPTS: "Across Three Continents," by Walter De Velder, with portions on his experiences in China, 1936–44; 3-page summary by De Velder of his experiences in China and publications, n.d.

3-MISCELLANEOUS COLLECTION ON CHINA MISSIONS, 1908–54, 30 items
PAMPHLETS/AUDIO-VISUAL MATERIALS: 30 miscellaneous articles and photos on China missions, 1908–54.

4-THE OLD CHINA HANDS-ORAL HISTORY PROJECT, 1976–77, 1.33 l.f.
ORAL HISTORIES/MANUSCRIPTS/AUDIO-VISUAL MATERIALS: Tapes and transcripts of oral histories with 17 retired missionaries, recorded and transcribed in 1976 and 1977, including photos and biographical sketches: William Angus, Ruth Broekema, Elizabeth G. Bruce, Jack and Joanne Hill, Johanna Hofstra, Theodore V. Oltman, Jesse Platz, Rose H. Talman, Alma Vander Meer, James D. Van Putten, Gordon J. and Bertha V. Van Wyk, Harold E. and Pearl Veldman, Jeannette Veldman, and Jenanne Walvoord.

5-JOHN AND FRANCES OTTE PAPERS, 1888–1910, .5 l.f.
Background note: For biographical notes, see Western Theological Seminary, Beardslee Library, 85 East 13th Street, Holland, MI, 49423. See also Netherlands Museum, 8 East Twelfth Street, Holland, MI, 49423.
CORRESPONDENCE/PAMPHLETS/MEMORABILIA/AUDIO-VISUAL MATERIALS: Ca. 50 pieces of correspondence, clippings, pamphlets, articles, and 2 photo albums about John Abraham Otte's work in China, 1888–1910.
MANUSCRIPTS: "Life of Dr. J. A. Otte," by Frances Otte, n.d.; student research papers, "Frances Otte, A Biography," by Paula Huey, n.d., and "A Big, Little Man," by Tom Dekker, n.d.
MEMORABILIA: Scrapbook by Frances Otte containing articles about China, n.d.; 2 issues of the *Annuals of the Messengers of Hope*, a Hope College alumni newsletter, containing letters by the Ottes about their work, n.d.

MI–110 Van Zoeren Library
Hope College
Holland MI 49423
(616) 392-5111
Carol Juth-Gavasso, Reference Librarian

1-GENERAL HOLDINGS
PAMPHLETS: *A Primer on Islam, and the Spiritual Needs of the Mohammedans of China*, by Samuel Marinus Zwemer, 1919.
SERIALS: *China*, 1947–51. *China Bulletin*, 1951–62. *China Notes*, 1962–67.

MI–115 NETHERLANDS MUSEUM
8 East Twelfth Street
Holland MI 49423
(616) 392-9084
Reid Van Sluys, Director, Holland Historical Trust

Finding aids: *A Guide to the Archives of the Netherlands Museum*, by Elton J. Bruins and Barbara Lampen, 1978.

1-FRANCES PHELPS OTTE PAPERS, 1907–15, ca. 1 l.f.
Background note: Frances Phelps Otte (1860–1950) was the wife of Johannes Abraham Otte, the first Reformed Church medical missionary to China. She served in China from 1887 to 1911. For biographical notes and materials on Johannes Otte, see Western Theological Seminary, Beardslee Library, 85 East 13th Street, Holland, MI, 49423. See also New Brunswick Theological Seminary, New Brunswick, NJ, 08901; and Hope College, Archives, Van Zoeren Library, Holland, MI, 49423.
MANUSCRIPTS: Sketch of Johannes Abraham Otte's life, n.d.
MEMORABILIA: Material on the China mission in *Messengers of Hope*, 1907–15, a magazine published by Hope College alumni in foreign missionary service; family memorabilia.

WESTERN THEOLOGICAL SEMINARY
MI–120 Beardslee Library
85 East 13th Street
Holland MI 49423
(616) 392-8555 Ext. 7
Elton J. Bruins, Archivist
Paul M. Smith, Librarian

Background note: For other materials relating to the Reformed Church in America, see also Hope College, Holland, MI, 49423; Netherlands Museum, Holland, MI, 49423; and New Brunswick Theological Seminary, 21 Seminary Place, New Brunswick, NJ, 08901.
Finding aids: *The Manuscript and Archival Holdings of Beardslee Library, Western Theological Seminary, Holland, Michigan*, by Elton J. Bruins (Holland, MI: Western Theological Seminary), 1970.

1-HARRY PETER BOOT PAPERS, 1909–60, 2 l.f.
Background note: Harry Peter Boot (1874–1961) was a Reformed Church in America missionary to China from 1903 to 1940.
MINUTES/RECORDS/REPORTS: Amoy Mission, annual reports, financial reports, statistical reports, 1911–60; China Information Committee, reports, 1940; F. B. Meyer visit, Amoy Mission, records, 1909; Mission to the Chinese after World War II, Hong Kong, and the Philippines, records, n.d.
CORRESPONDENCE: Folder of correspondence with family and letters concerning the finances of the Amoy Mission, 1909–60; box of miscellaneous correspondence.

MANUSCRIPTS: Folder of miscellaneous writings by Harry Peter Boot, n.d.
PAMPHLETS: Pamphlets on the Amoy Mission, 1911–60.
MAPS/DESIGNS/DRAWINGS: Folder of maps of China.
AUDIO-VISUAL MATERIALS: 2 boxes of photos of China, the Amoy Mission, and personnel, 1900–1940.
CHINESE LANGUAGE MATERIALS: Folder of unidentified materials, n.d.

2-HENRY PETER DE PREE PAPERS, 1907–43, 1 folder, 4 items
Background note: Henry Peter De Pree (1881–1969) was a Reformed Church in America missionary to China from 1907 to 1948. He was president and a professor at Fukien Theological Seminary from 1925 to 1946.
MEMORABILIA: Clippings from Reformed Church periodicals on students, the mission, and church buildings, n.d.
MAPS/DESIGNS/DRAWINGS: Map of the Amoy region, n.d.
AUDIO-VISUAL MATERIALS: Photos of students, the Amoy Mission, and church buildings, n.d.
CHINESE LANGUAGE MATERIALS: 4 personal notebooks, n.d.

3-WALTER DE VELDER PAPERS, 1929–50, 16 items
Background note: Walter De Velder (b. 1901) was a Reformed Church in America missionary to China from 1929 to 1950.
MEMORABILIA: Scrapbook compiled by Frances Phelps Otte containing correspondence, clippings, and articles about De Velder's experiences as a missionary in China, including items on John A. Otte.

4-FRANK ECKERSON PAPERS, 1941–49, 3 items
Background note: Frank Eckerson (1876–1949) was a Reformed Church in America missionary to China from 1903 to 1949.
CORRESPONDENCE: Copy of a letter from Luman J. Shafer, ca. 1941; copy of a letter from Eckerson to his family, 1947.
MEMORABILIA: Tribute to Eckerson after his death by Elizabeth G. Bruce, 1949.

5-TENA HOLKEBOER PAPERS, 1920–51, 10 items
Background note: Tena Holkeboer (1895–1965) was an educational missionary of the Reformed Church in America in China from 1920 to 1948.
MINUTES/RECORDS/REPORTS: Tung-an District, report, 1942.
CORRESPONDENCE: Correspondence with her family, n.d.
MANUSCRIPTS: "An Age on Age Telling," oration, 1920; "Comments on a Study Document on the China Issue," 1961; "Customs in Amoy," n.d.; "Dr. Sung's Revival Meetings in Amoy," 1935; "History of the First Protestant Church in China, After 100 Years," by Jin-gi Lin, n.d.; "Urging a Decision," talk, 1942; "What Is the Purpose of a Christian Education," n.d.; "Your Labor Is Not in Vain for the Lord," n.d.
PAMPHLETS: *Rooted and Built Up in Him: The Story of Our Educational Work in China*, n.a., n.d.

6-CLARENCE H. HOLLEMAN PAPERS, 1929–70, 23 items
Background note: Clarence H. Holleman (1890–1973) was a medical missionary at the Amoy Mission of the Reformed Church in America from 1919 to 1951. See also Claremont Colleges, Special Collections Department, Honnold Library, Eighth and Dartmouth Streets, Claremont, CA, 91711.

CORRESPONDENCE/MANUSCRIPTS: 23 letters and memoirs of Clarence H. Holleman, describing his work at the Amoy Mission and the Communist takeover.

7-JOHN A. OTTE PAPERS, 1888–1910, 16 items
Background note: John Abraham Otte (1861–1910) was a Reformed Church in America medical missionary to Amoy from 1888 to 1910. See also Hope College, Archives, Van Zoeren Library, Holland, MI, 49423; and Netherlands Museum, 8 East Twelfth Street, Holland, MI, 49423.
AUDIO-VISUAL MATERIALS: 2 photos albums of China, ca. 1900.
MEMORABILIA: 14 scrapbook leaves of personal and family clippings, ca. 1900.

8-REFORMED CHURCH IN AMERICA, BOARD OF FOREIGN MISSIONS PAPERS, 1857–1909, quantity undetermined
Background note: Originals of Reformed Church in America, Board of Foreign Missions correspondence are held by the Archives of the Reformed Church in America, New Brunswick Theological Seminary, 21 Seminary Place, New Brunswick, NJ, 08901.
CORRESPONDENCE: Microfilm copies of letters from secretaries of the Board of Foreign Missions to missionaries in the field including William R. Angus, William I. Chamberlain, Henry Cobb, C. H. Holleman, Johannes Abraham Otte, William Pohlman, Henry A. Poppen, F. M. Potter, and Luman J. Shafer.

9-REFORMED CHURCH IN AMERICA, CHINA MISSION RECORDS, 1856–1949, 8 reels microfilm
Background note: Originals of Reformed Church in America, Board of Foreign Missions correspondence are held by the Archives of the Reformed Church in America, New Brunswick Theological Seminary, 21 Seminary Place, New Brunswick, NJ, 08901.
CORRESPONDENCE: Microfilm copies of letters from missionaries in the field to the Board of Foreign Missions, 1856–1949, including discussion of Chinese civil war, communist activities, and mission affairs.

10-LUMAN JAY SHAFER, 1941, 1 item
Background note: Luman Jay Shafer was executive secretary of the Reformed Church in America Board of Foreign Missions from 1935 to 1955.
MINUTES/RECORDS/REPORTS: Report to the Board of Foreign Missions on the Deputation to Japan and China, 1941.

11-HENRY MICHAEL AND STELLA VEENSCHOTEN MATERIALS, 1940–51, 6 boxes
Background note: Henry M. (1892–1974) and Stella Elda (Girard) (1892–1962) Veenschoten served as missionaries to China from 1917 to 1951.
CORRESPONDENCE: Ca. 1 box of Veenschoten family correspondence, 1929–51; letters from Henry M. Veenschoten while a prisoner, n.d.; letter from a woman living in Communist China, n.d.
DIARIES: Diary kept by Henry M. Veenschoten as a prisoner, n.d.
MANUSCRIPTS: Notebook containing a hymnbook manuscript, n.d.
PAMPHLETS: Packet of miscellaneous printed matter, n.d.; printed matter on the Board of Foreign Missions, RCA, n.d.

MEMORABILIA: 2 notebooks containing clippings of hymns, n.d.; music for hymns translated into Chinese, n.d.; folder of materials on missionaries' churches, with photos, n.d.; small envelope of musical notations, n.d.; sermon materials and mission talks, n.d.; hymnbook, n.d.; business and financial papers, n.d.; miscellaneous papers, labeled "Board of World Missions, RCA," n.d.; packet of materials on Board of Foreign Missions, RCA, n.d.; furlough and retirement papers, n.d.; motor car records, n.d.; miscellaneous and personal papers of Henry M. Veenschoten, n.d.; envelope of materials on "I. O. K. Tch Girls' Middle School, 100th Anniversary," n.d.; a bag of film, n.d.

ORAL HISTORIES: Audio tape of interview with Henry M. Veenschoten, n.d.; audio tape, "Conversation with Father and Mother," n.d.

AUDIO-VISUAL MATERIALS: Audio tape of Amoy songs, n.d.; "Refugees' picture, Kulangsu, Amoy, 1932," a group photo; envelope of photos, labelled "Tang Poa Oa, 1st Chinese, Changchow," n.d.; photo of Stella Veenschoten and a Chinese students' choir, n.d.; 1 envelope each of photos of Chang Chow, Union Hospital in Chang Chow, Chinese churches and evangelism, and Sio Khe Hospital, n.d.; folder of Veenschoten family photos; 3 photos of Amoy harbor; photos of "Mission Conference," n.d.; group photo, n.d.; 6 envelopes of photos, n.d.; 2 photos of a Christmas pageant, n.d.; photos of missionary churches, n.d.; envelope of unidentified photos; 6 glass negatives, n.d.; audio tape of Christmas songs, n.d.; 3 audio tapes of hymns, n.d.; audio tape of Veenschoten sermon, n.d.; bundle of unidentified audio cassettes, n.d.; bundle of 3 unidentified magnetic tapes, n.d.; audio tape of memorial service for Stella Veenschoten, 1962; envelope of illustration materials, n.d.

SERIALS: *China Bulletin*, 1959–62. *China Notes*, 1962–73.

CHINESE LANGUAGE MATERIALS/MANUSCRIPTS: 4 folders of manuscripts of music and hymns, arranged by Stella Veenschoten, n.d.; "Church forms for liturgical use translated into Chinese," a notebook, n.d.; unidentified typewritten manuscript, n.d.; materials for a Chinese dictionary, n.d.

CHINESE LANGUAGE MATERIALS/MEMORABILIA/ AUDIO-VISUAL MATERIALS: Envelope containing pages of hymns and church music, n.d.; audio tape of part 1 of "Rev. Wurmbrand's message with Chinese translation," n.d.; "DEAS" in Chinese, n.d.; folder of printed materials in English and Chinese, n.d.; hymnbook edited by Stella Veenschoten, n.d.

12-JEANNETTE VELDMAN, 1909–63, 4 boxes
Background note: Jeannette Veldman (b. 1901) served as a Reformed Church in America missionary in Kulangsu, Amoy, from 1930 to 1951.

MINUTES/RECORDS/REPORTS: Hope Hospital, Kulangsu, Amoy, annual reports, 1946–52; procedures, n.d.; Alice Buryce, Amoy Mission, records and notebook, 1909–42; Jeannette Veldman, daily records, 1949–51.

CORRESPONDENCE: Ca. 50 letters from Jeannette Veldman to family and friends, 1929–51.

MANUSCRIPTS: "Fall of Amoy Island to Japan, 5/39," n.a., n.d.; "Furlough," a notebook by Jeannette Veldman, 1922–38; "Popcorn and Fellowship," by Jeannette Veldman, n.d.

PAMPHLETS: Packet of *China Calling* material, n.d.; *Chinese Boy Scout*, by the *Encyclopedia Britannica* Children's Series, n.d.; unidentified pamphlets, n.d.

MEMORABILIA: Academic credentials, n.d.; bundle of "Welcome Home" cards, 1951; travel documents, n.d.; 6 notebooks of notes and speaking engagements, 1939–40; assorted artifacts.

AUDIO-VISUAL MATERIALS: Photo of conference at Amoy, n.d.; 3 photos of Children's Home, n.d.

SERIALS: *China Notes*, 1963.

CHINESE LANGUAGE MATERIALS: Script of a play by nurses at Hope Hospital, 1939; brochures, n.d.; unidentified letter, n.d.; bundle of serials, n.d.; 2 unidentified books, n.d.; *Memorial Book for Miss Kittie Talmadge* (with translation), n.a., n.d.

13-ABBE LIVINGSTON WARNSHUIS PAPERS, 1906–58, 8 items
Background note: For biographical notes, see Union Theological Seminary, Archives, 3041 Broadway at Reinhold Niebuhr Place, New York, NY, 10027.

MINUTES/RECORDS/REPORTS: Records on the legal status of missions and missionaries in China, 1925.

MANUSCRIPTS: "Dr. A. Livingston Warnhuis, Ecumenical Servant, 1877–1958," student paper by Herman Harmelink III, 1962.

PAMPHLETS: Articles published by Warnshuis.

MEMORABILIA: Tribute by Norman Goodall, 1958.

14-GENERAL HOLDINGS
MINUTES/RECORDS/REPORTS: Records on the China mission of the Reformed Church in America in *The Mission Field*, 1888–1922.

PAMPHLETS: *China's Religious Policies and Christian Missions*, by Jonathan T'ien-en Chao, 1977; *The Chinese Church and Christian Missions*, by Jonathan T'ien-en Chao, 1977; collection of ca. 1,000 pamphlets including some by China missionaries of the Reformed Church in America, such as William I. Chamberlain, Henry N. Cobb, Tena Holkeboer, John Abraham and Frances Phelps Otte, Philip Wilson Pitcher, Henry A. Poppen, and Abbe Livingston Warnshuis.

ORAL HISTORIES: *China Missionaries Oral History Collection*, ed. by Cyrus H. Peake and Arthur L. Rosenbaum (Claremont Graduate School, Oral History Program), 1973. See ORAL HISTORIES Union List for the names of participants.

SERIALS: *China Christian Year Book*, 1911–12, 1923, 1929, 1931, 1938–39.

KALAMAZOO

KALAMAZOO COLLEGE
MI–125 Upjohn Library
Thompson and Academy Streets
Kalamazoo MI 49007
(616) 383-8499
Joan Hinz, Reference Librarian

1-GENERAL HOLDINGS
SERIALS: *Anking Newsletter*, 1937–48. *China Christian Advocate*, 1914–41. *China Christian Year Book*, 1910–39. *China Medical Journal*, 1887–1921. *China Mission Advocate*, 1839. *Fenchow*, 1919–36. *The Foochow Messenger*, 1903–40. *Four Streams: Bulletin of the Diocesan Association for Western China*, 1934–51. *Hainan Newsletter*, 1912–38, 1947–49. *West China Missionary News*, 1901–43.

DISSERTATIONS/THESES: *The Mission Compound in Modern

China: The Role of the United States Protestant Mission as an Asylum in the Civil and International Strife of China, 1900–1941, by Gladys Robina Quale, 1957.

WESTERN MICHIGAN UNIVERSITY
MI–130 Dwight B. Waldo Library
> Kalamazoo MI 49008
> (616) 383-4960
> Hans Engelke, Associate Director

1-GENERAL HOLDINGS
MINUTES/RECORDS/REPORTS: American Board of Commissioners for Foreign Missions, report of deputation to China, 1907. CHINESE LANGUAGE MATERIALS: *Fan tui Chi-tu chiao yün tung (The Anti-Christian Movement)*, comp. by the China Youth League Anti-Christian Alliance, n.d.

MOUNT PLEASANT

CENTRAL MICHIGAN UNIVERSITY
MI–135 Clarke Historical Library
> Mount Pleasant MI 48859
> (517) 774-3352
> William Miles, Coordinator, Reader Services

1-WILLIAM R. LONGSTREET, 1899–1901, 1 item
DIARIES: Diary of Isabella Longstreet, describing her missionary work in China, 1899–1901.

2-DORA E. VAN DEVENTER, ca. 1930, 1 item
MEMORABILIA/MAPS/DESIGNS/DRAWINGS/AUDIO-VISUAL MATERIALS: "China Missionaries," scrapbook containing a sketch map of Honan, photos, and clippings from Chinese newspapers, ca. 1930.

3-GENERAL HOLDINGS
PAMPHLETS: *To My Missionary Critics*, by Samuel Langhorne Clemens, in *North American Review*, 1901; *A Trip to China*, by Frances J. Baker, 1897.

SOUTHFIELD

MI–140 DUNS SCOTUS LIBRARY
> Franciscan Friars
> 20000 West Nine Mile Road
> Southfield MI 48075
> (313) 357-3070
> Gabriel Balassone, O.F.M., Director

Background note: In addition to the materials listed below, the *Provincial Chronicle* of St. John the Baptist Province of the Order of Friars Minor, Cincinnati, contains reports related to China missions from 1928 to the present, covering the entire range of Franciscan missions.

1-GENERAL HOLDINGS
MANUSCRIPTS: "A History of the Vicariate of Wuchang," by Bede Clancy, O.F.M., 1940.
PAMPHLETS: *The Passionists in China: A Series of Articles*, by Ronald Norris, C. P., 1942; *The Workings of the Divine Provi-*

dence in the Pacification of Kingchow, by the Apostolic Vicariate of South West Hupeh China, 1912.
SERIALS: Catholic University of Peking, *Bulletin*, 1928, 1931. *China Missionary Bulletin*, 1948–53. *Franciscans in China*, 1922–41. *Mission Bulletin*, 1954–60.
DISSERTATIONS/THESES: *Imperial Government and Catholic Missions in China during the Years 1784–1785*, by Bernward Henry Willeke, 1948. *The Negotiations between Ch'i-ying and Lagrené, 1844–1846*, by Angelus Francis J. Grosse-Aschhoff, 1950.

MINNESOTA

COLLEGEVILLE

ST. JOHN'S UNIVERSITY
MN–5   Alcuin Library
> Collegeville MN 56321
> (612) 363-2119
> Richard Oliver, O.S.B., Head Cataloguer

1-GENERAL HOLDINGS
PAMPHLETS: *Benedictine Mission to China*, by Wibora Muehlenbein, O.S.B., 1980; *Catholic Missions in China during the Middle Ages, 1294–1368*, by Paul Stanislaus Hsiang, 1949; *Franciscans in the Middle Kingdom: A Survey of Franciscan Missions in China from the Middle Ages to the Present Time*, by Otto Maas, O.F.M., 1938; *The Nestorian Tablet at Sianfu: A New English Translation of the Inscription and a History of the Stone*, by Ignatius Ying-ki (Ying Ch'ien-li) and Barry O'Toole, 1929; *The Publications of the Catholic University of Peking*, by Francis Clougherty, O.S.B., 1931; *Windows into China: The Jesuits and Their Books, 1580–1730*, by John Parker, 1977.
SERIALS: *Asia*, 1960, 1970. *Catholic Church in China*, 1928–47. Catholic University of Peking, *Bulletin*, 1926–30. *China Christian Year Book*, 1934–35.
DISSERTATIONS/THESES: *L'Euchologe de la mission de Chine: Editio princips 1628 et développements jusqu'à nos jours (contributions à l'histoire des livres de prières)*, by Paul Brunner, 1964. *The Mission Compound in Modern China: The Role of the United States Protestant Mission as an Asylum in the Civil and International Strife of China, 1900–1941*, by Gladys Robina Quale, 1957.

MANKATO

BETHANY LUTHERAN THEOLOGICAL SEMINARY
MN–10   Library
> 447 North Division Street
> Mankato MN 56001
> (507) 625-2977
> Melvina Aaberg, Secretary

1-GENERAL HOLDINGS
MANUSCRIPTS: ''The Chinese Term Question: Natural Knowledge Concerning God and the Application of This Doctrine to the Chinese Term Question,'' by Arnold H. Gebhardt, n.d.; ''A History of the Term Question Controversy in Our China Mission and the Chief Documents in the Case,'' by George O. Lillegard, 1930.
PAMPHLETS: *The Chinese Term Question*, by George Lillegard, 1929; *The Chinese Term Question: An Analysis of the Problem and Historical Sketch of the Controversy*, by George Lillegard, n.d.; *Our Task in China*, 1922.

MINNEAPOLIS

AUGSBURG COLLEGE
MN–15   George Sverdrup Library
731 21st Avenue South
Minneapolis MN 55454
(612) 330–1000
Margaret J. Anderson, Director

1-CHINESE RELIEF CORRESPONDENCE, 1920–21, 2 in.
CORRESPONDENCE: Correspondence concerning China relief work, 1920–21.

2-FRED DITMANSON COLLECTION, 1927–44, 1 in.
DIARIES: 2 diaries of Frederick Ditmanson, a Lutheran missionary in China, containing a description of a trip to Honan in 1927 and a narrative of events relating to the Sino-Japanese War, 1931–32.
MANUSCRIPTS: ''Peking Temples,'' by Frederick Ditmanson, n.d.; a narrative by Frederick Ditmanson of the seige of Luyi during the Sino-Japanese War, n.d.
FINDING AIDS: In-house inventory.

UNIVERSITY OF MINNESOTA

MN–20   James Ford Bell Library
462 Wilson Library
309 19th Avenue South
Minneapolis MN 55455–0414
(612) 624–1528
John Parker, Curator

1-GENERAL HOLDINGS
Background note: Bell Library is a special collection of works relating to the history of world commerce and exploration from the thirteenth to the eighteenth centuries, including extensive holdings of Jesuitica. In addition to the materials described below, the Bell Library has about 130 volumes of published correspondence from Jesuit missions in Asia during the seventeenth and eighteenth centuries, with items from China interspersed throughout, and approximately 90 volumes relating specifically to Jesuit missions in China during this period, including published correspondence from missionaries and works on the the rites controversy. Most of these works are in French, Italian, or Latin; a few are in Dutch, English, German, Portuguese, or Spanish. Representative titles include: *Histoire apologétique de la conduite des Jésuites de la Chine: Adressée à messieurs des missions étrangères*, by Gabriel

Daniel, 1700; *Letterae Societatis Iesv e Regno Sinarvm Annorvm MDCX. & XI. ad Clavdivm Aquauiuam eiusd. Societatis Praepositum Generalem*, by Nicolas Trigault, 1615; and *Lettere d'un dottore di teologia dell'Universitá di Parigi dell'ordine de' predicatori, intorno alle idolatrie e superstizione della China*, by Noël Alexandre, 1700.
MANUSCRIPTS: ''Relazione delli padri della Compagni di Gièsu di Pekin intorno a quanto opero e fece l'Ilmo Pevmo Patriarca Monsignore Carlo Tommaso Maillard di Tournon legata a Latere nell'imperio della Cina, e poi Emo Prete Cardinale della S.R. Chiesa morto relegato in Macao li otto del mese di Guigno 1710,'' by Antonio Thomas, ca. 1710.
PAMPHLETS: 16 pamphlets, 1610–1751, including works on the rites controversy, Jesuit martyrs in China, and Jesuit mission correspondence to Rome.

MN–25   Biomedical Library
University of Minnesota
Diehl Hall
Minneapolis MN 55455–0414
(612) 626–3260
Sherry Lynn Fuller, Director

1-GENERAL HOLDINGS
SERIALS: *China Medical Journal*, 1920–31. *China's Medicine*, 1966–68. *Peking Natural History Bulletin*, 1926–48.

MN–30   East Asia Library
University of Minnesota
S 30 Wilson Library
309 19th Avenue South
Minneapolis MN 55455
(612) 624–9833
Joseph Branin, Director, Humanities and Social Science Libraries

1-GENERAL HOLDINGS
CHINESE LANGUAGE MATERIALS/SERIALS: *Ching Feng*, 1970–77. *Lingnan Hsüeh-pao (Lingnan Journal)*, 1929–52. *Yenching Hsüeh-pao (Yenching Journal of Chinese Studies)*, 1927–41, 1946–51.

MN–35   Law Library
University of Minnesota
120 Law Building
Minneapolis MN 55455–0414
(612) 625–4309
Tom Woxland, Associate Director for Public Services

1-GENERAL HOLDINGS
SERIALS: *China Law Review*, 1922–37.

MN–40   O. Meredith Wilson Library
University of Minnesota
309 19th Avenue
Minneapolis MN 55455
(612) 624–5518
Joseph Branin, Director, Humanities and Social Science Libraries

1-GENERAL HOLDINGS
PAMPHLETS: *Deutsche Kulturbestrebungen in China; Vortrag Gehalten vor Geh. Legationsrat Dr. Knappe*, by Wilhelm Knappe, 1906; *Relation de ce qui s'est passé à la Chine en 1697, 1698, & 1699, à l'occasion d'un établissement que M. l'Abbé de Lyonne a fait à Nien-Tcheou, ville de la province de Tche-Kiang*, by Jean de Fontanoy, 1700.
SERIALS: China Christian Educational Association, *Bulletin*, 1928. *China Christian Year Book*, 1910–13, 1926–28, 1934–35, 1938–39. *China Monthly: The Truth about China*, 1939–50. *China's Millions* (London), 1875–76, 1880, 1886–88, 1892. *Chinese Recorder*, 1870–78, 1880–1923, 1925–40. *Chinese Repository*, 1832–51. *Monumenta Serica*, 1935–; monograph series, 1939–66.
DISSERTATIONS/THESES: *China Missions in Crisis: Bishop Laimbeckhoven and His Times, 1738–1787*, by Joseph Krahl, 1964. *Christian Colleges and the Chinese Revolution, 1840–1940: A Case Study in the Impact of the West*, by Loren William Crabtree, 1969. *Protestant Mission Schools for Girls in South China (1827 to the Japanese Invasion)*, by Mary Raleigh Anderson, 1943.

NEW BRIGHTON

BETHEL THEOLOGICAL SEMINARY

MN-45 Archival Center of the Baptist General Conference
3949 Bethel Drive
New Brighton MN 55112
(612) 638–6282
David Guston, Archivist

Background note: See also Baptist General Conference, Board of World Missions, 2002 South Arlington Heights Road, Arlington Heights, IL, 60005.

1-LINDSTEDT COLLECTION, 1910–53. ca. 3,000 items
Background note: August Lindstedt and his family served as missionaries of the Swedish Baptist General Conference in Vladivostok from 1916 to 1917, and among Russians in north China and Manchuria from 1917 to 1946.

Further information on the Lindstedts' work in China can be found in *The Standard* (until 1940, the *Svenska Standaret*), the Swedish Baptist General Conference newspaper, and in the Conference's annual reports.
MINUTES/RECORDS/REPORTS/CORRESPONDENCE: Ca. 2,500 letters in English, Russian, and Swedish to and from the Lindstedts, 1917–46, concerning the Russian Mission of the Swedish Baptist General Conference and affiliated institutions, including the Bethel Children's Orphanage in Harbin; statistical reports interfiled with the letters.
DIARIES: 20 day books belonging to August Lindstedt, 1910–46.
AUDIO-VISUAL MATERIALS: Ca. 500 photos of the Lindstedts, and of locations in north China and Manchuria, including Dairen and Harbin.
SERIALS: National Christian Council of China, *Bulletin*, 1932.
DISSERTATIONS/THESES: *A History of the Russian Mission of the Swedish Baptist General Conference of America*, by Lars Marwin Lindstedt, 1953.

MN-50 Bethel Theological Seminary Library
3949 Bethel Drive
New Brighton MN 55112
(612) 638–6183
Norris Magnuson, Director

1-GENERAL HOLDINGS
MINUTES/RECORDS/REPORTS: Christian Literature Society for China, annual reports, 1946–47.
SERIALS: *Bible for China*, 1926, 1928–31. *Challenger*, 1973–. *China and the Church Today*, 1979–86. *China Christian Year Book*, 1918–19, 1925, 1931, 1934–37. *The China Fundamentalist*, 1929–31, 1935. China Graduate School of Theology, *Bulletin*, 1972–84. *China Mission Advocate*, 1839. *China Notes*, 1962–64, 1966–. *China Prayer Letter*, 1978–. *China's Millions* (London), 1883, 1885–87. *Chinese around the World*, 1983–84. *Chinese Recorder*, 1909–15, 1917–41. *Chinese Repository*, 1833, 1846. *Chinese World Pulse*, 1977–83. *Ching Feng*, 1964–. *East Asia Millions* (Philadelphia), 1961–. *The Millions* (Philadelphia), 1952, 1954, 1957–60. *West China Messenger*, 1902–10. *West China Missionary News*, 1901, 1904–5, 1909, 1919, 1923–24, 1926–40.
DISSERTATIONS/THESES: *The Development of the Motive of Protestant Missions to China, 1807–1928*, by George B. Workman, 1928. *A Study of Frederik Franson: The Development and Impact of His Ecclesiology, Missiology, and Worldwide Evangelism*, by Edvard P. Torjeson, 1984.
CHINESE LANGUAGE MATERIALS/SERIALS: *Chung-kuo hsin t'u yüeh k'an (Chinese Christians Today)*, 1962–63, 1972–.

UNITED THEOLOGICAL SEMINARY OF THE TWIN CITIES
MN-55 Library
3000 Fifth Street NW
New Brighton MN 55112
(612) 633–4311
Arthur Merrill, Director

1-GENERAL HOLDINGS
SERIALS: *China Christian Year Book*, 1931–35. *Chinese Recorder*, 1923–34, 1937–39, 1941.

NORTHFIELD

CARLETON COLLEGE

MN-60 Archives
Northfield MN 55057
(507) 663–4270
Mark A. Greene, Archivist

Background note: In 1903, the Carleton Mission was established to support missionary activities by Carleton students. In 1904, the first student to receive support from the mission, Mary Reynolds (1904), went to China to teach English to members of the imperial family. In 1907, Watts Pye (1903) reinstituted a mission in Fenchow; Percy Watson (1903) joined Pye in 1909 to establish and run a mission hospital. Several Carleton alumni did work at the mission and hospital under the auspices of the Carleton Mission. In 1922, the Carleton-in-China program was initiated, wherein one or two juniors were selected every year to teach English at the new middle school in Fenchow for two years before returning to finish college. At this point, the Carleton Mission became the Carleton-in-China Board, the fund-raising and administrative body of the program. The Carleton-in-China program was discontinued after the return of its last representative in 1949.

In addition to the manuscript collection listed below, information on the Fenchow Mission, the Carleton Mission, the Carleton-in-China program, and the various individuals involved may be found in *The Carletonian*, the college newspaper, and the various forms of the Carleton alumni magazine. These publications are held by the Archives and are roughly indexed. The Archives also maintains a series of folders on alumni; many Carleton students involved with China are represented in this series with clippings, obituaries, alumni questionnaires, photos, and correspondence, some of which is from China. Scattered additional material relating to Carleton's missionary activity in China can be found in the Papers of the President's Office, 1909–62.

1-CARLETON-IN-CHINA COLLECTION, 1903–51, 1 l.f.
MINUTES/RECORDS/REPORTS: American Board of Commissioners for Foreign Missions: Fenchow Station, annual report, 1914; North China Mission, Shansi District, minutes of annual meeting, 1917; Peiping Station, report, 1937; Carleton-in-China: application materials and lists of applicants, 1927–37; constitution of the Board, n.d.; financial records, 1907–26; lists of representatives, 1916–44; minutes of the trustees and administrative records, 1903–51; Fenchow Hospital, annual report, 1930; Oberlin-in-China, application forms, n.d.; Oberlin-Shansi Memorial Association, administrative records, 1928–39; Article VII of the by-laws, n.d.

CORRESPONDENCE: Folder of letters concerning the work in China of the American Board of Commissioners for Foreign Missions, 1919–45; letter from Carleton-in-China representative William J. Bakken, n.d.; folder of correspondence of Carleton-in-China representative Sarah Beach, 1926–28; letter from Carleton-in-China representatives Carl and Bernice Brown, 1936; folder of correspondence of Carleton Mission representative Myron Burton, 1911–12; folder of Carleton College presidents' correspondence concerning Carleton-in-China, 1919–29, 1947–53; folder of correspondence of Carleton-in-China representative Jack Caton, 1938–39; letter from "Chek," a Chinese student at Carleton-in-China, to Axel E. Vestling, 1941; folder of correspondence of Carleton-in-China representative Laura Cross, 1947–51; folder of correspondence of American Board missionary Rowland Cross, relating to Carleton-in-China, 1935–43; fund-raising letter to Rowland Cross, 1938; letter from Rowland Cross and Alice B. Frame to the Prudential Committee of the American Board of Commissioners for Foreign Missions, 1938; letter from Lydia Lord Davis, executive secretary of the Oberlin-in-China Association, to Carleton College President Donald Cowling, 1945; folder of correspondence of Carleton-in-China representative Paul Clifford Domke, 1937–38; fund-raising letter from A. R. Edwards of the Central China Red Cross Committee to the dean of Carleton College, 1937; circular letter from Emery W. Ellis, Minnie Case Ellis, and Susan B. Tallman in Tsingtao, 1907; circular letter for children on Carleton-in-China from "G. E. K.," 1926; circular letter from Adelaide Hemingway, English secretary of Oberlin-in-Shansi, 1928; folder of correspondence of Carleton-in-China rep-

resentative Edwin Hertz, 1921–26; folder of correspondence of Carleton-in-China representative John Hlavacek, 1939–42; letters from Carleton Mission representative Vera Holmes, 1919–20; letter from Josie Horn, regarding Carleton-in-China alumna "Miss Cheng," 1928; folder of correspondence of Carleton-in-China representative Carl Huber, 1936; letter from Carl Huber to "Belle," giving a general description of Carleton-in-China, 1946; letter from Carleton-in-China representative Mary Carol Jones, 1929; letter from Walter Judd to Mrs. Axel E. Vestling, regarding Ming I Middle School, 1945; letter from Carleton-in-China representative Larry Krause, 1929; recruitment letter for Oberlin-in-China by Robert L. Kroc, chairman of the Student Shansi Committee, 1928; letter from Beatrice Liu to Axel E. Vestling, 1941; letter from Liu Teh-wei to the president of the Carleton College Student Council, appealing for funds, 1937; folder of correspondence of Carleton-in-China representative J. Rhodes Longley, 1939–41; letter from Carleton-in-China representative Harry S. Martin, 1938; letter from Harold S. Matthews to the Carleton-in-China Committee, 1940; folder of letters to and from Dean Philip Phenix of Carleton College, concerning Carleton-in-China, 1946–51; circular letter from Lucius Porter, Ming Hsien, on his meeting with Japanese officers, 1939; folder of correspondence of American Board missionary Watts O. Pye, relating to Carleton-in-China, 1919–25; folder of correspondence of Carleton Mission representative Mary Reynolds, 1905–6; folder of letters from Paul Reynolds of the Board of Home Missions, 1928–38; letter from Paul Reynolds to Jacob F. Balzer regarding Fenchow Middle School, 1928; letters from Carleton-in-China representative Edward Rosenow, 1929–30; fund-raising letter for Carleton Mission from Carleton College President William H. Salmon and Greg Huntington, 1907; letter from Carleton-in-China representative Everett Sandburg, 1929; circular letter from Lawrence Schilling at Anglo-Chinese College, 1938; folder of letters from B. C. Swen, principal of Ming I Middle School, 1914–38; folder of correspondence of American Board Mission representatives Percy and Clara Watson, 1909–34; folder of correspondence of Carleton-in-China representative Tom Wiener, 1941–43; letter from Carleton-in-China representative Ellis Yale, 1926; fund-raising letter for Carleton-in-China, n.a., 1937; fund-raising letters for Oberlin-in-China, 1927–28, n.d.

MANUSCRIPTS: "Carleton's Mission in China and Its Relationship to the Chinese Social Revolution," research paper by Laura Danielson, 1977; "Lu Ho Middle School, Sian, Shensi, China," by James A. Arthur and Harold W. Robinson, ca. 1944; "My Summary of the Political History of China from 1911 to 1949" and notes on John K. Fairbank's "Thumbnail History of China," by Myron Burton, n.d.; three untitled histories of Carleton-in-China, n.d.

PAMPHLETS: *Broadcasting from T'unghsien*, by Rowland M. Cross and Adelle Tenney Cross, 1936; brochure on Fenchow Middle School, n.a., n.d.; brochure on the Fenchow Mission by the American Board of Commissioners for Foreign Missions, n.d.; *The City of Fenchow and Its Counties: Items from the Work of the North China Mission of the American Board in Fenchow for the Year 1915*, n.a., 1915; *Facing China's Need*, n.a., 1914; *Fenchow: 1886–1936* (picture brochure), n.a., 1936; *An Urgent Call from China's Great Northwest*, n.a., n.d.; *The Work of Fenchow Station*, n.a., 1917.

MEMORABILIA: Folder of newspaper clippings, ca. 1906–1947; postcard and 2 posters depicting the Fenchow mission, n.d.

ORAL HISTORIES: 78-page transcript of a 1980 Midwest China Center oral history interview describing Paul Clifford Domke's work with the Carleton-in-China program, ca. 1937; transcript of a 1964 oral history interview describing Percy and Clara Watson's work as medical missionaries with Carleton-in-China from 1909 to 1934.

MAPS/DESIGNS/DRAWINGS: Folder of blueprints and plans relating to Carleton-in-China and the Fenchow mission, n.d.

AUDIO-VISUAL MATERIALS: Folder of photos of Carleton-in-China representatives, middle-school students, and the Fenchow mission, ca. 1930–1935.

SERIALS: *The Carletonian-in-China*, n.d. *China Bulletin* (Boston), 1937–38, 1944–45. *China Colleges*, 1938, 1943. *Dragon Tracks*, 1945. *Fenchow*, 1920. *IRC News Bulletin*, 1942. *Shansi Bulletin*, 1936.

FINDING AIDS: In-house contents list to Carleton-in-China Collection; in-house contents list to Papers of the President's Office, 1909–62; in-house index to Carleton student newspaper and Carleton alumni publications.

MN–65   Carleton College Library
Northfield MN 55057
(507) 663–4267
Richard Miller, Associate Librarian

1-GENERAL HOLDINGS
SERIALS: *China Notes*, 1968-.

ST. OLAF COLLEGE

MN–70   Archives
Rölvaag Memorial Library
Northfield MN 55057
(507) 663–3229
Joan R. Olson, Archivist

1-LARS W. BOE PAPERS, 1932–34, 11 items
Background note: Lars W. Boe was president of St. Olaf College from 1918 to 1942.
MINUTES/RECORDS/REPORTS: Contract for the resettlement in Brazil of Lutheran refugees from Harbin, 1934.
CORRESPONDENCE: 8 letters from W. Ulmer, in German, concerning the Harbin refugees, 1932–33.
MEMORABILIA: 2 newspaper clippings, one in German and one in English, on the Harbin refugees, 1933–34.

2-O. G. FELLAND PAPERS, 1912–15, 8 items
Background note: For biographical notes on Elsa Felland Armstrong, see Bentley Historical Library, Michigan Historical Collections, 1150 Beal Avenue, Ann Arbor, MI, 48109–2113. For biographical notes on Agnes Kittelsby, see Norwegian-American Historical Association below.
CORRESPONDENCE: 6 letters to and from China missionary Elsa Felland Armstrong from friends and family, 1912; letter from Armstrong to her parents, ca. 1915; letter from Agnes Kittelsby in China to "Link," 1915.

3-CLEMENS GRANSKOU PAPERS, 1921–74, 9 folders
Background note: President of St. Olaf College from 1943 to 1963, Clemens M. Granskou served as a Lutheran missionary at Kwang-

shan and Kikungshan in Honan from 1921 to 1927. See also American Lutheran Church, Archives, 2481 Como Avenue, St. Paul, MN, 55108.
MINUTES/RECORDS/REPORTS: Granskou's financial accounts, 1923–36; records relating to Granskou's participation in the Midwest China Center's oral history project (see Oral Histories Collection below).
CORRESPONDENCE: 3 letters from Granskou to John Mohn in Northfield, 1921–26, discussing Granskou's language training, his experiences as a missionary, and the political situation in China; 2 folders of letters by Granskou on China missions, 1922–44, including letters to his parents.
MANUSCRIPTS: "Greatness and Opportunity" (history of China and its relationship with the West), by Clemens Granskou, ca. 1971; "The Missionary in China—Past, Present, and Future," by George H. Dunne, S.J., 1973.
PAMPHLETS: *Kikungshan: A Guide to the Friends of the Summer Resort* (description of Kikungshan), n.a., 1925.
MEMORABILIA: 4 newspaper clippings describing Granskou's mission work, 1921–26; folder of magazine and newspaper clippings of articles on China missions, 1921–74; folder of draft addresses and clippings of articles written by Granskou on China missions, 1921–70.
MAPS/DESIGNS/DRAWINGS: Map of Shanghai published by the Shanghai YMCA, 1926.
SERIALS: Lutheran World Federation, *Information Letter* (LWF Marxism and China Study), 1972–73.
CHINESE LANGUAGE MATERIALS: Letter from Granskou to a "Miss Li," n.d.; calling cards with Granskou's address and Chinese name, n.d.
FINDING AIDS: In-house inventory.

4-MINA JORDETH HELLESTAD PAPERS, 1918–56, 47 items
Background note: Mina Jordeth Nold Hellestad served as a Lutheran missionary in China from 1910 to 1924, and from 1933 to 1940. Her husband, Oscar Hellestad, served as a Lutheran missionary in China from 1908 to 1940.
CORRESPONDENCE: Photocopies of 42 letters to and from the Hellestads, 1918–61; letter in Norwegian from their son, Einar Hellestad, to his grandmother in the United States, 1918.
DIARIES: Photocopy of Mina Hellestad's diary, 1940.
MEMORABILIA: Photocopies of an obituary of Mina Hellestad, 1956, and of clippings describing her experiences in China, ca. 1905, 1931.
FINDING AIDS: In-house inventory.

5-ORAL HISTORIES COLLECTION, 1976–80, 20 items
Background note: These transcripts were prepared by the Midwest China Study Resource Center. For further information, see the American Lutheran Church, Archives, 2841 Como Avenue, St. Paul, MN, 55108.
ORAL HISTORIES: Transcripts of interviews with Herman Bly, Ruth Gilbertson, Clemens Granskou, Agnes Holstad Hyde, Clara Jones, Lillian Landahl, David Lee, Estelle Lee Martin, Cora Martinson, Frida Nilsen, Lillian Olson Nelson, Iola Aalbue Peterson, Alma Roisum, Frederik Schiotz, Mabel Wold Sihler, Arne Sovik, Edgar Sovik, Edward Sovik, Gertrude Sovik, Borghild Roe Syrdal, Rolf Syrdal, and Waldo Wold.

6-PHOTOGRAPH COLLECTION, 1922–25, 1 folder
AUDIO-VISUAL MATERIALS: Photos of Chinese Christians

and St. Olaf graduates who served in China as missionaries, including Clemens Granskou and Agnes Kittelsby, most undated, except for a series of photos of Granskou's parish in Kwanghsien, 1922–25.

7-GENERAL HOLDINGS
MANUSCRIPTS: "St. Olaf Prepares for China: The Student Volunteer Movement for Foreign Missions," by Martha Termaat, 1981.

MN–75 Norwegian-American Historical Association
St. Olaf College
Rölvaag Memorial Library
Northfield MN 55057
(507) 663-3451
Charlotte Jacobson, Archivist

1-AGNES KITTELSBY PAPERS, 1914–18, 163 items
Background note: A 1900 graduate of St. Olaf College, Agnes Kittelsby (1880–1925) served as teacher and principal of the American School in Kikungshan, Honan, from 1914 to 1925.
CORRESPONDENCE: 160 letters describing Kittelsby's work and daily life at Kikungshan, 1914–18.
MANUSCRIPTS: 3 biographical sketches of Kittelsby written after her death, n.a.
FINDING AIDS: In-house inventory.

MN–80 Rölvaag Memorial Library
St. Olaf College
Northfield MN 55057
(507) 663-3224
Forrest E. Brown, Director

1-GENERAL HOLDINGS
MINUTES/RECORDS/REPORTS: Lutheran Church of China, report of annual meeting, 1928; Lutheran Church of China, Committee on Youth Work, report, 1946–49; Union Lutheran Conference, Kikungshan, reports on the Union Lutheran Council and committees, 1919.
PAMPHLETS: *They Carry On: Past and Present Experiences, and Future Needs and Hopes of the Lutheran Free Church Mission in China*, by Frederick Ditmanson and Arthur S. Olson, 1944; *The United Norwegian Lutheran Mission Field in China: A Short Sketch with Illustrations and Map*, by Ingvald Daehlin and Erik Sovik, 1911.
SERIALS: *China Christian Year Book*, 1917, 1928. *China Gleanings*, 1936–38. *Directory of Protestant Missions in China*, 1917. *Gleanings*, 1935. *Monumenta Serica*, 1966-.
DISSERTATIONS/THESES: *American Lutheran Mission Work in China*, by Rolf A. Syrdal, 1942.

ROSEVILLE

NORTHWESTERN COLLEGE
MN–85 McAlister Library
3003 North Snelling Avenue
Roseville MN 55113
(612) 631-5100
Mary Lou Hovda, Acquisitions Librarian

1-GENERAL HOLDINGS
PAMPHLETS: *American Bible Society in China: The Story of Eighty-two Years' Work*, by John R. Hykes, 1915; *Indigenous Ideals in Practice: Evangelistic Policy and Work in the Siaochang Field in North China*, by William Francis Rowlands, 1931.

ST. JOSEPH

ST. BENEDICT'S CONVENT
MN–90 Archives
St. Joseph MN 56734
(612) 363-5104
Sister Imogene Blatz, O.S.B., Archivist

Restrictions: All correspondence between the prioress and the Benedictine missionaries is confidential.
Background note: Benedictine nuns from Minnesota did mission work in Peking from 1930 to 1935, and in Kaifeng from 1935 to 1948, when they transferred their mission to Taiwan. The Archives have seven boxes of materials generated by the mission on Taiwan in addition to the items described below.
Finding aids: "Inventory of the Records of the Foreign Missions: Record Group 27," comp. by Imogene Blatz, O.S.B., 1985.

1-RECORDS OF ST. BENEDICT'S MISSION OFFICE, 1932–75, ca. 2 boxes
Background note: St. Benedict's Mission Office was founded in 1929 to raise money for the sisters' China mission effort.
MINUTES/RECORDS/REPORTS: Questionnaires from groups and individuals gathering data on the sisters' mission activities, including memos, reports, and publicity materials, 1940–74; St. Benedict's Mission Office, fund-raising records, 1942–75.
CORRESPONDENCE: .25 in. of circular letters from the Mission Office directors, Hilaria Finske, O.S.B., and Cleone Burnett, O.S.B., regarding China mission work and fund-raising efforts, 1932–43, 1949, 1955.
MANUSCRIPTS: "Outreach: Other Lands, Other Shores" (excerpt from the sisters' "Priory Study" dealing with foreign missions), n.a., 1973.
PAMPHLETS: Fund-raising brochures for foreign missions, n.d.
MEMORABILIA: Materials relating to departure ceremonies and itineraries for departing missionaries, 1939, n.d.
FINDING AIDS: In-house guide.

2-RECORDS OF THE CHINA/TAIWAN, R.O.C. MISSIONS, 1929–77, .5 box
MINUTES/RECORDS/REPORTS: American Benedictine Sisters in China, articles of incorporation, 1939; Chinese Mission Fund, expenditures, receipts, reports, statements, and summaries, 1929–54; miscellaneous chronologies, summaries, and reports relating to the sisters' China mission, 1929–75.
CORRESPONDENCE: .5 in. of letters between the prioress and Thomas Rice regarding the founding of a Chinese Benedictine community, 1945–48; letters from Lucy Chung, a student at the College of St. Benedict, concerning her life and problems after her return to Peking, 1932–40.
MEMORABILIA: .25 in. of clippings from Minneapolis, St. Cloud, and St. Paul newspapers, and from the *St. Procopius Abbey News Quarterly*, concerning the sisters' China mission, 1930–77.

3-RECORDS OF THE KAIFENG MISSION, 1935-70, 2.5 boxes
MINUTES/RECORDS/REPORTS: Agreement between St. Procopius Abbey and the Kaifeng Mission for the use of property in Kaifeng, 1941; Kaifeng Mission, annual lists of sisters, a chit book, and financial records, 1935-49; Office of the Prioress, government issuances, newsletters, and reports concerning the Benedictine mission in Kaifeng, 1933-48; Sisters of the Order of St. Benedict, claim forms, financial reports, instructions for filing claims, lists of property confiscated by the Japanese, notices, and proposed decisions on claims by the U.S. Foreign Claims Settlement Commission, 1935-71; Sisters of the Order of St. Benedict, affidavits, claim forms, English translations of deeds, instructions for filing claims, notices, and testimony regarding property claims against the Chinese Communists submitted to the U.S. Foreign Claims Settlement Commission, 1964-70.

CORRESPONDENCE: 2.5 in. of the prioress' correspondence, 1933-48, with Benedictine priests in Kaifeng, superiors of religious communities, and officials of the American Red Cross, Armed Services Forces, International Relief Committee, and National Catholic Welfare Conference concerning the transfer of the Benedictine mission from Peking to Kaifeng and the experiences of the sisters in Kaifeng during World War II; .25 in. of the prioress' correspondence with Joseph Tacconi (Vicar Apostolic in Kaifeng), 1933-39, concerning the transfer of the Benedictine mission from Peking to Kaifeng; .25 in. of letters written in response to the prioress' call for volunteers for the Kaifeng mission, 1937; 5 in. of letters to the prioress from missionaries in Kaifeng, 1935-48, including Vestina Bursken, O.S.B., Ronayne Gergen, O.S.B., Flora Goebel, O.S.B., Rachel Loulan, O.S.B., Wibora Muehlenbein, O.S.B., Mariette Pitz, O.S.B., Felicia Stager, O.S.B., Ursuline Venne, O.S.B., Francetta Vetter, O.S.B., Annelda Wahl, O.S.B., and Regia Zens, O.S.B., describing the establishment of the mission there, their experiences during World War II, their internment by the Japanese and subsequent repatriation, post-war rehabilitation of the mission, and the sisters' withdrawal to Shanghai during the Chinese civil war.

MEMORABILIA: Clippings from St. Cloud and St. Paul newspapers, 1936-47, describing the departure of missionaries for China, work of the mission in Kaifeng, the sisters' experiences during World War II, and the repatriation of Sr. Flora Goebel.

MAPS/DESIGNS/DRAWINGS: Maps submitted with property claims against the Chinese Communists, 1964-70.

AUDIO-VISUAL MATERIALS: 184 photos of the missionaries in catechetical work and work with dispensary patients, wounded soldiers, refugees, and children, as well as of the funeral of Rachel Loulan, O.S.B., and Kaifeng, 1935-41; photos and glass plates of buildings and properties belonging to the Kaifeng Mission, 1938-40; photos of buildings submitted with property claims against the Chinese Communists, 1964-70.

CHINESE LANGUAGE MATERIALS: Correspondence and miscellaneous documents concerning the sisters' damage claims against the Japanese, 1935-71; deeds and related materials concerning the mission's property in Kaifeng, 1938-40; photostatic copies of deeds submitted with property claims against the Chinese Communists, 1964-70.

4-RECORDS OF THE PEKING MISSION, 1929-35, 2 boxes
MINUTES/RECORDS/REPORTS: Peking Mission, chronicles, contracts, financial reports, and telegrams concerning the Women's College at Catholic University of Peking, 1929-35.

CORRESPONDENCE: 3 in. of letters concerning the Women's College at Catholic University of Peking between the prioress and such correspondents as Oswald Baker, O.S.B., Ildephonse Brandstetter, O.S.B., Bishop Joseph T. Busch, Terence Carroll, O.S.B., Francis Clougherty, O.S.B. (Apostolic Delegate in Peking), Celso Constantini (Apostolic Delegate to China), Alcuin Deutsch, O.S.B., Sylvester Healey, O.S.B., Carl P. Hensler, Boniface Martin, O.S.B., G. M. O'Toole, Basil Stegmann, O.S.B., Archabbot Aurelius Stehle, O.S.B., and Archbishop Samuel A. Stritch, 1929-35; 4 in. of letters to the prioress and other sisters from China missionaries, including Ronayne Gergen, O.S.B., Rachel Loulan, O.S.B., Wibora Muehlenbein, O.S.B., Donalda Terhaar, O.S.B., Francetta Vetter, O.S.B., and Regia Zens, O.S.B., 1930-35; .75 in. of letters to the prioress in response to her call for volunteers for the China mission, 1929.

AUDIO-VISUAL MATERIALS: 145 photos of Catholic University of Peking, Fu Jen Girls' Middle School and its students, missionaries, and people and buildings in Peking, 1930-35.

SERIALS: Catholic University of Peking, *Bulletin*, 1928, 1930. *Fu-Jen Magazine*, 1932-34. *Fu Jen News Letter*, 1931-32. *Peiping Mission Notes*, 1929-33. *Peking: News and Views of China*, 1931.

5-GENERAL HOLDINGS
MANUSCRIPTS: "Memoirs: A History of the Years Spent on the Chinese Mainland, the Transfer to Taiwan, and the Providential Beginning of Our Work in Japan," by Wibora Muehlenbein, O.S.B., 1962; "Our Apostolate in China and Taiwan," by Wibora Muehlenbein, O.S.B., 1968.

PAMPHLETS: *Benedictine Mission to China*, by Wibora Muehlenbein, O.S.B., 1980.

AUDIO-VISUAL MATERIALS: 4 photos of concentration camps, n.d.

ST. PAUL

AMERICAN LUTHERAN CHURCH
MN-95   Archives
2481 Como Avenue
St. Paul MN 55108
(612) 641-3205
Paul A. Daniels, Archivist, Luther Northwestern Theological Seminary, and Assistant Archivist, American Lutheran Church

Background note: In addition to the collections listed below, the American Lutheran Church Archives maintain biographical files on Norwegian-Americans who served as missionaries in China from 1889 to 1953, including Mr. and Mrs. Nels J. Aadland, Anna K. (Nilson) Aarkvisla, Mr. and Mrs. Albert Anderson, Marie Anderson, Mr. and Mrs. Palmer I. Anderson, Dr. and Mrs. Robert A. Anderson, Elsa Felland Armstrong, Mr. and Mrs. Oluf Asper, Dr. and Mrs. Olaf S. Behrents, Mr. and Mrs. Herman W. Bly, Mr. and Mrs. John M. Bly, E. O. Bøen, Mr. and Mrs. Einar Borg-Breen, Dr. Ragnhild Bottner, Anna Olsen Braafladt (Mrs. Louis Braafladt), Louis H. Braafladt, Frances Moore Braafladt (Mrs. Louis Braafladt), Mr. and Mrs. Olaf F. Braaten, Elma B. Carlson, Olive T. Christensen, Emma C. Hasle Daehlin (Mrs. Ingvald

Daehlin), Ingvald Daehlin, Nikoline Dahl Daehlin (Mrs. Ingvald Daehlin), Reidar A. Daehlin, Dr. and Mrs. O. E. Distad, Inga Dvergsness, Bertha M. (Gursli) Ege, Birgit Lappegaard Ekeland (Mrs. Tønnes Ekeland), Gudrid Lundebyy Ekeland (Mrs. Tønnes Ekeland), Tønnes Ekeland, Dr. and Mrs. Odd Eckfelt, Mathilda Elstad, Bergliot Evenson, Mr. and Mrs. H. S. Fauske, Dr. and Mrs. G. Nathanael Fedde, Marie Fugleskjel, Mr. and Mrs. Clemens Granskou, Mr. and Mrs. John E. Grønli, Lillian Groh, Mr. and Mrs. John B. S. Grindvik, Mr. and Mrs. J. M. O. Gudal, Mr. and Mrs. August W. Haugan, Mr. and Mrs. E. M. Hegge, Oscar O. Hellestad, Mina Jordeth Nold Hellestad, Otto Hesla, Alma Carlson Himle (Mrs. Thorstein Himle), Gidske Sigmundstad Himle (Mrs. Thorstein Himle), Thorstein Himle, Mina Hjeldness, Olive Hodnefield, Mr. and Mrs. George O. Holm, Lincoln Holman, Nellie Pederson Holman, Agnes Holstad, Mr. and Mrs. Lars Hompland, Berthina Horvik, Dr. and Mrs. J. M. J. Hotvedt, Mr. and Mrs. Irwin O. Jacobson, Christine L. Johnson, Agnes M. Kittelsby, Mr. and Mrs. Samson S. Klyve, Clara Kravig, Mr. and Mrs. Lyder S. J. Kristensen, Martha Kulberg, Alice Holmberg Landahl (Mrs. Carl Landahl), Carl W. Landahl, Lillian C. Landahl, Margaret C. Landahl, Thea Ronning Landahl (Mrs. Carl Landahl), Mr. and Mrs. N. Astrup Larsen, Sophie Malmin Larson, Mr. and Mrs. Thomas I. Lee, George O. Lillegaard, Mr. and Mrs. Karl A. O. Lillebergen, Mr. and Mrs. Andrew Martinson, Mr. and Mrs. Harold H. Martinson, Flora Moe, Bergitha L. Nelsen, Mr. and Mrs. Bert Nelson, Mr. and Mrs. Daniel Nelson, Sr., Mr. and Mrs. Daniel Nelson, Jr., Mary Nelson, Mr. and Mrs. Hans M. Nesse, Ole S. Nestegaard, Bertine Erickson Netland (Mrs. Sigvald Netland), Oline Hermanson Netland (Mrs. Sigvald Netland), Sigvald Netland, Frida Nilsen, Carrie Olson, Ingeborg Pederson, Clara Peterson, Therese Peterson, Hilda Petterson, Arna J. Quello, Ingeberg Richardson, Mr. and Mrs. Chester Ronning, Mr. and Mrs. Halvor N. Ronning, Mr. and Mrs. Talbert R. Ronning, Nora A. Rosvold, Aase Hagestande Rude, Thone Sandland, Lydia Kristensen Siqueland, Mr. and Mrs. John Skepstad, Dr. and Mrs. Casper C. Skinsnes, E. Grace Soderberg, Mr. and Mrs. Christian Stokstad, Mr. and Mrs. Gynther Storaasli, Helen Weeks Storvick, Mr. and Mrs. Edward Sovik, Mr. and Mrs. Erik Sovik, Mr. and Mrs. Knut S. Stokke, Mr. and Mrs. Rolf A. Syrdal, Mr. and Mrs. Joseph Tetlie, Agnes Thonstad, Mr. and Mrs. H. J. Thorpe, Mr. and Mrs. Peter E. Thorson, Marie Tjomsaas, Mr. and Mrs. Gustav Trygstad, Mr. and Mrs. Kristofer N. Tvedt, Therese Sheldahl Wee, Anna L. Wold (Mrs. Oscar Wold), Clara Simonson Wold (Mrs. Oscar Wold), Oscar R. Wold, and Sarah A. Xavier.

Scattered references to China missions can be found in the periodicals of the Synod for the Norwegian Evangelical Lutheran Church in America—*Lutheran Herald* (1906–17) and *Lutherske Kirketidende* (1911–17) and in the synod's annual reports (1913–16).

The oral histories described below were compiled by the Midwest China Study Resource Center (now the Midwest China Center) between 1976 and 1980. The original tapes and written transcripts of the oral history interviews are held by the American Lutheran Church Archives. Access to these materials is through the Archives.

Finding aids: *Oral History Summaries: A Guide to the Collection*, by Kurt Eric Johnson (St. Paul, MN: Midwest China Center), 1983.

1-ETHEL M. AKINS INTERVIEWS, 1976, 1 item
ORAL HISTORIES: 154-page transcript of interviews with Ethel M. Akins describing her experiences as an Augustana Synod missionary in Honan and Chungking, her memories of Feng Yü-hsiang and Sun Yat-sen, the establishment of Christian schools in Honan and Chungking, famine in 1942, and the Communist takeover of Hsuchang, Honan, in 1947.

2-ALICE K. ANDERSON INTERVIEWS, 1977, 1 item
ORAL HISTORIES: 78-page transcript of interviews describing Alice K. Anderson's experiences as a teacher at the American School-Kikungshan and at the Loyang Bible School, the journey from Loyang to Chengtu to escape the Japanese, famine relief work, and her views on the role of the missionaries in the 1940s.

3-CLARA ANDERSON INTERVIEW, 1979, 1 item
ORAL HISTORIES: 78-page transcript of an interview describing Clara Anderson's childhood in the Hauge Lutheran Mission compound in Fancheng (ca. 1916), and her return trip to China in 1923.

4-COLENA M. ANDERSON INTERVIEW, 1977, 1 item
ORAL HISTORIES: 57-page transcript of an interview describing Colena M. Anderson's work at the Shanghai American School and the University of Shanghai, the Nationalist takeover of Shanghai in 1927, the Shanghai Volunteer Corps, and her views on missionary leadership.

5-VIOLA ANDERSON INTERVIEWS, 1978, 1 item
ORAL HISTORIES: 84-page transcript of interviews discussing Viola Anderson's journeys to China in 1913 and 1923, her work in Fancheng as a Hauge Lutheran Synod missionary, the language school at the University of Nanking, her husband's work as headmaster of the Hauge Academy in Fancheng, anti-foreignism, and Norwegian missionaries in Laohokow, 1913–27.

6-ROBERT BALL INTERVIEW, 1978, 1 item
ORAL HISTORIES: 84-page transcript of an interview with Robert Ball describing his experiences as a Marine stationed in China and his encounters with Marist Brothers in Tientsin, ca. 1945.

7-KAY HAINES BEACH INTERVIEW, 1977, 1 item
ORAL HISTORIES: 40-page transcript of an interview describing Kay Beach's work with the Chinese Nationalist Relief and Rehabilitation Administration, ca. 1946.

8-HERMAN BLY INTERVIEWS, 1977, 1 item
ORAL HISTORIES: 128-page transcript of interviews with Herman Bly describing his work as a missionary of the Evangelical Lutheran Church in Kwangchow, Kaifeng, and Chengyang; efforts to raise ransom for kidnapped missionaries; relations between the Kuomintang and the Communists in the Kwangchow area; postwar Lutheran mission work in Honan; and Bly's journey out of China, 1926–46.

9-CARRIE McMULLEN BRIGHT INTERVIEW, 1976, 1 item
ORAL HISTORIES: 38-page transcript of an interview describing Carrie Bright's childhood among Southern Presbyterian missionaries in Hangchow and her education at the Shanghai American School, ca. 1913.

10-HEINZ BRUHL INTERVIEW, 1977, 1 item
ORAL HISTORIES: 76-page transcript of an interview describing Heinz Bruhl's work as a private physician in Hankow, his views on

mission hospitals and Chinese medicine, and the Hankow Rotary Club.

11-ERNEST CAHA INTERVIEW, 1977, 1 item
ORAL HISTORIES: 58-page transcript of an interview describing Ernest Caha's experiences in China as a naval officer and his work in helping to establish a YMCA hospital in Shanghai in 1912.

12-EMERY AND ELVERA TEED CARLSON NARRATIVE, 1978, 1 item
MANUSCRIPTS: 42-page narrative by Emery and Elvera Carlson discussing their work as Lutheran medical missionaries in Hsuchang, Chungking, and Kunming; famine in the early 1940s; and their experiences during the Sino-Japanese War.

13-H. MEAD CAVERT INTERVIEWS, 1979, 1 item
ORAL HISTORIES: 118-page transcript of interviews describing H. Mead Cavert's experiences as an Air Force serviceman in China from 1943 to 1945, YMCA work in Kunming, and a Maryknoll mission compound in Fukien.

14-CHANG YAU-WEH AND LAM YING INTERVIEW, 1977, 1 item
ORAL HISTORIES: 40-page transcript of an interview with Chang Yau-weh and Lam Ying discussing their conversion to Christianity, mission work in mainland China, and the Lutheran Church in Hong Kong.

15-BENEDICTUS CHAO INTERVIEW, 1977, 1 item
ORAL HISTORIES: 40-page transcript of an interview describing Benedictus Chao's experiences as a Trappist monk in China, relations with the Communists before and after World War II, and the Trappists' evacuation of China in 1949.

16-CHEUNG HIN-YAU INTERVIEW, 1977, 1 item
ORAL HISTORIES: 53-page transcript of an interview with Cheung Hin-yau discussing the arrest of his father, a Chinese Christian, by the Communists in 1957; his release from imprisonment in 1979, and the younger Cheung's views on mission work in China.

17-IVY CHOU INTERVIEW, 1976, 1 item
ORAL HISTORIES: 81-page transcript of an interview with Ivy Chou discussing her father's work in Christian education and giving her views on "rice" Christians, comparison of Marxism and Christianity, mission schools, and women as pastors.

18-LEILA PARTRIDGE CHRISTIANSON INTERVIEW, 1980, 1 item
ORAL HISTORIES: 94-page transcript of an interview describing Leila Partridge Christianson's work with the China Inland Mission in western Yunnan; the effects of the Japanese and the Communists on mission work; her memories of Shanghai, wartime Chungking, and post-war Lungling; and the medical risks of mission work.

19-DANIEL CHU INTERVIEW, 1979, 1 item
ORAL HISTORIES: 81-page transcript of an interview with Daniel Chu discussing his student days at Yale-in-China and Lutheran Theological Seminary in Shekow, his father's work as president of the Lutheran Church of China from 1932 to 1938, the elder Chu's imprisonment in 1927, anti-Christian sentiment, and Lutheran work in Chungking during World War II.

20-DOUGLAS CLIFFORD INTERVIEW, 1977, 1 item
ORAL HISTORIES: 74-page transcript of an interview with Douglas Clifford describing his work with the Friends Ambulance Unit in the late 1940s, his views on the Nationalist and Communist leaders during that period, and the rehabilitation of Hwa Mei Hospital in Chengchow.

21-ROWLAND CROSS INTERVIEW, 1977, 1 item
Background note: For biographical notes, see Hoover Institution, Archives, Stanford University, Stanford, CA, 94305–2323. See also Claremont Colleges, Honnold Library, Claremont, CA, 91711.
ORAL HISTORIES: 75-page transcript of interviews with Rowland Cross giving reminiscences on his work with the North China Mission, biographical information on prominent Chinese Christians, and his views on Y. T. Wu and the origins of the Three-Self Movement.

22-HELEN DEPASS DAHLIN INTERVIEW, 1977, 1 item
ORAL HISTORIES: 32-page transcript of an interview with Helen Depass Dahlin describing housing and education in Peking and Tientsin, and the relations between the foreign military, business, and missionary communities.

23-EARL DAHLSTROM INTERVIEW, 1977, 1 item
ORAL HISTORIES: 55-page transcript of an interview describing Earl Dahlstrom's work with the American School in Kikungshan during the 1940s, his opinions on Marcus Cheng, the work of the Covenant Missionary Society in China, the decision of the Covenant Mission Board to turn over control of the church to Chinese, and conditions in post-war China.

24-MORRIS BARNETT DEPASS INTERVIEW, 1976, 1 item
ORAL HISTORIES: 47-page transcript of an interview with former U.S. Army officer Morris Depass describing his experiences in China and giving his impressions of China missionaries, ca. 1923.

25-JACK DODDS INTERVIEW, 1977, 1 item
ORAL HISTORIES: 82-page transcript of an interview describing Jack Dodds' work with the Friends Ambulance Unit in Yenan during the 1940s, land reform in Communist areas, and his views on the Nationalists and the Communists.

26-PAUL CLIFFORD DOMKE INTERVIEW, 1977, 1 item
Background note: For biographical notes, see Hoover Institution, Archives, Stanford University, Stanford, CA, 94305.
ORAL HISTORIES: 78-page transcript of an interview describing Paul Domke's work with the Carleton-in-China program, ca. 1937; travels in Shansi, Shensi, and Peking; and the Carleton-in-China school in Fenchow.

27-ASTRID ERLING INTERVIEWS, 1978, 1 item
ORAL HISTORIES: 74-page transcript of interviews describing Astrid Erling's work as a medical missionary in Loyang, Chungking, and Kunming in the 1930s and 1940s; the revival movement of the 1930s; the Communist takeover of Loyang; and her views on the role of the single woman missionary.

28-DILLARD MARION EUBANK INTERVIEW, 1980, 1 item
ORAL HISTORIES: 70-page transcript of an interview describing Dillard Eubank's childhood in Huchow, his memories of the Boxer uprising, and the Shanghai American School (ca. 1900).

**29-EVANGELICAL LUTHERAN CHURCH/NORWEGIAN LUTH-
ERAN CHURCH OF AMERICA PAPERS, 1917–60, 4 volumes,
3 Hollinger boxes**

Background note: Scattered references to China missions can be
found in the minutes (1917–60), annual reports (1917–60), and
yearbooks (1936–44) of this denomination's Board of Foreign Missions, as well as in the periodicals *Lutheran Church Herald* (1917–
30), *Lutheran Herald* (1931–60; individual volumes indexed after
1939), and *Lutheraneren* (1917–56). There are also eight Hollinger boxes of materials concerning missions in Taiwan and Hong
Kong after 1953, as well as 1.5 linear feet of Evangelical Lutheran
Church mission correspondence to the Lutheran World Federation
regarding Taiwan and Hong Kong, 1954–56.
MINUTES/RECORDS/REPORTS: Lutheran Church of China,
reports, 1920–37; Lutheran Mission, property deeds in China,
1926–38; Lutheran Theological Seminary of China, reports,
1913–40; Lutheran United Mission, reports, 1921–40, 1947–48;
Missionary Home and Agency/Lutheran Board of Publications,
annual reports, 1921–24, 1933, 1936–38.
FINDING AIDS: Card file indexes for *Lutheran Herald* (1931–38)
and *Lutheraneren* (1927–30).

30-VIOLA I. FISCHER INTERVIEW, 1978, 1 item
ORAL HISTORIES: 77-page transcript of an interview describing
Viola Fischer's as a medical missionary in Hsuchang in the 1930s
and 1940s, and her views on the role of single women missionaries
in China.

**31-FOREIGN MISSION FIELDS COLLECTION (RG 9), 1917–49,
174 items**
Background note: In addition to the materials described below, this
collection contains ca. 100 works in Chinese, published in Taiwan
and Hong Kong after 1953.
CHINESE LANGUAGE MATERIALS: 174 books and pamphlets
(mostly in Mandarin script, with a few written in phonetic symbols), 1917–49, including works on the Augsburg Confession,
baptism, biblical studies, Christian apologetics, Christianity and
science, church history, evangelism, the 1932 constitution of the
Hsin I Hui (Lutheran Church of China), hymns, Martin Luther,
O. R. Wold, liturgy, the Lord's Supper, Luther's Catechism, Lutheran Church of China constitution, the Lutheran Youth Conference
at Kikungshan in 1947, the Reformation, religious education,
prayer, sermons, and theology.

32-JANE ARMOUR FOSTER INTERVIEW, 1977, 1 item
ORAL HISTORIES: 66-page transcript of an interview describing
Jane Foster's experiences in China in the 1930s and 1940s as the
wife of Episcopalian missionary John Foster and conditions at the
College of Chinese Studies.

33-JOHN FOSTER INTERVIEW, 1977, 1 item
Background note: For biographical notes, see Minnesota Historical
Society, Division of Archives and Manuscripts, 1500 Mississippi
Street, St. Paul, MN, 55101.
ORAL HISTORIES: 82-page transcript of an interview describing
John Burt Foster's work as a teacher at Boone College in Wuchang,
his role in Agnes Smedley's relief mission to the Eighth Route
Army in 1938, his reminiscences about Feng Yü-hsiang, and his
post-war work with the United States Information Agency in Han-
kow.

34-EMELINE FRANK INTERVIEW, 1979, 1 item
ORAL HISTORIES: 68-page transcript of an interview with Eme-
line Frank discussing evangelical work in China, conditions in
Kweichow, the Japanese bombing of Yuanling, her reminiscences
about Robert McClure, and her experiences raising a family in
China.

35-HENRY S. FRANK INTERVIEW, 1979, 1 item
ORAL HISTORIES: 63-page transcript of an interview describing
Henry Frank's work as a teacher in Lingnan University; civil
unrest in Canton in 1925; the campus, students, faculty, and trustees of Lingnan University; and financial support for mission work
in China.

36-HERBERT S. FRANK INTERVIEW, 1979, 1 item
ORAL HISTORIES: 66-page transcript of an interview describing
Herbert Frank's work as an Evangelical Brethren missionary in
Kweichow (ca. 1918), famine relief work, the problem of explain-
ing Christianity to the Chinese, and his journey out of China.

37-H. DANIEL FRIBERG INTERVIEW, 1979, 1 item
ORAL HISTORIES: 72-page transcript of an interview describing
H. Daniel Friberg's childhood in the mission compound at Loyang,
ca. 1908, his father's work as a medical missionary, his education
at the American School-Kikungshan, and his return to China to
work as an evangelist in Yuhsien from 1936 to 1941.

38-JOSEPH BERTIL FRIBERG INTERVIEWS, 1977, 1 item
ORAL HISTORIES: 86-page transcript of interviews with Joseph
Friberg discussing his father's work as a medical missionary in
Honan, ca. 1906, his childhood in Honan, ca. 1915, his education
at the American School-Kikungshan, and his return to China in
1976, including comments on Christianity in the People's Republic
of China.

39-ANNE EDWARDS FULTON INTERVIEW, 1979, 1 item
Background note: See also the Dwight Edwards Papers at Yale
Divinity School, Special Collections, 409 Prospect Street, New
Haven, CT, 06510.
ORAL HISTORIES: 120-page transcript of an interview describ-
ing Anne Fulton's childhood in China during the 1920s, her educa-
tion at the Peking American School, church services at Peking
Union Church, and departure from China after the Communist
takeover.

40-ROBERT BRANK FULTON INTERVIEWS, 1979, 1 item
Background note: See also the Records of the Yale-in-China Association collection at Yale University, Department of Manuscripts
and Archives, Sterling Memorial Library, 120 High Street, New
Haven, CT, 06520.
ORAL HISTORIES: 120-page transcript of interviews describing
Robert Fulton's work as a teacher with Yale-in-China during the
1940s, his teaching activities at Huachung and Yenching universities, his impressions of Sherwood Eddy and John Leighton Stuart,
his views on Christianity and Chinese modernization, and his departure from China in 1950.

41-ARIE GAALSWYK INTERVIEW, 1977, 1 item
ORAL HISTORIES: 55-page transcript of an interview with former U.S. Army officer Arie Gaalswyk describing his military
service in China during World War II and his contacts with China
missionaries.

42-RUTH GILBERTSON INTERVIEWS, 1978, 1 item
ORAL HISTORIES: 139-page transcript of interviews describing Ruth Gilbertson's experiences as a Lutheran educational missionary from 1919 to the 1940s, her work as a teacher at the American School-Kikungshan, her memories of Chiang K'ai-shek and Feng Yü-hsiang, and her internment by the Japanese during World War II.

43-CLEMENS GRANSKOU INTERVIEWS, 1976, 1 item
Background note: For biographical notes, see St. Olaf College, Archives, Rölvaag Memorial Library, Northfield, MN, 55057.
ORAL HISTORIES: 149-page transcript of interviews describing Clemens Granskou's experiences as a Lutheran missionary in China during the 1920s, his work at the American School-Kikungshan, his memories of Chiang K'ai-shek and Feng Yü-hsiang, his encounters with bandits and Nationalist troops, and his views on the impact of China missions on Christianity in America.

44-ELLA ODLAND GRANSKOU INTERVIEWS, 1977, 1 item
Background note: See Clemens Granskou Interviews above.
ORAL HISTORIES: 34-page transcript of interviews describing Ella Granskou's experiences as the wife of China missionary Clemens Granskou; her memories of Peking Language School, Kikungshan, Kwangshan, and Sinyang; the slaying of China missionary Bernard Hoff by bandits; and her journey out of China in 1927.

45-ANDERS B. HANSON INTERVIEWS, 1977, 1 item
ORAL HISTORIES: 105-page transcript of interviews describing Anders Hanson's experiences in Honan as the child of China missionaries, ca. 1917; his education at the American School-Kikungshan; post-war mission work in Honan and Kunming, 1946; and his expulsion from Honan by the Communists.

46-CONSTANCE TWEDT HANSON INTERVIEW, 1977, 1 item
ORAL HISTORIES: 77-page transcript of an interview describing Constance Hanson's work as a Lutheran medical missionary in Kioshan, Shanghai, Sinyang Nanking, and Kunming from 1945 to 1948; her memories of China missionary Daniel Nelson; and her evacuation to Hong Kong in 1948.

47-ORVIS HANSON INTERVIEW, 1976, 1 item
ORAL HISTORIES: 58-page transcript of an interview describing Orvis Hanson's work as a Lutheran educational missionary in China from 1947 to 1949, his experiences as principal of the American School-Kikungshan from 1948 to 1949, and his suggestions for church policies toward the People's Republic of China, and his views on anti-communist sentiment among missionaries.

48-HAUGE'S NORWEGIAN EVANGELICAL LUTHERAN SYNOD PAPERS, 1868–1917 ca. 100 items
Background note: Scattered references to Hauge's Synod mission activity in China can be found in the periodical *Budbaereren* (1868–1917) and a scrapbook entitled "The Mission Dove of Hauge's Synod, 1901–1917," compiled by the Women's Missionary Historical Department, Norwegian Lutheran Church of America, 1932.
MINUTES/RECORDS/REPORTS: China Mission Society and China Mission Board, minutes, 1894–1916; Director for China Missions, reports (part of Synod annual reports), 1875–87, 1889–1916; Norwegian Evangelical Lutheran China Mission Society in America, minutes and financial statements, 1893–1903; Norwegian Lutheran China Mission Society in America, minutes of the Board of Directors, 1893–1916.

49-HELEN HAYES INTERVIEW, 1977, 1 item
ORAL HISTORIES: 118-page transcript of interviews describing Helen Hayes' work as a Methodist missionary in Anhwei in the 1920s and 1930s, her experiences raising a daughter in China, civil unrest in China during her stay there, relief work, her work with Chinese Bible women, and her views on the People's Republic of China.

50-PAUL G. HAYES INTERVIEWS, 1977, 1 item
ORAL HISTORIES: 81-page transcript of interviews with Methodist missionary Paul Hayes, the husband of Helen Hayes, in which he describes his work as district superintendent and secretary in Anhwei, gives his views on fundamentalist and liberal approaches to mission work, and speculates on the future of mission work in China.

51-CATHERINE REYNOLDS HERTZ INTERVIEW, 1980, 1 item
ORAL HISTORIES: 44-page transcript of an interview describing Catherine Hertz's work in Fenchow as an American Board missionary, her departure from China in 1927, and the social relationships between Chinese and missionaries in Fenchow.

52-EDWIN HERTZ INTERVIEW, 1980, 1 item
ORAL HISTORIES: 56-page transcript of an interview describing Edwin Hertz's work as a teacher in the Carleton-in-China program and the response of the Chinese students in the program to Westerners, nationalism, and Christianity.

53-ELIZABETH HUGHES INTERVIEW, 1977, 1 item
ORAL HISTORIES: 82-page transcript of an interview describing Elizabeth Hughes' experiences with the Friends' Ambulance Unit in China from 1945 to 1948, conditions at Kutsing Hospital in Honan, and impressions from a stay at International Peace Hospital in Yenan, 1946.

54-AGNES HOLSTAD HYDE INTERVIEW, 1977, 1 item
ORAL HISTORIES: 34-page transcript of an interview describing Lutheran missionary Agnes Hyde's work at the American School-Kikungshan.

55-ANNA MOFFET JARVIS INTERVIEWS, 1977, 1 item
Background note: For biographical notes, see University of Oregon, Special Collections, Eugene, OR, 97403–1299.
ORAL HISTORIES: 157-page transcript of interviews describing Anna Jarvis' experiences as a Presbyterian missionary in China, ca. 1920–1950; her work as secretary-treasurer of the Presbyterian Mission in Nanking; the establishment of the Church of Christ in China, 1923; her views on liberalism and fundamentalism in Presbyterian theology; her memories of Pearl Buck's family; her evacuation to Hankow in 1937; her arrest by the Japanese after Pearl Harbor; the response of the church to Communism, 1946–48; and her views on the indigenization of the Chinese church and the future of Christianity in China.

56-CLARA JONES INTERVIEW, 1976, 1 item
ORAL HISTORIES: 124-page transcript of an interview describing Clara Jones' experiences as a Lutheran missionary in China, her culture shock after her arrival, the impact of World War II on Lutheran missions in China, missionaries' standard of living compared to the Chinese, the problems facing Chinese Christians, the

impact of China mission work on America, and her views of the future of China missions.

57-WALTER JUDD INTERVIEW, 1978, 1 item
ORAL HISTORIES: 127-page transcript of an interview describing Walter Judd's work as an American Board missionary in China, his observations on politics in China in the late 1920s, anti-foreignism and banditry, efforts to save the American Board hospital in Fenchow from bankruptcy in 1933, the Japanese occupation of China in the 1930s, and readjustment to American life after his return.

58-ALICE HOLMBERG LANDAHL LETTERS, 1899–1937, 1 l.f.
Background note: Alice Landahl (1879–1961) and her husband, Carl W. Landahl, were Hauge Synod missionaries in China from 1895 to 1936.
CORRESPONDENCE: Letters of Alice Landahl, 1899–1937 (originals in Norwegian, most of which have been translated).

59-LILLIAN LANDAHL INTERVIEW, 1978, 1 item
ORAL HISTORIES: 109-page transcript of an interview with Lillian Landahl describing the mission work of her father, Carl Landahl, in China, 1895–1936; her education at the American School-Kikungshan; mission stations at Taipingtien and Fancheng; the founding of the Lutheran seminary at Shekow; the mass baptism of Feng Yü-hsiang's soldiers; her work as a teacher at the American School-Kikungshan, ca. 1931; the evacuation of the school in 1938; and a return trip to China in 1946.

60-THYRA LAWSON INTERVIEWS, 1977, 1 item
ORAL HISTORIES: 87-page transcript of interviews describing Thyra Lawson's work as an Augustana Lutheran Synod missionary in Kiahsien and Loyang (ca. 1924), famine relief efforts, problems confronting Chinese Christians, mission work among Chinese Moslems, and her encounters with Communists after World War II.

61-THOMAS LEE PAPERS, 1947–61, 3 l.f.
Background note: Thomas Lee (1895–1980) was a Lutheran missionary in Honan from 1924 to 1949, and in Hong Kong from 1949 to 1953. Among his papers were a number of Chinese-language periodicals, which are listed among the Archives' GENERAL HOLDINGS
CORRESPONDENCE: Circular letters by Thomas Lee, 1947–58, discussing schools, hospitals, missionaries, the Enlarged Council of the Lutheran Church in China (1951), the Peking Christian Conference (1951), and his opposition to the Three-Self Movement; letters by Lee, 1953–61, discussing his opposition to the Three-Self Movement.

62-BEATRICE EXNER LIU INTERVIEW, 1977, 1 item
ORAL HISTORIES: 112-page transcript of an interview describing Beatrice Liu's experiences as an English teacher in Tientsin and Chungking in the 1930s, and her work with the International Relief Committee.

63-LUTHERAN FREE CHURCH PAPERS, 1911–63, ca. 2 Hollinger boxes
Background note: Scattered references to China missions can be found in the budgets, minutes, records, annual reports, and correspondence of the Lutheran Board of Missions (1911–62), and in the periodicals *Folkebladet* (1927–52) and *Lutheran Messenger*

(1948–50, 1954–63). There is also a box of materials relating to missions in Taiwan and Hong Kong after 1953.
MINUTES/RECORDS/REPORTS: Lutheran Board of Missions, property deeds and financial reports from China, n.d.; Lutheran Board of Missions, property deeds from Honan, n.d.
MAPS/DESIGNS/DRAWINGS: 7 maps of China and Lutheran mission fields in China, n.d.
CHINESE LANGUAGE MATERIALS: *A Record of Church Members in the Suichow District, 1918–1948*, 1948; 23 photostatic copies of deeds and other official documents, n.d.

64-NATHAN MA INTERVIEW, 1977, 1 item
ORAL HISTORIES: 62-page transcript of an interview with Nathan Ma discussing the work of his father, a Chinese Christian, Paulus Ma Pui-fan, as a Kuomintang official from 1937 to 1945; the escape of the Ma family from the mainland, 1949–50; Nathan Ma's life in Hong Kong and Taiwan; and his views on the future of Christianity in China.

65-DONALD MACINNIS INTERVIEWS, 1980, 1 item
ORAL HISTORIES: 110-page transcript of interviews describing Donald MacInnis' experiences as an English teacher at Anglo-Chinese College in Yangkow from 1940 to 1941; his service in the Air Force and the Office of Strategic Services in China during World War II; his work as a Methodist missionary and teacher at Fukien Christian University after the war; reminiscences about Kenneth Scott Latourette; his work as a Methodist missionary in Taiwan; and his work as director of the National Council of Churches' China Program and as director of the Midwest China Center.

66-HELEN MACINNIS INTERVIEW, 1979, 1 item
ORAL HISTORIES: 87-page transcript of an interview describing Helen MacInnis' work as an English teacher at Fukien Christian University (1948–49), the problems of missionary parents in China, the influence of single women missionaries, and her departure from China in 1949.

67-ESTELLE LEE MARTIN AND DAVID LEE INTERVIEW, 1979, 1 item
ORAL HISTORIES: 59-page transcript of an interview with Estelle Martin and David Lee describing their experiences as the children of China missionaries in the late 1940s; their education at the American School-Kikungshan; the evacuation of the school to Hankow in 1948; and their memories of Shanghai, Sinyang, and Hankow.

68-CORA MARTINSON INTERVIEWS, 1977–79, 1 item
ORAL HISTORIES: 172-page transcript of interviews describing Cora Martinson's experiences in China as the child of Lutheran missionaries (ca. 1902), her education at the American School-Kikungshan, mission work in Kioshan and Junan (1937–42), her return to China in 1947, and her reminiscences of John Sung.

69-FRANK MILES INTERVIEW, 1977, 1 item
ORAL HISTORIES: 48-page transcript of an interview describing Frank Miles' work with the Friends' Service Unit in Shensi, and his experiences at the International Peace Hospital in Yenan.

70-MISSION HERITAGE COLLECTION, 1890–1953, ca. 300 items
MEMORABILIA: Chinese artifacts, including clothing, jewelry, porcelains, silk posters, toys, vases, and other items collected by Lutheran missionaries to China.,

71-WIBORA MUEHLENBEIN INTERVIEW, 1978, 1 item
ORAL HISTORIES: 137-page transcript of an interview describing Wibora Muehlenbein's experiences as a Benedictine missionary at Fu Jen University and in Kaifeng, the work of the ecumenical International Relief Committee founded in 1937; her internment by the Japanese in Kaifeng, Weihsien and Peking; her views on Communism in China during the 1930s and 1940s; and the Benedictines' departure from China in 1948.

72-LILLIAN OLSON NELSON INTERVIEWS, 1977, 1 item
ORAL HISTORIES: 95-page transcript of interviews describing Lillian Nelson's work as a Lutheran medical missionary in Hsuchang and Kiahsien (1936–41), events subsequent to her departure from China, and her assessment of Chinese acupuncture.

73-RUSSELL E. NELSON INTERVIEWS, 1978, 1 item
ORAL HISTORIES: 237-page transcript of interviews describing Russell Nelson's experiences as a Lutheran missionary in Honan during the 1940s; teaching methods at the College of Chinese Studies in Peking; his work supervising ''orphaned'' German missions as South China Commissioner for the Lutheran World Federation after World War II; his work as a teacher at Lutheran Theological Seminary in Hupeh (1946–48), and the evacuation of the seminary to Hong Kong in 1948; reminiscences about Daniel Nelson, Peng Fu, and Wu Djen Ming; and his views on Chiang K'ai-shek, the Three-Self Movement, and the impact of China missions on Christianity in the United States.

74-FRIDA NILSEN INTERVIEWS, 1975, 1 item
ORAL HISTORIES: 250-page transcript of interviews describing Frida Nilsen's work as a Lutheran missionary and teacher at I Kwang High School in Honan in the 1920s, a bandit raid on the Honan mission compound, reminiscences about Feng Yü-hsiang, relations between various denominations in Honan, her views on the role of single women missionaries, and her opinions on the difference between government and mission schools in China.

75-MILDRED NORDLUND INTERVIEWS, 1980, 1 item
ORAL HISTORIES: 113-page transcript of interviews with Mildred Nordlund describing her parents' work with the China Inland Mission in Kansu (ca. 1891), her childhood in Sian and education at the American School-Kikungshan (ca. 1904), her work at the Covenant Mission hospital in Siangyang from 1930 to 1945, research at Peking Union Medical College, and her visit to China in 1980.

76-OLIVE OVERHOLT INTERVIEW, 1980, 1 item
ORAL HISTORIES: 47-page transcript of an interview describing Olive Overholt's experiences as a Methodist missionary in Foochow and Yenping from 1924 to 1950, her work as a teacher at the Anglo-Chinese College in Foochow, political unrest and anti-Americanism at Fukien Christian University, and her views on the future of mission work.

77-WILLIAM OVERHOLT INTERVIEW, 1980, 1 item
ORAL HISTORIES: 179-page transcript of an interview describing William Overholt's experiences as a Methodist missionary from 1925 to 1950, his work as a teacher at the Anglo-Chinese College, military unrest in Fukien in 1926, missions and agricultural work in Yenping, political unrest at Fukien Christian University after World War II, conditions at the university under the Communists, and his departure from China after the outbreak of the Korean War.

78-TRUMAN PENNEY INTERVIEWS, 1978, 1 item
ORAL HISTORIES: 112-page transcript of interviews describing Truman Penney's work with the Princeton-in-Peking program (ca. 1921), and the Chinese response to Christian missions, the YMCA, and Chinese Christian preachers.

79-IOLA AALBUE PETERSON INTERVIEW, 1979, 1 item
ORAL HISTORIES: 68-page transcript of an interview describing Iola Peterson's work as a Lutheran missionary and principal of the American School-Kikungshan in the 1930s, her experiences as a language student in Peking, and the evacuation of the school to Hong Kong in 1937 due to political unrest.

80-HENRY REFO INTERVIEW, 1980, 1 item
ORAL HISTORIES: 76-page transcript of an interview describing Henry Refo's experiences with the YMCA in China from 1920 to 1951, his work as a teacher at Canton Christian College (1920–39) and True Light Middle School (1939–42), his internment by the Japanese and repatriation on the *Gripsholm* in 1943, his views on the activities of Chinese Communists in 1925, his experiences during the Communist takeover of Canton in 1949, and his departure from China in 1951.

81-MURIEL LOCKWOOD REFO INTERVIEW, 1980, 1 item
ORAL HISTORIES: 57-page transcript of an interview describing Margaret Refo's experiences as a Methodist missionary and YMCA worker in China from 1919 to 1950, her work at the True Light Elementary School in Canton and the American School in Paak Hok Tung, and her views of the differing roles of single women and married missionaries.

82-ALMA ROISUM INTERVIEW, 1980, 1 item
ORAL HISTORIES: 42-page transcript of an interview describing Alma Roisum's trip to the American Board mission in Fenchow as secretary to Watts O. Pye (ca. 1925), and conditions at the Fenchow mission compound and hospital.

83-MAUD RUSSELL INTERVIEW, 1976, 1 item
ORAL HISTORIES: 101-page transcript of an interview describing Maud Russell's work with the YWCA in China, ca. 1917; her recollections of a trip to Yenan during World War II; revolutionary activity in Peking (1919), Sian, and Taiyuan; her trip to China in 1959; and her thoughts on the future of Sino-American relations.

84-RANDOLPH SAILER INTERVIEW, 1980, 1 item
ORAL HISTORIES: 126-page transcript of an interview describing Randolph Sailer's work as a Presbyterian missionary and teacher at Yenching University from 1923 to 1950, student activism at Yenching, his views on John Leighton Stuart's work as U.S. ambassador to China, the Communist takeover of Yenching University in 1949, and a return trip to China in 1973.

85-FREDERIK SCHIOTZ INTERVIEW, 1977, 1 item
ORAL HISTORIES: 55-page transcript of an interview describing Frederik Schiotz's visit to China in 1935, his work as executive secretary of the Commission on Orphaned Missions after World War II, attempts to establish a Lutheran university in China after World War II, and his work with the Lutheran Church in China from 1948 to 1950.

86-MABEL WOLD SIHLER INTERVIEWS, 1978–79, 1 item
ORAL HISTORIES: 292-page transcript of interviews with Mabel Wold Sihler describing the work of her parents, Oscar and Anna Wold, as Hauge Synod missionaries in Fancheng and Tszho, ca. 1898; their experiences during the Boxer Uprising; Hauge Synod orphanages in China; Oscar Wold's views on the Lutheran Church in China and Karl Ludwig Reichelt; Sihler's childhood and education at the American School-Kikungshan; and her memories of Feng Yü-hsiang, Anna Nelson, Agnes Kittelsby, and Grace Soderberg.

87-LEWIS AND MARGARET GARRETT SMYTHE INTERVIEW, 1977, 1 item
Background note: See also Claremont Colleges, Honnold Library, Claremont, CA, 91711.
ORAL HISTORIES: 54-page transcript of an interview with Lewis and Margaret Smythe describing Margaret Smythe's childhood in China; her parents' work as Disciples of Christ missionaries in Nantung-chow (ca. 1896); her experiences as a doctor in Nanking after 1949; Lewis Smythe's views on theological liberalism and conservatism in relation to mission work; and agricultural work at the University of Nanking.

88-ARNA QUELLO SOVIK INTERVIEWS, 1978, 1 item
ORAL HISTORIES: 89-page transcript of interviews describing Arna Sovik's work as a Lutheran missionary and nurse in Kioshan, Hwangchuan, Sinyang, and the American School-Kikungshan from 1923 to 1944; the work of Casper Skinsnes at Union Hospital in Sinyang; and her work in Fancheng after returning to China in 1946.

89-ARNE SOVIK INTERVIEW, 1978, 1 item
ORAL HISTORIES: 107-page transcript of an interview with Arne Sovik describing his work with the South Honan Lutheran Church and the National Student Relief Committee in Chungking, ca. 1944; his memories of Feng Yü-hsiang, Daniel Nelson, Jr., and Tom Lee; his views on extraterritoriality; and the work of his father, Edward Sovik, as a Lutheran pastor in Sinyang (ca. 1918).

90-EDGAR SOVIK INTERVIEW, 1977, 1 item
ORAL HISTORIES: 58-page transcript of an interview describing his work as manager of the Lutheran Church's Board of Publications and Lutheran Book Concern, controversies over the publication of articles in *Sin I Pao*, his dealings with the Communists as director of Lutheran Missions' Home and Agency, and his departure from China in 1950.

91-EDWARD SOVIK INTERVIEWS, 1976, 1 item
ORAL HISTORIES: 85-page transcript of interviews describing Edward Sovik's work in Honan, ca. 1925–1945; his memories of Daniel Nelson, Sr., Feng Yü-hsiang, and Chu Hao-jan; civil unrest in 1927; a missionary conference in Hankow in 1926; controversies in the Lutheran Church in China; and mission work in Hwangchuan and Fancheng after World War II.

92-GERTRUDE SOVIK INTERVIEWS, 1978, 1 item
ORAL HISTORIES: 448-page transcript of interviews with Gertrude Sovik describing her parents' experiences as Lutheran missionaries in Hupeh, 1905-ca. 1932; the Lutheran seminary at Shekow; her childhood and education at the American School-Kikungshan, ca. 1907; her memories of Joseph Aalbue and Agnes Kittelsby; civil unrest in 1926 and 1927; her work as a Lutheran

missionary and teacher at the American School-Kikungshan, 1935–41; her return to China to reopen the school in 1946; postwar conditions in Hankow and Sinyang; and moving the school to Hong Kong in 1947.

93-MARGARET STANLEY INTERVIEWS, 1977, 1 item
ORAL HISTORIES: 119-page transcript of interviews describing Margaret Stanley's work with the American Friends Service Committee in China, 1945–48; her experiences at Hwa Mei I Yüan in Chengchow; her work at International Peace Hospital in Yenan, 1947; her comparison of Nationalist- and Communist-controlled areas; and her return visit to China in 1972.

94-BORGHILD ROE SYRDAL INTERVIEWS, 1977, 1 item
ORAL HISTORIES: 83-page transcript of interviews describing Borghild Syrdal's experiences as a Lutheran missionary in China in the 1930s; a 1930 mission conference on Kikungshan; biographical information on Marie Anderson, Dora Wang, and the family of Chu Hao-jan; the activities of Communists in the Fancheng area; and the I Kwang Middle School.

95-ROLF SYRDAL INTERVIEWS, 1976, 1 item
ORAL HISTORIES: 121-page transcript of interviews describing Rolf Syrdal's work as a Lutheran missionary in China during the 1930s; his memories of the Bert Nelson affair, Chiang K'ai-shek, Feng Yü-hsiang, Peng Fu, gunboat policy, Communist activity in Fancheng, and anti-foreignism in Sinyang; his views on ecumenism in China; and his decision as the director of world missions of the Evangelical Lutheran Church to evacuate Lutheran missions from China in 1948.

96-MINNIE TACK INTERVIEWS, 1977, 1 item
ORAL HISTORIES: 97-page transcript of interviews describing Minnie Tack's experiences as a Lutheran missionary in China, 1921–44, 1947–49; her work at an orphanage and girls' school in Honan; her experiences in Honan and Yunnan after World War II; her encounters with Communists in Linju, Honan, in 1947; and her departure for Hong Kong in 1949.

97-DONALDA TERHAAR INTERVIEW, 1976, 1 item
ORAL HISTORIES: 40-page transcript of an interview describing Donalda Terhaar's experiences as a Benedictine missionary at Fu Jen University.

98-CHESTER TOBIN INTERVIEWS, 1978, 1 item
ORAL HISTORIES: 126-page transcript of interviews describing Chester Tobin's work with the YMCA in Shanghai in the 1920s and 1930s, his involvement in the organization of international athletic events, and the work of the international Shanghai Rotary Club.

99-UNITED NORWEGIAN LUTHERAN CHURCH OF AMERICA PAPERS, 1890–1917 ca. 70 items
Background note: Scattered references to China missions can be found in this denomination's annual reports (1890–1916), the records of its Board of Foreign Missions (1890–1917), and the periodicals *Lutheraneren* (1895–1916), *Lutersk Kirkeblad* (1891–1894), and *The United Lutheran* (1908–16).
MINUTES/RECORDS/REPORTS: Central China Union Theological Seminary, faculty minutes, 1913–52; China Mission Society, cash book, 1901–4; Mission Conferences on China Field, minutes, 1915–17; M. Saterlie (Foreign Mission Secretary), reports on trip to China, n.d.; United Norwegian Lutheran Church in America, minutes and reports, 1907–10, n.d.; records of contribu-

tions to support Chinese children, 1896–1901.

CORRESPONDENCE: 2 letters from Daniel Nelson, 1897; correspondence of M. Saterlie with China missionaries, including Erik Sovik, 1907–10; correspondence of M. Saterlie concerning China, n.d.

100-FRANKLIN WALLACE INTERVIEW, 1977, 1 item

ORAL HISTORIES: 53-page transcript of an interview describing Franklin Wallace's experiences as a professor at Lingnan University in the 1930s, a student demonstration at the university in 1934, and his attendance at a meeting of the China Science Society in Kwangsi in 1935.

101-C. C. WANG INTERVIEW, 1978, 1 item

ORAL HISTORIES: 60-page transcript of an interview with C. C. Wang describing his family's conversion to Christianity, his memories of Karl Ludwig Reichelt, and his views on Tao Fong Shan.

102-KATHERINE BOEYE WARD INTERVIEW, 1977, 1 item

Background note: See also Claremont Colleges, Honnold Library, Claremont, CA, 91711.

ORAL HISTORIES: 78-page transcript of an interview describing Katherine Ward's experiences as a Methodist missionary in China from 1924 to 1949; her work at Hwei Wen High School in Nanking, ca. 1928; and her views on extraterritoriality, Chiang K'ai-shek, Christian education in China, and prospects for mission work in the People's Republic of China.

103-AGNES BARTEL WIENEKE NARRATIVE, 1980, 1 item

MANUSCRIPTS: 62-page narrative describing Agnes Wieneke's experiences as a Mennonite missionary in Tsaohsien, Tsining, and Szechuan from 1932 to 1952, and her experiences with Communists and public trials in 1946.

104-MARVIN WILLIAMS INTERVIEW, 1978, 1 item

ORAL HISTORIES: 111-page transcript of an interview describing Marvin Williams' experiences as a teacher and radiologist at Peking Union Medical College, ca. 1935, and his assessment of missionary influence and the medical training policy at the college.

105-ORPHA WILLIAMS INTERVIEW, 1978, 1 item

ORAL HISTORIES: 60-page transcript of an interview describing Orpha Williams' work as librarian at North China Language School in the 1930s, her experiences living at Peking Union Medical College, her membership in the Peking Association of University Women and the Institute of Arts, and her views on the People's Republic of China.

106-WALDO WOLD INTERVIEW, 1978, 1 item

ORAL HISTORIES: 82-page transcript of an interview describing Waldo Wold's childhood in Shekow (ca. 1912), his education at the American School-Kikungshan and a comparison of the school's staff with that of the Shanghai American School, civil unrest in 1927, and his memories of Anna Lee Wold.

107-ERNST WOLFF INTERVIEW, 1979, 1 item

ORAL HISTORIES: 81-page transcript of an interview describing Ernst Wolff's childhood in Tientsin in the 1910s and 1920s, his father's experiences during the Boxer Uprising, life in the German Concession, his work in health and mining administration in the 1930s and 1940s, his memories of the Kuomintang-Communist civil war, and his departure from China in 1951.

108-WU MING-CHIEH INTERVIEWS, 1977, 1 item

ORAL HISTORIES: 67-page transcript of an interview describing Wu Ming-chieh's childhood in Honan (ca. 1916), his conversion to Christianity, his education at the Lutheran seminary in Shekow, the 1946 Annual Conference of the Lutheran Church of China, his views on organized religion in the People's Republic in China, the conflict between Christianity and traditional Chinese culture, and his work as a Lutheran pastor in Hong Kong.

109-MILDRED TEST YOUNG NARRATIVE, 1978, 1 item

ORAL HISTORIES: 116-page transcript of a taped narrative describing Mildred Young's experiences as a Methodist missionary and teacher in Yung Chun, Fukien, from 1920 to 1926; her views on Communist activity, Chinese customs, the Chinese diet, and women's rights; her memories of street preaching, vacations in China, and Chinese festivals; and her work with the Epworth League and the Peace Society.

110-GENERAL HOLDINGS

MANUSCRIPTS: "A Record of the Activities of the Finnish Missionary Society in Northwest Hunan, China, 1902–1952," by Ilma Ruth Aho, n.d.

PAMPHLETS: *A Brief History of the China Mission of Hauge's Norwegian Evangelical Lutheran Synod of America*, by Gustav Marius Bruce, 1916; *A Girls' School in China*, by Martha Kulberg, n.d.; *It Is the Lord*, by Alfred Berg Gjølseth, n.d.; *My Experience with the Bandits*, by Julien Olson Kilen, 1944; *Kinas Buddhister for Kristus! En Livsskildring og et Indlaeg for en Stor Sak*, by Karl L. Reichelt, 1921; *They Carry On: Past and Present Experiences and Future Needs and Hopes of the Lutheran Free Church Mission in China*, by Frederick Ditmanson, 1944; *The United Norwegian Lutheran Mission Field in China: A Short Sketch with Illustrations and Map*, by Ingvald Daehlin and Erik Søvik, 1911; *Why Should Our Home Church Continue Its China Mission*, by Erik A. Søvik, 1933.

AUDIO-VISUAL MATERIALS: "China, 1929," a film of visits to Lutheran sites in China by Gerald Giving; "China-Evangelism, 1936," a film by Andrew S. Burgess (also on videotape); "China-Lutheran Seminary at Shekow and Home Agency/Literature Program at Hankow, 1936," a film by Andrew S. Burgess (also on videotape); "China-Medical Mission, 1936," a film by Andrew S. Burgess (also on videotape); "China's Religions, 1936," a film by Andrew S. Burgess (also on videotape); "Lena Dahl Middle School for Girls (I Kwang), 1936," a film by Andrew S. Burgess (also on videotape); ca. 2,500 photos related to Lutheran mission work in China, 1890–1975.

SERIALS: *China Bulletin*, 1959. *China Gleanings*, 1920–22, 1926, 1932–38. *China News Letter*, 1946–59. *Kinamissionaeren*, 1891–1904. *Quarterly Notes on Christianity and Chinese Religion*, 1958–63.

DISSERTATIONS/THESES: *A History of the Evangelical Lutheran Church of America's Mission Policy in China*, by Roger Keith Ose, 1970.

CHINESE LANGUAGE MATERIALS/SERIALS: *Chung hua Chi-tu chiao ch'üan kuo tsung hui kung pao* (*Bulletin of the General Assembly of the Church of Christ in China*), 1950–52. *Chung-kuo chih sheng* (*China's Voice*), 1951–52. *Hsieh chin* (National Christian Council of China, *Bulletin*), 1950–51, 1954. *Hsin chiao hui* (*The New Church*), 1954–55. *Hsin chien she* (*New Construction*), 1950. *Hsin i ch'ing nien* (*Lutheran Youth*), 1952. *Hsin i pao*

(Journal of the Lutheran Church in China), 1917, 1921, 1923–31, 1949–51. *Hsin i t'ung hsün (Lutheran Newsletter)*, 1951–52. *Hsin wen t'ien ti*, 1951–52. *Hsüeh hsi (Study)*, 1950–51. *Shih shih shou ts'e pan yüeh k'an (Biweekly Handbook of Current Events)*, 1950–51. *T'ien feng chou k'an (T'ien Feng Weekly)*, 1950–51, 1955–57. *Tsung chiao chiao yü (Christian Education)*, 1949–51. *Tu li lun t'an (Independent Forum)*, 1951. *Tzu yu chen hsien (Freedom Front)*, 1951.

CHINESE LANGUAGE MATERIALS: 115 books and pamphlets from the papers of Thomas Lee and shelved in the Archives' general holdings, most written in the 1950s and concerning Christianity in the People's Republic, the Three-Self Movement, and Communist views on Chinese religion.

LUTHER NORTHWESTERN THEOLOGICAL SEMINARY
MN–100 Library
2375 Como Avenue
St. Paul MN 55108
(612) 641–3226
Ray Olson, Reference Librarian

1-GENERAL HOLDINGS
MINUTES/RECORDS/REPORTS: China Inland Mission, annual reports, 1950–56; Hauge Norwegian Evangelical Lutheran Synod, Board of China Mission, reports (in Norwegian), 1896–1900; Lutheran Church Council in Shekow, proceedings of annual meeting, 1922; Lutheran Church of China, annual reports, 1920–37; Lutheran Synod of Honan and Hupeh, annual report, 1924; Rheinische Missionsgesellschaft, annual report, 1921.
MAPS/DESIGNS/DRAWINGS: *Missionaries and Mission Stations of the China Inland Mission*, n.a., 1891.
SERIALS: *Challenger*, 1978. *China and the Church Today*, 1979–86. *China Bulletin* (New York), 1952–62. *China Christian Year Book*, 1910–19, 1923–26, 1928–29, 1934–35, 1938–39. *China Gleanings*, 1924–36. *China News Letter*, 1947–59. *China Notes*, 1962–. *China Perspectives*, 1977–80. *China Prayer Letter*, 1986–87. *China's Millions* (London), 1904, 1937–52. *Chinese Recorder*, 1896, 1904–41. *Ching Feng*, 1962–. *Directory of Protestant Missions in China*, 1916–17, 1919, 1923, 1927. *East Asia Millions* (Philadelphia), 1961–. *Kinamissionaeren*, 1891–1904. *Lutheran Literature Society for China Bulletin*, 1957–. *Millions* (Philadelphia), 1952–61.
DISSERTATIONS/THESES: *American Lutheran Mission Work in China*, by Rolf A. Syrdal, 1942. *Called to Be a Wife, a Mother, and a Missionary: The Correspondence of Alice Holmberg Landahl, 1899–1913*, by Christine E. Iverson, 1984. *China Missions in Crisis: Bishop Laimbeckhoven and His Times, 1738–1787*, by Joseph Krahl, 1964. *The Christian Approach to the Mind and Heart of Confucian China*, by Vernon E. Anderson, 1944. *Church and State in Republican China: A Survey History of the Relations between the Christian Churches and the Chinese Government, 1911–1945*, by Arne Sovik, 1952. *The Development of West China and Its Effect on Christian Missions*, by Arne Sovik, 1943. *The Hauge Synod Mission Enterprise in China*, by Talbert R. Ronning, 1930. *Imperial Government and Catholic Missions in China during the Years 1784–1785*, by Bernward H. Willeke, 1948. *Karl (Charles) Gutzlaff and His Mission: The First Lutheran Missionary to East Asian Countries and China*, by Scott Pan, 1985. *Protestantism and*

Nation-building in China: A Study of the Church during the Nationalist Decade, 1928–1937, by Cheng Hin-yau, 1981.

MINNESOTA HISTORICAL SOCIETY
MN–105 Division of Archives and Manuscripts
1500 Mississippi Street
St. Paul MN 55101
(612) 296–6980
Sue E. Holbert, Minnesota State Archivist
Dallas R. Lindgren, Head of Reference Services

Background note: In addition to the materials described below, the Minnesota Historical Society holds a large collection of the papers of Walter Judd, a Congregational medical missionary in China from 1925 to 1937, and later a Republican Congressman from Minnesota. The papers date from 1918 to 1962 and mostly cover his work in Congress, including his support of the Nationalists in the Chinese civil war and his opposition to the People's Republic of China. For papers relating to his mission work in China, see the Nebraska State Historical Society, 1500 R Street, Lincoln, NB, 68501; and the American Lutheran Church Archives, 2481 Como Avenue, St. Paul, MN, 55108.

1-KATHARINE GILTINAN BOWEN INTERVIEW, 1966, 1 item
ORAL HISTORIES: 31-page transcript of an interview with Katharine Giltinan Bowen, including information on her husband, Trevor, and his work as an administrator with the Rockefeller Medical Center in Peking, ca. 1935–50.

2-SENECA CUMMINGS AND FAMILY PAPERS, 1847–83, 21 items
Background note: Abby (Abigail) Stearns Cummings (Mrs. Seneca Cummings) was the sister of Lucy E. Hartwell, an American Board missionary at Foochow from 1852 until her death in 1883. For biographical notes and collections relating to Lucy Hartwell see Wheaton College, Marion B. Bebbie, 1901, Archives and Special Collections, Madeleine Clark Wallace Library, Norton, MA, 02766.
CORRESPONDENCE: 20 letters, 1847–53, written by Seneca and Abby Cummings to family members during their journey from the United States to Foochow via Hong Kong, and describing missionaries and mission work in China.
PAMPHLETS: *Memorial of Mrs. Lucy E. Hartwell of the American Board Mission at Foochow, China*, by C. Hartwell, 1883.

3-JOHN BURT FOSTER PAPERS, 1928–74, 7 boxes
Background note: John Burt Foster (b. 1911) was a missionary of the Protestant Episcopal Church in China from 1934 to 1942. From 1934 to 1940 he taught at Hua Chung College. In 1938 he worked at a Red Cross mission hospital for the Eighth Route Army in Shansi. After a furlough in the United States, he served as English secretary for the Chinese Industrial Cooperatives in south China (1941). From 1942 to 1947, he worked in China for the U.S. Office of War Information and the State Department. This collection also contains papers relating to academic work and his opposition to McCarthyism and the Vietnam War. See also American Lutheran Church Archives, 2481 Como Avenue, St. Paul, MN, 55108.
MINUTES/RECORDS/REPORTS: Central China College, annual report, 1934–35; Chinese Industrial Cooperatives, reports, 1939–40.

CORRESPONDENCE: 5 boxes of letters from Foster, 1934–47, to J. Thayer Addison, Pearl S. Buck, Bishop Alfred A. Gilman, Hubert Humphrey, John Wilson Wood, and various family members, describing his work at Hua Chung College; Christian colleges in China; his personal life and social activities; fellow missionaries; his membership in the Oxford Group Movement; his contacts with Chinese Communists, Eighth Route Army officers, and other prominent figures in Shansi, including Chou En-lai and Agnes Smedley; his views on Chinese politics and society; his association with Mme. Sun Yat-sen in refugee, relief, and medical work; conflicts with mission and college officials over his social activism; activities of the Red Cross, the Chinese Industrial Cooperatives, the China Defense League, and the Northwestern Partisan Relief Committee; the Sino-Japanese War; and post-war work for the U.S. Government.

DIARIES: 5 diaries by Foster, 1937–40, describing his contacts with the Eighth Route Army, his hospital work in Shanghai, and his views on Chinese Communism; diary and cashbook, 1944.

MANUSCRIPTS: Account of Foster's first few months as a missionary, n.d.; articles by Foster, 1939–42, on Chinese cooperatives, the Sino-Japanese War, the Eighth Route Army, China missions, and Chinese affairs; article on the Min-Chia (Pe-tso) tribe, n.d.; fragment of a semi-autobiographical story by Foster, n.d.; lecture notes, ca. 1934–1947; manuscript on cooperatives by W. An Jung, n.d.; "The People's Republic of China, August 1974: Impressions of a Visit after Forty Years," by Foster, 1974; typescript copy of the September-November 1938 portion of Foster's diaries.

PAMPHLETS: Leaflets of the Foreign Auxiliary of the Chinese Red Cross and the Chinese Industrial Cooperatives, n.d.; miscellaneous leaflets on the Sino-Japanese War, relief work, and post-war reconstruction, n.d.; 31 catalogued pamphlets and travel guides, 1937–48, on such topics as the China Defense League, the Chinese Industrial Cooperatives, Christian colleges in China, the Sino-Japanese War, and the so-called "Tanaka Memorial" of 1927.

MEMORABILIA: Essays and articles by Mme. Chiang K'ai-shek, Mao Tse-tung, and Mme. Sun Yat-sen, 1940; calling cards, Chinese currency, and miscellanous uncatalogued items, n.d.

MAPS/DESIGNS/DRAWINGS: Map of Peiping, n.d.

SERIALS: *District of Hankow: The Newsletter*, 1935–40. Uninventoried newsletters and bulletins from Christian colleges in China.

CHINESE LANGUAGE MATERIALS: Clippings and letters, n.d.; *Kuoyu New Testament*, 1940.

FINDING AIDS: In-house guide, including inventories of diaries and pamphlets.

4-HENRY GILBERT WHITE PAPERS, 1924–35, ca. 4 boxes
Background note: Henry Gilbert White was born in China in 1908, the son of Francis Johnstone and Ivy Edith (Thompson) White, Baptist missionaries in China from 1901 to 1935. He attended the Shanghai American School in the 1920s, returning to the United States in 1926. After studying forestry in college, he worked for the U.S. military in Japan and Korea after World War II, and was involved in economic development work in Asia through the 1960s.

CORRESPONDENCE: 62 letters from Henry White and his sisters to their parents in China, 1926–35, discussing Henry's education and employment, domestic life, and personal family matters; 53 letters from Francis and Ivy White in Shanghai and Tsingtao to

Henry and his sisters, 1926–35, discussing such topics as anti-Christian policies of the Nationalist regime in Canton, anti-foreignism, Communist influence, Japanese aggression in China, the parents' work at Shanghai College, their departure from China, and personal family matters; 7 letters from Francis White to Ivy White, 1924–35, discussing Chinese politics, mission work, and personal matters; 7 letters from Roberta, Henry's sister, to various correspondents, describing her husband's work as a teacher at Ginling and Yenching universities, 1932–35; letter from "Dolly" in Kuling to Ivy White, 1926; 2 letters from "Helen" in Peitaiho and Shaohsing to Francis and Ivy White, 1934–35; letter from "Mary" at Shanghai College to Ivy White on conditions in Shanghai, 1926; circular letter from Francis and Ivy White, 1927, discussing anti-Christian policies of the Nationalist regime in Canton and the registration of religious schools by the Peking government, with personal notes from Ivy White to Henry and Roberta appended; circular letter from Francis and Ivy White, 1928, discussing Chinese politics and conditions at Shanghai College; form letter from Carl M. Capen of the American Baptist Foreign Mission Society to all China missionaries, 1951, with a list of Chinese Baptist students appended.

MANUSCRIPTS: "Our Life," by Francis Johnstone and Ivy Edith White, 1935 (typed transcript, 1950); typescript of an untitled poem by Ivy White, 1931.

SERIALS: Shanghai American School, *S.A.S. Nooze*, 1924–26.

ST. PAUL SEMINARY
MN–110 Ireland Library
2260 Summit Avenue
St. Paul MN 55105
(612) 698–0323
Leo J. Tibesar, Director

1-GENERAL HOLDINGS
DISSERTATIONS/THESES: *American Missionaries and the Policies of the United States in China, 1898–1901*, by John M. H. Lindbeck, 1948. *Imperial Government and Catholic Missions in China during the Years 1784–1785*, by Bernward Henry Willeke, 1948.

UNIVERSITY OF MINNESOTA
MN–115 St. Paul Campus Libraries
1984 Buford Avenue
St. Paul MN 55108
(612) 624–6296
Richard Rohrer, Director, St. Paul Campus Libraries

1-GENERAL HOLDINGS
SERIALS: *Lingnan Science Journal*, 1922–51. *Peking Natural History Bulletin*, 1931–49?

MN–120 Young Men's Christian Association of the U.S.A. Archives
University of Minnesota
Social History Welfare Archives
2642 University Avenue
St. Paul MN 55114
(612) 627–4632
Andrea Hinding, Archivist
Dagmar Getz, Archivist

1-CHINA RECORDS, ca. 1890–1970s, 45 ft., ca. 1,000 items
Restrictions: The China Records are currently being processed and will not be open for research until 1988. Limited reference service will be provided in the meantime.

Background note: The China Records are part of the larger collection of historical records of the Young Men's Christian Association (YMCA) of the USA, which consists of ca. 10,000 volumes of books and journals; ca. 1,000 l.f. of historical records, about 300 l.f. of which document the YMCA's foreign work; ca. 1,500 photos; a special collection of pamphlets and other published material about men's and boy's societies dating from the early seventeenth century; and memorabilia.

In 1895 the first YMCA secretary, Willard Lyon, was sent to China in response to appeals from missionaries in Peking, Shanghai, and Chefoo, beginning fifty-five years of North American YMCA involvement in China. Approximately 150 secretaries served in about 40 associations throughout China.

The General Committee of China, Korea, and Hong Kong was founded in 1901. Headquarters were established in Shanghai the following year. In 1912 the name was changed to the National Committee of the Young Men's Associations of China. Fletcher Brockman was the first national secretary (1901–15), followed by C. T. Wang (1915–16), David Yui (1916–36), S. C. Leung (1936–49), and Y. C. Tu, who became general secretary after the communist revolution in 1949. After the revolution in 1949, the American YMCA continued to support Chinese YMCAs in Hong Kong and Taiwan. The YMCAs on mainland China continued to function for some years after the revolution.

Annual reports and report letters written by the foreign secretaries serving in China provide information on programs and activities of the National Committee and the local associations, such as religious education, physical education, student work, boys' work, industrial work, personnel, budgets, buildings, and the personal experiences of YMCA workers.

Correspondence between the foreign secretaries in China and officers of the International Committee in New York comprise the main part of the correspondence, including letters to supporters and personal letters. The reports and correspondence provide an account of the political climate and developments in China in addition to the information pertinent to YMCA activities.

Records of special programs sponsored or supported by the YMCA include work with Chinese laborers in France, mass education programs conducted by James Yen, programs of the lecture department headed by C. H. Robinson, and health education programs headed by W. W. Peter, as well as famine, flood, and war relief programs.

Photos depict activities of the health education campaigns and the lecture department, buildings, construction of buildings, inaugurations, conferences, special events, and life in China in general.

MINUTES/RECORDS/REPORTS/CORRESPONDENCE/PAMPHLETS / MAPS/AUDIO-VISUAL MATERIALS / SERIALS: Records documenting the YMCA work in China, including histories, annual reports, report letters, correspondence, minutes, records of specific programs and activities, building records (including some plans), financial records, biographical records, pamphlets, serials, maps, and photos.

MISSISSIPPI

CLEVELAND

DELTA STATE UNIVERSITY
MS-5   W. B. Roberts Library
Cleveland MS 38733
(601) 843–4440
Myra Macon, Director

1-GENERAL HOLDINGS
SERIALS: *Chinese Recorder*, 1868–1940. *Chinese Repository*, 1832–51.

CLINTON

MISSISSIPPI COLLEGE
MS-10   Leland Speed Library
West College Street
P. O. Box 51
Clinton MS 39056
(609) 925–3434
Alice Cox, Librarian, Mississippi Baptist Historical Commission

1-MISSISSIPPI BAPTIST HISTORICAL COLLECTION, 1877–1983, 4 items
Background note: In addition to the materials listed below, the collection contains articles on China missions in *The Baptist Record*, the weekly newspaper of the Mississippi Baptist Convention, including articles by Baptist medical missionary T. W. Ayers. See also Southern Baptist Convention Historical Commission, Library and Archives, 901 Commerce Street, Nashville, TN, 37203–3260; and Wallace Memorial Baptist Church, 701 Merchants Road, Knoxville, TN, 37912.
ORAL HISTORIES: 2 audio cassettes and a typed transcript of a 1983 interview with Cornelia Frances Leavell, a Baptist missionary in China and Hong Kong.
AUDIO-VISUAL MATERIALS: 38-page photo album of China by Pearl Caldwell, a Baptist missionary in China from 1910 to 1947.
FINDING AIDS: Card catalogue subject index to *The Baptist Record*, 1877–.

JACKSON

MILLSAPS COLLEGE
MS-15   J. B. Cain Archives
Millsaps-Wilson Library
Jackson MS 39210
(601) 354–5201
Gerry Reiff, Archivist

1-J. B. CAIN PAPERS, ca. 1850–1885, 2 folders
Background note: This partially processed collection contains information on James William Lambuth (1830–92), a Methodist missionary who was in China from 1854 to 1861, and from 1864 to 1886.
CORRESPONDENCE: Correspondence relating to James Lambuth's China mission work, n.d.
MANUSCRIPTS: "The Mission to China and the Lambuth Family," by J. B. Cain, n.d.

2-LAMBUTH-KELLEY PAPERS, ca. 1850–1885, 9 folders
Background note: David Campbell Kelley (1833–1909) was a Methodist missionary in China from 1852 to 1855. His daughter, Mary Isabella, married Walter Russell Lambuth (1854–1921), the son of James William Lambuth. Walter Lambuth was a Methodist missionary in China from 1877 to 1881 and from 1882 to 1885, and a bishop of the Methodist Episcopal Church, South, from 1910 to 1921. This collection is partially processed. See also Lambuth College, Luther L. Gobbel Library, Lambuth Boulevard, Jackson, TN, 38301; General Commission on Archives and History—The United Methodist Church, United Methodist Archives and History Center, 36 Madison Avenue, P. O. Box 127, Madison, NJ, 07940; and Vanderbilt University, Special Collections/Archives, Jean and Alexander Heard Library, Nashville, TN, 37240–0007.
MINUTES/RECORDS/REPORTS: Methodist Episcopal Mission, South, accounts from the China mission, 1861–72, and China mission account book, 1859–73; Soochow Hospital, report, 1884.
CORRESPONDENCE: Letter from James W. Lambuth in Shanghai, n.d.; folder of Lambuth family letters, n.d.
DIARIES: Diary of Mary Isabella Lambuth, n.d.
MANUSCRIPTS: "The China Mission and the Lambuth Family," n.a., n.d.; "Methodist Missions and the Lambuth Family," n.a., n.d.
CHINESE LANGUAGE MATERIALS: Folder of accounts from the China mission, 1869–70, 1873 (some English notes appended).

REFORMED THEOLOGICAL SEMINARY
MS–20   Seminary Library
5422 Clinton Boulevard
Jackson MS 39209
(601) 922–4988
Thomas G. Reid, Jr., Library Director

Background note: In addition to the items listed below, scattered references to China missions can be found in this library's holdings of the minutes of the General Assembly of the Orthodox Presbyterian Church (1936–84), the minutes of the General Assembly of the Presbyterian Church in the United States (1877–1982), and the minutes of the General Assembly of the Presbyterian Church in the United States of America (1789–1958).

1-GENERAL HOLDINGS
MINUTES/RECORDS/REPORTS: International Missionary Council, London, report of church history deputation to China, 1931–32.
SERIALS: *China Mission Year Book* 1910–39.

MISSOURI

COLUMBIA

UNIVERSITY OF MISSOURI, COLUMBIA

MO–5   Joint Collection, University of Missouri Western Historical Manuscript Collection and State Historical Society of Missouri Manuscripts
23 Elmer Ellis Library
Columbia MO 65201–5149
(314) 882–6028
James W. Goodrich, Director
Nancy Lankford, Associate Director

1-FRANK ELY ATWOOD PAPERS, 1926–29, 8 items
Background note: Frank Ely Atwood (1878–1943) was a Missouri attorney and an active layman in the Southern Baptist Church. The total collection consists of 1,243 folders, 15 volumes, 1888–1943.
CORRESPONDENCE: 8 letters between Atwood and Isaac Page and W. Alfred Schiehter of the China Inland Mission, 1926–27, and William B. Pettus, principal of the Yenching School of Chinese Studies, n.d.; correspondence concerning the Child Welfare Association of China and the North China Union Language School in Peking, n.d.

2-CARL CROW PAPERS, n.d., 2 items
Background note: Carl Crow (1883–1945) served as editor of the *China Press*, the first American daily in China, from 1911 to 1913. A resident of China again during the 1920s and 1930s, he founded and edited the *Shanghai Evening Post*, and later served as head of a Shanghai advertising agency until the Japanese invasion. This collection contains approximately 60 folders of China-related material; there may be further scattered references to China missions in addition to the items listed below. The total collection consists of 354 folders, 6 volumes, 1913–45.
MANUSCRIPTS: "American Saints and Chinese Sinners," by Carl Crow, n.d.; rough draft of "Americans Christianize the World," by Crow, n.d.

3-IVAN LEE HOLT PAPERS, ca. 1847–1962, ca. 20 folders
Restrictions: Permission for use must be obtained from Judge Ivan Lee Holt, Jr.
Background note: Ivan Lee Holt was a Methodist minister and bishop of North Texas (1939–44) and Missouri (1944–56). The total collection consists of 1,912 folders, 12 volumes, 12 records, and 1 card box, 1835–1967.
MINUTES/RECORDS/REPORTS: Reports on Methodism in China, ca. 1847–1947; reports on China missions, 1950.
CORRESPONDENCE: Correspondence concerning the church in China, ca. 1954–1962.

4-CURTIS FLETCHER MARBUT PAPERS, 1929, 1 item
Background note: The total collection consists of 184 folders and 12 volumes, 1852–1963, 1983.

CORRESPONDENCE: Letter from Presbyterian missionary H. G. C. Hallock in Shanghai, to Curtis Fletcher Marbut, a professor of geology at the University of Missouri and soil scientist with the U.S. Department of Agriculture, 1929.

5-MAURICE E. VOTAW PAPERS, 1922–77, ca. 55 folders
Background note: Maurice Votaw (1899–1981) was professor of journalism at St. John's University in Shanghai and an advisor to the Nationalist Ministry of Information. The total collection consists of 55 folders, 1909–78.
MINUTES/RECORDS/REPORTS/CORRESPONDENCE/MANUSCRIPTS/MAPS/DESIGNS/DRAWINGS/AUDIO-VISUAL MATERIALS: Ca. 54 folders of minutes, letters, literary productions, maps, photos, and published materials, 1922–77, most relating to Votaw's work in China.
ORAL HISTORIES: 35-page transcript of a 1977 interview describing Votaw's life, his views on China missions and their impact on the Chinese people, his work at St. John's University, Chinese and American journalism, the Sino-Japanese and Kuomintang-Communist conflicts, and U.S. China policy.

6-WOMAN'S SOCIETY OF CHRISTIAN SERVICE, METHODIST CHURCH, PAPERS, 1939–44, quantity undetermined
Background note: The total collection consists of 147 folders, 248 volumes, 1879–1971.
MINUTES/RECORDS/REPORTS: Woman's Foreign Missionary Society, lists of China missionaries and reports of unassigned field support in China, 1939–40.
SERIALS: *China Colleges*, 1944.

MO–10 Elmer Ellis Library
University of Missouri, Columbia
Columbia MO 65201–5149
(314) 882–4701
Mary Ryan, Reference Librarian

1-GENERAL HOLDINGS
SERIALS: *China Christian Year Book*, 1911, 1917, 1919, 1928–29. China International Famine Relief Commission, Publications, series A, 1922–36. *Lingnan Science Journal*, 1922–29, 1930–48. *Peking Natural History Bulletin*, 1930–31. *St. John's University Studies*, 1922. University of Nanking, College of Agriculture and Forestry, *Bulletin*, 1932–?
CHINESE LANGUAGE MATERIALS/SERIALS: Yen-ching ta hsüeh, *Hsiu wen hsüeh hsi* (Yenching University, *Journalism Study Series*), 1932; *Yen-ching hsüeh pao* (*Yenching Journal of Chinese Studies*), 1927–32.

CONCEPTION

CONCEPTION ABBEY AND SEMINARY
MO–15 Library
Conception MO 64433
(816) 944–2211
Aidan McSorley, O.S.B., Director

1-GENERAL HOLDINGS
SERIALS: Catholic University of Peking, *Bulletin*, 1926, 1928–31. *Fu-Jen Magazine*, 1932–33.

INDEPENDENCE

MO–20 HARRY S. TRUMAN LIBRARY
National Archives and Records Administration
24 Highway and Delaware
Independence MO 64050
(816) 833–1400
Benedict K. Zobrist, Director

1-WALTER H. JUDD INTERVIEW, 1976, 1 item
ORAL HISTORIES: 49-page transcript of an interview with Walter Judd, recorded for former members of Congress in 1976, focusing mainly on his work in Congress and political views, but including his observations on China and mission work.

2-HARRY S. TRUMAN PAPERS—GENERAL FILE, 1946, 1 item
CORRESPONDENCE: Draft of a fund-raising letter for the American Association for China Famine and Flood Relief by Wirt W. Hallam, 1946.

3-HARRY S. TRUMAN PAPERS—OFFICIAL FILE, 1946–48, 4 items
MINUTES/RECORDS/REPORTS: Memorandum from "C.G.R." to Edwin A. Locke, Jr., regarding a request from Gerald F. Winfield, promotion secretary of the China Christian Colleges Committee, that President Truman endorse a fund-raising campaign, 1946.
CORRESPONDENCE: Letter from Albert E. Greene, Sr., to President Truman, discussing the situation in China in light of correspondence received from China missionary Albert E. Greene, Jr., 1948; letter from Albert E. Greene, Jr., to his parents, describing the deteriorating economic and political situation in China during the civil war, 1948; open letter from Albert E. Greene, Jr., describing conditions at China Bible Seminary in Shanghai and Communist advances in the civil war, 1948.

4-HARRY S. TRUMAN PAPERS—PRESIDENT'S PERSONAL FILE, 1946, 1 item
MINUTES/RECORDS/REPORTS: Memorandum from W. D. Hassett to Edwin A. Locke, Jr., telling of President Truman's policy against endorsing charitable campaigns, and his decision not to endorse a fund-raising effort by the Associated Boards for Christian Colleges in China, 1946.

KANSAS CITY

CHURCH OF THE NAZARENE INTERNATIONAL HEADQUARTERS
MO–25 Nazarene Archives
6401 The Paseo
Kansas City MO 64131
(816) 333–7000 Ext. 437
Stan Ingersol, Archives Director
Lon Dagley, Curator of Special Collections

Background note: The first China mission work by a pre-Nazarene body began in 1902 when a band of students from Pasadena Bible College reopened a mission in Shantung which had previously been closed due to the Boxer Uprising. In 1905 the Hephzibah Faith

Missionary Association, which joined the Church of the Nazarene in 1948, began sending workers to help the China Inland Mission in Pingtichuan, Suiyuan. The Association purchased property and established its own China mission in 1920; it had 6 Chinese missionaries as late as 1940. The first official Church of the Nazarene mission in China opened in Chao Cheng, Shantung, in 1914. The mission also held meetings in Fanhsien, Juancheng, and Puchow. It also cooperated extensively with the National Holiness Association's China mission. In 1919 Tamingfu became the site for another Nazarene mission which developed into a focal point for all other Nazarene work in China. New missions were established in Puchow, Cheng An, and Kwangpingfu in the 1920s; Bresee Memorial Hospital and a Bible school were built in Taming during this time. The last of the Nazarene missionaries in China departed in 1949.

Many of the collections in the Archives, such as the J. B. Chapman papers and the R. T. Williams papers, have correspondence files arranged alphabetically. In addition to the correspondence listed below, letters from China missionaries may be in these files. The Archives also contain about 15 files of material relating to Nazarene mission work on Taiwan from 1959 to 1983.

1-JAMES B. CHAPMAN COLLECTION, 1921–35, 7 items

MINUTES/RECORDS/REPORTS: General Superintendent J. B. Chapman, report on trip to Japan and China, 1935; China Council, minutes, 1935.

CORRESPONDENCE: 3 letters from R. G. Fitz to J. B. Chapman, 1935; memorials of the China Missionary Council to the General Board, 1935.

MANUSCRIPTS: "The Past, Present and Future of the Church of the Nazarene [in China]," by Peter Kiehn, ca. 1921.

FINDING AIDS: In-house inventory.

2-DISTRICTS, FOREIGN MISSIONS—CHINA, 1917–82, ca. 20 files, 2 boxes

Restrictions: The Allen Yuan interview may not be used without permission from the World Mission Division. The 1981 "China letter" is restricted.

Background note: The China District was established about 1916–17. The Annual Mission Council began meeting in 1923. By 1941, the China District had been divided into the North China Field and the Kiangsi (South China) Field. The North China Field was closed in 1942, and the Kiangsi field was closed in 1949 when all the missionaries had to leave the country.

MINUTES/RECORDS/REPORTS: Annual District Assembly, proceedings, 1917–19, 1921; Annual Assembly and Annual Council, proceedings, reports, and district policy, 1921–26; J. E. Bates, Missionary Superintendent of the Orient, annual report to the Board of General Superintendents, 1925–26; Bresee Memorial Hospital, insurance and deeds, 1941, 1947–49; Chen Hsi Kui, China Trust Fund, financial statements about work in China, ca. 1930s; Mission Council, minutes, 1930–31, 1933–36, 1939–41.

CORRESPONDENCE: Letter from A. J. Smith, district treasurer, to the General Board of Foreign Missions concerning appropriations asked for at the China District Assembly, 1923; memo from Mary Scott concerning Bresee Memorial Hospital, n.d.; "China letter," 1981; letters about the China Trust Fund, ca. 1930s; letter from Peter Kiehn to Helen Temple, describing experiences in China and Taiwan, n.d.

MANUSCRIPTS: "The Legacy of Peter and Anna Kiehn," by Peter Kiehn, n.d.; "Mainland China" (describing China and mission work there), n.a., n.d.

MEMORABILIA: 2 glass candleholders purchased by Evelyn Eddy Engstrom in Peking in 1939.

ORAL HISTORIES: Taped interview with Allen Yuan, Nazarene national worker who was imprisoned in mainland China for over 20 years, 1982.

AUDIO-VISUAL MATERIALS: File of photos, ca. 1920, including pictures of buildings, famine-stricken Chinese, Mr. and Mrs. Peter Kiehn, and H. F. Reynolds; badly damaged photo of students of a Chinese Bible school, 1948; photos of the China District Annual Business Meeting, 1934, and the Tamingfu mission compound, n.d.; historical slides of China, n.d.; file of photos (mostly group pictures), 1939–48, including pictures of Evelyn Eddy Engstrom, R. G. Fitz, Hester Hayne, Arthur Moses, the Osborns, Mary Parnell, the Pattees, Ann Royal, Rhoda Schurman, Mary Scott, Ann Sutherland, the Varros, and the Wieses; 2 photos of Bresee Memorial Hospital, n.d.; group photo of China missionaries, 1940; group photo of China missionaries, including C. J. Kinne and Peter and Anna Kiehn, n.d.; photos of graduates of Bresee Memorial Hospital, ca. 1920s.

SERIALS: *The China Nazarene*, 1924–26.

FINDING AIDS: In-house inventory.

3-E.J. FLEMING PAPERS, 1931, 1 file

MINUTES/RECORDS/REPORTS: Bresee Memorial Hospital, financial reports, 1931.

CORRESPONDENCE: File of correspondence between R. G. Fitz, E. J. Fleming, and Peter Kiehn regarding Bresee Memorial Hospital, 1931.

4-GENERAL BOARD OF FOREIGN MISSIONS/DEPARTMENT OF FOREIGN MISSIONS, 1913–49, ca. 188 files

Background note: The general Missionary board was the earliest sending agency in the Church of the Nazarene and was responsible for both home and foreign missions. In 1915, these functions were separated and the General Board of Foreign Missions established. In 1923, all church boards were centralized under the General Board of the Church of the Nazarene and the Department of Foreign Missions was created as one of its division.

Further references to China may be found in the various general foreign mission records.

MINUTES/RECORDS/REPORTS: Bresee Memorial Hospital in Taming: property deed, 1926; fire insurance policy, 1941; information on Nazarene work in China in its missionary publication, *The Other Sheep*, 1913–74, renamed as *World Mission*, 1974-; General Board of Foreign Missions: annual reports on China missions, 1913, 1915–19, 1921–23; China field statistics, 1925, 1930–31, 1936–40; deeds and lists of mission property in Kiangsi, Hopei, and Shantung, 1947–49; General Superintendent J. B. Chapman, report on trip to Japan and China, 1935; National Holiness Mission of China, report on turning work over to the Church of the Nazarene, 1914; policies to govern the work in China, ca. 1919, 1922; questionnaires from the Tamingfu, Puchow, and Chao Cheng mission stations, 1920.

CORRESPONDENCE: File of administrative correspondence with the China field, including correspondence on forming a self-supporting district, 1932–35; file of administrative correspon-

dence with the China field, including telegrams telling of missionaries being held by the Japanese, and correspondence on the Kiehn dismissal, 1935–42; 2 files of correspondence of Pearl Denbo, 1915–19, 1921–22; 4 files of correspondence of Mr. and Mrs. O. P. Deale, 1917–26, 1928, 1931–33; 2 files of correspondence of Evelyn Eddy, 1937–41; 6 files of correspondence of R. G. Fitz, 1921–23, 1926, 1930–37; 4 files of correspondence of Catherine Flagler, 1931–41; 5 files of correspondence of Hester Hayne, 1921–24, 1930–43; 2 files of correspondence of Blanche Himes, 1919–23; file of correspondence of Bertie Haynes Karnes, 1934–35; 35 files of correspondence of Peter and Anna Kiehn, 1913–43; 5 files of correspondence of C. J. Kinne, 1920, 1923–24, 1927, 1930–32; 3 files of correspondence of Rev. and Mrs. Arthur Moses, 1939–44; file of correspondence of Margaret Needles, 1925–26; 10 files of correspondence of Rev. and Mrs. L. C. Osborn, 1919, 1923, 1925–26, 1928, 1930–36, 1938–44; 2 files of correspondence of Mary E. Pannell, 1930–32, 1935–42; 4 files of correspondence of J. W. Pattee, 1936–43; 8 files of correspondence of Rev. and Mrs. Geoffrey Royall, 1935–44; 2 files of correspondence of Rhoda Schurman, 1936–42; file of correspondence of Catherine Schmidt, 1917–20; 2 files of correspondence of Mary Scott, 1940–42; 2 files of correspondence of Glennie Sims, 1914–19, 1922–23, 1925–26, 1934–36; 11 files of correspondence of A. J. Smith, 1916–24, 1926–27; file of correspondence of Catherine Smith, 1922–24; 9 files of correspondence of Rev. and Mrs. F. C. Sutherland, 1920, 1922–44; unidentified letter of Helen Temple, n.d.; 4 files of correspondence of Myrl Thompson, 1930–39; 2 files of correspondence of Michael Varro, 1940–42; 3 files of correspondence of Ida Vieg, 1916–19, 1922–25, 1931–37; 2 files of correspondence of Dr. and Mrs. C. E. West, 1926, 1928; 8 files of correspondence of H. C. Wesche, 1935–43; 19 files of correspondence of Rev. and Mrs. H. A. Wiese, 1920–26, 1930–42.
MANUSCRIPTS: "Nazarene Mission in the Orient" (language unspecified), n.a., 1916–17.
PAMPHLETS: Brochures on an introduction to the Chinese language, n.d., interfiled with photos described below; brochure on plans to build P. F. Bresee Memorial Hospital in Tamingfu, published by the Nazarene Medical Missionary Union headed by C. J. Kinne, ca. 1920–1925; *Farmer Brown's Conversion*, by P. G. Fitz, n.d.
AUDIO-VISUAL MATERIALS: 6 files of China mission field photos, ca. 1930s, including photos of J. B. Chapman, R. G. Fitz, J. W. Goodwin, Mr. and Mrs. Peter Kiehn, mission stations, national workers, "Mrs. Staples," the Tamingfu compound, Michael Varro, W.M.S. chapters, Henry Wesche, Harry Wiese, and R. T. Williams; 2 photos taken during O. J. Nease's visit to the field, 1948; photo of Mr. and Mrs. Clarence J. Kinne of Bresee Memorial Hospital in Tamingfu, n.d.; historical missionary slides from China, n.d.; films by L. C. Osborn on work in China, 1936–47.
CHINESE LANGUAGE MATERIALS: Deeds for mission property in Kian, Kiangsi, 1947–49; W.M.S. course of study, rules, and goal, 1936, and monthly W.M.S. report blanks, n.d., interfiled with the photos.
FINDING AIDS: In-house inventory.

5-PETER AND ANNA KIEHN COLLECTION, ca. 1913, 4 items
Background note: Peter (b. 1885) and Anna Schmidt Kiehn served in Shantung from 1906 to 1912 under the China Mennonite Mission Society and from 1913 to 1948 under the Church of the Nazarene. In 1948 they moved to Taiwan and began an independent holiness Bible school and several Bible schools, two of which became affiliated with the Church of the Nazarene after 1956.
CORRESPONDENCE: Letter fragment written by Peter Kiehn, n.d.
MANUSCRIPTS: "The Legacy of Peter and Anna Kiehn," by Peter Kiehn, n.d.
AUDIO-VISUAL MATERIALS: Photo of Peter Kiehn on furlough in Kansas, ca. 1913; group photo of China missionaries, including Peter and Anna Kiehn, n.d.
FINDING AIDS: In-house inventory.

6-NAZARENE MEDICAL MISSIONARY UNION PAPERS, ca. 1920–1967, 8 items
Background note: The Nazarene Medical Missionary Union was founded by Clarence J. Kinne, manager of the Nazarene Publishing House, with the primary objective of enlisting lay support for building Bresee Memorial Hospital in Tamingfu. More extensive records on the hospital can be found in the collections of the Department of Foreign Missions and its correspondence with Kinne.
CORRESPONDENCE: Correspondence between Archivist R. R. Hodges, General Superintendent Hardy C. Powers, and missionary F. C. Sutherland regarding Hodges' research concerning Bresee Hospital, 1967.
MANUSCRIPTS: 2 copies of Hodges' typed research and research notes on Bresee Hospital, ca. 1967.
PAMPHLETS: *What Hath God Wrought* (showing progress of Bresee Hospital), n.a., ca. 1930s.
MEMORABILIA: Statement from Mrs. Paul Bresee regarding Nazarene Medical Missionary Union request that the future Board of Foreign Missions make arrangements for the building of Bresee Hospital, 1923; statement of support from the Board of General Superintendents for the Nazarene Medical Missionary Union's "week of self-denial" for Bresee Hospital, ca. 1920s.
FINDING AIDS: In-house inventory.

7-LEON C. AND EMMA D. OSBORN COLLECTION, 1919–73, ca. 23 files
Background note: Leon and Emma Osborn went to China in 1916 as independent missionaries. In 1919, they joined the Church of the Nazarene and served its church at Chao Cheng, Shantung, until 1942.
MINUTES/RECORDS/REPORTS: "Leon and Emma Osborn's Years of Service in the Church of the Nazarene," 1919–66 (4-page report containing biographical information on the Osborns' service in China).
DIARIES: 2 diaries of Emma Osborn, 1937–38, describing visits to the United States, travels in China and Japan, and military operations in and near the Osborns' locations.
MANUSCRIPTS: "Putting God's Word to the Test" (containing information on the Osborns' service in China), n.a., n.d.; poetry and a radio script by L. C. Osborn, 1930s, 1960s, and n.d.
MEMORABILIA: 2 of L. C. Osborn's personal Bibles, 1 with sermon outlines, n.d.; 2 of Emma Osborn's personal Bibles, one from Chao Cheng containing notes, clippings, quotations, and sermon notes, n.d.
ORAL HISTORIES: 2 copies of a taped narrative describing L. C. Osborn's detention by the Nationalists in 1928, recorded in 1973; 2 copies of a taped narrative describing L. C. Osborn's experiences

in 1941 and 1942; "The Healing of Mrs. Kung" (poor quality taped narrative by L. C. Osborn), n.d.
AUDIO-VISUAL MATERIALS: 6 films by L. C. Osborn on work in China, 1936–37, 1941; file of photos of the Osborn family, including some from China, 1923; 2 files of unidentified color slides, n.d.
FINDING AIDS: In-house inventory.

8-HIRAM F. REYNOLDS COLLECTION, 1913–26, ca. 17 files
Background note: Hiram F. Reynolds (1854–1938) was elected to the first board of General Superintendents in 1908 and served in that capacity until 1932. During these years he was also General Missionary Secretary (1908–14), and General Superintendent of Foreign Missions (1917–20), and more than any other single individual stamped the Church of the Nazarene with a missionary character. The collection documents every important development within the denomination up to 1932, including the opening of new mission fields. Total volume of the collection is about 11 c.f.
MINUTES/RECORDS/REPORTS: H. F. Reynolds, report on China, 1914; South China Holiness Mission, application and records, 1914; policy statement regarding the China mission, 1914.
CORRESPONDENCE: 7 files of China mission correspondence, 1913–15, 1917–18, 1922, 1923–26; file of correspondence with China missionary Peter Kiehn, 1923–26; 3 files of correspondence with Alice Galloway, regarding the union of the Pentecostal Mission work in China with the Church of the Nazarene, 1915–18; file of correspondence between Cora Snider and H. F. Reynolds, 1913; file of correspondence with Woodford Taylor of the National Holiness Mission in China, Peter Kiehn, P. F. Bresee, Leslie Gay, E. F. Walker, Herbert Hunt, and C. W. Ruth concerning the opening of Nazarene mission work in China, 1914; open letters from "Brother and Sister Monroe" (Mr. and Mrs. E. R. Munroe?), 1914.
MANUSCRIPTS: "Notes from Hudson Taylor's 'Spiritual Secrets,'" concerning the China Inland Mission, n.d.
PAMPHLETS: *Some of Our Holiness Preachers*, n.a., 1914; *What You Ought to Know About S.C.H.M.*, n.a., 1914.
MEMORABILIA: Articles on the situation in China and the departure of missionaries from China in "Things That Concern Zion," a regular feature in the serial *Herald of Holiness* from 1926 on.
AUDIO-VISUAL MATERIALS: Ca. 1 file of photos from China, n.d.; scrapbook of photos taken by Reynolds on missionary tours, 1913–14, including a few from China; 3 photo albums, containing negatives and positive prints, from missionary tours of China, 1914 and n.d.; photo of Reynolds on a conveyance in China, n.d.
FINDING AIDS: In-house inventory.

9-MARY SCOTT PAPERS, 1940–50, 3 items
CORRESPONDENCE: Unidentified letter, 1940; letter from H. A. Wiese to Mary Scott, 1950, concerning Mary Li, a Chinese national residing in the United States, and missions in China.
ORAL HISTORIES: Undated taped interview with Mary Scott describing her internment by the Japanese.

10-ROY T. WILLIAMS PAPERS, 1929, 65 items
Background note: Roy T. Williams (1863–1946) was a general superintendent in the Church of the Nazarene from 1916 to 1946. In 1929 Williams toured China as part of a survey of Nazarene missions world-wide.
AUDIO-VISUAL MATERIALS: 65 photos of missionaries, structures, congregations, and Chinese life, 1929.
FINDING AIDS: In-house inventory.

MO-30 KANSAS CITY PUBLIC LIBRARY
311 East 12th Street
Kansas City MO 64106
(816) 221–2685
Marilyn Pedram, Reference Librarian

1-GENERAL HOLDINGS
SERIALS: *China Christian Year Book*, 1924–25, 1928.

NAZARENE THEOLOGICAL SEMINARY
MO-35 Broadhurst Library
1700 East Meyer Boulevard
Kansas City MO 64030
(816) 333–6254
William C. Miller, Library Director

1-GENERAL HOLDINGS
DISSERTATIONS/THESES: *A History of Nazarene Missions in China*, by Clifton Cleve James, 1948.

PERRYVILLE

ST. MARY'S SEMINARY

MO-40 DeAndreis-Rosati Memorial Archives
1701 West St. Joseph Street
Perryville MO 63775
(314) 547–6533
Judy Kirn, Acting Librarian

Restrictions: St. Mary's Seminary is closed, but the Archives and Library are open to researchers by appointment. Papers of Provincials are restricted.
Background note: The DeAndreis-Rosati Memorial Archives is the principal repository for materials of the Vincentian community of priests and brothers of the Midwest Province, U.S.A. Vincentian missionaries from Europe first arrived in China in 1785. American Vincentians established missions in the Kanchow and Yukiang districts of Kiangsi province in the early 1920s.

In addition to the materials listed below, the Archives have extensive holdings of the periodicals, *Annales de la Congrégation de la Mission* (1834–1963), *Catalogue des Maisons et du personnel de la Congrégation de la Mission* (1853-), *The DeAndrein* (Seminary student newspaper, 1928–65), and *Vincentian* (1923–63), which contain information on Vincentian missions in China. Materials on the American Vincentians in China dates from 1920 to 1953.

1-GENERAL HOLDINGS
MINUTES/RECORDS/REPORTS: Annual reports of Superiors General Robert, Slattery, Souvay, and Verdier, n.d.; papers of Provincials Barr, Finney, Flavin, Stakelum, and Winne, n.d.
CORRESPONDENCE/MANUSCRIPTS/PAMPHLETS/MEMORABILIA: Folder of letters from missionary priest Louis Bereswill, 1932–45; folder of letters, papers, pamphlets, and memorabilia of Bishop Jean-Louis Clerc-Renaud, 1866–1935; folder of letters, papers, pamphlets, and memorabilia of missionary priest Leo Fox, n.d.; folder of letters, papers, pamphlets, and memorabilia of missionary priest John Meijer, n.d.; folder of letters, papers, pamphlets, and memorabilia of Bishop Paul Misner,

1891–1938; folder of letters, papers, pamphlets, and memorabilia of Bishop Charles Quinn, 1905–60; folder of letters, papers, pamphlets, and memorabilia of Bishop Edward Sheehan, 1888–1933.
AUDIO-VISUAL MATERIALS: 14 boxes of photo albums and loose photos, covering all aspects of mission life, n.d.; 100 reels of movie film, 1940s, in the Paul Lloyd Collection of Motion Picture Film.

MO–45   St. Mary's of the Barrens Library
St. Mary's Seminary
1701 West St. Joseph Street
Perryville MO 63775
(314) 547–6533
Judy Kirn, Acting Librarian

Background note: The library has two collections of books dealing with Vincentian missions in China: one consists of 150 works in French and Latin from the nineteenth century, dealing with the history of Catholic missions in China and Chinese culture, history, philosophy, and religion; the other consists of 125 volumes from the headquarters of the Vincentian mission in Shanghai, and contains works on language, religion, art, history, Christian missions, and relations with France.

1-GENERAL HOLDINGS
MANUSCRIPTS: "Vincentian Missions in China," a 112-page typescript describing Vincentian missions in Kiangsi from 1785 to 1900, n.a., n.d.
MEMORABILIA: Unprocessed collection of personal effects, souvenirs, and gifts from China missionaries, such as clothing, utensils, curios, and objects of art in the Edward T. Sheehan Museum in the library.
SERIALS: *Missions de Chine*, 1937, 1942. *Monumenta Serica*, n.d. *Variétés Sinologiques*, N 1–10, n.d.
DISSERTATIONS/THESES: *Diplomatic Correspondence Concerning the Chinese Missions of the American Vincentians, 1929–1934*, by Julius M. Schick, 1951.

ST. LOUIS

CONCORDIA HISTORICAL INSTITUTE
MO–50   Department of Archives and History
Lutheran Church—Missouri Synod
801 De Mun Avenue
St. Louis MO 63105
(314) 721–5934 Ext. 320
Kurt A. Bodling, Reference and Research Assistant

Restrictions: Access upon application.
Background note: In addition to the materials described below, the records of the Lutheran Church-Missouri Synod Board for Missions contains 22 boxes of materials related to missions in Hong Kong and Taiwan from 1953 to 1973.

1-EDWARD L. ARNDT PAPERS, 1886–1927, 3 boxes
Background note: Edward L. Arndt (1864–1929) founded the Evangelical Lutheran Mission for China in 1912. From 1913 to 1929 he served as a missionary in Hankow. This collection contains 2 folders of miscellaneous uncatalogued papers in addition to the materials listed below.

MINUTES/RECORDS/REPORTS: Mailing lists in German for "Missionsbriefe," 1886–1927.
CORRESPONDENCE: Folder of Arndt's correspondence, and miscellaneous "Missionsbriefe" donated by Arndt's son, Karl J., 1886–1927.
MANUSCRIPTS: Folder of Arndt's writings, 1886–1927; 7 notebooks and a bundle of miscellaneous sermons, 1886–1927.
AUDIO-VISUAL MATERIALS: 2 folders of photos, 1886–1927.

2-WILLIAM FREDERICK ARNDT PAPERS, n.d., 130 items
Background note: William Frederick Arndt (1880–1957) was a professor of New Testament exegesis at Concordia Seminary, ca. 1921.
CORRESPONDENCE: 22 letters concerning China missions, n.d.; 108 letters concerning the Chinese term question, n.d.

3-JOHN WILLIAM BEHNKEN PAPERS, 1938–47, 56 items
Background note: John William Behnken (b. 1884) was president of the Lutheran Church—Missouri Synod from 1935 to 1962.
CORRESPONDENCE: 56 letters relating to the Chinese term question, 1938–47.

4-LUDWIG ERNST FUERBRINGER PAPERS, n.d., 51 items
Background note: Ludwig Ernst Fuerbringer (1864–1947) was a teacher at Concordia Seminary from 1893 to 1943, and president of Concordia Seminary from 1931 to 1943.
CORRESPONDENCE: 46 letters on the Chinese term question, n.d.; 5 letters from Edward Arndt on the Chinese term question, n.d.

5-THEODORE GRAEBNER PAPERS, n.d., 83 items
Background note: Theodore Graebner (1876–1950) was a professor at Concordia Seminary, ca. 1913.
CORRESPONDENCE: 83 letters concerning China, n.d.

6-LUTHERAN CHURCH—MISSOURI SYNOD, BOARD FOR WORLD MISSIONS, RECORDS, 1898–1957, 104 boxes
MINUTES/RECORDS/REPORTS: Board of Foreign Missions: Anhwei province, reports, 1935; budgets for China missions, 1940–46; bulletins from China missionaries, n.d.; China accounts, 1945–49, 1951–53; China financial records, 1940–46; English conference on China missions, 1937, 1940–45, 1947; general records on China, 1931–57 and n.d.; records on disposition of property, n.d.; records on missions in Hankow; semi-annual reports on China, 1937–44; statistics relating to China missions, 1934–37, 1943, 1946–47, 1949–52; subsidy requests, 1936–52; China Committee, minutes, 1934–36; China General Conference: miscellaneous records, 1927–41; minutes, 1920–26, 1930–37, 1940–42, 1947–49, 1951–52; records of Hankow building projects, n.d.; rules and regulations, n.d.; statistics for missions, n.d.; treasurer's records, 1936–37, 1939, 1946–52; China Mission, ledger, 1936–50; copies of property deeds, 1934–37; Hankow Conference, minutes, 1919–27, 1933; Hankow Seminary, records, n.d.; Hupeh property records, n.d.; Information Service, records relating to China, n.d.; Kweifu property deeds, n.d.; Kweifu Station, minutes and reports, n.d.; library list for Hankow, 1914; miscellaneous reports on China, 1935–37, 1949; Norwegian conference on the Chinese term question, records, 1932; records from Ichang, n.d.; records of the deal for Shihnan Yamen, 1921–22; records of salary cuts, n.d.; records on missionaries who left service, 1926–28; records relating to missions at Shasi, n.d.; records relating to real estate, n.d.; report

on a visit to China, 1941; reports and minutes from Wanhsien, n.d.; salary records, 1939–40; Shanghai Conference, records, 1927; Shasi Conference, minutes, 1937; Shasi Station, minutes and reports, n.d.; Shasi Zion, records, n.d.; Shihnan Conference, minutes and reports, n.d.; studies on China missions, n.d.; survey of China missions, n.d.; Wanhsien Conference, records, n.d.; Wanhsien Middle School, records, 1945–47; Zion Cemetery, records, n.d.

CORRESPONDENCE: 24 letters of the Board of Foreign Missions regarding China missions, n.d.; ca. 146 letters of Martha Boss, 1941–51; 35 cables from China, n.d.; ca. 600 letters relating to the China General Conference, 1920–22, 1924–26, 1933–38, 1945–48, 1950–51; ca. 150 letters relating to the Hankow Conference, 1919–27, 1933; 22 letters relating to the Shasi Compound wall, 1935; 22 letters to the Chinese consulate, 1946, 1955–56; 343 letters of Anena Christensen relating to the term question, 1930, 1932–41; 80 letters of A. Cloeter, 1926–28; 55 letters of C. E. Dohrman, 1941–45; 204 letters of Ralph C. Egolf concerning China, 1942–45; 204 letters of John A. Fischer, 1923–32; 125 letters of P. Frillman, 1936–41; 473 letters of A. H. Gebhardt, 1918–37; 9 letters of A. H. Gebhardt concerning the Chinese term question, 1941; 38 letters of Hugo Gihring, 1918–20; 81 letters of Hedwig Gronbeck concerning Christianity in mainland China, 1950–57; 325 letters of Olive Gruen, 1937–57, n.d.; 196 letters of Leroy Haas on Christianity in mainland China, 1947–57; 295 letters of Herbert Hinz from China and Hong Kong, 1942–57; 179 letters of Wloert Hoeltje, 1945, 1947–51; 24 letters of Peter Kleid, 1923–25; 532 letters of H. Klein from China and Pueblo, Colorado, 1898–1929, 1934–36, 1939–43; 242 letters of A. T. Koehler, 1931–42; ca. 380 letters of Paul Kreyling, 1936–45, 1947–57; 32 letters of Norma Lenschow, 1947–48; 15 letters of Li Yen-nan, 1948; 253 letters of George O. Lillegard, 1921–25, 1929–35, including materials on the term question; 233 letters of Paul R. Martens, 1939–49; 200 letters of W. H. McLaughlin, 1929–37; 13 letters of Dorothy Meier, n.d.; 57 letters of Arnold Meyer, 1926–28; 239 letters of H. C. Meyer, 1939–42, 1944–45; 154 letters of L. Meyer, 1917–26; 179 letters of R. J. Muehl, 1931–43; 899 letters of R. J. Mueller, 1932–42, 1946–50; 42 letters of C. Nagel, 1925–28; 133 letters of N. W. Nero, 1931–35; 78 letters of Frieda Oelschlaeger, 1923–31; 87 letters of Marie Oelschlaeger, 1924–31; 49 letters relating to the Board's pension fund, 1946, 1949–51, 1954; 487 letters of Erhart Riedel, 1918–45; 260 letters of Frederick Schalow, 1947–56; 98 letters of Carl F. Schmidt, 1922–35; 100 letters of A. C. Scholz, 1921–30; 144 letters of Eugene Seltz, 1929–39; 720 letters of Gertrude Simon, 1926–57; 53 letters of Martin Simon, 1926–29; 129 letters of H. G. Theiss, 1926–27; 54 letters of Henry Walter Theiss, 1921–33; 650 letters of Elmer H. Thode, 1926–43, 1947–57; 45 letters of Michael Trinklein, 1955–57; 326 letters of Kurt E. Voss, 1939–45, 1947–48, 1950–57; 422 letters of G. M. Wenger, 1931–49; 197 letters of W. Werling, 1930–39; 290 letters of John Wilenius, 1945–54; 37 letters of S. Ylvisaker, 1926–27; 436 letters of A. H. Ziegler, 1925–49; 806 letters of E. C. Zimmerman, 1928–45; 690 letters of Max Zschiegner, 1923–42, 1948–57; 70 letters of Victor Zwintscher, 1947–57.

MANUSCRIPTS: "Natural Knowledge," by A. H. Gebhardt, 1937; "The Term Question," by A. W. Gebhardt, n.d.; 104 documents of A. W. Gebhardt relating to the term question, 1937–38; opinions on the term question from Hankow Seminary, E. W. A. Koehler, the faculty at Concordia Seminary, various China mis-

sionaries, and the Synodical conference, 1928, 1937–1938 and n.d.

PAMPHLETS: Ca. 1 folder of tracts and pamphlets on China from the Board of Foreign Missions, 1940s and 1950s.

MAPS/DESIGNS/DRAWINGS: 3 maps of China, n.d.; uninventoried maps from the Board of Foreign Missions, 1940s and 1950s.

AUDIO-VISUAL MATERIALS: 597 miscellaneous photos of China, n.d.; 49 photos of China Conference missionary families, 1930s; 24 photos of Anhwei, n.d.; 15 photos of Enshih, n.d.; 18 photos of the Han River District, n.d.; 334 photos of Hankow, n.d.; 6 photos of Hanyang, n.d.; 56 photos of Ichang, n.d.; 42 photos of Kuling, n.d.; 34 photos of Kweifu, n.d.; 16 photos of North Field, n.d.; 29 photos of Shanghai, n.d.; 137 photos of Wanhsien, n.d.; photo of Wuchang, n.d.

7-LUTHERAN CHURCH—MISSOURI SYNOD, BOARD OF DI-RECTORS, RECORDS, n.d., 1 box
CORRESPONDENCE: Letters pertaining to China missions and the term question, n.d.

8-LAWRENCE B. MEYER PAPERS, n.d., 10 items
Background note: Lawrence B. Meyer (b. 1890) served as a missionary in China from 1917 to 1926, and as director of Missionary Education and Publicity from 1926 to 1950.
CORRESPONDENCE: 10 letters on the term question, n.d.

9-JOHN THEODORE MUELLER PAPERS, n.d., 1 folder
Background note: John Theodore Mueller (b. 1888) was a Lutheran clergyman, educator, and author.
MINUTES/RECORDS/REPORTS: Shangdi-Shen Program, studies and thesis, n.d.

10-LOUIS JOHN SCHWARTZKOPF PAPERS, 1924–60, 355 items
Background note: Louis John Schwartzkopf (1896–1966) was a Lutheran minister and missionary in China.
CORRESPONDENCE: Letter from Hong Kong, 1952–53.
MANUSCRIPTS: Box of essays on the history and religion of China, 1944–45.
PAMPHLETS: Ca. 1 folder of pamphlets on China, n.d.
MEMORABILIA: Ca. 1 folder of articles on China, n.d.; 1 box of magazine and news clippings on China, n.d.

11-FRIEDA OELSCHLAEGER THODE PAPERS, n.d., .5 ft.
Background note: Frieda (Oelschlaeger) Thode and her husband, Elmer H. Thode, were missionaries in China during the 1920s and 1930s.
MANUSCRIPTS: Autobiography and an account of the Thodes' mission work, n.d.
AUDIO-VISUAL MATERIALS: Photos related to the Thodes' mission work, n.d.

12-WALTHER LEAGUE RECORDS, 1950–53, 1 folder
Background note: The Walther League was founded in 1893 as the youth organization of the Evangelical Lutheran Synodical Conference.
CORRESPONDENCE: China correspondence, 1950–53.

13-ELMER CHRISTIAN ZIMMERMAN PAPERS, 1927–53, ca. 450 items
Background note: Elmer Christian Zimmerman (1896–1985) was a missionary in China from 1928 to 1942, and an instructor in missions at Concordia Seminary after 1942.
MINUTES/RECORDS/REPORTS: Mission Board of the Synodi-

cal Conference, minutes and reports, n.d.; Norwegian Synod Pastorial (sic) Conference, report, 1932.
CORRESPONDENCE: Correspondence to the Mission Board of the Synodical Conference, n.d.; 93 letters concerning the Chinese term question, n.d.; letter from William Arndt to the Norwegian Synod, 1928; letter from Ludwig Fuerbringer to the Board of Missions, 1927; 2 letters from the Board of Missions to missionaries, 1928.
MANUSCRIPTS: "*God* in Hymns of Universal Praise," by H. C. Meyer, n.d.; "Legge's Arguments in Favor of *shangti* for *Elohim*," by George Lillegard, n.d.; document by E. W. A. Koehler on the theological aspects of the term question, 1923; document by E. W. A. Koehler on linguistic aspects of the term question, 1933; notes by E. W. A. Koehler, 1933, on a 1928 letter from William Arndt; 18 leaves of notes on the term question, n.d.; leaf of notes on the term question by A. Gebhardt, n.d.; 28 documents by various missionaries and Concordia Seminary faculty dealing with the term question and the faculty's opinions on it, 1927–29, n.d.

14-GENERAL HOLDINGS
CHINESE LANGUAGE MATERIALS: 30 shelf feet of Bibles, catechisms, hymnbooks, sermons, periodicals, and books from China, Taiwan, and Hong Kong.

DAUGHTERS OF CHARITY OF ST. VINCENT DE PAUL
MO–55   West Central Province Archives
Marillac Provincial House
7800 Natural Bridge Road
St. Louis MO 63121
(314) 382–2800
Sister Henrietta Guyot, D.C., Archivist

Background note: The China Collection relates to the two religious communities founded by St. Vincent de Paul: the Daughters of Charity (D.C.) and the Congregation of the Mission (C.M.), also known as the Priests of the Mission, the Vincentians, and the Lazarists. In 1697 the Vincentians sent a priest to China to prepare the way for mission work and to begin a seminary for the training of native priests. In 1847 the first Daughters of Charity embarked for China from France. The first American Daughter arrived in China in 1896 under the auspices of the French community. In 1922 and 1923, the two American Provinces established their own missions in Jaochow and Kiangsi, respectively. The sisters returned from China in 1948 after three attempts to maintain their missionary work in Kiangsi.

1-CHINA COLLECTION, 1921–70, ca. 400 items
CORRESPONDENCE/MEMORABILIA: 325 letters and several clippings, 1921–48, describing daily life and the various apostolates in east Kiangsi.
DIARIES: 8 composition books, describing daily life in China, including arranged marriages, baptisms, feast days, and evacuation after Pearl Harbor, ca. 1921–1941.
PAMPHLETS: *Sister Helen Ganel, D.C. (1901–1970)*, n.a., n.d.
AUDIO-VISUAL MATERIALS: Ca. 60 China photos, including some portraying American and European sisters, n.d.
ORAL HISTORIES: Interview with Bernice Szewczyk, D.C., on 3 audio cassettes, describing the war years in China from 1932 to 1949.

EDEN THEOLOGICAL SEMINARY
MO–60   Eden-Webster Libraries
Webster University
475 East Lockwood Avenue
St. Louis MO 63119
(314) 968–6950
Anne Moedritzer, Reference Librarian

1-GENERAL HOLDINGS
MANUSCRIPTS: "From Six to Sixty to Six: A Narrative of the China Mission of the Reformed Church in the United States and the Later Evangelical and Reformed Church," by Arthur Vale Casselman, 1951.
PAMPHLETS: *The Present Situation in China and Its Significance for Christian Missions*, n.a., 1925; foreign mission tracts, n.d.; pamphlets by W. E. Hoy on missions in China, n.d.
SERIALS: *China and the Gospel*, 1913. *China Christian Year Book*, 1915, 1918, 1931, 1934–39.
DISSERTATIONS/THESES: *The Protestant Missionary Approach in China*, by A. Vernon Kurz, 1946.

FRANCISCAN PROVINCE OF THE SACRED HEART
MO–65   Archives
St. Anthony of Padua Friary
3140 Meramec Street
St. Louis MO 63118–4339
(314) 353–3421
Barnabas Diekemper, O.F.M., Archivist

Restrictions: Letters of reference required for research. Personal files closed.
Background note: In addition to the materials listed below, references to the Sacred Heart Province's China missions can be found in Volumes 1 through 3 of the annals of the Sacred Heart Province (1925–28), and the periodicals *Around the Province* (1937–58), *Franciscan Herald* (1923–39), and *Franciscan Herald and Forum* (1956).

1-FRANCISCAN CHINESE MISSIONS OF THE SACRED HEART PROVINCE COLLECTION, 1881–1966, 5 l.f.
MINUTES/RECORDS/REPORTS: Catalogue of the college where Francis Middendorf, O.F.M., taught, n.d.; Chowtsun Mission Institution, records, n.d.; Diocese of Chowtsun, annals, 1925–35; Diocese of Chowtsun, constitution and by-laws, 1928; Kiangsu Mission Institution, records, n.d.; Tsinanfu Mission Institution, records, n.d.; Wuchang Mission Institution, records, n.d.
CORRESPONDENCE: 1 in. of China missionaries' correspondence, 1937–57; 7 in. of correspondence from Chowtsun, 1925–49; 1 in. of Franciscan Missionary Union correspondence, 1939–56; .25 in. of correspondence from Kiangsu, 1947; 2 in. of correspondence from Tsinanfu, 1920–47; 2 in. of correspondence from Wuchang, 1921–32; letters of Sacred Heart province missionaries in the Chowtsun Diocese, n.d.; 120 pages of letters of Franciscan China missionaries, 1930–33.

DIARIES: 13 diaries of Boniface Pfeilschifter, O.F.M., n.d.
MANUSCRIPTS: Autobiography of Fulgence Gross, O.F.M., n.d.; memoirs of Boniface Pfeilschifter, O.F.M., covering the period 1918 to 1955.
PAMPHLETS: *Bericht über das Franziskaner Vikariat Tsinanfu*, by Maurus Heinrich, O.F.M., 1946; *Franciscans in the Middle Kingdom: A Survey of Franciscan Missions in China from the Middle Ages to the Present Time*, by Otto Maas, O.F.M., 1938; *Lecture on Missiology*, by Ildephonse Rutherford, O.F.M., n.d.; *Six Months in China*, by Boniface Pfeilschifter, O.F.M., 1928–29.
MEMORABILIA: Cassock of Bernard Pfeilschifter, O.F.M.; newspaper clippings about Sacred Heart Province missionaries in the Chowtsun Diocese, n.d.; "A Franciscan and a Mission Scrapbook," by Pacific Hug, O.F.M., 1930–37.
MAPS/DESIGNS/DRAWINGS: *Das Apostolische Vikariat Tsinanfu*, by Vitalis Lang, O.F.M., n.d.
AUDIO-VISUAL MATERIALS: 2 in. of photos of Sacred Heart Province missionaries in the Chowtsun Diocese, n.d.; 1 in. of photos by Francis Middendorf, O.F.M., of Franciscan mission work in Wuchang; 2 in. of uncatalogued photos of missionaries and locations in China, n.d.; 45 in. of uncatalogued slides of China, n.d.
SERIALS: *Franciscans in China*, 1922–41. *Visits with the Missionaries*, n.d.
DISSERTATIONS/THESES: *The Constitution and Supreme Administration of Regional Seminaries Subject to the Sacred Congregation for the Propagation of the Faith in China*, by Marcian Mathis, O.F.M., 1953.

MO–70   ST. LOUIS PUBLIC LIBRARY
1301 Olive Street
St. Louis MO 63103
(314) 241-2288
Joan Collett, Librarian and Executive Director

1-GENERAL HOLDINGS
SERIALS: *China and the Gospel*, 1906–10. *China Christian Year Book*, 1928. *China Mission Year Book*, 1923, 1925.

ST. LOUIS UNIVERSITY
MO–75   Pius XII Memorial Library
3650 Lindell Boulevard
St. Louis MO 63108
(314) 658-3100
Brian Forney, Head Reference Librarian
Charles Ermatinger, Director, Vatican Microfilm Library

1-VATICAN MICROFILM LIBRARY, 1588–1892, 21 items
Background note: This collection contains microfilm reproductions of works in Latin, Italian, French, Dutch, and English on missions in China, including biographies of Catholic missionaries, histories, Jesuitica, materials on the rites controversy, and series of published correspondence from missions. Representative titles include *Compendiosa Narratione della Stato della Missione Cinese...*, by Prospero Intorcetta, 1672; *Dve lettere annve della Cina del 1610, e del 1611*, by Nicolas Trigault, 1615; and *Duo Responsa Centum Doctorum Sacrae Facultatis Theologicae Parisiensis ad Sinarum Quaesita in Sacra Congregatione S. Officii Propenenda*, n.a., 1700.
PAMPHLETS: *Lettera scritta da Monsignor Assessore del S[ant'] Offizio: al P[adre] General della Compagnia di Giesù li 11 ottobre 1710*, including a letter from Antonio Cardinal Banchieri to heads of other religious orders affected by the decree on Chinese rites, with their replies, 1710; *Observationes Reverendissimi Dominii D. Caroli Maigrot, Episcopi Canonensis et Vicarii Apostolici Fokiensis: in quaesita a patribus Societatis Jesu Sinarum Imperatori proposita i in responsum eiusdem Imperatoris*, by Charles Maigrot, 1701; *Riflessioni sopra la causa della Cina: doppo venuto in Europa il decreto dell'eminentissimo di Tournon*, by Tommaso Ceva, 1709; *Vergelyking van ket gedrag der Jesuiten, met het gedrag dat zy aan de Jansenisten verwyten...*, n.a., 1711.

2-GENERAL HOLDINGS
PAMPHLETS: *Missions et explorations portugaises: l'Oeuvre civilisatrice du Portugal depuis le XVe jusqu'au XIXe siècle*, by Augusto Ribeiro, 1900(?); *Catholic Missions in China during the Middle Ages, 1294–1368*, by Paul Stanislaus Hsiang, 1949.
DISSERTATIONS/THESES: *China Missions in Crisis: Bishop Laimbeckhoven and His Times, 1738–1787*, by Joseph Krahl, 1964. *Imperial Government and Catholic Missions in China during the Years 1784–1785*, by Bernward Henry Willeke, 1948. *Kilian Stumpf, 1655–1720; ein Würzburger Jesuit am Kaiserhof zu Peking*, by Sebald Reil, 1978. *Lorettine Education in China, 1923–1952: Educational Activities of the Sisters of Loretto in China, Hanyang, and Shanghai*, by Antonella Marie Gutterres, 1961. *The Negotiations between Ch'i-ying and Lagrené, 1844–1846*, by Angelus Francis J. Grosse-Aschhoff, 1950.

SOCIETY OF THE SACRED HEART
MO–80   National Archives
Villa Duchesne
801 South Spoede Road
St. Louis MO 63131
(314) 432-2021
Sister Mary Louise Padberg, R.S.C.J., National Archivist

Background note: From 1926 to 1952, the Congregation of the Religious of the Sacred Heart operated an elementary and secondary school and Aurora College for Women, affiliated with the Jesuit University of Shanghai (Aurora University, also called Chen tan ta-hsüeh). The Congregation has operated an elementary and secondary school in Taipei since 1960; the National Archives also contains materials pertaining to this institution.

The National Archives has custody of all of the Society's China materials in the United States. Further material, mostly letters, can be found at the Central Archives of the Congregation in Rome.

The National Archives has the following published materials which contain information on the Congregation's China mission: annual letters containing information about all of the Congregation's institutions worldwide and brief biographies of sisters who had died at each institution, including information on the Congregation's work in Shanghai from 1926 to 1952, the reasons for and progress of the foundation, the educational and missionary activities of the sisters, their views on life in Shanghai, their internment in the Convent of the Sacred Heart during World War II, and the events leading up to the departure of the mission from China; the Congregation's annual directory listing the sisters serving in each of its institutions, their principal occupations and responsibilities, and statistical information about the Congregation in each country; the monthly *Newsletter* published by the Motherhouse of the Congregation in Rome, containing information on the growth and development of the Shanghai institution against the background of the history of the period; the intra-Congregational periodical, *Caritas*; and the privately printed history, *The Society of the Sacred Heart in the Far East, 1908–1980*, by Margaret Williams, 1982.

1-CHINA COLLECTION, 1925-late 1970s, 38 items
CORRESPONDENCE: 27 letters from various sisters in Shanghai to families and friends in France, Rome, and the United States, describing their situation there, 1942–52.
MANUSCRIPTS: Account of an interview with Bishop Favre regarding the Boxer Uprising, 1901; account of a sister's journey through China, 1925; talk given by the last religious of the Sacred Heart to leave China, 1953.
PAMPHLETS: *Bulletin of Information—Aurora College for Women, 181 rue Bourgeat, Shanghai*, n.a., n.d.
MEMORABILIA: Newspaper article by one of the nuns interned in the Shanghai Convent describing their experiences there, 1946; newspaper clipping describing the departure of some of the sisters from Shanghai, 1949.
ORAL HISTORIES: Taped conversation with a teacher of English at Peking University in the late 1970s.
AUDIO-VISUAL MATERIALS: 5 photos of the buildings in Shanghai, n.d.

WASHINGTON UNIVERSITY

MO-85   East Asian Library
P.O. Box 1061
St. Louis MO 63130
(314) 889-5155
Sachiko Morrell, Librarian

Finding aids: *Research Sources for Chinese and Japanese Studies: A List of Serials in Humanities and Social Sciences Held by Washington University Libraries*, comp. by Ernest Tsai (St. Louis: Washington University Libraries), 1976.

1-GENERAL HOLDINGS
SERIALS: *China Notes*, 1970-. *Chinese Recorder*, 1868–1940. *Chinese Repository*, 1832–51. *Monumenta Serica*, 1935–47. *Yenching Journal of Social Studies*, 1938–50.
CHINESE LANGUAGE MATERIALS/SERIALS: *Chin-ling hsüeh pao (Nanking Journal)*, 1931–39. *Fu jen hsüeh chih (Fu jen Sinological Journal/Series Sinologica)*, 1928–47. *Yen-ching hsüeh pao (Yenching Journal of Chinese Studies)*, 1941–51.
CHINESE LANGUAGE MATERIALS: Books on the Bible, Catholic church, Gregorio Lopez, missions, and Matteo Ricci, and bibles.

MO-90   Freund Law Library
Washington University
Mudd Law Building
Campus Box 1120
St. Louis MO 63130
(314) 889-6459
Margaret McDermott, Reference Librarian

1-GENERAL HOLDINGS
SERIALS: *China Law Review*, 1922–40.

MO-95   John M. Olin Library
Washington University
Skinker and Lindell Boulevards
St. Louis MO 63130
(314) 889-5410
Kenneth L. Nabors, Humanities Librarian

1-GENERAL HOLDINGS
SERIALS: *China Christian Year Book*, 1912. *The Millions* (Philadelphia), 1877, 1879–82.
DISSERTATIONS/THESES: *The Missouri Evangelical Lutheran Mission in China, 1913–1948*, by Richard Henry Meyer, 1948.

MO-100   School of Medicine Archives
Washington University Medical Center
Box 8132
660 South Euclid Avenue
St. Louis MO 63110
(314) 534-0643
Paul Anderson, Archivist

1-E. V. COWDRY PAPERS, 1917-21, ca. 2 l.f.
Background note: Edmund Vincent Cowdry (1888–1975) was a professor at Peking Union Medical College (PUMC) from 1917 to 1921. From 1921 to 1928 he was an associate member of the Rockefeller Institute; he was associated with the Washington University School of Medicine in various capacities from 1928 to 1960. The collection, which totals 82 l.f. and covers the period from 1909 to 1975, is uninventoried. His later correspondence contains references to China, but these are not related to the China Medical Board, PUMC, or the Rockefeller Institute's China activities. See also Rockefeller University, Rockefeller Archive Center, Pocantico Hills, North Tarrytown, NY, 10591.
CORRESPONDENCE: Cowdry's correspondence relating to his work with the China Medical Board, PUMC, and Rockefeller Institute, Chinese medical education in general, and medical instruction at church-related schools, ca. 1917–1921.

2-PAUL H. STEVENSON PAPERS, 1922-66, ca. 4 document boxes
Background note: Paul Huston Stevenson (1890–1971) was a graduate of the Washington University School of Medicine and a clergyman of the Disciples of Christ. He served as superintendent of Luchowfu Christian Hospital (1918–20) and professor of anatomy at Peking Union Medical College (1920–37). He was involved in anthropological work in north China, including the discovery of "Peking man" at Chou-k'ou-tien in the 1920s.
MINUTES/RECORDS/REPORTS: Stevenson's field notes from Peking Union Medical College, 1922–23, 1935, and anthropometric summary sheets, ca. 1925–1932.

CORRESPONDENCE: Letter from Stevenson to Virginia L. Larsen, describing the Chinese-Tibetan borderlands, 1966; 2 letters from Stevenson to Harold M. Loucks, describing the embalming of Sun Yat-sen's body, 1965.

DIARIES: Tibetan Borderland diary, 1926; diary, 1941–42.

MANUSCRIPTS: "Contributions to the Physical Anthropology of the Eastern Asiatic Mainland: I. Detailed Anthropometric Measurements of the Chinese of the North China Plain," by Stevenson, n.d.; notes on Stevenson's participation in the embalming of Sun Yat-sen's body in 1925.

MEMORABILIA: Bulletin and admission card for the funeral of Sun Yat-sen at Peking Union Medical College, 1925; invitation to a conference with the Pansen (sic) Lama, sponsored by the International Institute (of China?), n.d.; notice to foreigners, Peking, 1925.

AUDIO-VISUAL MATERIALS: 11 photo albums from China, n.d.; 19 photos from China, 1925, 1929, and n.d., including photos of Stevenson, Dr. and Mme. Sun Yat-sen, Sun Fo, and the Chou-k'ou-tien site; lantern slides from China, n.d.

FINDING AIDS: In-house guide.

SPRINGFIELD

ASSEMBLIES OF GOD
MO–105   Archives
    1445 Boonville Avenue
    Springfield MO 65802
    (417) 862–2781
    Jodie Loutzenhiser, Assistant Archivist

Background note: References to China missions can be found in the denominational periodical, *Adullam News*, N 39 and 41, ca. 1942.

1-GENERAL HOLDINGS
MINUTES/RECORDS/REPORTS: North China District Council, minutes, 1940–41.

CORRESPONDENCE: 2 letters of Grace Agar, 1940; correspondence and clippings regarding the internment of A. Walker Hall by the Japanese, 1939–45.

DIARIES: Diary of Trans-Tibet Evangelistic Expedition, by Victor G. Plymire, 1927–28.

MANUSCRIPTS: "The Assemblies of God Missionary Effort in China, 1907–1952," by Joshua C. Yang, 1985; "Observations from the Field," by Victor G. Plymire, n.d.; photocopy of an untitled manuscript by Margaret H. Jamieson about China mission work, 1981; "Watchman, What of the Night" (about China missionary Leonard Bolton), by Elsie Bolton Ezzo, n.d.; "William Wallace Simpson: Pioneer Assemblies of God Missionary to China," by Joshua C. Yang, 1985.

PAMPHLETS: *Evangelizing West China*, by W. W. Simpson, ca. 1931; *Home of Onesiphorus*, by Leslie M. Anglin, 1936; *God's Faithfulness in Ningpo*, comp. by Nettie D. Nichols and Joshua Bang, 1938; *The Power of the Gospel in Shansi Province*, by Marie Stephany, ca. 1939; *Rejoice with Us!* (promotional flyer regarding Anglin's mission work), n.a., ca. 1935; *Salwin-Irrawaddy Gleanings* (describing J. C. and Lavada Morrison's experiences as missionaries in China, ca. 1920), n.a., n.d.

SERIALS: *Gleanings*, 1920.

NEBRASKA

BLAIR

DANA COLLEGE
NB–5   Archives
    C. A. Dana-Life Library
    Blair NB 68008
    (402) 426–4101 Ext. 119
    Sharon Jensen, Reference Librarian

1-GENERAL HOLDINGS
PAMPHLETS: *The China Mission*, by M. Saterlie, 1926.

LINCOLN

NEBRASKA STATE HISTORICAL SOCIETY
NB–10   Library
    1500 R Street
    Box 82554
    Lincoln NB 68501
    (402) 471–2926
    Andrea I. Paul, Reference Archivist

1-CHARLES HARRISON ARNOLD PAPERS AND SCRAPBOOKS, 1946–48, 6 folders, 2 items
Background note: Charles Harrison Arnold (1888–1966) was a medical missionary at West China Union University from 1946 to 1948.

MINUTES/RECORDS/REPORTS: Folder of rule sheets, reports, schedules, and courses of study from the hospital at West China Union University, n.d.

CORRESPONDENCE: 2 folders of letters from Arnold on his mission experiences in China, 1946–48.

DIARIES: Arnold's diary, including his experiences in China, 1946–48; diary by Mrs. Arnold during their voyage from China to England, 1948.

MEMORABILIA: Folder of lecture outlines by Arnold at West China Union University, 1946–48; scrapbook containing photos, clippings, mementos, passports, reports, and correspondence on Arnold's stay in China, 1946–48; brief biographical sketch of Charles Harrison Arnold, n.a., n.d.

2-FIRST CONGREGATIONAL UNITED CHURCH OF CHRIST OF FREMONT, NEBRASKA, 1910–55, 4 items
Background note: Ruth Mulliken, of the First Congregational United Church of Christ of Fremont, was a missionary to China from 1910 to 1942.

MANUSCRIPTS: Biographical sketch of Mulliken, n.a., n.d.; Mulliken's memoirs of her mission days, n.d.

PAMPHLETS: 2 church bulletins, "Service of Commission as a Missionary, Aug. 28, 1910," and "Memorial Service for Ruth Mulliken, May 7, 1950."

3-ARTHUR FOLSOM PAPERS, 1860–65, 1 volume, 5 items
Background note: Arthur Folsom (1833–1910) was a Presbyterian missionary to China from 1863 to 1869.

CORRESPONDENCE: 4 letters from Arthur and Mary Ann (Thomas) Folsom to her brother, John Thomas, on life and work in China, 1863, 1865.
DIARIES: Folsom's journal, 1860–63.
MEMORABILIA: Biographical sketch of Arthur and Mary Ann Folsom by their son, Ernest C. Folsom, 1939.

4-WALTER HENRY JUDD, 1927–28, quantity undetermined
CORRESPONDENCE: Letters from Walter Judd while a medical missionary in China, 1927–28.

5-H. M. LUCE PAPERS, 1901–4, quantity undetermined
CORRESPONDENCE: Letters to H. M. Luce of Garrison, Nebraska, from Methodist Episcopal Church China missionaries, 1901–4.
SERIALS: Methodist Episcopal Church in Fukien, *Bulletin*, 1903.

6-LAURA M. ULMER DIARIES, 1924–38, 2 volumes
Restrictions: Permission for publication of any part of this collection must be secured from the donor.
Background note: For biographical notes, see Hoover Institution, Archives, Stanford University, Stanford, CA, 94305-2323.
DIARIES: Laura M. White Ulmer's diaries on her mission experiences in China, 1924–38.

NEBRASKA WESLEYAN UNIVERSITY
NB–15 United Methodist Historical Center
50th and St. Paul Streets
Lincoln NB 68504
(402) 465–2175
Bernice M. Boilesen, Curator

Background note: See also General Commission on Archives and History—The United Methodist Church, United Methodist Archives and History Center, 36 Madison Avenue, P. O. Box 127, Madison, NJ, 07940.

1-GENERAL HOLDINGS
MINUTES/RECORDS/REPORTS: China Mission of the Evangelical Church, report, 1946; China mission, annual report, 1945; reports on China mission, n.d.; Women's Foreign Mission Society, report on China, n.d.; Yuhsien circuit, annual report, 1927; report by H. E. Voss to "Readers of the Messenger," 1926.
CORRESPONDENCE: Letter of appeal from Mr. and Mrs. Herman E. Voss, 1938; letter from Mr. and Mrs. Herman E. Voss to Nebraska Annual Conference of Evangelical Church, 1937; "Excerpts from Letters from China, 1939–1951, by Uniola V. Adams," ed. by Helen E. Adams, containing copies of 190 letters to her family covering her service in China as a nurse in Foochow; copies of letters from Voss to his wife, Sadie Dunkelberger Voss, and to C. Newton Dubs, 1926–27; annual letters from language school classmates after a year in the field, 1917; copies of letters from China from Sadie Voss, 1914–18.
MANUSCRIPTS: "The Changed Burden," by Mrs. C. C. Talbot, 1919; "How We Got Our First Chinese Pastor, His Oldest Son, and Family," n.a., n.d.; "Notes about Mission Work in Hunan and Kweichow China (Evangelical Church)," by C. C. Talbot, 1959; paper by William A. Voss (son of Mr. and Mrs. Herman E. Voss), 1984, on recollections of evacuation of missionaries in 1926 and 1927; "Reminiscences of the Early History of the China Mission of the Evangelical Church," by Herman E. Voss,

n.d.; "Missionary Evacuation from Yuhsien", by Herman E. Voss, ca. 1927; "My Hall of Memory," by Mary E. Myers, a classmate of Sadie Voss at language school, 1914–15, and nurse under the Evangelical and Reformed Church in Yoyang, n.d.
MANUSCRIPTS/PAMPHLETS/AUDIO-VISUAL MATERIALS: Articles, memoirs, and pictures of missionaries to China: Uniola Adams, Mr. and Mrs. J. J. Banbury, C. Newton and Emma Hasenpflug Dubs, Mr. and Mrs. Homer H. Dubs, Alma Ericksen, Earl and Marguerite Berkey, Pearl Fosnot, W. Max and Emily Gantry, Ovidia Hansing, Joel A. and Florence Smith, Clarence E. and Minnie Buswell Spore, Gerald V. Summers, Charles C. Talbott, Walter P. and Laura Ulmer, Mr. and Mrs. Herman E. Voss, and Ralph and Katherine Boeye Ward.
AUDIO-VISUAL MATERIALS: Photo of Changsha Girls' School, 1907.
MEMORABILIA: Wall hangings, slippers, chopsticks, and flag.
ORAL HISTORIES: Transcripts of interviews with Alma Ericksen and Margaret Seeck, printed in the conference paper, *The Nebraska Messenger*, n.d.

UNION COLLEGE
NB–20 Library
3800 South 48th Street
Lincoln NB 68506
(402) 488–2331 Ext. 401
Lawrence W. Onsager, Librarian

Background note: For other Seventh-Day Adventist materials, see also Andrews University, Berrien Springs, MI, 49104; General Conference of the Seventh-Day Adventists, Office of Archives and Statistics, 6840 Eastern Avenue, NW, Washington, DC, 20012; Loma Linda University, Loma Linda, CA, 92354; and Loma Linda University, Riverside, CA, 92515.

1-GENERAL HOLDINGS
DIARIES: "China Diary," 1906–7, by Jacob N. Anderson, the first Seventh-Day Adventist missionary appointed to China.
MANUSCRIPTS: "Thirty Years of Seventh-Day Adventist Missions in China," by Alton E. Hughes, 1932.
PAMPHLETS: *Catholic Church Activities in War Afflicted China*, by the China Information Committee, 1938(?); *An Hour with James Hudson Taylor, Pioneer Missionary to China*, by Theodore W. Engstrom, 1942.
SERIALS: *China Division Reporter*, 1931–38, 1943–45. *Far Eastern Division Outlook*, 1929–64.

UNIVERSITY OF NEBRASKA, LINCOLN
NB–25 Love Library
Lincoln NB 68588-0410
(402) 472–2526
Joseph G. Svoboda, University Archivist

1-RECORDS OF UNIVERSITY OF NEBRASKA YWCA, 1921–35, ca. 1 box
Background note: See also Young Women's Christian Association of America, National Board Archives, 726 Broadway, New York, NY, 10003.
MINUTES/RECORDS/REPORTS/CORRESPONDENCE: Reports, minutes of committee meetings, and correspondence of Nebraska-in-China, including material on Grace Coppock (General

Secretary of the National Committee, Shanghai), 1921–35.
MANUSCRIPTS: "Grace Coppock, A Person for Today," by Helen Thoburn, n.d.

2-GENERAL HOLDINGS
MINUTES/RECORDS/REPORTS: Cheeloo University, School of Medicine, report, 1923, 1930.
MANUSCRIPTS: "The Jesuits in China in the Last Days of the Ming Dynasty," by George H. Dunne, 1947.
SERIALS: *Chinese Recorder*, 1927–33. *Lingnan Science Journal*, 1922–50. University of Nanking, College of Agriculture and Forestry, *Bulletin*, 1924–26, 1932–36. *West China Missionary News*, 1899–1949.
DISSERTATIONS/THESES: *China and Educational Autonomy: The Changing Role of the Protestant Educational Missionary in China, 1807–1937*, by Alice Henrietta Gregg, 1945. *Protestant Mission Schools for Girls in South China (1827 to the Japanese Invasion)*, by Mary Raleigh Anderson, 1943. *A Survey of American Protestant Foreign Mission Colleges*, by S. P. Hieb, 1925.

SAINT COLUMBANS

COLUMBAN FATHERS
NB–30   Archives
St. Columbans NB 68056
(402) 291–1920
Paul Casey, Archivist

Background note: Founded by Edward J. Galvin in 1917, the St. Columbans Foreign Mission Society maintained a mission in Hanyang from 1920 to 1952. The files are not yet organized.

1-GENERAL HOLDINGS
MINUTES/RECORDS/REPORTS/CORRESPONDENCE: Ca. 2 l.f. of letters, reports and other documents relating to the Hanyang Mission of the St. Columbans Foreign Mission Society, ca. 1920- ca. 1952.
MANUSCRIPTS: "The History of Hanyang," by Abraham Shackleton, n.d.

NEW HAMPSHIRE

CONCORD

NH–5   NEW HAMPSHIRE HISTORICAL SOCIETY
30 Park Street
Concord NH 03301
(603) 225–3381
Stephen L. Cox, Manuscripts Curator

1-EDMUND ROBERTS PAPERS, 1832–33, 9 items
CORRESPONDENCE: 6 letters from Robert Morrison to Edmund Roberts concerning how to deal with the people of Cochin China and a draft of a letter from Roberts to Morrison, ca. 1832–33; letter of inquiry about papers of Robert Morrison, n.d.
MEMORABILIA: Copy of an advertisement for Morrison's translation of popular Chinese literature, n.d.

2-MARTHA A. WHEELER PAPERS, 1900–1901, 4 items
CORRESPONDENCE: Letter from T. T. Kin, Tientsin, to Martha A. Wheeler, Keene, New Hampshire, 1900; letter from George D. Wilder, North China Mission of the American Board, Tientsin, to Wheeler, concerning the siege of Tientsin and T. T. Kin (who was active in YMCA work), killed during the siege, 1901; letter from H. N. Woo to Wheeler, concerning Mrs. T. T. Kin and her sister, ca. 1901; letter from Mrs. Kin, Shanghai, to Wheeler, concerning Kin's death, 1901.

HANOVER

DARTMOUTH COLLEGE

NH–10   Archives
Hanover NH 03755
(603) 646–2037
Stanley W. Brown, Curator of Rare Books

1-DARTMOUTH-IN-CHINA, 1922–46, 1 folder
Background note: Beginning in 1922, the Dartmouth-in-China educational activities were mainly in Paotingfu in North China, under the sponsorship of the Dartmouth Christian Association and the direction of H. W. Robinson (1910), a representative of the American Board of Commissioners for Foreign Missions. Although many American universities supported college programs in China, Dartmouth's funding went mostly to elementary and secondary school education, including providing teachers and buildings for a rural school for boys in Kao-I and the Tung Jen Middle School in Paotingfu.
CORRESPONDENCE: Reprints of letters from Robinson, 1922; letter from Robinson to his wife reprinted in the *Dartmouth*, 1927.
MANUSCRIPTS: "A Dartmouth Reading Room in T'unghsien, China," by "Robbie" (Harold Robinson), n.d.
MEMORABILIA: Articles in Dartmouth *Alumni Magazine*: "A Dartmouth Hall in China," by Harold W. Robinson, n.d.; "Dartmouth in China," by Ralph B. Dwinnell, n.d.; "Ta-Te-Tung: Dartmouth in China—A Symposium," by Charles E. Butler, 1930; clippings from *Alumni Magazine*, including reprints of letters from Robinson, articles on Robinson, and short articles on Dartmouth-in-China programs, 1922–44; autobiographical article, 1922; clippings from the *Dartmouth*, 1924–36; clippings from local newspapers, 1937–46; *Dartmouth in China* brochures, 1925, 1926.

2-ROBERT WILLIAM MCCLURE ALUMNI FOLDER, 1931–47, 1 folder
Background note: Robert William McClure (1886–1965), a 1916 graduate of Dartmouth, was a missionary in China from 1916 to 1945. He and his wife taught at Foochow Christian College until 1937.
CORRESPONDENCE: Excerpt from a letter from McClure, reprinted in *The 1916 Balmacaan Newsletter*, 1947; letter from McClure dated 1931, reprinted in *Alumni Magazine*, 1932.
MEMORABILIA: Clipping about McClure's work in China, 1944; clipping from the Boston *Globe*, 1941, about reports to the American Board of Commissioners for Foreign Missions by Mc-

Clure and other missionaries in and around Foochow at the time of the Japanese occupation; clipping about Christian education in Fukien, by McClure in the *Shanghai Sunday Times*, 1931.

3-CHARLES DANIEL TENNEY ALUMNI FOLDER, 1904-ca. 1920, 1 folder

Background note: Charles Daniel Tenney (1857-1930), an 1878 graduate of Dartmouth, worked in China as a missionary under the American Board of Commissioners for Foreign Missions for three years, but resigned and shortly thereafter became tutor to the sons of Li Hung-chang. He organized the Anglo-Chinese School and was its principal from 1886 to 1895. In 1895, he became the first principal of Peiyang University in Tientsin, holding the post for 11 years. He later held several positions in the Chinese and American governments.

CORRESPONDENCE: Letter from Tenney, Tientsin, 1904, to "Professor" at Dartmouth.

MANUSCRIPTS: "History of the University," relating to the founding of Peiyang University in Tientsin and Tenney's presidency, n.d.; "Biographical Sketch of Dr. Charles D. Tenney, Former President of Peiyang University," n.a., n.d.; biographical essay on Tenney for the *Dictionary of American Biography*, by Esson M. Gale, n.d.; index of the Peiyang Government University alumni directory, n.d.

MEMORABILIA: Obituaries of Tenney, ca. 1930; clipping about Tenney's furlough to the United States in the *North China Star*, n.d. (ca. 1920); clipping about Tenney in *Christian Science Monitor*, 1918; clipping about Tenney in *Christian World*, 1909.

4-JOHN ROGERS THURSTON, 1901-4, quantity undetermined

Background note: John Rogers Thurston was a pastor of a church in Whitinsville, Massachusetts. His son was Lawrence Thurston, who served as a missionary in China. For biographical notes and other papers of Lawrence Thurston, see Yale University, Department of Manuscripts and Archives, Sterling Library, 120 High Street, New Haven, CT, 06520.

CORRESPONDENCE: Several letters regarding Lawrence Thurston, 1901-4.

NH-15   Dartmouth College Library
Hanover NH 03755
(603) 646-2235
Margaret Otto, Head Librarian

1-GENERAL HOLDINGS
SERIALS: *China Christian Year Book*, 1919, 1924-39. *Chinese Repository*, 1832-51.

MANCHESTER

NH-20   MONASTERY OF THE PRECIOUS BLOOD
700 Bridge Street
Manchester NH 03104
(603) 623-4264
Sister Mary Alice, Mother Superior

Background note: The Sisters Adorers of the Precious Blood first went to China in 1924, establishing a monastery in Sienhsien. They planned to transfer the monastery to Tientsin in 1948 at the site of the former British Hospital, but it was not realized because the superiors advised all the sisters to leave China. Most of the materials below are contained in 36 dated folders.

1-GENERAL HOLDINGS
CORRESPONDENCE: Correspondence, 1922-48, from Bishop Henri Lécroart, S.J., Precious Blood sisters, G. Debeauvais, S.J. (Provicaire and superior of the Chihli Mission), Piet Klok, S.J., François Xavier Chao, S.J., the bishop of Sienhsien, Patrick O'Connor (St. Columban's Missions in Shanghai), and Rt. Rev. Michael J. Read, National Catholic Welfare Conference; folder containing French originals and English translations labelled "official letters preceding China Foundation"; circular letter recounting experience of new recruits en route to China, 1929; copies of correspondence between Cordell Hull and John McCormack, regarding the U.S. government's responsibility for U.S. citizens in China, 1937; correspondence with John F. Stone, American vice-consul in Tientsin, 1937; correspondence relating to imprisonment of the sisters in Sienhsien and efforts to obtain their release, including a list of sisters, 1948; folder of correspondence relating to benefactors and donors to the China mission, 1945-48; circular letters from sisters in China, 1946-48; folder of post-war letters regarding efforts to contact sisters and establish their whereabouts in China, 1945-46, including correspondence with McCormack and George E. Stratemeyer; folder of letters relating to work at their mission in Japan, with occasional mention of native Chinese sisters, Jesuits, and missionaries who left China for Japan, ca. 1949-1950s; letter from B. A. Garside, 1948; French translations of letters and telegrams of T. C. Davis, Canadian ambassador to China, with the British consul in Tientsin and the Internuntiatura Apostolica in Sinis, 1948; correspondence with Arthur Ringwalt and Edward F. Kelly regarding evacuation of Chinese and foreign sisters, 1948; telegrams from McCormack and Hull on sisters' conditions in Sienhsien, 1937, 1943.

DIARIES: Journal of Sr. Tarsicius on her trip to China, with photo of her enclosed, 1931; "Star of the Sea," n.a., journal of trip from the United States to China via Japan, including arrival and installation in China, 1929; journal of Sr. Mary of the Good Shepherd on her trip to Sienhsien, 1929; journal by Sr. St. Jean de Dieu on trip from China to Portland, Oregon, with several returning sisters, 1931.

MANUSCRIPTS: "Memoirs of the Mission of Sienhsien through Troubled Waters, 1937-1948," by Sr. Mary of Calvary; "Necrologie Notice of Sister St. Catherine of Sienna," 1931, on the death of a native sister; "A Big Victory in One of the Nearby Villages, Potowchen," by André Joliet, S.J., 1935; lists of sisters in Sienhsien, 1937, 1942; "History of the Foundation in China," 1924; untitled manuscript including progress of the mission with excerpts of letters from China, 1922; manuscript on the establishment of the monastery in Sienhsien, n.d.; "Quelques Bribes Mensuelles, 1939"; "Some Echoes from Our Oriental Solitude," 1940; notes on discussion with Mr. Humble, Division of Chinese Affairs, Department of State, regarding the sisters' situation in Tientsin, 1948.

PAMPHLETS: *Etat de la mission au 1er juillet 1924*, containing a list of personnel and statistics for the Chihli Mission.

MEMORABILIA: Clippings on release of sisters, *L'Action Catholique* and *Tientsin Evening Journal*, 1948.

MAPS/DESIGNS/DRAWINGS: Map of the mission in South East Chihli, indicating the location of the monastery, n.d., in large photo album below.

AUDIO-VISUAL MATERIALS: Small photo album, 1925–48, containing photos of work in Hopeh, newly ordained native priests, Bishop Henri Lécroart, S.J., Mother St. Simon, Chihli Mission, Precious Blood missionaries, Chinese people and scenes, a Corpus Christi procession in Sienhsien, and the Sanctuary of the Monastery of the Precious Blood; large photo album, 1924–48, containing photos of the monastery in Sienhsien, foundresses of the monastery, Bishop Henri Lécroart, S.J., arrival in Sienhsien, a trip from Potowchen to Sienhsien, sisters, mission compound, chapel, construction of the monastery, interior views of the monastery, novitiate, British Hospital, Chinese sisters, and the last missionaries to China; photo of Bishop Henri Lécroart, S.J.
CHINESE LANGUAGE MATERIALS: Propagation of the Faith leaflet in the large photo album above, 1939; obituary of Bishop Lécroart; handwritten prayer.

NEW JERSEY

CLIFTON

PATERSON DIOCESE
NJ–5 Paterson Diocesan Archives
777 Valley Road
Clifton NJ 07013
(201) 334–4506
Raymond J. Kupke, Archivist

Background note: For additional material relating to the mission maintained by the Sisters of Charity of St. Elizabeth, see Sisters of Charity of St. Elizabeth, Generalate Archives, Convent Station, NJ, 07961.

1-GENERAL HOLDINGS
MINUTES/RECORDS/REPORTS/CORRESPONDENCE: Ca. 2 in. of reports and letters from the Sisters of Charity of St. Elizabeth to Thomas McLaughlin, Bishop of Paterson, describing the establishment of their mission at Yuanling, Hunan, and wartime conditions, 1937–47.
AUDIO-VISUAL MATERIALS: 2 photos of sisters standing in front of their convent after a Japanese bombing, n.d.

CONVENT STATION

COLLEGE OF SAINT ELIZABETH
NJ–10 Mahoney Library
Convent Station NJ 07961
(201) 539–1600
Sister Marie Rousek, S.C., Director of the Library

1-GENERAL HOLDINGS

SERIALS: *China Monthly*, 1939–49. *Les Missions de Chine*, 1942. *Les Missions de Chine et du Japon*, 1929. *Sign*, 1924–82.

SISTERS OF CHARITY OF ST. ELIZABETH
NJ–15 Generalate Archives
Convent Station NJ 07961
(201) 292–6543
Sister Elizabeth McLoughlin, S.C., Archivist

Restrictions: Access by appointment.
Background note: The Sisters of Charity of St. Elizabeth of New Jersey is an apostolic institute whose purpose is to show forth the love of Jesus Christ in serving those in need, especially the poor. Maintaining a mission in China until the Communist takeover, the Sisters of Charity served in Yuanling and Wuki, Hunan, from 1924 to 1951, when the Chinese Communists took over. Their work included a co-ed elementary school and a high school for girls, a hospital, a nursing school, dispensaries, orphanages, a catechumenate for women, and an embroidery school. In Yuanling the Sisters of Charity worked in conjunction with the Congregation of the Passion of the Eastern United States (Passionists). See also Congregation of the Passion of the Eastern United States, 110 Monastery Place, West Springfield, MA, 01089; and Paterson Diocese, Paterson Diocesan Archives, 777 Valley Road, Clifton, NJ, 07013.

Sister nurses also served in the U.S. 95th Station Hospital in Kunming, after being driven from Hunan by the Japanese. In 1980, a plaque was installed at the Sisters of Charity Generalate, by the China-Burma-India Veterans' Association (CBIVA) in recognition of this service. Medals were also awarded posthumously to Sister Mary Finan Griffin and Sister Maria Sebastian Curley, two Sisters of Charity who served in Kunming.

1-GENERAL HOLDINGS
MINUTES/RECORDS/REPORTS: 1 l.f. of reports on the Saint Therese Mission, Yuanling; Christ the King Mission, Wuki; by-laws, constitutions, and catalogues, 1924–54.
CORRESPONDENCE: 3 l.f. of correspondence on the Sisters of Charity mission activities, methods, problems, and accounts, 1924–51; letter detailing Sr. Maria Electa McDermott's death, Yuanling, 1941.
DIARIES: Diary of Sr. Mary Finan Griffin, 1924–33.
MANUSCRIPTS: Biography of Sr. Marie Devota Ross, n.d., in Sr. Mary Finan Griffin's scrapbook.
PAMPHLETS: *Lo Pa Hong: The Coolie of Saint Joseph*, by Paul Roberts, 1938; *Your Yuanling Catholic Hospital—1949*, in Sr. Mary Finan Griffin's scrapbook.
MEMORABILIA: 2.5 l.f. of scrapbooks containing: programs for Sisters of Charity ceremonial occasions such as departures for China, 1924, 1933, 1939, 1946; newspaper clippings on bombings of Yuanling, 1939–41, and on the expulsion from China of Sisters of Charity; Vicariate of Yuanling, spiritual ledger, 1940–41; script for TV show, "We the People," 1959, featuring Sr. Mary Finan Griffin and Sr. Mary Carita Pendergast on Sisters of Charity China mission and Communist takeover, covering 1924 to 1959.
ORAL HISTORIES: 9 cassette tapes by Sr. Theresa Beschel containing her account of Sisters of Charity China missions, 1924–51; Bishop Cuthbert M.O'Gara's account of his imprisonment in China, on 4 reel-to-reel tapes, 1951–54; interview with Jean Lynas, retired U.S. Army nurse, on Sisters of Charity work in China, on cassette tape.

MAPS/DESIGNS/DRAWINGS: Cloth maps of north, central, and southeast China, and Indo-China, U.S. Army Map Service, 1943; *Postal Map of Hunan District*, 1930; *The Complete Atlas of China*, (London: Edward Stanford, Ltd.), 1917; *Philips' Commercial Map of China with Handbook*, ed. by Sir Alexander Hosie (London: George Philip and Son, Ltd.), 1922.
AUDIO-VISUAL MATERIALS: 800 photos of people, places, and activities of Sisters of Charity mission, 1920–50; 9 slides of various artifacts used by or given to the mission; 16mm. film of departure for China of two Sisters of Charity, Easter Sunday, 1941; China-Burma-India Veterans' Association award of plaque for the work of the Sisters of Charity mission during World War II, on 2 tapes, 1980.
SERIALS: *Caritas*, 1933–43. *Hunan News*, 1950–54.
CHINESE LANGUAGE MATERIALS: 11 volumes on Catholic doctrine, missal, prayer, problem of labor, proofs of Catholic religion, Latin alphabet, Chinese language lessons, and Protestantism; newspaper clippings about bombings of Yuanling from 1939 to 1941; constitution of Sisters of Charity, 1949; *Daily Manual of Prayers for the Use of the Sisters of Charity*, 1949.
FINDING AIDS: General index.

ELMWOOD PARK

NJ–20 AMERICAN LEPROSY MISSIONS, INC.
1 Broadway
Elmwood Park NJ 07003
(201) 794–8650
Eugene Wilson, Director Program Finance

Background note: Materials are unorganized and uncatalogued.
1-GENERAL HOLDINGS
MINUTES/RECORDS/REPORTS: Information concerning leprosaria in Chekiang, Fukien, Hunan, Kansu, Kiangsi, Kiangsu, Kwangsi, Kwangtung, Kweichow, Shantung, Shensi, Sikang, Szechwan, Taiwan, and Yunnan provinces, including locations in Anfu, Anlung, Chaotung, Chengtu, Feng Tien, Foochow, Futsing, Hainan, Hanchung, Hangchow, Hankong, Hwang Shih, Kienow, Kiulungkiang, Kunming, Kutien, Lanchow, Linhsien, Lin Mei, Lo Ting, Loyuan, Lungchow, Mintsing, Mosimien, Nanchang, Nanning-Soeilok, Ngai Moon, Pakhoi, Putien, Salachi, Shanghai, Sheklung, Shimenk'an, Siaokan, Sinhwa, Taikam, Tenghsien, Tsam Kong, Tsinan, Tsingchow, Tsingyuen, Tungkun, Yenchowfu, Yenping, and Yuki, 1906–49.
Information concerning out-patient clinics in Chekiang, Fukien, Hunan, Hupeh, Kiangsu, Kwangsi, Kwangtung, Szechwan, and Yunnan provinces, including locations in Amoy, Canton, Changchow, Chaoyang, Chengtu, Chuanchow, Enshih, Fatshan, Foochow, Hangchow, Hankow, Hoihow, Hweian, Jukao, Kityang, Kongmoon, Kutien, Meihsien, Nanping, Nantungchow, Pao King, Putien, Sa Pu Shan, Shanghai, Shao Yang, Shima, Siaokan, Siu Tung, Swabue, Swatow, Taichow, Tali, Tongan, Tsingkiangpu, Tsingchow, Tsingtao, Tungkun, Weihsien, Wuchow, and Yi Yang, 1906–49.
CORRESPONDENCE/DIARIES: Miscellaneous correspondence and diaries of ALM missionaries.
AUDIO-VISUAL MATERIALS: Photos of the Rhenish mission in Tungkun and the Presbyterian mission in Hoihow.

ESSEX FELLS

NORTHEASTERN BIBLE COLLEGE
NJ–25 Lincoln Memorial Library
Essex Fells NJ 07021
(201) 226–1074
Mimi Mac Mullen, Assistant Librarian

Background note: The holdings at Northeastern Bible College reflect the school's rootage in Biblical theism. The college believes that world mission is one of the Biblical imperatives. Although the library holds no primary materials, its holdings of books show an unusual concentration on the China Inland Mission and biographies of missionaries and Chinese Christians who represent the theological stance of the college.

Subjects of the biographies include John and Jean Abernathy, John Arthur Anderson, Gladys Aylward, Mary Ball, Herman Becker, L. Nelson Bell, Rudolf Alfred Bosshardt, William Chalmers Burns, Sidney James Wells Clark, Francis Augustus Cox, David Davies, George Fox DeVol, Archibald Orr Ewing, Feng Yü-hsiang, James Outram Fraser, Henry Weston Frost, Archibald Edward Glover, Jonathan and Florence Rosalind Goforth, David Wells Herring, Dixon Edward Hoste, Frank Houghton, Hsi Sheng-mo, Jen Ch'eng-yuan, Margaret King, Isobel Selina Miller Kuhn, Herbert John Mason, Arthur and Wilda Mathews, Fred Mitchell, Charlotte Moon, Nee To-sheng, John Livingston Nevius, Sara Perkins, Casper C. Skinsnes, John and Elisabeth Stam, John Sung, Absalom Sydenstricker, J. Hudson and Maria Taylor, Mary Geraldine Taylor, Christiana Tsai, Wang Ming-dao, and John Elias Williams.

The China Inland Mission became the Overseas Missionary Fellowship after the establishment of the People's Republic of China. Its archives are at Wheaton College, Billy Graham Center Archives, Wheaton, IL, 60187. See also Overseas Missionary Fellowship, 404 South Church Street, Robesonia, PA, 19551.

1-GENERAL HOLDINGS
MINUTES/RECORDS/REPORTS: China Inland Mission, annual report, 1950.

LIBERTY CORNER

NJ–30 FELLOWSHIP DEACONRY, INC.
Box 204
Liberty Corner NJ 07938–0204
(201) 647–1777
Sister Rita Krohn, Deaconess

Background note: The Liberty Corner Mission serves in East Asia in partnership with the Marburger Mission, which is the foreign mission agency of the Deutscher Gemeinschaftsdiakonieverband in Germany, founded in 1899. Their work in China began as the Vandsburger Mission, working together with the Liebenzeller Mission within the China Inland Mission from 1909 to 1928. From 1929 to 1951, it was called the Yunnan Mission working independently within the China Inland Mission.

The Yunnan Mission Society founded the Dien Kwang School for Blind Girls in Kunming in 1929, in cooperation with several mission agencies. In 1934, a dental clinic was established at the mission, staffed by one of the few missionary dentists in China, Sister Kunigunde Brunner. The clinic serviced missionaries from all over China and U.S. servicemen stationed in Yunnan. During the Japanese occupation, when funds from Germany were not forthcoming, Brunner was commissioned to practice forensic dentistry, assisting in the identification of servicemen. During World War II, the school was evacuated to Anning and Yuki, during which time the property in Kunming was destroyed in 1940. They remained in Anning until the school was rebuilt in 1945, then returned to Kunming until 1951.

1-GENERAL HOLDINGS

MINUTES/RECORDS/REPORTS: Anning Station, annual report, 1942; Blind Girls' School, annual reports, 1942–44, 1946; Chengtong Station, annual report, 1939; China Inland Mission: Pato, reports, 1943–44: principles and practice, and blank application forms, n.d.; Yuki, annual report, 1943–44: Mission hospital at Yuki, annual report, 1943; record of mission work at Kunyang, 1942; Girls' Industrial Home, Oshan, annual report, 1942; Imen Station, annual report, 1939, 1942; Laopehchai Mission Station, annual report, 1941–42; Oshan Station, annual report, 1939, 1942; Pato Station, annual report, 1939; Pehcheng Station, annual report, 1939; Sinchai Station, annual report, 1939; Sinping Station, annual report, 1942; Yunnan Mission Society, reports, 1939–41, 1945–48, 1950; Children's Yunnan report, 1946.

CORRESPONDENCE: Bound volume of correspondence of Karoline Steinhoff, 1949–52, mostly on Japan, but containing mention of the China Inland Mission and Liebenzeller Mission, including letters from Edward C. Reber, West Point, to the U.S. consul in Frankfurt, attesting to the non-political nature of Steinhoff's work in China, 1952; 2 letters from Luise Töpfer, Oshan, 1939; letter from Barbara Deibel, Imen, 1939; bound volume of correspondence of Karoline Steinhoff and Kunigunde Brunner, 1949–50, containing circular letters and other letters regarding the Yunnan mission and speaking engagements in the United States, including such correspondents as Lina Reuter, Harold Brunner, Roger Howes of the China Inland Mission, China Inland Mission in Philadelphia, Milton Stauffer, Henry Brown, George Sutherland, Edgar Rue (Association for the Chinese Blind), King J. Coffman, Frank Houghton, and Edward C. Reber; bound volume of miscellaneous correspondence, 1939–45, containing letters to and from N. Arne Bendtz (War Prisoners Aid, World's Committee YMCA), Kunigunde Brunner, J. L. Dietrich, E. Fink, H. G. Gould (China Inland Mission), Anna Müller, Toni Radmer, Edward C. Reber, Lina Reuter, Karoline Steinhoff, and George Sutherland; bound volume of post–1951 China Inland Mission correspondence, including 12 letters of Hanna Liu, Oshan, 1952–54; circular letter regarding the progress of blind girls at the school, 1950; letters from Anna Müller, Kunming, 1948; circular letters of Maria Bido (1940), Kunigunde Brunner (1949, 1951), J. L. Dietrich (1940–41), Babette Fleischmann (1940), G. Guth (1942), Anna Müller (1939–40), Bertha Preisinger (1939), Lina Reuter (1944–51), Karoline Steinhoff (1949), and Yunnan Mission (1948–50); box of loose correspondence, 1949–51, containing 3 letters from Lina Reuter, 1951, regarding the continuation of the school after their departure, and other letters from correspondents including Lilly Benson, Esther Bower, Marion Bower, Kunigunde Brunner, the China Inland Mission, J. W. Decker, L. G. Dick, Babette Fleischmann, McKinley Gilliland, Myrtle Hinkhouse, Frank Houghton, Roger

Howes, Isobel Kuhn, W. G. Lewis, Paul Martens, Anna Müller, Johanna Ott, Frank E. Pulley (USMA Chaplain), Edgar H. Rue, Lina Reuter, B. Rink, Paula Schumm, and George Schmauss.

MANUSCRIPTS: Lists of Chinese working with the Yunnan Mission, n.d.; biographies of blind Chinese girls at the school; lists of American Lutheran servicemen who attended the Kunming Service Center, 1944–45; lists of supporters, 1949–50; biography with photo of Cheng Chi-ming, n.d.; list of sponsored children, 1952; China Children's Fund, list of adopted children and their sponsors, ca. 1952; "Bildererklärung," by J. Dietrich, 1936; "Abschrift," by A. Robisch, 1935; "6 Aufnahmen vom Bado-Bau," by J. Dietrich, 1936; "An die Hauseltern unserer Mutterhäuser von Altvandsburg, Neuvandsburg-Ost, Neuvandsburg-West, Hebron, Hensoltshöhe, Lachen, Tabor," by Georg Schmauss, 1951; "Folgende Chinabriefe gingen ein," by Georg Schmauss, 1949, listing China missionaries; "From the Blind Girls' School Diary," mimeograph, 1939; "Die Geschichte der Cheng Mei-li," by Anna Müller, ca. 1948; "Twenty-five Years in Kunming," by Annie Yü, n.d.

PAMPHLETS: *Götterleben in Yünnans Bergen*, by Lina Pfister, n.d.; *Handelt bis ich wiederkomme: Die Marburger Mission und ihre Geschichte*, 1965; *"Lord, That I Might Receive My Sight"*: *The Cry of Blind Girls in Yunnan, China*, by the Yunnan Mission Society, ca. 1947; *Auf Missionspfaden in China*, by Georg Schmauss, 1937; *The Story of Annie Yü and A Short History of the Blind Girls' School, Kunming (Yunnanfu), China*, n.d.; *25th Anniversary of the Missionary Work at Mosha, Yunnan, China*, by A. E. Pretel, ca. 1946.

MEMORABILIA: Yunnan Mission brochures, ca. 1934, 1949; conference of sisters in Kunming, program, 1936; China Inland Mission handbook, ca. 1953.

AUDIO-VISUAL MATERIALS: 2 envelopes of photos and brief biographies of blind girls needing supporters, 1948; bound volume of photos and biographies of blind girls supported, ca. 1948–1949; box of ca. 200 loose photos, ca. 1935–1951, of blind girls, Annie Yü, Kunigunde Brunner as a dentist, sisters at work, Dien Kwang School for Blind Girls, class photos, Chinese students, graduation ceremonies, faculty, missionaries and missionary families, Anna Müller, and Chinese people and scenes; envelope of negatives; small photo album of missionaries, n.d.; envelope of photos of Chinese scenes belonging to L. Pfister, n.d; printed photo of Frederick Brandauer of the Peking Union Language School, n.d.; envelope of photos, with a list of descriptions, sent to Lina Reuter by G. Guth, ca. 1949; photo of a Chinese youth, negative of a class photo, and letter to Lina Reuter, 1949; Chinese scroll.

SERIALS: *Missions-Nachrichten aus Yünnan*, 1945–51.

CHINESE LANGUAGE MATERIALS: Bible quotations on ribbons; miscellaneous handwritten Bible quotations; Religious Tract Society poster, "The Cross as a Gate," 1936; religious tract.

LINCOLN PARK

POCKET TESTAMENT LEAGUE
NJ–35   Archives
P. O. Box 368
Lincoln Park NJ 07035-0368
(201) 696–1900
Ernest C. Lubkemann, contact

Restrictions: Access by written request.

Background note: The Pocket Testament League, an interdenominational evangelical missionary ministry, was founded in 1893 by Helen Cadbury. She later married Charles M. Alexander, who, together with J. Wilbur Chapman, launched the Pocket Testament League as a worldwide movement in 1908. The Alexanders and evangelist J. Wilbur Chapman visited China in the early 1900s, but it was not until 1945 that the Pocket Testament League initiated its foreign missionary activities, beginning in China and moving to Taiwan after the Communist takeover.

The Pocket Testament League began its work with soldiers and students, receiving support from Chiang K'ai-shek, General George C. Marshall, and other government and military leaders. The evangelists soon expanded their work to the general public and worked closely with other mission organizations, including the China Inland Mission.

1-GENERAL HOLDINGS

MINUTES/RECORDS/REPORTS: "China," in Golden Jubilee booklet (1908–58), 1958.

CORRESPONDENCE: Several letters of introduction and recommendations for mission activity in China and Taiwan, including letters from Augustus W. Bennet, Chiang K'ai-shek, George C. Marshall, Luther D. Miller, Sun Li-jen, A. C. Wedemeyer, and various Chinese officials.

AUDIO-VISUAL MATERIALS: Several photos of mission activity in China, 1945–46.

MADISON

DREW UNIVERSITY

NJ–40 Drew University Library
Madison NJ 07940
(201) 377-3000
Susan Selinger, Theology Librarian

1-McCLINTOCK RARE BOOKS COLLECTION, 1894, 1 item
CHINESE LANGUAGE MATERIALS: New Testament in Mandarin, 1894.

2-GENERAL HOLDINGS
MINUTES/RECORDS/REPORTS: American Board of Commissioners for Foreign Missions, Foochow Mission, report, 1895–96; Central China Religious Tract Society, annual report, 1885–86, 1888–93, 1898, 1901–10, 1912, 1915; Chefoo Industrial Mission, report, 1905–6, 1908; China Continuation Committee, minutes, 1914, 1916–21; China International Famine Relief Commission, annual report, 1926; China Medical Board of New York, reports, 1964–66; Christian Literature Society for China, report, 1899, 1905–7, 1909–10; Educational Association of China, records, 1896; Foochow Medical Missionary Hospital, annual report, 1887; Hildesheim Missionary Society, report, 1911; Medical Missionary Society in China, report, 1832, 1861–66; Mission Among the Higher Classes in China, report, 1896–97, n.d. (14th–16th, 19th–20th); Mission to the Chinese Blind, annual report, 1892–94, 1899; National Christian Council of China on Church in China, 1926; North China College and Gordon Memorial Theological Seminary, catalogue, 1894–95; North China Tract Society, annual report, 1885–86, 1890–91, 1894, 1897, 1898; Peking Union

Medical College, annual report, 1916–17; Peking University, Board of Managers, minutes, 1909, 1911; Presbyterian Church in the U.S.A., Board of Foreign Missions, 1927; Society for the Diffusion of Christian and General Knowledge Among the Chinese, annual report, 1900, 1902; Tientsin Famine Relief Committee, 1890–91; West China Religious Tract Society, 1899–1902, 1904–5; West China Union University, report, 1910–11.

MANUSCRIPTS: "As I Look Back: Recollections of Growing Up in America's Southland and of Twenty-six Years in Pre-Communist China, 1888–1936," by Eugene E. Barnett, 1963–68.

PAMPHLETS: 46 titles, 1883–1937, including subjects such as Szechuan Riots, protest against the Chinese outrages, the Kucheng Massacre of 1895, and brief histories and reminiscences of the missionary situation in China.

MAPS/DESIGNS/DRAWINGS: Map of China among the pamphlets.

SERIALS: *China Bulletin*, 1952–62. *China Christian Year Book*, 1910–39. *China for Christ*, 1940–41. *China's Millions* (London), 1875–1916, 1941–52. *Chinese Missionary Gleaner*, 1853(?). *Chinese Recorder*, 1913–38. *Chinese Recorder and Educational Review*, 1939–41. *Chinese Recorder and Missionary Journal*, 1868–1912. *Chinese Repository*, 1832–51. *Ching Feng*, 1964–. *East Asia Millions* (Philadelphia), 1961–. *Educational Review*, 1915–38. *India's Women and China's Daughters*, 1896–1926. *Land of Sinim*, 1904, 1907–13. *Millions* (Philadelphia), 1952–61.

DISSERTATIONS/THESES: *American Lutheran Mission Work in China*, by Rolf Arthur Syrdal, 1942. *Chinese Christian Experience Psychologically and Theologically Considered*, by Mark Weber Brown, 1930. *The Covenant Missionary Society in China*, by Earl C. Dahlstrom, 1950. *Missionary Journalism in Nineteenth-century China: Young J. Allen and the Early "Wan kuo kung pao,"* 1886–1883, by Adrian Arthur Bennett, 1970. *A Program for the Church of Ping-tan Hsien, Fukien, China*, by Chang-tung Yang, 1935. *Prophet Sage and Wise Man: A Comparative Study of Intellectual Tradition in Ancient China and Israel*, by Nathaniel Yung-tse Yen, 1977. *A Symbolic Interactionist Approach to the Religious Stranger Concept: Protestant Missionaries in China, 1845–1900*, by Nishan J. Najarian, 1982.

NJ–45 General Commission on Archives and History— The United Methodist Church
United Methodist Archives and History Center Archives
36 Madison Avenue
P. O. Box 127
Madison NJ 07940
(201) 822-2787/2826
Charles Yrigoyen, Jr., General Secretary
William Beal, Archivist
Mark Shenise, Assistant Archivist

Restrictions: Many archival papers are under a 50-year limitation. Permission must be secured in writing from Marva Usher-Kerr, Records Manager, Central Records Room 1515, General Board of Global Ministries, United Methodist Church, 475 Riverside Drive, New York, NY, 10115.

Background note: The collections described below consist of records of the United Methodist Church dating back to the mid-eighteenth century. Some of the materials can be found under such antecedents as the Methodist Episcopal Church, South, the Methodist Protestant Church, the Methodist Church, the Evangelical Association, the United Evangelical Church, the Evangelical Church, the Church of the United Brethren in Christ, or the Evangelical United Brethren Church.

The General Board of Global Ministries is currently conducting a United Methodist China Missions History Project, which is collecting and organizing historical data, as well as compiling a collection of oral histories, which are stored in the Methodist Archives as they are completed. Contact the Archives Department for further details.

See also Church of the Brethren General Board, Brethren Historical Library and Archives, 1451 Dundee Avenue, Elgin, IL, 60120; Garrett Evangelical and Seabury-Western Theological Seminaries, United Library, 2121/22 Sheridan Road, Evanston, IL, 60201; Duke University, Divinity Library, Durham, NC, 27706; Emory University, Candler School of Theology, Pitts Theology Library, Atlanta, GA, 30322; Free Methodist Church of North America, Marston Historical Center, 901 College Avenue, Winona Lake, IN, 46590; Southern Methodist University, Perkins School of Theology, Bridwell Library, Dallas, TX, 75222; and United Theological Seminary, Library, 1810 Harvard Boulevard, Dayton, OH, 45406.

1-BOARD OF MISSIONS OF THE UNITED METHODIST CHURCH AND ITS, ANTECEDENTS, 1831-, 39 l.f.
MINUTES/RECORDS/REPORTS: Annual reports (yearbooks).

2-CHURCH OF THE UNITED BRETHREN IN CHRIST, 1905–11, 13,000 items
CORRESPONDENCE: 13,000 carbon copies of letters from executive offices to missionaries, 1905–11.

3-CORRESPONDENCE: BOARD OF MISSIONS, METHODIST CHURCH AND ITS ANTECEDENTS, 1912–65, ca. 55 c.f.
MINUTES/RECORDS/REPORTS/CORRESPONDENCE: Reports, minutes, and correspondence of the following institutions: Anglo-Chinese School, Associated Board for Christian Colleges in China, Bashford Memorial Bible School, Bureau of Construction for Foochow and Hinghwa, California College in China, Canton Union Christian College, Central China Conference, Chadwick Memorial Hospital, Chang Chow Church, Changchow Church, Changchow Hospital, Changli General Hospital, Changli Hui Wen Academy, Chengtu Conference, Chengtu Hospital, Chin Chin Middle School, China Centennial Committee, China Central Conference, China Christian Educational Association, China Committee, China Medical Association, China Medical Board, China Sunday School Union, Christian Literature Society for China, Christian Medical Council for Overseas Work, Chung Cheng Children's Home, Chungking Conference, Chungking High School, Chungking Hospital, Chungking Union Schools, College of Chinese Studies, East China Conference, East China Hospital, East China Union University, Foochow Conference, Foochow Methodist Mission, Foochow Union High School, Fukien Christian University, Fukien Conference, Fukien Construction Bureau, Fukien Union Theological College, Ginling College, Hangchow Christian University, Hinghwa Conference, Hopkins Memorial Hospital, Huchow General Hospital, Huchow University, insurance companies, Isabella Fisher Hospital, Kanhsien Union Christian Middle School, Kiangsi International Famine Relief Committee, Kiangsi-Anhui Christian Rural Service Union, Kien Yang Rural Service Union, Kuling Methodist Sanitorium, Lingnan University, McTyeire School, Methodist Hospital, Methodist Publishing House, Methodist Relief Fund, Methodist Union Hospital, Mission Book Company, Missionary Committee—Foochow, Moore Memorial Church, Mutao Union Junior Middle School, Mutoto Union Hospital, Nanchang Academy, Nanchang Hospital, Nanking Language School, Nanking Theological Seminary, Nanping Hospital, National Christian Council of China, National Missionary Conference China Continuation Committee, North China Christian Rural Service Union, North China Christian Broadcasting Association, North China Conference, North China Union Medical School for Women, Peking Academy, Peking American School, Peking High Primary School, Peking Theological Seminary, Peking Union Medical College, Peking University, Shantung Christian (Cheeloo) University, Shantung Conference, Shantung Mission, Sienyu Union Hospital, Sleeper Davis Hospital, Soochow University, South China Conference, South Fukien Conference, Standing Committee on Sunday Schools, Foochow Union High School, Stephenson Memorial Hospital, Tientsin Hui Wen School, Tsunhua Hui Wen Middle School, Tzechow Hospital, Union Architectural Service, Union Bible School for Women, Union Medical School for East China, Union Theological College, United Board for Christian Colleges in China, United Committee for Christian Universities of China, University of Nanking, West China Annual Conference, West China Conference, West China Union Theological College, West China Union University, West China Union University Middle School, West China University Hospital, Wiley Hospital, William Nast Academy, Women's Medical College for West China, Wuhu Hospital, Yenching Foundation, Yenching Hospital, Yenching University, and Yenping Conference; reports and correspondence of individuals including Edward J. Aeschliman, John F. Alman, Sidney R. Anderson, Frank A. Argelander, Reno W. Backus, Frederick Bankhardt, William C. Barrett, Helen E. Barton, J. W. Bashford, Joseph Beech, James H. H. Berckman, Marguerite L. Berkey, A. W. Billing, Mary E. Billing, Merlin A. Bishop, W. S. Bissonnette, George T. Blydenburgh, Mae Boucher, J. W. Bovyer, Arthur J. Bowen, Raymond R. Brewer, William N. Brewster, Harold N. Brewster, Mark W. Brown, Robert E. Brown, Fred R. Brown, Ernest B. Caldwell, Harry R. Caldwell, H. L. Canright, F. T. Cartwright, T. C. Chao, W. Y. Chen, Ernest H. Clay, Wray H. Congdon, Arthur B. Coole, Thomas H. Coole, Douglas Paul Coole, Esther Cooper, Earl Cranston, Walter M. Crawford, J. O. Curnow, George L. Davis, Walter W. Davis, Melissa J. Davis, Jackson Wesley Day, Louis R. Dennis, F. W. Dietrich, James L. Ding, Edward E. Dixon, Duncan F. Dodd, Gerald L. Downie, Clara Pearl Dyer, J. W. Dyson, Joseph Dyson, Margery K. Eggeston, Edwin R. Embree, James D. D. Endicott, J. B. Eyestone, Carl Felt, Eddy L. Ford, Pearl Fosnot, William A. Foster, C. W. Freeman, Glenn V. Fuller, Frank C. Gale, Elmer W. Galt, Frank D. Gamewell, Frank P. Gaunt, Evaline Gaw, W. Max Gentry, John McGregor Gibb, Jesse Earl Gossard, John Gowdy, Lyman L. Hale, Perry O. Hanson, Richard E. Hanson, Thomas A. Harris, Earl E. Harvey, Lewis F. Havermale, Robert Bruce Havighurst, Freeman C. Havighurst, Paul G. Hayes, E. Pearce Hayes, Willo M. Hecker, Ruth V. Hemenway, Earl R. Hibbard, Harry J. Hill, William T. Hobart,

Leland Holland, Gordon F. Hoople, Earl A. Hoose, Nehemiah S. Hopkins, George W. Hosslier, Edward H. Hume, Loren R. Humphrey, Paul Hutchinson, John Theron Illick, H. W. Irwin, Edward James, Bruce W. Jarvis, Allen O. Jernigan, Charles F. Johannaber, William R. Johnson, Paul E. Johnson, Edwin C. Jones, Tracey K. Jones, Oscar A. Guinn, Jr., Z. T. Kaung, J. L. Keeler, Claude R. Kellogg, Arthur C. Kenney, E. K. Knettler, Lillian Knobles, Oliver J. Krause, William H. Lacy, Walter N. Lacy, Henry V. Lacy, G. Carleton Lacy, William Irving Lacy, Creighton Lacy, B. F. Lawrence, Roxy Lefforge, Ruth R. Leitzel, Walter E. Libby, S. H. Liljestrand, Serene Loland, Allen P. Lovejoy, George D. Lowry, Donald MacInnis, Sarah Mabel Maclean, William A. Main, W. A. Main, Marian E. Manley, W. E. Manly, Arthur W. Martin, Herrymon Maurer, Francis J. McConnell, William A. McCurdy, Frank Rudd McDonald, George S. Miner, Hugh C. Morgan, Edgar K. Morrow, George B. Neumann, Eric M. North, William W. Overholt, Bromley Oxnam, B. H. Paddock, Robert Morris Paty, J. F. Peat, Edward C. Perkins, Robert Peterson, W. B. Pettus, Carlysle James Philips, Willis F. Pierce, Raymond F. Pilcher, John A. Pilley, Deanette Ploeg, Orvia Proctor, Frederick M. Pyke, James H. Pyke, C. Bertram Rape, Harry F. Rowe, Henry H. Rowland, Myra L. Sawyer, Karl W. Scheufler, William E. Schubert, Clair K. Searles, Margaret Seeck, Dwight Lamar Sheretz, Edith Simester, Willard J. Simpson, C. M. Lacy Sites, James E. Skinner, Dennis V. Smith, Herbert I. Smith, Margaret V. Stafford, Oscar G. Starrett, H. C. Steinheimer, Albert N. Steward, Lucy R. Stillman, F. Olin Stockwell, Everett M. Stowe, Ellen Studley, T. Janet Surdam, Roy E. Teele, Alice Terrell, Guy Thelin, May Belle Thompson, Frank M. Toothaker, R. L. Torrey, Charles G. Trimble, Clifford S. Trimmer, Amber Van, Gladys Venbert, Erma H. Wainner, Wallace Wang, Ralph A. Ward, Hyla S. Watters, Alice Weed, Ernest W. Weiss, Paul P. Wiant, Bliss Wiant, Alice Wilcox, Horace Williams, Edward J. Winans, George B. Workman, Harry W. Worley, George K. T. Wu, James M. Yard, and John W. Yost.
SERIALS: *China Christian Advocate*, 1932–41.
FINDING AIDS: Container checklist (accession # 73–43).

4-EVANGELICAL UNITED BRETHREN CHURCH BOARD OF MISSIONS, 1900–1961, 1.7 c.f.
MINUTES/RECORDS/REPORTS/PAMPHLETS: Board of Missions: reports, records, and other printed matter, 1912, 1916, 1918, 1923–24, 1927–30; legal papers, documents, 1921; China Mission: lists of missionary losses, 1927–28; minutes, 1908–23; proceedings of the annual meeting, 1926; treasurer's book, 1905–13; China Mission Committee, minutes and reports, 1932–49; East Hunan Mission, annual report, 1928; Indemnity funds for Chinese, 1922–23; South China Mission, minutes, 1947–49; 8 folders of miscellaneous materials on China, 1900–1961.
CORRESPONDENCE: 31 folders of Board of Mission correspondence, 1907–30, including H.C. Anderson, Regina Bigler, Pearl Bertch, Catherine Brunemeier, Clinton Burris, Frederick Davis, Sarah May Dick, Mable Drury, Irving Dunlap, Rose L. Fecker, Clifford Funk, Marie T. Hasenpflug, Elsie Bernice Heidenreich, Stanley Kintigh, Howard T. Kuist, Eunice Mitchell, Belle Myers, Cora F. Noberie, Arthur H. Sanders, E. W. and Lena M. Schmalzried, Martha Schroedter, W. E. Shambaugh, Charles Shoop, Ralph W. E. Spreng, Naomi K. Stoesser, Theodore and Esther Suhr, Charles C. Talbott, Walter P. Ulmer, E. B. Ward, and Mar-

tha Katherine Wolf; correspondence regarding burning and looting of Liling House, 1918.
MANUSCRIPTS: Biographies of missionaries of East Hunan and West Hunan-Kweichow Missions, by Charles H. Ream, n.d.
AUDIO-VISUAL MATERIALS/MAPS/DESIGNS/DRAWINGS/MEMORABILIA: 30 items of clippings and map pertaining to China mission, n.d.; photo of Siangta church, n.d.

5-INFORMATION FILES FROM THE LIBRARY OF THE GENERAL BOARD OF GLOBAL MINISTRIES, UNITED METHODIST CHURCH, 1889?–?, ca. 14 c.f.
MINUTES/RECORDS/REPORTS/PAMPHLETS: Reports, publications, and papers relating to Central China Conference and related institutions, China missions, Christian cause in China, College of Chinese Studies, East China Conference and related institutions, Family of Jesus Community, Foochow Conference and related institutions, medical missions, Ginling College, Hinghwa Conference and related institutions, Hwa Nan College, Kalgan Conference and related institutions, Kiangsi Conference and related institutions, Methodist work in China, mid-China Conference and related institutions, Nanking Theological Seminary, North China Conference and related institutions, Peking University, Shanghai American School, Shantung Conference and related institutions, Soochow University, West China Conference and related institutions, and Yenping Conference and related institutions; biographical files of Bishops James W. Bashford, Paul Bern, Lauress J. Birney, Hiram A. Boaz, Daniel Goodsell, John Gowdy, George R. Grose, Wilbur C. Hammaker, William L. Harris, Z. T. Kaung, G. Carlton Lacy, Walter R. Lambuth, Wilson Seeley Lewis, Willard F. Mallalieu, Enoch Marvin, Chih-ping Wang, Ralph A. Ward, Seth Ward, and Herbert Welch; biographical files, including Chiang K'ai-shek, Feng Yü-hsiang, Miner Searle Bates, Charles George Gordon, Jonathan Goforth, Kenneth Scott Latourette, Duncan Main, Sam Pollard, Samuel Isaac Joseph Schereschewsky, Charles Soong, John and Betty Stam, Helen Stam, and John Sung; biographical files on missionaries and domestic staff including Young J. Allen, Frank Argelander, Lucy Beach, Bliss and Helen Taylor Billings, Mark W. Brown, William B. Burke, Ralph Dieffendorfer, Clara Pearl Dyer, Eddy Lucius Ford, Frank Gamewell, Mary Ninde Gamewell, Perry O. Hanson, Virgil C. Hart, Laura Haygood, Walter A. Hearn, Bruce Jarvis, Claude Rupert Kellogg, James William Lambuth, Ida Belle Lewis Main, Nathan Sites, Albert N. Steward, Mary Stone, Alice Terrell, Moses C. White, Elizabeth Wood, and Harry W. Worley.
CORRESPONDENCE: 18-page letter from Esther B. Lewis (Mrs. Spencer Lewis) describing journey up the Yangtze, 1897, with photo of houseboat; missionary letters, mostly from Huchow, 1947–50; missionary letters relating to Kiangsi, Mid-China, North China, and Yenping Conferences, n.d.
MANUSCRIPTS: "Introduction to the Foochow Dialect," by Leo Chen and Jerry Norman, 1965; "Hwa Nan College," by Ethel Wallace, n.d.; "Social Work of the Methodist Church in China," by Alice Weed, 1947; bibliographies on China; notebook on the history of Nanking Theological Seminary, n.a., n.d.; notebook on the ministry of Wuhu Hospital, n.a., n.d.; untitled manuscript of James W. Bashford, n.d.; writings of G. Carleton Lacy, n.d.; writings and memoirs of Ralph A. Ward, n.d.; notebook of Mark W. Brown, "Hunting Trip to Yenchiaping," n.d.
PAMPHLETS: Miscellaneous publications of the University of Nanking, College of Agriculture and Forestry.

DIARIES: 19 diaries of Spencer Lewis, 1901–35, with index to each volume and appendices; diary of Walter R. Lambuth, 1911–14.

MAPS/DESIGNS/DRAWINGS: Map of the field of the Methodist Episcopal Church, South, in China, ca. 1937.

AUDIO-VISUAL MATERIALS: Photos of James W. Bashford, n.d.; photos of G. Carleton Lacy, n.d.

SERIALS: *China Talk*, 1978. Ginling College, *Bulletin*, 1919, 1931, 1933–35. Nanking Theological Seminary, *Bulletin*, 1913–16, 1930. *Tungwu Magazine*, 1937. University of Nanking, College of Agriculture and Forestry, *Agriculture and Forestry Notes*, 1926–27, 1931–36; *Agriculture and Forestry Series*, 1920–21, 1924; *Bulletin*, 1926; *Economic Facts*, 1936–37; *Miscellaneous Series*, 1924–25; *Special Report*, 1935. *University of Nanking Magazine*, 1910–12, 1915.

DISSERTATIONS/THESES: *The Development of Indigenous Leadership for Youth Work in China*, by Amber Lurrain Van, 1946. *An Educational Program for Young Adults Adaptable to the Christian Churches in China*, by I-hsin Liu, 1952. *The History of the Educational Work of the Methodist Episcopal Church in China: A Study of Its Development and Present Trends*, by Eddy Lucius Ford, 1936. *A Plan for Developing a Functional Curriculum in the Bible Teachers' Training School in Nanking, China, in the Postwar Era*, by Pearle McCain, 1946. *The Social Work Program of the Riverside Church as a Resource for a Social Work Program of an Urban Church in China*, by Angeline B. Y. Han, 1948.

CHINESE LANGUAGE MATERIALS: Unidentified publication of the University of Nanking, College of Agriculture and Forestry, 1920.

FINDING AIDS: Container checklist (accession # 79–16).

6-LEDGERS, 1842–1950, 76 l.f.

MINUTES/RECORDS/REPORTS: Mission Board financial transactions.

7-LETTERBOOKS: MISSIONARY SOCIETY OF THE METHODIST EPISCOPAL CHURCH 1884–1914, 1890–1910, 25 volumes

CORRESPONDENCE: Letterbook of incoming and outgoing letters, 1907–8, including Bishop [James] Bashford; 24 letterbooks on Central China, West China, North China and South China, 1890–1910, containing financial and other mission correspondence, of Carroll, Cheney, Fowles, Leonard McCabe, Jesse H. Baldwin, Palmer, Peck, Stuntz, and others.

FINDING AIDS: Index to each letterbook (accession # 73–44).

8-LETTERS FROM BOARD OF MISSIONS OF METHODIST EPISCOPAL CHURCH, SOUTH, 1896–1899, 11 volumes

CORRESPONDENCE: 11 letterbooks of Walter Lambuth, 1896–99 and n.d.

FINDING AIDS: Container checklist (accession # 73–45).

9-METHODIST EPISCOPAL CHURCH: SCRAPBOOKS, 1915–1940s, 9 c.f.

AUDIO-VISUAL MATERIALS: 23 scrapbooks, containing photos of Chinese people, scenes, and Methodist missions and missionaries, 1915–1940s.

10-METHODIST EPISCOPAL CHURCH, SOUTH: CORRESPONDENCE AND SUBJECT FILES OF THE BOARD OF MISSIONS 1817–1955, 1893–1940, 60 folders (ca. 1 c.f.)

MINUTES/RECORDS/REPORTS/CORRESPONDENCE: Correspondence, reports, and other materials relating to D.L. Anderson, 1909; Sidney R. Anderson, 1922–40; Anglo-Chinese College, 1911–17; J. H. H. Berckman, 1936–40; W. W. Blume, 1926; A. C. Bowen, 1893–1935; William B. Burke, 1909–40; E. Clayton Calhoun, 1937–40; Changchow General Hospital, n.d.; China Mission, minutes, 1931–34; Christian Education Association, 1927–29; John W. Cline, 1917–40; J. W. Dyson, 1925–40; W. A. Estes, 1924–40; J. B. Fearn, 1916; Frank C. Ferguson, 1929–38; Franklin A. Flatt, 1937–40; N. Gist Gee, 1915–18; John C. Hawk, 1911–40; T. A. Hearn, 1916–18; C. H. Hendry, 1918–35; J. L. Hendry, 1923–37; Huchow Union Hospital, 1910–28; Japan, 1927–34; Fred P. Manget, 1936–40; E. F. Moseley, 1898–1924; Walter B. Nance, 1914–39; Nanking Theological Seminary, 1914–21; W. H. Park, 1909–34; A. P. Parker, 1916–19; R. A. Parker, 1910; Vivian P. Patterson, 1920–39; E. C. Peters, 1908–27; Edward Philley, 1918–36; C. F. Reid, 1911; Religious Education Institute, 1908–36; Edmond L. Rice, 1927–40; W. B. Russell, 1919; Shanghai American School, 1928; D. L. Sheretz, 1923–40; J. A. B. Shipley, 1898–1915; Wesley M. Smith, 1924–40; John A. Snell, 1908–40; Hubert L. Sone, 1922–40; Soochow Hospital, 1908–31; Soochow University reorganization, 1927–28; Richard E. Strain, 1936–38; J. C. Thoroughman, 1928–40; Joseph W. Whiteside, 1898–1938; Rolfe Whitlow, 1929–39; Melville O. Williams, Jr., 1929–40; George B. Workman, 1929–40.

FINDING AIDS: Container checklist (accession # 73–25).

11-MISSIONARY CORRESPONDENCE, BOARD OF MISSIONS: METHODIST CHURCH AND ITS ANTECEDENTS, 1906–1967, quantity undetermined

CORRESPONDENCE: Correspondence indexed by name of missionaries, without geographic identification.

FINDING AIDS: Container checklist (accession # 73–5).

12-OUTGOING CORRESPONDENCE OF THE FIELD SECRETARIES, 1886–1910, 24 l.f.

CORRESPONDENCE: Replies of mission board field secretaries to missionaries overseas.

13-RECORDS OF THE GENERAL BOARD OF GLOBAL MINISTRIES, MISSIONARY CORRESPONDENCE: MISSIONARY SOCIETIES OF THE METHODIST EPISCOPAL CHURCH, 1840–1906; BOARD OF FOREIGN MISSIONS OF THE METHODIST EPISCOPAL CHURCH, 1907–1912, 1847–1912, ca. 3 c.f.

MINUTES/RECORDS/REPORTS: Chengtu University, constitution, n.d.; China Mission, annual reports, 1847–83; Kiangsi Church property, reports regarding reacquisition, 1902–4.

CORRESPONDENCE: 12 folders of letters of Bishop J. W. Bashford, 1894–1912; 2 folders of letters of D. H. Moore, 1900–1905; 1 folder each of letters of Bishops Earl Cranston, C. H. Fowler, Isaac W. Joyce, W. S. Lewis, W. F. Mallalieu, William X. Ninde, Henry Spellmeyer, and Isaac W. Wiley, 1850–1911; 1 folder of miscellaneous correspondence; ca. 3 boxes of correspondence, 1847–1912, with Foochow Church, Alden Speare Hospital, West China Union University, William Nast College, and Women's Foreign Missionary Society, and Methodist missionaries to China, including Jesse H. Baldwin, J. J. Banbury, Frederick Bankhardt, La Clede Barrow, Walter B. Batcheller, R. C. Beebe, Joseph Beech, W. S. Bissonnette, E. F. Black, J. H. Blackstone, W. E. Blackstone, Sarah M. Bosworth, A. J. Bowen, W. N. Brewster, Frederick Brown, Fred R. Brown, Mary E. Burns, H. Olin Cady, Harry R. Caldwell, H. L. Canright, T. H. Coole, J. D. Collins,

W. B. Cole, Walter M. Crawford, J. O. Curnow, W. H. Curtiss, George L. Davis, George R. Davis, Timothy, Donoghue, H. G. Dildine, Charles F. Ensign, J. B. Eyestone, John C. Ferguson, E. L. Ford, C. W. Freeman, F. D. Gamewell, J. McGregor Gibb, Jr., J. E. Gossard, John Gowdy, J. J. Gregory, O. F. and C. W. Hall, Perry O. Hanson, L. C. Hanzlik, E. H. Hart, V. C. Hart, Isaac T. Headland, Frederick G. Henke, W. T. Hobart, N. S. Hopkins, John R. Hykes, J. H. Irish, R. O. Irish, Harry W. Irwin (Wilbur Henry Irwin), J. Jackson, Edward James, E. R. Jellison, William R. Johnson, Ernest M. Johnstone, Edwin C. Jones, Ulric R. Jones, Kate E. Kauffman, Joseph L. Keeler, Claude R. Kellogg, Edwin M. Kent, Percy C. Knapp, John H. Korns, O. J. Krause, Carl F. Kupfer, Henry V. Lacy, Walter N. Lacy, William H. Lacy, B. F. Lawrence, Spencer Lewis, Edward S. Little, W. C. Longden, William A. Lovett, George D. Lowry, H. H. Lowry, J.H. McCartney, R. L. McNabb, R. S. Maclay, R. E. Maclean, W. A. Main, W. E. Manly, Arthur W. Martin, William S. Meek, Lilburn Merrill, E. M. Meuser, Q. A. Meyers, Mrs. William Millward, George S. Miner, J. J. Mullowney, J. F. Newman, Don W. Nichols, F. Ohlinger, Bernard H. Paddock, Ernest L. Paige, J. F. Peat, Mae Peregrine, L. W. Pilcher, N. J. Plumb, J. H. Pyke, C. Bertram Rape, Raymond C. Ricker, H. F. Rowe, Henry H. Rowland, Harvey Curtis Roys, Wallace B. Russell, Burton L. St. John, Francis B. Shelden, James Simester, N. Sites, J. E. Skinner, G. B. Smythe, Leslie Stevens, George A. Stuart, Marcus L. Taft, R. L. Torrey, F. H. Trimble, J. R. Trindle, John George Vaughan, George W. Verity, W. F. Walker, J. and L.M. Walley, L. N. Wheeler, Moses Clark White, M. C. Wilcox, Elrick Williams, Walter W. Williams, W. W. Williams, O. W. Willits, John F. Wilson, Wilbur F. Wilson, E. J. Winans, G. W. Woodhall, F. M. Woolsey, J. H. Worley, A. C. Wright, and John W. Yost.
FINDING AIDS: In-house container checklist (accession # 74-11).

14-WESLEYAN METHODIST MISSIONARY SOCIETY: MINUTES AND CORRESPONDENCE, 1829-1954, 1,760 microfiches
Background note: These materials are microfiche reproductions of the original archives, now housed in the Library of the School of Oriental and African Studies in London. The collection is divided into three components, two of which—the Wesleyan Methodist Missionary Society records and the Women's Work Collection—contain extensive materials concerning Methodist missions in China.
MINUTES/RECORDS/REPORTS: China Synod, minutes, 1853-1946; overseas schedules, China, 1923-46.
CORRESPONDENCE: 820 microfiches of letters in the Wesleyan Methodist Missionary Society records, divided into 11 series: Canton (1851-1905), China General (1936-45), China Miscellaneous (1924-34), Hunan (1907-45), Hupeh (1905-45), Ningpo (1933-46), North China (1933-45), South China (1905-45), South West China (1932-45), Wenchow (1933-45), and Wuchang (1876-1905); 281 microfiches of letters in the Women's Work Collection, divided into 3 series: Hunan, Hupeh, Ningpo, and Wenchow (1921-54); North, South, and South West China (1920-47); and Missionaries on Furlough (China, 1925-30).
MANUSCRIPTS: 330 microfiches of biographical materials and personal papers of Methodist missionaries in China, including David Hill, Samuel Pollard, and G. Stephenson, 1829-69.
FINDING AIDS: "Guide to the Methodist Missionary Society Archives," by Elizabeth Bennett (Microfiche Collection).

NJ-50 United Methodist Archives and History Center Historical Library
P. O. Box 127
Madison NJ 07940
(201) 822-2787/2826
Kenneth Rowe, Librarian

Background note: The Historical Library is a joint research library containing the collections of the General Commission on Archives and History, and the Wesley and Methodist Collections of Drew University.

1-GENERAL HOLDINGS
MINUTES/RECORDS/REPORTS: Evangelical Association, China Mission Committee, record book, 1905-17; Evangelical Church: China Mission Committee, minutes and reports, 1924-; China Mission, proceedings of the annual meeting, 1923-31, 1937, 1939, 1941; China Mission Conference, journal, 1923-27, 1929-31, 1937-39, 1941; Methodist Church (U.S.): China Central Conference, journal, 1941, 1947; address to the first session by bishops in China, 1941; Annual Conference journals: Central China (Mid-China), 1941, 1945-50; East China, 1940-45; Foochow, 1939-43, 1945-49; Hinghwa, 1939-49; Kalgan, 1939, 1947; Kiangsi, 1940, 1943, 1947-48; North China, 1940, 1947; Shantung, 1947; West China, 1939-41, 1946-47; West China (Woman's), 1940; Yenping, 1943, 1945-48, 1950.
Methodist Episcopal Church: Central Conference journals, China and East Asia, 1897-1920; Annual Conference journals: Central China, 1887-88, 1891-98, 1900-1939; Central China (Woman's), 1903-10, 1912-14, 1916-26, 1929-40; Chungking, 1925-35; Foochow, 1872, 1877-1939; Foochow (Woman's), 1896-97, 1903, 1909, 1910-13, 1915, 1917, 1922, 1926-31; Hinghwa, 1896-1939; Hinghwa (Woman's), 1899, 1904, 1908-10; Kiangsi, 1913-17, 1928-30, 1933-36; North China, 1892, 1896, 1898-1900, 1902, 1905, 1907-10, 1922, 1938-39; North China (Woman's), 1893-1940; Shantung, 1926-40; South Fukien, 1923-33; West China, 1895, 1899, 1903, 1905-7, 1909-15, 1917-23, 1926, 1928, 1931, 1934-36, 1938-39; yearbook, 1934; Yenping, 1917-32, 1934-40.
Methodist Episcopal Church-South, China Mission Annual Conference, journal, 1887-96, 1901-8, 1910-40; United Brethren Church, 1912; report on China of unidentified conference, 1943.
CORRESPONDENCE: 53 letters from J. Wesley Day, a Methodist missionary in China, to his friends at home, 1946-77.
MANUSCRIPTS: Photocopy of notebook of Bishop John Gowdy containing writings on China, n.d.; copy of manuscripts by Moses Clark White, pioneer missionary, relating to the founding of Methodist missions in Foochow, 1929; "Steps to the Kingdom, Harry Lee Canright, M.A., M.D., a Pioneer Medical Missionary in Chengtu, West China, Architect, Builder, and Physician of the Chengtu Hospital, One of the Founders of the West China Union University," n.a., n.d.; "Those Were Happy Years," by Alice Longden Smith, n.d.; untitled typescripts by Elmer T. Clark, n.d.
PAMPHLETS: 17 pamphlets, 1907-48, on Chinese Home Missionary Society, famine conditions, Laura Haygood, Mary McClellan Lambuth, Methodist work in China, Sino-Japanese war, Student Volunteer Movement, and women's missionary work; ca. 5 pamphlets by Frank Oldt, n.d.

AUDIO-VISUAL MATERIALS: Photo album and scrapbook of China by the United Brethren Board of Missions, ca. 1935.
SERIALS: *China Christian Advocate*, 1914–41. *China Talk*, 1977–85. *Chinese Evangelical Messenger*, 1914. *Educational Review*, 1926. *Foochow Witness*, 1902. *Fukien Witness*, 1903–9.
DISSERTATIONS/THESES: *American Missionaries and the Chinese Communists: A Study of Views Expressed by Methodist Episcopal Church Missionaries, 1921–1941*, by Milo Thornberry, 1974. *A History of the United Brethren Mission Work in China*, by Robert C. Painter, 1945. *The History of the Educational Work of the Methodist Episcopal Church in China*, by Eddy Lucius Ford, 1938.
CHINESE LANGUAGE MATERIALS/SERIALS: *Hwa mei chiao pao (Chinese Christian Advocate)*, 1911, 1917–20.

NJ-55 New Jersey Museum of Archaeology
Drew University
Madison NJ 07940
(201) 377-3000 Ext. 305
Robert Bull, Professor of Archaeology

1-NESTORIAN CROSSES, COLLECTION OF DREW UNIVERSITY, ca. 1260–1368, 525 items
Background note: The largest collection of Nestorian crosses in the United States, Drew's is the second largest in the world. The Museum also possesses a 12-foot high stone rubbing of the twelfth-century Sian-fu Nestorian monument, with Syriac and Chinese writing, dated 1780.
MEMORABILIA: 525 bronze Nestorian crosses dating from the Yüan dynasty (1260–1368), found in the Ordos district of the Shensi province, and ranging in size from an inch and half to a little over three inches; crosses are in a wide variety of shapes, including birds, flowers, rectangles, and stars, with decorations such as swastikas, concentric circles, triangles, and crosses.

NEW BRUNSWICK

NEW BRUNSWICK THEOLOGICAL SEMINARY

NJ-60 Archives of the Reformed Church in America
Gardner A. Sage Library
21 Seminary Place
New Brunswick NJ 08901
(201) 246-1779
Russell L. Gasero, Archivist

Background note: The Reformed Church in America maintained the Amoy Mission from 1842 until 1951 In the early period, the Reformed Church in America's China mission operated under the auspices of the American Board of Commissioners for Foreign Missions. See also Harvard University, Houghton Library, Manuscript Department, Cambridge, MA, 02138.

1-DAVID ABEEL PAPERS, 1830–46, 2 pamphlet boxes
Background note: An 1823 New Brunswick Theological Seminary graduate, David Abeel (1804–46) was a missionary in Canton in 1830, first with the Seaman's Friend Society, then with the American Board of the Reformed Church. He returned to Amoy under the auspices of the American Board from 1842 to 1845.
CORRESPONDENCE: Letters to Mrs. J. R. Schuyler, 1836, Phillip Schuyler, 1842, and Grace Schuyler, 1844; letter from W. J. Pehlman, 1846; list of correspondence by Abeel between 1827 and 1845.
DIARIES: Diary by Abeel, 1841–43.
MANUSCRIPTS: Sermon notes and outlines, 1843–44.
PAMPHLETS: *Farewell to the Missionary Abeel*, by George Washington Bethune, 1838; 19 sermons by Abeel, 1830, 1841–43.
CHINESE LANGUAGE MATERIALS: Unidentified book.

2-WILLIAM ANGUS PAPERS, ca. 1925–1950, 25 l.f.
Background note: William R. Angus (1901–84) was a Reformed Church in America missionary to South Fukien with the Amoy Mission from 1925 to 1951. These unprocessed papers cover the period from time of his graduation until the time he and his wife left China in 1951. See also Hope College, Archives, Van Zoeren Library, Holland, MI, 49423.

3-GENERAL HOLDINGS
MINUTES/RECORDS/REPORTS/CORRESPONDENCE: 2 reels of microfilmed documents concerning the Amoy and Borneo Missions of the American Board of Commissioners for Foreign Missions (ABCFM), including correspondence, diaries, and other papers, 1830–47; 5 boxes of materials relating to the Reformed Church in America Amoy Mission: disagreements within the mission, 1898–1905; financial reports, 1934–39; meeting minutes, 1918–50; mission reports, 1936–48; miscellaneous materials, 1856–1951, relating to China Continuation Committee, Foreign Missions Conference of North America—Committee of Reference and Counsel, and National Christian Council of China; Board of Foreign Missions: miscellaneous papers and correspondence, 1832–1926; deputation documents, 1915–16, 1929–30, 1940–41.
CORRESPONDENCE: 12 boxes of letters, 1856–1949, between members of the mission and secretaries of the Board of Foreign Missions concerning Chinese civil law, communist activities, and mission affairs, including correspondents William R. Angus, H. P. Boot, William I. Chamberlain, Henry Cobb, H. P. DePree, C. H. Holleman, E. Koeppe, J. Muilenberg, Johannes Abraham Otte, Philip Wilson Pitcher, William Pohlman, Henry A. Poppen, F. M. Potter, Luman J. Shafer, W. Vander Meer, G. Van Wyk, H. Veenschoten, W. de Velder, J. Veldman, and H. D. Voskuill.
MANUSCRIPTS: Autobiography by Elizabeth Gordon Bruce, 1970; biography of William J. Pohlman, n.a., n.d.; biographical sketch of Johannes Abraham Otte by his wife, Frances, n.d.
MEMORABILIA: Scrapbook of clippings and pamphlets on Johannes Abraham Otte, n.d.; scrapbook of clippings from the *Church Herald* on the Amoy mission, n.d.; 4 folders of memorabilia on Philip Wilson Pitcher, ca. 1885–1915; 9 folders of materials on Johannes Abraham Otte, ca. 1887–1910.
ORAL HISTORIES: "Old China Hands," oral histories recorded and transcribed in 1976 and 1977 with retired RCA missionaries William Angus, Ruth Broekema, Elizabeth G. Bruce, Jack and Joanne Hill, Johanna Hofstra, Theodore V. Oltman, Jesse Platz, Rose H. Talman, James D. Van Putten, Alma Vander Meer, Gordon J. and Bertha V. Van Wyk, Harold E. and Pearl Veldman, Jeannette Veldman, and Jenanne Walvoord.

NJ-65 Gardner A. Sage Library
New Brunswick Theological Seminary
21 Seminary Place
New Brunswick NJ 08901
(201) 247-5243
Russell L. Gasero, Archivist

Restrictions: Access by appointment.

1-ALUMNI COLLECTION, 1959, 1 item
DISSERTATIONS/THESES: *The Life and Work of David Abeel*, by Alvin John Poppen, 1959.

2-GENERAL HOLDINGS
MINUTES/RECORDS/REPORTS: Associated Boards for Christian Colleges in China, report, 1932; Australian Churchmen to China, report, n.d.; Board of Missionary Preparation, annual reports, 1914-15; China Colleges and United Board for Christian Colleges in China, miscellaneous documents, 1949-51; Joint Conference on the Correlation of Christian Higher Education in China, report, 1932; Layman's Mission, report by Pearl Buck, 1932; Presbyterian Church of Christ in China, minutes of the Council, 1907; Yunnan Mission, 1 box of miscellaneous documents, 1949.
CORRESPONDENCE: Correspondence to and from David Abeel, 1831-46, consisting of microfilmed selections from items relating to the Amoy and Borneo Missions in the American Board of Commissioners for Foreign Missions Collection at Harvard University (Houghton Library, Manuscript Department, Cambridge, MA, 02138).
MANUSCRIPTS: Bound volume of sermon notes and outlines, by David Abeel, 1843-44.
PAMPHLETS: *The Correlated Program as Adopted by the Council of Higher Education*, by the China Christian Educational Association, 1930, 1933; *"The Jesus I Know": A Chinese Book Written for Chinese Youth*, by E. R. Hughes, T. Z. Koo, and Y. T. Wu, 1930; *The North China Medical College for Women*, 1921; *Operation at One: A One-act Play of China*, by Maude Taylor Sarvis, 1935; *The Present Situation in China and Its Significance for Christian Missions*, 1925; *Yenching College*, 1921.
MAPS/DESIGNS/DRAWINGS: *Map of the Chinese Empire*, by Samuel Wells Williams, 1884, on cloth; "Missionary Map of Amoy and the Neighbouring Country," n.a., n.d., on cloth.
SERIALS: China Christian Educational Association, *Bulletin*, 1928, 1933. *China Christian Year Book*, 1926, 1928-29, 1931-35. *China Mission Year Book*, 1910-19, 1923-25. *Chinese Recorder*, 1913-41. *Chinese Repository*, 1832-44. *Ching Feng*, 1964-. *West China Missionary News*, 1939.
CHINESE LANGUAGE MATERIALS: 2 boxes of Chinese language lessons, notebooks, workbooks, and character diagrams, n.d.; 4 pamphlets of characters, 1930; 2 volumes of hymns used by the Church of Christ in China, n.d.; Romans, 1898; 2 Bibles in Amoy dialect, 1898 and 1959; translation of *The Life of David Abeel*, by Alvin John Poppen, 1963 (see DISSERTATIONS/THESES above).

RUTGERS UNIVERSITY

NJ-70 Special Collections and Archives
Archibald Stevens Alexander Library
New Brunswick NJ 08901
(201) 932-7204
Edward Skipworth, Library Associate

Finding aids: *A Guide to the Manuscript Collection of the Rutgers University Library*, comp. by Herbert F. Smith (New Brunswick: Rutgers University Library), 1964. *A Union List of New Jersey Annual Publications in the Library Collections of The New Jersey Historical Society and Rutgers University*, comp. by Ronald L. Becker and E. Richard McKinstry (New Brunswick: Rutgers University Libraries and the New Jersey Historical Society), 1977.

1-WILLIAM ELIOT GRIFFIS COLLECTION, 1887-1926, 4 folders
Background note: A Congregational minister, William Eliot Griffis taught in Japan for a number of years. His papers include materials relating to mission activity and conditions in China.
CORRESPONDENCE: Folder of correspondence sent and received by Griffis on Chinese history and missions in China, 1887-1926.
PAMPHLETS: Folder of mission publications relating to China.
MEMORABILIA: 2 folders of articles and clippings relating to mission schools, hospitals, personnel, and other general missionary activity; missionary articles on Chinese political situations, anti-missionary activity, and persecution in China.
CHINESE LANGUAGE MATERIALS: Bible, n.d.

NJ-75 Archibald Stevens Alexander Library
Rutgers University
New Brunswick NJ 08901
(201) 932-7509
Marianne Gaunt, Librarian

1-GENERAL HOLDINGS
MANUSCRIPTS: "Missions in China," by Henry Charles Cussler, 1893.
SERIALS: *China Christian Year Book*, 1912, 1919. *Chinese Recorder*, 1874-99, 1921-23. *Chinese Repository*, 1832-51. *Lingnaam Agricultural Review*, 1922-27. *Lingnan Science Journal*, 1927-28. *Monumenta Serica*, 1935-. Natural History Society of Fukien Christian University, *Proceedings*, 1929. *New Horizons*, 1934, 1937-40. *News of China*, 1942-49.
DISSERTATIONS/THESES: *American Protestant Missions and Communist China, 1946-1950*, by David J. Galligan, 1952.
CHINESE LANGUAGE MATERIALS/SERIALS: *Yenching hsüeh pao (Yenching Journal of Chinese Studies)*, 1927-35.

NEWARK

NJ-80 NEWARK ABBEY
528 Dr. Martin Luther King Boulevard
Newark NJ 07102
(201) 643-4800
Brother Augustine Curley, Librarian

Restrictions: Access by appointment.
Background note: Damien Smith was among the men of Newark Abbey at the Catholic University of Peking. St. Vincent Archabbey coordinated their activities. See also St. Vincent Archabbey and College Archives, Latrobe, PA, 15650.

1-GENERAL HOLDINGS
CORRESPONDENCE: 3 letters from Pope Pius XI to Archabbot Aurelius Stehle, O.S.B., of St. Vincent Archabbey, concerning efforts in behalf of the Catholic University of Peking, 1929; "Letter of His Excellency the Most Rev. Celso Constantini, Apostolic Delegate to China," n.d.
PAMPHLETS: 11 pamphlets about the American Benedictine Foundation, Catholic University of Peking, culture in mission fields, Peking Union Medical College, Peking Union Medical College-School of Nursing, radio broadcasting, selection of seminary students, and faculty and curriculum of the Catholic University of Peking, ca. 1929–33.
MEMORABILIA: Box of personal belongings of Damien Smith, a professor at the Catholic University of Peking; trunk of personal belongings of a brother who taught at the Catholic University of Peking.
MAPS/DESIGNS/DRAWINGS: Architectural plans of the Catholic University of Peking, ca. 1930.
AUDIO-VISUAL MATERIALS: 71 color stereopticon slides of persons and places connected with the Catholic University of Peking, 1929–32; group photo, possibly of seminarians, ca. 1930; photos of the Catholic University of Peking, ca. 1930.
SERIALS: Catholic University of Peking, *Bulletin*, 1926–30. *The Dragon*, 1933. *Mission News*, 1933.
CHINESE LANGUAGE MATERIALS: Catalogue, certificate, and pamphlet about the Catholic University of Peking, ca. 1930.

NJ–85   THE NEWARK MUSEUM
49 Washington Street
P. O. Box 540
Newark NJ 07101
(201) 733–6640
Margaret DiSalvi, Librarian
Valrae Reynolds, Curator of Oriental Collections

Background note: The Newark Museum's Tibetan Archive was founded with material obtained from Albert L. Shelton, M.D., of the Disciples of Christ Foreign Christian Missionary Society, which was active in the Sino-Tibetan border region, from 1904 to 1922. Subsequent Tibetan material was obtained from Robert B. Ekvall, Carter D. Holton, and M. G. Griebenow, all working for the Christian and Missionary Alliance (CMA) in Kansu and Tsinghai, from 1921 to 1949; and from Robert Roy Service, who was associated with the Young Men's Christian Association in Chengtu, Szechuan, from 1905 to 1921.
Finding aids: "The Newark Museum" in *A Survey of Tibetan Xylographs and Manuscripts in Institutions and Private Collections in the U.S. and Canada*, by Horace I. Poleman, 1961; *Catalogue of the Newark Museum Tibetan Collection*; catalogue of photograph prints.

1-CORRESPONDENCE FILES, 1902–40. ca. 1 file drawer
CORRESPONDENCE: Correspondence and notes relating to the Tibetan Archive, filed by the name of the donors/vendors, including: communications of Albert Shelton to the Museum, family, and friends, 1911–22; correspondence of CMA missionaries Robert B. Ekvall, Carter D. Holton, and M. G. Griebenow, 1920–40; correspondence of Robert Roy Service, 1902–21; correspondence from

the Museum's work with several Christian mission groups in organizing the 1923 exhibition "Everyday Life in China."

2-DOCUMENT COLLECTION, n.d., 1 item
MAPS/DESIGNS/DRAWINGS: *Map of the Chinese Empire*, by the China Inland Mission, London, n.d.

3-TIBETAN ARCHIVE, 12th century–1950, quantity undetermined
Restrictions: The photos described below are housed in the Museum Library; manuscripts and memorabilia are housed in the collections' vaults. Access to all materials is by appointment.
MANUSCRIPTS: 59 hand-written manuscripts, collected by Albert Shelton, of an inspirational or liturgical nature created by Tibetans during the 12th to 19th centuries, including prayer books, sutras, biographies of lamas, astrological handbooks, and books on other religious subjects; 10 manuscripts contributed by Carter D. Holton.
MEMORABILIA: Documents and hand-lettered silk scrolls recording political and religious interchanges between the Ch'ing emperors of China, the Lhasa government, and local Eastern Tibetan heads of state and church; large collections of paintings, images, costumes, objects used in ritual and everyday life, and other ethnographic artifacts, given or sold to the museum by Albert Shelton, Robert Ekvall, Carter Holton, and Robert Service.
AUDIO-VISUAL MATERIALS: Miscellaneous color and black and white photos of the area in and around Labrang, taken by Christian and Missionary Alliance missionaries W. D. Carlsen, Wayne Persons, and Gene Evans, 1949–50; 500 prints, slides, and negatives taken by Albert Shelton, 1904–22; M. G. Griebenow, 1922–40; and Shelton's colleague, Roderick A. MacLeod, 1917–27.

NEWTON

DON BOSCO COLLEGE
NJ–90   Library
Newton NJ 07860
(201) 383–3900 Ext. 32
Brother Damian McMahon, C.F.X., Librarian

Restrictions: Access by appointment.
Background note: The Salesians of St. John Bosco sent their first missionaries from Macao to China in 1910. Their first work began in the northern Canton area from which it spread to other places, especially with the assistance of the Salesian Sisters who first arrived in China in 1922. Don Bosco College is an institution of the New Rochelle, New York, Province of the Salesians.

1-GENERAL HOLDINGS
MINUTES/RECORDS/REPORTS: Reports on the China mission and Salesians in China in the *Salesian Bulletin*, 1892–1949 (Italian ed.), 1938 (Australian ed.), 1941 (Irish ed.), 1955–84 (U. S. ed.), 1968 (Philippines ed.), 1975 (British ed.); and in *Salesian Missions*, 1950–84.
MAPS/DESIGNS/DRAWINGS: Map of the "Vicariate Apostolic Shiuchow," 1919–39.
FINDING AIDS: *Index to the Salesian Bulletin*, 1892–1936.

PRINCETON

PRINCETON THEOLOGICAL SEMINARY
NJ-95 Robert E. Speer Library
Mercer Street and Library Place
Princeton NJ 08542
(609) 921-8092
James Armstrong, Librarian

1-AGNEW BAPTIST COLLECTION, n.d., 1 item
PAMPHLETS: *A Chinaman in Search of Baptism*, by [?] Angier, n.d.

2-SPEER MANUSCRIPTS COLLECTION, 1892–1943, 34 folders, 12 volumes
MINUTES/RECORDS/REPORTS/CORRESPONDENCE: 13 folders and 1 volume of reports and correspondence on topics including China missions, 1899–1908; China visits, 1896–97, 1926; cooperation and union in China, 1905–33; correspondence about China, 1892–1923; liquor and opium addiction, 1903; and the Sino-Japanese War, 1939–40.
MANUSCRIPTS: "Report on China and Japan of the Deputation Sent by the Board of Foreign Missions of the Missions of the Presbyterian Church in the U.S.A. to Visit These Fields," by Robert Elliott Speer, 1927.
MEMORABILIA: Ca. 16 folders and 4 scrapbooks of miscellaneous items relating to China in general, 1892–1943; cooperation and union in China, 1898–1911; liquor and opium addiction, 1903–6; Sino-Japanese war, 1932–42; and visits to China, 1896–97, 1915, 1921, 1926–27.
AUDIO-VISUAL MATERIALS: 5 photo albums and 2 folders of loose photos of China (and other East Asian countries), 1896–97 and n.d.
FINDING AIDS: In-house shelf list.

3-GENERAL HOLDINGS
MINUTES/RECORDS/REPORTS: Canton Christian College of Arts and Sciences and Agriculture, catalogue, 1917–26; Canton Union Theological College, catalogue, 1922–23; China Continuation Committee, minutes, 1915, 1917–19; Chinese Religious Tract Society, annual meeting, 1879–80; Chinese Tract Society, report, 1903; Christian Literature Society for China, 1889–91, 1893–94, 1902–3, 1917–18, 1920–27, 1933–34; Christian Medical Commission—China Health Care Study Group, report, 1974; Foreign Missions Conference of North America, address, 1928; International Missionary Council and Foreign Missions Conference of North America—Conference on Chinese Christian Education, report, 1925; Nanking Bible Training School and Affiliated Schools of Theology, catalogue, 1911–12; Nanking Theological Seminary: annual meeting of Board of Managers, 1923; Board of Founders, report on theological education, 1951–52; catalogue, 1907–8, 1923–24, 1943; Nanking Theological Seminary and Christian Council of China, survey of church behind the lines, 1941; North China Institute for Supervisors of Rural Work, reports of Tung Chow, 1935, and Anyang, 1937; North China Theological Seminary, catalogue, 1924; report, 1923–24; Peking University College of Theology, catalogue, 1917–18.

Presbyterian Church in the U.S.A.: Board of Foreign Missions, report, 1897, 1902; Board of Missionary Preparation, report, 1917; China Council, annual meeting, 1925, 1927; China missions, minutes and reports, 1807–77, 1879, 1888, 1897, 1899, 1926; Canton, reports, 1887–91, 1894, 1900–1901, 1903–5; Central China, reports, 1888–89, 1891–92, 1893–94, 1894–95, 1937; Central and Southern Synod, minutes, 1904; Hainan, reports, 1930–31; Hunan, minutes of annual meeting, 1915; Kiangan Mission, annual reports, 1913–16; North China, reports, 1908, 1909–10; Paotingfu, reports, 1921–22; Shantung, records, 1861–1913, 1930; Tengchow, annual report, 1925–26; Tenghsien, annual report, 1918; West Shantung, address and record of general meeting, 1905; United Brethren in Christ Foreign Missionary Society, report of foreign deputation, 1912.
DIARIES: "Diaries of Hunter Corbett, Presbyterian Missionary to China, 1863–1918…Chefoo, China."
MANUSCRIPTS: "Divie Bethune McCartee—Pioneer Missionary: A Sketch of His Career," by Henry William Rankin, 1902; "From Six to Sixty to Six: A Narrative of the China Mission of the Reformed Church in the United States and the Later Evangelical and Reformed Church," by Arthur Vale Casselman, 1951; "History of Nanking Theological Seminary, 1911 to 1961: A Tentative Draft," by Francis Wilson Price, 1961; "Life of J. L. Nevius," by his wife, n.d.; "Nestorian Manuscripts," containing prayers, songs/hymns, services for different occasions, treatises, histories, and ethics, n.d.
PAMPHLETS: 29 pamphlets, 1897–1978, including such topics as advice to missionaries, appeals for help in China, British Protestant Evangelists, Hunter Corbett, elementary schools, indigenous church movement in China, Jesuits in China, Nanking Theological Seminary, population and statistics of China, Presbyterian Hospital in Chefoo, sermons, Stam family, University of Nanking, Yale-in-China, and youth in China.
MAPS/DESIGNS/DRAWINGS: Map of China (Boston, 1888); *Atlas of China in Provinces*, by Thomas Cochrane (Shanghai: Christian Literature Society for China), 1913.
SERIALS: *Bible for China*, 1930–38. Canton Christian College of Agriculture, Publications, 1923. *China and the Church Today*, 1979–86. *China and the Gospel*, 1906–7, 1909–11, 1913, 1916, 1919, 1923, 1935, 1937, 1949–57. China Christian Educational Association, *Bulletin*, 1930–31, 1936. *China Christian Year Book*, 1910–39. *China Fundamentalist*, 1928, 1931–40. China Inland Mission, *List of Missionaries and Their Stations*, 1915, 1921. *China Mission Advocate*, 1839. *China Missionary Bulletin*, 1952–54. *China Notes*, 1974-. *China's Millions* (London), 1879, 1886–91. *China's Millions* (Philadelphia), 1904–7, 1910, 1921, 1932–61. *China's Millions* (Toronto), 1894–97, 1899–1900. *Chinese Christians Today*, 1976. *Chinese Recorder*, 1870–76, 1879–81, 1883, 1885, 1887–1903, 1905–7, 1909–41. *Chinese Repository*, 1832–40, 1842–43, 1845–51. *Chinese Theological Review*, 1985-. *Chinese World Pulse*, 1977–81. *Ching Feng*, 1964-. *Directory of Protestant Missions in China*, 1916, 1927. *East Asia Millions*, 1961-. *Hainan Newsletter*, 1918–19, 1922, 1924, 1932, 1935–37. *Land of Sinim*, 1904–5. *Maryknoll Mission Letters*, 1923–27. Methodist Episcopal Church in China, *Bulletin*, 1896–97, 1901–6, 1912–15, 1917, 1922. *Millions* (Philadelphia), 1952–60. *Mission Bulletin*, 1952–60. Nanking Theological Seminary, English Publications, 1940. Presbyterian Church in the U.S.A., *Special China Bulletin*, 1912. Southern Presbyterian Missions in China, *Bi-*

monthly Bulletin, 1918. *Variétés Sinologiques*, 1895–1902, 1911–19.

DISSERTATIONS/THESES: *Die Akkommodationsmethode des P. Matteo Ricci, S.I., in China*, by Johannes Bettray, 1955. *American Missionaries and the Chinese Communists: A Study of Views Expressed by Methodist Episcopal Church Missionaries, 1921–1941*, by Milo Lancaster Thornberry, Jr., 1974. *The Anti-Christian Movement in China, 1922–1927: With Special Reference to the Experience of Protestant Missions*, by Ka-che Yip, 1970. *The Basis of the Appeal in the United States for Protestant Missions to China (1830–1949)*, by Carlton Chung-chieh Wu, 1956. *Changes in the Christian Message for China by Protestant Missionaries*, by Lewis Strong Casey Smythe, 1928. *The China Inland Mission and Some Aspects of Its Work*, by Hudson Taylor Armerding, 1948. *China und die katholische Mission in Süd Shantung, 1882–1900*, by Jacobus Johannes Kuepers, 1974. *Christian Missions in China*, by Charles Sumner Estes, 1895. *Christianity and the Taiping Rebellion: An Historical and Theological Study*, by Philip L. Wickeri, 1974. *Christianity and Social Change: The Case in China, 1920–1950*, by Lee-ming Ng, 1971. *The Emergence of a Protestant Christian Apologetics in the Chinese Church During the Anti-Christian Movement in the 1920s*, by Wing-hung Lam, 1978. *How Shall the Chinese Church Continue Its Work under the Communist Government?*, by Tien-hsi Kao, 1950. *Die katholische Missionsmethode in China in neuester Zeit (1842–1912)*, by Johannes Beckmann, 1931. *Kilian Stumpf, 1655–1720: Ein Würzburger Jesuit am Kaiserhof zu Peking*, by Sebald Reil, 1978. *Lutheran Missions in a Time of Revolution: The China Experience, 1944–1951*, by Jonas Jonson, 1972. *The Missouri Evangelical Lutheran Mission in China, 1913–1948*, by Richard Henry Meyer, 1948. *Protestant Missions in Communist China*, by Creighton Lacy, 1953. *The Political Relevance of 'jen' in Early China and 'agape' in the Theology of Reinhold Niebuhr*, by Halk-jin Rah, 1975. *Protestant Christianity in China and Korea: The Problem of Identification with Tradition*, by Spencer John Palmer, 1964. *Seeking the Common Ground: Protestant Christianity, the Three-Self Movement, and China's United Front*, by Philip Wickeri, 1985. *Some Aspects of Chinese Popular Religion as They Indicate Missionary and Educational Method*, by Anne Marie Melrose, 1947. *A Study of the History of Mission Work for Koreans in South Manchuria and Its Relation to the Church in Korea*, by Allen DeGray Clark, 1939.

CHINESE LANGUAGE MATERIALS/SERIALS: *China Church Year Book*, 1914–36. *Chinese Christian Review*, 1903–4.

CHINESE LANGUAGE MATERIALS: Ca. 50 Bibles and Bible studies; Northern China Synod, minutes, with statistics of presbyteries, 1898–1903; *Hunter Corbett and the Presbyterian Church in Shantung*, by Martin T. Lien, 1940; *Religious Thought Movements in China during the Last Decade: A Source Book Specially Compiled for a Course of Study on Current Religious Thought in China for the Yenching School of Chinese Studies, North China Union Language School*, comp. by Neander C. S. Chang, 1927.

PRINCETON UNIVERSITY

NJ–100 Harvey S. Firestone Memorial Library
General Reference Division
Princeton University
Princeton NJ 08544
(609) 452-3180
Mary W. George, Head, General Reference Division

Restrictions: Access restricted.

1-GENERAL HOLDINGS

MINUTES/RECORDS/REPORTS: American Friends Service Committee, report on China policy, 1965; American Presbyterian Mission, report on Anting Hospital, Peking, 1890; China Continuation Committee, proceedings, 1916–17; Foreign Office of Great Britain, reports on China and foreign missions, 1860–1912; Peking United International Famine Relief Committee, report, 1922; St. John's University of Shanghai, catalogue, 1910–15; University of Nanking, catalogue, 1917–20; World Missionary Conference, China Continuation Committee, findings, 1913.

MANUSCRIPTS: "The Catholic Church in China," 1959(?), 1960.

PAMPHLETS: Pamphlets, 1888–1978, on subjects including the American Baptist mission at Kiangan, appeals for China of the National Cathedral Commission, Chinese civilization and culture, mission problems, polemic, and Princeton-in-China.

ORAL HISTORIES: *China Missionaries Oral History Collection*, ed. by Cyrus H. Peake and Arthur L. Rosenbaum (Claremont Graduate School, Oral History Program), 1973. See ORAL HISTORIES Union List for the names of participants.

MAPS/DESIGNS/DRAWINGS: *Atlas of the Chinese Empire...and a List of All Protestant Mission Stations*, by Edward Stanford (Philadelphia: China Inland Mission), 1908.

AUDIO-VISUAL MATERIALS: *Album des photographies de l'atlas*, by Émile Licent (Tientsin: Mission de Hsien Hsien), 1933; California College in China, recordings of language lessons, with flash cards and text, 1943.

SERIALS: American Friends Service Committee, *Bulletin on Work in China*, 1942–44. *Asian Folklore Studies*, 1952. Catholic University of Peking, *Bulletin*, 1926–34. *China Bulletin*, 1955–62. *China Christian Year Book*, 1910–39. *China Colleges*, 1941–47. China International Famine Relief Commission, Publications, series A, 1922–24, 1926, 1928–36; series B, 1930 (repr. 1980). *China Mission Advocate*, 1839. *China Monthly: The Truth about China*.1939–50. *China Notes*, 1962–81. *Chinese Recorder*, 1936–37. *Mission Bulletin*, 1955–58. *News of China*, 1942–49. *Peking Natural History Bulletin*, 1926–34, 1938–41. St. John's University of Shanghai, Department of Biology, *Biological Bulletin*, 1931–35. *UCR Envoy*, 1946–47. *United China Relief Series*, 1941. University of Nanking, College of Agriculture and Forestry, *Agriculture and Forestry Series*, 1924; Department of Agricultural Economics, *Economic Facts*, 1936–46. University of Nanking, *Newsletter*, 1946 (uncatalogued: bound within *China Colleges*). West China Border Research Society, *Journal*, 1922–39. Yenching University, Department of Biology, *Bulletin*, 1930; Department of Economics, *Yenching Index Numbers*, 1940; *Yenching Journal of Chinese Studies*, Monograph series, 1941; *Yenching Journal of Social Studies*, 1938–50; *Yenching Series on Chinese Industry and Trade*, 1932–37.

DISSERTATIONS/THESES: *Die Akkommodationsmethode des P. Matteo Ricci, S.I., in China*, by Johannes Bettray, 1955. *Apostolic Legations to China of the Eighteenth Century*, by Antonio Sisto Rosso, 1948. *The China Inland Mission and Some Aspects of Its Work*, by Hudson Taylor Armerding, 1948. *China's Opposition to Western Religion and Science during Late Ming and Early Ch'ing*, by George Ho Ching Wong, 1958. *Christian Missions in China*, by Charles Sumner Estes, 1895. *Missionary Conscience and the Comprehension of Imperialism: A Study of the Children of American*

Missionaries to China, 1900–1949, by Sarah Margaret Refo Mason, 1978. *The Negotiations between Ch'i-ying and Lagrené, 1844–1846*, by Angelus Francis J. Grosse-Aschhoff, 1950. *Peiping Municipality and the Diplomatic Quarter*, by Robert Moore Duncan, 1933. *The Political Reconstruction of China*, by Eu-yang Kwang, 1922.

NJ–105 Gest Oriental Library and East Asian Collections
Princeton University
Jones-Palmer Hall
Princeton NJ 08544
(609) 452–3182
Diane E. Perushek, Curator

1-GENERAL HOLDINGS
MINUTES/RECORDS/REPORTS: American Bible Society, Peiping sub-agency, exhibition catalogue, 1937; Congregation of Priests of the Mission in China, bibliography, 1933; North China Union Language School, catalogue of Western books in the library, 1931; Peking Union Medical College, dedication ceremonies and programme, 1921.
MANUSCRIPTS: "Memoirs of Eugene Epperson Barnett," 1963.
PAMPHLETS: *British Protestant Christian Evangelists and the 1898 Reform Movement*, by Leslie R. Marchant, 1975; *Ho Shen and Shu Ch'un-yuan: An Episode in the Past of the Yenching Campus*, by Willam Hung, 1910; *T'ang Love Stories: An Address before the Convocation of the North China Union Language School*, by S. Y. Shu, 1932; *Teaching Children in China at the Canton Christian College*, by H. B. Graybill, 1915.
MAPS/DESIGNS/DRAWINGS: *Der Jesuiten-Atlas der Kanghsi-Zeit, seine Entstehungsgeschichte nebst Namensindices für die Karten der Mandjurei, Mongolei, Ostturkestan und Tibet; mit Wiedergabe der Jesuiten-Karten in Originalgrösse*, by Walter Fuchs (Peking: Fu-jen University), 1943.
SERIALS: *Asian Folklore Studies*, 1942-. *China Mission Studies Bulletin*, 1979–84. *Chinese Repository*, 1832–51. *Collectanea Commissionis Synodalis*, 1928–36. *Directory of Protestant Missions in China*, 1934. *Monumenta Serica*, 1935–58, 1963, 1969–78. *Peking Natural History Bulletin*, 1926–35. *T'oung Pao*, 1890-. *Variétés Sinologiques*, 1896, 1902–3, 1906, 1909–34. West China Border Research Society, *Journal*, 1922–39. *Yenching Journal of Chinese Studies*, Monograph, 1936.
DISSERTATIONS/THESES: *Christianity in Communist China*, by Nancy K. Mak, 1980. *East and West: The Life and Times of Johann Adam Schall von Bell*, by Seth J. Masters, 1981. *Hudson Taylor and Timothy Richard: Faith in Practice*, by Fun N. Chau, 1978. *Russian (Greek Orthodox) Missionaries in China, 1689–1717: Their Cultural, Political, and Economic Role*, by Albert Parry, 1938.
CHINESE LANGUAGE MATERIALS/DISSERTATIONS/THESES: *Chi-tu chiao Chung-wen chi k'an chih tiao ch'a, 1950–1975 (An Examination of Chinese Christian Periodicals)*, by Pai Chia-ling, 1976.
CHINESE LANGUAGE MATERIALS: Bibles and commentaries in various dialects and languages including Chinese, Japanese, and Tibetan, 19th and 20th centuries; ca. 50 dictionaries, chrestomathies, grammars, and lexicons, by or to Christians in China, 1815–

1965; translations of French and Latin mission works, history, classics, and reference books.

NJ–110 Richard Halliburton Map Collection
Princeton University
Firestone Library
Princeton NJ 08544
(609) 452–3214
Lawrence Spellman, Curator, Maps Division

Background note: The division's historical section also holds maps of China dating from the sixteenth and seventeenth centuries, which were based on missionary and other surveys, although they were not always published by mission organizations. An example is a *Map of China* copied from a map prepared by J. B. d'Anville for Jean Baptiste du Halde's *Description of China* (1735). D'Anville relied on the surveys of missionaries such as Parennin, Nouvet, Régis, and Jartroux, among others, for this map. The text of a number of the maps listed is either partly or totally in Chinese.

1-GENERAL HOLDINGS
MAPS/DESIGNS/DRAWINGS: *China: Young People's Missionary Movement* (New York), 1907; *Map of China Prepared for the China Inland Mission*, China Inland Mission (London: China Inland Mission), 1894; *Map of China Showing the Stations of the China Inland Mission*, China Inland Mission (Philadelphia: China Inland Mission), 1911; *Map of the Chinese Empire Compiled from Native and Foreign Authorities*, by S. W. Williams (New York: J. M. Atwood), 1848; *The New Map of China Specially Prepared for Missionaries and Travellers* (Shanghai: Kwang Hsüeh Publishing House), 1936.

NJ–115 20th Century American Statecraft and Public Policy
Seeley G. Mudd Manuscript Library
Princeton University
Olden Street
Princeton NJ 08544
(609) 452–6345
Nancy Bressler, Curator of Public Affairs Papers

1-UNITED CHINA RELIEF—UNITED SERVICE TO CHINA ARCHIVES, 1941–66, 3 boxes, ca. 35 folders, 10 items,
Background note: United China Relief coordinated wartime relief efforts to China of secular as well as Christian organizations. The 1946 redesignation of United Service to China reflected extended peacetime activities. Confined to Taiwan after 1949, it became part of the American Bureau for Medical Aid to China in 1966. In addition to those items listed below, materials on Christianity in China are found scattered throughout records of the organization itself. See also New York Public Library, Manuscripts and Archives Section, Fifth Avenue and 42nd Street, New York, NY, 10018; and American Bureau for Medical Aid to China collection at Columbia University, Rare Book and Manuscript Library, Butler Library, 535 West 114th Street, New York, NY, 10027.
MINUTES/RECORDS/REPORTS: 2.5 boxes of the American Bureau for Medical Aid to China, Inc., 1941–66; box of the American Friends Service Committee, 1941–50; ca. 1 box of the Associated Boards for Christian Colleges in China, 1941–44; ca. 1 folder of each of the following, except where noted: Board of

Foreign Missions of the Presbyterian Church, 1941–50; Board of Missions and Church Extension of the Methodist Church, 1941–50; Business Women's Circle of the Presbyterian Church of Mount Holly, North Carolina, 1943–38; China Medical Board, Inc., 1943–46; Christian Medical Council for Overseas Work, 1943; ca. 2 folders of the Church Committee for China Relief, 1941–46; Church World Service, Inc., 1947–51; Institution for the Chinese Blind, Inc., 1942–49; Lingnan University, 1943–50; Maryknoll Fathers, 1943–48; Methodist Committee for Overseas Relief, 1942–47; National Catholic Welfare Conference, 1943–48; ca. 1 box of grant records from United Service to China's "One Million Dollar Fund" to the Church World Service, Dominican Sisters, Institute for the Chinese Blind, Maryknoll Fathers, and the United Board for Christian Colleges in China, 1943–48; United Board for Christian Colleges in China, 1947–66; United Service to China, China Office, 1948–50; Yale-in-China, 1942–49; Young Men's Christian Association, 1942–47; Young Women's Christian Association, 1943–49.

CORRESPONDENCE: Ca. 1 folder each of letters of Eugene Epperson Barnett, 1941–50; Pearl S. Buck, 1942–45; Fr. Devine, 1943–46; Dwight Edwards, 1946–51; Mrs. George A. Fitch, 1942–46; Sidney D. Gamble, 1941–55; B. A. Garside, 1942–50; Herbert E. House, 1942; Edward H. Hume, 1942–49; Walter H. Judd, 1943–50; Edwin C. Lobenstine, 1944–49; Mrs. Oswald B. Lord, 1946–55; Henry R. Luce, 1941–55; Mrs. Maurice Moore, 1946–63; Charles Stewart Mott, 1948–50; Bishop John F. O'Hara, 1942–46; W. B. Pettus, 1942–46; Aura E. Severinghaus, 1946–50; Archbishop Francis J. Spellman, 1942; and J. Leighton Stuart, 1946–50.

MEMORABILIA: Ca. 1 folder of radio scripts, 1942–47, including statements by Pearl S. Buck and Clare Booth Luce; ca. 1 folder of excerpts from addresses of Pearl S. Buck and Henry R. Luce, of the Writers' Committee Dinner of United China Relief, 1941; biographical information on Eugene Barnett, Miner Searle Bates, Pearl S. Buck, Mrs. Chu-sheng Yeh Cheng, Dwight Edwards, Welthy Honsinger Fisher, B. A. Garside, George A. Fitch, Emily Hahn, Edward Hume, Walter H. Judd, Mrs. Oswald Bates Lord, Clare Boothe Luce, Mildred Price, Ida Pruitt, Mary Stone, J. Leighton Stuart, Arnold B. Vaught, Frank Wilson, Bishop Paul Yu-pin, ca. 1941–ca. 1950.

AUDIO-VISUAL MATERIALS: Photos of Eugene E. Barnett, Pearl S. Buck, Dwight Edwards, B. A. Garside, Rufus M. Jones, Walter H. Judd, Henry R. and Clare Boothe Luce, Mrs. Maurice T. Moore, J. Leighton Stuart, and Arnold B. Vaught, ca. 1941–ca. 1950.

FINDING AIDS: In-house guide (NUCMC MS: 71–402, 468).

NJ-120 University Archives
Seeley G. Mudd Manuscript Library
Princeton University
Olden Street
Princeton NJ 08544
(609) 452-3213
Earle Coleman, University Archivist

1-UNIVERSITY ARCHIVES, 1800s–1900s, ca. 60 l.f.
Background note: The University Archives contains alumni records of classes in which all members are deceased. The Alumni Records and Mailing Office in New South Building holds records of classes with living members. Call in advance to check on avail-

ability and restrictions on these materials.
MINUTES/RECORDS/REPORTS/CORRESPONDENCE/AUDIO-VISUAL MATERIALS/MEMORABILIA: Primarily correspondence of the class secretary concerning each alumni's career and activities, clippings, circular letters from those on mission, graduation portraits, obituaries, and a few other items donated by relatives, such as maps of China.
FINDING AIDS: Alumni directories and *Princeton-in-China: A Resume of Fifty Years of Work by Princeton-in-Peking and Princeton-Yenching Foundation, 1898/99, 1948/49*, comp. by C. A. Evans, 1949 (in the Princeton-in-Asia Collection below).

2-PRINCETON-IN-ASIA COLLECTION, 1906–61, 2 boxes (8 in.)
Background note: Princeton-in-Asia began as Princeton-in-Peking. This organization financed Princeton student and alumni work with the Peking Young Men's Christian Association (YMCA). Reorganized as the Princeton-Yenching Foundation in 1930, it helped organize a Sociology Department at Yenching University. As Princeton-in-Asia, the Foundation supported schools outside the mainland and in other East Asian countries after 1949.
MINUTES/RECORDS/REPORTS: Princeton-in-Peking: budget, 1924–25; Executive Committee, minutes, 1924; Board of Trustees, minutes, 1924; constitution of the literary club, Peking School of Commerce and Finance, 1924; employment contract for J. T. Find, a professor with the Peking School of Commerce and Finance, 1924.
CORRESPONDENCE: Ca. .5 in. of correspondence, 1919–25, among the following individuals affiliated with Princeton-in-China: John G. Hibben, Robert Gailey, Robert Garrett, Dwight Edwards, John Stewart Burgess, and J. T. Find; ca. .5 in. of correspondence between Princeton-in-China, Princeton University, and the Peking YMCA, 1906–49; letter from Henry Winters Luce to Robert Garrett on Peking University, 1920; ca. .5 in. of fundraising letters from Princeton-in-Peking to Princeton University alumni, 1921–44.
MANUSCRIPTS: "Princeton-in-China: A Resume of Fifty Years of Work by Princeton-in-Peking and Princeton-Yenching Foundation, 1898–1899, 1948–1949," comp. by C. A. Evans, 1949; "Suggested Outline of the Principles and Practices of the Princeton University Center in China," 1921; reprints and typescript copies of such articles as "The Program of Community Work and Social and Civic Education of Princeton-in-Peking," by John Stewart Burgess, 1921, and "The American Stake in China," by John Stewart and Stella Fisher Burgess, 1927.
PAMPHLETS: Ca. 4 in. of various pamphlets, leaflets, and flyers on Princeton institutions and activities in China, 1916–28, including *The Princeton Work in Peking*, 1916, *The Princeton University Center in China*, 1918, and *A University in the Heart of the East*, 1920.
MEMORABILIA: News clippings about Princeton activities in China, 1920s; 2 semester grade books of J. T. Find, Peking School of Commerce and Finance, 1924; fund pledge cards, Princeton-in-Peking, 1924; term papers from students of J. T. Find, 1924–25; a term examination of the Peking School of Commerce and Finance, 1924.
AUDIO-VISUAL MATERIALS: 11 photos of Yenching University and Peking, ca. 1920s.
SERIALS: *China Colleges*, 1955. *New Horizons*, 1956, 1961. *Peking News*, 1921, 1924, 1925, 1927. *Princeton-in-Peking*,

1923. *Princeton-in-Peking Bulletin*, 1921–22. *Princeton Peking Gazette*, 1925–30. *The Princeton Work in Peking*, 1909–10, 1913. *Princeton-Yenching Gazette*, 1931, 1934, 1936–38. *Princeton-Yenching News*, 1941. *Yenching News*, 1931. *Yenching University Bulletin*, 1925.
CHINESE LANGUAGE MATERIALS: 5 Christmas-New Year greeting cards to J. T. Find of the Peking School of Commerce and Finance, 1924–25; *A View of the Work of the Social Science Club of Peking University*, n.a., 1924–25.

NJ–125 Manuscript Division

Rare Books and Manuscripts
Princeton University
Firestone Library
Princeton NJ 08544
(609) 452-3184
Jean Preston, Curator of Manuscripts

Finding aids: *LITMSS: An Indexed Catalog of Literary and Historical Manuscripts in Selected Manuscript Collections of Firestone Library* (Princeton University Library).

1-JOHN AND STELLA FISHER BURGESS PAPERS, 1900–1980, 2 boxes
Background note: A 1905 Princeton graduate, John Stewart Burgess (1883–1949) (JSB) served as a missionary to China with the Young Men's Christian Association (YMCA) of Peking and Japan and as secretary of the Princeton University Center in Peking. His wife, Stella Fisher Burgess (SFB), was secretary of the Peking Young Women's Christian Association (YWCA). See also Hoover Institution, Archives, Stanford University, Stanford, CA, 94305; Young Men's Christian Association of the U.S.A. Archives, University of Minnesota, Social History Welfare Archives, 2642 University Avenue, St. Paul, MN, 55114; and Young Women's Christian Association of America, National Board Archives, 726 Broadway, New York, NY, 10003.
MINUTES/RECORDS/REPORTS: "Contract between Mr. J. S. Burgess and the Te Chi Mu Chang-Mr. Su Jen Chu, prop.,…to build a house" for JSB, 1920; report by JSB to Princeton-in-Peking on his trip to England, 1921.
CORRESPONDENCE: Ca. 1 folder of letters among members of the Burgess family, 1899–1949; 1 letter each to F. S. Hughes, 1918; T. Chang Chin-shih, 1915; Dwight W. Edwards, 1914; W. A. P. Martin, 1912; and Hsü Pao Chien, 1915; envelope of condolences to the Burgess family on the death of JSB, 1949; circular letter by JSB as Secretary of Students of the YMCA of Peking, 1913; circular letter, "Peking as a Field for Social Service," 1914.
DIARIES: Diary by JSB, 1920s.
MANUSCRIPTS: "Autobiography," by JSB, 1940; "The Beggar Problem," by JSB, 1923; JSB opinion of World War II, 1942; "My Only Murder," by JSB, 1924?; "The Program of Community Work and Social and Civic Education of Princeton in Peking," by JSB, 1921; "The Shanghai Incident," by SFB, 1925; "Social Progress and Christian Faith," by JSB, n.d.; "A Sociological Study of the Two Canons I-Li and Li-ki," by Li An-che and SFB, 1927; "Teaching Opposition in the Orient," by JSB, 1916; "A Typical Mental Reaction of a Young Chinese to the Present Day Social and Political Phenomena in China," by Lü Hsun, 1928;

"Westerners' Adjustment to Chinese Life," by SFB, 1945–46; 3 stories by JSB, n.d.
PAMPHLETS: *Chinese Geography*, by JSB, 1937 (mimeographed); *Christians under the Chinese Communist State to June 1949*, by the General Assembly of the Church of Christ in China, Hong Kong, from *The Church*, n.d.; *Peking Studies in Social Science No. III—How to Study the Jinrickishaw Coolie*, by JSB, 1913; *Scientific Realism and Religious Idealism*, by Edwin G. Conklin, 1929; *Outline Study of Introduction to Christian Fundamentals*, by JSB, 1913.
MEMORABILIA: 22 folders of clippings, typescript articles, poems, stories, and speeches by Stella Fisher Burgess, 1900–1980; typed prayer, n.d.; obituaries of JSB, 1949; joke song by JSB about the Yenching faculty, 1924; folder of clippings of publications by JSB, n.d.; 5 *New York Times* clippings on civil war, 1929; clipping from *Bulletin of the National Christian Council* on the civil war, 1929; autobiographical sketch by SFB, 1954; datebook for SFB, 1900; folder of genealogies by SFB, n.d.; notes on life in Peking, by SFB, 1924; single-paragraph biographies of SFB students at Peking Normal University, 1924; 2 folders of SFB translations of Chinese poems, n.d.; book of poetry by SFB, n.d.; folder of published articles, by JSB, n.d.; 6 individual issues of popular serials containing articles by JSB and SFB: *Atlantic Monthly*, 1927; *Survey Graphic*, 1927; *The New Mandarin*, 1926; *North China Sunday News Magazine Supplement*, 1932; *Peking Daily News*, 1912, 1925; *China Weekly Review*, 1929.
MAPS/DESIGNS/DRAWINGS: Genealogical chart each for JSB and SFB, n.d.; map of the provinces of China (Chicago: Time-Life, Inc.), 1945; 4 handmade, mimeographed maps of China; map of China (Associated Boards for Christian Colleges in China), 1942.
AUDIO-VISUAL MATERIALS: Photo album of the Burgess family, home, students, and other people, n.d.; 32 photos of the Burgess family and home, n.d.; photo of JSB's students in China, n.d.; portrait of JSB, 1929 (ca. 20 copies); photo of the view from W. A. P. Martin's home, n.d.; photo of Peking, n.d., and 8 color (tinted) photos; photo album of the Temple of Heaven, Yenching University, the Summer Palace, the Great Wall, and a pottery works, n.d.; 30 photos of Yenching University, n.d.; group photo of the Department of Sociology of Yenching University, 1928; picture book of Yenching University and sights in Peking, n.d.; group photo of the College of Public Affairs of Yenching University, 1928.
CHINESE LANGUAGE MATERIALS: Unidentified letter, n.d.; card with Chinese for "Little Junior" (son of JSB and SFB who died in infancy), 1912–13; large envelope of letters to and from JSB, n.d.
Firestone Library finding data: AM 78-3 & 3a, 83–126. Loc: C 21: 4.

NJ–130 Rare Book Collections

Rare Books and Manuscripts
Firestone Library
Princeton University
Princeton NJ 08544
(609) 452-3185
Stephen Ferguson, Curator of Rare Books

Background note: Call numbers are designated in parentheses.
Finding aids: *Guide to Selected Special Collections of Printed*

Books and Other Materials in the Princeton University Library (Princeton), 1983.

1-GENERAL HOLDINGS
PAMPHLETS: Bound volume of pamphlets of papal legations, 1700–1709 (Ex 5552.999).
MAPS/DESIGNS/DRAWINGS: *Atlas général de la Chine; pour servir à la description générale de cet empire*, ed. by l'abbé Grosier, (Paris), 1785 (Ex 1724.613f).

NJ-135 General Holdings
>   Rare Books and Manuscripts
>   Firestone Library
>   Princeton University
>   Princeton NJ 08544
>   (609) 452-3184

Finding aids: LITMSS: An Indexed Catalogue, updated by computer every six months and available in the Manuscript Division. See also cross-indexes in the Manuscript Division catalogue.

1-PEARL S. BUCK, 1927–77, 72 boxes, 85 folders
Background note: This collection of Pearl S. Buck papers is mostly records and correspondence of business with publishers and producers. See also West Virginia Wesleyan College, Annie Merner Pfeiffer Library, Buckhannon, WV, 26201.
CORRESPONDENCE/MINUTES/RECORDS/REPORTS/MANUSCRIPTS: Correspondence, records, and drafts of Pearl S. Buck's publications and productions in books, magazines, newspapers, and television, scattered throughout various collections.
FINDING AIDS: Consult *LITMSS: An Indexed Catalogue*.

2-GAMBLE PHOTO ALBUMS, ca. 1918, 9 volumes
Background note: Sidney D. Gamble (1912) created this collection of photographs while traveling with Princeton-in-China in 1918. Jason Eyster of the Princeton-in-Asia office enlarged and framed fifty representative prints from the Gamble photo collection. Especially evocative of Chinese life and people of half a century ago, they are available for public display purposes. For information contact Jason Eyster, Princeton-in-Asia Program, 224 Palmer Hall, Princeton University, Princeton, NJ, 08544.
AUDIO-VISUAL MATERIALS: 9 photo albums of detailed studies of Chinese people, civilization and culture, Princeton-in-China, and missionaries, ca. 1918.
Firestone Library finding data: AM 21812. Loc: C 62: 6.

3-HENRY GALLOWAY COMINGO HALLOCK, 1922–25, 6 items
Background note: Henry Galloway Comingo Hallock was a missionary to China with Princeton-in-China from ca. 1919 to ca. 1941.
CORRESPONDENCE: 6 letters from Hallock, in Shanghai, to John Wright, 1922–25.

4-JOHN ALEXANDER MACKAY, 1965, 1 item
Restrictions: Permission required to quote or cite.
Background note: Clergyman and educator John Alexander MacKay served as secretary of the Presbyterian Board of Foreign Missions, 1932–36, and moderator of the General Assembly Presbyterian Church in the U.S.A., 1953–54.
ORAL HISTORIES: 50-page transcript of an oral history of John Alexander MacKay, including discussion of the admission of Communist China to the United Nations, 1965.

5-GRACE NEWTON PAPERS, 1887–1915, 1 box
Background note: Grace Newton (1860–1915) was a missionary under the North China Mission Society of the Presbyterian Church in the U.S.A. in Peking and Paotingfu from 1887 to 1909, and 1912 to 1915 (she traveled in Europe and the Middle East from 1910 to 1911).
CORRESPONDENCE: .75 box of Newton's correspondence with her family, 1887–1909, 1912–15.
DIARIES: 4 diaries on the Boxer Rebellion, 1900–1901.
MANUSCRIPTS: Ca. 1 folder of Newton's speeches and addresses, n.d.
AUDIO-VISUAL MATERIALS: Ca. 1 folder of photos of Newton and of China, 1887–1915.
Firestone Library finding data: AM 83–42. Loc.: Gen. mss.-N.

6-RICHARD H. RITTER, 1920–29, 1 item
Background note: Richard H. Ritter was a missionary to China with Princeton-in-China from 1920 to 1929.
MANUSCRIPTS: "Memories of Princeton Court in Peking," by Richard H. Ritter, ca. 1920.
Firestone Library finding data: AM 21330. Loc.: Gen. mss. (misc.).

7-THROOP AND MARTIN FAMILY PAPERS, 1830, 1 item
Background note: For biographical notes on David Abeel, see New Brunswick Theological Seminary, Archives of the Reformed Church in America, Gardner A. Sage Library, 21 Seminary Place, New Brunswick, NJ, 08901.
CORRESPONDENCE: Letter from David Abeel to D. Matthews, 1830.

SOUTH ORANGE

SETON HALL UNIVERSITY
NJ-140 University Archives
>   McLaughlin Library
>   405 South Orange Avenue
>   South Orange NJ 07079
>   (201) 761-9435
>   Msgr. William Field, Curator of Archives

1-GENERAL HOLDINGS
SERIALS: *China Christian Year Book*, 1919. China Inland Mission, *Occasional Papers*, 1872–75 (repr. 1973).
DISSERTATIONS/THESES: *The Jesuits in China in the Sixteenth and Seventeenth Centuries*, by R. Peter Bobrick, 1979.

TRENTON

NJ-145 FREE PUBLIC LIBRARY
>   120 Academy Street
>   Trenton NJ 08608
>   (609) 392-7188
>   Harold W. Thompson, Jr., Director

1-GENERAL HOLDINGS
AUDIO-VISUAL MATERIALS: "American Missionaries in Shanghai," photo showing missionaries in native dress strolling along a busy canal, 1912.
SERIALS: *China Mission Year Book*, 1925.

WAYNE

INTERNATIONAL MISSIONS, INC.
NJ–150 Library
Box 375
62 Sandra Lane
Wayne NJ 07470
(201) 696–4804
Bill K. Tarter, President

Background note: International Missions, Inc. (IMI) came into existence as an amalgamation of several Christian missions around the world, including the Oriental Boat Mission, which became part of IMI in 1966. The Oriental Boat Mission began in 1911 as the South China Boat Mission. It was founded by Florence Drew and her brother, Edward Drew, as an outreach to the poor and ostracized people living on boats in the harbors of Canton and other cities of South China. At its peak, the South China Boat Mission had 24 workers in three provinces, and it maintained 14 "gospel boats." When its missionaries were forced to leave in 1949, they shifted work to Hong Kong (and later also to Japan), changing the name to the Oriental Boat Mission.

1-GENERAL HOLDINGS
CORRESPONDENCE/MEMORABILIA/AUDIO-VISUAL MATERIALS: 80-page scrapbook containing correspondence, newspaper articles, brochures, and photos describing conditions in South China and the work of the South China Boat Mission, ca. 1909–1949.

WEST PATERSON

MISSIONARY SISTERS OF THE IMMACULATE CONCEPTION OF THE MOTHER OF GOD (MSIC)
NJ–155 Generalate Archives
48 Garden Avenue
West Paterson NJ 07424
(201) 279–1484
Sr. Lourdine Huang, Generalate Archivist

Background note: Most of the material is extensively catalogued. Each folder of correspondence contains a brief description of the contents of the letters. There are photos, letters, and printed materials which are not yet processed. China mission materials total about 20 l.f.

1-GENERAL HOLDINGS
MINUTES/RECORDS/REPORTS: *Chronicles of Our Congregation*, Book II, 1925–45 (day-to-day events in each MSIC province); 4 folders of Generalate chronicles regarding the MSIC's foundations in mainland China: Hungkialou, Shih-erh-li-chwang, Tientsin, and Peking; 2 lists of seminarians at Lintsing and Siaolu (filed with Mother Immaculata Tombrock's correspondence); articles and photos concerning MSIC missions in China in *Die Fran-*

ziskaner Missionen (yearbook of Franciscan missions worldwide) 1932, 1935–38, 1950, 1952–53, 1955, 1958, 1959; *Im Garten der Makellosen*, 1930–50; *Mission Bells*, 1935–47; *Mission Crumbs*, 1948–51; *Mosaic*, 1981–85 (MSIC newsletter).
CORRESPONDENCE: Folder of letters and telegrams about daily events in Tientsin, 1947–48; 6 folders of letters to and from MSIC sisters in China, and Fortunatus Baumgarten, Eduard Boedefeld, O.F.M., Mathias Faust, Gaspar Hu, Badurat Kaufmann, Joseph Lii, Peter Ly, Dominic Menke, Paulus Tchang, Joseph Tien, John Toung, Joannes Tsung, Josefo Tsung, Joseph Wang, and seminarians at St. Joseph's Seminary in Lintsing, 1937–51; 112 letters in English, German, Portuguese, and Latin to and from Mother Immaculata Tombrock, 1922–38, 1958.
MANUSCRIPTS: "A Critical Study of the History of the MSIC on Mainland China from 1931–1984," by Sr. Veneranda Bohlen.
MEMORABILIA: Folder of clippings, photos, and a day book of the Regional Superior concerning the foundation and development of the MSIC mission in Hungkialou, Shih-erh-li-chwang, Tientsin, and Peking, and about China in general, 1939–48.
ORAL HISTORIES: 3 tapes of interviews and personal reminiscences of Mother Immaculata Tombrock, recorded by Sr. M. Veneranda in 1978, including discussions of Mother Immaculata's study at St. Bonaventure, her second novitiate in preparation for mission work in China, the foundation and development of the MSIC mission in China, the training of native clergy at Hungkialou and Shih-erhli-chwang, MSIC foundations in Tientsin, Sheng Kung Girls' School, and leaving mainland China for Taiwan after the Communist takeover (transcriptions are contained in the MSIC newsletter, *Mosaic*, 1981–85).
AUDIO-VISUAL MATERIALS: Unprocessed collection of photos; films depicting MSIC work in convents, schools, and orphanages in China (also on videotape).
DISSERTATIONS/THESES: *The Life and Work of Msgr. De Besi in China*, by Veneranda Bohlen, 1950.
FINDING AIDS: In-house directory.

NEW MEXICO

ALBUQUERQUE

UNIVERSITY OF NEW MEXICO
NM–5 Library
Albuquerque NM 87131
(505) 277–4241
Beatrice A. Hight, Reference Department

1-GENERAL HOLDINGS
SERIALS: *Asian Folklore Studies*, 1964–78. *Folklore Studies*, 1942–63.

NEW YORK

ALBANY

ALBANY INSTITUTE OF HISTORY AND ART
NY–5   McKinney Library
125 Washington Avenue
Albany NY 12210
(518) 463–4478
Susan Safford, Librarian

1-HUGHSON FAMILY PAPERS, 1921–27, quantity undetermined
Background note: The Hughson family had a large lumber business in upstate New York. Before her 1929 marriage to Frank Hughson, Frances J. Heath, M.D., served as a medical missionary in Peking from 1921 to ca. 1927. She was associated with the Methodist mission, Sleeper Davis Memorial Hospital, Peking Union Medical College (PUMC), and the Union Medical College for Women.
MINUTES/RECORDS/REPORTS: Bank receipts for money credited to the account of PUMC, n.d.
CORRESPONDENCE: 194 letters from Frances J. Heath, during her work in Peking, including descriptions of political unrest and hostility toward foreigners, 1921–27.
MANUSCRIPTS: Mimeograph from the staff of Soochow University on the killing of Chinese students by foreign police, 1925.
MEMORABILIA: North China Union Language School, yearbook, 1922–23.
AUDIO-VISUAL MATERIALS: Several photos of Frances Heath.
FINDING AIDS: In-house finding list.

DAUGHTERS OF CHARITY OF ST. VINCENT DE PAUL
NY–10   De Paul Provincial House Archives
96 Menands Road
Albany NY 12204
(518) 462–5593
Sister Elaine Wheeler, D.C., Provincial Archivist

Background note: The company of the Daughters of Charity of St. Vincent de Paul was founded in France in 1633, spread throughout Europe, and sent its first missionaries to China from France in 1848. The first Americans went to China in the 1920s and left behind almost 250 native Chinese Daughters of Charity when forced to leave in 1952. The Sisters have always worked closely with the Vincentian (Congregation of the Mission) priests. See also Daughters of Charity of Saint Vincent de Paul, Saint Joseph's Provincial House, 333 South Seton Avenue, Emmitsburg, MD, 21727. The archives continues to acquire volumes of the denominational serial, *Annales de la Congrégation de la Mission*.

1-GENERAL HOLDINGS
MINUTES/RECORDS/REPORTS: Reports from the China mission in the following serials: *Annals of the Congregation of the Mission*, 1894–1926; *Annales de la Congrégation de la Mission*, 1834–95; *The Echoes of the Motherhouse* (continues as *The Echoes of the Community*), 1926-.

PAMPHLETS: "Ten Martyrs of Tien-tsin," repr. from *Lives of Deceased Sisters*, 1870.

THE NEW YORK STATE LIBRARY
NY–15   Manuscripts and Special Collections
Cultural Education Center
Empire State Plaza
Albany NY 12230
(518) 474–4461
James Corsaro, Senior Librarian, Manuscripts and Special Collections

1-BONNEY FAMILY PAPERS, 1851–71, 7 boxes
Restrictions: Use of the Bonney Family Papers requires written permission of the director of the Historic Cherry Hill Association, 523–1/2 South Pearl Street, Albany, NY, 12202.
Background note: Samuel William (1815–64) and Catherine Van Rensselaer Bonney (d. 1879) were missionaries in Canton and elsewhere in China from 1851 to 1871. Their family papers are part of the Historic Cherry Hill Papers.
MINUTES/RECORDS/REPORTS: Constitution and by-laws of *Steady Streams*, a children's mission aid organization, 1875–76; 2 items on 5-year adoptions of Chinese schoolgirls, 1854–60; a statement of Catherine Bonney's funds, 1866; Catherine Bonney's passport, 1866.
CORRESPONDENCE: 355 letters by the Bonney and Van Rensselaer families, 1851–62; 3 letters to the King of Siam, 1852–53; ca. 1 folder of letters between Catherine Bonney and her publisher on *Legacy of Historical Gleanings*, 1875.
DIARIES: 3 diaries and journals by Samuel Bonney: "epistolary journal," New York to Hong Kong, 1856, passage in the *N. B. Palmer*; 2 trip journals by Samuel Bonney: Canton to Shanghai, 1861, North River, 1863; 2 "Daily Journal(s)" by Samuel Bonney, 1864, 1879; journal by Samuel Bonney on his activities in America (probably on leave), n.d.
MANUSCRIPTS: Ca. 1,000 pages of drafts of *Legacy of Historical Gleanings*, by Catherine Bonney, ca. 1875; 2 volumes of ship's log abstracts, correspondence records, family and genealogy notes, addresses of ministers, notes on China, and rates of monetary exchange, by Samuel and Catherine Bonney, 1856–65; bound volume of "Verses and Rhymes," by Samuel Bonney, 1856–63; ca. 2 folders of religious sermons, lectures, notes, writings, scriptural quotations, and poems, by Samuel Bonney, 1851–64; "Family Record," by Samuel Bonney, n.d.
PAMPHLETS: *Notes of an Overland Trip into the Interior of Canton Province*, by John Preston, 1862; *The Late Rev. S. W. Bonney*, by "C. F. P.," 1864.
MEMORABILIA: Ca. 1 folder of newspaper clippings related to the *Legacy*, ca. 1875; advertisement for Mrs. Bonney's boarding school at Hong Kong, 1860; ca. 1 folder of miscellaneous clippings on China, n.d.; ca. 1 folder of letters, obituaries, funeral bills for Samuel and Catherine Bonney, 1864, 1879; bound volume of missionary autographs collected by Samuel and Catherine Bonney, 1844–69; "Seamen's Bethel Whampoa Dedication Hymn by John Bowring," n.d.
MAPS/DESIGNS/DRAWINGS: 3' by 5' manuscript map of Canton by D. Vrooman, 1855; 2 drawings of Samuel Bonney's tombstone.

AUDIO-VISUAL MATERIALS: Ca. 40 photos of the Bonney family, mission schools, Canton harbor, Pearl River, Peking Wall, and other unidentified people and places, ca. 1851-ca. 1864; 10 stereopticon slides of Canton and Peking, ca. 1860.
SERIALS: *Directory of Protestant Missions in China*, 1866.
CHINESE LANGUAGE MATERIALS: *Catechism about Christianity*, 1869; bound volume of religious phrases in Cantonese Chinese with English translation and Chinese pronunciation, by Samuel Bonney, 1855; sheet music for ''Jerusalem'' and ''The Lord's Prayer''; and ca. 1 folder of material on China, ca. 1860.
FINDING AIDS: In-house guide.

2-GENERAL HOLDINGS
MINUTES/RECORDS/REPORTS: International Institute of China, reports, 1926(?); Medical Missionary Society in China, report, 1845-47.
SERIALS: *China's Medicine*, 1968. *Chinese Medical Journal*, 1903-9, 1911-41, 1943-60, 1962-65, 1975; supplement, 1952. *Lingnan Science Journal*, 1927-42. *Peking Natural History Bulletin*, 1930-48.
CHINESE LANGUAGE MATERIALS/SERIALS: *Chung-hua i hsüeh tsa chih (Chinese Medical Journal)*, 1973-74.

THE UNIVERSITY AT ALBANY (State University of New York)
NY-20 University Libraries
400 Washington Avenue
Albany NY 12222
(518) 442-3568 (Director)
(518) 442-3544 (Special Collections)
Joseph Z. Nitecki, Director
Dorothy Christiansen, Acting Head,
  Special Collections

1-FRED R. BROWN PAPERS, 1910-48, 5 l.f.
Background note: A Methodist missionary to China from 1910 to 1931, Fred R. Brown (1888-1966) headed the Natural Science Department of William Nast College, Kiukiang, from 1910 to 1916. He then taught at Nanch'ang Academy, Nanch'ang, from 1917 to 1931, where he also served as acting principal (1918-19) and head of the Department of Natural Science (1927-31).
MINUTES/RECORDS/REPORTS: East Asia Conference, 1930, 1934, 1937; Kiangsi Annual Conference of the Methodist Episcopal Church, 1928-36, 1940, 1948; miscellaneous church and school records.
CORRESPONDENCE: Brown's weekly letters home, 1911-16, 1924-32, including letters to his wife, Clella, during the war period, 1927-28; correspondence related to mission matters, 1925-40.
MANUSCRIPTS/PAMPHLETS: Miscellaneous manuscripts and published versions of pamphlets by Fred and Clella Brown on pedagogical, religious, and political matters.
DIARIES: Diaries of journeys to and within China, to Japan, and to London, ca. 1910-1931.
MEMORABILIA: Notebooks on classroom lectures; clippings of newspaper articles on Brown's speeches and writings, mission school programs, and the political situation in China.
MAPS/DESIGNS/DRAWINGS: Hand-drawn maps of Amoy region and University of Amoy, 1930; printed maps of Kingtehchen, Nanch'ang, Shanghai, Kiangsi, and Fukien provinces, and Man-

churia; *The Cerographic Missionary Atlas*, by Sidney E. Morse and Co., 1848.
AUDIO-VISUAL MATERIALS: Several hundred negatives and prints of persons and places, concentrating on mission activities and buildings.
FINDING AIDS: Inventory list.

2-GENERAL HOLDINGS
DISSERTATIONS/THESES: *Imperial Government and Catholic Missions in China during the Years 1784-1785*, by Bernward Henry Willeke, 1948. *The Negotiations between Ch'i-ying and Lagrené, 1844-1846*, by Angelus Francis J. Grosse-Aschhoff, 1950.

ALFRED

ALFRED UNIVERSITY
NY-25 Herrick Memorial Library
Alfred NY 14802
(607) 871-2184
Norma Higgins, University Archivist

1-ALFRED AREA HISTORY COLLECTION, 1808-1952, quantity undetermined
Background note: John Fryer (b. 1839), though not a missionary, worked closely with missionaries and missionary organizations. He arrived in Hong Kong in 1861 to become principal of St. Paul's College until 1863, when he left to teach English in Hong Kong, Peking, and Shanghai. In 1866, he assumed the editorship of a Chinese-language newspaper, *The Mission News*. He later worked as a translator of scientific and technical materials for the Chinese government Translation Bureau in the Kiangnan Arsenal in Shanghai until 1896. At the same time, Fryer also compiled elementary textbooks condensed from British and American originals for missionary, government, and other schools, in cooperation with the General Missionary Conference in Shanghai. His wife, Eliza Nelson Fryer, an alumna of Alfred University, taught and performed administrative duties for the Seventh-Day Baptist Shanghai Mission.
MINUTES/RECORDS/REPORTS: Annual reports of the Seventh-Day Baptist Missionary Society's China Mission, 1845-1952, in *Seventh-Day Baptist Yearbook*, 1808-; reports on alumni in China in *The Alfred University* (quarterly newsletter, 1888-92), including ''Letter from the Shanghai Mission,'' by G. H. Fitz Randolph, 1890.
MANUSCRIPTS: ''Role of John Fryer in the Dissemination of Western Chemistry in 19th-century China,'' by Mel Gorman, 1974; ''A Beautiful Life,'' memoir of Eliza Nelson Fryer, published by her husband, John Fryer, for private circulation, with five sections on their life in China, 1912; ''Essay on Chinese Scientific Terminology, Its Present Discrepancies, and Means of Securing Uniformity,'' by John Fryer, 1890 (read at the General Missionary Conference at Shanghai, 1890).
PAMPHLETS: 4 pamphlets by Jay Crofoot: *Simplified Spelling in Shanghai*, *Localities in Shanghai*, *Four Addresses*, and *Souvenir of the Shanghai Union Language School*, 1912; *Conversational Exercises in Shanghai Dialect* by Jay Crofoot and F. Rawlinson, n.d.

2-ALFRED UNIVERSITY FACULTY AND ALUMNI RECORDS, n.d., 1 item

CORRESPONDENCE: Letter on teaching and political conditions in Foochow, China, by Willard J. Sutton of Fukien Christian University, n.d.
MEMORABILIA: "A Survey of the Chemical Translations of John Fryer in 19th-century China," by Mel Gorman in *Ambix*, 1977.
AUDIO-VISUAL MATERIALS: Photo of John Fryer, 1892.

AURORA

WELLS COLLEGE
NY–30 Library
Aurora NY 13026
(315) 364-3351
Marie Delaney, Director

1-GENERAL HOLDINGS
SERIALS: *China Christian Year Book*, 1917, 1924, 1936–37.

BATAVIA

NY–35 RICHMOND MEMORIAL LIBRARY
19 Ross Street
Batavia NY 14020
(716) 343-9550
Martha M. Spinnegan, Director
Kathleen M. Facer, Adult Services Librarian

1-MARY ELIZABETH WOOD COLLECTION, 1930–33, 1 file
Background note: See also Simmons College, Colonel Miriam E. Perry Goll Archives, 300 The Fenway, Boston, MA, 02115.
PAMPHLETS: Pamphlets on Boone Library triple anniversary celebration, 1930; informational brochure about Mary Elizabeth Wood Foundation, 1933.
MEMORABILIA: Obituaries of Mary Elizabeth Wood, 1931; invitation to memorial service held at Boone Library in Wuchang, 1931.
SERIALS: *Boone Library School Quarterly*, 1931 (Memorial to Wood issue).

BRONX

FORDHAM UNIVERSITY
NY–40 The Library
Bronx NY 10458
(212) 579-2415
Mary F. Riley, Chief Reference Librarian

Background note: In addition to the works listed below, the Fordham University Library holds a large collection of facsimiles of letters from Jesuit missions in China and Asia from the sixteenth century to the present, as well as a number of rare books on China by European authors.

1-GENERAL HOLDINGS
CORRESPONDENCE: "Avvisi del Giapone de gli anni MDLXXXII. LXXXIII et LXXXIV con alcuni altri della Cina dell' LXXXIII et LXXXIV. Cauati dalle lettere della Compagnia di Giesu riceuute il meme di dicembre MDLXXXV," 1586; "Avvisi della Cina et Giapone del fine dell' anno 1587," 1588; "Lettres des nouvelles missions de la Chine, 1841–1860," facsimile of manuscript.

BROOKLYN

BROOKLYN MUSEUM
NY–45 Art Reference Library
188 Eastern Parkway
Brooklyn NY 11238
(718) 638-5000 Ext. 308
Dierdre E. Lawrence, Librarian

1-GENERAL HOLDINGS
SERIALS: *Monumenta Serica*, monograph series, 1961.

NY–50 BROOKLYN PUBLIC LIBRARY
Grand Army Plaza
Brooklyn NY 11238
(718) 780-7712
Dorothy Nyren, Chief, Central Library

1-GENERAL HOLDINGS
MINUTES/RECORDS/REPORTS: World Missionary Conference, Edinburgh, 1910.
MAPS/DESIGNS/DRAWINGS: *Atlas of the Chinese Empire …Specially Prepared for the China Inland Mission*, by Edward Stanford, 1908.
SERIALS: *China Mission Year Book*, 1923–39. *Yenching Journal of Chinese Studies*, Monograph Series, 1936.

NY–55 MEDICAL RESEARCH LIBRARY OF BROOKLYN
State University of New York
450 Clarkson Avenue
Box 14
Brooklyn NY 11203
(718) 270-1041
Mary Doherty, Reference Librarian

1-GENERAL HOLDINGS
SERIALS: *China Medical Journal*, 1910–31.

BUFFALO

NY–60 BUFFALO AND ERIE COUNTY PUBLIC LIBRARY
Lafayette Square
Buffalo NY 14203
(716) 846-7108
Ruth Willet, Director, History Department

1-GENERAL HOLDINGS
SERIALS: *China Christian Year Book*, 1928, 1934–35. *Chinese Recorder*, 1924–32, 1941. *News of China*, 1942–49.

BUFFALO MUSEUM OF SCIENCE
NY-65 Research Library
Humboldt Parkway
Buffalo NY 14211-1293
(716) 896-5200
Shaun J. Hardy, Librarian

1-GENERAL HOLDINGS
SERIALS: Cheeloo University, *Journal*, 1934. *Lingnaam Agricultural Review*, 1922-26. *Lingnan Science Journal*, 1928-37. West China Border Research Society, *Journal*, 1939-40.

CANISIUS COLLEGE
NY-70 Andrew L. Bouwhuis Library
2001 Main Street
Buffalo NY 14208
(716) 883-7000 Ext. 253
Pat McGuinn, Reference Librarian

Background note: Bouwhuis Library received part of the recently discontinued Loyola Library of Jesuit materials at Fordham University, Bronx, NY, 10458. The materials are uncatalogued at present.

STATE UNIVERSITY OF NEW YORK AT BUFFALO
NY-75 Lockwood Library
Buffalo NY 14260
(716) 636-2820
Steve Roberts, Associate Director for Public Services

1-GENERAL HOLDINGS
SERIALS: China International Famine Relief Commission, Publications, series A, 1925, 1927, 1930-35; series B, 1930.

CLINTON

HAMILTON AND KIRKLAND COLLEGES
NY-80 Burke Library
Clinton NY 13323
(315) 859-4011
Frank K. Lorenz, Special Collections

1-GENERAL HOLDINGS
DIARIES: Diary of Justus Doolittle, missionary to China, ca. 1850-1873.
CHINESE LANGUAGE MATERIALS/SERIALS: *Yen-ching hsüeh pao (Yenching Journal of Chinese Studies)*, 1927-31.

GENEVA

HOBART AND WILLIAM SMITH COLLEGES
NY-85 Smith Library
Geneva NY 14456
(315) 789-5500
Eilene E. Moeri, Archivist

1-GENEVA COLLECTION, 1875-1970, 2 items
MINUTES/RECORDS/REPORTS/MANUSCRIPTS: Hobart

Missionary Society, reports, 1875, including information on their China mission.
DISSERTATIONS/THESES: *The Christian Missionary Movement and the Growth of Antiforeignism in Nineteenth-century China*, by Nancy Bernkopf, 1970.

ITHACA

CORNELL UNIVERSITY

NY-90 Department of Manuscripts and University Archives
John M. Olin Library
Room 101
Ithaca NY 14853-5301
(607) 256-3530
Kathleen Jacklin, Archivist

1-GEROW D. BRILL PAPERS, 1884-1924 , 3.2 c.f. (ca. 47 items)
Background note: Gerow D. Brill (1864-1931) was an agricultural economist who headed the Hupeh Agricultural College and Experimental Farm in Wuchang, and a scientific explorer for the U.S. Department of Agriculture from 1897 to 1901.
CORRESPONDENCE/MANUSCRIPTS: 45 letters and letter-impression copies of 2 reports to *The New York Times*, commenting on the activities and influence of both Protestant and Catholic missionaries, and mentioning the plight of missionaries in and around Chungking during the Boxer Rebellion, 1897-1900.
FINDING AIDS: In-house guide.

2-RICHARD HENRY EDWARDS: EDWARDS FAMILY PAPERS, 1913, 3 items
Background note: Richard Henry Edwards was a Congregational minister who served as pastor at the University of Wisconsin and director of Cornell United Religious Work. He was also involved in the YMCA and the Happy Valley Homes in Lisle, Broome County, New York.
CORRESPONDENCE: 3 letters from Sherwood Eddy, 1913, written on board ship to and from China and in Shanghai, describing his preaching mission to the Chinese in Hong Kong, Tientsin, Peking, Paotingfu, Shanghai, Foochow, and other cities, and expressing his hopes for the future of Christianity in the nation.

3-AUGUSTUS WARD LOOMIS PAPERS, 1844-49, .4 c.f. (20 items)
Restrictions: Access subject to prior use agreement.
Background note: Augustus Ward Loomis (1816-91) was a Presbyterian missionary in China from 1848 to 1849.
CORRESPONDENCE: 20 letters, 1848-49, from Loomis and his wife, Mary Ann, to relatives in New York, concerning their work in missions in Chusan and Ningpo, and their stay in Canton en route home.

4-HARRY HOUSER LOVE PAPERS, 1907-64, 1.5 c.f.
Background note: Harry Houser Love (1880-1966) was an agriculturalist and professor of plant breeding at Cornell University who served as consultant and lecturer at the University of Nanking.
MINUTES/RECORDS/REPORTS: 7 folders of materials, 1942-47, on Agricultural Missions, including student rosters, curriculum information on the school for missionaries sponsored by the

New York State College of Agriculture; mimeographed copy of papers relating to alumna Nina M. Stallings, concerning her work in Chengtu, 1943.

CORRESPONDENCE: Letters concerning American Protestant missionary work in China, including a Christmas letter from Frank W. Price, concerning his revisit to Nanking, 1939, and letters written from Shanghai after 1949; letters from Albert Mann regarding developments in China since 1911; circular letter from Nanking, reporting on student demonstrations and swift bans on demonstrations, n.d.; letters from B. A. Garside, G. Weidman Groff, and others; folder of official correspondence with John Elias Williams, n.d.; letter from Roy G. Wiggans, concerning the assault on Nanking and the killing of Dr. Williams, 1927; letters from Pearl and J. Lossing Buck, regarding Nanking, n.d.
FINDING AIDS: In-house guide.

5-HUGH ANDERSON MORAN PAPERS, 1919–47, 1 l.f.
Background note: For biographical notes, see Hoover Institution, Archives, Stanford University, Stanford, CA, 94305–2323.
MINUTES/RECORDS/REPORTS/CORRESPONDENCE: Uncatalogued materials concerning the Cornell-in-China program, 1919–47.

6-GEORGE DURAND WILDER PAPERS, ca. 1897–1976, 3 items
Background note: For biographical notes, see Bentley Historical Library, Michigan Historical Collections, 1150 Beal Avenue, Ann Arbor, MI, 48109–2113.
CORRESPONDENCE: Transcripts and summaries of letters George and Gertrude Wilder wrote home, 1941–43; folder of letters by George Wilder, written on his trip from China after being in the Weihsien Prison Camp in 1943.
MANUSCRIPTS: ''Random Jottings,'' by Gertrude Stanley Wilder, sketches of her childhood in China, education at Oberlin College, her return to China in 1893, marriage to Wilder, their home in Tungchou, transfer to Shantung, retirement in 1937, return to China in 1939, and internment by the Japanese in 1943, dated 1959, 1962; folder containing Ursula Wilder's (Mrs. Carroll C. Daniels) childhood recollections of China missions, n.d.
SERIALS: *The Watchman*, 1933.
FINDING AIDS: In-house guide.

7-WOMEN'S MEDICAL SOCIETY OF NEW YORK STATE RECORDS, 1907–66, 1 l.f. (28 items)
MINUTES/RECORDS/REPORTS: United Board of Christian Colleges in China, report on the fall of Tsinan and its effect on Cheeloo University, 1948.
CORRESPONDENCE: 25 letters and postcards, 1928–50, from the United Board of Christian Colleges in China, medical missionaries at Shantung Christian University, and Christian women medical students concerning the Society's financial backing for the education of these students.
DIARIES: Mimeographed log of the ''Migration of Cheeloo College of Medicine to Foochow,'' by Annie V. Scott, 1948.
SERIALS: Cheeloo University, *News Bulletin*, 1948.
FINDING AIDS: In-house guide.

8-GENERAL HOLDINGS
CORRESPONDENCE: Letter from John Heard in Canton to D. J. Kimball, concerning missionary efforts and Chinese education, 1846; letter to Sarah White, West Brookfield, Massachusetts, from her daughter, Adeline White Tracy, the wife of a missionary, de-

scribing Anglo-Chinese College in Malacca and efforts to teach Chinese girls in Singapore, 1836.

NY–95 Wason Collection
Cornell University
John M. Olin Library
Room 107 B
Ithaca NY 14853–5301
(607) 255–5759
Min-chih Chou, Curator

Background note: The Wason Collection is Cornell's library on East Asia. In addition to the European and Chinese-language materials listed below, there are 15 titles in Japanese relating to Christianity in China, including translations of Western studies on Christian missions and works by Japanese historians on Christianity in Manchuria.
Finding aids: *The Catalog of the Wason Collection on China and the Chinese, Cornell University Libraries* (Washington DC: Center for Chinese Research Materials, Association for Research Libraries), 1978, 7 V.

1-GENERAL HOLDINGS
MINUTES/RECORDS/REPORTS: Baptist Missionary Society, report of a deputation to China, 1919–20; Canton Christian College, report of the president, 1925(?); Central China Religious Tract Society, annual reports, 1886–87, 1904, 1907, 1909, 1913; China Inland Mission, annual reports, 1938, 1953–59; Christian Literature Society for China, annual report, 1917–18; Chung-hua ch'üan kuo Chi-tu chiao hsieh chin hui (National Christian Council of China), report of biennial meeting, 1935; College of Chinese Studies, booklists, 1931, 1933–34; course of study, 1911(?); Fukien Christian University, reports of the president and the dean, and minutes, 1930, 1932; Hua-chung ta hsüeh, catalogue, 1932–33; Lingnan University, College of Agriculture and Forestry, report, 1921–22; Mission catholique de Pékin, Bibliothèque de Pé-t'ang, catalogue, 1949; Morrison Education Society, Canton, annual reports, 1837–38, 1841–44; National Committee for Christian Religious Education in China, report of a deputation, 1931; North China Institute for Supervisors of Rural Work (Hua-pei Chi-tu chiao nung ts'un shih yeh ts'u chin hui), reports, 1935, 1937; North China Tract Society, constitution and by-laws, 188?; Peking Union Medical College, annual announcements, 1918–22, 1926–27; Po-chi i yüan (Canton Hospital), reports, 1914–23; Presbyterian Church in the U.S.A., China Council, annual report, 1919; Kiangan Mission, Nanking Station report, 1926–27; United Board for Christian Colleges in China, report of a survey of libraries of Christian colleges in China, 1947–48; United Board for Christian Higher Education in Asia, annual reports, 1947–76; University of Nanking, list of books in the library, 1937; West China Missionary Conference, report, 1908.
CORRESPONDENCE: Bound volume of letters from William P. Fenn, executive secretary of the United Board for Christian Higher Education in Asia, 1949-?; letter from Jean François Gerbillon to his father, 1686; carbon copy of letter by Baptist missionary Arthur Gostick Shorrock, in Lung Wan Shan, near Tai Yuan Fu, 1889; autograph letter and statement by Antoine Thomas, in Latin with English translation, 1687–1707.
MANUSCRIPTS: ''Apologia en la qual se responde á diversas calumnias que se escrevieron contra los padres de la Compañia de

Jesu de Japon, y de la China,'' by Alessandro Valignani, 1598; bibliography of works on or by John Fryer, 197?; ''Books on China in the University of Nanking Library: A Classified List,'' 1937; Chinese-Latin dictionary and grammar of the spoken and written Chinese language, for use by Catholic missionaries, ca. 19th century; ''Historia y relacion breue de la entrada en el reyno de China la mission que truxo de España nuestro Ho Comissario Fr. Buenaventura Ybañez,'' by Jaime Tarin, 1689; ''History of Nanking Theological Seminary, 1911 to 1961: A Tentative Draft,'' by Francis Wilson Price, 1961; index to letter journals of John Fryer, 1970(?); ''Indie Orientali'' (manuscript in Italian detailing the activities and expenses of Jesuit missionaries in China), ca.1784–1787; ''Jappam-China,'' by Antonio Francisco Cardim, 1849 transcript of an original manuscript written in 1649; ''Lessons to be Learned from the Experiences of Christian Missionaries in China,'' comp. by Harold S. Matthews, 1951; ''Lettres, mémoires, et renseignements, sur les juifs de la Chine,'' photocopies of manuscripts and drawings in the *Fonds Brotier*, V 123, of the Paris Jesuit archives, n.d.; ''Department of Biology, Yenching University,'' 1930(?).

PAMPHLETS: Most of the Wason Collection's pamphlets are organized into bound volumes and shelved with the book collections. The majority of pamphlets relating to China are found in two bound sets, *China and the Chinese-Pamphlets* (154 V), and *Pamphlets Relating to China* (20 V). Pamphlets on Christianity in China are also found in other bound collections of pamphlets, entitled: *Basel Missionsgesellschaft, British Parliamentary Papers: Missionaries in China, China Sunday School Union: Publications, Manchuria Pamphlets, Miscellaneous Maps, Charts, and Plans of China, Miscellaneous on China,* and *Pamphlets on China.* More pamphlets are shelved individually.

BASEL-MISSIONSGESELLSCHAFT, a bound volume of pamphlets containing items on William Chalmers Burns, William Carey, Jacob Henderson, Christian Martig, Phillip Winnes, and work in China.

BRITISH PARLIAMENTARY PAPERS: MISSIONARIES IN CHINA, 1868–1872, a bound volume containing 7 collections of reports, memoranda, and correspondence on missionaries in China.

CHINA AND THE CHINESE-PAMPHLETS

Background note: In addition to the items specified below this pamphlet collection includes items on the American Presbyterian Mission Press, ancestor worship, Anglo-Chinese calendar, Boxer Rebellion, Canton Christian College, China Inland Mission, China Medical Missionary Association, Chinese civilization and culture, China Famine Relief Fund, China Inland Mission, Chinese language instruction, Chinese term for God, Christian education, Christianity and Confucianism, Church Missionary Society, education of missionaries, famine, martyrs, medical missions, missions among Muslims, Nestorians, opium addiction, persecution of Christians, Timothy Richard, translations of the Bible, Wesleyan Methodist missionaries, and women missionaries.

[MINUTES/RECORDS/REPORTS]: American Board of Commissioners for Foreign Missions, 1831, 1837, 1848, 1857, 1859, 1862, 1867, 1868, 1870, 1892, 1896, 1907, 1920; American Tract Society, 1824; Baptist Missionary Society, 1892; Central China Famine Committee, 1907; Central China Presbyterian Mission, 1844–94; Foochow Missionary Hospital, 1909; General Association of Baptists (Kentucky), 1840; Kentucky and Foreign Bible Society, 1840; London Missionary Society, China Mission, report, 1866; London Mis-

sionary Society-Chinese Hospital at Peking, 1863; Malacca Mission Station and Anglo-Chinese College, 1830–31; Medical Missionary Society in China, 1838; Methodist Episcopal Church, South, 1908; Northern Baptist Convention, 1911; Opthalmic Hospital at Canton, 1827–32, 1834, 1838; Po-chi i yüan (Canton Hospital), 1914; Presbyterian Committee on Union, 1905; C. M. Ricketts, tour of mission stations at Pangkhau, Sin-hii, Kich-yang, and Mi-ow, 1879; Roberts' Fund and China Mission Society (Kentucky), 1840; Society for the Propagation of the Gospel in Foreign Parts, 1911, 1914; Young Men's Christian Associations, International Committee, 1898; Young Men's Christian Associations of China and Korea, 1907–12.

[CORRESPONDENCE]: Printed letters from the Bishop of Victoria to T. W. Meller, 1851; B. J. Bettelheim to Peter Parker, 1850, 1852; Lillian Ching to his (sic) family, 1838; Sr. Xavier Berkeley of the Sisters of Charity of St. Vincent de Paul to her family, 1905.

[SERIALS]: *China Medical Missionary Journal,* 1895.

[CHINESE LANGUAGE MATERIALS/SERIALS]: *Chin-ling shen hsüeh chih* (Nanking School of Theology, *Theological Quarterly*), 1915. *Hua t'u hsin pao* (Chinese Illustrated News), 1915–16. *Hwa mei chiao pao* (Chinese Christian Advocate), 1917. *The Monthly Herald,* 1915. *The Young People's Friend,* 1916.

[CHINESE LANGUAGE MATERIALS]: Bibles and portions of the Bible in Mandarin (1823, 1909, 1966), Hakka (1865), and Tibetan (1903); vocabulary to the New Testament, n.d.

CHINA SUNDAY SCHOOL UNION: PUBLICATIONS, a bound volume of pamphlets, containing items on Christian education by George Hamilton Archibald, 1912–16, and John Pilton Gregory, n.d.

MISCELLANEOUS ON CHINA, a bound volume of pamphlets, containing an inquiry into the Jews of Kaifeng by the London Society for Promoting Christianity among the Jews, and essays on China by James Hudson Taylor, n.d., and Robert Morrison, 1825.

MISCELLANEOUS MAPS, CHARTS, AND PLANS OF CHINA, a bound volume of pamphlets and maps, including:

[MAPS/DESIGNS/DRAWINGS]: *A New and Accurate Map of China, Drawn from Surveys Made by the Jesuit Missionaries, by Order of the Emperor,* by Emanuel Bowen, ca. late 1700s; *La Gran Tartaria diuisa nelle sue parti principali da Giacoma Cantelli da Vignola, conforme le relazioni che s'hanno da gl'Itinerarij de P. P. della Comp. di Giesù di Monsù Tauernier e dalle Raccolte di Monsù Theuenot e data in Luce da Gio,* by Giacomo Cantelli da Vignola, 1683; *Parte occidentale della China diuisa nelle sue Provincie, e dedicata al Molto Rev. Padre Antonia Baldigiani della Compagnia de Giesù,* by Marco Vincenzo Coronielli, ca. 1690; map of China prepared for the China Inland Mission by Edward Stanford, 1911.

MANCHURIA PAMPHLETS, a bound volume of pamphlets, containing *The Struggle for Manchuria: An Address before the Convocation of the North China Union Language School Cooperating with California College in China,* by Russell McCulloch Story, 1932.

PAMPHLETS ON CHINA, a bound volume of pamphlets containing *As the Chinese See Us,* by William Alexander Parsons Martin, n.d.; *The Religious Attitude of the Chinese Mind,* by William Alexander Parsons Martin, 1891; *Report on the China Missions of the American Board of Foreign Missions,* by Robert Elliott Speer, 1897; and the following relating to Christianity in China:

[MINUTES/RECORDS/REPORTS]: Peking University, calendar, 1896; Christian College in China, prospectus, 1886; Society for the Diffusion of Christian and General Knowledge among the Chinese, annual report, 1898.

PAMPHLETS RELATING TO CHINA

Background note: In addition to the items specified below, this pamphlet collection includes items on the American Board of Commissioners for Foreign Missions, ancestor worship, Anglo-Chinese calendar, Buddhism and Christianity, Chinese civilization and culture, Chinese language instruction, Chinese term for God, topography, Nestorians, Protestant missionaries, and the Taiping Rebellion.

[MINUTES/RECORDS/REPORTS]: American Board of Commissioners for Foreign Missions, 1867; Medical Missionary Society in China, annual meetings, 1838, 1841, 1845, 1848–49; Medical Missionary Society in China, hospital reports, 1839; Medical Missionary Society, Chinese Hospital at Macao, 1838; Medical Missionary Society in China, hospital at Ningpo, 1852; Medical Missionary Society in China, Ophthalmic Hospital at Canton, 1845, 1848–49; Protestant Episcopal Church in the U.S.A., Foreign Committee, 1854.

INDIVIDUAL PAMPHLETS. Approximately 200 pages of unbound pamphlets of the Wason Collection including those on the American Bible Society, Associated Boards for Christian Colleges in China, Buddhism and Christianity, Canton Christian College, Catholic missions in China, Chinese language instruction, Chinese term for God, Christian clergy, Christian Education Movement, Christianity in the People's Republic of China, church-government relations, Eastern Orthodox Church, Manchuria, missions in Tibet, United Board for Christian Higher Education in Asia, Yenching University, and Young Men's Christian Association-Foreign Division. Other pamphlets include:

[CORRESPONDENCE]: Letter from Robert Philip to Thomas Babington Macauley on missions and the Opium War, 1840.

[MAPS/DESIGNS/DRAWINGS]: Maps of Kwangtung and Hainan, 1933.

See CHINESE LANGUAGE MATERIALS for other pamphlets in the Wason Collection.

DIARIES: Carbon copy of a 62-page journal of a voyage to China by Arthur Gostick Shorrock, 1887.

MEMORABILIA: Game of Chinese radicals, 1920(?); scrapbook relating to China and Japan, comp. by William N. Hall of the Methodist Mission, Tientsin, containing clippings, illustrations, and maps, 1860–72.

ORAL HISTORIES: *China Missionaries Oral History Collection*, ed. by Cyrus H. Peake and Arthur L. Rosenbaum (Claremont Graduate School, Oral History Program), 1973, part I only. See ORAL HISTORIES Union List for the names of participants.

MAPS/DESIGNS/DRAWINGS: *Atlas des missions franciscaines en Chine*, by R. Hausermann (Paris: Procuré des missions franciscaines, 1915); *Atlas du haut Yangtse, de I-Tchang Fou à P'ing Chang Hien*, by Stanislas Chevalier, 1899; *Atlas of China in Provinces*, by Thomas Cochrane, 1913; *Atlas of the Chinese Empire*, by Edward Stanford (Philadelphia/London: China Inland Mission; Morgan and Scott, Ltd.), 1908; *Complete Atlas of China*, by Edward Stanford, 1917; map of China prepared for the China Inland Mission by Edward Stanford, 1899; *La mappemonde Ricci du Musée historique de Pékin*, by Augustin Bernard, 1928; *Nouvel atlas de la Chine, de la Tartarie chinoise et du Thibet...par les Jésuites missionnaires à la Chine*, ed. by Jean Baptiste Bourguignon d'Anville, to accompany J. B. Du Halde's *Description géographique, historique...de la Chine* (1736), 1737; *Shanghai Catholique*, by Mission de Nanking, 1933; maps, atlases, and other publications of Zika-wei Observatory, Shanghai, 1882–1934.

SERIALS: American Friends Service Committee: *Color and Background Material*, 1946–50; *Miscellaneous Bulletins*, 1946–47; *Periodic Summary*, 1946–50. *Anking Newsletter*, 1937–41, 1945, 1947–48. *Asia*, 1949–60. *Bulletin Catholique de Pékin*, 1913–48. Canton Christian College, *Agricultural Bulletin*, 1928; *Bulletin*, 1917, 1920–21, 1924–25, 1928. *Catholic Church in China*, 1928–32, 1936–45. *Cheeloo Monthly Bulletin*, 1935–37. *China*, 1947–52. *China Bulletin*, 1952–62. *China Christian Advocate*, 1914–30, 1932–41. China Christian Educational Association, *Bulletin*, 1928. *China Christian Year Book*, 1910–39. China Inland Mission: China Inland Mission/Overseas Missionary Fellowship, *Review*, 1951–64; *Occasional Papers*, 1872–75. China International Famine Relief Commission, Publications, series A, 1923–32; series B, 1923–?; series C, 1923–24; series E, 1932; series G, 1934–? *China Law Review*, 1922–37, 1940. *China Mission Advocate*, 1839. *China Monthly: The Truth about China*, 1939–50. *China Notes*, 1962–72. *The China Sunday School Journal*, 1913–19. *China's Young Men*, 1914–15. *Chinese-American Bulletin*, 1942–46. *Chinese and General Missionary Gleaner*, 1851–52. *Chinese Christian Intelligencer*, 1916. *Chinese Christians Today*, 1962–64. *Chinese Medical Journal*, 1905, 1907, 1910–13, 1915–44, 1949–66, 1975–76. *Chinese Medical Journal* (Chengtu ed.), 1942. *Chinese Recorder*, 1868–72, 1874–1941. *Chinese Repository*, 1832–49. *Ching Feng*, 1964–71. *The Christian Farmer*, 1935. College of Chinese Studies, *Bulletin*, 1947. *East Asia Millions* (London), 1875–1945, 1947–81. *East Asia Millions* (Philadelphia), 1896, 1906. *Educational Directory (and Year Book) of China*, 1914–18, 1921. *Educational Review*, 1907, 1909–11, 1914–38. *Fenchow*, 1919–36. *Folklore Studies*, supplement, 1952. *The Foochow Messenger*, 1903–40. *Fu Jen News Letter*, 1931–32. Hua Chung University, *Bulletin*, 1925. *Land of Sinim*, 1904–5. *The Light*, 1932–34, 1939–59. Lingnan University: *Science Bulletin*, 1930; Natural History Survey and Museum, *Special Publications*, 1942–50. *Lingnan Science Journal*, 1922–45, 1948. *Les Missions de Chine*, 1916–17, 1925–41. *Monumenta Serica*, 1935–71. Nanking Theological Seminary, English publications, 1940–41. Natural History Society, *Proceedings*, 1928–30. *New Horizons*, 1934–35, 1939, 1941–72. *Notes and Queries on China and Japan*, 1867–70. *Peking Natural History Bulletin*, 1926–41, 1948–50. Peking Union Medical College, *Contributions*, 1921–26. *Relations de Chine*, 1903–14, 1917–40. St. John's University, *Bulletin*, 1924. Shanghai American School, *Bulletin*, 1924–25, 1928. Shantung Christian University, *Bulletin*, 1924–25. *T'oung Pao*, 1890–1974. *Tung Wu Magazine*, 1935. *Understanding China Newsletter*, 1965–75. Université de l'Aurore (Chen Tan ta-hsüeh): *Bulletin*, 1933–49: *Fichier entomologique chinoise*, n.d.; *Monthly Bulletin*, 1946–48; *Notes de botanique chinoise*, 1931, 1933; *Notes d'entomologie chinoise*, 1929–49; *Notes de malacologie chinoise*, 1934–45. University of Nanking, *Bulletin*, 1920–21, 1924–25, 1931; *Newsletter*, 1944–46; College of Agriculture and Forestry: *Agricultural and Forestry Notes*, 1924; *Agriculture and Forestry Series*, 1923–24; *Bulletin*, 1933; *Miscellaneous Bulletin Series*, 1924–25; Women's College, *Bulletin*, 1931. *Variétés Sinologiques*, 1892–1903, 1905–6, 1909–16, 1918, 1920, 1922, 1924–25, 1932–34. West China Border Research Society, *Journal*, 1922–46. *Woman's Missionary Friend*, 1870–1918. *Woman's Work in the Far East*, 1877–87, 1890–1920. Yenching University: *Bulletin*, 1925, 1927, 1932; College of Natural Science, *Science Notes*, 1934–41; Department of Biology, *Bulletin*, 1930; Department of Sociology and Social Work, Publications, series C, 1929;

Social Research Series, 1930; *Yenching Index Numbers*, 1940–41; *Yenching Journal of Social Studies*, 1938–41, 1948–50.
DISSERTATIONS/THESES: *The American and British Missionary Concept of Chinese Civilization in the Nineteenth Century*, by James M. McCutcheon, 1959. *American Catholic China Missionaries, 1918–1941*, by Thomas A. Breslin, 1972. *American Catholic Missions and Communist China, 1945–1953*, by Virginia F. Unsworth, 1977. *The American Christian Press and the Sino-Japanese Crisis of 1931–1933: An Aspect of Public Response to the Breakdown of World Peace*, by Alden Bryan Pearson, 1968. *American Missionaries and the Chinese Communists: A Study of Views Expressed by Methodist Episcopal Church Missionaries, 1921–1941*, by Milo L. Thornberry, 1974. *Americans as Reformers in Kuomintang China, 1928–1937*, by James Claude Thomson, 1961. *The Anti-Christian Movement in China, 1922–1927, With Special Reference to the Experience of Protestant Missions*, by Ka-che Yip, 1970. *The Anti-Christian Persecution of 1616–1617 in Nanking*, by Edward Kelly, 1971. *Der Begriff Skandalon im Neuen Testament und der Wiederkehrgedanke bei Laotse*, by Lie Hwa-sun, 1973. *The Causes and Results of the Boxer Movement*, by Man Kwok-chaak, 1936. *Changes in the Christian Message for China by Protestant Missionaries*, by Lewis Strong Casey Smythe, 1928. *Chinese, Missionary, and International Efforts to End the Use of Opium in China, 1890–1916*, by Kathleen Lodwick, 1976. *Christian Colleges and the Chinese Revolution, 1840–1940: A Case Study in the Impact of the West*, by Loren William Crabtree, 1969. *A Christian's Inquiry into the Struggle Ethic in the Thought of Mao Tse-tung*, by Raymond L. Whitehead, 1972. *Church and State in Republican China: A Survey History of the Relations between the Christian Churches and the Chinese Government, 1911–1945*, by Arne Sovik, 1952. *An Enduring Encounter: E. T. Williams, China, and the United States*, by Dimitri Daniel Lazo, 1977. *The History of Baptist Missions in Hong Kong*, by Paul Yat-keung Wong, 1974. *A History of the Evangelical Lutheran Church of America's Mission Policy in China, 1890–1949*, by Roger Keith Ose, 1970. *Hsu Kuang-chi: Chinese Scientist and Christian (1562–1633)*, by Joseph King-hap Ku, 1973. *Issachar Jacox Roberts and American Diplomacy in China during the Taiping Rebellion*, by George Blackburn Pruden, 1977. *John Leighton Stuart: The Mind and Life of an American Missionary in China, 1876–1941*, by Shaw Yu-ming, 1975. *Die katholische Missionsmethode in China in neuester Zeit (1741–1912)*, by Johannes Beckmann, 1931. *The Life and Thought of W. A. P. Martin: Agent and Interpreter of Sino-American Contact in the Nineteenth and Early Twentieth Centuries*, by Ralph M. Covell, 1974. *The Mission Compound in Modern China: The Role of the United States Protestant Mission as an Asylum in the Civil and International Strife of China, 1900–1941*, by Gladys Robina Quale, 1957. *The Mission Enterprise of the Lutheran Church-Missouri Synod in Mainland China, 1913–1952*, by Roy A. Suelflow, 1971. *The Mission of Matteo Ricci, S.J.: A Case Study of an Effort at Guided Cultural Change in China in the Sixteenth Century*, by George L. Harris, 1967. *Missionary Conscience and the Comprehension of Imperialism: A Study of the Children of American Missionaries to China, 1900–1949*, by Sarah R. Mason, 1978. *Missionary Intelligence from China: American Protestant Reports, 1930–1950*, by Bruce Stephen Greenawalt, 1974. *Missionary Journalism in Nineteenth-century China: Young J. Allen and the Early "Wan kuo kung pao,"* by Adrian Arthur Bennett, 1970. *Oberlin-in-China, 1881–1951*, by Mary Tarpley Campfield, 1974. *Political Activities of the Christian Missionaries*

in the T'ang Dynasty, by Lam Ch'i-hung, 1975. *The Political Reconstruction of China*, by Eu-yang Kwang, 1922. *Protestant Christianity and Marriage in China*, by Calvin H. Reber, 1958. *Protestant Mission Schools for Girls in South China (1827 to the Japanese Invasion)*, by Mary Raleigh Anderson, 1943. *Protestant Missionary Activity in Hunan Province—China: History and Analysis, 1875–1912*, by James A. Bollback, 1981. *The Protestant Missionary Understanding of the Chinese Situation and the Christian Task from 1890 to 1911*, by C. William Mensendiek, 1958. *Protestant Missions in Communist China*, by Creighton Lacy, 1953. *Die Protestantische Christenheit in der Volksrepublik China und die Chinaberichterstattung in der deutschen evangelischen Missionsliteratur*, by Ilse Hass, 1974. *Reciprocal Change: The Case of American Protestant Missionaries to China*, by Paul Voninski, 1975. *Revolutionary Faithfulness: The Quaker Search for a Peaceable Kingdom in China, 1939–1951*, by Cynthia Letts Adcock, 1974. *The Role of the Christian Colleges in Modern China before 1928*, by Jessie Gregory Lutz, 1955. *Sino-American Relations, 1882–1885: The Mission of John Russell Young*, by Victoria M. Cha-tsu Siu, 1975. *Suomen lähetysseuran työ Kiinassa vuosina 1901–1926 (The Work of the Finnish Missionary Society in China in the Years 1901–1926)*, by Toivo Saarilahti, 1960. *Strangers in the House: J. Lewis Shuck and Issachar Roberts, First American Baptist Missionaries to China*, by Margaret M. Coughlin, 1972. *A Symbolic Interactionist Approach to the Religious Stranger Concept: Protestant Missionaries in China, 1845–1900*, by Nishan J. Najarian, 1982. *A Theological Dialogue between Christian Faith and Chinese Belief in the Light of "Sin": An Inquiry into the Apparent Failure of the Protestant Mission in Late Nineteenth-century China, Especially among Chinese Intellectuals*, by Christopher Chou, 1976.
CHINESE LANGUAGE MATERIALS/SERIALS: *Chiao yü chi k'an (China Christian Educational Quarterly)*, 1927–29. *Chin-ling hsüeh pao, (Nanking Journal)*, 1931–41. *Chin-ling shen hsüeh chih (Nanking Seminary Review)*, 1947–49. Chin-ling ta hsüeh, nung hsüeh yüan, *Pao kao*, 1928. *Chung-kuo hsin t'u yueh k'an (Chinese Christians Today)*, 1962–80. Hua-hsi hsieh ho ta hsüeh she hui hsüeh hsi, *Ch'i k'an* (West China Union University, Department of Sociology, *Periodical*), 1934. *Hua-hsi hsüeh pao (West China Union University Journal)*, 1933–34, 1936. *Ling nan*, 1919. *Ling-nan chou pao (Lingnan Weekly)*, 1939–40. *Ling-nan hsüeh pao (Lingnan Journal)*, 1929–37, 1947–52. *Ling-nan nung k'an (Lingnan Agricultural Journal)*, 1934. *Ling-nan ta hsüeh hsiao pao (Lingnan University Journal)*, 1935. Ling-nan ta hsüeh, Nung hsüeh nien pao (Lingnan University, *Agricultural Yearbook*), 1918. *T'ien chia pan yüeh k'an (The Christian Farmer)*, 1935. *T'ien feng*, 1948, 1953–63. *Tung hsi yang k'ao mei yüeh t'ung chi chuan (Eastern and Western Examiner)*, 1833–38. Tung-wu ta hsüeh, fa hsüeh lu, *T'ung hsüeh lu*, 1930-? *Yen-ching hsüeh pao (Yenching Journal of Chinese Studies)*, 1927–51. Yen-ching she hui k'o hsüeh (Yenching Social Sciences), 1948–49. Yen-ching ta hsüeh, T'u shu kuan pao (Yenching University, *Library Bulletin*), 1931–39. *Yen-ta nien k'an (The Yenchinian)*, 1928. *Yen-ta yu sheng (Yenching University Voice of Friendship)*, 1936–37. *Yen-ta yüeh k'an (Yenching University Monthly)*, 1927–28.
CHINESE LANGUAGE MATERIALS: Ca. 350 books and pamphlets, including translations of Western theological works into Chinese, biographies of missionaries and Chinese Christians, 43 translations of the Bible into various dialects (Mandarin, Cantonese, Fukienese, Hakka, Hwa Lisu, Amoy dialect, Swatow dialect,

and Wenchow dialect, 1813–1950); and works about ancestor worship, Gladys Aylward, the Bible, Chinese Christian Youth Association, Christian theology, Christianity in the People's Republic of China, church history, Christianity and Buddhism, Christianity and Confucianism, economics and public finance, Lingnan University, Southwest Society and Economics Research Institute, Robert M. Mateer, Society for the Promotion of Chinese Christian Religious Education, University of Nanking, Wu-han ch'ing nien hsieh hui (YMCA, Hankow), and Yenching University.

JAMAICA

ST. JOHN'S UNIVERSITY

NY–100 Library
Asian Collection
Grand Central and Utopia Parkways
Jamaica NY 11439
(718) 990–6735
Sister Marie Melton, Director of Libraries
Hou Ran Ferng, Asian Collection Librarian

1-GENERAL HOLDINGS
CHINESE LANGUAGE MATERIALS: 28 books on subjects including anti-foreign movements, Christian life (19th century), Christianity and Chinese modernization, Ch'ien-lung emperor and Christian missions, church history and missions, Cardinal Newman, relations between the K'ang-hsi emperor and Rome, Matteo Ricci, Stanislaus Lokuang, and Nestorians in China.

NY–105 University Archives
St. John's University
Grand Central and Utopia Parkways
Jamaica NY 11439
(718) 990–6161/6734
John E. Young, C.M., University Archivist

Background note: This collection mainly contains material concerning the activities of the Vincentian missionaries in China, from the Eastern Province of the Congregation of the Mission, with headquarters at St. Vincent's Seminary, 500 East Chelten Avenue, Philadelphia, PA, 19144.

1-CHINA MISSIONS COLLECTION, 1920–54, 33 l.f.
MINUTES/RECORDS/REPORTS: Financial and pastoral reports, n.d.; reports from the China mission in *Annals of the Congregation of the Mission*, 1895–1925; *Annales de la Congrégation de la Mission*, 1851–94, 1934–63; *The De Andrein*, 1931–64; *Heri-Hodie*, 1934–70; *Mémoires de la Congrégation de la Mission*, 1911–12; *The Miraculous Medal Magazine*, 1928; and *The Vincentian*, 1923–58.
CORRESPONDENCE: 414 letters of missionaries in China to the provincial superiors, 1920–54; 5 l.f. of missionaries' letters to families, friends, benefactors, confreres, etc., 1921–50.
DIARIES: "Sinfeng Chronicle," a typewritten daily account by a missionary on activities and events in Kiangsi province, 1929–41; excerpts from Sr. Vincent Louise DeLude's diary describing her departure from China, 1930.
MANUSCRIPTS: Typewritten notes on the Kiangsi mission, 1594–1838, by John E. McLoughlin, C.M., 1932; "Story of

Lungnan Mission from 1903 to 1910,'' by Felix Bonanate, C.M.; "Centenary of the Missions of Kiangsi,'' by J. G. Heijer, 1931; "History of the Sinfeng Mission,'' by Felix Bonanate, C.M.; "Kanchow Mission Survey,'' mimeograph by Congregation of the Mission novices in Connecticut, 1963.
PAMPHLETS: *The Systematic Destruction of the Catholic Church in China*, by Thomas J. Bauer, M.M., 1954; *Lebbe: Missioner Extraordinary*, 1946; *Father Lebbe: A Modern Apostle*, by Raymond De Jaegher, 1950; *Personnel List of Eastern Province Missionaries, 1921–1952*.
MEMORABILIA: Kanchow Jubilee booklet, 1921–46.
ORAL HISTORIES: Interviews on cassette by John W. Carven, C.M., with Congregation of the Mission priests who served in China between 1921 and 1953: Thomas P. Browne, Arthur J. Colby, Robert P. Crawford, Lawrence D. Curtis, Eugene Davis, Frederick P. Gehring, John J. Henry, Joseph J. Hill, John J. Lawlor, Vincent C. Loeffler, Frederick A. McGuire, Francis J. Melvin, Walter J. Menig, Paul Mottey, John J. Munday, Edward A. Murray, Charles J. O'Connor, Francis J. Stauble, and Edward W. Young, and Sr. Clara Groell, D.C.
MAPS/DESIGNS/DRAWINGS: Hand-drawn maps of the Vicariate of Kanchow, Kiangsi province, by Frederick Gehring, C.M., ca. 1935; 4 physical and political maps of China, by A. Richard and Long E. Greenwich, early 20th century.
AUDIO-VISUAL MATERIALS: Miscellaneous photos of persons and places in the Kiangsi Vicariate; photo albums about the consecration of Bishop James Edward Walsh, M.M., 1929; box of photos by Francis Moehringer, C.M., and Joseph Kennedy, C.M., depicting the Lungnan mission, n.d.
SERIALS: *Kanchow*, 1937–40. *Les Missions de Chine*, 1937. *Les Missions de Chine et du Japon*, 1931.
DISSERTATIONS/THESES: *Hsu Kuang-chi: Chinese Scientist and Christian (1562–1633)*, by Joseph King-hap Ku, 1973. *Maryknoll Sisters in China, 1921–1949*, by Patricia Hughes Ponzi, 1980. *Timothy Richard's Theory of Christian Missions to the Non-Christian World*, by Rita T. Johnson, 1966.
FINDING AIDS: In-house schedules.

MARYKNOLL

MARYKNOLL FATHERS AND BROTHERS

NY–110 Archives
Maryknoll NY 10545
(914) 941–7590
John Harrington, M.M., Archivist

Restrictions: Correspondence files are "closed,'' so they are not listed.
Background note: Founded in 1911, Maryknoll, the Catholic Foreign Mission Society of America, sent its first missionaries to China in 1918. A total of 241 priests, brothers, and lay missionaries served in China between 1918 and 1952. (This figure does not include Maryknoll sisters.)

1-GENERAL HOLDINGS
MINUTES/RECORDS/REPORTS: 400 boxes identified as "Miscellaneous A through Z,''including large sections on China, 1912-: General Council Minutes, General Council Visitations (reports of administrative visits), General Chapter Minutes, Inter-Chapter Assembly Minutes.

CORRESPONDENCE/DIARIES: 29 boxes containing "Diaries," i.e., daily logs of events and activities of the missioners and the mission,1901–52, from the following locations: Antung, Chakow, Chaoyangchun, Chikkai, Chikkung, Chiuling, Chongpu, Chungsun, Dairen, Di Ho, Erhpatan/Shanchengtze, Fachow, Fushun, Fushun/Hsinpin, Hingking, Hoighan, Hokshiha, Hong Kong, Hopei, Hsinpin, Kaying, Kiaotow, Kochow, Kongmoon, Kweilin, Laohukow, Linkiang, Lintaan, Loking, Loting, Lumchai, Lungwoh, Manchuria, Ngwa, Pakkai, Peiping, Pettochai, Pinglo, Pingnam, Samhopa, Sancian, Sanning, Shakchin, Shanchengtze, Siaoloc, South China, Sunchong, Sungkow, Sunwui, Taipathu, Tengchen, Toishan, Topong, Tsiahang, Tunghwa, Tungshek, Watlam, Wuchow, and Yeungkong.

CORRESPONDENCE/MANUSCRIPTS/PAMPHLETS/MEMORABILIA: 73 boxes of letters, sermons, clippings, and pamphlets, 1918–52, by and about Frederick C. Dietz, James N. Drought, Bishop Francis Xavier Ford, Bishop Raymond A. Lane, Bishop James E. Walsh, and Thomas F. Price.

MEMORABILIA: 5 boxes of scrapbooks, photo albums, souvenirs, and miscellaneous unshelved items.

ORAL HISTORIES: China History Project, consisting of 260 tapes and transcripts of American fathers, brothers and lay missionaries: A. J. Bagalawis, Thomas Brack, Donat Chatigny, John Comber, Timothy Daley, Charles Daly, Francis Daubert, Allan Dennis, Richard Downey, John Drew, John Driscoll, Paul Duchesne, Maurice Duffy, Joseph Early, Stephen Edmonds, William Eggleston, Herbert Elliot, Albert Fedders, Henry Felsecker, James E. Fitzgerald, Philip Furlong, Michael Gaiero, Raymond Gaspard, Howard Geselbracht, Sylvio Gilbert, Lloyd Glass, John Graser, Robert Greene, Joseph Hahn, John Heemskerk, Cyril Hirst, Raymond Hohlfeld, John Joyce, William Kaschmitter, Thomas Kiernan, Wenceslaus Knotek, William Kupfer, Edwin McCabe, Leo McCarthy, John McGinn, Frederick McGuire, Edward McGurkin, Michael McKeirnan, James McLaughlin, Francis MacRae, Edward Manning, John Mihelko, James T. Minning, John Moore, William Morrissey, Edward Mueth, Francis Mullen, Francis Murphy, Irwin Nugent, Michael O'Connell, Bernard Petley, William Pheur, Francis Pouliot, Joseph Pulaski, George Putnam, Carroll Quinn, Joseph Regan, Peter Reilly, Thaddeus Revers, Charles Schmidt, Robert Sheridan, Dennis Slattery, James Smith, Russell Sprinkle, John Tackney, Howard Trube, Joseph Van den Bogaard, John Velasco, John J. Walsh, Leo Walter, Edward Weis, Francis Wempe, Francis White, Bernard Wieland, Robert Winkels, Edward Youker, and Stanislaus Ziemba; and Chinese sisters, fathers, brothers, and lay missionaries who were associates of Maryknollers in China: Edith Au, Maureen Au, Philomena Chan, Rose Chan, Joachim Chen, Stephen Chen, Cheuk Chiu-yin, Cheuk Yee-chiu, Cheuk York-mong, Andrew Cheung, Paul Cheung, Rose Chin, Agnes Chow, Peter Chum, Chung Kwok-kwan, Jong Kin-shum, Pauline Koo, Joseph Lam, Rose Lam, Thomas Lau, Catherine Lee, Leatitia Lee, Paul Lei, Leung Kit-fong, Leung Wai-fan, Thomas Li, Joan Ling, Liu Hon-ching, Peter Ma, Protase Pai, Paul Pang, Qiu Runduan, Dominic Tang, Simeon To, Michael Tsa, David Tse, Eileen Tse, John Tse, Robert Tse, Peter Wong, Ruth Wong, John Wu, Wu Pak-seng, Xu Simeng, Paul Yang, Yau Chun-yuen, Joseph Yuen, and Yung Chi-tung.

MAPS/DESIGNS/DRAWINGS: Maps in both Chinese and English, mostly of Kwangtung and Kwangsi in the early 1900s.

CHINESE LANGUAGE MATERIALS: 5 boxes, primarily catechisms and instructional materials written by Maryknoll missioners, n.d.

FINDING AIDS: In-house directories.

NY–115 Library

Maryknoll Fathers and Brothers
Maryknoll NY 10545
(914) 941–7590
Arthur Brown, Librarian

1-GENERAL HOLDINGS

MINUTES/RECORDS/REPORTS: Reports on the China mission in *The Field Afar*, 1907-; United Board for Christian Colleges in China, report of a survey of the libraries of the Christian colleges, 1947–48.

MANUSCRIPTS: "The Missionary as China-Watcher: Samuel Wells Williams and the Chinese," by Murray A. Rubinstein, n.d.; "The Northeastern Connection: American Board Missionaries and the Formation of American Opinion Toward China, 1830–1860," by Murray A. Rubinstein, 1978; "Principal Events of the Maryknoll Wuchow Mission in Kwangsi, China," by John F. Donovan, 1976.

PAMPHLETS: *Nestorians in China: Some Corrections and Additions*, by Arthur Christopher Moule, 1940.

ORAL HISTORIES: *China Missionaries Oral History Collection*, ed. by Cyrus H. Peake and Arthur L. Rosenbaum (Claremont Graduate School, Oral History Program), 1973, part 1. See ORAL HISTORIES Union List for the names of participants.

SERIALS: *Annuaire des Missions Catholiques de Chine*, 1928–30, 1934–37, 1939–40. *Bulletin de la Société des Missions-Etrangères de Paris*, 1925–26, 1933, 1935–38, 1953–56, 1958–59, 1961. *China Christian Year Book*, 1925–26. *China Missionary Bulletin*, 1948–53. *Les Missions de Chine*, 1933–34, 1938, 1940. *Les Missions de Chine et du Japon*, 1916–17, 1923, 1925, 1927, 1929, 1931, 1933.

DISSERTATIONS/THESES: *The American Board in China: The Missionaries' Experiences and Attitudes, 1911-1952*, by Janet Elaine Heininger, 1981. *American Catholic Missions and Communist China, 1945-1953*, by Virginia Unsworth, 1976. *American Missionaries and the Policies of the United States in China, 1898-1901*, by John M. H. Lindbeck, 1948. *Apostolic Legations to China of the Eighteenth Century*, by Antonio Sisto Rosso, 1948. *A Brief History of the Missionary Work of the Maryknoll Fathers in China*, by Peter James Barry, M.M., 1977. *Catholic Activities in Kwangtung Province and Chinese Responses, 1848-1885*, by Jean-Paul Wiest, 1977. *The Confrontation: American Catholicism and Chinese Communism, 1945-1962*, by William C. Hearon, 1975. *An Image of the French Religious Protectorate in China, as Reflected in the Catholic and Moderate Press at the Time of the Third Republic*, by Lawrence Nemer, 1967. *Imperial Government and Catholic Missions in China during the Years 1784-1785*, by Bernward Henry Willeke, 1948. *An Investigation of the Modernizing Role of the Maryknoll Sisters in China*, by Mary Ann Schintz, 1978. *The Negotiations between Ch'i-ying and Lagrené, 1844-1846*, by Angelus Francis J. Grosse-Aschhoff, 1950. *Suffering in the Experience of the Protestant Church in China (1911-1980): A Chinese Perspective*, by Paul Cheuk-ching Szeto, 1980. *Zion's Corner: Origins of the American Protestant Missionary Movement in China, 1827-1839*, by Murray A. Rubinstein, 1976.

CHINESE LANGUAGE MATERIALS/DISSERTATIONS/ THESES: *A Brief History of the Missionary Work of the Maryknoll Fathers in China*, by Peter James Barry, M.M., 1977 (see also DISSERTATIONS/THESES above).

MARYKNOLL SISTERS OF ST. DOMINIC, INC.

NY-120 Maryknoll Sisters Archives
Maryknoll Sisters Center
Maryknoll NY 10545
(914) 941-7575
Dolores A.Rosso, Archivist

Restrictions: Access by appointment only. Since correspondence files are "closed," they are not listed. General historical records are not restricted. Administrative and special record groups are accessible by permission.

Background note: The Maryknoll Sisters of St. Dominic, Inc., was founded by Mary Josephine Rogers under the guidance of James A.Walsh, M.M., at Maryknoll, New York, in 1912. The focus of the congregation is foreign mission activities. Since 1921 the congregation has participated in educational programs on all levels, health related programs, community and social welfare programs, pastoral work, social action education, religious education and formation work. The first missions were in China. The sisters now serve in 28 countries around the world.

Finding aids: In-house directories, computer print-outs which retrieve data by subject, place, date, and personal name.

1-GENERAL HOLDINGS

MINUTES/RECORDS/REPORTS/DIARIES: 15 boxes containing Maryknoll Sisters Regional Assemblies, Asian World Section Meetings, and Pastoral Planning, 1921-; 19 boxes containing diaries, i.e., daily logs of events and activities of the missioners and the mission, 1921-68, listed by geographical location and archive box for the following locations: Antung, Chai Wan, Chiuling, Chungking, Dairen, Fushun, Hingning, Holy Spirit School, Homantin, Honan, Hopei, Kaying, Kowloon, Kunming, Kweichow, Kweilin, Laipo, Laitsui, Loting, Macao, Ngwa, Pakkai, Pettochai, Pingnam, Sancian, Shahokou, Shanghai, Shekhang, Shuichai, Siaoloc, Sungkow, Szwong, Tengshek, Tunghwa, Toishan, Yeungkong, Yunghui, Yunnan.

PAMPHLETS: 15 titles by Maryknoll missioners.

AUDIO-VISUAL MATERIALS: 7 boxes of photos of South China missions; 2 boxes of photos of Anthony Cotta and Vincent Lebbe in China; box of photos of Superior's visitations in South China, China missions in 1920s; 30 photo albums of Hong Kong and South China missions; several hundred unsorted and unidentified pictures of China, Hong Kong, Taiwan, and Manchuria; 11 films with reference to China;160 slides of Hong Kong; 1921-.

ORAL HISTORIES: The China History Project, 1927-50, containing 103 taped interviews, with transcriptions, of Maryknoll Sisters in South China: Jude Babione, Candida Maria Basto, Elizabeth Bauman, Monica Marie Bayle, Amata Brachtesende, Colombiere Bradley, Kathleen Bradley, Ann Carol Brielmaier, Mary de Ricci Cain, Veronica Marie Carney, Cecilia Carvalho, Agnes Cazale, Anne Clements, Cornelia Collins, Rita Claire Comber, Eucharista Coupe, Angela Marie Coveny, Henrietta Cunningham,

Rose Duchesne Debrecht, Agnes Devlin, Mary Diggins, Grace Doherty, Ruth Evans, Ann Mary Farrell, Virginia Flagg, Irene Fogarty, Godfrey Fuhr, Christella Furey, Mary Gerard Gallagher, Rose Bernadette Gallagher, Fabiola Gonyou, Therese Grondin, Antonia M. Guerrieri, Rose Benigna Hanan, Julia Hannigan, Corita Herrgen, Agnes Virginia Higgins, Mary Augusta Hock, Paulita Hoffman, Teresa Hollfelder, Marie Cor. Jaramillo, Margaret Jung, Joseph Marie Kane, Madeline Sophie Karlon, Rosalia Kettle, Theresa Killoran, Margaret Kim, Louise Kroeger, Miriam Lechthaler, Doretta Leonard, Jessie Lucier, Mary DeLellis McKenna, Mary Paul McKenna, Ignatius McNally, Lelia Makra, Ann Malone, Santa Maria Manning, F. de Sales Marsland, Mary Lou Martin, Barbara R. Mersinger, Miriam Xavier Mug, Frances Murphy, Catherine O'Hagan, Mary Angelica O'Leary, Agnes Regina Rafferty, Rita Marie Regan, Ruth Riconda, Moira Riehl, Edith Rietz, Corinne Rost, Dorothy Rubner, Mary Schafers, Gemma Shea, Kathleen Marie Shea, Beatrice Stapleton, Jean Theo. Steinbauer, Pauline Sticka, Herman Joseph Stitz, Paula Sullivan, Eunice Tolan, Magdalena Urlacher, Clara Venneman, Espiritu Venneman, Dorothy Walsh, Rosalie Weber, Celine Werner, and M. Chanel Xavier.

91 taped interviews of Maryknoll Fathers A. J. Bagalawis, Thomas Brack, Donat Chatigny, John Comber, Timothy Daley, Charles Daly, Francis Daubert, Allan Dennis, Richard Downey, John Drew, John Driscoll, Paul Duchesne, Maurice Duffy, Joseph Early, Stephen Edmonds, William Eggleston, Herbert Elliot, Albert Fedders, Henry Felsecker, James E. Fitzgerald, Philip Furlong, Michael Gaiero, Raymond Gaspard, Howard Geselbracht, Sylvio Gilbert, Lloyd Glass, John Graser, Robert Greene, Joseph Hahn, John Heemskerk, Cyril Hirst, Raymond Hohlfeld, John Joyce, William Kaschmitter, Thomas Kiernan, Wenceslaus Knotek, William Kupfer, Edwin McCabe, Leo McCarthy, John McGinn, Frederick McGuire, Edward McGurkin, Michael McKeirnan, James McLaughlin, Francis MacRae, Edward Manning, John Mihelko, James T. Minning, John Moore, William Morrissey, Edward Mueth, Francis Mullen, Francis Murphy, Irwin Nugent, Michael O'Connell, Bernard Petley, William Pheur, Francis Pouliot, Joseph Pulaski, George Putnam, Carroll Quinn, Joseph Regan, Peter Reilly, Thaddeus Revers, Charles Schmidt, Robert Sheridan, Dennis Slattery, James Smith, Russell Sprinkle, John Tackney, Howard Trube, Joseph Van den Bogaard, John Velasco, John J. Walsh, Leo Walter, Edward Weis, Francis Wempe, Francis White, Bernard Wieland, Robert Winkels, Edward Youker, and Stanislaus Ziemba.

49 taped interviews of Chinese people Edith Au, Maureen Au, Philomena Chan, Rose Chan, Joachim Chen, Stephen Chen, Cheuk Chiu-yin, Cheuk Yee-chiu, Cheuk York-mong, Andrew Cheung, Paul Cheung, Rose Chin, Agnes Chow, Peter Chum, Chung Kwok-kwan, Jong Kin-shum, Pauline Koo, Joseph Lam, Rose Lam, Thomas Lau, Catherine Lee, Leatitia Lee, Paul Lei, Leung Kit-fong, Leung Wai-fan, Thomas Li, Joan Ling, Liu Honching, Peter Ma, Protase Pai, Paul Pang, Qiu Runduan, Dominic Tang, Simeon To, Michael Tsa, David Tse, Eileen Tse, John Tse, Robert Tse, Peter Wong, Ruth Wong, John Wu, Wu Pak-seng, Xu Simeng, Paul Yang, Yau Chun-yuen, Joseph Yuen, and Yung Chitung.

Maryknoll Sisters Oral History Project, untranscribed cassette tapes of interviews with Maryknoll Sisters containing a segment on current mission activities in China in educational, medical, pastoral, and catechical work: M. Jude Babione, Marie Elise Baumann, Nancy Bone, Monica Marie Boyle, Edna Brophy, Veronica Marie Carney, Henrietta M. Cunningham, Grace Doherty, Ann Mary Farrell, Christella Furey, M. Dominic Guidera, Mary Ellen Kerrigan, M. Paul McKenna, Andree Normandin, Joan Catherine O'Hagan, Agnes Regina Rafferty, Gemma Shea, Beatrice Stapleton, Jean Theophane Steinbauer, M. Herman Joseph Stitz, Eunice Tolan, M. Richard Wenzel, and M. Chanel Xavier.

SERIALS: *Asia*, 1978–83.

DISSERTATIONS/THESES: *American Catholic Missions and Communist China, 1945–1953*, by Virginia Unsworth, 1976. *A Short History of the Missionary Work of the Maryknoll Fathers in China*, by Peter J. Barry, 1977. *Christianity in Modern China*, by Mary Lou Martin, 1975. *The Impact of Christianity on China in the Time of the Jesuits*, by Marya Roy, 1973. *An Investigation of the Modernizing Role of the Maryknoll Sisters in China*, by Mary Ann Schintz, 1978. *Maryknoll in Manchuria, 1927–1947: A Study of Accommodation and Adaptation*, by Kathleen Kelly, 1982. *Maryknoll Sisters in China, 1921–1949*, by Patricia Hughes Ponzi, 1980. *Some Elements of Truth Reflected in Chinese Religious Beliefs*, by Mariel Vitcavage, 1939. *Timothy Richard's Theory of Christian Mission to the Non-Christian World*, by Rita Therese Johnson, 1966.

NY–125 Rogers Library

Maryknoll Sisters of St. Dominic
Maryknoll NY 10545
(914) 941-7575
Patricia Noble, Librarian

1-GENERAL HOLDINGS

MINUTES/RECORDS/REPORTS: National Pastoral Workshops of the Catholic Church in the Republic of China, 1969–70.

CORRESPONDENCE/MANUSCRIPTS: Letter from Anthony Cotta to Cardinal Benedict Serafini concerning the condition of native clergy in China, 1916, with report on Council of Chala, 1914, from Anthony Cotta to Father Milon, C.M., Secretary General.

PAMPHLETS: *The Systematic Destruction of the Catholic Church in China*, by Thomas J. Bauer, 1954.

SERIALS: *Annuaire des missions Catholiques du Manchoukuo*, 1936. *Maryknoll Mission Letters*, 1942–46.

DISSERTATIONS/THESES: *American Catholic Missions and Communist China, 1945–1953*, by Virginia Unsworth, 1976. *A Short History of the Missionary Work of the Maryknoll Fathers in China*, by Peter J. Barry, 1977. *Timothy Richard's Theory of Christian Missions to the Non-Christian World*, by Rita Therese Johnson, 1966.

NEW YORK

AMERICAN BIBLE SOCIETY

NY–130 American Bible Society Archives

1865 Broadway
New York NY 10023
(212) 581-7400
Peter J. Wosh, Archivist

Background note: The American Bible Society (ABS) became involved in China mission work in 1833 by providing financial assistance to the American Board of Commissioners for Foreign Missions. In 1876 ABS actively participated in China mission work by establishing a China Agency administered by an ABS field representative. The Society united its offices with the British and Foreign Bible Society in 1933 in Hankow and began jointly administering mission work in China, later founding the China Bible House in 1936, in Shanghai. After the Revolution, relations between the Bible Societies and the new Chinese government became strained and were finally severed in 1951. Thereafter, the China Bible House was managed by a Chinese Board of Directors and joint mission work was carried on from a Hong Kong "Emergency Office."

Most of the materials in the ABS archives are uncatalogued. An inventory is available for researchers. Information on the ABS China missions work is also available in the ABS annual reports, *Bible Society Record* (the ABS magazine), and general correspondence of the ABS Corresponding Secretary (later General Secretary).

1-CHINA MISSION COLLECTION, 1815–1986, 18 reels microfilm, 8 l.f.

MINUTES/RECORDS/REPORTS: ABS China Agency (later the China Bible House), annual reports, including colportage narrative reports, 1879–1936; budgets, estimates, and financial reports, 1889–1955; China Advisory Council, minutes, 1933–37; China Bible House, annual reports, including colportage narrative reports, 1938–52; China Bible House, Executive Committee, minutes, 1937–51; Foreign Agencies Committee, minutes, 1931–53; National Christian Council of China, minutes, 1945–50.

CORRESPONDENCE: Correspondence of the Office of the Corresponding Secretary (after 1919, the Office of the General Secretary) with ABS China agents, colporteurs, and others, including discussion of administrative/personnel matters, Bible translations and versions, mission work in China, and political conditions in China (particularly on the Boxer Rebellion), 1878–1955.

DIARIES: "Diary of a Preaching Journey to the West Szechwan Mountains," by Peter Lo, 1923.

MANUSCRIPTS: 2 transcriptions of radio broadcasts: "Go Ye Therefore and Make Disciples of All Nations," by Ralph Mortensen, ABS China Agent (CBS "Church of the Air" series, 1942); "How the Hwa Lisu Tribe in Hunan Got the New Testament in Their Own Language," by A. B. Cooke, China Inland Mission ("China Bible House Hour" of the Christian Broadcasting Station, Shanghai, 1947).

MEMORABILIA: News clippings and articles on missions and political conditions in China, 1880–1955.

AUDIO-VISUAL MATERIALS: Ca. 100 photos, 1890s–1980s, of translators, missionaries, the China Bible House, and the Boxer Rebellion.

NY–135 American Bible Society Library

1865 Broadway
New York NY 10023
(212) 581-7400
Boyd Daniels, Director of Library Services

1-INTERNATIONAL DIVISION COLLECTION, 1978-, 11 titles
Background note: Although located in the International Division, the following serials are accessible through the library.
SERIALS: *China and Ourselves*, 1982-. *China and the Church Today*, 1980-86. *China Bulletin* (Rome), 1982-. *China News and Church Report*, 1984-. *China Notes*, 1978-. *China Study Project Bulletin*, 1979-. *China Talk*, 1980-. *Chinese Around the World*, 1979-. *Ching Feng*, 1981-85. *Pray for China Fellowship*, 1982-. *Tripod*, 1981-.

2-GENERAL HOLDINGS
MINUTES/RECORDS/REPORTS: Christian Vernacular Society of Shanghai, annual reports, 1894-95; Conference of Protestant Missionaries, Shanghai, reports, 1890; Council on Christian Literature for Overseas Chinese, annual reports, 1958, 1962; Shanghai Conference (British and Foreign Bible Society), memorandum regarding resolutions on editorial matters, by William Wright, 1890.
PAMPHLETS: 15 pamphlets, 1850-1972, on subjects including China missions, Christian literature, the Conference of Protestant Missionaries, George Hunter, David McGavin, Protestant missionaries, and translation of the Bible and scriptures.
MAPS/DESIGNS/DRAWINGS: *Atlas of the Chinese Empire: Containing Separate Maps of the Eighteen Provinces and of the Four Great Dependencies with an Index and a List of All Protestant Mission Stations, etc.*, by Edward Stanford (London: China Inland Mission), 1908.
CHINESE LANGUAGE MATERIALS: Phonetically-written catechism, with Chinese characters in parallel columns, n.d.; bibles and scripture translations; *Alphabet for Sight, Ten Minutes Study: The Lined Braille-Murray's Numeral Type*, by the Peking School for Chinese Blind, n.d.; *Chinese Primer in Murray's Numeral Type Mandarin Chinese: Composed by the Blind, for the Blind to Teach the Illiterate Sighted*, by the Peking School for Chinese Blind, n.d.

AMERICAN MUSEUM OF NATURAL HISTORY
NY-140 American Museum of Natural History Library
79th Street and Central Park West
New York NY 10024
(212) 873-4225
Nina J. Root, Chair, Department of Library Services
Carol Tucher, Senior Reference Librarian

Finding aids: Research Catalog of the Library of the American Museum Natural History: Classed Catalog (Boston: G. K. Hall, 1978), 4 V.

1-GENERAL HOLDINGS
MINUTES/RECORDS/REPORTS: English Methodist Free Church Mission, Report, Wenchow, 1898.
MANUSCRIPTS: "The Dawn of Life, or, Glimpses of the Life of a Sister in Chen-Tu," n.a., n.d.; paper on Chinese music, by Mrs. Timothy Richard, 1899.
PAMPHLETS: *The Nestorian Monument: An Ancient Record of Christianity in China*, by Paul Carus, 1909; *Translation of the Nestorian Inscription*, by A. Wylie, 1909.
MAPS/DESIGNS/DRAWINGS: *Map of China*, showing the sta-

tions of the China Inland Mission, n.d.
SERIALS: *Chinese Repository*, 1844-45. *Lingnan Science Journal*, 1922-51. Lingnan University, *Science Bulletin*, 1930-44; *Special Publication*, 1942-43. Natural History Society, *Proceedings*, 1928-30. *Peking Natural History Bulletin*, 1926-50. *South China Collegian*, 1904. University of Nanking, Plant Pathology Laboratory, *Contribution*, 1934. West China Border Research Society, *Journal*, 1922-46. West China Union University, *Museum Guidebook Series*, 1945. *Yenching Journal of Social Studies*, 1948. Yenching University, Department of Biology, *Bulletin*, 1930.
CHINESE LANGUAGE MATERIALS/SERIALS: *Chin-ling hsüeh pao (Nanking Journal)*, 1932-43.

COLUMBIA UNIVERSITY

Background note: The master card catalogue to all libraries (except Teachers' College) is in Butler Library. Each library also has its own card catalogue and may have titles not listed in the master catalogue.

NY-145 Burgess-Carpenter Classics Library
Columbia University
4th Floor East, Butler Library
New York NY 10027
(212) 280-4710
Eileen Glickstein, Instructional Librarian

1-GENERAL HOLDINGS
DISSERTATIONS/THESES: *The Anti-Christian Movement in China, 1922-1927: With Special Reference to the Experience of Protestant Missions*, by Ka-che Yip, 1970.

NY-150 Butler Library
General Library
Columbia University
535 West 114th Street
New York NY 10027
(212) 280-2241/2242
Eugene Sheehy, Head of Reference

1-GENERAL HOLDINGS
Background note: In addition to the materials listed below, Butler's General Library holds a significant number of books relating to Christian missions in China in the Romance, Germanic, and Slavic languages, as well as English, which date from 1700 through 1885. These books are by and about early missionaries to China and are not commonly found in other libraries.
MINUTES/RECORDS/REPORTS: International Institute of China, reports, 1908-9, 1912-13, 1919-23, 1926-27.
PAMPHLETS: *China: The Crisis in Its History: A Sermon Preached January 12th, 1902, in the First Congregational Church of Fall River, Mass.*, by W. W. Adams, 1902; *Das chinesische heidenthum: Ein vortrag im Göttinger frauenverein gehalten*, by A. W. Dieckhoff, 1859; *De Chinesiche kwestie*, by Henri Borel, 1900; *Far West in China*, by Stanton Lautenschlager, 1941; *A History of the Szechuen Riots (May-June, 1895)*, by Alfred Cunningham, 1895; *Iz kitaiskikh pisem (From Chinese Writings)*, by

Esper Esperovich Ukhtomskii, 1901; *Lettera di Monsignor Luigi de Cicé, nominate dalla S. Sede al vescovado di Sabula, ai RR. Padri gesuiti, sulle idolatrie e superstizioni della China*, 1700; *O padroado portuguez na China*, by A. Marques Pereira, 1873; *Relazioni di due martirj accaduti nel Su Tchuen, provincia della Cina*, 1840; *A Sermon Preached in Grace Church, New York, Oct. 31, 1877, on the Occasion of the Consecration of the Rev. Samuel I. J. Schereschewsky, D.D., as Missionary Bishop of Shanghai*, by William Bacon Stevens, 1877.

MAPS/DESIGNS/DRAWINGS: *Atlas des missions franciscaines en Chine*, by P. M. Chardin, 1915.

SERIALS: *China Christian Year Book*, 1911–13, 1915, 1917, 1919–29, 1931–39. China International Famine Relief Commission, Publications, series A, 1922–36; series B, 1924, 1930. *Directory of Protestant Missions in China*, 1919, 1921, 1923–29. *Variétés Sinologiques*, 1914, 1917. Yenching University, Department of Sociology and Social Work, Publications, series B, n.d.; *Social Research Series*, 1930.

DISSERTATIONS/THESES: *Die Anfänge der neuen Dominikanermission in China*, by B. M. Biermann, 1927. *Apostolic Legations to China of the Eighteenth Century*, by Antonio Sisto Rosso, 1948. *China and Educational Autonomy: The Changing Role of the Protestant Educational Missionary in China, 1807–1937*, by Alice Henrietta Gregg, 1946. *Christian Missions in China*, by Charles Sumner Estes, 1895. *The Foundations and Growth of Shantung Christian University, 1864–1917*, by William M. Decker, 1948. *Imperial Government and Catholic Missions in China during the Years 1784–1785*, by Bernward Henry Willeke, 1948. *The Negotiations between Ch'i-ying and Lagrené, 1844–1846*, by Angelus Francis J. Grosse-Aschhoff, 1950. *Physical Education in Protestant Christian Colleges and Universities of China*, by Kok A. Wee, 1937. *Protestant Mission Schools for Girls in South China (1827 to the Japanese Invasion)*, by Mary Raleigh Anderson, 1943.

NY–155 Law Library
Columbia University
435 West 116th Street
New York NY 10027
(212) 280–3922
Dorene Frenkl Robbie, Reference Librarian

1-GENERAL HOLDINGS
SERIALS: *China Law Review*, 1922–37.

NY–160 Augustus C. Long Health Sciences Library
Columbia University
701 West 168th Street
New York NY 10032
(212) 305–3688
Rachel Anderson, Librarian

1-GENERAL HOLDINGS
MINUTES/RECORDS/REPORTS: Cheeloo University, School of Medicine, report, 1934(?); China Medical Board of New York, report, n.d.; China Medical Missionary Association Conference, 1920; China Medical Association, special report, 1946.
SERIALS: *China Medical Journal*, 1907–31. *China Medical Missionary Journal*, 1887–1907. *China's Medicine*, 1966–68. *Chi-*

nese Medical Journal, 1932–44, 1947–60, 1962–66, 1979–; Chengtu ed., 1942; supplement, 1936–52. Peking Union Medical College, *Bibliography of the Publications from the Laboratories and Clinics*, 1915–25.

NY–165 Milbank Memorial Library
Teachers' College
Columbia University
525 West 120th Street
New York NY 10027
(212) 678–3494
Donna Barkman, Assistant Director, Collections

1-INTERNATIONAL COLLECTION, 1925–32, 6 items
PAMPHLETS: *Christian Education in China: A Statement of Educational Principles*, by the China Christian Educational Association, 1925; *A Correlated Program for Christian Higher Education in China*, by the China Christian Educational Association Council of Higher Education, 1928; *The Senior Returned Students: A Brief Account of the Chinese Educational Commission (1872–1881) under Dr. Yung Wing*, by Arthur G. Robinson, 1932.
SERIALS: China Christian Educational Association, *Bulletin*, 1928. *East China Studies in Education*, 1925, 1929.

2-JAMES EARL RUSSELL PAPERS, 1918–19, .5 in.
Background note: James Earl Russell was dean of Teachers' College from 1898 to 1927.
CORRESPONDENCE: Correspondence regarding West China Union University and a planned educational commission to China, 1918–19.

3-WILLIAM RUSSELL PAPERS, 1928–52, 1 in.
Background note: William F. Russell was dean of Teachers' College from 1927 to 1949.
CORRESPONDENCE: Correspondence with Chinese alumni of Teachers' College, including those involved in mission education; correspondence concerning China Union Universities and the Committee for Christian Colleges in China, 1928–52.

4-GENERAL HOLDINGS
MINUTES/RECORDS/REPORTS: China Christian Educational Association, records, 1900–8; China Educational Association, triennial report, 1893; Commission on Christian Education in China, report, 1910; International Institute of China, prospectus, 1910; Methodist Episcopal Church, Woman's Foreign Missionary Society, report of the girls' schools in Szechwan, n.d.; North China Educational Union, register of the union colleges, 1907.
SERIALS: *Educational Review*, 1908, 1914–37.
DISSERTATIONS/THESES: *The Boxer Indemnity Remissions and Education in China*, by Yam-tong Hoh, 1933. *China and Educational Autonomy: The Changing Role of the Protestant Educational Missionary in China, 1807–1937*, by Alice Henrietta Gregg, 1946. *Education of Christian Ministers in China*, by S. H. Leger, 1925. *A Method and Plan of Work for Developing a Program in Religious Education for Christian Secondary Schools for Girls in Szechuan, China*, by Katharine B. Hockin, 1948. *Methods of Developing Native Christian Leadership in China*, by Jesse B. Yaukey, 1930. *Physical Education in Protestant Christian Colleges and Universities of China*, by Kok A. Wee, 1937. *A Plan for Developing a Functional Curriculum in the Bible Teachers Train-*

ing School in Nanking, China, in the Post-war Era, by Pearle McCain, 1946. *The Promotion of the Economic Welfare of the Chinese People through the Protestant Churches in China*, by George Yuan-hsieh Geng, 1951.

NY-170 Philosophy Library
Columbia University
223 Butler Library
535 West 114th Street
New York NY 10027
(212) 280-3534
Eileen Glickstein, Reference Librarian

1-GENERAL HOLDINGS
DISSERTATIONS/THESES: *Protestant Christianity and Marriage in China*, by Calvin H. Reber, 1958. *The Protestant Missionary Understanding of the Chinese Situation and the Christian Task from 1890 to 1911*, by C. William Mensendiek, 1958.

NY-175 Rare Book and Manuscript Library
Columbia University
Butler Library, 6th Floor East
535 West 114th Street
New York NY 10027
(212) 280-2231
Kenneth A. Lohf, Librarian for Rare Books and Manuscripts

Restrictions: The library is available to Columbia University faculty and students, those in affiliated institutions, and researchers not affiliated with Columbia who are engaged in scholarly or publication projects. Non-Columbia undergraduates are required to apply in advance with letters from their faculty advisors. Permission to publish, cite, or quote materials is required in writing from the Librarian for Rare Books and Manuscripts.
Background note: In addition to the collections listed below, the Rare Book and Manuscripts Library also holds a small collection of books in the Romance languages dating from 1615 through 1865, most of which are by Jesuit missionaries.
Finding aids: For manuscript collections, a looseleaf collection of "Manuscript Descriptions" is available; for correspondence and other materials, a card catalog; and for oral histories, a separate card index.

1-ARTHUR J. ALLEN PAPERS, 1938-54, 110 items
Background note: Arthur J. and Netta Powell Allen were Episcopalian missionaries to China from the 1930s to 1951. See also Claremont Colleges, Special Collections Department, Honnold Library, Eighth and Dartmouth Streets, Claremont, CA, 91711.
CORRESPONDENCE: 110 letters from Arthur and Netta Allen, and from their son, Walter, who taught in China, to friends and relatives in the United States, describing social, cultural, and political conditions, 1938-54.

2-AMERICAN BUREAU FOR MEDICAL AID TO CHINA PAPERS, 1937-79, ca. 51,350 items
Background note: Founded in 1937, the American Bureau for Medical Aid to China gave assistance to Chinese medical and public health agencies and to medical colleges. In 1949, the Bureau transferred its work to Taiwan. The files of other relief organizations also in this collection are: Aid Refugee Chinese Intellectuals, 1954-69; American Emergency Committee for Tibetan Refugees, 1960-77; Free China Fund, 1954-63; United China Relief, 1941-46; and United Service to China, 1941-77. See also United China Relief collections at the New York Public Library, Manuscripts and Archives Section, Rare Books and Manuscripts Division, Fifth Avenue and 42nd Street, New York, NY, 10018; and Princeton University, 20th Century American Statecraft and Public Policy, Mudd Manuscript Library, Olden Street, Princeton, NJ, 08544.
MINUTES/RECORDS/REPORTS: Reports, minutes, committee files, membership records, financial records, and fund-raising records of the American Bureau for Medical Aid to China and of related organizations.
CORRESPONDENCE/MEMORABILIA: Correspondence and 5 scrapbooks.
AUDIO-VISUAL MATERIALS: Photo album; ca. 6,000 photos of Chinese medical institutions and personnel; 5 reel-to-reel tapes; 43 records, including speeches by Bureau supporters such as Pearl Buck and Mme. Chiang K'ai-shek.

3-EUGENE EPPERSON BARNETT PAPERS, 1910-40, ca. 59,100 items
Background note: Eugene Epperson Barnett (1888-1970) began 30 years of missionary service with the YMCA in 1910. Barnett was the founder and General Secretary of the Hangchow YMCA, 1910-21; National Student Secretary for the YMCA of China, 1921-23; and, concurrently, Associate General Secretary of the National Committee and Senior Secretary of the International Committee for YMCAs in China, 1923-36. He also served in several other religious and educational positions, including trusteeships of three Christian colleges in China. See also Young Men's Christian Association of the U.S.A. Archives, University of Minnesota, Social History Welfare Archives, 2642 University Avenue, St. Paul, MN, 55114; and Lyman Hoover Papers at Yale Divinity School, Special Collections, 409 Prospect Street, New Haven, CT, 06510.
MINUTES/RECORDS/REPORTS/CORRESPONDENCE/MANUSCRIPTS/MEMORABILIA/AUDIO-VISUAL MATERIALS: Material relating to Barnett's years in Japan and pre-communist China, his work as a lay leader in the Methodist Church, his leadership in the International YMCA, affiliations with the United Nations and other organizations, and his personal friends and family.
FINDING AIDS: In-house finding aid; "The Eugene Epperson Barnett Papers in the Columbia University Libraries: A Record of Thirty Years of Christian Service in China before World War II," by Bernard R. Crystal, 1984.

4-HENRY DEWITT BARNETT PAPERS, 1917-82, ca. 10,000 items
Background note: Henry DeWitt Barnett (b. 1917), son of Eugene Epperson Barnett, served as a YMCA executive in New York, 1946-65; as the Quaker International Affairs representative for East Asia with the American Friends Service Committee (AFSC) in Tokyo, 1965-71; and as the Hong Kong consultant to the Department of East Asia and the Pacific of the Division of Overseas Ministries of the Christian Church (Disciples of Christ), 1971-82. The collection focuses on materials after 1970.

MINUTES/RECORDS/REPORTS: Papers of organizations relating to church work in China, such as AFSC, United Board for Christian Higher Education in Asia, Canadian Council of Churches, Maryknoll Fathers, Christian Conference of Asia, Christian Church Division of Overseas Ministries; papers of organizations promoting Chinese-American relations; trip reports, 1977–82; speeches, 1974–82.

CORRESPONDENCE/MEMORABILIA: Family papers, clippings, notebooks, and miscellaneous unsorted papers, 1917–82; Henry Barnett's correspondence with his father, his brother, A. Doak Barnett, and other family members; correspondence and papers relating to missionaries in China, including Margaret Flory, George Hatem, Donald MacInnis, George E. Massey, and Peng Ming-min; correspondence with journalists.

AUDIO-VISUAL MATERIALS: Slides, filmstrip, and tape recordings.

5-CLAREMONT ORAL HISTORY PROGRAM OF CHINA MISSIONARIES, 1973, 2,941p.
ORAL HISTORIES: *China Missionaries Oral History Collection*, ed. by Cyrus H. Peake and Arthur L. Rosenbaum (Claremont Graduate School, Oral History Program), 1973. See ORAL HISTORIES Union List for the names of participants.
FINDING AIDS: ''The Claremont Missionaries: Summary and Evaluation of Findings,'' by Arthur Rosenbaum, 1973.

6-COLUMBIA ORAL HISTORY PROJECT, 1900–1950, 3 items
Background note: One of the most extensive oral history collections in the world, this collection contains interviews with Chinese political and military leaders, Americans with significant relations to China, and persons related to the Christian mission in China.
ORAL HISTORIES: Memoir of experiences of Abbe Livingston Warnshuis as a mission secretary in Amoy, with related papers, ca. 1940s; typescript account of Paul Frillman's service as a missionary before and during the Japanese occupation of 1936–41, as a military pilot with the Flying Tigers in Burma and China, 1941, and as a post-war China observer, ca. 1930s-late 1940s; 149-page account including Walter Judd's experiences as a missionary doctor from 1925 to 1931 and from 1934 to 1937.
FINDING AIDS: *The Oral History Collection of Columbia University*, ed. by Elizabeth B. Mason and Louis M. Starr (New York: Oral History Research Office), 1979. An expanded catalogue is currently being prepared under the direction of the East Asian Institute, Columbia University.

7-DONALD C. DUNHAM PAPERS, 1935, 1 item
Background note: This manuscript is contained in the Chinese Oral History Project Office files.
MANUSCRIPTS: ''The Influence of American Education in South China,'' submitted to the United States Department of State, 1935.

8-EDWARD HICKS HUME PAPERS, 1876–1928, 2 boxes
Background note: For biographical notes, see Yale University, Department of Manuscripts and Archives, Sterling Library, 120 High Street, New Haven, CT, 06520. See also Union Theological Seminary, Archives, 3041 Broadway at Reinhold Niebuhr Place, New York, NY, 10027.

MEMORABILIA / MANUSCRIPTS / PAMPHLETS / CHINESE LANGUAGE MATERIALS: Notes and transcripts of articles (some in Chinese periodicals), health reports, printed pamphlets, articles, etc., relating to medicine in China, including materials on Chinese beliefs about health and medical matters, and folk legends of the Chinese people.

9-J. HENG LIU PAPERS, 1923–60, 5 folders, 2 reels microfilm
Background note: The papers of Dr. Liu Jui-heng (1890–1961), who held several government positions in mainland China before 1949, are part of the Chinese Oral History Project Office files, which contains transcripts of the oral histories of prominent Chinese leaders. Dr. Liu's father was a preacher in a church which was part of the London Mission program. Dr. Liu studied at several Western-administered schools in China before his college studies at Harvard University and graduation from Harvard Medical College in 1913. After returning to China, he joined the staff of Peking Union Medical College (PUMC) in 1918 as an associate in surgery. He worked with Dr. James B. Murphy at the Rockefeller Institute on cancer research in the early 1920s. In 1923, he again returned to China, taking up the post of superintendent at PUMC before his appointment as Minister of Health (1929–30). Later, as director-general of the National Health Administration, he laid the foundation of Chinese national public health service. While living in the United States in the 1940s, he was associated with the American Bureau for Medical Aid to China until his move to Taiwan in 1949. See also Rockefeller University, Rockefeller Archive Center, Pocantico Hills, North Tarrytown, NY, 10591.
MINUTES / RECORDS / REPORTS / CORRESPONDENCE/ AUDIO-VISUAL MATERIALS: Lists of graduates of PUMC as of 1961; photocopies of files of China Medical Board; correspondence; photocopies of material concerning PUMC and its history; 2 reels of microfilmed records of Rockefeller Institute files, 1923–46.
ORAL HISTORIES: Typewritten account, covering Liu's youth, education, and professional history.

10-DMITRII MIKHAILOVICH MIKHAILOV MEMOIRS, 1970–73, 4 items
Background note: Dmitrii Mikhailovich Mikhailov (b. 1890?) served in the Imperial and White Russian armies before emigrating to China.
MANUSCRIPTS/AUDIO-VISUAL MATERIALS: Typescript memoir of his life, especially military experiences, with some notes on the Orthodox (Russian) Church in China, including 2 photos.

11-VALERII FRANTSEVICH SALATKO-PETRISHCHE PAPERS, 1930–76, ca. 200 items
Background note: Russian poet Valerii Frantsevitch Salatko-Petrishche (b. 1913) was in China from 1939 to 1943 as part of a Russian religious mission.
CORRESPONDENCE/MANUSCRIPTS/PAMPHLETS: Ca. 200 items of correspondence, manuscripts, and printed materials, relating especially to the Russian emigré colonies in Harbin, Shanghai, and Peking and to religious affairs in the Far East.

12-INNOKENTII NIKOLAEVICH SERYSHEV PAPERS, 1914–71, ca. 5,000 items
Background note: Innokentii Nikolaevich Seryshev (b. 1883) was a

Russian Orthodox priest who travelled extensively in Asia.
CORRESPONDENCE/PAMPHLETS/AUDIO-VISUAL MATE-
RIALS: Correspondence, photos of correspondents, and other
printed materials, ca. late 1920s.
MANUSCRIPTS: 5-volume autobiography of Seryshev's life and
travels, *V Zemnom plane moego vechnogo bytiia (In the Earthly
Plane of My Eternal Existence)*, including his time in China, 1922–
25.

13-GENERAL HOLDINGS
PAMPHLETS: *Abrégé historique des principaux traits de la vie de
Confucius, célèbre philosophe chinois; orné de 24 estampes in 4°
gravé par Helman, d'après des dessins originaux de la Chine,
envoyés à Paris par M. Amiot, missionnaire de Pékin et tirés du
cabinet de M. Bentin*, ca. 1787.

NY-180 School of Library Service Library
Columbia University
606 Butler Library
New York NY 10027
(212) 280-3543
Olha della Cava, Librarian

1-GENERAL HOLDINGS
SERIALS: *China Colleges*, 1946–55.

NY-185 School of Social Work Library
Columbia University
School of International Affairs
Lehman Library
420 West 118th Street
New York NY 10027
(212) 280-5087
Jerry Breeze, Librarian

1-GENERAL HOLDINGS
DISSERTATIONS/THESES: *The Social Work Program of the Riv-
erside Church as a Resource for a Social Work Program of an
Urban Church in China*, by Angeline B. Y. Han, 1948.

NY-190 Science Library
Columbia University
2990 Broadway
303 Mathematics
New York NY 10027
(212) 280-4712

1-GENERAL HOLDINGS
SERIALS: *Lingnan Science Journal*, 1927–28, 1936–37.

NY-195 C. V. Starr East Asian Library
Columbia University
Kent Hall
116th Street and Broadway
New York NY 10027
(212) 280-4318
Marsha I. Wagner, East Asian Librarian
Fran Lafleur, Chinese Curator/Bibliographer

**1-CHINESE LANGUAGE COLLECTION, 1300-, quantity undeter-
mined**
Background note: The Chinese language collection in the Starr
Library contains 250,000 volumes which focus mainly on Chinese
history, philosophy, and literature. Scattered among this extensive
collection are a few titles related to the Christian church in China
which are printed by Christian publishers and appear to be instructional materials for Chinese Christians. Some of the materials are
not catalogued and require assistance from the curator. A unique
preservation program currently in process has microfilmed 2,178
titles in this Chinese collection, comprising 350 serials, 1,828
monographs, and 22 newspaper items on 470 reels of microfilm.
CHINESE LANGUAGE MATERIALS/PAMPHLETS: Outline
of the Bible, 1919; the Gospel of St. Luke, romanized in Hainanese
dialect, 1916; 4 pamphlets dating from the 23rd to the 25th years of
the Tao-yuan emperor (ca. 1843–1845): *Court Permission to Practice Religion*; *Entering the Small Gate and Walking on the Narrow
Path*, a gospel tract; the Ten Commandments; and *Dialogue between Two Friends*, a primer probably written by Jesuits.

**2-CHINESE CHRISTIAN MONOGRAPH COLLECTION, 19th and
20th centuries, 16 reels microfilm**
CHINESE LANGUAGE MATERIALS: 313 books, mostly by
leading Chinese Christians and missionaries, including Miner
Searle Bates, Chang Lit-sen, Tzu-ch'en Chao, Chi-i Cheng, Karl
F. A. Gützlaff, Sung-kao Hsieh, Donald MacGillivray, Robert
Morrison, P. F. Price, and Wang Ming-tao, on such subjects as
church history, Christian ethics, theology, preaching, Cheeloo
School of Theology, Foochow YMCA, and comparisons of East-
ern and Western religions.
FINDING AIDS: *Chinese Christian Monograph Collection: An
Index to Chinese Christian Monographs Filmed from the Union
Theological Seminary Library Collection by the Board of Micro-
text, American Theological Library Association*, 1979.

**3-CHINESE CHRISTIAN SERIAL COLLECTION, 1877–1968, 55
reels microfilm**
CHINESE LANGUAGE MATERIALS/SERIALS: *Chan Wang
(Outlook)*, 1953–57, 1961–67. *Chen kuang (The True Light Review)*, 1925–35. *Chi-tu chiao sheng ho chou k'an (Christian
Sheng-ho Weekly)*, 1955. *Chi-tu chiao ts'ung k'an (Christianity
Series)*, 1943. *Chin-ling hsieh ho shen hsüeh chih (Chinling Journal of Theology)*, 1957. *Chin-ling shen hsüeh yuan hua hsi t'eh
k'an (Special Issues of the Nanking Theological Seminary Journal)*,
1945. *Chin pu (Progress)*, 1911–16. *Ch'ing nien chin pu (Youth
Progress)*, 1917–32. *China Bookman*, 1918–51. *Chüeh wu*, 1924–
25. *Chung hsi chiao hui pao (Missionary Review)*, 1896–98.
*Chung-hua chi-tu chiao chiao yü chi k'an (China Christian Educa-
tional Quarterly)*, 1925–36. *Chung-hua kuei chu*, 1923–41. *Chung-
kuo mu szu lin*, 1960. *En yu*, 1947–48, 1951. *Fu yin hsin pao (Gospel
Newsletter)*, 1877. *Hsi wang yüeh k'an (The Christian Hope)*,
1924–32. *Hsiang ts'un chiao hui (The Rural Church)*, 1940–42,
1946–47. *Hsiao hsi (News)*, 1930–50. *Hsieh chin (National Christian Council of China, Bulletin)*, 1930–31, 1943–54. *Hsien tai fo
hsüeh (Modern Buddhism)*, 1960. *Hsing hua (Chinese Christian
Advocate)*, 1904–27. *Hsüeh shu yüeh pao (Science Monthly)*,
1899. *Hua nien*, 1932–33. *Hua-pei nung lien t'ung hsün*, 1950-.
Hui hsün kung pao, 1930–54. *Kung yeh kai tsao*, 1926, 1929. *Nü
ch'ing nien (Young Women)*, 1930–35. *Shang-hai Kuang-tung
Chung-hua Chi-tu chiao hui yüeh pao (Cantonese Union Church*

Bulletin), 1917–24. Shen chao, 1932–34. Shen hsüeh chih (Theological Quarterly; Nanking Seminary Review), 1925–50. Sheng kung hui pao (Chinese Churchman), 1929. Tao-oan Kau-hoe Kong-po, 1923–67. Teng t'a, 1956–67. Tao sheng (The Preachers' Magazine), 1931–35. T'ien chia (The Christian Farmer), 1934–52. T'ien feng (Heavenly Wind), 1947–63. Tsung-chiao chiao-yü chi-k'an (Journal of Religious Education), 1937–40. T'ung wen pao (Chinese Christian Intelligencer), 1911. Wei li pao, 1956–58. Wei yin yüeh k'an, 1931–32. Young Sun, 1959–61. Ying Kuang, 1955–68.

FINDING AIDS: Chinese Christian Serial Collection: An Index to Chinese Christian Serials Filmed from the Union Theological Seminary Library Collection by the Board of Microtext, American Theological Library Association, 1979.

4-GENERAL HOLDINGS

MINUTES/RECORDS/REPORTS: "The Effects of the Sino-Japanese Conflict on American Educational and Philanthropic Enterprises in China," a preliminary report of the Institute of Pacific Relations, 1939.

PAMPHLETS: British Protestant Evangelists and the 1898 Reform Movement in China, by Leslie R. Marchant, 1975; China Consultation, 1958; The Harrowing of Hell in China: A Synoptic Study of the Role of Christian Evangelists in the Opening of Hunan Province, by Leslie R. Marchant, 1977; Nestorians in China: Some Corrections and Additions, by Arthur Christopher Moule, 1940; Selected Bibliography of Books, Pamphlets and Articles on Communist China and the Christian Church in China, comp. by Frank Wilson Price, 1958.

SERIALS: Asia, 1949–60. Catholic Church in China, 1928–41, 1947. Catholic University of Peking, Bulletin, 1926–34. China Mission Studies Bulletin, 1979–81. China Missionary, 1948–49. China Missionary Bulletin, 1949–50. China Monthly, 1939–50. China Notes, 1962–78, 1980. Chinese Medical Directory, 1930. Chinese Recorder and Missionary Journal, 1868–71, 1874–93, 1912–14, 1916–20, 1924–28, 1930–41. Chinese Repository, 1832–51. Ching Feng, 1957–67. Folklore Studies, 1942–47. Friends of Moslems, 1937–49. Monumenta Serica, 1935–80; monograph series, 1937–72. Moslems in China, 1942, 1946–47. University of Nanking, College of Agriculture and Forestry, Bulletin, 1932. West China Border Research Society, Journal, 1922–45. Yenching Journal of Chinese Studies, Monograph, 1932–50. Yenching Journal of Social Studies, 1939–50. Yenching News, 1934–36.

DISSERTATIONS/THESES: American Catholic Missions in China, by Luther Carrington Goodrich, 1927. The Anti-Christian Persecution of 1616–1617 in Nanking, by Edward T. Kelly, 1971. Fr. Terrence (Schreck), S.J., and His Work in China, 1576–1630, by Franz Emile Brem, 1950. La Politique missionaire de la France en Chine, 1842–1856, by Louis Tsing-sing Wei, 1960. Suomen Lähetysseuran työ Kiinassa vuosina, 1901–1926 (The Work of the Finnish Missionary Society in China, 1901–1926), by Toivo Saarilahti, 1960. Ying Lien-chih (1866–1926) and the Rise of Fu-jen, the Catholic University of Peking, by Donald Paragon, 1957.

CHINESE LANGUAGE MATERIALS/SERIALS: Ch'i nan hsüeh pao, 1936–37. Ch'i ta chi k'an, 1934–35. Ling-nan hsüeh pao (Lingnan Journal), 1929–36, 1947–52. She hui hsüeh chieh, 1936–38. Yen-ching she hui k'o hsüeh (Yenching Social Sciences), 1948–49.

GENERAL BOARD OF GLOBAL MINISTRIES
NY-200 Central Records
The United Methodist Church
475 Riverside Drive
Room 1515
New York NY 10015
(212) 870–3622
Marva Usher-Kerr, Records Manager
Loraine Harriott, Assistant Records Manager

Restrictions: Permission required.
Background note: The United Methodist Church was formed in 1968, in Dallas, Texas, by the union of the Methodist Church and the Evangelical United Brethren Church. The Methodist Church resulted in 1939 from the unification of three branches of Methodism—the Methodist Episcopal Church, the Methodist Episcopal Church, South, and the Methodist Protestant Church. The Methodist movement began in eighteenth-century England under the preaching of John Wesley, but the "Christmas Conference" of 1784 in Baltimore is regarded as the date on which the organized Methodist Church was founded as an ecclesiastical organization. It was there that Francis Asbury was elected the first bishop in this country. The Evangelical United Brethren Church was formed in 1946 with the merger of the Evangelical Church and the Church of the United Brethren in Christ, both of which had their beginnings in Pennsylvania in the evangelistic movement of the eighteenth and early nineteenth centuries. Philip William Otterbein and Jacob Albright were early leaders of this movement among the German-speaking settlers of the Middle Colonies. For other Methodist documents, see Drew University, General Commission on Archives and History of the United Methodist Church, United Methodist Archives and History Center, Archives, 36 Madison Avenue, P. O. Box 127, Madison, NJ, 07940.

1-BISHOPS' CORRESPONDENCE, 1847–1912, 34 reels microfilm
MINUTES/RECORDS/REPORTS/CORRESPONDENCE: Correspondence and reports on China mission work of the following bishops: J. W. Bashford, 1894–1912; C. H. Fowler, 1887–95; I. W. Joyce, 1896–97; W. S. Lewis, 1909–11; W. F. Mallalieu, 1892–93; P. H. Moore, 1900–1905; W. K. Ninde, 1894; H. Spellmeyer, 1906–7; J. W. Wiley, 1850–81; miscellaneous correspondence, 1873–1911; annual reports on China, 1847–83.
FINDING AIDS: In-house alphabetical index.

2-GENERAL FILE, 1917–55, 49 reels microfilm
MINUTES/RECORDS/REPORTS/CORRESPONDENCE: Correspondence and reports on China mission work of the following: American Board of Commissioners for Foreign Missions, 1929–48; American Bureau for Medical Aid to China, 1941–46; American Association for China Famine and Food Relief, 1941–46; American Mission to the Lepers, 1947–52; American Friends of the Chinese People, 1942; American Leprosy Missions, 1950–52; Aurora University for Women in Shanghai, n.d.; Association for the Chinese Blind, 1947–52; China Institute in America, 1952–53; United Service to China, 1941–48; miscellaneous correspondence

with Methodist and other missionaries to China, and a number of persons whose romanized names indicate Chinese origin.
FINDING AIDS: In-house alphabetical and chronological index.

3-MISSIONARY CORRESPONDENCE, 1911–49, 141 reels microfilm
MINUTES/RECORDS/REPORTS/CORRESPONDENCE: American relations with China, 1925–35; California Colleges in China, 1919–49; Canton Union Christian College, 1918–25; Central China Conference (Changchow Church, Changchow Hospital, East China Hospital, East China Union University, Huchow University, Methodist Hospital, Provisional Board of the Proposed East China Union University, Philander Smith Memorial), 1912–49; China Christian Advocate in China, 1932–41; China Christian Educational Association, 1933–49; China Conference, 1912–49; China Continuation Committee, 1947; China Continuation Committee of the National Missionary Conference of Shanghai, 1912–36; China Finance Committee, minutes, 1922–29; China Medical Board, 1917–25; China Sunday School Union, 1923–47; China Underwriters-China Conference, 1913–15; China Work Budgets, 1912–49; Christian Literature Society of China, 1916–49; College of Chinese Studies, 1918–45; East China Conference, 1912–49; Fukien Christian University, 1911–35; Ginling College, n.d.; Hangchow Christian College, 1925–49; Hinghwa Conference (Bible Women's Training School, Guthrie Memorial High School, Hinghwa Church, Kalgam Conference, Lankai-siong, Rebecca McCabe Orphanage, Richmond Methodist Hospital), 1912–49; Kiangsi Conference (Central Church Nanchang, Kanhsien Union Christian Middle School, Kiangsi-Anhwei Christian Rural Service Union, Nanchang Compound Welfare Committee), 1912–49; Lingnan University, 1926–49; Mid-China Field Commission, 1922–49; Mission Architects Bureau, 1921–24; National Christian Colleges in China, 1932–48; National Christian Council in China, 1925–49; National Health Administration, 1944–45; North China Conference (Changli General Hospital, Committee on Survey and Planning, Isabella Fisher Hospital, Medical Work in Peking, Methodist Hospital in Peking, Methodist Mission in Shantung, North China Christian Broadcasting Association, North China Religious Education, North China Vocational Training, Sleeper Davis Hospital, Tientsin Hui Wan School, Union Bible School for Women), 1912–49; North China Union Medical School, 1912–49; Peking Academy, 1925–47; Peking American School, 1920–48; Peking Theological Seminary, 1924–49; Peking Union Medical College, 1916–31; Peking Union Medical University, 1916–22; Peking University, 1890–1931; School for Missionary Children in China, 1912–40; Shanghai American School, 1912–49; Shanghai Residences, 1919–22; Sienyu Union Hospital, 1944–47; Soochow Conference (Changchow Church, Nutao Union Junior Middle School, Union High School in Foochow), 1912–49; Union Medical School in Shanghai, 1922–41; United Board for Christian Colleges in China, 1913–49; United Committee for Christian Universities of China, minutes, 1938–43; University of Nanking, 1912–49; West China Conference (Chengtu, Chungking, Chungking High School, Methodist Union Hospital, Middle School of West China University, Union Theological College at Chengtu, West China Union University Hospital), 1912–49; West China Union Middle School, 1939–49; West China Union Theological College, 1935–44; West China Union University, 1911–46; Women's Medical College, 1921–30; Yenching University, 1916–49; Yenping Conference (including Yenping Academy), 1912–49.
FINDING AIDS: In-house chronological index.

LUTHERAN COUNCIL IN THE U.S.A.
NY–205 Archives of Cooperative Lutheranism
360 Park Avenue South
New York NY 10010
(212) 532–6350
Alice M. Kendrick, Director of the LCUSA Records and Information Center
Helen M. Knubel, Archives Consultant

1-LUTHERAN WORLD CONVENTION RECORDS, 1944–59, 2 volumes
Background note: The Lutheran World Convention (1923–47), an international organization representing Lutheran denominations in over 20 nations, supervised relief and missionary efforts throughout the world.
MINUTES/RECORDS/REPORTS: Documents concerning the 1932 resettlement of 400 Lutheran refugees who had travelled from Siberia to Harbin.
SERIALS: *China News Letter*, 1947–59. *Chungking News Letter*, 1944–45. *Chungking Report*, 1945.

2-ORAL HISTORY COLLECTION, 1977–81, 4 items
Restrictions: The oral histories of Bernard Confer and Cordelia Cox are open to research. Researchers must get permission from the respondents to cite or quote from the oral histories of Albert Lueders or Reuben Lundeen.
Background note: The Oral History Collection of the Archives of Cooperative Lutheranism contains memoirs of 113 individuals involved with various cooperative Lutheran organizations and undertakings. The collection continues to grow, and a new oral history project, the ALC/AELC/LCA Oral History Project, is in progress.
ORAL HISTORIES: 1977 interview with Bernard Confer, an executive of Lutheran World Relief from 1946 to 1981, including discussion of relief work in Hong Kong; 1978 interview with Cordelia Cox, director of Lutheran Resettlement Service from 1948 to 1957, including discussion of refugees from China via Hong Kong; 1981 interview with Albert Lueders, a businessman in China from 1927 to 1946; 1980 interview with Reuben A. Lundeen, a Lutheran Church in America clergyman, including discussion of his childhood in China with missionary parents from 1920 to 1927.
FINDING AIDS: *The Oral History Collection of the Archives of Cooperative Lutheranism*, ed. by Alice M. Kendrick and Helen M. Knubel (New York: Lutheran Council in the USA), 1984.

METROPOLITAN MUSEUM OF ART
NY–210 Thomas J. Watson Library
Fifth Avenue at 82nd Street
New York NY 10028
(212) 879–5500
William B. Walker, Chief Librarian

1-GENERAL HOLDINGS
PAMPHLETS: *Anciennes relations des Indes et de la Chine*, by Eusèbe Renaudot, 1718; *The Nestorian Monument: An Ancient Record of Christianity in China*, by Paul Carus, 1909; *Painters among Catholic Missionaries and Their Helpers in Peking*, by John C. Ferguson (repr. from *Journal of the North China Branch of the Royal Asiatic Society*, 1934).

SERIALS: *Chinese Repository*, 1834–36. *Monumenta Serica*, 1935–83. West China Border Research Society, *Journal*, 1940. *Yenching Journal of Chinese Studies*, monograph series, 1933–41. CHINESE LANGUAGE MATERIALS/SERIALS: Yen-ching ta hsüeh, *T'u shu kuan pao* (Yenching University, *Library Bulletin)*, 1937–39. *Yen-ching hsüeh pao (Yenching Journal of Chinese Studies)*, 1930–32.

NEW SCHOOL FOR SOCIAL RESEARCH
NY–215 Library
65 Fifth Avenue
New York NY 10003
(212) 741–5600
Carmen Hendershott, Reference Librarian

1-GENERAL HOLDINGS
DISSERTATIONS/THESES: *The Taiping Rebellion: A Comparative Historical and Sociological Study of a Movement—From the Perspective of Intercivilizational Encounters and Missions*, by Robert H. T. Lin, 1977.

NEW YORK ACADEMY OF MEDICINE
NY–220 Library
2 East 103rd Street
New York NY 10029
(212) 876–8200
Brett Kirkpatrick, Head Librarian
Nighat Ispahany, Reference Librarian

1-GENERAL HOLDINGS
PAMPHLETS: *Address in Behalf of the China Mission*, by William Jones Boone, 1837; *The Medical Missionary Society in China*, by Thomas R. Colledge, 1838.
SERIALS: China International Famine Relief Commission Publications, series A, 1924, 1934. *China Medical Journal*, 1907–14, 1916–18, 1920–43. *China Medical Missionary Journal*, 1887–98, 1900, 1903. *China's Medicine*, 1966–68. *Chinese Medical Journal*, 1932–46, 1950–66, 1975–; Chengtu ed., 1942–45; supplement, 1936–40. *Chinese Repository*, 1836–37. *Lingnaam Agricultural Review*, 1922–23. *Lingnan Science Journal*, 1944–50. *Tsinan Medical Journal*, 1922–29.

NEW-YORK HISTORICAL SOCIETY
NY–225 Manuscript Department
170 Central Park West
New York NY 10024
(212) 873–3400
Thomas J. Dunnings, Jr., Curator of Manuscripts

1-GEORGE ALEXANDER PAPERS, 1895–1920, quantity undetermined
Background note: George Alexander was a Presbyterian minister.
REPORTS/CORRESPONDENCE: Correspondence and other papers relating to the foreign mission activities of the Presbyterian Church, including letters from Robert E. Speer, secretary of the Board of Foreign Missions, and reports of missionaries in China, 1895–1920.

2-E. C. BRIDGMAN, 1837, 1 item
Background note: For biographical notes, see Belchertown Historical Association, Stone House Museum, 20 Maple Street, Belchertown, MA, 01007.
CORRESPONDENCE: Letter from Elijah Coleman Bridgman, in Canton, to George Champion regarding a shipment of printed material about China, 1837.

3-BUTLER FAMILY COLLECTION, 1855–57, 19 items
Background note: Rev. William A. Macy (1824–59) was a missionary in China.
CORRESPONDENCE: 19 letters from William A. Macy, in Canton, Hong Kong, Whampoa, Macao, and Shanghai, to William A. Butler, New York City, 1855–57.

4-STEPHEN DECATUR WEEKS PAPERS, 1877–78, 1 volume
Background note: Stephen Decatur Weeks sailed from New York to Shanghai (probably on business), where he became seriously ill. He was treated at Shanghai General Hospital and then recuperated at the home of Rev. [Daniel?] Nelson, pastor of the American Church in Shanghai.
DIARIES: Diary of Weeks' journey and his stay in Shanghai, describing the people he met, Christmas celebrations, and life in Shanghai, 1877–78.

NEW YORK PUBLIC LIBRARY

NY–230 General Research Division
Fifth Avenue and 42nd Street
New York NY 10018
(212) 340–0827

Background note: The General Research Division maintains most of the library's general holdings in the humanities.

1-GENERAL HOLDINGS
MINUTES/RECORDS/REPORTS: American Board of Commissioners for Foreign Missions: Deputation, report, 1907; Foochow Mission, report, 1895–96, 1898; North China Mission, report, 1894; Prudential Committee, report, 1898; Baptist Zenana Mission, report, 1902–3; Canton Christian College, records, 1897; Central China Religious Tract Society, report, 1884, 1907; Central Presbyterian Church of New York City, General Missionary Committee, report, 1899–1900; China Inland Mission, report, 1904; China Mission at Amoy, report, 1853–64; Chinese Religious Tract Society, report, 1880–81, 1883; Christian Literature Society for China, report, 1887–1915; Church of England in China, report, 1893–97; International Institute of China, report, 1877–1929.

Methodist Episcopal Church: China Central Conference, minutes, 1892, 1897–99, 1901–2, 1907–9; Central China Women's Conference, minutes, 1898–1903; Foochow Conference, minutes, 1891–1908; report, 1891–1908; Foochow Women's Conference, minutes, 1896–1904; North China Conference, minutes, 1883, 1890–92, 1896–1909; North China Tract Society, report, 1884; National Christian Council of China, report, 1937; Presbyterian Church in the U.S.A., Board of Foreign Missions: Arthur Judson Brown, reports on 1902 and 1909 visits; Central China Mission Press, report, 1872–73, 1875; China campaign, report, 1913–14; China general, report, 1930; evaluation conference, report, 1926; Kiangan Mission, report, 1912, 1916, 1933; Robert E. Speer, report of deputation, 1926; South China Mission (Canton), report, 1890–92, 1894, 1896–97.

Protestant Episcopal Church in the U.S.A.: Missionary District of Hankow, report, 1905; Shanghai, report, 1901; Reformed Church in America: Women's Board of Foreign Missions, Amoy, report, 1901–2; Society of Earnest Workers for China, report, 1867–76, 1897–98, 1901–2; Young Men's Christian Association, China, report, 1915–16, 1918, 1922; Young Men's Christian Associations of China and Korea, report, 1908, 1911.

PAMPHLETS: Pamphlets, 1837–1952, on subjects including American Board of Commissioners for Foreign Missions in China, Catholic church in China, Chinese civilization and culture, Chinese language lessons, Christianity and the Chinese, Communism, Foreign Missions Conference of North America, Annie James, Jesuit missions in China, Mandana Eliza Doolittle Lyon, Methodist Episcopal Church missions in China, Sr. Marie de Sainte-Nathalie, Robert Morrison, opium, Presbyterian Church in Ireland, politics, role of women, Bishop Samuel I. J. Schereschewsky, and travel.

SERIALS: *Catholic Church in China*, 1922–47. Catholic University of Peking, *Bulletin*, 1926–34. *China Advent News*, 1903–6. China Christian Educational Association, *Bulletin*, 1924–25, 1928. China International Famine Relief Commission, *Bulletin*, 1923–36; *News Bulletin*, 1937–39; Publications, series A, 1923–37; series B, 1922–36; series G, 1934. *China Law Review*, 1922–35. *China Mission Advocate*, 1839. *China Mission Year Book*, 1910, 1912–39. *China Missionary*, 1948. *China Monthly*, 1939–50. *China's Millions* (London), 1881–1909. *China's Millions* (Toronto), 1893–1908. *Chinese Recorder*, 1870–1941. *Directory of Protestant Missions in China*, 1918, 1923, 1927. *Educational Review*, 1913–38. *Far East: A Magazine Devoted to the Conversion of China*, 1919–66. *Folklore Studies*, 1942–62. *Fu-Jen Magazine*, 1932–49. *Fu Jen News Letter*, 1931–32. *Ling-naam*, 1924–33. *Lingnan Science Journal*, 1922–48. Lingnan University, *Daily Meteorological Record*, 1919–37. *Maryknoll Mission Letters*, 1942–46. *Missionary Recorder*, 1867. *Missions de Chine*, 1916–19, 1923, 1927–31. Nanking Theological Seminary, *English Publications*, 1940. Natural History Society, *Proceedings*, 1929. *New Horizons*, 1934–60. *News of China*, 1942–46. *South China Collegian*, 1904–5. University of Nanking, College of Agriculture and Forestry, *Agriculture and Forestry Notes*, 1923–41; *Agriculture and Forestry Series*, 1923–24; *Bulletin*, 1926–36; *Special Report*, 1935. *USC Envoy*, 1946–47. West China Border Research Society, *Journal*, 1930–38. Yenching University, Department of Economics, *Index Numbers*, 1940–41; *Yenching Journal of Social Studies*, 1938–50; *Yenching Journal of Chinese Studies*, Monograph series, 1936; *Yenching Journal of Chinese Studies, Special Issue (Chuan-Hao)*, 1938; College of Public Affairs, *News Bulletin*, 1934–41; Department of Sociology and Social Work, Publications, series A, 1929–33; series B, 1930(?)–32(?); series C, 1930(?)–; *Social Research Series*, 1930; *Sociology Fellowship News*, 1930–32; *Yenching Political Science Series*, 1929–33; *Yenching Series on Chinese Industry and Trade*, 1934–38.

DISSERTATIONS/THESES: *Christian Missions in China*, by Charles Sumner Estes, 1895. *The Negotiations between Ch'i-ying and Lagrené, 1844–1846*, by Angelus Francis J. Grosse-Aschhoff, 1950. *The Protestant Missionary Understanding of the Chinese Situation and the Christian Task from 1890 to 1911*, by C. William Mensendiek, 1956.

CHINESE LANGUAGE MATERIALS/SERIALS: *Hwa Mei kiao pao* (*Chinese Christian Advocate*), 1903. *Kuo chi kung pao* (*International Journal*), 1929–. *Min sang hway paou* (*The Church Advocate*), 1893–97. *Missionary Review*, 1891–96. *Shang hsien t'ang chih shih* (International Institute of China, *Record*), 1911–13. University of Nanking, College of Agriculture and Forestry, Horticultural Association Library, *Publications*, 1924–35. *Yen-ching hsüeh pao* (*Yenching Journal of Chinese Studies*), 1927–40.

CHINESE LANGUAGE MATERIALS: 2 books on antiforeignism.

FINDING AIDS: *Dictionary Catalog of The Research Libraries of the New York Public Library*, by the New York Public Library, 1911–71 (Boston: G. K. Hall), 1979.

NY–235 Manuscripts and Archives Section
Rare Books and Manuscripts Division
New York Public Library
Fifth Avenue and 42nd Street
New York NY 10018
(212) 340–0804/0805
Susan Davis, Curator of Manuscripts and Archives

Finding aids: *Guide to the Research Collections of the New York Public Library*, comp. by Sam P. Williams (Chicago: American Library Association), 1975. *Bulletin of the New York Public Library* (1897-) contains detailed articles on New York Public Library collections. The *Dictionary Catalog of the Manuscript Division* (Boston: G. K. Hall), 1967, lists Manuscript Division holdings by catalogue card.

1-RACHEL BROOKS PAPERS, n.d., 1 item
Background note: Rachel Brooks (b. 1884) served as a missionary to China with the Young Men's Christian Association (YMCA).
MANUSCRIPTS: "The YMCA Government of China," by Rachel Brooks, recording her experiences as a field worker with the YMCA and the Central Christian (Disciples) Church, New York, n.d.

2-DOTY-DUBOIS FAMILY PAPERS, 1861-ca. 1865, ca. 6 folders
Background note: Elihu Doty was a missionary in Amoy from 1861 until at least 1865.
CORRESPONDENCE: Ca. 6 folders of letters by the missionary Elihu Doty and his daughter, Amelia C. Doty-Dubois, to Doty-Dubois family members on life and service as a missionary in Amoy, 1861-ca. 1865.
DIARIES: Log of distances covered daily by the ship *Kathay* from New York to Shanghai, China, 1861.

3-ROMAN CATHOLIC CHURCH—MISSIONS: CHINA, ca. 1735, 1 folio
CORRESPONDENCE: An account, ca. 1735, addressed to "Monsieur le Prieur Bouget," describing the experiences of six Jesuits who were sent by Louis XIV to China in early 1685.

4-CHARLES ERNEST SCOTT PAPERS, 1920, 1 item
Background note: Charles Ernest Scott was a missionary at the Presbyterian mission in Shantung from 1906 to 1918.
MANUSCRIPTS: "A Memorandum of Japan's Sinister Methods in Shantung, 1920," by Charles Ernest Scott.

5-UNITED CHINA RELIEF—NY RECORDS, 1928–47, 4 boxes
Background note: Founded by a number of organizations, United

China Relief coordinated prewar and wartime relief efforts to China. The 1946 redesignation of United Service to China reflected extended peacetime activities. After 1949, it became part of the American Bureau for Medical Aid to China. See also Princeton University, 20th Century American Statecraft and Public Policy, Seeley G. Mudd Manuscript Library, Olden Street, Princeton, NJ, 08544; and American Bureau for Medical Aid to China collection at Columbia University, Rare Book and Manuscript Library, Butler Library, 535 West 114th Street, New York, NY, 10027.

MINUTES/RECORDS/REPORTS: 26 folders of the China Aid Council on the following topics: Budget estimates, 1941–43; report, "Child Welfare in China," with collateral papers of the Child Welfare Planning Conference, Shanghai, 1946; China Child Welfare Service, minutes, 1946–47; reports on conditions in the Northwest of China, 1939–46; drugs and medicines, 1941–47; education, 1946; famine relief, 1943; medical aid (general), 1940–47; guerrillas, 1939–44; industrial development, 1941–44; labor, 1942–44; medical aid to China, 1938–41; medical instruments and ambulances, 1939–41; medicine in the Northwest, 1942–44; penicillin, 1944–46; "The Chinese Mass Education Movement—A Summary, 1942," by Y. C. James Yen; 3 folders on the China Defense League of United China Relief, 1938–44, n.d.; 3 folders of the Child Welfare Committee of United Service to China, Nanking and Shanghai, 1946–47; 13 folders of China Child Welfare on the following topics: China Nutritional Aid Council, 1939–44; miscellaneous, 1937–41; National Child Welfare Association, Shanghai, 1928–31, 1934–35; Shanghai Refugee Children Nutritional Aid Council, 1937–40.

CORRESPONDENCE: Ca. 2 folders by the China Nutritional Aid Council of China Child Welfare, 1939–44; ca. 3 folders by the Child Welfare Committee of United Service to China, 1946–47; ca. 1 folder by Mildred Price, secretary of the China Aid Council, China Child Welfare Service, Nanking, 1946–47; folder of correspondence by Mrs. Owen Roberts, secretary, and James A. Thomas of China Child Welfare, 1937–41; ca. 2 folders by J. S. Nagle and others of the National Child Welfare Association of China, with Garfield Huang, secretary at Shanghai, 1928–42; folder by Mrs. Owen Roberts with the Salvation Army at Peiping, 1937–39; folder by James A. MacKay of China Child Welfare and Mrs. Owen Roberts with the Shanghai Anti-Tuberculosis Association, 1940–43; folder by James A. MacKay with the Shanghai Public Hospital for Children, 1940–41; folder by James A. MacKay with the Shanghai Refugee Children Nutritional Aid Council, 1937–40; folder by Marion Yang of the National Health Administration, Chungking, with China Child Welfare, 1939–40.

MEMORABILIA: Ca. 2 folders of "clippings and printed emphemera" on Chinese women, n.d., medical aid, 1940–47, transportation and routes into China, n.d.; questionnaire on Robert Barnett's trip to China, 1942.

FINDING AID: In-house guide.

NY–240 Rare Book Section
    Rare Books and Manuscripts Division
    New York Public Library
    Fifth Avenue and 42nd Street
    New York NY 10018
    (212) 340–0820
    Francis O. Mattson, Curator of Rare Books

Background note: The Rare Book Division holds works on Christian missions including periodicals, publications and reports of societies and organizations, and publications about the missions themselves, dating from the late sixteenth through the eighteenth centuries. Among the titles issued by the American Board of Commissioners for Foreign Missions are catechisms, tracts, portions of the Gospels, the Bible, and other religious books in native dialects, some of which apply to China. Works relating to the Society of Jesus include letters from missions in the "East," "Jesuit Relations," which documents the order's early work in world missions, clerical lists and directories, and *Innocenta Victrix*, a block book in Chinese and Latin printed in Canton in 1671. The *Sessional Papers* of the Parliament of Great Britain occasionally contain materials concerning missionaries, such as *Correspondence Respecting the Attack on British Protestant Missionaries at Yang-chow-foo, August 1868* (London: Harrison and Sons), 1868–69, V 64.

NEW YORK UNIVERSITY

NY–245 Elmer Holmes Bobst Library
    70 Washington Square South
    New York NY 10012
    (212) 998–2560
    Ree DeDonato, Head Reference Librarian
    Lorraine Rutherford, Bibliographer

1-GENERAL HOLDINGS

PAMPHLETS: *Through China and Japan*, by R. N. P. Humfrey, 1932.

DISSERTATIONS/THESES: *American Catholic Missions and Communist China, 1945–1953*, by Virginia F. Unsworth, 1977. *A History of the Evangelical Lutheran Church of America's Mission Policy in China, 1890–1949*, by Roger Keith Ose, 1970. *The Problem of Missionary Education in China, Historical and Critical*, by Yau S. Seto, 1927. *Zion's Corner: Origins of the American Protestant Missionary Movement in China, 1827–1838*, by Murray Aaron Rubinstein, 1976.

NY–250 Stephen Chen Library of Fine Arts
    Institute of Fine Arts
    1 East 78th Street
    New York NY 10024
    (212) 772–5825
    Evelyn Samuel, Director

1-GENERAL HOLDINGS

PAMPHLETS: *Nestorians in China: Some Corrections and Additions*, by Arthur Christopher Moule, 1940; *The Ups and Downs of the Nestorian Church in China*, by Yoshiro Saiki, ca. 1950 (text in Japanese).

SERIALS: *Folklore Studies*, 1943–46.

NY–255 Frederick L. Ehrman Medical Library
    New York University Medical Center
    550 First Avenue
    New York NY 10016–6450
    (212) 340–5397
    Gilbert J. Clausman, Librarian

1-GENERAL HOLDINGS
SERIALS: *China Medical Journal*, 1921-31. *Chinese Medical Journal*, 1932-54, 1973-.

PROVINCIAL HOUSE OF MOST HOLY NAME PROVINCE OF FRANCISCAN FRIARS
NY-260 Provincial Archives
St. Francis Monastery
135 West 31st Street
New York NY 10001
(212) 736-8500
Cyprian Lynch, O.F.M., Archivist

1-PROVINCIAL ARCHIVES-MISSIONS, CHINA, 1912-52, 3 reels microfilm
MINUTES/RECORDS/REPORTS/CORRESPONDENCE: Holy Name Province, Order of Friars Minor, records of the China missions, including annual reports and correspondence between the Minister Provincial and individual missionaries, 1912-52.
CORRESPONDENCE: Letters of Sylvester Espelage about establishing an American Franciscan mission in Wuchang, 1920-22; correspondence concerning missions in Shansi province, 1924-28, and in Paoking, 1929-31.
MANUSCRIPTS: "Thirty-first Street to China; A History of American Franciscan Missions in China, 1913-1926," by Walter Hammon, n.d.
MEMORABILIA: Excerpts from *The Franciscan Provincial Annals*, and other publications on the China missions.
DISSERTATIONS/THESES: *Prefecture Apostolic of Shasi, 1913-1945*, by Raphael McDonald, 1945.

NY-265 SALVATION ARMY ARCHIVES AND RESEARCH CENTER
145 West Fifteenth Street
New York NY 10011
(212) 337-7427/7428
Thomas Wilsted, Archivist/Administrator

Restrictions: Official records are available 25 years after creation unless otherwise specified. Personal papers are subject to donor restrictions.
Background note: The Salvation Army Archives and Research Center was established in 1974 to serve as a center for Salvation Army historical material in the United States. The collection, which contain accounts of its mission in China which began with preliminary studies in 1898 by Colonel Rothweill and Brigadier Salter, is not organized geographically. The first mission was established in 1915.

1-GENERAL HOLDINGS
MINUTES/RECORDS/REPORTS: Occasional reports from and articles about Salvation Army work in China in Salvation Army serials: *All the World*, 1884-; *The Conqueror*, 1892-97; *The Salvation Army Year Book*, 1907-; *Social News*, 1911-21; and *War Cry*, London ed., 1879-, New York ed., 1881-.
CORRESPONDENCE: Correspondence of Lt. Colonel Anton A. Cedervall, 1921-50; correspondence of Mrs. Colonel Vernon Post, 1906-53, regarding the beginning of missionary work in

China, Chinese corps (churches) in San Francisco, and life in China following the Japanese occupation.
MEMORABILIA/AUDIO-VISUAL MATERIAL: Scrapbook and photo album of Mrs. Brigadier Ellen Brandt's experiences in China and Java, 1917-45; miscellaneous photos and publications by Lt. Colonel Anton A. Cedervall, 1921-50.

UNION THEOLOGICAL SEMINARY

NY-270 Archives
3041 Broadway at Reinhold Niebuhr Place
New York NY 10027
(212) 662-7100
Paul A. Byrnes, Chief Bibliographer and Archivist

Background note: John R. Mott founded the Missionary Research Library in 1914. Union Theological Seminary has housed it since 1929. In 1967, the Missionary Research Library's trustees turned over its administration to Union Theological Seminary. The Missionary Research Library's collections continue to grow under the care of Union Seminary's Burke Library.
Finding aids: "Union Theological Seminary Archives and Manuscripts: The Burke Library: An Index Guide," comp. by Paul A. Byrnes, 1986.

1-JULEAN H. ARNOLD, 1908-9, 1 box
MINUTES / RECORDS / REPORTS / PAMPHLETS / MAPS/ DESIGNS/DRAWINGS/AUDIO-VISUAL MATERIALS: Statistics, pamphlets, photos, and illustrations showing the nature and extent of American missionary enterprise in China, collected by Julean H. Arnold as an exhibit for the American Fleet visiting Amoy to accompany his dispatch to the Department of State.

2-WILLIAM ASHMORE PAPERS, 1868-79, 1 item
Background note: William Ashmore, Sr. (1824-1909), was a direct correspondent of the *Journal and Messenger*.
CORRESPONDENCE/MEMORABILIA: Scrapbook of newspaper articles and a letter from China, 1868-79.

3-JAMES WHITFORD BASHFORD DIARIES, 1904-18, 7 boxes
Background note: James Whitford Bashford (1849-1919) was a Methodist Episcopal missionary bishop in Shanghai and Peking from 1904 to 1918. See also General Commission on Archives and History—The United Methodist Church, United Methodist Archives and History Center, Archives, 36 Madison Avenue, P. O. Box 127, Madison, NJ, 07940.
DIARIES: 52 diaries describing Bashford's work, travels, interviews with public figures, and reflections upon reading, 1904-18.
MEMORABILIA: Notebook containing an index (not related to the diaries), n.d.; notebook containing notes on religions, land, people, and history of China, n.d.
AUDIO-VISUAL MATERIALS: Photo of Bashford, n.d.
FINDING AIDS: In-house inventory.

4-CHARLES LUTHER BOYNTON PAPERS, 1897-1942, 180 volumes and 1 box
Background note: For biographical notes see Claremont Colleges, Honnold Library, Special Collections Department, Claremont, CA, 91711. See also Hoover Institution on War, Revolution, and Peace, Archives, Stanford University, Stanford, CA, 94305.
MINUTES/RECORDS/REPORTS: International Committee YMCA, New York City, annual reports, 1907-12; alphabetical

and chronological lists of missionaries in China, 1807–1942; National Christian Council of China documents, n.d.; mission and church buildings in China, n.d.; data regarding mission stations, 1920s–early 1940s.
CORRESPONDENCE: Boynton's correspondence with family, friends, and missionaries, 1897–1902.
DIARIES: Boynton's diaries, 1897–1902.

5-MARGARET H. BROWN PAPERS, 1951, 1 item
Background note: Margaret H. Brown was a United Church of Canada missionary.
MANUSCRIPTS: "History of the Honan (North China) Mission [Presbyterian] of the United Church of Canada (1886–1951)," by Margaret H. Brown, 1951.

6-MARK W. BROWN PAPERS, 1932–65, 1 box
CORRESPONDENCE/PAMPHLETS/MEMORABILIA/AUDIO-VISUAL MATERIALS: Correspondence, clippings, sketches, photos, and pamphlets concerning the placement of a collection of Nestorian crosses in the New Jersey Museum of Archaeology at Drew University.

7-CATHOLIC UNIVERSITY, ART DEPARTMENT, PEKING, CHINA, 1937, 1 volume
AUDIO-VISUAL MATERIALS: Photo album containing 25 photos of an exhibition of Chinese Christian paintings, 1937.

8-CHINESE CHRISTIAN MONOGRAPH COLLECTION, 19th and 20th centuries, 16 reels microfilm
CHINESE LANGUAGE MATERIALS: 313 books, mostly by leading Chinese Christians and missionaries, including Miner Searle Bates, Chang Lit-sen, Tzu-ch'en Chao, Chi-i Cheng, Karl F. A. Gützlaff, Sung-kao Hsieh, Donald MacGillivray, Robert Morrison, P. F. Price, and Wang Ming-tao, on such subjects as church history, Christian ethics, theology, preaching, Cheeloo School of Theology, Foochow YMCA, and comparisons of Eastern and Western religions.
FINDING AIDS: *Chinese Christian Monograph Collection: An Index to Chinese Christian Monographs Filmed from the Union Theological Seminary Library Collection by the Board of Microtext, American Theological Library Association*, 1979.

9-CHINESE CHRISTIAN SERIAL COLLECTION, 1877–1968, 55 reels microfilm
CHINESE LANGUAGE MATERIALS/SERIALS: *Chan Wang (Outlook)*, 1953–57, 1961–67. *Chen kuang (True Light Review)*, 1925–35. *Chi-tu chiao sheng ho chou k'an (Christian Sheng-ho Weekly)*, 1955. *Chi-tu chiao ts'ung k'an (Series on Christianity)*, 1943. Chin-ling hsieh ho, *Shen hsüeh chih (Nanking Seminary Review)*, 1925–50. *Chin-ling shen hsüeh yuan hua hsi t'eh k'an (Special Issues of the Nanking Theological Seminary Journal)*, 1945. *Chin pu (Progress)*, 1911–16. *Ch'ing nien chin pu (Youth Progress)*, 1917–32. China Bookman, 1918–51. *Chüeh wu*, 1924–25. *Chung hsi chiao hui pao (Missionary Review)*, 1896–98. *Chung-hua chi-tu chiao chiao yü chi k'an (China Christian Educational Quarterly)*, 1925–36. *Chung-hua kuei chu*, 1923–41. *Chung-kuo mu szu lin*, 1960. *En yu*, 1947–48, 1951. *Fu yin hsin pao (Gospel Newsletter)*, 1877. *Hsi wang yüeh k'an (The Christian Hope)*, 1924–32. *Hsiang ts'un chiao hui (The Rural Church)*, 1940–42, 1946–47. *Hsiao hsi (News)*, 1930–50. *Hsieh chin* (National Christian Council of China, *Bulletin*), 1930–31, 1943–54. *Hsien tai fo hsüeh (Modern Buddhism)*, 1960. *Hsing hua (Chinese Christian*

Advocate), 1904–27. *Hsüeh shu yüeh pao (Science Monthly)*, 1899. *Hua nien*, 1932–33. *Hua-pei nung lien t'ung hsün*, 1950–. *Hui hsün kung pao*, 1930–54. *Kung yeh kai tsao*, 1926, 1929. *Nü ch'ing nien (Young Women)*, 1930–35. *Shang-hai Kuang-tung Chung-hua Chi-tu chiao hui yüeh pao (Cantonese Union Church Bulletin)*, 1917–24. *Shen chao*, 1932–34. *Sheng kung hui pao (Chinese Churchman)*, 1929. *Tao-oan kau hoe kong po*, 1923–67. *Teng t'a*, 1956–67. *Tao sheng (The Preachers' Magazine)*, 1931–35. *T'ien chia (The Christian Farmer)*, 1934–52. *T'ien feng (Heavenly Wind)*, 1947–63. *Tsung chiao chiao yü chi k'an (Journal of Religious Education)*, 1937–40. *T'ung wen pao (Chinese Christian Intelligencer)*, 1911. *Wei li pao*, 1956–58. *Wei yin yüeh k'an*, 1931–32. *Young Sun*, 1959–61. *Ying Kuang*, 1955–68.
FINDING AIDS: *Chinese Christian Serial Collection: An Index to Chinese Christian Serials Filmed from the Union Theological Seminary Library Collection by the Board of Microtext, American Theological Library Association*, 1979.

10-CHRISTIAN EVANGELISTIC AND RELIGIOUS EDUCATIONAL POSTERS, 1930–49, 1 box
MAPS/DESIGNS/DRAWINGS: Christian Evangelistic and Religious Educational posters, 1930–49.

11-CHRISTIAN SCROLLS AND BIBLE VERSES, 1930–49, 1 box
CHINESE LANGUAGE MATERIALS: Christian scrolls and bible verses, 1930–49.

12-HUNTER CORBETT AND HAROLD FREDERICK SMITH PAPERS, 1862–1948, 7 boxes
Background note: A pioneer missionary who laid the foundations of the Presbyterian mission in Shantung Province, Hunter Corbett (1835–1920) was a powerful advocate of the missionary enterprise. After his arrival in China in 1863, he founded the Yi Wen School (Boys' Academy/Hunter Corbett Academy) and organized the Temple Hill Church in Chefoo. Harold Frederick Smith (1885–1965), who married Corbett's daughter, May Nixon Corbett, taught at the Yi Wen School in Chefoo from 1910 to 1922 and at Cheeloo University from 1922 to 1930.
MINUTES/RECORDS/REPORTS: Cheeloo University, 1928–29, 1932; Cheeloo (University) rural institute, report, 1932; 3 reports on the rural program of the Council on Higher Education, 1928; report on the renaming of Hunter Corbett Academy as the Yi Wen School, 1926(?); China Missions of the Presbyterian Church in the U.S.A., statistics, 1929–30; Shantung Board of Christian Education, report, 1933; (Cheeloo) University sub-station, report, 1929; Shantung Presbyterian Mission (Peking Missionary Association), memorandum, 1925; Shantung Protestant University, Board of Directors, minutes, 1908; Tsinan Foreign School Association, School Board, minutes, 1926; Tsinan Foreign School Association, report, 1926; Tsinan Station, report, 1927–28; Christian Universities (of China), statistics, 1943; Yenching Alumni Association, charter and by-laws, 1926; Presbyterian missions at Chefoo and East Shantung, Hunter Corbett's personal reports, 1907–8.
CORRESPONDENCE: 2 letter copybooks by Hunter Corbett, 1865–69; ca. 1 folder of Corbett's and his family's correspondence, 1888–1948, with Arthur J. Brown, A. L. Carson, A. G. Corbett, Mr. and Mrs. George Cornwell, Irene Forsythe, John Fowler, John McGregor Gibb, Andrew Patton Happer, Stephen A. Hunter, Calvin W. Mateer, John R. Mott, Nan Pei Ling Church, and the Presbyterian Church of Chefoo; ca. 1 folder of other letters including William A. Adolph, Harold Balme, Harold Beame, Wil-

liam C. Booth, Arthur J. Brown, Hunter Corbett, George B. Cressey, F. F. Ellinwood, W. O. Elterich, B. A. Garside, O. M. Green, Charles F. Johnson A. T. Mills, Harold F. Smith, and "the Synod Committee (of the Presbyterian Church in the U.S.A.)."

DIARIES: 22 diaries of Hunter Corbett, 1862–1918; "Diary of Events in Tsinan and Vicinity, 1928," by Harold F. Smith.

MANUSCRIPTS: Notes on the Boxer Uprising of 1900, religions of China, n.d., and Chinese folktales, n.d., by Hunter Corbett; "Hunter Corbett's Answers to the Questions (for Corresponding Members of the World Mission Conference, Edinburgh, 1910)," by Hunter Corbett, 1909; "In Memoriam: Calvin Wilson Mateer, 1836–1908," by Hunter Corbett, 1908; "Note on Faculty Meeting (of Cheeloo University)," by Harold F. Smith, 1929; "Notes on Shantung Christian University," by Harold F. Smith, n.d.; "Protestant Higher Education in China: An Historical Sketch and Appraisal," by Kenneth Scott Latourette, n.d.; "The Tsinan Incident," n.a., 1928; "The Women's College [Yenching University]," n.a., n.d.

PAMPHLETS: 59 pamphlets, 1884–1949, on the American Presbyterian Mission, Anglo-Chinese College, anti-missionary riots, Boxer Uprising, Cheeloo University and School of Theology, Chifu School, Christian education, Christian colleges, Edinburgh 1910 World Missionary Conference, English Baptist Mission, Feng Yü-hsiang, Harriet Sutherland Corbett, Hunter Corbett, mission method, Peking Fellowship of Reconciliation, polemic, Presbyterian Hospital-Chefoo, Shanghai College, Shantung Christian University, Sun Yat-sen, travel, and William Ament Scott.

MEMORABILIA: 3 scrapbooks by Hunter Corbett, 1868–1906; obituary of Hunter Corbett in the *Chefoo Daily News*, 1920; "A Tribute to the Memory of Dr. Hunter Corbett," by W. O. Elterich in the *Presbyterian Banner*, 1920; "Translation of Boxer Placard in West City-Peking and Forwarded to Lord Salisbury by Sir C. McDonald," 1900; clipping on the Tsinan Incident, *Tsingta Times*, 1928.

MAPS/DESIGNS/DRAWINGS: "Plan Illustrating the Siege of Peking [during Boxer Rebellion]," *North China Daily News*, 1900; "Sketch Map of the Country between Taku and Peking," *North China Daily News*, 1900; *The Tsinan Incident May 1928*, pamphlet with maps, 1928; "Outline Study of Forty Centuries of Chinese History in Relation to the Ancestry of Jesus According to the Flesh," chart by Wilbert W. White, n.d.

AUDIO-VISUAL MATERIALS: 4 photos of Hunter Corbett, Temple Hill (Chefoo), and a Chinese baby's first birthday, ca. 1904–10; 2 pages of published photos of China missionaries and a page of pictures of Chinese Christians.

SERIALS: Cheeloo University: *Cheeloo Bulletin*, 1931; *Cheeloo Monthly Bulletin*, 1933; *Cheeloo Notes*, 1927; *Cheeloo Sketches*, 1927, 1929; Shantung Christian University, *Occasional Notes*, 1921–22, 1924. *Chefoo Station Bulletin*, 1922. *Progressive China*, 1929.

CHINESE LANGUAGE MATERIALS: A history of Tengchow College, 1913; children's hymnbook, 1906; 4 posters, 1900–1913, on the lunar and solar calendars, polemic, and orders of the Kwang Hsü emperor on conditions in Fu Shan County; 16 pamphlets, 1885–1948, on catechism, Chefoo Church of Christ in China, Chefoo Presbyterian Association School, China Christian Education Association Council on Public Health, China Medical Missionary Association, Chinese language instruction, Chinese mu-

sic, Great Massacre (Canton), Kwang Hsü emperor decrees, Nan Pei Ling Church, and polemic.

CHINESE LANGUAGE MATERIALS/SERIALS: *Cheeloo Education*, 1929. *Peking Women's Newspaper*, 1907–8.

FINDING AIDS: In-house inventory.

13-SAMUEL DODD DIARY, 1861–1958, 7 items
Background note: Samuel Dodd was a Presbyterian missionary to China from 1861 to 1877.

CORRESPONDENCE: Letter from Mary Dodd Craig to Letty Green, 1945, about the life of the her parents, Samuel and Sarah (Green) Dodd, in China.

MANUSCRIPTS: "Rambles in North China: Being an Account of a Trip during the Summer of 1873 by Rev. Samuel Dodd, through Shantung Province to Tien-tsin and Peking and Return," appendix to diary, n.d.; "Trial by Water," n.a., n.d.; "Preface to Diary of Rev. Samuel Dodd['s] Passage to and Life in China, 1861–1877, by J[ohn] N[evius] Dodd, from notes received from S. T. Dodd," 1958; "Continuation to Preface by S. T. Dodd to the Journal of Rev. Samuel Dodd, Missionary to China 1861–1877: Taken from Letters, By J. N. Dodd," n.d.

DIARIES: "The Journal of Rev. Samuel Dodd, Covering His Trip to and Life in China, 1861–1877: Copied and with Comments by His Son Samuel T. Dodd," n.d.

AUDIO-VISUAL MATERIALS: Photos in Dodd's diary of First Presbyterian Synod in China missionaries Hunter Corbett, "Wherry," David Lyon, "Leyenberger," John (Livingston) Nevius, and Samuel Dodd and his family; photo album of 39 photos illustrating scenes in S. T. Dodd's journal, 1922.

14-HARRISON SACKET ELLIOTT PAPERS, 1905–8, 1 box
Background note: From 1905 to 1908 Harrison Sacket Elliott served as secretary to James W. Bashford, a Methodist Episcopal missionary bishop in Shanghai and Peking from 1904 to 1918.

MINUTES/RECORDS/REPORTS: 21 reports and articles prepared by Elliott on aspects of mission work and Chinese civilization and culture for various publications, 1905–8.

CORRESPONDENCE: 148 letters on travel from Elliott to his family in the United States, 1905–8.

DIARIES: Diary of Elliott's trip through the Yangtze Gorges, 1907.

FINDING AIDS: In-house guide.

15-ALICE BROWNE FRAME COLLECTION, 1905–41, 1 box
Background note: Alice Seymour Browne (Mrs. Murray Frame) (1878–1941) was a missionary teacher under the ABCFM in Peking, Nanking (Ginling College), and Tungchow from 1905 to 1941. See also Mount Holyoke College, Williston Memorial Library, College History and Archives, South Hadley, MA, 01075–1493; University of Oregon, Special Collections, Eugene, OR, 97403–1299; and Matilda Calder Thurston Papers below. The collection is not yet catalogued.

CORRESPONDENCE: Letters of Alice Frame, some mimeographed, 1905–41.

16-GENERAL MISSIONARY CONFERENCE CLIPPINGS, 1890, 1 item
MEMORABILIA: Scrapbook containing 30 pages of clippings from the *North China Daily News* on the General Missionary Conference in Shanghai, China, 1890.

17-CHAUNCEY GOODRICH, n.d., 1 item
CHINESE LANGUAGE MATERIALS: Manuscript copy of Chauncey Goodrich's translation of the "Book of Daniel," n.d.

18-JOHN F. GOUCHER PAPERS, 1880–1922, 10 boxes
Background note: For biographical notes, see Goucher College, Julia Rogers Library, Towson, MD, 21204. See also Lovely Lane Museum, Library, 2200 St. Paul Street, Baltimore, MD, 21218.
MINUTES/RECORDS/REPORTS: Anglo-Chinese College/Foochow/Fukien Union College/Fukien Christian University: records, early organizing, 1911–17; Board of Trustees, minutes, reports, 1917–22; constitution and by-laws, 1918–22; mission schools in Fukien Province, statistics, n.d.; University of Nanking: constitution, records, 1906–21; Baille Colonization Scheme, reports, 1912–14; bulletins, catalogues, and reports, n.d.

Peking University: Provisional Board of Organization for Union in Higher Education in Chihli Province, records, 1912–13; Board of Trustees, minutes, 1916–22; Board of Trustees Executive Committee, minutes, 1916–22; Board of Managers, minutes, by-laws, 1917–22; annual reports by H. H. Lowry, 1912–13, 1918; annual report by J. Leighton Stuart, 1919–20.

West China Union University: Chengtu College Commission of Home Management, records, 1907; Temporary Board of Management, minutes, n.d.; early plans, 1906–20; constitution, 1908, 1910; Board of Governors, Executive Committee, minutes, by-laws, n.d.; University Senate, minutes, annual reports, 1912–22; Joint Commission, records, 1910; informal meeting of British members of the Board with Goucher, minutes, 1913; College of Medicine and Dentistry, records, n.d.; Union Theological College, reports, minutes, n.d.; Middle School, records, n.d.; West China Christian Educational Union, minutes, reports, 1906–19.

1 folder each of miscellaneous records, n.d. except where noted, of Canton Christian College, Carolyn Johnson Memorial Institute, Central China Christian Educational Union, China Centenary Missionary Conference (1907), China Institutional Union, China Sunday School Union (Shanghai), Christian Literature Society, Chungking Union High School, Committee for a (British) University in China, Committee on Christian Education in China, Continuation Committee of the Chinese National Mission Conference of 1913, East China Union Medical College, Goucher Day Schools (Nanchang), Goucher Primary School Unit-West China (Chengtu), Language Study Commission of the Methodist Publishing House (2 folders, 1901–19), Nanchang Academy, North China Methodist Mission, North China Union Women's College, Open Door Emergency Commission, Peking American School, Shanghai Baptist College, Shansi Union College, Shantung Christian University, South China Christian College for Women, statistics on mission schools in various provinces of China, Survey of Higher Education in China, Taianfu Middle School, Union School Movement, Union Theological College, Union Women's College for Central China, University of Hankow, West China Methodist Mission, West China Religious Tract Society, Wiley Institute (Peking), and William Nast College (Kiukiang).
CORRESPONDENCE: Box of Goucher's correspondence, 1880–1922, with James W. Bashford, Joseph Beech, William N. Brewster, Arthur John Bowen, Mr. and Mrs. Olin Cady, Harry Russell Caldwell, Benjamin Burgoyne Chapman, Clara M. Cushman, Charles Henry Fowler, Mr. and Mrs. Francis Dunlap Gamewell,

Perry O. and Ruth E. Hanson, Edgarton Haskell and V. C. Hart, Henry Theodore Hodgkin, George Heber Jones, Spencer Lewis, Wilson S. Lewis, Hiram Harrison Lowry, William Artyn Main, Wilson E. Manly, John H. McCartney, David Miller, Jacob Franklin Peat, Matthew Sites, J. R. Trinale, Ralph Ansel Ward, Lucius Nathan Wheeler, J. W. Wiley, John Wycliffe, and James Maxon Yard; folder of correspondence of American Baptist Missionary Union, n.d.; 3 folders of Anglo-Chinese College/Foochow/Fukien Union College/Fukien Christian University, 1880–1922; "Baille Colonization Scheme (University of Nanking)," 1912–14; ca. 2 folders of Methodist Publishing House, 1901–19; Peking University: H. H. Lowry, 1912–13, 1918, J. Leighton Stuart, 1919–20, and miscellaneous, n.d.; 3 folders of University of Nanking, 1906–21; West China Union University: J. L. Stuart, n.d., Henry T. Hodgkin, n.d., and miscellaneous, 6 folders, 1906–20; George B. Huntington, n.d.; West China Christian Education Union, ca. 1 folder, 1906–16; Young Men's Christian Association Student Volunteer Movement; box of Goucher's correspondence with the Board of Foreign Missions of the Methodist Church, Continuation Committee of the World Missionary Conference, Edinburgh (1910), the Epworth League, cooperation in Foreign Missions of the Federal Council of Churches, Foreign Missions Conference of North America, International Sunday School Association, Methodist Church Board of Education, Missionary Education Movement of the U.S. and Canada, Missionary Society of the Methodist Church, Mission Rooms of the Methodist Church, Missionary Society of the Methodist Church of Canada, National Council of Churches, Division of Foreign Missions, United and Federated Missionary Work, YMCA Student Volunteer Movement, and some personal business correspondence of Goucher, all n.d.; folder of miscellaneous correspondence, n.d.
MANUSCRIPTS: 2 folders of addresses by John F. Goucher, n.d.; list of educational institutions in Fukien and Foochow, n.d.
MEMORABILIA: Folder on Methodist Sunday School work, n.d.; folder of Peking University materials on medical education in Peking and North China, n.d.; "Ten Year History" and miscellaneous materials on West China Union University, 1919.
MAPS/DESIGNS/DRAWINGS: Maps and architectural drawings of the University of Nanking, n.d.; architectural plans, site sketches, and maps of West China Union University, n.d.; maps of China, n.d.
AUDIO-VISUAL MATERIALS: 5 folders of miscellaneous photos of missions and missionaries, n.d.; ca. 1 folder of photos of Fukien Christian University, n.d.; ca. 1 folder of photos of University of Nanking, n.d.; photo of Peking University President H. H. Lowry, n.d.
CHINESE LANGUAGE MATERIALS: Folder of lists of various schools and courses, n.d.
FINDING AIDS: In-house guide.

19-ALICE GREGG MANUSCRIPT, ca. 1946, 1 item
Background note: For biographical notes, see Winthrop College Archives, Dacus Library, Rock Hill, SC, 29733. See also Charleston County Library, South Carolina Room, 404 King Street, Charleston, SC, 29403-6466.
MANUSCRIPTS: 72 pages of 2 typescript chapters, "The Beginnings of Protestant Missions, 1867–95," and "The Victory of the New Learning, 1895–1901," plus preface and introduction to *China and Educational Autonomy: The Changing Role of the Prot-*

estant Educational Missionary in China, 1807–1937, published in 1946.

20-PAUL GOODMAN HAYES PAPERS, ca. 1920–1940, 3 volumes
Background note: Paul Goodman Hayes (b. 1890) was a Methodist Episcopal missionary to China.
MANUSCRIPTS: 3 loose-leaf binders containing hand-written biographical records of approximately 500 Chinese Christian and some non-Christian leaders and writers, ca. 1920–1940.
AUDIO-VISUAL MATERIALS: Ca. 10 portraits of Chinese Christians.

21-HIGHER EDUCATIONAL INSTITUTIONS IN CHINA, 1909–67, 1 box
Background note: See also Archives of the United Board for Christian Higher Education in Asia collection held by Yale Divinity School, Special Collections, 409 Prospect Street, New Haven, CT, 06510.
MINUTES/RECORDS/REPORTS/CORRESPONDENCE: Miscellaneous documents, including letters and reports, relating to Cheeloo University, Fukien Christian University, Huachung College, Lingnan University College of Medicine, Mukden Medical College, Nanking Theological Seminary, St. John's University School of Medicine, Yenching University, and the United Universities scheme.

22-EDWARD HICKS HUME PAPERS, 1913–55, 6 boxes
Background note: For biographical notes, see Yale University, Department of Manuscripts and Archives, Sterling Memorial Library, 120 High Street, New Haven, CT, 06520. See also Columbia University, Rare Book and Manuscript Library, Butler Library, 535 West 114th Street, New York, NY, 10027.
MINUTES/RECORDS/REPORTS: Yale-in-China president's report, 1935; "Report to the Committee of Reference and Counsel," 1936; list of students of the Chinese Educational Mission, 1954.
CORRESPONDENCE: Ca. 1,500 pages of letters concerning the publication of articles written by Edward Hicks Hume, 1913–55.
MANUSCRIPTS/MEMORABILIA: 5.5 boxes of manuscripts, typescripts, and clippings of addresses and articles appearing in *The Sun* (Baltimore, Maryland) and scholarly journals, 1913–55, including such subjects as the Canton army, Chiang K'ai-shek, Chinese civilization and culture, the Chinese medical figures Chang Chung-ching, Wang Ch'ing-jen, and Hua T'o, Christian colleges, communists, Harvey Cushing, international relations, libraries in China, missionenterprise, mission history, mission hospitals, mission medical schools, mission opportunity, missionary interests, native Chinese medical education and techniques, narcotics, Nationalists, National Medical College of Shanghai, religion, science, Sun Yat-sen, United China Relief, war, William Hector Park, William Henry Welch, Yung Wing, World Church, and Yenching University.
FINDING AIDS: In-house inventory.

23-TIMOTHY (TING FANG) LEW PAPERS, ca. 1920s–1950s, 7 boxes
Background note: Timothy (Ting Fang) Lew (1890–1947), a Protestant leader in China between 1920 and 1950, was a professor at Yenching and Peking universities. This collection is unprocessed.
CORRESPONDENCE: 7 boxes of correspondence with George Chen, Phillip De Vargas, Fred Field Goodsell, Theodore A. Green, Bishop Ronald O. Hall, H. H. Kung, Shuhsi Hsü, J. Latham-Stuart, S. J. McCauley, J. P. McCauley, and Charles A. Rowland.
MANUSCRIPTS: Lectures, articles, essays with the letters; "Bibliography of Published Writings of Timothy Lew, 1921–32," n.d.
CHINESE LANGUAGE MATERIALS: Translations of Lew's papers listed above; 16 pamphlets on Chinese Christian liturgy, edited by Lew, n.d.; biographical sketches of Timothy Lew and J. Leighton Stuart, n.d.

24-EDWIN CARLYLE LOBENSTINE, 1935, 1 item
Background note: Edwin Carlyle Lobenstine (1872–1958) was a Presbyterian missionary to China.
AUDIO-VISUAL MATERIALS: Photo album presented to Rev. and Mrs. E. C. Lobenstine on their retirement by the National Christian Council of China, 1935.

25-DAVID WILLARD LYON PAPERS, 1916–48, 2 boxes
Background note: See also Young Men's Christian Association of the U.S.A. Archives, University of Minnesota, Social History Welfare Archives, 2642 University Avenue, St. Paul, MN, 55114; and Lyman Hoover Papers at Yale Divinity School, Special Collections, 409 Prospect Street, New Haven, CT, 06510.
MINUTES/RECORDS/REPORTS: 16 folders of records of the YMCA of China, including: 4 folders of minutes, 11 folders of reports of YMCA groups, and 1 folder of statistical reports, 1916–48; records and reports of: China Christian Literature Council, 1918, 1921; Committee on Christian Literature, 1925–26; Christian Student Summer Conferences, 1933; Conference on Christian Literature, 1936; 4 folders on the Conference of Commissioners, 1932; National Student Christian Fellowship Conference, 1933; Shunhwachen Project, 1932–33; South Fukien Religous Tract Society, 1931; United Conference of YMCA and YWCA Student Secretaries, 1930; a list of (Christian Student) Summer Conferences; and photocopies of reports on visits to Chefoo, Mukden, and Tatung, probably by David Willard Lyon, n.d.
CORRESPONDENCE: 4 folders of YMCA correspondence, 1925–41; ca. 6 folders of Lyon's correspondence, 1927–39, with Arthur J. Allen, C. W. Allen, Clarence A. Barbour, Eugene Epperson Barnett, L. J. Birney, Harold D. Brown, John Wright Buckham, R. E. Chandler, T. C. Chao, Ch'uan Fang Lo, Bingham Dai, John C. De Korne, A. J. Fisher, Robert R. Gailey, W. Ernest Hocking, Henry T. Hodgkin, Leonard S. Hsu, E. R. Hughes, William Hung, D. T. Huntington, Rufus M. Jones, Arthur Jorgensen, Lewis Gaston Leary, Tong F. Lee, T. S. Lee, Hubert S. Liang, E. H. Lockwood, Bernard E. Meland, F. R. Millican, W. P. Merrill, John R. Mott, E. H. Munson, Lucius C. Porter, Francis Lister Hawks Pott, J. H. Ritson, Arthur Rugh, T. K. Shen, Frank V. Slack, William R. and Anna White Stewart, John Leighton Stuart, Tsai Chao Siu, Y. Y. Tsu, Gene Turner, Wong Kokshan, Andrew V. Wu, Y. T. Wu, Andrew C. Zenos, and N. Z. Zia.
DIARIES: "A Diary—Dodging War, Three Weeks on the Edge of War in China, August 11-September 1, 1937," by Arthur Rugh.
MANUSCRIPTS: 13 manuscripts, 1922–39, on Chinese philosophy, Christian Student Summer Conferences, Confucius, Foreign Division National Board YWCA, industry, polemic, war, and YWCA industrial work.
PAMPHLETS: *The Gest Chinese Research Library, McGill Uni-*

versity, 1931; *Forthcoming Conference on Religious Education at Hangchow College*, 1928.

MEMORABILIA: "Some Thoughts on the Literary Revolution," by Arthur W. Hummel, in *The New Mandarin*, n.d.; ca. 5 folders of articles by and about the YMCA in China and its work, by Lyon, Y. T. Wu, and others, 1928–39; clipping on water sports, 1925; 7 folders of printed and handwritten notes and articles by Lyon on Confucianism, mission methods and problems, 1927–45; 2 folders of study materials on Confucianism, 1926–27; 2 folders of proof sheets on *Religious Values in Confucianism*, by Lyon, 1927.

SERIALS: *China Bookman*, 1936. *China Mail*, 1937–38. Christian Literature Society for China, *Quarterly Link*, ca. 1934. Relief Work YMCA Refugee Civilians Fellowship, *Notes*, 1938.

CHINESE LANGUAGE MATERIALS: YMCA National Committee Report for 1924; enclosure, probably about Hangchow College, in a letter from Henry T. Hodgkin to Lyon, 1928; unidentified mimeographed document, n.d.

FINDING AIDS: In-house inventory.

26-HAROLD SHEPARD MATTHEWS, 1967, 1 item
Background note: For biographical notes, see Hoover Institution, Archives, Stanford University, Stanford, CA, 94305.
MANUSCRIPTS: "Some Historical Notes Pertaining to the Experiences of the North China American Board Mission, 1935–1960: This Being the Fourth Quarter of the One Hundred Years of Its History, Continuing the Story of Seventy-five Years of the American Board in North China, 1860–1935," by Harold Shepard Matthews, 1967.

27-JOHN R. MOTT PAPERS, 1911–39, 2.5 boxes, 1 folder
Background note: See also Yale Divinity School, Special Collections, 409 Prospect Street, New Haven, CT, 06510.
MINUTES/RECORDS/REPORTS: Ca. 1 folder of notes and minutes relating to the Shanghai National Conference, Christian Literature Section, Special Committee on Christian Literature, World Missionary Conference; ca. 1 folder, containing a record of discussions by representatives of Chinese educational institutions, Special Committee on Christian Education in the Mission Field, American Section, and the World Missionary Conference, n.d.; North China Educational Union, Board of Managers, statement on the development of higher education in Chihli, 1913; Canton Christian College, probable expenses, 1914; statement on Shantung Christian University, ca. 1914; program and report of conference on the "Situation in China," Committee of Reference and Counsel of the Foreign Missions Conference of North America, 1912.
CORRESPONDENCE: Letter from Henry R. Luce to Mott, on Christian education in China, 1913; letter from W. Oehler to Mott, Canton, 1915; 7 folders of correspondence with C. Y. Cheng, 1926–39; letter from Henry T. Hodgkin to Mott, 1912.
MANUSCRIPTS: "A Study in Survey and Occupation: The Province of Chekiang," by Alexander Miller, n.d.; "Memorandum on Suggested Approach to Chinese Government," n.a., n.d.; "Christian Education in China," n.a., n.d.; "Resolution Proposed for Presentation to the American Section of the Educational Committee of the Edinburgh Conference: Revised Form," 1913; 3 sets of Mott's notes, some on conferences with the Continuation Committee and "Prof. Monroe of Columbia," on Christian education, church, and government in China, 1912–13; "Some Notices about the Erudition of Our Pupils in Our Seminary in Respect of Our

Chinese Missionaries," probably by John R. Mott, 1913; 3 manuscripts on Christian education, literature, and the Chinese church and social reform by Mott, 1913–14.
PAMPHLETS: *China's Educational Problem*, by T. C. Chamberlain, n.d.; *Education*, by Francis Lister Hawks Pott, n.d.; biographical pamphlet on Pastor Ding, n.d.; *A Memorial for the Advancement of German Interests in China (addressing German language and schools in China)*, by the German Association of Shanghai, 1913; *Request for Intercessory Prayer of the Churches for China*, by the Committee of Reference and Counsel of the Foreign Missions Conference of North America, 1911.
MEMORABILIA: 2 descriptions of Shantung Christian University, n.a., n.d.; "A Church Outraged," *Shanghai Evening Post and Mercury*, 1915.
MAPS/DESIGNS/DRAWINGS: Maps of Shantung Province, Shantung Christian University, n.d., and Tsinan; artist's sketch of Shantung Christian University, ca. 1914.
FINDING AIDS: In-house inventory.

28-NATIONAL CHRISTIAN COUNCIL OF CHINA, ca. 1922–1946, 2 boxes
MINUTES/RECORDS/REPORTS/AUDIO-VISUAL MATERIALS: Miscellaneous documents, including committee minutes, reports, newsletter, and 4 photos (1922).

29-NESTORIAN TABLET, n.d., 1 item
MAPS/DESIGNS/DRAWINGS: Copy of a stone tablet at Sianfu, Shensi, reporting the introduction of Christianity into China in 634 A.D.

30-GEORGE NEWELL PAPERS, 1906–23, 1 folder
Background note: George Newell was a missionary under the American Board of Commissioners for Foreign Missions in Foochow during the 1920s.
MINUTES/RECORDS/REPORTS/CORRESPONDENCE: 26 report letters from Foochow Mission, 1906–11, and miscellaneous documents.
MANUSCRIPTS: "Some Notes and Other Things about the Foochow Union Normal and Middle School," by George Newell, 1922–23.

31-FRANK RAWLINSON PAPERS, 1924–37, 2 boxes
Background note: Frank Rawlinson (b. 1871) was a missionary to China with the Southern Baptist Convention from 1902 to 1921 and the American Board of Commissioners for Foreign Missions thereafter. He was editor of the *Chinese Recorder*.
CORRESPONDENCE: Box of letters to A. L. Warnshuis, 1924–28, and letters from China, 1937.
MANUSCRIPTS: "Revolution and Religion in Modern China," by Frank Rawlinson, 1928.
MEMORABILIA: Ca. 1 box of lecture notes on the naturalization of Christian education in China, 1932, 1936.

32-NATHAN SITES PAPERS, 1864–69, 3 volumes
Background note: Nathan Sites was a Methodist Episcopal missionary to China.
CORRESPONDENCE/DIARIES: 2 volumes of Sites' journal and correspondence, 1864–69.
MEMORABILIA: Scrapbook, 1864–69.

33-WILLIAM EDWARD SMITH PAPERS, 1897–1936, 10 boxes
Background note: William Edward Smith was a Canadian Method-

ist medical missionary in Jinghsien, Szechuan.

MINUTES/RECORDS/REPORTS: Church of Christ in China, Szechuan Synod, Chengtu, executive minutes, 1915, 1934; (Smith's) salary voucher, Canadian Methodist Missions, West China, 1922.

CORRESPONDENCE: 23 letters to and from "A. C. H.," "B. B.," Mabel A. Beatty, Chang Han, Wallace Crawford, A. Y. Crutche, James R. Cox, W. N. Fergusson, George M. Frank, Ernest Hibbard, Jean E. Holt, S. R. Johnston, R. O. Jolliffe, H. J. Lee, J. E. Egerton Shore, A. L. Smith, Ethelwyn Smith, J. W(ane?), "the other W. E.," and George A. Williams, 1912–36.

DIARIES: 44 diaries, 1897–1936.

PAMPHLETS: *The Bible Success Band in China*, by Charles Ernest Scott, n.d.

MEMORABILIA: Siberian Railway itinerary, 1912; "Proposed Union Course of Study in the Chinese Language," 1914; "Resolution to C[anadian] M[ethodist] M[issions] Executive re: Chinese Characters for the Name Canada," 1919; circuit examination time table, 1924; notes on the political conditions in China, 1928; list of stations of Evangelists and Probationers, n.d.

CHINESE LANGUAGE MATERIALS: "The Evangelist Report of Recommendations," n.d.

FINDING AIDS: In-house inventory.

34-STUDENT EVANGELISM IN GOVERNMENT UNIVERSITIES, NATIONAL CHRISTIAN COUNCIL OF CHINA PAPERS, 1946–49, 1 box

MINUTES/RECORDS/REPORTS/CORRESPONDENCE: Minutes, letters, and other documents, 1946–49.

35-MATILDA CALDER THURSTON PAPERS, 1902–55, 12 boxes

Background note: Protestant missionary Matilda Calder Thurston founded and was the first president of Ginling College, the first Christian women's college in China, from 1902 to 1943. See also Mount Holyoke College, Williston Memorial Library, College History and Archives, South Hadley, MA, 01075–1493. Her husband was Lawrence Thurston, the first missionary sent out by the Yale Foreign Mission Society. For papers of Lawrence Thurston, see Yale University, Department of Manuscripts and Archives, Sterling Library, 120 High Street, New Haven, CT, 06520.

MINUTES/RECORDS/REPORTS: 3 boxes on Ginling College, 1907–50: 5 folders of general records, 1923–50; 1 folder, except where noted, on Advisory Committee, Alumnae Association, Biology Department, Board of Control, Board of Founders, Business Manager, Candidate Committee Meeting, Child Guidance Service, Christmas, Class of 1927, Commencement, Conference Committee, Cooperating Committee for the Women's Union Christian Colleges in Foreign Fields, Curriculum, Easter, Education Department, Executive Committee, Experimental School, Extra-Curricular Activities Committee, 2 folders of faculty records (1927–46), Faculty Executive Committee, Faculty lists, faculty meeting, faculty retreat, financial records, Founder's Day, Georgia Grace Thomas Memorial Book Fund, Incorporation, Invitations, Joint Council, Library, Physical Education Department, Practice School, Publicity Committee, Red Cross, 9 folders of (Red Cross?) reports (1907–50), Rural Service Program, Schedule, Smith College, Statistics, Student Government Association, Students, Treasurer, 6 folders on the Twenty-Fifth Anniversary, Warship Services, and miscellaneous fragments; Ginling College, report, 1907–50.

1 folder (except where noted), n.d., of records of Ginling College faculty members Jane Thomas Bowies, Alice Seymour Browne, Alice L. Butler, Emily I. Case, Ruth Chester, C. Deng, Ada A. Grabill, 2 folders on Stella Marie Graves, Rebecca Griest, Edith C. Haight, Henry T. Hodgkin, Phoebe Hoh, Ming-sin Tang Hsueh, and 8 folders on Yi-fang Wu; 1 box, n.d., on the Chinese Women's Club of Shanghai, Conference of Christian Colleges and Universities, Conference on Church and Mission Administration, Council of Higher Education, Kiangan Mission Executive Committee, Nanking Women's Club, National Christian Council of China, United Christian Missionary Society, and Yangtsze Valley Student Conference; 18 folders of Thurston's miscellaneous personal records, 1910–55; unidentified document on Ming Teh Middle School for Girls, n.d.

CORRESPONDENCE: 4 boxes of Thurston's correspondence with the Calder and Thurston families, 1902–40; 2 boxes of correspondence, 1919–50, including such correspondents as the American Consulate General, John Earl Baker, Howard Barrie, Agnes Barry, John S. Barry, Mrs. Robert C. Beebe, Harlan P. Beach, Elizabeth R. Bender, A. J. Bowen, Jane Thomas Bowies, Eddy Brewer, Lydia Brown, Alice Butler, Russell Carter, Emily I. Case, Florence J. Chaney, Pin-dji Per Chen, Sanford Chen, Chen Shih, Chiu Li-ying, Ruth Chester, J. W. Creighton, Earl H. Cressy, Da Dzle, Mr. and Mrs. J. Horton Daniels, Mattie Dans, Djang Hsiang-lan, Mary F. Doan, Lois Anna Ely, Margaret Frame, Alice R. Fitch, Gilman Frost, Lulu Golisch, Ada Grabill, Stella Marie Graves, Rebecca Griest, Edith C. Haight, Eleanor M. Hinder, Margaret E. Hodge, Henry T. Hodgkin, Mrs. Houghton, Phoebe Hoh, Ming-sin Tang Hsueh, E. R. Hughes, Edward Hume, Paul Hutchinson, Mabel Jones, Kiangan Mission Executive Committee, Florence Kirk, Lillian Kirk, L. F. Koo, Mary Leaman, Marjorie B. Leavens, Jean R. Lingle, Liu En-lan, Edward Lobenstine, Helen M. Loomis, George W. Loos Jr., Eva Macmillan, Mrs. George Wilson McKee, Mao Yen-wen, Frederica Mead, Paul C. Meng, Luella Miner, Cornelia Mills, Mary Mills, W. Plumer Mills, Anna E. Moffet, Mereb Mossman, Mary Cole Murdoch, C. M. Myers, G. S. Myers, Y. T. Zee New, Miriam E. Null, V. K. Nyi, Alexander Paul, Lucy W. Peabody, Esther Pederson, Henry A. Perkins, Mrs. John B. Prest, Elsie M. Priest, Cora Reeves, Mrs. Charles K. Roys, David A. Robertson, Ted Romig, Logan H. Roots, William H. Sallmon, Caroline Savage, Katherine Schutze, Alice Seymour, Gratia Sharp, Mr. Smith, Dorothy Smith, Robert E. Speer, Ellen M. Studley, William Z. L. Sung, Mary Thayer, Helen Thomas, Mrs. Samuel Thorne, Jr., Mrs. F. J. Tooker, Mary Treudley, Tseh Yu, Mr. and Mrs. S. F. Tsen, Yeo Fu H. Tseu, Edna Turner, Florence G. Tyler, Minnie Vautrin, E. W. Wallace, A. L. Warnshuis, Hyla Watters, Clara E. Wells, Laura M. White, J. E. Williams, Andrew H. Woods, Blanche Wu, Yi-fang Wu, and Yu A-ji; folder of miscellaneous Ginling College correspondence, n.d.

DIARIES: 6 diaries by Minnie Vautrin, 1927–37; "Notes from a Nanking Diary," by Maude T. Sarvis, n.d.

PAMPHLETS: *Twenty-fifth Anniversary of Ginling College*, n.d.

MEMORABILIA: Folder of Thurston's addresses on Ginling College, n.d.; folder of material on Minnie Vautrin's death, n.d.; folder of biographical material on Yi-fang Wu, n.d.; obituary of Thurston, n.d.; 26 postcards, of Ginling College, n.d.; single issue of *The North China Herald*, 1927, and of *The China Press Weekly*, 1935.

MAPS/DESIGNS/DRAWINGS: 12 drawings, probably of Ginling

College, n.a., n.d.; folder of blueprints of Ginling College; 2 maps of Nanking.
AUDIO-VISUAL MATERIALS: 69 slides of China, missionary activity, and Asia, n.d.
SERIALS: 3 folders of unidentified Ginling College newsletters, n.d. *Nanking-Ginling News*, n.d.
FINDING AIDS: In-house inventory.

36-UNITED CHINA RELIEF, INC., 1943, 15 items
Background note: See also New York Public Library, Manuscripts and Archives Section, Rare Books and Manuscripts Division, Fifth Avenue and 42nd Street, New York, NY, 10018; Princeton University, 20th Century American Statecraft and Public Policy, Seeley G. Mudd Manuscript Library, Olden Street, Princeton, NJ, 08544; and American Board for Medical Aid to China collection at Columbia University, Rare Book and Manuscript Library, Butler Library, 535 West 114th Street, New York, NY, 19927.
MANUSCRIPTS: "Speaking of China," mimeographs of 15 radio broadcasts over station WQXR, New York, 1943.

37-ABBE LIVINGSTON WARNSHUIS PAPERS, 1900–1962, ca. 61 folders
Restrictions: Access restricted.
Background note: Abbe Livingston Warnshuis (1877–1958) was a Reformed Church in America missionary to China from 1900 to 1915. See also Western Theological Seminary, Beardslee Library, 85 East 13th Street, Holland, MI, 49423.
MINUTES/RECORDS/REPORTS: Folder of records on China famine relief, 1943–52; folder of minutes and records of the Committee on East China of the Foreign Missions Conference, 1943–44; 9 folders of minutes and records of the National Christian Council of China, 1921–40; 18 folders of records of the Nanking Theological Seminary Board of Founders, 1941–58; Reformed Church in America, Board of Missions: folder of records of the China Relief Committee, 1943–52; folder of records on the development of the Amoy mission, 1900–1915; folder of property records appeal of the Amoy mission, 1864, 1929; folder of records on Wilhelmina Hospital, Amoy, 1924; Shanghai police records, ca. 1915–20.
CORRESPONDENCE: Folder of Warnshuis' correspondence, 1908–1944, with Miner Searle Bates, B. F. Brissel, Sherwood Eddy, J. G. Fagg, W. B. Hill, J. A. Otte, and W. B. Van Staveren; 3 folders of Warnshuis' correspondence, 1899–1921, with W. I. Chamberlain and H. N. Cobb; 3 folders of letters concerning the China Continuation Committee, 1914–15; folder of quarterly letters, 1900–1915, by Warnshuis in Amoy; folder of "occasional" letters, 1916–17, by Warnshuis in Shanghai; folder of correspondence on Warnshuis' return to the Reformed Church in America Mission Board, 1919.
MANUSCRIPTS: Folder of Warnshuis' autobiographical notes prepared for the Oral History Research Office, 1955; 2 folders of sermons and reports on China, by Warnshuis, 1907–18, plus 1 folder of sermon material; folder of speeches and material on China, 1921; folder of addresses delivered in America, including "The Future of China," by Warnshuis, 1908; folder of manuscript and finished book, *Christian Ambassador, A Life of A. Livingston Warnshuis*, by Norman Goodall, n.d., and 2 folders of letter extracts and notes used by Goodall.
PAMPHLETS: *Dr. A. L. Warnshuis, Ecumenical Servant, 1877–1958*, by Herman Harmelink, 1962.

MEMORABILIA: 2 folders of background materials of the Committee on East China of the Foreign Missions Conference, 1943–44; 5 folders of datebooks, 1923–41, from Warnshuis' work in Shanghai and contacts with China; folder of biographical data, articles about Warnshuis, and *Who's Who in America* entry, n.d.; folder of material on the Reformed Church in America, Amoy mission centenary, 1942.
SERIALS: National Christian Council of China, *Bulletin*, 1921–40.
FINDING AIDS: In-house directory.

38-JOSEPH WHITESIDE DIARIES, 1899–1929, 6 boxes
Background note: Joseph Whiteside was a Methodist Episcopal missionary in Soochow, ca. 1900–1930.
DIARIES: 31 diaries, 1899–1929.
FINDING AID: In-house inventory.

39-M. T. YATES, 1878, 1 item
PAMPHLETS: *Ancestral Worship*, a revised edition of an essay read before the Missionary Conference, Shanghai, in 1877.

NY-275 The Burke Library

Union Theological Seminary
3041 Broadway at Reinhold Niebuhr Place
New York NY 10027
(212) 662-7100
Paul A. Byrnes, Chief Bibliographer
Seth E. Kasten, Reference Librarian

Background note: Burke Library of the Union Theological Seminary houses and administers the Missionary Research Library Collection. This collection is interfiled and listed below along with the general holdings of the Burke Library.
Finding aids: *Dictionary Catalog of the Union Theological Seminary* (Boston: G. K. Hall, 1960), 9 V. *Dictionary Catalog of the Missionary Research Library, New York* (Boston: G. K. Hall, 1968), 11 V. *American Missionaries in China: Books, Articles, and Pamphlets Extracted from the Subject Catalogue of the Missionary Research Library*, comp. by Clayton H. Chu (Cambridge: Harvard University Press), 1960.

1-GENERAL HOLDINGS
MINUTES/RECORDS/REPORTS: Administrators of mission boards having work in China, conference proceedings, 1925; Advent Girls' School, Nanking, catalogues, 1916, 1924; Alice Memorial and Affiliated Hospitals, Hong Kong, reports, 1920–22, 1924–25, 1932–34; American Association of China, annual report, 1919; American Baptist Convention Foreign Mission Society: East China Mission, bulletins, reports, minutes, and records, 1897, 1904–13, 1922, 1931–38; South China Mission, reports, minutes of conferences, minutes of Mission Reference Committee, annuals, and records, 1908, 1914–40; West China Baptist Mission, reports, constitution, and by-laws, 1911, 1913, 1918–36; American Bible Society: China Agency, Shanghai, report, 1925, Committee on Versions, report on Chinese version, 1850; Peking subagency, catalogue and supplement for 1937 exhibition of Bibles; American Board of Commissioners for Foreign Missions, reports on China missions, 1898, 1907, 1908, 1920–21; American Committee for China Famine Fund, reports, 1921, 1923; American Friends' Service Committee, report on trip to China by Lloyd

Balderston, n.d.; American Presbyterian Hospital, Hainan, report, 1930; American Presbyterian Hospital, Siangtan, Hunan, general reports, 1913, 1916–19; annual reports, n.d.; American Presbyterian Hospital, Weihsien, Shantung, reports, 1918–23; American University Club, Shanghai, constitution, 1917; Amoy Chinese Hospital, report, 1874; Anglican Communion in China and Hongkong (Chung-hua Sheng Kung Hui), report, 1909; reports of General Synod meetings, 1915, 1918, 1921, 1924, 1928, 1931; conference report and resolutions, 1909; Chekiang Diocese (Church Missionary Society Chekiang Mission), statistics, 1933; Anglo-Chinese Academy, Soochow, announcement, 1916–17; Anglo-Chinese College, Amoy, report, 1917–18, and prospectus, n.d.; Anglo-Chinese College, Foochow, reports and constitution, 1881, 1893–94, 1898–1900, 1907, 1909, 1911; Anglo-Chinese College, Shanghai, bulletin, 1909; Anglo-Chinese School, Ipoh, report, n.d.; Anki Red Cross Hospital, report, 1916; Anti-Narcotic Society, Tientsin (International Anti-Opium Association, Chihli Branch), quarterly reports, 1919–20; An Ting Hospital (Peking Hospital), reports, 1886, 1890; Anti-Opium League, annual reports, 1908, 1910; Associated Boards for Christian Colleges in China, memorandum on middle schools by Ralph C. Wells, 1945, planning committee report and papers, 1943–46; Association (Institution) for the Chinese Blind, reports, 1942–49; Association Secretarial School of China, catalogue, 1926; Augustana Mission in the Province of Honan, ten-year reports, 1905–25, and minutes of conferences in Honan, 1918–22, 1924–25, 1931, 1937–40; Baldwin School for Girls, Nanchang, catalogue, 1923; Baptist Church: China Baptist Conference, minutes, 1904–5, 1907, 1910; China Baptist Council, minutes and findings, 1930; China Baptist Publication Society, annual reports, 1902–6, 1909, 1911, 1913, 1918, 1920–23; Baptist Missionary Society: report of visit to China by W. Parker Gray and C. E. Wilson, 1929; report on China missions by W. Y. Fullerton and C. E. Wilson, 1908; Shansi report, 1925; Shensi report, 1925; Berlin Missionary Society in China, reports of mission school, 1866, 1895–95, 1903–4; Berlin Missionary Society in China, Kwangtung, order of worship, 1922; Bethel Mission, reports, 1920–28, 1930, silver anniversary, n.d.; Bethesda Hospital, annual reports and balance sheet, 1929–33, 1935–37; Bible, Book, and Tract Depot, Hongkong, reports, 1909–12; Bible Teachers' Training School for Women, Nanking, catalogues, reports, and minutes, 1913–35; Bixby Memorial General Hospital, Kityang, reports and letters, 1911, 1913–14, 1937–38; Book and Tract Society of China, report, 1886; Boone University, Wuchang, catalogues, reports, and announcements, 1907, 1909–24; Boys' Academy of the Reformed (Dutch) Church Mission in China, catalogue and special report, 1895, China Cities Evangelization Report, n.d.; Brethren Hospital, Shansi, report, 1921, 1923–24; Bridgman Academy, Peiping, report, 1936; Bridgman Memorial School, Shanghai, catalogue, 1914–18, 1923–24; British and Foreign Bible Society, reports on China, 1892–95, 1897–98, 1900, 1902–4, 1906, 1908, 1910–20, 1923–27, 1930–39; Manchukuo Agency, reports, 1936–37; Hongkong Auxiliary, reports and balance sheets, 1909, 1911, 1913–15, 1920, 1922; Canton Commercial Institute, catalogue, 1919–20; Canton Hospital, minutes, reports, and list of members, 1838–39, 1848–49, 1862–1939; reports, 1862–65, 1867–75, 1877–1933, 1939; Canton Hospital, South China Medical College lecture course, 1909; Canton Missionary Conference, report of the Board of Co-operation, 1920; Canton Union Language School, report and announcements, 1919–25; Canton Union Theological College, catalogue, 1918–19,

1929–30, prospectus, 1914, president's report, 1918–23; Central China Christian Educational Union, constitution and by-laws, 1910; Central China Famine Relief Committee, reports, 1906–7, 1910–12; Central China Teachers' College, catalogues, 1924, 1932–33; Central China Union Lutheran Theological Seminary, catalogues, 1913–14, 1916–17, 1920; Central China Wesleyan Methodist Lay Mission, reports, 1890, 1895; Changchow General Hospital, annual conference reports, 1918–22, 1925, 1934; Changpu Hospital, annual report, 1915–16; Chefoo Industrial Mission, report and letter, 1908, 1934; Cheeloo University: College of Arts and Science, catalogue, bulletin, and by-laws, 1931, 1937, University Hospital, report, 1936–38, Rural Institute, Lungshan Service Center, report, 1933, School of Medicine, reports and bulletins, 1915–38, 1949, 1952; Chengtu Eye, Ear, Nose, and Throat Hospital, six-year report, 1929–35; Chengtu Hospitals' Board, report, 1933–34; Chi Sue Girls' School, Shanghai, catalogue, 1914; Chin Fu Medical Work, reports, 1891–96; China Baptist Publication Society, reports, 1910; China Centenary Missionary Conference, reports and memorials, 1907; China Christian Educational Association: conference of missionary educators, 1927; reports, 1924–27, 1929–32, and a list of educational associations in China, n.d.; Chihli Province, courses of study for primary and middle schools, n.d.; Committee on Religious Education, bulletin, 1918; Council of Higher Education, minutes, reports, programs, and records, 1930, 1938, 1945; Council of Primary and Secondary Education, Shanghai, minutes, 1926, 1934; Council of Religious Education, records, n.d.; East China Educational Union, minutes, 1913–15; East and Central China Educational Association, records, n.d.; Fukien Province Branch, Preliminary Committee on Higher Christian Education, minutes and supplements, 1911, 1913, 1915–16; Hunan Christian Educational Association Branch, lists of societies doing educational work, 1913, 1915; Industrial and Agricultural Schools in China, records, n.d.; Kwangtung Educational Association Branch, reports and bulletins, 1912–13, 1915, 1921–24; miscellaneous papers, n.d.; North China Educational Union, minutes, constitution, and register of the Union College, 1907, 1912; Shanghai, miscellaneous reports, n.d.; Shantung and Honan Provinces Branch, minutes in English and Chinese, 1917–18, and records, n.d.; Union Schools in Korea and China, lists, 1915–16; West China Educational Union Branch, annual reports, 1913–15, 1917, 1922, 1924, and records, n.d.; West China Educational Union Branch, Committee in Primary and Secondary Education, proceedings, 1906–10; report to the National Christian Council, 1924; China Christian Literature Council: constitution, 1918, report, D. Willard Lyon, 1918; China Continuation Committee, findings of national conference, Shanghai, 1913, minutes of annual meetings, 1913–21, and records, n.d., report on evangelistic work in Manchuria by W. MacNaughtan, 1917, report on national and sectional conferences (including Manchuria), 1913; Christian Literature Council: report, 1921, Committee on Comity, report, n.d., Executive Committee, minutes, 1917–19, Kwangtung Christian Council Branch, minutes, 1914, Special Committee on a Forward Evangelistic Movement, bulletins, 1918, n.d., Special Committee on Survey and Occupation, records, n.d., Special Committee on Work for the Blind, bulletins, 1920–21, Special Committee on Work for Moslems, bulletins, 1918–19; China Foundation for the Promotion of Education and Culture, annual reports, 1926–40, information booklet, 1933; China Independent Mission, 1925, 1929; China Inland Mission: list of donations, 1883–84, list of missionaries and stations,

1893, 1914, 1936–41, press report, n.d., report of medical work, 1915, 1915–21, statement of policy, 1928, reports, 1904–59, Taichowfu, Chekiang, annual report, 1916, Jaochow, Kiangsi, reports, 1915, 1921–22, Hospital, report, 1920–21; lists of missions and statistics, 1893, 1914, 1936–37, 1939–41; press report, T'aichow, 1909; China International Famine Relief Commission: annual reports, 1922–36, and report on rural co-operative credit, 1926, Chihli province branch, report, 1924; Kiangsi province branch, annual report, 1925; China Medical Board of New York, annual reports, 1950–54; reports, 1914–19, 1921–25, 1950–52, 1954–55; China Medical Missionary Association: conference report, 1925, constitutions, 1905 and n.d., report by Robert C. Beebe, 1917; China Mennonite Mission Society, field report, 1922; China Missions Emergency Committee, report on China, 1907; Chinchew General Hospital, annual reports, 1915–18; Chinese Christian Curriculum Conference for South East Asia, report, 1960; Chinese Christian Literature Council, annual reports, 1952–63; Chinese Home Missionary Society, constitution, bulletins, 1909, n.d.; Chinese Hospital, Shanghai, annual reports, 1918, 1922, 1924; Chinese Medical Association, Missionary Division, prayer cycle, 1927, 1929–38, 1940–41, 1947–48; Chinese Students Famine Relief Committee, report, 1921; Chinese Tract Society, report, 1904–5, 1914; Chinkiang Girls' School, catalogue, 1912; Christian and Missionary Alliance, South China Branch, annual reports, 1912–24, 1916; Christian Churches in Szechwan, general conference report and program, 1925; Christian Churches (Disciples of Christ), International Convention, United Christian Missionary Society, China Mission, annual reports, 1924–27, 1929–30; Christian Educational Association of Shantung and Honan Provinces, reports, 1917–18; Christian Hospital, Shaohsing, annual reports, 1919–24, 1926–28, 1931–33, 1935, 1937, 1939–45; catalogue of Christian Literature in China, by J. Murdoch, 1882; Christian Literature Society for China (Society for the Diffusion of Christian and General Knowledge among the Chinese): annual reports, catalogue of publications, minutes, circulars, and a history, 1888–1943, 1946–48, minutes of the board of directors, 1938, 1940–41, 1948; London Committee, annual reports, 1903, 1908–9, 1915, Scotland Branch, annual report, 1914–15, and report of the Ladies' Branch, 1909; Chungking Men's Hospital (Chungking General Hospital/Syracuse-in-China Hospital), reports, 1892–93, 1895, 1897, 1899, 1901–5, 1908–12; Chungking Men's Hospital (Gould Memorial Hospital) and William Gamble Memorial Hospital for Women and Children, report, 1892–93, 1895, 1897, 1899, 1901–12; Church General Hospital, Wuchang, reports, 1921, 1923–25, 1929–30, 1937–40; Church Missionary Society, Hangchow Medical Mission, information booklet, n.d.; Church of Christ in China: 1927 constitution and 1938 revision, records, and report of the Commission on the Work of the Rural Church, 1936, General Assembly, reports, 1927, 1930, 1933, 1937, 1947, General Council, reports, 1928–33, 1935, 1946, Provisional General Assembly, minutes, 1922, 1925, miscellaneous papers, n.d.; records and publications of the General Assembly, 1927, 1932, 1938, 1944; Door of Hope, Shanghai, annual reports, 1900–1925, 1927–35; Church of England, Diocesan Association for Western China, financial reports and statements, 1934–39; Church of England, North China and Shantung Mission, reports, 1915–16; Church of England, Society for the Propagation of the Gospel in Foreign Parts, Diocese of Lucknow Board of Missions, annual reports, 1908–11, 1915; Church of England in Canada, Missionary Society, triennial reports and General Secretary's reports on the Chung-hua Sheng Kung Hui, Diocese of Honan, 1909, 1915, 1923, 1927–37; Church of Scotland Medical Mission (Rankine Memorial Hospital and Buchanan Memorial Hospital), annual reports, 1914–25, 1931–32; Church Training School for Bible Women, Soochow, report, 1916–17; Churches of Christ of the U.S.A., National Council, Research Committee of the Division of Foreign Missions, study of China missions, 1951; Commission on Christian Education in China, report, 1910; Committee for Christian Colleges in China, minutes, 1927–28; Community Church of Shanghai, annual reports, 1929–30, 1933; Conference of Mission Boards on China, records, 1925; Conference of Christian Colleges and Universities in China, report on medical education in China, 1912, sub-committee on Policy in China, draft memorandum, 1933; Conference on Christian Education in China, New York, 1925; Conference on Post War Missions in China, report, 1944; Congregational Christian Churches, American Board of Commissioners for Foreign Missions: Chinese Congregational Church of North China, Promotional Board, constitution, 1929; Fenchow Station, report, 1914; Foochow Mission, annual reports, constitution, by-laws, and minutes, 1895–1901, 1916–17, 1926, 1931; Foochow Station, Department of Religious Education, annual report, 1921; Foochow Mission, Ing Hok Station, annual reports of the Ing Hok Evangelization Company, 1897–1900, 1902, 1907, 1910–13, 1915, 1919; North China Congregational Union (North China Council, Congregational Union of Shansi, Shantung, and Chihli, North China Kung Li Hui), constitution, and minutes, 1914–41; North China Mission, minutes, standing rules, annual reports and Shantung district report, 1889–1914, 1918–21, 1923–41; North China Mission, Shansi District, Taiku Hsien Station, report, 1913–14; North China Mission, Tehchow Station, information booklet, 1940; Shansi Mission, annual reports, 1897, 1907–13; Correlated Program for Christian Higher Education in China, 1928; Council of Christian Publishers (United Christian Publishers), China, annual reports, 1944–49; Daily Vacation Bible Schools, China Association: national report, 1924, report, International Association on Schools in China, 1921; Danforth Memorial Hospital, reports, 1931, 1939, 1947; David Hill School for the Blind, Hankow, reports, 1922–24; Deutsche Medizinschule für Chinesen, annual report, 1912–13; Deutschen China-Allianz-mission, records and papers, n.d., and reports, 1908–14, 1917–18; Diocesan Association for Western China, financial report, 1924–29; Door of Hope and Children's Refuge Mission (Committee for Rescue Work in Shanghai—Shanghai Florence Crittenden Home), annual reports and records, 1900–1925, 1927–35; Douw Hospital for Women and Children, report, 1921; Dublin University Fuh-Kien Mission, Ladies Auxiliary report, and China's Children's Helping Band, report, 1911–12, and history, 1887–1911; East China Christian Colleges and Professional Schools, announcements of courses, 1926–27, 1929–30; Eastview Schools, Shenchow, catalogues, 1916–17; Ebenezer Mission, Miyang, Honan, reports, 1920, 1924; Educational Association of China, triennial meeting records, 1893–1900, triennial report, 1890–1909, and remarks, General Secretary of the Advisory Council on elementary education, 1914; Eliza Yates Memorial School for Girls, Shanghai, catalogues, 1917, 1919–20, 1922, 1925; Elisabeth Blake Hospital, Soochow, annual report, 1920–21, 1924; English Baptist Mission, Shantung Provincial Conference, report, 1926–27; Episcopal Church, China, handbook, 1925; Erskine Hospital, Changteho, Honan, report, 1915; Evangelical and Reformed Church, Board of International

Missions, report on middle schools in China, n.d.; Evangelical Church, China Mission, annual reports, 1916–18, 1927; Evangelistic Association of China, minutes, 1910; Everett Brown Chester Woman's Hospital and Training School for Nurses, Soochow, catalogue, 1914; Faber Hospital, Yingtau, annual report, 1909; Federation of Woman's Boards of Foreign Missions, report on Shanghai conference, 1920; First Presbyterian Church Society of Earnest Workers for China, and Society for the Support of the Lowrie High School at Shanghai, New York, annual report, 1882; Foochow College, catalogues, 1915–16, 1919, 1928, 1931; Foochow Girls' School, annual reports, 1859–1913, 1929–36; Foochow Hospital, bulletin, 1920; Foochow Hospital for Women and Children, reports, 1896, 1898; Foochow Missionary Hospital (Ponasang Missionary Hospital), annual reports, 1892–1904, 1908–14, 1916, 1919, 1923; Foochow Union High School, principal's report, n.d.; Foochow Union Medical College, papers, n.d.; Foreign Christian Missionary Society, Commission to the Far East, report, 1914; Foreign Missions Conference of North America, reports on visit to China by Frank Cartwright, 1946, and Christian education in China, 1927; Foreign Missions Conference, Committee on East Asia, 22 reports of study conferences on postwar work in China, 1944; Foreign Missions Conference of North America: 30th meeting, reports on China, 1923, China Committee, bulletins, minutes, news releases, ca. 1947, Commission on Christian Education in China, report, ca. 1910; Foreign Women's Home, Shanghai, annual reports and accounts, 1916–17; Forman Memorial Hospital, reports, 1931–32, 1934; Foster Hospital, Chowtsun, report, 1916; Friends Foreign Mission Association, report on China, 1916; Fuh Siang Union Girls' Middle School, announcements, papers, and booklet, 1931–33; Fukien Christian University, catalogues and presidents' reports, 1916–36, 1942, 1945; Fukien Union College of Liberal Arts, minutes, 1915; George C. Smith Girls' School, Soochow, catalogue, 1914, 1916–17, 1921; Ginling College, announcements, calendars, minutes, yearbooks, and reports, 1915–28, 1931, 1933–35, 1942; Department of Hygiene and Physical Education, reports, 1925, 1929–30, 1932; Griffith John College, Hankow, prospectuses, 1915–16, 1924–25; Hackett Medical College for Women (David Gregg Hospital), Turner Training Schools for Nurses, Canton, catalogues and reports, 1914–15, 1917–26, 1928–34; Hangchow Christian College, catalogues, announcements, minutes, and reports, 1911–30, 1936–37, 1940; Hangchow High School, catalogue, 1884; Hangchow Medical Mission, letter and reports, 1895, 1898, 1901–6, 1908, 1911, 1913–18; Hangchow Missionary Association, handbooks, 1931–34; Hangchow Union Evangelistic Committee, annual reports, 1916, 1920–23; Hangchow Union Girls' High School, catalogues, announcements, and minutes, 1912–25, 1929–32; Hanyang Hospital, annual reports, 1902, 1907, 1909–10, 1913; Hardy Training School, Yangchun, statement, n.d.; Harvard Medical School of China, reports, 1912–16; Harvard-Yenching Institute, certificate of incorporation, by-laws, and historical statement, 1928, 1935, 1940; Henry Lester Institute of Medical Research, Shanghai, report, 1936; Hildesheimer China-blinden-mission (Deutschen Blindermission unter dem Weiblichen Beschlecht in China), yearbooks, 1896–1928; Hill-Murray Mission to the Chinese Blind (Hill-Murray Institute for the Blind or Mission to the Chinese Blind and Illiterate), annual reports, 1887, 1889–95, 1898–1902, 1904–17, 1921, 1923–25, 1927, 1929, 1938; Hinghwa Biblical School, yearbook, 1909; Hongkong and New Territories Evangelization Society, reports, 1921, 1924; Hope Hospital of Hwaiyuan, reports, 1904–9; Hop-

kins Memorial Hospital (Peking Methodist Hospital), reports and histories, 1886–1936; Hospital and Dispensary at Tengchowfu, report, 1896; Hospitals of the Berlin Mission, annual report, 1906; Hsiang-Ya Hospital, annual reports, 1925–26; Hua Chung College (Central China College), Wuchang, general information, bulletins, and presidents' reports, 1924–25, 1927, 1929–49; Huchow General Hospital (Hunan Union Hospital), reports, 1916, 1928–35, 1937–38; Huchow Girls' Schools, catalogue, 1918; Huchow Woman's School, catalogues and prospectus, 1917–19, 1921, 1925; Hugh O'Neill Boy's High School, Tsingtau, statement, 1933; Hunan Bible Institute, Changsha, calendars, 1918–19, 1922–27, 1929–30; Hunan Missionary Union, conference report and constitution, 1903; Hunan Theological Seminary, Changsha, calendar, catalogue, and prospectus, 1914–15, 1925–26; Hunan-Yale College of Medicine, catalogues, 1916–21, 1923–24, 1926–27; Hunan-Yale School of Nursing, catalogues, 1913, 1920, 1922, 1924–25; Hwa Mei Hospital, Ningpo, annual reports and letters, 1913, 1915–16, 1920–22, 1925, 1932, 1940; Hwa Nan College, presidents' reports, 1929–34, 1942–43, 1946, Middle School Department, reports, 1920, 1924; Hwanghsien Hospitals, annual report, 1922; Ichowfu Men's Medical Work, report, 1908; Institute of Hospital Technology, headquartered at Union Hospital at Hankow, report, 1937; Institution for the Chinese Blind, Shanghai, reports, 1913–32, 1934–35; International Anti-Opium Association, Peking, annual reports, 1921–24; International Friends Institute, Chungking, annual reports, 1915, 1920–21; International Hospital, Hankow, report and statement of accounts, 1913; International Institute of China (Mission Among the Higher Classes of China), constitution, 1907; reports, 1894–1927; Institute of International Education, report on education in China, 1922; Irish Presbyterian Mission in Manchuria, reports, 1912–15, 1920, 1926–27, 1935, 1938–39; Japanese Christian delegation to China, report, 1957; Jefferson Academy, Tunghsien, catalogues and principal's report, 1921–25; Jenkins-Robertson Memorial Hospital, Shensi, report, 1925; John G. Kerr Hospital for the Insane, Canton, annual reports, 1898–1925; Joint Committee of Shanghai Woman's Organizations, annual report, constitution, and by-laws, 1926–27; Kahsing High School, catalogue, 1915, 1918; Kahsing Hospital, reports, 1906, 1924–25; Kiangsi International Famine Relief Committee, annual report, 1925; Kiating General Hospital, annual reports, 1932–35; Kingchow Theological Seminary, catalogues and one letter, 1923, 1933–34; Kuling American School (Anglo-American School at Kuling), announcements, 1911, 1923–25, 1931–34; Kuling Landrenters, minutes of annual meetings, 1899, 1901, 1903–4, 1906–12, 1917; Kuling Medical Mission, General Hospital and Tuberculosis Sanitorium, report, 1932–33; Kwangju Leper Colony, Christmas letter, 1925; Kwangtung Christian Educational Association, reports, 1920–23; Lao Ling Mission Hospital, annual report, 1924; League of Nations Health Organization, report on medical schools, 1931; Lester Chinese Hospital, Shanghai, records and annual report, 1930; Lingnan University, catalogues, financial statements, and presidents' reports, 1900–1903, 1905–13, 1915–31, 1934–35, 1942–43, 1946–48; London Mission College, Hankow, report of the high school, 1903; London Mission Hospital and Leper Colony at Hiao-Kan, reports, 1903, 1907; London Mission Hospitals in China, reports from Hankow, Wuchang, and Peking Hospitals, 1861–62, 1868, 1878, 1883, 1885–1893; London Mission Hospital at Siaochang, Hopei, reports, 1920, 1925, 1932; London Mission Hospital at Siao-Kan, reports, 1922–23; London Mission Medical School, Hankow, reports, 1902–3, 1907–8; London Mission Women's Hospital at Wuchang, report, 1903, 1907–8, 1913, 1922–23; London Missionary Society: report on deputation to China by W. Bolton and G. Cousins, 1903–4; report by Arthur Mitchell Chirgwin on a secretarial visit to China, 1938; Advisory Council in China, reports of annual meeting, 1915, 1922, 1926–30; Central China Mission, Hankow District Committee, reports, 1898, 1927, 1931; China Mission, reports by F. H. Hawkins, 1917, 1921, 1927–28; Tingchow Arthington Station, Fukien, annual reports, 1916, 1919–22; Wuchang, report, 1918; 3 reports on China missions and Peking Union Medical College by F. H. Hawkins, 1917, 1921, 1928; London Missions Hospitals, reports, 1889–1904; London Religious Tract Society, China mission records, n.d.; Lowrie Institute, Shanghai, catalogues, 1917–18, 1947; Lutheran Church of China: proposed constitutions for synods, districts, and local congregations, n.d., General Assembly, reports, 1920, 1928, 1931, 1934, 1937; Lutheran Church Council, minutes, 1921, 1928–37; Lutheran Theological Seminary (Central China Union Lutheran Theological Seminary), Shekow, Hupeh, catalogue, bulletin, annual reports, and minutes, 1914, 1916–17, 1920, 1931–32, 1949–50, 1952, 1954–56; Mackenzie Memorial Hospital (London Mission Hospital at Tientsin), reports 1919–25, 1933–34; McTyeire High School, catalogue, 1908, 1914–18, 1926–27; Mahan School, Yang chow, catalogues, 1914, 1918, 1924; Margaret Eliza Nast Memorial Hospital, Singju, Fukien, report, 1908; Margaret Hospital at Hankow, report, 1913, 1915–21, 1925; Margaret Williamson Hospital, Shanghai, manual and reports, 1926–28, 1930; Martyrs' Memorial Hospital, report, 1907–8; Mary Farnham School, Shanghai, catalogue, 1921, 1926–27; Mary Henry Hospital, Hainan, report, 1935–36; Mateer Memorial Hospital, annual report, 1893; Medhurst College, Shanghai, prospectus, 1912, 1917–18, 1923–24; Medical Committee of the (Presbyterian) Mission, statement and report, 1920; Medical Mission at Ningpo, reports, 1904, 1906–10, 1912–13, 1915–18, 1920–21; Medical Mission Hospital at Taichow, reports, 1910–11, 1913, 1917–18; Medical Missionary Society in China, reports, 1838–39, 1844–45, 1879, 1883–1893, 1898–1904; Mei Wa School, Canton, report, n.d.

Methodist Church, Board of Missions: Central China Conference, bulletin, minutes, and reports, 1940–41; East China Conference, minutes, 1940–41; Foochow Conference, yearbooks and minutes, 1939, 1946, 1948–49; Hinghwa Annual Conference, official journals, 1939–40; Kalgan Provisional Annual Conference, official journals, 1939, 1947; Kiangsi Annual Conference, journal, 1940, 1945, 1948; Mid-China Conference (Central China Conference), journals, 1947, 1950; North China Annual Conference, official journals, 1939–40, 1947; Shantung Annual Conference, records, 1939–40; West China Conference, yearbooks and journals, 1939, 1941, 1949; Woman's Division of Christian Service, North China Woman's Conference, annual report, 1939–40; Woman's Division of Christian Service, West China Conference, bulletin, 1941; Woman's Division of Christian Service, Yenping Annual Conference, official English journal, 1939; Yenping Woman's Conference, annual report, 1939–40.

Methodist Episcopal Church, Board of Foreign Missions: Central China Annual Conference/Central China Mission, minutes and records, 1888, 1892, 1894–1923, 1926–36, 1938–39; Chengtu West China Mission, minutes, 1927, 1929–34; Chungking West China Conference, 1925–26, 1929–35; Foochow Annual Confer-

ence, minutes, 1879, 1891, 1894–1916, 1918, 1920–27, 1930–35, 1937–38; Hinghwa Annual Conference/Mission Conference, minutes, 1896, 1900–1902, 1904–22, 1927–35, 1938; Kiangsi Annual Conference/Mission Conference, minutes, 1913–15, 1917–36, 1947; North China Conference/North China Mission, district reports and minutes, 1882–83, 1885, 1887–92, 1894–95, 1897–1932, 1938; Shantung Annual Conference, records, 1926–27, 1929–34, 1936–37; and records, n.d.; South Fukien Annual Conference/Mission Conference, minutes, 1923, 1925–26, 1929–33; West China Annual Conference, minutes, 1895, 1903–14; Yenping Conference, minutes, 1917–26, 1929–38.

Methodist Episcopal Church, Woman's Foreign Missionary Society: reports on schools in North China, Fukien, Szechwan, and the Yangtze valley by I. B. Lewis, 1921–22; Central China Woman's Conference, reports and minutes, 1888–1927, 1929–33, 1935–40; Chengtu Woman's Conference, report, 1926–30; Methodist Episcopal Church in China, program, 1920; Chungking and Chengtu Woman's Conferences, report, 1929; Chungking Woman's Conference, minutes, 1929; Foochow Woman's Conference, minutes and a copy of the "Foochow Mail," 1891, 1894–1931; Hinghwa Woman's Conference, minutes and reports, 1897–99, 1903–5, 1907–10, 1912–25, 1927, 1929–31; Kiangsi Woman's Conference, journal and reports, 1913–35; North China Woman's Conference, minutes, 1893–96, 1899, 1901–38; Shantung Woman's Conference, minutes, 1926–27, 1931–35; West China Woman's Conference, reports, 1911, 1913–25, 1931–36, 1938–39; Woman's Methodist Girls' High School, Nanking, catalogue and reports, 1923–25; Yenping Woman's Conference, reports, 1917–38.

Methodist Episcopal Church, South, Board of Missions: China annual conference, 50th anniversary report, 1886–1935; China conference executive council, minutes, 1936, 1939–40; China mission conference, minutes, 1890, 1892, 1894–95, 1912, 1914–15, 1917, 1919–38; China mission meeting, minutes, 1918, 1921; Central Council of the Methodist Episcopal Church, South, in China, minutes, 1928; Methodist Missionary Society, report on visit to Burma and China by Harold B. Rattenbury, 1939–40; reports and minutes of China mission conferences and councils, 1890, 1892, 1894–95, 1912, 1914–15, 1917–38, 1936, 1939–40; Foochow Woman's Conference, annual reports, 1902, 1911–12, 1918; Methodist Episcopal Church, North China Woman's Conference, minutes, 1902, 1906; West China Conference, minutes, n.d.

Ming Deh Girls' School, Nanking, report, 1935; Ming I Middle School, Fenchow, Shansi, report, 1932; Ming Sam School for Blind, Canton, reports, 1906–9, 1912–13, 1919, 1921–24, 1929–34, 1939; Morrison Education Society, minutes, 1837–38, 1841, 1844; Moukden Hospital, report, 1908, 1917; Moukden Medical College, annual reports, 1910–37, 1947–48; Nanchang Academy, report, 1929; Nanchang Hospital (Susan Toy Ensign Memorial Hospital), report, 1924–25; Nanking American School, catalogues, 1923–24, 1932–33; Nanking Bible Training School, minutes and catalogue, 1911–12; Nanking International Relief Committee, report, 1937–39; Nanking Theological Seminary, catalogues, faculty reports, and minutes, 1913–26, 1929, 1932–37, 1939, 1941, 1943–44, 1948–49, 1951; Nanking Theological Seminary: catalogue, 1916–19, 1922–26, 1929, 1943, 1948–49, 1951; minutes of annual meetings of the Board of Managers, 1925; 2 reports on evacuation of Nanking, the church in West China, and the church under Japanese occupation, 1940–41; Rural Church Department, survey, 1936; Nanking Union Church, annual report, 1922; Nanking Union Nurse School, report, 1909; Nanking University, catalogues, 1915–16, 1919–21, 1924–25, 1931, reports of the president and the treasurer, 1904, 1914, 1922–26; Nanking Woman's College and Girls' Boarding School, catalogue, 1912–13; Nantao Christian Institute, reports, 1922–24, 1928–1934; National Christian Conference in Shanghai, reports of commissions and resolutions, 1922; National Christian Council of China: annual reports, 1923–24; report on religious education in China, 1931; report on 1926 missionary conference; Conference on the People's Livelihood; miscellaneous reports and papers, 1922–46; report of delegation to International Missionary Council, 1928; reports and resolutions of annual meetings, 1925; constitution and by-laws, 1931, 1933; five-year report, 1922–27; reports on literacy work, 1930, 1933; report on Conference on Christianizing Economic Relations, 1927; report on conference of Christian workers in China, 1926, report on reorganization, 1928; Administrative Committee, minutes, 1929; Committee on the Church in Worship and Religious Education, minutes, 1927–29; Committee on Religious Education, minutes, 1923–30; Industrial Committee, programme, n.d.; report (sponsored jointly with Nanking Theological Seminary) on church in western China during wartime, 1941; National Committee for Christian Religious Education in China, reports, minutes, provisional constitution, booklets, budgets, and records, 1929–39, 1948; National Council of Churches in the U.S.A., Far Eastern Office Division of Foreign Missions: China Consultation, 1960; deputation of Australian churchmen to mainland China, report, 1957; National Leprosy Conference, Shanghai, minutes, 1932; New England Chinese Sunday School Workers Union, constitution, n.d.; New Territories Medical Benevolent Society, general and financial report, 1930; Ningpo Baptist Academy, catalogue, 1916–17; Norsk Lutherske Kinamissionsforbund (Norwegian Lutheran China Missions League), constitution, mutual guide, and yearbooks, 1895, 1898–99, 1907, 1910–11, 1913–20, 1925–26, 1928–29, 1936, 1939; Norske Evangelisk-Lutherske Frikerke, Kinamisjon (Norwegian Evangelical Lutheran Free Church, China Mission), 25th anniversary report, 1916–41; Norske Kinamisjon (Norwegian Mission in China), annual report, 1921; Norske Misjonsselskap (Norwegian Missionary Society), papers from China mission, 1912, 1918; North China American School, Tunghsien, catalogues and annuals, 1919–25; North China Christian Flood Relief Committee, report, 1918, 1920; North China Educational Union, register of the Union Colleges, 1907; North China Industrial Service Union, Peiping, report, 1933; North China Theological Seminary, reports, 1931–33; North China Union Bible Institute, catalogue, 1917–18; North China Union College, Tungchow, annual reports and courses of study, 1912, 1914–17; North China Union Language School, announcements of courses, calendars, prospectuses, yearbook, and annual reports, 1913–14, 1915–20, 1922–26, North China Union Medical College for Women, Peking, prospectuses, 1913, 1919, 1921; Norwegian Lutheran Church of America, Board of Foreign Missions, report of the Commission to China, 1929; Nurses Association of China, conference reports, 1926, 1928, 1930, 1934, 1936; Oberlin-in-China, calendars, 1921–25, 1948, 1950–57; Oberlin-Shansi Memorial Association, annual reports, 1948; Orthopedic Hospital of Shanghai, annual report, 1930–31; Pakhoi Leper Fund, report,

1907–8; Pakhoi Mission Hospital, report, 1920–21; Pangkiachwang Hospital, Shantung, report, 1909; Peking Academy, yearbooks and histories, 1932, 1935–36; Peking American School, annual announcements, 1922–25; Peking Association for the Relief of Destitute Native Women, annual reports, 1901–11; Peking Hospital, reports, 1861–64, 1874; Peking Medical Special School, regulations and schedule of courses, 1912; Peking Theological Seminary, reports, 1932–38; Peking Union Bible Training School for Women, bulletins and reports, 1823–24, 1922, 1929–33, 1937–38, 1948–50; Peking Union Medical College (Lockhart Union Medical College), announcements and reports, 1906–42, conference report, 1921, Hospital, reports, 1917–31, 1936, 1938–39, Hospital Social Service, report, 1927–29, Department of Religion and Social Work, report, 1925–26, School of Nursing, bulletin, 1929–30; Peking United International Famine Relief Commission, North China Famine of 1920–21, report on West Chihli Area, 1922, report on North China famine, 1922.

Peking University: announcements of courses, 1909, 1923–28; inutes of annual meeting of the Board of Managers, 1901–15, 1917–18; president's reports, 1909–10, 1912–13, 1923–27; College of Arts and Sciences for Men, and College of Arts and Sciences for Women, announcements of courses and bulletins, 1916–26; Department of History, special bulletin, 1923–24; Department of Leather Manufacture, announcements, 1923–24; Department of Sociology, announcement, 1923–25, 1929–30; School of Theology, announcements and catalogue, 1916, 1920–25.

Philander Smith Memorial Hospital, Nanking, annual report, 1890; Popular Education Program of Chefoo, report, 1923; premedical education, report on trip to South China, by W. W. Stifler, 1921; Presbyterian Board of Foreign Missions, report on China missions by Robert E. Speer, 1897; Presbyterian Church in Canada, Board of Foreign Missions, Canadian Presbyterian Mission in North Honan, annual reports, 1896, 1898, 1910; Presbyterian Church in Canada, Board of Foreign Missions, Western Division, annual report on work in northern Taiwan, 1912; Presbyterian Church in Canada, Board of Foreign Missions, Presbyterian Church in China, General Assembly, minutes and reports, 1916, 1918, 1922.

Presbyterian Church in China, General Assembly, minutes, 1923 (held contemporaneously with the Provisional General Assembly of the Church of Christ in China); Presbyterian Church in China, Provisional General Assembly, minutes, 1918; Presbyterian Church in China, Presbyterian Committee on Union, report, 1903; Presbyterian Church in the U.S., Executive Committee of Foreign Missions, report on China by Charles Darby Fulton, 1949; Presbyterian Church in the U.S., Mid-China Mission, minutes, 1925–27, and annual report, 1915; Presbyterian Church in the U.S., Mid-China Mission, Sinchang Field, report, 1903.

Presbyterian Church in the U.S.A., Board of Foreign Missions: Shanghai conference, report, 1926; report of delegation to China, 1946; reports on China missions by Robert Speer, 1897, and Arthur Judson Brown, 1901, 1909; Canton Mission, annual reports, 1886–94, 1896–97, 1900–1905; Central China Mission, annual convention reports (including station reports), minutes, rules, and station reports, 1888–89, 1891–1925, 1933–37; Hangchow Station, reports, 1907–8, 1926, 1937; Ningpo Station, annual report, 1933; Shanghai Station, annual reports, 1915–26, 1926, 1933, 1935–36; Soochow Station, 1926, 1938–39; China Council/China

Mission, minutes and reports, 1897, 1910–37, 1939–40, 1949–51; China Missions, Presbyterian Mission Press, annual reports, 1874–75, 1896, 1917–24; East China Mission, minutes, 1939–41; Hainan Mission, reports, 1893, 1906, 1912–30, 1932–37, 1939; Kiung Chow Station, reports, 1904–5, 1930–31; Kachek Station, report, 1930–31; Hangchow Station, report, 1907–8, 1926, 1937; Hunan Mission, minutes of annual meetings, 1915, 1917–30, 1932–38, 1940–41; station reports, 1906–7; Kiangan Mission, minutes and reports, 1905–38, 1940–41; Hwai-Yuen Station, reports, 1901–7, Nanking Station, station reports, 1914–15, 1926–41; Ningpo Station, 1933; North China Mission, annual reports, handbooks, and minutes of annual meetings, 1908–12, 1914–41; North Kiangsu Mission, minutes of annual meeting, 1912–27; Peking Mission, annual reports, 1904–5; Shanghai Mission, 1915–16, 1926, 1933, 1935–36; Shantung Mission, minutes, reports, and records, 1861–1916, 1918–34, 1936, 1938–41; Chefoo Station, reports and bulletins, 1890–1940; East Shantung Mission, annual reports, 1907; West Shantung Mission, reports, 1896–97, 1904–6; Ichowfu Station, annual reports, 1920–24, 1927–34; Soochow Station, 1926, 1938–39; Tengchow Station, station reports, 1917–18, 1922–27; Tsinan Station, annual reports, 1918, 1922–26, 1928–30, 1934–36; Tsingtao Station, station reports, 1902–3, 1919, 1922–24, 1927–28; Tsining Station, station reports, 1918–23, 1932–35, 1937–38; Weihsien Station, reports, 1921–26, 1928–34, 1939–40; Yihsien Station, station reports, 1922–26, 1933–39; South China Mission, annual report, 1907, 1910–13, 1922–24, 1935–36; minutes, 1912, 1914–30, 1932–39; reports, 1887–90, 1894, 1896, 1900–1901, 1903–4, 1930–31; Linchow Station, report, 1936; station reports: 1888–89, 1891–1923; minutes, 1894, 1896, 1903–6, 1908–24, 1933–37; Synod of Central and Southern China, minutes, 1902; Yunnan Mission, minutes, 1924; Kiulungkiang and Yuankiang Station, minutes, 1924–29; Synod of China, minutes, 1870–83, 1893.

Presbyterian Church of New Zealand, Canton Village Mission, annual report, 1910–11; Presbyterian Church of New Zealand, Chinese Mission, tour reports, 1909–11; Presbyterian Hospital at Changteh, reports, 1921–25, 1931, 1936; Presbyterian Union Theological Seminary, catalogues, 1907–8, minutes of the Board of Directors, 1907; Presbyterian Union Theological Seminary of Central China, minutes and bulletin, 1905, 1907–9, 1914; Princeton University Center in China, reports and bulletins, 1906–12, 1915–16; Princeton-Yenching Foundation, yearly survey, 1930–31; Protestant Episcopal Church in the U.S.A., National Council, Department of Missions, commission to China, report, 1927–28; Protestant Episcopal Church, District of Hankow, report of conference at Kuling, 1905; Protestant Episcopal Church, District of Shanghai, annual journals, 1914, 1916–17; Protestant Episcopal Church in the U.S.A., Board of Missions, report of the Commission to China, 1927–28; Prudential Committee of the American Board, report on deputation to China by Judson Smith, 1898; Red Cross, Canton International Red Cross, report, 1937–39; Red Cross, Shanghai International Red Cross, report, 1937–39; Red Cross China Committee for Central China, reports, 1938 and n.d.; Red Cross General Hospital, Shanghai, annual reports, 1915–17; Reformed Church in America, Board of Foreign Missions, report of Anthony Van Westenburg and Luman J. Shafer on deputation to China, 1946; Reformed Church in America, Woman's Board of Foreign Missions, yearbooks, 1901–18, Amoy, report, 1899–1916; Reformed Church in the United States, China mission, min-

utes of annual mission meeting, 1919; Reformed Presbyterian Church, Mission in China, report, 1895–1910; Religious Tract Society: reports on China, 1894–1904; Central China Religious Tract Society, records, n.d.; North China Tract Society, annual reports and catalogues, 1884, 1887, 1908–12; North Fukien Religious Tract Society, annual reports and catalogues, 1905, 1907, 1909, 1914–21; Chinese Religious Tract Society, Shanghai, annual reports, 1888–89, 1901, 1903, 1906–8, 1910–18; South China Religious Tract Society, Canton, annual reports, 1913, 1915; West China Religious Tract Society, annual reports, 1899, 1901–4, 1906, 1908, 1910–22; Religious Tract Society for China, Hankow, annual reports, 1884–1916, 1918–40; Religious Tract Society of London, catalogue of Chinese publications, 1892; Ren Gi Hospital, Tze Kung, annual report, 1939; "Report of the Deputation to China," by Edward C. Moore and James L. Barton, 1907; Riverside Girls' Academy, Ningpo, reports, 1923–25; Roberts Memorial Hospital, Tsangchow, report, 1919–20, 1923–24, 1932–33; Roman Catholic Church in China, Maryknoll-in-Kongmoon, decennial report, 1928; Rosenkranz Mission, yearbooks, 1916, 1919; Rulison Fish Memorial High School, Kiukiang, catalogue, 1910; Saint Agnes School, Anking, catalogue, n.d.; Saint Elizabeth's Hospital, Shanghai, annual report, 1937; Saint John's College, Church School for Boys, Shanghai, reports, 1892–96, 1898–1910, 1912–16; Saint John's University, Shanghai, catalogues and presidents' reports, 1900–1940; Saint John's University, Middle School, catalogue, 1929; Saint John's YMCA School, Shanghai, rules and regulations, 1917–18; Saint John's University, Pennsylvania Medical School, announcements and reports, 1910, 1914–15, 1920, 1924–25, 1929–33; Saint Luke's Hospital, Shanghai, by-laws and rules, 1922, annual reports, 1906, 1910, 1914, 1922, 1932–38, and statistics and financial statement, 1923; Saint Luke's and Saint Elizabeth's Hospitals, Shanghai, annual report, 1939; Saint Mary's Hall, Shanghai, catalogue, addresses, and announcements, 1913, 1922–26, 1930–31; Saint Paul's College, Hong Kong, annual, 1951; Saint Paul's Girls' College, Hong Kong, report, 1928; Saint Paul's School for Catechists, Kiangsu, rules and regulations, 1926; Schofield Memorial Mission Hospital, reports, 1906–10; (Charles Rogers Mills Memorial) School for Chinese Deaf Children, Chefoo, reports, 1902–3, 1909–37; Scientific medicine in Ting Hsien, annual report, 1933; Scott Thresher Memorial Hospital, Swatow, report, 1938; Seventh-Day Adventists, Mission Board, surveys, 1932–33, 1935, 1939; Shanghai American School, bulletins, handbooks, reports, and prospectuses, 1911–14, 1916–17, 1920–23, 1926–39; Shanghai College, annual catalogues, 1915–25, annual reports, catalogues, and minutes, 1907, 1909–28, 1930–31, president's report, 1923–32, reports, 1923–26; Shanghai College, Yangtsepoo Social Center, annual reports, 1919–21, 1928–29; Shanghai Mission to Ricksha Men, annual reports, 1915–30; Shanghai Union Language School, reports, 1912, 1952; Shantung Christian University, annual reports, 1911–12, 1915–16; reports, calendars, and minutes, 1905–13, 1916–32; School of Arts and Science, reports, 1928, 1931; School of Medicine, reports, 1915–30; School of Theology, reports, 1929, 1933; University Hospital, reports, 1919, 1922, 1930, 1932–33; Shantung Famine Relief Society, International Auxiliary, report, 1921; Siao Kan Medical Mission, report, 1911; Sienyu Christian Union Hospital, report, 1940; Soochow Academy, catalogue, 1929–30; Soochow Hospital, reports, 1883–88, 1905–6, 1913–19, 1924–25, 1928–31, 1933–35, 1937–40; Soochow University, catalogues, bulletins, announcements, and presidents' reports, 1900, 1910, 1915-16, 1919-26, 1929-30, 1934, 1937-40, 1942; Soochow University, Wu Dialect School, report, 1921-22; South China Alliance Press, report, 1915; South Fukien Missionary Conference, minutes, rules of order, and order of business, 1910-19, 1923; Southern Baptist Convention, Foreign Mission Board: minutes of conference on SBC missions in Japan and China, 1919; Central China Mission, reports, minutes, and reference books, 1905-6, 1909-10, 1913-18, 1922; North China Baptist Mission, yearbooks and minutes, 1903, 1911-12; South China Mission, reports and minutes, 1897-1900, 1907, 1909-11, 1913-16, 1918-20, 1924; West China Baptist Conference, annual reports, 1914-17; Statistics of Protestant Churches and Missions in China, 1934; Stephenson Memorial Hospital, Changchow, annual report, 1934; Stout Memorial Hospital, report, 1924; Student Volunteer Movement of China, undated constitutions and list of volunteers, 1916; Student Volunteer Movement of China, Student Volunteer Band of Peking University, yearly letters, 1914-17, 1921-22; Suifu Women's and Children's Hospital, report, 1924; Supervisory Committee for the Education for Chinese Girls, report, 1930; Svenska Missionen i Kina, reports, 1906, 1912-15, 1919-20, 1922; Svenska Mongol Missionen, records, 1897-1922; Swatow Academy, catalogues, 1917-19; Swatow Mission Hospitals, reports, 1894, 1913; Syracuse-in-China Hospital, reports, 1891-1932; Tainan Mission Hospital, report, 1915-16; Tainan Presbyterian Middle School, report, 1932; T'ai-yuan-fu Medical Mission, report, 1905; Talmage College (Amoy Union Middle School), report, 1914, and commemoration of 10th anniversary of Amoy Union Middle School, n.d.; Temple Hill English School, Chefoo, final report, 1918-20; Temple Hill Hospital, report, 1914-28, 1930; Tibetan Religious Literature Depot, reports, 1919-22; Tientsin Anglo-Chinese College, calendars and reports, 1902-25; Tientsin Hui Wen Academy, report, 1926; Tientsin Intermediate School for Chinese Boys, reports, 1899, 1902, 1912-13, 1916, 1933; Tingchow Boys' School, reports, 1924-25; Tooker Memorial Hospital, Soochow, report, 1913; Trinity College, Foochow, statement, n.d.; True Light Middle School, report, 1909-10, 1918, 1922; Tsehchow Mission, prospectus, financial statement, and circular letter, 1922-23, 1925; Tsinanfu Institute, reports, 1912-14, 1940; Tsingkiangpu General Hospital, reports, 1918-22; Tsingtao Lutheran Hospital, annual report, 1931; Tungkun Medical Missionary Hospital (Rheinische Missionsgesellschaft), reports, 1898-99, 1901-13, 1921-23; Union Church, Kulansu, Amoy, annual statement, 1922; Union Church, Shanghai, reports and accounts, 1925-26; Union Hospital at Hankow, reports, 1907, 1931-32; Union Medical College, Hankow, reports, 1910-12, 1914; Union Medical School, Shanghai, prospectus, 1924; Union Theological School, Foochow (Baldwin School of Theology), catalogues, 1909-10, 1916-17, 1921, 1924-25; Union Training School for Nurses, Peking, report, 1920; United Board for Christian Higher Education in Asia, minutes, reports, and records, 1935-66; United Brethren in Christ, Foreign Missionary Society, reports on East Asian missions, 1912-13; United Church of Canada, Woman's Missionary Society, West China Council, minutes of annual meetings and Workers' Conference of Sze-Chuan Branch, 1926, 1929-31; United Conference of Protestant Missionaries and Chinese Church Leaders of Kansu, report, 1924; United Evangelical Mission Hospital, report, 1920; United Free Church of Scotland, Manchuria Mission Council, abstracts of accounts and grants, 1926-27; United Methodist Mission, Lao Ling Mission Hospital, Chu Chia Tsai Tzu, Shantung, report, 1924; United Presbyterian Church of Scotland, report on medical missions in Manchuria, 1885; University of Hong Kong, School of Midwifery, report, 1932-33.

University of Nanking: College of Agriculture and Forestry, announcements, annual reports, catalogues, minutes, by-laws, presidents' and treasurers' reports, yearbooks, special bulletins, and commencement programs, 1892, 1910-27, 1931, 1935-37, 1942; College of Agriculture and Forestry, announcements and reports, 1914-15, 1918-34; College of Agriculture and Forestry, agricultural survey of Szechwan province, by John Lossing Buck, 1943; College of Agriculture and Forestry, rural economic surveys of Yenshan county, Chihli province, by John Lossing Buck, 1926; College of Agriculture and Forestry, Department of Agricultural Economics, report on 1931 flood; College of Agriculture and Forestry, Freeman Meteorological Observatory, records, 1895-1924, 1927; College of Agriculture and Forestry, Rural Workers' Training Course, reports, 1926-27, 1930; Department of Sericulture, annual reports, 1924-26; Department of Missionary Training, announcements and prospectus, 1911-15, 1918-26; Medical Department (East China Union Medical College), catalogues, course of study, and minutes, 1910-13; Department of Normal Training, catalogues, 1913, 1915; Summer School, bulletins, 1921-24; University Hospital, reports, 1917-23, 1925, 1928-36, 1940.

University of Shanghai, annual reports, bulletins, catalogues, announcements, 1930-37, 1939; Division of Religious Studies, course of study, 1936; Wayland Academy, Hangchow, catalogues, 1915-25; Wenshan Girls School, Foochow, bulletin, 1921; Wesleyan Methodist Church, Canton District, report, 1892; Wesleyan Mission, Central China, report, 1865-90, lay mission, report, 1890, 1893, and undated report on Hopeh; Wesleyan Missionary Society, Medical Missionary Hospital, Fatshan, report, 1892; West China Christian Educational Union, annual report, 1913; West China General Conference, report of the committee on ''The Worker,'' 1921; West China Missions Advisory Board, statistics, 1923-24; West China Union Normal School for Young Women, Chengtu, annual report, 1920, bulletin, n.d., and constitution, 1916; West China Union University: announcements and catalogues, 1913-17, 1919-39, 1942-43; annual reports, 1910-11, 1913, 1924-25, 1931-34, 1939, 1942; minutes of the Board of Directors, 1940; news bulletins, 1946, 1948; prospectus, 1910; reports of Board of Governors, 1926-28, 1931; College of Medicine and Dentistry, annual catalogues and reports, 1932-34, 1937-39, 1941-43; College of Religion, annual catalogue, 1931-32; Middle School, annual reports, 1917, 1930, 1932; Wiley General Hospital, annual reports, 1909, 1916-17, 1919, 1921-23, 1934; Wiley Institute, Peking, information bulletin, 1888; William Gamble Memorial Hospital for Women and Children, Chungking, report, 1915; William Nast College, Kiukiang, catalogues, yearbooks, and announcements, 1901, 1906-7, 1913-14, 1916-17, 1921-24; Williams Hospital, Pangkiakwang, Shantung Province, report, 1890; Williams-Porter Hospitals, Tehchow, annual report, 1939, broadcasting notes, ca. 1925; Willis F. Pierce Memorial Hospital (Foochow Christian Union Hospital), annual reports, 1935, 1937-38, 1941; Woman's Christian Medical College, Shanghai, announcements and bulletins, 1925-26, 1928, 1931-32; Woman's College of South China, Foochow, catalogues and handbooks, 1914, 1920, 1922, 1924-25, 1929-32, 1934-35; Woman's

Medical College of Soochow, announcements, 1916; Women's Christian Temperance Union, China, report, 1930; Women's International Friends Institute, report, 1909–10; Wuchang Union Normal School, prospectus, n.d.; Wuhu General Hospital, information booklet, letters, reports, and calendar, 1910, 1918–19, 1922, 1928, 1931–33, 1942; YWCA, China National Committee, 1925–26; YWCA of China, reports, staff yearbook, and records, 1911, 1915–16, 1919, 1922–23, 1926–28, 1930, 1933; YMCA of China: statement, Amoy, n.d.; Peking, report, 1917; Hangchow, annual report, 1920–22; Hongkong, annual reports, 1904, 1907; Nanchang, report, 1920; Shanghai, annual reports, by-laws, and constitution, 1907–8, 1913, 1915, 1919; Tientsin, annual reports, 1903, 1907, 1909, 1913; reports, and records, 1912–22, 1924–25, 1929, 1935–38; Evening School of Commerce, Shanghai, catalogues, 1914–17; documents of D. Willard Lyon, Secretary of the Foreign Department of the International Committee, 1895–; YMCA Normal School of Physical Education, Shanghai, catalogues, 1917–18, 1923–25; Summer Training School for Employees of the YMCA, report, 1914; YMCA of China and Korea, records and reports, 1906, 1908–9; YMCA of China, Korea, and Hongkong, annual and five-year reports, and constitution, 1902, 1904, 1907–12; YMCA Trade School, Chengtu, statement, n.d.; Yale-in-China, reports, 1910–17, 1922–25, 1939–46, 1951–53, 1967; (College of) Yale-in-China, Changsha, catalogues, 1906–8, 1913–14, 1921–23, 1925–26; Yale Mission College, reports, 1907–9, 1912–15; Yangchow Baptist Hospital, report, 1912; Yates Academy, Soochow, catalogues, 1914, 1916–19, 1922–26; Yenching University: alumni directory, 1929; annual reports of the president of the University, n.d.; directories, 1925, 1927–31; guidebooks for students, 1929–32; income and expenditure accounts, 1929–30; miscellaneous reports, 1921, 1926; programs of services, 1929; registrar's reports, 1928–31; College of Applied Social Sciences, announcements, 1929–30; College of Arts and Letters, reports, 1929–30, 1932–33; College of Natural Sciences, reports, 1929–30, 1932–33; College of Public Affairs, reports, 1930–35; Department of Biology, history, 1917–31; Department of Political Science, announcement, 1927–28; Graduate Division, announcement of courses, 1929–33; Institute of Religion, report, 1927; School of Chinese Studies, announcements and courses of study, 1925–33, 1947–48; School of Journalism, reports, 1932, 1936; School of Religion, announcements of courses, 1927–31; short courses for religious and social workers, 1930–33; writings and activities of faculty, 1932–34; president's reports, 1920–26; catalogues, 1916–18, 1920–21, 1925–26; Yihsien Industrial School, announcements and minutes, 1916, 1918; Youth and Religion Movement Mission, Southwest and West China, report, 1939; Yungchen Hospital, report, 1914–16.

CORRESPONDENCE: Letters from Alice Browne Frame, missionary in China (Woman's Board of Missions, Congregational Christian Churches), 1905–39; letters from Edith Fredericks of the Methodist Episcopal Church, Women's Foreign Missionary Society, in Kiangsi, 1936–39; letter from Frank A. Keller of the China Inland Mission in Changsha, 1909; letter from Henry J. Maier, secretary for the China Mennonite Mission Society, 1922; 2 letters from missionaries in Chengtu and Hong Kong to the Methodist Episcopal Church, Women's Foreign Missionary Society, 1896, 1938; 3 letters from China to Methodist Church, Board of Missions, 1946–48, and a letter from the board to China, 1948; letters from Mr. and Mrs. W. H. Oldfield of the Christian and Missionary Alliance, South China Branch, 1936–42; ca. 1 folder of war letters, Yenching University, 1938; ca. 1 folder of report letters by C. H. Robertson, YMCA in China, 1913–15; letter from Robbins Strong at Fukien Christian University to Congregational Christian Churches, American Board of Commissioners for Foreign Missions, 1949; circular letters from W. Reginald Wheeler, 1935–37; Kwangju Leper Colony, Christmas letter, 1925.

MANUSCRIPTS: 26 manuscripts, 1911–78, on subjects including agriculture, Eugene Epperson Barnett, Chinese medicine and modern science, Chinese Christians, Christian leaders, Church of Christ in China, economic welfare, education, German missionary literature, Alice H. Gregg, Hakkas, missionary administration, Nanking Theological Seminary, National Christian Conference (Shanghai, 1922), North China Mission, Reformed Church mission, social effects of missionary work, Southern Baptist Convention, theological education, and West China; "Directories of Missionaries in China," 1865, 1866, 1875, 1883, 1889, 1891; "List of Missionaries and Their Stations of the American Church Mission, 1911–1934, n.d.; "Missionaries to China, 1807–1942: A Chronological List," by Charles Luther Boynton, n.d.; National Christian Council of China, Conference on the People's Livelihood, papers and abstracts, 1931; libraries of the Christian colleges in China, survey by Charles B. Shaw, 1947–48.

PAMPHLETS: Ca. 500 pamphlets, 1834–1982, including such topics as agriculture in China, alphabetic and phonetic Chinese scripts, ABCFM Foochow Mission, American Baptist Foreign Mission Society, American Bureau for Medical Aid to China, Amoy Girls' School, Associated Boards for Christian Colleges, Basler Mission in China, Beacon Hill Farm (Foochow), Bible Union of China, Blind Children's Home and School (Kwai-ping), Boxer rebellion, Canadian Presbyterian Mission in North Honan, Canton Christian College (Lingnan University), Canton International Red Cross, Canton Union Theological College, Ch'iang min, Chentu Hospital and Chentu School, China Centenary Missionary Conference (Shanghai, 1907), China Christian Broadcasting Association, China Christian Educational Association, China Christian Literature Society, China Continuation Committee, China Inland Mission, China International Famine Relief Commission, China Sunday School Union, Chinese Bible and Book Society, Chinese Christian hymns, Chinese government policy toward missions, Chinese language instruction, Christian and Missionary Alliance, Christian education in China, Christian Hospital in Shaohsing, Christian martyrs in China, Christianity in contemporary China, Church Missionary Society, Church of Christ in China, Church of England Zenana Missionary Society, Church of the Nazarene in China, Congregational Christian Churches, Dartmouth in China, Disciples of Christ in China, economic conditions in China, English Methodist College (Ningpo), Evangelical Lutheran Synod/Board of Foreign Missions, extraterritoriality, Fowler University (Kiukiang), Good Shepherd Hospital (Dr. Nathan Sites' Memorial Hospital)—Ming-chiang, Grinnell-China Movement, Hangchow Medical Mission, Home of the Nazarene (Industrial Orphanage)—Chinkiang, Hopkins Memorial Hospital, Hwa Nan College, International Institute of China (Mission among the Higher Classes of China), Kuling American School, Kuling Estate Hospital, Kuomintang policy toward missions, Kwangju leper colony, literacy movement, London Missionary Society, Lutheran Church of China, mandatory religious instruction, Margaret Williamson Hospital (Shanghai), medical missions, Methodist Episcopal Church in China, missionary biography, missions in Canton, Chahar, Chinchow, Foochow, Fukien, Hainan, Hangchow,

Hankow, Honan, Hong Kong, Hunan, Jehol, Kansu, Kiangsi, Kiangsu, Manchuria, Moukden, Nanking, Ningpo, Peking, Shansi, Shantung, Siaochang, South China, Tibet, West China, and Yunnan, missions to Chinese Muslims, Moukden Hospital (United Free Church of Scotland Mission), name of God in Chinese, Nanchang Hospital (Susan Toy Ensign Memorial Hospital), Nanking International Relief Committee, Nanking Theological Seminary, National Christian Council of China, native Christians in China, North China Union Language School, opium traffic, Peking Union Medical College, persecution of Christians in China, Presbyterian Church in China, Presbyterian Church in Canada, Board of Foreign Missions, Presbyterian Church in the U.S.A., Central China mission, Protestant Episcopal Church in China, Presbyterian Hospital-Chefoo, Reformed Church in America, Woman's Board of Foreign Missions, Reformed Church in the U.S./Board of Foreign Missions, Rhenish Missionary Society, Roman Catholic Church in China, rural missions, Saint Agatha's Hospital (P'ing Yin), Saint Columban Chinese Mission Society, Saint Faith's School (Yangchow), Saint Hilda's School for Girls (Wuchang), St. John's University (Shanghai), San-miao orphanage, Shanghai Industrial Orphanage, Shansi Memorial Association, Shantung Christian University, Shaowu Station (Foochow Mission), Shunhwachen Rural Training Center, Si-ka-wei Station, Society of Friends in China, Soochow Hospital, Southern Baptist Convention/Foreign Mission Board, Sung Mei-ling (Mme. Chiang K'ai-shek), Svenska Missionsförbundet mission in Chinese Turkestan, Syracuse-in-China, Taylor Memorial Hospital and Hodge Memorial Hospital (Paoting), Tehchow Mission Station, Tibetan Forward Mission, Tientsin Anglo-Chinese College, training of missionaries, Training School for Bible Women (Hankow), Tsingtao Lutheran Hospital, Union Middle School (Canton), Union Hospital at Hankow, United Evangelical Hospital (Liling), United Committee for Christian Universities in China, Wai Hwei Kindergarten, West China Union University, Williams Hospital (Tehsien), women and missions, World War II and missions, Yale-in-China, Yenching University School of Chinese Studies, Yenching University School of Religion, and YWCA in China.

MEMORABILIA: Union Normal Training School, Foochow, clippings, n.d.; Wesley College, Wuchang, clippings, n.d.

MAPS/DESIGNS/DRAWINGS: *Atlas of China in Provinces...A Companion Work to "A Survey of the Missionary Occupation of China,"* by Thomas Cochrane (Shanghai: Christian Literature Society for China), 1913; *Charts, Showing the Progress of Missions in China: Prepared for the Student Volunteer Convention, Kansas City, 1914,* by David W. Lyon, 1914; China Christian Educational Association, map of nine affiliated associations, n.d.; map of China published by the Catholic Church of Ho-ch'ien-fu, n.d.; map of China showing the stations of the China Inland Mission (Toronto: China Inland Mission), n.d.; *Katholischer Missionsatlas,* by Karl Streit (Steyl Missionsdruckerei, 1906); *Province of Ssu-Ch'uan (Eastern Sheet)* (map showing location of mission stations), Topographical Section of the War Office (Great Britain), (London: E. Stanford), 1908.

AUDIO-VISUAL MATERIALS: 2 filmstrips, "Ever Faithful, Ever Sure: Christian Communities in China," by Gail Coulson and Jean Woo, 1983; 9 audio cassettes, "God's Call to a New Beginning," addresses at the International Christian Conference in Montreal, 1981; uncatalogued photos of people and places in China from the files of Isaac T. Headland, n.d.

SERIALS: Alden Speare Memorial Hospital, *Newsletter,* 1923.

American Baptist Foreign Mission Society, East China Mission, *Quarterly Bulletin,* 1911–31. American Friends Service Committee, *Bulletin on Work in China,* 1942–44. American Presbyterian Mission, Chefoo, *Newsletter,* n.d. Anglican Communion in China and Hongkong, Kiangsu Diocese, *Journal of Synod,* 1912–19, 1922–26, 1928–33; North China Diocese, *Journal of Synod,* 1917–23, 1925–26, 1928–32, 1934, 1936, 1939. *Anking News Letter,* 1922, 1925–41. *Anking-Hankow Newsletter,* 1944. *Asia,* 1948–60. Asia Christian Colleges Association, *Bulletin,* 1952-. *Bible for China,* 1925–37. Bible Union of China, *Bulletin,* 1921–25. *Bridge,* 1983-. *Bulletin of the East,* 1923–28. *Bulletin of the Hankow District,* 1903–4. Canton Christian College, Canton Christian College Club in America, *Quarterly,* 1916–17; *Newsletter,* 1912–14. Catholic University of Peking, *Bulletin,* 1928–30, 1936–37. *Central China Bi-monthly,* 1914–16. *Central China Record,* 1901–5. *Challenger,* 1982-. Charles Rogers Mills Memorial School for Chinese Deaf Children, Hangchow, *Letter,* 1914. Cheeloo University: *Cheeloo,* 1924–26; *Cheeloo Bulletin,* 1928–33; *Cheeloo Monthly Bulletin,* 1933–37, 1939–41. *Chefoo Station Bulletin,* 1922. *Chengtu Newsletter,* 1920–39. *China,* 1921. *China and Ourselves,* 1983-. *China and the Church Today,* 1979–86. *China and the Gospel,* 1918–37. *China Bulletin* (Rome), 1979-. *China Bulletin,* 1947–62. *China Christian Advocate,* 1914–41. China Christian Educational Association, *Bulletin,* 1924–39; Fukien Christian Educational Association Branch, *Journal,* 1908, 1918–19. *China Christian News Letter,* 1928–29. *China for Christ,* 1920. *China Fundamentalist and Anti-Bolshevik Bulletin,* 1928–29. China Graduate School of Theology, *Bulletin,* 1971-; *News Letter,* 1971-. China Independent Mission, Shanghai, *Letters,* 1925, 1929. China Information Committee, *News Releases* (Chungking), 1938–41. China Inland Mission, *List of Missionaries and Their Stations,* 1891, 1910, 1914, 1917, 1922–24; *Occasional Papers,* 1866–75. China International Famine Relief Commission, *Bulletin,* 1924, 1927–37; *News Bulletin,* 1935, 1937, 1939, Publications, series A, 1922–37; series B, 1923. *China Medical Journal,* 1907–31. *China Medical Missionary Journal,* 1887–1907. *China Methodist,* 1948–49. *China Mission Year Book,* 1910–39. *China Monthly,* 1940–41, 1943–46, 1948–50. *China News* (American Board of Commissioners for Foreign Missions), 1927. *China News* (China's Children Fund), 1949–50. *China News Letter* (Toronto), 1927. *China News Letter,* 1947–59. *China Notes,* 1958-. *China Prayer Letter,* 1979-. *China Spectrum,* 1983. China Study Project, *Bulletin,* n.d. *The China Sunday School Journal,* 1913–28, 1930–31, 1933–34. *China Talk,* 1983-. *China: The Quarterly Record,* 1903–4, 1908–9, 1911, 1913–15. *China Update: An Occasional Newsletter,* 1982-. *China-böte,* 1910, 1920, 1922–25. *Der Chinabote für den Amerikanischenfreunds Rheinischen Mission,* 1924, 1937–38. *China's Millions* (London), 1875. *China's Millions* (Toronto), 1892–1952. *China's Young Men,* 1876, 1906–16. *Chinese-American Bulletin,* 1942–46. *Chinese Anglicans in the Four Seas,* 1955, 1957. *Chinese around the World,* 1985-. *Chinese Christian Intelligencer,* 1916, 1920. *Chinese Christians Today,* 1962-. *Chinese Evangelist,* 1889–90. Chinese Medical Association, Council on Christian Medical Work, *Bulletin,* 1932–48. *Chinese Medical Directory,* 1941. *Chinese Medical Journal,* 1887–1951. *Chinese Missionary Gleaner,* 1856–59. *Chinese Newspaper Clippings on Religion,* 1984-. *Chinese Recorder,* 1912–38. *Chinese Recorder and Educational Review,* 1939–41. *Chinese Recorder and Missionary Journal,* 1868–1912. *Chinese Repository,* 1832–51. *Chinese World Pulse,* 1977, 1979-

83. *Ching Feng*, 1957-. Christian Churches (Disciples of Christ), International Convention, United Christian Missionary Society, China Mission, *Newsletter*, 1948. Christian Literature Society for China, *Link*, 1921-23, 1930-33, 1936-41; *Newsletter*, 1941, 1948. Christian Universities of China, *Bulletin*, 1932-50. *The Church: Bulletin (and Forum) of the Church of Christ in China*, 1935-50. Church Committee for China Relief, *Bulletin*, 1938-39. Committee on Relief in China, *Bulletin*, 1938. *Community Church*, 1923. *Day Star, or Message of Hope*, 1914. *Ding*, 1981-. *Directory of Protestant Missionaries in China, Japan, and Corea*, 1881-1913. District of Hankow, *Newsletter*, 1931-41. *East Asia Millions* (London), 1875-. *East Asia Millions* (Philadelphia), 1891-1943, 1947-61(?). *East China Studies in Education*, 1925-26. *ECF News*, 1983-. *Echoes from Inland China*, 1922-24. Educational Association of China, *Directory*, 1903, 1905; *Monthly Bulletin*, 1907-8. Educational Association of Fukien Province, *Journal*, 1906-20. *Educational Directory of China*, 1914-21. *Educational Review*, 1909-38. *The Evangel*, 1910-11, 1917-20, 1922. *Evangelical*, 1915-18, 1920. *Evangeliska stasien Missionen*, 1982-. *Evangelize China Fellowship News*, 1955-. *Far East*, 1925-50, 1960-. *Fenchow*, 1920-24, 1926, 1931. *Foochow College Quarterly*, 1923. *The Foochow Messenger*, 1903-17, 1922-27, 1929-31, 1934-40. *Foochow News*, 1924-28, 1930-40. *Foochow Trenches*, 1920, 1923. *Foochow Young Men*, 1908. *Four Streams*, 1919-60. *Free Wan-kan*, 1942-44. *Friend of China*, 1881-85, 1894-1916. *Fu Jen News Letter*, 1931. *Fuhkien Witness*, 1902-4, 1908-9. Fukien Christian University, *FCU News*, 1932; *Fukien Star*, 1924-25. *Gebetsanliegen der Canton-Blinden mission*, 1921-22. Ginling College: Ginling Association in America, *Newsletter*, 1958; *Ginling College Letter*, 1924, 1927; *Ginling College Magazine*, 1924-26, 1930. *Gleanings*, 1920-21. *Gleanings from South China*, 1906-8. *Glimpses from Central Honan*, 1923. *Gospel in China*, 1884-85. *The Green Year*, 1924-27. *The Green Year Supplement*, 1930-33. *The Green Years*, 1923, 1925, 1927-30. *Hainan News Letter*, 1923-25, 1927, 1930-38, 1948-49. *Have a Heart for China*, 1939-44. *Hinghwa*, 1918-19, 1921-24. Home of the Nazarene (Industrial Orphanage), *Letter*, 1927. *Homes of the East*, 1919. *Honan Messenger*, 1928-32. *Honan Quarterly*, 1932-41. I Fang School, *Newsletter*, 1938. *Information about China*, 1925-26. *Information Letter (LWF Marxism and China Study)*, 1972-. *Information Service* (Church of Christ in China), 1926-27, 1929-40. *Information Service of the Church of Christ in China*, 1946. *Intercessory Missionary*, 1906-7. International Anti-Opium Association, *Bulletin*, 1919-26. *Kina Missionären* (Augustana Synod), 1918-25. *Kina Missionären* (Norske Kinamission), 1923. *Kina och Japan*, n.d. *Kinamisjonaeren*, 1950-51. *Kineseren*, 1901, 1908, 1916, 1918-22, 1927-36. *Kochow Station Bi-monthly*, 1910-16. Kwang Hsüeh Publishing House, *Greetings*, 1935; *Letter*, 1937. Kwangsi Hunan Mission, *Newsletter*, 1911-12, 1919-20. *Lamp of China*, 1893-99. *Land of Sinim*, 1893-1918. *Liber Shanghaiensis*, 1915, 1919. *Liebenzeller Mission*, 1900-41, 1956-. *Lingnaam Agricultural Review*, 1922-26. *Lingnaam: The News Bulletin on Canton Christian College*, 1914, 1925. *Lingnan Journal*, 1930. *Lingnan Science Journal*, 1931. *The Linguist*, 1920-26. *Looking East at India's Women and China's Daughters*, 1881-86, 1888-1895, 1897-1901, 1905-57. *Looseleaves from Missionaries' Diaries*, 1917-21. *Lutheran Orient Mission*, 1915, 1917, 1920-?. *The Messenger*, 1888-96. Methodist Episcopal Church, *Bulletin*, 1896-1915. *The Millions* (London), 1952-64. *The Millions* (Philadelphia), 1952-61. *Missionary*

News Letters from China, 1937-53. *Missionary Recorder*, 1867. *Les Missions de Chine*, 1925, 1931, 1933, 1935-36, 1938-39. *Les Missions de Chine et du Japon*, 1916-17, 1919. *Missions-Bote*, 1892-1900, 1907-8, 1913, 1920-23, 1926-39, 1950-. *Missionsbote*, 1915-30. *Der Missionsbote aus der Deutscher Südsee*, 1908-9. *Missions-Nachrichten aus Yünnan*, 1950-56. *Missionstidningen Sinimsland*, 1946-. *Missionsvennen*, 1904-29, 1940-45. *Mr. Keyte's Bulletin*, 1923-26. *Mitteilungen das Berliner Frauen-Missionsvereins für China*, 1888-94, 1900-1919. *Mitteilungen das Berliner Vereins für Ärztliche mission*, 1908-20, 1924-27. *Nanking Bulletin of Church and Community*, 1922. Nanking Theological Seminary, *Bulletin*, 1939. National Christian Council of China, *Broadcast Bulletin*, 1938-41; *Bulletin*, 1922-37; *News*, 1948-50; *Newsletter*, 1942-44, 1947. National Committee for Christian Religious Education, *English Bulletin*, 1938-39; *Religious Education Fellowship*, 1923-25; *Religious Education Fellowship Bulletin*, 1932-50. Natural History Society, *Proceedings*, 1930. *New China*, 1931. *New East*, 1908-12, 1916, 1918-33. *New Horizons*, 1934-35, 1937-. *New Mandarin*, 1906. *News of China*, 1942-48. *Notes and Notices of the Nanking Union Church and Community*, 1933-34, 1939-41. *Peking News*, 1921-27. *Praise and Prayer*, 1934. *Prayer Cycle*, 1927, 1929-38, 1930-41, 1947-48. *Prayer Cycle and Newsletter for the Christian Missionary Society Chekiang Mission*, 1934. *Prayer Union Letter*, 1883-1917, 1924, 1926. Presbyterian Church in the U.S.A.: Central China Mission, *Quarterly*, 1905-7; Presbyterian Mission of South China, *Yeung Kong Station Bimonthly*, 1904-12. *Princeton-Peking Gazette*, 1925. *Religion in the People's Republic of China*, 1980-. *St. John's Echo*, 1902-19. *St. John's Review*, 1939. St. John's University, *Bulletin*, 1911. Shanghai American School, *Quarterly*, 1922, 1924-25. Shanghai Hebrew Mission, *Quarterly Bulletin*, 1940. *Shanghai Newsletter*, 1944. *Shanghai Young Men*, 1921. *Shansi Echoes*, 1889. *The Sign*, 1924-30. *South China*, 1937-39. *South China Alliance Tidings*, 1908-38. South China Boat Mission, *Bulletin*, 1918-19, 1923. *South China Collegian: An Anglo-Chinese Educational Monthly*, 1904-6. Southern Baptist Convention, Central China Mission, *Quarterly Bulletin*, 1906. Southern Presbyterian Missions in China, *Monthly Messenger*, 1903, 1909-18, 1923, 1925-26. *Tientsin Young Men*, 1905-14. *T'oung pao*, 1890-1921, 1925-26, 1929-34, 1936. *Tripod*, 1982-. *Trois Dix*, 1921. Tsehchow Mission, North, *Half-yearly Circular Letter*, 1924, 1926. *Tung Wu Magazine*, 1935, 1937. University of Nanking, College of Agriculture and Forestry, *Agriculture and Forestry Notes*, 1923-27, 1931-36; *Bulletin*, 1933; *Economic Facts*, 1936-38, 1943-46; *Miscellaneous Bulletin Series*, 1924-25. *University of Nanking Magazine*, 1909-16, 1918-19, 1923-25. University of Nanking, *Occasional Letter*, 1929. *Variétés Sinologiques*, 1893-94, 1922. *Voice*, 1912-13. West China Border Research Society, *Journal*, 1922-45. *West China Messenger*, 1902-8. *West China Missionary News*, 1901-43. *Westminster College Magazine*, 1917-18, 1923, 1925. *Woman's Work in the Far East*, 1877-87, 1890-1900, 1920-21. *The Word for God in Chinese*, 1914-16. *Wuchow Baptist Missioner*, 1920. Yale University: *Yale Alumni Weekly*, 1922; Yale-in-China, *Occasional Bulletin*, 1918-20, 1937-38; *Yali News Bulletin*, 1938-39, 1942-44; *Yali Quarterly*, 1916-38. Yenching University: *Bulletin*, 1921-27, 1929; Department of Sociology and Social Work, *Social Research Series*, 1930; *Yenching Biological News*, 1932; *Yenching Gazette*, 1932; *Yenching Journal*, 1927; *Yenching Journal of Social Studies*, 1938-40, 1948; *Yenching News*, 1931-35, 1938-41, 1944, 1946-47; *Yenta*

Journalism News, 1929, 1931. *Yenping Pagoda Herald*, 1918, 1924–36. *"Yes or No" Echoes*, 1924. *Yi (China Message)*, 1984-. *Young Asia*, 1930, 1949–52. *Young China* (New York), 1924. *Young China* (University of Illinois), 1920, 1924, 1930. Young Women's Christian Association of China: *News Items*, 1916–19; *YWCA Magazine*, 1922–23; *YWCA News*, 1926; *YWCA Outlook*, 1912. *Yung Chun Herald*, 1924, 1927, 1929. *Zhonglian*, 1984-. DISSERTATIONS/THESES: *Die Akkommodationsmethode des P. Matteo Ricci S.I. in China*, by Johannes Bettray, 1955. *American Lutheran Mission Work in China*, by Rolf Syrdal, 1942. *American Missionaries and the Chinese Communists: A Study of Views Expressed by Methodist Episcopal Church Missionaries, 1921–1941*, by Milo Lancaster Thornberry, 1974. *The Anti-Christian Movement in China, 1922–1927; With Special Reference to the Experience of Protestant Missions*, by Ka-che Yip, 1970. *Apostolic Legations to China of the Eighteenth Century*, by Antonio Sisto Rosso, 1948. *Applied Christianity and World Missions*, by Oswald J. Goulter, 1937. *The Background in the Four Books of the Confucian Classics for Chinese Christian Terms*, by Reidar Arnold Daehlin, 1943. *The Beginnings of the Protestant Church in China (1807–1860)*, by Wallace Chun-hsien Wang, 1940. *Changes in the Christian Message for China by Protestant Missionaries*, by Lewis Strong Casey Smythe, 1928. *The China Inland Mission and Some Aspects of Its Work*, by Hudson Taylor Armerding, 1948. *The Chinese Church: A Bridge to World Evangelization*, by Cyrus Onkwok Lam, 1983. *The Chinese Mind and the Missionary Approach*, by George Bell Workman, 1939. *Christian and National Influences in the Development of Modern Chinese Education*, by Katherine B. Hockin, 1947. *The Christian College Confronts Chinese Culture*, by Robert Johnston McMullen, 1936. *Christian Missions in China*, by Charles Sumner Estes, 1895. *Christianity and the New Life Movement in China*, by Christopher Tang, 1941. *A Christian's Inquiry into the Struggle Ethic in the Thought of Mao Tse-tung*, by Raymond Leslie Whitehead, 1972. *The Churches in Fukien: A Study of the Development of the Three Churches in North Fukien, China, and the Prospects of Church Unity*, by Liu Yu-ts'ang, 1950. *The Covenant Missionary Society in China*, by Earl C. Dahlstrom, 1950. *The Development of Indigenous Leadership for Youth Work in China*, by Amber Lurraine Van, 1946. *The Development of Some Significant Phases in Religious Education in China Since 1930*, by Dorothea M. Smith, 1942. *The Development of the Motive of Protestant Missions to China, 1807–1928*, by George Bell Workman, 1928. *The Disciples' Contribution to the Chinese Christian Movement*, by William K. C. Chen, 1930. *An Educational Approach to the Task of the Christian Worker in China*, by Pearle McCain, 1944. *The Emergence of a Protestant Christian Apologetics in the Chinese Church during the Anti-Christian Movement in the 1920s*, by Wing-hung Lam, 1978. *An Examination of Certain Chinese Institutions, Customs, Aesthetic Concepts, and Achievements, With a View to Determining How Far They Could Be Naturalized in the Practice and Teaching of the Christian Church in China*, by J. H. Pratt, 1935. *The Foundations and Growth of Shantung Christian University, 1864–1917*, by William M. Decker, 1948. *The History of Baptist Missions in Hong Kong*, by Paul Yat-keung Wong, 1974. *A History of the Development of the Chinese Indigenous Christian Church under the American Board in Fukien Province*, by Peter Siebert Goertz, 1933. *How Shall the Chinese Church Continue Its Work under the Communist Government?* by Kao Tien-hsi, 1950. *Hsu Kuang-chi: Chinese Scientist and Christian (1562–1633)*, by Joseph King-hap Ku,

1973. *Indigenous Materials in Chinese Christian Worship*, by Mary Ellen Hawk, 1945. *John Leighton Stuart: The Mind and Life of an American Missionary in China, 1876–1941*, by Yu-ming Shaw, 1975. *Joseph Samuel Adams of China: An Original Contribution to the History of Protestant World Missions in the Form of a Biographical Record of the Missionary Career of His Father*, by Archibald Guinness Adams, 1939. *Die katholische Missionmethode in China in neuester Zeit (1884–1912); geschichtliche Untersuchung über Arbeitsweisen, ihre Hindernisse und Erfolge*, by Johannes Beckmann, 1931. *The Life and Work of David Abeel*, by Alvin John Poppen, 1959. *Marcus Ch'eng, Apostle or Apostate? Relations with the Covenant Mission in China*, by O. Theodore Roberg, 1982. *Methods of Developing Native Christian Leadership in China*, by Jesse B. Yaukey, 1930. *The Mission Compound in Modern China: The Role of the United States Protestant Mission as an Asylum in the Civil and International Strife of China, 1900–1941*, by Gladys Robina Quale, 1957. *Missionary Administration in China*, by Edwin Marx, 1926. *The Missionary Factor in Anglo-Chinese Relations, 1891–1900*, by Edmund S. Wehrle, 1962. *The Missouri Evangelical Lutheran Mission in China, 1913–1948*, by Richard Henry Meyer, 1948. *Nestorian Christianity in China*, by Richard Hanson, 1930. *Physical Education in Protestant Christian Colleges and Universities of China*, by K. A. Wee, 1937. *Practical Evangelism: Protestant Missions and the Introduction of Western Civilization into China, 1820–1850*, by Suzanne Wilson Barnett, 1973. *A Project in Adult Religious Education for a Group of Educated Chinese Women*, by Margaret Cook Thomson, 1942. *The Protestant Church in Communist China, 1949–1958*, by James Herbert Kane, 1958. *Protestant Mission Schools for Girls in South China (1827 to the Japanese Invasion)*, by Mary Raleigh Anderson, 1943. *The Protestant Missionary Understanding of the Chinese Situation and the Christian Task from 1890 to 1911*, by C. William Mensendiek, 1958. *Protestant Missions in Communist China*, by Creighton Lacy, 1953. *The Relation of Church and Mission in the North China Mission of the Presbyterian Church in the U.S.A.*, by Wallace Chapman Merwin, 1938. *The Role in National Leadership of the East China Baptist Convention: Otherwise Known as the Chekiang-Shanghai Baptist Convention*, by Charles Ho, 1960. *The Shantung Presbyterian Mission*, by Howell Portman Lair, 1922. *The South Shensi Lutheran Mission*, by Sigurd Aske, 1951. *Suffering in the Experience of the Protestant Church in China: A Chinese Perspective*, by Paul Cheuk-ching Szeto, 1980. *A Survey of American Protestant Foreign Mission Colleges*, by S. P. Hieb, 1925. *Toward an Indigenous Church in China: A Study of Some Aspects of Chinese Protestantism's Concept of the Church, 1910–1950*, by Alden E. Matthews, 1952. *The Use of the Bible with Chinese Christian Youth*, by Florence W. Smith, 1945. *Winning Chinese Youth to Christ*, by Ellen M. Studley, 1956. CHINESE LANGUAGE MATERIALS/MINUTES/RECORDS/REPORTS: Anglo-Chinese College, Foochow, report, 1907; Anking and Fukien Dioceses, records, n.d.; China Medical Missionary Association, Publications Committee, list of medical publications, 1907; Chinese Christian student volunteer movement for church service, constitution, 1941; Literature Promotion Fund Projects, report of writers' conference, 1933; North China Christian Flood Relief Committee, interim reports, 1918, 1920; Yi Ying Boys' School, manuals, catalogues, and yearbooks, 1928–29, 1931, 1934. CHINESE LANGUAGE MATERIALS/SERIALS: *Amoy University Magazine*, 1931–32. *Chiao yü chi k'an (China Christian Edu-*

cational Quarterly), 1925–26, 1928–36. *Chi-tu chiao lun t'an* (*Christian Forum*), 1966–. Chin-ling hsieh ho, *Shen hsüeh chih* (*Nanking Seminary Review*), 1925–50. *Chin-ling hsüeh pao* (*Nanking Journal*), 1931–33. *Chin pu* (*Progress*), 1911–16. *China Bookman*, 1918–37, 1947–51. China Graduate School of Theology, *Bulletin*, 1979–80. *China Mission Yearbook*, 1924. *China's Young Men*, 1902–6, 1910–12, 1915–17. *Chinese Christian Advocate Weekly*, 1906–13. *Chinese Christian Serial Collection* (on microfilm; see Archives above). *Ching Feng*, 1958–. *En yen*, 1957. *Gospel Bell*, 1919, 1922–24, 1927. *Hsüeh shu yüeh pao* (*The Chinese Intercollegian*), 1897–99. *Hua Nien Weekly*, 1932–33. *Hui hsin*, 1949–50. *Hwa mei chiao [kiao] pao* (*Chinese Christian Advocate*), 1906–8. *Ling-nan hsüeh pao* (*Lingnan Journal*), 1929–31. *Lutheran*, 1913. *Tao Feng Christian Journal*, 1953–54. *T'ien Feng*, 1947–60, 1981–. *Tung kung*, 1924–41. *Wen she* (*Literature and Society*), 1925–28. *Yen-ching hsüeh pao* (*Yenching Journal of Chinese Studies*), 1927, 1929. *Yenching Social Sciences*, 1948. *Yüeh pao* (*Child's Paper*), 1890–99. *YWCA Monthly*, 1929, 1931–32, 1934.

CHINESE LANGUAGE MATERIALS: *Chinese Christian Monograph Collection* (on microfilm; see Archives above); *A Classified Index to the Chinese Literature of the Protestant Christian Churches in China*, by the Christian Publishers Association of China, 1933; ca. 25 items, 1887–1960, including Bibles, a bibliography of Chinese literature on agriculture, works on Chinese culture, dictionaries, a hymnal, polemics, translations of the Bible, and anthologies of stories.

YOUNG WOMEN'S CHRISTIAN ASSOCIATION OF AMERICA
NY–280 National Board Archives
726 Broadway
New York NY 10003
(212) 614–2700
Elizabeth Norris, YWCA Historian

Restrictions: Access by appointment.

1-NATIONAL BOARD PHOTOGRAPHS-RECORDS, 1890–1973, ca. 3,000 items
AUDIO-VISUAL MATERIALS: Ca. 3,000 photos taken by the publicity department of the YWCA of activities in China and the Near East, mostly from the 1920s and 1930s.

2-FLORENCE PIERCE PAPERS, 1926–62, quantity undetermined
Background note: Florence Pierce (1891–1974) was the executive secretary of student work in China and Singapore from 1925 to 1937 and from 1946 to 1950.
CORRESPONDENCE: Correspondence concerning the challenge of missionary work, including descriptions of travel through China, YWCA programs there in the 1930s, and the Chinese political situation during 1949 and 1950.
FINDING AIDS: Unpublished guide.

SUBJECT FILES: 1899–1970
Background note: The material on China in the Subject Files is contained on 5 reels of microfilm. Quantities on individual sections of the microfilm are unavailable.
Finding aids: "Inventory to the Record Files Collection of the National Board of the Young Women's Christian Association, 1978."

3-CHINA-AMERICAN STAFF CORRESPONDENCE AND REPORTS, 1907–50, quantity undetermined
MINUTES/RECORDS/REPORTS/CORRESPONDENCE: Reports and correspondence of: C. Adams, 1920; E. Anderson, 1921–33; V. Barger, 1922–29; M. Bagwell, 1929–33; M. Barnes, 1938–39; R. H. Barr, 1930–45; M. Belleville, 1918–19; F. Boss, 1921–23; E. Braden, n.d.; M. Brennecke, 1923–50; D. Brown, 1920–24; R. Brooks, 1921–24; J. Brown, 1925–36; M. Burton, 1922; H. Carter, 1920; B. Conde, 1907; M. Cross, 1923–27; I. Dean, 1925–36; N. Davis, 1920–27; M. Danuser, 1920–33; M. Dudley, 1928–44; E. Derry, 1920–25; E. Durfee, 1917–27; C. Eckert, 1931–33; N. Elliot, n.d.; E. Forbes, 1921–23; R. L. Fraser, 1918–29; W. Galbraith, n.d.; T. Gerlach, 1928–41; S. Glass, 1923–33; A. Grabill, 1920; M. Gill, 1925–30; B. Gleason, 1921–23; L. Haass, 1923–50; M. Hand, 1923; A. Harrison, 1921–26; E. Hartley, 1920–25; E. Hill, 1923; E. Hinder, 1926–32; L. Hinkley, 1921–48; E. Hiss, 1931–34; E. Hoag, 1925–31; A. Holmes, 1923–28; R. Hoople, 1920–28; E. Horjen, 1925; C. Hotchkiss, n.d.; R. Howes, 1920–22; W. Jacob, 1921–23; N. Jervis, 1923–25; M. Job, 1920–29; L. Johnson, 1927–41; E. Johnston, 1920–24; E. Kitchen, 1921–23; M. Klatt, 1921–27; H. Lacy, 1922–33; E. Lerrigo, 1946–47; G. Lowry, 1919–23; L. Lucchini, 1930–32; E. Luce, n.d.; M. Mack, 1920–25; M. MacKinley, 1919–36; C. MacKinnon, 1921–27; E. MacNeil, 1922–26; A. Mayhew, 1919–41; E. McCausey, 1918–24; J. McConnell, 1946; E. Morrison, 1921–24; L. Morrow, 1924–26; S. Most, 1922–25; C. Moyer, 1921; H. Murray, 1921; H. Myers, 1920–36; C. Neely, 1920–28; J. Newell, 1929; M. Owen, 1925–40; R. Packard, 1938–44; R. Parker, 1921–27; F. Pierce, 1927–33; P. Pollock, 1929–42; H. Rietveld, 1920–27; M. Russell, 1917–40; H. Rysdorp, 1920–22; C. Sargent, 1920–21; H. Scott, 1920–23; E. Scribner, 1922–24; E. Sawyer, 1920–25; A. Seescholtz, 1920–24; T. Severin, 1918–29; H. Smith, 1918–28; M. Speidel, 1920–25; A. Starrett, 1920–23; G. Steel-Brooke, 1917–33; G. Steinbeck, 1920–29; M. Streeter, 1923–28; M. Stroh, 1921–25; F. Sutton, 1922–24; N. Swann, 1920–31; H. Thoburn, 1921–32; C. Vance, 1920–31; J. Van Hengel, 1927–38; K. Vaughn, 1920–30; N. Waln, 1921–25; J. Ward, 1920–33; E. Wells, 1920–28; L. Wheeler, 1923; R. White, 1919–25; I. Wikander, 1919–26; E. Williams, 1914–25; F. Williams, 1925; K. Williams, 1920–23; L. Willis, 1920–31; E. Wright, 1920–21.
MINUTES/RECORDS/REPORTS: Reports by Grace Coppock, 1919–21, and a study by R. Dickinson, 1919.

4-CHINA-BACKGROUND HISTORY, 1914–50, quantity undetermined
MINUTES/RECORDS/REPORTS: National annual and interim reports, 1935–44; annual statistical reports, 1924–34; National Committee, annual reports, 1914–31; National constitution and policies, n.d.; National history, n.d.; National Committee, statements, 1949–50; convention reports, 1923, 1928, 1933.

5-CHINA-CORRESPONDENCE WITH NATIONAL GENERAL SECRETARY, 1906–26, quantity undetermined
CORRESPONDENCE: Correspondence with National General Secretaries Grace Coppock, 1906–21; A. Paddock, 1907–13; Shuching Ting, n.d.; Tsai Kwei, n.d.; R. Venable, 1922–26.

6-CHINA-FINANCE, n.d., quantity undetermined
MINUTES/RECORDS/REPORTS: National Committee Finance, n.d.; China Situation-Indemnity, n.d.; Ting Memorial, n.d.

7-CHINA-LEADERSHIP, 1922–50, quantity undetermined
MINUTES/RECORDS/REPORTS: National Committee, and staff, 1922–50; trainees from China, 1950.
CORRESPONDENCE: Correspondents include R. Buckwalter, n.d.; L. Haass, 1933–35; E. Hoag, 1925–28; G. Johnston, n.d.; F. Pierce, 1948; M. McKinley, n.d.; T. Severin, 1924; H. Thoburn, 1925; R. West, 1950.

8-MISCELLANEOUS CORRESPONDENCE, n.d., quantity undetermined
CORRESPONDENCE: Miscellaneous, unidentified correspondence, n.d.

9-CHINA-NANKING LANGUAGE SCHOOL, n.d., quantity undetermined
MINUTES/RECORDS/REPORTS: Nanking Language School, n.d.

10-CHINA-NATIONAL PROGRAM, 1923–50, quantity undetermined
MINUTES/RECORDS/REPORTS: National Committee, program, 1922–23; business and professional program, 1929–48; Girls' clubs, 1922–47; industrial program, 1922–48; pageants-Era Betzner, 1927–31; physical education, 1921–22; publications, 1922–31; religious education, 1923–48; rural program, 1927–43; student program, 1922–50; training program, 1926–40; War Emergency Program: National Committee, 1930, Sino-Japanese situation, 1937–39.

11-CHINA-NORTH CHINA UNION LANGUAGE SCHOOL, 1920–50, quantity undetermined
MINUTES/RECORDS/REPORTS: North China Union Language School, 1920, 1934–50.

12-CHINA-PROPERTY, 1915–44, quantity undetermined
MINUTES/RECORDS/REPORTS: Overall listings, n.d.; Canton property, n.d.; Foochow building, 1915–44; Hangchow-Mukden property, 1925–40; Peking lot, 1931–35; Shanghai building, 1922–36.

13-CHINA-STUDY OF THE YWCA OF CHINA, 1891–1930, quantity undetermined
MINUTES/RECORDS/REPORTS: China section of the *International Survey*, 1891–1930.

14-CHINA-STATUS OF WOMEN, 1939, quantity undetermined
PAMPHLETS: *Study on Status of Women*, n.a., 1939; *New Family Relations in China*, n.a., 1931; *With Centuries Behind It*, by Mrs. E. Barr, n.d.; *Changing Leadership*, by K. Vaughn, 1926; *The New Women of China*, n.a., 1924; *The Women's Rights Movement in China*, n.a., 1922; *Women and the Church*, by R. Cheng, n.a., 1922; *Report on China*, by E. Friedmann, 1920.

15-FOREIGN COUNTRIES-CHINA-MISCELLANEOUS, 1955–59, quantity undetermined
MINUTES/RECORDS/REPORTS: Miscellaneous, unidentified reports on China, 1955–59.

16-STUDENT WORK, 1940–51, quantity undetermined
MINUTES/RECORDS/REPORTS: Reports of the Chinese Student Christian Association, 1940–51.

17-WORLD EMERGENCY, 1940–46, quantity undetermined
MINUTES/RECORDS/REPORTS: YWCA records on its World Emergency Program in China, 1940–46.

18-THE YWCA OF CHINA RECORDS, 1912–52, 6 in.
MINUTES/RECORDS/REPORTS: Annual reports of the National Committee of the YWCA of China, reports on the status of women in China and the progress of the YWCA work there, and surveys of the associations.
CORRESPONDENCE: Correspondence of the American field staff concerning their adjustment to work in China, including travel narratives and descriptions of the life style, cultural habits, and political climate of the country.
PAMPHLETS/MEMORABILIA: Newsletters, posters, pamphlets, and material concerning rural and industrial programs offered by the YWCA.

19-GENERAL HOLDINGS
PAMPHLETS: File drawer of pamphlets, in English and Chinese, published by the National Board, the National YWCA of China, and other church-related organizations, 1890–1950.
SERIALS: *The Green Years*, 1899–1950.

NORTH TARRYTOWN

ROCKEFELLER UNIVERSITY

NY–285 Rockefeller Family Archives
Rockefeller Archive Center
Pocantico Hills
North Tarrytown NY 10591–1598
(914) 631–4505
Darwin H. Stapleton, Director

Background note: The Rockefeller Archive Center is the research repository for the archives of Rockefeller University, the Rockefeller Foundation, the Rockefeller family, related non-profit organizations, and persons associated with their endeavors. Holdings are divided into archives and manuscript collections. The archival materials are of organizations created by Rockefeller philanthropies. Manuscript collections are of individuals connected with Rockefeller activities. Holdings of the Rockefeller Archive Center total 13,000 feet and date from 1877 to the present. Guides to the archive and manuscript collections and photograph collections are available upon request.
Finding aids: *Archives and Manuscripts in the Rockefeller Archive Center* (New York: Rockefeller Archive Center), 1984. *Photograph Collections in the Rockefeller Archive Center* (New York: Rockefeller Archive Center), 1986.

1-OFFICE OF THE MESSRS. ROCKEFELLER—EDUCATIONAL INTERESTS (RG 2), 1912–51, 9 folders
MINUTES/RECORDS/REPORTS: Ca. 1 folder each of records relating to Rockefeller contributions to Canton Christian College, 1920–52; Lingnan University, 1924–29; Shanghai College, 1921–35; United Board for Christian Colleges in China, 1946–61; West China Union University, 1912; and Yenching University, 1921–51.
CORRESPONDENCE: Ca. 1 folder each of correspondence of Canton Christian College, 1920–52; Harvard Medical School, Shanghai, 1910–16; Lingnan University, 1924–29; Shanghai College, 1921–35; United Board for Christian Colleges in China, 1946–61; West China University, 1912; Women's Union Christian Colleges in the Orient, 1927–57; and Yenching University, 1921–51; correspondence with T. B. Appleget, Ernest D. Barton, Kenneth Chorley, F. Trubee Davison, Harry Emerson Fosdick, R. P.

Guesee, James M. Henry, Henry Robinson Luce, Henry Winters Luce, Fred Osborne, John D. Rockefeller, Jr., Henry P. Van Dusen, James Wood, Arthur Woods, and other Rockefeller representatives, concerning Rockefeller funding.
FINDING AIDS: In-house register.

2-OFFICE OF THE MESSRS. ROCKEFELLER—RELIGIOUS INTERESTS (RG 2), 1911-32, 3 folders
CORRESPONDENCE: 1 folder each of correspondence on John D. Rockefeller, Jr.'s pledge to Earl H. Cressy to assist with the Physics Apparatus Fund and to secure Primary School Supervisors for the East China Christian Educational Association, 1924-32; John R. Mott's plan for coordinating and unifying missionary activities, a Rockefeller Foundation pledge to coordinate efforts of missionary agencies, the China Medical Board's pledge to Ernest Burton's survey of education in China, and John D. Rockefeller, Jr.'s pledge to the Committee of Reference and Counsel of Foreign Missions Council of North America, 1911-29; and regarding John D. Rockefeller's support of D. Y. Tsien while a student in New York and subsequently as a social worker at the Yangtsepoo Social Center, 1924-29.

3-OFFICE OF THE MESSRS. ROCKEFELLER—ROCKEFELLER BOARDS COLLECTION—CHINA MEDICAL BOARD PAPERS (RG 2), 1914-61, 4 boxes
MINUTES/RECORDS/REPORTS: China Medical Commission, report to the China Medical Board, 1914; ca. 1 folder each of Peking Union Medical College (PUMC) records, 1916-58, describing acquisition of college, commemorative medal struck by China, progress reports, requests for aid, budgets, policy on appointments, investigation by Minister of Education, disintegrating political and military situation, closing of the college by the Japanese, internment of Americans, the question of creating a new PUMC in free China, descriptions of Japanese treatment of the college, restoration at the end of the war, replacement estimates, claims against the Japanese, refitting, and re-opening; memoranda, 1916-1921, on salaries, reconstruction of college; relations with architects, 1916-18; arrangements of Boards of Trustees of CMB and PUMC, 1934-36; release of those interned by the Japanese, 1942-45; arrangements with missionary boards controlling PUMC, and agreements with the London Missionary Society, 1915; incorporation, lease, and charter of PUMC, 1915-17; tenure of land by foreigners, 1915-26; PUMC reports, 1916-1922, on the CMB in China, Gedney Farms Conference, living conditions in Peking, pre-medical school, and scientific work in schools and colleges of the Nanking-Shanghai region; CMB records on the purchase of PUMC, relations with missionary societies, appropriations, PUMC policy, ca. 1914-1949; history of relations of Rockefeller Foundation, CMB and PUMC, 1936 financial rearrangement, and 1947 termination grant, 1935-47; relation of CMB to Rockefeller Foundation and John D. Rockefeller, III, after nationalization, 1954; relation of PUMC to missionary activities, and the status of the PUMC Department of Social and Religious Work, 1929-47; discussion of Roger Greene's recommendation for aid to mission hospitals in China, 1916-17; contract with St. John's University of Pennsylvania, Harvard School of Medicine, and Nanking Medical School on the creation of Shanghai Medical School, agreement with an architect, abandonment of plan, and disposal of property, 1916-24; program of the medical conference, PUMC, 1921.

CORRESPONDENCE: Folder of correspondence on the incorporation, lease, and charter of PUMC, 1915-17; folder of memoranda on estimates of CMB needs, thoughts on medical missions, and the spirit and teaching of Jesus, scholarships for Chinese nurses, a plan for development of hospitals in China, the conference agreements to form Peking Union Medical College, and memos on missionary work, 1915-21; John D. Rockefeller, Jr.'s letter to missionary boards explaining the CMB, 1915; ca. 1 folder of letters of gratitude from patients treated at PUMC, 1916-58.
MEMORABILIA: Folder of materials relating to retirement dinner for Edwin Lobenstine, 1945; John D. Rockefeller, Jr.'s address at the dedication of Peking Union Medical College, 1921.
MAPS/DESIGNS/DRAWINGS: Map of the Peking Union Medical College campus, 1921.
FINDING AIDS: In-house shelf list.

4-THE ROCKEFELLER FAMILY ARCHIVES—JOHN D. ROCKEFELLER OFFICE CORRESPONDENCE (series C O) (RG 1), 1879-94, 4 folders
CORRESPONDENCE: 1 folder each of correspondence relating to missionary work in China, with Julia Allen, 1892; Thomas Allen, 1880-87; A. H. Burlingham, 1881-94; and Samuel W. Duncan, 1879-94.

5-THE ROCKEFELLER FAMILY FILM COLLECTION, 1921, 1 reel film
AUDIO-VISUAL MATERIALS: "JDR, Jr., 1921-1943" (III 14.1 Fe 60), 1 reel, 16mm., black and white, silent and sound film, documenting John R. Rockefeller's trip to China with the officers of the China Medical Board, Abby Aldrich Rockefeller, and Babs Rockefeller for the 1921 dedication of Peking Union Medical College.
FINDING AIDS: In-house directory.

6-THE ROCKEFELLER FAMILY PHOTOGRAPH COLLECTION—JOHN DAVISON ROCKEFELLER, JR., FAMILY, 1921, 445 items
AUDIO-VISUAL MATERIALS: 206 black and white photos, hand-colored postcards, and 239 lantern slides of the 1921 dedication of Peking Union Medical College, Peking, and environs.

NY-290 Rockefeller Foundation Archives
Rockefeller University
Rockefeller Archive Center
Pocantico Hills
North Tarrytown NY 10591-1598
(914) 631-4505
Claire Collier, Archivist

1-CHINA MEDICAL BOARD COLLECTION, 1917-28, 96 boxes, 4 ledger cases
Background note: A division of the Rockefeller Foundation until its 1928 incorporation as the China Medical Board of New York, Inc., the China Medical Board (CMB) was established in 1914 to improve medical and hospital care in China. As part of this goal, the Board established Peking Union Medical College (PUMC) and made grants to missionary societies to advance their own medical facilities, universities, and hospitals.

SERIES 1.1
MINUTES/RECORDS/REPORTS: Applications, fellowships

and scholarships, 1913–18; appropriations and appointments, 1915–17; records of the China Continuation Committee of the National Missionary Conference in Shanghai, 1915–18; charter and by-laws, 1915–16; committees to China and reports, 1914–17; comptroller's records on PUMC building arrangements, 1915–18; executive committee, meetings, and dockets, 1914–18; hospitals and hospital equipment, 1916–17; medical and pre-medical education, 1912–18; mission hospitals, 1914–17; mission societies, 1914–18; public health, 1914–18; publications, 1917–18; press and publicity, n.d.; records of the resident director of the CMB, including PUMC construction, 1914–18; resident director, reports, n.d.; textbooks, 1914–18; treasurer, 1914–16; trustees, advisory committee, notices, and plans of the North China Union Language School, 1914–16; and work of missionaries, 1915–18.

American Baptist Foreign Mission Society (North), 1914–18; applications, 1915–16; American Board of Commissioners for Foreign Missions, 1914–18; applications, 1914–18; Baptist Missionary Society, London, 1914–16; China Inland Mission, London, 1914–16; China Medical Missionary Association, 1915–17; Christian Association of the University of Pennsylvania: St. John's University of Shanghai, 1914–18; Church Missionary Society, London, 1914–16; applications, 1914; Church of England in Canada, Missionary Society, n.d.; Church of England Zenana Missionary Society, n.d.; Church of Scotland, Foreign Mission Committee, 1915; Foreign Christian Missionary Society (Disciples), 1914–18; applications, 1915–18; Free Methodist Church of North America, 1918; Friends' Foreign Mission Association, London, 1914–15; Friends' Foreign Missionary Society of the Ohio Yearly Meeting, 1915–16; Interdenominational Board of Missionary Preparation, 1915–16; London Missionary Society, 1914–18; applications, 1915–17; Methodist Episcopal Church, American Baptist Church, and Southern Methodist Church, 1914–17; Methodist Episcopal Church, Board of Foreign Missions (North): applications, 1915–18; Methodist Episcopal Church, Board of Missions (South), 1914–18; applications, 1916–17; Methodist Episcopal Church, Women's Foreign Missionary Society (North), 1916; Missionary Society of the Methodist Church, Canada, 1915–18; applications, 1917–18; Presbyterian Church in Canada, Board of Foreign Missions, 1915–16; Presbyterian Church in Ireland, Foreign Mission Committee, 1914–18; Presbyterian Church in the U.S., Board of Foreign Missions (North), 1914–18; applications, 1915–18; Presbyterian Church in the U.S., Executive Committee of Foreign Missions (South), 1915–18; applications, 1915–18; Presbyterian Church of England, Foreign Mission Committee, 1914–18; Protestant Episcopal Church in the U.S., Domestic and Foreign Mission Society, 1914–18; applications, 1916; Reformed Church in America, Board of Foreign Missions, 1914–17; Reformed Church in the U.S., Board of Foreign Missions, 1914; Reformed Church in the U.S., Women's Missionary Society (German), 1915–18; Society for the Propagation of the Gospel in Foreign Parts, 1914–16; Southern Baptist Convention, Foreign Mission Board, 1914–18; applications, 1915; Student Volunteer Movement for Foreign Missions, 1916–17; United Free Church of Scotland, Foreign Mission Committee, 1914–18; Wesleyan Methodist Missionary Association, London, 1915; Yale Medical College and Yale Foreign Missionary Society, 1914–18; applications, 1918.

Records of mission hospitals and colleges: American Advent Mission Society hospital in Chaohsien, 1915–18; American Bap-

tist Church (North) mission hospitals in: Chaochow, 1914; Chaoyang, 1914; Hanyang, 1914; Kiating, 1914; Kinhwa, 1914–16; Kityang, 1914; Ningpo, 1914–16; Shaohsing, 1914–18; Swatow, 1914; Yachow, 1914; American Board mission hospitals: Fenchow, 1914–18; Foochow, 1914–17; Inghok, 1914; Lintsing, 1914–16; Pangchwang, 1914; Peking, 1914; Shaowu, 1914; Taikuhsien, 1914–18; Tehchow, 1915–18; and Tungchow, 1914–18; American Lutheran mission hospital in Kioshan, 1914–17; Boone University Medical School in Wuchang, 1914, 1916–17; Canadian Presbyterian Mission hospitals in Honan, 1915–17; Canton Christian College, Canton Hospital, Canton, 1914–18; China Inland Mission (London) hospitals: Chefoo, 1914; Chinkiang, 1914; Jaochow, 1914; Kaifeng, 1914; Kienchow, 1914; Lanchow, 1914; Pingyangfu, 1914; and Taichow, 1914; Church Missionary Society of London, hospitals in: Foochow, 1914–17; Funing, 1914; Futsing, 1914; Hinghwa, 1914; Hangchow, 1914–18; Kienning, 1914; Kweilin, 1914; Mienchuhsien, 1914–15; Nighteh [Ningteh], 1914; Ningpo, 1915; Pakhoi, 1914; Taichow, 1914–16; and Yunnanfu, 1917; Church of the Brethren Mission hospitals in Liaochou, 1918; and Pingtingchow, 1917–18; Church of England (Society for Propagation of the Gospel) Mission hospitals in: Peking, 1914; Pingtu, 1914; and Yenchowfu, 1914; Church of Scotland, Foreign Mission Committee, mission hospital in Ichang, 1913–16; English Baptist Mission (Baptist Missionary Society of London) hospitals in: Peichen, 1914; Sianfu, 1914–17; Taichow, 1914–15; Taiyuan, 1914–17; Tsingchowfu, 1914–15; and Tsowping, 1914; English Presbyterian (Presbyterian Church of England) Mission hospitals in: Changpu, 1914; Chaochow, 1914–18; Samhopa, 1914; Swahue [Swabue], 1914; Swatow, 1914–18; Tsuenchaufu, 1914; Wukingfu, 1914; and Yungchun, 1916; Foreign Christian Missionary Society (Disciples) hospitals in: Batang, 1917; Luchowfu, 1915–18; and Nantungchow, 1915–18; Foreign Mission Conference of North America, Survey of Higher Christian Education, 1915–18; Friends' Foreign Mission Association, hospitals: Suining, 1914–17; and Tungchwan, 1914; Friends' Foreign Missionary Society of the Ohio Yearly Meeting, hospital in Nanking, 1914–17; Fukien Christian University: Foochow, 1914–18 (Union University); Harvard Medical School of China, Shanghai, 1913–18; Huchow Union Hospital, Huchow, 1914–17; Hupeh Special Medical College, Wuchang, 1914–15; Irish Presbyterian mission hospitals: Chinchowfu, 1914; Fakumen, 1914; Kirin, 1914; Kwanchengtze, 1914; and Sinminfu, 1914; Kuling Medical Missionary Laboratory, Kuling, 1914–15; Kuling Library, Kuling, 1915 (Union); London Missionary Society hospitals: Hangchow, 1914; Hankow, 1914; Hong Kong, 1914; Shantung Road Hospital, Shanghai, 1914; Siaochang, 1916–17; Siaokan, 1914–16; Tientsin, 1917; Tingchow, 1914; Tsangchow, 1914–18; Tsaoshih, 1914; and Wuchang, 1914; Medical Missionary Society of Canton, n.d.; Methodist Church, Canada, Missionary Society, 1915–18; Chengtu, 1918; Methodist Episcopal Church, Women's Foreign Missionary Society hospitals: 1916; North China Union College for Women and Elizabeth Sleeper Davis Memorial Hospital, Peking, 1914–16; Isabella Fisher Hospital, Tientsin, 1914–17; Methodist Episcopal Mission (North) hospitals: Changli, 1914–15; Chengtu, 1914–15; Chinkiang, 1914; Chungking, 1914–16; Foochow (Matthew Magew Memorial Hospital), 1914–15; Foochow (Woolston Memorial Hospital), 1915; Haiteng, 1914; Hinghwa, 1914; Kiukiang, 1914–18; Kutien, 1914–15; Mintsinghsien, 1914–18; Nanchang, 1914–15; Nanking, 1914–17; Ngucheng, 1914–15; Peking, n.d.; Sienyu, 1914–15; Soochow, 1914–18; Tienfu, 1914–15; Wuhu,

1914–18; Yenping, 1914–18; Yungan, 1914; Methodist Episcopal Church (South): Soochow University, 1916–18; Peking University (Union University), Peking, 1914–17; Presbyterian Mission (North) hospitals: Canton, 1914; Changteh, 1914–18; Chefoo, 1914–18; Chenchow, 1914–16; Hengchow, 1914–16; Hwaiyuen, 1914–18; Ichowfu, 1914–16; Kachek, 1914; Kityang, 1914; Kiungchow, 1914; Kochow, 1914; Lienchow, 1914; Nansuchow, 1915–17; Nodoa (Hainan), 1914; Paotingfu, 1914–18; Peking, 1914; Peking, Women's hospital, 1914–15; Shuntefu, 1915–18; Siangtan, 1914–18; Soochow, 1914–16; Tengchow, 1914–15; Tenghsien, 1916; Tsinanfu, 1914–16; Tsining, 1914–16; Tsingtao, 1914; Weihsien, 1914–16; Yeungkong, 1914; Yihsien, 1914–16; Yuyao, 1915; and Yu Yiao, 1914; Presbyterian Mission (North) Training School for Nurses, Nanking, 1914; Presbyterian Mission (South) hospitals: Kashing, 1913–16; Soochow, 1915–16; Protestant Episcopal Church in the U.S. (American Church) mission hospitals: Anking, 1914–18; Shanghai, 1914–18; Wuchang, 1914–18; and Wusih, 1914–16; Reformed Church in America (Dutch) mission hospitals: Amoy, 1914–18, and Siokhe, 1914; Reformed Church in the U.S. (German) mission hospitals: Shenchow, 1914, and Yaochow, 1914–16; Roman Catholic Hospitals: Chumatien, 1914; Hankow, 1914; Kiukiang, 1914; and Laohokow, 1915; School for Blind Chinese Girls (Interdenominational), Moukden, 1914–15; Shanghai American School, 1916–18; Shanghai Baptist College, 1915–18; Shanghai Medical School, Harvard proposals and statistics, n.d.; Shantung Christian University, Union Medical College, Tsinan, 1914–18; Southern Baptist Convention mission hospitals: Chengchow, 1914–18; Hwangsien, 1914–18; Laichow, 1914–15; Liaoyang, 1915–16; Pingtu, 1914–16; Wuchow, 1914–17; Yangchow, 1915–18; and Yingtak, 1914; Tsing Hua College (YMCA), Peking, 1914–17; Tung Wah Hospital, Hong Kong, 1914; United Brethren Hospital (Foreign Missionary Society), Siulan, 1917; Union College, Ningpo, 1916; Union Medical College, Peking, 1914–18; Union Medical College and Hospital, Hankow, 1914; United Free Church of Scotland Mission hospitals: Ashiho, 1914; Chaoyangchen, 1914; Hulan, 1914–15; Ichang, 1913–16; Kaiyuan, 1914; Liaoyang, 1914; Moukden, 1914–18; Tiehling, 1914; and Yungling, 1914; University of Nanking: Nanking (Union University), 1914–18; statistics and reports, n.d.; Wesleyan Methodist Mission (London) hospitals: Anlu, 1914; Fatshan, 1914; Hankow, 1914; Pingkiang, 1914; Shiuchow, 1914; Tayeh, 1914; Teian, 1914; Wuchang, 1914; Wuchow, 1914; and Yungchow, 1914; Women's Union Mission hospital, Shanghai, 1914–18; Zangzok Dispensary, Zangzok, 1914.

CORRESPONDENCE: Correspondence, 1914–18, with John T. Anderson, T. W. Ayres, G. J. P. Barger, James L. Barton, Robert Beebe, Lloyd R. Boutwell, H. A. Boyd, John G. B. Branch, Arthur J. Brown, Nathan W. Brown, Wallace Buttrick, Jo Carr, S. H. Chester, Thomas Cochrane, Charles A. Coolidge, Stephen Corey, Douglas T. Davidson, Martha Davis, John R. Dickson, A. M. Dunlap, Nancy Smith Farmer, Simon Flexner, J. H. Franklin, Hanna Marie Fritzen, Helen R. Gage, Nina Gage, Frank D. Gamewell, James M. Gaston, Frederick Gates, Frank P. Gaunt, R. McLean Gibson, Frank J. Goodnow, J. S. Grant, Roger Greene, George B. Hantington, F. H. Hawkins, C. Judson Herrick, Walter G. Hiltner, N. S. Hopkins, Edward H. Hume, Allen C. Hutchinson, Mary L. James, E. M. Johnstone, George Heber Jones, Harry Pratt Judson, John H. Korns, Phyllis Kurtz, Claude M. Lee, Charles B. Lesher, Charles Lewis, Stephen C. Lewis, Charles S. Lincoln, Mr. and Mrs. Oliver T. Logan, O. Houghton Love,

George D. Lowry, P. L. McAll, Grace McBride, Franklin C. McLean, D. Duncan Main, Mabel Manderson, Fred P. Manget, Amy A. Metcalf, Lee M. Miles, R. Fletcher Moorshead, John R. Mott, Starr Murphy, O. G. Nelson, Frank Mason North, Elliott I. Osgood, W. H. Park, Francis W. Peabody, Ethel Polk, Jeanette Price, T. B. Ray, Paul Reinsch, Emma Robbins, Lillian D. Robinson, Wickliffe Rose, Marie Rustin, E. C. Sage, Florence Sayles, William M. Schultz, Charles W. Service, J. E. Skinner, John A. Snell, Robert E. Speer, Thornton Stearns, Mary Stone, William E. Strong, Harry B. Taylor, R. V. Taylor, Joseph O. Thompson, C. E. Tompkins, George T. Tootell, Francis F. Tucker, J. G. Vaughan, Paul Wakefield, William Welch, Stanley White, Amos P. Wilder, James W. Williams, James W. Wiltsie, Andrew H. Woods, John H. Wylie, and Mason P. Young.

SERIES 1.2

MINUTES/RECORDS/REPORTS: Records of CMB interaction with: American Advent Mission Society, 1919; American Advent Mission Hospital, Chaohsien, 1919; American Baptist Foreign Mission Society records on the political situation, labor contracts and unions, and a general strike, 1919–28; American Baptist Mission Hospitals: Ningpo, 1919–28; Shaohsing, 1919–28; Siufu, 1919–21; Swatow, 1925; and Yachow, 1919–23; Shanghai College, 1919–28; American Bible Society, 1927; American Board of Commissioners for Foreign Missions (2 folders), 1919–28; American Board Mission Hospitals: Fenchow, 1920–28; Foochow, 1925; Taikuhsien, 1919–24; Tehchow, 1919–26; and Tungchow, 1919–28; American Minister, 1922–25; Amherst College, 1925; Amoy University, 1923–28; Antioch College, 1922–26; Architectural Service Bureau (service to missionary organizations), 1918–28; Association for the Welfare of Children in China, 1928; Augustana Hospital, 1921–24; Southern Baptist Convention, 1919–28; Baptist Mission Hospitals (South): Chengchow, 1921–25; Hwangsien, 1920–28; Kaifeng, 1922–23; Laichowfu, 1920–25; Pingtu, 1921–23; Wuchow, 1919–25; and Yangchow, 1919–28; Baptist Missionary Society (English), 1920–25; Baptist Mission Hospitals (English): Chowtsun, 1922; Sianfu, 1921–25; and Taiyuanfu, 1920–24; Belgian Mission Institute, 1926; Beloit College, 1927; Benedictine Medical School, 1925; Board of Missionary Preparation, 1919; Boston University, 1922–24; British Charitable Hospital, 1921–26; Brown University, 1925; Canadian Methodist Mission, 1925; Canton Christian College, papers relating to the political situation, labor problems, boycott, and anti-Christian movement, 1919–26; Canton Hospital, hospital policy and hookworm, 1919–28; Carlton College, 1922–24; Catholic Church, 1921; Catholic Hospital Association, 1925; Central China University, 1923–27; China Society, YWCA, and factories of Shanghai, records on child labor, 1925; China Continuation Committee, 1919–20; China Christian Educational Association, 1919–28; China Inland Mission, 1921–26; China International Famine Policy Commission, 1922–27; China Medical Association, 1927–28; China Medical Board, 1920–23; China Medical Boat Fund, 1924–26; China Medical Missionary Association, medical literature and translations, 1919–26; China Union University, n.d.; Chinese Christian Education Association, 1926; Chinese Christian Union, 1925–26; Chinese Medical Students, 1920; Chinese Students Aid, 1927; Chinese Students Alliance, 1919–26; Chinese Students Christian Alliance, 1927; Chinese Students Club, 1924; Christian Colleges in China, 1923; Christian Education, 1923–29; Christian Reformed Church of America, 1920; Chung Hwa University, 1924–25; Chung Shan

University, 1927; Church of the Brethren, 1919–25; Church of the Brethren Mission Hospital, Pingtingchow, 1919–24; Church Missionary Society, 1922; Church of Scotland, 1920; Church of Scotland Mission Hospital, Ichang, 1919–28; Committee on Christian Education in China, 1920–21; Committee on Reference and Counsel of the Foreign Mission Conference of North America, 1919–28; Cooperation Among Missions, 1921; Cooperative Campaign Work, 1927; Copp Hospital, 1922; Cornell Clinic, 1922–26; Cornell College, 1923; Cornell University, 1920–28; Daily Vacation Bible Schools, 1922; Duke University, 1927; East China Christian Educational Association, 1923–28; education and educational institutions in China, 1919–28; Ensworth Methodist Hospital, 1922; Evangelical Lutheran Augustana Synod, 1922–24; records of exchange rates, exchange, and agreements with mission boards, 1918–26; famine relief, 1920–28; Federal Council of Churches, 1920–28; Fifth Avenue Presbyterian Church, 1921; Foreign Christian Missionary Society in Luchowfu and Nantungchow, 1919–23; Foreign Missions Conference, n.d.; Fordham University, 1920; Ginling College, 1919–28; Greater New York Federation of Churches, 1927; Grinnell College, 1923–24; Hackett Medical School, 1919–23; Hall Trust Fund, 1925–26; Hangchow Hospital, records relating to local events and political situation, 1919–27; Hankow Health Bureau, 1927; Hankow Hospital Union, 1926; Harbin Medical Society, 1921; Harkness Fund, 1927; Hartford Hospital, 1920–25; Harvard University, 1917–27; Hsin Kai Lu Hospital, 1922; Hsiang Shan Children's Home, 1925; Hsiang-Ya Medical College, records relating to provincial authority, student unrest, and the political situation, 1926–28; Huchow Union Hospital, 1919–28; Hupei Provincial Medical School, 1926; Infant's Hospital, 1922; Insane Asylum, Chulan, 1927–28; Institute of Social and Religious Research, 1924–25; Interchurch World Movement, 1920; International Association of Agricultural Missions, 1920; International Famine Relief Commission, 1923; International Institute of China, 1920–27; International Missionary Council, records relating to Christian education, anti-Christian feeling, Chinese education, tropical hygiene, indemnity funds, opium, and the political situation, 1924–28; Isolation Hospital, 1922; Johns Hopkins University, 1919–27; Joint Committee of Women's Colleges in the Orient, 1925; Kuling American School, 1926; Kuling Medical Missionary Association, 1922; Lehigh University, 1924; Library of the International Missionary Council, 1926; Lingnan University, 1927–28; London Missionary Society, 1919–27; London Mission hospitals: Hankow, 1927; Siaochang, 1919–28; Tientsin, 1919–24; and Tsangchow, 1919–27; Loyola University, 1922; Lying-in Hospital, 1919–23; Manchurian Medical College, 1925; Mass Education Movement, 1927–28; Maternity Hospital, Peking, 1925; Mayo Clinic (medical missionary training), 1920–23; McGill University, 1921–28; Methodist Episcopal Church, North, records relating to Christianity and religion, 1919–28; Methodist Episcopal Church, North: mission hospitals: Chinkiang, 1923–27; Eastern Asia, 1922–23; Foochow, 1921–27; Hinghwa, 1921–23; Kiukiang (Women's Foreign Missionary Society), 1915–25; Kutien, 1921–22; Nanchang, 1921–28; Dentistry School at Peking, 1919–27; Taianfu, 1921–25; Wuhu, 1919–28; and Yenping, 1919–25; Fukien Christian University, records relating to Union University, the political situation, religion, and student unrest, 1920–28; Tongshan Anglo-Christian College, 1920; Methodist Episcopal Church, Women's Foreign Missionary Society, 1924–27; Methodist Episcopal Women's Hospital, records relating to Sleeper Davis Hospital, 1917–27; Methodist Episcopal Women's Hospital, Tientsin, 1919–25; Methodist Episcopal Church, South, records relating to x-rays, transmission of funds, and real estate, 1919–28; Methodist Episcopal Church, South, mission hospital: Changchow, 1921–25; Soochow, records relating to the political situation, tapeworm, x-rays, buildings, and hookworm, 1919–26; Methodist Episcopal Church, South, Soochow University, 1922–28; Methodist Episcopal Church, Canada, 1919–28; Methodist Episcopal Church, Canada, mission hospitals: Chengtu, 1920–28; Chungchow, 1920–21; Chungking, 1921–23; and Tseliutsing, 1921–25; mission hospitals, 1916–26; Mission to Lepers, 1919–24; missions, 1923; mission colleges, 1922–23; Mokwang Home, 1919–20; Moukden Northeastern University, 1924–28; Mount Holyoke College, 1922; Mount Sinai Hospital, 1919–27; Museum of Comparative Zoology (Harvard University), 1925; Nankai College, records relating to student unrest, political situation, endowments, and gas plant, 1922–28; Nanking University Hospital, 1922; Nanyang College, 1923–27; National Christian Council, 1923–27; National Medical Missionary Association, 1922–25; National Student Council of the Episcopal Church, 1925; National Women's Christian Temperance Union, 1922; North China American School, 1922; North China Medical School for Women, 1922–23; North China Union Language School, 1919–24; Norwegian Lutheran Church of America, 1922–23; Norwegian Mission Hospitals: Kalgan, 1927; Kwangchow, 1922–25; and Yiyang, 1919–25; Ohio Wesleyan University, 1925; Pao Lee Hospital, 1919–25; Pennsylvania State College, 1924; Peking American School, 1920–27; CMB Peking office, records relating to Peking Union Medical College, finances, medicine, and politics, 1927–28; Peking Union Church, 1921–23; Peking Union Medical College, records relating to construction, advisory committee, carbon dioxide plant, charter, gas plant, thermostatic control, hygiene, insurance, pension, neurology, power plant, property, purchasing agent, refinite plant, refrigeration, religion, staff, water softener, water supply system, 1918–28; Peking University, records relating to Union University, political situation, buildings, curriculum, and staff, 1919–25; Peking Women's University, 1925; Peter Bent Brigham Hospital, 1919–27; records relating to the political situation, including relief for the wounded, anti-foreignism and anti-Christian agitation, student unrest and demonstration, student union, labor unrest, industrial disputes and strikes, racial animosity, banditry, tariff, and Chinese political factions, 1924–27; Presbyterian Church in the U.S.A., records relating to the political situation, famine relief, and exchange, 1919–28; Presbyterian Church in the U.S.A., North, mission hospitals: Changteh, 1919–28; Chefoo, 1919–28; Hengchow, 1919; Hwaiyuen, 1919–28; Kachek, 1919–27; J. G. Kerr Hospital, 1927; Korea, 1922–23; Paotingfu, 1919–28; Peking, 1920–28; Shuntefu, 1919–28; Weihsien, 1922–26; and Yihsien, 1920–25; Presbyterian Church, Shantung Christian University, records relating to Union University, political situation, endowment, student unrest, Boxer indemnity, food research, and merger, 1919–28; Presbyterian Church in the United States, South, 1919–27; Presbyterian Church in the United States, South, mission hospitals: Kashing, 1919–25; Soochow, 1920–26; Taichow, 1922–28; and Tsingkiangpu, 1920–27; Presbyterian Church, Canada, 1920–25; Presbyterian Church, Canada, mission hospitals: Changte chow, 1920–23; Hwaikingfu, 1922–27; Kai Kwong, 1925; Lungching tsun, 1921–27; and Weihwei, 1923–24; Presbyterian Church, England, 1924; Presbyterian Church, England, mission hospitals: Chuanchowfu, 1919–20; Swatow, 1919–25; and Wukingfu, 1923;

Presbyterian Hospital, 1924–26; records relating to pre-medical education, fellowships and policy, university pre-medical programs, summer institutes and science teaching, medical and scientific journals, visiting professors, Peking Union Medical College, political situation, indemnity fund, anti-Christian feeling, student and labor unrest, mission schools, educational standards and requirements, 1921–28; Princeton-in-Peking, 1922–27; Protestant Episcopal Church, 1919–28; Protestant Episcopal Church-St. John's University on political situation, student unrest, indemnity funds, and exchange, 1919–28; Protestant Episcopal Mission hospitals: Anking, 1924–27; Pakhoi, 1919–20; Shanghai, 1919–28; Wuchang, 1919–28; and Yunnanfu, 1919–20; Reformed Church in America, 1919–27; Reformed Church Mission Hospitals: Amoy, 1923–27; Shenchowfu, 1919–20; and Siokhe, 1921–25; Reformed Presbyterian Church, 1922; records of the resident director relating to the political situation, education, CMB administration and general policy, fellowships, PUMC property and construction, indemnity funds, mission hospitals, summer institute, Sino-Japanese relations, Pan-Pacific Congress, public health, research, immigration, foreign policy, exchange, famine relief, and narcotics, 1919–27; Seventh-Day Adventist Mission, 1922–27; Shanghai American School, 1919–25; Shanghai Medical School, 1919–26; Shanghai Union Medical College, 1927–28; Shanghai Union Medical College for Women, 1919–27; Shantung Road Hospital, 1925; Smith College, 1924; Society for the Propagation of the Gospel in Foreign Parts, 1924–26; Stone and Webster, records relating to PUMC construction, 1925–28; Student Relief Fund Committee, 1927; Student Volunteer Movement for Foreign Missions, 1921–28; Tooker Memorial Hospital, 1926–28; Tungchow, North China American School, 1922–26; Union College, 1922–27; Union Theological Seminary, 1925; United Brethren in Christ, 1920–24; United Brethren Mission Hospital, Siu Lam, 1923; United Christian Missionary Society, 1923–28; United Christian Mission hospitals: Luchowfu, 1920–28; Nantungchow, records relating to the political situation, X-ray, and fellowships, 1920–28; United Church of Canada, 1926–28; United Evangelical Lutheran Church, 1921–23; United Evangelical Missions Hospital, Leling, 1920–22; United Free Church of Scotland, 1925–26; United Free Church of Scotland Mission hospital: Hulan, 1921–22, and Moukden, 1919–27; United Lutheran Mission, Sinyangchow, 1926; Université l'Aurore, 1923–26; University of Nanking, records relating to the political situation, Boxer indemnity, anti-foreign feeling, pre-medical education, agricultural college, visiting professors, buildings, exchange, fellowships, science education, and the China Famine Fund, 1919–28; University of Nanking Hospital, records relating to the political situation, 1923–28; Vanderbilt in China, 1920; Wesley College, 1927; Wesleyan Mission Hospital, 1927; West China Union University, records relating to the political situation, fellowships, and translations, 1919–28; Women's American Baptist Foreign Missionary Society, 1920; Women's Christian College in the Orient, 1923; Woman's Hospital, 1919; Women's Medical College of Pennsylvania, 1919–25; Women's Union Christian Colleges, 1921; Yale Club, 1919–22; Yale Missionary Society, 1919–28; Yale Missionary Society/Hunan-Yale, records relating to the political situation, strikes, student unrest, pre-medical school and education, Chinese/American control of education, fellowships, indemnity, union universities, missionary societies, famine, buildings and equipment, 1918–26; Yale Missionary Society-Hunan Yale, Changsha, 1923–24; Yale Missionary Society, Wuhan, 1924; Yale University, 1919–28; Yenching School

of Chinese Studies, 1926–28; Yenching University, records relating to buildings, fellowships, immigration, and the political situation, 1926–28; Young Men's Christian Association, 1919–29; Young Women's Christian Association, 1921–25.

Series II, 5 boxes of accounts and financial records, 1915–30; Series III, Rockefeller Foundation Annual Reports and Minutes, containing minutes, 1916–28, and annual reports, 1913–26, of the China Medical Board and Peking Union Medical College.

MINUTES/RECORDS/REPORTS/MEMORABILIA: Folder of cable codes, 1921–24; ca. 1 folder each of various documents on China, 1926–27; Hangchow Hospital, 1919–27; and Putsi Hospital, 1922–25.

CORRESPONDENCE: Correspondence, 1919–28, of John Agar, Lucy Aldrich, Pastor Busch, Wallace Buttrick, Frank Cartwright, S. C. Chin, James J. Corbett, E. J. M. Dickson, Edwin R. Embree, Feng Yu-hsiang, J. Y. Ferguson, Galen Fisher, Mrs. Harold Fisher, Simon Flexner, Frederick T. Gates, L. C. Goodrich, John B. Grant, Roger Greene, John D. Hayes, Ruth Hemenway, L. J. Henderson, H. H. Johnson, Harry Pratt Judson, Wellington Koo, M. Laurentine, Stephen C. Lewis, P. K. Liang, John R. Mott, L. G. Myers, E. I. Osgood, Theodore H. Price, S. O. Pruitt, Paul Reinsch, Alfred Sao-Ke Sze, George E. Vincent, and William Welch; 6 folders of cables, 1919–28.

SERIALS: *China Medical Journal*, 1919–26. *China Mission Yearbook*, 1919.

CHINESE LANGUAGE MATERIALS: Folder of translated medical books, 1919–27.

FINDING AIDS: "The Archives of the China Medical Board and the Peking Union Medical College at the Rockefeller Archive Center: Some Sources on the Transfer of Western Science, Medicine, and Technology to China during the Republican Period," by Thomas Rosenbaum, 1987; in-house directory.

2-THE ROCKEFELLER FOUNDATION PHOTOGRAPH COLLECTION, Series 600 (Asia), Series 601 (China), 1909–50, 2,058 items

AUDIO-VISUAL MATERIALS: Series 600 (Asia), containing 132 photos to accompany Frederick T. Gates' 1909 report by the University of Chicago Educational Commission's Report to the Rockefeller Foundation on the state of education in the Far East, including Chinese society and culture, existing western schools, and scenic views of China; Series 601 (China), containing 1,926 photos of western medical schools in China, including American Presbyterian Mission Hospital, Boone Library School, Fukien Christian University, Methodist Episcopal Mission Hospital, Mokwang Home for Blind Girls Baptist Mission, Oberlin Shansi Memorial School, Peking Union Medical College, St. John's University, Shantung Christian University Medical School, University of Nanking, West China Union University, Yale-in-China, Yale Medical College, and Yenching University, showing buildings, students, faculty, and facilities; Mass Education Movement, National Flood Relief Commission, the Japanese invasion in the 1930s, student protests at Tsing-Hua University in the 1940s, and Chinese society and culture.

FINDING AIDS: In-house directory.

3-THE ROCKEFELLER FOUNDATION FILM COLLECTION, 1920–33, 6 reels motion picture film

AUDIO-VISUAL MATERIALS: "Peking and Its Environs," (II 50.6 Fb 4–6), scenes of Peking, 1920; "Eight Month Experiment," (II 50.6 Fb 7–9), of Peiping Psychopathic Hospital, 1933.

NY-295 Manuscript Collections

Rockefeller University
Rockefeller Archive Center
Pocantico Hills
North Tarrytown NY 10591–1598
(914) 631–4505

1-CONRAD W. ANNER COLLECTION, 1918–19, 2 folders, 1,402 items

Background note: Conrad W. Anner (1889–1960), an architect, was a draughtsman and supervisor of architectural work at Peking Union Medical College from 1919 to 1930.
MINUTES/RECORDS/REPORTS/CORRESPONDENCE: Folder of correspondence regarding Anner's employment at Peking Union Medical College; folder of reports, including "Programme of the Medical Conference, Peking Union Medical College, September 15–22, 1921," "Peking Union Medical College-Historical Sketch and Description of Buildings," 1922, and a report, "Specifications from the City of Peking to the Committee of Construction for the Peking National Library," n.d.
AUDIO-VISUAL MATERIALS: (Photograph Collection 1050) 1,402 photos, tinted lantern slides, and glass negatives documenting Anner's work at PUMC and his travels through China and Thailand, including architectural drawings of PUMC, building construction, western and Chinese construction workers, views of the campus, and the dedication of PUMC in 1921; views of Peking, people, including officials, workers, monks, peasants, merchants, and the countryside; drawings of the Old Summer Palace and photos of its ruins; aerial photos of an unidentified temple and city.
CHINESE LANGUAGE MATERIALS: "Peking National Library Building Construction Committee, Construction Bidding Handbook," 1928, and outline translation by David Kamen, 1987.
FINDING AIDS: In-house directory.

2-CLAUDE H. BARLOW PAPERS, 1919–28, ca. 1.5 boxes

Background note: A medical doctor and staff member of the International Health Division of the Rockefeller Foundation, Claude H. Barlow (1876–1968) was a medical missionary to China from 1908 to 1928 with the American Baptist Foreign Mission Society, during which time he was a surgeon and hospital supervisor in Shaohsing.
MINUTES/RECORDS/REPORTS: Peking Union Medical College, reports, 1927.
CORRESPONDENCE: Ca. 1 box of correspondence, 1919–28.
MAPS/DESIGNS/DRAWINGS: 2 maps concerning fluke in Chekiang Province, ca. 1928.
AUDIO-VISUAL MATERIALS: (Photograph Collection 1053) Ca. 25 photos of the China Fluke Study and portraits of Barlow with co-workers, ca. 1928.
MEMORABILIA: 3 undated articles by Barlow on medical problems in China: "Bilharzia Work in China," "Life Cycle of Fasciolopsis Buski (Human) in China," and "A Preliminary Note on the Life History of Clonorchis Sinensis in Chekiang Province, China."
FINDING AIDS: In-house directory.

3-WALLACE BUTTRICK PAPERS, ca. 1914–1917, ca. 1 folder

Background note: For biographical notes, see University of North Carolina at Chapel Hill, Southern Historical Collection, Wilson Library, Chapel Hill, NC, 27514–6080.
MINUTES/RECORDS/REPORTS: Summaries of Wallace Buttrick's activities with the China Medical Board, ca. 1914–1917.
FINDING AIDS: In-house directory.

4-CHINA MEDICAL BOARD OF NEW YORK, INC., COLLECTION, 1914–57, ca. 15 folders, 2,990 items

Background note: Incorporated from the China Medical Board in 1928, the China Medical Board of New York, Inc., made grants to missionary societies to advance their own medical facilities, universities, and hospitals.
MINUTES/RECORDS/REPORTS/CORRESPONDENCE: Ca. 1 folder each of material on the American Board of Missionary Hospitals, 1923; Canadian Mission Hospital, 1944; Christian Medical Association of India, 1931, 1934; Christian Medical Council for Overseas Work, 1939, 1946–51; Evangelical Lutheran Augustana Synod, 1934; Foreign Missions Conference of North America, 1929–30, 1945; London Missionary Society, 1915–54; Medical Missionary Association (London), 1915–26, 1935; Methodist Mission Hospital, Hunan and Ling-ling, 1943; Missionary Research Library, 1957; Shantung Christian University, 1931; Society for the Propagation of the Gospel in Foreign Parts, 1924–29, 1944; United Board for Christian Colleges in China, 1948–50; Young Men's Christian Association, 1946.

2 folders each of material, 1921–41, on American Baptist Foreign Missionary Society, American Board of Commissioners for Foreign Missions, Baptist Mission Society, China Inland Mission, Church Missionary Society, Church of the Brethren, Methodist Church (Canada), Methodist Episcopal Church, Presbyterian Church, Presbyterian Church of England, Protestant Episcopal Church, Reformed Church in America, Student Volunteer Movement for Foreign Missions, United Christian Missionary Society, United Evangelical Lutheran Church of America, United Free Church of Scotland, Wesleyan Methodist Missionary Society, and Women's Union Mission Society of America.
AUDIO-VISUAL MATERIALS: (Photograph Collection 1048) 2,990 photos, negatives, lantern slides, albums, and hand-colored postcards and prints, 1917–46, of PUMC, its construction, interior and exterior views of buildings, laboratories, wards, dispensaries, staff, staff quarters, students, classes, the Ying Compound, the Yu Wang Fu property, and Sun Yat-sen's funeral, albums of the National Flood Relief Commission's camp hospital, a Central Field Health Station, its public health classes and malaria control work, the City Psychopathic Hospital in Peking, and a Red Cross North China Field Hospital, showing patients, facilities, the Chinese army, and destruction by Japanese bombers.
FINDING AIDS: In-house directory.

5-ALFRED E. COHN PAPERS (RG 450 C661-U), 1927–53, 18 folders

Background note: A member of the China Medical Board of the Rockefeller Foundation, Alfred E. Cohn was a visiting professor at Peking Union Medical College in 1925.
MINUTES/RECORDS/REPORTS: China Medical Board/Peking Union Medical College (CMB/PUMC), 10 folders of amendments, annual reports, budget proposals, by-laws, financial reports, meeting dockets, minutes, and special accountant's reports, ca. 1940–53; Yu Wang Fu Association of the CMB/PUMC, 3 folders of address lists, 1927–53.
CORRESPONDENCE: 4 folders of Edwin Carlyle Lobenstine's correspondence concerning PUMC and the CMB, 1940–45; folder of Agnes M. Pearce's correspondence, 1940–51; folder of corre-

spondence relating to the Yu Wang Fu Association of the CMB/PUMC, ca. 1927–1951.
FINDING AIDS: In-house directory.

6-DAVISON FUND, INC., COLLECTION (II), ca. 1930s, 6 folders
MINUTES/RECORDS/REPORTS: 1 folder each of records of organizations to which the Davison Fund, Inc., made appropriations: American Baptist Foreign Mission Society Group Study of Jesus project at West China Union University, National Christian Council of China, and University of Nanking, College of Agriculture; American Bureau for Medical Aid to China, Inc.; Associated Boards for Christian Colleges in China; China Christian Broadcasting Association; Church Committee for China Relief; College of Chinese Studies; Congregational Projects: Foochow Union High School and Paoting Expanding Station Program-Hopei Province; Council on Medical Missions of the Chinese Medical Association; Lingnan University; Methodist Episcopal Church Board of Foreign Missions: Foochow Union High School; National Committee on Christian Religious Education; Women's American Baptist Foreign Mission Society: Mothercraft Work in China; YWCA, International Women's Service Building, Shanghai.

1 folder each of records of organizations to which the Davison Fund, Inc., declined to make appropriations: Church of Christ in China, Institution for the Chinese Blind, Lingnan University, Nanking Theological Seminary, Shanghai American School, and Union Theological Seminary, Foochow.
CHINESE LANGUAGE MATERIALS: Folder of records of Ting Li-ch'eng, of the American Baptist Foreign Mission Society, to which the Davison Fund, Inc., appropriated funds.
FINDING AIDS: In-house directory.

7-MARY E. FERGUSON PAPERS, 1891–1975, 3 c.f., 25 items
Background note: Mary E. Ferguson was registrar (1928–50), assistant secretary (1930, 1932), and secretary (1933–41, 1944–50) of the Peking Union Medical College; associate executive secretary (1950–60) of the United Boards for Christian Higher Education in China, and author of *China Medical Board and Peking Union Medical College*, 1970.
CORRESPONDENCE/MANUSCRIPTS: Notes, chapter drafts, and other material relating to the writing and publication of *China Medical Board and Peking Union Medical College* in 1970; correspondence with Raymond Fosdick, Harold H. Loucks, and Henry S. Houghton, and others relating to the publication of *China Medical Board and Peking Union Medical College*, n.d.
ORAL HISTORIES: 3 audio tapes of interviews with people connected with the China Medical Board and PUMC, Albert Dunlap, Paul Hodges, Henry S. Houghton, Stanley Wilson, and Anna D. Wolf, n.d.
AUDIO-VISUAL MATERIALS: (Photograph Collection 1046) 25 photos of PUMC, staff, health classes, nursing graduates, portraits of staff members, including Gertrude Hodgeman, C. Sidney Burwell, John R. Mott, and Anna D. Wolf, and the first health station in Peking, 1933.
FINDING AIDS: In-house directory.

8-SIMON FLEXNER PAPERS, 1914–22, quantity undetermined
Background note: For biographical notes, see the American Philosophical Society, Library, 105 South Fifth Street, Philadelphia, PA, 19106 (which holds the originals of the items in this microfilmed collection). The section in his papers on the China Medical

Board supplements the China Medical Board Collection listed above.
MINUTES/RECORDS/REPORTS: Documents relating to the China Medical Board: annual report including history and administration, 1918–19; proposed fellowships for nurses and paramedical staff at missionary hospitals, and aid to Chinese institutions, 1915; report on proposed establishment of medical school at Shanghai; 2 preliminary reports on the plans for and building of Peking Union Medical College (PUMC); election of trustees Simon Flexner, Frederick T. Gates, Wallace Buttrick, William H. Welch, John D. Rockefeller, Jerome Greene, and one representative of each missionary society; curricula vitae of physicians and nurses at PUMC, 1914; PUMC budgets, 1914, 1920–21; recommendation for a preparatory school for PUMC, 1917; report to trustees of Rockefeller Foundation, 1921–22; minutes of Rockefeller Foundation Executive Committee meetings; report of 1915 Special Commission to China on medical education in China, 1920; report on medical education in northern China, by William Welch, 1915; report on medical education in Hankow and Changsha, by Frederick Gates, 1915; report on medical education in southern China, by Simon Flexner, 1915; report on medical education of Chinese women, by Simon Flexner, n.d.
CORRESPONDENCE: Letters from Simon Flexner in Peking, 1915.
MAPS/DESIGNS/DRAWINGS: Blueprint of PUMC and surrounding properties.
FINDING AIDS: *Guide to the Archives and Manuscripts of the American Philosophical Society*, comp. by Whitfield J. Bell, Jr., and Murphy D. Smith (Philadelphia, 1966).

9-FREDERICK T. GATES PAPERS, 1910–17, 1 folder
Background note: A Baptist minister, Frederick T. Gates (1853–1929) was a trustee of the China Medical Board and Peking Union Medical College from 1914 to 1917.
CORRESPONDENCE: Correspondence on the policy of the China Medical Board, mission hospitals, Peking Union Medical College, and Gates' resignation from the Board of Trustees of the China Medical Board, including correspondents L. M. Bowers, Simon Flexner, J. J. Jesserand, Harry Pratt Judson, Frederick T. Gates, John D. Rockefeller, Sr., John D. Rockefeller, Jr., Charles W. Eliot, and Wallace Buttrick.
MANUSCRIPTS: Autobiography of Gates, published in 1977.
FINDING AIDS: In-house directory.

10-INTERNATIONAL EDUCATION BOARD, 1924–33, 7 folders
Background note: Incorporated in 1923, the International Education Board promoted educational and institutional improvement throughout the world until ending its activities in 1938.
MINUTES/RECORDS/REPORTS/CORRESPONDENCE: Records and correspondence on International Education Board appropriations: 6 folders of records and correspondence of C. H. Myers, H. H. Love, R. G. Wiggans, and John H. Reisner of Cornell University concerning fellowships and agricultural improvement programs at the University of Nanking, 1924–33 (see also Cornell University, Olin Library, Department of Manuscripts and University Archives, Ithaca, NY, 14853–5301); University of Nanking, 1926–32.
FINDING AIDS: In-house directory.

11-LOUISE PEARCE PAPERS (RG 450 P315), 1931–32, 1 folder
Background note: Louise Pearce (1885–1959) was a physician and

medical researcher with the Rockefeller Institute for Medical Research. In 1931 and 1932 she was a visiting professor of medicine at Peking Union Medical College (PUMC).
CORRESPONDENCE: Correspondence relating to Louise Pearce's leave of absence from the Rockefeller Institute for Medical Research, 1931–32, and her work at PUMC during that year.
FINDING AIDS: In-house directory.

12-THE LAURA SPELMAN ROCKEFELLER MEMORIAL, 1923, 6 folders
MINUTES/RECORDS/REPORTS: 4 folders on the National Christian Council in China, 1923, and the Jubilee Fund of Women's Christian Colleges in the Orient, n.d.; folder on the YMCA and Princeton-in-Peking, 1923–24.
CORRESPONDENCE: Correspondence of W. B. Pettus and the North China Union Language School, n.d.; folder of correspondence of W. B. Pettus, Roger S. Greene, and the North China Union Language School on curriculum, buildings, and equipment, 1920–25.
FINDING AIDS: In-house directory.

NYACK

ALLIANCE THEOLOGICAL SEMINARY
NY–300 Library
Nyack NY 10960
(914) 358–1710 Ext. 350
Sue Fedele, Librarian

Background note: Alliance Theological Seminary is affiliated with the Christian and Missionary Alliance (CMA), a Protestant denomination founded in 1887 by A. B. Simpson, which worked in China and Tibet from its inception. Denominational records, books about China, and other relevant materials are located at Christian and Missionary Alliance International Headquarters, A. B. Simpson Historical Library, Nyack, NY, 10960.

1-GENERAL HOLDINGS
SERIALS: *China and the Church Today*, 1979–86. *China Notes*, 1978-. *Ching Feng*, 1977-.
DISSERTATIONS/THESES: *A Theological Dialogue between Christian Faith and Chinese Belief in the Light of "Sin"—An Inquiry into the Apparent Failure of the Protestant Mission in Late Nineteenth-century China, Especially among Intellectuals*, by Christopher Chou, 1976.

CHRISTIAN AND MISSIONARY ALLIANCE
NY–305 A. B. Simpson Historical Library
Box C
Nyack NY 10960
(914) 353–0750
James A. Davey, Vice President for General Services

Background note: The Christian and Missionary Alliance (CMA) worked in Kwangsi, Hunan, Szechwan, and Tibet. The following collections are part of a larger, mostly unorganized collection housed in 8 file drawers in the library office.

1-B. H. ALEXANDER PAPERS, 1866–1968, 11 items
CORRESPONDENCE: Letter from Mrs. Edith Alexander to Howard Van Dyck, 1938, accompanying photos of the "Key of Changsha" (below).
MANUSCRIPTS: 2 typewritten drafts of a 1943 article by B. H. Alexander on missions in Changsha, 1898–1900, and the Japanese occupation of Changsha, 1938; Alexander's autobiography, 1948.
AUDIO-VISUAL MATERIALS: 6 photos of the "Key of Changsha," a ceremonial key presented to Alexander by Hunanese Christians on his return to Changsha in 1938.

2-BIRRELL PAPERS, 1934–36, 1 folder
Background note: Gordon Birrell was the son of CMA missionaries Matthew and Frances (Catlin) Birrell.
CORRESPONDENCE: Letters between Gordon Birrell and John Sawin, n.d.; brief excerpts from Agnes Birrell's letters from Szechwan, 1934–36.
MANUSCRIPTS: Biographical sketches of Gordon and Frances Birrell's children, Matthew, Marion, and Agnes; notes on Gordon Birrell's biography of his father, n.d.

3-WILLIAM CASSIDY MEMORABILIA, 1888, 5 items
Background note: CMA missionary William Cassidy (1854–88) died in Japan en route to Shanghai.
PAMPHLETS: Original and copies of a memorial pamphlet in Cassidy's honor, 1888.

4-MARY FUNK MEMORABILIA, 1889, 1980, 2 items
MINUTES/RECORDS/REPORTS: Photocopy of a "Report from China," by Mary Funk, in *The Christian and Missionary Alliance Weekly*, 1889.
MAPS/DESIGNS/DRAWINGS: Etching of Mary Funk, 1980.

5-ROBERT JAFFRAY PAPERS, 1896–ca. 1925, 1 file drawer
CORRESPONDENCE: Ca. 50 letters by CMA missionary Robert Jaffray while in Wuchow, 1896–ca. 1925.
CHINESE LANGUAGE MATERIALS: Books, commentaries, and scattered copies of *Bible Magazine*, all written by Jaffray.

6-ORA WOODBERRY INTERVIEW, 1962, 1 item
ORAL HISTORIES: Transcript of a taped interview in 1962, with Ora Woodberry, the daughter of China missionary John Woodberry, covering Woodberry's early life, the Boxer Rebellion, and missions in Shanghai, Tientsin, and Shansi.

7-WOODBERRY SISTERS FOLDER, 1966, 4 pages
MANUSCRIPTS: Brief biographies of CMA missionaries Ethel and Ora Woodberry from 1887 to 1966.

8-GENERAL HOLDINGS
MINUTES/RECORDS/REPORTS: Christian and Missionary Alliance Foreign Department, annual reports, including records of CMA work in China and Tibet until 1951; list of China missionaries of the CMA, 1887–1968; records and reports of CMA work in China and Tibet in *Bringing in the Sheaves: Gleanings from the Mission Fields of the Christian and Missionary Alliance*, 1898; *Quarter Centennial Forward Movement of the Christian and Missionary Alliance*, 1889–1914; and *The Christian and Missionary Alliance Weekly*, 1882–1950.
CORRESPONDENCE: 8 letters of J. O. Carlsen regarding the

writing of his book *In Search of a Miracle*, including such correspondents as Lowell Thomas, Louis L. King, and Thubten Jigme Norbu, ca. 1980–1981; transcriptions of letters, written by William Christie to his sister and her husband, 1891–1907, typed and bound in 1980, including such topics as Christie's voyage from San Francisco to Shanghai via Japan, and mission work in Shanghai, Wuhu, and Tibet.

MANUSCRIPTS: 72-page draft of J. O. Carlsen's book about mission work in Tibet, *In Search of a Miracle*; 5 or 6 notebooks of material for an untitled history of the work of the CMA in Central China by Paul Bartel, ca. 1978.

PAMPHLETS: 6 autobiographical and biographical pamphlets on Blind Chang, Feng Yü-hsiang, Pastor Chao, Timothy S. K. Dzao, and W. H. Oldfield, 1919–50; 12 pamphlets on the CMA mission in Northeast Tibet, Tibetan civilization and culture, the Hebron mission, martyrs, and polemic, 1903–74.

MEMORABILIA: Folder of reprints from the *Shanghai Mercury* on the Boxer Massacres, 1900; folder of "The Church in China under Communism," 1949–80, containing letters, articles, and periodicals collected by Paul Bartel and compiled chronologically by James A. Bollback, 1980; unprocessed file drawer containing correspondence, pamphlets and tracts, scrapbooks and other memorabilia, and mission magazines.

ORAL HISTORIES: 1 reel-to-reel tape by William Christie, primarily about the White Wolf Raiders, ca. 30 minutes, 1954 (also on cassette tape).

AUDIO-VISUAL MATERIALS: Autographed photo of Feng Yü-hsiang presented to A. C. Snead in the early 1920s, attached to the library copy of *Marshall Feng: The Man and His Work*, by Marcus Ch'eng (Shanghai: Kelly and Walsh, 1926); photos scattered among materials in the file drawer.

DISSERTATIONS/THESES: *The Ecclesiology of the Little Flock of China Founded by Watchman Nee*, by James Cheung, 1970. *Protestant Missionary Activity in Hunan Province—China: History and Analysis, 1875–1912*, by James Anthony Bollback, 1981.

CHINESE LANGUAGE MATERIALS: New Testament in Mandarin, n.d.; Bible, in Mandarin, n.d.; Bible, in romanized Amoy dialect, n.d.; unprocessed file drawer containing some Chinese language materials, including correspondence, pamphlets and tracts, scrapbooks and other memorabilia, mission magazines, and photos, ca. 1890-ca. 1950; Tibetan language materials, including *Stories from the Old Testament*, Tibetan Religious Literature Depot, n.d.; *Short Term of Christian Worship and Tibetan Catechism*, by Theodore Sorensen, China Inland Mission, n.d.

NYACK COLLEGE

NY–310 Rare Books and Archives
Shuman Hall
Nyack NY 10960
(914) 358-1710 Ext. 271
Jeffrey L. Brigham, Assistant Librarian for Technical Services

Background note: Nyack College is affiliated with the Christian and Missionary Alliance (CMA), a Protestant denomination founded in 1887 by A. B. Simpson, which worked in China and Tibet from its inception. See also Alliance Theological Seminary, Nyack, NY, 10960, and Christian and Missionary Alliance International Headquarters, A. B. Simpson Historical Library, Nyack, NY, 10960.

1-GENERAL HOLDINGS
AUDIO-VISUAL MATERIALS: Photo album of 34 photos and 2 loose photos of CMA missionaries, native Bible school students and Christian workers, refugees of the Boxer Uprising, Tibetan temple and priests, and scenes of Chinese daily life and countryside, n.d. [ca.1900].
SERIALS: *South China Alliance Tidings*, 1907-26.
CHINESE LANGUAGE MATERIALS: 60 leaves of a Tibetan Scripture portion, n.d.; Kuoyu Bible, 1936; *Mark: The Triumph of a Youthful Hero*, comp. by David G. Taylor, 1959 (bi-lingual); *Evangel Hymnal*, 1961; *Youth Hymns* (bi-lingual), n.d.

NY–315 Nyack College Library
Shuman Hall
Nyack NY 10960
(914) 358-1710 Ext. 271
Jeffrey L. Brigham, Assistant Librarian for Technical Services

1-GENERAL HOLDINGS
MINUTES/RECORDS/REPORTS: Reports from the Christian and Missionary Alliance work in China in *Alliance Witness*, 1894-.
MANUSCRIPTS: "Matthew Brown Birrell: Missionary to the Chinese: Jottings, An Autobiography," by Matthew Brown Birrell, 1981.
ORAL HISTORIES: *China Missionaries Oral History Collection*, ed. by Cyrus H. Peake and Arthur L. Rosenbaum (Claremont Graduate School, Oral History Program), 1973. See ORAL HISTORIES Union List for the names of participants.
SERIALS: *China Christian Year Book*, 1938-39.

PLATTSBURGH

STATE UNIVERSITY OF NEW YORK AT PLATTSBURGH
NY–320 Benjamin F. Feinberg Library
Plattsburgh NY 12901
(518) 564-3180
Joseph G. Swinyer, Special Collections

1-HYLA S. WATTERS, 1974, 1 item
ORAL HISTORIES: Transcript and tape of an interview with Hyla S. Watters, a medical missionary at Wuhu General Hospital in Anhui, 1974.

POUGHKEEPSIE

NY–325 ADRIANCE MEMORIAL LIBRARY
93 Market Street
Poughkeepsie NY 12601
(914) 485-4790
Kevin J. Gallagher, Local History Librarian

1-LOCAL HISTORY COLLECTION, ca. 1900–1910, 18 items
Background note: Items in the collection belonged to Guilford

Dudley, a prominent local banker active in area churches.
DIARIES: Diary on Foochow and Shanghai missions, 1910.
AUDIO-VISUAL MATERIALS: 17 photos of Dudley Memorial Church, other scenes, and individuals in Foochow, ca. 1900.
FINDING AIDS: Card catalogue.

VASSAR COLLEGE
NY-330 Library
Poughkeepsie NY 12601
(914) 452-7000
Bernice K. Lacks, Head Readers Services Librarian

1-GENERAL HOLDINGS
SERIALS: American Friends Service Committee, *Bulletin on Work in China*, 1942-44. *China Christian Year Book*, 1926, 1928. *China Mission Year Book*, 1913, 1916-19, 1924-25. China International Famine Relief Commission, Publications, series A, 1923-25, 1927-36; series B, 1926, 1929, 1931-32. *Chinese Recorder*, 1908-40. *News of China*, 1942-49. *United China Relief Series*, 1941.
DISSERTATIONS/THESES: *The Confrontation: American Catholicism and Chinese Communism, 1945-1952*, by William C. Hearon, 1975.

RENSSELAER

ST. ANTHONY-ON-HUDSON

NY-335 Province of the Immaculate Conception, O.F.M. Conv. Archives
St. Anthony-on-Hudson
Rensselaer NY 12144
(518) 463-2261
Andrew Ehlinger, O.F.M. Conv., Archivist

Background note: In 1925 the Conventual Franciscans revitalized a neglected Catholic mission in Hingan, Shensi. American friars from the Province of the Immaculate Conception participated in the work of this mission from 1931 until the outbreak of the Sino-Japanese war. Some foreign Franciscan friars remained in China until they were expelled in 1952; native friars are still there.

1-GENERAL HOLDINGS
CORRESPONDENCE: Ca. 3 files of letters to and from various officials of the Order and Province and the missionaries, 1931-37, 1952.
MANUSCRIPTS: "Account of the Escape from China of P. Maleddu and B. Permutti," by Carlo Cavallero, 1952; "China: Missionary history," n.a., n.d.; "Controversy Concerning the Chinese and Malabar Rites," by Raphael Huber, n.d.; "Conventual Missions in China," n.a., n.d.; "Independent Mission Field for Immaculate Conception and Our Lady of Consolation Provinces," (with map of China), n.a., n.d.; "Missions to the Mongols in Karakorum Mongolia," n.a., n.d.; "Plan for Mission Propaganda," n.a., n.d.
MEMORABILIA: "On the Communist Brutality towards Conventual Franciscan Missionaries" (Chinese Scroll), *The Catholic Sun*, 1952.

AUDIO-VISUAL MATERIALS: 125 pictures of Hingan mission, 1930s.

NY-340 Province of the Immaculate Conception, O.F.M. Conv. Library
St. Anthony-on-Hudson
Rensselaer NY 12144
(518) 463-2261
Peter D. Fehlner, O.F.M. Conv., Head Librarian

1-GENERAL HOLDINGS
MINUTES/RECORDS/REPORTS: Information on the missions in China during the 1920s and 1930s in the official commentaries and popular journals published by the Conventual Franciscans: *Acta Ordinis Fratrum Minorum*, 1882-; *Analecta Ordinis Fratrum Minorum Capucchinorum*, 1885-; *Commentarium Ordinis Fratrum Minorum Conventualium*, 1904-; *The Companion of St. Francis and St. Anthony*, 1936-65; and *The Minorite*, 1926-35 (superseded by *The Companion*).
DISSERTATIONS/THESES: *Imperial Government and Catholic Missions in China during the Years 1784-1785*, by Bernward Henry Willeke, 1948. *The Negotiations between Ch'i-ying and Lagrené, 1844-1846*, by Angelus Francis J. Grosse-Aschhoff, 1950.

ROCHESTER

NY-345 AMERICAN BAPTIST HISTORICAL SOCIETY
1106 South Goodman Street
Rochester NY 14620
(716) 473-1740
Susan Eltscher, Director of Library

Background note: The American Baptist Historical Society (ABHS) holds material relating to foreign missions of American Baptists. The foreign mission agency has been renamed several times. From 1814 to 1846, it was known as the General Missionary Convention of the Baptist Denomination in the United States for Foreign Missions. Subsequently, it was renamed as follows: the American Baptist Missionary Union (1846-1910); the American Baptist Foreign Mission Society (ABFMS)(1910-74); and the Board of International Ministries (1974-). Founded in 1871, the women's division, the Women's American Baptist Foreign Mission Society (WABFMS), complemented the work of the foreign board until 1955 when the two agencies were merged. American Baptist missions in China commenced in 1842 and closed in 1950. All archival materials not listed in this depository and originals of the correspondence listed below are located at the American Baptist Headquarters, Valley Forge, PA, 19481.

1-AMERICAN BAPTIST FOREIGN MISSION SOCIETY RECORDS, 1814-, ca. 130 l.f.
MINUTES/RECORDS/REPORTS: American Baptist Foreign Mission Society, Board of Managers and Executive Committee, minutes, 1814-; China field reports, 3 l.f.; reports on the China mission in denominational serials, *Along Kingdom Highways*, 1941-, and *American Baptist Magazine* (later, *Missions*), 1842-.
CORRESPONDENCE: Microfilm copies of ca. 100 l.f. of corre-

spondence from missionaries in the field to the home office, 1814-, arranged by mission field for 19th-century material and by author's name for 20th-century material.

AUDIO-VISUAL MATERIALS: About 250 slides and photos interfiled in general ABHS photo collection (not including photos in personal papers collections).

2-JOSEPH SAMUEL ADAMS, 1875-1920, 4 l.f.
Background note: Joseph Samuel Adams (1853-1912) served as an English Baptist missionary in Central China from 1878 to 1882. He became an ABFMS missionary in 1882 and began their Central China Mission in 1892.
MINUTES/RECORDS/REPORTS: Records of the closing of the Central China Baptist Mission (1913-20).
CORRESPONDENCE/DIARIES/AUDIO-VISUAL MATERIALS: Correspondence, diaries, and photos, 1875-1920.

3-WILLIAM ASHMORE, JR., 1851-1937, .1 c.f.
Background note: For biographical notes, see University of Oregon, Special Collections, Eugene, OR, 97403-1299.
CORRESPONDENCE/MANUSCRIPTS: Autobiography, letters, and other papers of William Ashmore, Jr., transcribed by his daughter.

4-CARL MAYO CAPEN, 1935, 1 items
Background note: Carl Mayo Capen (b. 1911) served in South China from 1935 to 1950.
DISSERTATION/THESES: *A History of the Baptist Mission at Swatow, China*, by Carl Mayo Capen, 1935.

5-SAMUEL COLGATE BAPTIST HISTORICAL COLLECTION, 1875-1939, 23 items
PAMPHLETS: 23 pamphlets, 1875-1939, on subjects including American Baptist Missionary Union, Baptist Missionary Society, Baptist missions, Frances E. Coombs, East China Baptist Mission, Miles J. Knowlton, Laura Nance Little, medicine, Northern Baptists in China, Southern Baptists in China, South China mission, Swatow mission, Timothy Richard, and West China mission.

6-PAUL F. CRESSEY, 1921-24, 2 volumes
Background note: Paul F. Cressey (1899-1969), an American Baptist missionary, was an English instructor at Swatow Academy from 1921 to 1924.
AUDIO-VISUAL MATERIALS: 2 photo albums of the Swatow Mission, 1921-24.

7-ANNIE CROWL, 1897-1914, 4 volumes
Background note: Annie Crowl (b. 1865) served as a WABFMS missionary in Central China from 1897 to 1915. She continued her work there from 1915 to 1928 sponsored variously by the Southern Baptists, the Society of Friends, and the London (Baptist) Missionary Society.
DIARIES: 4 volumes, 1897-1902, 1909-14.

8-WILLIAM DEAN, 1834-93, 14 items
Background note: William Dean (1807-95) served as a missionary in Hong Kong from 1842 to 1845 and from 1850 to 1853.
CORRESPONDENCE/MEMORABILIA: Correspondence and memorabilia, 1834-93.

9-JOHN WILLIAM DECKER, 1921-42, 9 l.f.
Background note: John William Decker (1890-1982) served as a

missionary in Chekiang from 1921 to 1935 and as ABFMS Foreign Secretary for China, Japan, and the Philippines from 1935 to 1942.
CORRESPONDENCE / MANUSCRIPTS / AUDIO-VISUAL MATERIALS: Correspondence, sermons and addresses, and photos, 1921-42.

10-SARA BODDIE DOWNER, 1930-50, 1 l.f.
Background note: For biographical notes, see Mount Holyoke College, Williston Memorial Library, College History and Archives South Hadley, MA, 01075-1493.
CORRESPONDENCE/DIARIES: Diaries and correspondence, 1930-50.

11-BEATRICE ERICSON, 1930-50, ca. 800 items
Background note: Beatrice Ericson (b. 1906) served as a WABFMS missionary in Swatow from 1931 to 1942 and in South China from 1946 to 1950.
CORRESPONDENCE/MEMORABILIA: Correspondence and memorabilia, 1930-50.

12-JAMES HENRY FRANKLIN, 1872-1961, quantity undetermined
Background note: James Henry Franklin (1872-1961) was foreign secretary of the ABFMS and later president of Crozer Theological Seminary.
MINUTES/RECORDS/REPORTS: Reports on trips to China in the early 1930s.

13-JOSIAH AND ELIZA ANN ABBOTT GODDARD, 1834-54, ca. 75 items
Background note: Josiah (1813-65) and Eliza Ann Abbott Goddard (1817-57) served in Ningpo from 1850 to 1854.
CORRESPONDENCE: Ca. 75 letters, 1834-54.

14-CLARA HOLLOWAY GROESBECK, 1885-1935, 13 items
Background note: For biographical notes, see University of Oregon, Special Collections, Eugene, OR, 97403-1299.
CORRESPONDENCE/DIARIES: Correspondence and diaries, 1885-1935.

15-WILLIE PAULINE HARRIS, 1923-50, ca. 250 items
Background note: Willie Pauline Harris (1897-1977) served as a WABFMS missionary nurse in Ningpo from 1923 to 1950.
CORRESPONDENCE/DIARIES: Correspondence and diaries, 1923-50.

16-VIOLA CAROLINE HILL, 1915-82, 1.3 l.f.
Background note: Viola Caroline Hill (b. 1887) served as a WABFMS missionary in East China from 1915 to 1949.
ORAL HISTORIES/AUDIO-VISUAL MATERIALS: Photos, 1915-28, and taped interview, 1982.

17-KENNETH GRAY HOBART, 1935-42, ca. 100 items
Background note: Kenneth Gray Hobart (b. 1893) served in South China between 1922 and 1944.
CORRESPONDENCE: Ca. 100 letters, 1935-42.

18-CLARA CHASE LEACH, 1916-46, 1 reel microfilm
Background note: For biographical notes and the original diaries, see American Baptist Headquarters, Valley Forge, PA, 19481.
DIARIES: Diaries, 1916-46.

19-GERTRUDE FLORENCE McCULLOCH, 1920-48, 3 l.f.
Background note: Gertrude Florence McCulloch (1890-1985)

was a Baptist missionary in Hangchow from 1919 to 1948. See also Bentley Historical Library, Michigan Historical Collections, 1150 Beal Avenue, Ann Arbor, MI, 48109–2113.
CORRESPONDENCE/AUDIO-VISUAL MATERIAL: Correspondence and photos, 1920–48.

20-MILDRED PROCTOR, 1922–49, ca. 35 items
Background note: Mildred Proctor (b. 1906) served as a WABFMS missionary in Shaohsing from 1934 to 1939 and from 1946 to 1949, in Ningpo from 1940 to 1941, and in Shanghai from 1941 to 1943.
CORRESPONDENCE/MEMORABILIA: Correspondence and memorabilia, 1922–49.

21-EDITH GRACE TRAVER, 1905–39, 4.75 l.f.
Background note: Edith Grace Traver (1881–1973) was a WABFMS missionary in South China from 1906 to 1939.
CORRESPONDENCE/MANUSCRIPTS/DIARIES/AUDIO-VISUAL MATERIALS: Correspondence, writings, diaries and photos, 1905–39.

22-WOMEN'S AMERICAN BAPTIST FOREIGN MISSION SOCI-ETY RECORDS, 1909–55, quantity undetermined
MINUTES/RECORDS/REPORTS: Women's American Baptist Foreign Mission Society (WABFMS), annual reports, 1913–55; *Our Work in the Orient* (annual report, with excerpts of missionary correspondence), 1909–28.
MEMORABILIA/PAMPHLETS: Miscellaneous publications, flyers, and pamphlets.

23-GENERAL HOLDINGS
MINUTES/RECORDS/REPORTS: Address on observations in China, by Foreign Secretary James H. Franklin, 1931; China Baptist Conference, 1905, 1907, 1913, 1916; China Baptist Council, 1924, 1930; South China Baptist Mission, annual report, 1908, 1911, 1916–20; South China Mission, Reference Committee, 1916–30 (inc.); West China Baptist Mission, annual report, 1910–11, 1913–15, 1923–25, 1929–32, 1934, 1936; West China, trip report by John William Decker, 1934.
MANUSCRIPTS: "Return Visit to China," by Raymond E. Stannard, 1982.
PAMPHLETS: 30 pamphlets, 1880–1957, on subjects including A Si, A Tui, Baptist Missionary Society, Baptist missions in China, Cyril Eustace Bousfield, Emma Brodbeck, Central China Mission, Chekiang-Shanghai Baptist Convention, Chinese revolutions, Frank Stockton Dobbins, East China Mission, field surveys, Elmer Alfred Fridell, Huchow Mission, infanticide, Kho-Khoi Mission, medical work, Augustus Inglesbe Nasmith, Ningpo Mission, North China mission (Shantung), Alice McLain Ross, Anna Kay Scott, Southern Baptist missions, Southern China Mission, Swatow Mission history, West China missions, and women's movements in China.
SERIALS: *China Mission Advocate*, 1839. *New East*, 1905–33.
DISSERTATIONS/THESES: *A Comparative History of the East China and South China Missions of the American Baptist Foreign Mission Society, 1833–1935*, by Kenneth Gray Hobart, 1937. *Southern Baptist Contributions to Missions in China: A Survey of Investments and Achievements*, by Park Harris Anderson, 1947.
CHINESE LANGUAGE MATERIAL: 2 China Baptist Publication Society pamphlets by Jacob Speicher, n.d.; bilingual edition of

China Has a Ten-Thousand-Mile Spiritual Wall, by Shao Yan Lee, 1945; 2 hymnbooks used in Baptist missions, ca. 1900, printed and manuscript.

COLGATE ROCHESTER-BEXLEY HALL-CROZER THEOLOGICAL SEMINARIES
NY–350 Ambrose Swasey Library
1100 South Goodman Street
Rochester NY 14620–2592
(716) 271–1320
Norman J. Kansfield, Director

1-GENERAL HOLDINGS
MINUTES/RECORDS/REPORTS: American Board of Commissioners for Foreign Missions, Board of Foreign Missions, report on a visit to China, Japan, and Korea by Arthur Judson Brown, 1909; Foreign Missions Conference, address on the missionary situation, 1928.
MANUSCRIPTS: "Chinese Ethical and Religious Culture," by Frank Joseph Rawlinson, 1930.
PAMPHLETS: *Address on Behalf of the China Mission*, by William J. Boone, 1837; *The Ceremonies of the Ch'uan Miao*, by David C. Graham, 1937; *The Missionary Situation in China*, by Henry Theodore Hodgkin, 1928; *The Medical Missionary Society in China*, by Thomas R. Colledge, 1838; box of 14 pamphlets labelled *Religious Drama: A Collection of Plays on China Missions*, n.d.; *The True Light That Lighteth*, by Robert F. Fitch, 1925.
AUDIO-VISUAL MATERIALS: *Brother, Are You Saved?*, audio cassette by David M. Stowe, 1972.
SERIALS: *China and the Gospel*, 1914. *China Mission Advocate*, 1839. *China's Millions* (Toronto), 1904–7, 1909, 1912, 1915. *China's Millions* (London), 1875–76, 1880–85, 1887, 1907–12, 1916–21, 1925–52. *Chinese Recorder*, 1868–76, 1878–84, 1891–1940. *Directory of Protestant Missionaries in China, Japan, and Korea*, 1918. *Directory of Protestant Missions in China*, 1918. *East Asia Millions* (London), 1965-. *The Millions* (London), 1953–64. Nanking Theological Seminary, English Publications, 1940. *New East*, 1905–33. *West China Missionary News*, 1921–40.
DISSERTATIONS/THESES: *American Protestant Missions and Communist China, 1946–1950*, by David J. Galligan, 1952. *Church and State in Republican China: A Survey History of the Relations between the Christian Churches and the Chinese Government, 1911–1945*, by Arne Sovik, 1952. *The Development of the Motive of Protestant Missions to China, 1807–1928*, by George Bell Workman, 1928. *Indications of Primitive Chinese Religion in the Confucian Classics*, by David Crockett Graham, 1919. *Lutheran Missions in a Time of Revolution: The China Experience, 1944–1951*, by Jonas Jonson, 1972. *The Mission Compound in Modern China: The Role of the United States Protestant Mission as an Asylum in the Civil and International Strife of China, 1900–1941*, by Gladys Robina Quale, 1957. *Principles and Methods of Community Church Work in China*, by Ts-chien Wu, 1925. *The Promotion of the Economic Welfare of the Chinese People through the Protestant Churches in China*, by George Yuan-hsieh Geng, 1951. *Protestant Christianity and Marriage in China*, by Calvin H. Reber, 1958. *The Protestant Missionary Understanding of the Chinese Situation and the Christian Task from 1890 to 1911*, by C. William Mensendiek, 1958. *Protestant Missions in Communist*

China, by Creighton Lacy, 1953.
CHINESE LANGUAGE MATERIALS/SERIALS: *Leprosy in China*, 1931, 1934(?)–1941.

UNIVERSITY OF ROCHESTER

NY-355 Edward G. Miner Library
School of Medicine and Dentistry
601 Elmwood Avenue
Rochester NY 14642
(716) 275-3364
Frances Rescher, Serials Librarian

1-GENERAL HOLDINGS
SERIALS: *China Medical Journal*, 1924–31. *Chinese Medical Journal*, 1932–55; Supplement, 1936, 1938, 1940, 1952.

NY-360 Rush Rhees Library
Department of Rare Books and Special Collections
University of Rochester
Wilson Boulevard
Rochester NY 14627
(716) 275-4477
Karl Kabelac, Manuscripts Librarian

1-HANFORD-MUNN FAMILY PAPERS, 1916–21, 6 items
Background note: Ruth (Hanford) Munn graduated from Wellesley College in 1909. Several of her college classmates became missionaries to China.
CORRESPONDENCE: 6 letters to Ruth Munn from former college classmates, Anna Brown Nipps and Martha Cecil Wilson, missionaries in China, writing from Hangchow, Peking, and Pei Tai Ho, 1916–21.

2-GENERAL HOLDINGS
SERIALS: China International Famine Relief Commission, Publications, series A, 1928–36, 1938. West China Border Research Society, *Journal*, 1922–34, 1936–37.
CHINESE LANGUAGE MATERIAL: 2 Bibles, 1963–64, and a book on the origin of anti-foreignism among Chinese gentry, 1966.

ST. BONAVENTURE

ST. BONAVENTURE UNIVERSITY

NY-365 Franciscan Institute
St. Bonaventure NY 14778
(716) 375-2105
Cyprian Lynch, O.F.M., Archivist

Background note: The Franciscan Institute is a center for learning, research, and publication related to the Franciscan movement. The Institute contains the major research collection for Franciscan studies in the United States. It also contains most of the holdings from the former library of Holy Name College, Washington, DC, including their rare book collection.

1-GENERAL HOLDINGS
MANUSCRIPTS: ''Biographical Sketches of Franciscans in

China,'' by Athanasius McInerney, O.F.M., 1944; ''Sources for a Biography of Fr. Basilio Brollo, O.F.M.,'' by Edmund Fox, O.F.M., 1944.
PAMPHLETS: *Franciscan Missionaries in China: Province of the Most Holy Name*, 1934.
SERIALS: *Apostolicum*, 1930-. *Franciscans in China*, 1924–42.
DISSERTATIONS/THESES: *The Negotiations between Ch'i-ying and Lagrené, 1844–1846*, by Angelus Francis J. Grosse-Aschhoff, 1950. *Prefecture Apostolic of Shasi*, by Raphael McDonald, O.F.M., 1945.

NY-370 Friedsam Memorial Library
Archive Collection
St. Bonaventure University
St. Bonaventure NY 14778
(716) 375-2323
Paul J. Spaeth, Director of Technical Services
Lorraine Welch, Archivist

1-GENERAL HOLDINGS
DISSERTATIONS/THESES: *The Life and Work of Msgr. De Besi in China*, by Veneranda Bohlen, 1950. *The Spanish Franciscans in the Province of Kiangsi, China, During the Years 1685–1813*, by Athanasius McInerney, O.F.M., 1949.

SYRACUSE

SYRACUSE UNIVERSITY

NY-375 Archives
E. S. Bird Library
George Arents Research Library for Special Collections
Syracuse NY 13210
(315) 423-2697/2585
Amy S. Doherty, University Archivist

Restrictions: Appointments required.

1-MEDICAL MISSIONARY PHOTOGRAPHS (RG 43), 1892–1936, 3 in.
Background note: Dr. Mary Luella Masters was a member of the Medical Missionary Association of China and served in Foochow beginning in 1892. She was affiliated with the Women's and Children's Hospital, and Foochow City Hospital.
MEMORABILIA/AUDIO-VISUAL MATERIALS: Mary Masters' scrapbook of her experiences in China, including photos of Chinese civilization and culture, accompanied by a holographic text, 1892–1936.

2-SYRACUSE-IN-CHINA COLLECTION (RG 62), 1920–56, 5 l.f.
Background note: The Syracuse-in-Asia Association, known as the Syracuse-in-China Association, served as a medical, religious, and educational mission prior to 1950.
MINUTES/RECORDS/REPORTS: 5 boxes, containing alumni records, 1937–47; constitution and minutes of meetings of the Association, 1921–34, 1936–49; financial records, 1925–52; general records of individual officers of the Association, 1941–53, and of Executive Secretary Ruth A. Hoople, 1941–52; reports by Syracuse-in-China representatives Don Flaherty and Tom Scott, 1947–50, and annual reports of the Student Board of Syracuse-in-China,

ca. 1947–52; student Syracuse-in-China organization, 1933–52, including records of the United Board for Christian Colleges in China Conference, 1949; and miscellaneous undated records relating to the origin and history of the Association.

CORRESPONDENCE: 3 boxes of correspondence of the Association, its Executive Committee and Executive Secretaries, Association representatives to China, China missionaries, the Board of Foreign Missions of the Methodist Church, Don Flaherty, Tom Gill, Helen Koo (Mrs. T. Z. Koo), Dr. Steinheimer, and Walker A. Taylor, relating to arrangements and needs of the program in China, West China Union University, the conditions met by representatives in China, and general organizational affairs, 1920–45; correspondence relating to the selection of an executive secretary, ca. 1941–53.

MANUSCRIPTS/AUDIO-VISUAL MATERIALS: 3 copies of a loose-leaf binder with text and photos entitled "Syracuse in China, Origins, Plans and Progress," 1924; "The Story of Syracuse in China," mimeograph, n.d.

PAMPHLETS/MEMORABILIA: Box of applications for post of representative to China, selection data, and recommendations, 1946–49, 1950, 1952, 1954; box of letters, programs, newspaper clippings, and miscellaneous materials used to publicize the Association, 1923–37, 1946, 1948–50; box of program/publicity material; 2 boxes of miscellaneous materials on subjects such as Chinese art, Oberlin-in-China, Yale-in-China, United China Relief, books, and films, 1936–56; box of promotional pamphlets of Syracuse-in-China, clippings, pamphlets, and journals relating to university and other medical, social, and educational programs, 1925–52.

MAPS/DESIGNS/DRAWINGS: Miscellaneous maps, n.d.

AUDIO-VISUAL MATERIALS: Photos of people, places, and events relating to Syracuse-in-China, n.d.

SERIALS: China International Famine Relief Commission, Publications, series A, 1922–36. *St. John's University Studies*, 1922. University of Nanking, College of Agriculture and Forestry, *Special Report*, 1935. *Yenching Journal of Chinese Studies*, Monograph, 1932.

DISSERTATIONS/THESES: *Reciprocal Change: The Case of American Protestant Missionaries to China*, by Paul Voninski, 1976.

FINDING AIDS: In-house inventory.

NY–380 Manuscript Division

E. S. Bird Library
George Arents Research Library for Special
  Collections
Syracuse University
Syracuse NY 13210
(315) 423–2697
Carolyn Davis, Manuscript Curator

1-NANKING INCIDENT COLLECTION, 1927, 1 in.
MINUTES/RECORDS/REPORTS: China Christian Educational Association, Shanghai, report, 1927.
MANUSCRIPTS: Descriptions of the Nanking Incident, including eye-witness accounts of the invasion of Nanking by the Nationalists, 1927.
SERIALS: University of Nanking *Newsletter*, 1928; *Occasional Letters*, 1927–28.

WEST POINT

UNITED STATES MILITARY ACADEMY
NY–385 Library Special Collections

West Point NY 10996–1799
(914) 938–2954
Marie T. Capps, Map and Manuscript Librarian

1-ANNIE ALLENDER GOULD PAPERS, 1889-ca. 1900, 19 items
Background note: Annie Allender Gould (1867–1900) graduated from Mount Holyoke College in 1892 and left for China in 1893. At the time of the Boxer Rebellion, she was a teacher, supervising the native Chinese teachers in the American Board School in Paotingfu. The collection includes the book, *In Memory of Miss Mary S. Morrill and Miss Annie Allender Gould, Martyrs of Paoting-fu, North China, July 1, 1900*, ed. by Alice M. Kyle, which contains biographical sketches and letters from 1889 to 1900. See also Mount Holyoke College, Williston Memorial Library, College History and Archives, South Hadley, MA, 01075; and Maine Historical Society, 485 Congress Street, Portland, ME, 04101.

CORRESPONDENCE/CHINESE LANGUAGE MATERIALS: 6 letters from Annie Gould to her family, describing the mission, work, and events in China, 1894–99; letter from Mary S. Morrill to Mrs. Gould, 1899; letter from Judson Smith to Annie Gould, 1893; 11 letters to the Gould family, one of which is written in Chinese (with the translation), informing them of the abduction and death of their daughter at the hands of the Boxers and expressing sympathy, ca. 1900.

NORTH CAROLINA

CHAPEL HILL

UNIVERSITY OF NORTH CAROLINA AT CHAPEL HILL

NC–5   **Walter Royal Davis Library**
Chapel Hill NC 27514
(919) 962–1301
James F. Govan, Director
Edward G. Martinique, Bibliographer, East Asian
  Resources

Finding aids: "Materials on East Asia in the Southern Historical Collection, Wilson Library, University of North Carolina at Chapel Hill," by Edward G. Martinique, in *Asian Resources in the Southeastern United States: Archival and Manuscript Resources on China and Japan in North Carolina*, ed. by Kenneth W. Berger, 1985.

1-NORTH CAROLINA ROOM, 1937, 1 item
PAMPHLETS: *Dr. George C. Worth*, ed. by Eliza Wright Murphy, 1937.

2-GENERAL HOLDINGS
DISSERTATIONS/THESES: *Missionary Intelligence from China: American Protestant Reports, 1930–1950*, by Bruce S. Greenawalt, 1974.

NC–10   Southern Historical Collection
University of North Carolina at Chapel Hill
Wilson Library, Room 024A
Chapel Hill NC 27514–6080
(919) 962–1345
Carolyn Wallace, Curator and Director
Richard Schrader, Reference Archivist

1-BAGLEY FAMILY PAPERS, 1931–36, 4 items
Background note: This collection contains correspondence of George C. Worth (1867–1937), a Presbyterian medical missionary in China from 1895 until his death and the founder of Gospel Hospital in Kiangyin.
CORRESPONDENCE: 3 letters from Worth to Belle Bagley and other family members, 1931–32, 1936, describing the Japanese invasion of China; letter from H. W. Jackson to Belle and Ethel Bagley informing them of Worth's death, 1936.

2-EUGENE EPPERSON BARNETT RECOLLECTIONS, 1959, 1 item
Background note: For biographical notes, see Columbia University, Rare Book and Manuscript Library, Butler Library, 535 West 114th Street, New York, NY, 10027.
MANUSCRIPTS: "As I Look Back," by Eugene Epperson Barnett, 1959, a 346-page typescript autobiography describing his life from 1888 to 1936.

3-WILLIAM BLOUNT BURKE PAPERS, 1879–97, 326 items
Background note: For biographical notes, see Emory University, Robert W. Woodruff Library, Special Collections Department, Atlanta, GA, 30322.
CORRESPONDENCE: 323 letters to Burke and his wife in Shanghai from his parents, Mr. and Mrs. J. W. Burke, discussing anti-Chinese legislation in the United States and anti-foreign disturbances in China.
MEMORABILIA: 2 scrapbooks entitled "Life Reflections," n.d.; sketch of the life of J. W. Burke by George G. Smith, n.d.
FINDING AIDS: In-house inventory.

4-BURNETT FAMILY PAPERS, 1912–26, quantity undetermined
CORRESPONDENCE: Letters from China missionary Mattie Buchanan, 1912–26, describing her work establishing clinics, Bible schools, and orphanages in Kowloon and Kwangtung, the 1911 Revolution, and a 1915 flood in Kwangtung.
FINDING AIDS: In-house guide.

5-WALLACE HENRY BUTTRICK BIOGRAPHY, 1940s–1960s, 1 item
Background note: A Baptist minister, Wallace Henry Buttrick (1853–1926) worked for the China Medical Board of the Rockefeller Foundation in Peking and Manchuria, ca. 1914, and was a trustee of the Rockefeller Foundation and secretary, president, and chairman of the General Education Board. See also Rockefeller Archive Center, Rockefeller University, Manuscript Collections, Pocantico Hills, North Tarrytown, NY, 10591–1598.
MANUSCRIPTS: "The Story of Wallace Henry Buttrick (1853–1926) and His Wife Sarah Isabella Allen (1853–1939)," a 473-page typescript biography written by their daughter, Caroline I. Buttrick, 1940s-early 1960s.
FINDING AIDS: In-house inventory.

6-FRANCIS ASBURY DICKINS PAPERS, 1875, 1 item
Background note: Francis Asbury Dickins (1804–79) worked for the U.S. War and Treasury Departments in the 1820s and 1830s. This collection contains a large quantity of materials from the Dickins and Randolph families, representing a period of over 200 years (1713–1934).
CORRESPONDENCE: Letter from an unidentified missionary in Hangchow, 1875.
FINDING AIDS: In-house inventory.

7-MARION DUDLEY PAPERS, 1927–59, 18 items
Background note: Marion Dudley worked for the YWCA in Kwangtung and Hong Kong from 1927 to 1931, and again from 1938 to 1941, when she was interned by the Japanese. She was released and returned to America in 1942. Her third stay in China lasted from 1943 to 1947.
CORRESPONDENCE: 14 letters from Marion Dudley in China to friends in the United States, 1927–31, 1939, 1942–47; 2 letters written after her return to the United States, 1954, 1959.
MANUSCRIPTS: 3 pages of biographical data written by Dudley in 1973.
MEMORABILIA/AUDIO-VISUAL MATERIALS: 2 scrapbooks of clippings and photos concerning Dudley's work in China, 1943–45; scrapbook of clippings and photos, some from China, 1927–55.
FINDING AIDS: In-house inventory.

8-JAMES McFADDEN GASTON PAPERS, 1928–35, 1 item
Background note: James McFadden Gaston was a surgeon in the Confederate Army. Later he practiced medicine in Brazil and Atlanta, Georgia. His son, James McFadden Gaston, Jr., was a medical missionary in China from 1912 to 1945.
DIARIES: Diary of James McFadden Gaston, Jr., 1928–35.
FINDING AIDS: In-house inventory.

9-WILLIAM PARSONS McCORKLE PAPERS, 1870s, quantity undetermined
Background note: William Parsons McCorkle (1855–1933) was a Presbyterian clergyman in Virginia and North Carolina.
CORRESPONDENCE: Letters from missionaries in Chekiang, 1870s.

10-McGAVOCK FAMILY PAPERS, ca. 1853, 1 item
CORRESPONDENCE: Letter from George M. Harris in Shanghai, ca. 1853, describing the Taiping Rebellion, his views on the future of Christianity in China, and the weakness of the Ch'ing dynasty.

11-WILLIAM NELSON PENDLETON PAPERS, 1854–70, 3 items
Background note: William Nelson Pendleton was an Episcopal clergyman and Confederate general.
CORRESPONDENCE: 3 letters from China missionary Robert Nelson, a distant relation of Pendleton's, describing missionary work in Shanghai, the Taiping Rebellion, the American attempt to purchase Chusan island in 1854, and Chinese intolerance toward foreigners, 1854, 1867, 1870.
FINDING AIDS: In-house inventory.

12-EDWIN McNEILL POTEAT PAPERS, 1925-29, ca. 50 items
Restrictions: Access by special permission only.
Background note: Edwin McNeill Poteat, Jr. (1892-1955), was a Baptist missionary in China and teacher at Shanghai Baptist College from 1917 to 1929. See also Wake Forest University, North Carolina Baptist Historical Collection, Z. Smith Reynolds Library, P. O. Box 7777, Reynolda Station, Winston-Salem, NC, 27109.
CORRESPONDENCE: Uncatalogued letters, discussing such topics as Chinese nationalism and its effect on missionary work, 1925-29.

CHARLOTTE

ADVENT CHRISTIAN GENERAL CONFERENCE
NC-15 Headquarters Archives
    P. O. Box 23152
    14601 Albemarle Road
    Charlotte NC 28212
    (704) 545-6161
    Harold R. Patterson, Director, Department of World
    Missions

Background note: The American Advent Mission Society, now the Department of World Missions of the Advent Christian General Conference is the denominational sending agency for the Advent Christian Church. For other materials on Advent Christian activity in China, their second mission field, see Aurora University, Phillips Library, 347 South Gladstone Avenue, Aurora, IL, 60507; and Berkshire Christian College, Carter Library, 200 Stockbridge Road, Lenox, MA, 01240.

1-CHINA INFORMATION AND OTHER FIELDS, 1884-1976, ca. 1 box
MINUTES/RECORDS/REPORTS: Account book on life insurance for missionaries, including China missionaries, n.d.; book of check stubs, 1955-56.
CORRESPONDENCE: Folder of correspondence from China missionaries, Wuhu Church compound, n.d.; letters from Sylvia Whitman in scrapbook (see MEMORABILIA below).
MANUSCRIPTS: "Information on Mission Work," including a small section on China with a map: "Advent Christian Mission Field in China," including Nanking, Wuhu, and Chao Hsien.
PAMPHLETS: *A Brief Sketch of the Medical Work of the American Advent Mission in Chao Hsien, China*," n.a., n.d.; memorial booklet for Joseph Wharton, missionary in Nanking and Wuhu; *Oriental Scenes*, n.d.; *Highlights of One Hundred Years*, by Doris Colby, 1966, with a list of China missionaries.
MEMORABILIA: Article about Wang Ming-tao, n.d.; envelope of leaflets about China; postcards of China and Japan, n.d.; scrapbook about Sylvia Whitman in China, 1946-48, with mention of Bertha Cassidy and some pictures of missionaries.
AUDIO-VISUAL MATERIALS: 2 photo albums, n.d.
DISSERTATIONS/THESES: *Floods, Famine, and Wars: A History of the Advent Christian Mission Work in China*, by David E. Dean, 1976.
CHINESE LANGUAGE MATERIALS: Folder of evangelistic tracts and posters, n.d.; Gospel of John, 1884; Buddhist prayer book.

DAVIDSON

DAVIDSON COLLEGE
NC-20 College Archives
    E. H. Little Library
    Davidson NC 28036
    (704) 892-1837
    Chalmers G. Davidson, College Archivist

1-ALUMNI FILES, n.d., quantity undetermined
MINUTES/RECORDS/REPORTS/CORRESPONDENCE/MEMORABILIA/AUDIO-VISUAL MATERIALS: Alumni reports, correspondence, clippings, autobiographies, photos, and other printed materials in alumni files of Davidson alumni who became missionaries to China: Augustus Rochester Craig (1917), John Wright Davis (1869), Palmer Clisby DuBose (1902), Francis Wilson Price (1915), Phillip Barbour Price (1917), Archibald Alexander McFadyen (1899), Wilson Plumer Mills (1903), Donald William Richardson (1902), Edgar A. Woods (1919), James Baker Woods, Jr. (1918), John Russell Woods (1918), and Charles William Worth (1920).

2-GENERAL HOLDINGS
SERIALS: *Chinese Recorder*, 1868-1940.

DURHAM

DUKE UNIVERSITY

NC-25 Biology-Forestry Library
    Durham NC 27706
    (919) 684-2381
    Bertha Livingstone, Librarian

1-GENERAL HOLDINGS
MINUTES/RECORDS/REPORTS: University of Nanking, College of Agriculture and Forestry, Experimental Station, annual reports, 1924-25, 1931-34.
SERIALS: *Lingnan Science Journal*, 1936-42. Peking Society of Natural History, *Bulletin*, 1926-30. University of Nanking, College of Agriculture and Forestry, *Bulletin*, 1932-35.

NC-30 Divinity School Library
    Duke University
    Durham NC 27706
    (919) 684-3691
    Donn Michael Farris, Librarian

1-PAMPHLET COLLECTION, 1926-48, 3 items
PAMPHLETS: *1847-1848: When the Methodists Came to China*, n.a., 1948; *The Situation in China: A Report to the Board of Foreign Missions of the Methodist Episcopal Church of an Official Visit*, n.a., n.d.
MAPS/DESIGNS/DRAWINGS: A map of China prepared for the China Inland Mission, n.a., 1926.

2-GENERAL HOLDINGS
MINUTES/RECORDS/REPORTS: China Continuation Committee, proceedings of the annual meeting, 1916-19; International Institute of China, reports, 1897-1909, 1911-24, 1927.

Methodist Episcopal Church: Central China Conference, minutes, 1909–12, 1916–17, 1919–22, 1926, 1932–33, 1936; Central China Mission Conference, minutes, 1888, 1905–6; Chungking West China Conference, minutes, 1925, 1928–29, 1933; Foochow Conference, minutes, 1891, 1897, 1902–3, 1907–8, 1911–13, 1915, 1917–23, 1927, 1932, 1939; Foochow Woman's Conference, minutes, 1905–12, 1920–24, 1929, 1931; Kiangsi Conference, minutes, 1913, 1916–21, 1923, 1925, 1927–33; North China Annual Conference, minutes, 1902, 1905–6, 1908–20, 1922, 1930, 1938; North China Woman's Conference, minutes and reports, 1906, 1908, 1910–12, 1921–24, 1931, 1938; West China Conference, minutes, 1915, 1920, 1922; West China Methodist Episcopal Mission, minutes, 1895, 1903, 1906–8; West China Mission Conference, 1908–13; Women's Foreign Missionary Society, Hinghwa Conference, minutes, 1921–25, 1931; Yenping Woman's Conference, 1920, 1922–30, 1935–39.

Methodist Episcopal Church, South, China Conference, minutes, 1897, 1909–12, 1916–18, 1920, 1924, 1926, 1930–32, 1936.

PAMPHLETS: *British Protestant Christian Evangelists and the 1898 Reform Movement in China*, by Leslie R. Marchant, 1975; *The Catholic Missions in China during the Middle Ages, 1294–1368*, by Paul Stanislaus Hsiang, 1949; *The Missionary Situation in China*, by Henry Theodore Hodgkin, 1928; *'Neath Changing Skies in China*, by Edith Couche, 1931; *Nestorians in China: Some Corrections and Additions*, by A. C. Moule, 1940; *The Present Situation in China and Its Significance for Christian Missions*, 1925; *1847–1848: When the Methodists Came to China*, 1948.
SERIALS: *China Christian Year Book*, 1910–39. *Monumenta Serica*, monograph series, 1943. Nanking Theological Seminary, English Publications, 1940. *The Story of the China Inland Mission*, 1904–37, 1940.
DISSERTATIONS/THESES: *American Missionaries and the Chinese Communists: A Study of Views Expressed by Methodist Episcopal Church Missionaries, 1921–1941*, by Milo Lancaster Thornberry, Jr., 1974. *Apostolic Legations to China of the Eighteenth Century*, by Antonio Sisto Rosso, 1948. *The China Inland Mission and Some Aspects of Its Work*, by Hudson Taylor Armerding, 1948. *China Missions in Crisis: Bishop Laimbeckhoven and His Times, 1738–87*, by Joseph Krahl, 1964. *Etude sur les missions nestoriennes en Chine au VIIe et au VIIIe siècles; d'après l'inscription syro-chinoise de Si-ngan-fou*, by Augustin Cleisz, 1880. *Imperial Government and Catholic Missions in China during the Years 1784–1785*, by Bernward Henry Willeke, 1948. *John Leighton Stuart: The Mind and Life of an American Missionary in China, 1876–1941*, by Shaw Yu-ming, 1975. *Die katholische Chinamission im Spiegel der Rotchinesischen Presse; Versuch einer missionarischen Deutung*, by Johannes Schütte, 1957. *Lutheran Missions in a Time of Revolution: The China Experience, 1944–1951*, by Jonas Jonson, 1972. *The Negotiations between Ch'i-ying and Lagrené, 1844–1846*, by Angelus Francis J. Grosse-Aschhoff, 1950. *La Politique missionnaire de la France en Chine, 1842–1896: l'ouverture des cinq ports chinois au commerce étranger et la liberté religieuse*, by Louis Tsing-sing Wei, 1960. *Revolutionary Faithfulness: The Quaker Search for a Peaceable Kingdom in China, 1939–1951*, by Cynthia Letts Adcock, 1974.

CHINESE LANGUAGE MATERIALS: *Ch'uan chiao shih yü chin tai Chung-kuo (Missionaries and Modern China)*, by Ku Ch'ang-sheng, 1981.

NC–35 East Campus Library
Duke University
Durham NC 27706–2500
(919) 684–3144
Betty Young, Librarian

1-GENERAL HOLDINGS
SERIALS: *Monumenta Serica*, monograph series, 1961.

NC–40 Law School Library
Duke University
Durham NC 27706–2580
(919) 684–2847
Richard Danner, Director

1-GENERAL HOLDINGS
SERIALS: *China Law Review*, 1922–31.

NC–45 Manuscript Department
Duke University
William R. Perkins Library
Durham NC 27706
(919) 684–3372
Ellen Gartrell, Assistant Curator for Reader Services

Background note: In addition to the materials listed below, scattered references to missions in China can also be found in the papers of Rufus Henry Jones (references to the Shanghai Baptist Mission) and Thomas Jerome Taylor.
Finding aids: *Guide to the Catalogued Collections in the Manuscript Department of the William R. Perkins Library, Duke University*, ed. by Richard C. Davis, Linda Angle Miller, Harry W. McKown, Jr., and Erma Paden Whittington (Santa Barbara, CA: Clio Books), 1980.

1-FREDERICK W. A. BRUCE PAPERS, 1860, 1 volume
MINUTES/RECORDS/REPORTS: Dispatches, including mention of China missions, 1860.

2-JOHN BOWRING PAPERS, n.d., quantity undetermined
Background note: Sir John Bowring (1792–1872) was a diplomat and governor of Hong Kong.
CORRESPONDENCE: Letters concerning missionary activity in China.

3-CAMPBELL FAMILY PAPERS, 1854–59, 3 items
CORRESPONDENCE: 3 letters from China missionary David C. Kelley, 1854–55, 1859.

4-ROBERT S. CHILTON, JR., PAPERS, n.d., quantity undetermined
Background note: Robert S. Chilton, Jr., was head of the U.S. State Department's Consular Bureau from 1897 to 1901.
CORRESPONDENCE: Letters from Hubbard T. Smith, U.S. consul at Canton, detailing persecution of missionaries, n.d.

5-PAUL HIBBERT AND MARY (KESTLER) CLYDE FAMILY PAPERS, 1930, 1 item
MEMORABILIA: Clipping, 1930.

6-MARTHA (FOSTER) CRAWFORD DIARIES, 1846–81, 7 volumes
Background note: Martha (Foster) Crawford (1830–93) and her husband, Tarleton Perry Crawford, were Southern Baptist mis-

sionaries in China from 1851 to 1892.
DIARIES: Diaries of Martha Crawford, containing observations on daily life in Shanghai and Tengchow, and comments on the Taiping Rebellion, 1846–81.
MANUSCRIPTS: A history of China missions, n.d.
PAMPHLETS: Several miscellaneous pamphlets, n.d.

7-CRONLY FAMILY PAPERS, 1937, 1 item
CORRESPONDENCE: Letter mentioning China missions, 1937.

8-THEODORE B. CUNNINGHAM, ca. 1875–1895, ca. 2 volumes
CORRESPONDENCE: Letterpress books containing copies of personal correspondence, mostly to family and friends, discussing aspects of life in Canton and Hong Kong, including the work of Christian missionaries, 1875–79, 1889–95.

9-DAVIDSON FAMILY PAPERS, 1882, quantity undetermined
CORRESPONDENCE: Letters mentioning the work of China missionary John W. Davis, 1882.

10-GALLAHER FAMILY PAPERS, 1890, 1 item
CORRESPONDENCE: Letter mentioning China missions, 1890.

11-ARTHUR R. GALLIMORE PAPERS, ca. 1933, 2 items
Background note: For biographical notes, see Wake Forest University, North Carolina Baptist Historical Collection, Z. Smith Reynolds Library, P. O. Box 7777, Reynolda Station, Winston-Salem, NC, 27109.
MANUSCRIPTS: "The New Work of the South China Mission among the Hakkas in Wai Chow," by Arthur R. Gallimore, ca. 1933.
AUDIO-VISUAL MATERIALS: Photo of Gallimore, ca. 1933.

12-MARY ZILPHA GILES PAPERS, 1912, 1 item
CORRESPONDENCE: Letter to Mary Zilpha Giles from a China missionary, 1912.

13-JOHN MEAD GOULD PAPERS, 1900, 2 items
CORRESPONDENCE: 2 letters mentioning China missions, 1900.

14-HALL FAMILY PAPERS, 1905–53, quantity undetermined
CORRESPONDENCE: Letters mentioning China missions, 1905, 1937, 1946–53.
AUDIO-VISUAL MATERIALS: Picture of Generalissimo and Mme. Chiang K'ai-shek, n.d.

15-HENRY SYDNOR HARRISON PAPERS, 1913, 1 item
CORRESPONDENCE: Letter mentioning China missions, 1913.

16-ROBERT WATTS HUDGENS PAPERS, 1962, 1 item
CORRESPONDENCE: Letter from John B. Griffing, 1962.

17-CATHERINE ELLA JONES PAPERS, 1852–63, 50 items
Background note: For biographical notes, see University of Virginia, Alderman Library, Manuscripts Department, Charlottesville, VA, 22901.
CORRESPONDENCE: 50 letters from Catherine Ella Jones, 1852–63.

18-THOMAS THWEATT JONES PAPERS, 1890, 1 item
CORRESPONDENCE: Letter mentioning China missions, 1890.

19-JOHN McINTOSH KELL PAPERS, 1854, 2 items
CORRESPONDENCE: 2 letters to Julia Blanche (Munroe) Kell (Mrs. John Kell), mentioning China missions, 1854.

20-GEORGE MACARTNEY, 1ST EARL MACARTNEY, PAPERS, 1795, 1 item
Background note: George Macartney was sent by the British government on an embassy to the Ch'ien-lung emperor, 1792–94.
CORRESPONDENCE: Letter mentioning China missions, 1795.

21-BESSIE N. MASON PAPERS, n.d., 1 item
CORRESPONDENCE: Letter from China missionary Ella Davidson, in Hangchow, to Bessie Mason, n.d. (ca. late 19th century).

22-NINA CORNELIA MITCHELL PAPERS, 1917–22, 7 items
CORRESPONDENCE: 7 letters mentioning China missions, 1917–18, 1920–22.

23-GEORGE OSBORN PAPERS, 1857, 1 item
CORRESPONDENCE: Letter to Methodist minister George Osborn from Henry Venn, secretary of a church missionary society, discussing treaty provisions for the protection of missions in China, 1857.

24-ALEXANDER SPRUNT AND SON, INC. PAPERS, 1909–21, 33 items
CORRESPONDENCE: 33 letters, including discussion of the Presbyterian mission at Kiangyin, 1909–10, 1919–21.

25-JAMES AUGUSTUS THOMAS PAPERS, n.d., quantity undetermined
MINUTES/RECORDS/REPORTS/CORRESPONDENCE/PAMPHLETS: Reports, correspondence, and printed material relating to the missionary schools, Navy YMCA, China relief efforts, and Yenching University, n.d. (ca. 1900–1920s).

26-TILLINGHAST FAMILY PAPERS, ca. 1860, quantity undetermined
CORRESPONDENCE: Correspondence and other papers relating to efforts to send Episcopalian missionaries to China, ca. 1860.

27-WILKES FAMILY PAPERS (DALTON COLLECTION), 1850, 1 item
CORRESPONDENCE: Letter mentioning China missions, 1850.

NC–50   University Archives
Duke University
William R. Perkins Library
Room 341
Durham NC 27706
(919) 684–5637
William E. King, University Archivist

1-CHARLES J. SOONG FILE, 1881–1943, 28 items
Background note: For biographical notes, see Vanderbilt University, Jean and Alexander Heard Library, Special Collections/Archives, Nashville, TN, 37240–0007.
MINUTES/RECORDS/REPORTS: Trinity College, grade book, 1884.
CORRESPONDENCE: Copies of the following: letter from Soong to "Miss Mattie," 1882; letter from Soong to Mr. Southgate, 1886; 2 letters from Soong to his son, T. V. Soong, 1915; letter from Arthur M. Harris to Franklin D. Roosevelt, 1942; letter from Roosevelt to T. V. Soong, 1942; letter from T. V. Soong to Roosevelt, 1942.
MEMORABILIA: "Charles J. Soong and His Daughter Will Visit City," newspaper article, 1904; "Charles Jones Soong and Cap-

tain Eric Gabrielson, United States Coast Guard: A Footnote to World History,'' n.a., 1943; ''Charles Jones Soong in America and China,'' excerpt from *The Chiangs of China* by Elmer T. Clark, 1943; ''Father and Mother Soong,'' article by Louise Roberts, 1942; ''Little Known Facts about Well-Known People,'' broadcast by Dale Carnegie about Mme. Chiang K'ai-shek, 1943; ''The Romance of Charlie Soong,'' article by Fred T. Barnett, 1942; ''The Story of Charlie Soong [at Trinity College],'' excerpt from *The Life of Braxton Craven* by Jerome Dowd, 1939.
AUDIO-VISUAL MATERIALS: Photo, ca. 1881.
FINDING AIDS: In-house catalogue.

2-MARQUIS LAFAYETTE WOOD PAPERS, 1856–93, 2 l.f.
Background note: Marquis Lafayette Wood (1829–1893), minister, educator, and president of Trinity College from 1883 to 1884, was a Methodist missionary in China from 1860 to 1866.
MINUTES/RECORDS/REPORTS: Account book, 1864–93.
CORRESPONDENCE: Journal of correspondence from Wood, 1865–66, including such correspondents as E. W. Sehon (Missionary Society of the Methodist Episcopal Church, South) and Charles Force Deems; letter from Wood to Brother Carpenter, 1886; letter from Wood to Andrew P. Tyler, 1892.
DIARIES: 8 diaries, 1860–67.
MEMORABILIA: A 2-page genealogy of the Wood family, n.d.
AUDIO-VISUAL MATERIALS: Portrait of Wood, n.d.
CHINESE LANGUAGE MATERIALS: Hymn book with psalms and church rituals, 1860; Methodist Episcopal Church, South, Chinese Mission, minutes of annual meeting, 1882–83 (both items are located in the Rare Book Room).
FINDING AIDS: In-house catalog.

NC–55   William R. Perkins Library
Duke University
Durham NC 27706
(919) 684-2373
Johannah Sherrer, Reference Librarian

1-GENERAL HOLDINGS
MANUSCRIPTS: ''Christian Higher Education in China: Contributions of the Colleges of Arts and Sciences to Chinese Life,'' by J. Dyke Van Putten, 1937.
PAMPHLETS: *The Story of the Kiangyin Hospital, China*, by Eliza Wright Murphy, 1930(?); *Windows into China: The Jesuits and Their Books, 1580–1730*, by John Parker, 1978.
ORAL HISTORIES: *China Missionaries Oral History Collection*, ed. by Cyrus H. Peake and Arthur L. Rosenbaum (Claremont Graduate School, Oral History Program), 1973. See ORAL HISTORIES Union List for the names of participants.
SERIALS: *China Christian Advocate*, 1916–18, 1920–24, 1931–40. China Christian Educational Association, *Bulletin*, 1924–28, 1933–39. *China Monthly: The Truth about China*, 1939–50. *China's Millions* (London), 1875–76, 1878–81, 1885–88, 1890–92, 1895–1913, 1918–21, 1924–27. *Chinese Recorder*, 1868–1941. *Chinese Repository*, 1832–45, 1847–49. *El Correo Sino-Annamita*, 1911–13. *Educational Review*, 1927–34. *Folklore Studies*, supplement, 1952. *Monumenta Serica*, 1935–83; monograph series, 1939, 1967. *Tung Wu Magazine*, 1937. *United China Relief Series*, 1941. West China Border Research Society, *Journal*, 1922–28, 1936, 1938. *Yenching Journal of Social Studies*, 1938–50.

DISSERTATIONS/THESES: *The American Christian Press and the Sino-Japanese Crisis of 1931–1933: An Aspect of Public Response to the Breakdown of World Peace*, by Alden B. Pearson, Jr., 1968. *Extracts from the Diary of Martha E. Foster Crawford, 1852–1854*, by Virginia M. Thompson, 1952. *J. Hudson Taylor and the China Inland Mission*, by Joseph Russell Andrews, 1950. *The London Missionary Society in India and China, 1798–1834*, by Laurence Kitzan, 1965. *Missionary Intelligence from China: American Protestant Reports, 1930–1950*, by Bruce Stephen Greenawalt, 1974.
CHINESE LANGUAGE MATERIALS: *Lin Le-chih tsai Hua shih yeh yü ''Wan kuo kung pao''* (*Young J. Allen in China: His Career and the ''Wan kuo kung pao''*), by Liang Yüan-sheng, 1978.

GREENSBORO

GUILFORD COLLEGE
NC–60   Friends Historical Collection
Guilford College Library
5800 West Friendly Avenue
Greensboro NC 27410
(919) 292-5511
Damon Hickey, Curator

Background note: This collection contains a complete run of the serial *Friends Missionary Advocate* (1885–1976), which has information on Friends' mission work in China.

1-GENERAL HOLDINGS
SERIALS: *Friends Oriental News*, 1908–62.

UNIVERSITY OF NORTH CAROLINA AT GREENSBORO
NC–65   Walter Clinton Jackson Library
1000 Spring Garden Street
Greensboro NC 27412-5201
(919) 379-5880
Nancy Fogarty, Head Reference Librarian

1-GENERAL HOLDINGS
SERIALS: *China Notes*, 1962-.

GREENVILLE

EAST CAROLINA UNIVERSITY
NC–70   East Carolina Manuscript Collection
J. Y. Joyner Library
Greenville NC 27834
(919) 757-6671
Donald R. Lennon, Coordinator of Special Collections

Finding aids: *Bulletin of the East Carolina Manuscript Collection*, Nos. 2–9; *Guide to Asian Studies Resources in the East Carolina Manuscript Collection*, by Donald R. Lennon (Greenville, NC: Joyner Library), 1985.

1-M. LOUISE AVETT INTERVIEW, 1932–70, 1 item
Background note: M. Louise Avett was a Methodist missionary in China from 1932 to 1945, and in Hong Kong from 1960 to 1970.

ORAL HISTORIES: 21-page transcript of an interview describing educational work in Soochow, Avett's transfer to Szechwan in 1941, conditions in Hong Kong during the 1960s, experiences in rural Szechwan, Chinese culture, and the Japanese invasion.

2-M. LOUISE AVETT PAPERS, 1930-49, 185 items
CORRESPONDENCE: 185 letters to M. Louise Avett's parents and siblings, 1930-49, including descriptions of her stay at Scarritt College; her work as a missionary at Changshu, Chengtu, Suining, and other localities; Chinese food, culture, and religion; travel in China; and conditions during the war.

3-EUGENE E. BARNETT MEMOIR, n.d., 1 item
Background note: For biographical notes, see Columbia University, Rare Book and Manuscript Library, Butler Library, 535 West 114th Street, New York, NY, 10027.
MANUSCRIPTS: 304-page typescript copy of Barnett's memoir recounting his childhood, education, and career as a YMCA official in China (1908-36), including descriptions of Hangchow and Shanghai, travel accounts, YMCA work, early Chinese Communism, confrontations between Communists and Nationalists, religion and ethical systems of China, Chinese views of Christianity, and the Japanese invasion of Manchuria.

4-HARRY V. BERNARD PAPERS, ca. 1911-1939, ca. 10 items
Background note: Harry V. Bernard (1879-1968) served in China as a businessman, diplomat, and coordinator of Western relief efforts.
MANUSCRIPTS: Writings and memoir material describing missionaries in China.

5-D. WILLARD BLISS PAPERS, 1835-1936, 2 items
MINUTES/RECORDS/REPORTS: Proceedings of a Baptist general convention in Richmond, Virginia, including reports of missionary activities in China, 1835.
MANUSCRIPTS: A brief history of missionary activity in Tengchow from 1861 to 1936.

6-ETHEL W. BOST DIARY, 1925, 1/5 reel microfilm
Background note: Ethel W. Bost was a Methodist missionary to China from 1925 to 1943, and was repatriated from a Japanese concentration camp in December 1943. From 1949 to 1969 she served as a missionary in Japan.
DIARIES: Microfilmed diary describing Bost's voyage to China from Vancouver, British Columbia, 1925.

7-VENETIA COX PAPERS, 1917-50, 196 items
Background note: Venetia Cox was an Episcopal missionary to China from 1917 to 1950, and taught music at a mission school in Hupei until 1937, when the school was forced to relocate in Kwangsi by the Japanese invasion. From 1937 to 1950, Cox and her colleagues travelled throughout the interior of China, at times along the Burma Road. In 1950 she was expelled from the mainland.
CORRESPONDENCE: Letters, 1917-50, including discussions of attempts to unify the church in China, banditry, Chinese methods of growing tobacco, footbinding, floods at Hankow (1930-32), the Japanese invasion, living conditions, student arrests, and unstable political conditions.
DIARIES: 3 diaries, 1917-20, 1938-39, including descriptions of Buddhist ceremonies, the effect of the Sino-Japanese war on missionary work, living conditions, Cox's meeting with President Hsu

Shih-chang, and the removal of the mission school from Wuchang during the Japanese invasion.
MEMORABILIA: Newspaper clippings concerning Cox's activities, n.d.
AUDIO-VISUAL MATERIALS: Uncatalogued photos, n.d.
CHINESE LANGUAGE MATERIALS: A music course book, n.d.
FINDING AIDS: In-house finding aid.

8-LULA M. DISOSWAY PAPERS, 1926-41, ca. 135 items
Background note: Lula M. Disosway (1897-1973) was an Episcopalian medical missionary in China from 1926 to 1941.
CORRESPONDENCE/DIARIES: Letters, a diary, and reports, 1926-41, including discussions of Disosway's work at St. Elizabeth's Hospital in Shanghai, high costs caused by the Sino-Japanese war, Chinese refugees from Yangchow, and problems caused by the prospects of war between Japan and the United States.
AUDIO-VISUAL MATERIALS: Photos of hospital staff and patients, and scenes from throughout China.
FINDING AIDS: In-house finding aid.

9-NORMAN PLAYER FARRIOR PAPERS, 1932-46, ca. 5 items
Background note: Norman Player Farrior (1890-1970) was a Presbyterian minister and missionary to Mexico from 1921 to 1924.
CORRESPONDENCE: Letters from other missionaries, including discussions of the Japanese invasion of China, the flight of missionaries in the interior, and Communism in China, 1932, 1946.

10-NELSON FEREBEE PAPERS, n.d., 1 item
MANUSCRIPTS: Memoir recounting Nelson Ferebee's service with the U.S. Navy (1872-1904), including an account of the rescue of three French missionaries from a mob in Canton.

11-QUENTIN GREGORY INTERVIEW, n.d., 1 item
Background note: Quentin Gregory was a tobacconist in China from 1908 to 1920, serving for a time as general inspector of sales in China for the British-American Tobacco Company.
ORAL HISTORIES: 8-page transcript of an interview containing descriptions of missionary attitudes toward businessmen in China and the aftermath of the Boxer Uprising, 1905-20.

12-OLA V. LEA PAPERS, 1893-1973, ca. 1,600 items
Background note: Ola V. Lea (1891-1979) was a Baptist missionary in China from 1925 to 1950, and a teacher of English at the University of Taiwan from 1950 to 1962. She taught in Soochow and Kaifeng until the outbreak of World War II, and served as dean of women at China Baptist Seminary in Soochow after the war.
CORRESPONDENCE: Letters, including discussions of missionary activities in China and Taiwan, 1928-50.
PAMPHLETS/AUDIO-VISUAL MATERIALS: Uncatalogued pamphlets and photos, n.d.
CHINESE LANGUAGE MATERIALS: Uncatalogued pamphlets, n.d.

13-JENNY LIND PAPERS, ca. 1930-1950, quantity undetermined
Background note: Jenny Lind was a Methodist missionary in China, Japan, and Brazil from 1924 to 1968.
CORRESPONDENCE/MANUSCRIPTS: Letters and personal notes, ca. 1930-1950, including discussions of Chiang K'ai-shek, Chinese customs, theatre, and politics, a Yangtze River flood, Japanese and Communist attacks, and health and disease in China.

14-PEARLE McCAIN INTERVIEW, n.d., 1 item
Background note: Pearle McCain was a Methodist missionary in China from 1929 to 1942, and from 1946 to 1949.
ORAL HISTORIES: 24-page transcript of an interview describing McCain's work in Peking, Shanghai, and Sungkiang, the Japanese invasion, travel, local customs, seminary work, the effect of World War II on China, McCain's personal views on the Communist government, her departure from China, and a return visit to Japan and Shanghai in 1980.

15-JANE GREGORY MARROW INTERVIEW, n.d., 1 item
Background note: Jane Gregory Marrow was born in Shanghai in 1905, the daughter of tobacconist Richard Henry Gregory. She remained in China until 1935.
ORAL HISTORIES: 39-page transcript of an interview containing descriptions of interaction between missionaries and the business community in China.

16-KATIE MURRAY INTERVIEW, n.d., 1 item
Background note: Katie Murray was a graduate of Woman's Missionary Union Training School in Louisville, Kentucky, and served as a missionary in mainland China from 1927 to 1944, and from 1946 to 1950. During the Sino-Japanese War she was involved in refugee relief work (1938–44). From 1954 to 1959 she was a missionary in Taiwan.
ORAL HISTORIES: 26-page transcript of an interview describing Murray's work in Chengchow (1927–44, 1946–50) and Taiwan (1954–59), mission schools, the Japanese invasion, refugee work, Murray's flight from China, conditions after World War II, Chinese attitudes toward foreigners, the breakdown of civil and moral authority in China, the Communist takeover, Chinese religion, marriage customs, warlords, and mountain tribes in Kwangsi.

17-KATIE MURRAY PAPERS, 1930–50, 357 items
Background note: See biographical notes above.
CORRESPONDENCE: Letters, ca. 1930–50, including discussion of Chinese social practices and customs, and various Protestant missionary activities.
DIARIES: Diaries, ca. 1930–50, containing discussions of China's war economy, the Japanese occupation of Chengchow, Murray's escape from China to Thailand after the Japanese attack on Chengchow (1944), and missionary work during the Communist occupation of Kwangsi in 1950.

18-SUSAN HERRING JEFFERIES TAYNTON PAPERS, 1896–1964, 270 items
Background note: Susan Taynton was the daughter of David Wells Herring, a Baptist missionary in China from 1885 to 1892, and from 1907 to 1929. In 1960, she wrote a biography of her father entitled *Papa Wore No Halo*.
CORRESPONDENCE/PAMPHLETS/MEMORABILIA/ AUDIO-VISUAL MATERIALS: Letters, pamphlets, clippings, and photographs, 1896–1964, including items concerning missionary work in China, theology, the Southern Baptist Foreign Mission Board, the Boxer Rebellion, and the publication of *Papa Wore No Halo*.
FINDING AIDS: In-house finding aid.

19-LUCY J. WEBB PAPERS, n.d., 1 item
Background note: Lucy J. Webb was a Methodist missionary in Shanghai from 1922 to 1943 and from 1946 to 1951. She was

interned by the Japanese for seven months in 1943.
MANUSCRIPTS: 281-page memoir describing Webb's experiences in China from 1921 to 1951, Chinese education, farming methods, industries, medicine, politics, religion, and social mores, the Japanese invasion, relief work, student uprisings, and the Communist takeover of China.

20-JESSIE L. WOLCOTT PAPERS, 1939–50, 90 items
Background note: Jessie L. Wolcott was a Methodist missionary in Nanking from 1922 to 1937, 1939 to 1941, and 1946 to 1951.
CORRESPONDENCE: Letters, describing her involvement in educational and relief work, economic conditions in and around Nanking, conditions under the Japanese occupation, the effects of worsening inflation under the Nationalists, and the impact of the U.S. Army on missionary activities, 1939–42, 1946–50.
MANUSCRIPTS: Travel accounts, providing information on conditions in areas untouched by the Sino-Japanese War and areas under Japanese military control, 1948.
FINDING AIDS: In-house finding aid.

LAKE JUNALUSKA

NC–75   WORLD METHODIST MUSEUM
World Methodist Building
P. O. Box 518
39 Lakeshore Drive
Lake Junaluska NC 28745
(704) 456–9432
Evelyn M. Sutton, Curator

1-BISHOP CORSON PAPERS, 1947–61, quantity undetermined
Background note: Fred Pierce Corson (1896–1985) was a Methodist bishop and church administrator. From 1947 to 1949 he represented the Methodist Council of Bishops at the centennial of Chinese Methodism; he travelled extensively in Asia during the late 1950s and early 1960s. His papers at the World Methodist Museum are only partially processed.
MANUSCRIPTS: "How Our Bishops Served the Chinese," by Bishop Otto Nall, n.d.; notebook on China, n.d.
AUDIO-VISUAL MATERIALS: Uncatalogued photos of Bishop Corson with President and Mme. Chiang K'ai-shek, n.d.

MONTREAT

NC–80   HISTORICAL FOUNDATION OF THE PRESBYTERIAN AND REFORMED CHURCHES
Montreat NC 28757
(704) 669–7061
Jerrold Lee Brooks, Executive Director
Robert Benedetto, Archivist

Background note: The Historical Foundation, incorporated in 1927, is the official repository of the former Presbyterian Church in the United States (PCUS). In addition to church records, the Historical Foundation holds important collections of manuscripts and papers of former missionaries to China, and a large number of secondary works on China, including histories of mission organizations, biographies and autobiographies of missionaries, and reference works on the Chinese language.

Finding aids: "A Review of Chinese and Japanese Resources for Research at the Historical Foundation of the Presbyterian and Reformed Churches," by Jerrold Lee Brooks, 1983.

1-HAROLD THOMAS BRIDGMAN PAPERS, 1923–41, 14 l.f.
CORRESPONDENCE/DIARIES/MEMORABILIA/AUDIO-VISUAL MATERIALS: Letters between Harold Thomas Bridgman and his wife, diaries, files, sermons, notes, and photos relating to Bridgman's work as a Presbyterian missionary in Yencheng, 1923–41.

2-FRANCIS AUGUSTUS BROWN, SR., PAPERS, 1914–54, 3.5 l.f.
Background note: Francis Augustus Brown, Sr., and his wife were Presbyterian missionaries in Suchowfu, Kiangsu, from 1914 to 1954.
CORRESPONDENCE/DIARIES/MANUSCRIPTS/MEMORABILIA/AUDIO-VISUAL MATERIALS: Letters, diaries, manuscripts for published articles and pamphlets, sermon notes, scrapbooks, and photo albums, 1914–54.

3-EDWARD SMITH CURRIE PAPERS, 1908–41, 28 l.f.
CORRESPONDENCE/DIARIES/MEMORABILIA/AUDIO-VISUAL MATERIALS: Uncatalogued letters of Edward Smith and Gay Wilson Currie, printed materials, and diaries, 1908–41; uncatalogued scrapbooks and photos related to their work as Presbyterian missionaries in Haichow, Kiangsu, from 1920 to 1941.

4-DAVIS FAMILY PAPERS, 1900–1961, 6 l.f.
Background note: Lowry Davis (1881–1962) and his wife, Mary Barnett Davis (1879–1949), served as educational missionaries in Kashing.
MINUTES/RECORDS/REPORTS/CORRESPONDENCE/DIARIES/MANUSCRIPTS/AUDIO-VISUAL MATERIALS: Account books; letters of Lowry and Mary Davis, 1900–1961; sermons and sermon notes, diaries, and photo albums relating to the Davis' work in Kashing, n.d.

5-JOHN WRIGHT DAVIS MANUSCRIPT, 1880, 1 item
CORRESPONDENCE: Letter of 1880 acknowledging a contribution toward the purchase of a lot in Soochow where John Wright Davis worked for over 30 years as a Southern Presbyterian missionary.

6-HAMPDEN COIT DuBOSE COLLECTION, n.d., 1 volume
Background note: Hampden Coit DuBose was a Southern Presbyterian missionary in Hangchow and Soochow in the 1870s and 1880s and the founder of the Yang Yoh Hang Church in Soochow.
MANUSCRIPTS: Lecture notes on China, n.d.

7-STACY CONRAD FARRIOR PAPERS, 1948–50, 3 l.f.
Background note: Stacy Conrad Farrior (1889–1975) and his wife, Kitty Caldwell (McMullen) Farrior, were Presbyterian missionaries in China from 1910 to 1950. Farrior served as principal of the Kashing and Chinkiang High Schools, and as treasurer of China Missions for the Presbyterian Church in the United States.
CORRESPONDENCE/MANUSCRIPTS/AUDIO-VISUAL MATERIALS: Letters describing the Farriors' escape from China, 1948–50; sermons, sermon notes, addresses, and photos, n.d., including items relating to women's work in the PCUS and the Shanghai Council of Church Women.

8-JENNIE GREENWOOD COLLECTION, n.d., 3 items
CORRESPONDENCE: 3 letters concerning the Mary Whittelsey Greenwood Memorial Chapel in Sinbeng (sic).

9-GEORGE ALEXANDER HUDSON PAPERS, 1957–61, 1 l.f.
DIARIES/MEMORABILIA/AUDIO-VISUAL MATERIALS: Diaries, 1957–61, including discussion of George Alexander Hudson's mission work in Kashing, ca. 1920s; China Mission postcards and photos, n.d.

10-JAMES FRANCIS JOHNSON MANUSCRIPT, 1884, 1 item
CORRESPONDENCE: Letter from James Francis Johnson describing affairs in Hangchow and the Chinese practice of foot-binding, 1884.

11-LEWIS HOLLADAY LANCASTER PAPERS, n.d., 3 in.
MINUTES/RECORDS/REPORTS/CORRESPONDENCE/MEMORABILIA: Uncatalogued letters, reports, articles and printed materials, and clippings, related to Lewis Holladay Lancaster's work as a Presbyterian missionary in Nanking.

12-LUCY LEGRAND LITTLE PAPERS, 1926–29, 1 in.
CORRESPONDENCE/MANUSCRIPTS/MAPS/DESIGNS/DRAWINGS: Letters between Lucy Legrand Little and her parents, Dr. and Mrs. Alexander Sprunt, n.d.; sermons, addresses, and articles relating to Little's work as co-founder of the Kiangyin Presbyterian mission station; maps of the China Protestant Missions, Soonchun Compound, 1929, and the Kiangyin mission field, 1926.

13-EDWARD MACK PAPERS, 1921–26, 68 items
Background note: Edward Mack was chairman of a commission of East Hanover Presbytery, Virginia, examining charges of unorthodoxy against John Leighton Stuart, who was a Presbyterian missionary to China, president of Yenching University, and later, U.S. Ambassador to China (1946–52).
MINUTES/RECORDS/REPORTS/CORRESPONDENCE: Letters and reports to East Hanover Presbytery collected by Mack, 1921–26.

14-ROBERT JOHNSTON McMULLEN COLLECTION, 1911-ca. 1945, 1 volume
MEMORABILIA/AUDIO-VISUAL MATERIALS: Scrapbook containing clippings and photos relating to Robert Johnston McMullen's work as a Presbyterian missionary in Hangchow and his return from Japanese internment during World War II, 1911-ca. 1945.

15-FLORENCE NICKLES COLLECTION, 1949, 1 volume
MEMORABILIA: Scrapbook describing Bible school students at the Woman's Bible Training School in Nanking, where Florence Nickles had been a teacher since 1915, and the destruction of Nanking by Communist soldiers, 1949.

16-BROWN CRAIG PATTERSON PAPERS, 1921–42, 1 l.f.
Background note: Brown Craig Patterson was a Presbyterian missionary in Sutsien and Tenghsien from 1891 to 1939, and a professor at the North China Presbyterian Theological Seminary.
MINUTES/RECORDS/REPORTS/CORRESPONDENCE/MEMORABILIA: Account books, scrapbooks, and cartes de visites of PCUS missionaries, 1921–42, including items relating to mission work in Sutsien; mimeographed missionary letters, n.d.;

scrapbook belonging to Mrs. Patterson, n.d.; supplement to the Tenghsien county history; correspondence relating to the North Kiangsu Mission, 1921–42, including 14 letters from Watson McMillan Hayes, president of the North China Theological Seminary.
MANUSCRIPTS: A history of Chinese missions from 1927 to 1933, n.d.

17-CRAIG HOUSTON PATTERSON PAPERS, n.d., 13 items
MANUSCRIPTS: 13 items containing Craig Houston Patterson's reminiscences about his experiences in China as a Presbyterian missionary in Sutsien, n.d.

18-PHOTO COLLECTION, ca. 1890–1940, 2 l.f.
AUDIO-VISUAL MATERIALS: Photos of PCUS missionaries and stations, hospitals, schools, and related organizations, 1890–1940.

19-PCUS BOARD OF WORLD MISSIONS, FIELDS: FAR EAST, 1868–1941, 8 l.f.
MINUTES/RECORDS/REPORTS: China Mission, minutes, 1868–95; Mid-China Mission, minutes, 1894–1941; North Kiangsu Mission, minutes, 1899–1940; miscellaneous mission station and hospital annual reports.

20-ANNIE E. RANDOLPH PAPERS, 1880s, 4 items
CORRESPONDENCE: 4 letters from Annie E. Randolph describing her experiences as a teacher in Hangchow in the 1880s.

21-SAFFORD FAMILY PAPERS, 1861–83, 1 l.f.
CORRESPONDENCE/DIARIES/MEMORABILIA: Letters and notebooks of Anna Cunningham Safford describing life in Soochow, 1861–83; 3 diaries of Safford, 1873–74, 1883.

22-ADDIE M. SLOAN MANUSCRIPT, 1916, 1 item
CORRESPONDENCE: Letter describing the work of Addie M. and Gertrude Lee Sloan in Soochow as Presbyterian educational missionaries, 1916.

23-EGBERT WATSON SMITH PAPERS, 1918–19, 12 items
Background note: Egbert Watson Smith (1862–1944) served as executive secretary of the Committee on Foreign Missions from 1912 to 1932, and field secretary of the Committee from 1932 to 1944. He visited mission stations in China in 1918 and 1919.
MINUTES/RECORDS/REPORTS: Minutes of meetings with missionaries at the following mission stations in China, 1918–19: Chinkiang, Haichow, Hwaianfu, Kashing, Kiangyin, Nanking, Soochow, Süchowfu, Sutsien, Taichow, Tsingkiangfu, and Yencheng.

24-HART MAXCY SMITH PAPERS, 1893–1943, 1 l.f.
CORRESPONDENCE/MANUSCRIPTS/CHINESE LANGUAGE MATERIALS: Letters, sermon notes, and printed materials in Chinese, 1893–1943, relating to Hart Maxcy Smith's work as a Presbyterian missionary in Soochow, the Japanese invasion of China, his internment by the Japanese, and other events in China during the 1920s and 1930s.

25-WADE HAMPTON VENABLE COLLECTION, 1893–1952, 14 volumes
DIARIES: 14 diaries relating to Wade Hampton Venable's work as a medical missionary in Kashing and as founder of the Kashing Hospital, 1893–1952.

26-HUGH WATT WHITE COLLECTION, n.d., 1 volume
MEMORABILIA: Scrapbook containing publications by Hugh Watt White, a Presbyterian missionary in Yencheng, on issues within the PCUS and the China Mission, n.d.

27-LOIS YOUNG PAPERS, 1917–41, .5 l.f.
CORRESPONDENCE: Letters from Lois Young to her family on topics such as Chinese culture, mission work, and her work as director of the Mary Thompson Stevens School for Girls in Suchowfu, 1917–41.

28-GENERAL HOLDINGS
MINUTES/RECORDS/REPORTS: Hangchow Christian College, bulletins, reports, and minutes, 1917–35; Hangchow Union Girls High School, announcements and reports, 1920–30; Nanking Theological Seminary, bulletins, catalogues, and minutes, 1917–25; Nanking University, charter, by-laws, and historical statement, n.d.; Nanking University Hospital, annual reports, n.d.; Shantung Christian University, reports, promotional items, and University and Medical School catalogues, 1917–40.
SERIALS: *China Christian Year Book*, 1911–14, 1916, 1918–19, 1923, 1929. *China Council Bulletin*, 1933. *The China Fundamentalist*, 1928–40. *China Mission Newsletter*, 1928–41. *China Notes*, 1962–77. *Chinese Recorder*, 1911–41. Southern Presbyterian Missions in China, *Bi-Monthly Bulletin*, 1899–1900, 1905–24.
CHINESE LANGUAGE MATERIALS: Uncatalogued books, including Bibles, hymnals, mission station minutes, and reports of schools, hospitals, and other organizations.

RALEIGH

NORTH CAROLINA DEPARTMENT OF CULTURAL RESOURCES
NC–85   **Division of Archives and History**
109 East Jones Street
Raleigh NC 27611
(919) 733–4867
William S. Price, Jr., Director
Jesse R. Lankford, Jr., Assistant State Archivist

Finding aids: *Guide to Private Manuscript Collections in the North Carolina State Archives*, ed. by Barbara T. Cain (Raleigh: North Carolina Department of Cultural Resources, Division of Archives and History), 1981.

1-DAVID WELLS HERRING LETTER, 1885, 1 item
Background note: For biographical notes see Susan Herring Jefferies Taynton Papers at East Carolina University, East Carolina Manuscript Collection, J. Y. Joyner Library, Greenville, NC, 27834.
CORRESPONDENCE: Letter from David Wells Herring, describing his voyage to China, 1885.

2-JOHN M. AND RUTH HODGES PAPERS, 1910, 1 item
CORRESPONDENCE: Letter from missionaries in China, 1910.

3-ELIZA MORING YATES LETTER, 1847, 1 item
Background note: For biographical notes on Matthew Tyson Yates,

see Wake Forest University, North Carolina Baptist Historical Collection, Z. Smith Reynolds Library, P. O. Box 7777, Reynolda Station, Winston-Salem, NC, 27109.

CORRESPONDENCE: Letter to Sarah C. Merritt from her sister, Eliza Moring Yates (Mrs. Matthew Tyson Yates), describing the Yates' voyage to China, 1847.

SALISBURY

CATAWBA COLLEGE

NC-90 Corriher-Linn-Black Library
>Salisbury NC 28144
>(707) 637-4484
>Betty Sell, Director

1-UNCATALOGUED MATERIALS—VAULT, 1926, 2 items
PAMPHLETS: *Huping Commencement Number*, Huping Christian College, 1926; *Our Mission in China Faced the Terrors of War*, Reformed Church in the U.S., Board of Foreign Missions, n.d.

2-GENERAL HOLDINGS
MANUSCRIPTS: "From Six to Sixty to Six: A Narrative of the China Mission of the Reformed Church in the United States and the Later Evangelical and Reformed Church," by Arthur Vale Casselman, 1953.
CHINESE LANGUAGE MATERIALS: 2 versions of the New Testament in Mandarin and English, 1923, 1939.

WAKE FOREST

SOUTHEASTERN BAPTIST THEOLOGICAL SEMINARY

NC-95 Seminary Library
>P. O. Box 752
>Wake Forest NC 27587-0752
>(919) 556-3101
>H. Eugene McLeod, Librarian

1-MANUSCRIPT COLLECTION, 1960, 2 items
MANUSCRIPTS: "Beginning in South China: A Story of the First Missionary Efforts of the Southern Baptist Convention, 1835–1945," by Arthur Raymond Gallimore, 1960; "Some Specimens of Chinese Literature and Journalism," comp. by Arthur Raymond Gallimore, n.d.

WINSTON-SALEM

WAKE FOREST UNIVERSITY

NC-100 North Carolina Baptist Historical Collection
>Room 207, Z. Smith Reynolds Library
>P. O. Box 7777, Reynolda Station
>Winston-Salem NC 27109
>(919) 761-5472
>John R. Woodard, University Archivist and Director, North Carolina Baptist Historical Collection

Background note: The North Carolina Baptist Historical Collection was established as a part of the Wake College library in 1885 and has been regarded as a special collection of the library since that time. Besides printed books and materials relating to North Carolina Baptists and Baptists in general, the collection began to acquire personal papers of Baptist missionaries, denominational leaders, and alumni.
Finding aids: "Missionaries' Papers and Other Sources in the North Carolina Baptist Historical Collection, Wake Forest University," by John Woodard, 1983.

1-THOMAS WILBURN AND SANFORD EMMETT AYERS PAPERS, ca. 1918–1949, ca. 20 items
Background note: Thomas Wilburn Ayers (1858–1954) was a medical missionary to China from 1900 to 1934. His son, Sanford Emmett Ayers (1899–1968), was also a medical missionary to China from 1921 to 1925, 1934 to 1941, and 1947 to 1955.
MANUSCRIPTS: Typescript biography of Thomas Ayers by Sanford Ayers, n.d.; typescript memoirs of Thomas Ayers, n.d.; notes for addresses, articles, reports, and a draft history of Southern Baptist medical missions in China, by Sanford Ayers, n.d.
DIARIES: Journal by Thomas Ayers, n.d.
AUDIO-VISUAL MATERIALS: Photos of Thomas Ayers and his medical staff, n.d.

2-THOMAS WILBURN AND SANFORD EMMETT AYERS PAPERS (MICROFILM), ca. 1900–1955, 1 reel microfilm
MANUSCRIPTS: Biographical materials concerning the Ayers family, n.d.; writings of Thomas Ayers and Sanford Ayers concerning their work, medical missions, and the Communist takeover of China, 1900–1955.

3-EXUM G. BECKWORTH PAPERS, n.d., 1 item
AUDIO-VISUAL MATERIALS: Photo of China missionary David Wells Herring, n.d.

4-GEORGE PLEASANT BOSTICK PAPERS, 1884–1905, 10 items
Background note: George Pleasant Bostick (1858–1926) and his wife, Mary J. Thornton Bostick, served as Southern Baptist missionaries in China from 1889 to 1892. Bostick served again from 1912 to 1926.
MANUSCRIPTS: 2 notebooks, ca. 1884–1886.
DIARIES: 3 diaries, 1898–1899 and n.d.
AUDIO-VISUAL MATERIALS: 5 photos of family members and Chinese, 1905.

5-WILLIS RICHARD CULLOM PAPERS, 1935–54, ca. 40 items
Background note: Willis Richard Cullom (1867–1963) was a Baptist minister and professor of religion at Wake Forest College.
CORRESPONDENCE: 7 letters between Cullom and Wade Dobbins Bostick, 1934–57; 11 letters between Cullom and Arthur R. Gallimore, 1939–49, 1954; 4 letters between Cullom and Arthur Samuel Gillespie, 1945–47; several letters from David Wells Herring, 1935–36; 11 letters between Cullom and Sophie Stephens Lanneau, 1936–37; 8 letters between Cullom and Charles Alexander Leonard, ca. 1948–1962; letter from Edwin McNeill Poteat, 1948.

6-CHARLES BENNETT DEANE PAPERS, 1956, 6 items
Background note: For biographical notes on Edwin McNeill Poteat, Jr., see William Louis Poteat Papers below.
CORRESPONDENCE: Letter from John Burder Hipps, 1956; 5 letters from Edwin McNeill Poteat, Jr., n.d.

7-ALVADA GUNN DURHAM PAPERS, 1920–84, 60 items
Background note: Alvada Gunn Durham was a Southern Baptist missionary to China from 1920 to 1926.
CORRESPONDENCE: 33 letters from Durham to the J. W. Holmes family, 1920–26, 1984.
MANUSCRIPTS: An article by Durham, n.d.
AUDIO-VISUAL MATERIALS: 24 photos of Durham, fellow missionaries, other co-workers, and Chinese, 1920–26.
CHINESE LANGUAGE MATERIALS: 2 Chinese Bible cards, n.d.

8-ARTHUR RAYMOND GALLIMORE PAPERS, 1908–44, 7 items
Background note: Arthur Raymond Gallimore (1885–1955) and his wife, Gladys (Stephenson) Gallimore, were Southern Baptist missionaries in China from 1918 to 1947. See also Duke University, Manuscript Department, William R. Perkins Library, Durham, NC, 27706.
PAMPHLETS: 2 pamphlets, 1928, 1939.
MEMORABILIA: Scrapbook on Baptist journalism, 1928–41; 2 scrapbooks containing miscellaneous materials, ca. 1908–1944.
AUDIO-VISUAL MATERIALS: Photo of Arthur R. Gallimore, n.d.
CHINESE LANGUAGE MATERIALS: Chinese scroll, n.d.

9-ARTHUR SAMUEL GILLESPIE PAPERS, 1941–52, 36 items
Background note: Arthur Samuel Gillespie (1902–52) was a Southern Baptist missionary in China from 1931 to 1952.
CORRESPONDENCE/MANUSCRIPTS/AUDIO-VISUAL MATERIALS: Letters, an unpublished biography of Gillespie, and photos, 1941–52.

10-GEORGE WASHINGTON GREENE PAPERS, n.d., quantity undetermined
Background note: George Washington Greene (1852–1911) was a Southern Baptist missionary to China from 1891 to 1911.
MANUSCRIPTS: Biographical information on Greene, n.a., n.d.
PAMPHLETS: Miscellaneous polemical pamphlets, 1893.
AUDIO-VISUAL MATERIALS: A framed portrait of Greene, n.d.

11-SOPHIE STEPHENS LANNEAU PAPERS, 1907–50, 2,122 items
Background note: Sophie Stephens Lanneau (1880–1963) served as an educational missionary to China from 1907 to 1951. She founded the Wei Ling Girls' Academy in Soochow (1911), and was interned by the Japanese in 1942. After being repatriated to the United States in 1943, she returned to China in 1946, remaining until 1950.
CORRESPONDENCE/MANUSCRIPTS/MEMORABILIA/ AUDIO-VISUAL MATERIALS: Letters, writings, scrapbooks, and photos, 1907–50.

12-CHARLES ALEXANDER LEONARD PAPERS, 1944–69, 540 items
Background note: Charles Alexander Leonard (1882–1973) served

as a Southern Baptist missionary in China from 1910 to 1924, and in Manchuria from 1936 to 1937.
CORRESPONDENCE/MANUSCRIPTS: Letters concerning Leonard's published autobiography, *Repaid a Hundredfold* (1969), and drafts of the book, 1944–69.

13-HENRY HUDSON McMILLAN PAPERS, 1942, 10 items
Background note: Henry Hudson McMillan (1885–1959) was a Southern Baptist missionary in China from 1913 to 1951.
MANUSCRIPTS: Biographical files of Henry Hudson McMillan and Leila Memory McMillan, 1942.

14-NORWOOD FAMILY PAPERS, 1985, 2 items
MANUSCRIPTS: A biography, with family information and a supplement, of Evan Wilkins Norwood, a Southern Baptist missionary in China from 1923 to 1928, comp. by Charles Stephens Norwood, 1985.

15-JESSE COLEMAN AND REBECCA OWEN PAPERS, 1900–1943, 13 items
Background note: Jesse Coleman and Rebecca Owen were Southern Baptist missionaries in China from 1899 to 1911.
MANUSCRIPTS/MEMORABILIA: Sermon outline, n.d.; ''A Pilgrimage'' and ''The Old Story in Tsin,'' by Jesse Coleman Owen, n.d.
PAMPHLETS: *The Bible and Wine*, by Jesse Coleman Owen, 1943; 2 copies of an unidentified evangelistic pamphlet, n.d.; *Shantung Christian University, Wei Hsien*, 1909.
AUDIO-VISUAL MATERIALS: 6 photos of the Owens, Pingtu Institute, and an unidentified group of Chinese, 1900, 1935, and n.d.
CHINESE LANGUAGE MATERIALS: Bible, 1900.

16-WILLIAM LOUIS POTEAT PAPERS, 1894–1938, 18 items, 2 folders
Background note: William Louis Poteat (1856–1938) was president of Wake Forest College and the uncle of Edwin McNeill Poteat, Jr. For biographical notes on Edwin McNeill Poteat, Jr., see University of North Carolina at Chapel Hill, Southern Historical Collection, Wilson Library, Chapel Hill, NC, 27514-6080.
MINUTES/RECORDS/REPORTS: Shanghai College, catalogues, 1911–12, 1916.
CORRESPONDENCE: Letter, 1894, and a postcard, 1896, from China missionary Leroy Norcross Chappel; 3 letters from China missionary George Washington Greene, 1897–1903; letter from George William Greene about a proposed biography of his father, George Washington Greene, 1926; letter from China missionary John Burder Hipps, 1931; 5 letters between Poteat and Charles Alexander Leonard, 1907–35; 4 letters from Sophie Stevens Lanneau, 1927–38; 2 folders of correspondence with Poteat's nephews, China missionaries Edwin McNeill Poteat, Jr., and Gordon Poteat, 1909, 1920–36; 2 letters from China missionary Wade Dobbins Bostick, 1932, 1934.
SERIALS: *Shanghai College Bulletin*, 1923–25.

17-JEHU LEWIS SHUCK PAPERS, 1848, 1 item
Background note: For biographical notes, see Virginia Baptist Historical Society, University of Richmond, Boatwright Memorial Library, Box 95, Richmond, VA, 23173.

CORRESPONDENCE: Letter to Mrs. William Graham, 1848, including discussion of the Cantonese, the Shanghai Baptist Church, Chinese anti-foreign activities, provincial governors, and the Chinese Emperors.

18-EZRA FRANCIS TATUM PAPERS, 1915–37, 10 items
Background note: Ezra Francis Tatum (1847–1937) was a Southern Baptist missionary in Shanghai and Yangchow from 1888 to 1934.
CORRESPONDENCE: Letter from Ezra Francis Tatum to his daughter, Alice Joy Tatum, 1915; letter from Tatum to Pattie Moore, 1927.
MANUSCRIPTS: Biographical sketch of Alice Mabel Flagg Tatum (Mrs. Ezra Tatum), by her daughter, Alice Joy Tatum, n.d.; genealogical notes on Ezra Tatum's family, n.d.; obituary of Ezra Tatum, 1937.
AUDIO-VISUAL MATERIALS: 3 photos of Tatum and his family, n.d.

19-W. M. WINGATE PAPERS, 1878, 2 items
CORRESPONDENCE: 2 letters from Matthew Tyson Yates, 1878.

20-MATTHEW TYSON YATES PAPERS, 1847–88, 44 items
Background note: Matthew Tyson Yates (1819–88) was the first Southern Baptist missionary in China from North Carolina, serving from 1846 to 1888.
CORRESPONDENCE: 39 letters between Yates and family members, 1847–88.
PAMPHLETS: *Our Central China Mission*, n.a., n.d.
AUDIO-VISUAL MATERIALS: 4 photos, n.d.
MEMORABILIA: Biographical materials, n.d.

21-GENERAL HOLDINGS
SERIALS: *Voice*, 1925–39.

NC–105 University Archives
Wake Forest University
Z. Smith Reynolds Library
P. O. Box 7777, Reynolda Station
Winston-Salem NC 27109
(919) 761-5472
John R. Woodard, University Archivist and Director, North Carolina Baptist Historical Collection

1-PRESIDENT'S RECORDS, 1944–47, 1 file
CORRESPONDENCE: Letters to and from Arthur Gillespie, 1944–47.

NC–110 Z. Smith Reynolds Library
Wake Forest University
P. O. Box 7777, Reynolda Station
Winston-Salem NC 27109
(919) 761-5480
Merrill G. Berthrong, Director

1-GENERAL HOLDINGS
DISSERTATIONS/THESES: *Sophie Stevens Lanneau: Southern Baptist Missionary to Soochow, China, 1907-1950*, by Carolyn Howard Carter, 1974.

NORTH DAKOTA

ELLENDALE

TRINITY BIBLE COLLEGE
ND–5 Fred J. Graham Library
50 Sixth Avenue South
Box 74
Ellendale ND 58436
(701) 349–3621
Esther Zink, Director

1-TBI ARCHIVE, 1942, 2 items
PAMPHLETS: *An Hour with James Hudson Taylor: Pioneer Missionary to China*, by Theodore Wilhelm Engstrom, 1942; *An Hour with John and Betty Stam: Martyred Missionaries to China*, by Theodore Wilhelm Engstrom, 1942.

OHIO

ALLIANCE

MOUNT UNION COLLEGE
OH–5 Library
Alliance OH 44601
(216) 821–5320 Ext. 260
Joanne Houmard, Serials Librarian

1-GENERAL HOLDINGS
SERIALS: *China Mission Year Book*, 1912–15. *Chinese Recorder*, 1923.

ATHENS

OHIO UNIVERSITY

OH–10 Department of Archives and Special Collections
Vernon R. Alden Library
Park Place
Athens OH 45701-2978
(614) 593-2710
George W. Bain, Head, Archives and Special Collections

1-ANDREW STRITMATTER COLLECTION, ca. 1873–1880, 20 items
Background note: For biographical notes, see Harvard University, Harvard-Yenching Library, 2 Divinity Avenue, Cambridge, MA, 02138.
CORRESPONDENCE: Ca. 20 transcripts of letters from Andrew Stritmatter, a Methodist missionary in China from 1873 to 1880.

OH–15 Vernon R. Alden Library
Ohio University
Park Place
Athens OH 45701-2978
(614) 593-2693
Nancy Rue, Head of Reference

1-GENERAL HOLDINGS
PAMPHLETS: *British Protestant Christian Evangelists and the 1898 Reform Movement in China*, by Leslie R. Marchant, 1975; *The Harrowing of Hell in China: A Synoptic Study of the Role of Christian Evangelists in the Opening of Hunan Province*, by Leslie R. Marchant, 1977.
SERIALS: *China Mission Year Book*, 1911, 1925. *Chinese Recorder*, 1924–26. *Chinese Repository*, 1832–51.
DISSERTATIONS/THESES: *The Negotiations between Ch'i-ying and Lagrené, 1844–1846*, by Angelus Francis Grosse-Aschhoff, 1950.

BEREA

BALDWIN-WALLACE COLLEGE
OH–20 Ritter Library
57 East Bagley Road
Berea OH 44017
(216) 826-2204
Richard D. Densmore, Head Public Services Librarian

1-METHODIST HISTORICAL COLLECTION, 1907–40, 2 items
SERIALS: *China Christian Advocate*, 1940 (General Conference Special All China Number).
CHINESE LANGUAGE MATERIALS: *Chinese Hymnal*, by H. Blodget and C. Goodrich (North China Mission of the American Board of Commissioners for Foreign Missions), 1907.

BOWLING GREEN

BOWLING GREEN STATE UNIVERSITY
OH–25 Center for Archival Collections
Jerome Library
Bowling Green OH 43403-0175
(419) 372-2411
Ann M. Bowers, Assistant Director/University Archivist

1-GRACE McCLURG CARSON PAPERS, 1912–26, ca. 39 folders
Background note: Grace McClurg Carson taught at the Methodist mission in Hinghwa from 1910 to 1926. The items listed below are part of a larger collection.
MINUTES/RECORDS/REPORTS: Account ledger of the mission

and financial reports for Hinghwa City Primary and Day schools, 1924–26; records on Carson, 1910–26.
CORRESPONDENCE: 6 folders of correspondence from Carson in China, 1910–26; postcards from Carson, 1910–26; folder of correspondence from Ruth McClurg, 1917–22, n.d.
DIARIES: Ca. 2 folders of Carson's diary, 1910–25.
MANUSCRIPTS: Ca. 1 folder of stories by Carson, 1907, 1912, 1924–25; "History of the Hinghwa Women's Foreign Missionary Society," by Carson, 1871–1925.
PAMPHLETS: Folder of printed materials on the Foochow Mission and Hinghwa Conference, 1897, 1939; *Story of the Foochow Foreign Cemeteries*, n.d. (pre-1926).
MEMORABILIA: 2 scrapbooks containing miscellaneous items on China, 1914, n.d.; folder of scrapbook items on China, 1916, 1923, 1961, and n.d.
MAPS/DESIGNS/DRAWINGS: Bi-lingual map of China, 1938; 2 wood-cut prints and a drawing on red paper, n.d.; folder of paper dolls; folder of stencils of daily activities of the Chinese; folder of miscellaneous drawings, n.d.
AUDIO-VISUAL MATERIALS: 2 group photos of the Hinghwa Mission, n.d.; folder of postcards of China, n.d.; 10 folders of photos of the Hinghwa Mission, its personnel, Chinese people, civilization, and culture, 1902–25; oversize group photo of the Hinghwa Mission, n.d.; audio tapes containing a "letter" in Chinese from a military student and Chinese songs.
CHINESE LANGUAGE MATERIALS: Bible; hymnal; rice culture booklet; writing instructions for missionaries, n.d.; folder of clippings, pamphlets, and other Chinese items, 1913, 1948, 1959, 1964, 1969, n.d.

CANTON

MALONE COLLEGE
OH–30 Archives Section
Everett L. Cattell Library
515 25th Street NW
Canton OH 44709
(216) 489-0800 Ext. 393
Esther Hess, Acquisitions Librarian

Background note: The Friends Ohio Yearly meeting sent its first missionary to China, Esther H. Butler, in 1887. The Friends China Mission was established in 1890 in the Nanking-Luho area. By 1940 there were over 1,000 members. The Ohio Yearly meeting moved its China Mission to Taiwan in 1953.

1-GENERAL HOLDINGS
CORRESPONDENCE: File drawer and 1/3 of a file box of correspondence of Friends Foreign Mission Society Board with Friends missionaries to China, 1887–1953 (both mainland and Taiwan): John and Barbara Brantingham, Edith Esther Butler, Eva Carmichal, Carson W. and Vercia P. Cox, Annie L. Crowl, Charles E. and Leora DeVol, George and Isabella DeVol, William Ezra and Frances H. DeVol, Wilbur A. and Julia Estes, Freda Farmer, Lucy A. Gaynor, Freda Girsberger, Mary A. Hill, Martha B. Hixon, Margaret A. Holme, Ella Ruth Hutson, Amanda Kirkpatrick, Li Yun Tsao, Charles A. and Elsie V. Matti, Emily R. Moore, Howard and Mary Evelyn Moore, Rachel Mostrom, Effie Murray, Roberta Naylor, R. Ethel Naylor, Emma D. Oliver, Eva

Pennington, Oona Mae Robbins, Harriet Shimer, Lenna M. Stanley, Matilda Stewart, John and Geraldine Williams, Walter R. and Myrtle M. Williams, Mary Wood, and Russell and Esther Zinn. AUDIO-VISUAL MATERIALS: 2 boxes of slides and pictures of Friends missions and missionaries in Taiwan and China, 1887–1986.
SERIALS: *Friends Oriental News*, 1908–63.

CINCINNATI

OH–35   LLOYD LIBRARY
917 Plum Street
Cincinnati OH 45202
(513) 721-3707
Rebecca A. Perry, Librarian

1-GENERAL HOLDINGS
SERIALS: *Chinese Medical Journal*, supplement, 1938–40. Fukien Christian University, *Biological Bulletin*, 1939–47. *Lingnaam Agricultural Review*, 1922–27. *Lingnan Science Journal*, 1927–50. *Peking Natural History Bulletin*, 1926–40.

PROVINCE OF ST. JOHN THE BAPTIST

OH–40   Archives
10290 Mill Road
Cincinnati OH 45231
(513) 825-7544
Leonard Foley, O.F.M., Archivist

Background note: The Franciscan Province of St. John the Baptist maintained a mission in the Wuchang-Hankow area from ca. 1920 to 1953.

1-GENERAL HOLDINGS
MINUTES/RECORDS/REPORTS: Articles and references to the Wuchang mission in the *Provincial Chronicle*, 1928–53.
CORRESPONDENCE: Ca. 1 folder each of correspondence from ca. 30 missionaries of the Franciscan Province of St. John the Baptist in China, including Elgar Mindorff, Sigfrid Schneider, Bishop Rembert Kowalski, and Floribert Blank, ca. 1920–1953.
MANUSCRIPTS: Articles by Province of St. John the Baptist missionaries in China, 1930–53.

OH–45   William Faber Franciscana Library
Province of St. John the Baptist
10290 Mill Road
Cincinnati OH 45231
(513) 825-7544
Leonard Foley, O.F.M., Archivist

1-FRANCISCANA, 1923–72, 10 items
MANUSCRIPTS: "Highlights of the Wuchang Mission, 1930–1953, St. John the Baptist Province, Cincinnati, Ohio, U.S.A.," by Leonard Foley, O.F.M., n.d.
PAMPHLETS: *China in Chains*, by Raphael Montaigne, O.F.M., 1958; *A Franciscan Bishop Tells His Story*, by Rembert Kowalski, O.F.M., 1972; *Franciscans in the Middle Kingdom: A Survey of Franciscan Missions in China from the Middle Ages to the Present Time*, by Otto Maas, O.F.M., 1938; *Die Franziskanermission in*

China vom Jahre 1900 bis zur Gegenwart, by Otto Maas, O.F.M., 1934; *John of Montecorvino, First Archbishop of Peking*, by George Barry O'Toole, 1929; *Now It Can Be Told!*, by Elgar Mindorff, O.F.M., 1944; *Sistema Italiano di transcrizione dei suoni Cinesi*, by Luigi Vannicelli, O.F.M., 1942; *Aus unserer Mission in Hunan (China) Jahresbotschaft aus der apostolischen Präfektur Yungchow*, by the Franziskaner-Missionen, 1935.
SERIALS: *Franciscans in China*, 1923–41.

OH–50   PUBLIC LIBRARY OF CINCINNATI
800 Vine Street
Library Square
Cincinnati OH 45202–2071
(513) 369-6000
James R. Hunt, Director-Librarian

1-GENERAL HOLDINGS
MAPS/DESIGNS/DRAWINGS: *Atlas of the Chinese Empire...with a List of All Protestant Mission Stations, etc., Specially Prepared for the China Inland Mission*, by Edward Stanford (London and Philadelphia: Morgan and Scott), 1908.
SERIALS: Catholic University of Peking, *Bulletin*, 1928–31. *China Mission Year Book*, 1911–12.
DISSERTATIONS/THESES: *China and Educational Autonomy: The Changing Role of the Protestant Educational Missionary in China, 1807–1937*, by Alice Henrietta Gregg, 1945. *Protestant Mission Schools for Girls in South China (1827 to the Japanese Invasion)*, by Mary Raleigh Anderson, 1943. *The Use of Material from China's Spiritual Inheritance in the Christian Education of Chinese Youth*, by Warren Horton Stuart, 1932.

ST. THOMAS INSTITUTE FOR ADVANCED STUDIES
OH–55   Library
1842 Madison Road
Cincinnati OH 45206
(513) 861-3460
M. Virgil Ghering, O.P., Librarian

1-GENERAL HOLDINGS
MANUSCRIPTS: "Hunan Mission Memories, 1924–1953," by William Westhoven, C.P., 1982–83.

SISTERS OF NOTRE DAME DE NAMUR
OH–60   Ohio Province Archives
The Provincial House
701 East Columbia Avenue
Cincinnati OH 45215
(513) 821-7448
Agnes Immaculata, S.N.D.N., Provincial Archivist

Background note: The Sisters of Notre Dame de Namur maintained the Good Counsel Girls' Middle School in Wuchang from 1929 to 1949. *History of the Notre Dame Mission in Wuchang, China 1926–1951*, by Sister Mary Francesca Lanahan, S.N.D.N., 1984, describes the mission.

1-GENERAL HOLDINGS
MINUTES/RECORDS/REPORTS: Box of deeds, documents, as-

sessments of property involving land and buildings, 1929–50, and financial accounts, 1929–55.
CORRESPONDENCE: 5 volumes of collected letters from Sister missionaries in China to the Ohio Province, 1929–52; box of official correspondence, 1926–47.
DIARIES: "Annals—Community and School," 1929–51; "Community Journal," 1929–43.
PAMPHLETS: *People's Republic of China and the Christian Churches*, by Margaret Francis Loftus, S.N.D.N., 1982; *People's Republic of China and the Christian Churches*, by Ann Brennan and Margaret Francis Loftus, S.N.D.N., 1984.
AUDIO-VISUAL MATERIALS: 40 slides of missionaries, students, and buildings; 350 photos of missionary sisters, Chinese staff members, students, buildings, travel, and scenes, 1929–49.
MEMORABILIA: Ca. 1/2 box of clippings about China, the sisters' mission in Wuchang, and various aspects of missionary work in China, 1929–49.
SERIALS: *Drawnet*, 1929–42.

UNIVERSITY OF CINCINNATI
OH–65   Central Library
University and Woodside
Cincinnati OH 45221
(513) 475–2218
Virginia Parr, Reference Librarian

1-GENERAL HOLDINGS
ORAL HISTORIES: *China Missionaries Oral History Collection*, ed. by Cyrus H. Peake and Arthur L. Rosenbaum (Claremont Graduate School, Oral History Program), 1973. See ORAL HISTORIES Union List for the names of participants.
SERIALS: Catholic University, College of Education, *Publications*, 1939–40. *China Monthly*, 1939–47. *Lingnan Science Journal*, 1936–42. *Monumenta Serica*, 1948–83.
DISSERTATIONS/THESES: *Etude sur les missions nestoriennes en Chine au VIIe et au VIIIe siècles, d'après l'inscription syrochinoise de Si-Ngan-Fou*, by Augustin Cleisz, 1880. *Simon of Saint-Quentin and the Dominican Mission to the Mongols, 1245–1248*, by Gregory Guzman, 1968.

CLEVELAND

CASE WESTERN RESERVE UNIVERSITY

OH–70   Special Collections
Freiberger Library
11161 East Boulevard
Cleveland OH 44106
(216) 368–2993
Susan Hanson, Head, Special Collections

1-AMBROSE SWASEY PAPERS, 1916–17, 10 folders
Background note: Cleveland industrialist Ambrose Swasey (1846–1937) supported Christian mission work in China through donations to Canton Christian College, the University of Nanking, and the YMCA. The Swasey Papers, which span 1880–1935, total 35 boxes (15 l.f.).
CORRESPONDENCE: 9 folders of correspondence from Swasey on China, missions, travel, and Canton Christian College, 1916–17 and n.d.

AUDIO-VISUAL MATERIALS: Folder of photos of Canton Christian College and University of Nanking, n.d.
FINDING AIDS: In-house register.

2-GENERAL HOLDINGS
PAMPHLETS: *Prayers for Daily Use*, by Eric H. Liddell, n.d.; *The Sermon on the Mount: Notes for Sunday School Teachers*, by Eric H. Liddell, 1936–37.

OH–75   Freiberger Library
Case Western Reserve University
11161 East Boulevard
Cleveland OH 44106
(216) 368–3530
Gail Reese, Head Reference Librarian

1-GENERAL HOLDINGS
SERIALS: *China Christian Year Book*, 1911. *Yenching Journal of Social Studies*, 1938–49.

CLEVELAND HEALTH SCIENCES
OH–80   Allen Memorial Library
11000 Euclid Avenue
Cleveland OH 44106
(216) 368–3640
Lydia Holian, Associate Librarian

1-GENERAL HOLDINGS
MANUSCRIPTS: "The Story of Christian Nursing in China," by Gladys E. Stephenson, ca. 1955.
SERIALS: *China Medical Journal*, 1910–31. *China's Medicine*, 1966–68. *Chinese Medical Journal*, 1932–44, 1947–48, 1952, 1957–66; supplement, 1936. Lingnan University, *Science Bulletin*, 1934.

OH–85   CLEVELAND PUBLIC LIBRARY
325 Superior Avenue
Cleveland OH 44114–1271
(216) 623–2800
Joan L. Sorger, Head of Main Library

1-GENERAL HOLDINGS
PAMPHLETS: *Le nestorianisme et l'inscription de Kara-Balgassoun*, by Edouard Chavannes, 1897; *Nestorians in China: Some Corrections and Additions*, by Arthur Christopher Moule, 1940.
MAPS/DESIGNS/DRAWINGS: *Atlas of the Chinese Empire*, by Edward Stanford (Philadelphia: Morgan and Scott), 1908.
SERIALS: *China Christian Year Book*, 1910–15, 1917–39. *China's Millions* (London), 1875–95. *Chinese Recorder*, 1939–41. *Folklore Studies*, 1942–62. *Fu Jen Newsletter*, 1931–32. *Monumenta Serica*, monograph series, 1937-. *Variétés Sinologiques*, 1895–1902, 1913, 1932–34.

OH–90   WESTERN RESERVE HISTORICAL SOCIETY
10825 East Boulevard
Cleveland OH 44106
(216) 721–5722
John J. Grabowski, Curator of Manuscripts

1-JONATHAN HALE FAMILY PAPERS (Mss. 3115), 1893–99, 10 items
CORRESPONDENCE: 10 letters from C. W. Price and Eva Hale to C. O. Hale describing daily life at the mission school in Fenchowfu, 1893–99.

2-VERTICAL FILE, 1863–1914, 9 items
CORRESPONDENCE: 2 letters from Daniel Vrooman to George Ladd, telling of his ministry in Canton, 1863.
MAPS/DESIGNS/DRAWINGS: 6 blueprints of the University of Nanking, consisting of site plans and sections for the campus, topographical drawings, floor plans, and elevations for the medical school, a hospital, and a dispensary, by Perkins, Fellows, and Hamilton, Architects, 1914 (acc. no. 34–62, no. 82).
MEMORABILIA: An article by Vrooman on the phonetic alphabet for Cantonese dialect, 1363.

COLUMBUS

OH-95   OHIO HISTORICAL SOCIETY
1985 Velma Avenue
Columbus OH 43211
(614) 466–1500
Gary J. Arnold, Head of Reference Services,
Archives—Library Division

1-CHARLES A. JONES COLLECTION (P-205), 1919, 2 boxes
Background note: Charles A. Jones traveled to China in 1919 on the staff for the Advancement of the Methodist Centenary Movement. The following materials are contained in Series II of the collection.
MINUTES/RECORDS/REPORTS/MAPS/DESIGNS/DRAWINGS: Folder of documents of the Methodist Episcopal Missions in Foochow and North China, including graphs recording contributions and organization of the missions, 1919.
AUDIO-VISUAL MATERIALS: 2 boxes of photos from Jones' trip to China, consisting of 7 folders of individual and group portraits of Western and Chinese people in candid poses and varying styles of dress; 1 folder each of photos of agriculture, transport, silk farming, miscellaneous trades, agricultural implements and produce, parades, boats, statues, churches, general views, exterior and interior details of temples, shrines, scenic views of buildings, ruins, 2 folders of river views and 2 of other scenic views, including views of the ocean crossing, Peking and Shanghai, and 1 folder of miscellaneous photos; unidentified group photo.

2-VERTICAL FILE MATERIAL, 1845–97, 3 folders
CORRESPONDENCE: Letter from J. J. Roberts, in Canton, to J. L. Smith, Grandville, Ohio, transmitting to the Society of Religious Inquiry a proclamation opening China to missionaries, 1845 (VFM 737); letter from an unknown missionary in China to "Brother Adams," 1863 (VFM 2240); folder of letters from Jennie Pond and Earnest R. Atwater, missionaries in China, to friends and family concerning their work, 1888–97 (VFM 2002).

OHIO STATE UNIVERSITY

OH-100   Agriculture Library
45 Agriculture Administration Building
2120 Fyffe Road
Columbus OH 43210
(614) 422–6125
Mary P. Key, Librarian

1-GENERAL HOLDINGS
SERIALS: *Lingnan Science Journal*, 1922–48.

OH-105   Health Sciences Library
Ohio State University
376 West 10th Avenue
Columbus OH 43210–1240
(614) 422–9810
Pamela Bradigan, Head of Reference

1-GENERAL HOLDINGS
SERIALS: *China's Medicine*, 1966–68. *Chinese Medical Journal*, 1923–25, 1931–32, 1941, 1943, 1947–51, 1955–60, 1962–66.

OH-110   William Oxley Thompson Memorial Library
Ohio State University
1858 Neil Avenue Mall
Columbus OH 43210–1286
(614) 292–6175
William J. Studer, Director

1-COUNCIL FOR WORLD MISSION ARCHIVES, CENTRAL CHINA, 1843–1940, 1,275 microfiches
MINUTES/RECORDS/REPORTS: Council for World Mission, Central China, mission reports, 1866–1940.
CORRESPONDENCE: Incoming letters, 1843–1927; incoming and outgoing letters, 1928–39.
DIARIES: Journals, 1889–96.

2-COUNCIL FOR WORLD MISSION ARCHIVES, FUKIEN, 1845–1939, 372 microfiches
MINUTES/RECORDS/REPORTS: Council for World Mission, Fukien, mission reports, 1866–1939.
CORRESPONDENCE: Incoming letters, 1845–1927; incoming and outgoing letters, 1928–39.

3-COUNCIL FOR WORLD MISSION ARCHIVES, SOUTH CHINA, 1803–1939, 580 microfiches
MINUTES/RECORDS/REPORTS: Council for World Mission, South China, mission reports, 1866–1939.
CORRESPONDENCE: Incoming letters, 1803–1927; incoming and outgoing letters, 1928–39.
DIARIES: Journals, 1807–42.

4-GENERAL HOLDINGS
MINUTES/RECORDS/REPORTS: Presbyterian Board of Foreign Missions, report, 1897; National Christian Conference, report, 1926.
PAMPHLETS: *The Missionary Situation in China*, by Henry Theodore Hodgkin, 1928; *Russian (Greek Orthodox) Missionaries in China, 1689–1917: Their Cultural, Political, and Economic Role*, by Albert Parry, 1940.

ORAL HISTORIES: *China Missionaries Oral History Collection*, ed. by Cyrus H. Peake and Arthur L. Rosenbaum (Claremont Graduate School, Oral History Program), 1973. See ORAL HISTORIES Union List for the names of participants.

SERIALS: *Anking Newsletter*, 1937–48. *China Christian Advocate*, 1914–41. *China Christian Year Book*, 1910–39. China Inland Mission, *Occasional Papers*, 1872–75. *China Mission Advocate*, 1839. *China Monthly*, 1940–49. *Chinese Medical Journal*, 1887–1921. *Chinese Recorder*, 1919–27, 1930, 1934, 1937–41. *Educational Review*, 1907–38. *Fenchow*, 1919–36. *The Foochow Messenger*, 1903–40. *Four Streams*, 1934–51. *Hainan Newsletter*, 1912–49. *Lingnan Science Journal*, 1922–50. *News of China*, 1943–49. *OMS Outreach*, 1903–75. *West China Missionary News*, 1901–43.

DISSERTATIONS/THESES: *The Changing Attitudes of the American Protestant Missionaries Toward the Unequal Treaties with China*, by Robert Milton Fessenden, 1971. *A Church for China: A Problem in Self-identification, 1919–1937*, by Katherine Kennedy Reist, 1983. *Growth and Change in Protestant Missionary Education in Nineteenth-century China*, by Beverly Sue Abbott, 1974. *Reciprocal Change: The Case of American Protestant Missionaries to China*, by Paul Voninski, 1975.

CHINESE LANGUAGE MATERIALS/SERIALS: *Chiao hui hsin pao (Church News)*, 1868–74. *Wan kuo kung pao (The Globe Magazine: A Review of the Times)*, 1874–1907 (repr. 1968). Yenching ta hsüeh, *T'u shu kuan pao* (Yenching University, *Library Bulletin*), 1931–39.

CHINESE LANGUAGE MATERIALS: 8 books, 1901–81, on Young J. Allen, anti-Christian movements, anti-foreignism, bibliography of the history of Christianity in China, Catholic missions in China, church-state relations, missionary biography, and missions in modern China.

ST. MARY OF THE SPRINGS MOTHERHOUSE
OH–115 Congregational Archives
North Nelson and Johnstown Roads
Columbus OH 43219
(614) 252–2137
Mary McCaffrey, O.P., Congregational Archivist

Background note: The China mission of the Dominican Sisters was interwoven with that of the Dominican Fathers of St. Joseph Province, U.S.A. Some of the sisters' papers may be found in the Dominican House of Studies, Province of St. Joseph Archives, 487 Michigan Avenue, NE, Washington, DC, 20017.

1-GENERAL HOLDINGS
MINUTES/RECORDS/REPORTS: St. Mary of the Springs convent, inventory, n.d.; Chinese mission volunteers, records, n.d.; annual financial reports, 1936–47; ship travel arrangements, 1940–42, 1946–47; departures for China, records, 1935, 1937–38, 1940–41, 1946–47; return from China, records, 1944, 1949; official documents, 1935–40; Chinese scholarships, 1943–49.
CORRESPONDENCE: A set of letters from sisters in China, 1937–47; correspondence between Sisters of St. Mary of the Springs China Mission and benefactors of mission, 1935–44; Central Hanover Bank, 1941; Chinese government, 1939–41, 1946; Department of State, 1936–47; Diocesan offices, 1936–45; immigration officials, 1949; Propagation of Faith, 1935–48; relief

agencies, 1940–41, 1944–49; relief, east-west, 1942–43, and miscellaneous, n.d.; folder of letters from sisters in hospital training to Mother Stephanie, 1938; Mae Lyons' personal letters, 1937–47; 4 volumes of letters from Mother Stephanie, in China, 1938–47; correspondence from Bishops Aguirre and Prat, 1922; letters of a trip from Columbus, Ohio, to China, 1935, n.a.; 19 folders of correspondence of China mission with Motherhouse, 1934–49; folder of correspondence with the Dominican fathers, 1937–44; folder of correspondence from Chinese postulants/novices, n.d.
MANUSCRIPTS: "The American Congregation of Dominican Tertiaries of the Blessed Virgin Mary: 1830–1840," by Frederica Kearney, O.P., n.d.; "History of Our Mission in China," n.a., n.d.; "Reflections of Catherine Malya Chen, O.P., on a Visit to Her Homeland, China," ca. 1980; "Return from China," by Srs. Felicia and Rosamund, n.d.; "St. Mary of the Springs: Its History and Spirit, 1830–1850," by Estelle Casalandra, O.P.; "Short History of Kienning-Fu," by William F. Cassidy, n.d.; "Three Came Home," by Fathers Gordon, Joyce, and Hyde, n.d.
PAMPHLETS: Folder of booklets, n.d.; Sr. Estelle's account of the Chinese Mission.
MEMORABILIA: 4 Chinese panels, n.d.; 2 folders of souvenirs of China; folder of miscellaneous memorabilia; departure ceremonies, 1935, 1937–38; notices of deaths of Srs. Hildegarde, 1936, Leocadia, 1937, and James Luke Devine, O.P., 1947; clippings, 1930s–1950s.
MAPS/DESIGNS/DRAWINGS: Blueprint of the Convent in China, n.d.
AUDIO-VISUAL MATERIALS: 2 photo albums of the St. Mary of the Springs China mission; ca. 100 photos relating to the mission; 6 short films of departure ceremonies; "Dominican Mission Endeavor in China," 3 audio recordings by James Luke Devine, O.P., n.d.

DAYTON

UNITED THEOLOGICAL SEMINARY
OH–120 Library
1810 Harvard Boulevard
Dayton OH 45406
(513) 278–5817 Ext. 120
Richard R. Berg, Assistant Librarian

Background note: See also Church of the Brethren General Board, Brethren Historical Library and Archives, 1451 Dundee Avenue, Elgin, IL, 60120; and General Commission on Archives and History—The United Methodist Church, United Methodist Archives and History Center, Archives, 36 Madison Avenue, P. O. Box 127, Madison, NJ, 07940.

1-EUNICE MITCHELL BENNETT PAPERS, 1922–33, 3 volumes
AUDIO-VISUAL MATERIALS: 3 photo albums of mission work in China of the Church of the United Brethren in Christ, 1922–33.

2-CHURCH OF THE UNITED BRETHREN IN CHRIST, 1800–1946, 119 volumes
MINUTES/RECORDS/REPORTS: Reports on China in the Board of Foreign Mission report, 1854–1946; Foreign Missionary Society reports, n.d.; and General Conference proceedings, 1800–1946; Foreign Missionary Society, report of a visit to China, 1912; report of the Foreign Deputation, 1911–12; report of the Episcopal

visit to mission fields in the Orient, 1936–37; reports on China in denominational periodicals, *Search Light*, 1895–1905; *Missionary Advance*, 1905–8; and *Woman's Evangel*, 1882–1946.

3-SCHUYLER COLFAX ENCK, 1912–58, 31 items
DIARIES: Schuyler Colfax Enck's diaries, 1912, 1929–58.
MEMORABILIA: Scrapbook of clippings, etc., by Enck on his United Brethren Church Mission Deputation trip to China and the Orient, 1936–37.

4-EVANGELICAL ASSOCIATION OF NORTH AMERICA, 1859–1922, 18 volumes
MINUTES/RECORDS/REPORTS: Sections on China in the reports of the Board of Foreign Missions, n.d.

5-EVANGELICAL CHURCH, 1923–41, 59 volumes
MINUTES/RECORDS/REPORTS: Evangelical Church: China Conference, minutes, 1937–38; China Mission, proceedings, 1923–27, 1929, 1930–31, 1937–39, 1941; General Conference, proceedings, 1923–46; yearbook, 1923–46; Commission to the Orient, report, 1929–30, 1936–37; reports on China in denominational periodicals, *Evangelical Missionary World*, 1923–46.

6-EVANGELICAL UNITED BRETHREN CHURCH, 1946–68, 50 volumes
MINUTES/RECORDS/REPORTS: Central China Mission Council, minutes, 1948; Board of Missions, 1946–66; reports on China in denominational periodicals, *Missionary Year Book*, 1947–61, and *World Evangel*, 1946–68.

7-MISSIONARY LETTERS, 1908–47, 14 items
CORRESPONDENCE: 14 letters from missionaries of the United Brethren in Christ Church and of the Evangelical United Brethren Church, Paul S. and Frances Mayer, Anna Kammerer Ranck, Elsie I. Reik, and Gerald R. and Sylvia Zimmer, 1908–47.

8-CHARLES AND KATHRYN SHOOP PAPERS, 1895–1938, 1 volume
CORRESPONDENCE/AUDIO-VISUAL MATERIALS/MEMORABILIA: Album containing correspondence, photos, and other printed matter relating to mission work in China of the Church of the United Brethren in China, 1895–1938.

9-UNITED EVANGELICAL CHURCH, 1892–1922, 16 volumes
MINUTES/RECORDS/REPORTS: Reports on China in denominational periodicals, *Missionary Gem*, 1904–22, and *Missionary Tidings*, 1892–1922.

10-SAMUEL G. ZIEGLER PAPERS, n.d., 2 items
MANUSCRIPTS: Chapters on missions in China in manuscripts of 2 unpublished works on the history of missions of the Church of the United Brethren in Christ, n.d.

11-GENERAL HOLDINGS
MINUTES/RECORDS/REPORTS: American Board of Commissioners for Foreign Missions, Foochow Missionary Hospital, annual report, 1916; Canton Union Theological College, president's report, 1924–25; Christian Conference of Asia, consultation with church leaders from China, 1981; Church of Christ in China: General Assembly, digest of important actions, 1927, 1937; Hong Kong Council, annual report and supplementary reports, 1964–65; ten-year development plan, 1967(?); Kwangtung Synod, annual report, 1953; Consultation of World Evangelization, report on Chinese, 1980; Lingnan Refugee Camp, report of medical service,

1938–41; National Christian Council of China, annual report, 1924–25; South China Chinese Language Institute, yearbook, 1940; World Conference of Christian Youth, reports of the Chinese delegates, 1939.
MANUSCRIPTS: "Information about China: For Those Interested," by the Foreign Missions Conference of North America, 1925.
PAMPHLETS: *An Adventure in Church Union in China: Origin, Nature, and Task of the Church of Christ in China*, n.d. (post–1941); *The Beginnings of the Women's Department of the Canton Christian College*, 1915; *The Church of Christ in China: Church Unity in China and Church and Mission Cooperation*, 1938; *Let Us Unite!: The Church of Christ in China and Church Unity in China*, ca. 1937; *The People and Church in China: A Guide to Prayer*, comp. by the China Program of the National Council of the Churches of Christ in the U.S.A., 1983; *The Present Situation in China and Its Significance for Christian Missions*, 1925 (?); *Rehabilitation and Expansion Campaign*, by the Church of Christ in China, Kwangtung Synod, n.d.; *The Story of Yale in China*, 1945; *The Suffering "Middle Kingdom": A Student Appeal*, by Canton Christian College Students, English Publications Committee, 1925; *Teaching Children in China at the Canton Christian College*, 1915.
AUDIO-VISUAL MATERIALS: *Ever Faithful, Ever Sure: Christian Communities in China*, a filmstrip and audio cassette with script, by Gail V. Coulson and Jean Woo for the China Program, Division of Overseas Ministries, National Council of the Churches of Christ in the U.S.A., 1983.
SERIALS: *Bridge*, 1983-. *China and the Church Today*, 1979–86. *China Christian Educational Association, Bulletin*, 1928. *China Christian Yearbook*, 1926–39. *China Mission Yearbook*, 1910–25. *China Notes*, 1962-. *Chinese Recorder*, 1921–41.
DISSERTATIONS/THESES: *China Missions in Crisis: Bishop Laimbeckhoven and His Times, 1738–1787*, by Joseph Krahl, 1964. *The Chinese Renaissance and Its Relation to and Effects upon Protestant Missions*, by Paul Vincent Cunkle, 1946. *The History and Development of the Central China Mission of the Evangelical United Brethren Church*, by Frederick W. Brandauer, 1953. *A History of the United Brethren Mission Work in China*, by Robert C. Painter, 1945. *Protestant Christianity and Marriage in China*, by Calvin H. Reber, 1958.

UNIVERSITY OF DAYTON

OH–125 Marian Library
300 College Park Avenue
Dayton OH 45469
(513) 229-4214
Theodore Koehler, S.M., Director

Background note: In addition to the materials listed below, information on the China mission can be found in the following serials: *Annalen der Gesellschaft zur Verbreitung des Glaubens*, 1834–1914; *Annales de l'Oeuvre de la Sainte-Enfance*, 1849–60; *Annales de la Propagation de la Foi*, 1842–73; *Annals of the Propagation of the Faith*, 1885–1923; and *Die Katholischen Missionen*, 1874–1898.

1-GENERAL HOLDINGS
SERIALS: *Apostolicum*, 1941.

OH-130 Marianist Community (Cincinnati Province) Archives
University of Dayton
Roesch Library
300 College Park Avenue
Dayton OH 45469
(513) 229-2724
Bernard Laurinaitis, S.M., Archivist

Background note: The Society of Mary (Cincinnati Province) maintained mission work in China during the 1930s and early 1940s in Hankow, where Marianist Brothers founded the Sangtze Middle School (also called the Sacred Heart School) in 1935, and in Tsinanfu, where brothers worked at the Li Ming School and Te Yü Middle School, located at the Catholic Mission.

1-GENERAL HOLDINGS
MINUTES/RECORDS/REPORTS: Sangtze Middle School (Sacred Heart College): house annals and council minutes, ca. 1935-1943; account book, 1935-42; Catholic Mission of Hankow and the Cincinnati Province of the Society of Mary, 2 contracts regarding Sacred Heart Middle School, 1935, 1940; Li Ming School, annals, ca. 1935-1943.
CORRESPONDENCE: Large envelope of correspondence from Joseph Janning, S.M., concerning Li Ming School, 1933-36; letter from Janning, in Peking, 1939; large envelope of correspondence from Janning and Dario Angarini, S.M., to Society of Mary Provincial Superiors, concerning Sangtze Middle School, 1935-1943.
MANUSCRIPTS: Manila envelope of manuscripts by Br. Francis McCulken, concerning Sangtze Middle School, ca. 1935-1943; "Christmas and New Year Greetings from the Brothers of Mary in China," by Joseph Bruder, 1938.
PAMPHLETS: *A Brief Pictorial of Marianist Missions in China*, n.d.; Sangtze Middle School spiritual bulletin, ca. 1935.
MEMORABILIA: Tearsheet from *China Light*, 1934, with a biography of William Joseph Chaminade, S.M., founder of the Society of Mary; "China Looks to America's Catholic Youth," by Joseph McCoy, S.M., in *Catholic Universe Bulletin*, 1944; 2 scrapbooks on China and some loose papers, by Lillian Schlund, sister of Herman Schlund, S.M., 1937.
SERIALS: *Digest of the Synodal Commission of Peiping, China*, 1933-37.

DELAWARE

OHIO WESLEYAN UNIVERSITY

OH-135 United Methodist Archives Center
Beeghly Library
Delaware OH 43015
(614) 369-4431 Ext. 214
Susan Cohen, Associate Curator

Background note: See also General Commission on Archives and History—The United Methodist Church, United Methodist Archives and History Center, Archives, 36 Madison Avenue, P. O. Box 127, Madison, NJ, 07940.

1-GENERAL HOLDINGS
MINUTES/RECORDS/REPORTS: Methodist Episcopal Church: Annual Missionary Report, 1825-1906; Board of Foreign Missions, 1907-39; Board of Missions and Church Extension, journal of the annual meeting, 1940-69; Central China Mission, Na-chang district, report, 1900; Eastern Asia Central Conference, address of Bishops Herbert Welch, L. J. Birney, G. R. Grose, and W. E. Brown, 1928; Methodist Episcopal Church, South, China Mission Annual Conference, minutes, 1917; Missionary Society, annual report, 1847, 1855, containing reports on China missions including extracts of missionary correspondence; United Methodist Church, Board of Global Ministries, journal of the annual meeting, 1970-76.
MANUSCRIPTS: "Founding and Early History of Our China Mission at Foochow, 1847 to 1853...Being an Address Delivered at Boston, Massachusetts, September, 1887," by Moses Clark White, 1887.
CORRESPONDENCE/CHINESE LANGUAGE MATERIALS: Bound volume of correspondence to Bishop Edward Thomson (the first president of Ohio Wesleyan University) from missionaries and native mission leaders in China, 1864-65, including letters in Chinese.
DIARIES: Journal of Moses Clark White describing his work in the China Mission in Foochow and his work in the United States, 1845-59.
SERIALS: *Foochow News*, 1940.

OH-140 Beeghly Library
Ohio Wesleyan University
Delaware OH 43015
(614) 369-4431 Ext. 360
Lois J. Szudy, Head of Technical Services

1-GENERAL HOLDINGS
MINUTES/RECORDS/REPORTS: China Continuation Committee, proceedings and minutes, 1915-19.
PAMPHLETS: *China Centennial Documents*, a bound volume of pamphlets by J. W. Bashford, 1907.
SERIALS: *China Christian Year Book*, 1938-39. *China Mission Advocate*, 1839. *Chinese Recorder*, 1901, 1911-41.

FREMONT

RUTHERFORD B. HAYES PRESIDENTIAL CENTER
OH-145 Library
Spiegel Grove
Fremont OH 43420-2796
(419) 332-2081
Janice L. Haas, Reference Librarian

1-LUCY E. KEELER COLLECTION, 1904-38, ca. 10 items
Background note: For biographical notes on George A. Fitch, see Harvard University, Harvard-Yenching Library, 2 Divinity Avenue, Cambridge, MA, 02138.
CORRESPONDENCE: A few letters to Lucy Keeler from Fitch family members (Alice, James F., Sr., Minnie E., and Robert F.), ca. 1906; 3 letters from George A. Fitch, published in the *Fremont News*, 1938.

AUDIO-VISUAL MATERIALS: 2 photos of Ningpo College, n.d.; 2 photos of Fitch children, Margaret, Katherine, and Elliot, Ningpo, 1904.
FINDING AIDS: In-house guide.

2-OHLINGER FAMILY COLLECTION, 1870–1911, 211 items
Background note: Methodist Episcopal missionaries Bertha and Franklin Ohlinger worked in China from 1870 to 1887 and from 1895 to 1911. In 1881, they established the Anglo-Chinese College in Foochow.
CORRESPONDENCE: Letter of introduction from Ohlinger for Uong De Ci, 1913; telegram from Bertha Ohlinger to Franklin Ohlinger, ca. 1889; 46 post cards from Gustav Ohlinger to his parents, 1894–1907; 15 Ohlinger family letters, 1886–1907; letter from Nathan Sites to Ohlinger, 1891; letter from W. N. Brewster to Ohlinger, n.d.
MANUSCRIPTS: "Experiences in Life of Noted Missionary to China," 1908; 1-page biography of Ohlinger (with photo), ca. 1908; "Bertha Schweinfurth Ohlinger [Mrs. Franklin]," n.a., n.d.; "Commonplace Book," by Franklin Ohlinger, 1870–1910; 12 typed sermons by Ohlinger, n.d.
MEMORABILIA: Foochow Girls' College, graduation program, 1910; "China, the Empire and China, the Republic," handbill for stereopticon lecture by Franklin Ohlinger, ca. 1913–1918; 28 galley proofs from Shanghai newspapers, 1904–5(?); United States flag flown at Ohlinger's homes in Foochow and Shanghai, 1896–1908; scale used for mailing in China; certificate of baptism for Gustav Schweinfurth Ohlinger, 1877; article by Ohlinger, in *T'oung Pao*, 1901; 6 clippings, n.d.; 1 reel microfilm of Franklin Ohlinger's articles in *Ideal Scrapbook*, 1885–1917; 1 reel microfilm of Franklin Ohlinger's articles in *Blätter Scrapbook*, 1876–97; 1 reel microfilm of Bertha Ohlinger's articles in *Centennial Scrapbook*, 1876–97.
AUDIO-VISUAL MATERIALS: 60 photos of Ohlinger's experiences in China, 1870–87, 1895–1911; photo of Ohlinger's brothers and sisters, n.d.; photo of Ohlinger, 1908; 3 miscellaneous photos, n.d.; colored slides by Ohlinger, n.d.
SERIALS: *Chinese Recorder*, 1870, 1874.
CHINESE LANGUAGE MATERIALS: Translation of *An Indian Priestess: The Life of Chundra Lela*, by Ada Lee, 1903; *Hymns and Tunes for Use by the Foochow Mission of the Methodist Episcopal Church*, 1893; *Cáng Cio Séng Si Beng Mi Buo La Ung*, 1907; *Sing Iok Cu*, 1900; translations of 8 books on American history, biography, and theology by Franklin Ohlinger, 1885–1915.
FINDING AIDS: In-house guide.

3-GENERAL HOLDINGS
PAMPHLETS: *Sia Sek Ong and the Self-Support Movement in Our Foochow Mission: A Story of His Life and Work Related by Himself*, by Sia Sek Ong, n.d.; *To the Mecca of Inner Mongolia, by George A. Fitch as Retold from His Letters by His Wife, Geraldine T. Fitch*, by George A. Fitch, 1931.

GLENDALE

OH–150 SOCIETY OF THE TRANSFIGURATION
495 Albion Avenue
Glendale OH 45246
(513) 771–5291
Sister Librarian/Archivist

Background note: An Anglican community of women, the Society of the Transfiguration engaged in educational work (kindergarten and primary school) and industrial work for women, and maintained an out-patient clinic and ward for sick women, as well as an orphanage for abandoned babies in China from 1914 to 1949. Appointments recommended.

1-GENERAL HOLDINGS
CORRESPONDENCE/DIARIES/MANUSCRIPTS/PAMPHLETS: Uncatalogued letters, diaries, articles, and other items relating to the work of Society of the Transfiguration missionaries in China, 1914–48.

GRANVILLE

DENISON UNIVERSITY
OH–155 University Archives
William Howard Doane Library
P. O. Box L
Granville OH 43023
(614) 587–6399
Florence W. Hoffman, University Archivist

1-FACULTY-PERSONAL PAPERS: KIRTLEY F. MATHER, 1914–49, 158 items
CORRESPONDENCE: 58 letters to Kirtley F. Mather, Clinton Neyman, and the "Council" (a club organized in their undergraduate years by Kirtley F. Mather and his friends), from fellow members and China missionaries Archibald G. and Olive Mason Adams, 1914–24; 96 letters to Kirtley F. Mather, Clinton Neyman, and the "Council" from China missionaries Leslie B. and Marion Venn Moss, 1915–21.
MANUSCRIPTS: "Mini-autobiographies" of Leslie and Marion Moss, with their letters, ca. 1916.
MAPS/DESIGNS/DRAWINGS: Watercolor from China, with the letters of Leslie and Marion Moss, 1949.
MEMORABILIA: Death notice of Leslie and Marion Moss, 1949.

2-GENERAL PUBLICATIONS AND BIOGRAPHIES FILE, 1868–1978, 30 items
CORRESPONDENCE: 9 letters from American Baptist missionary William Ashmore, Sr., to [?] Ewart, Ebenezer Thresher, and Dr. Osgood, 1868–1899.
MANUSCRIPTS: Original manuscript and typescript of "Sea Journal, Voyage of the Sailing Ship, *Channing*," New York to Hong Kong, by Martha Sanderson Ashmore (Mrs. William Ashmore, Sr.), 1851; sketch of the life of Eliza Ann Dunlevy Ashmore (the second Mrs. William Ashmore, Sr.), by C. H. Daniels, ca. 1885.
PAMPHLETS: *Studies in Theology in the Orient*, by William Ashmore, Sr., n.d., in William Ashmore, Sr.'s file.
MEMORABILIA: Obituary of Russel E. Adkins, of the Baptist South China mission, *Denison Alumnus*, 1936; 5 reprints from the *Chinese Recorder*, by William Ashmore, Sr., 1897–99, in William Ashmore, Sr.'s file; obituary of John L. Bjelke, missionary in South China, *Denison Alumnus*, 1974; 3 notes in the *Denison Alumnus*, by Daniel Sheets Dye, 1918, 1938, 1976; obituary of Dye, *Denison Alumnus*, 1978; 4 English-language reprints from Chinese journals, n.d., in Dye's file; obituary of Robert A. Vick, who died in plane crash on the way to a mission station in China,

Denison Alumnus, 1947; article about Vick, *Young People*, 1947.
AUDIO-VISUAL MATERIALS: Large framed photo of William
Ashmore, Sr., n.d.

**3-UNIVERSITY RELATIONS AND DEVELOPMENT—10Lx—
ALUMNI, 1962, 1 item**
MINUTES/RECORDS/REPORTS: List of eminent alumni, sec-
tion E, including China missionaries, 1962.

LIMA

ALLEN COUNTY HISTORICAL SOCIETY
OH-160 Elizabeth M. MacDonnell Memorial Library
620 West Market Street
Lima OH 45801
(419) 222-9426
Raymond F. Schuck, Curator
Anna B. Selfridge, Assistant Curator, Manuscripts and
Archives

1-GENERAL HOLDINGS
PAMPHLETS: Pamphlet prepared by F. Stanley Carson, Methodist missionary in Hinghwa, consisting of reproductions of drawings by an unknown artist on the subject of Chinese rice culture,
n.d.
MEMORABILIA: 2 newspaper clippings reproducing letters from
Grace McClurg Carson, Methodist missionary in Hinghwa, ca.
1913.
CHINESE LANGUAGE MATERIALS: Reprint of the *K'ang-hsi
chun hsing Cheng-chiao lu* (*Decree of the K'ang-hsi Emperor
Granting Toleration to Christianity*), 1835; translation of the Gospel of Mark, n.d.

MOUNT SAINT JOSEPH

SISTERS OF CHARITY MOTHERHOUSE
OH-165 Archives
5701 Delhi Pike
Mount Saint Joseph OH 45051
(513) 244-4624
Laura Marie Watson, S.C., Archivist

Background note: The Sisters of Charity of Cincinnati began their
service in China at the request of the Franciscan Fathers. They
agreed to take charge of a small hospital in Wuchang. Six sisters
arrived in 1928. As time went on, their work broadened to include
an orphanage, school, dispensary, and training school for nurses.
Additional sisters were sent from the United States and Chinese
women began to join the congregation. A novitiate was opened in
China and eventually 20 Chinese women entered the congregation.
In 1937, a new orphanage was built in San Kiang Kow, but after
1937, the area was occupied by Japanese troops. The American
sisters were interned after Pearl Harbor, first at the hospital compound and later in Shanghai, until the end of the war. The Chinese
sisters remained in Wuchang during the war. The hospital was
rebuilt after the war and construction continued even after the
decision was made to withdraw the sisters. They left China in 1948
and 1949.

1-GENERAL HOLDINGS
MINUTES/RECORDS/REPORTS: Records of the opening of the
Sisters of Charity China mission, including the agreement between
the community and Sylvester Espelage, O.F.M., 1928; St. Vincent
Orphanage, San Kiong Ko, St. Joseph Hospital, Wuchang, Hupeh,
records, ca. 1928-1949.
CORRESPONDENCE: 4 file boxes of letters from sisters in Chi-
na, sisters from other communities in China, Chinese sisters and
students, and others, 1926-51, including letters of Bishop Bur-
chard, O.F.M., Cosmas Chang, Bishop Vitus Chang, S.V.D.,
Joseph Henkels, S.V.D., Bishop Rembert Kowalski, O.F.M.,
Bonaventure Kuo, Madian Schneider, O.F.M., Sigfrid Schneider,
O.F.M., Alphonse Schnusenberg, O.F.M., Fr. Seraphim,
O.F.M., Leon Sullivan, O.F.M., and Bishop Joseph Yuen; folder
of letters of Mother Irenaea and Sylvester Espelage, O.F.M., relating to the opening of the mission, 1928; an album book of letters
from Sr. Mary Roberta Cahill (the first local superior in Wuchang),
Sr. Mary Alban Kennedy, and Sr. Mary James Mullen, 1928-32;
"Travelettes," a series of letters by Sr. Mary Evangelist Mahan on
the journey from Mount St. Joseph to Wuchang, 1928.
MANUSCRIPTS: Annotations of the sisters' China correspondence, i.e., booklets of dates and synopses of letters and other
materials; "History of Sisters of Charity in Wuchang, Hupeh,
China," by Helen Therese Walsh, S.C., and Marguerite Schuler,
S.C., 1934; "Shade of His Hand Outstretched: History of the
Sisters of Charity in China, 1933-49," by Jean Pierre King, S.C.,
and Edward Mary North, S.C., 1961; "Up River to Wuchang—
Memoirs of S. Marie Amadea," 1960.
ORAL HISTORIES: Tapes and transcripts of interviews conduct-
ed in 1967 with Sisters of Charity former China missionaries: Srs.
Mary Gerard Cheng, Francis Roberta Chin, Teresa Mary Chiou,
Maria Chow, Mary Theophane Costanza, Ann Majella Dunn,
Frances Maria Hautman, Marie Amadea Heaney, Marie Alphonse
I, Mary Alban Kennedy, Mary Concepta Kraus, Maurice Clet
Ling, Paul Vincent Liu, Lucia Mao, Joseph Ignatius Owyang,
Hildegarde Sumner, Martha Seton Tsai, and Columba Yuan.
AUDIO-VISUAL MATERIALS: 5 photo albums and small box of
loose photos of the Sisters of Charity China mission, Chinese
civilization and culture, clergy, sisters, and native Chinese sisters,
1928-50.
SERIALS: *Lotus Leaves*, 1929-51.

OBERLIN

OBERLIN COLLEGE
OH-170 Archives
420 Mudd Learning Center
Oberlin OH 44074
(216) 775-8285 Ext. 246
Roland M. Baumann, Archivist

**1-GEORGE NELSON ALLEN COLLECTION (30/67), 1891-93, 5
items**
CORRESPONDENCE: 5 letters from Mary Ament to Carrie Allen, 1891-93.
FINDING AIDS: In-house box list.

2-WILLARD L. BEARD (30/76), 1910-25, 1 box
Background note: Willard L. Beard (d. 1947) served as a mission-

ary in Foochow from 1907 to 1947. His daughter, Phebe, accompanied him to China as a missionary in 1921.

CORRESPONDENCE: Beard family correspondence, 1910–25; ca. 20 letters from Beard and his daughter, Phebe, Foochow, 1921–23, some of which describe struggle between factions for control of the area.

AUDIO-VISUAL MATERIALS/MEMORABILIA: Photos of China and missionary activities and miscellaneous memorabilia.

3-ARTHUR N. BROWN PAPERS (30/122), ca. 1916-ca. 1945, ca. 2 in.

CORRESPONDENCE: Letters from China missionary Philip Dutton to Arthur N. Brown, ca. 1916–ca. 1945.

4-ELLSWORTH C. CARLSON COLLECTION (30/176), 1939–81, 5 boxes

Restrictions: Access by appointment.

Background note: Shansi Memorial Association trustee Ellsworth C. Carlson taught in China from 1939 to 1943. See also Shansi Memorial Association below.

MINUTES/RECORDS/REPORTS: Shansi Memorial Association, records, 1939–81 (mostly post-1960s).

FINDING AIDS: In-house box list.

5-PAUL LEATON CORBIN PAPERS (30/49), 1904–35, 3 l.f. (7 boxes)

Background note: Paul Leaton Corbin (1875–1936) was a missionary under the American Board of Commissioners for Foreign Missions (ABCFM) in Shansi from 1904 to 1932. He assisted in rebuilding the Oberlin Mission in Shansi that had been destroyed during the Boxer Uprising in 1900 and later worked with H. H. Kung in establishing and developing the Oberlin memorial schools in Shansi.

MINUTES/RECORDS/REPORTS: American Board of Commissioners for Foreign Missions, North China Mission, Shansi district, minutes, 1908–19, 1926; Prudential Committee, report of the deputation to China, 1907; Canton Union Theological College, president's report, 1914–15; Oberlin Shansi Memorial Schools Agricultural Department, report to the Boards of managers and trustees, 1931; Shansi District Association, Literature Committee, report, 1918; minutes, 1918–19; minutes of other organizations, 1904–35; report of inspection of elementary schools in Taiku, 1919; report of a special committee on a Forward Evangelistic Movement, ca. 1918; report on evangelistic work in Taiku, 1928; reports on plague, 1919; report of the proceedings of the Tentative Committee on Federation, Shansi province, 1908; Soochow University, report by Chinese staff on killing of Chinese students in the International Settlement, 1925; Tokyo Chinese YMCA, report, 1914; reports, 1907–31 and n.d., on American Board missionaries, single women, trip to Shansi, disturbance at North China Union College, churches in Asia, graduation exercises of the Oberlin Shansi memorial schools, visit to a "*tao yuan*," famine relief work, trip to Sutsien field, and American military protection for missionaries.

CORRESPONDENCE: 5 folders of circular letters to Corbin from China missionaries, 1908–35.

MANUSCRIPTS: Folder of unspecified manuscripts.

MEMORABILIA: 6 boxes of miscellaneous printed matter on China and missionary work.

FINDING AIDS: Partial box list.

6-HOWARD C. CURTIS FAMILY PAPERS (50/59), ca. 1900, 4 folders

MEMORABILIA: Printed matter relating to China missionary James Goldsbury, ca. 1900.

7-LYDIA LORD DAVIS COLLECTION (30/80), 1889–1940, 6 boxes

Background note: Lydia Lord Davis accompanied her husband, Francis W. Davis, to China as missionary under the American Board of Commissioners for Foreign Missions (ABCFM) in 1889. She founded the first girls' school in Shansi under the ABCFM. After Francis W. Davis' death in the Boxer Uprising of 1900, Lydia Lord Davis became a fund-raiser in the Oberlin area for Congregational mission work and executive secretary of the Shansi Memorial Association, 1929–41. She made a return trip to China in 1924.

CORRESPONDENCE: Letters between Lydia Lord Davis and her parents, 1889–98; ca. 125 letters to Lydia Lord Davis, ca. 1889–1897, from China missionaries Jennie Pond Atwater, Rowena Bird, Jennie Rowland Clapp, P. F. Edwards, Dr. and Mrs. James Goldsbury, Vesta Greer, Anna C. Merritt, Mary Louise Partridge, Eva Price, D'Etta Hewett Thompson, Myrtle H. Wanger, Maggie Whitaker, Emily Whitchurch, and Alice Moon Williams; several letters from Francis Davis, 1899–1900; letters to Lydia Lord Davis on her husband's death; letters to Lydia Lord Davis on her work, ca. 1920–1940; letters to Judson Smith and the ABCFM, 1899–1905.

MANUSCRIPTS: Davis' notebooks, 1889–99; "Letters to My Grandchildren: The Story of Our Family," by Lydia Lord Davis, 1944.

MEMORABILIA/AUDIO-VISUAL MATERIALS: Memoranda, printed matter, and photos, 1890–1938.

FINDING AIDS: In-house box list.

8-LEWIS AND LOIS GILBERT LETTERS (30/138), 1925–41, 16 volumes

Background note: Lewis (1898–1978) and Lois (d. 1969) Gilbert were missionaries to China from 1925 to 1941. They taught at Yale-in-China from 1925 to 1927, when they were evacuated, and returned to China in 1929 and were stationed in Shantung until 1941. The originals of this collection are held by Yale Divinity School, Special Collections, 409 Prospect Street, New Haven, CT, 06520 (Record Group #8).

CORRESPONDENCE: 16 spiral bound volumes of typescript copies of letters from Lewis and Lois Gilbert in China, 1925–41.

9-GRADUATE SCHOOL OF THEOLOGY (Group 11), 1925, 1 item

CORRESPONDENCE: Letter from J[ohn] L[eighton] Stuart to Edward Increase Bosworth, 1925.

10-THOMAS WESLEY GRAHAM COLLECTION (30/86), 1920–27, 4 items

CORRESPONDENCE: 4 letters to Thomas Wesley Graham, dean of the Graduate School of Theology, from China missionaries Raymond Buker, Horton Daniels, and Myra L. Sawyer, 1920–27.

FINDING AIDS: In-house box list.

11-EDWIN MICHAEL HOFFMAN COLLECTION (30/69), 1919–74, 2 boxes

Restrictions: Available only on microfilm.

Background note: Edwin M. Hoffman (d. 1977) was a YMCA worker before World War I. He served in Harbin from 1919 to 1920 because of the American Expeditionary Force's presence in Siberia.

CORRESPONDENCE: Ca. 80 letters from Hoffman in Harbin, mainly to his family, commenting on YMCA work, American troops, and native peoples, 1919–20; miscellaneous letters to Hoffman, including one by H. H. Kung, 1926; several letters written by Hoffman with recollections of the 1918–20 period, 1972–74.

DIARIES: Journal by Hoffman commenting on Manchurian customs and photos taken in Manchuria.

AUDIO-VISUAL MATERIALS: Photos of Manchuria and Irkutsk, Lake Baikal; descriptions and drawings of birds.

MEMORABILIA: Newspaper clippings, n.d.

FINDING AIDS: In-house box list.

12-HENRY CHURCHILL KING: GENERAL COLLECTION (2/611), 1910, 2 boxes

Background note: This collection is also available on microfilm.

CORRESPONDENCE: Box of letters from Oberlin President Henry Churchill King, on tour in China, to Mrs. King, 1910.

AUDIO-VISUAL MATERIALS: Box of photos taken by King on tour in China, 1910.

FINDING AIDS: In-house box list.

13-LIBRARY-MISCELLANEOUS, 1896–1905, 1 box

CORRESPONDENCE/MEMORABILIA/AUDIO-VISUAL MATERIALS: Letters, clippings, and photos on Boxer Rebellion martyrs, 1896–1905.

14-GRACE E. McCONNAUGHEY LETTERS (30/160), 1910–60, 5 in.

Background note: Grace E. McConnaughey (1882–1978) was a Congregational missionary in Shansi from 1910 to 1928, mostly as principal of a girls' school in Fenchow.

CORRESPONDENCE: Letters from McConnaughey in China, 1912–28.

MANUSCRIPTS: "Amazing Grace," prepared from McConnaughey's letters by her niece, Grace E. McConnaughey Murray, n.d.; "A Short Sketch of the Life of Grace McConnaughey," 1960.

AUDIO-VISUAL MATERIALS: Several photos by McConnaughey in China, 1910–28.

15-IRVING W. METCALF PAPERS (30/9), 1882–1934, 2 l.f., 4 in.

CORRESPONDENCE: Mimeographed and personal letters from missionaries in China, 1882–1934; letter from C. R. Hager in South China, ca. 1900–1920; 4 letters and 3 postcards from Chauncey Marvin Cady, 1882; letter from H. H. Kung, 1926.

MEMORABILIA: 2 printed items from Chauncey Marvin Cady.

FINDING AIDS: In-house box list.

16-MARGARET PORTIA MICKEY COLLECTION (30/26), 1914–40, 2 boxes

Background note: Margaret Portia Mickey (b. 1889) was a missionary teacher in north China under the American Board of Commissioners for Foreign Missions.

CORRESPONDENCE: Ca. 1.25 boxes of letters from Mickey on mission, 1914–20; 4 folders of letters from Mickey's mother, 1917–18; folder of letters unsigned or written by others, 1917–19; folder of miscellaneous letters, 1918, 1935, 1940, and n.d.

MANUSCRIPTS: Essays on medical work, floods, women's work, work in rural areas, schools, and other subjects, n.d.

PAMPHLETS: Miscellaneous printed matter, n.d.

CHINESE LANGUAGE MATERIALS: Unidentified written materials.

17-OBERLIN SHANSI MEMORIAL ASSOCIATION—GENERAL FILES, ca. 1904–1980, ca. 15 l.f.

Background note: Some older files are still held by the Oberlin Shansi Memorial Association (OSMA) main office.

MINUTES/RECORDS/REPORTS: Oberlin Shansi Memorial Association (OSMA): Board of Managers, minutes and correspondence, 1919–37; Conference on Industrial and Agricultural Education in Shansi, 1933; executive board and trustees, minutes, 1945–85; executive committee, 1944–79; executive secretary reports, 1915–80; finance committee meeting minutes, 1954–64; financial reports, 1948–72; financial statements and auditor's certificates, 1960–80; minutes, 1907–40; program planner's reports, 1973–80; representative's reports to trustees, 1933–79; Shansi Mission, reports, 1908–19; treasurer's reports, 1936–80; trustee meeting minutes, 1944–77; Union of North China and Shansi Missions, 1911–25; Chinese educational regulations, 1937; record on evacuation, 1927; Industrial Department, 1933; Shansi Building for Oberlin, 1931; Shansi Educational reorganization, 1918–19; evangelistic reports by Wynn Fairfield on Taiku, 1912–16; financial records relating to Ming Hsien budget, reports, etc. 1950.

CORRESPONDENCE: Ca. 10 boxes of OSMA correspondence, 1882–1971, with organizations and individuals including American colleges, American Board of Commissioners for Foreign Missions, Associated Boards for Christian Colleges in China, Gertrude M. Cheney, China representatives, Chinese students, Church World Service, Paul L. Corbin, Lydia Lord Davis, Wynn C. Fairfield, Far Eastern Joint Office, Joseph W. Hamilton, Mr. and Mrs. John W. Hamlin, Everett D. Hawkins, Roger R. Hawkins, Adelaide Hemingway, W. A. Hemingway, Hu Shih, George D. Hubbard, Francis S. Hutchins, Harold B. Ingalls, Mr. and Mrs. Richard G. Irwin, Walter H. Judd, Liu Lan-hua, Robert P. Louis, Y. P. Mei, Luella Miner, Ming Hsien alumni, J. Clayton Miller, Raymond R. Moyer, OSMA representatives, Walter S. Phillips, W. O. Pye, Jane E. Smith, Robbins Strong, H. B. Thurston, Samuel E. Wilson, We K'e-ming, United Board for Christian Colleges in China, United China Relief, F. B. Warner, and J. B. Wolfe; correspondence and other materials on institutions in Asia surveyed by Fairfield, 1955; correspondence regarding withdrawal of old representatives and sending new ones, 1938–39.

MANUSCRIPTS: Fairfield's notes for writing history of the first 50 years in Shansi, n.d.; unspecified essays, 1928–30.

PAMPHLETS: Printed matter, 1945–49 and n.d.

AUDIO-VISUAL MATERIALS: Films by John Hamlin, n.d.: "One of Dr. Mei's Last Morning Assemblies Here," "Family," "John Francis: Wedding," "A Peiping Funeral on Teng Shih Kin in January," and untitled (1938); unspecified photos.

MAPS/DESIGNS/DRAWINGS: Map of Fenchow Mission compound, n.d.

SERIALS: *Dragon Tracks*, 1938–46. *OSMA Newsletter*, 1949–81.

FINDING AIDS: In-house inventory.

18-CHAUNCEY N. POND—MISSIONARY LETTERS, 1892–1916, 11 folders

Background note: The collection totals 3 boxes, 1852–1919.

MINUTES/RECORDS/REPORTS: Folder of copies of letters and accounts, ca. 1895–1900.

CORRESPONDENCE: 7 folders of letters sent to or collected by

Chauncey Pond, 1892–1910; [Jennie Pond?] Atwater, 1892–98; I. J. Atwood, 1897; Louise Partridge, 1893–1900; Rowena Bird, 1893–98; Eva Price, 1897–1900; and miscellaneous, 1874–1910 and n.d.
MEMORABILIA: 2 folders of material removed from scrapbooks, consisting of letters from missionaries, clippings, and photos, mostly about Shansi, 1904–16, and n.d.; folder of printed matter on China, ca. 1889–1901.

19-SHANSI MEMORIAL ASSOCIATION—FINANCIAL RECORDS, 1908–40; OBERLIN CHINA BAND, 1881–84; MISCELLANEOUS PHOTOS, ca. 1890–1935, 1881–1935, 2 boxes, 1 volume
MINUTES/RECORDS/REPORTS: Oberlin China Band, ledger and minutes of the recording secretary, 1881–84; Shansi Memorial Association, 8 ledgers of income and expenditures, 1908–40; ledger of Shansi investments, 1933–39.
CORRESPONDENCE: Folder of ''Oberlin-Taiku Correspondence,'' 1909, 1918–28; folder of correspondence relating to the ''Hall Fund,'' 1919–28, a large donation to the Shansi Memorial Association; ''National City Bank,'' financial correspondence, 1929–32; folder of ''American Board,'' letters of transmittal through the American Board of Commissioners for Foreign Missions, 1908–34; folder of ''Contribution Correspondence,'' letters of transmittal, 1908–28.
AUDIO-VISUAL MATERIALS: Photo albums and loose photos of the Shansi Memorial Association, ca. 1890–1935.

20-SHANSI MEMORIAL ASSOCIATION—LETTERS FROM SHANSI REPS, 1951–67, 2 boxes
CORRESPONDENCE: Letters from Shansi Memorial Association representatives, 1951–67.

21-SHANSI MEMORIAL ASSOCIATION—MISCELLANEOUS PUBLICATIONS AND PRINTED MATERIAL, 1906–78, 3 boxes
MINUTES/RECORDS/REPORTS: Shansi District Association, Taiku, minutes, 1924–26; Shansi Mission, annual reports, 1906–14; North China Mission, annual reports, 1914–15.
CORRESPONDENCE: Miscellaneous letters, n.d.
PAMPHLETS: Brochures and pamphlets relating to commencements and other events of Oberlin-in-China and Oberlin-in-Shansi, 1920s–1970s, n.d.
SERIALS: *Dragon Tracks*, 1938–46. *Oberlin-in-China*, 1949–57. *Oberlin-Shansi Memorial Association Newsletter*, 1958–78.
CHINESE LANGUAGE MATERIALS: Unidentified manuscript.

22-SHANSI MEMORIAL ASSOCIATION—MISCELLANY, 1900–1903, 1 box
CORRESPONDENCE: Letters regarding H. H. Kung and Fei Ch'i-hao visit to the United States, 1900–1903.
CHINESE LANGUAGE MATERIALS: Box of greetings and tributes to H. H. Kung on his 60th birthday.

23-SHANSI MEMORIAL ASSOCIATION—PHOTO SLIDES AND NEGATIVES; MOTION PICTURES, 1921-ca. 1930s, quantity undetermined
AUDIO-VISUAL MATERIALS: Glass slides received from the Shansi Memorial Association, 1921-ca. 1930s, believed to have been taken by Ted Forbes, 1924–26; George D. Hubbard, 1921; and W. A. Hemingway, n.d.; motion picture film of China, ca. 1930s.

24-GEORGE L. AND MARY ALICE MOON WILLIAMS COLLECTION, 1891–1960, 6 boxes
Background note: George L. Williams (1858–1900) arrived in China in 1892, and was killed in the Boxer Uprising of 1900. His wife, Mary Alice (Moon) Williams (1860–1952), returned to China from 1909 to 1912 and 1935 to 1937. Their daughter, Gladys M. Williams (1893–1981), was also a missionary in China from 1917 to 1952. She taught at the Alice M. Williams School, in Taiku, Shansi, named for her mother.
MINUTES/RECORDS/REPORTS: Unidentified reports and minutes, 1895–1912.
CORRESPONDENCE: 5 boxes of letters from George and Alice Williams describing missionary life, 1891–1900; letters written by missionaries to each other and to people in the United States, n.d.
MANUSCRIPTS: Accounts of the events of 1900; account of events in China in 1912(?) by C. H. Fay (Fei), n.d.; notes and notebook on Shansi events, by Alice Williams, 1889–91.
DIARIES: Diary by Alice Williams of her 1909–12 trip to China.
AUDIO-VISUAL MATERIALS/MEMORABILIA: Box of photos, ca. 1890–1950, maps, and miscellany, from Alice Williams' trips to China; printed matter, ca. 1906–1960, including information about missionaries such as Alma Atzel, Hazel F. Bailey, Lucy P. Bement, Paul Leaton Corbin, Katharine P. Crane, Helen Dizney, Philip D. Dutton, Howard S. Galt, Sarah Boardman Clapp (Mrs. Chauncey Goodrich), Flora K. Heebner, Dr. and Mrs. Willoughby Hemingway, Gertrude E. Kellogg, Maryette H. Lum, James Hamilton McCann, Lou Vera McReynolds, Luella Miner, Alzine C. Munger, Esther Ethel Nelson, Clara A. Nutting, Watts O. Pye, William Satterthwaite, Josephine C. Walker, Cora May Walton, and Dr. and Mrs. Leonard Fisk Wilbur.
CHINESE LANGUAGE MATERIALS: Unidentified correspondence.
FINDING AIDS: In-house box list.

25-WRITINGS ABOUT OBERLIN PEOPLE, ca. 1923, 2 items
CORRESPONDENCE: Part of a letter from Emily Bostwick, containing information about Oberlin people in China, ca. 1923.
MANUSCRIPTS: ''Appreciations of Cora Walton Sledge,'' comp. by Geraldine Searle McLellan, n.d.

26-WRITINGS BY OBERLIN PEOPLE, 1900–1901, quantity undetermined
CORRESPONDENCE: Letter by Rowena Bird, Shansi, on Boxer Uprising, 1900; letters and memoranda on the Boxer Uprising, n.a., 1901.
MEMORABILIA: Printed information relating to H. H. Kung and martyrs of the Boxer Uprising, 1900.

27-GENERAL HOLDINGS
MAPS/DESIGNS/DRAWINGS: ''General Plan Oberlin in China at Taiku, Shansi,'' 2 drawings by Henry K. Murphy, 1929, 1931; map of the Tungchow Mission, 1912.

OH–175 Main Library
Mudd Learning Center
Oberlin College
Oberlin OH 44074
(216) 775-8285
Ray English, Head of Reference

1-GENERAL HOLDINGS

MINUTES/RECORDS/REPORTS: American Board of Commissioners for Foreign Missions: China deputation, general report, 1898, 1907; Fenchow Station, annual report, 1912–14; Foochow Mission, annual report, 1845–1901; Work for Women and Children, Foochow, report, 1901; Lintsing Station, annual report, 1913–14; North China Mission, annual report, 1833–1914; minutes, 1914, 1934, 1936, 1938–40; North China Mission, Chihli district, annual report, 1913–14; North China Mission, Kung Li Hui Council, minutes, 1934, 1936, 1938–41; Shansi Mission, annual report, 1897, 1905–18; Shansi Mission, Taikuhsien Station, report, 1913–14; Shantung district, annual report, 1913–14; Shaowu Mission, annual report, 1900.

American Presbyterian Mission in Canton, report, 1890–91; China Continuation Committee, report, 1917–18; Christian Literature Society for China, annual report, 1912–13, 1919–20; Church Missionary Society and Dispensary, Pakhoi, report, 1892; Ing Hok (The Valley of Everlasting Happiness), report, 1912–13; International Institute of China, report, 1897, 1902–7; Methodist Episcopal Church in China, program of advance, 1920; Methodist Episcopal Church: Fuhkien province, Women's Conference, session records, 1900–1911; Hing-Hua Women's Conference, minutes, 1899; Women's Conference, minutes, 1901–15.

North China Educational Union, register of union colleges, 1907; Oberlin-in-Shansi Memorial Association, financial statement, 1920–27, letter and annual report, 1920, 1922, 1927; Ponasang Missionary Hospital, Foochow, annual report, 1904; Presbyterian Church in the U.S.A., Central China mission, summary of the annual reports, 1892–93; Society for the Diffusion of Christian and General Knowledge among the Chinese, annual report, 1896–97.

MANUSCRIPTS: Photocopy of "Diary of Rosewell Hobart Graves," 1854; "An Annotated Bibliography of Selected Missionary Periodicals Concerning China in the Oberlin College Library," by David A. Schlesinger, 1982.

PAMPHLETS: 56 pamphlets, 1985–1934, on American Board of Commissioners for Foreign Missions mission in China, anti-Christian movement, F. K. Bement, L. P. Bement, Boxers, Chinese church, merchants, ministry, and schools, Congregationalists, M. L. Corbin, P. L. Corbin, country parish, Dartmouth-in-China, Jeannette O. Ferris, Charles Hartwell, Interchurch World Movement of North America, International Institute, Ada (Haven) Mateer, medical missions, missionary education, method, and stories, Robert Morrison, Robert Nelson, Oberlin Shansi Memorial Association, Presbyterian Church of England China mission, Presbyterian Church in the U.S.A. Board of Foreign Missions and Women's Board of Foreign Missions, South China Girls' School, Protestant missionaries, Reformed Church in U.S.—Shenchowfu Station, Theological and Bible Training School in Fenchow, Mark William Williams, and the Women's Board of Missions.

AUDIO-VISUAL MATERIALS: Package of photos associated with the Kinnears, who were China missionaries, showing anti-opium activities and a training school, ca. 1905–1906.

SERIALS: *China and the Gospel*, 1904–20. *China Christian Advocate*, 1914–41. *China Christian Year Book*, 1926–31. China Inland Mission, *Occasional Papers*, 1866–?. China International Famine Relief Commission, Publications, series A, 1924–30, 1932–36; series B, 1926, 1929–30. *China Medical Journal*, 1907–

31. *China Medical Missionary Journal*, 1887–1907. *China Mission Year Book*, 1910–25. *China's Millions* (London), 1875–80, 1882–84, 1886–1921. *China's Millions* (Toronto), 1895–96, 1906–7, 1910, 1914, 1925. *China's Young Men*, 1906, 1909–10. *Chinese Recorder*, 1868–1941. *Directory of Protestant Missions in China*, 1916–17, 1923–25. *Educational Review*, 1907–8, 1909–38. *The Foochow Messenger*, 1903–8, 1925–26. *Johannean*, 1924. West China Border Research Society, *Journal*, 1922–23, 1940. *West China Missionary News*, 1901–43.

DISSERTATIONS/THESES: *Oberlin-in-China, 1881–1951*, by Mary Tarpley Campfield, 1974.

CHINESE LANGUAGE MATERIALS/SERIALS: *China's Young Men*, 1906–16 (inc.).

OH–180 Special Collections
Oberlin College
Mudd Learning Center
Oberlin OH 44074
(216) 775–8285
Dina Schoonmaker, Curator

1-GENERAL HOLDINGS

MINUTES/RECORDS/REPORTS: Oberlin Shansi Memorial Association, Board of Trustees, minutes, 1929–30.

CORRESPONDENCE: Letter from I. J. Atwood, 1904; a letter each from missionaries of the Shaowu Mission of the American Board, Leona Lloyd Burr, Edwin D. Kellogg, Jeanie Graham McClure, and Josephine C. Walker, 1920.

MANUSCRIPTS: "Princeton Work in Peking Young Men's Christian Associations," by John Stewart Burgess, 1911; "Shaowu to Foochow, in Perils Oft," by Frances Katherine Bement, Lucy P. Bement, and Grace A. Funk, n.d.; "Shaowu Letter," by Frances Katherine Bement, 1909.

PAMPHLETS: *Brief History of the South China Mission of the American Board*, by C. A. Nelson, 1911; *History of the Mei-Wa School of the American Chinese Educational Commission, Canton, China*, by C. A. Nelson, 1935; *A Letter from Shansi*, by K'ung Hsiang-hsi, n.d.; *In Loving Remembrance: "The Noble Army of Martyrs Praise Thee..."*, by the American Board of Commissioners for Foreign Missions, 1900; *Medical Work for Women in Shaowu, China: The Shao-wu Hospital*, by Frances Katherine Bement, n.d.; *A Message to the Churches*, by Chauncey Goodrich, 1901(?); *New Conditions in China*, by C. A. Stanley, 1904; *New Oberlin Beginnings in Shansi*, by Alice Williams, 1907.

SERIALS: *Chinese Repository*, 1832–51.

DISSERTATIONS/THESES: *Christianity and China: A Study of Church and State*, by Robbins Strong, 1938. *An Experiment in Teaching the Christian Religion by Life Situations in Fan Village, China*, by Mabel Ellis Hubbard, 1938.

OXFORD

MIAMI UNIVERSITY
OH–185 Edgar W. King Library
Oxford OH 45056
(513) 529–2944
Richard H. Quay, Social Science Librarian

1-GENERAL HOLDINGS
PAMPHLETS: *Hangchow Journal of 1870*, by David Nelson Lyon, 1936; *Mother of Seven: Reminiscences*, by Mandana E. Lyon, 1937.
SERIALS: *China Christian Year Book*, 1928.
CHINESE LANGUAGE MATERIALS: *Chung-kuo kuan shen fan chiao ti yüan yin (The Origin and Cause of the Anti-Christian Movement by Chinese Officials and Gentry, 1860–1874)*, by Lü Shih-ch'iang, 1966.

TOLEDO

OH-190 TOLEDO-LUCAS COUNTY PUBLIC LIBRARY
325 Michigan Street
Toledo OH 43624
(419) 255-7055
James C. Marshall, Head, Local History and Genealogy Department

1-GENERAL HOLDINGS
CORRESPONDENCE: 7 volumes of carbon copies of letters from medical missionary William W. Peter about life in China, 1912.

WILMINGTON

WILMINGTON COLLEGE
OH-195 Archives
Quaker Collection
Sheppard Arthur Watson Library
Wilmington OH 45177
(513) 382-6661
Ina E. Kelley, Archivist/Curator

1-GENERAL HOLDINGS
MINUTES/RECORDS/REPORTS: American Churches and China Relief, record and prospect, n.d.; American Friends Service Committee: delegation to China, report, 1972; working part on China policy, report, 1964–65.
PAMPHLETS: *A Challenge from Chengtu*, by D. M. Gill and P. M. Pullen, 1936; *China at the Parting of the Ways*, by the University of China Committee, Friends Service Council, n.d.; *Friends in the Villages of West China*, by the Friends Service Council, 1935; *Friends' Schools in China*, by Harry T. Silcock, n.d.; *History of Friends' Work in China*, n.a., 1904(?); *Inside China*, by Sven Linquist, n.d.; *Peace in China*, by William Hanson, 1955; *Quaker Mission to China: W. Grigor McClelland's Diary, 26th September–29th October, 1955*, by W. Grigor McClelland, 1955; *Through the Gorges and Beyond: Friends' Work in West China*, by the Friends Service Council, 1932; *West China Union University*, by R. J. Davidson, et. al., 1934.
DISSERTATIONS/THESES: *Revolutionary Faithfulness: The Quaker Search for a Peaceable Kingdom in China, 1939–1951*, by Cynthia Letts Adcock, 1974.

WOOSTER

COLLEGE OF WOOSTER
OH-200 Andrews Library
Wooster OH 44691
(216) 263-2155
Denise Monbarren, Reference Librarian

1-GENERAL HOLDINGS
MINUTES/RECORDS/REPORTS: Presbyterian Church in the U.S.A., Central China mission, station reports, 1900, 1903.
PAMPHLETS: *Across the Desert of Gobi: A Narrative of an Escape During the Boxer Uprising, June to September, 1900*, by Mark Williams, 1901.
MAPS/DESIGNS/DRAWINGS: *Atlas of China in Provinces*, by Thomas Cochrane (Shanghai: Christian Literature Society for China), 1913.
SERIALS: *Chinese Recorder*, 1916–18, 1928–32. *Chinese Recorder and Missionary Journal*, 1869–71, 1874–78, 1886, 1891–92, 1901–8.
DISSERTATIONS/THESES: *Reciprocal Change: The Case of American Protestant Missionaries to China*, by Paul Voninski, 1975.

OKLAHOMA

ENID

PHILLIPS UNIVERSITY
OK-5 John Rogers Graduate Seminary Library
University Station
Box 2218
Enid OK 73702-2218
(405) 237-4433
John L. Sayre, Director of University Libraries
Marilee J. Pralle, Public Services Supervisor

1-GENERAL HOLDINGS
MINUTES/RECORDS/REPORTS: Central China Christian Missionary Conventions, reports, 1889–90, 1891–92, 1895–96, 1898, 1900–1924, 1926.
PAMPHLETS: *The China Christian Mission: Completing Fifty Years of Service*, by Elliott I. Osgood, n.d.; *Far West in China*, by Stanton Lautenschlager, 1944; *The Lone Pine Principal: A Sketch of Emma A. Lyon's Work in the Christian Girls' School, Nanking, China*, by Eva May Dye, 1922; *Missions in Far Eastern Cultural*

Relations, by Miner Searle Bates, 1943; *The Present Situation in China and Its Significance for Christian Missions*, n.a., 1925; *On God's Errand: Report of the China Inland Mission*, n.a., 1924.
MEMORABILIA: Central China Christian Mission, handbook, 1907, 1917.
ORAL HISTORIES: 54-page typescript of an interview with Oswald J. Goulter for the *China Missionaries Oral History Project*, Claremont Graduate School, Oral History Program, 1971.
SERIALS: *China and the Gospel*, 1912, 1916. *China Mission Year Book*, 1910, 1919, 1923. *Directory of Protestant Missions in China*, 1921, 1923.
DISSERTATIONS/THESES: *The Development of the Motive of Protestant Missions to China, 1807–1928*, by George Bell Workman, 1928.
CHINESE LANGUAGE MATERIALS: 2 Chinese hymnals, 1895, 1912; translation of *Come Wind, Come Weather, the Present Experience of the Church in China*, by Leslie Theodore Lyall, 1961.

TULSA

ORAL ROBERTS UNIVERSITY
OK–10 **Messick Learning Resources Center**
7777 South Lewis Avenue
Tulsa OK 74171
(918) 495–6894
Oon-chor Khoo, Theology Librarian

1-GENERAL HOLDINGS
AUDIO-VISUAL MATERIALS: "Underground Evangelism Presents, 'Missions China '74,'" audio cassette by L. Joe Bass, 1974.
SERIALS: *East Asia Millions* (Philadelphia), 1964–70.

OREGON

CORVALLIS

OREGON STATE UNIVERSITY
OR–5 **William Jasper Kerr Library**
Corvallis OR 97331
(503) 754–3331
Kristine Rankka, Religious Studies Librarian

1-GENERAL HOLDINGS
SERIALS: *Fukien Agricultural Journal*, 1947–51. *Lingnan Science Journal*, 1922–48. *News of China*, 1943–49. *Peking Natural History Bulletin*, 1930–50. University of Nanking, College of Agriculture and Forestry, *Bulletin*, 1926–36. Yenching University, Department of Biology, *Bulletin*, 1930.

EUGENE

NORTHWEST CHRISTIAN COLLEGE
OR–10 **Learning Resource Center**
828 East 11th Street
Eugene OR 97401
(503) 343–1641
Sue Rhee, Library Director

1-GENERAL HOLDINGS
MINUTES/RECORDS/REPORTS: Consultation on World Evangelization, report, 1980.
AUDIO-VISUAL MATERIALS: *Missions Ahead*, audio cassette by Samuel H. Moffett, n.d.
SERIALS: *China's Millions* (London), 1886, 1890.

UNIVERSITY OF OREGON

OR–15 **Special Collections**
Eugene OR 97403–1299
(503) 686–3068
Hilary Cummings, Manuscripts Curator

Finding aids: *Catalogue of Manuscripts in the University of Oregon Library*, comp. by Martin Schmitt, 1971.

1-EDITH F. ABEL COLLECTION, 1916–44, 5 items
CORRESPONDENCE/MEMORABILIA: 2 letters from Edith F. Abel, 1941, 1944; clipping from *Sheridan Post*, containing Abel's first letter from China, 1916.
AUDIO-VISUAL MATERIALS: Photo album containing captioned snapshots of Ngucheng school, n.d.
SERIALS: *Foochow News*, 1938.
FINDING AIDS: In-house inventory.

2-WILLIAM ASHMORE FAMILY PAPERS, 1881–1937, quantity undetermined
Background note: William Ashmore, Jr. (1851–1937), was a Baptist missionary in Swatow between 1880 and 1926. See also American Baptist Historical Society, 1106 South Goodman Street, Rochester, NY, 14620. For papers of his father, William Ashmore, Sr., see Union Theological Seminary, Archives, 3041 Broadway at Reinhold Niebuhr Place, New York, NY, 10027.
CORRESPONDENCE: Correspondence of Ashmore with family members, 1892–1937; ca. 1,300 letters of Lida Scott Ashmore in Swatow to William Ashmore, between 1881 and 1934; extracts of Lida Ashmore's letters to Edith Ashmore, n.d.
MANUSCRIPTS: "My Life Story," by Lida Scott and William Ashmore, Jr., 1925.
DIARIES: Diaries of Lida Scott Ashmore, 1919–28; diaries of Edith Ashmore, 1895, 1907.
MEMORABILIA: Biographical data on William Ashmore, Jr., assembled by Edith Ashmore Hensolt, including sermons, docu-

ments, and notes on Bible translations; scrapbook of Lida Ashmore, containing Chinese paper samples, and other items, n.d.; clippings concerning American Baptists in China.
MAPS/DESIGNS/DRAWINGS: Oil paintings by Lida Ashmore of North China, Swatow, Hakka boats, and other subjects, n.d.
AUDIO-VISUAL MATERIALS: Loose photos of Ashmore family and views of China, n.d.
FINDING AIDS: In-house register.

3-HAZEL M. ATWOOD PAPERS, 1933–50, 1 box
Background note: Hazel M. Atwood (b. 1891) was a Congregational missionary nurse from 1921 until the 1940s at the Willis F. Pierce Memorial Hospital (formerly, the Foochow Christian Union Hospital) in Foochow.
MINUTES/RECORDS/REPORTS: American Board of Commissioners for Foreign Missions, reports, miscellaneous newsletters, and other printed materials on China, including "Notes on Reports of Conferences with Chou En-lai, 1941–51; Helen H. Smith, miscellaneous reports, bulletins, programs, and other printed materials, n.d.; Willis F. Pierce Memorial Hospital, annual reports, constitution, by-laws, minutes of Trustees, 1894–1950.
CORRESPONDENCE: 5 letters from Atwood, 1933–50; 16 letters to Atwood, 1927–50, from correspondents including the American Board of Commissioners for Foreign Missions, Lora G. Dyer, Helen Gold, Eula B. Lee and William E. Strong, Alden and Derrith Matthews, Harold and Grace Matthews, Arthur E. St. Clair, Ruth Van Kirk, Mary I. Ward, and Paul P. Wiant; 4 letters from Henry V. Lacy regarding group hospitalization, 1935–38.
MANUSCRIPTS: "Wenshaw on Trek," by Helen H. Smith, n.d.
MEMORABILIA: Miscellaneous biographical material, including certificate of registration, folding card of Foochow missionaries, and clipping, n.d.
SERIALS: *China Bulletin*, 1957–60. *China Notes*, 1964–65. *The Foochow Messenger*, 1927, 1936–38. National Christian Council of China, *Broadcast Bulletin*, 1940–41. *News of China* (United China Relief), 1942–43.

4-FREDERICK BANKHARDT, 1936–49, 8 volumes, 7 items
Background note: Frederick Bankhardt was associated with the Yenping Mission of the Methodist Episcopal Church. See also General Commission on Archives and History—The United Methodist Church, United Methodist Archives and History Center, Archives, 36 Madison Avenue, P. O. Box 127, Madison, NJ, 07940.
CORRESPONDENCE: 7 unidentified letters.
DIARIES: Personal diaries, reflecting spiritual problems peculiar to missionaries, 1936–39, 1941, 1947–49.

5-ARTHUR AND MABEL BILLING COLLECTION, 1935–60, ca. 400 items
Background note: Arthur (1877–1960) and Mabel Billing were Methodist Episcopal missionaries connected with the Union High School, Foochow.
MINUTES/RECORDS/REPORTS: Foochow Conference of the Methodist Church, yearbook and official minutes, 1945–49; International Cooperative Society of Foochow, by-laws, 1939; unidentified mission newsletters and Christmas circular letters.
CORRESPONDENCE: 360 letters to and from the Billings, 1935–60, including such correspondents as Gene Ayer, Grant Chandler, Conrad Fisher, Loren R. Humphrey, Henry V. Lacy, Methodist Church Board of World Missions and Board of World Peace,

Martha Noble, Guy A. Thelin, and Paul P. Wiant.
PAMPHLETS: 5 pamphlets of Foochow Union High School, n.d.
SERIALS: *Foochow News*, 1939, 1941.
DISSERTATIONS/THESES: *A Preview by a Prospective Teacher in a Chinese Rural High School of the Potential Relationship of Its Activities with the Family and Community Life*, by Portia Billings Foster, a study of Union High School, n.d.
CHINESE LANGUAGE MATERIALS: Chinese lessons for illiterates, n.d.
FINDING AIDS: In-house inventory.

6-MAE BOUCHER PAPERS, 1926–49, 1 box
Background note: Mae Boucher was a missionary nurse of the Methodist Episcopal Church in Yenping.
MINUTES/RECORDS/REPORTS: Alden Speare Memorial Hospital, Yenping, annual report, 1923.
CORRESPONDENCE: 61 letters from Frederick Bankhardt and Frank T. Cartwright, n.d., and to Boucher's family, 1926–30; 3 circular letters from Esther Ling and K. W. Scheufler, 1927–28; 2 annual letters, including information on activities of the Methodist mission in Yenping, 1928–30.
DIARIES/MEMORABILIA/AUDIO-VISUAL MATERIALS: Diary, 1926; 2 photo albums, n.d.
SERIALS: *Yenping Pagoda Herald*, 1927, 1931.
FINDING AIDS: Partial inventory.

7-HOMER V. BRADSHAW, 1955, 1 item
Background note: For biographical notes, see Presbyterian Historical Society, Archives and Library, 425 Lombard Street, Philadelphia, PA, 19147.
MINUTES/RECORDS/REPORTS: Mimeograph of report to the Presbyterian Board of Foreign Missions, "Behind Bars behind the Iron Curtain," 1955, concerning the seizure of the Presbyterian missionaries in Linhsien between 1949 and 1955.

8-HENRY OLIN CADY, 1866–1904, 1 folder
Background note: Henry Olin Cady (1856–1916) was a Methodist Episcopal missionary to China. He went to China in 1886, was one of the founders of the West China Mission, and was stationed in Chungking and Chengtu.
CORRESPONDENCE: Photocopy reproductions of typed excerpts from ca. 300 original letters, later destroyed, which were intended to form an epistolary history of the West China Mission, mostly from Cady's mother, Cady, his wife, Hattie Yates Cady, and other missionaries, 1866–1904.

9-ELIZABETH CARLYLE, 1937–38, 10 items
Background note: Elizabeth Carlyle was a nurse at the Isabella Fisher Hospital, Tientsin.
CORRESPONDENCE: 10 letters from Carlyle to her mother, describing the conquest of Tientsin by the Japanese, 1937–38.

10-MONONA L. CHENEY COLLECTION, 1918–40, quantity undetermined
Background note: Monona L. Cheney was a missionary teacher of the Methodist Episcopal Church. She went to China in 1918, taught at the Keen School in Tientsin in 1920, at Gamewell School in Peking from 1924 to 1926, and at Yenching University from 1926 to 1930.
CORRESPONDENCE: 266 letters from Cheney to her family, 1918–30; letter from Ida Frantz to Cheney, n.d.; letter from Myra Jaquet to Cheney, 1944.

MANUSCRIPTS: "A Sunday Picnic," by Cheney, 1932; "Love Never Fails," a sermon by Dean Chao Tze-ch'en of Yenching University School of Religion, 1927.
PAMPHLETS: *China in Western Literature: Fragments from Some Well-known Writers*, by Philippe de Vargas, 1940; *William C. Hunter's Books on the Old Canton Factories*, by Philippe de Vargas (repr. *Yenching Journal of Social Studies*, 1939).
AUDIO-VISUAL MATERIALS: Photos of Chinese life, n.d.
SERIALS: *China Bulletin*, 1937. *China Christian Advocate*, 1937.
CHINESE LANGUAGE MATERIALS: Pamphlet on Mary Porter Gamewell School and other pamphlets.
FINDING AIDS: In-house inventory.

11-ARTHUR BRADDEN COOLE PAPERS, 1908–74, 1.5 l.f.
Background note: Arthur Bradden Coole (b. 1900) was a missionary under the Methodist Episcopal Church in Tientsin (1924–37), Peking (1938–41), and Chungking (1944–46). His father, Thomas Henry Coole (1868–1930), was a medical missionary in Kutien, Fukien, from 1906 to 1914 and 1923 to 1930; his older brother, Douglas, also served in China.
MINUTES/RECORDS/REPORTS: Methodist missionaries meetings, minutes, 1937–64.
CORRESPONDENCE: 952 letters from Arthur and Ella Coole, 1908–74; 1,391 personal and official letters to Arthur and Ella Coole, 1921–73, with boards and individuals representing the Methodist Episcopal Church, particularly the Board of Foreign Missions, such as Frank T. Cartwright, and with family members; 91 letters from Thomas and Cora Coole, 1908–48; 66 letters to Thomas and Cora Coole, 1888–1946; miscellaneous telegrams of Thomas and Cora Coole, n.d.
DIARIES: Journal of Thomas and Cora Coole, n.d.
MANUSCRIPTS: Autobiography of Arthur Coole, n.d.; "The Fruits of Fukien, China," n.d.; "Levanda and Arthur Yin Meet Their Death," n.d.; "O. J. Krause, A Man Who Lived His Christianity," n.d.; "A Trouble Shooter for God in China," published in 1976; book review of *Chinese Banknotes*, by Ward Smith and Brian Matravers, n.d.; book review of *Chinese Cash*, by Oliver Cress Will, n.d.; folder of essays and speeches written by Arthur Coole's students and other faculty in China, n.d.; notebook of Thomas and Cora Coole, n.d.
PAMPHLETS: Tearsheet of "A Heathen Artist's Apology," n.d.; folder of miscellaneous pamphlets and newsletters regarding Chinese academics, school, etc., n.d.; miscellaneous pamphlets of Thomas and Cora Coole, n.d.
MEMORABILIA/AUDIO-VISUAL MATERIALS/MAPS/DESIGNS/DRAWINGS: Folder of biographical information on Arthur Coole, including clippings, a photo, and resume, n.d.; scrapbook, including expenses, maps, clippings, and receipts from ship travel form China to New York, 1929; folder of loose clippings on Arthur Coole, including his missionary work, n.d.; reviews of Arthur Coole's books on Chinese coins, n.d.; folder of biographical information on Thomas Coole, including clippings, photo, and articles, n.d.
FINDING AIDS: In-house inventory.

12-SYDNEY ARTHUR DAVIDSON, JR., PAPERS, 1934–39, 2 folders
CORRESPONDENCE/MANUSCRIPTS: Letters, essays, interviews, and reports on Chinese life, sent to the *Brockton Enterprise* and other newspapers, by Sydney Arthur Davidson, Jr., a teacher of English at Anglo-Chinese College in Foochow.

13-ELIZA ANNE HUGHES DAVIS, 1897–1920, 1 folder
CORRESPONDENCE: 79 letters to Eliza Anne Hughes Davis, including family members, George Hughes, and Jennie V. Hughes, who was principal of Knowles Bible Training School, Kiukiang, Kiangsi, sponsored by the Woman's Foreign Missionary Society, Methodist Episcopal Church.

14-CLARENCE BURTON DAY, 1914–44, ca. 130 items
Background note: Clarence Burton Day was a Presbyterian missionary teacher, first in Ningpo, then at Hangchow College, from 1915 to 1943 and 1948 to 1951. From 1947 to 1948 he taught at Forman Christian College in Lahore.
CORRESPONDENCE: 60 letters to and from Clarence Day, 1927–42.
MANUSCRIPTS: "Meditations of T. F. Day, 1935," in a notebook.
DIARIES: 20 diaries of Clarence Day, 1914–24, 1927, 1929–33, 1935–40, 1942–44.
MEMORABILIA: Travel permits, tickets, immunization forms, menus from the *Gripsholm*, n.d.
AUDIO-VISUAL MATERIALS/MAPS/DESIGNS/DRAWINGS: Photo album, n.d.; loose passport photos of family; 38 illustrations and colored photos, n.d.
FINDING AIDS: Partial inventory.

15-CLARA PEARL DYER, 1901–58, ca. 130 items, 9 volumes
Background note: Clara Pearl Dyer was a missionary teacher under the Methodist Episcopal Church at the Alderman School, Changli, Hopei.
MINUTES/RECORDS/REPORTS: 12 unidentified conference reports.
CORRESPONDENCE: 100 letters to and from Dyer, 1901–65.
DIARIES: 9 diaries of Dyer, 1932–37, 1942, 1944, 1946–47, 1949–52, 1954–58.
MANUSCRIPTS: "Boys' and Girls' Names in Chinese," by Shun-hsin Chi, n.d.; "By Peking Cart," a poem by Dyer, n.d.; "The Changliar," 1914; "Improved Sweet Potato and Better Wheat Project," n.d.; "Let's Try Chinese," n.d.; "Slides on our Work in Kiukiang," description by Edith Fredericks, n.d.; "Some Chinese Feasts," n.d.; "Two Men in a Crowd: A Dramatization for Lent or Easter," n.d.
PAMPHLETS: "A Chinese Pollyanna" and "Story of Golden Pearl," from *Woman's Missionary Friend*, 1913; *70th Anniversary Woman's Foreign Missionary Society, Methodist Episcopal Church*, n.d.
MAPS/DESIGNS/DRAWINGS/AUDIO-VISUAL MATERIALS: Photos and postcards; sketchings and paintings by Dyer, n.d.
FINDING AIDS: In-house inventory.

16-HUBERT HENRY FARNHAM, 1924–40, 53 items
Background note: The son of Hubert Henry Farnham, Vernon L. Farnham (b. 1897), was an Evangelical Church missionary in Nanking, Changsha, and Liling.
CORRESPONDENCE: 53 letters from Vernon L. Farnham to his father, 1924–40, including detailed descriptions and comments on mission work and China politics.

17-SARAH FARIS PAPERS, n.d., 1 item
MANUSCRIPTS: "The Increase: The True Story of a Buddhist Conversion to Christianity in the City of Yangchow," by Sarah Faris, n.d.

18-ALZO JOHN FISHER, 1894–1962, quantity undetermined
Background note: Alzo John Fisher (1877–1967) was a Presbyterian missionary associated with the Church of Christ in China.
MINUTES/RECORDS/REPORTS: 3 folders of loose papers, including reports and newsletters from various missions in South China, mimeographed or carbon copies of minutes of missionary meetings, and other documents relating to the organization of the Church of Christ in China; American Presbyterian Church in Canton, annual reports, 1894, 1895, 1905; Christian Family Service Center, report, n.d.; Church of Christ in China: annual report, 1947; Bible Training School, report, 1948; Committee on Christianizing the Home, report, 1940; Committee on Further Procedure, report on closer relationships of general interdenominational agencies, 1944; General Assembly, important actions, 1937, 1949; records and minutes, 1932; National Christian Council of China, biennial report, 1937–46; Pearl River Masonic Lodge, minutes, 1939; Presbyterian Church in the U.S.A., Board of Foreign Missions, report of the deputation to China, 1946; Seung Kei, report, 1940; South China Mission survey, ca. 1929–1930; Union Normal and Middle School, report, 1937–45, 1949; report of the principal, 1948; United Board for Christian Higher Education in Asia, annual report, 1967–68.
CORRESPONDENCE: 15 letters from Alzo John Fisher, 1940–51; 45 incoming letters, 1940–61, from correspondents including M. S. Ady, George Anderson, E. Bruce Copland, W. B. Djang, Margaret Frame, J. Stewart Kunkle, Ma Yi-ying, Mildred Tsui, and Wu Yick Wan; mimeographed letters from missionaries, n.d.; 29 circular letters, 1932–57, written by Merrill Ady, Lois Armentrout, Hal Clark, Grace Darling, A. J. Fisher, J. Elliott Fisher, Paddy Jansen, Hattie MacCurdy, Wallace Merwin, Florence F. Pike, Herbert Pommerenke, Ronald D. Rees, Lloyd Ruland, Alice Schaffer, Sonia Tomara, C. T. Tsai, and Bill Upchurch.
MANUSCRIPTS: Research notes, fragments, and two drafts of "Building a Christian Church in China: A Record of the Origin, Organization, and History of the Church of Christ in China," by Fisher, written mostly after 1941 while he was under house arrest in Shanghai; "Presbyterianism in China," written by Fisher for Clifford Drury's unpublished "400 Years of Presbyterianism," with research materials and fragments; "Synods of the Church of Christ in China, Chapter II," by Fisher, n.d.; vignettes, sermons, magazine article, and address to South China Mission Meeting of 1922; manuscripts by W. H. Dobson, most undated: "Christianity and Communism in China," "Historical Sketch of Canton Station and Chinese Churches of Presbyterian Origin in Canton," "History of the South China Mission," "History of the True Light Seminary, Prepared for Mission Meeting" (1935), "Ninety Years in Cathay," "Rehabilitation Plan of the Kwangtung Synod"; speeches; folder of loose papers relating to South China Mission, including notes, memos, reports, etc.
PAMPHLETS: *An Adventure in Church Union in China: Origin, Nature, and Task of the Church of Christ in China*, by Fisher, 1944; *Leung Ah Faat: Hero of the Christian Faith, First Ordained Minister of the Protestant Church in China*, by Fisher, 1962; *Life and Work of the Christian in China*, by Fisher, 1942; *Reconstruction of Our Mission Work*, n.d.; student publications; leaflets; broadsides; publications relating to the Canton Committee for Justice to China, 1938; ca. 30 pamphlets, 1925–50, on the Church of Christ in China, Christianity in China, True Light School, and other topics; folder of copies of pamphlets, broadsides, and periodicals.

DIARIES: 7 pages of David S. Tappan's diary, written in Canton, 1942.
MEMORABILIA: Clippings and issues of magazines, relating to Chinese communism and Chiang K'ai-shek, 1925–49; postcards, poster, and miscellaneous clippings.
AUDIO-VISUAL MATERIALS: Photo of Christian funeral, with description, n.d.; 8 photo-portraits, n.d.
SERIALS: *China Bulletin*, 1956–58. *China Notes*, 1969. *Chinese Recorder*, 1941. *The Church*, 1941–50. Fati Theological College, *Bulletin*, 1911–12. *Information Service*, Church of Christ in China, Kwangtung Synod, 1940–46. *A Monthly Cycle of Prayer*, 1949. *Prayer Cycle*, 1949. *True Light YMCA Newsletter*, 1922–24.
CHINESE LANGUAGE MATERIALS: *The Progress*, 1938; *The War Illustrated*, n.d.; miscellaneous publications, including missionary booklets, broadsides, and periodicals.
FINDING AIDS: In-house inventory.

19-MURRAY SCOTT FRAME, 1910–16, quantity undetermined
Background note: Murray Scott Frame went to Peking as a missionary for the Congregational Church in 1910. He was married to Alice Seymour Browne in 1913.
CORRESPONDENCE: Letters from Murray Frame to his mother, Mrs. N. S. Frame, and sister, Margaret, 1910–16; 7 letters from Alice Frame to Margaret Frame, n.d.

20-EDWARD E. GIFFEN, 1894–96, 46 items
Background note: Edward E. and Bertha Giffen were missionaries under the China Inland Mission in Hankow.
CORRESPONDENCE: 46 letters from the Giffens to family members, 1894–96, reflecting their missionary zeal, a desire for martyrdom, and Bertha Giffen's illness.

21-RUTH A. GRESS, 1939–58, 1 box
Background note: Ruth A. Gress was a Methodist missionary in Nanping, Fukien, where she taught at the Chien Ching Middle School starting in 1939.
CORRESPONDENCE: 65 letters from Gress to her family in North Dakota, 1939–42; 3 letters of Ethel Wallace from Nanping, 1945–46; 10 printed letters from Nanping missionaries, 1939–45.
MANUSCRIPTS: "Lessons to Be Learned from the Experiences of Christian Missions in China," by Harold S. Matthews, 1941.
MEMORABILIA: Miscellaneous mementos, including a Chinese song book.

22-ADAM AND CLARA GROESBECK, 1897–1939, quantity undetermined
Background note: Adam and Clara Groesbeck were Baptist missionaries under the ABFMS in Kwangtung from 1897 to 1927 and 1931 to 1935. They were first assigned to Ungkung, later to Chaochowfu, and then to Chaoyang in 1904. Adam Groesbeck performed administrative duties for the South China Mission; Clara Holloway Groesbeck (1867–1956) taught at the boys' school in Chaoyang. See also American Baptist Historical Society, 1106 South Goodman Street, Rochester, NY, 14620.
MINUTES/RECORDS/REPORTS: Executive Committee, 1936; Reference Committee, minutes, 1919–21, 1929–30, 1939; South China Mission (?), annual reports, 1905–22, 1931–39; 30 unidentified reports; legal documents; miscellaneous accounts.
CORRESPONDENCE: 60 outgoing letters, 1897–1939; 200 incoming letters, 1865–1939 (mostly 1930s), from correspondents including Carl M. Capen, Howard R. Chapman, Chau Yau-pik,

P. Clark, Randolph L. Howard, Ethel L. and George Hylbert, Frank W. Padelford, A. G. Page, and C. C. Siam; 8 circular letters, 1934–40; 48 circular letters by Adam Groesbeck, 1903–12, 1919–22, 1932–33.

DIARIES: 8 diaries of Adam Groesbeck, on the political situation in China and church issues, 1897–1903, 1920–22, 1926–27, 1936; 5 diaries of Clara Groesbeck on family matters, 1902–5, 1910–24.

MANUSCRIPTS: 13 personal and address notebooks, n.d.; sermons, church-related articles, and outlines by Adam Groesbeck; account of the Groesbecks' work in China by Tracy Groesbeck, n.d.

PAMPHLETS: Published materials on missions and the church in China.

MEMORABILIA: Magazine and newspaper articles about Adam Groesbeck, n.d.; biographical materials; folder of miscellaneous memorabilia, including maps.

AUDIO-VISUAL MATERIALS: 2 folders of family photos, 2 folders and 2 albums of photos relating to the mission, 33 matted photos of Chinese people and streets, 118 glass slides of Chaoyang and Ungkung Missions, and 3 glass negative plates.

CHINESE LANGUAGE MATERIALS: Folder of miscellaneous items.

FINDING AIDS: In-house inventory.

23-ARTHUR M. GUTTERY PAPERS, 1919–81, 3 boxes
Background note: Arthur M. Guttery (1885–1981) was an organizer and missionary for the YMCA in China and the United States. He went to Hankow with his wife, Myrtle, in 1913. From 1913 to 1928, he served as general secretary for the YMCA and helped to organize and establish the program in Wuhan. Photos and broadsides from the collection have been removed and are available upon request. See also Young Men's Christian Association of the U.S.A. Archives, University of Minnesota, Social History Welfare Archives, 2642 University Avenue, St. Paul, MN, 55114.

CORRESPONDENCE: Folder of correspondence, 1919–81, mostly to family in the United States.

MANUSCRIPTS: Sermons, religious addresses and notes, essays and notes on China, and notes on YMCA activities; "Excerpts from Reports and Letters Concerning YMCA Work in China," by Guttery, n.d.; "The Influence and Leadership of God in the Life of One YMCA Secretary," Guttery's memoirs, 1975; "Memoirs," Vol. II, by Eugene Epperson Barnett, n.d.; "Memoirs," by Ethan T. Colton, 1968; "Vignette of China That Was, 1915–1945," by Annie Laurie and Lawrence Todnem, 1974; "Boyhood and Early Domestic and China YMCA Experiences," by Clifford W. Petitt, 1977.

ORAL HISTORIES: "Jean Fritz (Daughter) Speaking on Arthur Guttery," an audio cassette, n.d.

FINDING AIDS: In-house inventory.

24-IRENE FORSYTHE HANSON PAPERS, 1921–76, ca. 3.25 c.f.
Background note: Irene Forsythe Hanson (b. 1898) was a Presbyterian missionary in China for 25 years. She went to Tsingtao in 1926 and returned to the United States in 1951. The following year she married Perry O. Hanson, who had also been a missionary in China. Photographs have been removed from the collection to the Photograph Collection.

CORRESPONDENCE: 16 folders of letters from Irene Forsythe in China, 1926–51; folder of letters to friends, n.d.

MANUSCRIPTS: 32 folders of manuscripts, most undated, including "Breaking Through," "Mother Fan," published as *Cheng's Mother* (1943), and "The Wheelbarrow and the Comrade," published in 1972.

PAMPHLETS/MAPS/DESIGNS/DRAWINGS/MEMORABILIA: 2 boxes of printed matter and subject files, including maps, religious teaching aids, statistics of the China missions (1929–30), miscellaneous newsletters, publicity, pamphlets, and clippings; hand-painted volume presented in remembrance of Forsyth's days in China, n.d.

DIARIES: Diary of Irene Forsythe, 1927–31.

MEMORABILIA: 3 folders of greeting cards, n.d.

SERIALS: *Have a Heart for China*, 1940–41, 1943. *News of China*, 1943–44, 1946.

CHINESE LANGUAGE MATERIALS: Folder of unidentified letters, n.d.

FINDING AIDS: In-house inventory.

25-BARBARA M. HAYES: JOHN DAVID HAYES BIOGRAPHY, 1973, 1 item
Background note: John David Hayes (1893–1957) was the executive chairman of the American Presbyterian Mission in Peking, where he was also active in community affairs, flood and famine relief, and education at the university level. He and his wife, Barbara (Kelman) Hayes, were appointed by the Board of Foreign Missions to the China Mission in 1917. After two years' internment by the Japanese from 1943 to 1945 and a short leave in the United States, he returned to China to serve with the Church of Christ in Kweichow. Hayes was interned by the Chinese Communists in 1950 and released the following year. The original copy of this collection is at the Presbyterian Historical Society, Archives and Library, 425 Lombard Street, Philadelphia, PA, 19147; a second photocopy is at Yale Divinity School, Special Collections, 409 Prospect Street, New Haven, CT, 06510 (Record Group #8).

MANUSCRIPTS: 200-page biography of Hayes by his wife, Barbara M. Hayes, through which is interspersed written and printed materials by and about Hayes, 1973.

26-EMILY HOBART, 1884–1928, 63 items
Background note: Emily Hobart was the wife of William Hatfield Hobart, a Methodist missionary in Peking and Tsun Hua.

CORRESPONDENCE: 63 letters to her parents, brother, and sisters, describing daily occupations and scenes in China, 1884–99, 1912, 1927–28.

27-ANITA R. IRWIN PAPERS, 1938–56, 14 items
MINUTES/RECORDS/REPORTS: "The Advantage of Communism in China in Relation to the Church," report by Ben T. Cowles, 1956(?).

CORRESPONDENCE: 6 missionary letters and 3 press releases by the Committee on Relief in China by the Foreign Missions Conference, describing the Japanese invasion, 1938; 2 missionary letters from Shanghai describing the conflict between Communist and Nationalist forces, 1949(?); 2 letters and copies of messages describing the imprisonment of Americans by the Japanese in the Philippines, n.d.

FINDING AIDS: In-house inventory.

28-MYRA ANNA JAQUET PAPERS, 1913–43, 1 folder
Background note: Myra Anna Jaquet was a teacher in the Methodist mission, Peking, and principal of the Gamewell School in

Peking. She was interned by the Japanese and repatriated aboard the *Gripsholm* in 1943.

CORRESPONDENCE/MANUSCRIPTS/AUDIO-VISUAL MATERIALS: Letters, notebooks illustrated with photos describing the work of a mission teacher, and a letter about her voyage aboard the *Gripsholm*, 1913–43.

29-BRUCE W. JARVIS PAPERS, 1927–28, 1.5 l.f.

Background note: Bruce W. Jarvis (1885–1970) was a medical missionary in Peking (1923–29), Foochow (1931–37 and 1946–49), and Chengtu (1944–46). His wife, Anna Moffet Jarvis (b. 1892), was in Nanking from 1920 to 1945 as secretary of Ming Deh School and treasurer of the Presbyterian mission. She later worked in Chengtu and Foochow. See also American Lutheran Church, Archives, 2481 Como Avenue, St. Paul, MN, 55108.

MINUTES/RECORDS/REPORTS: Nanking Station, report, 1928–29.

CORRESPONDENCE: 52 letters to Anna Moffet, 1927–28; 11 letters of Colonel and Mrs. W. P. Moffet, Anna Moffet's parents, 1927–28, relating to her experiences in the Nanking Incident; 9 miscellaneous letters, 1927–28.

MANUSCRIPTS: 14 manuscripts, most by Moffet, relating to Nanking, Ginling College, and trips to Chinese cities, 1927–28.

PAMPHLETS: *Statement to Chinese Friends*, 1927; *Story of 80 Years in Protestant Missions in Nanking, China, 1867–1947*; *Through Faith to Power*, 1927.

MEMORABILIA/AUDIO-VISUAL MATERIALS/CORRESPONDENCE/MANUSCRIPTS: Scrapbook of clippings on the Nanking Incident, 1927–28; scrapbook containing photos, letters, and miscellaneous memoirs of Moffet's years in Nanking.

AUDIO-VISUAL MATERIALS: Photos of the mission, children of the mission, and Chinese scenery, n.d.

CHINESE LANGUAGE MATERIALS: *Proclamation of Western Missionaries of Nanking to the Chinese Christians in Nanking*, 1927.

FINDING AIDS: In-house inventory.

30-CHARLES F. JOHNSON, 1878–1904, 5 volumes

Background note: Charles F. Johnson was a Presbyterian medical missionary to China.

CORRESPONDENCE: Letterpress books, 1900–1904, to Johnson's father and individuals associated with Presbyterian missions, such as Frank H. Chalfant, George F. Fitch, Charles W. Hand, and James B. Neal, from Shanghai, Tsingtao, and Ichow-fu, describing the Boxer Uprising and re-establishment of the missions.

DIARIES: Johnson's diary, 1878–79.

31-EDWIN DWIGHT KELLOGG, 1930–31, 15 items

Background note: Edwin Dwight Kellogg (1882–1952) was a Congregational missionary in China.

CORRESPONDENCE: Copies of 15 letters from Canton and Foochow, 1930–31.

32-HENRY VEERE LACY, 1913–50, 1 l.f.

Background note: Henry Veere Lacy (b. 1886) was a Methodist Episcopal missionary teacher, evangelist, and administrator in Fukien from 1912 to 1952. His wife, Jessie Ankeny Lacy, went to Fukien in 1909 as a missionary teacher for the Methodist Episcopal Church. Louise Ankeny, her sister, was also a teacher in China.

CORRESPONDENCE: Ca. 400 letters, including letters of Henry Lacy to his friends and family in the United States; letters of Jessie Lacy to her parents and relatives, 1909–49; letters to Jessie Lacy from missionary friends, n.d.; and letters to Jessie Lacy from Louise Ankeny, 1920–26.

33-BERTHA E. MAGNESS PAPERS, 1916–41, 122 items

CORRESPONDENCE: 20 letters from Bertha E. Magness, 1916–21; 13 letters to Magness, 1919–41.

MANUSCRIPTS: "Historical Sketch of the Former United Brethren Church in China," n.d.

AUDIO-VISUAL MATERIALS: 87 captioned photos of scenes of daily activities in Chinese cities, villages, and countryside, 1916–21.

CHINESE LANGUAGE MATERIALS: Unidentified newspaper.

FINDING AIDS: In-house inventory.

34-IDA BELLE (LEWIS) MAIN PAPERS, 1895–1978, quantity undetermined

Background note: Ida Belle (Lewis) Main (1887–1969) was a Methodist missionary teacher. She went to Tientsin in 1910, and to Shanghai in 1923 as assistant secretary of education for the Methodist Church in China. In 1926 she became president of Hwa Nan College, Foochow, and returned to Shanghai in 1930 as secretary of the China Christian Education Association. Between 1937 and 1941 she worked with refugees in Shanghai, and returned to Foochow in 1946 to act as president of Hwa Nan College until 1949. Photographs originally in the collection have been removed to the Photograph Collection.

CORRESPONDENCE: 5 folders of letters to her family from China, 1911–13, 1918–22, 1925–33, 1939, 1946–49.

MANUSCRIPTS: Memoirs and other miscellaneous writings by Main on families in China and the schools with which she was associated.

PAMPHLETS/MEMORABILIA: Printed materials on Hwa Nan College, newspapers, and memorabilia, n.d.

DIARIES: Main's diaries for 1910, 1914, 1921, 1935–36, 1939, 1941, 1949–51, 1965, and loose pages.

FINDING AIDS: In-house inventory.

35-PAUL C. MELROSE, 1929–51, 1 box

Background note: Paul C. Melrose, son of missionary parents, was born in Hainan. In 1916 he and his wife, Esther Agnew Melrose, came to Hainan as missionaries of the Presbyterian Church, stationed in Nodoa, where they remained until 1944. See also Hoover Institution, Archives, Stanford University, Stanford, CA, 94305.

CORRESPONDENCE: 7 letters from Esther Melrose, 1929–44; letter from Paul Melrose, 1941; letters to Paul and Esther Melrose from Eva Keyser and Esther Morse, 1948–51.

MANUSCRIPTS: 14 manuscripts by Paul or Esther Melrose, 1946–49, on post-war Canton, Hainan, Hong Kong, Nodoa, and other post-war subjects.

PAMPHLETS: Incomplete booklet about the Chiangmai Leper Asylum; "Christians under the Chinese Communist State," supplement to *The Church*, 1949.

DIARIES: 9 logs, recording daily events, expenses, weather, etc., 1932–37, 1941–42, 1949.

SERIALS: *Hainan Newsletter*, 1924, 1937.

FINDING AIDS: In-house inventory.

36-MARGARET M. MONINGER, 1920–39, 43 items

Background note: For biographical notes, see Presbyterian

Historical Society, Archives and Library, 425 Lombard Street, Philadelphia, 19147.
MINUTES/RECORDS/REPORTS: Church of Christ in China, General Assembly, report, 1933.
CORRESPONDENCE: 3 letters from Margaret M. Moninger, 1925, 1939; letter to Moninger from A. W. Halsey, 1920.
MANUSCRIPTS: "Aboriginal Tribes of China," by Margaret Moninger, n.d., including 8 photos; "Chinese Parallels to Greek and Roman Customs," by Margaret Moninger, 1929; "Hainan Mission Song," by Margaret Moninger, n.d.; "Hainan Notes as Illuminating Certain Scripture Passages," holograph of a notebook, by Margaret Moninger, n.d.; "Hainanese Colloquial Dictionary," by Iap Hi-soang and Margaret M. Moninger, ca. 1933–35; "Heart Throbs from Hainan, China," by Margaret Moninger, n.d.; "Humoresque Hainan," by Margaret Moninger, 1923.
PAMPHLETS: 15 pamphlets on Hainan, n.d.
MEMORABILIA: Tearsheets from scrapbook of Moninger articles on Hainan and poems, 1919–35; calendars made by Moninger, containing photos of Hainan, 1935.
AUDIO-VISUAL MATERIALS: 3 photo albums of Hainan, n.d.
SERIALS: *Hainan Newsletter*, 1932–33.
FINDING AIDS: In-house inventory.

37-ESTHER MORSE PAPERS, 1929–63, 3 l.f.

Background note: Esther Morse (1898–1976) was a Presbyterian missionary doctor at the Hainan Mission from 1930 to 1943 and 1946 to 1953.
MINUTES/RECORDS/REPORTS: Report on internment under the Japanese, n.d.; salary accounts and missionary assignment information, 1930–63.
CORRESPONDENCE: Typewritten copies of 673 outgoing letters in binders, 1930–53; newsletters and personal correspondence, including newsletters of Alice Bixby, 1933–35.
MANUSCRIPTS: "China, Now," 1973, draft and revisions, including map of Chinese empire; untitled manuscript on missionary work, 1969; notebook containing names and dates of missionaries assigned by the Presbyterian Church, n.d.; language study notebooks.
PAMPHLETS: Hainan Church of the Church of Christ in China, 19th anniversary publication, n.d.; *Story of the Tibetan Bible*, by the British and Foreign Bible Society, n.d.
DIARIES: Diaries, 1925–47; folder of loose diary sheets, 1937–39, including description of mission work and the Japanese attack on Hainan; folder of typed copies of 1931 diaries.
MEMORABILIA: 163 Chinese banknotes, n.d.; Chinese cards and calendar; scrapbooks, 1907–76; Chinese wall hangings.
AUDIO-VISUAL MATERIALS: 9 photo albums and loose photos of China.
SERIALS: *China Notes*, 1967–75. *Hainan Newsletter*, 1918, 1929–38, 1948. *Lingnan Science Journal*, 1932, 1934. *A Monthly Cycle of Prayer*, 1931, 1950. *Prayer Cycle*, 1931–32.
CHINESE LANGUAGE MATERIALS: Calling card of Esther Morse; Chinese Medicinal Certificate.
FINDING AIDS: In-house inventory.

38-JAY CHARLES OLIVER PAPERS, 1906–45, quantity undetermined

Background note: Jay Charles Oliver (b. 1886) was an administrator with the YMCA in China beginning in 1916, first in Hangchow, then in Shanghai. He was repatriated aboard the *Gripsholm*, but returned to China after 1945. See also Claremont Colleges, Special Collections Department, Honnold Library, Eighth and Dartmouth Streets, Claremont, CA, 91711; Young Men's Christian Association of the U.S.A. Archives, University of Minnesota, Social History Welfare Archives, 2642 University Avenue, St. Paul, MN, 55114; and Lyman Hoover Papers at Yale Divinity School, Special Collections, 409 Prospect Street, New Haven, CT, 06510.
MINUTES/RECORDS/REPORTS: YMCA documents: Impressions of World's YWCA Council Meeting, Hangchow, report, 1947; Ninth National Conference of Association Secretaries of China, report, 1947; administrative reports by Oliver to the International Committee of the YMCA, 1917–49; Harold Round's reports on YMCA situation in Chinese cities, n.d.; excerpt from report by Oliver on trip to Peking, 1948; "Digest of Reports and Prepared Materials Presented in the Fall Setting-up Conference of the National Committee of the YMCA's of China," by Oliver, 1948; YMCA reports by E. E. Barnett, Hangchow and Shanghai, 1916–27; Hangchow YMCA, annual report, 1916–17; 10 miscellaneous reports, n.d.; medical records of Jay and Lucile Priscilla (Cummings) Oliver, n.d.; 5 reports by Oliver relating to the Rotary Club, n.d.; report on a visit to West China by J. W. Decker, submitted to American Baptist Foreign Mission Society, Board of Managers, 1934.
CORRESPONDENCE: 200 outgoing and 46 incoming letters of Jay C. Oliver and his wife, Lucile Oliver, with relatives and friends, 1946–60; 12 folders of outgoing letters, 1906–52; 16 folders of incoming letters from family members, 1913–40; 45 incoming letters, 1949–53; 4 folders of miscellaneous incoming letters, n.d.; 10 folders of YMCA correspondence and documents, 1916–45; 1 box of correspondence and documents relating to Oliver's service with the Inspectorate of Salt Revenue, 1934–36; 3 folders of letters and documents relating to Chapei Civil Assembly Center and the *Gripsholm* voyage; folder of report letters by Oliver to YMCA constituency, 1917–47; Grand Lodge of Free and Accepted Masons of China, 40 letters, 1953–60; 2 letters relating to Rotary Club, n.d.
MANUSCRIPTS: "Biography of a Manuscript (code sinaiticus)," by Arthur Rinden, n.d.; "The China Movement Faces a New Challenge," by Y. C. Tu, 1948; 2 notebooks of Jay Oliver, 1906–7; speeches on China by Lucile Oliver, 1943–47; "Selected Readings from Shorter Bible (Charles Foster Kent)," by Oliver, n.d.; "A Shanghai Refugee Camp," by Oliver, 1938; "Significant Trends in Hangchow Churches," by Oliver (repr. *Chinese Recorder*), 1934.
PAMPHLETS: *A Sound Table of the Hangchow Dialect*, by Henry W. Moule, 1908.
DIARIES: Diaries and letters of trip to China and return of Oscar A. and Frances Corinne Sheldon Oliver (parents of Jay Oliver), 1920–21.
MEMORABILIA: 2 folders of clippings, 1947–51; miscellaneous notes, programs, brochures, travel guides, reprints, university literary publications and catalogues, and other items.
SERIALS: *Assembly Times*, internment camp paper, 1943.
FINDING AIDS: In-house inventory.

39-GEORGE E. PARTCH, 1936, 1 item

MANUSCRIPTS: "Shanghai Mission History," by George E. Partch, 1936 (concerning the Presbyterian church mission and South Gate church).

40-HERBERT H. POMMERENKE PAPERS, 1923–46, 1 l.f.
Background note: For biographical notes, see Presbyterian Historical Society, Archives and Library, 425 Lombard Street, Philadelphia, PA, 19147.
CORRESPONDENCE: 734 letters, mostly from Herbert H. Pommerenke and his wife, Jean, to his parents, discussing Chinese social life and customs, politics, and mission matters, 1923–46.
PAMPHLETS: Printed newsletters by W. H. Dobson, medical missionary, 1931–40.

41-JAMES HOWELL PYKE, 1900–1951, 1 box
Background note: James Howell Pyke (1845–1924) went to China as a Methodist missionary starting in 1873, serving for 51 years, mainly in the North China Mission, Peking. His son, Frederick Merrill Pyke, was also a missionary in North China.
CORRESPONDENCE: 168 letters, mostly by Pyke family members, describing missionary life and personal matters, 1900–1951.

42-ELSIE I. REIK, 1922–27, 239 items
CORRESPONDENCE: 227 letters from Elsie I. Reik, a Methodist missionary teacher at Hwa Nan College, Foochow, to her family in Milwaukee, Wisconsin, describing her work and experiences, 1922–27; 11 letters from Reik, 1931–57.
SERIALS: *China Bulletin*, 1929. *China Christian Advocate*, 1929.

43-ROLAND AND ESTHER SCHAEFER COLLECTION, 1914–68, ca. 50 items
MINUTES/RECORDS/REPORTS: Unidentified reports, mission newsletters from Fukien and Kiangsi, form letters, and annual letters.
CORRESPONDENCE: 31 letters to and from Roland and Esther Schaefer, 1914–68.
MEMORABILIA: Photocopy of a newspaper article about evacuation of missionaries from Foochow in 1927.
MAPS/DESIGNS/DRAWINGS: Unidentified map.
AUDIO-VISUAL MATERIALS: Photo album containing pictures of the mission school and medical facilities in Kuling, personal photos of the Schaefer family, other missionaries, and views of Kuling; loose photos of the Schaefers, other missionaries, and views in Yenping and Foochow.
SERIALS: *China Colleges*, 1940–42. *Foochow News*, 1939.
CHINESE LANGUAGE MATERIALS: 2 unidentified letters, a broadside, a copy of a newspaper and pictorial journal (ca. 1911), and miscellaneous items.
FINDING AIDS: In-house inventory.

44-FREDERICK AND MYRA SCOVEL, 1930–70, quantity undetermined
Background note: Frederick Gilman (1902–1985) and Myra Scott Scovel (b. 1905) spent about 30 years in the overseas mission of the United Presbyterian Church. They worked in China from 1930 to 1951, before going to India. In 1930 they went to Bachman Hunter Hospital in Tsining and remained there for 15 years until they were repatriated in 1943 after internment by the Japanese. In 1946 they worked at Hope Hospital in Huaiyuan, then transferred to Hackett Medical Center in Canton in 1948 where they stayed until their return to the United States in 1951. The collection contains materials on their later careers in India, as well as after their overseas service, in addition to the materials listed below.
CORRESPONDENCE: 56 letters from Frederick and Myra Scovel, and Mrs. Carl W. Scovel (Frederick Scovel's mother, who was with them in Tsining and Huaiyuan), 1930–50.
MANUSCRIPTS/CORRESPONDENCE: Manuscripts, proofs, publicity, and correspondence relating to Myra Scovel's books, including *The Chinese Ginger Jar*, published in 1962; "A Letter from China," by Myra Scovel, 1964; book proposal for "Toward Understanding China and the Chinese People," 1969–70.
PAMPHLETS: *China Consultation*, ed. by Earle H. Ballou, 1960.
DIARIES: 6 diaries of Frederick Scovel, 1933, 1937, 1945–46, 1959, n.d.; carbon copy of part of a journal by Myra Scovel during their internment, 1941–42.
MEMORABILIA: Folder of biographical material, n.d.
FINDING AIDS: In-house inventory.

45-EDITH SHUFELDT, 1922–25, 1 folder
PAMPHLETS/MEMORABILIA: Mementos of Edith Shufeldt, a Methodist missionary teacher in Peking, including clippings, programs, and broadsides.

46-EDITH WINIFRED SIMESTER, 1945–46, 1 volume, 15 items
CORRESPONDENCE: Letterbook containing transcriptions of letters from Edith Winifred Simester, a Methodist Episcopal missionary teacher at Anglo-Chinese College, Foochow, to her mother, 1945–46; 15 letters from former students to Simester, n.d.

47-JAMES EDWARDS AND SUSAN LAWRENCE SKINNER PAPERS, 1892–1958, quantity undetermined
Background note: James Edwards Skinner (1867–1959) was a medical missionary under the Methodist Episcopal Church in Kutien, Fukien, and Yenping.
MINUTES/RECORDS/REPORTS: Reports by James Skinner, n.d.; Hwa Nan College, Foochow, annual report, 1926–29; Methodist Church: Central China Conference, address, 1941; Foochow Conference, minutes, 1933, 1937–38, 1948–49; Foochow Woman's Conference, minutes, 1927; Yenping Conference, minutes, 1923, 1927–29, 1937–39; Yenping Woman's Conference, minutes, 1936, 1938; Wiley General Hospital, Kutien, annual report, 1935.
CORRESPONDENCE: 238 letters from James E. Skinner, 1892–1954; 114 letters from Susan Lawrence Skinner, 1922–48; 450 letters to James and Susan Skinner, 1919–58, from correspondents including Frederick Bankhardt, Gerald Downie, Bruce and Anna Jarvis, Kong Sin Ching, Kuan Pin Lin, Carleton Lacy, Lewis Luke, B. H. Paddock, Geraldine Skinner, Henry Skinner, Lawrence and Clara Skinner, and Paul Wiant; 102 letters from James Skinner relating to medical supplies, particularly antigen.
MANUSCRIPTS: Notes on his career, articles, and memos by James Skinner; biographical sketches by Susan Skinner, n.d.; "A Short History of the Lawrence Family," by Frederick S. Skinner, n.d.; memorial on William Artyn Main by B. H. Paddock, 1945; eulogy for James Skinner by Dr. C. E. Trimble, 1959; other notes and records, n.d.
PAMPHLETS: *From Foochow to the Nation*, by Frank T. Cartwright, 1923; *Hwa Nan's Celebration of Lydia A. Trimble's Jubilee*, n.d.; *The Reconstruction of Ngo-li Ding*, by A. W. Billing, 1935; *Six Chinese Melodies*, 1949; *William Artyn Main: Biography*, by Ida Belle Main, n.d.
DIARIES: Diary of James E. Skinner, 1942; 8 diaries of Susan Skinner, 1924–25, 1928–31, 1934; folder of photocopies of Susan Skinner's diaries, 1903, 1920–25, 1927–28, 1934, 1939, 1942.
MEMORABILIA: Newsclippings, n.d.
AUDIO-VISUAL MATERIALS: 2 photo albums and 2 loose pho-

tos, n.d.; loose photo of Dr. and Mrs. John Gowdy, n.d.
SERIALS: *Bamboo Baz-zoo*, 1917. *China Bulletin*, 1955–56. *Foochow News*, 1929–36, 1940. *Yenping Pagoda Herald*, 1932–36.
FINDING AIDS: In-house inventory.

48-DENNIS V. SMITH, 1915–26, 165 items
Background note: For biographical notes see University of Michigan, Bentley Historical Library, 1150 Beal Avenue, Ann Arbor, MI, 48109–3482.
CORRESPONDENCE: 165 letters from Dennis and Hazel Littlefield Smith, Peking, to his parents, commenting on social and political conditions in China, 1915–16, 1923–26.

49-MYRTLE A. SMITH, 1921–47, 111 items
CORRESPONDENCE: 111 letters from Myrtle A. Smith, a Methodist Episcopal missionary teacher in Kutien, Fukien, to her parents and friends, describing her experiences, and from fellow teachers to Smith, 1921–25, 1930–38, 1940, 1947.
AUDIO-VISUAL MATERIALS: Photos of Kutien and Foochow, n.d.

50-MYRA L. SNOW, 1928–44, 14 items
CORRESPONDENCE: 12 letters from Myra L. Snow, a teacher at the Methodist Mission, Tientsin, describing her school experiences and reactions to the Chinese, 1928–30; letters from Lora Battin, 1937, and Myra Jaquet to Snow, 1944, describing the Japanese invasion and life in a concentration camp.

51-RUSSELL H. STEININGER, 1920–76, 11 items
Background note: Russell H. Steininger was associated with the Yenping Mission of the Methodist Episcopal Church, and with the Fukien Construction Bureau, Foochow.
CORRESPONDENCE: 3 letters from Russell Steininger, in China, referring to mission matters and Chinese customs, 1920–21; 2 letters from Steininger, 1927, 1976; 5 letters from Frederick Bankhardt, 1927; letter from Lucerne Hoddinott, 1928.

52-DAVID S. AND LUELLA R. TAPPAN PAPERS, 1913–66, .75 c.f. (3 boxes)
Background note: David Stanton Tappan II (1880–1968) was a missionary in Hainan between 1906 and 1949. He founded the Hainan Christian Middle School, served as executive secretary to the Presbyterian Mission in Hainan, and was an advisor to the Hainan Synod.
MINUTES/RECORDS/REPORTS: Hainan Christian Middle School, report, n.d.; report on Kiungchow Evangelistic work, 1939; Kiungchow Station, report on educational work, 1939.
CORRESPONDENCE: 4 folders of correspondence, 1921–65.
DIARIES: 12 diaries, mostly written by Luella Tappan, 1913, 1921–66; diary fragments, 1941–43.
MANUSCRIPTS: Drafts of *Hainan Reporter*; manuscript on women in China, war, and other subjects.
PAMPHLETS: Miscellaneous publications.
MEMORABILIA: Clippings and news articles on the Tappans' mission in China.
SERIALS: *Hainan Newsletter*, 1929–49. *Hainan Reporter*, 1947–49.
FINDING AIDS: In-house inventory.

53-LYREL G. TEAGARDEN PAPERS, 1921–51, ca. 150 items
Background note: Lyrel G. Teagarden (b. 1894) served as a mis-

sionary teacher in Luchowfu from 1920 to 1951 under the Disciples of Christ.
CORRESPONDENCE: 102 letters from Teagarden, primarily to her mother and to Myrle Cunningham Pultz, 1921–50; 20 letters to Teagarden, 1922–54; 11 unidentified letters, 1923–51.
MANUSCRIPTS: "The Little Black House," a fictionalized 614-page account of her experiences from 1924 to 1944; manuscripts by Teagarden on Christian education in China, n.d.
DIARIES/MEMORABILIA: Clippings, day-journals, and memorabilia, n.d.; unspecified newsletters.
FINDING AIDS: In-house inventory.

54-GRACE TERRELL COLLECTION, 1931–66, quantity undetermined
Background note: Grace Terrell was a Methodist missionary in Tientsin.
CORRESPONDENCE: Letter from Grace Terrell to Ruth Owen, 1966; letter from Grace Terrell to Emma Wilson, 1953; 3 unidentified letters; 313 letters to Grace and Larry Terrell, 1931–67; 204 letters to Adah Kirkpatrick, 1962–66; 3 letters to Grace Kirkpatrick, 1931; 22 miscellaneous letters; 14 circular letters of Kirkpatrick family, 1929–62; 44 letters between Larry and Grace Terrell, 1931–33.
MANUSCRIPTS: Articles by Grace Terrell, n.d.
DIARIES: 14 diaries of Grace Terrell, 1917–59, with scattered entries, notes, and sketches.
MEMORABILIA: 5 folders of greeting cards, n.d.; folder of clippings on family events, n.d.; miscellaneous mementos.
MAPS/DESIGNS/DRAWINGS: Folder of sketches and paintings by Mrs. E. G. Kirkpatrick Terrell, n.d.
AUDIO-VISUAL MATERIALS: Photo album and 3 folders of photos of relatives and friends, n.d.
FINDING AIDS: Preliminary inventory.

55-GEORGE T. TOOTELL PAPERS, 1913–59, ca. 2 l.f.
Background note: George Thomas Tootell (b. 1886) was a Presbyterian medical missionary in Hunan province. See also Claremont Colleges, Honnold Library, Claremont, CA, 91711.
CORRESPONDENCE: 1,077 letters from George T. Tootell, 1913–45; 96 letters to Tootell, 1913–49, including such correspondents as Bachman Hunter Hospital (F. Scovel) and Presbyterian Mission Hospital (F. Newman and R. Kepler).
MANUSCRIPTS: 512-page memoir, 1913–59.

56-FRANK M. TOOTHAKER PAPERS, 1918–67, quantity undetermined
Background note: Frank Morey Toothaker (b. 1891) was a Methodist missionary in Yenping.
MINUTES/RECORDS/REPORTS: Methodist Episcopal Church, Yenping Conference, minutes, 1918, 1920–22; report, n.d.; personal financial accounts, 1920–37.
CORRESPONDENCE: 205 letters to Frank M. Toothaker, 1917–67, from correspondents including Frank A. Argelander, Frederick Bankhardt, Harry R. Caldwell, Frank T. Cartwright, Martha Huffaker Chen, Carleton Lacy, Karl W. Scheufler, Russell Steininger, and Paul Wiant; 100 letters from Toothaker, 1918–49; 36 letters from the Board of Missions to Toothaker, 1924–31; 8 miscellaneous letters, 1920–49; 20 letters regarding actions by missionaries after the revolution, 1949–50; 3 newsletters, n.d.
MANUSCRIPTS: Form letter to contributors, 1920; "China's Revolution," n.d.; "Chinese Idea of God," 1918; "Hymn for

China,'' n.d.; ''Purple Mountain Picnic,'' n.d.; ''Wednesday Night Prayer Meeting,'' n.d.; statement of informal meeting, n.d.; letters to the editor of H. G. C. Hallock, 1928; statements regarding actions by missionaries after the revolution, 1949–50; untitled story, n.d.
PAMPHLETS: Methodist Episcopal Church, Board of Foreign Missions publications; *Letter from Madame Chiang Kai-shek to Boys and Girls Across the Ocean*, 1940; *Reconstruction of Ngo-li Ding*, 1935.
DIARIES: 9 volumes of irregular and sketchy accounts of appointments, meetings, and events, 1918–26.
MEMORABILIA/MAPS/DESIGNS/DRAWINGS/AUDIO-VISUAL MATERIALS: Miscelleneous items, including funeral notice, fragment of a Bible, maps, scrolls, poems, clippings, and photos.
SERIALS: *Yenping Pagoda Herald*, 1927.
CHINESE LANGUAGE MATERIALS: Social Customs Improving Society Club, Yenping, rules, n.d.; answers to Buddhist prayers, n.d.
FINDING AIDS: In-house inventory.

57-CHARLES GARNET TRIMBLE PAPERS, 1914–64, 1 folder
Background note: Charles Garnet Trimble (b. 1884) was a medical missionary first associated with the Methodist Mission in Foochow in 1914, then with the Alden Speare Hospital in Yenping.
CORRESPONDENCE: 96 letters, including circular letters to mission friends and associates, 1930–64; and letters from Edith Alford Trimble (Mrs. Charles Trimble), 1914–20, describing her life in China.

58-GEORGE WILSON VAN GORDER, ca. 1925–1928, 9 volumes, 1 folder
Background note: George Wilson Van Gorder (1889–1969) was a professor and surgeon at Peking Union Medical School from 1919 to 1928.
MANUSCRIPTS: 8 bound volumes of typed narrative and x-ray case histories of surgical cases, ca. 1925–1928.
MEMORABILIA: Folder of biographical materials.
AUDIO-VISUAL MATERIALS: Photo album of surgical photos, n.d.
FINDING AIDS: In-house inventory.

59-WILLIAM MOSES WELCH, 1914–17, quantity undetermined
CORRESPONDENCE: Letters to William Moses Welch, a Methodist clergyman, from Mr. and Mrs. Kenneth Duncan, missionaries at Canton Christian College, 1914–17.

60-PAULINE E. WESTCOTT PAPERS, 1901–49, 15 items
MINUTES/RECORDS/REPORTS: Chefoo Club, articles of association and by-laws, 1914; Methodist Church: Foochow Conference, yearbook and minutes, 1946; Hinghua Conference, minutes, 1901; Hinghwa Annual Conference, 1942, 1946–49; Hinghwa Conference, annual report, 1912; Hinghwa Women's Conference, minutes, 1909; Keen School, student annual, 1927; Tsinanfu Club, rules and by-laws, 1915; Women's Foreign Missionary Society (Pacific Branch), annual report, 1940; 70th anniversary, records, n.d.
PAMPHLETS: *The China Home Missionary Society*, by Mary Ninde Gamewell, 1942; *Straws from the Hinghwa Harvest*, 1910; *The Ting Hsien Experiment in 1934*, 1934.
SERIALS: *Foochow News*. 1935.
FINDING AIDS: In-house inventory.

61-LAURA MAUDE WHEELER PAPERS, 1930–66, ca. 2 boxes
Background note: Laura Maude Wheeler (1874–1966) was a Methodist missionary teacher in north China, stationed in Peking and Tientsin, from 1903 to 1948. She was interned at the Civilian Civic Center in Weihsien from 1943 to 1945. Photographs originally in the collection have been removed to the Photograph Collection.
MINUTES/RECORDS/REPORTS: Gamewell School, yearbook, 1930; Methodist Episcopal Church, North China Conference, Tientsin District, report, 1931; Peking Higher Primary School, yearbook and 60th anniversary publication, 1870–1930; form letter from the Board of Foreign Missions, 1941.
CORRESPONDENCE: 62 incoming letters, 1947–66.
MANUSCRIPTS: Recollections written retrospectively from a personal diary which is not in the collection, containing personal accounts of travels, historical subjects, biographical portraits, and accounts of internment; lesson plans on Japan, the Apostles (some instructions in Chinese), and education; 16 typescripts of short pieces on Chinese money, villages, Mongolia, Peking Theological College, Peking churches, and other subjects, n.d.
DIARIES: Diary of Laura Wheeler, 1938; holograph of journal on Wheeler's work in China, 1938.
PAMPHLETS/MEMORABILIA: 2 home-made booklets: ''Chinese Cave Temples,'' by Marie Adams, 1934, and ''How We Got Our Bible,'' by Marie Adams, n.d.; *Impressive Service: The Story of the Christian College of China*, 1937; *Hua Nan College*, 1937; Peking Union Church reunion, 1954; *Recollections of My Chinese Days*, by Laura Wheeler, 1948; 31 Chinese scrolls; miscellaneous mementos; folder of miscellaneous materials.
MAPS/DESIGNS/DRAWINGS: Map of Tientsin, by Noah Fields Drake, 1902.
AUDIO-VISUAL MATERIALS: 34 large photos of missionary staff, students, religious scenes, and historical sites, n.d.; 62 small photos of scenery, Chinese people, and missionaries, n.d.; small photo album of the mission and life in China, n.d.; medium photo album of Chinese art, n.d.; large photo album of mission, staff, and classes in China, n.d.; 14 slides of China, n.d.; book of negatives of photos of mission campus, n.d.; ''Children of the Flower Kingdom,'' 40-frame film strip, n.d.
CHINESE LANGUAGE MATERIALS: 37 catechism cards, n.d.
FINDING AIDS: In-house inventory.

OR–20   University of Oregon Library
Eugene OR 97403-1299
(503) 686-3096
William Z. Schenk, Collection Development Librarian

1-RARE BOOK COLLECTION, ca. 1900, 1 item
PAMPHLETS: *Thrilling Experiences of Missionaries of the China Inland Mission, in Chihli Province, North China, during the ''Boxer'' Troubles of 1900: A Personal Narrative of Persecutions, . . . of Mr. Green...and Escape at Last by Arrival of Foreign Troops*, by Mr. and Mrs. Greene, ca. 1900.

2-GENERAL HOLDINGS
MINUTES/RECORDS/REPORTS: Methodist Episcopal Church: China Central Conference, official minutes, 1925, 1945; North China Conference, official journal, 1947–48; North China Woman's Conference, 1922, 1925, 1927–29, 1932–33; National Christian Council of China, report of a conference with Christian workers, 1926.

MANUSCRIPTS: "As I Look Back: Recollections of Growing Up in America's Southland and of Twenty-six Years in Pre-Communist China, 1888–1936," by Eugene Epperson Barnett, 1964(?); "Christian Missions in China," by Edward Wilson Wallace, 1929; "Fifteen Years among the Hakkas of South China," by F. J. Wiens, n.d.

PAMPHLETS: *Across Asia's Back Door*, by Earl R. Hibbard, 1967; *The American Bible Society in China*, by J. R. Hykes, 1916; *Learning for Living: Stories from a Chungking Boarding School*, by Florence F. Jack, 1944(?); *The Missionary Situation in China*, by H. T. Hodgkin, 1928; *Windows into China: The Jesuits and Their Books, 1580–1730*, by John Parker, 1978; *Yale in China*, 1923.

SERIALS: *China Bulletin*, 1952–62. *China Christian Advocate*, 1927–41. China Christian Educational Association, *Bulletin*, 1928. *China Christian Year Book*, 1936–37. China International Famine Relief Commission, *Bulletin*, 1923–36; Publications, series A, 1922–36; series B, 1926–28. *China Mission Year Book* 1917–19. *China Monthly*, 1939–50. *Chinese Recorder*, 1924–41. *Lingnan Science Journal*, 1929, 1932–42, 1945, 1948. *Monumenta Serica*, 1935–45, 1948–76, 1979–83. National Christian Council of China, *Bulletin*, 1932–37. *West China Missionary News*, 1935. *Yenching Index Numbers*, 1940–41. *Yenching Journal of Social Studies*, 1938–41.

DISSERTATIONS/THESES: *Die Akkomodationsmethode des P. Matteo Ricci S.I. in China*, by Johannes Bettray, 1955. *China and Educational Autonomy: The Changing Role of the Protestant Educational Missionary in China, 1807–1937*, by Alice Henrietta Gregg, 1945. *China Missions in Crisis: Bishop Laimbeckhoven and His Times, 1738–1787*, by Joseph Krahl, 1964. *An Experiment in Teaching the Christian Religion by Life Situations in Fan Village, China*, by Mabel Ellis Hubbard, 1938. *Suomen lähetysseuran työ Kiinassa vuosina, 1901–1926 (The Work of the Finnish Missionary Society in China in the Years 1901–1926)*, by Toivo Saarilahti, 1960. *Temple Community and Village Cultural Integration in North China: Evidence from "Sectarian Cases" (chiao an) in Chihli, 1860–1895*, by Charles Albert Litzinger, 1983. *Timothy Richard's Influence on the Missionary Movement and Chinese Reform in Late Ch'ing China*, by Bert Hideo Kikuchi, 1969.

CHINESE LANGUAGE MATERIALS/SERIALS: *Chiao hui hsin pao (The Church News)*, 1868–74 (repr. 1968). *Chin-ling hsüeh pao (Nanking Journal)*, 1931–41(?). *Wan kuo kung pao (The Globe Magazine: A Review of the Times)*, 1868–1906. *Yen-ching hsüeh pao (Yenching Journal of Chinese Studies)*, 1927–34, 1949–51.

CHINESE LANGUAGE MATERIALS: 4 books, 1948–69, on anti-Christian movements, Catholic missions, and Methodist missions.

NEWBERG

GEORGE FOX COLLEGE
OR–25   Shambaugh Library
Newberg OR 97132
(503) 538-8383
Dawn Ulmer, Reference Librarian

Background note: Since George Fox College is affiliated with the Evangelical Friends Association, the Shambaugh Library has a significant concentration in Quaker materials.

1-QUAKER COLLECTION, 1896–76, 5 items
MINUTES/RECORDS/REPORTS: Reports on Quaker China mission work, some of it as correspondence, in *Friends Missionary Advocate*, 1939–76, and *Friends World News: News Bulletin of the Friends World Committee for Consultation*, 1939–; Conference on Friends' Foreign Missions, Darlington, England, report, 1896.

PAMPHLETS: *Events in Old Cathay*, by Elsie V. Matti, 1980; *The Overseas and International Service of British and Irish Friends in the Twentieth Century (to 1961): A Condensed Record in Chronological Order*, by Bernard G. Lawson, 1961.

PORTLAND

WESTERN CONSERVATIVE BAPTIST SEMINARY
OR–30   Cline-Tunnell Library
5511 S. E. Hawthorne Boulevard
Portland OR 97215
(503) 233-8561
Robert Krupp, Director

1-GENERAL HOLDINGS
PAMPHLETS: *The Challenge of Independent Nosuland*, by Ralph R. Covell, ca. 1950; *The Far East, Nationalist, Militarist, Communist, or Christian*, by Stanley High, 1932; *Trophies of Grace and How They Are Won*, by the Conservative Baptist Foreign Mission Society, ca. 1952.

SERIALS: *China and the Church Today*, 1979–86. *China Notes*, 1984-. *China Prayer Letter*, 1984-. *Chinese Around the World*, 1983-. *Chinese Theological Review*, 1985-. *Christianity in China: Historical Studies*, 1986-.

DISSERTATIONS/THESES: *The Role of the Chinese Church in World Missions*, by Henry T. Ang, 1985.

WESTERN EVANGELICAL SEMINARY
OR–35   George Hallauer Memorial Library
4200 S. E. Jennings Avenue
Portland OR 97222
(503) 654-5182
Nobel V. Sack, Archivist

1-GENERAL HOLDINGS
SERIALS: *China and the Church Today*, 1983–86. *China Prayer News*, 1984–86. *Ching Feng*, 1966–86. *Pray for China Fellowship*, 1983–87.

SALEM

WESTERN BAPTIST COLLEGE
OR–40   Library
5000 Deer Park Drive S.E.
Salem OR 97301
(503) 581-8600
J. Richard Muntz, Librarian

Background note: In addition to the materials listed below, the library holds a significant collection of published works by and about Watchman Nee (Nee To-sheng).

1-GENERAL HOLDINGS
MANUSCRIPTS: ''Lessons to be Learned from the Experiences of Christian Missions in China,'' comp. by Harold S. Matthews, 1951.
PAMPHLETS: *David Hill, a Missionary Saint*, by Arthur H. Robins, n.d.
SERIALS: *China Christian Year Book*, 1915. *Chinese Recorder*, 1922–23, 1925, 1933. *East Asia Millions* (Philadelphia), 1932-.
DISSERTATIONS/THESES: *An Analysis of Watchman Nee's Doctrine of Dying and Rising with Christ as It Relates to Sanctification*, by Robert Kingston Wetmore, 1983.

PENNSYLVANIA

BADEN

ST. JOSEPH CONVENT
PA–5 Sisters of St. Joseph Archives
Baden PA 15005
(412) 869–2151
Sister Helen Marie Shrift, C.S.J., Archivist

Restrictions: Access by appointment.
Background note: The Sisters of St. Joseph was founded in France around 1650. The Sisters of St. Joseph of Pittsburgh was founded at Ebensburg, Pennsylvania, in 1869, and moved to Baden in 1901. In 1926, the Passionist Fathers requested assistance for their missionary work in China. Sisters of St. Joseph were sent to China from 1926 to 1948, to work in the areas of Shenchow and Chihkiang (Yuanchow) in Hunan. The collection is not fully processed. See also Congregation of the Passion of the Eastern United States (Passionists), Mother of Sorrows Retreat House, West Springfield, MA, 01089.

1-GENERAL HOLDINGS
CORRESPONDENCE: Letters to and from sisters, including correspondence with Superiors, 1925–48.
MANUSCRIPTS: ''Events and Places in China,'' by the sisters in China.
PAMPHLETS: *New Bamboo Shoots*, by Msgr. Eugene E. Fahy, S.J., 1954 (a collection of reprints of articles from *Sign* magazine, published from 1926 to 1948).

DIARIES: Diary by Sr. Clarissa Stattmiller, 1927, who died of malaria in July of that year.
MEMORABILIA: 6 scrapbooks containing unpublished narratives, articles from *Sign* magazine, news clippings, and letters.
AUDIO-VISUAL MATERIALS: 3 photo albums of areas in China where the sisters worked and travelled, including photos of Chinese people.
SERIALS: *The Little Design in China*, 1946–49.

BETHLEHEM

MORAVIAN COLLEGE
PA–10 Reeves Library
Bethlehem PA 18018
(215) 861–1544
John Thomas Minor, Director

1-GENERAL HOLDINGS
MINUTES/RECORDS/REPORTS: Midwest China Consultation, 1979.
SERIALS: *China Notes*, 1969-.

BRYN MAWR

BRYN MAWR COLLEGE
PA–15 Canaday Library
Bryn Mawr PA 19010
(215) 645–5000
James Tanis, Director
Leo M. Dolenski, Manuscripts Librarian

1-MARGARET BAILEY SPEER PAPERS, 1925–43, 1.5 l.f.
Restrictions: Access restricted.
Background note: Sponsored by the Board of Foreign Missions of the Presbyterian Church of the U.S.A., Margaret Bailey Speer, a Bryn Mawr graduate, went to China in the late summer of 1925 to teach at the Women's College at Yenching University in Peking. She later served as dean of the Women's College. Interned by the Japanese in 1941, she returned to the United States in 1943.
MINUTES/RECORDS/REPORTS/CORRESPONDENCE: Correspondence to her parents containing detailed accounts of the political chaos prior to World War II, along with accounts of academic life at Yenching, 1925–43.
FINDING AIDS: Unpublished guide.

2-ANDREW HENRY WOODS PAPERS, 1891–1956, 6 volumes
Restrictions: Access restricted.
Background note: Andrew Henry Woods (1872–1956) spent about twenty years in China as a neurologist and founded the medical department at Canton Christian College. In 1919, he was recruited by the Rockefeller Foundation to head the Department of Neurology at the new Peking Union Medical College. He returned from China in 1928.
DIARIES: 6 diaries, including his education, work in China, and relations with friends and family, 1891–1956.

3-GENERAL HOLDINGS
SERIALS: *News of China*, 1942–49.
DISSERTATIONS/THESES: *Revolutionary Faithfulness: The*

Quaker Search for a Peaceable Kingdom in China, 1939–1951, by Cynthia Letts Adcock, 1974.

CARLISLE

DICKINSON COLLEGE
PA–20 Boyd Lee Spahr Library
Carlisle PA 17013
(717) 245–1399
Martha Slotten, Archivist and Curator of Special Collections

1-DICKINSON-IN-CHINA PAPERS, 1921–36, ca. 5 files
Background note: Dickinson College maintained an academic relationship with West China Union University in Chengdu, Sichuan, from 1921 to 1933. Raymond R. Brewer, a 1916 Dickinson graduate, was supported by the project from 1921 to 1927.
MINUTES/RECORDS/REPORTS: Constitution and other papers of the Dickinson College Extension Board; Fourth Annual Report, by Raymond Brewer, 1925.
CORRESPONDENCE: 100 letters, with correspondents including Dickinson College presidents Mervin Grant Filler, James Henry Morgan, and Karl Waugh, and representatives of the Board of Missions of the Methodist Church, 1921–27.
MANUSCRIPTS: "Dickinson-in-China, 1921–1933," by Leslie Lax, 1977.
MEMORABILIA: File of clippings from the college paper, *The Dickinsonian*, providing a full account of the project, 1921–36.
FINDING AIDS: "A Bibliography of a Missionary Campaign; Dickinson-in-China, 1921–1936," by Leslie Lax, 1977.

2-GENERAL HOLDINGS
SERIALS: *Educational Review*, 1916–38.

CARLISLE BARRACKS

DEPARTMENT OF THE ARMY
PA–25 U.S. Army Military History Institute
Carlisle Barracks PA 17013
(717) 245–3601
Richard J. Sommers, Archivist-Historian

1-COLONEL LAWRENCE B. BIXBY PAPERS, ca. 1971, 1 item
MANUSCRIPTS: Biography of Colonel Lawrence B. Bixby's grandfather, Dr. Moses Homan Bixby, a Baptist missionary in Burma from 1853 to 1856 and 1861 to 1868, who believed that his ministry in northeastern Burma would open a route for missionaries to enter western China.
FINDING AIDS: *Bibliography 13: Oral History*, by Roy S. Barnard, 2 V, 1976–77. *Holdings of the Military History Research Manuscript Collection*, by Richard J. Sommers, 2 V, 1972–75.

2-CHAPLAIN LESLIE R. GROVES, SR., PAPERS, 1900, 1 box
CORRESPONDENCE/DIARIES: Typescript diary and family letters of Chaplain Leslie R. Groves, Sr., who accompanied the 14th U.S. Infantry Regiment in China from July to November, 1900, during the Boxer Rebellion.

3-U.S. ARMY IN CHINA PAPERS, 1900–1949, quantity undetermined
CORRESPONDENCE/MANUSCRIPTS/DIARIES: Letters, diaries, and memoirs of approximately 40 U.S. Army officers and soldiers who served in China during the Boxer Rebellion, the garrisoning of Tientsin by the 15th U.S. Infantry Regiment during World War II, and the civil war between the Chinese Nationalists and the Chinese Communists, containing references to missionaries and their work in China between 1900 and 1949.

CLARKS SUMMIT

BAPTIST BIBLE COLLEGE
PA–30 Library
538 Venard Road
Clarks Summit PA 18411
(717) 587–1172
David C. McClain, Head Librarian

1-GENERAL HOLDINGS
DISSERTATIONS/THESES: *The Baptist Problem of the Indigenous Church in China*, by Frank T. Woodward, 1934.

ELIZABETHTOWN

ELIZABETHTOWN COLLEGE
PA–35 Zug Memorial Library
Elizabethtown PA 17022
(717) 367–1151
Ann M. Carper, Director

Background note: The Church of the Brethren, founded in 1708 in Schwarzenau, Germany, entered the American colonies in 1719 and settled at Germantown, Pennsylvania. The major collections of this denomination are held at the Church of the Brethren General Board, Brethren Historical Library and Archives, 1451 Dundee Avenue, Elgin, IL, 60120.

1-CHURCH OF THE BRETHREN CHINA FILES, 1933–48, quantity undetermined
MINUTES / RECORDS / REPORTS / CORRESPONDENCE: Printed reports, correspondence, and policy statements about the denomination's work in China.
SERIALS: *Star of Cathay*, 1933–34, 1936, 1939–48.

ERIE

GANNON UNIVERSITY

PA–40 Diocese of Erie Archives
Nash Library
University Square
Erie PA 16541
(814) 871–7562
Sr. Gertrude Marie Peterson, Archivist

Background note: See also Maryknoll Fathers and Brothers, Archives, Maryknoll, NY, 10545.

1-BISHOP GANNON COLLECTION, 1926-37, 11 items
DIARIES: 17-page account of the fall of Shanghai to the Japanese, by the Maryknoll Sisters in nearby Pei Chow, 1937.
CORRESPONDENCE: 7 letters from Rev. William J. Downs to Bishop John Mark Gannon, written from Kaying via Swatow, 1926-30.
MANUSCRIPTS: "Maryknoll in Kaying Aug. 1, 1928-Aug. 1, 1929."
AUDIO-VISUAL MATERIALS: Photo of Rev. Downs; photo of a Maryknoll Sisters' school in Hong Kong.

PA-45   Gannon University Archives
Nash Library
University Square
Erie PA 16541
(814) 871-7554
Grace A. Davies, Archivist

1-BISHOP GANNON COLLECTION, 1926-61, quantity undetermined
MINUTES/RECORDS/REPORTS: Personnel and statistical report of the Catholic Foreign Mission Society of America (Maryknoll), 1946; 2 historical accounts of the Maryknoll Movement, 1926, 1961; China reports in the *Annals of the Society for the Propagation of the Faith*, 1922.

GETTYSBURG

LUTHERAN THEOLOGICAL SEMINARY
PA-50   A. R. Wentz Library
Gettysburg PA 17325
(717) 334-6286
Donald N. Matthews, Librarian

1-GENERAL HOLDINGS
SERIALS: *China News Letter*, 1947-56. *Chinese Recorder*, 1912-17, 1920-21, 1923-24, 1927-28, 1930-41.

GIBSONIA

PITTSBURGH BIBLE INSTITUTE
PA-55   Archives
R. D. #1, Box 391
Gibsonia PA 15044
(412) 935-1329
David Vogel, Director

Background note: The Evangelization Society of the Pittsburgh Bible Institute sent out missionaries to several foreign countries, including China, where it had workers in Szechuan and Hupei, and later also Hong Kong and Taiwan.

1-GENERAL HOLDINGS
MINUTES/RECORDS/REPORTS: Occasional, brief reports from or about ca. 14 missionaries and several native workers in China, Hong Kong, and Taiwan in the Institute's periodical, *The Record of Faith*, 1911, 1922, 1924, 1945, 1948, and other dates.

GLADWYNE

DEACONESS COMMUNITY OF THE LUTHERAN CHURCH IN AMERICA
PA-60   Archives
801 Merion Square Road
Gladwyne PA 19035-1599
(215) 642-8838
Sister Louise Burroughs, Archivist

1-GENERAL HOLDINGS
MINUTES/RECORDS/REPORTS: "Place of service files" containing reports from the Board of World Missions, Augustana Synod Mission in China, conference in Hsuchang, 1946; annual conference in Hankow, 1948; Emergency conference at Hsuchang and Hankow, minutes, 1947-48.
MINUTES/RECORDS/REPORTS/CORRESPONDENCE: Personal files of the following deaconesses who served in China: Sr. Thyra Lawson, 1912-49; Sr. Ingeborg Nystul, 1906-48; Sr. Elvira Persson, 1914-27, 1932-38, 1946-48; Sr. Myrtle Anderson, 1936-43, 1947-48; Sr. Astrid Erling, 1932-49.
MANUSCRIPTS: Typescript autobiographies of Srs. Thyra Lawson, Ingeborg Nystul, and Elvira Persson.
MEMORABILIA: Silk embroidered hanging presented to Sr. Thyra Lawson by the Chinese church in Hong Kong, bearing inscription in Chinese, 1954.
AUDIO-VISUAL MATERIALS: Photos of each of the deaconesses.

GROVE CITY

GROVE CITY COLLEGE
PA-65   Henry Buhl Library
Grove City PA 16127
(412) 458-6600
Diane Grundy, Librarian

1-JAMES AND ALEXANDER WAITE CORRESPONDENCE, 1907-12, 73 items
Background note: This collection deals specifically with the policies and personnel practices of the Presbyterian China Mission from 1907 through 1912. The correspondence revolves around James and Alexander Waite, twin brothers, who were expelled from mission service in China by the Board of Foreign Missions of the Presbyterian Church in the U.S.A. More than half of the letters were written to Isaac Ketler, president of Grove City College, to enlist his help in seeking the reinstatement of the Waite brothers. The Waites also forwarded letters from their friends and colleagues. The file therefore contains letters from Presbyterian missionaries in China to executives of the Board of Foreign Missions, notably Arthur Judson Brown and Robert E. Speer. This correspondence is now available on computer diskettes, with an index.
MINUTES/RECORDS/REPORTS: "Overture by Presbytery of Clarion to the General Assembly on Behalf of the Waite Brothers," n.d., enclosed with undated letter from James Waite to Isaac Ketler; "To the Members of the West Shantung Mission," a 28-page review of the action taken against the Waite brothers, by

Alexander Waite, 1907, enclosed with a letter from him to Isaac Ketler, 1912.

CORRESPONDENCE: 71 letters to or from Roy Allison, George A. Blackburn, Arthur Judson Brown, C. R. Callender, Howard Campbell, W. R. Cunningham, Mabel M. Dodd, W. Clifton Dodd, M. Fitch, Margaretta Franz, William Clement Isett, Charles F. Johnson, Isaac Ketler, Charles Lyon, John Murray, Harry G. Romig, Lucy A. Romig, Robert E. Speer, Alexander and Edna Waite, James Waite, John Waite, and J. Stanley White.

FINDING AIDS: "Working Calendar of Correspondence Exchanged by Dr. Isaac Ketler, President of Grove City College, with James and Alexander Waite, Expelled from the China Inland Mission by the Board of Foreign Missions of the Presbyterian Church in the U.S.A.," by Diane Grundy.

HATFIELD

BIBLICAL THEOLOGICAL SEMINARY
PA-70   Library
200 North Main Street
Hatfield PA 19440
(215) 368-5000
James C. Pakala, Librarian

1-GENERAL HOLDINGS
PAMPHLETS: Boxer Uprising in Chihli, accounts of the church in Manchuria, and findings of the World Missionary Conference held in Shanghai, 1913.

SERIALS: *Agricultural Missions*, 1937–41. *Directory of Protestant Missions in China, Japan, and Corea*, 1912.

DISSERTATIONS/THESES: *Changes in Missionary Policy Entailed in the Development of an Indigenous Chinese Church*, by Uri G. Chandler, 1946. *Christian Education in New-born China*, by Yi Ying Ma, 1941. *A Comparison of the Work of Robert Morrison and Jonathan Goforth with Special Reference to Their Contribution to Protestant Missions in China*, by Russel R. Van Vleet, 1949. *A Course of Bible Stories for Use in Teaching Christian Women of Rural South China*, by Margaret Jane Edwards, 1937. *Drama as a Means of Evangelism in China*, by Anne L. Winn, 1944. *The Effect of the Recent Westward Migration on the Program of the Church in China*, by Beth Blackstone, 1942. *Fifty Years of Covenanter Evangelism in South China*, by Orlena Marie Lynn, 1948. *A History of the Baptist Mission at Swatow (Kakchieh), China*, by Carl Capen, 1935. *The Influence of Christian Student Movements in the Colleges and Universities of China and Japan*, by Anne Marie Beguin, 1948. *James Hudson Taylor, Christian Statesman*, by Frank J. Kline, 1936. *Lay Leadership Training for Rural Women of the China Inland Mission in West Szechwan*, by Marion Elinor Cleveland, 1938. *Orientation Program for Christian Missionary Nurses for China*, by Lucy Rebecca Stillman, 1941. *The Picture of Student Living and Thinking in China and Its Implications for Christian Student Work*, by Gwendolyn Wong, 1948. *Present Movements in China Bearing upon the Post-war Program of the Christian Church*, by Gladys E. Marth, 1945. *Present Policies of the China Inland Mission Compared with the Policies of Missions Established by James Hudson Taylor*, by Merilie Robertson, 1955. *Problems of Christian Education in Western Hunan, China*, by Lucile Hartman, 1946. *Proposed Plans for the Revision of the Program of Religious Education for the Sixth to the Ninth Grades, Miller Seminary, Siu Laam, China*, by Myrtle M. Lefever, 1931. *A Proposed Program of Primary Christian Education in Rural China*, by Shirley E. Ginns, 1946. *Selection and Adaptation of Extra-Biblical Stories for Use in Christian Education of Chinese Girls of Intermediate Age*, by Miriam Ellen Null, 1943. *A Study of Curriculum Trends in the Christian Education Programs of Selected Mission Schools in China*, by Katharine Whitney Hand, 1941. *Study of the Chinese Industrial Cooperatives with an Evaluation of Their Significance to the Christian Church*, by Robert Cameron Urquhart, 1949. *A Study of Typical Life Problems Faced by Three Outstanding Missionary Wives of the Nineteenth Century*, by Mable Busch Bontrager, 1948. *A Suggested Program of Direct Evangelism for the Missionary in Present-day China as Based upon a Study of the Most Effective Methods*, by Clifford E. Chaffee, 1944. *A Suggested Program of Evangelization for South Fukien Province, China*, by Christina Wang, 1940.

HAVERFORD

HAVERFORD COLLEGE
PA-75   James P. Magill Library
Haverford PA 19041
(215) 896-1175
Edwin B. Bronner, Librarian and Curator of the Quaker Collection
Diana Alten, Manuscripts Cataloger

Background note: Additional collections of the Religious Society of Friends' China mission documents are located at the archives of the American Friends Service Committee, 1501 Cherry Street, Philadelphia, PA, 19102; Malone College, Everett L. Cattell Library, 515 25th Street NW, Canton, OH, 44709; and Swarthmore College, Friends Historical Library, Swarthmore, PA, 19081.

Finding aids: *The Quaker Collection of the Haverford College Library*, Haverford College, 1963. An index to the Rufus Jones papers is under preparation.

1-QUAKER COLLECTION-CHINA DOCUMENTS, 1907–63, quantity undetermined
CORRESPONDENCE: Letters of Morris Wistar Wood, regarding his teaching of Bible at Canton Christian College and recording his general impressions of the Canton area, 1921–22; letters of William Warder Cadbury, regarding the University Medical School, Canton Hospital, and Lingnan University, 1907–1940s; letters to Rufus Matthew Jones, chairman of the American Friends Service Committee, from China mission field workers, 1917–27, 1934–44; correspondence relating to the China visit of members of the Laymen's Foreign Missionary Inquiry, including Rufus Jones, 1931; letter from Roderick Scott, regarding his teaching at the newly organized Fukien Union Arts College, 1918; letter from Robert L. Simkin, regarding the organization of the Friends Foreign Mission Association and West China Union University, 1918.

MANUSCRIPTS: "Friends in China," by the American Friends' Board of Missions, 1941(?); "Quaker Relations with China," a brief history of Quaker missionary and relief work in China, by J. Duncan Wood, 1963.

PAMPHLETS: 34 pamphlets describing the work and history of the Society of Friends in China, medical practice, and West China Union University.

DIARIES: Holograph journal by Rufus Jones, written during a lecture tour of the Orient, in which he records his impressions of his contacts with Wellington Koo, Tsai Ting Kang, and C. Y. Cheng, as well as comments on the secular and religious life of China.

AUDIO-VISUAL MATERIALS: Photos, especially of Canton, by M. Wistar Wood, 1921–22.

SERIALS: *The Foochow Messenger*, 1937. *Friends Centre Bulletin*, 1939–40.

LANCASTER

EVANGELICAL AND REFORMED HISTORICAL SOCIETY

PA–80   Lancaster Central Archives and Library
Philip Schaff Library
Lancaster Theological Seminary
555 West James Street
Lancaster PA 17603
(717) 393–0654 Ext. 29
Florence M. Bricker, Archivist

Background note: This is the major collection of documents related to the China mission of the Reformed Church in the United States (mission agency: Board of Foreign Missions), which became the Evangelical and Reformed Church (Board of International Missions) in 1934, which united with the General Council of the Congregational Churches in 1957 to become the United Church of Christ (Board of World Ministries).

Approximately 50 Reformed Church in the U.S. (later, Evangelical and Reformed Church) missionaries served in China, and the Archives preserves material by and about them: correspondence, particularly to the denominational mission board; articles by and clippings about them; portraits and family photos; and various medical, financial, and personal records. Several of the larger collections of papers are mentioned in detail below. Other Evangelical and Reformed China missionaries, whose papers are in the Archives, but not listed below, are: W. F. Adams, Helen B. Ammerman, J. Albert Beam, George W. Bachman, William H. and Elizabeth Jane (Teitsworth) Daniels, Marion P. (Johnson) Firor, Mr. and Mrs. F. Karl Heinrichsohn, Paul E. Keller, Horace R. Lequear, Rebecca M. Messimer, Elizabeth J. Miller, J. W. Owen, Mr. and Mrs. Hesser Ruhl, Jacob George Rupp, Esther I. Sellemeyer, Tasie Shaak, George Randolph and Esther Snyder, Lewis R. Thompson, Alice E. Traub, and Minerva Stout Weil.

1-BARTHOLOMEW MISSION LIBRARY, 1910–60, quantity undetermined
Background note: The materials in this collection belonged to Allen Revellen Bartholomew, who had a keen interest in missions and in China, to which he made a trip in 1910.
MINUTES/RECORDS/REPORTS: Evangelical and Reformed Church, China mission: Executive committee minutes and annual mission meeting minutes, 1920, 1922, 1924, 1929–30, 1932–37; report, 1938–39.

PAMPHLETS: *Holding Out at Huping*, by Edwin Allen Beck, 1939; *Memoirs of China*, by Minerva S. Weil, 1954 (?); *Our Work of Evangelism in Japan and China*, by Jacob G. Rupp, 1922 (?).
SERIALS: *China Christian Year Book*, 1910–11, 1913, 1916, 1918–24, 1926, 1929–39. *Quarterly Notes on Christianity and Chinese Religion*, 1959–60.
CHINESE LANGUAGE MATERIALS: Chinese hymnbook, ca. 1933.

2-EDWIN A. BECK PAPERS, 1905–60, 17 folders
Background note: Edwin Allen Beck (1875–1960) served in China with his wife, Etta Irene (Poling) Beck (1878–1967). During his 35 years in China (1906–41), Beck specialized in agricultural missions and public health work.
MINUTES/RECORDS/REPORTS/CORRESPONDENCE: Reports and letters, n.d.
MANUSCRIPTS: Folder of manuscripts, including the original and a revision of "The China Story, 1938–41," by Edwin Beck, n.d.
MEMORABILIA: Folder of articles reporting on mission work, war conditions, Beck's travel, and the stoning of evangelist Chen Djou-tsing in 1927; biographical sketch of Edwin Beck, by Jacob B. Wagner, 1961.
AUDIO-VISUAL MATERIALS: Ca. 15 photos of Edwin Beck and his family.

3-KARL HERBERT BECK PAPERS, 1914–61, 9 folders
Background note: Karl Herbert Beck (1890–1976) was a China missionary with his wife, Meta M. (Bridenbaugh) Beck (who had arrived in China in 1911), from 1914 to 1935 and from 1940 to 1952. He was the last Evangelical and Reformed missionary to leave China.
CORRESPONDENCE/MEMORABILIA: 7 folders of personal reports to Arthur Vale Casselman and other mission executives, letters, and clippings, 1917–53.
MANUSCRIPTS: Folder of typescripts by Karl Beck, describing his work in China, famine and relief, conferences, and agricultural missions.
AUDIO-VISUAL MATERIALS: 13 photos of Karl and Meta Beck and their family, 1919-ca. 1955.

4-JONAS AND OLIVE BUCHER PAPERS, 1905–57, 16 folders
Background note: Jonas Frank and Olive (Miller) Bucher worked with the Evangelical and Reformed Church's Eastview schools in Hunan, where Mr. Bucher was principal.
MINUTES/RECORDS/REPORTS/CORRESPONDENCE: 4 folders of reports, 1932–57; 7 folders of correspondence, 1905–33; folder of personal reports, n.d.
MANUSCRIPTS: Sketch of the Boys' School work of the Shenchow station, by Jonas Bucher, n.d.; "Four Primary Stories from China," by Olive Bucher, for use by Sunday School teachers, n.d.; 2 folders of miscellaneous articles by Olive Bucher and her daughters, Mary and Olive; memoir by Olive Bucher.

5-CHINA MISSION COLLECTION, 1900–1952, 7 boxes
MINUTES/RECORDS/REPORTS: 7 boxes of materials from and about the China mission of the Evangelical and Reformed Church: 1.5 boxes of minutes and financial reports (including Hong Kong), 2 boxes of materials pertaining to schools and colleges in China, and 3.5 boxes of topical and miscellaneous files on the China mission.

6-CHINA—SOCIAL LIFE AND CUSTOMS (RG 41), n.d., 2 boxes
MINUTES/RECORDS/REPORTS: Records of Eastview Boys' School, Hua Chung College, Ziemer Memorial Girls' School, Abounding Grace Hospitals, Hoy Memorial Hospital, and other institutions related to the China mission of the Reformed Church in the U.S. and the Evangelical and Reformed Church.
MANUSCRIPTS/PAMPHLETS: Materials concerning evangelistic work, places and customs, rural life, thinking under Communism, and travel.
AUDIO-VISUAL MATERIALS: Unspecified number of photos relating to the denominational China mission work.

7-WARD HARTMAN PAPERS, 1936–58, 4 folders
Background note: Ward Hartman (1882–1967) served with his wife, Frieda (Plack) Hartman, as a missionary of the Evangelical and Reformed Church. He was in China from 1911 to 1949, when he went to Hong Kong. In his last years in China he was president of the Evangelical and Reformed China Mission.
CORRESPONDENCE/MEMORABILIA: Letters and reports, especially to and from denominational mission executives such as Arthur Vale Casselman, F. A. Goetsch, Reginald Helfferich, and John H. Poorman, regarding the work in China and Hong Kong, his finances, and travels to the United States; miscellaneous telegrams, travel and financial papers, trip diaries, and medical records.

8-WILLIAM EDWIN HOY PAPERS, 1905–52, 15 folders
Background note: William Edwin Hoy was a missionary in China from 1887 to 1927.
CORRESPONDENCE/AUDIO-VISUAL MATERIALS: Correspondence, including hand-written letters, and photos by William Hoy.

9-MAP AND SCROLL COLLECTION, ca. 1926, 8 items
MAPS/DESIGNS/DRAWINGS: Missionary map of China and Japan, n.d.; 4 maps, including Eastern Hunan and China mission stations, issued by the Board of Foreign Missions, Reformed Church in the U.S., n.d.
MEMORABILIA: 2 Chinese scrolls, one presented to the Board of Foreign Missions by Chinese teachers in Shenchow, the other probably presented to a woman missionary by the students of Eastview School, Hunan.

10-MARY EDNA MYERS PAPERS, 1914–67, 9 folders
Background note: Mary Edna Myers (1886–1978) was an Evangelical and Reformed missionary nurse in China from 1914 to 1953.
MINUTES/RECORDS/REPORTS/CORRESPONDENCE: Correspondence, reports, health and financial records, and articles by Mary Myers.

11-WILLIAM A. REIMERT PAPERS, 1901–49, 2 folders
Background note: William Anson Reimert was martyred in China in 1920.
CORRESPONDENCE/AUDIO-VISUAL MATERIALS: Letters and photos by Reimert and his wife.

12-HOWARD KELLER SHUMAKER COLLECTION (RG 19), n.d., 1 box
Background note: Howard Keller Shumaker was a medical missionary in Canton under the United Brethren Church.
CORRESPONDENCE: Personal letters and correspondence relating to Shumaker's work as a medical missionary in Canton.
PAMPHLETS: English language tracts.
MEMORABILIA: Miscellaneous items, including a complimentary banner.
AUDIO-VISUAL MATERIALS: Unspecified number of photos.

13-GENERAL HOLDINGS
MINUTES/RECORDS/REPORTS: Evangelical and Reformed Church, China mission reports by Arthur Vale Casselman, 1938–39; Board of Foreign Missions, Shenchow station minutes, 1919–37; Eastview Schools, Shenchow, catalogue, n.d.; ca. 63 China mission deeds for Chenlingchi, Hwa Yang, Linhsiang, San Hsien, Shenchow (including Eastview Schools and outstations), Yang Lou Szi, and Yoyang (including Ziemer Girls School, Huping Middle School and College, and Tah Chien Kia).

Reformed Church in the U.S.: Board of Foreign Missions, financial reports from the China missions, 1905–6; minutes of the regular annual meeting, 1916–24, 1926, 1928–35, 1947–48; China Mission, minutes, 1916–48; China Mission, Shenchow station, bound volume of original typewritten minutes, 1919–37.

Photostats of miscellaneous deeds; property registrations and lists of miscellaneous assets, Yoyang; Synod of the East, Classis of Hunan, minutes, 1910–20; United Board for Christian Colleges in China, minutes, n.d.; United Board for Christian Colleges in China, Huachung University Committee, minutes, 1947–49; Kwangsi Famine Relief Fund, report, ca. 1900; reports of religious work in China by interdenominational agencies, n.d.
MANUSCRIPTS: Description of China by Mrs. Hesser Ruhl, a missionary of the Reformed Church, intended to accompany [missing] slides, n.d.; "From Six to Sixty to Six: A Narrative of the China Mission of the Reformed Church in the United States and the Later Evangelical and Reformed Church," by Arthur Vale Casselman, 1951 (published under the title, *It Happened in Hunan*); "Memoirs of Hsiang-Si Mission," by Karl H. Beck, 1970; "Meaningful Moments in the Experience of an American Who Lived in China," by Grace Walborn Snyder, 1940; "And They Also Came," by Margaret C. Young, a history of the work of native Chinese missionaries to Hawaii, 1976; "Lessons to be Learned from the Experiences of Christian Missions in China...1951," with 49 articles and a complete packet of research papers for the Willingen Conference; 3 scrapbooks of Otto G. Reuman, containing materials used in educational work, items about the activity of a missionary Masonic Lodge, pamphlets in English and Chinese, and material on missionary life in Foochow, ca. 1919–1925.
PAMPHLETS: *The Lynx Becomes a Link: A Brief Report on a Trip to the China Mission Stations of the Evangelical and Reformed Church*, by Dobbs Frederick Ehlman, 1947(?); *Our Work of Evangelism in Japan and China*, by Jacob George Rupp, 1923(?); *Holding Out at Huping*, by Edwin Allen Beck, n.d.; *On to China! The Needs of China Vividly Portrayed*, by William Edwin Hoy, 1899; miscellaneous pamphlets about the work and missionaries of the Reformed Church in the U.S. in China.
MEMORABILIA: 3 scrapbooks of Otto G. Reuman, containing invitations and programs used in educational mission work espe-

cially in Foochow, including Daily Vacation Bible Schools, the YMCA and YWCA, and a missionary Masonic Lodge, ca. 1919–1925; bulletins from farewell services of various missionaries of the Reformed Church in the U.S.

AUDIO-VISUAL MATERIALS: Photos of a China mission by Arthur Vale Casselman, 1903; 4 photo albums of persons in Huping, by F. Mildred Bailey (Mrs. Ben Webber), n.d.; "China," a 16 mm. color film by Paul V. Taylor, n.d.; "Views of China," a photo album by Allen Revellen Bartholomew, 1910; photo album by Bartholomew, 1910; unidentified slides of China and Japan by Paul R. Gregory; filmstrip of China by Paul V. Taylor, 1948; miscellaneous unidentified materials in China missions picture files.

SERIALS: *China Christian Year Book*, 1931, 1938–39. *China Mission News*, 1901–2. *Chinese Recorder*, 1908–11, 1924–36, 1938–40. *Huping*, 1924–26.

CHINESE LANGUAGE MATERIALS: Miscellaneous pamphlets in the scrapbooks of Otto G. Reuman (see above), ca. 1919–25; catechism, trans. by Henry Blodget, 1882(?); *I Believe*, by Nevin Cowger Harner, trans. by L. Haui, 1966.

FRANKLIN AND MARSHALL COLLEGE
PA–85 Shadek-Fackenthal Library
P. O. Box 3003
Lancaster PA 17604
(717) 291–4224
Kathleen Moretto Spencer, Director

1-GENERAL HOLDINGS

MINUTES/RECORDS/REPORTS: China Educational Commission, 1921–22.

MANUSCRIPTS: "From Six to Sixty to Six: A Narrative of the China Mission of the Reformed Church in the United States and the Later Evangelical and Reformed Church," by Arthur Vale Casselman, 1951.

SERIALS: *China Christian Year Book*, 1919, 1925–26.

CHINESE LANGUAGE MATERIALS: 2 Chinese-English dictionaries, chrestomathy, and grammar/conversation and phrase book, printed by Christian institutions.

LANCASTER THEOLOGICAL SEMINARY
PA–90 Philip Schaff Library
555 West James Street
Lancaster PA 17603
(717) 393–0654
Anne-Marie Salgat, Director of Library Services

Background note: Lancaster Theological Seminary is a seminary of the United Church of Christ, which formed when the Evangelical and Reformed Church and the General Council of the Congregational Christian Chruches merged in 1961. Before 1932, the Evangelical and Reformed Church had been known as the Reformed Church in the United States. The major collections of documents for these denominations are held by the Evangelical and Reformed Historical Society, Central Archives and Library, Schaff Library, 555 West James Street, Lancaster, PA 17603.

1-GENERAL HOLDINGS

MINUTES/RECORDS/REPORTS: Evangelical and Reformed Church, China mission, report, 1938–39.

MANUSCRIPTS: "From Six to Sixty to Six: A Narrative of the China Mission of the Reformed Church in the U.S. and the Later Evangelical and Reformed Church," by Arthur Vale Casselman, 1951.

PAMPHLETS: *Memoirs of China*, by Minerva S. Weil, 1956(?); *We Look at the China Mission of the Reformed Church in the United States*, by the Department of Missionary ducation, Board of Foreign Missions, 1932–33.

SERIALS: *Chinese Recorder*, 1903–14, 1917–20, 1922–41.

LATROBE

SAINT VINCENT ARCHABBEY AND COLLEGE
PA–95 Archives
Latrobe PA 15650
(412) 539–9761
Omer Kline, O.S.B., Archivist

Restrictions: Access by written request.
Background note: Saint Vincent Archabbey is the founding house of the American Cassinese Federation of the Benedictines. In 1925, American Benedictines founded the Catholic University of Peking, known popularly as Fu Jen Catholic University. It was transferred to the Society of the Divine Word in 1933, discontinued in 1949, and re-established in Taiwan in 1963. See also Newark Abbey, 528 Dr. Martin Luther King Boulevard, Newark, NJ, 07102.

1-THE CATHOLIC UNIVERSITY OF PEKING, CHINA COLLECTION, 1914–73, 9 boxes

MINUTES/RECORDS/REPORTS: Extract from a report to the Vatican on Catholic China Missions (in French), by Père Vincent Lebbe, n.d.; report of the University, n.d.; lists of American Catholic clergy in China and of faculty at the University, n.d.; Benedictine Abbey, Peking, n.d.; confidential Inspectors' Report on the University, to the Ministry of Education, 1927; miscellaneous notes and documents pertaining to the history of the University, to the Medical School, and to duties of University officials, n.d.; University constitution, n.d.; China (war) claims, 1973; reports on the China debt and its solution, n.d.; records of court trials involving the University and the Benedictines, n.d.

CORRESPONDENCE: Ca. 2 boxes of letters of Archabbot Aurelius Stehle, O.S.B., 1923–29, including correspondents Msgr. Stanislaus Jarlin, C.M., and Vincent Ying, K.S.G.; ca. 1 folder of letters of P. Valentine Köhler, O.S.B., n.d.; correspondence of Alfred Koch, O.S.B., 1931–33, including petitions to the pope and correspondence with Ildephonse Brandstetter, Amleto Cicognani, Francis Clougherty, Celso Constantini, Alcuin Deutsch, Gregory Feige, Fumasoni-Biondi, P. Gerhard, Columban Gross, Cardinal Hayes, Sylvester Healey, Ernest Helmstetter, Carl P. Hensler, Valentine Koehler, Cardinal Pacelli, Cardinal Seredi, Cardinal Spellman, Basil Stegmann, Samuel Stritch, and Louis B. Ward; ca. 3 boxes of miscellaneous letters, ca. 1917–33, including correspondents Pope Benedict XV, Ildephonse Brandstetter, Francis Clougherty, Alcuin Deutsch, Earl S. Dickens, Aidan Germain, Adalbert Gresnicht, Columban Gross, Placidus Houtmeyers, Dr. E. H. Ingram, Msgr. Stansislaus Jarlin, Theodore F. MacManus, Boniface Martin, Donald Murphy, H. H. Nu, Brendan O'Connor, Barry O'Toole, Leopold Probst, Placidus Rattenberger, Charles Rauth, Gregory Schramm, Callistus Stehle, Rt. Rev. Fidelis de Stotzingen, Magnus Straten, Bishop Tacconi, Antonius Teh'enn, Nicholas Tsu, William Cardinal Van Rossum, Hugh Wilt, and Vincent Ying, K.S.G.; folder of miscellaneous cablegrams, n.d.; box of letters pertaining to the history and needs of the University and the Benedictines, including fund-raising materials and letters of thanks, 1924–31.

MANUSCRIPTS: "Exhortation to Study," by Vincent Ying, K.S.G., 1917; "A Short History of the Catholic University of Peking," n.d.; "The Catholic University of Peking, China," by P. Hugh Wilt, O.S.B., 1930; history of Fu Jen [the University], by Hugh Wilt, O.S.B., n.d.; "Memoir," by Fr. Anthony Cotta to Cardinal Serafini, 1917; "Seen on the Streets of Peking," by Columban Gross, O.S.B., 1930.

MEMORABILIA: Résumé of endeavors by Archabbot Alfred Koch, O.S.B.; miscellaneous clippings and articles about the University, Benedictines in China and the United States, and other subjects, ca. 1914–1934.

MAPS/DESIGNS/DRAWINGS: Map of University property and other miscellaneous maps, n.d.

SERIALS: Catholic University of Peking, *Bulletin*, 1926–31. *Fu Jen Magazine*, 1932–35. *Fu Jen News Letter*, 1931. *Mission News*, 1933. *Peking Magazine*, 1931. *Peking News and Views of China*, 1931.

CHINESE LANGUAGE MATERIALS: 9 bulletins bearing the stamp "Ying Lien Tche, Directeur de l'Impartial, Tientsin, China": homilies, biography of Li Chih-tsao of the Ming Dynasty, writings of Adam Schall, *Messages from the Pope* calligraphed by Chen Hong, and an essay on John of Montecorvino in the Yuan Dynasty.

FINDING AIDS: "Peking University (China) VPK 32561 Collection."

LEWISBURG

BUCKNELL UNIVERSITY
PA-100 Ellen Clarke Bertrand Library
Lewisburg PA 17837
(717) 524-1493
George M. Jenks, Special Collections Librarian

1-CAROLINE BEEGLE DIARY, 1942, 1 volume
Background note: Caroline Beegle was a Presbyterian missionary nurse.
DIARIES: Diary by Beegle, recording her life and thoughts as a prisoner in a Japanese detention center and her experience of becoming "liberated" to board the ship *Gripsholm*, which carried repatriated prisoners to the United States, 1942.

2-GENERAL HOLDINGS
SERIALS: *China Christian Year Book*, 1926, 1928, 1931. *New East*, 1908–10, 1926–33. *News of China*, 1943–49.

MEADVILLE

ALLEGHENY COLLEGE
PA-105 Pelletier Library
North Main Street
Meadville PA 16355
(814) 724-3769
Stella K. Edwards, Special Collections

Restrictions: Access by appointment.

1-HARRIET LINN BEEBE LETTERS, 1885–1903, quantity undetermined
Background note: Harriet Linn Beebe (Mrs. Robert C. Beebe) graduated from Allegheny College in 1880.
CORRESPONDENCE: Letters written by Harriet Linn Beebe from Philander Smith Memorial Hospital in Nanking and other places in China, to her parents and relatives in the United States, 1885–1903.

2-GENERAL HOLDINGS
MINUTES/RECORDS/REPORTS: China Centennial Commission, Board of Foreign Missions of the Methodist Episcopal Church, 1907–8.

MYERSTOWN

EVANGELICAL CONGREGATIONAL CHURCH HISTORICAL SOCIETY
PA-110 Evangelical School of Theology Library-Historical Archives
Myerstown PA 17067
(717) 866-7581
Creighton Christman, Archivist

Restrictions: Access by appointment.
Background note: The Evangelical Congregational Church was organized by Jacob Albright in the early 19th century as the Evangelical Association. A division in 1891 resulted in the organization of the United Evangelical Church in 1894. There was an attempt to reunite in 1922, but a section of the United Evangelical Church remained apart, taking the name of Evangelical Congregational Church in 1928. The Evangelical Association merged with the United Brethren Church in 1946, forming the Evangelical United Brethren Church.

The first mission to China was opened in Hunan province by C. Newton Dubs in 1900. There were 65 missionaries in China in 1928 affiliated with the United Evangelical Church or the Evangelical Association, but by 1949, they had all returned to the United States. See also Church of the Brethren General Board, Brethren Historical Library and Archives, 1451 Dundee Avenue, Elgin, IL, 60120; and General Commission on Archives and History—The United Methodist Church, United Methodist Archives and History Center, Archives, 36 Madison Avenue, P. O. Box 127, Madison, NJ, 07940.

1-BISHOP W. F. HEIL PAPERS, 1890s–1920s, 20 folders
CORRESPONDENCE: Correspondence related to the denomination's mission in China, arranged alphabetically by the name of the writer.

NORTHAMPTON

MARY IMMACULATE SEMINARY
PA–115 Library
>
> Northampton PA 18067
> (215) 262–7866
> Kathleen Kokolus, Librarian

Background note: The Congregation of the Mission (now called "Vincentians" in the United States and "Lazaristes" in Europe) began as a religious community under Vincent de Paul in 1625. Its first missionaries entered China in 1699. The Vincentians have a sister religious community called the Daughters of Charity of St. Vincent de Paul. The Vincentian mission in China worked in the provinces of Hebei, Zhejiang, and Jiangxi. Additional documents are located at Daughters of Charity of St. Vincent de Paul, St. Joseph's Provincial House Archives, 333 South Seton Avenue, Emmitsburg, MD, 21727; Daughters of Charity of St. Vincent de Paul, De Paul Provincial House, 96 Menands Road, Albany, NY, 12204; and St. John's University, Grand Central and Utopia Parkways, Jamaica, NY, 11439.

1-GENERAL HOLDINGS
MINUTES/RECORDS/REPORTS/CORRESPONDENCE: Records, reports, and letters printed in *Annals of the Congregation of the Mission* in both English (1894–1925) and French (1835–1963) sets.
PAMPHLETS: *An Historical Survey of Our Province's Missions in China, Panama, and the Southern United States*, by St. Vincent de Paul Unit, 1950; *Life of Blessed Francis Regis Clet*, by G. Paillart, n.d.; *Sinarum beatificationis seu declarationis martyrii ven. servi Dei Francisci Clet*, 1899.
SERIALS: *Le Bulletin Catholique de Pekin*, 1927–35. *China Missionary*, 1949. *China Missionary Bulletin*, 1950–53. *Les Missions de Chine*, 1942.
FINDING AIDS: In-house schedules

OVERBROOK

AMERICAN CATHOLIC HISTORICAL SOCIETY
PA–120 Archives and Historical Collection
>
> Saint Charles Seminary
> Ryan Memorial Library
> Overbrook PA 19151
> (215) 839–3760 Ext. 283
> Joseph J. Casino, Archivist

1-GENERAL HOLDINGS
MINUTES/RECORDS/REPORTS/PAMPHLETS: 2 pamphlets about the Association of the Holy Childhood, including descriptions of infanticide in China and the association's progress, 1843, 1860; pamphlet appealing for funds for the Catholic University of Peking, by the Benedictines' Station O.S.B. Broadcasting, Pittsburgh, 1925; pamphlet containing a short history of the Catholic University of Peking, with congratulatory letters, n.d.; pamphlet describing plans for the first Maryknoll seminary in China, in Kongmoon, 1925.
CORRESPONDENCE: Letter from Joseph A. Skelly of German-town, Pennsylvania to the subscribers to the magazine *The Miraculous Medal*, explaining how subscriptions to the magazine help missionary work in China, n.d.
SERIALS: Catholic University of Peking, *Bulletin*, 1927–28.

PARADISE

PA–125 AMBASSADORS FOR CHRIST, INC.
>
> P. O. Box AFC
> Paradise PA 17562
> (717) 687–8564
> David Chow, Director
> James Brubaker, Administrator

1-LEAMAN FAMILY AND CHRISTIANA TSAI PAPERS, ca. 1870–1985, 10 boxes
Background note: This collection is extensive but incompletely processed. In 1874, Charles Leaman went to Nanking as a missionary unattached to a mission board, supported by his family. He married fellow missionary Lucy Crouch, and they had two daughters, Mary A. and Lucy A. Leaman. The Leaman family worked for some time under the auspices of the American Presbyterian Mission. Together, Mary and Lucy founded and directed a Presbyterian school for girls in Nanking. One of their students, who took the name Christiana Tsai, later became a colleague in the work of the school and in Mary's lifelong work on a phonetic Chinese Bible. Despite suffering from cerebral malaria and being confined to a darkened room from 1931 until her death in 1984, Christiana Tsai conducted evangelistic services in her room and carried on other forms of mission work in China and, after 1949, in the United States.
MINUTES/RECORDS/REPORTS: Folder marked "Tsai Papers—Mission Reports, 1924–54," containing: American Consulate Intelligence Committee, 1924; China Bible Seminary, 1940; China Missions Phonetics Committee, Shanghai, minutes, 1946; Colportage Association of China, 1928; Presbyterian Church in the U.S.A., Board of Foreign Missions, China Mission, reports, 1932, 1941–43, 1954; Nanking Station, reports, 1929–30, 1934–35. [See also CORRESPONDENCE/MEMORABILIA.]
CORRESPONDENCE/MANUSCRIPTS/MEMORABILIA: Correspondence from Charles Leaman while in school at Princeton University, ca. 1870, and from Charles and his wife, Lucy, in Nanking; 3 diplomas from the Presbyterian School for Girls at Nanking, including 1 signed by Lucy and Mary A. Leaman, 1909; 40 letters from Christiana Tsai and/or Mary A. Leaman, in Nanking, to Henry Leaman, Mary W. Leaman (cousin of Mary A. and Lucy), and Lucy A. Leaman in Pennsylvania, together with Chinese postcards and unused stationery engraved with scenes of China, 1923–24; box of correspondence from Tsai in Nanking; 3 folders marked "Tsai and Leaman Papers, ca. 1910–1949," containing: 3 of Mary's report cards and the 1913 commencement program from Mary Baldwin Seminary, the last will and testament of Mary A. Leaman, 2 expense books from the Leaman sisters' work in China, hand-drawn Chinese phonetic charts, a typewritten autobiographical manuscript, "Christiana's Three Talks," and letters/reports of the Leaman sisters and Tsai concerning the girls' school, the Chinese Phonetic Bible Project, and other aspects of the work in China, especially to and from family in Pennsylvania; 2 folders marked "Tsai Papers—Others in China, 1932–57," con-

taining occasional correspondence and reports of Paul H. Bartel, Ruth M. Brittain, Richard P. Butrick, J. Calvitt Clarke, Ellen Dresser, Ellen Drummond, Jane A. Hyde, Kathryn S. Judd, Florence L. Logan, Leslie and Kathryn Lyall, Hattie R. Mac-Curdy, James and Awrie Montgomery, Miriam E. Null, F. Frank Price, Helen G. Struthers, George Sutherland, Leland Wang, Grace Wells, Lillian C. Wells, and Marion Wilcox, and 3 reports of trips to China made by W. J. Drummond in 1927 (Nanking), 1932, and 1935; 3 boxes of correspondence, clippings, and other materials, including letters about Tsai's family and friends remaining in China, 1949-ca. 1984; notebook of reviews of *Queen of the Dark Chamber*, ca. 1953-1956; 2 folders of letters to and from Tsai, mostly regarding distribution of her book, 1953-74; 3 folders marked "Christiana Tsai Papers, 1949-85," containing: a few letters to and from Mary A. Leaman, clippings about Tsai, messages and brief autobiographical sketches by her, and her correspondence, especially regarding the Chinese Phonetic Bible project, her book (including several letters from former China missionaries such as Frank Childs, Mrs. Charles Gibbs, Viola C. Hill, Mrs. Charles Lewis, Jenny Lind, and Catharine T. Woods), and evangelistic work conducted in her home (among seamen, Chinese students, and Chinese dignitaries).

MANUSCRIPTS/PAMPHLETS: Box of teaching aids, including copies of a teaching manual for use in West China with *Szechwan Phonetic Primer and Chart* (1944), ca. 1945; ca. 20 copies of "How Great is Thy Goodness," by Christiana Tsai, n.d.; miscellaneous tracts in English and Chinese; 3 small boxes of manuscript material from *Queen of the Dark Chamber*, by Christiana Tsai, ca. 1950-1953.

AUDIO-VISUAL MATERIALS: 4 boxes of photos depicting the work of the Leaman sisters and Tsai in Nanking, and their later life in the United States, ca. 1928-1970(?).

SERIALS: *Chinese Recorder*, 1925.

CHINESE LANGUAGE MATERIALS: Box of miscellaneous tracts, hymnals, and periodicals, including *Companion*, 1952-53, and *The Bible Magazine*, 1948, 1952-53; 2 folders of tracts, pamphlets, letters, and reports; folder of letters in romanized Chinese, 1907-9.

PENNSBURG

PA-130 SCHWENKFELDER LIBRARY
Seminary Avenue
Pennsburg PA 18073
(215) 679-3103
Claire E. Conway, Librarian

Background note: The Schwenkfelder Church of the United States of America established a mission in Tai Ku, Shansi, in 1882. Its missionaries were killed in the Boxer Uprising of 1900. The mission was re-established in 1904 by Flora K. Heebner. She was later joined by Daisy (Gehman) Fairfield and Gladys Williams, whose parents had been killed by the Boxers.

1-GENERAL HOLDINGS
MINUTES/RECORDS/REPORTS: 2 l.f. of records and correspondence of the Schwenkfelder Church's American Board of Home and Foreign Missions, including the Tai Ku Mission, 1904-47; articles and letters about the work of missionaries at Tai Ku in *The Schwenckfeldian*, 1904-47.

CORRESPONDENCE / MEMORABILIA / DIARIES / PAMPHLETS: 3 boxes of letters from Flora K. Heebner to her mother, 1904-34; letters of Gladys Williams and Mabel Reiff, 1947; Nettie M. Senger letters, 1935-45; box of miscellaneous letters, diaries, and pamphlets, including letters and diaries of Daisy Gehman, Mabel Reiff, and Gladys Williams; box of miscellaneous pamphlets from and about the mission at Tai Ku; miscellaneous pamphlets mixed in with above boxes of correspondence.

AUDIO-VISUAL MATERIALS: 60 black and white glass slides, some hand-colored, of the mission work in Tai Ku.

PHILADELPHIA

THE ACADEMY OF NATURAL SCIENCES OF PHILADELPHIA
PA-135 Library
19th and the Parkway
Logan Square
Philadelphia PA 19103
(215) 299-1093
Carol Spawn, Manuscript/Archives Librarian

Finding aids: *Guide to the Manuscript Collections of the Academy of Natural Sciences of Philadelphia*, by Vania T. Phillips (Philadelphia, 1963).

1-WILLIAM WARDER CADBURY PAPERS (MS coll. 732), 1892-1952, 65 items
Background note: William Warder Cadbury (1877-1959) was a Philadelphia Quaker who spent his professional life as a medical missionary in Canton. His second wife, Catharine Balderston Jones, was the sister of Rufus Jones, who co-founded the American Friends Service Committee with Cadbury's brother, Henry Cadbury. In 1898 William Cadbury graduated from Haverford College. After his medical studies, he left for Canton in 1909 to begin his missionary career, supported by members of the Society of Friends in Philadelphia. He became an instructor in materia medica and therapeutics at the University Medical School in Canton, which was sponsored by the Christian Association of the University of Pennsylvania. When this school moved to Shanghai in 1914, he continued teaching at the Hackett Medical College for Women in Canton. He soon joined two other missionary organizations, becoming chief of internal medicine at Canton Hospital and physician to Canton Christian College, which later became Lingnan University. Dr. Cadbury was made the first chief of staff there and remained chief of internal medicine throughout his service in China. In 1930, when the hospital and Hackett Medical College were united with Lingnan University under Chinese direction, Dr. Cadbury was appointed Superintendent of the Hospital. In 1935, he and his niece, the Quaker author Mary Hoxie Jones, published a centennial history of Canton Hospital. During the Japanese occupation, Cadbury continued to live in his home on the Lingnan campus, studying plants and orchids until 1943 when he was moved to an internment camp. He was repatriated in 1943 on the *Gripsholm*.

MANUSCRIPTS: "The Glory of Spring Time, Lingnan University," "A Walk on Christmas Day in My Lingnan University, Canton, China," "The Orchids of Kwangtung, South China," and "Recollections of My Orchid Garden in Canton, China," by Cadbury, n.d.; 23 pages of notes of addresses by Cadbury, n.d.; typed carbon copy of 5-volume *History of European Botanical Discoveries in China*, by E. Bretschneider, 1898; list of plants growing on the Lingnan University campus and in the vicinity, 1947; mimeo articles on trees, shrubs and vines of Lingnan University and of Shanghai, n.d.; 60 pages of data on ferns of Kwangtung, Kwangsi, and Hong Kong.

MEMORABILIA: "William W. Cadbury, M.D., Quaker Missionary and Orchidologist in China," in *Frontiers* (annual of the Academy), 1980; notebook on trees, flowers, flowering plants and ferns, with English, Latin, and Chinese names, with descriptions; notebook on weeds and roadside plants of South China, 1948.

MAPS/DESIGNS/DRAWINGS/CHINESE LANGUAGE MATERIALS: Large map of Lingnan University and surrounding area, showing location of different plants collected by Cadbury, in Chinese, n.d.; large map of Cadbury's garden on the Lingnan University campus, marking location of various trees and plants, n.d.

2-MARION HERBERT DUNCAN PAPERS (MS coll. 64B), 1933–67, 78 items

Background note: Marion Herbert Duncan (b. 1896) went to Tibet in 1921 and remained in Batang with the Tibetan Christian mission of the Church of Christ. The mission closed in 1932 after the battle of Batang and he returned to the United States the following year. The following material relates to his second trip to China as part of Brooke Dolan's expedition beginning in 1935.

CORRESPONDENCE/MANUSCRIPTS: Correspondence with Brooke Dolan II, the Academy, and Ernst Schaefer, and related papers concerning Duncan's participation in the Dolan Expedition to West China and Tibet, 1934–36.

3-ADELE MARION FIELDE PAPERS (MS coll. 341), 1884–1916, 59 items

Background note: Adele Marion Fielde (1839–1916) was a Baptist missionary and naturalist who served in Swatow. She studied biology at the Academy of Natural Sciences, where she met Edward J. Nolan, librarian of the Academy. Her chief works were on entomology, in particular on the senses, activities, and behavior of ants. The materials below date mostly from her second trip to China, 1885 to 1892.

CORRESPONDENCE: Correspondence with E. J. Nolan, from China.

MEMORABILIA: Obituary in *Entomological News*, 1916.

AUDIO-VISUAL MATERIALS: 3 photoportraits of Fielde in MS Coll. 457.

4-GENERAL HOLDINGS

SERIALS: *Chinese Repository*, 1836–38, 1844–48. *Lingnan Science Journal*, 1922–50. Lingnan University: *Science Bulletin*, 1930, 1934–35; Lingnan Natural History Survey and Museum, *Special Publication*, 1942–50. Natural History Society, *Proceedings*, 1928–30. *Peking Natural History Bulletin*, 1926–41. West China Border Research Society, *Journal*, 1923–46. Yenching University, Department of Biology, *Bulletin*, 1930.

AMERICAN FRIENDS SERVICE COMMITTEE
PA–140 Archives

    1501 Cherry Street
    Philadelphia PA 19102
    (215) 241–7044
    Jack Sutters, Archivist

Background note: The American Friends Service Committee (AFSC), a Quaker organization involved in peace, social justice, and humanitarian service, had contact with missionaries when it forwarded money for disaster relief in the 1920s and 1930s. British Friends had formed ambulance units in Europe and other fighting zones in 1939. In 1941 a Friends Ambulance Unit representative asked the AFSC to provide personnel and financial assistance to the China effort about to be undertaken. A small number of American personnel were sent to assist in this service. Also at this time, the United China Relief (UCR) was formed, and the AFSC was invited to participate. The United China Relief became one of the chief sources of funding for the Friends Ambulance Unit. Following the conclusion of World War II, larger numbers of young Americans were sent by the AFSC to join the China work. In 1946, since the Friends Ambulance Unit service was being terminated with the end of the war, the AFSC took over administration of the mixed group of nationalities, and the program was renamed the Friends Relief Service (FRS). At this time, the FRS undertook to work on both sides of the lines during the Civil War. Additional documents relating to the Religious Societies of Friends are located at Haverford College, James P. Magill Library, Haverford, PA, 19041; and at Swarthmore College, Friends Historical Library, Swarthmore, PA, 19081.

1-FILES, FOREIGN SERVICE: CHINA, 1922–52, quantity undetermined

MINUTES/RECORDS/REPORTS: Reports of war-time activity of the Friends Ambulance Unit, Friends Relief Service, and the United China Relief; reports of Friends who served as missionaries or who were in China in relation to their work, 1922–52.

CORRESPONDENCE: Several letters from Arnold Vaught, an American Friend appointed by British Friends as a missionary in China, to Clarence Pickett, executive secretary of the American Friends Service Committee, 1930s and early 1940s.

AUDIO-VISUAL MATERIALS: Several hundred photos pertaining to the Friends' work in China, dated mostly in the 1940s.

SERIALS: American Friends Service Committee, *Bulletin on Work in China*, 1942–44.

AMERICAN PHILOSOPHICAL SOCIETY
PA–145 Library

    105 South Fifth Street
    Philadelphia PA 19106
    (215) 627–0706
    Beth Carroll-Horrocks, Manuscripts Librarian
    Roy E. Goodman, Reference Librarian

1-SIMON FLEXNER PAPERS, 1914–22, 12 files

Background note: Simon Flexner was a trustee of the China Medical Board, and his papers include one section on that organization. The China Medical Board, predecessor of the China Medical Board, Inc., was a division of the Rockefeller Foundation until 1928, when it was incorporated as a separate entity. The China Medical Board, Inc., was the organization through which the Rockefeller Foundation undertook a comprehensive plan for the improvement of medical and hospital care in China. The China Medical Board, Inc. made grants to missionary societies to advance their own medical facilities, universities, and hospitals. See also the Rockefeller University, Rockefeller Archive Center,

Manuscript Collections, Pocantico Hills, North Tarrytown, NY, 10591-1598.

MINUTES/RECORDS/REPORTS: China Medical Board: annual report, including history and administration, 1918-19; proposed fellowships for nurses and para-medical staff at missionary hospitals, and aid to Chinese institutions, 1915; report on proposed establishment of medical school at Shanghai; 2 preliminary reports on the plans for and building of Peking Union Medical College (PUMC); election of trustees Wallace Buttrick, Simon Flexner, Frederick T. Gates, Jerome Greene, John D. Rockefeller, William H. Welch, and one representative of each missionary society; curricula vitae of physicians and nurses at PUMC, 1914; PUMC budgets, 1914, 1920-21; recommendation for a preparatory school for PUMC, 1917; report to trustees of Rockefeller Foundation, 1921-22; minutes of Rockefeller Foundation Executive Committee meetings; report of 1915 Special Commission to China on medical education in China, 1920; report on medical education in northern China, by William Welch, 1915; report on medical education in Hankow and Changsha, by Frederick Gates, 1915; report on medical education in southern China, by Simon Flexner, 1915; report on medical education of Chinese women, by Simon Flexner, n.d.

CORRESPONDENCE: Letters from Simon Flexner from Peking, 1915.

MAPS/DESIGNS/DRAWINGS: Blueprint of PUMC and surrounding properties.

FINDING AIDS: *A Guide to Selected Files of the Professional Papers of Simon Flexner at the American Philosophical Society Library*, by Margaret Miller, 1979.

2-BASILE DE GLEMONA COLLECTION, 18th century, 1 volume
Background note: Basile de Glemona was an Italian missionary and Chinese scholar.

MANUSCRIPTS/CHINESE LANGUAGE MATERIALS: "Dictionarium linguae Sinensis" (in Chinese and French), by Basile de Glemona, 18th century.

3-VICTOR GEORGE HEISER PAPERS, 1894-1966, quantity undetermined
Background note: Victor George Heiser (1873-1972) was a physician who worked in Asia and the Philippines and created an international awareness of public health realities and needs.

MINUTES/RECORDS/REPORTS/CORRESPONDENCE: Material on the China Medical Board (see Simon Flexner Papers above) and public health in China.

FINDING AIDS: In-house inventory.

4-EUGENE LINDSAY OPIE PAPERS, ca. 1919-1950, quantity undetermined
Background note: Eugene Lindsay Opie (1873-1971) was a pathologist with a deep interest in China and Chinese medicine.

MINUTES/RECORDS/REPORTS/CORRESPONDENCE: Material relating to United China Relief, the American Bureau for Medical Aid to China, the International Health Division of the Rockefeller Foundation, the Rockefeller Institute, and Chinese medicine.

FINDING AIDS: In-house finding aid.

5-OSWALD HOPE ROBERTSON PAPERS, 1918-68, 1 folder
Background note: Oswald Hope Robertson (1886-1966) was a physician and educator.

MINUTES/RECORDS/REPORTS/CORRESPONDENCE/ MEMORABILIA: Papers relating to Peking Union Medical College (PUMC), 1918-68.

MAPS/DESIGNS/DRAWINGS: Map of Peking marking the location of various missions and PUMC, 1920s.

FINDING AIDS: In-house finding aid.

6-GENERAL HOLDINGS
PAMPHLETS: 2 letters on the Chinese system of writing, by Karl Friedrich August Gützlaff, reprinted from *Transactions of the American Philosophical Society*, 1840.

SERIALS: *Chinese Recorder and Missionary Journal*, 1870. *Chinese Repository*, 1832-34. *El Correo Sino-Annamita ó Correspondencia de las Misiones del Sagrado Orden de Predicatores en Formosa, China, Tung King y Filipinas*, 1891, 1912.

CHINESE LANGUAGE MATERIALS/SERIALS: *Chinese Magazine*, 1837-39.

CHINESE LANGUAGE MATERIALS: Gospel and Epistles of John in Japanese (with Chinese title), a New Testament, missionary tracts, periodicals, and a Chinese almanac; Chinese texts of the writings of Karl Gützlaff, on Jesus Christ; topography, history, customs, etc. of the Chinese; eternal life; history of England; history of the Jews; right and wrong; commerce; Chinese writing; universal history; and turning misery to happiness, 1803-51.

BIBLE PRESBYTERIAN CHURCH
PA-150 Independent Board of Presbyterian Foreign Missions Archives
246 West Walnut Lane
Philadelphia PA 19144
(215) 438-0511
Earle R. White, General Secretary

Restrictions: Access by appointment.
Background note: The Independent Board of Presbyterian Foreign Missions was formed in 1933 by Presbyterian missionaries dissatisfied with theological currents in the Presbyterian Church in the U.S.A. Some early members of the Independent Board, such as Egbert W. Andrews and Richard B. and Polly Gaffin, soon left and joined the fledgling Presbyterian Church of America (later called the Orthodox Presbyterian Church). The Independent Board continued to function and became the foreign mission arm of the Bible Presbyterian Church, which carried on its China mission principally in eastern Shantung and Shanghai.

One of the leaders of the Independent Board in China was Albert Baldwin Dodd (1877-1972), who had been a Presbyterian Church in the U.S.A. missionary for 32 years starting in 1903. He served the Independent Board from 1935 to 1942 and from 1946 to 1948 in Shantung, and from 1955 to 1960 in Taiwan. Before joining the Independent Board, Dodd had helped found North China Theological Seminary in 1919, where his wife, Mabel Beatrice (Mennie) Dodd, served as dean of women. For other documents concerning some of the people mentioned below, see Orthodox Presbyterian Church, Committee on Foreign Missions, Archives, 7401 Old York Road, Philadelphia, PA, 19126.

1-GENERAL HOLDINGS
MINUTES/RECORDS/REPORTS/CORRESPONDENCE: Ca. 100 reports, letters, and articles, published in *The Independent Board Bulletin* (after 1944, continued as *Biblical Missions*), 1935-

51, by Independent Board missionaries Henry and Betty Coray, Richard and Polly Gaffin, Egbert Andrews, Ruth Brack, Albert and Mabel Dodd, and William McIlwaine, concerning the history of Presbyterian missions in China, reasons for joining the Independent Board, evangelistic and relief work in China, conditions during warfare, Shantung Theological Seminary, and attitudes toward other Christian groups there, especially other Presbyterian missions and the China Inland Mission.

MANUSCRIPTS/MEMORABILIA: "Biblical Missions—China," a folder containing articles from *The Independent Board Bulletin* (*Biblical Missions*) by and about Albert and Mabel Dodd, Henry Coray, Donald and Louise H. (Reicke) Hunter, and Mr. and Mrs. John M. L. Young, and "Albert B. Dodd: Highlights from the Life of a Missionary Warrior," by Maurine Gordon, for the Foreign Missions Committee of the Women's Synodical of the Bible Presbyterian Church, 1977.

AUDIO-VISUAL MATERIALS: Miscellaneous photos used for publication in *The Independent Board Bulletin.*

COLLEGE OF PHYSICIANS OF PHILADELPHIA
PA–155 Library

19 South Twenty-second Street
Philadelphia PA 19103
(215) 561–6050
Andrea Kenyon, Head of Reference Services
Tom Horrocks, Curator, Historical Collections

Background note: Canton Hospital, founded in 1835 by Peter Parker as an ophthalmic hospital, was the first medical missionary hospital in China. Owned by the Medical Missionary Society, it was staffed by physicians from the American Presbyterian mission beginning in 1855. Both the hospital and the society became related to Canton Christian College, founded by the Presbyterians in 1886, and known as Lingnan University to the Chinese. In 1926, the college officially changed its name to Lingnan University, now known as Zhongshan University. South China Medical College, started in 1862 by the Presbyterians, was connected to both Canton Christian College and Canton Hospital.

1-GENERAL HOLDINGS

MINUTES/RECORDS/REPORTS: Bound reports: Canton Hospital, 1876–78; Medical Missionary Society in China, Canton, reports, 1845–47, 1858–75, 1879–80; minutes of annual meetings, 1850–51, 1854–56; and report by John Graham Kerr, 1855–56; bound reports: Canton Hospital, 1836, 1838, 1845; Medical Missionary Society in China, 1838, 1841–42, 1845; the Medical Missionary Society's (Ophthalmic) Hospital, Macao, 1827–32, 1838, 1841–42; China-Medico-Chirurgical Society, 1845–46; Canton International Red Cross Executive Committee, 1938–39.

Miscellaneous reports: American Presbyterian Mission, Canton, 1890; Canton Hospital, 1908–9, 1924–41; Canton Hospital, Canton Medical Missionary Society, and Canton Medical Missionary Union, 1917–19; Canton Medical College for Women, catalogue, 1910–11; Canton Ophthalmic Hospital, reports by Peter Parker, 1845–47; China Medical Association, list of members, 1929; China Medical Board, Rockefeller Foundation, 1914–17, together with Peking Union Medical College, 1914–51; China Medical Missionary Association, constitution, 1924; Hospital for Chinese at the American Episcopal Mission, Shanghai, 1882–86;

Ling Naam Hospital and Canton Christian College, 1925; Lingnan University, College of Medicine, report, 1928–30; Lingnan University, Medical Department, Hospital, and Infirmary, 1928–30; Lingnan University, Sun Yat-sen Medical College, n.d.; Medical Missionary Society in China, reports, minutes, and addresses, 1838, 1841, 1843, 1845, 1860, 1882, 1885–86, 1889–93, 1895; Ophthalmic Hospital, Macao, 1827–32; Peiping Union Medical College, 1918–23; annual report, 1908–9, 1921–28; Department of Pathology, 1928–29; dedication ceremonies and medical conference, 1921; director's report, 1916–17, 1926–27; program, medical conference, 1921; Rockefeller Foundation, China Medical Commission, 1914; Saint Luke's Hospital for Chinese, Shanghai, 1919, 1930–36; Shantung Christian University, School of Medicine, Tsinan, prospectus for 1910(?); annual report, 1918–19; Shaohsing Christian Hospital, 1909, 1914–16, 1919–20, 1923–25, 1928; T'ai-yüen Fu medical mission, Shansi, 1884–86.

PAMPHLETS: *An Additional Fragment of Medical Work in China*, by Mary H. Fulton, 1889; *Canton Committee for Justice*, 1937; *For Shantung and for China*, by Shantung Christian University, 1920; *A Fragment of Medical Work in China*, by Mary H. Fulton, 1888; *Medical Missionaries in Relation to the Medical Profession*, by John Graham Kerr, 1890; *Medicine in China*, 1914; *Plague in the Orient with Special Reference to the Manchurian Outbreaks*, by Wu Lien-têh, 1921; *Some Introductory Lectures on General Histology*, by Cornelius Ubbo Ariëns Kappers, 1923.

SERIALS: *China Medical Journal*, 1909–31. *China Medical Missionary Journal*, 1887–98, 1900–1908. *China's Medicine*, 1966–68. *Chinese Medical Directory*, 1932. *Chinese Medical Journal*, 1932–66, 1973-; Chengtu ed., 1945.

CHINESE LANGUAGE MATERIALS: Canton Hospital, reports, 1864, 1867, 1869, 1886, 1891; translations of 6 standard medical reference books and textbooks.

EASTERN BAPTIST THEOLOGICAL SEMINARY
PA–160 Austin K. DeBlois Library

City Line and Lancaster Avenue
Philadelphia PA 19151
(215) 896–5000
Thomas Gilbert, Director
R. David Koch, Associate Librarian for Technical Services

1-GENERAL HOLDINGS

SERIALS: *China Christian Year Book*, 1913, 1916. *China Notes*, 1967-. *East Asia Millions* (Philadelphia), 1965-.

PA–165 FREE LIBRARY OF PHILADELPHIA

Logan Square
Philadelphia PA 19103
(215) 686–5322
Keith Doms, Director

1-GENERAL HOLDINGS

PAMPHLETS: *Institutions Connected with the American Church Mission in China*, by G. F. Mosher, 1914; *Windows into China: The Jesuits and Their Books, 1580–1730*, by John Parker, 1978. SERIALS: *China Christian Year Book*, 1910, 1913–17, 1923–25, 1928–39. *China Monthly*, 1939–50. *Directory of Protestant Missions in China*, 1916.

PA-170 HISTORICAL SOCIETY OF PENNSYLVANIA

1300 Locust Street
Philadelphia PA 19107
(215) 732-6200
Theresa Snyder, Director

Restrictions: Restricted to graduate and post-graduate researchers.
Finding aids: *Guide to the Manuscript Collections of the Historical Society of Pennsylvania*, 2nd ed., 1949.

1-GRATZ COLLECTION, 1830-44, 3 items
CORRESPONDENCE: Letter from David Abeel to I. Matthews about his work in China and Siam, from Canton, 1830; letter from James Legge to Samuel H. Cox, regarding political and religious life in China, from Malacca, 1842; letter from Samuel Wells Williams to Benjamin Selmian on the need for Anglo-Chinese school books and medical missionaries, 1844.

2-GENERAL HOLDINGS
CORRESPONDENCE: Letter from Pearl Buck to Harrold E. Gillingham, urging him to contribute to China Relief efforts, New York, 1941.

PA-175 LIBRARY COMPANY OF PHILADELPHIA

1314 Locust Street
Philadelphia PA 19107-5698
(215) 546-3181
John C. Van Horne, Librarian
Fred Lapsansky, Head of Reference
James Green, Curator of Rare Books

Background note: Most of the books about China in the Library Company's holdings were acquired during the height of American trade with China during the late eighteenth and nineteenth centuries. A large number of reprints of English works on China were printed by Philadelphian publishers; many of these can be found in the Library Company's holdings. A significant portion of these books are accounts of the establishment and development of Christianity in China.
Finding aids: *China on Our Shelves: An Exhibition of Books about China Acquired by the Library Company of Philadelphia Mostly before and during the Heyday of the American China Trade, 1784-1840* (Philadelphia: The Library Company of Philadelphia), 1984.

1-GENERAL HOLDINGS
PAMPHLETS: *The Medical Missionary Society in China, Address, with Minutes and Proceedings*, by Thomas R. Colledge, 1838.
MAPS/DESIGNS/DRAWINGS: Atlas to *A Description of the Empire of China* by Jean Baptiste du Halde, London, 1738-41; *Novvs atlas sinensis*, by Martino Martini (Amsterdam: Apud Joannem Blaeu), 1659.
SERIALS: *China's Millions* (London), 1876-?. *Chinese Repository*, 1832-51.
CHINESE LANGUAGE MATERIALS: Old Testament, Genesis to Ruth, 1854; children's bible picture book in Foochow dialect, 1873.

LUTHERAN THEOLOGICAL SEMINARY
PA-180 Krauth Memorial Library

7301 Germantown Avenue
Philadelphia PA 19119
(215) 248-4616
David J. Wartluft, Director
John E. Peterson, Curator

Background note: The former United Lutheran Church in America began mission work in China about 1925 when it took over the work of the Berlin Society. The Swedish Lutheran Church (Augustana Synod) was also involved in the China mission. The Norwegian Lutherans in America were the most active Lutherans in China.

1-GENERAL HOLDINGS
MINUTES/RECORDS/REPORTS: Christian Literature Society for China, annual reports, 1910-16; Evangelical Lutheran Augustana Synod of North America, China mission field report, Hunan, n.d.; Lutheran World Convention, American Section, Chungking report, by Daniel Nelson, 1946.
PAMPHLETS: *Addresses on China*, by the Foreign Missions Conference of North America, 1927; *Christian Missions in China*, 1927; *Missionary Situation in China: An Address Delivered at the Foreign Missions Conference of North America*, by H. T. Hodgkin, 1928.
SERIALS: *China Christian Year Book*, 1928-29, 1931-39. *China Mission Year Book*, 1912-14, 1924-26. *Chinese Recorder*, 1874, 1927-32. *Lutheran Literature Society for China Bulletin*, 1968-.
CHINESE LANGUAGE MATERIALS: Bilingual edition of *China Has a Ten-Thousand-Mile Spiritual Wall*, by Shau Yan Lee, 1946.

MEDICAL COLLEGE OF PENNSYLVANIA AND HOSPITAL
PA-185 Archives and Special Collections on Women in Medicine

3300 Henry Avenue
Philadelphia PA 19129
(215) 842-7124
Sandra L. Chaff, Director of Archives and Special Collections on Women in Medicine

Background note: The Woman's Medical College of Pennsylvania (which became The Medical College of Pennsylvania and Hospital in 1970) educated many women physicians who served as missionaries abroad, especially in China and India. The first graduate to go to China, Lucinda L. (Strittmater) Coombs, left the United States in 1873.
Finding aids: *Women in Medicine: A Bibliography of the Literature on Women Physicians*, ed. by Sandra L. Chaff (Metuchen, NJ: Scarecrow Press), n.d.

1-AMERICAN MEDICAL WOMEN'S ASSOCIATION COLLECTION, n.d., 1.5 l.f.
CORRESPONDENCE/MANUSCRIPTS/PAMPHLETS: Uncatalogued materials regarding schools and hospitals in China.

2-AMERICAN WOMEN'S HOSPITAL SERVICE COLLECTION, 1938-41, 50 items
CORRESPONDENCE: 50 letters relating to American Women's Hospital Service activities in China, 1938-41.

3-MEDICAL COLLEGE OF PENNSYLVANIA ARCHIVES COLLECTION, n.d., 5.5 l.f.
CORRESPONDENCE/MANUSCRIPTS/PAMPHLETS: Missionary alumnae folders of correspondence, news clippings, brochures, reprints, and pamphlets; annual announcements containing student information offering scholarships to women aspiring to missionary work; transactions of the Alumnae Association, many of which contain reports from women physicians in missionary service; student lists of alumnae missionaries working in China.
MEMORABILIA: Items collected by alumnae who travelled in China in the late 19th century.

4-MISSIONARIES COLLECTION, n.d., 1.5 l.f.
CORRESPONDENCE/MANUSCRIPTS/PAMPHLETS: Correspondence and lists of missionary alumnae; pamphlets, catalogues, and reprints about hospitals and schools in China.

5-PHOTO COLLECTION, n.d., ca. 150 items
AUDIO-VISUAL MATERIALS: Ca. 150 photos of alumnae of the Medical College of Pennsylvania, and of organizations and buildings related to missionary activities in China; clinical photos of patients' maladies, including foot-binding.

6-BERTHA EUGENIA LOVELAND SELMON COLLECTION, n.d., .5 l.f.
CORRESPONDENCE/MANUSCRIPTS/PAMPHLETS: Materials regarding Bertha Selmon's 21 years as a medical missionary in Shanghai.

ORTHODOX PRESBYTERIAN CHURCH
PA-190 Committee on Foreign Missions Archives
  7401 Old York Road
  Philadelphia PA 19126
  (215) 635-0700
  Donald G. Buchanan, Jr., General Secretary

Restrictions: Access by appointment.
Background note: The Orthodox Presbyterian Church (OPC) was formed in 1936, as the Presbyterian Church of America, by ministers of the Presbyterian Church in the U.S.A. who perceived serious doctrinal error in that denomination. The name was changed to the Orthodox Presbyterian Church in 1939. The denomination appointed its first missionaries in 1937, some of whom were drawn from the Independent Board of Presbyterian Foreign Missions that had formed several years earlier and still exists today (see also Bible Presbyterian Church, Independent Board of Presbyterian Foreign Missions, Archives, 246 West Walnut Lane, Philadelphia, PA, 19144).

The material in this collection is particularly concerned with relations between OPC missionaries and those of other mission groups, including the China Inland Mission, China Inter-Varsity Fellowship, various theological seminaries, and the missions of other Presbyterian denominations.

1-EGBERT W. ANDREWS PAPERS, 1937-50, 4 in.
Background note: Egbert W. Andrews was an OPC missionary in Harbin, Manchoukuo (Manchuria), from 1937 to 1945, in Shanghai from 1945 to 1948, and then in Taiwan. In Shanghai he also served as district secretary of China Inter-Varsity Fellowship.
MINUTES/RECORDS/REPORTS: "An Open Door in Manchoukuo," annual report of the OPC missionaries in Harbin, 1939-40; North China Theological Seminary Home Council, minutes, 1942.
CORRESPONDENCE: Financial records, reports, telegrams, and correspondence of Egbert Andrews, including letters to and from OPC mission executives Robert S. Marsden and John P. Galbraith, on subjects such as relations with other missions and the work of North China Theological Seminary, 1937-50.
MEMORABILIA: Miscellaneous clippings about Andrews, ca. 1940-50.

2-CHINA COLLECTION, ca. 1944-1946, 1 folder
MINUTES/RECORDS/REPORTS: Memorandum on the opening of East China Theological Seminary, Soochow, by the Spiritual Bread World Evangelistic Society, n.d.
CORRESPONDENCE: Letter from T. F. Tsiang, director general of the Chinese National Relief and Rehabilitation Administration, to Robert T. Henry, director of the American Advisory Committee, Chungking, 1945; letter from David H. Adeney in Nanking to Robert S. Marsden, concerning the work of China Inter-Varsity Fellowship, 1946.
MANUSCRIPTS: "A Preliminary Survey of the Possible Fields of Labor for the China Mission of the Orthodox Presbyterian Church," by Egbert W. Andrews, 1944.

3-RICHARD AND POLLY GAFFIN PAPERS, 1937-49, 1 in.
Background note: Richard B. and Polly Gaffin were OPC missionaries in Tsingtao, Shantung, then in Shanghai, and finally in Taiwan. They were in China from 1937 to 1941 and 1947 to 1949.
CORRESPONDENCE: Correspondence, including reports to mission executives John P. Galbraith and Robert S. Marsden, covering subjects such as the differences between the Student Christian Movement and Inter-Varsity Fellowship, relations with seminaries in China, and relations with missionaries of other denominations and groups.

4-BRUCE F. HUNT PAPERS, 1938-42, 1 in.
Background note: Bruce Finley Hunt served with his wife as an OPC missionary in Harbin, Manchoukuo (Manchuria), from 1936 to 1942. In late 1941, he was arrested by the Japanese for refusing to worship at Shinto shrines and for encouraging fellow Christians to do likewise. This small amount of material is part of a larger collection that highlights his later years in Korea. See also Wheaton College, Billy Graham Center Archives, Wheaton, IL, 60187.
MINUTES/RECORDS/REPORTS/CORRESPONDENCE: Miscellaneous correspondence and financial records.
MANUSCRIPTS: 2 typewritten "statements" by Hunt, concerning his imprisonment and trial in the fall of 1941, and his treatment after Pearl Harbor.

5-GENERAL HOLDINGS
MINUTES/RECORDS/REPORTS: Miscellaneous reports from the China missionaries in the *Guardian*, 1937-49; brief annual reports in *Minutes of General Assembly, Orthodox Presbyterian Church*, 1938-49.

PHILADELPHIA MUSEUM OF ART
PA-195 Library
Benjamin Franklin Parkway
Box 7646
Philadelphia PA 19191-7647
(215) 763-8100
Barbara Sevy, Librarian

1-GENERAL HOLDINGS
SERIALS: Catholic University of Peking, *Bulletin*, 1928.

PRESBYTERIAN HISTORICAL SOCIETY
PA-200 Archives and Library
425 Lombard Street
Philadelphia PA 19147
(215) 627-1852
William Miller, Director
Gerald Gillette, Research Historian
Frederick Heuser, Archivist

Restrictions: 75-year restrictions are in effect on manuscript material; researchers should inquire for use within these limits.
Background note: Since its founding in 1852, the Presbyterian Historical Society (PHS) has collected documents related to the Presbyterian and Reformed churches in the United States and its ecclesiastical connections throughout the world. The PHS is also the official archive for the National Council of Churches in the U.S.A., whose collection contains many important documents related to China.

The Presbyterian Church (U.S.A.) is the result of several mergers throughout its history, the most recent being that of June 1983, between the United Presbyterian Church in the U.S.A. (northern) and the Presbyterian Church in the U.S. (southern). The archives of the two churches in the last merger have not yet been combined. The archives of the former Presbyterian Church in the U.S. are housed at the Historical Foundation of the Presbyterian and Reformed Church, Montreat, NC, 28757.

The American agencies responsible for missionary work beyond the boundaries of the United States evolved through different names (some coterminous) through various stages of church history. The starting dates of these agencies are as follows: United Foreign Missionary Society, 1817; Western Foreign Missionary Society, 1831; Board of Foreign Missions, 1837; Women's Foreign Missionary Society, 1838; Ladies' Board of Missions, 1879; Women's General Missionary Society, 1883; Commission on Ecumenical Mission and Relations, 1958; General Assembly Mission Council, 1973.

The first Presbyterian missionaries to China were appointed in 1837. In 1935, during the peak of the foreign missionary enterprise, the number of Presbyterian missionaries in China was 377, or 28 percent of all Presbyterian foreign missionaries. China continued to be the largest part of Presbyterian foreign mission work until the renewal of the Sino-Japanese conflict in 1942. The number of missionaries gradually diminished to none by 1952, as the administration of the People's Republic of China consolidated its power over the Chinese mainland.

1-BIOGRAPHICAL FILES, 1837-1949, quantity undetermined
Restrictions: Closed for an initial period of 75 years. Permission for use is at the discretion of the Presbyterian Historical Society.
MINUTES/RECORDS/REPORTS: Personnel files on individuals associated with the American Presbyterian and Reformed Churches, including candidates for missionary service in China and administrators in headquarters offices in the United States.

2-HOMER VERNON BRADSHAW PAPERS (RG 188), 1937-57, .5 c.f.
Background note: Homer Vernon Bradshaw (b. 1899) was appointed by the Board of Foreign Missions as a medical missionary to the South China Mission in 1928. His entire career was spent at Lin hsien Station, where he headed the medical staff of the Van Norden Memorial Hospital for Men and the Brooks Memorial Hospital for Women. He also taught at the Hackett Medical College in Canton. From 1942 to 1945, he served in the U.S. Air Force as a flight surgeon with Chennault's Flying Tigers. After the war, he returned to missionary work in China until 1951, when he and his wife, Wilda (Hockenberry) Bradshaw, were incarcerated by the Chinese Communists until 1955. See also Claremont Colleges, Special Collections Department, Honnold Library, Eighth and Dartmouth Streets, Claremont, CA, 91711.
CORRESPONDENCE: Incoming and outgoing correspondence relating to his stay in China, 1937-51.
MEMORABILIA: Miscellaneous items, 1942-55.

3-ARCHIE R. CROUCH PAPERS, 1924-82, ca. 1 box
MINUTES/RECORDS/REPORTS: Mimeographed and offset statements and reports, 1947-81, relating to the church and Communism, the church in China, National Christian Council of China, the Presbyterian Church in the U.S.A., and visits to China.
CORRESPONDENCE: Bound volume of clippings, printed circular letters, and carbons of letters to supporting groups and friends, written by Archie and Ellen Crouch from the East China Mission, 1936-41; 32 letters regarding a gift from the Mark Waltz family in Cambria, California, which was used for a ward in the Presbyterian Mission Hospital in Hengyang, Hunan, 1946-49.
MANUSCRIPTS: Miscellaneous manuscripts, ca. 1939-1982, including book notes and reviews, stories, and papers on Chinese Communists, the People's Republic of China, China and the church, Manchuria, Ningpo, McCartee Hospital in Yuyao, Riverside Academy for Girls, mission schools, and Lolo (Nosu) social customs; academic papers relating to China and the Christian mission in China, 1941-82, including preliminary papers on China mission documents in libraries and archives of the United States.
PAMPHLETS: Miscellaneous pamphlets on China, ca. 1940s-1978; 6 dramas, 1924-40, n.d.
MEMORABILIA: "Return from China on *Tatuta Maru*," a bound volume of clippings on the Crouches, 1941-52; "Mission to China," a bound volume of "Ricksha Rambles" columns by Archie Crouch, published in *The Cambrian* (Cambria Pines, California), 1937-41, 1944-46.
SERIALS: *China Notes*, 1976. *The Church*, 1948.
CHINESE LANGUAGE MATERIALS: Manuscript regarding inscription for Waltz memorial plaque and manuscript of a leaflet for presentation of the plaque, n.d. (see CORRESPONDENCE above).

4-FEDERAL COUNCIL OF CHURCHES, DEPARTMENT OF INTERNATIONAL JUSTICE AND GOODWILL FILES (RG 18 NCC), 1907–50, 5 folders

Background note: In 1911 the Federal Council of Churches established a Commission on Peace and Arbitration to organize a conference of American, British, and German church leaders for a peaceful settlement of international disputes. The commission was renamed the Commission on International Justice and Goodwill in 1916, and the Department of International Justice and Goodwill in 1932. In 1941 a parallel Commission on a Just and Durable Peace was established and worked so closely with the Department of International Justice and Goodwill that their records overlap. In 1947 the two commissions were merged. When the Federal Council of Churches became part of the new National Council of Churches of Christ in the U.S.A. in 1950, the Department of International Justice and Goodwill became the Department of International Affairs. The files date primarily from 1940 to 1950.
MINUTES/RECORDS/REPORTS/CORRESPONDENCE/PAMPHLETS/MEMORABILIA: Documents pertaining to Aid to China, Foreign Missions Conference, and the Christian Basis for Reconstruction; financial statements, speeches, programs, and clippings, 1920–50.
FINDING AIDS: Guide to Record Group 18.

5-SAMUEL RANKIN GAYLEY PAPERS, 1856, 3 folders

Background note: Samuel Rankin Gayley (1828–1862) was appointed by the Board of Foreign Missions to the Shanghai Mission in 1856. He served at Tengchow and died in China in 1862.
DIARIES: Journal (with transcript) describing his journey from New York to Shanghai in 1856, including his observations on Chinese culture and relations with missionaries from other denominations; incomplete undated diary describing his journey to Hangchow.

6-FRANCIS PATRICK GILMAN PAPERS (RG 56), 1885–1918, 2 c.f.

Background note: Francis Patrick Gilman (1853–1918) was appointed by the Board of Foreign Missions to the Hainan Mission in 1885. He died in China in 1918.
CORRESPONDENCE: Letters relating to his wife, Mary White Gilman, 1903.
DIARIES/MEMORABILIA: Miscellaneous diaries and notebooks.
AUDIO-VISUAL MATERIALS: Photo of Gilman.
FINDING AIDS: In-house guide to Record Group 56.

7-JOHN DAVID HAYES PAPERS, 1949–57, 3 folders

Background note: For biographical notes, see University of Oregon, Special Collections, Eugene, OR, 97403–1299.
CORRESPONDENCE: Correspondence mainly from John David Hayes to his family, 1949–57.

8-JAMES McCLURE HENRY PAPERS (RG H5), 1948–49, 1 folder

Background note: James McClure Henry was a Presbyterian missionary to China for the Covenant Christian Endeavor Society from 1909 to 1919. At that time he joined the staff of Lingnan University (Canton Christian College), serving as president from 1924 to 1927 and as provost from 1927 to 1948.
CORRESPONDENCE: 2 letters between Edward L. R. Elson, pastor of the National Presbyterian Church in Washington, DC, and Olin D. Wannamaker, American director of the Board of Trustees of Lingnan University, concerning James McClure Hen-

ry's visit to the National Presbyterian Church, 1949; 3 letters between Henry and Elson concerning an invitation to Henry read in a church service, 1949; letter from Elson to Lloyd S. Ruland of the Board of Foreign Missions of the Presbyterian Church in the U.S.A., concerning Henry's status as a missionary, 1949; letter from Henry to Elson concerning the visit of Gerald Winfield, a missionary to China from the United Board for Christian Colleges, to the National Presbyterian Church in Washington, DC, 1949; copy of a letter from a staff member of the Cheeloo University Hospital concerning war and conditions in China, 1948.
MEMORABILIA: Biographical sketch of James McClure Henry, 1948.
SERIALS: *Latest News of Christian Colleges in China*, 1948. *Lingnan (Canton Christian College)*, 1948.

9-CHARLES A. KILLIE PAPERS, 1889–1907, 1 folder

Background note: Charles A. Killie (1856–1916) was appointed to the Shantung Mission in 1889 by the Board of Foreign Missions. In 1899 he was transferred to Peking in the North China Mission, where he taught and performed evangelistic work until his death.
MINUTES/RECORDS/REPORTS/CORRESPONDENCE: Miscellaneous newsletters, reports, and correspondence, 1889–1907.

10-KWEICHOW MISSION PAPERS, 1960–70, 1 folder

CORRESPONDENCE: Correspondence of the Kweichow Mission Fund, Church of Christ in China, 1960–70.

11-LAUTENSCHLAGER FAMILY PAPERS, 1922–52, 2 folders

Background note: Roy S. (1889–1978) and Harriet Grace (Miller) Lautenschlager (b. 1889) were appointed by the Board of Foreign Missions to the East China Mission in 1922. They were assigned to Hangchow Christian College, where Lautenschlager taught and later headed the Political Science and History Department. In 1937, the Sino-Japanese war forced the college to close, but it later reopened in Shanghai, where Lautenschlager served as professor of political science from 1939 to 1942. Interned by the Japanese in 1942 and released the following year, Lautenschlager returned with his family to Hangchow in 1947. They left China in 1951.
MINUTES/RECORDS/REPORTS/CORRESPONDENCE/MEMORABILIA: Family correspondence, including miscellaneous reports and clippings, 1922–52.

12-McCARTEE FAMILY PAPERS (RG 177), 1854–1906, .5 c.f.

Background note: Divie Bethune McCartee (1820–1900) was appointed by the Board of Foreign Missions as a medical missionary to China in 1843. He went to Ningpo in 1844, engaging in medical and evangelistic work. In 1853, he married fellow missionary Juana M. Knight. McCartee performed consular services in Shanghai until a regular consular service was established there in 1857. The McCartees returned to Ningpo in 1865, then were transferred to the Shanghai mission in 1872. McCartee resigned shortly thereafter to join the Shanghai consular staff as interpreter and assessor in the Mixed Court.
CORRESPONDENCE: Outgoing correspondence of the McCartees relating to their missionary experiences and McCartee's consular service, 1854–1906.

13-JASPER SCUDDER McILVAINE PAPERS, 1858–81, 3 folders

Background note: Jasper Scudder McIlvaine (1844–81) was appointed by the Board of Foreign Missions to the China mission in

1868. Initially stationed in Peking, he served in various places within Shantung until his death.
CORRESPONDENCE: Letters from McIlvaine to his family, 1858–81.

14-MILLICAN FAMILY PAPERS (RG 199), 1907–50, 4 boxes
Restrictions: Access to some of these materials is closed for 25 years.
Background note: Frank R. (1883–1961) and Aimee Boddy Millican (1884–1974) were appointed by the Free Methodist Church as missionaries to China in 1907 and served as evangelists in Hunan until 1915. The following year they were appointed to the China Mission of the Presbyterian Church, U.S.A., and served until 1964. From 1917 to 1929, Frank Millican served as principal of the Presbyterian Boys' High School and later vice-principal of the Union Middle School, while Aimee Millican engaged in evangelistic work with Chinese women. In 1930, they were assigned to the Christian Literature Society in Shanghai, where Rev. Millican translated, edited, and supervised the distribution of Christian literature, while Mrs. Millican was instrumental in starting a Christian Broadcasting Station. During World War II, Rev. Millican was interned by the Japanese until 1945. After the war, the Millicans returned to Shanghai, but were transferred to the Philippines in 1950.

Their daughter, Edith (1914–85), earned a medical degree from Women's Medical College in Philadelphia and was appointed to the China Council of the Presbyterian Church in the U.S.A. in 1941. She went to China in 1943, ministering to war victims and refugees in Hengyang, Kweiyang, Pichieh, and Kweichow. From 1946 to 1948, she was in charge of the Chenhsien Hospital in Hunan. She left China in 1948.
CORRESPONDENCE: 2 boxes of correspondence between Frank and Aimee Millican, documenting their missionary experiences, 1917–1950; box of Edith Millican's correspondence, documenting church work in China during and following the conclusion of World War II, 1945–48.
MEMORABILIA: Clippings, notebooks, certificates, citations, and other miscellaneous items.
AUDIO-VISUAL MATERIALS: 21 folders of photos relating to the Millican family and their mission work in China.
FINDING AID: In-house guide to Record Group 199.

15-MARY MARGARET MONINGER PAPERS, 1915–18, 4 folders
Background note: Mary Margaret Moninger (1891–1950) was appointed by the Board of Foreign Missions to the China mission in 1915 and served there until 1942. She taught and performed evangelistic work at Kachek, Kiungchow, and Hoihow Stations. She also wrote, edited, and translated a number of Chinese language items. See also University of Oregon, Special Collections, Eugene, OR, 97403–1299.
CORRESPONDENCE: Correspondence from Moninger to her family, 1915–18.

16-NATIONAL COUNCIL OF THE CHURCHES OF CHRIST IN THE U.S.A., DIVISION OF OVERSEAS MINISTRIES, EAST ASIA COMMITTEE (RG 8), 1920–72, 5.5 boxes
Background note: East Asia (China, Japan, Korea, and the Philippines) was the greatest focus of missionary activity of the churches of the United States. Most of the work was unilateral between the

various churches of the United States and their respective mission organizations in China. However, as united projects developed, they were administered out of united offices in the United States with counterparts in China, Hong Kong, and Taiwan. These records reflect the following evolution of the united administrative organizations:
1940s–1960s—Foreign Missions Conference of North America, Division of Foreign Missions, Far Eastern Joint Office, China Committee.
1965–69—National Council of the Churches of Christ in the U.S.A., Division of Overseas Ministries, Asia Committee, China Committee.
1969—National Council of the Churches of Christ in the U.S.A., Division of Overseas Ministries, Department of East Asia and the Pacific, China Program.
MINUTES/RECORDS/REPORTS/CORRESPONDENCE: Ballou study, Christian missions in China, n.d.; California College in China, n.d.; China Christian Education Association, n.d.; China Committee, minutes, 1962–68; China Consultation, reports, 1955–62; correspondence pertaining to *China Notes*, n.d.; China Program, reports, 1967–72; China Study Project, papers and correspondence, n.d.; Chinese Student and Alumni Services, n.d.; Christian Literature Society for China, n.d.; Christian Study Centre on Chinese Religion and Culture, 1958–72; Church of Christ in China, n.d.; College of Chinese Studies, North American Council, minutes and reports, 1923–66; Council of Christian Publishers, 1946–51; East China Christian Rural Service Union, n.d.; Far Eastern (Joint) Office of the Foreign Missions Conference of North America Committee on the Far East, 1943–64; Lutheran World Relief, n.d.; National Committee for Christian Religious Education in China, n.d.; National Christian Council, correspondence and reports, 1946–50, 1948; North China Christian Rural Service Union, n.d.; North China Union Language School, minutes, n.d.; Peking British Cemetery, n.d.; Peking Methodists, Ch'en report, n.d.; Peking Union Church, n.d.; Princeton Inn Conference, 1940s; Shanghai American School, Board of Trustees, minutes, 1920–50, 1961–66; minutes, reports, and correspondence, 1927–67; Shanghai Municipal Cemetery, n.d.; Special Committee on Approaches to China, 1951–61; World Council of Churches, China reports, n.d.; miscellaneous correspondence, reports, and articles, 1920–66; directories of China missionaries, n.d.
MANUSCRIPTS: "History of Nanking Theological Seminary," by F. W. Price, n.d.; "Lessons Learned from China," n.d.
SERIALS: *China Bulletin*, 1950–66. *China Notes*, 1967–72. *Quarterly Notes on Christianity and Chinese Religion*, 1957–63.
FINDING AIDS: In-house guide to Record Group 8, 1979.

17-POMMERENKE FAMILY PAPERS (RG 193), 1907–80, 2 c.f.
Background note: Herbert (1900–1978) and Jean (Macpherson) Pommerenke (b. 1895) served as missionaries in China until their retirement in 1970. Jean Macpherson was appointed by the Board of Foreign Missions in 1920 and began her career as a teacher in the True Light School in Canton. Herbert Pommerenke served as a volunteer teacher at Canton Christian College in Canton from 1924 to 1927. They married in 1927. In 1930, they were assigned to the Yeungkong Station, and in 1934 they were transferred to Kochow, Kwangtung, where they taught and performed evangelistic work.

Herbert Pommerenke taught at Union Theological Seminary in Canton during 1937 and 1938, before reassignment to Yeungkong. They were interned under the Japanese occupation in the late 1930s, returning to China in 1943 to do relief work in Chengtu. In 1946 they moved to Canton to assist with postwar rehabilitation and remained there until they were forced to leave China in 1948. They returned again in 1955, when Mr. Pommerenke became treasurer of the mission field office and pastor of a church comprised of Chinese refugees from the former Presbyterian mission on Hainan Island. See also University of Oregon, Special Collections, Eugene, OR, 97403-1299.

CORRESPONDENCE/MEMORABILIA: Correspondence with family, 1907–80; miscellaneous items relating to their stay in China and mission work, 1900–1960s.

18-PRESBYTERIAN CHURCH IN THE U.S.A., BOARD OF FOREIGN MISSIONS, DOMESTIC MISSIONS-FOREIGN MISSIONS DOMESTIC CORRESPONDENCE, 1829–95 (RG 31), 67.5 c.f.

Background note: Most of the materials originally in this record group have been removed and are filed in the library (see GENERAL HOLDINGS).

MINUTES/RECORDS/REPORTS/CORRESPONDENCE: Mostly incoming material, late 1830s–1895.

FINDING AIDS: In-house chronological guide to Record Group 31; 150 indexes interspersed throughout the collection.

19-PRESBYTERIAN CHURCH IN THE U.S.A., BOARD OF FOREIGN MISSIONS, CORRESPONDENCE AND REPORTS, 1837–1911, 54 reels microfilm

MINUTES/RECORDS/REPORTS/CORRESPONDENCE: Presbyterian Church in the U.S.A., Board of Foreign Missions, incoming and outgoing missions correspondence, and missionary and station reports on China (some of which overlap with the material in the record groups), including some early files from the American Board of Commissioners for Foreign Missions, 1837–1911, and index to microfilm.

FINDING AIDS: Calendars immediately preceding the sequences of records on 3 reels of microfilm; these calendars have also been printed.

20-PRESBYTERIAN CHURCH IN THE U.S.A., BOARD OF FOREIGN MISSIONS, SECRETARIES' FILES (RG 82), 1890–1955, 106.5 c.f.

Background note: See also United Presbyterian Church in the U.S.A., Commission on Ecumenical Mission and Relations, Secretaries' Files, China Mission, 1956–67 (RG 129), below.

MINUTES/RECORDS/REPORTS/CORRESPONDENCE: Bible Union League, 1920–23; Canton Christian College, n.d.; Canton Hospital, 1916–42; Central China Mission, 1911–12, 1919–25; Central China Teachers College, 1923–33; Chefoo School for the Deaf, 1910–46; Chihli School for Missionaries' Children, n.d.; China Campaign, 1911–12; China Child Welfare, 1930; China Christian Educational Association, 1927; China Council, 1920–31; China Famine Fund, 1921–23; China Famine Relief, 1928–30; China Famine Relief Committee, n.d.; China Union Universities, 1922–32; Christian Colleges in China, 1930–40; Christian Higher Education in China, 1923–30; Christian Literature Society for China, 1911–24, 1936–45; Church of Christ in China, 1926–28, 1934–38; East China Mission, 1940–42; Famine Loan Mission,

1936; Ginling College, 1922–25, 1933–44; Hackett Medical College (Canton), 1912–46; Hainan Mission, 1912, 1918–20, 1922–25, 1941–42; Hamilton Memorial Building, 1906–17; Hangchow Christian College, 1911–46; Hangchow Union Girls' School, 1912–35; Hengchow Hospital (Hengyang, Hunan), 1908–45; Hoi How Hospital (Hainan), 1917–46; Hunan Mission, 1911–20; Institute of Engineering Practice, 1935; Kiangan Mission, 1919–20, 1922–25, 1941–43; Kuling American School for Missionary Children, 1917–18, 1921–43; Ming Sam School (Canton), 1909–47; Mission Press (Shanghai), 1891–1932; Nanking Theological Seminary, 1930–46; Nanking (University) Hospital, 1909–31; Nantao Christian Institute (Shanghai), 1921–28; National Christian Council of China, 1927–29; Ningpo School, 1921–40; North China American School, 1922–33; North China Union Language School, 1921–26; North China Mission, 1911, 1919, 1921–23, 1925, 1941–42; Peking Language School, 1927–29; Peking Union Medical College, 1920–35; Peking University, 1911–27; Presbyterian Church in China, Provisional Assembly, 1914–25; Shanghai American School, 1918–22, 1926–32, 1935–40; Shantung Christian University, 1903–47; Shantung Mission, 1906–43, 1945; South China Mission, 1911–12, 1918–40, 1942, 1947–50; Tenghsien Station, 1911–40; True Light Middle School, 1918–28; True Light Seminary (Canton), 1909–33; Tsinanfu Station, n.d.; Tungchou Chihli School for Missionary Children, 1912–17; Union Medical School (Shanghai), 1922–25; Union Normal School (Canton), 1921–39; Union Theological Seminary (Canton), 1919–25; University of Nanking, 1906–32, 1935–40; Weihsien Hospital (Shantung), 1918–41; West China Mission, 1942; Yale-in-China Association, 1922–46; Yenching University, 1924–45; Yeungkong, 1921–47; Yunnan Mission, 1922–25.

MANUSCRIPTS: Biography of Charles Lewis, n.d.; address by Mme. Chiang K'ai-shek, 1937; ''The Kuomintang and Religion,'' by A. R. Kepler, 1930; ''Directory of Missions in China, 1950.''

AUDIO-VISUAL MATERIALS: Unidentified photos.

SERIALS: Cheeloo University: *Cheeloo Bulletin*, 1927–29, 1931–46; *Cheeloo Weekly Bulletin*, 1926, 1928–29.

FINDING AIDS: In-house guide to Record Group 82, 1977.

21-HENRY VAN VLECK RANKIN PAPERS (RG 176), 1842–63, 1 c.f.

Background note: Henry Van Vleck Rankin (1825–1863) was appointed by the Board of Foreign Missions in 1848 and served in Ningpo until his death in 1863.

CORRESPONDENCE/DIARIES/MEMORABILIA: Correspondence, diaries, and miscellaneous items relating to his work in China, 1842–63.

22-MYRLE MARIE (FOSTER) SEATON, 1924–52, 30 items

MINUTES/RECORDS/REPORTS/CORRESPONDENCE/MANUSCRIPTS/MEMORABILIA: Correspondence, clippings, bulletins, and other papers relating to the American Presbyterian Mission, Hainan, 1924–52.

23-HARRIET STROH PAPERS (RG 187), 1918–42, 1.5 c.f.

Background note: Harriet Stroh (b. 1896) was appointed to the China Mission in 1919. She taught at the Girls' School in Hwaiyuan (1920–27 and 1933–37) and at the North China American School (1927–28). She did evangelistic work in Paoting (1928–29), Hwaiyuan (1929–31), and Showchow (1935–36). During the Sino-Japanese war, she was engaged in refugee work in Hwaiyuan. She resigned from mission work in 1942.

CORRESPONDENCE/MEMORABILIA/AUDIO-VISUAL MA-
TERIALS: Correspondence, photos, and miscellaneous items relating to her missionary experiences in China, 1918–42.

**24-UNITED BOARD FOR CHRISTIAN HIGHER EDUCATION IN
ASIA, 1959–71, 1 folder**
Background note: See also the Center for Research Libraries, 5721
Cottage Grove Avenue, Chicago, IL, 60637; and Yale Divinity
School, Special Collections, 409 Prospect Street, New Haven, CT,
06510.,
MINUTES/RECORDS/REPORTS/PAMPHLETS: Reports, pub-
licity materials, and other papers, 1959–71.

**25-UNITED PRESBYTERIAN CHURCH IN THE U.S.A., COMMIS-
SION ON ECUMENICAL MISSION AND RELATIONS, SECRE-
TARIES' FILES, 1892–1965 (RG 81), ca. 1912–1965, ca. 20 folders**
Background note: These files contain more than 1,500 folders,
some of which have materials related to China in addition to the
ones noted below.
MINUTES/RECORDS/REPORTS/CORRESPONDENCE: Chi-
na Inland Mission, n.d.; Far East, 1929–30, 1936, 1946, 1949–50;
Gripsholm, 1942–42; Japanese and Chinese Students' Christian
Federation, 1926–42; Henry Little, trip to Asia, 1939–40; John C.
Smith, 1948; Robert E. Speer, trip to Asia, 1898; United Board for
Christian Higher Education in Asia, 1962–65; Stanley White,
1912–13.
FINDING AIDS: In-house guide to Record Group 81.

**26-UNITED PRESBYTERIAN CHURCH IN THE U.S.A., COMMIS-
SION ON ECUMENICAL MISSION AND RELATIONS, SECRE-
TARIES' FILES, CHINA MISSION (RG 129), 1893–1963, ca. 20
folders**
Background note: See also Presbyterian Church in the U.S.A.,
Board of Foreign Missions, Secretaries' Files, China Mission
1890–1955 (RG 82), above.
MINUTES/RECORDS/REPORTS/CORRESPONDENCE: As-
sociated Mission Treasurers, 1921; Central China Mission, rules,
1934; China Committee, minutes, 1959; China Council, constitution and handbook, n.d.; Church of Christ in China, 1956–62; East
China Mission, historical material and general rules, n.d.; Hainan
Mission, historical materials, rules, n.d., and annual report, 1893;
Kiangan Mission, survey and rules, n.d.; Linhsien, 1949–55; list
of medical schools in China, 1966; Nanking Theological Seminary, 1956–61; North China Mission, historical materials and
rules, n.d.; Restoration Fund, 1948; Shantung Mission, historical
material and rules, n.d.; South China Mission, historical materials,
rules, and constitution, n.d.; West China Mission in Yunnan, constitution and terms of service, n.d.; miscellaneous reports and
statements.
MANUSCRIPTS: "U.S. Gunboats on the Yangtze: History and
Political Aspects, 1842–1922," by E. Mowbry Tate, n.d.;
"Shanghai Station History, 1895–1936," by George Partch, n.d.
FINDING AIDS: In-house guide to Record Group 129.

27-VAN DYCK FAMILY PAPERS, 1926–49, 3 folders
Background note: David Bevier (1892–1963) and Anna Richardson Van Dyck (b. 1895) were appointed to the China mission in
1918 and were assigned to Hwaiyuan. In 1927, they left China for a
few months due to the political situation, but returned, relocating
to Tsingtao. They returned to Hwaiyuan in 1928, and from 1933 to
1940 they worked in the Showchow field at Anhwei. Mr. Van Dyck

returned to Hunan in 1943, but was forced to leave China in 1949.
REPORTS/CORRESPONDENCE/AUDIO-VISUAL MATERI-
ALS: Correspondence, reports, and photos relating to their stay in
China, 1926–49.

28-GENERAL HOLDINGS
MINUTES/RECORDS/REPORTS: American Bible Society,
1826–1974; American Board of Commissioners for Foreign Missions, 1825–1945; American Presbyterian Mission Press: 1868,
1874–75, 1891–94, 1896–1907, 1909–24; catalogues, 1887, 1893,
1902; Amoy Mission, 1899; Associated Mission Treasurers, annual reports, 1931, 1934, 1936; Australian Churchmen, deputation
to mainland China, report, 1957; Bible Seminary for Women,
annual reports, 1938–39; Canton Christian College, catalogues,
1918–26; president's report, 1902–4, 1910–12, 1924; Canton
Missionary Conference, report, 1919–20; Canton Union Theological College, catalogues, 1918–19; Central China, Presbyterian Conference, proceedings, 1901; Central China Religious Tract
Society, annual reports, 1884, 1893–96, 1901–2, 1904–5, 1909,
1911, 1915; Chapei Presbyterian Church, appeal, 1933; Chefoo
School for the Deaf (Shantung), 1938; China Christian Literature
Council, constitution, 1918; China Committee, special mission to
China, report, 1946; China Continuation Committee of the National Missionary Conference, proceedings, 1913–21; China Inland Mission, reports, 1922–49; China International Famine Relief Commmission, constitution, by-laws, and regulations, 1925;
China Medical Missionary Association, 1918–47; Chinese Tract
Society, annual reports, 1901–5, 1910–12; Christian Literature
Society for China, annual reports, 1917–21, 1941–45, 1946–47;
minutes, 1937, 1940; Church of Christ in China, constitution,
1932, 1936; manifesto, 1930; address, 1930; doctrinal basis, n.d.;
minutes and reports, 1927, 1933; General Assembly, important
actions, 1937, 1946; minutes and reports, 1930; General Council,
minutes and reports, 1928–29, 1931–32; Church of Christ in China, border service, 1940; Commission for the Investigation of the
Shakee Massacre (Kwangtung), report, 1925; Conference of Missionary Societies in Great Britain and Ireland, report, 1934; Conference on Federation, records, 1905; Door of Hope and Children's Refuge (Shanghai), annual report, 1937; Evangelical
Church, Board of Missions, Commission to the Orient, report,
1930; Foreign Missions Conference of North America, Committee
of Reference and Counsel, papers, 1912; Hangchow Union Evangelistic Committee, reports, 1921, 1924–25; Hoi Poh Hospital,
reports, 1934–35; International Institute of China, regulations,
1897; International Missionary Council, China delegation, report,
1928; International Missionary Council, China Continuation
Committee, findings, 1913, 1915, 1919, 1923; Layman's Foreign
Mission Inquiry, special China report, 1933; London Missionary
Society, reports, 1921, 1938; Medical Missionary Society in China, reports, 1864, 1879; Mission Architects and Engineers, conference report, 1921; National Christian Council of China, conference report, 1922, 1926–27, 1933, 1937; biennial reports, 1931–
35, proposals, 1928; North China Union Language School, newsletter, 1929; Presbyterian Church of Christ in China, minutes of
council, 1907; general assembly minutes, 1922.

Presbyterian Church in the U.S.A., China Council, 1910–51;
mission reports: Canton, annual report, 1886–1905; Central China, annual reports, 1923–32; station reports, 1893–1904, 1889–
1933; general rules, 1892, 1897, 1906, 1924, 1934; minutes,

1891–1940; policy and organization, n.d.; Changtek, reports, 1925; Chefoo, annual reports, 1903–9, 1913–28, 1930, 1932–33, 1935, 1939; memo, 1926; newsletter, 1915; East China, minutes, 1937–41, 1942–49; Hainan, annual reports, 1894, 1905, 1907; minutes, 1913–40, 1948; rules, 1907, 1923; station reports, 1910, 1913; Hangchow, annual reports, 1926, 1932–33, 1936–37; Hunan, annual reports, 1939–42, 1946; minutes, 1907–8. 1911–14, 1948; station reports, 1915, 1927–28; Hwaiyuan, annual reports, 1907, 1923–24, 1927–47; Ichowfu, 1923–34; Kiangan, minutes, 1906–41; station reports, 1906–17, 1922; Kiung-chow (Hainan), n.d.; Kwangtung, 1907–17; Kwangtung Synod, report, 1940; Lienchow, reports, 1902, 1914, 1936; Linhsien, report, 1950–55; Nanking, reports, 1946; station reports, 1927, 1929–37, 1940–41; Ningpo, reports, 1909–11, 1919; catalogue, 1951; North China, annual station report, 1906; annual personal reports, 1909; reports, 1908–11, 1914; general rules, 1933; minutes, 1911–41; newsletter, 1940; Paotingfu, annual reports, 1922, 1925, 1933–36; Peking, annual reports, 1904–5, 1917, 1924, 1928, 1932; evangelistic report, 1924; Shanghai, annual reports, 1926, 1933, 1936, 1938; general workers group, minutes, 1939–40; Shantung, address, 1930; minutes, 1911–41; records, 1861–1913; rules, 1889, 1912–13, 1923, 1930; Soochow, annual reports, 1926, 1933–38; South China, annual reports, 1910–14, 1922–24, 1936–39; constitution and by-laws, 1910; minutes, 1912–41, 1948; Tengchow, annual report, 1926; Tenghsien-Yihsien, annual report, 1936; Tsinan, annual report, 1924–25, 1936–37; Tsining, annual reports, 1919–23, 1932–38; Tsingtao, annual reports, 1901, 1918–19, 1921–24, 1928; Weihsien, annual reports, 1919, 1922, 1924–25, 1931–32, 1936; West Shantung, annual report, 1906–7; Yeung Kong, report, 1914; Yunnan, annual report, 1922; report, 1918–19; station report, 1924–34; Kiulikiang and Yuankiang, report, 1930–31.

Presbyterian Committee on Union, 1905; Presbyterian Mission in the U.S.A. (Shanghai), Evaluation Conference, findings, 1926; Presbyterian Mission Press, 1867–68, 1872, 1922–26, 1929; catalogue, 1885, 1910; Protestant Episcopal Church in the U.S.A., Commission to China, report, 1927–28. Reformed Presbyterian Church of North America, China mission, reports, 1895–1910; Religious Tract Society in China, annual reports, 1876–1935, 1939–40; Shanghai Southern Presbyterian Mission, 1914, 1917; Shantung Christian University (Tsinan), 1924; Shantung Cities Evangelization Project, annual report, 1921–22, 1924–25, 1927; Siangtan Community Guild (Hunan), yearbook, 1918–19; United Board for Christian Higher Education in Asia, annual reports, 1938, 1941, 1948–58, 1970–75; West China Annual Conference, 1912–49; West China Missionary Conference (Chengtu), report, 1908; West China Union University, Board of Governors, minutes, n.d.; West China Union Middle School, 1913–26; Woman's Board of Foreign Missions of the Presbyterian Church (formerly Ladies' Board of Missions) Annual Reports, 1871–1923; Woman's Foreign Missionary Society of the Presbyterian Church Annual Reports, 1872–1923; Woman's Occidental Board of Foreign Missions, 1876–1920; Yale-in-China Association, report, 1951.

MANUSCRIPTS: 30 titles, 1902–70, on the American Presbyterian Mission in Hangchow, Board of Foreign Missions of the Presbyterian Church, China and the Far East, church and state in Manchuria, Church of Christ in China, Communist China, famine, Hong Kong, Hwaiyuan, Kiangnan, W. A. P. Martin, Nestorians,

Peking, Reformed Church in the United States, Sino-Japanese conflict, student patriotic movement, Wuhan Missionary prayer meeting, and Yunnan.

PAMPHLETS: Ca. 200 pamphlets, 1852–1978, on ancestor worship, James Hillcoat Arthur, asylum for the insane, Baptist missions, Bernard John Bettelheim, William Jones Boone, J. Clarence Burns, Catholic church, Frank Herring Chalfant, Bishop della Chiesa, China Seminary conference, Chinese church, Chinese empire, Christian colleges, Christian missionaries and Chinese officials, Christians in China, church unity, College of Chinese Studies, Congregationalists in China, Hunter Corbett, Isabella Ruth (Eakin) Dodd, engineering mission work, English-speaking Chinese Christians, evangelism, famine, farm ownership and tenancy, John Ashley Fitch, Hainan, Hainan Mission, Hainanese Miao, Hakka, Hangchow, home life, Hunan relief, Hwaiyuan, Indians of South China, indigenous church, William F. Junkin, Kwangtung geography, William Lane, Lienchow martyrs, Manchuria, martyrs, Julia Brown Mateer, Grace Burroughs Mather, medical missions, Annetta Thompson Mills, mission history, mission methods, missionary reports on Communist China, missions, Nanking, National Christian Council of China, National YWCA, Nestorians, New Life movement, Nosu tribes, Harriet Newell Noyes, opium, John A. Otte, Peking, persecution of missionaries, politics, population, Presbyterian missions, Protestant captives, Protestant martyrs, public opinion, refugees, Lloyd S. Ruland visit to China (1939–40), relief work, rural China, rural economy, rural population, Samkong, Peter Y. F. Shih, Siaochang, siege of Peking, Sino-Japanese war, H. Taples Smith, Robert E. Speer visit to China (1897), Cornelia Spencer, John and Betty Stam, student patriotic movements, study books, Sun Yat-sen, Swatow, Absalom Sydenstricker, Tai, J. Hudson Taylor, Mary Dorothy (Fine) Twinem, Union Christian College, West China, women, women in the Chinese mission, Women's Union Christian Colleges, word for God in Chinese, Eleanor M. Wright, Yao society, Yenshan county (Chihli), and Yunnan harvest feasts.

DIARIES: "Letters from China, 1920–1949," by Anna Moffet Jarvis, containing a day-by-day account of the Christian community during the Chiang K'ai-shek takeover of Nanking in 1927, the Sino-Japanese battles of 1937–49, and the Nationalist-Communist conflicts from 1927 to 1949.

MEMORABILIA: Package of newsletters, articles, and photos, collected by Albert Andrew Fulton concerning the North China Mission and Canton, 1916–19; scrapbook of clippings collected by Herbert E. House from "religious exchanges" during the Boxer Rebellion, 1900.

ORAL HISTORIES: Interview, recorded off the air from *The Tonight Show*, with Sara Perkins and Christina Sevilla, by Howard Jones, ca. 1956; *Future of the Church in China: Interview with Dr. Lloyd S. Ruland and Gerald F. Winfield*, audio cassette, 1950; interview with Sara Perkins and George Lord on audio cassette, 1956; *Missionary Nurse in China Prison*, interview with Sara Perkins, recorded in 1955; interview with John D. and Barbara M. Hayes, recorded off the air from the television program, *Journey Through Life*, ca. 1950s; interview with John David Hayes on Communist prison life in China, on reel-to-reel tape, n.d.; interview of Henry D. Jones on audio cassette, 1978; China experiences and reminiscences of Andrew Todd Roy, ca. 1930 to 1972, a Radio Hong Kong tape recording of broadcast interviews in 1970.

MAPS/DESIGNS/DRAWINGS: Sketch map of Nanking, n.d.;

PCUSA, Board of Foreign Missions maps of China missions, 1915; South China, n.d.; Hupeh and Hunan provinces, n.d.; Ichowfu Field, preaching stations, and cart roads, n.d.; missions in Chihli province, comp. by C. H. Fenn (negative only), 1899; "Map of China Mission Stations and Other Points at Which Our Missionaries Are Located," by the PCUSA, Board of Foreign Missions, 1932.

AUDIO-VISUAL MATERIALS: Photo album by Paul and Clara Doltz from a journey to Japan, China, and Korea, 1905; 27 pages of photos, with inscriptions, of missionaries and friends at Nanking Mission Station, presented to J. Horton and Helen (Dunn) Daniels, 1923; 6 photos of missionaries and scenes in China, ca. 1891–1894, by William R. Fairies, Wei Hien Mission, Shantung; "A Nation Is Born," motion picture film by the Nanking YMCA, ca. 1950; 5 slides of Kuling School, by the PCUSA, Board of Foreign Missions, with narrator's script, n.d.; "Letter from China," 16 mm. motion picture film by the PCUSA, Board of Foreign Missions, ca. 1948.

SERIALS: *Canton Committee for Justice to China*, 1937–38. *Central China Bi-monthly*, 1914–16. *Central China Presbyterian Mission Quarterly*, 1905–6. *Chefoo Station Bulletin*, 1922–27. *Cheung Chow Beacon*, 1936. *China Bulletin*, 1952–53, 1959–61. China Inland Mission, *Occasional Papers*, 1868–72. *China Mission Year Book*, 1910–39. *China Notes*, 1967–72. *China's Millions* (Philadelphia), 1910–50. *China's Millions* (London), 1875–1903. *Chinese Recorder*, 1870–1941. *Chinese Repository*, 1833, 1836–40, 1847, 1851. Christian Literature Society for China, *Newsletter*, 1941. *Community Service*, 1923–27. *Directory of Protestant Missionaries in China, Japan, and Corea*, 1902, 1904–5, 1907–8, 1910, 1912, 1914, 1917. *Directory of Protestant Missions in China*, 1916, 1918–21, 1923–24, 1927–28, 1930, 1932–33, 1935–37, 1939–40. *Educational Review*, 1909–11, 1913–14, 1917–18, 1921–30. *Fati Theological College Bulletin*, 1911–12. *The Foochow Messenger*, 1914. *Friends of Moslems*, 1928, 1930–31. *The Green Year*, supplement, 1925. *Hainan Newsletter*, 1912–38, 1947–49. *Information Service*, 1958. *Information Service of the Church of Christ in China*, 1936–37, 1939–40, 1946–47. *A Monthly Cycle of Prayer*, 1911–16, 1919–23, 1925–35, 1938–40, 1948–50. *Nantao Christian Institute Bulletin*, 1922. National Christian Council of China, *Bulletin*, 1922–31. National Committee for Christian Religious Education, *Religious Education Fellowship Bulletin*, 1940–41. *New East*, 1905–9. *New Horizons*, 1938–45, 1948–55, 1957–66, 1970. *New Mandarin*, 1926. *Prayer Cards of Central China Presbyterian Mission*, 1895, 1898, 1900, 1904. Presbyterian Church in the U.S.A., *Yeung Kong Station Bi-monthly*, 1903–12. *Princeton-Yenching Gazette*, 1936. *Quarterly of the Central China Mission*, 1905–7. *Shantung Mission Bulletin*, 1930. Southern Presbyterian Mission in China, *Bi-monthly Bulletin*, 1914, 1917. University of Nanking, College of Agriculture and Forestry, *Bulletin*, 1926; *University of Nanking Magazine*, 1910. West China Border Research Society, *Journal*, 1922–25. *Woman's Work in the Far East*, 1894, 1897–1911. *Work in China*, 1888. *Yenching News*, 1948.

DISSERTATIONS/THESES: *J. Lossing Buck, American Missionary: The Application of Scientific Agriculture in China, 1915–1944*, by James Pugh, 1973. *Presbyterians in the Church of Christ in China*, by David Jefferson McGown, 1947. *A Program for the Christian Church in the Building of New Rural Communities in China*, by Ralph M. Galt, 1941. *The Relation of Church and

Mission in the North China Mission of the Presbyterian Church in the U.S.A., by Wallace C. Merwin, 1938. *William Alexander Parsons Martin, Missionary to China, 1850–1916*, by Mary Edna Boggs, 1948.

CHINESE LANGUAGE MATERIALS/SERIALS: *Hua t'u hsin pao (Chinese Illustrated News)*, 1891, 1900–1901.

CHINESE LANGUAGE MATERIALS: Letter from the Presbyterian Church in China, Provincial Assembly, to the General Assembly of the Presbyterian Church in the U.S.A., 1919.

RELIGIOUS SOCIETY OF FRIENDS
PA–205 Philadelphia Yearly Meeting Library
1515 Cherry Street
Philadelphia PA 19102
(215) 241–7000
Mary V. Davidson, Librarian

1-GENERAL HOLDINGS
PAMPHLETS: *Quaker Mission to China: W. Grigor McClelland's Diary, 26th September–29th October, 1955*, by W. Grigor McClelland, n.d.

TEMPLE UNIVERSITY
PA–210 Samuel Paley Library
Berks and 13th Streets
Philadelphia PA 19122
(215) 787–8240
James Myers, Librarian

1-CONWELLANA-TEMPLANA COLLECTION, TEMPLE AUTHOR REPRINTS, JOHN STEWART BURGESS PAPERS, 1910–44, 40 items
Background note: For biographical notes, see Princeton University, Firestone Library, Rare Books and Manuscripts, Manuscript Division, Princeton, NJ, 08544.
PAMPHLETS: 40 articles and reprints by John Stewart Burgess, 1910–44, relating to social science in China, social work in China, the church in China, Chinese culture, and comments on the Princeton University Center in China, reprinted from *China's Young Men*, the *Chinese Recorder*, the *Chinese Social and Political Science Review*, *The Christian Century*, *The Intercollegian*, *The New Republic*, *Peking Daily News*, *Peking Leader Press*, *Peking Studies in Social Service*, *Princeton Alumni Weekly*, *Social Forces*, *Sociology and Social Research*, *Survey*, *Survey Graphic*, and *World Affairs Interpreter*.
FINDING AIDS: Typed chronological list of 25 uncatalogued articles (15 articles are catalogued).

2-GENERAL HOLDINGS
MANUSCRIPTS: "The Mission Work of the Presbyterian Church in the United States in China, 1867–1952," by James Edwin Bear, Jr., 1963–71 (microfilm of original typescript at Union Theological Seminary in Virginia, Richmond, VA, 23227).
SERIALS: *China Christian Year Book*, 1926, 1934–35. *China Monthly: The Truth about China*, 1942–49. *Chinese Recorder*, 1922–23, 1926–31, 1934. *Yenching Journal of Social Studies*,

1938–41. Yenching University, Department of Sociology and Social Work Publications, series A, 1932; series C, n.d.; *Social Research Series*, 1930.

DISSERTATIONS/THESES: *The History and Development of the Central China Mission of the Evangelical United Brethren Church*, by Frederick W. Brandauer, 1953. *Missionary Mother and Radical Daughter: Anna and Ida Pruitt in China, 1887–1939*, by Marjorie King, 1985. *The Other May Fourth Movement: The Chinese "Christian Renaissance," 1919–1937*, by Samuel D. Ling, 1980.

CHINESE LANGUAGE MATERIALS: Lesson outlines and files of educational administration. 1974; outlines of imperial memorials concerning Christianity, 1902.

UNIVERSITY OF PENNSYLVANIA
PA–215 Van Pelt Library
Philadelphia PA 19104
(215) 243-3205
Nancy Cheng, Oriental Bibliographer

1-GENERAL HOLDINGS
PAMPHLETS: *Catalogue of Publications by Protestant Missionaries in China*, 1876.

MAPS/DESIGNS/DRAWINGS: *Missions Catholiques en Chine*, by J. B. Prudhomme, 1936, containing maps and a chart showing ecclesiastical regions, Catholic population by province, and the increase in Chinese priests from 1900 to 1935.

SERIALS: China Christian Educational Association, *Bulletin*, 1925–26. *Chinese Recorder*, 1868–78. *Chinese Repository*, 1832–51. *Ching Feng*, 1964–73. *Educational Review*, 1926–33. *Folklore Studies*, 1942-. *Lingnan Science Journal*, 1922–41. Lingnan University, *Science Bulletin*, 1930–31. *Monumenta Serica*, 1935-. Nanking Theological Seminary, English publications, 1940. *Variétés Sinologiques*, 1895–1902, 1909, 1912, 1914, 1917. West China Border Research Society, *Journal*, 1922, 1924–45(?). Yenching University: *Yenching Journal of Social Studies*, 1938-; Monograph, 1936; Supplement, n.d.

DISSERTATIONS/THESES: *The American Missionaries' Outlook on China, 1830–1860*, by Earl Cranston, 1934. *American Missions and American Diplomacy in China, 1830–1900: A Study of the Relations of American Missionaries, American Missions, and the American Missionary Movement to the Official Relations between the United States and China to 1900*, by Allen Thomas Price, 1932. *China and Educational Autonomy: The Changing Role of the Protestant Educational Missionary in China*, by Alice Henrietta Gregg, 1945. *The Chinese Indigenous Church Movement, 1919–1927: A Protestant Response to the Anti-Christian Movements in Modern China*, by Jonathan Chao, 1986. *Christian Missions in China*, by C. S. Estes, 1895. *An Eighteenth-century Frenchman at the Court of the K'ang-hsi Emperor: A Study of the Early Life of Jean François Foucquet*, by John W. Witek, 1973. *G. W. von Leibniz und die China-mission*, by Franz Rudolf Merkel, 1920. *Imperial Government and Catholic Missions in China during the Years 1784–1785*, by Bernward Henry Willeke, 1948. *The Negotiations between Ch'i-ying and Lagrené, 1844–1846*, by Angelus Francis J. Grosse-Aschhoff, 1950. *La Politique missionaire de la France en Chine, 1842–1856: l'ouverture des cinq ports chinois au commerce étranger et à la liberté religieuse*, by Louis

Tsing-sing Wei, 1960. *Protestant Mission Schools for Girls in South China (1827 to the Japanese Invasion)*, by Mary Raleigh Anderson, 1943. *La Rencontre et le conflit entre les idées des missionnaires chrétiens et les idées des Chinois en Chine depuis la fin de la dynastie des Ming*, by Liang Si-ing, 1940.

CHINESE LANGUAGE MATERIALS: 6 books on Chinese church history, Christianity and Christian missions, Young J. Allen, and religious thought movements in China, 1927–77.

WESTMINSTER THEOLOGICAL SEMINARY
PA–220 Library
Chestnut Hill
Philadelphia PA 19118
(215) 887-5511
Robert Kepple, Librarian
Grace Mullen, Archivist

1-J. GRESHAM MACHEN PAPERS, 1920s–1930s, 1 l.f.
Background note: John Gresham Machen was a professor of New Testament at Princeton Theological Seminary from 1906 until 1929. In 1929, he left Princeton and was instrumental in the founding of Westminster Theological Seminary, where he taught until his death in 1937. During the 1920s and 1930s Machen was involved in the Fundamentalist/Modernist controversy that raged in the Presbyterian Church in the U.S.A. He was interested in documenting what was happening during this period in the foreign mission fields, particularly China.

CORRESPONDENCE: Correspondence of J. Gresham Machen with missionaries and others in China to document the type of teaching and work in China during the 1920s and early 1930s.

FINDING AIDS: The collection is inventoried. A guide is in preparation.

2-GENERAL HOLDINGS
SERIALS: China Inland Mission, *Occasional Papers*, 1872–75. *China Notes*, 1971-. *Chinese Recorder*, 1871–72, 1909–10, 1923–24.

DISSERTATIONS/THESES: *American Missionaries and the Chinese Communists: A Study of Views Expressed by Methodist Episcopal Church Missionaries, 1921–1941*, by Milo Lancaster Thornberry, Jr., 1974. *Timothy Richard's Theory of Christian Missions to the Non-Christian World*, by Rita Thérèse Johnson, 1966.

PHOENIXVILLE

VALLEY FORGE CHRISTIAN COLLEGE
PA–225 Library
Phoenixville PA 19460
(215) 935-0450
Dorsey Reynolds, Librarian

1-GENERAL HOLDINGS
PAMPHLETS: *Evangelizing West China*, by W. W. Simpson, 1931(?); *God's Faithfulness in Ningpo*, comp. by Nettie D. Nichols and Joshua Bang, n.d.

PITTSBURGH

CAPUCHIN FRANCISCAN FRIARS
PA–230 Province of St. Augustine of the Capuchin Order Library
220 Thirty-seventh Street
Pittsburgh PA 15201
(412) 682–6430
Francis Fugini, O.F.M. Cap., Archivist

1-GENERAL HOLDINGS
CORRESPONDENCE: Letters from Capuchins in Kansu province: 31 letters to and from Rudolph Blockinger, O.F.M. Cap., Tsinchow, 1925-51; 9 letters from Agatho Rolf, O.F.M. Cap., Tsinchow, 1925-1929; 4 letters from Gabriel McCarthy, O.F.M. Cap., Tsinchow, 1925-1929; 8 letters from Most Rev. Salvator P. Walleser, O.F.M. Cap., bishop of Tienshui, 1918-29 (in German); 2 letters from Most Rev. Gratian Grimm, O.F.M. Cap., bishop of Tienshui, 1949-50 (in German).
MANUSCRIPTS: "The Capuchin Mission in China, 1922-1952," by Rudolph Blockinger, O.F.M. Cap., 1958.

PA–235 CARNEGIE LIBRARY OF PITTSBURGH
4400 Forbes Avenue
Pittsburgh PA 15213–4080
(412) 622–3127
Robert P. Croneberger, Director
Robert M. Repp III, Head, Reference Department

1-GENERAL HOLDINGS
CORRESPONDENCE/PAMPHLETS: Letters written from China by John of Montecorvino and Andrew of Perugia, ca. 13th century, in Latin with translation, repr. from the *Royal Asiatic Society Journal*, 1914.
MAPS/DESIGNS/DRAWINGS: *Atlas of the Chinese Empire, Containing Separate Maps of the Eighteen Provinces of China Proper, Together with an Index to All the Names on the Maps and a List of All Protestant Mission Stations, &c., Specially Prepared for the China Inland Mission*, by Edward Stanford, 1908.
SERIALS: *Yenching Journal of Social Studies*, Monograph, 1936.

PITTSBURGH THEOLOGICAL SEMINARY
PA–240 Clifford E. Barbour Library
616 North Highland Avenue
Pittsburgh PA 15206
(412) 362–5610
Dikran Y. Hadidian, Director
Mary Ellen Scott, Archivist

1-GENERAL HOLDINGS
MINUTES/RECORDS/REPORTS: American Presbyterian Mission at Shantung, annual station reports: Chefoo Station, 1925, 1930-36, 1938-39; Tengchow Station, 1922; Vihsien Station, 1932; Foreign Missions Conference of North America, addresses on China, 1927; General Mission Meeting, Shantung Mission (Tsingtao), addresses and discussions, 1930; Presbyterian Church in the U.S.A., China Council, 1918, 1920.
CORRESPONDENCE: Letters of B. Craig Patterson from Suchien, n.d.

MANUSCRIPTS: "A College and an Empire," Shantung Union College, n.d.
PAMPHLETS: Reprint of article in the *Peking & Tientsin Times* about murders in Shansi, 1900; letter in pamphlet form by Mary J. Bergen from Shantung Union College, 1906; program for the celebration of the 50th anniversary (1882-1932) of Samuel Hayes' missionary service.
ORAL HISTORIES: *China Missionaries Oral History Collection*, ed. by Cyrus H. Peake and Arthur L. Rosenbaum (Claremont Graduate School, Oral History Program), 1973. See ORAL HISTORIES Union List for the names of participants.
SERIALS: *China Christian Year Book*, 1918-19, 1923-26, 1928-29, 1931-37. *Ching Feng*, 1964-.
DISSERTATIONS/THESES: *The Work of the American Presbyterian Mission from 1918 to 1941 toward the Lessening of Adult Illiteracy in Shantung Province, China*, by Horace Edward Chandler, 1943.

REFORMED PRESBYTERIAN THEOLOGICAL SEMINARY
PA–245 Library
7418 Penn Avenue
Pittsburgh PA 15208
(412) 731–8690
Rachel George, Librarian

1-"HEAVENLY WIND"—RED CHINA PROTESTANT PRO-COMMUNIST PAPERS AND OTHER BOOKS AND MAGAZINES, n.d., 2 l.f.
MINUTES/RECORDS/REPORTS/CHINESE LANGUAGE MATERIALS: Papers in English and Chinese including Protestant pro-Communist and Protestant anti-Communist writings.

2-SOUTH CHINA REFORMED PRESBYTERIAN MISSION PAPERS, 1895-1954, 2 l.f.
MINUTES/RECORDS/REPORTS: Research materials from South China Reformed Presbyterian Mission used by Alice Robb to write *Hoi Moon* (1970), 1895-1954.

3-GENERAL HOLDINGS
MINUTES/RECORDS/REPORTS: Folder of reports on closed communion, a principle of the Reformed Presbyterian Church of North America not adopted by the Chinese church; folder of reports on the split in the church in China after the missionaries were forced to leave.
CORRESPONDENCE/MEMORABILIA: Folder of correspondence and miscellaneous items of Mrs. E. J. M. Dickson, including South China letters, and excerpts and copies from *Olive Trees* magazine, 1899-1949; uncatalogued letters of Johannes Geerhardus Vos, who served in Manchuria from 1931 to 1942, including clippings and miscellaneous ephemera, some in Chinese, n.d.
DISSERTATIONS/THESES: *Fifty Years of Covenanter Evangelism in South China*, by Orlena Marie Lynn, 1948.

UNIVERSITY OF PITTSBURGH
PA–250 East Asian Library
Hillman Library (Third Floor)
Pittsburgh PA 15260
(412) 624–4457/0259
Thomas Kuo, Director

1-GENERAL HOLDINGS

CHINESE LANGUAGE MATERIALS: 23 volumes, 1917–74, on Young J. Allen, American missions in China, the anti-Christian movement of 1860–74, Catholic church government, Christian life, Christianity and Christians in China, early collections of Christian literature, historical sources of Christianity in China, relations with foreign countries (involving Christian missions), and the Taiping Rebellion.

PA–255 Health Sciences Library

University of Pittsburgh
Scaife Hall
Pittsburgh PA 15260
(412) 624-2521
June B. Bandamere, Acting Director

1-GENERAL HOLDINGS

SERIALS: *Chinese Medical Journal*, 1943–44.

PA–260 Hillman Library

University of Pittsburgh
Pittsburgh PA 15260
(412) 624-4434
Ann Woodsworth, Director
Charles Aspon, Director, Special Collections

1-GENERAL HOLDINGS

PAMPHLETS: *Far West in China*, by Stanton Lautenschlager, 1944.
ORAL HISTORIES: *China Missionaries Oral History Collection*, ed. by Cyrus H. Peake and Arthur L. Rosenbaum (Claremont Graduate School, Oral History Program), 1973. See ORAL HISTORIES Union List for the names of participants.
SERIALS: *China Christian Year Book*, 1932–33. *Directory of Protestant Missions in China*, 1916. *Folklore Studies*, 1942–47.
DISSERTATIONS/THESES: *American Catholic China Missionaries, 1918–1941*, by Thomas A. Breslin, 1974. *The New China: An Eastern Version of Messianic Hope*, by Lee Seung-ik, 1982. *The Work of the American Presbyterian Mission from 1918 to 1941 toward the Lessening of Adult Illiteracy in Shantung Province, China*, by Horace Edward Chandler, 1943.

ROBESONIA

PA–265 OVERSEAS MISSIONARY FELLOWSHIP

404 South Church Street
Robesonia PA 19551
(215) 693-5881
Daniel W. Bacon, Home Director

Restrictions: Access by appointment.
Background note: The Overseas Missionary Fellowship (OMF) began as a branch of the China Inland Mission (CIM) in 1951, after CIM missionaries left China. Overseas Missionary Fellowship became the mission's official name in 1952. The China Inland Mission, which had been founded by J. Hudson Taylor in 1865 in England, sent its first missionaries from the United States and the CIM to Wheaton College, Billy Graham Center Archives, Wheaton, IL, 60187.

The published material of the CIM archives is located in OMF's Permanent Reference Library, while most of the unpublished material (memorabilia, photos, etc.) is kept in a separate room.

1-CHINA INLAND MISSION ARCHIVES, 1866–1977, quantity undetermined

MINUTES/RECORDS/REPORTS: "Report of a Journey of Investigation Made by Mark E. Botham on the Invitation of the Special Committee on Work for Moslems," by Mark E. Botham, ca. 1920s; China Inland Mission (CIM), annual reports, 1904–59; Marcus Ch'eng's verbatim report and newspaper reports, prayer meeting in the Lyceum Theatre, Shanghai, 1926; Chungking Theological Seminary, report, 1945.
CORRESPONDENCE: 6 boxes of candidates' files.
MANUSCRIPTS: "Memoirs of Cyril Faulkner," 1977; "Years That Are Past," by Henry W. Frost, n.d., which was the basis of the book *By Faith—Henry W. Frost and the CIM* (1938) by Howard and Mary Taylor; untitled manuscript by Henry Frost describing the work in China, 1930s.
PAMPHLETS: *After Forty Years*, by Marcus Ch'eng, n.d.; *China and Mohammed*, by Olive M. Botham, 1948; *The Hospital of Benevolence and Compassion [in Liangshan, Szechwan]*, by Evelyn M. Barber, n.d.; *An Hour with James Hudson Taylor, Pioneer Missionary to China*, by Theodore W. Engstrom, 1942; *An Hour with John and Betty Stam, Martyred Missionaries to China*, by Theodore W. Engstrom, 1942; *Introducing Students of the Chungking Theological Seminary*, by Marcus Ch'eng, n.d.; *Light Shineth in Darkness*, by Dorothy Beugler, 1940; *The Two Roads: An Explanatory Pamphlet to be Used in Conjunction with Posters*, by Charlotte F. Tippett, 1932.
MEMORABILIA: 3 boxes of Chinese clothing and other memorabilia, including a banner presented to Joy Leister when she left China, and a Chinese flag; bag of Chinese hats and brooms; CIM guest books, Philadelphia, 1903–51.
MAPS/DESIGNS/DRAWINGS: *Complete Atlas of China*, by Edward Stanford (London: China Inland Mission and Edward Stanford, Ltd.), 1917; *Complete Map of China Prepared for the China Inland Mission* (London: China Inland Mission and Edward Stanford, Ltd.), 1923; *A Map of China Prepared for the China Inland Mission* (London: Stanford's Geographical Establishment), 1923; *Map of China Showing the Stations of the China Inland Mission* (London: China Inland Mission), 1911; *Map of China Showing the Stations of the China Inland Mission* (London: China Inland Mission), 1926; *Map of China Showing the Stations of the China Inland Mission* (Toronto: China Inland Mission), n.d.
AUDIO-VISUAL MATERIALS: Box of glass negatives by J. Hudson Taylor, n.d.; 60 slides taken by Lucile Opperman, n.d.; 80 slides taken by Ian and Helen Anderson, n.d.
SERIALS: *China and the Gospel*, 1904–36. *China Christian Year Book*, 1928, 1931, 1934–35. China Inland Mission, *Field Bulletin*, 1939–52; *Occasional Papers*, 1866–75. *China Mission Year Book*, 1917, 1919, 1923–25. *China's Millions*, (London) 1875–1952; (Australian ed.) 1935–53, 1971, 1975–84; (Philadelphia) 1893–1952; (American supp.) 1891–92. *Directory of Protestant Missionaries in China, Japan, and Corea*, 1912. *Directory of Protestant*

Missions in China, 1919–21, 1923–24, 1928–34, 1936–37, 1939. *Friends of Moslems*, 1927–49. West China Border Research Society, *Journal*, 1922–25, 1932–34, 1936, 1938, 1942, 1944–45. *Yenching Journal of Social Studies*, 1938–41. *Young China*, 1927–50.

CHINESE LANGUAGE MATERIALS: Box marked "Old manuscripts in a tribal language prepared when CIM was in China," n.d. (apparently pre-1900); *The Acts of Hudson Taylor*, by Hu-tai Sheng, 1904; *Biography of Hudson Taylor*, by Howard and Mary Taylor, trans. S. M. Hu, 1950s(?); *Margaret King's Vision*, by Mary Taylor, trans. Mary Woo, 1936; *Outlines of Church History*, by Nina E. Gemmell, n.d.; "The Two Roads: An Exposition of No. 3250A, of the "Preaching by Pictures' Series of Posters," by Charlotte F. Tippet; 4 hymn books, including *The C.I.M. Hymnary*, 1922; *Daily Light*, n.d.; *The Kuoyü Bible Commentary*, by F. C. H. Dreyer, n.d.; *The Mandarin Bible Commentary*, by F. C. H. Dreyer, n.d.; 11 Hwa Miao, Nosu, and Mandarin New and Old Testament Bibles.

FINDING AIDS: Card files.

2-PERMANENT LIBRARY, 1878–1980, 3 titles
SERIALS: *China's Millions* (London), 1878, 1885–1949. *The Millions* (Philadelphia), 1954–80. *Young China*, 1927, 1930–32, 1937–41.

3-PHOTOGRAPH COLLECTION, ca. 1888–1951, ca. 2 l.f., 2 in.
MANUSCRIPTS/MEMORABILIA/AUDIO-VISUAL MATERIALS: "OMF Historical," a folder containing: "Wang Ming-tao," by David H. Adeney, n.d.; "Declaration of Trust," by J. Hudson Taylor, 1894; 10 photos of John and Isobel Kuhn, n.d.; photo of the China Inland Mission's farewell meeting in Toronto for its first 20 missionaries from North America, 1888; photos of J. Hudson Taylor, Betty Stam, Howard and Mary Geraldine (Guinness) Taylor, and Mr. and Mrs. Herbert Taylor; "Pre-OMF Portraits: Worthies," a folder containing: CIM valedictory service program for commissioning new missionaries, ca. 1940s; photos of J. Hudson Taylor's funeral, 1905, and of the tomb of his wife, Maria, taken by the sister of Harold Marshall, n.d.; ca. 20 photos of J. Hudson Taylor by himself and with other missionaries, n.d.; photos of Bishop Frank Houghton, H. M. Griffin, Mrs. Robert Porteous, George K. Harris, George W. Gibb, Oswald Sanders, and D. E. Hoste, n.d.; 2 l.f. of photos depicting civilization, culture, people, war, relief efforts, and mission work in China.
ORAL HISTORIES: Typescript of an oral interview of Helen E. and Ralph C. Scoville, by Catherine Damato, n.d.
SERIALS: *China's Millions* (Philadelphia), 1927.

SWARTHMORE

SWARTHMORE COLLEGE
PA-270 Friends Historical Library
   Swarthmore PA 19081
   (215) 447-7496
   J. William Frost, Director
   Albert W. Fowler, Associate Director

Background note: Additional documents of the Religious Society of Friends (Quakers) are located at Haverford College, James P. Magill Library, Haverford, PA, 19041, and the American Friends Service Committee Archives, 1501 Cherry Street, Philadelphia, PA, 19102.
Finding aids: *Guide to the Manuscript Collections of the Friends' Historical Library of Swarthmore College*, 1982.

1-ELKINTON FAMILY PAPERS, 1914–15, 1 folder
Background note: Joseph Elkinton (1859–1920), a Quaker minister, travelled to China, Japan, and Korea in 1914–15 representing the Philadelphia Monthly Meeting (Orthodox).
CORRESPONDENCE: Letter of introduction from W. J. Bryan of the U.S. State Department to U.S. diplomatic and consular officers in Japan and China, 1915; responses to Elkinton's trip from Chinese friends, 1915.
MEMORABILIA: Passport to China, Korea, and Japan, 1914.
FINDING AIDS: "Elkinton Family Papers Checklist."

2-FRIENDS OPPORTUNITY IN THE ORIENT PAPERS, 1922–24, quantity undetermined
Background note: Friends Opportunity in the Orient was an unofficial organization of the Hicksite Quakers in the Philadelphia area. Funds were collected and sent to Canton Christian College and Canton Hospital, in part to support Margaret Hallowell (Riggs) Augur, a Quaker teacher there.
MINUTES/RECORDS/REPORTS: Canton Hospital, annual report, 1922; Friends Opportunity in the Orient, treasurer's report, 1924.
CORRESPONDENCE: Letters, mostly from or about Margaret Hallowell Augur, 1923–24.

3-HAVILLAND FAMILY PAPERS, 1913, 1 item
CORRESPONDENCE: Copy of an epistle from the Szechwan Yearly Meeting of Friends, addressed to Friends overseas, 1913.

4-GENERAL HOLDINGS
MINUTES/RECORDS/REPORTS: Records of peace activities of Quaker meetings, 1827–1947, including views and activities of Friends in China.
PAMPHLETS: *Friends in China*, 1941.
DISSERTATIONS/THESES: *J. Lossing Buck, American Missionary: The Application of Scientific Agriculture in China, 1915–1944*, by James Pugh, 1973.

UNIVERSITY PARK

PENNSYLVANIA STATE UNIVERSITY
PA-275 Penn State Room
   Pattee Library
   University Park PA 16802
   (814) 865-7931
   Leon J. Stout, Head, Penn State Collection Archives

Background note: The Penn State collections are part of the record of the Penn State College Mission to China which was centered at Lingnan University in Canton. Lingnan University was founded by the American Presbyterian Mission in 1885 as the Christian College of China, later renamed Canton Christian College, now called Zhongshan University.

The Penn State College Mission to China grew out of the appointment of a Penn State graduate, George Weidman Groff, as a

missionary teacher in Canton by the Presbyterian Board of Foreign Missions in 1907. Trained as an agriculturalist and committed to teaching agriculture, he began that work as soon as he arrived. His friends at Penn State developed financial support for his work and organized the Penn State College Mission to China in 1911 to administer the finances and the program. Lingnan University's School of Agriculture was founded in 1921, with Groff as dean. Penn State exchanged students with Lingnan and sent livestock and seed for use in the program. See also Lingnan University collections at Harvard University, Harvard-Yenching Library, 2 Divinity Avenue, Cambridge, MA, 02138; and Yale Divinity School, Special Collections, 409 Prospect Street, New Haven, CT, 06510.
Finding aids: "Resources on Twentieth-century China in Special Collections at the Pennsylvania State University Libraries," ed. by Leon J. Stout, 1977.

1-WALTER L. FUNKHOUSER PAPERS, 1919–22, 800 items
Background note: A graduate of Pennsylvania State University, Walter L. Funkhouser was a professor of animal husbandry at Lingnan University.
CORRESPONDENCE/DIARIES: Letters and diary describing his life and work in Canton, 1919–22.
AUDIO-VISUAL MATERIALS: 200 photos of life in and around Canton, 1919–22.

2-GEORGE WEIDMAN GROFF PAPERS, 1910–58, 77 l.f.
MINUTES/RECORDS/REPORTS/CORRESPONDENCE/ MANUSCRIPTS: George Groff's published and unpublished works, and material relating to his interest in increasing Western knowledge of Chinese plant life, including a *Chinese Index to Botanical Names of Kwangtung Plants*, and copies of early works on Chinese botany (some as early as 11th century).
FINDING AIDS: *Report on the G. Weidman Groff Collection*, by Henry S. Brunner (University Park, PA), 1961.

3-PENN STATE-IN-CHINA COLLECTION, 1910–58, 5.5 l.f.
MINUTES/RECORDS/REPORTS/CORRESPONDENCE: American Board of Trustees, 1910–58; Penn State-in-China Committee (successor to the Penn State College Mission to China), 1910–58; correspondence between George Weidman Groff and his Penn State associates: Dean of Agriculture Ralph Watts, Professor of Agricultural Education Henry S. Brunner, and Richard E. Pride (who succeeded Groff as professor of horticulture at Lingnan University).
FINDING AIDS: Scope and content notes.

4-GENERAL HOLDINGS
MINUTES/RECORDS/REPORTS: American Board of Commissioners for Foreign Missions, annual reports, 1810–21, 1827, 1834–45, 1847–1901, 1903–39, 1941–56; Federation of Woman's Boards of Foreign Missions of North America, report of deputation to China, 1920; Presbyterian Church in the U.S.A., Board of Foreign Missions, annual reports, 1838–1950.
CORRESPONDENCE: Letter from Justus Doolittle, in Foochow, to James Calder of Hillsdale, Michigan, describing his situation, having lost his position as translator for A. Heard & Co., and requesting aid to publish a two-volume *Vocabulary and Handbook of the Chinese Language*, 1871.
MANUSCRIPTS: Repr. of typescript of "An Agricultural Survey of Szechwan Province, China: A Summary and Interpretation . . . of a full report in Chinese by the Szechwan rural economics survey

committee of the Farmer's Bank of China, in cooperation with the Department of Agricultural Economics, University of Nanking...," by John Lossing Buck, 1943.
PAMPHLETS: *Far West in China*, by Stanton Lautenschlager, 1944.
ORAL HISTORIES: *China Missionaries Oral History Collection*, ed. by Cyrus H. Peake and Arthur L. Rosenbaum (Claremont Graduate School, Oral History Program), 1973. See ORAL HISTORIES Union List for the names of participants.
SERIALS: China Christian Educational Association, *Bulletin*, 1928. *Chinese Repository*, 1832–51. *Lingnan Science Journal*, 1922–50. Lingnan University: *Bulletin*, 1908–21; *Daily Meteorological Record*, 1919–23; *Science Bulletin*, 1930–31, 1944. *Peking Natural History Bulletin*, 1931-. *T'oung Pao*, 1890–1962, 1970-. Yenching University, Department of Biology, *Bulletin*, 1930.
CHINESE LANGUAGE MATERIALS: Book on the origin of anti-Christian activities, 1966.

VALLEY FORGE

PA–280 AMERICAN BAPTIST HEADQUARTERS
American Baptist Board of International Ministries
Valley Forge PA 19481
(215) 768-2000
Priscilla Shaw, Librarian

Restrictions: Most materials are closed to the public; researchers should inquire regarding access.
Background note: The American Baptist Board of International Missions was previously known as: the General Missionary Convention of the Baptist Denomination in the United States for Foreign Missions (1814–46), the American Baptist Missionary Union (1845–1910), and the American Baptist Foreign Mission Society (1910–74). The Women's American Baptist Foreign Mission Society was founded in 1871, and in 1955 it was integrated with the American Baptist Foreign Mission Society. American Baptist missions in China began in 1842 and closed in 1950. See also the American Baptist Historical Society, 1106 South Goodman Street, Rochester, NY, 14620; and the American Baptist Historical Society, American Baptist Archives Center, Valley Forge, PA, 19481.

1-CLARA LEACH COLLECTION, 1916–49, quantity undetermined
Background note: A graduate of Wellesley College and Temple University, Clara Chase Leach (1888–1981) became a doctor in the early 1900s. She began work as a missionary doctor in China in 1916 under the auspices of the American Baptist Women's Foreign Missionary Society, working in a missionary hospital in Kityang, South China from 1916 to 1931 and from 1934 to 1941. Interned by the Japanese in 1941, she was later returned to the United States on the *Gripsholm* in a prisoner exchange. After the war she returned to China, remaining there until she was forced out in 1949. Microfilm copies of her diaries are held by the American Baptist Historical Society, 1106 South Goodman Street, Rochester, NY, 14620; and University of Vermont, Bailey/Howe Library, Burlington, VT, 15405-0036.
CORRESPONDENCE/DIARIES/MEMORABILIA: Correspondence and diaries relating to her missionary service in China, 1916–28, 1935–49; several boxes of miscellaneous items, including native costumes.

AMERICAN BAPTIST HISTORICAL SOCIETY
PA–285 American Baptist Archives Center
P. O. Box 851
Valley Forge PA 19482–0851
(215) 768–2000
Beverly Carlson, Archivist, Interim Administrator

Background note: American Baptist Foreign Mission Society (ABFMS) presence in China spans the years from 1834 to 1954. See also the American Baptist Historical Society, 1106 South Goodman Street, Rochester, NY, 14620.

1-RECORDS OF THE AMERICAN BAPTIST FOREIGN MISSION SOCIETY, 1842–1950, quantity undetermined
MINUTES/RECORDS/REPORTS: 3 l.f. of field reports from China; Commission to Central China, report, 1911; China policy, 1912; Yangtzepoo Social Center of Shanghai College, report, 1921; report on postwar problems, 1948.
CORRESPONDENCE: Correspondence of all China missionaries, included both in the China section of the Missionary Candidate Files and on microfilm (not organized geographically), 1842–1950.
PAMPHLETS: Miscellaneous pamphlets about mission work in China.
MEMORABILIA: Miscellaneous printed matter and clippings relating to conditions between 1900 and 1950 and the Huchow mission.
AUDIO-VISUAL MATERIALS: Photos of missionaries and mission fields.
SERIALS: *China Mission Advocate*, 1839.

2-GENERAL HOLDINGS
MINUTES/RECORDS/REPORTS: East China Conference, 1919–26; East China, minutes, 1886–1939; Ginling College, catalogues, 1915–35; Nanking Seminary, 1916–41; Shaohsing Hospital, 1911–45; South China, minutes, 1908–40; South China Baptist Annual, 1916–20; South China Mission, Reference Committee, minutes, 1921–30; University of Nanking, catalogues, 1914–31; University of Nanking, 1913–34; University of Shanghai, reports, 1909–41; West China Baptist missions, 1915–36; West China Conference Director, 1925–28; West China, minutes, 1910–50; West China Union University, catalogues, 1910–33; West China Union University, reports, 1910–39; *Our Work in the Orient*, (annual reports on China of the women's branch of ABFMS), 1909–28; Yearbook of the Northern Baptist Convention, China reports, 1909–49; Yearbook of the American Baptist Convention, China reports, 1950–85; China reports in the denominational serials *Baptist Missionary Review*, 1895–1957; *Christian Higher Education*, 1924–37; and *Christian Middle Schools*, 1925–39.
CORRESPONDENCE/AUDIO-VISUAL MATERIALS: 16 boxes of correspondence and photos, n.d.; 19 boxes of letters and reports from China, 1938–49; letters from American Baptist Foreign Missionary Society missionaries in China, n.d.
SERIALS: American Baptist Foreign Mission Society, *Quarterly Bulletin*, 1917–25. *China Bulletin*, 1937, 1952–62. *Shanghai Baptist College Bulletin*, 1907–36. University of Nanking, College of Agriculture and Forestry, *Report of Agriculture and Forestry*, 1920–44. *University of Shanghai Bulletin*, 1937–40. *West China Missionary News*, 1932–35, 1939.

RHODE ISLAND

PROVIDENCE

BROWN UNIVERSITY

RI–5   John Carter Brown Library
College Green
Providence RI 02912
(401) 863–2725

1-GENERAL HOLDINGS
PAMPHLETS: *Windows into China: The Jesuits and Their Books, 1580–1730*, by John Parker, 1978.

RI–10   Brown University Archives
Brown University
The John Hay Library
Providence RI 02912
(401) 863–2148
Martha L. Mitchell, University Archivist

Background note: In addition to the materials listed below, the Brown University Archives may hold papers on the Brown-in-China program in collections of individuals affiliated with the university.

1-GENERAL HOLDINGS
MANUSCRIPTS: List of Brown alumni who became missionaries, 1807–1934, including China missionaries.
PAMPHLETS: *Brown in China*, 1922.
MEMORABILIA: Clippings on Brown-in-China in *Brown Alumni Monthly*, 1917, 1923, 1926.
DISSERTATIONS/THESES: *The Protestant Church in Communist China, 1949–1958*, by James Herbert Kane, 1958. *The Reaction of Western Commentators to the Taiping Rebellion, with a Concentration on the Writings of Leading Nineteenth-century Protestant Missionaries: A Study in Comparative Historiography*, by Daniel Peter Altieri, 1971.
CHINESE LANGUAGE MATERIALS: *How Would Hydro-electrical Development Improve the Economic Life of the People?*, by Tan Kuei-chun, 1948; *A Social Survey of the Village of Sung-Ka-Hong, China, 1923–24*, by Yu Chang-ching, 1924 (a study by students at Shanghai College, published by Brown-in-China).

RI–15   The John Hay Library
Brown University
20 Prospect Street
Providence RI 02912
(401) 863–2146
Barbara Filipac, Manuscripts
Jennifer B. Lee, Curator of Printed Books

1-BAPTIST COLLECTION, 1896–1910, 10 items
MINUTES/RECORDS/REPORTS: China Baptist Publication Society, Canton, report, 1902, 1910; Eastern China Baptist Mission Conference, Shanghai, minutes, 1904, 1907, 1909–10; Kakchie, Swatow Mission, annual report, 1902.
PAMPHLETS: *Pope and Pagan*, by William Ashmore (repr. *Baptist Missionary Review*), n.d.; *Flatly Contradicted (Outrages on the American Baptist Mission at Kho-khoi)*, by William Ashmore, 1897; *Outrages on the American Baptist Mission at Kho-khoi (near Swatow)*, by William Ashmore, 1896.

2-CHARLES DAVIS JAMESON PAPERS (MS 83.2), ca. 1900, 2 items
Background note: Charles Davis Jameson (1855–1927) was an engineer who worked and travelled in China during the Boxer Rebellion.
CORRESPONDENCE: Letter to Jameson from J[onathan] Goforth, J. MacKenzie, L. Craigie Hood, [?] Leslie, and "Jno. Griffith" (Griffith John?), ca. 1900.
MANUSCRIPTS: "A Trip from Tientsin via Te Chow, Ling Ching, Wai Hui, Hwai King, Chang Tien, Yellow River, Yangtze Hsien, Nan Yang Fu, Fancheng, Anlu, and Hankow, to Shanghai; During the Boxer Disturbances," including discussion of the role of missionaries, 1900.
FINDING AIDS: In-house inventory.

3-METCALF COLLECTION, 1837–72, 4 items
PAMPHLETS: *Hope for China! or, Be Not Weary in Well-doing*, by Griffith John, 1872; *Sermon in Salem, Jan. 26, 1812, for the Benefit of the Translations of the Scriptures into the Languages of India and China*, by William Johns, n.d.; *China as a Mission Field*, by Miles Justin Knowlton, n.d.; *Address in Behalf of the China Mission*, by W. J. Boone, 1837.

4-GENERAL HOLDINGS
MANUSCRIPTS: "The Great Crisis in China: Century of China Missions, 1807–1907," by William Ashmore, n.d.; Chinese dictionary by Ba[r]ilico de [C]lemona, transcribed by Abel Xaverius, 1726(?); "West of the Yangtze Gorges," by Joseph Taylor, 1944.
PAMPHLETS: *Baptist Mission in China*, by E. F. Merriam, 1894; *A Bibliography of the History of Christianity in China, A Preliminary Draft*, by Jonathan T'ien-en Chao, 1970.
DISSERTATIONS/THESES: *The Negotiations between Ch'i-ying and Lagrené, 1844–1846*, by Angelus Francis Grosse-Aschhoff, 1950. *The Reaction of Western Commentators to the Taiping Rebellion, with a Concentration on the Writings of Leading Nineteenth-century Protestant Missionaries: A Study in Comparative Historiography*, by Daniel Peter Altieri, 1971.
CHINESE LANGUAGE MATERIALS: New Testament, 1936.

RI–20 John D. Rockefeller, Jr., Library
Brown University
10 Prospect Street
Providence RI 02912
(401) 863-2167
(401) 863-2171 (Chinese Collection)
Carol Tatian, Reference Librarian
Wen-kai Kung, Curator, Chinese Collection

1-CHINESE COLLECTION, 1868–1978, 17 items
CHINESE LANGUAGE MATERIALS: 15 volumes on anti-foreignism, churches, Christianity, Matteo Ricci, and missions, 1928–78.
CHINESE LANGUAGE MATERIALS/SERIALS: *Chiao hui hsin pao (Church News)*, 1868–74. *Wan kuo kung pao (The Globe Magazine: A Review of the Times)*, 1874–1907.

2-GENERAL HOLDINGS
SERIALS: Catholic University of Peking, College of Education, Publications, 1939. China Christian Educational Association, *Bulletin*, 1928. *China Christian Year Book*, 1923–24, 1926. China International Famine Relief Commission, Publications, series A, 1927–31. *Chinese Repository*, 1832–51. *The Church in China*, 1894–98. *Lingnan Science Journal*, 1928–29. *New East*, 1909–23, 1925–33. *Yenching Political Science Series*, 1931.
CHINESE LANGUAGE MATERIALS/SERIALS: Yen-ching ta hsüeh, *T'u shu kuan pao* (Yenching University, *Library Bulletin*), n.d.

PROVIDENCE COLLEGE
RI–25 Phillips Memorial Library
Providence RI 02918
(401) 865-2242
Malinda Carpenter, Reference Librarian

1-GENERAL HOLDINGS
DISSERTATIONS/THESES: *American Catholic Missions and Communist China, 1945–1953*, by Virginia F. Unsworth, 1977.

RHODE ISLAND COLLEGE
RI–30 James P. Adams Library
Providence RI 02908
(401) 456-9653
Sally M. Wilson, Assistant Librarian, Special Collections

1-HELEN HAZARD BACON PAPERS, 1918–24, 5 folders
Background note: Helen Hazard Bacon (1861–1925) was the wife of a prominent entrepreneur-industrialist, Nathaniel Terry Bacon. She was involved in a number of civic and charitable activities, including contributions to religious organizations such as the American-Chinese Educational Commission, which operated a school in Canton.
MINUTES/RECORDS/REPORTS/CORRESPONDENCE/PAMPHLETS: American-Chinese Educational Commission, 1918–24, including a small number of pamphlets on missions.
FINDING AIDS: *Register of the Papers of Nathaniel Terry Bacon*.

RHODE ISLAND HISTORICAL SOCIETY
RI–35 Library
121 Hope Street
Providence RI 02906
(401) 331-0448
Harold E. Kemble, Curator of Manuscripts

1-CHARLES NICHOLL TALBOTT PAPERS, 1834–51, 15 items
Background note: Charles Nicholl Talbott (1802–74), a merchant

in silk and tea in Canton, was a Presbyterian and a strong supporter of missionary activities and of the American Bible Society. He provided financial support in New York and abroad, routinely carrying missionaries to China (in particular, to the river city of Lintin) in ships owned or chartered by his firm. His partner, David W. Olyphant, gave free passage to Robert Morrison, the first Protestant missionary in China.

CORRESPONDENCE: 5 letters from Elijah Coleman Bridgman, concerning travel and missionary activity in China, 1834–51; letter from James T. Dickinson, concerning testimony about Alexander V. Fraser, Master of the brig, *Himmaleh*, 1837; 6 letters from Charles William King, including reports on missionary work, 1837; letter from Joshua Leavitt, concerning the editor of the *New York Evangelist*, S. J. Roberts, a missionary requesting passage to China, 1836; letter from David W. C. Olyphant, commenting on missionary work, 1836; letter from Peter Parker, asking Talbott to forward a portrait of Quinqua(?) to Professor Silliman in New Haven, 1836.

FINDING AIDS: In-house inventory.

SOUTH CAROLINA

CHARLESTON

CHARLESTON COUNTY LIBRARY
SC–5   **South Carolina Room**
404 King Street
Charleston SC 29403-6466
(803) 723-1645
Jan Buvinger, Director

1-GENERAL HOLDINGS
Background note: For biographical notes on Alice H. Gregg, see Winthrop College, Archives, Dacus Library, Rock Hill, SC, 29733. See also Union Theological Seminary, Archives, 3041 Broadway at Reinhold Niebuhr Place, New York, NY, 10027.
MANUSCRIPTS: "*Hsin hsin yin*: Heart Touch Hearts: Reminiscences about China and Missioner Alice H. Gregg, 1916–1950," comp. and ed. by Archibald J. Sampson, 1978.

SOUTH CAROLINA HISTORICAL SOCIETY
SC–10   **Archives**
Fireproof Building
100 Meeting Street
Charleston SC 29401
(803) 723-3225
Harlan Greene, Archivist

1-LEILA FAYSSOUX DAVIDSON WILKINSON PAPERS, 1920s, 90 items
Background note: Leila Fayssoux Davidson Wilkinson (1881–1970) was a missionary in China in the 1920s.
CORRESPONDENCE: 14 letters from Wilkinson in China to various correspondents, 1923–24.
DIARIES: Diary, 1924.
AUDIO-VISUAL MATERIALS: 75 photos of China, 1920s.

CLEMSON

CLEMSON UNIVERSITY
SC–15   **Robert Muldrow Cooper Library**
Clemson SC 29631
(803) 656-3026
Joseph F. Boykin, Director

1-GENERAL HOLDINGS
SERIALS: *Lingnan Science Journal*, 1922–48. *Monumenta Serica*, 1935–47.

COLUMBIA

LUTHERAN THEOLOGICAL SOUTHERN SEMINARY
SC–20   **Lineberger Memorial Library**
4201 North Main Street
Columbia SC 29203
(803) 786-5150
W. Richard Fritz, Librarian

1-GENERAL HOLDINGS
SERIALS: *Bridge*, 1983–. *China and the Church Today*, 1979. China Graduate School of Theology *Bulletin*, 1972–82. *Chinese Christians Today*, 1972–74, 1981–82.

UNIVERSITY OF SOUTH CAROLINA
SC–25   **South Caroliniana Library**
Columbia SC 29208
(803) 777-5183
Herbert J. Hartsook, Curator of Manuscripts

1-FRANCIS CLEVELAND JOHNSON PAPERS, 1846–50, 7 items
CORRESPONDENCE: 7 letters from Francis Cleveland Johnson to his father, William Bullein Johnson, 1846–50.

2-MILLS FAMILY PAPERS, 1942–49, 27 items
Background note: The Mills Family papers consist of 484 items (1895–1970). Wilson Plumer Mills (1883–1959) was a Presbyterian missionary in China.
CORRESPONDENCE: 7 letters, 6 of which are from Wilson Mills to his brother, James Edward Mills, 1943–44, including discussions of Wilson Mills' repatriation from internment by the Japanese; 12 letters from Wilson Mills' wife, Cornelia, to various family members, 1942–43, 1949, including discussions of Wilson Mills' repatriation from internment by the Japanese and conditions for missionaries in China in 1949.

PAMPHLETS: *To the Relatives and Friends of Our China Missionaries*, a series of 8 bulletins issued by the Board of Foreign Missions of the Presbyterian Church in the United States of America, 1942–43.

3-HENRY MIDDLETON PARKER, JR. PAPERS, 1859, 4 items
Background note: Henry Middleton Parker, Jr., was a Protestant Episcopal lay missionary in Africa and the son of China missionary Henry Middleton Parker, Sr. (1831–61). This collection of papers contains a total of 66 items (1859–78, 1943).
CORRESPONDENCE: Letter appointing Henry Middleton Parker, Sr., as a missionary to China, and 3 letters from Parker, Sr., in China to his son, 1859 and n.d.

GREENVILLE

FURMAN UNIVERSITY
SC–30   James Buchanan Duke Library
Greenville SC 29613
(803) 294–2191
J. Glenwood Clayton, Director of Special Collections

1-BAPTIST HISTORICAL COLLECTION, 1921, 2 items
PAMPHLETS: *The China Baptist Centennial, 1836–1936: Historical and Miscellaneous Notes*, a bound collection of 6 pamphlets, n.a., n.d.
CHINESE LANGUAGE MATERIALS: Translation of *The Course of Christian History*, by William J. McGlothlin, 1921.

2-GENERAL HOLDINGS
SERIALS: *China Mission Year Book*, 1924. *Chinese Recorder*, 1910.

ROCK HILL

WINTHROP COLLEGE
SC–35   Archives
Dacus Library
Rock Hill SC 29733
(803) 323–2131 Ext.28
Ronald J. Chepesiuk, Head of Special Collections

1-ALICE HENRIETTA GREGG PAPERS, 1930–67, ca. 500 items
Background note: Alice Henrietta Gregg (1893–1978) was a 1914 graduate of Winthrop College and a missionary in China from 1916 to 1950. See also Charleston County Library, South Carolina Room, 404 King Street, Charleston, SC, 29403–6466; and Union Theological Seminary, Archives, 3041 Broadway at Reinhold Niebuhr Place, New York, NY, 10027.
CORRESPONDENCE/MEMORABILIA: Scrapbook containing letters and biographical information, 1950–67.
MANUSCRIPTS/PAMPHLETS/MAPS/DESIGNS/DRAWINGS/AUDIO-VISUAL MATERIALS: Dissertation notes on Chinese culture, pamphlets, magazines, dedication book, charts, drawings, and photos, some relating to Gregg's stay in China.

SOUTH DAKOTA

MITCHELL

UNITED METHODIST CHURCH COMMITTEE ON ARCHIVES AND HISTORY
SD–5   Library
1331 West University Avenue
Mitchell SD 57301
(605) 996–6552
Bette Fillmore, Archivist

1-GENERAL HOLDINGS
PAMPHLETS: *Marie and Missions in China: Survey of Service of Marie Brethorst in West China under the Women's Foreign Missionary Society of the Methodist Church*, comp. by O. B. Dunbar, Vera Ford Knox, and Violet Sanders, 1928; *When the Methodists Came to China, 1847–1948*, by the Methodist Church in the United States, 1949.

SIOUX FALLS

AUGUSTANA COLLEGE

SD–10   Archives of the Episcopal Diocese of South Dakota
The Center for Western Studies
Mikkelsen Library
Box 727
Sioux Falls SD 57197
(605) 336–4007
Harry F. Thompson, Archivist

FINDING AIDS: *Guide to the Archives of the Episcopal Church in South Dakota*, n.d.

1-WILLIAM HOBART HARE PAPERS, 1892, ca. 1 box
Background note: William Hobart Hare, Episcopal Bishop of South Dakota, documented the condition of Anglican missions while serving as missionary bishop to China in 1892.
MINUTES/RECORDS/REPORTS/CORRESPONDENCE/PAMPHLETS/MEMORABILIA/AUDIO-VISUAL MATERIALS: Reports, correspondence, notes, printed materials, notes, clippings, and photos by Hare while in China, 1892.

SD–15   Mikkelsen Library
Augustana College
2111 South Summit Avenue
Sioux Falls SD 57197
(605) 336–4921
Ronelle Thompson, Director

1-NORWEGIAN COLLECTION, 1910, 2 items
PAMPHLETS: *The United Norwegian Lutheran Mission Field in China: A Short Sketch with Illustrations and Map*, by Ingvald Daehlin and Erik Sovik, 1911.
MAPS/DESIGNS/DRAWINGS: *Atlas over Norske Missioner: Karter over Norske Missionsfelter, Fortegnelse over Missionsstationer og Missionsarbeidere*, by O. F. Olden, 1910.

SIOUX FALLS COLLEGE
SD-20   Norman B. Mears Library
22nd and Prairie
Sioux Falls SD 57101
(605) 331-6660
Evelyn Olson, Archivist

1-GENERAL HOLDINGS
SERIALS: *China Christian Year Book*, 1911.

TENNESSEE

CHATTANOOGA

TENNESSEE TEMPLE UNIVERSITY
TN-5   Cierpke Memorial Library
1815 Union Avenue
Chattanooga TN 37404
(615) 493-4251
Sarah Patterson, Director

1-GENERAL HOLDINGS
MINUTES/RECORDS/REPORTS: China Inland Mission, annual reports, 1946, 1949.

CLEVELAND

HAL BERNARD DIXON, JR., PENTECOSTAL RESEARCH CENTER
TN-10   William G. Squires Library
260 11th Street NE
P. O. Box 3448
Cleveland TN 37311-0670
(615) 472-2111
Clyde R. Root, Special Collections Librarian

Background note: The Church of God mission was initiated by Jennie B. Rushin in 1914. Interrupted by the Chinese civil war in 1927, the mission was re-established in 1936 by Paul C. Pitt, who brought Bethel (Bethany) Mission (Free Methodist Church, Canada) into the Church of God. All Church of God missionaries were evacuated in 1949.

1-CHINA MISSION COLLECTION, ca. 1914-ca. 1949, quantity undetermined
MINUTES/RECORDS/REPORTS/CORRESPONDENCE/ AUDIO-VISUAL MATERIALS: Records, reports, and correspondence of Church of God missionaries in China, ca. 1914-ca. 1949; 1 reel microfilm of correspondence from Paul C. Pitt, n.d.; records of the China mission in the Church of God publication, *Church of God Evangel*.

JACKSON

LAMBUTH COLLEGE
TN-15   Luther L. Gobbel Library
Lambuth Boulevard
Jackson TN 38301
(901) 427-1500 Ext. 290
Ann Phillips, Archivist

1-WALTER RUSSELL LAMBUTH PAPERS, 1921-77, 2 items
Background note: For biographical notes, see Millsaps College, Millsaps-Wilson Library, J. B. Cain Archives, Jackson, MS, 39210.
MINUTES/RECORDS/REPORTS: Siberia-Manchuria Mission, annual meeting, minutes, 1921.
MANUSCRIPTS: Biography of Bishop Lambuth by J. Joel Stowe, Jr., 1977.

JEFFERSON CITY

CARSON-NEWMAN COLLEGE
TN-20   Library
Russell Street
Jefferson City TN 37760
(615) 475-9061 Ext. 335
Stanley Benson, Director

1-GENERAL HOLDINGS
PAMPHLETS: *Ida Deaver Lawton of China: Happily Ever After*, by Sadie (Lawton) Holloway, 1954; pamphlets about Lottie Moon: *Big Love Heart*, 1950(?); *Faithful unto Death*, by Miriam Robinson, (?); and *Her Lengthened Shadow*, by Lucy Hamilton Howard, 1950(?).
AUDIO-VISUAL MATERIALS: *Journey Home: Lottie Moon of China*, videocassette by the Southern Baptist Convention, Foreign Mission Board, 1983(?).
DISSERTATIONS/THESES: *Education of Women by Baptists in South China*, by Pauline Frances Brammer, 1947. *Protestant Mission Schools for Girls in South China (1827 to the Japanese Invasion)*, by Mary Raleigh Anderson, 1943.

KNOXVILLE

KNOX COUNTY PUBLIC LIBRARY SYSTEM
TN-25 Calvin M. McClung Historical Collection
Lawson McGhee Library
500 West Church Avenue
Knoxville TN 37902–2505
(615) 523–0781
Steve Cotham, Head, McClung Historical Collection

1-ANNA GAY McCLUNG COLLECTION, 1868–71, 5 folders
Restrictions: Access by appointment.
Background note: E. B. Inslee (1822–71) was a missionary in China from 1856 to 1865, and from 1867 to 1870.
CORRESPONDENCE: Letters of E. B. Inslee, 1868, 1871; miscellaneous correspondence, n.d.
MANUSCRIPTS/MEMORABILIA: "A Complete Life" biography of E. B. Inslee by Mary D. Gay, n.d.; uncatalogued notes, articles, and clippings, belonging to E. B. Inslee, n.d.
PAMPHLETS: *The Missionary Survey*, n.a., 1915; *101 Questions and Answers About China and Our China Missions*, n.a., n.d.; *The Story of the Hangchow Girls' School*, by Mary S. Matthews, n.d.; *The Union Girls' School at Hangchow*, by Mary S. Matthews, n.d.
CHINESE LANGUAGE MATERIALS: Unidentified pamphlet, n.d.

UNIVERSITY OF TENNESSEE, KNOXVILLE
TN-30 Agriculture-Veterinary Medicine Library
Knoxville TN 37996–4500
(615) 974–4273
Don Jett, Director

1-GENERAL HOLDINGS
SERIALS: *Liagnaam Agricultural Review*, 1922–27. *Lingnan Science Journal*, 1927–28, 1942, 1945, 1948.

TN-35 WALLACE MEMORIAL BAPTIST CHURCH
701 Merchants Road
Knoxville TN 37912
(615) 688–4343
Jane R. Powell, Researcher

Restrictions: Access by appointment.
Background note: William L. Wallace, native of Knoxville, was a medical missionary to China from 1935 until his death in a Communist prison in 1951. He was chief surgeon of Stout Memorial Hospital in Wuchow. The church, formed in 1953, is named in his honor. Since 1985, the church has been collecting material relating to Dr. Wallace, his work in China, and the South China Mission. The collection continues to grow and is currently uncatalogued.

In addition to the materials listed below, the collection contains folders of information, including biographies, photographs, correspondence, anecdotes, and manuscripts on the following missionaries who served in China and had some relationship to Dr. Wallace or his work: John A. Abernathy, Jewell Abernathy, Mary C. Alexander, Sanford E. Ayers, Winnie B. Ayers, Mansfield Bailey, Ethel Bailey, Clifford Irene Barratt, Euva Bausum, Robert L.

Bausum, Louella Beddoe, Robert E. Beddoe, James D. Belote, Martha Belote, Sarah K. Bigham, Blanche Bradley, Irene Branum, Catharine Bryan, Eugene Kay Bryan, Frances A. Bryan, John Nelson Bryan, Leta Rue Bryan, Nelson A. Bryan, Ruth Bryan, Baker James Cauthen, Eloise Glass Cauthen, Lora Clement, Inabelle Coleman, Marie Conner, Charles P. Coward, Marian P. Coward, Addie Estelle Cox, Margaret Crawley, Winston Crawley, Charles L. Culpepper, Charles L. Culpepper, Jr., Donal Culpepper, Ola Culpepper, Ida Davis, Robert C. Davis, Jr., Flora E. Dodson, Ruth Ford, Ronald W. Fuller, Margaret Fuller, Arthur Gallimore, Gladys Gallimore, Ed Galloway, Betty Galloway, Arthur S. Gillespie, Pauline Gillespie, Mary Frances Gould, Eva Graves, Rosewell H. Graves, Jessie Green, Lydia E. Greene, Blanche Groves, Elizabeth Hale, Fern Harrington, Ann Harris, Clifton E. Harris, Floyd Flora Hawkins, Alice J. Hayes, C. A. Hayes, Everley Hayes, James A. Herring, Mary Herring, Nan Trammell Herring, Eugene Hill, Louise Hill, Corrine Hollis, James D. Hollis, Frances Hudgens, Edith (Highfill) Humphrey, J. H. Humphrey, Sallie M. James, Pearl Johnson, Virginia Lake, Deaver Lawton, Dorothy Lawton, Geraldine Lawton, Olive Lawton, Cornelia Leavell, George Leavell, Millie Lovegren, Julia Lowe, Helen L. McCullough, Archibald M. MacMillan, Margaret K. MacMillan, Molly McMinn, Charles E. Maddry, Frank K. Means, Dell Mewshaw, Robert Mewshaw, John H. Miller, William Donald Moore, Anne Moore, Agnes Morgan, Carter Morgan, Cleo Morrison, Katie Murray, Buford L. Nichols, Mary Frances Nichols, Lucy Wright Parker, Auria Pender, Ruth Pettigrew, Nelle Putney, Mary Quick, Oz J. Quick, Grace E. Rankin, Manley W. Rankin, Miriam Rankin, Samuel G. Rankin, Janet Ray, Rex Ray, Bettie Ricketson, Robert F. Ricketson, D. Rudolph Russell, Joy D. Russell, Mary H. Sampson, Annie M. Sandlin, Joel R. Saunders, Mabel E. Saunders, Mary Lucile Saunders, Lenora Scarlett, Lois Jorine Short, Margie Shumate, Lucy Smith, Grace Snuggs, Harold Snuggs, Hattie Stallings, Reba C. Stewart, Greene W. Strother, Martha Strother, Mattie Vie Summer, Ethel Fay Taylor, L. A. Thompson, Pauline Thompson, Lorene Tilford, Mary Bryson Tipton, Mary Nelle Tipton, W. H. Tipton, Betty M. Vaught, Cecil S. Ward, Gertrude Ward, Lila Florence Watson, Philip E. White, Mattie M. White, James T. Williams, Laurie S. Williams, Thelma Williams, Frank Woodward, and Mabel Woodward.

See also Southern Baptist Convention, Foreign Mission Board, Box 6767, 3806 Monument Avenue, Richmond, VA, 23230; Southern Baptist Convention Historical Commission, Library and Archives, 901 Commerce Street, Nashville, TN, 37203–3260; and Virginia Baptist Historical Society, University of Richmond, Boatwright Memorial Library, Box 95, Richmond, VA, 23173.

1-BILL WALLACE COLLECTION, 1905–85, quantity undetermined
MINUTES/RECORDS/REPORTS: Southern Baptist Convention, Foreign Mission Board, South China Mission, annual reports, 1905–51.
CORRESPONDENCE: Correspondence and information from friends and co-workers, n.d.; copies of correspondence from Everley Hayes, n.d.
MANUSCRIPTS: Background materials on the making of the film, "Bill Wallace of China," supplied by Gregory Walcott, n.d.; unpublished biography of Wallace by Nelle Davidson, n.d.; "China Project Bibliography," by Frank K. Means, ca. 1983.

MEMORABILIA/AUDIO-VISUAL MATERIALS: Miscellaneous Wallace family memorabilia; missionary albums and directories, 1935–52; general information on Wallace family and friends; memorials to Wallace; tributes, press releases, articles, and speeches, 1935–85; photos from Everley Hayes, n.d.; miscellaneous information on Lucy Wright Parker, n.d.; box of mounted photos, n.d.; ''Bill Wallace of China,'' on video cassette, n.d.; audio cassettes from friends of Wallace, including missionaries, doctors, nurses, and family, with transcripts; audio cassette and transcript of memorial service for Wallace, 1985; colored slides, photos, and newspaper articles of the memorial service, 1985.
MAPS/DESIGNS/DRAWINGS: Folder of miscellaneous maps of China.
ORAL HISTORIES: Interviews or audio cassettes, some with transcripts, including Eloise Glass Cauthen, Marie Conner, Winston Crawley, Charles L. Culpepper, Ruth Ford, Betty Galloway, Everley Hayes, Eugene Hill, Deaver Lawton, Dorothy Lawton, Cornelia Leavell, Millie Lovegren, Agnes and Carter Morgan, Lucy Wright Parker, Samuel G. Rankin, Mary Lucile Saunders, and Frank Woodward.

MEMPHIS

MEMPHIS THEOLOGICAL SEMINARY
TN–40   Library
> 168 East Parkway South
> Memphis TN 38104
> (901) 458-8232
> Bobbie E. Oliver, Administrative Librarian

1-GENERAL HOLDINGS
MINUTES/RECORDS/REPORTS: China Continuation Committee, minutes of annual meeting, 1914, 1916; Christian Literature Society for China, annual report, 1910–16, 1940; Church of Christ in China, minutes of annual meeting, 1932; Committee on the Constitution for a General Assembly of the Presbyterian Churches in China, report, 1916; Conference on Federation, Peking, records, 1905; Foreign Missions Conference of North America, Conference on the Situation in China, papers, 1912; Joint Council on Extension Service to the Rural Church of the North China Area (Northern Section)/Nanking Theological Seminary, Rural Church Department, report, n.d.; National Christian Council of China, reports, 1922–23, 1935; Shanghai Missionary Conference, 1890.
MANUSCRIPTS: ''It Happened in Hunan,'' by Arthur Vale Casselman, 1951.
PAMPHLETS: *The Christian Country Life Movement*, by Fu-liang Chang, 1930; *Christians Courageous in China*, by Lucy Fish Miller, n.d.; *East and West and the Novel: Sources of the Early Chinese Novel*, by Pearl Buck (address at the North China Union Language School), 1932; *The Making of a Christian College in China*, by the Trustees of the Christian College in China, n.d.; *Missionsanfänge in Hochwan und Wusheng*, by Ursula von Reiswitz, 1949; *Presbyterian Work in China*, comp. by Constance M. Hallock, n.d.; *Virginia School, Huchow, China*, n.a., 1926; *When the West Came to the East*, by W. Sheldon Ridge, 1935.
SERIALS: *China Christian Year Book*, 1910–11, 1913–19, 1923–29, 1931, 1934–35, 1938–39. *Directory of Protestant Missions in China*, 1939. Yenching University, Department of Sociology and Social Work, Publications, series C, 1924.

NASHVILLE

DISCIPLES OF CHRIST HISTORICAL SOCIETY
TN–45   Library and Archives
> 1101 Nineteenth Avenue, South
> Nashville TN 37212
> (615) 327-1444
> David I. McWhirter, Director of the Library and Archives

Background note: These materials are only partially catalogued. See also Bethany College, T. W. Phillips Memorial Library, Bethany, WV, 26032.

1-DIVISION OF OVERSEAS MISSIONS, CHINA DEPARTMENT RECORDS, 1886–1956, 51 boxes
MINUTES/RECORDS/REPORTS: Associated Boards for Christian Colleges in China, administrative reports, 1933–43; Bible Teachers' Training School, records, 1920–22; Bible Union of China, records, 1923–24; Chichow Mission, records, 1937–40; China administrative minutes, 1945–50; China Conference of Missionaries, records, 1950.

China Department: administrative and financial records for Chinese national students, 1948–50; budget, 1949–51; famine fund records, 1921–28; general records, 1946–51; miscellaneous conference minutes, 1944; miscellaneous records and correspondence, 1915–20, 1928–31, 1935–43; records concerning relief work, 1927–31; records for various missionary conferences, 1941–45; records of staff conference, 1951; report to the trustees, 1950; reports on repatriation, personal property losses, and postwar reconstruction of China missions, 1940–44; reports on ''the present situation in China,'' 1928–29; uncatalogued personnel records, n.d.; uncatalogued records concerning Tibet and Batang, n.d.; China Property Survey, Division of Overseas Ministries, uncatalogued transit notes, n.d.; China Union Universities, records, 1923–24, 1928–31; Christian Middle School, uncatalogued records, n.d.; Church of Christ in China: records of Hofei Mission Station, 1937–42; records of Nantung Mission Station, 1937–38; records of Nantungchow Mission Station, 1914–19; College of Christian Studies, uncatalogued records, n.d.; Community House, South Gage, 1921–27; Crusade for a Christian World, records, 1947–50; Gifts for China, uncatalogued records, n.d.; Ginling College, records and newsletters, 1921–31, 1935–43; James McCallum, Secretary of the China Mission, records, 1948–49; Medical Board, records, 1914–28; Mission Secretary, records, 1947–48; Mission Council Administrative Committee, 1945–49; Nanking Mission, records, 1886–1941; Nanking Theological Seminary, records, 1928–29, 1931, and n.d.; Nantungchow Christian Hospital, report, 1937; Nantungchow School, records, 1918–19; National Christian Council of China, uncatalogued records, n.d.; Secretary-Treasurer of the China Mission, records, 1928–42, 1950–51; Shanghai American Schools, records, 1918–31 and n.d.; Virgil Sly, report on the Orient, 1949–51; Treasurer of the China Mission, records, 1948–50; University of Nanking, records, 1928–30 and n.d.; Anwei, Hofei, and Weihu Missions, records, 1933–38.
CORRESPONDENCE: Associated Boards for Christian Colleges in China, correspondence, 1933–43; China Department, general correspondence, 1921–24, 1951; China Department Secretary,

correspondence, 1917–32; Edwin Marx, China Department Secretary, correspondence, 1933–47, including letters describing the evacuation of missionaries from China and conditions during the Sino-Japanese War; Nanking Theological Seminary, correspondence, 1955–56; letters between Alexander Paul and S. J. Corey, 1927; letters from C. W. Plopper to the treasurer's office, 1922–24; United Board for Christian Colleges, uncatalogued correspondence, n.d.; 21 boxes of partially inventoried letters by China missionaries, n.d., including letters from Lillian Abbott, Mrs. E. H. Barnum, Miner Searle Bates, J. Edwin Carothers, Susan Carothers, Douglas Corpron, Grace Chapman Corpron, Nancy Fry, Mr. and Mrs. Frank Garrett, Irene Gouchen, Oswald Goulter, Cammie Gray, George Hagman, Ruby Hagman, Howard Holyrod, Madge Holyrod, W. Remfry Hunt, Lawrence Lew, Emma A. Lyan, Eva McCallum, James Henry McCallum, Ruth McElroy, Edwin Marx, Nora Baird Marx, Vincoe Paxton, Caroline Ritchey, George Ritchey, Lilliath Robbins, Guy Walter Sarvis, Katherine Schutze, Charles Settlemyer, Joseph M. Smith, Winnifred Smith, Lewis S. C. Smythe, Pauline Starn, Paul Stevenson, Stella Tremaine, Minnie Vautrin, and Grace N. Young; correspondence concerning Alexander Paul's trip to China, 1939–41; miscellaneous uncatalogued letters, 1946–50; uncatalogued letters concerning students, n.d.
PAMPHLETS: Uncatalogued pamphlets, n.d.
MAPS/DESIGNS/DRAWINGS: Uncatalogued rubbings, 1948; uncatalogued maps, n.d.
AUDIO-VISUAL MATERIALS: 687 partially inventoried photos of missionaries, China Relief workers, mission buildings, schools, hospitals, and scenes from West China and Hong Kong, n.d.; uncatalogued photos for the China Property Survey, Division of Overseas Ministries, n.d.
SERIALS: Ginling College, *Newsletter* (uncatalogued). National Christian Council of China, *Bulletin* (uncatalogued). Uncatalogued mission newsletters, n.d. University of Nanking, College of Agriculture and Forestry, *Agriculture and Forestry Notes*, 1924–25, 1939–40; *Miscellaneous Bulletin Series*, 1925.
FINDING AIDS: In-house partial inventory.

SCARRITT GRADUATE SCHOOL
TN–50 Virginia Davis Laskey Library
1008 19th Avenue, South
Nashville TN 37203-4466
(615) 340-7479
Dale Bilbrey, Librarian

1-GENERAL HOLDINGS
MINUTES/RECORDS/REPORTS: British Quaker Mission to the People's Republic of China, report, n.d.; Christian Literature Society for China, reports, 1887–1947; Methodist Episcopal Church, South, China Annual Conference, minutes, 1900, 1921, 1928–29, 1931–33, 1939; National Committee for Christian Religious Education in China, report, 1935; Presbyterian Church in the U.S.A.: China Council, minutes, 1910; Shantung Mission Council, minutes of the annual meeting, 1911–25.
CORRESPONDENCE: Printed letter from Clara and Charles Ernest Scott regarding the martyrdom of John and Betty Stam, 1936.
MANUSCRIPTS: "China Log," by Annie Eloise Bradshaw, n.d.
PAMPHLETS: *The Chinese Church Rides the Storm*, by R. Orlando Jolliffe, 1946; *Far West in China*, by Stanton Lautenschlager,

1941; *New Life in Fan Village, North China*, by Mrs. Hugh Hubbard, n.d.; *The Story of the Years in China*, by Mrs. J. P. Cobb, n.d.; *What Christian Approach to the Chinese?*, by Hubert Reynolds, 1969; *When the Methodists Came to China, 1847/1848–1947/1947*, n.d.
MEMORABILIA: "The Siege in Peking," an album of clippings, maps, and pictures comp. by Mary Porter Gamewell, 1900.
AUDIO-VISUAL MATERIALS: Photo album of J. W. Lambuth family, showing home life, mission work, and scenes of China, ca. late 19th century.
SERIALS: *China Christian Year Book*, 1910–37. *China Notes*, 1966–80. *China Talk*, 1976–82. *China's Millions* (Toronto), 1893.
DISSERTATIONS/THESES: *The Significance of Rural Reconstruction in China for the Philosophy of Missions*, by Martha Amie Snell, 1937.

SOUTHERN BAPTIST CONVENTION HISTORICAL COMMISSION
TN–55 Library and Archives
901 Commerce Street, Suite 400
Nashville TN 37203-3260
(615) 244-0344
Bill Sumners, Archivist

Background note: The first missionary appointed by the Foreign Mission Board of the Southern Baptist Convention after its organization in 1845 was sent to China. In the years that followed, the Southern Baptists organized and developed four missions in China: the South China Mission (1845), the Central China Mission (1847), the North China Mission (1859), and the Interior China Mission (1904).

In addition to the materials listed below, the Historical Commission Library and Archives received about 200 l.f. of uncatalogued missionary correspondence from the headquarters of the Foreign Mission Board in Richmond, Virginia, in 1987. See also Southern Baptist Convention, Foreign Mission Board, Box 6767, 3806 Monument Avenue, Richmond, VA, 23230; and Virginia Baptist Historical Society, University of Richmond, Boatwright Memorial Library, Box 95, Richmond, VA, 23173.

1-BAPTIST MISSIONARY SOCIETY ARCHIVES, 1860–1914, 8 reels microfilm
Restrictions: Literary rights for these materials are retained by the Baptist Missionary Society. To obtain permission to cite these materials, researchers should contact the Society at 93/97 Gloucester Place, London, W1H 4AA, England.
Background note: This collection is a microfilm reproduction of the Archives of the Baptist Missionary Society of England (1792–1914), currently housed in London.
MINUTES/RECORDS/REPORTS: Baptist Missionary Society, application forms and references for all missionary candidates, 1881–1914; Baptist Missionary Society, China Committee, records, 1884–1914; Baptist Missionary Society, China, Ceylon and France Sub-Committee, minute books, 1861–67; Baptist Missionary Society, China Sub-Committee, 1884–1914.
CORRESPONDENCE/DIARIES: Correspondence and journals of Jennie Beckinsale, 1898–1913; journals and 5 letters from Herbert Dixon, 1887–88, including information about Timothy Rich-

ard; journal and letter from George Edwards, 1916; journals and 86 letters of George Farthing, 1887–1900, including discussions of mission finances, missions in Shansi, and Timothy Richard; 3 letters from Richard Glover (Baptist minister in Bristol) to Alfred Henry Baynes (secretary of the Baptist Missionary Society), discussing the health of Herbert S. Jenkins; 9 letters from Francis H. James, including discussions of famine relief work and Timothy Richard; 5 letters from Herbert S. Jenkins, 1903–4; 316 letters, 4 telegrams, and journals of Alfred G. Jones, 1868, 1877–1905, with such correspondents as Clement Bailhache (secretary of the Baptist Missionary Society), Alfred Henry Baynes, Richard Glover, Timothy Richard, and Arthur DeC. Sowerby, discussing famine relief work, mission finances, missions in Shantung, and the political situation in China; journal and letter of R. F. Laughton to Alfred Henry Baynes concerning finances at the Chefoo mission, 1868; uncatalogued correspondence and journal of M. Lewis, Baptist missionary to China, 1912–14; journal and correspondence of E. F. Kingdon, 1864–67; 4 letters from Mary Richard (Mrs. Timothy Richard) to Albert Henry Baynes, 1895, including discussion of Chinese officials' hostility to missionaries; 227 letters to and from Timothy Richard, 1877–78, 1883–99, 1901–5, with such correspondents as Albert Henry Baynes, Richard Glover, Alfred G. Jones, William Muirhead, and Sir Harry Parkes (British consul in China), discussing the Boxer Uprising, famine relief work, missions in Shansi, missions in Shantung, the persecution of Chinese Christians, and translations of the Bible.
MANUSCRIPTS: 18 papers prepared by, or commenting on, Timothy Richard, 1894; unpublished description of Timothy Richard's work in Shansi by Mary Richards, 1887.
DIARIES: Diaries of Timothy Richard, 1888–92, 1895, 1897–1903.
MEMORABILIA: Insurance policy issued in Shanghai for E. F. Kingdon, 1867; press cuttings on Herbert S. Jenkins, 1904.
FINDING AIDS: "Baptist Missionary Society: Papers Relating to China, 1860–1914," by Mary M. Evans, 1965.

2-WILLIAM OWEN CARVER PAPERS, 1933–46, ca. 1 l.f.
Background note: William Owen Carver was a professor of Christian missions at Southern Baptist Theological Seminary in Louisville, Kentucky. His son, George Alexander Carver, was a Baptist missionary in China from 1933 to 1946. This collection is only partially processed.
MINUTES/RECORDS/REPORTS: Associated Board of Christian Colleges in China, minutes, 1933–45; University of Shanghai, bulletins, 1934–39; University of Shanghai, Board of Directors, minutes and reports, 1934–43.
CORRESPONDENCE: Uncatalogued correspondence from Carver's trip to China, 1923; uncatalogued letters to Carver from his son, George Carver, n.d.

3-FOREIGN MISSION BOARD RECORDS, 1874–1950, 1.5 l.f.
MINUTES/RECORDS/REPORTS: All-China Baptist Seminary Committee (China Baptist Theological Seminary), minutes, 1939; Central China Mission, annual reports, Executive Committee minutes and annual reports, minutes, reference books, and records, 1901–7, 1909–20, 1922–32, 1934–39, 1941–42, 1946, 1948–49; Interior China Mission, constitution and by-laws, Educational Committee reports, Executive Committee reports, field reports, Medical Committee reports, minutes, and records, 1903, 1916–20, 1922–41, 1947; Interior China Mission, Honan-Anhwei Bap-

tist Bible School, report, 1934; Interior China Mission, Kaifeng Baptist Boy's School, minutes, 1924; Interior China Mission, Kaifeng Baptist Industrial School for Women, records, 1917; Interior China Mission, Pochow Station, minutes and field report, 1935, 1938; Interior China Mission, Shih Yu Bible Institute, report, 1934; North China Mission, Executive Committee reports, financial reports, minutes, reference books, and resolutions, 1909–17, 1919–25, 1927–28, 1931–40; South China Mission, annual meeting minutes and records, Executive Committee minutes, mission meeting minutes, and report books, 1874, 1907–10, 1912–20, 1922–23, 1925–42, 1946–49; South China Mission, Kweilin Baptist Hospital, reports, 1932–33; South China Mission, China Baptist Publication Society, meeting minutes, 1934.
FINDING AID: In-house inventory.

4-FRANK HARTWELL LEAVELL PAPERS, 1929–36, 9 folders
Background note: Frank Hartwell Leavell (1884–1949) was an organizer and leader of Southern Baptist youth and student activities from 1913 to 1949. He visited China and Japan in 1936. His brother, George Leavell, was a medical missionary in Wuchow from 1912 to 1935.
CORRESPONDENCE: Folder of letters to Frank Leavell from his brother, George, 1929–34; 6 folders of letters concerning Leavell's trip to China, 1936, including such correspondents as Charles L. Culpepper, Sr., and James T. Williams.
DIARIES: Diary concerning Leavell's trip to China, 1936.
MANUSCRIPTS: "An Appreciation of the Youth of China," by Frank Leavell, n.d.; notebooks concerning Leavell's trip to China, 1936.
MEMORABILIA: Scrapbook of materials about the University of Shanghai, 1936.

5-PEYTON STEPHENS PAPERS, 1890–1941, 1 l.f.
Background note: Peyton Stephens (1865–1950) and his wife, Mary Thompson Stephens (d. 1963), were Southern Baptist missionaries in north China from 1893 to 1923.
MINUTES/RECORDS/REPORTS: Constitution of the Hwe Ching (Chefoo) Baptist Church, 1895; North China Baptist Mission, resolution of appreciation to Peyton Stephens, 1922.
CORRESPONDENCE: 4 letters to and from the Stephenses, n.d.
MANUSCRIPTS: 2 folders containing Stephens' autobiography and autobiographical notes, n.d.; 2 folders of notes on China by Peyton and Mary Stephens, n.d.; "Glimpses and Echoes from the Bedside of Mrs. Charlotte N. Hartwell, Sept.-Oct. 1903," n.a., 1903 (manuscript about the death of Charlotte Hartwell); folder of historical notes on Manchuria, n.d.; folder of sermons and devotional notes, n.d.; "Story of Going to China," by Mary Stephens, n.d.
MEMORABILIA: Folder of clippings belonging to Mary Stephens, n.d.
AUDIO-VISUAL MATERIALS: Scrapbook of photos of the North China Baptist Mission, 1923; 5 folders of photos of the Hartwell family, other Baptist missionaries in China, buildings in North China, and the Stephens family, n.d.; scrapbook of photos of life in China, 1897.
CHINESE LANGUAGE MATERIALS: 3 unidentified Chinese documents, n.d.; Bible, n.d.
FINDING AIDS: In-house inventory.

6-GENERAL HOLDINGS
SERIALS: *China Mission Advocate*, 1839.

TENNESSEE STATE LIBRARY AND ARCHIVES
TN–60   Archives and Manuscripts Section
403 Seventh Avenue North
Nashville TN 37219
(615) 741-2764
Marylin Bell, Archivist III

Background note: See also General Commission on Archives and History—The United Methodist Church, United Methodist Archives and History Center, 36 Madison Avenue, P. O. Box 127, Madison, NJ, 07940.
Finding aids: *Guide to the Microfilmed Manuscript Holdings of the Tennessee State Library and Archives*, ed. by Sara J. Harwell (Nashville: Tennessee State Library and Archives), 1983.

1-HARRY RUSSELL CALDWELL PAPERS, ca. 1930-ca. 1960, 1 reel microfilm
Background note: Harry Russell Caldwell (b. 1876) was a naturalist and Methodist missionary in Yenpingfu in the 1900s and 1910s.
MANUSCRIPTS: Microfilm reproduction of articles, sermons, notes on natural history, book manuscripts, and an autobiography by Caldwell, including references to his work in China, and Chinese life and customs.

2-FRANCES DURRETT COLLECTION, ca. 1901–1931, quantity undetermined
Background note: Frances Durrett's parents, Albert C. (1865–1951) and Johnnie Sanders Bowen (1867–1926), were Methodist missionaries in China from 1901 to 1931. This collection is unprocessed.
CORRESPONDENCE/MEMORABILIA/AUDIO-VISUAL MATERIALS: Letters, photos, and a scrapbook, n.d.
DIARIES: Journal of Johnnie Sanders Bowen, n.d.

VANDERBILT UNIVERSITY

TN–65   Divinity Library
419 21st Avenue South
Nashville TN 37240–0007
(615) 322–2865
William Hook, Reference Librarian
Dorothy Ruth Parks, Director

1-GENERAL HOLDINGS
MINUTES/RECORDS/REPORTS: China Continuation Committee, proceedings of the annual meeting, 1917; Educational Association of China, records, 1902.
MANUSCRIPTS: "The Jesuits in China in the Last Days of the Ming Dynasty," by George Dunne, S.J., 1947.
PAMPHLETS: *Die Kirche Chinas unter dem Kreuz*, by Karl Hartenstein and Jakob Keck, 1952.
SERIALS: *China's Millions* (London), 1883. *Land of Sinim*, 1905.
DISSERTATIONS/THESES: *Chinese Political Thought and the Christian Movement*, by T. F. Wu, 1925. *Christianity and China: A Study of Church and State*, by Robbins Strong, 1938. *An Experiment in Teaching the Christian Religion by Life Situations in Fan Village, China*, by Mabel Ellis Hubbard, 1938. *The Fellowship of Goodness: A Study in Contemporary Chinese Religion*, by John Cornelius De Korne, 1941. *The Lost Churches of China: A Study of the Contributing Factors in the Recurring Losses Sustained by*

Christianity in China during the Past Thirteen Hundred Years, by Leonard M. Outerbridge, 1951. *Political Status of Missionaries in China*, by Benjamin Bock-on Kwok, 1934. *Some Phases of the Administration of Christian Education for Boys in China*, by Ulin W. Leavell, 1921.

TN–70   Special Collections/Archives
Vanderbilt University
Jean and Alexander Heard Library
Nashville TN 37240–0007
(615) 322–2807
Marice Wolfe, Head of Special Collections and University Archivist

1-FLETCHER AND MARY BROCKMAN COLLECTION, ?–1956, ca. 100 items
CORRESPONDENCE: 6 letters between Mary Brockman and John Keith Benton, dean of the Divinity School, concerning the disposition of her collection of Oriental art, 1956.
MANUSCRIPTS: "The Rhyme of the Rickshaman" (poem), n.a., n.d.; notes on Chinese art, n.d.
PAMPHLETS: *Dedication, Peking Union Medical College, 1921*, n.a., 1921; *Madonna and Child with Lotus Flower*, n.a., n.d.; *We Fight for China (1937–1943)* (YMCA publication), n.a., n.d.
MEMORABILIA: Ca. 80 items collected by Fletcher and Mary Brockman during their stay in China, including clothing, coins, kitchen ware, paintings, post cards, scrolls, statuettes, toys and a portfolio of Chinese Christian art, "The Life of Christ by Chinese Artists."
AUDIO-VISUAL MATERIALS: Ca. 10 photos of Chinese art, persons, and places, n.d.
FINDING AIDS: Inventory of the collection of art objects.

2-KWANSEI GAKUIN VISIT 9/86, 1986, quantity undetermined
Background note: For biographical notes on James Lambuth, see Millsaps College, J. B. Cain Archives, Millsaps-Wilson Library, Jackson, MS, 39210. See also Lambuth College, Luther L. Gobbel Library, Lambuth Boulevard, Jackson, TN, 38301.
CORRESPONDENCE/MANUSCRIPTS: Correspondence and typescripts relating to Kwansei Gakuin University representatives' visit to the United States regarding materials on Methodist missions in Japan, including lists of correspondence and writings by James and Mary Lambuth from China in the 1880s.

3-CHARLIE SOONG (RG 935), 1931–81, quantity undetermined
Background note: Charles Jones (Yao-ju) Soong was a student at the Vanderbilt University School of Religion from 1882 to 1885. Soong joined the Methodist Church in North Carolina and attended Trinity College (now Duke University) for a brief period under the patronage of Julian S. Carr, wealthy tobacco manufacturer and Methodist layman. A convert to Methodism, he was the father of Soong Mei-ling (Mme. Chiang K'ai-shek), Soong Ch'ing-ling (Mme. Sun Yat-sen), and other children who became prominent public figures in Republican China. See also Duke University, University Archives, William R. Perkins Library, Durham, NC, 27706.
CORRESPONDENCE: Ca. 50 letters and several inter-office memos to and from Vanderbilt University administrators regarding requests for materials on Charles Soong, and discussion of honoring Soong at Vanderbilt, 1931–80.

MEMORABILIA: Clippings on Charlie Soong and his family, 1931–81; 3 news releases from Vanderbilt University, containing newspaper articles by and about the Soongs, 1943; credit reports on T. L. Soong and T. V. Soong, 1969; T. V. Soong biography from Howard Boorman's *Biographical Dictionary of Republican China*, n.d. (ca. 1970); other miscellaneous fragments on Soong.

4-JOHN JAMES TIGERT IV COLLECTION, 1886, 2 items
Background note: See Kwansei Gakuin Visit collection above.
CORRESPONDENCE: Letter from Mary Lambuth, in Shanghai, to Bishop Holland N. McTyeire, 1886; letter from James William Lambuth, in Shanghai, to Bishop McTyeire, 1886.

TEXAS

AUSTIN

TX-5 ARCHIVES AND HISTORICAL COLLECTIONS OF THE EPISCOPAL CHURCH
606 Rathervue Place
P. O. Box 2247
Austin TX 78768
(512) 472–6816
V. Nelle Bellamy, Archivist
Elinor Hearn, Librarian

Restrictions: References requested.
Background note: In addition to the collections described below, there are scattered references to China missions in the following collections: Domestic and Foreign Missionary Society, Annual Proceedings and Reports, 1835–1951, and Minutes, 1822–1918; National Council, Annual Reports, 1919–52, and Minutes, 1919–52; Executive/National Council Records: Overseas Department Records, 1950–66; and in *The Spirit of Missions*, a periodical of the Domestic and Foreign Missionary Society, 1836–1949. An oral history project on Episcopalian missions in China is in progress; access to these materials will be available when the project is completed. Personnel files on missionaries are also held in the archives; however, they are closed.

The archives hold collections of private papers, currently closed, of the following individuals: Deaconess Evelyn Ashcroft, Bishop William Jones Boone and family, Emeline Bowne, Louise Boynton, Elizabeth M. Buchanan, John L. Coe, Marian Gardner Craighill, Leslie Fairfield, Alice H. Gregg, Mary Tyng Higgins, Claude L. Pickens, Deaconess Katharine Putnam, Deaconess Ger-

trude Stewart, Bishop Andrew Y. Y. Tsu, Walworth and Ethel Tyng, Maurice E. Votaw, J. M. Wilson, Martha Wilson, and Y. K. Yen and family.

1-FREDERICK ROGERS GRAVES PAPERS, 1880–1961, 2.5 l.f.
Background note: Frederick Rogers Graves (1858–1940) was an Episcopal missionary in Wuchang from 1881 to 1893 and missionary bishop of Shanghai from 1893 to 1937. He helped found the Chung-hua Sheng Kung Hui, and served as chair of its House of Bishops from 1915 to 1926.
MINUTES/RECORDS/REPORTS: American Church Mission, list of publications, 1923, 1933; rules of the mission, 1928; Church Missionary Society Conference, Shanghai, resolutions, 1908; Graves' records books, containing a register of business and official acts, and a list of his confirmands, 1897–1937; Graves' legal documents, 1921, 1940; House of Bishops, Shanghai, minutes, 1938; "Statement of English Missionaries on the Subject of Episcopal Jurisdiction in Shanghai," 1906.
CORRESPONDENCE: Ca. 1.2 l.f. of letters to and from Graves, 1880–1940, including Graves' letter press books, 1887–98, and letters to various family members; letters regarding Graves after his death, 1940, 1951.
DIARIES: 4 in. of Graves' diaries, 1881–1939.
MANUSCRIPTS: 4 in. of undated manuscripts by Graves and "F. R. Graves and the China Mission," by his daughter, Lucy, 1961.
MEMORABILIA: 3 in. of clippings, 1881–1941, and scrapbooks, n.d.
AUDIO-VISUAL MATERIALS: 3 in. of photos of Graves, his family, Chang Ah-seu (president of the Shanghai Women's Auxiliary), Church of the Nativity in Wuchang, St. John's University, 1863–1939 and n.d.; portrait painted by John Hubbard Rich, 1926.
FINDING AIDS: Indices to the Graves' papers by Lucy Graves; in-house inventory.

2-NATIONAL COUNCIL/DOMESTIC AND FOREIGN MISSION-ARY SOCIETY, CHINA RECORDS, 1835–1951, 319 boxes (80 l.f.)
Background note: The China Records are divided according to period (1835–1901, 1901–10, and 1910–51) and missionary district (Anking, Hankow, and Shanghai). This collection contains miscellaneous uninventoried materials in addition to the items listed below.
MINUTES/RECORDS/REPORTS: American Church Mission, account sheets, bills, invoices, and treasury letters, 1835–1901; Anglican Communion in China and Hong Kong, conference report and resolutions, 1909; Anglican Communion in China and Hong Kong, records of Bishops' Conferences, 1899, 1903, 1907; William J. Boone, documents concerning his election to the Shanghai Episcopate, n.d.; Herbert Bruton, report, 1913; China Mission, report of the Third Conference, 1899; Chung-hua Sheng Kung Hui, certificate of incorporation, 1912, and records of K. Michael Chang, Quentin K. Huang, Newton Liu, T. Lindel Tsen, and Y. Y. Tsu, 1935–51; Church General Hospital, Hankow, reports by Logan H. Roots, 1911–21; Church General Hospital, Women's Committee, accounts, receipts, pledge cards, pledge updating sheets, publicity materials, and treasurers' papers, 1916–21; Elizabeth Cooper, report, 1912–13; Lillis Crummer, report, ca. 1900s; Diocese of Anking, treasurers' reports, 1919–30, 1936; Diocese of Hankow, provisional constitution and canons, 1910; Diocese of Hankow, Bishops' Conference records, conference reports, prop-

erty records, and treasurers' papers, 1905, 1909–50; Stephen Dodson, reports, ca. 1900s; Domestic and Foreign Missionary Society, Foreign Committee/Foreign Sub-committee, reports on China, 1835–1901; Rosa Elwin, reports, ca. 1900s; Episcopal "Jurisdiction" and "Ritualism" controversies, documents, 1882–83 and n.d.; uninventoried papers of the Foreign Secretary concerning missions in China, n.d.; J. W. Fell, reports, 1913–14; Robert Greisser, report, 1913; Susan H. Higgins, report, ca. 1910s; Home Office records concerning missions in China, n.d.; T. K. Hu, reports, 1913–14; Huang Sui-chiang, reports, 1913–14; James Jackson, reports, 1912–14; C. W. Kaster, report, 1912; Carl F. Lindstrom, reports, 1898–1901; Liu Yin-tsung, report, 1904; Carolyn Macadam, report, 1901; Missionary District of Shanghai, conference reports, 1902, 1904–6, 1908; Thomas Nelson, report, 1911–12; John W. Nichols, confirmation list, 1934–37; Louise L. Phelps, reports, 1913–14; Ida Porter, report, ca. 1910s; A. H. Standring, reports, 1911–30; Z. S. Sung, reports, 1914; Synod of the Chinese Church in the Province of Kiangsu, constitution and by-laws, 1903; Evelyn A. Tabor, reports, 1913–14; Tai Tiao-hou, report, 1914. T. F. Ts'en, report, 1913; Dudley Tyng, reports, 1913–14; Maurice Votaw, reports, 1922–51; Martha Waddill, report, 1914; Wang Hsuin-i, report, 1914; F. K. Woo, reports, 1912–14; Woo Hoong Neck (Woo Hong Neok?), report, 1912–14; Wu Ching-chang, reports, 1904, 1912–14; Yu Tsen-sheng, report, 1904.

CORRESPONDENCE: Correspondence to and from Episcopal missionaries in Anking: 84 letters of Elizabeth Barber, 1917–24; 5 letters of Bertha Beard, 1924; 12 letters of Mother Beatrice Martha, 1929; 13 letters of Theodore Bliss, 1917–19; 82 letters of Emeline Bovne, 1922–50; 5 letters of Mildred Buchanan, 1927; 128 letters of Mildred S. Capron, 1921–33; 2 letters of Norah Carnie, 1924; 57 letters of Robin Ch'en, 1940–50; 22 letters of Laura E. Clark, 1937–46; 12 letters of Meta B. Connell, 1923–29; 19 letters of Sr. Constance Anna, 1922–46; 630 letters of Lloyd R. Craighill, 1917–50; 45 letters of Marian Gardner Craighill, 1921–48; 11 letters of E. Louise Cummings, 1924, 1927; 9 letters of Carol Davis, 1926; 7 letters of Sr. Deborah Ruth, 1917–21; 9 letters of Kimber Den, 1950; 12 letters of Paul B. Denlinger, 1946–48; 1 letter of C. B. Eagan, 1921; 44 letters of Sr. Edith Constance, 1918–26; 6 letters of Sr. Eleanor Mary, 1926–27; 9 letters of MacCarlyle Fellows, 1923; 28 letters of Elizabeth F. Fueller, 1921–27; 1 letter of Alexandra Gerecht, 1925; 4 letters of P. C. Gilmore, 1924–26; 200 letters of Amos Goddard, 1916–27; 16 letters of R. A. Goodwin, 1917–19; 33 letters of Vincent H. Gowen, 1917–26; 275 letters of Alice Gregg, 1920–52; 1 letter of Lillian Harris, 1927; 11 letters of Jeanie V. Heald, 1917–19; 2 letters of Virginia Hebbert, 1947; 18 letters of Sr. Helen Veronica, 1918–31; 53 letters of Alden Hewitt, 1916–21; 3 letters of Henry D. Holt, 1924; 84 letters of Sallie E. Hopwood, 1910–19; 1 letter of Quentin K. Y. Huang, 1930; 2,215 letters of Daniel T. Huntington, 1910–50; 7 letters of V. E. Huntington, 1919–29; 2 letters of Sr. Isabel, 1936, 1939; 5 letters of James Jackson, 1917–18; 3 letters of Alice Jeffer, 1920–24; 12 letters of Lucy Kent, 1920–26; 4 letters of Mary Kent, 1922; 291 letters of B. Woodward Lanphear, 1917–52; 1 letter of Marian Lanphear, 1942; 3 letters of Mina Lanphear, 1951; 15 letters of George Laycock, 1941–45; 71 letters of Alan W. S. Lee, 1917–33; 265 letters of Edmund J. Lee, 1912–33; 27 letters of Lucy Lee, 1919–27; 1 letter of Jenny Lind, 1924; 79 letters of Carl F. Lindstrom, 1917–27; 49 letters of Julia Lindstrom, 1920–23; 5 letters of Faith Liu, 1947–48; 30 letters of

Sr. Louise Magdalene, 1936–45; 5 letters of Annie J. Lowe, 1920; 236 letters of F. E. Lund, 1916–33; 12 letters of Julia McBee, 1917; 5 letters of William McCarthy, 1917–19; 45 letters of Richard H. Mead, 1923–27; 107 letters of Margaret K. Monteiro, 1920–49; 31 letters of Blanche Myers, 1924–50; 38 letters of Hannah B. Ogden, 1920–27; 88 letters of Mary L. Ogden, 1916–26; 8 letters of Mary A. Parke, 1938–39; 54 letters of Katherine Phelps, 1927–29; 36 letters of Henri B. Pickens, 1941–49; 1 letter of Esta Pickets, 1924; 3 letters of Laliah Pingree, 1926–27; 19 letters of Caroline Pitcher, 1922–27; 73 letters of James Pott, 1917–24; 27 letters of Charles D. Reid, 1920–26; 42 letters of Kathleen Rigby, 1919–21; 15 letters of Sr. Ruth Magdalene, 1922–27; 5 letters of John Schaad, 1923; 3 letters of Margaret Schaad, 1922–23; 25 letters of Harry M. Schaffer, 1922–27; 114 letters of John K. Shryock, 1917–28; 102 letters of T. L. Sinclair, 1918–30; 37 letters of Elita W. Smith, 1916–22; 5 letters of Elizabeth Spencer, 1920; 2 letters of Albert H. Stone, 1926; 10 letters of Lila Stroman, 1924–30; 20 letters of Alicia Booth Taylor, 1918–51; 790 letters of Harry B. Taylor, 1910–33, 1936–38; 18 letters of E. K. Thurlow, 1913–18; 11 letters of Leonard Tomlinson, 1920–33; 220 letters of Sada C. Tomlinson, 1910–32; 25 letters of Mollie E. Townsend, 1926; 12 letters of P. Lindel Tsen, 1919–29; 12 letters of R. W. Watts, 1923; 27 letters of Anne Louise Wharton, 1917–20; 11 letters of Hannah J. Williams, 1923; 68 letters of Velma E. Woods, 1917–26; 2 letters of E. L. Woodward, 1910–13; 6 unidentified letters, n.d.

Correspondence to and from Episcopal missionaries in Hankow: 195 letters of Arthur Allen, 1932–51; 12 letters of Netta Allen, 1938–52; 9 letters of Walter P. Allen, 1948–50; 12 letters of Roy Allgood, 1935–38; 10 letters of Charlotte Anderson, 1927; 29 letters of Mother Anita Mary, 1926–50; 10 letters of Elizabeth Armour, 1906; 7 letters of Sr. Augusta, 1936–38; 28 letters of J. Gilbert Baker, 1941–50; 8 letters of Lucy Baker, 1910; 1 letter of George F. Bambach, 1906; 2 letters of Pearson Bannister, 1906; 10 letters of Elizabeth Barber, 1904–8; 23 letters of Christine Barr, 1924–29; 9 letters of Catherine Bennett, 1922–27; 1 letter of Dorothy Bergamini, 1939; 69 letters of John Bergamini, 1919–46; 1 letter of G. P. Bickford, Jr., 1922; 14 letters of Anstiss B. Bishop, 1920–26; 16 letters of Helen Cory Bliss, 1921–23; 69 letters of Theodore Bliss, 1917–27; 2 letters of E. E. Booth, 1935–37; 17 letters of Robert Boreland, 1905–6; 2 letters of Mrs. Robert Boreland, 1902; 3 letters of Louise Boynton, 1931–34; 1 letter of Alice Barlow Brown, 1924; 48 letters of Annie Brown, 1920–30; 18 letters of Bonnie Brown, 1925–50; 49 letters of F. Crawford Brown, 1924–50; 56 letters of Elizabeth Buchanan, 1916–27; 19 letters of Robert Bundy, 1922–29; 19 letters of Anne E. Byerly, 1904–8, 1913–19, 1925, 1927; 43 letters of Geraldine Cabot, 1921–32; 47 letters of Eva S. Carr, 1922–27; 13 letters of Gertrude Carter, 1901–05; 4 letters of Elizabeth Cheshire, 1909; 12 letters of Morton Y. T. Chu, 1924–32; correspondence of the Church General Hospital, Women's Committee, Hankow, 1916–21; 149 letters of Alice M. Clark, 1902–7, 1912–35; 69 letters of Coral Clark, 1925–44; 245 letters of Julia Clark, 1914–51; 74 letters of John L. Coe, 1923–51; 47 letters of Mary Coe, 1938–46; 132 letters of Albert S. Cooper, 1908–24; 1 letter of Elizabeth Cooper, ca. 1912–13; 129 letters of Frances J. M. Cotter, 1917–27; 6 letters of Ida Cotter, 1922–24; 104 letters of Caroline Couch, 1918–38; 151 letters of Venetia Cox, 1917–50; 16 letters of Mary E. S. Dawson, 1922–32; 1 letter of Madeleine Day, 1922; 25

letters of Emily W. Deis, 1917–19; 116 letters of Frederick Deis, 1910, 1912–24; 202 letters of Elise Dexter, 1918–39; 31 letters of Aimee B. Drake, 1918–22; 2 letters of Edward Fitzgerald, 1907; 27 letters of Pauline Flint, 1920–26; box of letters of the Foreign Secretary and Treasurer, 1901–10; 40 letters of George Foster, 1917–24; 36 letters of John B. Foster, 1935–43; 11 letters of Dorothy Fowler, 1921; 54 letters of J. Earl Fowler, 1921–31; 19 letters of Henrietta Gardiner, 1917–27; 1 letter of Elisa G. Gardner, 1920; 6 letters of Norman F. Garrett, 1934–36; 5 letters of Benjamin S. Garvey, 1921–26; 14 letters of Alice Gates, 1905; 2 boxes of letters to and from the General Secretary of the Domestic and Foreign Missionary Society, 1910–27; 3 letters of Sr. Geraldine, 1937–39; 48 letters of Nelson D. Gifford, 1926–28; 797 letters of Alfred Gilman, 1902–10, 1912–48; 147 letters of Gertrude Gilman, 1905–10, 1917–36; 55 letters of Mary Glenton, 1903–8, 1910–17; 14 letters of Amos Goddard, 1902–10; 26 letters of Conrad H. Goodwin, 1915–17; 11 letters of Robert A. Goodwin, 1910, 1921; 55 letters of Hazel Gosline, 1925–50; 84 letters of Francis A. Gray, 1921–24; 1 letter of G. Francis S. Gray, 1947; 8 letters of Harold S. Gray, 1922–26; 1 letter of Mary B. Gray, 1923; 2 letters of Rebecca Halsey, 1908; 277 letters of Edith Hart, 1914–27; 8 letters of Elizabeth Hart, 1906; 14 letters of W. F. Hayword, 1914–20; 21 letters of Charles A. Higgins, 1937–42; 26 letters of Susan H. Higgins, 1905–10, 1912–17; 30 letters of Theodore Hobbie, 1917, 1921–29; 22 letters of George Hoisholt, 1917–19; 23 letters of T. G. Hollander, 1909–10; 9 letters of Sallie Hopwood, 1910; 20 letters of C. H. Horner, 1920–24; 136 letters of C. Fletcher Howe, 1912–30; 1 letter of J. C. L. Hsu, 1930; 2 letters of Harvey F. D. Huang, 1929; 1 letter of W. K. Huang, 1905; 34 letters of Violet L. Hughes, 1918–28; 66 letters of Daniel T. Huntington, 1902–10; 1 letter of M. C. Huntington, 1903; 66 letters of Grace Hutchins, 1913–26; 1 letter of Edith M. Hutton, 1947; 4 letters of Sophia Igo, 1926–27; 21 letters of Charlotte Ingle, 1904–10; 48 letters of James Addison Ingle, 1901–3; 7 letters of J. Catherine Jackson, 1905–6; 16 letters of James Jackson, 1901–10; 2 letters of W. Jacob, 1934–35; 304 letters of Mary James, 1913–47; 4 letters of Ellen Jarvis, 1922; 5 letters of Frances A. Jenner, 1931–34; 2 letters of Sr. Joan Mary, 1921; 59 letters of Nina G. Johnson, 1917–49; 1 letter of Iris Johnston, 1939; 1 letter of Alice B. Jordan, 1927; 14 letters of Edith Kay, 1910, 1913–19; 61 letters of A. S. Kean, 1914–27; 16 letters of Ada W. Kean, 1921–26; 1 letter of Elizabeth Kemp, 1935; 12 letters of Frances Kemp, 1927–39, 1945; 143 letters of Robert A. Kemp, 1914–50; 3 letters of Frances Kennicott, 1922–26; 1 letter of Lucy Kent, 1924; 59 letters of Ruth Kent, 1910, 1914–20; 1 letter of Samuel C. Kuo, 1932; 13 letters of Hazel Kuyers, 1922–24; 9 letters of Mary Kwei, 1931–32; 1 letter of Paul Kwei, 1938; 14 letters of Dorothy Langman, 1920–21; 8 letters of Lau Yun Jin, 1908; 85 letters of E. J. Lee, 1901–10; 4 letters of Mark Li, 1927–40; 26 letters of Arthur C. Lichtenberger, 1926–32; 12 letters of Graham Y. L. Lieo, 1951–52; 4 letters of C. F. Lindstrom, 1901–6; 5 letters of Edward S. H. Ling, 1928; 2 letters of Charlotte Littell, 1904–9; 15 letters of Edward Littell, 1926–29; 40 letters of Helen Littell, 1918; 26 letters of John S. Littell, 1924–27; 346 letters of S. Harrington Littell, 1901–10, 1913–29; 8 letters of Marion Little, 1923; 1 letter of Nelson E. P. Liu, 1935; 3 letters of Newton Y. L. Liu, 1931–40; 20 letters of Annie J. Lowe, 1922–35; 1 letter of S. C. Y. Lowe, 1927; 16 letters of Helen R. L. Ludlow, 1918; 255 letters of Theodore R. Ludlow, 1912–20; 1 letter of Carl H. Lui, 1933; 32 letters of F. E.

Lund, 1902–10; 54 letters of Rigina G. Lustgarten, 1926–30; 13 letters of William McCarthy, 1902–10; 24 letters of J. A. McDonald, 1918–20; 13 letters of J. Patrick H. McGinnis, 1949–51; 75 letters of John MacWillie, 1905–18; 96 letters of Paul Maslin, 1910–33; 17 letters of Stella Maslin, 1910, 1924–27; 8 letters of T. P. Maslin, 1903–5; 12 letters of Eva Mathewson, 1922–27; 12 letters of Arthur G. Melvin, 1924–27; 12 letters of Beatrice Merrins, 1921–28; 80 letters of Edward M. Merrins, 1912–28; 7 letters of Frances E. Merrill, 1922–26; 2 letters of Bertha Meyers, 1922; 106 letters of Everard P. Miller, 1908, 1912–44; 30 letters of Lucy Fish Miller, 1917–44; 35 letters of Ida Jean Morrison, 1914–23; 53 letters of Walter P. Morse, 1939–51; 8 letters of John Mowrey, 1925–27; 52 letters of James A. Muller, 1917–20; 16 letters of Ann B. Mundelein, 1927; 3 letters of W. S.T. Neville, 1923–25; 1 letter of Nelson T. S. Ngou, 1928; 61 letters of Harry G. Nichols, 1917–22; 7 letters of Mary R. Ogden, 1905; 4 letters of Johanna Olsson, 1941–47; 8 letters of Joseph E. Olsson, 1932–37; 6 letters of P. A. Osgood, 1902–6; 18 letters of Alice H. Peavey, 1917–18; 31 letters of Katherine Phelps, 1905–18; 13 letters of Louise Phelps, 1908–10; 1 letter of Grace D. Phillips, 1935; 128 letters of Claude Pickens, 1926–39, 1941–51; 1 letter of Mabel Piper, 1925; 3 letters of Caroline J. Porter, 1922; 2 letters of Julia E. Prichard, 1917–18; 17 letters of Marie Jarvey Ravenel, 1924–27; 7 letters of Charles D. Reid, 1920; 12 letters of Louise M. Reiley, 1931–47; 33 letters of Howard Richards, 1905–10; 1 letter of Mary S. Richards, 1933; 1 letter of Cornelia M. Richardson, 1926; 19 letters of Margaret C. Richey, 1924–27; 71 letters of Emily L. Ridgely, 1910, 1913–17; 4 letters of Louise Ridgely, 1902–08; 359 letters of Lawrence B. Ridgely, 1901–10, 1912–31; 28 letters of Elsie W. Riebe, 1917–51; 3 letters of Kathleen L. Rigby, 1918; 6 letters of Margaret Roberts, 1925–28; 38 letters of Eliza McCook Roots, 1902–10, 1916–34; 2 letters of Frances B. Roots, 1933–34; 4,288 letters of Logan H. Roots, 1901–38; 66 letters of Logan H. Roots, Jr., 1932–54; 2 letters of Marie-Lou Roots, 1935–38; 162 letters of Katherine Scott, 1913–23; 3 letters of Samuel T. Y. Seng, 1927–36; 4 letters of Margaret Sheets, 1948–51; 2 letters of Anne Catherine Sherman, 1929–30; 389 letters of Arthur M. Sherman, 1902–30; 5 letters of Martha Sherman, 1909, 1917, 1927, 1938; 8 letters of R. B. Shipman, 1905; 61 letters of Mabel Sibson, 1917–28; 1 letter of Alan W. Simms, 1924; 1 letter of Margaret P. Smith, 1924; 1 letter of Joanette A. Snellgrave, 1922; 4 letters of J. H. Snoke, 1925; 191 letters of Edmund Souder, 1917–37; 2 letters of Martha Souder, 1924; 20 letters of Thacher Souder, 1917–22; 7 letters of James Sowerby, 1909; 3 letters of Margaret Spurr, 1930–33; 14 letters of Alfred B. Starratt, 1947–50; 72 letters of Edith G. Stedman, 1920–27; 174 letters of Gertrude Stewart, 1904–44; 2 letters of Winfred Stewart, 1926–28; 12 letters of Percy R. Stockman, 1907–10; 16 letters of Albert H. Stone, 1925–37; 1 letter of Alexander Tao-ling, 1928; 2 letters of Anna Tattershall, 1908; 28 letters of Harry B. Taylor, 1904–10; 13 letters of Walter A. Taylor, 1924–27; 2 letters of Mrs. Walter A. Taylor, 1927; 11 letters of Margaret Tetley, 1926–36; 87 letters of Olive Bird Tomlin, 1917–50; 20 letters of Sada Tomlinson, 1907–10; 7 letters of Lillian B. Towner, 1920–23; 1 letter of Albert Tsang, 1927; 8 letters of James J. Tsang, 1930–39; 159 letters of Stephen H. S. Tsang, 1927–39, 1947–52; 1 letter of Archie Tsen, 1908; 1 letter of H. W. Tseng, 1928; 3 letters of Samuel S. L. Tseng, 1935; 1 letter of Dorothy Tso, 1933; 1 letter of Eugene Turner, 1932; 5 letters of Dudley Tyng, 1908–10; 2 letters of Ethel Tyng, 1919–24; ca. 400 letters of Walworth Tyng,

1912–50; 24 letters of Richard S. Underwood, 1923–33; 98 letters of Mother Ursula Mary, 1922–50; 26 letters of A. R. Van Meter, 1902–6; 4 letters of Estelle Villey, 1905; 5 letters of Deward R. Van Sant, 1950–51; 1 letter of R. T. Viguers, 1935; 10 letters of Hilda Waddington, 1936–48; 2 letters of Dorothea Wakeman, 1934–36; 7 letters of Olive Lindsay Wakefield, 1923–27; 74 letters of Paul Wakefield, 1924–30; 38 letters of Edward Walker, 1914–21; 5 letters of Flora Walker, 1917–18; 1 letter of Alexander Wang, 1927; 2 letters of Paul Wang, 1927–28; 17 letters of Marian DeC. Ward, 1923–26; 9 letters of Catharine Ward, 1947–50; 20 letters of Paul Ward, 1947–50; 62 letters of C. Mc. Wassell, 1914–25; 4 letters of Mrs. C. Mc. Wassell, 1920; 120 letters of Francis C. M. Wei, 1926–51; 1 letter of Lillian Weiderhammer, 1950; 2 letters of Millie Weir, 1926–27; 26 letters of Charles Wells, 1925; 11 letters of Ethel Wheeler, 1908–10; 16 letters of Charles H. Whiston, 1932–37; 3 letters of Ada Whitehouse, 1913–17; 1 letter of Thomas F. Wiesen, 1924; 5 letters of Agnes Williston, 1919–24; 19 letters of Jessie C. Wilson, 1924–27; 100 letters of John A. Wilson, Jr., 1906–9, 1912–26; 4 letters of Carmen Wolff, 1947–50; 527 letters of Mary Elizabeth Wood, 1901–31; 261 letters of Robert E. Wood, 1902–10, 1912–51; 182 letters of Edmund L. Woodward, 1902–10; 2 letters of Leighton Yang, 1927–28; 2 letters of Louise Yao-Hsiung, 1928; 2 letters of Benjamin C. L. Yen, 1931; 2 letters of Theo Young, 1926.

Correspondence to and from Episcopal missionaries in Shanghai: 16 letters of Eugelius F. Alsop, 1914–18; 479 letters of Benjamin L. Ancell, 1899–1910, 1913–33; 84 letters of Frances Cattell Ancell, 1910, 1917–38; 31 letters of George H. Appleton, 1882–85; 29 letters of Evelyn Ashcroft, 1937–51; 30 letters of Margaret Bailey, 1917–23; 3 letters of Ernest K. Banner, 1924–27; 3 letters of Catharine C. Barnaby, 1925; 38 letters of Daniel M. Bates, 1877–1933; 2 letters of Margaret Bates, 1917; 65 letters of Margaret E. Bender, 1905–10, 1920–26; 7 letters of James W. Bennett, 1924; 15 letters of Frances Berg, 1920–23; 13 letters of John Van Wie Bergamini, 1939, 1946; 2 letters of Yvette Bissett, 1917; 8 letters of Annie E. Boone, 1908; 215 letters of Henry W. Boone, 1880–1911; 74 letters of Henrietta Boone, 1877–92; 945 letters of William J. Boone, 1837–91; 14 letters of Robert Boreland, 1898–1901; 146 letters of William F. Borrman, 1916–27; 12 letters of Elizabeth Boyd, 1881; 3 letters of Stephanie Bradford, 1922; 25 letters of Grace Brady, 1925–50; 122 letters of M. Althea Bremer, 1917–51; 1 letter of Alice B. Brown, 1923; 8 letters of Annie Brown, 1917–27; 4 letters of Bonnie Crawford Brown, 1927; 6 letters of Francis C. Brown, 1927; 8 letters of Robert E. Browning, 1908–10; 37 letters of Martha Bruce, 1882–85; 91 letters of Albert C. Bunn, 1874–87; 2 letters of Elizabeth Bunn, 1875–77; 11 letters of Olive R. Burl, 1925–27; 1 letter of Eleanor Buse, 1926; 21 letters of Edward K. Buttles, 1881–82; 9 letters of Anne E. Byerly, 1900–1; 16 letters of T. Bowyer Campbell, 1918; 2 letters of Gertrude Carter, 1901; 19 letters of E. Maude Cartwright, 1909, 1919–27; 2 letters of Elizabeth Chambers, 1933; 4 letters of K. S. Francis Chang, 1935–36; 5 letters of Annie W. Cheshire, 1909; 10 letters of Elizabeth Chisholm, 1917–18; 5 letters of E. Virginia Chiswell, 1900–1901; 1 letter of Chu Yu Tang, ca. 1895; letters concerning the Chung-hua Sheng Kung Hui (American Church Mission), 1937; 23 letters of H. Clinton Collins, 1893–1900; 7 letters of Jeannette R. Conover, 1860–63; 17 letters of Julia K. Cook, 1924–27; 9 letters of Emily G. Cooper, 1903–8, 1917; 50 letters of Frederick C. Cooper, 1898–1900,

1902–9; 1 letter of George W. Cooper, 1897; 40 letters of Gwendolin L. Cooper, 1920–44; 6 letters of Merbyn C. Cooper, 1920–21; 3 letters of Caroline Couch, 1924; 6 letters of Richard Corsa, 1950; 42 letters of Frances A. Cox, 1921–41; 43 letters of Lillis Crummer, 1894–1910; 1 letter of Henry Cummings, 1844; 31 letters of John F. Davidson, 1924–27; 7 letters of Emily W. Davis, 1920–23; 3 letters of Floy Shelly Davis, 1926; 1 letter of Eli Day, 1905; 9 letters of E. Catherine Deahl, 1924; 67 letters of William A. Deas, 1880–91; 11 letters of Lula M. Disosway, 1926–38; 95 letters of Stephen Dodson, 1888–1901, 1903–9, 1917–24; letters to and from the Domestic and Foreign Missionary Society's Foreign Committee/Foreign Secretary and Treasurer, 1835–1910; 1 letter of Dong Tsing Oong, 1908; 3 letters of James T. Doyen, 1860–61; 1 letter of Jane Doyen, 1860; 93 letters of Louise J. Duncan, 1923–38; 6 letters of Thomas Drumm, 1891–94; ca. 60 letters of Edward R. Dyer, 1917–38; 14 letters of Mrs. Edward R. Dyer, 1917–23; 14 letters of Williette Eastham, 1902; 7 letters of Gertrude Eby, 1949; 34 letters of Rosa M. Elwin, 1904–8, 1914–19; 139 letters of John Ely, 1918–37; 31 letters of Mrs. John Ely, 1919–21; 6 letters of Leslie Fairfield, 1937–49; 22 letters of Elizabeth Falk, 1921–50; 43 letters of Lawrence Fawcett, 1921–25; 104 letters of Lydia Fay, 1851–78; 4 letters of MacCarlyle Fellows, 1928–29; 6 letters of M. W. Fish, 1854–56; 81 letters of Ernest H. Forster, 1920–50; 14 letters of Lilian Fredericks, 1902–10; 101 letters of Caroline Fullerton, 1910, 1919–39; 31 letters of Ellen Fullerton, 1908, 1912–27; 6 letters of Mary Gates, 1898–1901; 12 letters of James H. George, 1905–9; 6 letters of Alexandra Gerecht, 1925; 17 letters of Althea Gill, 1917–23; 160 letters of J. M. B. Gill, 1908–10, 1912–24; 1 letter of Eliza Gillette, 1845; 8 letters of Lila Gilmore, 1941–43; 2 letters of Mary Glenton, 1899–1901; 12 letters of Isabel Gold, 1923–24; 2 letters of R. A. Goodwin, 1922; 2 letters of O. W. Gott, 1918; 14 letters of Richardson Graham, 1843–49; 33 letters of Elizabeth Graves, 1919–28; ca. 6,000 letters of Frederick R. Graves, 1881–1908, 1912–40; 29 letters of Josephine Graves, 1884–1901, 1904–5, 1917–19; 52 letters of Lucy Graves, 1917–37; 48 letters of Stephen Green, 1919–49; 19 letters of George S. Greshem, 1920–23; 1 letter of Esther Griffith, 1886; 15 letters of Anne M. Groff, 1925–52; 23 letters of Sumner Guerry, 1921–27; 14 letters of Robert A. Guesser, 1909–10; 1 letter of Helen Hales, 1922; 95 letters of Louise Hammond, 1917–43; 8 letters of Francis R. Hanson, 1835–38; 5 letters of Charles W. Harbison, Jr., 1943–47; 6 letters of Weston Harding, 1907–8; 12 letters of Blanche M. Harris, 1923–27; 6 letters of Henrietta Harris, 1875–77; 21 letters of Marie Haslep, 1888–96; 9 letters of Paul Hartzell, 1917–18; 6 letters of A. A. Hayes, 1862–74; 28 letters of Florence C. Hayes, 1922–27; 7 letters of Maude Henderson, 1903–6; 55 letters of Mary A. Hill, 1905–10, 1912–27; 10 letters of Amy Ho, 1947; 63 letters of Augustus Hoehing, 1867–77; 8 letters of Henrietta Hoehing, 1874–77; 1 letter of Sam Hokking, 1926; 4 letters of Henry D. Holt, 1924; 10 letters of Esther L. Houghton, 1921–25; 8 letters of Eliza Hoyt, 1874–78; 60 letters of Samuel R. Hoyt, 1871–80; 3 letters of Edmund Hsu, 1941; 4 letters of Edward Hubbell, 1860; 61 letters of Daniel Huntington, 1895–1901; 1 letter of M. C. Huntington, 1901; 1 letter of Josephine Hutchinson, 1922; 1 letter of Addison Ingle, 1903; 87 letters of James A. Ingle, 1891–1901, 1903; 2 letters of James Jackson, 1900–1906; 26 letters of Fleming James, 1902–6; 8 letters of Rebecca James, 1902–3; 6 letters of H. H. Jeffery, 1910–26; 68 letters of William H. Jefferys, 1900–1910; 5 letters of Catherine Jones, 1853–56; 21 letters of Emma

Jones, 1844–76; 40 letters of Alice B. Jordan, 1917–25; 51 letters of Louise Jordan, 1926–35; 5 letters of Caroline Keith, 1856–61; 61 letters of Cleveland Keith, 1846–62; 4 letters of Tracy Kelley, 1910; 32 letters of Edmund Harrison King, Jr., 1920–35; 10 letters of Kiung Yong, 1855–74; 1 letter of K. M. Koo, 1927; 1 letter of Mary Kwei, 1927; 41 letters of Anne Lamberton, 1924–47; 2 letters of E. W. Lane, 1925; 19 letters of Sara E. Lawson, 1882–84; 406 letters of Claude Lee, 1905–9, 1912–47; 20 letters of Mary Lee, 1918–47; 25 letters of Laura Lenhart, 1917–39; 1 letter of Ruth Leonard, 1923; 23 letters of John Liggins, 1854–59; 119 letters of Charles F. S. Lincoln, 1898–1900, 1902–9, 1912–25; 6 letters of Wilamette Lincoln, 1908, 1917; 6 letters of Carl F. Lindstrom, 1898–1901; 17 letters of S. H. Littell, 1898–1900; 69 letters of Arthur H. Locke, 1882–93; 16 letters of Henry Lockwood, 1835–59; 5 letters of Charles Long, 1947–49; 4 letters of Annie Lowe, 1910; 8 letters of Franz E. Lund, 1898–1900; 1 letter of William McCarthy, 1901; 14 letters of Eliza L. McCook, 1899–1900; 157 letters of Josiah C. McCracken, 1920–43; 4 letters of Viola McGoldrick, 1924–25; 57 letters of Harley F. MacNair, 1920–27; 17 letters of Edith McNulty, 1919–38; 317 letters of Henry A. McNulty, 1909–40; 55 letters of C. R. McRae, 1902–10; 238 letters of Cameron F. McRae, 1899–1901, 1910–38; 27 letters of Sarah McRae, 1908–9, 1917–28; 11 letters of Florence McRay, 1893–99; 8 letters of Faith Magee, 1925–38; 245 letters of John Magee, 1914–42; 21 letters of Robert A. Magill, 1921–28; 4 letters of J. N. Major, 1907; 16 letters of Arthur Mann, 1903–7; 23 letters of K. T. Mao, 1946–50; 1 letter of Frances Markley, 1926; 15 letters of Charlotte Mason, 1899–1900; 45 letters of Robert Massie, 1891–96; 27 letters of Percy Mathews, 1888–96; 15 letters of Harrison Matsinger, 1925–27; 7 letters of Matilda A. Matton, 1919–20; 1 letter of Joseph Meade, 1910; 54 letters of Edward M. Merrins, 1891–98, 1917–30; 2 letters of Ellen Miller, 1917; 36 letters of Lillian Minhinnick, 1920–26; 9 letters of James A. Mitchell, 1917–19; 83 letters of Marian Mitchell, 1903–9, 1919–27; 7 letters of Laura Moffett, 1926–27; 117 letters of Harold H. Morris, 1910–30; 14 letters of Fanny S. Mosher, 1900, 1905, 1917–18; 6 letters of Gertrude Mosher, 1896–1900; 273 letters of Gouverneur Frank Mosher, 1898–1920; 15 letters of Angie M. Myers, 1906–10; 45 letters of Mary C. Nelson, 1854–80; 182 letters of Robert Nelson, 1849–80; 48 letters of Rose Nelson, 1860–81; 1 letter of Thomas Nelson, 1911–12; 1 letter of Neok Woo Hong, 1875 (see "Woo Hong Neok" below); 7 letters of Alfred Newberry, 1919; 7 letters of Elizabeth Nichols, 1910–11; 344 letters of John W. Nichols, 1902–38; 31 letters of Julia Nichols, 1917–27; 30 letters of J. Randall Norton, 1917–51; 11 letters of Margaret S. Norton, 1921–24; 5 letters of H. S. Osburn, 1910; 12 letters of Pauline A. Osgood, 1898–1901; 66 letters of Theodora Paine, 1905–7, 1917–27; 9 letters of Lewis Palen, 1904; 12 letters of Carrie Palmer, 1904–10; 39 letters of Giles Palmer, 1900–1908; 3 letters of Henry Parker, 1860–61; 288 letters of Sidney Partridge, 1882–1900; 6 letters of Eugene C. Peck, 1922–26; 2 letters of Carey Perry, 1943; 12 letters of Charles E. Perry, 1932–49; 23 letters of Julian Petit, 1917–18; 1 letter of Laliah Pingree, 1926; 6 letters of Anne A. Piper, 1922–24; 7 letters of Edith Piper, 1909; 11 letters of Mabel P. Piper, 1920–24; 18 letters of John T. Points, 1851–58; 2 letters of Robert Pollard, 1923, 1926; 13 letters of Ida Porter, 1908–9, 1912–19; 18 letters of David Porterfield, 1924–27; 8 letters of Margaret H. Porterfield, 1922–27; 50 letters of Williard H. Porterfield, 1917–28; 7 letters of Henry Post, 1909; 3 letters of David G. Poston, 1933–36; 8

letters of Elizabeth Pott, 1922–26; 18 letters of Emily Pott, 1919–26; 1,357 letters of Francis Lister Hawks Pott, 1886–1907, 1912–47; 75 letters of James H. Pott, 1924–49; 31 letters of Olivia Pott, 1920–27; 1 letter of Soo-ngoo Wong Pott (Mrs. F. L. H. Pott), 1910; 63 letters of Walter Pott, 1919–41; 5 letters of William S. A. Pott, 1919–22; 15 letters of Louise H. Powers, 1922–28; 1 letter of Thomas Protheroe, 1885; 114 letters of Rea G. Pumphrey, 1918–26; 3 letters of Henry M. Purdon, 1860; 9 letters of Jessie A. Purple, 1884; 63 letters of Katharine Putnam, 1917–50; 27 letters of J. Lambert Rees, 1893–1904; 30 letters of Sarah H. Reid, 1909, 1917–29; 46 letters of Alice Reimer, 1917–24; 151 letters of Carl F. Reimer, 1917–29; 18 letters of Geraldine R. Rennie, 1920–30; 8 letters of Sarah Taylor Rhett, 1904; 23 letters of Margaret C. Richey, 1927–51; 26 letters of Annette B. Richmond, 1898–1900, 1906–7, 1916–17; 14 letters of Lawrence B. Ridgely, 1898–1901; 33 letters of Donald Roberts, 1919–50; 18 letters of Dorothy Roberts, 1919–49; 6 letters of Frances Roberts, 1942–43; 4 letters of John Roberts, 1937–41; 18 letters of Josephine Roberts, 1800–1882; 1,021 letters of William P. Roberts, 1918–51; 22 letters of Logan H. Roots, 1896–1901; 1 letter of Edith R. Ross, 1925; 1 letter of Gladys M. Ross, 1937; 7 letters of Hans Rottenstein, 1949; 24 letters of Julia Russell, 1925–27; 16 letters of T. H. P. Sailer, 1919–20; 2 letters of Gladys A. Saleeby, 1948; 64 letters of Edgar L. Sanford, 1917–29; 5 letters of Rollins Sawyer, 1909; 6 letters of Anna Sayres, 1882; 1 letter of Rosa Sayres, 1879; 101 letters of William Sayres, 1878–86; 341 letters of Samuel Schereschewsky, 1861–1901; letters about Samuel Schereschewsky, 1927–37; 285 letters of Susan M. Schereschewsky, 1870–1901, 1907–9; 20 letters of Louise H. Schleicher, 1920–27; 17 letters of Lawrence Schultz, 1923–27; 14 letters of Warren A. Seager, 1921–26; 4 letters of John F. Seaman, 1870–71; 59 letters of Gertrude Selzer, 1923–50; 20 letters of Bishop T. K. Shen, 1930–49; 11 letters of Arthur M. Sherman, 1894–1901; 7 letters of Bessie Sims, 1944–49; 10 letters of T. Lowry Sinclair, 1907; ca. 600 letters of Samuel E. Smalley, 1889–1910, 1917; 20 letters of Anne Piper Smith, 1926–38; 14 letters of Dudley D. Smith, 1861–63; 113 letters of Hollis S. Smith, 1922–40; 4 letters of Mary J. Smith, 1920–23; 2 letters of Elsie Snoke, 1922; 37 letters of John H. Snoke, 1920–24; 4 letters of Fanny Sowerby, 1888–89; 83 letters of Herbert Sowerby, 1882–1900; 14 letters of Phineas D. Spalding, 1846–49; 56 letters of Esther A. Spencer, 1882–91; 47 letters of A. H. Standring, 1911–30; 10 letters of William Standring, 1905–10; 18 letters of George Nye Steiger, 1906, 1919; 9 letters of Anna Stevens, 1881–82; 10 letters of Juliet Stevens, 1901, 1904; 6 letters of Fanny Stewart, 1898; 8 letters of Gertrude Stewart, 1927; 5 letters of Albert H. Stone, 1926–27; 1 letter of Edna Stone, 1918; 2 letters of Alice J. Street, 1919; 18 letters of Francis Stricker, 1874–76; 4 letters of George N. Steiger, 1906; 3 letters of Suang Ting Kia, 1874–77; 3 letters of Frances C. Sullivan, 1921–23; 25 letters of Philip B. Sullivan, 1922–46; 14 letters of William Z. L. Sung, 1946; 129 letters of Edward W. Syle, 1844–63; 1 letter of T. H. Tai, 1902; 19 letters of Sterling J. Talbot, 1920–21; 103 letters of H. J. Taylor Walter, 1917–39; 1 letter of C. T. Teng, 1926; 8 letters of E. M. Thomson, 1917; 639 letters of Elliott H. Thomson, 1860–1910, 1917; 67 letters of Jeanette Thomson, 1871–87; 21 letters of M. Helen Thompson, 1883–84; 105 letters of Montgomery H. Throop, III, 1907–9, 1917–48; 8 letters of Ann Torrence, 1908; 2 letters of Mollie E. Townsend, 1930–31; 2 letters of A. C. S. Triveh, 1950–51; 28 letters of Archie T. L. Tsen, 1928–41; 1 letter of P. T. Tsu, 1908;

169 letters of A. W. Tucker, 1906–10, 1915–37; 1 letter of B. D. Tucker, 1906. 8 letters of Ellis N. Tucker, 1925–26, 1949–50; 7 letters of Percy Urban, 1910; 23 letters of Helen Van Voast, 1936–51; 43 letters of Maurice Votaw, 1922–51; 44 letters of M. P. Walker, 1902–10; 13 letters of Rachel Walker, 1927–43; 6 letters of Lily F. Ward, 1894–97; 2 letters of Susan Waring, 1857, 1866; 1 letter of Charley Warnock, 1901; 1 letter of Y. C. Wei, 1939; 2 letters of Anna Jean Weigel, 1924; 30 letters of W. Harold Weigel, Jr., 1922–28; 2 letters of Millie E. Weir, 1922–24; 39 letters of Laura P. Wells, 1921–49; 31 letters of Channing Moore Williams, 1855–75; 1 letter of Ethel Williams, 1920; 9 letters of Helen Wilson, 1923–27; 14 letters of J. M. Wilson, 1931–48; 2 letters of Martha Wilson, 1937–38; 225 letters of Robert C. Wilson, 1902–10, 1912–27; 9 letters of Sarah Rhett Wilson, 1926–27; 24 letters of Roger Wolcott, 1916–18; 31 letters of Wong Kong Chai, 1859–86; 1 letter of S. N. Wong, 1887–88; 34 letters of Woo Hong Neok, 1873–1910; 6 letters of Elizabeth Wood, 1899–1901; 18 letters of Robert Wood, 1898–1901; 4 letters of Sarah Woodard, 1905–6; 12 letters of Edmund Woodward, 1895–1901; 7 letters of Henry Woods, 1844–46; 5 letters of Emma T. Wray, 1853–54; 13 letters of Mary L. Wright, 1926–27; letters of W. William Yen, 1900–1901; 161 letters of Yen Yung Kiung, 1872–1901; 9 letters of Yen Zu Soong, 1874–88; 3 letters of Thomas Yocum, 1860; 9 letters of Theo Young, 1925–26; 3 letters of B. S. Yu, 1937–42. DIARIES: Diary of Cleveland Keith, 1849–53; diaries of John Roberts, ca. 1940; fragments from a journal of Edward W. Syle, 1848–51; uninventoried journals interfiled with the correspondence, 1835–1952. MANUSCRIPTS: Biography of Samuel Schereschewsky, 1937; 13 sermons by Cleveland Keith, n.d.; 2 manuscripts by Annette B. Richmond, n.d.; obituary of Soo-Ngoo Wong Pott, n.a., 1918; historical notes of H. N. Woo, n.d. PAMPHLETS: *The Term Question*, n.a., 1877; uninventoried pamphlets relating to the Diocese of Anking, n.d.; uninventoried pamphlets relating to the Diocese of Hankow, n.d. MEMORABILIA: Post cards from China, ca. 1910; folder of unofficial papers of E. M. Thomson, 1917. MAPS/DESIGNS/DRAWINGS: *Property of American Church Mission, Shanghai District*, 17 plates, 1909. AUDIO-VISUAL MATERIALS: Uninventoried photos relating to the Diocese of Anking, n.d.; uninventoried photos relating to the Diocese of Hankow, n.d. SERIALS: *The Church in China*, 1894–99. *District of Anking Newsletter*, 1920–43. *District of Hankow Newsletter*, 1920–50. *District of Shanghai Newsletter*, 1915–49. CHINESE LANGUAGE MATERIALS: Untitled pamphlet, 1908. FINDING AIDS: In-house inventory; indices for all of the three chronological divisions of records.

3-NATIONAL COUNCIL/DOMESTIC AND FOREIGN MISSIONARY SOCIETY, CHINA RECORDS ADDITION, 1845–1951, 2.5 l.f.
MINUTES/RECORDS/REPORTS: American Church Mission, China, rules and regulations, 1889–1908; American Protestant Episcopal Mission at Shanghai, minutes of committee meetings, 1857–59; Bishop William J. Boone, record book, 1898–1941; China Mission Diocese of Shanghai, records of the Standing Committee, 1880–84; Commission of the Department of Missions to Confer with the Bishops in China, report, 1927–28; Hua Chung College, minutes of the Board of Trustees, 1943–49; miscella-

neous records on the registration of schools and education in China, 1928–29; Mission of the Protestant Episcopal Church of the U.S. at Shanghai, parish register, 1845–1913; Missionary District of Shanghai, lists of missionaries with biographical details, 1859–1951; Missionary District of Shanghai, Council of Advice, minutes, 1913–25; Missionary Jurisdiction of Shanghai, minutes of the Standing Committee, 1902–13; Woman's Auxiliary to the Board of Missions, China Branch, journal, 1893–1908. CORRESPONDENCE: Letter press book of Bishop William J. Boone, 1887–88; letter press book of the Shanghai Protestant Episcopal Mission, 1869–80. MANUSCRIPTS: Notebook written by Edward W. Syle and Elliott H. Thomson, containing facts about China, description of temples in the Shanghai area, an 1861 list of communicants connected with the Shanghai Episcopal church, and accounts of the church, 1846–58, 1860–68; notebook containing lists of arrivals and departures of missionaries, 1910–23; ''Opinion of Council Concerning Certain Administrative Responsibilities of the National Council,'' n.a., n.d.; outline of Philippians prepared for the Diocese of Kiangsu Third Young People's Conference, n.a., n.d.; notebook on stations and persons by Bishop Graves, 1897–1912. PAMPHLETS: Liturgy of prayer for the consecration of Emmanuel Church in Yangchow, 1924; liturgy of prayer for the building of a church, 1933. AUDIO-VISUAL MATERIALS: Photo of the consecration of Emmanuel Church in Yangchow, 1924; photo of the ceremony marking the inauguration of self-support of All Saints Church in Shanghai, 1933; photo of the Church Conference for Christian Fellowship, Yangchow, Diocese of Shanghai, 1936; photo of the Young People's Summer Conference, St. John's University, Diocese of Shanghai, 1940. CHINESE LANGUAGE MATERIALS: Gospel of Matthew in Shanghai colloquial dialect, copied by Jeannette R. Conover on her first voyage to China, 1853. FINDING AIDS: In-house inventory.

4-NATIONAL COUNCIL/DOMESTIC AND FOREIGN MISSIONARY SOCIETY, AND EXECUTIVE COUNCIL OF THE EPISCOPAL CHURCH IN THE U.S.A., PUBLICATIONS, 1885–1944, 104 items
Background note: In addition to the materials listed below, this collection contains pamphlets, books, and study guides relating to Episcopal missions in China, including items on Benjamin Ancell, Anglo-American School (Kuling), Central China Teachers' College (Wuchang), Central Theological School, Chung-hua Sheng Kung Hui (Nanking), Church General Hospital (Wuchang), Episcopal Mission at Changsha, Grace Church (Anking), St. Faith's School (Yangchow), St. James' Hospital (Anking), School for Catechists and Clergy (Shanghai), Soochow Academy (boys' school in Soochow), and Wuchang Normal School. MINUTES/RECORDS/REPORTS: Bishop Boone Memorial School, report, 1885, 1909; Boone University, report, 1913–15; missions in China, annual report of the bishops, 1913; St. John's College, report, 1885, 1901; St. John's University, report, 1907–8, 1912–16; report of the president, 1917–18; St. Mary's Hall, report, 1901; St. Mary's Orphanage, report, 1912. CORRESPONDENCE: Letter from the American Church Mission, Ichang, 1909. FINDING AIDS: In-house inventory.

**5-NATIONAL COUNCIL/DOMESTIC AND FOREIGN MISSION-
ARY SOCIETY, HOUSE OF BISHOPS, CHINA, MINUTES OF
MEETINGS, 1912–43, 1 reel microfilm**
MINUTES/RECORDS/REPORTS: House of Bishops, China,
minutes, 1912–43.

**6-NATIONAL COUNCIL/DOMESTIC AND FOREIGN MISSION-
ARY SOCIETY, PHOTOGRAPH COLLECTIONS: CHINA,
1912–35, 9 l.f.**
AUDIO-VISUAL MATERIALS: Mostly undated photos, includ-
ing Bible Women's Training School, Soochow; Boone College,
Wuchang; Central Theological School, Nanking; Elizabeth Bunn
Memorial Hospital, Wuchang; Chinese agriculture and livestock;
Chinese art; Chinese bridges, gates, and arches; Chinese Chris-
tians and their families; Chinese clergy from Hankow and
Shanghai; Chinese Medical Missionary Association Conference;
Chung-hua Sheng Kung Hui General Synods; Church General
Hospital, Wuchang; the consecration of Bishop Alfred Gilman in
Hankow, 1925; the consecration of Bishop Daniel Huntington in
Anking, 1912; coolies and ricksha men; the Dowager Empress;
Episcopalian cathedrals, chapels, and churches in Anking, Han-
kow, Hanyang, Ichang, Kinkiang, Kuling, Miaochien, Nanchang,
Nanking, Shanghai, Soochow, Taihu, Tsingpoo, Woosung, Wu-
chang, Wuhu, Wusih, and Yangchow; famine victims and relief
work; Fukai Yamen Refugee Camp, Wuchang; Ginling College,
Nanking; Grace Church, Anking; the Great Wall; High Commer-
cial School, Hankow; Hunan Middle School; Imperial palaces in
Peking; James Addison Ingle in Anking and Hankow; Kuling
American School; Mahan School, Yangchow; Medical Social Service, Wuchang; Ming tombs in Nanking and Peking; mission con-
ferences at Anking, Hankow, and Shanghai; Nationalist soldiers;
public gatherings and exhibits in connection with the New Life
Movement; the Red Cross in Hankow and Tientsin; St. Andrew's
Hospital, Wusih; St. Elizabeth's Hospital, Shanghai; St. Faith's
School, Yangchow; St. Hilda's School, Wuchang; St. James' Hos-
pital, Anking; St. John's University, Shanghai; St. Lois' School,
Hankow; St. Luke's Hospital, Shanghai; St. Mary's Orphanage,
Shanghai; St. Matthew's School, Nanchang; St. Peter's Day
School, Shanghai; St. Peter's Hospital, Wuchang; Salley Stuart
Memorial School, Anking; Rosa Sayre Day School, Shanghai;
scenes of village life; Soochow Academy; temples and pagodas in
Anking, Changsha, Peking, and Shanghai; Trinity Chapel, Ank-
ing; Trinity Girls' School, Changsha; Trinity College, Canton;
Women's Auxiliary District Conference, Shanghai; and Yüan
Shih-k'ai.
FINDING AIDS: In-house inventory.

7-FRANCIS LISTER HAWKS POTT PAPERS, 1883–1947, 7 l.f.
Background note: Francis Lister Hawks Pott (1864–1947) was an
Episcopal missionary in China from 1886 to 1941, president of St.
John's College from 1888 to 1896 and of St. John's University
from 1896 to 1941, and a leading figure of the Chung-hua Sheng
Kung Hui. This collection contains miscellaneous uncatalogued
materials in addition to the items listed below.
MINUTES/RECORDS/REPORTS: Pott's legal documents,
1887–1948; Pott's memoranda, resolutions, lists, and reports,
1909–38 and n.d.
CORRESPONDENCE: .75 l.f. of letters to and from Pott, 1883–
1934.
DIARIES: .5 l.f. of diaries written by Pott, 1895–1947.

MANUSCRIPTS: 1.5 l.f. of articles and lectures written by Pott,
1892–1939 and n.d.; 3.75 l.f. of sermons and addresses written by
Pott, 1883–1947 and n.d.
MEMORABILIA: Pott's personal notes, 1898–1931; newspaper
clippings, 1904–47; and other personal items, 1905–29.
FINDING AIDS: In-house inventory; bibliography of Pott's writings from 1887 to 1946, comp. by V. L. Wong.

AUSTIN PRESBYTERIAN THEOLOGICAL
SEMINARY
TX–10 Stitt Library
106 East 27th Street
Austin TX 78705
(512) 472-6736
Calvin Klemt, Librarian

1-GENERAL HOLDINGS
PAMPHLETS: *The Apostle of China, Father Lebbe*, by Raymond
J. De Jaegher, 1954; *The Awakening of China: In Relation to the
Modern Missionary Programme*, by Harold Balme, 1920; *The
Bible and China*, by Will H. Hudspeth, 1952; *China in Chains*, by
Raphael Montaigne, 1958; *Karl Ludvig Reichelt*, by Sverre Holth,
1952.
SERIALS: *Ching Feng*, 1982-.
DISSERTATIONS/THESES: *Etude sur les missions nestoriennes
en Chine, au VIIe et au VIIIe siècles, d'après l'inscription Syro-
Chinoise de Si-ngan-fou*, by Augustin Cleisz, 1880. *The Mission
Compound in Modern China: The Role of the United States Protes-
tant Mission as an Asylum in the Civil and International Strife of
China, 1900–1941*, by Gladys Robina Quale, 1957. *Protestant
Christianity and Marriage in China*, by Calvin H. Reber, 1958.
*The Protestant Missionary Understanding of the Chinese Situation
and the Christian Task from 1890 to 1911*, by C. William Mensen-
diek, 1958.

UNIVERSITY OF TEXAS AT AUSTIN
TX–15 The General Libraries
Box P
Austin TX 78713–7330
(512) 471-3811
Harold W. Billings, Director
John Tongate, Head Librarian, Reference Services
   Department

1-GENERAL HOLDINGS
SERIALS: *Monumenta Serica*, 1935-.
CHINESE LANGUAGE MATERIALS/SERIALS: *Yen-ching
hsüeh pao (Yenching Journal of Chinese Studies)*, 1927–51.

DALLAS

SOUTHERN METHODIST UNIVERSITY
TX–20 Bridwell Theology Library
Dallas TX 75275
(214) 692-3441
Roger Loyd, Associate Director

1-METHODIST MISSIONARY SOCIETY ARCHIVES, 1829–1946, 1,760 microfiches

Background note: These materials are microfiche reproductions of the original archives, now housed in the Library of the School of Oriental and African Studies in London. The collection is divided into three components, two of which—the Wesleyan Methodist Missionary Society records and the Women's Work Collection—contain extensive materials concerning Methodist missions in China.

MINUTES/RECORDS/REPORTS: China Synod, minutes, 1853–1946; overseas schedules, China, 1923–46.

CORRESPONDENCE: 820 microfiches of letters in the Wesleyan Methodist Missionary Society records, divided into 11 series: Canton (1851–1905), China General (1936–45), China Miscellaneous (1924–34), Hunan (1907–45), Hupeh (1905–45), Ningpo (1933–46), North China (1933–45), South China (1905–45), South West China (1932–45), Wenchow (1933–45), and Wuchang (1876–1905); 281 microfiches of letters in the Women's Work Collection, divided into 3 series: Hunan, Hupeh, Ningpo, and Wenchow (1921–54), North, South, and South West China (1920–47), and Missionaries on Furlough (China, 1925–30).

MANUSCRIPTS: 330 microfiches of biographical materials and personal papers of Methodist missionaries in China, including David Hill, Samuel Pollard, and G. Stephenson, 1829–69.

FINDING AIDS: Microfiche reproductions of typescript correspondence inventories.

2-GENERAL HOLDINGS

MINUTES/RECORDS/REPORTS: Methodist Church, China Central Conference, journal, 1947; reports from a deputation of Australian churchmen to the People's Republic of China, 1956; British Quaker Mission to the People's Republic of China, Society of Friends, London Yearly Meeting, report, 1956.

MANUSCRIPTS: "Educational Crisis in China, 1926: Material Bearing on the Matter of Registration of Christian Schools with the Chinese Government Authorities," comp. by the Chinese Christian Educational Association, 1926; "History of Nanking Theological Seminary, 1911 to 1961: A Tentative Draft," by Francis Wilson Price, 1961; "Work and Progress in China of the Methodist Episcopal Church, South, from 1848–1907," 1907.

PAMPHLETS: *The American Bible Society in China*, by John R. Hykes, 1916; *A Brief Summary of the China Inland Mission for the Past Year, Presented at the Annual Meetings in North America, Autumn of 1930*, by Robert Hall Glover, n.d.; *Documents Relating to the History of the Franciscan Missions in Shantung, China*, by Bernward H. Willeke, 1947; *The Gospel Liberating China; Or, the Present Situation in China and Our Relation to It*, by Young J. Allen, 1906; *A Handbook of the China Inland Mission*, n.a., n.d.; *The Interpretation of Clause Five of the Government Regulations for the Registration of Mission Schools*, by Timothy Tingfang Lew, 1926; *Windows into China: The Jesuits and Their Books, 1530–1730*, by John Parker, 1978.

SERIALS: *Bridge: Church Life in China Today*, 1983-. *China and the Church Today*, 1984–86. *China Bulletin*, 1947–58. *China Christian Year Book*, 1916, 1923–26, 1928–29, 1931–39. *China Notes*, 1962–72. *China Talk*, 1976-. *Chinese Christian Intelligencer*, 1916. *Chinese Christians Today*, 1962–64. *Chinese Recorder*, 1920–41. *Chinese Repository*, 1832–51. *Ching Feng*, 1964-. *Mission Bulletin*, 1958–59. *Quarterly Notes on Christianity and Chinese Religion*, 1960–63.

DISSERTATIONS/THESES: *Die Akkommodationsmethode des P. Matteo Ricci S.I. in China*, by Johannes Bettray, 1955. *Christianity and Communism in China and Korea*, by Myong-gul Son, 1959. *Die katholische Chinamission im Spiegel der rotchinesischen Presse; Versuch einer missionarischen Deutung*, by Johannes Schütte, 1957. *Nationalism and Christianity in China*, by Fongkwei Yeh, 1934. *Student Opinion and Christian Missions in China*, by Elna Lucy Martin, 1931.

FORT WORTH

SOUTHWESTERN BAPTIST THEOLOGICAL SEMINARY
TX–25 A. Webb Roberts Library
P. O. Box 22000–2E
Fort Worth TX 76122
(817) 923–1921
Robert Phillips, Associate Director for Reader Services
Ben Rogers, Archivist, Texas Baptist Historical Collection

1-BAPTIST MISSIONARY SOCIETY ARCHIVES, 1860–1914, 8 reels microfilm

Restrictions: Literary rights for these materials are retained by the Baptist Missionary Society. To obtain permission to cite these materials, researchers should contact the Society at 93/97 Gloucester Place, London, W1H 4AA, England.

Background note: This collection is a microfilm reproduction of the Archives of the Baptist Missionary Society of England (1792–1914), currently housed in London.

MINUTES/RECORDS/REPORTS: Baptist Missionary Society, application forms and references for all missionary candidates, 1881–1914; Baptist Missionary Society, China Committee, records, 1884–1914; Baptist Missionary Society, China, Ceylon and France Sub-Committee, minute books, 1861–67; Baptist Missionary Society, China Sub-Committee, 1884–1914.

CORRESPONDENCE/DIARIES: Correspondence and journals of Jennie Beckinsale, 1898–1913; journals and 5 letters from Herbert Dixon, 1887–88, including information about Timothy Richard; journal and letter from George Edwards, 1916; journals and 86 letters of George Farthing, 1887–1900, including discussions of mission finances, missions in Shansi, and Timothy Richard; 3 letters from Richard Glover (Baptist minister in Bristol) to Alfred Henry Baynes (secretary of the Baptist Missionary Society), discussing the health of Herbert S. Jenkins; 9 letters from Francis H. James, including discussions of famine relief work and Timothy Richard; 5 letters from Herbert S. Jenkins, 1903–4; 316 letters, 4 telegrams, and journals of Alfred G. Jones, 1868, 1877–1905, with such correspondents as Clement Bailhache (secretary of the Baptist Missionary Society), Alfred Henry Baynes, Richard Glover, Timothy Richard, and Arthur DeC. Sowerby, discussing famine relief work, mission finances, missions in Shantung, and the political situation in China; journal and letter of R. F. Laughton to Alfred Henry Baynes concerning finances at the Chefoo mission, 1868; uncatalogued correspondence and journal of M. Lewis, Bap-

tist missionary to China, 1912–14; journal and correspondence of E. F. Kingdon, 1864–67; 4 letters from Mary Richard (Mrs. Timothy Richard) to Albert Henry Baynes, 1895, including discussion of Chinese officials' hostility to missionaries; 227 letters to and from Timothy Richard, 1877–78, 1883–99, 1901–5, with such correspondents as Albert Henry Baynes, Richard Glover, Alfred G. Jones, William Muirhead, and Sir Harry Parkes (British consul in China), discussing the Boxer Uprising, famine relief work, missions in Shansi, missions in Shantung, the persecution of Chinese Christians, and translations of the Bible.
MANUSCRIPTS: 18 papers prepared by, or commenting on, Timothy Richard, 1894; unpublished description of Timothy Richard's work in Shansi by Mary Richards, 1887.
DIARIES: Diaries of Timothy Richard, 1888–92, 1895, 1897–1903.
MEMORABILIA: Insurance policy issued in Shanghai for E. F. Kingdon, 1867; press cuttings on Herbert S. Jenkins, 1904.
FINDING AIDS: "Baptist Missionary Society: Papers Relating to China, 1860–1914," by Mary M. Evans, 1965.

2-TEXAS BAPTIST HISTORICAL COLLECTION, 1894–1937, 2 c.f.
MINUTES/RECORDS/REPORTS: China Baptist Publication Society, Canton, annual reports, 1905–6; Eliza Yates Memorial School, catalogue, 1919–20; Kaifeng Baptist College, catalogue, 1921; Southern Baptist Convention, Central China Mission, minutes, 1925–26, 1928–29; Southern Baptist Convention, North China Mission, 1934; Southern Baptist Convention, South China Mission, annual reports, 1904, 1909.
CORRESPONDENCE: Letter from P. H. Anderson, Canton, to J. B. Gambrell, Dallas, Texas, 1909; letter from G. P. Bostie, Pingtu, to J. M. Carroll, Lampasas, Texas, 1894; letter from H. F. Buckner, Yinglak, to Baptist General Convention of Texas, Dallas, Texas, n.d.; letter from R. E. L. Meshaw, Kweilin, to J. B. Gambrell, Dallas, Texas, 1905; letter from Grace A. H. Mills to Mrs. R. T. Bryan, 1923; letter from J. M. Oxner, Pingtu, to J. B. Gambrell, Dallas, Texas, 1905; letter from Mrs. J. M. Oxner, Pingtu, to Mrs.Bobo, n.d.; 9 letters from W. Eugene Sallee, Kaifeng, to Baptist General Convention of Texas, 1907–28; 20 letters from J. R. Saunders, Yong-tak-hia, Canton, to Baptist General Convention of Texas, 1899–1921; circular letter from Jacob Gould Schurman, Peking, about Kaifeng Baptist College, 1923.
MEMORABILIA: Scrapbook of letters, tributes, and other items commemorating W. Eugene Sallee, 1931.
AUDIO-VISUAL MATERIALS: 40 photos of Chinese Baptist churches and congregations, mission schools, and individuals, 1907–36; glass slides of Chinese landscape, n.d.

3-GENERAL HOLDINGS
SERIALS: *China Christian Year Book*, 1911–19, 1923–25, 1926, 1928–29, 1931–39. *China's Millions* (London), 1879, 1881–85, 1887, 1925, 1927–31, 1934. *China's Millions* (Philadelphia), 1908–18, 1920–44, 1946–52.
DISSERTATIONS/THESES: *A Program of Christian Education in Baptist Schools in China*, by Cherry Y. K. Chang, 1955. *Sin in the Chinese Religions*, by Charles L. Culpepper, 1945. *Teaching the Christian Faith in the Chinese Educational Context*, by Jack L. Gentry, 1971.
CHINESE LANGUAGE MATERIALS/SERIALS: *Chin hui t'ung hsun* (*Baptist Bulletin*), 1947–48.

TEXAS CHRISTIAN UNIVERSITY
TX–30 Burnett Library
Brite Divinity School
P. O. Box 32904
Texas Christian University Station
Fort Worth TX 76129
(817) 921-7106
Robert A. Olsen, Librarian

1-GENERAL HOLDINGS
MINUTES/RECORDS/REPORTS: Shantung Missionary Conference, records, 1893, 1898.
CORRESPONDENCE: Bound volume of correspondence from China missionary Katherine Schutze, 1935–40.
MANUSCRIPTS: "The American Board in China, 1830–1950: Review and Appraisal," by Fred Field Goodsell, 1969; "History of Nanking Theological Seminary, 1911 to 1961: A Tentative Draft," by Francis Wilson Price, 1961; "The Mission Work of the Presbyterian Church in the United States in China, 1867–1952," by James Edwin Bear, 1963–73 (microfilm copy of original manuscript in Union Theological Seminary in Virginia, Archives, 3401 Brook Road, Richmond, VA, 23227); "Notes on the Chronological List of Missionaries to China and the Chinese, 1807–1942," by Charles Luther Boynton (microfilm copy of original manuscript at Union Theological Seminary, 3041 Broadway, New York, NY, 10027).
PAMPHLETS: *The China Christian Mission*, by Elliott I. Osgood and Edwin Marx, 1935; *An Hour with James Hudson Taylor, Pioneer Missionary to China*, by Theodore W. Engstrom, 1942; *An Hour with John and Betty Stam, Martyred Missionaries to China*, by Theodore W. Engstrom, 1942.
DISSERTATIONS/THESES: *Christian Missions and Foreign Relations in China: An Historical Study*, by Clifford Merrill Drury, 1932. *The Development of the Motive of Protestant Missions to China, 1807–1928*, by George Bell Workman, 1928.

HOUSTON

HOUSTON PUBLIC LIBRARY
TX–35 Special Collections
500 McKinney Avenue
Houston TX 77002
(713) 236-1313 Ext. 292, 293
Donna Grove, Curator, Special Collections
Ellen Hanlon, Assistant, Special Collections

1-MILSAPS COLLECTION, 1892–1920, 31 items
Background note: John Milsaps (d. 1932) was a Houston native who became a major in the Salvation Army. He donated books, pamphlets, and diaries gathered and written during his extensive travels.
MINUTES/RECORDS/REPORTS: Chinese Religious Tract Society, annual report, 1893; Federation of Women's Boards of Foreign Missions, report of a deputation concerning a conference at Shanghai, 1920.
DIARIES: 50 pages from a diary of John Milsaps, describing his travels in China, 1899–1900.
PAMPHLETS: 17 pamphlets, 1892–1914, and n.d., including a series entitled *The Mission Crisis in China*, ca. 1900, and pam-

phlets on the Boxer Uprising, famine in South China, and the use of Chinese music in evangelization.

CHINESE LANGUAGE MATERIALS: Baptist hymn book, 1875; translation of John Bunyan's *Pilgrim's Progress*, 1870-71; Gospel of Matthew in Mandarin, written in a numeric character set designed by China missionary W. H. Murray, 1899; pamphlets on Christianity, 1863, 1867, 1883, 1893, 1898, and n.d.

CHINESE LANGUAGE MATERIALS/SERIALS: *Hua t'u hsin pao* (*The Chinese Illustrated News*), 1899. *Wan kuo kung pao* (*The Globe Magazine: A Review of the Times*), 1899.

FINDING AIDS: In-house inventory.

2-PAMPHLET COLLECTION, 1893-1901, 16 items
PAMPHLETS: Pamphlets published by the China Inland Mission, Chinese Religious Tract Society, the Christian and Missionary Alliance, Foreign Missions Board of the Presbyterian Church in the U.S.A., and the Young People's Missionary Movement, 1893, 1899-1901, and n.d., including items on the Boxer Uprising, persecution of missionaries and Chinese Christians, and the use of Chinese music in evangelization.

SERIALS: *Directory of Protestant Missions in China*, 1899.

RICE UNIVERSITY
TX-40 Fondren Library
Woodson Research Center
P. O. Box 1892
Houston TX 77251-1892
(713) 527-4022
Nancy L. Boothe, Director, Woodson Research Center

1-HARRIS MASTERSON, JR., PAPERS, 1911-16, ca. 1.5 l.f.
Background note: Harris Masterson, Jr. (1881-1935), was an Episcopal clergyman and missionary. This collection is unprocessed.

MINUTES/RECORDS/REPORTS/CORRESPONDENCE/ MANUSCRIPTS/PAMPHLETS/MEMORABILIA: Reports, meeting agendas, correspondence, sermons, lectures, programs, circular letters, pamphlets, postcards, and greeting cards, relating to Masterson's work with Boone University and the Wuhan YMCA, 1911-16.

JACKSONVILLE

BAPTIST MISSIONARY ASSOCIATION THEOLOGICAL SEMINARY
TX-45 Kellar Library
1410 East Pine Street
Jacksonville TX 75766-9633
(214) 586-2501 Ext. 8
James Blaylock, Director

1-GENERAL HOLDINGS
PAMPHLETS: *How to Study China through a College Window*, by Saxon Rowe Carver, 1938; *Southern Baptists in China*, n.d.
AUDIO-VISUAL MATERIALS: *Journey Home: Lottie Moon of China*, on videocassette, 1984.
SERIALS: China Graduate School of Theology, *Bulletin*, 1980-83, 1985-86. *Chinese Around the World*, 1983-86.

SAN ANTONIO

TRINITY UNIVERSITY
TX-50 Elizabeth Coates Maddux Library
715 Stadium Drive
San Antonio TX 78284
(512) 736-8121
Richard Hume Werking, Director
Katherine D. Pettit, Head, Department of Archives and Special Collections

1-WILLIAM M. KELLY PAPERS, 1924-35, 41 items
Restrictions: Access by appointment only.
Background note: William M. Kelly, an 1897 graduate of Trinity University, was a missionary in China from 1897 to 1909. After studying medicine at the University of London and Harvard University, he returned to China to work as a medical missionary from 1910 to 1942. Samuel Lee Hornbeak was president of Trinity University from 1908 to 1920.

CORRESPONDENCE: 39 letters between Kelly and Dr. Samuel Lee Hornbeak, including discussion of Chinese art and culture, famine relief, medical missions, and Kelly's travels in China, 1924-35; 2 letters from Kelly to Kate Spencer, 1931, n.d.
FINDING AIDS: In-house inventory.

WACO

BAYLOR UNIVERSITY
TX-55 J. M. Dawson Institute of Church-State Relations
Box 380
Waco TX 76798-0356
(817) 755-1510
James E. Wood, Jr., Director

1-GENERAL HOLDINGS
Background note: With the exception of the papers by Jonathan Chao, Zhang Chunjiang, and Mark E. Matheson, the manuscripts listed below were papers presented at the Conference on Church and State in the Modern Experience of China, Baylor University, June 27-28, 1985.

MANUSCRIPTS: "Contemporary Perspectives," by H. J. Kung, 1985; "An Examination of Religious Freedom in the People's Republic of China," by Mark E. Matheson, 1985; "Historical Perspectives," by P. Richard Bohr, 1985; "In Retrospect: The Mission School," by C. K. Zhang, 1985; "The Missionary," by L. Gerald Fielder, 1985; "Recent Political and Church Events in China and Their Implications for China Ministries," by Jonathan Chao, n.d.; "Role of Christianity in the Development of Modern China," by Zhang Chunjiang, 1985; "Theme Interpretation: Religion and the State in Historical and International Perspective," by James E. Wood, Jr., 1985.

SERIALS: *China and the Church Today*, 1980-86. *China Prayer Letter* (Hong Kong), 1982-83, 1986-. *China Prayer Letter* (San Jose, CA), 1982-84.

DISSERTATIONS/THESES: *Ritual as Ideology in an Indigenous Chinese Christian Church*, by Morris Aaron Fred, 1975.

CHINESE LANGUAGE MATERIALS/SERIALS: *Zhongguo yu jiaohui* (*China and the Church*), 1986-.

TX-60 Moody Memorial Library
Baylor University
CSB 356
Waco TX 76798-0356
(817) 755-3590
Sue Margaret Hughes, Director
Janet Sheets, Head of Reference Services

1-GENERAL HOLDINGS
MINUTES/RECORDS/REPORTS: Eliza Yates Girls' School, yearbook, 1926.
ORAL HISTORIES: *China Missionaries Oral History Collection*, ed. by Cyrus H. Peake and Arthur L. Rosenbaum (Claremont Graduate School, Oral History Program), 1973. See ORAL HISTORIES Union List for the names of participants.
SERIALS: *China Christian Year Book*, 1910-19, 1923-25, 1928-29, 1931-39. *China's Millions* (Philadelphia), 1911-47. *Chinese Recorder*, 1910-41.
DISSERTATIONS/THESES: *China Missions in Crisis: Bishop Laimbeckhoven and His Times, 1738-1787*, by Joseph Krahl, 1964. *Protestant Mission Schools for Girls in South China (1827 to the Japanese Invasion)*, by Mary Raleigh Anderson, 1943. *Missionary Conscience and the Comprehension of Imperialism: A Study of the Children of American Missionaries to China, 1900-1949*, by Sarah R. Mason, 1978. *The Protestant Missionary in China: The Career of Annie Jenkins Sallee, 1905-1930*, by David Hubert Hattox, 1977.

UTAH

LOGAN

UTAH STATE UNIVERSITY
UT-5 Merrill Library
Logan UT 84322-3000
(801) 750-2678
Warren Babcock, Reference Librarian

1-GENERAL HOLDINGS
SERIALS: *Lingnan Science Journal*, 1929, 1937-48.

PROVO

BRIGHAM YOUNG UNIVERSITY
UT-10 Harold B. Lee Library
Provo UT 84602
(801) 378-4301
Gail King, Curator, Asian Collection

1-GENERAL HOLDINGS
MINUTES/RECORDS/REPORTS: American Board of Commissioners for Foreign Missions, Foochow Mission, annual report, 1897; China Inland Mission, annual reports, 1948, 1951.
MANUSCRIPTS: "Christianity and Revolution: J. Harry Giffin, An American Baptist in South China, 1904-1934," by Loren W. Crabtree, 1984; "Nineteenth-century Christian Missions in China," by Dennis A. Kastens, 1977.
PAMPHLETS: *Has Christianity Come to China to Stay?*, by Frank R. Millican, 1935, and *Training of Missionaries*, by the National Christian Council of China, 1935, in a binder entitled "College of Chinese Studies"; *An Hour with Jonathan and Rosalind Goforth, Missionaries to China*, by Theodore Wilhelm Engstrom, 1943; *In War and Peace: Showchow, China*, 1939; *Msgr. Gauthier et le vicariat du Tong-King méridional*, n.a., 1879; *North of the Yellow River: Six Decades in Honan, 1888-1949*, by W. Harvey Grant, 1948; *Windows into China: The Jesuits and Their Books, 1580-1730*, by John Parker, 1978.
SERIALS: *China and the Gospel*, 1906-17. China Inland Mission, *Occasional Papers*, 1872-75. *China Notes*, 1970-78. *China's Millions* (London), 1879-80, 1895. *Chinese Christians Today*, 1962-73, 1976-. Chinese Church Research Center, *Occasional Papers*, 1979, 1981. *Chinese Recorder*, 1868-72, 1874-76, 1878-79, 1888, 1892, 1903, 1916-23, 1925, 1930-34, 1937, 1941. *Lingnan Science Journal*, 1922-48. *Les Missions de Chine*, 1938-39. *Variétés Sinologiques*, 1917.
DISSERTATIONS/THESES: *China Missions in Crisis: Bishop Laimbeckhoven and His Times, 1738-1787*, by Joseph Krahl, 1964. *Chinese Christianity since 1949: Implications for the Church of Jesus Christ of Latter-day Saints*, by Bruce J. M. Dean, 1981. *An Historical Overview of the Missionary Activities of the Church of Jesus Christ of Latter-day Saints in Continental Asia*, by Robert Clayton Patch, 1949. *Protestant Mission School for Girls in South China (1827 to the Japanese Invasion)*, by Mary Raleigh Anderson, 1943. *The Negotiations between Ch'i-ying and Lagrené, 1844-1846*, by Angelus Francis J. Grosse-Aschhoff, 1950. *A Q-sort Comparison between Cultural Experiences of Chinese and Cultural Perceptions of Returned Latter-day Saint Missionaries from the United States Who Had Been Assigned to Chinese Missions*, by Gary G. Y. Chu, 1974.

SALT LAKE CITY

CHURCH OF JESUS CHRIST OF LATTER-DAY SAINTS
UT-15 Historical Department
East Wing
50 East North Temple Street
Salt Lake City UT 84150
(801) 531-2745
Grant Allen Anderson, Manager, Library Services

Background note: In addition to the materials listed below, the Historical Department also holds records of mission work in Hong Kong and Taiwan.

1-GENERAL HOLDINGS
ORAL HISTORIES: Oral interview with Tsang Shiu-ngo Sheila Hsia, describing her early life in China, conversion, and church activities in Hong Kong and Singapore, n.d.
DISSERTATIONS/THESES: *Chinese Christianity since 1949: Im-

plications for the Church of Jesus Christ of Latter-day Saints, by Bruce J. M. Dean, 1981. *An Historical Overview of the Missionary Activities of the Church of Jesus Christ of Latter-day Saints in Continental Asia*, by Robert Clayton Patch, 1949. *A Q-sort Comparison between Cultural Experiences of Chinese and Cultural Perceptions of Returned Latter-day Saint Missionaries from the United States Who Had Been Assigned to Chinese Missions*, by Gary G. Y. Chu, 1974.

UNIVERSITY OF UTAH

UT–20 Manuscripts Department
Marriott Library
Salt Lake City UT 84112
(801) 581-8863
Nancy V. Young, Manuscripts Librarian

1-MADELINE R. McQUOWN PAPERS (Ms. 143), 1852, 1 item
MANUSCRIPTS: 2-page typescript by Mormon missionary James Lewis, who travelled to China in 1852 in an unsuccessful attempt to recruit new members for the Mormon church.

UT–25 Marriott Library
University of Utah
Salt Lake City UT 84112
(801) 581-6273
Paul Mogren, Reference Librarian

1-GENERAL HOLDINGS
PAMPHLETS: *Jesuit Letters from China, 1583-1584*, ed. and trans. by M. Howard Rienstra, 1986; *Windows into China: The Jesuits and Their Books, 1580-1730*, by John Parker, 1978.

VERMONT

BURLINGTON

UNIVERSITY OF VERMONT
VT–5 Bailey/Howe Library
Burlington VT 05405-0036
(802) 656-2138
Connell Gallagher, University Archivist and Curator of Manuscripts

1-HENRY C. BROWNELL PAPERS, 1911–42, 6 l.f.
Background note: Henry C. Brownell (d. 1970) taught at Lingnan University, Canton. He was in Canton from 1911 to 1942. His papers are as yet unprocessed. See also Lingnan University collections at Harvard University, Harvard-Yenching Library, 2 Divinity Avenue, Cambridge, MA, 02138; and Yale Divinity School, Special Collections, 409 Prospect Street, New Haven, CT, 06510.
MINUTES/RECORDS/REPORTS: Canton Christian College, catalogues, 1919-24; illustrated bulletin, 1944; Lingnan University calendar, 1930.
CORRESPONDENCE: Correspondence with family and friends, 1925-50; letters to Brownell from friends, missionaries, and students in China, 1950s-1960s; letters from Brownell in China, 1950s; letters from Lee Hung Suen, 1958.
DIARIES: 2 diaries on Japanese occupation of Canton, 1938-40.
PAMPHLETS: Pamphlets and brochures on China in general and Lingnan University, 1920-50.
MEMORABILIA: "Nowadays in China" by Brownell, *Vermont Alumni Weekly*, 1927; "Six Months behind Barbed Wire," *Vermont Alumni News*, 1942; miscellaneous articles by Brownell; miscellaneous newsletters and clippings, n.d.; list of plants on Lingnan University campus, 1947; Lingnan University staff list, n.d.
AUDIO-VISUAL MATERIALS: Photos, including students and family, ca. 1910-1950.
SERIALS: *Canton Christian College Bulletin*, 1910-11. *Canton Committee for Justice to China Bulletin*, 1938. *China Bulletin*, 1954-62. *China Talk*, 1945. *Educational Review*, 1911.

2-CLARA LEACH PAPERS, 1916–49, 1 reel microfilm
Background note: For biographical notes and the originals of this collection, see American Baptist Headquarters, American Baptist Board of International Ministries, Valley Forge, PA, 19481.
DIARIES: Set of diaries of Clara Leach, 1916-49.

3-GENERAL HOLDINGS
MINUTES/RECORDS/REPORTS: American Board of Commissioners for Foreign Missions, Foochow mission, report by Dwight Goddard, 1896; North China mission, report, 1903-10.
PAMPHLETS: *China under the Shadow of War*, by the Presbyterian Church in the U.S.A. Board of Foreign Missions, 1939; *Facing the Future of the Missionary Movement*, by Edward Hicks Hume, 1927; *The Record of Ten Years of Church Progress in China*, by Frederick Rogers Graves, 1903; *The Students of China for Christ*, by Robert Ellsworth Lewis, 1898; *Windows into China: The Jesuits and Their Books, 1580-1730*, by John Parker, 1978.
SERIALS: *China Christian Year Book*, 1919, 1926, 1928. China Inland Mission, *Occasional Papers*, 1872-75. *Chinese Recorder*, 1938-40.
DISSERTATIONS/THESES: *Protestant Mission Schools for Girls in South China (1827 to the Japanese Invasion)*, by Mary Randolph Anderson, 1943.

MONTPELIER

VT–10 VERMONT HISTORICAL SOCIETY
109 State Street, Pavilion Building
Montpelier VT 05602
(802) 828-2291
Reidun D. Nuquist, Librarian

1-GENERAL HOLDINGS
Background note: For biographical notes on Clara Leach, see American Baptist Headquarters, Valley Forge, PA, 19481.
PAMPHLETS: *Clara C. Leach: In Quietness and Confidence Shall Be Your Strength, Isaiah 30: 15* [excerpts from her diaries and letters], by Clara Chase Leach, 1981.

VIRGINIA

ALEXANDRIA

VIRGINIA THEOLOGICAL SEMINARY
VA-5   Bishop Payne Library
Alexandria VA 22304
(703) 370-6602
Jack H. Goodwin, Librarian

1-GENERAL HOLDINGS
MINUTES/RECORDS/REPORTS: National Council of the Churches of Christ in the U.S.A., Division of Foreign Missions, China consultation, 1958; St. Andrew's Hospital, Wusih, report, 1938–39; St. James Hospital, Anking, 1936.
SERIALS: *Anking Newsletter*, 1939–41. *China Christian Year Book*, 1911–13, 1924, 1929. *District of Shanghai Newsletter*, 1940–41. Nanking Theological Seminary, English Publications, 1941.
DISSERTATIONS/THESES: *Christianity and the Chinese Republic*, by Graham Yu Ling Lieo, 1926. *The Development of the Motive of Protestant Missions to China, 1807–1928*, by George Bell Workman, 1928. *Lutheran Missions in a Time of Revolution: The China Experience, 1944–1951*, by Jonas Jonson, 1972. *Political Activities of the Christian Missionaries in the T'ang Dynasty*, by Lam Ch'i-hung, 1975. *The Relation between Christian Missions and Economic Imperialism in China in the Nineteenth Century*, by Henri Batcheller Pickens, 1937.

ASHLAND

RANDOLPH-MACON COLLEGE
VA-10   Walter Hines Page Library
Ashland VA 23005
(804) 798-8372
Dan T. Bedsole, Director
Nancy B. Newins, Reference Librarian/Archivist

1-GENERAL HOLDINGS
MINUTES/RECORDS/REPORTS: China Annual Conference of the Methodist Episcopal Church, South (Golden Jubilee, 1886–1935), Shanghai, 1935.

BLACKSBURG

VIRGINIA POLYTECHNICAL INSTITUTE AND STATE UNIVERSITY
VA-15   University Libraries
Blacksburg VA 24601
(703) 961-5593
Paul M. Gherman, Director

1-GENERAL HOLDINGS
SERIALS: *Peking Natural History Bulletin*, 1930–41.

BRIDGEWATER

BRIDGEWATER COLLEGE
VA-20   Alexander Mack Memorial Library
Bridgewater VA 22812
(703) 828-2501 Ext. 510
Ruth Greenawalt, Director

Background note: See also Church of the Brethren General Board, Brethren Historical Library and Archives, 1451 Dundee Avenue, Elgin, IL, 60120; General Commission on Archives and History—The United Methodist Church, United Methodist Archives and History Center, Archives, 36 Madison Avenue, P. O. Box 127, Madison, NJ, 07940; and United Theological Seminary, Library, 1810 Harvard Boulevard, Dayton, OH, 45406.

1-GENERAL HOLDINGS
MINUTES/RECORDS/REPORTS: China Famine Relief of the American Red Cross, 1921; Foreign Missions Conference of North America: Jubilee Meeting of the Conference of Foreign Mission Boards in Canada and the United States (1944), Fifty-seventh Annual Meeting (1950), Sixth Meeting of the Division Assembly/Sixty-second Annual Meeting (1955); Shansi Plague Prevention Bureau, 1918.
MANUSCRIPTS: "Excerpts from My Life in China," by Nettie M. Senger, n.d.; "Minor M. Myers: A Brief Biography," 1969(?).
PAMPHLETS: *Brethren Missions in China*, by Ron Nolley, 1973.
MEMORABILIA: Notebook by Minor Myers on his experiences in missions and relief, n.d.; special China issues of *The Gospel Messenger*, every August from 1930 to 1950.
AUDIO-VISUAL MATERIALS: Photo of Brethren Hospital in Shansi just before its opening in November, 1923.
SERIALS: *Star of Cathay*, 1940, 1942, 1947–48.
DISSERTATIONS/THESES: *Brethren Rural Reconstruction in China, 1920–1950*, by Bradley Kent Geisert, 1975.

CHARLOTTESVILLE

UNIVERSITY OF VIRGINIA

VA-25   Manuscripts Department
Alderman Library
Charlottesville VA 22901
(804) 924-3025
Ray W. Frantz, Jr., University Librarian
Edmund Berkeley, Jr., Curator of Manuscripts and University Archivist
Ann L. S. Southwell, Manuscripts Cataloger

1-AMERICAN CATHOLIC MISSIONARIES TO CHINA INTERVIEWS (7155a), 1971-72, 8 reels tape
Background note: See also Maryknoll Fathers and Brothers, Archives, Maryknoll, NY, 10545; and Maryknoll Sisters of St. Dominic, Inc., Maryknoll Sisters Archives, Maryknoll Sisters Center, Maryknoll, NY, 10545.
ORAL HISTORIES: Interviews by Thomas Breslin with Jesuit,

Franciscan, and Maryknoll missionary priests and sisters Candida Maria Basto, Rita Claire Comber, Dulcissima Dessel, Paul J. Duchesne, C. Stephen Dunker, Albert V. Fedders, Angelica Frisch, Francis Lynch, J. F. Magner, Brice Moran, Albert R. O'Hara, Francis J. O'Neill, Protase Pai, Boniface Pfeilschifter, Peter Reilly, Hubertine Rempe, Moira Riehl, and James Thornton, discussing such topics as motives and training of missionaries, mission work, relations with local governments, inhabitants, Chinese clergy and missionaries of other denominations, and life under Japanese and Communist occupation.

2-AMERICAN MISSIONS IN CHINA COLLECTION (9928), 1973, 7 items
MANUSCRIPTS: Papers on missionary methods and problems, written for a graduate seminar on American missions in China taught by Suzanne W. Barnett: "The Boxer Rebellion: Did It Influence Missionary Attitudes?"by Mary Jane Conger; "Brethren Rural Reconstruction in China, 1920–1950," by Bradley Kent Geisert; "Christianity and Feng Yü-hsiang," by Thomas A. Creamer; "John Foster Dulles' Missionary Perspective on China," by Christine Coffey; "The Missionary Goes to Washington: The Career of Walter Judd, China Missionary and Congressman," by Daniel F. Gillespie; "Pearl S. Buck: Cultural and Humanitarian Missionary," by Shannon Foster; and "Reverend Arthur Henderson Smith and American Missionary Response to a Changing China (1890–1910)," by Minerva M. Taylor.

3-PEARL BUCK PAPERS (7795a), 1933, 1 item
CORRESPONDENCE: Letter from Pearl Buck to James V. Barrett on the success of missions in China, 1933.

4-COLLINS DENNY PAPERS (2672f), 1886–87, 1 volume
MEMORABILIA: Scrapbook containing clippings and articles describing Collins Denny's tour of mission inspection to China and the Far East, 1886–87.

5-JONES FAMILY PAPERS (8557), 1852–63, 56 items
Background note: Catherine Ella Jones was an Episcopal missionary in Shanghai. See also Duke University, Manuscript Department, William R. Perkins Library, Durham, NC, 27706.
CORRESPONDENCE: Letters of Catherine Ella Jones, written to her sisters, chronicling mission life and work and current events, 1852–63.

6-ULIN W. LEAVELL PAPERS (5675), 1921, 1 item
DISSERTATIONS/THESES: *Some Phases of the Administration of Christian Education for Boys in China*, by Ulin W. Leavell, 1921.

7-NANKING INCIDENT COLLECTION (3550), 1927, 2 items
MANUSCRIPTS: 2 eyewitness accounts of the Nanking Incident, by Harry and Jeannie Clemons after they fled the city in 1927.

8-WILLIAM NELSON PAGE PAPERS (6851), 1852, 1 item
CORRESPONDENCE: Letter from Rose Nelson to friends on her year in a Shanghai mission, 1852.

9-TAYLOR FAMILY PAPERS (9965), 1905–06, 1 item
Background note: John Cowder Taylor was the father of Harry Baylor Taylor (see below).
MANUSCRIPTS: Excerpt of Harry B. Taylor's letters from China to John Cowder Taylor, 1905-6.

10-TAYLOR FAMILY PAPERS (9965-a), 1868–1967, 10 l.f.
Background note: A medical missionary of the Protestant Episcopal Church, Harry Baylor Taylor (1882–1967) received his medical degree from the University of Virginia in 1902, first went to China in 1905, and served at St. James Hospital in Anking from 1907 to 1950. He witnessed the great damage done to the hospital, one of the first nursing schools in China, during the Nanking Incident. Repatriated in 1943 after a year of protective custody following the closing of St. James Hospital by the Japanese, Taylor returned to the hospital in 1947. He remained until the end of 1950, when the Communists closed the hospital.
MINUTES/RECORDS/REPORTS: St. James Hospital, report, 1936.
CORRESPONDENCE: 17 boxes of Taylor family correspondence, 1904–51, on the Communist occupation, famine relief, Japanese conquest, life in Anking, local life and customs, medical and surgical work, missionary compound activities, 1911 revolution, 1927 occupation by Nationalist Southern Army, Panay incident, summer vacations in Kuling, China, and Taylor's 1942–43 imprisonment by the Japanese; telegram advising immediate evacuation of women and children from Anking, n.d.; letter from Mrs. Gilman of Changsha to her family, 1911; letter from David W. K. Au, T. C. Bau, and others to "Missionary Societies and Missionaries," 1948.
DIARIES: 7 folders and a manuscript of Harry B. Taylor's diary, 1906, 1931–46; medical diary of Harry B. Taylor, 1948–50; Alma B. Taylor's health record and diary of her children, 1924–32.
MANUSCRIPTS: 10 typescripts by Harry B. Taylor on Anking, Christmas in 1937, Kuling, the Panay incident, P'ei-en Tutorial School, polemic, and St. James Hospital, 1906-ca. 1939; "Sunrise over Anking," by Emeline Bowne, Isabella Colson, Blanche Meyers, and Harry B. Taylor, 1938; 3 typescript issues of newsletter, *Anking Ch'ing Pao (Air Raid Alarm)*, by Robin Ch'en, Alice Gregg, Blanche Meyers, and Harry B. Taylor, 1937–38; typescript material sent to R. A. Bridges, St. Stephen's Church, Erwin, North Carolina, by Alma Taylor in 1941; "Landing at Anking," by J. K. Shyrock, 1925; "Religion in its Biological Aspects," a sermon by Rev. Needham, 1928; "St. James Hospital, Anking," by Blanche E. Meyers, 1940; "Notes from Anking," and "St. James Hospital, Anking, China," n.a., n.d.; "Taylor Story," by [?] Larkin for *The Progress*, 1943; 68 manuscripts and typescripts of speeches by Alma and Harry B. Taylor, 1939–45, and n.d.; Harry B. Taylor's medical notebook and 7 accompanying notes, 1945 and n.d.; 9 manuscripts of articles on medical topics by Harry B. Taylor and L. F. Si Se, ca. 1930–1942 and n.d.; 2 photocopies of Harry B. Taylor's autobiography, published as *My Cup Runneth Over*, n.d.
PAMPHLETS: 15 printed items on mission work in China and St. James Hospital, 1904–61; 25 printed items on medicine and surgery, ca. 1923–1941; *19 Missionaries along the Yangtze*, by the Younger Generation, 1925; *The Diocese of Anking*, by Rt. Rev. Daniel Trumbull Huntington, Bishop of Anking, 1943.
MEMORABILIA: 4 account notebooks of Harry B. Taylor, ca. 1940–64; 40 accounts, cancelled checks, and receipts of the Taylor family, 1923–50; bullets and shrapnel removed from Chinese patients at St. James Hospital, 1937–38; 4 Chinese handbills, n.d.; chronology of Harry B. Taylor, n.d.; 146 newspaper clippings on China, religion, and the Taylor family, 1905–51; Harry B. Taylor's Certificate of Repatriation, 1943; copy of Helen Wickham Tay-

lor's birth report, 1919; 2 lists of code words used by Taylor in correspondence, 1940; 99 greeting cards, n.d.; 15 mailing lists and addresses, n.d.; receipt bearing messages written by various people, 1938; 2 needlework handkerchiefs; notebook of Bible verses, probably by Harry B. Taylor, 1942; 2 notes on Harry B. Taylor, n.a., 1898–1910; governmental regulations proclaimed by the Peoples' Liberation Army after the liberation of Anking, n.d.; 26 poems and songs, ca. 1919–47 and n.d.; 40 prayers, hymns, and inspirational notes, 1935–46 and n.d.; "Proclamation from the Anking Garrison Commander of the Imperial Japanese Army," 1941; red ribbon with "T. I. L. K. A.," printed on it, 1901–8; "Regulations for Aliens," 1941; 4 programs for Field Days for Missions in China at St. Mark's Episcopal Church, Shreveport, Louisiana, by Alma and Harry B. Taylor, 1940–41; 6 items for a promotional campaign for Lenten offering, including service of dedication, an (open) letter from Alma Taylor, and a play, "Have a Heart for China," 1941; 7 Japanese propaganda posters, ca. 1938; sack inscribed with Chinese figures and a large red sun, n.d.; 30 school reports of Taylor children, 1929–47; 116 school papers, essays, and exams of the Taylor children, 1930–46; wing fabric from a crashed Japanese airplane, 1938; 30 miscellaneous programs, 1936–52 and n.d.; 2 folders of miscellaneous printed and other material, 1911–62.

MAPS/DESIGNS/DRAWINGS: Map of China prepared for China Inland Mission, 1911; map of central China, showing the American Dioceses of the Chinese Holy Catholic Church, n.d.

AUDIO-VISUAL MATERIALS: Ca.130 photos of Harry B. Taylor and family, 1904–49; 16 photos of St. James Hospital, staff members, hospital scenes, and Anking, 1927–41; 32 photos of "The Walking Trip," 1937; 37 photos of various scenes in China and America, n.d.; 60 photos of Taylor friends and acquaintances from China and America, 1931–46, and n.d.; 4 photos of General and Mrs. Yang Sen, 1938; 25 envelopes of negatives, n.d.

SERIALS: *Anking Newsletter*, 1944. *District of Anking Newsletter*, 1925–41. *District of Hankow: The Newsletter*, 1934–41. *District of Shanghai Newsletter*, 1930–41. *Free Wan-Kan*, 1942–44.

CHINESE LANGUAGE MATERIALS: 2 Chinese flash cards and a syllabary of the national phonetic signs, n.d.

FINDING AIDS: In-house directory.

11-WITHROW FAMILY PAPERS (38–148), 1882, 15 items
CORRESPONDENCE: Sympathy notes to the father of China missionary Evelyn Withrow Houston, who died in 1882; fragment of a letter from Evelyn Houston, n.d.

12-GENERAL HOLDINGS
CORRESPONDENCE/MEMORABILIA: Plaque of Sun Yat-sen and Abraham Lincoln presented to Henry and Jeannie Clemons by Feng Yu Heieng (Feng Yü-hsiang) in 1945, together with Feng's covering letter.

VA–30   Alderman Library
University of Virginia
Charlottesville VA 22901
(804) 924-3025
Ray W. Frantz, Jr., University Librarian

1-GENERAL HOLDINGS
MINUTES/RECORDS/REPORTS: China Baptist Publication Society, annual report, 1922; Chinese Religious Tract Society, annual report, 1885–86; International Institute of China, constitution, 1907, reports, 1903, 1906, 1927; Methodist Episcopal Church, South, Mission Conferences on China, minutes, 1887–88, 1926–28; Presbyterian Church in the U.S.A., Kiangan mission, minutes of the Executive Committee and Annual Meeting, 1927; President and Treasurer of the University of Nanking, report, 1925–26; Shanghai American Episcopal Mission Hospital for Chinese, annual report, 1885–86.

PAMPHLETS: *A Message from China to the Women's Missionary Society of the Methodist Episcopal Church, South*, by Laura Askew Haygood, 1885.

ORAL HISTORIES: *China Missionaries Oral History Collection*, ed. by Cyrus H. Peake and Arthur L. Rosenbaum (Claremont Graduate School, Oral History Program), 1973. See ORAL HISTORIES Union List for the names of participants.

MAPS/DESIGNS/DRAWINGS: *Atlas of the Chinese Empire*, comp. by Edward Stanford (London and Philadelphia: The China Inland Mission), 1908; *Complete Atlas of China...*, by Edward Stanford (London and Philadelphia: The China Inland Mission), 1917; *A Map of China, Prepared for the China Inland Mission, 1911...* (London: China Inland Mission and Edward Stanford), 1911; map of China, prepared by Stanford's geographical establishment in London for the China Inland Mission, n.d.

SERIALS: *Bulletin on China's Foreign Relations*, 1932–35. *China Bulletin*, 1951–62. *China Christian News Letter*, 1928. *The China Fundamentalist*, 1928–32. China Inland Mission, *Occasional Papers*, 1872–75. China International Famine Relief Commission, Publications, series A, 1922–36. *China Monthly*, 1939–50. *China Notes*, 1962–75. *Educational Review*, 1923, 1927–29. *Nanking Church Bulletin*, 1916–33. *Nanking Church Notes and Notices*, 1933–37, 1939–40. National Christian Council of China, *Bulletin*, 1932–33. *News of China*, 1943–49. University of Nanking, College of Agriculture and Forestry, *Agriculture and Forestry Notes*, 1931–32, 1939–41; *Bulletin*, 1932–36; *Special Report*, 1934. University of Nanking, Department of Botany, Plant Pathology Laboratory, *Contribution*, 1930–34. *University of Nanking Magazine*, 1922–28. Yenching University, *Social Research Series*, 1930; *Yenching Journal of Social Studies*, 1938–41.

DISSERTATIONS/THESES: *American Catholic China Missionaries, 1918–1941*, by Thomas A. Breslin, 1972. *Brethren Rural Reconstruction in China, 1920–1950*, by Bradley Kent Geisert, 1975. *Christian Colleges and the Chinese Revolution, 1840–1940: A Case Study in the Impact of the West*, by Loren William Crabtree, 1969. *The Disordered Society: American Catholics Look at China, 1900–1937*, by Thomas A. Breslin, 1969. *Evangelizing China: Four Centuries of Failure*, by Li Guang-zhao, 1983. *Missionaries and Revolutionary Change: China, 1949–1951*, by Edith C. Maynard, 1972. *Missionary Views of China and Japan, 1890–1899*, by Mary Jane Conger, 1975. *Oberlin-in-China, 1881–1951*, by Mary Tarpley Campfield, 1974. *Strangers in the House: J. Lewis Shuck and Issachar Roberts, First American Baptist Missionaries to China*, by Margaret M. Coughlin, 1972.

CHINESE LANGUAGE MATERIALS/SERIALS: *Chin-ling hsüeh pao (Nanking Journal)*, 1931–39. *Hwa mei chiao pao (Chinese Christian Advocate)*, 1934–40. *Organ of Soochow University College of Arts and Sciences*, 1935. University of Nanking, College of Arts, Publications, Series A, *Studies in the Humanities*, 1936. University of Nanking, Institute of Chinese Cultural Studies, Publications, Series A, 1931–32. University of Nanking Library, *Publications*, 1924–35. *Yen-chiag hsüeh pao (Yenching Journal of Chinese Studies)*, 1927–37.

CHINESE LANGUAGE MATERIALS: Agricultural index, books on geography, literature, local history, regional gazetteers in the University of Nanking Library, the Sacred Edict, and anti-Christian activities of Chinese officials; pamphlet on the library of the University of Nanking.

VA–35   Law School Library
University of Virginia
Charlottesville VA 22901
(804) 924–3384
Marsha Rogers, Archivist

1-GENERAL HOLDINGS
PAMPHLETS: *Endorsements of the International Institute of China*, 1897.

HARRISONBURG

EASTERN MENNONITE COLLEGE AND SEMINARY
VA–40   Menno Simons Historical Library and Archives
Harrisonburg VA 22801-2462
(703) 433–2771
Grace I. Showalter, Librarian

Background note: See also Bethel College, Mennonite Library and Archives, North Newton, KS, 67117-9998; Center for Mennonite Brethren Studies, 4824 East Butler, Fresno, CA, 93727; and Goshen College, Archives of the Mennonite Church, 1700 South Main Street, Goshen, IN, 46526.

1-GENERAL HOLDINGS
MINUTES/RECORDS/REPORTS: China General Conference Mennonite Mission, 1924; West China Mission, Mennonite Brethren Church of North America, 1949; Mennonite China mission, 1913, 1940.
PAMPHLETS: 7 pamphlets on Mennonite missions and student movements in China, by and about H. J. and Maria Brown, Mrs. S. J. Goering, Joseph Daniel Graber, and E. G. Kaufman, 1924–49.

HOLLINS COLLEGE

HOLLINS COLLEGE
VA–45   Fishburn Library
Hollins College VA 24020
(703) 362–6237
Anthony B. Thompson, Archivist and Assistant for
Special Collections

1-SPECIAL COLLECTION, 1840–1913, 3 items
Background note: Charlotte Moon attended Hollins College. For biographical notes, see First Baptist Church, Lottie Moon Room, 114 West Cherokee Avenue, Cartersville, GA, 30120. See also Virginia Baptist Historical Society, University of Richmond, Boatwright Memorial Library, Box 95, Richmond, VA, 23173.

CORRESPONDENCE: Letter from Charlotte Moon in Tengchow, to Matty Cocke at Hollins College, 1912, relating to Hollins College catalogue and pictures sent by Matty Cock; letter from Cynthia Aldine Miller to Mrs. Francis H. Smith, 1913.
MANUSCRIPTS: 3 leaves from unpublished "Life of Lottie Moon," by Cynthia Aldine Miller, n.d.

LEXINGTON

VA–50   GEORGE C. MARSHALL RESEARCH FOUNDATION
P. O. Box 1600
Lexington VA 24450
(703) 463–7103
John N. Jacob, Archivist

1-FRANK W. PRICE PAPERS, 1929–49, 4 boxes
Background note: For biographical notes, see Union Theological Seminary in Virginia, Archives, 3401 Brook Road, Richmond, VA, 23227.

The collection is organized into six series: general correspondence, correspondence with the Chiang family, materials concerning the Chiangs (not correspondence), materials on the general situation in China during Frank W. Price's stay there, materials relating to the Foreign Affairs Bureau, and miscellanea.
MINUTES/RECORDS/REPORTS: Report concerning missionaries in Communist areas, 1941; certificate granting Price permission to travel, 1943; memoranda concerning the Foreign Affairs Bureau of the National Military Council, Republic of China, 1944–45; proposed plan for Chinese-speaking American personnel in War Service in China.
CORRESPONDENCE: Box of correspondence, including letters to and from the following individuals and organizations: Dean Acheson, Carsun Chang, Chang Chih-chung, Chang Chun, Daniel S. K. Chang, Chang Kia-ngau, M. H. Chang, P. H. Chang, Y. Z. Chang, Theodore Chen, Chiang K'ai-shek and Mme. Chiang (Soong Mei-ling), Chiang Mon-ling, Ch'ien Tien-ho, Chu Chia-hua, Feng Yü-hsiang, Randall Gould, Han Li-wu, Ho Hao-jo, Patrick Hurley, George Kao, Wellington Koo, Ku Cheng-kang, Li Huang, Liu Chieh, H. Loomis, Lung Yun, George C. Marshall, William Martin, National Christian Council, L. C. Ning, W. P. M. Plumer, San Min Chu I Youth Corps, K. C. Shale, George Shively, Shao Tzu-cheng, J. P. Slaybaugh, T. V. Soong, C. T. Sung, Tan Chuen Yu, Edgar C. Tang, Hollington Tong, Tso Yung-szu, M. T. Z. Tyau, Arthur H. Vandenburg, Walter Walkinshaw, Mme. Chengting T. Wang, Wang Chung-hui, Wang Shih-chieh, Albert C. Wedemeyer, F. C. Wu, P. Y. Yüan, and O. K. Yui, 1929–49; 10 pages of letters concerning the Foreign Affairs Bureau of the National Military Council, Republic of China, 1944–45.
DIARIES: 18 pages of journals and diaries on Price's experiences in China, 1937–46.
MANUSCRIPTS: 55 pages of notes on Generalissimo and Mme. Chiang K'ai-shek, 1930–45; 18 pages of transcriptions of Generalissimo and Mme. Chiang K'ai-shek's and radio addresses, 1944–45; 34 pages of notes on "the general situation in China," 1939–47.
PAMPHLETS: *My Testimony and My Religion*, by Generalissimo and Mme. Chiang K'ai-shek, 1937; *Democracy Reaps the Whirl-*

wind, 1940; speeches by Chiang K'ai-shek, 1944–5; *Notes on Madame Chiang*, by E. Hahn, in *American Mercury*, 1944; *The Future of Chinese Democracy: Nine Questions Asked by Collier's and Answered by Generalissimo Chiang K'ai-shek*, 1945; *Madame Chiang K'ai-shek at the Front*, by Charlotte T. Brown, n.d.
MEMORABILIA: Box of news clippings on Chiang K'ai-shek and the political situation in China, 1930–45; medical exam report, 1948; Hong Kong Fire Insurance Co., Ltd., 1933.
AUDIO-VISUAL MATERIALS: Photo of Chiang K'ai-shek, n.d.
CHINESE LANGUAGE MATERIALS: *Tzu Shih Ching Hua* (*Essentials and Ornamentals from Philosophical and Historical Texts*), 3 V, n.d.; *P'ei Wen Yun Fu* (*Famous Quotations and Literary Allusions, for Use by Chinese Scholars and Writers*), 16 V, n.d.
FINDING AIDS: In-house inventory.

WASHINGTON AND LEE UNIVERSITY
VA–55 Library
Lexington VA 24450
(703) 463-8640
Barbara J. Brown, Director of the Library
Erin Foley, Special Collections Librarian

1-MATTHEW HALE HOUSTON PAPERS, 1861–93, 19 items
CORRESPONDENCE: 17 letters from Matthew Hale Houston to his brother, William Wilson Houston, and 2 to Mary Houston (Mrs. William Houston), concerning Matthew Houston's experiences as a missionary in China.

2-JAMES LEWIS HOWE PAPERS, 1916, 4 items
Background note: James Lewis Howe was a professor of chemistry at Washington and Lee University.
CORRESPONDENCE: Letters to Howe from Randolph T. Shields, n.d.; Phillip Francis Price, 1916; Rev. John W. Paxton, 1916; and C. F. S. Lincoln, at St. John's College, Shanghai, on missions in China, n.d.

3-GENERAL HOLDINGS
PAMPHLETS: *China Mission Studies (1550–1800): Directory*, by David E. Mungello, 1978.
ORAL HISTORIES: *China Missionaries Oral History Collection*, ed. by Cyrus H. Peake and Arthur L. Rosenbaum (Claremont Graduate School, Oral History Program), 1973. See ORAL HISTORIES Union List for the names of participants.
SERIALS: *The China Fundamentalist*, 1930–31, 1934–40.

LYNCHBURG

RANDOLPH-MACON WOMEN'S COLLEGE
VA–60 Robert C. Watts Rare Book Room
Lipscomb Library
Lynchburg VA 24503
(804) 846-7392 Ext.242
Ruth Ann Edwards, Director

1-PEARL S. BUCK COLLECTION, 1911–72, 120 items
Background note: Emma Edmunds White and Pearl S. Buck (1892–1973) were classmates (Class of 1914) and lifelong friends.
CORRESPONDENCE: 101 letters from Pearl S. Buck to Emma Edmunds White, covering personal, political, and literary topics, 1911–72.

MANUSCRIPTS: 8 folders of uncatalogued biographical material, brochures, journal articles, and other items, about Pearl Buck, her birthplace, and the Pearl S. Buck Foundation, 1939–73.
AUDIO-VISUAL MATERIALS: Uncatalogued photos of Pearl S. Buck, from student days until her death.

2-GENERAL HOLDINGS
SERIALS: *News of China* (United China Relief), 1943–49.

RICHMOND

SOUTHERN BAPTIST CONVENTION, FOREIGN MISSION BOARD
VA–65 Archives Center
Box 6767
3806 Monument Avenue
Richmond VA 23230
(804) 353-0151
Edith Jeter, Archivist/Analyst
Rebecca M. Wills, Records Manager
Isabelle R. Peterson, Data Administration Coordinator

Restrictions: Correspondence of retired missionaries is restricted for their lifetime and for 25 years beyond. Correspondence of resigned missionaries is restricted for 50 years beyond age 65. Release of mission minutes and reports must be approved by the area director or his administrative assistant.
Background note: The Foreign Mission Board (FMB) is the Southern Baptist sending agency. China was its first mission field. Programs include evangelism and church growth, schools and student work, publications, hospitals and health care, and benevolent ministries. See also Southern Baptist Convention Historical Commission, Library and Archives, 901 Commerce Street, Nashville, TN, 37203-3260; and Wallace Memorial Baptist Church, 701 Merchants Road, Knoxville, TN, 37912.

1-BAKER J. CAUTHEN'S GENERAL CORRESPONDENCE FILES, 1888–1979, quantity undetermined
Background note: Baker J. Cauthen was secretary to the Orient of the Southern Baptist Convention. He was in China until about 1954.
MINUTES/RECORDS/REPORTS: Treasurer's office, financial statements relating to Lottie Moon Christmas Offering, 1964–67; records relating to "Lottie Moon Christmas Offering," 1888–1968.
CORRESPONDENCE: Folder of correspondence with Chinese nationals, 1952–53; folder of correspondence relating to the China mission field, n.d. (1950s–1960s); correspondence between H. C. Goerner and Rankin, Sadler, and [Charles] Maddry, 1943–51.
PAMPHLETS: Foreign Mission Board pamphlets on China, n.d.
SERIALS: *China Bulletin*, 1952–62.
FINDING AIDS: In-house inventory.

2-MISSIONS RECORD SERIES, 1845-, 1500 l.f.
MINUTES/RECORDS/REPORTS/CORRESPONDENCE: Records on beginning of work in China, mainland missions, and All-China Seminary, n.d.; All-China Southern Baptist Missionary Conference, minutes, 1935; Associated Boards for Christian Colleges in China, 12 folders of reports and records, 1933–47; Associ-

ation for the Chinese Blind, 1931–51; box of materials relating to Central China including, evangelism work, medical work, property, schools, and historical information, 1896–1940; China Baptist Convention, 1948; China Baptist Publication Society, reports and information, 1905–50; deed, 1910; China Baptist Theological Seminary, 1947–48; catalogues, 1940–41; China Commission, 1929–30; China's Children Fund, Inc., 1950–51; 4 folders on China in general, 1950–51, n.d.; China mission minutes and reports: Central China, 1901–49; Interior China, 1903–47; North China, 1909–40; South China, 1874–1950; China relief, n.d.; Church Committee for China Relief, 1938–39; China Information Service (Frank Price), 1937–39; Conference on Mainland China, 1964; First Baptist Church (Old North Gate), minutes, 1847; "For Christ in China," n.d.; Foreign Mission Board, meeting notes, 1849–50, 1852–53, 1855, 1877; reports from B. J. Cauthen, 1949(?); Free China, 1942–45; Hartwell-Crawford case, photocopies of China Committee reports and other papers, n.d.; Lottie Moon offering, records, clippings, and other papers, 1961–74; National Christian Council of China, report, 1938; box of materials relating to North China, including evangelistic work, medical work, property, schools, 1901 FMB report by J. B. Hartwell, and miscellaneous, 1901–36; North China Baptist Theological Seminary and Bible School, catalogue, 1935; Primary and Junior Baptist Women's Bible School, 1938–39; 7 boxes of material relating to Shanghai Baptist College and Seminary, including constitutions, minutes, reports, newsletters, correspondence, articles, publications, property appraisals, historical data, and other items, 1900–1961; Shanghai annuals, 1916, 1918, 1921–31, 1933–34, 1940–41, 1947; Shanghai Baptist College, catalogues, 1910–36; annual reports, 1909–41; Shanghai Baptist College and Seminary, minutes of the board of trustees, 1918–27; Shanghai College, Conference of Christian Colleges and Universities in China, report, 1926; materials relating to South China, including deeds, historical information, Kweilin trouble, property, annual report (1932–33), schools, and miscellaneous, n.d.; South China Mission, statistical table, 1916; Tai Kam Leper Island, 1934–36; Union Conference of American Baptist Missionaries in China, report, 1905; University of Shanghai, catalogue, 1936; minutes, 1934, 1936; Board of founders, n.d.; project file folder on Bill Wallace, 1965; Warren Memorial Hospital, report, 1934; Wei Ling Girls' Academy, Soochow, report, 1924–25; Yangtzepoo Social Center, annual report, n.d.; Yates Academy, catalogue, n.d.; purchase of war surplus, records, n.d.; relocation of missionaries, 1948–52; unspecified reports and pamphlets, 1921–37; 6 folders of miscellaneous property deeds, n.d.; 8 envelopes of property deeds, including mission property in Tengchow, Tung Shan compound, Dr. Hartwell's residence in Tengchow, True Light Building, China Baptist Publication Society, Baptist headquarters of China, Women's Missionary Union (WMU) headquarters, Pingtu medical and other property, First Baptist Hospital (later, Warren Memorial Hospital), Stout Memorial Hospital, Wuchow, and an 1850 deed for mission property which is the oldest extant deed for such a purchase in China, 1850–1903; 5 packets of deeds for property in Kwangsi province, n.d.; 9 packets of deeds, building permits, leases, and other documents for property in Shantung province, including Tsingtao, Tsinan, Tsining, Chefoo, Manchuria, and Talien, n.d.; 10 packets of deeds and other documents for property in Kiangsu province, including Kiangyin, Chinkiang, Yangchow, Nanking, and Shanghai, n.d.; 10 packets of deeds and other documents for property in North China, including Laichow,

Tsinan, Laiyang, Honan province, Kaifeng, Anhui province, and Chengchow, n.d.; 10 packets of deeds and other documents for property in South China, including Canton, Kwangtung province, and Shiuchow, n.d.; 13 packets of deeds for property unspecified in Kiangsu province, n.d.; reports on China in denominational periodicals, *The Commission*, 1856–61, 1938–; *The Foreign Mission Journal*, 1869–1916; *Home and Foreign Fields*, 1916–36; and *The Southern Baptist Missionary Journal*, 1846–51.

CORRESPONDENCE: 45 copybooks of correspondence of Foreign Mission Board presidents, 1845–1914, including A. M. Poindexter, W. H. Smith, J. B. Taylor, H. A. Tupper, and R. J. Willingham; letter from M. Dean, regarding T. P. Crawford and G. W. Burton en route to Shanghai, 1852; 2 folders of China correspondence to Willingham and Ray, n.d.; general correspondence, 1920–59, including the Associated Boards for Christian Colleges, Baptist Convention, Central China Mission, China Children's Fund, China Baptist Publication Society, China Inland Mission, Chinese nationals, Christian Educational Association, Church Committee for China Relief, Church World Service, Inabelle G. Coleman, College of Chinese Studies, Frontier Mission, Herman Liu Memorial Home for Refugee Children, Cordell Hull, Edward H. Hume, Institution for the Chinese Blind, Interior China Mission, Joshua Jensen, R. S. Jones, Leung Kwong Baptist Hospital, Roberta Ma, Mokwang Home for Blind Girls, North China Mission, South China Mission, Tai Kam Leper Work, University College of Medicine, University of Shanghai, and miscellaneous; letters from native workers, 1850–1923; box of correspondence with Chinese nationals, 1946–57; letter from Alice Armstrong to T. P. Bell, n.d.; letter from Mary Lib Fuqua, 1949.

MANUSCRIPTS: Biographies of John and Jewell Abernathy, Mary Charlotte Alexander, Clifford Irene Barratt, the Bausum-Lord family, Jeannette Beall, Robert Beddoe, Edward M. and Nell Lawrence Bostick, Mary Demarest, Flora Elizabeth Dodson, John Wilson and Maudie Fielder, Rosewell H. Graves, Blanche Groves, Lettie Hamlett, John Burder and Margaret Hipps, Helen Hsu, Lillie Mae Hundley, John Edward Jackson, Belle Johnson, Margaret Jung, Virginia Lake, Edith D. Larson, Olive Ailene Lawton, Charles and Evelyn Leonard, Francis P. Lide, Herman C. E. Liu, Julia Lowe, Helen McCullough, Leila Memory McMillan, Rose Marlowe, Lottie Moon, J. Walton and Minnie Foster Moore, Katie Murray, Buford and Mary Frances Nichols, Lucy Wright Parker, M. Theron Rankin, Rex Ray, Olive Pauline Riddell, Hannah Fair Sallee, Joel Roscoe Saunders, Henrietta Hall and Jehu Lewis Shuck, Drure and Elizabeth Stamps, John Stout, Martha Strother, Edna Teal, William Lindsey Wallace, Josephine Ward, Charles and Louise Westbrook, and J. T. Williams; folder of articles written by missionaries on Interior China, n.d.; folder of articles written by missionaries on Manchuria, n.d.; "China Project Bibliography," by Frank K. Means, ca. 1983; transcript of "China—A Baptist Perspective," a chapel service, by Baker J. Cauthen, J. Winston Crawley, Eugene L. Hill, and James D. Belote, 1972; transcript of Student Conference on World Missions, 1979; transcript of symposium with Keith Parks, Mary Lois Kirksey, Bill Smith, Burt Dyson, and G. Dean Dickens, 1982; "A Century of Grace," by Jane Lide (on J. B. Hartwell), n.d.; "Contributed in Full: The Life of Arthur Samuel Gillespie," by Pauline Pittard Gillespie, 1973; "Critical Moments in the History of Christianity in China," by H. F. MacNair, 1925; "Dug up out of the Past," by Charles G. McDaniel (on J. Lewis Shuck), n.d.; "Fifty Years in South China: Report of Jubilee Celebration, 1856–1906," n.a.;

"Henrietta Hall Shuck, Beulah Wong—Pioneers in Christian Education in Hong Kong," by Lila Watson, n.d.; "History of Nanking Theological Seminary," by Frank Wilson Price, 1961; "History of South China Mission," by A. R. Gallimore, n.d.; "Medical Mission Work in China," by Sanford E. Ayers, n.d.; "Pui Ching Middle School, Hong Kong: Photographs and History," by the Foreign Mission Board, n.d.; "Recollections, Reveries, and Reflections: A Collection of Clippings and Articles Written by Edgar L. Morgan, Missionary to North China, 1905-1932"; "The Shantung Revival," by C. L. Culpepper, n.d.; "They of Sinim," n.a., n.d.; songs of Chinese children, n.d.; untitled manuscript by Mary K. Crawford, n.d.; Floyd North's research materials on the University of Shanghai, n.d.; "West of the Yangtze Gorges," by Joseph Taylor, 1936.

PAMPHLETS: *China Consultation*, 1958; articles and pamphlets on China, ca. 1936, n.d.; booklets on Chinese writing, n.d.; pamphlets of United China Relief, n.d.; pamphlets and clippings on the Taiping Rebellion, 1853-54.

MEMORABILIA/CORRESPONDENCE: 6 folders of miscellaneous clippings and correspondence, 1850-1917, 1936-40, 1950-53, and n.d.; postcard album, ca. 1925-1930; articles on medical work, n.d.; clippings from *Dallas Morning News*, 1945; miscellaneous printed materials on University of Shanghai, n.d.; folder of articles on Interior China, 1933-40; folder of articles on Manchuria, 1935-39; folder of articles and bulletins on China, 1935-40; articles on North China, 1933-40; articles on Central China, 1930-40; articles on South China, 1933-39, n.d.; newspaper clippings and pamphlets, n.d.; WMU materials on Annie Armstrong and Lottie Moon, n.d.; articles and letters of Lottie Moon, n.d.; letters of J. Lewis Shuck, 1837-52; clippings on the return of the *Gripsholm*, ca. 1940s; articles, pamphlets, and biographical information on M. Theron Rankin, n.d.

DIARIES: 10 diaries of Attie T. Bostick, 1925-41; diary of Mary Thornton (Mrs. G. P. Bostick), n.d.; unidentified diary (may have belonged to Attie Bostick); diary of Edgar L. Morgan, n.d.

ORAL HISTORIES: Oral histories (some with transcripts) of F. Catharine Bryan, Ruth Lucille Ford, Martha Franks, Lois C. Glass, Jessie L. Green, Eugene Hill, Rose Marlowe, Lucy Wright Parker, Auria Pender, Olive Pauline Riddell, Lucy Smith, Harold and Grace Snuggs, Lorene Tilford, Lila Watson, Wilma Weeks, and Frank Woodward; "The Shantung Revival," interview with Charles L. Culpepper, Sr., 1982; interview with Baker J. and Eloise Cauthen, 1979; transcripts of interviews with Baker J. and Eloise Cauthen, 1983.

MAPS/DESIGNS/DRAWINGS: Folder of China maps, n.d.; preliminary blueprints and maps of North China, ca. 1916-35; blueprints of Tungshan compound, Stout Memorial Hospital and adjacent property, Jining Road Church, Shantung province properties, and Harbin properties (with deeds, see MINUTES/RECORDS/REPORTS above), n.d.

AUDIO-VISUAL MATERIALS: Cassette of memorial service for Lucy Smith, 1981; filmstrips: *The Lottie Moon Christmas Offering*, 1952, 1956, 1958, and *Where the Gospel Speaks Chinese*, 1970; slide sets: *Lottie Moon Christmas Offering: Typical Projects*, 1958, *Lottie Moon—Virginia Sites*, 1961, *Lottie Moon—China Years*, 1961, *Lottie Moon Christmas Offering*, 1966, *Miss Lottie Moon*, 1967; audio cassette: *China, A Baptist Perspective*, 1972; multi-media: "Orient Report," 1966, and "The Lottie Moon Christmas Offering," 1971; motion pictures: *New Life for China*, 1948, and *The Lottie Moon Story*, 1960; photos: *Journey Home:*

Lottie Moon of China, 1983; audio recordings: "China—Past, Present, and Future," by Baker J. Cauthen, J. Winston Crawley, and Eugene L. Hill, 1971 (transcript also); "China," by Eugene L. Hill, 1971; "Historical Background of the Communist Takeover," by James D. Belote, 1971, "Update on China," n.a., 1971; "Trip to China," by Dr. and Mrs. Baker J. Cauthen, 1980 (transcript also); photo album of University of Shanghai, 1946-47; "Lottie Moon in Pictures," n.d.; photo albums of China, compiler unknown, n.d.

SERIALS: China Christian Educational Association, *Bulletin*, 1924. *Directory of Protestant Missions in China*, 1918. *New East*, 1910, 1927. Shanghai Baptist College, *Bulletin*, 1918-21, 1925.

DISSERTATIONS/THESES: *A Critical Examination of the National Christian Council of China*, by Milledge T. Rankin, 1928. *The Place of Education in the Religious Education of China*, by James Toy Williams, 1921.

CHINESE LANGUAGE MATERIALS: Unidentified books and paper gods; hymnals, 1913 and n.d.; hymns belonging to Thelma Williams, n.d.; printed materials and banners, some of the Foreign Mission Board, n.d.; unidentified newspapers; "The Inner Story of Catholicism," by F. C. H. Dreyer, n.d.; packet of old Chinese pictures of men, n.d.; printing block and dictionary, n.d.; sheet music, 1938.

FINDING AIDS: In-house box inventories.

3-OVERSEAS DIRECTOR'S FILES, 1950s-, quantity undetermined

MINUTES/RECORDS/REPORTS: Baptist Union Middle School, 1936; report on the history of Baptist work, n.d.; miscellaneous records on mission work and personal property losses.

PAMPHLETS: *China Consultation*, 1958.

SERIALS: *China Bulletin*, 1956-59. *China Notes*, 1960-77.

VA-70   Jenkins Research Library

Southern Baptist Convention, Foreign Mission Board
P. O. Box 6767
3806 Monument Avenue
Richmond VA 23230
(804) 353-0151
Kathryn K. Purks, Resource Manager, Research and Planning Office

1-GENERAL HOLDINGS

MINUTES/RECORDS/REPORTS: Educational Association of China, records of the second triennial meeting, 1896; state Baptist annuals of individual church work in China, 1845-.

PAMPHLETS: *Adventuring with Rose: The Story of Rose Marlowe, Southern Baptist Missionary to China and Japan*, by Anna Mae Smith, 1964; *The Bible and China*, by Will H. Hudspeth, n.d.; *The Chinese Church Rides the Storm*, by R. Orlando Jolliffe, 1946; *God Still Lives in China*, by the China Bible Fund, 1975; *Tales from Free China*, by Robert B. McClure, 1941.

SERIALS: *Bridge*, 1983-87. *China and the Church Today*, 1981-86. *China Christian Year Book*, 1926-39. *China Mission Year Book*, 1910-25. *China News and Church Report*, 1983-87. *China Notes*, 1980-87. *China Prayer Letter*, 1982-85. *China Study Project Bulletin*, 1982-86. *Chinese around the World*, 1983-87. *Chinese Theological Review*, 1985-86. *Ching Feng*, 1985-87. *Directory of Protestant Missions in China*, 1924.

DISSERTATIONS/THESES: *The Chinese Indigenous Church Movement, 1919-1927: A Protestant Response to Anti-Christian Movements in Modern China*, by Jonathan Chao, 1986. *The Gospel Mission Movement within the Southern Baptist Convention*, by Adrian Lamkin, 1980. *The History of Southern Baptist Missions in Hong Kong*, by Paul Yat-keung Wong, 1974. *Issachar Jacox Roberts and American Diplomacy in China during the Taiping Rebellion*, by George Blackburn Pruden, Jr., 1977. *Protestant Mission Schools for Girls in South China (1827 to the Japanese Invasion)*, by Mary Raleigh Anderson, 1943. *Seeking the Common Ground: Protestant Christianity, the Three-Self Movement, and China's United Front*, by Philip Lauri Wickeri, 1985.

CHINESE LANGUAGE MATERIALS: Bibles and hymnbooks, 1924-71.

VA-75   Resource Coordination, Office of Communications and Public Relations

Southern Baptist Convention, Foreign Mission Board
P. O. Box 6767
3806 Monument Avenue
Richmond VA 23230
(804) 353-0151
Victoria M. Bleick, Manager, Resource Coordination

Restrictions: Access by appointment through the Archives Center or Jenkins Research Library. Consult staff for access and other restrictions.

1-GENERAL HOLDINGS
ORAL HISTORIES: Oral histories recorded in 1970s of missionaries who served in China in the 1930s-1940s (see ORAL HISTORIES under Archives above).

AUDIO-VISUAL MATERIALS: Ca. 4,000 photos of the work of the Southern Baptist missionaries in China, 1847-1947; 4 motion pictures about China or missionaries who served in China: *New Life for China*, 1948; *The Lottie Moon Story*, 1960; *Journey Home: Lottie Moon of China*, 1983-84; and *Winter is Past*, 1986; photoprint files of missionaries who served in China.

FINDING AIDS: Limited finding aids available.

UNION THEOLOGICAL SEMINARY IN VIRGINIA

VA-80   Archives

3401 Brook Road
Richmond VA 23227
(804) 355-0671 Ext. 272
John B. Trotti, Head Librarian

1-JAMES E. AND MARGARET W. BEAR PAPERS, 1873-1975, 36 boxes, 28 volumes
Background note: James E. Bear (1893-1977) was a Presbyterian missionary to China and then Royster Professor of Christian Missions at Union Theological Seminary.

MANUSCRIPTS/MEMORABILIA: Background research documents for "Mission Work of the PCUS in China, 1867-1930," by James Bear.

ORAL HISTORIES: 41-page transcript of oral history interview with James E. Bear by Henry M. Goodpasture, 1975.

2-FRANK PRICE PAPERS, 1939-65, 13 boxes
Background note: Francis (Frank) Wilson Price (1896-1974) was a Presbyterian missionary who served in China from 1923 to 1952 as an educator at Nanking Theological Seminary and West China Union University. He was also a friend and adviser to Chiang K'ai-shek, and an adviser to the Foreign Affairs Bureau of the National Military Council. See also George C. Marshall Research Foundation, P.O. Box 1600, Lexington, VA, 24450.

MINUTES/RECORDS/REPORTS: Nanking Theological Seminary in West China, catalogue, 1943.

MANUSCRIPTS: Scripts of radio talks from China to America, 1937-43; transcribed notes of Asian trip, n.d.

PAMPHLETS: *Shunhwachen Rural Training Center of Nanking Theological Seminary*; *Wartime Survey of Social and Religious Conditions and the Christian Church in Szechwan Province, West China*.

DISSERTATIONS/THESES: *The Rural Church in China*, by Frank W. Price, 1938.

CHINESE LANGUAGE MATERIALS: *Li Lao Erh, Rural Religious Picture Series*.

VA-85   Seminary Library

Union Theological Seminary in Virginia
3401 Brook Road
Richmond VA 23227
(804) 355-0671 Ext. 311
Martha B. Aycock, Reference Librarian

1-GENERAL HOLDINGS
MINUTES/RECORDS/REPORTS: China Sunday School Association, annual report, 1957; Church of Christ in China, General Assembly, minutes, records, and reports of meetings, 1931-32, 1950; Presbyterian Church in the U.S., Board of Foreign Missions, annual reports of mission fields to General Assembly, 1879-1972; Mid-China Mission, Executive Committee of Foreign Missions, minutes, 1899-1941; North Kiangsu Mission, Executive Committee of Foreign Missions, minutes of annual meetings, 1898-1937, 1940; Presbyterian Church in the U.S.A., Central China Mission, annual station reports, 1890-1905, 1911-12, 1915-16, 1918-23; Hainan Mission, minutes, 1920, 1937-39, 1948; North China Mission, minutes of annual meetings, 1919-20, 1934, 1936, 1938-41.

CORRESPONDENCE: "Letters from China: Missionary Correspondence Letters of James E. and Margaret W. Bear, 1923-1929" (150-page typescript and microfilm of original letters), 1959; "The Mission Work of the Presbyterian Church in the United States in China, 1867-1952," by James E. Bear, 1963-71, 5 volumes, typescript and microfilm.

PAMPHLETS: 67 pamphlets from the China Sunday School Association, including subjects such as Mme. Chiang K'ai-shek, Christian education in China, Christianity in the People's Republic of China, medical missions, and rural missions in China.

SERIALS: *China and the Church Today*, 1982-84. *China Bulletin* (New York), 1951-62. *China Bulletin* (Rome), 1979-84. *China Christian Year Book*, 1910-12, 1923-24, 1931, 1934-39. *China Colleges*, 1948-53. *China Council Bulletin*, 1920-29. *The China Fundamentalist*, 1928-40. *China News* (Atlanta), 1981-83. *China Notes*, 1962-84. *China Prayer Letter*, 1982-84. *China Talk*,

1981–84. *China Update*, 1983–84. *China's Millions* (London), 1894–1928. *Chinese Around the World*, 1983–84. *Chinese Recorder*, 1870–1941. *Ching Feng*, 1977–85. *Educational Review*, 1927–32.

VA–90 VIRGINIA BAPTIST HISTORICAL SOCIETY
University of Richmond
Boatwright Memorial Library
Box 95
Richmond VA 23173
(804) 289–8434
Fred Anderson, Executive Director
Darlene Slater, Research Assistant

Restrictions: Access by appointment.
Background note: The collections listed below are not fully processed. See also Southern Baptist Convention, Foreign Mission Board, P. O. Box 6767, 3806 Monument Avenue, Richmond, VA, 23230; and Southern Baptist Convention Historical Commission, Library and Archives, 901 Commerce Street, Nashville, TN, 37203–3260; and Wallace Memorial Baptist Church, 701 Merchants Road, Knoxville, TN, 37912.

1-OLIVE ELLIOTTE BAGBY PAPERS, 1905–81, 1 box
Background note: Olive Elliotte Bagby (1888–1983) was a missionary to China in the early 1900s.
CORRESPONDENCE/MEMORABILIA: Uncatalogued news clippings and letters.
DIARIES: 7 diaries, 1905–7, 1923–81.

2-CHARLOTTE (LOTTIE) DIGGES MOON PAPERS, 1887–1908, 15 items
Background note: For biographical notes, see First Baptist Church, Lottie Moon Room, 114 West Cherokee Avenue, Cartersville, GA, 30120. See also Hollins College, Fishburn Library, Hollins College, VA, 24020.
CORRESPONDENCE: 15 letters, 1887–1908.

3-T. BRONSON RAY PAPERS, 1922, 1 item
Background note: T. Bronson Ray (1868–1934) was foreign secretary of the Foreign Mission Board of the Southern Baptist Convention from 1914 to 1927.
MINUTES/RECORDS/REPORTS: Report on China missions, 1922.

4-I. J. ROBERTS JOURNAL, 1848, 1 volume
DIARIES: Journal by I. J. Roberts, Canton, 1848.

5-HENRIETTA HALL AND JEHU LEWIS SHUCK PAPERS, 1835–63, 1 box
Background note: Jehu Lewis Shuck (1812(?)–63) and his wife, Henrietta Hall Shuck (1817–44), went to China as missionaries in 1835. He served as an appointee of the Triennial Convention from 1835 to 1846, and as the first Southern Baptist missionary in China from 1846 to 1853. Henrietta Hall Shuck died in China. See also Wake Forest University, North Carolina Baptist Historical Collection, Z. Smith Reynolds Library, P. O. Box 7777, Reynolda Station, Winston-Salem, NC, 27109.
CORRESPONDENCE/DIARIES: Letters to Jehu Lewis Shuck, 1846–53, 1862–63, and Henrietta Hall Shuck, 1835–44, from correspondents including Yong Seen Sang, a Chinese convert to Christianity, and journal notes, 1835–1840s.

6-MARGIE SHUMATE PAPERS, 1914–56, 1 box
CORRESPONDENCE: Uncatalogued letters, 1914–28, 1956.

7-ROBERT JOSIAH WILLINGHAM PAPERS, 1908, 1 volume
Background note: Robert Josiah Willingham (1854–1914) was corresponding secretary of the Foreign Mission Board of the Southern Baptist Convention from 1894 to 1914.
DIARIES: Journal of Willingham's visit to Asia, 1908.

8-GENERAL HOLDINGS
MINUTES/RECORDS/REPORTS: American Southern Baptist Convention, South China Mission, annual report, 1897, 1899; China Baptist Publication Society, annual reports, 1903–6, 1908, 1910, 1919–20; Chinese Tract Society, report, 1905; Edinburgh World Missionary Conference, National Conference, Shanghai, report by J. R. Mott, 1913; Southern Baptist Convention, South China Mission, annual report, 1909; statistical table, 1909.
MANUSCRIPTS: "Lottie Moon, Missionary to North China," by Joy Eubank, 1945; typescript by Blanche White, based on letters and journals of Jehu Lewis Shuck from 1849 to 1851.
PAMPHLETS: 16 pamphlets, 1888–1948, on topics including the China Baptist Publication Society, Chinese folk songs, King Chow Temple, Lottie Moon, Pooi To Middle School (Canton), Shanghai Baptist College, Shanghai Temple, Southern Baptist missions, and the University of Shanghai.
MEMORABILIA: "China Vast and Mysterious," clipping by Curtis Lee Laws, 1925; "Matthew T. Yates, Missionary," clipping from the *Biblical Recorder*, by R. J. Willingham, 1895.
AUDIO-VISUAL MATERIALS: University of Shanghai class photo, n.d.
SERIALS: *China Mission Advocate*, 1839. *China's Young Men*, 1904–5. *Chinese Christians Today*, 1962. *Chinese Recorder*, 1872, 1889. *Chinese Repository*, 1849–51.
DISSERTATIONS/THESES: *Southern Baptist Missions in China 1945–1951*, by Garnett Lee White, 1967.

VA–95 VIRGINIA STATE LIBRARY
Richmond VA 23219–3491
(804) 786–8929
Ella Gaines Yates, State Librarian
William R. Chamberlain, Assistant Director
  for the General Library

Finding aids: *Catalogue of Virginia Library Resources, 1983 Edition* (Richmond: Virginia State Library), 1984.

1-GENERAL HOLDINGS
SERIALS: American Friends Service Committee, *Bulletin on Work in China*, 1942–44.

STAUNTON

MARY BALDWIN COLLEGE
VA–100 Archives
Staunton VA 24401
(703) 887–7085
William Pollard, Archivist and Librarian

Background note: The materials in these collections are related to activities and missions of First Presbyterian Church of Staunton, Virginia, and Mary Baldwin College and Seminary. The Seminary had a number of graduates involved in China missions during the late nineteenth and early twentieth centuries. The college faculty and students financially supported missionaries and reported on their activities in college publications. The college's archives are as yet unprocessed; the items listed below are a small sample of the total collection.

The archives contain information on the following College/Seminary graduates who were involved in China missions: Irene McIlwaine (faculty member), Pauline DuBose Little, Ellen Bell Magill, Cornelia Morgan, Bessie Woods Smith, Josephine Underwood Woods, Lily Underwood Woods, Ida Albaugh Vousden, and Nellie Van Lear Webb.

Agnes Lacy Woods Harnsberger and Nettie DuBose Junkin were involved with the Martha D. Riddle School for Girls in Hwaianfu, which received financial support from the College. An 1883 graduate of Augusta Female Seminary, Sophie Peck Graham, was also involved in the School. Another Mary Baldwin alumna, Jeanne Woodbridge, is recorded to have been in Shanghai.

1-GENERAL HOLDINGS
MINUTES/RECORDS/REPORTS: Accounts of fund-raising by students for missions and the Martha D. Riddle School.
CORRESPONDENCE: Uncatalogued letters sent by missionaries to the college.
AUDIO-VISUAL MATERIALS: Photos of the Martha D. Riddle School for Girls in Hwaianfu.

WILLIAMSBURG

THE COLLEGE OF WILLIAM AND MARY
VA–105 Earl Gregg Swem Library
Williamsburg VA 23185
(804) 253–4407 (Reference)
(804) 253–4550 (Manuscripts)
D. W. Moore, Reference Coordinator
Margaret Cook, Curator of Manuscripts and Rare Books

1-ROBERT NELSON PAPERS, 1845–85, ca. 550 items
Background note: Robert Nelson was a missionary to Shanghai from the Protestant Episcopal Church in the U.S.A. from 1851 to 1881.
MINUTES/RECORDS/REPORTS: List of Chinese confirmed by Bishop Schereschewsky in the Church of Our Savior at Hong Kew, 1879; building permit issued to Nelson, Shanghai, 1879; resolution approving Nelson's resignation as missionary, Foreign Committee of the Domestic and Foreign Missionary Society of the Protestant Episcopal Church in the U.S.A., 1881; chit book, 1894; Nelson's accounts, 1868–85; table showing number of English, American, and German missionaries in China, 1807–74.
CORRESPONDENCE: Letters to Robert Nelson from correspondents including William Henry Brooks, Domestic and Foreign Missionary Society of the Protestant Episcopal Church in the U.S.A., A. A. Hayes, James Johnston, William H. Kinckle, John

MacLeod, R. N. Morburn, Mrs. Robert Nelson, James Stoddard, E. W. Syle, E. H. Thomson, J. K. Wight, Women's Christian Temperance Union, and Hoong N. Woo, 1846–85.
MANUSCRIPTS: "The Ritualistic Character of the China Mission," by Robert Nelson, 1882; notes, drafts, complete and incomplete sermons, Robert Nelson, 1845–84; comments by T. P. Crawford, E. H. Thomson, Charles R. Mills, C. W. Mateer, E. W. Syle, [Joseph] Edkins, [Henry] Blodget, [Andrew] Happer, D. James Legge, R. H. Graves, S. L. Baldwin, and D. Z. Sheffield, on Nelson's review of D. James Legge's essay, "Confucianism in Relation to Christianity," 1877.
PAMPHLETS: *Augustine W. Tucker, Doctor in China*, by Beverley D. Tucker, 1961.
MEMORABILIA: Clipping from *Christian Observer*, 1877, about D. James Legge's article "Confucianism in Relation to Christianity"; program, hymns, and directory of members of Missionary Conference in Shanghai, 1877; concert program of Shanghai Temperance Society, 1878.
AUDIO-VISUAL MATERIALS: Photo of Robert Nelson.
FINDING AIDS: In-house directory.

2-GENERAL HOLDINGS
SERIALS: *Chinese Recorder*, 1869–77, 1919, 1922–30.

WINCHESTER

SHENANDOAH COLLEGE AND CONSERVATORY
VA–110 Howe Library
Winchester VA 22601
(703) 665–4553
Jennie M. Robertson, Curator, Evangelical United Brethren Collection

Background note: This collection contains materials from the United Brethren in Christ and the Evangelical United Brethren Church. The United Brethren in Christ began in 1800 among Germans in Pennsylvania, Maryland, and Virginia who were led by men inspired by Methodist beliefs and practices. The Evangelical United Brethren Church came into existence in 1946 when the United Brethren in Christ merged with the Evangelical Church, which was also German in constituency and Methodist in orientation. In 1968 the Evangelical United Brethren Church merged with the Methodist Church to form the United Methodist Church. See also Church of the Brethren General Board, Brethren Historical Library and Archives, 1451 Dundee Avenue, Elgin, IL, 60120; General Commission on Archives and History—The United Methodist Church, United Methodist Archives and History Center, Archives, 36 Madison Avenue, P. O. Box 127, Madison, NJ, 07940; and United Theological Seminary, Library, 1810 Harvard Boulevard, Dayton, OH, 45406.

1-EVANGELICAL UNITED BRETHREN COLLECTION, ca. 1900–1950, quantity undetermined
MINUTES/RECORDS/REPORTS/AUDIO-VISUAL MATERIALS: Reports, correspondence, and photos from the denomination's work in China in denominational reports and periodicals: General Conference of the United Brethren in Christ, 1873–1946; *The Woman's Evangel*, 1916–17; *The Evangel*, 1918–46; and *The World Evangel*, 1947–50.

WASHINGTON

BELLINGHAM

WESTERN WASHINGTON UNIVERSITY
WA-5   Mabel Zoe Wilson Library
Bellingham WA 98225
(206) 676-3050
Diane C. Parker, Director of Libraries
Wayne V. Richter, Library Specialist, East Asia

Background note: In addition to the materials listed below, the Wilson Library holds a large number of reprints of mission imprints, with a particular concentration in works on minority nationalities.

1-GENERAL HOLDINGS
SERIALS: Catholic University of Peking: *Bulletin*, 1934; College of Education, Publications, 1939-40. *Folklore Studies*, 1942-58, 1962; supplement, 1952. *Lingnan Science Journal*, 1939. *Monumenta Serica*, 1935-47, 1954-56, 1961-; monograph series, 1937, 1941-45, 1947, 1969-71. Nanking Theological Seminary, English Publications, 1940. *Variétés Sinologiques*, 1894, 1896, 1905, 1912, 1922, 1932, 1932-34.

KIRKLAND

NORTHWEST COLLEGE OF THE ASSEMBLIES OF GOD
WA-10   Hurst Library
11102 N.E. 53rd Street
Box 579
Kirkland WA 98033
(206) 822-8266 Ext. 255
Ruth Petty, Librarian

1-GENERAL HOLDINGS
PAMPHLETS: *An Hour with John and Betty Stam: Martyred Missionaries to China*, by Theodore Wilhelm Engstrom, 1942.
DISSERTATIONS/THESES: *The Protestant Missionary Understanding of the Chinese Situation and the Christian Task from 1890 to 1911*, by C. William Mensendiek, 1958.

PULLMAN

WASHINGTON STATE UNIVERSITY

WA-15   Holland Library
Pullman WA 99164-5610
(509) 335-2691
Barbara E. Kemp, Head, Humanities/Social Sciences
  Public Services

1-GENERAL HOLDINGS
MANUSCRIPTS: "Chinese Communists and Mission Properties," n.a., 1926.
SERIALS: *Chinese Recorder*, 1891, 1893, 1914, 1916, 1920, 1922-27, 1929-32, 1934-38.
DISSERTATIONS/THESES: *The Policy of the American State Department toward Missionaries in the Far East*, by Harold James Bass, 1937.
CHINESE LANGUAGE MATERIALS: *The Origin and Cause of the Anti-Christian Movement by Chinese Officials and Gentry, 1860-1874*, by Lü Shih-ch'iang, 1966.

WA-20   Manuscripts, Archives, and Special Collections
Washington State University
Pullman WA 99164-5610
(509) 335-6692
Christian Frazza, Manuscripts Librarian

1-THOMAS EDWARD LAFARGUE PAPERS, ca. 1878-1941, 2 boxes
Background note: See also Harvard University, Houghton Library, Manuscripts Department, Cambridge, MA, 02138. For biographical notes on Arthur G. Robinson, see Marian Rider Robinson Papers in the Wellesley College Archives, Margaret Clapp Library, Wellesley, MA, 02181.
CORRESPONDENCE: 42 letters with Arthur G. Robinson and others, regarding Thomas Edward LaFargue's attempt to communicate with surviving members of the Chinese Educational Mission and the exchange of sources with Robinson, n.d.; 2 letters from Sik Yak Foo, written en route to China from the United States, 1881-82; unidentified letters from Chinese students, collected by LaFargue and Robinson.
MANUSCRIPTS: "China's First Hundred," by Thomas Edward LaFargue, on the Chinese Educational Mission, published in 1942; "The Senior Returned Students," an account of the Chinese Educational Mission, by Arthur G. Robinson, ca. 1932; biographical information on individual Chinese students; miscellaneous notes, transcriptions of source materials, address lists, lists of photos, and other materials.
MEMORABILIA: Clippings, reprints, miscellaneous magazines, and other source material, including articles of Fred G. Blakeslee and Arthur Robinson, 1896-1939; ca. 100 notecards used in writing *China's First Hundred*.
AUDIO-VISUAL MATERIALS: Individual and group photos of students of the Chinese Educational Mission, 1878-1938, many used in *China's First Hundred*; 37 printed illustrations from *China's First Hundred*.
FINDING AIDS: In-house inventory.

2-JAMES P. LEYNSE PAPERS, n.d., 2 items
Background note: James P. Leynse (b. 1890), a missionary under the Dutch Reformed Church, served at the Presbyterian Mission in Peking from 1920 to 1949. He worked with the Peking Poor Relief Committee, operating mission kitchens for the poor.
MANUSCRIPTS: "Beauty for Ashes," his autobiography, n.d.; "Fly the Dragon," a novel, n.d.
FINDING AIDS: In-house finding aid.

SEATTLE

SEATTLE PACIFIC UNIVERSITY
WA–25   Weter Memorial Library
3307 Third Avenue West
Seattle WA 98119
(206) 281–2228
Laura Arksey, Humanities Librarian

1-GENERAL HOLDINGS
MANUSCRIPTS: "Fifty Years of Seattle Pacific College's Foreign Missionary Influence," a student paper by Paul Yardy, 1942, containing sections on missionaries to China.
PAMPHLETS: *The Indigenous Church: Evangelistic and Church Planting Work at the Big End*, by Sidney J. W. Clark, 192?.
DISSERTATIONS/THESES: *The Role of the Minister in Chinese Christian Preaching*, by John W. Silva, 1967.

WA–30   SEATTLE PUBLIC LIBRARY
1000 Fourth Avenue
Seattle WA 98104
(206) 625–4896
Michael Moffit, Religion Librarian

1-GENERAL HOLDINGS
SERIALS: *China Christian Year Book*, 1919–39. China International Famine Relief Commission, Publications, series A, 1922–36.

UNIVERSITY OF WASHINGTON

WA–35   East Asia Library
322 Gowen Hall, DO–27
Seattle WA 98195
(206) 543–4490
Karl K. Lo, East Asian Librarian

1-GENERAL HOLDINGS
MINUTES/RECORDS/REPORTS: United Board for Christian Higher Education in Asia, annual reports, 1970–82.
PAMPHLETS: *America's Contribution to Chinese Democracy: The Christian Colleges in China*, 1939. *British Protestant Christian Evangelists and the 1898 Reform Movement in China*, by Leslie R. Marchant, 1975; *Ernst Faber's Scholarly Mission to Convert the Confucian Literati in the Late Ch'ing Period: A Study of the German Literary Mission's Use of the Science of Hermeneutics, of the Art of Translation, and of the Human Input into Information Technology to Induce Protestant Christian Reform in China*, by Leslie R. Marchant, 1984; *The Harrowing of Hell in China: A Synoptic Study of the Role of Christian Evangelists in the Opening of Hunan Province*, by Leslie R. Marchant, 1977; *The United Board for Christian Higher Education in Asia*, by Nathan M. Pusey, 1979–80; chapters from *Western Thought in Russia and China*, by Donald W. Treadgold, 1968, entitled, "Christian Humanism: The Jesuits (1582–1774)," "Christian Modernism: Sun Yat-sen, 1896–1923," and "Christian Pietism: The Fundamentalist Protestants, 1807–1900."
SERIALS: *China Law Review*, 1922–40. *China Monthly: The Truth about China*, 1939–41. *New Horizons*, 1972–83. *St. John's University Studies*, 1922. University of Nanking, *Economic Facts*, 1936–46. *Variétés Sinologiques*, 1932–34.

DISSERTATIONS/THESES: *An Eighteenth-century Frenchman at the Court of the K'ang-hsi Emperor: A Study of the Early Life of Jean François Foucquet*, by John W. Witek, 1973. *K'ung Tzu or Confucius: The Jesuit Interpretation of Confucianism*, by Paul A. Rule, 1972. *The Negotiations between Ch'i-ying and Lagrené, 1844–1848*, by Angelus Francis Grosse-Aschhoff, 1950.
CHINESE LANGUAGE MATERIALS/SERIALS: *Chin-ling hsüeh pao (Nanking Journal)*, 1931–41. *Fu jen hsüeh chih (Fu Jen Sinological Journal)*, 1928–47. *Hsin yang yü sheng huo (Faith and Life)*, 1953–65. *Teng t'a (Lighthouse)*, 1957–66. *Yen-ching hsüeh pao (Yenching Journal of Chinese Studies)*, 1927–51. Yen-ching ta hsüeh, *Shih hsüeh nien pao* (Yenching University, *Historical Annual*), 1934–40. Yen-ching ta-hsüeh, tsung chiao hsüeh yuan, *Ts'ung shu*, 1941–52.
CHINESE LANGUAGE MATERIALS: 41 volumes, 1924–81, on Young J. Allen, anti-Christian movement among Chinese gentry and officials, Catholic church in China, Chinese Catholics, Christian literature, Christians in China, education, Jesuits, the K'ang-hsi and Ch'ien-lung emperors and Catholic missionaries, Gregorio Lopez, medical missions, Protestant missionaries in China, relations between the K'ang-hsi emperor and Rome, Matteo Ricci, sectarian cases, Taiping Rebellion, and theology, and publications of the University of Nanking (Chin-ling ta hsüeh), including an agricultural index to serials in Chinese and English.

WA–40   Manuscripts and University Archives Division
University of Washington Libraries, FM–25
Seattle WA 98195
(206) 543–1879
Karyl Winn, Head
Janet Ness, Specialist, Manuscripts Section

Finding aids: Comprehensive Guide to the Manuscripts Collection and to the Personal Papers in the University Archives, comp. by Marilyn Priestley, 1980.

1-LEON BOCKER PAPERS, 1919–21, ca. 10 items
Background note: Leon Bocker was a member of the Associated Mission Treasurers in China, a group formed by several Protestant mission societies to facilitate the handling of mission money in China.
MINUTES/RECORDS/REPORTS/PAMPHLETS/MEMORABILIA: By-laws, agreements, reprints, clippings, and other materials, relating to his activities as a member of the Associated Mission Treasurers in China, 1919–21.

2-HERBERT GOWEN PAPERS, 1914–25, 9 folders
Background note: Herbert Gowen's son, Vincent Edward Gowen, taught at St. Paul's High School in Anking and was a missionary under the American Church mission in Wuhu. This collection—which is in the University Archives—primarily contains the papers of Herbert Gowen, an Episcopalian minister and missionary who founded the Chinese mission in Hawaii; one of his students in Hawaii was Sun Yat-sen.
CORRESPONDENCE: Letters from Vincent Edward Gowen, Wuhu, to Herbert Gowen, 1914–25.
FINDING AIDS: Preliminary in-house inventory.

3-MEAD FAMILY PAPERS, 1896–1937, 11 folders
MINUTES/RECORDS/REPORTS/MEMORABILIA: 3 folders in papers of Frederica Mead, containing reports, ephemera, and

miscellaneous items, relating to Ginling College, 1913–37 and n.d.

CORRESPONDENCE: 144 letters of Frederica Mead, relating to Ginling College, 1914–24; 21 letters to Margaret Platt Mead and Marie Louise Myers Mead (Mrs. Frederick Mead), relating to Ginling College, 1896–1937; 4 letters to Marie Mead, relating to the YMCA in China, 1927–28; 3 letters from Claude and Margaret Thomson, Nanking, 1933–34.

FINDING AIDS: In-house inventory.

4-LUELLA MINER PAPERS, 1884–1935, ca. 1 l.f.

Background note: Luella Miner (1861–1935) went to China in 1887 under the American Board of Commissioners for Foreign Missions. She was a teacher at Luho Academy in Tungchou starting in 1888, and in 1905 founded the North China Union College there, acting as its president until 1920. From 1923 until her death, she was professor of Religious Education at Cheeloo Theological School in Tsinan. One of her students, H. H. Kung, went on to become the Finance Minister of China.

MINUTES/RECORDS/REPORTS: Report on bound feet, by Li Ting Jung, 1894.

CORRESPONDENCE: Ca. 600 letters from Luella Miner, mostly to her parents, Mr. and Mrs. D. L. Miner, and her sisters, Edith, Stella, and Carrie, 1884–1925; typescripts of letters, 1901–21; letters from Mary Ament, n.d., Chauncey Goodrich, 1888, and Cousin "Vie" to D. L. Miner, 1897; letter to Mrs. Flagg from Lyman Cody containing a tribute to Miner, 1935.

MANUSCRIPTS: Speech by Mrs. Fay, n.d.

DIARIES: Typescripts of journal, 1901–21.

MEMORABILIA: 6 clippings on the Boxer Rebellion and the Siege of Peking, 1900; issue of *Peiping Chronicle*, containing a tribute to Miner, 1935.

SERIALS: *Mission Mirror*, 1935 (containing a tribute to Miner).

FINDING AIDS: In-house inventory.

5-STRONG FAMILY PAPERS, 1934–50, ca. 10 in.

Background note: See also Oberlin College, Archives, 420 Mudd Learning Center, Oberlin, OH, 44074; and Young Men's Christian Association of the U.S.A. Archives, University of Minnesota, Social History Welfare Archives, 2642 University Avenue, St. Paul, MN, 55114.

CORRESPONDENCE/MANUSCRIPTS: Correspondence between Tracy and Edith Strong and their children, including over 100 letters and writings from their son, Robbins Strong, who taught at Oberlin-in-Shansi from 1934 to 1937, and worked for the YMCA in China from 1948 to 1950.

6-GENERAL HOLDINGS

ORAL HISTORIES: *China Missionaries Oral History Collection*, ed. by Cyrus H. Peake and Arthur L. Rosenbaum (Claremont Graduate School, Oral History Program), 1971–72. See ORAL HISTORIES Union List for the names of participants.

WA–45   Resource Sharing Program
University of Washington Libraries
Suzallo Library
Seattle WA 98195
(206) 543-0242

1-GENERAL HOLDINGS

MINUTES/RECORDS/REPORTS: Chin-ling ta hsüeh (University of Nanking), reports, minutes, and other materials, 1906–52 (3 reels microfilm); Fu-chien hsieh ho ta hsüeh (Fukien Christian University), reports, minutes, and other materials, 1917–? (on microfilm); Presbyterian Board of Foreign Missions, report on the China missions, 1897; Yen-ching ta hsüeh (Yenching University), reports, minutes, and other materials, n.d. (7 reels microfilm).

MANUSCRIPTS: "Christian Missions in China," by Edward Wilson Wallace, n.d.; "An Experiment in the Registration of Vital Statistics in China," by Ch'i-ming Ch'iao, 1938; "The Jesuits in China in the Last Days of the Ming Dynasty," by George H. Dunne, S.J., 1947.

PAMPHLETS: *Jesuit Letters from China, 1583–1584*, ed. and trans. by M. Howard Rienstra, 1986; *Briefve relation de la Chine, et de la notable conversion des personnes royales de cet estat*, by Michał Boim, 1696; *China, Her Future and Her Past: Being a Charge Delivered to the Anglican Clergy in Trinity Church, Shanghae, on Oct. 20, 1853*, by George Smith, 1854; *De Chineesche kwestie*, by Henri Borel, 1900; *Critical Moments in the History of Christianity in China*, by Harley Farnsworth MacNair, 1925(?); *The Missionary Question in China: How to Lessen the Recurrence of Anti-Christian and Anti-foreign Riots*, by Christopher Thomas Gardner, 1894(?); *La nouvelle mission du Kiangnan (1840–1922)*, by Joseph de la Servière, 1925; *The Political Obstacles to Missionary Success in China*, by Alexander Michie, 1901; *Review of the Introduction of Christianity into China and Japan*, by John H. Gubbins, 1888; *Windows into China: The Jesuits and Their Books, 1580–1730*, by John Parker, 1978; *Yuen-ming-yuen: L'Oeuvre architecturale des anciens jésuites au XVIIIe siècle*, by Maurice Adam, 1936.

SERIALS: *Asian Folklore Studies*, 1942–86; supplement, 1952-. Catholic University of Peking, *Bulletin*, 1926–34. *China Christian Year Book*, 1912, 1917–18, 1928, 1931, 1936–37. China International Famine Relief Commission, Publications, series A, 1922–36. *China Law Review*, 1922–40. *Chinese Recorder*, 1870–1890, 1909–10, 1915, 1918, 1920–21, 1924–25, 1927, 1929–41. *Chinese Repository*, 1832–51. *Ching Feng*, 1958–67, 1978–79, 1983. *India's Women and China's Daughters*, 1896–1939. *Lingnan Science Journal*, 1922–48. *Looking East*, 1951–57. *Looking East at India's Women and China's Daughters*, 1940–50. *Monumenta Serica*, 1935-; monograph series, 1937–61, 1972, 1985. Nanking Theological Seminary, English publications, 1940–41. Natural History Society, *Proceedings*, 1929–30. *News of United China Relief*, 1943–49. *Peking Natural History Bulletin*, 1926–50. *Variétés Sinologiques*, 1901–37. West China Border Research Society, *Journal*, 1922–45. Yenching University: Department of Sociology and Social Work, *Social Research Series*, 1930; *Yenching Index Numbers*, 1940; *Yenching Journal of Social Studies*, 1938–41, 1948–50.

DISSERTATIONS/THESES: *Die Akkommodationsmethode des P. Matteo Ricci, S.I., in China*, by Johannes Bettray, 1955. *Catholic Activities in Kwangtung Province and Chinese Responses, 1848–1885*, by Jean-Paul Wiest, 1977. *The Catholic Implantation at Canton: French Missionary Work, 1848–1860*, by Jean-Paul Wiest, 1972. *China Missions in Crisis: Bishop Laimbeckhoven and His Times, 1738–1787*, by Joseph Krahl, 1964. *China's Opposition to Western Religion and Science during Late Ming and Early*

Ch'ing, by George Ho-ching Wong, 1958. *Missionary Educators and the Chinese Nationalist Revolution, 1925–1928*, by John Otto Mason, 1970.

WALLA WALLA

WHITMAN COLLEGE
WA–50   Archives
   Penrose Memorial Library
   345 Boyer Avenue
   Walla Walla WA 99362
   (509) 527–5191
   Arley D. Jonish, Library Director

1-ROSS R. BRATTAIN, 1901–10, 124 items
CORRESPONDENCE: 12 letters to Ross R. Brattain, a missionary, from his wife, Ottilie Hauser Brattain, in Shanghai and Amoy, 1901, 1908–10.
AUDIO-VISUAL MATERIALS: 112 lantern slides of China, n.d.

2-DAVID CROCKETT GRAHAM COLLECTION, 1919–86, ca. 6 in.
Background note: For biographical notes, see Smithsonian Institution, Archives, 900 Jefferson Drive, SW, Washington, DC, 20560.
CORRESPONDENCE: Ca. .75 in. of correspondence between David Crockett Graham and Howard S. Brode, professor of botany, Whitman College, concerning items Graham presented to Whitman College and to the Smithsonian Institution, 1919–32.
MEMORABILIA/CORRESPONDENCE/PAMPHLETS: Ca. 5 in. of clippings, letters, and other printed materials about Graham, his work in China, and his professional career, n.d.
DISSERTATIONS/THESES: *David Crockett Graham: Anthropologist, Collector, and Missionary in China*, by Susan R. Brown, 1986.

YAKIMA

WA–55   YAKIMA VALLEY MUSEUM AND HISTORICAL ASSOCIATION
   2105 Tieton Drive
   Yakima WA 98902
   (509) 248–0747
   Frances A. Hare, Archivist

1-MARTHA WILEY PAPERS, 1900–1947, ca. 4 boxes
Background note: Martha Wiley (1874–1969) was a missionary of the Congregational Church in Foochow from 1900 to 1947. She taught at Foochow College. This collection of her papers is only partially processed. See also Claremont Colleges, Honnold Library, Claremont, CA, 91711.
CORRESPONDENCE: Letters from Martha Wiley to her family describing her travels in China, her work as a teacher, and factional politics in Foochow, 1900–1947.
MANUSCRIPTS: Notebooks of Wiley's lessons for her students, n.d.; autograph books, n.d.
MEMORABILIA: Wiley's personal papers, including passports and college diplomas, n.d.; artifacts sent by Wiley from China to her family, including brass pieces, clothing, porcelain, and scrolls.

AUDIO-VISUAL MATERIALS: Uncatalogued photos of Wiley's students, n.d.
CHINESE LANGUAGE MATERIALS: Bible in Foochow dialect prepared by Emily S. Hartwell, a colleague of Wiley's, 1900–1908.

WEST VIRGINIA

BETHANY

BETHANY COLLEGE
WV–5   T. W. Phillips Memorial Library
   Bethany WV 26032
   (304) 829–7321
   Jonas Barciauskas, Director

Background note: The founder of Bethany College, Alexander Campbell, also founded the Disciples of Christ. See also Disciples of Christ Historical Society, Library and Archives, 1101 Nineteenth Avenue, South, Nashville, TN, 37212.

1-GENERAL HOLDINGS
MINUTES/RECORDS/REPORTS: Reports on the China mission in Disciples of Christ denominational periodicals: *The Christian*, 1874–82; *The Christian-Evangelist*, 1882–1958; *The Evangelist*, 1865–82; *The Gospel Echo*, 1863–72; *The Gospel Echo and Christian*, 1872–73.
SERIALS: *China Christian Year Book*, 1910, 1912, 1919.
FINDING AIDS: *Christian-Evangelist Index, 1863–1958* (V II, 1962, indexes the above denominational periodicals).

BUCKHANNON

WEST VIRGINIA WESLEYAN COLLEGE
WV–10   Annie Merner Pfeiffer Library
   Buckhannon WV 26201
   (304) 473–8000
   Ben F. Crutchfield, Director of Library Services

Restrictions: For permission to use the Pearl S. Buck Manuscript Collection contact the Pearl S. Buck Birthplace Foundation, Inc., Box 126, Hillsboro, WV, 24946.

1-PEARL S. BUCK MANUSCRIPTS, 1930–70, 75 boxes (54 l.f.)
Background note: The property of the Pearl S. Buck Birthplace Foundation, Inc., the Pearl S. Buck Manuscripts collection will housed at West Virginia Wesleyan College until the opening of the Foundation's archives in Hillsboro.

CORRESPONDENCE/MEMORABILIA: 2 uncatalogued boxes of letters and other miscellaneous papers.
MANUSCRIPTS: 323 manuscripts, typescripts, carbons, and galleys (ca. 64 boxes) of drafts of Pearl S. Buck's books, representing 75 of her books, many in more than one draft; articles, speeches, dramas, short stories, book reviews, introductions, and epilogues; typescript for *Our Life and Work in China*, by Absalom Sydenstricker, 1930.
DISSERTATIONS/THESES: *The Pearl S. Buck Manuscripts: The Harvest of Half a Century*, by Mary Lee Welliver, 1977.
CHINESE LANGUAGE MATERIALS: 2 speeches written both in Chinese and English, by Pearl S. Buck.
FINDING AIDS: *The Works of Pearl S. Buck: A Bibliography*, by Lucille S. Zinn, 1979.

MORGANTOWN

WEST VIRGINIA UNIVERSITY
WV-15   Library
    West Virginia and Regional History Collection
    Main Campus
    Morgantown WV 26505
    (304) 293-3660 (Reference)
    (304) 293-3536 (West Virginia Collection)
    Harold M. Forbes, Associate Curator, West Virginia
        and Regional History Collection
    Clifford Hamrick, Reference Librarian

1-JULIA A. BONAFIELD PAPERS, 1888-1943, quantity undetermined
Background note: Julia A. Bonafield (1863-1956) grew up in West Virginia and later went to the Girls' School in Foochow to serve as a missionary teacher from 1888 to 1943.
MEMORABILIA: Clippings concerning her career, 1888-1943.
AUDIO-VISUAL MATERIALS: Photo of Bonafield as a schoolgirl, n.d.

2-HARVEY WALKER HARMER PAPERS, 1929-40, 17 items
Background note: Harvey Walker Harmer (1865-1961) was a lawyer, Republican state senator, and local historian from Clarksburg, West Virginia.
MINUTES/RECORDS/REPORTS: 3 newsletters from Methodist missionaries, 1939-40.
CORRESPONDENCE: 14 letters from Methodist missionaries in Foochow, Hinghwa Mountain, Peitaiho, Peking, Sienyu (Fukien), Suining, and Tientsin, 1939-40.

3-WILLIAM PRICE PAPERS, 1912, 1 item
CORRESPONDENCE: Mimeographed copy of a letter from Fannie Ni Torrance (Mrs. A. A. Torrance), in Tsinan, to Miss Lowrie of the Women's Foreign Missionary Society of the Presbyterian Church, Philadelphia, concerning the looting in Tsinan and work on the missionary station there, 1912.

4-GENERAL HOLDINGS
SERIALS: *Lingnan Science Journal*, 1922-41.
DISSERTATIONS/THESES: *The Pearl S. Buck Manuscripts: The Harvest of Half a Century*, by Mary Lee Welliver, 1977.
CHINESE LANGUAGE MATERIALS/SERIALS: *Yen-ching hsüeh pao*, 1927-29.

WISCONSIN

DE PERE

SAINT NORBERT COLLEGE
WI-5   Todd Wehr Library
    De Pere WI 54115
    (414) 337-3280
    Sally Cubitt, Acquisitions Librarian

Background note: See also Maryknoll Fathers and Brothers, Archives, Maryknoll, NY, 10545.

1-GENERAL HOLDINGS
AUDIO-VISUAL MATERIALS: *I Saw Him in the Rice Fields*, a videotape about Bishop James E. Walsh, by Maryknoll World Films, n.d.

JANESVILLE

SEVENTH DAY BAPTIST HISTORICAL SOCIETY
WI-10   Library
    3120 Kennedy Road
    P. O. Box 1678
    Janesville WI 53547
    (608) 752-5055
    Janet Thorngate, Librarian
    Don A. Sanford, Historian

Background note: The Seventh Day Baptist Missionary Society founded missions in Shanghai (1847) and Liuho (1902). The annual reports of the Shanghai and Liuho missions can be found in the *Seventh Day Baptist Yearbook*, 1847-1950. Letters and articles on missionaries, mission churches, schools, and medical work were published in the weekly, *Sabbath Recorder*, 1857-1950.

1-CHINA MISSION COLLECTION, 1847-1950, 3 files
CORRESPONDENCE/MEMORABILIA/MAPS/DESIGNS/DRAWINGS/AUDIO-VISUAL MATERIALS: Uncatalogued letters, memorabilia, maps, drawings, photos, slides, films, and recordings, 1847-1950.
DIARIES: Journals of Solomon Carpenter and Nathan Wardner, the first Seventh Day Baptist missionaries in China, 1846-76.

2-SEVENTH DAY BAPTIST MISSIONARY SOCIETY RECORDS, 1845-1944, 9 volumes
MINUTES/RECORDS/REPORTS: Seventh Day Baptist Missionary Society, records of evangelistic, educational, and medical work in Shanghai and Liuho, 1845-1944.

3-GENERAL HOLDINGS
SERIALS: *China Mission Bulletin*, 1934-48.

LA CROSSE

FRANCISCAN SISTERS OF PERPETUAL ADORATION GENERALATE

WI-15   Archives
St. Rose Convent
912 Market Street
La Crosse WI 54601
(608) 782-5610
Grace McDonald, F.S.P.A., Archivist

Background note: Founded in the United States in 1849 by a group of six tertiary women from Ettenbeuren, Bavaria, the Franciscan Sisters of Perpetual Adoration began missionary work in Wuchang in 1928.

1-CHINA (WUCHANG, HUPEH), 1928-49, 5 boxes
MINUTES/RECORDS/REPORTS: Franciscan Sisters of Perpetual Adoration, information work sheet on sisters in China (with private correspondence below); financial accounts relating to World War II property claims in China, 1928-40 (pursuant to a public law of 1962).
CORRESPONDENCE: Letters from Bishop Sylvester Espelage, O.F.M., and other Catholic clerics to Mother Ludovica Keller, 1926-29; letters from Sisters of Saint Francis of Assisi in China, 1933-45; box of letters from the sisters in China to Reverend Mothers Seraphine Kraus, 1928-40, Engelberta Kamp, 1940-46, and Rose Kreibich, 1946-43; private letters between Franciscan Sisters of Perpetual Adoration authorities and sisters in China, 1929-48; correspondence relating to Hwang-shih-kang mission, 1936; letters relating to the native community of sisters in China, 1945; letters from the U.S. Army concerning sisters interned by the Japanese, 1943; letters concerning World War II property claims in China, 1966-79; correspondence and photos by and relating to Sr. Stella Smith in Matsu, 1971-79; miscellaneous correspondence regarding China mission.
DIARIES: Diary account of missionaries' first trip to China, by Sr. Dominica Urbany, et. al., 1928.
MANUSCRIPTS: "Memoirs of China," by Sr. Rosibia Thienel, 1984; "My China Experiences," by Sr. Charitina Craigen, 1981; "My Trip to Red China," by Sr. Dominica Chen, 1973.
MEMORABILIA: Miscellaneous materials on plans and departures of sisters to China, 1928; excerpts from letters of the sisters in China as newsletters to the Community, 1929-47; scrapbook of newspaper clippings on the sisters in China, 1928-53; single issue of the *People's Herald*, Tsingtao, 1946; "The Story of Matsu," 2 scrapbooks by Sr. Stella Smith containing photos and narrative, 1971-79.
ORAL HISTORIES: "China Experience," cassette tape by Sr. Maxine Frank, Wuchang, 1933-48, and by Sr. Stella Smith, Matsu, 1971-79; "Experiences as Missionary to China, 1939-1948," cassette tape by Sr. Optata Fries, 1985; "Experiences in Wuchang during the Japanese Occupation of China, 1939-1945 and 1945-1949," and "Visit to China, 1973, 1978," cassette tape by Sr. Dominica Chen, 1978.
AUDIO-VISUAL MATERIALS: Loose photos of China donated by Rev. Siegfried, O.F.M., n.d.; "China," photo album on F.S.P.A. mission, 1928-1940s; "Some Days in China," photo album on F.S.P.A. mission work in Safang and Wuchang, 1933; photo album by Mother Rose Kreibach and Sr. Enrico Pudenz, on the death of Sr. Dominica Urbany in 1936, Mother Seraphine

Kraus' visit, preparations in New Orleans, voyage on ship, and scenes in China, 1947; photo album containing photos of Chinese infants baptized and named for Mother Seraphine Kraus; loose photos of F.S.P.A. missionaries and Chinese aspirants, 1936.
SERIALS: *Franciscans in China*, 1924, 1926-36, 1941.

MADISON

STATE HISTORICAL SOCIETY OF WISCONSIN

WI-20   Archives Division
816 State Street
Madison WI 53706
(608) 262-3421
Harold L. Miller, Reference Archivist

1-DEXTER FAMILY PAPERS, 1923-24, 3 folders
Background note: Harriet Harmon Dexter taught at the Normal School for Men in Hofeihsien, Anhwei, from 1923 to 1924.
CORRESPONDENCE: 2 folders of letters from Dexter, 1923-24.
DIARIES: Dexter's diary, 1923-24.
FINDING AIDS: In-house guide.

2-ROGER S. GREENE PAPERS, ca. 1916-1927, quantity undetermined
Background note: For biographical notes see Harvard University, Houghton Library, Manuscript Department, Cambridge, MA, 02138. See also Rockefeller University, Rockefeller Archive Center, Pocantico Hills, North Tarrytown, NY, 10591.
CORRESPONDENCE/MANUSCRIPTS: Correspondence and writings of Roger S. Greene relating to his work with the China Medical Board, ca. 1916-1927.

3-FREDERICK O. LEISER PAPERS, 1905-14, ca. 1 box
Background note: See also Young Men's Christian Association of the U.S.A. Archives, University of Minnesota, Social History Welfare Archives, 2642 University Avenue, St. Paul, MN, 55114.
CORRESPONDENCE: Letters from Frederick O. Leiser, 1909-10, 1913.
DIARIES: Diaries by Leiser, 1909-10, 1913.
MANUSCRIPTS: "Reminiscences of Frederick O. Leiser of His Experiences in Hongkong and Canton, China, as a Representative of the International Committee of the Young Men's Christian Association from 1905 to 1914," by Frederick O. Leiser, n.d.

4-MADISON CHINA AID COUNCIL, 1938-44, 1 box
Background note: An affiliate of United China Relief, the Madison China Aid Council assisted in China relief work during World War II. See also United China Relief collections at the New York Public Library, Manuscripts and Archives Section, Rare Books and Manuscripts Division, Fifth Avenue and 42nd Street, New York, NY, 10018; and Princeton University, 20th-Century American Statecraft and Public Policy, Mudd Manuscript Library, Olden Street, Princeton, NJ, 08544. Collections on Yale-in-China and Hsiang-Ya hospital are at Yale University, Department of Manuscripts and Archives, Sterling Memorial Library, 120 High Street, New Haven, CT, 06520.
MINUTES/RECORDS/REPORTS/CORRESPONDENCE/MEMORABILIA: Madison China Aid Council, financial records, correspondence, and miscellaneous materials, 1938-44; extracts of letters from Phillips Greene, medical director of Hsiang-Ya Hospital in Changsha, and his wife, Ruth, describing their experiences in China, 1938-44.

WI-25   Historical Library
State Historical Society of Wisconsin
816 State Street
Madison WI 53706
(608) 262-3421
Michael Edmonds, Special Collections Librarian

1-GENERAL HOLDINGS
PAMPHLETS: *Augustine W. Tucker: Doctor in China*, by Beverley D. Tucker, 1961; *The Awakening of China*, by Theodore Roosevelt, 1908; *Banquet of the Committee Representing the Conference of Foreign Missions Boards and Societies in the United States and Canada: Hotel Astor, Evening of Thursday the Fourteenth of January at Seven O'Clock MCMIX*, 1909; *A Brief Memorial of My Missionary Children, Rev. Calvin Wight and His Sister, Frannie E. Wight, Who Both Died of Pneumonia at Chinan-fu, China*, by Joseph Kingsbury Wight, 1899; *Concerning Beggars and the Trade School at Ichang, China*, by D. T. Huntington, 1908; *Historical Sketch of China Mission, 1834-1884*, n.a., 1885; *Schereschewsky of China*, by Massey H. Shepherd, 1962.
SERIALS: American Friends Service Committee, *Bulletin on Work in China*, 1942-44.
DISSERTATIONS/THESES: *Missionary Intelligence from China: American Protestant Reports, 1930-1950*, by Bruce S. Greenawalt, 1974.

WI-30   Iconographic Collections
State Historical Society of Wisconsin
816 State Street
Madison WI 53706
(608) 262-9581
Myra Williamson, Reference Librarian

1-GENERAL HOLDINGS
MEMORABILIA: Postcard with scenes of Union Medical College, Peking, 1918 (Lot 2744).
AUDIO-VISUAL MATERIALS: 40 photos of people and scenes at Canton Christian College and the Canton YMCA, and in Canton and Hong Kong, 1906-14 (Lot 489).

UNIVERSITY OF WISCONSIN-MADISON

WI-35   Health Sciences Library
1305 Linden Drive
Madison WI 53706
(608) 262-2376
Virginia Holtz, Director

1-GENERAL HOLDINGS
SERIALS: *Chinese Medical Journal*, 1910-31.

WI-40   Law Library
University of Wisconsin-Madison
Law Building, 5th floor
Madison WI 53706
(608) 262-3394
Anita Morse, Director

1-GENERAL HOLDINGS
SERIALS: *China Law Review*, 1922-37.

WI-45   Memorial Library
University of Wisconsin-Madison
728 State Street
Madison WI 53706
(608) 262-8271
Jean Thompson, Reference Librarian
Chester Wang, East Asian Bibliographer

1-GENERAL HOLDINGS
MANUSCRIPTS: "As I Look Back: Recollections of Growing Up in America's Southland and of Twenty-six Years in Pre-Communist China, 1888-1936," by Eugene E. Barnett, 1963-68.

PAMPHLETS: *China Mission Studies (1550-1800) Directory*, ed. by David E. Mungello, 1978.

SERIALS: *China Bulletin*, 1954-62. *China Christian Year Book*, 1910-12, 1914-39. China International Famine Relief Commission, Publications, series A, 1922-36. *China Notes*, 1962-81. *Chinese Recorder*, 1868-1941. *Monumenta Serica*, 1935-; Monograph series, 1939-. Yenching University, Department of Biology, *Bulletin*, 1930.

DISSERTATIONS/THESES: *Die Akkommodationsmethode des P. Matteo Ricci, S.I., in China*, by Johannes Bettray, 1955. *The American Board in China: The Missionaries' Experiences and Attitudes, 1911-1952*, by Janet Elaine Heininger, 1981. *The American and British Missionary Concept of Chinese Civilization in the Nineteenth Century*, by James Miller McCutcheon, 1959. *China and Educational Autonomy: The Changing Role of the Protestant Educational Missionary in China, 1807-1937*, by Alice Henrietta Gregg, 1945. *Imperial Government and Catholic Missions in China during the Years 1784-1785*, by Bernward Henry Willeke, 1948. *An Investigation of the Modernizing Role of the Maryknoll Sisters in China*, by Mary Ann Schintz, 1978. *Lutheran Missions in a Time of Revolution: The China Experience, 1944-1951*, by Jonas Jonson, 1972. *The Mission Enterprise of the Lutheran Church-Missouri Synod in Mainland China, 1913-1952*, by Roy Arthur Suelflow, 1971. *Protestant Mission Schools for Girls in South China (1827 to the Japanese Invasion)*, by Mary Raleigh Anderson, 1943.

CHINESE LANGUAGE MATERIALS: *Chung-kuo kuan shen fan chiao ti yüan yin (The Origins of Anti-foreignism in the Chinese Bureaucracy)*, by Lü Shih-ch'iang, 1966; *Chung-kuo T'ien-chu chiao chiao ch'uan chiao shih (History of Catholic Missions in China)*, by P. M. d'Elia, 1968; *Chung-kuo T'ien-chu chiao shih lun yeh (Studies in the History of Chinese Catholicism)*, by Fang Hao, 1944; *T'ien-chu chiao shih liu shih chi tsai Hua ch'uan chiao chih (A History of Sixteenth Century Catholic Missions in China)*, by Henri Bernard, trans. by Hsiao Ch'un-hua, 1964.

WI-50   University System Archives
University of Wisconsin-Madison
Memorial Library
Room 443F
728 State Street
Madison WI 53706
(608) 263-5629
Nancy Kunde, Archivist

1-GENERAL HOLDINGS
MINUTES/RECORDS/REPORTS/CORRESPONDENCE/
AUDIO-VISUAL MATERIALS/MEMORABILIA: Ca. 1 folder
each on University of Wisconsin alumnae and China missionaries
James Whitford Bashford (1876); Jennie M. Field (Mrs. James
Bashford) (1882); and Mary Dunwiddie (1880), containing correspondence, school records, portraits, clippings, and obituaries.
FINDING AIDS: *General Catalogue of the Officers and Graduates of the University of Wisconsin from Its Organization in 1849 to
1892*, comp. by David B. Frankenburger (Madison, WI: University of Wisconsin), 1892; alumni directories.

MEQUON

CONCORDIA COLLEGE
WI–55 Library
12800 North Lake Shore Drive
Mequon WI 53092
(414) 243–5700
David O. Berger, Librarian

1-GENERAL HOLDINGS
PAMPHLETS: *The Chinese Term Question*, by George O. Lille-
gard, 1929; *Foreign Missions in China*, by Frederick Brand, 1927;
*Our China Mission (China Missions of the Evangelical Lutheran
Synod of Missouri, Ohio, and Other States)*, 1926.

MILWAUKEE

MARQUETTE UNIVERSITY
WI–60 Department of Special Collections
Memorial Library
1415 West Wisconsin Avenue
Milwaukee WI 53233
(414) 224–7256
Robert V. Callen, S.J., Archivist

1-JESUITICA COLLECTION, 1953, 1 item
Background note: This collection also contains ca. 20 books concerning missions in China, as well as extensive holdings of *Lettres
édifiantes et curieuses* and *Annales de la propagation de la foi*.
PAMPHLETS: *La mission de Pékin vers 1700: Etude de géographie missionnaire*, by Joseph Dehergre, 1953.

2-GENERAL HOLDINGS
SERIALS: *China Monthly*, 1941–50.

WI–65 MILWAUKEE PUBLIC LIBRARY
814 West Wisconsin Avenue
Milwaukee WI 53233–2385
(414) 278–3000
Donald J. Sager, Librarian

1-GENERAL HOLDINGS
SERIALS: *China Christian Year Book*, 1917, 1923–39. *China
Monthly*, 1939–46, 1948–49.

WI–70 ST. FRANCIS CONVENT
Sisters of the Third Order of St. Francis
3221 South Lake Drive
Milwaukee WI 53207
(414) 744–1160
Jeanine Greusser, O.S.F., Archivist

Background note: Approximately 10 American sisters and 24 Chinese sisters of the Third Order of St. Francis maintained a mission
in Tsinanfu from 1929 to 1948.

**1-CHINA MISSION COLLECTION, ca. 1929–1948, quantity unde-
termined**
MINUTES/RECORDS/REPORTS/CORRESPONDENCE: Ca.
10 folders of reports and correspondence relating to mission work
in China.
MANUSCRIPTS: "The History of Sisters of the Third Order of
St. Francis in Tsinanfu," by Sr. Julian Alderson, n.d.
AUDIO-VISUAL MATERIALS: Unspecified photos and slides.
ORAL HISTORIES: Oral histories of pioneers of the mission, Srs.
Julian Anderson, Esther Muench, and Veronica Schurell, 1970s.
MEMORABILIA: 2 scrapbooks, Chinese Bible, and several pray-
er books.

SCHOOL SISTERS OF SAINT FRANCIS
GENERALATE
WI–75 Archives
1501 South Layton Boulevard
Milwaukee WI 53215–0006
(414) 384–4105
Barbara Misner, S.C.S.C., Archivist

Restrictions: Access by appointment.
Background note: The China Mission of the Sisters of Saint Francis
was initiated in 1923 by Mother M. Alfons. They opened a school
for upper class Chinese girls in 1931. The mission was expanded in
1934 with a part-time school for the poor and again in 1937 with a
primary school. The Japanese army closed the school and interned
the sisters in 1941. The schools reopened in 1945 during the Chinese civil war, but in 1949 the sisters moved to Taiwan.

1-IRENE (Sr. FIDES) BETHKE, 1933–49, 7 folders
Background note: Sr. Fides (Irene) Bethke taught music at St.
Joseph Middle School in Tsingtao from 1933 to 1949.
MANUSCRIPTS: A paper written by Sr. Fides Bethke as part of
learning Chinese language, n.d.; folder of essays, a speech, and an
annotated manuscript on the S.S.S.F. mission, n.d.; 2 folders of
music education materials, music students' assignments and 3
manuscripts in Chinese and English, n.d.
PAMPHLETS: Ca. 1 folder of printed matter relating to Sr. Fides'
arrival in China, 1933; ca. 1 folder of printed matter relating to her
Chinese language and culture lessons, n.d.; ca. 1 folder of printed
matter on music for church and secular occasions, n.d.; ca. 1
folder of printed matter relating to prayer, n.d.
MEMORABILIA: Ca. 1 folder of Sr. Fides' Chinese language and
culture lessons, n.d.; ca. 1 folder of music materials for church and
secular occasions; 2 prayer booklets, n.d.

CHINESE LANGUAGE MATERIALS: Folder of official documents relating to Sr. Fides' arrival in China, 1933.
FINDING AIDS: In-house inventory.

2-GERTRUDE (Sr. EUSTELLA) BUSH, 1931-77, 1 box

Background note: Sr. Eustella (Gertrude) Bush helped found the St. Joseph Middle School in Tsingtao in 1931. She remained in China until 1949.
MINUTES/RECORDS/REPORTS: St. Joseph Middle School, regulations and program for 1931; St. Joseph Middle School, annual reports, 1936-39; St. Theresa's Club, member list and financial records, 1938-41, n.d.; primary and middle school statistics, 1939-41, n.d.; inventory of St. Joseph School at time of the Japanese takeover, 1941-42; rosters and passbooks (financial records) of Catholic laity and missionaries in Japanese confinement, 1942-44; folder of financial records and orders of the S.S.S.F. store, 1946-49, n.d.; 2 folders of S.S.S.F. daily and monthly financial records, 1938-42; folder of invoices and miscellaneous financial records, 1943-48, n.d.
CORRESPONDENCE: Letter from Vincent Lebbe, 1931; ca. 1 folder of letters concerning Japanese takeover of St. Joseph School, 1941-42; folder of letters to School Sisters in concentration camp, 1942-44; 33 folders of correspondence with Mother Corona Wirfs, various School Sisters, Adolph J. Klink, Thomas Cardinal Tien, August Olbert, H. G. Pinger, John Weig, Raymond de Jaegher, Jesuits, Order of Friars Minor, Society of the Divine Word, Franciscan Missionaries of Mary, Hijas of Jesus, Holy Ghost Sisters, Hospital Sisters of Saint Francis, Order of Saint Francis of Assisi, Order of Saint Francis of the Holy Family, Religious of the Sacred Heart, Sisters of Providence, Sisters of Adoration Convent, various clergy and religious, laity, U.S. servicemen, U.S. government, Chinese government, U.S. military and Swiss consulate, United Nations Relief and Rehabilitation Administration, Bush family, Hazel Zimmerman, the S.S.S.F. store, and boys' orphanage; circular letter from Raymond de Jaegher, 1977.
MANUSCRIPTS: "Account of Beginning of Tsingtao Mission," probably by Sr. Eustella Bush, n.d.; "Civil Assembly Center: S.S.S.F. Activities," by Sr. Eustella Bush, 1942-44, n.d.; "Communism," by Sr. Eustella Bush, n.d.; "History of St. Joseph Middle School," by Sr. Eustella Bush, 1931-34, n.d.; "Our Mission Work in Shansi, China before and after the Occupation, Including the Story of Repatriation," by Sr. Eustella Bush, 1942; "Vow of Perfection," by Sr. Eustella Bush, ca. 1942; Yin Yuan Yi's statement, n.d.
PAMPHLETS: Ca. 1 folder of printed matter on St. Joseph Middle School, n.d.; ca. 1 folder of printed matter about School Sisters' work in China before and after the Japanese invasion, 1942; *Truth about China's Crisis*, by Louis Maloof, 1949.
MEMORABILIA: Folder of notes about Sr. Eustella Bush's collection, n.d.; ca. 1 folder of publicity about St. Joseph Middle School, n.d.; announcement of evacuation, by the Imperial Japanese Navy, 1942; folder of newspaper clippings, n.d.
AUDIO-VISUAL MATERIALS: Watercolor painting of a room at the Civil Assembly Center (Japanese concentration camp), probably the sisters' room, n.d.
SERIALS: *China Missionary*, 1948-49.
CHINESE LANGUAGE MATERIALS: Folder of unidentified correspondence.
FINDING AIDS: In-house inventory.

3-CHINA (MS 015), 1915-62, 4.5 boxes

MINUTES/RECORDS/REPORTS: Memorandum of agreement of Bishop Georg Weig with School Sisters of Saint Francis, 1929; contract between Franciscan missionaries of Mary and School Sisters of Saint Francis, 1939; St. Joseph Middle School, folder of general data, 1931-49; report of St. Joseph Primary and Middle School, 1942; folder of data on former Tsingtao students at St. Joseph Middle School, 1936-46; St. Joseph Middle School Annuals, 1935, 1938-39; academic records of St. Joseph Middle School, 1931-47; St. Joseph Middle School, 1 reel microfilm, n.d.; School Sisters of Saint Francis: rosters of volunteers for China, 1933, 1939; 2 folders of reports of teachers on their work, 1935; report of Tsingtao Mission, 1936-39, 1941, 1946-47; folder of records of orders and shipments from China and from Milwaukee, 1937-47; lists and prices of gifts sent to the Motherhouse, 1946-48; Marie Anna Chen's scholastic records, 1945-53.
CORRESPONDENCE: 1 folder apiece of administrative correspondence: from Fumasoni-Biondi to Archbishop Messmer, 1924; John Weig to Mother Stanislaus Hegner, 1928-41; Bishop Peter Walleser, O.F.M. Cap., to Mother Stanislaus, 1929-40; Bishop Georg Weig to Mother Stanislaus, 1929-41; various bishops and clergy to Mother Stanislaus, 1932-41; Mother Stanislaus to Bruno Hagspiel, 1936-41; Bishop Weig with Mother Corona Wirfs, 1937; National Catholic Welfare Conference to Mother Stanislaus, 1937-39; various telegrams and letters from Mother Corona regarding the sisters' voyage to China, 1939; Sr. Confirma Ruhlman, O.S.F., and others to Mother Stanislaus regarding the voyage to and arrival in China, 1939; Bishop Weig to A. J. Klink, 1936; Mother Corona, summary of mission, 1930-45, 1961; opening of St. Joseph Middle School, 1931; scholarships from Holy Cross College to School Sisters of Saint Francis, 1939-40; letters from Sr. Eustella Bush to Mother Stanislaus, concerning Donatilla Lorenz and Richard Lee, 1938-39; correspondence from Verna Vasen to Mother Corona, aboard the *Gripsholm*, 1943-44; Thomas Cardinal Tien to Mother Corona, 1945-46; Chumatien, Roman Catholic Mission, to Mother Corona, 1946-47; John Weig, S.V.D., to Mother Corona, 1946-48; J. P. Ryan, M.M., to Mother Corona, 1944; Federal Security Agency, U.S. Office of Education, to Mother Corona, 1947; Sr. Hiltrudis Kappes to Mother Corona, 1946; Sr. Adolph Chou to Mother Corona, 1949; Sr. Eustella Bush to Mother Corona, 4 folders, 1945-52; school supplies and books, 1936-46; correspondence concerning gifts sent to the Motherhouse, 1946-48; correspondence on transfer of money and taxes on China properties, 1946-50; folder of condolences from sisters in China, on death of Pope Pius XI, 1939; Paul Christ to Mother Corona, 1950; Paul Christ to the Sisters of Tsingtao, 1950; Maria Elfleda, F.M.M., to Sr. Mario Tsung about Communist China, 1952; Sr. Eustella Bush to Sr. Valencia Van Driel on China papers, 1962; correspondence from various sisters, 1942-47, n.d.; 2 reels microfilm of correspondence of St. Joseph's Middle School, 1931-47, including Mother Corona's visit, 1936.
MANUSCRIPTS: "Catholic Mission and Life in China," by various sisters and Paul Conrad, n.d.; "China in Tsingtao," by Blanda Johns, n.d.; "Chinese Food and Its Preparation," by Sr. Turibia Soehnlein, O.S.F., 1936; "Letters from Our Missionaries," by various sisters in China, 1931-41; "Our Mission in China, 1929-1949," by Sr. Eustella Bush, n.d.; "Summary of Mission," by Mother Corona Wirfs, 1930-45, 1961; account of Mother Corona's visit, 1937; folder of accounts of concentration

camp life by Sisters of Saint Francis, 1944; "Life under the Japanese, June 11, 1942-Sept. 27, 1945," n.a.; Sr. Eustella Bush's account of concentration camp, 1945; "Need for Missionaries," n.d.; "My Home Leave," by Sr. Eustella Bush, O.S.F., ca. 1941; "Confrontation of Church and Communism," n.d.; "A Visit to China," by Mother Corona Wirfs, O.S.F., 1937.
PAMPHLETS: *Adveniat Regnum Tuum: The Story of China's First Cardinal*, by Louis Maloof, 1946; magazine article on Joseph Lo Pa Hong, 1938.
AUDIO-VISUAL MATERIALS: Several hundred photos of mission life, people, and places in China; art photos; bound photos entitled, "Visit of Mother Corona to Tsingtao, 1936: The Mission and the People," "Institutions, S.S.S.F.: Black and White Photos of Tsingtao, China, along with Other Institutions of the S.S.S.F.," "China," ca. 1936 (ca. 300 photos of people, places, and sights in China and 30 labeled postcard pictures of the "nature gods"), "China Days" (delicate cutwork by Chinese school children and ink drawings by unidentified artist), "St. Joseph Middle School, Tsingtao, China," ca. 1930s (ca. 180 photos of buildings, people and places in China).
MEMORABILIA: Folder of newspaper clippings of first staff of St. Joseph Middle School, 1931; St. Joseph Middle School, school song, n.d.; folder of St. Joseph Middle School monthly newspapers, 1934-37; accounts of the death of George and John Weig, 1941, 1948; folder of correspondence codes for World War II, 1942; printed matter included in a folder of correspondence from Verna Vasen to Mother Corona Wirfs, aboard the *Gripsholm*, 1943-44; death notice of Bishop Peter Walleser, O.F.M. Cap.; folder of printed matter on Thomas Cardinal Tien's visit to the United States, 1946; obituary of Joseph Lo Pa Hong, 1938; graduation program of Aurora College for Women, 1941; Olympic Games edition of *Far East*, 1935; program of sacred concert in honor of Thomas Cardinal Tien, n.d.; radio sketches and recitations in Chinese and English, 1947; religion books used at St. Joseph Middle School, n.d.; clipping from *Catholic Herald Citizen* on Communist takeover, 1979; holy cards and other items, some inscribed; ca. 100 post cards of scenes in Tsingtao and other parts of China; album of ca. 150 postcard pictures, some captioned in Chinese and English.
CHINESE LANGUAGE MATERIALS: 4 volumes of American catechetical texts, trans. by Sr. Adolph Chou, O.S.F., and criticism, 1939-40, 1948; 9 folders of Chinese school books, n.d.; Chinese language edition of *Mass Prayers*, by E. F. Garesche, S.J., n.d.; *Highway to Heaven* series, trans. by Sr. Adolph Chou, S.S.S.F.; Chinese hymnals, n.d.; other books; *In Memory of the West Country Story and the Weakness of the King*, trans. by Sr. Mario Tsung, n.d.
FINDING AIDS: In-house inventory.

4-Sr. CALLISTA MESSMER, 1943-45, 1 folder
CORRESPONDENCE: Ca. 1 folder of letters from Sr. Callista Messmer to Herr Pater Flesch, Mary Sun, C. Nourry, S. M. Mario, S. Lindskog, S. Agerina, and unknown, 1943-45.
CHINESE LANGUAGE MATERIALS: 2 cards to Sr. Callista, n.d.
FINDING AIDS: In-house inventory.

5-PHOTOGRAPHS, 1915-71, ca. 1,000 items
AUDIO-VISUAL MATERIALS: Ca. 1,000 photos of Chinese civilization, culture, and people, and the S.S.S.F. mission, missionaries, and activities, 1915-71; 25 art prints and pictures, some about Christmas.
FINDING AIDS: In-house inventory.

6-CECILIA (Sr. CONFIRMA) RUHLMAN, 1941-42, 4 folders
MINUTES/RECORDS/REPORTS: St. Joseph Middle School, Tsingtao, report, 1941-42; official documents, ca. 1 folder, 1942, n.d.
DIARIES: Diary on repatriation from Japanese captivity, 1942.
MANUSCRIPTS: "Religions in China: Untitled Speech to U.S. High School students," n.d.
PAMPHLETS: Ca. 1 folder of printed matter, 1942, n.d.
MAPS/DESIGNS/DRAWINGS: Map illustrating repatriation from captivity (with diary above), 1942.
MEMORABILIA: Ca. 1 folder of clippings, 1942, n.d.
FINDING AIDS: In-house inventory.

NASHOTAH

WI-80 NASHOTAH HOUSE
2777 Mission Road
Nashotah WI 53058-9990
(414) 646-3371
Lynn Feider, Librarian

1-GENERAL HOLDINGS
SERIALS: *China Christian Year Book*, 1934-35.
CHINESE LANGUAGE MATERIALS: Old and New Testaments, n.d.

WYOMING

LARAMIE

UNIVERSITY OF WYOMING
WY-5 William Robertson Coe Library
Box 3334, University Station
Laramie WY 82071
(307) 766-6505
William O. Van Arsdale, Collection Development

1-GENERAL HOLDINGS
SERIALS: *China Christian Year Book*, 1927. *China Medical Journal*, 1918-21. *Peking Natural History Bulletin*, 1930-41.

Union Lists

This list of serials uses the *Union List of Serials in the Libraries of the United States and Canada* of the Library of Congress as a model for standardized format. However, since the system for recording serial holdings varies widely from repository to repository, the *Guide* uses the verbatim information in the repository records, even where this may seem to contradict the dates of publication. Example:

TITLE: Subtitle. Publisher, Place of publication. Date of issue.
    Title changes or other detail.
        Institution—Repository/Library (Repository Index Code/Collection Number): holdings (Volumes and numbers, then dates).

Abbreviations and Symbols

[ ] Incomplete
? uncertain
| | closed entry
     continues to receive

Months

Ja	January	Jl	July
F	February	Ag	August
Mr	March	S	September
Ap	April	O	October
My	May	Nv	November
Je	June	D	December

Serial Titles

ADVENT CHRISTIAN MISSIONS. Boston. V 1–61, 1920–79.
Yale Divinity School Library (CT–55/2): V 1–61, 1920–79.

AGRICULTURAL EXTENSION SERVICE BULLETIN. *See* Catholic University of Peking.

AGRICULTURAL MISSIONS MIMEOGRAPH SERIES. Agricultural Missions, New York.
Biblical Theological Seminary Library (PA–70/1): N 75, 86, 98, 104, 105, 108–10, 115, 135–39, 141, 144, 1937–41. Harvard Divinity School—Andover-Harvard Theological Library (MA–95/1): N 14, 47, 72, 79, 83, 84, 86, 87, 88, 98, 99, 105, 118, 119, 127, 132, 137, 139, 140, 141, 151, 156, 157, 174, 175, 205; ca. 1935–50.

AGRICULTURE AND FORESTRY NOTES. *See* University of Nanking.

AGRICULTURE AND FORESTRY SERIES. *See* University of Nanking.

ALDEN SPEARE MEMORIAL HOSPITAL NEWSLETTER. Alden Speare Memorial Hospital, Yenping.
Union Theological Seminary—Burke Library (NY–275/1): 1923.

American Baptist Foreign Mission Society
QUARTERLY BULLETIN. American Baptist Foreign Mission Society. East China Mission.
American Baptist Historical Society—American Baptist Archives Center (PA–285/2): 1917–25. Union Theological Seminary—Burke Library (NY–275/1): Nv 1911, Nv 1912, 1913–31.

AMERICAN CHURCH MISSION NEWSLETTER. Episcopal Church (?). Hankow.
Graduate Theological Union Library (CA–15/1): 1911.

American Friends Service Committee
BULLETIN ON WORK IN CHINA. American Friends Service Committee, Philadelphia, PA. N 1–17, Ja 1942-Mr 1944.
American Friends Service Committee—Archives (PA–140/1): N 1–17, 1942–44. Boston Public Library (MA–30/2): N 1–17, 1942–44. California State Library (CA–230/1): N 1–17, 1942–44. Earlham College—Lilly Library (IN–100/1): N 1–17, Ja 1942–44. Harvard University—Widener Library (MA–155/1): N 1–17, 1942–44. Indiana State Library (IN–65/1): N 1–17, 1942–44. Louisville Free Public Library (KY–40/1): N 1–17, 1942–44. New York Public Library—General Research Division (NY–230/1): N 1–?, 1942–?. Princeton University—Firestone Library (NJ–100/1): N 1–17, 1942–44. State Historical Society of Wisconsin—Historical Library (WI–25/1): N 1–17, 1942–44. Union Theological Seminary—Burke Library (NY–275/1): N 1–17, 1942–44. University of California, Berkeley—General Library (CA–70/1): N 1–17, 1942–44. University of Chicago—Regenstein Library (IL–85/1): N 1–17, 1942–44. Vassar College Library (NY–330/1): N 1–17, 1942–44. Virginia State Library (VA–95/1): N 1–17, 1942–44.

COLOR AND BACKGROUND MATERIAL. N 1–, 1946–.
Cornell University—Wason Collection (NY–95/1): N 1, 5, 7, 10–11, 13–15, 1946–50.

MISCELLANEOUS BULLETINS. American Friends Service Committee, Philadelphia, PA.
Cornell University—Wason Collection (NY–95/1): Ja, Mr, My 1946, D 1947.

PERIODIC SUMMARY. American Friends Service Committee, Philadelphia, PA. N 1–, Nv 1946–.
Cornell University—Wason Collection (NY–95/1):

N 1–3, 5–9, 11, 1946–50.

AMERICAN JESUITS IN CHINA. San Jose, CA.
California Province of the Society of Jesus Archives (CA–195/1): 1949.
Georgetown University—Woodstock Theological Center Library (DC–70/4): V 1, Mr, Nv 1952.

American Presbyterian Mission.
NEWSLETTER. American Presbyterian Mission, Chefoo.
Union Theological Seminary—Burke Library (NY–275/1): n.d.

Anglican Communion in China and Hongkong (Chung-hua Sheng Kung Hui).
JOURNAL OF SYNOD. Kiangsu Diocese. N 1–23?, 19??–33?.
Union Theological Seminary—Burke Library (NY–275/1): N 7–23, 1912–19, 1922–26, 1928–33.
JOURNAL OF SYNOD. North China Diocese. N 1–17(?), 1917–39(?).
Union Theological Seminary—Burke Library (NY–275/1): N 1–17, 1917–23, 1925–26, 1928–32, 1934, 1936, 1939.

ANIMUS. Central China Mission, Methodist Episcopal Church, Nanking.
Garrett-Evangelical and Seabury-Western Theological Seminaries—United Library (IL–110/1): V 2, N 8; V 3, N 2, 4, 8, 10; V 4, N 1, 1899–1901.

ANKING NEWSLETTER. American Episcopal Diocese of Anking, Wuhu, Anhwei. V 5–22, 1922–41 (irregular).
Title varies: DISTRICT OF ANKING NEWSLETTER, 1938–41. Continued by FREE WAN-KAN, 1942.
Center for Research Libraries (IL–25/4): V 2, N 4; V 21, N 4; V 22, N 1–2; 1945, 1947–48.
Cornell University—Wason Collection (NY–95/1): V 18, N 1–7; V 19, N 1–3; V 20, N 1–5; V 21, N 1–4; V 22, N 1; n.s. V 2, N 4; V 21, N 4; V 22, N 1–2; 1937–41, 1945, 1947–48.
Kalamazoo College—Upjohn Library (MI–125/1): 1937–48.
Ohio State University—Thompson Memorial Library (OH–110/4): 1937–48.
Stanford University—Green Library (CA–305/1): V 18–22, n.s., V 2, 21–22, 1937–41, 1945, 1947–48.
Union Theological Seminary—Burke Library (NY–275/1): V 5–22; D 1922; Je 1925; Mr, Je, Nv-D 1926; Ja-Je 1927; Ja, Ap, Je, D 1928; Ja-Jl, Nv-D 1929; Ja, Mr, My, O, D 1930; Ja, Mr, My, S, Nv 1931; Ja, Mr, My, S, Nv 1932; Ja, My, S, Nv 1933; Ja, Mr, My, S, Nv 1934; Ja, Mr, My, S, Nv 1935; Ja, Mr, My, S, Nv 1936; Ja-Ap, S, Nv 1937; Ja, Mr, My, S, D 1938; Ja, Mr, My, S, Nv 1939; Ja, Mr, My, O, D 1940; Mr, Je, O 1941.
University of Virginia—Manuscripts Department (VA–25/10): V 2, N 4, D 1944.
Wheaton College—Graham Center Library (IL–205/1): V 18–22, 1937–48.
Yale Divinity School Library (CT–55/2): V 2–13, 15–16, 18, 20–22, n.s. V 2, 21–22, 1920–41, 1945, 1947–48.

ANKING NEWSLETTER. St. John's University of Shanghai. N

1–, 1939–.
Virginia Theological Seminary—Payne Library (VA–5/1): 1939–41.

ANKING-HANKOW NEWSLETTER. n.p.
Union Theological Seminary—Burke Library (NY–275/1): F 1944.

ANNALES DE L'OBSERVATOIRE ASTRONOMIQUE DE ZO-SE. *See* Zi-ka-wei Observatoire, Shanghai.

ANNUAIRE DES MISSIONS CATHOLIQUES DE CHINE. Bureau Sinologique de Zi-ka-wei, Shanghai. V 1–, 1901–.
Title varies: ANNUAIRE DE L'OBSERVATOIRE DE ZI-KA-WEI, ser. 1, 1901–22; MISSIONS, SEMINAIRES, ECOLES…EN CHINE, ser. 2, 1922–32; ANNUAIRE DES MISSIONS CATHOLIQUES DE CHINE, ser. 3, 1933–47; ANNUAIRE DE L'EGLISE CATHOLIQUE, 1947–.
Catholic University of America—Mullen Library (DC–20/1): V 1–47, 1901–47(?).
Maryknoll and Brothers Fathers Library (NY–115/1): 1928–30, 1934–37, 1939–40.
Yale Divinity School Library (CT–55/2): 1924–41.

ANNUAIRE DES MISSIONS CATHOLIQUES DE MAN-CHOUKUO. Imprimerie de la Mission Catholique, Moukden.
Maryknoll Sisters of St. Dominic—Rogers Library (NY–125/1): 1936.

APOSTOLICUM: Periodicum Pastorale et Ascelicum pro Missionariis. Shanghai. V 1–12?, 1930–42?
St. Bonaventure University—Franciscan Institute (NY–365/1): V 1, N 2, 1930–.
University of Dayton—Marian Library (OH–125/1): V 12, N 1–11, Ja-Nv 1941.

ARTS AND LETTERS NEWS. *See* Yenching University, Peking.

ASIA. Synodal Commission, Catholic Church in China, Hong Kong. V 12–, 1960– (monthly except July and August).
Continues in part COLLECTANEA COMMISSIONIS SYNODALIS. Title varies: CHINA MISSIONARY, Ja 1948-Je 1949; LE MISSIONAIRE DE CHINE, S 1949-Jl 1953; CHINA MISSIONARY BULLETIN, S 1953-D 1959; ASIA, Ja 1960–.
Catholic Theological Union Library (IL–20/1): V 12, 1960.
Catholic University of America—Mullen Library (DC–20/1): V 12, N 1, Ja 1960.
Columbia University—Starr East Asian Library (NY–195/4): V 1–12, S 1949-D 1960.
Cornell University—Wason Collection (NY–95/1): V 1, N 1–3; V 2, N 4, 6–9; V 3; V 4, N 2, 4–10; V 5–12; 1949–60.
Georgetown University—Woodstock Theological Center Library (DC–70/4): 1948–60.
Maryknoll Sisters of St. Dominic Archives (NY–120/1): 1978–83.
Northwestern University Library (NY–115/1): V 4, N 1–3; V 5–12, 1952–1960.
St. John's University—Alcuin Library (MN–5/1): V 12, 18–19, 1960, 1970.
St. Mary of the Lake Seminary—Feehan Memorial Li-

brary (IL–130/1): V 12, 1960.

Union Theological Seminary—Burke Library (NY–275/1): V 1–12, 1948–60.

University of Chicago—Regenstein Library (IL–85/1): V 9–12, 1957–60.

University of Delaware—Morris Library (DE–5/2): V 18, Aut 1970.

University of Kansas—Watson Library (KS–35/3): V 1, N 4–7; V 2, N 1–6; V 4, N 1–10; V 5, N 1–10; V 6, N 1–10; V 7, N 1–10; V 8, N 2–10; V 9, N 1–10; V 10, N 1–2, 4–10; V 11, N 1–10; V 12, N 1–10; 1948–49, 1952–60.

University of Southern California—Von Kleinsmid Center Library (CA–190/2): N 1, 1964.

Yale Divinity School Library (CT–55/2): V 1–12, 1948–60.

ASIA CHRISTIAN COLLEGES ASSOCIATION BULLETIN. Asia Christian Colleges Association, London. N 1–, 1952–.

Title varies: CHRISTIAN UNIVERSITIES OF CHINA BULLETIN, N 214, 16–40, 1932–4?; CHINA CHRISTIAN UNIVERSITIES BULLETIN, ??.

Union Theological Seminary—Burke Library (NY–275/1): N 1–, 1952–.

ASIAN FOLKLORE STUDIES. Catholic University of Peking, Museum of Oriental Ethnology, Peking. V 12–, 1953–.

Continues FOLKLORE STUDIES. Publisher varies: 1942–52, Catholic University of Peking, Museum of Oriental Ethnology, Peking; 1953–56, S. V. D. Research Institute; 1958–, Society for Asian Folklore.

Catholic Theological Union Library (IL–20/1): V 37–, 1978–.

Princeton University—Firestone Library (NJ–100/1): V 11, N 1, 1952.

Princeton University—Gest Oriental Library (NJ–105/1): 1942–.

Stanford University—Green Library (CA–305/1): V 1–, 1942–.

University of California, Berkeley—Anthropology Library (CA–25/1): V 1–, 1942–.

University of Chicago—Regenstein Library (IL–85/1): V 1–, 1942–.

University of New Mexico Library (NM–5/1): V 23, N 1; V 24–33; V 34, N 2–V 37, N 2; 1964–78.

University of Washington Libraries (WA–45/1): V 1–5; V 6, N 1; V 7–25; V 26, N 1; V 27–30; V 31, N 1; V 32–45; 1942–86.

ASIAN FOLKLORE STUDIES. SUPPLEMENT. *See* FOLKLORE STUDIES. SUPPLEMENT.

ASIATIC DIVISION MISSION NEWS. Asiatic Division, General Conference of the Seventh-Day Adventists, Shanghai. V 3–6, 1914–17.

Continues NEWSLETTER FOR THE ASIATIC DIVISION, 1914. Continued as ASIATIC DIVISION OUTLOOK, 1917.

General Conference of Seventh-Day Adventists Archives (DC–40/1): V 3–6, 1914–17.

Loma Linda University—Radcliffe Memorial Library (CA–135/1): V 3–5, 1914–16.

ASIATIC DIVISION OUTLOOK. Asiatic Division, General Conference of the Seventh-Day Adventists, Shanghai. V 6–13, 1917–24.

Continues ASIATIC DIVISION MISSION NEWS, 1917. Continued as FAR EASTERN DIVISION OUTLOOK, 1924.

Andrews University—White Library (MI–50/1): V 7, 1918.

General Conference of Seventh-Day Adventists Archives (DC–40/1): V 6–13, 1917–24.

Loma Linda University—Radcliffe Memorial Library (CA–135/1): V 6, N 15, 22; V 7, N 1–3, 9–12, 21–22; V 8, N 6–8, 21–22; V 9, N 7–14, 17–18 23–24; V 10, N 11, 19–20; V 11, N 3–4, 10–11; V 12, N 1, 5–6; V 13, N 2–4, 6–7; 1917–24.

ASSEMBLY TIMES. Chapei Civil Assembly Center, Chapei.

University of Oregon—Department of Special Collections (OR–15/38): V 1, N 1–16, 1943.

AUSBREITUNG-EVANGELIUMS IN TANGSHAN. General Conference Mennonite Mission (?), Crimmitschau.

Title varies: MISSIONS-NACHRICHTEN AUS TANGSHAN, 1920–28; AUSBREITUNG-EVANGELIUMS IN TANGSHAN, 1928; VERKÜNDIGT DAS EVANGELIUM NACHRICHTEN AUS CHINA, 1929–38; NACHRICHTEN AUS CHINA, 1938–41.

Bethel College—Mennonite Library and Archives (KS–55/8): N 28, Ap 1928.

BAMBOO BAZ-ZOO. Camp of the Cicada Chorus, Yenping. V 1, N 1, 1917.

University of Oregon—Department of Special Collections (OR–15/47): V 1, N 1, Ag 1917.

BAMBOO WIRELESS. Manila.

California Province of the Society of Jesus Archives (CA–195/1): V 1, N 1–V 8, N 2, O 1952–F 1958.

Bethel Mission of China, Pasadena, California
NEWSLETTER OF BETHEL MISSION OF CHINA, INC. Pasadena, California.

Asbury Theological Seminary—Fisher Library (KY–90/1): Ag 1950, Jl 1959–Spr 1974.

BIBLE FOR CHINA. Bible Union of China, Shanghai. N 1–, 1921–37 (irregular).

Title varies: BULLETIN OF THE BIBLE UNION OF CHINA, N 1–17, 1925; BIBLE FOR CHINA, N 18–.

Bethel Theological Seminary Library (MN–50/1): N 25, 34, 37, 40, 44–49, F 1926; Mr 1928; Ja, Jl 1929; Mr 1930–Ja 1931.

Columbia Theological Seminary—Campbell Library (GA–35/1): N 6, 10, 14, 25, 34–57, 1922, 1932.

Emory University—Pitts Theology Library (GA–15/5): N 26, My 1926.

Princeton Theological Seminary—Speer Library (NJ–95/3): N 43–90, 1930–38.

San Francisco Theological Seminary Library (CA–235/2): N 18–?, 1925–27.

Union Theological Seminary—Burke Library (NY–275/1): N 18–86, 88, 1925–37.

Bible Union of China, Shanghai
BULLETIN. Bible Union of China, Shanghai. 1921–25.

Title varies: BULLETIN OF THE BIBLE UNION OF CHINA, N 1-17, 1925; BIBLE FOR CHINA, N 18-.
Emory University—Pitts Theology Library (GA-15/5): V 1, 1921.
San Francisco Theological Seminary Library (CA-235/2): V 1, N 1-17, Ja 1921-25.
Union Theological Seminary—Burke Library (NY-275/1): V 1, N 1-17, 1921-25.

BIMONTHLY BULLETIN. *See* Southern Presbyterian Mission in China.

BIOLOGICAL BULLETIN. *See* Fukien Christian University, Shanghai.

BIOLOGICAL BULLETIN. *See* St. John's University of Shanghai.

BOLETIM ECLESIASTICO DA DIOCESE DE MACAU. Diocese of Macao, Macao.
Indiana University—University Libraries (IN-20/2): D 1941; S, D 1960; My, O 1961; Nv 1963.
Yale Divinity School Library (CT-55/2): V 55-77, 1957-79.

BOONE LIBRARY SCHOOL QUARTERLY. Boone Library School, Wuchang.
Richmond Memorial Library (NY-35/1): V 3, N 3, S 1931.

BOONE REVIEW. The Boone School, Wuchang.
Essex Institute—Phillips Library (MA-210/2): 1908.

BIBLIOGRAPHY OF PUBLICATIONS FROM THE LABORATORIES AND CLINICS. *See* Peking Union Medical College, Peking.

BRIDGE. Tao Fong Shan Ecumenical Centre, Hong Kong. N 1, S 1983.
Asbury Theological Seminary—Fisher Library (KY-90/1): N 6, N 8-, Jl 1984-.
Emory University—Pitts Theology Library (GA-15/5): N 1-, 1983-.
Fuller Theological Seminary—McAlister Library (CA-205/1): N 1-10, 13, 15-20, 1983-86.
Graduate Theological Union Library (CA-15/2): N 1-, S 1983-.
Harvard Divinity School—Andover-Harvard Theological Library (MA-95/2): N 1-, 1983-.
Harvard University—Harvard-Yenching Library (MA-125/6): N 1-, 1983-.
Institute for Chinese-Western Cultural History (CA-245/7): N 1-, 1983-.
Lutheran Theological Southern Seminary—Lineberger Memorial Library (SC-20/1): N 1-, 1983-.
Southern Baptist Convention—Jenkins Research Library (VA-70/1): 1983-87.
Southern Methodist University—Bridwell Theology Library (TX-20/2): N 1, N 5-, 1983-.
Trinity Evangelical Divinity School Library (IL-90/1): N 7-, 1984-.
Union Theological Seminary—Burke Library (NY-275/1): N 1-, 1983-.
United Theological Seminary Library (OH-120/11): N 1-, 1983-.

Wheaton College—Graham Center Library (IL-205/1): N 1, N 8-, Ja 1983, Nv 1984-.

BROADCAST BULLETIN. *See* National Christian Council of China.

BROADCASTS. *See* National Christian Council of China.

BUGLE CALL. Sisters of Providence, s.l.
Sisters of Providence Archives (IN-105/2): Ap 1923.

BULLETIN AEROLOGIQUE. *See* Zi-ka-wei Observatoire, Shanghai.

LE BULLETIN CATHOLIQUE DE PEKIN. Lazarists, Peking. V 1-, D 1913- (annual).
Cornell University—Wason Collection (NY-95/1): V 1-35, 1913-48.
Library of Congress—General Reading Room Division (DC-120/1): V 23-24; S-O, D 1936; Ap-My 1937.
Mary Immaculate Seminary Library (PA-115/1): V 14, N 166-72; V 15, N 174-84; V 16, N 185-86, 188-96; V 17, N 197-203; V 18, N 117-20; V 19, N 221-26, 228-32; V 20, N 233; V 21, N 251, 254, 256; V 22, N 258, 261, 262; 1927-35.

BULLETIN DE LA SOCIETE DES MISSIONS-ETRANGERES DE PARIS. Imprimerie de la Société des Missions Etrangères de Paris. Nazareth-Hong Kong. V 1-, 1922-.
Maryknoll Fathers and Brothers Library (NY-115/1): 1925-26, 1933, 1935-38, 1953-56, 1959-59, 1961.

BULLETIN DE L'UNIVERSITE DE L'AURORE. *See* Université de l'Aurore, Shanghai.

BULLETIN DES OBSERVATIONS. *See* Zi-ka-wei Observatoire, Shanghai.

BULLETIN MENSUEL DE L'OBSERVATOIRE MAGNETIQUE ET METEOROLOGIQUE DE ZI-KA-WEI. *See* Zi-ka-wei Observatoire, Shanghai.

BULLETIN OF THE DIOCESAN ASSOCIATION FOR WESTERN CHINA. The Association, London. N 132, 1937.
Cover title: FOUR STREAMS. Continues BULLETIN OF THE DIOCESE OF WESTERN CHINA. Continued by NEWSLETTER OF THE DIOCESAN ASSOCIATION FOR WESTERN CHINA.
Center for Research Libraries (IL-25/4): N 132-165, 1937-46.
Stanford University—Green Library (CA-305/1): Series 1, N 121-173, Series 2, N 1-13, ?-1951, 1951-57.
Wheaton College—Graham Center Library (IL-205/1): N 121-178, 1934-51.
Yale Divinity School Library (CT-55/2): N 132-178, 1937-51.

BULLETIN OF THE DIOCESE OF WESTERN CHINA. The Diocese, London.
Continued by BULLETIN OF THE DIOCESAN ASSOCIATION FOR WESTERN CHINA.
Center for Research Libraries (IL-25/4): N 121-131, 1934-37.
Yale Divinity School Library (CT-55/2): N 121-131, 1934-37.

BULLETIN OF THE EAST. China Educational Association.
  Union Theological Seminary—Burke Library (NY–275/1): Ja, F 1923; Mr, My, Ag 1924; Mr, Ap 1925; D 1927; Nv 1928.

BULLETIN OF THE HANKOW DISTRICT. American Church Mission, Protestant Episcopal Church of the U.S.A., Hankow. V 1, N 1–9, Mr 1903-Ja 1904 (irregular).
  Union Theological Seminary—Burke Library (NY–275/1): V 1, N 1–9, Mr 1903-Ja 1904.

BULLETIN OF THE HOPEI BIBLE SCHOOL. General Conference Mennonite Mission, Kaichow, Hopei.
  Associated Mennonite Biblical Seminaries Library (IN–25/3): 1932–33.
  Bethel College—Mennonite Library and Archives (KS–55/13): 1932–33.

BULLETIN OF THE INTERNATIONAL ANTI-OPIUM ASSOCIATION. *See* International Anti-opium Association.

BULLETIN OF THE TIENTSIN BIBLE SEMINARY. Tientsin Bible Seminary, Tientsin.
  Taylor University Archives (IN–110/1): 1938–39.

BULLETIN ON CHINA'S FOREIGN RELATIONS. University of Nanking. Nanking. V 1, N 1–11, O 1931–35?; University of Nanking, Foreign Relations Association. V 1, N 12-V 3, N 1, 1932-Ja 1935 (irregular).
  Harvard University—Widener Library (MA–155/1): V 1–3, N 1, 1931–35.
  University of Virginia—Alderman Library (VA–30/1): V 1, N 6–7, 9–19, 21; V 2, N 1–4, 6, 7; V 3, N 1; 1932–35.
  Yale Divinity School—Special Collections (CT–50/25): V 1, N 1–3, 6–21; V 2, N 1–7; V 3, N 1; 1931–35.
  Yale University—Sterling Memorial Library (CT–80/1): V 1–10, 12–21, 1931–35.

BULLETIN ON WORK IN CHINA. *See* American Friends Service Committee.

CALL TO PRAYER. National Holiness Missionary Society. 1900-. Place of publication varies: Chicago, Illinois, 1900–30; Marion, Indiana, 1931-.
  World Gospel Mission Archives (IN–75/1): V 1-, 1900-.

CAMPUS LIFE. Hangchow Christian College, Chekiang. V 1, 1930(?).
  Yale Divinity School—Special Collections (CT–50/25): n.v., N 2–3, 5; n.v., N 1, 3–4; V 2, N 8–10; V 3, N 2; 1930–34.

Canton Christian College, Canton
  AGRICULTURAL BULLETIN.
    Cornell University—Wason Collection (NY–95/1): N 4, 1928.
  BULLETIN.
    Cornell University—Wason Collection (NY–95/1): N 10, 12, 25, 26, 30, 36, 37, 41, 1917, 1920–21, 1924–25, 1928.
    University of Vermont—Bailey/Howe Library (VT–5/1): 1910–11.
    Yale Divinity School Library (CT–55/1): N 2–8, 10,

12, 15–16, 18–19, 23–26, 30, 32, 34, 37, 38, 41, 43, 1909–30.
  NEWSLETTER.
    Union Theological Seminary—Burke Library (NY–275/1): N 8, 10–11, 13, 1912–14.
    Yale Divinity School Library (CT–55/1): 1915–19.
  PUBLICATIONS. College of Agriculture.
    Princeton Theological Seminary—Speer Library (NJ–95/3): 1923.
  QUARTERLY. Canton Christian College Club in America.
    Union Theological Seminary—Burke Library (NY–275/1): My, D 1916; Ap, Jl 1917.

CANTON COMMITTEE FOR JUSTICE TO CHINA. Presbyterian Church in the U.S.A., South China Mission, Canton.
  Presbyterian Historical Society—Archives and Library (PA–200/28): N 4, 7, D 1937, Ap 1938.
  San Francisco Theological Seminary Library (CA–235/2): N 5, F 1938.
  University of Vermont—Bailey/Howe Library (VT–5/1): 1938.

CARITAS. Sisters of Charity of Saint Elizabeth, Convent Station, NJ. V 1-, 1933-.
  Congregation of the Passion of the Eastern United States—Chronicle Office (MA–255/1): 1933–43, 1966–67 (inc.).
  Sisters of Charity of Saint Elizabeth—Generalate Archives (NJ–15/1): V 1–10, Je 1933-O 1943.

THE CARLETONIAN-IN-CHINA. Carleton-in-China, Fenchow.
  Carleton College Archives (MN–60/1): V 1, N 2, n.d.

CATHOLIC CHURCH IN CHINA. Catholic Church in China, Synodal Commission, Collectanea Commissionis Synodalis, Peking. V 1–19, N 7/12, My 1928-Jl/D 1947.
  Title varies: CHINA MISSIONARY—LE MISSIONNAIRE DE CHINE, Ja 1948-Je 1949; CHINA MISSIONARY BULLETIN, S 1949-Jl 1953; MISSION BULLETIN, S 1953-D 1959; ASIA, Ja 1960-. *See also* COLLECTANEA COMMISSIONIS SYNODALIS and DIGEST OF THE SYNODAL COMMISSION OF PEIPING.
    Columbia University—Starr East Asian Library (NY–195/4): V 1–13, [14], [19], 1928–41, 1947.
    Cornell University—Wason Collection (NY–95/1): V 1–5, 9–18, 1928–32, 1936–45.
    New York Public Library—General Research Division (NY–230/1): My 1922-D 1947 (inc.).
    St. John's University—Alcuin Library (MN–5/1): V 1–5, 10–14, 19, 1928–47.
    Yale Divinity School Library (CT–55/2): V 1–14, 18–19, 1928–41, 1945–46.

CATHOLIC REVIEW. California Jesuits, Shanghai.
  California Province of the Society of Jesus Archives (CA–195/1): 1941–49.

Catholic University of Peking
  AGRICULTURAL EXTENSION SERVICE BULLETIN. Catholic University of Peking, Peking.

Harvard University—Harvard-Yenching Library (MA–125/6): N 2, 1948.

Yale University—Sterling Memorial Library (CT–80/1): N 2, 1948.

BULLETIN. Catholic University of Peking, Peking. N 1–9, S 1926-N 1934.

Suspended 1932–33. N 7–9 have added title: FU JEN YING-WEN HSÜEH PAO. N 9 in English, French, German, and Chinese. Index to V 1–9 in V 9.

American Catholic Historical Society—Archives and Historical Collection (PA–120/1): Mr, S 1927; My 1928.

Asbury Theological Seminary—Fisher Library (KY–90/1): N 1–9, 1926–34.

Boston Public Library (MA–30/2): N 1–6, 8, 1926–32, 1934.

Catholic University of America—Mullen Library (DC–20/1): N 1–9, 1926–31, 1934.

Columbia University—Starr East Asian Library (NY–195/4): N 1–9, S 1926-Nv 1934.

Conception Abbey and Seminary Library (MO–15/1): N 1, 4–8, 1926, 1928–31.

Duns Scotus Library (MI–140/1): N 5, 8, O 1928, D 1931.

Harvard University—Gutman Library (MA–120/1): N 1–7, 1926–30.

Harvard University—Harvard-Yenching Library (MA–125/6): N 1–9, 1926–34.

Harvard University—Widener Library (MA–155/1): N 1–7, 1926–30.

Iowa State University Library (IA–5/1): N 1–9, 1926–34.

Johns Hopkins University—Eisenhower Library (MD–10/1): N 1, 4, 7–8, 1926, 1928, 1930–31.

Library of Congress—General Reading Rooms Division (DC–120/1): N [1–9], 1926–31, 1934.

New York Public Library—General Research Division (NY–230/1): N 1–9, S 1926-N 1934.

Newark Abbey (NJ–80/1): N 1–7, S 1926-O 1928, Jl 1929, D 1930.

Philadelphia Museum of Art Library (PA–195/1): N 4, My 1928.

Princeton University—Firestone Library (NJ–100/1): N 1–9, 1926–34.

Public Library of Cincinnati (OH–50/1): N 5–8, 1928–31.

St. Benedict's Convent Archives (MN–90/4): N 4–5, 7, 1928, 1930.

St. John's University—Alcuin Library (MN–5/1): N 1–7, S 1926-D 1930.

Saint Vincent Archabbey and College Archives (PA–95/1): S 1926; Mr, S 1927; My, O 1928; Jl 1929; D 1930; D 1931.

Sisters of Providence Archives (IN–105/6): S 1926, My 1928.

Smithsonian Institution—Freer Gallery of Art Library (DC–160/2): N 4–5, 7–8; My, O 1928; D 1930; D 1931.

Stanford University—Green Library (CA–305/1): N 4, 1928.

Union Theological Seminary—Burke Library (NY–275/1): 1928–30, 1936–37.

University of Arizona Library (AZ–5/1): N 1–9, 1926–34.

University of Illinois at Urbana-Champaign Library (IL–185/1): N 1–9, 1926–34.

University of Washington Libraries (WA–45/1): N 1, 3–9, 1926–34.

Western Washington University—Wilson Library (WA–5/1): N 9, 1934 (repr. 1978?).

Yale Divinity School Library (CT–55/1): 1926–31.

Yale University—Sterling Memorial Library (CT–80/1): N 1–9, 1926–34.

PUBLICATIONS. Catholic University of Peking, College of Education, Peking. V 1, 1939.

Brown University—Rockefeller Library (RI–20/2): V 1, 1939.

Catholic University of America—Mullen Library (DC–20/1): V 1, 1939.

Detroit Public Library (MI–55/1): V 1–2, 1939–40.

Stanford University—Green Library (CA–305/1): V 1, 1939–40.

University of California at Los Angeles—University Research Library (CA–185/1): V 1, 1939–40.

University of Cincinnati—Central Library (OH–65/1): V 1–2, 1939–40.

Western Washington University—Wilson Library (WA–5/1): V 1, 1939–40.

See also ASIAN FOLKLORE STUDIES, DRAGON, FOLKLORE STUDIES, FU-JEN MAGAZINE, FU-JEN NEWS LETTER, THE LIGHT, MISSION NEWS, and MONUMENTA SERICA.

CENTRAL CHINA BI-MONTHLY. Presbyterian Mission Press, Shanghai.

Presbyterian Historical Society—Archives and Library (PA–200/28): V 1, N 1-V 3, N 3, Ja 1914-Je 1916.

Union Theological Seminary—Burke Library (NY–275/1): Ja-F, My-Je, S-D 1914; 1915; Ja-Je 1916.

CENTRAL CHINA CHRISTIAN. Central China Mission, Nanking. V 1–10, Ja 1900-D 1909.

Christian Church (Disciples of Christ) Library (IN–55/1): V 1–10; Ja, Ap-D 1900; 1901; Ja-S, Nv-D 1902; 1903; Ja-Nv 1904; 1905–8; Ja-Nv 1909.

Christian Theological Seminary Library (IN–60/2): V 7, N 1, Ja 1906.

First Christian Church—Fall Memorial Library (KY–25/2): V 7, N 1, Ja 1906.

CENTRAL CHINA PRESBYTERIAN MISSION QUARTERLY. n.p.

Presbyterian Historical Society—Archives and Library (PA–200/28): Jl 1905, Ja 1906.

CENTRAL CHINA RECORD. Methodist Episcopal Church, Central China Mission, Nanking. V 1–?, 1898–?

Garrett-Evangelical and Seabury-Western Theological Seminaries—United Library (IL–110/1): V 4, N 2–12; V 5, N 1–8, 10–12; V 6, N 1–2, 6–12; V 7, N 1–10; V 8, N 1–3; 1901–5.

Union Theological Seminary—Burke Library

(NY–275/1): Ag-S, Nv-D 1901; Mr, My 1902; Mr-Ap, My-D 1903; 1904; Ja-My 1905.

CENTRAL CHINA YEAR BOOK. Methodist Episcopal Church, Central China Conference.

> Garrett-Evangelical and Seabury-Western Theological Seminaries—United Library (IL–110/1): 1911.

CHALLENGER. Chinese Christian Mission, Petaluma, CA. Continues CHINESE CHRISTIANS TODAY.

> American Baptist Seminary of the West Library (CA–10/1): F 1973.
>
> Bethel Theological Seminary Library (MN–50/1): V 12-, 1973-.
>
> Emory University—Pitts Theology Library (GA–15/5): F, Mr 1977.
>
> Luther Northwestern Theological Seminary Library (MN–100/1): 1978.
>
> Union Theological Seminary—Burke Library (NY–275/1): 1982-.

Charles Rogers Mills Memorial School for Chinese Deaf Children

> LETTER. Charles Rogers Mills Memorial School for Chinese Deaf Children, Hangchow.
>
> > Union Theological Seminary—Burke Library (NY–275/1): D 1914.

Cheeloo (Shantung Christian) University

BULLETIN. Cheeloo University, School of Medicine.

> Library of Congress—General Reading Rooms Division (DC–120/1): 1920-21, 1932.

BULLETIN.

> Cornell University—Wason Collection (NY–95/1): N 32, 38, 47, 1924-25.
>
> Harvard Divinity School—Andover-Harvard Theological Library (MA–95/2): N 29-88, 1922-32.

CHEELOO. Shantung Christian University, Tsinan. V 1, 1924.

> Harvard Divinity School—Andover-Harvard Theological Library (MA–95/1): V 1, N 3; V 2, N 4, O 1924, D 1925.
>
> Union Theological Seminary—Burke Library (NY–275/1): 1924-26.

CHEELOO BULLETIN. Cheeloo University, Tsinan. 1927-.

> Harvard Divinity School—Andover-Harvard Theological Library (MA–95/1): N 263, 310, 1930-31.
>
> Harvard Divinity School—Andover-Harvard Theological Library (MA–95/2): D 1927-My 1939 (inc.).
>
> Presbyterian Historical Society—Archives and Library (PA–200/20): 1927-29, 1931-46.
>
> Union Theological Seminary—Archives (NY–270/12): N 321, Je 1931.
>
> Union Theological Seminary—Burke Library (NY–275/1): 1928-33.

CHEELOO COLLEGE OF MEDICINE BULLETIN. Cheeloo University, College of Medicine, Foochow. N 1, 1948.

> Harvard Divinity School—Andover-Harvard Theological Library (MA–95/1): N 1, Nv 1948.

CHEELOO MAGAZINE.

> Yale Divinity School—Special Collections

(CT–50/25): V 1, N 1, 3-4; V 2, N 1-4; V 3, 1-2; 1924-26.

CHEELOO MONTHLY BULLETIN. Tsinan.

> Cornell University—Wason Collection (NY–95/1): N 22-36, 38, O 1935-Ap 1937, Je 1937.
>
> Harvard Divinity School—Andover-Harvard Theological Library (MA–95/1): V 8, N 1, Je 1946.
>
> Union Theological Seminary—Archives (NY–270/12): N 1, S 1933.
>
> Union Theological Seminary—Burke Library (NY–275/1): N 1, 3-20, 22-38, 41-45, 51-57, 64-71, 1933-37, 1939-41.
>
> Yale Divinity School—Special Collections (CT–50/25): N 1-38, 41-45, 51-57, 61-71, n.s. V 8, N 1, 1933-41, 1946.

CHEELOO NEWS. New York.

> Yale Divinity School—Special Collections (CT–50/25): 1944-45.

CHEELOO NOTES. Shantung Christian University, Office of the Board of Governors, London.

> Harvard Divinity School—Andover-Harvard Theological Library (MA–96/1): N 16, 19, O 1928, O 1929.
>
> Union Theological Seminary—Archives (NY–270/12): N 11, O 1927.
>
> Yale Divinity School—Special Collections (CT–50/25): N 4, 7, 1926.

CHEELOO SCHOOL OF THEOLOGY BULLETIN. Cheeloo University, Tsinan.

> Harvard Divinity School—Andover-Harvard Theological Library (MA–95/1): N 65, 1933.

CHEELOO SKETCHES. Shantung Christian University, New York. V 1, N 1, Mr 1927.

> Harvard Divinity School—Andover-Harvard Theological Library (MA–95/1): V 1, N 1, 2; V 3, N 1; Mr, My 1927, Ja 1929.
>
> Union Theological Seminary—Archives (NY–270/12): V 1, N 1-2; V 3, N 1; Mr-My 1927, Ja 1929.
>
> Yale Divinity School—Special Collections (CT–50/25): V 1, N 1-3; V 3, N 1; 1927, 1929.

CHEELOO WEEKLY BULLETIN.

> Presbyterian Historical Society—Archives and Library (PA–200/20): 1926, 1928-29.
>
> Yale Divinity School—Special Collections (CT–50/25): N 9-18, 21-44, 46-48, 82-87, 89-93, 95-96, 99-150, 152-201, 203-4, 206-212, 214-241, 243-266, 268, 270-73, 275-80, 282-92, 294-97, 318, 325-29, 331-336, 338-402, 550-58, n.s. N 1, 13, n.s. N 1-2, 1923-30, 1932-33, 1937, 1948-49.

JOURNAL. Cheeloo University, Tsinan. V 1-8, D 1932-Je 1937?

> Buffalo Museum of Science—Research Library (NY–65/1): N 3, 5, D 1934.

NEWS BULLETIN. College of Arts and Sciences, Tsinan.

> Cornell University—Department of Manuscripts and University Archives (NY–90/7): N 1, Nv 1948.
>
> Yale Divinity School—Special Collections (CT–50/25): 1948-49.

OCCASIONAL NOTES. Cheeloo University, Tsinan. N 1-, 1920?-.

Harvard Divinity School—Andover-Harvard Theological Library (MA–95/1): 1922, 1924.
Union Theological Seminary—Archives (NY–270/12): N 1–2, 4–5, 9; Jl, Nv 1921; Je, O 1922; Ja 1924.
Yale Divinity School—Special Collections (CT–50/25): N 1–2, 4–9, 1921–24.

SHANTUNG CHRISTIAN UNIVERSITY BULLETIN. Tsinan.
Cornell University—Wason Collection (NY–95/1): N 32, 38, 47, 1924(?), 1925.
Yale Divinity School—Special Collections (CT–50/25): N 1, 3, 5–7, 9, 11, 13–14, 16–21, 23–24, 28–29, 32, 34, 36–38, 41–42, 45–49, 53–54, 56–57, 59, 67–69, 72–75, 77, 79, 82–85, 88–89, 91, 93, 95–96, 98, 102, 105, 1917–36, 1940–42.

CHEFOO STATION BULLETIN. Chefoo.
Presbyterian Historical Society—Archives and Library (PA–200/28): N 2–11, Ja 1922–F 1927.
Union Theological Seminary—Archives (NY–270/12): N 3–4, F–Mr 1922.
Union Theological Seminary—Burke Library (NY–275/1): Je 1922.

Chen tan ta-hsüeh. *See* Université de l'Aurore.

CHENGTU NEWSLETTER. N 1–43, 19?–1929; renumbered, N 1–15(?), 1930–1939(?).
Formerly TOKYO NEWSLETTER.
Union Theological Seminary—Burke Library (NY–275/1): N 30–33, 35–43, n.s., N 1–15, 1920–39.

CHEUNG CHOW BEACON. Hong Kong.
Presbyterian Historical Society—Archives and Library (PA–200/28): N 6, Mr 1936.

Ch'i lu ta hsüeh, Tsinan. *See* Cheeloo (Shantung Christian) University.

CHINA. Foreign Missions Conference of North America, New York. Far Eastern Joint Office, China Committee. N 1–124, 1947–52.
Boston University—School of Theology Library (MA–35/1): 1947–48, 1950–52.
Cornell University—Wason Collection (NY–95/1): N 1–124, 1947–52.
Hope College—Van Zoeren Library (MI–110/1): N 1–116, 1947–51.

CHINA. National Christian Conference.
Union Theological Seminary—Burke Library (NY–275/1): N 4, O 1921.

CHINA ADVENT NEWS. A. C. Mission Monthly. Shanghai. V 1–3, 1903–6.
New York Public Library—General Research Division (NY–230/1): V 1–3, 1903–6 (inc.).

CHINA AID COUNCIL NEWSLETTER. China Aid Council, New York.
Title varies: V 1–2, N 2, 1938–O 1939, NEWS; V 2, N 3–V 4, N 3, BULLETIN.

Goshen College—Archives of the Mennonite Church (IN–35/6): V 1–11, 1938–49.

CHINA AND OURSELVES: Newsletter of the Canada China Programme. Canada China Programme, Canadian Council of Churches, Toronto, Ottawa.
American Bible Society Library (NY–135/1): 1982–.
Asian Studies Newsletter Archives (MD–40/1): N 1–, 1976–.
Denver Conservative Baptist Seminary—Thomas Library (CO–10/3): N 24, 30, 34–48, 1981–86.
Union Theological Seminary—Burke Library (NY–275/1): N 1–, 1983–.
Wheaton College—Graham Center Library (IL–205/1): N 24–, F 1981–.

CHINA AND THE CHURCH TODAY. Chinese Church Research Center, Hong Kong. V 1–, 1979– (bimonthly).
Ceased with V 8, N 5, O 1986. Merged with CHINA PRAYER LETTER, D 1986.
Alliance Theological Seminary Library (NY–300/1): V 1–8, 1979–86.
American Bible Society Library (NY–135/1): Mr 1980–86.
Asbury Theological Seminary—Fisher Library (KY–90/1): V 1; V 2, N 2–3, 6; V 3–5; V 6, N 2–6; V 7–8; 1979–86.
Asian Studies Newsletter Archives (MD–40/1): 1979–86.
Associated Mennonite Biblical Seminaries Library (IN–25/3): 1979–85.
Baylor University—Dawson Institute of Church-State Relations (TX–55/1): V 2–8, 1980–86.
Bethel Theological Seminary Library (MN–50/1): V 1–8, 1979–86.
Catholic Theological Union Library (IL–20/1): V 3–8, 1981–86.
Denver Conservative Baptist Seminary—Thomas Library (CO–10/3): V 1–8, 1979–86.
Emory University—Pitts Theology Library (GA–15/5): V 1–7; V 8, N 1–5, 1979–O 1986.
Fuller Theological Seminary—McAlister Library (CA–205/1): V 1–8, 1979–86.
Gordon-Conwell Theological Seminary—Goddard Library (MA–230/4): N 1–3, 5–6, 1979.
Graduate Theological Union Library (CA–15/2): 1987–.
Institute for Chinese-Western Cultural History (CA–245/7): V 1–, 1979–.
International Christian Graduate University—International School of Theology Library (CA–240/1): V 7, N 4, 6; V 8, N 1–5; Ag, D 1985, F–O 1986.
Luther Northwestern Theological Seminary Library (MN–100/1): 1979–86.
Lutheran Theological Southern Seminary—Lineberger Memorial Library (SC–20/1): V 1, N 1–2, 5–6, 1979.
Princeton Theological Seminary—Speer Library (NJ–95/3): 1979–86.
Reformed Bible College Library (MI–95/1): V 1–2, N 3; V 3, N 3–V 8, N 5, 1979–86.
Southern Baptist Convention—Jenkins Research Library (VA–70/1): V 3, N 4; V 4, N 6; V 5, N 1; V 6, N 3–6; V 7, N 1, 4–5; V 8, N 1, 3; 1981–86.

Southern Baptist Theological Seminary—Boyce Centennial Library (KY–50/2): V 1–7, [8], 1979–86.
Southern Methodist University—Bridwell Theology Library (TX–20/2): V 6–8, 1984–86.
Trinity Evangelical Divinity School Library (IL–90/1): V 1–8, 1979–86.
Union Theological Seminary—Burke Library (NY–275/1): V 1–8, 1979–86.
Union Theological Seminary in Virginia Library (VA–85/1): V [4], 5–6, 1982–84.
United Theological Seminary Library (OH–120/11): V 1–8, 1979–86.
Western Conservative Baptist Seminary—Cline-Tunnell Library (OR–30/1): V 1–8, 1979–86.
Western Evangelical Seminary—Hallauer Memorial Library (OR–35/1): V 5, N 2-V 8, N 1, My 1983-F 1986.
Wheaton College—Graham Center Library (IL–205/1): V 1–8, 1979–86.
World Vision International—Research and Information Division (CA–200/1): 1979–81, 1985–86.
Yale Divinity School Library (CT–55/2): V 4–5, 1982–83.

CHINA AND THE GOSPEL: An Illustrated Report of the China Inland Mission. China Inland Mission, London.
1904–5 as LAND OF SINIM.
American Baptist Seminary of the West Library (CA–10/1): 1909.
Biola University—Rose Memorial Library (CA–130/4): 1910.
Brigham Young University—Lee Library (UT–10/1): 1906–17.
Claremont Colleges—Honnold Library (CA–85/1): 1908.
Colgate Rochester Theological Seminaries—Swasey Library (NY–350/1): 1914.
Eden Theological Seminary—Eden-Webster Libraries (MO–60/1): 1913.
Emory University—Pitts Theology Library (GA–15/5): 1906, 1908, 1912–55.
Harvard Divinity School—Andover-Harvard Theological Library (MA–95/2): 1913.
North Park College and Theological Seminary—Wallgren Library (IL–65/1): 1906–8.
Oberlin College—Main Library (OH–175/1): 1904–20.
Overseas Missionary Fellowship (PA–265/1): 1904–36.
Phillips University—Rogers Graduate Seminary Library (OK–5/1): 1912, 1916.
Princeton Theological Seminary—Speer Library (NJ–95/3): 1906–7, 1909–11, 1913, 1916, 1919, 1923, 1935, 1937, 1949–57.
St. Louis Public Library (MO–70/1): 1906–10.
Union Theological Seminary—Burke Library (NY–275/1): 1918–37.
University of Chicago—Regenstein Library (IL–85/1): 1905–30.

THE CHINA BOOKMAN. Christian Publishers' Association of China, Shanghai. V 1, 1919.
Emory University—Pitts Theology Library (GA–15/5): V 1–11, 18–21, 25–26, 1918–28, 1935–38, 1948–49.
San Francisco Theological Seminary Library

(CA–235/2): V 25, N 4; V 27, N 4; Nv 1948, Jl 1950.
Union Theological Seminary—Archives (NY–270/25): V 19, N 1–2, 6; F, Mr, Jl 1936.
Yale Divinity School Library (CT–55/2): V 1; V 2, N 5; V 8–10; V 11, N 1; V 14–19; V 20, N 1–8; V 21; V 22, N 1; V 24, N 1; V 25–27; 1919, 1925–28, 1931–39, 1947–50.
Yale Divinity School—Special Collections (CT–50/2): 1922–37.

CHINA BULLETIN. American Board of Commissioners for Foreign Missions, Boston.
Carleton College Archives (MN–60/1): N 8–24, 71, 74, S 1937-Jl 1938, D 1944-Nv 1945.
Harvard Divinity School—Andover-Harvard Theological Library (MA–95/2): N 2–74A, Jl 1937-F 1946.

CHINA BULLETIN. Centre for Chinese Studies, Pontifical Urban University, Rome. V 1-, Mr 1979- (quarterly).
American Bible Society Library (NY–135/1): 1982-.
Asian Studies Newsletter Archives (MD–40/1): V 1, N 1-, 1979-.
Catholic Theological Union Library (IL–20/1): V 5-, 1983-.
Institute for Chinese-Western Cultural History (CA–245/7): V 1-, 1979-.
Union Theological Seminary—Burke Library (NY–275/1): V 1, N 1, My 1979-.
Union Theological Seminary in Virginia Library (VA–85/1): V 1–6, 1979–84.
Wheaton College—Graham Center Library (IL–205/1): V 2, N 2-, Je 1980-.

CHINA BULLETIN. National Council of Churches of Christ in the U.S.A., Far Eastern Office, Division of Foreign Missions, New York. N 1–124, 1947–52; n.s. V 2–12, N 6, Ja 1952-Je 1962 (issued about 20 times a year, 1952–56).
Continues CHINA, 1952. Continued by CHINA NOTES, S 1962. Publisher name varies: Foreign Missions Conference of North America, Far Eastern Joint Office, China Committee (1947–52).
American Baptist Historical Society—American Baptist Archives Center (PA–285/2): 1937, 1952–62.
American Lutheran Church Archives (MN–95/110): V 9, 1959.
Andover Newton Theological School—Trask Library (MA–180/2): V 5–7, 1955–57.
Andrews University—White Library (MI–50/1): 1947–62.
Associated Mennonite Biblical Seminaries Library (IN–25/3): V 3–13, 1952–62.
Boston University—School of Theology Library (MA–35/1): V 2–12, 1952–62.
Christian Theological Seminary Library (IN–60/2): V 2–12, N 6, F 1952-Je 1962.
Cornell University—Wason Collection (NY–95/1) : V 2–12, 1952–62.
Drew University Library (NJ–40/2): V 2–12, 1952–62.
Emory University—Pitts Theology Library (GA–15/5): N 1–124, n.s., V 2–12, N 6, 1947–62.
Garrett-Evangelical and Seabury-Western Theological Seminaries—United Library (IL–110/1): N 1–124, n.s. V

[2–3], 4–10, [11], 12, 1951–62.

Graduate Theological Union Library (CA–15/2): V 1–12, 1947–62.

Harvard Divinity School—Andover-Harvard Theological Library (MA–95/1): V 2–12, 1952–62 (inc.).

Harvard Divinity School—Andover-Harvard Theological Library (MA–95/2): N 1–124, n.s., V 2, N 1–V 12, N 6, 1947–62.

Harvard University—Harvard-Yenching Library (MA–125/6): V 2–12, 1952–62.

Hoover Institution Library (CA–300/1): 1947–62.

Hope College—Van Zoeren Library (MI–110/1): N 117–124, n.s. V 2–12, 1951–62.

Los Angeles Public Library (CA–150/1): 1959–67.

Luther Northwestern Theological Seminary Library (MN–100/1): V 2–12, 1952–62.

Moody Bible Institute Library (IL–55/1): 1979–89 (current 10 years).

Northwestern College—Ramaker Library (IA–45/2): V 3–12, 1952–62.

Presbyterian Historical Society—Archives and Library (PA–200/16): 1950–66 (inc.).

Presbyterian Historical Society—Archives and Library (PA–200/28): V 2, N 1–2, 4–5, 7–9, 11–15, 17–19; V 3, N 1–5, 7–9, 12–14; V 9–11; 1952–53, 1959–61.

Princeton University—Firestone Library (NJ–100/1): V 5, N 6–V 6, N 11; V 6, N 13–15, 17–18, 20; V 7, N 1–15, 17–20; V 8–V 11, N 6, 1955–62.

Southern Baptist Convention—Archives Center (VA–65/1): 1952–62.

Southern Baptist Convention—Archives Center (VA–65/3): 1956–59.

Southern Baptist Theological Seminary—Boyce Centennial Library (KY–50/2): V [9–10], 11–12, 1959–62.

Southern Methodist University—Bridwell Theology Library (TX–20/2): N 1–124, n.s. V 2–8, 1947–58.

Union Theological Seminary—Burke Library (NY–275/1): V 1–12, N 6, 1947–62.

Union Theological Seminary in Virginia Library (VA–85/1): V [1–5], 6–10, [11], 12, 1951–62.

University of Chicago—Regenstein Library (IL–85/1): V 1–12, N 6, 1947–62.

University of Illinois at Urbana-Champaign—University Archives (IL–180/1): V 3, 1952.

University of Oregon—Department of Special Collections (OR–15/3): V 7, N 7–23; V 8, N 3–20, 22; V 9, N 1–23; V 10, N 1–9; 1957–60.

University of Oregon—Department of Special Collections (OR–15/10): V 24, N 2, F 1937.

University of Oregon—Department of Special Collections (OR–15/18): My, Nv, D 1956; Mr–Nv 1957; S 1958.

University of Oregon—Department of Special Collections (OR–15/42): V 16, N 2, F 1929.

University of Oregon—Department of Special Collections (OR–15/47): V 5, N 12–22; V 6, N 1, 3–9, 13, 15, 18, 21, 1955–56.

University of Oregon Library (OR–20/2): V 2, N 1–2, 4–7, 10, 12; V 3–6; V 7, N 2–12; V 8–10; V 11, N 1–5, 8–12; V 12, 1952–62.

University of Vermont—Bailey/Howe Library (VT–5/1):

1954–62.

University of Virginia—Alderman Library (VA–30/1): V [1–12], 1951–62.

University of Wisconsin-Madison—Memorial Library (WI–45/1): V 4, N 1–V 12, N 6, 1954–62.

Western Theological Seminary—Beardslee Library (MI–120/11): 1959–62.

Yale Divinity School Library (CT–55/2): V 1–12, 1947–62.

Yale Divinity School—Special Collections (CT–50/22): 1950–52.

CHINA CHRISTIAN ADVOCATE. Methodist Publishing House, Shanghai. V 1–29(?), 1914–41(?).

Baldwin-Wallace College—Ritter Library (OH–20/1): Mr 1940.

Boston University—School of Theology Library (MA–35/1): V 18–21, 23, 26–29, 1931–41.

Center for Research Libraries (IL–25/4): V 1–11; V 12, N 2–12; V 13; V 14, N 1–22, 25–52; V 15, N 1–11; V 16–17; V 19, N 8–10, 12; V 20; V 21, N 1, 10–11; V 23, N 2–12; V 24, N 3, 5, 7–12; V 25–29; 1914–41.

Cornell University—Wason Collection (NY–95/1) : V 1–11; V 12, N 2–12; V 13; V 14, N 1–22; V 15, N 1–11; V 16–17; V 19, N 7–10, 12; V 20; V 21, N 1–3, 5, 7–12; V 22, N 1, 10; V 23, N 2–12; V 24, N 3, 5, 7–12; V 25–29; 1914–30, 1932–41.

Drew University—United Methodist Archives (NJ–45/3): 1932–41.

Drew University—United Methodist Historical Library (NJ–50/1): V 1–29 (inc.), 1914–41.

Duke University—Perkins Library (NC–55/1): V 1–4, 7–10, 18–28, 1916–18, 1920–24, 1931–40.

Emory University—Pitts Theology Library (GA–15/5): V 1–4, 12–23, 25–29, 1914–18, 1925–36, 1938–41.

Garrett-Evangelical and Seabury-Western Theological Seminaries—United Library (IL–110/1): V 1–19, 1914–41.

Gordon-Conwell Theological Seminary—Goddard Library (MA–230/4): V 1–29, 1914–41.

Graduate Theological Union Library (CA–15/2): V 1–29, 1914–41.

Harvard University—Widener Library (MA–155/1): V 1–11; V 12, N 2–12; V 13–15, N 11; V 16–17; V 19, N 1–7, 11; V 21, N 4, 6; V 22, N 2–9, 12; V 23, N 1; V 24, N 1–2, 4, 6; V 25–29, N 11; 1914–30, 1932, 1934–41.

Hoover Institution Archives (CA–290/16): V 24, N 10, O 1937.

Hoover Institution Library (CA–300/1): V 1–29, N 10–11, F 1914–Nv 1941.

Iowa State University Library (IA–5/1): V 1–17, 19–29, 1914–41.

Kalamazoo College—Upjohn Library (MI–125/1): V 1–29, 1914–41.

Oberlin College—Main Library (OH–175/1): 1914–41.

Ohio State University—Thompson Memorial Library (OH–110/4): V 1–29, 1914–41.

Stanford University—Green Library (CA–305/1): V 1–29, N 10–11, 1914–41.

Union Theological Seminary—Burke Library (NY–275/1): V 1–27, 1914–41.

University of Oregon—Department of Special Collections (OR–15/10): V 24, N 2, F 1937.
University of Oregon—Department of Special Collections (OR–15/42): V 16, N 2, F 1929.
University of Oregon Library (OR–20/2): V 13–27, 1927–41 (inc.).
Wheaton College—Graham Center Library (IL–205/1): V 1–29, 1914–41.
Yale Divinity School Library (CT–55/2): V 1–29, 1914–29, 1931–41.

China Christian Educational Association

BULLETIN. China Christian Educational Association, Shanghai. N 1, 1924–.

Brown University—Rockefeller Library (RI–20/2): N 20, 1928.
Claremont Colleges—Asian Studies Collection (CA–75/2): N 6, 25, 1925, 1928–29.
Columbia University—Milbank Library (NY–165/1): N 20, 1928.
Connecticut College—Shain Library (CT–85/1): N 18, 1926.
Cornell University—Wason Collection (NY–95/1) : N 20, 1928.
Duke University—Perkins Library (NC–55/1): N 1–2, 4–6, 8–14, 16–17, 20, 24, 31, 33, 37, 39–40, 43, 1924–28, 1933–39.
Emory University—Pitts Theology Library (GA–15/5): N 16, 18, 20, 24, 30, 1926–28, 1932–33.
Graduate Theological Union Library (CA–15/2): N 20, 1928.
Harvard Divinity School—Andover-Harvard Theological Library (MA–95/1): N 1, 40, 1922, 1936.
Harvard Divinity School—Andover-Harvard Theological Library (MA–95/2): N 31–37, 1933–36.
Harvard University—Harvard-Yenching Library (MA–125/6): N 20, 1928.
Hoover Institution Library (CA–300/1): N 14, 20, 1926, 1928.
Library of Congress—General Reading Rooms Division (DC–120/1): N 3, 5, 17–18, 29, 31, 33, 35–37, 1924–26, 1932–36.
New Brunswick Theological Seminary—Sage Library (NJ–65/2): N 20, 24, 30, 1928, 1933.
New York Public Library—General Research Division (NY–230/1): N 1–2, 4–11, 20, 1924–25, 1928.
Pennsylvania State University—Penn State Room (PA–275/4): N 20, 1928.
Princeton Theological Seminary—Speer Library (NJ–95/3): N 27–28, 37, 1930–31, 1936.
Smith College—Neilson Library (MA–190/1): N 16, 1926.
Southern Baptist Convention—Archives Center (VA–65/2): n.v., 1924.
Southern Baptist Theological Seminary—Boyce Centennial Library (KY–50/2): N 18, 1926.
Stanford University—Green Library (CA–305/1): N 20, 1928.
Union Theological Seminary—Burke Library (NY–275/1): N 1–43, 1924–39.

U.S. Department of Education—Educational Research Library (DC–180/1): N 1–3, 6–10, 16, 28, 30, 1924–26, 1929, 1931, 1933.
United Theological Seminary Library (OH–120/11): N 20, 1928.
University of Chicago—Regenstein Library (IL–85/1): N 18, 20, 1926, 1928.
University of Illinois at Urbana-Champaign Library (IL–185/1): N 3–4, 12, 14, 16, 18, 20, 1924, 1926, 1928.
University of Minnesota—Wilson Library (MN–40/1): N 20, 1928.
University of Oregon Library (OR–20/2): N 20, 1928.
University of Pennsylvania—Van Pelt Library (PA–215/1): N 5, 12, 1925–26.
Wellesley College—Clapp Library (MA–245/1): N 16, 20, 1926, 1928.
Yale Divinity School Library (CT–55/1): N 1–2, 4–6, 8–9, 11, 15–20, 24–29, 32, 1924–33.
Yale Divinity School Library (CT–55/2): N 20, 1928.
Yale Divinity School—Special Collections (CT–50/25): 1924–26, 1928–34, 1937–40.

JOURNAL. China Christian Educational Association, Fukien Christian Education Association Branch, Fukien. V 1-?, 1908-?

Union Theological Seminary—Burke Library (NY–275/1): V 1, N 3; V 2, N 3, 4, 1908, 1918–19.

CHINA CHRISTIAN NEWS LETTER. United Christian Missionary Society, Shanghai. V 1-, 1927(?)-.

Union Theological Seminary—Burke Library (NY–275/1): Mr, Nv, D 1928; Ja 1929.
University of Virginia—Alderman Library (VA–30/1): V 2, N 5–6, My–Je 1928.
Yale Divinity School Library (CT–55/2): V 2, N 5–6, 1928.

CHINA CHRISTIAN YEAR BOOK. National Christian Council of China, Christian Literature Society, Kwang Hsüeh Publishing House, Shanghai. V 14–21, 1926–39 (annually, 1928–29; biennially, 1926–27, 1931–39).

Title varies: CHINA MISSION YEAR BOOK, 1910–25.

Andover Newton Theological School—Trask Library (MA–180/2): V 14–21, 1926–39.
Andrews University—White Library (MI–50/1): 1911, 1917, 1919.
Asbury Theological Seminary—Fisher Library (KY–90/1): V 1–21, 1910–39.
Associated Mennonite Biblical Seminaries Library (IN–25/3): V 12, 1924.
Bangor Theological Seminary—Moulton Library (ME–5/1): V 12–14, 1924–26.
Baylor University—Moody Memorial Library (TX–60/1): V 1–13, 15–21, 1910–19, 1923–25, 1928–29, 1931–39.
Bethany and Northern Baptist Theological Seminaries Library (IL–135/1): V 15, 17, 1928, 1931.
Bethany College—Phillips Memorial Library (WV–5/1): V 1, 3, 10, 1910, 1912, 1919.
Bethel Theological Seminary Library (MN–50/1): V 9–

10, 13, 17, 19–20, 1918–19, 1925, 1931, 1934–37.

Biola University—Rose Memorial Library (CA–130/4): 1910–35.

Boston Public Library (MA–30/2): V 7, 11–, 1916, 1923–26, 1928–29, 1931–33.

Boston University—School of Theology Library (MA–35/1): 1911, 1916, 1919, 1923–25.

Brandeis University Library (MA–235/1): 1911.

Brown University—Rockefeller Library (RI–20/2): 1923–24, 1926.

Bucknell University—Bertrand Library (PA–100/2): 1926, 1928, 1931.

Buffalo and Erie County Public Library (NY–60/1): 1928, 1934–35.

Butler University—Irwin Library (IN–50/1): V 1, 16–17, 1910, 1926–27.

Calvin College and Seminary Library (MI–85/1): V 2–6, 8, 18–20, 1911–16, 1918, 1928–38.

Case Western Reserve University—Freiberger Library (OH–75/1): V 2, 1911.

Center for Research Libraries (IL–25/4): V 14–21, 1926–39.

Central Baptist Theological Seminary Library (KS–20/1): V 7–8, 10, 14, 16, 1916–17, 1919, 1926, 1929.

Christian Church (Disciples of Christ) Library (IN–55/1): V 1–17, 21, 1910–31, 1938–39.

Christian Theological Seminary Library (IN–60/2): V 1, 3–19, 21, 1910, 1912–35, 1938–39.

Claremont Colleges—Asian Studies Collection (CA–75/3): 1910–39.

Claremont Colleges—Honnold Library (CA–85/1): 1910–39.

Cleveland Public Library (OH–85/1): V 1–6, 8–21, 1910–15, 1917–39.

Columbia University—Butler Library (NY–150/1): V 2–4, 6, 10–20, 1911–13, 1915, 1917, 1919–29, 1931–39.

Cornell University—Wason Collection (NY–95/1) : V 1–21, 1910–39.

Dartmouth College Library (NH–15/1): V 10, 12–21, 1919, 1924–39.

Detroit Public Library (MI–55/1): V 12–16, 1924–28.

Drew University Library (NJ–40/2): V 1–21, 1910–39.

Duke University—Divinity School Library (NC–30/2): V 1–21, 1910–39.

Eastern Baptist Theological Seminary—DeBlois Library (PA–160/1): 1913, 1916.

Eden Theological Seminary—Eden-Webster Libraries (MO–60/1): V 6, 9, 17, 29–21, 1915, 1918, 1931, 1934–39.

Emory University—Pitts Theology Library (GA–15/5): 1910–39.

Evangelical and Reformed Historical Society—Schaff Library (PA–80/1): V 1–2, 4, 7, 9–12, 14, 16–20; 1910–11, 1913, 1916, 1918–24, 1926, 1929–39.

Evangelical and Reformed Historical Society—Schaff Library (PA–80/13): 1931, 1938–39.

Florida Southern College—Roux Library (FL–20/1): V 17, 1931.

Franklin and Marshall College—Shadek-Fackenthal Library (PA–85/1): 1919, 1925–26.

Free Library of Philadelphia (PA–165/1): 1910, 1913–17, 1923–25, 1928–39.

Fuller Theological Seminary—McAlister Library (CA–205/1): V 1–21, 1910–39.

General Theological Library (MA–60/1): 1926, 1928–29, 1931.

Georgetown University—Lauinger Library (DC–60/1): 1925.

Gordon-Conwell Theological Seminary—Goddard Library (MA–230/4): V 1–21, 1910–39.

Graduate Theological Union Library (CA–15/2): 1926–39.

Greenville College—Dare Library (IL–120/1): V 2, 1911.

Harvard Divinity School—Andover-Harvard Theological Library (MA–95/2): V 2–5, 7–16, 19–21, 1911–14, 1916–29, 1934–39.

Harvard University—Harvard-Yenching Library (MA–125/6): V 14, 1926.

Harvard University—Widener Library (MA–155/1): V 14–21, 1926–39.

Historical Foundation of the Presbyterian and Reformed Churches (NC–80/28): 1911–14, 1916, 1918–19, 1923, 1929.

Hoover Institution Library (CA–300/1): V 1–19, 21, 1910–35, 1938–39.

Iowa State University Library (IA–5/1): V 1–21, 1910–39.

Kalamazoo College—Upjohn Library (MI–125/1): V 1–21, 1910–39.

Kansas City Public Library (MO–30/1): V 12–13, 15, 1924–25, 1928.

Library of Congress—General Reading Rooms Division (DC–120/1): 1911–19, 1923–39.

Luther College Archives (IA–15/2): 1913–19, 1923–26, 1928–29.

Luther Northwestern Theological Seminary Library (MN–100/1): V 1–16, 19, 21, 1910–19, 1923–26, 1928–29, 1934–35, 1938–39.

Lutheran Theological Seminary—Krauth Memorial Library (PA–180/1): 1928–29, 1931–39.

Maryknoll Fathers and Brothers Library (NY–115/1): 1925–26.

Memphis Theological Seminary Library (TN–40/1): V 1–2, 4–13, 14–17, 19, 21, 1910–11, 1913–19, 1923–26, 1928–29, 1931, 1934–35, 1938–39.

Miami University—King Library (OH–185/1): 1928.

Milwaukee Public Library (WI–65/1): V 8, 11–21, 1917, 1923–39.

Mount Holyoke College—Williston Memorial Library (MA–225/1): V 4–21, 1913–39.

Nashotah House (WI–80/1): V 16, 1934–35.

New Brunswick Theological Seminary—Sage Library (NJ–65/2): 1926, 1928–29, 1931–35.

New Orleans Baptist Theological Seminary—Christian Library (LA–15/1): V 14–20, 1926, 1928–29, 1931–37.

Northwestern University Library (IL–115/1): V 12–15, 17–19, 21, 1924–28, 1930–35, 1940.

Nyack College Library (NY–315/1): 1938–39.

Oberlin College—Main Library (OH–175/1): 1926–31.

Ohio State University—Thompson Memorial Library (OH–110/4): V 1–21, 1910–39.

Ohio Wesleyan University—Beeghly Library (OH–140/1): 1938–39.

Overseas Missionary Fellowship (PA–265/1): 1928, 1931, 1934–35.

Pittsburgh Theological Seminary—Barbour Library (PA–240/1): V 9–20, 1918–19, 1923–26, 1928–29, 1931–37.

Princeton Theological Seminary—Speer Library (NJ–95/3): 1910–39.

Princeton University—Firestone Library (NJ–100/1): 1910–39.

Rutgers University—Alexander Library (NJ–75/1): 1912, 1919.

St. John's University—Alcuin Library (MN–5/1): V 19, 1934–35.

St. Louis Public Library (MO–70/1): V 15, 1928.

St. Olaf College—Rölvaag Memorial Library (MN–80/1): V 8, 15, 1917, 1928.

Scarritt Graduate School—Laskey Library (TN–50/1): 1910–37.

School of Theology at Claremont Library (CA–90/1): 1911–12, 1916–23, 1931.

Seattle Public Library (WA–30/1): V 10–11, 14, 16, 21, 1919–39.

Seton Hall University—McLaughlin Library (NJ–140/1): 1919.

Sioux Falls College—Mears Library (SD–20/1): V 2, 1911.

Southern Baptist Convention—Jenkins Research Library (VA–70/1): 1926–39.

Southern Baptist Theological Seminary—Boyce Centennial Library (KY–50/2): V 1–5, 7–21, 1910–14, 1916–39.

Southern Methodist University—Bridwell Theology Library (TX–20/2): V 7, 11–21, 1916, 1923–26, 1928–29, 1931–39.

Southwestern Baptist Theological Seminary—Roberts Library (TX–25/3): V 1–21, 1911–19, 1923–25, 1926, 1928–29, 1931–39.

Stanford University—Green Library (CA–305/1): V 1–21, 1910–39.

Temple University—Paley Library (PA–210/2): 1926, 1934–35.

Trinity Evangelical Divinity School Library (IL–90/1): V 20, 1936–37.

Union Theological Seminary in Virginia Library (VA–85/1): 1910–12, 1923–24, 1931, 1934–39.

United Theological Seminary Library (OH–120/11): V 14–21, 1926–39.

United Theological Seminary of the Twin Cities Library (MN–55/1): V 17–19, 1931–35.

University of California at Los Angeles—University Research Library (CA–185/1): 1931.

University of California, Berkeley—General Library (CA–70/1): V 1–3, 7, 11, 14–15, 20–21, 1910–12, 1916, 1923, 1926–28, 1931, 1936–39.

University of California, Davis, Library (CA–110/2): 1911–12, 1914–17, 1919, 1923–26, 1929, 1931.

University of California, Santa Barbara—Department of Special Collections (CA–270/1): 1912–13, 1918, 1928, 1931, 1934–35.

University of Chicago—Regenstein Library (IL–85/1): V 1–20, 1910–37.

University of Georgia Libraries (GA–5/1): V 14, 19, 1926, 1934–35.

University of Hawaii—Hamilton Library (HI–15/1): 1915, 1936–37.

University of Hawaii—Hamilton Library (HI–15/2): 1926–39.

University of Illinois at Urbana-Champaign Library (IL–185/1): V 2, 4–6, 12, 16, 18–21, 1911, 1913–15, 1924, 1929, 1932–39.

University of Iowa Libraries (IA–40/1): 1917, 1919, 1926, 1938–39.

University of Kansas—Watson Library (KS–35/3): 1910–14, 1923–25.

University of Massachusetts at Amherst Library (MA–15/2): 1928–29, 1931.

University of Michigan—Hatcher Graduate Library (MI–25/1): V 14–21, 1926–39.

University of Minnesota—Wilson Library (MN–40/1): V 1–4, 14–15, 19–21, 1910–13, 1926–28, 1934–35, 1938–39.

University of Missouri-Columbia—Ellis Library (MO–10/1): V 2, 8, 10, 15–16, 1911, 1917, 1919, 1928–29.

University of Notre Dame Memorial Library (IN–95/1): V 1–21, 1910-1939.

University of Oregon Library (OR–20/2): V 20, 1936–37.

University of Pittsburgh—Hillman Library (PA–260/1): 1932–33.

University of Redlands—Armacost Library (CA–210/1): 1918, 1923, 1925–26, 1928–29, 1936–37.

University of Southern California—Von Kleinsmid Center Library (CA–190/2): 1932–33.

University of Vermont—Bailey/Howe Library (VT–5/3): 1919, 1926, 1928.

University of Washington Libraries (WA–45/1): V 3, 8–9, 15, 17, 20, 1912, 1917–18, 1928, 1931, 1936–37.

University of Wisconsin-Madison—Memorial Library (WI–45/1), V 1–3, 5–21, 1910–12, 1914–39.

University of Wyoming—Coe Library (WY–5/1): 1927.

Vassar College Library (NY–330/1): V 14–15, 1926, 1928.

Virginia Theological Seminary—Payne Library (VA–5/1): 1911–13, 1924, 1929.

Washington University—Olin Library (MO–95/1): V 3, 1912.

Wellesley College—Clapp Library (MA–245/1): 1928–29.

Wells College Library (NY–30/1): V 8, 12, 20, 1917, 1924, 1936–37.

Western Baptist College Library (OR–40/1): 1915.

Western Kentucky University—Helm-Cravens Library (KY–10/1): V 11–20, 1923–36.

Western Theological Seminary—Beardslee Library (MI–120/14): V 2–3, 11, 16, 17, 21, 1911–12, 1923, 1929, 1931, 1938–39.

Wheaton College—Buswell Library (IL–195/1): 1929.

Wheaton College—Graham Center Library (IL–205/1): V 1–21, 1910–39.

Yale Divinity School Library (CT–55/2): V 1–21, 1910–39.

Yale Divinity School—Special Collections (CT–50/2): 1928–29, 1932–37.

Yale University—Sterling Memorial Library (CT–80/1): V 1–5, 7–21, 1910–14, 1916–19, 1923–39.

CHINA CIRCULAR BULLETIN. n.p.

Harvard Divinity School—Andover-Harvard Theological Library (MA–95/2): V 52, N 1–6, 1951–52.

CHINA COLLEGES. United Board for Christian Higher Education in Asia, New York. V 1–20, Je 1934- (quarterly).

Title varies: NEW HORIZONS FOR THE CHINA COLLEGES, THE CHINA COLLEGES FIND NEW HORIZONS, Je 1952-D 1955. Publisher name varies: Associated Boards for Christian Colleges in China, Je 1934-Je 1947; United Board for Christian Colleges in China, S 1947-D 1955. Continued as NEW HORIZONS, V 21, N 1, My 1953.

Asian Studies Newsletter Archives (MD–40/1): V 16, N 3-V 20, N 3, 1949–53.

Carleton College Archives (MN–60/1): V 5, N 1; V 10, N 4; O 1938, Je 1943.

Columbia University—School of Library Service Library (NY–180/1): V [14–22], O 1946-Jl 1955.

Francis A. Countway Library of Medicine (MA–55/1): V 1–3, 1934–37.

Harvard Divinity School—Andover-Harvard Theological Library (MA–95/1): V 19, N 1, O 1951.

Harvard Divinity School—Andover-Harvard Theological Library (MA–95/2): V 19, N 1-V 35, N 1, O 1951-Spr 1966.

Harvard University—Harvard-Yenching Library (MA–125/6): V 14, N 3, 4, V 15, N 1, 4–5, 1947–48.

Harvard University—Widener Library (MA–155/1): V 1, N 1–3; V 2, N 1; V 3, N 1; V 5, N 1; V 7, N 1–2; V 8, N 1–3; V 9, N 1–2; V 10, N 3–4; V 11; V 12, N 1–3; V 13–14; V 15, N 1–2, 4–5; V 16–17; V 18, N 1, 3–4; V 19; V 20, N 1–3; V 21, N 3; V 22; V 23, N 1; 1934–35, 1937–38, 1940–55.

Hoover Institution Library (CA–300/1): V 1, 3, 5–16, 1934–35, 1937–48.

Princeton University—Firestone Library (NJ–100/1): V 7–14, Spring 1941-Je 1947.

Princeton University—University Archives (NJ–120/2): V 23, N 3, D 1955.

Union Theological Seminary in Virginia Library (VA–85/1): V 16–20, 1948–53.

University of Illinois at Urbana-Champaign Library (IL–185/1): V 1, N 1–3; V 2, N 1; V 5, N 1–3; V 6, N 1–2; V 8, N 1–3; V 9, N 1–2; V 10, N 3–4; V 11–18; V 34, N 3; V 35, N 1–3; V 36, N 1; V 37, N 1; V 38, N 1; V 39, N 1–2; V 40, N 1–3; V 41, N 1–3; V 42, N 1–3; V 43, N 1–3, V 44, N 1–3; V 45, N 1–3; V 46, N 1–3; V 47, N 1–3; V 48, N 1, 3; V 49, N 1, 3; V 52, N 1; Je, O 1934-Spr 1935; Aut 1935; O-Nv 1938; Mr, S 1939; Mr, Aut 1940; Spr, D 1941; Mr, Je, O, D 1942; Mr, Je, O 1943-F 1951.

University of Missouri-Columbia—Joint Collection-Western Historical Manuscript Collection and State Historical

Society of Missouri Manuscripts (MO–5/6): V 11, N 2, 1944.

University of Oregon—Department of Special Collections (OR–15/43): V 7, N 2; V 8, N 2–3; V 9, N 2; 1940–42.

Wellesley College Archives (MA–240/3): Nv 1938-D 1954 (inc.).

Wheaton College—Graham Center Library (IL–205/1): V [1–9], 1934–42.

Yale Divinity School—Special Collections (CT–50/25): V 1, N 1–3; V 2, N 1; V 3, N 1; V 5, N 1–3; V 6, N 1–2; V 7, N 1–2; V 8, N 1–3; V 9, N 1–2; V 10, N 3–4; V 11, N 1–2, 4; V 12, N 1–4; V 13, N 1–4; V 14, N 1–2, 4; V 15, N 1–4; 1934–35, 1937–48.

Yale Divinity School—Special Collections (CT–50/26): V 15, N 3–5; V 16, N 1–2; V 21, N 1–3; V 22, N 1–4; 1948–55.

CHINA CONTINUATION COMMITTEE BULLETIN. n.p.

Emory University—Pitts Theology Library (GA–15/5): N 2, 11–13, n.d.

CHINA COUNCIL BULLETIN. The China Council, Presbyterian Church in the U.S.A., Shanghai. N 1-?, 1920-?

Historical Foundation of the Presbyterian and Reformed Churches (NC–80/28): N 144–145, Ag-Nv 1933.

Union Theological Seminary in Virginia Library (VA–85/1): N 1–100, Nv 1920–29.

CHINA DIVISION REPORTER. China Division, General Conference of Seventh-Day Adventists, Shanghai. V 1–20, 1931–51. Not published 1942–47.

Andrews University—White Library (MI–50/1): V 1–6, [7], 8, [9], 10–15, 1931–45.

General Conference of Seventh-Day Adventists Archives (DC–40/1): V 1–20, 1931–51.

Loma Linda University Library (CA–220/1): V 1–16, N 1, 1931–51.

Loma Linda University—Radcliffe Memorial Library (CA–135/1): V 1–6; V 7, N 1–7, 10–12; V 8–10; V 11, N 1–9, 11; V 12, N 1–4; V 13, N 2–12; V 14–15; V 16, N 1; 1931–41, 1947–51.

Union College Library (NB–20/1): V 1–7, 12–14, 1931–38, 1943–45.

CHINA EVANGELICAL SEMINARY NEWS BULLETIN. China Evangelical Seminary, Lexington, MA.

Gordon-Conwell Theological Seminary—Goddard Library (MA–230/4): N 65-, 1978-.

Trinity Evangelical Divinity School Library (IL–90/1): N 47, 61–69, 71-, Je 1975, My 1977-O 1978, 1979-.

CHINA EVANGELISM. Seventh-Day Adventists. n.p.

Loma Linda University—Radcliffe Memorial Library (CA–135/1): 1977–80.

CHINA FOR CHRIST: Bulletin of the China-for-Christ Movement. China-For-Christ Movement, Shanghai. N 1, Ja 1920.

Union Theological Seminary—Burke Library (NY–275/1): N 1, Ja 1920.

CHINA FOR CHRIST. National Christian Council of China, Shanghai.

Drew University Library (NJ–40/2): N 208–12, 215–16, 1940–41.

THE CHINA FUNDAMENTALIST. Christian Fundamentals League of China, Yencheng. V 1–12, 1928–40 (quarterly).
Continues THE CHINA FUNDAMENTALIST AND ANTI-BOLSHEVIK BULLETIN.
Bethel Theological Seminary Library (MN–50/1): V 2–4, 8, 1929–31, 1935.
Columbia Theological Seminary—Campbell Library (GA–35/1): V 1, N 2–4; V 3, N 2–4; V 4–8; 1928–29, 1930–36.
Emory University—Pitts Theology Library (GA–15/5): V 6–7, 9, 1933–35, 1937.
Garrett-Evangelical and Seabury-Western Theological Seminaries—United Library (IL–110/1): V 2, N 3–4; V 3; V 5, N 1–3; V 6; 1930–34.
Historical Foundation of the Presbyterian and Reformed Churches (NC–80/28): V 1–12, 1928–40.
Hoover Institution Library (CA–300/1): V 8, 1936.
Princeton Theological Seminary—Speer Library (NJ–95/3): Nv 1928; Jl-D 1931; Ja-Mr, Jl-D 1932; 1933–38; Wint 1939; Ap-Je 1940.
Trinity Evangelical Divinity School Library (IL–90/1): V 5–6, O 1932-S 1933.
Union Theological Seminary in Virginia Library (VA–85/1): V [1–3], 4–11, [12], 1928–40.
University of Virginia—Alderman Library (VA–30/1): V [1–4], 1928–32.
Washington and Lee University Library (VA–55/3): V 3–4, N 1–4; V 6, N 4; V 7–11, N 1–4; V 12, N 1–2, 1930–31, 1934–40.
Yale Divinity School Library (CT–55/2): V 2–12, 1929–40.

CHINA FUNDAMENTALIST AND ANTI-BOLSHEVIK BULLETIN. Christian Fundamentals League of China, Shanghai. V 1, 1928.
Moody Bible Institute Library (IL–55/1): V 1, N 1, My 1928.
Union Theological Seminary—Burke Library (NY–275/1): V 1, N 1–4; V 2, N 1–3, 1928–29.

CHINA GLEANINGS. Lutheran United Missions, Honan. 1923-.
Title varies: also, GLEANINGS.
American Lutheran Church Archives (MN–95/110): V 2, N 1–2, 4; V 3, N 2; V 4, N 1–3; V 7, N 2–3; V 9–15; 1920–22, 1926, 1932–38.
Luther Northwestern Theological Seminary Library (MN–100/1): V 6–15, 1924–36.
St. Olaf College—Rölvaag Memorial Library (MN–80/1): V 13–15, 1936–38.

China Graduate School of Theology, Philadelphia, PA
BULLETIN (English edition). China Graduate School of Theology, Philadelphia, PA.
American Baptist Seminary of the West Library (CA–10/1): N 5, 1972.
Andrews University—White Library (MI–50/1): N 5–84 (inc.), 1972–82.
Asian Studies Newsletter Archives (MD–40/1): 1982- (inc.).
Baptist Missionary Association Theological Seminary—Kellar Library (TX–45/1): N 57–72, 74–84, 91, 110, 113, 121, 124, Je 1980-Ap 1981, Je 1981-

Nv 1982, Je 1983, Ja, Ap, D 1985, Mr 1986.
Bethel Theological Seminary Library (MN–50/1): N 6–17, 19–22, 26–84, 1972–84.
Gordon-Conwell Theological Seminary—Goddard Library (MA–230/4): N 42–66, 68–84, 1978.
Lutheran Theological Southern Seminary—Lineberger Memorial Library (SC–20/1): N 4–84, 1972–82.
San Francisco Theological Seminary Library (CA–235/2): N 9, 13–15, 33, 37, D 1973-?.
Union Theological Seminary—Burke Library (NY–275/1): N 1-, 1971-.
NEWS LETTER. China Graduate School of Theology, Philadelphia, PA. V 1-, 1971-.
Union Theological Seminary—Burke Library (NY–275/1): V 1, N 2, 1971-.

CHINA HEUTE: Informationen über Religion und Christentum im chinesischen Raum. Steyler Mission, Sankt Augustin, Federal Republic of Germany. N 1, 1982.
Asian Studies Newsletter Archives (MD–40/1): N 1-, 1982-.
Catholic Theological Union Library (IL–20/1): 1985-.

CHINA INDEPENDENT MISSION LETTERS. China Independent Mission, Shanghai. 1925?–29?.
Union Theological Seminary—Burke Library (NY–275/1): 1925, 1929.

CHINA INFORMATION COMMITTEE NEWS RELEASES (CHUNGKING).
Union Theological Seminary—Burke Library (NY–275/1): N 146–366, Je 1938-Nv 1941.

China Inland Mission/Overseas Missionary Fellowship
FIELD BULLETIN. China Inland Mission.
Overseas Missionary Fellowship (PA–265/1): V 1, N 1-V 14, N 3, 1939–52.
DIRECTORY.
Wheaton College—Graham Center Archives (IL–200/50): 1900–1937, 1939–50, 1952.
LIST OF MISSIONARIES AND THEIR STATIONS. China Inland Mission, Shanghai Mercury, Shanghai.
Princeton Theological Seminary—Speer Library (NJ–95/3): 1915, 1921.
Union Theological Seminary—Burke Library (NY–275/1): 1891, 1910, 1914, 1917, 1922–24, 1936–37, 1939–41.
Wheaton College—Graham Center Library (IL–205/1): 1912–21.
MONTHLY NOTES. China Inland Mission.
Wheaton College—Graham Center Archives (IL–200/50): 1896–1938.
Wheaton College—Graham Center Archives (IL–200/73): n.d.
OCCASIONAL PAPERS. China Inland Mission, London. V 1–7, N 1–39, Ja 1866–75.
Issued January 1866-May 1868 as CHINA INLAND MISSION OCCASIONAL PAPER. Reprinted in 1973 in Taipei: Ch'eng-wen Publishing Co.
Brigham Young University—Lee Library (UT–10/1):

1872–75 (repr. 1973).

Cornell University—Wason Collection (NY–95/1): 1872–75 (repr. 1973).

Essex Institute—Phillips Library (MA–210/2): V 1–2, N 1–13, V 5–8, N 23–39, 1866–75.

Harvard University—Widener Library (MA–155/1): V 1–7, 1866–75.

Hoover Institution Library (CA–300/1): N 31–39, 1872–75.

Iowa State University Library (IA–5/1): 1872–75 (repr. 1973).

Oberlin College—Main Library (OH–175/1): N 1–76, 1866–?.

Ohio State University—Thompson Memorial Library (OH–110/4): 1872–75 (repr. 1973).

Overseas Missionary Fellowship (PA–265/1): N 1–39, 1866–75.

Presbyterian Historical Society—Archives and Library (PA–200/28): N 14–31, 1868–72.

Seton Hall University—McLaughlin Library (NJ–140/1): 1872–75 (repr. 1973).

Union Theological Seminary—Burke Library (NY–275/1): 1866–75.

University of Vermont—Bailey/Howe Library (VT–5/3): N 1872-Mr 1975 (repr. 1973).

University of Virginia—Alderman Library (VA–30/1): N 1872-Mr 1975 (repr. 1973).

Westminster Theological Seminary Library (PA–220/2): 1872–75 (repr. 1973).

REVIEW. London, Philadelphia.

Title varies: 1903–59, REPORT.

Cornell University—Wason Collection (NY–95/1): 1951–64.

Yale Divinity School Library (CT–55/2): 1903–45, 1947–65.

See also CHINA AND THE GOSPEL, LAND OF SINIM, CHINA'S MILLIONS, EAST ASIA MILLIONS, THE MILLIONS, and THE STORY OF THE CHINA INLAND MISSION.

China International Famine Relief Commission

BULLETIN. China International Famine Relief Commission, New York. V 1–14, O 1923-D 1936.

Text in Chinese and English.

Claremont Colleges—Honnold Library (CA–85/1): V 1, N 2–3, 5–6; V 2, N 1–5; V 3, 1–5; V 4, N 1–5; V 5, N 1–4; V 6, N 1–4; V 7, N 1–3, 5; V 8, N 4; V 9, N 2–4; V 10, N 1–3, 5; V 11, N 1–5; V 12, N 1–12; V 13, N 1–9, 12; V 14, N 1–3; 1923–26.

Harvard University—Widener Library (MA–155/1): V 3, N 1–2, 5; V 4, N 1, 3, 5; V 5, N 1–5; 1925–28.

New York Public Library—General Research Division (NY–230/1): V 1–14, O 1923-D 1936.

Stanford University—Green Library (CA–305/1): V 7, 1929.

Union Theological Seminary—Burke Library (NY–275/1): V 1, N 5, n.v.; V 7, N 1–4; V 8, N 1–2, 4–5; V 9, N 1–5; V 10, N 1–5; V 11, N 1–5; V 12, N 1–12; V 13, N 1–7, 10–12; V 14, N 1–3; 1924, 1927–36.

University of Oregon Library (OR–20/2): V 1–14, O 1923-D 1936.

NEWS BULLETIN. China International Famine Relief Commission, Shanghai. V 1–, Jl 1935-.

Claremont Colleges—Honnold Library (CA–85/1): V 1, N 1–3; V 2, 1–4; V 3, N 1–8; V 4, N 1–3; 1935–39.

New York Public Library—General Research Division (NY–230/1): 1937–39.

Union Theological Seminary—Burke Library (NY–275/1): V 1, N 2; V 3, N 2; V 4, N 1–3, Jl 1935, F 1937, F-Mr 1939.

University of Arizona Library (AZ–5/3): V 4, N 3, Mr 1939.

University of California at Los Angeles—University Research Library (CA–185/1): V 1, N 1; V 4, N 1–3, 1935, 1938–39.

Yale University—Sterling Memorial Library (CT–80/1): V 3–4, 1937–39.

PUBLICATIONS. China International Famine Relief Commission, New York.

SERIES A. Annual Reports. N 1–, 1922–42.

Boston Public Library (MA–30/2): N 1, 5, 7, 11, 12, 19, 26, 28, 30, 34, 36, 40, 42, 1922–24, 1926, 1929–34.

Brown University—Rockefeller Library (RI–20/2): N 19, 23, 26, 28, 30, 1927–31.

Center for Research Libraries (IL–25/4): N 47, 1936.

Claremont Colleges—Honnold Library (CA–85/1): N 1, 4–7, 11–12, 14, 16, 18–23, 25–26, 28–30, 32, 34–42, 44–48, 50–51, 1923–37.

Columbia University—Butler Library (NY–150/1): N 1–5, 12, 16, 19, 23, 26, 28, 30, 34, 36, 40, 42, 45, 50, 1922–36.

Cornell University—Wason Collection (NY–95/1) : N 1–13, 16–23, 25–32, 34–41, 1923–32.

Detroit Public Library (MI–55/1): N 1, 5, 7, 12, 19, 23, 26, 28, 30, 34, 36, 40, 42, 45, 50, 1921–24, 1926–36.

Harvard Divinity School—Andover-Harvard Theological Library (MA–95/1): N 1–?, 1923–?.

Harvard University—Harvard-Yenching Library (MA–125/6): N 1, 5, 11, 12, 16, 19, 21, 23, 25, 26, 28, 30, 32, 34, 36, 38, 40, 42, 45, 47, 50, 1923–32, 1934–37.

Hoover Institution Library (CA–300/1): 1922, 1926, 1928, 1930–36.

Johns Hopkins University—Eisenhower Library (MD–10/1): N 1, 4–7, 9, 11–12, 16–19, 21–23, 25–32, 34–36, 40, 42, 45, 47, 50, 1923–37.

Library of Congress—General Reading Rooms Division (DC–120/1): N [1–47], 1922–35(?).

Michigan State University Library (MI–75/1): N 1–?, 1922–36.

New York Academy of Medicine Library (NY–220/1): N 12, 42, 1924, 1934.

New York Public Library—General Research Division (NY–230/1): 1923–37 (inc.).

Oberlin College—Main Library (OH–175/1): N 7, 12, 16, 19, 23, 26, 28, 34, 36, 40, 42, 45, 47, 50, 1924–30, 1932–36.

Princeton University—Firestone Library (NJ–100/1): 1922–24, 1925, 1928–36.

Seattle Public Library (WA–30/1): N 1–50, 1922–36.

Smith College—Neilson Library (MA–190/1): N 1, 5, 7, 12, 16, 19, 23, 26, 28, 30, 34, 36, 40, 42, 45, 1922–35.

Stanford University—Green Library (CA–305/1): N 1–45, 1922–36.

State University of New York at Buffalo—Lockwood Library (NY–75/1): 1925, 1927, 1930–35.

Syracuse University—Archives (NY–375/2): N 1–45, 1922–36.

Union Theological Seminary—Burke Library (NY–275/1): N 1, 5, 7, 11–12, 16, 19, 23, 26, 28, 30, 34, 36, 40, 42, 45, 50, 1922–37.

University of Arizona Library (AZ–5/3): N 12, 16, 19, 28, 30, 40, 45, 50, 1924–26, 1929–30, 1933–36, 1938.

University of California at Los Angeles—University Research Library (CA–185/1): N 38, 1934.

University of California, Berkeley—General Library (CA–70/1): N 1, 4, 5, 7, 9, 11, 12, 14, 16, 19, 21, 23, 25, 26, 28, 30, 32, 34, 36, 38, 40, 42, 45, 47, 50, 1922–36.

University of Chicago—Regenstein Library (IL–85/1): N 1–50, 1922–36.

University of Illinois at Urbana-Champaign Library (IL–185/1): N 4, 30, 34, 36, 40, 42, 45, 47, 50, 1923, 1931–37.

University of Michigan—Hatcher Graduate Library (MI–25/1): N [1–50], 1922–36.

University of Missouri-Columbia—Ellis Library (MO–10/1): 1922–36.

University of Oregon Library (OR–20/2): N 1, 5, 12, 14, 16, 19, 23, 26, 28, 30, 34, 36, 40, 42, 45, 47, 50, 1922–36.

University of Rochester—Rhees Library (NY–360/2): N 26, 28, 30, 34, 36, 40–41, 45, 50, 1928–36, 1938.

University of Southern California—Von Kleinsmid Center Library (CA–190/2): N 1–50, 1922–36.

University of Virginia—Alderman Library (VA–30/1): N [1–50], 1922–36.

University of Washington Libraries (WA–45/1): N 1, 5, 12, 16, 19, 23, 26, 28, 30, 34, 36, 40, 42, 45, 50, 1922–36.

University of Wisconsin-Madison—Memorial Library (WI–45/1): N 1–2, 5, 12, 16, 19, 23, 26, 28, 30, 34, 36, 40, 42, 45, 47, 50, 1922–36.

Vassar College Library (NY–330/1): 1923–25, 1927–36.

Yale Divinity School Library (CT–55/1): N 34, 45, 47, 50, 1932, 1936–37.

Yale University—Sterling Memorial Library (CT–80/1): N 1, 5, 7, 11–12, 16, 19, 23, 26, 28, 30, 34, 36, 40, 42, 45, 47, 50, 1923–37.

SERIES B. N 1, 1922–.

Boston Public Library (MA–30/2): N 3, 10, 1923–24.

Claremont Colleges—Honnold Library (CA–85/1): N 10–11, 14–15, 17–19, 22–23, 28–31, 36–37, 41, 49, 51, 1924–26, 1928–31, 1933.

Columbia University—Butler Library (NY–150/1): N 10, 37, 1924, 1930.

Cornell University—Wason Collection (NY–95/1) : N 1–20, 22–23, 25, 28–50, 52–54, 56–59, 61–63, 65–70, 72, 83, 1923-?

Detroit Public Library (MI–55/1): N 22, 41, 1926, 1930.

Harvard Divinity School—Andover-Harvard Theological Library (MA–95/1): N 38, 1930.

Harvard Divinity School—Andover-Harvard Theological Library (MA–95/2): N 47, 1931.

Harvard University—Harvard-Yenching Library (MA–125/6): N 3, 1923.

Harvard University—Widener Library (MA–155/1): N 2–3, 38, 41, 47, 49, 1923, 1930–31.

Library of Congress—General Reading Rooms Division (DC–120/1): N [1–41], 1922–30(?).

Mount Holyoke College—Williston Memorial Library (MA–225/1): N 19, 41, 1926, 1930.

New York Public Library—General Research Division (NY–230/1): 1922–36 (inc.).

Oberlin College—Main Library (OH–175/1): N 19, 36, 41, 1926, 1929–30.

Princeton University—Firestone Library (NJ–100/1): N 37, 1930 (repr. 1980).

Smith College—Neilson Library (MA–190/1): N 3, 19, 41, 1923, 1930.

Stanford University—Green Library (CA–305/1): N [2–44], 1922–30(?).

State University of New York at Buffalo—Lockwood Library (NY–75/1): N 37, 1930 (repr. 1980).

Union Theological Seminary—Burke Library (NY–275/1): N 2–3, 1923.

University of California at Los Angeles—University Research Library (CA–185/1): N 61, 1935.

University of California, Berkeley—General Library (CA–70/1): N 1, 3, 8–10, 18–15, 18, 19, 22, 28–30, 36 38, 41, 61, 1922–35.

University of California, Davis, Library (CA–110/2): N 37, 1930 (repr. 1980).

University of Chicago—Regenstein Library (IL–85/1): N 6–69, 1924–34.

University of Illinois at Urbana-Champaign Library (IL–185/1): N 3, 8–10, 15, 18–19, 28–30, 36–38, 41, 47, Jl 1923, S 1923-My 1924, Ag 1924, F-Ap 1926, Ap-Jl 1928, Nv 1929-Ap 1930, Je 1930, Ap 1931.

University of Michigan—Hatcher Graduate Library (MI–25/1): N 3, [10–19], 36, 41, 1923–26, 1929–30.

University of Oregon Library (OR–20/2): N 22, 28–29, 1926–28.

Vassar College Library (NY–330/1): N 19, 36, n.v., 1926, 1929, 1931–32.

Wellesley College—Clapp Library (MA–245/1): N 10, 1924.

Yale University—Sterling Memorial Library (CT–80/1): N 3, 10, 19, 36–37, 41, 1923–24, 1926, 1929–30, 1977.

SERIES C. N 1–3, 1923–24?
    Cornell University—Wason Collection (NY-95/1): N 1, 3, 1923–24.
SERIES E. N 1–12, 1932–36?
    Boston Public Library (MA-30/2): N 4, 1932.
    Cornell University—Wason Collection (NY-95/1): N 1–4, 1932.
    Harvard University—Widener Library (MA-155/1): N 4, 1932.
    Library of Congress—General Reading Rooms Division (DC-120/1): N 4, 1932.
    University of California, Berkeley—General Library (CA-70/1): N 4, 1932.
    University of Michigan—Hatcher Graduate Library (MI-25/1): N 4, 1932.
SERIES G. N 1–?, 1934–?
    Cornell University—Wason Collection (NY-95/1): N 1–13, 1934–?
    New York Public Library—General Research Division (NY-230/1): N 1, 1934.

CHINA LAW REVIEW (in English and Chinese). Soochow University, Department of Law, Shanghai. V 1, Ap 1922–.
    California State Library (CA-230/1): V 1–10, N 1, Ap 1922-Je 1937.
    Claremont Colleges—Honnold Library (CA-85/1): V 1, 1922–24.
    Columbia University—Law Library (NY-155/1): V 1–10, N 1, Ap 1922-Je 1937.
    Cornell University—Wason Collection (NY-95/1) : V 1–10, N 12, 1922–37, 1940.
    Duke University—Law School Library (NC-40/1): V 1–9, 1922–31.
    Georgetown University—Dennis Law Library (DC-55/1): V6, 1928.
    Harvard University—Law Library (MA-135/1): V 1–6, 1922–33.
    Indiana University—University Libraries (IN-20/2): V 1–10, 1922–40.
    Johns Hopkins University—Eisenhower Library (MD-10/1): V 1–4, 1925–29.
    Library of Congress—General Reading Rooms Division (DC-120/1): 1922, 1937–40.
    Los Angeles County Law Library (CA-140/1): V 1–10, 1922–37.
    Louisiana State University—Law Center Library (LA-5/1): V 1–10, 1922–40.
    New York Public Library—General Research Division (NY-230/1): Ap 1922-F 1935.
    University of California at Los Angeles—Law Library (CA-170/1): V 1–9, Ap 1922-Mr 1937.
    University of California, Berkeley—Law Library (CA-60/1): 1922-Mr 1937.
    University of California, Davis—Law Library (CA-105/1): V 1–10, 1922–24, 1937–40.
    University of Chicago—Law Library (IL-80/1): V 1–10, N 2, 1922–40.
    University of Illinois at Urbana-Champaign—Law Library (IL-175/1): V 1- 10, 1922–40.
    University of Michigan—Law Library (MI-30/1): V 1–10, 1922–40.
    University of Minnesota—Law Library (MN-35/1): V 1–10, N 1, 1922–37.
    University of Washington—East Asia Library (WA-35/1): V 1–10, 1922–40.
    University of Washington Libraries (WA-45/1): V 1–10, 1922–40.
    University of Wisconsin-Madison—Law Library (WI-40/1): V 1–10, 1922–37.
    Washington University—Freund Law Library (MO-90/1): V 1–10, 1922–40.
    Yale University—Law Library (CT-70/1): V 1–10, 1922–40.

CHINA LETTER. American Jesuits in China, San Francisco. Continues YOUR CHINA LETTER, 1955.
    Georgetown University—Woodstock Theological Center Library (DC-70/4): V 4–12, Ja 1955-Nv 1963.
    Graduate Theological Union Library (CA-15/2): 1955–66.

CHINA LETTER OF THE AMERICAN JESUITS TO THEIR FRIENDS IN THE STATES. Zi-ka-wei, Shanghai.
    California Province of the Society of Jesus Archives (CA-195/1): N 1–41, D 1929-Aut 1941.

CHINA MAIL. Foreign Division, National Board of YWCA.
    Union Theological Seminary—Archives (NY-270/25): V 1–6, S 1937-My 1938.

CHINA MEDICAL JOURNAL. China Medical Missionary Association, Shanghai.
Continues CHINA MEDICAL MISSIONARY JOURNAL. Continues as CHINESE MEDICAL JOURNAL.
    Center for Research Libraries (IL-25/4): V 21, N 3-V 45, 1907–31.
    Cleveland Health Sciences—Allen Memorial Library (OH-80/1): V 24–45, 1910–31.
    College of Physicians of Philadelphia Library (PA-155/1): V 23–28; V 29, N 2–3; V 30–45; 1909–31.
    Columbia University—Long Health Sciences Library (NY-160/1): V 21, N 3-V 45, 1907–31.
    Francis A. Countway Library of Medicine (MA-55/1): V 21, N 3–4, 6; V 22–27; V 28, N 1, 6; V 29–46; 1907–32.
    Francis A. Countway Library of Medicine—Rare Book and Manuscript Department (MA-50/4): V 21, N 3; V 22–27; 1907–14.
    Graduate Theological Union Library (CA-15/2): V 21, N 3-V 36, My 1907–22.
    Harvard University—Widener Library (MA-155/1): V 21, N 3–4, 6-V 35, N 6, 1907–21.
    Indiana University—School of Medicine Library (IN-70/1): V 31, N 6; V 32, N 1; V 33, N 4; V 42–45, 1917–19, 1928–31.
    Iowa State University Library (IA-5/1): V 1–11, 15, 19, 20–35, 1887–1921.
    Kalamazoo College—Upjohn Library (MI-125/1): V 1–35, 1887–1921.
    Los Angeles County Medical Association Library (CA-145/1): V 42, 45, 1928, 1931.
    Medical Research Library of Brooklyn (NY-55/1): V 24, N 1–5; V 25, N 1–4; V 26, N 4; V 27, N 1–2; V 28, N 5–6;

V 29, N 3–6; V 30, N 1–4; V 31, N 1, 4, 6; V 32–41; V 42, N 1–7, 9–11; V 43–45; 1910–31.

National Library of Medicine (MD–35/2): V 21–36, 1907–22.

New York Academy of Medicine Library (NY–220/1): V 21, N 4; V 22, N 2–4; V 23–27; V 29, N 2–4; V 30; V 31, N 1–5; V 33–45; 1907–14, 1916–18, 1920–43.

New York University—Ehrman Medical Library (NY–255/1): V 35–45, 1921–31.

Oberlin College—Main Library (OH–175/1): V 21, N 3–V 45, My 1907–31.

Rockefeller University—Rockefeller Archive Center (NY–290/1): 1919–26.

Stanford University—Lane Medical Library (CA–310/1): V 27, 30–45, 1913, 1916–31.

Union Theological Seminary—Burke Library (NY–275/1): V 21, N 3–V 45, 1907–31.

University of Michigan—Asia Library (MI–10/1): V 21, N 4–5; V 34, N 1–5; V 35, N 1–3, 5–6; V 36, N 3; V 37–67; V 68, N 110; V 69–72; V 75–84; V 85, N 1, 3, 7–9; 1907, 1920–54, 1957–64, 1965.

University of Minnesota—Biomedical Library (MN–25/1): V 34–39; V 40, N 1–9, 11–12; V 41, N 1–3, 5–12; V 42, N 1–6; V 43, N 1–10; V 44; V 45, N 4, 11–12; 1920–31.

University of Rochester—Miner Library (NY–355/1): V 38–45, 1924–31.

University of Wyoming—Coe Library (WY–5/1): V 32–35, 1918–21.

Wheaton College—Graham Center Library (IL–205/1): V 1–35, 1887–1921.

Yale Divinity School Library (CT–55/2): V 21–35, 1907–21.

Yale University—Medical Library (CT–75/1): V 21, N 3–V 45, 1907–31.

CHINA MEDICAL MISSIONARY JOURNAL. China Medical Missionary Association, Shanghai.

Continued as CHINA MEDICAL JOURNAL. Index to V 1–9 bound with V 9–10.

Center for Research Libraries (IL–25/4): V 1–21, N 2, 1887–1907.

College of Physicians of Philadelphia Library (PA–155/1): V 1–12; V 13, N 1–3; V 14–22; 1887–98, 1900–1908.

Columbia University—Long Health Sciences Library (NY–160/1): V 1–V 21, N 2, 1887–1907.

Cornell University—Wason Collection (NY–95/1): V 9, N 4, D 1895.

Emory University—Pitts Theology Library (GA–15/5): V 6–9, 14–15, 1892–95, 1900–1901.

Essex Institute—Phillips Library (MA–210/2): V 1–3; V 4, N 1–3, 1887–90.

Francis A. Countway Library of Medicine (MA–55/1): V 1, N 1–2; V 2, N 3–4; V 3–4; V 5, N 1, 3–4; V 6; V 7, N 1–2, 4; V 8, N 1–2, 4; V 9–13; V 14, N 4; V 15–17; V 18, N 1, 3–4; V 19, N 1–5; V 20, N 2–6; V 21, N 1–2, 4; 1887–1907.

Francis A. Countway Library of Medicine—Rare Book and Manuscript Department (MA–50/4): V 1–21, 1887–1907.

Graduate Theological Union Library (CA–15/2): V 1, N 1–V 21, N 2, Mr 1887–Mr 1907.

Harvard University—Widener Library (MA–155/1): V 1, N 1–2; V 2, N 3–4; V 3; V 4, N 1, 3–4; V 5, N 1, 3–4; V 7; V 8, N 2, 4; V 9–11; V 15; V 20–21, N 2; 1887–91, 1893–97, 1901, 1906–7.

National Library of Medicine (MD–35/2): V 1–21, 1887–1907.

New York Academy of Medicine Library (NY–220/1): V 1, N 1–2; V 2, N 3; V 3, N 1–2, 4; V 4, N 1–3; V 5, N 1–4; V 6, N 1–4; V 7; V 8, N 1–2, 4; V 9–10; V 11, N 1–2; V 13, N 1–3; V 16, N 2–3; 1887–98, 1900, 1903.

Oberlin College—Main Library (OH–175/1): V 1–21, N 2, 1887–1907.

Stanford University—Lane Medical Library (CA–310/1): V 1, N 1; V 2, N 3; V 5; V 6, N 2, 4; V 7, N 2–4; V 8, N 2, 4; V 9, N 1, 4; V 10; V 11, N 2; 1887–88, 1891–97.

Union Theological Seminary—Burke Library (NY–275/1): V 1, N 1–V 21, N 2, 1887–1907.

Yale Divinity School Library (CT–55/2): V 1, N 1–V 5; V 7–11; V 15; V 19–V 21 N 2; 1887–1907.

Yale University—Medical Library (CT–75/1): V 1–4; V 8, N 1–2, 4; V 12, N 2; V 14–21, N 2; 1887–90, 1894, 1898, 1900–1907.

CHINA MEDICAL SCHOOL NEWS. Medical Philanthropies, Inc.

Loma Linda University—Radcliffe Memorial Library (CA–135/1): 1950–52.

CHINA METHODIST. N 1–9(?), 1948–49(?).

Union Theological Seminary—Burke Library (NY–275/1): N 1–9; Ap-Je, Ag-O, D 1948; Je, S 1949.

CHINA MISSION ADVOCATE. Boston. V 1, 1839.

American Baptist Historical Society (NY–345/23): 1839.

American Baptist Historical Society—American Baptist Archives Center (PA–285/1): 1839.

Andover Newton Theological School—Trask Library (MA–180/2): V 1, 1839.

Bethel Theological Seminary Library (MN–50/1): V 1, 1839.

Center for Research Libraries (IL–25/4): V 1, N 1–12, 1839.

Central Baptist Theological Seminary Library (KS–20/1): V 1, 1839.

Colgate-Rochester Theological Seminaries—Swasey Library (NY–350/1): V 1, N 1–2, Ja-D 1839.

Cornell University—Wason Collection (NY–95/1): V 1, 1839.

Denver Conservative Baptist Seminary—Thomas Library (CO–10/3): V 1, 1839.

Graduate Theological Union Library (CA–15/2): V 1, 1839.

Harvard University—Widener Library (MA–155/1): V 1, 1839.

Iowa State University Library (IA–5/1): V 1, 1839.

Kalamazoo College—Upjohn Library (MI–125/1): V 1, 1839.

New York Public Library—General Research Division (NY–230/1): V 1, 1839.

Ohio State University—Thompson Memorial Library

(OH–110/4): V 1, 1839.
Ohio Wesleyan University—Beeghly Library (OH–140/1): V 1, 1839.
Princeton Theological Seminary—Speer Library (NJ–95/3): V 1, 1839.
Princeton University—Firestone Library (NJ–100/1): V 1, 1839.
Southern Baptist Convention Historical Commission—Library and Archives (TN–55/6): V 1, 1839.
Southern Baptist Theological Seminary—Boyce Centennial Library (KY–50/2): V 1, 1839.
Stanford University—Green Library (CA–305/1): V 1, 1839.
University of Kentucky—King Library (KY–30/1): V 1, 1839.
University of Maryland—McKeldin Library (MD–45/2): V 1, 1839.
Virginia Baptist Historical Society (VA–90/8): V 1, 1839.
Wheaton College—Graham Center Library (IL–205/1): V 1, 1839.
Yale Divinity School Library (CT–55/2): V 1, N 1–2, 1839.

CHINA MISSION BULLETIN. Seventh Day Baptist Mission, Shanghai.
Seventh Day Baptist Historical Society Library (WI–10/3): 1934–48.

CHINA MISSION NEWS. Presbyterian Mission Press, Shanghai.
Evangelical and Reformed Historical Society—Schaff Library (PA–80/13): N 4, 7, 1901–2.

CHINA MISSION NEWS LETTER. United Christian Missionary Society, Nanking.
Yale Divinity School Library (CT–55/2): 1927–29, 1940–42, 1948–49.

CHINA MISSION NEWSLETTER. Presbyterian Church in the U.S. N 1–128, S 1928–S 1941.
Historical Foundation of the Presbyterian and Reformed Churches (NC–80/28): N 1–128, S 1928–S 1941.

CHINA MISSION NEWSLETTER. n.p.
Hartford Seminary Foundation Archives (CT–10/2): 1947–48.

CHINA MISSION STUDIES BULLETIN. Cedar Rapids, IA. V 1–, 1979–.
Asian Studies Newsletter Archives (MD–40/1): V 1–, 1979–.
Columbia University—Starr East Asian Library (NY–195/4): V 1–4, 1979–81.
Coe College—Stewart Memorial Library (IA–10/1): V 1–, 1979–.
Emory University—Pitts Theology Library (GA–15/5): V 1–7, 1979–85.
Fuller Theological Seminary—McAlister Library (CA–205/1): V 1–8, 1979–86.
Harvard University—Harvard-Yenching Library (MA–125/6): 1979–.
Institute for Chinese-Western Cultural History (CA–245/7): V 1–, 1979–.
Loyola University of Chicago—Cudahy Memorial Library

(IL–45/2): V 1–, 1979–.
Princeton University—Gest Oriental Library (NJ–105/1): V 1–6, 1979–84.
University of California, Berkeley—General Library (CA–70/1): V 1–, 1979–.
University of Hawaii—Hamilton Library (HI–15/1): V 1–, 1979–.
Yale Divinity School Library (CT–55/2): V 1–5, 1979–83.

CHINA MISSION YEAR BOOK. Christian Literature Society for China, Kwang Hsüeh Publishing Housing, Shanghai. V 1–13, 1910–25 (annual).
Title varies: 1926–39, CHINA CHRISTIAN YEAR BOOK. Suspended 1920–22. Publisher varies: Christian Literature Society for China and the China Continuation Committee, 1919; Christian Literature Society and the National Christian Council of China, 1923–25.
American Baptist Seminary of the West Library (CA–10/1): 1915, 1924.
American Congregational Association Library (MA–25/3): V 3–9, 11–12, 1912–18, 1923–24.
Andover Newton Theological School—Trask Library (MA–180/2): V 1–13, 1910–25.
Bates College—Ladd Library (ME–15/1): 1910.
Berea College—Special Collections (KY–5/2): 1910–15, 1918, 1923, 1925, 1938–39.
Bethel College—Mennonite Library and Archives (KS–55/13): 1917–19, 1923–24.
Brooklyn Public Library (NY–50/1): V 11–21, 1923–39.
Center for Research Libraries (IL–25/4): V 1–13, 1910–25.
Essex Institute—Phillips Library (MA–210/2): V 1, 1910.
Furman University—Duke Library (SC–30/2): V 12, 1924.
Garrett-Evangelical and Seabury-Western Theological Seminaries—United Library (IL–110/1): V 3, 1912.
General Theological Library (MA–60/1): 1912–14, 1917, 1919–20, 1923–25.
Gordon College—Winn Library (MA–250/2): 1911, 1913.
Graduate Theological Union Library (CA–15/2): 1910–25.
Harvard University—Widener Library (MA–155/1): V 1–13, 1910–25.
Iliff School of Theology—Taylor Library (CO–15/1): 1911, 1917–19, 1925–26, 1928–29, 1931–37.
Indiana University—University Libraries (IN–20/2): V 8, 1917.
Lindsey Wilson College—Murrell Library (KY–20/2): V 2, 1911.
Los Angeles Public Library (CA–150/1): V 9–21, 1918–39.
Lutheran Theological Seminary—Krauth Memorial Library (PA–180/1): 1912–14, 1924–26.
Mount Union College Library (OH–5/1): V 3–5, 1912–15.
New Brunswick Theological Seminary-Sage Library (NJ–65/2): 1910–19, 1923–25.
New Orleans Baptist Theological Seminary—Christian

Library (LA–15/1): V 2, 7, 10, 11–13, 1911, 1916, 1919, 1923–25.

New York Public Library—General Research Division (NY–230/1): V 1, 3–21, 1910, 1912–39.

Oberlin College—Main Library (OH–175/1): 1910–25.

Ohio University—Alden Library (OH–15/1): V 2, 13, 1911, 1925.

Overseas Missionary Fellowship (PA–265/1): 1917, 1919, 1923–25.

Phillips University—Rogers Graduate Seminary Library (OK–5/1): V 1, 10–11, 1910, 1919, 1923.

Presbyterian Historical Society—Archives and Library (PA–200/28): 1910–39.

Public Library of Cincinnati (OH–50/1): V 2–3, 1911–12.

Reformed Theological Seminary Library (MS–20/1): V 1–21, 1910–39.

Rockefeller University—Rockefeller Archive Center (NY–290/1): 1919.

St. Louis Public Library (MO–70/1): V 11, 13, 1923, 1925.

Southern Baptist Convention—Jenkins Research Library (VA–70/1): 1910–25.

Trenton Free Public Library (NJ–145/1): V 13, 1925.

Union Theological Seminary—Burke Library (NY–275/1): 1910–39.

United Theological Seminary Library (OH–120/11): V 1–13, 1910–25.

University of Arizona Library (AZ–5/3): V 1–5, 1910–14.

University of Georgia Libraries (GA–5/1): V 2, 1911.

University of Massachusetts at Amherst Library (MA–15/2): 1919.

University of Michigan—Hatcher Graduate Library (MI–25/1): V 1–2, 4, 6, 9–10, 13, 1910–11, 1913, 1915, 1918–19, 1925.

University of Oregon Library (OR–20/2): V 8–10, 1917–19.

Vassar College Library (NY–330/1): V 4, 7–10, 12–13, 1913, 1916–19, 1924–25.

Wellesley College—Clapp Library (MA–245/1): 1917–23.

Wesleyan University—Special Collections and Archives (CT–30/15): 1924.

Yale Divinity School Library (CT–55/2): 1910–25.

Yale Divinity School—Special Collections (CT–50/2): 1910–19, 1923–26.

CHINA MISSIONARY: Le Missionaire de Chine. Synodal Commission, Catholic Church in China, Shanghai. V 1–2, N 6, Ja 1948-Ag 1949.

Continues in part CATHOLIC CHURCHES IN CHINA. Title varies: CHINA MISSIONARY—LE MISSIONAIRE DE CHINE, Ja 1948-Je 1949; CHINA MISSIONARY BULLE-TIN, S 1949-Jl 1953; MISSION BULLETIN, S 1953-D 1959; ASIA, Ja 1960-.

Catholic Theological Union Library (IL–20/1): V 1–6, 1948–53.

Catholic University of America—Mullen Library (DC–20/1): V 1–2, N 6, 1943–49.

Columbia University—Starr East Asian Library (NY–195/4): V 1–2, N 6, Mr 1948-Je 1949.

Harvard University—Harvard-Yenching Library (MA–125/6): V 1, N 4–7; V 2, N 1–6; 1948–49.

Mary Immaculate Seminary Library (PA–115/1): V 2, N 1–6, 1949.

New York Public Library—General Research Division (NY–230/1): 1948.

St. Mary of the Lake Seminary—Feehan Memorial Library (IL–130/1): V 1, N 1-V 2, N 6, 1948–49.

School Sisters of Saint Francis—Generalate Archives (WI–75/2): V 1, N 1–6; V 2, N 1–2, 1948–49.

Trinity Evangelical Divinity School Library (IL–90/1): V 1–2, 1948–49.

Wheaton College—Graham Center Library (IL–205/1): V 2, N 1–6, Ja-Je 1949.

CHINA MISSIONARY BULLETIN. Synodal Commission, Catholic Church in China, Shanghai. S 1949-Jl 1953.

Title varies: CHINA MISSIONARY—LE MISSIONAIRE DE CHINE, Ja 1948-Je 1949; CHINA MISSIONARY BUL-LETIN, S 1949-Jl 1953; MISSION BULLETIN, S 1953-D 1959; ASIA, Ja 1960+.

Catholic University of America—Mullen Library (DC–20/1): V 2–5, N 6, Ja 1950-Jl 1953.

Columbia University—Starr East Asian Library (NY–195/4): S 1949-F 1950.

Congregation of the Passion of the Eastern United States—Chronicle Office (MA–255/1): 1949–60.

Duns Scotus Library (MI–140/1): V 1–5, 1948–53.

Harvard University—Harvard-Yenching Library (MA–125/6): V 4/5, N 1–10; V 5/6, N 1–3, 1952–53.

Mary Immaculate Seminary Library (PA–115/1): V 2–5, N 6, 1950–53.

Maryknoll Fathers and Brothers Library (NY–115/1): 1948–53.

Princeton Theological Seminary—Speer Library (NJ–95/3): V 4, N 12, V 5–6, N 6; D 1952-Ag 1954.

St. Mary of the Lake Seminary—Feehan Memorial Library (IL–130/1): V 2–5, N 6, 1950–53.

Trinity Evangelical Divinity School Library (IL–90/1): V 2–5, 1950–53.

Wheaton College—Graham Center Library (IL–205/1): V [2–5], 1949–53.

Yale Divinity School—Special Collections (CT–50/2): 1948–63.

CHINA MONTHLY: The Truth about China. New York. V 1–11, N 3, D 1939-Mr 1950.

Asbury Theological Seminary—Fisher Library (KY–90/1): V 1–11, 1939–50.

Boston Public Library (MA–30/2): V 1–11, 1939–50.

Catholic University of America—Mullen Library (DC–20/1): V7–10, 1947–49.

College of Saint Elizabeth—Mahoney Library (NJ–10/1): V 1–10, D 1939-O 1949.

Columbia University—Starr East Asian Library (NY–195/4): V 1, [2–3], 4, 9, [10–11], 1939–50.

Cornell University—Wason Collection (NY–95/1) : V 1–11, 1939–50.

Duke University—Perkins Library (NC–55/1): V 1, N 1,

6–11; V 2, N 1–8, 10–11; V 3–11; 1939–50.

Free Library of Philadelphia (PA–165/1): V [1], V 2–10, V 11, N 3, 1939–50.

Harvard University—Widener Library (MA–155/1): V 1–11, N 3, 1939–50.

Indiana University—University Libraries (IN–20/2): V 1, N 1–V 2, N 12; V 3, N 2–3; V 4; V 6, N 1–V 11, N 3; 1939–50.

Iowa State University Library (IA–5/1): V 3–11, 1941–50.

Johns Hopkins University—Eisenhower Library (MD–10/1): V 1–11, 1939–50.

Library of Congress—General Reading Rooms Division (DC–120/1): V [1–8], D 1939–Mr 1941, D 1944–S 1946, 1949–50.

Marquette University—Department of Special Collections (WI–60/2): V 3–6; V 7, N 7–V 10, N 6; V 10, N 8–10; V 11, N 1–2; 1941–50.

Michigan State University Library (MI–75/1): V 2, 6–11, 1940, 1946–50.

Milwaukee Public Library (WI–65/1): V 1–7, 9–10, N 4, D 1939–Ap 1946, 1948–49.

New York Public Library—General Research Division (NY–230/1): V 1–11, 1939–50.

Northwestern University Library (IL–115/1): V 1, N 6, 8–11; V 2, N 1–11; V 3, N 1–11; V 4–7, 1939–47.

Ohio State University—Thompson Memorial Library (OH–110/4): V 1, N 6–11; V 2–10, N 1–4; 1940–49.

Princeton University—Firestone Library (NJ–100/1): V 1–8, D 1939–Mr 1950.

Temple University—Paley Library (PA–210/2): V 4–10, 1942–49.

Union Theological Seminary—Burke Library (NY–275/1): V 1, N 1–6, 8–11; V 2; V 3, N 8; V 4, N 9–11; V 5; V 6, N 1–11; V 8, N 4–11; V 9, N 11; V 10, N 1; 1940–41, 1943–46, 1948–50.

University of Arizona Library (AZ–5/3): V 1–8, 1939–47.

University of California, Berkeley—Center for Chinese Studies Library (CA–45/1): V 8–10, 1946–49.

University of California, Berkeley—General Library (CA–70/1): V 1–3, N 3; V 4, N 3–V 10, N 1; V 10, N 4–V 11, N 3; 1939–50.

University of Chicago—Regenstein Library (IL–85/1): V 1–11, N 3, 1939–50.

University of Cincinnati—Central Library (OH–65/1): V 1–8, 1939–47(?).

University of Illinois at Urbana-Champaign Library (IL–185/1): V 1, N 6–11; V 2, N 1–V 3, N 11; V 4, N 1–V 5, N 11; V 6, N 1–V 9, N 11; V 10, N 1–7, 10–11; V 11, N 1–3, My 1940–Ag 1949, Nv 1949–Mr 1950.

University of Maryland—McKeldin Library (MD–45/2): V 6–11, 1944–50.

University of Minnesota—Wilson Library (MN–40/1): V 1–11, 1939–50.

University of Oregon Library (OR–20/2): V 1–11, D 1939–Mr 1950.

University of Virginia—Alderman Library (VA–30/1): V 1–11, 1939–50.

University of Washington—East Asia Library (WA–35/1): V 1, N 1, 3–4, 6–9, 11–V 2, N 1–2, D 1939–Ja 1941.

Wellesley College—Clapp Library (MA–245/1): V 3, N 6–V 11, N 3, My 1942–Mr 1950.

Yale University—Sterling Memorial Library (CT–80/1): V 1–11, 1939–50.

THE CHINA NAZARENE. Church of the Nazarene, China Mission.

Church of the Nazarene International Headquarters—Nazarene Archives (MO–25/2): Mr, D 1924; S 1925; Mr 1926.

CHINA NEWS. American Board of Commissioners for Foreign Missions, Boston. N 1, 1927.

Harvard Divinity School—Andover-Harvard Theological Library (MA–95/1): N 1–5, 1927.

Harvard Divinity School—Andover-Harvard Theological Library (MA–95/2): N 1, 3–5, 1927.

Union Theological Seminary—Burke Library (NY–275/1): N 1–5, Ap, My 1927.

Yale Divinity School Library (CT–55/2): N 1–5, 1927.

CHINA NEWS. Division of International Mission, General Assembly Mission Board, Presbyterian Church in the U.S., later Presbyterian Church (U.S./U.S.A.), Atlanta, GA. V 1–, O 1981– (quarterly).

Continued by CHINA NEWS UPDATE.

Asian Studies Newsletter Archives (MD–40/1): V 1–5, O 1981–86.

Union Theological Seminary in Virginia Library (VA–85/1): V 1–, O 1981–83.

CHINA NEWS. China's Children Fund, Richmond, VA.

Union Theological Seminary—Burke Library (NY–275/1): V 7, N 2–3, 1949–50.

CHINA NEWS AND CHURCH REPORT. Chinese Church Research Centre, Shatin, Hong Kong.

American Bible Society Library (NY–135/1): 1984–.

Asbury Theological Seminary—Fisher Library (KY–90/1): N 59, 64–66, 189, 191–, Je–Jl 1984, Ja 1987–.

Asian Studies Newsletter Archives (MD–40/1): N 1–, 1983–.

Reformed Bible College Library (MI–95/1): N 1–67, 73–93, 95, 98–99, 101–, Ag 1984–.

Southern Baptist Convention—Jenkins Research Library (VA–70/1): 1983–87.

CHINA NEWS LETTER. Board of Foreign Missions and the Woman's Missionary Society of the United Church of Canada, Toronto. V 1, N 1–3, My–O 1929 (occasionally).

Union Theological Seminary—Burke Library (NY–275/1): V 1, N 1–3, My, Je, O 1927.

CHINA NEWS LETTER. Lutheran World Federation, Kowloon, Hongkong. V 2–10, Ja 1947–Mr 1959 (irregular).

American Lutheran Church Archives (MN–95/110): V 1–2, N 2–5, 7; V 3, N 3–6; V 4, N 1–6; V 5, 3–6; V 6, N 3–6; V 7, N 1–6; V 8, N 1–2; V 9, N 3–12; V 10, N 1–2, 1946–59.

Associated Mennonite Biblical Seminaries Library (IN–25/3): 1948–51.

Luther Northwestern Theological Seminary Library (MN–100/1): V 2–10, 1947–59.

Lutheran Church in America Archives (IL–50/1): 1949–56.

Lutheran Council in the U.S.A.—Archives of Cooperative Lutheranism (NY–205/1): 1947–59.

Lutheran Theological Seminary—Wentz Library (PA–50/1): V [2], 3–4, [5], 6–7, [8], 9, 1947–56.

Union Theological Seminary—Burke Library (NY–275/1): V 2, N 1–V 10, N 2, Ja 1947–Mr 1959.

Wheaton College—Graham Center Archives (IL–200/46): 1947.

CHINA NEWS UPDATE. New York, Atlanta.
 Continues CHINA UPDATE: NEWS IN BRIEF.
 Asian Studies Newsletter Archives (MD–40/1): Jl 1986-.

CHINA NEWSLETTER. n. p.
 Bethel College—Mennonite Library and Archives (KS–55/3): V 4, N 1–2, 1949

 Claremont Colleges—Asian Studies Collection (CA–75/2): 1947–49.

 Harvard Divinity School—Andover-Harvard Theological Library (MA–95/2): N 1–55, 1944–51.

CHINA NEWSLETTER. *See* National Christian Council of China.

CHINA NOTES. National Christian Council of China, East Asia Office, Division of Overseas Ministries, New York. V 1–, 1951-.
 Continues CHINA BULLETIN, 1962. Renumbered V 1–, S 1962- (quarterly). Title of publisher varies: also China Committee, Far Eastern Office. Division of Foreign Missions.
 Alliance Theological Seminary Library (NY–300/1): V 16, N 2–, 1978-.

 American Bible Society Library (NY–135/1): 1978-.

 Andover Newton Theological School—Trask Library (MA–180/2): 1962–68.

 Andrews University—White Library (MI–50/1): V 1, N 2; V 2, N 3, 5; V 4–5; V 6, N 2, 4; V 7; V 8, N 1, 3–4; V 9, N 1–3; V 10, N 2–4; V 11–12; V 13, N 1–2, 4; V 14, N 1, 4; V 15–17; V 18, N 1. 3–4; V 19–23; 1962–64, 1966–85.

 Asbury Theological Seminary—Fisher Library (KY–90/1): V 1–, 1962-.

 Asian Studies Newsletter Archives (MD–40/1): V 8, N 1-, 1970-.

 Associated Mennonite Biblical Seminaries Library (IN–25/3): V 1–,1962-.

 Bethel College—Mennonite Library and Archives (KS–55/13): V 18, N 3–V 23. N 3, 1980–85.

 Bethel Theological Seminary Library (MN–50/1): V 1–3, 5-, 1962–64, 1966-.

 Boston University—School of Theology Library (MA–35/1): V 1–22, 1962–84.

 Brigham Young University—Lee Library (UT–10/1): V 8–16, N 1, 1970–78.

 Carleton College Library (MN–65/1): V 6, N 4–, 1968-.

 Columbia University—Starr East Asian Library (NY–195/4): V 1–14, 16, S 1962–Fall 1976, Winter 1977/78–Fall 1980.

 Cornell University—Wason Collection (NY–95/1): V 1–

10, 1962–72.

Denver Conservative Baptist Seminary—Thomas Library (CO–10/3): V 1–14, N 1; V 16, N 3; V 17, N 4; V 18, N 1, 3; V 19, N 1-, 1962–76, 1978-.

Eastern Baptist Theological Seminary—Deblois Library (PA–160/1): V 6–, 1967-.

Emory University—Pitts Theology Library (GA–15/5): V 1–23, 1962–84.

Fuller Theological Seminary—McAlister Library (CA–205/1): V 3–24 (inc.), 1964–86.

Garrett-Evangelical and Seabury-Western Theological Seminaries—United Library (IL–110/1): V 1–7, 1962–69.

Graduate Theological Union Library (CA–15/2): V 1-, S 1962-.

Harvard Divinity School—Andover-Harvard Theological Library (MA–95/2): V 1, N 1–2, 5; V 2, N 2–5; V 3–22, 1962–84.

Harvard University—Harvard-Yenching Library (MA–125/6): V 1–22, 1962–83.

Harvard University—Widener Library (MA–155/1): V 1-, 1962-.

Historical Foundation of the Presbyterian and Reformed Churches (NC–80/28): V 1–15, 1962–77.

Hoover Institution Library (CA–300/1): V 1–12, 1962–74.

Hope College—Van Zoeren Library (MI–110/1): V 1–5, 1962–67.

Kentucky Mountain Bible Institute—Gibson Library (KY–75/1): V 8-, 1970-.

Library of Congress—General Reading Rooms Division (DC–120/1): V 1–6, 1962–68.

Luther Northwestern Theological Seminary Library (MN–100/1): V 1-, 1962-.

Moravian College—Reeves Library (PA–10/1): V 1, N 8-, 1969-.

Northwestern College—Ramaker Library (IA–45/2): V 1–5, 1962–67.

Presbyterian Historical Society—Archives and Library (PA–200/3): V 15, N 3, Summer 1976.

Presbyterian Historical Society—Archives and Library (PA–200/16): V 6–10, 1967–72.

Presbyterian Historical Society—Archives and Library (PA–200/28): 1967–72.

Princeton Theological Seminary—Speer Library (NJ–95/3): V 12-, 1974-.

Princeton University—Firestone Library (NJ–100/1): V 1–19, S 1962–Fall 1981.

Scarritt Graduate School—Laskey Library (TN–50/1): V 4–17, 1966–80.

Southern Baptist Convention—Archives Center (VA–65/3): 1960–77.

Southern Baptist Convention—Jenkins Research Library (VA–70/1): 1980–87 (scattered issues).

Southern Baptist Theological Seminary—Boyce Centennial Library (KY–50/2): V 1-, 1962-.

Southern Methodist University—Bridwell Theology Library (TX–20/2): V 1–10, 1962–72.

Trinity Evangelical Divinity School Library (IL–90/1): V 1–14; V 15, N 1–3; V 16–17, N 1–2; V 18, N 3; V 20, N

1–4; V 21–; 1962–.

Union Theological Seminary—Burke Library (NY–275/1): V 8, 1958–.

Union Theological Seminary in Virginia Library (VA–85/1): V 1–14, [15], 16–19, [20–21], 22, 1962–84.

United Theological Seminary Library (OH–120/11): V 1–, 1962–.

University of California at Los Angeles—University Research Library (CA–185/1): V 6–, 1967–.

University of California, Riverside, Library (CA–225/1): V 1–5; V 6, N 4; V 7–, 1962–.

University of Chicago—Regenstein Library (IL–85/1): V 1–10, 1962–72.

University of Hawaii—Hamilton Library (HI–15/1): 1968–.

University of North Carolina at Greensboro—Jackson Library (NC–65/1): V 1–, 1962–.

University of Notre Dame Memorial Library (IN–95/1): V 1–, 1962–.

University of Oregon—Department of Special Collections (OR–15/3): V 2, N 4–5; V 3, N 2; 1964–65.

University of Oregon—Department of Special Collections (OR–15/18): Fall, Wint 1969.

University of Oregon—Department of Special Collections (OR–15/37): V 5, N 1–4; V 6, N 1–4; V 7, N 1–4; V 8, N 1–4; V 9, N 1–4; V 10, N 1–4; V 11, N 1, 3–4; V 12, N 1–2; V 13, N 4; 1967–75.

University of Southern California—Von Kleinsmid Center Library (CA–190/2): V 1–12; V 13, N 2–4; V 14, N 2–4; V 15; V 16, N 2–3; V 17, N 3–4; V 18, N 1–2; V 19–22; 1962–84.

University of Virginia—Alderman Library (VA–30/1): V 1–13, 1962–75.

University of Wisconsin-Madison—Memorial Library (WI–45/1): V 1, N 1–2, 4–5; V 2, N 2–5; V 3–4; V 5, N 1, 3–4; V 6; V 7, N 2; V 8, N 3–4; V 9–18; V 19, N 1; 1962–81.

Washington University—East Asian Library (MO–85/1): V 9–, 1970–.

Wellesley College—Clapp Library (MA–245/1): V 4, N 1–, 1966–.

Western Conservative Baptist Seminary—Cline-Tunnell Library (OR–30/1): V 23, N 2–, 1984–.

Western Theological Seminary—Beardslee Library (MI–120/11): 1962–73.

Western Theological Seminary—Beardslee Library (MI–120/12): Je 1963.

Westminster Theological Seminary Library (PA–220/2): V [10], 11–, 1971–.

Wheaton College—Graham Center Library (IL–205/1): V 1, N 2, 4–V 3, N 3; V 4, N 1–V 5, N 3; V 6, N 1–2, 4–V 10, N 1; V 10, N 3–V 11, N 3; V 12, N 1–3; V 13, N 1, 4–V 15, N 2, 4–V 16, N 3; V 17, N 2–; 1962–.

World Vision International—Research and Information Division (CA–200): current year only.

Yale Divinity School Library (CT–55/2): V 1–21, 1962–83.

CHINA PERSPECTIVES. Midwest China Study Resource Center, St. Paul, MN.

Luther Northwestern Theological Seminary Library (MN–100/1): 1977–80.

CHINA PRAYER LETTER. Chinese Church Research Center, Hong Kong. N 1–, 1979– (bi-monthly, 1979–82; monthly, 1982–).

Numbering irregular: N 25, 27 repeated, N 28 omitted; issues from Ja 1983 unnumbered. Continues in part CHINA AND THE CHURCH TODAY.

Asian Studies Newsletter Archives (MD–40/1): N 1–, 1978–.

Baylor University—Dawson Institute on Church-State Relations (TX–55/1): O 1982–F 1983, 1986–.

Bethel Theological Seminary Library (MN–50/1): 1978–.

International Christian Graduate University—International School of Theology Library (CA–240/1): N 76–, D 1986–.

Luther Northwestern Theological Seminary Library (MN–100/1): 1986–87.

Southern Baptist Convention—Jenkins Research Library (VA–70/1): 1982–85.

Trinity Evangelical Divinity School Library (IL–90/1): N 70–74, 78–, 1986–.

Union Theological Seminary—Burke Library (NY–275/1): 1979–.

Union Theological Seminary in Virginia Library (VA–85/1): 1982–84.

Western Conservative Baptist Seminary—Cline-Tunnell Library (OR–30/1): F 1984–.

Wheaton College—Graham Center Library (IL–205/1): N 4–7, 19, 25–76, 79, 82–, 1979–.

World Vision International—Research and Information Division (CA–200): current year only.

CHINA PRAYER LETTER. San Jose, CA.

Baylor University—Dawson Institute on Church-State Relations (TX–55/1): Jl–O 1982; Ja, Ap–Je, Ag–O, D 1983; Ja–F 1984.

CHINA PRAYER NEWS. Chinese Church Research Center, Hong Kong.

Western Evangelical Seminary—Hallauer Memorial Library (OR–35/1): S 1984–My 1986.

CHINA RELIEF NOTES. Mennonite Central Committee. V 1–4(?), 1945–48(?).

Continues CHINA SHEET, 1945–My 1946.

Associated Mennonite Biblical Seminaries Library (IN–25/3): V 1–4, 1945–48.

Bethel College—Mennonite Library and Archives (KS–55/13): V 1, N 7–V 4, N 1, Je 1946–D 1948.

Center for Research Libraries (IL–25/4): V 1, N 5–V 3, N 2; V 3, N 4–V 4, N 1, 1946–48.

CHINA SHEET. Mennonite Central Committee. 1945–46.

Continued as CHINA RELIEF NOTES, Je 1946.

Bethel College—Mennonite Library and Archives (KS–55/13): V 1, N 1–6, ? 1945–My 1946.

CHINA SPECTRUM. Midwest China Center, St. Paul, MN. V 1–, 1981–.

Union Theological Seminary—Burke Library (NY–275/1): Spring 1983.

World Vision International—Research and Information Division (CA–200): current year only.

CHINA STUDY PROJECT BULLETIN. China Study Project, Tunbridge Wells, Kent, England.
American Bible Society Library (NY–135/1): 1979-.
Emory University—Pitts Theology Library (GA–15/5): V 1, N 1, Ap 1986-.
Southern Baptist Convention—Jenkins Research Library (VA–70/1): N 20–21, 23–29, D 1982-Ja 1986.
Union Theological Seminary—Burke Library (NY–275/1): n.d.

THE CHINA SUNDAY SCHOOL JOURNAL. China Sunday School Union, Shanghai. V 1, 1913.
Cornell University—Wason Collection (NY–95/1): V 1, N 1, 3–12; V 2; V 3, N 2, 6–9, 11–12; V 4, N 1–7, 9–12; V 5–6; V 7, N 1–4; 1913–19.
Emory University—Pitts Theology Library (GA–15/5): V 1–10, 12–18, 1913–28.
Harvard Divinity School—Andover-Harvard Theological Library (MA–95/1): N 6, Summ 1928.
San Francisco Theological Seminary Library (CA–235/2): V 16, Fall, Wint, 1927.
Union Theological Seminary—Burke Library (NY–275/1): V 1–11, 18; V 19, N 11; V 20, N 6; V 22, N 2; V 23, N 6; 1913–28, 1930–31, 1933–34.
Yale Divinity School Library (CT–55/2): V 1–19, 22–23, 1913–28, 1930, 1933–34.

CHINA TALK. China Liaison Office, World Division, Board of Global Ministries, United Methodist Church, Hong Kong. V 1-, 1976- (bimonthly).
American Bible Society Library (NY–135/1): 1980-.
Asian Studies Newsletter Archives (MD–40/1): V 1, N 5-, 1976-.
Boston University—School of Theology Library (MA–35/1): V 1–10, 1976–85 (inc.).
Drew University—United Methodist Archives (NJ–45/5): V 3, N 1–2, My 1978.
Drew University—United Methodist Historical Library (NJ–50/1): V 2–10, 1977–85 (inc.).
Emory University—Pitts Theology Library (GA–15/5): V 1–7, 1975–82.
Institute for Chinese-Western Cultural History (CA–245/7): V 9, N 2-, 1984-.
Scarritt Graduate School—Laskey Library (TN–50/1): V 1–6 (inc.), 1976–82.
Southern Methodist University—Bridwell Theology Library (TX–20/2): V 1, N 5; V 2, N 2–5; V 3, N 1, 5; V 4–5; V 6, N 1–4; V 7, N 1–4; V 8, N 1–5; V 9-; 1976-.
Union Theological Seminary—Burke Library (NY–275/1): V 7, S 1983.
Union Theological Seminary in Virginia Library (VA–85/1): V [6], 7–9, 1981–84.

CHINA TALK. n.p. St. Paul, MN.
University of Vermont—Bailey/Howe Library (VT–5/1): 1945.

CHINA: The Quarterly Record. Christian Literature Society for China.

Harvard University—Widener Library (MA–155/1): 1912–13, 1915.
Union Theological Seminary—Burke Library (NY–275/1): N 3–10, 25–27, 37, 43, 45–50, 1903–4, 1908–9, 1911, 1913–15.
Yale Divinity School Library (CT–55/2): N 13, 34–50, 1905, 1911–15.

CHINA UPDATE: An Occasional Newsletter. J. Spae, Oud-Haverlee, Belgium. V 1-, 1982-.
Catholic Theological Union Library (IL–20/1): V 2-, 1983-.
Fuller Theological Seminary—McAlister Library (CA–205/1): V 3–18, 1983–86.
Institute for Chinese-Western Cultural History (CA–245/7): V 1-, 1982-.
Union Theological Seminary—Burke Library (NY–275/1): V 1, O 1982-.
Yale Divinity School Library (CT–55/2): 1983–84.

CHINA UPDATE: News in Brief. China Program Associates, Program Agency, United Presbyterian Church, U.S.A., New York. N 1-, F 1981 (irregular).
Continues as CHINA NEWS UPDATE.
Asian Studies Newsletter Archives (MD–40/1): N 1–17, 1981–86.
Trinity Evangelical Divinity School Library (IL–90/1): N 15–16, Ja-Jl 1985.
Union Theological Seminary in Virginia Library (VA–85/1): 1983–84.

CHINA UPDATE: The Yale-China Association Newsletter. New Haven, Connecticut.
Continues YALE-CHINA NEWSLETTER.
Asian Studies Newsletter Archives (MD–40/1): V 1, N 1-, 1979-.

DE CHINABODE. Rotterdam.
Yale Divinity School Library (CT–55/2): N 40, 81–88, 1908–21.

CHINA-BOTE. Deutsche China-Allianz Mission, Barmen. V 1, 1892.
Continued by MISSIONS-BOTE, 1952-.
Union Theological Seminary—Burke Library (NY–275/1): O 1910, Ag 1920, Ag 1922, Jl-Ag 1923, Ag 1924, Je-Ag 1925.
Yale Divinity School Library (CT–55/2): V 16–20, 1908–12.

DER CHINABOTE FÜR DEN AMERIKANISCHEN FREUNDESKREIS DER RHEINSCHEN MISSION IN CHINA. Tungkun.
Union Theological Seminary—Burke Library (NY–275/1): V 1, N 3; V 2, N 1, 3; 1924, 1937–38.
Yale Divinity School Library (CT–55/2): V 2(?), N 1–3, 1937–38.

THE CHINA-HOME BOND. China Mission of the General Conference of Mennonites, Kai Chow, Hopei. V 1, S 1939.
Associated Mennonite Biblical Seminaries Library (IN–25/3): 1939–41.
Bethel College—Mennonite Library and Archives

(KS–55/13): V 1–3, 1939–41.
  Harvard Divinity School—Andover-Harvard Theological
  Library (MA–95/2): V 1, N 4–5; V 2, N 1–8; V 3, N 1–6;
  S 1939-Nv 1940, Apr 1941-S 1941.

CHINA'S MEDICINE. Chinese Medical Association, Peking.
  Ceased publication N 12, 1968. Continues CHINESE MEDI-
  CAL JOURNAL which was continued by CHINA'S MEDI-
  CINE which reverted to CHINESE MEDICAL MISSION-
  ARY JOURNAL in 1973. The chronological sequence is
  CHINA MEDICAL MISSIONARY JOURNAL, V 1–21, N
  2, 1887-O 1909; CHINA MEDICAL JOURNAL, V 21, N 3-
  V 45, N 12, N 1909-D 1931; CHINESE MEDICAL JOUR-
  NAL, 1932–66; CHINA'S MEDICINE, 1966-N 12, 1968;
  CHINESE MEDICAL JOURNAL, 1968-.
    Cleveland Health Sciences—Allen Memorial Library
    (OH–80/1): 1966–68.
    College of Physicians of Philadelphia Library
    (PA–155/1): O 1966-D 1968.
    Columbia University—Long Health Sciences Library
    (NY–160/1): N 1–12, O 1966-D 1968.
    Francis A. Countway Library of Medicine (MA–55/1):
    1966–68.
    Indiana University—University Libraries (IN–20/2):
    1966.
    Los Angeles County Medical Association Library
    (CA–145/1): 1966–68.
    National Library of Medicine (MD–35/2): 1966–68.
    New York Academy of Medicine Library (NY–220/1): V
    85, N 10-V 87, 1966–68.
    New York State Library (NY–15/2): V 3, N 4–12, 1968.
    Ohio State University—Health Sciences Library
    (OH–105/1): 1966–68.
    Stanford University—Lane Medical Library (CA–310/1):
    1966–68.
    University of California at Los Angeles—Biomedical Li-
    brary (CA–160/1): 1966–68.
    University of California, Berkeley—Biology Library
    (CA–40/1): O-D 1966, 1968.
    University of California, Davis—Health Sciences Library
    (CA–95/1): N 1–12, O 1966-D 1968.
    University of Illinois at Urbana-Champaign Library
    (IL–185/1): 1966–68.
    University of Louisville—Kornhauser Health Sciences Li-
    brary (KY–60/1): 1966–72.
    University of Maryland—McKeldin Library (MD–45/2):
    1966–67.
    University of Michigan—Asia Library (MI–10/1): V 1–3;
    1966–68.
    University of Minnesota—Biomedical Library
    (MN–25/1): 1966–68.
    Yale University—Medical Library (CT–75/1): 1966–68.

CHINAS MILLIONEN VEREINIGT MET DEM MISSIONS-
  BOTEN AUS DER DEUTSCHEN SÜDSEE. Liebenzeller
  Mission, Wurttburg. V 1, 1900.
    Continued by MITTEILUNGEN DER LIEBENZELLER
    MISSION.
      Yale Divinity School Library (CT–55/2): V 1–7, 11–18,
      21–41, 1900–1906, 1910–17, 1920–40.

CHINA'S MILLIONS (American Supplement).
  Overseas Missionary Fellowship (PA–265/1): 1891–92.

CHINA'S MILLIONS (Australia/New Zealand edition). Mel-
  bourne, Australia. 1935–87.
    Overseas Missionary Fellowship (PA–265/1): 1935–71,
    1975–84.

CHINA'S MILLIONS. China Inland Mission. V 1–22, 1875–92;
  n.s. V 1–34, 1893–1926, (volume numbering reverts) V 52-,
  1926-Mr 1952(?) (monthly).
    Place of publication varies: London, 1875–1976; Sevenoaks,
    Kent, 1977-. Continued by THE MILLIONS, 1952–64; con-
    tinued in turn by EAST ASIA MILLIONS, 1964-.
      American Congregational Association Library
      (MA–25/3): 1875–90, 1891, N 1–5, 7–10; 1892, N 1–2,
      4, 6–7, 9, 11; 1893–94; 1895, N 1–10, 12; 1896–1902;
      1903, N 3, 6; 1903; 1904, N 3–12; 1904–6; 1907, 1–8,
      10–12; 1908; 1909, N 1–6, 8–12; 1910; 1911, N 5–7,
      9, 12; 1912, N 1–2; 1913, N 7; 1914, N 11; 1915, N
      1–2.
      Bethel Theological Seminary Library (MN–50/1): 1883,
      1885–87.
      Biola University—Rose Memorial Library (CA–130/4):
      1886–88.
      Boston Public Library (MA–30/2): N 1–54, 79–114,
      1875–79, 1882–84.
      Brigham Young University—Lee Library (UT–10/1):
      1879–80, 1895.
      Cleveland Public Library (OH–85/1): V 1–20, 1875–95.
      Colgate Rochester Theological Seminaries—Swasey Li-
      brary (NY–350/1): V 1; V 5, N 63–65; V 6, N 70–72, 78;
      V 7, N 79–81, 83–90; V 8, N 91–102; V 9, N 103–108,
      110–113; V 10, N 2–5; V 33–38, 42–47, 51–78; 1875–76,
      1880–85, 1887, 1907–12, 1916–21, 1925–52.
      Drew University Library (NJ–40/2): V 1–24, 49–60,
      1875–1916, 1941–52.
      Duke University—Perkins Library (NC–55/1): V 1–22,
      n.s. V 9–21, 26–29, 32–35, 1875–76, 1878–81, 1885–88,
      1890–92, 1895–1913, 1918–21, 1924–27.
      Emory University—Pitts Theology Library (GA–15/5): V
      17, 55–68, 1892, 1929–42.
      Essex Institute—Phillips Library (MA–210/2): 1875–99,
      1902–16.
      Garrett-Evangelical and Seabury-Western Theological Se-
      minaries—United Library (IL–110/1): V 8, N 2, 5–6, 8–9;
      V 9, 1, 3–6, 8–12; V 10, N 1–2, 9–10; V 11, N 7–12; V
      12, N 3, 5–6, 9–10, 12; V 13, N 1–2, 6, 8–9, 11; V 14, N
      1, 3–12; V 30, N 9; V 34, N 3–5; V 53, N 1–12; V 60–61;
      1883–89, 1904, 1908, 1927, 1934–35.
      Harvard Divinity School—Andover-Harvard Theological
      Library (MA–95/2): V 1–75, N 5, Jl 1875-My 1952.
      Library Company of Philadelphia (PA–175/1): V 2-?,
      1876-?.
      Luther Northwestern Theological Seminary Library
      (MN–100/1): V 12, 39–60, 1904, 1937–52.
      Moody Bible Institute Library (IL–55/1): n.v., V 40, 42–
      60, 1886–87, 1891–92, 1895, 1902–3, 1906, 1932, 1934–
      52.
      New York Public Library—General Research Division
      (NY–230/1): 1881–1909 (inc.).

Northwest Christian College—Learning Resource Center (OR-10/1): 1886, 1890.

Oberlin College—Main Library (OH-175/1): n.v., V 1-5, 7-9, 11-14, 16-44, n.s. V 27-29, 1875-80, 1882-84, 1886-1921.

Overseas Missionary Fellowship (PA-265/1): 1875-1952.

Overseas Missionary Fellowship (PA-265/2): 1878, 1885-1949.

Presbyterian Historical Society—Archives and Library (PA-200/28): V 1-17, n.s. V 1-9, V 28-29, 1875-1903.

Princeton Theological Seminary—Speer Library (NJ-95/3): V 4, 11-16, 1879, 1886-91.

San Francisco Theological Seminary Library (CA-235/2): 1875-93, 1950-52.

Southwestern Baptist Theological Seminary—Roberts Library (TX-25/3): V 4, 6-10, 12; V 51, N 5; V 53-54; V 55, N 1-3; V 57, N 1; V 60; 1879, 1881-85, 1887, 1925, 1927-31, 1934.

Union Theological Seminary—Burke Library (NY-275/1): N 1-6, Jl-D 1875.

Union Theological Seminary in Virginia Library (VA-85/1): V [9-36], 1894-1928.

University of California, Berkeley—General Library (CA-70/1): 1881.

University of Hawaii—Hamilton Library (HI-15/2): N 1-78, 1875-1981.

University of Illinois at Urbana-Champaign Library (IL-185/1): V 59, 1933.

University of Iowa Libraries (IA-40/1): 1875-99.

University of Minnesota—Wilson Library (MN-40/1): 1875-76, 1880, 1886-88, 1892.

Vanderbilt University—Divinity Library (TN-65/1): N 91-102, 1883.

Wheaton College—Graham Center Library (IL-205/1): V 1-17, n.s. V 1-7, 22-60, 1875-99, 1914-52.

CHINA'S MILLIONS (North American ed.). China Inland Mission. V 1-, 1893-1952(?) (monthly).

Place of publication varies: Philadelphia, 1932-74; Robesonia, 1974-. Continued by THE MILLIONS (North American edition), V 61, N 4, Ap 1952-; *see also* EAST ASIA MILLIONS.

Asbury Theological Seminary—Fisher Library (KY-90/1): V 60, N 1-3, 1952.

Associated Mennonite Biblical Seminaries Library (IN-25/3): V 59, F-S 1951.

Baylor University—Moody Memorial Library (TX-60/1): V 15-55, 1911-47.

Bethany and Northern Baptist Theological Seminaries Library (IL-135/1): n.s. V [33, 38], 39-60, 1925, 1930-52.

Claremont Colleges—Honnold Library (CA-85/1): n.s. V 1, N 6; V 2, N 2, 4, 6-12; V 21, N 2, 4-5, 7, 9; V 22, N 2-8, 10-12; V 23, N 2-9, 11-12; V 24, N 7-12; V 25-27; V 28, N 1-7, 9-12; V 29, N 1, 10-12; V 30, N 1-3, 5-7, 9-11; V 31, N 2-12; V 32, N 1-22; V 33-40; V 41, N 1-3, 5-12; V 42-44; V 46; V 57, N 5-6, 11; 1893-94, 1913-36, 1938, 1949.

Garrett-Evangelical and Seabury-Western Theological Seminaries—United Library (IL-110/1): V 1-3, 5, 7-12, 16-60, N 3, 1893-1952.

Goucher College—Rogers Library (MD-70/2): V 1-2, 9-10, 12, 1893-94, 1901-2, 1904.

Library of Congress—General Reading Rooms Division (DC-120/1): 1903-4, 1919, 1924-61.

Moody Bible Institute Library (IL-55/1): V 1-17; n.s. V 3, 10-11, 14, 40-60, 1893-1910, 1933-52.

Overseas Missionary Fellowship (PA-265/1): 1893-1952.

Overseas Missionary Fellowship (PA-265/3): D 1927.

Presbyterian Historical Society—Archives and Library (PA-200/28): V 18-58, 1910-50.

Princeton Theological Seminary—Speer Library (NJ-95/3): 1904-7, 1910, 1921, 1932-61.

Southwestern Baptist Theological Seminary—Roberts Library (TX-25/3): V 16-26, 28-32; V 33, N 1-4, 6-12; V 34-36; V 37, N 1-7, 8-12; V 38, N 1-5, 7-12; V 39-40; V 41, N 1-9, 11-12; V 42-51; V 52, N 1-2; V 54, N 1-9, 11-12; V 55-58; V 59, N 1-4, 10-12; V 60, N 1-3; 1908-1918, 1920-44, 1946-52.

Wheaton College—Graham Center Archives (IL-200/15): 1934-47.

Wheaton College—Graham Center Archives (IL-200/25): 1926.

Wheaton College—Graham Center Archives (IL-200/50): V 46-48, 1938-40.

Yale Divinity School—Special Collections (CT-50/2): 1899-1937.

CHINA'S MILLIONS (North American ed.). China Inland Mission, Toronto. 1891-1932.

American Congregational Association Library (MA-25/3): V 20, N 12, 1915(?).

Biola University—Rose Memorial Library (CA-130/4): 1895-1901, 1932-34, 1937-52.

Colgate Rochester Theological Seminaries—Swasey Library (NY-350/1): V 12, N 10-11; V 13, N 1-8, 10-12; V 14, N 1-2, 6-10; V 15, N 3, 7; V 17, N 8, 11; V 20, N 1, 3; 1904-7, 1909, 1912, 1915.

Essex Institute—Phillips Library (MA-210/2): 1893-96, 1898, 1901, 1903-40.

Fuller Theological Seminary—McAlister Library (CA-205/1): V 45-60 (inc.), 1937-52.

Gordon-Conwell Theological Seminary—Goddard Library (MA-230/4): V 50-60, 1942-52.

Harvard Divinity School—Andover-Harvard Theological Library (MA-95/2): n.s. N 1-12; (ser. 3) n.s. V 2, N 1-V 5, N 2; V 5, N 6; V 6, N 1-12; V 7, N 1-V 10, N 4, 8; V 11, N 4; Ja-D 1893, Ja 1894-F 1897, Je 1897, Ja-D 1898, Ja 1899-Apr 1902, Ag 1902, Apr 1903.

New York Public Library—General Research Division (NY-230/1): 1893-1908 (inc.).

Oberlin College—Main Library (OH-175/1): V [3-4], 14-15, 18, 22, 33, 1895-96, 1906-7, 1910, 1914, 1925.

Princeton Theological Seminary—Speer Library (NJ-95/3): 1894-97, 1899-1900.

Scarritt Graduate School—Laskey Library (TN-50/1): 1893.

Union Theological Seminary—Burke Library (NY-275/1): V 17, N 12, n.s. V 1, N 1-V 60, N 3, 1892-1952.

CHINA'S YOUNG MEN. Association Press of China, Shanghai. V 1, 1906.
> Continues CHINESE INTERCOLLEGIAN.
>> Yale Divinity School Library (CT–55/2): V 1–11, 1906–16.

CHINA'S YOUNG MEN. Shanghai. V 1–19, N 10, Je 1896-Ja 1917. V 1–10, 1896–1914, volumes renumbered V 1-, 1914-.
> Cornell University—Wason Collection (NY–95/1): V 10, n 2–3, 5, 1914–15.
> Garrett-Evangelical and Seabury-Western Theological Seminaries—United Library (IL–110/1): V 3, N 1, 4–12; V 4–6; V 7, N 1–4; V 9, N 1–6, 9–12; V 10, N 1–9; V 11, N 1–6, 1908–16.
> Oberlin College—Main Library (OH–175/1): V 1, N 1; V 4, N 1, 3–4; V 5, N 1–3; 1906, 1909–10.
> Union Theological Seminary—Burke Library (NY–275/1): Je 1876; Ap, Jl, O 1906; Ja, Ap, Jl, O 1907; F, My, Ag, Nv 1908; F, My, Ag, Nv 1909; F, My, Jl, O 1910; Ja, Ap, Jl, O 1911; Ja, Ap, Jl, O 1912; Ja-Je, S-D 1913; Ja-Je 1914; Ja-Je 1915; Ja-Je 1916.
> Virginia Baptist Historical Society (VA–90/8): V 7, N 3, 4, 6, 8; V 8, N 1, 3, 1904–5.

CHINE, CEYLAN, MADAGASCAR. Jésuites français du nord et de l'est, Lille. V 1, 1898.
> Title varies: 1899–1901, CHINE ET CEYLON; 1902–48, CHINE, CEYLON, MADAGASCAR; 1944–46, PROCURE DES MISSIONS DE CHINE, CEYLON, MADAGASCAR.
>> Georgetown University—Woodstock Theological Center Library (DC–70/4): V 1, N 1; V 3–4, 8, 22, 27–28; Nv 1898, 1901–2, 1906, 1920, 1925–26.
>> Harvard University—Widener Library (MA–155/1): V 1–5, 7 bis, 8 bis, 1898–1905.

CHINE, MADAGASCAR. Jésuites français du nord et de l'est, Lille. V 1, 1898.
> Title varies: 1899–1901, CHINE ET CEYLON; 1902–48, CHINE, CEYLON, MADAGASCAR; 1944–46, PROCURE DES MISSIONS DE CHINE, CEYLON, MADAGASCAR.
>> Yale Divinity School Library (CT–55/2): V 2–134, n.s. V 2–185, 1899–1939, 1944–82.
>> Yale Divinity School—Special Collections (CT–50/2): 1949.

CHINESE ADVOCATE: Organ of the Chinese Sunday Schools. New York. V 1, 1890.
> Essex Institute—Phillips Library (MA–210/2): V 1, N 1, My 1890.

CHINESE-AMERICAN BULLETIN. Catholic Foreign Mission Society of America, Maryknoll, New York. V 1-, Ja 1942- (bimonthly September to May).
> Cornell University—Wason Collection (NY–95/1): V 1–3; V 4, N 1, 4; V 5, N 1–4; 1942–46.
> Union Theological Seminary—Burke Library (NY–275/1): V 1, N 4-V 4, N 1; V 4, N 4-V 5, N 4; 1942–46.

CHINESE AND GENERAL MISSIONARY GLEANER. Partridge and Oakey, London. V 1–2, Je 1851-My 1853.
> Cornell University—Wason Collection (NY–95/1): V 1–2, 1851–52.

CHINESE ANGLICANS IN THE FOUR SEAS: A Periodical Review of the Mission of the Anglican Communion amongst the Chinese Diaspora. N 1, 2, 1955, 1957.
> Union Theological Seminary—Burke Library (NY–275/1): N 1–2, 1955, 1957.

CHINESE AROUND THE WORLD. Chinese Coordination Centre of World Evangelism, Hong Kong.
> American Bible Society Library (NY–135/1): 1979-.
> Baptist Missionary Association Theological Seminary—Kellar Library (TX–45/1): Mr-Ap 1983, Je 1983-Ap 1984, Je 1984-Je 1986.
> Bethel Theological Seminary Library (MN–50/1): 1983–84.
> Biola University—Rose Memorial Library (CA–130/4): Ja, Je, S 1984; Ja 1985.
> Fuller Theological Seminary—McAlister Library (CA–205/1): 1983, F 1986.
> International Christian Graduate University—International School of Theology Library (CA–240/1): F 1983; Mr-My, Ag, O, D 1985; F, Je 1986-.
> Southern Baptist Convention—Jenkins Research Library (VA–70/1): 1983–87.
> Union Theological Seminary—Burke Library (NY–275/1): F 1985-.
> Union Theological Seminary in Virginia Library (VA–85/1): 1983–84.
> Western Conservative Baptist Seminary—Cline-Tunnell Library (OR–30/1): F 1983-.
> Wheaton College—Graham Center Library (IL–205/1): V 2, N 2, 5, 9–11; V 3, N 1, 3–7, 10; V 4, N 1, 5–8; V 5-; 1980-.
> World Vision International—Research and Information Division (CA–200/1): 1979-.

CHINESE BACK TO JERUSALEM EVANGELISTIC BAND.
> Free Methodist Church—Marston Memorial Historical Center (IN–120/5): N 9, Je 1949.

CHINESE CHRISTIAN DIGEST. Chinese for Christ, Inc., Los Angeles. V 1, 1962.
> Gordon-Conwell Theological Seminary—Goddard Library (MA–230/4): V 1, N 1, 1962.

CHINESE CHRISTIAN INTELLIGENCER. Shanghai. V 1, 1916.
> Cornell University—Wason Collection (NY–95/1): V 1, 1916.
> Southern Methodist University—Bridwell Theology Library (TX–20/2): V 1, 1916.
> Union Theological Seminary—Burke Library (NY–275/1): 1916, 1920.

CHINESE CHRISTIANS TODAY (CHUNG-KUO HSIN T'U YÜEH K'AN). Chinese Christian Mission, Detroit. V 1–3, N 5, F 1962-My 1964.
> Continued by CHALLENGER.
>> Andrews University—White Library (MI–50/1): V 11, N 5, 8–12; V 12, N 1–4, 6–12; V 13, N 1, 4, 6, 11–12; V 14; V 15, N 2–10; V 16, N 1–2, 4–12; V 17–18; V 19, N 2, 4, 6, 9–12; V 20, N 1–7, 9–12; V 21, N 1–3, 5–12; V 22–24, V 25, N 1–11; 1972–86.

Associated Mennonite Biblical Seminaries Library (IN–25/3): V 1, 2, 10, 15–, 1962–63, 1972, 1977-.

Bethel College—Mennonite Library and Archives (KS–55/3): V 1, N 1–3, 5–11; V 2, N 2, 4; 1962–63.

Biola University—Rose Memorial Library (CA–130/4): V 19, N 7, 12, Jl, D 1980.

Brigham Young University—Lee Library (UT–10/1): V 1, N 3, 5–8, 11; V 2, N 1–4, 12; V 3, N 3–12; V 4, N 3, 5–9, 11–12; V 5, N 1–5, 7–12; V 6, N 1–2, 4, 7–8, 10, 12; V 7–8; V 9, N 1–5, 7–12; V 10, N 1, 3–5, 7–12; V 11–12, 15–19; V 20, N 1–3, 5–12; V 21–; 1962–73, 1976-

Cornell University—Wason Collection (NY–95/1): V 1–3, F 1962-My 1964.

Lutheran Theological Southern Seminary—Lineberger Memorial Library (SC–20/1): V 11–13, 20–21, N 3; 1972–74, 1981–82.

Princeton Theological Seminary—Speer Library (NJ–95/3): 1976.

Southern Methodist University—Bridwell Theology Library (TX–20/2): V 1, N 1, 4–11; V 2, N 2, 4; V 3, N 5; 1962–64.

Trinity Evangelical Divinity School Library (IL–90/1): V 11, N 6–7, 9–12; V 12, N 1, 3–5, 7–8; V 13, N 1–2, 4–6, 8–12; V 14–18, N 1–4, 6–12; V 19–23, N 1–3; V 24, N 12; V 25–; 1972-.

Union Theological Seminary—Burke Library (NY–275/1): V 1–, 1962-.

University of California, Davis, Library (CA–110/2): 1986-.

Virginia Baptist Historical Society (VA–90/8): V 1, N 8–10, S-Nv 1962.

Chinese Church Research Center, Hong Kong

OCCASIONAL PAPERS. Chinese Church Research Center, Hong Kong. N 1, 1979.

Brigham Young University—Lee Library (UT–10/1): N 3–5, 7, 10–11, 1979, 1981.

Fuller Theological Seminary—McAlister Library (CA–205/1): N 1, 1979.

CHINESE CHURCHES TODAY. Chinese Coordination Center of World Evangelism, Hong Kong.

Fuller Theological Seminary—McAlister Library (CA–205/1): 1982–86.

Wheaton College—Graham Center Library (IL–205/1): Jl 1979-.

World Vision International—Research and Information Division (CA–200): current year only.

CHINESE EVANGELICAL MESSENGER. n.p., Hunan. V 1, 1914.

Drew University—United Methodist Historical Library (NJ–50/1): V 1, 1914.

CHINESE EVANGELIST. New York. V 1, N 9–11, 1888–89.

Boston Public Library (MA–30/2): 1888–89.

Union Theological Seminary—Burke Library (NY–275/1): Ap, S 1889, F-Ap 1890.

Yale Divinity School Library (CT–55/2): V 2, 1889–90.

CHINESE FOR CHRIST INC. NEWSLETTER.

Gordon-Conwell Theological Seminary—Goddard Library (MA–230/4): V 2, N 3–5; V 3, N 1; V 4, N 1–3; V 5, N 1, 1960–63.

Chinese Medical Association

BULLETIN. Chinese Medical Association, Council on Christian Medical Work, Shanghai.

Title varies: OCCASIONAL LEAFLET, 1932–41; BULLETIN OF THE COUNCIL ON CHRISTIAN MEDICAL WORK, 1947–48.

Harvard Divinity School—Andover-Harvard Theological Library (MA–95/2): V 10, N 37; V 11, N 40; V 13, N 42; Nv 1947, Jl 1948, Ja 1949.

National Library of Medicine (MD–35/2): V 10–12, N 36–45, S 1947-O 1949.

Union Theological Seminary—Burke Library (NY–275/1): N 1–34, 36–38, 40–41, 1932–48.

OCCASIONAL LEAFLET. Chinese Medical Association, Council on Medical Missions, Shanghai. V 1–9, N 1–35, D 1932-Nv 1941.

Issue for Ap 1941 called also BULLETIN; issue for Nv 1941 called MEDICAL MISSION BULLETIN. Issues for D 1932-O 1934 have no volume numbering but constitute V 1–2. Index for V 6–8, 1938–40, in V 8. Continues as THE BULLETIN OF THE ASSOCIATION'S COUNCIL ON CHRISTIAN MEDICAL WORK, 1947. Issued jointly with the National Christian Council of China.

Harvard Divinity School—Andover-Harvard Theological Library (MA–95/1): V 3, N 14; V 4, N 19; V 6, N 27, O 1935, Je 1936, Nv 1938.

National Library of Medicine (MD–35/2): V [1]–9, N 1–35, D 1932-Nv 1941.

CHINESE MEDICAL DIRECTORY. China Medical Association, Shanghai. 1928-.

Continues MEDICAL GUIDE, WITH CLASSIFIED LIST OF MEDICAL SUPPLIERS, V 1, 1928.

Center for Research Libraries (IL–25/4): 1932, 1936.

College of Physicians of Philadelphia Library (PA–155/1): 1932.

Columbia University—Starr East Asian Library (NY–195/4): 1930.

Los Angeles County Medical Association Library (CA–145/1): V 3, 1932.

National Library of Medicine (MD–35/2): V 1–4, 1928–34.

Union Theological Seminary—Burke Library (NY–275/1): 1941.

University of Chicago—Crerar Library (IL–70/1): 1928, 1930.

CHINESE MEDICAL JOURNAL (English). China Medical Missionary Association, Peiping Union Medical College, Peiping, Shanghai. V 1–, 1887- (monthly).

Publisher and place of publication varies: currently published by People's Medical Publishers, Peking; V 61–62, 1943–44, published in Washington, D.C. Title varies: CHINA MEDICAL MISSIONARY JOURNAL, V 1–21, N 2, 1887-O 1909; CHINA MEDICAL JOURNAL, V 21, N 3-V 45, N 12, N 1909-D 1931.

Center for Research Libraries (IL–25/4): V 84–85, N 9, 1965–66.

Cleveland Health Sciences—Allen Memorial Library (OH–80/1): V 46–63, 65–66, 70, 75–85, 1932–44, 1947–48, 1952, 1957–66.

College of Physicians of Philadelphia Library (PA–155/1): V 46–70; V 71, N 1, 3–6; V 72–85; n.s. V 1–2; n.s. V 1–; 1932–66, 1973–.

Columbia University—Long Health Sciences Library (NY–160/1): V 46–58; V 59, N 1–6; V 61–62, 65, 69–71, 73–83; V 84, N 7–12; V 85; V 92, N 1–; 1932–44, 1947–60, 1962–66, n.s., 1979–.

Cornell University—Wason Collection (NY–95/1): V 19, N 5; V 21, N 4; V 24–27, 29–61; V 62, N 1–2; V 67–68; V 69, N 1–4; V 70, N 9–12; V 71, N 4–6; V 72; V 73, N 1–4, 6; V 74–85, n.s. V 1–2; 1905, 1907, 1910–13, 1915–44, 1949–66, 1975–76.

Francis A. Countway Library of Medicine (MA–55/1): V 46–85, n.s. V 1–4, n.s. V 92, 1932–66, 1973–79.

Garrett-Evangelical and Seabury-Western Theological Seminaries—United Library (IL–110/1): V 19, N 2–4, 6; V 20; V 21, N 1–4, 6; V 22; V 23, N 2–6; V 24–25; 1905–11.

Georgetown University—Dahlgren Medical Library (DC–50/1): V 61–62, 81–85, 1943–44, 1962–66.

Harvard University—Harvard-Yenching Library (MA–125/6): V 71–76, 79–85, 1953–66.

Indiana University—School of Medicine Library (IN–70/1): V 46–59; V 60, N 1–6; V 61–69, 75–85, n.v.; 1932–51, 1957–66, 1973–75, 1979, 1983–.

Iowa State University Library (IA–5/1): V 92–, 1979–.

Library of Congress—General Reading Rooms Division (DC–120/1): 1908–14, 1916, Jl 1937-Je 1939, Ja-Je 1941, 1945, 1950–57.

Los Angeles County Medical Association Library (CA–145/1): V 46, N 3–11; V 48, N 9–12; V 49, N 7–9, 11; V 50, N 7–8, 10–12; V 51–54; V 55, N 1–3, 5; V 56, N 1, 3–6; V 57, N 2, 6; V 58–59; V 60, N 1–3; V 61; V 62, N 1–4; V 63, N 2; V 65; V 66, N 1–10, 12; V 67; V 68, N 1–4, 9–12; V 69–71; V 72, N 7–12; V 73–85; n.s., V 1–4; V 92; V 93, N 1–3, 5–12; V 94, N 1–11; V 95–96; V 97, N 1–11; V 98, N 2–9; V 99, N 4–8; 1932, 1934–41, 1943–45, 1947–66, 1973–.

National Library of Medicine (MD–35/2): V 46–85, 1932–66.

New York Academy of Medicine Library (NY–220/1): V 46–62, 66–85, n.s., V 1–4, 92–, 1932–46, 1950–66, 1975–.

New York State Library (NY–15/2): V 17, index; V 18, N 1; V 19, N 1; V 20, N 5–6; V 21, N 1, 3–6; V 22, N 1, 3–6; V 23, N 4–6; V 25, N 3–6; V 26; V 27, N 1–5; V 28–34; V 35, N 1–4, 6; V 36, N 1, 3–4; V 37–39; V 40, N 1–5, 8; V 41, N 7–12; V 42, N 1–3, 9–11; V 43, N 7–8, 10–12; V 44; V 45, N 6; V 46–54; V 55, N 1–3; V 57, N 6, V 58, N 4–6; V 59, N 6; V 60, N 1, 3; V 61–69; V 70, N 9–12; V 71, N 1–5; V 72, N 4, 6; V 73, N 4; V 74–75; V 76, N 1–2, 4–6; V 77, N 1, 3–6; V 78, N 2–3; V 80, N 2–6; V 81, N 9; V 82, N 6, 10–12; V 83–84; n.s. V 1; 1903–9, 1911–41, 1943–60, 1962–65, 1975.

New York University—Ehrman Medical Library (NY–255/1): V 4672, n.s. V 1, 1932–54, 1973–.

Ohio State University—Health Sciences Library (OH–105/1): V 37, N 2–12; V 38; V 39, N 1–5; V 45, N 8–11; V 46, N 1–6, 8; V 59; V 60, N 1–3; V 61; V 65–69; V 73–77; V 78, N 1, 4–6; V 79–80; V 81, N 1–4, 6; V 82–85; 1923–25, 1931–32, 1941, 1943, 1947–51, 1955–60, 1962–66.

Ohio State University—Thompson Memorial Library (OH–110/4): V 1–35, 1887–1921.

Stanford University—Green Library (CA–305/1): V 1–35, N 6, Mr 1887-Nv 1921.

Stanford University—Lane Medical Library (CA–310/1): V 46–67, [68], 69, [70], 73–81, [82–85], n.s. V 1–4, n.s. V 92–, 1932–52, 1955–66, 1973–.

Union Theological Seminary—Burke Library (NY–275/1): V 1–69, N 4, Mr 1887–1951.

University of California at Los Angeles—Biomedical Library (CA–160/1): 1932–34, 1937–52, 1954–66, (n.s.) 1975–.

University of California, Berkeley—Biology Library (CA–40/1): V 82–85, n.s., V 3, N 3-V 4, N 4, 1963–66, 1977–78.

University of California, Davis—Health Sciences Library (CA–95/1): V 74–84, n.s., V 1–4, n.s. V 92–, 1956–65, 1975–.

University of California, San Francisco—Medical Library (CA–250/2): 1924–.

University of California, Santa Barbara, Library (CA–275/2): n.s. V 1–4, 92–, 1975–.

University of Chicago—Crerar Library (IL–70/1): V 45–85, 1931–66, 1973–.

University of Georgia Libraries (GA–5/1): V 51–69, 91–, 1937–51, 1978–.

University of Illinois at Urbana-Champaign Library (IL–185/1): V 22; V 23, N 6; V 24–61, 65–69; V 70, N 9–12; V 71, N 4–6; V 72, N 4–6; V 73, N 1–4; V 74, N 4–6; V 75–79; V 80, N 1–6; V 84; V 85, N 1–9; 1908–41, 1943, 1947–60, 1965–66.

University of Louisville—Kornhauser Health Sciences Library (KY–60/1): V 46–, 1932- (inc.).

University of Maryland—McKeldin Library (MD–45/2): V 70, 74–75, 77–85, 1952, 1956–57, 1959–66.

University of Michigan—Asia Library (MI–10/1): V 1–4; n.s. V 92, N 5; V 93–98; 1975–78, 1980–85.

University of Pittsburgh—Health Sciences Library (PA–255/1): V 61–, 1943–44.

University of Rochester—Miner Library (NY–355/1): V 46–47; V 48, N 1–2; V 49, N 1–2; V 50, N 1–2; V 51; V 52, N 1–2, 6; V 53–59; V 60, N 1–3; V 61–63; V 64, N 3–12; V 65–71; V 72, N 1, 3–6; V 73; 1932–55.

University of Wisconsin-Madison—Health Sciences Library (WI–35/1): V 24, 26, 31, 33, 41–45, 1910–31.

Yale Divinity School Library (CT–55/2): V 1, 7–11, 15, 22–69, 1887, 1893–97, 1901, 1908–51.

Yale University—Medical Library (CT–75/1): n.s. V 1–4, 92, 1975–78, 1979–.

CHINESE MEDICAL JOURNAL (Chengtu edition). China Medical Missionary Association, Chengtu. V 61A–63A, N 5, O 1942-O 1945.

    V 61A also called V 1–.

College of Physicians of Philadelphia Library (PA–155/1): [V 63A], 1945.

Columbia University—Long Health Sciences Library (NY–160/1): V 61A, 1942.

Cornell University—Wason Collection (NY–95/1): V 61A, N 1, O 1942.

Francis A. Countway Library of Medicine (MA–55/1): V 61A, N 1; V 62A; V 63A, N 1, 5; 1942–45.

New York Academy of Medicine Library (NY–220/1): 1942–45.

Stanford University—Lane Medical Library (CA–310/1): V 61A–63A, 1942–45.

CHINESE MEDICAL JOURNAL. Foreign ed. Peking/Shanghai/Peking. 1932–66.

Continued as CHINA'S MEDICINE.

Francis A. Countway Library of Medicine (MA–55/1): V 46–84; V 85, N 1–9, 1932–66.

Yale University—Medical Library (CT–75/1): V 46–81, 83–85, 1932–66.

CHINESE MEDICAL JOURNAL. SUPPLEMENT. V 1, 1936.

Cleveland Health Sciences—Allen Memorial Library (OH–80/1): V 1, 1936.

Columbia University—Long Health Sciences Library (NY–160/1): V 1–4, 1936–52.

Francis A. Countway Library of Medicine (MA–55/1): V 1–3, 1936–40.

Lloyd Library (OH–35/1): V 2–3, 1938–40.

Los Angeles County Medical Association Library (CA–145/1): 1936, 1952.

New York Academy of Medicine Library (NY–220/1): V 1–3, 1936–40.

New York State Library (NY–15/2): 1952.

Stanford University—Lane Medical Library (CA–310/1): V 1–3, 1936–40.

University of California at Los Angeles—Biomedical Library (CA–160/1): 1936.

University of Chicago—Crerar Library (IL–70/1): V 1–3, 1936–40.

University of Illinois at Urbana-Champaign Library (IL–185/1): V 1, 3, 1936, 1940.

University of Louisville—Kornhauser Health Sciences Library (KY–60/1): V 1–3, 1936–40.

University of Rochester—Miner Library (NY–355/1): V 1–3, 16, 1936, 1938, 1940, 1952.

THE CHINESE MISCELLANY. Mission Press, Shanghai. N 1–4, 1849–50.

Yale University—Department of Manuscripts and Archives (CT–60/33): N 1–3, 1849.

CHINESE MISSIONARY GLEANER. London. V 1, 1851.

Continues THE GLEANER IN THE MISSIONARY FIELD.

Drew University Library (NJ–40/2): V 3, N 35, 1853(?).

Union Theological Seminary—Burke Library (NY–275/1): 1856–59.

Yale Divinity School Library (CT–55/2): V 1–2, n.s. V 1–2, 1851–55.

CHINESE NEWSPAPER CLIPPINGS ON RELIGION. Tao Fong Shan Har Ecumenical Centre, Hong Kong. V 1–, 1979-.

Union Theological Seminary—Burke Library (NY–275/1): V 5-, 1984-.

CHINESE RECORDER. China Editorial Board, Shanghai. V 1–, My 1868-. V 43, N 2-V 69, F 1912-D 1938 (monthly).

Continues MISSIONARY RECORDER AND MISSIONARY JOURNAL. Title varies: CHINESE RECORDER AND MISSIONARY JOURNAL, Je 1870-Ja 1912. Absorbed EDUCATIONAL REVIEW (Shanghai) in 1938 to form CHINESE RECORDER AND EDUCATIONAL REVIEW. Publisher and place of publication varies: Rozario, Marcel & Co, Foochow, 1869–72; American Presbyterian Mission Press, 1874–1941. Suspended from Je 1872-D 1873. Index: V 1–20, 1868–89, includes index to MISSIONARY RECORDER.

Ambassadors for Christ (PA–125/1): V 56, N 3, 1925.

Andover Newton Theological School—Trask Library (MA–180/2): V 37–40, 53–72, 1906-9, 1922–41.

Andrews University—White Library (MI–50/1): V 40, N 11–12; V 41; V 42, N 1–3, 5–7, 9–12; V 44, N 1–7, 9–11; V 45, N 4–12; V 46, N 1–2, 4–7, 9–12; V 47, N 8; V 48, N 1, 3–4; 6–12; V 49, N 2–12; V 50; V 51, N 1–11; V 52, N 6; V 53; V 54, N 1–9, 11–12; V 55; V 56, N 1–2, 4–6, 8–10; V 58, N 1–7, 9–12; V 59–60; V 61, N 1, 3–4, 6–12; V 62, N 11; V 64, N 1–2, 4–8, 10–12; V 65, N 2–12; V 66–67; V 68, N 1–3, 5–9, 11–12; V 70, N 2–5, 8, 12; V 71, N 1–2, 4, 9–11; V 72, N 5–6, 8, 10; 1909–11, 1913–25, 1927–31, 1933–37, 1939–41.

Associated Mennonite Biblical Seminaries Library (IN–25/3): V 3, [6–8], [9–11], [18–48], 1871, 1874–76, 1878–80, 1887–1917.

Bangor Theological Seminary—Moulton Library (ME–5/1): V 58–62, 1927–31.

Baylor University—Moody Memorial Library (TX–60/1): V 41–72, 1910–41.

Berea College—Special Collections (KY–5/2): V 3–4, 54–64; V 66, N 8; V 67–68; V 69, N 1, 4–6; 1870–71, 1923–33, 1935–38.

Bethany and Northern Baptist Theological Seminaries Library (IL–135/1): V 46–54; V 55, N 1–3, 5–12; V 58–63; V 64, N 1, 4–7, 9–10, 12; V 65, N 1–3, 5–12; V 66; V 67, N 1–4, 6–8, 10; V 68, N 5-V 71, N 6; 1915–24, 1927–40.

Bethel Theological Seminary Library (MN–50/1): V 40–46, 4872, 1909–15, 1917–41.

Boston University—School of Theology Library (MA–35/1): V 1–72, 1868–1941.

Brigham Young University—Lee Library (UT–10/1): V 1, N 7–11; V 3–4; V 5, N 1–6; V 6, N 4–5; V 7, N 2, 4–5; V 9, N 2–4, 6; V 10, N 1, 3–6; V 19, 23, 34; V 47, N 8, 10–12; V 48, N 1–3, 5–12; V 49; V 50, N 2, 5–6, 8, 10–12; V 51, N 1–3, 6–12; V 52, N 1–10, 12; V 53, N 2–12; V 54, N 1–11; V 56; V 58, N 1–4, 8–12; V 62, N 1–7, 9, 11–12; V 63, N 1–4, 7–12; V 64, N 1–11; V 65, N 2–12; V 68, N 1–4, 8; V 72, N 3; 1868–72, 1874–76, 1878–79, 1888, 1892, 1903, 1916–23, 1925, 1930–34, 1937, 1941.

Buffalo and Erie County Public Library (NY–60/1): 1924–32, 1941 (inc.).

Calvin College and Seminary Library (MI–85/1): V 52–72, 1921–41.

Central Baptist Theological Seminary Library (KS–20/1): V 23–27, 54–71, 1892–96, 1923–40.

Christian Theological Seminary Library (IN–60/2): V 1–72, 1869–1941.

Claremont Colleges—Honnold Library (CA–85/1): V 1–72, 1868–1941.

Cleveland Public Library (OH–85/1): V 70–71; V 72, N 1–10; 1939–40, Ja-O 1941.

Colgate-Rochester Theological Seminaries—Swasey Library (NY–350/1): V 1–7, 9–15, 17–72, 1868–76, 1878–84, 1891–1940.

College of William and Mary—Swem Library (VA–105/2): V 2–8, V 50, N 9, V 53, N 10-V 61, 1869–77, S 1919, O 1922–30.

College of Wooster—Andrews Library (OH–200/1): V 47–48, [49], 59–60, [61–63], 1916–18, 1928–32.

Cornell University—Wason Collection (NY–95/1): V 1–12; V 13, N 2–6; V 14–15; V 26, N 1–10, 12; V 27–29; V 30, N 1–6, 8, 10–12; V 31, N 2, 5–8, 10–12; V 32; V 33, N 2–12; V 34, N 1–2, 4–12; V 35–36; V 37, N 2–12; V 38–44; V 45, N 3–4, 6–12; V 46–55; V 56, N 1–10, 12; V 57; V 58, N 2–12; V 59–71; V 72, N 1–11; 1868–72, 1874–1941.

Davidson College Archives (NC–20/2): 1868–1940.

Delta State University—Roberts Library (MS–5/1): V 1–71, 1868–1940.

Denver Conservative Baptist Seminary—Thomas Library (CO–10/3): V 1–72, 1868–1941.

Drew University Library (NJ–40/2): V 44–69, 1913–38.

Duke University—Perkins Library (NC–55/1): V 1–71; V 72, N 1–10; 1868–1941.

Emory University—Pitts Theology Library (GA–15/5): V 1–5, 7–8, 16–17, 29–72, 1868–74, 1876–77, 1885–86, 1898–1941.

Evangelical and Reformed Historical Society—Schaff Library (PA–80/13): V 39–42, 55–67, 69–71, 1908–11, 1924–36, 1938–40.

Florida State University—Strozier Library (FL–25/1): V 3, 5–8, 10, 12–17, 19–72, 1870–71, 1874–77, 1879, 1881–86, 1888–1941.

Fuller Theological Seminary—McAlister Library (CA–205/1): V 15–43, 1884–1912.

Furman University—Duke Library (SC–30/2): V 41, 1910.

Garrett-Evangelical and Seabury-Western Theological Seminaries—United Library (IL–110/1): V 43, N 2-V 44, N 10; V 45–52, N 11; V 53–69; 1912–39.

Graduate Theological Union Library (CA–15/2): V 34–71, 1903–40.

Harvard Divinity School—Andover-Harvard Theological Library (MA–95/2): V 1, N 3, 7–9, 11; V 2, N 9; V 3, N 1-V 7, N 6; V 8, N 3-V 9, N 6; V 14, N 1-V 26, N 2; V 39, N 1–12; V 41, N 1-V 43, N 1–12; V 45, N 1-V 48, N 12; V 51, N 1–8, 10-V 62, N 12; V 64, N 1-V 65, N 12; V 66, N 7-V 71; 1868–78, 1883–95, 1908, 1910–12, 1914–17, 1920, 1925–31, 1933–36, 1939–40.

Harvard University—Harvard-Yenching Library (MA–125/6): V 4, N 8, 10–12; V 13, N 2–6; V 24, N 2; V 33, N 2–4, 6, 9, 11; V 34, N 2, 6–7; V 36, N 6, 10; V 37, N 3–6, 8; 1872, 1882, 1893, 1902–3, 1905–6.

Harvard University—Widener Library (MA–155/1): V

1–46; V 47, N 1–3, 5–6; V 48–71; V 72, N 1–10; 1868–1941.

Historical Foundation of the Presbyterian and Reformed Churches (NC–80/28): V 42–72, 1911–41.

Indiana University—University Libraries (IN–20/2): F 1912-D 1938.

Johns Hopkins University—Eisenhower Library (MD–10/1): V 56, N 11; V 57, N 5–12; V 58; V 59, N 1–4; 1925–28.

Lancaster Theological Seminary—Schaff Library (PA–90/1): V 34, N 1, 9; V 35, N 1–3, 5–6, 8–12; V 36, N 4, 8–9; V 37, N 5–6, 10–12; V 38, N 1, 4–12; V 39–43; V 44, N 1–2, 4–10, 12; V 45, N 1, 3, 11;.V 48; V 49, N 2, 4–6, 9–12; V 50, N 1–4, 6–9, 11–12; V 51; V 53, 2–5, 7–8, 10–12; V 54–71; V 72, N 1–10; 1903–14, 1917–20, 1922–41.

Luther Northwestern Theological Seminary Library (MN–100/1): V 27, [35–38], 39–40, [41–43], 44–45, [46–47], 48–49, [50], 51–71; V 72, N 1–11; 1896, 1904–41.

Lutheran Theological Seminary—Krauth Memorial Library (PA–180/1): My-Je 1874, Ag 1927-Je 1932.

Lutheran Theological Seminary—Wentz Library (PA–50/1): V [43–47], 48, [51], 52, 54, [55], 58–59, [61–62], 63–67, [68], 69–71, [72], 1912–17, 1920–21, 1923–24, 1927–28, 1930–41.

Michigan State University Library (MI–75/1): V 43–72, 1912–41.

Mount Holyoke College—Williston Library (MA–225/1): V 62, [67], 68–71, [72], 1931, 1937–41.

Mount Union College Library (OH–5/1): V 54, F-Ap 1923.

New Brunswick Theological Seminary—Sage Library (NJ–65/2): V [44], 45–71, [72], 1913–41.

New York Public Library—General Research Division (NY–230/1): 1870–1941 (inc.).

North Park College and Theological Seminary—Wallgren Library (IL–65/1): V 34, 36–72, 1903, 1905–41.

Oberlin College—Main Library (OH–175/1): V 1–72, N 10, 1868-O 1941.

Ohio State University—Thompson Memorial Library (OH–110/4): V 50–58; V 61, N 2–12; V 65, 68; V 69, N 1–2; V 70, N 1, 3–12; V 71, N 2–12; V 72, N 1–10; 1919–27, 1930, 1934, 1937–41.

Ohio University—Alden Library (OH–15/1): Ja 1924-D 1926.

Ohio Wesleyan University—Beeghly Library (OH–140/1): V 32, 42–72, 1901, 1911–41.

Presbyterian Historical Society—Archives and Library (PA–200/28): 1870–1941.

Princeton Theological Seminary—Speer Library (NJ–95/3): V 2, N 10; V 3, N 1-V 5, N 4; V 5, N 7-V 7; V 10–12, 14, 16; V 18, 5–10; V 19-V 20, N 11; V 21, N 1–6, 8–12; V 22, N 1–6, 8–12; V 23-V 26, N 3; V 26, N 6–7, 9–12; V 27-V 31, N 8; V 31, N 10–12; V 32-V 34, N 6; V 34, N 8–12; V 36–38; V 40–72, N 6, V 72, N 8–11; 1870–76, 1879–81, 1883, 1885, 1887–1903, 1905–7, 1909–41.

Princeton University—Firestone Library (NJ–100/1): V

66–67, My 1936-Ap 1937.

Rutgers University—Alexander Library (NJ–75/1): 1874–99, 1921–23.

Rutherford B. Hayes Presidential Center Library (OH–145/2): V 3, N 5; V 5, N 1; O 1870, Ja-F 1874.

San Francisco Theological Seminary Library (CA–235/2): Mr 1870-O 1941.

Southern Baptist Theological Seminary—Boyce Centennial Library (KY–50/2): V [1–2], 3–26, [27], 28, [29–31], 32–36, 41–72, 1868–1905, 1910–41.

Southern Methodist University—Bridwell Theology Library (TX–20/2): V 51–72, 1920–41.

Temple University—Paley Library (PA–210/2): V [53–54, 57–62, 65], 1922–23, 1926–31, 1934.

Union Theological Seminary—Burke Library (NY–275/1): V 43–69, 1912–38.

Union Theological Seminary in Virginia Library (VA–85/1): V 3–5, 12, 14–15, 18–26, [27], 28–36, [37], 38–71, [72], 1870–1941.

United Theological Seminary Library (OH–120/11): V 52–72, 1921–41.

United Theological Seminary of the Twin Cities Library (MN–55/1): V 54–65, 68–70, 72, 1923–34, 1937–39, 1941.

University of Arizona Library (AZ–5/3): V 1–72, 1868–1941.

University of California, Berkeley—Bancroft Library (CA–35/12): V 1, N 1–3, My-Jl 1868.

University of California, Berkeley—General Library (CA–70/1): V 1–72, 1868–1941.

University of California, Davis, Library (CA–110/2): V 18, 24–26, 1887, 1893–95.

University of California, Santa Barbara—Department of Special Collections (CA–270/1): V 6, 1874.

University of Chicago—Regenstein Library (IL–85/1): V 3–71, 1870–1940.

University of Delaware—Morris Library (DE–5/2): V 1–72, 1867–1941.

University of Georgia Libraries (GA–5/1): V 1–71, 1868–1940.

University of Hawaii—Hamilton Library (HI–15/2): 1874–1941.

University of Illinois at Urbana-Champaign Library (IL–185/1): V 56–57, 70–72, 1925–26, 1939–41.

University of Iowa Libraries (IA–40/1): 1868–1941.

University of Kansas—Watson Library (KS–35/3): V 43, N 9–10; V 44, N 3–4; V 46–51; V 56, N 11–12; V 57, N 2–3, 5–12; V 58; V 59, N 1–5, 7–12; V 60, N 6–11; V 61, N 1, 3–12; V 62, N 1–7; 1912–13, 1915–20, 1925–31.

University of Maryland—McKeldin Library (MD–45/2): 1868–1940.

University of Michigan—Hatcher Graduate Library (MI–25/1): V 7, 22–28, 30–39, 42–72, 1876–1941.

University of Minnesota—Wilson Library (MN–40/1): V 3–9, 11–54, 56–72, N 1–10, 1870–78, 1880–1923, 1925–40.

University of Nebraska, Lincoln—Love Library (NB–25/2): V 58, N 2–3, 5–6, 8–9, 11–12; V 59–60; V 61, N 1–3, 5–12; V 62, N 1–10, 12; V 63, N 1–9, 11–12; V 64; 1927–33.

University of Notre Dame—Memorial Library (IN–95/1): V 1–72, 1868–1941.

University of Oregon—Department of Special Collections (OR–15/18): Mr 1941.

University of Oregon Library (OR–20/2): V 55–72, 1924–41.

University of Pennsylvania—Van Pelt Library (PA–215/1): V 1–9, 1868–78.

University of Vermont—Bailey/Howe Library (VT–5/3): V 69–71, 1938–40.

University of Washington Libraries (WA–45/1): V 3–21, 40–41, 46, 49, 51–52, 55–56, 58, 60–71; V 72, N 1–11; 1870–90, 1909–10, 1915, 1918, 1920–21, 1924–25, 1927, Ja-Je 1929, Ag 1929-Nv 1941.

University of Wisconsin-Madison—Memorial Library (WI–45/1): V 1–72, 1868–1941.

Vassar College Library (NY–330/1): V 39–71, 1908–40.

Virginia Baptist Historical Society (VA–90/8): V 4, N 11–12, V 20, N 5, Ap-My 1872, My 1889.

Washington State University—Holland Library (WA–15/1): V 22, 24, [45], [47], [51], 53–54, [55], 56, [57–58], [60–61], 62–63, 65–67, [68–69], 1891, 1893, 1914, 1916, 1920, 1922–27, 1929–32, 1934–38.

Washington University—East Asian Library (MO–85/1): V 1–71, 1868–1940.

Wellesley College—Clapp Library (MA–245/1): V 1, N 2-V 71, Je 1868-D 1940.

Western Baptist College Library (OR–40/1): V 53, N 9; V 54, N 3, 12; V 56, N 4–5, 9; V 64, N 10, 12; 1922–23, 1925, 1933.

Westminster Theological Seminary Library (PA–220/2): V 4, 40–41, 54–55; 1871–72, 1909–10, 1923–24.

Wheaton College—Bebbie Archives and Special Collections (MA–200/3): 1868–1940.

Wheaton College—Graham Center Library (IL–205/1): V 1–61, [62–72], 1868–1941.

Yale Divinity School Library (CT–55/2): V 1–72, 1868–1941.

Yale Divinity School—Special Collections (CT–50/2): 1871–1911, 1922–29, 1932–40.

Yale Divinity School—Special Collections (CT–50/15): 1931–40.

Yale University—Sterling Memorial Library (CT–80/1): V 1–59, 64, 70, 1868–1928, 1933, 1939.

CHINESE RECORDER AND EDUCATIONAL REVIEW. China Editorial Board, Shanghai.

Drew University Library (NJ–40/2): V 70–71, 1939–41.

Garrett-Evangelical and Seabury-Western Theological Seminaries—United Library (IL–110/1): V 70–72, 1939–41.

Indiana University—University Libraries (IN–20/2): 1939–40.

Union Theological Seminary—Burke Library (NY–275/1): V 70–72, 1939–41.

CHINESE RECORDER AND MISSIONARY JOURNAL. Shanghai.

American Antiquarian Society (MA–265/1): Ag 1869; F-Mr 1870-S 1871; Je-D 1874; Mr 1875-O 1878.

American Philosophical Society Library (PA–145/6): V 2,

N 10, Mr 1870.

College of Wooster—Andrews Library (OH–200/1): V 2–3, 5–6, [7], 8, [9], 17, 22–23, 32–35, [36–39], 1869–71, 1874–78, 1886, 1891–92, 1901–8.

Columbia University—Starr East Asian Library (NY–195/4): V 1–3, 5–24, 37, [43–60], 61–70, [71], 1868–71, 1874–93, 1912–14, 1916–20, 1924–28, 1930–41.

Drew University Library (NJ–40/2): V 2–43, 1868–1912.

Essex Institute—Phillips Library (MA–210/2): V 1, N 2–5, 7–12; V 2 N 1–7, 9–12; V 3–7; V 8, N 1, 4,; V 9–25; V 26, N 3–12; V 27–30; V 31, N 1–2, 4–12; V 32–60; V 61, N 1–7, 9, 11–12; V 62, N 1–8, 10–12; V 63; 1868–1932.

Fuller Theological Seminary—McAlister Library (CA–205/1): V 43, N 2-V 61, 1912–30.

Garrett-Evangelical and Seabury-Western Theological Seminaries—United Library (IL–110/1): V 3–12, 17, 19–34; V 35, N 1–2, 4, 5–12; V 36–43, N 1, 1870–81, 1886, 1888–1912.

Gordon-Conwell Theological Seminary—Goddard Library (MA–230/4): V 1–63, N 3, 8, 10; V 68, N 9; V 71, N 10, 12, 1868–1932, 1937, 1940.

Harvard University—Harvard-Yenching Library (MA–125/6): V 53, N 6, 1922.

Indiana Universities—University Libraries (IN–20/2): Je 1868-Ja 1912.

Stanford University—Green Library (CA–305/1): V 1–14, 16–72, 1868–1941.

Union Theological Seminary—Burke Library (NY–275/1): V 143, 1868–1912.

CHINESE REPOSITORY. Canton. V 1–20, My 1832-D 1851.
Index V 1–20.

Academy of Natural Science of Philadelphia Library (PA–135/4): V 5–6, 13–17, My 1836-Ap 1838, Ja 1844-D 1848.

American Antiquarian Society (MA–265/1): V 1–2, [3–4], 5–11, 1832–36, 1842.

American Congregational Association Library (MA–25/3): V 1, N 1–11; V 2–15, V 16, N 1–10; V 17, V 18, N 1–10, 12; V 19, N 1, 3, 9; V 20, N 2–12; 1832–51.

American Museum of Natural History Library (NY–140/1): V 13–14, 1844–45.

American Philosophical Society Library (PA–145/6): V 1-[3], 1832–34.

Amherst College—Special Collections (MA–10/1): 1832–48, 1850–51.

Andover Newton Theological School—Trask Library (MA–180/2): V 4–5, 1836–37.

Bethel Theological Seminary Library (MN–50/1): V 2, 15, 1833, 1846.

Boston College—Burns Library (MA–170/1): V 1–20, 1832–51.

Boston Public Library (MA–30/2): V 1–6, 8, 10–15, [16], 1832–38, 1840, 1842–46.

Boston University—School of Theology Library (MA–35/1): V 1–20, 1832–51.

Brown University—Rockefeller Library (RI–20/2): V 1–20, 1832–51.

Catholic University of America—Special Collections Section (DC–25/2): V2–20, My 1833-Ap 1851.

Claremont Colleges—Honnold Library (CA–85/1): V 1–20, 1832–51.

Columbia University—Starr East Asian Library (NY–195/4): V 1–20, My 1832-D 1851.

Cornell University—Wason Collection (NY–95/1): V 1–18, 1832–49.

Dartmouth College Library (NH–15/1): V 1–20, 1832–51.

Delta State University—Roberts Library (MS–5/1): V 1–20, 1832–51.

Drew University Library (NJ–40/2): V 1–20, 1832–51.

Duke University—Perkins Library (NC–55/1): V 1–14, 16–18, 1832–45, 1847–49.

Emory University—Pitts Theology Library (GA–15/5): V 1–20, 1832–51.

Emory University—Woodruff Library (GA–25/1): V 3–4, V 9–10, 20, 1834–36, 1840–41, 1851.

Essex Institute—Phillips Library (MA–210/2): V 1–19, 1832–50.

Field Museum of Natural History Library (IL–40/1): V 1–20, 1832–51.

Garrett-Evangelical and Seabury-Western Theological Seminaries—United Library (IL–110/1): V 1–20, 1832–51.

Graduate Theological Union Library (CA–15/2): V 1–20, 1833–51.

Harvard Divinity School—Andover-Harvard Theological Library (MA–95/2): V 1–20, 1832–51.

Harvard University—Harvard-Yenching Library (MA–125/6): V 1–20, 1832–51.

Harvard University—Widener Library (MA–155/1): V 1–20, 1832–51.

Hoover Institution Library (CA–300/1): V 1–20, 1832–51.

Indiana University—University Libraries (IN–20/2): V 1–20, 1832–51.

Iowa State University Library (IA–5/1): V 1–20, My 1832-D 1851.

Johns Hopkins University—Peabody Institute Library (MD–20/1): V 1–20, 1832–51.

Library Company of Philadelphia (PA–175/1): V 1–20, 1832–51.

Library of Congress—Rare Book Division (DC–110/1): V 1–20, 1832–51.

Library of the Boston Athenaeum—Rare Book Room (MA–65/1): V 1–20, 1832–51.

Louisville Presbyterian Theological Seminary Library (KY–45/1): V 1–20, My 1832-D 1851.

Metropolitan Museum of Art—Watson Library (NY–210/1): V 3–4, My 1834-Ap 1836.

National Library of Medicine (MD–35/1): V 17, N 3, Mr 1848.

New Brunswick Theological Seminary—Sage Library (NJ–65/2): V [1–13], 1832–44.

New York Academy of Medicine Library (NY–220/1): V 4–5, 1836–37.

Oberlin College—Special Collections (OH–180/1): V 1–20, 1832–51.

Ohio University—Alden Library (OH–15/1): V 1–20, 1832–51.

Peabody Museum—Phillips Library (MA–215/2): V 1–

20, 1832–51.

Pennsylvania State University—Penn State Room (PA–275/4): 1832–51 (repr.).

Presbyterian Historical Society—Archives and Library (PA–200/28): V 2, 4–8, 14–16, 20, 1833, 1836–40, 1847, 1851.

Princeton Theological Seminary—Speer Library (NJ–95/3): V 1–V 2, N 10; V 2, N 12–V 4, N 10; V 5, N 1, 7–V 9; V 11–12; V 14–16, N 2; V 16, N 4–10; V 17, N 1–5, 7–9, 11–12; V 18–20; 1832–40, 1842–43, 1845–51.

Princeton University—Gest Oriental Library (NJ–105/1): 1832–51.

Rutgers University—Alexander Library (NJ–75/1): V 1–20, 1832–51.

San Francisco Theological Seminary Library (CA–235/2): 1833–51.

School of Theology at Claremont Library (CA–90/1): V 1–15, 1832–46.

Southern Baptist Theological Seminary—Boyce Centennial Library (KY–50/2): V 1–20, My 1832–D 1851.

Southern Methodist University—Bridwell Theology Library (TX–20/2): V 1–20, 1832–51.

Stanford University—Green Library (CA–305/1): V 1–20, 1832–51.

Stanford University—Special Collections (CA–315/3): V 1–20, 1832–51.

Trinity College—Watkinson Library (CT–20/1): V 2–12; V 13, N 1–5, 8–12; V 20, N 6; 1833–44, 1851.

Union Theological Seminary—Burke Library (NY–275/1): 1832–51.

University of California at Los Angeles—University Research Library (CA–185/1): V 1–20, 1832–51.

University of California, Berkeley—General Library (CA–70/1): V 2–12, 14–20, 1833–43, 1845–51.

University of California, Davis, Library (CA–110/2): V 1–20, 1832–51.

University of Chicago—Regenstein Library (IL–85/1): V 1–20, 1832–51.

University of Illinois at Urbana-Champaign Library (IL–135/1): V 1–20, 1833–51.

University of Michigan—Hatcher Graduate Library (MI–25/1): V 1–20, 1832–51.

University of Minnesota—Wilson Library (MN–40/1): V 1–20, 1832–51.

University of Pennsylvania—Van Pelt Library (PA–215/1): 1832–51.

University of Redlands—Armacost Library (CA–210/3): V 1–11, 1832–43.

University of Washington Libraries (WA–45/1): V 1–20, 1832–51.

Virginia Baptist Historical Society (VA–90/8): V 18, N 1–3, 7–10; V 19, N 4–5, 8–12; V 20, N 1–7; 1849–51.

Washington University—East Asian Library (MO–85/1): V 1–20, 1832–51.

Wellesley College—Clapp Library (MA–245/1): V 1–20, My 1832–D 1851.

Wheaton College—Graham Center Library (IL–205/1): V 1–20, 1832–51.

Yale Divinity School Library (CT–55/2): V 1–19, 1832–50.

Yale University—Sterling Memorial Library (CT–80/1): V 1–20, 1832–51.

CHINESE THEOLOGICAL REVIEW. Foundation for Theological Education in Southeast Asia, Holland, MI. 1985–.

Graduate Theological Union Library (CA–15/2): 1985–.

Princeton Theological Seminary—Speer Library (NJ–95/3): 1985–.

Southern Baptist Convention—Jenkins Research Library (VA–70/1): 1985–86.

Southern Baptist Theological Seminary—Boyce Centennial Library (KY–50/2): V 1–, 1985–.

Western Conservative Baptist Seminary—Cline-Tunnell Library (OR–30/1): V 1–, 1985–.

CHINESE WORLD PULSE. Evangelical Missions Information Service, Wheaton, IL. V 1–7, N 4, 1977–83.

Merged with other world mission periodicals to form PULSE, 1984–.

Asbury Theological Seminary—Fisher Library (KY–90/1): V 1, N 1; V 2, N 1; V 3, N 1–2; V 4, N 1–2; V 5, N 1–2, 4; V 7, N 1–4; O 1977–Nv 1983.

Bethel Theological Seminary Library (MN–50/1): V 1–7, 1977–83.

Biola University—Rose Memorial Library (CA–130/4): V 5, N 1, Mr 1981.

Denver Conservative Baptist Seminary—Thomas Library (CO–10/3): V 1–7, 1977–83.

Gordon-Conwell Theological Seminary—Goddard Library (MA–230/4): V 1, N 1; V 2, N 1; V 3, N 1, 2; V 4, N 1–3; V 5, N 1–4; 1977–81.

Princeton Theological Seminary—Speer Library (NJ–95/3): 1977–81.

Reformed Bible College Library (MI–95/1): V 2, N 4; V 4, N 1–2; V 5, N 4; V 6, N 1–3; My 1978; Ja, My 1980; D 1981; Mr, Jl 1982.

Southern Baptist Theological Seminary—Boyce Centennial Library (KY–50/2): V 1–7, 1977–83.

Trinity Evangelical Divinity School Library (IL–90/1): V 1, N 1, V 2, N 1, V 3–7, O 1977, My 1978–83.

Union Theological Seminary—Burke Library (NY–275/1): V 1, 3–7, 1977, 1979–83.

Wheaton College—Graham Center Library (IL–205/1): V 1, N 1; V 2, N 1; V 3, N 1–2; V 4, N 1–3; V 5, N 1–V 6, N 2–3; V 7, N 1–4; 1977–83.

World Vision International—Research and Information Division (CA–200/1): 1971.

CHINESE Y'S MEN'S BULLETIN. *See* Young Men's Christian Association, Shanghai.

CHINESEGRAMS. Chinese Brethren Fellowship, Chicago.

Church of the Brethren General Board—Brethren Historical Library and Archives (IL–105/11): N 1–85, 1931–66.

CHING FENG (English edition). Christian Study Centre on Chinese Religion and Culture, Hong Kong. V 8–, winter 1964– (quarterly).

Title varies: V 1–7, QUARTERLY NOTES ON CHRISTIANITY AND CHINESE RELIGION AND CULTURE. Publisher name varies: Christian Study Centre on Chinese Religion and Culture. Chinese edition also exists.

Alliance Theological Seminary Library (NY–300/1): V 20, N 2-, 1977-.

American Bible Society Library (NY–135/1): 1981–85.

Andover Newton Theological School—Trask Library (MA–180/2): V 5-, 1961-.

Andrews University—White Library (MI–50/1): V 8; V 9, N 1–3; V 10–16; V 17, N 2, 3; V 18, N 1–3, 1964–75.

Asbury Theological Seminary—Fisher Library (KY–90/1): V 8; V 9, N 1–3; V 10–23; V 24, N 1–4; V 25, N 1–4; V 26, N 1–4; V 27, N 1–4; V 28, N 1–4; V 29, N4-; 1964-

Associated Mennonite Biblical Seminaries Library (IN–25/3): V 8–28, 1964–84.

Austin Presbyterian Theological Seminary—Stitt Library (TX–10/1): V 25-, 1982-.

Bethel Theological Seminary Library (MN–50/1): V 8-, 1964-.

Boston University—School of Theology Library (MA–35/1): V 8–27, 1964–84.

Claremont Colleges—Asian Studies Collection (CA–75/2): V 8, N 3–4, Summer 1964.

Columbia University—Starr East Asian Library (NY–195/4): V 10–22, Mr 1957-Winter 1966/67.

Cornell University—Wason Collection (NY–95/1): V 8–14, 1964–71.

Denver Conservative Baptist Seminary—Thomas Library (CO–10/3): V 8–29, 1964–86.

Drew University Library (NJ–40/2): V 8-, 1964-.

Emory University—Pitts Theology Library (GA–15/5): V 8–26, 1964–83.

Fuller Theological Seminary—McAlister Library (CA–205/1): V 9–29, 1966–86.

Garrett-Evangelical and Seabury-Western Theological Seminaries—United Library (IL–110/1): V 8-, 1964-.

Gordon-Conwell Theological Seminary—Goddard Library (MA–230/4): V [8–9], 10–15, [16–17], [19–20], 21-, 1964–74, 1976-.

Harvard Divinity School—Andover-Harvard Theological Library (MA–95/2): V 8-, 1964-.

Harvard University—Harvard-Yenching Library (MA–125/6): V 1-, 1957-.

Library of Congress—General Reading Rooms Division (DC–120/1): 1968–86.

Louisville Presbyterian Theological Seminary Library (KY–45/1): V 19–27, 1976–84.

Luther Northwestern Theological Seminary Library (MN–100/1): V 6-, 1962-.

New Brunswick Theological Seminary—Sage Library (NJ–65/2): V 8, N 1, Winter 1964-.

North Park College and Theological Seminary—Wallgren Library (IL–65/1): V 8–22, 1964–79.

Pittsburgh Theological Seminary—Barbour Library (PA–240/1): V 8-, 1964-.

Princeton Theological Seminary—Speer Library (NJ–95/3): V 8-, 1964-.

San Francisco Theological Seminary Library (CA–235/2): V 19, N 3–4; V 22, N 2, 1976, 1979.

Southern Baptist Convention—Jenkins Research Library (VA–70/1): 1985–87.

Southern Methodist University—Bridwell Theology Library (TX–20/2): V 8-, 1964-.

Trinity Evangelical Divinity School Library (IL–90/1): V 8, N 1, 3–4; V 9, N 1–3; V 10-; 1964-.

Union Theological Seminary—Burke Library (NY–275/1): V 1, N 1-, Mr 1957-.

Union Theological Seminary in Virginia Library (VA–85/1): V [20], 21–27, 1977–85.

University of California, Santa Barbara, Library (CA–275/2): V 8–19, 1964–76 (inc.).

University of Chicago—Regenstein Library (IL–85/1): V 8-, 1964-.

University of Illinois at Urbana-Champaign—University Archives (IL–180/1): V 14, 1971.

University of Pennsylvania—Van Pelt Library (PA–215/1): V [8]–16, 1964–73.

University of Washington Libraries (WA–45/1): V 2, N 2–4; V 3, N 1, 3–4; V 4, N 1, 3–4; V 5, N 1–2; V 6; V 7, N 1, 4; V 8–10; V 21, N 4-V 26; My 1958-D 1963, 1964–67, 1978–79, 1983.

Western Evangelical Seminary—Hallauer Memorial Library (OR–35/1): V 9–29, 1966–86 (inc.).

Wheaton College—Graham Center Library (IL–205/1): V 8, N 1, 3-V 11, N 1, 3-V 16, N 4, V 17, N 2-; 1964-.

Yale Divinity School Library (CT–55/2): V 1–4, 7–27, 1957–60, 1963–84.

Yale Divinity School—Special Collections (CT–50/2): 1965–72.

CHING I DIGEST. Ching I Middle School, Kaifeng.
Sisters of Providence Archives (IN–105/2): 1940–42.

Christian Churches (Disciples of Christ), International Convention, United Christian Missionary Society, China Mission
NEWSLETTER. Christian Churches (Disciples of Christ), International Convention, United Christian Missionary Society, China Mission.
Union Theological Seminary—Burke Library (NY–275/1): D 1948.

CHRISTIAN COLLEGES IN CHINA PROGRESS BULLETIN.
Associated Boards for Christian Colleges in China, New York.
Yale Divinity School—Special Collections (CT–50/25): V 6, N 1–3, 1942–43.

CHRISTIAN COLLEGES NEWSLETTER. Hwasipa, Chengtu. N 1, 1943.
Yale Divinity School—Special Collections (CT–50/25): N 1, 1943.

THE CHRISTIAN FARMER. North China Christian Rural Service Union, Literature Department, Tsinan. V 1, 1934. Special English issue, V 2, N 15, Ag 1935.
Cornell University—Wason Collection (NY–95/1): V 2, N 15, Ag 1935.
Harvard Divinity School—Andover-Harvard Theological Library (MA–95/2): V 2, N 15, Ag 1935.

CHRISTIAN INDUSTRY. National Christian Council of China, Industrial Committee, Shanghai. N 1–12, 1924–28(?).
Luther College Archives (IA–15/1): N 8, Jl 1926.

Christian Literature Society for China
LINK. Christian Literature Society for China. N

1–46, 1921?–1941.
Continued as NEWS LETTER of the C. L. S. of China, 1941.
Emory University—Pitts Theology Library (GA–15/5): N 30–31, 1937.
Union Theological Seminary—Burke Library (NY–275/1): N 5–7, 10–11, 15–16, 19, 21, 29–46, 1921–23, 1930–33, 1936–41.

MONTHLY LINK. Christian Literature Society for China, Shanghai.
    Harvard Divinity School—Andover-Harvard Theological Library (MA–95/2): N 31, 41–42, F 1937, Ap-Ag 1939.
    University of Kansas—Watson Library (KS–35/3): n.s. N 31–35, 1937

NEWSLETTER. Christian Literature Society for China. n.s., N 1-, 1941-.
    Continues LINK, 1941. Continued as NEWS FLASHES, 1948.
    Presbyterian Historical Society—Archives and Library (PA–200/28): N 1, Mr 1941.
    Union Theological Seminary—Burke Library (NY–275/1): n.s., N 1, Mr 1941, Jl 1948.

PERIODICAL LINK. Christian Literature Society for China, Shanghai.
    Harvard Divinity School—Andover-Harvard Theological Library (MA–95/1): N 29, Ag 1936.

QUARTERLY LINK. Christian Literature Society for China.
    Union Theological Seminary—Archives (NY–270/25): Je 1934.

CHRISTIAN UNIVERSITIES OF CHINA BULLETIN. China Christian Universities Association, London, [1931–50] (two or three times a year).
Title varies: CHINA CHRISTIAN UNIVERSITIES BULLETIN, N 43, 44, 1950. Continued by ASIA CHRISTIAN COLLEGE ASSOCIATION BULLETIN.
    Harvard Divinity School—Andover-Harvard Theological Library (MA–95/1): N 19, S 1938.
    Union Theological Seminary—Burke Library (NY–275/1): N 2–14, 16–40, 43–44, Ja 1932–50.

CHRISTIANITY IN CHINA: Historical Studies. Springfield, Missouri. V 1, 1985.
    Asian Studies Newsletter Archives (MD–40/1): V 1, N 1, 1985-.
    Western Conservative Baptist Seminary—Cline-Tunnell Library (OR–30/1): V 1, N 2- My 1986-.

CHUNGKING NEWS LETTER. Lutheran World Federation, Chungking, 1944–45.
    Lutheran Council in the U.S.A.—Archives of Cooperative Lutheranism (NY–205/1): 1944–45.

CHUNGKING REPORT. Lutheran World Federation, Chungking. 1945.
    Lutheran Council in the U.S.A.—Archives of Cooperative Lutheranism (NY–205/1): 1945.

THE CHURCH: Bulletin (and Forum) of the Church of Christ in China. Church of Christ in China, Shanghai (Chungking, Peking). V 1-, 1935- (irregular).
    Claremont Colleges—Asian Studies Collection

(CA–75/2): V 4, N 1, F 1950.
Harvard Divinity School—Andover-Harvard Theological Library (MA–95/1): V 4, N 4, O-Nv 1950.
Harvard Divinity School—Andover-Harvard Theological Library (MA–95/2): Nv 1935, My-Ag 1936, Ja 1947, F, O 1948, Ag 1949, Ap-Nv 1950.
Presbyterian Historical Society—Archives and Library (PA–200/3): V 2, N 1, F 1948.
San Francisco Theological Seminary Library (CA–235/2): V 1, N 8; V 2, N 1–2; V 3, N 1; V 4, N 1–4; Je 1947; F, O 1948; Ag 1949; 1950.
Union Theological Seminary—Burke Library (NY–275/1): V 1, N 1–8; V 2, N 1–2; V 3, N 1; V 4, N 1–4; 1935–50.
University of Oregon—Department of Special Collections (OR–15/18): 1941–45, S 1946; Ja, Je, 1947; F, O 1948; Je 1949 (supplement); F, Ap 1950.

Church Committee for China Relief
BULLETIN.
    Continues as HAVE A HEART FOR CHINA.
    Union Theological Seminary-Burke Library (NY–275/1): N A1-A17, 1938–39.

THE CHURCH IN CHINA. Shanghai. V 1–6, N 5, 1894-D 1899.
    Archives and History Collection of the Episcopal Church (TX–5/2): V 1–6, 1894–99.
    Brown University—Rockefeller Library (RI–20/2): V 1, N 2–3, 6; V 2, N 7–8, 10–11; V 3, N 1, 4–7, 9–11; V 4; V 5; 1894–98.

Church of Christ in China. See INFORMATION SERVICE.

THE CLASPED HANDS. Methodist Episcopal Church, East City, Peking; Tsunhua, Hopei. V 1, 1931.
    Wesleyan University—Special Collections and Archives (CT–30/4): V 1, N 1, n.v., Ap 1931, Jl 1934.

COLLECTANEA COMMISSIONIS SYNODALIS (Latin, English, French and Chinese). Synodal Commission, Catholic Church in China, Peking. V 1–19, 1928–47 (10 times per year).
Continued in part as: CHINA MISSIONARY—LE MISSIONAIRE DE CHINE, Ja 1948, and TO SHENG (Chinese), S 1949. Title varies: CHINA MISSIONARY—LE MISSIONAIRE DE CHINE, Ja 1948-Je 1949; CHINA MISSIONARY BULLETIN, S 1949-Jl 1953; MISSION BULLETIN, S 1953-D 1959; ASIA, Ja 1960-. See also CATHOLIC CHURCH IN CHINA.
    Catholic Theological Union Library (IL–20/1): V 1–19, 1928–47.
    Catholic University of America—Mullen Library (DC–20/1): V 1–19, 1928–46, Jl-D 1947.
    Johns Hopkins University—Eisenhower Library (MD–10/1): V 1, N 1–4; V 2–4, 1928–31.
    Princeton University—Gest Oriental Library (NJ–105/1): V 1–9, 1928–36.

College of Chinese Studies, Peking
BULLETIN.
    Cornell University—Wason Collection (NY–95/1): 1947.
MISCELLANEOUS PUBLICATIONS. 1934–41.
    University of California, Berkeley—General Library

(CA–70/1): V 1–2, 1934–41.

COLLEGE OF SCIENCE NEWSLETTER. *See* West China Union University.

COLOR AND BACKGROUND MATERIAL. *See* American Friends Service Committee.

Committee on Relief in China (F.M.C.)
BULLETIN. Committee on Relief in China (F.M.C.). N 1–9, Mr 1938-Je 1938.
> Union Theological Seminary—Burke Library (NY–275/1): N 1–9, Mr-Je 1938.

COMMUNITY CHURCH. Community Church of Shanghai. N 1–(?), 1923(?)–?.
> Union Theological Seminary—Burke Library (NY–275/1): N 6–26, 1923.

COMMUNITY SERVICE. Community Church of Shanghai.
> Presbyterian Historical Society—Archives and Library (PA–200/28): My 1923-My 1927.

COMPOSITION BULLETIN. *See* Fukien Christian University, Shanghai.

CONTRIBUTION. *See* University of Nanking, Nanking.

CONTRIBUTIONS. *See* Peking Union Medical College.

EL CORREO SINO-ANNAMITA: O, Correspondencia de las Misiones del Sagrado Orden de Predicadores en Formosa, China, Tung-king y Filipinas. Manila. 1866-.
> American Philosophical Society Library (PA–145/6): V 25, 38, 1891, 1912.
> Duke University—Perkins Library (NC–55/1): V 37–39, 1911–13.
> Harvard University—Widener Library (MA–155/1): V 1–41, 1866–1916 (inc.).
> University of California, Berkeley—General Library (CA–70/1): V 23, 33, 1889, 1905.
> Yale Divinity School Library (CT–55/2): V 20–25, 27–29, 1886–91, 1893–95.

DAILY METEOROLOGICAL RECORD. *See* Lingnan University, Canton.

DAILY METEOROLOGICAL RECORDS. *See* University of Nanking, Nanking.

DANZIGER EVANGELISCHER MISSIONS-VEREIN FÜR CHINA. Danzig.
> Yale Divinity School Library (CT–55/2): 1852–78.

DAY STAR, OR MESSAGE OF HOPE. n.p.
> Union Theological Seminary—Burke Library (NY–275/1): Ap 1914.

DIGEST OF THE SYNODAL COMMISSION OF PEIPING, CHINA. (Latin, English, French and Chinese). Synodal Commission, Catholic Church in China, Peking. V 1–19, 1928–47 (10 times per year).
> Continued as: COLLECTANEA COMMISSIONIS SYNODALIS, 1937–48; CHINA MISSIONARY—LE MISSIONAIRE DE CHINE, Ja 1948; and TO SHENG (Chinese), S 1949. Title varies: CHINA MISSIONARY—LE MISSIONAIRE DE CHINE, Ja 1948-Je 1949; CHINA MISSIONARY BULLETIN, S 1949-Jl 1953; MISSION BULLETIN, S 1953-

D 1959; ASIA, Ja 1960-. *See also* CATHOLIC CHURCH IN CHINA.
> University of Dayton—Marianist Community Archives (OH–130/1): V 5, N 1, 12; V 6–8: V 9, N 1–5: Ja, D 1933, 1934–36, Ja-My 1937.

DING. Holy Spirit Study Center, Hong Kong. V 1, 1981. Continued by TRIPOD.
> Institute for Chinese-Western Cultural History (CA–245/7): V 1, 1981.
> Union Theological Seminary—Burke Library (NY–275/1): V 1-, 1981-.

Diocesan Association for Western China, BULLETIN. *See* BULLETIN OF THE DIOCESAN ASSOCIATION FOR WESTERN CHINA.

Diocese of Macao. *See* BOLETIM ECLESIASTICO DA DIOCESE DE MACAU.

DIRECTORY OF PROTESTANT MISSIONARIES IN CHINA, JAPAN, AND COREA. The Hong Kong Daily Press Office, Hong Kong. V 1–11, 1881–1913.
> Biblical Theological Seminary Library (PA–70/1): 1912.
> Claremont Colleges—Asian Studies Collection (CA–75/3): 1912, 1917.
> Colgate-Rochester Theological Seminaries—Swasey Library (NY–350/1): 1918.
> Overseas Missionary Fellowship (PA–265/1): V 11, 1912.
> Presbyterian Historical Society—Archives and Library (PA–200/28): 1902, 1904–5, 1907–8, 1910, 1912, 1914, 1917.
> Union Theological Seminary—Burke Library (NY–275/1): V 1–11, 1881–1913.

DIRECTORY OF PROTESTANT MISSIONS IN CHINA. American Methodist Episcopal Mission Press, Foochow.
> American Antiquarian Society (MA–265/1): 1866.
> New York State Library—Manuscripts and Special Collections (NY–15/1): 1866.

DIRECTORY OF PROTESTANT MISSIONS IN CHINA. China Continuation Committee, Shanghai.
> American Congregational Association Library (MA–25/3): 1916.
> Biola University—Rose Memorial Library (CA–130/4): 1920, 1930.
> Christian Church (Disciples of Christ) Library (IN–55/1): 1919, 1923.
> Claremont Colleges—Asian Studies Collection (CA–75/3): 1916–19, 1923, 1928, 1930, 1939.
> Colgate-Rochester Theological Seminaries—Swasey Library (NY–350/1): 1918.
> Columbia University—Butler Library (NY–150/1): 1919, 1921, 1923–29.
> Emory University—Pitts Theology Library (GA–15/5): 1916–17, 1921, 1924, 1930, 1932.
> Essex Institute—Phillips Library (MA–210/2): 1918.
> Florida Southern College—Roux Library (FL–20/1): 1930.
> Free Library of Philadelphia (PA–165/1): 1916.
> Hoover Institution Library (CA–300/1): 1916, 1930.
> Luther Northwestern Theological Seminary Library

(MN–100/1): 1916–17, 1919, 1923, 1927.

Memphis Theological Seminary Library (TN–40/1): 1939.

New York Public Library—General Research Division (NY–230/1): 1918, 1923, 1927.

Oberlin College—Main Library (OH–175/1): 1916–17, 1923–25.

Overseas Missionary Fellowship (PA–265/1): 1919–21, 1923–24, 1928–34, 1936–37, 1939.

Phillips University—Rogers Graduate Seminary Library (OK–5/1): 1921, 1923.

Presbyterian Historical Society—Archives and Library (PA–200/28): 1916, 1918–21, 1923–24, 1927–28, 1930, 1932–33, 1935–37, 1939–40.

Princeton Theological Seminary—Speer Library (NJ–95/3): 1916, 1927.

Princeton University—Gest Oriental Library (NJ–105/1): 1934.

San Francisco Theological Seminary Library (CA–235/2): 1927.

Southern Baptist Convention—Archives Center (VA–65/2): 1918.

Southern Baptist Convention—Jenkins Research Library (VA–70/1): 1924.

University of Chicago—Regenstein Library (IL–85/1): 1916–17, 1928, 1930.

University of Hawaii—Hamilton Library (HI–15/2): 1923.

University of Massachusetts at Amherst Library (MA–15/2): 1930.

University of Michigan—Hatcher Graduate Library (MI–25/1): 1926.

University of Pittsburgh—Hillman Library (PA–260/1): 1916.

University of Southern California—Von Kleinsmid Center Library (CA–190/2): 1929.

Yale Divinity School Library (CT–55/2): 1916, 1921, 1923–24, 1926–30, 1932–36, 1940, 1950.

DIRECTORY OF PROTESTANT MISSIONS IN CHINA. Presbyterian Mission Press, Shanghai.

Houston Public Library (TX–35/2): 1899.

DIRECTORY OF PROTESTANT MISSIONS IN CHINA. United Christian Publishers, Chengtu.

Boston University—School of Theology Library (MA–35/1): 1921.

Graduate Theological Union Library (CA–15/2): 1916.

St. Olaf College—Rölvaag Memorial Library (MN–80/1): 1917.

Southern Baptist Theological Seminary—Boyce Centennial Library (KY–50/2): 1943.

DISTRICT OF ANKING NEWSLETTER. American Episcopal Diocese of Anking, Chung-hua Sheng Kung Hui, Anking. Continued by FREE WAN-KAN, 1941. Title varies: ANKING NEWSLETTER.

Archives and Historical Collections of the Episcopal Church (TX–5/2): 1920–43.

Center for Research Libraries (IL–25/4): V 18, N 1–7; V 19, N 1–3; V 20, N 1–5; V 21, N 1–4; V 22, N 1; 1937–

41.

Graduate Theological Union Library (CA–15/2): V 18–22, N 1; n.s., V 2, N 4–V 22, N 2, 1937–41, 1945(?)–48.

Iowa State University Library (IA–5/1): V 18–22, 1937–48.

University of Virginia—Manuscripts Department (VA–25/10): V 5–21, Mr 1925–Je 1941.

DISTRICT OF HANKOW: The Newsletter. Chung-hua Sheng Kung Hui, Hankow. 1920(?).

Archives and Historical Collections of the Episcopal Church (TX–5/2): 1920–50.

Minnesota Historical Society—Division of Archives and Manuscripts (MN–105/3): 1935–40.

Union Theological Seminary—Burke Library (NY–275/1): V 11, N 2, 5–7; V 12, N 1–8, 10–V 16, N 5, 7–V 17, N 7–8; V 18, N 3–4; V 19, N 1–3, 5–7; V 21, N 1; 1931–41.

University of Virginia—Manuscripts Department (VA–25/10): Mr 1934–Je 1941.

DISTRICT OF SHANGHAI NEWSLETTER. St. John's University of Shanghai, Shanghai.

Archives and Historical Collections of the Episcopal Church (TX–5/2): 1915–49.

University of Virginia—Manuscripts Department (VA–25/10): Mr 1930–Ag 1941.

Virginia Theological Seminary—Payne Library (VA–5/1): V 26, N 7–12; V 27, N 2–5, Nv 1940–Ja 1941, Mr–Ap 1941.

DRAGON. Catholic University of Peking, Peking. V 1–, 1933–(?).

Newark Abbey (NJ–80/1): V 1, N 1, Spr 1933.

DRAGON FLAG. St. John's University, Shanghai.

Yale Divinity School—Special Collections (CT–50/25): 1904, 1907.

DRAGON TRACKS. Oberlin-Shansi Memorial Association, Oberlin. V 1, 1938.

Continues as OBERLIN SHANSI MEMORIAL ASSOCIATION NEWSLETTER.

Carleton College Archives (MN–60/1): V 7, N 2, Summ 1945.

Harvard Divinity School—Andover-Harvard Theological Library (MA–95/1): V 3, N 4, Mr 1941.

Harvard Divinity School—Andover-Harvard Theological Library (MA–95/2): V 6, N 3, V 7, N 1–3, Fall 1944, Spr 1945–Wint 1946.

Oberlin College Archives (OH–170/17, OH–170/21): V 1, N 1–V 8, N 1, Nv 1938–Spr 1946.

DRAWNET. Sisters of Notre Dame de Namur, Ohio Province, Cincinnati, Ohio. V 1–13, 1929–42.

Quarterly. Devoted to the China mission.

Sisters of Notre Dame de Namur—Ohio Province Archives (OH–60/1): V 1–13, 1929–42.

EAST ASIA MILLIONS. China Inland Mission, Philadelphia. My 1961–.

Title varies: CHINA'S MILLIONS, 1892–1952; THE MILLIONS, 1953–61.

Asbury Theological Seminary—Fisher Library

(KY–90/1): V 69, N 5-, 1961-.

Associated Mennonite Biblical Seminaries Library (IN–25/3): V 69–94, 1959–84.

Bethany and Northern Baptist Theological Seminaries Library (IL–135/1): V 69, N 5–10; V 70, N 1–3, 5–11; V 71–80, N 1–11; V 81, N 1–6; V 82, N 2–V 86, N 5; 1961–78.

Bethel Theological Seminary Library (MN–50/1): V 69, N 5-, My 1961-.

Biola University—Rose Memorial Library (CA–130/4): 1961–70; Mr, My, Ag 1985; Ja, Ap 1986.

Claremont Colleges—Asian Studies Collection (CA–75/2): V 79, N 6–8, Je-S 1971.

Cornell University—Wason Collection (NY–95/1): 1896, 1906.

Drew University Library (NJ–40/2): V 69, N 5-, 1961- (inc.).

Eastern Baptist Theological Seminary—DeBlois Library (PA–160/1): V 73-, 1965-.

Emory University—Pitts Theology Library (GA–15/5): V 57–86, 88–90, 1949–78, 1980–82.

Fuller Theological Seminary—McAlister Library (CA–205/1): V 69, N 5-, 1961-.

Garrett-Evangelical and Seabury-Western Theological Seminaries—United Library (IL–110/1): V 70–92, 1961–84.

Gordon-Conwell Theological Seminary—Goddard Library (MA–230/4): V 62, N 1-, 1954-.

Harvard Divinity School—Andover-Harvard Theological Library (MA–95/2): V 67–90, 1959–82.

Harvard University—Widener Library (MA–155/1): V 69, N 5-, 1961-.

Luther Northwestern Theological Seminary Library (MN–100/1): V 69, N 5-, My 1961-.

Moody Bible Institute Library (IL–55/1): 1979–89 (current 10 years).

Oral Roberts University—Messick Learning Resources Center (OK–10/1): V 72–78, 1964–70.

Princeton Theological Seminary—Speer Library (NJ–95/3): V 69-, 1961-.

Southern Baptist Theological Seminary—Boyce Centennial Library (KY–50/2): V [55], 56-, 1947-.

Trinity Evangelical Divinity School Library (IL–90/1): V 69–85; V 86, N 1–4, 6; V 87-; 1961-.

Union Theological Seminary—Burke Library (NY–275/1): V 1; n.s. V 1–51; V 55, N 11; V 56–69; 1891–1943, 1947–61(?).

Western Baptist College Library (OR–40/1): V 40-, 1932-.

Yale Divinity School Library (CT–55/2): V 1–93, 1892–1985.

EAST ASIA MILLIONS. Overseas Missionary Fellowship, London. V 92-, 1965-.

Title varies: CHINA'S MILLIONS, 1875–1952; THE MILLIONS, 1952–64.

Colgate-Rochester Theological Seminaries—Swasey Library (NY–350/1): V 92, N 2–12; V 93–94; V 95, N 1–2, 4–12; V 96–100; V 101, N 1–6, 10–12; V 102-; 1965-.

Cornell University—Wason Collection (NY–95/1): V 1–71, 73–98; V 99, N 1–5, 7–12; V 100–107, 1875–1945, 1947–81.

Harvard Divinity School—Andover-Harvard Theological Library (MA–95/2): V 92–111, 1965–84.

Union Theological Seminary—Burke Library (NY–275/1): V 1-, 1875-.

University of Illinois at Urbana-Champaign Library (IL–185/1): V 100–111, 1973–84.

Yale Divinity School Library (CT–55/2): V 1–17, n.s. V 1–106, 1875–1979.

EAST CHINA CHRISTIAN EDUCATIONAL ASSOCIATION BULLETIN. Shanghai. 1923-.

Yale Divinity School Library (CT–55/2): 1923–28.

EAST CHINA STUDIES IN EDUCATION. East China Christian Educational Association, Shanghai. 1925–29.

Columbia University—Milbank Library (NY–165/1): N 1, 2, 5; 1925, 1929.

Union Theological Seminary—Burke Library (NY–275/1): N 2–3, 1926.

ECF NEWS. Evangelize China Fellowship, Los Angeles, CA.

Asbury Theological Seminary—Fisher Library (KY–90/1): V 3–21; V 22, N 1–3; V 23; V 24, N 1; V 25–27; V 28–30; V 32, N 5, 7-; 1957-.

Los Angeles Public Library (CA–150/1): V 15, N 2, Je 1970.

Union Theological Seminary—Burke Library (NY–275/1): 1983-.

ECHOES FROM INLAND CHINA. Ebenezer Mission, Miyang, Honan.

Union Theological Seminary—Burke Library (NY–275/1): V 1, N 1; V 2, N 1–2; V 3, N 1; 1922–24.

ECONOMIC FACTS. *See* University of Nanking.

ECONOMIC WEEKLY. *See* University of Nanking.

Educational Association of China

DIRECTORY. Educational Association of China, Methodist Publishing House, Shanghai. V 1-, 1903-.

Title varies: MISSION EDUCATIONAL DIRECTORY.

Claremont Colleges—Asian Studies Collection (CA–75/3): 1910.

Essex Institute—Phillips Library (MA–210/2): 1910.

Harvard University—Widener Library (MA–155/1): 1905.

Hoover Institution Library (CA–300/1): 1910.

Southern Baptist Theological Seminary—Boyce Centennial Library (KY–50/2): 1910.

Union Theological Seminary—Burke Library (NY–275/1): 1903, 1905.

MONTHLY BULLETIN. Shanghai. N 1–18, 1907–8.

Continued as EDUCATIONAL REVIEW.

Graduate Theological Union Library (CA–15/2): N 1–17, My 1907-D 1908.

Union Theological Seminary—Burke Library (NY–275/1): N 1–17, My 1907-D 1908.

Yale Divinity School Library (CT–55/2): N 1–17, 1907–8.

EDUCATIONAL ASSOCIATION OF FUKIEN PROVINCE JOURNAL. Educational Association of Fukien Province, Foochow.

Title reads: EDUCATIONAL ASSOCIATION OF FUKIEN PROVINCE JOURNAL, V 1–2, N 2, 1906–17; FUKIEN CHRISTIAN EDUCATIONAL ASSOCIATION JOURNAL, V 2–3, N 5, 1918–20.

Harvard Divinity School—Andover-Harvard Theological Library (MA–95/2): V 1, N 2, 6, S 1907, Ag 1911.

Union Theological Seminary—Burke Library (NY–275/1): V 1–2, 1906–20.

THE EDUCATIONAL DIRECTORY OF CHINA: A Reference Book for All Interested in Western Education in China. The Educational Directory of China Publishing Company, Shanghai. V 1–, 1914–.

Title varies: THE EDUCATIONAL DIRECTORY AND YEAR BOOK OF CHINA, 1914–.

Cornell University—Wason Collection (NY–95/1): V 1–5, 7, 1914–18, 1921.

Essex Institute—Phillips Library (MA–210/2): 1914.

Union Theological Seminary—Burke Library (NY–275/1): V 1–7, 1914–21.

Yale Divinity School Library (CT–55/2): 1917, 1921.

EDUCATIONAL REVIEW. China Christian Educational Association, Shanghai. V 1–30, 1907–38 (quarterly).

Title varies: MONTHLY BULLETIN OF THE CHINA CHRISTIAN EDUCATIONAL ASSOCIATION, V 1, 1907. Merged into CHINESE RECORDER, 1938.

Berea College—Special Collections (KY–5/2): V 18, N 1–2; V 19, N 3; V 20–24; V 25, N 1, 3–4; V 27, N 1; 1926–33, 1935.

Center for Research Libraries (IL–25/4): V 2–4, 6–30, 1909–38.

Claremont Colleges—Honnold Library (CA–85/1): V 8–30, 1916–38.

Columbia University—Milbank Library (NY–165/4): V 1–6, [7–30], 1908, 1914–37.

Cornell University—Wason Collection (NY–95/1): V 1, N 1, 4–5; V 2; V 3, N 12; V 4, N 5–6; V 6–15; V 16, N 1, 3–4; V 17–30; 1907, 1909–11, 1914–38.

Dickinson College—Spahr Library (PA–20/2): V [8–30], 1916–38.

Drew University Library (NJ–40/2): V 7–30, 1915–38 (inc.).

Drew University—United Methodist Historical Library (NJ–50/1): V 18, 1926.

Duke University—Perkins Library (NC–55/1): V 21–22; V 23, N 1–3; V 24, N 2–4; V 25, N 1–3; V 26, N 1–2; 1927–34.

Emory University—Pitts Theology Library (GA–15/5) (GA–15/5): V 2–30 1909–38.

Garrett-Evangelical and Seabury-Western Theological Seminaries—United Library (IL–110/1): V 6, N 2–4; V 7–30, 1914–38.

Graduate Theological Union Library (CA–15/2): V 2–30, 1909–38.

Harvard University—Widener Library (MA–155/1): V 2–30, N 4, 1909–38.

Hoover Institution Library (CA–300/1): V 1–4, 6–30, 1907–11, 1913–38.

Iowa State University Library (IA–5/1): V 1–4, 6–30, 1907–38.

Library of Congress—General Reading Rooms Division (DC–120/1): V 7–9, 11, 23–30, 1915–38.

New York Public Library—General Research Division (NY–230/1): V 5–30, 1913–38.

Oberlin College—Main Library (OH–175/1): 1907–8, 1909–38.

Ohio State University—Thompson Memorial Library (OH–110/4): V 1–30, 1907–38.

Presbyterian Historical Society—Archives and Library (PA–200/28): V 2–4, 6–7, 10–11, 14–30, 1909–11, 1913–14, 1917–18, 1921–30.

San Francisco Theological Seminary Library (CA–235/2): V 26, N 2, Ap 1934.

Stanford University—Green Library (CA–305/1): V 1–4, 6–30. 1907–11, 1913–38.

Union Theological Seminary—Burke Library (NY–275/1): V 2, N 1–V 30, N 4, 1909–38.

Union Theological Seminary in Virginia Library (VA–85/1): V [14], 21–22, [23–24], 1927–32.

University of California, San Diego, Library (CA–125/2): V 12, N 3; V 13, N 1; V 15, N 4; V 21, N 3–4; V 22, N 1–2, 4; V 23, N 1–2, 4; V 24, N 1, 3; V 25, N 2–3; V 26, N 1; V 29, N 4; 1920–37.

University of Illinois at Urbana-Champaign Library (IL–185/1): V 16, N 1, 3–4; V 17–30, 1924–38.

University of Notre Dame—Memorial Library (IN–95/1): V 1–30, 1907–38.

University of Pennsylvania—Van Pelt Library (PA–215/1): V [18]–25, 1926–33.

University of Vermont—Bailey/Howe Library (VT–5/1): 1911.

University of Virginia—Alderman Library (VA–30/1): V 15, N 3; V 19, N 4–12; V 20; V 21, N 1–2, 4–12; Mr 1923, Ap–D 1927, 1928, Ja–F, Ap–D 1929.

Yale Divinity School Library (CT–55/2): V 1–2, 6–30, 1907–9, 1913–38.

Yale Divinity School—Special Collections (CT–50/2): 1907–10, 1920–38.

Yale University—Sterling Memorial Library (CT–80/1): V 2, 6–9, 13–14, 16–30, 1909, 1914–17, 1921–22, 1924–38.

ELECTRIC MESSAGES: The Official Organ of the OMS working in Japan, Korea, China. n.p.

Continued by ORIENTAL MISSIONARY STANDARD, 1914. Continues ELECTRIC MESSAGES FROM JAPAN, 1908.

Asbury Theological Seminary—Special Collections (KY–85/1): V 7–V 12, N 9, 1908–14.

EN CHINE AVEC LES SOEURS MISSIONNAIRES NOTRE DAME DES ANGES. Sherbrooke, Quebec. 1939–.

Yale Divinity School Library (CT–55/2): 1939–45.

ENGLISH BULLETIN. *See* National Committee for Christian Religious Education in China.

ENGLISH PUBLICATIONS. *See* Nanking Theological Seminary.

EPISTOLA FAMILIAE MISSIONIS. Shanghai.
California Province of the Society of Jesus Archives
(CA–195/1): N 19–39, O 1949-Mr 1950.

THE EVANGEL. Organ of the Evangel Mission, Shin Hing, South
China. V 1(?)-, 1907(?)-.
Union Theological Seminary—Burke Library
(NY–275/1): V 3–4, 10–13, 15, 1910–11, 1917–20, 1922.

EVANGELICAL. United Evangelical Church.
Union Theological Seminary—Burke Library
(NY–275/1): 1915–18, 1920.

EVANGELISCHER REICHSBOTE. Hauptverein für die evangelische mission in China zu Berlin, Berlin. V 1, 1851.
Yale Divinity School Library (CT–55/2): V 1–15, 17–23,
1851–65, 1867–73.

EVANGELISKA ÖSTASIEN MISSIONEN. Evangeliska Östasien
Missionen, Stockholm, Sweden.
Union Theological Seminary—Burke Library
(NY–275/1): 1982-.

THE EVANGELIST: and Miscellanea Sinica. Albion Press, Macao.
Essex Institute—Phillips Library (MA–210/2): N 2, 1833.

EVANGELIZE CHINA FELLOWSHIP NEWS. Evangelize Chi-
na Fellowship, Los Angeles, CA. V 1-, 1955-.
Union Theological Seminary—Burke Library
(NY–275/1): V 1, N 1, O 1955-.

FALL LEAVES. North China American School, Tunghsien.
Harvard Divinity School—Andover-Harvard Theological
Library (MA–95/1): N 1, Nv 1932.

FAR EAST: A Magazine Devoted to the Conversion of China.
Chinese Mission Society, Omaha, Nebraska. V 1, 1876.
Catholic University of America—Mullen Library
(DC–20/1): V 44, N 1–8; V 45, N 3–4, 6, 12; V 46, N 2–
3, 5, 7–9, 11–12; V 47; V 48, N 1, 3–7, 11–12; V 50, N 2,
7–9; V 51; V 52, N 1–3, 5–12; V 53–56; V 57, N 1, 3–5,
7–9, 11; V 58, N 1–7, 9–11; V 59; V 60, N 1; V 61–65; V
67–77; V 80–81; 1920–24, 1926–41, 1943–53, 1956–57.
Library of Congress—General Reading Rooms Division
(DC–120/1): 1896–98.

FAR EAST: The Magazine of the Chinese Mission Society. Chi-
nese Mission Society, St. Columbans, Nebraska. V 1, 1917.
Marygrove College Library (MI–65/1): V 11–12, 1928–
29.
New York Public Library—General Research Division
(NY–230/1): V 2, N 12; V 3, N 10-V 49; D 1919, O 1920–
66.
St. John's Seminary Library (MA–85/1): V 20–27, 1937–
44.
St. Mary of the Lake Seminary—Feehan Memorial Li-
brary (IL–130/1): V 29–37, 1946–54.
Union Theological Seminary—Burke Library
(NY–275/1): 1925–50 (inc.), 1960-.

FAR EAST. Maynooth Mission to China, Naven, Ireland. V 1,
1915(?).
St. John's Seminary Library (MA–85/1): V 19–26, 1936–
43.

FAR EAST: A Monthly Illustrated Journal. Shanghai. V 1, 1870;
n.s. V 1, 1876.
Yale Divinity School Library (CT–55/2): n.s. V 1–4, Jl
1876–78.

FAR EASTERN DIVISION NEWSLETTER. Far Eastern Divi-
sion, General Conference of Seventh-Day Adventists.
Loma Linda University—Radcliffe Memorial Library
(CA–135/1): S-D 1980, 1981-S 1985.

FAR EASTERN DIVISION OUTLOOK. Far Eastern Division,
General Conference of Seventh-Day Adventists, Shanghai. V
13-, 1924-.
Continues ASIATIC DIVISION OUTLOOK, 1924. Place of
publication varies: Baguio, Philippines, 1924(?)–36; Kuala
Lampur, Singapore, 1936-.
Andrews University—White Library (MI–50/1): V [16–
17], 18–24, [25], 26, [29–31]-, 1926–36, 1939-.
Columbia Union College—Weis Library (MD–65/1):
1948-.
General Conference of Seventh-Day Adventists Archives
(DC–40/1): V 13-, 1924-.
Loma Linda University Library (CA–220/1): V 12, N 10–
11, 13, 15; V 16, N 9–12; V 17–19; V 20, N 1–7, 9, 11; V
21, N 1, 3–5, 8–12; V 22, N 1–5, 12; V 23, N 2, 6, 12; V
24, N 1–3; V 25, N 2; V 26, N 1–2, 4–7, 9, 11, 13, 15–17,
21; V 27, N 1, 7–13; V 28, N 1–3, 5–10; V 29, N 4–5; V
30, N 2, 5–6; V 31, N 1–10; V 32, N 1–6; V 33, N 1–8; V
34-; 1923, 1927–42, 1944-.
Loma Linda University—Radcliffe Memorial Library
(CA–135/1): V 13, N 8, 10, 12; V 14; V 15, N 3–7, 10–
12; V 16, N 1–5, 7, 9–12; V 17–22; V 23, N 1–6, 8–12, V
24–26; V 27, N 3–5, 11–13; V 28, N 2, 9–10; V 29, N 5–
7, 11; V 30, N 6, 8–10; V 31, N 2–10; V 32–67; n.v.;
1924–41, Ap-Nv 1944, 1945-O 1985.
Union College Library (NB–20/1): V 18–53, 1929–64.

FAR EASTERN DIVISION VOICE. n.p.
Loma Linda University—Radcliffe Memorial Library
(CA–135/1): V 7–12, 1981–85.

FAR EASTERN PROMOTER. n.p.
Loma Linda University—Radcliffe Memorial Library
(CA–135/1): V 3, N 2–6, 1925.

FATI THEOLOGICAL COLLEGE BULLETIN. Canton.
Presbyterian Historical Society—Archives and Library
(PA–200/28): 1911–12.
University of Oregon—Department of Special Collections
(OR–15/18): 1911–12.

FELLOWSHIP NOTES. *See* Young Men's Christian Association,
Shanghai.

FENCHOW. American Board of Commissioners for Foreign Mis-
sions, Fenchow Station, Fenchow, Shansi. V 1–19, Ag 1919-D
1936 (irregular).
Andover Newton Theological School—Trask Library
(MA–180/2): V 1–19; Ag 1919-D 1936(?).
Carleton College Archives (MN–60/1): V 2, N 2–3, O-D
1920.
Center for Research Libraries (IL–25/4): V 1–7, N 4; V 8,

N 1-2; V 9; V 10, N 2-5; V 14-19; 1919-36.

Cornell University—Wason Collection (NY-95/1): V 1-19, N 1, Ag 1919-D 1936.

Essex Institute—Phillips Library (MA-210/2): V 5, N 2-5, V 6, N 1, 1923-24.

Harvard Divinity School—Andover-Harvard Theological Library (MA-95/1): V 19, N 1, D 1936.

Harvard Divinity School—Andover-Harvard Theological Library (MA-95/2): 1919-35 (inc.).

Iowa State University Library (IA-5/1): V 1-19, 1919-36.

Kalamazoo College—Upjohn Library (MI-125/1): V 1-19, 1919-36.

Ohio State University—Thompson Memorial Library (OH-110/4): V 1-19, Ag 1919-D 1936.

Stanford University—Green Library (CA-305/1): V 1-19, N 1, 1919-36.

Union Theological Seminary—Burke Library (NY-275/1): V 1-5, 7, 11; F, Ap, Ag, O, D 1920; F, Ap, O, D 1921; F, Ap, Ag, O, D 1922; F, Ap, Ag, O, D 1923; F 1924; Je 1926; Mr 1931.

Wheaton College—Graham Center Library (IL-205/1): V 1-19, 1919-36.

Yale Divinity School Library (CT-55/2): V 1-7, 9-11, 14-19, 1919-26, 1928-36.

FICHIER ENTOMOLOGIQUE CHINOISE. *See* Université de l'Aurore, Shanghai.

FIELD BULLETIN. *See* China Inland Mission.

FOLKLORE STUDIES. V 1-, 1942-.
Continued by ASIAN FOLKLORE STUDIES, 1963. Publisher varies: Catholic University of Peking, Museum of Oriental Ethnology, Peking, 1942-53; S.V.D., Tokyo, 1953-63.

Center for Research Libraries (IL-25/4): V 1; V 6, pt. 1; V 16-21, 1942, 1947, 1957-62.

Claremont Colleges—Honnold Library (CA-85/1): V 1-5, 1942-46.

Cleveland Public Library (OH-85/1): V 1-21, 1942-62.

Columbia University—Starr East Asian Library (NY-195/4): V 1-5, 1942-47.

Field Museum of Natural History Library (IL-40/1): V 1-5, 1942-47.

Georgetown University—Lauinger Library (DC-60/1): N7, 10-12, 14-20, 1948, 1951-53, 1955-61.

Harvard University—Harvard-Yenching Library (MA-125/6): V 1-6, 10, 1942-47, 1951.

Indiana University—University Libraries (IN-20/2): V 1-26, 28-, 1942-.

New York Public Library—General Research Division (NY-230/1): V 1-20, 1942-62.

New York University—Fine Arts Library (NY-250/1): V 2-5, 1943-46.

University of California at Los Angeles—University Research Library (CA-185/1): V 1-21, 1942-62.

University of California, Berkeley—General Library (CA-70/1): V 1-19, 1942-60.

University of California, Davis, Library (CA-110/1): V 1-6, 1942-52.

University of California, Santa Barbara, Library (CA-275/2): V 1-6, 1942-47.

University of Maryland—McKeldin Library (MD-45/1): V 1-6, 11, 1942-47, 1952.

University of Michigan—Hatcher Graduate Library (MI-25/1): V 1-42, 1942-83.

University of New Mexico Library (NM-5/1): V 1-5; V 6, N 1; V 7-22, 1942-63.

University of Pennsylvania—Van Pelt Library (PA-215/1): V 1, 1942-.

University of Pittsburgh—Hillman Library (PA-260/1): V 1-5, 1942-47.

Western Washington University—Wilson Library (WA-5/1): V 1-17, 21, 1942-58, 1962.

Yale University—Sterling Memorial Library (CT-80/1): V 1-21, 1942-62.

FOLKLORE STUDIES. SUPPLEMENT. Catholic University of Peking, Museum of Oriental Ethnology. N 1, 1952.

Cornell University—Wason Collection (NY-95/1): N 1, 1952.

Duke University—Perkins Library (NC-55/1): N 1, 1952.

Harvard University—Harvard-Yenching Library (MA-125/6): N 1, 1952.

Stanford University—Green Library (CA-305/1): N 1-, 1952-.

University of California, Berkeley—Anthropology Library (CA-25/1): N 1, 1952.

University of California, Berkeley—General Library (CA-70/1): N 1, 1952.

University of California, Santa Barbara, Library (CA-275/2): N 1, 1952.

University of Washington Libraries (WA-45/1): N 1-, 1952-.

Western Washington University—Wilson Library (WA-5/1): N 1, 1952.

FOOCHOW COLLEGE QUARTERLY. Foochow College, Fukien.

Harvard Divinity School—Andover-Harvard Theological Library (MA-95/1): V 3, N 1, Ja 1924.

Union Theological Seminary—Burke Library (NY-275/1): Ja 1923.

FOOCHOW GOODWILL TRENCHES. n.p.

Harvard Divinity School—Andover-Harvard Theological Library (MA-95/2): V 3, N 4; V 4, N 6, 1923-24.

THE FOOCHOW MESSENGER. American Board of Commissioners for Foreign Missions, Foochow. V 1-, Nv 1903-Spring 1940. Quarterly 1904-11, irregular from 1912. Suspended, 1917-21. Volumes renumbered from V 1, starting 1922.

Amherst College Archives (MA-5/3): V 1, N 1-2, 4; V 1, N 1-2; Nv 1903; Ja, Ap 1904; Ja, Ap 1905.

Andover Newton Theological School—Trask Library (MA-180/2): V 1-37(?), 1903-17, 1922-40.

Center for Research Libraries (IL-25/4): V 1-7, N 1; n.s. V 3, N 1-V 8, N 1; Nv 1903-Nv 1923; Mr 1924-Ja 1929; O 1929-Spr 1940.

Claremont Colleges—Asian Studies Collection (CA-75/2): Ja 1912; Je 1913; Je 1916; Ja, Je 1925; Ja, O

1926; 1928; O 1929; Summ 1936; Summ 1937; Summ 1938; Summ, Wint 1939; Spr 1940.

Cornell University—Wason Collection (NY–95/1): 1903–40.

Emory University—Pitts Theology Library (GA–15/5): V 1–5, 7–14, n.s. V 5, 7–8, 1903–8, 1910–17, 1926, 1928–29.

Gordon-Conwell Theological Seminary—Goddard Library (MA–230/4): 1903–40.

Graduate Theological Union Library (CA–15/2): 1903–40.

Harvard Divinity School—Andover-Harvard Theological Library (MA–95/1): V 1, N 2, Je 1922.

Harvard Divinity School—Andover-Harvard Theological Library (MA–95/2): V 1–14, 19–28, 32–37, 1903–17, 1922–31, 1935–40.

Harvard University—Widener Library (MA–155/1): 1903–17, 1922–40.

Haverford College—Magill Library (PA–75/1): Summer 1937.

Iowa State University Library (IA–5/1): 1903–40.

Kalamazoo College—Upjohn Library (MI–125/1): 1903–40.

Library of Congress—General Reading Rooms Division (DC–120/1): Ja-Ap 1909; centennial 1910; Ap, O 1911; Ja-S 1912; Mr-O 1913; Ap, O 1914; Ja-Je 1915; Mr-Je 1916.

Oberlin College—Main Library (OH–175/1): V 1–5, n.s., V 4–5, 1903–8, 1925–26.

Ohio State University—Thompson Memorial Library (OH–110/4): 1903–40.

Presbyterian Historical Society—Archives and Library (PA–200/28): Ap 1914.

Stanford University—Green Library (CA–305/1): V 1–37, 1903–40.

Union Theological Seminary—Burke Library (NY–275/1): n.v., V 1, N 1–2; V 2, N 2; V 3, N 1–3; V 4, N 1–3; V 5, N 1–3; V 6, N 1–2; V 7, N 1; V 8, N 1–3; V 9, N 1; n.v.; Nv 1903; Ja, Ap, Jl, O 1904; Ja, Ap, Jl, O 1905; Ja, Ap, Jl, O 1906; Ja, Ap, Jl, O 1907; Ja, Ap, Jl, O 1908; Ja, Ap, Jl, 1909; Ja 1910; Ja, Ap, O 1911; Ja, My, S 1912; Mr, Je, O 1913; Ap, O, 1914; Ja, Je, O, 1915; Mr, Je, O, 1916; F, Je, O, 1917; Ap, Je 1922; Ag 1923; Mr, Je, O, 1924; Ja, Je, O, 1925; Ja, Je, O, 1926; Ja, Je, 1927; S 1929; Ja, Ap, Je, 1930; Ja 1931; Spr 1934; Spr, Aut 1935; Spr, Summ, Aut 1936; Spr 1937; Spr, Aut 1938; Summ, Aut 1939; Summ, Aut 1940.

University of Oregon—Department of Special Collections (OR–15/3): Ja 1927; Summ, Aut 1936; Summ 1937; Wint, Spr 1938.

Wheaton College—Graham Center Library (IL–205/1): V 1–37, 1903–40.

Yale Divinity School Library (CT–55/2): 1903–7, 1909–17, 1922–30, 1935–40.

FOOCHOW NEWS. Methodist Episcopal Mission, Foochow. V 1, 1924.

Garrett-Evangelical and Seabury-Western Theological Seminaries—United Library (IL–110/1): V 12, N 1, 1938.

Hoover Institution Archives (CA–290/16): V 5, N 3–5; V 6, N 1; V 8, N 3; V 9, N 2–4; V 10, N 1–2; V 11, N 1–3; V 12, N 1; n.v.; 1931–32, 1934–40.

Lovely Lane Museum Library (MD–25/3): Summer 1940.

Lovely Lane Museum Library (MD–25/4): V 11, N 1; V 12, N 1; Mr 1937, Nv 1938, anniversary pictorial supplement (n.d.).

Ohio Wesleyan University—United Methodist Archives Center (OH–135/1): Summer 1940.

Union Theological Seminary—Burke Library (NY–275/1): V 1, N 1, 4; V 2, N 3–4; V 3, N 1; V 4, N 4–5; V 5, N 2–3; V 6, N 1; V 7, N 1–2; V 8, N 4; V 9, N 1; V 11, N 1, 8; 1924–28, 1930–38, Summer 1939, Summer 1940.

University of Oregon—Department of Special Collections (OR–15/1): Nv 1938.

University of Oregon—Department of Special Collections (OR–15/5): Wint 1939, Aut 1941.

University of Oregon—Department of Special Collections (OR–15/43): Wint 1939.

University of Oregon—Department of Special Collections (OR–15/47): V 4, N 2; V 5, N 1–5; V 6, N 1–2; V 7, N 1–2; V 8, N 3; V 9, N 1, 3; V 11, N 1; V 12, N 1; 1929–35, My 1936, Summ 1940, anniversary pictorial supplement (n.d.).

University of Oregon—Department of Special Collections (OR–15/60): V 9, N 3, Ag 1935.

University of the Pacific—Fry Research Library (CA–320/1): Summer 1940.

Wesleyan University—Special Collections and Archives (CT–30/5): 1940.

Yale Divinity School Library (CT–55/2): V 2–6, 9, 12, 1927–32, 1935, 1938–41.

FOOCHOW TRENCHES. n.p.

Union Theological Seminary—Burke Library (NY–275/1): F 1920, Nv 1923.

FOOCHOW WITNESS. Methodist Publishing House, Foochow. V 1, 1902.

Continues as FUHKIEN WITNESS, 1903.

Drew University—United Methodist Historical Library (NJ–50/1): V 1, N 1–4, S-D 1902.

FOOCHOW YOUNG MEN. n.p.

Union Theological Seminary—Burke Library (NY–275/1): Nv 1908.

FOR CHRIST IN CHINA. For Christ in China, Chinese Christian Mission, Kunming.

San Jose Bible College Archives (CA–255/1): My 1947, F 1948, Mr 1949.

FOUR STREAMS: Newsletter of the Diocesan Association for Western China. Ashford, Kent.

Title varies: BULLETIN OF THE DIOCESAN ASSOCIATION FOR WESTERN CHINA. Continued by NEWSLETTER OF THE DIOCESAN ASSOCIATION FOR WESTERN CHINA, 1951.

Center for Research Libraries (IL–25/4): N 167–178, ser. 2, N 1; Jl 1947-Ja 1951, Jl 1951.

Kalamazoo College—Upjohn Library (MI–125/1): N 121–178, 1934–51.

Ohio State University—Thompson Memorial Library (OH–110/4): N 121(?)–178, 1934–51.

Union Theological Seminary—Burke Library (NY–275/1): Ja 1919; Mr, Je, S, D, 1920; Ap, Jl, O, 1921; Ja, Ap, Jl, O, 1922; Ja, Ap, Jl, O, 1923; 1924–60.

Yale Divinity School Library (CT–55/2): V 121–177; n.s. V 1–13; ser. 3, V 1–4; 1934–59.

FRANCISCANS IN CHINA. Franciscans, Wuchang. V 1–20, N 1, 0 1922–Ja 1942 (monthly).

Index V 1–3, 1922–25.

Catholic Theological Union Library (IL–20/1): V 1–20, 1922–42.

Catholic University of America—Mullen Library (DC–20/1): V 2–7, 1923–27.

Duns Scotus Library (MI–140/1): V 1–19, 1922–41.

Franciscan Province of the Sacred Heart—Archives (MO–65/1): V1–19, 1922–41.

Franciscan Sisters of Perpetual Adoration—Generalate Archives (WI–15/1): V 3, N 3; V 5, N 1–7, 10; V 6, N 1–9; V 7, N 1–11; V 8, N 1–10; V 9–12; V 13, N 1–3; V 14, N 3–12; V 15, N 1–2; V 19, N 1, 8; D 1924; D 1926; Ja–Ap, Jl–Ag, O–D 1927; Ja–Je O–D 1928; 1928–34; D 1935–S–Nv 1936; Ja, Ag 1941.

Province of St. John the Baptist—Faber Franciscana Library (OH–45/1): 1923–41.

St. Bonaventure University—Franciscan Institute (NY–365/1): V [1]–20, 1922–42.

Wheaton College—Graham Center Library (IL–205/1): V [1–18], 1922–40.

Yale Divinity School Library (CT–55/2): V 1–19, 1923–41.

FREE WAN–KAN. National Council of Protestant Episcopal Church, Overseas Department, New York. V 1–4, 1942–44 (mimeographed)

Continues DISTRICT OF ANKING NEWSLETTER (ANKING NEWSLETTER). V 2, N 4 has a supplement.

Union Theological Seminary—Burke Library (NY–275/1): V 1–4, 1942–44.

University of Virginia—Manuscripts Department (VA–25/10): 1942–F 1944.

Yale Divinity School Library (CT–55/2): V 1–2, 1942–44.

FRIEND OF CHINA. n.p.

Union Theological Seminary—Burke Library (NY–275/1): D 1881; Ja, Mr 1882; My, Jl–O, D 1884; F–Je, S, D 1885; Ag, 1894; My, Jl 1895; Jl 1896; Ja 1897; Ap 1898; Jl, O 1899; O 1900; Ja, Jl 1901; O 1902; Je 1908; Je, O 1909; O 1919; Jl 1913; Ja 1916.

FRIENDS' CENTRE BULLETIN. Friends' Centre, Shanghai. 1939–40.

Haverford College—Magill Library (PA–75/1): N 1–3, Ap 1939–Nv 1940.

FRIENDS OF MOSLEMS: The Quarterly Newsletter. Society of Friends of the Moslems in China, Hankow. V 1–, 1927– (quarterly).

V 1 as its QUARTERLY NEWSLETTER.

Columbia University—Starr East Asian Library (NY–195/4): V 11, 14, 15–16, 17–23, Ap 1937, Ja 1940, Ja 1941–Ja 1942, Ja 1943–O 1949.

Harvard University—Harvard-Yenching Library (MA–125/3): 1927–36.

Harvard University—Harvard-Yenching Library (MA–125/6): V 1, N 2–V 10, N 4, Jl 1927–O 1936.

Overseas Missionary Fellowship (PA–265/1): V 1, N 2–V 23, N 4, Jl 1927–O 1949.

Presbyterian Historical Society—Archives and Library (PA–200/28): V 2, N 4; V 5, N 2–4, 1928, 1930–31.

Yale Divinity School Library (CT–55/2): V 1–25, 1927–51.

FRIENDS ORIENTAL NEWS. American Friends Mission, Nanking. V 1–55, 1908–63.

Merged with EVANGELICAL FRIEND Ag 1962 to become EVANGELICAL FRIEND AND ORIENTAL NEWS.

Asbury Theological Seminary—Fisher Library (KY–90/1): V 37–51, 1948–62.

Guilford College—Friends Historical Collection (NC–60/1): V 1–51, 1908–62.

Malone College—Archives Section (OH–30/1): V 1–55, 1908–63.

FU-JEN MAGAZINE. Catholic University of Peking, Peking. V 1–, Mr 1932–.

V 3 omitted in numbering. Continues FU JEN NEWS LETTER, Mr 1932.

Conception Abbey and Seminary Library (MO–15/1): V 1, N 1–6, Mr 1932–D 1933.

Hoover Institution Library (CA–300/1): V 1, 1932–33.

Library of Congress—General Reading Rooms Division (DC–120/1): V 1–12, Mr 1932–35.

New York Public Library—General Research Division (NY–230/1): V 1, [2], 4–18, 1932–Je 1949.

St. Benedict's Convent Archives (MN–90/4): V 4–12, My 1932–Ja 1934.

Saint Vincent Archabbey and College Archives (PA–95/1): My–Je, S–O, D 1932; Ja–F 1933; Ja–F, S–O 1934; Ja 1935.

University of Illinois at Urbana-Champaign Library (IL–185/1): V 2, N 3–6; V 4–17, N 1–3; V 18, N 2, My–O 1934, D 1934–Je 1939; S, D 1939; Ap, Je, S, D 1940; 1941–S 1948; Je 1949.

FU JEN NEWS LETTER. Catholic University of Peking, Peking. N 1–12, Mr 1931–F 1932.

Continued as FU-JEN MAGAZINE, Mr 1932. N 7/8 issued in 1 number.

Cleveland Public Library (OH–85/1): N 1–12, Mr 1931–F 1932.

Cornell University—Wason Collection (NY–95/1): N 1–12, Mr 1931–F 1932.

Harvard University—Widener Library (MA–155/1): N 1–12, 1931–32.

Hoover Institution Library (CA–300/1): N 1–12, 1931–32.

Library of Congress—General Reading Rooms Division (DC–120/1): N 1–12, Mr 1931–F 1932.

New York Public Library—General Research Division (NY–230/1): N 4–12, 1931–F 1932.

St. Benedict's Convent Archives (MN–90/4): N 2–12, Ap

1931-F 1932.
Saint Vincent Archabbey and College Archives (PA–95/1): Mr-Nv 1931.
Union Theological Seminary—Burke Library (NY–275/1): D 1931.
University of Illinois at Urbana-Champaign Library (IL–185/1): N 1–12, 1931–32.
Yale University—Sterling Memorial Library (CT–80/1): N 1–12, 1931–32.

Fu jen ta hsüeh. *See* Catholic University of Peking.

FUHKIEN WITNESS. *See* FUKIEN WITNESS.

FUKIEN AGRICULTURAL JOURNAL. Fukien Christian University, College of Agriculture, Foochow.
Iowa State University Library (IA–5/1): V 10–12, 1948–51.
Kansas State University—Farrell Library (KS–45/1): V 9–11, 1947–50.
Michigan State University Library (MI–75/1): V 4, 9–11, 1942, 1947–50.
Oregon State University—Kerr Library (OR–5/1): V 9–12, 1947–51.
University of Illinois at Urbana-Champaign Library (IL–185/1): V 9, N 3-V 12, N 2, 1948–51.
Yale Divinity School—Special Collections (CT–50/25): V 9–11, 1947–50.

Fukien Christian University, Natural History Society, PROCEEDINGS. *See* Natural History Society.

Fukien Christian University, Shanghai
BIOLOGICAL BULLETIN. V 1–6(?), 1939–47.
Field Museum of Natural History Library (IL–40/1): V 1, 1939.
Lloyd Library (OH–35/1): V 1–6, 1939–47.
Smithsonian Institution—National Museum of Natural History Branch Library (DC–175/1): V 5, Ap 1947.
University of Michigan—Natural Sciences Library (MI–40/1): N 1, 1939.
COMPOSITION BULLETIN. Fukien Christian University, Department of English.
Harvard Divinity School—Andover-Harvard Theological Library (MA–95/1): n.s. 1923, N 3, 1923.
FCU FAMILY NEWSLETTER IN AMERICA. Fukien Christian University, Foochow.
Hoover Institution Archives (CA–290/29): 1951–54, 1956.
Yale Divinity School—Special Collections (CT–50/25): N 6, 1956.
FCU NEWS. Fukien Christian University, Foochow.
Harvard Divinity School—Andover-Harvard Theological Library (MA–95/2): My 1930, Ja 1932.
Hoover Institution Archives (CA–290/29): My 1930.
Union Theological Seminary—Burke Library (NY–275/1): Ja 1932.
Yale Divinity School—Special Collections (CT–50/25): Mr 1930, Ja 1932.
FUKIEN LEAFLET. Fukien Christian University, Foochow. N 1, 1935.

Harvard Divinity School—Andover-Harvard Theological Library (MA–95/1): N 1, 1935.
Yale Divinity School—Special Collections (CT–50/25): N 1, 1935.
FUKIEN NEWS. Fukien Christian University, Foochow.
Harvard Divinity School—Andover-Harvard Theological Library (MA–95/1): Jl 1934, Spr 1937.
Hoover Institution Archives (CA–290/29): Jl 1934, Spring 1937.
Yale Divinity School—Special Collections (CT–50/25): Jl 1934, Spr 1937.
FUKIEN STAR. Fukien Christian University, Foochow. V 1, 1922.
Harvard Divinity School—Andover-Harvard Theological Library (MA–95/1): V 1, N 2–3, Ap-Je 1922.
Union Theological Seminary—Burke Library (NY–275/1): V 2; V 3, N 1–2; V 4, N 1; F, Ap 1924; Je, Nv 1924; Je 1925.
Wesleyan University—Special Collections and Archives (CT–30/6): V 3, N 2, Nv 1924.
Yale Divinity School—Special Collections (CT–50/25): V 2, N 2–4; V 3, N 1–2; V 4, N 1; 1923–25.
FUKIEN VOICE. Fukien Christian University, English Club, Foochow. V 1, Ja 1935.
Yale Divinity School—Special Collections (CT–50/25): V 1, N 1, 1935.
NEWS.
Union Theological Seminary—Burke Library (NY–275/1): 1932.
SCIENCE JOURNAL. Foochow. V 1-, 1938-.
Continues Natural History Society, PROCEEDINGS, 1938.
Iowa State University Library (IA–5/1): V 1, 1938.
Smithsonian Institution—National Museum of Natural History Branch Library (DC–175/1): V 1, Je 1938.
WEEKLY BULLETIN.
Yale Divinity School—Special Collections (CT–50/25): 1933-38.

FUKIEN WITNESS. Methodist Publishing House, Foochow. S 1902-D 1909(?).
Continues FOOCHOW WITNESS, V 1, N 1–4.
Drew University—United Methodist Historical Library (NJ–50/1): V 1–6, Ja 1903-D 1909.
Garrett-Evangelical and Seabury-Western Theological Seminaries—United Library (IL–110/1): V 4, N 4, 1905.
Harvard Divinity School—Andover-Harvard Theological Library (MA–95/2): Ja-Jl 1908.
Union Theological Seminary—Burke Library (NY–275/1): S 1902; Ja-F, Ag 1903; F 1904; D 1908; My 1909.

GEBETSANLIEGEN DER CANTON-BLINDEN MISSION. n.p.
Union Theological Seminary—Burke Library (NY–275/1): Jl 1921, Ja 1922.

Ginling College

BULLETIN. Board of Directors, Nanking.
> Drew University—United Methodist Archives (NJ–45/5): 1919, 1931, 1933–35.
> Mount Holyoke College—College History and Archives (MA–220/21): 1920, 1925, 1928.
> Smith College—College Archives (MA–185/6): n.v., N 4–8, 1915, 1919, 1922, 1925, 1928, 1931, 1933–35.
> University of California, Berkeley—General Library (CA–70/1): 1920–35.
> Yale Divinity School Library (CT–55/1): 1915, 1919–20, 1922, 1925, 1928, 1931, 1933–35.

GINLING ASSOCIATION IN AMERICA NEWSLETTER. Ginling College, New York. N 1, 1951.
> Smith College—College Archives (MA–185/6): N 2–3, 13, 1951–52, 1954, 1957.
> Union Theological Seminary—Burke Library (NY–275/1): N 16, Special issue, Summer, 1958.
> Yale Divinity School—Special Collections (CT–50/25): N 1–26, 1951–64.

GINLING NEWS. Ginling College, Chengtu.
> Yale Divinity School—Special Collections (CT–50/25): Ja, Apr 1942, S 1945.

LETTER. Ginling College, Nanking. N 1, 1924.
> Mount Holyoke College—College History and Archives (MA–220/21): Series I, N 4, Nv 1925.
> Smith College—College Archives (MA–185/6): Series I, N 1–3, 1924–25.
> Union Theological Seminary—Burke Library (NY–275/1): Series I, N 1–2, Jl, Nv 1924, Nv 1927.
> Yale Divinity School—Special Collections (CT–50/25): Series I, N 1–5, 1924–26.

MAGAZINE. Ginling College, Nanking. V 1, 1924.
> Emory University—Pitts Theology Library (GA–15/5): V 1–2, 5, 1924–26, 1929.
> Mount Holyoke College—College History and Archives (MA–220/21): V 1, N 1; V 4, N 2; Je 1924, Je 1928.
> Smith College—College Archives (MA–185/6): V 1, N 1–4; V 2, N 1–3; V 4, N 2; V 5, N 1; 1924–26, 1928–29.
> Union Theological Seminary—Burke Library (NY–275/1): V 1, N 1–2; V 2, V 7, N 1; 1924–26, 1930.
> Yale Divinity School—Special Collections (CT–50/25): V 1, N 1–4; V 2, N 1–3; V 4, N 1–2; V 5, N 1–2; V 7, N 1; 1924–30.

NEWS LETTER. Ginling College, Nanking.
> Disciples of Christ Historical Society Library and Archives (TN–45/1): uncatalogued.
> Mount Holyoke College—College History and Archives (MA–220/21): Jl 1934.
> Yale Divinity School—Special Collections (CT–50/25): Jl 1934.

GLEANINGS. Lutheran United Mission, Honan and Hupeh Provinces, China.
Title varies: CHINA GLEANINGS.
> Luther College Archives (IA–15/1): V 4, N 1, Ag 1922.

> St. Olaf College—Rölvaag Memorial Library (MN–80/1): V 12, 1935.

GLEANINGS. South China Holiness Mission, Canton, China.
> Assemblies of God Archives (MO–105/1): V 1, N 2, Mr 1920.
> Union Theological Seminary—Burke Library (NY–275/1): D 1920; Mr, Jl, O 1921.

GLEANINGS FROM SOUTH CHINA. Bible Missionary Society. V 1–?, 1905(?)–?.
> Union Theological Seminary—Burke Library (NY–275/1): V 2, N 1; V 3, N 1; V 4, N 1; 1906–8.

GLIMPSES FROM CENTRAL HONAN. n.p.
> Union Theological Seminary—Burke Library (NY–275/1): Nv 1923.

GOSPEL IN CHINA. Foreign Mission Committee of the Presbyterian Church of England.
> Union Theological Seminary—Burke Library (NY–275/1): D 1884, Ja-Ap, Jl, D 1885.

THE GREEN YEAR. Young Women's Christian Association.
> Union Theological Seminary—Burke Library (NY–275/1): Ja, Mr-Je, O-D 1924; Ja, Mr-Jl, Nv 1925; Ja, Ap, O 1926; O 1927.

THE GREEN YEAR SUPPLEMENT. Young Women's Christian Association.
> Presbyterian Historical Society—Archives and Library (PA–200/28): Jl 1925.
> Stanford University—Green Library (CA–305/1): 1925.
> Union Theological Seminary—Burke Library (NY–275/1): My, Jl, Nv 1930; F, My, O, D 1931; Mr, Ap, 1932; D 1933.

THE GREEN YEARS. National Board and National YWCA in China, New York. 1899–1950.
> Union Theological Seminary—Burke Library (NY–275/1): O-D 1923; Mr, Jl 1925; Jl 1927; Ja, Mr, Nv 1928; D 1929; My 1930.
> Young Women's Christian Association of America—National Board Archives (NY–280/19): 1899–1950.

HAINAN NEWSLETTER. American Presbyterian Mission, Haichow, Hainan. 1912–49.
> Center for Research Libraries (IL–25/4): V 1, N 1–5, S 1912-D 1914, D 1915–1949.
> Graduate Theological Union Library (CA–15/2): S 1912-Christmas 1949.
> Hoover Institution Archives (CA–290/21): D 1914; F, Ag 1917; Ja, Ap, Jl, Nv 1918; Mr, Jl, Nv 1919; F, Jl, Nv 1920; Je, S 1921; Summ, Aut 1922; Spr, Aut 1923; Spr, Summ 1924; Spr 1925; Summ, Aut 1926; Spr 1927; Wint 1930–31; Spr 1931; Spr, Aut, Christmas 1932; Christmas 1933; Spr 1934; Spr, Christmas 1935; Spr, Christmas 1936; Centennial, Aut 1937; Summ, Aut, Christmas 1938; Christmas 1947; Christmas 1948; Christmas 1949.
> Iowa State University Library (IA–5/1): 1912–38, 1947–49.
> Kalamazoo College—Upjohn Library (MI–125/1): 1912–38, 1947–49.
> Ohio State University—Thompson Memorial Library (OH–110/4): V 1–27, 1912–49.

Presbyterian Historical Society—Archives and Library (PA–200/28): 1912–38, 1947–49.

Princeton Theological Seminary—Speer Library (NJ–95/3): Ap 1918; Nv 1919; Summ 1922; Christmas 1924; Spr 1932; Spr, Aut, Christmas 1935; Spr, Aut, Christmas 1936; Centennial Number 1937.

San Francisco Theological Seminary Library (CA–235/2): 1922–38, 1947–49.

Stanford University—Green Library (CA–305/1): 1912–49.

Union Theological Seminary—Burke Library (NY–275/1): Summ, Aut 1923; Je, D 1924; D 1925; Spr 1927; Wint, Spr, Aut 1930; Aut 1931; Spr, Aut, Christmas 1932; Spr, Aut, Christmas 1933; Spr, Aut, Christmas 1934; Spr, Aut, Christmas 1935; Spr, Aut, Christmas 1936; Spr, Aut, Christmas 1937; Spr, Aut, Christmas 1938; Aut, Christmas 1948; Christmas 1949.

University of Oregon—Department of Special Collections (OR–15/35): Christmas 1924; Aut 1937.

University of Oregon—Department of Special Collections (OR–15/36): Aut 1932; Spr 1933.

University of Oregon—Department of Special Collections (OR–15/37): Ap 1918, Wint 1929–30; Spr, Aut 1930; Wint 1930–31; Spr 1931; Spr, Aut, Christmas 1932; Spr, Aut, Christmas 1933; Spr, Christmas 1934; Spr, Aut, Christmas 1935; Spr, Aut, Christmas 1936; Centennial Number 1937; Summ, Aut, Christmas 1938; Christmas, n.d.; Christmas 1948.

University of Oregon—Department of Special Collections (OR–15/52): Wint 1929–Au 1932, Spr 1933–Wint 1935, Spr 1936–1949.

Wheaton College—Graham Center Library (IL–205/1): V 1–63, 1919–49.

Yale Divinity School Library (CT–55/2): 1912–49.

HAINAN REPORTER. n.p.
University of Oregon—Department of Special Collections (OR–15/52): 1947–49.

HAN YANG SPECIAL. n.p.
Sisters of Loretto Archives (KY–65/1): 1924–29.

HAVE A HEART FOR CHINA. Church Committee for China Relief, s.l.
Continues BULLETIN OF THE CHURCH COMMITTEE FOR CHINA RELIEF.
Union Theological Seminary—Burke Library (NY–275/1): N 18–30, 32, 34–40, 44, 45, 49, 50, 51–53, 55–56, 1939–44.
University of Oregon—Department of Special Collections (OR–15/24): N A–25, 26, 31, 45, O–Nv 1940, Ap 1941, F 1943.

THE HERALD OF THE RICE FIELDS. Fratres of the Old Mission, Santa Barbara, CA.
Mission Santa Barbara—Archives (CA–260/1): V 1, N 6–8; V 2, N 1–7, 1929–31.

HERE AND NOW. American Board of Commissioners for Foreign Missions, North China Mission, Tientsin.
Harvard Divinity School—Andover-Harvard Theological Library (MA–95/1): N 2, 4–5, 7, 1923, 1925–26.

Harvard Divinity School—Andover-Harvard Theological Library (MA–95/2): N 1–2, 4–9, 1922–30.

HINGHWA. Methodist Episcopal Church, Hinghwa Mission, Hinghwa.
Essex Institute—Phillips Library (MA–210/2): V 5, N 3; V 6, N 3–4; V 7, N 1–4; 1922–24.
Union Theological Seminary—Burke Library (NY–275/1): Ja, Jl, O 1918; Ja, Ap, Jl 1919; O 1921; Ja, Ap, Jl 1922; Ja, Ap, Jl 1923; Ja, Mr 1924.

Home of the Nazarene (Industrial Orphanage), Chinkiang
LETTER. Home of the Nazarene (Industrial Orphanage) Chinkiang, N 1–?, O 1927–?.
Union Theological Seminary—Burke Library (NY–275/1): N 1, O 1927.

HOMES OF THE EAST. Church of England Zenana Missionary Society.
Union Theological Seminary—Burke Library (NY–275/1): N 62, 1919.

HONAN GLIMPSES. Augustana Mission, Shekow and Hankow. Mr 1922-Mr 1927.
Continues GLIMPSES OF CENTRAL HONAN. Merged with FOREIGN MISSIONARY, Rock Island, IL, 1927.
Lutheran Church in America Archives (IL–50/1): 1922–27.

HONAN MESSENGER. V 1(?)–18, 1914?–32.
Continued as HONAN QUARTERLY, 1932.
Union Theological Seminary—Burke Library (NY–275/1): V 14–18, 1928–32.

HONAN QUARTERLY. V 1–9, 1932–41.
Continues HONAN MESSENGER, 1932.
Union Theological Seminary—Burke Library (NY–275/1): V 1, N 1–3, n.v., 1932–41.

Hsü-chia-hui kuan hsiang t'ai. *See* Zi-ka-wei Observatoire, Shanghai.

Hua Chung University, Wuchang
BULLETIN. Hua chung University, Wuchang.
Cornell University—Wason Collection (NY–95/1): 1925.
HUA CHUNG COLLEGE BULLETIN. Huachung College.
Yale Divinity School—Special Collections (CT–50/25): V 4, N 33; V 5, N 11–15; V 6, N 14; V 7, N 2–3; V 8, N 2–7, 15–20, 47–50; V 9, N 1–2, 6, 35; 1937, 1939–41.
HUA CHUNG COLLEGE NEWS. Huachung College, Hsichow, Yunnan.
Yale Divinity School—Special Collections (CT–50/25): V 1, N 1, 3–4; V 2, N 1; 1940–41.
Yale University—Manuscripts and Archives (CT–60/32): V 1, N 1–4, 1940–41.
HUA CHUNG NEWS. Huachung College.
Yale Divinity School—Special Collections (CT–50/25): N 1–3, 1938.
HUA CHUNG NEWSLETTER. Huachung University, Wuchang, Hupeh.
Yale Divinity School—Special Collections (CT–50/25): V 1, N 1–12; V 2, N 1–16; V 3, N 5–7,

14; V 4, N 2, 7–8, 12–14; V 5, N 4–5; V 6, N 2–3; 1947–50.

HUA MING NEWS SERVICE. Catholic Central Bureau of China. Suspended in 1949. Continued by MISSION CHRONICLE. California Province of the Society of Jesus Archives (CA–195/1): Ap-My 1949.

HUA NAN NEWS. Hwa Nan College, Yenping, Fukien.
Yale Divinity School—Special Collections (CT–50/25): V 1, N 1–4; V 2, N 1; 1939.

HUNAN BIBLE INSTITUTE BULLETIN. Hunan Bible Institute, Changsha. Reprinted by Wayne Co., Hong Kong.
Biola University—Rose Memorial Library (CA–130/1): 1949–50.

HUNAN NEWS. Congregation of the Passion, Hong Kong. (weekly) 1949–56.
Congregation of the Passion of the Eastern United States—Chronicle Office (MA–255/1): 1949–56 (inc.).
Sisters of Charity of Saint Elizabeth—Generalate Archives (NJ–15/1): Je 1950-S 1954 (inc.).

HUNAN-YALE BULLETIN. Changsha. N 1, 1932.
Yale University—Manuscripts and Archives (CT–60/32): N 1, 1932.

HUPING. Huping Christian College, Yochow, Hunan.
Published monthly during the college year.
Evangelical and Reformed Historical Society—Schaff Library (PA–80/15): V 7, N 4-V 10, D 1924-Ja 1926.

I FANG SCHOOL NEWSLETTER. I Fang School, Changsha. N 1-, 1938-.
Union Theological Seminary—Burke Library (NY–275/1): N 2–4, 6–13, 1938.

INDIA'S WOMEN AND CHINA'S DAUGHTERS. Zenana Missionary Society, Church of England, London. V 16, N 115-V 59, N 635, Ja 1896-D 1939.
Title varies: V 1–15, INDIA'S WOMEN; V 16–59, INDIA'S WOMEN AND CHINA'S DAUGHTERS; V 60-, LOOKING EAST AT INDIA'S WOMEN AND CHINA'S DAUGHTERS.
Drew University Library (NJ–40/2): V 16–46, 1896–1926.
Emory University—Pitts Theology Library (GA–15/5): V 1, 8–9, 32–36, 40–58, 1881, 1888–89, 1912–16, 1920–38.
Garrett-Evangelical and Seabury-Western Theological Seminaries—United Library (IL–110/1): V 17, N 1–7, 9–12; V 8-V 18, N 12; V 19, N 5, 7–12; V 20-V 21, N 3, 5, 7, 12; V 22, N 1, 3–4; V 48, N 1–7, 9–12; V 49-V 59, N 12; 1897–1902, 1928–39.
University of Washington Libraries (WA–45/1): V 16–59, 1896–193.

INFORMATION ABOUT CHINA: Weekly Bulletin for the Missionary Conference of North America.
Union Theological Seminary—Burke Library (NY–275/1): N 1, 5–12, 14–17, 19–21, 1925–26.

INFORMATION LETTER (LWF MARXISM AND CHINA STUDY). *See* Lutheran World Federation.

INFORMATION SERVICE. Church of Christ in China, Hong Kong Council, Hong Kong.
Presbyterian Historical Society—Archives and Library (PA–200/28): N 8, My 1958.
Union Theological Seminary—Burke Library (NY–275/1): n.v.; V 4, N 1–3; V 5, N 1–3; V 6, N 1, 3; V 7, N 1, 2; V 8, N 1; V 9–11, 12, N 1; V 13, N 1; V 14, N 1; 1926–27, 1929–40.

INFORMATION SERVICE. Church of Christ in China, n.l.
Harvard Divinity School—Andover-Harvard Theological Library (MA–95/2): N 26–31, 34, 36, 55, 60, D 1959-My 1960, Ag 1960, O 1960, Jl 1962, F 1963.

INFORMATION SERVICE OF THE CHURCH OF CHRIST IN CHINA. Church of Christ in China, Kwangtung Synod, Canton. 1936–47.
Presbyterian Historical Society—Archives and Library (PA–200/28): F, Ag 1936; Jl 1937; S 1939; D 1940; Je 1946; Mr 1947.
San Francisco Theological Seminary Library (CA–235/2): V 11, N 1, Jl 1937.
Union Theological Seminary—Burke Library (NY–275/1): N 1–3, 1946.
University of Oregon—Department of Special Collections (OR–15/18): 1940–46.

INTERCESSORY MISSIONARY. Kiungchow Union Mission.
Union Theological Seminary—Burke Library (NY–275/1): D 1906, Ja, Je 1907.

International Anti-opium Association, Peking
BULLETIN. V 1–6(?), 1919–26(?).
Union Theological Seminary—Burke Library (NY–275/1): V 1, N 3–5, 7–10; V 2, N 1–2, n.v.; V 3, N 2; V 4, N 1; V 5, N 1; V 6, N 1, 1919–26.

IRC NEWS BULLETIN. International Relief Committee.
Carleton College Archives (MN–60/1): N 3, Nv 1942.

JOHANNEAN. St. John's University, Shanghai.
Emory University—Pitts Theology Library (GA–15/5): V 3–4, 1917–18.
Library of Congress—General Reading Rooms Division (DC–120/1): V 10, 1924.
Oberlin College—Main Library (OH–175/1): V 10, 1924.

JOURNAL OF ORIENTAL STUDIES. *See* MONUMENTA SERICA

JOURNAL OF SINOLOGICAL STUDIES. *See* Yenching University.

JOURNAL OF SYNOD. *See* Anglican Communion in China and Hong Kong (Chung-hua Sheng Kung Hui).

KAKCHIEH WEAKLY NEWS. American Baptist Mission, Kakchieh.
Yale Divinity School—Special Collections (CT–50/14): V 1, N 1–2, 1914.

KANCHOW. n.p.
St. John's University Archives (NY–105/1): V 1–3, O 1937-Je 1940.

KINAMISSIONAEREN. The American Norwegian China Mission Society, Madison, MN. V 1–14, 1891–1904.
Place of publication varies: Faribault, MN, 1891–99; Atwater, MN, 1899. Publisher varies: Augsburg Publishing House, United Norwegian Lutheran Church.
American Lutheran Church Archives (MN–95/110): V 1–2, N 1–4, 6–14, 16, 18–20, 22–24; V 3, N 1–8, 18–24; V 5–14, N 1–8, 12, 1891–1904.
Luther College Archives (IA–15/2): V 1–5, 1891–95.
Luther Northwestern Theological Seminary Library (MN–100/1): V 1–14, 1891–1904.

KINA MISSIONAEREN. Norske Kinamission, s.l.
Union Theological Seminary—Burke Library (NY–275/1): F 1923.

KINA MISSIONÄREN. Augustana Synod China Mission, s.l.
Union Theological Seminary—Burke Library (NY–275/1): D 1918, 1919–D 1925?.

KINA MISSIONÄREN. China Mission Society, Rock Island, IL (monthly, in Swedish).
Augustana College—Swenson Swedish Immigration Research Center (IL–150/2): V 21, N 5; V 22, N 8, 11; My 1923; Ag, Nv 1924.

KINA OCH JAPAN. n.p.
Union Theological Seminary—Burke Library (NY–275/1): n.d.

KINAMISJONAEREN. Norske Kinamisjon, Oslo.
Union Theological Seminary—Burke Library (NY–275/1): Ag 1950–Nv 1951.

KINESEREN. Norksk Lutherne Kinamissionsforbund.
Union Theological Seminary—Burke Library (NY–275/1): 1901, 1908, 1916, 1918–22, 1927–36.

KITAISKII BLAGOVIESTNIK: Ezhemiesiachoe Izdanie Rossiskoi Dukhovnoi Missii v Kitae (Russian Religious Missions in China). Missiia, Peking.
University of California, Berkeley—General Library (CA–70/1): 1936, 1941.

KOCHOW STATION BI-MONTHLY. South China Mission, Kochau.
Continues KO CHAU FIELD BI-MONTHLY BULLETIN, 19?–12.
Union Theological Seminary—Burke Library (NY–275/1): N 42–45, 47–48, 51–52, 55, 57–59, 63, 69, 71, 1910–16.

Kwang Hsüeh Publishing House, Shanghai
GREETINGS. Kwang Hsüeh Publishing House, Shanghai.
Union Theological Seminary—Burke Library (NY–275/1): 1935.
LETTER. Kwang Hsüeh Publishing House, Shanghai.
Union Theological Seminary—Burke Library (NY–275/1): 1937.

Kwangsi Hunan Mission
NEWSLETTER. Kwangsi Hunan Mission.
Not published in 1921.
Union Theological Seminary—Burke Library (NY–275/1): n.v., N 55–57, 1911–12, 1919–20.

LAMP OF CHINA. n.p. 1893(?)–99(?).
Union Theological Seminary—Burke Library (NY–275/1): 1893–99.

LAND OF SINIM. North China and Shantung Mission. N 1, 1893.
Continued by CHINA AND THE GOSPEL.
American Baptist Seminary of the West Library (CA–10/1): 1905.
Claremont Colleges—Honnold Library (CA–85/1): 1904.
Cornell University—Wason Collection (NY–95/1): 1904–5.
Drew University Library (NJ–40/2): 1904, 1907–13.
Emory University—Pitts Theology Library (GA–15/5): 1904.
Princeton Theological Seminary—Speer Library (NJ–95/3): 1904–5.
Southern Baptist Theological Seminary—Boyce Centennial Library (KY–50/2): 1904.
Union Theological Seminary—Burke Library (NY–275/1): 1893–1912, Ja-Mr, My-D 1913, 1914–18.
Vanderbilt University—Divinity Library (TN–65/1): 1905.
Yale Divinity School Library (CT–55/2): N 1, V 1–61, 1893–1951.

LATEST NEWS FROM CHINA COLLEGES. Associated Boards for Christian Colleges in China, New York.
Yale Divinity School—Special Collections (CT–50/25): 1945–46, 1948–49.

LATEST NEWS OF CHRISTIAN COLLEGES IN CHINA. Associated Boards for Christian Colleges in China, New York.
Presbyterian Historical Society—Archives and Library (PA–200/8): Nv-D 1948.

LAY TRAINING BULLETIN. *See* National Committee for Christian Religious Education.

LETTERS FROM CHINA. n.p.
Hoover Institution Library (CA–300/1): V 1–5, 1948–49.

LETTRES DES NOUVELLES MISSIONS DE CHINE. n.p. 1842–68.
Georgetown University—Woodstock Theological Center Library (DC–70/4): V 2–3, 1843–44.

LIBER SHANGHAIENSIS. Shanghai College, Shanghai. V 1–, 1915–.
Union Theological Seminary—Burke Library (NY–275/1): V 1, 4, 1915, 1919.

LIEBENZELLER MISSION (CHINAS MILLIONEN). Monateschrift für China und sein Freunde. 1900–1956(?).
Union Theological Seminary—Burke Library (NY–275/1): 1900, Mr-D 1901, 1902, Ja-O 1903, 1904–20, Ja-My 1921, My-D 1922, Ja-Nv 1923, 1924, Ja-Nv 1925, 1926–40, Ja-My 1941, 1956–?

THE LIGHT. Catholic University of Peking, Peking. V 1–18, N 2, Mr 1932–Je 1949. S.V.D. CATHOLIC UNIVERSITIES, 1949–.
Title varies: FU-JEN MAGAZINE, V 1–18, N 2, Mr/Ap 1932–Je 1949; THE LIGHT OF FAITH AND SCIENCE, V

18, N 3-V 20, N 1, S 1949-Mr 1951. Supersedes FU JEN NEWS LETTER. Suspended Mr-D 1933.

> Cornell University—Wason Collection (NY–95/1): V 1–2, 8–28, 1932–34, 1939–59.
>
> Yale Divinity School Library (CT–55/2): V 1–36, 1932–67.

LINGNAAM: The News Bulletin of Canton Christian College. New York. V 1, 1924.

> Title varies: LINGNAN.
>
> Hoover Institution Library (CA–300/1): V 10, N 1–2, Ja 1938.
>
> New York Public Library—General Research Division (NY–230/1): Ag 1924-O 1933 (inc.).
>
> Presbyterian Historical Society—Archives and Library (PA–200/8): V 14, N 2, Aut 1948.
>
> Union Theological Seminary—Burke Library (NY–275/1): V 1, N 1–2; V 11, N 3, 21; 1914, 1925.
>
> Yale Divinity School Library (CT–55/2): V 1–2, 4–7, 9, 1924–25, 1927–31, 1936.
>
> Yale Divinity School—Special Collections (CT–50/25): V 1, N 1, 1924.

LINGNAAM AGRICULTURAL REVIEW. Lingnan University, Canton. V 1–, D 1922–.

> Title varies: LINGNAAM AGRICULTURAL REVIEW, D 1922-Jl 1927. Continued by LINGNAN SCIENCE JOURNAL.
>
> Buffalo Museum of Science—Research Library (NY–65/1): V 1, N 1–2; V 2, N 1–2; V 3, N 1–2; V 4, N 1–2; V 5, N 1–4; 1922–26.
>
> Detroit Public Library (MI–55/1): V 2–3, Jl 1924-Ap 1926.
>
> Harvard University—Arnold Arboretum Library (MA–100/1): V 1–4, 1922–27.
>
> Harvard University—Museum of Comparative Zoology Library (MA–140/1): V 1–4, 1922–27.
>
> Lloyd Library (OH–35/1): V 1–4, 1922–27.
>
> New York Academy of Medicine Library (NY–220/1): V 1, N 1, 2, V 2, N 2, 1922–23.
>
> Rutgers University—Alexander Library (NJ–75/1): D 1922-Jl 1927.
>
> Trinity College Library (CT–25/1): V 1–4, 1922–27.
>
> Union Theological Seminary—Burke Library (NY–275/1): V 1, N 1–2; V 2, N 1–3; V 3, N 1; 1922–26.
>
> University of California at Los Angeles—Biomedical Library (CA–160/1): V 3–4, 1925–27.
>
> University of Tennessee, Knoxville—Agriculture-Veterinary Medicine Library (TN–30/1): V 1–5, 1922–27.
>
> Yale Divinity School—Special Collections (CT–50/25): V 1–4, 1922–27.

LINGNAN. *See* LINGNAAM.

LINGNAN: A Monthly Magazine. Lingnan University, Hong Kong. V 1, Ap 1941.

> Yale Divinity School—Special Collections (CT–50/25): V 11, N 1, V 12, N 1–2, V 13, N 1, 3, V 14, N 1, V 15, N 1, 1944, 1946–49.
>
> Yale University—Sterling Memorial Library (CT–80/1): V 1, N 1–3, 1941.

LINGNAN JOURNAL. Lingnan University, Canton. V 1–12, N 1, D 1929-Je 1952.

> Publisher varies: 1929–37 by the University; 1947–50 by the University's Institute of Chinese Studies. Suspended 1938–46.
>
> Union Theological Seminary—Burke Library (NY–275/1): V 1, N 2, 4, My, S 1930.
>
> University of Michigan—Asia Library (MI–10/1): V 1–8, 1929–37, 1949–52.

LINGNAN NEWS. Lingnan University.

> Yale Divinity School—Special Collections (CT–50/25): V 15, N 2; V 16, N 1–2; 1949–50.

LINGNAN SCIENCE JOURNAL. Lingnan University, Canton. V 1–, D 1922–.

> Title varies: LINGNAAM AGRICULTURAL REVIEW, D 1922-Jl 1927. Suspended Ja-My 1930, Je-D 1941, Ag 1942-Ag 1945. Publisher and place of publication varies: College of Agriculture, Canton Christian College, V 1–2; Lingnan Agricultural College, Canton Christian College, V 3. Index V 1–14 (1922–34) in V 14. In English and Chinese.
>
> Academy of Natural Sciences of Philadelphia Library (PA–135/4): V 1–23, N 2, 1922–50.
>
> American Museum of Natural History Library (NY–140/1): V 1–23, 1922–51.
>
> Brigham Young University—Lee Library (UT–10/1): V 3–22, 1922–48.
>
> Brown University—Rockefeller Library (RI–20/2): V 6–7, 1928–29.
>
> Buffalo Museum of Science—Research Library (NY–65/1): V 6, N 1–4; V 7–8; V 9, N 1–4; V 10, N 1–4; V 11, N 1–4; V 12–14; V 15, N 1–4; V 16, N 1–2; 1928–37.
>
> Center for Research Libraries (IL–25/4): V 9, N 1–2; V 10, N 2–3; V 14, N 4-V 17, N 3; V 18–19, 22; Je 1930, Ag 1931, O 1935-Ag 1938, 1939–40, 1948.
>
> Claremont Colleges—Honnold Library (CA–85/1): V 1–21, 1922–45.
>
> Clemson University—Cooper Library (SC–15/1): V 1–22, 1922–48.
>
> Columbia University—Science Library (NY–190/1): V 5, 15–16, N 1927-Ap 1928, 1936–37.
>
> Cornell University—Wason Collection (NY–95/1): V 1–22, 1922–45, 1948.
>
> Detroit Public Library (MI–55/1): V 15, N 2–3; V 16–18; V 19, N 1–3; V 20, N 2–4; V 21, N 1–4; 1936–40, 1942, 1945.
>
> Duke University—Biology-Forestry Library (NC–25/1): V 15–22, 1936–42.
>
> Field Museum of Natural History Library (IL–40/1): V 1–22, 1922–42, 1945, 1948.
>
> Harvard University—Arnold Arboretum Library (MA–100/1): V 5–23, 1927–50.
>
> Harvard University—Harvard-Yenching Library (MA–125/6): V 12–18, 21, 1933–39, 1945.
>
> Harvard University—Museum of Comparative Zoology Library (MA–140/1): V 5–6, 1927–28.
>
> Harvard University—Peabody Museum (MA–145/1): V 18, N 3, 1939.
>
> Indiana University—University Libraries (IN–20/2): V 18–20, 21–22, 1939–41, 1945, 1948.

Iowa State University Library (IA–5/1): V 1–22, 1922–48.

Kansas State University—Farrell Library (KS–45/1): V 1–22, 1922–48.

Library of Congress—General Reading Rooms Division (DC–120/1): D 1922-Je 1923; Ap 1926; Je 1929-O 1931; Mr-Nv 1932; F-O 1933; Ja-O 1934; Ja-O 1935; Ja-Nv 1936; 1937–42.

Lloyd Library (OH–35/1): V 5–23, N 2, 1927–50.

Louisiana State University—Middleton Library (LA–10/1): V 5–6, 8; V 9, N 1–2; V 11, N 3; V 13; V 14, N 3; V 15–19; V 20, N 2–4; V 21–22; V 23, N 1–2; 1926–27, 1929–30, 1932, 1934, 1936–42, 1945, 1948–49.

Marine Biological Laboratories Library (MA–260/1): V 1–23, 1922–50.

Michigan State University Library (MI–75/1): V 1–23, 1922–45.

New York Academy of Medicine Library (NY–220/1): V 17–19, 20, N 2–4, V 21–22, 23, N 1–2, 1944–50.

New York Public Library—General Research Division (NY–230/1): V 1–4, [5–6], 7–20, D 1922–48 (inc.).

New York State Library (NY–15/2): V 5–22, 1927–42.

Ohio State University—Agriculture Library (OH–100/1): V 1–22, 1922–48.

Ohio State University—Thompson Memorial Library (OH–110/4): V 1–23, 1922–50.

Oregon State University—Kerr Library (OR–5/1): V 1–22, D 1922–1948.

Pennsylvania State University—Penn State Room (PA–275/4): N 1–19, 21–23, 1922–50.

Purdue University—Humanities, Social Science, and Education Library (IN–115/1): V 2–7, 21, 1924–29, 1945.

Rutgers University—Alexander Library (NJ–75/1): V 5–6, Ag 1927–28.

Smithsonian Institution—National Museum of Natural History Branch Library (DC–175/1): V 1–23, N 2, 1922–50.

Stanford University—Green Library (CA–305/1): V 1–23, 192250.

Trinity College Library (CT–25/1): V 5–22, 1927–48.

Union Theological Seminary—Burke Library (NY–275/1): Ja, Ag, O 1931.

University of Arizona Library (AZ–5/3): V 1–2, 15–17, 20–23, 1922–23, 1936–38, 1941–48.

University of California at Los Angeles—Biomedical Library (CA–160/1): V 5–22, 1927–48.

University of California, Berkeley—Biology Library (CA–40/1): V 1–21, 23, N 1–2, 1922–45, 1950.

University of California—Northern Regional Library Facility (CA–215/1): V 1–5, N 2; V 7–8; V 9, N 3; V 10, N 4; V 18–22, 1922–48.

University of Chicago—Regenstein Library (IL–85/1): V 5–23, 1927–50.

University of Cincinnati—Central Library (OH–65/1): V 15–20, 1936–42.

University of Georgia Libraries (GA–5/1): V 1–23, 1922–50.

University of Idaho—Special Collections (ID–5/2): V 1–21, 1922–45.

University of Illinois at Urbana-Champaign Library

(IL–185/1): V 1–23, N 2, D 1922-D 1950.

University of Maryland—McKeldin Library (MD–45/2): V 1–22, 1922–48.

University of Massachusetts at Amherst Library (MA–15/2): 1922–42.

University of Michigan—Hatcher Graduate Library (MI–25/1): V 1–22, 1922–48.

University of Minnesota—St. Paul Campus Libraries (MN–115/1): V 1–23, N 1–3, 1922–51.

University of Missouri-Columbia—Ellis Library (MO–10/1): V 1–7, 9–22, 1922–29, 1930–48.

University of Nebraska, Lincoln—Love Library (NB–25/2): V 1–23, 1922–50.

University of Notre Dame—Memorial Library (IN–95/1): V 1–21, 1922–45.

University of Oregon—Department of Special Collections (OR–15/37): 1932, 1934.

University of Oregon Library (OR–20/2): V 7–8; V 9, N 3/4-V 22; 1929, 1932–42, 1945, 1948.

University of Pennsylvania—Van Pelt Library (PA–215/1): V 1–19, 1922–41.

University of Tennessee, Knoxville—Agriculture-Veterinary Medicine Library (TN–30/1): V 6, V 20, N 2–4, V 21, N 1–4, V 22, N 1–4, 1927–28, 1942, 1945, 1948.

University of Washington Libraries (WA–45/1): V 1–22, 1922–48.

Utah State University—Merrill Library (UT–5/1): V 7–8, 16–22, 1929, 1937–48.

West Virginia University Library (WV–15/4): V 1–19, 1922–41.

Western Washington University—Wilson Library (WA–5/1): V 18, N 3–4, 1939 (repr. 1978?).

Yale Divinity School—Special Collections (CT–50/25): V 5, N 1–2; V 7–10; V 11, N 1–2; V 13, N 2; V 14–15; V 16, N 1; V 18–19; V 20, N 2–4; V 21–22; V 23, N 1–2; 1927, 1929–50.

Yale University—Kline Science Library (CT–65/1): V 1–22, 1922–42, 1945, 1948.

Lingnan University, Canton

BULLETIN. 1908-.

> Pennsylvania State University—Penn State Room (PA–275/4): N 1–31, 1908–21.
>
> University of California, Berkeley—General Library (CA–70/1): 1909–35.

DAILY METEOROLOGICAL RECORD. Lingnan University, Freeman Meteorological Observatory, Canton. 1919-.

> Library of Congress—General Reading Rooms Division (DC–120/1): 1921–26.
>
> New York Public Library—General Research Division (NY–230/1): 1919-Mr 1937.
>
> Pennsylvania State University—Penn State Room (PA–275/4): 1919–23.

SCIENCE BULLETIN. Lingnan University, Canton. V 1-, 1930–44.

> Academy of Natural Sciences of Philadelphia Library (PA–135/4): N 1, 6–7, 1930, 1934–35.
>
> American Museum of Natural History Library (NY–140/1): V 1–8, 10, 1930–44.
>
> Cleveland Health Sciences—Allen Memorial Library

(OH–80/1): N 6, My 1934.

Cornell University—Wason Collection (NY–95/1): N 1, 1930.

Field Museum of Natural History Library (IL–40/1): N 10, 1944.

Harvard University—Arnold Arboretum Library (MA–100/1): N 1–9, 1930–40.

Iowa State University Library (IA–5/1): V 1–8, 10, 1930–36, 1944.

Library of Congress—General Reading Rooms Division (DC–120/1): V 1, 6–7, 1930, 1936–37.

Pennsylvania State University—Penn State Room (PA–275/4): N 1–2, 10, 1930–31, 1944.

Smithsonian Institution—Botany Library (DC–155/1): V 1, 1930.

Smithsonian Institution—National Museum of Natural History Branch Library (DC–175/1): V 10, 1944.

University of California, Berkeley—Biology Library (CA–40/1): N 1–10, 1930–44.

University of Michigan—Hatcher Graduate Library (MI–25/1): V 1–7, 1930–35.

University of Pennsylvania—Van Pelt Library PA–215/1): V 1–2, 1930–31.

SPECIAL PUBLICATION. Lingnan University, Lingnan Natural History Survey and Museum. N 1–13, Ja 1942–Ap 1950.

Academy of Natural Sciences of Philadelphia Library (PA–135/4): N 1–13, 1942–50.

American Museum of Natural History Library (NY–140/1): N 1–3, 1942–43.

Cornell University—Wason Collection (NY–95/1): N 1–13, Ja 1942–Ap 1950.

Library of Congress—General Reading Rooms Division (DC–120/1): N 6, 9–12, 1947(?), 1948(?)–50.

THE LINGUIST. Nanking Language School, Department of Missionary Training, University of Nanking, Nanking.

Union Theological Seminary—Burke Library (NY–275/1): 1920–26.

Yale Divinity School—Special Collections (CT–50/25): 1922–24.

LINK. *See* Christian Literature Society for China.

LIST OF MISSIONARIES AND THEIR STATIONS. *See* China Inland Mission.

THE LITTLE DESIGN IN CHINA. Sisters of St. Joseph, Baden, PA.

St. Joseph Convent—Sisters of St. Joseph Archives (PA–5/1): Jl 1946–Je 1949.

LOOKING EAST. Zenana Missionary Society, Church of England, London. V 71, N 1–V 77, N 6, Ja 1951–O 1957.
Title varies: V 1–15, INDIA'S WOMEN; V 16–59, INDIA'S WOMEN AND CHINA'S DAUGHTERS; V 60–71, LOOKING EAST AT INDIA'S WOMEN AND CHINA'S DAUGHTERS; V 71–77, LOOKING EAST; absorbed by C. M. S. OUTLOOK.

Garrett-Evangelical and Seabury-Western Theological Seminaries—United Library (IL–110/1): V 60–77, 1940–57.

University of Washington Libraries (WA–45/1): V 71–77,

N 6, 1951–57.

LOOKING EAST AT INDIA'S WOMEN AND CHINA'S DAUGHTERS. Zenana Missionary Society, Church of England, London. V 60, N 1–V 70, N 10, Ja 1940–D 1950.
Title varies: V 1–15, INDIA'S WOMEN; V 16–59, INDIA'S WOMEN AND CHINA'S DAUGHTERS; V 60–71, LOOKING EAST AT INDIA'S WOMEN AND CHINA'S DAUGHTERS; V 71–77, LOOKING EAST; absorbed by C. M. S. OUTLOOK.

Emory University—Pitts Theology Library (GA–15/5): V 60–77, 1940–57.

Union Theological Seminary—Burke Library (NY–275/1): V 1–6, 6–15, 17–21, 25–77, 1881–86, 1888–1895, 1897–1901, 1905–57.

University of Michigan—Hatcher Graduate Library (MI–25/1): V 1, 3–8, 13–14, 1880–81, 1883–88, 1893–94.

University of Washington Libraries (WA–45/1): V 60–70, N 10, 1940–50.

Yale Divinity School Library (CT–55/2): V 2–3, 19–20, 22–24, 31–77, 1882–83, 1899–1900, 1902–4, 1911–57.

LOOSE LEAVES FROM MISSIONARIES' DIARIES. American Board of Commissioners for Foreign Missions, Foochow. Continues FOOCHOW MESSENGER.

Claremont Colleges—Asian Studies Collection (CA–75/2): N 5, 1919.

Harvard Divinity School—Andover-Harvard Theological Library (MA–95/2): N 1–10, 1917–21.

Union Theological Seminary—Burke Library (NY–275/1): S-O, D 1917; Jl, D 1918; Ja-Mr, My 1919; F My, D 1920; F, Jl-Ag, 1921.

LOTUS LEAVES. Sisters of Charity, Mount St. Joseph, OH. 1929–51.

Sisters of Charity Motherhouse Archives (OH–165/1): 1929–51.

LUTHERAN LITERATURE SOCIETY FOR CHINA BULLETIN. Lutheran Literature Society for China, Northfield, MN. V 1, 1957.

Luther Northwestern Theological Seminary Library (MN–100/1): V 1–, 1957–.

Lutheran Church in America Archives (IL–50/1): 1958–63.

Lutheran Theological Seminary—Krauth Memorial Library (PA–180/1): V 12, N 3, 1968–.

LUTHERAN ORIENT MISSION. Hamilton, OH; Northfield, MN. V 1, 1910.

Emory University—Pitts Theology Library (GA–15/5): V 29, N 1, 3–5; V 30, N 2–5; V 31, N 1–5; V 32, N 1–2; V 34, N 2, 5; V 35, N 3–5; V 36, N 2–5; V 37, N 1–5; V 38, N 1–5; V 39, N 1–4; V 40, N 2, 4–5; V 41, N 2–7; V 42, N 1–10; V 43, N 2, 5–6, 9; V 44, N 1–4, 6–12; V 45, N 1–9; 1941–44, 1946–57.

Union Theological Seminary—Burke Library (NY–275/1): Mr-Ap 1915; D 1917; Ap, Je, D 1920; Ja, Mr-Ap, O-D 1921; 1922–?.

Lutheran World Federation
INFORMATION LETTER (LWF MARXISM AND CHINA

STUDY). Lutheran World Federation, Department of Studies, Geneva. V 1-. 1972-.

> Asbury Theological Seminary—Fisher Library (KY-90/1): V 1-, 1972-.
> Emory University—Pitts Theology Library (GA-15/5): N 18-31, 1977-80.
> St. Olaf College Archives (MN-70/3): N 1, 3, 5; S 1972; F, Ag 1973.
> Union Theological Seminary—Burke Library (NY-275/1): N 1, S 1972-.

MARYKNOLL MISSION LETTERS. Catholic Foreign Mission Society of America, Maryknoll, New York. V 1-, 1923-.
Continues MARYKNOLL MISSION LETTERS, CHINA, 1923-27. Suspended 1928-41.

> Andrews University—White Library (MI-50/1): 1923, 1943.
> Boston College—Burns Library (MA-170/1): 1942-46.
> Catholic University of America—Mullen Library (DC-20/1): 1927, Ja 1942, 1943, 1946.
> Harvard University—Widener Library (MA-155/1): 1923-27.
> Library of Congress—General Reading Rooms Division (DC-120/1): 1929-49.
> Maryknoll Sisters of St. Dominic—Rogers Library (NY-125/1): 1942-46.
> New York Public Library—General Research Division (NY-230/1): 1942-46.
> Princeton Theological Seminary—Speer Library (NJ-95/3): V 1-2, 1923-27.
> St. John's Seminary Library (MA-85/1): V 1, 1923.

MEI HUA PAI SO. North China American School, Tunghsien.
> Harvard Divinity School—Andover-Harvard Theological Library (MA-95/1): V 1, N 2, D 1932.

THE MESSENGER. n.p., Shanghai.
> Union Theological Seminary—Burke Library (NY-275/1): Jl-D 1888, F-D 1889, 1890-96.

Methodist Episcopal Church in China
BULLETIN.
> Princeton Theological Seminary—Speer Library (NJ-95/3): 1896-97, 1901-6, 1912-15, 1917, 1922.

Methodist Episcopal Church in Fukien
BULLETIN. Methodist Episcopal Church, Fukien. N 1-69(?), 1896-1915(?).
> Nebraska State Historical Society Library (NB-10/5): 1903.
> Union Theological Seminary—Burke Library (NY-275/1): N 1-69; Nv 1896; Ja-Je 1897; Mr, Nv 1898; Ag-Nv 1899; 1900-1; Ja-O 1902; Ja, Ap-Jl 1903; Ja-O 1904; Ja, Ap, Jl, O 1905; Ja, Ap, Jl, O-D 1906; Ja-Je, O-D 1907; 1908-9; Ja-S, Nv 1910; Je, Nv 1911; Je, D 1912; Jl 1913; F, Je 1914; Ja 1915.

THE MILLIONS. China Inland Mission, London. N 1, 1875.
> Colgate-Rochester Theological Seminaries—Swasey Library (NY-350/1): V 79-91, 1953-64.
> Harvard Divinity School—Andover-Harvard Theological Library (MA-95/2): V 78, N 6-V 91, N 19, Je 1952-D 1964.

> Moody Bible Institute Library (IL-55/1): V 60, 1952.
> Union Theological Seminary—Burke Library (NY-275/1): V 60, N 5-V 73, N 12, Je 1952-D 1964.
> University of Kansas—Watson Library (KS-35/3): V 6, 1880.
> Wellesley College—Clapp Library (MA-245/1): N 1-102, Jl 1875-D 1883.

THE MILLIONS. China Inland Mission, Philadelphia. 1952-64.
Continues CHINA'S MILLIONS. Continued by EAST ASIA MILLIONS.

> Asbury Theological Seminary—Fisher Library (KY-90/1): V 60, N 4-12; V 61-68; V 69, N 1-4; 1952-61.
> Associated Mennonite Biblical Seminaries Library (IN-25/3): V 60, N 4-V 69, N 4, 1952-61.
> Bethany and Northern Baptist Theological Seminaries Library (IL-135/1): V 60, N 4-V 63; V 64, N 1-6, 8-12; V 65-69, N 4; 1952-61.
> Bethel Theological Seminary Library (MN-50/1): V 60, 62, 65-68, 1952, 1954, 1957-60.
> Biola University—Rose Memorial Library (CA-130/4): 1953-60.
> Drew University Library (NJ-40/2): V 60, N 4-V 69, N 4, 1952-61.
> Emory University—Pitts Theology Library (GA-15/5): V 60, N 4-V 69, N 4, 1952-61.
> Fuller Theological Seminary—McAlister Library (CA-205/1): V 60, N 4-V 69, N 4, 1952-61.
> Garrett-Evangelical and Seabury-Western Theological Seminaries—United Library (IL-110/1): V 60, N 4-V 69, N 4, 1952-61.
> Gordon-Conwell Theological Seminary—Goddard Library (MA-230/4): V 60, N 4-V 61, N 6, V 62-V 69, N 4, 1952-61.
> Harvard Divinity School—Andover-Harvard Theological Library (MA-95/2): V 67, N 1-V 69, N 4, Ja 1959-Apr 1961.
> Harvard University—Widener Library (MA-155/1): V 67, N 1-V 69, N 4, Ja 1959-Apr 1961.
> Luther Northwestern Theological Seminary Library (MN-100/1): V 60, N 4-V 69, N 4, 1952-61.
> Moody Bible Institute Library (IL-55/1): V 60-69, 1952-61.
> Overseas Missionary Fellowship (PA-265/2): 1954-80.
> Princeton Theological Seminary—Speer Library (NJ-95/3): V 59-68, 1952-60.
> Union Theological Seminary—Burke Library (NY-275/1): V 60, N 4-V 69, N 4, Ap 1952-Ap 1961.
> University of Michigan—Hatcher Graduate Library (MI-25/1): 1875-77.
> Washington University—Olin Library (MO-95/1): 1877, 1879-82.

MISCELLANEOUS BULLETIN SERIES. *See* University of Nanking.

MISCELLANEOUS BULLETINS. *See* American Friends Service Committee.

MISCELLANEOUS PUBLICATIONS. *See* College of Chinese Studies, Peking.

MISSION BULLETIN. Catholic Church in China, Synodal Commission, Hong Kong, Shanghai. S 1953-D 1959 (10 per year). Continues CHINA MISSIONARY BULLETIN. Continued as ASIA, Ja 1960. Title varies: CHINA MISSIONARY—LE MISSIONAIRE DE CHINE, Ja 1948-Je 1949; CHINA MISSIONARY BULLETIN, S 1949-Jl 1953; MISSION BULLETIN, S 1953-D 1959; ASIA, Ja 1960-. Articles in English and French.

 Catholic Theological Union Library (IL-20/1): V 5, N 6-V 11, 1953-59.
 Catholic University of America—Mullen Library (DC-20/1): V5-6, 8-9, 1953-54, 1956-57.
 Duns Scotus Library (MI-140/1): V 6-12, 1954-60.
 Garrett-Evangelical and Seabury-Western Theological Seminaries—United Library (IL-110/1): V 5, N 7-V 11, N 10, 1953-59.
 Graduate Theological Union Library (CA-15/2): N 3-11, 1951-59.
 Princeton Theological Seminary—Speer Library (NJ-95/3): D 1952-60.
 Princeton University—Firestore Library (NJ-100/1): V 7; V 8, N 1-6, 8-10; V 9-10, N 3; 1955-Mr 1958.
 St. Mary of the Lake Seminary—Feehan Memorial Library (IL-130/1): V 5, N 7-V 11, 1953-59.
 Southern Methodist University—Bridwell Theology Library (TX-20/2): V 10-11, 1958-59.
 Trinity Evangelical Divinity School Library (IL-90/1): V 6-8, 1954-56.

MISSION CHRONICLE. Catholic Central Bureau, Shanghai. Continues HWA MING NEWS SERVICE. Continued by EPISOTOLA FAMILIAE MISSIONIS.

 California Province of the Society of Jesus Archives (CA-195/1): N 1-18, Je-O 1949.

MISSION MIRROR. North China Mission, Peking.

 Harvard Divinity School—Andover-Harvard Theological Library (MA-95/2): My, S 1932; My, Nv 1933; O 1934; 1935; Jl-D 1936; O 1937; Nv 1938; 1939; Je 1941; Mr 1942.
 University of Washington—Manuscripts and University Archives Division (WA-40/4): 1935.

MISSION NEWS. Catholic University of Peking, Peking. V 1-, 1933-?

 Newark Abbey (NJ-80/1): V 1, N 1-2, 1933.
 Saint Vincent Archabbey and College Archives (PA-95/1): F, Mr 1933.

MISSION NEWS JOTTINGS. American Jesuits in China, San Francisco.

 California Province of the Society of Jesus Archives (CA-195/1): V 1, N 1-V 4, N 11, My 1949-Nv 1952.

MISSIONARIORUM MINISTERIA ET OPERA IN PROVINCIA KIANG-NAN AB ANNO MDCCCXLVII AD MDCCCLXXXI (1847-1881). Zi-ka-wei.

 Georgetown University—Woodstock Theological Center Library (DC-70/4): 1881.

MISSIONARY NEWS LETTERS FROM CHINA. Women's American Baptist Foreign Mission Society.

 Union Theological Seminary—Burke Library

(NY-275/1): 1937-53.

MISSIONARY RECORDER: A Repository of Intelligence from Eastern Missions. American Presbyterian Mission Press, Foochow. V 1, N 1-12, Ja-D 1867. Recommenced in My 1868 as CHINESE RECORDER AND MISSIONARY JOURNAL.

 Boston University—School of Theology Library (MA-35/1): V 1, 1867.
 Claremont Colleges—Honnold Library (CA-85/1): V 1, 1867.
 Denver Conservative Baptist Seminary—Thomas Library (CO-10/3): V 1, 1867.
 Essex Institute—Phillips Library (MA-210/2): V 1, 1867.
 Graduate Theological Union Library (CA-15/2): V 1, 1867.
 Harvard Divinity School—Andover-Harvard Theological Library (MA-95/2): N 1-3, 11-12, 1867.
 New York Public Library—General Research Division (NY-230/1): V 1, N 1-12, 1867.
 San Francisco Theological Seminary Library (CA-235/2): V 1, N 1-12, 1867.
 Stanford University—Green Library (CA-305/1): V 1, 1867.
 Union Theological Seminary—Burke Library (NY-275/1): V 1, N 1-12, Ja-D 1867.
 University of California, Berkeley—General Library (CA-70/1): V 1, N 1-5, 8-9, Ja-My, Ag-S, 1867.
 Yale Divinity School Library (CT-55/2): V 1, N 1-3, 1867.
 Yale University—Sterling Memorial Library (CT-80/1): V 1, N 1-3, 1867.

LES MISSIONS DE CHINE. Lazaristes du Pétang, Procure des Lazaristes, Shanghai. V 1-, 1916-. Title varies: MISSIONS DE CHINE ET DU JAPON, V 1-10, 1916-23.

 Brigham Young University—Lee Library (UT-10/1): 1938-39.
 Catholic University of America—Mullen Library (DC-20/1): V1, 6-10, 15-16, 1916, 1925-33, 1938-41.
 College of St. Elizabeth—Mahoney Library (NJ-10/1): 1942.
 Cornell University—Wason Collection (NY-95/1): V 1-2, 6-16, 1916-17, 1925-41.
 Library of Congress—General Reading Rooms Division (DC-120/1): 1940-41.
 Mary Immaculate Seminary (PA-115/1): 1942.
 Maryknoll Fathers and Brothers Library (NY-115/1): 1933-34, 1938, 1940.
 New York Public Library—General Research Division (NY-230/1): 1916-19, 1923, 1927-31.
 St. John's University Archives (NY-105/1): 1937.
 St. Mary's Seminary—St. Mary's of the Barrens Library (MO-45/1): 1937, 1942.
 Union Theological Seminary—Burke Library (NY-275/1): 1925, 1931, 1933, 1935-36, 1938-39.
 Yale Divinity School Library (CT-55/2): V 1-3, 5-12, 15, 1916-17, 1919, 1923, 1925, 1927, 1929, 1931, 1933-35, 1938-39.

LES MISSIONS DE CHINE ET DU JAPON. Imprimerie des Lazaristes, Peking. 1916.

> College of Saint Elizabeth—Mahoney Library (NJ–10/1): 1929.
>
> Georgetown University—Woodstock Theological Center Library (DC–70/4): 1929.
>
> Harvard University—Widener Library (MA–155/1): 1916, 1919, 1929.
>
> Johns Hopkins University—Eisenhower Library (MD–10/1): V 10, 1933.
>
> Maryknoll Fathers and Brother Library (NY–115/1): 1916–17, 1923, 1925, 1927, 1929, 1931, 1933.
>
> St. John's University Archives (NY–105/1): 1931.
>
> Union Theological Seminary—Burke Library (NY–275/1): 1916–17, 1919.
>
> University of Chicago—Regenstein Library (IL–85/1): 1927.
>
> University of Delaware—Morris Library (DE–5/2): V 1–2, 4, 1916–17, 1919.

MISSIONS EN CHINE ET AU CONGO. Congrégation du coeur immaculé de Marie, Scheut-les-Bruxelles. N 1, F 1889.

> Continued by MISSIONS DE SCHEUT. Title varies: MONDE ET MISSION.
>
> Indiana University—University Libraries (IN–20/2): 1902–3.
>
> University of California, Berkeley—General Library (CA–70/1): V 1–131, 1889–99.

MISSIONS-BOTE. Allianz-China-Mission, Wuppertal-Barmen. V 1–60(?), 1892–1952(?).

> Continues CHINA-BOTE, S-O 1952.
>
> Union Theological Seminary—Burke Library (NY–275/1): V 1–9, 10–19, 22–27; V 28, N 5, 8; V 29, N 4, 8; V 30, N 6; V 31, N 4, 6; V 32–47; V 58–59; V 60–?; 1892–1900, 1907–8, 1913, 1920–23, 1926–39, 1950-.

MISSIONSBOTE. n.p. V 1–24, 1915–39.

> Union Theological Seminary—Burke Library (NY–275/1): V 1–15, 1915–30.

DER MISSIONSBOTE AUS DER DEUTSCHER SÜDSEE. n.p. 1908–9.

> Continued as part of CHINA'S MILLIONS.
>
> Union Theological Seminary—Burke Library (NY–275/1): My 1908, My 1909.

MISSIONS-NACHRICHTEN AUS TANGSHAN. n.p., Tangshan. N 1, 1920.

> Title varies: MISSIONS-NACHRICHTEN AUS TANGSHAN, 1920–28; AUSBREITUNG-EVANGELIUMS IN TANGSHAN, 1928; VERKUNDIGT DAS EVANGELIUM NACHRICHTEN AUS CHINA, 1929–38; NACHRICHTEN AUS CHINA, 1938–41.
>
> Bethel College—Mennonite Library and Archives (KS–55/8): N 1–9, 11–27, Mr 1920-Ja 1928.

MISSIONS-NACHRICHTEN AUS YÜNNAN. Ländli, Oberägeri, Switzerland.

> Fellowship Deaconry (NJ–30/1): O 1945, O-D 1946, 1947–49, Ja-O, D 1950, Ja-My 1951.

MISSIONS-NACHRICHTEN AUS YÜNNAN. Marburger Mission, Marburg.

> Title varies: to V 23 (1952) as MISSIONS-NACHRICHTEN AUS YÜNNAN; V 23, N 5–6 (1952)-, as MARBURGER MISSIONS NACHRICHTEN.
>
> Union Theological Seminary—Burke Library (NY–275/1): 1950–56.

MISSIONSTIDNINGEN SINIMS LAND: Organ für Svenska Missionen Kina och Japan. Svenska Missionen i Kina, Stockholm.

> Union Theological Seminary—Burke Library (NY–275/1): V 54–, 1946-.
>
> Yale Divinity School Library (CT–55/2): V 30–86, 1925–81.

MISSIONSVENNEN. Norske Missionsalliance, North China. V 1–44(?), 1900–1944(?).

> Union Theological Seminary—Burke Library (NY–275/1): n.v.; N 1–11; V 39, N 1, 7–8, 11; V 40, N 1, 4–12; V 41; V 42, N 2–10; V 43, N 1, 4–7, 9; V 44; 1904–29, 1940–45.

MR. KEYTE'S BULLETIN. Baptist Missionary Society(?), Peking.

> Union Theological Seminary—Burke Library (NY–275/1): N 16–18, 20–28, 1923–26.

MITTEILUNGEN DAS BERLINER FRAUEN-MISSIONSVEREINS FÜR CHINA. Berliner Frauen-Missionsvereins für China, 1888–93, 3rd qt 1894, 1900–1908 (3 or 4 times a year).

> Succeeded by DER CHINA-BOTE which was succeeded by AUS ZWEIWELTEN.
>
> Union Theological Seminary—Burke Library (NY–275/1): 1888–93; Jl 1894; 1900–1903; Ap, Jl, O 1904; Ja, Ap, Jl 1905; Ja 1906; 1907–13; Ap, Jl, D 1914; Ja, Jl, D 1915; 1916; Ja, Ap 1917; Ja 1918; Ap, D 1919.

MITTEILUNGEN DAS BERLINER VEREINS FÜR ARZTLICHE MISSION. n.p.

> Union Theological Seminary—Burke Library (NY–275/1): Je, Ag, O, D 1908; D 1909; Ja, Mr, My, Jl, S, Nv 1910; Ja, Mr, My, Jl, S, Nv 1911; Ja, Mr, Jl, S, Nv 1912; Ja, F, My, Je, S, Nv 1913; Ja, Mr, My, Jl-S, D 1914; Ap, Je, O 1915; My, O 1916; My, O 1917; Mr, O 1918; Je, O 1919; S 1920; 1924; Ja, Mr, My, Ag 1925; Ja, Mr, My, Ag 1926; Ja, Mr 1927.

MONDE ET MISSION. Congrégation du coeur immaculé de Marie, Bruxelles. N 1, 1889.

> Title varies: MISSIONS EN CHINE ET AU CONGO, 1889-; MISSIONS DE SCHEUT, –1963. Suspended Je 1915-My 1919.
>
> Northwestern University Library (IL–115/1): 1899–1971.
>
> Yale Divinity School Library (CT–55/2): V 1–14, 35–?, 1889–1902, 1927–75.

MONOGRAPH SERIES. *See* West China Union University.

MONTHLY BULLETIN. *See* Educational Association of China.

MONTHLY BULLETIN. *See* Université de l'Aurore, Shanghai.

A MONTHLY CYCLE OF PRAYER. Presbyterian Church in the U.S.A., Board of Foreign Missions.

Presbyterian Historical Society—Archives and Library (PA–200/28): 1911–16, 1919–23, 1925–35, 1938–40, 1948–50.

University of Oregon—Department of Special Collections (OR–15/18): 1949.

University of Oregon—Department of Special Collections (OR–15/37): 1931, 1950.

MONTHLY LINK. *See* Christian Literature Society for China.

MONTHLY MESSENGER. *See* Southern Presbyterian Mission in China.

MONTHLY NOTES. *See* China Inland Mission.

MONUMENTA SERICA: Journal of Oriental Studies of the Catholic University of Peking. Catholic University of Peking, Divine Word Society, V 1–, 1935–48, Peking; S.V.D. Research Institute, 1949/55–, Tokyo.

Continued as MONUMENTA SERICA: Journal of Oriental Studies, 1949/55.

Biola University—Rose Memorial Library (CA–130/4): V 1–24, 31–, 1935–65, 1974–.

Catholic University of America—Mullen Library (DC–20/1): V 1, pt.1; V 2, pt.1; V 3, pt.1; V 4, pt. 1; V 6–7, 14–20, 22–27, 29–38; 1935–38, 1940–41, 1949–55, 1957–62, 1964–76.

Claremont Colleges—Honnold Library (CA–85/1): V 1–, 1935–.

Clemson University—Cooper Library (SC–15/1): V 1–12, 1935–47.

College of the Holy Cross—Dinand Library (MA–280/1): V 13–35, 1948–83.

Columbia University—Starr East Asian Library (NY–195/4): V 1–34, 1935–80.

Cornell University—Wason Collection (NY–95/1): V 1–30, 1935–71.

Duke University—Perkins Library (NC–55/1): V 1–35, 1935–83.

Emory University—Woodruff Library (GA–25/1): V 19, 1954.

Field Museum of Natural History Library (IL–40/1): V 1–6, V 11, V 13–35, 1935–41, 1946, 1948–83.

Georgetown University—Lauinger Library (DC–60/1): V 1–, 1935–.

Iowa State University Library (IA–5/1): V 1–, 1935–.

Metropolitan Museum of Art—Watson Library (NY–210/1): V 1–35, 1935–83.

Museum of Fine Arts—Hunt Library (MA–70/1): V 1–, 1935–.

Princeton University—Gest Oriental Library (NJ–105/1): V 1–17, 22, 28–33, 1935–58, 1963, 1969–78.

Rutgers University—Alexander Library (NJ–75/1): V 1–, 1935–.

St. Mary's Seminary—St. Mary's of the Barrens Library (MO–45/1): n.d.

St. Olaf College—Rölvaag Memorial Library (MN–80/1): V 25–, 1966–.

Smithsonian Institution—Freer Gallery of Art Library (DC–160/2): V 1–, 1935–.

Stanford University—Green Library (CA–305/1): V 1–, 1935–.

University of Arizona Library (AZ–5/3): V 1–, 1935–.

University of California at Los Angeles—University Research Library (CA–185/1): V 1–33, 1935–78.

University of California, San Diego, Library (CA–125/2): V 1–35, 1935–83.

University of California, Berkeley—East Asiatic Library (CA–55/1): V 1–11, 13, 1935–46, 1948–.

University of California, Berkeley—News Department (CA–65/1): V 12, 1947.

University of California, Davis, Library (CA–110/2): V 1–, 1935–.

University of California, Santa Barbara, Library (CA–275/2): V 13–, 1948–.

University of Chicago—Regenstein Library (IL–85/1): V 1–, 1935–.

University of Cincinnati—Central Library (OH–65/1): V 13–35, 1948–83.

University of Iowa Libraries (IA–40/1): V 13–, 1948–.

University of Minnesota—Wilson Library (MN–40/1): V 1–, 1935–.

University of Oregon Library (OR–20/2): V 1–10, 12–32, 34–35, 1935–45, 1948–76, 1979–83.

University of Pennsylvania—Van Pelt Library (PA–215/1): V 1–, 1935–.

University of Texas at Austin—General Libraries (TX–15/1): V 1–, 1935–.

University of Washington Libraries (WA–45/1): V 1–11, 13–, 1935–.

University of Wisconsin-Madison—Memorial Library (WI–45/1): V 1–, 1935–.

Washington University—East Asian Library (MO–85/1): V 1–12, 1935–47.

Western Washington University—Wilson Library (WA–5/1): V 1–12, 19–21, 26–, 1935–47, 1954–56, 1961–.

Yale University—Sterling Memorial Library (CT–80/1): V 1–35, 1935–83.

MONUMENTA SERICA: Monograph Series. Catholic University of Peking, Divine Word Society, V 1–, 1937–.

Brooklyn Museum—Art Reference Library (NY–45/1): N 14, 1961.

Cleveland Public Library (OH–85/1): V 1–, 1937–.

Columbia University—Starr East Asian Library (NY–195/4): V 1–12, 14–16, 1937–72.

Duke University—Divinity School Library (NC–30/2): N 4, 1943.

Duke University—East Campus Library (NC–35/1): N 14, 1961.

Duke University—Perkins Library (NC–55/1): N 2, 12, 1939, 1967.

Emory University—Woodruff Library (GA–25/1): N 2, 1939 (repr. 1969).

Harvard University—Widener Library (MA–155/1): N 13, 1948.

Stanford University—Green Library (CA–305/1): N 3–47, 9, 12–15, 1942–43, 1945–46, 1948, 1961, 1966.

University of California, Berkeley—East Asiatic Library (CA–55/1): V 1–13, 15–, 1937–.

University of Iowa Libraries (IA–40/1): V 2–4, 7–8, 12–15, 72, 1939–67.

University of Minnesota—Wilson Library (MN–40/1): V 2; V 3, N 2; V 4, 7–8, 12–15, 1939–66.

University of Washington Libraries (WA–45/1): N 1–14, 16–17, 1937–61, 1972, 1985.

University of Wisconsin-Madison—Memorial Library (WI–45/1): V 2–12, 14–, 1939-.

Western Washington University—Wilson Library (WA–5/1): N 1–2, 5–6, 11–12, 14, 16, 1937, 1941–44, 1945 (repr. 1964), 1947, 1969–71.

Yale University—Sterling Memorial Library (CT–80/1): N 1–11, 13–14, 1937, 1939, 1941–48, 1961.

MOSLEMS IN CHINA. Society of Friends in China, London.

Columbia University—Starr East Asian Library (NY–195/4): S 1942, Summer 1946, Spring, Nv 1947.

MUSEUM GUIDEBOOK. *See* West China Union University.

MUSEUM OF ARCHEOLOGY, ART, AND ETHNOLOGY, TRANSLATION SERIES. *See* West China Union University.

NACHRICHTEN AUS CHINA. n.p., Tangshan

Title varies: MISSIONS-NACHRICHTEN AUS TANG-SHAN, 1920–28; AUSBREITUNG-EVANGELIUMS IN TANGSHAN, 1928; VERKUNDIGT DAS EVANGELIUM NACHRICHTEN AUS CHINA, 1929–38; NACHRICHTEN AUS CHINA, 1938–41.

Bethel College—Mennonite Library and Archives (KS–55/8): V 19, N 4-V 22, N 1, O 1938–41.

NANKING BULLETIN OF CHURCH AND COMMUNITY. University of Nanking.

Union Theological Seminary—Burke Library (NY–275/1): N 22, Ap 1922.

Yale Divinity School—Special Collections (CT–50/25): N 355–356, 1925.

NANKING CHURCH BULLETIN. Nanking Church, Nanking. V 1-, 1916.

University of Virginia—Alderman Library (VA–30/1): V 1–9, 1916–33.

NANKING CHURCH NOTES AND NOTICES. Nanking Church, Nanking. n 1–85, J 1933–41? (weekly).

Annual Report issued as a supplement. Continues the weekly issue of the NANKING BULLETIN, which continued independently as a monthly publication. Title varies: NANKING NOTES AND NOTICES; NOTES AND NOTICES OF THE NANKING UNION CHURCH AND COMMUNITY. Suspended summer, 1937-Mr 1939. Mr 1939-D 1940 called emergency issues and renumbered.

University of Virginia—Alderman Library (VA–30/1): N 1–127, 131, 132, 159, 160, 169–72, 175–78, 228–29, n.s. N 1–54, 1933–37, 1939–40.

NANKING NOTES AND NOTICES. University of Nanking, Shanghai.

Title varies: NANKING CHURCH NOTES AND NOTICES.

Yale Divinity School—Special Collections (CT–50/25): N 2, 1939.

Nanking Theological Seminary

BULLETIN. Nanking Theological Seminary, Shanghai. N 1–5, 1939.

Drew University—United Methodist Archives (NJ–45/5): 1913–16, 1930.

Union Theological Seminary—Burke Library (NY–275/1): N 1–5, Mr, My, Je, S, D 1939.

Yale Divinity School Library (CT–55): uncatalogued.

Yale Divinity School—Special Collections (CT–50/27): 1916–17.

ENGLISH PUBLICATIONS. Nanking Theological Seminary, Nanking. N 1–4, 1940-?

Colgate-Rochester Theological Seminaries—Swasey Library (NY–350/1): N 1, 1940 (repr. 1969).

Cornell University—Wason Collection (NY–95/1): N 1–2, 1940–41.

Duke University—Divinity School Library (NC–30/2): N 1, 1940 (repr. 1969).

Emory University—Woodruff Library (GA–25/1): N 1, 1940.

Harvard Divinity School—Andover-Harvard Theological Library (MA–95/2): N 1, 1940.

Iliff School of Theology—Taylor Library (CO–15/1): N 1, 1940.

Library of Congress—General Reading Rooms Division (DC–120/1): N 1, 4, 1940.

Loma Linda University—Radcliffe Memorial Library (CA–135/1): N 1, 1940.

New York Public Library—General Research Division (NY–230/1): N 1, 1940.

Princeton Theological Seminary—Speer Library (NJ–95/3): N 2, 1940.

Southern Baptist Theological Seminary—Boyce Centennial Library (KY–50/2): N 1, 1940.

Stanford University—Green Library (CA–305/1): N 4, 1940.

University of California at Los Angeles—University Research Library (CA–185/1): N 1, 4, 1940.

University of California, Berkeley—General Library (CA–70/1): N 1, 4, 1940.

University of Iowa Libraries (IA–40/1): N 1, 4, 1940.

University of Michigan—Hatcher Graduate Library (MI–25/1): N 4, 1940.

University of Pennsylvania—Van Pelt Library (PA–215/1): N 1, 4, 1940.

University of Washington Libraries (WA–45/1): N 1–2, 1940–41.

Virginia Theological Seminary—Payne Library (VA–5/1): N 2, 1941.

Western Washington University—Wilson Library (WA–5/1): N 1, 1940 (repr. 1969).

Yale Divinity School Library (CT–55/1): N 4, 1940.

Yale Divinity School Library (CT–55/2): N 1–2, 1940–41.

Yale University—Sterling Memorial Library (CT–80/1): N 2, 4, 1940–41.

NANKING UNIVERSITY. *See* University of Nanking.

NANKING-GINLING NEWS. n.p.

Union Theological Seminary—Archives (NY–270/35): n.d.

NANTAO CHRISTIAN INSTITUTE BULLETIN. n.p.
> Presbyterian Historical Society—Archives and Library (PA–200/28): F 1922.

National Christian Council of China
> BROADCAST BULLETIN. National Christian Council of China, Shanghai. 1938–41.
>> Christian Church (Disciples of Christ) Library (IN–55/1): Ser. 5, N 17–ser. 6, N 12, 16–50, Ja 1941–Ag 1942.
>> Union Theological Seminary—Burke Library (NY–275/1): N 1–44; ser. 3, N 1–4; ser. 4, N 1–42; ser. 5, N 1–50; ser. 6, N 1–12; Mr-Je 1938, Jl 1939-Jl 1940, S 1940-Nv 1941.
>> University of Oregon—Department of Special Collections (OR–15/3): V 4, N 39; V 5, N 17, 28, 31, 34–39, 41; 1940–41.
>
> BROADCASTS. National Christian Council of China, Shanghai.
>> Harvard Divinity School—Andover-Harvard Theological Library (MA–95/2): Ja-Je 1938.
>
> BULLETIN. National Christian Council of China, Shanghai. N 1–61, 1922-Mr 1937.
>> Title varies: 1940–41 NATIONAL CHRISTIAN COUNCIL BROADCAST BULLETIN.
>> Andover Newton Theological School—Trask Library (MA–180/2): V 1–61, 1922–37.
>> Bethel Theological Seminary—Archival Center of the Baptist General Conference (MN–45/1): N 39, Ja 1932.
>> Center for Research Libraries (IL–25/4): N 30–38, 40–59, 61, Nv 1928-Mr 1937.
>> Disciples of Christ Historical Society—Library and Archives (TN–45/1): uncatalogued.
>> Graduate Theological Union Library (CA–15/2): N 1–61, Nv 1922-Mr 1937.
>> Harvard Divinity School—Andover-Harvard Theological Library (MA–95/2): 1930–40.
>> Luther College Archives (IA–15/1): N 18–20, Mr, Je, S 1926.
>> Presbyterian Historical Society—Archives and Library (PA–200/28): N 1–38, 1922–31.
>> San Francisco Theological Seminary Library (CA–235/2): N 1–61(?), 1922–37.
>> Union Theological Seminary—Archives (NY–270/37): n.v., ca. 1921–40.
>> Union Theological Seminary—Burke Library (NY–275/1): N 1–61, N 1922-Mr 1937.
>> University of Chicago—Regenstein Library (IL–85/1): N 1–61, Nv 1922-Mr 1937.
>> University of Florida Libraries (FL–15/1): N 1–61, 1922–37.
>> University of Illinois at Urbana-Champaign—University Archives (IL–180/5): 1931–32.
>> University of Oregon Library (OR–20/2): N 39–61, Ja 1932-Mr 1937.
>> University of Virginia—Alderman Library (VA–30/1): N 4, 46, 1932–33.
>> Wheaton College—Graham Center Library (IL–205/1): N 1–61, 1922–37.

> Yale Divinity School Library (CT–55/2): N 1–61; ser. II, N 1–44; ser. III, N 1–4; ser. IV, N 1–42; ser. V, N 1–30; ser. VI, N 1–10; 1922–41.
>> Yale Divinity School—Special Collections (CT–50/27): 1925.
>
> CHINA NEWS LETTER. National Christian Council of China.
>> Christian Church (Disciples of Christ) Library (IN–55/1): O, Nv 1941.
>
> DAY BY DAY. National Christian Council of China.
>> Christian Church (Disciples of Christ) Library (IN–55/1): D 1941-S 1942.
>
> NEWS. National Christian Council of China, Shanghai. V 1, 1948.
>> Harvard Divinity School—Andover-Harvard Theological Library (MA–95/2): V 1, N 5–6; V 2, N 1–2, 4–5; V 3, N 10; 1948, 1950.
>> Union Theological Seminary—Burke Library (NY–275/1): V 1, N 1–7; V 2, N 1–10; V 3, N 1–10; 1948–50.
>
> NEWSLETTER. National Christian Council of China, Shanghai. V 1, My 1950-.
>> Supersedes the English edition of the Council's BULLETIN.
>> National Library of Medicine (MD–35/2): V 1-, 1950-.
>> Union Theological Seminary—Burke Library (NY–275/1): Ap, My 1942; Je, S, Nv 1943; Ap 1944; O 1947.
>
> OVERSEAS NEWSLETTER.
>> Harvard Divinity School—Andover-Harvard Theological Library (MA–95/1): N 46, Ja 1947.
>
> SPECIAL ORIENT BULLETIN. National Christian Council of China.
>> Christian Church (Disciples of Christ) Library (IN–55/1): N 1–29, Ja 1942-F 1943.

National Committee for Christian Religious Education
> BULLETIN. Christian Literature Society for China, Shanghai. N 1, 1935.
>> Harvard Divinity School—Andover-Harvard Theological Library (MA–95/1): N 1, 3, 5, 1935–37.
>
> ENGLISH BULLETIN. National Committee for Christian Religious Education in China, Shanghai.
>> Harvard Divinity School—Andover-Harvard Theological Library (MA–95/1): N 5, Ja 1935.
>> Union Theological Seminary—Burke Library (NY–275/1): N 8–9, 1938–39.
>
> LAY TRAINING BULLETIN. Christian Literature Society, Shanghai.
>> Southern Baptist Theological Seminary—Boyce Centennial Library (KY–50/2): N 1–2, 1935.
>
> RELIGIOUS EDUCATION FELLOWSHIP.
>> Union Theological Seminary—Burke Library (NY–275/1): V 1, N 1–10; V 2, N 1–9, S 1923-Je 1924, S 1924-My 1925.
>
> RELIGIOUS EDUCATION FELLOWSHIP BULLETIN. National Committee for Christian Religious Education in China, Shanghai.
>> Harvard Divinity School—Andover-Harvard The-

ological Library (MA–95/2): Aut 1933, F 1936, My 1937, Ap 1938, Ja-Aut 1939, Ja 1948, Jl 1950.
Presbyterian Historical Society—Archives and Library (PA–200/28): N 16, 1940–41.
Union Theological Seminary—Burke Library (NY–275/1): N 1–29, 1932–50.

Natural History Society, Fukien Christian University, Shanghai

PROCEEDINGS. Natural History Society (Po Wu Hsüeh Hui), Fukien Christian University, Shanghai. Je 1928–30.
Continued as Fukien Christian University, SCIENCE JOURNAL, 1930.

Academy of Natural Sciences of Philadelphia Library (PA–135/4): V 1–3, Je 1928-Ag 1930.
American Museum of Natural History Library (NY–140/1): V 1–3, 1928–30.
Cornell University—Wason Collection (NY–95/1): V 1–3, 1928–30.
Field Museum of Natural History Library (IL–40/1): V 1–3, 1928–30.
Harvard Divinity School—Andover-Harvard Theological Library (MA–95/1): V 1, 3, Ja 1928, Ag 1930.
Harvard University—Museum of Comparative Zoology Library (MA–140/1): V 2, 1929.
Iowa State University Library (IA–5/1): V 1–3, 1928–30.
New York Public Library—General Research Division (NY–230/1): V 2, 1929.
Rutgers University—Alexander Library (NJ–75/1): V 2, 1929.
Smithsonian Institution—National Museum of Natural History Branch Library (DC–175/1): V 1–3, 1928–30.
Union Theological Seminary—Burke Library (NY–275/1): 1930.
University of Michigan—Hatcher Graduate Library (MI–25/1): V 1–3, 1928–30.
University of Washington Libraries (WA–45/1): V 2–3, 1929–30.

NEW CHINA. Yenching University, Journalism Club, Peking. V 1-, F 1931- (monthly).
Union Theological Seminary—Burke Library (NY–275/1): V 1, N 4, F 1931.

NEW EAST. China Baptist Publication Society, Canton. V 1–27, N 2, 1905-Ap 1933.
American Baptist Historical Society (NY–345/23): 1905–33.
Brown University—Rockefeller Library (RI–20/2): V 4–6, 8–9, 11–17, 19–26, V 27, N 1–2, 1909–23, 1925–33.
Bucknell University—Bertrand Library (PA–100/2): V [4], 5, [6, 22–27]; 1908–10, 1926–33.
Colgate-Rochester Theological Seminaries—Swasey Library (NY–350/1): V 1–2, [3–4], 5–27, 1905–33.
Harvard University—Widener Library (MA–155/1): V 4, N 3–4, V 5–7, 1909–12.
Presbyterian Historical Society—Archives and Library (PA–200/28): V 1–4, 1905–9.

Southern Baptist Convention—Archives Center (VA–65/2): My 1910; Ap, Je 1927.
Southern Baptist Theological Seminary—Boyce Centennial Library (KY–50/2): V 1–3, [4–5], [8–9, 11], 12–25, [26], 1905–10, 1913–14, 1916–33.
Union Theological Seminary—Burke Library (NY–275/1): V 3, N 3–4; V 5, N 1–4; V 6–7; V 11, N 1; V 13, N 1–6; V 14, N 6; V 15, N 1–3, 6; V 16, N 2–3, 5–6; V 17, N 1–6; V 18, N 1–6; V 19, N 1–6; V 20–27; 1908–12, 1916, 1918–33.
Yale Divinity School Library (CT–55): uncatalogued.

NEW HORIZONS. United Board for Christian Higher Education in Asia, New York. V 1-, Je 1934- (quarterly).
Title varies: CHINA COLLEGES, V 1–23, N 3, Je 1934-My 1952; THE SPIRIT OF THE CHINA COLLEGES CARRIES ON, V 19, N 1–3; NEW HORIZONS FOR THE CHINA COLLEGES, V 19, N 4-V 20, N 3; and THE CHINA COLLEGES FIND NEW HORIZONS, V 21, N 1-V 23, N 3; also other variations. Agency name varies: United Board for Christian Colleges in China, S 1947-D 1955; Associated Boards for Christian Colleges in China, Je 1934-Je 1947.
Asian Studies Newsletter Archives (MD–40/1): V 21, N 1-, O 1953-.
Cornell University—Wason Collection (NY–95/1): V 1, N 2–3; V 5, N 3; V 6, N 1; V 7, N 2; V 8, N 1–3; V 9, N 1–2; V 10, N 3; V 11, N 1–2, 4; V 12–39; 1934–35, 1939, 1941–72.
Emory University—Pitts Theology Library (GA–15/5): V 20–21, 25–27, 29–44, 1952, 1954, 1958–77.
Library of Congress—General Reading Rooms Division (DC–120/1): V 1–10, 1934–44.
New York Public Library—General Research Division (NY–230/1): 1934–60.
Presbyterian Historical Society—Archives and Library (PA–200/28): V 5, N 2; V 6, N 1; V 7, N 1; V 8, N 1–3; V 9, N 1–2; V 10, N 3–4; V 11, N 1–2; V 12, N 3–4; V 15, N 5; V 16, N 1–4; V 17, N 1–4; V 18, N 1, 3–5; V 19, N 1–4; V 20, N 1–3; V 21, N 2–3; V 22, N 1–4; V 23, N 1, 3; V 24, N 2–4; V 25, N 1–5; V 26, N 1–4; V 27, N 1–2; V 28, N 2–3; V 29, N 1–2; V 30, N 1; V 31, N 1; V 32, N 2–3; V 33, N 1–2; V 34, N 3; V 35, N 1; V 38, N 1; 1938–45, 1948–55, 1957–66, 1970.
Princeton University—University Archives (NJ–120/2): V 24, N 1; V 29, N 1; Nv 1956, Aut 1961.
Rutgers University—Alexander Library (NJ–75/1): 1934, 1937–40.
San Francisco Theological Seminary Library (CA–235/2): V 13, N 1–3; V 14, N 1, 3–4; V 15, N 2, 4; V 16, N 1–2, 4; V 17, N 1–4; V 18, N 1, 3, 5; V 19, N 1–4; V 21, N 1–2; V 22, N 1, 1945–55.
Union Theological Seminary—Burke Library (NY–275/1): V 1, N 1–3; V 2, N 1; V 3, N 1; V 5, N 1–3; V 6, N 1–2; V 7, N 1–2; V 8, N 1–3; V 9, N 1–2; V 10, N 3; V 11, N 1–2, 4; V 12, N 1–4; V 13, N 1–4; V 14, N 1–4; V 15, N 1–5; V 16, N 1–4; V 17, N 1–4; V 18, N 1–5; V 19, N 1–4; V 20, N 1–3; V 21, N 1–3; V 22, N 1–4; V 23, N 1–5; V 24, N 1–4; V 25, N 1–5; V 26, N 1–4; V 27, N 1–3; V 28, N 1–2; 1934–35, 1937-.
University of California, Berkeley—General Library

(CA–70/1): V 48–, 1982–.

University of Illinois at Urbana-Champaign Library (IL–185/1): V 34, N 3; V 35, N 1–3; V 36, N 1; V 37, N 1; V 38, N 1; V 39, N 1–2; V 40, N 1–3; V 41, N 1–3; V 42, N 1–3; V 43, N 1–3, V 44, N 1–3; V 45, N 1–3; V 46, N 1–3; V 47, N 1–3; V 48, N 1, 3; V 49, N 1, 3; V 52, N 1; Winter 1965; Spring 1966; Summer, Winter 1967; Winter 1968; Fall 1969; Fall 1970; Fall 1971; Spring, Fall 1972; F, Je, S 1973; F, J, O 1974; F, Je, O 1975; F, Je, O 1976; F, Je, O 1977; F, Je, O 1978; F, Je, O 1979; F, Je, O 1980; Je, O 1981; Je 1982; O 1984.

University of Washington—East Asia Library (WA–35/1): V 39, N 2; V 40, N 1–3; V 41, N 1–2; V 43, N 1, 3; V 44, N 1–2; V 45, N 3; V 46, N 3; V 47, N 1, 3; V 50, N 2; 1972–83.

Yale Divinity School—Special Collections (CT–50/25): V 20, N 1, 3; V 21, N 3; V 22, N 2; V 23, N 2–5; V 24, N 1–4; V 25, N 4; 1952–58.

Yale Divinity School—Special Collections (CT–50/26): V 23, N 1–2, 4–5; V 24, N 2–4; V 25, N 1–5; V 26, N 1; V 27, N 1; V 28, N 1; V 29, N 1; V 39, N 1–2; V 40, N 1–3; V 41, N 1–2; V 42, N 1–3; V 43, N 1–3, 1955–61, 1972–76.

Yale University—Sterling Memorial Library (CT–80/1): V 1, 5–11, 13–14, 19–27, 39–40, 1934–35, 1938–44, 1945–47, 1952–59, 1972.

NEW MANDARIN. Yenching University, College of Chinese Studies, Peking. V 1, 1926.

Emory University—Pitts Theology Library (GA–15/5): V 1, 1926.

Harvard Divinity School—Andover-Harvard Theological Library (MA–95/2): V 1, N 1–3, Je-Je 1926.

Harvard University—Widener Library (MA–155/1): V 1, Ja-Je 1926.

Presbyterian Historical Society—Archives and Library (PA–200/28): V 1, N 3, 1926.

Union Theological Seminary—Burke Library (NY–275/1): V 1, N 1–3, Ja, Mr, Je 1906.

University of California, Berkeley—General Library (CA–70/1): V 1, N 1–3, Ja-Je 1926.

Yale Divinity School Library (CT–55/2): V 1, N 1–3, 1926.

Yale Divinity School—Special Collections (CT–50/25): V 1, N 1–3, 1926.

NEWS BULLETIN. *See* West China Union University.

NEWS BULLETIN. *See* Yenching University.

NEWS BULLETIN OF THE YALE COLLEGIATE SCHOOL AND HOSPITAL. Changsha.

Yale University—Manuscripts and Archives (CT–60/32): 1912.

NEWS ITEMS. *See* Young Women's Christian Association.

NEWS OF CHINA. United China Relief, Inc., New York. V 1–8, N 3, S 1942-Je 1949.

Continues NEWSLETTER. Title varies: NEWS, S 1942-D 1943. Suspended Jl 1946-My 1947. V 3, N 5 (My 6, 1944) incorrectly called N 6. Running title: NEWS OF UNITED CHINA RELIEF.

Boston Public Library (MA–30/2): V 1–8, 1942–49.

Bryn Mawr College—Canaday Library (PA–15/3): V 1–8, 1942–49.

Bucknell University—Bertrand Library (PA–100/2): V [2], 1943–49.

Buffalo and Erie County Public Library (NY–60/1): 1942–49 (inc.).

Emory University—Pitts Theology Library (GA–15/5): V 2–3, 1943–44.

Johns Hopkins University—Eisenhower Library (MD–10/1): V 1, N 1–5; V 6, N 1–2, 4–7; V 7, N 2–4; V 8, N 1–3; 1942–49.

Library of Congress—General Reading Rooms Division (DC–120/1): 1945, 1948–49.

New York Public Library—General Research Division (NY–230/1): V 1–4, 1942–46.

Ohio State University—Thompson Memorial Library (OH–110/4): V 2–8, 1943–49.

Oregon State University—Kerr Library (OR–5/1): V 2, N 2-V 8, N 3, 1943-Je 1949.

Princeton University—Firestone Library (NJ–100/1): V 1–8, N 3, S 1942-Je 1949.

Randolph-Macon Women's College—Watts Rare Book Room (VA–60/2): V 2–8, 1943–49.

Rutgers University—Alexander Library (NJ–75/1): V 1–8, S 1942-Je 1949.

San Francisco Theological Seminary Library (CA–235/2): V 2, N 2–12; V 3, N 2–12; V 4, N 1; V 7, N 1; V 8, N 1–3; 1943–45, 1948–49.

Smith College—Neilson Library (MA–190/1): V 2, N 2-V 8, N 3, F 1943-Je 1949.

Union Theological Seminary—Burke Library (NY–275/1): V 1, N 2; V 3–6; V 7, N 1–6; V 8, N 5, 8–11; V 9, N 4, 6, 11; 1942–48.

University of California, Berkeley—General Library (CA–70/1): V 1–8, N 3, 1942–49.

University of Oregon—Department of Special Collections (OR–15–3): V 1, N 4; V 2, N 1, 6–7, 9; 1942–43.

University of Oregon—Department of Special Collections (OR–15/24): V 2, N 2; V 3, N 9; V 5, N 1, 4; F 1943, S 1944, Ja, Ap 1946.

University of Virginia—Alderman Library (VA–30/1): V 2, [3–4, 6–8], 1943–45, 1947–49.

University of Washington Libraries (WA–45/1): V 2–8 (inc.), 1943–49.

Vassar College Library (NY–330/1): V 1–8, 1942–49.

NEWS OF UNITED CHINA RELIEF. *See* NEWS OF CHINA.

NEWSLETTER FOR THE ASIATIC DIVISION. Asiatic Division, General Conference of Seventh-Day Adventists, Shanghai. V 1–2, 1912–14.

Continued as ASIATIC DIVISION MISSION NEWS, 1914.

General Conference of Seventh-Day Adventists Archives (DC–40/1): V 1–2, 1912–14.

Loma Linda University—Radcliffe Memorial Library (CA–135/1): V 1, N 8; V 2, N 2–12; 1913–14.

NEWSLETTER OF THE DIOCESAN ASSOCIATION FOR WESTERN CHINA. The Association, Ashford, Kent. N 1, 1951–.

Continues BULLETIN OF THE DIOCESAN ASSOCIATION FOR WESTERN CHINA.
>   Iowa State University Library (IA–5/1): N 121–165, 167–178, 1934–51.
>   Yale Divinity School Library (CT–55/2): N 1-n.s. N 4, 1951–59.

NORSK MISJONSTIDENDE. Norwegian Mission, Stavanger. V 1, 1847.
>   Title varies: 1847–1928, NORSK MISJONSTIDENDE. Continued by MISJONSTIDENDE. Ceased 1983.
>   Yale Divinity School Library (CT–55/2): V 3–9, 13–14, 16, 18–24, 26–32, 34–36, 39–66, 74–96, 103–112, 114–138, 1848–54, 1858–59, 1861, 1863–69, 1871–77, 1879–81, 1884–1911, 1919–41, 1948–57, 1959–83.

NORTH CHINA AMERICAN SCHOOL BULLETIN. Tunghsien.
>   Yale Divinity School Library (CT–55/1): 1919–23.

NORTH CHINA UNION COLLEGE BULLETIN. Tungchou.
>   Harvard Divinity School—Andover-Harvard Theological Library (MA–95/2): N 3–4, 6–7, Ja-Jl 1914, Jl 1915, My 1916.

NOTES AND NOTICES OF THE NANKING UNION CHURCH AND COMMUNITY. University of Nanking.
>   Title varies: NANKING CHURCH NOTES AND NOTICES; NANKING NOTES AND NOTICES.
>   Hoover Institution Archives (CA–290/4): 1941.
>   Union Theological Seminary—Burke Library (NY–275/1): N 1–21, 25–30, 44–79, 1933–34, 1939–41.
>   Yale Divinity School—Special Collections (CT–50/25): N 722–731, 733, 735–737, 744, 747–758, 1940–41.

NOTES AND QUERIES ON CHINA AND JAPAN. Hong Kong. V 1–4, N 10; Ja 1867-Nv 1870.
>   Cornell University—Wason Collection (NY–95/1): V 1–4, N 8, 1867–70.
>   Stanford University—Green Library (CA–305/1): V 1–4, N 1, 1867–70.

NOTES DE BOTANIQUE CHINOISE. *See* Université de l'Aurore, Shanghai.

NOTES D'ENTOMOLOGIE CHINOISE. *See* Université de l'Aurore, Shanghai.

NOTES DE MALACOLOGIE CHINOISE. *See* Université de l'Aurore, Shanghai.

NOTES D'ORNITHOLOGIE. *See* Université de l'Aurore, Shanghai.

NOTES DE METEOROLOGIE PHYSIQUE. *See* Zi-ka-wei Observatoire, Shanghai.

NURSE IN CHINA. Yale-in-China Association, New Haven, CT. V 1, 1946.
>   Free Methodist Church—Marston Memorial Historical Center (IN–120/5): Jl 1946.
>   Yale University—Manuscripts and Archives (CT–60/32): V 1, N 2; V 2, N 1–2, 1946–47.

OBERLIN-IN-CHINA. Oberlin-Shansi Memorial Association, Oberlin.
>   Asian Studies Newsletter Archives (MD–40/1): N 1–13, Spr 1949-Spr 1956.
>   Harvard Divinity School—Andover-Harvard Theological Library (MA–95/1): F, Nv 1948.
>   Oberlin College Archives (OH–170/21): 1949–57.

OBERLIN SHANSI MEMORIAL ASSOCIATION NEWSLETTER. Oberlin.
>   Continues DRAGON TRACKS.
>   Asian Studies Newsletter Archives (MD–40/1): N 14-, Winter 1957-.
>   Harvard Divinity School—Andover-Harvard Theological Library (MA–95/1): F 1938.
>   Oberlin College Archives (OH–170/17): 1949–81.
>   Oberlin College Archives (OH–170/21): 1958–78.

OCCASIONAL LEAFLET. *See* Chinese Medical Association.

OCCASIONAL LETTERS. *See* University of Nanking.

OCCASIONAL PAPERS. *See* China Inland Mission.

OCCASIONAL PAPERS. *See* Chinese Church Research Center, Hong Kong.

OEUVRES DE LA MISSION DE KIANGNAN. 1891–1912.
>   Georgetown University—Woodstock Theological Center Library (DC–70/4): 1891–1912.

OFFPRINT SERIES. *See* West China Union University.

OMS OUTREACH. Oriental Missionary Society, n.p. V 1-, 1903-.
>   Title varies: ELECTRIC MESSAGES, 1903–14; ORIENTAL MISSIONARY STANDARD, 1914–44; ORIENTAL AND INTER-AMERICAN MISSIONARY STANDARD, 1944–49; MISSIONARY STANDARD, 1949–73.
>   Ohio State University—Thompson Memorial Library (OH–110/4): V 1–72, 1903–75.

ORIENTAL AND INTER-AMERICAN STANDARD. Oriental Missionary Society, Los Angeles.
>   Continues ORIENTAL MISSIONARY STANDARD, 1944. Continued by MISSIONARY STANDARD.
>   Asbury Theological Seminary—Special Collections (KY–85/1): V 43, N 10-12; V 44–48, 1944–49.
>   Wheaton College—Graham Center Library (IL–205/1): 1946–49.

ORIENTAL MISSIONARY STANDARD. Oriental Missionary Society.
>   Continues ELECTRIC MESSAGES. Continues as ORIENTAL AND INTERAMERICAN MISSIONARY STANDARD.
>   Asbury Theological Seminary—Special Collections (KY–85/1): V 12, N 1-V 19; V 21–24; V 25, N 1–6, 8–12; V 26, N 1–2, 5, 9–12; V 27; V 28, N 3–12; V 29, N 1–11; V 30, N 1–2; V 31; V 32, N 2–12; V 33, N 1–2, 10–12; V 34, N 1–7, 9–12; V 35–40; V 41, N 1; V 42, N 2, 5–6, 9; V 43; V 44, N 1–3; V 45, N 4–9; 1914–44.

OUR CHILDREN'S OWN MAGAZINE. n.p.
>   Asbury Theological Seminary—Special Collections (KY–85/1): V 1–10, 20–21, 28, 30, 33–43, 45, 48–49, 60–89, n.s. V 1, N 2–6; V 2; V 3, N 1–3, 5–6; V 4; 1929–41, 1944–55.

OUR PRAYER CIRCLE BULLETIN. n.p.

Asbury Theological Seminary—Special Collections (KY–85/1): N 1–3, 5, 8–13, 15–19, 23, 28, 31, 36, 38–41, 44–47, 49–55, 57, 64, 66–67, 71, n.v., 1933–39, 1941.

OVERSEAS NEWSLETTER. *See* National Christian Council of China.

PEIPING MISSION NOTES. n.p.

St. Benedict's Convent Archives (MN–90/4): 1929–33.

PEKING MAGAZINE. Peking.

Continues PEKING NEWS AND VIEWS OF CHINA.

Saint Vincent Archabbey and College Archives (PA–95/1): Jl–Ag 1931.

PEKING NATURAL HISTORY BULLETIN. Yenching University, Department of Biology and Peking Society of Natural History, Peking. V 1–, 1926–.

Continues Yenching University, Department of Biology, BULLETIN V 1–4, 1926–Ag 1930. Suspended 1942–48. Index V 1–10, 1925–36. Title varies: 1930, Yenching University, Department of Biology, BULLETIN was combined with the PEKING SOCIETY OF NATURAL HISTORY BULLETIN under the new title PEKING NATURAL HISTORY BULLETIN, which is numbered in continuation of the BULLETIN of the Society. V 1–4 (1926–30) include proceedings and lists of members of the society. Index to V 1–10 with V 10–11.

Academy of Natural Sciences of Philadelphia Library (PA–135/4): V 1–16, 1926–41.

American Museum of Natural History Library (NY–140/1): V 1–19, N 1, 1926–50.

Claremont Colleges—Honnold Library (CA–85/1): V 1–14, 1926–40.

Cornell University—Wason Collection (NY–95/1): V 1–18, 1926–41, 1948–50.

Field Museum of Natural History Library (IL–40/1): V 1–3, part 2; V 4–5, parts 2–4; V 6–16, part 1; V 17, parts 1–3; 1926–41, 1948–49.

Harvard University—Museum of Comparative Zoology Library (MA–140/1): V 1–17, 1926–41, 1948–49.

Harvard University—Peabody Museum (MA–145/1): V 2, part 2, 1927.

Harvard University—Widener Library (MA–155/1): V 3, part 2, 1928.

Iowa State University Library (IA–5/1): V 1–17, 1926–49.

Library of Congress—General Reading Rooms Division (DC–120/1): 1926–33, S 1933–Je 1935, S 1935–Je 1936, S 1936–Je 1937, S 1937–Je 1939, S 1939–Je 1940, S 1940, Je, S 1941, S 1948–Je 1950, S 1950.

Lloyd Library (OH–35/1): V 1–15, 1926–40.

Marine Biological Laboratories Library (MA–260/1): V 1–19, N 1, 1926–50.

Michigan State University Library (MI–75/1): V 1–18, 1926–50.

New York State Library (NY–15/2): V 5–17, 1930–48.

Oregon State University—Kerr Library (OR–5/1): V 5–18, S 1930–Je 1950.

Pennsylvania State University—Penn State Room (PA–275/4): V 5–, 1931–.

Princeton University—Firestone Library (NJ–100/1): V 1–8, [13]–14, [15–16], 1926–34, 1938–S 1941.

Princeton University—Gest Oriental Library (NJ–105/1): V 1–5; V 6, parts 1–3; V 7, parts 2–4; V 8; V 9, parts 1–3; 1926–35.

Purdue University—Humanities, Social Science, and Education Library (IN–115/1): V 5–16, 1930–41.

Smithsonian Institution—National Museum of Natural History Branch Library (DC–175/1): V 1–16, N 1, 1926–41.

University of California at Los Angeles—Biomedical Library (CA–160/1): V 1–16, 1926–41.

University of California, Berkeley—Biology Library (CA–40/1): V 1–17, 1926–49.

University of California, Berkeley—Earth Sciences Library (CA–50/1): V 3–4, 1928–30.

University of Illinois at Urbana-Champaign Library (IL–185/1): V 1–10, part 4; V 12–16, part 1; 1926–Je 1936, S 1937–S 1941.

University of Kansas—Watson Library (KS–35/3): V [5–18], 1930–49.

University of Michigan—Museum Libraries (MI–35/1): V 1–17, 1926–49.

University of Minnesota—Biomedical Library (MN–25/1): V 1–16, 1926–48.

University of Minnesota—St. Paul Campus Libraries (MN–115/1): V 5–16, V 17, part 1, 1931–49 (?).

University of Missouri-Columbia—Ellis Library (MO–10/1): V 6, 1930–31.

University of Washington Libraries (WA–45/1): V 1–18, 1926–50.

University of Wyoming—Coe Library (WY–5/1): V 5–16, N 1, S 1930–S 1941.

Virginia Polytechnic Institute and State University Libraries (VA–15/1): V5–14, 1930–41.

Yale University—Kline Science Library (CT–65/1): V 1–19, 1926–41, 1948–51.

PEKING NEWS. Peking University, New York. N 1, 1921.

Continued as YENCHING NEWS, 1933.

Princeton University—University Archives (NJ–120/2): n.v., N 12, 17, 21, 1921, F 1924, F 1925, My 1927.

Union Theological Seminary—Burke Library (NY–275/1): O, D 1921; F, Ap, O, D 1922; F, Ap, O, D 1923; F, Ap, Ag, D 1924; F, Ap, Nv 1925; Je 1926; My 1927.

Wellesley College Archives (MA–240/4): N 2, O 1921.

Yale Divinity School—Special Collections (CT–50/25): N 1–21; V 7, N 3; V 8, N 1–3; V 9, N 1; 1921–30.

PEKING NEWS AND VIEWS OF CHINA. Peking. V 1–4, Jl–O 1931.

Continued as PEKING MAGAZINE.

St. Benedict's Convent Archives (MN–90/4): Jl–S 1931.

Saint Vincent Archabbey and College Archives (PA–95/1): Jl 1931.

Peking Society of Natural History

BULLETIN.

Title varies: 1930, Yenching University, Department of Biology, BULLETIN was combined with the PEKING SOCIETY OF NATURAL HISTORY BULLETIN under the new title PEKING NATURAL HISTORY BULLE-

TIN, which is numbered in continuation of the BULLE-
TIN of the Society.
> Duke University—Biology-Forestry Library
> (NC–25/1): V 1–4, 1926–30.
> Harvard University—Arnold Arboretum
> (MA–100/1): V 1–3, 5–15; V 16, N 1; V 17; 1926–
> 41, 1947–48.
> University of Chicago—Regenstein Library
> (IL–85/1): V 1–2, 1926–27.

PEKING UNION CHURCH BULLETIN. Peking Union Church,
Peking.
> Harvard Divinity School—Andover-Harvard Theological
> Library (MA–95/1): N 57, O 1928.

Peking Union Medical College
BIBLIOGRAPHY OF THE PUBLICATIONS FROM THE
LABORATORIES AND CLINICS. Peking Union Medical
College, Peking. V 1-?, 1915–32.
> Center for Research Libraries (IL–25/4): 1925–29,
> 1932–38.
> Columbia University—Long Health Sciences Library
> (NY–160/1): 1915–25.
> Iowa State University Library (IA–5/1): 1915–33,
> 1939–40.
> University of Chicago—Regenstein Library
> (IL–85/1): V 1-?, 1915–32.

CONTRIBUTIONS. Department of Anatomy, Peking Union
Medical College, Washington, DC. 1918–20.
> University of California, Berkeley—Biology Library
> (CA–40/1): 1918–20.

CONTRIBUTIONS. Department of Pharmacology, Peking
Union Medical College, Peking. V 1–6, 1921–26.
> Center for Research Libraries (IL–25/4): V 1–6,
> 1921–26.
> Cornell University—Wason Collection (NY–95/1):
> V 1–6, 1921–26.
> Iowa State University Library (IA–5/1): V 1–6,
> 1921–26.
> University of California, Berkeley—Biology Library
> (CA–40/1): V 1–2, 1921–22.
> University of Chicago—Regenstein Library
> (IL–85/1): V 1–6, 1921–26.

PEKING UNIVERSITY. *See* Yenching University.

PERIODIC SUMMARY. *See* American Friends Service Committee.

PERIODICAL LINK. *See* Christian Literature Society for China,
Shanghai.

PHOENIX. St. Mary's Hall, Shanghai.
> Garrett-Evangelical and Seabury-Western Theological Se-
> minaries—United Library (IL–110/1): V 8, 1926.

PRAISE AND PRAYER. China Annual Conference of the Free
Methodist Church.
> Free Methodist Church—Marston Memorial Historical
> Center (IN–120/5): D 1927; Ja, Ap, Jl 1928; Mr 1929; My
> 1930; Ap, Nv 1931; S 1932; Je 1933; F, D 1934; Ag 1935;
> F 1937.

PRAISE AND PRAYER. Kaifeng.
> Union Theological Seminary—Burke Library
> (NY–275/1): V 2, N 12, D 1934.

PRAY FOR CHINA FELLOWSHIP. Overseas Missionary Fellowship, Berkeley, CA.
> American Bible Society Library (NY–135/1): 1982-.
> Western Evangelical Seminary—Hallauer Memorial Li-
> brary (OR–35/1): O 1983–87.
> World Vision International—Research and Information
> Division (CA–200): current year only.

PRAYER CARDS OF CENTRAL CHINA PRESBYTERIAN
MISSION. Presbyterian Church in the U.S.A. Board of Foreign
Missions.
> Presbyterian Historical Society—Archives and Library
> (PA–200/28): 1895, 1898, 1900, 1904.

PRAYER CYCLE. Missionary Division, Chinese Medical Association, Shanghai.
> None issued 1941–47. Chinese Medical Association called
> China Medical Association before 1912.
> Union Theological Seminary—Burke Library
> (NY–275/1): 1927, 1929–38, 1940–41, 1947–48.
> University of Oregon—Department of Special Collections
> (OR–15/18): 1949.
> University of Oregon—Department of Special Collections
> (OR–15/37): 1931–32.

PRAYER CYCLE AND NEWSLETTER FOR THE CHRISTIAN
MISSIONARY SOCIETY CHEKIANG MISSION.
> Union Theological Seminary—Burke Library
> (NY–275/1): Ag-O 1934.

PRAYER UNION LETTER OF THE WESLEYAN MISSION OF
SOUTH AND CENTRAL CHINA. N 1–151(?), 1883–1917(?).
> Union Theological Seminary—Burke Library
> (NY–275/1): N 1–17, 19–77, 80–83, 85–90, 92–98, 100,
> 102–149, 151, 170, 175, 1883–1917, 1924, 1926.

PREACH THE GOSPEL: Mission Reports from Tangshan. n.p.
> Bethel College—Mennonite Library and Archives
> (KS–55/8): V 1, N 1, n.d.; V 1, N 2; V 2, N 1–3; V 3, N 1;
> Nv 1939-Ja 1941.

Presbyterian Church in the U.S.A.
QUARTERLY. Central China Mission, Presbyterian Church
in the U.S.A.
> Union Theological Seminary—Burke Library
> (NY–275/1): 1905-6, Ap, Jl, O 1907.
SPECIAL CHINA BULLETIN. Presbyterian Church in the
U.S.A. Board of Foreign Missions. New York.
> Princeton Theological Seminary—Speer Library
> (NJ–95/3): 1912.
YEUNG KONG STATION BIMONTHLY. Presbyterian Mis-
sion of South China. N 1–50(?), 1905(?)–11(?).
> Presbyterian Historical Society—Archives and Li-
> brary (PA–200/28): D 1903-Ja 1912.
> Union Theological Seminary—Burke Library
> (NY–275/1): N 6–8, 11–14, 25–26, 29, 34–36, 39,
> 46–48, 50, 52, 1904–12.

PRINCETON-IN-PEKING. Peking University, Peking. V 1, N 1,
Ap 1923.
> Princeton University—University Archives (NJ–120/2):
> V 1, N 1, Ap 1923.

PRINCETON-IN-PEKING BULLETIN. Princeton University, Princeton, NJ. V 1, N 1, Je 1921.

> Princeton University—University Archives (NJ–120/2): V 1, N 1; V 2, N 6; Je 1921, Nv 1922.

PRINCETON PEKING GAZETTE. Princeton-Yenching Foundation, New York. V 1-, 1925–29.

> Continued by PRINCETON-YENCHING NEWS.
> Princeton University—University Archives (NJ–120/2): V 1, N 1–4; V 2, N 1, EXTRA; V 2, N 1–4, EXTRA; V 3, N 2–3; V 4, N 3–4; F, O 1925; F, Ap, O, D 1926; Ja, Ap, O, D 1927; F, O 1928; Nv 1929; Nv 1930.
> Union Theological Seminary—Burke Library (NY–275/1): V 1, O 1925.
> Yale Divinity School—Special Collections (CT–50/25): 1925–29.

THE PRINCETON WORK IN PEKING. Princeton-in-Peking, New York. 1909(?)–1913(?).

> Princeton University—University Archives (NJ–120/2): N 9, 13, 17, Ap 1909–10, 1913.

PRINCETON-YENCHING GAZETTE. Princeton-Yenching Foundation, New York. 1939–50.

> Continues PRINCETON-YENCHING NEWS.
> Presbyterian Historical Society—Archives and Library (PA–200/28): V 6, N 3–4, Je 1936.
> Princeton University—University Archives (NJ–120/2): V 5, N 1, 4; V 6, N 3–4; V 7, N 1–3; F 1931; D 1934; Je, D 1936; Je 1937; My, D 1938.
> Yale Divinity School—Special Collections (CT–50/25): 1930–39.

PRINCETON-YENCHING NEWS. Princeton-Yenching Foundation, New York. V 1-, 1930–38.

> Continues PRINCETON PEKING GAZETTE. Continued by PRINCETON-YENCHING GAZETTE. Title varies: PRINCETON PEKING GAZETTE, 1925–29; PRINCETON-YENCHING NEWS, 1930–38; PRINCETON-YENCHING GAZETTE, 1939–1950.
> Princeton University—University Archives (NJ–120/2): Je 1941.
> Yale Divinity School—Special Collections (CT–50/25): 1942–54.

PROCEEDINGS. *See* Natural History Society, Fukien Christian University.

PROGRESSIVE CHINA. Chinese Aid Society(?).

> Union Theological Seminary—Archives (NY–270/12): V 1, N 1, Ja 1929.

PUBLIC AFFAIRS. *See* Yenching University.

PUBLICATIONS. *See* China International Famine Relief Commission.

PUBLICATIONS. *See* University of Peking.

PUBLICATIONS. *See* Yenching University.

QUARTELBERICHTE DER CHINESISCHEN STIFTUNG.

> Yale Divinity School Library (CT–55/2): V 1–2, 1850–51.

QUARTERLY BULLETIN. *See* American Baptist Foreign Mission Society.

QUARTERLY BULLETIN. *See* Shanghai Hebrew Mission.

QUARTERLY BULLETIN. *See* Southern Baptist Convention, Central China Mission.

QUARTERLY LINK. *See* Christian Literature Society for China.

QUARTERLY NEWS. *See* Yenching University.

QUARTERLY NOTES ON CHRISTIANITY AND CHINESE RELIGION. Tao Fong Shan Ecumenical Centre, Hong Kong. Series 1–7, 1957–D 1963.

> Continues as CHING FENG.
> American Lutheran Church Archives (MN–95/110): ser. 2, N 3–4; ser. 3, N 1–2; ser. 4, N 1–4; ser. 5, N 1–4; ser. 6, N 1–4; ser. 7, N 1, 3–4; 1958–63.
> Andover Newton Theological School—Trask Library (MA–180/2): ser. 5, V 2, ser. 6-ser. 7, 1961–63.
> Emory University—Pitts Theology Library (GA–15/5): V 1–7, 1957–63.
> Evangelical and Reformed Historical Society—Schaff Library (PA–80/1): ser. 3, N 2; ser. 4, N 1–2; Ag 1959, Mr-Jl 1960.
> Harvard Divinity School—Andover-Harvard Theological Library (MA–95/1): ser. 4, N 4; ser. 5, N 2; D 1960, Je 1961.
> Harvard Divinity School—Andover-Harvard Theological Library (MA–95/2): ser. 2, N 2-ser. 3, N 1, 3/4-ser. 4, N 1, 3-ser. 7, N 4, My 1958-Mr 1959, D 1959-Mr 1960, O 1960-D 1963.
> Harvard University—Harvard-Yenching Library (MA–125/6): 1957–63.
> Presbyterian Historical Society—Archives and Library (PA–200/16): 1957–63.
> Southern Methodist University—Bridwell Theology Library (TX–20/2): ser. 4, N 1–4; ser. 5–7, 1960–63.
> Wheaton College—Graham Center Library (IL–205/1): V 1, N 1, 3; V 2, N 2–4; V 3–7; 1957–63.

QUARTERLY OF THE CENTRAL CHINA MISSION.

> Presbyterian Historical Society—Archives and Library (PA–200/28): 1905–7.

RELATIONS DE CHINE: Kiang-Nan. Paris, V 1-, 1903–7; ser. 2, 1908-. (Volume and series numbering irregular.)

> Continues RELATIONS DE LA MISSION DU KIANG-NAN. V 13–14 (1915–16) not published.
> Cornell University—Wason Collection (NY–95/1): V 1–12, 15–23; V 24, N 1, 3; V 27, N 1, 3–4; V 28, N 2–4; V 29, N 2–4; V 30, N 2–4; V 30; V 32, N 2–4; V 33; V 34, 2–4; V 35–36; V 37, N 1–3; V 38; 1903–14, 1917–40.
> Florida State University—Strozier Library (FL–25/1): 1903–7.
> Georgetown University—Woodstock Theological Center Library (DC–70/4): V23–36, 1925–38.
> University of Michigan—Hatcher Graduate Library (MI–25/1): V 1, 3–18, ser. 2, V 1–12, 1903–10.
> Yale Divinity School Library (CT–55/2): V 19–38, 1921–40.

RELIEF WORK YMCA REFUGEE CIVILIANS FELLOWSHIP NOTES.
>>Union Theological Seminary—Archives (NY-270/25): 1938.

RELIGION IN THE PEOPLE'S REPUBLIC OF CHINA. China Study Project. Tunbridge Wells, Kent, England.
>>Emory University—Pitts Theology Library (GA-15/5): N 14-19, 1984-85.
>>Union Theological Seminary—Burke Library (NY-275/1): Jl 1980-.
>>World Vision International—Research and Information Division (CA-200): current year only.
>>Yale Divinity School Library (CT-55/2): V 2-12, 1980-83.

RELIGIOUS EDUCATION: A Journal for Promoting Educational Methods in Religion. National Committee for Christian Religious Education in China, Shanghai. V 1, 1937.
>>Yale Divinity School Library (CT-55/2): V 1-4, 1937-40.

RELIGIOUS EDUCATION FELLOWSHIP. *See* National Committee for Christian Religious Education.

RELIGIOUS EDUCATION FELLOWSHIP BULLETIN. *See* National Committee for Christian Religious Education.

REVUE MENSUELLE. *See* Zi-ka-wei Observatoire, Shanghai.

SAINT JOHN'S ECHO. St. John's University, Shanghai. V 1, 1890.
>>Claremont Colleges—Asian Studies Collection (CA-75/2): V 40, N 2, Jl 1929.
>>Emory University—Pitts Theology Library (GA-15/5): V 4-19, 23, 26, 1893-1908, 1912, 1915.
>>Union Theological Seminary—Burke Library (NY-275/1): 1902; Ap, Je, Ag, O, D 1903; Ap 1904; 1905; Mr, Je, Ag, O, D, 1907; Ap, Je, Ag, O, D 1908; 1909-10; Ja, Mr-Je, S-D 1911; Ja, Mr-Je, S-D 1912; Ja-F, Ap-Je, O-D 1913; F-Ap, Nv-D 1914; Ja, Ap, Je, S, Nv-D, 1915; Ja, Mr-Je, S-Nv 1916; Ja-Je, S-D 1918; Ja 1919.
>>Yale Divinity School Library (CT-55/2): V 1-36, 1890-1925.
>>Yale Divinity School—Special Collections (CT-50/25): V 11, N2, V 12, N 1, V 15, 1-3, V 16, N 4, 1900-1901, 1904-5.

ST. JOHN'S REVIEW. St. John's University, Hong Kong.
>>Union Theological Seminary—Burke Library (NY-275/1): Ja-Ap 1939.

St. John's University of Shanghai
BIOLOGICAL BULLETIN. St. John's University of Shanghai, Department of Biology, Shanghai. 1931-35.
Title varies: Department of Biology, BULLETIN.
>>Harvard University—Museum of Comparative Zoology Library (MA-140/1): N 2, 1935.
>>Princeton University—Firestone Library (NJ-100/1): N1-2, 1931-35.
>>University of California, Berkeley—Biology Library (CA-40/1): V 1-2, 1931-35.
BULLETIN. St. John's University, Shanghai. N 1, 1911.
>>Cornell University—Wason Collection (NY-95/1): N 17, 1924.

>>Emory University—Pitts Theology Library (GA-15/5): N 1-3, 1911-15.
>>Harvard Divinity School—Andover-Harvard Theological Library (MA-95/2): N 1-2, My 1911-Jl 1912.
>>Union Theological Seminary—Burke Library (NY-275/1): My 1911.
STUDIES. St. John's University. N 1, 1922.
>>Boston Public Library (MA-30/2): 1922.
>>Harvard University—Widener Library (MA-155/1): 1922.
>>Mount Holyoke College—Williston Library (MA-225/1): 1922.
>>Syracuse University Archives (NY-375/2): 1922.
>>University of California, Berkeley—General Library (CA-70/1): N 1, 1922.
>>University of Illinois at Urbana-Champaign Library (IL-185/1): N 1, 1922.
>>University of Missouri-Columbia—Ellis Library (MO-10/1): N 1, 1922.
>>University of Washington—East Asia Library (WA-35/1): 1922.
>>Wellesley College—Clapp Library (MA-245/1): 1922.
See also DRAGON FLAG.

SCIENCE BULLETIN. *See* Lingnan University, Canton.

SCIENCE JOURNAL. *See* Fukien Christian University.

SCIENCE NOTES. *See* Yenching University.

SELECTED CONTRIBUTIONS. *See* Peking Union Medical College.

THE SHANGHAI. Shanghai Baptist College and Theological Seminary, Shanghai.
>>Essex Institute—Phillips Library (MA-210/2): V 6, 1921.

Shanghai American School, Shanghai
BULLETIN. Shanghai American School, Shanghai.
>>Cornell University—Wason Collection (NY-95/1): V 3, 7, 1924-25, 1928.
QUARTERLY. Shanghai American School, Shanghai.
>>Union Theological Seminary—Burke Library (NY-275/1): V 1; V 3, N 1; V 4, N 2, extra N 1-2; 1922, 1924-25.
S.A.S. NOOZE. Shanghai American School, Shanghai.
Volume numbering irregular; V 6 begins D 18, 1925, but reverts back to V 5 F 26, 1926.
>>Minnesota Historical Society—Division of Archives and Manuscripts (MN-105/5): V 4, N 2-5, 7, 9; V 5, N 7, 10-17, 21-22, 24-28, 30; O 1924-Ja 1925, Ap 1925, O 1925-My 1926.

SHANGHAI BAPTIST COLLEGE BULLETIN. American Presbyterian Mission Press, Shanghai.
>>American Baptist Historical Society—American Baptist Archives Center (PA-285/2): 1907-36.
>>Southern Baptist Convention—Archives Center (VA-65/2): 1918-21, 1925.

SHANGHAI COLLEGE BULLETIN. Shanghai.
>>Wake Forest University—North Carolina Baptist Historical Collection (NC-100/16): V 17-19, 1923-25.

Shanghai Hebrew Mission
QUARTERLY BULLETIN. Shanghai Hebrew Mission.
Union Theological Seminary—Burke Library (NY–275/1): Jl 1940.

SHANGHAI NEWSLETTER. American Church Mission, Shanghai. V ?, 1940-.
Title varies: –1940, DISTRICT OF SHANGHAI NEWSLETTER.
Union Theological Seminary—Burke Library (NY–275/1): F 1944.
Yale Divinity School Library (CT–55/2): V 14, N 1, 19; V 26, N 9–10; 1928, 1940, 1944.

SHANGHAI SPECTATOR. University of Shanghai, Shanghai.
Yale Divinity School—Special Collections (CT–50/25): V 6, N 3, 1947.

SHANGHAI YOUNG MEN. YMCA of China, Shanghai.
San Francisco Theological Seminary Library (CA–235/2): V 23, N 43, D 1924.
Union Theological Seminary—Burke Library (NY–275/1): F 1921.
Yale Divinity School—Special Collections (CT–50/27): 1917–18.

SHANSI BULLETIN. American Board of Commissioners for Foreign Missions, Boston.
Carleton College Archives (MN–60/1): N 2–5, Mr 1936.
Harvard Divinity School—Andover-Harvard Theological Library (MA–95/2): N 3–5, n.s. N 1–2, 1930, 1936, 1948.

SHANSI ECHOES. American Board of Commissioners for Foreign Missions. V 1–?, 1889–?.
Union Theological Seminary—Burke Library (NY–275/1): V 1, N 3, Mr 1889.

Shantung Christian University. *See* Cheeloo University.

SHANTUNG MISSION BULLETIN. American Presbyterian Mission, Chefoo.
Presbyterian Historical Society—Archives and Library (PA–200/28): N 2, D 1930.

SHAOWU BULLETIN. Shaowu Mission, Shaowu.
Harvard Divinity School—Andover-Harvard Theological Library (MA–95/2): O 1921, Ja-S 1922, Ap-S 1923, Ja-S 1924, Ja-S 1925, Ja-Ap, D 1926.

SIGN. Passionist Fathers, Union City, NJ. V 1–61, Ag 1921-My 1982.
Catholic Theological Union Library (IL–20/1): V 1–61, 1921–82.
College of Saint Elizabeth—Mahoney Library (NJ–10/1): V 4–61, O 1924-My 1982.
Congregation of the Passion of the Eastern United States—Chronicle Office (MA–255/1): V 1–61, Ag 1921-My 1982.
Emory University—Pitts Theology Library (GA–15/5): V 10–11, 13–61, 1930–82.
Union Theological Seminary—Burke Library (NY–275/1): V 3, N 12; V 4; V 6, N 11–12; V 7–9; V 10, N 4–8; 1924–30.

SINICA FRANCISCANA. Collegium Bonaventura, Quaracchi-Firenze. 1929.
Santa Barbara Mission—Institute for Franciscan Studies (CA–265/1): V 1–5, 1929–54.
Yale Divinity School Library (CT–55/2): V 1–8, 1929-.

SOCIAL RESEARCH SERIES. *See* Yenching University.

SOCIAL SCIENCES QUARTERLY. *See* Yenching University.

SOCIOLOGY FELLOWSHIP NEWS *See* Yenching University.

SOUTH CHINA. Victoria Diocesan and Missionary Association. V 1–3(?), 1937–39(?).
Union Theological Seminary—Burke Library (NY–275/1): V 1, N 1; V 2, N 1; V 3, N 1, 3; 1937–39.

THE SOUTH CHINA ALLIANCE TIDINGS. Christian and Missionary Alliance, Wuchow. V 1, 1907.
Nyack College—Rare Books and Archives (NY–310/1): V 1, N 3-V 20, N 2, 1907–26.
Union Theological Seminary—Burke Library (NY–275/1): Jl, D 1908; Ap, Jl 1909; F, Je 1910; F, Je, Ag, D 1911; F-Mr, Je, Ag, O, D 1912; F-Ag, Nv-D 1913; 1914–15; Mr-D 1916; 1917–19; Ja-O 1920; 1921–38.
Yale Divinity School—Special Collections (CT–50/27): 1914.

SOUTH CHINA BOAT MISSION BULLETIN. South China Boat Mission.
Union Theological Seminary—Burke Library (NY–275/1): Ap, Ag 1918; F, S 1919; My 1923.

SOUTH CHINA COLLEGIAN: An Anglo-Chinese Educational Monthly. Canton. V 1–2, N 8/9, O 1904-Ja 1906.
American Museum of Natural History Library (NY–140/1): V 1, N 5, 1904.
New York Public Library—General Research Division (NY–230/1): V [1–2], 1904–5.
Union Theological Seminary—Burke Library (NY–275/1): V 1, N 1–5, 6–8; V 2, N 1–6, 10; V 3, N 7, 1904–6.
University of California at Los Angeles—University Research Library (CA–185/1): V 1, 1904.

SOUTH CHINA COLLEGIAN. Macao; Martinsburg, WV. 1904–6.
Chinese title: LINGNAN HSÜEH-SHENG CHIEH.
Yale Divinity School Library (CT–55/2): V 1, 1904.

Southern Baptist Convention, Central China Mission
QUARTERLY BULLETIN. Central China Mission, Southern Baptist Convention.
Union Theological Seminary—Burke Library (NY–275/1): N 2, O 1906.

Southern Presbyterian Missions in China
BI-MONTHLY BULLETIN. Southern Presbyterian Missions in China. Shanghai. V 1–6, 1899–1904; n.s. V 1–14, 1905–24.
Continued by MONTHLY MESSENGER.
Historical Foundation of the Presbyterian and Reformed Churches (NC–80/28): V 1, N 3; V 2, N 3; n.s. V 1–14; 1899–1900, 1905–24.
Presbyterian Historical Society—Archives and Li-

brary (PA–200/28): V 6, N 2; V 9, N 2; Nv–D 1914, Mr–Ap 1917.

Princeton Theological Seminary—Speer Library (NJ–95/3): V 10, N 70–74, 1918.

MONTHLY MESSENGER. Southern Presbyterian Missions in China. V 1–6, 1899–1904; n.s., V 1–14, 1905–24. Continues BI-MONTHLY BULLETIN.

Union Theological Seminary—Burke Library (NY–275/1): n.v., N 18–21, 23, 24, 26, 28, 30–33, 35, 38, 39, 42–73, 86, 88, 89, 96, 97, 99, 100, 102, 103, 109, 1903, 1909–18, 1923, 1925–26.

SPECIAL ORIENT BULLETIN. *See* National Christian Council of China.

SPECIAL PUBLICATION. *See* Lingnan University.

STAR OF CATHAY. China Missions of the Church of the Brethren, Elgin, IL. Irregular. 1933–.

American Baptist Seminary of the West Library (CA–10/1): V 6, N 1, Summer, 1946.

Church of the Brethren General Board—Brethren Historical Library and Archives (IL–105/11): V 1, N 1–3; V 2, N 1–2; V 3, N 1; V 4, N 1; V 5, N 1; V 6, N 1; V 7, N 1; 1933–35, 1939–48.

Bridgewater College—Mack Memorial Library (VA–20/1): V 2, N 2; V 4, N 1; V 7, N 1; 1940, 1942, 1947–48.

Elizabethtown College—Zug Memorial Library (PA–35/1): Christmas issues 1933–34, 1936, 1939–48.

STAR OF CATHAY. Church of the Brethren in China, Shansi. V 1, 1939?

McPherson College—Miller Library (KS–40/1): V 3, N 1, 1940–41.

Manchester College—Funderberg Library (IN–85/1): V 2, 1939–40.

Yale Divinity School Library (CT–55/2): V 2–7, 1940–48.

THE STORY OF THE CHINA INLAND MISSION. China Inland Mission, London.

Biola University—Rose Memorial Library (CA–130/4): 1935, 1937, 1940, 1942, 1945–46, 1949–55, 1957.

Duke University—Divinity School Library (NC–30/2): 1904–37, 1940.

San Francisco Theological Seminary Library (CA–235/2): 1950.

University of Illinois at Urbana-Champaign Library (IL–185/1): 1914–40, 1942–47, 1949–51.

STUDIA SERICA. *See* West China Union University, Chengtu.

THE SUTSIEN TOWER. n.p.

Santa Barbara Mission—Archives (CA–260/1): V 2, N 9–12; V 3, N 2–12; V 4, N 2–6; 1942–43.

SZECHUAN WEEKLY BULLETIN. n.p.

Hoover Institution Library (CA–300/1): V 73–158, 1936–38.

TAIKU REFLECTOR. Taiku. N 1, 1932.

Harvard Divinity School—Andover-Harvard Theological Library (MA–95/1): N 1, Spr 1932.

THE TIBETAN MISSIONARY. Tibetan Mission, Pa-an, West China.

San Jose Bible College Archives (CA–255/1): V 2, N 8–9; V 3, N 3–4, 6–8, S–D 1946, Je–D 1947, Mr–D 1949.

TIENTSIN YOUNG MEN. Young Men's Christian Association, Tientsin?

Union Theological Seminary—Burke Library (NY–275/1): 1905–14.

THE TORCH. Dominican Fathers, Somerset, OH; New York. V 1–50, 1916–66.

Catholic University of America—Mullen Library (DC–20/1): V 12, N 11; V 13, N 1–2, 7, 9; V 15; V 16, N 12; V 17, N 1; V 19, N 8; V 20–21, 26–27, 29–30, 31–37, 39–40; 1927–37, 1941–43, 1945–53, 1955–56.

T'OUNG PAO: ou, Archives concernant l'histoire, les langues, la géographie et l'ethnographie de l'Asie orientale. V 1–10, 1890–99; Ser. 2, V 1–, 1900–.

Cornell University—Wason Collection (NY–95/1): V 1–60, 1890–1974.

Emory University—Pitts Theology Library (GA–15/5): ser. 1, V 1–10, ser. 2, V 1–54, 1890–1944.

Hartford Seminary Foundation—Archives (CT–10/1): V 25, N 5, 1928.

Pennsylvania State University—Penn State Room (PA–275/4): V 1–10, ser. 2, V 1–ser. 2, V 49, V 56–, 1890–1962, 1970–.

Princeton University—Gest Oriental Library (NJ–105/1): V 1–, 1890–.

Smithsonian Institution—Freer Gallery of Art Library (DC–160/2): V 1–, 1890–.

Union Theological Seminary—Burke Library (NY–275/1): ser. 1, V 1–10; ser. 2, V 1–20; V 24, N 1–5; V 25, N 1–5; V 26, N 1–5; V 27, N 1–5; V 28, N 1–5; V 29, N 1–5; V 30, N 1–2; V 31, N 1–3; V 32, N 2–3; 1890–1921, 1925–26, 1929–34, 1936.

University of California, Berkeley—East Asiatic Library (CA–55/1): V 1–10; ser. 2, V 1–, 1890–.

TRIPOD. Holy Spirit Study Centre, Hong Kong. V 2–, 1981–. Continues DING.

American Bible Society Library (NY–135/1): 1981–.

Emory University—Pitts Theology Library (GA–15/5): 1984–85.

Union Theological Seminary—Burke Library (NY–275/1): V 2–, 1982–.

TROIS DIX. Fukien Christian University.

Union Theological Seminary—Burke Library (NY–275/1): O 1921.

TRUE LIGHT REVIEW. China Baptist Publication Society, Canton. V 1–?, 1902?–?.

Southern Baptist Theological Seminary—Boyce Centennial Library (KY–50/2): V 35, 1937.

TRUE LIGHT YMCA NEWSLETTER. n.p.

University of Oregon—Department of Special Collections (OR–15/18): 1922–24.

TRUTH AND LIFE. Peking. Special English issue.

Harvard Divinity School—Andover-Harvard Theological Library (MA–95/2): F 1927.

Tsehchow Mission, North China

HALF-YEARLY CIRCULAR LETTER, Tsehchow Mission, North China.

> Union Theological Seminary—Burke Library (NY-275/1): Je 1924, Je 1926.

TSINAN MEDICAL JOURNAL. Tsinan. V 1–9, 1921–29.

> New York Academy of Medicine Library: (NY-220/1) V 2–9, 1922–29.

TSINAN MEDICAL REVIEW. Shantung Christian University, Medical Department, Tsinan. V 1, 1921.

> Yale Divinity School—Special Collections (CT–50/25): V 1, N 1, 1921.

TUNG WU MAGAZINE. Soochow University, International Relations Club

> Cornell University—Wason Collection (NY–95/1): V 3, N 2, Jl 1935.
>
> Drew University—United Methodist Archives (NJ–45/5): 1937.
>
> Duke University—Perkins Library (NC–55/1): V 5, Ap 1937.
>
> Lovely Lane Museum Library (MD–25/4): V 3, N 4, Nv 1935.
>
> Union Theological Seminary—Burke Library (NY–275/1): 1935, 1937.
>
> Yale Divinity School—Special Collections (CT–50/25): 1937.

UCR ENVOY: The Monthly Messenger to United China Relief Chairmen. *See* USC ENVOY: The Monthly Messenger to United Service to China Chairmen.

UNDERSTANDING CHINA NEWSLETTER (LIAO CHIEH CHUNG-KUO PAO). American Friends Service Committee, Pacific Southwest Region, Pasadena, CA. V 1–12, 1965–76.

> Asian Studies Newsletter Archives (MD–40/1): V 1, N 1– V 12, N 1, 1965–76.
>
> Cornell University—Wason Collection (NY–95/1): V 1– 11, 1965–75.

UNITED CHINA RELIEF SERIES. United China Relief, Chungking. N 1–, 1941-.

> Duke University—Perkins Library (NC–55/1): N 1–21, 1941.
>
> Princeton University—Firestone Library (NJ–100/1): 1941.
>
> Vassar College Library (NY–330/1): N 1–14, 16–21, 1941.

Université de l'Aurore, Shanghai

BULLETIN DE L'UNIVERSITE DE L'AURORE (French and Chinese). Jesuits, Université de l'Aurore, Shanghai. N 1– 19, 1909–19, Series 2, N 1–40, 1919–40, Series 3, V 1–, 1940- (semi-annually).

> Cornell University—Wason Collection (NY–95/1): Ser. 2, N 27–40; ser. 3, V 1–10; 1933–49.
>
> Harvard University—Harvard-Yenching Library (MA–125/6): V 27–40, ser. 3, V 1–10, 1933–49.
>
> Harvard University—Widener Library (MA–155/1): Ser. 3, V 3, N 1; V 6, N 4; V 7–8; V 9, N 33–36; V 10, N 40; 1942, 1945–49.

University of Notre Dame—Memorial Library (IN–95/1): Ser. 3, V 8, N 29–32; V 9, N 33–34; V 10, N 37, 40; 1947–49.

FICHIER ENTOMOLOGIQUE CHINOISE. N 1-, 193?-.

> Cornell University—Wason Collection (NY–95/1): N 1–59, n.d.

MONTHLY BULLETIN. Chen Tan Ta Hsüeh (Université l'Aurore), Ching Chi Yen Chiu Shih (Economic Research Department), Shanghai. N 1–22, O 1946-Nv 1948.

> Cornell University—Wason Collection (NY–95/1): N 1–22, O 1946-Nv 1948.
>
> Harvard University—Widener Library (MA–155/1): N 1–22, 1946–48.
>
> University of California at Los Angeles—University Research Library (CA–185/1): N 1–22, 1946–48.

NOTES DE BOTANIQUE CHINOISE. Chen Tan Ta Hsüeh (Université l'Aurore), Musée Heude, Imprimerie de T'ou-se-we, Shanghai. N 1-, O 1931-.

> Cornell University—Wason Collection (NY–95/1): N 1, 3, 1931, 1933.
>
> Field Museum of Natural History Library (IL–40/1): N 1–8, 1931–46.

NOTES D'ENTOMOLOGIE CHINOISE. Chen Tan Ta Hsüeh (Université l'Aurore), Musée Heude, Shanghai. V 1-, 1929/34-.

> Cornell University—Wason Collection (NY–95/1): V 1–10, V 11, N 1–2, V12–13, 1929/34–49.
>
> Field Museum of Natural History Library (IL–40/1): V 1–11, 1929–47.

NOTES DE MALACOLOGIE CHINOISE. Chen Tan Ta Hsüeh (Université l'Aurore), Musée Heude, Shanghai. V 1-, Jl 1934-.

> Cornell University—Wason Collection (NY–95/1): V 1, 1934–45(?).

NOTES D'ORNITHOLOGIE. Chen Tan Ta Hsüeh (Université l'Aurore), Musée Heude, Shanghai.

> Field Museum of Natural History Library (IL–40/1): N 1–2, 1943, 1946.
>
> University of California, Berkeley—Biology Library (CA–40/1): N 1, 1943.

University of Nanking

AGRICULTURE AND FORESTRY NOTES. University of Nanking, College of Agriculture and Forestry, Nanking. N 1– 42, Nv 1923-Nv 1936; n.s. N 1-, 1937- (irregular publication).

> Suspended Mr 1927-Nv 1931.
>
> Claremont Colleges—Asian Studies Collection (CA–75/2): N 8, 10–11, 13–14, 16, 18–21, 23, 25, Je 1924-F 1927.
>
> Cornell University—Wason Collection (NY–95/1): N 1, O 1924.
>
> Disciples of Christ Historical Society—Library and Archives (TN–45/1): N 7, 12–14, n.s. N 4, 7–10, 1924–25, 1939–40.
>
> Drew University—United Methodist Archives (NJ–45/5): N 20–23, 25–39; Ja-My, S-O 1926; Ja-F 1927; O 1931-Ja 1932; Je 1932-Ja 1936.
>
> Emory University—Pitts Theology Library

(GA-15/5): N 5, 14, 17–19, 21–25, 28, 31–32, 34–35, 1925, 1934.

Harvard University—Arnold Arboretum (MA-100/1): N 6–11, 14–16, 18–23, 27, 29–33, 35–39, n.s., N 8–11, 1924–26, 1932–36, 1940–41.

Harvard University—Widener Library (MA-155/1): N 10, 18, 20–21, 25, 33, 35–39, n.s. N 1–4, 11–13, 1924–27, 1934–36, 1938–41.

Iowa State University Library (IA-5/1): N 27–30, 1932–33.

Library of Congress—General Reading Rooms Division (DC-120/1): N 36–39, 1935–36.

New York Public Library—General Research Division (NY-230/1): Nv 1923-Ap 1941 (inc.).

Union Theological Seminary—Burke Library (NY-275/1): N 1–39, 1923–27, 1931–36.

University of California, Berkeley—General Library (CA-70/1): N 3, 5–14, 16–39; ser. 2, N 4, 7, 10–11; 1924–36, 1939–41.

University of California, Davis, Library (CA-110/2): N 3–5, 7–13, 1924–41.

University of Michigan—Hatcher Graduate Library (MI-25/1): N 8, 15–39, 1924–36.

University of Virginia—Alderman Library (VA-30/1): N 3, 22, 32, n.s., 3, 6, 8, 10, 11, 1931–32, 1939–41.

Yale Divinity School—Special Collections (CT-50/25): N 1–43, n.s. N 1–13, 1923–27, 1931–41.

AGRICULTURE AND FORESTRY SERIES. University of Nanking, College of Agriculture and Forestry, Nanking. V 1, 1920-.

Claremont Colleges—Asian Studies Collection (CA-75/2): V 1, N 1, F 1920.

Cornell University—Wason Collection (NY-95/1): N 6–7, 9, 1923–24.

Drew University—United Methodist Archives (NJ-45/5): V 1, N 1–2, 4, 9, F, Ag 1920, F 1921, My 1924.

Emory University—Pitts Theology Library (GA-15/5): V 1, N 7, 1923.

Harvard University—Arnold Arboretum (MA-100/1): V 1, N 4–5, 9, 1921–24.

Harvard University—Widener Library (MA-155/1): V 1, N 7, 9, 1924.

Library of Congress—General Reading Rooms Division (DC-120/1): V 1, N 4, 6–7, 9, 1920.

New York Public Library—General Research Division (NY-230/1): 1923–24 (inc.).

Princeton University—Firestone Library (NJ-100/1): V 1, N 7, Jl 1924.

University of California, Berkeley—General Library (CA-70/1): V 1, Ag 1920-My 1925.

University of California, Davis, Library (CA-110/2): V 1, N 1–22, 1920–26.

University of Chicago—Regenstein Library (IL-85/1): N 1–48, 1932–36.

University of Illinois at Urbana-Champaign Library (IL-185/1): V 1, N 2–4, 9; Ag, D 1920; F 1921; My

1924.

BULLETIN. University of Nanking, College of Agriculture and Forestry, Nanking. N 1–18, 1924–36; n.s. N 1-, Ap 1932-.

Title varies: N 12–16 also known as the College's CIRCULAR.

California State Library (CA-230/1): n.s. N 1, 1932.

Catholic University of America—Mullen Library (DC-20/1): n.s. N 5, 1932.

Claremont Colleges—Asian Studies Collection (CA-75/2): N 7, 10–12, 15, 1926.

Columbia University—Starr East Asian Library (NY-195/4): n.s. N 1, 1932.

Cornell University—Wason Collection (NY-95/1): n.s. N 3, 1933.

Drew University—United Methodist Archives (NJ-45/5): N 10, 13, 15, 16, 1926.

Duke University—Biology-Forestry Library (NC-25/1): N 1–11, 15–17, 19, 21–41, 1932–35.

Field Museum of Natural History Library (IL-40/1): n.s. N 2–11, 17–48, 1933–36.

Harvard University—Arnold Arboretum (MA-100/1): V 6, N 7; V 7, N 4, 8–9; V 8, N 2; n.s., N 2–10, 12–47; 1923–27, 1931–34, n.s. 1933–37.

Harvard University—Farlow Reference Library (MA-110/1): n.s. N 2–48, 1933–36.

Harvard University—Widener Library (MA-155/1): N 13, 15, n.s. N 1–48, 1926, 1932–36.

Iowa State University Library (IA-5/1): N 12–16, n.s. N 1–51, 1926, Ap 1932–35.

Johns Hopkins University—Eisenhower Library (MD-10/1): n.s. V 1, Ap 1932.

Kansas State University—Farrell Library (KS-45/1): N 13–16, n.s., N 9–48, 1926, 1933–36.

Library of Congress—General Reading Rooms Division (DC-120/1): n.s., N 1–48, 53–54, 1932, 1934–36, 1938–41.

Michigan State University Library (MI-75/1): N 13–14, n.s., N 2–6, 9–48, 1926, 1932–36.

New York Public Library—General Research Division (NY-230/1): N 12–15, n.s., N 1–48, N 12–15, n.s. N 1–48, 1926–36.

Oregon State University—Kerr Library (OR-5/1): N 13–15, n.s. N 2–48, 1926–36.

Presbyterian Historical Society—Archives and Library (PA-200/28): N 13, 15; Je, Nv 1926.

San Francisco Theological Seminary Library (CA-235/2): N 13, Je 1926.

Stanford University—Green Library (CA-305/1): N 13, n.s. 3–41, 1926, 1933–35.

Union Theological Seminary—Burke Library (NY-275/1): N 3, 1933.

University of California at Los Angeles—University Research Library (CA-185/1): N 2–10, 12–48, 1932–36.

University of California, Berkeley—General Library (CA-70/1): N 11–16, n.s. N 1–48, 53, Mr-D 1926, Ap 1932-F 1938.

University of Chicago—Regenstein Library (IL-85/1): N 1–48, 1932–36.

University of Georgia Libraries (GA-5/1): N 13, 22,

27–35, 42–48, 1926, 1934–36.

University of Illinois at Urbana-Champaign Library (IL–185/1): N 13–16, n.s. N 1–48, Je-D 1926, Ap 1932-D 1936.

University of Iowa Libraries (IA–40/1): N 5, 1933.

University of Michigan—Natural Sciences Library (MI–40/1): N 12, 14–15, n.s., N 1–41, 43–46, ser. 3, N 3, 5, 8, 11, 14–42, 47–48, 1924–36.

University of Missouri-Columbia—Ellis Library (MO–10/1): N 2–25, 1932-?.

University of Nebraska, Lincoln—Love Library (NB–25/2): N 12–16, n.s., N 9–10, 12–47, 1924–26, 1932–36.

University of Virginia—Alderman Library (VA–30/1): n.s. N 1, 3–4, 8, 12-, 1932–36.

Yale Divinity School Library (CT–55/1): V 5, N 5; V 6, N 5, 12, 17; V 7, N 4, 8–10; V 8, N 2; 1920–21, 1923–27, 1931, 1934.

Yale Divinity School—Special Collections (CT–50/25): 1933–35.

Yale University—Sterling Memorial Library (CT–80/1): V 13–16, n.s., N 1, ser. 3, V 1–6, 1926, 1932, 1933–34.

BULLETIN. University of Nanking, Women's College, Nanking.

Cornell University—Wason Collection (NY–95/1): V 7, 1931.

BULLETIN. Department of Missionary Training.

Emory University—Pitts Theology Library (GA–15/3): V 6, N 2, 1921.

BULLETIN. Department unknown.

Claremont Colleges—Asian Studies Collection (CA–75/2): V 7, N 5, 1926–27.

Cornell University—Wason Collection (NY–95/1): V 6, N 5, 18; V 7, N 1, 3–4, 7, 9; V 8, N 1; 1920–21, 1924–25, 1931.

University of California, Berkeley—General Library (CA–70/1): 1915–34.

BULLETIN ON FOREIGN RELATIONS. *See title.*

CONTRIBUTION. University of Nanking, Botany Department, Plant Pathology Laboratory, Nanking. N 1, 1930-.

Title varies: ITS PAPERS.

American Museum of Natural History Library (NY–140/1): N 30, 1934.

University of Illinois at Urbana-Champaign Library (IL–185/1): N 25, 30, 1933(?), 1934.

University of Michigan—Natural Sciences Library (MI–40/1): N 25, 30, 1932, 1936.

University of Virginia—Alderman Library (VA–30/1): N 21–23, 25, 30–31, 35, 39–40, 1930–34.

DAILY METEOROLOGICAL RECORDS.

Claremont Colleges—Asian Studies Collection (CA–75/2): N 9, O-D 1925.

Yale Divinity School—Special Collections (CT–50/25): 1925.

ECONOMIC FACTS. University of Nanking, College of Agriculture and Forestry, Department of Agricultural Economics, Nanking and Chengtu. N 1–55, 1936–46 (irregular).

In English and Chinese.

Drew University—United Methodist Archives (NJ–45/5): 1936–37.

Harvard University—Widener Library (MA–155/1): N 1–6, 1936–37.

Iowa State University Library (IA–5/1): N 1–55, 1936–46.

Princeton University—Firestone Library (NJ–100/1): N 1–55, S 1936-Ap 1946.

Union Theological Seminary—Burke Library (NY–275/1): N 1–4, 6–11, 16, 23, 47, 55, 1936–38, 1943–46.

University of California, Berkeley—General Library (CA–70/1): V 1–11, 13–55, 1936–46.

University of Washington—East Asia Library (WA–35/1): V 1–4, N 1–55, S 1936-Ap 1946 (repr. 1980).

Yale Divinity School—Special Collections (CT–50/25): N 13, 16–18–25, 47–55, 1939, 1943, 1945–46.

ECONOMIC WEEKLY. Department of Agricultural Economics, College of Agriculture and Forestry, Chengtu.

Yale Divinity School—Special Collections (CT–50/25): N 1–20, 22, 24–25, 27–28, 33–34, 36–61, 63–70, 72–76, 78–86, 88–102, 1947–49.

THE LINGUIST. *See title.*

MISCELLANEOUS BULLETIN SERIES. University of Nanking, Nanking. N 1–16, 1924-D 1926?

Claremont Colleges—Asian Studies Collection (CA–75/2): N 3–6, D 1924-Ap 1925.

Cornell University—Wason Collection (NY–95/1): N 1, 5, 1924–25.

Disciples of Christ Historical Society—Library and Archives (TN–45/1): N 5, F 1925.

Drew University—United Methodist Archives (NJ–45/5): N 1, 4–5, S, D 1924, F 1925.

Harvard University—Widener Library (MA–155/1): N 1, 1924.

Union Theological Seminary—Burke Library (NY–275/1): N 1–3, 5–6, 1924–25.

University of California, Berkeley—General Library (CA–70/1): N 1, 5, S 1924, F 1925.

University of California, Davis, Library (CA–110/2): N 1, 4–5, 1924–25.

University of Michigan—Hatcher Graduate Library (MI–25/1): N 3–6, 1924–25.

NEWSLETTER. Associated Boards of Christian Colleges in Asia, University of Nanking, Nanking.

Cornell University—Wason Collection (NY–95/1): Ja-Ap 1944, Ja-Mr, S-D 1945, Ap-My 1946.

NEWSLETTER. University of Nanking, Department of Agricultural Economics, Chengtu.

Princeton University—Firestone Library (NJ–100/1): Mr 1946.

Syracuse University—Manuscript Division (NY–380/1): 1928.

OCCASIONAL LETTERS. University of Nanking.

Syracuse University—Manuscript Division (NY–380/1): N 5–11, 1927–28.

Union Theological Seminary—Burke Library (NY–275/1): N 11, Je 1929.

REPORT OF AGRICULTURE AND FORESTRY.

American Baptist Historical Society—American Baptist Archives Center (PA–285/2): 1920–44.

SPECIAL REPORT. University of Nanking, Nanking. N 1–12, Mr 1934-Jl 1936(?).
> Drew University—United Methodist Archives (NJ–45/5): N 2, F 1935.
> Harvard University—Widener Library (MA–155/1): N 3–4, 1935.
> Library of Congress—General Reading Rooms Division (DC–120/1): N 3–4, 1935.
> New York Public Library—General Research Division (NY–230/1): N 2–4, 1935.
> Syracuse University Archives (NY–375/2): N 2, 1935.
> University of California, Berkeley—General Library (CA–70/1): N 3–4, Mr-Ag 1935.
> University of Chicago—Regenstein Library (IL–85/1): V 3–4, 12, 1935–36.
> University of Illinois at Urbana-Champaign Library (IL–185/1): N 3–4, Mr, Ag 1935.
> University of Virginia—Alderman Library (VA–30/1): N 2, 1934.
> Yale Divinity School—Special Collections (CT–50/25): N 1–4, 1934–35.

UNIVERSITY OF NANKING MAGAZINE. University of Nanking, Nanking. V 1–19, 1909-? (publication varies).
> Center for Research Libraries (IL–25/4): V 1, N 1–4, 6–9; V 2, N 4–8; V 4, N 1–4; V 5, N 5–8; V 6, N 1, 3–11; V 7, N 1–4; V 8–10, N 1–2, 4; V 11, N 1–2, Ja-N 1910; Ja-N 1911, My-D 1912, F-My 1913, O 1913-Ja 1914, Mr 1914-My 1915, O 1915-Je 1916, Ag 1916 (special no.), D 1916-Je 1918, O 1918-Je 1919, O-D 1919.
> Drew University—United Methodist Archives (NJ–45/5): 1910–12, 1915.
> Presbyterian Historical Society—Archives and Library (PA–200/28): My 1910.
> Union Theological Seminary—Burke Library (NY–275/1): D 1909; Ja, Mr-My, S-Nv 1910; Ja, Mr, My, Ag-S, Nv 1911; Ja-My, S-D 1912; 1913; Ja, Mr-Je, O-D 1914; Ja, Mr-Je, O 1915; Ja, Ap, Je, Ag 1916; O 1918; Je, O, D 1919; Je 1923; F, Je 1924; Ap, Nv 1925.
> University of Iowa Libraries (IA–40/1): 1910.
> University of Virginia—Alderman Library (VA–30/1): V 12, N 1; V 13, N 1–2; V 14, N 1; V 15, N 2; V 16, N 1; 1922–28.
> Yale Divinity School Library (CT–55): uncatalogued.
> Yale Divinity School—Special Collections (CT–50/25): V 1, N 1, 6–7; V 2, N 1–3, 6; V 3, N 1–4; V 4, N 1; V 5, N 5; V 6, N 1–5; V 7, N 2; V 9, N 4–5; V 12, N 2–4; V 13, N 1–2; V 17, N 1; 1909–14, 1916, 1918, 1922–24, 1930.
> Yale Divinity School—Special Collections (CT–50/27): 1919.

University of Peking, Peking
> BULLETIN. University of Peking, College of the Arts.
>> Yale Divinity School Library (CT–55/1): 1895–1925.

PUBLICATIONS. University of Peking, College of Education. N 1, 1939.
> Harvard University—Widener Library (MA–155/1): N 1–2, 1939–40.

UNIVERSITY OF SHANGHAI BULLETIN. n.p.
> American Baptist Historical Society—American Baptist Archives Center (PA–285/2): 1937–40.

USC ENVOY: The Monthly Messenger to United Service to China Chairmen. United Service to China, New York. V 1, 1946–47. Jl 1946 as UCR ENVOY: The Monthly Messenger to United China Relief Chairmen.
> Center for Research Libraries (IL–25/4): V 1, N 1–5, 7–9, Jl 1946-Mr 1947.
> Johns Hopkins University—Eisenhower Library (MD–10/1): V 1, N 3–4, 6–9, 1946–47.
> New York Public Library—General Research Division (NY–230/1): V 1, N 1–8, Jl 1946-Ja 1947.
> Princeton University—Firestone Library (NJ–100/1): V 1, N 1–12, 1946–47.

VARIETES SINOLOGIQUES. Imprimerie de la Mission Catholique, Shanghai; Institute of Jesuit Sources, St. Louis, MO; Ricci Institute, Taipei.
> Brigham Young University—Lee Library (UT–10/1): N 47, 1917.
> Calvin College and Seminary Library (MI–85/1): n.s. N 72, 1985.
> Cleveland Public Library (OH–85/1): N 7, 12, 30, 35, 59–60, 1895–1902, 1913, 1932–34.
> College of the Holy Cross—Dinand Library (MA–280/1): n.s. N 72, 1985.
> Columbia University—Butler Library (NY–150/1): N 38, 47, 1914, 1917.
> Cornell University—Wason Collection (NY–95/1): N 1–4, 6–8, 11–14, 19–21, 24–25, 28–29, 33, 37, 43, 50, 52–56, 59–60, 1892–1903, 1905–6, 1909–16, 1918, 1920, 1922, 1924–25, 1932–34.
> Denver Conservative Baptist Seminary—Thomas Library (CO–10/3): n.s. N 6, 1985.
> Earlham College—Lilly Library (IN–100/1): n.s. N 72, 1985.
> Emory University—Pitts Theology Library (GA–15/2): N 16, 54, 1899, 1922.
> Emory University—Pitts Theology Library (GA–15/5): N 24, 47, 1905, 1917.
> Emory University—Woodruff Library (GA–25/1): N 47, 1917.
> Essex Institute—Phillips Library (MA–210/2): 1901–19.
> Florida State University—Strozier Library (FL–25/1): N 1–25, 29, 55, 1892–1938 (?).
> Georgetown University—Woodstock Theological Center Library (DC–70/4): N 59–60, 1932 (repr. 1971).
> Hartford Seminary Foundation—Archives (CT–10/1): N 20, 1902.
> Harvard University—Harvard-Yenching Library (MA–125/6): n.s. N 72, 1985.
> Princeton Theological Seminary—Speer Library (NJ–95/3): N 7, 12, 20, 32–36, 39, 41–42, 44–46, 48–49, 51, 1895–1902, 1911–19.

Princeton University—Gest Oriental Library (NJ–105/1): N 8, 10, 13, 16, 21–22, 25, 27, 29, 31–32, 34–36, 38–39, 41–42, 44–49, 51, 57, 59–60, 61, 1896, 1902–3, 1906, 1909–34.

St. Mary's Seminary—St. Mary's of the Barrens Library (MO–45/1): N 1–10, n.d.

Santa Clara University—Orradre Library (CA–280/1): N 59–60, 1932–34.

Smithsonian Institution—Freer Gallery of Art Library (DC–160/2): N 8, 10, 27, 29, 32, 34, 36, 39, 41–42, 44–46, 48–49, 51–52, 57, 1895–98, 1909–29.

Stanford University—Green Library (CA–305/1): N 1–66, 67–, 1892–1938, 1982–.

Union Theological Seminary—Burke Library (NY–275/1): N 3, 5, 34, 1893–94, 1922.

University of California, Berkeley—East Asiatic Library (CA–55/1): N 5, 9, 1894, 1896.

University of California, Berkeley—General Library (CA–70/1): N 1–66, n.s., 1–65, 1892–1938, n.d.

University of Notre Dame—Memorial Library (IN–95/1): N 38, 1914.

University of Pennsylvania—Van Pelt Library (PA–215/1): N 7, 12, 17, 19–20, 38, 47, 1895–1902, 1909, 1912, 1914, 1917.

University of Washington—East Asia Library (WA–35/1): N 59–60, 1932–34 (repr. 1976).

University of Washington Libraries (WA–45/1): N 1–60, 63–65, 1901–37 (inc.).

Western Washington University—Wilson Library (WA–5/1): N 5–6, 9, 24, 33, 53, 58–60, 1894 (repr. 1971), 1896 (repr. 1971), 1905 (repr. 1967), 1912 (repr. 1978?), 1922, 1932, 1932–34 (repr. 1976).

Yale Divinity School Library (CT–55/1): N 7, 12, 20, 38, 1895–1902, 1914.

VERKUNDIGT DAS EVANGELIUM NACHRICHTEN AUS CHINA. Crimmitschau.
Title varies: MISSIONS-NACHRICHTEN AUS TANG-SHAN, 1920–28; AUSBREITUNG-EVANGELIUMS IN TANGSHAN, 1928; VERKUNDIGT DAS EVANGELIUM NACHRICHTEN AUS CHINA, 1929–38; NACHRICHTEN AUS CHINA, 1938–41.
Bethel College—Mennonite Library and Archives (KS–55/8): N 29–30; n.s. V 10–18, V 19, N 1–3, Ja 1929–1938.

VISITS WITH THE MISSIONARIES. Published by Franciscan missionaries in China. 1 issue, n.d.
Franciscan Province of the Sacred Heart Archives (MO–65/1): n.d.

VOICE. Shanghai Baptist College, Shanghai. V 1, 1911.
Union Theological Seminary—Burke Library (NY–275/1): Je, Nv 1912, Mr, Je, O-Nv 1913.
Wake Forest University—North Carolina Baptist Historical Collection (NC–100/21): V [14–19], 1925–39.

THE WATCHMAN. Paotingfu.
Cornell University—Department of Manuscripts and University Archives (NY–90/6): V 10, N 1, Mr 1933.

WEEKLY BULLETIN. See Fukien Christian University, Shanghai.

West China Border Research Society, Chengtu
JOURNAL OF THE WEST CHINA BORDER RESEARCH SOCIETY. West China Union University, Chengtu. V 1–16, 1922–45.
V 12–16 issued in 2 series: Series A: General; Series B: Natural Sciences.
Academy of Natural Sciences of Philadelphia Library (PA–135/4): Ser. B, V 12, 14–16, 1923–46.
American Museum of Natural History Library (NY–140/1): V 1–16, 1922–46.
Buffalo Museum of Science—Research Library (NY–65/1): V 11, 1939; ser. B, V 12, 1940.
Columbia University—Starr East Asian Library (NY–195/4): V 1–16, 1922–45.
Cornell University—Wason Collection (NY–95/1): V 1–16, 1922–46.
Duke University—Perkins Library (NC–55/1): 1922–28, 1936, 1938.
Emory University—Pitts Theology Library (GA–15/5): V 3–4, 1926–31.
Field Museum of Natural History Library (IL–40/1): V 1–11; ser. A: V 12–16; ser. B: V 12–13, 15–16; 1922–42, 1944–46.
Harvard University—Fine Arts Library (MA–115/1): V 11, 1939.
Harvard University—Harvard-Yenching Library (MA–125/6): V 1–16, 1922–45; supplement, V 8, 1937.
Harvard University—Museum of Comparative Zoology Library (MA–140/1): V 1–3, 5–6; ser. B, V 12, 15; 1922–29, 1932–34, 1940, 1945.
Harvard University—Peabody Museum (MA–145/1): V 1–16, 1922–45.
Harvard University—Widener Library (MA–155/1): V 1–9, 1922–37.
Iowa State University Library (IA–5/1): V 11–16, 1939–46.
Library of Congress—General Reading Rooms Division (DC–120/1): V 1–10, 1922–32.
Metropolitan Museum of Art—Watson Library (NY–210/1): Ser. A, V 12, 1940.
New York Public Library—General Research Division (NY–230/1): 1930–38 (inc.).
Northwestern University Library (IL–115/1): V 1–9; ser. A, V 15, 1922–37, 1944.
Oberlin College—Main Library (OH–175/1): V 1–2, 11–12, 1922–23; ser. B, 1940.
Overseas Missionary Fellowship (PA–265/1): V 1–2, 5–6, 8, 10; ser. A, V 14–16, 1922–25, 1932–34, 1936, 1938, 1942, 1944–45.
Presbyterian Historical Society—Archives and Library (PA–200/28): 1922–25.
Princeton University—Firestone Library (NJ–100/1): V 1–11, 1922–39.
Princeton University—Gest Oriental Library (NJ–105/1): V 1–11, 1922–39.
Stanford University—Lane Medical Library (CA–310/1): V 5, 1932.
Union Theological Seminary—Burke Library (NY–275/1): V 1–16, 1922–45.

University of California, Berkeley—General Library (CA–70/1): V 1–16, 1922–46.

University of Chicago—Regenstein Library (IL–85/1): 1922–45.

University of Illinois at Urbana-Champaign Library (IL–185/1): V 2–11; ser. A, V 13–15; ser. B, V 12–16; 1924–46.

University of Michigan—Hatcher Graduate Library (MI–25/1): V 1–16, 1922–45.

University of Pennsylvania—Van Pelt Library (PA–215/1): V 1, 3–16, 1922, 1924–45 (?).

University of Rochester—Rhees Library (NY–360/2): V 1–8, 1922–34, 1936–37.

University of Washington Libraries (WA–45/1): V 1–12; ser. A, V 15–16, 1922–45; ser. B, V 15, 1945.

Yale Divinity School—Special Collections (CT–50/25): V 1–2; ser. B, V 9, 12; 1922–23, 1939–40.

Yale University—Sterling Memorial Library (CT–80/1): V 1–8, 11–15, 1922–36, 1939–44; V 5, supplement, 1932.

WEST CHINA MESSENGER. West China Mission of the Methodist Episcopal Church, Chungking. V 1–9, 1902–10(?).

Bethel Theological Seminary Library (MN–50/1): V 1–9, 1902–10.

Boston University—School of Theology Library (MA–35/1): V 2, N 5, 1903.

Union Theological Seminary—Burke Library (NY–275/1): V 1–7, 1902–8.

WEST CHINA MISSIONARY NEWS. West China Missionary News Publication Committee, Chengtu. V 1–45, 1899–1945.

American Baptist Historical Society—American Baptist Archives Center (PA–285/2): 1932–35, 1939.

Bethel Theological Seminary Library (MN–50/1): V 3, 6–7, 11, 21, 25–26, 28–41, 1901, 1904–5, 1909, 1919, 1923–24, 1926–40.

Boston University—School of Theology Library (MA–35/1): V 40–41, 43, 45, 1938–43.

Center for Research Libraries (IL–25/4): V 3, N 2, 5–10; V 4–5; V 6, N 3–12; V 7, 9; V 10, N 4, 8–9, 12; V 11, N 5; V 12, N 5–12; V 13–28, N 7; V 28, N 9–12; V 29–V 30, N 7; V 30, N 9–12; V 31–40, N 8; V 40, N 10–V 45; 1901–43.

Claremont Colleges—Asian Studies Collection (CA–75/3): V 9, N 3; V 10, N 2; V 11, N 1; V 12, N 11; V 13, N 1, 3–12; V 14, N 3–12; V 15–16, N 5; V 16, N 7–V 17, N 7; V 17, N 9–V 20, N 9; V 20, N 11–V 23, N 11; V 24, N 1–V 25, N 4; V 25, N 11–V 30, N 7; V 30, N 9–V 36, N 6; V 36, N 9–V 42, N 10; V 43, N 1–2, 11–12; V 44, N 1–8; V 45; 1907–43.

Colgate-Rochester Theological Seminaries—Swasey Library (NY–350/1): V 23, N 1–7, 11; V 24–28; V 29, N 1–9, 11–12; V 30, N 2–12; V 31, N 1–9, 11–12; V 32; V 33, N 1–11; V 34–35; V 36, N 1–9, 11–12; V 37; V 38, N 1, 3–12; V 39–41; V 42, N 1–5; 1921–40.

Emory University—Pitts Theology Library (GA–15/5): V 20–41, 43, 1918–42.

Graduate Theological Union Library (CA–15/2): V 1–45, N 5–12, 1899–1943.

Harvard University—Harvard-Yenching Library

(MA–125/6): V 35, N 2, 11; V 36, N 5, 7–8, 12, 1933–34.

Harvard University—Widener Library (MA–155/1): V 3, N 1–2, 5–10; V 4, 1–3, 6, 9, 11; V 5, N 3–5, 7–8, 10–12; V 6, N 3–12; V 7–9; V 10, N 4, 6, 8–9, 12; V 11, N 5; V 12, N 5–12; V 13–27; V 28, N 1–7, 9–12; V 29; V 30, N 1–7, 9–12; V 31–39; V 40, N 1–8, 10–12; 1901–43.

Iowa State University Library (IA–5/1): V [3–45], 1901–43.

Kalamazoo College—Upjohn Library (MI–125/1): V 1–45, 1901–43.

Library of Congress—General Reading Rooms Division (DC–120/1): V 17; V 18, N 4–6; V 19, N 5–6, 11–12; V 22; V 26, N 1–9, 11; V 27, N 2; V 28, N 11; 1915–17, 1920, 1924–26.

New Brunswick Theological Seminary—Sage Library (NJ–65/2): V 40(?), Mr 1939.

Oberlin College—Main Library (OH–175/1): V [3–45], 1901–43.

Ohio State University—Thompson Memorial Library (OH–110/4): V 3–45, 1901–43.

Southern Baptist Theological Seminary—Boyce Centennial Library (KY–50/2): V 31–41, 1931–41.

Stanford University—Green Library (CA–305/1): V 1–45, 1899–1943.

Union Theological Seminary—Burke Library (NY–275/1): V 2–43, 1901–43.

University of Nebraska, Lincoln—Love Library (NB–25/2): V 1–51, 1899–1949.

University of Oregon Library (OR–20/2): V 37, 1935.

Wheaton College—Graham Center Library (IL–205/1): V 1–45, 1901–43.

Yale Divinity School Library (CT–55/2): V 1–45, 1899–1943.

Yale Divinity School—Special Collections (CT–50/24): V 28, N 7–8, 1926.

West China Union University, Chengtu

COLLEGE OF SCIENCE NEWSLETTER. Chengtu.

Yale Divinity School—Special Collections (CT–50/25): N 12, 4, 1940–42.

MONOGRAPH SERIES. Hwasipa, Chengtu. N 1, 1946.

Harvard University—Harvard-Yenching Library (MA–125/6): N 1, 1946.

MUSEUM GUIDEBOOK SERIES. N 1, 1945.

American Museum of Natural History Library (NY–140/1): N 2, 7, 1945.

Field Museum of Natural History Library (IL–40/1): N 1–2, 6–7, 10, 1945, 1947.

Harvard University—Fine Arts Library (MA–115/1): N 1–2, 7, 9, 1945.

Harvard University—Harvard-Yenching Library (MA–125/6): N 1–3, 6–7, 9, 1945.

Harvard University—Peabody Museum (MA–145/1): N 1–11, 1943–47.

Smithsonian Institution—Freer Gallery of Art Library (DC–160/2): N 1–, 1945–.

MUSEUM OF ARCHEOLOGY, ART AND ETHNOLOGY, TRANSLATION SERIES.

Harvard University—Peabody Museum (MA–145/1): N 2, 1946.

NEWS BULLETIN.
> Yale Divinity School—Special Collections (CT–50/25): V 1, N 1–4; V 2, N 1–3; V 3, N 2–3; V 4, N 3; V 5, N 1–3; V 6, N 1–2; 1946–48.

OFFPRINT SERIES.
> Harvard University—Harvard-Yenching Library (MA–125/6): N 8, 1945.

> Harvard University—Peabody Museum (MA–145/1): N 8, 1945.

STUDIA SERICA. West China Union University, Chinese Cultural Studies Research Institute, Chengtu. V 1-, 1940- (in Chinese and English).
> Field Museum of Natural History Library (IL–40/1): V 1, N 1–3, 1940–41.

> Yale Divinity School—Special Collections (CT–50/25): V 1, part 1, 1940.

WESTMINSTER COLLEGE MAGAZINE. Chinchow. V 1–7(?), 1917–25(?).
> Union Theological Seminary—Burke Library (NY–275/1): V 1, N 1; V 2, N 1–2; V 6, N 1–2; V 7, N 1; 1917–18, 1923, 1925.

WOMAN'S MISSIONARY FRIEND. Boston. V 1–73, N 7, 1869-Ag 1940.
> Title varies: HEATHEN WOMAN'S FRIEND, 1869-Je 1896.
> Cornell University—Wason Collection (NY–95/1): V 2, N 11–12; V 3, N 5; V 4, N 7, 11–12; V 5, N 2, 9–12; V 6, N 2–12; V 7, N 2–12; V 8, N 2–5, 7–8, 10–12; V 12, N 7, 10; V 13–15; V 16, N 1–9, 11–12; V 17–50; 1870–1918.

WOMAN'S WORK IN THE FAR EAST. American Presbyterian Mission Press, Shanghai. V 1–42, 1877–87, 1890–1921.
> Title varies: WOMAN'S WORK IN CHINA, V 1–10. Publication suspended 1888–89.
> Cornell University—Wason Collection (NY–95/1): V 1–41, 1877–87, 1890–1920.
> Presbyterian Historical Society—Archives and Library (PA–200/28): V 15, N 1, V 18–32, Ag 1894, 1897–1911.
> Union Theological Seminary—Burke Library (NY–275/1): V 1–42, 1877–87, 1890–1900, 1920–21.

THE WORD FOR GOD IN CHINESE. Commercial Press, Shanghai. V 1, 1914.
> Biola University—Rose Memorial Library (CA–130/1): V 1, N 1–2, 5, S-O, 1914, Ja 1915.
> Union Theological Seminary—Burke Library (NY–275/1): S-D 1914, Ja-F, Ap, O-D 1915, Ja 1916.

WORK IN CHINA. American Presbyterian Mission Press, Shanghai. V 1, 1888.
> Presbyterian Historical Society—Archives and Library (PA–200/28): V 1, N 1, Ja 1888.

WUCHOW BAPTIST MISSIONER. Southern Baptist. Wuchow.
> Union Theological Seminary—Burke Library (NY–275/1): Jl, O 1920.

Yale University, New Haven
> YALE ALUMNI WEEKLY. Yale-in-China.
> > Union Theological Seminary—Burke Library (NY–275/1): N 26, 1922.
> YALE-CHINA NEWSLETTER. New Haven.
> > Continued by CHINA UPDATE: The Yale-China Association Newsletter.
> > Asian Studies Newsletter Archives (MD–40/1): 1965–79 (inc.).

YALE-IN-CHINA NEWSLETTER. Yale-in-China Association, New Haven.
> Yale University—Manuscripts and Archives (CT–60/32): 1924, 1963–73.

YALE-IN-CHINA NEWSLETTER TO CONTRIBUTORS. Yale-in-China Association, New Haven.
> Yale University—Manuscripts and Archives (CT–60/32): 1937–38.

YALE-IN-CHINA: Occasional Bulletin. Changsha. N 1, 1918.
> Union Theological Seminary—Burke Library (NY–275/1): S 1918; S 1919; Ap 1920; D 1937; Ja, Ap, S 1938.
> Yale University—Manuscripts and Archives (CT–60/32): N 1–4 and unnumbered, 1918–20, 1937–38.

YALE-IN-CHINA OCCASIONAL NOTES. Changsha.
> Yale University—Manuscripts and Archives (CT–60/32): 1904–5.

THE YALE-IN-CHINA STUDENT. Changsha. V 1, 1917.
> Yale University—Manuscripts and Archives (CT–60/32): V 1, N 1–7, 1917–21.

YALE MISSION IN CHINA NEWSLETTER. New Haven.
> Yale University—Manuscripts and Archives (CT–60/32): 1908–9.

YALI NEWS. New Haven/Changsha.
> Yale University—Manuscripts and Archives (CT–60/32): 1934.

YALI NEWS BULLETIN. New Haven.
> Union Theological Seminary—Burke Library (NY–275/1): Je, O, D 1938; Ja, Ap, Je 1939; Ja, Ap, My 1942; My, D 1943; D 1944.
> Yale University—Manuscripts and Archives (CT–60/32): 1938–49, 1951–57.

YALI QUARTERLY. Yale College in China, Changsha; Yale-in-China Association, Yale University, New Haven. V 1–22, O 1916-N 1938.
> Union Theological Seminary—Burke Library (NY–275/1): V 1, N 3-V 22, N 1, 1916–38.
> Yale University—Manuscripts and Archives (CT–60/32): V 1, N 1–5, V 2, N 1, 3–4, V 3, N 1–2, N 12–17, V 6, N 1–3, V 7, N 1, V 8–11, V 12, N 3–4, V 13, N 1–3, V 14, V 15, N 1–2, V 16, N 1–2, V 17, N 2–3, V 18, N 1–3, V 19, N 1–3, V 20, V 21, N 1, V 22, N 1, 1916–38.

YENCHING GAZETTE. *See* Yenching University.

YENCHING INDEX NUMBERS. *See* Yenching University.

YENCHING JOURNAL OF CHINESE STUDIES. *See* Yenching University.

YENCHING JOURNAL OF SOCIAL STUDIES. *See* Yenching University.

YENCHING NEWS LETTER. *See* Yenching University.

YENCHING POLITICAL SCIENCE SERIES. *See* Yenching University.

Yenching University

ARTS AND LETTERS NEWS. College of Arts and Letters, Peking.
>> Yale Divinity School—Special Collections (CT–50/25): V 1, N 1, 1941.

BULLETIN. Yenching University, Peking.
>> Cornell University—Wason Collection (NY–95/1): V 7, N 12, 21, 30; V 9, N 15, 15A, 50; V 10, N 21; V 17, N 20, 24–26; 1925, 1927, 1932.
>> Harvard Divinity School—Andover-Harvard Theological Library (MA–95/2): V 19, N 15-V 25, N 14, Ja 1927-O 1940.
>> Harvard University—Harvard-Yenching Library (MA–125/6): V 10, 17–19, 21, 25, 27, 1927–28, 1932–37, 1940–41, 1947–48.
>> Princeton University—University Archives (NJ–120/2): 1925.
>> Union Theological Seminary—Burke Library (NY–275/1): 1921–27, 1929.
>> University of California, Berkeley—General Library (CA–70/1): 1925–48.

BULLETIN. Department of Biology, Peking. V 1, N 1–4, Ja-Jl 1930.
>> Continued as PEKING NATURAL HISTORY BULLETIN, 1930.
>> Academy of Natural Sciences of Philadelphia Library (PA–135/4): V 1, N 1–4, Ja-Jl 1930.
>> American Museum of Natural History Library (NY–140/1): V 1, N 1–4, 1930.
>> Cornell University—Wason Collection (NY–95/1): V 1, 1930.
>> Harvard University—Museum of Comparative Zoology Library (MA–140/1): V 1, N 1–4, 1930.
>> Kansas State University—Farrell Library (KS–45/1): V 1, 1930.
>> Library of Congress—General Reading Rooms Division (DC–120/1): V 1, N 1–4, Ja-Jl 1930.
>> Marine Biological Laboratories Library (MA–260/1): V 1, N 1–4, 1930.
>> Oregon State University—Kerr Library (OR–5/1): V 1, 1930.
>> Pennsylvania State University—Penn State Room (PA–275/4): 1930.
>> Princeton University—Firestone Library (NJ–100/1): V 1, Ja-Je 1930.
>> Smithsonian Institution—National Museum of Natural History Branch Library (DC–175/1): V 1, 1930.
>> University of California, Berkeley—Biology Library (CA–40/1): V 1, 1930.
>> University of Wisconsin-Madison—Memorial Library (WI–45/1): V 1, N 1–2, 1930.

JOURNAL OF SINOLOGICAL STUDIES. Yenching University, Peking, V 1, 1923.
>> Harvard University—Harvard-Yenching Library (MA–125/6): V 1, N 1, 1923.

NEWS BULLETIN. Yenching University, College of Public Affairs, Peking. N 1–3, Je 1934-Ap 1935; n.s. V 1, 1935-?
>> Title varies: PUBLIC AFFAIRS...OCCASIONAL NEWS, 1934-Ap 1935; QUARTERLY NEWS, Nv 1935-My 1937.

New York Public Library—General Research Division (NY–230/1): Je 1934-Nv 1941.
>> Yale Divinity School—Special Collections (CT–50/25): V 3, N 2–3; V 4, N 1–2; V 5, N 1–3; 1938–40.

OCCASIONAL PAPERS. N 1, 1939.
>> Harvard University—Harvard-Yenching Library (MA–125/6): N 1-?, 1939-?.

PEKING UNIVERSITY MAGAZINE.
>> Yale Divinity School—Special Collections (CT–50/25): V 1, N 1–2, 1919–20.

PUBLIC AFFAIRS. College of Public Affairs, Peking.
>> Yale Divinity School—Special Collections (CT–50/25): N 1–3, 1934–35.

PUBLICATIONS. Series A. Yenching University, Department of Sociology and Social Work, Peking.
>> New York Public Library—General Research Division (NY–230/1): 1929–33.
>> Temple University—Paley Library (PA–210/2): N 32, 1932.

PUBLICATIONS. Series B. Department of Sociology.
>> Columbia University—Butler Library (NY–150/1): N 24, n.d.
>> Harvard Divinity School—Andover-Harvard Theological Library (MA–95/1): N 30, 1932.
>> New York Public Library—General Research Division (NY–230/1): 1922–36.

PUBLICATIONS. Series C. [Monographs and Books]. Department of Sociology and Social Work. N 1–41, 1929(?)-33(?).
>> Cornell University—Wason Collection (NY–95/1): N 21, 1929.
>> Hoover Institution Library (CA–300/1): N 21, 24, 26, 1929–30, 1933.
>> Memphis Theological Seminary Library (TN–40/1): N 6, 1924.
>> New York Public Library—General Research Division (NY–230/1): N 6, 20–21, 23–27, 29–33, 37–41, 1930(?)-?.
>> Stanford University—Green Library (CA–305/1): N 21, 26, 1929, 1933.
>> Temple University—Paley Library (PA–210/2): N 20, 24, n.d.
>> University of Chicago—Regenstein Library (IL–85/1): N 21, 24, 1929–30.

QUARTERLY NEWS. College of Public Affairs, Peking.
>> Yale Divinity School—Special Collections (CT–50/25): V 1, N 1–3; V 2, N 1–3; V 3, N 1; 1935–37.

SCIENCE NOTES. Yenching University, College of Natural Science, Peking. N 1–17, 1934–41.
>> Cornell University—Wason Collection (NY–95/1): N 1–17, 1934–41.
>> Harvard Divinity School—Andover-Harvard Theological Library (MA–95/1): N 2–6, 9–10, 12, 14, Je 1934-Nv 1935, Nv 1936-My 1937, S 1938, Nv 1939.
>> Yale Divinity School—Special Collections (CT–50/25): N 1–17, 1934–41, 1947.

SOCIAL RESEARCH SERIES. Yenching University, Department of Sociology and Social Work, Peking. V 1, 1930.

Columbia University—Butler Library (NY-150/1): V 1, 1930.

Cornell University—Wason Collection (NY-95/1): V 1, 1930.

Harvard University—Widener Library (MA-155/1): V 1, 1930.

Hoover Institution Library (CA-300/1): V 1, 1930.

Johns Hopkins University—Eisenhower Library (MD-10/1): V 1, 1930.

New York Public Library—General Research Division (NY-230/1): V 1, 1930.

Stanford University—Green Library (CA-305/1): V 1, 1930.

Temple University—Paley Library (PA-210/2): V 1, 1930.

Union Theological Seminary—Burke Library (NY-275/1): V 1, 1930.

University of California, Berkeley—Anthropology Library (CA-25/1): V 1, 1930.

University of California, Berkeley—General Library (CA-70/1): V 1, 1930.

University of Michigan—Hatcher Graduate Library (MI-25/1): V 1, 1930.

University of Virginia—Alderman Library (VA-30/1): V 1, 1930.

University of Washington Libraries (WA-45/1): V 1, 1930.

Wellesley College—Clapp Library (MA-245/1): V 1, 1930.

SOCIAL SCIENCES QUARTERLY. Yenching University, Peking. V 1, 1922.

Harvard University—Harvard-Yenching Library (MA-125/6): V 1-3, 1922-25.

SOCIOLOGY FELLOWSHIP NEWS. Yenching University, Department of Sociology and Social Work, Peking. N 1-11, 1930-32(?)

Library of Congress—General Reading Rooms Division (DC-120/1): N 3-4, Mr-Ap 1930.

New York Public Library—General Research Division (NY-230/1): N 4-11, 1930-32 (inc.).

Yale Divinity School—Special Collections (CT-50/25): N 2, 4-6, 1930.

YENCHING BIOLOGICAL NEWS. Department of Biology, Yenching University, Peking.

Union Theological Seminary—Burke Library (NY-275/1): Ja 1932.

YENCHING CATALYST.

Yale Divinity School—Special Collections (CT-50/25): F 1945, S 1946.

YENCHING FACULTY BULLETIN.

Yale Divinity School—Special Collections (CT-50/25): 1928-34, 1936-41, 1945-46 (inc.).

YENCHING FORTNIGHTLY.

Yale Divinity School—Special Collections (CT-50/25): 1945-46.

YENCHING GAZETTE.

Claremont Colleges—Honnold Library (CA-85/1): V 1, N 26-123, Ja 1932-My 1933 (inc.).

Union Theological Seminary—Burke Library (NY-275/1): V 1, N 20-103, Ap-Je, 1932.

Yale Divinity School—Special Collections (CT-50/25): Ja-Mr 1932; supplement, S 1931.

YENCHING INDEX NUMBERS. Yenching University, Department of Economics, Peking. V 1, 1940-?

Continues ACADEMIA SINICA, Institute of Social Sciences, Yenching University, monthly index numbers of the cost of living in Peking.

Cornell University—Wason Collection (NY-95/1): V 1, N 4-12; V 2, N 2-4, 6-8, 1940-41.

Harvard University—Widener Library (MA-155/1): V 1, N 1-8, 10; V 2, N 1-4, 6-8, 1940-41.

New York Public Library—General Research Division (NY-230/1): V 1-2, 1940-41.

Northwestern University Library (IL-115/1): V 1, N 1-10; V 2, N 1-4, 6-8, 1940-41.

Princeton University—Firestone Library (NJ-100/1): V 1, N 1-4, Ja-Ap 1940.

University of Oregon Library (OR-20/2): V 1, N 1-12; V 2, N 1-8, Ja 1940-Ag 1941.

University of Washington Libraries (WA-45/1): V 1, N 1-4, Ja-Ap 1940.

Yale Divinity School—Special Collections (CT-50/25): V 1, N 1-12; V 2, N 1-8; n.v.; 1940-41, 1947-48.

YENCHING JOURNAL.

Union Theological Seminary—Burke Library (NY-275/1): Je, D 1927.

YENCHING JOURNAL OF CHINESE STUDIES (YENCHING HSÜEH PAO). Monograph (English edition of YENCHING JOURNAL OF CHINESE STUDIES). Yenching University, Harvard-Yenching Institute, Peking. V 1, 1932-.

Boston Public Library (MA-30/2): V 12, 1936.

Brooklyn Public Library (NY-50/1): V 12, 1936.

Columbia University—Starr East Asian Library (NY-195/4): V 1-16, 18, 1932-50.

Metropolitan Museum of Art—Watson Library (NY-210/1): N 1-3, 5-6, 17, 1933-41.

New York Public Library—General Research Division (NY-230/1): V 12, 1936.

Princeton University—Firestone Library (NJ-100/1): V 17, 1941.

Princeton University—Gest Oriental Library (NJ-105/1): V 12, 1936.

Syracuse University Archives (NY-375/2): V 1, 1932.

YENCHING JOURNAL OF CHINESE STUDIES (YENCHING HSÜEH PAO). Special Issue. Yenching University, Harvard-Yenching Institute. V 1, Ja 1932-.

New York Public Library—General Research Division (NY-230/1): V 6, 1938.

YENCHING JOURNAL OF CHINESE STUDIES. Supplement. Yenching University, Peking. N 1, 1932.

Harvard University—Harvard-Yenching Library (MA-125/6): N 1, 1932.

Harvard University—Widener Library (MA-155/1): N 1, 1932.

Stanford University—Green Library (CA-305/1): N 1, 1932.

YENCHING JOURNAL OF SOCIAL STUDIES (English). Yenching University, Peking. V 1-, Je 1938-50 (semi-annually).

Suspended Ag 1941-Ag 1948.

American Museum of Natural History Library (NY-140/1): V 4, N 1, 1948.

Case Western Reserve University—Freiberger Library (OH-75/1): V 1-4, 1938-49.

Catholic University of America—Mullen Library (DC-20/1): V1-6, 1938-41, 1948-49.

Claremont Colleges—Honnold Library (CA-85/1): V 1-3, 1938-41.

Columbia University—Starr East Asian Library (NY-195/4): V 2-3, [5], Jl 1939-Jl-1950.

Cornell University—Wason Collection (NY-95/1): V 1-5, N 1, 1938-41, 1948-50.

Duke University—Perkins Library (NC-55/1): V 1-5, 1938-50.

Emory University—Pitts Theology Library (GA-15/5): V 1, N 1-2; V 2, N 2, 1938-39.

Field Museum of Natural History Library (IL-40/1): V 1-3, N 2, 1938-41.

Harvard University—Harvard-Yenching Library (MA-125/6): V 1-5, 1938-41, 1948-50.

Harvard University—Widener Library (MA-155/1): V 1-5, 1938-50.

Hoover Institution Library (CA-300/1): V 1, N 1-V 3, N 3; V 4, N 1-2; V 5, N 7; 1938-41, 1948-50.

Iowa State University Library (IA-5/1): V 1-5, 1938-48, 1950.

Johns Hopkins University—Eisenhower Library (MD-10/1): V 1, N 1, V 2-4; V 5, N 1; 1938-50.

New York Public Library—General Research Division (NY-230/1): V 1-11, 1938-50.

Northwestern University Library (IL-115/1): V 1, 1938-39.

Overseas Missionary Fellowship (PA-265/1): V 1, N 1-V 3, N 2, Je 1938-Ag 1941.

Princeton University—Firestone Library (NJ-100/1): V 1-5, N 1, Je 1938-Jl 1950.

Stanford University—Green Library (CA-305/1): V 1-5, 1938-50.

Temple University—Paley Library (PA-210/2): V 1-3, 1938-41.

Union Theological Seminary—Burke Library (NY-275/1): V 1-2; V 3, N 1-2; V 4, N 1; 1938-40, 1948.

University of Arizona Library (AZ-5/3): V 1-3, 1938-41.

University of California, Berkeley—General Library (CA-70/1): V 1-5, N 1, 1938-50.

University of California, Davis, Library (CA-110/2): V 1-5, N 1, 1938-50.

University of California, Santa Barbara, Library (CA-275/2): V 1-5, 1938-50.

University of Chicago—Regenstein Library (IL-85/1): V 1-5, 1938-50.

University of Illinois at Urbana-Champaign Library (IL-185/1): V 1-5, 1938-50.

University of Oregon Library (OR-20/2): V 1-3, Je 1938-Ag 1941.

University of Pennsylvania—Van Pelt Library (PA-215/1): V 1-, 1938-.

University of Virginia—Alderman Library (VA-30/1): V 1-2; V 3, N 1, 2, 1938-41.

University of Washington Libraries (WA-45/1): V 1-3; V 4, N 1-2; V 5, N 1; Je 1938-Ag 1941, 1948-50.

Washington University—East Asian Library (MO-85/1): V 1-5, 1938-50.

Wellesley College—Clapp Library (MA-245/1): V 4-5, N 1, Ag 1948-Jl 1950.

Yale Divinity School—Special Collections (CT-50/26): 1938-40.

Yale University—Sterling Memorial Library (CT-80/1): V 1-5, 1938-50.

YENCHING JOURNAL OF SOCIAL STUDIES. Monograph. V 1, 1932.

Carnegie Library of Pittsburgh (PA-235/1): V 16, 1936.

University of Pennsylvania—Van Pelt Library (PA-215/1): V 12, 1936.

University of Southern California—Von Kleinsmid Center Library (CA-190/2): N 20, 24, ca. 1936 (?).

YENCHING JOURNAL OF SOCIAL STUDIES. Supplement. V 1, 1932.

Abstracts in English of articles in YENCHING JOURNAL OF SOCIAL STUDIES.

University of Pennsylvania—Van Pelt Library (PA-215/1): n.d.

YENCHING NEWS. Yenching University, New York.

Title varies: -1931, PEKING NEWS.

Columbia University—Starr East Asian Library (NY-195/4): V 1-2, S 1934-Je 1936.

Harvard Divinity School—Andover-Harvard Theological Library (MA-95/2): Ap 1922-Nv 1950.

Harvard University—Harvard-Yenching Library (MA-125/6): V 17, 20, 22-29, 1938, 1941, 1944-50.

Presbyterian Historical Society—Archives and Library (PA-200/28): V 26, N 2; V 27, N 1; Je, Nv 1948.

Princeton University—University Archives (NJ-120/2): V 10, N 3, Nv 1931.

San Francisco Theological Seminary Library (CA-235/2): V 25, N 1, Nv 1946.

Union Theological Seminary—Burke Library (NY-275/1): N 1931; D 1932; Ap 1933; Ap 1934; Ap 1935; D 1938; D 1939; D 1941; Ja 1944; Nv 1946; Nv 1947.

Yale Divinity School—Special Collections (CT-50/25): V 10, N 1-3; V 11, N 1-2; V 12, N 1; V 13, N 1; V 14, N 1; V 15, N 1-2; V 16, N 1-2; V 17, N 1; V 18, N 1; V 19, N 1; V 20, N 1; V 21, N 1; V 22, N 1-2; V 23, N 1-2; V 24, N 1; V 25, N 1-2; V 26, N 1-2; V 27, V 1-2; V 28, N 1-2; V 29, N 1; 1931-41, 1943-50.

YENCHING NEWS. Peking.

Yale Divinity School—Special Collections (CT-50/25): V 1, N 43-74, 78-93; V 2, N 1-3, 15, 30-44, 46-56, 71-72; V 3, N 1, 3, 5, 11-59; V 4, 3-

25; V 5, 1–34; V 6, 1–27, 29–34; V 7, N 1–34; V 8, N 1–14; V 9, N 6; V 10, N 11–12; V 11, N 1–12, 19–20, 22, 24, 26–27, 29–30; 1935–41, 1943–45.

YENCHING NEWS LETTER. Yenching University, Peking.
Yale University—Sterling Memorial Library (CT–80/1): 1936.

YENCHING POLITICAL SCIENCE SERIES. Yenching University, Peking. N 1–20, 1930–33?
Brown University—Rockefeller Library (RI–20/2): N 13, 1931.
Harvard University—Widener Library (MA–155/1): N 1, 6, 8–19, 1929–32.
New York Public Library—General Research Division (NY–230/1): 1929–33.

YENCHING SERIES ON CHINESE INDUSTRY AND TRADE. Yenching University, Peking. V 1–4, 1932–38(?).
Harvard University—Baker Library (MA–105/2): V 2–3, 1933–34.
Harvard University—Widener Library (MA–155/1): V 4, 1937.
New York Public Library—General Research Division (NY–230/1): V 3–4, 1934–38.
Princeton University—Firestone Library (NJ–100/1): V 1–4, 1932–37.
University of Chicago—Regenstein Library (IL–85/1): V 1, 3, 1930, 1934.

YENTA JOURNALISM NEWS. Department of Journalism.
Union Theological Seminary—Burke Library (NY–275/1): Nv 1929, Ja, Jl 1931.
Yale Divinity School—Special Collections (CT–50/25): N 7, 1934.

YENPING PAGODA HERALD. Methodist Episcopal Church, Yenping Conference, Yenping. 1917–.
Union Theological Seminary—Burke Library (NY–275/1): 1918, 1924–36.
University of Oregon—Department of Special Collections (OR–15/6): F, Nv 1927, Ap 1931.
University of Oregon—Department of Special Collections (OR–15/47): V 1, N 2; V 2, N 1–3; V 4, N 3; Mr 1932, Ap 1933, S 1934, S 1935, My 1936.
University of Oregon—Department of Special Collections (OR–15/56): Nv 1927.

"YES OR NO" ECHOES. Young Men's Christian Association.
Union Theological Seminary—Burke Library (NY–275/1): N 1–11, 19–23, 23–27, Nv–D 1924.

YEUNGKONG STATION BIMONTHLY. See Presbyterian Church in the U.S.A.

YI (CHINA MESSAGE). Hong Kong. (English edition)
Graduate Theological Union Library (CA–15/2): 1987–.
Union Theological Seminary—Burke Library (NY–275/1): 1984–.

YMCA. See Young Men's Christian Association of China.

YWCA. See Young Women's Christian Association of China.

YOUNG ASIA: Junior Publication of the China Inland Mission. China Inland Mission, Philadelphia, PA. V 1–26, 1927–52.

Monthly, except July and August.
Continues YOUNG CHINA, V 26, N 4, Ap 1952.
Union Theological Seminary—Burke Library (NY–275/1): V 4, N 8; V 23, N 10–V 26; Ag 1930, D 1949–D 1952.

YOUNG CHINA. Chinese Students (Association), University of Illinois.
Union Theological Seminary—Burke Library (NY–275/1): N 1920; Mr 1924; Ag 1930.

YOUNG CHINA: The Magazine of the Comradeship of China, The Young People's Department of the China Inland Mission. China Inland Mission, Toronto. (North American edition)
Overseas Missionary Fellowship (PA–265/1): V 1–24, 1927–50.
Overseas Missionary Fellowship (PA–265/2): 1927, 1930–32, 1937–41.
Wheaton College—Graham Center Archives (IL–200/50): V 5, Mr 1931.

YOUNG CHINA. World Association of Daily Vacation Bible Schools, New York. V 1–?, 1924–?.
Union Theological Seminary—Burke Library (NY–275/1): V 1, N 9, F 1924.

Young Men's Christian Association of China, Shanghai
CHINESE Y'S MEN'S BULLETIN. Globe Publishing Co., Shanghai.
Yale Divinity School—Special Collections (CT–50/15): N 810, 1946.
FELLOWSHIP NOTES. Office of the National Committee of the Young Men's Christian Associations of China, Shanghai.
Yale Divinity School—Special Collections (CT–50/15): 1930–31, 1933, 1935 (inc.).

Young Women's Christian Association of China
NEWS ITEMS. Young Women's Christian Association of China. V 1–5(?), 1916–19(?).
Union Theological Seminary—Burke Library (NY–275/1): V 1, 3–5, 1916–19.
YWCA MAGAZINE. Young Women's Christian Association of China, Shanghai.
Union Theological Seminary—Burke Library (NY–275/1): Ap, Je, O, N 1922; Ja, Mr–Je 1923.
YWCA NEWS. Young Women's Christian Association of China. Canton.
Union Theological Seminary—Burke Library (NY–275/1): V 3, Ja 1926.
YWCA OUTLOOK. Young Women's Christian Association of China.
Union Theological Seminary—Burke Library (NY–275/1): Ap 1912.

YOUR CHINA LETTER. American Jesuits in China, San Francisco. V 1, Ja 1952.
Continued by CHINA LETTER.
California Province of the Society of Jesus Archives (CA–195/1): V 1, N 1–V 3, N 12, Spring 1952–D 1954.
Georgetown University—Woodstock Theological Center Library (DC–70/4): V 1–3, 1952–54.
Graduate Theological Union Library (CA–15/2): V 2, N 3–5, 7–9, 11–12; V 3, N 4, 7–8, 11–12; 1953–54.

YUNGCHUN HERALD. Methodist Episcopal Church, Conferences, Fukien. V 1, Je 1924.
> Garrett-Evangelical and Seabury-Western Theological Seminaries—United Library (IL–110/1): V [1–2, 4–9], 1924–33.
> Union Theological Seminary—Burke Library (NY–275/1): Je, O 1924, Nv 1927, Nv 1929.

THE YUNNAN CHRISTIAN. For Christ in China, Chinese Christian Mission, Kunming.
> San Jose Bible College Archives (CA–255/1): V 1, N 1–3; V 2, N 1, Je 1947, Je 1948, Nv 1948, Mr 1949.

ZHONGLIAN. China Catholic Communication, Singapore. V 1, Jl 1981.
> Emory University—Pitts Theology Library (GA–15/5): V 1, 1981–85.
> Institute for Chinese-Western Cultural History (CA–245/7): N 16-, Mr 1985-.
> Union Theological Seminary—Burke Library (NY–275/1): 1984-.

Zi-ka-wei Observatoire, Shanghai

ANNALES DE L'OBSERVATOIRE ASTRONOMIQUE DE ZO-SE.
> University of California, Berkeley—Astronomy Library (CA–30/1): V 17, 19–20; V 21, N 4, 7; V 22, N 1; 1929, 1936–40, 1942.

BULLETIN AEROLOGIQUE. Observatoire météorologique de Zi-ka-wei, Hankow, et Zi-ka-wei. V 1, 1931.
> University of California, Berkeley—General Library (CA–70/1): V 1–13, Ja 1931-Jl 1937.

BULLETIN DES OBSERVATIONS. Imprimerie de la mission catholique, Shanghai.
> Title varies: BULLETIN MENSUELLE, V 3–26.
> University of California, Berkeley—General Library (CA–70/1): V 1–14, 18–19, 21–26, 36(?), 37–64, 1874–88, 1892–93, 1895–1900, 1910(?), 1911–38.

BULLETIN DES OBSERVATIONS. Fasc. A: Magnétisme Terrestre. Imprimerie de la mission catholique à l'orphelinat de T'ou-se-we, Shanghai.
> Continues in part BULLETIN DES OBSERVATIONS. Continued by She shan kuan hsiang t'ai, OBSERVATIONS MAGNETIQUES.
> Center for Research Libraries (IL–25/4): V 31–33, 1905–7.

BULLETIN DES OBSERVATIONS. Fasc. B: Météorologie, 1906–7. Imprimerie de la mission catholique à l'orphelinat de T'ou-se-we, Shanghai.
> Continues in part BULLETIN DES OBSERVATIONS. Combined with BULLETIN DES OBSERVATIONS. Fasc. C: Sismologie to re-form BULLETIN DES OBSERVATIONS.
> Center for Research Libraries (IL–25/4): V 32–33, 1906–7.

BULLETIN DES OBSERVATIONS. Fasc. C: Sismologie. Imprimerie de la mission catholique à l'orphelinat de T'ou-se-we, Shanghai.
> Continues in part BULLETIN DES OBSERVATIONS. Combined with BULLETIN DES OBSERVATIONS. Fasc. B: Météorologie to re-form BULLETIN DES OBSERVATIONS.
> Center for Research Libraries (IL–25/4): V 31, 1905.

BULLETIN MENSUEL DE L'OBSERVATOIRE MAGNETIQUE ET METEOROLOGIQUE DE ZI-KA-WEI. Imprimerie de la mission catholique à l'orphelinat de T'ou-se-we, Shanghai.
> Continued by: BULLETIN DES OBSERVATIONS.
> Center for Research Libraries (IL–25/4): V 8–11, 13–14, 19, 1882–85, 1887–88, 1893.

NOTES DE METEOROLOGIE PHYSIQUE. Observatoire de météorologie de Zi-ka-wei, Shanghai. 1934–39.
> University of California, Berkeley—General Library (CA–70/1): V 1–9, 1934–39.

REVUE MENSUELLE. Observatoire de météorologie de Zi-ka-wei, Shanghai.
> University of California, Berkeley—General Library (CA–70/1): N 1–421, 1913–40.

Oral Histories

Repositories which hold the "China Missionaries Oral History Collection" are listed on page 500, following the list of individuals below.

Adolph, Harold: Wheaton College—Graham Center Archives (IL-200/1)

Ady, Merrill Steele: *See* "China Missionaries Oral History Collection"

Akins, Ethel M.: American Lutheran Church Archives (MN-95/1)

Allen, Netta Powell: *See* "China Missionaries Oral History Collection"

Anderson, Alice K.: American Lutheran Church Archives (MN-95/2)

Anderson, Clara: American Lutheran Church Archives (MN-95/3)

Anderson, Colena M.: American Lutheran Church Archives (MN-95/4)

Anderson, John Peter: Andrews University—Adventist Heritage Center (MI-45/1)

Anderson, Julian: St. Francis Convent (WI-70/1)

Anderson, Viola: American Lutheran Church Archives (MN-95/5)

Andrews, John Nevins: *See* "China Missionaries Oral History Collection"

Angus, William: Hope College Archives (MI-105/4)
New Brunswick Theological Seminary—Archives of the Reformed Church of America (NJ-60/3)

Au, Edith: Maryknoll Fathers and Brothers Archives (NY-110/1)
Maryknoll Sisters of St. Dominic—Maryknoll Sisters Archives (NY-120/1)

Au, Maureen: Maryknoll Fathers and Brothers Archives (NY-110/1)
Maryknoll Sisters of St. Dominic—Maryknoll Sisters Archives (NY-120/1)

Avett, M. Louise: East Carolina University—East Carolina Manuscript Collection (NC-70/1)

Babione, Jude: Maryknoll Fathers and Brothers Archives (NY-110/1)
Maryknoll Sisters of St. Dominic—Maryknoll Sisters Archives (NY-120/1)

Bagalawis, A. J.: Maryknoll Fathers and Brothers Archives (NY-110/1)
Maryknoll Sisters of St. Dominic—Maryknoll Sisters Archives (NY-120/1)

Baker, James Chamberlain: *See* "China Missionaries Oral History Collection"

Ball, Robert: American Lutheran Church Archives (MN-95/6)

Bartel, Susan Schultz: Center for Mennonite Brethren Studies—Archives and Historical Library (CA-115/1)
Wheaton College—Graham Center Archives (IL-200/5)

Basto, Candida Maria: Maryknoll Sisters of St. Dominic—Maryknoll Sisters Archives (NY-120/1)
University of Virginia—Manuscripts Department (VA-25/1)

Bauman, Elizabeth: Maryknoll Sisters of St. Dominic—Maryknoll Sisters Archives (NY-120/1)

Baumann, Marie Elise: Maryknoll Sisters of St. Dominic—Maryknoll Sisters Archives (NY-120/1)

Bayle, Monica Marie: Maryknoll Sisters of St. Dominic—Maryknoll Sisters Archives (NY-120/1)

Beach, Kay Haines: American Lutheran Church Archives (MN-95/7)

Beals, Zephaniah Charles: Aurora University—Phillips Library (IL-10/1)

Bear, James E.: Union Theological Seminary in Virginia Archives (VA-80/1)

Beschel, Theresa: Sisters of Charity of St. Elizabeth—Generalate Archives (NJ-15/1)

Bly, Herman: American Lutheran Church Archives (MN-95/8)
St. Olaf College Archives (MN-70/5)

Bone, Nancy: Maryknoll Sisters of St. Dominic—Maryknoll Sisters Archives (NY-120/1)

Bowen, Katharine Giltinan: Minnesota Historical Society—Division of Archives and Manuscripts (MN-105/1)

Boyle, Monica Marie: Maryknoll Sisters of St. Dominic—Maryknoll Sisters Archives (NY-120/1)

Brachtesende, Amata: Maryknoll Sisters of St. Dominic—Maryknoll Sisters Archives (NY-120/1)

Brack, Thomas: Maryknoll Fathers and Brothers Archives (NY-110/1)

Maryknoll Sisters of St. Dominic—Maryknoll Sisters Archives (NY–120/1)

Bradley, Colombiere: Maryknoll Sisters of St. Dominic—Maryknoll Sisters Archives (NY–120/1)

Bradley, Kathleen: Maryknoll Sisters of St. Dominic—Maryknoll Sisters Archives (NY–120/1)

Bradshaw, Homer Vernon: *See* "China Missionaries Oral History Collection"

Brennan, John: California Province of the Society of Jesus Archives (CA–195/1)

Brielmaier, Ann Carol: Maryknoll Sisters of St. Dominic—Maryknoll Sisters Archives (NY–120/1)

Bright, Carrie McMullen: American Lutheran Church Archives (MN–95/9)

Broekema, Ruth: Hope College Archives (MI–105/4)
New Brunswick Theological Seminary—Archives of the Reformed Church of America (NJ–60/3)

Brophy, Edna: Maryknoll Sisters of St. Dominic—Maryknoll Sisters Archives (NY–120/1)

Browne, Thomas P.: St. John's University Archives (NY–105/1)

Bruce, Elizabeth G.: Hope College Archives (MI–105/4)
New Brunswick Theological Seminary—Archives of the Reformed Church of America (NJ–60/3)

Bruhl, Heinz: American Lutheran Church Archives (MN–95/10)

Bryan, F. Catharine: Southern Baptist Convention—Archives (VA–65/2)

Buck, Pearl Sydenstricker: Louisville Presbyterian Theological Seminary Library (KY–45/1)

Caha, Ernest: American Lutheran Church Archives (MN–95/11)

Cain, Mary de Ricci: Maryknoll Sisters of St. Dominic—Maryknoll Sisters Archives (NY–120/1)

Campbell, Louise: Yale Divinity School—Special Collections (CT–50/6)

Carlson, Carol: Wheaton College—Graham Center Archives (IL–200/9)

Carlson, Robert Dean: Wheaton College—Graham Center Archives (IL–200/10)

Carney, Veronica Marie: Maryknoll Sisters of St. Dominic—Maryknoll Sisters Archives (NY–120/1)

Carvalho, Cecilia: Maryknoll Sisters of St. Dominic—Maryknoll Sisters Archives (NY–120/1)

Cassidy, Bertha: Aurora University—Phillips Library (IL–10/1)

Cauthen, Baker J.: Southern Baptist Convention—Archives (VA–65/2)

Cauthen, Eloise Glass: Southern Baptist Convention—Archives (VA–65/2)
Wallace Memorial Baptist Church (TN–35/1)

Cavert, H. Mead: American Lutheran Church Archives (MN–95/13)

Cazale, Agnes: Maryknoll Sisters of St. Dominic—Maryknoll Sisters Archives (NY–120/1)

Chan, Philomena: Maryknoll Fathers and Brothers Archives (NY–110/1)
Maryknoll Sisters of St. Dominic—Maryknoll Sisters Archives (NY–120/1)

Chan, Rose: Maryknoll Fathers and Brothers Archives (NY–110/1)
Maryknoll Sisters of St. Dominic—Maryknoll Sisters Archives (NY–120/1)

Chang, Yau-weh: American Lutheran Church Archives (MN–95/14)

Chao, Benedictus: American Lutheran Church Archives (MN–95/15)

Chatigny, Donat: Maryknoll Fathers and Brothers Archives (NY–110/1)
Maryknoll Sisters of St. Dominic—Maryknoll Sisters Archives (NY–120/1)

Chen, Dominica: Franciscan Sisters of Perpetual Adoration Generalate (WI–15/1)

Chen, Joachim: Maryknoll Fathers and Brothers Archives (NY–110/1)
Maryknoll Sisters of St. Dominic—Maryknoll Sisters Archives (NY–120/1)

Chen, Stephen: Maryknoll Fathers and Brothers Archives (NY–110/1)
Maryknoll Sisters of St. Dominic—Maryknoll Sisters Archives (NY–120/1)

Cheng, Mary Gerard: Sisters of Charity Motherhouse Archives (OH–165/1)

Cheuk Chiu-yin: Maryknoll Fathers and Brothers Archives (NY–110/1)
Maryknoll Sisters of St. Dominic—Maryknoll Sisters Archives (NY–120/1)

Cheuk Yee-chiu: Maryknoll Fathers and Brothers Archives (NY–110/1)
Maryknoll Sisters of St. Dominic—Maryknoll Sisters Archives (NY–120/1)

Cheuk York-mong: Maryknoll Fathers and Brothers Archives (NY–110/1)
Maryknoll Sisters of St. Dominic—Maryknoll Sisters Archives (NY–120/1)

Cheung, Andrew: Maryknoll Fathers and Brothers Archives (NY–110/1)
Maryknoll Sisters of St. Dominic—Maryknoll Sisters Archives (NY–120/1)

Cheung Hin-yau: American Lutheran Church Archives (MN–95/16)

Cheung, Paul: Maryknoll Fathers and Brothers Archives (NY–110/1)
Maryknoll Sisters of St. Dominic—Maryknoll Sisters Archives (NY–120/1)

Chin, Francis Roberta: Sisters of Charity Motherhouse Archives (OH–165/1)

Chin, John C. (*Chin Chung-an*): Wheaton College—Graham Center Archives (IL–200/11)

Chin, Rose: Maryknoll Fathers and Brothers Archives (NY–110/1)
Maryknoll Sisters of St. Dominic—Maryknoll Sisters Archives (NY–120/1)

Chiou, Teresa Mary: Sisters of Charity Motherhouse Archives (OH–165/1)

Chou, Ivy: American Lutheran Church Archives (MN–95/17)

Chow, Agnes: Maryknoll Fathers and Brothers Archives (NY–110/1)
Maryknoll Sisters of St. Dominic—Maryknoll Sisters Archives (NY–120/1)

Chow, Maria: Sisters of Charity Motherhouse Archives (OH–165/1)

Christianson, Leila Partridge: American Lutheran Church Archives (MN–95/18)

Christie, William: Christian and Missionary Alliance—Simpson Historical Library (NY–305/8)

Chu, Daniel: American Lutheran Church Archives (MN–95/19)

Chum, Peter: Maryknoll Fathers and Brothers Archives (NY–110/1)
Maryknoll Sisters of St. Dominic—Maryknoll Sisters Archives (NY–120/1)

Chung Kwok-kwan: Maryknoll Fathers and Brothers Archives (NY–110/1)
Maryknoll Sisters of St. Dominic—Maryknoll Sisters Archives (NY–120/1)

Clementia, Sister: Hospital Sisters of the Third Order of St. Francis—St. Francis Convent Archives (IL–155/1)

Clements, Anne: Maryknoll Sisters of St. Dominic—Maryknoll Sisters Archives (NY–120/1)

Clifford, Douglas: American Lutheran Church Archives (MN–95/20)

Clifford, John W.: California Province of the Society of Jesus Archives (CA–195/1)

Colby, Arthur J.: St. John's University Archives (NY–105/1)

Collins, Cornelia: Maryknoll Sisters of St. Dominic—Maryknoll Sisters Archives (NY–120/1)

Comber, John: Maryknoll Fathers and Brothers Archives (NY–110/1)
Maryknoll Sisters of St. Dominic—Maryknoll Sisters Archives (NY–120/1)

Comber, Rita Claire: Maryknoll Sisters of St. Dominic—Maryknoll Sisters Archives (NY–120/1)
University of Virginia—Manuscripts Department (VA–25/1)

Confer, Bernard: Lutheran Council in the U.S.A.—Archives of Cooperative Lutheranism (NY–205/2)

Conner, Marie: Wallace Memorial Baptist Church (TN–35/1)

Costanza, Mary Theophane: Sisters of Charity Motherhouse Archives (OH–165/1)

Coupe, Eucharista: Maryknoll Sisters of St. Dominic—Maryknoll Sisters Archives (NY–120/1)

Coveny, Angela Marie: Maryknoll Sisters of St. Dominic—Maryknoll Sisters Archives (NY–120/1)

Cowman, Lettie: Asbury Theological Seminary—Special Collections (KY–85/1)

Cox, Cordelia: Lutheran Council in the U.S.A.—Archives of Cooperative Lutheranism (NY–205/2)

Cranston, Earl: *See* "China Missionaries Oral History Collection"

Cranston, Mildred (Welch): *See* "China Missionaries Oral History Collection"

Crawford, Robert P.: St. John's University Archives (NY–105/1)

Crawley, Winston: Wallace Memorial Baptist Church (TN–35/1)

Cross, Rowland McLean: American Lutheran Church Archives (MN–95/21)
See also "China Missionaries Oral History Collection"

Crossett, Margaret Rice Elliott: Wheaton College—Graham Center Archives (IL–200/15)

Crossett, Vincent Leroy: Wheaton College—Graham Center Archives (IL–200/15)

Crumpsacker, Anna: Church of the Brethren General Board—Brethren Historical Library and Archives (IL–105/1)

Culpepper, Charles L., Sr.: Southern Baptist Convention—Archives (VA–65/2)
Wallace Memorial Baptist Church (TN–35/1)

Cunningham, Henrietta: Maryknoll Sisters of St. Dominic—Maryknoll Sisters Archives (NY–120/1)

Curtis, Lawrence D.: St. John's University Archives (NY–105/1)

Dahlin, Helen Depass: American Lutheran Church Archives (MN–95/22)

Dahlstrom, Earl: American Lutheran Church Archives (MN–95/23)

Daley, Timothy: Maryknoll Fathers and Brothers Archives (NY–110/1)
Maryknoll Sisters of St. Dominic—Maryknoll Sisters Archives (NY–120/1)

Daly, Charles: Maryknoll Fathers and Brothers Archives (NY–110/1)
Maryknoll Sisters of St. Dominic—Maryknoll Sisters Archives (NY–120/1)

Daubert, Francis: Maryknoll Fathers and Brothers Archives (NY–110/1)
Maryknoll Sisters of St. Dominic—Maryknoll Sisters Archives (NY–120/1)

Davis, Eugene: St. John's University Archives (NY–105/1)

Debrecht, Rose Duchesne: Maryknoll Sisters of St. Dominic—Maryknoll Sisters Archives (NY–120/1)

Dennis, Allan: Maryknoll Fathers and Brothers Archives (NY–110/1)
Maryknoll Sisters of St. Dominic—Maryknoll Sisters Archives (NY–120/1)

Depass, Morris Barnett: American Lutheran Church Archives (MN–95/24)

Dessel, Dulcissima: University of Virginia—Manuscripts Department (VA–25/1)

Devlin, Agnes: Maryknoll Sisters of St. Dominic—Maryknoll Sisters Archives (NY–120/1)

Deward, Ralph: California Province of the Society of Jesus Archives (CA–195/1)

Diggins, Mary: Maryknoll Sisters of St. Dominic—Maryknoll Sisters Archives (NY–120/1)

Dizney, Helen: *See* "China Missionaries Oral History Collection"

Dodds, Jack: American Lutheran Church Archives (MN–95/25)

Doherty, Grace: Maryknoll Sisters of St. Dominic—Maryknoll Sisters Archives (NY–120/1)

Domke, Paul Clifford: American Lutheran Church Archives (MN–95/26)
Carleton College Archives (MN–50/1)

Downey, Richard: Maryknoll Fathers and Brothers Archives (NY–110/1)
Maryknoll Sisters of St. Dominic—Maryknoll Sisters Archives (NY–120/1)

Drew, John: Maryknoll Fathers and Brothers Archives (NY–110/1)
Maryknoll Sisters of St. Dominic—Maryknoll Sisters Archives (NY–120/1)

Driscoll, John: Maryknoll Fathers and Brothers Archives (NY–110/1)
Maryknoll Sisters of St. Dominic—Maryknoll Sisters Archives (NY–120/1)

Duchesne, Paul J.: Maryknoll Fathers and Brothers Archives (NY–110/1)
Maryknoll Sisters of St. Dominic—Maryknoll Sisters Archives (NY–120/1)
University of Virginia—Manuscripts Department (VA–25/1)

Duffy, Maurice: Maryknoll Fathers and Brothers Archives (NY–110/1)

Maryknoll Sisters of St. Dominic—Maryknoll Sisters Archives (NY–120/1)

Dunker, C. Stephen: University of Virginia—Manuscripts Department (VA–25/1)

Dunlap, Albert: Rockefeller University—Rockefeller Foundation Archives (NY–295/7)

Dunn, Ann Majella: Sisters of Charity Motherhouse Archives (OH–165/1)

Early, Joseph: Maryknoll Fathers and Brothers Archives (NY–110/1)

Maryknoll Sisters of St. Dominic—Maryknoll Sisters Archives (NY–120/1)

Ebeling, William: Biola University—Rose Memorial Library (CA–130/3)

Edmonds, Stephen: Maryknoll Fathers and Brothers Archives (NY–110/1)

Maryknoll Sisters of St. Dominic—Maryknoll Sisters Archives (NY–120/1)

Eggleston, William: Maryknoll Fathers and Brothers Archives (NY–110/1)

Maryknoll Sisters of St. Dominic—Maryknoll Sisters Archives (NY–120/1)

Ekvall, Emma: Wheaton College—Graham Center Archives (IL–200/17)

Ekvall, Robert Brainerd: Wheaton College—Graham Center Archives (IL–200/18)

Elliot, Herbert: Maryknoll Fathers and Brothers Archives (NY–110/1)

Maryknoll Sisters of St. Dominic—Maryknoll Sisters Archives (NY–120/1)

Elliott, Eleanor Ruth: Wheaton College—Graham Center Archives (IL–200/20)

Embery, Doris: Wheaton College—Graham Center Archives (IL–200/21)

Erikson, Alma: Nebraska Wesleyan University—United Methodist Historical Center (NB–15/1)

Erling, Astrid: American Lutheran Church Archives (MN–95/27)

Erny, Esther: Asbury Theological Seminary—Special Collections (KY–85/1)

Erny, Eugene: Asbury Theological Seminary—Special Collections (KY–85/1)

Eubank, Dillard Marion: American Lutheran Church Archives (MN–95/28)

Evans, Ruth: Maryknoll Sisters of St. Dominic—Maryknoll Sisters Archives (NY–120/1)

Fahy, Eugene: California Province of the Society of Jesus Archives (CA–195/1)

Faries, McIntyre: University of California, Berkeley—Bancroft Library (CA–35/4)

Farrell, Ann Mary: Maryknoll Sisters of St. Dominic—Maryknoll Sisters Archives (NY–120/1)

Faulkner, Cyril: *See* "China Missionaries Oral History Collection"

Fedders, Albert V.: Maryknoll Fathers and Brothers Archives (NY–110/1)

Maryknoll Sisters of St. Dominic—Maryknoll Sisters Archives (NY–120/1)

University of Virginia—Manuscripts Department (VA–25/1)

Felsecker, Henry: Maryknoll Fathers and Brothers Archives (NY–110/1)

Maryknoll Sisters of St. Dominic—Maryknoll Sisters Archives (NY–120/1)

Fischer, Viola I.: American Lutheran Church Archives (MN–95/30)

Fitzgerald, James E.: Maryknoll Fathers and Brothers Archives (NY–110/1)

Maryknoll Sisters of St. Dominic—Maryknoll Sisters Archives (NY–120/1)

Fitzwilliam, Jennie: Wheaton College—Graham Center Archives (IL–200/25)

Flagg, Virginia: Maryknoll Sisters of St. Dominic—Maryknoll Sisters Archives (NY–120/1)

Flavey, Mark A.: California Province of the Society of Jesus Archives (CA–195/1)

Fogarty, Irene: Maryknoll Sisters of St. Dominic—Maryknoll Sisters Archives (NY–120/1)

Ford, Ruth Lucille: Southern Baptist Convention—Archives (VA–65/2)

Wallace Memorial Baptist Church (TN–35/1)

Foster, Jane Armour: American Lutheran Church Archives (MN–95/32)

Foster, John: American Lutheran Church Archives (MN–95/33)

Foster, John Hess: Colby College—Miller Library (ME–25/2)

Frame, Helen Nowack: Wheaton College—Graham Center Archives (IL–200/27)

Frank, Emeline: American Lutheran Church Archives (MN–95/34)

Frank, Henry S.: American Lutheran Church Archives (MN–95/35)

Frank, Herbert S.: American Lutheran Church Archives (MN–95/36)

Frank, Maxine: Franciscan Sisters of Perpetual Adoration Generalate (WI–15/1)

Franks, Martha: Southern Baptist Convention—Archives (VA–65/2)

Friberg, H. Daniel: American Lutheran Church Archives (MN–95/37)

Friberg, Joseph Bertil: American Lutheran Church Archives (MN–95/38)

Fries, Optata: Franciscan Sisters of Perpetual Adoration Generalate (WI–15/1)

Frillman, Paul: Columbia University—Rare Book and Manuscript Library (NY–175/6)

Frisch, Angelica: University of Virginia—Manuscripts Department (VA–25/1)

Fuhr, Godfrey: Maryknoll Sisters of St. Dominic—Maryknoll Sisters Archives (NY–120/1)

Fuller, Glenn V.: *See* "China Missionaries Oral History Collection"

Fulton, Anne Edwards: American Lutheran Church Archives (MN–95/39)

Yale Divinity School—Special Collections (CT–50/7)

Fulton, Robert Brank: American Lutheran Church Archives (MN–95/40)

Yale Divinity School—Special Collections (CT–50/7)

Furey, Christella: Maryknoll Sisters of St. Dominic—Maryknoll Sisters Archives (NY–120/1)

Furlong, Philip: Maryknoll Fathers and Brothers Archives (NY–110/1)
Maryknoll Sisters of St. Dominic—Maryknoll Sisters Archives (NY–120/1)

Gaalswyk, Arie: American Lutheran Church Archives (MN–95/41)

Gaiero, Michael: Maryknoll Fathers and Brothers Archives (NY–110/1)
Maryknoll Sisters of St. Dominic—Maryknoll Sisters Archives (NY–120/1)

Gallagher, Mary Gerard: Maryknoll Sisters of St. Dominic—Maryknoll Sisters Archives (NY–120/1)

Gallagher, Rose Bernadette: Maryknoll Sisters of St. Dominic—Maryknoll Sisters Archives (NY–120/1)

Galloway, Betty: Wallace Memorial Baptist Church (TN–35/1)

Garvey, Justin: Congregation of the Passion of the Eastern United States (Passionists)—Chronicle Office (MA–255/1)

Gaspard, Raymond: Maryknoll Fathers and Brothers Archives (NY–110/1)
Maryknoll Sisters of St. Dominic—Maryknoll Sisters Archives (NY–120/1)

Gehring, Frederick P.: St. John's University Archives (NY–105/1)

Geselbracht, Howard: Maryknoll Fathers and Brothers Archives (NY–110/1)
Maryknoll Sisters of St. Dominic—Maryknoll Sisters Archives (NY–120/1)

Gieser, Paul Kenneth: Wheaton College—Graham Center Archives (IL–200/30)

Gilbert, Sylvio: Maryknoll Fathers and Brothers Archives (NY–110/1)
Maryknoll Sisters of St. Dominic—Maryknoll Sisters Archives (NY–120/1)

Gilbertson, Ruth: American Lutheran Church Archives (MN–95/42)
St. Olaf College Archives (MN–70/5)

Glass, Lloyd: Maryknoll Fathers and Brothers Archives (NY–110/1)
Maryknoll Sisters of St. Dominic—Maryknoll Sisters Archives (NY–120/1)

Glass, Lois C.: Southern Baptist Convention—Archives (VA–65/2)

Gonyou, Fabiola: Maryknoll Sisters of St. Dominic—Maryknoll Sisters Archives (NY–120/1)

Goulter, Oswald John: Phillips University—Rogers Graduate Seminary Library (OK–5/1)
See also "China Missionaries Oral History Collection"

Granskou, Clemens: American Lutheran Church Archives (MN–95/43)
St. Olaf College Archives (MN–70/5)

Granskou, Ella Odland: American Lutheran Church Archives (MN–95/44)

Graser, John: Maryknoll Fathers and Brothers Archives (NY–110/1)
Maryknoll Sisters of St. Dominic—Maryknoll Sisters Archives (NY–120/1)

Green, Jessie L.: Southern Baptist Convention—Archives (VA–65/2)

Greene, Robert: Maryknoll Fathers and Brothers Archives (NY–110/1)

Maryknoll Sisters of St. Dominic—Maryknoll Sisters Archives (NY–120/1)

Gregory, Quentin: East Carolina University—East Carolina Manuscript Collection (NC–70/11)

Groell, Clara: St. John's University Archives (NY–105/1)

Grondin, Therese: Maryknoll Sisters of St. Dominic—Maryknoll Sisters Archives (NY–120/1)

Groves, Blanche: Women's Missionary Union Archives (AL–10/2)

Guerrieri, Antonia M.: Maryknoll Sisters of St. Dominic—Maryknoll Sisters Archives (NY–120/1)

Guidera, M. Dominic: Maryknoll Sisters of St. Dominic—Maryknoll Sisters Archives (NY–120/1)

Guttery, Arthur M.: University of Oregon—Special Collections (OR–15/23)

Hahn, Joseph: Maryknoll Fathers and Brothers Archives
Maryknoll Sisters of St. Dominic—Maryknoll Sisters Archives (NY–120/1)

Hanan, Rose Benigna: Maryknoll Sisters of St. Dominic—Maryknoll Sisters Archives (NY–120/1)

Hannigan, Julia: Maryknoll Sisters of St. Dominic—Maryknoll Sisters Archives (NY–120/1)

Hanson, Anders B.: American Lutheran Church Archives (MN–95/45)

Hanson, Constance Twedt: American Lutheran Church Archives (MN–95/46)

Hanson, Orvis: American Lutheran Church Archives (MN–95/47)

Hautman, Frances Maria: Sisters of Charity Motherhouse Archives (OH–165/1)

Hayes, Barbara M.: Presbyterian Historical Society—Archives and Library (PA–200/28)

Hayes, Edward Pearce: See "China Missionaries Oral History Collection"

Hayes, Egbert M.: See "China Missionaries Oral History Collection"

Hayes, Everley: Wallace Memorial Baptist Church (TN–35/1)

Hayes, Helen: American Lutheran Church Archives (MN–95/49)

Hayes, John David: Presbyterian Historical Society—Archives and Library (PA–200/28)

Hayes, Paul G.: American Lutheran Church Archives (MN–95/50)

Heaney, Marie Amadea: Sisters of Charity Motherhouse Archives (OH–165/1)

Heemskerk, John: Maryknoll Fathers and Brothers Archives (NY–110/1)
Maryknoll Sisters of St. Dominic—Maryknoll Sisters Archives (NY–120/1)

Heininger, Alfred Dixon: See "China Missionaries Oral History Collection"

Henry, John J.: St. John's University Archives (NY–105/1)

Herrgen, Corita: Maryknoll Sisters of St. Dominic—Maryknoll Sisters Archives (NY–120/1)

Hersey, John: Radcliffe College—Schlesinger Library (MA–165/7)

Hertz, Catherine Reynolds: American Lutheran Church Archives (MN–95/51)

Hertz, Edwin: American Lutheran Church Archives (MN–95/52)

Higgins, Agnes Virginia: Maryknoll Sisters of St. Dominic—Maryknoll Sisters Archives (NY–120/1)

Hill, Eugene: Southern Baptist Convention—Archives (VA–65/2)

Wallace Memorial Baptist Church (TN–35/1)

Hill, Jack: Hope College Archives (MI–105/4)

New Brunswick Theological Seminary—Archives of the Reformed Church of America (NJ–60/3)

Hill, Joanne: Hope College Archives (MI–105/4)

New Brunswick Theological Seminary—Archives of the Reformed Church of America (NJ–60/3)

Hill, Joseph J.: St. John's University Archives (NY–105/1)

Hill, Viola Caroline: American Baptist Historical Society (NY–345/16)

Hirst, Cyril: Maryknoll Fathers and Brothers Archives (NY–110/1)

Maryknoll Sisters of St. Dominic—Maryknoll Sisters Archives (NY–120/1)

Hock, Mary Augusta: Maryknoll Sisters of St. Dominic—Maryknoll Sisters Archives (NY–120/1)

Hockman, Robert: Wheaton College—Graham Center Archives (IL–200/36)

Hockman, Winifred: Wheaton College—Graham Center Archives (IL–200/36)

Hodges, Paul: Rockefeller University—Rockefeller Foundation Archives (NY–290/7)

Hoffman, Paulita: Maryknoll Sisters of St. Dominic—Maryknoll Sisters Archives (NY–120/1)

Hofstra, Johanna: Hope College Archives (MI–105/4)

New Brunswick Theological Seminary—Archives of the Reformed Church of America (NJ–60/3)

Hohlfeld, Raymond: Maryknoll Fathers and Brothers Archives (NY–110/1)

Maryknoll Sisters of St. Dominic—Maryknoll Sisters Archives (NY–120/1)

Holleman, Clarence H.: *See* "China Missionaries Oral History Collection"

Hollfelder, Teresa: Maryknoll Sisters of St. Dominic—Maryknoll Sisters Archives (NY–120/1)

Houghton, Henry S.: Rockefeller University—Rockefeller Foundation Archives (NY–290/7)

Houle, John: California Province of the Society of Jesus Archives (CA–195/1)

Houston, Lyda Suydam: *See* "China Missionaries Oral History Collection"

Hsia, Tsang Shiu-ngo Sheila: Church of Jesus Christ of Latter-day Saints—Historical Department (UT–15/1)

Hsio, Anna: Asbury Theological Seminary—Special Collections (KY–85/1)

Hsu Hua: Loma Linda University—Radcliffe Memorial Library (CA–135/1)

Pacific Union College—Nelson Memorial Library (CA–5/1)

Hughes, Elizabeth: American Lutheran Church Archives (MN–95/53)

Hunt, Bruce Finley: Wheaton College—Graham Center Archives (IL–200/38)

Hutchins, Louise Gilman: Berea College—Special Collections (KY–5/1)

Radcliffe College—Schlesinger Library (MA–165/2)

Hyde, Agnes Holstad: American Lutheran Church Archives (MN–95/54)

St. Olaf College Archives (MN–70/5)

Hylbert, Ethel Lacey: *See* "China Missionaries Oral History Collection"

I, Marie Alphonse: Sisters of Charity Motherhouse Archives (OH–165/1)

Ikenberry, Ernest Leroy: Church of the Brethren General Board—Brethren Historical Library and Archives (IL–105/11)

See also "China Missionaries Oral History Collection"

Jaramillo, Marie Cor.: Maryknoll Sisters of St. Dominic—Maryknoll Sisters Archives (NY–120/1)

Jarvis, Anna Moffet: American Lutheran Church Archives (MN–95/55)

Jefferies, Lee: Asbury Theological Seminary—Special Collections (KY–85/1)

Johnson, Lydia: *See* "China Missionaries Oral History Collection"

Johnson, Nelson Trusler: Yale University—Department of Manuscripts and Archives (CT–60/14)

Jones, Clara: American Lutheran Church Archives (MN–95/56)

St. Olaf College Archives (MN–70/5)

Jones, Francis Price: *See* "China Missionaries Oral History Collection"

Jones, Lucile Williams: *See* "China Missionaries Oral History Collection"

Jones, Henry D.: Presbyterian Historical Society—Archives and Library (PA–200/28)

Jong Kin-shum: Maryknoll Fathers and Brothers Archives (NY–110/1)

Maryknoll Sisters of St. Dominic—Maryknoll Sisters Archives (NY–120/1)

Joyce, John: Maryknoll Fathers and Brothers Archives (NY–110/1)

Maryknoll Sisters of St. Dominic—Maryknoll Sisters Archives (NY–120/1)

Judd, Walter: American Lutheran Church Archives (MN–95/57)

Columbia University—Rare Book and Manuscript Library (NY–175/6)

Dwight D. Eisenhower Library (KS–5/5)

Harry S. Truman Library (MO–20/1)

Jung, Margaret: Maryknoll Sisters of St. Dominic—Maryknoll Sisters Archives (NY–120/1)

K'an, Clara Li: Church of the Brethren General Board—Brethren Historical Library and Archives (IL–105/1)

K'an, Kenneth: Church of the Brethren General Board—Brethren Historical Library and Archives (IL–105/1)

Kane, James Herbert: Wheaton College—Graham Center Archives (IL–200/40)

Kane, Joseph Marie: Maryknoll Sisters of St. Dominic—Maryknoll Sisters Archives (NY–120/1)

Kane, Winnifred: Wheaton College—Graham Center Archives (IL–200/40)

Karlon, Madeline Sophie: Maryknoll Sisters of St. Dominic—Maryknoll Sisters Archives (NY–120/1)

Kaschmitter, William: Maryknoll Fathers and Brothers Archives (NY–110/1)

Maryknoll Sisters of St. Dominic—Maryknoll Sisters Archives (NY–120/1)

Kellogg, Claude Rupert: *See* "China Missionaries Oral History Collection"

Kennedy, Mary Alban: Sisters of Charity Motherhouse Archives (OH–165/1)

Kerrigan, Mary Ellen: Maryknoll Sisters of St. Dominic—Maryknoll Sisters Archives (NY–120/1)

Kettle, Rosalie: Maryknoll Sisters of St. Dominic—Maryknoll Sisters Archives (NY–120/1)

Kiernan, Thomas: Maryknoll Fathers and Brothers Archives (NY–110/1)
Maryknoll Sisters of St. Dominic—Maryknoll Sisters Archives (NY–120/1)

Kilbourne, Edwin L.: Asbury Theological Seminary—Special Collections (KY–85/1)

Killoran, Theresa: Maryknoll Sisters of St. Dominic—Maryknoll Sisters Archives (NY–120/1)

Kim, Margaret: Maryknoll Sisters of St. Dominic—Maryknoll Sisters Archives (NY–120/1)

Kingman, Harry Lees: University of California, Berkeley—Bancroft Library (CA–35/6)

Klaeser, Albert: California Province of the Society of Jesus Archives (CA–195/1)

Knotek, Wenceslaus: Maryknoll Fathers and Brothers Archives (NY–110/1)
Maryknoll Sisters of St. Dominic—Maryknoll Sisters Archives (NY–120/1)

Koo, Pauline: Maryknoll Fathers and Brothers Archives (NY–110/1)
Maryknoll Sisters of St. Dominic—Maryknoll Sisters Archives (NY–120/1)

Kraus, Mary Concepta: Sisters of Charity Motherhouse Archives (OH–165/1)

Kroeger, Louise: Maryknoll Sisters of St. Dominic—Maryknoll Sisters Archives (NY–120/1)

Kupfer, William: Maryknoll Fathers and Brothers Archives (NY–110/1)
Maryknoll Sisters of St. Dominic—Maryknoll Sisters Archives (NY–120/1)

Lam, Joseph: Maryknoll Fathers and Brothers Archives (NY–110/1)
Maryknoll Sisters of St. Dominic—Maryknoll Sisters Archives (NY–120/1)

Lam, Rose: Maryknoll Fathers and Brothers Archives (NY–110/1)
Maryknoll Sisters of St. Dominic—Maryknoll Sisters Archives (NY–120/1)

Lam Ying: American Lutheran Church Archives (MN–95/14)

Landahl, Lillian: American Lutheran Church Archives (MN–95/59)
St. Olaf College Archives (MN–70/5)

Latimer, Mary Lee Nelson: *See* "China Missionaries Oral History Collection"

Lau, Thomas: Maryknoll Fathers and Brothers Archives (NY–110/1)
Maryknoll Sisters of St. Dominic—Maryknoll Sisters Archives (NY–120/1)

Lawlor, John J.: St. John's University Archives (NY–105/1)

Lawson, Tyra: American Lutheran Church Archives (MN–95/60)

Lawton, Deaver: Wallace Memorial Baptist Church (TN–35/1)

Lawton, Dorothy: Wallace Memorial Baptist Church (TN–35/1)

Leavell, Cornelia Frances: Mississippi College—Speed Library (MS–10/1)
Wallace Memorial Baptist Church (TN–35/1)

Lechthaler, Miriam: Maryknoll Sisters of St. Dominic—Maryknoll Sisters Archives (NY–120/1)

Lee, Catherine: Maryknoll Fathers and Brothers Archives (NY–110/1)
Maryknoll Sisters of St. Dominic—Maryknoll Sisters Archives (NY–120/1)

Lee, David: American Lutheran Church Archives (MN–95/67)
St. Olaf College Archives (MN–70/5)

Lee, Leatitia: Maryknoll Fathers and Brothers Archives (NY–110/1)
Maryknoll Sisters of St. Dominic—Maryknoll Sisters Archives (NY–120/1)

Lei, Paul: Maryknoll Fathers and Brothers Archives (NY–110/1)
Maryknoll Sisters of St. Dominic—Maryknoll Sisters Archives (NY–120/1)

Leonard, Doretta: Maryknoll Sisters of St. Dominic—Maryknoll Sisters Archives (NY–120/1)

Leung Kit-fong: Maryknoll Fathers and Brothers Archives (NY–110/1)
Maryknoll Sisters of St. Dominic—Maryknoll Sisters Archives (NY–120/1)

Leung Wai-fan: Maryknoll Fathers and Brothers Archives (NY–110/1)
Maryknoll Sisters of St. Dominic—Maryknoll Sisters Archives (NY–120/1)

Li, Thomas: Maryknoll Fathers and Brothers Archives (NY–110/1)
Maryknoll Sisters of St. Dominic—Maryknoll Sisters Archives (NY–120/1)

Ling, Joan: Maryknoll Fathers and Brothers Archives (NY–110/1)
Maryknoll Sisters of St. Dominic—Maryknoll Sisters Archives (NY–120/1)

Ling, Maurice Clet: Sisters of Charity Motherhouse Archives (OH–165/1)

Little, Marie Huttenlock: Wheaton College—Graham Center Archives (IL–200/43)

Liu, Beatrice: American Lutheran Church Archives (MN–95/62)

Liu Hon-ching: Maryknoll Fathers and Brothers Archives (NY–110/1)
Maryknoll Sisters of St. Dominic—Maryknoll Sisters Archives (NY–120/1)

Liu Jui-heng: Columbia University—Rare Book and Manuscript Library (NY–175/9)

Liu, Paul Vincent: Sisters of Charity Motherhouse Archives (OH–165/1)

Loeffler, Vincent C.: St. John's University Archives (NY–105/1)

Loftus, John Joseph: *See* "China Missionaries Oral History Collection"

Lord, George: Presbyterian Historical Society—Archives and Library (PA–200/28)

Lovegren, Millie: Wallace Memorial Baptist Church (TN–35/1)

Lucier, Jessie: Maryknoll Sisters of St. Dominic—Maryknoll Sisters Archives (NY–120/1)

Lueders, Albert: Lutheran Council in the U.S.A.—Archives of Cooperative Lutheranism (NY–205/2)

Lundeen, Reuben A.: Lutheran Council in the U.S.A.—Archives of Cooperative Lutheranism (NY–205/2)

Lynas, Jean: Sisters of Charity of St. Elizabeth—Generalate Archives (NJ–15/1)

Lynch, Francis: University of Virginia—Manuscripts Department (VA–25/1)

Ma, Nathan: American Lutheran Church Archives (MN–95/64)

Ma, Peter: Maryknoll Fathers and Brothers Archives (NY–110/1)
Maryknoll Sisters of St. Dominic—Maryknoll Sisters Archives (NY–120/1)

McCabe, Edwin: Maryknoll Fathers and Brothers Archives (NY–110/1)
Maryknoll Sisters of St. Dominic—Maryknoll Sisters Archives (NY–120/1)

McCaine, Pearle: East Carolina University—East Carolina Manuscript Collection (NC–70/14)

McCallum, James Henry: *See* "China Missionaries Oral History Collection"

McCarthy, Charles: California Province of the Society of Jesus Archives (CA–195/1)

McCarthy, Leo: Maryknoll Fathers and Brothers Archives (NY–110/1)
Maryknoll Sisters of St. Dominic—Maryknoll Sisters Archives (NY–120/1)

McCormick, Mary Colmcille: *See* "China Missionaries Oral History Collection"

McGinn, John: Maryknoll Fathers and Brothers Archives (NY–110/1)
Maryknoll Sisters of St. Dominic—Maryknoll Sisters Archives (NY–120/1)

McGuire, Frederick A.: Maryknoll Fathers and Brothers Archives (NY–110/1)
Maryknoll Sisters of St. Dominic—Maryknoll Sisters Archives (NY–120/1)
St. John's University Archives (NY–105/1)

McGurkin, Edward: Maryknoll Fathers and Brothers Archives (NY–110/1)
Maryknoll Sisters of St. Dominic—Maryknoll Sisters Archives (NY–120/1)

MacInnis, Donald: American Lutheran Church Archives (MN–95/65)

MacInnis, Helen: American Lutheran Church Archives (MN–95/66)

MacKay, John Alexander: Princeton University—Rare Books and Manuscripts—General Holdings (NJ–135/1)

McKeirnan, Michael: Maryknoll Fathers and Brothers Archives (NY–110/1)
Maryknoll Sisters of St. Dominic—Maryknoll Sisters Archives (NY–120/1)

McKenna, Mary DeLellis: Maryknoll Sisters of St. Dominic—Maryknoll Sisters Archives (NY–120/1)

McKenna, Mary Paul: Maryknoll Sisters of St. Dominic—Maryknoll Sisters Archives (NY–120/1)

McLaughlin, James: Maryknoll Fathers and Brothers Archives (NY–110/1)
Maryknoll Sisters of St. Dominic—Maryknoll Sisters Archives (NY–120/1)

McNally, Ignatius: Maryknoll Sisters of St. Dominic—Maryknoll Sisters Archives (NY–120/1)

MacRae, Francis: Maryknoll Fathers and Brothers Archives (NY–110/1)
Maryknoll Sisters of St. Dominic—Maryknoll Sisters Archives (NY–120/1)

Magner, J. F.: University of Virginia—Manuscripts Department (VA–25/1)

Makra, Lelia: Maryknoll Sisters of St. Dominic—Maryknoll Sisters Archives (NY–120/1)

Malone, Ann: Maryknoll Sisters of St. Dominic—Maryknoll Sisters Archives (NY–120/1)

Manning, Edward: Maryknoll Fathers and Brothers Archives (NY–110/1)
Maryknoll Sisters of St. Dominic—Maryknoll Sisters Archives (NY–120/1)

Manning, Santa Maria: Maryknoll Sisters of St. Dominic—Maryknoll Sisters Archives (NY–120/1)

Mao, Lucia: Sisters of Charity Motherhouse Archives (OH–165/1)

Marlowe, Rose: Southern Baptist Convention—Archives (VA–65/2)

Marrow, Jane Gregory: East Carolina University—East Carolina Manuscript Collection (NC–70/15)

Marsland, F. de Sales: Maryknoll Sisters of St. Dominic—Maryknoll Sisters Archives (NY–120/1)

Martin, Estelle Lee: American Lutheran Church Archives (MN–95/67)
St. Olaf College Archives (MN–70/5)

Martin, Mary Lou: Maryknoll Sisters of St. Dominic—Maryknoll Sisters Archives (NY–120/1)

Martinson, Cora: American Lutheran Church Archives (MN–95/8)
St. Olaf College Archives (MN–70/5)

Melvin, Francis J.: St. John's University Archives (NY–105/1)

Menig, Walter J.: St. John's University Archives (NY–105/1)

Mersinger, Barbara R.: Maryknoll Sisters of St. Dominic—Maryknoll Sisters Archives (NY–120/1)

Mihelko, John: Maryknoll Fathers and Brothers Archives (NY–110/1)
Maryknoll Sisters of St. Dominic—Maryknoll Sisters Archives (NY–120/1)

Miles, Frank: American Lutheran Church Archives (MN–95/69)

Miller, Harry: Loma Linda University—Radcliffe Memorial Library (CA–135/1)

Minning, James T.: Maryknoll Fathers and Brothers Archives (NY–110/1)
Maryknoll Sisters of St. Dominic—Maryknoll Sisters Archives (NY–120/1)

Moon, Lottie: Women's Missionary Union Archives (AL–10/2)

Moore, John: Maryknoll Fathers and Brothers Archives (NY–110/1)
Maryknoll Sisters of St. Dominic—Maryknoll Sisters Archives (NY–120/1)

Moran, Brice: University of Virginia—Manuscripts Department (VA–25/1)

Morgan, Agnes: Wallace Memorial Baptist Church (TN–35/1)

Morgan, Carter: Wallace Memorial Baptist Church (TN–35/1)

Morrissey, William: Maryknoll Fathers and Brothers Archives (NY–110/1)
Maryknoll Sisters of St. Dominic—Maryknoll Sisters Archives (NY–120/1)

Mottey, Paul: St. John's University Archives (NY–105/1)

Moynan, Mary Goforth: Wheaton College—Graham Center Archives (IL–200/47)

Muehlenbein, Wibora: American Lutheran Church Archives (MN–95/71)

Muench, Esther: St. Francis Convent (WI–70/1)

Mueth, Edward: Maryknoll Fathers and Brothers Archives (NY–110/1)
Maryknoll Sisters of St. Dominic—Maryknoll Sisters Archives (NY–120/1)

Mug, Miriam Xavier: Maryknoll Sisters of St. Dominic—Maryknoll Sisters Archives (NY–120/1)

Mullen, Francis: Maryknoll Fathers and Brothers Archives (NY–110/1)
Maryknoll Sisters of St. Dominic—Maryknoll Sisters Archives (NY–120/1)

Munday, John J.: St. John's University Archives (NY–105/1)

Murphy, Edward: California Province of the Society of Jesus Archives (CA–195/1)

Murphy, Frances: Maryknoll Sisters of St. Dominic—Maryknoll Sisters Archives (NY–120/1)

Murphy, Francis: Maryknoll Fathers and Brothers Archives (NY–110/1)
Maryknoll Sisters of St. Dominic—Maryknoll Sisters Archives (NY–120/1)

Murray, Edward A.: St. John's University Archives (NY–105/1)

Murray, Katie: East Carolina University—East Carolina Manuscript Collection (NC–70/16)

Nelson, Lillian Olson: American Lutheran Church Archives (MN–95/72)
St. Olaf College Archives (MN–70/5)

Nelson, Russell E.: American Lutheran Church Archives (MN–95/73)

Nilsen, Frida: American Lutheran Church Archives (MN–95/74)
St. Olaf College Archives (MN–70/5)

Nordlund, Mildred: American Lutheran Church Archives (MN–95/75)

Normandin, Andree: Maryknoll Sisters of St. Dominic—Maryknoll Sisters Archives (NY–120/1)

Nugent, Irwin: Maryknoll Fathers and Brothers Archives (NY–110/1)
Maryknoll Sisters of St. Dominic—Maryknoll Sisters Archives (NY–120/1)

O'Connell, Michael: Maryknoll Fathers and Brothers Archives (NY–110/1)
Maryknoll Sisters of St. Dominic—Maryknoll Sisters Archives (NY–120/1)

O'Connor, Charles J.: St. John's University Archives (NY–105/1)

O'Gara, Cuthbert M.: Sisters of Charity of St. Elizabeth—Generalate Archives (NJ–15/1)

O'Hagan, Joan Catherine: Maryknoll Sisters of St. Dominic—Maryknoll Sisters Archives (NY–120/1)

O'Hara, Albert: California Province of the Society of Jesus Archives (CA–195/1)
University of Virginia—Manuscripts Department (VA–25/1)

O'Leary, Mary Angelica: Maryknoll Sisters of St. Dominic—Maryknoll Sisters Archives (NY–120/1)

O'Neill, Francis J.: University of Virginia—Manuscripts Department (VA–25/1)

Oliver, Jay Charles: *See* "China Missionaries Oral History Collection"

Oltman, Theodore V.: Hope College Archives (MI–105/4).
New Brunswick Theological Seminary—Archives of the Reformed Church of America (NJ–60/3)

Osborn, Leon C.: Church of the Nazarene International Headquarters—Nazarene Archives (MO–25/7)

Overholt, Olive: American Lutheran Church Archives (MN–95/76)

Overholt, William: American Lutheran Church Archives (MN–95/77)

Owyang, Joseph Ignatius: Sisters of Charity Motherhouse Archives (OH–165/1)

Pai, Protase: Maryknoll Fathers and Brothers Archives (NY–110/1)
Maryknoll Sisters of St. Dominic—Maryknoll Sisters Archives (NY–120/1)
University of Virginia—Manuscripts Department (VA–25/1)

Pang, Paul: Maryknoll Fathers and Brothers Archives (NY–110/1)
Maryknoll Sisters of St. Dominic—Maryknoll Sisters Archives (NY–120/1)

Parker, Lucy Wright: Southern Baptist Convention—Archives (VA–65/2)
Wallace Memorial Baptist Church (TN–35/1)

Pender, Auria: Southern Baptist Convention—Archives (VA–65/2)

Penney, Truman: American Lutheran Church Archives (MN–95/78)

Perkins, Sara: Presbyterian Historical Society—Archives and Library (PA–200/28)

Peterson, Iola Aalbue: American Lutheran Church Archives (MN–95/79)
St. Olaf College Archives (MN–70/5)

Petley, Bernard: Maryknoll Fathers and Brothers Archives (NY–110/1)
Maryknoll Sisters of St. Dominic—Maryknoll Sisters Archives (NY–120/1)

Pfeilschifter, Boniface: University of Virginia—Manuscripts Department (VA–25/1)

Pheur, William: Maryknoll Fathers and Brothers Archives (NY–110/1)
Maryknoll Sisters of St. Dominic—Maryknoll Sisters Archives (NY–120/1)

Phillippe, Garnett: Asbury Theological Seminary—Special Collections (KY–85/1)

Phillips, Thomas: California Province of the Society of Jesus Archives (CA–195/1)

Platz, Jesse: Hope College Archives (MI–105/4)
New Brunswick Theological Seminary—Archives of the Reformed Church of America (NJ–60/3)

Pope, Gerald: California Province of the Society of Jesus Archives (CA–195/1)

Pouliot, Francis: Maryknoll Fathers and Brothers Archives (NY–110/1)
Maryknoll Sisters of St. Dominic—Maryknoll Sisters Archives (NY–120/1)

Pruitt, Ida: Radcliffe College—Schlesinger Library (MA–165/5)

Pulaski, Joseph: Maryknoll Fathers and Brothers Archives (NY–110/1)
Maryknoll Sisters of St. Dominic—Maryknoll Sisters Archives (NY–120/1)

Putnam, George: Maryknoll Fathers and Brothers Archives (NY–110/1)

Maryknoll Sisters of St. Dominic—Maryknoll Sisters Archives (NY–120/1)

Qiu Runduan: Maryknoll Fathers and Brothers Archives (NY–110/1)

Maryknoll Sisters of St. Dominic—Maryknoll Sisters Archives (NY–120/1)

Quimby, Paul: Loma Linda University—Radcliffe Memorial Library (CA–135/1)

Pacific Union College—Nelson Memorial Library (CA–5/1)

Quinn, Carroll: Maryknoll Fathers and Brothers Archives (NY–110/1)

Maryknoll Sisters of St. Dominic—Maryknoll Sisters Archives (NY–120/1)

Rafferty, Agnes Regina: Maryknoll Sisters of St. Dominic—Maryknoll Sisters Archives (NY–120/1)

Rankin, Samuel G.: Wallace Memorial Baptist Church (TN–35/1)

Reed, Alice Clara: *See* "China Missionaries Oral History Collection"

Refo, Henry: American Lutheran Church Archives (MN–95/80)

Refo, Muriel Lockwood: American Lutheran Church Archives (MN–95/81)

Regan, Joseph: Maryknoll Fathers and Brothers Archives (NY–110/1)

Maryknoll Sisters of St. Dominic—Maryknoll Sisters Archives (NY–120/1)

Regan, Rita Marie: Maryknoll Sisters of St. Dominic—Maryknoll Sisters Archives (NY–120/1)

Reilly, Peter: Maryknoll Fathers and Brothers Archives (NY–110/1)

Maryknoll Sisters of St. Dominic—Maryknoll Sisters Archives (NY–120/1)

University of Virginia—Manuscripts Department (VA–25/1)

Rempe, Hubertine: University of Virginia—Manuscripts Department (VA–25/1)

Renich, Helen Torrey: Wheaton College—Graham Center Archives (IL–200/55)

Revers, Thaddeus: Maryknoll Fathers and Brothers Archives (NY–110/1)

Maryknoll Sisters of St. Dominic—Maryknoll Sisters Archives (NY–120/1)

Riconda, Ruth: Maryknoll Sisters of St. Dominic—Maryknoll Sisters Archives (NY–120/1)

Riddell, Olive Pauline: Southern Baptist Convention—Archives (VA–65/2)

Riehl, Moira: Maryknoll Sisters of St. Dominic—Maryknoll Sisters Archives (NY–120/1)

University of Virginia—Manuscripts Department (VA–25/1)

Rietz, Edith: Maryknoll Sisters of St. Dominic—Maryknoll Sisters Archives (NY–120/1)

Roisum, Alma: American Lutheran Church Archives (MN–95/82)

St. Olaf College Archives (MN–70/5)

Rost, Corinne: Maryknoll Sisters of St. Dominic—Maryknoll Sisters Archives (NY–120/1)

Rouleau, Francis: California Province of the Society of Jesus Archives (CA–195/1)

Rowley, Grace May: Claremont Colleges—Asian Studies Collection (CA–75/2)

See also "China Missionaries Oral History Collection"

Roy, Andrew Todd: Presbyterian Historical Society—Archives and Library (PA–200/28)

Rubner, Dorothy: Maryknoll Sisters of St. Dominic—Maryknoll Sisters Archives (NY–120/1)

Rude, James: California Province of the Society of Jesus Archives (CA–195/1)

Rudin, Harry: Yale University—Department of Manuscripts and Archives (CT–60/32)

Ruland, Lloyd S.: Presbyterian Historical Society—Archives and Library (PA–200/28)

Russell, Maud: American Lutheran Church Archives (MN–95/83)

Rutledge, Arthur: California Province of the Society of Jesus Archives (CA–195/1)

Sailer, Randolph: American Lutheran Church Archives (MN–95/84)

Yale Divinity School—Special Collections (CT–50/7)

Salzman, Esther I.: Wheaton College—Graham Center Archives (IL–200/56)

Saunders, Mary Lucile: Wallace Memorial Baptist Church (TN–35/1)

Sawyer, Helen Irvin: Wheaton College—Graham Center Archives (IL–200/57)

Sawyer, Malcolm: Wheaton College—Graham Center Archives (IL–200/57)

Schafers, Mary: Maryknoll Sisters of St. Dominic—Maryknoll Sisters Archives (NY–120/1)

Schiotz, Frederik: American Lutheran Church Archives (MN–95/85)

St. Olaf College Archives (MN–70/5)

Schmidt, Charles: Maryknoll Fathers and Brothers Archives (NY–110/1)

Maryknoll Sisters of St. Dominic—Maryknoll Sisters Archives (NY–120/1)

Schoerner, Katherine Hastings: Wheaton College—Graham Center Archives (IL–200/58)

Schoerner, Otto: Wheaton College—Graham Center Archives (IL–200/59)

Schubert, William E.: Yale Divinity School—Special Collections (CT–50/7)

Schurell, Veronica: St. Francis Convent (WI–70/1)

Scott, Agnes (Kelly): *See* "China Missionaries Oral History Collection"

Scott, Mary: Church of the Nazarene International Headquarters—Nazarene Archives (MO–25/9)

Scott, Roderick: *See* "China Missionaries Oral History Collection"

Scoville, Helen E. and Ralph C.: Overseas Missionary Fellowship (PA–265/3)

Seeck, Margaret: Nebraska Wesleyan University—United Methodist Historical Center (NB–15/1)

Sellon, Lena: Berkshire Christian College—Carter Library (MA–175/1)

Service, John Stewart: University of California, Berkeley—Bancroft Library (CA–35/10)

Sevilla, Christina: Presbyterian Historical Society—Archives and Library (PA–200/28)

Shea, Gemma: Maryknoll Sisters of St. Dominic—Maryknoll Sisters Archives (NY–120/1)

Shea, Kathleen Marie: Maryknoll Sisters of St. Dominic—Maryknoll Sisters Archives (NY–120/1)

Sheridan, Robert: Maryknoll Fathers and Brothers Archives (NY–110/1)
Maryknoll Sisters of St. Dominic—Maryknoll Sisters Archives (NY–120/1)

Sihler, Mabel Wold: American Lutheran Church Archives (MN–95/86)
St. Olaf College Archives (MN–70/5)

Simkin, Margaret Timberlake: *See* "China Missionaries Oral History Collection"

Slattery, Dennis: Maryknoll Fathers and Brothers Archives (NY–110/1)
Maryknoll Sisters of St. Dominic—Maryknoll Sisters Archives (NY–120/1)

Small, Elizabeth Stair: Wheaton College—Graham Center Archives (IL–200/61)

Smith, Gertrude: Wheaton College—Graham Center Archives (IL–200/17)

Smith, Helen: Yale Divinity School—Special Collections (CT–50/7)

Smith, Howard: Wheaton College—Graham Center Archives (IL–200/17)

Smith, James: Maryknoll Fathers and Brothers Archives (NY–110/1)
Maryknoll Sisters of St. Dominic—Maryknoll Sisters Archives (NY–120/1)

Smith, Lucy: Southern Baptist Convention—Archives (VA–65/2)

Smith, Stella: Franciscan Sisters of Perpetual Adoration Generalate (WI–15/1)

Smythe, Lewis Strong Casey: American Lutheran Church Archives (MN–95/87)
See also "China Missionaries Oral History Collection"

Smythe, Margaret Garrett: American Lutheran Church Archives (MN–95/87)
See also "China Missionaries Oral History Collection"

Snuggs, Grace: Southern Baptist Convention—Archives (VA–65/2)

Snuggs, Harold: Southern Baptist Convention—Archives (VA–65/2)

Sovik, Arna Quello: American Lutheran Church Archives (MN–95/88)

Sovik, Arne: American Lutheran Church Archives (MN–95/89).
St. Olaf College Archives (MN–70/5)

Sovik, Edgar: American Lutheran Church Archives (MN–95/90)
St. Olaf College Archives (MN–70/5)

Sovik, Edward: American Lutheran Church Archives (MN–95/91)
St. Olaf College Archives (MN–70/5)

Sovik, Gertrude: American Lutheran Church Archives (MN–95/92)
St. Olaf College Archives (MN70/5)

Sprinkle, Russell: Maryknoll Fathers and Brothers Archives (NY–110/1)
Maryknoll Sisters of St. Dominic—Maryknoll Sisters Archives (NY–120/1)

Stanley, Louise Claire (Hathaway): University of Michigan—Bentley Historical Library (MI–10/9)
See also "China Missionaries Oral History Collection"

Stanley, Margaret: American Lutheran Church Archives (MN–95/93)

Stapleton, Beatrice: Maryknoll Sisters of St. Dominic—Maryknoll Sisters Archives (NY–120/1)

Stauble, Francis J.: St. John's University Archives (NY–105/1)

Steinbauer, Jean Theophane: Maryknoll Sisters of St. Dominic—Maryknoll Sisters Archives (NY–120/1)

Steurt, Marjorie Rankin: *See* "China Missionaries Oral History Collection"

Sticka, Pauline: Maryknoll Sisters of St. Dominic—Maryknoll Sisters Archives (NY–120/1)

Stitz, Herman Joseph: Maryknoll Sisters of St. Dominic—Maryknoll Sisters Archives (NY–120/1)

Stockwell, F. Olin: *See* "China Missionaries Oral History Collection"

Sullivan, Paula: Maryknoll Sisters of St. Dominic—Maryknoll Sisters Archives (NY–120/1)

Sumner, Hildegarde: Sisters of Charity Motherhouse Archives (OH–165/1)

Sundquist, Ruth: Wheaton College—Graham Center Archives (IL–200/64)

Suttie, Melvin: Wheaton College—Graham Center Archives (IL–200/65)

Syrdal, Borghild Roe: American Lutheran Church Archives (MN–95/94)
St. Olaf College Archives (MN–70/5)

Syrdal, Rolf: American Lutheran Church Archives (MN–95/95)
St. Olaf College Archives (MN–70/5)

Szewczyk, Bernice: Daughters of Charity of St. Vincent de Paul—West Central Province Archives (MO–55/1)

Tack, Minnie: American Lutheran Church Archives (MN–95/96)

Tackney, John: Maryknoll Fathers and Brothers Archives (NY–110/1)
Maryknoll Sisters of St. Dominic—Maryknoll Sisters Archives (NY–120/1)

Talman, Rose H.: Hope College Archives (MI–105/4)
New Brunswick Theological Seminary—Archives of the Reformed Church of America (NJ–60/3)

Tang, Dominic: California Province of the Society of Jesus Archives (CA–195/1)
Maryknoll Fathers and Brothers Archives (NY–110/1)
Maryknoll Sisters of St. Dominic—Maryknoll Sisters Archives (NY–120/1)

Terhaar, Donalda: American Lutheran Church Archives (MN–95/97)

Thomson, Diana: Radcliffe College—Schlesinger Library (MA–165/7)

Thomson, James C., Jr.: Radcliffe College—Schlesinger Library (MA–165/7)

Thornton, James: University of Virginia—Manuscripts Department (VA–25/1)

Tilford, Lorene: Southern Baptist Convention—Archives (VA–65/2)

To, Simeon: Maryknoll Fathers and Brothers Archives (NY–110/1)
Maryknoll Sisters of St. Dominic—Maryknoll Sisters Archives (NY–120/1)

Tobin, Chester: American Lutheran Church Archives (MN–95/98)

Tolan, Eunice: Maryknoll Sisters of St. Dominic—Maryknoll Sisters Archives (NY–120/1)

Tombrock, Immaculata: Missionary Sisters of the Immaculate Conception of the Mother of God—Generalate Archives (NJ–155/1)

Tootell, George Thomas: *See* "China Missionaries Oral History Collection"

Topping, William Hill: *See* "China Missionaries Oral History Collection"

Torrey, Reuben Archer, III: Wheaton College—Graham Center Archives (IL–200/71)

Trube, Howard: Maryknoll Fathers and Brothers Archives (NY–110/1)
Maryknoll Sisters of St. Dominic—Maryknoll Sisters Archives (NY–120/1)

Tsa, Michael: Maryknoll Fathers and Brothers Archives (NY–110/1)
Maryknoll Sisters of St. Dominic—Maryknoll Sisters Archives (NY–120/1)

Tsai, Martha Seton: Sisters of Charity Motherhouse Archives (OH–165/1)

Tse, David: Maryknoll Fathers and Brothers Archives (NY–110/1)
Maryknoll Sisters of St. Dominic—Maryknoll Sisters Archives (NY–120/1)

Tse, Eileen: Maryknoll Fathers and Brothers Archives (NY–110/1)
Maryknoll Sisters of St. Dominic—Maryknoll Sisters Archives (NY–120/1)

Tse, John: Maryknoll Fathers and Brothers Archives (NY–110/1)
Maryknoll Sisters of St. Dominic—Maryknoll Sisters Archives (NY–120/1)

Tse, Robert: Maryknoll Fathers and Brothers Archives (NY–110/1)
Maryknoll Sisters of St. Dominic—Maryknoll Sisters Archives (NY–120/1)

Urlacher, Magdalena: Maryknoll Sisters of St. Dominic—Maryknoll Sisters Archives (NY–120/1)

Van Baak, Edward: Calvin College and Seminary Archives (MI–80/9)

Van den Bogaard, Joseph: Maryknoll Fathers and Brothers Archives (NY–110/1)
Maryknoll Sisters of St. Dominic—Maryknoll Sisters Archives (NY–120/1)

Van Putten, James D.: Hope College Archives (MI–105/4)
New Brunswick Theological Seminary—Archives of the Reformed Church of America (NJ–60/3)

Van Wyk, Bertha V.: Hope College Archives (MI–105/4)
New Brunswick Theological Seminary—Archives of the Reformed Church of America (NJ–60/3)

Van Wyk, Gordon J.: Hope College Archives (MI–105/4)
New Brunswick Theological Seminary—Archives of the Reformed Church of America (NJ–60/3)

Vander Meer, Alma: Hope College Archives (MI–105/4)
New Brunswick Theological Seminary—Archives of the Reformed Church of America (NJ–60/3)

Vaskco, Stephen: California Province of the Society of Jesus Archives (CA–195/1)

Veenschoten, Henry M.: Western Theological Seminary—Beardlee Library (MI–120/11)

Veenschoten, Stella Elda: Western Theological Seminary—Beardslee Library (MI–120/11)

Velasco, John: Maryknoll Fathers and Brothers Archives

(NY–110/1)
Maryknoll Sisters of St. Dominic—Maryknoll Sisters Archives (NY–120/1)

Veldman, Harold E.: Hope College Archives (MI–105/4)
New Brunswick Theological Seminary—Archives of the Reformed Church of America (NJ–60/3)

Veldman, Jeannette: Hope College Archives (MI–105/4)
New Brunswick Theological Seminary—Archives of the Reformed Church of America (NJ–60/3)

Veldman, Pearl: Hope College Archives (MI–105/4)
New Brunswick Theological Seminary—Archives of the Reformed Church of America (NJ–60/3)

Venneman, Clara: Maryknoll Sisters of St. Dominic—Maryknoll Sisters Archives (NY–120/1)

Venneman, Espiritu: Maryknoll Sisters of St. Dominic—Maryknoll Sisters Archives (NY–120/1)

Votaw, Maurice E.: University of Missouri, Columbia—Joint Collections (MO–5/5)

Wallace, Franklin: American Lutheran Church Archives (MN–95/100)

Waller, Anne Thomson: Radcliffe College—Schlesinger Library (MA–165/7)

Walling, Norman: California Province of the Society of Jesus Archives (CA–195/1)

Walsh, Dorothy: Maryknoll Sisters of St. Dominic—Maryknoll Sisters Archives (NY–120/1)

Walsh, John J.: Maryknoll Fathers and Brothers Archives (NY–110/1)
Maryknoll Sisters of St. Dominic—Maryknoll Sisters Archives (NY–120/1)

Walter, Leo: Maryknoll Fathers and Brothers Archives (NY–110/1)
Maryknoll Sisters of St. Dominic—Maryknoll Sisters Archives (NY–120/1)

Walvoord, Jenanne: Hope College Archives (MI–105/4)
New Brunswick Theological Seminary—Archives of the Reformed Church of America (NJ–60/3)

Wang, C. C.: American Lutheran Church Archives (MN–95/101)

Ward, Katherine Bertha (Boeye): American Lutheran Church Archives (MN–95/102)
See also "China Missionaries Oral History Collection"

Warner, Elizabeth Howard: Wheaton College—Graham Center Archives (IL–200/74)

Warnshuis, Abbe Livingston: Columbia University—Rare Book and Manuscript Library (NY–175/6)
Yale University—Department of Manuscripts and Archives (CT–60/29)

Watson, Clara: Carleton College Archives (MN–60/1)

Watson, Lila: Southern Baptist Convention—Archives (VA–65/2)

Watson, Percy: Carleton College Archives (MN–60/1)

Watters, Hyla S.: State University of New York at Plattsburgh—Feinberg Library (NY–320/1)

Weber, Rosalie: Maryknoll Sisters of St. Dominic—Maryknoll Sisters Archives (NY–120/1)

Weeks, Wilma: Southern Baptist Convention—Archives (VA–65/2)

Weis, Edward: Maryknoll Fathers and Brothers Archives (NY–110/1)
Maryknoll Sisters of St. Dominic—Maryknoll Sisters Archives (NY–120/1)

Wempe, Francis: Maryknoll Fathers and Brothers Archives (NY–110/1)
Maryknoll Sisters of St. Dominic—Maryknoll Sisters Archives (NY–120/1)

Wenzel, M. Richard: Maryknoll Sisters of St. Dominic—Maryknoll Sisters Archives (NY–120/1)

Werner, Celine: Maryknoll Sisters of St. Dominic—Maryknoll Sisters Archives (NY–120/1)

White, Francis: Maryknoll Fathers and Brothers Archives (NY–110/1)
Maryknoll Sisters of St. Dominic—Maryknoll Sisters Archives (NY–120/1)

White, Marcellus: Congregation of the Passion of the Eastern United States (Passionists)—Chronicle Office (MA–255/1)

Wieland, Bernard: Maryknoll Fathers and Brothers Archives (NY–110/1)
Maryknoll Sisters of St. Dominic—Maryknoll Sisters Archives (NY–120/1)

Wieneke, Agnes Bartel: American Lutheran Church Archives (MN–95/103)

Wiley, Martha: *See* "China Missionaries Oral History Collection"

Williams, Marvin: American Lutheran Church Archives (MN–95/104)

Williams, Orpha: American Lutheran Church Archives (MN–95/105)

Wilson, Martha: Yale Divinity School—Special Collections (CT–50/13)

Wilson, Stanley: Rockefeller University—Rockefeller Foundation Archives (NY–290/7)

Winance, Eleutherius: *See* "China Missionaries Oral History Collection"

Winans, Pearl Beatrice (Fosnot): *See* "China Missionaries Oral History Collection"

Winfield, Gerald F.: Presbyterian Historical Society—Archives and Library (PA–200/28)

Winkels, Robert: Maryknoll Fathers and Brothers Archives (NY–110/1)
Maryknoll Sisters of St. Dominic—Maryknoll Sisters Archives (NY–120/1)

Wold, Waldo: American Lutheran Church Archives (MN–95/106)
St. Olaf College Archives (MN–70/5)

Wolf, Anna D.: Rockefeller University—Rockefeller Foundation Archives (NY–290/7)

Wolff, Ernst: American Lutheran Church Archives (MN–95/107)

Wong, Peter: Maryknoll Fathers and Brothers Archives (NY–110/1)
Maryknoll Sisters of St. Dominic—Maryknoll Sisters Archives (NY–120/1)

Wong, Ruth: Maryknoll Fathers and Brothers Archives (NY–110/1)
Maryknoll Sisters of St. Dominic—Maryknoll Sisters Archives (NY–120/1)

Woodberry, Ora: Christian and Missionary Alliance—Simpson Historical Library (NY–305/6)

Woodward, Frank: Southern Baptist Convention—Archives (VA–65/2)
Wallace Memorial Baptist Church (TN–35/1)

Wu, John: Maryknoll Fathers and Brothers Archives (NY–110/1)
Maryknoll Sisters of St. Dominic—Maryknoll Sisters Archives (NY–120/1)

Wu Ming-chieh: American Lutheran Church Archives (MN–95/108)

Wu Pak-seng: Maryknoll Fathers and Brothers Archives (NY–110/1)
Maryknoll Sisters of St. Dominic—Maryknoll Sisters Archives (NY–120/1)

Xavier, M. Chanel: Maryknoll Sisters of St. Dominic—Maryknoll Sisters Archives (NY–120/1)

Xu Simeng: Maryknoll Fathers and Brothers Archives (NY–110/1)
Maryknoll Sisters of St. Dominic—Maryknoll Sisters Archives (NY–120/1)

Yang, Paul: Maryknoll Fathers and Brothers Archives (NY–110/1)
Maryknoll Sisters of St. Dominic—Maryknoll Sisters Archives (NY–120/1)

Yau Chun-yuen: Maryknoll Fathers and Brothers Archives (NY–110/1)
Maryknoll Sisters of St. Dominic—Maryknoll Sisters Archives (NY–120/1)

Youker, Edward: Maryknoll Fathers and Brothers Archives (NY–110/1)
Maryknoll Sisters of St. Dominic—Maryknoll Sisters Archives (NY–120/1)

Young, Edward W.: St. John's University Archives (NY–105/1)

Young, Grace Hsuen: Aurora University—Phillips Library (IL–10/1)

Young, Mildred Test: American Lutheran Church Archives (MN–95/109)

Yuan, Allen: Church of the Nazarene International Headquarters—Nazarene Archives (MO–25/2)

Yuan, Columba: Sisters of Charity Motherhouse Archives (OH–165/1)

Yuen, Joseph: Maryknoll Fathers and Brothers Archives (NY–110/1)
Maryknoll Sisters of St. Dominic—Maryknoll Sisters Archives (NY–120/1)

Yung Chi-tung: Maryknoll Fathers and Brothers Archives (NY–110/1)
Maryknoll Sisters of St. Dominic—Maryknoll Sisters Archives (NY–120/1)

Ziemba, Stanislaus: Maryknoll Fathers and Brothers Archives (NY–110/1)
Maryknoll Sisters of St. Dominic—Maryknoll Sisters Archives (NY–120/1)

ORAL HISTORIES

China Missionaries Oral History Collection

Photocopies or microform copies of the original transcripts are held by the following repositories:

Baylor University—Moody Memorial Library (TX-60/1)

Biola University—Rose Memorial Library (CA-130/4)

Claremont Colleges—Special Collections Department (CA-80/1-4, 6-10, 12-30, 32-47)

Columbia University—Rare Book and Manuscript Library (NY-175/5)

Cornell University—Wason Collection (NY-95/1)

Duke University—Perkins Library (NC-55/1)

Eastern Kentucky University—Crabbe Library (KY-70/1)

Emory University—Woodruff Library (GA-25/1)

Fuller Theological Seminary—McAlister Library (CA-205/1)

Iowa State University Library (IA-5/1)

Maryknoll Fathers and Brothers Library (NY-110/1)

Northwestern University Library (IL-115/1)

Nyack College Library (NY-310/1)

Ohio State University—Thompson Memorial Library (OH-110/4)

Pennsylvania State University—Penn State Room (PA-275/4)

Pittsburgh Theological Seminary—Barbour Library (PA-240/1)

Princeton University—Firestone Memorial Library (NJ-100/1)

Stanford University—Green Library (CA-305/1)

University of California, Berkeley—Bancroft Library (CA-35/2)

University of California, Santa Cruz—McHenry Library (CA-285/1)

University of Chicago—Regenstein Library (IL-85/1)

University of Cincinnati—Central Library (OH-65/1)

University of Georgia Libraries (GA-5/1)

University of Hawaii—Hamilton Library (HI-15/1)

University of Louisville—Ekstrom Library (KY-55/1)

University of Maryland—McKeldin Library (MD-45/2)

University of Notre Dame—Memorial Library (IN-95/1)

University of Pittsburgh—Hillman Library (PA-260/1)

University of Virginia—Alderman Library (VA-30/1)

University of Washington—Manuscripts and University Archives (WA-40/6)

Washington and Lee University Library (VA-55/3)

Western Theological Seminary—Beardslee Library (MI-120/14)

Wheaton College—Graham Center Archives (IL-200/12)

Yale Divinity School—Special Collections (CT-50/7)

Dissertations/Theses

ABBOTT, Beverly Sue. *Growth and Change in Protestant Missionary Education in Nineteenth-century China*. Ohio State University (M.A.), 1974, 89p.

    Ohio State University—Thompson Memorial Library (OH–110/4)

ADAMS, Archibald Guinness. *Joseph Samuel Adams of China: An Original Contribution to the History of Protestant World Missions in the Form of a Biographical Record of the Missionary Career of His Father*. Union Theological Seminary (Th.D.), 1939, 2 V.

    Union Theological Seminary—Burke Library (NY–275/1)

ADCOCK, Cynthia Letts. *Revolutionary Faithfulness: The Quaker Search for a Peaceable Kingdom in China, 1939-1951*. Bryn Mawr College (Ph.D.), 1974, 316p.

    Bryn Mawr College—Canaday Library (PA–15/3)
    Cornell University—Wason Collection (NY–95/1)
    Duke University—Divinity School Library (NC–30/2)
    Stanford University—Green Library (CA–305/1)
    University of California, Santa Barbara, Library (CA–275/2)
    Whittier College—Wardman Library (CA–330/1)
    Wilmington College Archives (OH–195/1)

AHO, Ilma Ruth. *A Record of the Activities of the Finnish Missionary Society in Northwest Hunan, China, 1902-1952*. University of California, Berkeley (M.A.), 1953, 390p.

    Suomi College—Finnish American Historical Archives (MI–100/1)
    University of California, Berkeley—General Library (CA–70/1)

ALTIERI, Daniel Peter. *The Reaction of Western Commentators to the Taiping Rebellion, with a Concentration on the Writings of Leading Nineteenth-century Protestant Missionaries: A Study in Comparative Historiography*. Brown University (A.M.), 1971, 58p.

    Brown University Archives (RI–10/1)
    Brown University—Hay Library (RI–15/4)

ANDERSON, Mary Raleigh. *Protestant Mission Schools for Girls in South China (1827 to the Japanese Invasion)*. Columbia University (Ph.D.), 1943, 365p.

Bangor Theological Seminary—Moulton Library (ME–5/1)
Baylor University—Moody Memorial Library (TX–60/1)
Brigham Young University—Lee Library (UT–10/1)
Carson-Newman College Library (TN–20/1)
Catholic University of America—Mullen Library (DC–20/1)
Central Baptist Theological Seminary Library (KS–20/1)
Columbia University—Butler Library (NY–150/1)
Cornell University—Wason Collection (NY–95/1)
Garrett-Evangelical and Seabury-Western Theological Seminaries—United Library (IL–110/1)
Indiana University—University Libraries (IN–20/2)
Johns Hopkins University—Eisenhower Library (MD–10/1)
Loma Linda University Library (CA–220/1)
New Orleans Baptist Theological Seminary—Christian Library (LA–15/1)
Northern Illinois University Libraries (IL–95/1)
Public Library of Cincinnati (OH–50/1)
Southern Baptist Convention—Jenkins Research Library (VA–70/1)
Southern Baptist Theological Seminary—Boyce Centennial Library (KY–50/2)
Stanford University—Green Library (CA–305/1)
Stetson University—DuPont-Ball Library (FL–10/1)
Union Theological Seminary—Burke Library (NY–275/1)
University of California, Berkeley—General Library (CA–70/1)
University of Chicago—Regenstein Library (IL–85/1)
University of Georgia Libraries (GA–5/1)
University of Maryland—McKeldin Library (MD–45/2)
University of Minnesota—Wilson Library (MN–40/1)
University of Nebraska—Love Library (NB–25/2)
University of Pennsylvania—Van Pelt Library (PA–215/1)
University of Vermont—Bailey/Howe Library (VT–5/3)
University of Wisconsin-Madison Memorial Library (WI–45/1)

ANDERSON, Ora Margaret. *Present Day Mission Work in Rural China*. Kennedy School of Missions (M.A.), 1934, 104p.

    Hartford Seminary Foundation—Case Memorial Library (CT–15/7)

ANDERSON, Park Harris. *Southern Baptist Contributions to Missions in China: A Survey of Investments and Achievements*. New Orleans Baptist Theological Seminary (Th.D.), 1947, 143p.

American Baptist Historical Society (NY–345/23)

New Orleans Baptist Theological Seminary—Christian Library (LA–15/1)

Wheaton College—Graham Center Library (IL–205/1)

ANDERSON, Park Harris. *A Survey of Southern Baptist Medical Missions to China*. New Orleans Baptist Theological Seminary (Th.M.), 1946, 23p.

New Orleans Baptist Theological Seminary—Christian Library (LA–15/1)

ANDERSON, Vernon E. *The Christian Approach to the Mind and Heart of Confucian China*. Luther Northwestern Theological Seminary (M.A.), 1944, n.p.

Luther Northwestern Theological Seminary Library (MN–100/1)

ANDREWS, Joseph Russell. *J. Hudson Taylor and the China Inland Mission*. Duke University (B.D.), 1950, 95p.

Duke University—Perkins Library (NC–55/1)

ANG, Henry T. *The Role of the Chinese Church in World Missions*. Grace Theological Seminary (M.Div.), 1985, 92p.

Grace College and Theological Seminary—Morgan Library (IN–125/1)

Western Conservative Baptist Seminary—Cline-Tunnell Library (OR–30/1)

Wheaton College—Graham Center Library (IL–205/1)

ARMERDING, Hudson Taylor. *The China Inland Mission and Some Aspects of Its Work*. University of Chicago (M.A.), 1948, 202p.

Duke University—Divinity School Library (NC–30/2)

Princeton Theological Seminary—Speer Library (NJ–95/3)

Princeton University—Firestone Library (NJ–100/1)

Stanford University—Green Library (CA–305/1)

Trinity Evangelical Divinity School Library (IL–90/1)

Union Theological Seminary—Burke Library (NY–275/1)

University of Chicago—Regenstein Library (IL–85/1)

Wheaton College—Department of Special Collections (IL–190/1)

Wheaton College—Graham Center Library (IL–205/1)

ARNOLD, John William. *Pioneer Protestant Educational Missionaries to China, 1807–1857*. Yale Divinity School (S.T.M.), 1948, 177p.

Yale Divinity School—Special Collections (CT–50/23)

ARTHUR, Brenton Joffre Kitchener. *The Influence of the Mongol Invasion on the Russian Church Indirect and Negative Rather Than Direct and Positive*. Gordon Divinity School (B.D.), 1944, 80p.

Gordon-Conwell Theological Seminary—Goddard Library (MA–230/3)

ASKE, Sigurd Olaf. *An Analysis of Religion as Found in the Works of Hsun-tzu*. Kennedy School of Missions (M.A.), 1949, 155p.

Hartford Seminary Foundation—Case Memorial Library (CT–15/7)

ASKE, Sigurd Olaf. *The South Shensi Lutheran Mission*. Hartford Seminary Foundation (Ph.D.), 1951, 316p.

Emory University—Pitts Theology Library (GA–15/5)

Hartford Seminary Foundation—Case Memorial Library (CT–15/7)

North Park College and Theological Seminary—Wallgren Library (IL–65/1)

Stanford University—Green Library (CA–305/1)

Union Theological Seminary—Burke Library (NY–275/1)

Yale Divinity School Library (CT–55/2)

ATWOOD, Elmer Bugg. *Outlines of a History of Missions in China*. Southern Baptist Theological Seminary (Th.D.), 1911, 156p.

Southern Baptist Theological Seminary—Boyce Centennial Library (KY–50/2)

Wheaton College—Graham Center Library (IL–205/1)

AU-YEUNG, Thomas M. C. *Chinese Family Mission-church: A Contextualized Model for Holistic Christian Mission in Mainland China*. Fuller Theological Seminary (D.Miss.), 1985, 357p.

Fuller Theological Seminary—McAlister Library (CA–205/1)

BACON, Daniel W. *The Influence of Hudson Taylor on the Faith Missions Movement*. Trinity Evangelical Divinity School (D.Miss.), 1983, 199p.

Trinity Evangelical Divinity School Library (IL–90/1)

BALLOU, Earle Hoit. *Ancestor Worship and the Progress of Christianity in China*. Hartford Theological Seminary (B.D.), 1916, n.p.

Hartford Seminary Foundation—Case Memorial Library (CT–15/7)

BARNETT, Suzanne Wilson. *Practical Evangelism: Protestant Missions and the Introduction of Western Civilization into China, 1820–1850*. Harvard University (Ph.D.), 1973, 444p.

Harvard University—Harvard-Yenching Library (MA–125/6)

Harvard University—Pusey Library (MA–150/3)

Harvard University—Widener Library (MA–155/1)

Union Theological Seminary—Burke Library (NY–275/1)

BARRY, Peter James. *A Brief History of the Missionary Work of the Maryknoll Fathers in China*. National University of Taiwan (M.A.), 1977, 226p.

Maryknoll Fathers and Brothers Library (NY–115/1)

Maryknoll Sisters of St. Dominic—Archives (NY–120/1)

Maryknoll Sisters of St. Dominic—Rogers Library (NY–125/1)

BARSS, Gordon D. *The Early Eastward Spread of Christianity*. Andover Newton Theological School (B.D.), 1949, 50p.

Andover Newton Theological School—Trask Library (MA–180/2)

BARTEL, Paul Henry. *The Chinese Bible: Being a Historical Survey of Its Translation*. University of Chicago (M.A.), 1946, 133p.

Bethel College—Mennonite Library and Archives (KS–55/13)

University of Chicago—Regenstein Library (IL–85/1)

BARTEL, Paul Henry. *The Use of Literature in the Protestant Missionary Enterprise Among the Chinese People*. Fuller Theological Seminary (B.Div.), 1962, n.p.

Wheaton College—Graham Center Library (IL–205/1)

BASS, Harold James. *The Policy of the American State Department toward Missionaries in the Far East*. State College of Washington (Ph.D.), 1937, 462p.

Washington State University—Holland Library (WA–15/1)

BAUDIMENT, Louis. *François Pallu, Principal fondateur de la Société des missions étrangères (François Pallu, Principal Founder of the Foreign Mission Society)*. Paris (thesis), 1934, 481p.

Harvard University—Widener Library (MA–155/1)

BECKMANN, Johannes. *Die katholische Missionmethode in China in neuester Zeit (1884-1912); geschichtliche Untersuchung über Arbeitsweisen, ihre Hindernisse und Erfolge (Catholic Mission Policy and Methods in China in the Most Recent Period (1884-1912): An Historical Inquiry into Work Methods, Their Drawbacks, and Successes).* Münster (thesis), 1931, 202p.

Cornell University—Wason Collection (NY-95/1)

Graduate Theological Union Library (CA-15/2)

Harvard Divinity School—Andover-Harvard Theological Library (MA-95/2)

Harvard University—Widener Library (MA-155/1)

Princeton Theological Seminary—Speer Library (NJ-95/3)

Union Theological Seminary—Burke Library (NY-275/1)

University of Chicago—Regenstein Library (IL-85/1)

University of Michigan—Hatcher Graduate Library (MI-25/1)

BEGUIN, Anne Marie. *The Influence of Christian Student Movements in the Colleges and Universities of China and Japan.* Biblical Seminary in New York (M.R.E.), 1948, 84p.

Biblical Theological Seminary Library (PA-70/1)

BEHNKE, Donna Alberta. *Politics and Prayer: A Study of the Advent Christian Denomination's Mission Efforts in China.* Northwestern University (M.A.), 1971, n.p.

Aurora University—Phillips Library (IL-10/5)

Garrett-Evangelical and Seabury-Western Theological Seminaries—United Library (IL-110/1)

Northwestern University Library (IL-115/1)

BENNETT, Adrian Arthur, III. *John Fryer and the Introduction of Western Science and Technology into Nineteenth-century China.* University of California, Davis (M.A.), 1966, 176p.

University of California, Davis—Department of Special Collections (CA-100/1)

BENNETT, Adrian Arthur, III. *Missionary Journalism in Nineteenth-century China: Young J. Allen and the Early "Wan kuo kung pao," 1868-1883.* University of California, Davis (Ph.D.), 1970, 417p.

Boston University—School of Theology Library (MA-35/1)

Cornell University—Wason Collection (NY-95/1)

Drew University Library (NJ-40/2)

Emory University—Woodruff Library (GA-25/1)

Garrett-Evangelical and Seabury-Western Theological Seminaries—United Library (IL-110/1)

Stanford University—Green Library (CA-305/1)

University of California, Davis—Department of Special Collections (CA-100/1)

Yale University—Sterling Memorial Library (CT-80/1)

BERNKOPF, Nancy. *The Christian Missionary Movement and the Growth of Antiforeignism in Nineteenth-century China.* William Smith College (B.A.), 1970, n.p.

Hobart and William Smith Colleges—Smith Library (NY-85/1)

BERRY, Frances Audrey. *The Effects of the War on the Future of Our Mission Work in China.* New Orleans Baptist Theological Seminary (M.R.E.), 1945, 10p.

New Orleans Baptist Theological Seminary—Christian Library (LA-15/1)

BETTRAY, Johannes. *Die Akkommodationsmethode des P. Matteo Ricci S.I. in China (The Accommodation Method of P. Matteo Ricci, S.J., in China).* Pontificia Universita Gregoriana, Rome (thesis), 1955, 411p.

Catholic Theological Union Library (IL-20/1)

Catholic University of America—Mullen Library (DC-20/1)

Garrett-Evangelical and Seabury-Western Theological Seminaries—United Library (IL-110/1)

Indiana University—University Libraries (IN-20/2)

Newberry Library (IL-60/2)

Princeton Theological Seminary—Speer Library (NJ-95/3)

Princeton University—Firestone Library (NJ-100/1)

St. Mary of the Lake Seminary—Feehan Memorial Library (IL-130/1)

Southern Methodist University—Bridwell Theology Library (TX-20/2)

Union Theological Seminary—Burke Library (NY-275/1)

University of California at Los Angeles—University Research Library (CA-185/1)

University of California, Berkeley—General Library (CA-70/1)

University of Chicago—Regenstein Library (IL-85/1)

University of Michigan—Hatcher Graduate Library (MI-25/1)

University of Oregon Library (OR-20/2)

University of Washington Libraries (WA-45/1)

University of Wisconsin-Madison Memorial Library (WI-45/1)

Yale Divinity School Library (CT-55/2)

BIERMANN, Benno M. *Die Anfänge der neuen Dominikanermission in China (The Beginnings of the New Dominican Mission in China).* Münster (thesis), 1927, 236p.

Columbia University—Butler Library (NY-150/1)

Harvard Divinity School—Andover-Harvard Theological Library (MA-95/2)

Harvard University—Widener Library (MA-155/1)

Stanford University—Green Library (CA-305/1)

BLACKSTONE, Beth. *The Effect of the Recent Western Migration on the Program of the Church in China.* Biblical Seminary in New York (M.R.E.), 1942, 82p.

Biblical Theological Seminary Library (PA-70/1)

BOARDMAN, Eugene P. *Biblical Influence upon the Ideology of the T'ai-p'ing Rebellion.* Harvard University (Ph.D.), 1946, n.p.

Harvard University—Pusey Library (MA-150/3)

BOBRICK, R.Peter. *The Jesuits in China in the Sixteenth and Seventeenth Centuries.* Seton Hall University (M.A.), 1979, 65p.

Seton Hall University Archives (NJ-140/1)

BODIN, Thomas. *The Young Men's Christian Association in China, Hong Kong, and Korea.* Institute and Training School of Young Men's Christian Associations (YMCA Certificate), 1906, 15p.

George Williams College Library (IL-100/1)

BOGGS, Mary Edna. *William Alexander Parsons Martin, Missionary to China, 1850-1916.* Presbyterian College of Christian Education (M.A.), 1948, 64p.

Presbyterian Historical Society—Archives and Library (PA-200-28)

BOHLEN, Veneranda. *The Life and Work of Msgr. De Besi in China.* St. Bonaventure's College (M.A.), 1950, 90p.

Missionary Sisters of the Immaculate Conception of the Mother of God—Generalate Archives (NJ-155/1)

St. Bonaventure University—Friedsam Library (NY-370/1)

BOHR, Paul Richard. *Famine in China and the Missionary: Timothy Richard as Relief Administrator and Advocate of National*

Reform. Harvard Divinity School (B.D.), 1971, 368p.

Harvard Divinity School—Andover-Harvard Theological Library (MA-95/2)

BOHR, Paul Richard. *The Politics of Eschatology: Hung Hsiu-ch'uan and the Rise of the Taipings, 1837–1853.* University of California, Davis (Ph.D.), 1978, 413p.

University of California, Davis—Department of Special Collections (CA-100/1)

BOLLBACK, James Anthony. *Protestant Missionary Activity in Hunan Province—China: History and Analysis, 1875–1912.* Cornell University (M.A.), 1981, 146p.

Christian and Missionary Alliance—Simpson Library (NY-305/8)

Cornell University—Wason Collection (NY-95/1)

BONTRAGER, Mable Busch. *A Study of Typical Life Problems Faced by Three Outstanding Missionary Wives of the Nineteenth Century.* Biblical Seminary in New York (M.R.E.), 1948, 87p.

Biblical Theological Seminary Library (PA-70/1)

BRAMMER, Pauline Frances. *Education of Women by Baptists in South China.* New Orleans Baptist Theological Seminary (M.R.E.), 1947, 28p.

Carson-Newman College Library (TN-20/1)

New Orleans Baptist Theological Seminary—Christian Library (LA-15/1)

Wheaton College—Graham Center Library (IL-205/1)

BRANDAUER, Frederick W. *The History and Development of the Central China Mission of the Evangelical United Brethren Church.* Temple University (S.T.D.), 1953, 263p.

Temple University—Paley Library (PA-210/2)

United Theological Seminary Library (OH-120/11)

BREM, Franz Emile. *Fr. Terrence (Schreck), S.J., and His Work in China, 1576–1630.* Columbia University (M.A.), 1950, n.p.

Columbia University—Starr East Asian Library (NY-195/4)

BRESLIN, Thomas A. *American Catholic China Missionaries, 1918–1941.* University of Virginia (Ph.D.), 1972, 296p.

Cornell University—Wason Collection (NY-95/1)

Emory University—Woodruff Library (GA-25/1)

Stanford University—Green Library (CA-305/1)

University of California, Santa Barbara, Library (CA-275/2)

University of Chicago—Regenstein Library (IL-85/1)

University of Hawaii—Hamilton Library (HI-15/2)

University of Pittsburgh—Hillman Library (PA-260/1)

University of Virginia—Alderman Library (VA-30/1)

BRESLIN, Thomas A. *The Disordered Society: American Catholics Look at China, 1900–1937.* University of Virginia (M.A.), 1969, 113p.

University of Virginia—Alderman Library (VA-30/1)

BROWN, Mark Weber. *Chinese Christian Experience Psychologically and Theologically Considered.* Drew University (Ph.D.), 1930, n.p.

Drew University Library (NJ-40/2)

BROWN, Susan R. *David Crockett Graham: Anthropologist, Collector, and Missionary in China.* Whitman College (Senior thesis), 1986, n.p.

Whitman College Archives (WA-50/2)

BRUNNER, Paul. *L'Euchologe de la mission de Chine; Editio princeps 1628 et développements jusqu'à nos jours; contribution à l'histoire des livres de prières (The Eucharist of the Mission in China: The First Edition of 1628 and Developments to the Present; Contribution to the History of Prayer Books).* Trier (thesis), 1964, 368p.

St. John's University—Alcuin Library (MN-5/1)

University of California, Berkeley—General Library (CA-70/1)

Yale Divinity School Library (CT-55/2)

BUNCE, H. Ross. *A Brief History of the Young Men's Christian Association of China, with Particular Emphasis on Its Department of Physical Education.* Institute and Training School of Young Men's Christian Associations (YMCA Certificate), 1914, 43p.

George Williams College Library (IL-100/1)

BURKHOLDER, Marion Olin. *A Study of Southern Methodist Schools in China.* Emory University (B.D.), 1937, 51p.

Emory University—Pitts Theology Library (GA-15/5)

BÜRKLER, Franz Xaver. *Die Sonn- und Festtagsfeier in der Katholischen Chinamission; eine geschichtlich-pastorale Untersuchung (The Sunday and Holiday Celebrations in the Catholic China Mission: An Historical-pastoral Treatise).* Institutum Missionale Scientificum, Rome (thesis), 1942, n.p.

Catholic University of America—Mullen Library (DC-20/1)

Yale Divinity School Library (CT-55/2)

BURNETT, George Chester. *Mary Ann Aldersey and the Beginning of Christian Schools for Women in China.* University of California, Davis (M.A.), 1975, 149p.

University of California, Davis—Department of Special Collections (CA-100/1)

CAMPFIELD, Mary Tarpley. *Oberlin-in-China, 1881–1951.* University of Virginia (Ph.D.), 1974, 393p.

Cornell University—Wason Collection (NY-95/1)

Oberlin College—Main Library (OH-175/1)

Stanford University—Green Library (CA-305/1)

University of Iowa Libraries (IA-40/1)

University of Virginia—Alderman Library (VA-30/1)

Wheaton College—Graham Center Library (IL-205/1)

CAPEN, Carl. *A History of the Baptist Mission at Swatow (Kakchieh), China.* Biblical Seminary in New York (S.T.B.), 1935, 90p.

American Baptist Historical Society (NY-345/4)

Biblical Theological Seminary Library (PA-70/1)

CARTER, Carolyn Howard. *Sophie Stevens Lanneau: Southern Baptist Missionary to Soochow, China, 1907–1950.* Wake Forest University (M.A.), 1974, n.p.

Wake Forest University—Reynolds Library (NC-110/1)

CHA, Ho Won. *God's Communication Media on Church Growth in Korea and Mission Broadcasting toward Iron Walls.* Fuller Theological Seminary (D. Min.), 1983, 177p. (In Korean, with extended summary in English).

Fuller Theological Seminary—McAlister Library (CA-205/1)

CHAFFEE, Clifford E. *A Suggested Program of Direct Evangelism for the Missionary in Present-day China as Based upon a Study of the Most Effective Methods.* Biblical Seminary in New York (S.T.M.), 1944, 118p.

Biblical Theological Seminary Library (PA-70/1)

CHANDLER, Horace Edward. *The Work of the American Presbyterian Mission from 1918 to 1941 toward the Lessening of Adult Illiteracy in Shantung Province, China.* University of Pittsburgh (Ph.D.), 1943, 192p.

Pittsburgh Theological Seminary—Barbour Library (PA-240/1)

University of Pittsburgh—Hillman Library (PA-260/1)

CHANDLER, Uri G. *Changes in Missionary Policy Entailed in*

the Development of an Indigenous Chinese Church. Biblical Seminary in New York (S.T.B.), 1946, 107p.

Biblical Theological Seminary Library (PA–70/1)

CHANG, Cherry Y. K. *A Program of Christian Education in Baptist Schools in China*. Southwestern Baptist Theological Seminary (Ph.D.), 1955, 215p.

Southwestern Baptist Theological Seminary—Roberts Library (TX–25/3)

CHANG Lit-sen. *The Fallacy of Pantheism in Respect to the Personality of God*. Gordon Divinity School (B.D.), 1958, 71p.

Gordon-Conwell Theological Seminary—Goddard Library (MA–230/3)

CHANG Tien-be. *The Opportunity of the Young Men's Christian Association Service of Physical Education in the Reconstruction of Chinese Society*. Young Men's Christian Association College (Bachelor of Physical Education), 1920, 50p.

George Williams College Library (IL–100/1)

CHAO, Jonathan. *The Chinese Indigenous Church Movement, 1919–1927: A Protestant Response to Anti-Christian Movements in Modern China*. University of Pennsylvania (Ph.D.), 1986, 376p.

Southern Baptist Convention—Jenkins Research Library (VA–70/1)

University of Pennsylvania—Van Pelt Library (PA–215/1)

CHAPPELL, Rachel Mostrom. *The Missionary Approach to the Religions of China*. Wheaton College (M.A.), 1946, n.p.

Wheaton College—Department of Special Collections (IL–190/1)

Wheaton College—Graham Center Library (IL–205/1)

CHAU Fun N. *Hudson Taylor and Timothy Richard: Faith in Practice*. Princeton University (B.A.), 1978, n.p.

Princeton University—Gest Oriental Library (NJ–105/1)

CHEN Chang-yu. *A Program of Religious Education for Christian Churches in China*. Hartford Theological Seminary (B.D.), 1926, n.p.

Hartford Seminary Foundation—Case Memorial Library (CT–15/7)

CHEN Hsien-ping. *The History of Christian Missions in China and Preparation for New Beginnings*. Columbia Theological Seminary (Th.M.), 1973–74, 196p.

Columbia Theological Seminary—Campbell Library (GA–35/1)

CHEN Kuan-yu. *A Century of Chinese Christian Education: An Analysis of the True Light Seminary and Its Successors in Canton and Hong Kong*. University of Connecticut (Ph.D.), 1972, 313p.

Emory University—Pitts Theology Library (GA–15/5)

Stanford University—Green Library (CA–305/1)

University of Connecticut—Babbidge Library (CT–90/1)

Wheaton College—Graham Center Library (IL–205/1)

CHEN, Samuel Kun-kang. *A Study of the Development of Christian Education in China*. Asbury Theological Seminary (M.R.E.), 1955, 110p.

Asbury Theological Seminary—Fisher Library (KY–90/1)

CHEN Wei-cheng. *The Educational Work of the Missionaries in China*. University of Michigan (Ph.D.), 1910, n.p.

University of Michigan—Hatcher Graduate Library (MI–25/1)

CHEN, William K.C. *The Disciples' Contribution to the Chinese Christian Movement*. College of the Bible (M.R.E.), 1930, 90p.

Union Theological Seminary—Burke Library (NY–275/1)

CHEN, Wilson Wei-sing. *The Prospect of Student Christian Work in Communist China*. Andover Newton Theological School (Th.M.), 1950, 103p.

Andover Newton Theological School—Trask Library (MA–180/2)

CHENG Hin-yau. *Protestantism and Nation-building in China: A Study of the Church during the Nationalist Decade, 1928–1937*. Luther Northwestern Theological Seminary (M.A.), 1981, n.p.

Luther Northwestern Theological Seminary Library (MN–100/1)

CHENG, Timothy Chih-tien. *The Scope, Organization, and Program of the Christian School of China*. Boston University (M.R.E.), 1925, 104p.

Boston University—School of Theology Library (MA–35/1)

CHEUNG, James Mo-oi. *The Ecclesiology of the "Little Flock" of China Founded by Watchman Nee*. Trinity Evangelical Divinity School (M.A.), 1970, 130p.

Christian and Missionary Alliance—Simpson Historical Library (NY–305/8)

Trinity Evangelical Divinity School Library (IL–90/1)

CHEUNG, Pauline Fei Ha. *A Survey of Chinese Baptist Missions of the Northern and Southern Boards in the United States*. Baptist Bible Institute (M.C.T.), 1940, 33p.

New Orleans Baptist Theological Seminary—Christian Library (LA–15/1)

CHOA, Alexander T. K. *Jesus and the Oriental Mind*. Gordon College of Theology and Missions (B.D.), 1931, 49p.

Gordon-Conwell Theological Seminary—Goddard Library (MA–230/3)

CHOU, Charles Shwee Lin. *The Cultural and Religious Heritage of China as Related to the Communication of the Christian Faith*. Pacific School of Religion (M.R.E.), 1967, 248p.

Graduate Theological Union Library (CA–15/2)

CHOU, Christopher. *A Theological Dialogue between Christian Faith and Chinese Belief in the Light of "Sin": An Inquiry into the Apparent Failure of the Protestant Mission in Late 19th-century China, Especially among Chinese Intellectuals*. Lutheran School of Theology at Chicago (S.T.D.), 1976, 127p.

Alliance Theological Seminary Library (NY–300/1)

Cornell University—Wason Collection (NY–95/1)

Denver Conservative Baptist Seminary—Thomas Library (CO–10/3)

Emory University—Pitts Theology Library (GA–15/5)

Fuller Theological Library—McAlister Library (CA–205/1)

Wheaton College—Graham Center Library (IL–205/1)

CHOU, Po-chin. *Present Day Problems in Chinese Christianity*. Berkeley Baptist Divinity School (B.D.), 1926, 24p.

Graduate Theological Union Library (CA–15/2)

CHOW, Timothy Yu-hsi. *A Comparison of Jesus and Confucius as Ethical Teachers*. Boston University (M.R.E.), 1952, 104p.

Boston University—School of Theology Library (MA–35/1)

CHU, Fred Meichong. *A Policy and Program for Physical Development of the Young Men's Christian Association in China*. Young Men's Christian Association College (Bachelor of Physical Education), 1918, 73p.

George Williams College Library (IL–100/1)

CHU, Gary G. Y. *A Q-sort Comparison between Cultural Experiences of Chinese and Cultural Perceptions of Returned Latter-Day Saint Missionaries from the United States Who Had Been Assigned to Chinese Missions*. Brigham Young University (M.A.), 1974, n.p.

Brigham Young University—Lee Library (UT–10/1)

Church of Jesus Christ of Latter-Day Saints—Historical Department (UT–15/1)

CHU Li-chih. *Hsi fang ch'uan chiao shih tsai Hua tsao ch'i ti pao yeh t'an t'ao (Newspaper Publishing among Early Western Missionaries in China).* Chinese Cultural Institute (Chung-kuo wen-hua hsüeh-yuan) (M.A.), 1977, 183p.

University of Hawaii—Hamilton Library (HI–15/1)

Yale University—Sterling Memorial Library (CT–80/1)

CHUN, Lola. *American Influence in Chinese Higher Education Since 1900.* University of California, Berkeley (M.A.), 1948, 137p.

University of California, Berkeley—General Library (CA–70/1)

CLARK, Allen DeGray. *A Study of the History of Mission Work for Koreans in South Manchuria and Its Relation to the Church in Korea.* Princeton Theological Seminary (Th.M.), 1939, 116p.

Princeton Theological Seminary—Speer Library (NJ–95/3)

CLEISZ, Augustin. *Etude sur les missions nestoriennes en Chine au VIIe et au VIIIe siècles d'après l'inscription Syro-Chinoise de Si-ngan-fou (A Study of the Nestorian Missions in China in the 7th and 8th Centuries, According to the Syro-Chinese Inscription of Hsi-an-fu).* Paris (B.Th.), 1880, 92p.

Austin Presbyterian Theological Seminary—Stitt Library (TX–10/1)

Duke University—Divinity School Library (NC–30/2)

University of Cincinnati—Central Library (OH–65/1)

Yale Divinity School Library (CT–55/2)

CLEMENTS, Charles Everleigh. *The Bible Institute of Los Angeles in China: An American Missionary Experience as Viewed from the Stewart Papers.* California State University, Fullerton (M.A.), 1975, 551p.

Biola University—Rose Memorial Library (CA–130/4)

California State University, Fullerton, Library (CA–120/1)

Emory University—Woodruff Library (GA–25/1)

CLEVELAND, Marion Elinor. *Lay Leadership Training for Rural Women of the China Inland Mission in West Szechwan.* Biblical Seminary in New York (M.R.E.), 1938, 106p.

Biblical Theological Seminary Library (PA–70/1)

COCHRANE, Ruth L. *An Outline History of Medical Missions in China.* Woman's Missionary Union Training School (M.R.E.), 1939, 64p.

Southern Baptist Theological Seminary—Boyce Centennial Library (KY–50/2)

COHEN, Paul Andrew. *Chinese Hostility to Christianity: A Study in Intercultural Conflict, 1860–1870.* Harvard University (Ph.D.), 1960, 113p.

Harvard University—Harvard-Yenching Library (MA–125/6)

Harvard University—Pusey Library (MA–150/3)

Harvard University—Widener Library (MA–155/1)

University of California at Los Angeles—University Research Library (CA–185/1)

CONGER, Mary Jane. *Missionary Views of China and Japan, 1890–1899.* University of Virginia (M.A.), 1975, 103p.

University of Virginia—Alderman Library (VA–30/1)

COOK, Robert Lawrence. *Missionary Power and Civil Authority in China: The Crisis of 1900.* Harvard University (Honors thesis), 1970, n.p.

Harvard University—Widener Library (MA–155/1)

COUGHLIN, Margaret M. *Strangers in the House: J. Lewis Shuck and Issachar Roberts, First American Baptist Missionaries to China.* University of Virginia (Ph.D.), 1972, 332p.

Cornell University—Wason Collection (NY–95/1)

Emory University—Woodruff Library (GA–25/1)

Stanford University—Green Library (CA–305/1)

University of California, Santa Barbara, Library (CA–275/2)

University of California, Santa Cruz—McHenry Library (CA–285/2)

University of Hawaii—Hamilton Library (HI–15/2)

University of Virginia—Alderman Library (VA–30/1)

Wheaton College—Graham Center Library (IL–205/1)

COVELL, Ralph M. *The Life and Thought of W. A. P. Martin: Agent and Interpreter of Sino-American Contact in the Nineteenth and Early Twentieth Centuries.* University of Denver (Ph.D.), 1974, 604p.

Cornell University—Wason Collection (NY–95/1)

Stanford University—Green Library (CA–305/1)

University of Denver—Penrose Library (CO–20/1)

CRABTREE, Loren William. *Christian Colleges and the Chinese Revolution, 1840–1940: A Case Study in the Impact of the West.* University of Minnesota (Ph.D.), 1969, 482p.

Cornell University—Wason Collection (NY–95/1)

Emory University—Pitts Theology Library (GA–15/5)

University of Minnesota—Wilson Library (MN–40/1)

University of Virginia—Alderman Library (VA–30/1)

CRANSTON, Earl. *The American Missionaries' Outlook on China, 1830–1860.* Harvard University (Ph.D.), 1931, 327p.

Harvard University—Pusey Library (MA–150/3)

Harvard University—Widener Library (MA–155/1)

University of Pennsylvania—Van Pelt Library (PA–215/1)

CROCKER, Marion Sandow. *The Socio-economic Conditions of China as a Mission Field.* Woman's Missionary Union Training School (M.R.E.), 1935, 45p.

Southern Baptist Theological Seminary—Boyce Centennial Library (KY–50/2)

CULPEPPER, Charles L. *Sin in the Chinese Religions.* Southwestern Baptist Theological Seminary (Th.D.), 1945, 176p.

Fuller Theological Seminary—McAlister Library (CA–205/1)

Southwestern Baptist Theological Seminary—Roberts Library (TX–25/3)

CUNKLE, Paul Vincent. *The Chinese Renaissance and Its Relation to and Effects upon Protestant Missions.* United Theological Seminary (M.Div.), 1946, 77p.

United Theological Seminary Library (OH–120/11)

DAEHLIN, Reidar Arnold. *The Background in the Four Books of the Confucian Classics for Chinese Christian Terms.* Union Theological Seminary (M.A.), 1943, 200p.

Union Theological Seminary—Burke Library (NY–275/1)

DAHLSTROM, Earl Carl. *The Covenant Missionary Society in China.* Hartford Seminary Foundation (Ph.D.), 1950, 291p.

Drew University Library (NJ–40/2)

Emory University—Pitts Theology Library (GA–15/5)

Evangelical Covenant Church—Covenant Archives and Historical Library (IL–35/3)

Fuller Theological Seminary—McAlister Library (CA–205/1)

Hartford Seminary Foundation—Case Memorial Library (CT–15/7)

Union Theological Seminary—Burke Library (NY–275/1)

DAHLSTROM, Earl Carl. *Some Aspects of the Religion of the Former Han Dynasty as Found in the Annals Section of the*

Dynastic History. Kennedy School of Missions (M.A.), 1949, 183p.

    Hartford Seminary Foundation—Case Memorial Library (CT–15/7)

DAVIS, George Lowry. *The Chinese University of the Past and the Future*. Boston University (S.T.B.), 1902, 9p.

    Boston University—School of Theology Library (MA–35/1)

DAY, Clarence Burton. *Peasant Religion in Northern Chekiang*. Hartford Theological Seminary (Ph.D.), 1930, 376p.

    Hartford Theological Seminary—Case Memorial Library (CT–15/7)

DEAN, Bruce J. M. *Chinese Christianity Since 1949: Implications for the Church of Jesus Christ of Latter-Day Saints*. Brigham Young University (M.A.), 1981, 105p.

    Brigham Young University—Lee Library (UT–10/1)

    Church of Jesus Christ of Latter-Day Saints—Historical Department (UT–15/1)

DEAN, David E. *Floods, Famine and Wars: A History of the Advent Christian Mission Work in China*. Berkshire Christian College (A.B.), 1976, 115p.

    Advent Christian General Conference—Headquarters Archives (NC–15/1)

    Aurora University—Phillips Library (IL–10/5)

    Berkshire Christian College—Carter Library (MA–175/1)

DECKER, William M. *The Foundations and Growth of Shantung Christian University, 1864–1917*. Columbia University (M.A.), 1948, 128p.

    Columbia University—Butler Library (NY–150/1)

    Union Theological Seminary—Burke Library (NY–275/1)

DE KORNE, John Cornelius. *The Fellowship of Goodness (Tung Shan She): A Study in Contemporary Chinese Religion*. Kennedy School of Missions (Ph.D.), 1941, 109p.

    Calvin College and Seminary Library (MI–85/1)

    Hartford Seminary Foundation—Case Memorial Library (CT–15/7)

    Vanderbilt University—Divinity Library (TN–65/1)

DETRICK, Robert H. *Henry Andrea Burgevine in China: A Biography*. Indiana University (Ph.D.), 1968, 258p.

    Indiana University—University Libraries (IN–20/2)

DONALDSON, Mary Lois. *Facing Family Problems with Chinese Youth*. Kennedy School of Missions (M.A.), 1938, 117p.

    Hartford Seminary Foundation—Case Memorial Library (CT–15/7)

DOWNS, Jacques. *The American Community in Canton, 1784–1844*. Georgetown University (Ph.D.), 1961, 390p.

    Georgetown University—Lauinger Library (DC–60/1)

DRAKE, George F. *The Missionary and Western Education in Nineteenth-century China*. University of California, Berkeley (M.A.), 1959, 92p.

    University of California, Berkeley—General Library (CA–70/1)

DRAKE, Richard Bryant. *Missionary Status and Influence in Early Nineteenth-century China*. University of Chicago (A.M.), 1950, 127p.

    University of Chicago—Regenstein Library (IL–85/1)

DRURY, Clifford Merrill. *Christian Missions and Foreign Relations in China: An Historical Study*. University of Edinburgh (thesis), 1932, 432p.

    Texas Christian University—Burnett Library (TX–30/1)

    Wheaton College—Graham Center Library (IL–205/1)

DUNCAN, Robert Moore. *Peiping Municipality and the Diplo-*

matic Quarter. Yenching University (Ph.D.), 1933,146p.

    Princeton University—Firestone Library (NJ–100/1)

DUNN, Clyde H. *T. C. Chao's Struggle for a Chinese Christianity*. Emory University (M.A.), 1974, 120p.

    Emory University—Woodruff Library (GA–25/1)

DUNNE, George Harold. *The Jesuits in China in the Last Days of the Ming Dynasty*. University of Chicago (Ph.D.), 1944, 698p.

    University of Chicago—Regenstein Library (IL–85/1)

    University of Redlands—Armacost Library (CA–210/1)

    Wheaton College—Graham Center Library (IL–205/1)

    Yale Divinity School Library (CT–55/2)

EAVENSON, Ira Dennis. *The Bible Growing a Christian Culture in China*. Southern Baptist Theological Seminary (Ph.D.), 1928, 136p.

    Southern Baptist Theological Seminary—Boyce Centennial Library (KY–50/2)

    Wheaton College—Graham Center Library (IL–205/1)

EDWARDS, Margaret Jane. *A Course of Bible Stories for Use in Teaching Christian Women of Rural South China*. Biblical Seminary in New York (M.R.E.), 1937, 143p.

    Biblical Theological Seminary Library (PA–70/1)

ENSIGN, Samuel James Russell. *The Influence of the Chinese Renaissance upon Protestant Christianity in China*. Kennedy School of Missions (M.A.), 1930, 46p.

    Hartford Seminary Foundation—Case Memorial Library (CT–15/7)

ESTES, Charles Sumner. *Christian Missions in China*. Johns Hopkins University (Ph.D.), 1895, 61p.

    Andover Newton Theological School—Trask Library (MA–180/2)

    Boston Public Library (MA–30/2)

    Brandeis University Library (MA–235/1)

    Columbia University—Butler Library (NY–150/1)

    Harvard Divinity School—Andover-Harvard Theological Library (MA–95/2)

    Harvard University—Widener Library (MA–155/1)

    Johns Hopkins University—Eisenhower Library (MD–10/1)

    New York Public Library—General Research Division (NY–230/1)

    Northwestern University Library (IL–115/1)

    Princeton Theological Seminary—Speer Library (NJ–95/3)

    Princeton University—Firestone Library (NJ–100/1)

    Union Theological Seminary—Burke Library (NY–275/1)

    University of California, Berkeley—General Library (CA–70/1)

    University of Chicago—Regenstein Library (IL–85/1)

    University of Michigan—Hatcher Graduate Library (MI–25/1)

    University of Pennsylvania—Van Pelt Library (PA–215/1)

    Yale Divinity School Library (CT–55/2)

FARBER, Mark Sherman. *The Middle Kingdom Revisited: The Validity of S. Wells Williams' Book and Its Sources*. University of California, Davis (M.A.), 1972, 153p.

    University of California, Davis—Department of Special Collections (CA–100/1)

FAST, Aganetha Helen. "*Folkways and Religion," Translations of Chapters Nine and Ten from "Ting-Hsien, a Social Survey."* Hartford Seminary Foundation (M.A.), 1936, 173p.

    Associated Mennonite Biblical Seminaries Library (IN–25/3)

    Hartford Seminary Foundation—Case Memorial Library (CT–15/7)

FERM, Deane William. *Sherwood Eddy: Evangelist and YMCA Secretary*. Yale University (Ph.D.), 1954, 457p.

  Yale University—Sterling Memorial Library (CT–80/1)

FESSENDEN, Robert Milton. *The Changing Attitudes of the American Protestant Missionaries toward the Unequal Treaties with China*. Ohio State University (M.A.), 1971, 50p.

  Ohio State University—Thompson Memorial Library (OH–110/4)

FISCH, Edwin William. *A Survey of Sunday School Work in China from 1930 to 1945*. Wheaton College (M.A.), 1947, n.p.

  Wheaton College—Department of Special Collections (IL–190/1)

  Wheaton College—Graham Center Library (IL–205/1)

FLEMING, Peter, S.J. *Chosen for China: The California Jesuits in China, 1928–1957, A Case Study in Mission and Culture*. Graduate Theological Union (Ph.D.), 1986, n.p.

  California Province of the Society of Jesus Archives (CA–195/1)

  Graduate Theological Union Library (CA–15/2)

FORD, Eddy Lucius. *The History of the Educational Work of the Methodist Episcopal Church in China: A Study of Its Development and Present Trends*. Northwestern University (Ph.D.), 1936, 294p.

  Drew University—United Methodist Archives (NJ–45/5)

  Drew University—United Methodist Historical Library (NJ–50/1)

  Garrett-Evangelical and Seabury-Western Theological Seminaries—United Library (IL–110/1)

  Northwestern University Library (IL–115/1)

  Yale Divinity School Library (CT–55/1)

FORD, Rosalie Judith. *Matteo Ricci, S.J. in China, 1583–1610: A Case Study of a Precursor in Educational Anthropology*. University of Connecticut (Ph.D.), 1985, 258p.

  University of Connecticut—Babbidge Library (CT–90/1)

FORSYTHE, Sidney Alexander. *Missionaries and Chinese: A Descriptive Case Study of the Response of American Board Missionaries to Selected Aspects of the Setting of Their Work, 1895–1905*. Harvard University (Ph.D.), 1963, 182p.

  Harvard University—Pusey Library (MA–150/3)

  Harvard University—Widener Library (MA–155/1)

FOSS, Theodore Nicholas. *A Jesuit Encyclopedia for China: A Guide to Jean-Baptiste du Halde's "Description...de la Chine" (1735)*. University of Chicago (Ph.D.), 1979, 731p.

  Institute for Chinese-Western Cultural History (CA–245/7)

  University of Chicago—Regenstein Library (IL–85/1)

FOSTER, Portia Billings. *A Preview by a Prospective Teacher in a Chinese Rural High School of the Potential Relationship of Its Activities with the Family and Community Life*. University unknown (M.A.), n.d., 65p.

  University of Oregon—Department of Special Collections (OR–15/5)

FRED, Morris Aaron. *Ritual as Ideology in an Indigenous Chinese Christian Church*. University of California, Berkeley (Ph.D.), 1975, 248p.

  Baylor University—Dawson Institute of Church-State Relations (TX–55/1)

  University of California, Berkeley—General Library (CA–70/1)

GAGE, Brownell. *The American College in the Orient: A Study of the Transplanting of a National Institution with Special Refer-*

ence to the College of Yale in China. Yale University (Ph.D.), 1924, 203p.

  Yale University—Sterling Memorial Library (CT–80/1)

GALLIGAN, David J. *American Protestant Missions and Communist China, 1946–1950*. Rutgers University (Ph.D.), 1952, 159p.

  Colgate-Rochester Theological Seminaries—Swasey Library (NY–350/1)

  Rutgers University—Alexander Library (NJ–75/1)

GALT, Ralph M. *A Program for the Christian Church in the Building of New Rural Communities in China*. Yenching University, School of Religion (B.D.), 1941, 164p.

  Presbyterian Historical Society—Archives and Library (PA–200/28)

GARRETT, Shirley Stone. *The Salvation of China: Urban Reform and the Chinese YMCA*. Harvard University (Ph.D.), 1966, n.p.

  Harvard University—Pusey Library (MA–150/3)

  Harvard University—Widener Library (MA–155/1)

GATES, Alan Frederick. *Christianity and Animism: China and Taiwan*. Fuller Theological Seminary (D.Miss.), 1971, 343p.

  Fuller Theological Seminary—McAlister Library (CA–205/1)

  Wheaton College—Graham Center Library (IL–205/1)

GEISERT, Bradley Kent. *Brethren Rural Reconstruction in China, 1920–1950*. University of Virginia (M.A.), 1975, 98p.

  Bridgewater College—Mack Memorial Library (VA–20/1)

  Church of the Brethren General Board—Brethren Historical Library and Archives (IL–105/11)

  University of Virginia—Alderman Library (VA–30/1)

GENG, George Yuan-hsieh. *The Promotion of the Economic Welfare of the Chinese People through the Protestant Churches in China*. Columbia University Teachers' College (Ed.D.), 1951, 244p.

  Colgate-Rochester Theological Seminaries—Swasey Library (NY–350/1)

  Columbia University—Milbank Library (NY–165/4)

GENTRY, Jack L. *Teaching the Christian Faith in the Chinese Educational Context*. Southwestern Baptist Theological Seminary (Th.D.), 1971, n.p.

  Southwestern Baptist Theological Seminary—Roberts Library (TX–25/3)

  Wheaton College—Graham Center Library (IL–205/1)

GIEDT, Emanuel Herman. *The Planting of Protestant Christianity in the Province of Kwangtung, China*. Yale University (Ph.D.), 1936, 309p.

  Yale Divinity School Library (CT–55/2)

  Yale University—Sterling Memorial Library (CT–80/1)

GIFFIN, Alice Marjorie. *Reaching the Heart of China through the Home*. Woman's Missionary Union Training School (M.R.E.), 1939, 64p.

  Southern Baptist Theological Seminary—Boyce Centennial Library (KY–50/2)

GING, Woodrow. *Nestorianism in the T'ang Dynasty (618–906 A.D.)*. Kennedy School of Missions (Ph.D.), 1930, 286p.

  Hartford Seminary Foundation—Case Memorial Library (CT–15/7)

GINNS, Shirley E. *A Proposed Program of Primary Christian Education in Rural China*. Biblical Seminary in New York (M.R.E.), 1946, 94p.

  Biblical Theological Seminary Library (PA–70/1)

GLÜER, Winfried. *Christliche Theologie in China: T. C. Chao,*

1918-1956 (Christian Theology in China: T. C. Chao, 1918-1956). Ruhr Universität (thesis), 1978, 300p.

> Fuller Theological Seminary—McAlister Library (CA-205/1)
>
> Stanford University—Green Library (CA-305/1)

GOERTZ, Peter Siebert. *A History of the Development of the Chinese Indigenous Christian Church under the American Board in Fukien Province*. Yale University (Ph.D.), 1933, 394p.

> Bethel College—Mennonite Library and Archives (KS-55/13)
>
> Union Theological Seminary—Burke Library (NY-275/1)
>
> Yale University—Sterling Memorial Library (CT-80/1)

GOODRICH, Luther Carrington. *American Catholic Missions in China*. Columbia University (M.A.), 1927, 64p.

> Columbia University—Starr East Asian Library (NY-195/4)

GOULTER, Oswald J. *Applied Christianity and World Missions*. Union Theological Seminary (M.A.), 1937, 46p.

> Union Theological Seminary—Burke Library (NY-275/1)

GRAHAM, David Crockett. *Indications of Primitive Chinese Religion in the Confucian Classics*. University of Chicago (M.A.), 1919, 25p.

> Colgate-Rochester Theological Seminaries—Swasey Library (NY-350/1)
>
> University of Chicago—Regenstein Library (IL-85/1)

GRAHAM, David Crockett. *Religion in Szechuan Province*. University of Chicago (Ph.D.), 1927, 83p.

> University of Chicago—Regenstein Library (IL-85/1)

GREENAWALT, Bruce Stephen. *Missionary Intelligence from China: American Protestant Reports, 1930-1950*. University of North Carolina at Chapel Hill (Ph.D.), 1974, 375p.

> Catholic Theological Union Library (IL-20/1)
>
> Cornell University—Wason Collection (NY-95/1)
>
> Duke University—Perkins Library (NC-55/1)
>
> Emory University—Woodruff Library (GA-25/1)
>
> State Historical Society of Wisconsin—Historical Library (WI-25/1)
>
> University of California, Santa Barbara, Library (CA-275/2)
>
> University of North Carolina at Chapel Hill—Davis Library (5/2)
>
> University of Notre Dame—Memorial Library (IN-95/1)
>
> Wheaton College—Graham Center Library (IL-205/1)

GREGG, Alice Henrietta. *China and Educational Autonomy: The Changing Role of the Protestant Educational Missionary in China, 1807-1937*. Columbia University (Ph.D.), 1945, 285p.

> Columbia University—Butler Library (NY-150/1)
>
> Columbia University—Milbank Library (NY-165/4)
>
> Detroit Public Library (MI-55/1)
>
> Johns Hopkins University—Eisenhower Library (MD-10/1)
>
> Public Library of Cincinnati (OH-50/1)
>
> University of Michigan—Hatcher Graduate Library (MI-25/1)
>
> University of Nebraska—Love Library (NB-25/2)
>
> University of Notre Dame—Memorial Library (IN-95/1)
>
> University of Oregon Library (OR-20/2)
>
> University of Pennsylvania—Van Pelt Library (PA-215/1)
>
> University of Wisconsin-Madison—Memorial Library (WI-45/1)

GROSSE-ASCHHOFF, Angelus Francis J. *The Negotiations between Ch'i-ying and Lagrené, 1844-1846*. Columbia University (Ph.D.), 1950, 196p.

> Brigham Young University—Lee Library (UT-10/1)
>
> Brown University—Hay Library (RI-15/4)
>
> Catholic Theological Union Library (IL-20/1)
>
> Catholic University of America—Mullen Library (DC-20/1)
>
> Columbia University—Butler Library (NY-150/1)
>
> Duke University—Divinity School Library (NC-30/2)
>
> Duns Scotus Library (MI-140/1)
>
> Emory University—Pitts Theology Library (GA-15/5)
>
> Harvard Divinity School—Andover-Harvard Theological Library (MA-95/2)
>
> Johns Hopkins University—Eisenhower Library (MD-10/1)
>
> Maryknoll Fathers and Brothers Library (NY-115/1)
>
> New York Public Library—General Research Division (NY-230/1)
>
> Ohio University—Alden Library (OH-15/1)
>
> Princeton University—Firestone Library (NJ-100/1)
>
> St. Anthony-on-the-Hudson—Province of Immaculate Conception Library (NY-340/1)
>
> St. Bonaventure University—Franciscan Institute (NY-365/1)
>
> St. Louis University—Pius XII Memorial Library (MO-75/2)
>
> St. Mary of the Lake Seminary—Feehan Memorial Library (IL-130/1)
>
> Stanford University—Green Library (CA-305/1)
>
> University at Albany (SUNY) Libraries (NY-20/2)
>
> University of Arizona Library (AZ-5/3)
>
> University of California, Berkeley—General Library (CA-70/1)
>
> University of Chicago—Regenstein Library (IL-85/1)
>
> University of Hawaii—Hamilton Library (HI-15/2)
>
> University of Kansas—Watson Library (KS-35/3)
>
> University of Notre Dame—Memorial Library (IN-95/1)
>
> University of Pennsylvania—Van Pelt Library (PA-215/1)
>
> University of Washington—East Asia Library (WA-35/1)
>
> Yale Divinity School Library (CT-55/2)
>
> Yale University—Sterling Memorial Library (CT-80/1)

GUTTERRES, Antonella Marie. *Lorettine Education in China, 1923-1952: Educational Activities of the Sisters of Loretto in China, Hanyang, and Shanghai*. St. Louis University (A.M.), 1961, 142p.

> St. Louis University—Pius XII Memorial Library (MO-75/2)
>
> Sisters of Loretto Archives (KY-65/1)

GUZMAN, Gregory. *Simon of Saint-Quentin and the Dominican Mission to the Mongols, 1245-1248*. University of Cincinnati (Ph.D.), 1968, n.p.

> University of Cincinnati—Central Library (OH-65/1)

HALE, Elizabeth Neal. *The Development of Interdenominational and International Cooperation in China: A Study in Missionary Congresses*. Woman's Missionary Union Training School (M.R.E.), 1932, 58p.

> Southern Baptist Theological Seminary—Boyce Centennial Library (KY-50/2)

HAN, Angeline B. Y. *The Social Work Program of the Riverside Church as a Resource for a Social Work Program of an Urban Church in China*. Columbia University (M.A.), 1948, 100p.

> Columbia University—School of Social Work Library (NY-185/1)
>
> Drew University—United Methodist Archives (NJ-45/5)

HAND, Katharine Whitney. *A Study of Curriculum Trends in the Christian Education Programs of Selected Mission Schools in China*. Biblical Seminary in New York (M.R.E.), 1941, 125p.

> Biblical Theological Seminary Library (PA-70/1)

HANSON, Eric Osborne. *The Chinese State and the Catholic Church: The Politics of Religion within the Confucian-sectarian Dynamic.* Stanford University (Ph.D.), 1976, 279p.

Stanford University—Green Library (CA-305/1)

University of Notre Dame—Memorial Library (IN-95/1)

HANSON, Richard. *Nestorian Christianity in China.* Union Theological Seminary (M.A.), 1930, 52p.

Union Theological Seminary—Burke Library (NY-275/1)

HARRIS, George L. *The Mission of Matteo Ricci, S.J.: A Case Study of an Effort at Guided Cultural Change in China in the Sixteenth Century.* Catholic University of America (Ph.D.), 1967, 246p.

Catholic University of America—Mullen Library (DC-20/1)

Cornell University—Wason Collection (NY-95/1)

Johns Hopkins University—Eisenhower Library (MD-10/1)

Stanford University—Green Library (CA-305/1)

Wheaton College—Graham Center Library (IL-205/1)

HARRIS, Hendon Mason. *Indigenous Churches in China.* Southern Baptist Theological Seminary (Th.D.), 1927, 250p.

Southern Baptist Theological Seminary—Boyce Centennial Library (KY-50/2)

Wheaton College—Graham Center Library (IL-205/1)

HART, H. D. *The Missionary Life and Work of W. R. Lambuth.* Emory University (B.D.), 1924, 37p.

Emory University—Pitts Theology Library (GA-15/5)

HARTMAN, Lucile. *Problems of Christian Education in Western Hunan, China.* Biblical Seminary in New York (M.R.E.), 1946, 116p.

Biblical Theological Seminary Library (PA-70/1)

HASS, Ilse. *Die Protestantische Christenheit in der Volksrepublik China und die Chinaberichterstattung in der Deutschen evangelischen Missionsliteratur (Protestant Christianity in the People's Republic of China and Reportorial Coverage of China in German Evangelical Missionary Literature).* Hamburg (thesis), 1974, 314p.

Cornell University—Wason Collection (NY-95/1)

Graduate Theological Union Library (CA-15/2)

University of Illinois at Urbana-Champaign Library (IL-185/1)

University of Michigan—Hatcher Graduate Library (MI-25/1)

Yale Divinity School Library (CT-55/2)

HATTOX, David Hubert. *The Protestant Missionary in China: The Career of Annie Jenkins Sallee, 1905-1930.* Baylor University (M.A.), 1977, 110p.

Baylor University—Moody Memorial Library (TX-60/1)

HAVERMALE, Lewis Frederick. *The Transfer of the Functions of Christian Missions and the Assumption Thereof by the Chinese Church.* University of Chicago (A.M.), 1932, 295p.

University of Chicago—Regenstein Library (IL-85/1)

HAWK, Mary Ellen. *Indigenous Materials in Chinese Christian Worship.* Union Theological Seminary (M.A.), 1945, n.p.

Union Theological Seminary—Burke Library (NY-275/1)

HAWKES, Jean McCown. *Women in a Changing China: The YWCA.* University of Michigan (Senior thesis), 1971, 64p.

University of Michigan—Hatcher Graduate Library (MI-25/1)

Yale Divinity School—Special Collections (CT-50/7)

HAWKINS, John N. *Francis Lister Hawks Pott—1864-1947: China Missionary and Educator.* Peabody College (thesis), 1971, 26p.

Yale Divinity School—Special Collections (CT-50/7)

HEARON, William C. *The Confrontation: American Catholicism and Chinese Communism, 1945-1952.* Vassar College (B.A.), 1975, 155p.

Maryknoll Fathers and Brothers Library (NY-115/1)

University of Georgia Libraries (GA-5/1)

Vassar College Library (NY-330/1)

HEININGER, Janet Elaine. *The American Board in China: The Missionaries' Experiences and Attitudes, 1911-1952.* University of Wisconsin, Madison (Ph.D.), 1981, 358p.

Denver Conservative Baptist Seminary—Thomas Library (CO-10/3)

Maryknoll Fathers and Brothers Library (NY-115/1)

University of Wisconsin-Madison Memorial Library (WI-45/1)

Wheaton College—Graham Center Library (IL-205/1)

HIEB, S. P. *A Survey of American Protestant Foreign Mission Colleges.* University of Nebraska (M.A.), 1925, 49p.

Union Theological Seminary—Burke Library (NY-275/1)

University of Nebraska—Love Library (NB-25/2)

HINES, George Estel. *American (Northern) Baptist Work in East China.* Northern Baptist Theological Seminary (B.D.), 1951, 91p.

Bethany and Northern Baptist Theological Seminaries Library (IL-135/1)

HO, Charles. *The Role in National Leadership of the East China Baptist Convention: Otherwise Known as the Chekiang-Shanghai Baptist Convention.* Berkeley Baptist Divinity School (B.D.), 1960, 90p.

Graduate Theological Union Library (CA-15/2)

Union Theological Seminary—Burke Library (NY-275/1)

HO Hoi-lap. *Protestant Missionary Publications in Modern China, 1912-1949: A Study of Their Programs, Operations, and Trends.* University of Chicago (Ph.D.), 1979, 273p.

University of Chicago—Regenstein Library (IL-85/1)

Wheaton College—Graham Center Library (IL-205/1)

HOBART, Kenneth Gray. *A Comparative History of the East China and South China Missions of the American Baptist Foreign Mission Society, 1833-1935: A Study of the Intensive vs. the Extensive Policy in Mission Work.* Yale University (Ph.D.), 1937, 772p.

American Baptist Historical Society (NY-345/23)

American Baptist Seminary of the West Library (CA-10/1)

Yale Divinity School Library (CT-55/2)

Yale University—Sterling Memorial Library (CT-80/1)

HOCKIN, Katharine B. *Christian and National Influences in the Development of Modern Chinese Education.* Union Theological Seminary (M.A.), 1947, 112p.

Union Theological Seminary—Burke Library (NY-275/1)

HOCKIN, Katharine B. *A Method and Plan of Work for Developing a Program in Religious Education for Christian Secondary Schools for Girls in Szechuan, China.* Columbia University Teachers' College (Ed.D.), 1948, 338p.

Columbia University—Milbank Library (NY-165/4)

HOH Yam-tong. *The Boxer Indemnity Remissions and Education in China.* Columbia University Teachers' College (Ph.D.), 1933, 485p.

Columbia University—Milbank Library (NY-165/4)

HOLDEN, Reuben Andrus. *An Educational Experience in China: The Story of the Development of Yale-in-China.* Yale University (Ph.D.), 1951, 307p.

Yale University—Sterling Memorial Library (CT-80/1)

HSIANG, Paul Stanislaus. *The Catholic Missions in China during the Middle Ages, 1294–1368*. Catholic University of America (S.T.D.), 1949, 213p.

Catholic University of America—Mullen Library (DC-20/1)
Wheaton College—Graham Center Library (IL-205/1)

HSIEH Ching-shen. *The Christian Church in Rural China*. Hartford Theological Seminary (S.T.M.), 1942, 120p.

Hartford Seminary Foundation—Case Memorial Library (CT-15/7)

HSÜ Hsiang-ch'u. *L'Oeuvre de T'ang T'ai-tsong (The Work of T'ang T'ai-tsong)*. Université l'Aurore, Shanghai (Ph.D.), 1924, 154p.

Field Museum of Natural History Library (IL-40/1)

HU Kuo-t'ai. *Tsao ch'i Mei-kuo chiao hui tsai Hua chiao yü shih yeh chih chien li (The Establishment of Early American Educational Missions in China)*. Taiwan National University (M.A.), 1980, 145p.

University of California, Santa Barbara, Library (CA-275/2)

HUANG, Carol Shu Ngo. *Aspects of Religious Education in China with Particular Reference to Developments in the Hinghwa Annual Conference*. Emory University (M.A.), 1948, 129p.

Emory University—Woodruff Library (GA-25/1)

HUANG Chao-hung. *Ch'ing mo yü Hua hsi chiao shih chih cheng lun chi ch'i ying hsiang (The Political Commentaries of Western Missions in China and Their Influence on Late Ch'ing Government)*. National Political University (Kuo-li cheng chih ta-hsüeh) (M.A.), 1970, 344p.

Yale University—Sterling Memorial Library (CT-80/1)

HUBBARD, Mabel Ellis. *An Experiment in Teaching the Christian Religion by Life Situations in Fan Village, China*. Oberlin College (M.A.), 1938, 87p.

American Congregational Association Library (MA-25/3)
Bangor Theological Seminary—Moulton Library (ME-5/1)
Graduate Theological Union Library (CA-15/2)
Oberlin College—Special Collections (OH-180/1)
University of Oregon Library (OR-20/2)
Vanderbilt University—Divinity Library (TN-65/1)
Yale Divinity School Library (CT-55/2)

HUNTER, Jane Harlow. *Imperial Evangelism: American Women Missionaries in Turn-of-the-Century China*. Yale University (Ph.D.), 1981, n.p.

Yale University—Sterling Memorial Library (CT-80/1)

HUTCHISON, Anna M. *China and Her People*. Bethany Biblical Seminary (B.S.L.), 1919, 13p.

Bethany and Northern Baptist Theological Seminaries Library (IL-135/1)

HYATT, Irwin Townsend, Jr. *Patterns at Tengchow: Life Experiences of Three American Missionaries in East Shantung Province, China, 1864–1882*. Harvard University (Ph.D.), 1969, 195p.

Harvard University—Harvard-Yenching Library (MA-125/6)
Harvard University—Pusey Library (MA-150/3)
Harvard University—Widener Library (MA-155/1)

IMLER, William A. *The Evangelistic Campaigns of Sherwood Eddy in India and China, 1896–1931*. Yale Divinity School (M.S.T.), 1953, 107p.

Yale Divinity School Library (CT-55/2)
Yale Divinity School—Special Collections (CT-50/23)

IVERSON, Christine E. *Called to Be a Wife, a Mother, and a Missionary: The Correspondence of Alice Holmberg Landahl,* *1899–1913*. Luther Northwestern Theological Seminary (M.A.), 1984, n.p.

Luther Northwestern Theological Seminary Library (MN-100/1)

JAMES, Clifton Cleve. *A History of Nazarene Missions in China*, Nazarene Theological Seminary (B.D.), 1948, 151p.

Nazarene Theological Seminary—Broadhurst Library (MO-35/1)

JAMES, Violet B. *Why Christianity Failed to Take Root in the Soil of China*. Wheaton College (M.A.), 1978, n.p.

Wheaton College—Department of Special Collections (IL-190/1)

JOHNSON, Rita Thérèse. *Timothy Richard's Theory of Christian Missions to the Non-Christian World*. St. John's University (Ph.D.), 1966, 332p.

Denver Conservative Baptist Seminary—Thomas Library (CO-10/3)
Graduate Theological Union Library (CA-15/2)
Maryknoll Sisters of St. Dominic—Archives (NY-120/1)
Maryknoll Sisters of St. Dominic—Rogers Library (NY-125/1)
St. John's University Archives (NY-105/1)
Westminster Theological Seminary Library (PA-220/2)
Wheaton College—Graham Center Library (IL-205/1)

JOHNSSON, Stephen Henning. *The Influence of American Missionaries in China upon the Foreign Policy of the United States, 1931–1941*. Georgetown University (M.A.), 1956, 233p.

Georgetown University—Lauinger Library (DC-60/1)
Stanford University—Green Library (CA-305/1)

JONES, Clara. *The Cross in Conquest over China*. University unknown, 1958, 164p.

Yale Divinity School—Special Collections (CT-50/7)

JONES, Maud Risher. *A Study of Some Phases of the Christian Religious Education of Adults in China*. Hartford School of Religious Education (B.R.E.), 1929, n.p.

Hartford Seminary Foundation—Case Memorial Library (CT-15/7)

JONSON, Jonas. *Lutheran Missions in a Time of Revolution: The China Experience, 1944–1951*. Uppsala (thesis), 1972, 230p.

Andrews University—White Library (MI-50/1)
Associated Mennonite Biblical Seminaries Library (IN-25/3)
Calvin College and Seminary Library (MI-85/1)
Colgate-Rochester Theological Seminary—Swasey Library (NY-350/1)
Denver Conservative Baptist Seminary—Thomas Library (CO-10/3)
Duke University—Divinity School Library (NC-30/2)
Fuller Theological Seminary—McAlister Library (CA-205/1)
Graduate Theological Union Library (CA-15/2)
Harvard University—Widener Library (MA-155/1)
Johns Hopkins University—Eisenhower Library (MD-10/1)
Princeton Theological Seminary—Speer Library (NJ-95/3)
University of California, Berkeley—General Library (CA-70/1)
University of Chicago—Regenstein Library (IL-85/1)
University of Illinois at Urbana-Champaign Library (IL-185/1)
University of Kansas—Watson Library (KS-35/3)
University of Wisconsin-Madison Memorial Library (WI-45/1)

Virginia Theological Seminary—Payne Library (VA-5/1)

KANE, James Herbert. *The Protestant Church in Communist China, 1949-1958*. Brown University (M.A.), 1958, 352p.

Brown University Archives (RI-10/1)

Harvard Divinity School—Andover-Harvard Theological Library (MA-95/2)

Union Theological Seminary—Burke Library (NY-275/1)

Wheaton College—Graham Center Library (IL-205/1)

KAO Tien-hsi. *How Shall the Chinese Church Continue Its Work under the Communist Government?* Princeton Theological Seminary (Th.M.), 1950, 146p.

Princeton Theological Seminary—Speer Library (NJ-95/3)

Union Theological Seminary—Burke Library (NY-275/1)

KAUFMAN, John E. *The Beginning and Growth of the Educational Mission Work in China of the Mennonite General Conference of North America*. Witmarsum Theological Seminary (Ph.D.), 1924, 57p.

Associated Mennonite Biblical Seminaries Library (IN-25/3)

Bethel College—Mennonite Library and Archives (KS-55/13)

KELLY, Colleen Adele. *The Educational Philosophy and Work of Welthy Honsinger Fisher in China and India: 1906-1980*. University of Connecticut (Ph.D.), 1983, 484p.

University of Connecticut—Babbidge Library (CT-90/1)

KELLY, Edward T. *The Anti-Christian Persecution of 1616-1617 in Nanking*. Columbia University (Ph.D.), 1971, 372p.

Columbia University—Starr East Asian Library (NY-195/4)

Cornell University—Wason Collection (NY-95/1)

University of Michigan—Hatcher Graduate Library (MI-25/1)

KELLY, Kathleen. *Maryknoll in Manchuria, 1927-1947: A Study of Accommodation and Adaptation*. University of Southern California (Ph.D.), 1982, 568p.

Maryknoll Sisters of St. Dominic—Archives (NY-120/1)

Mount St. Mary's College—Coe Library (CA-155/1)

University of Southern California—Von Kleinsmid Center Library (CA-190/2)

KIKUCHI, Bert Hideo. *Timothy Richard's Influence on the Missionary Movement and Chinese Reform in Late Ch'ing*. University of Oregon (M.A.), 1969, 115p.

University of Oregon Library (OR-20/2)

KIM, Sung-hae. *The Righteous and the Sage: A Comparative Study on the Ideal Images of Man in Biblical Israel and Classical China*. Harvard Divinity School (Th.D.), 1981, 471p.

Harvard Divinity School—Andover-Harvard Theological Library (MA-95/2)

KING, Marjorie. *Missionary Mother and Radical Daughter: Anna and Ida Pruitt in China, 1887-1939*. Temple University (Ph.D.), 1985, 461p.

Temple University—Paley Library (PA-210/2)

Wheaton College—Graham Center Library (IL-205/1)

KITZAN, Laurence. *The London Missionary Society in India and China, 1798-1834*. University of Toronto (Ph.D.), 1965, 242p.

Duke University—Perkins Library (NC-55/1)

Stanford University—Green Library (CA-305/1)

KLINE, Frank J. *James Hudson Taylor, Christian Statesman*. Biblical Seminary in New York (S.T.B.), 1936, 138p.

Biblical Theological Seminary Library (PA-70/1)

KOO, Daniel C. *A Practical Program for Character Training in Yuih Dzae Academy (A Baptist Mission School in China)*. Andover Newton Theological School (M.R.E.), 1935, 56p.

Andover Newton Theological School—Trask Library (MA-180/2)

KORSON, Thomas Eliot. *Congregational Missionaries in Foochow during the 1911 Revolution*. Harvard University (Honors Thesis), 1963, 63p.

Harvard Divinity School—Andover-Harvard Theological Library (MA-95/2)

KRAHL, Joseph. *China Missions in Crisis: Bishop Laimbeckhoven and His Times, 1738-1787*. Pontificia Universit*a Gregoriana (thesis), 1964, 383p.

Baylor University—Moody Memorial Library (TX-60/1)

Brigham Young University—Lee Library (UT-10/1)

Calvin College and Seminary Library (MI-85/1)

Catholic Theological Union Library (IL-20/1)

Duke University—Divinity School Library (NC-30/2)

Garrett-Evangelical and Seabury-Western Theological Seminaries—United Library (IL-110/1)

Graduate Theological Union Library (CA-15/2)

Indiana University—University Libraries (IN-20/2)

Luther Northwestern Theological Seminary Library (MN-100/1)

St. Louis University—Pius XII Memorial Library (MO-75/2)

St. Mary of the Lake Seminary—Feehan Memorial Library (IL-130/1)

United Theological Seminary Library (OH-120/11)

University of California at Los Angeles—University Research Library (CA-185/1)

University of Chicago—Regenstein Library (IL-85/1)

University of Minnesota—Wilson Library (MN-40/1)

University of Oregon Library (OR-20/2)

University of Washington Libraries (WA-45/1)

KU, Joseph King-hap. *Hsu Kuang-chi: Chinese Scientist and Christian (1562-1633)*. St. John's University, NY (Ph.D.), 1973, 171p.

Cornell University—Wason Collection (NY-95/1)

St. John's University Archives (NY-105/1)

Union Theological Seminary—Burke Library (NY-275/1)

Wheaton College—Graham Center Library (IL-205/1)

KUEPERS, Jacobus Joannes Antonius Mathias. *China und die katholische Mission in Süd-Shantung, 1882-1900: die Geschichte einer Konfrontation (China and the Catholic Mission in South Shantung, 1882-1900: The Story of a Confrontation)*. Nijmegen (thesis), 1974, 232p.

Harvard University—Harvard-Yenching Library (MA-125/6)

Princeton Theological Seminary—Speer Library (NJ-95/3)

University of Arizona Library (AZ-5/3)

Yale Divinity School Library (CT-55/2)

KUNOS, Jeno. *Working Out a New Approach to Chinese Social Units, Particularly Village and Clan*. Kennedy School of Missions (M.A.), 1948, 194p.

Hartford Seminary Foundation—Case Memorial Library (CT-15/7)

KURZ, A. Vernon. *The Protestant Missionary Approach in China*. Eden Theological Seminary (B.Div.), 1946, 68p.

Eden Theological Seminary—Eden-Webster Libraries (MO-60/1)

KWANG Eu-yang. *The Political Reconstruction of China*. St. John's University of China (M.A.), 1922, 190p.

Cornell University—Wason Collection (NY-95/1)

Princeton University—Firestone Library (NJ-100/1)

KWOK, Benjamin Bock-on. *Political Status of Missionaries in China*. Vanderbilt University, School of Religion (B.D.), 1934, 125p.

Vanderbilt University—Divinity Library (TN-65/1)

KWOK, David C. P. *Timothy Richard's Contribution to the Christian Church in China*. Berkeley Baptist Divinity School (M.A.), 1957, 86p.
  Graduate Theological Union Library (CA–15/2)

LACY, Creighton Boutelle. *Protestant Missions in Communist China*. Yale University (Ph.D.), 1953, 670p.
  Colgate-Rochester Theological Seminaries—Swasey Library (NY–350/1)
  Cornell University—Wason Collection (NY–95/1)
  Graduate Theological Union Library (CA–15/2)
  Princeton Theological Seminary—Speer Library (NJ–95/3)
  Stanford University—Green Library (CA–305/1)
  Union Theological Seminary—Burke Library (NY–275/1)
  Wheaton College—Graham Center Library (IL–205/1)
  Yale Divinity School Library (CT–55/2)
  Yale University—Sterling Memorial Library (CT–80/1)

LAIR, Howell Portman. *The Shantung Presbyterian Mission*. Union Theological Seminary (S.T.M.). 1922, 72p.
  Union Theological Seminary—Burke Library (NY–275/1)

LAM Ch'i-hung. *Political Activities of the Christian Missionaries in the T'ang Dynasty*. University of Denver (Ph.D.), 1975, 254p.
  Cornell University—Wason Collection (NY–95/1)
  University of Denver—Penrose Library (CO–20/1)
  Virginia Theological Seminary—Payne Library (VA–5/1)
  Wheaton College—Graham Center Library (IL–205/1)

LAM, Cyrus On-kwok. *The Chinese Church: A Bridge to World Evangelization*. Fuller Theological Seminary, School of World Mission (D.Miss), 1983, 283p. (in Chinese and English).
  Emory University—Pitts Theology Library (GA–15/5)
  Fuller Theological Seminary—McAlister Library (CA–205/1)
  Union Theological Seminary—Burke Library (NY–275/1)
  Wheaton College—Graham Center Library (IL–205/1)

LAM Wing-hung. *The Emergence of a Protestant Christian Apologetics in the Chinese Church during the Anti-Christian Movement in the 1920s*. Princeton Theological Seminary (Ph.D.), 1978, 353p.
  Fuller Theological Seminary—McAlister Library (CA–205/1)
  Princeton Theological Seminary—Speer Library (NJ–95/3)
  Union Theological Seminary—Burke Library (NY–275/1)
  Yale Divinity School Library (CT–55/2)

LAMKIN, Adrian, Jr. *The Gospel Mission Movement within the Southern Baptist Convention*. Southern Baptist Theological Seminary (Ph.D.), 1980, 242p.
  Fuller Theological Seminary—McAlister Library (CA–205/1)
  Southern Baptist Convention—Jenkins Research Library (VA–70/1)
  Southern Baptist Theological Seminary—Boyce Centennial Library (KY–50/2)
  Wheaton College—Graham Center Library (IL–205/1)

LAU, Albert S. L. *The New Life Movement and Its Significance to the Christian Church of China*. Berkeley Baptist Divinity School (Th.B.), 1940, 66p.
  Graduate Theological Union Library (CA–15/2)

LAZO, Dimitr Daniel. *An Enduring Encounter: E. T. Williams, China, and the United States*. University of Illinois at Urbana-Champaign (Ph.D.), 1977, 407p.

Cornell University—Wason Collection (NY–95/1)
Stanford University—Green Library (CA–305/1)
University of Illinois at Urbana-Champaign Library (IL–185/1)

LEAVELL, Ulin W. *Some Phases of the Administration of Christian Education for Boys in China*. George Peabody College (M.A.), 1921, 109p.
  University of Virginia—Manuscripts Department (VA–25/6)
  Vanderbilt University—Divinity Library (TN–65/1)

LEE, Mavis Shoa-ling. *A Collection of Hymns for Use in Chinese Churches, Centers, and Schools in China*. Berkeley Baptist Divinity School (Th.M.), 1951, n.p.
  Graduate Theological Union Library (CA–15/2)

LEE, Peter Hsing-hsien. *A Study of Progressive Christian Education in Light of the Needs of China*. Southern Baptist Theological Seminary (Ph.D.), 1950, 166p.
  Southern Baptist Theological Seminary—Boyce Centennial Library (KY–50/2)

LEE, Samuel Mau-cheng. *A Comparative Study of Leadership Selection Processes among Four Chinese Leaders*. Fuller Theological Seminary, School of World Mission (D.Miss.), 1985, 408p.
  Emory University—Pitts Theology Library (GA–15/5)
  Fuller Theological Seminary—McAlister Library (CA–205/1)

LEE, Seung-ik. *The New China: An Eastern Version of Messianic Hope*. University of Pittsburgh (Ph.D.), 1982, 270p.
  Emory University—Pitts Theology Library (GA–15/5)
  University of Pittsburgh—Hillman Library (PA–260/1)

LEE LIM, Guek-eng Violet. *Cognitive Processes and Linguistic Forms in Old Testament Hebrew and Chinese Cultures: Implications for Translation*. Fuller Theological Seminary (Ph.D.), 1986, 464p.
  Fuller Theological Seminary—McAlister Library (CA–205/1)

LEFEVER, Myrtle M. *Proposed Plans for the Revision of the Program of Religious Education for the Sixth to the Ninth Grades, Miller Seminary, Siu Laam, China*. Biblical Seminary in New York (M.R.E.), 1931, 99p.
  Biblical Theological Seminary Library (PA–70/1)

LEFFORGE, Roxy. *Some Guiding Principles for Christian Education in China Today*. Boston University School of Theology (D.R.E.), 1933, 457p.
  Boston University—School of Theology Library (MA–35/1)
  Yale Divinity School Library (CT–55/2)

LEGER, Samuel Howard. *Education of Christian Ministers in China: An Historical and Critical Study*. Columbia University (Ph.D.), 1925, 118p.
  Columbia University—Milbank Library (NY–165/4)
  Emory University—Pitts Theology Library (GA–15/5)
  Harvard Divinity School—Andover-Harvard Theological Library (MA–95/2)
  Yale Divinity School Library (CT–55/2)

LENNOX, William Gordon. *A Comparative Study of Missionary Families in Japan, China, and a Selected Group in America*. University of Denver (M.A.), 1921, 121p.
  University of Denver—Penrose Library (CO–20/1)

LI, Anthony C. *The History of Privately Controlled Higher Education in the Republic of China*. Catholic University of America (Ph.D.), 1954, 157p.
  Catholic University of America—Mullen Library (DC–20/1)

California (Th.M.), 1952, 281p.

    Drew University—United Methodist Archives (NJ–45/5)

    University of Southern California—Von Kleinsmid Center Library (CA–190/2)

LI Ching-lien. *The Renaissance in China in the Twentieth Century (Especially with Reference to Education and Religion)*. Hartford School of Religious Education (M.A.), 1930, 125p.

    Hartford Seminary Foundation—Case Memorial Library (CT–15/7)

LI Guang-zhao. *Evangelizing China: Four Centuries of Failure*. University of Virginia (M.A.), 1983, 113p.

    University of Virginia—Alderman Library (VA–30/1)

LI Gwan-fang. *The Contribution of Religious Education to the Democratization of China*. Boston University (M.R.E.), 1927, 153p.

    Boston University—School of Theology Library (MA–35/1)

LIANG Si-ing. *La Rencontre et le conflit entre les idées des missionnaires chrétiens et les idées des Chinois en Chine depuis la fin de la dynastie des Ming (The Encounter and the Conflict between Christian Missionary Thought and the Thought of the Chinese in China Since the End of the Ming Dynasty)*. Université de Paris (thesis), 1940, 159p.

    Harvard University—Widener Library (MA–155/1)

    University of Michigan—Hatcher Graduate Library (MI–25/1)

    University of Pennsylvania—Van Pelt Library (PA–215/1)

    Yale Divinity School Library (CT–55/2)

LIDE, Francis Pugh. *The Training of an Efficient Native Leadership for the Christian Churches of China*. Southern Baptist Theological Seminary (Ph.D.), 1928, 125p.

    Southern Baptist Theological Seminary—Boyce Centennial Library (KY–50/2)

LIE Hwa-sun. *Der Begriff Skandalon im neuen Testament und der Wiederkehrgedanke bei Laotse (The Concept of Scandal in the New Testament and the Recurring Thought of Lao-tse)*. Frankfurt am Mein (thesis), 1973, 252p.

    Cornell University—Wason Collection (NY–95/1)

LIEO, Graham Yu Ling. *Christianity and the Chinese Republic*. Virginia Theological Seminary (B.D.), 1926, n.p.

    Virginia Theological Seminary—Payne Library (VA–5/1)

LIN, Robert Hsiang Teng. *The Taiping Revolution: A Comparative Historical and Sociological Study of a Movement from the Perspective of Intercivilizational Encounters and Missions*. New School for Social Research (Ph.D.), 1977, 201p.

    New School for Social Research Library (NY–215/1)

LINDBECK, John M. H. *American Missionaries and the Policies of the United States in China, 1898–1901*. Yale University (Ph.D.), 1948, 539p.

    Catholic Theological Union Library (IL–20/1)

    Maryknoll Fathers and Brothers Library (NY–115/1)

    St. Paul Seminary—Ireland Library (MN–110/1)

    Wheaton College—Graham Center Library (IL–205/1)

    Yale Divinity School Library (CT–55/2)

    Yale University—Sterling Memorial Library (CT–80/1)

LINDBERG, David Lloyd. *The Oriental Educational Commission's Recommendations for Mission Strategy in Higher Education*. University of Chicago (Ph.D.), 1972, 214p.

    University of California, Santa Barbara, Library (CA–275/2)

    University of Chicago—Regenstein Library (IL–85/1)

    Wheaton College—Graham Center Library (IL–205/1)

LINDQUIST, Harry Maurice. *North China Villages: A Comparative Analysis of Models in the Published and Unpublished Writings of Arthur Henderson Smith, American Missionary to China*. University of Kansas (Ph.D.), 1967, 259p.

    University of Kansas—Watson Library (KS–35/3)

LINDSTEDT, Lars Marwin. *A History of the Russian Mission of the Swedish Baptist General Conference of America*. Bethel Theological Seminary (B.D.), 1953, n.p.

    Bethel Theological Seminary—Archival Center of the Baptist General Conference (MN–45/1)

LING, Samuel D. *The Other May Fourth Movement: The Chinese "Christian Renaissance," 1919–1937*. Temple University (Ph.D.), 1980, 222p.

    Fuller Theological Seminary—McAlister Library (CA–205/1)

    Temple University—Paley Library (PA–210/2)

    Wheaton College—Graham Center Library (IL–205/1)

LITZINGER, Charles Albert. *Temple Community and Village Cultural Integration in North China: Evidence from "Sectarian Cases (chiao an)" in Chihli, 1860–1865*. University of California, Davis (Ph.D.), 1983, 288p.

    University of California, Davis—Department of Special Collections (CA–100/1)

    University of Oregon Library (OR–20/2)

LIU I-hsin. *An Educational Program for Young Adults Adaptable to the Christian Churches in China*. University of Southern California (Th.M.), 1952, 281p.

    Drew University—United Methodist Archives (NJ–45/5)

    University of Southern California—Von Kleinsmid Center Library (CA–190/2)

LIU Yu-ts'ang. *The Churches in Fukien: A Study of the Development of the Three Churches in North Fukien, China, and the Prospects of Church Unity*. Union Theological Seminary (S.T.M.), 1950, 142p.

    Union Theological Seminary—Burke Library (NY–275/1)

LO Ka-man. *The Missions' Responsibilities toward the Reopening of China*. Trinity Evangelical Divinity School (M.A.), 1971, 113p.

    Trinity Evangelical Divinity School Library (IL–90/1)

LODWICK, Kathleen Lorraine. *Chinese, Missionary, and International Efforts to End the Use of Opium in China, 1890–1916*. University of Arizona (Ph.D.), 1976, 309p.

    Cornell University—Wason Collection (NY–95/1)

    Stanford University—Green Library (CA–305/1)

    University of Arizona Library (AZ–5/3)

LUKE, Handel Hing-tat. *A History of Seventh-Day Adventist Higher Education in the China Mission, 1888–1980*. Andrews University (Ed.D.), 1983, 289p.

    Andrews University—White Library (MI–50/1)

    Denver Conservative Baptist Seminary—Thomas Library (CO–10/3)

    Loma Linda University Library (CA–220/1)

    Loma Linda University—Radcliffe Memorial Library (CA–135/1)

    Pacific Union College—Nelson Memorial Library (CA–5/1)

    Wheaton College—Graham Center Library (IL–205/1)

LUNDY, Robert Fielden. *The Missionary Policy of the Methodist Episcopal Church, South, in China, 1848–1911*. Emory University (B.D.), 1944, 163p.

    Emory University—Pitts Theology Library (GA–15/5)

LUOMA, John Kenneth Reynold. *The Anti-missionary Movement in China, 1922–1927: A Case Study of the Effect of Modernization on the Attitude toward Christian Missions*. Hartford Seminary Foundation (M.A.), 1970, 63p.

Hartford Seminary Foundation—Case Memorial Library (CT-15/7)

LUTZ, Jessie Gregory. *The Role of Christian Colleges in Modern China before 1928*. Cornell University (Ph.D.), 1955, 375p.

    Cornell University—Wason Collection (NY-95/1)

    University of California, Santa Cruz—McHenry Library (CA-285/2)

LYNN, Orlena Marie. *Fifty Years of Covenanter Evangelism in South China*. Biblical Seminary in New York (M.R.E.), 1948, 156p.

    Biblical Theological Seminary Library (PA-70/1)

    Reformed Presbyterian Theological Seminary Library (PA-245/3)

MA Yi-ying. *Christian Education in New-born China*. Biblical Seminary in New York (M.R.E.), 1941, 79p.

    Biblical Theological Seminary Library (PA-70/1)

McCAIN, Pearle. *An Educational Approach to the Task of the Christian Worker in China*. Union Theological Seminary (M.A.), 1944, 81p.

    Union Theological Seminary—Burke Library (NY-275/1)

McCAIN, Pearle. *A Plan for Developing a Functional Curriculum in the Bible Teachers Training School in Nanking, China, in the Post-war Era*. Columbia University Teachers' College (Ph.D.), 1946, 174p.

    Columbia University—Milbank Library (NY-165/4)

    Drew University—United Methodist Archives (NJ-45/5)

McCUTCHEON, James Miller. *The American and British Missionary Concept of Chinese Civilization in the Nineteenth Century*. University of Wisconsin (Ph.D.), 1959, 294p.

    Cornell University—Wason Collection (NY-95/1)

    Emory University—Woodruff Library (GA-25/1)

    Stanford University—Green Library (CA-305/1)

    University of Hawaii—Hamilton Library (HI-15/1)

    University of Wisconsin-Madison Memorial Library (WI-45/1)

    Wheaton College—Graham Center Library (IL-205/1)

McDONALD, Raphael. *Prefecture Apostolic of Shasi, 1913-1945*. St. Bonaventure College (M.A.), 1945, 86p.

    Provincial House of Most Holy Name Province of Franciscan Friars—Provincial Archives (NY-260/1)

    St. Bonaventure University—Franciscan Institute (NY-365/1)

McGOWN, David Jefferson. *Presbyterians in the Church of Christ in China*. Yale University (B.A.), 1947, n.p.

    Presbyterian Historical Society—Archives and Library (PA-200/28)

McINERNEY, Athanasius. *The Spanish Franciscans in the Province of Kiangsi, China, during the Years 1685-1813*. St. Bonaventure College (M.A.), 1949, 91p.

    St. Bonaventure University—Friedsam Library (NY-370/1)

McKAY, Moira Jane. *Faith and Facts in the History of the China Inland Mission, 1832-1905*. University of Aberdeen (M.Litt.), 1981, 452p.

    Fuller Theological Seminary—McAlister Library (CA-205/1)

    Wheaton College—Graham Center Library (IL-205/1)

McKIBBEN, C. R. *A History of the Educational Development of China*. Emory University (B.D.), 1922, 33p.

    Emory University—Pitts Theology Library (GA-15/5)

McMULLEN, Robert Johnston. *The Christian College Confronts Chinese Culture*. Union Theological Seminary (M.A.), 1936, 53p.

Union Theological Seminary—Burke Library (NY-275/1)

McMULLEN, Robert Johnston. *Lessons for China Missionaries from Paul, the Herald of the Gospel*. Southern Baptist Theological Seminary (Ph.D.), 1930, 166p.

    Southern Baptist Theological Seminary—Boyce Centennial Library (KY-50/2)

    Wheaton College—Graham Center Library (IL-205/1)

McMURRY, Francis P. *The China Tractor Boys*. University of Maryland (M.A.), 1969, 65p.

    Church of the Brethren General Board—Brethren Historical Library and Archives (IL-105/11)

    University of Maryland—McKeldin Library (MD-45/2)

MAK, Nancy K. *Christianity in Communist China*. Princeton University (Senior thesis), 1980, n.p.

    Princeton University—Gest Oriental Library (NJ-105/1)

MAN Kwok-chaak. *The Causes and Results of the Boxer Movement*. Lingnan University (thesis), 1936, 130p.

    Cornell University—Wason Collection (NY-95/1)

MARTH, Gladys E. *Present Movements in China Bearing upon the Post-war Program of the Christian Church*. Biblical Seminary in New York (M.R.E.), 1945, 139p.

    Biblical Theological Seminary Library (PA-70/1)

MARTIN, Elna Lucy. *Student Opinion and Christian Missions in China*. Southern Methodist University (B.D.), 1931, 54p.

    Southern Methodist University—Bridwell Theology Library (TX-20/2)

MARTIN, John P. *A Critical Survey of French Sinology, 1870-1900*. Georgetown University (M.A.), 1966, 105p.

    Georgetown University—Lauinger Library (DC-60/1)

MARTIN, Mary Lou. *Christianity in Modern China*. Mundelein College (M.A.), 1975, 82p.

    Maryknoll Sisters of St. Dominic—Archives (NY-120/1)

MARX, Edwin. *Missionary Administration in China*. Union Theological Seminary (B.D.), 1926, 57p.

    Union Theological Seminary—Burke Library (NY-275/1)

MASON, John Otto. *Missionary Educators and the Chinese Nationalist Revolution, 1925-1928*. University of Washington (M.A.), 1970, 194p.

    University of Washington Libraries (WA-45/1)

MASON, Sarah Margaret Refo. *Missionary Conscience and the Comprehension of Imperialism: A Study of the Children of American Missionaries to China, 1900-1949*. Northern Illinois University (Ph.D.), 1978, 428p.

    Andrews University—White Library (MI-50/1)

    Baylor University—Moody Memorial Library (TX-60/1)

    Cornell University—Wason Collection (NY-95/1)

    Emory University—Woodruff Library (GA-25/1)

    Northern Illinois University Libraries (IL-95/1)

    Princeton University—Firestone Library (NJ-100/1)

    Stanford University—Green Library (CA-305/1)

    Wheaton College—Graham Center Library (IL-205/1)

MASTERS, Seth J. *East and West: The Life and Times of Johann Adam Schall von Bell*. Princeton University (Senior thesis), 1981, n.p.

    Princeton University—Gest Oriental Library (NJ-105/1)

MATHIS, Marcian J. *The Constitution and Supreme Administration of Regional Seminaries Subject to the Sacred Congregation for the Propagation of the Faith in China*. Catholic University of America (Ph.D.), 1953, 172p.

    Catholic University of America—Mullen Library (DC-20/1)

    Dominican House of Studies Library (DC-30/1)

    Franciscan Province of the Sacred Heart—Archives (MO-65/1)

(MO–65/1)

MATTHEWS, Alden E. *Toward an Indigenous Church in China: A Study of Some Aspects of Chinese Protestantism's Concept of the Church, 1910–1950.* Union Theological Seminary (S.T.M.), 1952, 138p.

    Union Theological Seminary—Burke Library (NY–275/1)

MATTHEWS, Harold Shepard. *The Influence of the Modern Christian Missionaries on Social Conditions of China.* University of Chicago (A.M.), 1920, 35p.

    University of Chicago—Regenstein Library (IL–85/1)

MAYNARD, Edith. *Missionaries and Revolutionary Change: China, 1949–1951.* University of Virginia (M.A.), 1972, 101p.

    University of Virginia—Alderman Library (VA–30/1)

MEGGINSON, William James. *The Rural Work of American Protestant Missionaries in China, 1911–1937.* George Washington University (M.A.), 1968, 277p.

    George Washington University—Gelman Library (DC–45/2)
    Yale Divinity School Library (CT–55/2)
    Yale Divinity School—Special Collections (CT–50/2)

MELROSE, Anne Marie. *Some Aspects of Chinese Popular Religion as They Indicate Missionary and Educational Method.* Princeton Theological Seminary (M.R.E.), 1947, 74p.

    Princeton Theological Seminary—Speer Library (NJ–95/3)

MENSENDIEK, C. William. *The Protestant Missionary Understanding of the Chinese Situation and the Christian Task from 1890 to 1911.* Columbia University (Ph.D.), 1958, 335p.

    Austin Presbyterian Theological Seminary—Stitt Library (TX–10/1)
    Boston University—School of Theology Library (MA–35/1)
    Colgate-Rochester Theological Seminaries—Swasey Library (NY–350/1)
    Columbia University—Philosophy Library (NY–170/1)
    Cornell University—Wason Collection (NY–95/1)
    Denver Conservative Baptist Seminary—Thomas Library (CO–10/3)
    Emory University—Woodruff Library (GA–25/1)
    New York Public Library—General Research Division (NY–230/1)
    Northwest College of the Assemblies of God—Hurst Library (WA–10/1)
    Stanford University—Green Library (CA–305/1)
    Union Theological Seminary—Burke Library (NY–275/1)
    University of California, Santa Barbara, Library (CA–275/2)
    University of Chicago—Regenstein Library (IL–85/1)
    University of Hawaii—Hamilton Library (HI–15/2)
    University of Notre Dame—Memorial Library (IN–95/1)
    Wheaton College—Graham Center Library (IL–205/1)
    Yale Divinity School Library (CT–55/2)

MERKEL, Franz Rudolf. *G. W. Liebniz und die China-mission (G. W. Liebniz and the China Mission).* Göttingen (dissertation), 1920, 254p.

    University of California at Los Angeles—Department of Special Collections (CA–165/1)
    University of Pennsylvania—Van Pelt Library (PA–215/1)

MERRIAM, G. H. *Protestant Missions in China.* Clark University (M.A.), 1927, 215p.

    Clark University—Goddard Library (MA–270/1)

MERWIN, Wallace C. *The Relation of Church and Mission in the North China Mission of the Presbyterian Church in the U.S.A.* Union Theological Seminary (S.T.M.), 1938, 86p.

    Presbyterian Historical Society—Archives and Library

(PA–200/28)

    Union Theological Seminary—Burke Library (NY–275/1)

METZNER, Hans Wolfgang. *Roland Allen, sein Leben und Werk; kritischer Beitrag zum Verständnis von Mission und Kirche (Roland Allen, His Life and Work: A Critical Contribution to the Understanding of Mission and Church).* Heidelberg (thesis), 1970, 298p.

    Yale Divinity School Library (CT–55/2)

MEYER, Richard Henry. *The Missouri Evangelical Lutheran Mission in China, 1913–1948.* Washington University (M.A.), 1948, 57p.

    Princeton Theological Seminary—Speer Library (NJ–95/3)
    Union Theological Seminary—Burke Library (NY–275/1)
    University of Chicago—Regenstein Library (IL–85/1)
    Washington University—Olin Library (MO–95/1)
    Yale Divinity School Library (CT–55/2)

MIAO, Estelle. *A Survey of Religious Education in Chinese Christian Schools.* Berkeley Baptist Divinity School (M.A.), 1950, 70p.

    Graduate Theological Union Library (CA–15/2)

MINAMIKI, George Hisaharu. *The Modern Phase and Conclusion of the Chinese Rites Controversy.* University of Notre Dame (Ph.D.), 1977, 270p.

    Denver Conservative Baptist Seminary—Thomas Library (CO–10/3)
    Emory University—Pitts Theology Library (GA–15/5)
    Stanford University—Green Library (CA–305/1)
    University of Notre Dame—Memorial Library (IN–95/1)

MINNEN, Johannes Maarten van. *Accomodatie in de Chinese Zendingagescheidenis (Accommodation in the History of Chinese Missions).* Vrije Universiteit, Amsterdam (thesis), 1951, 190p.

    Calvin College and Seminary Library (MI–85/1)
    Harvard University—Widener Library (MA–155/1)
    Yale Divinity School Library (CT–55/2)

MINNICH, Herbert Spenser. *Devolution of Missionary Administration in China.* Northwestern University (M.A.), 1926, 95p.

    Bethany and Northern Baptist Theological Seminaries Library (IL–135/1)
    Church of the Brethren General Board—Brethren Historical Library and Archives (IL–105/11)
    Garrett-Evangelical and Seabury-Western Theological Seminaries—United Library (IL–110/1)
    Manchester College—Funderberg Library (IN–85/1)
    Northwestern University Library (IL–115/1)

MOFFETT, Samuel Hugh. *The Relation of the Board of Foreign Missions of the Presbyterian Church in the United States of America to the Missions and Church Connected with It in China.* Yale University (Ph.D.), 1945, n.p.

    Yale Divinity School Library (CT–55/2)
    Yale University—Sterling Memorial Library (CT–80/1)

MORRIS, John Glenn. *Christianity and Social Change in China, 1912–1942.* Southern Baptist Theological Seminary (Ph.D.), 1946, 175p.

    Southern Baptist Theological Seminary—Boyce Centennial Library (KY–50/2)
    Wheaton College—Graham Center Library (IL–205/1)

MOSS, C. G. G. *Missionary Participation in the Diplomacy of the United States in China: A Study of the Work of the Missionaries Bridgman, Parker, and Martin.* Yale University (M.A.), 1926, 84p.

Yale Divinity School—Special Collections (CT–50/20)

MURPHY, Alice Eugenia. *The Training of Laymen for Christian Service in North China*. Kennedy School of Missions (M.A.), 1938, 123p.

Hartford Seminary Foundation—Case Memorial Library (CT–15/7)

NAJARIAN, Nishan J. *A Symbolic Interactionist Approach to the Religious Stranger Concept: Protestant Missionaries in China, 1845–1900*. Drew University (Ph.D.), 1982, 548p.

Cornell University—Wason Collection (NY–95/1)

Denver Conservative Baptist Seminary—Thomas Library (CO–10/3)

Drew University Library (NJ–40/2)

Emory University—Pitts Theology Library (GA–15/5)

Wheaton College—Graham Center Library (IL–205/1)

NAPIER, Augustus Young. *The Challenge of China to America*. Southern Baptist Theological Seminary (Th.D.), 1922, 139p.

Southern Baptist Theological Seminary—Boyce Centennial Library (KY–50/2)

Wheaton College—Graham Center Library (IL–205/1)

NEGRON, Richard Edward. *The Jesuit Mission of Matteo Ricci: Christianity and the Chinese World View*. University of California, Davis (M.A.), 1984, 102p.

University of California, Davis—Department of Special Collections (CA–100/1)

NELSON, Daniel. *A Compendium of Basic Characters in Chinese Christian Thought*. Hartford Seminary Foundation (Ph.D.), 1943, 98p.

Hartford Seminary Foundation—Case Memorial Library (CT–15/7)

NEMER, Lawrence. *An Image of the French Religious Protectorate in China, as Reflected in the Catholic and Moderate Press at the Time of the Third Republic*. Catholic University of America (M.A.), 1967, 118p.

Catholic University of America—Mullen Library (DC–20/1)

Maryknoll Fathers and Brothers Library (NY–115/1)

NG, Lee-ming. *Christianity and Social Change: The Case in China, 1920–1950*. Princeton Theological Seminary (Th.D.), 1971, 279p.

Emory University—Pitts Theology Library (GA–15/5)

Fuller Theological Seminary—McAlister Library (CA–205/1)

Graduate Theological Union Library (CA–15/2)

Princeton Theological Seminary—Speer Library (NJ–95/3)

University of California at Los Angeles—University Research Library

University of California, Santa Barbara, Library (CA–275/2)

Wheaton College—Graham Center Library (IL–205/1)

NULL, Miriam Ellen. *Selection and Adaptation of Extra-Biblical Stories for Use in Christian Education of Chinese Girls of Intermediate Age*. Biblical Seminary in New York (M.R.E.), 1943, 165p.

Biblical Theological Seminary Library (PA–70/1)

O'NEILL, Joseph Patrick. *The American Protestant Missionary Movement: Its Impact on China*. Harvard University (Honors thesis), 1969, n.p.

Harvard University—Widener Library (MA–155/1)

ONSTOTT, Daniel. *China's Crisis*. Boston University (S.T.B.), 1894, 13p.

Boston University—School of Theology Library (MA–35/1)

OPPENHEIM, Raymond L. *The First Nestorian Mission to China:*

A Discussion of the History and Strategy of China's Earliest Christian Missionaries. Church Divinity School of the Pacific (M.A.), 1969, 103p.

Graduate Theological Union Library (CA–15/2)

OSE, Roger Keith. *A History of the Evangelical Lutheran Church of America's Mission Policy in China, 1899–1949*. New York University (Ph.D.), 1970, 247p.

American Lutheran Church Archives (MN–95/110)

Cornell University—Wason Collection (NY–95/1)

Denver Conservative Baptist Seminary—Thomas Library (CO–10/3)

Emory University—Pitts Theology Library (GA–15/5)

Graduate Theological Union Library (CA–15/2)

New York University—Bobst Library (NY–245/1)

University of Chicago—Regenstein Library (IL–85/1)

Wheaton College—Graham Center Library (IL–205/1)

OUTERBRIDGE, Leonard Mallory. *The Lost Churches of China: A Study of Contributing Factors in the Recurring Losses Sustained by Christianity in China during the Past Thirteen Hundred Years*. University of Chicago (Ph.D.), 1952, 222p.

University of Chicago—Regenstein Library (IL–85/1)

Vanderbilt University—Divinity School Library (TN–65/1)

OUTERBRIDGE, Leonard Mallory. *The Transformation of Religious Concepts in North China*. University of Chicago (A.M.), 1933, 137p.

University of Chicago—Regenstein Library (IL–85/1)

PADELFORD, Norman Judson. *The Legal Status of Alien Religious Property Situated in China*. Harvard University (Ph.D.), 1929, n.p.

Harvard University—Law School Library (MA–135/1)

Harvard University—Pusey Library (MA–150/3)

Harvard University—Widener Library (MA–155/1)

PAGE, Kirby. *The Young Men's Christian Associations of China*. University of Chicago (M.A.), 1916, 132p.

George Williams College Library (IL–100/1)

University of Chicago—Regenstein Library (IL–85/1)

PAI Chia-ling. *Chi-tu chiao Chung-wen chi k'an chih tiao ch'a, 1950–1975 (An Examination of Chinese Christian Periodicals, 1950–1975)*. China Graduate School of Theology (M.A.), 1976, 73p.

Princeton University—Gest Oriental Library (NJ–105/1)

University of Chicago—Regenstein Library (IL–85/1)

PAINTER, Robert C. *A History of the United Brethren Mission Work in China*. United Theological Seminary (M.Div.), 1945, 126p.

Drew University—United Methodist Historical Library (NJ–50/1)

United Theological Seminary Library (OH–120/11)

PALMER, Spencer John. *Protestant Christianity in China and Korea: The Problem of Identification with Tradition*. University of California, Berkeley (Ph.D.), 1964, 199p.

Emory University—Woodruff Library (GA–25/1)

Princeton Theological Seminary—Speer Library (NJ–95/3)

University of California, Berkeley—General Library (CA–70/1)

Wheaton College—Graham Center Library (IL–205/1)

PAN, Scott. *Karl (Charles) Gutzlaff and His Mission: The First Lutheran Missionary to East Asian Countries and China*. Luther Northwestern Theological Seminary (M.A.), 1985, n.p.

Luther Northwestern Theological Seminary Library (MN–100/1)

PARAGON, Donald. *Ying Lien-chih (1886–1926) and the Rise of Fu-jen, the Catholic University of Peking*. Columbia University (M.A.), 1957, 82p.

    Columbia University—Starr East Asian Library (NY-195/4)

PARRY, Albert. *Russian (Greek Orthodox) Missionaries in China, 1689–1917: Their Cultural, Political, and Economic Role*. University of Chicago (Ph.D.), 1938, 140p.

    Hoover Institution—East Asian Collection (CA-295/1)

    Princeton University—Gest Oriental Library (NJ-105/1)

    University of Chicago—Regenstein Library (IL-85/1)

    University of Hawaii—Hamilton Library (HI-15/2)

PATCH, Robert Clayton. *An Historical Overview of the Missionary Activities of the Church of Jesus Christ of Latter-Day Saints in Continental Asia*. Brigham Young University (M.A.), 1949, 217p.

    Brigham Young University—Lee Library (UT-10/1)

    Church of Jesus Christ of Latter-Day Saints—Historical Department (UT-15/1)

PATERNO, Roberto Montilla. *The Yangtze Valley Anti-missionary Riots of 1891*. Harvard University (Ph.D.), 1967, 712p.

    Harvard University—Pusey Library (MA-150/3)

    Harvard University—Widener Library (MA-155/1)

    Stanford University—Green Library (CA-305/1)

PEARSON, Alden Bryan. *The American Christian Press and the Sino-Japanese Crisis of 1931–1933: An Aspect of Public Response to the Breakdown of World Peace*. Duke University (Ph.D.), 1968, 309p.

    Cornell University—Wason Collection (NY-95/1)

    Duke University—Perkins Library (NC-55/1)

PHILLIPS, Clifton Jackson. *Protestant America and the Pagan World: The First Half Century of American Board of Commissioners for Foreign Missions, 1810–1860*. Harvard University (Ph.D.), 1954, n.p.

    Harvard University—Pusey Library (MA-150/3)

PICKENS, Henri Batcheller. *The Relation between Christian Missions and Economic Imperialism in China in the Nineteenth Century*. Virginia Theological Seminary (B.D.), 1937, 61p.

    Virginia Theological Seminary—Payne Library (VA-5/1)

POMMERENKE, Herbert Henry. *The Idea of the Church in the Minds of Protestant Missionaries to China*. Kennedy School of Missions (S.T.M.), 1937, 138p.

    Hartford Seminary Foundation—Case Memorial Library (CT-15/7)

PONZI, Patricia Hughes. *Maryknoll Sisters in China, 1921–1949*. St. John's University (M.A.), 1980, 120p.

    Maryknoll Sisters of St. Dominic—Archives (NY-120/1)

    St. John's University Archives (NY-105/1)

POPPEN, Alvin John. *The Life and Work of David Abeel*. Union Theological Seminary in New York (S.T.M.), 1959, 154p.

    New Brunswick Theological Seminary—Sage Library (NJ-65/1)

    Union Theological Seminary—Burke Library (NY-275/1)

POTTS, Anna Hortense. *Songs of Chinese Children: The Religious Education of Youth in the New China*. University of Chicago (M.A.), 1927, 76p.

    Claremont Colleges—Asian Studies Collection (CA-75/2)

    University of Chicago—Regenstein Library (IL-85/1)

POWERS, George C. *The Maryknoll Movement*. Catholic University of America (M.A.), 1926, 167p.

    Catholic University of America—Mullen Library (DC-20/1)

    Mount St. Mary's College—Special Collections (MD-55/1)

PRATT, J. H. *An Examination of Certain Chinese Institutions, Customs, Aesthetic Concepts, and Achievements, with a View to Determining How Far They Could Be Naturalized in the Practice and Teaching of the Christian Church in China*. Oxford University (B.L.), 1935, 158p.

    Union Theological Seminary—Burke Library (NY-275/1)

PRICE, Allen Thomas. *American Missions and American Diplomacy in China, 1830–1900: A Study of the Relations of American Missionaries, American Missions, and the American Missionary Movement to the Official Relations between the United States and China to 1900*. Harvard University (Ph.D.), 1932, 751p.

    Harvard University—Pusey Library (MA-150/3)

    Harvard University—Widener Library (MA-155/1)

    University of Maryland—McKeldin Library (MD-45/2)

    University of Pennsylvania—Van Pelt Library (PA-215/1)

PRICE, Frank W. *The Rural Church in China*. Yale University (Ph.D.), 1938, 296p.

    Union Theological Seminary in Virginia Archives (VA-80/2)

    Yale University—Sterling Library (CT-80/1)

PROCTOR, John Thomas. *Methods of Mission Work in China*. University of Chicago (D.B.), 1896, 30p.

    University of Chicago—Regenstein Library (IL-85/1)

PRUDEN, George Blackburn, Jr. *Issachar Jacox [i.e., Jacob] Roberts and American Diplomacy in China during the Taiping Rebellion*. American University (Ph.D.), 1977, 333p.

    American University Library (DC-5/1)

    Cornell University—Wason Collection (NY-95/1)

    Southern Baptist Convention—Jenkins Research Library (VA-70/1)

    Stanford University—Green Library (CA-305/1)

PUGH, James. *J. Lossing Buck, American Missionary: The Application of Scientific Agriculture in China, 1915–1944*. Swarthmore College (thesis), 1973, 104p.

    Presbyterian Historical Society—Archives and Library (PA-200/28)

    Swarthmore College—Friends Historical Library (PA-270/4)

PURNOMO, David H. *Evangelism in the Chinese Church*. Mennonite Brethren Biblical Seminary (M.Div.), 1981, 66p.

    Center for Mennonite Brethren Studies—Archives and Historical Library (CA-115/1)

QUALE, Gladys Robina. *The Mission Compound in Modern China: The Role of the United States Protestant Mission as an Asylum in the Civil and International Strife of China, 1900–1941*. University of Michigan (Ph.D.), 1957, 311p.

    Austin Presbyterian Theological Seminary—Stitt Library (TX-10/1)

    Colgate-Rochester Theological Seminaries—Swasey Library (NY-350/1)

    Cornell University—Wason Collection (NY-95/1)

    Emory University—Woodruff Library (GA-25/1)

    Graduate Theological Union Library (CA-15/2)

    Harvard Divinity School—Andover-Harvard Theological Library (MA-95/2)

    Kalamazoo College—Upjohn Library (MI-125/1)

    St. John's University—Alcuin Library (MN-5/1)

    Stanford University—Green Library (CA-305/1)

    Union Theological Seminary—Burke Library (NY-275/1)

    University of California, Santa Cruz—McHenry Library (CA-285/2)

    University of Hawaii—Hamilton Library (HI-15/2)

    University of Michigan—Hatcher Graduate Library

(MI–25/1)

    Wheaton College—Graham Center Library (IL–205/1)

    Yale Divinity School Library (CT–55/2)

RABE, Valentin Hanno. *The American Protestant Foreign Mission Movement, 1880–1920*. Harvard University (Ph.D.), 1965, n.p.

    Harvard University—Pusey Library (MA–150/3)

    Harvard University—Widener Library (MA–155/1)

RAH Halk-jin. *The Political Relevance of 'jen' in Early China and 'agape' in the Theology of Reinhold Niebuhr*. Princeton Theological Seminary (Ph.D.), 1975, 268p.

    Princeton Theological Seminary—Speer Library (NJ–95/3)

RANKIN, Milledge Theron. *A Critical Examination of the National Christian Council of China*. Southern Baptist Theological Seminary (Th D.), 1928, 127p.

    Southern Baptist Convention—Archives (VA–65/2)

    Southern Baptist Theological Seminary—Boyce Centennial Library (KY–50/2)

    Wheaton College—Graham Center Library (IL–205/1)

REAMEY, G. S. *The Present Religious Situation in China*. Emory University (B.D.), 1922, 40p.

    Emory University—Pitts Theology Library (GA–15/5)

REBER, Calvin H., Jr. *Protestant Christianity and Marriage in China*. Columbia University (Ph.D.), 1958, 403p.

    Austin Presbyterian Theological Seminary—Stitt Library (TX–10/1)

    Colgate-Rochester Theological Seminaries—Swasey Library (NY–350/1)

    Columbia University—Philosophy Library (NY–170/1)

    Cornell University—Wason Collection (NY–95/1)

    Emory University—Woodruff Library (GA–25/1)

    United Theological Seminary Library (OH–120/11)

    University of Hawaii—Hamilton Library (HI–15/1)

    Wheaton College—Graham Center Library (IL–205/1)

    Yale Divinity School Library (CT–55/2)

REED, James Elden. *The Missionary Mind and American Far Eastern Policy, 1911–1915*. Harvard University (Ph.D.), 1976, n.p.

    Harvard University—Pusey Library (MA–150/3)

    Harvard University—Widener Library (MA–155/1)

REGIER, Marie Johanna. *Cultural Interpretation in a Local Community in China*. University of Chicago (M.A.), 1936, 128p.

    University of Chicago—Regenstein Library (IL–85/1)

REIFF, Mabel Heebner. *The New Life Movement in China*. Kennedy School of Missions (M.A.), 1945, 67p.

    Hartford Seminary Foundation—Case Memorial Library (CT–15/7)

REIL, Sebald. *Kilian Stumpf, 1655–1720 ein Würzburger Jesuit am Kaiserhof zu Peking (Kilian Stumpf, 1655–1720: A Würzburger Jesuit at the Royal Court in Peking)*. Würzburg (thesis), 1978, 207p.

    Princeton Theological Seminary—Speer Library (NJ–95/3)

    St. Louis University—Pius XII Memorial Library (MO–75/2)

    Yale Divinity School Library (CT–55/2)

REIST, Katherine Kennedy. *A Church for China: A Problem in Self-identification, 1919–1937*. Ohio State University (Ph.D.), 1972, 235p.

    Ohio State University—Thompson Memorial Library (OH–110/4)

RINDEN, Arthur Owen. *Christian Education of Adults in China*. Yale University (Ph.D.), 1941, 418p.

    Yale University—Sterling Memorial Library (CT–80/1)

RITTER, Richard H. *Franciscans at the Court of the Khan: An Essay in World Unity*. Hartford Theological Seminary (S.T.M.), 1937, 281p.

    Hartford Seminary Foundation—Case Memorial Library (CT–15/7)

RO, Young Chan. *A Search for a Dialogue between the Confucian "Sincerity" and the Christian "Reality": A Study of the Neo-Confucian Thought of Lee Yu-lok and the Theology of Heinrich Ott*. University of California, Santa Barbara (Ph.D.), 1982, 502p.

    University of California, Santa Barbara, Library (CA–275/2)

ROBERG, O. Theodore. *Marcus Ch'eng, Apostle or Apostate? Relations with the Covenant Mission in China*. North Park Theological Seminary (M.A.), 1982, 181p.

    Evangelical Covenant Church—Covenant Archives and Historical Library (IL–35/3)

    North Park College and Theological Seminary—Wallgren Library (IL–65/1)

    Union Theological Seminary—Burke Library (NY–275/1)

ROBERTSON, Merilie. *Present Policies of the China Inland Mission Compared with the Policies of Missions Established by James Hudson Taylor*. Biblical Seminary in New York (M.R.E.), 1955, 64p.

    Biblical Theological Seminary Library (PA–70/1)

ROBINSON, Lewis Stewart. *Double-edged Sword: Christianity and Twentieth-century Chinese Fiction*. University of California, Berkeley (Ph.D.), 1982, 568p.

    University of California, Berkeley—General Library (CA–70/1)

RONNING, Ella Gryting. *A Study of the Experiences of Chinese Children and Their Implications for Religious Education*. Kennedy School of Missions (M.A.), 1947, 147p.

    Hartford Seminary Foundation—Case Memorial Library (CT–15/7)

RONNING, Talbert Rorem. *The Hauge Synod Mission Enterprise in China*. Luther Northwestern Theological Seminary (M.A.), 1930, n.p.

    Luther Northwestern Theological Seminary Library (MN–100/1)

RONNING, Talbert Rorem. *The Spiritual Awakening in the Lutheran Churches of China*. Kennedy School of Missions (M.A.), 1947, 118p.

    Hartford Seminary Foundation—Case Memorial Library (CT–15/7)

ROSSO, Antonio Sisto. *Apostolic Legations to China of the Eighteenth Century*. Columbia University (Ph.D.), 1948, 502p.

    Andrews University—White Library (MI–50/1)

    Catholic University of America—Mullen Library (DC–20/1)

    Columbia University—Butler Library (NY–150/1)

    Duke University—Divinity School Library (NC–30/2)

    Harvard University—Widener Library (MA–155/1)

    Johns Hopkins University—Eisenhower Library (MD–10/1)

    Maryknoll Fathers and Brothers Library (NY–115/1)

    Northwestern University Library (IL–115/1)

    Princeton University—Firestone Library (NJ–100/1)

    Union Theological Seminary—Burke Library (NY–275/1)

    University of California, Berkeley—General Library (CA–70/1)

    University of Michigan—Hatcher Graduate Library (MI–25/1)

    University of Notre Dame—Memorial Library (IN–95/1)

Yale University—Sterling Memorial Library (CT–80/1)

ROY, Marya. *The Impact of Christianity on China with Concentration on the Time of the Jesuits*. University of Hawaii (M.A.), 1973, n.p.

Maryknoll Sisters of St. Dominic—Archives (NY–120/1)

University of Hawaii—Hamilton Library (HI–15/2)

RUBINSTEIN, Murray Aaron. *Zion's Corner: Origins of the American Protestant Missionary Movement in China, 1827–1839*. New York University (Ph.D.), 1976, 497p.

Emory University—Woodruff Library (GA–25/1)

Maryknoll Fathers and Brothers Library (NY–115/1)

New York University—Bobst Library (NY–245/1)

Stanford University—Green Library (CA–305/1)

University of California, Santa Cruz—McHenry Library (CA–285/2)

Wheaton College—Graham Center Library (IL–205/1)

RULE, Paul A. *K'ung-tze or Confucius: The Jesuit Interpretation of Confucianism*. Australian National University (thesis), 1972, 498p.

University of Washington—East Asia Library (WA–35/1)

SAARILAHTI, Toivo. *Suomen lähetysseuran työ Kiinassa vuosina, 1901–1926 (The Work of the Finnish Missionary Society in China in the Years 1901–1926)*. Helsinki (thesis), 1960, 283p.

Columbia University—Starr East Asian Library (NY–195/4)

Cornell University—Wason Collection (NY–95/1)

Hoover Institution Library (CA–300/1)

University of Oregon Library (OR–20/2)

Yale Divinity School Library (CT–55/2)

SALTERS, Myrtle Carolyn. *Present Opportunity for the Missionary in China*. Woman's Missionary Union Training School (M.R.E.), 1934, 31p.

Southern Baptist Theological Seminary—Boyce Centennial Library (KY–50/2)

SAUNDERS, Mary Lucile. *Training Native Christian Leaders in China*. Woman's Missionary Union Training School (M.R.E.), 1937, 93p.

Southern Baptist Theological Seminary—Boyce Centennial Library (KY–50/2)

SCHAEFFER, Mary. *The Religious Background of the Chinese Villager and Its Implication to Mission Work*. Bethany Biblical Seminary (M.R.E.), 1942, 117p.

Bethany and Northern Baptist Theological Seminaries Library (IL–135/1)

SCHICK, Julius M. *Diplomatic Correspondence Concerning the Chinese Missions of the American Vincentians, 1929–1934*. Catholic University of America (M.A.), 1951, 98p.

Catholic University of America—Mullen Library (DC–20/1)

St. Mary's Seminary—St. Mary's of the Barrens Library (MO–45/1)

SCHINTZ, Mary Ann. *An Investigation of the Modernizing Role of the Maryknoll Sisters in China*. University of Wisconsin-Madison (Ph.D.), 1978, 561p.

Maryknoll Fathers and Brothers Library (NY–115/1)

Maryknoll Sisters of St. Dominic—Archives (NY–120/1)

University of Wisconsin-Madison Memorial Library (WI–45/1)

SCHLYTER, Herman. *Karl Gützlaff als Missionar in China (Karl Gützlaff as a Missionary in China)*. Lund (dissertation), 1946, 318p.

Johns Hopkins University—Eisenhower Library (MD–10/1)

University of Chicago—Regenstein Library (IL–85/1)

SCHÜTTE, Johannes. *Die katholische Chinamission im Spiegel der rotchinesischen Presse; Versuch einer missionarischen Deutung (The Catholic China Mission in the Mirror of the Red Chinese Press: An Attempt at a Missionary Interpretation)*. University of Münster (dissertation), 1957, 394p.

Catholic University of America—Mullen Library (DC–20/1)

Duke University—Divinity School Library (NC–30/2)

Hoover Institution Library (CA–300/1)

Southern Methodist University—Bridwell Theology Library (TX–20/2)

University of California, Berkeley—General Library (CA–70/1)

University of Chicago—Regenstein Library (IL–85/1)

University of Hawaii—Hamilton Library (HI–15/2)

SEABURY, Warren Bartlett. *Certain Fundamental Religious Characteristics of the Chinese with a Brief Reference to the Proper Application of Christianity to Them*. Hartford Theological Seminary (B.D.), 1903, n.p.

Hartford Seminary Foundation—Case Memorial Library (CT–15/7)

SEBES, Joseph Schobert. *The Treaty of Nerchinsk (Nipchu), 1689: A Case Study of the Initial Period of Sino-Russian Diplomatic Relations, Based on the Unpublished Diary of Father Thomas Pereyra of the Society of Jesus*. Harvard University (Ph.D.), 1958, n.p.

Harvard University—Pusey Library (MA–150/3)

Harvard University—Widener Library (MA–155/1)

SENGER, N. M. *Interpretation of Christianity to China*. Bethany Biblical School (B.D.), 1923, 79p.

Bethany and Northern Baptist Theological Seminaries Library (IL–135/1)

SENN, Pauline Poy-ling. *An Estimate of the Applicability of the Christian Message to Modern China*. Gordon College of Theology and Missions (B.D.), 1939, 55p.

Gordon-Conwell Theological Seminary—Goddard Library (MA–230/3)

SETO, Yau S. *The Problem of Missionary Education in China, Historical and Critical*. New York University (Ph.D.), 1927, 110p.

New York University—Bobst Library (NY–245/1)

Stanford University—Green Library (CA–305/1)

SHA, Philip Shung-tse. *The Bases and Tactics of the Anti-Vatican Movement in Communist China*. Georgetown University (Ph.D.), 1960, 241p.

Georgetown University—Lauinger Library (DC–60/1)

SHAO, Luther Ching-san. *Religious Liberty and Christian Education in China*. Yale University (Ph.D.), 1934, 69p.

Yale University—Sterling Memorial Library (CT–80/1)

SHAW Yu-ming. *John Leighton Stuart: The Mind and Life of an American Missionary in China, 1876–1941*. University of Chicago (Ph.D.), 1975, 374p.

Cornell University—Wason Collection (NY–95/1)

Duke University—Divinity School Library (NC–30/2)

Fuller Theological Seminary—McAlister Library (CA–205/1)

Union Theological Seminary—Burke Library (NY–275/1)

University of California, Santa Barbara, Library (CA–275/2)

University of Chicago—Regenstein Library (IL–85/1)

University of Notre Dame—Memorial Library (IN–95/1)

Wheaton College—Graham Center Library (IL–205/1)

Yale Divinity School Library (CT–55/2)

SHEN, Joseph Stephen. *A History of the Southern Methodist Church in China*. Emory University (B.D.), 1925, 47p.

    Emory University—Pitts Theology Library (GA–15/5)

SHENG, David. *A Study of the Indigenous Elements in Chinese Christian Hymnody*. University of Southern California (D.M.A.), 1964, 568p.

    University of Southern California—Von Kleinsmid Center Library (CA–190/2)

SHEPHERD, Charles Reginald. *The Situation in China from a Sociological Point of View*. Southern Baptist Theological Seminary (Th.D.), 1913, 135p.

    Southern Baptist Theological Seminary—Boyce Centennial Library (KY–50/2)

    Wheaton College—Graham Center Library (IL–205/1)

SHERMAN, James Charles. *Missionary Activities as a Cause of the Boxer Rebellion*. University of Arizona (M.A.), 1966, 146p.

    University of Arizona Library (AZ–5/3)

SHRADER, Ralph Raymond. *Some Adjustment Problems of Chinese High School Students*. University of Chicago (M.A.), 1933, 229p.

    University of Chicago—Regenstein Library (IL–85/1)

    Yale Divinity School Library (CT–55/2)

SHULTZ, James Harold. *A Study of the Christian Church [ching chiao] in T'ang China: A.D. 618 to 906*. University of Southern California (M.A.), 1970, 120p.

    Loma Linda University—Radcliffe Memorial Library (CA–135/1)

    University of Southern California—Von Kleinsmid Center Library (CA–190/2)

SIBLEY, Janna. *Breaking the Bonds of Womanhood: Perspectives on the History, Ideology, and Courage of American Women Missionaries*. Hampshire College (B.A.), 1985, 83p.

    Mount Holyoke College—College History and Archives (MA–220/37)

SILVA, John W. *The Role of the Minister in Chinese Christian Preaching*. Seattle Pacific College (M.A.), 1967, n.p.

    Seattle Pacific University—Weter Memorial Library (WA–25/1)

SINCLAIR, Thomas Lowry. *Some Chinese Roads to Christianity: Or, Some Elements in Chinese Religion Which May Be Used as a Basis for the Teaching of Christianity*. Kennedy School of Missions (M.A.), 1926, 74p.

    Hartford Seminary Foundation—Case Memorial Library (CT–15/7)

SIU, Victoria M. Cha-tsu. *Sino-American Relations, 1882–1885: The Mission of John Russell Young*. Georgetown University (Ph.D.), 1975, 669p.

    Cornell University—Wason Collection (NY–95/1)

    Georgetown University—Lauinger Library (DC–60/1)

SMITH, C. L. *Early History of Christian Propaganda*. Clark University (M.A.), 1911, 106p.

    Clark University—Goddard Library (MA–270/1)

SMITH, Charles Stanley. *The Development of Protestant Theological Education in China: In the Light of the History of the Education of the Clergy in Europe and America*. Yale University (Ph.D.), 1938, n.p.

    Boston University—School of Theology Library (MA–35/1)

    Princeton Theological Seminary—Speer Library (NJ–95/3)

    Yale Divinity School Library (CT–55/1)

    Yale University—Sterling Memorial Library (CT–80/1)

SMITH, Dorothea. *The Development of Some Significant Phases in Religious Education in China Since 1930*. Union Theological Seminary (M.A.), 1942, 45p.

    Union Theological Seminary—Burke Library (NY–275/1)

SMITH, Florence W. *The Use of the Bible with Chinese Christian Youth*. Union Theological Seminary (M.A.), 1945, 40p.

    Union Theological Seminary—Burke Library (NY–275/1)

SMITH, Henry D., Jr. *Edwin McNeill Poteat: A Study of His Life and Work*. New Orleans Baptist Theological Seminary (Th.D.), 1963, n.p.

    New Orleans Baptist Theological Seminary—Christian Library (LA–15/1)

SMYTHE, Lewis Strong Casey. *Changes in the Christian Message for China by Protestant Missionaries*. University of Chicago (Ph.D.), 1928, 298p.

    Cornell University—Wason Collection (NY–95/1)

    Harvard Divinity School—Andover-Harvard Theological Library (MA–95/2)

    Princeton Theological Seminary—Speer Library (NJ–95/3)

    Union Theological Seminary—Burke Library (NY–275/1)

    University of Chicago—Regenstein Library (IL–85/1)

    Wheaton College—Graham Center Library (IL–205/1)

    Yale Divinity School Library (CT–55/2)

SNELL, Martha Amie. *The Significance of Rural Reconstruction in China for the Philosophy of Missions*. Scarritt College for Christian Workers (M.A.), 1937, 206p.

    Scarritt Graduate School—Laskey Library (TN–50/1)

SON, Myong-gul. *Christianity and Communism in China and Korea*. Southern Methodist University (M.S.T.), 1959, 121p.

    Southern Methodist University—Bridwell Theology Library (TX–20/2)

SONNACK, Iver A. *The Development of Protestant Higher Education in China*. Yale Divinity School (S.T.M.), 1951, 160p.

    Yale Divinity School—Special Collections (CT–50/23)

SOVIK, Arne. *Church and State in Republican China: A Survey History of the Relations between the Christian Churches and the Chinese Government, 1911–1945*. Yale University (Ph.D.), 1952, 400p.

    Colgate-Rochester Theological Seminaries—Swasey Library (NY–350/1)

    Cornell University—Wason Collection (NY–95/1)

    Luther Northwestern Theological Seminary Library (MN–100/1)

    Wheaton College—Graham Center Library (IL–205/1)

    Yale University—Sterling Memorial Library (CT–80/1)

SOVIK, Arne. *The Development of West China and Its Effect on Christian Missions*. Luther Northwestern Theological Seminary (M.A.), 1943, n.p.

    Luther Northwestern Theological Seminary Library (MN–100/1)

STANNARD, Ely Martin. *Social Implications of the Teaching of Agriculture in the Mission Schools of China*. University of Chicago (A.M.), 1925, 77p.

    University of Chicago—Regenstein Library (IL–85/1)

STEVEN, Walter T. *The Role of Religion in Chinese Education under the Manchus, 1644–1908*. New York University (M.A.), 1927, 55p.

    Biblical Theological Seminary Library (PA–70/1)

STILLMAN, Lucy Rebecca. *An Orientation Program for Christian Missionary Nurses for China*. Biblical Seminary in New York (M.R.E.), 1941, 211p.

    Biblical Theological Seminary Library (PA–70/1)

STRONG, Robbins. *Christianity and China: A Study of Church and State*. Oberlin College (A.M.), 1938, 163p.

    Oberlin College—Special Collections (OH–180/1)

    Vanderbilt University—Divinity Library (TN–65/1)

STUART, Warren Horton. *The Use of Material from China's Spiritual Inheritance in the Christian Education of Chinese Youth*. Yale University (Ph.D.), 1932, n.p.

    Emory University—Pitts Theology Library (GA–15/5)

    Public Library of Cincinnati (OH–50/1)

    Southern Baptist Theological Seminary—Boyce Centennial Library (KY–50/2)

    Yale University—Sterling Memorial Library (CT–80/1)

STUDLEY, Ellen M. *Winning Chinese Youth to Christ*. Union Theological Seminary (B.D.), 1956, 156p.

    Union Theological Seminary—Burke Library (NY–275/1)

    Yale Divinity School—Special Collections (CT–50/2, CT–50/25)

SUELFLOW, Roy Arthur. *The Mission Enterprise of the Lutheran Church-Missouri Synod in Mainland China, 1913-1952*. University of Wisconsin (Ph.D.), 1971, 392p.

    Cornell University—Wason Collection (NY–95/1)

    Graduate Theological Union Library (CA–15/2)

    Stanford University—Green Library (CA–305/1)

    University of California, Santa Barbara, Library (CA–275/2)

    University of Chicago—Regenstein Library (IL–85/1)

    University of Wisconsin-Madison Memorial Library (WI–45/1)

    Wheaton College—Graham Center Library (IL–205/1)

SWEETEN, Alan Richard. *Community and Bureaucracy in Rural China: Evidence from "Sectarian Cases (chiao an)" in Kiangsi, 1860-1895*. University of California, Davis (Ph.D.), 1980, 345p.

    University of California, Davis—Department of Special Collections (CA–100/1)

SYRDAL, Rolf Arthur. *American Lutheran Mission Work in China*. Drew University (Ph.D.), 1942, 545p.

    Drew University Library (NJ–40/2)

    Gordon-Conwell Theological Seminary—Goddard Library (MA–230/3)

    Luther Northwestern Theological Seminary Library (MN–100/1)

    St. Olaf College—Rölvaag Memorial Library (MN–80/1)

    Union Theological Seminary—Burke Library (NY–275/1)

SZETO, Paul Cheuk-ching. *Suffering in the Experience of the Protestant Church in China (1911-1980): A Chinese Perspective*. Fuller Theological Seminary (D.Miss.), 1980, 277p.

    Emory University—Pitts Theology Library (GA–15/5)

    Fuller Theological Seminary—McAlister Library (CA–205/1)

    Maryknoll Fathers and Brothers Library (NY–115/1)

    Union Theological Seminary—Burke Library (NY–275/1)

    Wheaton College—Graham Center Library (IL–205/1)

TAI, James Shih-chia. *Gospel and Culture*. Fuller Theological Seminary (D.Miss.), 1974, 394p. (In Chinese and English).

    Fuller Theological Seminary—McAlister Library (CA–205/1)

TANG, Christopher. *Christianity and the New Life Movement in China*. San Francisco Theological Seminary (Th.D.), 1941, 263p.

    San Francisco Theological Seminary Library (CA–235/2)

Union Theological Seminary—Burke Library (NY–275/1)

TENG Yuan-chung. *Americans and the Taiping Tien Kuo: A Case of Cultural Confrontation*. Georgetown University (Ph.D.), 1961, 238p.

    Georgetown University—Lauinger Library (DC–60/1)

THOMPSON, Virginia M. *Extracts from the Diary of Martha E. Foster Crawford: Edited, with Notes, an Introduction, and Some Critical Historical Comments on the Role of Mrs. Crawford as a Christian Emissary from the United States to China*. Duke University (A.M.), 1952, 135p.

    Duke University—Perkins Library (NC–55/1)

THOMSON, James Claude. *Americans as Reformers in Kuomintang China, 1928-1937*. Harvard University (Ph.D.), 1961, 453p.

    Cornell University—Wason Collection (NY–95/1)

    Harvard University—Pusey Library (MA–150/3)

    Harvard University—Widener Library (MA–155/1)

THOMSON, Margaret Cook. *A Project in Adult Religious Education for a Group of Educated Chinese Women*. Union Theological Seminary (M.A.), 1942, 29p.

    Union Theological Seminary—Burke Library (NY–275/1)

THONG, Chan-kei. *The House-Church Movement in China: A Biblical Model for Church Growth*. International School of Theology (M.A.), 1985, 89p.

    International Christian Graduate University—International School of Theology Library (CA–240/1)

    Wheaton College—Graham Center Library (IL–205/1)

THORNBERRY, Milo Lancaster, Jr. *American Missionaries and the Chinese Communists: A Study of Views Expressed by Methodist Episcopal Church Missionaries, 1921-1941*. Boston University (Th.D.), 1974, 427p.

    Asbury Theological Seminary—Fisher Library (KY–90/1)

    Boston University—School of Theology Library (MA–35/1)

    Cornell University—Wason Collection (NY–95/1)

    Drew University—United Methodist Historical Library (NJ–50/1)

    Duke University—Divinity School Library (NC–30/2)

    Emory University—Pitts Theology Library (GA–15/5)

    Fuller Theological Seminary—McAlister Library (CA–205/1)

    Princeton Theological Seminary—Speer Library (NJ–95/3)

    Union Theological Seminary—Burke Library (NY–275/1)

    University of California, Santa Barbara, Library (CA–275/2)

    Westminster Theological Seminary Library (PA–220/2)

    Wheaton College—Graham Center Library (IL–205/1)

TJANDRA, Lukas. *The Responsibility and Prospects of Overseas Chinese Christians to Evangelize Mainland China When It Reopens*. Trinity Evangelical Divinity School (M.A.), 1973, 116p.

    Trinity Evangelical Divinity School Library (IL–90/1)

    World Vision International—Research and Information Division (CA–200/1)

TORJESEN, Edvard P. *A Study of Fredrik Franson: The Development and Impact of His Ecclesiology, Missiology, and Worldwide Evangelism*. International College (Ph.D.), 1984, 855p.

    Bethel Theological Seminary Library (MN–50/1)

    Trinity Evangelical Divinity School Library (IL–90/1)

TSANG, David Kwai. *A Chinese Adaptation of "Discipling the Nations," by Richard T. De Ridder*. Fuller Theological Seminary (M.A.), 1976, 297p. (In Chinese).

    Fuller Theological Seminary—McAlister Library (CA–205/1)

TSANG, David Kwai. *A New Missiological Approach to Chinese Confucianism.* Fuller Theological Seminary (D.Miss.), 1977, 317p. (In Chinese and English).

    Fuller Theological Seminary—McAlister Library (CA–205/1)

TSAO Lien-chih. *The Development and History of the Seventh-Day Adventist Church in China Since the Communist Take-over.* Loma Linda University (M.A.), 1975, 88p.

    Loma Linda University Library (CA–220/1)

    Loma Linda University—Radcliffe Memorial Library (CA–135/1)

TSHIA, Charles P. *A Study of the Young Men's Christian Association in China.* Young Men's Christian Association College (Bachelor of Association Science), 1924, 43p.

    George Williams College Library (IL–100/1)

TUCKER, Sara Waitstill. *The Canton Hospital and Medicine in Nineteenth-century China, 1835–1900.* Indiana University (Ph.D.), 1982, 316p.

    Indiana University—University Libraries (IN–20/2)

TURNBLADH, Edwin Theodore. *Louis the Fourteenth's Jesuit Missionary Company to China in 1685.* University of California, Berkeley (M.A.), 1930, 111p.

    University of California, Berkeley—General Library (CA–70/1)

TWINEM, Jessie Marguerite. *Toward a Religious Program for Youth in North China.* Kennedy School of Missions (M.A.), 1938, 103p.

    Hartford Seminary Foundation—Case Memorial Library (CT–15/7)

TYLER, Ernest Delbert. *Missionary and Manchu.* University of Kansas (M.A.), 1930, 381p.

    University of Kansas—Watson Library (KS–35/3)

UDY, James Stuart. *Attitudes within the Protestant Churches of the Occident towards the Propagation of Christianity in the Orient: An Historical Survey.* Boston University (Ph.D.), 1952, 422p.

    Boston University—School of Theology Library (MA–35/1)

UNSWORTH, Virginia F. *American Catholic Missions and Communist China, 1945–1953.* New York University (Ph.D.), 1977, 217p.

    Cornell University—Wason Collection (NY–95/1)

    Fuller Theological Seminary—McAlister Library (CA–205/1)

    Maryknoll Fathers and Brothers Library (NY–115/1)

    Maryknoll Sisters of St. Dominic—Archives (NY–120/1)

    Maryknoll Sisters of St. Dominic—Rogers Library (NY–125/1)

    New York University—Bobst Library (NY–245/1)

    Providence College—Phillips Memorial Library (RI–25/1)

    Stanford University—Green Library (CA–305/1)

    Wheaton College—Graham Center Library (IL–205/1)

URQUHART, Robert Cameron. *A Study of the Chinese Industrial Cooperatives with an Evaluation of Their Significance to the Christian Church.* Biblical Seminary in New York (S.T.B.), 1949, 116p.

    Biblical Theological Seminary Library (PA–70/1)

VAN, Amber Lurraine. *The Development of Indigenous Leadership for Youth Work in China.* Union Theological Seminary (S.T.M.), 1946, 83p.

    Drew University—United Methodist Archives (NJ–45/5

    Union Theological Seminary—Burke Library (NY–275/1)

VAN PUTTEN, J. Dyke. *Christian Higher Education in China:*

Contributions of the Colleges of Arts and Sciences to Chinese Life. University of Chicago (Ph.D.), 1934, 472p.

    University of Chicago—Regenstein Library (IL–85/1)

VAN VLEET, Russel R. *A Comparison of the Work of Robert Morrison and Jonathan Goforth with Special Reference to Their Contribution to Protestant Missions in China.* Biblical Seminary in New York (S.T.B.), 1949, 67p.

    Biblical Theological Seminary Library (PA–70/1)

VITCAVAGE, Muriel. *Some Elements of Truth Reflected in Chinese Religious Beliefs.* Manhattanville College (M.A.), 1939, 42p.

    Maryknoll Sisters of St. Dominic—Archives (NY–120/1)

VONINSKI, Paul. *Reciprocal Change: The Case of American Protestant Missionaries to China.* Syracuse University (Ph.D.), 1975, 203p.

    College of Wooster—Andrews Library (OH–200/1)

    Cornell University—Wason Collection (NY–95/1)

    Emory University—Woodruff Library (GA–25/1)

    Ohio State University—Thompson Memorial Library (OH–110/4)

    Stanford University—Green Library (CA–305/1)

    Syracuse University—Archives (NY–370/2)

    University of California, Santa Barbara, Library (CA–275/2)

    Wheaton College—Graham Center Library (IL–205/1)

WANG, Christina. *A Suggested Program of Evangelization for South Fukien Province, China.* Biblical Seminary in New York (M.R.E.), 1940, 180p.

    Biblical Theological Seminary Library (PA–70/1)

WANG, H. I. *The Significance of the Anti-Christian Movement in China Today.* Boston University (S.T.M.), 1925, 50p.

    Boston University—School of Theology Library (MA–35/1)

WANG Man-p'ing. *I pa ch'i ling nien T'ien-chin chiao an chih yen chiu (The Tientsin Massacre of 1870).* National Taiwan University (M.S.), 1975, 240p.

    University of California, Berkeley—East Asiatic Library (CA–55/1)

    Yale University—Sterling Memorial Library (CT–80/1)

WANG Shu-hwai. *The Educational Association of China, 1890–1912: Its History and Meaning in the Missionary Education in China.* University of Hawaii (M.A.), 1963, 202p.

    University of Hawaii—Hamilton Library (HI–15/2)

WANG, Wallace Chun-hsien. *The Beginnings of the Protestant Church in China (1807–1860).* Union Theological Seminary (S.T.M.), 1940, 116p.

    Union Theological Seminary—Burke Library (NY–275/1)

WEE, Kok A. *Physical Education in Protestant Christian Colleges and Universities of China.* Columbia University Teachers' College (Ph.D.), 1937, 105p.

    Columbia University—Butler Library (NY–150/1)

    Columbia University—Milbank Library (NY–165/4)

    Union Theological Seminary—Burke Library (NY–275/1)

WEEKS, Wilma Jesseline. *The Kindergarten in the South China Mission.* Woman's Missionary Union Training School (M.R.E.), 1936, 39p.

    Southern Baptist Theological Seminary—Boyce Centennial Library (KY–50/2)

WEHRLE, Edmund S. *The Missionary Factor in Anglo-Chinese Relations, 1891–1900.* University of Chicago (Ph.D.), 1962, 285p.

    Union Theological Seminary—Burke Library (NY–275/1)

    University of Chicago—Regenstein Library (IL–85/1)

    University of Hawaii—Hamilton Library (HI–15/2)

WEI, Louis Tsing-sing. *La Politique missionaire de la France en Chine, 1842–1856: l'ouverture des cinq ports chinois au commerce étranger et la liberté religieuse (The Missionary Politics of France in China, 1842–1856: The Opening of the Five Chinese Ports to Foreign Trade and Religious Freedom).* Paris (thesis), 1960, 630p.

> Columbia University—Starr East Asian Library (NY–195/4)
> Duke University—Divinity School Library (NC–30/2)
> Emory University—Pitts Theology Library (GA–15/5)
> Harvard University—Widener Library (MA–155/1)
> University of California, Berkeley—General Library (CA–70/1)
> University of Chicago—Regenstein Library (IL–85/1)
> University of Maryland—McKeldin Library (MD–45/2)
> University of Michigan—Hatcher Graduate Library (MI–25/1)
> University of Notre Dame—Memorial Library (IN–95/1)
> University of Pennsylvania—Van Pelt Library (PA–215/1)
> Yale Divinity School Library (CT–55/2)
> Yale University—Sterling Memorial Library (CT–80/1)

WELLIVER, Mary Lee. *The Pearl S. Buck Manuscripts: The Harvest of Half a Century.* West Virginia University (M.A.), 1977, 76p.

> West Virginia University Library (WV–15/4)
> West Virginia Wesleyan College—Pfeiffer Library (WV–10/1)

WEN Shun-t'ien. *Ma-li-no hui tsai Hua ch'uan chiao chien shih (A Short History of Maryknoll Missions in China).* Taiwan National University (M.A.), 1977, 247p.

> University of California at Los Angeles—Rudolph Oriental Library (CA–180/1)
> University of Southern California—Von Kleinsmid Center Library (CA–190/1)

WEST, Philip. *Yenching University and American-Chinese Relations, 1917–1937.* Harvard University (Ph.D.), 1971, n.p.

> Harvard University—Harvard-Yenching Library (MA–125/6)
> Harvard University—Pusey Library (MA–150/3)
> Harvard University—Widener Library (MA–155/1)

WETMORE, Robert Kingston. *An Analysis of Watchman Nee's Doctrine of Dying and Rising with Christ as It Relates to Sanctification.* Trinity Evangelical Divinity School (Master of Theology), 1983, 101p.

> Trinity Evangelical Divinity School Library (IL–90/1)
> Western Baptist College Library (OR–40/1)

WHITE, Garnett Lee. *Southern Baptist Missions in China.* University of Richmond (M.A.), 1967, 95p.

> Virginia Baptist Historical Society (VA–90/8)
> Wheaton College—Graham Center Library (IL–205/1)

WHITEHEAD, Raymond Leslie. *A Christian's Inquiry into the Struggle Ethic in the Thought of Mao Tse-tung.* Union Theological Seminary (Ph.D.), 1972, 334p.

> Cornell University—Wason Collection (NY–95/1)
> Union Theological Seminary—Burke Library (NY–275/1)

WHITENER, Sterling Hegnauer. *The Interpretation of History in Chinese Christianity.* Yale Divinity School (S.T.M.), 1952, 139p.

> Yale Divinity School Library (CT–55/2)

WICKERI, Philip Lauri. *Christianity in China and the Taiping Rebellion: An Historical and Theological Study.* Princeton Theological Seminary (M.Div.), 1974, 135p.

> Princeton Theological Seminary—Speer Library (NJ–95/3)

WICKERI, Philip Lauri. *Seeking the Common Ground: Protestant Christianity, the Three-Self Movement, and China's United Front.* Princeton Theological Seminary (Ph.D.), 1985, 598p.

> Emory University—Pitts Theology Library (GA–15/5)
> Graduate Theological Union Library (CA–15/2)
> Princeton Theological Seminary—Speer Library (NJ–95/3)
> Southern Baptist Convention—Jenkins Research Library (VA–70/1)

WIDMER, Eric George. *The Russian Ecclesiastical Mission in Peking during the Eighteenth Century.* Harvard University (Ph.D.), 1970, 358p.

> Harvard University—Harvard-Yenching Library (MA–125/6)
> Harvard University—Pusey Library (MA–150/3)
> Harvard University—Widener Library (MA–155/1)

WIENS, Abraham K. *The Work of the Mennonite Missions in China.* University of Southern California (M.A.), 1951, 155p.

> Biola University—Rose Memorial Library (CA–130/4)
> Center for Mennonite Brethren Studies—Archives and Historical Library (CA–115/1, CA–115/2)
> University of Southern California—Von Kleinsmid Center Library (CA–190/2)

WIEST, Jean-Paul. *Catholic Activities in Kwangtung Province and Chinese Responses, 1848–1885.* University of Washington (Ph.D.), 1977, 334p.

> Harvard University—Harvard-Yenching Library (MA–125/6)
> Maryknoll Fathers and Brothers Library (NY–115/1)
> University of Washington Libraries (WA–45/1)
> Wheaton College—Graham Center Library (IL–205/1)

WIEST, Jean-Paul. *The Catholic Implantation at Canton: French Missionary Work, 1848–1860.* University of Washington (M.A.), 1972, 188p.

> University of Washington Libraries (WA–45/1)

WILEY, James Hundley. *Christianizing Chinese Sex Relations: The Fight for Monogamy in China.* Southern Baptist Theological Seminary (Ph.D.), 1929, 152p.

> Southern Baptist Theological Seminary—Boyce Centennial Library (KY–50/2)

WILLEKE, Bernward Henry. *Imperial Government and Catholic Missions in China during the Years 1784–1785.* Columbia University (Ph.D.), 1948, 227p.

> Catholic Theological Union Library (IL–20/1)
> Catholic University of America—Mullen Library (DC–20/1)
> Columbia University—Butler Library (NY–150/1)
> Duke University—Divinity School Library (NC–30/2)
> Duns Scotus Library (MI–140/1)
> Hartford Seminary Foundation—Case Memorial Library (CT–15/7)
> Harvard Divinity School—Andover-Harvard Theological Library (MA–95/2)
> Luther Northwestern Theological Seminary Library (MN–100/1)
> Maryknoll Fathers and Brothers Library (NY–115/1)
> Northern Illinois University Libraries (IL–95/1)
> St. Anthony-on-the-Hudson—Province of Immaculate Conception Library (NY–340/1)
> St. Louis University—Pius XII Memorial Library (MO–75/2)
> St. Mary of the Lake Seminary—Feehan Memorial Library (IL–130/1)
> St. Paul Seminary—Ireland Library (MN–110/1)
> Trinity College Library (CT–25/1)

University at Albany (SUNY) Libraries (NY–20/2)

University of California, Berkeley—General Library (CA–70/1)

University of California, Santa Cruz—McHenry Library (CA–285/2)

University of Michigan—Hatcher Graduate Library (MI–25/1)

University of Notre Dame—Memorial Library (IN–95/1)

University of Pennsylvania—Van Pelt Library (PA–215/1)

University of Wisconsin-Madison Memorial Library (WI–45/1)

Yale Divinity School Library (CT–55/2)

Yale University—Sterling Memorial Library (CT–80/1)

WILLIAMS, James Toy. *The Place of Education in the Religious Redemption of China.* Southern Baptist Theological Seminary (Th.D.), 1921, 137p.

Southern Baptist Convention—Archives (VA–65/2)

Southern Baptist Theological Seminary—Boyce Centennial Library (KY–50/2)

Wheaton College—Graham Center Library (IL–205/1)

WINDEMILLER, Duane A. *The Psychodynamics of Change in Religious Conversion and Communist Brainwashing with Particular Reference to the Eighteenth-century Evangelical Revival and the Chinese Thought Control Movement.* Boston University (Ph.D.), 1960, 186p.

Boston University—School of Theology Library (MA–35/1)

WINN, Anne L. *Drama as a Means of Evangelism in China.* Biblical Seminary in New York (M.R.E.), 1944, 125p.

Biblical Theological Seminary Library (PA–70/1)

WITEK, John W. *An Eighteenth-century Frenchman at the Court of the K'ang-hsi Emperor: A Study of the Early Life of Jean François Foucquet.* Georgetown University (Ph.D.), 1973, 753p.

Florida State University—Strozier Library (FL–25/1)

Georgetown University—Lauinger Library (DC–60/1)

University of Hawaii—Hamilton Library (HI–15/1)

University of Michigan—Hatcher Graduate Library (MI–25/1)

University of Pennsylvania—Van Pelt Library (PA–215/1)

University of Washington—East Asia Library (WA–35/1)

WONG, George Ho Ching. *China's Opposition to Western Religion and Science during Late Ming and Early Ch'ing.* University of Washington (Ph.D.), 1958, 199p.

Fuller Theological Seminary—McAlister Library (CA–205/1)

Princeton University—Firestone Library (NJ–100/1)

University of Washington Libraries (WA–45/1)

Wheaton College—Graham Center Library (IL–205/1)

WONG, Gwendolyn. *The Picture of Student Living and Thinking in China and Its Implications for Christian Student Work.* Biblical Seminary in New York (M.R.E.), 1948, 73p.

Biblical Theological Seminary Library (PA–70/1)

WONG, Joseph Chi-choi. *A Comparative Study of the Concept of God in Chinese Thought and Christian Theology as Represented by Selected Evangelical Theologians.* Trinity Evangelical Divinity School (M.Th.), 1979, 275p.

Trinity Evangelical Divinity School Library (IL–90/1)

WONG, Paul Yat-keung. *The History of Baptist Missions in Hong Kong.* Southern Baptist Theological Seminary (Ph.D.), 1974, 368p.

Cornell University—Wason Collection (NY–95/1)

Southern Baptist Convention—Jenkins Research Library (VA–70/1)

Southern Baptist Theological Seminary—Boyce Centennial Library (KY–50/2)

Union Theological Seminary—Burke Library (NY–275/1)

Wheaton College—Graham Center Library (IL–205/1)

WONGSO, Peter. *Essential Knowledge of Missionary Work* (a Chinese adaptation of "Understanding Christian Missions," by J. Herbert Kane). Fuller Theological Seminary (M.A.), 1976, 270p. (In Chinese).

Fuller Theological Seminary—McAlister Library (CA–205/1)

WOODWARD, Frank T. *The Baptist Problem of the Indigenous Church in China.* Southern Baptist Theological Seminary (Ph.D.), 1934, 129p.

Baptist Bible College Library (PA–30/1)

Southern Baptist Theological Seminary—Boyce Centennial Library (KY–50/2)

Wheaton College—Graham Center Library (IL–205/1)

WORKMAN, George Bell. *The Chinese Mind and the Missionary Approach.* Union Theological Seminary (S.T.M.), 1939, 317p.

Union Theological Seminary—Burke Library (NY–275/1)

WORKMAN, George Bell. *The Development of the Motive of Protestant Missions to China, 1807–1928.* Yale University (M.A.), 1928, 215p.

Bethel Theological Seminary Library (MN–50/1)

Colgate-Rochester Theological Seminaries—Swasey Library (NY–350/1)

Fuller Theological Seminary—McAlister Library (CA–205/1)

Graduate Theological Union Library (CA–15/2)

Phillips University—Rogers Library (OK–5/1)

Texas Christian University—Burnett Library (TX–30/1)

Union Theological Seminary—Burke Library (NY–275/1)

Virginia Theological Seminary—Payne Library (VA–5/1)

Wheaton College—Graham Center Library (IL–205/1)

Yale Divinity School Library (CT–55/2)

WORLEY, Harry Wescott. *The Central Conference of the Methodist Episcopal Church: A Study of the Mission Field to the Development of Church Organization.* Yale University (Ph.D.), 1938, 37p.

Yale Divinity School Library (CT–55/2)

Yale University—Sterling Memorial Library (CT–80/1)

WU, Carlton Chungchieh. *The Basis of the Appeal in the United States for Protestant Missions to China (1830–1949).* Princeton Theological Seminary (Th.M.), 1956, 108p.

Princeton Theological Seminary—Speer Library (NJ–95/3)

WU Chao-kwang. *The Legal and Political Aspects of the Missionary Movement in China.* Johns Hopkins University (Ph.D.), 1928, 285p.

Brandeis University Library (MA–235/1)

Johns Hopkins University—Eisenhower Library (MD–10/1)

WU, David Chusing. *The Employment of Chinese Classical Thought in Matteo Ricci's Theological Contextualization in Sixteenth-century China.* Graduate Theological Union (Th.D.), 1983, 270p.

Graduate Theological Union Library (CA–15/2)

WU Ming-yung. *A Study of Paul's First Epistle to the Corinthians in the Light of Conditions in China.* Woman's Missionary Union Training School (M.R.E.), 1933, 18p.

Southern Baptist Theological Seminary—Boyce Centennial Library (KY–50/2)

WU, T. F. *Chinese Political Thought and the Christian Movement.* Vanderbilt University (M.A.), 1925, 96p.

Vanderbilt University—Divinity Library (TN–65/1)

WU Ts-chien. *Principles and Methods of Community Church Work in China.* Rochester Theological Seminary (B.D.), 1925, 23p.

Colgate-Rochester Theological Seminaries—Swasey Library (NY–350/1)

YANG, Bill Tung Chuan. *A Chinese Adaptation of "Church Growth and the Word of God."* Fuller Theological Seminary (M.A.), 1974, 84p. (In Chinese).

Fuller Theological Seminary—McAlister Library (CA–205/1)

YANG, Bill Tung Chuan. *A Study of Mission for Chinese Churches.* Fuller Theological Seminary (D.Miss.), 1975, 169p. (In Chinese and English).

Fuller Theological Seminary—McAlister Library (CA–205/1)

YANG Chang-tung. *A Program for the Church of Ping-tan Hsien, Fukien, China.* Drew University (Ph.D.), 1935, n.p.

Drew University Library (NJ–40/2)

YAUKEY, Jesse B. *Methods of Developing Native Christian Leadership in China.* Columbia University Teachers' College (M.A.), 1930, 29p.

Columbia University—Milbank Library (NY–165/4)

Union Theological Seminary—Burke Library (NY–275/1)

YEH Fong-kwei. *Nationalism and Christianity in China.* Southern Methodist University (B.D.), 1934, 74p.

Southern Methodist University—Bridwell Theology Library (TX–20/2)

YEN, Nathaniel Yung-tse. *Prophet Sage and Wise Man: A Comparative Study of Intellectual Tradition in Ancient China and Israel.* Drew University (Ph.D.), 1977, 338p.

Drew University Library (NJ–40/2)

Emory University—Pitts Theology Library (GA–15/5)

YIP, Ka-che. *The Anti-Christian Movement in China, 1922–1927: With Special Reference to the Experience of Protestant Missions.* Columbia University (Ph.D.), 1970, 358p.

Columbia University—Burgess-Carpenter Classics Library (NY–145/1)

Cornell University—Wason Collection (NY–95/1)

Graduate Theological Union Library (CA–15/2)

Princeton Theological Seminary—Speer Library (NJ–95/3)

Stanford University—Green Library (CA–305/1)

Union Theological Seminary—Burke Library (NY–275/1)

University of Hawaii—Hamilton Library (HI–15/2)

University of Maryland—McKeldin Library (MD–45/2)

University of Notre Dame—Memorial Library (IN–95/1)

Wheaton College—Graham Center Library (IL–205/1)

YOON, Yee-heum. *A Comparative Study of the Religious Thought of Chi-tsang and H. Richard Niebuhr: A Comparison and Contrast of the Buddhist and Christian.* Northwestern University (Ph.D.), 1979, 273p.

Emory University—Pitts Theology Library (GA–15/5)

Northwestern University Library (IL–115/1)

YOUNG, John Dragon. *Christianity and Confucianism: The Writings of Matteo Ricci (1552–1610) and Yang Kuang-hsien (1597–1669).* University of California, Davis (M.A.), 1972, 129p.

University of California, Davis—Department of Special Collections (CA–100/1)

YOUNG, John Dragon. *Confucianism and Christianity: The Jesuits, Their Converts, and Their Critics, 1552–1669.* University of California, Davis (Ph.D.), 1976, n.p.

University of California, Davis—Department of Special Collections (CA–100/1)

YOUNG, Joseph. *Reflection on the Expansion of the Christian Movement among the Chinese People.* Fuller Theological Seminary (M.A.), 1974, 234p. (In Chinese).

Fuller Theological Seminary—McAlister Library (CA–205/1)

YÜAN Min-pao. *Des Systèmes Agraires en Chine (Chung-kuo nung yeh chih t'u k'ao/ Agrarian Systems in China).* In French and Chinese. Université de Changhai (L'Aurore), 1922, 155p.

University of Michigan—Asia Library (MI–10/1)

ZI, Dung-hwe. *The Idea of God in the Chinese Classics.* Hartford Theological Seminary (Ph.D.), 1930, 461p.

Hartford Seminary Foundation—Case Memorial Library (CT–15/7)

ZIA, Z. K. *The Confucian Civilization.* Boston University (M.A.), 1924, 52p.

Boston University—School of Theology Library (MA–35/1)

Bibliography

ALLISON, WILLIAM HENRY. *Inventory of Unpublished Material for American Religious History in Protestant Church Archives and Other Repositories*. Washington, D.C.: Carnegie Institution, 1910.

AMERICAN ANTIQUARIAN SOCIETY. *Catalogue of the Manuscript Collections of the American Antiquarian Society*. 4 V. Boston: G. K. Hall & Co., 1979.

————. *A Dictionary Catalog of American Books Pertaining to the Seventeenth through the Nineteenth Centuries: Library of the American Antiquarian Society*. 20 V. Westport, CT: Greenwood, 1971.

American Council on Education, ed. *American Universities and Colleges*. New York, Berlin: Walter de Gruyter, 1983.

American Library Directory, 1984 Edition. New York, London: R. R. Bowker Company, 1984.

American Library Directory, 1987–88 Edition. New York, London: R. R. Bowker Company, 1987.

American Museum of Natural History. *Research Catalog of the Library of the American Museum Natural History: Classed Catalog*. 4 V. Boston: G. K. Hall, 1978.

American Theological Library Association. *Chinese Christian Monograph Collection: An Index to Chinese Christian Monographs Filmed from the Union Theological Seminary Library Collection by the Board of Microtext, American Theological Library Association*. 1979.

————. *Chinese Christian Serial Collection: An Index to Chinese Christian Serials Filmed from the Union Theological Seminary Library Collection by the Board of Microtext, American Theological Library Association*. 1979.

ASH, LEE, and WILLIAM G. MILLER. *Subject Collections: A Guide to Special Book Collections and Subject Emphases as Reported by University, College, Public, and Special Libraries and Museums in the United States and Canada*. New York: R. D. Bowker, 1985.

Association of Asian Studies. *Bibliography of Asian Studies*. 11 V. Ann Arbor: Association for Asian Studies, 1965–81.

————. *Cumulative Bibliography of Asian Studies, 1941–1965. Author Bibliography*. 4 V. Boston: G. K. Hall, 1969. *Subject Bibliography*. 4 V. Boston: G. K. Hall, 1970.

BARNETT, SUZANNE WILSON, and JOHN KING FAIRBANK. *Christianity in China: Early Protestant Missionary Writings*. Cambridge: Harvard University Press, 1984.

BARROW, JOHN G. *A Bibliography of Bibliographies in Religion.* Ann Arbor: Edwards Brothers, 1969.

BEACH, HARLAN P., ed. *A Geography and Atlas of Protestant Missions.* New York: Student Volunteer Movement for Foreign Missions, 1903.

BECKER, RONALD L. and E. RICHARD MCKINSTRY, comps. *A Union List of New Jersey Annual Publications in the Library Collections of The New Jersey Historical Society and Rutgers University.* New Brunswick: Rutgers University Libraries and the New Jersey Historical Society, 1977.

BELL, WHITFIELD J., JR., and MURPHY D. SMITH, comps. *Guide to the Archives and Manuscript Collections of the American Philosophical Society.* Philadelphia: The American Philosophical Society, 1966.

BENNETT, ELIZABETH. "Guide to the Methodist Missionary Society Archives." n.p., n.d.

BERGER, KENNETH W., ed. *Asian Resources in the Southeastern United States: Archival and Manuscript Resources on China and Japan in North Carolina.* Occasional Papers of the Southeast Conference, Association of Asian Studies. Series on Asian Resources in the Southeastern United States, N 1, 1985.

BERTON, PETER and EUGENE WU. *Contemporary China: A Research Guide.* Edited by Howard Koch, Jr. Stanford, CA: Hoover Institution on War, Revolution, and Peace, 1967.

BLANCHARD, MONICA J. *A Guide to the Far Eastern Holdings of the Institute of Christian Oriental Research (ICOR) Library.* Washington, D.C.: Catholic University of America, 1986.

BOISCLAIR, REGINA A. "American Roman Catholic Missioners in China: A Bibliography Drawn from the Resources of Yale University and Maryknoll Seminary." Yale Divinity School, 1979.

BOXER, C. R. *Catalogue of Philippine Manuscripts in the Lilly Library.* Bloomington, IN: Asian Studies Research Institute, 1968.

BROOKS, JERROLD LEE. "A Review of Chinese and Japanese Resources for Research at the Historical Foundation of the Presbyterian and Reformed Churches." 1983.

BRUINS, ELTON J. *The Manuscript and Archival Holdings of Beardslee Library, Western Theological Seminary, Holland, Michigan.* Holland, MI: Western Theological Seminary, 1978.

BRUINS, ELTON J. and BARBARA LAMPEN. *A Guide to the Archives of the Netherlands Museum.* 1978.

BRUNNER, HENRY S. "Report on the G. Weidman Groff Collection." University Park, PA: Pennsylvania State University, 1961.

BYRNES, PAUL A. *Current Periodicals in the Missionary Research Library: A Subject List.* New York: Missionary Research Library, 1972.

Catholic University of America. *Catalog of the Oliveira Lima Library.* Boston: G. K. Hall, 1970.

Center for Research Libraries. *The Center for Research Libraries Catalogue: Monographs.* 5 V. Chicago: The Center for Research Libraries, 1969.

————. *The Center for Research Libraries Catalogue: Serials.* 2 V. Chicago: The Center for Research Libraries, 1972.

————. *The Center for Research Libraries Catalogue: Serials, First Supplement.* Chicago: The Center for Research Libraries, 1978.

CHAFF, SANDRA L., ed. *Women in Medicine: A Bibliography of the Literature on Women Physicians.* Metuchen, N.J.: Scarecrow Press, 1977.

Check List of Periodicals in Nine Theological Libraries of Southeastern Pennsylvania. Philadelphia: Theological Seminary Libraries of Southeastern Pennsylvania, 1970.

Chicago Area Theological Library Association. *Union List of Serials.* Chicago: Chicago Area Theological Library Association, 1974.

Chicago Cluster of Theological Schools, comp. *Union List of Current Periodicals*. Chicago: Office of the Library Program, Chicago Cluster of Theological Schools, 1979.

China Inland Mission: List of Missionaries and Their Stations. Shanghai: China Inland Mission, 1915, 1921.

CHU, CLAYTON H., comp. *American Missionaries in China: Books, Articles, and Pamphlets Extracted from the Subject Catalogue of the Missionary Research Library*. Cambridge: Harvard University Press, 1960.

Ci Hai: Yu ci fen ce. Shanghai: Ci Shu Publishing House, 1980.

Claremont University Center. *Claremont Graduate School Oral History Program: A Bibliography*. 1978.

CLARK, ALEXANDER P. *The Manuscript Collections of the Princeton University Library: An Introductory Survey*. Princeton: Princeton University Library, 1958.

COCHRANE, THOMAS. *Survey of the Missionary Occupation of China*. Shanghai: Christian Literature Society for China, 1913.

Comprehensive Dissertation Index: 1861–1972. 5 V. Ann Arbor, MI: Xerox University Microfilms, 1973.

Comprehensive Dissertation Index: 1983 Supplement. Ann Arbor, MI: Xerox University Microfilms, 1984.

Comprehensive Dissertation Index: Ten-Year Cumulation, 1973–1982. 6 V. Ann Arbor, MI: Xerox University Microfilms, 1984.

Comprehensive Dissertation Index: Ten-Year Cumulation, 1972–1982. Author Index. 6 V. Ann Arbor, MI: University Microfilms International, 1983.

Comprehensive Dissertation Index. 1983 Supplement. Author Index. Ann Arbor, MI: University Microfilms International, 1984.

CONN, CHARLES W. *Like a Mighty Army: A History of the Church of God*. Cleveland, TN: Pathway Press, 1977.

Cornell University. *The Catalog of the Wason Collection on China and the Chinese, Cornell University Libraries*. 7 V. Washington, D.C.: Center for Chinese Research Materials, Association for Research Libraries, 1978.

CRAIG, TRACEY LINTON, comp. *Directory: Historical Societies and Agencies in the United States and Canada, 1973–1974*. Nashville: American Association for the State and Local Workers, 1982.

DeLONG, RUSSELL V., and MAXWELL TAYLOR. *Fifty Years of Nazarene Missions. Volume II: History of the Fields*. Kansas City, MO: Beacon Hill Press, 1955.

DENNIS, JAMES S. *Centennial Survey of Foreign Missions: A Statistical Supplement to "Christian Missions and Social Progress," Being a Conspectus of the Achievements and Results of Evangelical Missions in All Lands at the Close of the Nineteenth Century*. New York, Chicago, Toronto: Fleming H. Revell Company, 1902.

DEUTRICH, MABEL E. "American Church Archives—An Overview." In *The American Archivist*, V 24, N 4 (O 1961), pp. 387–402.

A Directory of Information Resources in the United States: Social Sciences. Revised ed. Washington, D C.: Library of Congress, 1973.

Directory of Protestant Missions in China, 1916. Edited by Charles L. Boynton. Shanghai: Christian Literature Society Book Depot, n.d.

Directory of Protestant Missions in China, 1927. Edited by the National Christian Council of China. Shanghai: Kwang Hsüeh Publishing House, n.d.

The Directory of Religious Organizations in the United States. 2nd ed. Falls Church, VA: McGrath Publishing Company, 1982.

DONAT, NAFI. "The Archives of the Case Memorial Library." Hartford Seminary Foundation, 1972.

East Carolina University, J. Y. Joyner Library. *Bulletin of the East Carolina Manuscript Collection*, N 2–9.

EKELAND, T., ALBERT ANDERSON, and OLIVE T. CHRISTENSEN, eds. *White Unto Harvest:*

A Survey of Lutheran United Mission, the China Mission of Norwegian Lutheran Church of America. Minneapolis: Board of Foreign Missions, 1919.

ELLIOTT, CLARK A., comp. *A Descriptive Guide to the Harvard University Archives*. Cambridge: Harvard University Library, 1976.

EMMERICH, HENRICUS, S.V.D., ed. *Atlas Missionum a Sacra Congregatione de Propaganda Fide Depedentium*. Vatican City, 1958.

Encyclopedia of Southern Baptists. 2 V. Nashville: Broadman Press, 1958.

————. *Volume III: Supplement*. Nashville: Broadman Press, 1971.

————. *Volume IV: Supplement*. Nashville: Broadman Press, 1982.

EVANS, C.A., comp. "Princeton-in-China: A Resumé of Fifty Years of Work by Princeton-in-Peking and Princeton-Yenching Foundation, 1898–99, 1948–49," 1949.

EWING, WILLIAM S., comp. *Guide to the Manuscript Collections in the William L. Clements Library*. Ann Arbor: Clements Library, 1953.

FAIRBANK, JOHN K., ed. *The Missionary Enterprise in China and America*. Cambridge: Harvard University Press, 1974.

FAIRBANK, JOHN K., and LIU KWANG-CHING. *Modern China: A Bibliographical Guide to Chinese Works, 1898–1937*. Cambridge: Harvard University Press, 1950.

Fleming Library, Southwestern Baptist Theological Seminary. *Union List of Baptist Serials*. Fort Worth, TX: NEMAC Publishers, 1960.

Freer Gallery of Art. *Dictionary Catalog of the Library of the Freer Gallery of Art*. Boston: G. K. Hall, 1967.

Gazetteer of Chinese Geographic Names. Washington, D.C.: Military Intelligence Division, 1945. Reprint of a publication compiled by the Information Bureau, Japanese Foreign Office.

GLENN, E. N., comp. *Church Directory of the Churches of Christ of the United States and Canada. Revised and Enlarged*. Cincinnati: F. L. Rowe, 1932.

GOLDSTEIN, JONATHAN. "Documents in the Atlanta Regional Archives." In *Committee on East Asian Libraries Bulletin*, N 74 (Je 1984), pp. 19–23.

GRUBER, KATHERINE, ed. *Encyclopedia of Associations*. 5 V. Detroit: Gale Research, 1980–86.

Guide to the Archives of the Episcopal Church in South Dakota. Sioux Falls, SD: Center for Western Studies, Archives of the Episcopal Diocese of South Dakota, n.d.

HALE, RICHARD W., ed. *Guide to Photocopied Historical Materials in the United States and Canada*. Ithaca: American Historical Association/Cornell University Press, 1961.

HAMEROCH, PHILLIP M., ed. *A Guide to Archives and Manuscripts in the United States*. New Haven, CT: Yale University Press, 1961.

HAMILTON, KENNETH G. "The Moravian Archives at Bethlehem, Pennsylvania." In *The American Archivist*, V 24, N 4 (O 1961), pp. 415–424.

HARMON, NOLAN B., ed. 2 V. *The Encyclopedia of World Methodism*. Nashville: United Methodist Publishing House, 1974.

Harvard University Library. *Widener Shelflist, 14: China, Japan, and Korea*. Cambridge: Harvard University Library, 1968.

HARWELL, SARA J., ed. *Guide to the Microfilmed Manuscript Holdings of the Tennessee State Library and Archives*. Nashville: Tennessee State Library and Archives, 1983.

Haverford College. *The Quaker Collection of the Haverford College Library*. 1963.

Hawaiian Children's Mission Society. *A Guide to the Manuscript Collections in the Hawaiian Mission Children's Society Library*. Honolulu, 1980.

HINDING, ANDREA, ed.; Ames Sheldon Bower, assoc. ed.; Clarke A. Chambers, consulting ed. 2 V. *Women's History Sources: A Guide to Archives and Manuscript Sources in the United States*. New York, London: R. R. Bowker, 1979.

Historical Records Survey, Division of Professional and Service Projects, Work Projects Administration. *Inventory of the Church Archives in New York City: Lutheran*. New

York: The Historical Records Survey, 1940.

Historical Society of Pennsylvania. *Guide to the Manuscript Collections of the Historical Society of Pennsylvania.* 2nd ed., 1949.

HOLMES, RUTH E. V., comp. *Bibliographical and Historical Description of the Rarest Books in the Oliveira Lima Collection at the Catholic University of America.* Washington, D.C.: Catholic University of America, 1926.

HOLMIO, ARMAS K. E. *The Finnish Missionary Society, 1859–1950.* Hancock, MI: Finnish Lutheran Book Concern, 1950.

Hoover Institution on War, Revolution, and Peace. "Hoover Institution Archives Holdings on China." 1986.

Interdocumentation Company, Switzerland. "Guide to the Methodist Missionary Society Archives." n.d.

International Bulletin of Missionary Research. Special issues on China Mission History. V 9, N 2–3, Apr–Jl 1985.

Iowa State University. Library. *Serials Catalog.* Ames, IA: Library, Iowa State University, 1986.

JACQUET, CONSTANT A., JR. *Yearbook of American and Canadian Churches, 1984.* Nashville: Abingdon, 1984.

Johns Hopkins University. *Archives and Manuscripts: The Alan Mason Chesney Medical Archives, the Johns Hopkins Medical Institutions.* Baltimore, MD: The Johns Hopkins University, 1980.

JOHNSON, KURT ERIC. *Oral History Summaries: A Guide to the Collection.* St. Paul, MN: Midwest China Center, 1983.

KENDRICK, ALICE M., and HELEN M. KNUBEL, eds. *The Oral History Collection of the Archives of Cooperative Lutheranism.* New York: Lutheran Council in the U.S.A., 1984.

KIM, HONG N. *Scholars' Guide to Washington, D.C., for East Asian Studies (China, Japan, Korea, and Mongolia).* Washington, D.C.: Smithsonian Institution Press for the Woodrow Wilson International Center for Scholars, 1979.

KRAHN, CORNELIUS, MELVIN GINGERICH, and ORLANDO HARMS, eds. *The Mennonite Encyclopedia: A Comprehensive Reference Work on the Anabaptist-Mennonite Movement.* Scottsdale, PA: The Mennonite Publishing House, 1955.

LAI, JOHN YUNG-HSIANG, comp. *Catalog of Protestant Missionary Works in Chinese, Harvard-Yenching Library.* Cambridge: Harvard University Press, 1980.

LANAHAN, SISTER MARY FRANCESCA, S.N.D.N. *History of the Notre Dame Mission in Wuchang, China, 1926–1951.* Cincinnati: Sisters of Notre Dame de Namur, 1984.

LENNON, DONALD R. *Guide to Asian Studies Resources in the East Carolina Manuscript Collection.* Greenville, NC: Joyner Library, 1985.

LESLIE, DONALD D., COLIN MACKERRAS, and WANG GUNGWU, eds. *Essays on the Sources of Chinese History.* Columbia, SC: University of South Carolina Press, 1975.

LIETZ, PAUL S., ed. *Calendar of Philippine Documents in the Ayer Collection of the Newberry Library.* Chicago: The Newberry Library, 1956.

LIND, WILLIAM E. "Methodist Archives in the United States." In *The American Archivist.* V 24, N 4 (O 1961), pp. 435–440.

LINDEMANN, RICHARD H. F. "A Guide to Manuscript Sources for China, Japan, and Korea." 1983.

————. "Resources in the Woodruff Library, Emory University." In *Committee on East Asian Libraries Bulletin*, N 74 (Je 1984), pp. 24–28.

————. "Resources on China, Japan, and Korea in Special Collections, Woodruff Library, Emory University." In *Asian Resources in the Southeastern United States: Archival and Manuscript Resources on East Asia in Georgia*, edited by Kenneth W. Berger, 1985.

BIBLIOGRAPHY

LIU KWANG-CHING. *Americans and Chinese: A Historical Essay and a Bibliography.* Cambridge: Harvard University Press, 1963.

Lloyd Library and Museum. *Catalog of the Periodical Literature of the Lloyd Library and Museum.* Cincinnati: Lloyd Library, 1981.

LODWICK, KATHLEEN, comp. *The Chinese Recorder Index: A Guide to Christian Missions in Asia, 1867–1941.* 2 V. Wilmington, DE: Scholarly Resources, 1986.

LÖWENTHAL, RUDOLF, et al. *The Religious Periodical Press in China.* 2 V. Peiping: Synodal Commission in China, 1940.

LUNDEEN, JOEL W. *Preserving Yesterday for Tomorrow: A Guide to the Archives of the Lutheran Church in America.* Chicago: Archives of the Lutheran Church in America, 1977.

LUST, JOHN. *Index Sinicus: A Catalogue of Articles Relating to China in Periodicals and Other Collective Publications, 1920–1955.* Compiled by Werner Eichhorn. Cambridge, England: W. Heffner, 1964.

MACAVOY, THOMAS T. "Catholic Archives and Manuscript Collections." In *The American Archivist,* V 24, N 4 (O 1961), pp. 409–414.

McCUTCHEON, JAMES M., comp. *China and America: A Bibliography of Interactions, Foreign and Domestic.* Honolulu: University Press of Hawaii, 1972.

McDONALD, DONNA, ed. *Historical Societies and Agencies in the United States and Canada.* Nashville: The American Association for State and Local History, 1978.

MACGILLIVRAY, D., ed. *A Century of Christian Missions in China (1807–1907): Being the Centenary Conference Historical Volume.* Shanghai: American Presbyterian Mission Press, 1907.

MARCHANT, LESLIE R. *A Guide to the Archives and Records of Protestant Christian Missions from the British Isles to China, 1796–1914.* Perth: University of Western Australia Press, 1966.

MARTINIQUE, EDWARD G. "Materials on East Asia in the Southern Historical Collection, Wilson Library, University of North Carolina at Chapel Hill." In *Asian Resources in the Southeastern United States: Archival and Manuscript Resources on China and Japan in North Carolina,* edited by Kenneth W. Berger, n.p., 1985.

————. "Materials on East Asia in the Southern Historical Collection, Wilson Library, University of North Carolina at Chapel Hill." In *Committee on East Asian Libraries Bulletin,* N 69 (O 1982), pp. 1–11.

MASON, ELIZABETH B. and LOUIS M. STARR, eds. *The Oral History Collection of Columbia University.* New York: Oral History Research Office, 1979.

MATHEWS, R. H. *Mathews' Chinese-English Dictionary.* Revised American Edition. Cambridge: Harvard University Press, 1947. (reprint of *A Chinese-English Dictionary Compiled for the China Inland Mission.* Shanghai: China Inland Mission and Presbyterian Mission Press, 1931.)

MATTHEWS, DONALD N., ed. *Union List of Periodicals of the Members of the Washington Theological Consortium and Contributing Institutions.* 3rd ed. Lancaster, PA: Pridemark Press, 1976.

————. *Union List of Periodicals of the Southeastern Pennsylvania Theological Library Association.* Gettysburg, PA: Lutheran Theological Seminary, 1977.

MECKLER, ALAN M. and RUTH McMULLIN, comps. and eds. *Oral History Collections.* New York, London: R. R. Bowker Company, 1975.

MENKUS, BELDEN. "The Baptist Sunday School Board and Its Records." In *The American Archivist,* V 24, N 4 (O 1961), pp. 441–444.

Michigan Historical Records Survey, Division of Community Service Programs, Work Projects Administration. *Inventory of the Church Archives of Michigan. Churches of God: Michigan Assemblies.* Detroit, MI: The Michigan Historical Records Survey Project, 1941.

MICKELSON, ARNOLD R., ed.; ROBERT C. WIEDERAENDERS, assoc. ed. *A Biographical*

Directory of Clergymen of the American Lutheran Church. Minneapolis: Augsburg Publishing House, 1972.

Missionary Research Library. *Dictionary Catalog of the Missionary Research Library, New York*. 11 V. Boston: G. K. Hall, 1968.

Missions Advanced Research and Communication Center. *Mission Handbook: North American Protestant Ministries Overseas*. 12th ed. Monrovia, CA: Missions Advanced Research and Communication Center, 1980.

MUMPER, SHARON E. "Christianity and China/Chinese: A Periodical Bibliography." Wheaton Graduate School, 1982.

NATHAN, ANDREW J. *Modern China, 1840–1972: An Introduction to Sources and Research Aids*. Ann Arbor: University of Michigan Press, 1973.

National Archives and Records Administration. *Historical Materials in the Dwight D. Eisenhower Library*. Abilene, KS: Dwight D. Eisenhower Library, 1984.

National Archives and Records Service. *Catalog of National Archives Film Publications*. 1974.

————. *Guide to the National Archives of the United States*. 1974.

————. *Motion Pictures in the Audiovisual Archives Division of the National Archives*, by Mayfield S. Bray and William T. Murphy. 1972.

————. *Still Pictures in the Audiovisual Archives Division of the National Archives*, by Mayfield S. Bray. 1972.

National Geographic Atlas of the World, Melville Bell Grosvenor, editor-in-chief; James M. Darley, chief cartographer. Washington, D.C.: National Geographic Society, 1963.

National Historical Publications and Records Commission, ed. *Directory of Archives and Repositories in the United States*. 1983 ed. Washington, D.C.: National Archives and Records Service, General Services Administration, 1983.

————. *The NHPRC Guide/Data Base: A Manual for Cooperating Projects, 1979*. Washington, D.C.: National Historical Publications and Records Commission, 1979.

National Union Catalog 1963–1967: Music and Phonorecords, V 1–2. Ann Arbor, MI: J. W. Edwards, 1969.

NEUFELD, DON F. ed. *Seventh-Day Adventist Encyclopedia*. Washington, D.C.: Review and Herald Publishing Association, 1966.

New Jersey Historical Records Survey Program, Research and Records Section, Division of Community Service Programs, Work Projects Administration. *Inventory of the Church Archives of New Jersey: Baptist Bodies*. Newark, N.J.: The Historical Records Survey, 1938.

————. *Inventory of the Church Archives of New Jersey: Baptist Bodies: Seventh-Day Adventist Supplement*. Newark, N.J.: The Historical Records Survey, 1939.

————. *Inventory of the Church Archives of New Jersey: Congregational Christian Churches*. Newark, N.J.: The Historical Records Survey, 1941.

New York Public Library. *Dictionary Catalog of the Manuscript Division*. Boston: G. K. Hall, 1967.

————. *Dictionary Catalog of The Research Libraries of the New York Public Library, 1911–71*. Boston: G. K. Hall, 1979.

————. *Guide to the Research Collections of the New York Public Library*. Compiled by Sam P. Williams. Chicago: American Library Association, 1975.

Newark Museum. *Catalogue of the Newark Museum Tibetan Collection*. n.d.

Newberry Library. *Catalogue of the Greenlee Collection, The Newberry Library, Chicago*. Boston: G. K. Hall and Co., 1970.

NUNN, G. RAYMOND, ed. *Asia and Oceania: A Guide to Archival and Manuscript Sources in the United States*. New York: Mansell, 1985.

ORR, CLARA E. *Directory of Christian Colleges in Asia, Africa, the Middle East, the*

Pacific, Latin America, and the Caribbean. New York: Missionary Research Library, 1961.

O'TOOLE, JAMES M. *Guide to the Archives of the Archdiocese of Boston.* New York: Garland Publishing, Inc., 1982.

Papers of the American Board of Commissioners for Foreign Missions: Guide to the Microfilm Collection, Units 1–2. Woodbridge, CT: Research Publications, Inc., 1985.

PERSON, LAURA. *Cumulative List of Doctoral Dissertations and Masters' Theses in Foreign Missions and Related Subjects as Reported by the Missionary Research Library in the Occasional Bulletin, 1950–1960.* New York: Missionary Research Library, 1961.

PETERSON, JOHN, OLAF LYSNES, and GERALD GIVING, eds. *A Biographical Directory of Pastors of the Evangelical Lutheran Church.* Minneapolis: Augsburg Publishing House, 1952.

PHILLIPS, VANIA T. *Guide to the Manuscript Collections of the Academy of Natural Sciences of Philadelphia.* Philadelphia: Academy of Natural Sciences, 1963.

PIERSON, ROSCOE M., comp. *A Union List of Periodicals Currently Received by Protestant Theological Libraries in Kentucky, Ohio, and Indiana.* Lexington, KY: Bosworth Memorial Library, The College of the Bible, 1957.

PLAYFAIR, G. M. H. *The Cities and Towns of China: A Geographical Dictionary.* 2nd ed. Shanghai: Kelly and Walsh, Ltd., 1910.

POLEMAN, HORACE I. *A Survey of Tibetan Xylographs and Manuscripts in Institutions and Private Collections in the U.S.and Canada.* 1961.

PRIESTLEY, MARILYN, comp. *Comprehensive Guide to the Manuscripts Collection and to the Personal Papers in the University Archives.* Seattle: University of Washington, 1980.

Princeton University. *Guide to Selected Special Collections of Printed Books and Other Materials in the Princeton University Library.* 1983.

————. *LITMSS: An Indexed Catalog of Literary and Historical Manuscripts in Selected Manuscript Collections of Firestone Library.* Princeton: Princeton University Library, updated every 6 months.

Radcliffe College, Schlesinger Library. *The Manuscript Inventories and the Catalogs of Manuscripts, Books, and Periodicals.* 10 V. 2nd ed. Boston: G. K. Hall, 1984.

REESE, ED, ed. *A Guide to Churches, Denominations, Missionary Societies, Church Publications, Christian Schools.* Wheaton, IL: Church League of America, 1975.

REYNOLDS, MICHAEL M. *Guide to Theses and Dissertations: An Annotated International Bibliography of Bibliographies.* Detroit: Gale Research Co., 1975.

Rhode Island College. *Register of the Papers of Nathaniel Terry Bacon.* n.d.

Rockefeller Archive Center. *Archives and Manuscripts in the Rockefeller Archive Center.* New York: Rockefeller Archive Center, 1984.

————. *Photograph Collections in the Rockefeller Archive Center.* New York: Rockefeller Archive Center, 1986.

ROUSE, RUTH. ''Hints to Research Workers in the John R. Mott Library.'' Yale Divinity School, 1945.

RUOSS, G. MARTIN. *A World Directory of Theological Libraries.* Metuchen, NJ: The Scarecrow Press, Inc., 1968.

SAHLI, NANCY. *Directory of Archives and Manuscript Repositories in the United States.* Washington, D.C.: National Archives and Records Service, General Services Administration, 1978.

SAVORD, RUTH, and PEARL M. KEEFER. *Union List of Periodicals in Special Libraries of the New York Metropolitan District.* New York: H. W. Wilson for the New York Special Libraries Association, 1931.

SCHIFF, JUDITH ANN, comp. ''Primary Sources for the Study of China in the Department of Manuscripts and Archives, Yale University Library.'' 1984.

SCHMITT, MARTIN, comp. *Catalogue of Manuscripts in the University of Oregon Library*. 1971.

SCHULTZ, SALINA GERHARD, comp. *Schwenckfeldiana*. Norristown, PA: Board of Publications of the Schwenckfeldiana Church, 1947.

SHEEHY, EUGENE P., comp. *Guide to Reference Books*. 9th ed. Chicago: American Library Association, 1976.

SHULMAN, FRANK JOSEPH. ''Bibliography of Newsletter-type Publications Available Within the Asian Studies Newsletter Archives.'' 1984.

————. *Doctoral Dissertations on Asia: An Annotated Bibliographical Journal of Current International Research*. 4 V. Ann Arbor: Association for Asian Studies, 1975–81.

————. *Doctoral Dissertations on China, 1971–1975: A Bibliography of Studies in Western Languages*. Seattle: University of Washington Press, 1978.

————, and LEONARD H. D. GORDON. *Doctoral Dissertations on China: A Bibliography of Studies in Western Languages, 1945–1970*. Seattle: University of Washington Press, 1972.

SKINNER, G. WILLIAM. *Modern Chinese History: An Analytical Bibliography*. 3 V. Stanford, CA: Stanford University Press, 1973.

SMITH, HERBERT F., comp. *A Guide to the Manuscript Collection of the Rutgers University Library*. New Brunswick: Rutgers University Library, 1964.

Smith College. ''Papers on Asia in the Smith College Archives,'' n.d.

Smithsonian Archives. *Guide to the Smithsonian Archives*. Washington, D.C.: Smithsonian Institution Press, 1983.

Smithsonian Institution. *Catalog to Manuscripts at the National Anthropological Archives*. Washington, D.C.: Smithsonian Institution, 1975.

————. *Dictionary Catalog of the Freer Gallery of Art*. Washington, D.C.: Smithsonian Institution, 1967.

————. *Guide to the Smithsonian Archives*. Washington, D.C.: Smithsonian Institution, 1978.

Society of American Archivists. *Religious Archives in the United States and Canada: A Bibliography*. Chicago: Society of American Archivists, 1984.

STALKER, JOHN C., comp. *The Jesuit Collection in the John J. Burns Library of Boston College*. 1986.

STOUT, LEON J., ed. ''Resources on Twentieth-century China in Special Collections at the Pennsylvania State University Libraries.'' 1977.

STREIT, F. C. *Catholic World Atlas: Containing a Geographical and Statistical Description with Maps of the Holy Roman Catholic Church with Historical and Ethnographical Notes*. Paderborn: St. Boniface Press, 1929.

STREIT, ROBERT (V 1–12, 15–21); DINDINGER, JOHANNES (V 6–12, 15–21); ROMMERSKIRCHEN, J. (V 13–14, 22–30); KOWALSKY, N. (V 13–14); and METZLER, J. (V 22–30). 30 V. In *Bibliotheca Missionum* (V 1—Münster I.W.: Verlag der Aschendorffer Buchhandlung; V 2–11—Aachen: Franziskus Xaverius Missionsverein; V 12, 15–21—Freiburg: Herder; V 13–14, 22–30—Rom: Herder), 1916–74.

STUART, KAREN A. ''The 'Golden Chain: ' Manuscripts on East Asia at the Maryland Historical Society.'' Unpublished paper presented at the Tenth Annual Meeting of the Mid-Atlantic Region/Association of Asian Studies, University of Maryland, 1981.

SUELFLOW, AUGUST R., comp. *A Preliminary Guide to Church Records Repositories*. s.l.: Church Archives Committee, Society of American Archivists, 1969.

TANIS, NORMAN E., DAVID L. PERKINS, and JUSTINE PINTO. *China in Books: A Basic Bibliography in Western Languages*. Greenwich, CT: Jai Press, 1979.

Theological Libraries Group. *CORECAT*. Compiled by Richard Spoor. Pomona, CA: Autographics, Inc., 1986.

THOMAS, EVANGELINE, C.S.J. *Women Religious History Sources: A Guide to Repositories in the United States.* New York, London: R. R. Bowker Company, 1983.

THOMPSON, LAURENCE G. *Studies of Chinese Religion: A Comprehensive and Classified Bibliography of Publications in English, French, and German Through 1970.* Encino, CA: Dickenson Publishing Co., 1976.

TIEDEMANN, R. G. *A Brief Guide to Archival and Manuscript Sources Relating to Protestant and Roman Catholic Missions to China, 1800–1865.* London, 1985.

TIEN, H.C., RONALD HSIA, and PETER PENN. *Gazetteer of China.* Kowloon: Oriental Book Company, 1961.

TITUS, EDNA BROWN, ed., and the Joint Committee on the Union List of Serials. 5 V. 3rd ed. *Union List of Serials in the Libraries of the United States and Canada.* New York: H. W. Wilson Company, 1965.

TROLLIET, P. *Noms propres de géographie, d'histoire, et de littérature modernes de la Chine.* Paris: Ecole Nationale des Langues Orientales, n.d.

TSAI, ERNEST, comp. *Research Sources for Chinese and Japanese Studies: A List of Serials in Humanities and Social Sciences Held by Washington University Libraries.* St. Louis: Washington University Libraries, 1976.

TSIEN, TSUEN-HSUIN, and JAMES K. M. CHENG, comps. *China: An Annotated Bibliography of Bibliographies.* Boston: G. K. Hall, 1978.

Ulrich's International Periodicals Directory. 24th ed. New York: R. R. Bowker, 1986.
''A Union List of Adventist Serials.'' Berrien Springs, MI: Andrews University, James White Library, 1978.

Union Theological Seminary, NY. *Dictionary Catalog of the Union Theological Seminary.* 9 V. Boston: G. K. Hall, 1960.

United States Board on Geographic Names. *Gazetteer of the People's Republic of China.* Washington, D.C.: Defense Mapping Agency, 1979.

U.S. Department of Health, Education, and Welfare. *Author/Title Catalog of the Department Library.* 1965. (supp. 1972).

————. *Author/Title Catalog of the Department Library. Supplement.* 1972.

U.S. Library of Congress. 8 V. *Bibliography of Cartography.* Boston, G. K. Hall, 1973, 1980.

————. *Bibliography of Cartography, First Supplement.* 2 V. Boston: G. K. Hall, 1980.

————. *The Catalog of Books Represented by Library of Congress Printed Cards Issued (August, 1898-July 1942).* 167 V. Washington, D.C.: Library of Congress.

————. *The Catalog of Books Represented by Library of Congress Printed Cards Issued. Supplement: August 1, 1942-December 31, 1947.* 42 V. Washington, D.C.: Library of Congress.

————. *Checklist of Archives: In the Japanese Ministry of Foreign Affairs, Tokyo, Japan, 1868-1945: Microfilmed for the Library of Congress, 1949–1951.* Compiled by Cecil H. Uyehara. Washington, D.C.: Library of Congress Photoduplication Service, 1954.

————. *Checklist of Microfilm Reproductions of Selected Archives of the Japanese Army, Navy, and Other Government Agencies*, by John Young. Washington, D.C.: Georgetown University Press, 1959.

————. *Chinese Collections in the Library of Congress: Excerpts from the Annual Reports of the Librarian of Congress, 1898–1971.* Compiled by Ping-kuen Yu. 3 V. Washington, D.C.: Center for Chinese Research Materials, Association of Research Libraries, 1974.

————. *Chinese Cooperative Catalog*, 1975-82.

————. *Chinese-English and English-Chinese Dictionaries in the Library of Congress*, by Robert Dunn. 1977.

————. *Chinese Periodicals in the Library of Congress*, by Han-chu Huang. 1979.

————. *Combined Indexes to the Library of Congress Classification Schedules.* Compiled by Nancy Olson. 15 V. Washington, D.C.: U.S. Historical Documents Institute, 1974-.

————. *A Descriptive Catalog of Rare Chinese Books in the Library of Congress*. 2 V. Compiled by Chung-min Wang; edited by T. L. Yuan. 1957.

————. *Early Motion Pictures: The Paper Print Collection in the Library of Congress*, by Kemp R. Niver. Washington, D.C.: Library of Congress, 1985.

————. *Far Eastern Languages Catalog*. 22 V. Boston: G. K. Hall and Co., 1972.

————. *Geography and Map Division: A Guide to Its Collections and Services*. Washington, D.C.: Library of Congress, 1975.

————. *A Guide to the Collections of Recorded Folk Music and Folklore in the Library of Congress*. 1986.

————. *Guide to the Special Collections of Prints and Photographs in the Library of Congress*, by Paul Vanderbilt. Washington, D.C.: Library of Congress, 1955.

————. *Handbook of Manuscripts in the Library of Congress*. Washington, D.C.: Library of Congress, 1918.

————. *Index to the Calvin Coolidge Papers*. Washington, D.C.: Library of Congress, 1965.

————. *The Library of Congress Author Catalog: A Cumulative List of Works Represented by Library of Congress Cards, 1948–52*. 24 V. Washington, D.C.: Library of Congress.

————. *Library of Congress Catalog-Books: Subjects, A Cumulative List of Works Represented by Library of Congress Printed Cards*, 1945–74 (reprint cumulations for 1950–59 from Rowan and Littlefield; 1960–77 from J. W. Edwards; 1978-present, LC Cataloging Distribution Service Division).

————. *Library of Congress Subject Catalog*. Washington, D.C.: Library of Congress, 1975-, quarterly issues with an annual cumulation.

————. *List of Geographical Atlases in the Library of Congress, with Bibliographical Notes*. 8 V. Washington, D.C.: Library of Congress, 1908–74.

————. *List of Manuscript Collections in the Library of Congress to July 1931*, by Curtis W. Garrison. 1932.

————. *List of Manuscript Collections Received in the Library of Congress, July 1931 to July 1938*, by C. Percy Powell. 1939.

————. *National Union Catalog-Audiovisual Materials*. 1977-.

————. *The National Union Catalog of Manuscript Collections*. 1959–61—Ann Arbor: J. W. Edwards Company, 1962. 1962—Hamden, CT: Shoe String Press, 1964. 1963–83—Washington, D.C.: U.S. Library of Congress, 1965–83.

————. *National Union Catalog: Reference and Related Services*. Washington, D.C.: Library of Congress, 1973.

————. *New Serial Titles: A Union List of Serials Commencing Publication After December 31, 1949*. New York, London: R. R. Bowker Company, 1973.

————. *Rare Book Division: A Guide to its Collections and Services*. 1965.

————. *Some Guides to Special Collections in the Rare Book Division*. 1974.

————. *Special Collections in the Library of Congress, A Selective Guide*, by Annette Melville. Washington, D.C.: Library of Congress, 1980.

————. *Union List of Serials in the Libraries of the United States and Canada*. 3rd ed. New York: H. W. Wilson Co., 1965.

U.S. Library of Congress and American Library Association. *The National Union Catalog of Pre-1956 Imprints*. V 1–704. Chicago: Mansell, 1968.

U.S. National Library of Medicine. *Biomedical Serials, 1950–1960, A Selective List of Serials in the National Library of Medicine*. Compiled by Lela M. Spanier. Washington, D.C.: U.S. Department of Health, Education, and Welfare, Public Health Service, 1962.

————. *Index of NLM Serial Titles, 1984*. Bethesda, MD: National Library of Medicine, 1985.

————. *National Library of Medicine Catalog, 1950–54.* 6 V. Washington, D.C.: Judd and Detweiler, Inc., 1960.

————. *National Library of Medicine Catalog, 1960–64.* 5 V. Washington, D.C.: Library of Congress, 1961–65.

U.S. Navy Department, Hydrographic Office. *Gazetteer (No. 15): China Coast.* Washington, D.C.: U.S. Government Printing Office, 1945.

U.S. Surgeon General's Office. *Index Catalogue of the Library of the Surgeon General's Office.* 4th series. 11 V. Washington, D.C.: U.S. Government Printing Office, 1936–55.

University of California, Berkeley. East Asiatic Library. *Author-Title Catalog.* 13 V. Boston: G. K. Hall, 1968.

————. *First Supplement: Author Catalog.* 2 V. Boston: G. K. Hall, 1973.

————. *First Supplement: Subject Catalog.* 2 V. Boston: G. K. Hall, 1973.

————. *Subject Catalog.* 6 V. Boston: G. K. Hall, 1968.

University of Chicago Library. *Author-Title Catalog of the Chinese Collection.* 8 V. Boston: G. K. Hall, 1973.

————. *Author-Title Catalog of the Chinese Collection: First Supplement.* 4 V. Boston: G. K. Hall, 1981.

————. *Classified Catalog and Subject Index of the Chinese and Japanese Collections.* 6 V. Boston: G. K. Hall, 1973.

————. *Classified Catalog and Subject Index of the Chinese and Japanese Collections: First Supplement.* 4 V. Boston: G. K. Hall, 1981.

————. *Far Eastern Serials.* Chicago: University of Chicago Library, 1977.

Virginia State Library. *Catalogue of Virginia Library Resources, 1983 Edition.* Richmond, VA: Virginia State Library, 1984.

WALEY-COHEN, JOANNA. "Bibliography on English-language Source Material at Yale University for the Study of Chinese History." Yale University, 1985.

WEICHERDING, ROBERT, ed. *The Official Catholic Directory.* Wilmette, IL: P. J. Kennedy and Sons, 1985.

Who's Who in the Methodist Church. New York/Nashville: Abingdon Press, 1966.

WINFREY, DORMAN H. "Protestant Episcopal Church Archives." In *The American Archivist,* V 24, N 4 (O 1961), pp. 431–434.

Wisconsin Historical Records Survey, Division of Professional and Service Projects, Work Projects Administration. *Inventory of the Church Archives of Wisconsin. Churches of the United Brethren in Christ.* Madison, WI: The Wisconsin Historical Records Survey Project, 1940.

WOODARD, JOHN. "Missionaries' Papers and Other Sources in the North Carolina Baptist Historical Collection, Wake Forest University." 1983.

Young Women's Christian Association. "Inventory to the Record Files Collection of the National Board of the Young Womens' Christian Association, 1978."

YUAN TUNG-LI. *A Guide to Doctoral Dissertations by Chinese Students in America, 1905–1960.* Washington, D.C.: 1961.

ZINN, LUCILLE S. *The Works of Pearl S. Buck: A Bibliography,* 1979.

Indexes

Subject Index

Titles of churches and mission organizations changed from time to time, and they were often used in abbreviated or ad hoc form in the mission documents. This index uses the titles as they appear in the library records. For current titles see the latest edition of *The Yearbook of American and Canadian Churches* edited by the Office of Research of the National Council of the Churches of Christ in the U.S.A., 475 Riverside Drive, New York, NY 10115.

SUBJECT INDEX

543

Personal Names Index

This index lists all individuals named in the collections. Married women are listed under their married names, with cross references under the maiden name (indicated in parentheses), where known. Since this index reproduces the library records without alteration, some variant spellings may occur where it was not possible to determine the correct version. See also Union List of Oral Histories and Union List of Dissertations.

Citations use Index Codes as indicated in each entry and collection. Example: McClurg, Ruth, OH-25/1: OH = Ohio; 25 = institutional code (in this case, Bowling Green State University); 1 = collection number (here, the Grace McClurg Carson Papers). Citations without a collection number refer to the background notes for the insitution (e.g., TN-35).

Information in brackets was obtained from sources other than the collection inventories. The "b" listed after a collection number indicates that the citation contains biographical information.

"Agnes," KY-30/1
A Si, NY-345/23
A Tui, NY-345/23
Aadland, Mr. and Mrs. Nels J., MN-95
Aalbue, Joseph, MN-95/92
Aandahl, Eliot, IA-15/1
Aarkvisla, Anna K. (Nilson), MN-95
Aasgaard, J. A., IA-15/1
Abbey, Katherine J. *See* Vanderbeek, Katherine J.
Abbott, [?], ME-10/1
Abbott, Eliza Ann. *See* Goddard, Eliza Ann (Abbott)
Abbott, Lillian, TN-45/1
Abeel, David, NJ-60/1b, NJ-65/1, NJ-65/2, NJ-135/7, NY-275/1, PA-170/1
Abel, Edith F., OR-15/1
Abel-Remusat, Jean Pierre, DC-25/2
Abernathy, Jean (Mrs. John), NJ-25
Abernathy, Jewell (Mrs. John A.), TN-35, VA-65/2
Abernathy, John, NJ-25
Abernathy, John A., TN-35, VA-65/2
Acheson, Dean, VA-50/1
Acquaviva, Claudio, IL-60/2
Adam, Maurice, CA-185/1, WA-45/1
Adams, A. S., CT-50/14
Adams, Archibald, CT-50/7
Adams, Archibald Guinness, OH-155/1
Adams, Arthur, CT-50/7
Adams, C., NY-280/3
Adams, Carrie (Mrs. Roy), KY-85/1
Adams, Elizabeth, KY-85/1
Adams, Eva. *See* Macmillan, Eva (Adams)

Adams, Helen E., NB-15/1
Adams, Joseph Samuel, NY-275/1, NY-345/2b
Adams, Mabel, CT-50/14
Adams, Marie, CT-50/7, IN-40/1, OR-15/61
Adams, Olive Mason (Mrs. Archibald Guinness), OH-155/1
Adams, Roy, KY-85/1
Adams, Uniola V., NB-15/1
Adams, W. F., PA-80
Adams, W. W., NY-150/1
Addison, James Thayer, MN-105/3
Adeney, David H., PA-190/2, PA-265/2
Adkins, Russel E., OH-155/2
Adlam, Edith , CA-235/1
Adolph, Harold, IL-200/1, IL-200/50
Adolph, Paul, IL-200/44, IL-200/50
Adolph, Vivian (Mrs. Paul), IL-200/44, IL-200/50
Adolph, William A., NY-270/12
Ady, Lucile (Meloy) (Mrs. Merrill Steele), CT-50/7
Ady, Merrill Steele, CA-75/2, CA-80/1, CT-10/2, CT-50/2, CT-50/7, OR-15/18
Aeschliman, Edward J, NJ-45/3
Agar, Grace, MO-105/1
Agar, John, NY-290/1
Agerina, S., WI-75/4
Aggola, L. Leona, IN-75/1
Agnes Clare, Sr., IN-105/6
Agnew, Esther. *See* Melrose, Esther (Agnew)
Aguirre, Bishop, OH-115/1
Aho, Ilma Ruth, MN-95/110
Ainsworth, William Newman, GA-10/1
Akins, Ethel M., MN-95/1

Albaugh, Ida. *See* Vousden, Ida (Albaugh)
Albert, Martin, CT-50/7
Albright, Anne M., IL-105/11
Albright, Jacob, NY-200
Aldersey, M., CT-50/9, IL-25/1, IL-200/14, KS-35/1
Aldersey, Mary Ann, CA-100/1
Aldrich, Abby. *See* Rockefeller, Abby (Aldrich)
Aldrich, Lucy, NY-290/1
Aleni, Julio, IN-15/1
Alexander, B. H., NY-305/1
Alexander, Charles M., NJ-35
Alexander, George, NY-225/1
Alexander, Mary Charlotte, TN-35, VA-65/2
Alexander, Edith, NY-305/1
Alexandre, Noel, IL-45/1, MN-20
Alfons, Mother M., WI-75
Alford, Edith. *See* Trimble, Edith (Alford)
Allder, James R., CA-130/1
Allen, Arthur J., CA-80/2, GA-20/1, NY-270/25, TX-5/2, NY-175/1**b**
Allen, Benjamin F., CT-50/14
Allen, Bertha H., CA-20/1
Allen, Bertha Harding. *See* St. Clair, Bertha Harding (Allen)
Allen, C. W., NY-270/25
Allen, Carrie, OH-170/1
Allen, Catherine B., AL-10/2
Allen, Edgar, GA-20/1
Allen, George Nelson, OH-170/1
Allen, Julia, NY-285/4
Allen, Julia F., MA-220/2**b**
Allen, Malvina, GA-20/1
Allen, Mary (Mrs. Young J.), GA-20/1
Allen, Netta (Powell) (Mrs. Arthur J.), CA-80/2, NY-175/1**b**, TX-5/2
Allen, Roland, CT-55/2
Allen, Sarah Isabella. *See* Buttrick, Sarah Isabella (Allen)
Allen, Thomas, NY-285/4
Allen, Walter, NY-175/1
Allen, Walter P., TX-5/2
Allen, Young John, AZ-5/1, CA-100/1, CA-110/1, CA-180/1, CA-190/1, CA-275/1, CA-305/1, CT-55/2, CT-80/1, GA-15/1, GA-15/3, GA-20/1**b**, GA-25/1, HI-15/1, IL-85/1, IL-110/1, IL-170/1, IN-20/1, MA-35/1, MI-10/1, NC-55/1, NJ-40/2, NJ-45/5, NY-95/1, OH-110/4, PA-215/1, PA-250/1, TX-20/2, WA-35/1
Alley, Rewi, MA-165/5
Allgood, Roy, TX-5/2
Allison, Roy, PA-65/1
Allyn, Harriett M., MA-220/3
Alman, John F., NJ-45/3
Alperin, David, IA-25/1
Alsop, Bugelius F., TX-5/2
Alsup, Alice, CT-50/7
Altman, Ruth Peabody. *See* Greene, Ruth Peabody (Altman)
Amadea, S. Marie, OH-165/1
Ament, Mary (Penfield) (Mrs. William Scott), OH-170/1, WA-40/4
Ament, Mildred May. *See* Rowland, Mildred May (Ament)
Ames, Herman, MD-15/1
Amiot, M., NY-175/13
Ammerman, Helen B., PA-80
Ancell, Benjamin Lucius, TX-5/2, TX-5/4
Ancell, Frances Cattell (Mrs. Benjamin Lucius), TX-5/2
Anderson, Alice K., MN-95/2
Anderson, Charlotte, TX-5/2
Anderson, Clara, MN-95/3
Anderson, Colena M., MN-95/4
Anderson, D. L., NJ-45/10
Anderson, David, CT-60/32
Anderson, Dr. and Mrs. Robert A., MN-95
Anderson, E., NY-280/3
Anderson, George, OR-15/18
Anderson, H. C., NJ-45/4
Anderson, Helen (Mount) (Mrs. Ian), IL-200/3**b**, PA-265/1
Anderson, Ian Rankin, IL-200/3**b**, PA-265/1
Anderson, Jacob N., NB-20/1

Anderson, John Arthur, NJ-25
Anderson, John Peter, MI-45/1
Anderson, John T., NY-290/1
Anderson, Marie, MN-95, MN-95/94
Anderson, Mr. and Mrs. Palmer I., MN-95
Anderson, Mr. and Mrs. Matthew G., IL-200/50
Anderson, Mr. and Mrs. Albert, MN-95
Anderson, Mrs. Carl L., CT-50/7
Anderson, Myrtle, PA-60/1
Anderson, Olive (Mrs. Sid), CA-320/1
Anderson, P. H., TX-25/2
Anderson, Paul B., IL-180/1
Anderson, R. K., CT-50/2
Anderson, Sidney R., GA-10/1, NJ-45/3, NJ-45/10
Anderson, Sr. Julian, WI-70/1
Anderson, Viola, MN-95/5
Andreassen, Einar C., IA-15/1
Andrew of Perugia, PA-235/1
Andrews, Egbert W., PA-150, PA-150/1, PA-190/1**b**, PA-190/2
Andrews, Grace A. (Funk) (Mrs. H. Edwin V., 2nd wife), CT-50/7, OH-180/1
Andrews, J. CA-75/2
Andrews, John Nevins, CA-80/3
Angarini, Dario, OH-130/1
Angelita, Marcelo, IL-60/1
Angelus, Fr., CA-260/1
Angier, [?], NJ-95/1
Anglin, Leslie M., MO-105/1
Angus, William R., IA-45/2, MI-105/1, MI-105/4, MI-120/8, NJ-60/2**b**, NJ-60/3
Anita Mary, Mother, TX-5/2
Ankeny, Louise, OR-15/32**b**
Anner, Conrad W., NY-295/1**b**
Anspach, P. E., IA-15/1
Anspach, Paul P., IL-50/1
Anville, Jean Baptiste Bourguignon d', NJ-110, NY-95/1
Appleget, T. B., NY-285/1
Appleton, C. F., IN-120/6
Appleton, George H., TX-5/2
Appleton, Laura, IN-120/4, IN-120/5, IN-120/6
Archibald, George Hamilton, NY-95/1
Argelander, Frank A., CA-290/1**b**, NJ-45/3, NJ-45/5, OR-15/56
Armacost, R. L. CA-75/2
Armentrout, Lois, CT-10/2, OR-15/18
Armour, Elizabeth, TX-5/2
Armstrong, Alice, VA-65/2
Armstrong, Annie, VA-65/2
Armstrong, Arthur Edward Marriott, MI-15/1**b**
Armstrong, Elsa (Felland) (Mrs. Arthur), MI-15/1**b**, MN-70/2, MN-95
Armstrong, Susan, MA-95/1
Arndt, Edward L., MO-50/1**b**, MO-50/4
Arndt, Karl J., MO-50/1
Arndt, William Frederick, MO-50/2**b**, MO-50/13
Arnold, Charles Harrison, NB-10/1**b**
Arnold, Julean H, MA-195/5, NY-270/1
Arnold, Mrs. Charles, NB-10/1
Arthur, James A., MN-60/1
Arthur, James Hillcoat, PA-200/28
Asbury, Francis, NY-200
Ashcraft, E. P., IN-120/1, IN-120/5
Ashcraft, Harriet (Mrs. E. P.), IN-120/1, IN-120/5
Ashcroft, Evelyn, TX-5, TX-5/2
Ashmore, Edith. *See* Hensolt, Edith (Ashmore)
Ashmore, Eliza Ann (Dunlevy) (Mrs. William, Sr., 2nd wife), OH-155/2
Ashmore, Lida Scott (Mrs. William, Jr.), OR-15/2
Ashmore, Martha Sanderson (Mrs. William, Sr., 1st wife), OH-155/2
Ashmore, William, Sr., CT-50/12, CT-50/14, NY-270/2**b**, OH-155/2, RI-15/1, RI-15/4
Ashmore, William, Jr., NY-345/3, OR-15/2**b**
Asper, Mr. and Mrs. Oluf, MN-95
Atherton, Frank, HI-20/1
Atkinson, Virginia M., AL-5/1

Bartel, Nellie (Mrs. Henry C.), CA–115/1
Bartel, Paul, KS–55/8, NY–305/8
Bartel, Paul H., PA–125/1
Bartel, Susan (Schultz) (Mrs. Loyal), CA–115/1, IL–200/5b
Barth, Karl, CA–290/29
Bartholomew, Allen Revellen, PA–80/1, PA–80/13
Bartholomew, Bob, CT–50/14
Bartlett, Myrth, CT–50/7
Bartlett, Samuel Colcord, HI–15/2, MA–30/2
Barton, Ernest D., NY–285/1
Barton, Helen E., NJ–45/3
Barton, James L., CT–50/22, NY–275/1, NY–290/1
Bashford, James Whitford, CT–50/16, CO–15/1, IN–10/1, MA–35/1, MD–25/1, NJ–45/3, NJ–45/5, NJ–45/7 NJ–45/13, NY–200/1, NY–270/3b, NY–270/14, NY–270/18, OH–140/1, WI–50/1
Bashford, Jennie M. (Field) (Mrs. James), WI–50/1
Basile de Gemona, DC–70/3
Basile de Glemona, PA–145/2b
Basilio da Gemona, CA–165/1
Basilio da G[l]emona, IN–10/5
Bass, L. Joe, OK–10/1
Bastiannini, P. Giovanni, CA–265/1
Basto, Candida Maria, NY–120/1, VA–25/1
Batcheller, Walter B., NJ–45/13
Batdorf, Charles William, CA–35/1
Bates, Daniel M., TX–5/2
Bates, J. E., MO–25/2
Bates, Margaret, TX–5/2
Bates, Miner Searle, CA–90/1, CT–10/2, CT–50/17, CT–50/25, CT–50/2b, CT–60/32, HI–15/2, IN–60/2, MA–155/1, MA–195/5, NJ–45/5, NJ–115/1, NY–195/2, NY–270/8, NY–270/37, OK–5/1, TN–45/1
Battin, Lora, OR–15/50
Bau, Ming-chien Joshua, CT–50/2
Bau, T. C., CT–50/13, VA–25/10
Bauer, Thomas J., NY–105/1, NY–125/1, IL–20/1, IL–130/1, IN–60/2, MA–280/1
Bauman, Elizabeth, NY–120/1
Baumann, Marie Elise, NY–120/1
Baumgarten, Fortunatus, NJ–155/1
Baumgartner, Fannie (Chapman), IN–30/1
Bausum, Euva Evelyn (Majors) (Mrs. Robert Lord), CT–50/7, TN–35
Bausum, Robert Lord, CT–50/7, TN–35
Bausum family, VA–65/2
Bayle, Monica Marie, NY–120/1
Baynes, Alfred Henry, IL–200/4, TN–55/1, TX–25/1
B., B., NY–270/33
Beach, Frederick P., CT–50/7, MA–95/1
Beach, Harlan Page, CT–50/3b, CT–50/17, CT–50/22, CT–60/13, CT–60/24, CT–60/32, NY–270/35
Beach, Kay Haines, MN–95/7
Beach, Lucy (Ward) (Mrs. Harlan Page), CT–50/3b, NJ–45/5
Beach, Ruth P. (Ward) (Mrs. Frederick P.), MA–220/55b
Beach, Sarah, MN–60/1
Beall, Jeannette, VA–65/2
Beals, Effie Pinkham (Mrs. Zephaniah Charles, 3rd wife), IL–10/1
Beals, Zephaniah Charles, IL–10/1b, IL–10/2, IL–10/3
Beam, J. Albert, PA–80
Beame, Harold, NY–270/12
Bean, Ruth M., IN–35/5
Bear, James Edwin, CA–205/1, CT–50/7, MI–85/1, TX–30/1, VA–80/1b, VA–85/1
Bear, James Edwin, Jr., PA–210/2
Bear, Margaret W. (Mrs. James Edwin), CT–50/7, VA–80/1, VA–85/1
Bear, Tom, IN–120/4
Beard, Bertha, TX–5/2
Beard, Flora, MA–95/1
Beard, Mary L., MA–220/6b
Beard, Phebe, OH–170/2b
Beard, Willard Livingston, CT–10/2, CT–15/5, CT–50/7, MA–95/1, OH–170/2b
Beaton, Kenneth J., CT–50/2
Beatrice Martha, Mother, TX–5/2

Beattie, Nellie E. (Hartwell) (Mrs. Andrew), CT–50/13b
Beatty, Mabel A., NY–270/33
Beauvolier, Antoine, IN–15/1
Beck, Edwin Allen, PA–80/1, PA–80/2b, PA–80/13
Beck, Etta Irene (Poling) (Mrs. Edwin), PA–80/2b
Beck, Karl Herbert, CT–50/2, CT–50/7, PA–80/3, PA–80/13
Beck, Meta M. (Bridenbaugh) (Mrs. Karl), PA–80/3b
Becker, Auguste (Mrs. Herman), IL–200/50
Becker, Herman, IL–200/50, NJ–25
Beckinsale, Jennie, IL–200/4, TN–55/1, TX–25/1
Beckworth, Exum G., NC–100/3
Beddoe, Louella, TN–35
Beddoe, Robert E., TN–35, VA–65/2
Beebe, Harriet Linn (Mrs. Robert Case), NY–270/35, PA–105/1b
Beebe, Robert Case, CT–10/2, NJ–45/13, NY–275/1, NY–290/1
Beech, Joseph, CT–30, CT–30/1, NJ–45/3, NJ–45/13, NY–270/18
Beech, Katharine, CT–30/1
Beech, Miriam, CT–30/1
Beede, B. Willis, MA–95/1
Beegle, Caroline, PA–100/1b
Beets, Henry, MI–80/1b
Behnken, John William, MO–50/3b
Behrents, [Olaf?], IA–15/1
Behrents, Dr. and Mrs. Olaf S., MN–95
Belcher, H. B., MA–95/1
Belcher, Harold, CT–50/7
Belcher, Marian (Mrs. Harold), CT–50/7
Belknap, Charlotte. *See* Reynolds, Charlotte (Belknap)
Bell, E. Hope, CT–50/9, IL–25/1, IL–200/14, KS–35/1
Bell, Ellen. *See* Magill, Ellen (Bell)
Bell, Florence, MA–240
Bell, L. Nelson, CT–50/7, NJ–25
Bell, T. P., VA–65/2
Bellsmith, Florence Rosalind. *See* Goforth, Florence Rosalind (Bellsmith)
Belleville, M., NY–280/3
Belote, James D., TN–35, VA–65/2
Belote, Martha, TN–35
Bement, F. K., OH–175/1
Bement, Frances Katherine, OH–180/1
Bement, L. P., OH–175/1
Bement, Lucy P., OH–170/24, OH–180/1
Bender, Elizabeth R., NY–270/35
Bender, Margaret E., TX–5/2
Bendtz, N. Arne, NJ–30/1
Benedict XV, Pope, PA–95/1
Bennet, [Daniel?], IL–25/1, IL–200/14, KS–35/1
Bennet, Augustus W., NJ–35/1
Bennett, Adrian Arthur, CA–80/48, CO–10/3, CT–80/1
Bennett, Catherine, TX–5/2
Bennett, Eunice Mitchell, OH–120/1
Bennett, James W., TX–5/2
Benson, J. L., IA–15/1
Benson, Lilly, NJ–30/1
Benson, Nels, IA–15/1
Bentin, M., NY–175/13
Benton, John Keith, TN–70/1
Benton, Ruth, IN–75/1
Berckman, James H. H., NJ–45/3, NJ–45/10
Bercowitz, Nathaniel, CT–10/2
Bereswill, Louis, MO–40/1
Berg, Frances, TX–5/2
Bergamini, Dorothy, TX–5/2
Bergamini, J. V. W., CT–60/32
Bergamini, John Van Wic, TX–5/2
Bergen, Mary J., PA–240/1
Berkeley, Sr. Xavier, NY–95/1
Berkey, Earl, NB–15/1
Berkey, Marguerite L. (Mrs. Earl), NB–15/1, NJ–45/3
Berlew, Herman D., CT–30/4
Bern, Paul, NJ–45/5
Bernard, Augustin, NY–95/1
Bernard, Harry V., NC–70/4b
Bernard, Henri, WI–45/1

Brown, Clella E. (McDonnell) (Mrs. Frederick R., 2nd wife), NY–20/1
Brown, Cora M., KS–10/1
Brown, D., NY–280/3
Brown, F. A., CT–50/9, IL–25/1, IL–200/14, KS–35/1
Brown, F. C., CT–50/26
Brown, F. Crawford, TX–5/2
Brown, Fanny Pomeroy, CT–50/7
Brown, Francis Augustus, Sr., NC–80/2b
Brown, Francis C., TX–5/2
Brown, Frank A., GA–35/1
Brown, Fred R., CT–50/16, NJ–45/3, NJ–45/13, NY–20/1b
Brown, Frederick, NJ–45/13
Brown, Harold D., NY–270/25
Brown, Harry, IL–205/1
Brown, Heinrich Jacob, KS–55/1b
Brown, Henry, NJ–30/1
Brown, Henry J., CA–115/1, IN–25/1, KS–55/2b, KS–55/3, KS–55/13, VA–40/1
Brown, J., NY–280/3
Brown, John Crosby, CT–60/32
Brown, Julia. See Mateer, Julia (Brown)
Brown, Lydia. See Hipps, Lydia (Brown)
Brown, Margaret H., CT–10/2, CT–50/2, NY–270/5b
Brown, Maria (Mrs. Henry J.), CA–115/1, IN–25/1, KS–55/2, KS–55/13, VA–40/1
Brown, Mark W., NJ–45/3, NJ–45/5, NY–270/6
Brown, Mr. and Mrs. H. J., KS–55, VA–40
Brown, Mrs., CT–50/16
Brown, Nathan Worth, NY–290/1
Brown, Robert E., NJ–45/3
Brown, Ruby E. (Higgins) (Mrs. Leroy C.), MA–220/27
Brown, Velva V., CT–50/7
Brown, Viette I. See Sprague, Viette I. (Brown)
Brown, W. E., OH–135/1
Brown, William Adams, MA–230/4
Browne, Alice Seymour. See Frame, Alice Seymour (Browne)
Browne, Emily G. See Cooper, Emily G.
Browne, Thomas P., NY–105/1
Brownell, Henry C., VT–5/1b
Browning, Margaret. See Leavens, Margaret (Browning)
Browning, Robert E., TX–5/2
Brubaker, Leland S., IL–105/7
Bruce, Elizabeth Gordon, CT–50/7, MI–105/4, MI–120/4, NJ–60/3
Bruce, Frederick W. A., NC–45/1
Bruce, Gustav Marius, MN–95/110
Bruce, Martha, TX–5/2
Bruder, Joseph, OH–130/1
Bruhl, Heinz, MN–95/10
Brune family, MD–30/1
Brunemeier, Catherine, NJ–45/4
Brunger, Harry A., CT–50/7
Brunner, Harold, NJ–30/1
Brunner, Henry S., PA–275/3
Brunner, Kunigunde, NJ–30, NJ–30/1
Bruno, F. F., MA–75/1
Bruton, Herbert, TX–5/2
Bryan, Catharine, TN–35
Bryan, Eugene Kay, TN–35
Bryan, F. Catharine, VA–65/2
Bryan, Frances A., TN–35
Bryan, John Nelson, TN–35
Bryan, Leta Rue, TN–35
Bryan, Mamie (Sallee) (Mrs. Robert Thomas), KY–15/1, TX–25/2
Bryan, Nelson A., TN–35
Bryan, Robert Thomas, KY–50/2
Bryan, Ruth, TN–35
Bryan, W. J., PA–270/1
Buchanan, Elizabeth M., TX–5, TX–5/2
Buchanan, Mattie, NC–10/4
Buchanan, Mildred, TX–5/2
Bucher, Henry H., CT–10/2
Bucher, Jonas Frank, PA–80/4b
Bucher, Mary, PA–80/4

Bucher, Olive (Miller)(Mrs. Jonas Frank), PA–80/4b
Buchman, Frank N. D., DC–90/6
Buck, David D., CA–45/1, MA–25/3
Buck, John Lossing, CA–70/1, CA–185/1, CT–50/2, MA–155/1, MI–10/1, NY–90/4, NY–275/1, PA–200/28, PA–270/4, PA–275/4
Buck, Mina Van Cleave, CT–50/7
Buck, Pearl (Sydenstricker) (Mrs. John Lossing), CA–210/2, CT–15/1, CT–50/6, CT–60/30, DC–90/4, DE–10/1, IL–200/47, IL–200/55, KY–45/1, MA–130/2, MA–195/5, MI–10/1, MN–95/55, MN–105/3, NJ–65/2, NJ–115/1, NJ–135/1, NY–90/4, NY–175/2, PA–170/2, TN–40/1, VA–25/2, VA–25/3, VA–60/1b, WV–10/1, WV–15/4
Buckham, John Wright, NY–270/25
Buckner, H. F., TX–25/2
Buckwalter, R., NY–280/7
Budde, Lambert, MA–255/1
Buell, Constance, MA–95/1
Buettner, Milton, IN–5/1
Buglio, Louis, IL–85/1
Buhler, Gertrude. See Wiens, Gertrude (Buhler)
Buker, Raymond, OH–170/10
Bundy, Gladys (Wilson) (Mrs. Robert E.), CT–50/7
Bundy, Robert E., CT–50/7, TX–5/2
Bunn, Albert C., TX–5/2
Bunn, Elizabeth, TX–5/2
Bunts, Alexander Taylor, MA–50/3
Bunyan, John, IL–85/1, TX–35/1
Burchard, Bishop, OH–165/1
Burdon, J. S., HI–15/2
Burgess, Andrew S., MN–95/110
Burgess, John Stewart, CA–290/5, CT–50/26, MD–15/2, NJ–120/2, NJ–125/1b, OH–180/1, PA–210/1
Burgess, Stella (Fisher) (Mrs. John Stewart), CA–290/5, NJ–120/2, NJ–125/1
Burgevine, Henry Andrea, IN–20/2
Burke, James Cobb, GA–20/2
Burke, John, GA–20/2
Burke, Mr. and Mrs. J. W., NC–10/3
Burke, Leila, GA–20/2
Burke, William Blount, CA–15/2, GA–20/2, NC–10/3, NJ–45/5, NJ–45/10
Burket, Everett Stanley, CT–50/6
Burket, Margaret Larue (Campbell) (Mrs. Everett), CT–50/6b
Burkey, Kathryn, IN–30/1
Burkey, Lydia, IN–30/1
Burkholder, Lawrence J., CT–50/2
Burl, Olive R., TX–5/2
Burlingame, Anson, CT–60/30
Burlingham, A. H., NY–285/4
Burnett, Cleone, MN–90/1
Burnett family, NC–10/4
Burns, J. Clarence, PA–200/28
Burns, Mary E., NJ–45/13
Burns, William C., DC–80/2
Burns, William Chalmers, NJ–25, NY–95/1
Burr, Leona Lloyd, OH–180/1
Burris, Clinton, NJ–45/4
Burroughs, Grace. See Mather, Grace (Burroughs)
Bursken, Vestina, MN–90/3
Burton, Ernest DeWitt, IL–75/1, IL–75/2b, NY–285/2
Burton, G. W., VA–65/2
Burton, M., NY–280/3
Burton, Margaret E., IL–75/2
Burton, Marion Leroy, MA–185/19
Burton, Myron, MN–60/1
Burtschy, Conradin, KY–80/1
Burtt, Edwin Palmer, ME–25/1b
Burtt, Lucy R., MA–95/1
Burwell, C. Sidney, NY–295/7
Buryce, Alice, MI–120/12
Busch, Bishop Joseph T., MN–90/4
Busch, Pastor, NY–290/1
Buse, Eleanor, TX–5/2
Bush, Richard C. Jr., IL–180/1

Bush, Sr. Eustella (Gertrude), WI-75/2**b**, WI-75/3
Bushnell, Horace, CT-15/2
Bushnell, Samuel Clarke, CT-60/4**b**, CT-60/32
Buswell, Ina. *See* Johnson, Ina (Buswell)
Buswell, Laura S., CT-50/16
Buswell, Minnie. *See* Spore, Minnie (Buswell)
Butler, Alice L., NY-270/35
Butler, Charles E., NH-10/1
Butler, E. S., CT-50/14
Butler, Edith Esther, OH-30/1
Butler, Esther H., OH-30
Butler, Rosa May, CT-50/7
Butler, William A., NY-225/3
Butrick, Richard P., PA-125/1
Buttles, Edward K., TX-5/2
Buttrick, Sarah Isabella (Allen) (Mrs. Wallace), NC-10/5
Buttrick, Caroline I., NC-10/5
Buttrick, Wallace Henry, NC-10/5**b**, NY-290/1, NY-295/3, NY-295/8, NY-295/9, PA-145/1
Byerly, Anne E., TX-5/2

Cable, Alice Mildred, CA-205/1
Cabot, Geraldine, TX-5/2
Cadbury, Catharine Balderston (Jones) (Mrs. W. W.), MA-155/1, PA-135/1**b**
Cadbury, Helen, NJ-35
Cadbury, Henry, PA-135/1
Cadbury, William Warder, MA-155/1, PA-75/1, PA-135/1**b**
Cady, Henry Olin, NJ-45/1, OR-15/8**b**
Cady, Chauncey Marvin, OH-170/15
Cady, Hattie (Yates) (Mrs. Henry), OR-15/8
Cady, Mr. and Mrs. Olin, NY-270/18
Caha, Ernest, MN-95/11
Cahill, Father, IN-105/6
Cahill, Mary Roberta, OH-165/1
Cain, J. B., MS-15/1
Cain, Mary de Ricci, NY-120/1
Cairns, Robert, MA-275/1
Calder, James, PA-275/4
Calder, Matilda S. *See* Thurston, Matilda S. (Calder)
Caldwell, Ernest B., NJ-45/3
Caldwell, Harry Russell, NJ-45/3, NJ-45/13, NY-270/18, OR-15/56, TN-60/1**b**
Caldwell, Mary W., CT-50/7
Caldwell, Oliver J., CT-50/25
Caldwell, Pearl, MS-10/1
Calhoun, E. Clayton, NJ-45/10
Callender, C. R., PA-65/1
Calverly, E. E., CT-15/1
Calvin, John, IL-85/1
Cameron, Allen Noah, IL-200/23
Cameron, Jennie (Williams) (Mrs. Allen Noah), IL-200/23
Cammann, Schuyler V. R., CT-50/24
Campbell, Louise, CT-50/6**b**
Campbell, Alexander, WV-5
Campbell, David Miles, CT-50/6**b**
Campbell, Dorothy McBride, CT-50/6**b**
Campbell family, NC-45/3
Campbell, George, CT-50/6**b**
Campbell, Howard, PA-65/1
Campbell, Isabella C., CA-130/4
Campbell, Jennie (Wortman) (Mrs. George), CT-50/6**b**
Campbell, Kenneth, CT-50/6
Campbell, Margaret Larue. *See* Burket, Margaret Larue (Campbell)
Campbell, T. Bowyer, TX-5/2
Candler, Asa Griggs, GA-20/1
Candler, Warren Akin, GA-20, GA-20/1
Cannon, Walter Bradford, MA-50/1
Canright, Harry Lee, NJ-45/3, NJ-45/13, NJ-50/1
Cantelli da Vignola, Giacomo, NY-95/1
Capen, Carl Mayo, MN-105/4, NY-345/4**b**, OR-15/22
Capen, Edward Warren, CT-10/2, CT-15/2, CT-15/4, CT-15/5, CT-50/14

Capen, Lydia, CT-10/2
Capen, Samuel, CT-15/2
Capillas, Francisco, IL-60/1
Capron, Mildred S., TX-5/2
Cardim, Antonio Francisco, IL-60/2, NY-95/1
Cardoso, Juan, DC-65/1
Carey, William, NY-95/1
Carlberg, Ernest, IL-200/50
Carlberg, Gustav, IL-50/1
Carleton, Miss, MA-195/5
Carleton, Mary Elaine, CT-50/7
Carlsen, J. O., NY-305/8
Carlsen, W. D., NJ-85/3
Carlson, Alma. *See* Himle, Alma (Carlson)
Carlson, Ellsworth C., OH-170/4
Carlson, Carol (Mrs. Edwin), IL-200/9**b**
Carlson, Edwin, IL-200/9**b**
Carlson, Elma B., MN-95
Carlson, Elvera (Mrs. Emery), MN-95/12
Carlson, Emery, MN-95/12
Carlson, Robert Dean, IL-200/10**b**
Carlyle, Elizabeth, OR-15/9**b**
Carmichal, Eva, OH-30/1
Carnegie, Dale, NC-50/1
Carney, Veronica Marie, NY-120/1
Carnie, Norah, TX-5/2
Carothers, J. Edwin, TN-45/1
Carothers, Susan, TN-45/1
Carpenter, Solomon, WI-10/1
Carpenter, A. G., CA-130/1
Carpenter, Brother, NC-50/2
Carr, Eva S., TX-5/2
Carr, Jo, NY-290/1
Carr, Julian S., NC-50/1
Carr, Ruth M. (White) (Mrs. Clarence), CT-50/7
Carroll, [?], NJ-45/7
Carroll, J. M., TX-25/2
Carroll, Terence, MN-90/4
Carson, A[rthur] L., NY-270/12
Carswell, Helen Charlotte (Lotta). *See* Hume, Helen Charlotte (Carswell)
Carter, Edward C., MA-50/1
Carson, F. Stanley, CT-50/7, OH-160/1
Carson, Grace (McClurg) (Mrs. F. Stanley), OH-25/1**b**, OH-160/1
Carter, Gertrude, MA-240, TX-5/2
Carter, H., NY-280/3
Carter, Russell, NY-270/35
Cartwright, E. Maude, TX-5/2
Cartwright, F. T., NJ-45/3
Cartwright, Frank Thomas, CA-190/1, CT-15/5, MA-95/1, NY-275/1, NY-290/1, OR-15/6, OR-15/11, OR-15/47, OR-15/56
Cartwright, Frank, Sr., family,, IL-200/39
Carus, Paul, NY-140/1, NY-210/1
Carvalho, Cecilia, NY-120/1
Carven, John W., NY-105/1
Carver, William Owen, TN-55/2**b**
Carver, George Alexander, TN-55/2**b**
Carver, Saxon Rowe, TX-45/1
Cary, Alice, MA-95/1
Casalandra, Estelle, OH-115/1
Case, Emily Ingersoll. *See* Mills, Emily Ingersoll (Case)
Casselman, Arthur Vale, CT-50/2, CT-60/32, GA-15/5, MO-60/1, NC-90/2, NJ-95/3, PA-80/3, PA-80/7, PA-80/13, PA-85/1, PA-90/1, TN-40/1
Cassidy, Bertha, IL-10/1, IL-10/2, IL-10/3, IL-10/5, NC-15/1
Cassidy, William, NY-305/3**b**
Cassidy, William F., DC-30/1, OH-115/1
Catlin, Frances. *See* Birrell, Frances (Catlin)
Caton, Jack, MN-60/1
Cauthen, Baker James, TN-35, VA-65/1, VA-65/2
Cauthen, Eloise (Glass) (Mrs. Baker James), TN-35, TN-35/1, VA-65/2
Cavallero, Carlo, NY-335/1
Cavert, H. Mead, MN-95/13
Cazale, Agnes, NY-120/1

Ch'i-ying, AZ–5/3, CA–70/1, CA–305/1, CT–55/2, CT–80/1, DC–20/1, GA–15/5, HI–15/2, IL–20/1, IL–85/1, IL–130/1, IN–95/1, KS–35/3, MA–95/2, MD–10/1, MI–140/1, MO–75/2, NC–30/2, NJ–100/1, NY–20/2, NY–115/1, NY–150/1, NY–230/1, NY–340/1, NY–365/1, OH–15/1, PA–215/1, RI–15/4, UT–10/1, WA–35/1
Chiang K'ai-shek, AR–5/1, CA–290/30, CA–320/1, CT–25/1, CT–50/10, CT–50/16, CT–50/21, CT–60/32, IL–200/40, IL–200/55, MA–125/1, MN–95/42, MN–95/43, MN–95/73, MN–95/95, MN–95/102, NC–45/14, NC–70/13, NC–75/1, NJ–35, NJ–35/1, NJ–45/5, NY–270/22, OR–15/18, PA–200/28, VA–50/1, VA–80/2
Chiang K'ai-shek, Mme. (Soong Mei-ling), AR–5/1, CA–320/1, CT–50/16, CT–60/32, GA–20/1, IL–200/40, MA–40/1, MA–240/4, MN–105/3, NC–45/14, NC–50/1, NC–75/1, NY–175/2, NY–275/1, OR–15/56, PA–200/20, TN–70/3, VA–50/1, VA–85
Chiang Mon-lin(g), VA–50/1
Ch'iao Ch'i-ming, CA–110/2. WA–45/1
Ch'ien-lung emperor, AZ–5/1, HI–15/1, IN–20/1, NC–45/20, NY–100/1, WA–35/1
Ch'ien T'ung, DC–160/2
Ch'ien Tien-ho, VA–50/1
Chiesa, Bernardino della, IN–10/5
Chik, Mrs., MA–195/5
Childs, Frank, PA–125/1
Chilton, Robert S., Jr., NC–45/4
Chin, John C. (Chin Chung-an), IL–200/11
Chin, Francis Roberta, OH–165/1
Chin, Miss, MA–195/5
Chin, Rockwood Q. P., CT–60/32
Chin, Wesley, CT–60/32
Chin, Rose, NY–110/1, NY–120/1
Chin, S. C., NY–290/1
Ching, Lillian, NY–95/1
Ching, Julia, CT–50/2
Ching Jung-lin, MA–95/1
Chiou, Teresa Mary, OH–165/1
Chirgwin, Arthur Mitchell, NY–275/1
Chisholm, Elizabeth, TX–5/2
Chiswell, E. Virginia, TX–5/2
Chiu Li-ying, NY–270/35
Chiu, Mrs. Y. T., IN–45/1
Chiu, Yan Tze (Y. T. Chiu), IN–45/1b
Chorley, Kenneth, NY–285/1
Chou, Ivy, MN–95/17
Chou En-lai (Zhou Enlai), IL–200/40, MA–255/1, MN–105/3, OR–15/3
Chou, Sr. Adolph, WI–75/3
Chow, Agnes, NY–110/1, NY–120/1
Chow Chang Hung, MA–215/2
Chow, Maria, OH–165/1
Chow, Nancy, MA–230/3
Christ, Paul, WI–75/3
Christensen, Anena, MO–50/6
Christensen, Olive T., MN–95
Christian, Agnes (Mrs. Leonard), CT–10/2
Christian, Leonard, CT–10/2
Christianson, Leila Partridge, MN–95/18
Christie, William, NY–305/8
Ch'ü Ang-lai, GA–15/3
Chu Chia-hua, VA–50/1
Chu, Daniel, IL–50/1, MN–95/19
Chu, H. R. (Chu Hao-ran/Chu Hao-jan), IA–15/1, MN–95/91, MN–95/94
Chu, Morton Y. T., TX–5/2
Chu Yu-tang, TX–5/2
Ch'uan Fang-lo, NY–270/25
Ch'üan, James, MA–25/2
Chuang-tzu, CT–15/5
Chue, Harriet, CT–10/2
Chum, Peter, NY–110/1, NY–120/1
Chung Jung-kuang, CT–80/1
Chung Kwok-kwan, NY–110/1, NY–120/1
Chung, Lucy, MN–90/2
Cibot, Pierre Martial, GA–15/3
Cicognani, Amleto, PA–95/1

Ciu Do Gieng, CT–30/2
Cixi, Empress Dowager. *See* Tz'u Hsi, Empress Dowager
Clack, Douglas, IL–10/3
Clancy, Bede, MI–140/1
Clapp, Jennie Rowland, OH–170/7
Clapp, Sarah Boardman. *See* Goodrich, Sarah Boardman (Clapp)
Clapp, Margaret, MA–240/4
Clarissa, Sr., MA–255/1
Clark, Alice M., TX–5/2
Clark, Brooks, CT–50/14
Clark, Coral, TX–5/2
Clark, Elmer T., NJ–50/1
Clark, Elsie. *See* Krug, Elsie (Clark)
Clark, Hal, OR–15/18
Clark, Irving B., CT–50/7
Clark, Julia Adeline, MA–185/2b, TX–5/2
Clark, Laura E., TX–5/2
Clark, P., OR–15/22
Clark, Sidney James Wells, CO–10/3, IN–25/3, NJ–25, WA–25/1
Clarke family, CA–315/2
Clarke, J. Calvitt, PA–125/1
Clarke, J. Eric G., CA–315/2b
Clarke, Ruth Elliott (Johnson) (Mrs. J. Eric G.), CA–315/2b
Clay, Ernest H., NJ–45/3
Clemens, Samuel Langhorne, MI–135/3
Clement, Lora, TN–35
Clement XI (Gian Francesco Albani), Pope, CT–60/5, DC–25/1
Clementia, Sr., IL–155/1
Clements, Anne, NY–120/1
Clements, Charles Everleigh, CA–130/3
Clements, Marjorie, CT–50/9, IL–25/1, IL–200/14, KS–35/1
Clemons, Harry, VA–25/7, VA–25/12
Clemons, Jeannie (Mrs. Harry), VA–25/7, VA–25/12
Clemons, William Harry, CT–30/3
Clerc-Renaud, Jean-Louis, MO–40/1
Clet, François Régis, MD–50/1, PA–115/1
Cleveland, F. A., MA–195/5
Cliff, Howard, IL–200/50
Cliff, May (Mrs. Howard), IL–200/50
Clifford, Douglas, MN–95/20
Clifford, John W., CA–195/1
Cline, John W., NJ–45/10
Cline, John Wesley, AR–5/1
Cloeter, A., MO–50/6
Clougherty, F. H., IN–105/2
Clougherty, Father, IN–105/11
Clougherty, Francis, MN–5/1, MN–90/4, PA–95/1, PA–95/1
Clyde, Mary (Kestler) (Mrs. Paul Hibbert), NC–45/5
Clyde, Paul Hibbert, NC–45/5
Coan, Titus, HI–10/3
Cobb, Adelia. *See* Hallock, Adelia (Cobb)
Cobb, Alice, GA–20/1
Cobb, H. N., NY–270/37
Cobb, Henry N[itchie], MI–120/8, MI–120/14, NJ–60/3
Cobb, Mrs. J. P., TN–50/1
Cochran, Henry J., CT–50/26
Cochran, Jacqueline, KS–5/2
Cochran, William, CA–235/1
Cochrane, Thomas, IN–20/2, NJ–95/3, NY–95/1, NY–275/1, NY–290/1, OH–200/1
Cocke, Matty, VA–45/1
Cody, Lyman, WA–40/4
Coe, John L., CT–50/25, TX–5, TX–5/2
Coe, Mary, TX–5/2
Coffey, Christine, VA–25/2
Coffman, King J., NJ–30/1
Cogswell, Harriet. *See* Meyer, Harriet (Cogswell)
Cohn, Alfred E., IL–75/7, NY–295/5b
Colby, Arthur J., NY–105/1
Colby, Doris, IL–10/4, NC–15/1
Colder, James, DC–90/1b
Cole, Rufus, IL–75/7
Cole, W[infred] B[ryan], NJ–45/13
Coleman, Inabelle G., TN–35, VA–65/2

Colgate, Samuel, NY-345/5
Colledge, Thomas Richardson, MA-50/4, MA-215/2, MD-35/1, NY-220/1, NY-350/1, PA-175/1
Collie, David, DC-30/2
Collins, Judson Dwight, MI-5/1, MI-15/2b, MI-60/4
Collins, Sr. Berchmans, IN-105/2, IN-105/6
Collins, Cornelia, NY-120/1
Collins, H. Clinton, TX-5/2
Collins, J. D., NJ-45/13
Colson, Isabella, VA-25/10
Colton, Ethan T., OR-15/23
Colvin, Harold, CT-50/15
Colvin, Reba (Mrs. Harold), CT-50/15
Comber, John, NY-110/1, NY-120/1
Comber, Rita Claire, NY-120/1, VA-25/1
Comstock, Ada. See Notestein, Ada (Comstock)
Conard, C., CA-135/1
Conde, B., NY-280/3
Condit, Ira M., CA-125/1
Confer, Bernard, NY-205/2
Confucius, KY-90/L, MA-35/1, NY-175/13, WA-35/1
Congdon, Pearl, IN-75/1
Congdon, Wray H., NJ-45/3
Conger, Mary Jane, VA-25/2
Conger, Sarah Pike, MA-45
Conklin, Edwin G., NJ-125/1
Connell, Meta B., TX-5/2
Conner, Marie, TN-35, TN-35/1
Conover, Jeannette R., TX-5/2, TX-5/3
Conrad, Paul, WI-75/3
Constance Anna, Sr., TX-5/2
Constantini, Celso, IL-20/1, MN-90/4, NJ-80/1, PA-95/1
Cook, Alice B., MA-95/1
Cook, Alice H. See Millner, Alice H. (Cook)
Cook, Elmer L., CA-20/1
Cook, Julia K., TX-5/2
Cook, Margaret. See Thomson, Margaret (Cook)
Cooke, A. B., NY-130/1
Cooke, Allyn, IL-200/50
Cooke, Leila (Mrs. Allyn), IL-200/50
Coole, Arthur Bradden, CT-50/7, KS-10/1, NJ-45/3, OR-15/11b
Coole, Cora (Mrs. Thomas), OR-15/11
Coole, Douglas Paul, KS-10/1, NJ-45/3, OR-15/11b
Coole, Ella (Endres) (Mrs. Arthur), KS-10/1, OR-15/11
Coole, Polly, KS-10/1
Coole, Thomas Henry, KS-10/1, NJ-45/3, NJ-45/13, OR-15/11b
Cooley, Mr. and Mrs. Clifford, IN-75/1
Coolidge, Calvin, DC-90/2
Coolidge, Charles A., NY-290/1
Coombs, Frances E., NY-345/5
Coonradt, Ralph, CT-10/2
Cooper, Albert S., TX-5/2
Cooper, Elizabeth, TX-5/2
Cooper, Emily. See Pott, Emily (Cooper)
Cooper, Emily G[eorgiana] (Browne) (Mrs. F. Clement), TX-5/2
Cooper, Esther, NJ-45/3
Cooper, Frederick C., TX-5/2
Cooper, George W., TX-5/2
Cooper, Grady L., IL-50/1
Cooper, Gwendolin L., TX-5/2
Cooper, Merbyn C., TX-5/2
Copland, E. Bruce, OR-15/18
Coppock, Grace, CT-50/27, NB-25/1, NY-280/3, NY-280/5
Coray, Betty (Mrs. Henry), PA-150/1
Coray, Henry, PA-150/1
Corbett, A. G., NY-270/12
Corbett, Charles, CT-10/2
Corbett, Charles H., CT-15/5
Corbett, Harriet (Sutherland) (Mrs. J. Hunter, 3rd wife?), NY-270/12
Corbett, [J.] Hunter, NJ-95/3, NY-270/12b, PA-200/28
Corbett, James J., NY-290/1
Corbett, May Nixon. See Smith, May Nixon (Corbett)
Corbin, M. L., OH-175/1
Corbin, Paul Leaton, OH-170/5b, OH-170/17, OH-170/24, OH-175/1

Cordell, Bessie, IN-30/1, IN-75/1, IN-80/1
Cordier, Henri, DC-160/2
Corey, Catherine, IN-40/5
Corey, Stephen Jared, IN-55/1, NY-290/1, TN-45/1
Cormack, J[ames] G., CT-50/2
Cornaby, William Arthur, IL-110/1
Cornwell, Mr.and Mrs.George, NY-270/12
Cornwell, William M., CA-290/6b
Coronielli, Marco Vincenzo, NY-95/1
Corpron, Douglas S., CT-10/2, CT-50/7, TN-45/1
Corpron, Grace Chapman, TN-45/1
Corsa, Richard, TX-5/2
Corson, Fred Pierce, NC-75/1b
Cortmeyer, Clara, IN-75/1
Corwin, Edward S., CT-50/26
Cory, Abram Edward, IN-60/1b, IN-65
Cory, Edwin, CA-130/1
Cory, Edwin, CA-130/1
Cory, Eleanor (Mrs. Edwin), CA-130/1
Costanza, Mary Theophane, OH-165/1
Cotta, Anthony, NY-120/1, NY-125/1, PA-95/1
Cotta, Antoine, CT-80/1
Cotter, Frances J. M., TX-5/2
Cotter, Ida, TX-5/2
Couch, Caroline, TX-5/2
Couche, Edith, NC-30/2
Coulson, Gail V., NY-275/1, OH-120/11
Coulter, Caroline E. (Mrs. Moses), IL-75/5b
Coulter, John M., IL-75/5
Coulter, Moses S., IL-75/5b
Coupe, Eucharista, NY-120/1
Couplet, Philippe, CA-245/5
Cousins, G[eorge], NY-275/1
Cousland, Philip B., MD-35/2
Covell, Ralph R., CA-205/1, CO-10/1, OR-30/1
Coveny, Angela Marie, NY-120/1
Coveyou, Walter, MA-255/3
Coward, Charles P., TN-35
Coward, Marian P., TN-35
Cowdry, Edmund Vincent, MO-100/1b
Cowen, H., MA-195/5
Cowles, Ben T., OR-15/27
Cowling, Donald, MN-60/1
Cowman, Charles, KY-85/1
Cowman, Lettie (Mrs. Charles), KY-85/1
Cox, Addie Estelle, TN-35
Cox, Angie W., MA-45/2
Cox, Carson W., OH-30/1
Cox, Cordelia, NY-205/2
Cox, Frances A., TX-5/2
Cox, Francis Augustus, NJ-25
Cox, James R., NY-270/33
Cox, Lilian E., MD-35/2
Cox, Samuel H., PA-170/1
Cox, Venetia, NC-70/7b, TX-5/2
Cox, Vercia P. (Mrs. Carson W.), OH-30/1
Crabtree, Loren W., UT-10/1
Craig, Augustus Rochester, NC-20/1
Craig, Mary Dodd, NY-270/13
Craigen, Charitina, WI-15/1
Craighill, Lloyd R[utherford], CT-50/16, TX-5/2
Craighill, Marian (Gardner) (Mrs. Lloyd R.), CT-50/7, TX-5, TX-5/2
Cram, W. O., GA-10/1
Crane, Katharine P., OH-170/24
Cranston, Earl, CA-80/7, NJ-45/3, NJ-45/13
Cranston, Mildred (Welch) (Mrs. Earl), CA-80/8
Craven, Braxton, NC-50/1
Crawford, Martha E. (Foster) (Mrs. Tarleton Perry), NC-45/6b, NC-55/1
Crawford, Mary K., VA-65/2
Crawford, O. C., CT-10/2, CT-50/7
Crawford, Robert P., NY-105/1
Crawford, Tarleton Perry, NC-45/6b, VA-65/2, VA-105/1
Crawford, Wallace, NY-270/33
Crawford, Walter M., NJ-45/3, NJ-45/13

Crawley, J. Winston, VA–65/2
Crawley, Margaret, TN–35
Crawley, Winston, TN–35, TN–35/1
Creamer, Thomas A., VA–25/2
Creighton, J.W., NY–270/35
Cressey, George B., CT–50/25, NY–270/12
Cressey, Marion H. (Chatfield) (Mrs. George B.), CT–15/5, MA–220/15b
Cressey, Paul F., NY–345/6b
Cressy, Earl Herbert, CT–10/2, CT–15/3, CT–15/5, CT–50/22, CT–50/25, NY–270/35, NY–285/2
Cressy, Mrs., CT–15/3
Crim, Bessie M., IL–205/1
Cripe, Winifred E., IL–105/7
Crisler, C. C., CA–135/1
Crofoot, Jay, NY–25/1
Cronly family, NC–45/7
Crook, Edith Loree, CT–50/7
Crooks, Grace A., IN–40/5
Cross, Adelle (Tenney) (Mrs. Rowland McLean), MN–60/1
Cross, Helen C. (Silsby) (Mrs. Robert C.), CT–50/7
Cross, Laura, MN–60/1
Cross, M., NY–280/3
Cross, Rowland McLean, CA–75/2, CA–80/5, CA–80/9, CA–130/1, CA–290/7, CT–50/15, MA–95/1, MN–60/1, MN–95/21
Crossett, Margaret Rice Elliott (Mrs. Vincent), IL–200/15b, IL–200/20
Crossett, Vincent Leroy, IL–200/15b
Crouch, Archie R., CT–10/2, CT–50/2, CT–50/4, CT–50/24, PA–200/3
Crouch, Ellen (Gibbs) (Mrs. Archie R.), PA–200/3
Crouch, Lucy A. *See* Leaman, Lucy A. (Crouch)
Crouse, Moses C., IL–10/3
Crow, Carl, MO–5/2b
Crowl, Annie L., NY–345/7b, OH–30/1
Cruikshank, E. W., MA–50/1
Crummer, Lillis, TX–5/2
Crumpacker, F. H., KS–40/1
Crumpsacker, Anna, IL–105/1, IL–105/11
Crutche, A. Y., NY–270/33
Cuddeback, Margaret, MI–60/3
Culbertson, Matthew Simpson, CA–35/3b
Culbertson, Michael Simpson, CA–235/2
Culley, Miss, MA–195/5
Cullis, Charles, CT–35/1
Cullom, Willis Richard, NC–100/5
Culpepper, C. L., VA–65/2
Culpepper, Charles L., Jr., TN–35, TN–35/1
Culpepper, Charles L., Sr., TN–55/4, VA–65/2
Culpepper, Donal, TN–35
Culpepper, Ola, TN–35
Cummings, Abigail (Abby) (Stearns) (Mrs. Seneca), MN–105/2
Cummings, E. Louise, TX–5/2
Cummings, Henry, TX–5/2
Cummings, Lucile Priscilla. *See* Oliver, Lucile Priscilla (Cummings)
Cummings, Seneca, MN–105/2
Cunha, Simao da, IL–60/2
Cunningham, Theodore B., NC–45/8
Cunningham, Alfred, NY–150/1
Cunningham, Edwin S., IA–15/1
Cunningham, Henrietta M., NY–120/1
Cunningham, Laura, IL–200/50
Cunningham, W. R., PA–65/1
Cunnyngham, W. G. E., GA–20/1
Curley, Maria Sebastian, NJ–15
Curnow, J. O., NJ–45/3, NJ–45/13
Curran, Jean Alonzo, MA–50/2b, MA–50/4, MA–95/1
Currie, Edward Smith, NC–80/3
Currie, Gay Wilson (Mrs. Edward Smith), NC–80/3
Curtis, Howard C., OH–170/6
Curtis, Edith, CT–50/7
Curtis, Lawrence D., NY–105/1
Curtiss, W. H., NJ–45/13
Cushing, Dorothy, MA–95/1
Cushing, Harvey, NY–270/22
Cushman, Vera (Scott), MA–185/13

Cushman, Clara M., NY–270/18
Cussler, Henry Charles, NJ–75/1

Da Dzle, NY–270/35
Daehlin, Emma C. (Hasle) (Mrs. Ingvald), MN–95
Daehlin, Ingvald, MN–80/1, MN–95, MN–95/110, SD–15/1
Daehlin, Nikoline (Dahl) (Mrs. Ingvald), MN–95
Daehlin, Reidar A., MN–95
Dahl, Nikoline. *See* Daehlin, Nikoline (Dahl)
Dahlin, Helen (Depass), MN–95/22
Dahlstrom, Earl C., CT–10/2, MN–95/23
Dai, Bingham, NY–270/25
Daley, Timothy, NY–110/1, NY–120/1
Dalheimer, John J., CA–195/1
Daly, Charles, NY–110/1, NY–120/1
Damato, Catherine, PA–265/2
Dana, Arnold G., CT–60/32
Dana, James Dwight, CT–60/30
Daniel, Gabriel, MN–20
Daniels, C[aroline] H., OH–155/2
Daniels, Elizabeth Jane (Teitsworth) (Mrs. William H.), PA–80
Daniels, Helen (Dunn) (Mrs. J. Horton), CA–235/1, NY–270/35, PA–200/28
Daniels, J. Horton, CA–235/1, NY–270/35, OH–170/10, PA–200/28
Daniels, Mrs. Charles H., MA–195/3
Daniels, Ursula (Wilder) (Mrs. Carroll C.), NY–90/6
Daniels, William H., PA–80
Danielson, Laura, MN–60/1
Dans, Mattie, NY–270/35
Danuser, M., NY–280/3
Darley, Mary E., IL–110/1
Darling, Grace. *See* Phillips, Grace (Darling)
Darnall, Trissa. *See* Smith, Trissa (Darnall)
Daubert, Francis, NY–110/1, NY–120/1
Davidson, Douglas T., NY–290/1
Davidson, Ella, NC–45/21
Davidson family, NC–45/9
Davidson, John F., TX–5/2
Davidson, Nelle, TN–35/1
Davidson, R. J., OH–195/1
Davidson, Robert John, CT–80/1
Davidson, Sydney Arthur, CT–50/7
Davidson, Sydney Arthur, Jr., OR–15/12
Davies, Dr., MA–195/5
Davies, David, NJ–25
Davies, L. J., IA–15/1
Davies, Llewellyn James, MI–25/1
Davis, Carol, TX–5/2
Davis, Eliza Anne Hughes, OR–15/13
Davis, Emily W., TX–5/2
Davis, Eugene, NY–105/1
Davis, Floy Shelly, TX–5/2
Davis, Francis W., OH–170/7
Davis, Frederick, NJ–45/4
Davis, George L., NJ–45/3, NJ–45/13
Davis, [George] Lowry, NC–80/4b
Davis, George R[itchie], NJ–45/13
Davis, Helen A. *See* Chandler, Helen A. (Davis)
Davis, Ida, TN–35
Davis, Jerome, CA–35/6
Davis, John W., NC–45/9
Davis, John Wright, NC–20/1, NC–80/5
Davis, Lydia Lord (Mrs. Francis W.), MN–60/1, OH–170/7b, OH–170/17
Davis, Martha, NY–290/1
Davis, Mary Barnett (Mrs. Lowry), NC–80/4b
Davis, Melissa J., NJ–45/3
Davis, N., NY–280/3
Davis, Robert C., Jr.,, TN–35
Davis, Russell, CA–130/1
Davis, T. C., NH–20/1
Davis, Walter W., NJ–45/3
Davison, F. Trubee, NY–285/1

Dodds, Marguerite, MA–220/18**b**
Dodge, Adelia M. *See* Starrett, Adelia M. (Dodge)
Dodson, Flora Elizabeth, TN–35, VA–65/2
Dodson, Stephen, TX–5/2
Doherty, Grace, NY–120/1
Dohrman, C. E., MO–50/6
Dolan, Brooke, II, PA–135/2
D'Olive, W. C., CA–75/2
Doltz, Clara (Mrs. Paul), PA–200/28
Doltz, Paul, PA–200/28
Dominique, Sr., CT–80/1
Domke, Paul Clifford, CA–290/8**b**, MN–60/1, MN–95/26
Donaghy, Frederick, MA–275/1
Donaldson, Fred F. G., CT–15/5
Donaldson, Mary L., CT–10/2
Dong Tsing-oong, TX–5/2
Donoghue, Timothy, NJ–45/13
Donovan, John F., NY–115/1
Doolittle, Justus, NY–80/1, PA–275/4
Doolittle, Mandana Eliza. *See* Lyon, Mandana Eliza (Doolittle)
Doré, Henri, DC–160/2
Doty, Elihu, NY–235/2**b**
Doty-Dubois, Amelia C., NY–235/2
Douglas, Carole, IL–10/3
Douglass, Enid H., CA–35/2, CA–80, CA–80/48
Dowd, Jerome, NC–50/1
Dowd, Rachel, CT–60/15
Downer, Sara Boddie, MA–220/20**b**, NY–345/10
Downey, Richard, NY–110/1, NY–120/1
Downie, Gerald L., NJ–45/3, OR–15/47
Downs, William J., PA–40/1
Doyen, James T., TX–5/2
Doyen, Jane, TX–5/2
Dozier family, CA–80/5
Dozier, Leila. *See* Boynton, Leila (Dozier)
Drake, Aimee B., MA–195/3, TX–5/2
Drake, Noah Fields, OR–15/61
Dresser, Ellen, PA–125/1
Drew, Edward, NJ–150
Drew, Florence, CT–50/7, NJ–150
Drew, John, NY–110/1, NY–120/1
Dreyer, Edith G., IL–200/44
Dreyer, F. C. H., PA–265/1, VA–65/2
Dreyer, Frederick, IL–200/50
Dreyer, Gertrude C., IL–200/50
Driscoll, John, NY–110/1, NY–120/1
Drought, James N., NY–110/1
Drumm, Thomas, TX–5/2
Drummond, Ellen, PA–125/1
Drummond, W. J., PA–125/1
Drury, Clifford, OR–15/18
Drury, Mable, NJ–45/4
DuBose, Hampden Coit, NC–80/6**b**
DuBose, Nettie Lambuth. *See* Junkin, Nettie Lambuth (DuBose)
DuBose, Palmer Clisby, NC–20/1
DuBose, Pauline McAlpine. *See* Little, Pauline (DuBose)
Dubs, C. Newton, NB–15/1
Dubs, Emma (Hasenpflug) (Mrs. C. Newton), NB–15/1
Dubs, Homer, GA–15/5
Dubs, Mr. and Mrs. Homer H., NB–15/1
Duchesne, Paul J., NY–110/1, NY–120/1, VA–25/1
Dudgeon, John, CT–50/9, IL–25/1, IL–200/14, KS–35/1, MD–35/2
Dudley, Guilford, NY–325/1
Dudley, M., NY–280/3
Dudley, Marion, NC–10/7**b**
Duff, James Arthur, CA–290/9**b**
Duffield, [?], MI–60/2
Duffy, Maurice, NY–110/1, NY–120/1
Dugout, Ignatius Henri, DC–70/4
Dulles, Eleanor Lansing, KS–5/3
Dulles, John Foster, KS–5/3**b**, VA–25/2
Dunbar, O. B., SD–5/1
Duncan, Marion Herbert, PA–135/2**b**

Duncan, Louise J., TX–5/2
Duncan, Mr. and Mrs. Kenneth, OR–15/59
Duncan, Samuel W., NY–285/4
Dunham, Donald C., NY–175/7
Dunham, Helen. *See* MacEachron, Helen (Dunham)
Dunkelberger, Sadie. *See* Voss, Sadie (Dunkelberger)
Dunker, C. Stephen, VA–25/1
Dunlap, A. M., NY–290/1
Dunlap, Albert, NY–295/7
Dunlap, Irving, NJ–45/4
Dunlevy, Eliza Ann. *See* Ashmore, Eliza (Dunlevy)
Dunn, Ann Majella, OH–165/1
Dunn, Helen. *See* Daniels, Helen (Dunn)
Dunn, Marvin, IL–200/16**b**
Dunn, Miriam J. (Toop) (Mrs. Marvin), IL–200/16**b**
Dunne, George H., MN–70/3, NB–25/2, TN–65/1, WA–45/1
Dunwiddie, Mary, WI–50/1
Durfee, E., NY–280/3
Durham, Alvada Gunn, NC–100/7**b**
Durrett, Frances, TN–60/2
Dutton, Philip D., MA–95/1, OH–170/3, OH–170/24
Dvergsness, Inga, MN–95
Dwight, A. L., IL–35/3
Dwight, Albert, IL–35/1
Dwinnell, Ralph B., NH–10/1
Dye, Daniel Sheets, OH–155/2
Dye, Eva May, OK–5/1
Dyer, Clara Pearl (Ryant), NJ–45/3, NJ–45/5, OR–15/15**b**
Dyer, Edward R., TX–5/2
Dyer, Lora Genevieve, CT–15/5, MA–95/1, MA–185/3, MA–195/3, OR–15/3
Dyer, Mrs. Edward R., TX–5/2
Dykstra, Harry A. MI–80/3
Dykstra, Simon A., MI–80/3
Dyson, Burt, VA–65/2
Dyson, J. W., CT–50/26, NJ–45/3, NJ–45/10
Dyson, Joseph, NJ–45/3
Dzao, Timothy S. K., NY–305/8

Eagan, C. B., TX–5/2
Eakin, Isabella Ruth. *See* Dodd, Isabella Ruth (Eakin)
Early, Joseph, NY–110/1, NY–120/1
Earp, Carlyle Reede, MD–25/2
Eastham, Williette, TX–5/2
Eaton, J. S., CT–35/2
Ebeling, William, CA–130, CA–130/3
Eby, Gertrude, TX–5/2
Eby, Kermit, IL–75/6**b**, IN–25/3
Eckard, Leighton W., CT–50/7
Eckerson, Frank, MI–120/4**b**
Eckerd, Helen Nevius. *See* Yerkes, Helen Nevius (Eckerd)
Eckert, C., NY–280/3
Eckfelt, Dr. and Mrs. Odd, MN–95
Eddy, Evelyn, MO–25/4
Eddy, G. S., CT–50/27
Eddy, George Sherwood, CT–10/2, CT–15/4, CT–50/10**b**, CT–50/21, CT–50/22, CT–50/23, CT–55/2, CT–80/1, ME–10/2, MN–95/41, NY–90/2, NY–270/37
Eddy, Mary Baker, MA–45, MA–45/7
Edgar, Fr., CA–260/1
Edgar, J[ames]Huston, DC–150/2
Edith Constance, Sr., TX–5/2
Edkins, [Joseph?], VA–105/1
Edkins, Joseph, DC–80/2
Edmonds, Stephen, NY–110/1, NY–120/1
Edmunds, C. K., MD–15/1
Edmunds, Charles K., CA–80/11**b**, MA–125/4, MA–155/1
Edwards, Richard Henry, NY–90/2**b**
Edwards, A. R., MN–60/1
Edwards, Anna C., MA–220/32, MA–220/49
Edwards, Anne. *See* Fulton, Anne (Edwards)
Edwards, Dwight Woodbridge, CT–10/2, CT–50/11**b**, CT–50/15, CT–50/26, NJ–115/1, NJ–120/2, NJ–125/1

Feiner, Berea St. John, IL–200/23**b**
Felicia, Sr., OH–115/1
Fell, J. W., TX–5/2
Felland, Elsa. *See* Armstrong, Elsa (Felland)
Felland, O. G., MN–70/2
Fellegrino da Città, CA–265/1
Fellows, MacCarlyle, TX–5/2
Felsecker, Henry, NY–110/1, NY–120/1
Felt, Carl, NJ–45/3
Feng, Helen, MA–240/6
Feng Sien Hsii, MI–15/3
Feng Yu Heieng (Feng Yü-hsiang), VA–25/12
Feng Yü-hsiang, CT–50/10, CT–50/21, CT–55/2, IL–85/1, IL–200/21, IL–200/47, MA–165/4, MI–10/1, MN–95/1, MN–95/33, MN–95/42, MN–95/43, MN–95/59, MN–95/74, MN–95/86, MN–95/89, MN–95/91, MN–95/95, NJ–25, NJ–45/5, NY–270/12, NY–290/1, NY–305/8, VA–25/2, VA–50/1
Fenn, C. H., PA–200/28
Fenn, Courtney Hughes (Mrs. Henry), CT–50/7, CT–50/11
Fenn, S. P., CT–50/21
Fenn, William P., CA–235/1, CT–50/2, CT–50/11, CT–50/25, CT–50/26, NY–95/1
Ferebee, Nelson, NC–70/10
Ferguson, Frank C., NJ–45/10
Ferguson, J. Y., NY–290/1
Ferguson, John C[alvin] (Chên Yü-kuang), CT–50/7, DC–160/2, NJ–45/13, NY–210/1
Ferguson, Mary E., NY–295/7**b**, IL–75/7
Fergusson, W. N., NY–270/33
Ferrari, Barthelemy, CA–165/1
Ferris, Helen, CA–15/2
Ferris, Jeannette O., OH–175/1
Fessenden, Frances, MA–185/19
Fessler, Donald R., IA–25/1
Fetzer, Bertha A., MI–60/3
Feuser, Guenther, IL–180/1
Field, Jennie M. *See* Bashford, Jennie M. (Field)
Fielde, Adele Marion, CT–50/12, MD–30/3, PA–135/3**b**
Fielder, John Wilson, VA–65/2
Fielder, L. Gerald, TX–55/1
Fielder, Maudie (Mrs. John Wilson), VA–65/2
Filler, Mervin Grant, PA–20/1
Filley, Jennie. *See* Judson, Jennie (Filley)
Find, J. T., NJ–120/2
Fine, Mary Dorothy. *See* Twinem, Mary Dorothy (Fine)
Fink, E., NJ–30/1
Finney, [?], MO–40/1
Finske, Hilaria, MN–90/1
Firman, Helen. *See* Sweet, Helen (Firman)
Firor, Marion P. (Johnson), PA–80
Fischbacher, Olive (Mrs. Theodore), IL–200/24
Fischbacher, Theodore, IL–200/24
Fischer, John A., MO–50/6
Fischer, Viola I., MN–95/30
Fish, M. W., TX–5/2
Fisher, Alzo John, CT–10/2, CT–50/7, NY–270/25, OR–15/18**b**
Fisher, Conrad, OR–15/5
Fisher, Galen M., NY–290/1
Fisher, J. Elliott, OR–15/18
Fisher, Lizzie M., IN–40/5
Fisher, Mrs. A. F., MA–195/5
Fisher, Mrs. Harold, NY–290/1
Fisher, Stella. *See* Burgess, Stella (Fisher)
Fisher, Welthy Honsinger, CT–50/8, CT–90/1, NJ–115/1
Fitch, Alice, OH–145/1
Fitch, Alice R., NY–270/35
Fitch, Elliot, OH–145/1
Fitch, George A[shmore], CT–50/15, MA–125/1**b**, NJ–115/1, OH–145/1, OH–145/3
Fitch, George F., OR–15/30
Fitch, Geraldine T[ownsend] (Mrs. George A.), CT–50/15, MA–125/1**b**, OH–145/3
Fitch, James F., Sr., OH–145/1

Fitch, Jeannette. *See* Kepler, Jeannette (Fitch)
Fitch, John Ashley, PA–200/28
Fitch, Katherine, OH–145/1
Fitch, M., PA–65/1
Fitch, Margaret, OH–145/1
Fitch, Minnie E., OH–145/1
Fitch, Mrs. George A., NJ–115/1
Fitch, Robert F., NY–350/1, OH–145/1
Fitz, R. G., MO–25/1, MO–25/3, MO–25/4
Fitzgerald, Edward, TX–5/2
Fitzgerald, James E., NY–110/1, NY–120/1
Fitzwilliam, Francis Julius, IL–200/25**b**
Fitzwilliam, Jennie (Kingston) (Mrs. Francis Julius), IL–200/25**b**
Flagg, Herbert W., IL–200/26
Flagg, Alice Mabel. *See* Tatum, Alice Mabel (Flagg)
Flagg, Minnie E. (Green) (Mrs. Herbert W.), IL–200/26
Flagg, Mrs., WA–40/4
Flagg, Virginia, NY–120/1
Flagler, Catherine, IN–75/1, MO–25/4
Flaherty, Don, NY–375/2
Flatt, Franklin A., NJ–45/10
Flavey, Mark A., CA–195/1
Flavin, [?], MO–40/1
Fleischmann, Babette, NJ–30/1
Fleming, E.J., MO–25/3
Fleming, Rebecca, IN–75/1
Flesch, Herr Pater, WI–75/4
Flexner, Simon, IL–75/7, MA–50/4, MD–5/1, NY–290/1, NY–295/8, NY–295/9, PA–145/1**b**
Flint, Pauline, TX–5/2
Flory, Margaret, NY–175/4
Flory, Minnie. *See* Bright, Minnie (Flory)
Flory, Wendell, IL–105/7
Fogarty, Irene, NY–120/1
Foley, Frederick, CA–195/1, CA–245/2
Foley, Leonard, OH–45/1
Folsom, Arthur, NB–10/3
Folsom, Ernest C., NB–10/3
Folsom, Mary Ann (Thomas) (Mrs. Arthur), NB–10/3
Fong Ping, CA–165/1
Fong, Rowena, MA–240/6
Fontanoy, Jean de, MN–40/1, CA–185/1
Foote, Andrew Hull, CT–45/1
Foote, Paulina, CA–115/1
Forbes, E., NY–280/3
Forbes, Ted, OH–170/23
Ford, Eddy Lucius, NJ–45/3, NJ–45/5, NJ–45/13
Ford, Francis Xavier, NY–110/1
Ford, Ruth, TN–35, TN–35/1
Ford, Ruth Lucille, VA–65/2
Forster, Ernest H., TX–5/2
Forsythe, Irene. *See* Hanson, Irene (Forsythe)
Fosdick, Harry Emerson, CA–35/6, NY–285/1
Fosdick, Raymond, NY–295/7
Fosnot, Pearl. *See* Winans, Pearl (Fosnot)
Foss, L. C., IA–15/1
Foss, Theodore, CA–245/3
Foster, Anna E., CT–50/6, CT–50/12**b**
Foster, Clara (Hess) (Mrs. John Marshall), CT–50/12**b**
Foster, Elizabeth B. (Mrs. John Barton), CT–50/12
Foster, Erin, ME–25/6
Foster, Frank Clifton, CT–50/12, ME–25/2
Foster, George, TX–5/2
Foster, Helen. *See* Snow, Helen (Foster)
Foster, Helen (Thomas) (Mrs. John Hess), ME–25/2, NY–270/35
Foster, Jane Armour, MN–95/32
Foster, John, CA–245/5, KS–20/1, MN–95/32, MN–95/33
Foster, John B., TX–5/2
Foster, John Barton, CT–50/12**b**
Foster, John Burt, MN–105/3**b**
Foster, John Hess, CT–50/12**b**, CT–60/15, CT–60/32, ME–25/2
Foster, John Marshall, CT–50/12**b**, ME–25/2

Foster, Martha. *See* Crawford, Martha (Foster)

Foster, Mary Louise, MA–185/4

Foster, Mary Parke, KS–5/3b

Foster, Mr. and Mrs. John Barton, CT–50/12

Foster, Myrle Marie. *See* Seaton, Myrle Marie (Foster)

Foster, Shannon, VA–25/2

Foster, William A., NJ–45/3

Foucquet, Jean François, DC–60/1, FL–25/1, HI–15/1, MI–25/1, PA–215/1, WA–35/1

Fourmont, Barbara, IL–10/3

Fowler, C. H., NJ–45/13, NY–200/1

Fowler, Charles Henry, NY–270/13

Fowler, Dorothy, TX–5/2

Fowler, J. Earl, TX–5/2

Fowler, John, NY–270/12

Fowler, Mabel B., MA–45/1

Fowles, [?], NJ–45/7

Fox, Charles James, CA–35/6

Fox, Edmund, NY–365/1

Fox, Leo, MO–40/1

Frame, Alice Seymour (Browne) (Mrs. Murray Scott), CT–10/2, CT–50/7, MA–220/12, MN–60/1, NY–270/15b, NY–270/35, NY–275/1, OR–15/19

Frame, Helen (Nowack) (Mrs. Raymond), IL–200/27, IL–200/34b

Frame, Margaret, MA–195/5, NY–270/35, OR–15/18, OR–15/19

Frame, Mrs. N. S., OR–15/19

Frame, Murray Scott, OR–15/19b

Frame, Raymond, IL–200/27

Francis, John, OH–170/17

Frank, Cyprian, MA–255/5

Frank, Emeline, MN–95/34

Frank, George M., NY–270/33

Frank, Henry S., MA–125/4, MN–95/35

Frank, Herbert S., MN–95/36

Frank, Maxine, WI–15/1

Franklin, J. H., NY–290/1

Franklin, James Henry, NY–345/12, NY–345/23

Franks, Martha, VA–65/2

Franson, F., IL–150/1

Franson, Frederik, IL–90/1, IL–200/28b, MN–50/1

Frantz, Ida, OR–15/10

Franz, Margaretta, PA–65/1

Fraser, Alexander V., RI–35/1

Fraser, J. O., IL–200/50

Fraser, James Outram, NJ–25

Fraser, Mrs. J. O., IL–200/25

Fraser, R. L., NY–280/3

Fredericks, Edith, NY–275/1, OR–15/15

Fredericks, Lilian, TX–5/2

Freeman, Albert L., CT–35/1

Freeman, C. W., NJ–45/3, NJ–45/13

Freeman, Norman, CT–60/13

French, Mary Grace. *See* Dilley, Mary Grace (French)

French, Orville and Eileen, KY–85/1

Freri, J., DC–10/1

Frey, Emerson, IL–200/29b

Frey, Grace (Mrs. Emerson), IL–200/29b

Frey, Helen Virginia, MA–185/19

Friberg, H. Daniel, MN–95/37

Friberg, Joseph Bertil, MN–95/38

Fridell, Elmer Alfred, NY–345/23

Fried, Morton H., CT–50/2

Friedericksen, Kathleen (Hockman), IL–205/1

Friedmann, E., NY–280/14

Fries, Optata, WI–15/1

Frillman, Paul, CA–290/10b, MO–50/6, NY–175/6

Frisch, Angelica, VA–25/1

Fritz, Jean, OR–15/23

Fritzen, Hanna Marie, NY–290/1

Frost, Caroline, MA–95/1

Frost, Gilman, NY–270/35

Frost, Henry, CA–130/1, IL–200/50

Frost, Henry Weston, NJ–25, PA–265/1

Fry, Nancy, TN–45/1

Fryer, Eliza Ann (Nelson) (Mrs. John), NY–25/1b

Fryer, John, CA–100/1, MD–15/2, NY–25/1b, NY–25/2, NY–95/1

Fuchs, Walter, NJ–105/1

Fueller, Elizabeth F., TX–5/2

Fuerbringer, Ludwig Ernst, MO–50/4b, MO–50/13

Fugleskjel, Marie, MN–95

Fuhr, Godfrey, NY–120/1

Fuller, Glenn V., CA–80/13, NJ–45/3

Fuller, Leslie E., CA–80/5

Fuller, Margaret, TN–35

Fuller, Ronald W., TN–35

Fullerton, Caroline, TX–5/2

Fullerton, Ellen, TX–5/2

Fullerton, W. Y., NY–275/1

Fulton, Albert Andrew, PA–200/28

Fulton, Anne (Edwards) (Mrs. Robert Brank), CT–50/7, MN–95/39

Fulton, Charles Darby, NY–275/1

Fulton, James, CT–30/8

Fulton, John Farquhar, MA–50/3

Fulton, Mary H., MD–35/2, PA–155/1

Fulton, Robert Brank, CT–10/2, CT–50/7, MA–220/12, MN–60/1, NY–270/15b, NY–270/35, NY–275/1, OR–15/19

Fumasoni-Biondi, PA–95/1, WI–75/3

Funk, Clifford, NJ–45/4

Funk, Grace A. *See* Andrews, Grace A. (Funk)

Funk, Mary A., NY–305/4

Funkhouser, Walter L., PA–275/1

Fuqua, Mary Lib, VA–65/2

Furey, Christella, NY–120/1

Furlong, Philip, NY–110/1, NY–120/1

Fuson, Chester Garfield, CT–50/7

Fuson, Phebe (Meeker) (Mrs. Chester Garfield), CT–50/7

Gaalswyk, Arie, MN–95/41

Gabiani, Jean-Dominiques, CA–245/5

Gabrielson, Eric, NC–50/1

Gaffin, Polly (Mrs. Richard B.), PA–150, PA–150/1, PA–190/3b

Gaffin, Richard B., PA–150, PA–150/1, PA–190/3b

Gage, Brownell, CT–60/32

Gage, Helen R., NY–290/1

Gage, Nina, MA–240, NY–290/1

Gaiero, Michael, NY–110/1, NY–120/1

Gailey, Robert R., CT–50/11, CT–50/26, NJ–120/2, NY–270/25

Gain, Leopold, DC–70/4

Galbraith, John P., PA–190/1, PA–190/3

Galbraith, W., NY–280/3

Gale, Esson McDowell, MI–15/4, NH–10/3

Gale, F[rancis] C[lair], CT–50/16

Gale, Frank C., NJ–45/3

Gale, Grant, IA–25/1

Gallagher, Mary Gerard, NY–120/1

Gallagher, Rose Bernadette, NY–120/1

Gallaher family, NC–45/10

Gallatin, Grace Thompson. *See* Seton, Grace Thompson (Gallatin)

Gallimore, A. R., VA–65/2

Gallimore, Arthur Raymond, NC–45/11, NC–95/1, NC–100/5, NC–100/8b, TN–35

Gallimore, Gladys E. (Stephenson) (Mrs. Arthur Raymond), NC–100/8b, OH–80/1, TN–35

Gallimore, Mr. and Mrs. Arthur Raymond, KY–50/2

Galloway, Alice, MO–25/8

Galloway, Betty, TN–35, TN–35/1

Galloway, Charles Betts, GA–20/1, GA–20/3

Galloway, Ed, TN–35

Galt, Curtis M., CT–50/7

Galt, Elmer W., CT–10/2, MA–95/1, NJ–45/3

Galt, Howard S., CT–50/7, MA–95/1, OH–170/24

Galt, Howard Spilman, MA–155/1

Galt, Mabel (Moore) (Mrs. Curtis M.), CT–50/7

Galvin, Edward J., KY–65/1, NB–30

Gamble, James N., MD–25/2

Gamble, Sidney D., CT–50/7, CT–50/26, NJ–115/1, NJ–135/2

Gamble, William, CA-75/3, DC-80/2**b**, DC-105/1
Gambrell, J. B., TX-25/2
Gamewell, F. D., NJ-45/13
Gamewell, Francis Dunlap, DC-90/3**b**
Gamewell, Frank D., MI-60/1, NJ-45/3, NJ-45/5, NY-290/1
Gamewell, Mary (Ninde) (Mrs. Frank D., 2nd wife), NJ-45/5, OR-15/60
Gamewell, Mary Q. (Porter) (Mrs. Frank D., 1st wife), CT-50/7, TN-50/1
Gamewell, Mr. and Mrs. Francis Dunlap, NY-270/18
Gander, Donald, CA-260/1
Gandhi, Mohandas, CA-35/6
Ganel, Helen, MO-55/1
Gannon, John Mark, PA-40/1
Gantry, Emily (Mrs. W. Max), NB-15/1
Gantry, W. Max, NB-15/1
Gardiner, Angelus, IL-155/1
Gardiner, Henrietta, TX-5/2
Gardner, Christopher Thomas, CA-70/1, WA-45/1
Gardner, Elisa G., TX-5/2
Gardner, Marian. *See* Craighill, Marian (Gardner)
Garesche, E. F., WI-75/3
Garrett, Frank, CT-50/7
Garrett, Mr. and Mrs. Frank, TN-45/1
Garrett, Margaret. *See* Smythe, Margaret (Garrett)
Garrett, Norman F., TX-5/2
Garrett, Robert, NJ-120/2
Garrett, Verna Waugh (Mrs. Frank), CT-50/7
Garside, B. A., CT-15/5, CT-50/11, CT-50/26, MA-95/1, MA-240/4, NH-20/1, NY-90/4, NY-270/12
Garside, Bettis Alston, CA-290/11**b**
Garvey, Benjamin S., TX-5/2
Garvey, Justin, MA-255/1
Gaspard, Raymond, NY-110/1, NY-120/1
Gaston, James M., NY-290/1
Gaston, James McFadden, NC-10/8
Gaston, James McFadden, Jr., NC-10/8**b**
Gately, Joseph, MD-50/1
Gates, Alice, TX-5/2
Gates, Carl, MA-95/1
Gates, Frederick, NY-290/1
Gates, Frederick T., NY-290/1, NY-290/2, NY-295/8, NY-295/9**b**, PA-145/1
Gates, Mary, TX-5/2
Gaudissart, R., CA-260/1
Gaulke, David, IN-5/1
Gaunt, Frank P., NJ-45/3, NY-290/1
Gauthier, Msgr., UT-10/1
Gaw, Evaline, NJ-45/3
Gay, Leslie, MO-25/8
Gay, Mary D., TN-25/1
Gayley, Samuel Rankin, PA-200/5**b**
Gaynor, Lucy A., OH-30/1
Gebhardt, A., MO-50/13
Gebhardt, A. H., MO-50/6
Gebhardt, Arnold H., MN-10/1
Gee, N. Gist, NJ-45/10
Gehman, Daisy. *See* Fairfield, Daisy (Gehman)
Gehring, Frederick P., NY-105/1
Geiger, Maynard, CA-260/1
Geisert, Bradley Kent, VA-25/2
Gemmell, Nina E., PA-265/1
Gentry, W. Max, NJ-45/3
George, James H., TX-5/2
Geraldine, Sr., TX-5/2
Gerber, Lena, IN-30/1
Gerbillon, Jean François, DC-160/2, NY-95/1
Gerecht, Alexandra, TX-5/2
Gergen, Ronayne, MN-90/3, MN-90/4
Gerhard, P., PA-95/1
Gerlach, T., NY-280/3
Germain, Aidan, PA-95/1
Geselbracht, Howard, NY-110/1, NY-120/1
Gherardini, Giovanni, DC-90/5

Gibb, George W., PA-265/2
Gibb, J. McGregor, Jr., NJ-45/13
Gibb, John McGregor, NJ-45/3, NY-270/12
Gibbs, Ellen. *See* Crouch, Ellen (Gibbs)
Gibbs, Hazel M., ME-25
Gibbs, Mrs. Charles, PA-125/1
Gibson, R. McLean, NY-290/1
Giedt, E. H., CT-50/2
Giedt, Emanuel Herman, CT-50/14, KY-50/2
Gieser, Paul Kenneth, IL-200/30**b**
Giffen, Bertha (Mrs. Edward E.), OR-15/20**b**
Giffen, Edward E., OR-15/20**b**
Giffin, J. Harry, UT-10/1
Giffin, Jean (Mrs. Raymond H.), CT-50/7
Giffin, Raymond H., CT-50/7
Gifford, Nelson D., TX-5/2
Gih, Andrew, IL-90/1
Gihring, Hugo, MO-50/6
Gilbert, Josephine Cowin, CT-50/7
Gilbert, Lewis Loder, CT-10/2, CT-50/7, OH-170/8**b**
Gilbert, Lois (Chandler) (Mrs. Lewis Loder), CT-10/2, CT-50/7, OH-170/8**b**
Gilbert, Sylvio, NY-110/1, NY-120/1
Gilbertson, Ruth, MN-70/5, MN-95/42
Gilchrist, Huntington, ME-10/2**b**
Giles, Br., CA-260/1
Giles, Mary Zilpha, NC-45/12
Gill, Althea, TX-5/2
Gill, D. M., OH-195/1
Gill, J. M. B., TX-5/2
Gill, M., NY-280/3
Gill, Tom, NY-375/2
Gillespie, Arthur Samuel, NC-100/5, NC-100/9**b**, NC-105/1, TN-35, VA-65/2
Gillespie, Daniel F., VA-25/2
Gillespie, Miln, CA-75/2
Gillespie, Pauline (Pittard), TN-35, VA-65/2
Gillett, P. L., CT-15/5
Gillette, Charles, MA-95/1
Gillette, Charles L., CT-10/2
Gillette, Eliza Jane. *See* Bridgman, Eliza Jane (Gillette)
Gilliland, McKinley, NJ-30/1
Gillingham, Harrold E., PA-170/2
Gilman, Alfred, TX-5/2, TX-5/6
Gilman, Alfred A., MN-105/3
Gilman, Bishop [Alfred], KY-5/2, MA-40/1
Gilman, Francis Patrick, PA-200/6
Gilman, Gertrude, TX-5/2
Gilman, Louise. *See* Hutchins, Louise (Gilman)
Gilman, Mary (White) (Mrs. Francis Patrick), PA-200/6
Gilman, Mrs., VA-25/10
Gilmore, Lila, TX-5/2
Gilmore, P. C., TX-5/2
Gilmour, James, CA-130/4, IL-205/1
Ging, Woodrow, CT-10/2
Giovanni da Montecorvino, CA-265/1
Giovanni di Pian del Carpine, CA-265/1
Girard, Stella Elda. *See* Veenschoten, Stella Elda (Girard)
Girsberger, Freda, OH-30/1
Giving, Gerald, MN-95/110
Gjølseth, Alfred Berg, MN-95/110
Glass, Eloise. *See* Cauthen, Eloise (Glass)
Glass, Lloyd, NY-110/1, NY-120/1
Glass, Lois C., VA-65/2
Glass, S., NY-280/3
Glass, Sally, MA-195/5
Glasser, A. F., MI-95/1
Gleason, B., NY-280/3
Glenk, Edith, IN-75/1
Glenton, Mary, TX-5/2
Gloss, Anna M., IN-40/5
Glover, Archibald Edward, NJ-25
Glover, Richard, IL-200/4, TN-55/1, TX-25/1

Glover, Robert Hall, TX-20/2
Go, Mrs., MI-60/3
Goddard, Amos, TX-5/2
Goddard, Dean, CT-50/7
Goddard, Dwight, VT-5/3
Goddard, Eliza Ann (Abbott) (Mrs. Josiah), NY-345/13b
Goddard, Francis Wayland, GA-15/5
Goddard, J., CA-10/1
Goddard, Josiah, NY-345/13b
Goddard, O. E., GA-10/1
Goddard, Steven G., MI-60/3
Godshall, Dr., MA-195/5
Goebel, Flora, MN-90/3
Goering, Mrs. S. J., VA-40/1
Goering, Pauline, IN-25/3
Goering, Samuel Joseph, KS-55/5b
Goerner, H. C., VA-65/1
Goertz, Helen Riesen, KS-55/6
Goertz, Peter Siebert, KS-55/6b
Goetsch, F. A., PA-80/7
Goforth family, IL-210/1
Goforth, [Florence] Rosalind (Bellsmith) (Mrs. Jonathan, 2nd wife), FL-5/1, IL-200/31b, IL-200/47, IL-205/1, IL-210/1, NJ-25, UT-10/1
Goforth, Jonathan, CA-130/4, FL-5/1, IL-200/31b, IL-200/47, NJ-25, NJ-45/5, PA-70/1, RI-15/2, UT-10/1
Goforth, Mary. See Moynan, Mary (Goforth)
Gold, Helen, OR-15/3
Gold, Isabel, TX-5/2
Gold, Ralph G., CT-15/5, CT-50/7
Goldman, Merle, CT-50/2
Goldsbury, Dr. and Mrs. James, OH-170/7
Goldsbury, James, OH-170/6
Golisch, Lulu, NY-270/35
Gonçalves, Joaquim Affonso, DC-15
Gonyou, Fabiola, NY-120/1
Good, Rev. and Mrs. Harold, IN-75/1
Goodall, Norman, MI-120/13, NY-270/37
Goodnow, Frank J., MD-15/1, MD-15/3, MD-15/4, NY-290/1
Goodpasture, Henry M., VA-80/1
Goodrich, C., MA-95/2, OH-20/1
Goodrich, Chauncey, CT-50/7, NY-270/17, OH-180/1, WA-40/4
Goodrich family, CT-60/8
Goodrich, Grace. See Smith, Grace (Goodrich)
Goodrich, L. C., NY-290/1
Goodrich, Luther Carrington, CA-210/2, CT-10/2, CT-50/7, CT-50/25
Goodrich, Sarah Boardman (Clapp) (Mrs. Chauncey, 3rd wife), CT-50/7, OH-170/24
Goodrich, William Henry, CT-60/8
Goodsell, Daniel, NJ-45/5
Goodsell, Fred Field, CA-15/2, CA-75/2, CT-50/7, CT-50/21, MA-25/2b, NY-270/23, TX-30/1
Goodspeed, Edgar J., IL-75/2
Goodwin, Conrad H., TX-5/2
Goodwin, J. W., MO-25/4
Goodwin, Robert A., TX-5/2
Gordon, Charles George, NJ-45/5
Gordon, Fr., OH-115/1
Gordon, Maurine, PA-150/1
Gordon-Cumming, Constance Frederica, MA-30/2
Gorman, Mel, NY-25/1, NY-25/2
Gosline, Hazel, TX-5/2
Gossard, J. E., NJ-45/13
Gossard, Jesse Earl, NJ-45/3
Gott, O. W., TX-5/2
Gotwald, Luther A., IL-50/1
Gouchen, Irene, TN-45/1
Goucher, John Franklin, MD-25/1, MD-25/2, MD-70/1b, NY-270/18
Goucher, Mrs., MD-25/2
Gould, Annie Allender, MA-220/22, MD-25/1, ME-20/1, NY-385/1b,
Gould, H. G., NJ-30/1
Gould, John Mean, NC-45/13
Gould, Mary Frances, TN-35

Gould, Mrs., NY-385/1
Gould, Randall, VA-50/1
Goulter, Oswald John, CA-80/14, CT-10/2, OK-5/1, TN-45/1
Gouveia, Antonio de, IN-15/1
Goux, Mrs., MI-60/3
Gowdy, Bishop and Mrs. John, MD-25/1
Gowdy, Dr. and Mrs. John, OR-15/47
Gowdy, Elizabeth Thompson, CT-30/5
Gowdy, John, CT-30/5, IL-110/1, MA-95/1, NJ-45/3, NJ-45/5, NJ-45/13, NJ-50/1
Gowen, Herbert, WA-40/2
Gowen, Vincent Edward, WA-40/2b
Gowen, Vincent H., TX-5/2
Graber, C. L., IN-35/9
Graber, Joseph D., IN-35/2, IN-35/3
Graber, Joseph Daniel, IN-25/3, KS-15/1, VA-40/1
Grabill, A., NY-280/3
Grabill, Ada A., NY-270/35
Grady, M. Pauline, IL-140
Graebner, Theodore, MO-50/5b
Graham, Alicia May (Morey) (Mrs. David Crockett), DC-150/2
Graham, David Crockett, CT-50/24, DC-145/1, DC-150/1, DC-150/2b, DC-150/3, DC-150/5, DC-160/2, DC-165/1, DC-170/1, NY-350/1, WA-50/2
Graham, Mrs.William, NC-100/17
Graham, Richardson, TX-5/2
Graham, Sophie Peck, VA-100/1
Graham, Thomas Wesley, OH-170/10
Granger, Walter, DC-65/2
Granskou, Clemens M., IA-15/1, MN-70/3b, MN-70/5, MN-70/6, MN-95/43, MN-95/44
Granskou, Ella (Odland) (Mrs. Clemens M.), MN-95/44
Granskou, Mr. and Mrs. Clemens, MN-95
Grant, J. S., NY-290/1
Grant, John B., NY-290/1
Grant, Lawrence, KY-85/1
Grant, Margaret (Mrs. Lawrence), KY-85/1
Grant, W. Harvey, MA-125/4, UT-10/1
Graser, John, NY-110/1, NY-120/1
Gratia, Sr. Marie, IN-105/1, IN-105/6, IN-105/8, IN-105/9, IN-105/11
Gratz, [?], PA-170/1
Graves, Edith, IN-120/5
Graves, Elizabeth, TX-5/2
Graves, Eva, TN-35
Graves, Frederick Rogers, TX-5/1b, TX-5/2, VT-5/3
Graves, Jane W[ormeley] (Morris) (Mrs. Rosewell H.), MD-30/2
Graves, Josephine, TX-5/2
Graves, Lucy J., CT-50/7, TX-5/1, TX-5/2
Graves, Rosewell Hobart, KY-50/2, MD-30/2b, OH-175/1, TN-35, VA-65/2, VA-105/1
Graves, Stella Marie, NY-270/35
Gray, Cammie, KS-10/1, TN-45/1
Gray, Frances (Mrs. Luther Newton Budden), MA-240
Gray, Francis A., TX-5/2
Gray, G. Francis S., TX-5/2
Gray, Harold S., TX-5/2
Gray, Harold Studley, MI-15/5b
Gray, Mary B., TX-5/2
Gray, Minnie Moore, CA-130/1
Gray, W. Parker, NY-275/1
Graybill, H[enry] B[lair], NJ-105/1
Grayson, Dorothy D. (formerly Mrs. Harold N. Brewster), CT-50/7
Green, Jessie, TN-35
Green, Jessie L., VA-65/2
Green, John Dryer, IN-120/5
Green, Katharine R., MA-220/23b
Green, Letty, NY-270/13
Green, Lydia (Mrs. Norman Edwards), IN-120/5
Green, Minnie E. See Flagg, Minnie E. (Green)
Green, Norman Edwards, IN-120/5
Green, O. M., CA-35/6, NY-270/12
Green, Sarah. See Dodd, Sarah (Green)
Green, Stephen, TX-5/2

Green, Theodore A., NY-270/23
Greene, Albert E., Sr., MO-20/3
Greene, Albert E., Jr., MO-20/3
Greene, George Washington, NC-100/10b, NC-100/16
Greene, George William, NC-100/16
Greene, Jerome, NY-295/8, PA-145/1
Greene, Kate (Mrs. Roger), MA-130/2
Greene, Lydia E., TN-35
Greene, Mr. and Mrs., OR-20/1
Greene, Phillips, family, CT-60/32
Greene, Phillips Foster, CT-60/9b, WI-20/4
Greene, Dr. and Mrs. Phillips, CT-50/25
Greene, Robert, NY-110/1, NY-120/1
Greene, Roger Sherman, CT-50/12, CT-60/32, IA-15/1, MA-50/1,
    MA-130/2, NY-285/3, NY-290/1, NY-295/12, WI-20/2
Greene, Ruth Peabody (Altman) (Mrs. Phillips), CT-60/9b, WI-20/4
Greene, Theodore Chase, MA-50/3
Greenlee, [?], IL-60/2
Greenwell, Florentine, KY-65/1
Greenwich, Long E., NY-105/1
Greenwood, Jennie, NC-80/8
Greer, Vesta, OH-170/7
Gregg, Alice Henrietta, NY-270/19, NY-275/1, SC-5/1, SC-35/1b,
    TX-5, TX-5/2, VA-25/10
Gregory, J. J., NJ-45/13
Gregory, John Pilton, NY-95/1
Gregory, Miriam, IN-75/1
Gregory, Paul R., PA-80/13
Gregory, Quentin, NC-70/11b
Gregory, Richard Henry, NC-70/15
Greisser, Robert, TX-5/2
Grenfell, Wilfred T[homasson], CT-60/10
Greshem, George S., TX-5/2
Gresnicht, Adalbert, PA-95/1
Gress, Ruth A., OR-15/21b
Griebenow, M. G., NJ-85, NJ-85/1, NJ-85/3
Griest, Rebecca, NY-270/35
Griffen, Thomas, CT-60/32
Griffin, H. M., PA-265/2
Griffin, J. B., CT-50/26
Griffin, Mary Finan, NJ-15, NJ-15/1
Griffin, Pansy P., CT-50/7
Griffing, John B., NC-45/16
Griffis, William Eliot, NJ-70/1b
Griffith, Esther, TX-5/2
Griggs, Frederick, MI-45/2b
Grimm, Gratian, PA-230/1
Grindvik, Mr. and Mrs. John B. S., MN-95
Griswold, B. H., MD-15/2
Grønli, Mr. and Mrs. John E., MN-95
Groell, Clara, MD-50/1, NY-105/1
Groesbeck, Adam, OR-15/22b
Groesbeck, Clara (Holloway) (Mrs. Adam), NY-345/14, OR-15/22b
Groesbeck, Gertrude, IN-120/5
Groesbeck, Tracy, OR-15/22
Groff, Anne M., CT-50/7, TX-5/2
Groff, George Weidman, NY-90/4, PA-275, PA-275/2, PA-275/3
Groh, Lillian, MN-95
Gronbeck, Hedwig, MO-50/6
Grondin, Therese, NY-120/1
Grose, G. R., OH-135/1
Grose, George R., NJ-45/5
Grosier, abbé, NJ-130/1
Gross, Columban, PA-95/1
Gross, Daniel, MA-95/1
Gross, Fulgence, MO-65/1
Grosvenor, Thomas George, CT-60/30
Groves, Blanche, AL-10/2, TN-35, VA-65/2
Groves, Leslie R., DC-125/2
Groves, Leslie R., Sr., PA-25/2
Grubb, Violet M., CA-205/1
Gruen, Olive, MO-50/6
Grussinger, Sr. Margaretta, IN-105/6

Guangxu emperor, NY-270/12
Gubbins, John H., WA-45/1
Gudal, Mr. and Mrs. J. M. O., MN-95
Guerreiro, Fernao, IL-60/2
Guerrero, Jerónimo, IN-10/4
Guerrieri, Antonia M., NY-120/1
Guerry, Sumner, TX-5/2
Guesee, R. P., NY-285/1
Guesser, Robert A., TX-5/2
Guidera, M. Dominic, NY-120/1
Guilhermy, Elesban de, DC-70/4
Guinn, Oscar A., Jr., NJ-45/3
Guinness, G. Whitfield, IL-200/44
Guinness, Mary Geraldine. *See* Taylor, Mary Geraldine (Guinness)
Gulick, Luther Halsey, HI-10/2
Gulley, Esther, IN-75/1
Gunn, Selksar M., CA-290/12
Gursli, Bertha M. *See* Ege, Bertha M. (Gursli)
Guth, G., NJ-30/1
Guthrie, Anne, CT-10/2
Gutteres, Antonella Marie, KY-65/1
Guttery, Arthur M., IL-180/1, OR-15/23b
Guttery, Myrtle (Mrs. Arthur M.), OR-15/23
Gutzall, Mary, MI-20/2
Gützlaff, Karl Friedrich August (Charles), CA-15/2, CT-55/2, DC-80/2,
    IL-85/1, MA-95/1, MA-250/1, MD-10/1, MI-60/5, MN-100/1,
    NY-195/2, NY-270/8, PA-145/6
Gwong, Moy, IL-105/6

Ha, Miss, MA-195/5
Haag, Howard Lee, CT-60/11b, IL-180/1
Haas, Leroy, MO-50/6
Haas, Lillian, MA-195/5
Haass, L., NY-280/3, NY-280/7
H., A. C., NY-270/33
Haden, Thomas Henry, GA-20
Hager, C[harles] R[obert], OH-170/15
Haggard, [?], CT-50/14
Haggerty, Theodata, IN-105/2, IN-105/3, IN-105/5
Hagman, George, TN-45/1
Hagman, Ruby, TN-45/1
Hagspiel, Bruno, IN-105/2, IN-105/6, WI-75/3
Hahn, E., VA-50/1
Hahn, Emily, NJ-115/1
Hahn, Joseph, NY-110/1, NY-120/1
Haight, Edith C., NY-270/35
Haist, Virginia. *See* Huntington, Virginia (Haist)
Halde, Jean Baptiste du, CA-245/7, DC-25/2, IL-85/1, NJ-110,
    NY-95/1, PA-175/1
Hale, C. O., OH-90/1
Hale, Eva, OH-90/1
Hale, Elizabeth, TN-35
Hale, Jonathan, family, OH-90/1
Hale, Lyman L., NJ-45/3
Hales, Helen, TX-5/2
Hall, Anne. *See* Starrett, Anne (Hall)
Hall, Henrietta. *See* Shuck, Henrietta (Hall)
Hall, Jessie, MA-240
Hall, A. Walker, MO-105/1
Hall, Anne G. *See* Starrett, Anne G. (Hall)
Hall, C. W., NJ-45/13
Hall, Elmer Edgar, CA-35/1
Hall family, NC-45/14
Hall, James W., CT-50/7
Hall, Lawrence K., KS-10/1
Hall, O. F., NJ-45/13
Hall, Ronald O., NY-270/23
Hall, William N[elthorpe], NY-95/1
Hallam, Wirt W., MO-20/2
Halling, F. R., MA-45/2
Hallock, Adelia (Cobb), MA-185/19
Hallock, Constance M., TN-40/1

Hallock, H. G. C., CT-10/2, CT-50/14, MO-5/4, OR-15/56
Hallock, Henry Galloway Comingo, CT-50/7, NJ-135/3
Halsey, A. W., OR-15/36
Halsey, Marion (Spencer), MA-185/5b
Halsey, Rebecca, TX-5/2
Hamilton, Clarence, CT-15/3
Hamilton, E. H., GA-35/1
Hamilton, Joseph W., OH-170/17
Hamlett, Lettie, VA-6/2
Hamlin, John, OH-170/17
Hamlin, Mr. and Mrs. John W., OH-170/17
Hammaker, Wilbur Emory, CT-50/16, NJ-45/5
Hammon, Walter, CA-265/1, NY-260/1
Hammond, Louise, TX-5/2
Hampton, Emma, AL-10/1
Han Li-wu, VA-50/1
Han Yü-shan, CT-50/2
Hanan, Rose Benigna, NY-120/1
Hand, Charles W., OE-15/30
Hand, Katharine W., CT-50/7
Hand, M., NY-280/3
Hanford, Ruth. See Munn, Ruth (Hanford)
Hannigan, Julia, NY-120/1
Hansing, Ovidia, NB-15/1
Hanson, Anders B., MN-95/45
Hanson, Constance Twedt, MN-95/46
Hanson, Francis R., TX-5/2
Hanson, Irene (Forsythe) (Mrs. Perry O., 2nd wife), NY-270/12, OR-15/24b
Hanson, Orvis, MN-95/47
Hanson, Perry O., NJ-45/3, NJ-45/5, NJ-45/13, NY-270/18, OR-15/24
Hanson, Raymond, IL-110/1
Hanson, Richard E., NJ-45/3
Hanson, Ruth E. (Mrs. Perry O., 1st wife?), NY-270/18
Hanson, William, OH-195/1
Hansrote, Hazel Groves, MD-60/1
Hantington, George B., NY-290/1
Hanzlik, L. C., NJ-45/13
Happer, [Andrew?], VA-105/1
Happer, Andrew Patton, CT-60/30, MA-125/4, MI-20/1, NY-270/12
Harbison, Charles W. Jr., TX-5/2
Harbison, Sr. Elizabeth Cecile, IN-105/2, IN-105/5, IN-105/6
Harbison, Sr. Mary Elizabeth, IN-105/11
Harder, Agnes. See Wiens, Agnes (Harder)
Harder, Tina. See Dick, Tina (Harder)
Harding, Weston, TX-5/2
Hare, Hobart Amory, MD-35/2
Hare, William Hobart, SD-10/1b
Harmelink, Herman, III, MI-120/13, NY-270/37
Harmer, Harvey Walker, WV-15/2
Harmon, Mr., MA-155/1
Harner, Nevin Cowger, PA-80/13
Harnsberger, Agnes Lacy (Woods), VA-100/1
Harriet, CT-10/2
Harrington, Fern, TN-35
Harris, Arthur M., NC-50/1
Harris, George M., NC-10/10
Harris, Willie Pauline, NY-345/15b
Harris, Ann, TN-35
Harris, Blanche M., TX-5/2
Harris, Clifton E., TN-35
Harris, George K[auffelt], CT-10/2, PA-265/2
Harris, Winifred (Mrs. George K.), CT-10/2
Harris, Henrietta, TX-5/2
Harris, Lillian, TX-5/2
Harris, Thomas A., NJ-45/3
Harris, William L., NJ-45/5
Harrison, A., NY-280/3
Harrison, Everett, CA-130/3
Harrison, Henry Sydnor, NC-45/15
Harrison, Robert T., CA-130, CA-130/1, CA-130/4
Hart, E. H., NJ-45/13
Hart, Edgarton Haskell, NY-270/18

Hart, Edith, TX-5/2
Hart, Elizabeth, TX-5/2
Hart, Robert, GA-20/1
Hart, V. C., NJ-45/13, NY-270/18
Hart, Virgil C[hittenden], NJ-45/5
Hartenstein, Karl, TN-65/1
Hartigan, Sr. Mary Liguori (Mary Loretta), IN-105/2, IN-105/4
Hartley, E., NY-280/3
Hartman, Frieda (Plack) (Mrs. Ward), PA-80/7b
Hartman, Ward, PA-80/7b
Hartshorn, Harold, CA-80/5
Hartt, Mrs. A. W., MA-50/1
Hartwell, Anna Burton, CT-50/13b
Hartwell, Charles Norris, CT-10/2, CT-50/13b, MA-5b, MA-5/2b, MA-5/3, MA-200/1, MA-200/2, MN-105/1, OH-175/1
Hartwell, Charlotte W. (Mrs. Jesse Boardman, 2nd wife), TN-55/5
Hartwell, Eliza (Jewett) (Mrs. Jesse Boardman, 1st wife), CT-50/13
Hartwell, Emily Susan, CA-20/1, CT-50/7, MA-200/1b, MA-220/25, WA-55/1
Hartwell, Hannah Louisa (Plimpton) Peet (Mrs. Lyman B. Peet [lst]; Mrs. Charles [2nd], 2nd wife), CT-60/12, MA-220/40b, MA-220/41
Hartwell, J. B., VA-65/2
Hartwell, Jesse Boardman, Jr., CT-50/13b
Hartwell, Lottie N. See Ufford, Lottie N. (Hartwell)
Hartwell, Lucy Estabrook (Stearns) (Mrs. Charles, 1st wife), MA-200/1, MA-200/2b, MA-210/2, MA-220/49, MN-105/1
Hartwell, Mrs. [Lucy?], MA-5/2
Hartwell, Nellie E. See Beattie, Nellie E. (Hartwell)
Hartzell, Paul, TX-5/2
Harvey, Earl E., NJ-45/3
Hasenpflug, Emma. See Dubs, Emma (Hasenpflug)
Hasenpflug, Marie T., NJ-45/4
Hasle, Emma C. See Daehlin, Emma C. (Hasle)
Haslep, Marie, TX-5/2
Hassell, Jean (Mrs. Jean), KY-85/1
Hassell, Richard, KY-85/1
Hassett, W. D., MO-20/4
Hatem, George, NY-175/4
Hathaway, Louise Claire. See Stanley, Louise Claire (Hathaway)
Haugan, Mr. and Mrs. August W., MN-95
Haugh, Gertrude. See Sibley, Gertrude (Haugh)
Haui, L., PA-80/13
Hauser, Ottilie. See Brattain, Ottilie (Hauser)
Hausermann, R., DC-10/1, NY-95/1
Hausske, Albert Carl, CT-50/7
Hautman, Frances Maria, OH-165/1
Haven, Ada. See Mateer, Ada (Haven)
Haven, William, CA-130/1
Haverkamp, William C., MI-80/5
Havermale, Lewis F., NJ-45/3
Havighurst, Freeman C., KS-10/1, NJ-45/3
Havighurst, Robert Bruce, NJ-45/3
Havilland family, PA-270/3
Hawk, John C., NJ-45/10
Hawkins, Everett D., OH-170/17
Hawkins, F. H., CT-50/9, IL-25/1, IL-200/14, KS-35/1, NY-275/1, NY-290/1
Hawkins, Floyd Flora, TN-35
Hawkins, Roger R., OH-170/17
Hawley, J. W., CT-10/2, MA-95/1
Hayes, A. A., TX-5/2, VA-105/1
Hayes, Alice J., TN-35
Hayes, Barbara M. (Kelman) (Mrs. John David), OR-15/25b, PA-200/7, PA-200/28
Hayes, C. A., TN-35
Hayes, Cardinal, PA-95/1
Hayes, E. Pearce, NJ-45/3
Hayes, Edward Pearce, CA-80/15
Hayes, Egbert M., CA-80/16
Hayes, Estella, IL-200/50
Hayes, Everley, TN-35, TN-35/1
Hayes, Florence C., TX-5/2
Hayes, Helen (Mrs. Paul Goodman), MN-95/49, MN-95/50

Hayes, John David, CT–50/7, MA–195/5, NY–290/1, OR–15/25**b**, PA–200/7, PA–200/28
Hayes, Paul Goodman, CT–10/2, MN–95/50, NJ–45/3, NY–270/20**b**
Hayes, Rev. and Mrs. John D., DC–140
Hayes, Rutherford, CT–60/30
Hayes, Samuel, PA–240/1
Hayes, Watson McMillan, CT–50/7, NC–80/16
Haygood, Atticus Greene, GA–20/1, GA–20/4**b**
Haygood, Laura Askew, GA–20/1, GA–20/4**b**, NJ–45/5, NJ–50/1, VA–30/1
Hayne, Hester, MO–25/2, MO–25/4
Hayward, Harold Dewey, IL–200/33
Hayward, Helen M. (Mrs. Harold Dewey), IL–200/33
Hayward, Victor E. W., IN–25/3
Hayword, W. F., TX–5/2
He Shen. *See* Ho Shen
Headland, Isaac T[aylor], NJ–45/13, NY–275/1
Heald, Jeanie V., TX–5/2
Healey, Sylvester, MN–90/4, PA–95/1
Heaney, Marie Amadea, OH–165/1
Heard, John, NY–90/8
Heard, Paul F., DC–95/2
Hearn, T. A., NJ–45/10
Hearn, Thomas A., GA–10/1
Hearn, Walter Anderson, GA–10/1**b**, NJ–45/5
Heath, Frances J. *See* Hughson, Frances J. (Heath)
Hebbert, Virginia, TX–5/2
Hecker, Willo M., NJ–45/3
Heebner, Flora K., KS–55/13, MA–95/1, OH–170/24, PA–130, PA–130/1
Heemskerk, John, NY–110/1, NY–120/1
Heerema, Elisabeth, MI–80/3
Hegge, Mr. and Mrs. E. M., MN–95
Hegner, Mother Stanislaus, WI–75/3
Heidenreich, Elsie Bernice, NJ–45/4
Heigham, Beverly, MA–95/1
Heijer, J. G., NY–105/1
Heil, W. F., PA–110/1
Heininger, A. D., IA–25/1
Hein-inger, Alfred Dixon, CA–80/17
Heinrich, Maurus, MO–65/1
Heinrichs, Sara, CA–115/1
Heinrichsohn, Mr. and Mrs. F. Karl, PA–80
Heiser, Victor George, PA–145/3**b**
Heisey, Mrs. Walter J., CT–50/7, IL–105/11
Helen Veronica, Sr., TX–5/2
Helfferich, Reginald, CT–50/26, PA–80/7
Hellestad, Einar, MN–70/4
Hellestad, Mina Jordeth (Nold) (Mrs. Oscar O.), MN–70/4**b**, MN–95
Hellestad, Oscar O., MN–70/4, MN–95
Helman, [?], NY–175/13
Helmstetter, Ernest, PA–95/1
Helsby, Esther, KY–85/1
Helsby, Meredith, KY–85/1
Helsby, Christine, KY–85/1
Hembold, Elizabeth (Rue), CT–50/7
Hemenway, Ruth V., MA–195/1, NJ–45/3, NY–290/1
Hemingway, Adelaide, MN–60/1, OH–170/17
Hemingway, Dr. and Mrs. Willoughby, OH–170/24
Hemingway, Mary E. (Williams) (Mrs. Willoughby), CT–10/2
Hemingway, W[illoughby] A[nson], OH–170/17, OH–170/23
Henderson, Jacob, NY–95/1
Henderson, Katherine L. *See* Read, Katherine L. (Henderson)
Henderson, L. J., NY–290/1
Henderson, Maude, TX–5/2
Hendry, C. H., NJ–45/10
Hendry, J. L., NJ–45/10
Hening, S. E., CA–80/5
Henke, Frederick G[oodrich], NJ–45/13
Henkels, Joseph, OH–165/1
Henry, B[enjamin] C., MA–125/4
Henry, J. M., MA–195/5
Henry, James M., MA–125/4, NY–285/1

Henry, James McClure, DC–140, PA–200/8**b**
Henry, John J., NY–105/1
Henry, Robert T., PA–190/2
Henry, Sr. Joseph, IN–105/11
Hensler, Carl P., MN–90/4, PA–95/1
Hensolt, Edith (Ashmore), OR–15/2
Heppner, Helen (Quiring), CA–115/1
Hermanson, Oline. *See* Netland, Oline (Hermanson)
Herrgen, Corita, NY–120/1
Herrick, C. Judson, NY–290/1
Herrick, W. B., CT–50/14
Herring, David Wells, NC–70/18**b**, NC–85/1, NC–100/3, NC–100/5, NJ–25
Herring, James A., TN–35
Herring, Mary, TN–35
Herring, Nan Trammell, TN–35
Hersey, John, MA–165/7
Hertz, Catherine Reynolds, MN–95/51
Hertz, Edwin, MN–95/52, MN–60/1
Hesla, O. E., IA–15/1
Hesla, Otto, MN–95
Hess, Clara. *See* Foster, Clara (Hess)
Hess, Esther Marguerite (Nowack) (Mrs. Lawrence), IL–200/34**b**, IL–200/44
Hess, Lawrence, IL–200/34**b**, IL–200/44
Hewey, Clarissa, CT–50/13
Hewitt, Alden, TX–5/2
Hibbard, Earl R., CT–10/2, CT–50/7, NJ–45/3, OR–20/2
Hibbard, Ernest, NY–270/33
Hibben, John G., NJ–120/2
Higgins, Agnes Virginia, NY–120/1
Higgins, Charles A., TX–5/2
Higgins, Mary Tyng, TX–5
Higgins, Ruby E. *See* Brown, Ruby E. (Higgins)
Higgins, Susan H., TX–5/2
High, Stanley, OR–30/1
Highbaugh, Irma, KS–10/1, MA–195/5
Highfill, Edith. *See* Humphrey, Edith (Highfill)
Highland, Augusta, IL–50/1
Hildegarde, Sr., OH–115/1
Hildreth, Ellison Story, CT–50/14**b**
Hildreth, Lottie Rowe (Lane) (Mrs. Ellison Story), CT–50/14**b**, MA–220/33
Hill, David, CT–50/19, IL–25/2, IL–110/1, IL–200/45, KS–35/2, NJ–45/14, OR–40/1, TX–20/1
Hill, E., NY–280/3
Hill, Esther (Mrs. Howard), KY–85/1
Hill, Eugene, TN–35, TN–35/1, VA–65/2
Hill, Harry J., NJ–45/3
Hill, Howard, KY–85/1
Hill, Jack, MI–105/4, NJ–60/3
Hill, Joanne (Mrs. Jack), MI–105/4, NJ–60/3
Hill, Joseph J., NY–105/1
Hill, Louise, TN–35
Hill, Mary, IN–75/1
Hill, Mary A., OH–30/1, TX–5/2
Hill, Polly (Dexter) (Mrs. Lewis W.), MA–40/1
Hill, Viola C., MI–60/3, PA–125/1
Hill, Viola Caroline, NY–345/16**b**
Hill, W. B., NY–270/37
Hilscher, Harris G., CT–50/7
Hiltner, Frederica (Mead), MA–185/7, NY–270/35, WA–40/3
Hiltner, Walter G., NY–290/1
Hilty, Elizabeth, IN–30/1
Hilty, Minnie, IN–30/1
Himes, Blanche, MO–25/4
Himle, Alma (Carlson) (Mrs. Thorstein), MN–95
Himle, Gidske (Sigmundstad) (Mrs. Thorstein), MN–95
Himle, Thorstein, MN–95
Hinder, E., NY–280/3
Hinder, Eleanor M., NY–270/35
Hines, William, CT–50/15
Hinkey, Rhoda. *See* Lugibihl, Rhoda (Hinkey)

Lewis, M., IL–200/4, TN–55/1, TX–25/1
Lewis, Mrs. Charles, PA–125/1
Lewis, Ralph C., CA–235/1
Lewis, Robert Ellsworth, VT–5/3
Lewis, Spencer, NJ–45/5, NJ–45/13, NY–270/18
Lewis, Stephen C., NY–290/1
Lewis, W. G., NJ–30/1
Lewis, W. S., NJ–45/13, NY–200/1
Lewis, Wilson S., NY–270/18
Lewis, Wilson Seeley, CT–50/7, NJ–45/5
Leyenberger, [?], NY–270/13
Leynse, James P., CA–235/1, CT–50/7, WA–20/2**b**
Li An-che, NJ–125/1
Li, C. N., IA–15/1
Li Chen-nan, CT–60/32
Li Chih-tsao, IL–85/1, MI–10/1, PA–95/1
Li, Ching-lien, CT–10/2
Li Huang, VA–50/1
Li Hung-chang, MA–95/1, MA–155/1, NH–10/3
Li, Mark, TX–5/2
Li, Mary, MO–25/9
Li Shih-yüeh, IN–20/2
Li, Agnes Joan, IN–105/6, IN–105/11
Li, Thomas, NY–110/1, NY–120/1
Li Ting Jung, WA–40/4
Li Yen-nan, MO–50/6
Li Yun-tsao, OH–30/1
Li, Miss, MN–70/3
Liang A-fa, MI–10/1
Liang Ch'i-ch'ao, CT–50/2
Liang Ch'uan-ch'in, CT–10/2
Liang, Hubert S., NY–270/25
Liang, P. K., NY–290/1
Liao Chung-k'ai, CT–50/2
Libby, Walter E., NJ–45/3
Licent, Emile, NJ–100/1
Lichtenberger, Arthur C., TX–5/2
Liddell, Eric, CT–50/9, IL–25/1, IL–200/14, KS–35/1
Liddell, Eric H., OH–70/2
Lide, Francis P., VA–65/2
Lide, Jane, VA–65/2
Lien, Martin T., NJ–95/3
Lieo, Graham Y. L., TX–5/2
Liggins, John, TX–5/2
Lii, Joseph, NJ–155/1
Liljestrand, S. H., NJ–45/3
Lillebergen, Mr. and Mrs. Karl A. O., MN–95
Lillegard, George, MO–50/13
Lillega[a]rd, George O., IA–15/1, MN–10/1, MN–95, MO–50/6, WI–55/1
Lim, Micheline, MA–240/6
Lim, Robert S. K., MA–50/1
Lima, Manoel de Oliveira, DC–15
Lin, C. J., CT–15/5, MA–95/1
Lin Ching-jin, CT–50/2
Lin, David, CA–135/1
Lin, Jin-gi, MI–120/5
Lin King Ching, MA–215/2
Lincoln, Abraham, VA–25/12
Lincoln, C. F. S., VA–55/1
Lincoln, Charles F. S., TX–5/2
Lincoln, Charles S., NY–290/1
Lincoln, Wilamette, TX–5/2
Lind, Jenny, CT–10/2, CT–50/7, NC–70/13**b**, PA–125/1, TX–5/2
Lindberg, Sten, IL–5/1
Lindholm, Paul R., GA–15/3
Lindsay, Henrietta, CA–35/6
Lindskog, S., WI–75/4
Lindstedt, August, MN–45/1**b**
Lindstrom, C. F., TX–5/2
Lindstrom, Carl F., TX–5/2
Lindstrom, Julia, TX–5/2

Ling, Edward S. H., TX–5/2
Ling, Esther, OR–15/6
Ling, Joan, NY–110/1, NY–120/1
Ling, Maurice Clet, OH–165/1
Ling, Samuel D., IL–205/1
Lingle, Jean [Richardson Ritchie] (Mrs. William Hill), CA–75/2, NY–270/35
Lingle, Mrs. [Jean?], CT–15/5
Lingle, W. H., CT–50/12
Lingle, William Hill, CA–75/2
Linn, Harriet. *See* Beebe, Harriet (Linn)
Linquist, Sven, OH–195/1
Linus, Mother Mary, KY–65/1
Lis Yin Shan Yen, MI–80/4
List, Augusta, MA–240
Littell, Charlotte, TX–5/2
Littell, Edward, TX–5/2
Littell, Helen, TX–5/2
Littell, John S., TX–5/2
Littell, S. Harrington, TX–5/2
Little, Lucy Legrand, NC–80/12
Little, Edward S., NJ–45/13
Little, Henry, PA–200/25
Little, Laura (Nance), NY–345/5
Little, Marie (Huttenlock), IL–200/43
Little, Marion, TX–5/2
Little, Pauline [McAlpine] (DuBose) (Mrs. Lacy L.), VA–100/1
Littlefield, Hazel. *See* Smith, Hazel (Littlefield)
Littlefield, Josiah L., MI–15/8
Littmarck, Tore, IL–180/1
Liu, Beatrice Exner, MN–60/1, MN–95/62
Liu Chieh, VA–50/1
Liu En-lan, NY–270/35
Liu, Faith, TX–5/2
Liu, Hanna, NJ–30/1
Liu, Herman, MA–195/5
Liu, Herman C. E., VA–65/2
Liu Hon-ching, NY–110/1, NY–120/1
Liu, J. H., MA–50/1
Liu Jui-heng, MA–50/4, NY–175/9
Liu Lan-hua, OH–170/17
Liu, Miss, MA–195/5
Liu, Nelson E. P., TX–5/2
Liu, Newton Y. L., TX–5/2
Liu, Paul Vincent, OH–165/1
Liu, Stephen C., CT–60/32
Liu Teh-wei, MN–60/1
Liu Toi-ching, MA–195/5
Liu Yin-tsung, TX–5/2
Lo Pa Hong, Joseph, NJ–15/1, WI–75/3
Lo, Peter, NY–130/1
Lobelli, Giovanni, DC–70/3
Lobenstine, E. C., CA–290/3, CT–15/5, MA–50/1, MA–195/5
Lobenstine, Edward, NY–270/35
Lobenstine, Edwin, CT–60/32, NY–285/3
Lobenstine, Edwin C., CT–50/7, NJ–115/1
Lobenstine, Edwin Carlyle, MA–230/4, NY–270/24, NY–295/5
Lobinger, Judge, MI–60/1
Locke, Arthur H., TX–5/2
Locke, Edwin A., Jr., MO–20/3, MO–20/4
Lockhart, [?], CT–50/9, IL–25/1, IL–200/14, KS–35/1
Lockwood, E. H., NY–270/25
Lockwood, Henry, TX–5/2
Lockwood, W. W., IL–180/1
Loeffler, Vincent C., NY–105/1
Loehr, George R., Jr., GA–20/1
Loehr, George R., Sr., GA–20/1
Loew, Cora, IN–45/1
Loewen, Esko, IN–25/2
Loftus, John Joseph, CA–80/27
Loftus, Margaret Francis, OH–60/1
Logan, Alice L., MA–240

McCallum, [?], CA–75/2
McCammon, Don, IN–35/2, IN–35/5
McCammon, Dorothy (Mrs. Don), IN–35/2, IN–35/5
McCann, J. H., MA–95/1
McCann, James, MA–95/1
McCann, James Hamilton, OH–170/24
McCartee, Divie Bethune, DC–80/2, DC–170/1, MI–60/2, NJ–95/3, PA–200/12
McCartee, Juana M. (Knight) (Mrs. Divie), PA–200/12b
McCarthy, Charles, CA–195/1
McCarthy, Edward, IN–105/2
McCarthy, Gabriel, PA–230/1
McCarthy, Leo, NY–110/1, NY–120/1
McCarthy, William, TX–5/2
McCartney, J. H., CT–50/24, NJ–45/13
McCartney, John H., NY–270/18
McCauley, J. P., NY–270/23
McCauley, S. J., NY–270/23
McCausey, E., NY–280/3
McClain, Helen B., CA–235/1
McClellan, Mary. *See* Lambuth, Mary (McClellan)
McClelland, W. Grigor, CA–125/1, DE–5/1, OH–195/1, PA–205
McClung, Anna Gay, TN–25/1
McClure, Jeanie Graham (Mrs. Robert W.), CT–50/7, OH–180/1
McClure, R. W., MA–95/1
McClure, Robert, MN–95/34
McClure, Robert B., KY–5/2, VA–70/1
McClure, Robert Baird, CA–205/1, GA–25/1
McClure, Robert William, NH–10/2b
McClure, William, IL–200/21
McClurg, Grace. *See* Carson, Grace (McClurg)
McClurg, Ruth, OH–25/1
McConaughy, James Lukens, CT–30/7b
McConnaughey, Grace E. *See* Murray, Grace E. (McConnaughey)
McConnell, Francis J., NJ–45/3
McConnell, J[ohn], NY–280/3
McCook, Eliza L., TX–5/2
McCorkle, William Parsons, NC–10/9
McCormack, John, NH–20/1
McCormick, Cyrus H., CT–50/26
McCormick, Mary Colmcille, CA–80/29
McCoy, Joseph, OH–130/1
McCoy, Katherine, KY–85/1
McCracken, Josiah C., TX–5/2
McCracken, Josiah Calvin, CT–50/7
McCreery, Caroline, CA–235/1
McCulken, Francis, OH–130/1
McCulloch, Gertrude Florence, CT–50/7, MI–15/6, NY–345/19b
McCullough, Helen L., TN–35, VA–65/2
MacCurdy, Hattie R., OR–15/18, PA–125/1
McCurdy, William A., CT–50/7, NJ–45/3
McCutcheon, James, CT–50/7
McDaniel, Charles G., VA–65/2
McDermott, Maria Electa, NJ–15/1
McDermott, Timothy, MA–255/2
McDonald, Jessie, IL–200/44b
McDonald, Frank Rudd, NJ–45/3
McDonald, J. A., TX–5/2
McDonald, Jane, KY–65/1
McDonald, C., NY–270/12
McDonnell, Clella E. *See* Brown, Clella E. (McDonnell)
MacEachron, Helen (Dunham) (Mrs. Paul), IA–25/1
MacEachron, Paul, IA–25/1
MacElroy, Edward, CA–300/1
McElroy, Ruth, TN–45/1
McFadden, Agatha, IN–105/2, IN–105/5
McFadyen, Archibald Alexander, NC–20/1
McFerrin, John B., GA–20/1
McGavin, David, NY–135/2
McGavock family, NC–10/10
McGavock, Mrs. D. H., GA–20/1
McGill, Alexander Taggart, MI–20/1
MacGillivray, Donald, CT–15/5, CT–50/2, NY–195/2, NY–270/8

McGinn, John, NY–110/1, NY–120/1
McGinnis, J. Patrick H., TX–5/2
McGlothlin, William J., SC–30/1
McGoldrick, Viola, TX–5/2
MacGown, Marian G. *See* Evans, Marian G. (MacGown)
McGuire, Frederick, NY–110/1, NY–120/1
McGuire, Frederick A., NY–105/1
McGurkin, Edward, NY–110/1, NY–120/1
McGwingan, Maude M., CA–20/1
Machen, John Gresham, PA–220/1b
McIlvaine, Jasper Scudder, PA–200/13b
McIlwaine, Irene, VA–100/1
McIlwaine, William, PA–150/1
McInerney, Athanasius, NY–365/1
MacInnis, Donald, CT–50/2, MI–95/1, MN–95/65, NJ–45/3, NY–175/4
MacInnis, Helen (Mrs. Donald), MN–95/66
Mack, Edward, NC–80/13b
Mack, Isabella. *See* Patton, Isabella (Mack)
Mack, M., NY–280/3
MacKay, George Leslie, CA–130/4
McKay, James, MI–60/3
MacKay, James A., NY–235/5
MacKay, John Alexander, NJ–135/4
MacKay, Raymond C., IA–15/1
McKee, Elizabeth, CA–235/1
McKee, Mrs. George Wilson, NY–270/35
MacKenzie, Dr., MA–195/5
MacKenzie, J., RI–15/2
McKeirnan, Michael, NY–110/1, NY–120/1
McKenna, M. Paul, NY–120/1
McKenna, Mary DeLellis, NY–120/1
McKenna, Mary Paul, NY–120/1
McKinley, M., NY–280/7
MacKinley, M., NY–280/3
McKinley, William, DC–90/7
MacKinnon, C., NY–280/3
Macklin, W. E., CT–10/1
Macklin, William Edward, KY–25/1b
McLaughlin, James, NY–110/1, NY–120/1
McLaughlin, Thomas, NJ–5/1
McLaughlin, W. H., MO–50/6
Maclay, R. S., NJ–45/13
McLean, Franklin C., IL–75/1, IL–75/7b, MD–5/1, NY–290/1
McLean, Helen (Vincent) (Mrs. Franklin), IL–75/1
Maclean, R. E., NJ–45/13
Maclean, Sarah Mabel, NJ–45/3
McLean, Winfield A., CT–50/7
McLellan, Geraldine Searle, OH–170/25
MacLeod, John, VA–105/1
MacLeod, Roderick A., NJ–85/3
McLoughlin, John E., NY–105/1
MacManus, Theodore F., PA–95/1
MacMillan, Archibald M., TN–35
Macmillan, Eva (Adams), MA–185/10, MA–240/4, NY–270/35
McMillan, Henry Hudson, NC–100/13b
McMillan, Leila (Memory) (Mrs. Henry), NC–100/13, VA–65/2
MacMillan, Margaret K., TN–35
McMinn, Molly, TN–35
McMullen, Kitty Caldwell. *See* Farrior, Kitty Caldwell (McMullen)
McMullen, Robert Johnston, NC–80/14
McNabb, R. L., NJ–45/13
MacNair, Florence Wheelock (Ayscough) (Mrs. Harley Farnsworth), CA–210/2b
MacNair, H. F., CT–50/2, VA–65/2
MacNair, Harley F., TX–5/2
MacNair, Harley Farnsworth, CA–210/1, CA–210/2b, MA–125/6, WA–45/1
McNally, Ignatius, NY–120/1
MacNaughtan, W[illiam], NY–275/1
MacNeil, E., NY–280/3
McNulty, Edith, TX–5/2
McNulty, Henry A., TX–5/2
Macpherson, Jean. *See* Pommerenke, Jean (Macpherson)

McQuown, Madeline E., UT–20/1
McRae, C. R., TX–5/2
McRae, Cameron F[arquhar], TX–5/2
MacRae, Francis, NY–110/1, NY–120/1
McRae, Sarah [Nicoll Woodward] (Mrs. Cameron Farquhar), TX–5/2
McRay, Florence, TX–5/2
McReynolds, Lou Vera, OH–170/24
McRoberts, Duncan, KY–85/1
McTyeire, Enoch Mather, GA–20/1
McTyeire, Holland N., TN–70/4
MacWillie, John, TX–5/2
Macy, William A., NY–225/3b
Macy, William Allen, CT–60/8
Maddry, [Charles], VA–65/1
Maddry, Charles E., TN–35
Madsen, Richard P., IL–205/1
Magalhaes, Gabriel de, DC–10, DC–65/1
Magan, P. T., CA–135/1
Magee, Faith, TX–5/2
Magee, John, TX–5/2
Magill, Ellen (Bell) (Mrs. Orrin), CT–50/15, VA–100/1
Magill, Orrin, CT–50/15
Magill, Robert A., TX–5/2
Magner, J. F., VA–25/1
Magness, Bertha E., OR–15/33
Mahan, Mary Evangelist, OH–165/1
Mahoney, Mrs. L., IN–105/2
Mahy, G. Gordon, CA–235/1
Mahy, G. Gordon, Jr., CT–10/2
Maiden, Daisy V. (Mrs. Boone), IN–5/1
Maier, Henry J., NY–275/1
Maier, Mr. and Mrs. Henry, IN–30/1
Maigrot, Charles, MO–75/1
Maillard de Tournon, Charles Thomas, CA–245, CA–245/6, CT–60/5, IL–60/1, IL–75/4, IN–10/3, IN–10/4, IN–10/5
Maillard di Tournon, Carlo Tommaso, MN–20/1
Main, Dr. [Duncan?], IA–25/1
Main, D. Duncan, GA–15/5, NJ–45/5, NY–290/1
Main, Ida Belle (Lewis) (Mrs. William A.), MA–195/5, NJ–45/5, OR–15/34, OR–15/47
Main, W. A., NJ–45/3, NJ–45/13
Main, William A., NJ–45/3
Main, William Artyn, NY–270/18, OR–15/47
Major, J. N., TX–5/2
Majors, Euva Evelyn. *See* Bausum, Euva Evelyn (Majors)
Makra, Lelia, NY–120/1
Malatesta, Edward, CA–245
Maleddu, P., NY–335/1
Mallalieu, W. F., NJ–45/13, NY–200/1
Mallalieu, Willard F., NJ–45/5
Malmin, O. G., IA–15/1
Malmin, R., IA–15/1
Malone, Ann, NY–120/1
Maloney, Anthony, MA–255/1
Maloof, Louis, WI–75/2, WI–75/3
Manderson, Mabel, NY–290/1
Maness, Mary, KY–85/1
Manget, Fred P., GA–40/1, NJ–45/10, NY–290/1
Manget, Mrs. V. E., GA–20/6
Manley, Marian E., NJ–45/3
Manly family, CT–50/7
Manly, W. E., NJ–45/3, NJ–45/13
Manly, Wilson E., NY–270/18
Mann, Albert, NY–90/4
Mann, Arthur, TX–5/2
Mann, Mary, IN–40/5
Manning, Edward, NY–110/1, NY–120/1
Manning, Santa Maria, NY–120/1
Manson, Patrick, MD–35/2
Mao, K. T., TX–5/2
Mao, Lucia, OH–165/1
Mao Tse-tung. *See* Mao Zedong
Mao Zedong, MA–255/1, MN–105/3, NY–95/1, NY–275/1

Mao Yen-wen, NY–270/35
Marbut, Curtis Fletcher, MO–5/4
March, A. W., CT–50/7
March, Arthur W., CA–235/1
Marchant, Leslie Ronald, CA–275/2, CT–80/1, IL–85/1, IL–185/1, KY–90/1, MA–230/4, MI–25/1, NC–30/2, NJ–105/1, NY–175/4, OH–15/1, WA–35/1
Marias, Eunice, KY–85/1
Marie de Sainte-Nathalie, Sr., NY–230/1
Mario, S. M., WI–75/4
Marita, Mother Ann, KY–65/1
Marius, Fr., CA–260/1
Markley, Frances. *See* Roberts, Frances (Markley)
Marlowe, Rose, KY–50/2, VA–65/2, VA–70/1
Marr, Marjorie Smith, MA–45/2, MA–45/10
Marrow, Jane Gregory, NC–70/15b
Marsden, Robert S., PA–190/1, PA–190/2, PA–190/3
Marshall, Charles K., GA–20/1
Marshall, George C., NJ–35, NJ–35/1, VA–50/1
Marshall, Harold, PA–265/2
Marshall, Kendric Nicols, MA–240/4
Marsland, F. de Sales, NY–120/1
Marston, Margaret. *See* Sherman, Margaret (Marston)
Martens, Paul R., MO–50/6, NJ–30/1
Martig, Christian, NY–95/1
Martin, Anna M., MI–60/3
Martin, Arthur W., NJ–45/3, NJ–45/13
Martin, Boniface, MN–90/4, PA–95/1
Martin, Elizabeth Ellen, CT–50/7
Martin, Emma Estelle, CT–50/7
Martin, Estelle Lee, MN–70/5, MN–95/67
Martin, F., GA–15/3
Martin family, NJ–135/7
Martin, Harold Harber, GA–20/5
Martin, Harry S., ME–5/1, MN–60/1
Martin, Mary. *See* Richard, Mary (Martin)
Martin, Mary Lou, NY–120/1
Martin, W. A. P., CA–305/1, CO–20/1, CT–50/20, IL–85/1, MI–10/1, NJ–125/1, NY–95/1, PA–200/28
Martin, William, VA–50/1
Martin, William Alexander Parson, CT–60/30, DC–80/2, NY–95/1, PA–200/28
Martini, Martino, IN–15/1, PA–175/1
Martinson, Cora, MN–70/5, MN–95/68
Martinson, Harold, CT–10/2
Martinson, Mr. and Mrs. Andrew, MN–95
Martinson, Mr. and Mrs. Harold H., MN–95
Marvin, Enoch, NJ–45/5
Marx, Edwin, CA–75/2, TN–45/1, TX–30/1
Marx, Nora Baird, TN–45/1
Mary Elise, Sr., IN–105/2, IN–105/5, IN–105/11
Mary Evangela, Sr., IN–105/6
Mary Margaretta, Sr., IN–105/11
Mary of Calvary, Sr., NH–20/1
Mary of the Good Shepherd, Sr., NH–20/1
Masen, Herbert J., IA–15/1
Masland, John W., CT–50/2
Maslin, Paul, MA–195/5, TX–5/2
Maslin, Stella, TX–5/2
Maslin, T. P., TX–5/2
Mason, Bessie, NC–45/21
Mason, Charlotte, TX–5/2
Mason, Herbert John, NJ–25
Massey, George E., NY–175/4
Massie, Robert, TX–5/2
Masters, Frederic J., CA–165/1
Masters, Luella M., IN–40/5
Masters, Mary Luella, NY–375/1b
Masterson, Harris, Jr., TX–40/1b
Mateer, Ada (Haven) (Mrs. Calvin Wilson, 2nd wife), OH–175/1
Mateer, C.W., VA–105/1
Mateer, Calvin, CT–50/21
Mateer, Calvin W., NY–270/12

Mateer, Calvin Wilson, CT–60/30, NY–270/12
Mateer, Julia [Ann] (Brown) (Mrs. Calvin Wilson, 1st wife), CT–50/21, PA–200/28
Mateer, Robert M., NY–95/1
Mather, Grace (Burroughs) (Mrs. William Arnot), MA–220/13**b**, PA–200/28
Mather, Kirtley F., OH–155/1
Mather, Ruth, MI–60/3
Mather, William A[rnot], CT–15/2
Matheson, Mark E., TX–55/1
Mathews, Arthur, NJ–25
Mathews, Percy, TX–5/2
Mathews, Wilda (Mrs. Arthur), NJ–25
Mathewson, Eva, TX–5/2
Matravers, Brian, OR–15/11
Matsinger, Harrison, TX–5/2
Matson, Edla, IL–35/3
Matson, Esther, IL–35/1
Matson, P., IL–150
Matson, Peter, IL–35/1, IL–35/3
Matthews, Alden, MA–95/1, OR–15/3
Matthews, D., NJ–135/7
Matthews, Derrith (Mrs. Alden), OR–15/3
Matthews, Grace (Mrs. Harold), OR–15/3
Matthews, Harold S., CA–305/1, CO–20/1, CT–50/20, IL–85/1, MI–10/1, NJ–125/1, NY–95/1, PA–200/28
Matthews, Harold Shepard, CA–290/19**b**, NY–270/26**b**
Matthews, I., PA–170/1
Matthews, Mary S., TN–25/1
Matthews, Mrs. Harold, IA–25/1
Matti, Charles A. OH–30/1
Matti, Elsie V. (Mrs. Charles A.), OR–25/1, OH–30/1
Mattie, Miss, NC–50/1
Matton, Matilda A., TX–5/2
Mattox, Elmer L., CA–290/20**b**
Maurer, Herrymon, NJ–45/3
Maxim, Hiram Stevens, MA–30/2
Maya, Mathias da, IN–15/1
Mayer, Frances (Mrs. Paul S.), OH–120/7
Mayer, Lucy Rider, IN–40/5
Mayer, Paul S., OH–120/7
Mayhew, A., NY–280/3
Mayhew, Abbie, MA–240
Mayo, Ruth, CO–10/2**b**
Mayou, Matthias, MA–255/1
Mead family, CT–50/7, IL–180/1
Mead, Frederica. *See* Hiltner, Frederica (Mead)
Mead, Lucy Irene, MA–210/1
Mead, Margaret Platt, WA–40/3
Mead, Marie Louise (Myers) (Mrs. Frederick), WA–40/3
Mead, Richard H., TX–5/2
Meade, Joseph, TX–5/2
Meadows, Clyde, IN–45/1
Means, Alexander, GA–20/1
Means, Frank K., TN–35, TN–35/1, VA–65/2
Medhurst, [?], CT–50/9, IL–25/1, IL–200/14, KS–35/1
Medhurst, C. Spurgeon, MD–15/7
Medhurst, Walter, IL–85/1
Medhurst, Walter Henry, CT–20/1, CT–55/2, DC–80/2
Medlicox, Mrs., MA–95/1
Meebold, Louise, MA–95/1
Meek, William S., NJ–45/13
Meeker, Phebe. *See* Fuson, Phebe (Meeker)
Megan, Thomas M., IN–105/2
Mei, Y. P., OH–170/17
Meier, Dorothy, MO–50/6
Meijer, John, MO–40/1
Meister, Hans, MD–35/2
Meland, Bernard E., NY–270/25
Meller, T. W., NY–95/1
Mellow, Frances M. (Mrs. James H.), IL–200/50
Mellow, James H., IL–200/50
Meloy, Lucile. *See* Ady, Lucile (Meloy)

Melrose, Esther (Agnew) (Mrs. Paul), OR–15/35**b**
Melrose, Paul C., CA–290/21, CT–10/2, OR–15/35**b**
Melvin, Arthur G., TX–5/2
Melvin, Francis J., NY–105/1
Memory, Leila. *See* McMillan, Leila (Memory)
Mencius, KY–50/1
Mencken, H. L., IL–180/5
Mendizábal, Rufo, DC–70/4
Mendoza, Juan Gonzalez de, DC–110
Menezes, Francisco Xavier de, 1N–10/5
Meng Hsiao-ch'ih, CT–80/1
Meng, Paul C., NY–270/35
Menig, Walter J., NY–105/1
Menke, Dominic, NJ–155/1
Mennie, Mabel Beatrice. *See* Dodd, Mabel Beatrice (Mennie)
Menzi, Margaret (Wilder), MI–15/7
Merrell, Charlotte E., CT–50/7
Merriam, E. F., RI–15/4
Merrill, Frances E., TX–5/2
Merrill, Lilburn, NJ–45/13
Merrill, W. P., NY–270/25
Merrins, Beatrice, TX–5/2
Merrins, Edward M., TX–5/2
Merritt, Anna C., OH–170/7
Merritt, Sarah L., NC–85/3
Mersinger, Barbara R., NY–120/1
Merwin, W. C., CT–10/2
Merwin, Wallace C., CA–235/1, CT–50/2, CT–50/7, CT–50/11, MA–95/1, OR–15/18
Meshaw, R. E. L., TX–25/2
Messimer, Rebecca M., PA–80
Messmer, Archbishop, WI–75/3
Messmer, Sr. Callista, WI–75/4
Metcalf, [?], RI–15/3
Metcalf, Amy A., NY–290/1
Metcalf, Irving W., OH–170/15
Metzner, Theodore E., MA–45/3
Meuser, E. M., NJ–45/13
Mewshaw, Dell, TN–35
Mewshaw, Robert, TN–35
Meyer, Arnold, MO–50/6
Meyer, F. B., MI–120/1
Meyer, H. C., MO–50/6, MO–50/13
Meyer, Harriet (Cogswell) (Mrs. Paul C.), MA–220/16**b**
Meyer, L., MO–50/6
Meyer, Lawrence B., MO–50/8**b**
Meyer, William, CT–10/2
Meyers, Bertha, TX–5/2
Meyers, Blanche, VA–25/10
Meyers, Q. A., NJ–45/13
Miao, Chester, CT–50/2
Michie, Alexander, MA–30/2, WA–45/1
Mickey, Margaret Portia, OH–170/16**b**
Middendorf, Francis, MO–65/1
Middleton, R. W., IL–200/73
Mihelko, John, NY–110/1, NY–120/1
Mikhailov, Dmitrii Mikhailovich, NY–175/10**b**
Miles, Frank, MN–95/69
Miles, Mildred D., MA–240
Miles, Lee M., NY–290/1
Miller, Alexander, NY–270/27
Miller, Arleta, KY–85/1
Miller, Cynthia Aldine, VA–45/1
Miller, David, NY–270/18
Miller, Elizabeth J., PA–80
Miller, Ellen, TX–5/2
Miller, Everard P., TX–5/2
Miller, Geneva, KS–10/1
Miller, H. W., CA–135/1
Miller, Harriet Grace. *See* Lautenschlager, Harriet Grace (Miller)
Miller, Harry, CA–135/1
Miller, Isobel Selina. *See* Kuhn, Isobel Selina (Miller)
Miller, Iva M., CA–290/22**b**

Morse, Sidney Edwards, CT–60/18**b**
Morse, Walter P., TX–5/2
Mortensen, Ralph, NY–130/1
Moseley, E. F., NJ–45/10
Moseley, [?], IL–200/53
Moses, Arthur, MO–25/2
Moses, Rev. and Mrs. Arthur, MO–25/4
Mosher, Fanny S., TX–5/2
Mosher, G. F., PA–160/1
Mosher, Gertrude, TX–5/2
Mosher, Gouverneur Frank, TX–5/2
Moss, Leslie B., OH–155/1
Moss, Marion Venn (Mrs. Leslie B.), OH–155/1
Mossman, Mereb, NY–270/35
Most, S., NY–280/3
Mostrom, Rachel, OH–30/1
Mott, Charles Stewart, NJ–115/1
Mott, J. R., IL–75/2, VA–90/8
Mott, John R., CT–50/10, CT–50/14, CT–50/15, CT–50/17, CT–50/21,
    CT–50/27, NY–270, NY–270/12, NY–270/25, NY–270/27,
    NY–285/2, NY–290/1, NY–295/7
Mottey, Paul, NY–105/1
Moule, A. C., HI–15/2, NC–30/2
Moule, Arthur Christopher, CA–125/2, DC–160/2, IL–85/1, IN–20/2,
    NY–115/1, NY–175/4, NY–250/1, OH–85/1
Moule, Arthur Evans, GA–15/3
Moule, George Evans, CA–110/2
Moule, Henry W., OR–15/38
Moule, Ven Archdeacon, CA–235/1
Mount, Helen. *See* Anderson, Helen (Mount)
Mowrey, John, TX–5/2
Moy Ling, IN–45/1
Moyer, C., NY–280/3
Moyer, Elgin Sylvester, IL–105/6
Moyer, Raymond R., OH–170/17
Moynan, Mary (Goforth), IL–200/47**b**
Muehl, R. J., MO–50/6
Muehlenbein, Wibora, MN–5/1, MN–90/3, MN–90/4, MN–90/5,
    MN–95/71
Mueller, John Theodore, MO–50/9**b**
Mueller, R. J., MO–50/6
Muench, Esther, WI–70/1
Muenzenmayer, Naomi, KS–10/1
Mueth, Edward, NY–110/1, NY–120/1
Mug, Miriam Xavier, NY–120/1
Muilenberg, J., NJ–60/3
Muirhead, William, DC–80/2, GA–15/3, IL–200/4, TN–55/1, TX–25/1
Mullen, Francis, NY–110/1, NY–120/1
Mullen, Sr. Mary James, OH–165/1
Müller, Anna, NJ–30/1
Muller, James A., TX–5/2
Muller, James Arthur, MA–125/6
Mulliken, Ruth, NB–10/2**b**
Mullowney, J. J., NJ–45/13
Mumper, Sharon E., IL–205/1, MI–90/1
Munday, John J., NY–105/1
Mundelein, Ann B., TX–5/2
Mungello, David E., CA–75/3, HI–15/1, IL–185/1, VA–55/3, WI–45/1
Munger, Alzine C., OH–170/24
Munn, Ruth (Hanford), NY–360/1**b**
Munroe, Elbridge, KY–85/1
Munroe, Florence, KY–85/1
Munroe, Julia Blanche. *See* Kell, Julia Blanche (Munroe)
Munroe, Minnie (Mrs. Elbridge), KY–85/1
Munson, E. C., DE–10/1
Munson, E. H., NY–270/25
Murdoch, J., NY–275/1
Murdoch, Margaret, CA–235/1
Murdoch, Mary Cole, NY–270/35
Murphy, Alice E., CT–10/2
Murphy, Donald, PA–95/1
Murphy, Edward, CA–195/1

Murphy, Eliza Wright, NC–55/1
Murphy, Frances, NY–120/1
Murphy, Francis, NY–110/1, NY–120/1
Murphy, Henry K., OH–170/27
Murphy, James B., NY–175/9
Murphy, Starr, NY–290/1
Murray, Edward A., NY–105/1
Murray, Effie, OH–30/1
Murray, Florence, IN–120/5
Murray, Grace E. (McConnaughey), OH–170/14**b**
Murray, H., NY–280/3
Murray, John, PA–65/1
Murray, Katie, NC–70/16**b**, NC–70/17, TN–35, VA–65/2
Murray, Lucy H. (Booth) (Mrs. Everett E.), MA–220/7**b**
Murray, Mrs. E. E., CA–235/1
Murray, W. H., TX–35/1
Myers, Mary Edna, PA–80/10**b**
Myers, Miss, MA–195/5
Myers, Angie M., TX–5/2
Myers, Angie Martin, MA–185/11
Myers, Belle, NJ–45/4
Myers, Blanche, TX–5/2
Myers, C. H., NY–295/10
Myers, C. M., NY–270/35
Myers, G. S., NY–270/35
Myers, George W., IL–180/3
Myers, H., NY–280/3
Myers, L. G., NY–290/1
Myers, Mary E., NB–15/1
Myers, Marie Louise. *See* Mead, Marie Louise (Myers)
Myers, Minor M., VA–20/1
Myers, Ray, CA–130/1
Myers, Ruth L., IN–40/5

Nadal, Geronimo, IN–15/1
Nagakubo, Sekisui, DC–85/2
Nagel, C., MO–50/6
Nagle, J. S., NY–235/5
Nagle, J. Stewart, IN–40/5
Naish, C. G., CT–80/1
Nall, Otto, NC–75/1
Nance, Laura. *See* Little, Laura (Nance)
Nance, W. B., GA–10/1
Nance, Walter B., NJ–45/10
Nasmith, Augustus Inglesbe, CA–300/1, CT–50/7, NY–345/23
Navarrete, Domingo Fernández, IL–60/2
Naylor, R. Ethel, OH–30/1
Naylor, Roberta, OH–30/1
Neal, James B., OR–15/30
Neall, Beatrice, CA–5/1, CA–220/1
Neall, Ralph, CA–5/1, CA–220/1
Nease, O. J., MO–25/4
Nebel, Dale, IN–35/10
Nee, Brother, NJ–25
Nee, Gilbert Chibee, FL–5/1
Nee, Watchman (Nee To-sheng), FL–5, IL–90/1, IL–200/40, KS–25/1,
    NY–305/8, OR–40, OR–40/1
Needham, Rev., VA–25/10
Needles, Margaret, MO–25/4
Neely, C., NY–280/3
Neiderhiser, Martha. *See* Parker, Martha (Neiderhiser)
Neilson, Frances, CA–130/1
Nelsen, Bergitha L., MN–95
Nelson, Anna, MN–95/86
Nelson, Bert, MN–95/95
Nelson, C. A., OH–180/1
Nelson, Charles, CT–50/7
Nelson, Clara, KY–85/1
Nelson, [Daniel?], NY–225/4
Nelson, Daniel, IL–200/46, MI–15/1, MN–95/46, MN–95/73,
    MN–95/99, PA–180/1
Nelson, Daniel, Jr., MN–95/89

Nelson, Daniel, Sr., MN-95/91
Nelson, E. A., CT-50/7
Nelson, Edward, IL-35/1
Nelson, Eliza Ann. *See* Fryer, Eliza Ann (Nelson)
Nelson, Esther Ethel, OH-170/24
Nelson, Jennie (Mrs. Charles), CT-50/7
Nelson, Lillian Olsen, MN-70/5, MN-95/72
Nelson, Mary, MN-95
Nelson, Mary C., TX-5/2
Nelson, Mary Lee. *See* Latimer, Mary Lee (Nelson)
Nelson, Mr. and Mrs. Bert, MN-95
Nelson, Mr. and Mrs. Daniel, Sr., MN-95
Nelson, Mr. and Mrs. Daniel, Jr., MN-95
Nelson, Mrs. Robert, VA-105/1
Nelson, Nels Christian, CA-35/1
Nelson, O. G., NY-290/1
Nelson, Philip W., IL-200/48
Nelson, Robert, NC-10/11, OH-175/1, TX-5/2, VA-105/1b
Nelson, Rose, TX-5/2, VA-25/8
Nelson, Russell, CT-10/2
Nelson, Russell E., MN-95/73
Nelson, Thomas, TX-5/2
Nelson, Valley, MA-95/1
Neok Woo Hong. *See* Woo, Hong Neok
Nero, N. W., MO-50/6
Ness, J. A. E., IA-15/1
Nesse, Mr. and Mrs. Hans M., MN-95
Nestegaard, O. S., IA-15/2
Nestegaard, Ole S., MN-95
Netland, Bertine (Erickson) (Mrs. Sigvald), MN-95
Netland, Oline (Hermanson) (Mrs. Sigvald), MN-95
Netland, Sigvald, MN-95
Neufeld, Talitha, KS-55/2, KS-55/13
Neumann, George E., NJ-45/3
Neville, W. S. T., TX-5/2
Nevius, J. L., NJ-95/3
Nevius, John Livingston, DC-80/2, NJ-25, NY-270/13
New, Y. T. Zee (Mrs. Way-sung), CT-50/7, NY-270/35
Newberry, Alfred, TX-5/2
Newell, Ada, MA-240
Newell, George, NY-270/30b
Newell, Harriet, MA-130/1
Newell, J., NY-280/3
Newman, Cardinal, NY-100/1
Newman, Elizabeth, CA-235/1
Newman, F., OR-15/55
Newman, Frank W., CA-235/1
Newman, J. F., NJ-45/13
Newton, Earle, IN-75/1
Newton, Eva (Mrs. Earle), IN-75/1
Newton, Grace, NJ-135/5b
Neyman, Clinton, OH-155/1
Ng Kam Yan, CT-60/17
Ngou, Nelson T. S., TX-5/2
Nicholas II, Czar, MD-50/1
Nichols, Buford, VA-65/2
Nichols, Buford L., TN-35
Nichols, Don W., NJ-45/13
Nichols, Elizabeth, TX-5/2
Nichols, Harry G., TX-5/2
Nichols, John Howard, MA-105/1b
Nichols, John W., TX-5/2
Nichols, Julia, TX-5/2
Nichols, Mary Frances (Mrs. Buford), TN-35, VA-65/2
Nichols, Nettie D., MO-105/1, PA-225/1
Nichols, Ruthvan Beebe, CT-30/9
Nickerson, Florence, IN-40/5
Nickles, Florence, NC-80/15
Niebuhr, H. Richard, GA-15/5, IL-115/1
Niebuhr, Reinhold, IL-85/1, NJ-95/3
Nilsen, Frida, MN-70/5, MN-95, MN-95/74
Nilson, Anna. *See* Aarkvisla, Anna K. (Nilson)
Nilssen, J. E., IA-15/1

Ninde, Mary. *See* Gamewell, Mary (Ninde)
Ninde, W. K., NY-200/1
Ninde, William X., NJ-45/13
Ning, L. C., VA-50/1
Nipps, Anna Brown, NY-360/1
Nixon, Richard, IL-200/22
Noberie, Cora F., NJ-45/4
Noble, Martha, OR-15/5
Nolan, Edward J., PA-135/2
Nold, Mina Jordeth. *See* Hellestad, Mina Jordeth (Nold)
Nollen, John Scholte, IA-25/1
Nolley, Ron, VA-20/1
Noordhoff, Jeane, IA-45/2
Norbu, Thubten Jigme, NY-305/8
Nordlund, Mildred, MN-95/75
Noreen, Emma B., MA-95/1
Norelius, Jessie P., CT-60/32
Norman, Jerry, NJ-45/5
Normandin, Andree, NY-120/1
Norris, Ronald, MI-140/1
North, Eric, CT-50/26
North, Eric M., NJ-45/3
North, Floyd, VA-65/2
North, Frank Mason, NY-290/1
Northen family, GA-40/1
Norton, J. Randall, TX-5/2
Norton, Margaret S., TX-5/2
Norton, Richard B., CT-10/2
Norwood, Charles Stephens, NC-100/14
Norwood, Evan Wilkins, NC-100/14
Notestein, Ada (Comstock), MA-185/12
Nourry, C., WI-75/4
Nouvet, [?], NJ-110
Nowack, Esther Marguerite. *See* Hess, Esther Marguerite (Nowack)
Nowack, Helen. *See* Frame, Helen (Nowack)
Nowack, Katherine (Plantz) (Mrs. William Henry), IL-200/27, IL-200/34b
Nowack, Ruth, IL-200/34b, IL-200/40
Nowack, William Henry, IL-200/27, IL-200/34b, IL-200/49
Nowlin, Mabel, MA-195/5
Nowlin, Mabel Ruth, CT-50/7
Noyes, Harriet Newell, PA-200/28
Nu, H. H., PA-95/1
Nugent, Irwin, NY-110/1, NY-120/1
Null, Miriam E., NY-270/35, PA-125/1
Nutting, Clara A., CT-10/2, OH-170/24
Nyi, V. K., NY-270/35
Nyland, Dorothy, CT-50/7
Nyman, William G., CA-130/1
Nystul, Ingeborg, PA-60/1

Oberholtzer, Isaiah Ebersole, IL-105/7
O'Connell, Joannes, MD-50/1
O'Connell, Maureen, KY-65/1
O'Connell, Michael, NY-110/1, NY-120/1
O'Connell, William Henry Cardinal, MA-75/1
O'Connor, Brendan, PA-95/1
O'Connor, Charles J., NY-105/1
O'Connor, Doloretta Marie, KY-65/1
O'Connor, Patrick, NH-20/1
Odland, Ella. *See* Granskou, Ella (Odland)
O'Donovan, Winifred Patrice, IN-105/2
Odoric of Pordenone, MA-210/2
Oehler, W., NY-270/27
Oelschlager, Frieda. *See* Thode, Frieda (Oelschlager)
Oelschlaeger, Marie, MO-50/6
O'Gara, Cuthbert M., MA-255/4, NJ-15/1
Ogden, Hannah B., TX-5/2
Ogden, Mary L., TX-5/2
Ogden, Mary R., TX-5/2
Ogden, Nancy Hamilton, GA-20/5b
O'Hagan, Catherine, NY-120/1
O'Hagan, Joan Catherine, NY-120/1

O'Hara, Albert, CA–195/1
O'Hara, Albert R., VA–25/1
O'Hara, John F., NJ–115/1
Ohlinger, Bertha (Schweinfurth) (Mrs. Franklin), CT–50/7, OH–145/2**b**
Ohlinger, F., NJ–45/13
Ohlinger, Franklin, CT–50/7 , OH–145/2**b**
Ohlinger, Gustav, OH–145/2
Olbert, August, WI–75/2
Olden, O. F., SD–15/1
Oldfield, Mr. and Mrs. W. H., NY–275/1
Oldfield, W. H., NY–305/8
Oldt, Frank, NJ–50/1
O'Leary, Mary Angelica, NY–120/1
Oliver, Emma D., OH–30/1
Oliver, Frances Corinne (Sheldon) (Mrs. Oscar A.), OR–15/38
Oliver, Jay C., CT–50/15
Oliver, Jay Charles, CA–80/30, OR–15/38**b**
Oliver, Lucile Priscilla (Cummings) (Mrs. Jay Charles), CT–50/15, OR–15/38
Oliver, Oscar A., OR–15/38
Olsen, Anna. *See* Braafladt, Anna (Olsen)
Olsen, Olga. *See* Robinson, Olga (Olsen)
Olson, Arthur S., MN–80/1
Olson, Carrie, MN–95
Olsson, Johanna, TX–5/2
Olsson, Joseph E., TX–5/2
Oltman, Theodore V., MI–105/4, NJ–60/3
Olyphant, David W., RI–35/1
O'Neill, Francis J., VA–25/1
O'Neill, Mary Evangela, IN–105/2, IN–105/6
Openshaw, Henry James, CT–50/7
Openshaw, Lona (Van Valkenburgh) (Mrs. Henry James), CT–50/7
Opie, Eugene Lindsay, PA–145/4**b**
Opperman, Lucile, PA–265/1
Orense, Pedro, IN–10/3
Orlini, P. M. Alfonso, CA–265/1
Orr, William, CA–130/1
Osborn, Betty (Mrs. George), CT–50/15
Osborn, Emma D. (Mrs. Leon C.), MO–25/7**b**
Osborn family, MO–25/2
Osborn, George, CT–50/15, NC–45/23
Osborn, Rev. and Mrs. L. C., MO–25/4
Osborn, Leon C., MO–25/7**b**
Osborne, Fred, NY–285/1
Osburn, H. S., TX–5/2
Ose, Roger Keith, MI–50/1
Osgood, Dr., OH–155/2
Osgood, E. I., NY–290/1
Osgood, Elliott I., NY–290/1, OK–5/1, TX–30/1
Osgood, Pauline A., TX–5/2
O'Shea, John, MD–50/1
Osler, William, MD–35/2
Ostrom, Alvin, MA–105/1
Ostrom, Sue (Mrs. Alvin), MA–105/1
O'Toole, Barry, MN–5/1, PA–95/1
O'Toole, G. M., MN–90/4
O'Toole, George Barry, OH–45/1
Ott, Heinrich, CA–275/2
Ott, Johanna, NJ–30/1
Otte, Frances (Phelps) (Mrs. John Abraham), MI–105/5, MI–115/1**b**, MI–120/3, MI–120/14, NJ–60/3
Otte, J. A., NY–270/37
Otte, John A., KY–90/1, MI–80/9, MI–120/3, MI–120/7**b**, PA–200/28
Otte, John Abraham, MI–105/5, MI–120/14
Otte, Johannes Abraham, CT–55/2, MI–115/1, MI–120/8, NJ–60/3
Otterbein, Philip William, NY–200
Overholt, Olive, MN–95/76
Overholt, William, MN–95/77
Overholt, William W., NJ–45/3
Owen, J. W., PA–80
Owen, Jesse Coleman, NC–100/15**b**
Owen, M., NY–280/3
Owen, Rebecca (Mrs. Jesse Coleman), NC–100/15**b**

Owen, Ruth, OR–15/54
Owens, Rachel, CA–235/1
Owyang, Joseph Ignatius, OH–165/1
Oxnam, Bromley, NJ–45/3
Oxnam, Garfield Bromley, CA–35/6
Oxner, J. M., TX–25/2
Oxner, Mrs. J. M., TX–25/2

P'ang, Chih-kun, MA–95/1
P'i Huei, GA–15/3
Pacelli, Cardinal, PA–95/1
Packard, R., NY–280/3
Paddock, A., NY–280/5
Paddock, B. H., NJ–45/3, OR–15/47
Paddock, Bernard H., NJ–45/13
Paddock, Estelle, CT–50/27
Padelford, Frank W., OR–15/22
Page, Arthur Hartstein, ME–25
Page, William Nelson, VA–25/8
Page, A. G., OR–15/22
Page, Isaac, MO–5/1
Page, Kirby, CA–35/6, MI–15/5
Pai, Protase, NY–110/1, NY–120/1, VA–25/1
Paige, Ernest L., NJ–45/13
Paillart, G., PA–115/1
Paine, Theodora, TX–5/2
Palen, Lewis, TX–5/2
Pallu, François, MA–155/1
Palmer, [?], NJ–45/7
Palmer, Carrie, TX–5/2
Palmer, Giles, TX–5/2
Palmer, K. R., IA–15/1
Pang, Paul, NY–110/1, NY–120/1
Pannabecker, S. F., CA–115/2, KS–55/13
Pannabecker, Samuel Floyd, IL–110/1, IN–25/3
Pannell, Mary E., MO–25/4
Parennin, [?], NJ–110
Park, Alphonse, CT–60/17
Park, Margarita. *See* Sheretz, Margarita (Park)
Park, Robert E., IL–180/5
Park, W. H., NJ–45/10, NY–290/1
Park, William Hector, GA–20/1, NY–270/22
Parke, Mary A., TX–5/2
Parker, A. P., NJ–45/10
Parker, Alice Maria, CA–80/5
Parker, Daryl M., CT–50/7
Parker, Henry, TX–5/2
Parker, Henry Middleton, Jr., SC–25/3
Parker, Henry Middleton, Sr., SC–25/3**b**
Parker, John, CA–185/1, CO–20/1, IL–85/1, IN–95/1, KS–35/3, MA–15/2, MA–30/2, MA–215/2, MA–225/1, MA–235/1, MA–245/1, MA–280/1, MN–5/1, NC–55/1, OR–20/2, PA–165/1, RI–5/1, TX–20/2, UT–10/1, UT–25/1, VT–5/3, WA–45/1
Parker, Lucy Wright, TN–35, TN–35/1, VA–65/2
Parker, Martha (Neiderhiser) (Mrs. Daryl M.), CT–50/7, IL–105/11
Parker, Peter, CT–30/8, CT–50/20, CT–55/1, CT–60/13, CT–60/30, MA–5**b**, MA–50/4, MD–35/1, NY–95/1, PA–155, PA–155/1, RI–35/1
Parker, R., NY–280/3
Parker, R. A., NJ–45/10
Parker, Susie, MA–205/1
Parkes, Harry, IL–200/4, TN–55/1, TX–25/1
Parks, Keith, VA–65/2
Parnell, Mary, MO–25/2
Parry, Albert, IL–85/1, OH–110/4
Parsons, Elmer, IN–120/5
Parsons, R. Keith, GA–15/5
Partch, George, PA–200/26
Partch, George E., OR–15/39
Partridge, Louise, OH–170/18
Partridge, Mary Louise, MA–220/38**b**, OH–170/7
Partridge, Sidney, TX–5/2
Paschal, Fr., CA–260/1

Paterson, Marion B. *See* Blydenburgh, Marion B. (Paterson)
Paton, David M., CT–50/15
Paton, David MacDonald, MA–95/2, MA–155/1
Patriarch of Antioch, CT–60/5
Pattee, J. W., MO–25/4
Pattees, MO–25/2
Patterson, B. Craig, PA–240/1
Patterson, Brown Craig, NC–80/16**b**
Patterson, Craig Houston, NC–80/17
Patterson, Mrs. Brown, NC–80/16
Patterson, Vivian P., NJ–45/10
Pattillo, W. P., GA–20/1
Patton, Isabella (Mack) (Mrs. Charles E.), MA–185/13
Patton, Lulu, MA–195/5
Paty, Robert Morris, NJ–45/3
Paul, Alexander, NY–270/35, TN–45/1
Paul, Charles, CT–10/1**b**
Paxson, Ruth, MI–15/1
Paxton, J. Hall, CT–60/32
Paxton, John W., VA–55/2
Paxton, Vincoe, TN–45/1
Peabody, Francis W., NY–290/1
Peabody, Lucy W., NY–270/35
Peake, Cyrus H., CA–35/2, CA–80/48, CA–130/4, CA–205/1, CA–235/1, CA–305/1, GA–5/1, GA–25/1, HI–15/1, IA–5/1, IL–85/1, IL–115/1, IL–220/12, IN–95/1, KY–55/1, KY–70/1, MD–45/2, MI–120/14, NC–55/1, NJ–100/1, NY–95/1, NY–115/1, NY–175/5, NY–315/1, OH–65/1, OH–110/4, PA–240/1, PA–260/1, PA–275/4, TX–60/1, VA–30/1, VA–55/3, WA–40/6
Pearce, Agnes M., MA–50/1, NY–295/5
Pearce, Louise, NY–295/11**b**
Peat, J. F., NJ–45/3, NJ–45/13
Peat, Jacob Franklin, NY–270/18
Peavey, Alice H., TX–5/2
Peck, [?], NJ–45/7
Peck, Eugene C., TX–5/2
Pederson, Esther, NY–270/35
Pederson, Ingeborg, MN–95
Pederson, Nellie. *See* Holman, Nellie (Pederson)
Pedersen, Thyra, MA–165/4**b**
Pedroche, Cristóbal, IL–60/1
Peet, Caroline (Koerner) (Mrs. Lyman B., 2nd wife), MA–220/32
Peet, Ellen L. *See* Hubbard, Ellen L. (Peet)
Peet, Hannah Louisa (Plimpton). *See* Hartwell, Hannah Louisa (Plimpton) Peet
Peet, Lyman B., MA–180/1
Pehlman, W. J., NJ–60/1
Peill, Sidney George, LA–15/1
Peña, José, CA–195
Pender, Auria, TN–35, VA–65/2
Pendergast, Mary Carita, NJ–15/1
Pendleton, Ellen, MA–240/4
Pendleton, William Nelson, NC–10/11
Penfield, Mary. *See* Ament, Mary (Penfield)
Penfield, Paul, CT–60/32
Peng Fu, MN–95/73, MN–95/95
Peng Ming-min, NY–175/4
Penn, Erwin S., CT–60/32
Penney, Truman, MN–95/78
Pennington, Eva, OH–30/1
Perboyre, John Gabriel, MD–50/1
Peregrine, Mae, NJ–45/13
Pereira, A. Marques, NY–150/1
Pereira, Feliciano Antonio Marques, IN–15/1
Pereira, Thomas, DC–65/1
Pereyra, Thomas, MA–150/3, MA–155/1
Perine, Florence, IN–40/5
Perkins, Edward C., NJ–45/3
Perkins, Elizabeth S., CT–50/7
Perkins, Henry, CT–10/2
Perkins, Henry A., NY–270/35
Perkins, Henry Poor, CA–185/1
Perkins, Sara, NJ–25, PA–200/28

Permutti, B., NY–335/1
Perrin, Marion P., MA–240
Perry, Carey, TX–5/2
Perry, Charles E., TX–5/2
Perry, Elizabeth, CT–50/2
Perry, Matthew, CT–60/30
Persons, Wayne, NJ–85/3
Persson, Elvira, PA–60/1
Peter, Eleanor Elizabeth (Whipple) (Mrs. William Wesley), CT–50/7
Peter, W. W., MN–120/1
Peter, William W., OH–190/1
Peter, William Wesley, MD–35/2
Peters, E. C., NJ–45/10
Peterson, Clara, MN–95
Peterson, Ellen Josephine, ME–25
Peterson, Iola Aalbue, MN–70/5, MN–95/79
Peterson, Lily, IN–120/5, IN–120/6**b**
Peterson, Mattie, IN–120/4, IN–120/5, IN–120/6**b**
Peterson, N. B., IN–120/5
Peterson, Robert, NJ–45/3
Peterson, Stephen L., CT–50/24
Peterson, Therese, MN–95
Petit, Julian, TX–5/2
Petitt, Clifford W., OR–15/23
Petley, Bernard, NY–110/1, NY–120/1
Petterson, Hilda, MN–95
Pettigrew, Ruth, TN–35
Pettus, John De F., CT–10/2
Pettus, Sarah F. (Mrs. William B.), CT–10/2
Pettus, W. B., CT–10/2, CT–15/5, CT–50/11, NJ–45/3, NJ–115/1, NY–295/12
Pettus, William Bacon, CA–80/31, CA–290/24**b**, CT–10/2, MO–5/1
Pettus, William Winston, CA–235/1, CT–60/19**b**
Pfeilschifter, Boniface, MO–65/1, VA–25/1
Pfister, Lina, NJ–30/1
Pfister, Louis, DC–70/4
Pflauger, L. E., IL–200/50
Phelps, Dryden Linsley, CT–50/7
Phelps, Frances. *See* Otte, Frances (Phelps)
Phelps, Isabella, MA–95/1, MA–240
Phelps, Katherine, TX–5/2
Phelps, Louise L., TX–5/2
Phenix, Philip, MN–60/1
Pheur, William, NY–110/1, NY–120/1
Philip, Robert, NY–95/1
Philips, Carlysle James, NJ–45/3
Philley, Edward, NJ–45/10
Phillippe, Elma, KY–85/1
Phillippe, Garnett, KY–85/1
Phillips, Edward, MA–95/1
Phillips, Grace D., TX–5/2
Phillips, Grace (Darling), CT–50/7, OR–15/18
Phillips, Thomas, CA–195/1
Phillips, Walter S., OH–170/17
Pickens, Claude L., Jr., CT–50/15, MA–125/2**b**, TX–5
Pickens, Henri B., TX–5/2
Pickens, N. Elizabeth (Zwemer) (Mrs. Claude L.), CT–50/15, MA–125/2
Pickets, Esta, TX–5/2
Pickett, Christine Hubbard, CT–50/7
Pickett, Clarence, PA–140/1
Pierce, F., NY–280/3, NY–280/7
Pierce, Florence M., CT–50/7, NY–280/2**b**
Pierce, George Foster, GA–20/1
Pierce, Gussie M., IL–10/5
Pierce, H. F., MD–5/1
Pierce, Ruth, IN–40/5
Pierce, Willis F., NJ–45/3
Pierson, Isaac, MA–95/1
Pike, Florence, CA–235/1
Pike, Florence F., OR–15/18
Pilcher, L. W., NJ–45/13
Pilcher, Leander William, MI–60/4
Pilcher, Raymond F., NJ–45/3

Revers, Thaddeus, NY–110/1, NY–120/1
Reynolds, Hiram F., MO–25/8b
Reynolds, Charlotte (Belknap) (Mrs. Paul Russell), CT–50/7
Reynolds, H. F., MO–25/2
Reynolds, Hubert, TN–50/1
Reynolds, Johanna Madson, CT–50/24
Reynolds, Mary, MN–60/1
Reynolds, Paul, MN–60/1
Reynolds, Paul R., MA–95/1
Reynolds, Paul Russell, CT–50/7
Rhett, Charlotte. *See* Ingle, Charlotte (Rhett)
Rhett, Sarah Taylor, TX–5/2
Rhodes, Alexandre de, CA–70/1, DC–10
Ribeiro, Augusto, MO–75/2
Ricci, Matteo, CA–15/2, CA–70/1, CA–100/1, CA–165/1, CA–185/1,
    CA–245/5, CA–305/1, CT–55/2, CT–80/1, DC–20/1, DC–85/2,
    IL–20/1, IL–60/2, IL–85/1, IL–110/1, IL–130/1, IL–205/1, IN–20/1,
    IN–20/2, MD–10/1, MI–10/1, MI–25/1, MO–85/1, NJ–95/3,
    NJ–100/1, NY–95/1, NY–100/1, NY–275/1, OR–20/2, RI–20/1,
    TX–20/2, WA–35/1, WA–45/1, WI–45/1
Ricci, Matthaei, DC–25/1
Ricci, Matthew, DC–70/4
Ricci, Victorio, IN–15/1
Rice, Edmond L., NJ–45/10
Rice, Mildred (Mrs. Rolland), KY–85/1
Rice, Rolland, KY–85/1
Rice, Thomas, MN–90/2
Rice, William North, CT–30/15
Rich, John Hubbard, TX–5/1
Richard, A., NY–105/1
Richard, Mary (Martin) (Mrs. Timothy, 1st wife), IL–200/4, TN–55/1,
    TX–25/1
Richard, Mrs. Timothy, CA–75/2, NY–140/1
Richard, Timothy, CA–15/2, CA–75/3, CA–85/1, CO–10/3, GA–15/3,
    GA–20/1, IL–85/1, IL–200/4, IL–205/1, IN–20/1, MA–95/2,
    MA–240/6, NJ–105/1, NY–95/1, NY–105/1, NY–120/1, NY–125/1,
    NY–345/5, OR–20/2, PA–220/2, TN–55/1, TX–25/1
Richards, Howard, CT–60/21b, TX–5/2
Richards, Mary S., TX–5/2
Richardson, Agnes (Mrs. Robert Price), CT–50/7
Richardson, Cornelia M., TX–5/2
Richardson, Donald William, NC–20/1
Richardson, Ingeberg, MN–95
Richardson, Robert Price, CT–50/7
Richert, Marie, CA–115/1
Richert, Sophie, CA–115/1
Richey, Margaret C., TX–5/2
Richmond, Annette B., TX–5/2
Ricker, Raymond C., NJ–45/13
Ricketson, Bettie, TN–35
Ricketson, Robert F., TN–35
Riconda, Ruth, NY–120/1
Riddell, Olive Pauline, VA–65/2
Ride, Lindsay, HI–15/1
Rider, Marian. *See* Robinson, Marian (Rider)
Ridge, W. Sheldon, TN–40/1
Ridgely, Emily L., TX–5/2
Ridgely, Lawrence B., TX–5/2
Ridgely, Louise, TX–5/2
Riebe, Elsie W., TX–5/2
Riedel, Erhart, MO–50/6
Riehl, Moira, NY–120/1, VA–25/1
Rienstra, M. Howard, ME–5/1, MI–85/1, UT–25/1, WA–45/1
Rietveld, H., NY–280/3
Rietveld, Harriet, CA–290/27
Rietveld, Harriet A., CT–50/7
Rietz, Edith, NY–120/1
Rigani, Sr. Monica Marie, IN–105/2
Rigby, Kathleen L., TX–5/2
Riggs, Margaret Hallowell. *See* Augur, Margaret Hallowell (Riggs)
Rijnhart, Patros, CT–10/1
Riley, Joseph Harvey, DC–150/3
Rinden, Arthur O., CT–50/22, MA–95/1, OR–15/38

Rinden, Gertrude (Jenness) (Mrs. Arthur O.), CT–50/22, MA–95/1,
    MA–220/29b
Ringwalt, Arthur, NH–20/1
Rink, B., NJ–30/1
Rinker, Rosalind, KY–85/1
Ritchey, Caroline, TN–45/1
Ritchey, George, TN–45/1
Ritsher, Cynthia, MI–15/9
Ritson, J. H., NY–270/25
Ritter, Emma (Mrs. Richard), MA–95/1
Ritter, Mr. and Mrs., CT–15/5
Ritter, Richard H., CT–15/5, CT–50/7, MA–95/1, NJ–135/6
Robb, Alice, PA–245/2
Robbins, Emma, NY–290/1
Robbins, Lilliath, TN–45/1
Robbins, Oona Mae, OH–30/1
Robert, [?], MO–40/1
Roberts, Charles, CA–130, CA–130/1, CA–130/3, IN–30/1
Roberts, Florence (Suter) (Mrs. Charles), IN–30/1
Roberts, Donald, TX–5/2
Roberts, Dorothy, TX–5/2
Roberts, Edmund, NH–5/1
Roberts, Frances (Markley) (Mrs. William Payne), TX–5/2
Roberts, I. J., KY–50/2, VA–90/4
Roberts, Issachar Jacox, CA–275/2, CA–285/2, CA–305/1, DC–5/1,
    GA–25/1, HI–15/2, IL–205/1, MI–10/1, NY–95/1, VA–30/1, VA–70/1
Roberts, J. J., OH–95/2
Roberts, James Hudson, CT–15/6b
Roberts, John, TX–5/2
Roberts, Josephine, TX–5/2
Roberts, Louise, NC–50/1
Roberts, Margaret, TX–5/2
Roberts, Mrs. Owen, NY–235/5
Roberts, Paul, NJ–15/1
Roberts, S. J., RI–35/1
Roberts, William P[ayne], TX–5/2
Roberts, William P., and family, CT–50/7
Robertson, C. H., NY–275/1
Robertson, David A., NY–270/35
Robertson, James T., IN–25/1
Robertson, O. H., MA–50/1
Robertson, Oswald Hope, PA–145/5b
Robins, Arthur H., OR–40/1
Robinson, A., IL–200/50
Robinson, Arthur Greenwood, MA–130/3, MA–240/5b, ME–25/3,
    NY–165/1, WA–20/1
Robinson, C. H., MN–120/1
Robinson, Charles, MA–95/1
Robinson, David, IL–180/1
Robinson, G. Canby, MA–50/1
Robinson, H. W., CT–10/2
Robinson, Harold W., MN–60/1, NH–10/1
Robinson, Henry, MA–180/1
Robinson, Hugh Laughlin, ME–25
Robinson, J., IL–200/50
Robinson, Jay, CT–50/7
Robinson, Laura, IL–200/50
Robinson, Lillian D., NY–290/1
Robinson, Marian (Rider) (Mrs. Arthur Greenwood), MA–240/5b,
    ME–25/3
Robinson, Mary, CT–10/2
Robinson, Miriam, TN–20/1
Robinson, Olga (Olsen) (Mrs. Hugh Laughlin), CT–50/7
Robisch, A., NJ–30/1
Rockefeller, Abby (Aldrich), NY–285/5
Rockefeller, Babs, NY–285/5
Rockefeller, John D., NY–285/4, NY–295/8, PA–145/1
Rockefeller, John Davison, Jr., NY–285/1, NY–285/2, NY–285/3,
    NY–285/6, NY–295/9
Rockefeller, John D., Sr., NY–295/9
Rockefeller, John D., III, NY–285/3
Rockefeller, John R., NY–285/5
Rockefeller, Laura (Spelman), NY–295/12

Rockwood, Charles Parkman, CT–60/22**b**
Rodriguez, Simon, DC–65/1
Roe, Borghild. *See* Syrdal, Borghild (Roe)
Roe, Herman, IA–15/1
Rogers, Mary Josephine, NY–120
Rogner, Clementia, KY–65/1
Rohlfs, Mae, CT–50/7
Roisum, Alma, MN–70/5, MN–95/82
Rolf, Agatho, PA–230/1
Rolvaag, O. E., IA–15/1
Romano, Oriolo, CA–260/1
Romig, Harry G., PA–65/1
Romig, Lucy, CA–235/1
Romig, Lucy A., PA–65/1
Romig, Ted, NY–270/35
Ronning, Mr. and Mrs. Chester, MN–95
Ronning, Mr. and Mrs. Halvor N., MN–95
Ronning, Mr. and Mrs. Talbert R., MN–95
Ronning, Thea. *See* Landahl, Thea (Ronning)
Rood, Paul, CA–130/1
Roosevelt, Eleanor, MA–125/1
Roosevelt, Franklin D., NC–50/1
Roosevelt, Theodore, WI–25/1
Root, Helen I., IN–120/5
Roots, Eliza McCook, TX–5/2
Roots, Frances B., TX–5/2
Roots, Logan H., NY–270/35
Roots, Logan H., Jr., TX–5/2
Roots, Logan Herbert, MA–40/1, TX–5/2
Roots, Marie-Lou, TX–5/2
Rosamund, Sr., OH–115/1
Rose, Wickliffe, NY–290/1
Roseberry, Anna Ruth, KS–10/1
Rosenbaum, Arthur L., CA–35/2, CA–80/48, CA–130/4, CA–205/1, CA–235/2, CA–305/1, GA–5/1, GA–25/1, HI–15/1, IA–5/1, IL–85/1, IL–115/1, IL–200/12, IN–95/1, KY–55/1, KY–70/1, MD–45/2, MI–120/14, NC–55/1, NJ–100/1, NY–95/1, NY–115/1, NY–175/5, NY–315/1, OH–65/1, OH–110/4, PA–240/1, PA–260/1, PA–275/4, TX–60/1, VA–30/1, VA–55/3, WA–40/6
Rosenow, Edward, MN–60/1
Ross, Alice McLain, NY–345/23
Ross, Edith R., TX–5/2
Ross, Gladys M., TX–5/2
Ross, Marie Devota, NJ–15/1
Rosso, Sisto, CT–15/5
Rost, Corinne, NY–120/1
Rosvold, Nora A., MN–95
Roth, Mr. and Mrs. Ezra G., IN–30/1
Rothe, Jean B., CT–50/7
Rothweill, Colonel, NY–265
Rottenstein, Hans, TX–5/2
Rouleau, Francis A., CA–195/1, CA–245, CA–245/5, CA–245/6
Round, Harold, OR–15/38
Rounds, Alice Chamberlain Darrow, CT–60/2
Rouse, Ruth, CT–50/27
Roux, François, GA–15/5
Rowe, H. F., NJ–45/13
Rowe, Harry F., NJ–45/3
Rowland, Charles A., NY–270/23
Rowland, Henry H., NJ–45/3, NJ–45/13
Rowland, Henry Hosie, CT–50/7
Rowland, Marion Jean, CT–50/7
Rowland, Mildred May (Ament) (Mrs. Henry Hosie), CT–50/7
Rowlands, W. F., CO–10/3
Rowlands, William Francis, CA–205/1, MN–85/1
Rowley, Grace M., CA–75/2, CA–235/1
Rowley, Grace May, CA–80/33
Rowley, Mary, CA–75/2
Rowlin, M. R., IL–105/9
Roy, Andrew, CT–50/15
Roy, Andrew Todd, PA–200/28
Roy, Margaret (Mrs. Andrew), CT–50/15
Royal, Ann, MO–25/2

Royall, Rev. and Mrs. Geoffrey, MO–25/4
Royall, W. W., GA–20/1
Roys, Harvey Curtis, NJ–45/13
Roys, Mrs.Charles K., NY–270/35
Rubinstein, Murray A., CT–50/2
Rubner, Dorothy, NY–120/1
Rudd, Herbert, IL–180/5
Rude, Aase Hagestande, MN–95
Rude, James, CA–195/1
Rudin, Harry, CT–60/32
Rue, Edgar H., NJ–30/1
Rue, Elizabeth. *See* Hembold, Elizabeth (Rue)
Rue, Margaret Mary, CT–50/7
Rugh, Arthur, NY–270/25
Rugh, Dwight, CT–50/15, CT–50/17, CT–50/25, CT–60/32
Rugh, Gertrude (Mrs. Dwight), CT–50/15
Ruhl, Mr. and Mrs. Hesser, PA–80
Ruhl, Mrs. Hesser, PA–80/13
Ruhlman, Cecilia (Sr. Confirma), WI–75/3, WI–75/6
Ruland, Lloyd, OR–15/18
Ruland, Lloyd S., CT–10/2, PA–200/8, PA–200/28
Rulison, S. A., MI–60/5
Rullman, J. A. C., MI–80/9
Rupp, Jacob G., PA–80/1
Rupp, Jacob George, PA–80, PA–80/13
Rushin, Jennie B., TN–10
Russell, Bertrand, CA–35/6
Russell, D. Rudolph, TN–35
Russell, Grace Louise, MA–185/19
Russell, James Earl, NY–165/2**b**
Russell, Joy D., TN–35
Russell, Julia, TX–5/2
Russell, M., NY–280/3
Russell, Maud, MN–95/83
Russell, Sr. Francis de Sales, IN–105/2, IN–105/6, IN–105/9
Russell, W. B., NJ–45/10
Russell, Wallace B., NJ–45/13
Russell, William F., NY–165/3**b**
Rustin, Marie, NY–290/1
Ruth, C. W., MO–25/8
Ruth Magdalene, Sr., TX–5/2
Rutherford, Ildephonse, MO–65/1
Rutledge, Arthur, CA–195/1
Ryan, J. P., WI–75/3
Ryant, Clara Pearl. *See* Dyer, Clara Pearl (Ryant)
Ryding, I. S. W., IN–120/5
Ryding, I. Stanley, IN–120/5
Rysdorp, H., NY–280/3

Sá, Manuel de, IN–10/5
Sadler, [?], VA–65/1
Sadlo, Jan, DC–95/2
Saeki, P. Yoshio, MA–125/6
Safford, Anna Cunningham, NC–80/21
Sage, E. C., NY–290/1
Saiki, Yoshiro, NY–250/1
Sailer, Randolph C., CT–50/2, CT–50/7, MA–95/1, MN–95/84
Sailer, T. H. P., CT–50/26, TX–5/2
St. Bernard, IL–85/1
St. Catherine of Sienna, Sr., NH–20/1
St. Clair, Arthur E., OR–15/3
St. Clair, Bertha Harding (Allen) (Mrs. Arthur E.), CT–50/7
St. Francis, Sr., IN–105/2
St. Jean de Dieu, Sr., NH–20/1
St. John, Burton, IL–50/1
St. John, Burton L., NJ–45/13
St. John, Lucy Ann. *See* Knowlton, Lucy Ann (St. John)
St. Simon, Mother, NH–20/1
St. Vincent de Paul, MO–55
Salatko-Petrishche, Valerii Frantsevitch, NY–175/11**b**
Saleeby, Gladys A., TX–5/2
Salisbury, Lord, NY–270/12
Sallee, Annie Jenkins, TX–60/1

Sallee, Hannah Fair, VA–65/2
Sallee, Mamie. *See* Bryan, Mamie (Sallee)
Sallee, W. Eugene, TX–25/2
Sallmon, William H., CT–60/32, NY–270/35
Salmon, Frances (King) (Mrs. Robert J.), CT–50/7
Salmon, Robert J., CT–50/7
Salmon, William H., MN–60/1
Salter, Brigadier, NY–265
Saltmarsh, Alice I., IL–200/50
Salzman, Esther I., IL–200/56b
Sammann, Mary Edna, MA–45/2
Sampson, Archibald J., SC–5/1
Sampson, Mary H., TN–35
Sandburg, Everett, MA–95/1, MN–60/1
Sanders, Al, CA–130/2
Sanders, Arthur H., NJ–45/4
Sanders, Morris B., CT–60/32
Sanders, Oswald, PA–265/2
Sanders, Violet, SD–5/1
Sanderson, Abbie G., CT–50/7
Sanderson, Abbie Gertrude, ME–25
Sanderson, Miss, MA–195/5
Sanderson, Martha. *See* Ashmore, Martha (Sanderson)
Sandland, Thone, MN–95
Sandlin, Annie M., TN–35
Sanford, Edgar L., TX–5/2
Santa Maria, Antonio de, IN–10/4
Santoro, Egidio, CA–260/1
Sargent, C., NY–280/3
Sargent, Clyde B., CT–10/2
Sargent, Clyde Bailey, CA–290/28b
Sarvis, Guy Walter, TN–45/1
Sarvis, Maude T., NY–270/35
Sarvis, Maude Taylor, NJ–65/2
Sassen, Augusta, CA–80/5
Saterlie, M., IA–15/1, MN–95/99, NB–5/1
Satterthwaite, William, OH–170/24
Saunders, J. R., TX–25/2
Saunders, Joel R., TN–35
Saunders, Joel Roscoe, VA–65/2
Saunders, Mabel E., TN–35
Saunders, Mary Lucile, TN–35, TN–35/1
Saunders, Mr. and Mrs. J. R., CA–130/1
Savage, Caroline, NY–270/35
Savage, Ruth C. *See* Tewksbury, Ruth C. (Savage)
Sawin, John, NY–305/2
Sawtelle, Henry Allen, ME–25/4b
Sawyer, E., NY–280/3
Sawyer, Helen (Irvin) (Mrs. Malcolm), IL–200/57
Sawyer, Malcolm, IL–200/57
Sawyer, Myra L., MA–95/1, NJ–45/3, OH–170/10
Sawyer, Rollins, TX–5/2
Sayles, Florence, NY–290/1
Sayre, Geneva, IN–120/3, IN–120/4, IN–120/5
Sayres, Anna, TX–5/2
Sayres, Rosa, TX–5/2
Sayres, William, TX–5/2
Scarlett, Lenora, TN–35
Scarritt, Nathan, GA–20/1
Schaad, John, TX–5/2
Schaad, Margaret, TX–5/2
Schaefer, Ernst, PA–135/2
Schaefer, Esther (Mrs. Roland), OR–15/43
Schaefer, Roland, OR–15/43
Schafers, Mary, NY–120/1
Schaffer, Alice, OR–15/18
Schaffer, Harry M., TX–5/2
Schaffer, Pearl, IN–120/4, IN–120/5, IN–120/6
Schall, Adam, IL–45/1, MI–10/1, PA–95/1
Schall von Bell, Johann Adam. *See* Schall, Adam
Schalow, Frederick, MO–50/6
Schell, Esther, IL–200/32
Schereschewsky, Samuel Isaac Joseph, MA–125/6, ME–10/1, NJ–45/5,

NY–150/1, NY–230/1, TX–5/2, VA–105/1, WI–25/1
Schereschewsky, Susan M[ary] (Waring) (Mrs. Samuel Isaac Joseph), TX–5/2
Scherick, Rilla, CT–15/5
Scheufler, K. W., OR–15/6
Scheufler, Karl W., NJ–45/3, OR–15/56
Schiehter, W. Alfred, MO–5/1
Schilling, Lawrence, MN–60/1
Schiotz, Frederik, MN–70/5, MN–95/85
Schleicher, Louise H., TX–5/2
Schlesinger, David A., OH–175/1
Schlosser, Frances, IN–120/5
Schlosser, John (son of Mary Schlosser), IN–120/5
Schlosser, Mary, IN–120/5, IN–120/6
Schlund, Herman, OH–130/1
Schlund, Lillian, OH–130/1
Schmalzried, E. W., NJ–45/4
Schmalzried, Lena M. (Mrs. E. W.), NJ–45/4
Schmauss, George, NJ–30/1
Schmidt, Anna. *See* Kiehn, Anna (Schmidt)
Schmidt, Carl F., MO–50/6
Schmidt, Catherine, MO–25/4
Schmidt, Charles, NY–110/1, NY–120/1
Schmidt, Mary, CA–115/1
Schmitz, DeMontfort, IL–155/1
Schmüser, A., CT–15/5
Schneider, Madian, OH–165/1
Schneider, Sigfrid, OH–40/1, OH–165/1
Schneiders, Nicholas, KY–80/1
Schnusenberg, Alphonse, OH–165/1
Schoeffler, V. A., IN–90/1
Schoerner, Katherine Hastings (Dodd) (Mrs. Otto), IL–200/58b, IL–200/59
Schoerner, Otto Frederick, IL–200/40, IL–200/50, IL–200/58, IL–200/59b
Schofield, Robert Harold Aynsworth, MA–30/2
Scholz, A.C., MO–50/6
Schoyer, B. Preston, CT–60/32
Schrader, Elizabeth (Mrs. Ralph), MA–95/1
Schrader, Ralph, MA–95/1
Schrag, Jonathan, KS–55/13
Schramm, Gregory, PA–95/1
Schroedter, Martha, NJ–45/4
Schubert, William E., CT–50/7, NJ–45/3
Schuler, Marguerite, OH–165/1
Schulman, Irwin J., CT–50/2
Schultheis, Frederick Dwight, CA–185/1
Schultz, Sr. Francis, IN–105/2, IN–105/10
Schultz, J. Harold, CA–135/1
Schultz, Lawrence, TX–5/2
Schultz, Sister St. Francis, IN–105/2, IN–105/6, IN–105/11
Schultz, Susan. *See* Bartel, Susan (Schultz)
Schultz, Valentine, IN–105/10
Schultz, William M., NY–290/1
Schumm, Paula, NJ–30/1
Schurell, Veronica, WI–70/1
Schurman, Jacob Gould, TX–25/2
Schurman, Rhoda, MO–25/2, MO–25/4
Schutze, Katherine, NY–270/35, TN–45/1, TX–30/1
Schuurman, M., MI–80/9
Schuyler, Grace, NJ–60/1
Schuyler, Mrs. J. R., NJ–60/1
Schuyler, Phillip, NJ–60/1
Schwarcz, Vera, CT–50/2
Schwartzkopf, Louis John, MO–50/10b
Schwarz, George, DC–65/1
Schweinfurth, Bertha. *See* Ohlinger, Bertha (Schweinfurth)
Schwepker, Paul, CA–130/2
Scott, Agnes (Kelly) (Mrs. Roderick), CA–75/2, CA–80/34, CA–80/45, CA–290/29, MA–95/1
Scott, Anna Kay, NY–345/23
Scott, Annie V., MA–95/1, NY–90/7
Scott, Charles E., DE–10/1

Scott, Charles Ernest, CT-10/2, CT-60/23, NY-235/4, NY-270/33, TN-50/1
Scott, Clara (Mrs. Charles Ernest), TN-50/1
Scott, Francis H., CA-235/1
Scott, H., NY-280/3
Scott, Katherine, CT-50/7, TX-5/2
Scott, Katherine E., MA-195/3
Scott, Mary, MA-240, MO-25/2, MO-25/4, MO-25/9
Scott, Roderick, CA-75/2, CA-80/35, CA-80/45, CA-290/29b, T-10/2, MA-95/1, MA-125/1, MA-195/5, PA-75/1
Scott, Tom, NY-375/2
Scott, Vera. See Cushman, Vera (Scott)
Scott, William Ament, NY-270/12
Scott, William Anderson, CA-235/2
Scovel, F., OR-15/55
Scovel, Frederick Gilman, CA-235/1, OR-15/44b
Scovel, Mrs. Carl W., OR-15/44
Scovel, Myra Scott (Mrs. Frederick Gilman), CA-235/1, OR-15/44b
Scoville, Helen E. (Mrs. Ralph C.), IL-200/60b, PA-265/2
Scoville, Ralph C., IL-200/60b, PA-265/2
Scribner, E., NY-280/3
Se, L. F. Si, VA-25/10
Seabury, Warren Bartlett, CT-60/13, CT-60/24b, CT-60/32
Seager, Warren A., TX-5/2
Seaman, John F., TX-5/2
Searles, Clair K., NJ-45/3
Sears, Stella, CA-75/2
Seaton, Myrle Marie (Foster), PA-200/22
Seaton, Stuart P., CT-50/7
Sebastian, Fr., CA-260/1
Seeck, Margaret, CT-10/2, NB-15/1, NJ-45/3
Seely, Albert, MA-240/4
Seescholtz, A., NY-280/3
Seescholtz, Anne, CT-50/27
Sehon, E. W., NC-50/2
Selden, Charles C[ard], CT-50/7
Selden, Mrs. Charles C., CA-235/1
Selden, Gertrude (Thwing) (Mrs. Charles Card), CT-50/7
Sell, Ralph, CT-10/2
Sellemeyer, Esther I., CT-50/7, PA-80
Selles, Albert H., MI-80/3
Sellew, Walter A., IN-120/7b
Sellon, Lena, MA-175/1
Selmian, Benjamin, PA-170/1
Selmon, Bertha Eugenia Loveland, PA-185/6
Selsbee, Elizabeth, CT-50/7
Seltz, Eugene, MO-50/6
Selzer, Gertrude, TX-5/2
Semmedo, Alvaro, DC-15
Seng, Samuel T. Y., TX-5/2
Senger, Nettie Mabelle, CT-10/2, CT-15/5, CT-50/7, IL-105/9, IL-105/11, PA-130/1, VA-20/1
Sequeira, Luis de, IN-15/1
Serafini, Benedict, NY-125/1
Serafini, Cardinal, PA-95/1
Seraphim, Fr., OH-165/1
Seredi, Cardinal, PA-95/1
Service, Charles W., NY-290/1
Service, Grace Josephine (Boggs) (Mrs. Robert Roy), CA-35/9b, CA-35/10
Service, John Stewart, CA-35/10b
Service, Robert Roy, CA-35/9, CA-35/10, NJ-85, NJ-85/1, NJ-85/3
Servière, Joseph de la, WA-45/1
Seryshev, Innokentii Nikolaevich, NY-175/12b
Seton, Grace Thompson (Gallatin), MA-195/4
Settlemyer, Charles, TN-45/1
Severin, T., NY-280/3, NY-280/7
Severin, Theresa, MA-240
Severinghaus, Aura E., NJ-115/1
Sevilla, Christina, PA-200/28
Sewall, Carolyn T., MA-220/44b
Seward, Anna. See Pruitt, Anna (Seward)
Seward, William Henry, CT-60/30

Seward family, MA-165/5
Seybold, Clement, MA-255/3
Seydell, Mildred, GA-20/9
Seymour, Alice, NY-270/35
Shaak, Tasie, PA-80
Shackleton, Abraham, NB-30/1
Shafer, Luman J., MI-120/4, MI-120/8, NJ-60/3, NY-275/1
Shafer, Luman Jay, MI-120/10b
Shale, K. C., VA-50/1
Shambaugh, W. E., NJ-45/4
Shanahan, Cormac, MA-255/1
Shang Him Yung, GA-25/1
Shanley, Grace Clare, KY-65/1
Shantz, William, IN-30/1, IN-80/1
Shao Tzu-cheng, VA-50/1
Sharp, Gratia, NY-270/35
Sharpe, Annie Elizabeth. See Torrance, Annie Elizabeth (Sharpe)
Shaw, C. K., CT-50/16
Shaw, Charles B., MA-95/1, NY-275/1
Shaw, Ella C., CT-50/7
Shaw, Ernest T., CT-50/7
Shaw, J. L., CA-135/1
Shea, Gemma, NY-120/1
Shea, Kathleen Marie, NY-120/1
Shearer, Mary, CT-15/5
Sheehan, Edward, MO-40/1
Sheets, Margaret, TX-5/2
Sheffield, D. Z., MA-240/6, VA-105/1
Sheld, Dr., MA-195/5
Shelden, Francis B., NJ-45/13
Sheldon, Frances Corinne. See Oliver, Frances Corinne (Sheldon)
Shelton, Albert L., NJ-85, NJ-85/1, NJ-85/3
Shen, Anne, MA-240/6
Shen, T. K., NY-270/25, TX-5/2
Sheng, Hu-tai, PA-265/1
Shepard, Birse, MA-45/10
Shepard, Cora. See Boynton, Cora (Shepard)
Shepard, Mary W. See Voskuil, Mary W. (Shepard)
Shepherd, Clara (Mrs. George), CA-75/2, MA-95/1
Shepherd, George, CA-75/2, MA-95/1
Shepherd, George W., CT-10/2
Shepherd, George William, CA-290/30b
Shepherd, Massey H., WI-25/1
Sheretz, D. L., NJ-45/10
Sheretz, Dwight Lamar, CT-50/7, NJ-45/3
Sheretz, Margarita (Park) (Mrs. Dwight Lamar), CT-50/7
Sheridan, Robert, NY-110/1, NY-120/1
Sherman, Capt., MA-215/1
Sherman, Anne Catherine, TX-5/2
Sherman, Arthur M., CT-50/7, TX-5/2
Sherman, John, DC-90/7
Sherman, Margaret (Marston) (Mrs. Arthur), CT-50/7
Sherman, Martha, TX-5/2
Sherman, Martha L., MA-220/46b
Shields, Dr., MA-195/5
Shields, R. T., MA-55/1
Shields, Randolph, CT-50/25
Shields, Randolph T., CT-50/7, VA-55/2
Shih, C. C., IL-105/9
Shih, Peter Y. F., CT-10/2, PA-200/28
Shimer, Harriet, OH-30/1
Shipley, J. A. B., NJ-45/10
Shipman, R. B., TX-5/2
Shirk, Helen M., IL-50/1
Shively, George, VA-50/1
Shock, Laura, IN-45/1
Shoemaker, Samuel Moor, MD-30/4b
Shoop, Charles, NJ-45/4, OH-120/8
Shoop, Kathryn (Mrs. Charles), OH-120/8
Shore, J. E. Egerton, NY-270/33
Shorrock, Arthur Gostick, NY-95/1
Short, Lois Jorine, TN-35
Shortall, Marie Patricia, IN-105/2, IN-105/6

Shove, John D., CT–60/32
Shrader, Elizabeth T. (Mrs. Ralph R.?), CT–50/7
Shreve, Ina, KY–85/1
Shryock, John K., TX–5/2
Shu Ch'un-yuan, NJ–105/1
Shu, Grace, CT–50/26
Shu, S. Y., NJ–105/1
Shuck, Henrietta (Hall) (Mrs. Jehu Lewis), VA–65/2, VA–90/5b
Shuck, Jehu Lewis, CA–275/2, CA–285/2, CA–305/1, GA–25/1, HI–15/2, IL–205/1, NC–100/17, NY–95/1, VA–30/1, VA–65/2, VA–90/5b, VA–90/8
Shufeldt, Edith, OR–15/45
Shumaker, Howard Keller, PA–80/12b
Shumate, Margie, VA–90/6, TN–35
Shyrock, J. K., VA–25/10
Sia Sek Ong, OH–145/3
Siam, C. C., OR–15/22
Siam, King of, NY–15/1
Siao, Joseph, CA–280/1
Sibley, Gertrude (Haugh) (Mrs. Horace), CT–50/7
Sibley, Horace, CT–50/7
Sibson, Mabel, TX–5/2
Siegfried, Rev., WI–15/1
Sigmundstad, Gidske. *See* Himle, Gidske (Sigmundstad)
Sihler, Mabel (Wold), MN–70/5, MN–95/86
Sik Yak Foo, WA–20/1
Silcock, H. T., CA–125/1
Silcock, Harry T., OH–195/1
Silliman, Professor, RI–35/1
Silsby, Helen C. *See* Cross, Helen C. (Silsby)
Silsby, John Alfred, CT–50/7
Silvestri, P. C., CA–260/1
Simam de Graças de Felice Acclamaçao del Rey, Padre, IL–60/2
Simester, Edith Winifred, CT–50/7, NJ–45/3, OR–15/46
Simester, James, NJ–45/13
Simkin, Margaret (Timberlake) (Mrs. Robert), CA–75/2, CA–80/36
Simkin, Robert L., CA–75/2, PA–75/1
Simmons, John W., GA–20/1
Simms, Alan W., TX–5/2
Simon, Gertrude, MO–50/6
Simon, Martin, MO–50/6
Simon of Saint-Quentin, OH–65/1
Simons, Charles D., CA–195/1
Simonson, Clara. *See* Wold, Clara (Simonson)
Simpson, A. B., IL–200/28
Simpson, Alice, CA–75/2
Simpson, Willard, CA–75/2
Simpson, Willard J., CT–50/7, NJ–45/3
Simpson, William Wallace, MO–105/1, PA–225/1
Sims, Bessie, TX–5/2
Sims, Glennie, MO–25/4
Sinclair, T. Lowry, TX–5/2
Sing, Joseph C. D., CT–10/2
Singleterry, George, IL–10/3
Singleterry, Orrin O., IL–10/3
Siqueland, Lydia Kristensen, MN–95
Sites, C. M. Lacy, NJ–45/3
Sites, Clement M. Lacy, CT–10/2, CT–15/5
Sites, Evelyn M. (Worthley) (Mrs. Clement M. Lacy), CT–10/2, CT–15/5, CT–50/7, MA–220/60b
Sites, Matthew, NY–270/18
Sites, N., NJ–45/13
Sites, Nathan, NJ–45/5, NY–270/32b, OH–145/2
Sites, Virginia, VA–65/2
Skelly, Joseph A., PA–120/1
Skepstad, Mr. and Mrs. John, MN–95
Skinner, Clara (Mrs. Lawrence), OR–15/47
Skinner, Geraldine, OR–15/47
Skinner, Henry, OR–15/47
Skinner, J. E., NJ–45/13, NY–290/1
Skinner, James E., NJ–45/3
Skinner, James Edwards, OR–15/47b

Skinner, Lawrence, OR–15/47
Skinner, Susan Lawrence (Mrs. James), OR–15/47
Skinsnes, Casper C., IA–15/1, MN–95/88, NJ–25
Skinsnes, Dr. and Mrs. Casper C., MN–95
Slack, Harry Richmond, MD–30/1b
Slack, Elizabeth Blanchard Randall, MD–30/1
Slack, Frank V., NY–270/25
Slater, Philip, CT–50/7
Slater, Phyllis (Mrs. Philip), CT–50/7
Slattery, [?], MO–40/1
Slattery, Dennis, NY–110/1, NY–120/1
Slaybaugh, J. P., VA–50/1
Sledge, Cora Walton, OH–170/25
Sloan, Addie M., NC–80/22
Sloan, Gertrude Lee, NC–80/22
Sloan, Mr., IL–200/67
Small, Elizabeth Stair, IL–200/61
Smalley, Samuel E., TX–5/2
Smart, Ninian, CA–205/1
Smedal, G., IA–15/1
Smedley, Agnes, MN–95/33, MN–105/3
Smit, Albert H., MI–80/3, MI–80/9
Smith, A. L., NY–270/33
Smith, A. J., MO–25/2, MO–25/4
Smith, Alice Longden, NJ–50/1
Smith, Anna Mae, VA–70/1
Smith, Anne Piper, TX–5/2
Smith, Arthur, MA–95/1
Smith, Arthur H., CT–50/21, CA–80/5
Smith, Arthur Henderson, CT–60/30, GA–15/5, KS–35/3, VA–25/2
Smith, B. Ward, CT–50/7
Smith, Bessie Woods, VA–100/1
Smith, Bill, VA–65/2
Smith, C. Stanley, CA–235/1
Smith, Catherine, MO–25/4
Smith, Damien, NJ–80, NJ–80/1
Smith, Dennis V., MI–15/8b, NJ–45/3, OR–15/48
Smith, Dorothy, NY–270/35
Smith, Dudley D., TX–5/2
Smith, E. H., MA–95/1
Smith, Edward H., CT–10/2
Smith, Edward Huntington, CT–50/22
Smith, Egbert W., GA–35/1
Smith, Egbert Watson, NC–80/23b
Smith, Elita W., TX–5/2
Smith, Elleroy, CT–50/7
Smith, Elleroy M., CT–10/2
Smith, Ethelwyn, NY–270/33
Smith, Florence (Mrs. Joel A.), NB–15/1
Smith, Florence W., CT–10/2
Smith, George, WA–45/1
Smith, George G., NC–10/3
Smith, George Gilman, GA–20/1
Smith, Gertrude, (Mrs. Howard), IL–200/17
Smith, Grace (Goodrich), CT–50/7
Smith, Grace W. (Thomas) (Mrs. Edward), CT–50/22b
Smith, H., NY–280/3
Smith, H. Alexander, CT–50/26
Smith, H. Taples, PA–200/28
Smith, May Nixon (Corbett) (Mrs. Harold Frederick), NY–270/12
Smith, Harold F., NY–270/12b
Smith, Harold Frederick, NY–270/12
Smith, Harriet H., MA–220/47b
Smith, Hart Maxcy, CT–50/7, NC–80/24
Smith, Hazel (Littlefield) (Mrs. Dennis), MI–15/8b, OR–15/48
Smith, Helen, CT–50/14, MA–95/1
Smith, Helen H., OR–15/3, MA–220/48
Smith, Helen Huntington, CT–50/22b
Smith, Herbert I., NJ–45/3
Smith, Hollis S., TX–5/2
Smith, Hope Braithwaite, CA–80/5
Smith, Howard, IL–200/17

Scott, Charles Ernest, CT-10/2, CT-60/23, NY-235/4, NY-270/33, TN-50/1
Scott, Clara (Mrs. Charles Ernest), TN-50/1
Scott, Francis H., CA-235/1
Scott, H., NY-280/3
Scott, Katherine, CT-50/7, TX-5/2
Scott, Katherine E., MA-195/3
Scott, Mary, MA-240, MO-25/2, MO-25/4, MO-25/9
Scott, Roderick, CA-75/2, CA-80/35, CA-80/45, CA-290/29b, T-10/2, MA-95/1, MA-125/1, MA-195/5, PA-75/1
Scott, Tom, NY-375/2
Scott, Vera. *See* Cushman, Vera (Scott)
Scott, William Ament, NY-270/12
Scott, William Anderson, CA-235/2
Scovel, F., OR-15/55
Scovel, Frederick Gilman, CA-235/1, OR-15/44b
Scovel, Mrs. Carl W., OR-15/44
Scovel, Myra Scott (Mrs. Frederick Gilman), CA-235/1, OR-15/44b
Scoville, Helen E. (Mrs. Ralph C.), IL-200/60b, PA-265/2
Scoville, Ralph C., IL-200/60b, PA-265/2
Scribner, E., NY-280/3
Se, L. F. Si, VA-25/10
Seabury, Warren Bartlett, CT-60/13, CT-60/24b, CT-60/32
Seager, Warren A., TX-5/2
Seaman, John F., TX-5/2
Searles, Clair K., NJ-45/3
Sears, Stella, CA-75/2
Seaton, Myrle Marie (Foster), PA-200/22
Seaton, Stuart P., CT-50/7
Sebastian, Fr., CA-260/1
Seeck, Margaret, CT-10/2, NB-15/1, NJ-45/3
Seely, Albert, MA-240/4
Seescholtz, A., NY-280/3
Seescholtz, Anne, CT-50/27
Sehon, E. W., NC-50/2
Selden, Charles C[ard], CT-50/7
Selden, Mrs. Charles C., CA-235/1
Selden, Gertrude (Thwing) (Mrs. Charles Card) CT-50/7
Sell, Ralph, CT-10/2
Sellemeyer, Esther I., CT-50/7, PA-80
Selles, Albert H., MI-80/3
Sellew, Walter A., IN-120/7b
Sellon, Lena, MA-175/1
Selmian, Benjamin, PA-170/1
Selmon, Bertha Eugenia Loveland, PA-185/6
Selsbee, Elizabeth, CT-50/7
Seltz, Eugene, MO-50/6
Selzer, Gertrude, TX-5/2
Semmedo, Alvaro, DC-15
Seng, Samuel T. Y., TX-5/2
Senger, Nettie Mabelle, CT-10/2, CT-15/5, CT-50/7, IL-105/9, IL-105/11, PA-130/1, VA-20/1
Sequeira, Luis de, IN-15/1
Serafini, Benedict, NY-125/1
Serafini, Cardinal, PA-95/1
Seraphim, Fr., OH-165/1
Seredi, Cardinal, PA-95/1
Service, Charles W., NY-290/1
Service, Grace Josephine (Boggs) (Mrs. Robert Roy), CA-35/9b, CA-35/10
Service, John Stewart, CA-35/10b
Service, Robert Roy, CA-35/9, CA-35/10, NJ-35, NJ-85/1, NJ-85/3
Servière, Joseph de la, WA-45/1
Seryshev, Innokentii Nikolaevich, NY-175/12b
Seton, Grace Thompson (Gallatin), MA-195/4
Settlemyer, Charles, TN-45/1
Severin, T., NY-280/3, NY-280/7
Severin, Theresa, MA-240
Severinghaus, Aura E., NJ-115/1
Sevilla, Christina, PA-200/28
Sewall, Carolyn T., MA-220/44b
Seward, Anna. *See* Pruitt, Anna (Seward)
Seward, William Henry, CT-60/30

Seward family, MA-165/5
Seybold, Clement, MA-255/3
Seydell, Mildred, GA-20/9
Seymour, Alice, NY-270/35
Shaak, Tasie, PA-80
Shackleton, Abraham, NB-30/1
Shafer, Luman J., MI-120/4, MI-120/8, NJ-60/3, NY-275/1
Shafer, Luman Jay, MI-120/10b
Shale, K. C., VA-50/1
Shambaugh, W. E., NJ-45/4
Shanahan, Cormac, MA-255/1
Shang Him Yung, GA-25/1
Shanley, Grace Clare, KY-65/1
Shantz, William, IN-30/1, IN-80/1
Shao Tzu-cheng, VA-50/1
Sharp, Gratia, NY-270/35
Sharpe, Annie Elizabeth. *See* Torrance, Annie Elizabeth (Sharpe)
Shaw, C. K., CT-50/16
Shaw, Charles B., MA-95/1, NY-275/1
Shaw, Ella C., CT-50/7
Shaw, Ernest T., CT-50/7
Shaw, J. L., CA-135/1
Shea, Gemma, NY-120/1
Shea, Kathleen Marie, NY-120/1
Shearer, Mary, CT-15/5
Sheehan, Edward, MO-40/1
Sheets, Margaret, TX-5/2
Sheffield, D. Z., MA-240/6, VA-105/1
Sheld, Dr., MA-195/5
Shelden, Francis B., NJ-45/13
Sheldon, Frances Corinne. *See* Oliver, Frances Corinne (Sheldon)
Shelton, Albert L., NJ-85, NJ-85/1, NJ-85/3
Shen, Anne, MA-240/6
Shen, T. K., NY-270/25, TX-5/2
Sheng, Hu-tai, PA-265/1
Shepard, Birse, MA-45/10
Shepard, Cora. *See* Boynton, Cora (Shepard)
Shepard, Mary W. *See* Voskuil, Mary W. (Shepard)
Shepherd, Clara (Mrs. George), CA-75/2, MA-95/1
Shepherd, George, CA-75/2, MA-95/1
Shepherd, George W., CT-10/2
Shepherd, George William, CA-290/30b
Shepherd, Massey H., WI-25/1
Sheretz, D. L., NJ-45/10
Sheretz, Dwight Lamar, CT-50/7, NJ-45/3
Sheretz, Margarita (Park) (Mrs. Dwight Lamar), CT-50/7
Sheridan, Robert, NY-110/1, NY-120/1
Sherman, Capt., MA-215/1
Sherman, Anne Catherine, TX-5/2
Sherman, Arthur M., CT-50/7, TX-5/2
Sherman, John, DC-90/7
Sherman, Margaret (Marston) (Mrs. Arthur), CT-50/7
Sherman, Martha, TX-5/2
Sherman, Martha L., MA-220/46b
Shields, Dr., MA-195/5
Shields, R. T., MA-55/1
Shields, Randolph, CT-50/25
Shields, Randolph T., CT-50/7, VA-55/2
Shih, C. C., IL-105/9
Shih, Peter Y. F., CT-10/2, PA-200/28
Shimer, Harriet, OH-30/1
Shipley, J. A. B., NJ-45/10
Shipman, R. B., TX-5/2
Shirk, Helen M., IL-50/1
Shively, George, VA-50/1
Shock, Laura, IN-45/1
Shoemaker, Samuel Moor, MD-30/4b
Shoop, Charles, NJ-45/4, OH-120/8
Shoop, Kathryn (Mrs. Charles), OH-120/8
Shore, J. E. Egerton, NY-270/33
Shorrock, Arthur Gostick, NY-95/1
Short, Lois Jorine, TN-35
Shortall, Marie Patricia, IN-105/2, IN-105/6

Smith, Hubbard T., NC–45/4
Smith, Iona, CT–50/7
Smith, J. L., OH–95/2
Smith, James, NY–110/1, NY–120/1
Smith, Jane E., OH–170/17
Smith, Joel A., NB–15/1
Smith, John C., PA–200/25
Smith, Joseph M., TN–45/1
Smith, Judson, IL–200/62b, MA–30/2, MA–95/1, NY–385/1, OH–170/7
Smith, Lucy, TN–35, VA–65/2
Smith, Mabelle (Mrs. Elleroy), CT–50/7
Smith, Margaret (Jones) (Mrs. Hart Maxcy), CT–50/7
Smith, Margaret E., CT–50/7
Smith, Margaret P., TX–5/2
Smith, Mary J., TX–5/2
Smith, Miss, MA–195/5
Smith, Mr., NY–270/35
Smith, Mr. and Mrs. B. W., IL–180/1
Smith, Mrs. Francis H., VA–45/1
Smith, Myrtle A., OR–15/49
Smith, Olga Lucille, MA–185/14b
Smith, Osborne L., GA–20/1
Smith, Oswald, IL–200/47
Smith, Oswald J., IL–200/40
Smith, Ralph, CA–130/3
Smith, Ralph D., CA–130/1
Smith, Robert Ashton, CT–60/32
Smith, Stella, WI–15/1
Smith, Trissa (Darnall) (Mrs. B. Ward), CT–50/7
Smith, W. H., VA–65/2
Smith, Ward, OR–15/11
Smith, Wesley M., NJ–45/10
Smith, William Edward, NY–270/33b
Smith, Winnifred, TN–45/1
Smythe, G. B., NJ–45/13
Smythe, Lewis Strong Casey, CA–75/2, CA–80/37, CT–10/2, CT–50/2, MN–95/87, TN–45/1
Smythe, Margaret (Garrett) (Mrs. Lewis Strong Casey), CA–80/38, CT–10/2, MN–95/87
Snead, A. C., NY–305/8
Snell, John A., NJ–45/10, NY–290/1
Snellgrave, Joanette A., TX–5/2
Snider, Cora, MO–25/8
Snoke, Elsie, TX–5/2
Snoke, John H., TX–5/2
Snow, Edgar, MA–165/5
Snow, Helen (Foster) (Mrs. Edgar), MA–165/5
Snow, Myra L., OR–15/50
Snuggs, Grace (Mrs. Harold), TN–35, VA–65/2
Snuggs, Harold, TN–35, VA–65/2
Snyder, Calvin F., IN–30/1, IN–80/1
Snyder, Phoebe (Brenneman) (Mrs. Calvin), IN–30/1, IN–80/1
Snyder, Dorothy Jean, CA–235/1
Snyder, Esther (Mrs. George Randolph), PA–80
Snyder, George Randolph, PA–80
Snyder, Grace Walborn, PA–80/13
Soderberg, E. Grace, MN–95, MN–95/86
Soehnlein, Turibia, WI–75/3
Soetens, C., CA–290/17
Sokolsky, George, CT–50/25
Sollenberger, Howard, IL–105/7
Sollman, Miss, MA–195/5
Somervell, W. H., CT–50/9, IL–25/1, IL–200/14, KS–35/1
Sone, Hubert L., NJ–45/10
Soong, Charles, NJ–45/5
Soong, Charles Jones (Yao-ju), NC–50/1, TN–70/3b
Soong Ch'ing-ling. See Sun Yat-sen, Mme. (Soong Ch'ing-ling)
Soong family, AR–5/1, MI–10/1
Soong Mei-ling. See Chiang K'ai-shek, Mme. (Soong Mei-ling)
Soong, T. L., TN–70/3
Soong, T. V., NC–50/1, TN–70/3, VA–50/1
Sorensen, Theodore, NY–305/8

Sorenson, Sigurd T., IA–15/1
Souder, Edmund, TX–5/2
Souder, Martha, TX–5/2
Souder, Thacher, TX–5/2
Southgate, Mr., NC–50/1
Souvay, [?], MO–40/1
Sovik, Arna Quello, MN–95/88
Sovik, Arne, MN–70/5, MN–95/89
Sovik, Edgar, MN–70/5, MN–95/90
Sovik, Edward, IA–15/1, MN–70/5, MN–95/89, MN–95/91
Søvik, Erik, IA–15/1, MN–80/1, MN–95/99, MN–95/110, SD–15/1
Sovik, Gertrude, MN–70/5, MN–95/92
Søvik, Mr. and Mrs. Erik, MN–95
Sovik, Mr. and Mrs. Edward, MN–95
Sowerby, Arthur, DC–150/4b
Sowerby, Arthur DeC., IL–200/4, TN–55/1, TX–25/1
Sowerby, Arthur de Carle, DC–150/4b
Sowerby, Fanny, TX–5/2
Sowerby, Herbert, TX–5/2
Sowerby, James, TX–5/2
Spalding, Phineas D., TX–5/2
Speak, Celia Belle. See Steward, Celia Belle (Speak)
Speaks, Margaret, DC–100/1
Speer, Margaret Bailey, MA–195/5, MA–240/4, PA–15/1b
Speer, Robert E., NY–225/1, NY–230/1, NY–270/35, NY–275/1, NY–290/1, PA–65/1, PA–200/25, PA–200/28
Speer, Robert Elliott, NJ–95/2, NY–95/1
Speer, William, CA–235/2
Speicher, Jacob, NY–345/23
Speicher, Mrs., MA–195/5
Speidel, M., NY–280/3
Spellman, Francis J., NJ–115/1
Spellman, Cardinal, PA–95/1
Spellmeyer, H., NY–200/1
Spellmeyer, Henry, NJ–45/13
Spelman, Laura. See Rockefeller, Laura (Spelman)
Spencer, Cornelia, PA–200/28
Spencer, Elizabeth, TX–5/2
Spencer, Esther A., TX–5/2
Spencer, Kate, TX–50/1
Spencer, Marion. See Halsey, Marion (Spencer)
Spicer, Miss, MA–195/5
Spicer, W. A., CA–135/1
Spore, Clarence E., NB–15/1
Spore, Minnie (Buswell) (Mrs. Clarence E.), NB–15/1
Sprague, Viette I. (Brown) (Mrs. William P., 2nd wife), MA–220/11b
Spreckley, J. W., CT–50/7
Spreng, Ralph W. E., NJ–45/4
Springer, Charles Oliver "Dick," IL–200/63
Springer, Marion Elizabeth (Mrs. Charles Oliver), IL–200/63
Sprinkle, Russell, NY–110/1, NY–120/1
Sprunt, Alexander, NC–45/24
Sprunt, Dr. and Mrs. Alexander, NC–80/12
Spurr, Margaret, TX–5/2
Stafford, Margaret V., NJ–45/3
Stafford, Russell, MA–95/1
Stafford, Russell Henry, CT–10/2
Stager, Felicia, MN–90/3
Stakelum, [?], MO–40/1
Stalker, Hugh Lyle, MA–50/3
Stallings, Hattie, TN–35
Stallings, N. M., IL–105/9
Stallings, Nina M., NY–90/4
Stam, Elizabeth (Betty) (Mrs. John), CA–130/4, GA–35/1, IL–200/21, IL–200/30, IL–200/40, IL–200/47, IL–205/1, KY–50/2, MA–125/1, MI–85/1, ND–5/1, NJ–25, NJ–45/5, PA–200/28, PA–265/1, PA–265/2, TN–50/1, TX–30/1, WA–10/1
Stam family, NJ–95/3
Stam, Helen Priscilla, GA–35/1, NJ–45/5
Stam, John, CA–130/4, GA–35/1, IL–200/21, IL–200/30, IL–200/40, IL–200/47, IL–205/1, KY–50/2, MA–125/1,

MI–85/1, ND–5/1, NJ–25, NJ–45/5, PA–200/28, PA–265/1, TN–50/1, TX–30/1, WA–10/1
Stamps, Drure, VA–65/2
Stamps, Elizabeth (Mrs. Drure), VA–65/2
Standring, A. H., TX–5/2
Standring, William, TX–5/2
Standring, Ann (Torrence) (Mrs. William H.), MA–240, TX–5/2
Stanford, Edward, CA–175/1, CA–210/1, CA–305/1, DC–160/2, GA–15/5, IA–30/1, IL–65/1, IL–85/1, KY–35/1, MA–30/2, MA–155/1, MI–25/1, MI–55/1, NJ–100/1, NY–50/1, NY–95/1, NY–135/2, OH–50/1, OH–85/1, PA–235/1, PA–265/1, VA–30/1
Stanley, Mr., MA–195/5
Stanley, C. A., OH–180/1
Stanley, Charles A., CA–80/39, MA–240/6
Stanley, Flora Bonsack, CA–205/1, MA–155/1
Stanley, Gertrude. *See* Wilder, Gertrude (Stanley)
Stanley, Lenna M., OH–30/1
Stanley, Louise Claire (Hathaway) (Mrs. Charles A.), CA–80/39, MI–15/9
Stanley, Margaret, MN–95/93
Stannard, Mrs. Raymond E., CT–50/7
Stannard, Raymond E., NY–345/23
Staples, Mrs., MO–25/4
Stapleton, Beatrice, NY–120/1
Starn, Pauline, TN–45/1
Starr, Edward Comfort, CT–60/25
Starratt, Alfred B., TX–5/2
Starrett, A., NY–280/3
Starrett, Adelia M. (Dodge) (Mrs. Oscar G., 2nd wife), CT–50/7, MA–220/19**b**
Starrett, Anne G. (Hall) (Mrs. Oscar G., 1st wife), MA–220/24**b**
Starrett, Oscar G., NJ–45/3
Stattmiller, Clarissa, PA–5/1
Stauble, Francis J., NY–105/1
Stauffer, Milton, MA–25/2, NJ–30/1
Stearns, Abigail. *See* Cummings, Abigail (Stearns)
Stearns, Lucy E. *See* Hartwell, Lucy E. (Stearns)
Stearns, Thornton, NY–290/1
Stedman, Edith G., MA–165/6**b**, TX–5/2
Steel-Brooke, G[ertrude], NY–280/3
Steele, William B., CT–10/2
Stefler, Susan Reed, MA–20/1
Stegmann, Basil, MN–90/4, PA–95/1
Stehle, Aurelius, MN–90/4, NJ–80/1, PA–95/1
Stehle, Callistus, PA–95/1
Steiger, George Nye, CA–185/1, MD–10/1, TX–5/2
Steinbauer, Jean Theophane, NY–120/1
Steinbeck, G., NY–280/3
Steinheimer, Dr., NY–375/2
Steinheimer, H. C., NJ–45/3
Steinheimer, Karl, KS–10/1
Steinhoff, Karoline, NJ–30/1
Steininger, Russell H., OR–15/51**b**, OR–15/56
Stephanie, Mother, OH–115/1
Stephany, Marie, MO–105/1
Stephens, Peyton, TN–55/5**b**
Stephens, Mary Thompson (Mrs. Peyton), TN–55/5**b**
Stephenson, G., CA–285/1, CT–50/19, IL–25/2, IL–200/45, KS–35/2, NJ–45/14, TX–20/1
Stephenson, Gladys. *See* Gallimore, Gladys (Stephenson)
Steurt, Marjorie (Rankin) (Mrs. Roy), CA–75/2, CA–80/40, MA–220/42**b**
Stevens, Anna, TX–5/2
Stevens, Helen, MA–50/1
Stevens, Juliet, TX–5/2
Stevens, Leslie, NJ–45/13
Stevens, William Bacon, NY–150/1
Stevenson, D. D., MA–195/5
Stevenson, J. Ross, DE–10/1
Stevenson, P. H., MA–195/5
Stevenson, Paul, TN–45/1
Stevenson, Paul Huston, MO–100/2**b**
Stevenson, William Fleming, FL–15/1

Steward, Albert N., NJ–45/3, NJ–45/5
Steward, Albert Newton, CT–50/7
Steward, Celia Belle (Speak) (Mrs. Albert Newton), CT–50/7
Stewart, Anna White (Mrs. William R.), CT–10/2, NY–270/25
Stewart, Arthur, CA–80/5
Stewart family, MD–30/2
Stewart, Fanny, TX–5/2
Stewart, Gertrude (Mrs. Arthur), CA–80/5, TX–5, TX–5/2
Stewart, Jean, CT–10/2
Stewart, Lyman, CA–120/1, CA–130**b**, CA–130/1, CA–130/3, CA–130/4
Stewart, Mary W., CA–130/1
Stewart, Matilda, OH–30/1
Stewart, Milton, CA–130**b**, CA–130/1, CA–130/3, GA–25/1
Stewart, Reba C., TN–35
Stewart, William [Ramsey], CT–10/2, NY–270/25
Stewart, Winfred, TX–5/2
Stewart, [?], IL–200/53
Sticka, Pauline, NY–120/1
Stifler, W. W., NY–275/1
Stillman, Lucy R., NJ–45/3
Stirewalt, Catherine, CT–50/7
Stitz, Herman Joseph, NY–120/1
Stockman, Percy R., TX–5/2
Stockwell, Eugene, CT–50/7
Stockwell, F. Olin, CA–80/41, CT–30/1, CA–320/1, NJ–45/3
Stoddard, James, VA–105/1
Stoesser, Naomi K., NJ–45/4
Stokes, Anson Phelps, CT–50/21, CT–50/25, CT–60/13, CT–60/26**b**, CT–60/32, MA–50/4
Stokke, Mr. and Mrs. Knut S., MN–95
Stokstad, Mr. and Mrs. Christian, MN–95
Stone, Albert H., TX–5/2
Stone, Edna, TX–5/2
Stone, John F., NH–20/1
Stone, Mary, IL–200/11, IL–200/23, IN–40/5, MA–195/4, NJ–45/5, NJ–115/1, NY–290/1
Stone, Merry, IL–10/3
Storaasli, Mr. and Mrs. Gynther, MN–95
Storrs, Charles L[ysander], CT–10/2
Storrs, Mary (Mrs. Charles L.), CT–10/2
Storvick, Helen Weeks, MN–95
Story, Russell McCulloch, NY–95/1
Stotzingen, Fidelis de, PA–95/1
Stout, John, VA–65/2
Stowe, David M., NY–350/1
Stowe, E. M., MA–95/1
Stowe, Everett M., CT–50/7, NJ–45/3
Stowe, J. Joel, Jr., TN–15/1
Strain, Richard E., NJ–45/10
Strand, Alma, IL–150/1**b**
Stratemeyer, George E., NH–20/1
Straten, Magnus, PA–95/1
Street, Alice J., TX–5/2
Streeter, M., NY–280/3
Strehlow, Shirli, IL–105/11
Stricker, Francis, TX–5/2
Stringham, James A., CA–235/1
Stritch, Samuel A., MN–90/4, PA–95/1
Stritmatter, Andrew, MA–125/5**b**, OH–10/1
Stroh, Harriet, PA–200/23**b**
Stroh, M., NY–280/3
Stroman, Lila, TX–5/2
Strong, Anna Louise, CA–125/1
Strong, Edith (Mrs. Tracy), WA–40/5
Strong, Robbins, NY–275/1, OH–170/17, WA–40/5
Strong, Tracy, CT–10/2, WA–40/5
Strong, W. E., MA–95/1
Strong, William E., NY–290/1, OR–15/3
Strother, Greene W., TN–35
Strother, Martha, TN–35, VA–65/2
Struthers, Ernest, MA–95/1
Struthers, Helen G., PA–125/1
Stryker, Minnie, CT–50/7, MA–220/50**b**

Stuart, [?], IL–200/53
Stuart, Deaconess, MA–195/5
Stuart, George A., NJ–45/13
Stuart, John Leighton, CA–205/1, CA–210/2, CA–275/2, CA–290/24,
　CA–290/31, CT–10/2, CT–15/5, CT–15/7, CT–50/7, CT–50/8,
　CT–50/11, CT–50/25, CT–50/26, CT–55/2, CT–60/15, CT–60/32,
　IL–85/1, IL–205/1, IN–95/1, MA–50/1, MA–95/1, MA–240/4,
　MI–10/1, MN–95/41, MN–95/84, NC–30/2, NC–80/13, NJ–115/1,
　NY–95/1, NY–270/18, NY–270/23, NY–270/25, NY–275/1,
　OH–170/9
Stuart, Margery, IL–200/6
Stuart, Warren Horton, CT–50/7
Stub, H. G., IA–15/1
Stub, J. A. O., IA–15/1
Stubbs, Clifford Morgan, CT–50/7
Stucki, John Calvin, CT–50/7
Stucki, Marie (Mrs. John Calvin), CT–50/7
Studley, Elizabeth, MA–200/1
Studley, Ellen, NJ–45/3
Studley, Ellen M., NY–270/35
Studley, Ellen Masia, IN–40/3b
Stumpf, Kilian, CT–55/2, MO–75/2, NJ–95/3
Stuntz, [?], NJ–45/7
Sturton, Stephen Douglas, CA–190/1
Su Jen Chu, NJ–125/1
Suang Ting-kia, TX–5/2
Suhr, Esther (Mrs. Theodore), NJ–45/4
Suhr, Theodore, NJ–45/4
Sullivan, Frances C., TX–5/2
Sullivan, Leon, OH–165/1
Sullivan, Paula, NY–120/1
Sullivan, Philip B., TX–5/2
Summer, Mattie Vie, TN–35
Summers, Gerald V., NB–15/1
Summers, James, DC–80/2
Sumner, Hildegarde, OH–165/1
Sun, Anne Koopman, MA–45/2
Sun Fo, MO–100/2
Sun Li-Jen, NJ–35/1
Sun, Mary, WI–75/4
Sun Tsun-ying, IL–105/9
Sun Yat-sen, CT–50/16, CA–35/6, CA–180/1, CT–50/21, MN–95/1,
　MO–100/2, NY–270/12, NY–270/22, NY–295/4, PA–200/28,
　VA–25/12, WA–35/1, WA–40/2
Sun Yat-sen, Mme. (Soong Ch'ing-ling), MN–105/3, MO–100/2,
　TN–70/3
Sundquist, Hjalmar, IL–35/3
Sundquist, Ruth, IL–200/64
Sung, C. T., VA–50/1
Sung, Dr., MI–120/5
Sung, John (Shang-chieh), MI–10/1, MN–95/68, NJ–25, NJ–45/5
Sung Mei-ling. See Chiang K'ai-shek, Mme. (Soong Mei-ling)
Sung, William Z. L., NY–270/35, TX–5/2
Sung, Z. S., TX–5/2
Surdam, T. Janet, CT–10/2, NJ–45/3
Suter, Florence. See Roberts, Florence (Suter)
Sutherland, Ann, MO–25/2
Sutherland, Catharine E., IL–205/1
Sutherland, F. C. , MO–25/6
Sutherland, Rev. and Mrs. F. C., MO–25/4
Sutherland, George, NJ–30/1, PA–125/1
Sutherland, Harriet. See Corbett, Harriet (Sutherland)
Suttie, Melvin, IL–200/65
Sutton, F., NY–280/3
Sutton, Willard J., NY–25/2
Swain, Clara, CA–90/1
Swain, Robert, CA–290/24
Swann, N., NY–280/3
Swanson, J. F., IL–90/1
Swasey, Ambrose, OH–70/1b
Sweet, Helen (Firman) (Mrs. Lennig), CT–50/15
Sweet, Lennig, CT–50/7, CT–50/15
Swen, B. C., MN–60/1

Swenson, Victor E., IA–15/1
Swift, Ernest J., CT–10/2
Sydenstricker, Absalom, CT–50/2, NJ–25, PA–200/28, WV–10/1
Sydenstricker, Pearl. See Buck, Pearl (Sydenstricker)
Syle, E. W., VA–105/1
Syle, Edward W., TX–5/2, TX–5/3
Syrdal, Borghild (Roe) (Mrs. Rolf), MN–70/5, MN–95/94
Syrdal, Rolf, MN–70/5, MN–95/95
Syrdal, Mr. and Mrs. Rolf A., MN–95
Sze, Alfred Sao-ke, NY–290/1
Sze-tu, Duncan, MA–240/6
Szewczyk, Bernice, MO–55/1
Szto, Paul, MI–95/1

T. Chang Chin-shih, NJ–125/1
Tabor, Evelyn A., TX–5/2
Tacconi, Joseph, IN–105/2, MN–90/3, PA–95/1
Tack, Minnie, MN–95/96
Tackney, John, NY–110/1, NY–120/1
Taft, Frances, MA–240
Taft, Marcus L., NJ–45/13
Tai, A. L., CA–135/1
Tai, T. H., TX–5/2
Tai Tiao-hou, TX–5/2
Talbot, C. C., NB–15/1
Talbot, Louis, CA–130/1
Talbot, Sterling J., TX–5/2
Talbott, Charles C., NB–15/1, NJ–45/4
Talbott, Charles Nicholl, RI–35/1b
Talbott, Mrs. C. C., NB–15/1
Tallman, Susan B., MN–60/1
Talmadge, Kittie, MI–120/12
Talmage, J[ohn] V[an] N[est], MA–105/1
Talmage, M. E., MA–105/1
Talman, Rose H., MI–105/4, NJ–60/3
Tan Chuen Yu, VA–50/1
Tan Kuei-chun, RI–10/1
Tang, Dominic, CA–195/1, NY–110/1, NY–120/1
Tang, Edgar C., VA–50/1
T'ang T'ai-tsong, IL–40/1
Tanner, Matthias, DC–65/1
Tao-ling, Alexander, TX–5/2
Tao-yuan emperor, NY–195/1
Tappan, David S., OR–15/18
Tappan, David Stanton, II, CT–50/7, OR–15/52b
Tappan, Luella R. (Mrs. David), CT–10/2, OR–15/52
Tarin, Jaime, NY–95/1
Tarsicius, Sr., NH–20/1
Tate, Mowbry, PA–200/26
Tatlow, T., CT–50/27
Tattershall, Anna, TX–5/2
Tatum, Alice Joy, NC–100/18
Tatum, Alice Mabel (Flagg) (Mrs. Ezra), NC–100/18
Tatum, Ezra Francis, NC–100/18b
Taylor, Alice (Mrs. James Hudson, II), IN–120/5
Taylor, Alicia Booth, TX–5/2
Taylor, Alma (Booth) (Mrs. Harry Baylor), VA–25/10
Taylor, Charles, GA–15/5
Taylor, Clyde W., IL–200/23
Taylor, David G., NY–310/1
Taylor, Ethel Fay, TN–35
Taylor, F. Howard, IL–200/50, PA–265/1, PA–265/2
Taylor, Frederick, MA–50/4
Taylor, Harry B., NY–290/1, TX–5/2
Taylor, Harry Baylor, VA–25/9, VA–25/10b
Taylor, Helen. See Billings, Helen (Taylor)
Taylor, Helen Wickham, VA–25/10
Taylor, Herbert John, IL–200/50, IL–200/66
Taylor, Hudson, IL–90/1, IL–200/50
Taylor, J. B., MA–195/5, VA–65/2
Taylor, James Hudson, AZ–5/1, CA–130/4, CA–235/1, CT–50/21,
　IA–40/1, IL–35/4, IL–200/3, IL–200/21, IL–200/23, IL–200/28,
　IL–200/36, IL–200/67, IL–205/1, MI–95/1, MO–25/8, NB–20/1,

NC–55/1, ND–5/1, NJ–25, NJ–105/1, NY–95/1, PA–70/1, PA–200/28, PA–265, PA–265/1, PA–265/2, TX–30/1
Taylor, James Hudson II, IN–120/5
Taylor, J. Hudson's mother, IL–200/50
Taylor, Jane (Mrs. Herbert), IL–200/50
Taylor, John Cowder, VA–25/9
Taylor, Joseph, CT–50/2, GA–15/5, IL–110/1, MA–25/2, MA–95/2, MA–180/2, RI–15/4, VA–65/2
Taylor, Maria (Mrs. James Hudson), NJ–25
Taylor, Mary Geraldine (Guinness) (Mrs. F. Howard), NJ–25, PA–265/1, PA–265/2,
Taylor, Minerva M., VA–25/2
Taylor, Mr. and Mrs. Herbert, PA–265/2
Taylor, Mrs. Walter A., TX–5/2
Taylor, Paul V., PA–80/13
Taylor, R. V., NY–290/1
Taylor, Walker A., NY–375/2, TX–5/2
Taylor, Woodford, MO–25/8
Taylor, Thomas Jerome, NC–45
Taynton, Susan Herring Jefferies, NC–70/18
Tchang, Paulus, NJ–155/1
Teagarden, Lyrel G., CT–50/7, OR–15/53b
Teal, Edna, VA–65/2
Teele, Roy E., NJ–45/3
Teh'enn, Antonius, PA–95/1
Teilhard de Chardin, Pierre, DC–65/2, DC–65/3, DC–70, DC–70/1, DC–160/2, MA–130/2
Teitsworth, Elizabeth Jane. *See* Daniels, Elizabeth Jane (Teitsworth)
Tellier, P. de, DC–25/1
Temple, Helen, MO–25/2, MO–25/4
Teng, C. T., TX–5/2
Teng, S. Y., CT–50/2, CT–60/32
Tenney, Charles Daniel, NH–10/3b
Tenney, Adelle. *See* Cross, Adelle (Tenney)
Tenney, Helen Margaret (Jaderquist), IL–200/68b
Terani, Mrs. Steve, CT–50/7
Terhaar, Donalda, MN–90/4, MN–95/97
Termaat, Martha, MN–70/7
Terrell, [?], CT–50/9, IL–25/1, IL–200/14, KS–35/1
Terrell, Alice, NJ–45/3, NJ–45/5
Terrell, Grace (Mrs. Larry), OR–15/54b
Terrell, Larry, OR–15/54
Terrell, Mrs. E. G. Kirkpatrick, OR–15/54
Terrill, Richard Baker, IL–110/1
Terry, Myron E., CT–50/7
Tetley, Margaret, TX–5/2
Tetlie, Joseph, IA–15/1
Tetlie, Mr. and Mrs. Joseph, MN–95
Tewksbury, M. Gardner, CT–50/7
Tewksbury, Ruth C. (Savage) (Mrs. M. Gardner), MA–220/43b
Thayer, Mary V., CT–50/25, NY–270/35
Theiss, H. G., MO–50/6
Theiss, Henry Walter, MO–50/6
Thelander, Roy F., IA–15/1
Thelin, Guy A., MA–95/1, NJ–45/3, OR–15/5
Theodore, Sr., IN–105/2
Thiele, Edwin R., CT–15/5
Thienel, Rosibia, WI–15/1
Thoburn, H., NY–280/3, NY–280/7
Thoburn, Helen, NB–25/1
Thode, Elmer H., MO–50/6, MO–50/11b
Thode, Frieda (Oelschlaeger) (Mrs. Elmer), MO–50/6, MO–50/11b
Thomas, Antoine, IL–60/2, IN–15/1, NY–95/1
Thomas, Antonio, MN–20/1
Thomas, Eunice, MA–95/1
Thomas, Grace. *See* Smith, Grace W. (Thomas)
Thomas, Helen. *See* Foster, Helen (Thomas)
Thomas, James A., NY–235/5
Thomas, James Augustus, NC–45/25
Thomas, John, NB–10/3
Thomas, Lowell, NY–305/8
Thomas, Mary Ann. *See* Folsom, Mary Ann (Thomas)
Thomas, Winburn, CT–50/15

Thompson, Annetta. *See* Mills, Annetta (Thompson)
Thompson, C. J., LA–15/1
Thompson, D'Etta Hewett, OH–170/7
Thompson, Ivy Edith. *See* White, Ivy Edith (Thompson)
Thompson, Joseph O., NY–290/1
Thompson, K. K., CT–50/13
Thompson, L. A., TN–35
Thompson, Lewis R., PA–80
Thompson, M. Helen, TX–5/2
Thompson, May Belle, NJ–45/3
Thompson, Myrl, MO–25/4
Thompson, Pauline, TN–35
Thompson, Seal, MA–240
Thompson, Phyllis, IL–200/24
Thompson, Winifred. *See* Hockman, Winifred (Thompson)
Thomson, Anne. *See* Waller, Anne (Thomson)
Thomson, Charles, IL–200/69
Thomson, Claude, WA–40/3
Thomson, Diana, MA–165/7
Thomson, E. H., VA–105/1
Thomson, E. M. (Mrs. E. H.), TX–5/2
Thomson, Edward, OH–135/1
Thomson, Elliott H., TX–5/2, TX–5/3
Thomson, J. O., CT–50/2
Thomson, James C., Jr., MA–165/7
Thomson, James Claude, CA–235/1, MA–165/7b
Thomson, Jeanette, TX–5/2
Thomson, Joseph Oscar, CT–50/7
Thomson, Margaret (Cook) (Mrs. James Claude), CA–235/1, MA–165/7b, MA–185/15, WA–40/3
Thonstad, Agnes, MN–95
Thorne, Lois Anna, GA–15/5
Thorne, Mrs. Samuel, Jr., NY–270/35
Thornton, James, VA–25/1
Thornton, Mary J. *See* Bostick, Mary (Thornton J.)
Thoroughman, J. C., NJ–45/10
Thorpe, Mr. and Mrs. H. J., MN–95
Thorson, Peter E., IA–15/1
Thorson, Mr. and Mrs. Peter E., MN–95
Thresher, Ebenezer, OH–155/2
Throop family, NJ–135/7
Throop, Montgomery H[unt], III, TX–5/2
Thurlow, E. K., TX–5/2
Thurston, John Rogers, NH–10/4b
Thurston, H. B., OH–170/17
Thurston, John Lawrence, CT–60/24, CT–60/27b
Thurston, Lawrence, CT–60/32, NH–10/4
Thurston, Matilda S. (Calder) (Mrs. Lawrence), CA–235/1, CT–10/2, CT–60/15, MA–220/14, NY–270/35b
Thurston, Mrs., MA–195/5
Thwing, Edward Payson, CT–50/7
Thwing, Gertrude. *See* Selden, Gertrude (Thwing)
Thwing, Susan M. (Waite) (Mrs. Edward P.), MA–220/53b
Tien, Joseph, NJ–155/1
Tien, Thomas Cardinal, IN–105/6, WI–75/2, WI–75/3
Tien, Z. M., CT–50/12
Tigert, John James, IV, TN–70/4
Tilford, Lorene, TN–35, VA–65/2
Tillinghast family, NC–45/26
Tilson, Jonathan, DC–45/1b
Timberlake, Margaret. *See* Simkin, Margaret (Timberlake)
Ting Li-ch'eng, NY–295/6
Ting Me Iung, CT–50/7
Ting, Miss, MA–195/5
Ting, Shu-ching, NY–280/5
Tippett, C. F., MA–35/1
Tippett, Charlotte F., PA–265/1
Tipton, Mary Bryson, TN–35
Tipton, Mary Nelle, TN–35
Tipton, W. H., TN–35
Tjomsaas, Marie, MN–95
To, Simeon, NY–110/1, NY–120/1
Tobin, Chester, MN–95/98

Ufford, A. Frank, CT–50/13
Ufford, Lottie (Hartwell) (Mrs. Frank), CT–50/13b, MA–240
Ukhtomskii, Esper Esperovich, NY–150/1
Uline, Mary, MA–95/1
Ulmer, Laura M. (White) (Mrs. Walter P.), CA–290/32b, NB–10/6, NB–15/1, NY–270/35
Ulmer, W., MN–70/1
Ulmer, Walter P., NB–15/1, NJ–45/4
Underwood, Josephine. *See* Woods, Josephine (Underwood)
Underwood, Richard S., TX–5/2
Uong De Ci, OH–145/2
Upchurch, Bill, OR–15/18
Urban, Percy, TX–5/2
Urbany, Dominica, WI–15/1
Urlacher, Magdalena, NY–120/1
Ursula Mary, Mother, TX–5/2

Valdemar, [?], IA–15/1
Valignani, Alessandro, NY–95/1
Van, Amber, NJ–45/3
Van Baak, Edward, MI–80/9, MI–95/1
Van Benschoten, Frederika, CT–30/10
Vance, C., NY–280/3
Vance, Roland, CT–60/32
Van den Bogaard, Joseph, NY–110/1, NY–120/1
Vandenburg, Arthur H., VA–50/1
Vander Meer, Alma, MI–105/4, NJ–60/3
Vander Meer, W., NJ–60/3
Vanderbeek, Katherine J. (Abbey) (Mrs. Horace), MA–220/1b
Vanderslice, Mary E. *See* Edwards, Mary E. (Vanderslice)
Van Deusen, Mrs. Courtland, CA–235/1
Van Deventer, Dora E., MI–135/2
Van Doren, Helen, MA–220/52b
Van Driel, Valencia, WI–75/3
Van Dusen, Henry Pitney, CT–50/2, CT–50/15, CT–50/17, NY–285/1
Van Dyck, Anna Richardson (Mrs. David Bevier), PA–200/27b
Van Dyke, David B., CT–10/2
Van Dyck, David Bevier, PA–200/27b
Van Dyck, Howard, IL–200/53, NY–305/1
Van Evera, Kepler, CA–235/1
Van Evera, Pauline W. (Mrs. Kepler), CA–235/1
Van Gorder, George Wilson, OR–15/58b
Van Hengel, J., NY–280/3
Van Kirk, Ruth, CT–50/14, OR–15/3
Van Meter, A. R., TX–5/2
Van Meter, John B., MD–70/1
Vannicelli, Luigi, OH–45/1
Van Putten, J. Dyke, IL–115/1, MA–35/1, MI–25/1, MI–105/4, NC–55/1, NJ–60/3
Van Rensselaer, Catherine. *See* Bonney, Catherine (Van Rensselaer)
Van Reken, Henry Everett, MI–80/3
Van Rossum, William Cardinal, PA–95/1
Van Sant, Deward R., TX–5/2
Van Slyke, Donald D., IL–75/7, MA–50/1
Van Staveren, W. B., NY–270/37
Van Valkenburgh, Lona. *See* Openshaw, Lona (Van Valkenburgh)
Van Voast, Helen, TX–5/2
Van Westenburg, Anthony, IN–25/1, NY–275/1
Van Wyk, Bertha V. (Mrs. Gordon J.), MI–105/4, NJ–60/3
Van Wyk, Gordon J., MI–105/4, NJ–60/3
Varg, Paul A., CT–50/2
Vargas, Philippe de, CT–50/27, OR–15/10
Varo, Francisco, CA–165/1
Varro, Michael, MO–25/4
Varros, MO–25/2
Vasen, Verna, WI–75/3
Vaskco, Stephen, CA–195/1
Vaughan, J. G., CT–50/16, NY–290/1
Vaughan, John George, NJ–45/13
Vaughn, K., NY–280/14, NY–280/3
Vaught, Arnold B., NJ–115/1, PA–140/1
Vaught, Betty M., TN–35
Vautrin, Wilhelmina (Minnie), CT–50/7, NY–270/35, TN–45/1

Veenschoten, H., NJ–60/3
Veenschoten, Henry M., MI–120/11b
Veenschoten, Stella Elda (Girard) (Mrs. Henry M.), MI–120/11b
Velasco, John, NY–110/1, NY–120/1
Veldman, Harold E., MI–105/4, NJ–60/3
Veldman, J., NJ–60/3
Veldman, Jeannette, MI–105/4, MI–120/12b, NJ–60/3
Veldman, Miss, MA–195/5
Veldman, Pearl (Mrs. Harold E.), MI–105/4, NJ–60/3
Venable, R., NY–280/5
Venable, Wade Hampton, NC–80/25
Venbert, Gladys, NJ–45/3
Venn, Henry, NC–45/23
Venne, Ursuline, MN–90/3
Venneman, Clara, NY–120/1
Venneman, Espiritu, NY–120/1
Verbiest, Ferdinand, DC–85/1, IL–60/2, IN–15/1, KS–30/1
Verdier, [?], MO–40/1
Verity, George W., NJ–45/13
Vestling, Axel E., MN–60/1
Vestling, Mrs. Axel E., MN–60/1
Vetter, Francetta, MN–90/3, MN–90/4
Vick, Robert A., OH–155/2
Vieg, Ida, MO–25/4
Viguers, R. T., TX–5/2
Villey, Estelle, TX–5/2
Vincent de Lude, Sr., MD–50/1
Vincent, George E., NY–290/1
Vincent, Helen, *See* McLean, Helen (Vincent)
Vinson, John W., GA–35/1
Vogel, Ezra F., CT–50/2
Von Gunten, Eliza, IN–30/1
Vos, Johannes Geerhardus, PA–245/3
Voskuil, Mary W. (Shepard) (Mrs. Henry J.), MA–220/45b
Voskuill, H. D., NJ–60/3
Voss, Bernard J., MI–80/3
Voss, Herman E., NB–15/1
Voss, Kurt E., MO–50/6
Voss, Sadie (Dunkelberger) (Mrs. Herman E.), NB–15/1
Voss, William A., NB–15/1
Votaw, M. E., CT–50/26
Votaw, Maurice E., MO–5/5b, TX–5, TX–5/2
Voth, Matilda (Kliew), IN–25/3
Voth, William C., KS–55/12
Vousden, Ida (Albaugh), VA–100/1
Vreeland, H. H., CT–60/15
Vrooman, D., NY–15/1
Vrooman, Daniel, OH–90/2

W(ane?), J., NY–270/33
Waddill, Martha, TX–5/2
Waddington, Hilda, TX–5/2
Wagner, Augusta F., MA–240
Wagner, Jacob B., PA–80/2
Wagner, Maria M., CA–75/2, CA–235/1
Wahl, Annelda, MN–90/3
Wahlquist, D. R., CA–185/1
Wainner, Erma H., NJ–45/3
Waite, Alexander, PA–65/1
Waite, Edna (Mrs. Alexander), PA–65/1
Waite, James, PA–65/1
Waite, John, PA–65/1
Waite, Susan M. *See* Thwing, Susan M. (Waite)
Wakefield, Olive Lindsay, TX–5/2
Wakefield, Paul, MI–15/8, NY–290/1, TX–5/2
Wakeman, Dorothea, TX–5/2
Walcott, Gregory, TN–35/1
Waldenstrom, N. P., IL–35/1
Walker, E. F., MO–25/8
Walker, Edward, TX–5/2
Walker, Flora, TX–5/2
Walker, Geoffrey K., CT–60/32
Walker, Josephine C., OH–170/24, OH–180/1

Weig, Georg, WI–75/3
Weig, John, WI–75/2, WI–75/3
Weigel, Anna Jean, TX–5/2
Weigel, W. Harold, Jr., TX–5/2
Weigle, Luther A., CT–50/21, CT–60/32
Weigle, Luther Allan, CT–50/17
Weigle, Richard D., CT–60/32
Weil, Minerva Stout. *See* White, Minerva Stout (Weil)
Weir, Millie, TX–5/2
Weis, Edward, NY–110/1, NY–120/1
Weiss, Ernest W., NJ–45/3
Weist, Georgia, CT–50/7
Welch, Herbert, CT–50/16, NJ–45/5, OH–135/1
Welch, Mildred. *See* Cranston, Mildred (Welch)
Welch, W. H., MA–50/4
Welch, William, NY–290/1
Welch, William H., NY–295/8, PA–145/1
Welch, William Henry, CT–60/13, MD–5/1, MD–5/2b, NY–270/22
Welch, William Moses, OR–15/59
Welcher, Amy, CT–50/7
Wells, Edith May, MA–185/17
Wells, Laura P., MA–220/56b
Wells, Charles, TX–5/2
Wells, Clara E., NY–270/35
Wells, E., NY–280/3
Wells, Grace, PA–125/1
Wells, Laura P., TX–5/2
Wells, Lillian C., PA–125/1
Wells, Ralph C., NY–275/1
Welsh, E., IL–200/50
Welton, Felix B., CT–50/7
Welton, Frances (Mrs. Felix), CT–50/7
Wempe, Francis, NY–110/1, NY–120/1
Wenger, G. M., MO–50/6
Wentworth, Erastus, CT–30, CT–30/11
Wenzel, M. Richard, NY–120/1
Werling, W., MO–50/6
Werner, Celine, NY–120/1
Wesche, H. C., MO–25/4
Wesche, Henry, MO–25/4
Wesley, John, GA–15/1, GA–15/3, IL–85/1, IN–20/1, NY–200
West, Anna, MA–165/3
West, Dr. and Mrs. C. E., MO–25/4
West, Mrs. D. K., CA–235/1
West, R., NY–280/7
Westbrook, Charles Hart, CT–50/7, VA–65/2
Westbrook, Louise (Mrs. Charles Hart), CT–50/7, VA–65/2
Westcott, Pauline E., OR–15/60
Westhoven, William, MA–255/5, OH–55/1
Westman, Knut B., IA–15/1
Westmore, Alexander, DC–150/2
Weston, Beryl Audrey, IL–205/1
Westra, Rena D., MI–80/8
Wharton, Anne Louise, TX–5/2
Wharton, Joseph, IL–10/3, IL–10/4b, NC–15/1
Whatstone, Harold, IL–50/1
Wheeler, Ethel, TX–5/2
Wheeler, Frances O., IN–40/5
Wheeler, L., NY–280/3
Wheeler, L. N., NJ–45/13
Wheeler, Laura Maude, OR–15/61b
Wheeler, Lucius Nathan, NY–270/18
Wheeler, Martha A., NH–5/2
Wheeler, W. Reginald, CT–10/2, CT–60/32, NY–275/1
Wheeler, William Reginald, GA–15/3
Wherry, [?], NY–270/13
Whipple, Eleanor Elizabeth. *See* Peter, Eleanor Elizabeth (Whipple)
Whiston, Charles H., TX–5/2
Whitaker, Louise (Mrs. R. B.), MA–95/1
Whitaker, Maggie, OH–170/7
Whitaker, R. B., MA–95/1
Whitchurch, Emily, OH–170/7
White, Anna. *See* Stewart, Anna (White)

White, Blanche, VA–90/8
White, Emma Edmunds, VA–60/1b
White, Francis, NY–110/1, NY–120/1
White, Francis Johnstone, MN–105/4
White, Henry Gilbert, MN–105/4b
White, Herbert C., CA–5/1
White, Hugh Watt, NC–80/26
White, Ivy Edith (Thompson) (Mrs. Francis Johnstone), MN–105/4
White, J. Stanley, PA–65/1
White, Laura M. *See* Ulmer, Laura M. (White)
White, Marcellus, MA–255/1
White, Mary. *See* Gilman, Mary (White)
White, Mary Culler, CT–50/7, GA–10/1
White, Mattie M., TN–35
White, Minerva Stout (Weil) (Mrs. John Leslie), CT–50/7, PA–80, PA–80/1, PA–90/1
White, Moses C., NJ–45/5
White, Moses Clark, CT–30/13, NJ–45/13, NJ–50/1, OH–135/1
White, Philip E., TN–35
White, R., NY–280/3
White, Ralph M., CA–235/1
White, Roberta, MN–105/4
White, Ruth M. *See* Carr, Ruth M. (White)
White, Sarah, NY–90/8
White, Stanley, NY–290/1, PA–200/25
White, W. C., CA–135/1
White, Wilbert W., NY–270/12
White, William Clarence, CA–135/1
White, William Wesber, KY–85/2b
Whitehead, Raymond L., CT–50/2
Whitehouse, Ada, TX–5/2
Whitener, Sterling Wilfong, CT–50/7
Whiteside, Joseph, NY–270/38b
Whiteside, Joseph W., NJ–45/10
Whiting, Clara Husted, CT–50/7
Whiting, Samuel M., CT–35/2
Whitlow, Rolfe, NJ–45/10
Whitman, Sylvia, NC–15/1
Whittlesey, Roger B., DE–10/1
Wiant, Bliss, CT–50/7, CA–320/1, NJ–45/3
Wiant, Mildred (Mrs. Bliss), CA–320/1
Wiant, Paul P., NJ–45/3, OR–15/3, OR–15/5, OR–15/47, OR–15/56
Wiant, Mr., MA–195/5
Wickes, Dean, MA–95/1
Wickes, Fanny, CT–50/14
Wickings, H. F., MA–35/1
Wickman, Irma, IN–120/5
Wiebe, Katie Funk, CA–115/1, KS–55/13
Wiedlocher, Magdalene, IL–155/1
Wieland, Bernard, NY–110/1, NY–120/1
Wieneke, Agnes Bartel, MN–95/103
Wiener, Tom, MN–60/1
Wiens, Abraham K., CA–115/1
Wiens, Agnes (Harder) (Mrs. Frank J., 1st wife), CA–115/1
Wiens, Agnes (Koop) (Mrs. Frank J., 2nd wife), CA–115/1
Wiens, Anna (Mrs. Roland), CA–115/1
Wiens, Bernard, CA–115/1
Wiens, F. J., OR–20/2
Wiens, Frank J., CA–115/1
Wiens, Gertrude (Buhler) (Mrs. Abraham), CA–115/1
Wiens, Roland, CA–115/1
Wiens, Sarah (Mrs. Bernard), CA–115/1
Wiese, H. A., MO–25/9
Wiese, Harry, MO–25/4
Wiese, Rev. and Mrs. H. A., MO–25/4
Wiesen, Thomas F., TX–5/2
Wieses, MO–25/2
Wiggans, R. G., NY–295/10
Wiggans, Roy G., NY–90/4
Wight, Calvin, WI–25/1
Wight, Frannie E., WI–25/1
Wight, J. K., VA–105/1
Wight, Joseph Kingsbury, WI–25/1

Wolcott, Jessie L., NC–70/20**b**
Wolcott, Roger, TX–5/2
Wold, Anna L. (Mrs. Oscar), MN–95, MN–95/86
Wold, Anna Lee, MN–95/106
Wold, Clara (Simonson) (Mrs. Oscar), MN–95
Wold, Mabel. *See* Sihler, Mabel (Wold)
Wold, O. R., IA–15/1, MN–95/31
Wold, Oscar R., MN–95, MN–95/86
Wold, Waldo, MN–70/5, MN–95/106
Wolf, Anna D., NY–295/7
Wolf, Martha Katherine, NJ–45/4
Wolf, Sr. Agnes Loyola, IN–105/2, IN–105/6, IN–105/11, IN–105/12
Wolf, Sister Ann Colette, IN–105/2, IN–105/13
Wolfe, J. B., OH–170/17
Wolfe, Jesse B., CT–50/7
Wolfe, John R., MA–215/2
Wolferz, Louis E., CT–10/2
Wolferz, Katherine (King) (Mrs. Louis E.), CT–10/2
Wolff, Carmen, TX–5/2
Wolff, Ernst, MN–95/107
Wong, Beulah, VA–65/2
Wong, Kei Tin (?), CA–35/12
Wong Kok-shan, NY–270/25
Wong Kong-chai, TX–5/2
Wong, Lucy, MA–195/5
Wang Ming-dao, NJ–25
Wong, Peter, NY–110/1, NY–120/1
Wong Ping San, KY–50/2
Wong, Priscilla, MA–195/5
Wong, Ruth, NY–110/1, NY–120/1
Wong, S. N., TX–5/2
Wong, Soo-Ngoo. *See* Pott, Soo-Ngoo (Wong)
Woo, F. K., TX–5/2
Woo, Francis H., HI–5/1
Woo, H. N., NH–5/2, TX–5/2
Woo Hong-neok, TX–5/2
Woo, Hoong N., VA–105/1
Woo Hoong Neck (Woo Hong Neok?), TX–5/2
Woo, Jean, NY–275/1, OH–120/11
Woo, Mary, PA–265/1
Woo, S. M., MA–55/1
Wood, Annie L. (Kentfield) (Mrs. Clarence M.), MA–220/31**b**
Wood, Bernie, IN–120/4, IN–120/5
Wood, Chester Frank, ME–25/5**b**
Wood, Elizabeth, NJ–45/5, TX–5/2
Wood, J. Duncan, PA–75/1
Wood, James, NY–285/1
Wood, James E., Jr., TX–55/1
Wood, John Wilson, MN–105/3
Wood, Marquis Lafayette, NC–50/2**b**
Wood, Mary, OH–30/1
Wood, Mary Elizabeth, MA–80/1**b**, NY–35/1, TX–5/2
Wood, Morris Wistar, PA–75/1
Wood, Muriel. *See* Bowrey, Muriel (Wood)
Wood, Myfanwy, MA–195/5
Wood, Robert, MA–80/1, TX–5/2
Wood, Robert E., TX–5/2
Woodard, Sarah, TX–5/2
Woodberry, Ethel, NY–305/7
Woodberry, John, NY–305/6
Woodberry, Mrs. J., CA–130/1
Woodberry, Ora, NY–305/6, NY–305/7
Woodbridge, Jeanne (Mrs. Samuel Isett, 1st wife), VA–100/1
Woodhall, G. W., NJ–45/13
Woodhead, H. G. W., CT–50/2
Woods, Agnes Lacy. *See* Harnsberger, Agnes Lacy (Woods)
Woods, Andrew H., NY–270/35, NY–290/1
Woods, Andrew Henry, PA–15/2
Woods, Arthur, NY–285/1
Woods, Catharine T., MA–220/58**b**, PA–125/1
Woods, Catherine, CA–235/1
Woods, Edgar A., NC–20/1

Woods, Emily (Mrs. Harry), KY–85/1
Woods, Harry, KY–85/1
Woods, Henry, TX–5/2
Woods, James Baker, Jr., NC–20/1
Woods, John Russell, NC–20/1
Woods, Josephine (Underwood) (Mrs. Henry McKee, 1st wife), VA–100/1
Woods, Lily Underwood, VA–100/1
Woods, Martha D., MA–220/59**b**
Woods, Velma E., TX–5/2
Woodsmall, Ruth, MA–195/5
Woodward, E. L., TX–5/2
Woodward, Edmund L., TX–5/2
Woodward, Frank, TN–35, TN–35/1, VA–65/2
Woodward, Mabel, TN–35
Woollen, Betsy, MD–70/1
Woolsey, F. M., NJ–45/13
Workman, George B., NJ–45/3, NJ–45/10
Worley, Harry, CT–10/2
Worley, Harry W., NJ–45/3, NJ–45/5
Worley, Harry Westcott, CT–50/7
Worley, Harry Wiltsie, CT–10/2
Worley, J. H., NJ–45/13
Worley, Zela W. (Mrs. Harry Wiltsie), CT–10/2, CT–50/7
Worth, Charles William, NC–20/1
Worth, George C., NC–10/1**b**, NC–5/1
Worthley, Evelyn M. *See* Sites, Evelyn M. (Worthley)
Wortman, Jennie. *See* Campbell, Jennie (Wortman)
Wray, Emma T., TX–5/2
Wright, A. C., NJ–45/13
Wright, E., NY–280/3
Wright, Eleanor, CA–235/1, CT–50/7
Wright, Eleanor M., PA–200/28
Wright, Elizabeth C., CT–5/1, CT–10/2
Wright, Elizabeth Curtis, CT–50/7, MA–185/18
Wright, Harrison King, CT–10/2
Wright, John, NJ–135/3
Wright, Joseph K., IL–200/75
Wright, Mary L., TX–5/2
Wright, Mr. and Mrs. Harrison K., CT–10/2
Wright, Quincy, MA–95/1
Wright, Randall S., IL–10/3
Wright, William, IL–200/75, NY–135/2
Wu, Andrew V., NY–270/25
Wu, Blanche, NY–270/35
Wu, C. F., CT–50/26
Wu, Ch'i-yu, MA–95/1
Wu Ching-chang, TX–5/2
Wu Djen Ming, MN–95/73
Wu, F. C., VA–50/1
Wu, George K. T., NJ–45/3
Wu, John, NY–110/1, NY–120/1
Wu Lien-têh, CA–210/2, PA–155/1
Wu Ming-chieh, MN–95/108
Wu, Mrs., MA–195/5
Wu Pak-seng, NY–110/1, NY–120/1
Wu Shêng-tê, CA–55/1
Wu, Y. T., CT–50/2, CT–50/10, CT–50/15, MN–95/21, NJ–65/2, NY–270/25
Wu Yi-fang, CT–50/21, MA–195/5, NY–270/35
Wu Yick Wan, OR–15/18
Wurley, Mrs., MA–195/5
Wurmbrand, Rev., MI–120/11
Wyckoff, Ellen Gertrude, CT–50/7
Wyckoff, Helen Grace, CT–50/7
Wycliffe, John, NY–270/18
Wylie, A., NY–140/1
Wylie, Alexander, DC–80/2
Wylie, John H., NY–290/1

Xaverius, Abel, RI–15/4
Xavier, M. Chanel, NY–120/1
Xavier, Sarah A., MN–95

Repository Index